Mastercan
Version 7

Su-Chen Jonathon Lin, Ph.D.
Professor of Computer-Aided Manufacturing
College of Technology
Eastern Michigan University

F.C. Tony Shiue, Ph.D.
Professor of Computer-Aided Design
College of Technology
Eastern Michigan University

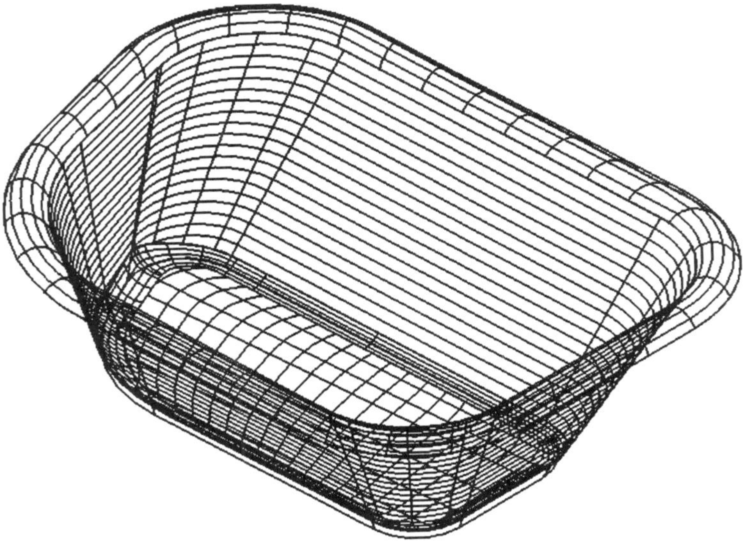

Scholars International Publishing Corp.
Ann Arbor, Michigan

Mastercam Version 7
Scholar's International Publishing Corp., 1998

Warning and Disclaimer

The authors and the publisher have made every effort to assure that the information provided is as accurate and complete as possible. However, the narrative and examples provided were developed on our computers and different configurations may create unforeseen anomalies.

This book is sold "as is" without warranty of any kind, either expressed or implied, respecting the contents of this book, including but not limited to implied warranties for the book's quality, performance, merchantability, or fitness for any particular purpose. The authors and the publisher shall have neither liability or responsibility to any purchaser or any other person or entity with respect to any liability, loss or damages in connection with or arising from the information contained in this book.

Scholars staff:
Marketing manager: Grace Lin
Chief editor: Jonathon Lin
Project editor: Karen L. Sterzik
Project manager: Jacob Cheu
Illustrator: Jacob Cheu
Cover designer: Jasha Chen
Printer/Binder: Bookcrafters, Chelsea Michigan
Printed and bound in the United States of America
99 200 - - 10 9 8 7 6 5 4

To request more information on this publication, contact:

Scholars International Publishing Corp.
2675 Georgetown Blvd.
Ann Arbor MI 48105
Phone: (734) 930-0813 or FAX:(734) 741-1927
Internet: WWW. Scholarsbook.com

Lin, SuChen Jonathon, and F.C. Tony Shiue
Mastercam Version 7
Includes index.
ISBN 1-886552-11-8

Mastercam 7

Preface

CAD/CAM technology has emerged as one of the major driving forces in our modern manufacturing industry. Due to the increased computer power and the advancement of CAD/CAM software, manual CNC programming has been replaced by CAD/CAM programming in recent years. Mastercam CNC programming software has become the leading PC-based CAM software due to its power and ease of use.

Mastercam software is widely used in industry and schools. It has become a leading tool for teaching CNC programming. Additionally, there is a need for a comprehensive text to teach students of all skill levels to effectively use Mastercam. This text is intended to be used to teach CAD/CAM/CNC with Mastercam software in schools and in industrial training classes. It is also a valuable reference for all levels of Mastercam users.

This text is written for Mastercam Version 7. It covers most of important features and functionalities in Mastercam Version 7. Three new chapters have been added in addition to many significant changes throughout the book to reflect the new features in Version 7. Readers should find this new text a valuable learning tool for mastering CNC programming with Mastercam software.

This book is suited for a two-semester course. It is appropriate for industrial technology, engineering technology, and engineering courses at many levels; universities and colleges, junior colleges, trade schools, high schools, as well as for courses offered by industry.

The following is a list of suggested topics to be covered in two semesters:

First semester:

Chapters 1 and 2: CNC programming and machining fundamentals
Chapters 3 through 10: 2-D toolpath programming
Chapter 19: Engraving artworks
Chapters 20 through 22: Lathe programming
Chapter 24: File conversion

Second semester:

Chapters 11 through 18: 3-D (surfaces) toolpath programming
Chapters 23: Mill-turn programming
Chapter 25: Post processor customization

Chapters 3, 5, 6, and 24 were written by Dr. Fuh-Cwo (Tony) Shiue.

Su-Chen Jonathon Lin

Mastercam 7

Acknowledgements

The author is indebted to many persons and organizations for their help and contributions in making this book into a reality. First, I wish to express my sincere appreciation to Iven May of CNC Software, Inc. He is the person who initiated the book idea and gave numerous suggestions toward making it possible. His three colleagues in the Educational Division of CNC Software, Dan Newby, Rick Meyers, and Mike Freimann, also provided a lot of assistance and especially helped by reviewing the manuscript. Mike has given a lot of suggestions in Operations Manager function.

Special thanks are due to Jack, Brian and Mark Summers who provided Mastercam software and helped tremendously in marketing the book to Mastercam users. Because they are so friendly and easy to work with, they make the project progress smoothly.

Thanks are extended to Scholars staff. Dr. Jacob Cheu, the project manager, prepared several hundred illustrations using AutoCAD and Mastercam. Without his great skill and care, the book would never have been finished. Joshua Chen, art and cover designer, created artworks and provided assistance to develop chapter 19. His work is very appreciated. I greatly appreciate the excellent work Ms. Karen Sterzik has contributed to this book in editing and using PageMaker to do the page layout design. This is the nineth book Karen has done for Scholars.

I am greatly indebted to my dear wife, Grace, for her patient and continuous support. Your great skill in running the business has made Mastercam books widely distributed. I am also grateful to my son, Andrew, and daughter, Carol, for their support. I will do my best to stay longer time at home to enjoy your youth years.

A credit needs to be given also to Delmar Publishers, Inc. for granting me their permission to use the following twelve figures and tables:

Figure 1.2 Direct numerical control
Figure 1.3 Distributive numerical control
Figure 2.6 Toolholder system for machining centers
Figure 2.11 Insert identification system
Figure 2.20 Drilling
Figure 2.21 Milling
Figure 2.22 Turning
Figure 2.9 Unit horsepower required for drilling AISI 1112 steels
Figure 2.10 Approximate conversion factor for unit horsepower required to drill other materials
Figure 2.11 Unit horsepower for milling
Figure 2.12 Unit horsepower for turning various materials
Figure 7.39 Pocket cutting direction

All the above illustrations are Reproduced by Permission.

COMPUTER NUMERICAL CONTROL: FROM PROGRAMMING TO NETWORKING

By Jonathon Lin, Delmar Publishers Inc., Albany, New York, Copyright 1994

Machine photographs are provided by the following companies:
Bridgeport Machines, Inc., Leadwell CNC Machines Mfg. Co., Mori Seiki Co., Ltd., Okuma Machinery, Inc.,and Peddinghaus Corp.

Mastercam 7

Table of Contents

Table of Contents

14 3D Toolpath I: Generated from Wireframe Models

15 3D Toolpaths II: Generated from Surface Models

16 Multiaxis Machining

17 3D Toolpath Editing

18 3D Toolpath Planning

19 Engraving Artworks

20 Creating Part Geometry for Lathes

Table of Contents

21 Job Setup and Tool Definition

22 Lathe Programming

23 Mill-Turn Toolpaths

24 File Conversion

25 Post Processor Customization

Chapter 1

CNC Programming Fundamentals

Objectives:

1. Understand the basic concepts required in CNC programming and operation.
2. Be aware of the career opportunities in NC related jobs.
3. Know NC programming words and commands.
4. Be familiar with CNC machines and their axes designation.
5. Know various reference zero points in CNC programming.

1.1 NC, CNC and DNC, What are they ?

Four terms are often used in describing the emerging technology dealt with in this book:

- numerical control (NC)
- computer numerical control (CNC),
- direct numerical control (DNC)
- distributive numerical control (DNC).

Numerical Control (NC)

Numerical control (NC) is a technique for controlling machine tools or processes by using coded command instructions. The NC controller interprets these instructions and then converts them into two types of control signals: **motion control signals** and **miscellaneous control signals** (Figure 1.1).

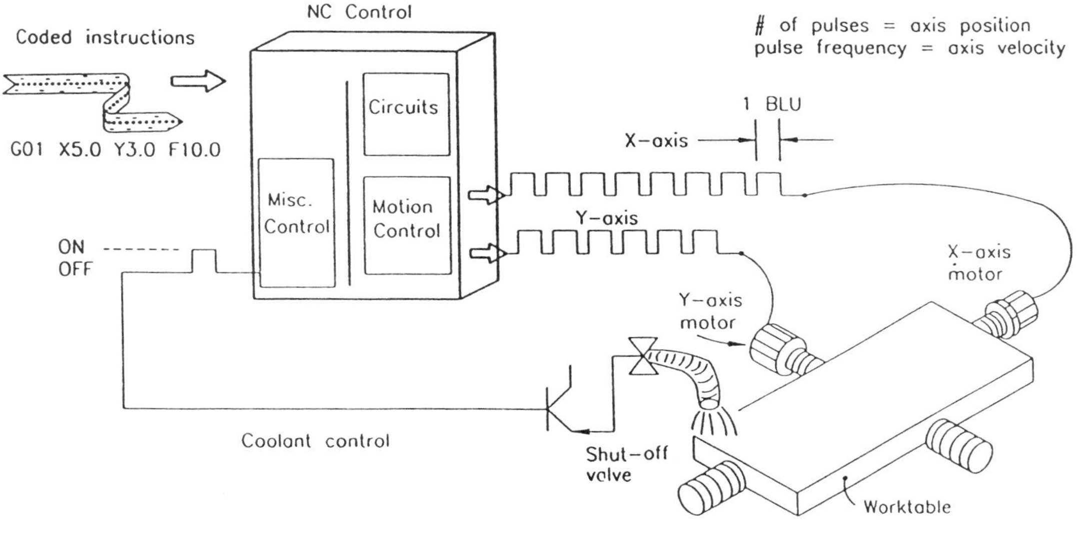

Figure 1.1 Numerical control

Motion control signals are a series of electric pulse trains that are used to control the position and the speed of the machine table and spindle. Each pulse activates a motion of one basic length-unit (BLU) which is the minimum increment size of the NC control system. The typical increment for one BLU in the old generation of NC controls is 0.001in. (or 0.01 mm), while in modern CNC controls, the increment resolution can reach 0.0001 in. (or 0.001 mm). The number of pulses transmitted to each axis determines the incremental axis position, and the frequency of these pulses regulates the axis speed.

Miscellaneous control functions are a set of on/off signals to implement the control of the speed and direction of the spindle rotation, control of coolant supply, selection of cutting tool, automatic clamping and unclamping, etc.

NC is often referred to as the older generation of numerical control technology. NC systems are hard-wired controls in which most functions are implemented by electronic hardware based upon digital circuit technology.

Computer Numerical Control (CNC)

Computer numerical control (CNC) is the numerical control system in which a dedicated, stored program computer is built into the control to perform basic and advanced NC functions. CNC controls are also referred to as soft-wired NC systems because most of their control functions are implemented by the *control software programs.* All numerical control machines manufactured since the seventies are of CNC type. The control signals in CNC systems are in the form of binary words. Each word contains a fixed number of bits, 32 bits or 64 bits are commonly used. Each bit of data produces one BLU motion in the controlled axis. Theoretically a 32-bit word could represent one of up to 2^{32} = 4,294,967,296 different axial positions. If the system resolution is, for example, BLU = 0.0001 in., this number can represent up to 429,969 in. possible motions, which is more than enough for all types of applications.

Direct Numerical Control (DNC)

Direct numerical control uses a shared computer to simultaneously control the operation of a group of NC machine tools (Figure 1.2). The main tasks performed by the computer are to program and edit part programs as well as download part programs to NC machines. The idea of direct numerical control began in the mid-1960s in Cincinnati Milacron and General Electric. In 1970 about a half-dozen vendors marketed their DNC systems.

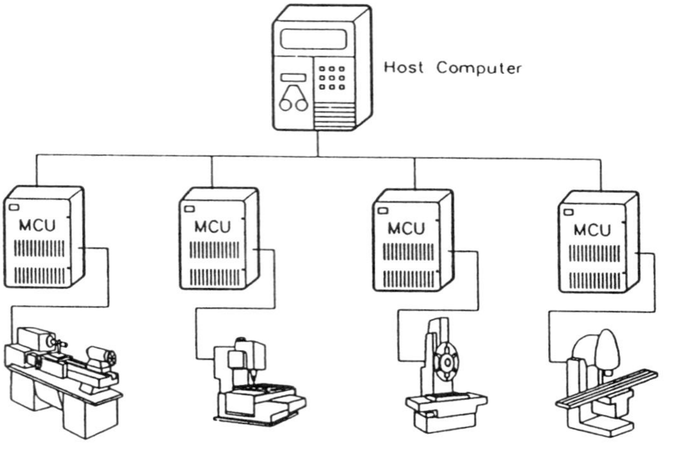

Figure 1.2 Direct numerical control (Source: S. C. Jonathon Lin, Computer Numerical Control: From Programming to Networking, 1994.Courtesy of Delmar Publishers, Inc.)

Direct numerical control was not widely used in industry mainly due to two reasons. The industry could not afford the expensive mainframe computers which could cost as much as a million dollars each. The other reason was the introduction of CNC in 1970s. The capacity of stored memory and enhanced intelligence of the built-in low cost dedicated computer replaced the desirable features of the DNC systems.

Distributive Numerical Control (DNC)

The main concept of distributive numerical control is to use a network of computers to coordinate the operation of a group of CNC machine tools (Figure 1.3). This new form of DNC systems began to evolve in the early 1980s and grew with the development of computer and communication technologies. Today many CNC machines, together with robots, programmable logic controllers and other computer-based controllers, have been integrated into DNC systems to make automated manufacturing systems possible.

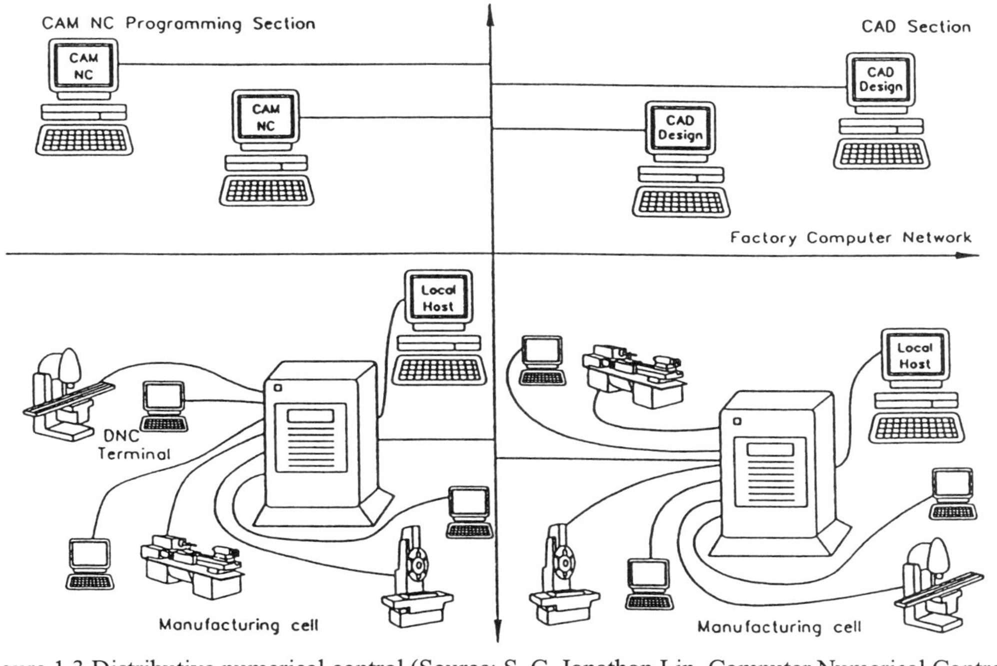

Figure 1.3 Distributive numerical control (Source: S. C. Jonathon Lin, Computer Numerical Control: From Programming to Networking, Courtesy of Delmar Publishers, Inc.)

1.2 Advantages and Limitations of CNC

The main advantages of using CNC technology are to **reduce product cost, improve product quality, and facilitate production planning and control**. These benefits can be realized through these **nine** causes:

- Increased productivity
- Reduced production costs
- Facilitation of complex machining operations
- Improved production planning and control
- Facilitation of flexible automation
- High accuracy and repeatability
- Reduced indirect operating costs
- Greater flexibility
- Lower operator skill requirement

Three main drawbacks of using CNC technology include **high initial investment, high maintenance requirement, and not cost-effective for low productions runs**.

1.3 CNC Operations

The orgnizational structure for implementing computer numerical control operations varies throughout the industry. The larger the operation, the greater the need for organization. The functions found within a CNC group are the same no matter how large the group is; the only difference is how those functions are delegated. A small shop might have only one or two people performing all of the NC department functions, while a medium to large operation will divide the NC functions into groups or even assign them to departments (Figure 1.4):

- NC shop management
- NC part programming
- Tool and fixture design
- Machine maintenance
- NC machine operation

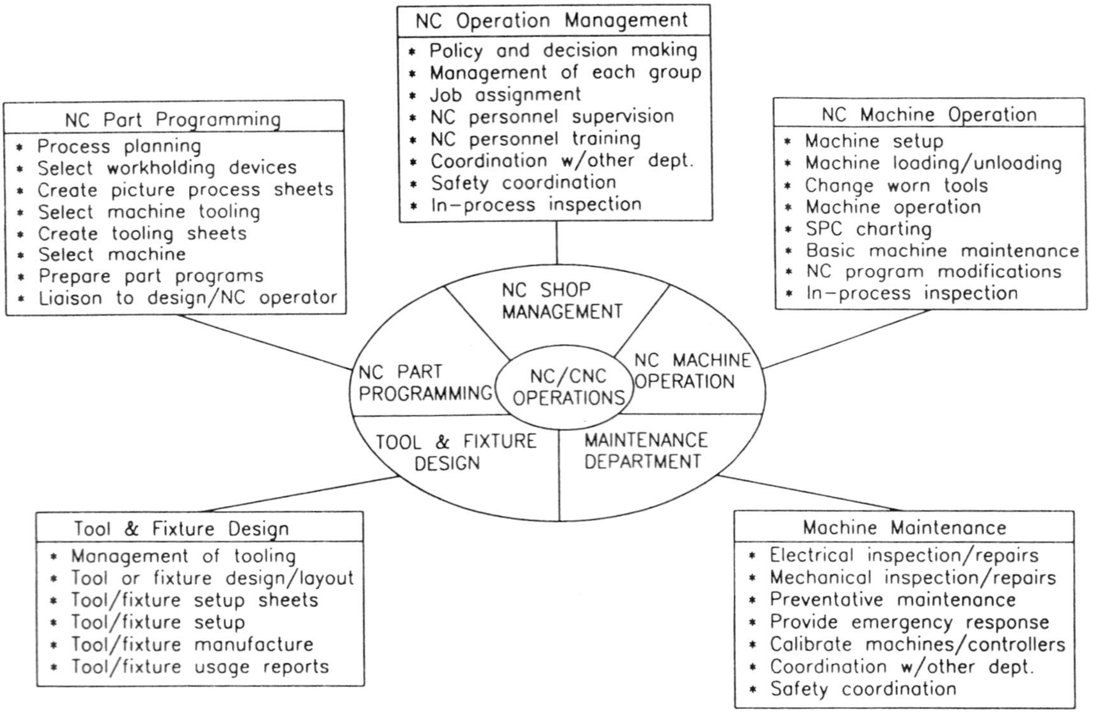

Figure 1.4 NC/CNC operations

1.4 Career Opportunities

There are about three hundred thousand NC related jobs available to service 170,000 NC/CNC machine tools in the U.S. industry today. The demand for NC related personnel has increased in a very steady pace as industry moves further into automated manufacturing. The job titles associated with NC personnel may appear as NC manager or supervisor, process planner, part programmer, tool designer, tool maker, machine setup person, machine operator, or maintenance person. The major responsibilities, required job skills, as well as education and experience of each job title are summarized in Table 1.1.

Table 1.1 CNC Career Opportunities

Job Title	Responsibility	Required Job Skills	Education/Experience
NC manager or supervisor	• Oversee NC operations • NC personnel hiring, training and job assignment • Coordination with other departments • Evaluate and acquire new CNC machine tools and CAD/CAM software	— Management skills — Machining knowledge — NC programming and operation background	4-year college degree with several years of manufacturing experience
Process planner	• Determine what machining processes to be used, with what sequence, and in what machines • Select cutting tools and workholders and fixtures • Prepare operation sheets and tooling sheets	— Overall knowledge of machining, tooling, and capability of available equipment — Good background in manufacturing and CNC	At least 2-year college degree, 4-year college degree preferred
Part programmer	• Prepare part programs • Prepare NC documents concerning setup instructions • Prepare process plan if needed	— Good command at math, geometry and trigonometry — Sound knowledge of machining — Blue-print reading — Computer skills — Use of CAD/CAM software	2-year college degree or vocational technical school
Tool designer	• Select standard tooling • Design special-purpose tooling	— Good command at locating and clamping knowledge — Knowledge of tool making — Understanding of standard tooling and fixturing	At least 2-year college degree with tool and machine experience 4-year college degree preferred
Tool maker	• Assemble and preset standard tooling • Make special-purpose tooling • Repair damaged tooling items	— Highly skilled in machining — Knowledge in CNC — Print reading and making	4-year apprenticeship program
Machine setup person	• Set up fixture and cutting tools on the machine • Coordinate the machine • Determine and enter offset and compensation values • Correct errors in tooling and program • Tryout run the program	— Good knowledge in machining and tooling — Understanding of part program and machine functions	Machinist experience with extensive CNC knowledge
Machine operator	• Load and unload workpieces • Monitor machining in progress • Finished part inspection • SPC charting • Regular check-up	— General knowledge of machining	Technical programs in vocational technical school, area occupational school, community college

1.5 CNC System Elements

A typical CNC system consists of the following **six** elements shown in Figure 1.5:

- •Part program
- •Program input device
- •Machine control unit
- •Drive system
- •Machine tool
- •Feedback system

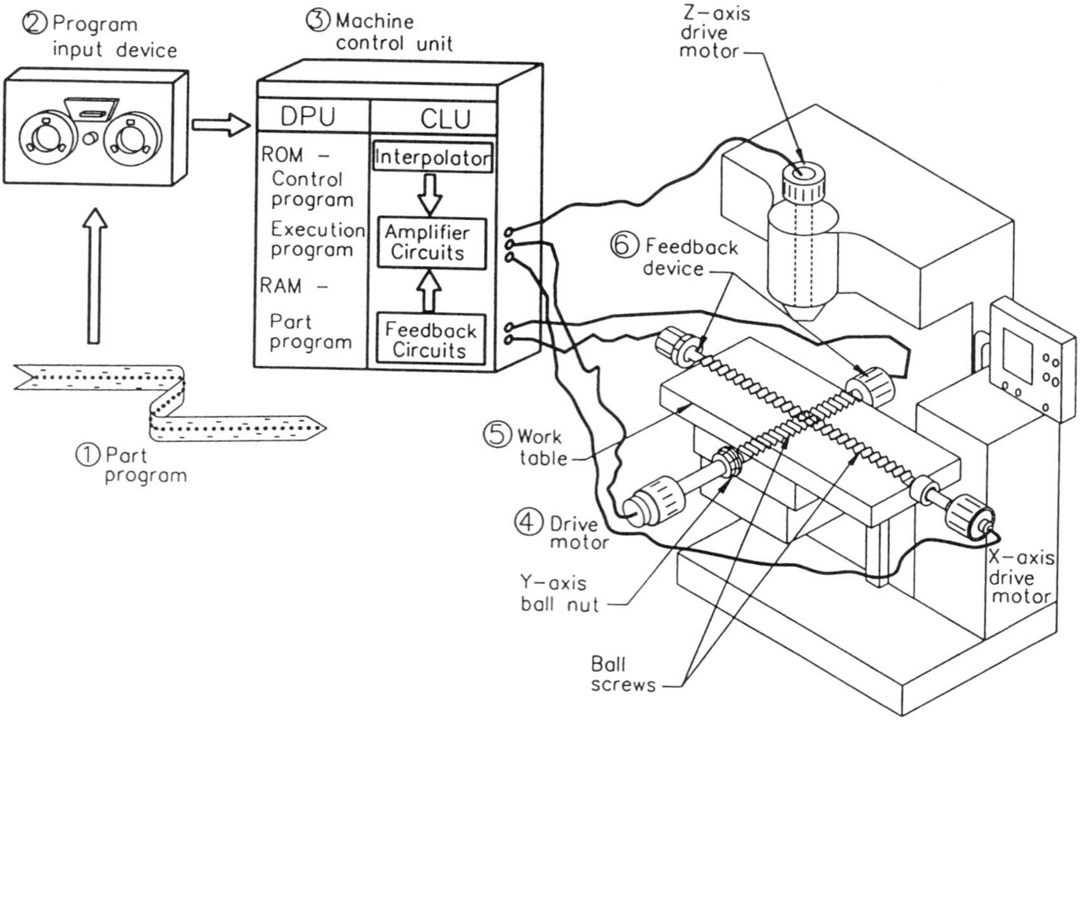

Figure 1.5 CNC system elements

Part Program

A part program is a series of coded instructions required to produce a part. It controls the movement of the machine tool and the on/off control of auxiliary functions such as spindle rotation and coolant. The coded instructions are composed of letters, numbers and symbols and are arranged in a format of functional blocks as in the following example.

N10 G01 X5.0 Y2.5 F15.0

- F15.0 — Feed rate (15 in/min)
- Y2.5 — Y-coordinate (2.5")
- X5.0 — X-coordinate (5.0")
- G01 — Linear interpolation mode
- N10 — Sequence number

Program Input Device

The program input device is the mechanism for part programs to be entered into the CNC control. **Three** commonly used program input devices are **punch tape reader, magnetic tape reader, and computer via RS-232-C communication.**

Machine Control Unit

The machine control unit (MCU) is the heart of a CNC system. It is used to perform the following functions:

- Read coded instructions
- Decode coded instructions
- Implement interpolations (linear, circular, and helical) to generate axis motion commands
- Feed axis motion commands to the amplifier circuits for driving the axis mechanisms
- Receive the feedback signals of position and speed for each drive axis
- Implement auxiliary control functions such as coolant or spindle on/off, and tool change

Drive System

A drive system consists of **amplifier circuits, drive motors, and ball lead-screws**. The MCU feeds control signals (position and speed) of each axis to the amplifier circuits. The control signals are augmented to actuate drive motors which in turn rotate the ball lead-screws to position the machine table.

Machine Tool

CNC controls are used to control various types of machine tools. Regardless of which type of machine tool is controlled, it always has a **slide table and a spindle to control of position and speed.** The machine table is controlled in the X and Y axes, while the spindle runs along the Z axis.

Feedback System

The feedback system is also referred to as the *measuring system*. It uses position and speed transducers to continuously monitor the position at which the cutting tool is located at any particular time. The MCU uses the difference between reference signals and feedback signals to generate the control signals for correcting position and speed errors.

1.6 CNC Applications and Machines

CNC technology has been successfully applied to almost every aspect of the manufacturing industry. Their applications are often classified in these five categories:

- Chip removal (metal cutting)
- Grinding
- Unconventional machining
- Fabrication
- Special-purpose applications

The machines controlled by CNC can be classified into the following **eight** categories:

- CNC mills and machining centers
- CNC lathes and turning centers
- CNC EDMs
- CNC grinding machines
- CNC cutting machines (laser, plasma, electron, or flame)
- CNC fabrication machines (sheet metal punch press, bending machine, or press brake)
- CNC welding machines
- CNC coordinate measuring machines

Figures 1.6 to 1.14 show some typical CNC controlled machine tools used in industry.

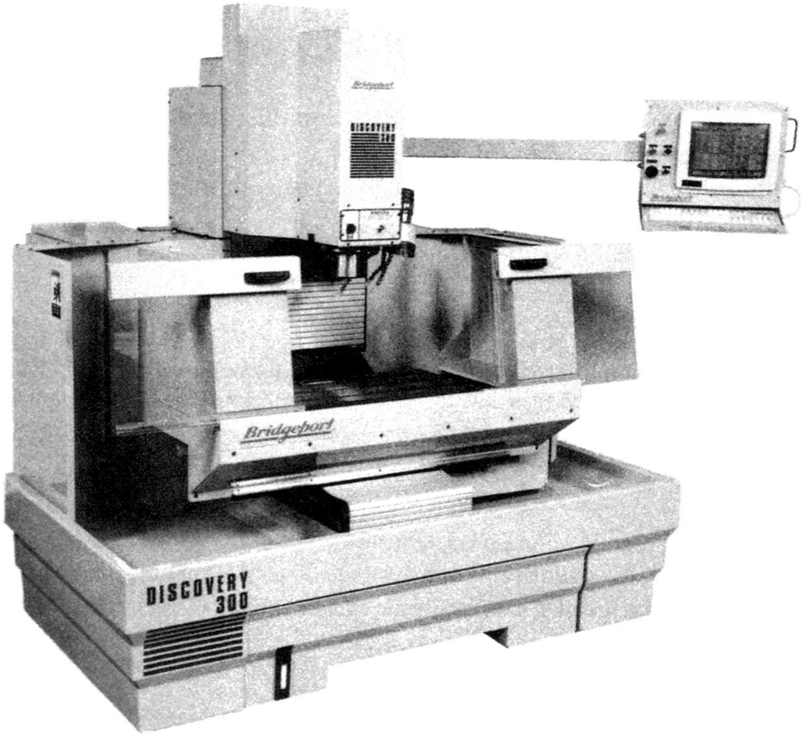

Figure 1.6 CNC milling machine (Courtesy of Bridgeport Machines, Inc.)

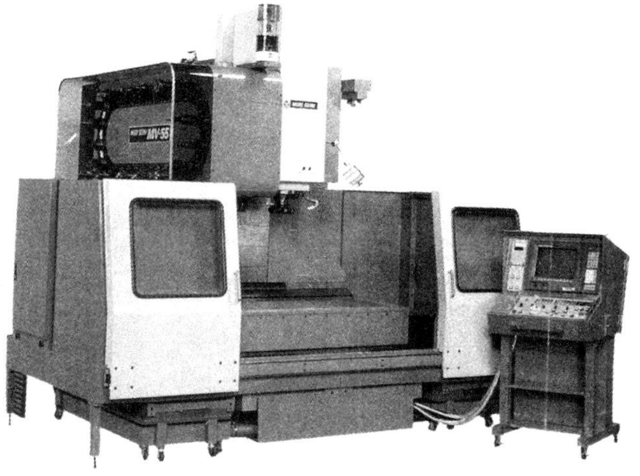

Figure 1.7 CNC Vertical machining center (Courtesy of Mori Seiki Co., LTD.)

Figure 1.8 CNC Horizontal machining center (Courtesy of Mori Seiki Co.,LTD.)

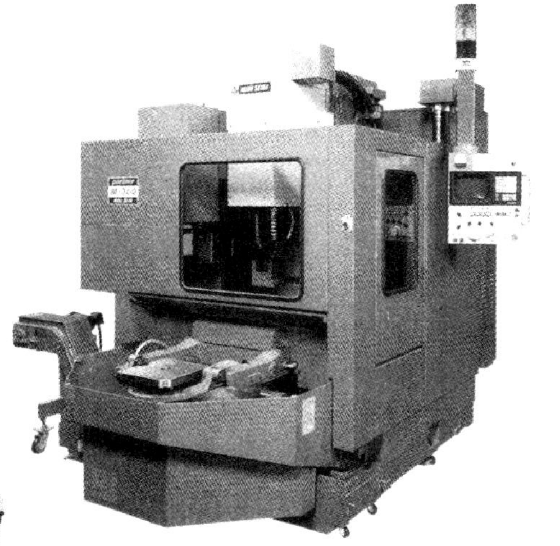

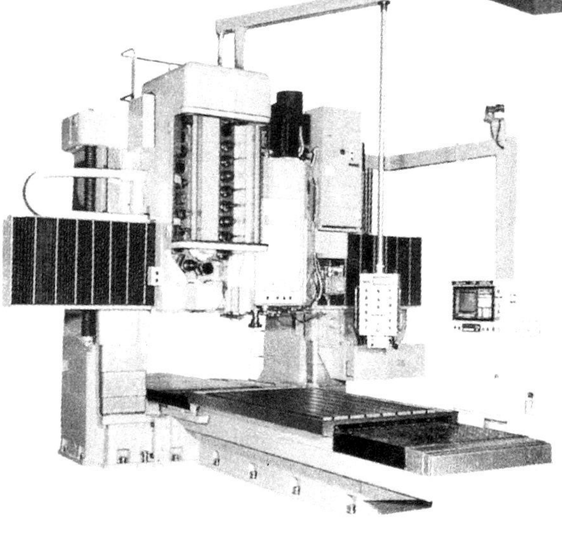

Figure 1.9 Double-column machining center (Courtesy of Okuma Machinery, Inc.)

Figure 1.10 CNC Turning center (Courtesy of Leadwell CNC Machines Mfg. Corp.)

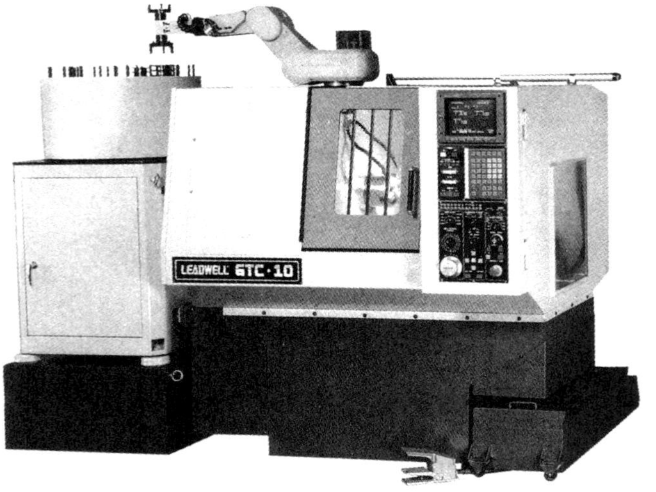

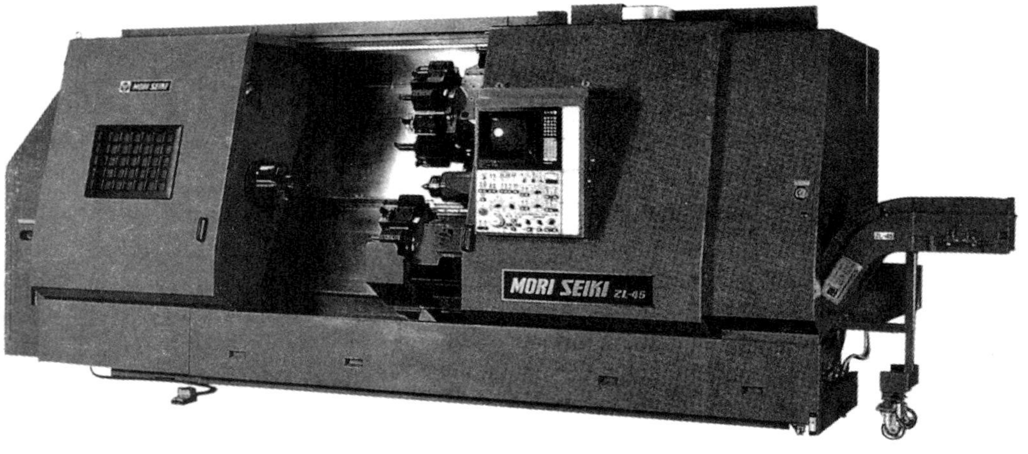

Figure 1.11 CNC Dual turret turning center (Courtesy of Mori Seiki Co., LTD.)

Figure 1.12 Heavy-duty CNC lathe (Courtesy of Mori Seiki Co., LTD.)

Figure 1.13 CNC Measuring machine (Courtesy of Okuma Machinery, Inc.)

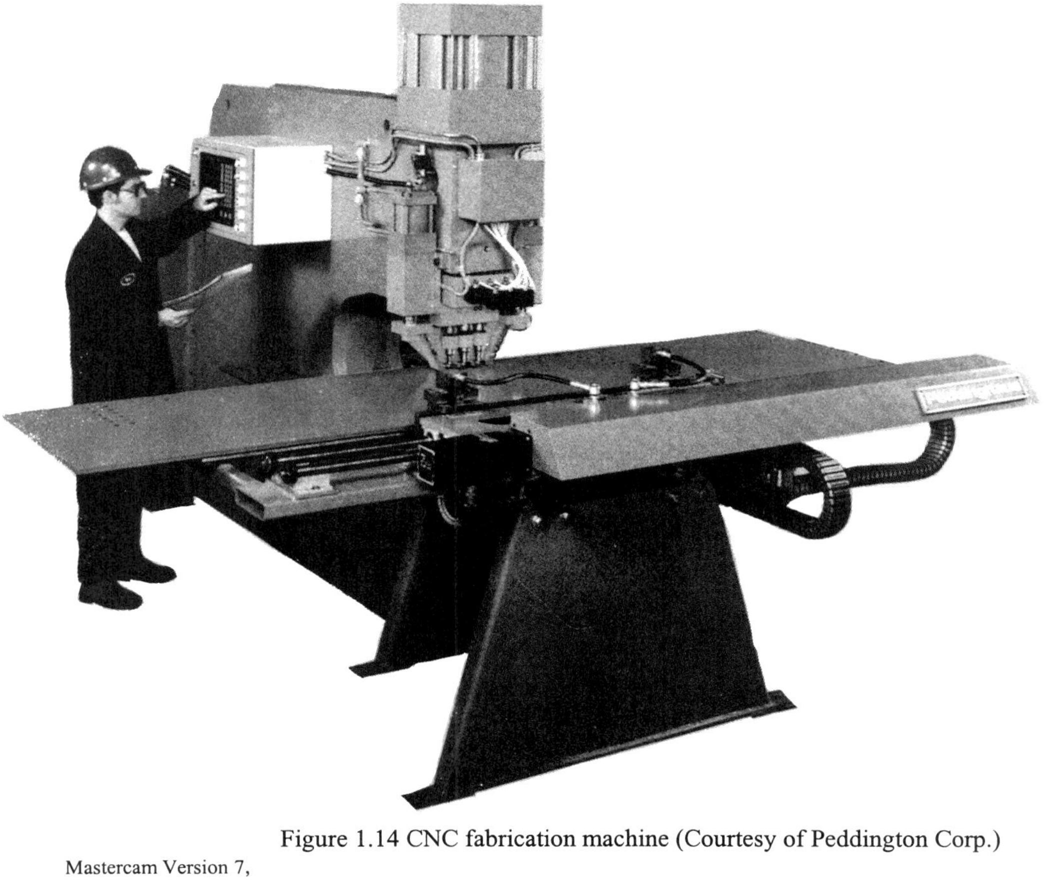

Figure 1.14 CNC fabrication machine (Courtesy of Peddington Corp.)

1.7 NC Coding Systems

There are **two** coding systems used in NC/CNC controls: **EIA and ASCII standards.** The EIA coding system is established by the EIA standard 244-B. This code was widely adopted in North America before the ASCII code was established. The hole pattern assignment of EIA codes is given in the **left column** of the Figure 1.15.

ASCII is an acronym for the American Standard Code for Information Interchange. It refers to the code used to represent common keyboard characters. The ASCII NC code for punched tape was established by the RS-358-B standard. It is also referred to as the ISO code. The hole pattern of ASCII codes is given in the **right column** of Figure 1.15.

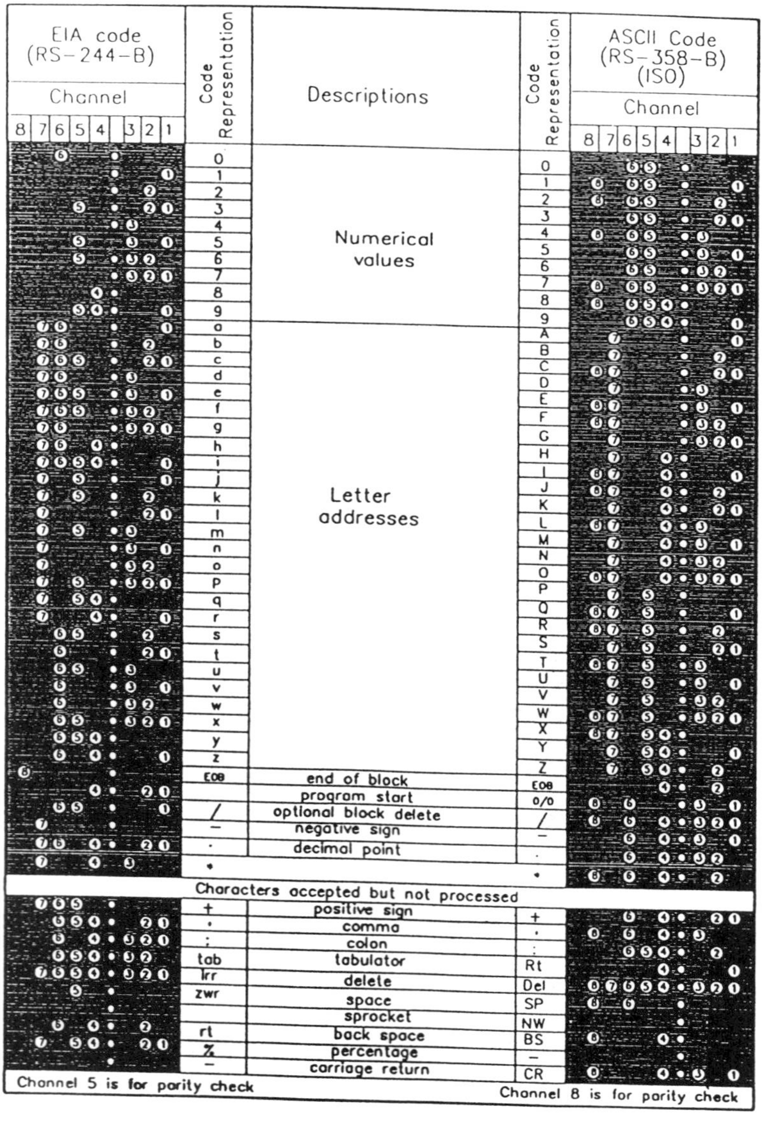

Figure 1.15 EIA and ASCII NC Coding systems

1.8 NC Addresses

An address is the letter at the beginning of each word which defines the meaning or purpose of the numerical data. The addresses used in NC programming have been specified by ANSI's EIA RS-274-B standard. Most of the letters are assigned to a unique function, but some have two functions. The NC addresses can be classified into the seven groups according to their functionality; refer to Table 1.2.

Table 1.2 NC Addresses

Address Type	Description	Illustration
1. Dimension		
a. Primary linear dimensions		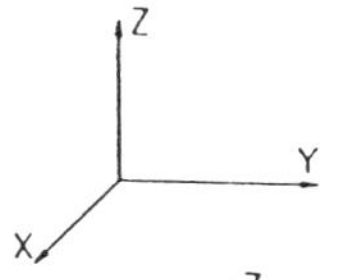
X	Primary X motion dimension	
Y	Primary Y motion dimension	
Z	Primary Z motion dimension	
b. Secondary linear dimensions		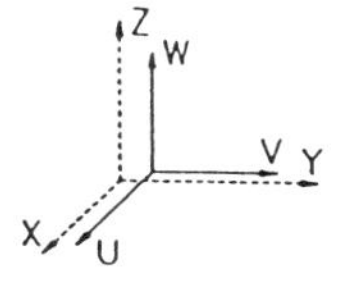
U	Secondary dimension parallel to X axis	
V	Secondary dimension parallel to Y axis	
W	Secondary dimension parallel to Z axis	
c. Tertiary linear dimensions		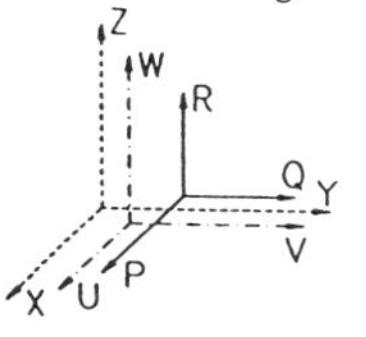
P	Third dimension parallel to X axis	
Q	Third dimension parallel to Y axis	
R	Third dimension parallel to Z axis	
d. Primary rotary dimensions		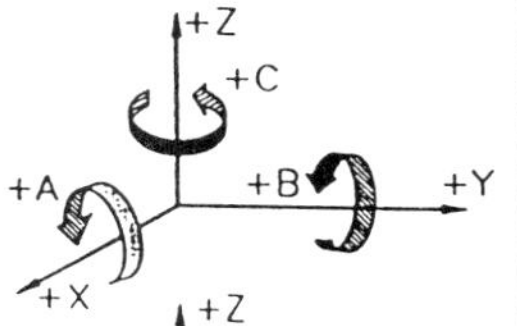
A	Angular dimension around X axis	
B	Angular dimension around Y axis	
C	Angular dimension around Z axis	
e. Special rotary dimensions		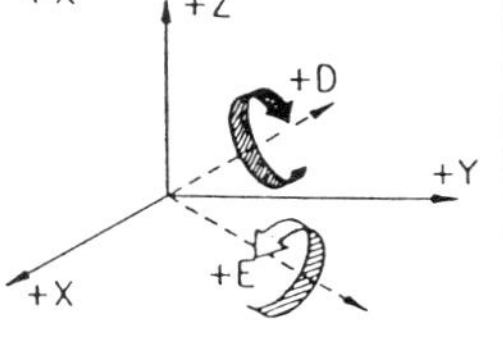
D	Angular dimension around a special axis or line	
E	Angular dimension around a special axis or line	
2. Arc center		
I	X dimension for circular arc center	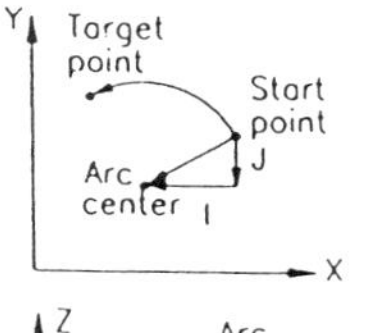
J	Y dimension for circular arc center	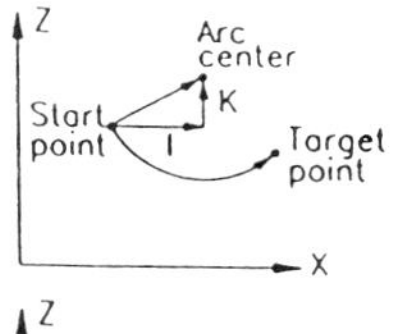
K	Z dimension for circular arc center	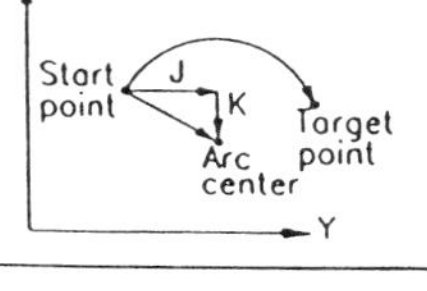

Table 1.2 (Continued)

Address Type		Description	Illustration
3. Feed			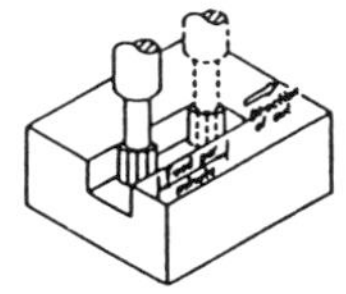
	F	Primary feed function (applied to the main slide table)	
	E	Secondary feed function (applied to the second slide table)	
	D	Third feed function (applied to the third slide table)	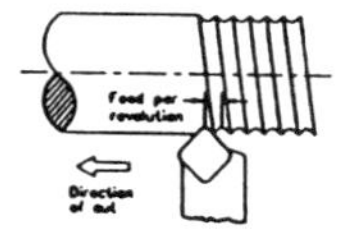
4. Thread pitches			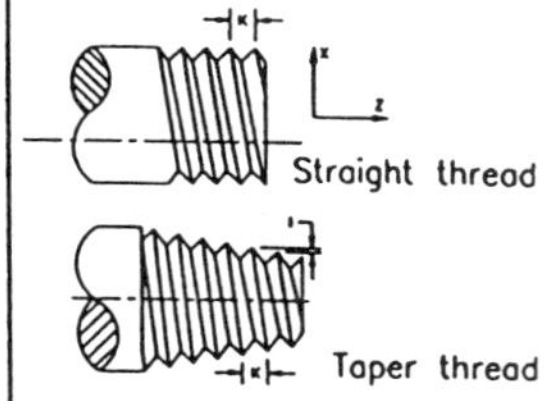
	I	Thread pitch in the X axis	
	J	Thread pitch in the Y axis	
	K	Thread pitch in the Z axis	
5. Preparatory functions	GXX		A preparatory function is defined by the address G followed by two digits to specify the control mode of the operation. (see Tables 1.4 and 1.5 for detail)
a. Motion commands		G00, G01, G02, and G03	
b. Plane selection commands		G17, G18, and G19	
c. Cutter compensation commands		G40, G41, and G42	
d. Tool length offset commands		G43–G49	
e. Fixed cycle commands		G80–G89	
f. Unit selection commands		G20 (or G70) and G21 (or G71)	
g. Positioning system commands		G90 and G91	
h. Coordinate system setting commands		G92, G54–G59	
6. Miscellaneous function	MXX		A miscellaneous function is defined by the address M followed by two digits to specify the type of machine control. (see Table 1.6 for detail)
a. Program stop		M00 and M01	
b. End of program		M02 and M30	
c. Spindle rotation		M03, M04, and M05	
d. Tool change		M06	
e. Coolant control		M07; M08, and M09	
7. Other functions			
	N	Sequence number of program block	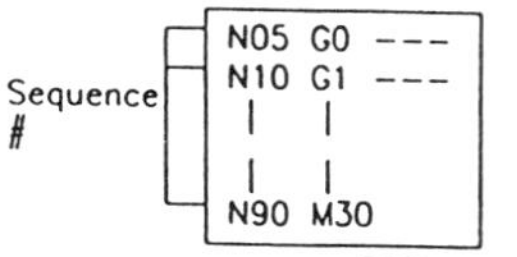
	S	Spindle speed function	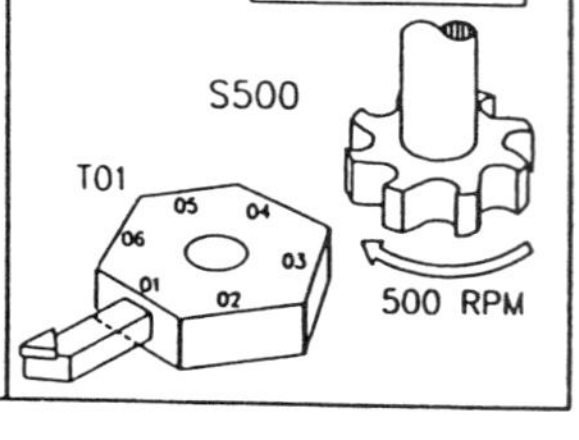
	T	Tool function	

1.9 NC Words

NC part programs are coded instructions that are organized into functional blocks. Each **block** consists of one or more NC words. An **NC word** is a collection of characters that begins with an address followed by numbers. A **character** is one byte (8 bits) of information representing a number, letter, or symbol. The sequence and arrangement of NC words in part programs must follow a certain pattern that is called the **tape format** or program format.

An NC word is the collection of characters arranged in a certain order to cause a special action by an NC machine. NC words always begin with a letter address followed by a numerical value. Table 1.3 lists seven groups of NC words.

Table 1.3 NC words

NC Words	Description	Typical Examples
1. Dimension words	Specify coordinates of a tool path.	X10.5 Y4.5 Z-1.0
2. Arc center words	Indicate coordinates of an arc center.	I3.0 J1.5 or R3.5
3. Feed words	Specify the feed rate of machining.	F15.0
4. Preparatory words	Specify command modes, the information of the block to be executed.	G90 G1 G2 G43
5. Miscellaneous words	Indicate control modes such as program stop, spindle rotation, tool change, coolant control, end of program, etc.	M0 M3 M6 M7M30
6. Spindle words	Specify spindle rotation speed in RPM	S3000
7. Tool words	Indicate the tool number to be selected	T5

Preparatory Words

The term "preparatory" in NC means that it "prepares" the control system to be ready for implementing the information that follows in the next block of instructions. A **preparatory function** is designated in a program by the word address G followed by two digits. Preparatory functions are also called **G-codes** and they specify the control mode of the operation. On the next page, Table 1.4 illustrates **eight groups** of commonly used G-codes in CNC milling machines. Following that, Table 1.5 lists the G-codes for CNC turning machines.

Table 1.4 G-Codes for Milling

Command Group	G-code	Function and Command statement	Illustration
Tool motion	G00	Rapid traverse G00 Xx Yy Zz	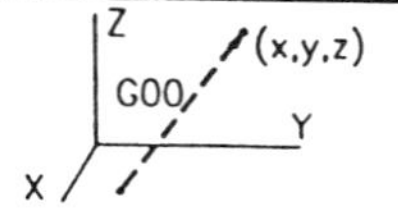
	G01	Linear interpolation G01 Xx Yy Zz Ff	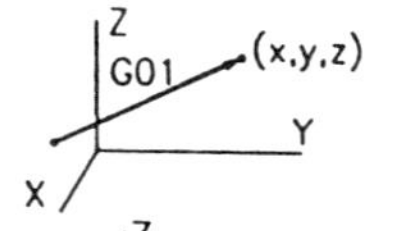
	G02	Circular interpolation in clockwise direction G02 Xx Yy Ii Jj G02 Xx Zz Ii Kk G02 Yy Zz Jj Kk	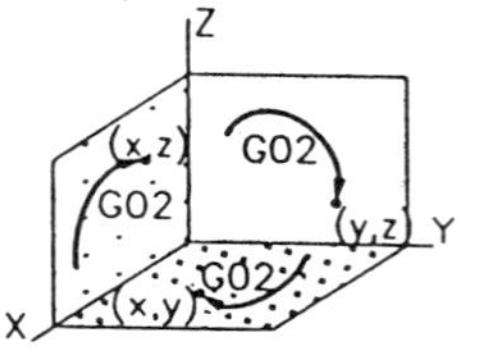
	G03	Circular interpolation in counter-clockwise direction G03 Xx Yy Ii Jj G03 Xx Zz Ii Kk G03 Yy Zz Jj Kk	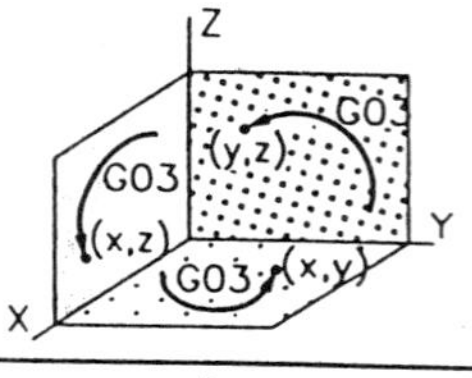
Plan selection	G17	XY-plane selection	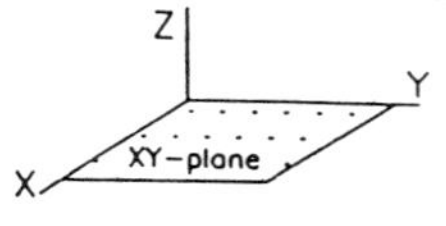
	G18	ZX-plane selection	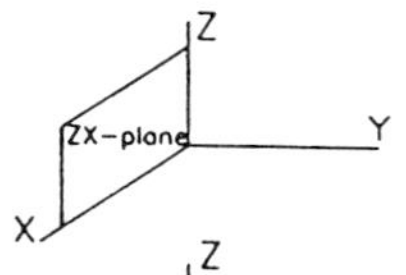
	G19	YZ-plane selection	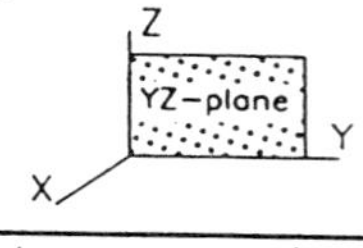
Unit selection	G20 or G70	Inch unit selection G20 or G70	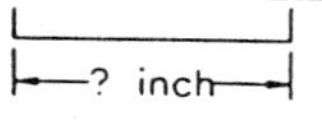
	G21 or G71	Metric unit selection G21 or G71	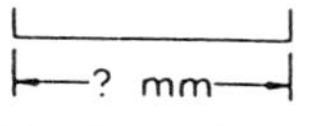
Offset and compensation	G40	Cutter diameter compensation cancel G40 G0 (or G1) Xx Yy	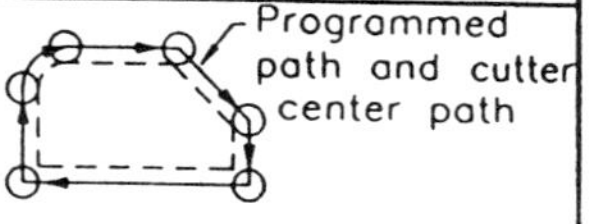
	G41	Cutter diameter compensation left G41 G0 (or G1) Xx Yy Dd	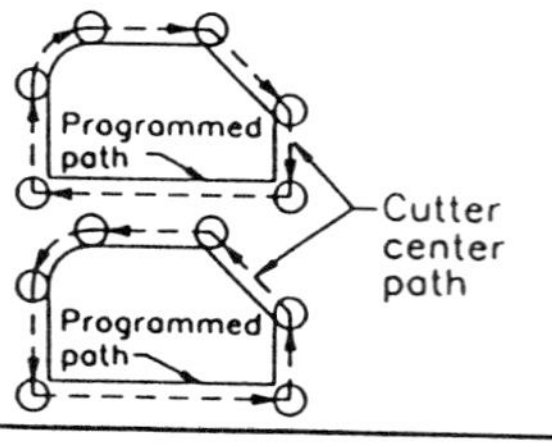
	G42	Cutter diameter compensation right G42 G0 (or G1) Xx Yy Dd	

Mastercam Version 7,
Scholar's International Publishing Corp., 1998

Table 1.4 (Continued)

Command Group	G-code	Function and Command statement	Illustration
	G43	Tool length offset G43 Hh	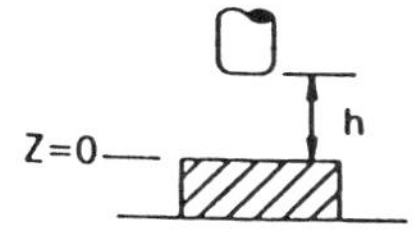
Positioning system	G90	Absolute positioning system G90 Xx Yy Zz	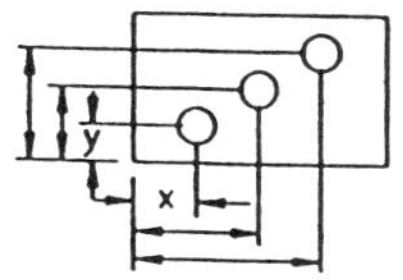
	G91	Incremental positioning system G91 Xx Yy Zz	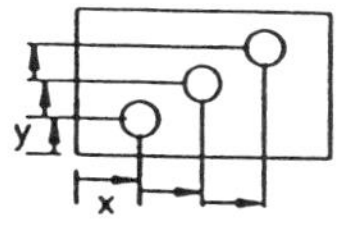
Feed unit selection	G94	Feed per minute system G94 Ff	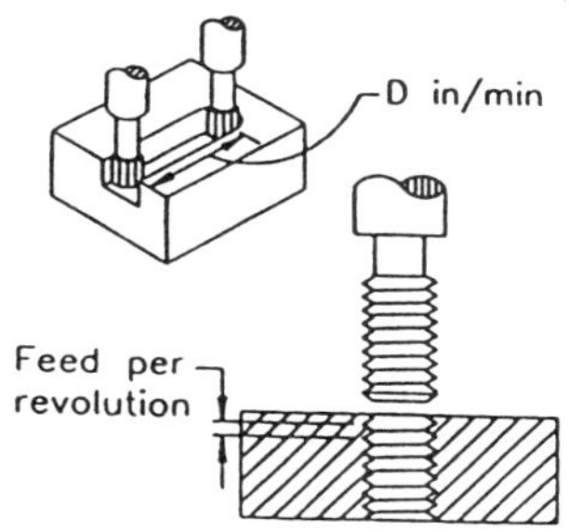
	G95	Feed per revolution system G95 Ff	
Work Coordinate Definition	G92	Absolute zero setting G92 Xx Yy Zz	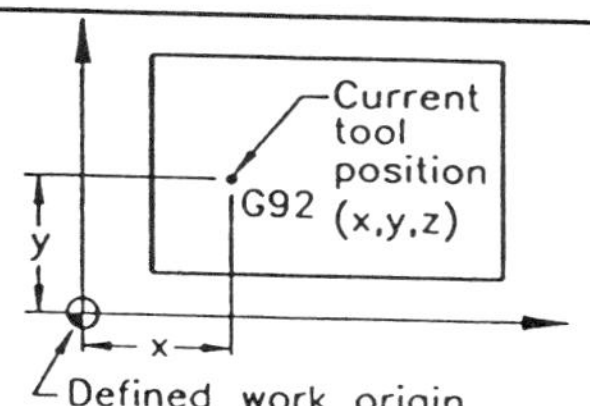
	G54 – G59	Work Coordinate setting G54 Xx Yy Zz	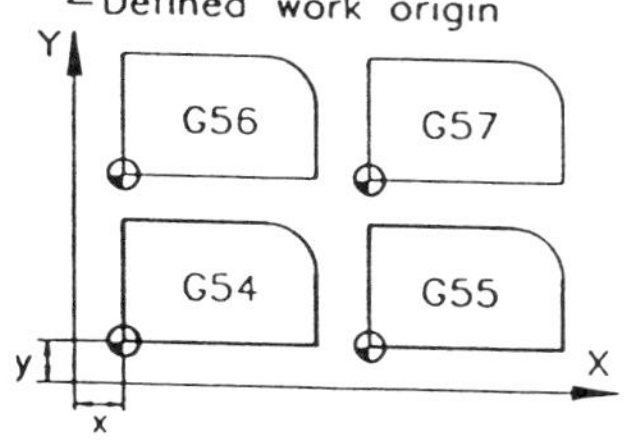
Fixed cycles selection	G80 –	Fixed cycle cancel	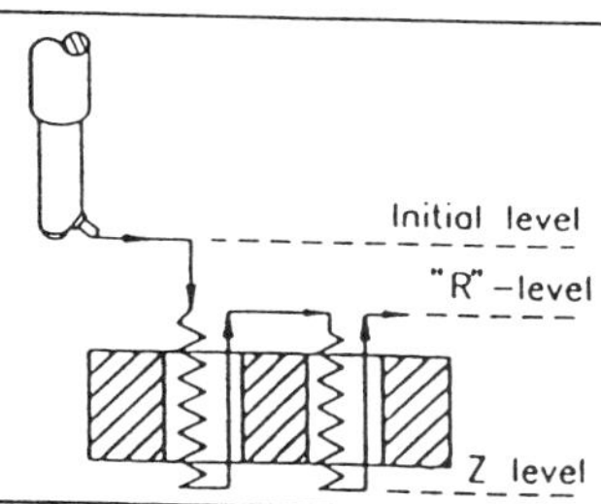
	G81 – G89	Fixed cycle G99/G98 G8_ Xx Yy Zz Rr Ff Qq Pp	

Table 1.5 G-Codes for Turning

Command Group	G-code	Function and Command Statement	Illustration
1. Tool motion	G00	Rapid traverse G00 Xx Zz	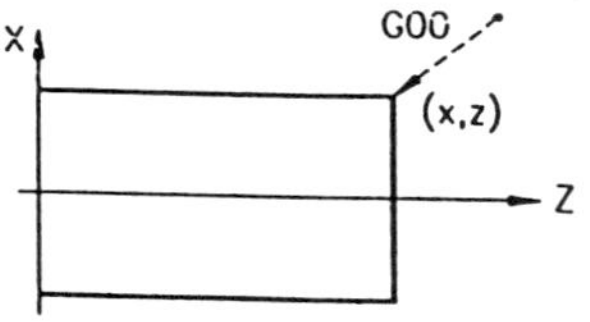
	G01	Linear interpolation G01 Xx Zz	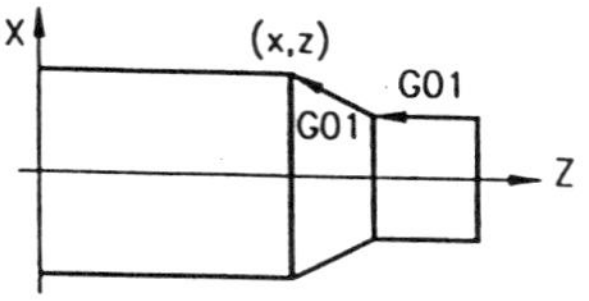
	G02	Circular interpolation in clockwise direction a. IJK method G02 Xx Zz Ii Kk b. R–method G02 Xx Zz Rr	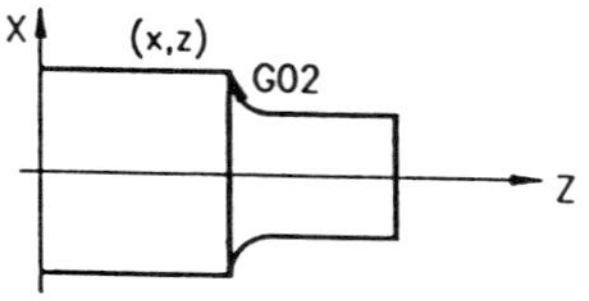
	G03	Circular interpolation in counter–clockwise direction a. IJK method G03 Xx Zz Ii Kk b. R–method G03 Xx Zz Rr	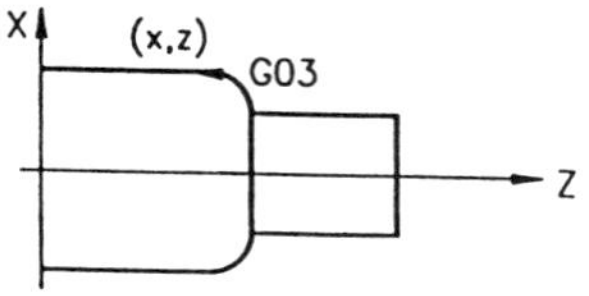
2. Work coordinate definition	G50 or G92 in some controls	(Work zero setting) G50 Xx Zz	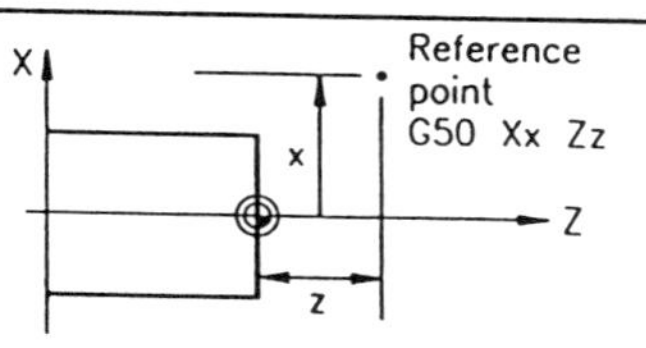
3. Spindle speed control	G50 G96 G97	Maximum spindle speed G50 Ss in RPM Constant surface speed setting G96 Ss in FPM Fixed spindle speed G97 Ss in RPM	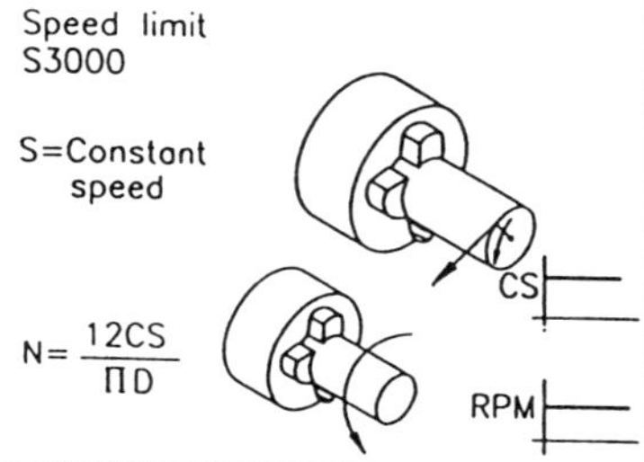
4. Unit selection	G20/G70 G21/G71	Inch unit selection Metric unit selection	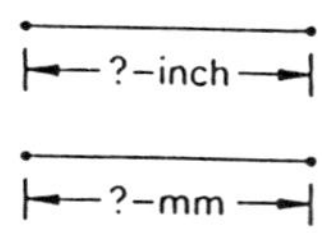

Table 1.5 (Continued)

Command Group	G-code	Function and Command Statement	Illustration
5. Feed Unit Selection	G98	Feed per minute	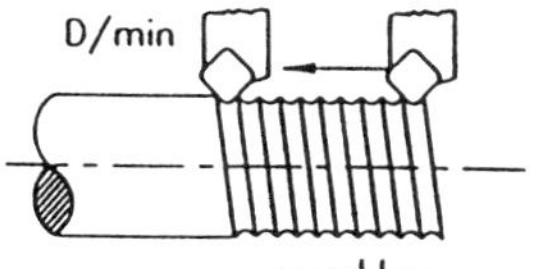
	G99	Feed per revolution	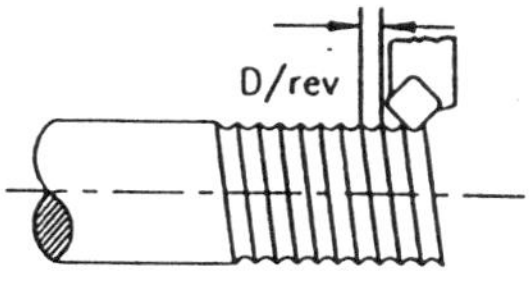
6. Tool nose radius compen-sation	G40	Tool nose radius compensation cancel G40 G0/G1 Xx Zz	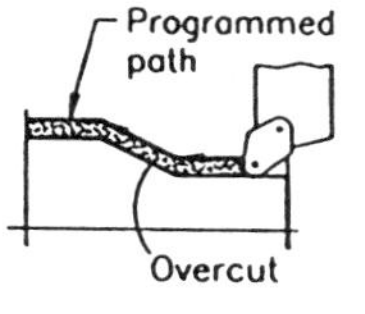
	G41	Tool nose radius compensation left G41 G0/G1 Xx Zz Txxxx	
	G42	Tool nose radius compensation right G42 G0/G1 Xx Zz Txxxx	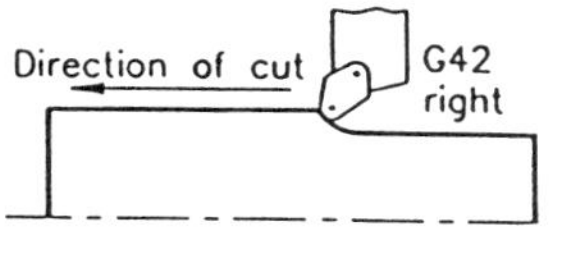
7. Fixed cycles A. Single cycles	G90 G94	Generate one pass of four toolpath moves	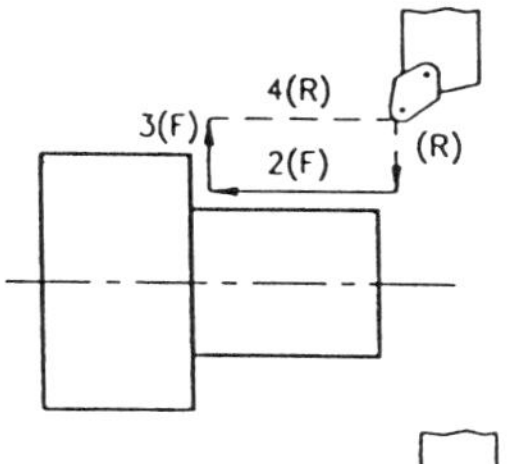
B. Multiple-pass cycles	G71 G72	Generate multiple passes of four toolpath moves	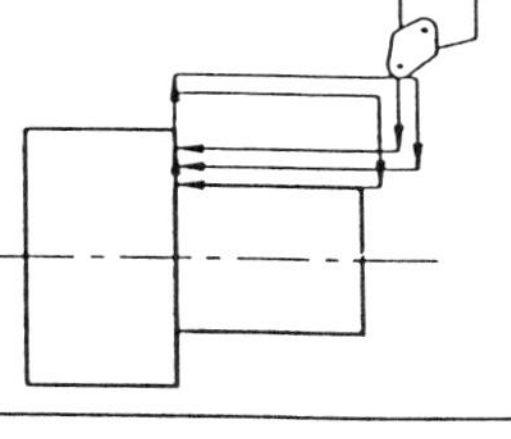

Miscellaneous Words

Miscellaneous functions use the address letter M followed by two digits. They perform a group of instructions such as coolant on/off, spindle on/off, tool change, program stop, or program end. They are often referred to as machine functions or **M-functions**. Table 1.6 illustrates common M-functions used in both milling and turning machines.

Table 1.6 Miscellaneous Functions

Function Group	M-function	Function and Command statement	Illustration
Program Stop	M00	Program stop	Stop M00
	M01	Optional stop	Opt Stop M01
Spindle Control	M03	Spindle on (rotation in clockwise direction)	 CW M03
	M04	Spindle on (rotation in counter-clockwise direction)	 CCW M04
	M05	Spindle off	 M05
Tool Change	M06	Too change to the specified tool number T__ M06	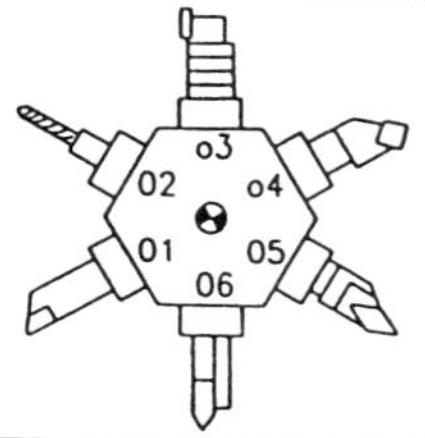
Coolant Control	M07	Coolant on (midst)	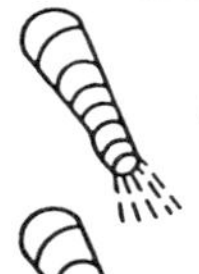 M07
	M08	Coolant on (flood)	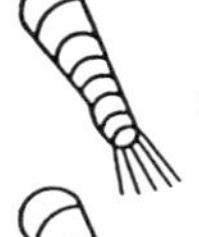 M08
	M09	Coolant off	 M09
End of Program	M02	End of program and tape rewind	Oxxx N1 ... N2 ... N3 ... N4 ... ... M30 — or M02
	M30	End of program and memory return	

1.10 NC Functional Blocks

NC controls simultaneously execute **all NC words contained in a block**. Therefore, NC blocks are normally organized according to their tasks. Table 1.7 gives some common functional blocks used in part programming.

Table 1.7 CNC functional blocks

Functional Block	Explanation	Typical Examples
1. Safety feature	Set the control to proper operating modes at the beginning of a part program. This block is also used after a tool change.	G90 G80 G40 G17
2. Coordinate system setting	Define the work zero point.	G92 Xx Yy Zz G54
3. Tool length offset	Offset the difference between the programmed tool length and the acutal tool length.	G43 Hh
4. Tool motion	Generate tool paths to machine the workpiece.	G0 Xx Yy Zz G1 Xx Yy Zz G2/G3 Xx Yy Zz
5. Cutter diameter compensation	Offset the cutter in a specified direction by a given amount of distance.	G41/G42 Xx Yy Hh/Dd G40 Xx Yy
6. Fixed cycle	Generate a series of tool paths to perform hole operations.	G8_ Xx Yy Zz Rr Ff
7. Tool change	Select a tool and cause a tool change.	Tt M6
8. Spindle control	Command spindle rotation speed and direction.	Ss M3/M4 M5
9. Reference point return	Return the tool to the machine home position.	G91 G28 Z0 G91 G28 X0 Y0
10. Program end	Specify the end of part program	M2 M30

1.11 NC Programming Methods

NC part programming methods can be classified into two main categories: **manual programming and computer-assisted programming**. In the manual method, a part program is prepared by manually inputting the coded instructions into the controller by either using a tape-punching unit, via manual data input (MDI) mode on the CNC unit, or using a computer with a text editor.

The computer-assisted NC programming method uses a computer to help automatically generate the tool path for producing a part. It can appear in one of the following three forms:

- NC processor languages (APT, Compact II, etc.)
- CAD/CAM NC software systems
- Conversational programming software as part of the CNC unit

Using NC processor languages to generate part programs is gradually being replaced by CAD/CAM software. More than one-third of the plants use CAD/CAM software systems to generate part programs. This approach is gaining ground and eventually will become the major method of NC programming. Conversational programming, also referred to as interactive programming, has found use in about one-fifth of plants. This type of programming software is provided by the CNC unit builder and is part of the CNC unit. This method is adequate for programming simple workpieces.

1.12 CNC Control Systems

CNC controls can be either a **point-to-point system or a continuous path system**. The point-to-point (PTP) control moves the tool to the programmed point, normally in rapid traverse, without engaging the workpiece. Once the programmed point is reached, machining is then executed in the Z axis direction.

The PTP sytem is also called the positioning system because its exact tool path normally cannot be controlled. Depending on the control type, the PTP tool path (Figure 1.16) may follow one of the following three modes:

- Axial path (Figure 1.16a)
- 45° line path (Figure 1.16b)
- Linear path (Figure 1.16c)

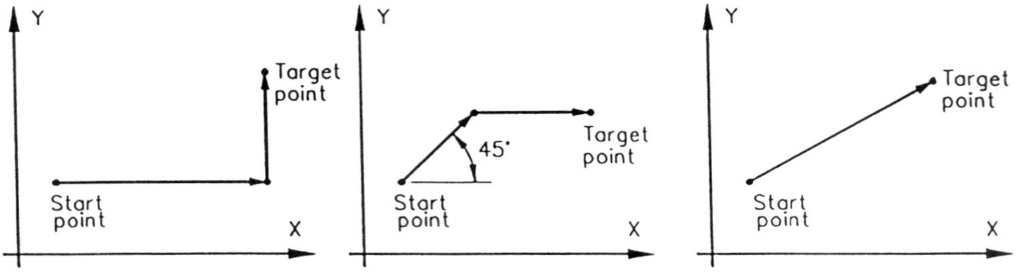

a. axial path b. 45° line path c. linear path

Figure 1.16 PTP tool path

PTP systems are typically used in drilling machines, punch presses, and spot welders which require positioning in the XY-plane in rapid traverse mode while executing machining in the Z axis (see Figure 1.17). PTP control systems are less expensive and are simple in control structure. They are also easy to maintain.

The continuous path control system is also called the contouring system. A **contouring system** is capable of synchronizing two or more axial drives to produce a prescribed path. Depending on the control type, a contouring system can be one of these four types: **2-D contouring, 2½-D contouring, 3-D contouring and 4-D contouring.**

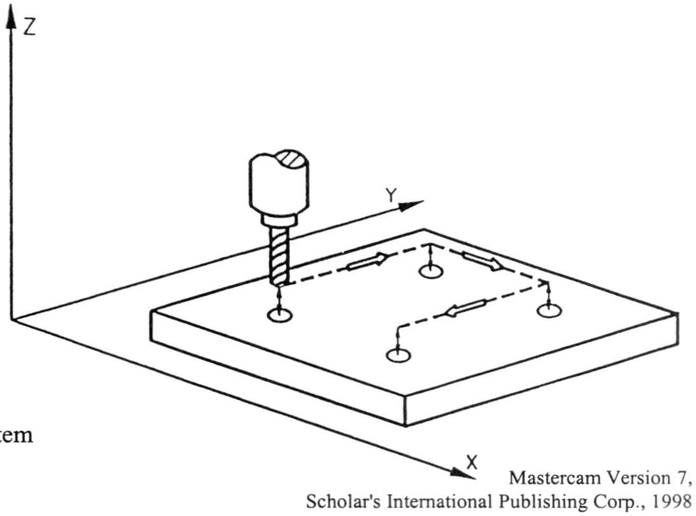

Figure 1.17 Application of a PTP system

Mastercam Version 7,
Scholar's International Publishing Corp., 1998

2-D Contouring Control

A 2-D contouring system implements linear and circular tool paths in the two-axis (XY-) plane (Figure 1.18). The third (Z) axis is controlled independently of the other two axes. Contouring can be implemented in only one plane, in most cases the XY-plane (in a 2-D system). In other words, a 2-D contouring system can synchronize the feed of only two axes simultaneously. In practice, the feeding to desired depth in the Z axis should be made before contouring in the XY-plane.

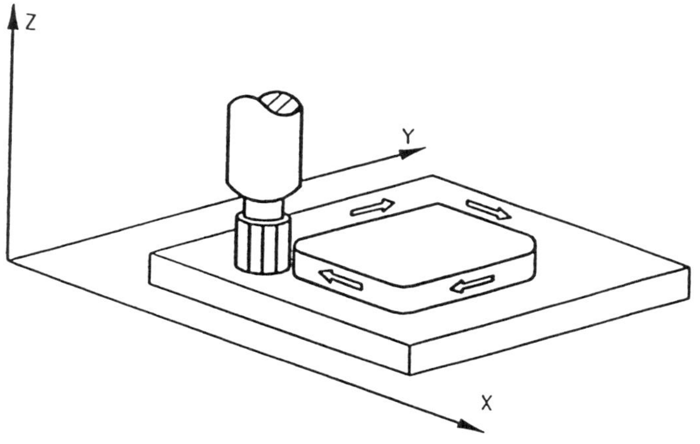

Figure 1.18 2-D contouring

2½-D Contouring Control

In a 2½-D contouring system, **any two** of three axes can be controlled simultaneously. Thus, the contouring can be implemented either in the XY-plane, ZX-plane, or YZ-plane. In practice, the feed can be executed in any one of the three axis, then followed by contouring in any two-axis plane. Figure 1.19 shows contouring in the ZX- and YZ- planes, respectively.

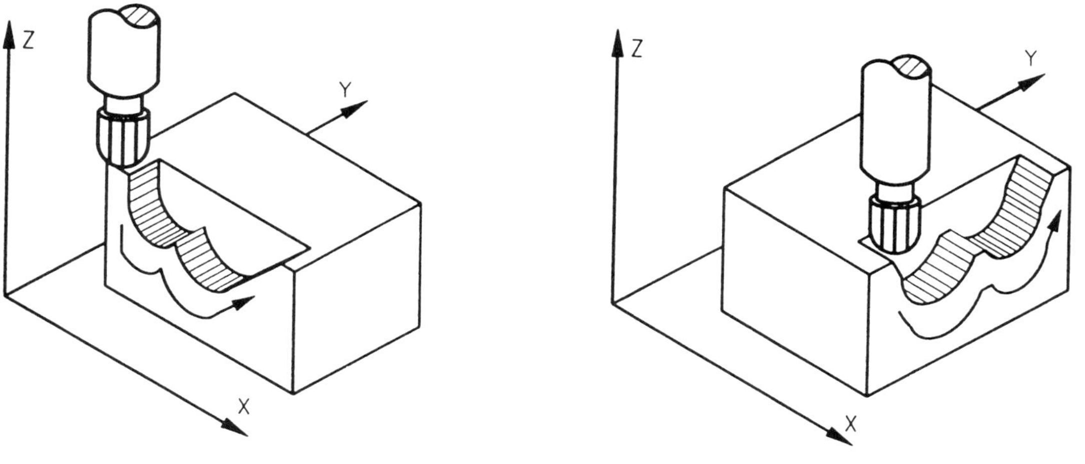

a. in the ZX- plane

b. in the YZ- plane

Figure 1.19 2 ½-D Contouring

3-D Contouring Control

A 3-D contouring system is capable of synchronizing **three axes** simultaneously to produce linear and circular tool paths in 3-D space. It can be used to produce any 3-D surface as shown in Figure 1.20.

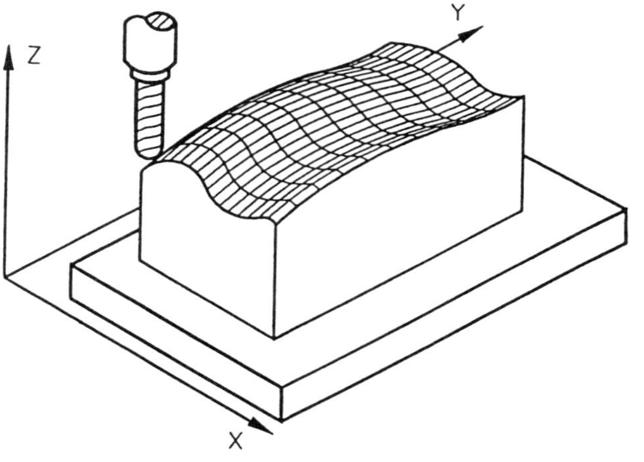

Figure 1.20 3-D contouring

4-D Contouring Control

Some controls furnish an additional axial control for the regular 3-axial control system. The fourth axial control is normally the **rotary axis** which is used for indexing the rotary table. Figure 1.21 shows a 4-D contouring example.

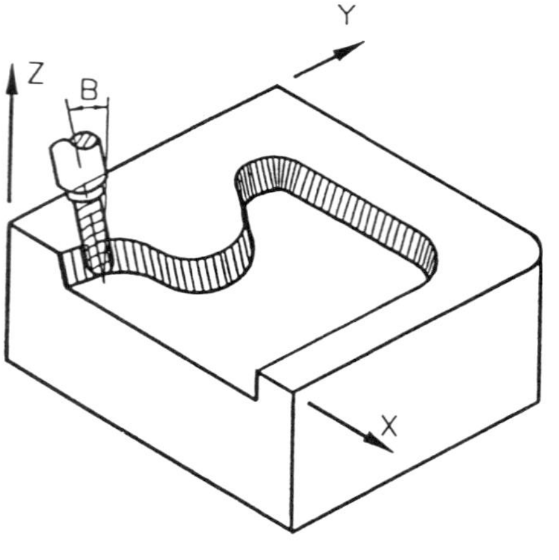

Figure 1.21 4-D contouring

1.13 CNC Drive Systems

The CNC drive systems can be either **open loop or closed loop** type. The main difference between the two systems depends on whether the system has a **feedback loop** to insure the accuracy of system performance.

Open Loop System

No feedback loop is used in open loop drive systems. The drive motor acts upon the control commands from the machine control unit (MCU). The system simply assumes the machine table will reach the target position. There is no way for the MCU to know the actual performance of the system. An open loop system is very sensitive to the load resistance. Position and velocity error may occur when a heavy cutting resistance is encountered. Figure 1.22 shows an open loop CNC drive system. Open loop drives are typically used in PTP systems in which the cutting tool does not engage with the workpiece during positioning. They can also be used in light-loaded cutting machines. Open loop systems are less expensive, but they are prone to load resistances during machining.

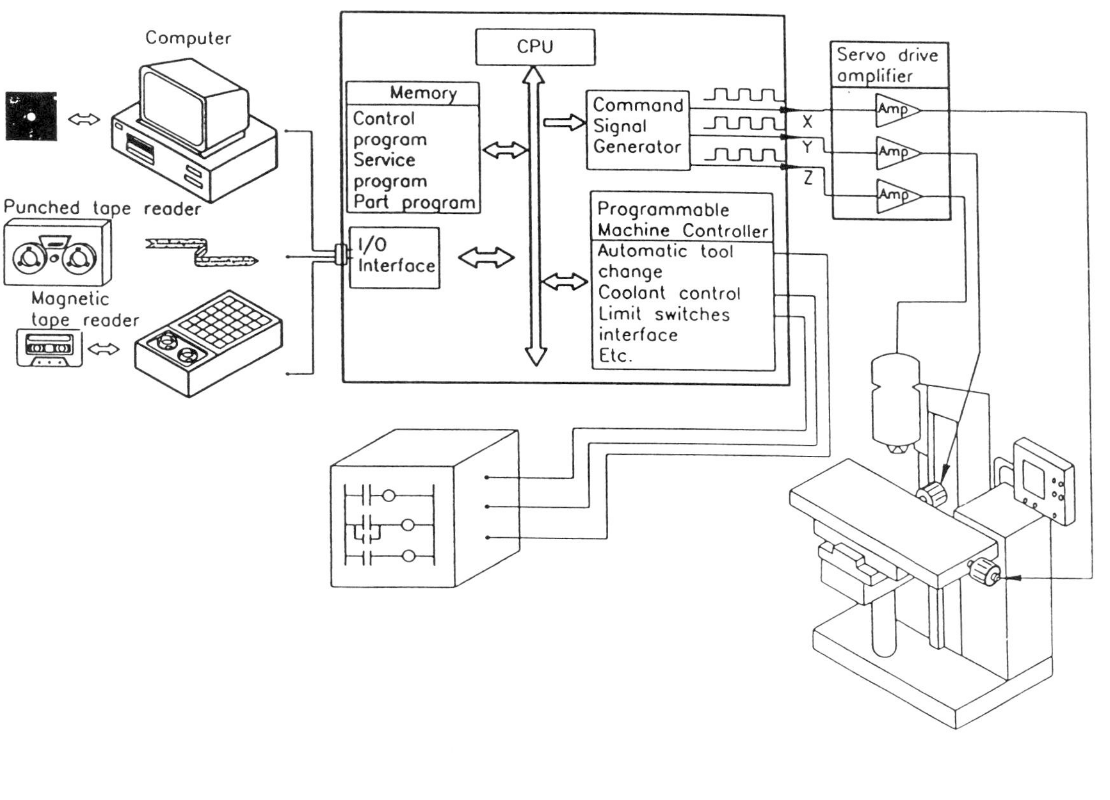

Figure 1.22 An open loop CNC drive system

Closed Loop System

With closed loop drive systems, feedback sub-systems are used to monitor the actual output and correct any discrepancy between desired and actual system performance. Feedback sub-systems may be either an analog or digital type. **Analog systems** measure the variation of physical systems such as position and velocity in voltage level. Tachometers are typically used to measure the velocity, while resolvers for position.

There are two feedback loops in CNC drive systems: **position loop and velocity loop** (Figure 1.23). The **position loop** is the outer loop that consists of a comparator, an amplifier ciurcuit, a velocity loop, a resolver, and a resolver interface. In operation, the comparator receives the reference signal from CNC control and the position feedback signal from the resolver. The difference of these two signals represents the existing positional error. The comparator produces the positional error signal and feeds this signal to the amplifier to drive the servo motor for correcting the error.

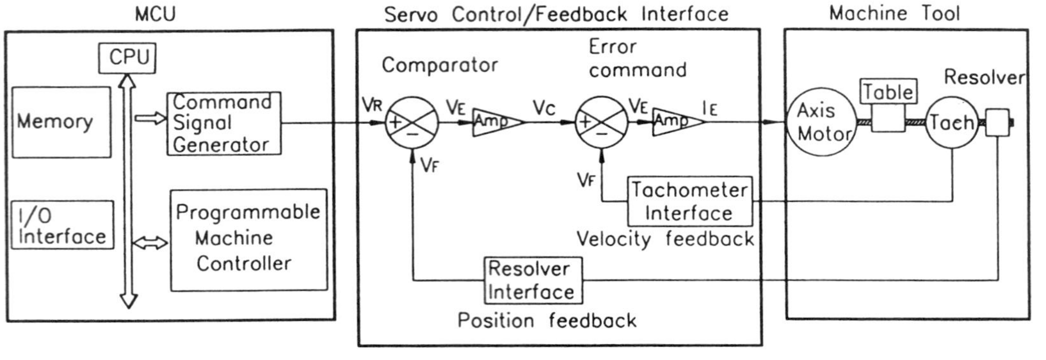

Figure 1.23 Analog type closed loop CNC drive system

The **velocity loop** is the sub-loop within the position loop. It consists of a comparator, an amplifier circuit, a tachometer attached to either the leadscrew or the servo motor, and a tachometer interface.

Digital feedback systems (Figure 1.24) use a digital position transducer to measure the position. Encoders are popular digital position transducers. An up-down counter and a digital-to-analog converter are used in place of the comparator and amplifier. The velocity loop in a digital feedback system is the same as that found in the analog feedback system.

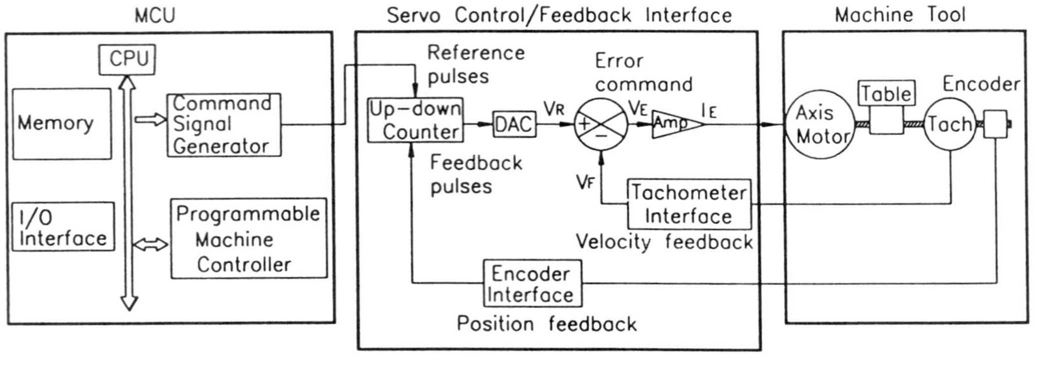

Figure 1.24 Digital type closed loop CNC drive system

1.14 CNC Interpolations

CNC controls use various forms of interpolation to execute contouring tool paths. **Interpolation** is the process of producing a series of intermediate data points between given coordinate positions. The interpolation points are implemented by various types of CNC control interpolators.
The **two** main functions provided by an interpolator are:

Compute intermediate coordinate positions along the programmed path

Compute the axial velocity of an individual axis along the contour path

CNC controls furnish the following **five** possible types of interpolations:

- Linear interpolation
- Circular interpolation
- Helical interpolation
- Parabolic interpolation
- Cubic interpolation

All modern CNC controls furnish linear, circular, and helical interpolation; very few controls support parabolic and cubic interpolations.

Linear Interpolation

Linear interpolation moves the tool from the starting point to the target point along a straight line. Linear interpolation can be implemented in a 2-D plane or 3-D space. It is used in two categories of applications: machine lines (Figure 1.25) and on the following page, approximate irregular curves (Figure 1.26) and surfaces (Figure 1.27).

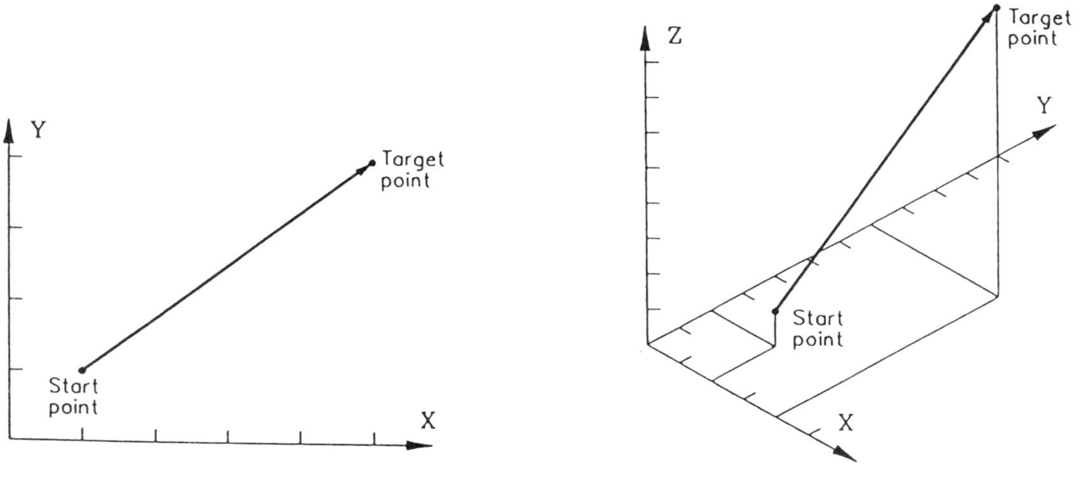

a. in 2-D b. in 3-D

Figure 1.25 Straight line cutting

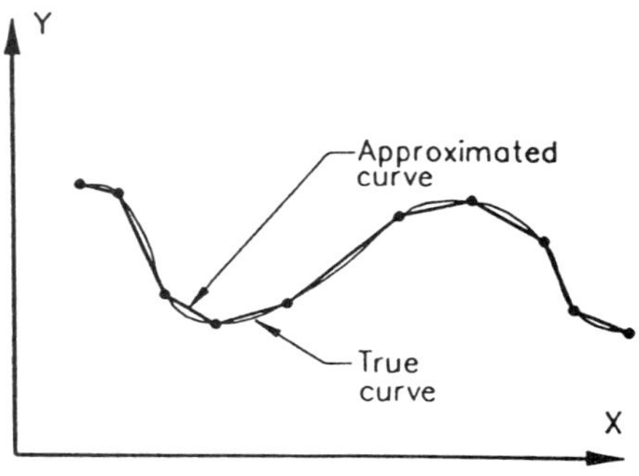

Figure 1.26 Cutting irregular curve

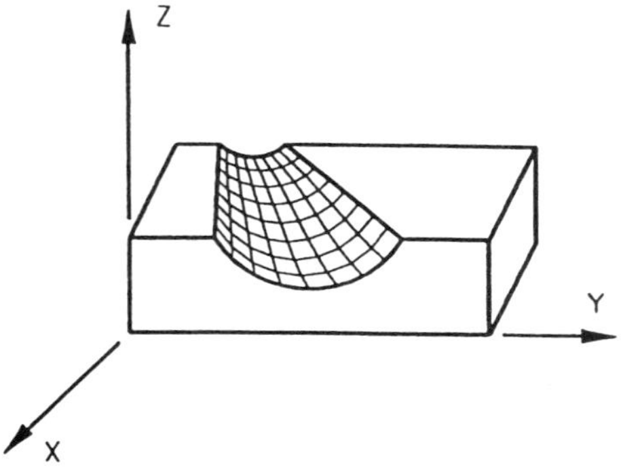

Figure 1.27 Surface cutting

Circular Interpolation

Circular interpolation is programmed to cut circular arcs in one of three principal planes (XY-plane, ZX-plane, or YZ-plane) (Figure 1.28).

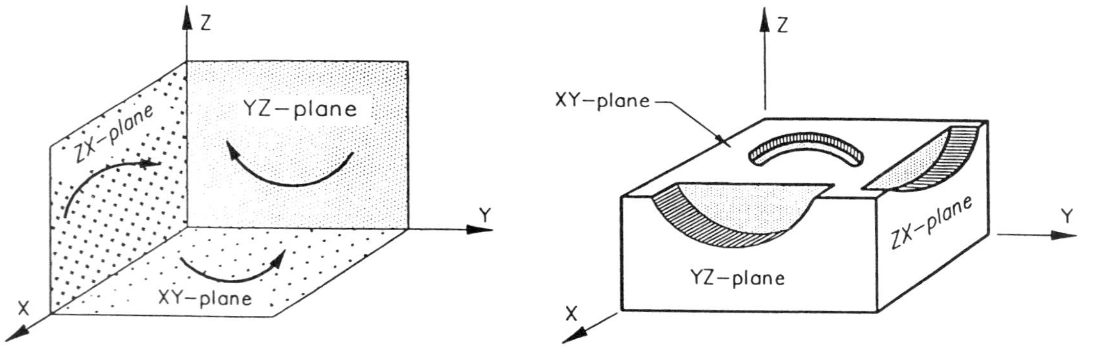

Figure 1.28 Circular interpolation

Helical Interpolation

Helical interpolation combines the two-axis circular interpolation and a linear interpolation in the third axis. It can be used in the following three configurations:

- •Circular arc in XY-plane and linear interpolation in Z axis (Figure 1.29**a**)
- •Circular arc in ZX-plane and linear interpolation in Y axis (Figure 1.29**b**)
- •Circular arc in YZ-plane and linear interpolation in X axis (Figure 1.29**c**)

Mastercam Version 7,
Scholar's International Publishing Corp., 1998

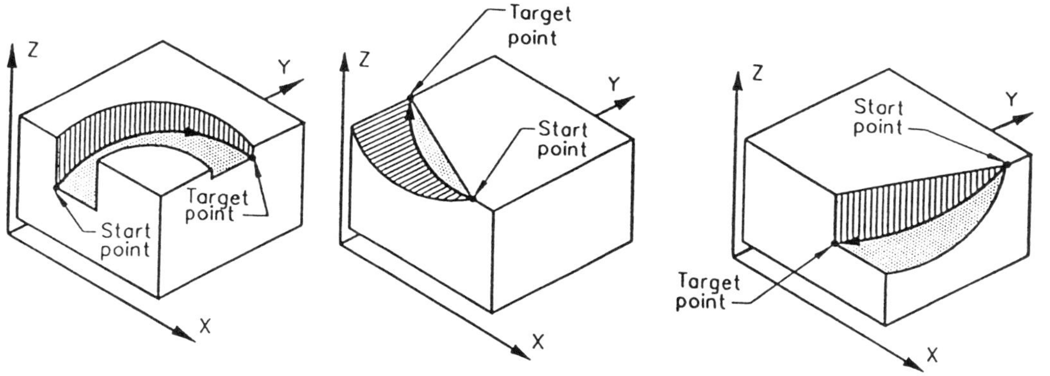

a. Arc in the XY-plane b. Arc in the ZX-plane c. Arc in the YZ-plane

Figure 1.29 Helical interpolation

Parabolic Interpolation

Parabolic interpolation uses three non-collinear points to approximate curves that are of free form (Figure 1.30). It is mainly used in mold and die making where free form designed, rather than precisely defined shapes, are preferred. The use of two or more successive parabolic interpolations can approximate higher-order curves (Figure 1.31). The advantage of using parabolic interpolation is the reduction of programmed points by as much as 50 times that required by the linear interpolation mode.

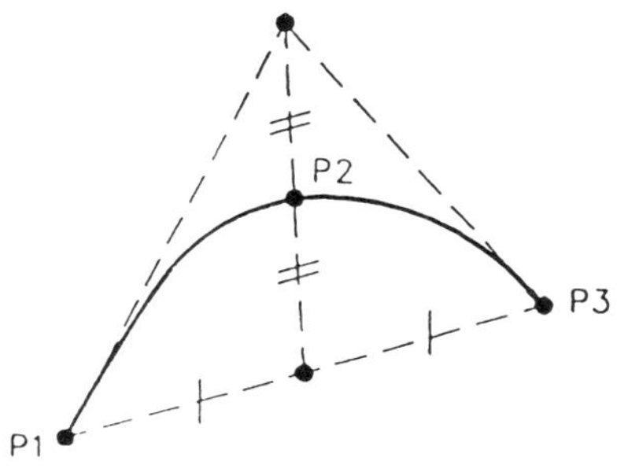

Figures 1.30 Parabolic interpolation

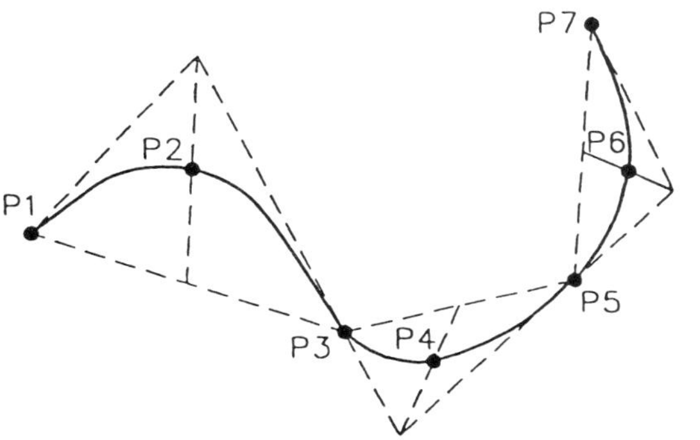

Figure1.31 Parabolic interpolation of a higher order curve

Cubic Interpolation

Cubic interpolation approximates the surfaces defined by third-order geometry. It involves the motion of three axes to machine complex shapes such as automobile sheet metal dies.

1.15 Machine Axes Designation & Direction

The EIA-267-B standard specifies fourteen axes for describing the linear and rotary motions of CNC machines. This includes nine linear axes and five rotary axes. The nine linear axes are further divided into the following three groups: (Figure 1.32)

- Primary linear axes (X,Y, and Z)
- Secondary linear axes (U, V, and W)
- Tertiary linear axes (P, Q, and R)

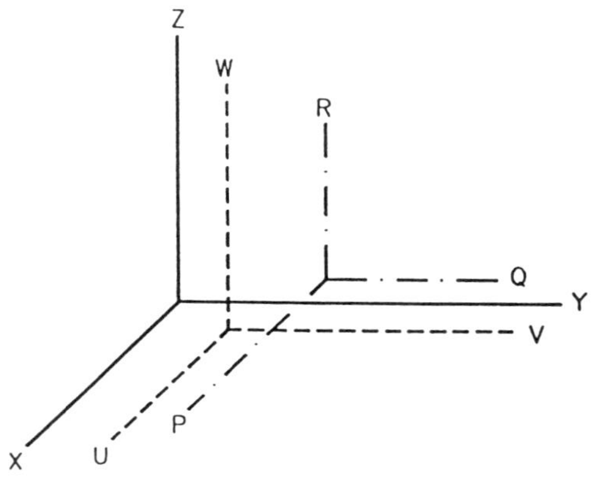

Figure 1.32 Nine linear axes

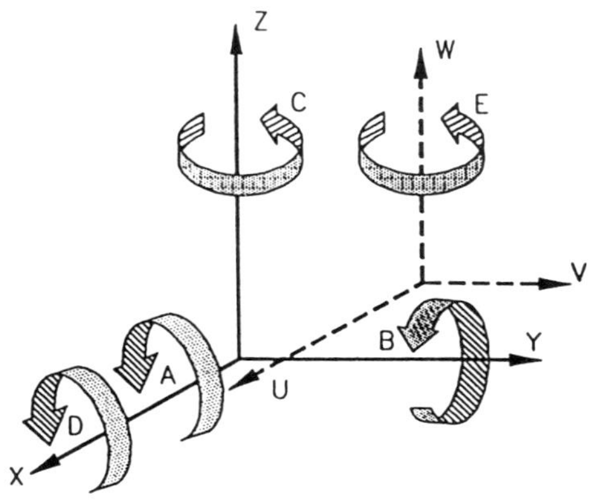

Figure 1.33 Five rotary axes

The primary axes (X, Y, and Z) are assigned to the primary slide table. The secondary linear axes (U, V, and W) are added to the primary axes for defining the movement of the second moving slide or spindle. Similarly, the tertiary linear axes (P, Q, and R) are used to represent the linear motion of the third slide or spindle.

The five rotary axes consist of three primary rotary axes (A, B, and C) and two special axes (D and E) (Figure 1.33). Their definitions are:

Axis A:	**rotary motion around the primary linear axis X**
Axis B:	**rotary motion around the primary linear axis Y**
Axis C:	**rotary motion around the primary linear axis Z**
Axis D:	**rotary motion around any linear axis**
Axis E:	**rotary motion around any linear axis**

Machine Axes Designation

Machine axes are designated according to the "right-hand rule". When the thumb of right hand points in the direction of the positive X axis, the index finger points toward the positive Y axis, and the middle finger toward the positive Z aixs. Figure 1.34 shows the right-hand rule applied to vertical machines, while Figure 1.35 applies to horizontal machines.

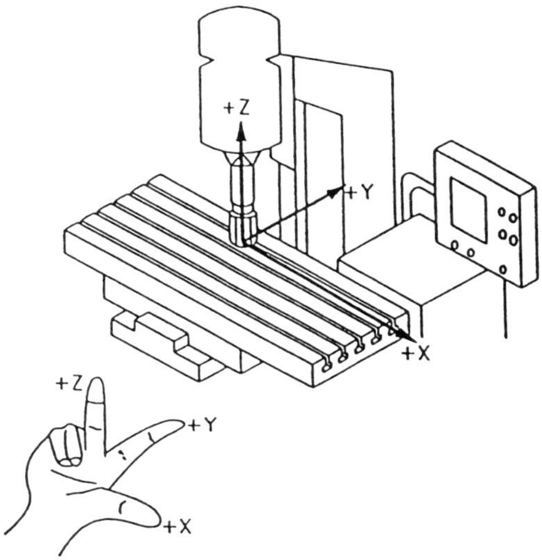

Figures 1.34 Right hand rule: vertical machine

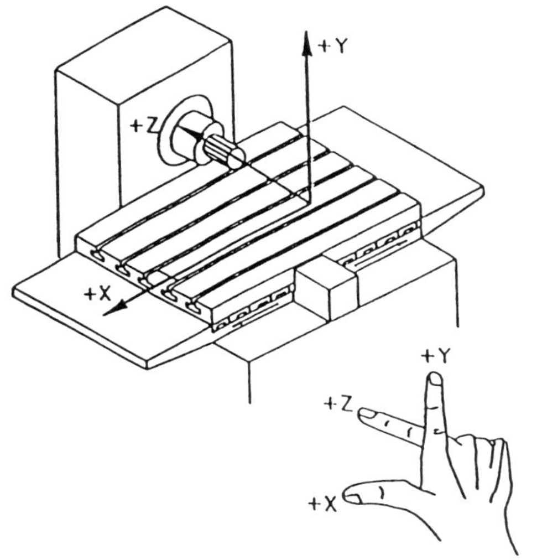

Figure 1.35 Right hand rule: horizontal machine

Direction of Machine Axes

CNC controls use the positive (+) and negative (-) sign to indicate the motion direction of the machine axes. This is how we define the directions.

+Z direction: is the direction which increases the distance between the workpiece and the cutting tool.
-Z direction: is in the opposite direction of +Z.

+X direction: (a) In vertical machines, it is the direction to the right when observed *from* the spindle *toward* its supporting column.
(b) In horizontal machines, it is pointed to the right when viewed *from* the spindle axis *toward* the workpiece.
-X direction: is in the opposite direction of +X.

+Y direction: follows the right-hand rule: when the thumb points *toward* the +X axis and the middle finger is directed *toward* the +Z axis, the index finger points in the direction of the +Y axis.
-Y direction: is in the opposite direction of +Y.

1.16 Reference Zero Points

Reference zero points are the base or starting points that are chosen as the reference for calculating the coordinates of the other points. Also, reference zero points are called the **zero points**. CNC controls use the following **four** types of reference zero points to facilitate the programming of tool paths:

- Machine zero point
- Reference return point
- Work zero point
- Program zero point

Machine Zero Point

The machine zero point is the origin of the machine coordinate system. It is set by the machine tool manufacturer and can not be changed.

The machine zero is labelled with an **M** and represented by this symbol:

The location of the machine zero point varies from manufacturer to manufacturer. For turning machines, the machine zero is normally located at the center of the spindle end face (Figure 1.36). In milling machines, the machine zero is usually at the extreme limit of each axis travel (Figure 1.37).

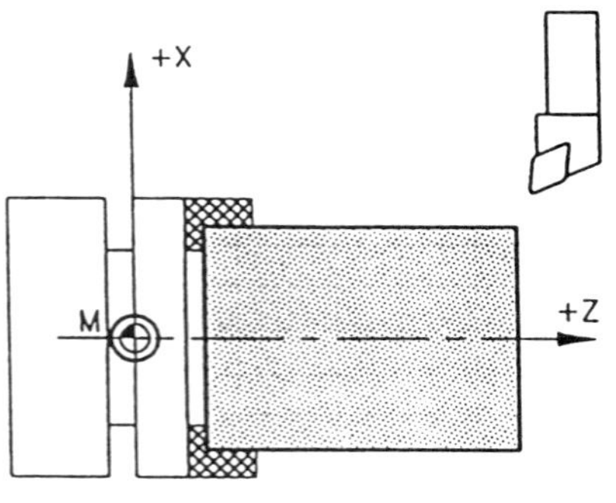

Figures 1.36 Machine zero point of a turning machine

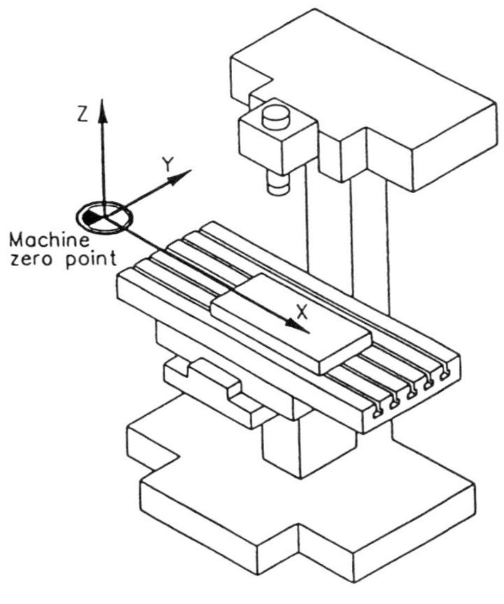

Figure 1.37 Machine zero point of a milling machine

Normally the machine zero is not directly used as the reference point for writing part programs. It may be used in one of the following **three** applications:

- **Initial setup of the machine**
- **As the reference point for other reference points such as reference return points, work zeros, and program zeros**
- **As the tool change position**

Reference Return Point

Reference return points are the locations to which the machine table or the spindle is returned. They are identified by the letter **R** and are represented by the symbol: 

Some CNC controls allow defining up to four reference return points. Normally, the machine zero is set to be the first reference return point in milling machines (Figure 1.38). The second, third, and fourth reference return points are specified by setting their parameter values. They can be set at any convenient location within the work envelope. In turning machines, the reference return point is located in the extreme end of the work envelope (Figure 1.39)

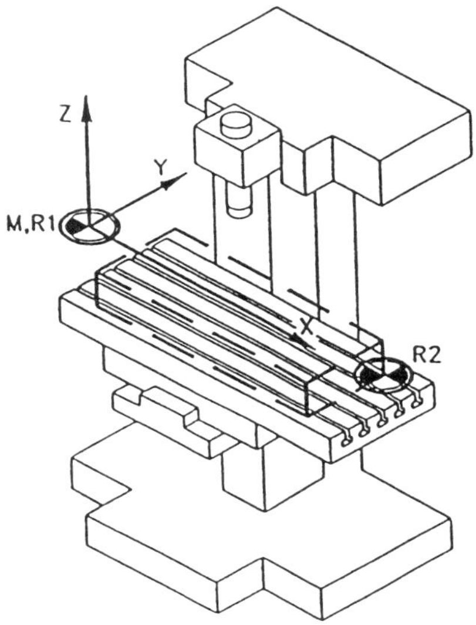

Figures 1.38 Reference return point of a milling machine

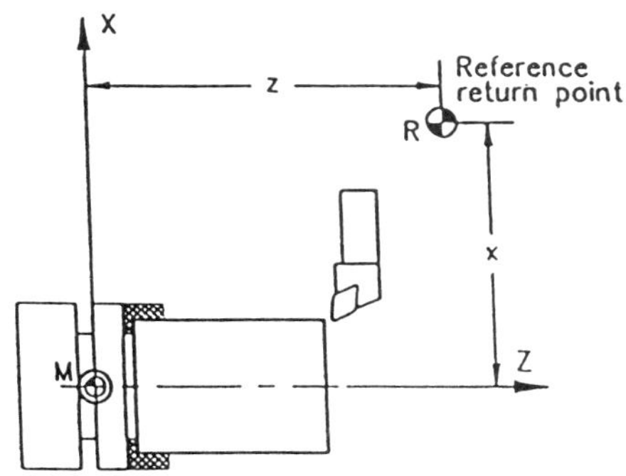

Figure 1.39 Reference return point of a turning machine

The location of the first reference return point is precisely predetermined in each moving axis in relation to the machine zero point. Because of this, it can be used for **calibrating and regulating** the measuring system of the slide table and spindle.

Specifically, the reference point is used in **four** situations:

1. **When the control is powered up, all axes <u>always</u> must be positioned at the reference return point to calibrate the measuring system.**
2. **The machine must be re-positioned to the reference return point for reestablishing the proper coordinate values in situations such as losing the current position data due to electrical failure or improper operation.**
3. **All axes must be retracted to the reference point before the tool change can take place.**
4. **At the end of the part program, all axes must be retracted to the reference return point to reset the control system for re-running the part program or running a new part program.**

Work Zero Point

A work zero point is the origin of the workpiece's coordinate system. It is used to determine the work's coordinate system in relation to the machine zero point. The work's zero points are often referred to as setup points because they are the locations for setting up the workpiece on the machine table. Some CNC controls allow the use of multiple work zero points in one machine setup or operation. The work zero point is labelled by **W** and represented by the symbol: 

The work zero point can be chosen by the programmer at any convenient location within the working envelope of the machine. It is recommended that you place the work zero point in a way that it can be easily located and measured on the workpiece. Figure 1.40 shows two common methods of choosing the work zero point for turnings and Figure 1.41 shows milling examples.

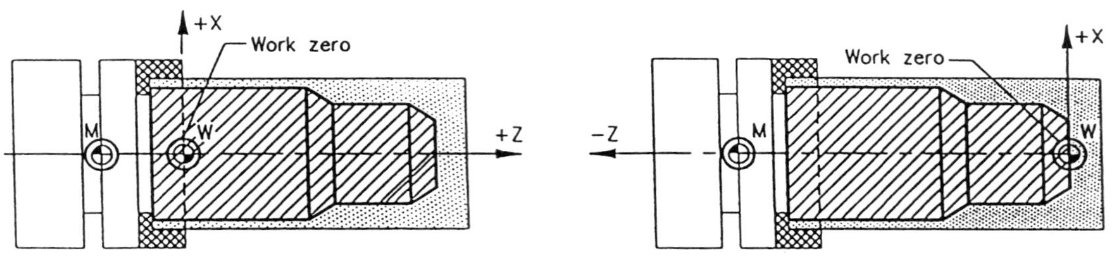

a. located at the chuck face   b. located at right workpiece face

Figures 1.40 Selecting work zero for turning

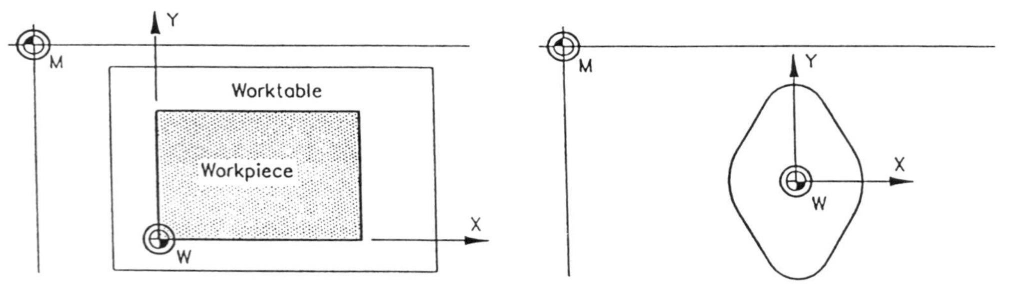

a. located at intersecting point of two datum surfaces b. located at workpiece center

Figure 1.41 Selecting work zero for milling

Program Zero Points

A program zero point is the **origin** of the part program. It is used to locate all other points in the part program. Therefore, it must be chosen before any programming can proceed. The program zero point is labelled by P and represented by the symbol: 

The program zero point normally coincides with the work zero point. However, it can be located at any convenient position. On the next page, Figure 1.42 shows the situation of the program zero point and the work zero point coinciding, while these two points are located separately in Figure 1.43.

Mastercam Version 7,
Scholar's International Publishing Corp., 1998

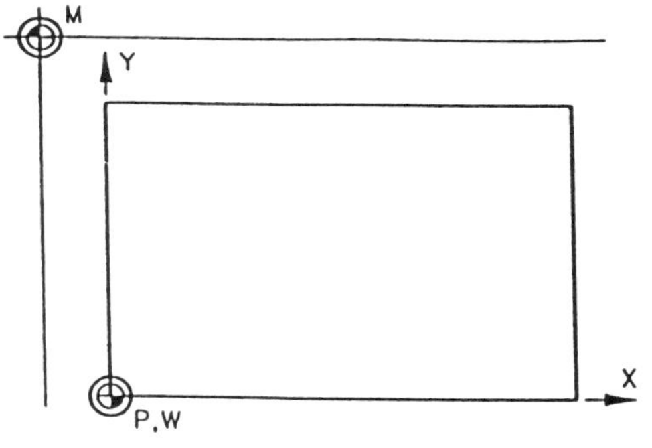

Figures 1.42 Program zero point and work zero point coincide

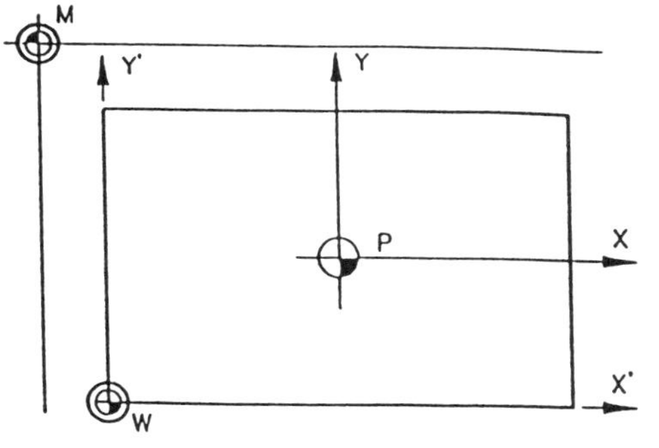

Figure 1.43 Separate program zero point and work zero point

It is possible to define multiple program zero points to facilitate the programming of workpieces with complex features. The **first** program zero point is the **program zero** and the **second** program zero point and **all succeeding points** are referred to as the **local zero point**. Figure 1.44 illustrates using two zero points to write a part program.

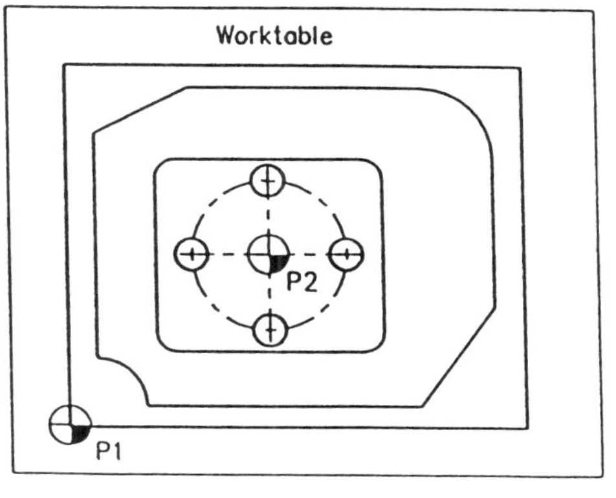

Figure 1.44 Multiple program zero points

1.17 Positioning Systems

We use a positioning system to determine the locations of the positioning points on the workpiece to which the cutting tool is moved. Two methods of positioning systems are used in NC part programming:

- absolute positioning system and
- incremental positioning system.

Absolute Positioning System

We always measure the dimension data of all positions from a **fixed reference point** in the absolute positioning system. In fact, this point is the program zero point. The absolute positioning system is sometimes referred to as the reference positioning system. Figure 1.45 shows an example using absolute positioning system.

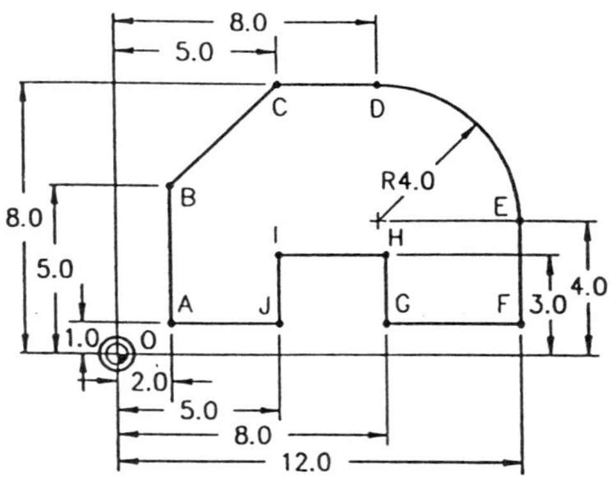

Figure 1.45 Absolute positioning system

Incremental Positioning System

When using the incremental positioning system, the dimension data of a point always refers to the immediately **preceding** point. Each position is measured in relation to the previous one and the coordinate system shifts from point to point. Some important features of the incremental positioning system are given below:

> **a. The program zero point is used as the reference point only for the first programmed point.**
> **b. The plus (+) and minus (-) sign should be used to indicate the direction of tool motion even though points may be located only in the first quadrant.**
> **c. The positioning sequence of the tool path affects the dimension data of a point. This feature is illustrated in Figure 1.46.**

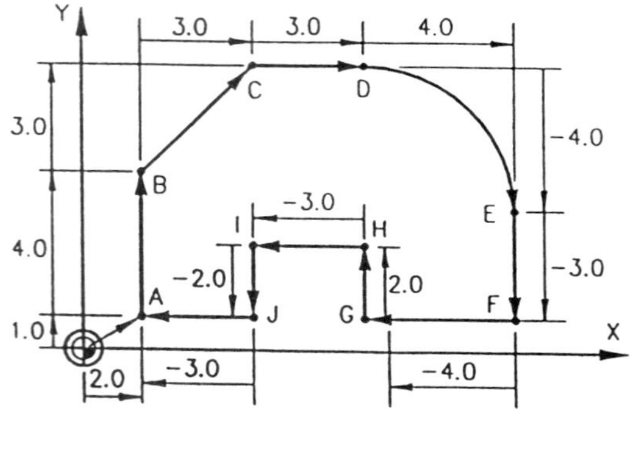

a. Clockwise sequence

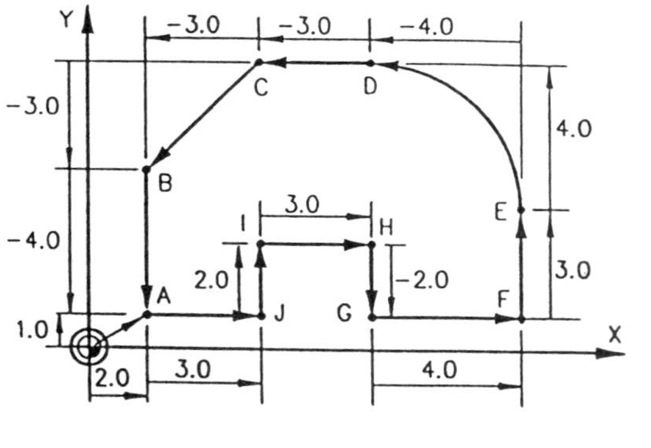

b. Counter-clockwise sequence

Figure 1.46 Incremental positioning system

Selection of the Positioning System

Using the **absolute positioning system** in part programming is recommended for the following **two** reasons:

1. **The positioning error encountered with an individual point has no effect on subsequent positions.**
2. **The absolute system is easier to use to trace the cutter locations for checking errors because all dimensions are referenced to the same fixed point.**

The **incremental positioning system** is preferred when common patterns (holes, pockets, or contour patterns) in a workpiece are repeated several times. **Three** main disadvantages of using the incremental positioning system are:

1. **Any positioning error will be continued throughout the rest of the program. A positioning error of 1.0" in H1 as shown in Figure 1.47 below, for example, is carried to all succeeding programming positions.**
2. **A compound error is progressively accumulated if more than one error is encountered in a part program. Figure 1.48 below depicts this feature. A positioning error of 0.5" in H1 continues on to H2. An additional error of 1.5" is encountered in H3, the accumulated error of 2.0" then appears throughout the rest of the program.**
3. **It is very difficult to check for any position error, especially in large part programs.**

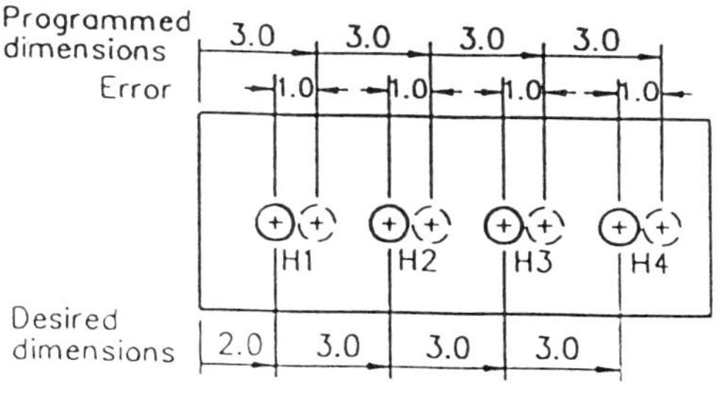

Figure 1.47 A position error is extended to all succeeding programming positions

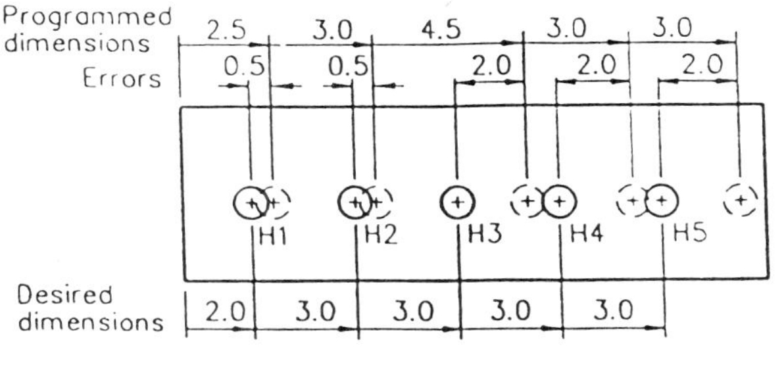

Figure 1.48 Accummulated errors

Chapter 2

Machining Fundamentals

Objectives:

1. Be familiar with the machining processes performed by CNC milling and turning machines.
2. Know cutting tools and tooling systems for CNC machines.
3. Select machining parameters for various machining processes.
4. Provide useful tips for various machining processes.

2.1 CNC Milling Processes

CNC milling machines and machining centers are used to perform **six** types of machining processes. Table 2.1 illustrates these six types of machining processes on the following two pages.

- Facing
- Profiling
- Pocketing
- Slot cutting
- Hole machining
- 3-D surface machining

2.2 CNC Turning Processes

CNC turning machines and turning centers implement the following **ten** types of machining processes:

- Facing
- Profiling
- Drilling
- Threading
- Cutting off
- Turning
- Grooving
- Boring
- Chamfering
- Milling

All ten processes are illustrated in Table 2.2 on the following pages 2-4 and 2-5.

Table 2.1 Milling Processes

Process Type	Tool	Illustration
1. Facing Producing flat surfaces	Face mill for larger surfaces End mill for small surfaces	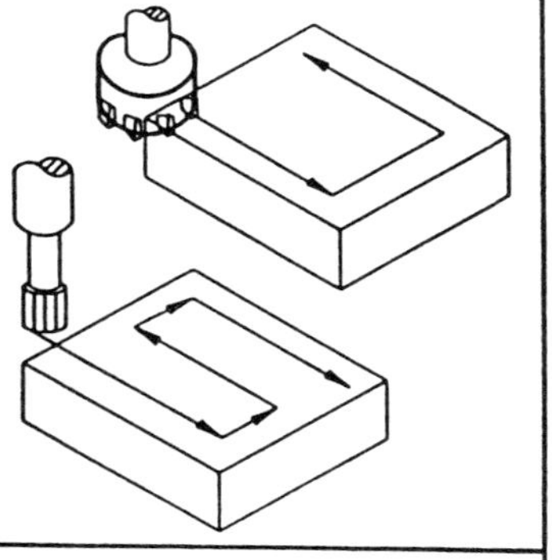
2. Profiling Producing part contours	End mill	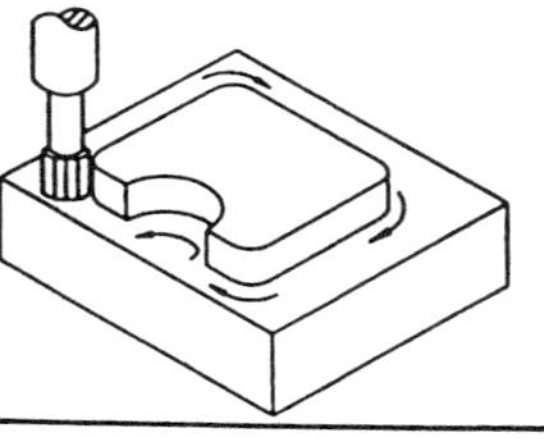
3. Pocketing Removing the material enclosed by a closed boundary	End mill	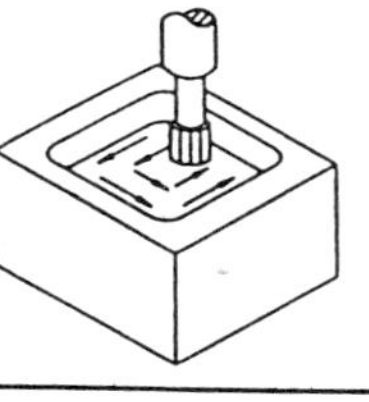
4. Slot cutting Producing various types of slots	End mill	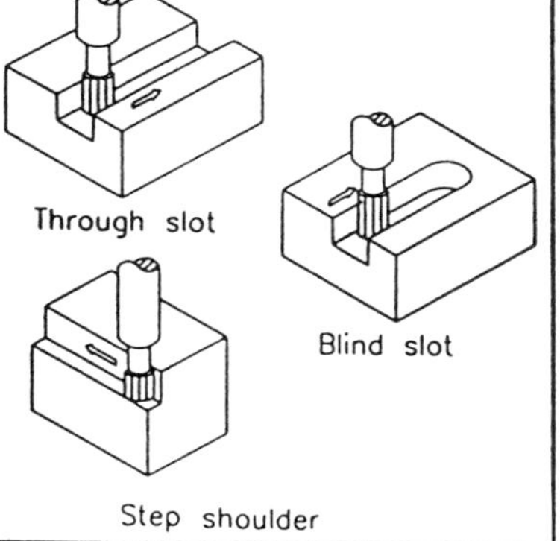
5. Hole machining a. Drilling	Drill	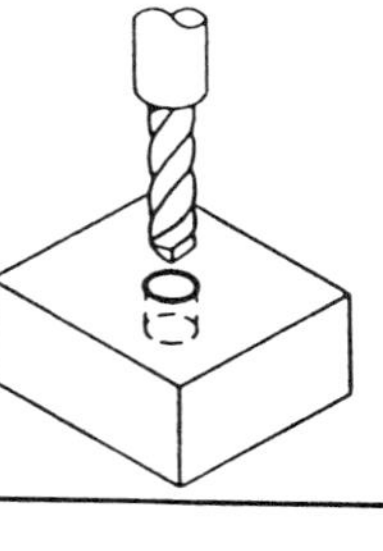

Table 2.1 (Continued)

Process Type	Tool	Illustration
b. Countersinking	Countersink tool	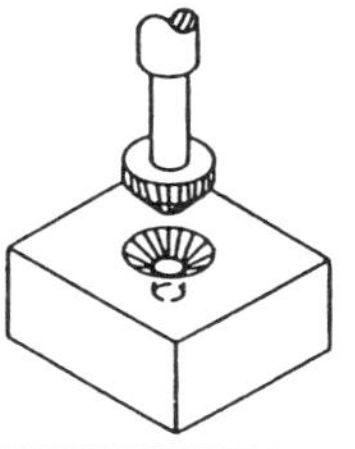
c. Counterboring	Counterbore tool	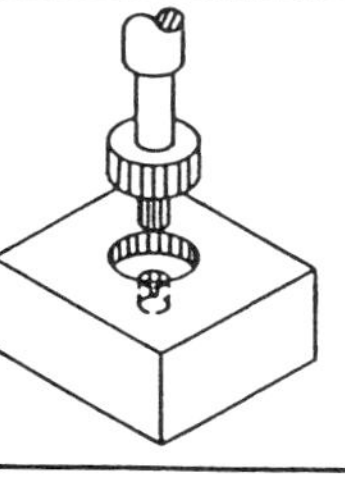
d. Boring	Boring tool	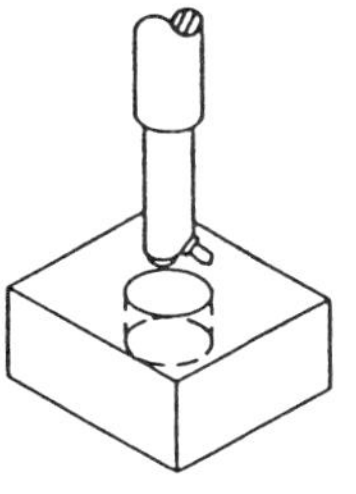
e. Tapping	Tap	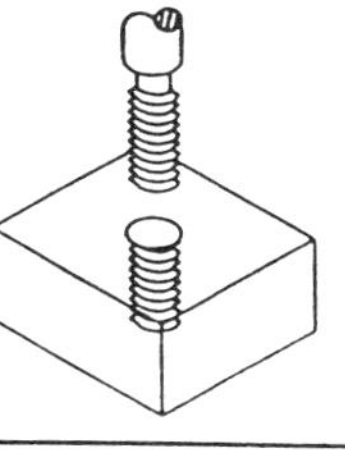
f. Reaming Producing smooth and precise holes	Reamer	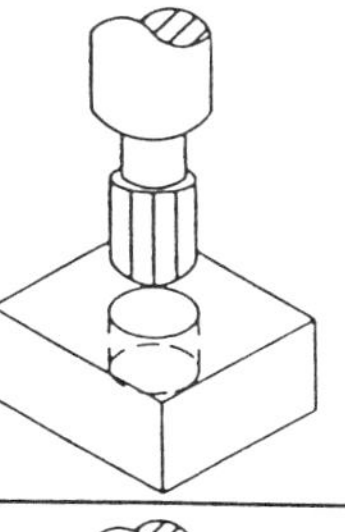
6. 3-D Surface machining Cutting various types of surfaces	Ball-end mill	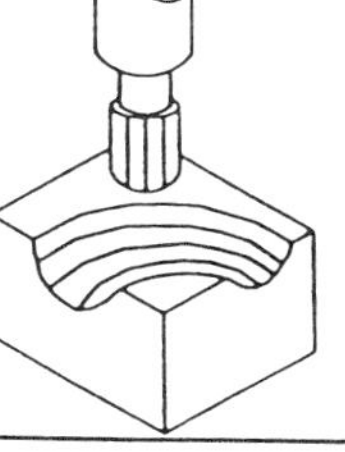

Table 2.2 Turning Machining Processes

Process Type	Tool	Illustration
1. Facing: Producing flat end face a. Facing to center b. Facing to shoulder	Facing tool	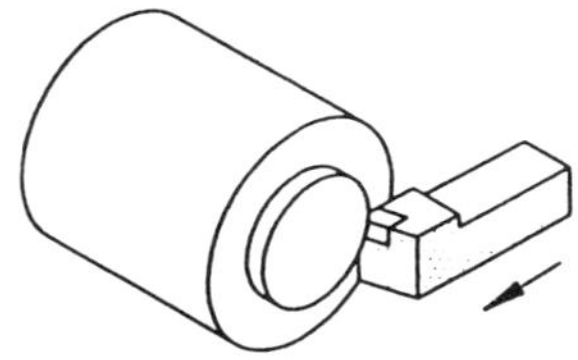
2. Turning: Producing line profiles a. Straight turning	Turning tool	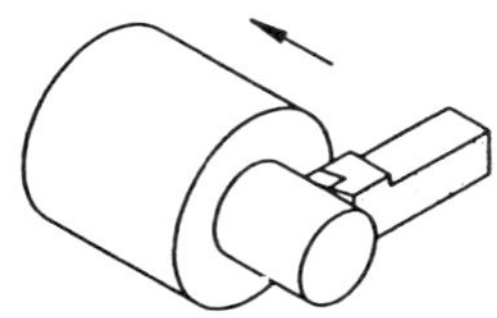
b. Taper turning		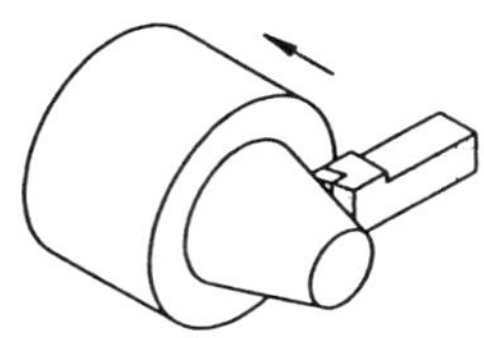
3. Profiling Producing external line and circular profiles	Profiling tool	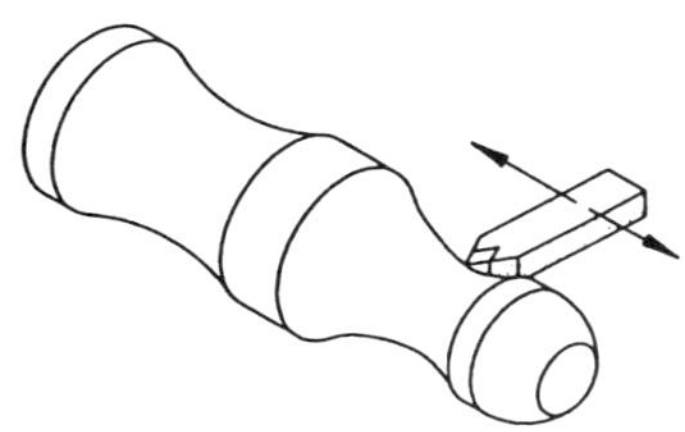
4. Grooving: Cutting various forms of grooves a. Side grooving	Grooving tool	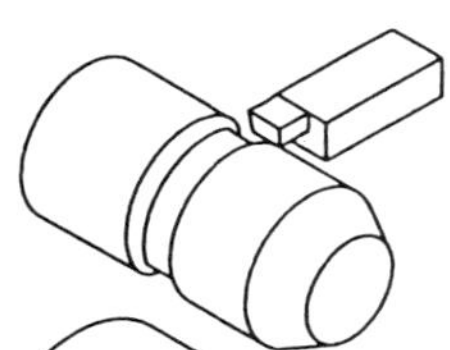 Side grooving
b. Face grooving		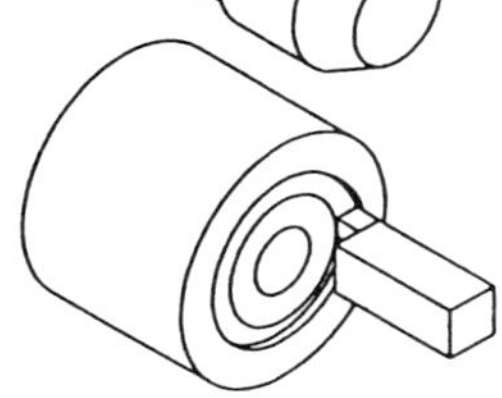 Face grooving
5. Drilling Producing holes in the spindle axis	Drill	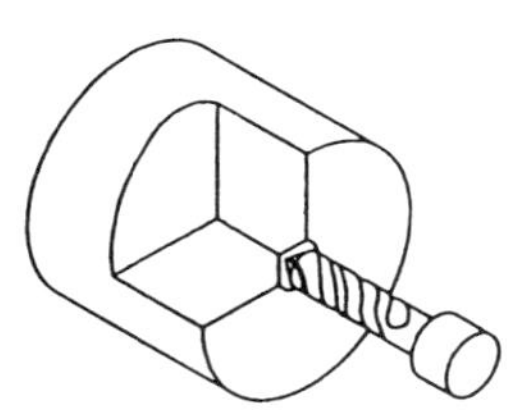

Table 2.2 (Continued)

Process Type	Tool	Illustration
6. Boring Producing internal line and circular profiles	Boring tool	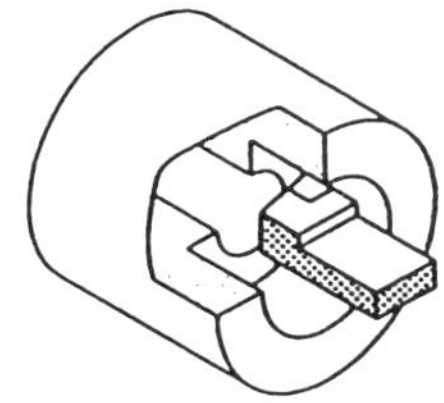
7. Threading: Cutting various thread forms a. External thread	Threading tool	External thread 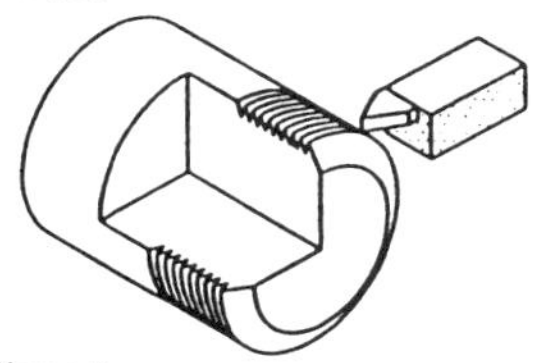
b. Internal thread		Internal thread 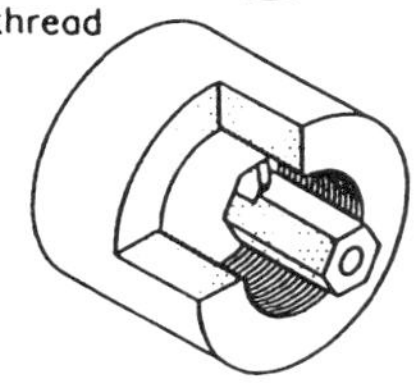
8. Chamfering Generating chamfers at sharp corners	Chamfering tool	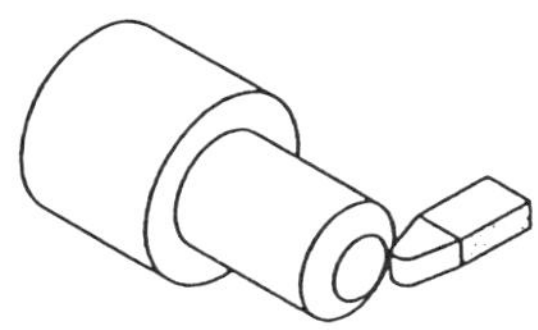
9. Cutting off Separating the workpiece from the stock	Cut–off tool	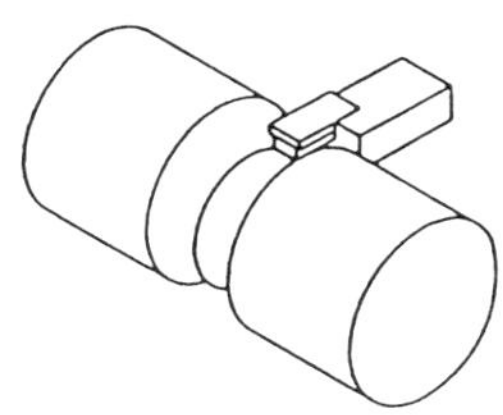
10. Milling Producing slots and surfaces	End mill	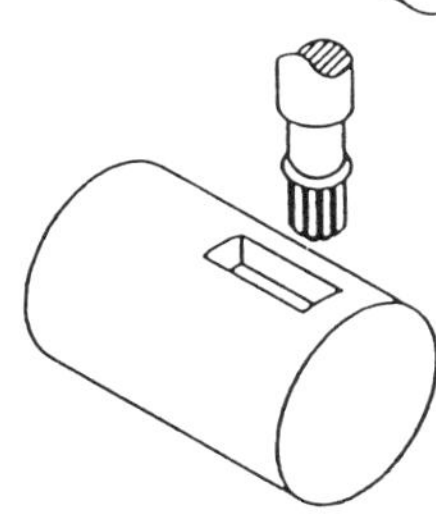

2.3 Cutting Tool Materials

Required Properties of Cutting Tool Materials

Three important properties of any cutting tool material are:

1. Wear resistance (resistance to the various wear mechanism)
2. Toughness (the ability to absorb energy and withstand plastic deformation without fracturing under compressive loading)
3. Hot hardness (the ability to resist stresses and maintain hardness and cutting efficiency at elevated temperatures)

Cutting Tool Materials

The common cutting tool materials used for CNC machining are **high speed steel (HSS), tungsten carbides, cermets, ceramics, and polycrystalline.** Table 2.3 summarizes the characteristics and applications of various cutting tool materials.

Table 2.3 Characteristics and applications of various cutting tool materials

Material	Principal Characteristics	Typical Applications	Advantages
HSS	Tougher than carbides	Low speed machining, and interrupted cuts.	Lower cost than carbide, longer tool life, better surface finish.
Uncoated carbide	Very tough, excellent edge wear resistance.	Roughing to finishing virtually any material including iron, steel, stainless steel, high temperature alloy, non ferrous metals and non- metallic materials.	Higher cutting speed than HSS and tougher than coated carbides.
PVD coated carbide	Very tough, good thermal shock resistance and crater resistance. High retained edge strength. Excellent resistance to buildup on the cutting edge.	Machining of steels, high temperature alloys, stainless steels, difficult to machine materials, aluminum, carbon and alloy steels.	Permit speeds to be increased up to 15% when compared to uncoated with no loss of tool life.
Cermet	Excellent resistance to wear, shock and heat.	Finishing operations on malle able cast irons, carbon steels, alloy steels, stainless steels, and aluminum alloys.	Up to 20 times the tool life of conventional carbide grades.
Ceramics (alumina base)	High hardness, excellent chemical wear resistance.	For high speed rouging and finishing of cast irons and steels.	Better finishes at higher machining rates.
Ceramics (silicon base)	High hardness plus high fracture toughness and thermal shock esistance.	Roughing and finishing operations on cast irons.	Machining speeds up to 5000 sfm and beyond.
Polycrystalline diamond (PCV)	Hardness of diamond plus toughness, excellent wear resistance.	Roughing to finishing operations on aluminum and other soft or abrasive non-ferrous or non-metallic materials.	Better than 30 times the tool life of carbide, even on high silicon aluminum.
Cubic born nitride (CBN)	Exceptional hardness, excellent wear resistance and mechanical shock resistance.	High speed machining on hardened ferrous materials in the 50 65 Rc (480 740 Bhn) range.	Provide many times the edge life of carbide, eliminate the need for costly alternative grinding operations.

ANSI and ISO Carbide Grade Classifications

There are two commonly used classification systems for carbide cutting tools:

ANSI system and ISO system.

ANSI System

The ANSI carbide classification system was initiated in the U.S. automotive industry and more commonly used in the United States. It is also called U.S. **C-system** because it uses the letter C with a numeric digit ranging from 1 to 8 to indicate the carbide grade (Table 2.4)

Table 2.4 ANSI Carbide Classification System

Class	Class	Material to be cut	Application	Characteristics of cutting	Characteristics of carbide
C1	Tungsten	Cast iron, nonferrous metals, and nonmetallics	Roughing cuts	Increasing cutting speed (↓); Increasing feed rate (↑)	Increasing hardness & wear resistance (↓); Increasing strength (↑)
C2	Tungsten		General-purpose		
C3	Tungsten		Finishing		
C4	Tungsten		Roughing cuts		
C5	Tungsten	Steels and steel alloys	Tungsten	Increasing cutting speed (↓); Increasing feed rate (↑)	Increasing hardness & wear resistance (↓); Increasing strength (↑)
C6	Titanium		General-purpose		
C7	Tungsten Titanium and Tantalum in varying amounts		Finishing		
C8			Fine finishing		

Carbide tools are classified into **two** major categories. One category is composed of the **straight tungsten carbides** (classes 1 to 4), which are hard and have very good wear resistance. They are best suited to machining cast iron, non-ferrous metals, and some nonmetallic materials that are abrasive. The second category (classes 5 to 8) includes the combinations of **tungsten and tantalum or titanium carbide**. These carbides are generally used for machining steels. They are resistant to cratering, which is a serious problem when tungsten carbide is used to machine steels.

ISO System

The ISO (International Organization for Standardization) system is based on the ISO Standard 513-1975(E) which is widely used in Europe. It uses **three** main categories: **P, M, and K** (Table 2.5 on the next page).

P category:	**for machining**	**ferrous metals with long chips**
M category:	**for machining**	**(1) ferrous metals with long or short chips** **(2) non-ferrous metals**
K category:	**for machining**	**(1) ferrous metals with short chips** **(2) non-ferrous metals** **(3) non-metallic materials**

Table 2.5 ISO Carbide Classification System

Symbol and color	Broad material categories to be cut	Class	Application	Characteristics of cutting	Characteristics of carbide
P (Blue)	Ferrous metals with long chips	P01	Finish turning and boring under vibration free operations	↑ Increasing cutting speed; ↓ Increasing feed rate	↑ Increasing wear resistance; ↓ Increasing toughness
		P10	Turning, copying, threading and milling of light roughing and finishing		
		P20	Turning, copying and milling at medium cutting speeds		
		P30	Turning and milling under heavy feeds and shocks		
		P40	Turning, planning and milling under unfavorable conditions		
		P50	Machining operations demanding very tough carbide		
M (Yellow)	Ferrous metals with long and short chips	M10	Finish turning alloy steels and cast iron	↑ Increasing cutting speed; ↓ Increasing feed rate	↑ Increasing wear resistance; ↓ Increasing toughness
		M20	General grade for machining of alloy steels and gray cast iron		
	Nonferrous metals	M30	Rough machining of tough materials		
		M40	Turning and parting off of mild steel, nonferrous metals and light alloys		
K (Red)	Ferrous metals with short chips	K01	Finish turning, boring and milling of very hard materials, abrasive plastics and ceramics		
	Nonferrous metals	K10	Turning, milling, drilling, and boring of malleable cast iron, nonferrous alloys, plastics, rubber, etc.		
	Nonmetallic materials	K20	Machining of copper, brass, and aluminum demanding tough carbide		
		K30	Rough machining of soft cast iron, low tensile steel in unfavorable conditions		
		K40	Machining of wood and nonferrous metals in unfavorable conditions		

Table 2.6 Relationship between ANSI and ISO Carbide Classification Systems

	Carbide grade		
ISO	P01 P05 P10 P20 P25 P30 P40 P50	M10 M20 M30 M40	K01 K05 K10 K20 K30 K40
ANSI	C8 C7 C6 C5		C4 C3 C2 C1

Increasing toughness →

← Increasing hardness

Note that both ISO and ANSI designation systems for various types and grades of cutting tool materials are not precise. They can only serve as a general guide in selecting cutting tool materials for specific applications. Cutting tool manufacturers often use their own classification systems with ANSI and ISO equivalent grades for their products.

Cutting Tool Material Selection

Selecting proper cutting tool materials for a specific machining application can provide significant advantages including **increased productivity, improved quality, and reduced costs**. The following factors should be carefully considered in selecting cutting tool materials:

1. Type of material to be machined (ferrous or non-ferrous type)

Select grade C5 - C8 for steel materials

Select grade C1 - C4 for cast iron, non-ferrous metals, and non-metallic materials

---

2. Machining types

Roughing:	**C1 for non-steel materials** **C5 for steel materials**
General Purpose:	**C2 for non-steel materials** **C6 for steel materials**
Finishing:	**C3 for non-steel materials** **C7 for steel materials**
Precision boring and fine finishing:	**C4 for non-steel materials** **C8 for steel materials**

Figure 2.1 is a comparision chart of the cutting speed range for various cutting tool materials for machining different metals.

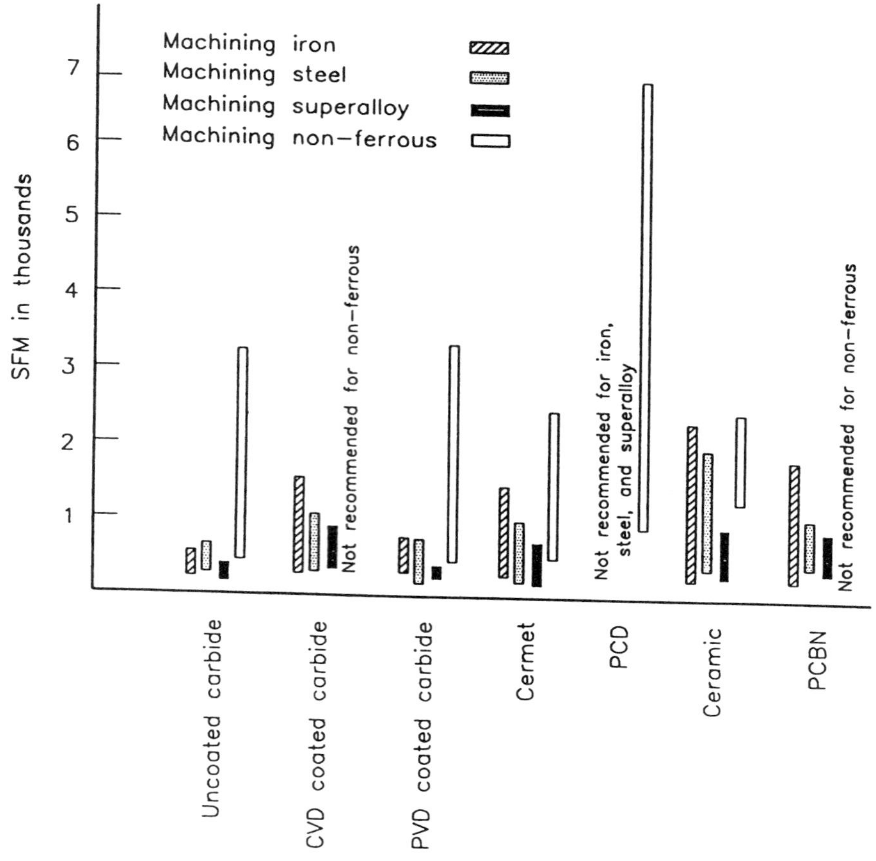

Figure 2.1

2.4 Tooling for Milling

A typical tooling system for machining centers consists of the **four** major components; **automatic tool changer, toolholders, adaptors, and cutting tools.** Any tooling system for CNC machine tools must meet the following **three** requirements:

- capable of holding multiple tools
- automatic tool change to shorten tool change time
- interchangeability

Automatic Tool Changer

An automatic tool changer (ATC) facilitates the quick change of tools in and out of the machine spindle. The tools are stored in the **automatic tool magazine** which is an indexable storage component part of the machine tool. The tools can be selected and changed under the control of the part program. Figure 2.2 on the following page shows a machining center with a chain type of ATC.

Figure 2.2 A chain type of automatic tool changer

Toolholders

Toolholders are used to facilitate the switching of a broad range of cutting tools in and out of the spindle automatically. A toolholder consists of **five** basic components (Figure 2.3):

1. Tapered shank
2. Flange
3. Retention knob
4. Opposed slots
5. Adaptor

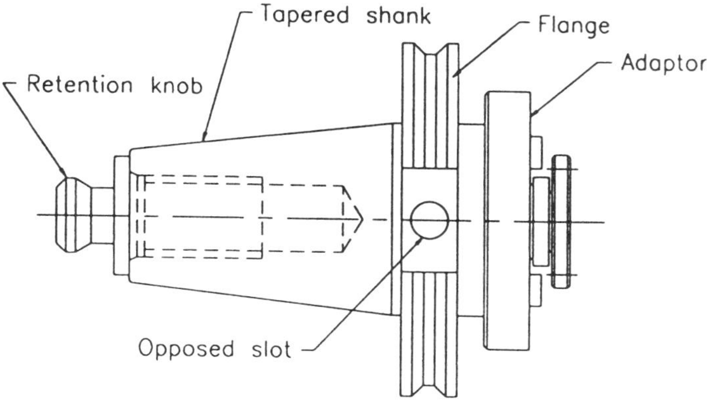

Figure 2.3

Tapered Shank

The tapered shank fits the toolholder to the spindle. The ANSI standard defines **six basic taper shank sizes** including #30, #35, #40, #45, #50, and #60. Larger machines use toolholders that have larger shank taper numbers. The taper of the shank is made to 3.5 in./ft (or a ratio of 7:24).

Taper Shank No.	Type of Machine
#60	**Very large machines**
#50	**Medium size machines (20 to 50 HPs)**
#40	**Small size machines**
#30	**Very small machines**

Flange Type

The flange allows the toolholder to be grabbed by the tool gripper or the machine spindle. There are **two** commonly used flange types: **V-flange and BT-flange** (Figure 2.4). V-falnges are often referred to as Caterpillar V-flanges. They use inch threads for the retention knob and are used to hold inch-dimensioned cutting tools. BT-flanges have metric threads for the retention knob, but their adaptors can be designed to accommodate a wide range of inch-dimensioned cutting tools. BT-flange holders are widely used in Japanese and European made machining centers.

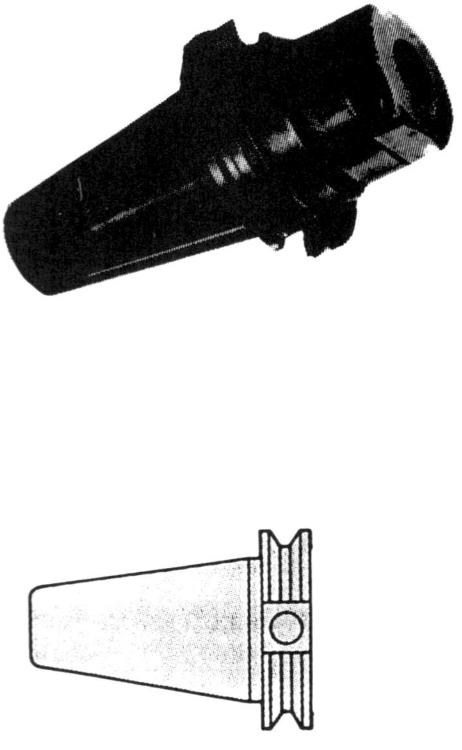

Figure 2.4a V-flange

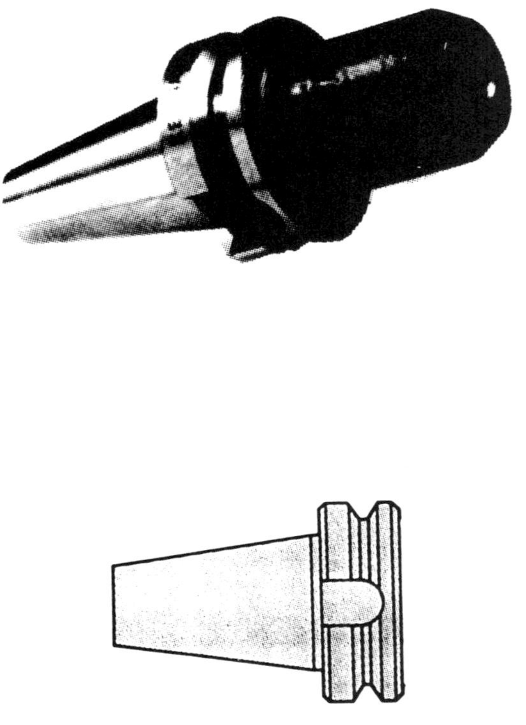

Figure 2.4b BT-flange

Retention Knob

The retention knob allows the locking drawbar of the spindle to pull the toolholder firmly into the spindle and to release the toolholder automatically (Figure 2.5). Retention knobs are made in various styles and sizes. They are not necessarily interchangeable. Only use the retention knobs that are specified by the machine tool manufacturer.

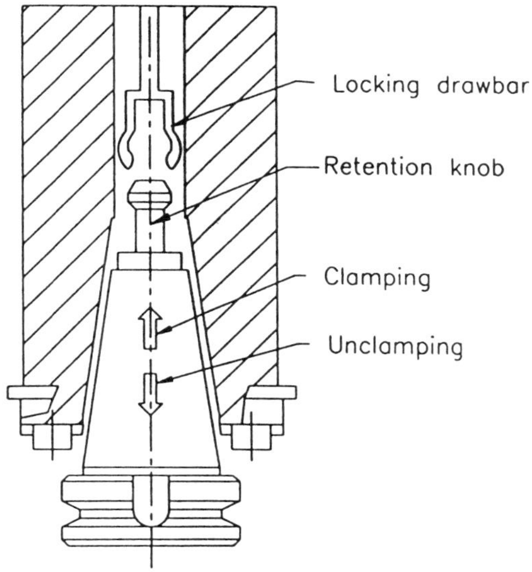

Figure 2.5

Adaptors

Adaptors are designed with various configurations to accommodate different types and sizes of cutting tools. Toolholders are often named according to their adaptor type. Commonly used adaptors include; **end mill holders, face mill holders, tap holders, collet holders, boring bar holders, Morse taper holders, Jacob taper holders, and straight shank holders.** Figure 2.6 on the next page shows a toolholder selection chart. There is no established standard for specifying the configuration and size of adaptors.

2.5 Tooling System for Turning

The tooling system for turning centers consists of **six** basic components (Figure 2.7):

1. Turret head
2. Mounting blocks
3. Mounting plates
4. Tool holders
5. Sleeves and sockets
6. Inserts or cutting tools

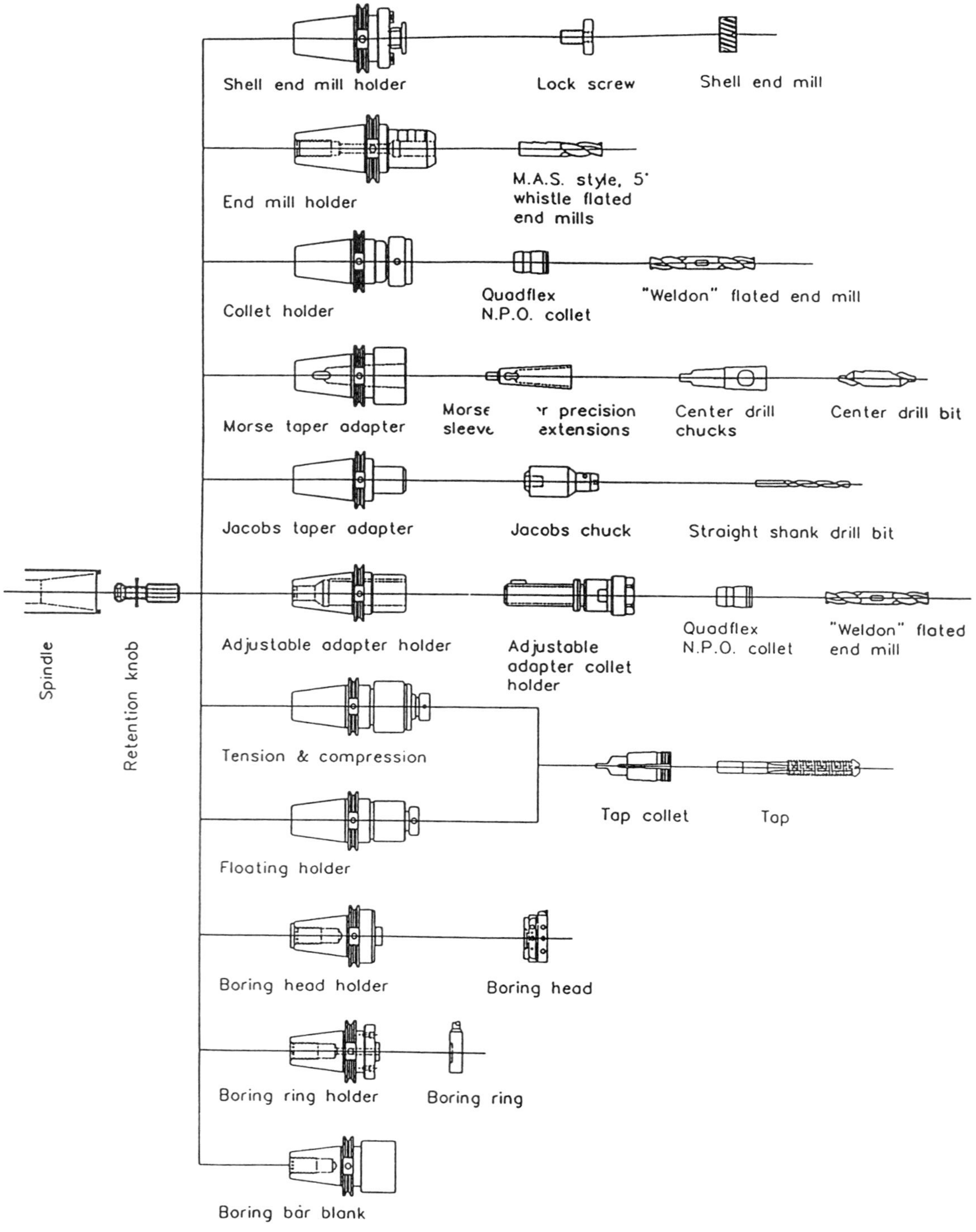

Figure 2.6 Tooling system for milling machines (Source: S.C. Jonathon Lin, Computer Numerical Control: From Programming to Networking, 1994. Courtesy of Delmar Publishers, Inc.)

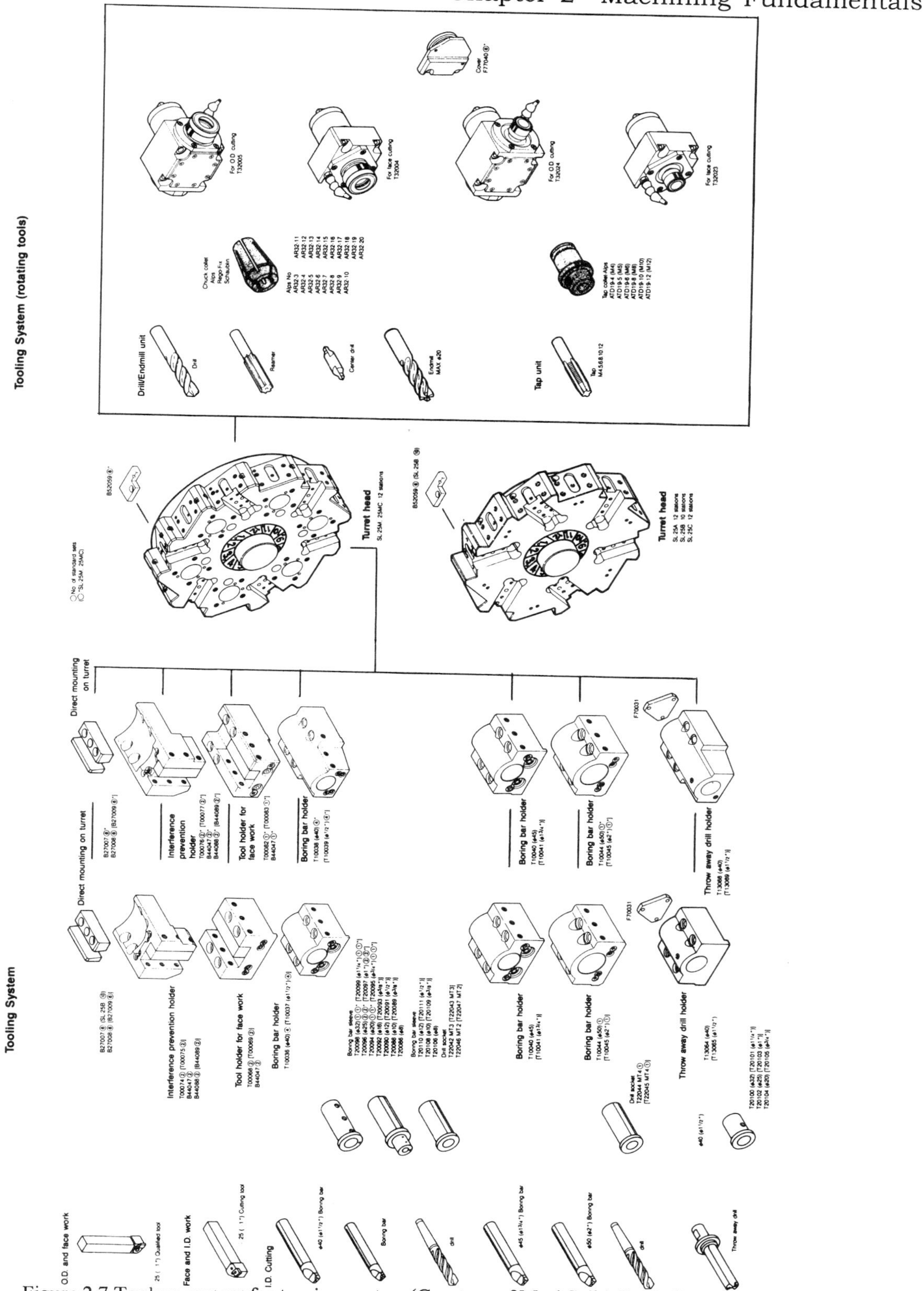

Figure 2.7 Tooling system for turning centers (Courtesy of Mori Seiki Co. Ltd.)

A turret head provides from 6 to 12 tool stations that can be automatically indexed by the control. Depending on the type of cutting tool used, mounting plates or mounting blocks are needed to attach the cutting tools to turret head. Normally, tools for OD turning and facing operations use mounting plates. Boring tools and drills use mounting blocks. Usually sleeves or sockets are needed to allow for different tool shank size. Figure 2.8 shows a 12-station turret head with a variety of cutting tools. Some turning centers provide simultaneous 3-axis control (X, Z, and spindle angular orientation). The spindle C axis can give as small as 0.001° of spindle rotation. Spindle axis control combined with rotating tools allows the machine to turn, bore, drill, mill, tap, and ream the workpiece in any direction in one machine setup. These turning centers have simultaneous 3-axis control which allows the machining of the rotating tools and they are often referred to as mill-turn. Figure 2.9 shows a turret used in a mill turn.

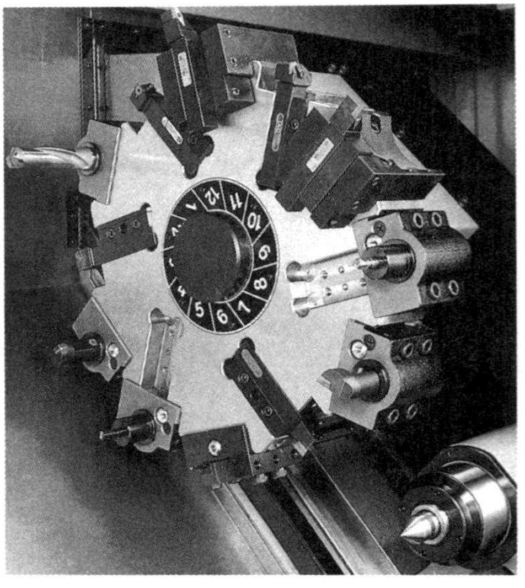

Figure 2.8

Figure 2.9

(Source of Photographs: Mori Seiki Co. Ltd.)

2.6 Inserts Identification and Selection

Indexable inserts are widely used in CNC machines. They are made with various shapes and sizes (Figure 2.10). The ANSI standard provides an identification system to describe the features of inserts. The identification consists of up to 10 symbol codes. Each code defines a feature of the insert (Figure 2.11). The first 7 symbols are mandatory, the following 2 symbols are optional, and the last symbol is for the manufacturer's use. The ISO standard basically follows the ANSI standard except the dimensions are specified in millimeters.

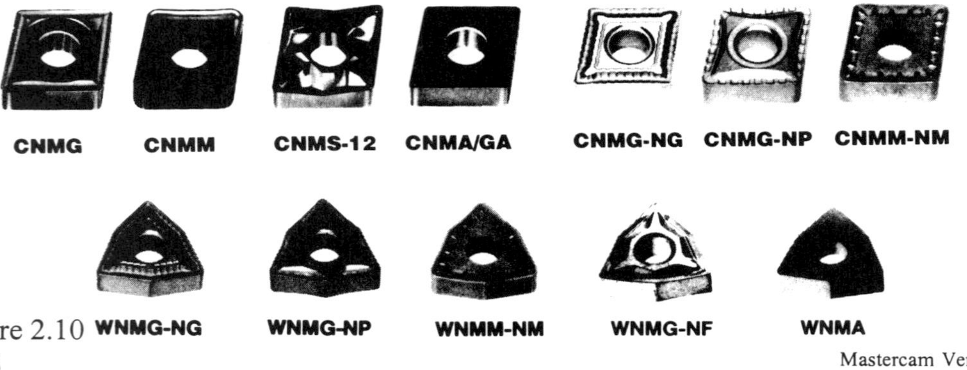

Figure 2.10

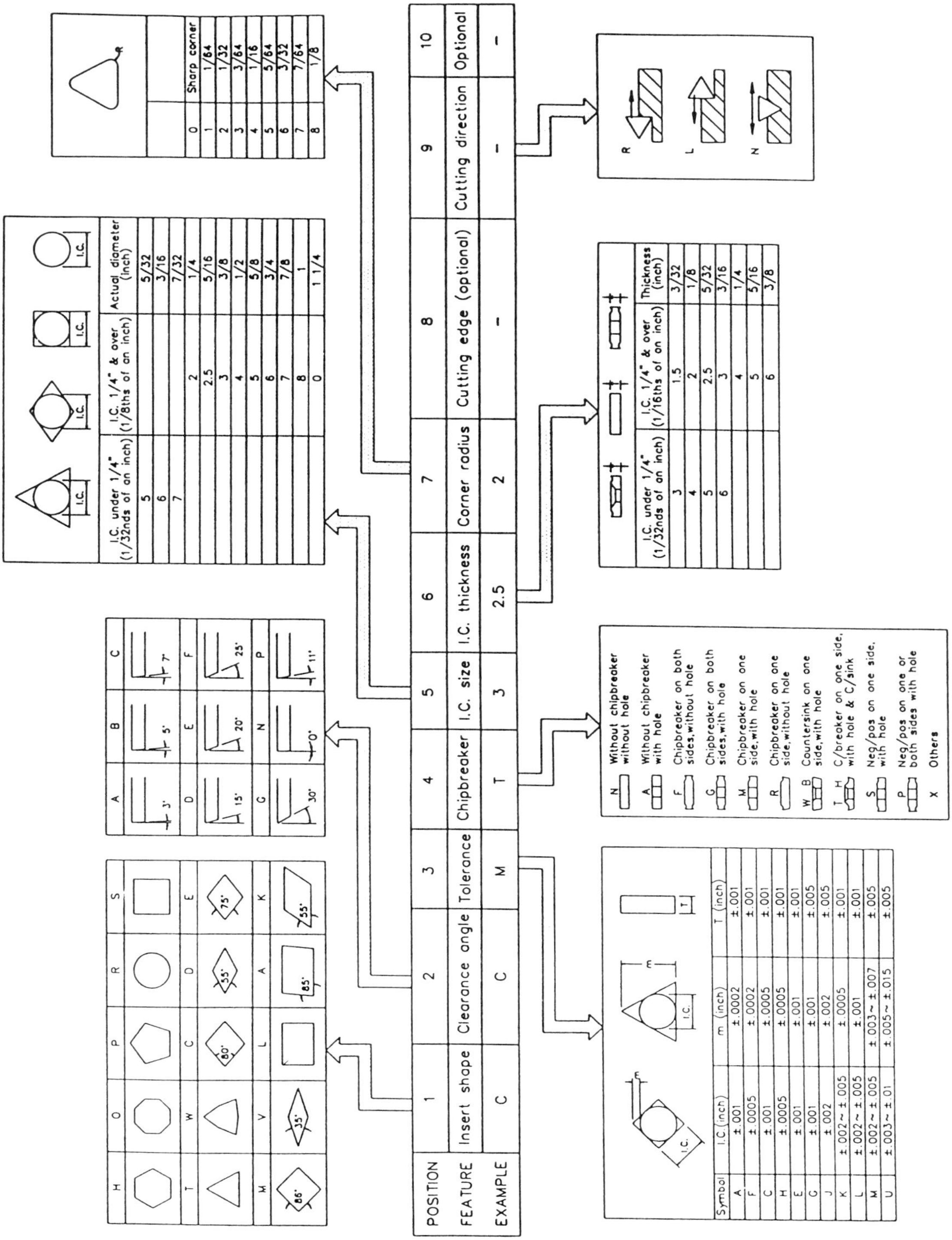

Figure 2.11 Insert identification system (Source: S.C. Jonathon Lin, Computer Numerical Control: From Programming to Networking, 1994. Courtesy of Delmar Publishers Inc.)

Insert Selection

Several factors must be carefully considered in selecting proper inserts for specific applications. These factors include **insert shape, insert size, and chip breaker.**

Insert Shape

Inserts are made in various shapes. The insert shape affects **insert strength, insert angle, maximum number of cutting edges available, power consumption, and versatility**. The larger the included insert angle, the stronger the insert. A round insert is the strongest, while the 35° diamond insert is the weakest type.

The inserts with more sides provide a greater number of cutting edges. A hexagonal shaped insert has six cutting edges, while a triangle shape only furnishes three edges. The cutting edges of those inserts with a zero clearance angle are twice those with a non-zero clearance angle. The zero clearance triangle inserts, for example, have 6 possible edges.

The more commonly used insert types in turning applications include:

80° diamond shape:	**for OD turning, ID boring, and facing**
55° diamond shape:	**for OD turning, profiling, and ID boring**
35° diamond shape:	**for OD profiling and ID profiling**
60° shape:	**for OD turning, ID boring, and facing**
Round shape:	**for OD turning, and ID boring**

Insert Size

Three dimensions used to describe the insert size are the **inscribed circle (IC), thickness (T), and nose radius (R)** (Figure 2.12).

Figure 2.12

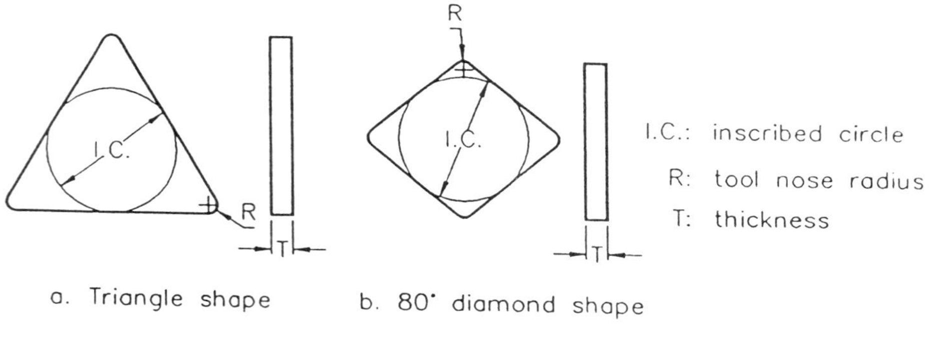

The selection of IC size depends on the maximum depth of cut to be taken. The rule of thumb is that the maximum cutting edge engagement is one-half the insert edge length. The cutting edge length is normally longer than the IC size except for square and round inserts as shown in Figure 2.13. The cutting edge length of commonly used inserts can be computed from the formulas given in Table 2.7.

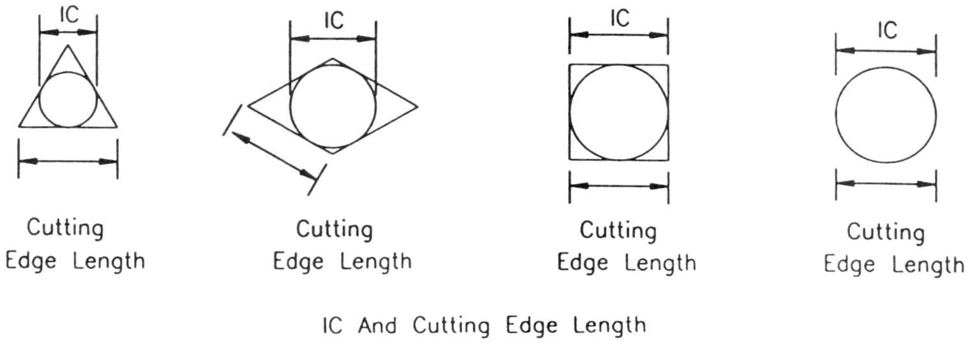

Figure 2.13

Table 2.7 The cutting edge length of various insert shapes

Insert Shape	Cutting Edge Length (L)
Square	L = IC
Round	L = IC
Triangle	L = 1.732 IC
80° diamond	L = 1.015 IC
55° diamond	L = 1.221 IC
35° diamond	L = 1.744 IC

Insert Thickness

The factors affecting the selection of insert thickness are the **feed rate** and the **cutting edge engagement**. The nomograph shown in Figure 2.14 provides a reference guide for selecting the insert thickness to meet the strength requirement. To use this nomograph, connect a line between the selected feed rate and the actual maximum cutting edge engagement. This line intersects with the insert thickness line at one point which is the proper insert thickness. Two scales are given in the insert thickness line, one for regular cuts and the other for interrupted cuts.

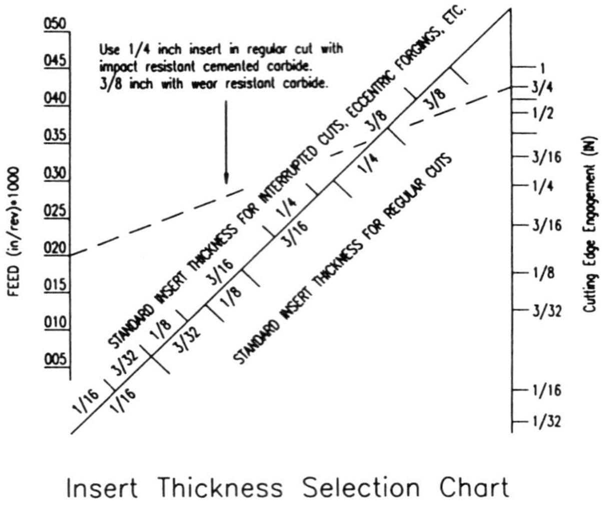

Figure 2.14

Insert Nose Radius

The selection of insert nose radius for an operation is mainly determined by two factors: **feed rate and required surface finish.** The surface finish (or roughness) is normally expressed by an arithmetic average (AA) value or the root mean square (RMS) value. Figure 2.15 provides a nomograph for selecting the proper insert nose radius based on the given feed rate and the required surface finish either in AA or RMS value.

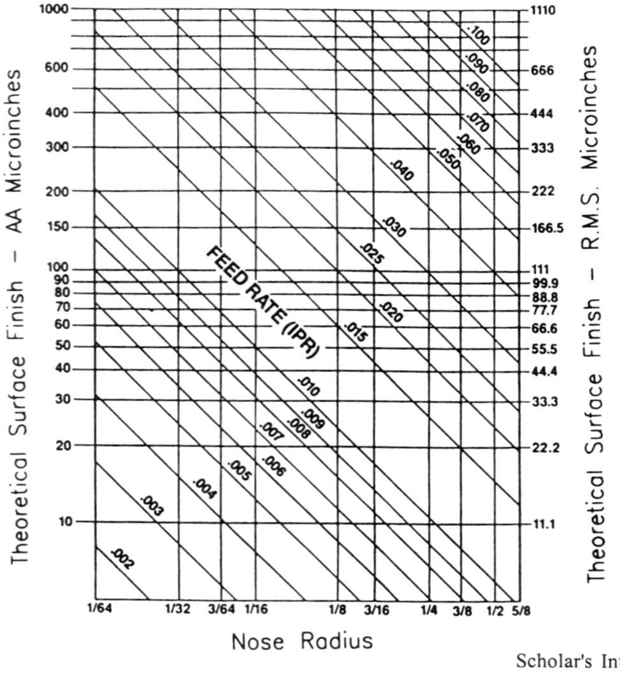

Figure 2.15

Mastercam Version 7,
Scholar's International Publishing Corp., 1998

Follow these steps to select the nose radius using the nomograph:

1. Locate the required surface finish (AA or RMS) on the vertical line.
2. Follow the horizontal line corresponding to the desired surface finish to the point at which the line intersects the diagonal line representing the feed rate.
3. Project a line from this point downward to the nose radius scale.
4. If this line falls between two values, select the larger value.
5. If no available nose radius generates the required finish, reduce the feed rate.

Chip Breakers

Follow these **two** guidelines when selecting the proper chip breaker:

a. No chip breaker is required for:
- interrupted cuts
- turning brittle materials such as cast iron

b. Chip breakers are needed for turning tough, stringy matrials such as steels, aluminum, and non-ferrous materials.

2.7 Toolholders

The ANSI standard for insert toolholder identification system is given in Figure 2.17 on the next page. The ANSI identification system describes the following features of an insert toolholder:

1. Clamping method
2. Insert shape
3. Holder style
4. Rake angle
5. Hand of tool
6. Shank size
7. Insert IC size
8. Qualified condition

An insert toolholder is specifically designed to match only one insert shape and size. Therefore, it is very important to choose the right insert toolholder for a particular job. There are **five factors** to be considered in selecting an insert toolholder. They are:

1. Holder style
2. Insert shape and size
3. Rake angle
4. Shank dimension
5. Hand type

The **lead angle** defines the style of the insert toolholder. The lead angle is also referred to as the side cutting edge angle. It is formed between the side cutting edge and one of the principal axis (Figure 2.17). **Three** types of lead angle are **negative lead angle, zero lead angle, and positive lead angle** (Figure 2.18 on page 2-23).

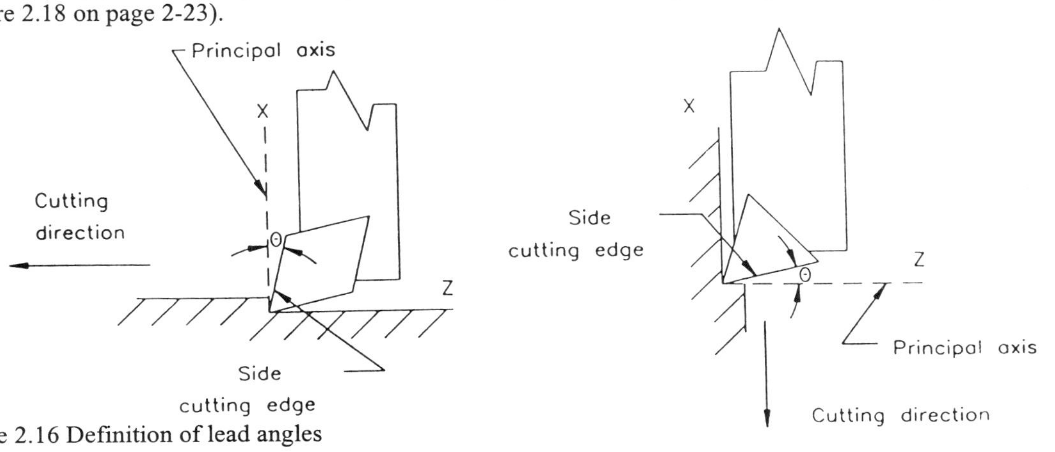

Figure 2.16 Definition of lead angles

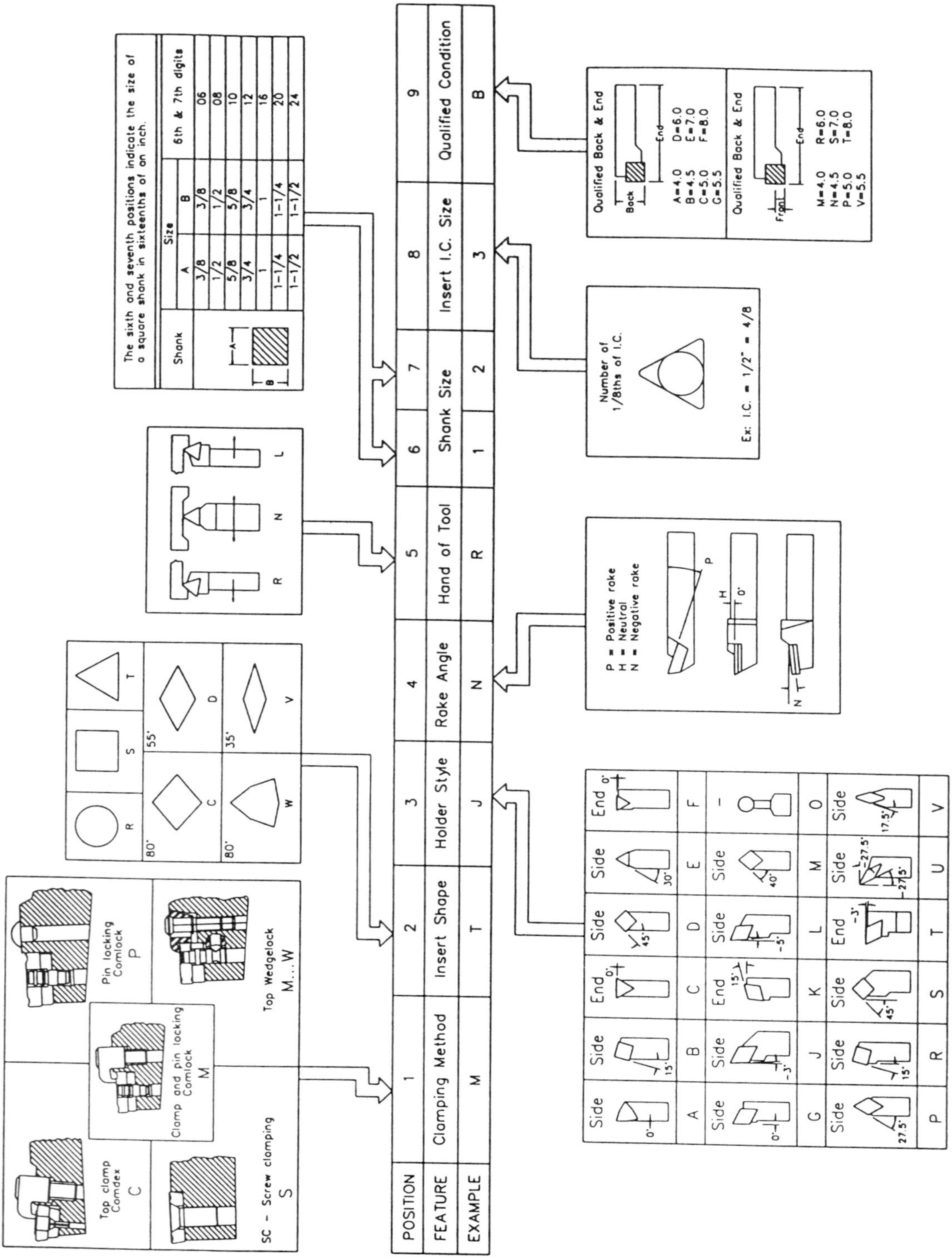

Figure 2.17 Insert toolholder identification system

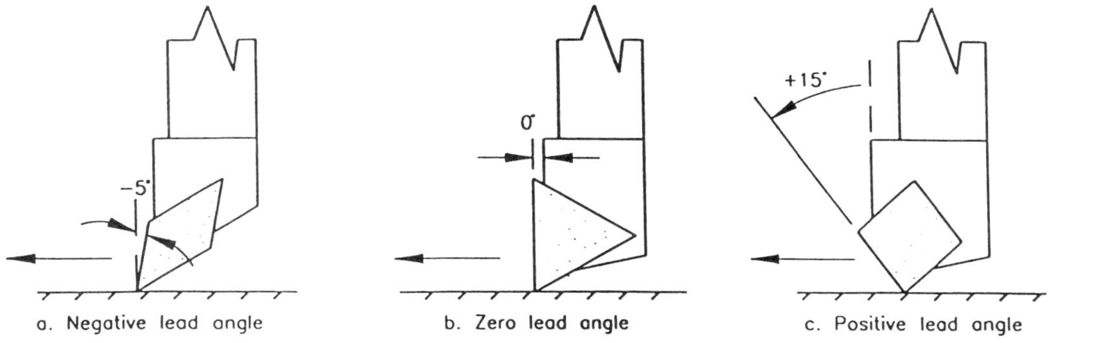

Figure 2.18 Three types of lead angles

The other important angle to be considered in selecting a toolholder type is the **profile** angle. The profile angle is the maximum slope angle that the combination of insert and toolholder can produce in profiling (Figure 2.19). A profile angle can be calculated from the following formula:

Profile angle = 90° + lead angle - insert angle

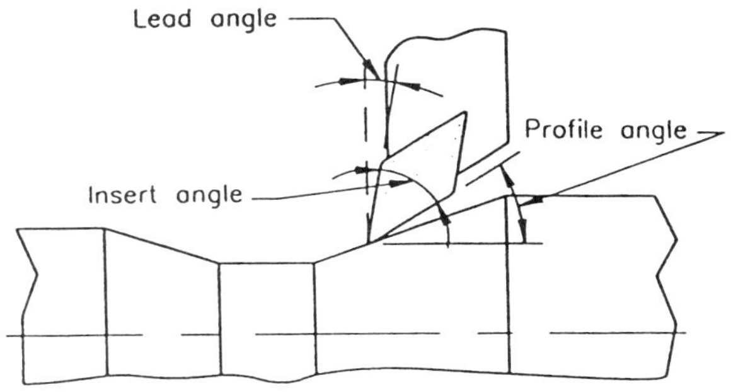

Figure 2.19

In practice, the maximum profile angle to be produced should be at least *2° smaller* than the computed profile angle.

Boring Bar Indentification System

A boring bar identification system is actually very similar to that of regular toolholders. The main difference is that a bar composition code is added to the beginning of the identification codes. The bar composition indicates what materials are in the boring bar. Two common boring bar materials are **steel (S)** and **carbide (C)**. The sixth and seventh positions specify the cross section of the shank for regular toolholders, and they are used to represent the bar diameter for boring bars.

The selection of boring bars for specific applications depends on the following seven factors:

1. Bar compositon
2. Boring bar style
3. Minimum bore diameter
4. Bar diameter
5. Insert shape and size
6. Hand type
7. Rake angle

Table 2.8 on the next two pages presents a list of combinations of toolholder styles and inserts commonly used in industry. Their typical applications are also included.

2.8 Machining Parameters

Three variables that dictate the efficiency of a machining process include **cutting speed, feed rate, and depth of cut**. These three variables are often referred to as machining parameters. The following factors should be carefully considered in selecting machining parameters:

- Operating capacity of the cutting tool
- Machine's available spindle horsepower
- Machinability of the workpiece material
- Rigidity of the part and fixture

Cutting Speed and Spindle Speed

Cutting speed, also called surface speed, refers to the speed at which the cutting edge of the tool passes over the surface of the workpiece. The cutting speed of a machining operation can be determined by the following two formulas:

$$CS = \frac{\pi \cdot D \cdot N}{12} \quad \text{(unit: FPM in inch units)}$$

$$CS = \frac{\pi \cdot D \cdot N}{1000} \quad \text{(unit: MPM in metric units)}$$

where CS = surface cutting speed, feet/minute (FPM) or meter/minute (MPM)
D = diameter of the rotating part, either the cutting tool or workpiece, in. or mm
N = RPM (rotation speed at which workpiece or cutter will turn)

In drilling (Figure 2.20) and milling (Figure 2.21), the diameter of the rotating part refers to the cutter diameter. In turning (Figure 2.22), the diameter represents the workpiece major diameter.

Table 2.8 Selection of Indexable Insert Holders

Operation Pattern	Holder Illustration	Holder Style	Insert Shape	Applications
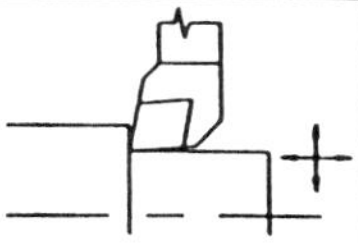	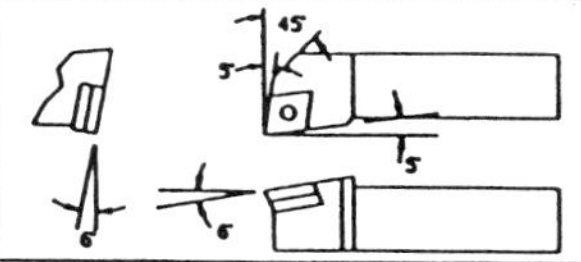	L −5°	C 80° diamond	• OD turning • Facing
	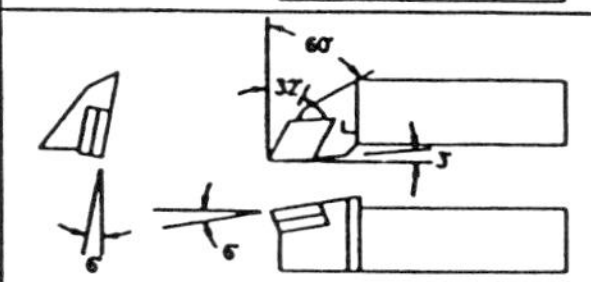	J −3°	D 55° diamond	• OD turning • Profiling with a max. of 30° profile angle
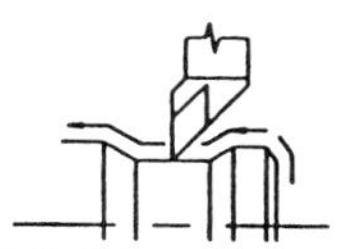	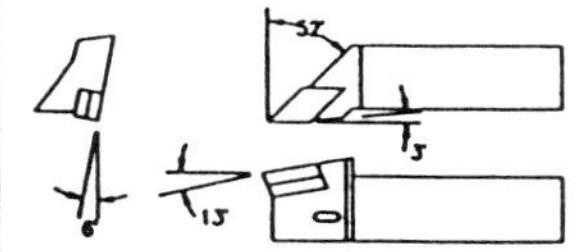	J −3°	V 35° diamond	• OD Profiling with a max. of 50° profile angle
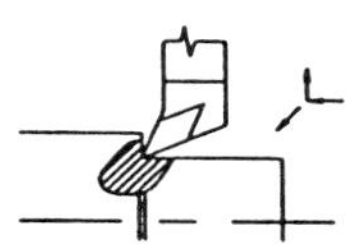	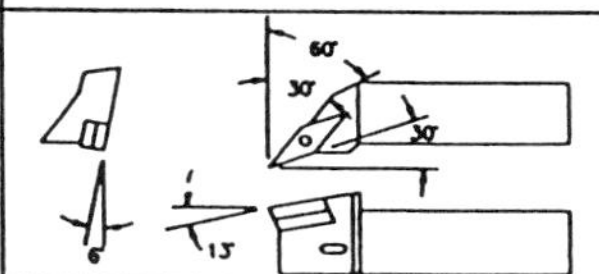	T	V 35° diamond	• Turning and undercutting
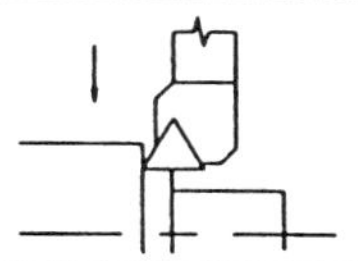	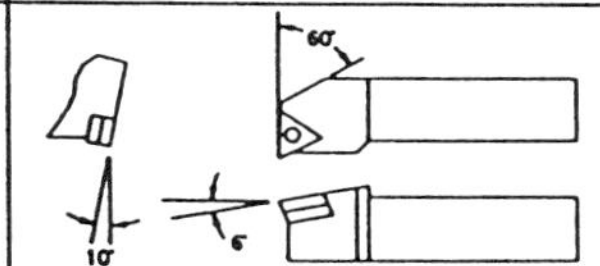	F 0°	T 60°	• Facing with square shoulder cutting
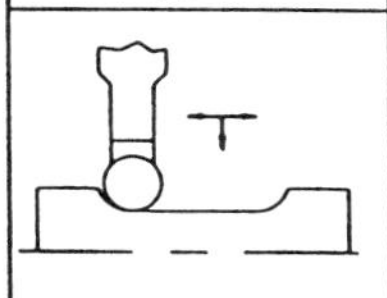	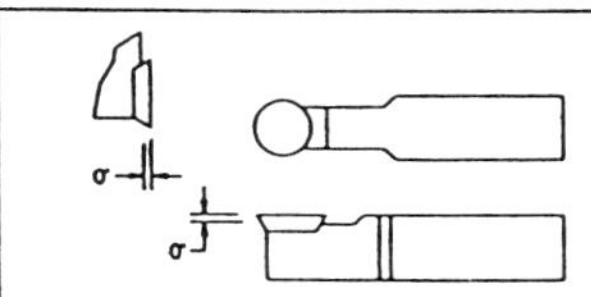	N	R round	• Profiling
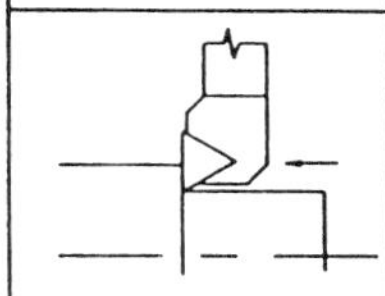	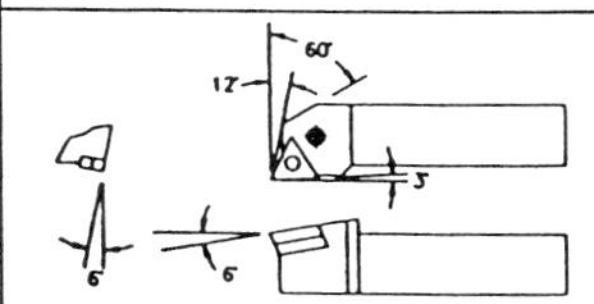	J −3°	T 60°	• OD turning with Square shoulder cutting
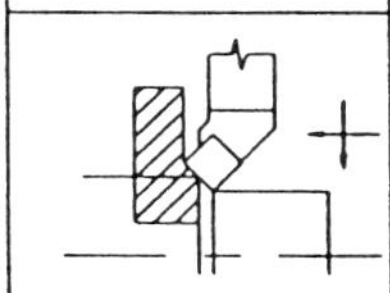	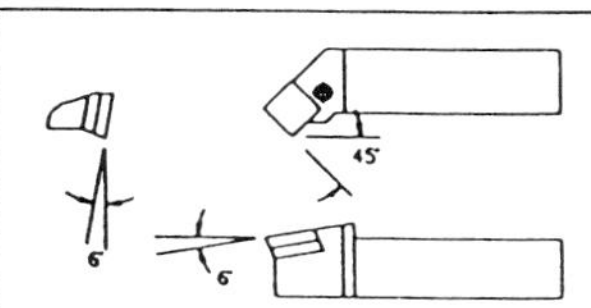	D 45°	T 90° square	• OD turning Facing
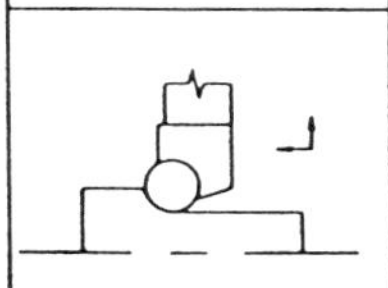	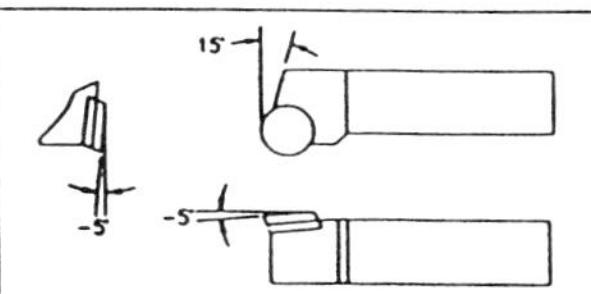	G 0°	R round	• OD turning Facing

Table 2.8 (Continued)

Operation Pattern	Holder Illustration	Holder Style	Insert Shape	Applications
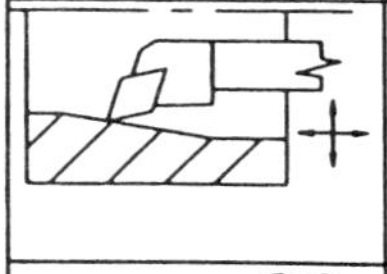	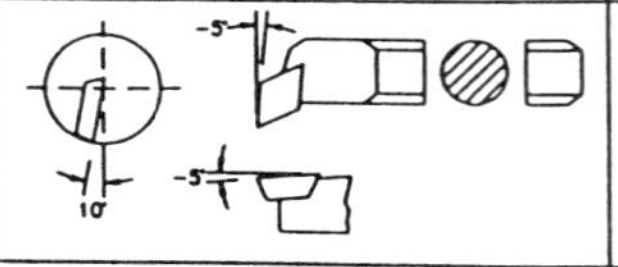	L −5°	C 80° diamond	• Straight surfaces and boring profiles positive
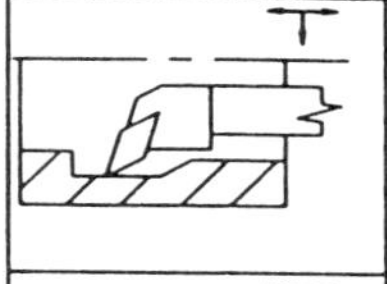	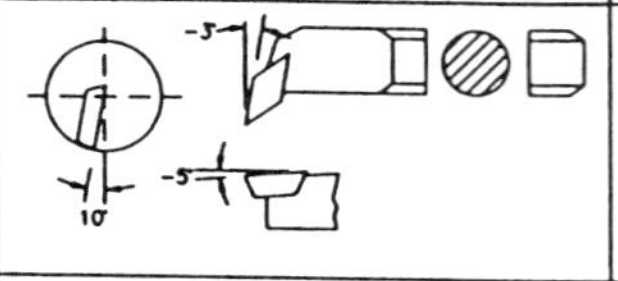	J −3°	D 55° diamond	• Boring internal profiles with the max. profile angle of 30°
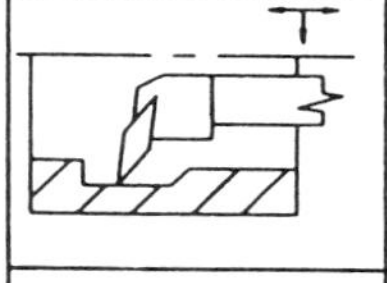	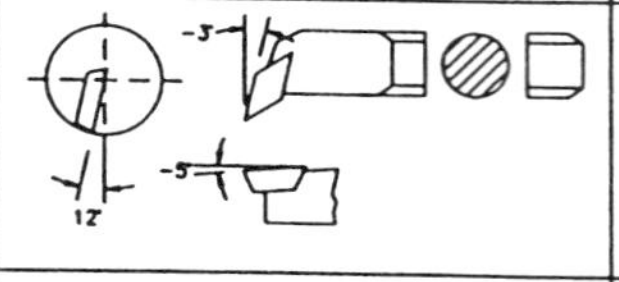	J −3°	V 35° diamond	• Boring internal profiles with the max. profile angle of 50°
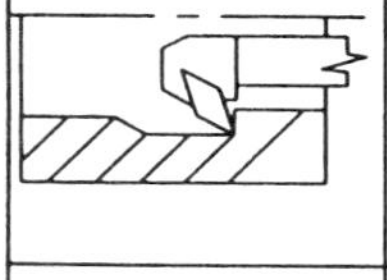	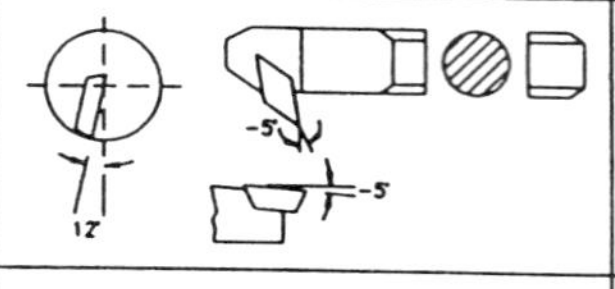	L −5°	V 35° diamond	• Back boring internal profiles
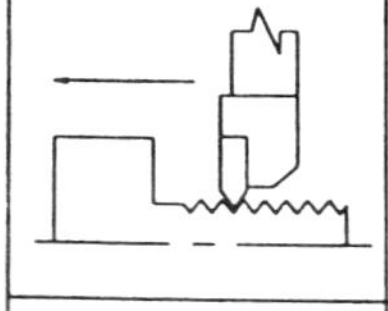	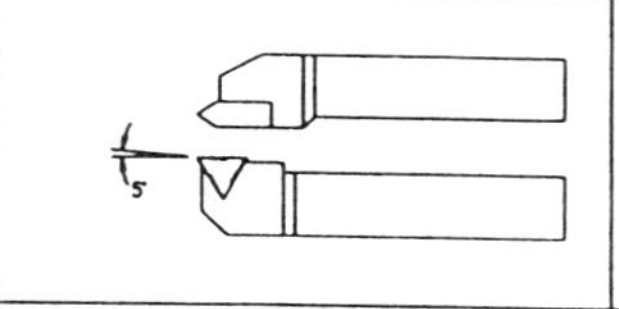	Vertical	Threading insert	• External threads cutting
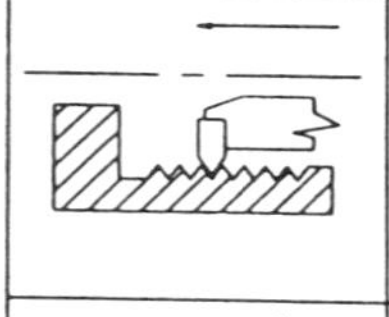	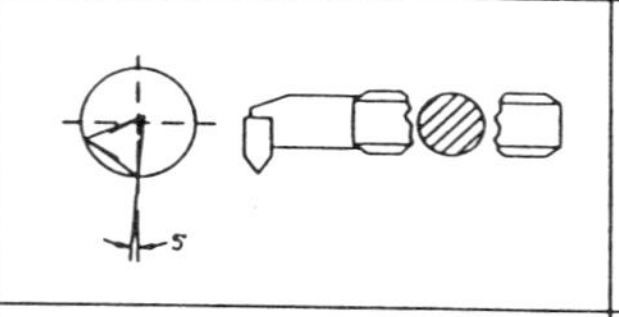	Horizontal	Threading insert	• Internal threads cutting
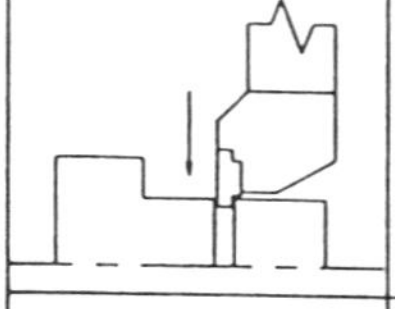	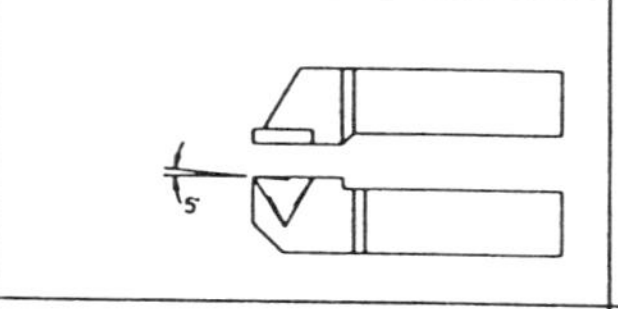	Vertical	Grooving insert	• External grooves cutting
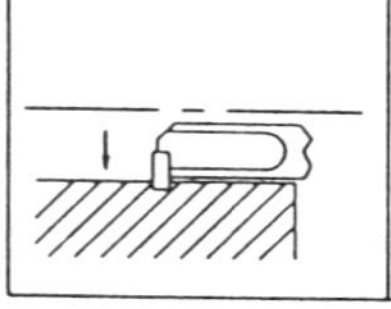	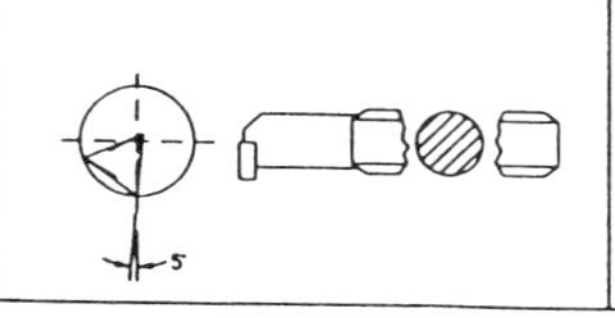	Horizontal	Grooving insert	• Internal grooves cutting

Mastercam Version 7,
Scholar's International Publishing Corp., 1998

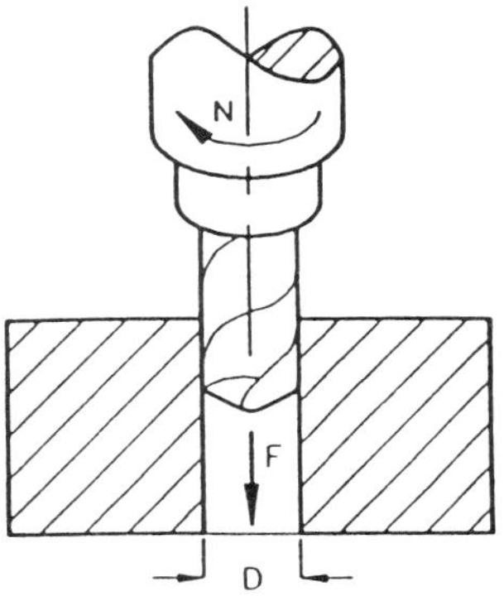

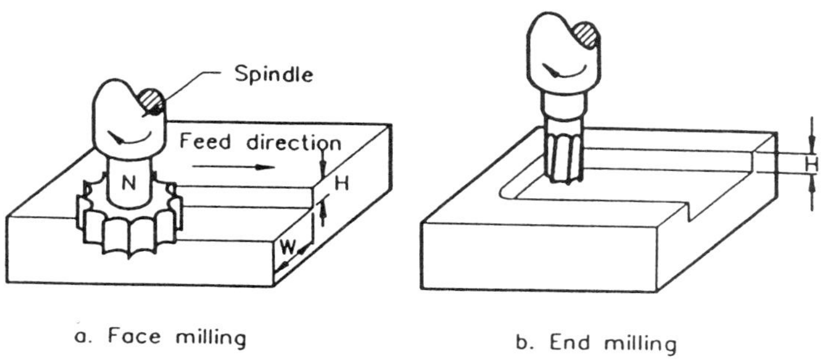

Figure 2.20 Drilling | Figure 2.21 Milling

(Source: S.C. Jonathon Lin, Computer Numerical Control: From Programming to Networking, 1994. Courtesy of Delmar Publishers, Inc.)

The surface cutting speed at which a material is machined is a given quantity and is normally obtained from a machining data handbook or experience. We can use the given surface cutting speed value to find the spindle speed by re-arranged the above two formulas as follows:

$$N = \frac{12 \cdot CS}{\pi \cdot D} \quad \text{(Inch unit)}$$

$$N = \frac{1000 \cdot CS}{\pi \cdot D} \quad \text{(Metric unit)}$$

where N = rotation speed in RPM

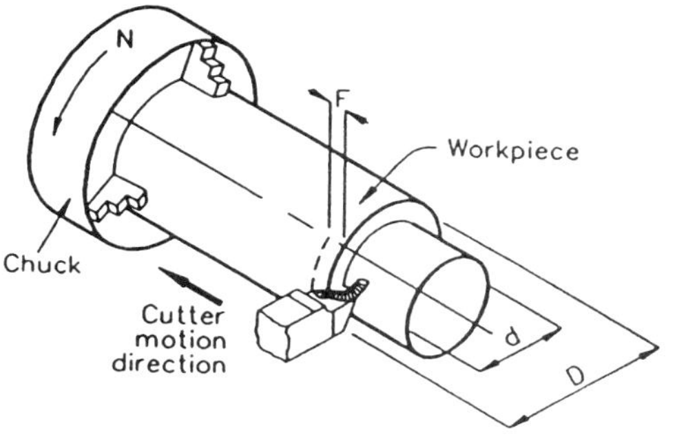

Figure 2.22 Turning (Source: S.C. Jonathon Lin, Computer Numerical Control: From Programming to Networking, 1994. Courtesy of Delmar Publishers, Inc.)

Feed Rate

The **feed** is the movement of the cutting tool in the cutting direction. The **feed rate** is the speed of feed that is normally specified by the following **three** units:

- **Feed per tooth, inches per tooth (IPT) or millimeters per tooth (MMPT)**
- **Feed per revolution, inches per revolution (IPR) or millimeters per revolution (MMPR)**
- **Feed per minute, inches per minute (IPM) or millimeters per minute (MMPM)**

The feed rate *recommended* by machining handbooks or cutting tool manufacturers is normally given in feed per tooth. However, the feed is *programmed* in the units of feed per revolution or feed per minute in NC machines.

The following three formulas can be used to convert the feed rate from feed per tooth to feed per revolution or feed per minute:

$$f_r = f_t \cdot T$$

$$f_m = f_r \cdot N$$

$$f_m = f_t \cdot T \cdot N$$

where f_r = feed per revolution (unit: IPR or MMPR)
f_t = feed per tooth (or flute) (unit: IPT or MMPT)
f_m = feed per minute (unit: IPM or MMPM)
T = number of teeth (or flutes) of the cutter
N = RPM

Depth of Cut

Depth of cut is the distance the cutter penetrates into the workpiece and is measured in the direction perpendicular to the cutter motion direction. The depth of cut is mainly determined by two factors: **available spindle horsepower** and **rigidity of cutter and machine.**

Material Removal Rate

The material removal rate refers to the amount of material removed per unit time. It is normally expressed in the units of **cubic inch per minute** or **cubic meter per minute**. The formulas to compute the material removal rate for three commonly used machining processes are given below:

1. **For Drilling** (see Figure 2.20):

$$MRR = \frac{\pi \cdot D^2 \cdot f_r \cdot N}{4}$$

where MRR = material removal rate, in^3/min.
D = drill diameter, inches
f_r = feed rate, IPR
N = spindle speed, RPM

2. **For Milling** (see Figure 2.21):

$$MRR = W \cdot H \cdot f_m$$

where W = width of cut, inches
H = depth of cut, inches
f_m = feed rate, inches/minute

3. **For Turning** (see Figure 2.22):

$$MRR = \frac{\pi \cdot (D^2 - d^2) \cdot f_r \cdot N}{4}$$

where D = original (major) diameter of workpiece
d = diameter after cut
f_r = feed (IPR)
N = revolutions per minute

Horsepower Requirement

It is important to know the required power for machining a workpiece under a set of machining conditions. The required horsepower in machining can not exceed the machine spindle power rating. The unit horsepower concept is widely used to calculate the required power for machining a workpiece. The amount of power needed to remove 1 cubic inch per minute of a certain material is called the **unit horsepower** (UHP). It is determined experimentally and is provided in tables for practical use.

The required horsepower can be obtained from the following formula:

$$HP_c = UHP \cdot MRR \cdot C$$

where HP_c = required horsepower at cutter
UHP = unit horsepower
MRR = material removal rate
C = feed correction factor

Tables 2.9 and 2.10 give the unit horsepower for drilling various materials. Tables 2.11 and 2.12 on the next page provide unit horsepower for milling, and turning operations, respectively.

Drill Size, in.	Feed, ipr										
	0.001	0.002	0.004	0.006	0.008	0.010	0.013	0.016	0.020	0.025	0.030
1/8	1.63	1.63	1.22	1.22							
1/4	1.43	1.32	1.17	1.02	0.94	0.86					
3/8	1.40	1.22	1.09	1.02	0.91	0.85					
1/2	1.38	1.07	1.03	0.98	0.86	0.83	0.78	0.75	0.71		
3/4	1.36	1.13	1.02	0.94	0.90	0.86	0.78	0.74	0.70		
1	1.27	1.08	0.99	0.89	0.83	0.82	0.74	0.72	0.70	0.66	
1 1/4	1.22	1.06	0.92	0.87	0.80	0.77	0.72	0.69	0.65	0.62	
1 1/2	1.24	1.02	0.88	0.83	0.78	0.74	0.70	0.67	0.62	0.59	
1 3/4	1.25	1.04	0.85	0.83	0.78	0.71	0.70	0.65	0.62	0.58	
2	1.18	0.99	0.88	0.80	0.76	0.70	0.66	0.64	0.61	0.57	0.55
2 1/2	—	—	—	—	0.71	0.67	0.63	0.61	0.54	0.56	0.53
3	—	—	—	—	—	—	—	0.61	0.57	0.52	0.52

Table 2.9 Unit horsepower required for drilling AISI 1112 steels (Source: S.C. Jonathon Lin, Computer Numerical Control: From Programming to Networking, 1994. Courtesy of Delmar Publishers, Inc.)

Material	Factor
AISI 1020	1.6
AISI 1035	1.3
1.99% C Tool Steel	1.7
AISI 3150	1.6
Gray Cast Iron	0.5
Malleable Iron	0.6
Stainless Steel	
AISI 416 free-machining martensitic	1.2
AISI 303 free-machining austenitic	1.6
AISI 304 austenitic	1.8
17-7 PH precipitation-hardened austenitic	2.0
4340 Steel heat-treated to 240,000-260,000 psi	2.3

Table 2.10 Approximate conversion factor for unit horsepower required to drill other materials (Source: S.C. Jonathon Lin, Computer Numerical Control: From Programming to Networking, 1994. Courtesy of Delmar Publishers,Inc.)

Material	UHP	Material	UHP
Magnesium	0.25	Stainless	
Aluminum	0.25	Free machining	1.0
Copper	0.5	Other	1.7
Brass	0.4	Titanium	
Bronze	0.5	Under 100,000 psi	1.3
Malleable iron	1.0	100,000–135,000 psi	1.7
Cast iron		135,000 and over	2.5
Ferrite	0.7	High–tensile alloys	
Pearlitic	1.0	180,000–220,000 psi	2.0
Chilled	0.7	220,000–260,000 psi	2.5
Steel		260,000–300,000 psi	3.3
Up to 150 BHN	1.4	High–temperature alloys	
300 BHN	1.7	Ferritic low alloys	1.7
400 BHN	2.0	Austenitic alloys	2.0
500 BHN	2.5	Nickel–based alloys	2.5
		Cobalt–based alloys	2.5

Table 2.11 Unit horsepower for milling (Source: S.C. Jonathon Lin, Computer Numerical Control: From Programming to Networking, 1994. Courtesy of Delmar Publishers, Inc.)

(a) Ferrous Metals and Alloys

Materials	BHN					
	150–175	176–200	201–250	251–300	301–350	351–400
	Unit Horsepower (UHP)					
AISI						
1010–1025	0.58	0.67				
1030–1055	0.58	0.67	0.80	0.96		
1060–1095			0.75	0.88	1.00	
1112–1120	0.50					
1314–1340	0.42	0.46	0.50			
1330–1350		0.67	0.75	0.92	1.10	
2015–2115	0.67					
2315–2335	0.54	0.58	0.62	0.75	0.92	
2340–2350		0.50	0.58	0.70	0.83	1.00
2512–2515	0.50	0.58	0.67	0.80	0.92	
3115–3130	0.50	0.58	0.70	0.83	1.00	
3160–3450		0.50	0.62	0.75	0.87	1.00
4130–4345		0.46	0.58	0.70	0.83	1.00
4615–4820	0.46	0.50	0.58	0.70	0.83	0.87
5120–5150	0.46	0.50	0.62	0.75	0.87	1.00
52100		0.58	0.67	0.83	1.00	
6115–6140	0.46	0.54	0.67	0.83	1.00	
6145–6195		0.70	0.83	1.00	1.20	1.30
Plain cast iron	0.30	0.33	0.42	0.50		
Alloy cast iron	0.30	0.42	0.52			
Malleable cast iron	0.42					
Cast steel	0.62	0.67	0.80			

(b) High–Temperature Alloys

Material	BHN	UHP	Material	BHN	UHP	Material	BHN	UHP
A286	165	0.82	Hastelloy B	230	1.10	Ti–150A	340	0.65
A286	285	0.93	Inco 700	300	1.12	U–500	375	1.10
Chromoloy	200	0.78	Inco 702	230	1.10	4340	200	0.78
Chromoloy	310	1.18	M–252	230	1.10	4340	340	0.93
			M–252	310	1.20			

(c) Nonferrous Metals and Alloys

Material	UHP	Material	UHP	Material	UHP
Brass		Bronze		Aluminum	
Hard	0.83	Hard	0.83	Cast	0.25
Medium	0.50	Med.	0.50	Hard	0.33
Soft	0.33	Soft	0.33	Monel	1.00
Free–machining	0.25	Copper	0.90	Zinc(die cast)	0.25

Table 2.12 Unit horsepower for turning various materials (Source: S.C. Jonathon Lin, Computer Numerical Control: From Programming to Networking, 1994. Courtesy of Delmar Publishers, Inc.)

The feed correction factor C is used to compensate for the effect of feed on horsepower because **high** feed rates require **less** unit horsepower. Figure 2.23 shows the feed correction factors.

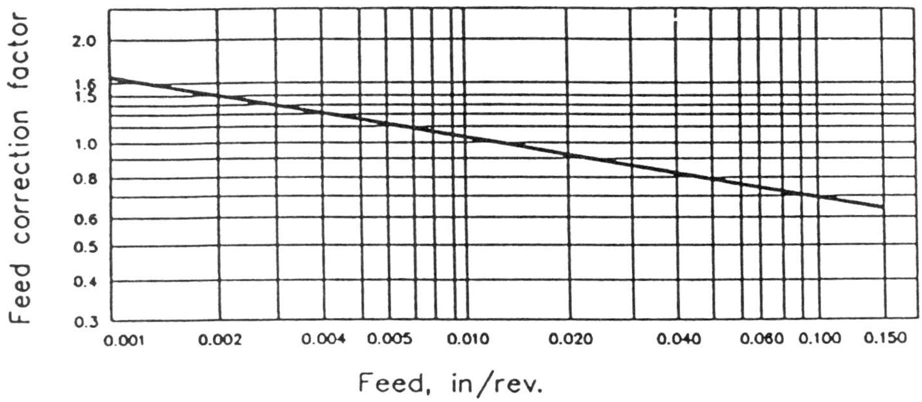

Adjustment for lead angle as follows:

If tool cuts with a lead angle of	Reduce the actual feed by this amount and use the feed correction factor for the finer feed
30°	10%
45°	30%
60°	50%
If the depth of cut is less than the nose radius	30%

Figure 2.23 Feed conversion facator
(Source: Application Data Manual, Courtesy of Carboloy Inc., a Seco Tools Company)

The efficiency of the machine must be considered when calculating the required horsepower because power is needed to overcome friction in the machine. The formula for calculating the required horsepower at the spindle motor is:

$$HP_m = \frac{HP_c}{E}$$

where HP_m = required horsepower at the spindle motor
E = machine efficiency

2.9 Face Milling

Face milling is normally used in two situations:

1. where a large amount of material must be removed in a short period of time
2. a good surface finishing is required.

Cutter Size

When possible, use a larger effective diameter to shorten the machining time. The larger the flat surface to be machined, the larger the effective diameter should be used.

The cutter height determines the allowable maximum depth of cut. The depth of cut should be smaller than the cutter height.

Cutting Width Selection

The selection of cutting width is dictated by two considerations, **tool life and machining efficiency**. The *larger* the cutting width, the *shorter* the tool life and the *better* the machining efficiency. Cutting width must be chosen in such a way that it produces efficient machining, yet tool life is not significantly sacrificed. The engage angle, the angle between the initial contact point and the exit point (Figure 2.24), is often used to relate the cutting width to tool life.

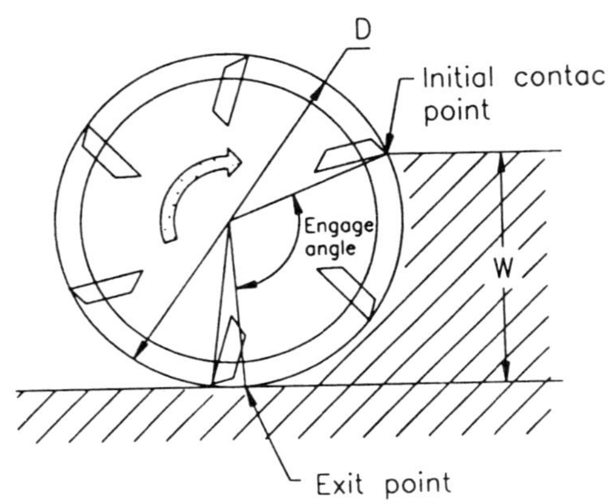

Figure 2.24 Engage angle

Figure 2.25 shows the relationship between the **ratio of W/D to the engage angle.** The engage angle ranges from 0 to 180° depending on the amount of cutting width. The engage angle is 180° for W/D = 1, and 90° for W/D = 0.5.

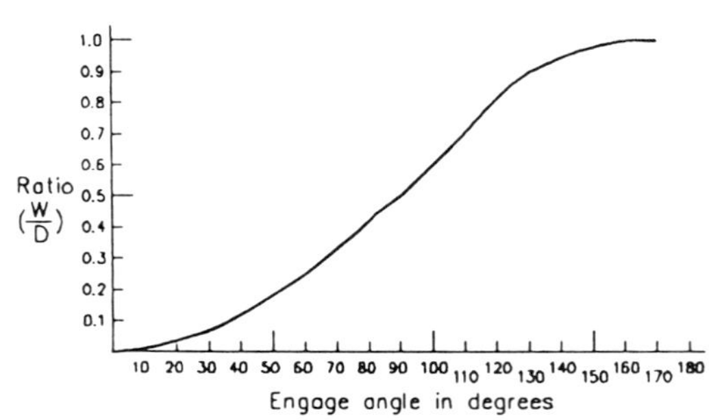

Figure 2.25

Figure 2.26 shows how the engage angle affects the tool life. Tool life decreases drastically after the engage angle exceeding 105°. Also, note that the relationship between the tool life and the engage angle varies from one material to another.

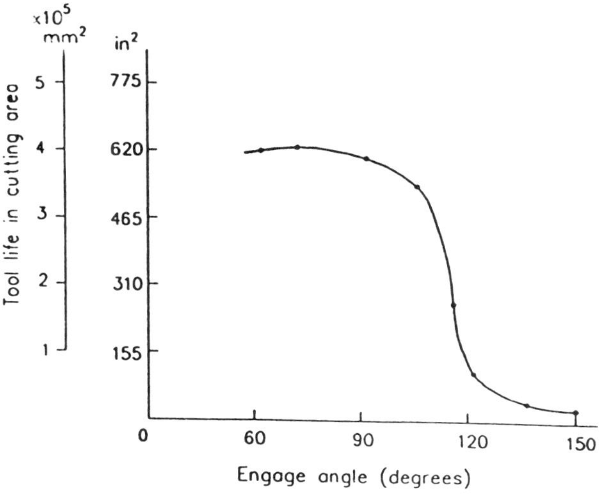

Figure 2.26 ☞

The following two rules are used to determine the maximum cutting width in face milling:

W = (.6) D (for face milling steels)

W = (.75) D (for face milling cast irons)

where W = cutting width
D = diameter of face mill

The maximum depth of cut for most face milling operations is **0.1 in.** and the feed rate is approximately **0.001 - 0.01 in./revolution.**

2.10 End Milling

End mills can be used to perform five types of operations: plunge milling, peripheral shoulder milling, slot milling, pocket milling, and profile milling (Table 2.13) on the next page.

Table 2.13 End Milling Operations

Operation Type	Features	Application	Illustration
1. Plunge milling	Repeatly plunges to a predetermined depth retracts, then advances and plunges again. The maximum cutting force acts in the axial (Z) direction where the machine is strongest.	Rapidly remove large quantity of material.	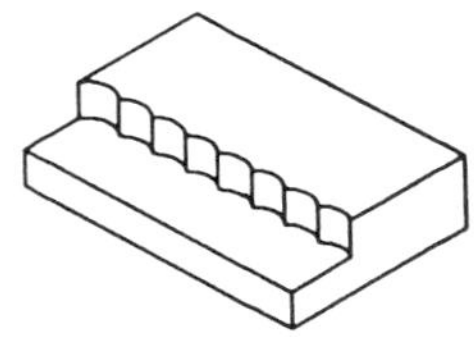
2. Peripheral shoulder milling	Uses end mill's to produce side edges shoulders or steps.	The maximum width of cutter engagement is 3D/4 where D is the cutter diameter.	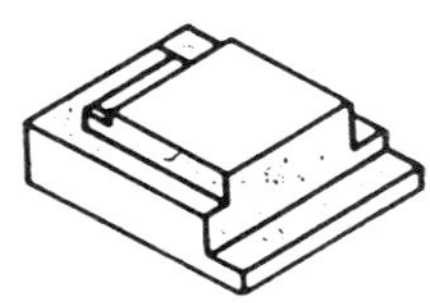
3. slot milling	Uses cutter's side edges to produce blind slot and through slot.	To cut various forms of slots.	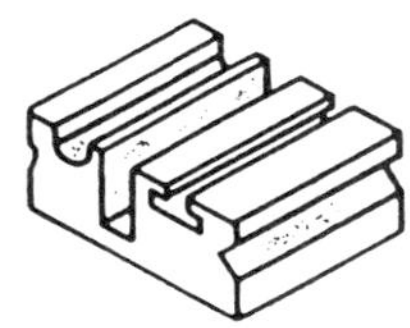
4. Pocket milling	Takes a zig zag or spiral out pattern of cuts in sequence.	To produce a deep cavity.	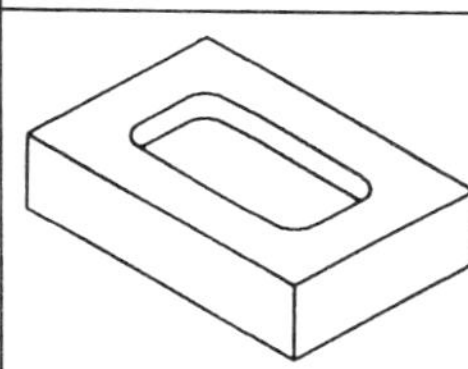
5. Profile milling	Takes the cutter along a predetermined contour.	To machine part profiles that consist of a series of lines and arcs.	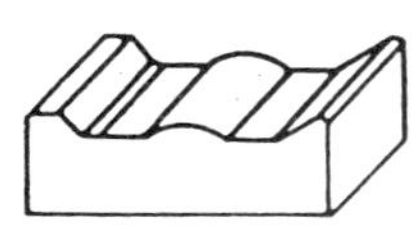

End Mills Selection

End mills are made in various forms, configurations, number of flutes, and end face center types. End mills are availbale in three forms: **solid end mills, carbide-tipped end mills and indexable inserts.** Solid end mills are made from high speed steel or sintered cabide. They are double or single ended. Carbide-tipped end mills have carbide inserts brazed on the tool body to form the cutting edges. In CNC applications, the end mills with indexable inserts are the most widely used.

End mills are made in a variety of configurations including straight end mills for general purpose applications, waved-formed end mills for roughing operation, ball end mills for machining dies, molds, and surfaces, and shell end mills for producing deep slots, shoulders, or profiles (Figure 2.27 on the next page)

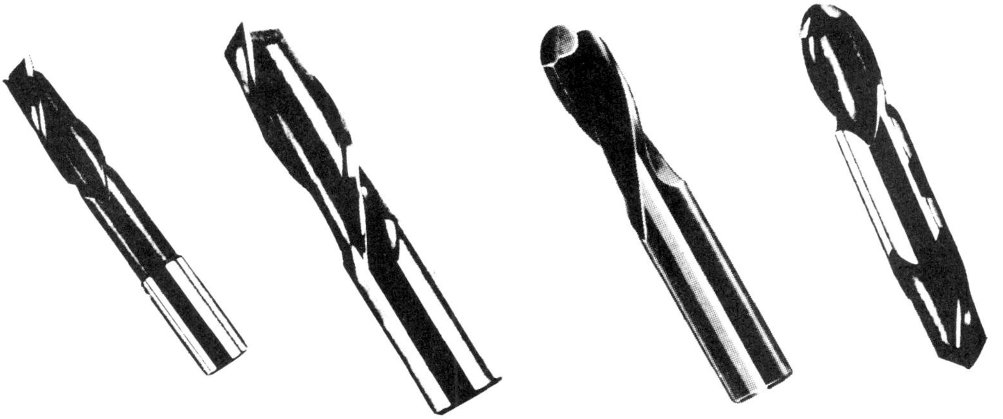

Figure 2.27 Various forms of end mills

End mills have two, three, four, or more flutes to allow for the removal of chips. The fewer the number of flutes means the bigger the cutting pocket.

The end face center of an end mill can be made as either a cutting type or hole type. End mills with a **center cutting** type, have one or two end-cutting edges extending past the center of the cutter (Figure 2.28) so that they can be used for plunging purposes. With the **center hole** type (Figure 2.29), no end-cutting edge is extended to the center of the cutter, therefore, they can not be used to perform plunging operations.

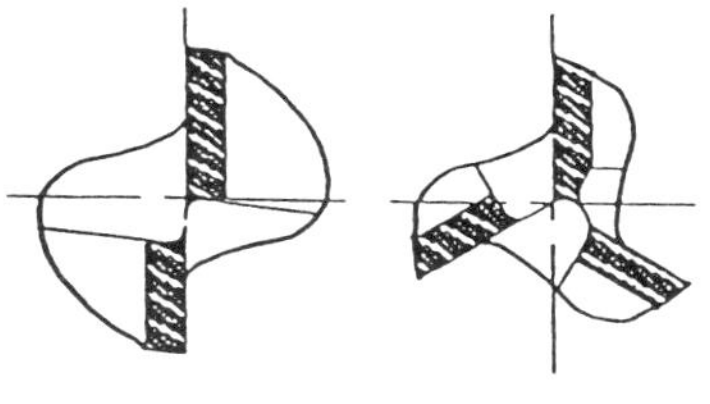

Figure 2.28 Center cutting type

Figure 2.29 Center hole type

The following criteria are used to select end mills for a particular application:

1. **Use end mills with 30° helical angle for general applications. Use 40°-45° helical angle and 15° of axial helical angle at the end face to perform heavy cuttings.**

2. **Use end mills with waved-shaped cutting edges for roughing cuts to obtain rapid metal removal.**

3. **Select end mills with a smaller number of flutes for roughing cuts because they provide larger cutting pockets. Tools with a larger number of flutes are used for finishing cuts.**

4. **Choose tools with the end face of center cutting type for cutting involving plunging. Tools with the end face of center hole type can perform only side cutting.**

The **width of cut** for end milling operations affects the tool life. The maximum width of cut is 75 percent of the cutter diameter (or 3D/4).

2.11 Milling with Ball End Mills

A ball end mill, also known as spherical end mill or ball nose end mill, has a semi-sphere at the tool end. Ball end mills are used extensively in the machining of dies, molds, and workpieces with complex surfaces in the automotive, aerospace, and defense industries.

Effective diameter is the main factor used in the calculation of the required spindle speed. Effective diameter is defined as the **actual diameter of the cutter at the axial depth-of-cut line** (Figure 2.30). The effective diameter is affected by two parameters: **tool radius and axial depth of cut**.

The effective diameter can be calculated from:

$$D_E = 2[R^2-(R-H)^2]^{1/2}$$

where D_E = effective diameter
R = tool radius
H = axial depth of cut

The **effective** radius replaces the cutter radius when calculating the cutting speed for ball end milling. The formula becomes:

$$CS = \frac{\pi \cdot D_E \cdot N}{12}$$

where D_E = effective diameter (in.)
CS = cutting speed (feet/minute)
N = rotation speed (revolution/minute)

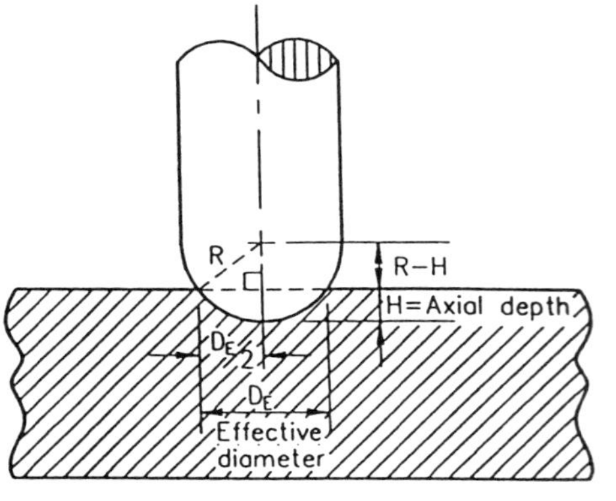

Figure 2.30

When a cutter with a non-flat end, such as a ball end mill, is used to cut a surface in a zigzag pattern, an uncut strip is created between the two cutting passes (Figure 2.31). The height of these undesirable strips is called cusp height.

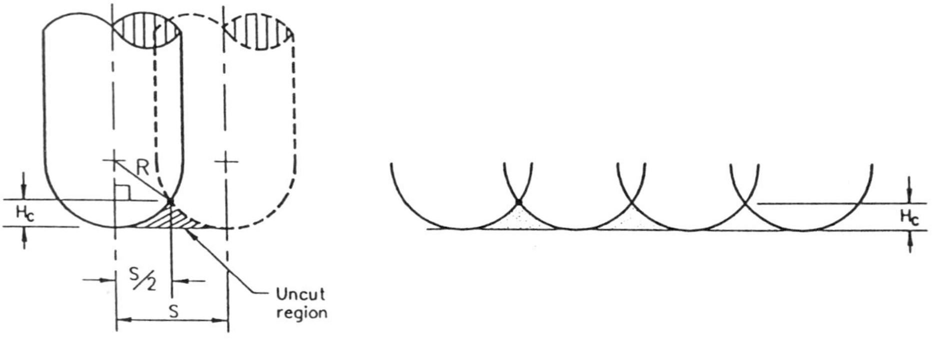

Figure 2.31

Mastercam Version 7,
Scholar's International Publishing Corp., 1998

The cusp height can be calculated from

$$H_C = R - [R^2 - (S/2)^2]^{1/2}$$

or

$$S = 2[R^2 - (R - H_C)^2]^{1/2}$$

where H_c = cusp height (in.)
R = tool nose radius (in.)
S = stepover value between two cutting passes (in.)

2.12 Drilling Operations

Drilling is the process to produce holes or enlarge existing holes. Commonly used drilling operations include drilling, center drilling, countersinking, and counterboring.

Factors to Be Considered in Drilling

1. Initial condition of holes:

The initial state of holes may have one of three forms:

- Casted holes or forged holes in which rough hole dimension has been formed. These holes can be produced by using a correct-size drill or a two-flute end mill.
- Pre-drilled holes in which holes, normally of large diameter, have been drilled by a small drill. The final drilling is done by using a correct size of drill.
- Blank stock. Drilling holes on blank stock may require using more than one drill depending on the size, accuracy, and surface roughness of the holes.

2. Required accuracy of holes

Drilling tends to produce oversized holes with a dislocation of hole centers. Hole oversize and runout are two parameters in measuring the hole accuracy. When the required accuracy of hole, with respect to diameter and runout, is within ±0.005 in., a center drilling is required to locate the hole center.

3. Hole size

The hole **diameter** decides the number of drillings required to produce the hole. Generally speaking, a 1 in. diameter is used as the critical dimension. Only one drilling is required for any hole size that is smaller than **1 in.** of diameter. To drill a 1¼ in. hole, for example, requires two drillings, first drilling with a 3/8 in. drill and then a final drilling with 1¼ in. drill to produce the finished size.

4. Hole depth

Only one drilling pass is required to drill shallow holes. As the depth of hole **increases**, peck drilling is used to clear chips and avoid packing. Peck drilling is recommended when the depth of hole is greater than three to four times the diameter of drills. The distance (depth) of each peck ranges from ½ to 1½ times the drill diameter,depending upon the chip formation and rate of drill breakage encountered.

Note: that the cutting speed and feed rate for drilling deep holes should be reduced according to the ratio of hole depth to drill diameter.

Safety, drill lip, and penetration distance

In drilling with NC machines, the tool moves rapidly to the reference level (**R**) and then feeds into the workpiece until it reaches the hole bottom. **Three** distances should be carefully determined to optimize NC use: **safety, drill lip, and penetration distance** (Figure 2.32).

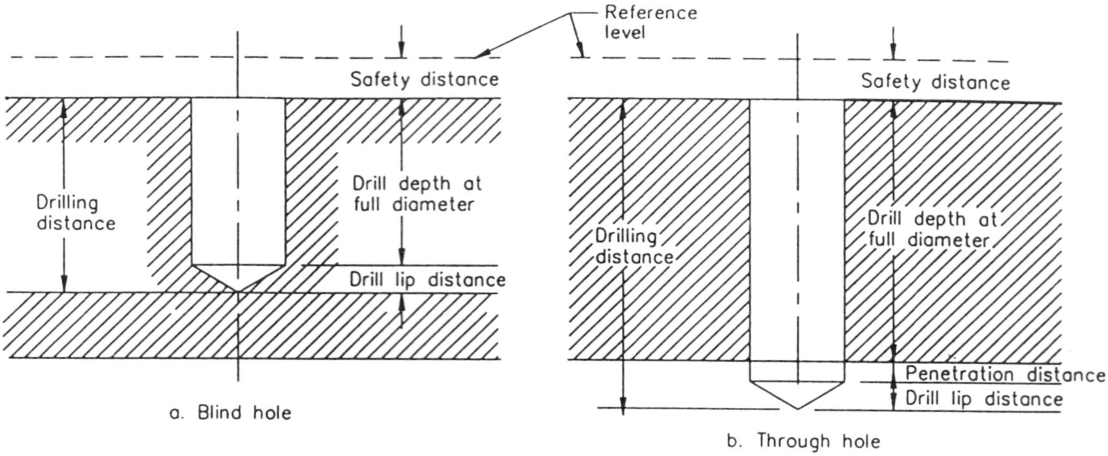

Figure 2.32 Drilling distances

Safety distance

The safety distance is measured from the reference (R) level to the work surface and should be as short as possible to increase NC efficiency. The safety distance is determined by the surface condition of the workpiece and is calculated as follows:

L_S = 0.15 in. (or 4 mm) for flat casted, and machined surfaces
L_S = 0.2 in. (or 5 mm) for rough surfaces

Drill lip distance

The drill point angle is generally ground to 118° or 59° on each side of the centerline. The drill lip distance can be calculated from:

$$L_L = \frac{D}{2(\tan 59°)}$$

or $$L_L = 0.3\ D$$

where D = drill diameter (in. or mm)
L_L = drill lip distance (in. or mm)

Penetration distance

Penetration distance is the allowance that permits the drill to move to extra depth to remove the burs produced during the time when the drill penetrated through the hole. Generally speaking, the penetration distance is equal to the safety distance that is:

L_P = 0.15 in. (or 4 mm) for flat casted, and machined surfaces

L_P = 0.2 in. (or 5 mm) for rough surfaces

The drilling distance of a blind hole consists of **three** components: **safety distance, depth at full diameter, and depth of drill lip** (Figure 2.32a).

$$L = L_S + L_D + L_L$$

where L = drilling distance
L_S = safety distance
L_D = drill depth at full diameter
L_L = depth of drill lip

The drilling distance for a through hole is the sum of **four** components (Figure 2.32b) and can be found from:

$$L = L_S + L_D + L_P + L_L$$

where L_D = depth of hole

L_P = penetration distance

2.13 Boring Operations

Boring is a precision machining process for producing internal holes by removing metal with single-point tools or tools with multiple cutting edges. Common applications for boring include the enlarging or finishing of existing holes that were drilled, pierced, casted, or forged. Boring operations can be of **two** categories; **single-stage** (Figure 2.33) **and multiple-stage** (Figure 2.34).

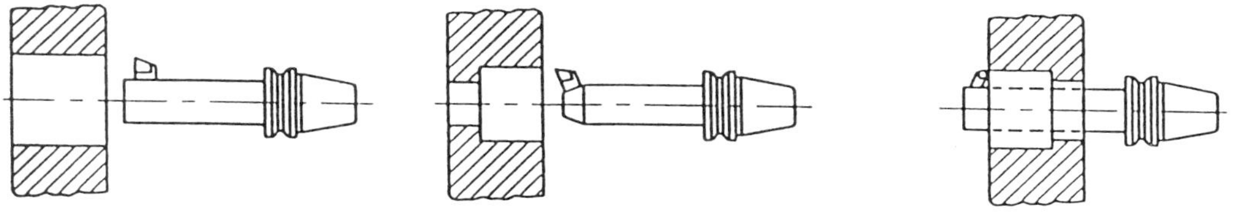

a. through hole b. Blind hole c Back hole

Figures 2.33Single stage boring operations

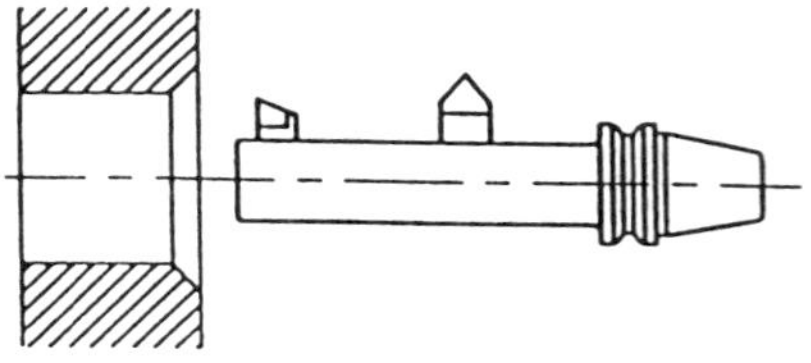

a. Boring and chamfering

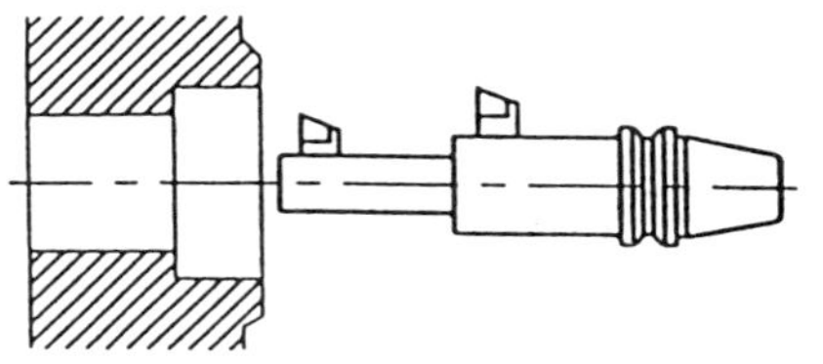

b. Boring two-step hole

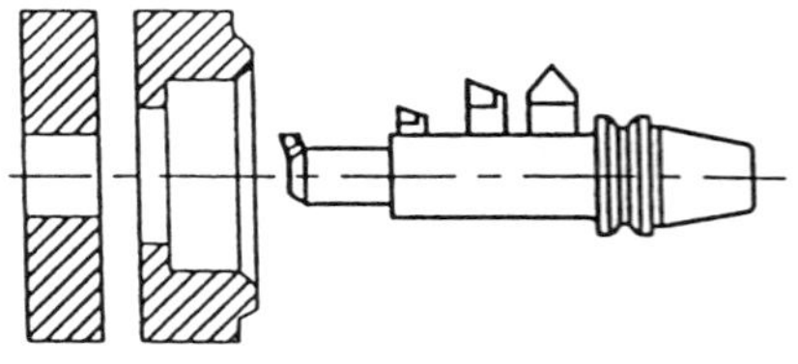

c. Boring three-step hole and chamfering

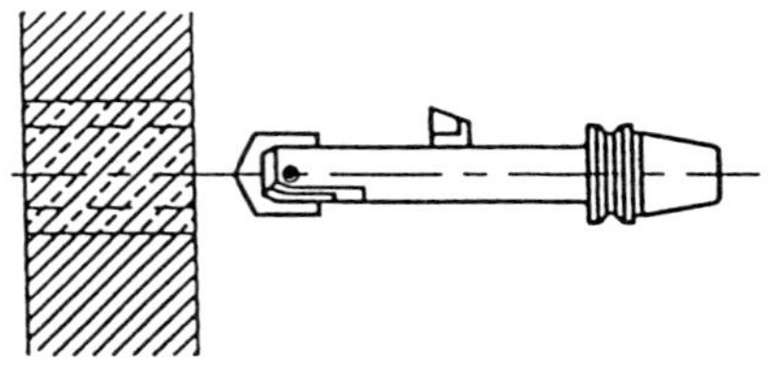

d. Spade drilling and boring

Figure 2.34 Multiple stage boring operaitons

Boring bars are made of various sizes and types. The most common type is the single-stage boring bar that is a round boring bar with one cutting edge mounted at the end of the bar to perform a single-diameter boring operation. The ratio of length to diameter of the shank (L/D) is the main measure of the boring capability for a boring bar. As a general rule, a L/D ratio of 4 - 5 would provide a stable machining under normal boring conditions. Chatter may occur when this ratio is larger than 5. Actually, chatter results from the deflection of the boring bar that is subjected to the cutting resistant force. The larger the cutting resistant force, the larger the deflection results. In some critical applications, this deflection must be kept within an allowable limit.

Selection of Feed and Depth of Cut

The selection of feed and depth of cut depends on the following factors:

1. Deflection should not exceed 0.001 in. (or 0.02 mm).

2. Use the formula, $F = (8HR)^{1/2}$
to determine the feed for the required surface roughness,
where H = surface roughness (in.),
R = tool nose radius (in.)
F = feed (in./rev).

3. Depth of cut for rough borings ranges from 0.04 - 0.24 in. (1 - 6 mm).
Use 0.02 - 0.04 in. (0.5 - 1 mm) for finish borings.

2.14 Tapping Operations

Tapping is a process of using a tap to produce internal threads in existing holes by a combination of axial and rotary motions. CNC milling machines use hand taps, spiral-pointed taps, spiral-fluted taps, and metric taps for cutting straight threads.

Tap selection

Several types of taps are used in CNC machines to produce internal threads. Table 2.14 on the next page summarizes various tap types and their applications.

Tap drill selection

A tap drill is used to produce the minor diameter of the internal threads. The percentage of thread engagement, or thread height, is an important factor in determining the tap drill size. Figure 2.35 illustrates the definition of thread height percentage. Table 2.15 gives a range of thread height percentage for general applications of classes 1B and 2B.

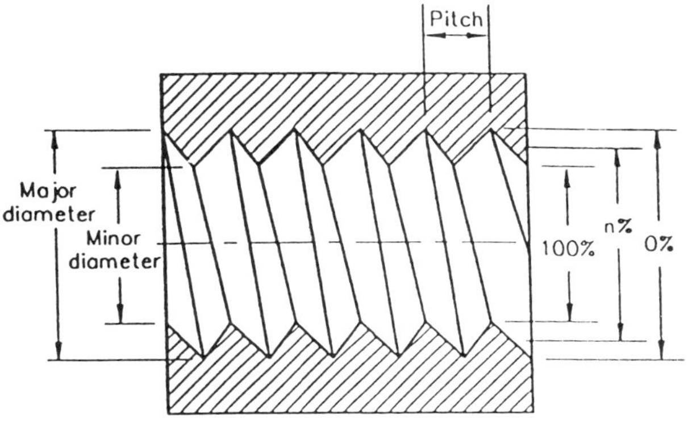

Figure 2.35

Table 2.15 Thread height percentages for various thread sizes

Thread Size	Thread Height, %
#0 to #12	53 to 65
1/4 to 1/2"	64 to 66.5
1/2 to 1"	64 to 67
1 to 2"	66 to 71

Note that the **tougher** the material, the less percentage of thread should be produced. The **closer** the tolerance, the greater percentage of thread is required.

The tap hole diameter can be roughly calculated by the formula:

$$D = D_M - P$$

where D = tap hole diameter
D_M = tap major diameter
P = thread pitch

Table 2.14 Tap Types and Their Applications

Tap Type	Feature	Application	Illustration
A. Hand Tap			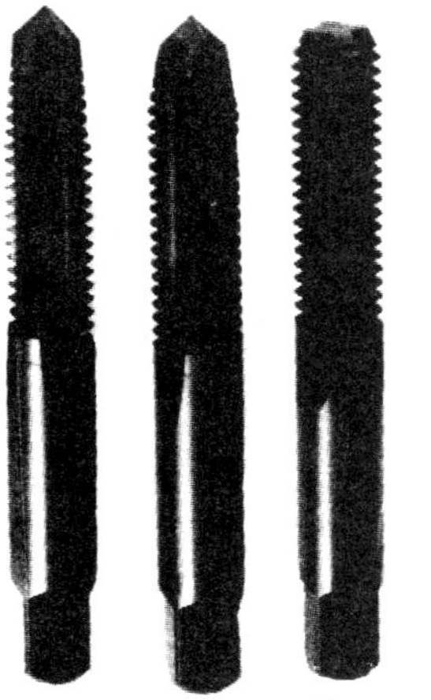
1. Taper Tap	Having first 8 to 10 threads chamfered.	For starting the threads in a deep hole or for tapping through holes.	
2. Plug Tap	Having a 3 to 5 thread chamfer length.	Tapping through holes, general tapping application.	
3. Bottoming Tap	Having only 1 thread chamfer length.	Tapping blind holes where limited lengths of imperfect threads are allowed. They should be used only a taper or plug tap has been used to thread a blind hole as far as possible.	
B. Spiral-pointed tap	Having a left-hand spiral flute at the point to force the chips ahead of the tap. More rigid than conventional taps. Low cutting resistance.	Tapping short through holes in mild steel and stainless steel where chips do not easily break. Produce high precision threads.	
C. Spiral-fluted taps			
1. Spiral-flute taps	Having right hand helical flutes with a helix angle ranging from 25° to 35° to increase lifting action in ejecting chips backward.	Tapping blind holes where chips have to be ejected backward through the open end of the hole.	
2. Fast spiral-flute taps	45°-60° helix angle to increase lifting action in ejecting chips backward.	Tapping deep blind holes in materials that produce long curling chips.	

The following formulas are used to calculate the tap drill size when the thread height percentage is considered:

Unified Threads:

$$D = D_M - \frac{2 \cdot H \cdot Q}{100}$$

$$H = 0.6495\ P$$

$$P = 1/N$$

or

$$D = D_M - 0.01299 \times (Q/N)$$

where D = tap drill size (diameter)
D_M = major diameter of tap (threads)
H = thread height
P = thread pitch
Q = thread height percentage
N = number of threads per in.

Metric threads:

$$D = D_M - \frac{2 \cdot H \cdot Q}{100}$$

$$H = 0.6403\ P$$

or

$$D = D_M - 0.01281\ P \cdot Q$$

Depth of tap holes

The depth of tap holes must be deep enough to allow the tap to produce threads to the desired depth. In tapping blind holes, the depth of holes is the sum of the **four** distances: **thread length, deceleration length, clearance length, and drill tip length** (Figure 2.36).

$$L = L_l + L_d + L_c + L_t$$

$$L_t = 0.3\ D$$

where L = depth of tap hole
L_l = thread length
L_d = deceleration length (1 -2 thread pitch)
L_c = clearance length (0.5 thread pitch)
L_t = drill tip length
D = tap drill diameter

Figure 2.36

2.15 Turning Operation

Turning is an improtant machining process for producing external and internal profiles and surfaces on a turning machine. Several important factors should be considered in turning operation are presented in this section. They include **feed selection, depth of cut, error resulting from off center of the cutter, and chip breaker.**

Feed selection and surface roughness

Feed is one of important factors in determining the machining efficiency. The selection of feed for turning is mainly governed by the required surface roughness. The theoretical formula for calculating the roughness is: (Figure 2.37):

$$H = R - (R^2 - (F/2)^2)^{1/2}$$

where H = surface roughness (in. or mm)
R = tool nose radius (in. or mm)
F = feed (in./rev or mm/rev)

This equation can be expanded as:

$$H^2 - 2RH = -F^2/4$$

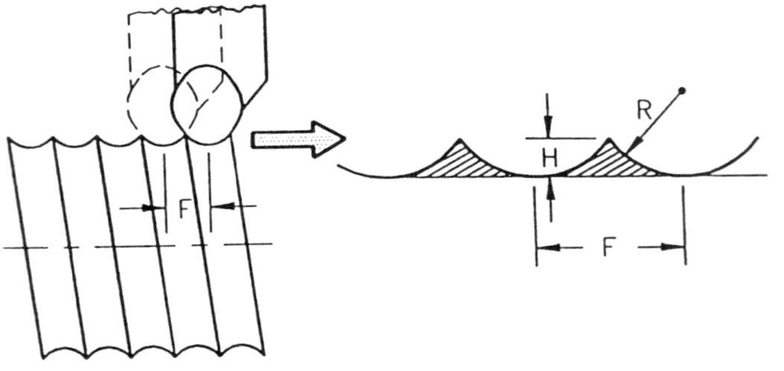

Figure 2.37

Since the value of H is very small, the term H^2 can be overlooked and the equation becomes:

$$H = \frac{F^2}{8R}$$

or $$F = (8RH)^{1/2}$$

The surface roughness can be improved either by **reducing** the feed rate or by **increasing** the tool nose radius. It is preferred to use a larger tool nose radius to obtain better roughness than to reduce the feed rate because chips may congest on the insert tip and cause damage to the surface when too small a feed is used.

Depth of cut and deflection

Generally speaking, the depth of cut for roughing all materials, excluding stainless steels, is about 0.15 in. (4 mm). Roughing stainless steels uses 0.1 in. depth of cut.

The deeper cut requires a larger cutting force. The cutting resistant force causes the workpiece to be deflected. This deflection produces chatter when the workpiece rotates at a relatively high speed. When this deflection is greater than 0.001 in. (or 0.02mm), chatter may be severe enough to make the surface finish requirements impossible to obtain.

Error resulted from off center of the cutter

In most cases, we like to have the cutter tip located at the center in turning operations. The turned diameter is slightly larger than the programmed dimension when the tip of the cutter is off center by a distance (Figure 2.38 on the next page).

The resultant diameter error can be calculated from:

$$\Delta X = (X^2 + Y^2)^{1/2} - X$$

where ΔX = error amount
X = X-coordinate of the programmed point
Y = amount of center offset

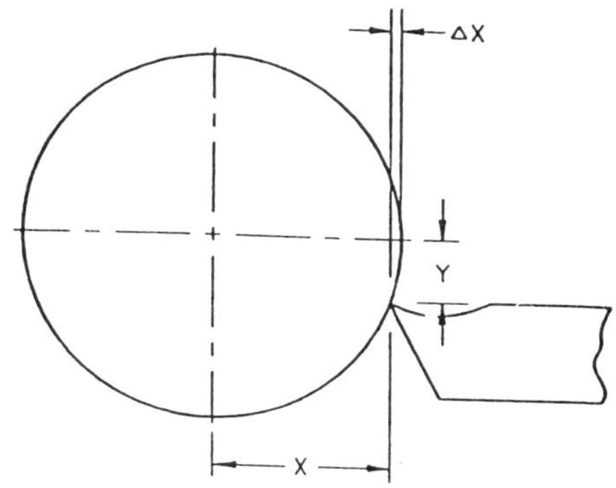

Figure 2.38

Chip breaker

Chips should be broken into pieces or curled into small coils to facilitate the removal from the workpiece and the cutter. When turning brittle materials such as cast iron and intermittent cuttings, the chips are automatically broken, so no chip breaker is required. A chip breaker must be given to the cutter which is used to turn the stingy, tough materials such as steels, aluminum, and so on. Chip breakers can appear in various forms. Figure 2.39 illustrates the basic principle of a chip breaker.

The theoretical radius of curled chips can be determined by two variables: **width of the chip breaker (W) and depth of the chip breaker (H)**, and can be calculated by using the relationship of two similar triangles ABD and ACB.

$$\frac{AC}{AB} = \frac{AB}{AD}$$

Since $AC = 2R$, $AD = H$, and $AB = (H^2 + W^2)^{1/2}$

Therefore, $2RH = H^2 + W^2$

or $$R = \frac{W^2}{2H} + \frac{H}{2}$$

where W = width of the chip breaker
H = depth of the chip breaker
R = radius of curled chips

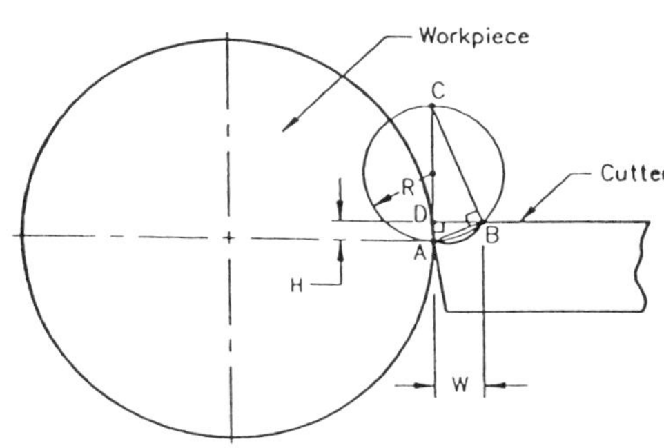

Figure 2.39

The actual chip size is also affected by the feed used in cutting. Larger feed causes chips to be broken easily, whereas smaller feed reduces the effect of chip breaking.

Chapter 3

Mastercam Environments

Objectives:

1. Start the Mastercam program.
2. Understand screen menus and how to move from one screen to another.
3. Know the function of the SAVE, FILE and EXIT commands.

3.1 Launching Mastercam (Windows 95)

There are only two steps needed to start Mastercam Mill Version 7 running under Windows 95.

Step 1. If you have created a shortcut icon on the screen, double click on it.

Figure 3.1

Step 2. Click on the Start box, then Programs, Mastercam and finally Mastercam Mill v7.0

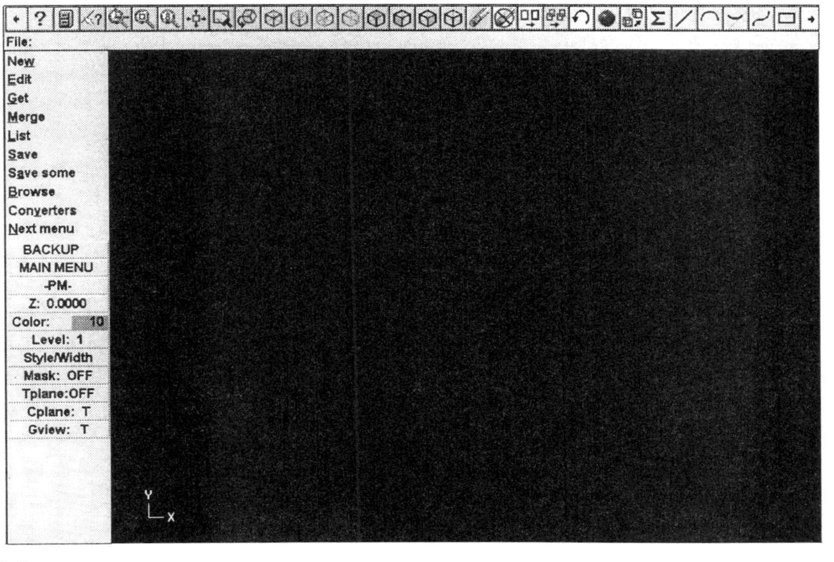

Figure 3.2

3.2 Changing the Size of the Window

To maximize the Mastercam window to the full screen, click the maximize button on the title bar as shown in Figure 3.3.

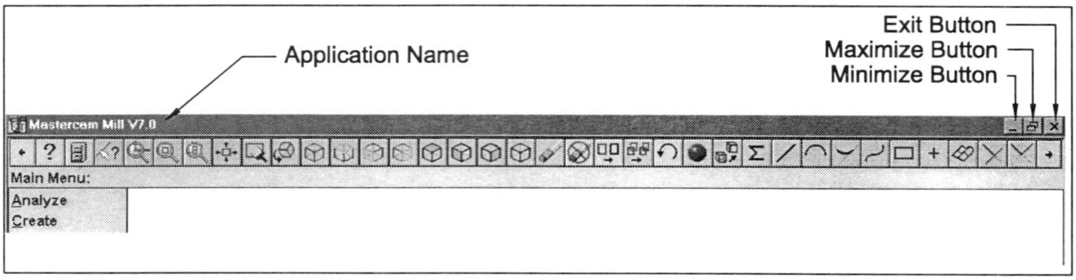

Figure 3.3 The Title Bar of Mastercam

To minimize the Mastercam window to an icon, click the minimize button on the title bar shown in Figure 3.3 above.

To change the size of the window, follow this procedure:

1. Point to the Mastercam border, or corner, and the pointer will change to a two headed arrow.
2. Press and hold the pick (left) mouse button while dragging the corner or border of the Mastercam screen.
3. Release the pick button when you have the desired window size.

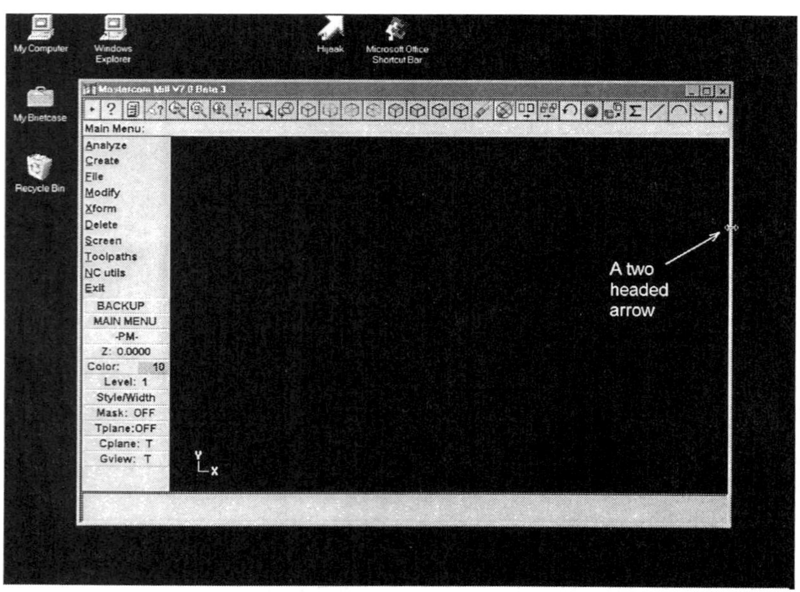

Figure 3.4

Moving a Window

To move a window, position your mouse pointer in the bar at the top of your window that contains the application name (or the title bar), press the pick button, and keep the button down. Drag the window to its new position, and release the pick button.

3.3 Mastercam Screen

After you enter Mastercam, the system will display the Mastercam screen which is divided into **four sections**: a graphics display, a tool bar, a screen menu and a system response area (see Figure 3.5).

Graphics Display Area

This is the working area where your drawing geometry can be created, retrieved or modified.

Toolbar Area

The toolbar is a row of buttons across the top of the screen. These buttons either have an icon or a number to identify them. To get a description of a toolbar icon, move your mouse cursor onto the button, or let the mouse cursor rest over the icon and Mastercam will automatically identify the button. Click any mouse button to activate the icon command.

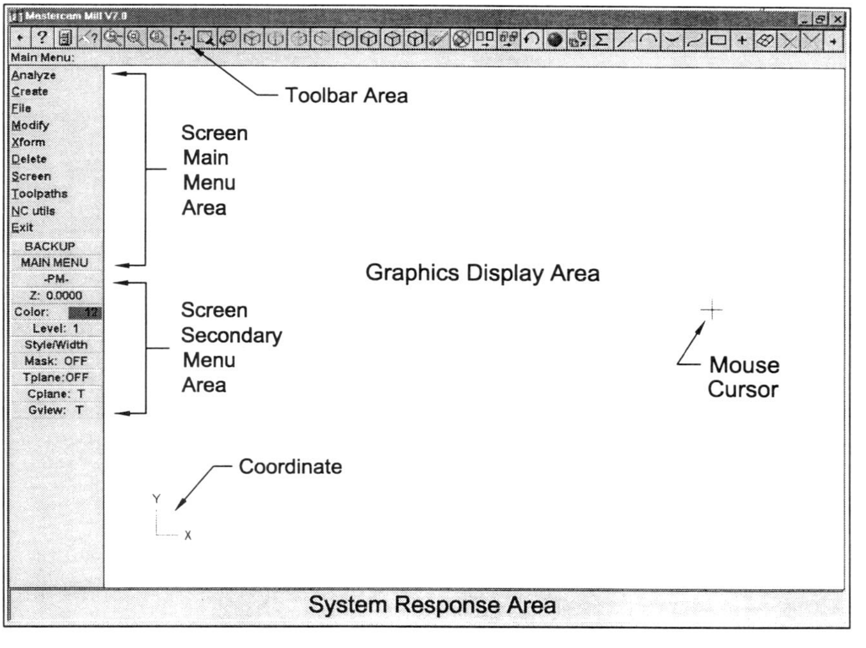

Figure 3.5 Mastercam Screen Display

Screen Menu Area

This area is located at the left of the screen and consists of a main menu and a secondary menu. The **main menu** is used to select the system's main functions such as create, modify, or toolpaths. The **secondary menu** is used to change the system's param eters such as the Z depth or color which is frequently revised by the user. All the commands used in Mastercam can be selected from this area.

System Response Area

One or two text lines at the bottom of the screen indicate the status of the commands. This is where you will receive messages from Mastercam. Watch this area carefully; it might require some input from the keyboard.

Selecting a Menu Option

In Mastercam, there are **two** ways to select a menu option from the Screen Menu area:

1. Moving the mouse or pointing devices into the menu area. After the desired menu box is highlighted, press any mouse button to activate the command.
2. Pressing the first capital letter of the command.

The first menu to appear on the Mastercam main menu screen is the Mastercam **Root Menu**. It is shown in the previous Figure 3.5. Some of these menu items have a more detailed submenu from which an item must be selected. A brief description of the commands available from the main menu and secondary menu is listed on Table 3.1 and 3.2.

Table 3.1 The Main Menu

Main Item	Description
Analyze	Displays coordinate and database information for selected object such as point,line, arc, spline, surface or dimension on the screen. It is helpful to identify objects that had already been created. For example, it can be used to determine the angle of an existing line or the radius of a specified circle.
Create	Creates geometry to the drawing database and draws it on the Graphics Display Area. These geometries include line, arc, circle, rectangle, etc.
File	Manipulates disk **files** such as SAVE, GET, CONVERT, TRANSMIT, or RECEIVE.
Modify	Modifies screen geometry with the fillet, trim, break and join commands.
Xform	Transforms already created geometry with the mirror, rotate, scale, and offset commands.
Delete	Deletes an entity or group of entities from the screen and the system's database.
Screen	Plots or views the drawing geometry, shows the number of drawing entities, zooms in and out, changes the viewport number and configuration.
Toolpaths	Creates NC toolpaths using drill, contour, pocket, etc.
NC utils	Manipulates and processes NC toolpaths.
Exit	Exits Mastercam.
BACKUP*	Brings the main menu item to its upper level.
MAIN MENU*	Brings the main menu item to its root page.
*	Refer to section 3.5 for short-cut keys.

Table 3.2 The Secondary Menu

Main Item	Description
-PM-	Drafting global parameters. This has three subpages. Double-click to activate it.
Z: 0.0000	Displays and changes the current working depth.
Color 10	Sets the current system default color.
Level 1	Sets the current system active level.
Style/Width	Sets the line style and line width.
Mask: OFF	Sets the system masking level.
Tplane: OFF	Sets a tool plane.
Cplane: T	Sets a construction plane.
Gview: T	Changes the graphic view. Note that the graphic view can be independent of the construction plane.

The menu, command, and option structure of Mastercam is a *tree* (or *hierarchy*) arrangement. For example, the actual tree arrangement to Create a Rectangle using the 2 points option is shown in Figure 3.6.

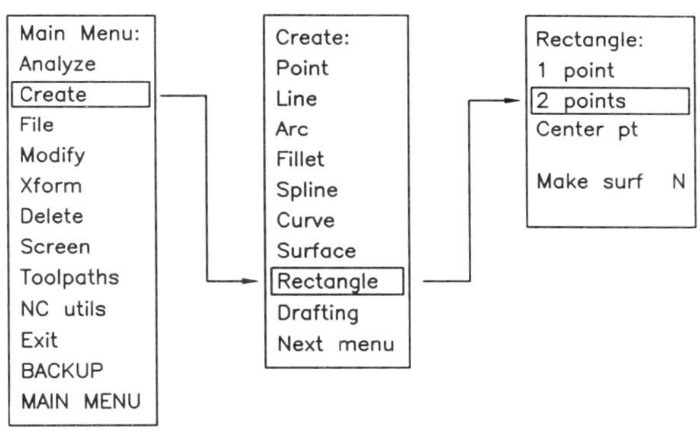

Figure 3.6 The tree arrangement of the CREATE menu

Select the **Create** menu with your mouse pointer. The menu changes and now consists of the submenu of **Create**. Select **Rectangle** and the menu changes to the submenu of **Rectangle**. Select **2 points** to activate the option. Notice the prompts in the system response area. It provides important information for you to follow through.

To conserve space and still allow you to access the commands properly, the convention used in this book for the command selections shown in Figure 3.6 will be indicated as,

Create → Rectangle → 2 points

The entire Mastercam command hierarchy is organized systematically. Take your time to review it. You will have more opportunity to learn and practice some of the screen commands in the upcoming chapters.

3.4 Exiting Mastercam

To exit Mastercam, follow the steps shown here. The same steps also apply to the DOS version.

Step 1. Go to the root page of the main menu.
Select MAIN MENU

Step 2. Select the Exit option.
Select Exit

Step 3. Confirm to exit Mastercam.
Select Yes

3.5 Using Mastercam Navigation Commands

Understanding Mastercam navigation commands is essential to operating the system effectively. In section 3.3, we explained how to select a menu option from the Screen Menu Area. To speed up the drawing construction, other commands such as accepting the default value and short-cut keys are described as follows:

Default Values

In Mastercam, the default value set up by the system (or from previous user input) is indicated in a dialog box in the system response area, e.g.,

Enter the radius
0.5

If you decide to use this default value, you don't have to re-type it and the value can be accepted in two ways: (a) press the (Enter) key, or
(b) press the left mouse button.

If you want to change the default value at any time, you don't have to erase the old value, just type the new value in its place.

BACKUP and MAIN MENU

BACKUP backs up one menu level at a time and **MAIN MENU** jumps back to main menu options are used constantly and are available from every menu option. You can use mouse to select the option or use the following **short-cut keys.**

Menu option	Key(s)
BACKUP	Esc
MAIN MENU	Press Esc key continuously

Mastercam short-cut keys

Fifteen short-cut keys have special uses in Mastercam.

Key	Function
Alt -A	Opens the AutoSave window
Alt-B	Toggles the toolbar display/hide
Alt-C	Run C-Hook application program[*1]
Alt-D	Drafting global parameters
Alt-F	Set menu fonts
Alt-H	Display on-line help
Alt-L	Set current line style
Alt-M	Lists the Mastercam memory allocations
Alt-O	Operation Manager
Alt-P	Toggles Mastercam prompt area display/hide
Alt-S	Display surface
Alt-U	Undo
Alt-W	Set viewport windows
PageUp/PageDown	Zoom in/zoom out
Cursor Arrows	Pans over geometry

[*1] C-Hook programs are a customized application program written by CNC Software Inc. or other professionals using Watcom C/C++32 and the Mastercam C-Hooks library.

Mastercam function keys

Nineteen function keys have special uses in Mastercam. Using Mastercam's short-cut commands and function keys is a fast way to step into an operation and can reduce your drawing time remarkably.

	Function Key	Alt + Function key
F1	Zoom	Fit to extents of the screen
F2	Zoom Previous or Scale by 0.5	Scale by 0.8
F3	Repaint	Analyze at Cursor Position
F4	Analyze	Exit Mastercam
F5	Delete	Delete Window
F6	File	Edit File
F7	Modify	(Blank)
F8	Create	Configuration
F9	Display System Information	Draw Axes
F10	Display execute function window	Display execute function window

3.6 Getting Help

If you need help for a Mastercam function key, use the **Alt-H** keys, select **Search**, and type **Default Special Key Assignments**. A detail help screen is displayed. See Figure 3.7.

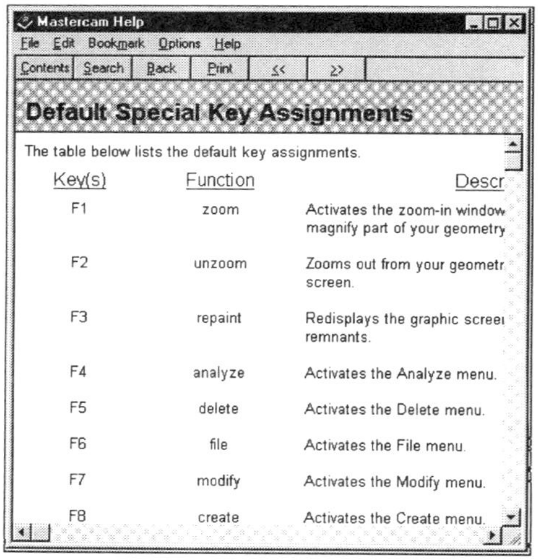

Figure 3.7 Mastercam Function Key Help Screen

In Mastercam Version 7.0, you will notice that the on-line help screen can be accessed by pressing Alt-H. This on-line help, shown in Figure 3.8 is related to the Screen Main Menu option and, provides you with information in great detail. Therefore, it is highly recommended to step into this new utility. You can select a topic with the mouse or double-click the control-menu box at the upper-left corner to exit the help. An example showing help on Xform → Translate is shown in Figure 3.9 .

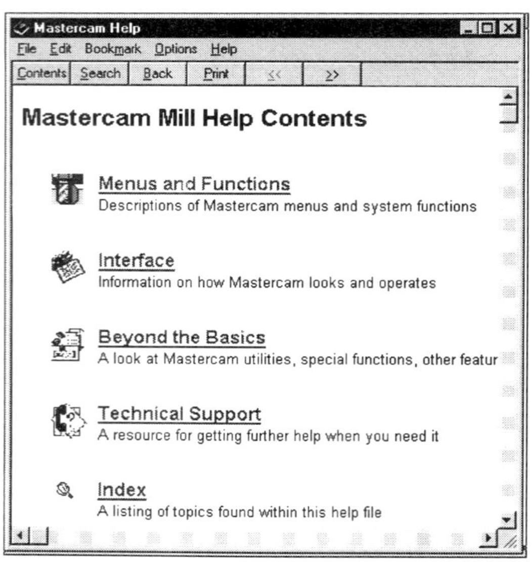

Figure 3.8

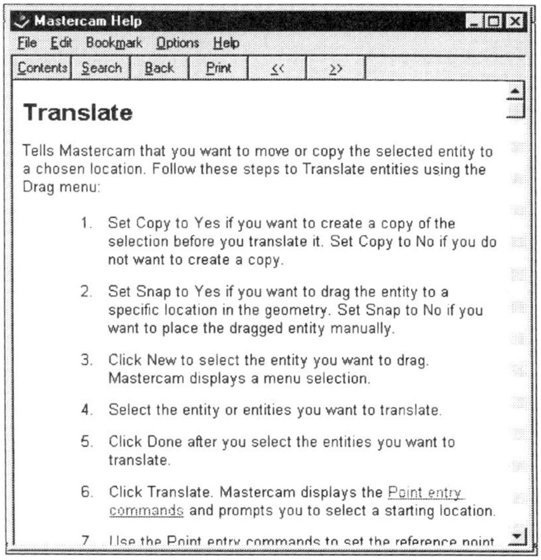

Figure 3.9

3.7 Setting System Configuration

In Mastercam, common system's default values such as Allocations, Tolerances, NC settings and CAD settings are stored in a configuration file (*.CFG). This configuration file is either MILL7.CFG for English units or MILL7M.CFG for metric units. If you want to customize these default startup settings for Mastercam, use the following command sequences:

MAIN MENU → Screen → Configure

The System Configuration dialog box appears as shown on the next page as Figure 3.10.

⌛**Tip** Backing up all the configuration files (*.CFG) to a floppy will help you to recover the original settings.

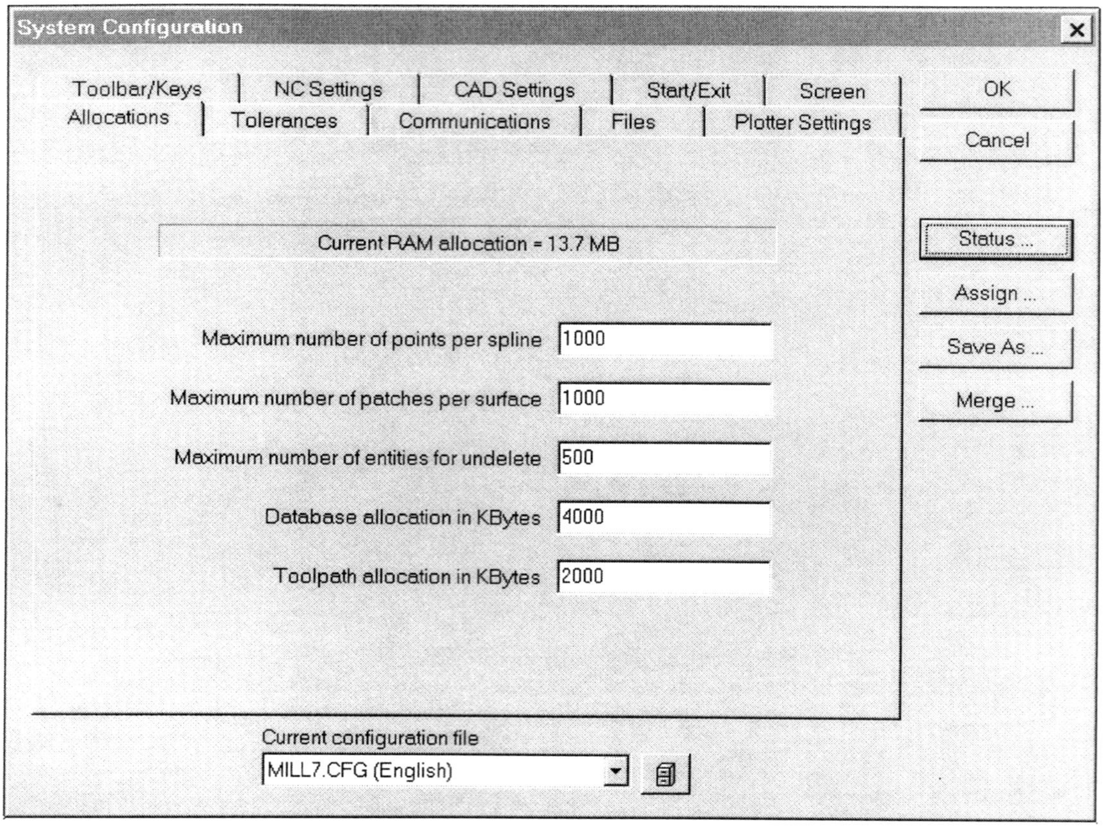

Figure 3.10

The dialog box is divided into three sections: **button options, tab options** and **current configuration file** options. Next, each section and their options are explained in more detail.

Button Option

OK Close the System Configuration dialog box to implement the updates. When you choose this option, the system prompts the following message:

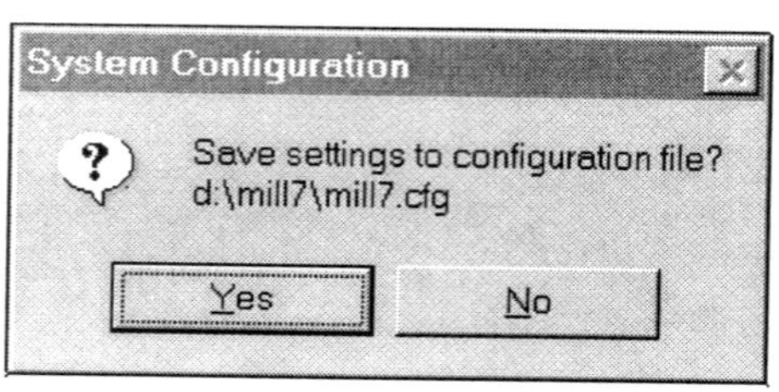

Choosing **Yes** will implement the changes and save them to the current configuration file.

Choosing **No** will implement the changes for the current Mastercam session only, but not save them to the configuration file.

Cancel Exit the System Configuration dialog box without saving or implementing the changes.

Status Let you view which sections of the configuration information have been modified. The modified section has a mark in the check box. Deselecting the check box will undo the changes in that section. See Figure 3.11.

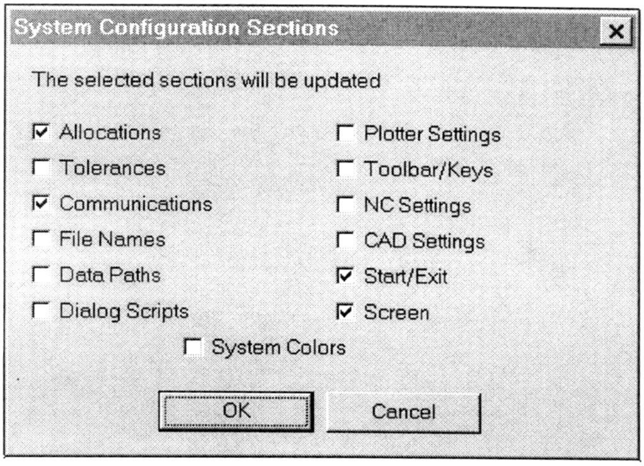

Figure 3.11

Assign – Assign any configuration file to a post (*.PST) file. The default post processor file is MILL7.CFG for English units or MILL7M.CFG for metric units.

Merge – Merge configuration information from other files with the current configuration file.

Tab Option

There are ten tabs in the dialog box, each representing a page of configuration parameters.

Allocations – Set maximum values for certain Mastercam features such as number of points per spline, number of points per surface, number of entities for undelete, database allocation in Kbytes and toolpath allocation in Kbytes. See Figure 3.12.

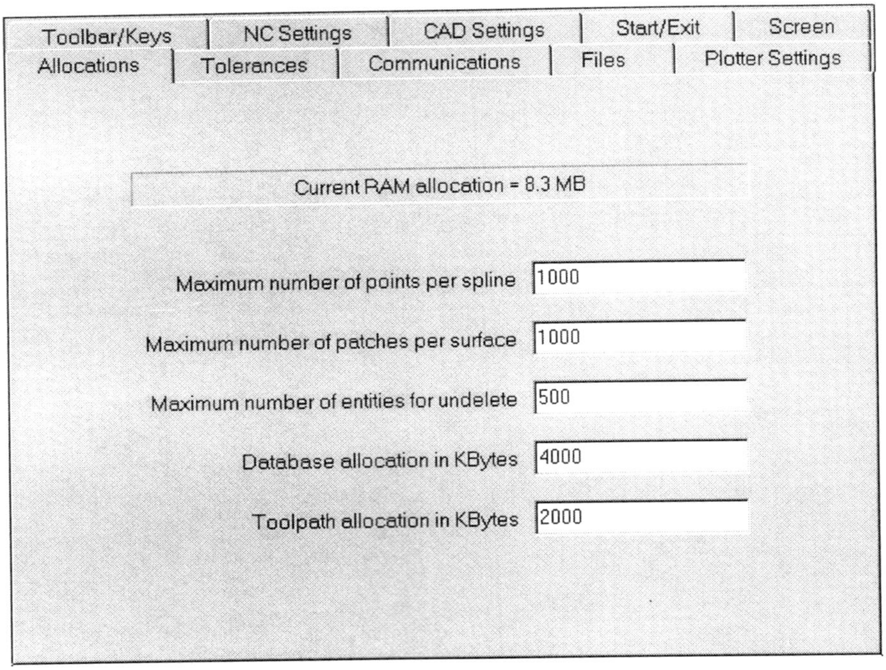

Figure 3.12

Tolerances – Set the default tolerances values for different areas of Mastercam.

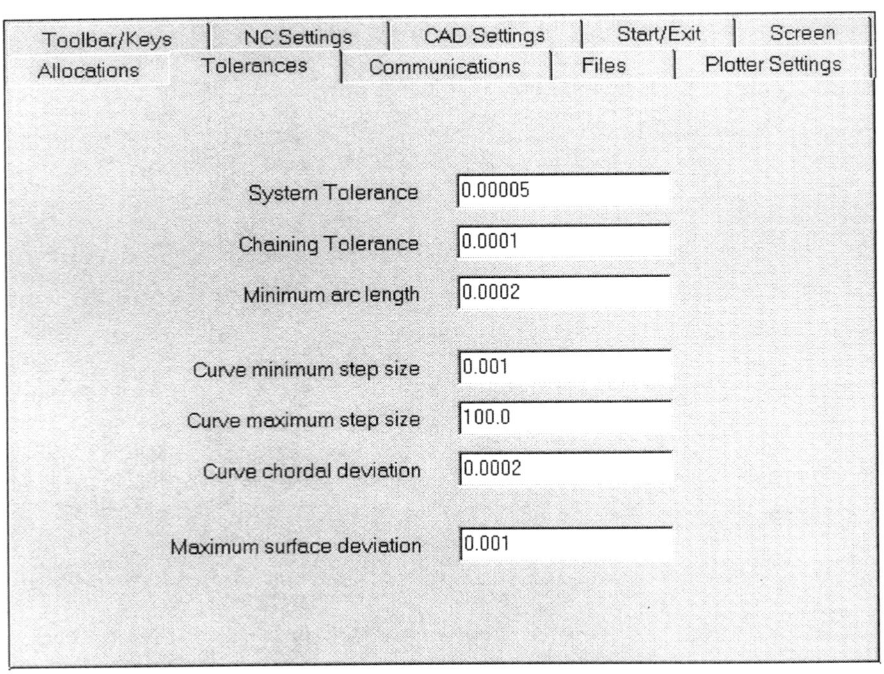

Figure 3.13

Communication – Set the default communication settings with CNC control and other peripheral devices as shown here.

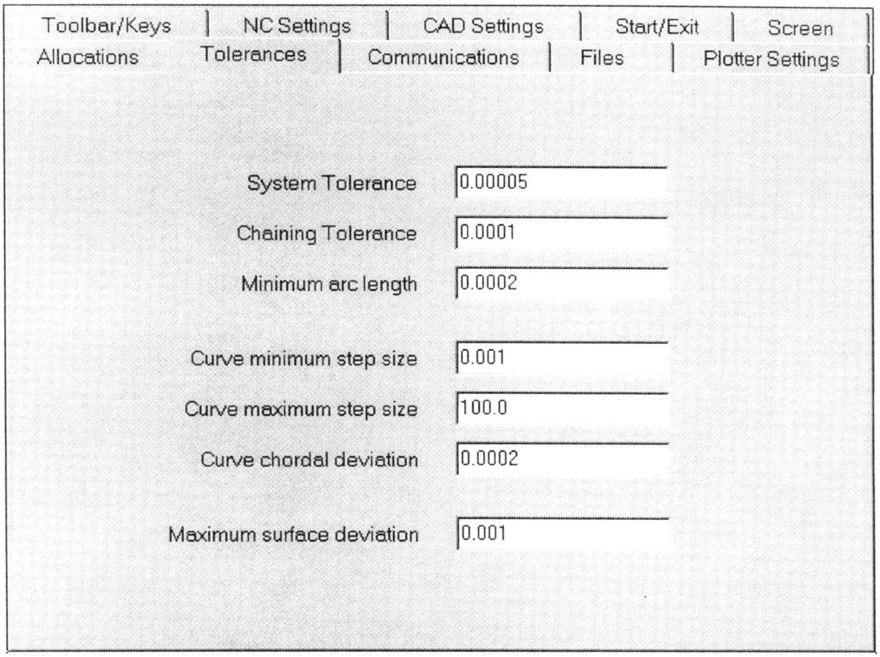

Figure 3.14

Files – Set the default values for files and directories used by Mastercam. See Figure 3.15.

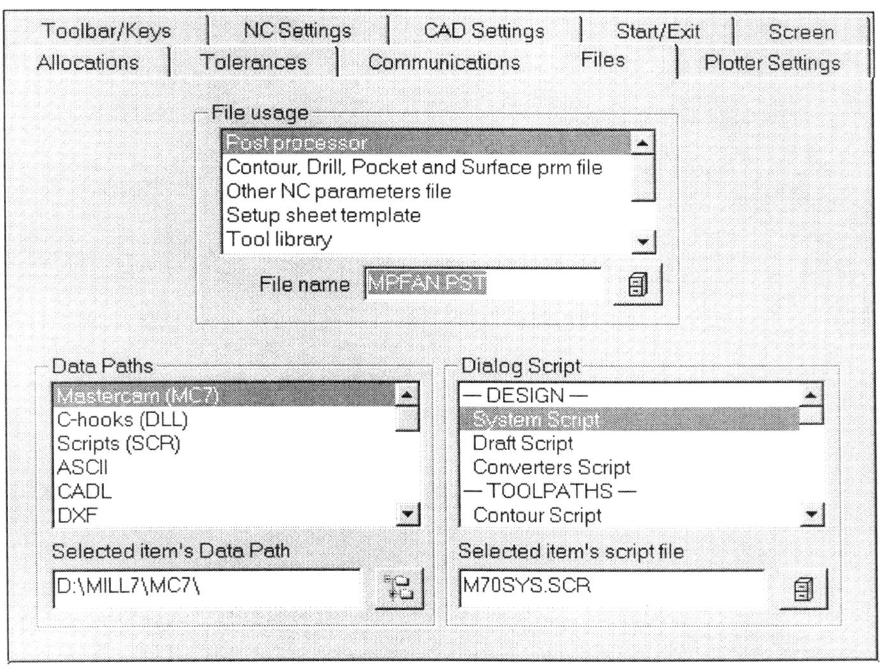

Figure 3.15

Plotter Settings – Set default values for plotter parameters. When selected, it opens a page of non-Windows driver parameters. If you select the Use Windows driver check box at the lower-left corner of the dialog box, the dialog box updates to the Windows driver parameters. The following Figure 3.16 shows the non-Windows driver parameters for plotter settings.

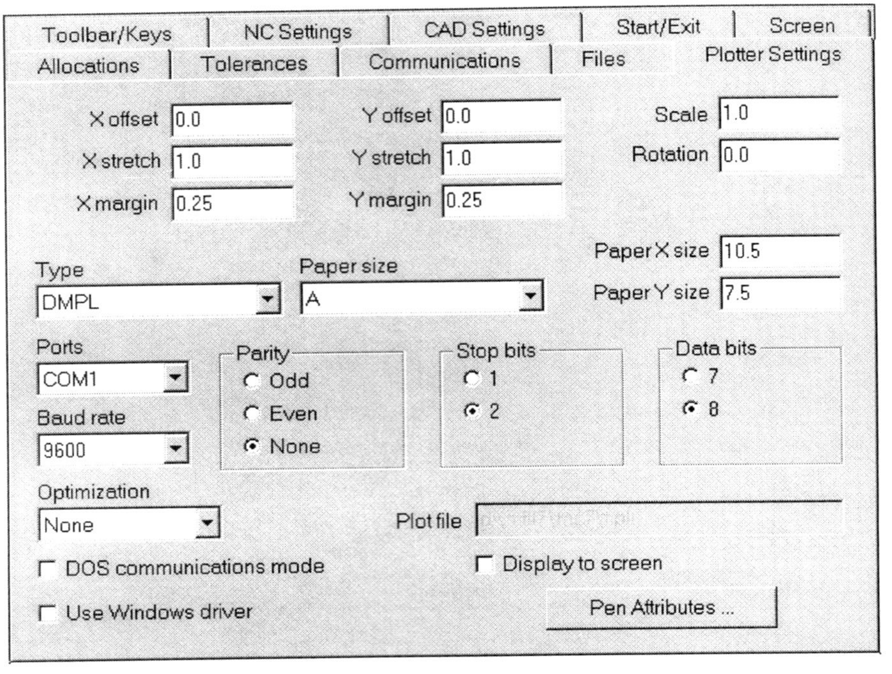

Figure 3.16

The following Figure 3.17 shows the Windows driver parameters for plotter settings.

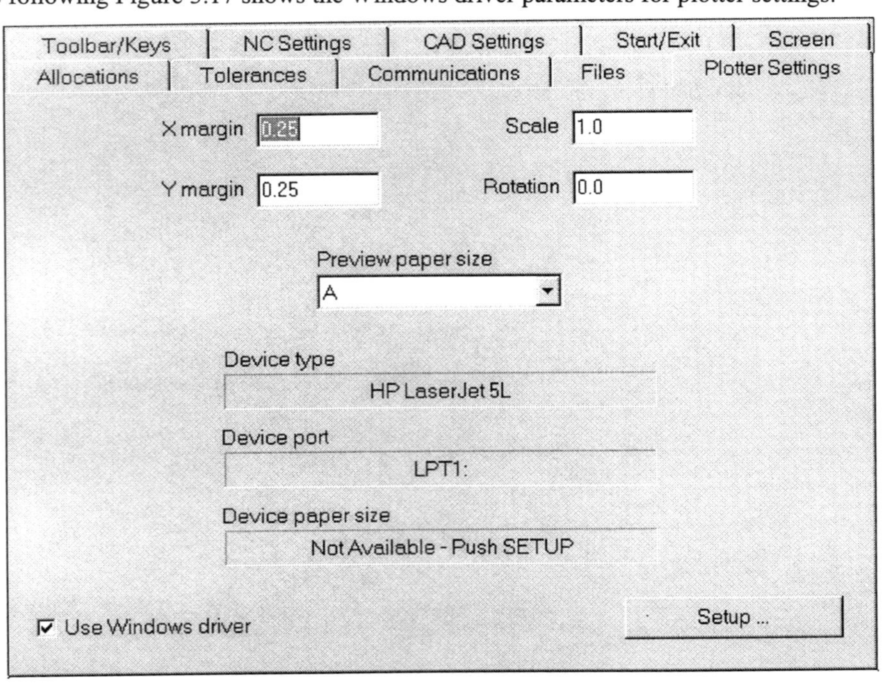

Figure 3.17

Toolbar/Keys – Assign function keys (F1 – F10), Alt keys (excluding system keys such as Alt + F3), or toolbar buttons to functions, C-hooks, and macros. A maximum of 50 keys and 99 buttons can be assigned. See Figure 3.18.

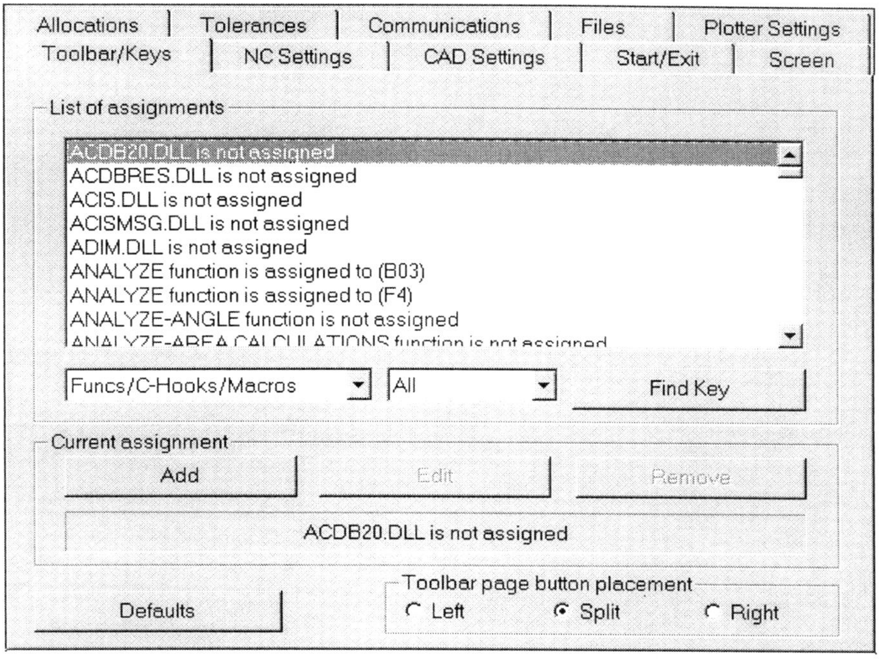

Figure 3.18

NC Settings – Set parameters for generating NC data through Mastercam. See Figure 3.19.

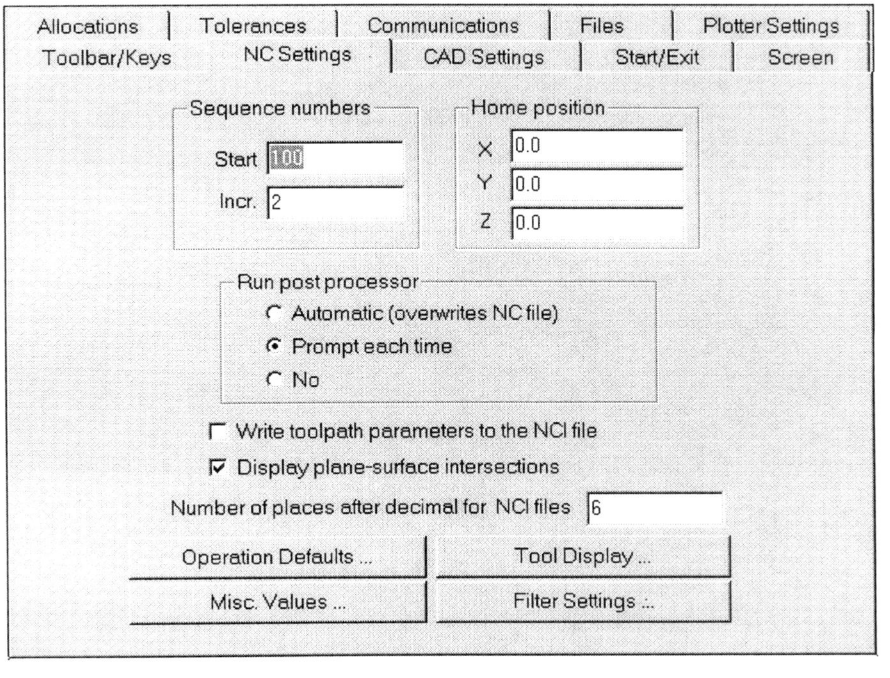

Figure 3.19

CAD Settings – Set the default Design parameter values such as Spline/Surface creation type, Drafting settings, IGES write setting, etc. Refer to Figure 3.20.

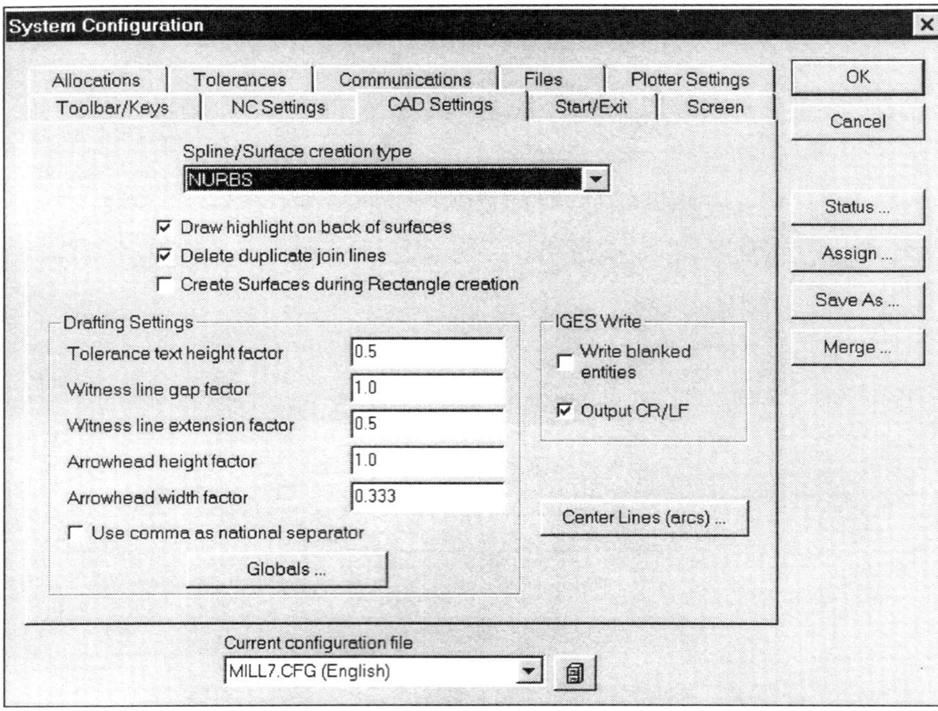

Figue 3.20

Start/Exit – Set the default values that the system uses when you start and/or exit Mastercam. These default values include startup configuration file, default construction plane, editor name, C-hooks settings and autosave setting. See Figure 3.21.

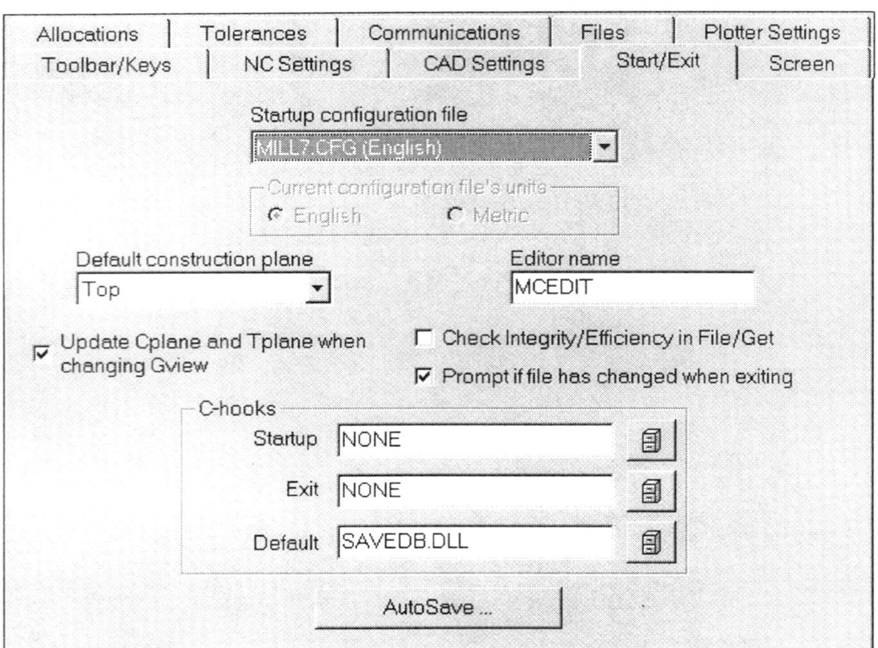

Figure 3.21

Screen – Set the appearance of different areas of Mastercam's screen display. It includes menu font, default view configuration, default point entry mode, toolbar visible at system startup, etc.

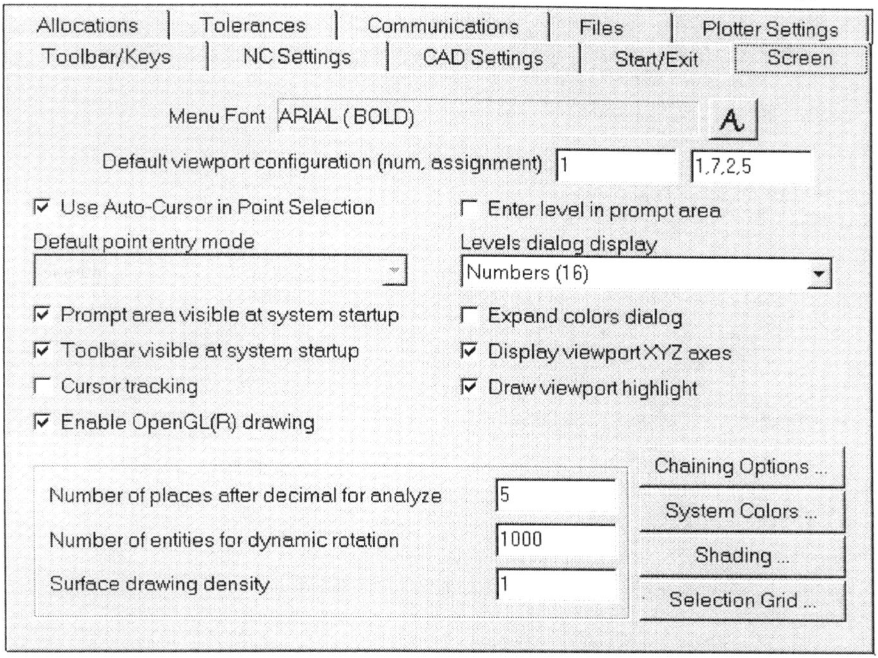

Figure 3.22

Current configuration file options

By selecting the drop-down check mark, you can select the current configuration file for Mastercam. For example, you can select MILL7M.CFG if you are using metric units. See Figure 3.23.

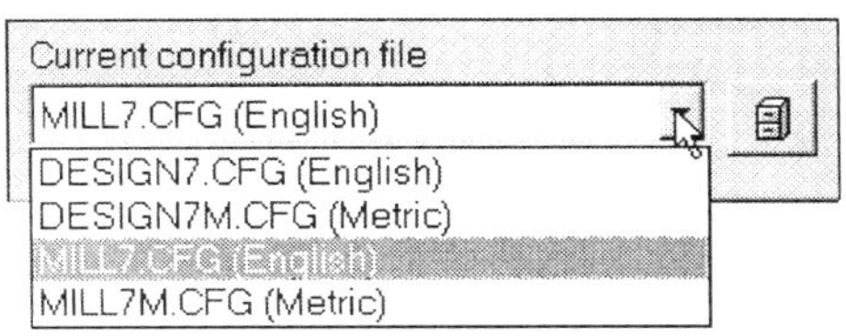

Figure 3.23

Example

In the following example, you will practice the essential commands introduced in this chapter to work with Mastercam. You will enter the Mastercam environment, complete a simple drawing as shown in Figure 3.24, save the drawing and retrieve it. Don't worry about exact sizes or dimensions, but do try to make them look as much like the drawing as possible.

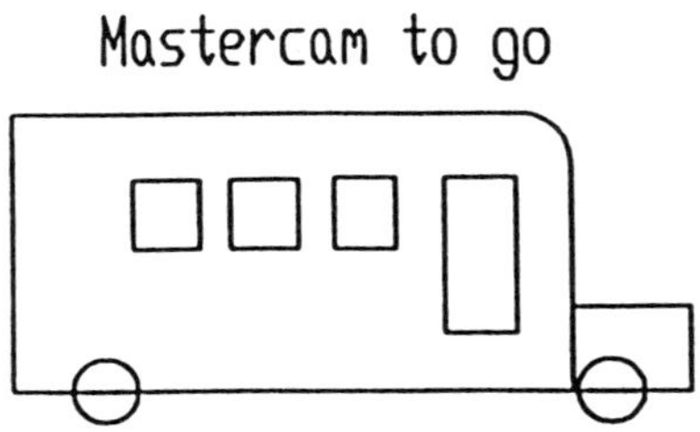

Figure 3.24 Example drawing: Mastercam to go

In the process of creating this drawing, you will learn to use the mouse, select the screen menu commands and enter other input from the keyboard. This hands-on experience is important for you to be familiar with Mastercam and its applications. The learning objectives can be itemized as:

- Entering Mastercam
- Analyzing the drawing entities
- Creating a simple geometry
- Saving to a file
- Exiting Mastercam
- Restarting Mastercam
- Retrieving previous file

Step 1. Entering Mastercam

Follow the procedures shown in Section 3.2.

Step 2. Analyzing the drawing entities

In order to construct the drawing, the first procedure is to identify the drawing entities as shown in Figure 3.25, and the construction sequences. Although this chapter does not cover this procedure, it is important to include it in your practice before you start constructing your drawing.

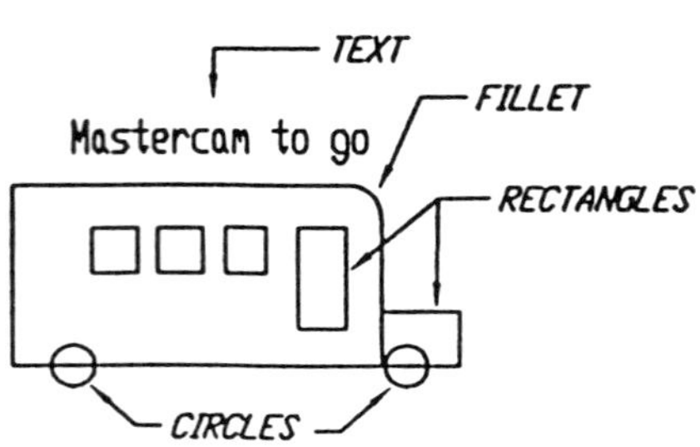

Figure 3.25

Step 3. Creating a simple geometry

For steps 4 through 9, you should refer to the pick points shown in Figure 3.26.

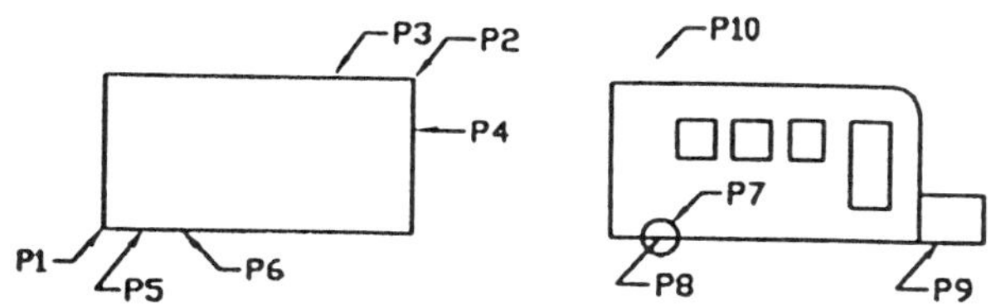

Figure 3.26 Pick points for the example drawing

Step 4. Create a rectangle

Select the menu items:

Main Menu → Create → Rectangle → 2 points

(Notice and switch to the prompt in the System Response Area)

Enter the lower left corner: Pick **P1**

Enter the upper right corner: Pick **P2**

Step 5. Create a fillet

Select the menu items:

Main Menu → Create → Fillet

(Notice the default values in the System Response Area)

Select an entity: Pick **P3**

Select another entity: Pick **P4**

Step 6. Create a circle

Select the menu items:

Main Menu → Create → Arc → Circ 2 pts

(Notice the prompt in the System Response Area)

Enter the first point: Pick **P5**

Enter the second point: Pick **P6**

Step 7. Create rectangles

Follow Step 4 and create the rest of the five rectangles using rectangle commands.

Step 8. Copy a circle

Select the menu items:

Main Menu → Xform → Translate

Select an entity: Pick **P7**

Select the menu items:

Done → Between pts

(Notice the pop-up dialog box on screen)

Enter the points to translate from: Pick **P8**

Enter the points to translate to: Pick **P9**

Set the Translate menu as shown:☞

Select **Done** to return from the Translate menu.

Step 9. Create a text note

Select the menu items:
Main Menu → Create → Drafting → Note → Keyin
(Notice the prompt in the System Response Area)
Text: Enter **Mastercam to go**
Enter **line 2** (press Enter when done): press **Enter**
Create note: Indicate text position: Pick **P10**
Press **ESC** to end this function

Step 10. Saving to a file

Main Menu → File → Save
Enter file name (Drive:\MILL7\MC7\T.MC7): Enter **BUS**

Step 11. Exiting Mastercam

Main Menu → Exit → Yes

Step 12. Restarting Mastercam

Follow the procedures outlined in Section 3.2.

Step 13. Retrieving previous file

Main Menu → File → Get
Enter file name (Drive:\MILL7\MC7\T.MC7): Enter **BUS**
Note: The drawing you just created in this example should appear much like Figure 3.24. at the top of page 3-10.

Exercises

Review and practice the essential commands presented in the previous example.

1. Turn on your computer and load Mastercam to access the drawing editor.

2. Begin a new drawing using your own variables.
   Draw six connected lines. (Hint: Create → Line → Multi → sKetch)
   Draw two rectangle boxes.
   Draw four circles.
   Draw two text notes.
   Delete a line, a rectangle box, a circle, and a text note.

3. Save the drawing as **EX** and exit Mastercam.

4. Enter Mastercam and load **EX**.

5. Explain the overall purpose of the Graphics Display Area, Toolbar Area, System Response Area and Screen Menu Area in Mastercam.

6. Briefly describe the ways to select a menu option.

7. What is the short-cut function key for DELETE?

8. Briefly explain the purpose of the following commands: Create, Modify, Xform

Chapter 4

Mastercam Process Overview

Objectives:

1. Provide an overview of CAD/CAM NC programming.
2. Use a simple example to step through the main tasks of CAD/CAM NC programming.
3. Be familiarized with the process of CAD/CAM NC programming.

4.1 CAD/CAM NC Programming Process

The intent of this chapter is to provide an overview of the processing steps required to generate NC codes in a CAD/CAM system. CAD/CAM NC programming involves **three** major components: **CAD, CAM, and a postprocessor**. Figure 4.1 illustrates the CAD/CAM NC programming steps. Each step indicates the input data and output data. Studying the part drawing is the first step of the process. We need to identify what part features need to be produced and determine the size of the raw material. From these, we should be able to determine how much material needs to be removed. The next step is to create a CAD drawing. The main task of the CAD program is to create the part geometry of the final finished part and its raw material shape if necessary.

The CAM program requires **two** types of input data, **part geometry and machining data**, to generate the tool path to machine the part. The output of the CAM program is a generic file called a cutter location data file (NCI) which contains the coordinate values of a series of cutter paths, machining information such as feed rate, spindle speed, coolant control command, etc. The postprocessor converts the NCI file into NC codes readable to CNC controllers. Since CNC controllers vary from vendor to vendor, this requires us to create a dedicated postprocessor for a particular CNC controller/machine combination. We need to know which CNC machine will be used for machining the part in order to select the appropriate postprocessor.

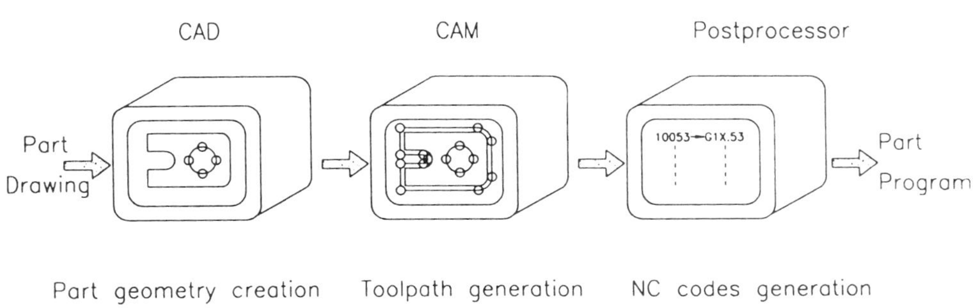

Figure 4.1

4.2 Mastercam Process Overview

This section presents the step-by-step procedure that generates the toolpath to machine a simple part shown in Figure 4.2. This exercise will help you to understand the overall process of CAD/CAM NC programming.

The project involves creating a 6" x 4" rectangle, a blind slot, and four holes. The contour module is used to generate the toolpaths for the outer profile, and the drill module is used for generating the toolpaths for drilling four holes.

Note: If the working envelope of your machine is smaller than 6" x 4", scale all the dimensions by one-half.

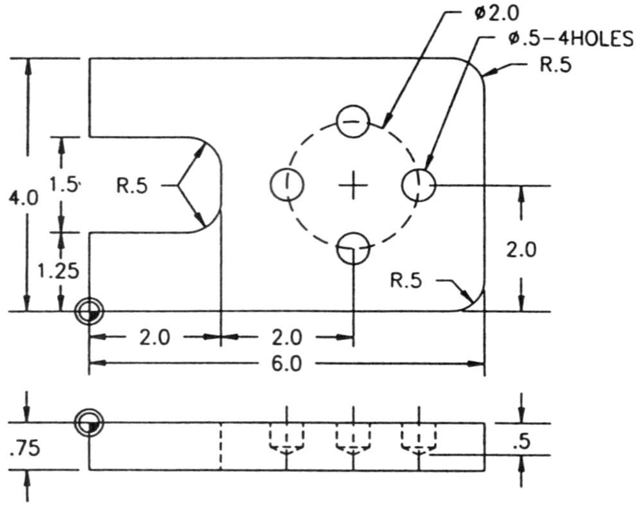

Figure 4.2

Tips: Creating part geometry:

1. Create a rectangle with 6" x 4" dimensions.
2. Create two horizontal lines and one vertical line.
3. Break the left vertical line of the rectangle into two pieces. This allows the line to be trimmed.
4. Add four fillets.
5. Trim the left vertical line of the rectangle and two horizontal lines.
6. Create four circles.
7. Define material stock toolpaths → Top setup → select by selecting any material you want or accept the default material.

Tips: Generating toolpaths:

1. Use the contour module to generate the toolpaths for the outer profile with a 1" end mill.
2. Use the drill module to generate the toolpaths for drilling four holes with a 0.5" drill.
3. Set the NC parameters according to the following tooling and machining specifications:

Tool No.	Tool Dia.	Feedrate	Plunge Rate	Spindle Speed
1	1.0"	15.0 ipm	10.0 ipm	3000 rpm
2	0.5"	15.0 ipm	-	1500 rpm

Step 1. Enter Mastercam Mill. Following the procedure given in Chapter 3.

Step 2. Create a rectangle.

Select **MAIN MENU →Create → Rectangle → 1 point**
Enter the lower left corner: **0,0** ←
Enter the width: **6** ←
Enter the height: **4** ←
Press **ALT + F1** simultaneously then press **F2** to fit the drawing to the screen as in Figure 4.3.

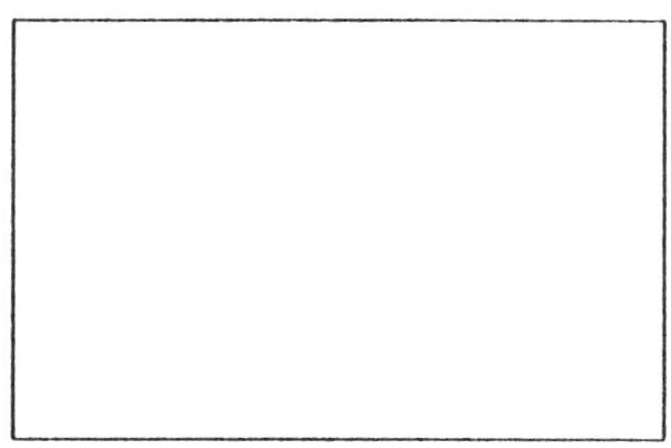

Figure 4.3

Step 3. Create two horizontal lines and one vertical line.

Select **MAIN MENU → Create → Line → Endpoints**
Specify the first endpoint: **-0.5, 2.75** ←
Specify the second endpoint: **2.5, 2.75** ← to complete the first line
Specify the first endpoint: **-0.5, 1.25** ←
Specify the second endpoint: **2.5,1.25** ← to complete the second line
Specify the first endpoint: **2.0, 3.0** ←
Specify the second endpoint: **2.0, 1** ← to complete the third line
The three lines should add to the drawing as shown in Figure 4.4.

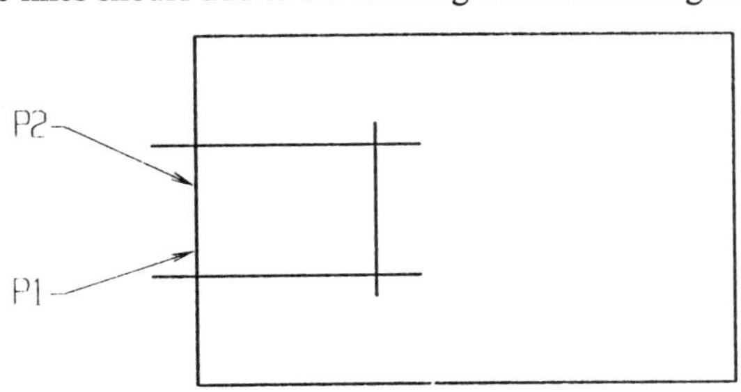

Figure 4.4

Step 4. Break the left vertical line of the rectangle into two pieces.

Use the pick points in Figure 4.4 on the previous page.

Select **MAIN MENU → Modify → Break → 2 pieces**

Select an entity: pick **P1** ←

Enter the breakpoint: pick **P2** ←

The left vertical line is broken into two pieces, but you may not see this on the screen. The new drawing should look identical to Figure 4.4 which is redrawn in Figure 4.5.

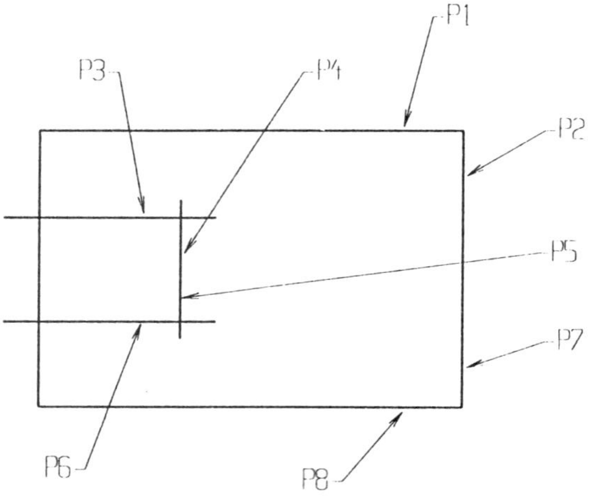

Figure 4.5

Step 5. Add four fillets using the pick points in Figure 4.5.

Select **BACKUP → BACKUP → Fillet → Radius**

Enter the fillet radius: **0.5** ←

Pick points **P1** and **P2** to complete the first fillet

Sequentially pick points at **P3 - P8** to complete the three remaining fillets

The four fillets should appear as in Figure 4.6.

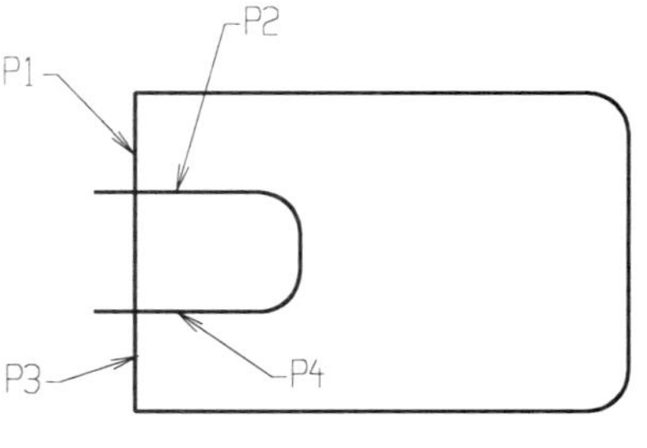

Figure 4.6

Step 6. Trim the left vertical line of the rectangle and two horizontal lines using the pick points in Figure 4.6.

Select **BACKUP → Trim → 2 entities**

Select the entity to trim: pick **P1**

Select the entity to trim to: pick **P2** to trim the upper half of the vertical line

Select the entity to trim: pick **P3**

Select the entity to trim to: pick **P4** to complete the trimming

The trimmed drawing should look like Figure 4.7 on the next page.

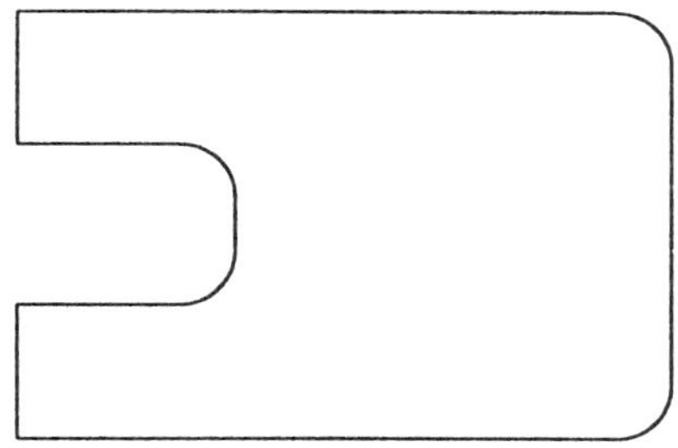

Figure 4.7

Step 7. Create four circles.

Select **MAIN MENU** → **Create** → **Arc** → **pt Dia cir**
Enter the center point: **5,2** ←
Enter the diameter: **.5** ←
Enter the center point: **4,3** ←
Enter the diameter (0.5): press ← to accept the default value
Enter the center point: **3,2** ←
Enter the diameter (0.5): press ←
Enter the center point: **4,1** ←
Enter the diameter (0.5); press ←
The four circles are added to the drawing as shown in Figure 4.8.

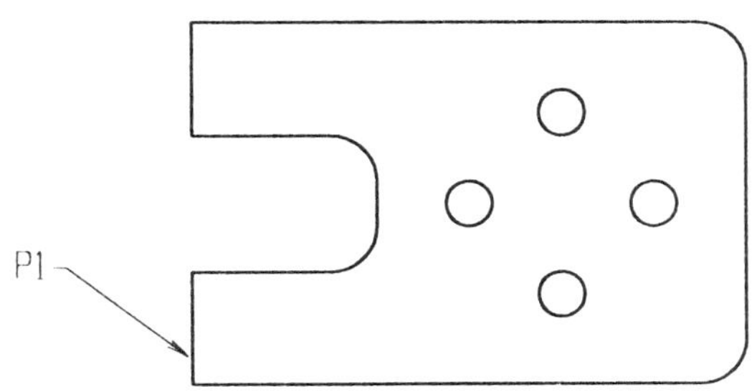

Figure 4.8

Step 8. Initiate the Contour module to generate the toolpath for the outer profile.

Select **MAIN MENU** → **Toolpaths** → **Contour**
Enter file name (C:\NC\NCI\T.NCI): **overview** ←
Define contour 1: select **Chain** from the chaining method menu
Select the first entity in the contour: pick **P1**
Note: The chaining diamond will go in the clockwise direction
Select **Close** → **Done** to complete the contour chaining
Use the pick point in Figure 4.8.

Step 9. Select a 1" end mill.

Click the right mouse button, then select **Get tool from library**
The tool manager dialog box with a list of tools should appear as below.

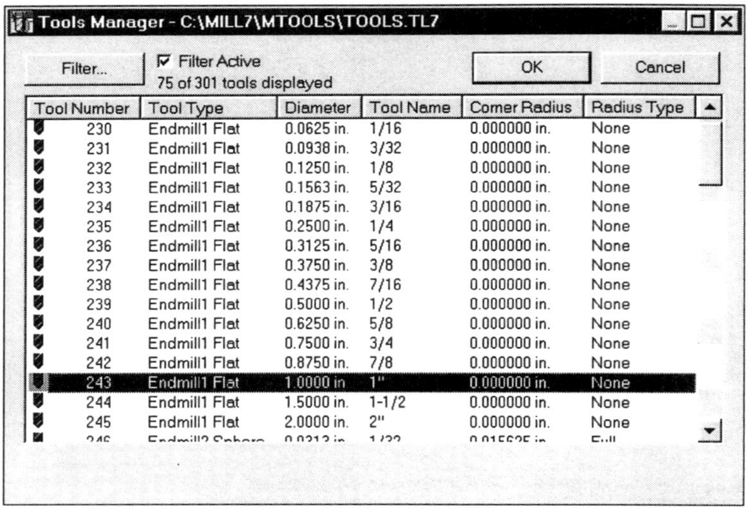

From the Tool Manager list, select **END_MILL_FLAT**
Select **OK**

Step 10. Select a material.

Click on the right mouse button, then select the "Job setup" option
The Job Setup screen will appear as below

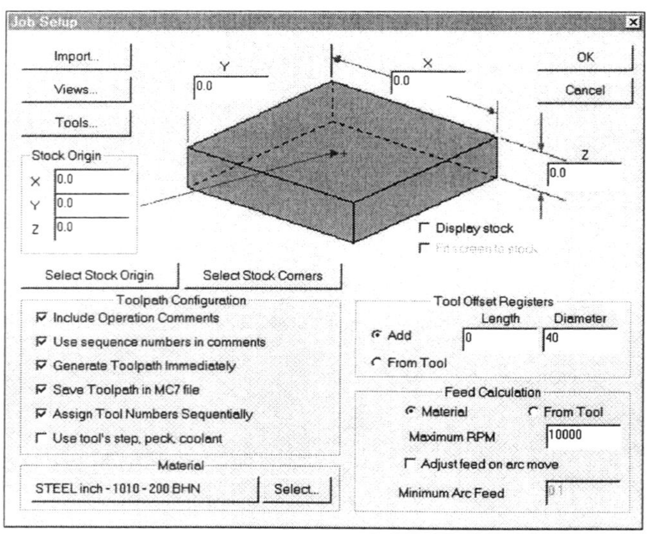

Click **Select** from the bottom of the "Material Selection: menu.
The "Material list: screen is shown below
Select **ALUMINUM inch - 2024 → OK**

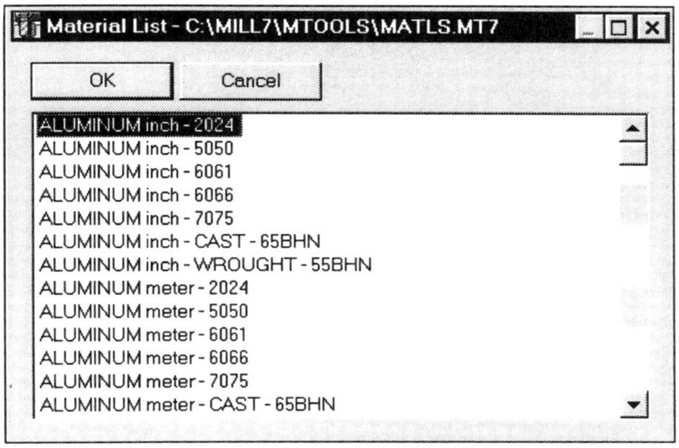

Step 11. Define the tool holder.

Use the right mouse button to click on the **tool icon** of "Endmill"
Set the parameters as below

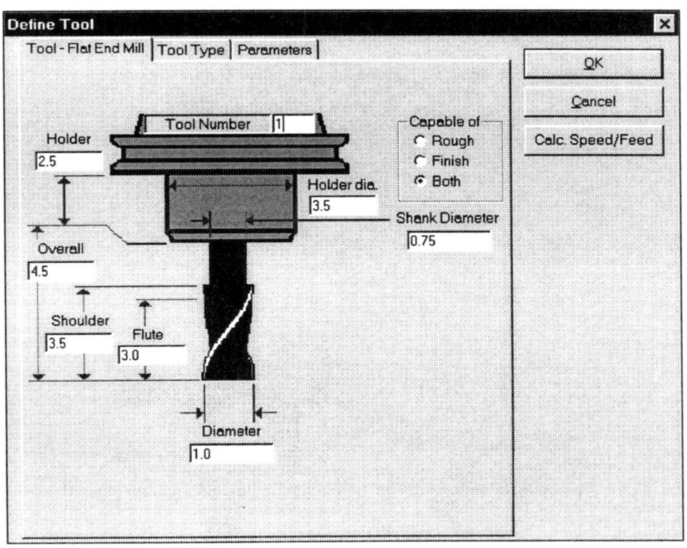

Step 12. Define the tooling and machining parameters.

Select the **parameters button** to open the parameters menu.

Set the parameters as below

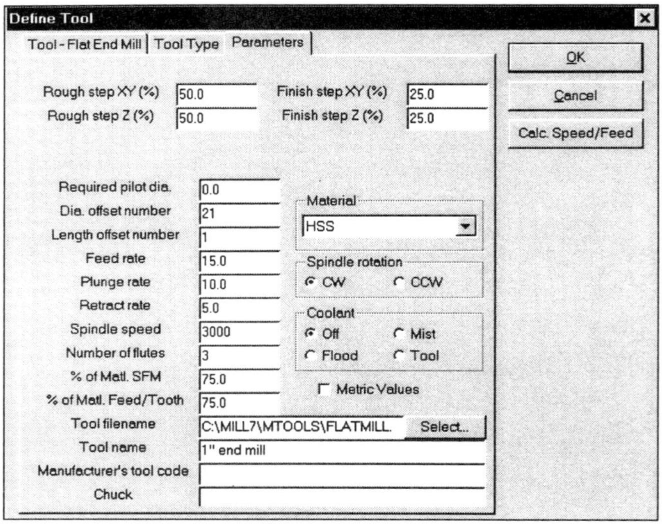

Select **OK**

Step 13. Define tool parameter.

Set the tool parameters as below

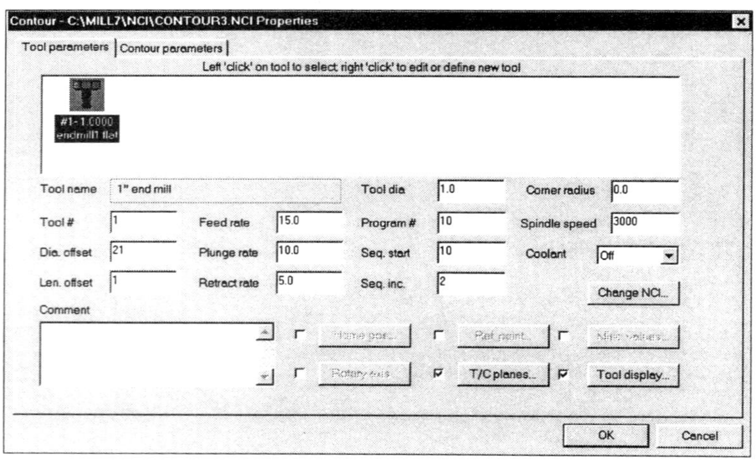

Step 14. Define the contour parameters.

Select the **Contour Parameters** button

Set the parameters as below

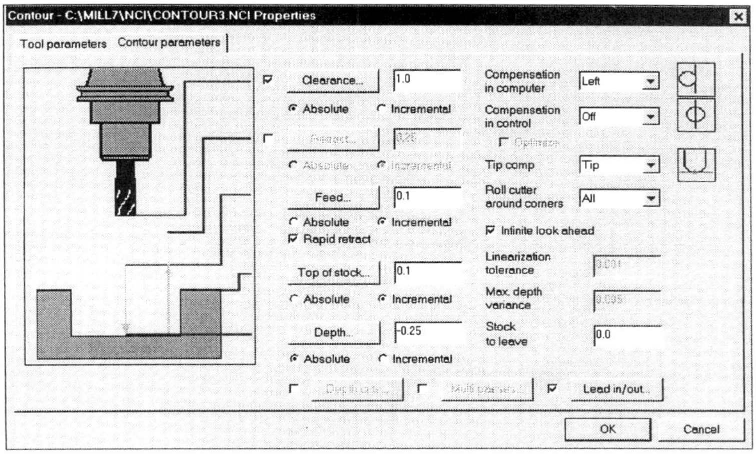

Step 15. Define lead In/Out parameters

Select the **Leadin/out** button

Set the parameters as below

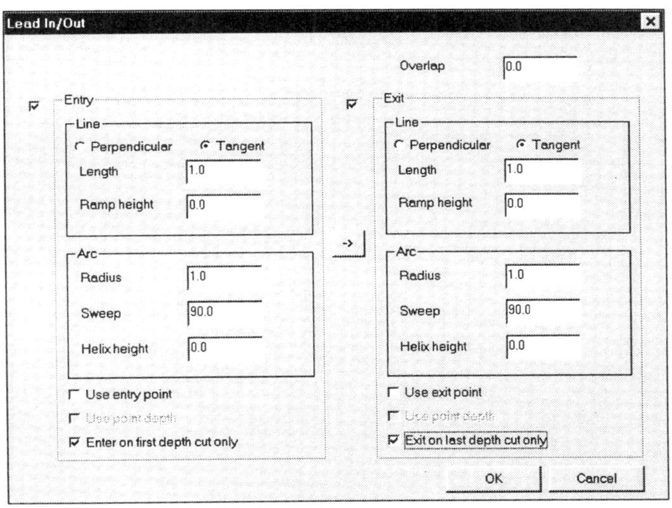

Select **OK → OK**

The toolpaths should appear as in Figure 4.9.

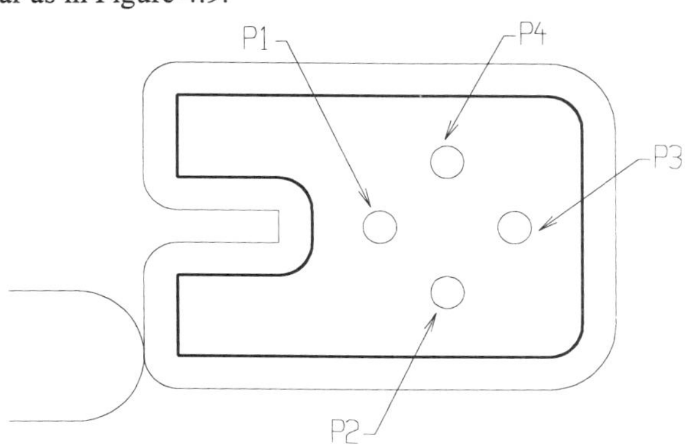

Figure 4.9

Step 16. Initiate the Drill module.

Use the pick points in Figure 4.10.

Select **Drill**

Select **Manual** from the Select points menu

Select **Center** from the point menu

Sequentially pick **P1, P2, P3,** and **P4,**
then press **Esc** to complete the points selection

Select **BACKUP → Done**

Step 17. Set a 1/2" Drill.

Click the right mouse button, then select **Get tool from library**

Select **tool #141** (1/2" drill) as shown below.

Set the Drill parameters to the following settings:

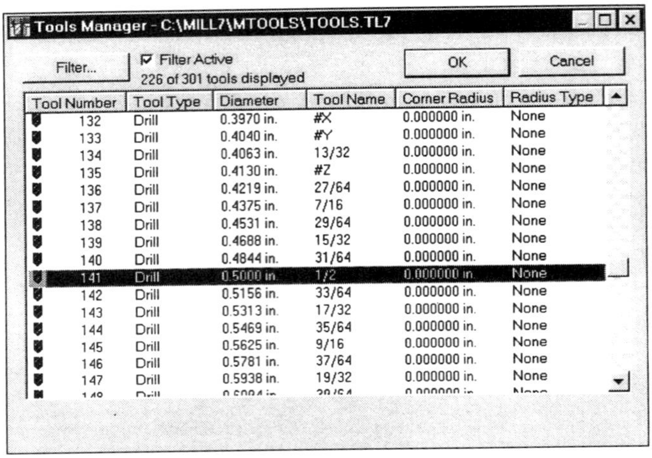

Select **OK**

Step 18. Define the tool holder.

Use the right mouse button to click on the tool icon of the drill

Set the Define Tool parameters as below:

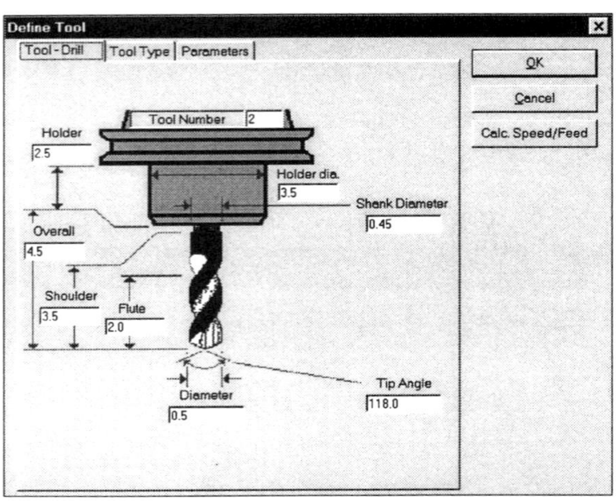

Step 19. Define the machinery parameters

Select the **parameters** button

Set the parameters as below.

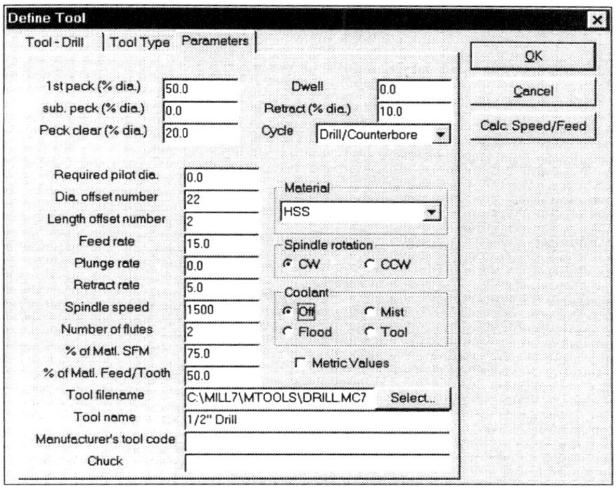

Select **OK**

Step 20. Set the tool parameters as below.

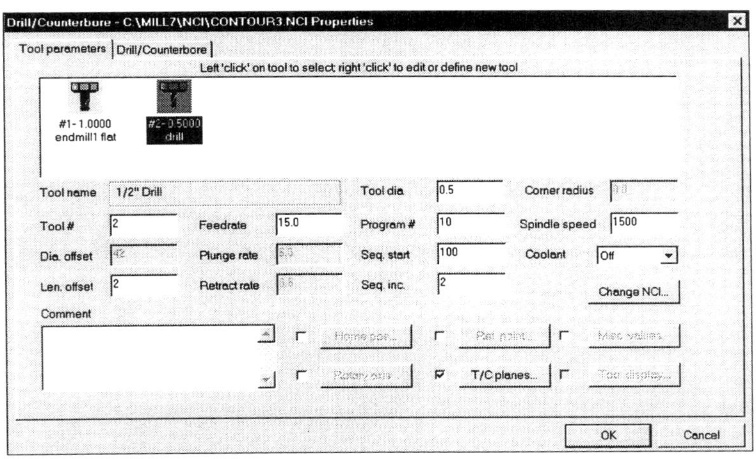

Step 21. Define the drill parameters

Click on the tool icon of drill

Set the parameters as below

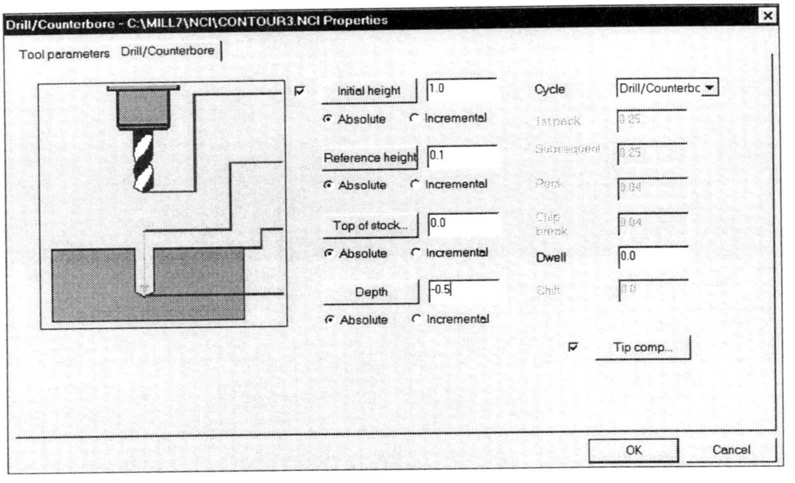

Select **OK → OK**
The drilling toolpaths are added to the drawing as shown in Figure 4.10.

Step 22. Change to isometric view

Select **Gview** from the Secondary menu
Select **Isometric** from the Gview menu
Press **Alt** + **F1** simultaneously
then press **F2** to fit the drawing on the screen if necessary.

The drawing should look like Figure 4.11.

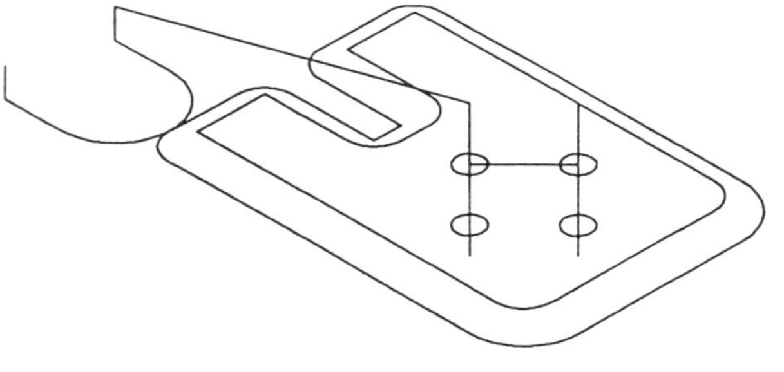

Figure 4.11

Step 23. Select the post processor.

Select **MANI MENU → NC utils → Post Proc → Change**
Filename: **mpfan.pst**
Select **Open**

Step 24. Run the post processor to convert the toolpath file (.NCI) into the NC codes (.NC).

Select **Run → Open**
Filename: **Overview**

The part program should appear on the screen

Exit the list program by clicking the Close box **[X]**

Step 25. List the NC codes

Select **MAIN MENU → File → Edit →NC**

File3name: **Overview**

The program generated from this process is listed below.

Note: Due to different configurations in post processors, your program might be slightly different.

The part program generated from this process is listed below:

```
%
O0010
(PROGRAM NAME - CONTOUR3)
(DATE=DD-MM-YY - 29-05-98 TIME=HH:MM - 15:51)
(1" ENDMILL TOOL - 1 DIA. OFF. - 21 LEN. - 1 DIA. - 1.)
N10G20
N12G0G40G49G80G90
/N14G91G28Z0.
/N16G28X0.Y0.
/N18G92X0.Y0.Z0.
N20T1M6
N22G0G90X-2.5Y-1.S3000M3
N24G43H1Z1.
N26Z.2
N28G1Z-.25F10.
N30X-1.5F15.
N32G3X-.5Y0.J1.
N34G1Y1.25
N36G2X0.Y1.75I.5
N38G1X1.5
N40Y2.25
N42X0.
N44G2X-.5Y2.75J.5
N46G1Y4.
N48G2X0.Y4.5I.5
N50G1X5.5
N52G2X6.5Y3.5J-1.
N54G1Y.5
N56G2X5.5Y-.5I-1.
N58G1X0.
N60G2X-.5Y0.J.5
N62G3X-1.5Y1.I-1.
N64G1X-2.5
N66G0Z1.
N68M5
N70G91G28Z0.
N72M01
(1/2" DRILL TOOL - 2 DIA. OFF. - 42 LEN. - 2 DIA. - .5)
N74T2M6
N76G0G90X3.Y2.S1500M3
N78G43H2Z1.
N80G98G81Z-.6502R.1F15.
N82X3.9959Y.9792
N84X5.0167Y2.
N86X3.9959Y3.0058
N88G80
N90M5
N92G91G0G28Z0.
N94M30
%
```

Exercises

1. What are the three major components involved in CAD/CAM NC programming?

2. What should be included in generating CAD drawing?

3. What are the two types of data that should be entered into any CAM program to generate NC toolpath?

4. Describe the output of the CAM program.

5. Explain the main task performed in a postprocessor.

6. Explain why a dedicated postprocessor is needed for a unique combination of CNC controller/machine.

Chapter 5

Basic (2D) Geometry Construction

Objectives:

1. Understand the function of POINT, LINE, ARC, CIRCLES, RECTANGLE, CHAMFER, SPLINE, ELLIPSE, POLYGON and LETTERS commands.
2. Practice using Mastercam **CREATE** commands to construct entities on screen.
3. Construct part geometries using basic create commands.

Overview

The part geometry of the final finished part and its raw material shape should be defined in the CAD program. This geometric file is then used in the CAM program to generate the toolpaths for producing the part. An accurate and complete CAD geometry model is very essential in implementing any CAD/CAM software for producing a part program. The focus of this chapter is to show how to use Mastercam's CAD functions to create basic 2D part geometries. The commands presented in this chapter include Point, Line, Arc, Circles, Rectangle, Chamfer, Spline, Ellipse, Polygon and Letters. Advanced geometry modification functions are presented in chapter 6. 3D wireframe geometric model construction is covered in chapter 11.

5.1 Create Menu

Mastercam groups geometry entity construction functions under the Create menu. To create a geometric entity, we have to follow a proper cascaded menu sequence which starts at the MAIN MENU, followed by the Create menu and necessary sub-menus. Figure 5.1 shows a cascaded sequence for the Create function.

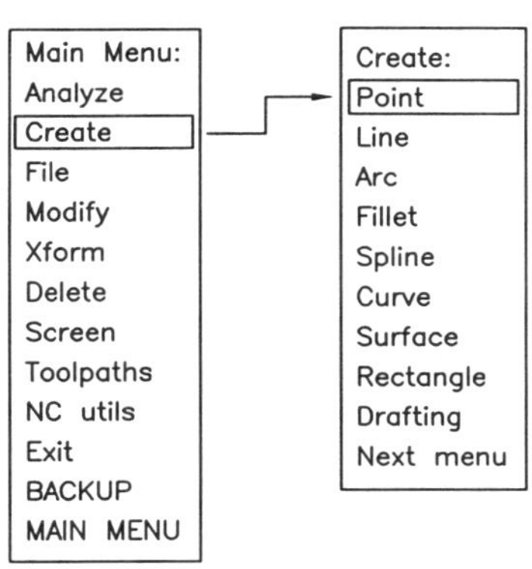

Figure 5.1: Menu for Create

5.2 Point and The Point Submenu

The **Point** command marks points on the drawing with a plus (+) mark. These points can be used as reference points for other geometric constructions when needed.

Select **Create → Point** from the main menu and you will see the following options (Figure 5.2).

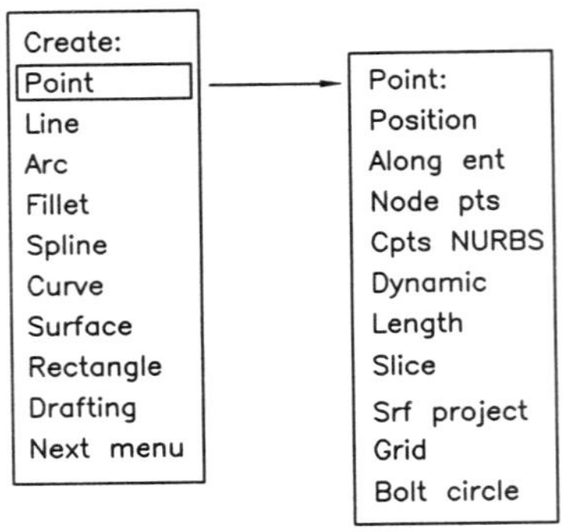

Figure 5.2: Menu for Point

A brief description for the POINT options follows:

Point option	**Description**	
Position:	Create a point by selecting from the following submenu	
	Value:	<Refer to the next table for detailed descriptions of these options.>
	Center:	
	Endpoint:	
	Intersec:	
	Midpoint:	
	Point:	
	Last:	
	Relative:	
	sKetch:	
Along ent:	Create a series of points along an entity with equal distance	
Node pts:	Recall the node points used to create a parametric spline curve	
Cpts NURBS:	Recall the control points of NURBS curve or 3-D surface	
Dynamic:	Create points along an existing entity using the pointing device	
Length:	Create a point on an entity by a given distance from the end point.	
Slice*:	Create points at intersections of planes with non-coplanar lines, arcs and splines.	
Srf project*:	Create points on a surface by projecting them directly onto the surface	
Grid*:	Create a grid array of points.	
Boltcircle*:	Create points in a bolt circle	

Note: * indicates this topic will not be discussed in this chapter.

Create → Point → Position

Use the Position command to create points on the screen. As shown in Figure 5.3, there are

ten options available and they will be referred as the **<using position menu>** in the future.

Position:

Value:	Enter coordinates.
Center:	Select an entity which has a geometric center, e.g., arc, circle.
Endpoint:	Select an entity which has end points, e.g., line, arc, spline, etc. Pick a location closest to the end point you intend to select.
Intersec:	Select two entities which have an intersection point, e.g., line-line, line-arc, etc.
Midpoint:	Select an entity which has a midpoint.
Point:	Select an existing point.
Last:	Select the last point created.
Relative:	Create a point by giving a relative distance to an existing point. Input the distance as either Rectangular or Polar coordinates.
Quadrant:	Create a point by picking a quadrant position on an existing arc.
sKetch:	Use the mouse to pick the point to be created.

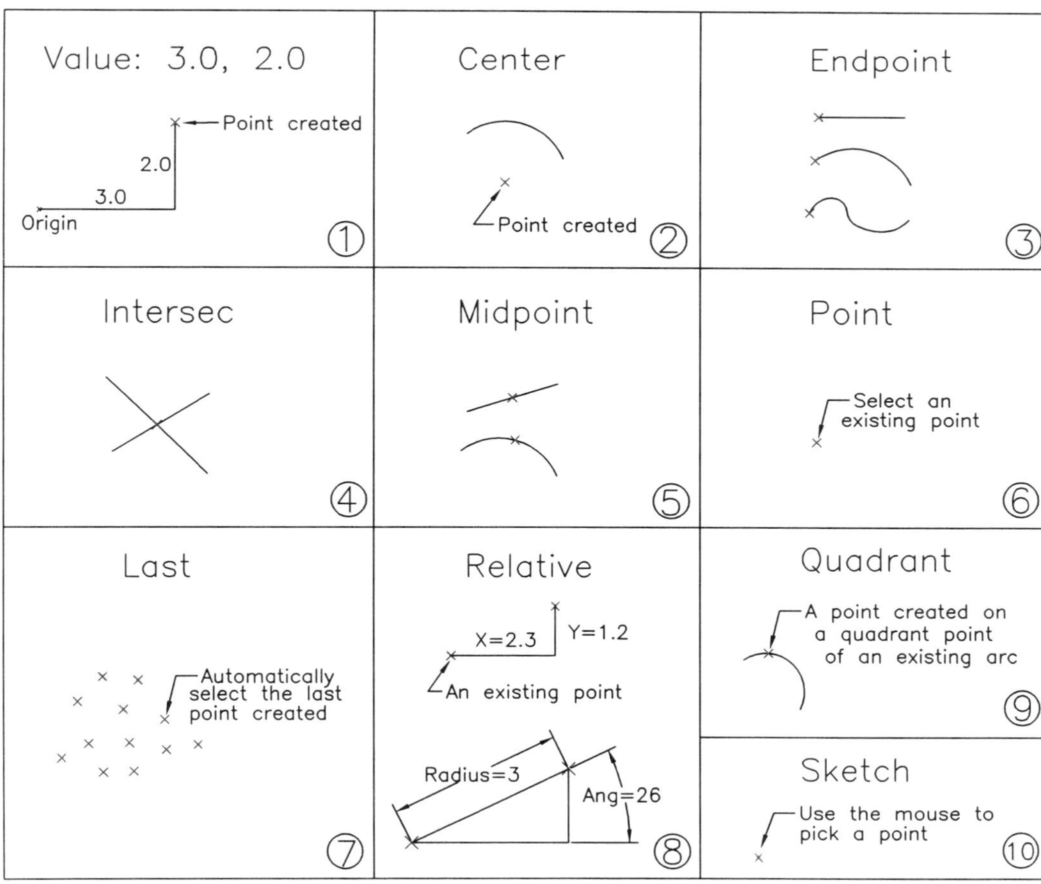

Figure 5.3 Mastercam position menu

Create → Point → **Along ent**

Create a series of points along an entity with equal distance between the points.

Procedure:

Create an entity such as line, arc, circle, fillet or spline.

Select an entity

Use the mouse to select an entity including line, arc, circle, fillet or spline.

Enter the number of points to create (def val): **6** ↵

Note: **def val** stands for default value from the system, see section **3.5** for more detailed information. The points created are spaced at an equal distance along the entity selected as shown in Figure 5.4.

Tip

If you want to break an entity into 3 equal sections, this is the command you can use. The number of points to create should be set to 4.

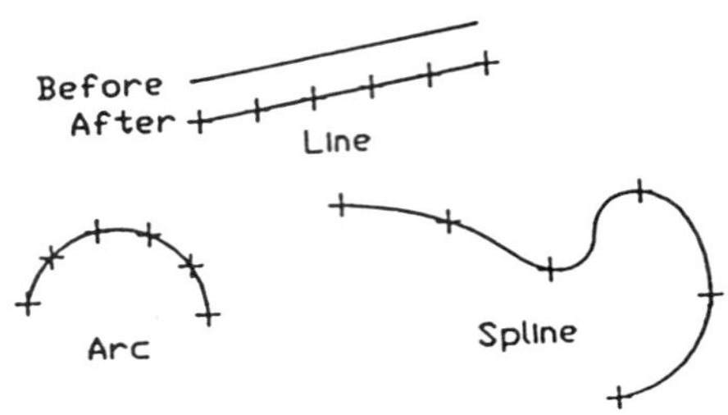

Figure 5.4

Create → Point → **Node pts**

Recall the node points used to create a parametric spline curve (Figure 5.5).

Procedure:

Create a parametric spline curve. Refer to Section 5.6 for the steps in the construction of a parametric spline curve.

Select a parametric spline.

Tips

1. These points are the node points used to define the spline.
2. If a wrong entity is selected, (other than parametric spline), the system will respond "try again". Use the **Esc** key to quit the selection.

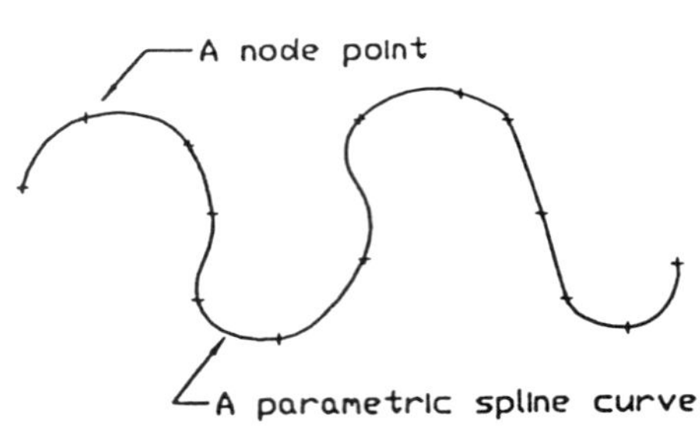

Figure 5.5

Create → Point → **Cpts NURBS**

Recall the control points of NURBS curve or 3-D surface.

Procedure:

Create a NURBS spline.
Refer to Section 5.6 for the construction of a NURBS curve.
Select a NURBS curve (or a 3-D surface).

Tips

1. These points are the control points used to define the curve or surface (Figure 5.6).
2. If you select a wrong entity (other than NURBS curve or surface), the system will response "try again". Use the Esc key to quit the selection.

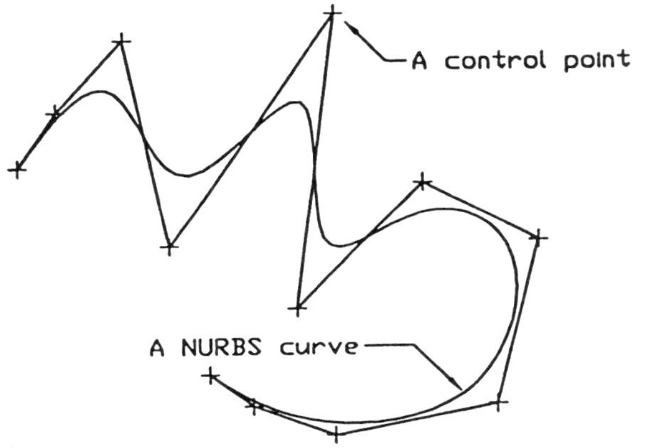

Figure 5.6

Create → Point → **Dynamic**

Create points along an existing entity with the mouse or pointing device (Figure 5.7).

Procedure:

Select an entity such as line, circle or spline.
Move the mouse around the entity and then click the left mouse button to create a point (press Esc when done).

Note: You can use this function to create as many points as you want in any position along the entity selected.

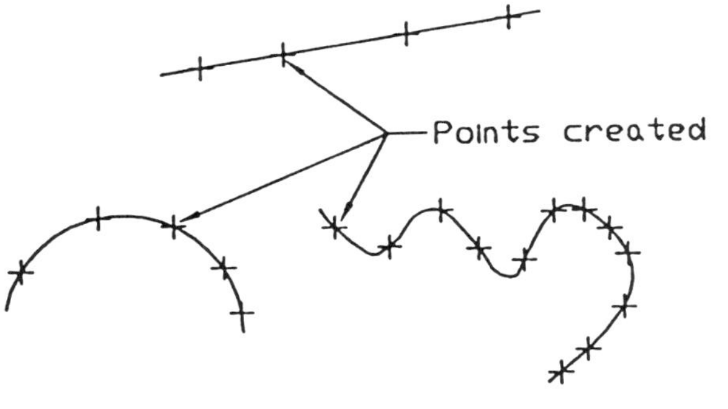

Figure 5.7

Create → Point → **Length**
Create a point on an entity at given distance from the end point. (Figure 5.8).
Procedure:
Create an entity such as a line, arc, etc.
Select an entity: Pick at **P1**
Length = **1.5**↵
Press **ESC** to quit

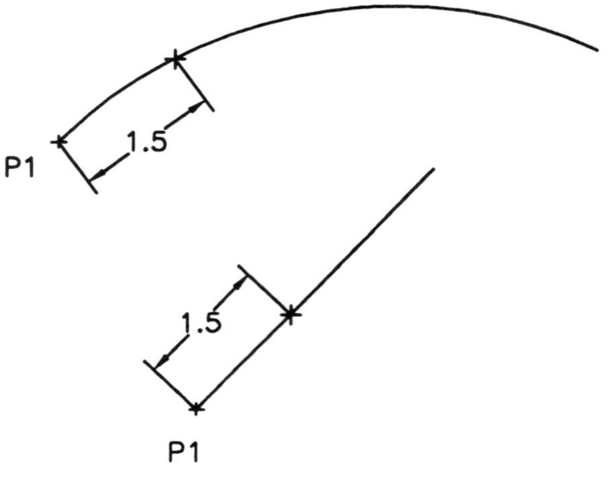

Figure 5.8

5.3 Line and Its Submenu

The **Line** command draws lines on the screen. These lines can be horizontal, vertical, or with any other orientation. It can be used to construct geometries such as those shown in Figure 5.9.

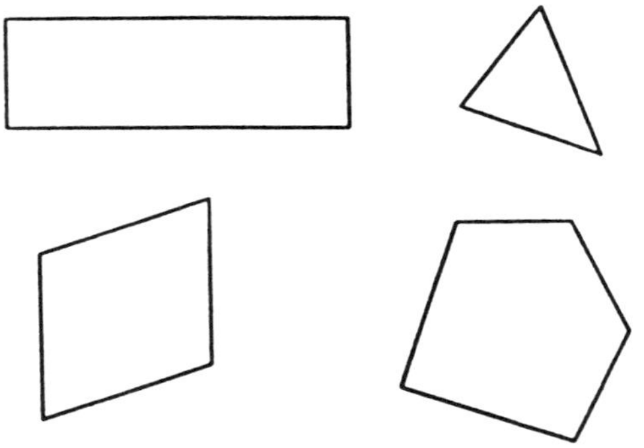

Figure 5.9

Select **Create → Line** from the main menu and you will see the following submenu options.

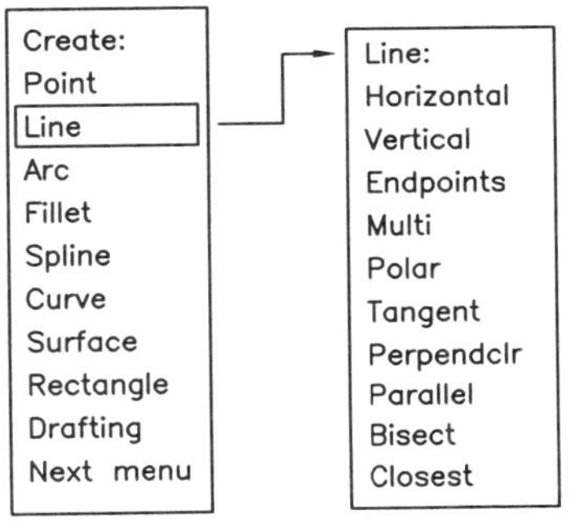

Figure 5.10: Submenu options for Line

In the LINE submenu, there are **ten** options. A brief description of each option is given below and its examples are provided in Figure 5.11.

Line option	Description
Horizontal:	Create a horizontal line.
Vertical:	Create a vertical line.
Endpoints:	Create a line by specifying its two endpoints.
Multi:	Construct multi-line segments by specifying segment endpoints.
Polar:	Create a line using polar coordinate.
Tangent:	Create a line which is tangent to an arc or arcs.
Perpendclr:	Create a line which is perpendicular to a line or an arc.
Parallel:	Create a line that is parallel to reference a line.
Bisect:	Create a line that bisects the angle formed by two intersecting lines.
Closest:	Create a line that is closest to the next entity.

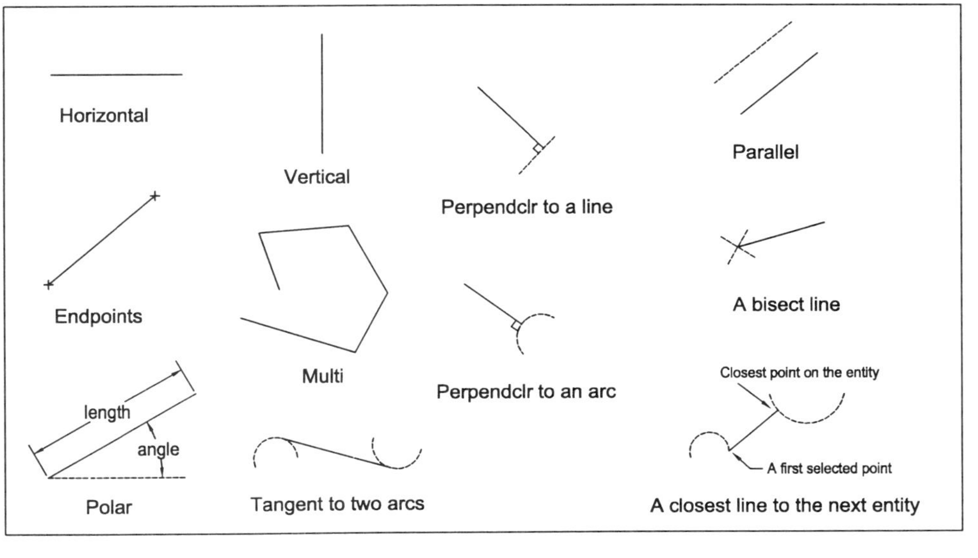

Figure 5.11

Note: The default line style and line width can be changed by picking the Style/Width button from the Menu Area (See Figure 3.3). The available line styles are solid, hidden, center, phantom and Zbreak.

Create → Line → **Horizontal**

Create a horizontal line (Figure 5.12).

Procedure:

Specify the first endpoint <using position menu>: Pick at **P1**
Specify the second endpoint <using position menu>: Pick at **P2**
Enter the y coordinate (def val): **3.0** ↵
(Press Esc to quit this procedure.)

Note: The default value inside the dialog box is the Y coordinate of the first selected endpoint.

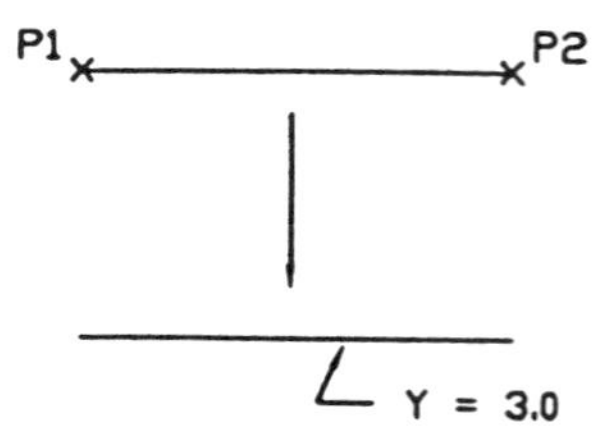

Figure 5.12

Create → Line → **Vertical**

Create a vertical line (Figure 5.13).

Procedure:

Specify the first endpoint <using position menu>: Pick at **P1**
Specify the second endpoint <using position menu>: Pick at **P2**
Enter the x coordinate (def val): **3.0** ↵
(Press Esc to quit this procedure.)

Note: The default value inside the dialog box is the X coordinate of the first selected endpoint.

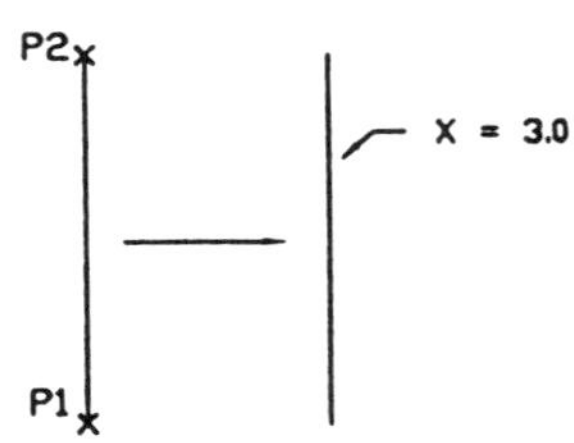

Figure 5.13

Create → Line → **Endpoints**

Create a line by specifying its two endpoints (Figure 5.14).

Procedure:

Specify the first endpoint <using position menu>: Pick at **P1**
Specify the second endpoint <using position menu>: Pick at **P2**

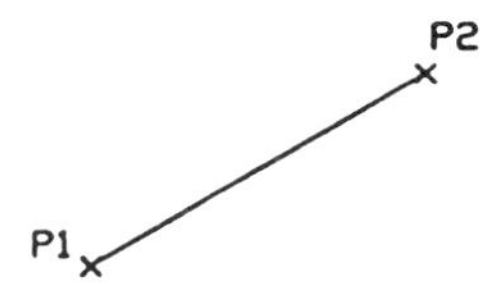

Figure 5.14

Create → Line → **Multi**

Construct multi-line segments by specifying their segment endpoints (Figure 5.15).

Procedure:

Select endpoint 1 <using position menu>: Pick at **P1**
Select endpoint 2 <using position menu>: Pick at **P2**
Select endpoint 3 <using position menu>: Pick at **P3**
Continue with endpoint selection(s): Pick at **P4**, **P5** and **P6**
Select **BACKUP** or press **Esc** key to exit the selection.

Note: As of Mastercam V7.0, the **UNDO** key will undo only the last line segment created.

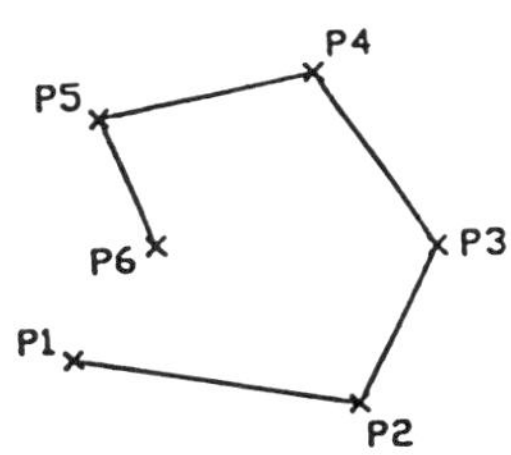

Figure 5.15

Create → Line → **Polar**

Create a line using polar coordinate (Figure 5.16).

Procedure:

Specify an endpoint <using position menu>: Pick at **P1**
Enter the angle in degrees (def val): **30**↵
Enter the line length (def val): **2.5** ↵

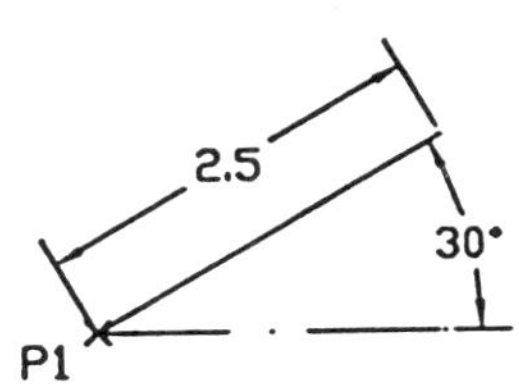

Figure 5.16

Create → Line → **Tangent**

Create a line which is tangent to an arc or arcs. It has **three** options:

Angle:	Create a line with a specified angle and length and tangent to an arc.
2 arcs:	Create a line tangent to two arcs

Point: Create a line tangent to an arc through a specified point.

Create → Line → Tangent → **Angle**

Create a line with a specified angle and length tangent to an arc.

Procedure:

Create an arc or a circle similar to the one shown in Figure 5.17.
(Refer to section 5.4 for the construction of arcs.)
Select an arc: Pick at **P1**
Enter the angle in degrees (def val): **30**↵
Enter the line length (def val): **2.0** ↵
Select line to keep: **Pick** the correct line segment.

Note: There are two line segments created in this procedure. Choose the one you want to keep.

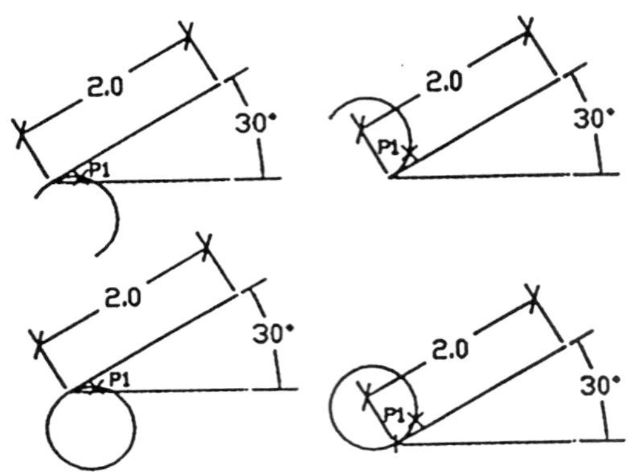

Figure 5.17

Create → Line → Tangent → **2 arcs**

Create a line tangent to two arcs (Figure 5.18).

Procedure:

Create two arcs.
Select an arc: Pick at **P1**
Select another arc: Pick at **P2**

Tip	There are several possibilities when a line is tangent to two arcs. In procedure 1 and 2, choose the points close to the arcs where you want the line to be created.

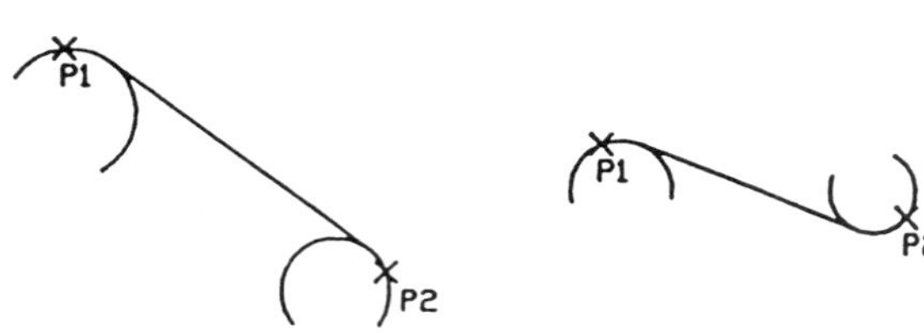

Figure 5.18

Create → Line → Tangent → **Point**

Create a line tangent to an arc or a spline through a specified point (Figure 5.19).

Procedure:

Create an arc.
Select arc or spline: Pick at **P1**
Specify an endpoint <using position option>: Pick at **P2**
Enter the line lenght (def val): ↵

Note: The default value is calculated automatically from the tangent point to P2.

> **Tip** Generally speaking, there are two possibilities in this case. In procedure 1, choose the points close to the arcs where you want the line to be tangent to.

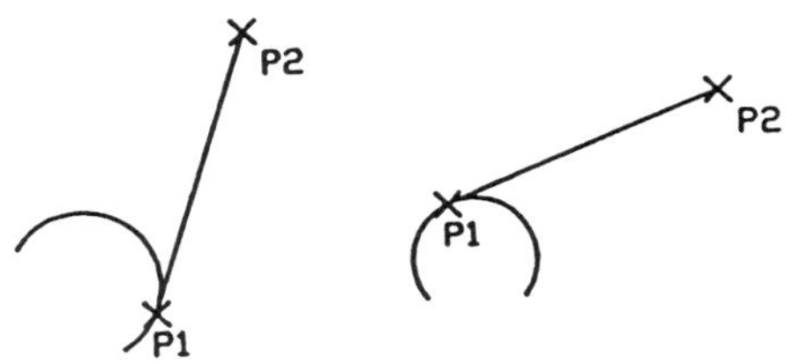

Figure 5.19

Create → Line → **Perpendclr**

Create a line which is perpendicular to a line, arc, spline, or NURBS curve through a point.
It has **two** options:

Point:	Create a line perpendicular to another line, arc, spline NURBS curve through a point.
Arc:	Create a line perpendicular to an existing line and tangent to an existing arc.

Create → Line → Perpendclr → **Point**

Create a line perpendicular to another line, arc, spline, or NURBS curves through a point (Figure 5.20a).

Procedure:

Create a line or an arc.
Select a line or an arc: Pick at **P1**
Specify an endpoint <using position menu>: Pick at **P2**
Enter the line length (def val): ↵

Note: As shown in Figure 5.20a, in some cases the line created does not have an explicit intersection with the line or the arc selected. Mastercam will automatically extend the line or the arc to calculate intersected point.

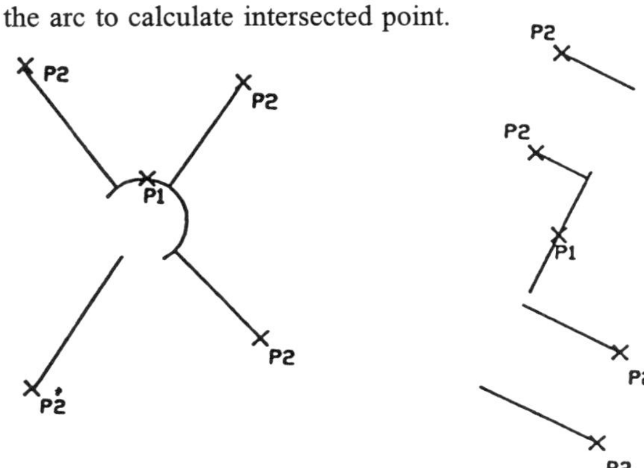

Figure 5.20

Create → Line → Perpendclr → **Arc**

Create a line perpendicular to an existing line and tangent to an existing arc. (Figure 5.20b)

Procedure:

Create a line and an arc.
Select a line: Pick at **P1**
Select an arc to place a perpendicular line tangent to: Pick at **P2**
Enter the length of the perpendicular line (def val): ←
Select which line to keep: Pick at **P3**

> **Tip** Again, there are two possibilities. Mastercam will ask you to choose the one you want to keep.

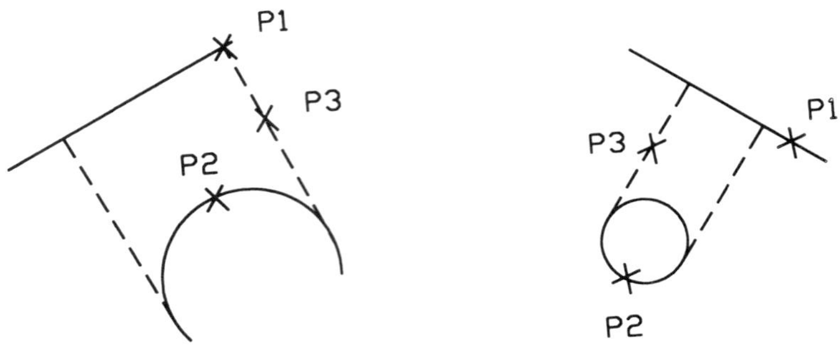

Figure 5.20b

Line Exercise

Using the LINE Command and your mouse, draw each of the following objects as shown in Figure 5.21. Don't worry about exact sizes, but do try to make them look like these drawings as much as possible. Practice the various options covered in this section.

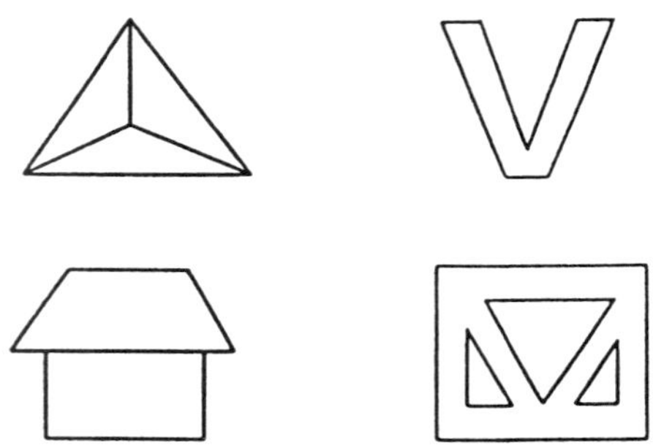

Figure 5.21

Practice LINE commands to draw the the objects shown in Figure 5.22.

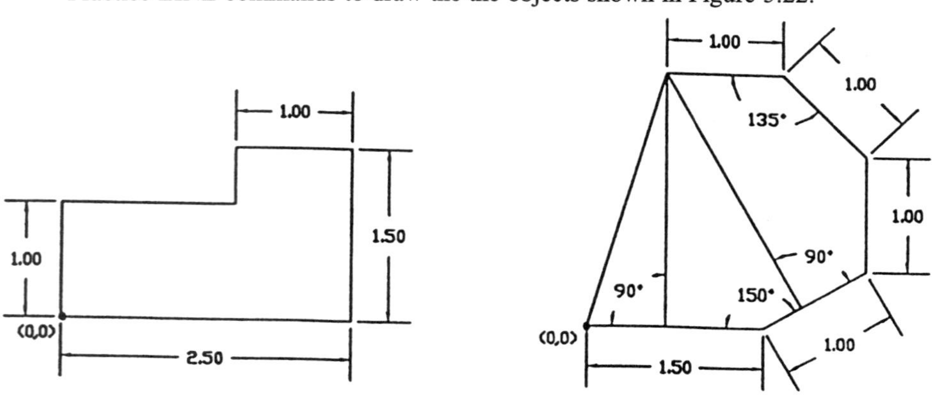

Figure 5.22

5.4 Arc and the Arc Submenu

The Arc command is used to create arcs and circles. Figure 5.23 shows some of the arcs and circles that will be created in this section. Mastercam provides **four** methods to create arcs and **five** methods for drawing circles.

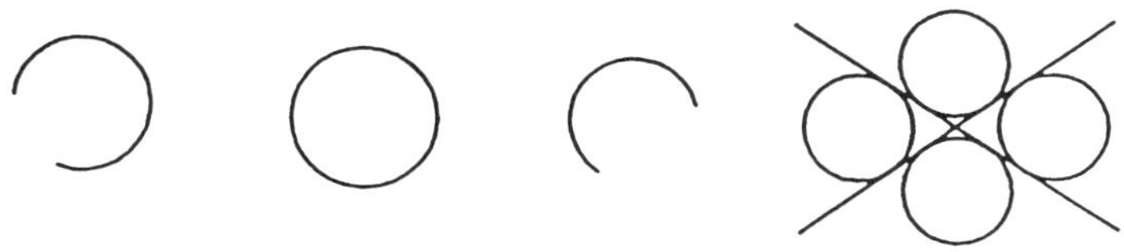

Figure 5.23

In Mastercam, these arcs and circles can be created using several options. Select **Create → Arc** from the main menu and you will see the following **Arc submenu**. A short description of each menu item follows.

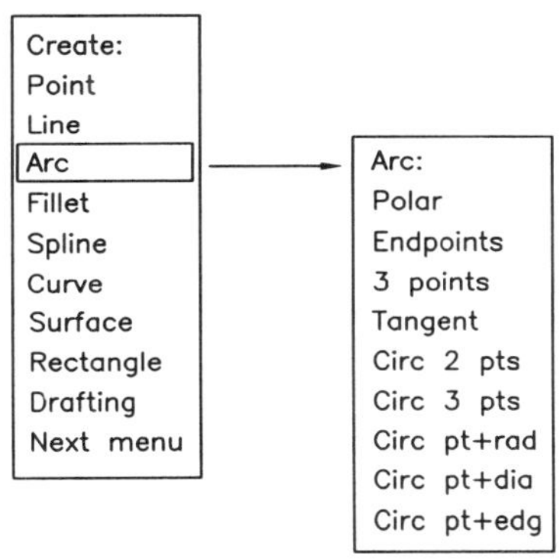

Figure 5.24: Submenu for arc

Arc option	Description
Polar:	Create an arc using polar coordinates
Endpoint:	Create an arc with known two endpoints and its radius.
3 points:	Create an arc with known 3 points
Tangent:	Create an arc that passes through tangent points of select entities
Circ 2 pts:	Create a circle by giving two diameter points
Circ 3 pts:	Create a circle that passes through 3 known points
Circ pt + Rad:	Create a circle with a given center point and a radius
Circ pt + Dia:	Create a circle with a given center point and a diameter
Circ pt + edg:	Create a circle with a given center point and a point on the circumference

Create → Arc → Polar

Create an arc using polar coordinates. In Mastercam, there are **four** options under polar. These are explained in the following procedures. They are:

Center pt	Sketch	Start pt	End pt

Create → Arc → Polar → **Center pt**

Create an arc with a given center point, radius, initial and final angles. The angles are entered from the keyboard.

Procedure:

Enter the center point <using position menu>: **0,0** ←
Enter the radius (def val): **1.5** ←
Enter the initial angle (def val): **30** ←
Enter the final angle (def val): **280** ←

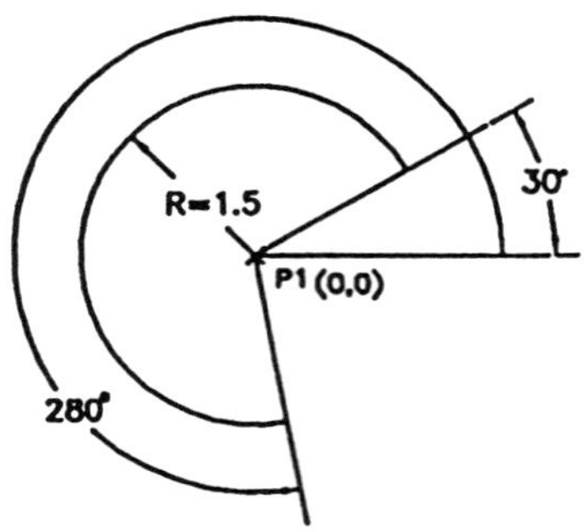

Figure 5.25

Create → Arc → Polar → **Sketch**

Create an arc with a given center point, radius, initial and final angles. The angles are selected by the mouse.

Procedure:

Enter the center point <using position menu>: Pick at **P1**
Enter the radius (def val): **1.5** ←
Sketch the initial angle: Pick at **P2**
Sketch the final angle: Pick at **P3**

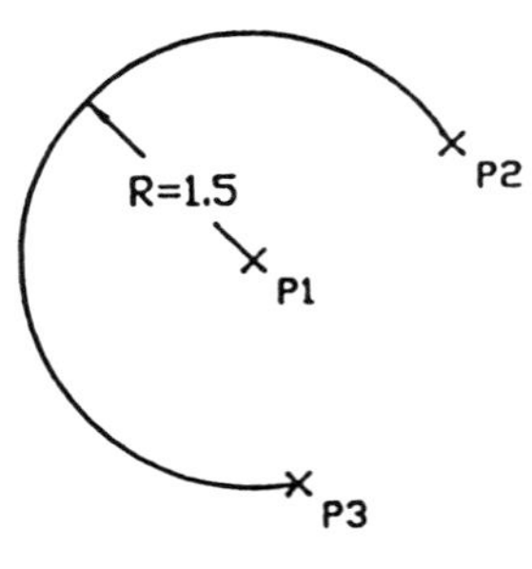

Figure 5.26

Create → Arc → Polar → **Start pt**

Create an arc with given starting point, radius, initial and final angles. The angles are entered from the keyboard.

Procedure:

Enter the start point <using position menu>: Pick at **P1**
Enter the radius (def val): **1.0** ←
Enter the initial angle (def val): **30** ←
Enter the final angle (def val): **280** ←

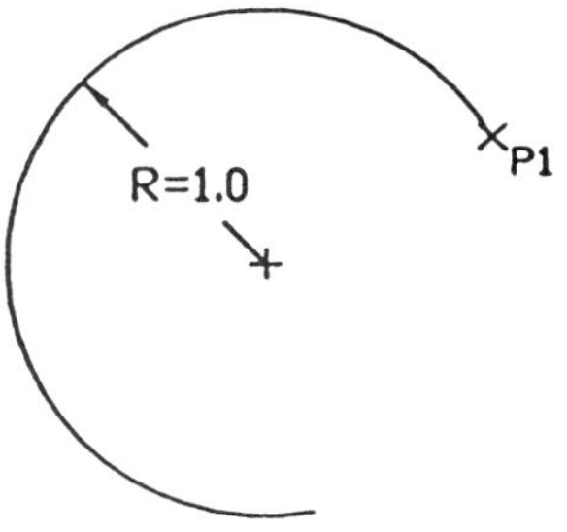

Figure 5.27

Create → Arc → Polar → **End pt**

Create an arc with a given end point, radius, initial and final angles. The angles are entered from the keyboard.

Procedure:

Enter the end point <using position menu>: Pick at **P1**
Enter the radius (def val): **1.0** ←
Enter the initial angle (def val): **30** ←
Enter the final angle (def val): **280** ←

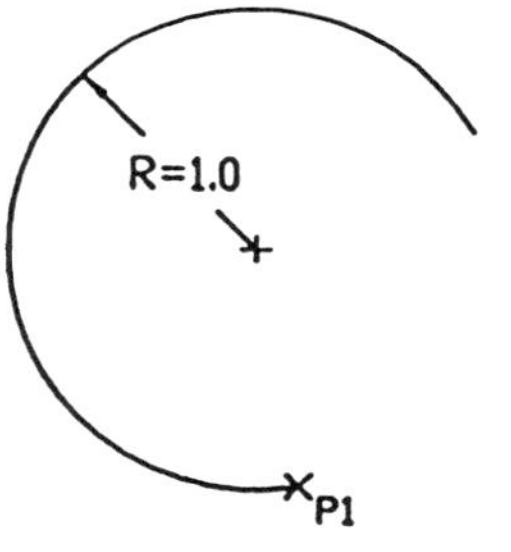

Figure 5.28

Create → Arc → **Endpoints**

Create an arc with two given endpoints and a radius. In general, there is more than one possible choice for the arc. You will have chance to pick the desired one.

Procedure:

Enter the first point <using position menu>: Pick at **P1**
Enter the second point <using position menu>: Pick at **P2**
Enter the radius (def val): **1.0** ←
Select an arc: Pick at **P3** <pick the desired arc>

> **Tip** In this example, there are four possible arcs to be selected. To pick the desired arc, you need to use the mouse to select a point closest to the arc.

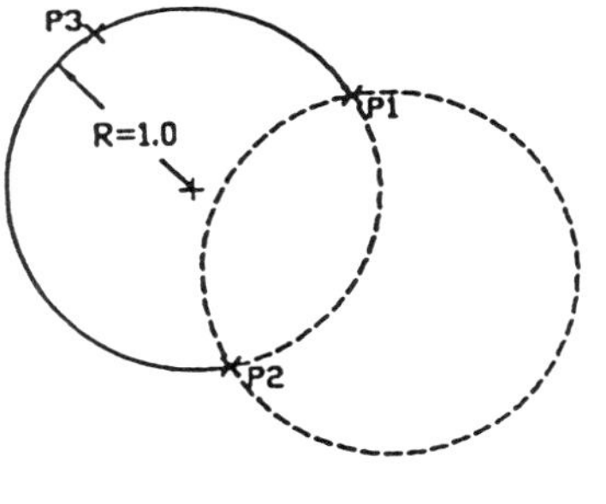

Figure 5.29

Create → Arc → **3 points**

Create an arc that passes through three points selected. The first and third points become the endpoints of the arc.

Procedure:

Enter the first point <using position menu>: Pick at **P1**
Enter the second point <using position menu>: Pick at **P2**
Enter the third point <using position menu>: Pick at **P3**

Note: These three points should not be on the same line.

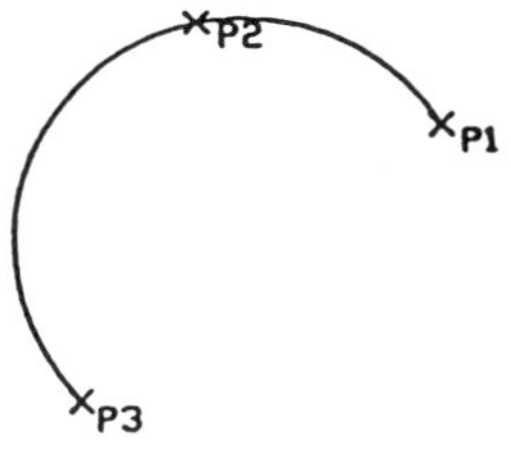

Figure 5.30

Create → Arc → **Tangent**

Create an arc tangent to one, two, or three lines or arcs. There are **six** options under tangent:

1 entity:	Create a 180-degree arc which is tangent to a selected entity.
2 entities:	Create a 360 degree arc that is tangent to two selected entities.
3 entities:	Create an arc that passes through three tangent points of three selected entities.
Center line:	Create a 360 degree arc that is tangent to a line and has its center point on another line.
Point:	Create an arc that is tangent to an entity through another entity.
Dynamic:	Create an arc that is tangent at a selected point on an entity.

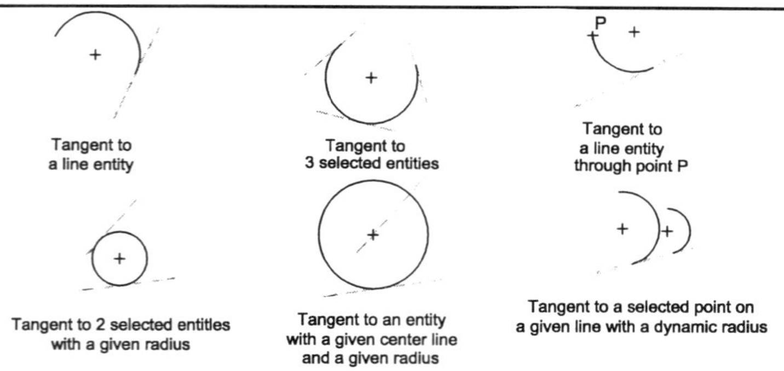

Figure 5.31

Create → Arc → Tangent → **1 entity**

Create a 180-degree arc which is tangent to a selected entity.

Procedure:

Create a line entity.
Select the entity that the arc is to be tangent to: Pick at **P1**
Specify the tangent point: Pick at **P2**
Enter the radius (def val): **1.0** ←
Select an arc: Pick at **P3**

Tip In this example, there are four possible choices. To pick the desired arc, you need to use the mouse and pick on the desired arc.

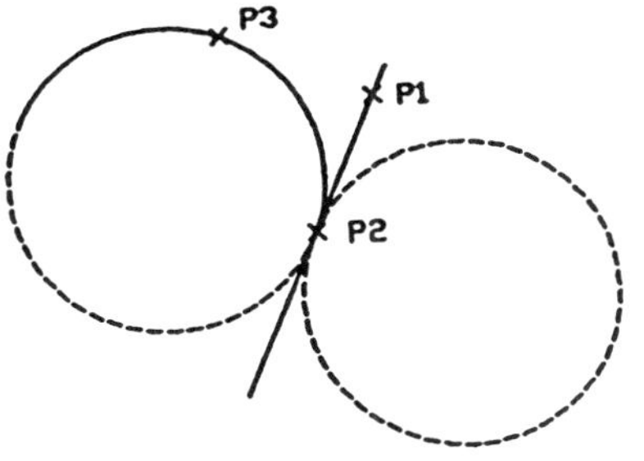

Figure 5.32

Create → Arc → Tangent → 2 entities

Create an arc that is tangent to two selected entities.

Procedure:

Create 2 lines and/or two arcs.
Enter radius: 1.0 ←
Select the first entity: Pick at **P1**
Select the second entity: Pick at **P2**

Tips 1. Select each entity near its tangent point.

2. If the entered radius value is too large, Mastercam displays multiple circular arcs so that you can select the desired one.

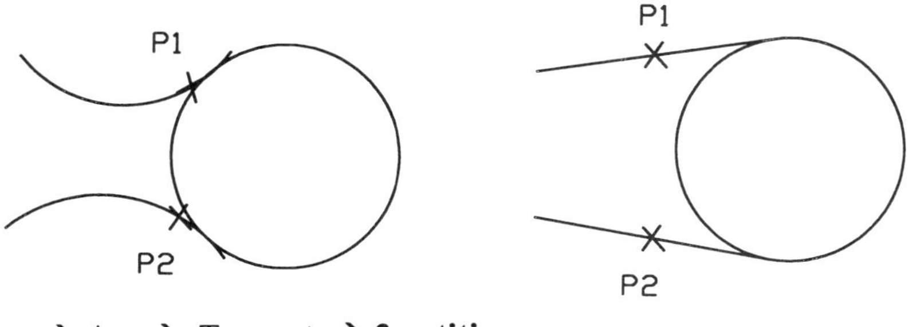

Figure 5.33

Create → Arc → Tangent → 3 entities

Create an arc that passes through three tangent points of three selected entities. The arc will start at the first entity and end at the third entity.

Procedure:

Create 3 lines and/or three arcs.
Select the first entity: Pick at **P1**
Select the second entity: Pick at **P2**
Select the third entity: Pick at **P3**

⌛**Tips** 1. Select each entity near its tangent point.

2. The order of the selection will determine the arc direction.

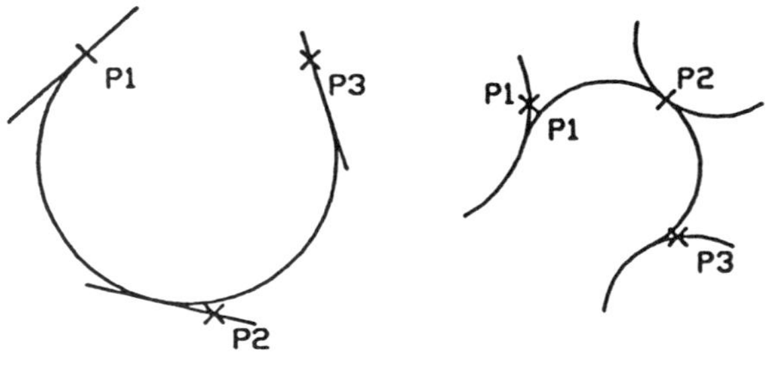

Figure 5.34

Create → Arc → Tangent → **Center line**

Create a 360-degree arc that is tangent to one line with its centerpoint on another line.

Procedure:

Create two non-parallel lines.
Select a line that will be tangent to the circle: Pick at **P1**
Select the line to contain the center of the circle: Pick at **P2**
Enter the radius of the circle: **2.0** ←
Select which arc to keep: Pick at **P3**

⌛**Tips** 1. In this example, there are two choices. Pick on the desired arc to keep at the last step.

2. The tangen line and the center line cannot be parallel.

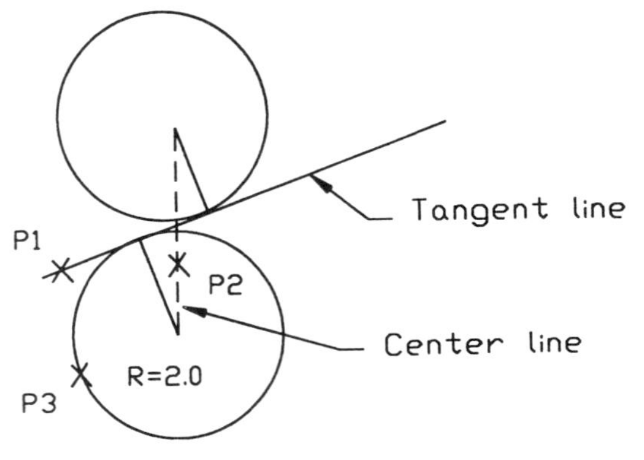

Figure 5.35

Create → Arc → Tangent → **Point**

Create an arc that is tangent to an entity and passes through a point.

Procedure:

Create a line and/or an arc.
Select the entity that the arc is to be tangent to: Pick at **P1**

Enter the thru point: Pick at **P2**
Enter the radius (def val): **1.0** ←
Select an arc: Pick at **P3**

Tips 1. Select each entity near its tangent point.

2. If there is more than one possible choice, use the mouse to select a point on the closest arc.

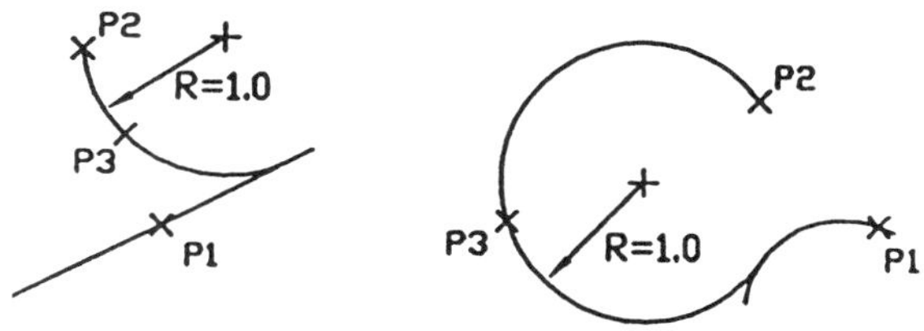

Figure 5.36

Create → Arc → Circ 2 pts

Create a circle by giving two points which lie 180-degree apart on its circumference; or in other words, pick the endpoints of the circle's diameter.

Procedure:

Enter the first point <using position menu>: Pick at **P1**
Enter the second point <using position menu>: Pick at **P2**

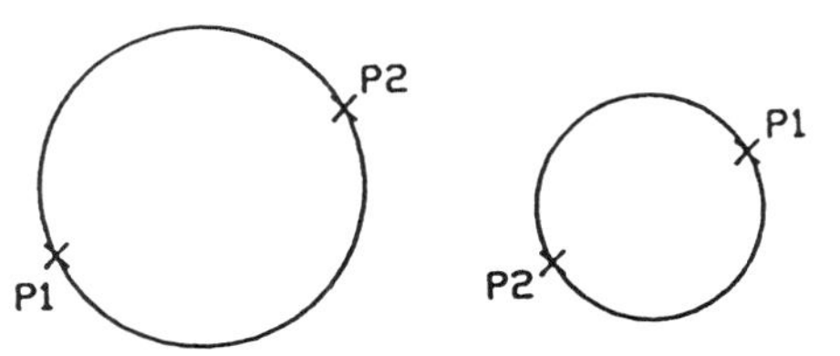

Figure 5.37

Create → Arc → Circ 3 pts

Create a circle by specifying three points on its circumference. These three points should **not** be in a straight line. The selection order is not important.

Procedure:

Enter the first point <using position menu>: Pick at **P1**
Enter the second point <using position menu>: Pick at **P2**
Enter the third point <using position menu>: Pick at **P3**

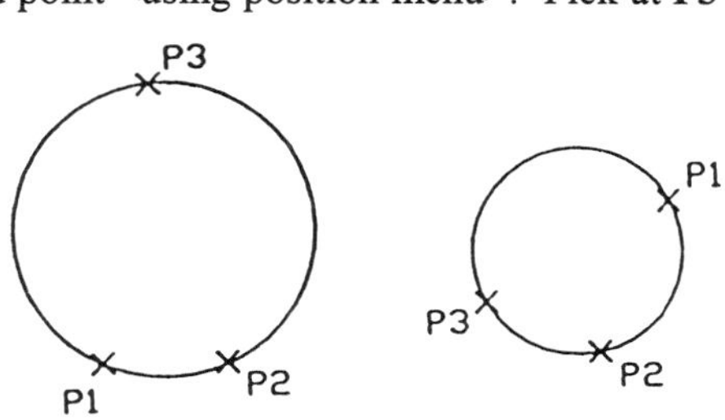

Figure 5.38

Create → Arc → Circ pt+ rad

Create a circle with a given center point and a radius.

Procedure:

Enter the center point <using position menu>: Pick at **P1**

Enter the radius (def val): **1.0** ←

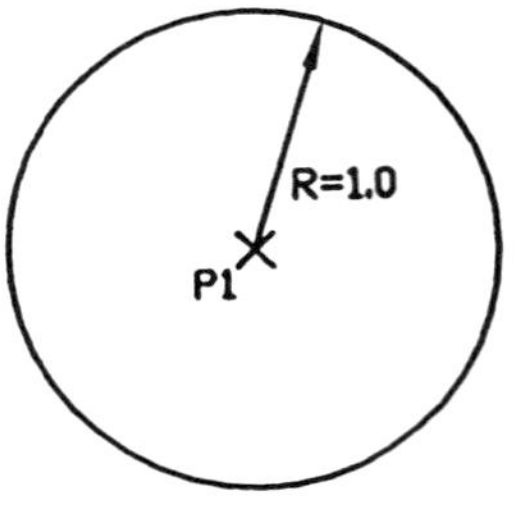

Figure 5.39

Create → Arc → Circ pt+ dia

Create a circle with a given center point and a diameter.

Procedure:

Enter the center point <using position menu>: Pick at **P1**

Enter the diameter (def val): **2.0** ←

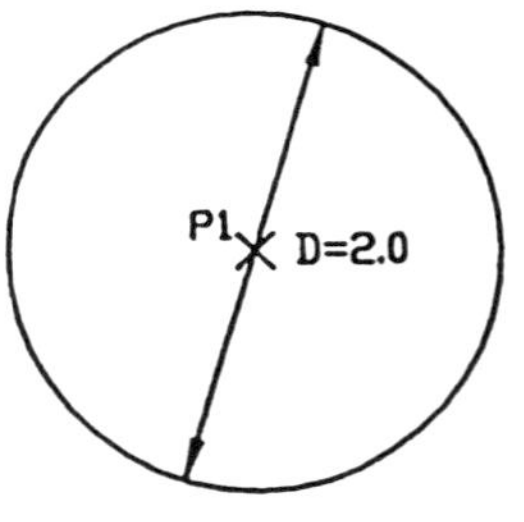

Figure 5.40

Create → Arc → Circ pt+ edg

Create a circle with a given center point and a point on the circumference.

Procedure:

Enter the center point <using position menu>: Pick at **P1**

Enter the edge point <using position menu>: Pick at **P2**

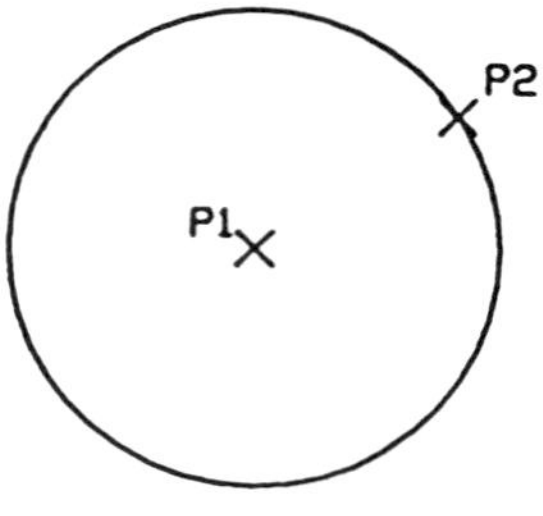

Figure 5.41

Example: Arc and Circle Exercise

Using the ARC Command and your mouse, draw each of the following objects. Don't worry about exact sizes, but do try to make them look as much as these drawings as possible. Practice the various options covered in this section.

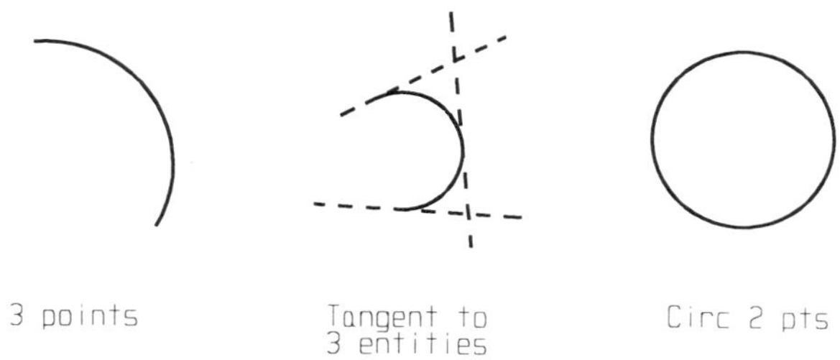

Figure 5.42

Practice using ARC command to draw the following objects.

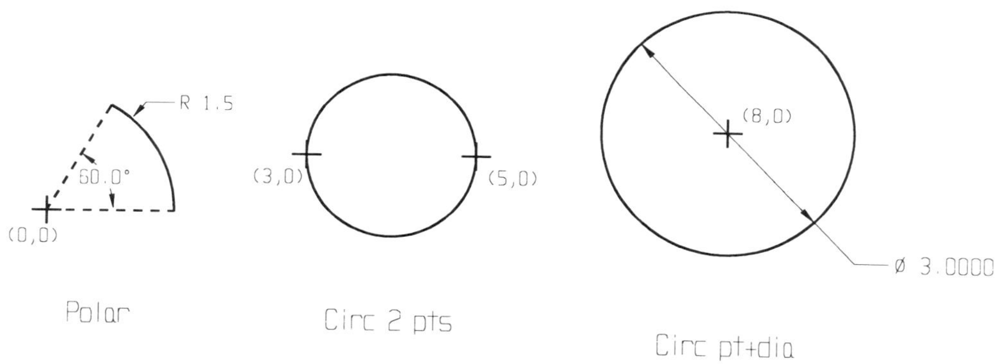

Figure 5.43

5.5 Fillet and the Fillet Submenu

The menu sequence for Fillet command is **Create → Fillet.**

Create one or more fillets for two or more entities by specifying the following **four** fillet parameters:

Radius:	Change to a new radius.
Angle<180:	Toggle the angle option. The angle options can be greater than 180-degrees (L), less than 180-degrees (S), or a full circle (F).
Trim:	Toggle the trim option to either keep (N) or delete (Y) the trimmed line after filleting.
Chain:	Create one or more fillets by chaining several entities at once.

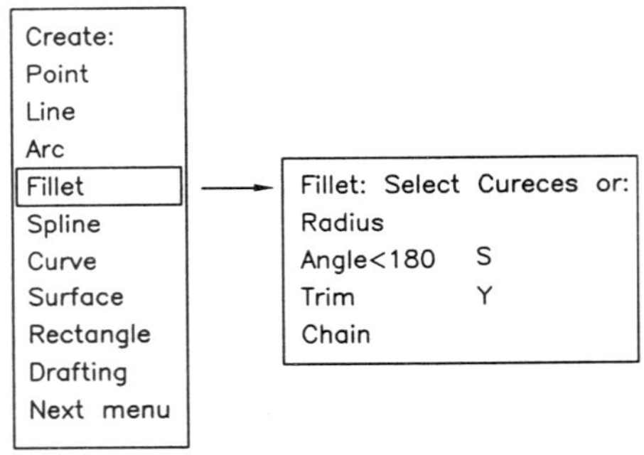

Figure 5.44: Submenu for Fillet

Create a fillet between two lines.

Procedure:

Create two lines.

Choose and change fillet parameters (radius, angle and trim options) if needed.

Select the first entity: Pick at **P1**

Select the second entity: Pick at **P2**

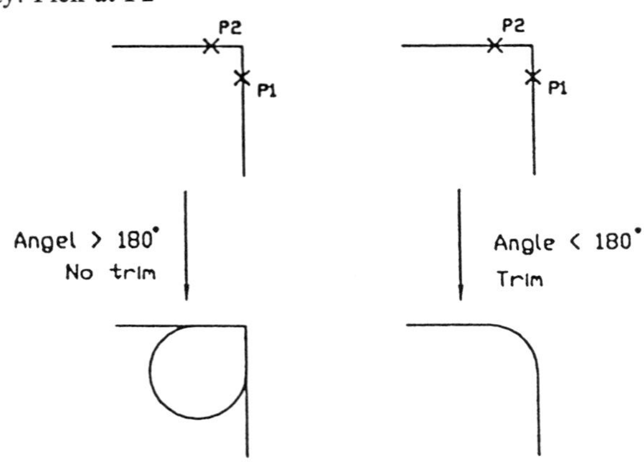

Figure 5.45

Create several fillets by chaining several entities at once.

Procedure:

Create several lines using **Create→ Line→ Multi.**

Choose and change fillet parameters (radius, angle and trim options) if needed.

Select **Chain**

Select the first entity in the chain: Pick at **P1**

Select **Done**

Refillet at existing fillets? Select **No (If necessary, you can select Yes and change the fillet.)**

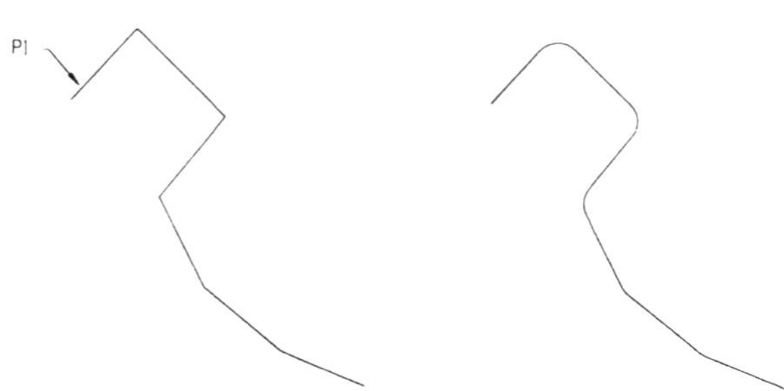

Figure 5.46

5.6 Spline and the Spline Submenu

In Mastercam, the Spline command creates a smooth spline curve that passes through all the node points selected, and there are **two** spline curve options: **Parametric spline** (Type P) and **NURBS spline** (Type N). The user is able to toggle this option by selecting the first option (Type) in the menu (Figure 5.47).

A parametric spline curve is a flexible strip which can be held by weights so that it passes through each of the given points. Corresponding to a draftman's spline, the present mathematical procedure requires that both the slope and the curvature be the same on both sides of the node points.

NURBS is abbreviated from Non-Uniform Rational B-Spline curve or surface. In general, NURBS is smoother than the regular spline curve and may be edited more easily by pulling its control points (see section 6.2.6 and Figure 6.14). It is a useful tool to generate curves and surfaces for the automotive industry.

There are four ways to generate a spline curve:

Manual:	Manually select all the points for the spline curve.
Automatic:	Automatically select the points for the spline curve.
Curves:	Create a spline from existing entities.
Blend:	Create a spline that smoothly joins two arcs, curves, or lines.

The menu sequence for spline is **Create → Spline.**

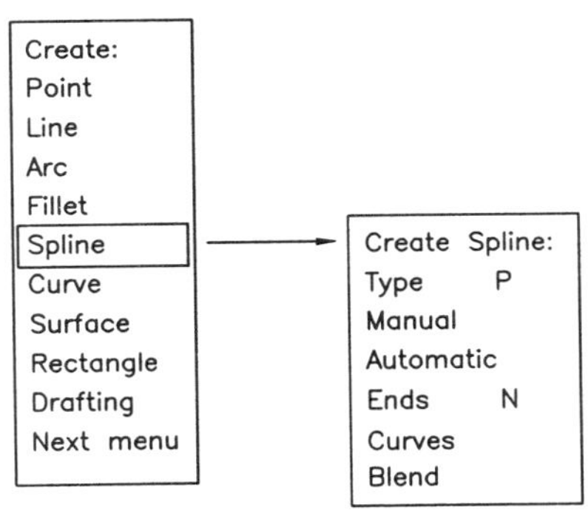

Figure 5.47: Submenu for Spline

The **Ends** option in the menu allows you to modify the slope of the spline at the start and end points. The default value is **N.**

Tips 1. Default maximum value of 1000 node points can be changed in the MILL7.CFG file using **Screen → Configure → Allocations → Maximum number of points per spline.**

2. To generate a closed spline curve, pick the same point for the first and last node points for the curve.

Create → Spline → **Manual**

Manually select all the points for the spline curve. The user needs to select all the points in a proper order.

Procedure:

Select all the node points <using position menu>: Pick at **P1**, **P2**, **P3**, etc.
Select BACKUP or Press <ESC> to finish selection and create the spline.

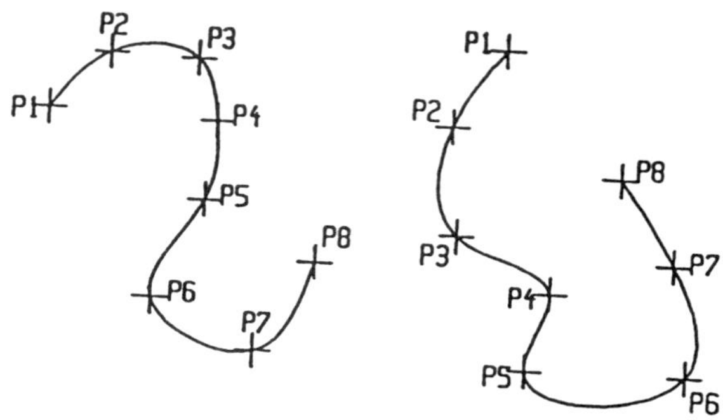

Figure 5.48

Create → Spline → **Automatic**

Automatically select the points for the spline curve. The user needs to select the first, second, and last point on the curve. The system will automatically select other points which stay within the system's curve tolerance.

1. The first, second and last point should be existing points created by the **Create → Point** command.
2. Use the **Create → Spline → Manual** option if it doesn't work as you desired.

Procedure:

Create several points as shown in Figure 5.49
Select the first point: Pick at **P1**
Select the second point: Pick at **P2**
Select the last point: Pick at **P3**

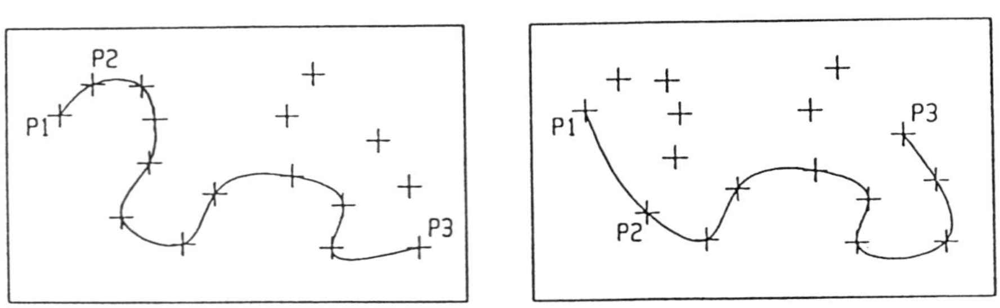

Figure 5.49

When a curve's geometry changes dramatically, create more points around that area to better control the direction of the spline. This is shown in Figure 5.50 on the next page.

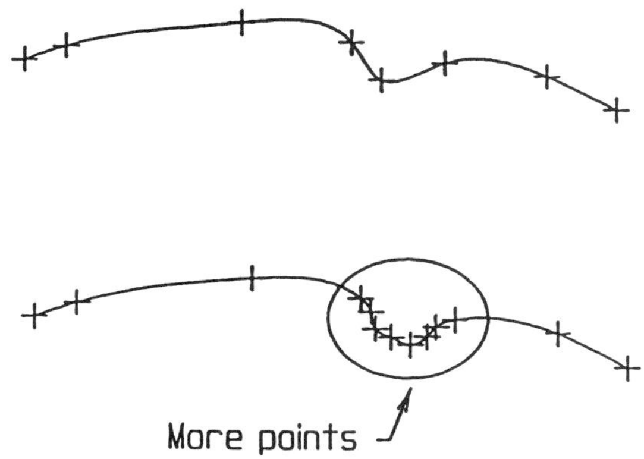

Figure 5.50

A comparison of a NURBS and a parametric spline curve created by the same points are shown in Figure 5.51. Notice the difference at the beginning and ending point.

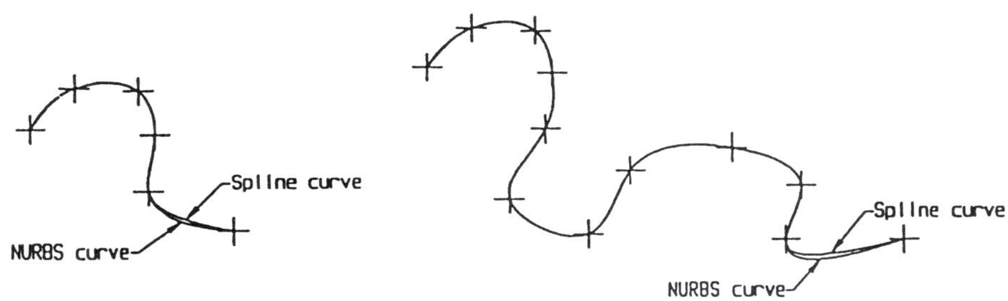

Figure 5.51

Create → Spline → **Curves**

Create a spline from existing entities. You can create a spline from any existing curve or combination of curves; including arcs, lines or splines. If you want to create a spline from only one entity, click the **Single** option. Click **Chain** if you want to create a spline from several entities connected to each other at their endpoints.

> **Tip** You can use Analyze (F4) to check on the new curve.

Create → Spline → Curves → **Chain**

Create a spline from several entities connected to each other at their endpoints.

Procedure:

Create multi-line segments shown in Figure 5.52 using

Create → Line → Multi→ sKetch

Select Curve(s) for spline creation: Pick at **P1**

Select **Done → Do it**

<the original line segments are converted to a NURBS curve.>

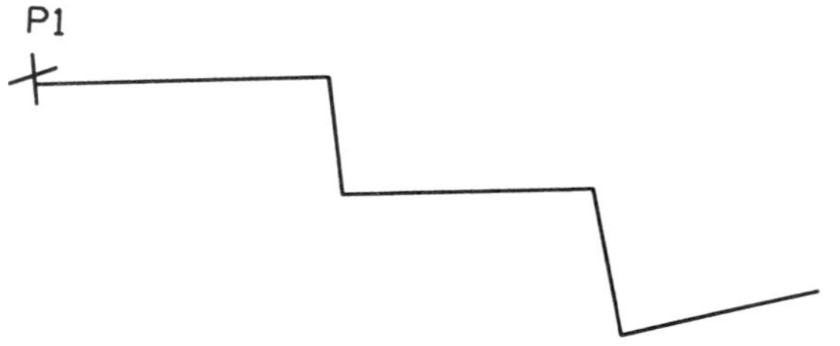

Figure 5.52

Create → Spline → Curve → Chain → **Single**

Create a spline from a single entity such as an arc or a line.

Procedure:

Create an arc or line as shown in Figure 5.53.

Select curve(s) for spline creation: Pick at **P1**

Select **Done** → **Do it** <The original arc or line is converted to NURBS>

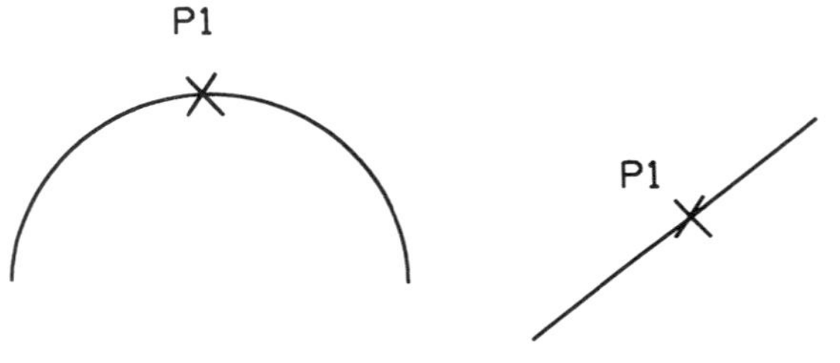

Figure 5.53

5.7 Curve and Surface

Figure 5.54 shows the submenus of the Curve and Surface options. The Curves feature in Mastercam can be used to create a number of curve types on surfaces of existing entities. The Surface function will be covered in chapters 11 and 12.

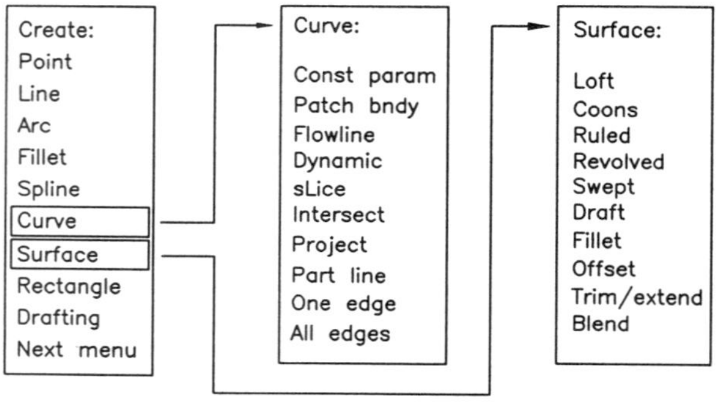

Figure 5.54 Submenus for Curve and surface

5.8 Rectangle and the Rectangle Submenu

The rectangle menu sequence is **Create → Rectangle.**
In Mastercam, there are **four** options to generate a rectangle:

1 point:	Create a rectangle by giving corner point, the width and the height.
2 points:	Create a rectangle by giving its two corner points.
Center:	Create a rectangle by giving its center point, width and height.
Make surf:	A toggle option to create a rectangular surface by giving the rectangle's two corner points. Cross lines are created within the rectangle.

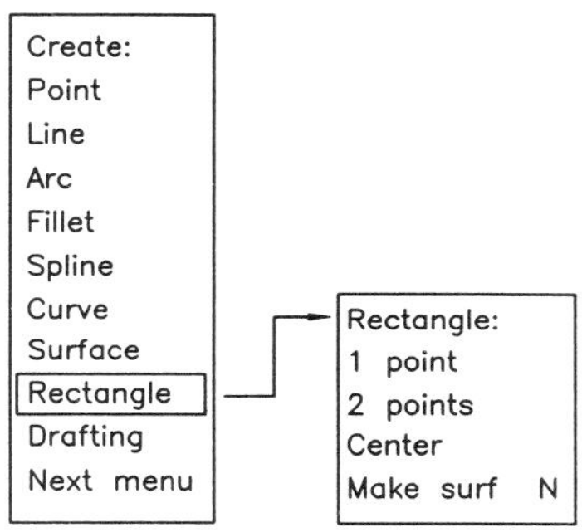

Figure 5.55: Submenu for Rectangle

Create → Rectangle → **1 point**

Create a rectangle by giving corner point, the width and the height.

Procedure:

Enter the lower left corner <using position menu>: Pick at **P1**
Enter the width <def val>: **3.0** ←
Enter the height <def val>: **2.0** ←

Tip The width and the height can be negative values. If both of them are negative, the point selected in Procedure 1 becomes the upper right corner.

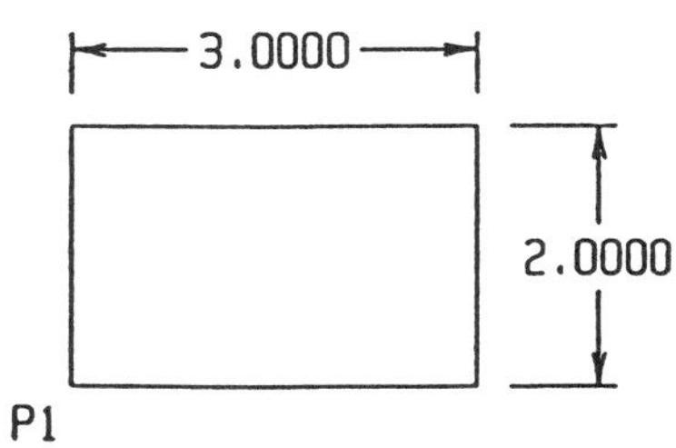

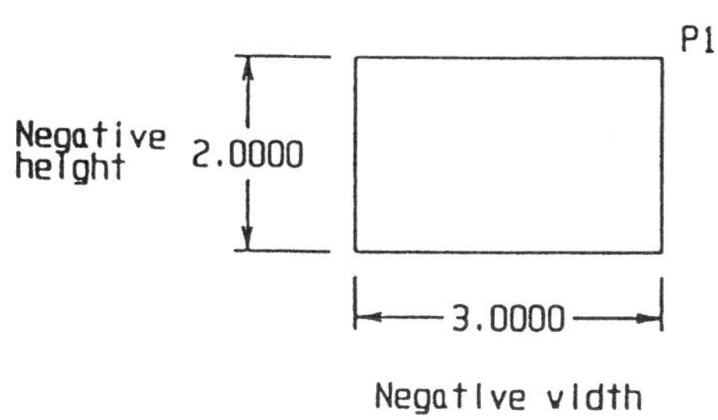

Figure 5.56

Figure 5.57

Create → Rectangle → **2 points**

Create a rectangle by giving its two corner points.

Procedure:

Enter the lower left corner <using position menu>: Pick at **P1**
Enter the upper right corner <using position menu>: Pick at **P2**

The selection sequence is not that important. For example, you can select the upper right corner first, then, the lower left corner.

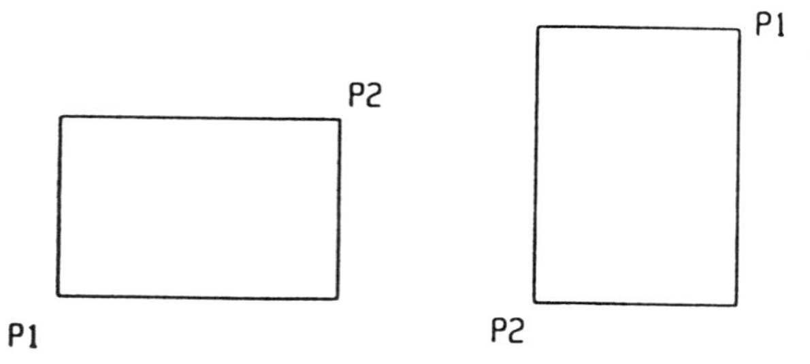

Figure 5.58

Create → Rectangle → **Center**

Create a rectangle by giving a center point, width and height.

Procedure:

Enter the center point: Pick at **P1**
Enter the width <def val>: **3.0** ←
Enter the height <def val>: **2.0** ←

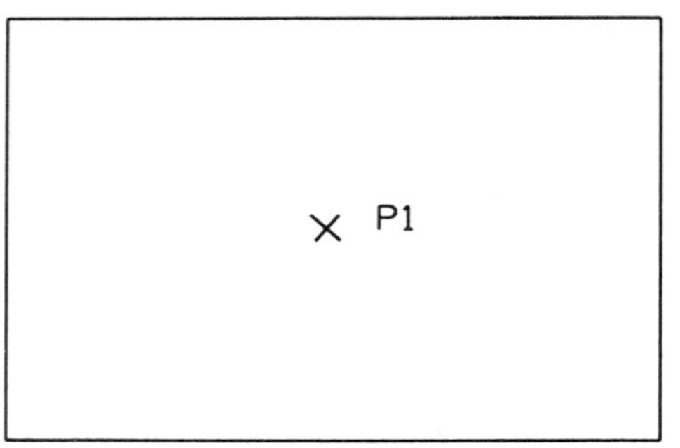

Figure 5.59

Create → Rectangle → **Make surf(Y)**

Create a rectangle and make it into a surface using option **1 point**, **2 points** or **Center**. When **Make surf** is on **(Y)**, there is another toggle option, **Surf type**, for you to choose either NURBS **(N)** or parametric **(P)** surface. The following procedure allows you to create a rectangular NURBS surface using the 2 point option.

Procedure:

Toggle **Surf type** to **N**
Select **2 points**
Enter the lower left corner <using position menu>: pick at **P1**
Enter the upper right corner <using position menu>:pick at **P2**

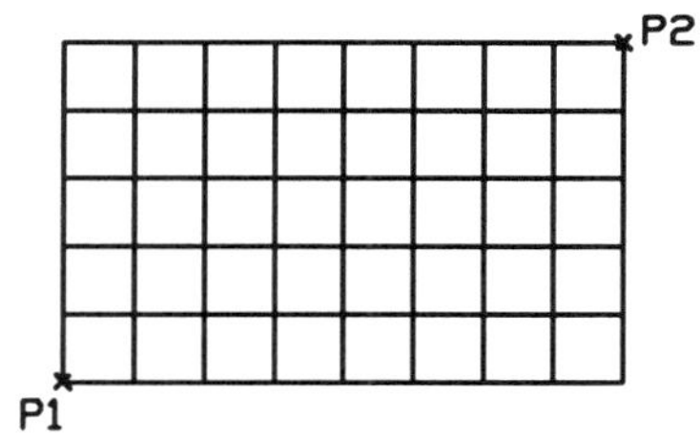

Figure 5.60

Note: To **turn off** the surface option for rectangle; toggle the **Make surf** option to **N**.

5.9 Chamfer and the Chamfer Submenu

The chamfer menu sequence is **Create → Next menu → Chamfer**. This command is used to create a chamfer between two non-parallel lines with two given distances. There is an option under the Chamfer command to change the chamfer distance:

Distances:	To change the default chamfer distance(s) of the chamfer. In general, there are two distances can be changed. The first distance related to the first picked point (**P1**), and the second distance related to the second picked point (**P2**).

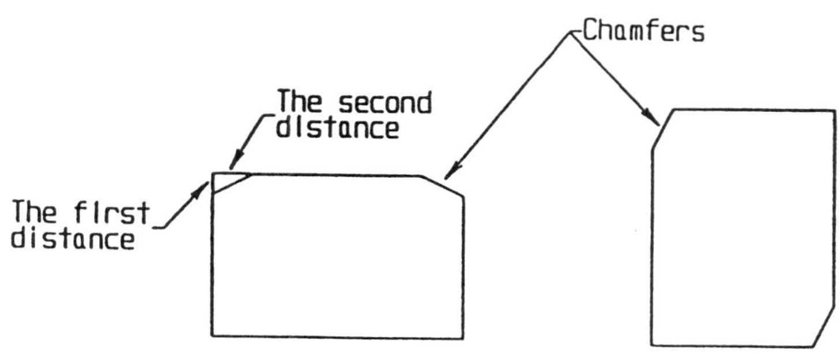

Figure 5.61

Tips 1. The chamfer command operates very similar to the Fillet command.

2. To change the distances, select Distances or enter D at the keyboard, and specify the first and second chamfer distance.

Note: The system prompts the following message for default values in the System Response Area:

first distance = (def value)
second distance = (def val)
(Make sure the first distance = 0.25 and the second distance = 0.50)

Procedure:

Create a rectangle.
Select the first line: Pick at **P1**
Select the second line: Pick at **P2**

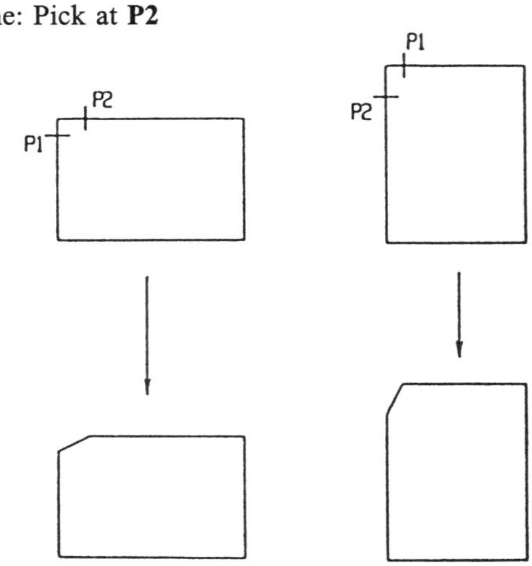

Figure 5.62

5.10 Letters and the Letter Submenu

Letter geometries can be useful for cutting letters on plaques. In Mastercam, there are two methods to create these letter geometries. The first method creates the geometry using Mastercam's **Letters** command. This command lets you use Windows standard Truetype fonts as geometry, create geometry from the current Mastercam drafting fonts, or continue to use Version 5.0 and 5.5 GE3 lettering fonts.

With the second method you create a "**Note**" in Drafting, and then change its attributes and reposition it. The details of these two methods are described in this section.

Method 1: Using the Letters Command

The letters command sequence is **Create → Next menu → Letters.**

The sub menu for Lettering includes **three** options:

TrueType(R):	Use the Windows standard TrueType fonts and convert them to geometry.
Drafting:	Create geometry from the current Mastercam drafting font.
MC7/GE3	**Use Mastercam's existing MC7 or GE3 lettering fonts.**

Create → Next menu → Letters → **True Type (R)**

Create geometry from standard TrueType fonts. Review Windows documentation for more information about TrueType fonts.

Procedure:

After this item is selected, Mastercam displays the Standard Windows font dialog box.

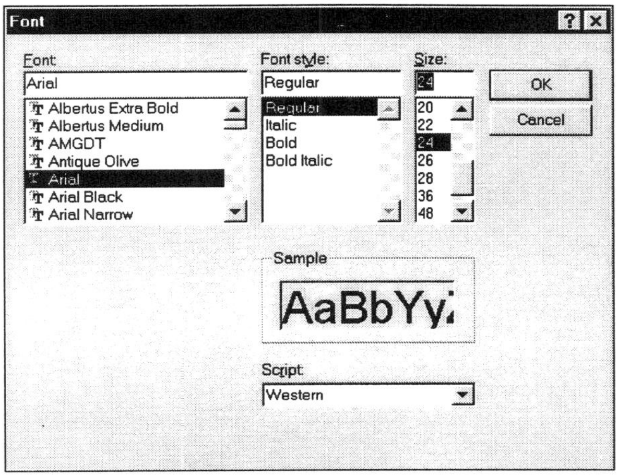

Figure 5.63 Standard Windows font dialog box

Select the **font** and the **font style.** Ignore the font size and select **OK.**
Enter letters: **Mastercam** ←
Enter letter height (def val): **2.0** ←
Selection a direction for the TrueType letters:
Note: The system will give you **four** options described in Figure 5.64.

Horizontal:	Write letters in the horizontal direction
Vertical:	Write the letters in the vertical direction
Top of arc:	Write letters on top of an arc
Btm of arc:	Write on the bottom of an arc.

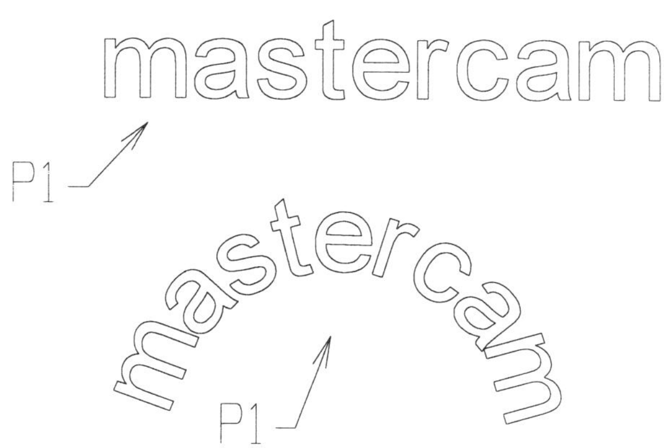

Figure 5.64 Letter orientations

Enter letter spacing (def val): **2.0** ←

Note: The system will have different prompts after this step. There is one more step for horizontal and vertical letters, and two more steps for top arc and bottom arc letters.

For horizontal and vertical letters:
Enter starting location of letters: Pick at **P1**

For top and bottom arc letters:
Enter coordinates of arc center: Pick at **P1**
Enter arc radius: **4.0** ←

Create → Next menu → Letters → **Drafting**

Create geometry from the current Mastercam drafting font.

Procedure:
Enter letters: **Mastercam** ←
Enter starting location of letters: Pick at **P1**

Figure 5.65

Note: The current Mastercam drafting font can be changed by picking -PM- (Drafting Global Parameters) from the Menu Area. The available drafting fonts are Stick, Roman, European, Swiss, Hartford, Old English, Palatino and Dayville.

Create → Next menu → Letters → **MC7/GE3**

Create Mastercam version 5.0 and 5.5 GE3 letter geometry. As shown in Figure 5.66 below, there are **four** font styles available in Mastercam 5.0 and 5.5. Be sure these font styles are installed on your computer before you attempt to use them. For example, the box font can be installed in C:\MILL7\BOX directory. Note that these font files have no TrueType equivalent and create only upper case letter geometries. For more details, see your Mastercam version 5.0 and 5.5 documentation.

Box:	Box font
bLock:	Block font
Roman:	Roman font
Slant:	Slant font

Figure 5.66

Procedure:
Enter the path for the letters: **C:\MILL7\BLOCK** ←
Enter the default letter width (def val): **0.8** ←
Enter letter height (def val): **1.0** ←
Enter letter spacing (def val): **0.2** ←
Write letters on an arc (Y/N)?
Select **Yes** to accept an arc letter.
Select **No** to accept a line letter.

Note: The system will have different prompts after this step. There are **four** more steps for arc letters and **two** more steps for line letters.

For arc letters
Enter coordinates of arc center: Pick at **P1**
Enter arc radius (def val): **5.0** ←
Write on top or bottom of the arc: Select **Top** or **Bottom** ←

Note: Refer to Figure 5.67 for the type of arc.
Enter letters: **ARC LETTERS** ←

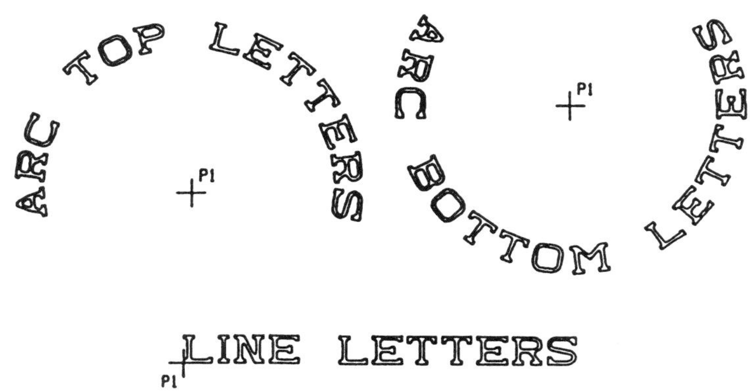

Figure 5.67 Arc and line letters

For line letters
Enter starting location of letters: Pick at **P1**
Enter letters: **LINE LETTERS** ←

Method 2: Using Note and Modify Commands

In this method, you will create a string of letters using the "Note" command in Drafting.

Procedure:
1. Create a string of letters using the "Note" command in the drafting section.
2. Change the attributes including the height, aspect ratio, font type and spacing.
3. Convert the Note into chains of geometry entities by using
   Modify → Break → Note/Let → Geometry → Entity commands.
4. Reposition the letters string to a new position, if necessary.

In the following example, we are creating a letter geometry (Mastercam) using a European font with height = 0.5, aspect = 0.6 and spacing = 0.25.

The sequence is **Create** → **Drafting** → **Note** → **Keyin**
Text: **Mastercam** ←
Enter line 2 (press Enter when done): ←
Select a Point: Pick **P1**
Text: Press **<ESC>** when done

Figure 5.68

Select **BACKUP** → **Globals edit** → Select the note just created → **Done**
In the Drafting Global Parameters pop-up:
Select Note Text Height: **0.5**
Select down arrow symbol, scroll to **European font**

Select **Character Display**

Select Character Aspect: **0.6**
Click on **Change**
Select Extra Char Spacing: **0.25**
Select **Done** → **Done**
(Notice the changes in System Response Area: Attribute style: **European**)

Figure 5.69

Select **MAIN MENU** → **Modify** → **Break** → **Note/lel** → **Geometry** → **Entity**
Select note: Pick at **the note**
Select Done :(After this step the note is turned into geometry. You
Note: Use the **Analyze** (F4) key to see if the original note has changed to geometries.

5.11 Ellipse and Ellipse Submenu

The ellipse menu sequence is **Create → Next menu → Ellipse.**

An ellipse or an elliptical arc can be created by specifying the following **five parameters** in addition to the center point:

A radius:	Set the ellipse's X-axis radius.
B radius:	Set the ellipse's Y-axis radius.
Start angle:	Set the starting angle.
End angle:	Set the ending angle.
Rot angle:	Set the angle of rotation about the X-axis direction.
Center Point:	Set the center of the ellipse.

Mastercam displays the ellipse after you set the center point.

Tips 1. Mastercam displays information about the ellipse in the System Response Area.

2. All the angles are measured in degrees in the counterclockwise direction.

Procedure: Example 1
Adjust the ellipse with these following specifications:

A (X-axis radius) = **3.0**
B (Y-axis radius) = **1.5**
Start angle = **30.0**

End angle = **300.0**
Rotation angle = **0.0**

Select **Center Point**
Enter the center point: Pick at **P1**

Procedure: Example 2
Adjust the ellipse with these following specifications:

A (X-axis radius) = **3.0**
B (Y-axis radius) = **1.5**
Start angle = **0.0**

End angle = **360.0**
Rotation angle = **15.0**

Select **Center Point**
Enter the center point: Pick at **P1**

Figure 5.70

5.12 Polygon and Polygon Submenu

The polygon sequence is **Create → Next menu → Polygon**

To create a polygon in Mastercam, you need to specify the following **five parameters** with a given center point.

No. sides:	Set the number of sides for the polygon.
Radius:	Set the distance from the center of the polygon to its edge. See Meas crnr for more information.
Start Angle:	Set the starting angle of the polygon about the X-axis direction.
Meas crnr Y:	A toggle switch to measure the radius distance. **Y**: Radius distance is measured from the center to the apex of a corner. **N**: Radius distance is measured from the center to the midpoint of a flat side.
Make NURBS N:	A toggle switch to make the polygon to be a single NURBS curve or multi-line entities. **Y**: Create the polygon as a single NURBS curve. **N**: Create the polygon as multi-line segments.
Center pt:	Set the center of the polygon. Mastercam displays the polygon after you set the centerpoint.

Tips 1. Mastercam displays information about your polygon in the System Response Area.

2. The starting angle is measured in degrees in the counterclockwise direction.

Procedure: Example 1
Adjust the polygon #1 with the following specifications:

Polygon number of sides = **5**
Polygon radius = **1.0**
Polygon starting angle = **0.0**
Measure Radius to **Corner**
Create **Lines**

Select **Center Point**
Enter the center point Pick at **P1**

Procedure: Example 2
Adjust the polygon#2 with the following specifications:

Polygon number of sides = **5**
Polygon radius = **1.0**
Polygon starting angle = **30.0**
Measure Radius to **Flat**
Create **NURBS spline**

Select **Center Point**
Enter the center point Pick at **P1**

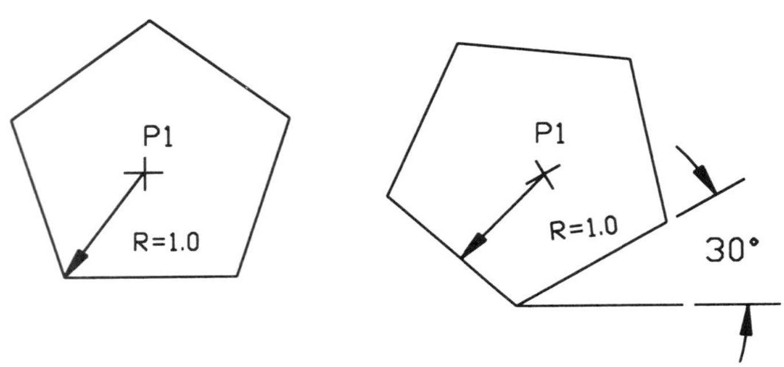

Figure 5.71

5.13 2-D Geometry Construction Project

In the following five projects, you will practice a combination of commands introduced in this chapter. A step by step procedure is provided. Save each project under the file name specified. You will retrieve these files to generate the toolpaths for producing the part in chapters 7 and 8. 1

Project 1.

Create a part geometry as shown in Figure 5.72. Save the file as **contour1.** This file will be used in project 1 of chapter 7.

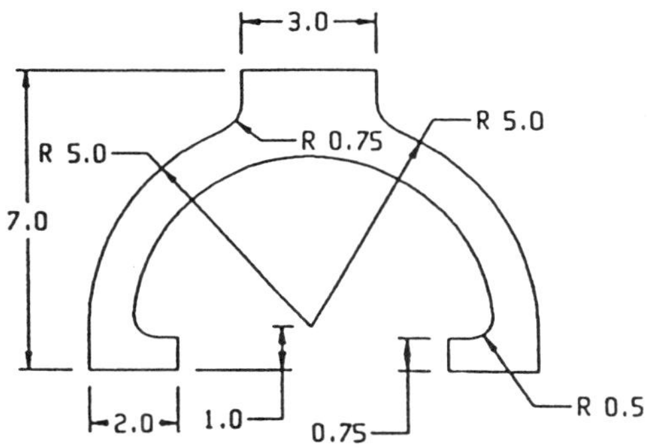

Figure 5.72

Tips 1. The geometry is symmetrical about the Y-axis. Create one-half of the geometry and then use the Mirror command (see section 6.3.1) to create the other half.
2. The basic geometry consists of two rectangles, two arcs and two fillets.

Step 1. Create two rectangles.

Select **MAIN MENU → Create → Rectangle → 2 points**
Enter the lower left corner: **3,-1** ←
Enter the upper right corner: **5,-.25** ← for the first rectangle
Enter the lower left corner: **0,6** ←
Enter the upper right corner: **1.5,5** ← for the second rectangle

Press Alt and F1 simultaneously, then F2 to fit the geometry on the screen

The two rectangles should appear as Figure 5.73.

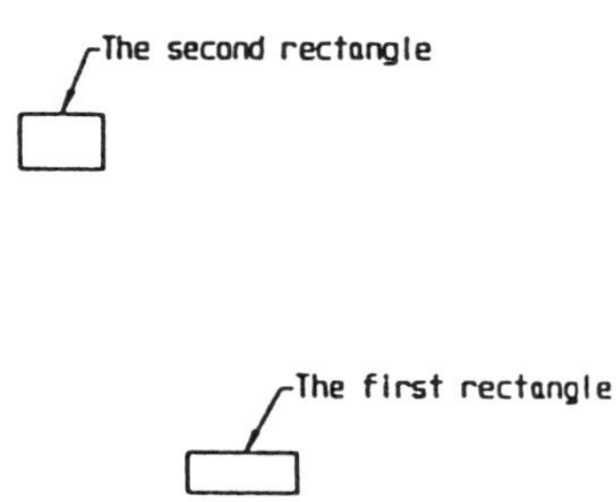

Figure 5.73

Step 2. Create two arcs.

Select **MAIN MENU** → **Create** → **Arc** → **Polar** → **Center pt**
Enter the center point: **0,0** ←
Enter the radius: **5** ←
Enter the initial angle: **0** ←
Enter the final angle: **90** ← for the first arc
Enter the center point: **0,0** ←
Enter the radius: **4** ←
Enter the initial angle: **0** ←
Enter the final angle: **90** ← for the second arc

The new drawing becomes Figure 5.74

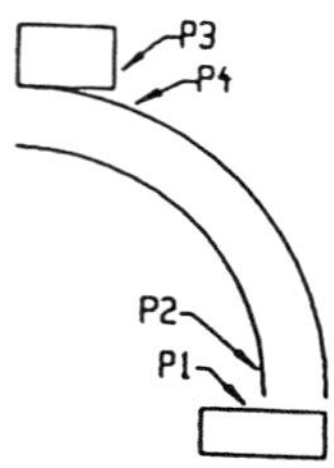

Figure 5.74

Step 3. Create two fillets using the pick points in Figure 5.74.

Select **MAIN MENU** → **Create** → **Fillet** → **Radius**
Enter the fillet radius: **0.5**

Note: Make certain the other two options are correct. If the fillet angle is less than 180; trim to fillet.

Select an entity: Pick at **P1**
Select another entity: Pick at **P2**
Select **Radius**
Enter the radius: **0.75** ←
Select an entity: Pick at **P3**
Select another entity: Pick at **P4**

The two fillets are added as shown in Figure 5.75.

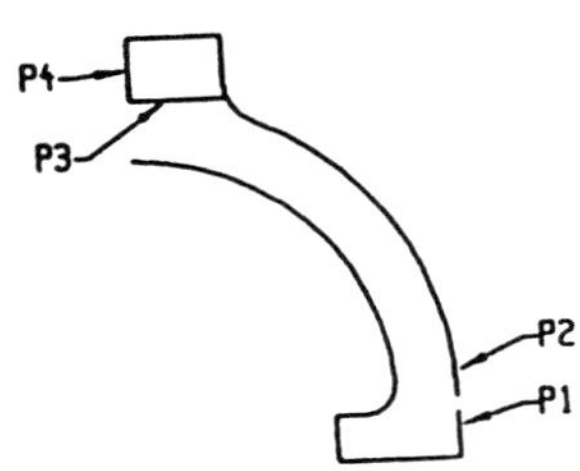

Figure 5.75

Step 4. Trim and delete the unnecessary lines using the pick points in Figure 5.75 on the last page.

Select **MAIN MENU → Modify → Trim → 1 entity**
Select the entity to trim: Pick at **P1**
Select the entity to trim to: Pick at **P2**
Select **MAIN MENU → Delete**
Select an entity or: Pick at **P3**
Select an entity or: Pick at **P4**
The half geometry should look like Figure 5.76.

Figure 5.76

Step 5. Mirror about the Y axis.

Select **MAIN MENU→Xform→ Mirror→ All→Entities→Done→Y axis→Copy →Done**
The complete geometry appears as Figure 5.77.

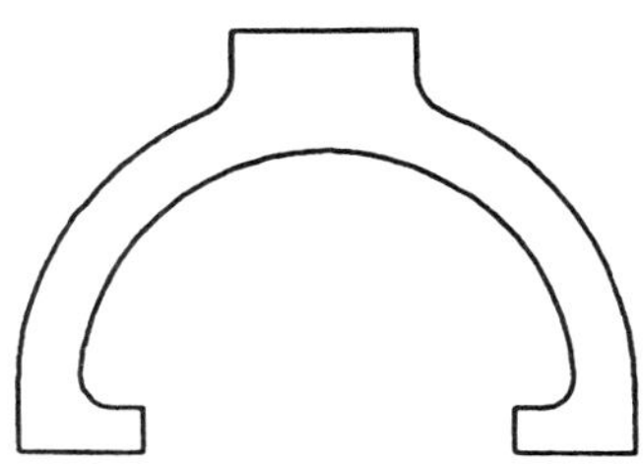

Figure 5.77

Step 6. Save to a file.

Select **MAIN MENU → File → Save**
Enter file name: **contour1**

2 Project 2.

Create a part geometry as shown in Figure 5.78. Save the file as **contour3**. This file will be used to generate the toolpaths for contouring in project 3 of chapter 7.

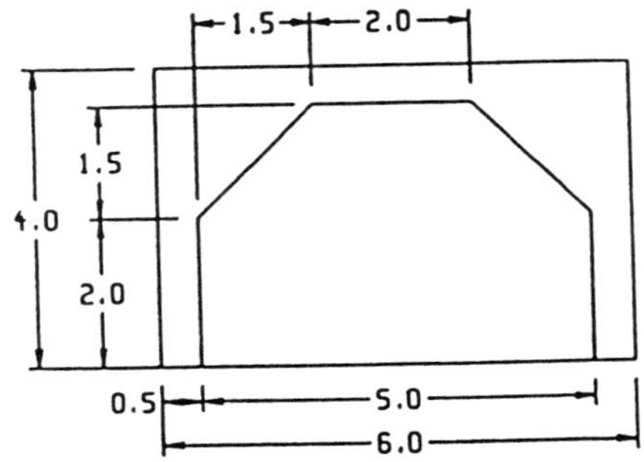

Figure 5.78

> **Tips** 1. This geometry can be created using a rectangle and several lines.
>
> 2. The coordinates of keypoints are shown in Figure 5.79.

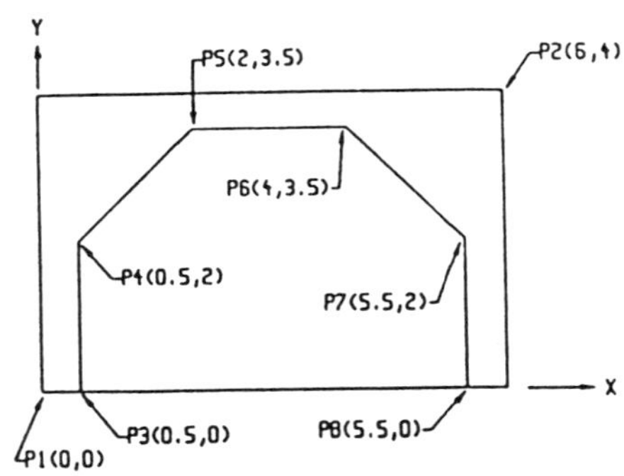

Figure 5.79

Step 1. Create a rectangle.

Select **MAIN MENU →Create → Rectangle → 2 points**
Enter the lower left corner: **0,0** ←
Enter the upper right corner: **6,4** ←

Step 2. Create five lines.

Select **MAIN MENU → Create → Line → Multi**
Specify endpoint 1: Enter **0.5,0** ←
Specify endpoint 2: Enter **0.5,2** ←
Specify endpoint 3: Enter **2,3.5** ←
Specify endpoint 4: Enter **4,3.5** ←
Specify endpoint 5: Enter **5.5,2** ←
Specify endpoint 6: Enter **5.5,0** ←

Step 3. Save to a file.

Select **MAIN MENU → File → Save**
Enter file name: **contour3**

Project 3. 3

Construct a geometry as shown in Figure 5.80. Save the file as **pocket1**. This file will be used to generate the toolpaths for pocketing in project 5 of chapter 7.

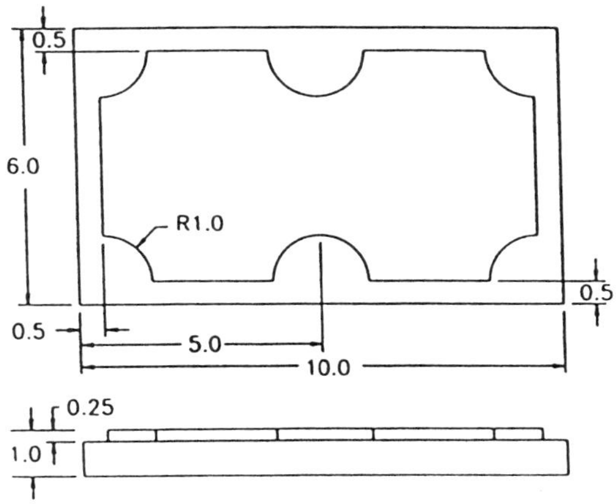

Figure 5.80

> **Tips** 1. Create two rectangles and six circles.
>
> 2. Break the two horizontal lines of the inside rectangle into two pieces to allow for the trimming of the two circles in the middle.
> 3. Trim the six circles and four lines using 3 entities command.

Step 1. Create two rectangles.

Select **MAIN MENU** → **Create** → **Rectangle** → **2 points**
Enter the lower left corner: **0,0** ←
Enter the upper right corner: **10,6** ← for the first rectangle
Enter the lower left corner: **0.5,0.5** ←
Enter the upper right corner: **9.5,5.5** ← for the second rectangle
Press **Alt** + **F1** simultaneously and then **F2** to fit the drawing in the screen
The two rectangles should look like Figure 5.81.

Figure 5.81

Step 2. Create six circles.

Select **MAIN MENU** → **Create** → **Arc** → **Circ pt+rad**
Enter the center point: **0.5,0.5** ←
Enter the radius: **1** ←
Enter the center point: **5,0.5** ←
Enter the radius: **1** ←

Enter the center point: **9.5,0.5** ←
Enter the radius: **1** ←
Enter the center point: **0.5,5.5** ←
Enter the radius: **1** ←
Enter the center point: **5,5.5** ←
Enter the radius: **1** ←
Enter the center point: **9.5,5.5** ←
Enter the radius: **1** ←

The six circles are added as shown in Figure 5.82.

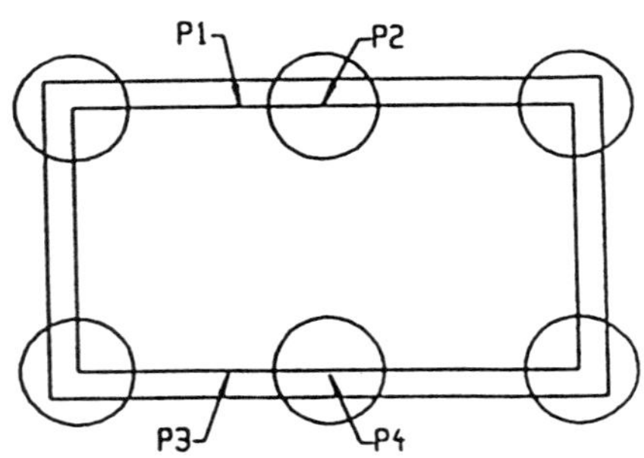

Figure 5.82

Step 3. Break two horizontal lines of the inside rectangle into two pieces.

Use the pick points in Figure 5.82.
Select **MAIN MENU → Modify → Break → 2 pieces**
Select an entity: pick at **P1**
Enter the break point: pick at **P2** to break the first line
Select an entity: pick at **P3**
Enter the break point: pick at **P4** to break the second line
After breaking two lines the drawing still looks the same as before breaking.
This drawing is redrawn in Figure 5.83.

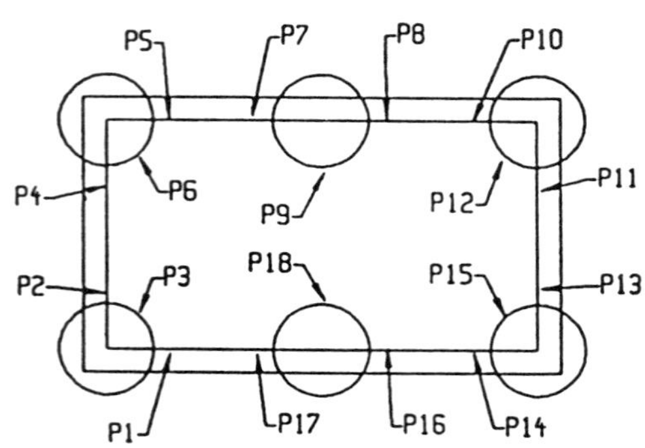

Figure 5.83

Step 4. Trim the six circles using the pick points in Figure 5.83.

Select **MAIN MENU → Modify → Trim → 3 entities**
Select the first entity to trim: pick at **P1**
Select the second entity to trim: pick at **P2**
Select the entity to trim to: pick at **P3** to complete the trimming of first circle

Sequentially pick at **P4 - P18** to complete the trimming of the remaining five circles

The final geometry should look like Figure 5.84.

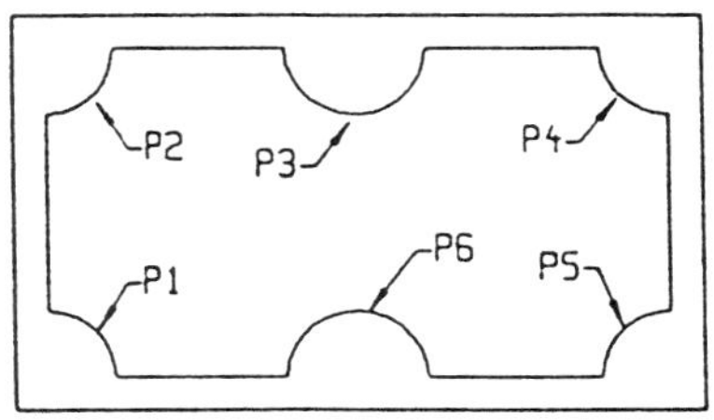

Figure 5.84

Step 5. Save the file (pocket1).

Select **MAIN MENU → File → Save**
Enter file name: **pocket1**

Note: Continue steps 6 and 7 to add six points for another project.

Step 6. Create six points at the center of each arc.

Use the pick points labeled in Figure 5.84 above.
Select **MAIN MENU → Create → Point → Position → Center**
Specify a point: pick at **P1** to create the first point
Select **Center** option, then sequentially pick at **P2 - P6** to create the remaining five points
The six points are added as shown in Figure 5.85.

Figure 5.85

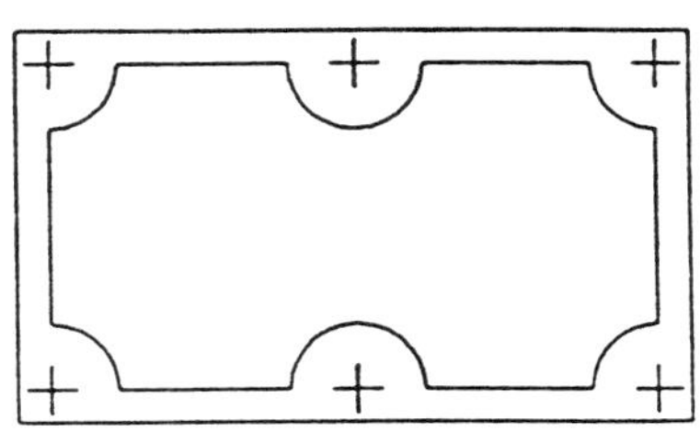

Step 7. Save to another file (drill2).

Select **MAIN MENU → File → Save**
Enter file name: **drill2**

Note: The geometry file **drill2** is used to drilling and tapping six holes in project 8 of chapter 7.

4 Project 4.

Create a rectangle and four points as shown in Figure 5.86. Save this file as **drill3**. This file will be used in project 9 of chapter 7.

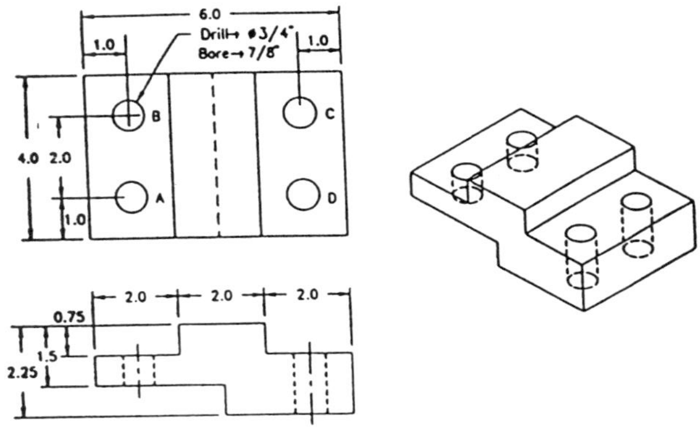

Figure 5.86

This geometry consists of a rectangle and four points. The coordinates of keypoints are shown in Figure 5.87.

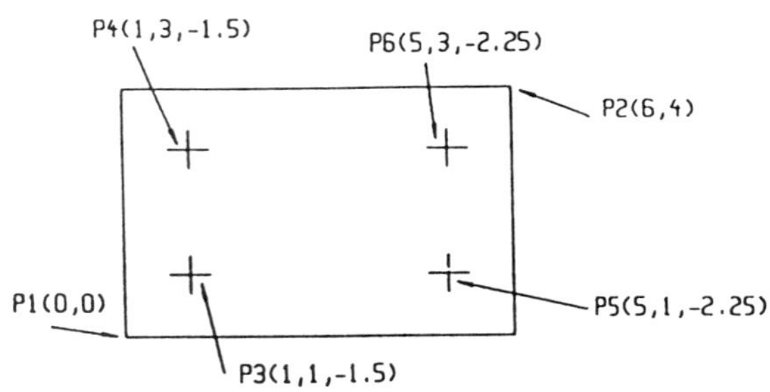

Figure 5.87

Step 1. Create a rectangle.

Select **MAIN MENU** → **Create** → **Rectangle** → **2 points**
Enter the lower left corner: **0,0** ←
Enter the upper right corner: **6,4** ←

Step 2. Create four points.

Select **MAIN MENU** → **Create** → **Point** → **Position** → **Value**
Enter coordinates: **1,1, 0** ←
Enter coordinates: **1,3, 0** ←
Enter coordinates: **5,1, 0** ←
Enter coordinates: **5,3, 0** ←

Step 3. Save to a file.

Select **MAIN MENU** → **File** → **Save**
Enter file name: **drill3**

Project 5.

Use the Letters command to create a geometry as shown in Figure 5.88. This geometry consists of two circles and five strings of letters in **three** true type fonts; MS LineDraw, Arial, and TimesNew Roman. Use these three fonts to create letters as follows:

1. EASTERN MICHIGAN UNIVERSITY
   Font = MS LineDraw (Regular)
   Height = 0.3
   Spacing = 0.05
   Arc Radius=2.45
2. INDUSTRIAL TECHNOLOGY
   Font = MS LineDraw (Regular)
   Height = 0.3
   Spacing = 0.05
   Arc Radius=2.5
3. CAD CAM
   Font=Arial (Regular)
   Height=0.4
   Spacing=0.1
   Arc Radius=1.4
4. CNC
   Font=Arial (Bold Italic)
   Height=0.6
   Spacing=0.15
   Starting point= (-1,-.3)
5. YES
   Font=Times New Roman (Regular)
   Height=0.6
   Spacing=0.2
   Arc Radius=1.4

Figure 5.88

Tips 1. Use different levels and colors for different groups of geometry and letters.

2. The letter strings EASTERN MICHIGAN UNIVERSITY and INDUSTRIAL TECHNOLOGY can be changed to your school name and department name.

Step 1. Create two circles

Select **MAIN MENU → Create → Arc → Circ pt+dia**
Enter the center point: **0,0** ←
Enter the diameter: **6**←
Enter the center point: **0,0** ←
Enter the diameter: **4.5** ←

The two circles appear as Figure 5.89.

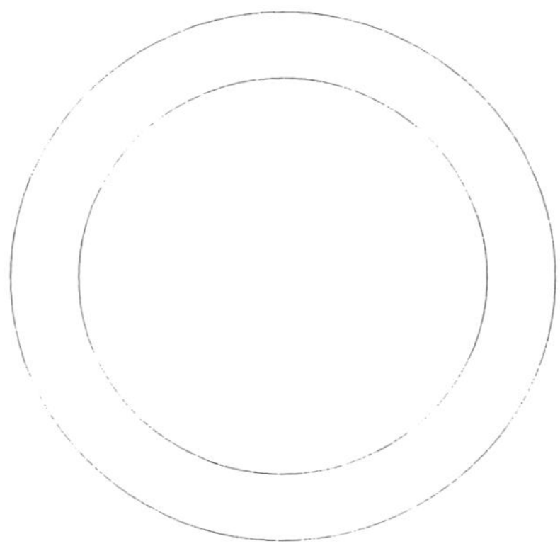

Figure 5.89

Step 2. Create a string of MS LineDraw letters using level 2 and color 12.

Select **Level** then enter **2** ←
Select **Color** then enter **12** ←
Select **MAIN MENU → Create → Next menu → Letters → Truetype (R)→ MSLineDraw → Regular → OK**
Enter letters: **EASTERN MICHIGAN UNIVERSITY** (or your school name)
Enter letter height: **0.3** ←
Select **Top of arc**
Enter letter spacing: **0.05** ←
Enter coordinates of arc center: **0,0**←
Enter arc radius: **2.45** ←

Step 3. Create a string of MS LineDraw letters in the bottom arc.

Select **Truetype (R) → MS LineDraw → Regular → OK**
Enter letters: **INDUSTRIAL TECHNOLOGY** (or your department name)
Enter letter height: **0.3** ←
Select **Btm of arc**
Enter letter spacing: **0.05** ←
Enter coordinates of arc center: **0,0** ←
Enter arc radius: **2.5**←

Two strings of MS LineDraw letters should look like Figure 5.90.

Figure 5.90

Step 4. Change level to 3 and color to 13.

Select **Level** then enter **3** ←
Select **Color** then enter **13** ←

Step 5. Create a string of Arial letters on an arc.

Select **Truetype (R)→ Arial → Regular → OK**
Enter letters: **CAD CAM** ←
Enter letter height: **0.4** ←
Select **Top of arc**
Enter letter spacing: **0.1** ←
Enter coordinates of arc center: **0,0** ←
Enter arc radius: **1.4** ←

The letter string of Arial font appears as Figure 5.91.

Figure 5.91

Step 6. Create the letters string CNC along a line.

Select **Truetype (R) → Arial Bold Italic → OK**
Enter letters: **CNC** ←
Enter letter height: **0.6** ←
Select **Horizontal**
Enter letter spacing: **0.15** ←
Enter starting location of letters: **-1,-0.3** ←

The CNC letters are added as in Figure 5.92.

Figure 5.92

Step 7. Create the letters string YES along a bottom arc.

Select **Truetype → Times New Roman → Regular → OK**
Enter letters: **YES ←**
Enter letter height: **0.6 ←**
Select **Btm of arc**
Enter letter spacing: **0.2 ←**
Enter coordinates of arc center: **0,0 ←**
Enter arc radius: **1.4 ←**

The final drawing should look like Figure 5.93.

Figure 5.93

Step 8. Save to a file.

Select **MAIN MENU → File → Save**
Enter file name: **letter2**

Project 6. Change the letter CNN from level 3 and color 13 to level 4 and color 14.

Step 1. Retrieve the file **LETTER2.MC7** saved in Project 5.
Select **MAIN MENU → File → Get**
Specify File Name to Read: Letter2.mc7

The file should appear as Figure 5.93.

Step 2. Changing the current settings to level 4 and color 14.
Select **Level** then enter 4
Select **Color** then enter 14
Select **MAIN MENU → Screen → Ch colors**
Select entity to change: Select Window
Enter the first window corner: pick P1 (Figure 5.94)
Enter the second window corner: Pick P2 (Figure 5.94)

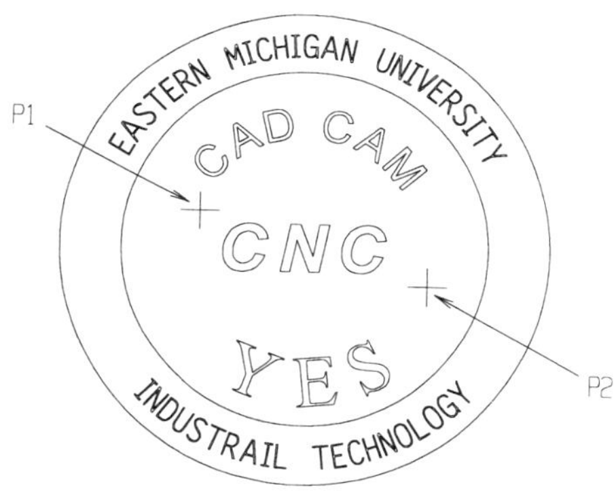

The letter CNC should be changed to color 14.

Select **MAIN MENU → Screen → Chg levels**
Select entity to change: Select **Window**
Enter the first window corner: Pick P1 (Figure 5.94)
Enter the second window corner: Pick P2 (Figure 5.94)

The letter CNC should be changed to level 4. You can verify the change using Analyze (F4) command. You do not need to save this project into a file.

5.14 Exercises

1. Use a drawing to show how Mastercam uses cascaded menus for creating geometry entities.

2. A point can be defined in Mastercam with how many options ?

3. How many options can be used to create a line in Mastercam?

4. Describe how the feature of the Multi command creates lines.

5. Describe the difference between arcs and circles.

6. How many options can define an arc in Mastercam?

7. How many options can define a circle in Mastercam?

8. What are the three fillet parameters? Describe, with drawings, how these three parameters change the fillets.

9. What is a spline?

10. What is the minimum number of points required to define a spline?

11. What are two common types of curves for 2-D geometry in Mastercam?

12. What is the full name of NURBS?

13. Describe the major difference between splines and NURBS curves.

14. Use a drawing to show how Mastercam creates a rectangle with (a)one point and (b)two points options.

15. Describe the procedure used in Mastercam for creating a Windows Truetype font letter geometry.

Problems

16. Create the geometry shown in Figure 5.95. Save the file as **contour8.** This file is used in problem 66 of chapter 7.

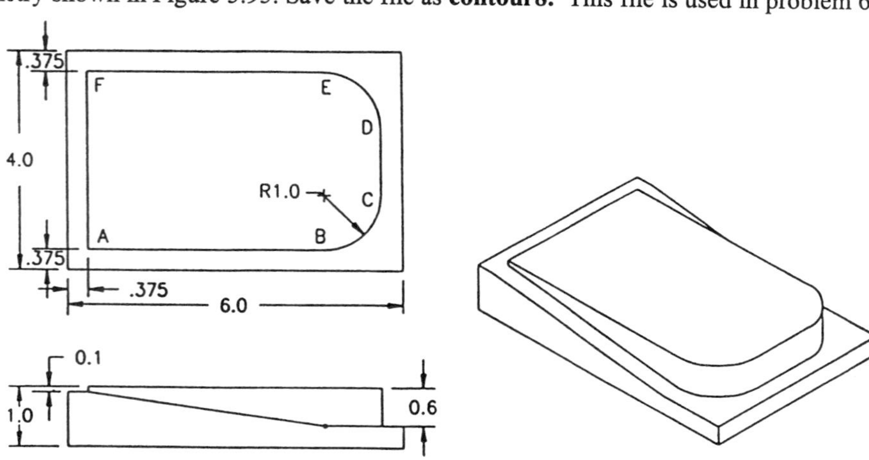

Figure 5.95

Mastercam Version 7,
Scholar's International Publishing Corp., 1998

18. Create the geometry shown in Figure 5.95. Save the file as **drill4.** This file is used in problem 71 of chapter 7.

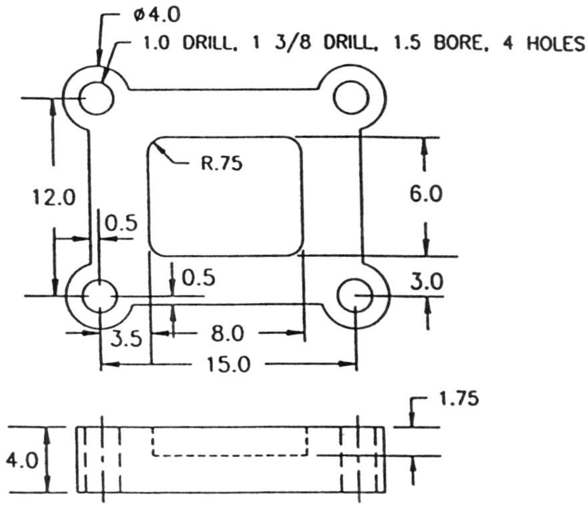

Figure 5.95

19. Create the geometry shown in Figure 5.96. Save the file as **comb2**. This file is used in problem 73 of chapter 7.

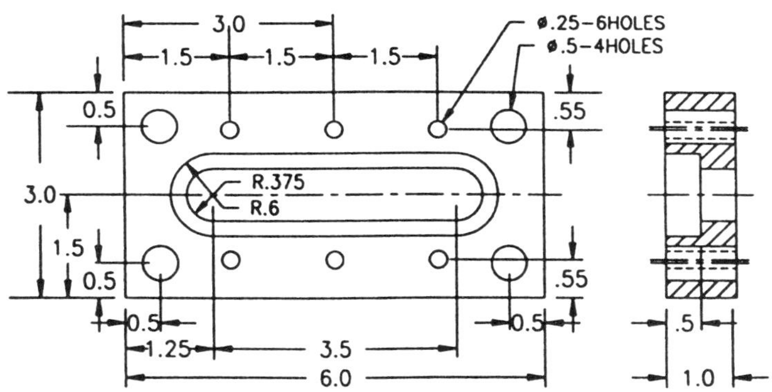

Figure 5.96

20. Create the part geometry shown in Figure 5.97. and save the files as **trans2.** This file is used later in problem 19 of chapter 8.

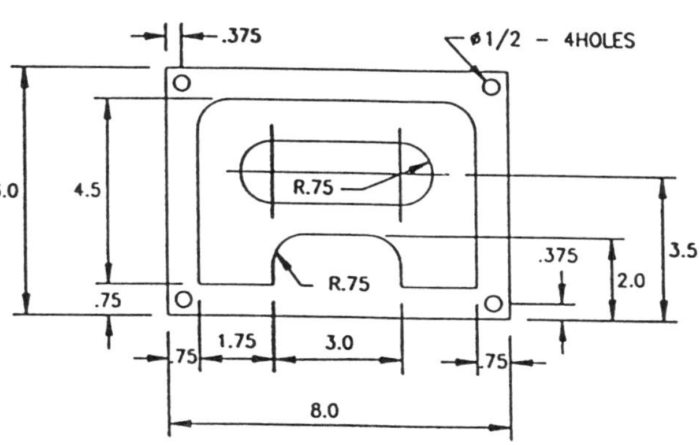

Figure 5.97

21. Create the geometry and letter strings as shown in Figure 5.98. Save the file as letters4 which will be used in problem 77 in chapter 7. Replace the string EMU IT with your school name and department name. Some helpful tips are listed.

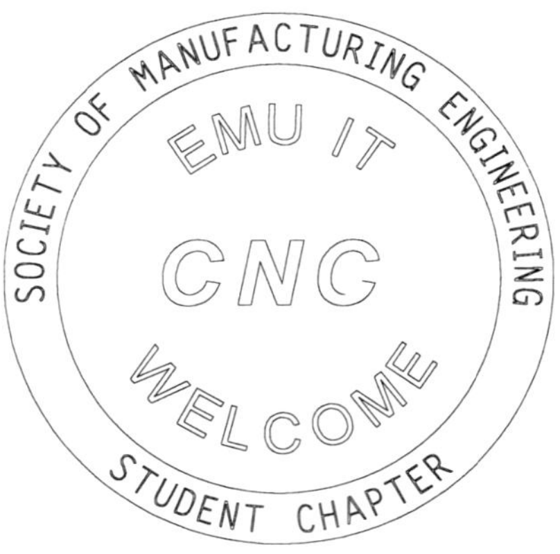

Figure 5.98

1. The geometry file is organized by level and color as below:

Two circles:	level 1 and color 10
Box font:	level 2 and color 12
Roman font:	level 3 and color 13
Block font:	level 4 and color 14

2. Box font: SOCIETY OF MANUFACTURING ENGINEERING and STUDENT CHAPTER

Roman font:	EMU IT and WELCOME
Block font:	CNC

3. Height,spacing, radius, and starting point:

Box font:	height = 0.5"	Spacing = 0.15"	Radius = 4.25"
Roman font:	height = 0.75"	Spacing = 0.2"	Radius = 2.5"
Block font:	height = 1.0"	Spacing = 0.25"	Starting point is (-2.1,-0.3)

Chapter 6

Modify Existing Geometry

Objectives:

1. Understand the features of geometry modification functions and know when to apply them.
2. Apply geometry modification functions, Delete, Modify, and Xform, to simplify the geometric creation process.

Overview

The geometry creation functions presented in chapter 5 are used to produce simple part geometries. It will be very time consuming, if not impossible, to use those basic functions to create complex part geometries. Like most CAD software, Mastercam provides a variety of functions to modify existing geometric entities. All of these modifying functions make geometric construction easier and faster. Three groups of modifying functions are covered in this chapter including delete, modify, and Xform.

6.1 Delete Function

The delete function is used for removing a single entity or a group of entities from the screen and the system's database. Select **Delete** from the main menu (or press **F5** on the keyboard), and you will have an option to select an entity or use its submenu options shown in Figure 6.1.

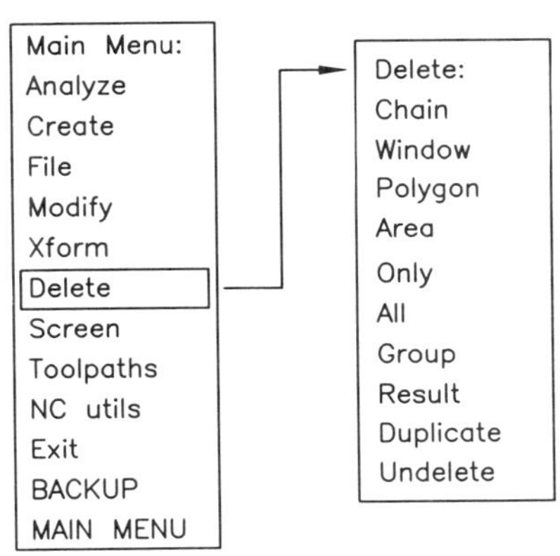

Figure 6.1: Submenu for Delete

The submenu options for Delete can be described as follows:

Chain -	deletes a chain of connected entities.
Window -	deletes all the entities either inside or outside a defined rectangular window **Alt-F5** is a shortcut key for this operation.
Polygon -	deletes all the entities inside, intersected, or outside a defined polygon.
Area-	deletes all Color mask, Level mask, Plane mask, Ignore mask, Set start of chain from point entities, and Entity mask.
Only -	deletes only a certain type of entities such as points, lines, splines, etc. User selection is required.
All -	deletes all entities of a certain type. User selection is not required.
Group -	deletes the current group defined by the Xform→ Group function.
Result -	deletes the result of the transformed entities.
Duplicate -	deletes duplicate entities occupying the same space.
Undelete -	undeletes previously deleted entities.

Undelete

Undelete recreates the deleted entities in the order they were deleted. This function is under the submenu of Delete, and it includes **three** options: **Single**, **Number** and **All**.

Single -	restores the single entity that was most recently deleted.
Number -	restores a number of entities that were most recently deleted.
All -	restores all the previously deleted entities of a certain type. You may choose to undelete all arcs, all points, all splines, all surfaces, etc.

6.2 Modify Functions

A group of modifying functions are grouped under the **Modify** menu. They are used to change existing entities. Select Modify from the main menu and you will have the submenu options shown in Figure 6.2.

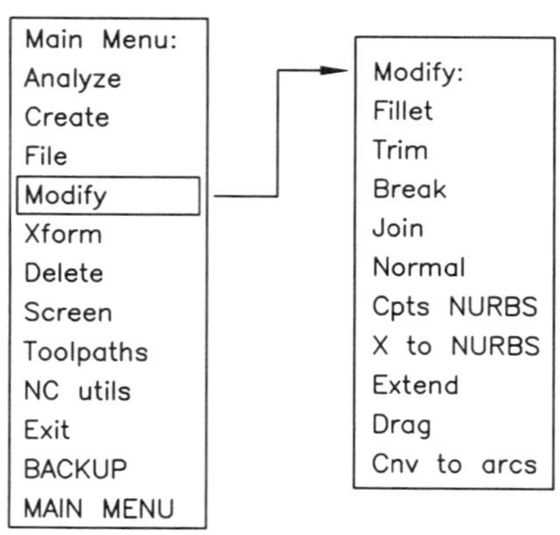

Figure 6.2: Submenu for Modify

The submenu options for **Modify** can be described as follows:

Fillet -	creates a fillet between two intersected entities.
Trim -	trims up to three entities to specified boundaries.
Break -	divides entities (lines, arcs, or splines) into two or more segments.
Join -	joins two segments into one entity. It undoes what break does.
Normal -	modifies the normal directions of a 3-D surface.
Cpts NURBS -	modifies the control points of a NURBS curve.
X to NURBS	transforms arcs or lines into NURBS format.
Extend -	extend a line or arc by a desired length
Drag -	dynamically drags (moves or copies) entities on screen.
Cnv to arcs	convert circular spline or NURBS to an arc.

Fillet Function

This function is used to create a fillet between two entities. The procedures for filleting are the same as shown in section 5.5. Figure 6.3 shows two filleting examples.

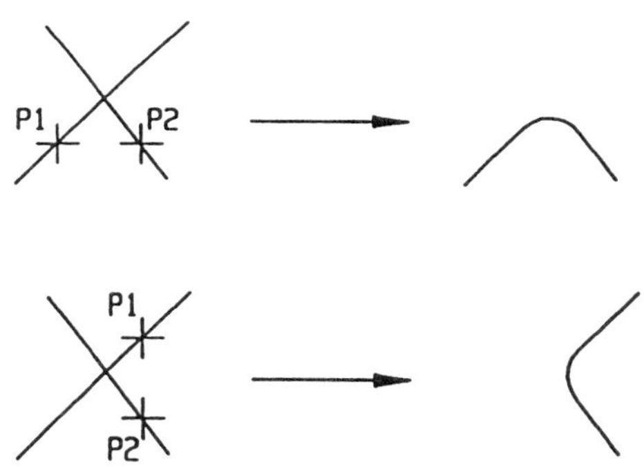

Figure 6.3

Trim Function

The Trim function is used to trim up to three entities to a specified boundaries. The trimming can trim or extend entities to their intersection points. **Eight** options are available:

1 entity-	trims an entity by selecting the entity and an entity to trim to.
2 entities-	trims two entities at the same time at their intersection point.
3 entities-	trims three entities in the same time at their intersection point(s).
To point-	trims or extends the selected entity to a point selected.
Many -	trims several entities at once.
Close arc -	converts any arc to a full circle.
Divide -	trims a line or curve between two other lines or curves.
Surface-	trims surfaces. This topic will not be discussed in this chapter.

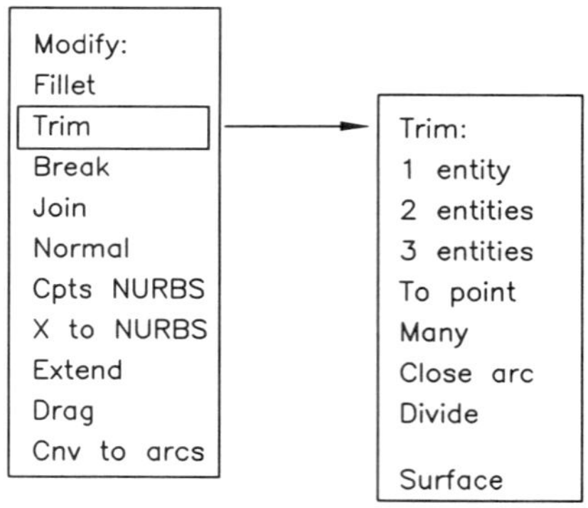

Figure 6.4

1 Entity Trimming

Menu selection sequence is **Modify → Trim → 1 entity**.

This function trims an entity by selecting the segment of the object you wish to retain first, then pick the entity you wish to trim to.

Procedure: (Figure 6.5)

1. Select the entity to trim: Pick at **P1**
2. Select the entity to trim to: Pick at **P2**

Tip On step 1, pick the segment of the entity you wish to retain first.

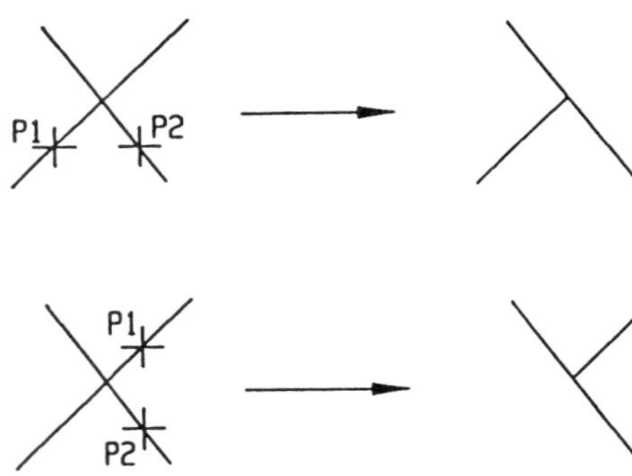

Figure 6.5

2 Entities Trimming

Menu selection sequence is **Modify → Trim → 2 entities.**

This function trims two entities simultaneously to their intersection point.

Procedure: (Figure 6.6)

1. Select the entity to trim: Pick at **P1**
2. Select the entity to trim to: Pick at **P2**

Tips 1. These two entities need to have an intersection point.

2. Pick the segments to be kept on both entities.

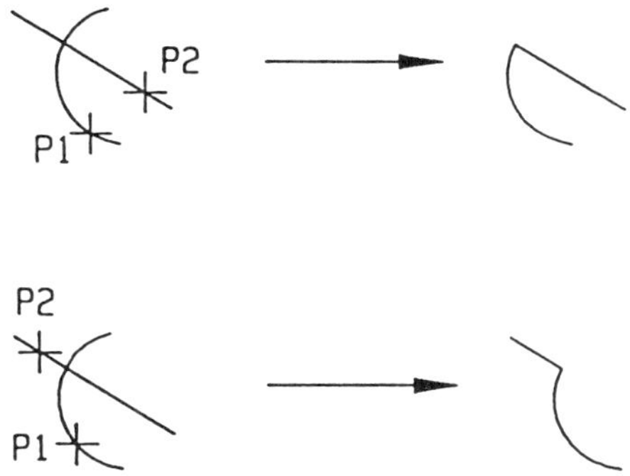

Figure 6.6

3 Entities Trimming

Menu selection sequence is **Modify → Trim → 3 entities.**

This function trims three entities simultaneously to their intersection points.
Procedure: (Figure 6.7)
1. Select the first entity to trim: Pick at **P1**
2. Select the second entity to trim: Pick at **P2**
3. Select the third entity to trim: Pick at **P3**

Tips 1. These three entities need to intersect with one another at three different points.

2. The first two entities will become the boundaries of the third entity.

3. Pick the segments to be kept on these three entities.

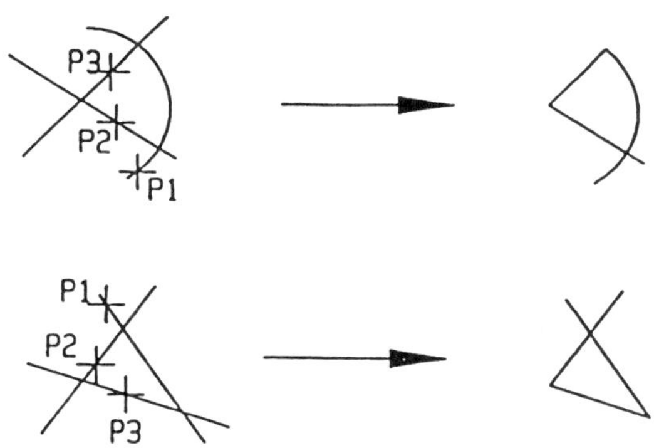

Figure 6.7

Trimming An Entity To a Point

Menu selection is **Modify → Trim → To point.**

This command trims or extends the selected line or arc entity to a point selected. The selected entity will be trimmed at or extended to the point where the perpendicular relationship occurs.
Procedure: (Figure 6.8 on the next page)
1. Select Line or Arc entity to TRIM/EXTEND: Pick at **P1**
2. Indicate TRIM/EXTEND location <position option>: Pick at **P2**

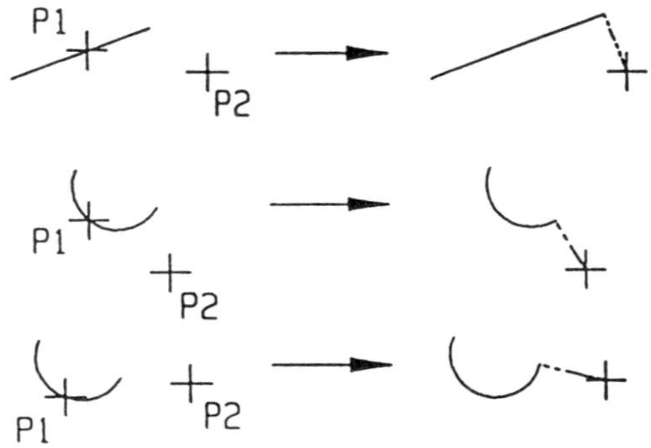

Figure 6.8

Trimming Many Entities at a time

Menu select is **Modify → Trim → Many**

This command trims several entities at once.

Procedure: (Figure 6.9)

1. Select Curves to trim <entity selection options>: Sequentially pick at P1 - P6.
2. Select Done
3. Select Trimming Curve: Pick at P7
4. Indicate Side of Trimming Curve: Pick at P8

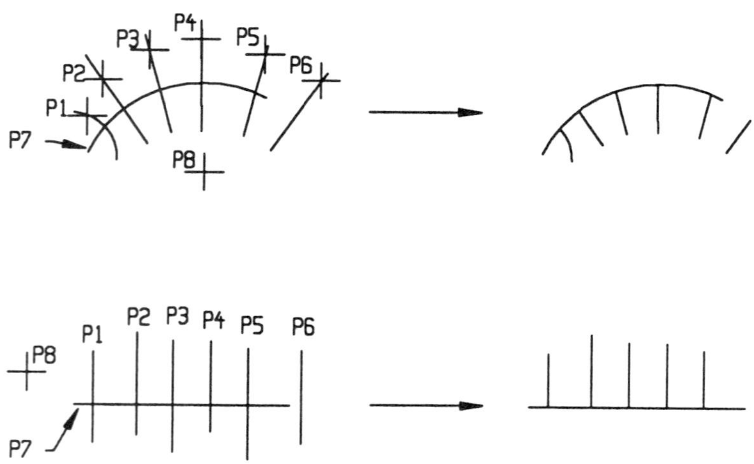

Figure 6.9

Convert an Arc to a Full Circle

Menu select is **Modify → Trim → Close arc**

This command converts an arc to a full circle.

Procedure: (Figure 6.10)

1. Select an Arc to convert to a full circle: Pick at **P1**

1

Figure 6.10

Trimming a Curve Between Two Other Curves

Menu select is **Modify → Trim → Divide**

This command trims a line or curve between two other lines or curves.

Procedure: (Figure 6.11)

1. Select curve to divide: Pick at **P1**
2. Select first dividing curve: Pick at **P2**
3. Select second dividing curve: Pick at **P3**

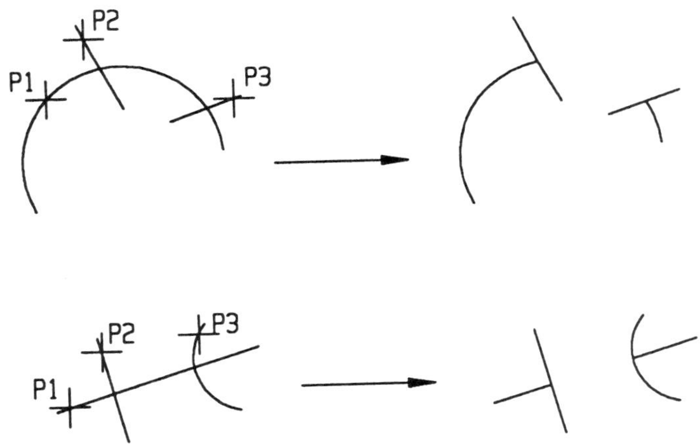

Figure 6.11

Project 1. Filleting and Trimming

Create the geometry shown in Figure 6.12a. Save the file as **array1**. This file is used in project 6 of chapter 8 to generate a set of toolpaths to produce three pockets as shown in Figure 6.12b.

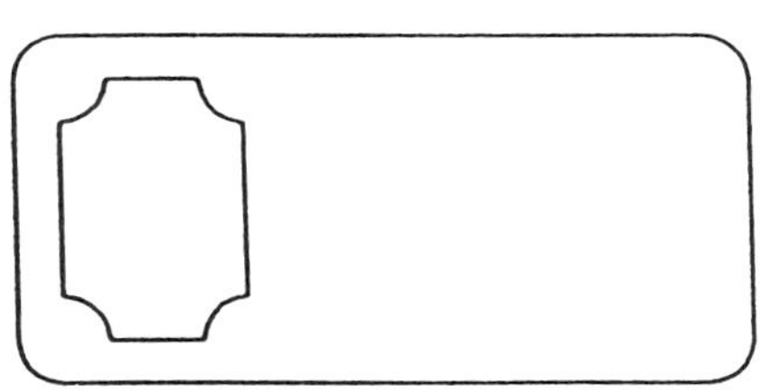

Figure 6.12a

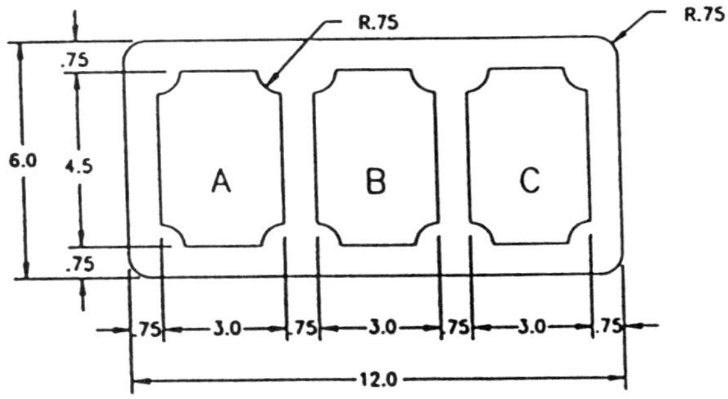

Figure 6.12.b

Tips 1. Create two rectangles.

2. Add four fillets at the corners of the outer rectangle.

3. Create four circles at the corners of the inside rectangle.

4. Use Trim → 3 entities commands to trim the four circles to their desired arcs.

Step 1. Create two rectangles.

Select **MAIN MENU** → **Create** → **Rectangle** → **2 points**
Enter the lower left corner: **0,0** ←
Enter the upper right corner: **12,6** ← for the outer rectangle
Enter the lower left corner: **0.75,0.75** ←
Enter the upper right corner: **3.75,5.25** ← for the inside rectangle

Press **Alt** and **F1** simultaneously to fit the drawing.

The two rectangles appear as Figure 6.13.

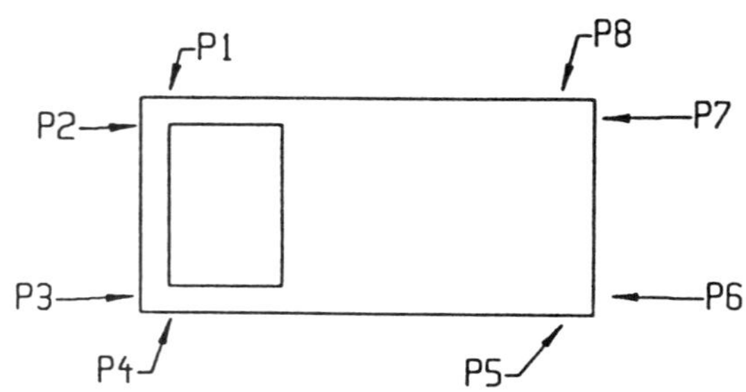

Figure 6.13

Step 2. Create four fillets at corners of outer rectangle. Use the pick points in Figure 6.13.

Select **MAIN MENU → Create → Fillet → Radius**
Enter the first radius: **0.75 ←**

Note: Make sure the other two parameters' settings are correct. The fillet angle is less than 180; trim to fillet.

Select an entity: pick at **P1**
Select another entity: pick at **P2** to complete the first fillet
Sequentially pick at **P3 - P8** to complete the remaining three fillets

The four fillets are added as in Figure 6.14.

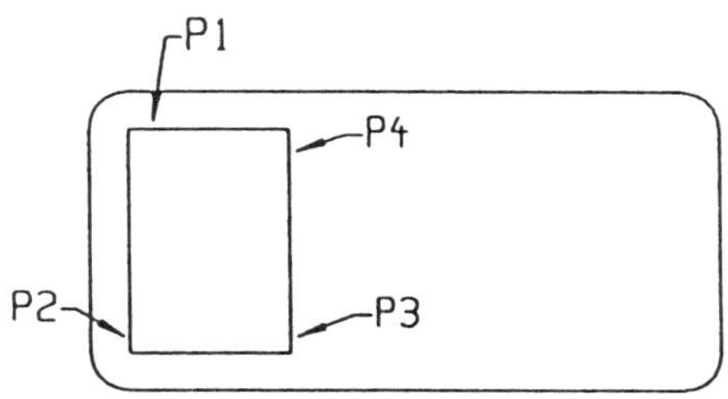

Figure 6.14

Step 3. Create four circles at corners of the inner rectangle.

Use the pick points from the Figure 6.14 above.
Select **MAIN MENU → Create → Arc → Cir pt + rad → Endpoint**
Enter the center point: Pick at **P1**
Enter the radius: **0.75 ←** to complete the first circle
Enter the center point: Pick at **P2**
Enter the radius: **0.75 ←** for the second circle
Enter the center point: Pick at **P3**
Enter the radius: **0.75 ←** for the third circle
Enter the center point: Pick at **P4**
Enter the radius: **0.75 ←** for the fourth circle

Four circles are added as in Figure 6.15.

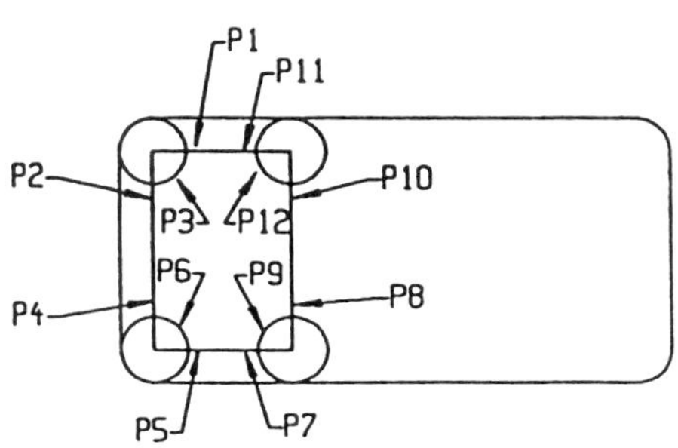

Figure 6.15

Step 4. Trim four circles to become arcs. Use the pick points in Figure 6.15.

Select **MAIN MENU → Modify → Trim → 3 entities**
Select the first entity to trim: pick at **P1**
Select the second entity to trim: pick at **P2**
Select the entity to trim to: pick at **P3** to complete the trimming of the first corner
Sequentially pick at **P4 - P12** to trim the remaining three corners

The final drawing should look like Figure 6.16.

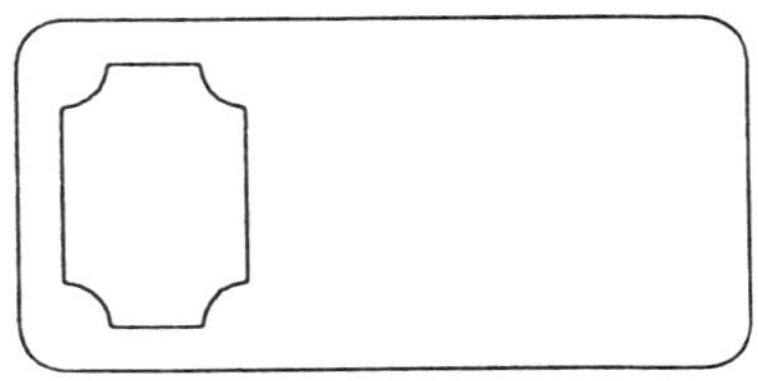

Figure 6.16

Step 5. Save to a file (array1).

Select **MAIN MENU → File → Save**
Enter file name: **array1**

Break Function

This function separates an entity into two or more entities. The new entities can be different from the original entity type. The options under Break are:

2 pieces-	breaks lines, arcs, splines and NURBS curve into two pieces.
At length -	breaks a line, arc or spline at a distance along the entity.
Mny pieces-	breaks lines, arcs, splines and NURBS curve into more than two pieces.
At inter	breaks lines, arcs, splines and NURBS curve into two pieces.
Spl to arc	breaks spline into many pieces.
Note/let -	breaks a note into geometry.
Hatch/line-	breaks a crosshatch entity into line segments.
Cdata/line-	breaks a copious data entity into points or line segments.
Breakcir-	not available.

Tip These new line and arc segments are difficult to distinguish on screen. Use **Analyze** (F4) command to examine these segments.

Join Function

Join combines two separated entities together to become a new entity.

Tips

1. NURBS or parametric curves can not be joined unless they were originally created as the same entity.
2. Note that these two entities have to be compatible. The system checks the database for each entity and tries to join them together. An error message displays if the two entities selected are not compatible. For example:
   "Cannot join the lines - they are not collinear."

"Cannot join the arcs - they do not have the same center and radius."

Normal Function

This function is used to change the normal direction of surfaces.

Cpts NURBS Function

This function modifies the control points of NURBS curves and surfaces, and creates a new NURBS curve and surface.

Procedure: (Figure 6.17)

1. Select a NURBS curve or surface: Pick at **P1**
   The yellow control points and red control lines will appear on screen.
2. Select a control point: Pick at **P2**
3. Modify NURBS Cpts: Select **Dynamic**

Dynamic -dynamically drag the control point and see the new curve in blue. Point entry - input, or select, a new XYZ coordinates for the control points.

4. Enter the starting point: Pick at **P2** again.
5. Move to **P3** and press the mouse button.

Tip **F3** key to repaint the drawing.

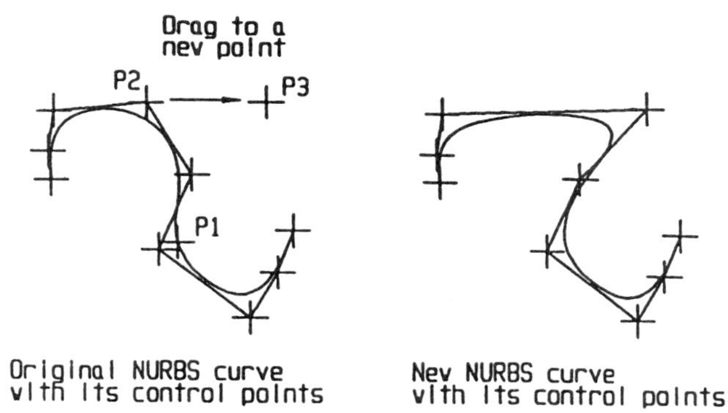

Figure 6.17.

X to NURBS Function

This function converts lines, arcs, splines and surfaces to the NURBS format. The new entities are saved to the drawing database as NURBS curves.

Procedure:

1. Select line arc, spline, or surface to convert to NURBS.
2. Select **Done**

Tip Use **Analyze** (F4) to confirm the changes.

Extend Function

This function allows the user to extend a line or arc by a desired length. The user types in the desired length and selects a line or arc near the endpoint to direct the extension.

Drag Function

This function dynamically moves or copies drawing entities when given the new location. Drag helps you see the results of the command before it is finished.

Cnv to arcs

This function converts a circular spline or NURBS to an arc.

Procedure:

1. Select splines
2. Select **Done**
3. Select **Do it**

6.3 Xform Functions

Mastercam provides ten very useful editing functions to change the position, orientation, and size of exiting geometries. These **ten** functions are mirror, rotate, scale, scalexyz, translate, offset, ofs ctour and group. They are grouped under the Xform command. The submenu of Xform is shown in Figure 6.18 on the next page.

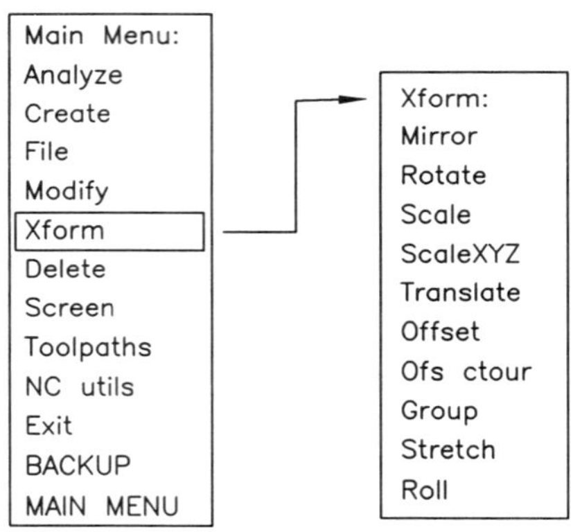

Figure 6.18

The ten editing functions are described below:

Mirror - produces a mirror image of a drawing, detail, or part.
Rotate- rotates the selected entities about any point.
Scale - scales the selected entities to increase or decrease their sizes.
Scale XYZ - scales the selected entities by the given x, y and z values.
Ofs ctour - offsets several connected lines or arcs by chaining their entities.
Translate - moves or copies objects to new location(s).
Offset - moves or copies a line or arc away from itself in a perpendicular direction with an offset distance to the line or arc.
Group - selects and defines a group of entities to be transformed. The selected entities will be highlighted in red.
Stretch - translates entities and stretch lines relative to a selection windows.
Roll - rolls and wraps entities as though around a cylinder or unwraps rolled entities.

Entity Selection Option and Its Procedures

When Mirror, Rotate, Scale, Translate or Offset is selected, the following **entity selection option** will appear on the Main Menu Area. You can select an entity one after another, use chain, window, or combine different options in the menu. The selected entity will be highlighted in white. You can select **Done** to finish the selection process and proceed to the next step, or select **Unselected** to abort the selected entities

Unselect - clears the current selected group.
Chain - selects a group of entities that are chained together.
Window - selects all the entities that are inside or outside the window.
Polygon - selects all the entities defined by a polygon-shaped window.
Area- has two options; mode and Options.
Only - selects a group of entities with a specific entity type, i.e., lines, arcs, etc. select the specific kind of entity one after another to add into the database.
All - selects a group of entities of a specific type, i.e., lines, arcs, splines,etc. The options automatically selects all the entities in that particular entity type.
Group - retrieves and selects the current group from the database.
Results - shows the current result.
Intr wndw - selects all the entities that are either inside or intersect with the window, or outside or intersect with the window.
Ungroup (Y/N) - sets this switch to Y to ungroup entities or N to group them.
Done- finish the selection process and proceed to the new step.

Transformation Parameters

Mastercam uses different dialog boxes with different parameters to perform a transformation. An example for rotate is shown in the following figure.

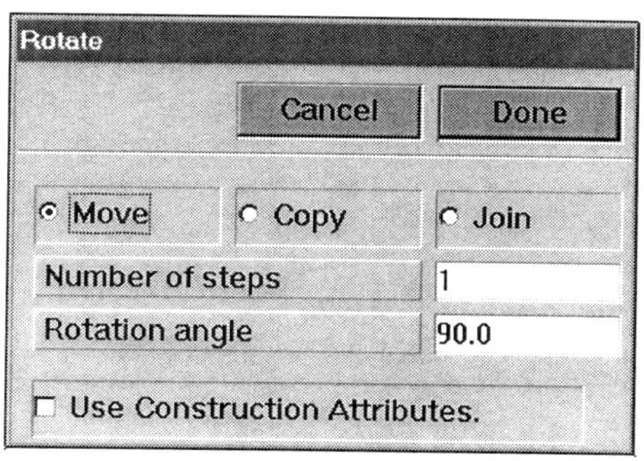

Figure 6.19

Number of Steps - specifies the number of steps to be performed by the transformation function.
Move - moves the original entities.
Copy - copies the original entities.
Join - joins the new transformed entities to original entities at their end points.
Rotation Angle - specifies the angle of rotation.

Mirror Function

2 This function produces a **mirror** image of selected entities about the X axis, Y axis, an existing line, or 2 points. It is best suited for those parts that have identical features being symmetrical about an axis or a line.

Procedure: (Figure 6.20)

1. Entity selection option: Pick at **P1**
2. Entity selection option: Select **Done**
3. Mirror about: Select **Line**

X axis -	mirrors with respect to X axis.
Y axis -	mirrors with respect to Y axis.
Line -	mirrors with respect to an existing line. The system will prompt after this selection.
2 Points -	mirrors with respect to two selected points.

4. Select line to mirror across: Pick at **P2**
5. Select **Copy → Done** from the pop-up dialog box.

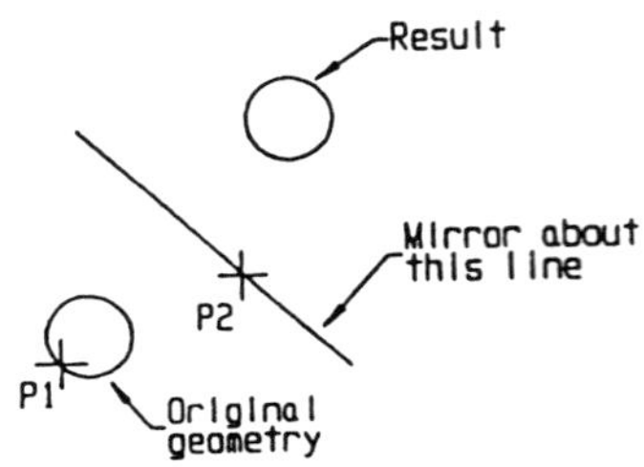

Figure 6.20: Mirroring an entity about an existing line

Tips 1. Select **Move → Done** or **Copy → Done** in step 5 to delete or retain the original entities.
2. Use the **Repaint** (F3) command to see the complete drawing after modification.

Project 2. Mirroring

Create a hexagon and a rectangle as shown in Figure 6.21. Save the file as **scale1**. This file is used in project 4 of chapter 8 to generate a set of toolpaths for pocketing three hexagons at different depths.

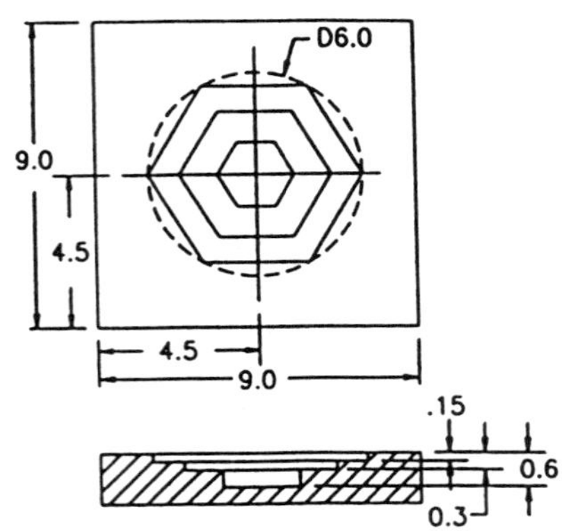

Figure 6.21

Tips 1. Create three sides of upper half of hexagon.

2. Mirror the three sides of hexagon about the X-axis to form the hexagon.

Step 1. Create two lines.

Select **MAIN MENU** → **Create** → **Line** → **Polar**
Specify an endpoint: **3,0** ←
Enter the angle in degree: **120** ←
Enter the length: **3** ←
Specify an endpoint: **-3,0** ←
Enter the angle in degree: **60** ←
Enter the length: **3** ←

The drawing appears as Figure 6.22.

Figure 6.22

Step 2. Create another line using the pick points in Figure 6.22.

Select **BACKUP** → **Endpoints** → **Endpoint**
Specify the first endpoint: Pick at **P1**
Specify the second endpoint: Pick at **P2**

The new drawing becomes Figure 6.23.

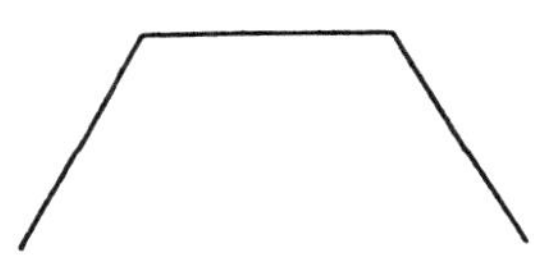

Figure 6.23

Step 3. Mirror about X axis.

Select **MAIN MENU** → **Xform** → **Mirror** → **All** → **Entities** → **Done** → **X axis** → **Copy** →**Done**

The hexagon appears as in Figure 6.24.

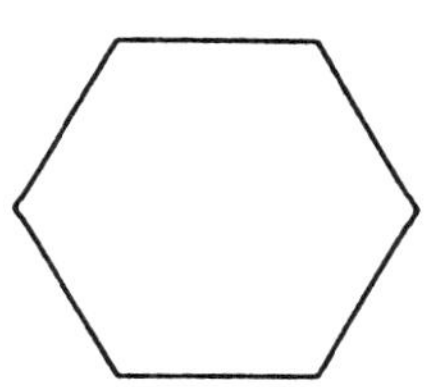

Figure 6.24

Step 4. Create a rectangle.

3 Select **MAIN MENU → Create → Rectangle → 2 points**
Enter the lower left corner: **-4.5,-4.5 ←**
Enter the upper right corner: **4.5,4.5 ←**

The final drawing shall look like Figure 6.25.

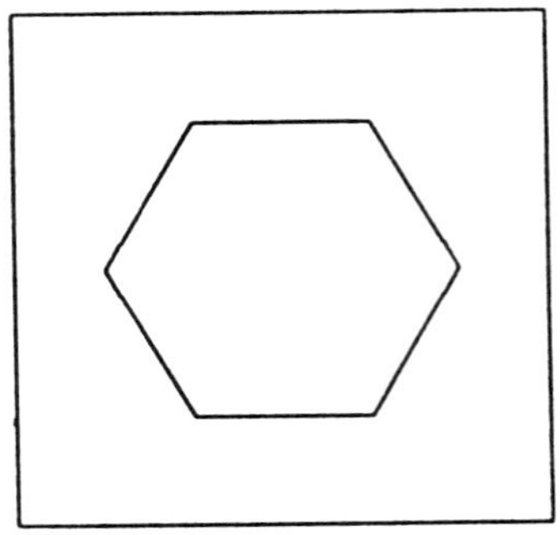

Figure 6.25

Step 5. Save to a file (scale1).

Select **MAIN MENU → File → Save**
Enter file name: **Scale1**

Project 3. Mirroring

Create a geometry as shown in Figure 6.26. Save the file as **contour2.** This file is used in project 2 of chapter 7 to generate the toolpaths to cut the internal profile.

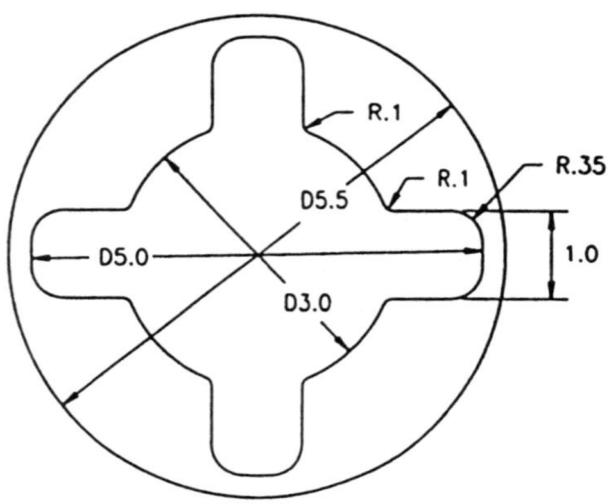

Figure 6.26

Tips 1. Create three 45° construction arcs and one construction line at 45° with the X axis.

2. Add two fillets to form the basic profile.

3. Mirror the basic profile about the 45° line to form a quarter of the part profile.

4. The quarter profile is then mirrored twice to complete the final part profile. The first time mirror about the Y axis. The second time mirror about the X axis.

Step 1. Create three 45° arcs.

Select **MAIN MENU → Create → Arc → Polar → Center pt**
Enter the center point: **0,0** ←
Enter the radius: **2.75** ←
Enter the initial angle: **0** ←
Enter the final angle: **45** ←
Enter the center point: **0,0** ←
Enter the radius: **2.5** ←
Enter the initial angle: **0** ←
Enter the final angle: **45** ←
Enter the center point: **0,0** ←
Enter the radius: **1.5** ←
Enter the initial angle: **0** ←
Enter the final angle: **45** ←

The three 45° arcs are shown in Figure 6.27.

Figure 6.27

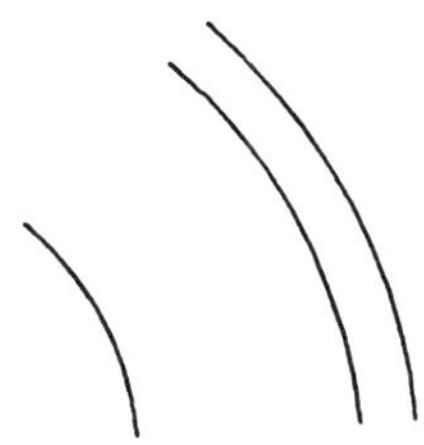

Step 2. Create a horizontal line at y = 0.5 and a 45° line.

Select **MAIN MENU → Create → Line → Endpoints**
Specify the first endpoint: Enter **0,0.5** ←
Specify the second endpoint: Enter **2.5,0.5** ←
Specify the first endpoint: Enter **0,0** ←
Specify the second endpoint: Enter **3,3** ←

Two lines are added as in Figure 6.28.

Figure 6.28

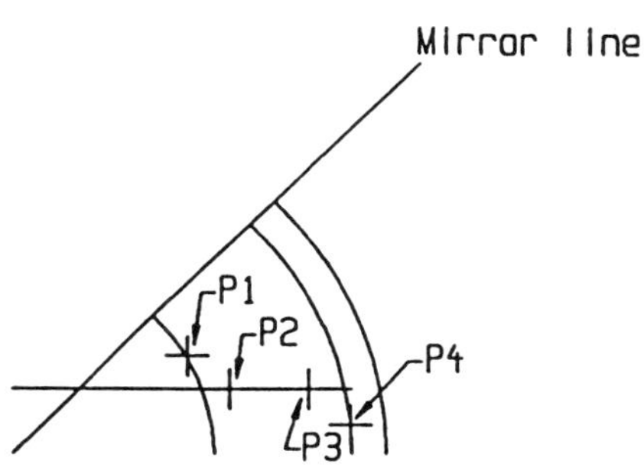

Step 3. Create two fillets using the pick points in Figure 6.28.

Select **MAIN MENU → Create → Fillet → Radius**
Enter the fillet radius: **0.1** ←

Note: Be sure the other two options are correct. The fillet angle is less than 180; trim to the fillet.

Select an entity: pick at **P1**
Select another entity: pick at **P2**

Select **Radius**
Enter the radius: **0.35** ←
Select an entity: pick at **P3**
Select another entity: pick at **P4**

Two fillets are added as in Figure 6.29.

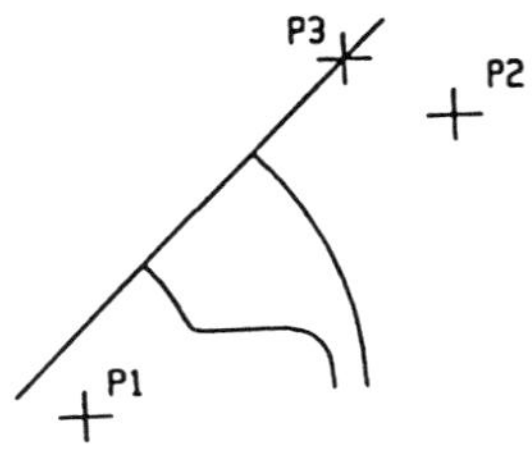

Figure 6.29

Step 4. Mirror the basic profile about the 45° line using the pick points in Figure 6.29.

Select **MAIN MENU** → **Xform** → **Mirror** → **Window** → **Inside**
Select the first corner: pick at **P1**
Select the second corner: pick at **P2**
Select **Done** → **Line**
Select line about which to mirror: pick at **P3**
Select **Copy**→ **Done**
The mirrored profile should look like Figure 6.30.

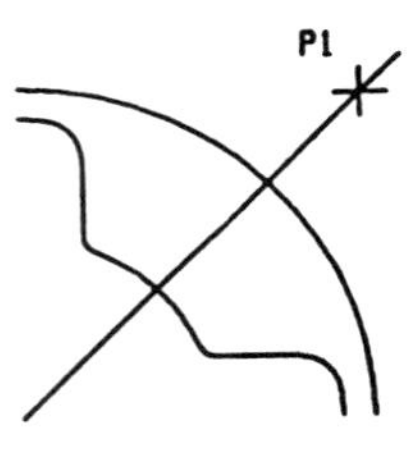

Figure 6.30

Step 5. Delete the mirror line using the pick point in Figure 6.30.

Select **MAIN MENU** → **Delete**
Select an entity or: pick at **P1**

The new drawing appears as Figure 6.31.

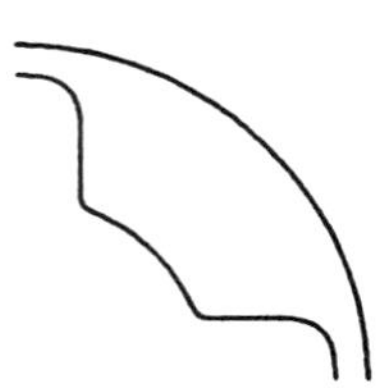

Figure 6.31

Step 6. Complete the geometry by using the Mirror command twice.

4

Select **MAIN MENU → Xform → Mirror → All → Entities → Done → Y axis → Copy → Done→ All → Entities → Done → X axis→Copy → Done**

The final drawing should resemble Figure 6.32.

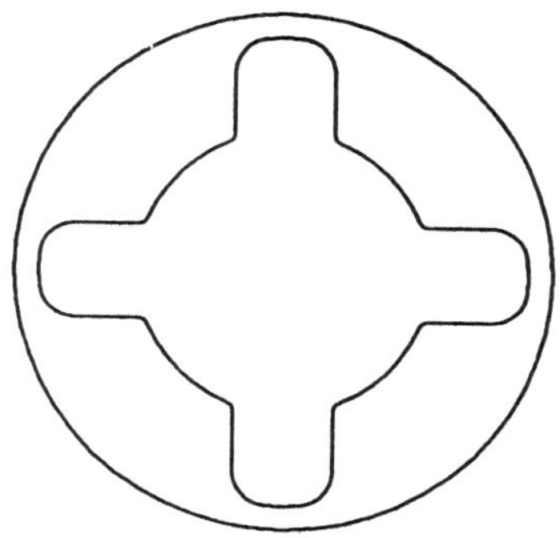

Figure 6.32

Step 7. Save to a file.

Select **MAIN MENU → File → Save**
Enter file name: **contour2**

Project 4. Mirroring

Create a geometry as shown in Figure 6.33. Save the file as **rotate1.** This file is used in project 3 of chapter 8 to generate toolpaths.

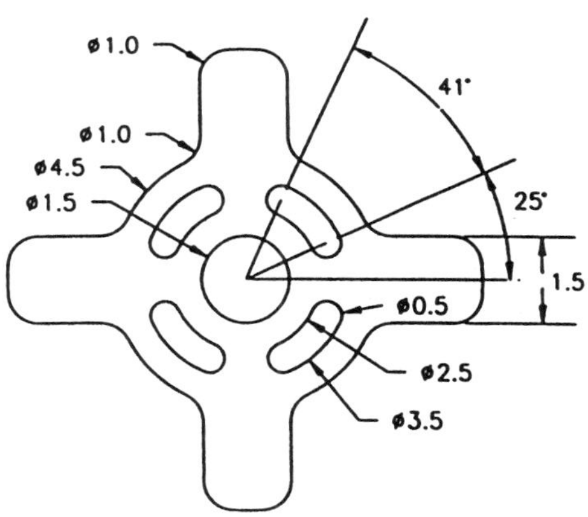

Figure 6.33

Tips 1. Create a basic profile that encompasses 45° of the profile.

2. Mirror the basic profile about the 45° line to complete a profile of 90°.

3. Mirror the profile of 90° about the Y axis to generate another profile of 180°.

4. Mirror the 180° profile about the X axis to complete the geometry.

Step 1. Create five circles.

Select **MAIN MENU → Create → Arc → Circ pt + rad**
Enter the center point: **0,0** ←
Enter the radius: **4.0** ←
Enter the center point: **0,0** ←
Enter the radius: **2.25** ←
Enter the center point: **0,0** ←
Enter the radius: **1.75** ←
Enter the center point: **0,0** ←
Enter the radius: **1.25** ←
Enter the center point: **0,0** ←
Enter the radius: **0.75** ←

Step 2. Create a 45° line.

Select **MAIN MENU → Create → Line → Polar**
Specify an endpoint: Enter **0,0** ←
Enter angle in degrees: **45** ←
Enter the line length: **4.5** ←

The drawing should look like Figure 6.34.

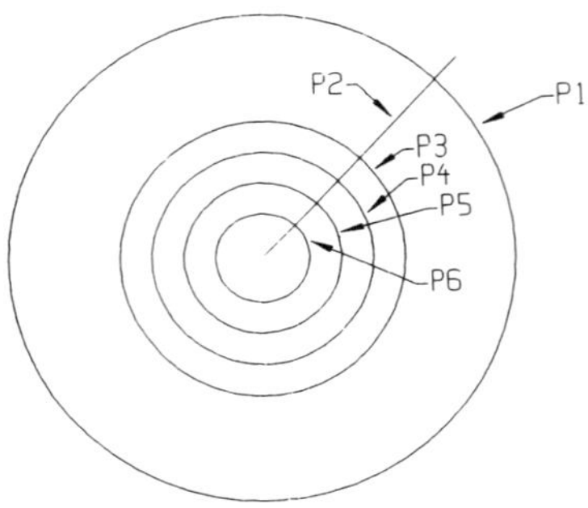

Figure 6.34

Step 3. Trim the circles to the line. Use pick points in Figure 6.34.

Select **MAIN MENU → Modify → Trim → 1 entity**
Select the entity to trim: pick at **P1**
Select the entity to trim to: pick at **P2**
Select the entity to trim: pick at **P3**
Select the entity to trim to: pick at **P2**
Select the entity to trim: pick at **P4**
Select the entity to trim to: pick at **P2**
Select the entity to trim: pick at **P5**
Select the entity to trim to: pick at **P2**
Select the entity to trim: pick at **P6**
Select the entity to trim to: pick at **P2**

These trimmed arcs should appear as Figure 6.35.

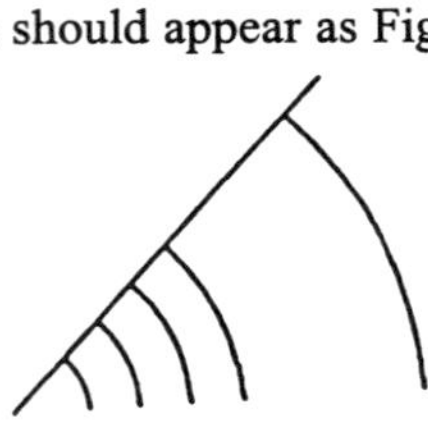

Figure 6.35

Tip Step 3 can be done by the following procedures:

Select **MAIN MENU → Modify → Trim → Many→ All →Arcs →Done**
Select trimming curve: pick at **P2**
Indicate side of the trimming curve: pick at **P2**

Step 4. Create two lines for fillets.

Select **MAIN MENU → Create → Line → Polar**
Specify an endpoint: Enter **0,0** ←
Enter angle in degrees: **25.0** ←
Enter the line length: **2.5** ←
Select **BACKUP → Endpoints**
Specify the first endpoint: Enter **2.25,.75** ←
Specify the second endpoint: Enter **4,.75** ←

The two lines are added as in Figure 6.36.

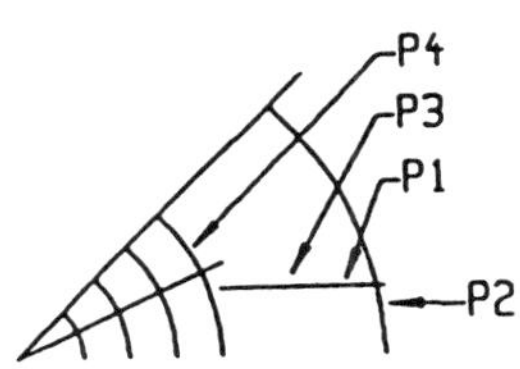

Figure 6.36

Step 5. Create two fillets using the pick points in Figure 6.36.

Select **MAIN MENU → Create → Fillet → Radius**
Enter the fillet radius: **0.5** ←

Note: Make sure the other two options are correct. The fillet angle is less than 180; trim to fillet.

Select an entity: pick at **P1**
Select another entity: pick at **P2**
Select an entity: pick at **P3**
Select another entity: pick at **P4**

The new drawing becomes Figure 6.37.

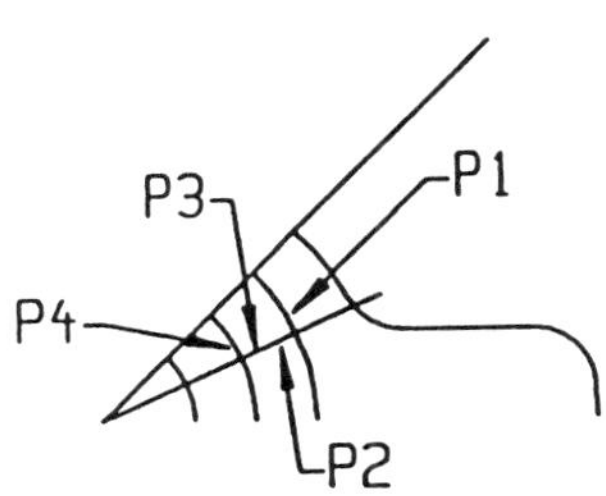

Figure 6.37

Step 6. Trim entities using the pick points in Figure 6.37.

Select **MAIN MENU → Modify → Trim → 2 entities**
Select the entity to trim: pick at **P1**
Select the entity to trim to: pick at **P2**
Select the entity to trim: pick at **P3**
Select the entity to trim to: pick at **P4**

The drawing should look like Figure 6.38.

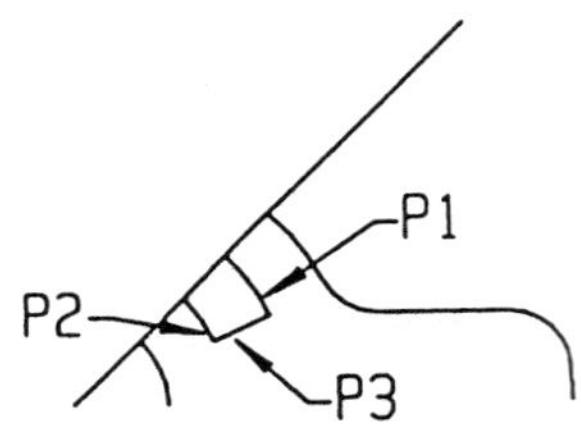

Figure 6.38

Step 7. Create an arc and delete a line using the pick points in Figure 6.38.

Select **MAIN MENU → Create → Arc → Endpoints → Endpoint**
Enter the first point: pick at **P1**
Enter the second point: pick at **P2**
Enter the radius: **0.25** ←
Select an arc: pick at the bottom arc
Select **MAIN MENU → Delete**
Select an entity or: pick at **P3**

The arc should appear in Figure 6.39.

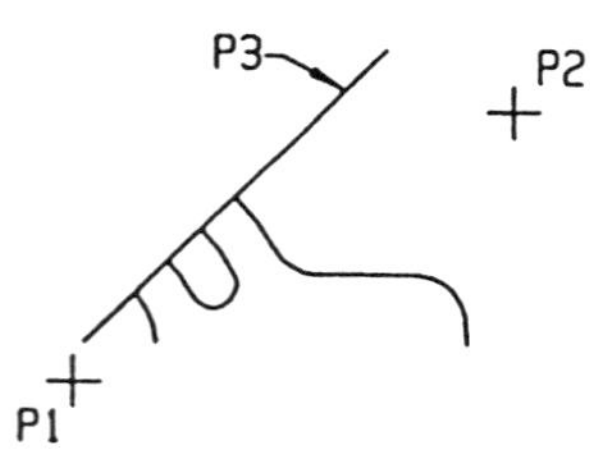

Figure 6.39

Step 8. Mirror about the 45° line. Use the pick points in Figure 6.39.

Select **MAIN MENU → Xform → Mirror → Window →Inside**
Select the first corner: pick at **P1**
Select the second corner: pick at **P2**
Select **Done → Line**
Select line about which to mirror: pick at **P3**
Select **Copy → Done**

The mirrored drawing should look like Figure 6.40 on the next page.

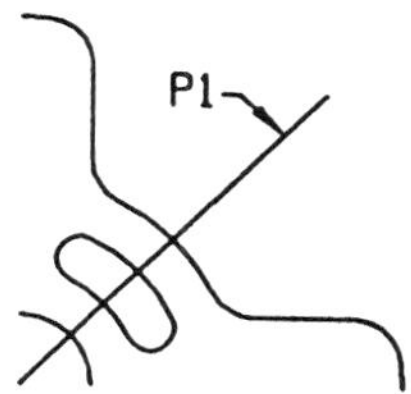

Figure 6.40

Step 9. Delete the 45° line using the pick point in Figure 6.40.

Select **MAIN MENU → Delete**
Select an entity or: pick at **P1**
The new drawing becomes Figure 6.41.

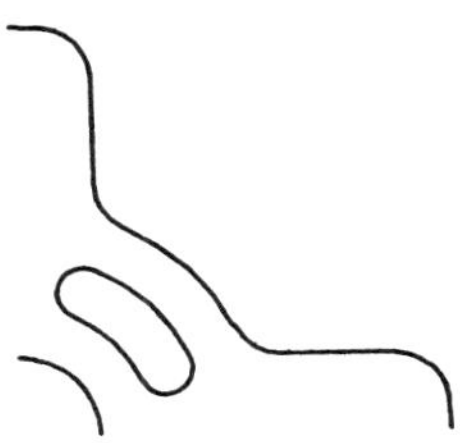

Figure 6.41

Step 10. Mirror all entities twice. The first time about the Y axis and second time about the X axis.

Select **MAIN MENU → Xform → Mirror → All → Entities →Done → Y axis → Copy → Done → All → Entities → Done → X axis → Copy → Done**

The final drawing should resemble Figure 6.42.

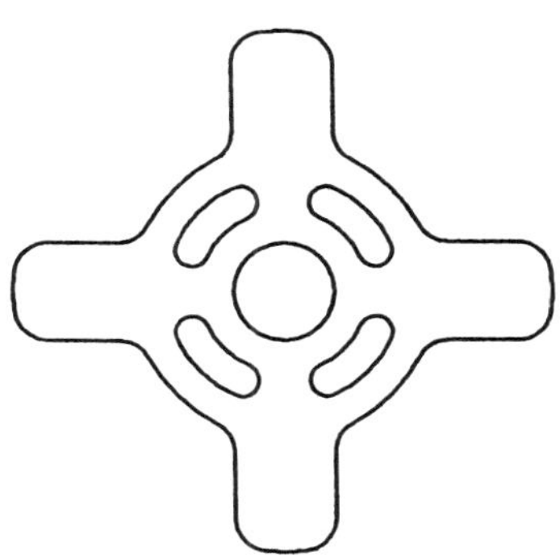

Figure 6.42

Step 11. Save to a file.

Select **MAIN MENU → File → Save**
Enter file name: **rotate1**

5

Project 5. Mirroring

Create a part geometry as shown in Figure 6.39. Save the file as **pocket2**. This file is used in project 6 of chapter 7 to generate a set of toolpaths for pocketing the internal profile with an island.

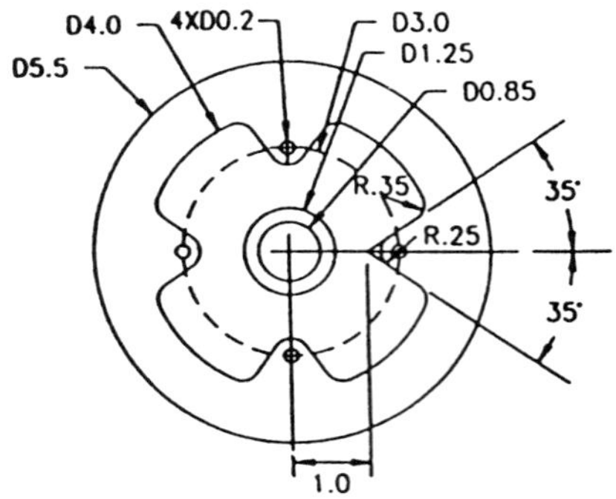

Figure 6.43

Tips 1. Create a basic (partial) profile. This basic profile is then mirrored about a 45° line from the +X axis to form a quarter profile.
2. Mirror the quarter profile twice, first with the Y axis and then with the X axis.

3. Create the remaining seven circles.

Step 1. Create a circle.

Select **MAIN MENU → Create → Arc → Circ pt + dia**
Enter the center point: **0,0** ←
Enter the diameter: **4** ←

Step 2. Create two lines for fillets and two lines for trimming and mirroring.

Select **MAIN MENU → Create → Line → Polar**
Specify an endpoint: **1.0,0** ←
Enter angle in degrees: **35** ←
Enter the line length: **1.5** ←
Specify an endpoint: **1.0,0** ←
Enter angle in degrees: **-35** ←
Enter the line length: **1.5** ←
Specify an endpoint: **0,0** ←
Enter angle in degrees: **45** ←
Enter the line length: **3** ←
Specify an endpoint: **0,0** ←
Enter angle in degrees: **0** ←
Enter the line length: **3** ←

The drawing should look like Figure 6.44 on the next page.

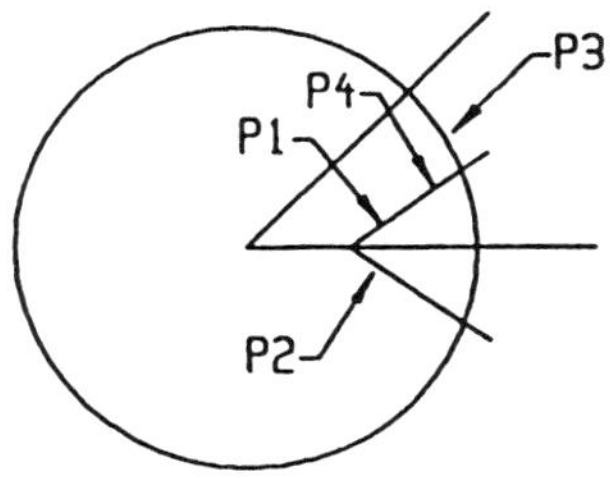

Figure 6.44

Step 3. Create two fillets. Use the pick points in Figure 6.44.

Select **MAIN MENU → Create → Fillet → Radius**
Enter the fillet radius: **0.25 ←**
Select an entity: pick at **P1**
Select another entity: pick at **P2**
Select **Radius**
Enter the fillet radius: **0.35 ←**
Select an entity: pick at **P3**
Select another entity: pick at **P4**

The new drawing appears as Figure 6.45.

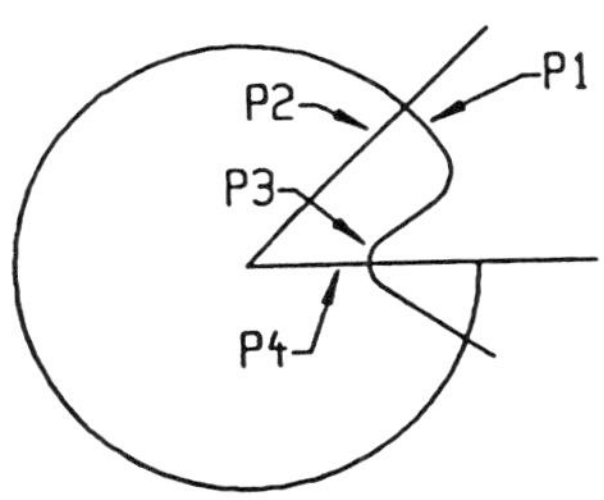

Figure 6.45

Step 4. Trim entities using the pick points in Figure 6.45 above.

Select **MAIN MENU → Modify → Trim → 1 entity**
Select the entity to trim: pick at **P1**
Select the entity to trim to: pick at **P2**
Select the entity to trim: pick at **P3**
Select the entity to trim to: pick at **P4**

The trimmed geometry appears as Figure 6.46.

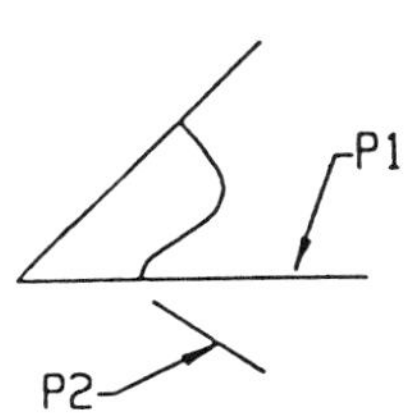

Figure 6.46

Step 5. Delete two construction entities using the pick points in Figure 6.46.

Select **MAIN MENU → Delete**
Select an entity: pick at **P1**
Select an entity: pick at **P2**

New drawing with the basic profile should resemble Figure 6.47.

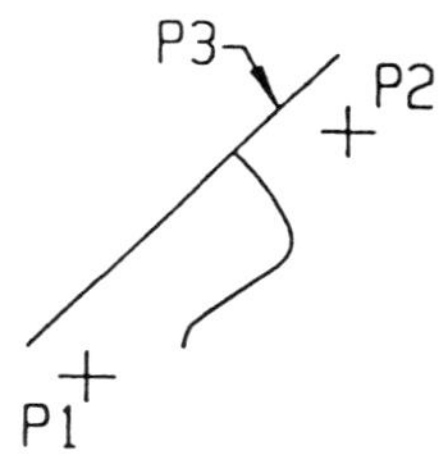

Figure 6.47

Step 6. Mirror the basic profile about the 45° line.

Use the pick points marked in Figure 6.47.
Select **MAIN MENU → Xform → Mirror → Window → Inside**
Select the first corner: pick at **P1**
Select the second corner: pick at **P2**
Select **Done → Line**
Select line about which to mirror: pick at **P3**
Select **Copy → Done**

The new profile becomes as shown in Figure 6.48.

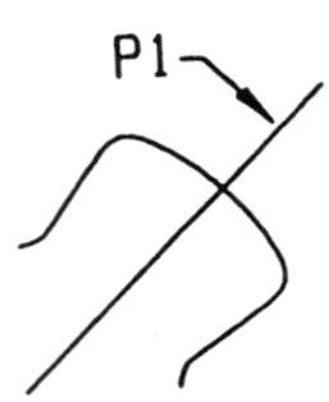

Figure 6.48

Step 7. Delete the 45° construction line using the pick point in Figure 6.48.

Select **MAIN MENU → Delete**
Select an entity or: pick at **P1**

The profile should resemble Figure 6.49.

Figure 6.49

Step 8. Mirror the profile twice.

Select **MAIN MENU → Xform → Mirror → All → Entities → Done → Y axis → Copy → Done →All → Entities → Done → X axis→Copy → Done**

The complete profile should look like Figure 6.50.

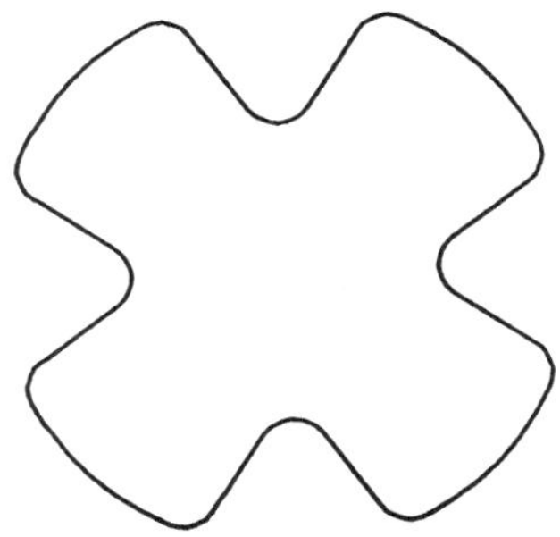

Figure 6.50

Step 9. Create the remaining seven circles.

Select **MAIN MENU → Create → Arc → Circ pt + dia**
Enter the center point: **0,0** ←
Enter the diameter: **5.5** ←
Enter the center point: **0,0** ←
Enter the diameter: **1.25** ←
Enter the center point: **0,0** ←
Enter the diameter: **0.85** ←
Enter the center point: **1.5,0** ←
Enter the diameter: **0.2** ←
Enter the center point: **0,1.5** ←
Enter the diameter: **0.2** ←
Enter the center point: **-1.5,0** ←
Enter the diameter: **0.2** ←
Enter the center point: **0,-1.5** ←
Enter the diameter: **0.2** ←

The seven circles are added as in Figure 6.51.

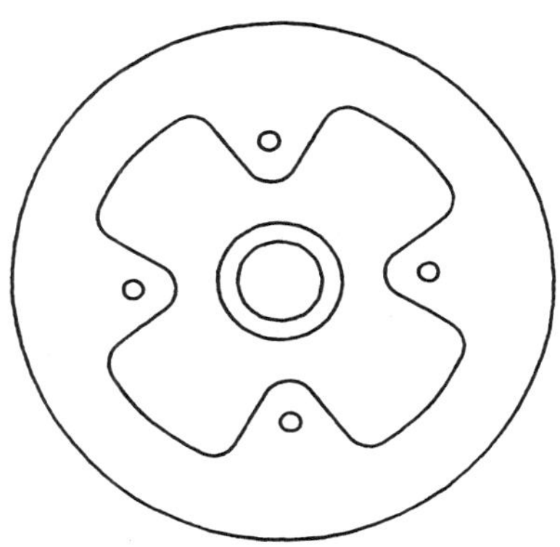

Figure 6.51

Step 10. Save to a file.

Select **MAIN MENU → File → Save**

Enter file name: **pocket2**

6 Rotate Function

The rotate function moves or copies existing entities by rotating about the origin or any given point. It is best suited to generating geometries for identical patterns or features that are symmetrical about a point.

Procedure: (Figure 6.52)

1. Entity selection option: pick at **P1**
2. Entity selection option: select **Done**
3. Rotate about: select **Point**

Origin - system origin or Construction origin. Point - for a specific point with a <position options>.

4. Enter the point to rotate about: Pick at **P2**
5. Select **Rotation angle** option in the dialogue box = **90** ←
   (Make sure the Number of steps =1.)
6. Select **Copy** → **Done**

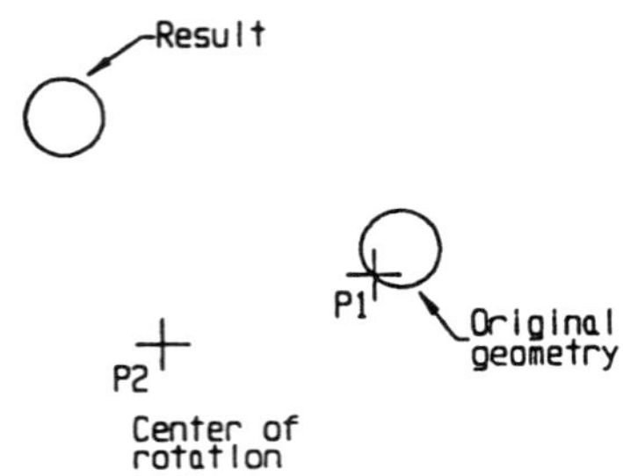

Figure 6.52: Rotating an entity about an existing point for 90-degree

Project 6. Rotating

Create the geometry as shown in Figure 6.53a. Save the file as **mirror1**. This geometry file is used in project 2 of chapter 8 to generate the toolpaths to cut the four pockets shown in Figure 6.53b.

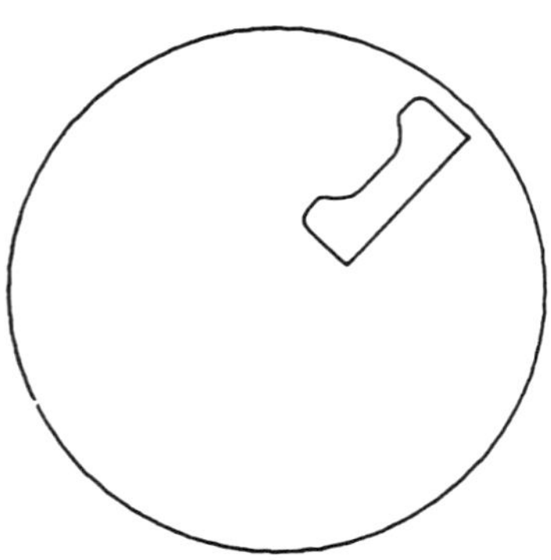

Figure 6.53a

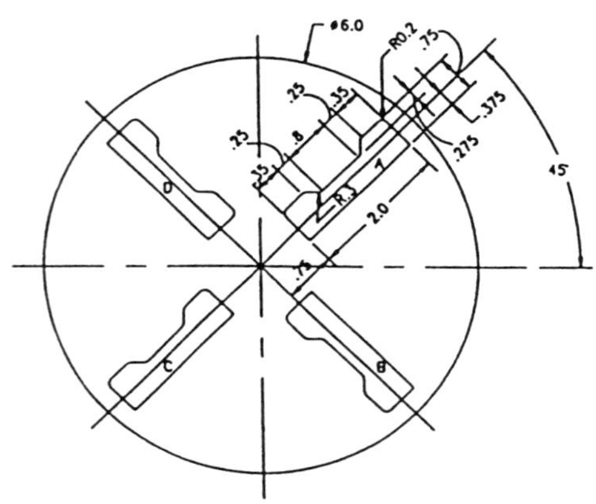

Figure 6.53b

Mastercam 7,
Scholar's International Publishing Corp., 1998

⌛**Tips** 1. Create the entities of the pocket profile in the +X direction. Then rotate them 45° in the counterclockwise direction.
2. Use the Multi line command to create the basic pocket profile consisting of eight lines. Their end coordinates are illustrated in Figure 6.54 on the next page.

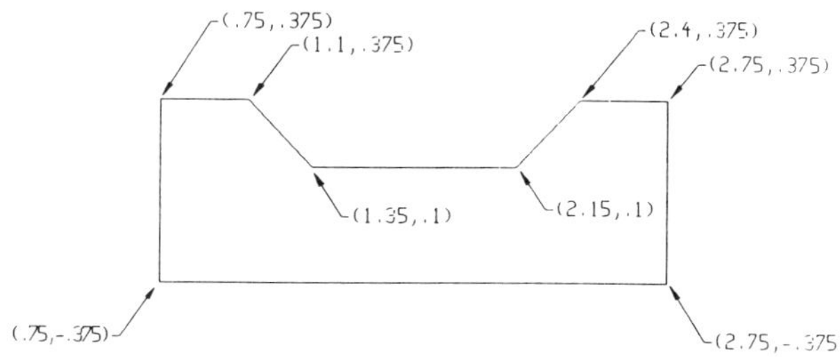

Figure 6.54

Step 1. Create eight lines

Select **MAIN MENU → Create → Line → Multi**
Specify endpoint 1: Enter **.75,-.375** ←
Specify endpoint 2: Enter **2.75,-.375** ←
Specify endpoint 3: Enter **2.75,.375** ←
Specify endpoint 4: Enter **2.4,.375** ←
Specify endpoint 5: Enter **2.15,.1** ←
Specify endpoint 6: Enter **1.35,.1** ←
Specify endpoint 7: Enter **1.1,.375** ←
Specify endpoint 8: Enter **.75,.375** ←
Specify endpoint 9: Enter **.75,-.375** ←

The basic pocket profile appears as Figure 6.55.

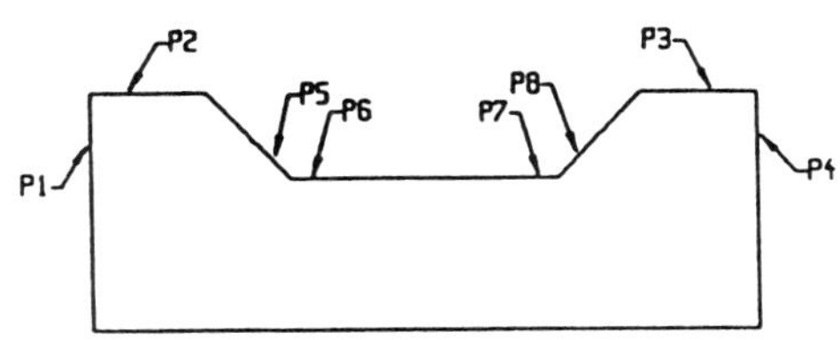

Figure 6.55

Step 2. Create four fillets using the pick points in Figure 6.55.

Select **MAIN MENU → Create → Fillet → Radius**
Enter the fillet radius: **0.15** ←

Note: Make sure the other two options are correct. The fillet angle is less than 180; trim to fillet.

Select an entity: Pick at **P1**
Select another entity: Pick at **P2**
Select an entity: Pick at **P3**
Select another entity: Pick at **P4**
Select **Radius**
Enter the fillet radius: **0.3** ←
Select an entity: Pick at **P5**
Select another entity: Pick at **P6**
Select an entity: Pick at **P7**

Select another entity: Pick at **P8**
The four fillets are added to the drawing as shown in Figure 6.56 below.

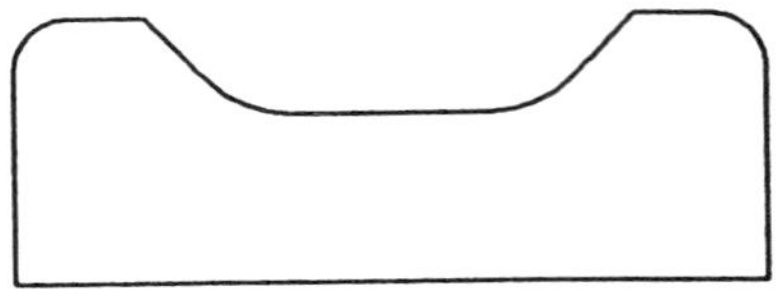

Figure 6.56

Step 3. Rotate the geometry for 45° in counterclockwise direction about the origin.

Select **MAIN MENU → Xform → Rotate → All → Entities → Done → Origin**
Select Rotation angle option in the dialog box: **45 ←**
(Make sure the Number of steps = 1)
Select **Move →Done**

The rotated geometry entities are shown in Figure 6.57.

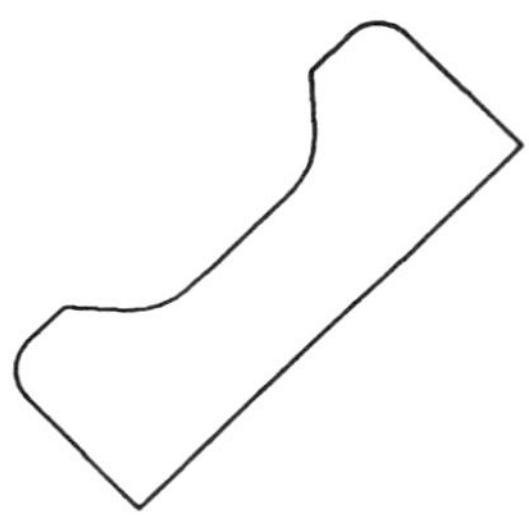

Figure 6.57

Step 4. Create an outside circle.

Select **MAIN MENU → Create → Arc → Circ pt+dia**
Enter the center point: **0,0 ←**
Enter the diameter: **6 ←**

The complete drawing should resemble Figure 6.58.

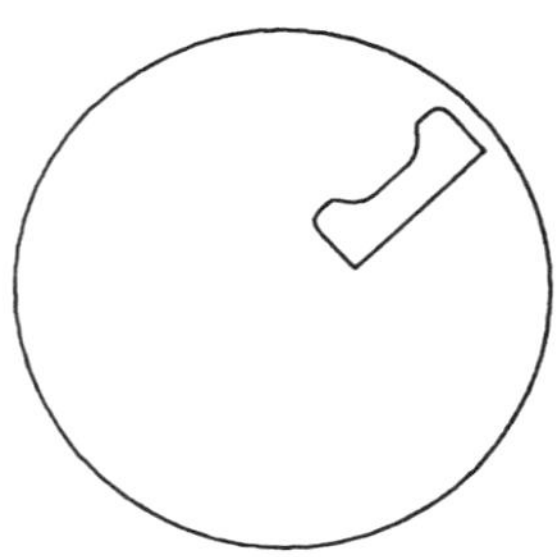

Figure 6.58

Step 5. Save to a file.

Select **MAIN MENU → File → Save**
Enter file name: **mirror1**

Project 7. Rotating

Use the basic create commands and the rotate function to create a geometry as shown in Figure 6.59a. The file is saved as **trans1**. This file is used in project 5 of chapter 8 to generate a set of toolpaths for producing three pockets as shown in figure 6.59b.

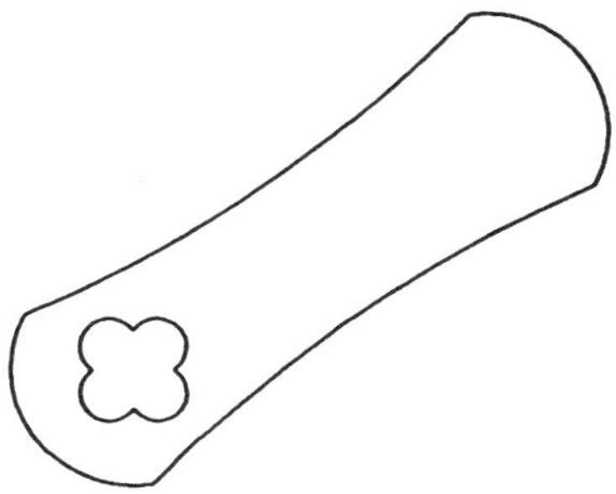

Figure 6.59a

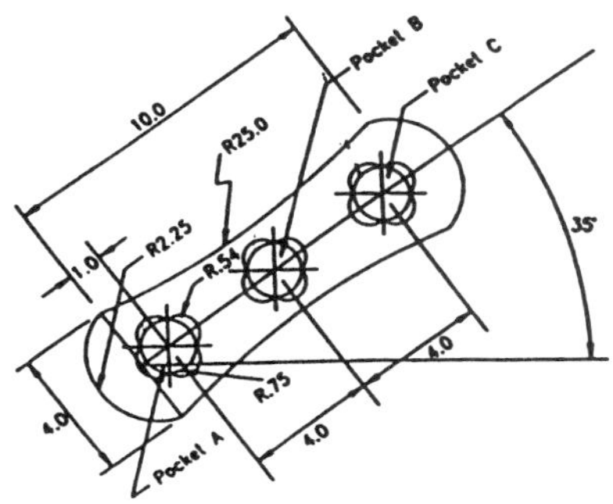

Figure 6.59b

> **Tips** 1. Create the outer curved profile in the X direction. This profile is then rotated 35° in the counterclockwise direction to its desired location.
> 2. Create a construction circle and two construction lines to create an arc. This arc is then rotated by 90° to three other locations.

Step 1. Create a construction rectangle.

Select **MAIN MENU → Create → Rectangle → 2 points**
Enter the lower left corner: **0,-2** ←
Enter the upper right corner: **10,2** ←

Note: Press Alt-F1 (Fit) to see the whole geometry

The rectangle should appear as Figure 6.60.

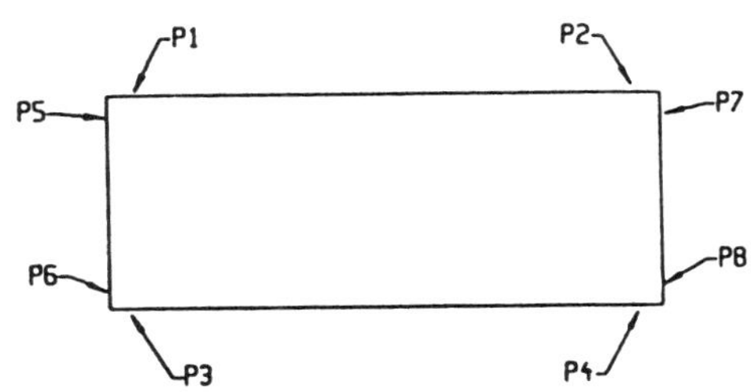

Figure 6.60

Step 2. Create four arcs using the pick points in Figure 6.60.

Select **MAIN MENU → Create → Arc → Endpoints → Endpoint**
Enter the first point: Pick at **P1**
Enter the second point: Pick at **P2**
Enter the radius: **25** ←
Select an arc: Pick at the correct arc *Note:* there are four choices

Step 2, continued.

Enter the first point: Pick at **P3**
Enter the second point: Pick at **P4**
Enter the radius: **25** ←
Select an arc: Pick at the correct arc
Enter the first point: Pick at **P5**
Enter the second point: Pick at **P6**
Enter the radius: **2.25** ←
Select an arc: Pick at the correct arc
Enter the first point: Pick at **P7**
Enter the second point: Pick at **P8**
Enter the radius: **2.25** ←
Select an arc: Pick at the correct arc

The four arcs are added as in Figure 6.61.

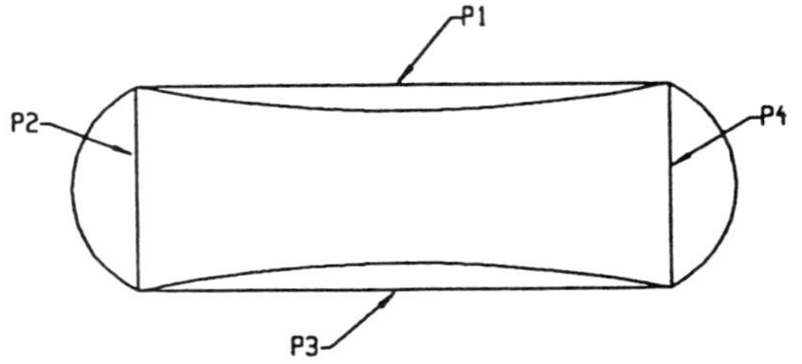

Figure 6.61

Step 3. Delete the rectangle using the pick points in Figure 6.61.

Select **MAIN MENU** → **Delete**
Select an entity or: pick at **P1**
Select an entity or: pick at **P2**
Select an entity or: pick at **P3**
Select an entity or: pick at **P4**

The outer profile should look like Figure 6.62.

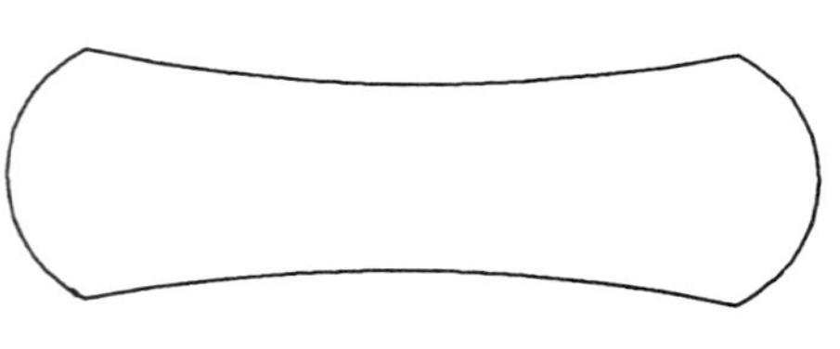

Figure 6.62

Step 4. Create a construction circle.

Select **MAIN MENU** → **Create** → **Arc** → **circ pt +rad**
Enter the center point: **1,0** ←
Enter the radius: **.75** ←

The circle is added as in Figure 6.63.

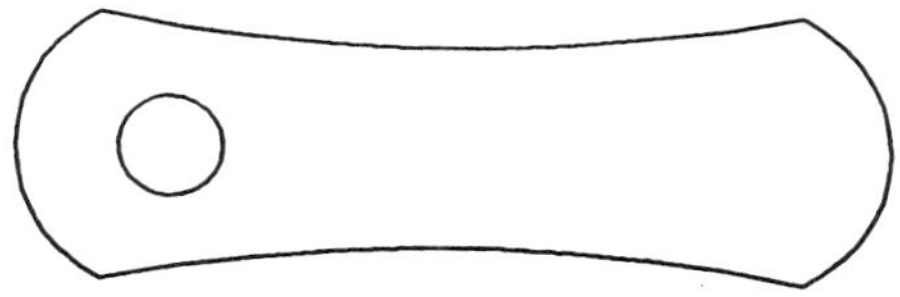

Figure 6.63

Step 5. Rotate all entities for 35° in the counterclockwise direction.

Select **MAIN MENU → Xform → Rotate → All → Entities → Done → Point**
Enter the point to rotate about: **1,0 ←**
Select the Rotation angle option in the dialog box= **35 ←**
(Make sure the Number of steps = 1)
Select **Move →Done**

The rotated geometry becomes Figure 6.64.

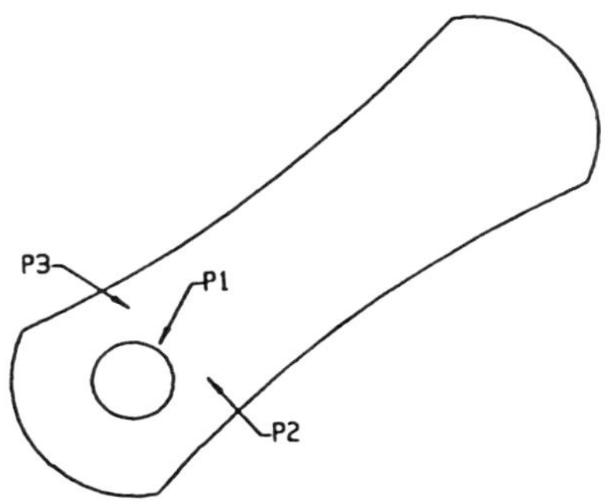

Figure 6.64

Step 6. Create two construction lines. Use the pick points in Figure 6.64.

Select **MAIN MENU → Create → Line → Horizontal → Center**
Specify the first endpoint: pick at **P1**

Specify the second endpoint: pick at **P2**
Enter the Y coordinate: 0 ←
Select **BACKUP → Vertical → Center**
Specify the first endpoint: Pick at **P1**
Specify the second endpoint: Pick at **P3**
Enter the X coordinate: 1 ←

The two lines are added as in Figure 6.65.

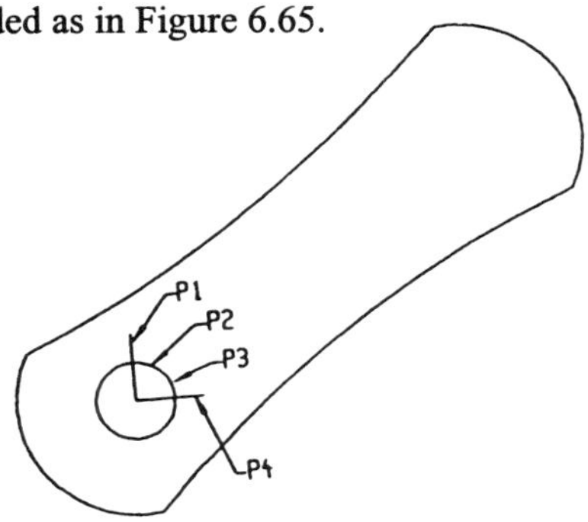

Figure 6.65

Step 7. Create an arc using the pick points in Figure 6.65 on the previous page.

Select **MAIN MENU → Create → Arc → Endpoints → Intersec**
Enter the first point: pick at **P1**
Enter the first point: pick at **P2**
Select **Intersec**
Enter the second point: pick at **P3**
Enter the second point: pick at **P4**
Enter the radius: **.54** ←
Select an arc: Pick at the outside one on the upper-right corner
Note: there are four choices

The arc is added as in Figure 6.66.

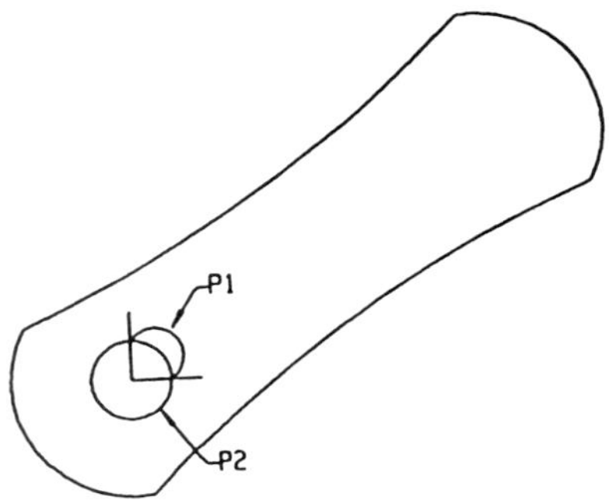

Figure 6.66

Step 8. Rotate the arc by 90° to other three locations.

Use the pick points in Figure 6.66.
Select **MAIN MENU → Xform → Rotate**
Pick at **P1** to select the arc to be rotated
Select **Done → Point → Center**
Pick at **P2**
Select Rotation angle option in the dialog box = **90** ←
Select the Number of steps option in the dialog box = **3** ←
Select **Copy → Done**

Three arcs are added as shown in Figure 6.67.

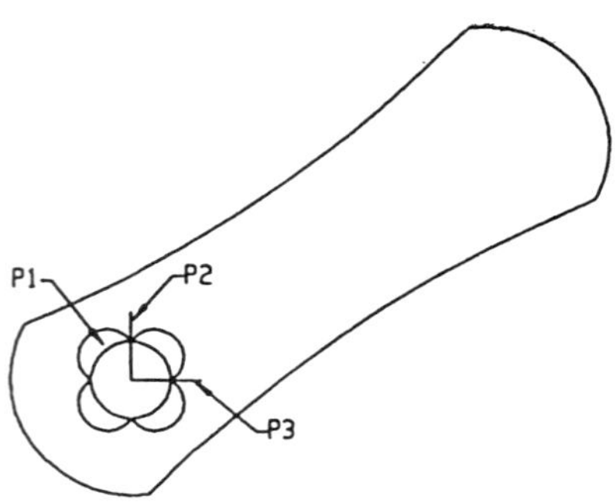

Figure 6.67

Step 9. Delete a construction circle and two construction lines. Use the pick points in Figure 6.67.

Select **MAIN MENU → Delete**
Select an entity or: pick at **P1**
Select an entity or: pick at **P2**

Select an entity or: pick at **P3**
The final drawing should look like Figure 6.68.

Figure 6.68

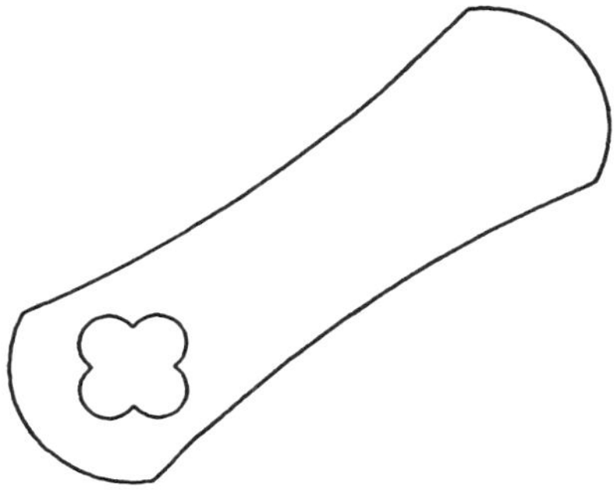

Step 10. Save to a file.

Select **MAIN MENU** → **File** → **Save**
Enter file name: **trans1**

Project 8. Rotating

Create 24 circles and 24 points at their centers (Figure 6.69). Three construction circles are added to show their positions. Save the file as **drill1**. This file will be used to generate the drilling toolpaths in project 7 of chapter 7.

Figure 6.69

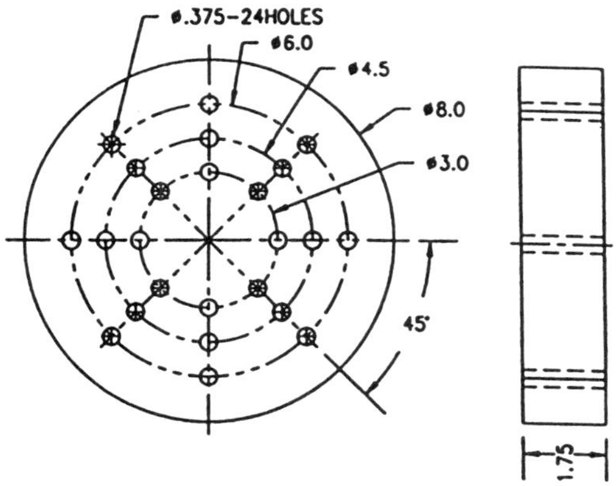

Tips 1. Create 3 circles and three points at their centers in the X axis.

2. Rotate these 3 circles and 3 points by 45° to the other 7 locations.

3. Construct three construction circles. Set the line type to hidden.

Step 1. Create three circles.

Select **MAIN MENU** → **Create** → **Arc** → **Circ pt+dia**
Enter the center point: **1.5,0** ←
Enter the diameter: **0.375** ←
Enter the center point: **2.25,0** ←
Enter the diameter: **0.375** ←
Enter the center point: **3,0** ←
Enter the diameter: **0.375** ←

Three arcs appear as in figure 6.70.

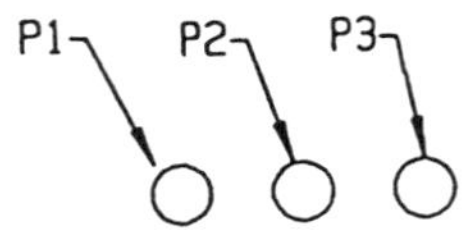

Figure 6.70

Step 2. Create points at the center of the circles using the pick points in Figure 6.70.

Select **MAIN MENU → Create → Point → Position → Center**
Define the three points: Pick at **P1**
Select Center again, then pick at **P2**
Select Center again, then pick at **P3**

Three points are added as in Figure 6.71.

Figure 6.71

Step 3. Rotate these six entities 45° about the origin, seven times.

Select **MAIN MENU → Xform → Rotate → All → Entities → Done → Origin**
In the pop-up dialog box:

Number of steps: **7**
Rotation angle: **45**

Select **Copy → Done**

Twenty-four circles are created as shown in Figure 6.72.

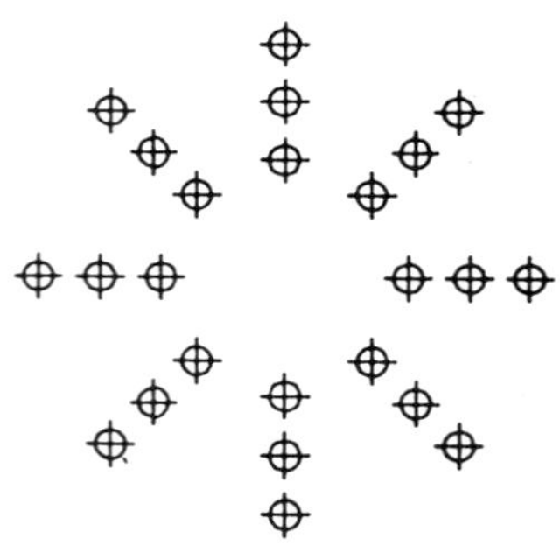
Figure 6.72

Step 4. Create three construction circles.

Double-click to select **-Style/Width-** from the left Menu
Select the line style parameter to **hidden**
Select **OK** to complete the setting
Select **MAIN MENU →Create → Arc → Circ pt +dia**
Enter the center point: **0,0** ←
Enter the diameter: **3** ←
Enter the center point: **0,0** ←
Enter the diameter: **4.5** ←
Enter the center point: **0,0** ←

Enter the diameter: **6.0** ←
The final drawing should resemble Figure 6.73.

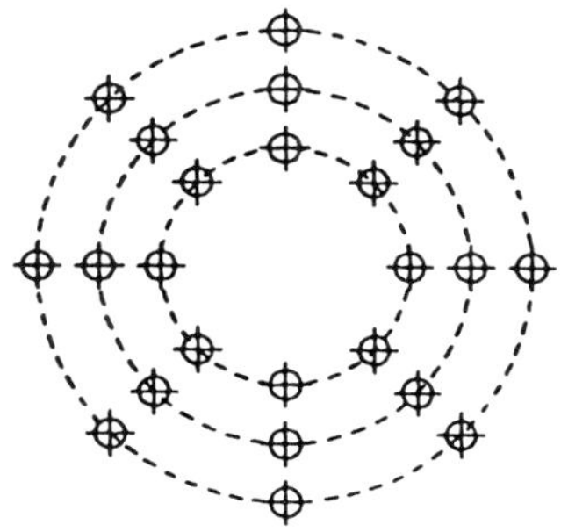

Figure 6.73

Step 5. Save to a file.

Select **MAIN MENU → File → Save**
Enter file name: **drill1**

Scale Function

The scale function increases or decreases the sizes of geometry entities by a specified scale factor. Two important factors to be determined in scaling are the scaling center and the scaling factor. The scaling center is the point from which the scaling of the geometric entity starts. The scaling factor determines the size.

Scaling factor > 1	enlarges the entity size
Scaling factor = 1	sizes do not change
Scaling factor < 1	reduces the entity size

Procedure: (Figure 6.74)

1. Entity selection option (see section 6.3): Pick at **P1**
2. Entity selection option: Select **Done**
3. Scale about: Select **Point**

   Origin - system origin or Construction origin.
   Point - for a specific point with a <position options>.

4. Enter the point for scaling: Pick at **P2**
5. Adjust the parameters in the pop-up dialog box:

   Number of steps = 1
   Scale factor = 2.0

6. Select **Copy → Done**

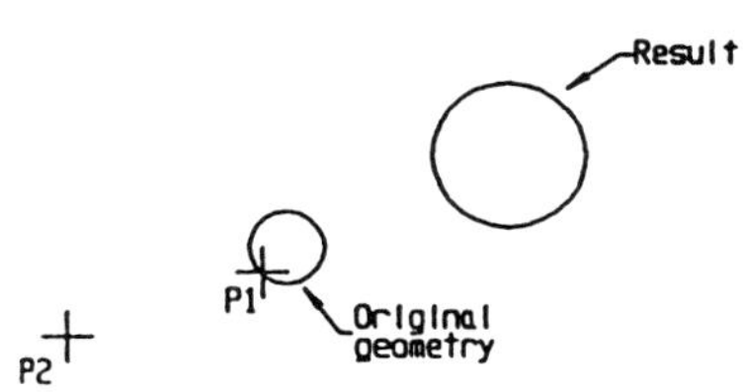

Figure 6.70: Scaling an entity about an existing point for a factor of 2

ScaleXYZ Function

The scaleXYZ is the other scale function and is similar to the Scale discussed in section 6.3.3. It gives the user an opportunity to specify the x, y and z scale factors individually. By adjusting the scale factors properly, it is possible to transform a circle into an ellipse.

Procedure: (Figure 6.75)

1. Select entities to scale <entity selection options>: Pick at **P1**
2. Select **Done → Point → Center**
3. Enter the point to scale about: Pick at **P1**
4. In the dialog box:

Number of steps: **1**
X scale factor: **0.5**
Y scale factor: **2.0**
Z scale factor: **1.0**

5. Select **Move → Done**
6. Press <Enter> to continue: ←

Note: The original circle was converted to a NURBS curve.

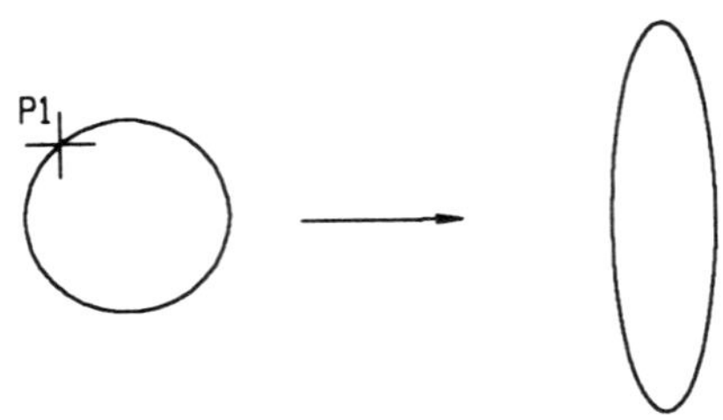

Figure 6.75

Translate Function

The translate function moves or copies the selected geometric entities to new locations.

Procedure: (Figure 6.76 on the next page)

1. Entity selection option (see section 6.3): Pick at **P1**
2. Entity selection option: Select **Done**
3. Translate: Refer to Figure 6.71 to select **an appropriate method**

Rectang -	enters a rectangular (Cartesian) coordinate vector for the X and Y translation.
Polar -	enters a polar coordinate vector for the translation.
Between pts -	selects the beginning and ending points for the translation.
btween Vws -	translates the entities between viewport.

For Rectang

4. Enter the translation vector: **1,0.5** ←

For Polar

4a. Enter the translation distance: **1.5** ←
4b. Enter the translation angle: **30** ←

For Btween pts

4a. Enter the point to translate from <position option>: Pick at **P2**

4b. Enter the point to translate to <position option>: Pick at **P3**

5. In the pop-up dialog box:

Number of steps = **1** Select **Copy** →**Done**

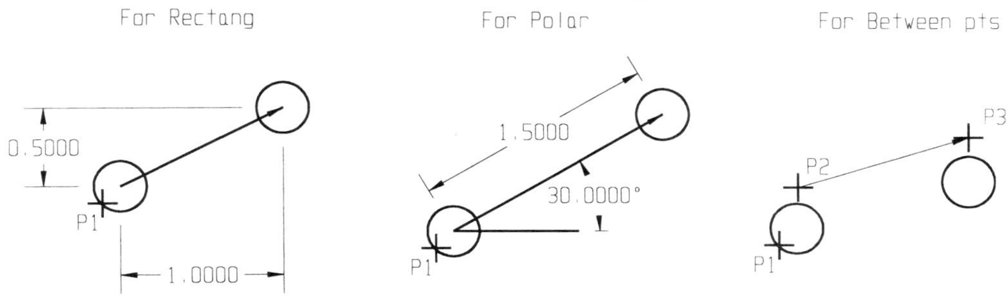

Figure 6.76: Translating using different methods

Project 9. Translating

Copy the inside pocket contour of the drawing shown in Figure 6.77a to two locations by using the **Translate →** **Rectang** commands. The file for Figure 6.77a is **array1** which is cre-
ated in project 1 of this chapter. The complete part geometry is shown in Figure 6.77b.

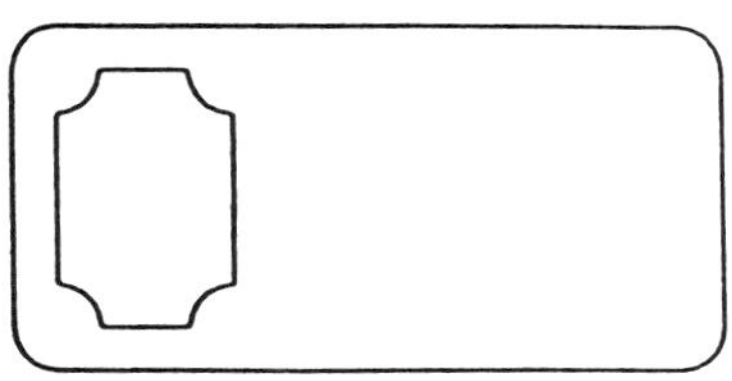

Figure 6.77a

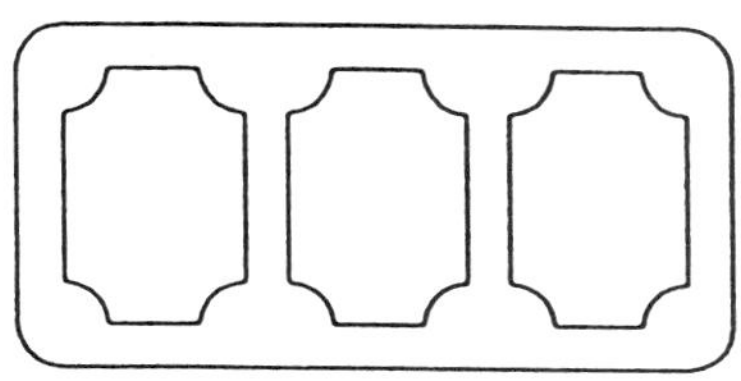

Figure 6.77b

Tips 1. Use the file array1 which is created in project 1 of this chapter.

2. Use Xform → Translate → Rectang commands to copy the pocket profile.

3. Set the number of steps to 2.

Step 1. Load the geometry file array1.

Select **MAIN MENU →** **File → Get**

Enter file name: **array1**

Select **Yes** to save the current part

The part geometry should appear as Figure 6.78 on the next page.

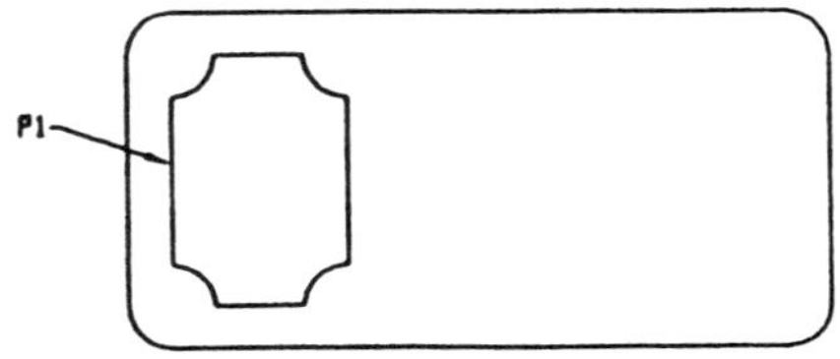

Figure 6.78

Step 2. Initiate the Translate command.

Select **MAIN MENU → Xform →Translate → Chain**

Step 3. Define the contour using the pick point in Figure 6.78.

Pick at **P1**
Select **Done**
Select → Done (again)

Step 4. Define Translate parameters.

Select **Rectang**
Enter the translation vector: **X3.75 ←**
In the pop-up dialog box:

Set the Number of steps = **2**
Select **Copy →Done**

The two translated profiles are shown in Figure 6.79.

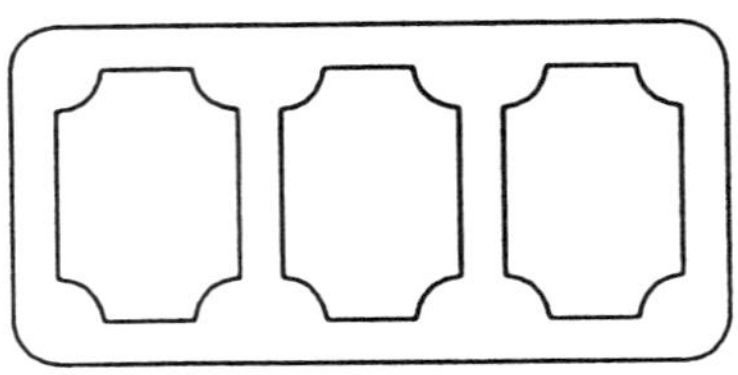

Figure 6.79

Offset Function

The offset function moves or copies a line, arc, spline, or curve away from itself in a perpendicular direction with an offset distance to the selected entity. *Note:* this function only works for a single entity.

Procedure: (Figure 6.80)
In the pop-up dialog box:

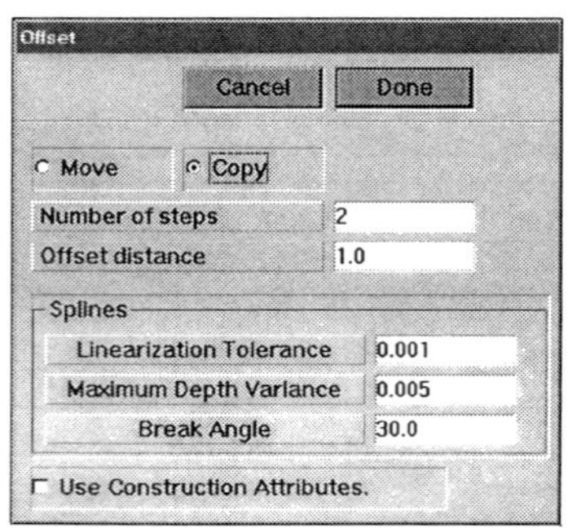

2. Select **Done**
3. Select the line, arc, spline, or curve to offset: Pick at **P1**
4. Indicate the offset direction: Pick at **P2**

Note: In general, there are two perpendicular directions. Indicate the appropriate direction using the mouse.

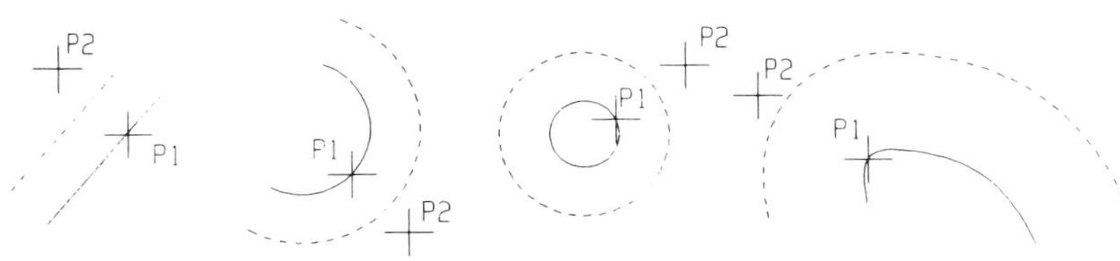

Figure 6.80

Ofs ctour Function

This option allows the user to offset several connected lines or arcs by chaining the entities. The process is similar to the toolpath contour function. This function will offset only lines and arcs.

Procedure: (Figure 6.81)
1. Chaining method: Select **Chain**
2. Select the first entity in the contour: Pick at **P1**
3. Select → **Done**
4. In the dialog box:

Offset distance: **0.5** Corners: **None** Side: **Right** Select **Copy** →**Done**

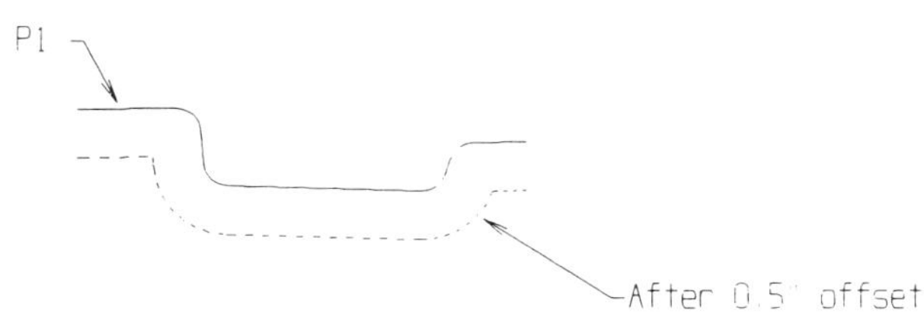

Figure 6.81

Group Parameter

Group selects and defines a collection of entities to be used in Xform. The last Group is saved in the database and can be used in other Xform functions such as Mirror, Rotate, Scale, ScaleXyz and Translate. Note that Offset can not take advantage of Group since it only works with a single entity.

When **Group** is selected, these Group Entity Selection Options appear on the Main Menu Area:	
New -	clears the existing groups.
Entity -	adds or deletes a single entity to or from the database.
Chain -	adds or deletes a group of entities to or from the database.
Only -	adds or deletes a specific type of entities to or from the database.
All -	adds or deletes all entities of a specific type to or from the database.
Results -	shows the current selected group in Magenta.
Window -	selects all the entities that are inside or outside the window to or from thedatabase.
Polygon-	selects all the entities defined by a polygon-shaped window.
Area-	not yet available.
UnGroup (Y/N) -	toggles the system to group (add) or ungroup (delete) the selected entities for previous operations.

You can combine different methods to select the entities for the group, then select **Backup** to exit and save the database.

6.4 Exercises

1. What does the delete function do?
2. What does the undelete function do?
3. What does the trim function do?
4. Describe the difference between the following three trim commands:
   1 entity
   2 entities
   3 entities
5. Describe what the break function does?
6. Describe what the join function does?
7. List the first six editing functions under the Xform command.
8. List the five transformation parameters and describe what they are.
9. When should you use the mirror function?
10. When should you use rotate function?

11. Explain how to use the scale function to increase or decrease the size of geometry entities.

12. When should you use the translate function.

13. When should you use the offset function.

14. Create the geometry shown in Figure 6.82. Save the file as **contour5**. This file is used in problem 63 of chapter 7.

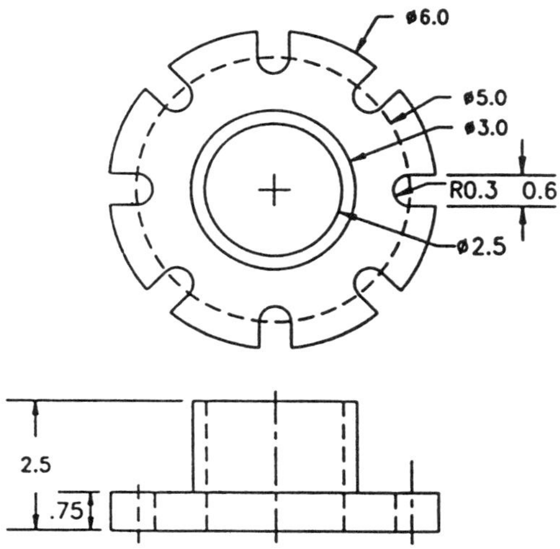

Figure 6.82

15. Create the geometry shown in Figure 6.83 and save the file as **contour6**. This file is used to generate the toolpath in problem 64 of chapter 7.

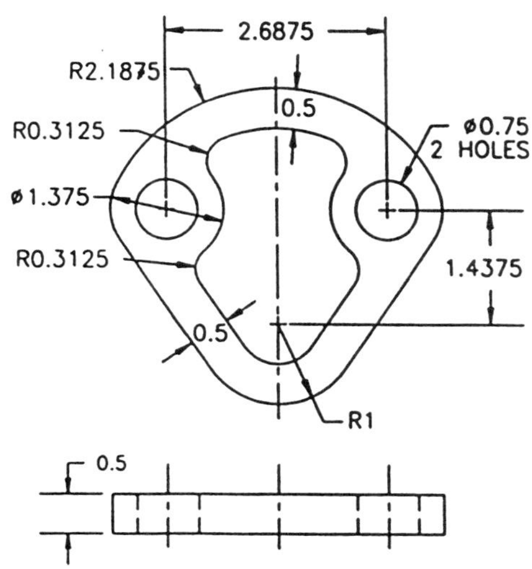

Figure 6.83

16. Create the part geometry as shown in Figure 6.84. Save the file as **contour7**. This part geometry is used to generate the toolpath for problem 65 in chapter 7.

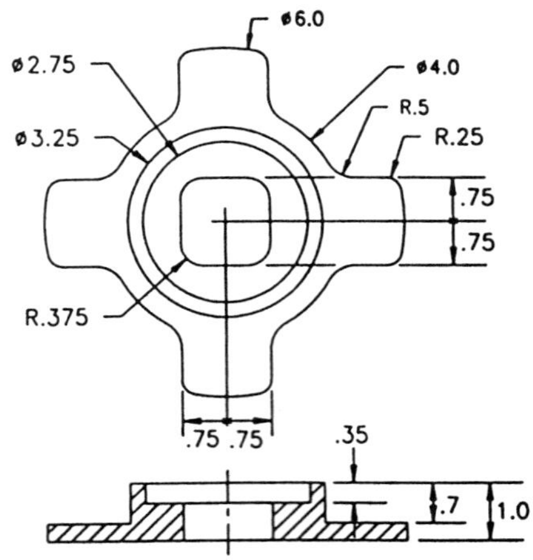

Figure 6.84

17. Create the part geometry for Figure 6.85. Save the geometry file as **pocket3**. This geometry file is used to generate the pocketing toolpath for problem 68 in chapter 7.

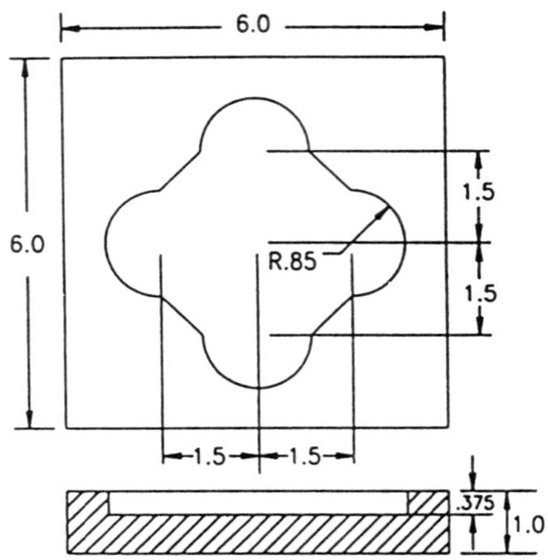

Figure 6.85

18. Create the geometry shown in Figure 6.86. Save the geometry as **pocket4**. This file is used to generate the pocketing toolpaths in problem 69 of chapter 7.

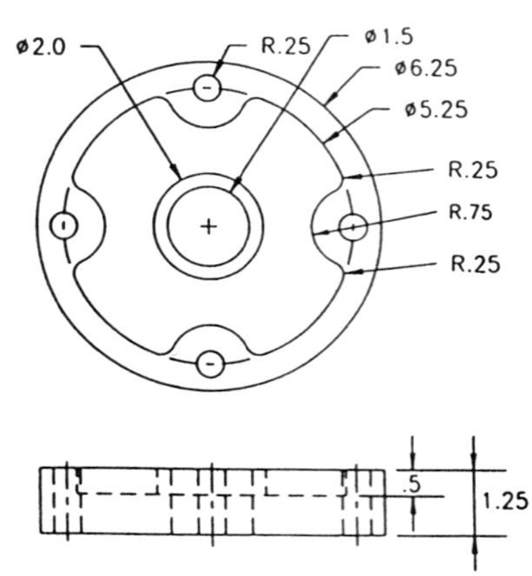

Figure 6.86

19. Create the part geometry as shown in Figure 6.87 and save the file as **pocket5**. This geometry will be used to generate the toolpath for pocketing with an island in problem 70 of chapter 7.

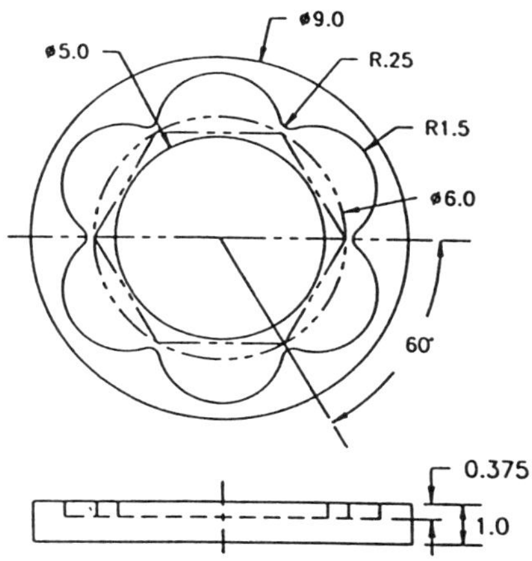

Figure 6.87

20. Create the part geometry shown in Figure 6.89. Save the file as **comb1**. This geometry will be used to generate the toolpaths for contouring, pocketing, and drilling in problem 72 of chapter 7.

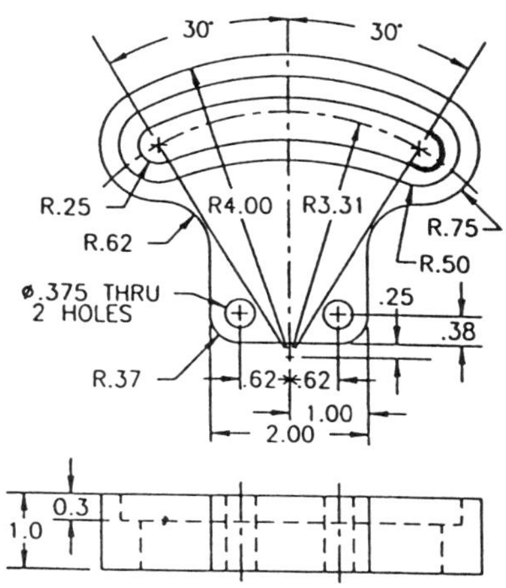

Figure 6.88

21. Create the part geometry shown in Figure 6.89 and save the file as **comb3**. The file is used to generate the toolpaths in problem 74 of chapter 7.

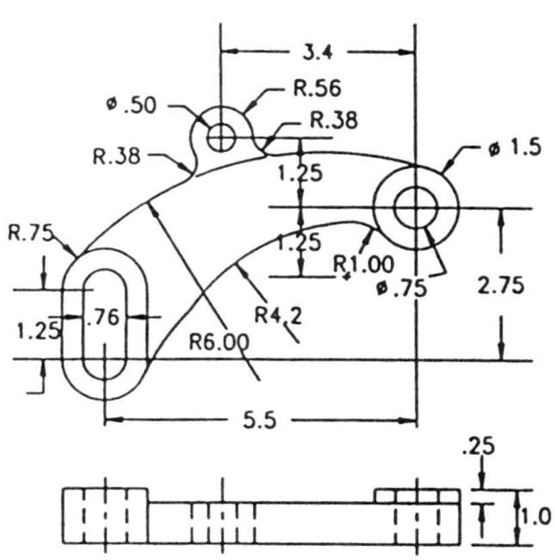

Figure 6.89

22. Create the geometry as shown in Figure 6.90 and save this file as **comb4**. This geometry is used to generate the toolpaths in problem 75 of chapter 7.

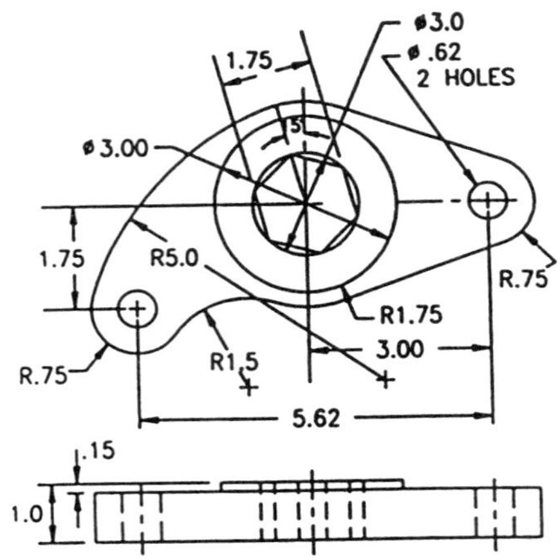

Figure 6.90

23. Create the part geometry shown in Figure 6.91 and save the file as **rotate2**. This geometry is used to generate the toolpaths in problem 16 of chapter 8.

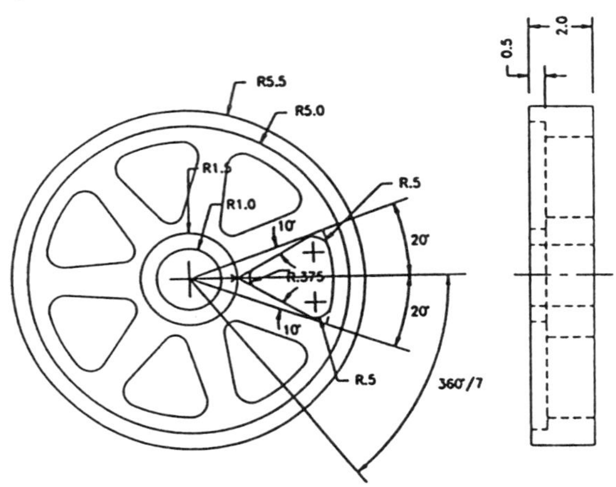

Figure 6.91

24. Create the part geometry shown in Figure 6.92 and save the file as **mirror2**. The file is used to generate a set of toolpaths to machine one part and then copy to machine another part by using the mirror function in problem 17 of chapter 8.

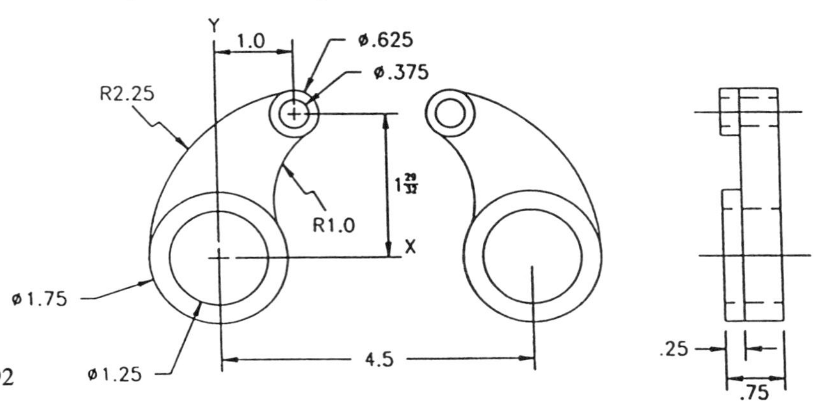

Figure 6.92

Chapter 7
2D Toolpath Generation: From Print to Part

Objectives:

1. Identify five types of 2D toolpath modules and know when to use them.
2. Define common tool parameters used in 2D toolpath modules.
3. Apply five 2D toolpath modules to generate NC programs for producing parts.

7.1 2D Toolpath Modules

Mastercam provides three groups of toolpath modules for generating toolpaths: **2D modules**, **3D modules**, and **multiple-axis modules**. Use 2D modules to generate toolpaths for machining workpieces in a 2D plane, 3D toolpath modules for machining various forms of 3D surfaces, and multiple-axis for machining complex parts. This chapter presents 2D toolpath modules. Mastercam has five 2D toolpath modules: **contour, pocket, drill, circmill**, and **point**. Table 7.1 summaries the features and applications of these 2D toolpath modules.

Table 7.1 Toolpath Module Features

Module	Description	Application	Illustration
Contour	Generate the toolpaths along a series of geometric entities chained as a contour. Required geometry: lines, arcs, or splines.	Cutting external and internal part profiles.	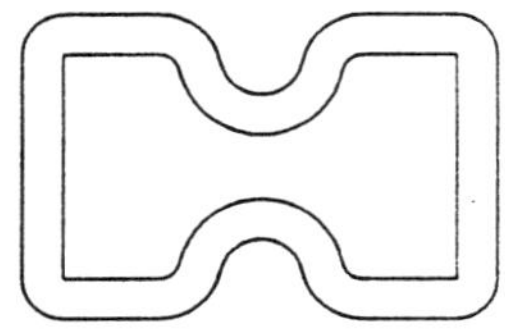
Pocket	Generate the toolpaths to remove the material by a closed contour. Required geometry: closed boundary	Cutting pockets Facing large flat Surfaces.	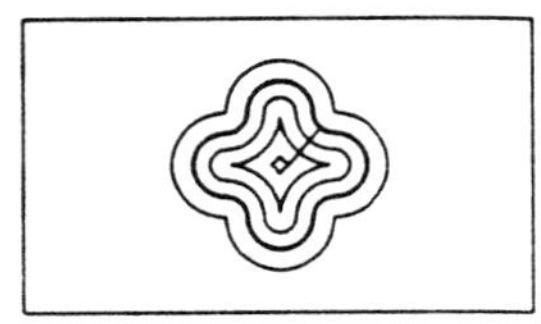
Drill	Generate the toolpaths to perform drilling, boring, or tapping holes. Required geometry: points	Drilling Boring Tapping	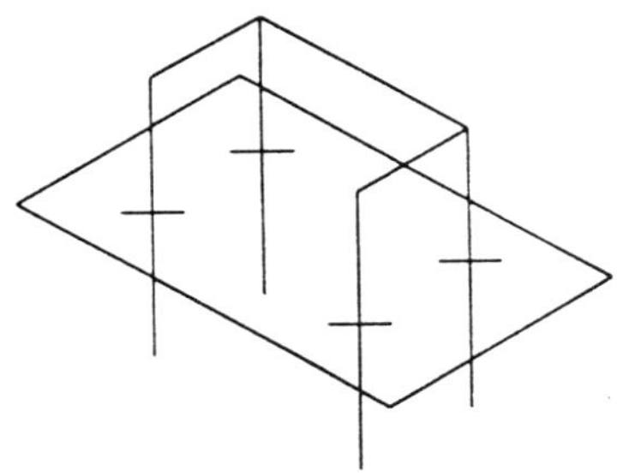
Circmill	Generate the toolpaths to cut a complete circle with an entry arc, two 180-degrees arcs, and an exit arc.	Cut the internal shape of a circle.	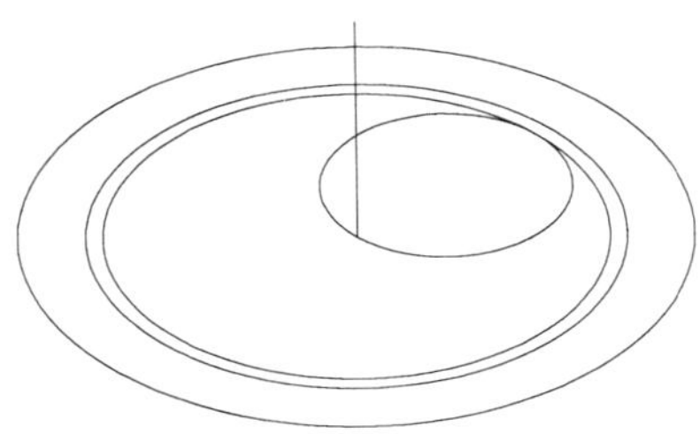
NC Point	Generate a toolpath by selecting points or entities.	Move the cutter to any specified locations.	

7.2 Tool Definition

Mastercam uses various types of parameters to define the information required to generate toolpaths. These parameters can be classified into three groups: **tool definition, tool parameters** and **module specific parameters**. Tool definition allows the user to define a new tool, select an existing tool from the tool library, or edit an existing tool. Tool parameters are also referred to as common parameters because they are commonly used in all toolpath modules, while module specific parameters are unique to the particular module and are not applicable to any other modules. This section focuses on how to define a new tool, select a tool from tool library, and edit an existing tool.

Tools Manager

Mastercam uses Tools Manager dialog box to define, select, or edit a tool. The empty Tools Manager dialog box appears below.

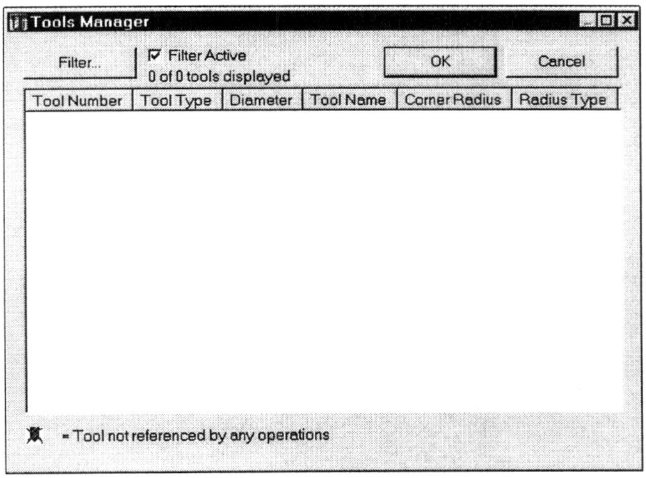

- **Select Toolpaths → Tools to open the Tools Manager dialog box.**

- Click the right mouse button to bring up the tools manager option as below.
  The top three options will be dimmed out if no existing tools in the active file.

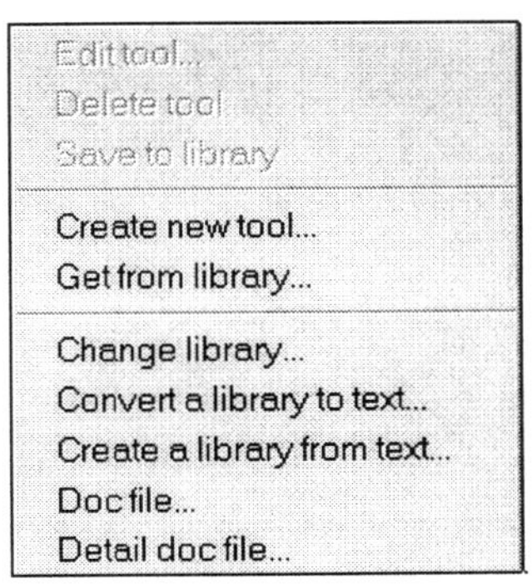

The tools manager options are described below:

Edit tool:	edit an existing tool used in the project.
Delete tool:	delete an existing tool used in the project.
Save to library:	save the tool you create or modify to the tool library.
Create new tool:	define a new tool.
Get from library:	retrieve an existing tool from the tool library.
Change library:	select a new tool library.
Convert a library to text:	export the current tool library from a TL7 file to a TXT file.
Create a library from text:	import a new tool library from a TXT file to a TL7 file.
Doc file:	create a document listing all tools in the current job or the current tool library.
Detail doc file:	create a document listing detail information of all tools in the current job or the current tool library.

Creating A New Tool

Creating a new tool involves using three sets of dialog box: **tool type, tool/holder definition**, and **tool parameters**. Their dialog boxes are shown below.

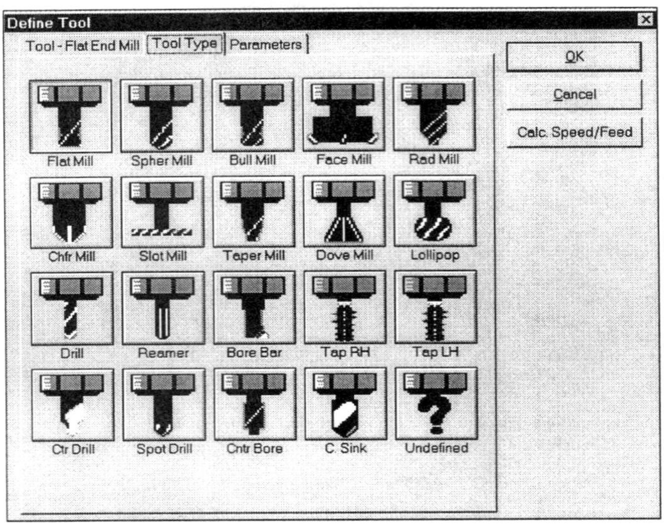

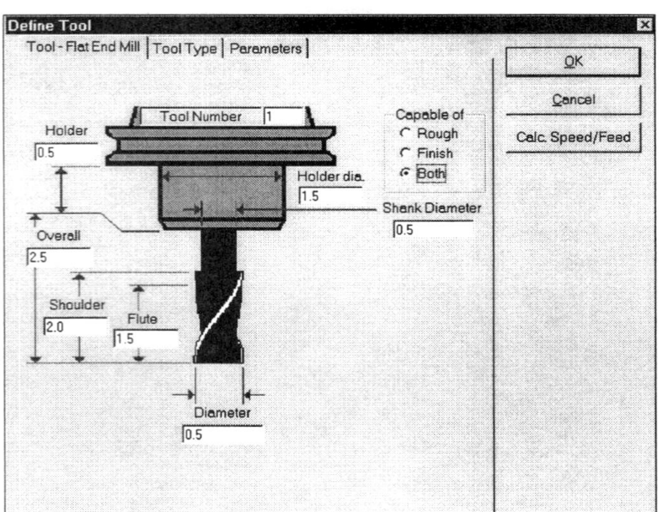

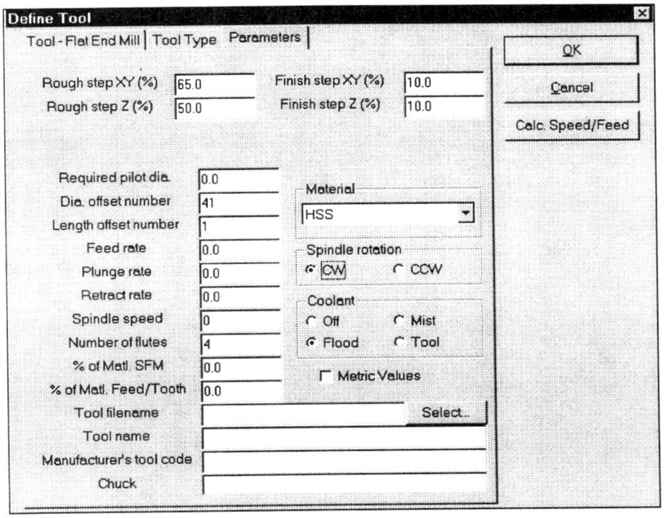

Tool type

Click the "Tool Type" tag in the Define Tool menu to open the tool type dialog box. Mastercam provides twenty tool types to choose from. The "Tool Type" selection menu appears.

Tool/Holder definition

Click "Tool-tool type" tag on the top of the Define Tool menu to open the Tool/Holder dialog box. Different tool/holder dialog boxes may appear for different tool types. Three sets of data are defined in this dialog box: **tool size, holder size**, and **machining type**. We use a spherical end mill as an example. The tool/holder dialog box of a spherical end mill should appear as below.

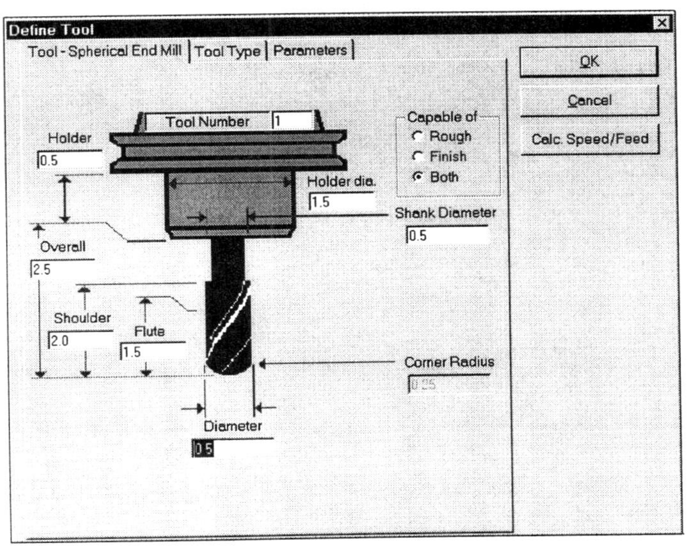

Tool size parameters

Mastercam uses the following parameters to fully define a tool:

Diameter:	specify the cutter diameter.
Corner radius:	specify the corner radius of the tool.
Shank diameter:	specify the shank diameter of the tool.
Flute:	specify the flute length (effective length) of the tool.
Shoulder:	specify the length from the tip to the shoulder of the tool.
Overall:	specify the length from the tip of the tool to the end face of the holder.

Holder size parameters

Mastercam uses the following parameters to define a holder:

Holder diameter:	specify the diameter of the holder.
Holder:	specify the length measured from the flange face to the holder end face.
Tool number:	specify the tool number used to identify this tool.

Machining type

In some tool types Mastercam provides a "Capable of" parameter to indicate the machining type a particular tool is capable of performing. It has the following three options:

Rough:	the tool is capable of roughing cut only.
Finish:	the tool is capable of finish cut only.
Both:	the tool is capable of both roughing and finishing cuts.

Tool Parameters

Mastercam uses a set of parameters in "Parameters" dialog box to define machining data and other related information for a tool. The "Parameters" dialog box is shown below.

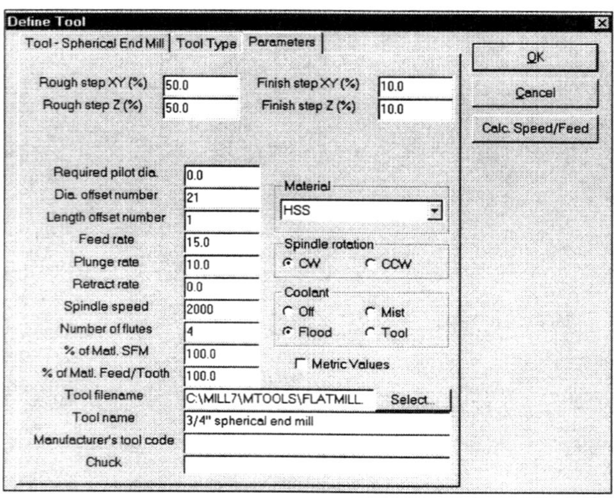

The parameters for defining machining data and tooling information are described below.

Rough step XY (%) This parameter specifies the percentage of tool's diameter engagement with the workpiece in roughing cuts. In other words, it specifies the stepover value of roughing passes. A 1-inch flat end mill with 60% of rough step XY value, for example, will have 0.6" stepover distance for roughing passes.

Finish step XY (%) This parameter specifies the percentage of tool's diameter engagement with the workpiece in finishing cuts. It indicates the stepover value of finishing passes. A 1-inch flat end mill with 10% of finish step XY value, for example, will have 0.1" stepover distance for finishing passes.

Rough step Z (%) This parameter specifies the depth of cut in Z-direction for roughing passes. It is expressed as the percent of tool's diameter. A 1-inch flat end mill with 50% of rough step Z value will have 0.5" depth of cut for roughing passes.

Finish step Z (%) This parameter specifies the depth of cut in Z-direction for finishing passes. It is expressed as the percent of tool's diameter. A 1-inch flat end mill with 10% of finish step Z value will have 0.1" depth of cut for finishing passes.

Required pilot dia. This parameter is used to specify the diameter of pilot hole required for this particular tool. Pilot holes are normally needed for tapping, boring, drilling large holes, or milling a pocket.

Material This parameter is used to select the tool material. It has the following six options:

HSS:	high speed steel tool
Carbide:	carbide tool
C Carbide:	coated carbide tool
Ceramic:	ceramic tool
Borzon:	borzon tool
Unknown:	tool material to be defined

% of Matl. SFM This parameter indicates the default cutting speed in the percentage of suggested surface speed from the database. The surface speed is mainly determined by the tool material and the type of material to be cut.

% of Matl. Feed/Tooth This parameter specifies the default feed rate in the percentage of suggested feed rate from the database. The feed rate is mainly determined by the tool material, type of material to be cut, depth of cut, tool diameter, etc.

Tool filename This parameter selects the tool geometry file to be displayed. Mastercam provides a list of tool geometry files for you to select as below.

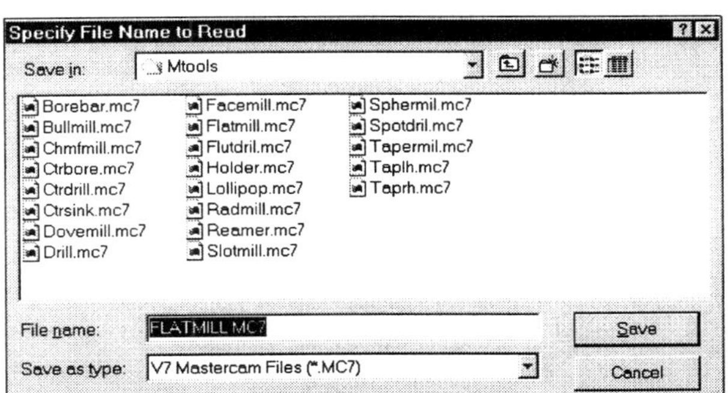

Select the Select button to bring up the "Specify File Name to Read" menu

Tool name This parameter is used to enter a name for the tool. You can enter any descriptive comment for the tool.

Spindle rotation This parameter is used to specify the spindle rotation either in clockwise (CW) direction or counterclockwise (CCW) direction.

Coolant This parameter specifies the coolant control mode to be one the following four modes:

Off:	turn coolant off.
Mist:	turn coolant on in mist mode.
Flood:	turn coolant on in flood mode.
Tool:	turn coolant on through the tool.

Creating a new tool

There are two ways to access the utility for creating a new tool. One way is to use the Tools command under the Toolpaths function. The other way is to access on the fly.

The procedure for creating a new tool using Tools command is:

1. Select Toolpaths → Tools to open the Tools Manager dialog box
2. Click the right mouse button to open the tools manager menu, then select Create new tool
3. Select Tool Type from Define Tool dialog box

The Tool Type dialog box should appear as below.

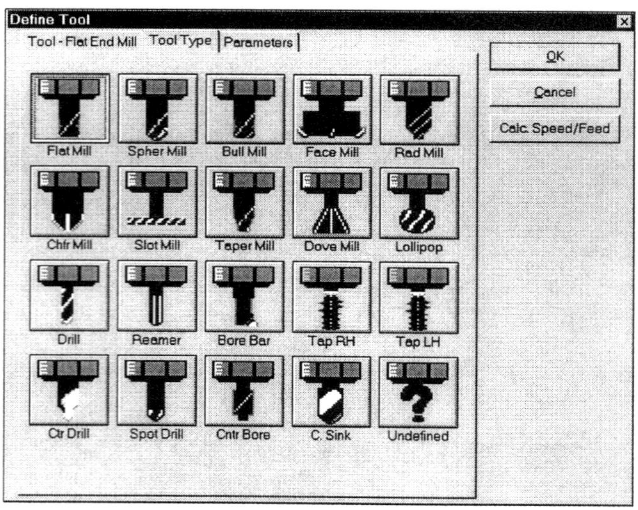

Select Flat Mill from the dialog box. The flat mill definition dialog box should appear. Define the tooling information for tool and tool holder as below.

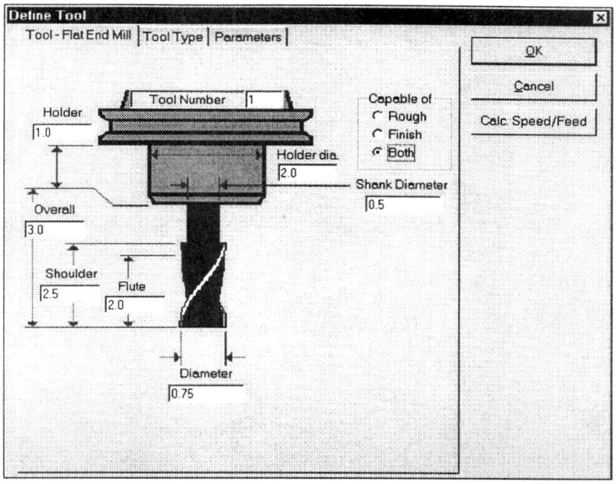

Click the Parameters tag to open the parameters dialog box. Define the parameters as below.

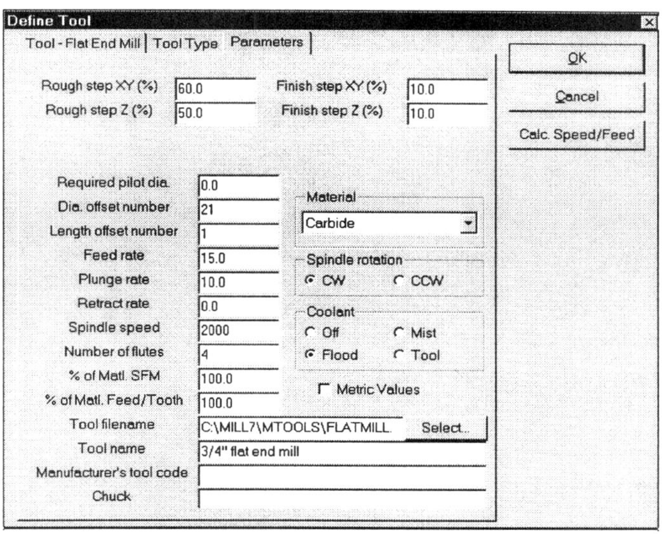

Select the OK button from the Define tool dialog box. The system will return back to Tools Manager dialog box as below.

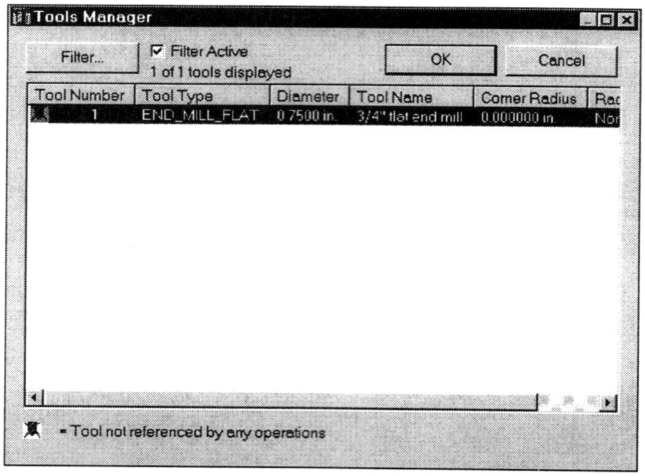

The procedure for creating a new tool using on the fly method is:

1. Select Toolpaths → Contour (or one of toolpath module)
   The system will prompt for entering File Name: T.NCI
2. Chain the contour profile.
   A contour properties dialog box will appear. It may contain exiting tools as shown below or may be empty depending on whether tools have been added.

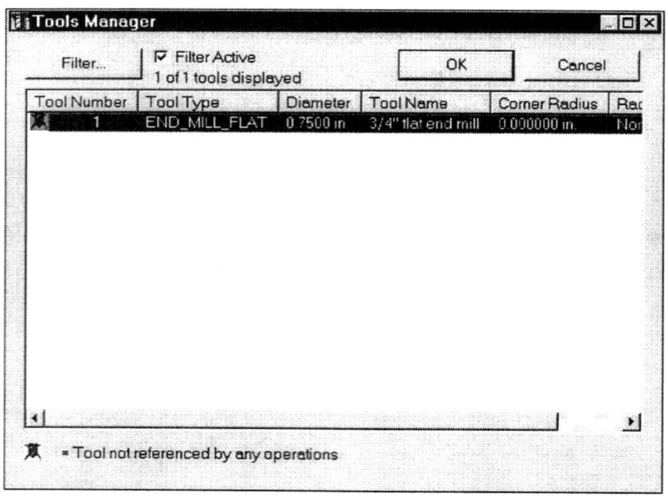

3. Click the right mouse button to open the tools manager menu. Select "Create new tool" to open the Define Tool dialog box.
4. Repeat the steps 4 – 6 in the previous section to define a new tool.

The procedure for selecting a tool from tool library

Follow these steps to retrieve an existing tool from tool library:

1. Select Toolpaths → Tools to open the Tools Manager dialog box.
2. Click right mouse button to bring up the Tools Manager menu.
3. Select "Get from library" to open the tool list as below.

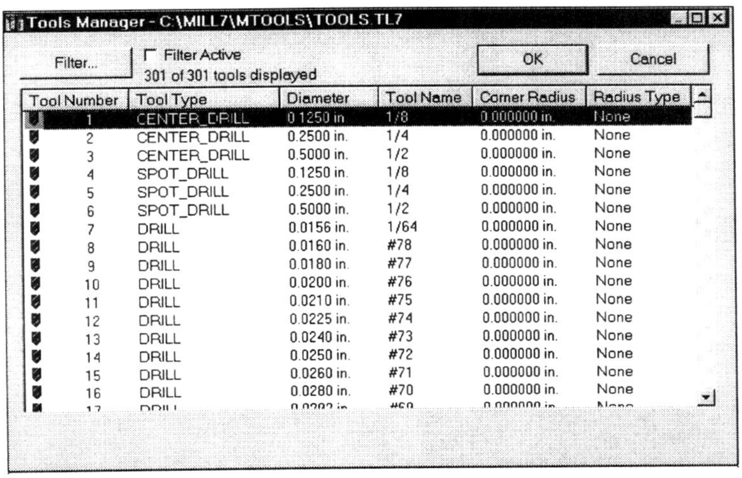

4. Scroll the tool list to find the one you want "1-in flat end mill", then select OK. The tool is retrieved to the Tool Manager dialog box as below.

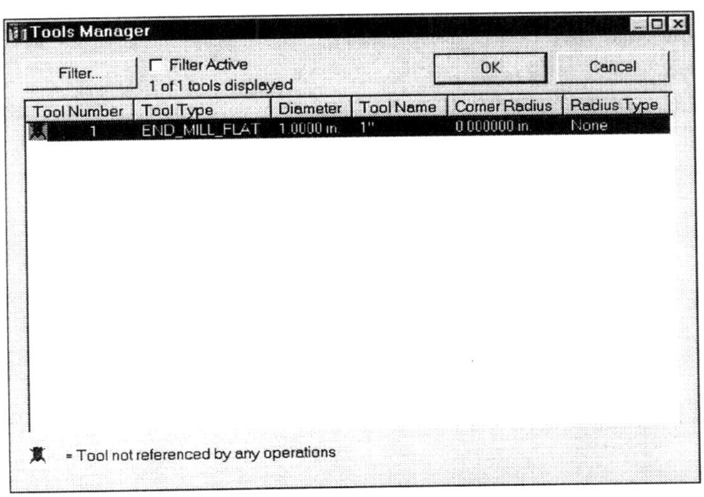

5. Repeat steps 2 – 4 to retrieve another tool (1/2" drill). Two tools are now shown in Tools Manager dialog box as below.

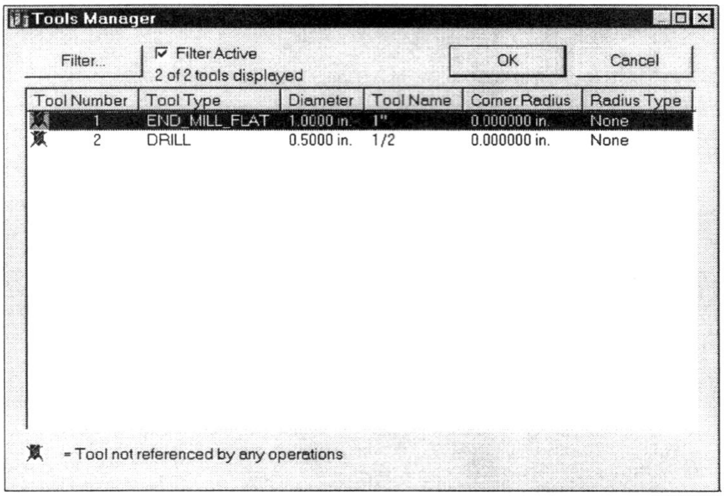

The procedure for editing an exiting tool

Tools in Tools Manager dialog box can be modified.

1. Place the mouse on the tool to be modified in "Tools Manager" dialog box (1" flat end mill in this example), then click the right mouse button.
2. Select "Edit Tool" from Tools Manager menu. The Define Tool menu should appear as below.

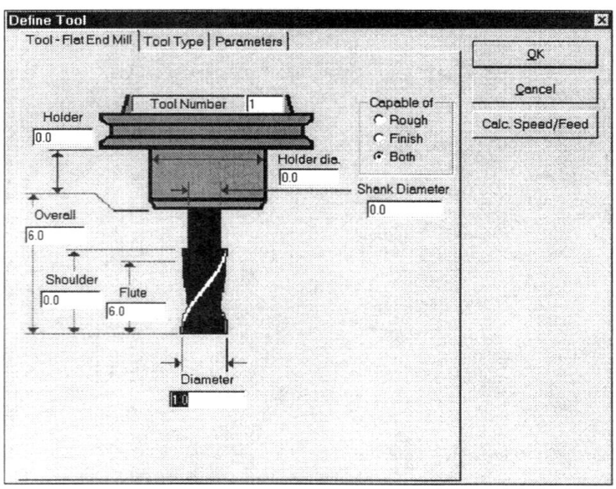

3. Redefine the tool and holder parameters as below.

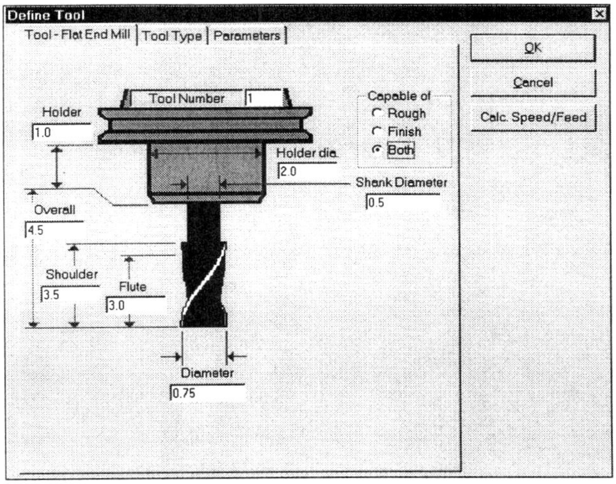

4. Select "Parameters" tag to open the Parameters dialog box as below.

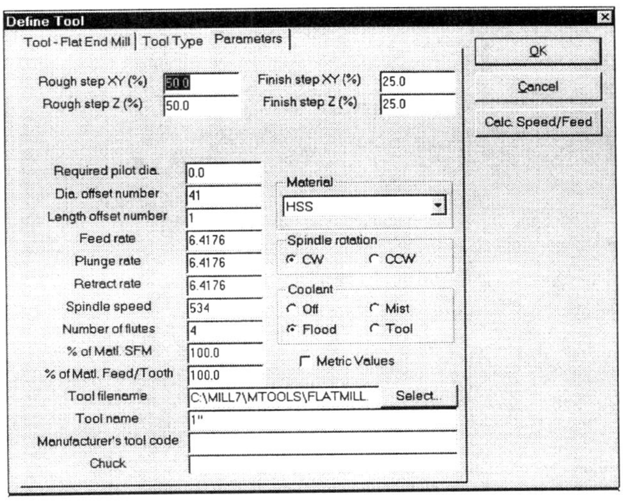

5. Redefine the machining data and tooling information as below.

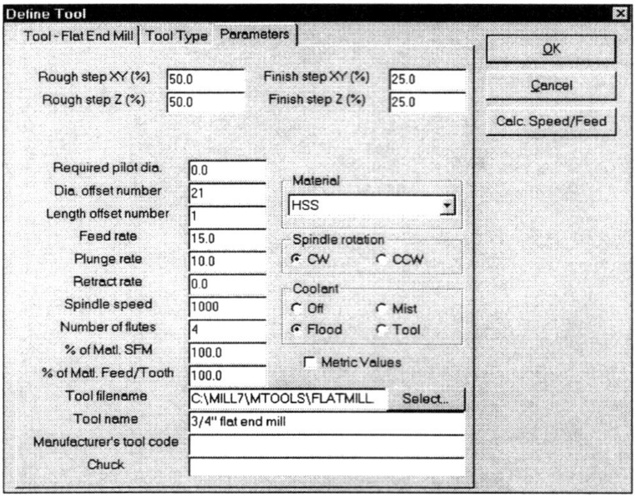

6. Select OK to complete the tool editing and return to Tools Manager dialog box. The old "1-in flat end mill now has been changed to ¾" flat end mill as below.

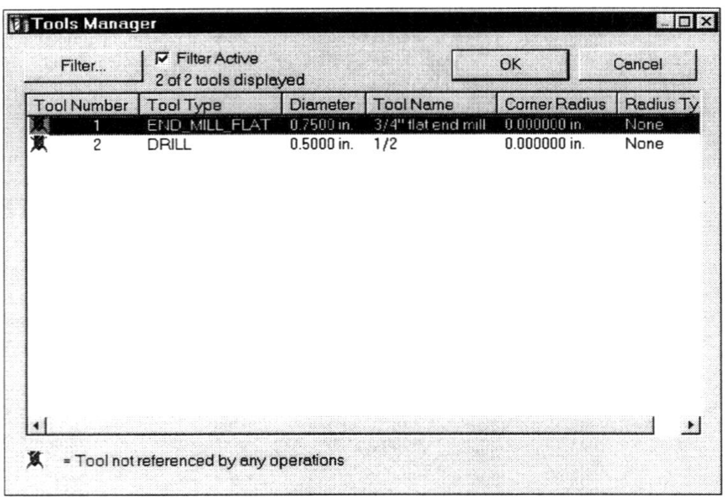

7.3 Operations Manager

After toolpaths have been generated, they can be graphically verified, post-processed to generate NC codes, and regenerated based on new machining data and tooling information. Mastercam groups these operation functions under the "Operations Manager" dialog box. The four functions included in the Operations Manager dialog box are:

Backplot:	generating backplot of selected toolpaths on the screen.
Post:	converting toolpath location data to NC program.
N-See 2000:	executing toolpath verification.
Regen Path:	regenerating the toolpath based on the new parameters.

The procedure to open the Operations Manager dialog box:

1.Select Toolpaths → Operations

2. The Operations Manager dialog box with existing toolpaths data should appear as below.

7.4 Backplot Function

The backplot function redisplays the toolpaths in a given mode. The backplot menu appears as shown here.

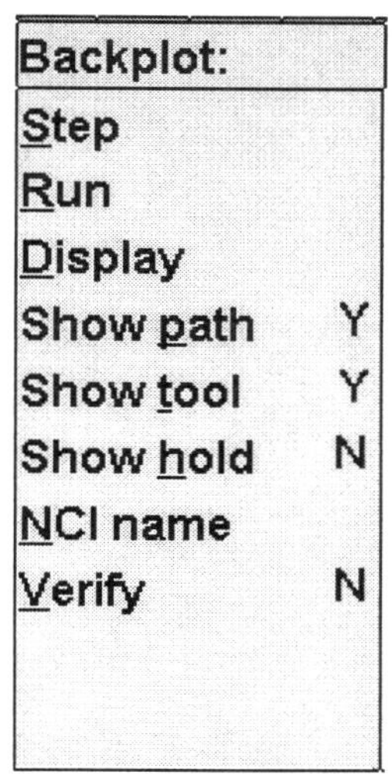

Execution mode

The backplot can be implemented in the following two modes:

Step:	tool moves one increment when the Step command is selected once. You need to continually select the Step command to complete the backplot of toolpaths.
Run:	tool continues to run until the end of the entire toolpaths.

Show path:	leave a trace of tool center along the toolpaths after backplotting (Figure 7.1).
Show tool:	show the cutting tool during backplotting (Figure 7.2).
Show hold:	show the tool holder during backplotting (Figure 7.3).
Verify:	leave a trace of shade for showing the material to be removed (Figure 7.4).

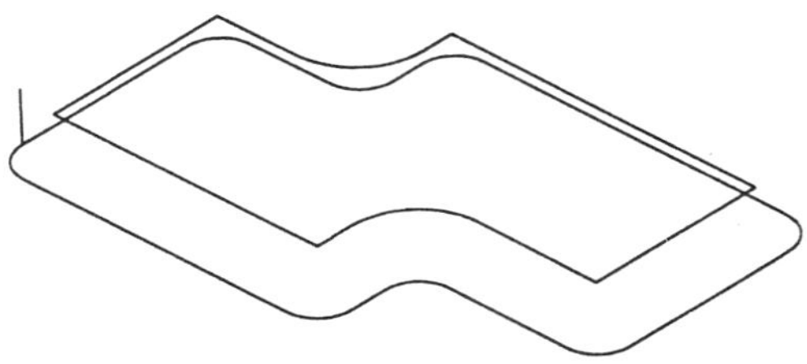

Figure 7.1

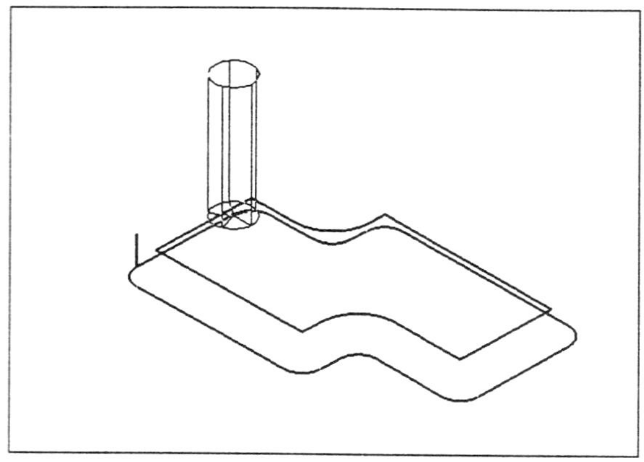

Figure 7.2

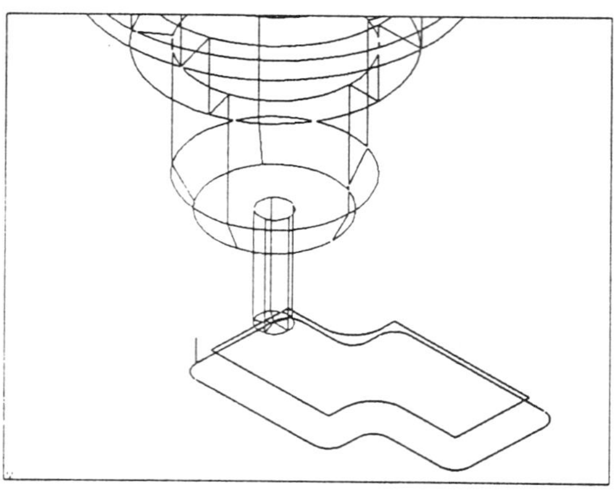

Figure 7.3

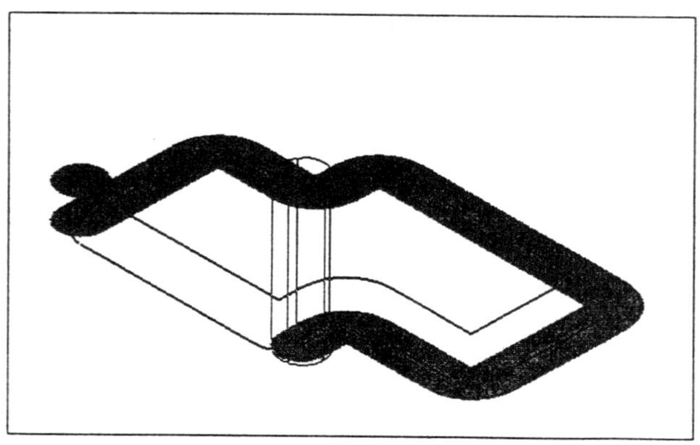

Figure 7.4

Display mode

Mastercam provides various parameters to display the tool and toolpaths. The backplot display parameters menu is shown below.

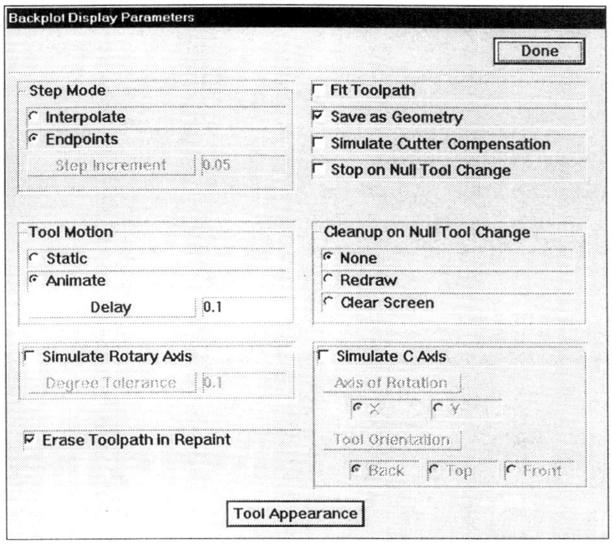

Step mode

Tool display can be set to one of the following two modes (Figure 7.5):

Interpolate:	tool is shown at increments of specified step size (Figure 7.5a).
Endpoints:	tool is shown at each endpoint of the toolpath (Figure 7.5b).

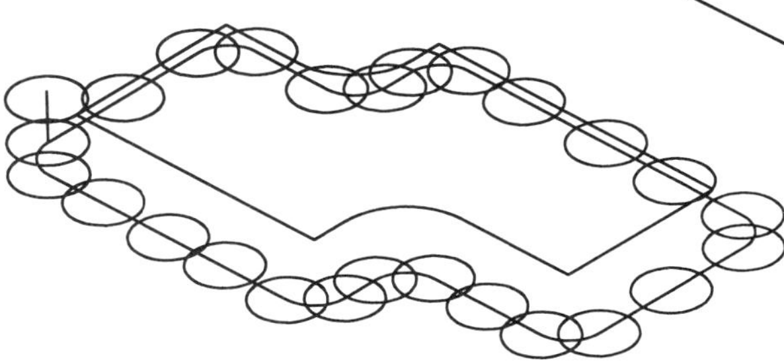

Figure 7.5a

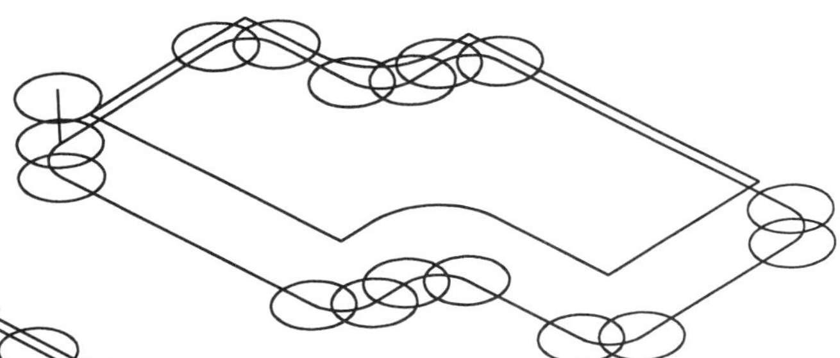

Figure 7.5b

The Step Increment option allows you to specify the step distance for the tool display.

Tool motion

The display parameters allow us to select the display mode for tool and toolpath. The tool motion can be shown in animated mode or static mode. In animated mode, the tool will appear and disappear at each point along the toolpath and as if it were moving. In static mode, the tool will appear at every point along the toolpaths and will not be erased.

The system uses the Delay function to allow for specifying how long the tool will be displayed each time it appears on the screen. Use delay of 0.0 for large files.

The remaining backplot display parameters are briefly described as below:

Simulate Rotary Axis: wrap geometry on a cylinder for rotary axis toolpaths.
Erase Toolpath in Repaint: remove the displayed backplot from the graphics window when the screen refreshes.
Fit Toolpath: display the entire toolpath on the screen.
Save as Geometry: create geometry from the backplot toolpath moves.
Stop on Null Tool Change: instruct the system to stop at each tool change and null tool change while implementing the backplot.
Cleanup on Null Tool Change: select the operation mode for refreshing the screen during each null tool change.
Simulate C Axis: Simulate the motion of a C axis for a rotary axis toolpath.

Tool Appearance

Click the Tool Appearance button at the bottom of the Backplot Display Parameters dialog box to bring up the Tool Appearance Parameters dialog box as below.

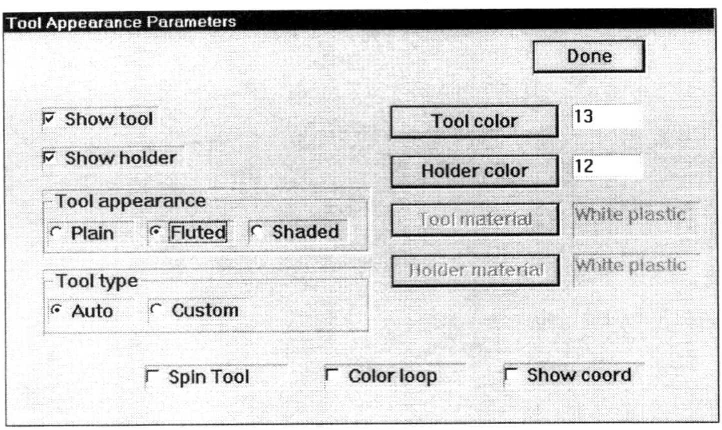

The following two parameters are used to specify whether tool and/or holder are to be shown during backplotting.

Show tool: show the cutting tool during the backplot.
Show holder: show the toolholder during the backplot.

Tool appearance

This parameter is used to define how a cutting appears during backplotting. It has the following three modes:

Plain: the cutting tool is shown in plain straight shape (Figure 7.6a).
Fluted: the flutes of cutting tool is shown (Figure 7.6b).
Shaded: the cutting tool is shown in shaded mode (Figure 7.6c).

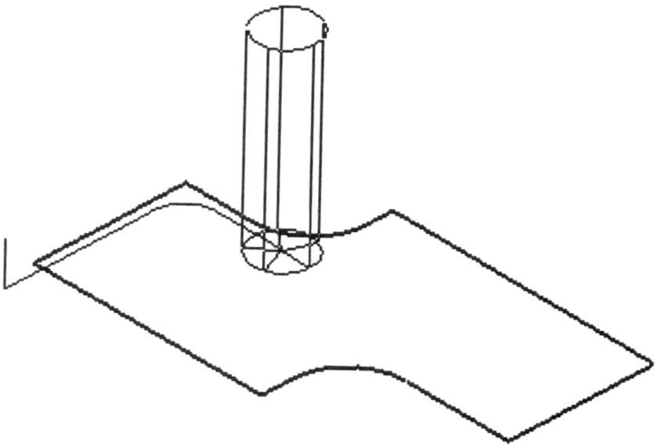

Figure 7.6a Plain

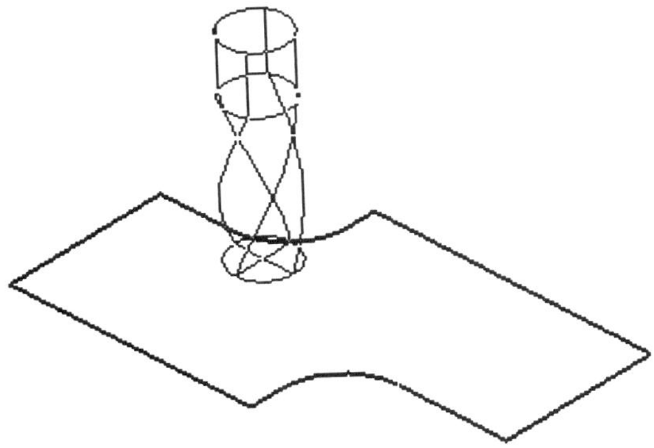

Figure 7.6b Fluted

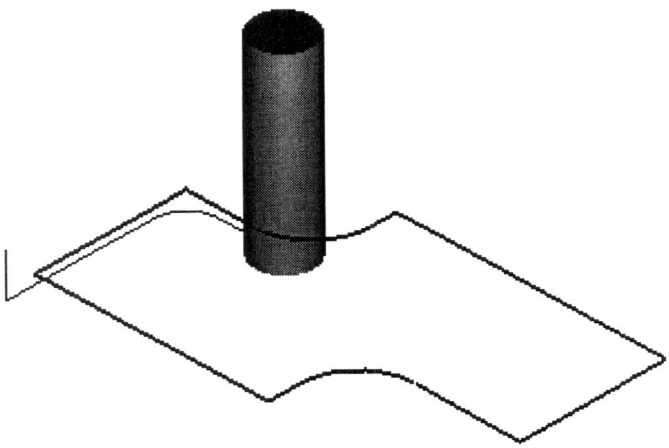

Figure 7..6c Shaded

Colors for tool and holder

The display color for tool and tool holder can be selected by either the color type or material type. The two options for tool and holder each are briefly described below:

Tool color:	select a color to display the cutting tool.
Holder color:	select a color to display the tool holder.
Tool material:	select a color to display the cutting tool material.
Holder material:	select a color to display the tool holder material.

The material type dialog box is shown here.

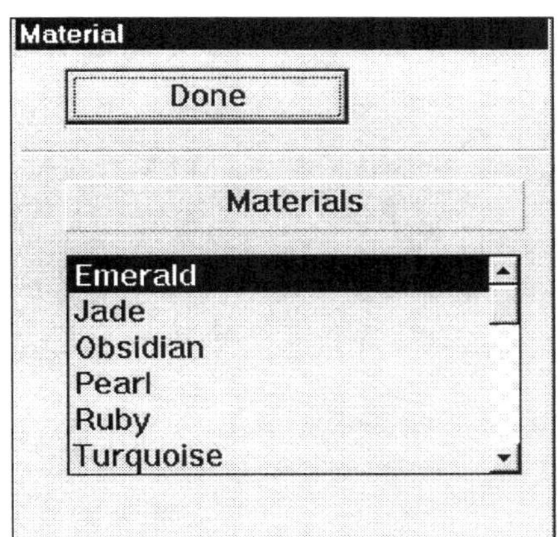

Other parameters related to tool appearance:

Spin Tool:	spin the tool during backplotting.
Color loop:	display the backplot path in color.
Show coord:	display the coordinate values of the backplot path.

7.5 N-See Verification

The N-See 2000 function is a powerful solid-model NC verification tool for Mastercam. This function uses the NCI file as the input to show the toolpath and the finished part in solid model form. Toolpath verification is very important in NC programming for the following reasons:

- Detect potential errors in part programs before they are used in tryout run.
- Simulate graphically the machining of the part programs.
- Eliminate the need for tryout run.
- Reduce the production lead time from design to part.
- Reduce costs.

N-See 2000 provides the following three verification modes for you to choose from:

Preview: provide tool animation while verifying the toolpath verification for the selected NCI file(s) (Figure 7.7).
Turbo: provide toolpath verification without showing tool animation for the selected NCI file(s) (Figure 7.8).
Verify: create very accurate results that can be easily manipulated by rotating, sectioning, and zooming for detailed inspection. This mode does not come with all systems.

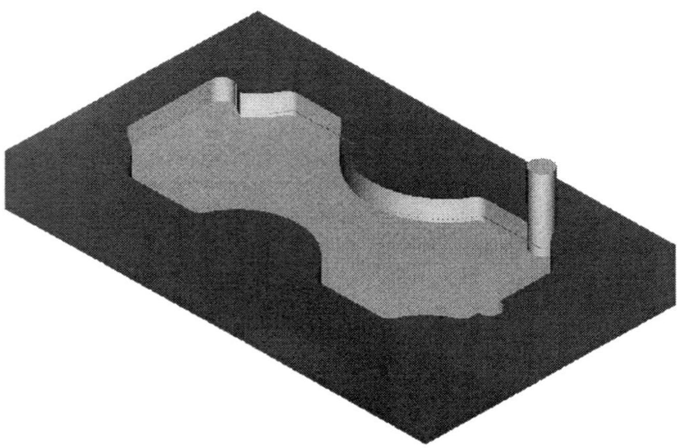

Figure 7.7

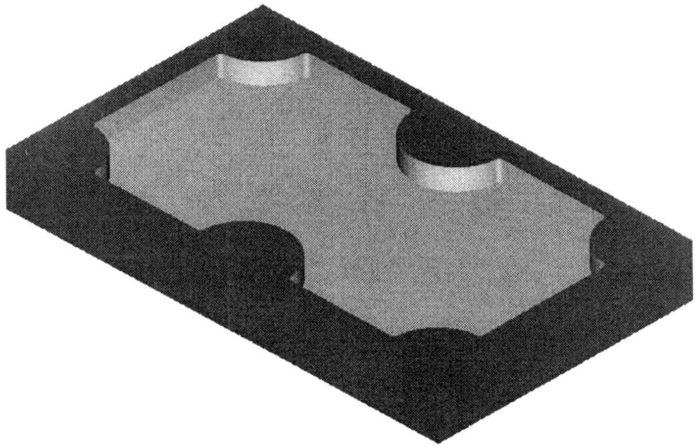

Figure 7.8

The N-See 2000 function can be initiated in two ways: from **Operations Manager mode** or from **NC utilities mode**.

The procedure Initiated from Operations Manager mode:

1. Select "Operations" to open Operations Manager menu
2. Select "N-See 2000" button to open N-See function
3. Select "Preview" or "Turbo" mode from "Select mode for current job" menu, then select OK
4. The raw material block model should appear on the screen. Select "Do it" to verify the toolpath

The procedure Initiated from NC Utilities mode:

1. Select NC utils → N-See 2000
2. Select Yes to "Operations have been modified. Create the NCI text file?"
3. Select "Preview" or "Turbo" mode from "Select mode for current job" menu, then select OK
4. The raw material block model should appear on the screen. Select "Do it" to verify the toolpath

7.6 Job Setup

The job setup function is used to define the workpiece setup information. Its dialog box is given below.

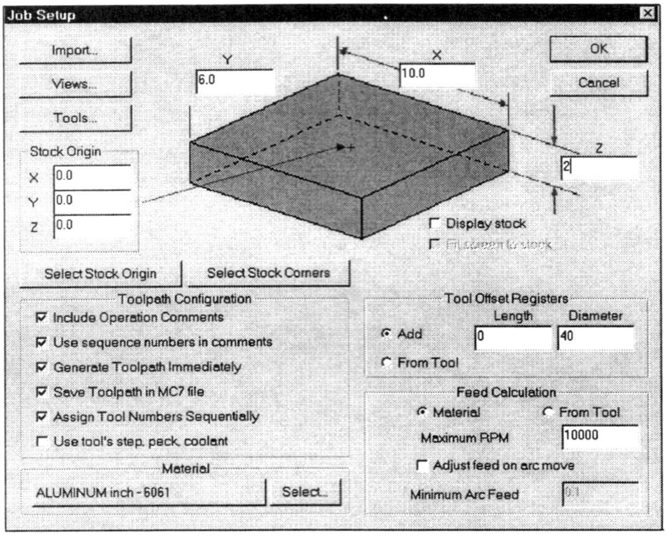

Stock Origin and Size

You can define the stock origin in two ways; pick a corner or center and pick at any location. There are ten possible locations that can be selected as the stock origin including eight locations at corners and two at the center of top and bottom surfaces. A small cross-mark with an arrow is used to indicate the corner or center you pick as the stock origin.

There are two buttons can be used to define the origin and corners:

Select Stock Origin:	use one of point entry methods to define the stock origin.
Select Stock Corners:	use one of point entry methods to define the stock corners.

The stock size are fully defined by its X, Y, and Z dimensions as shown in Figure 7.9.

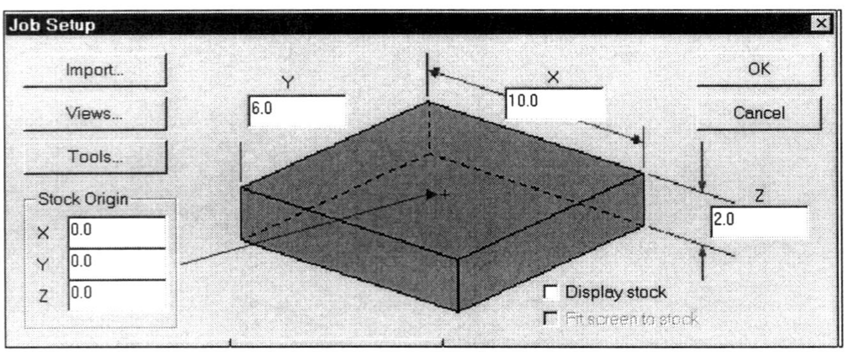

Figure 7.9

Material selection

The job setup also includes material type. Click the Select button in the Material section to bring up a material list as below.

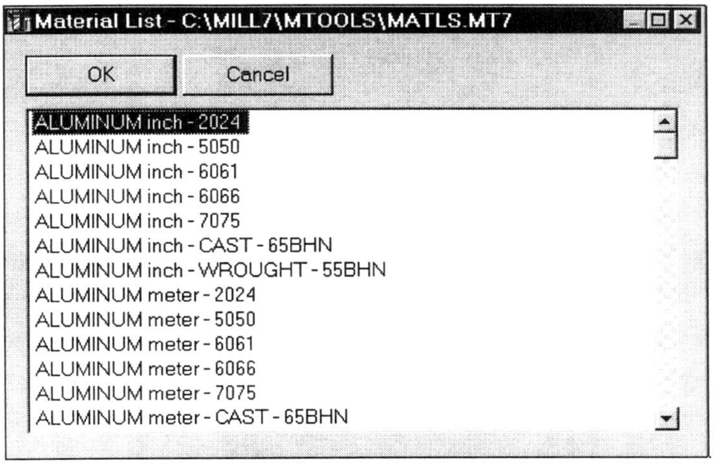

Tool Offset Registers

The register numbers for tool length offset and diameter compensation can be specified either in the job setup dialog box or directly taken from tooling information as shown below.

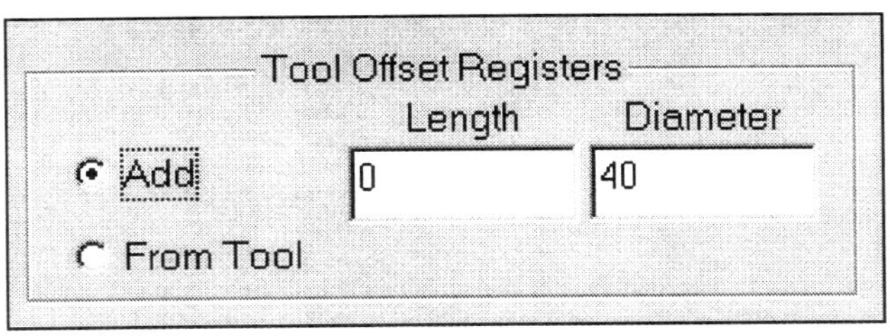

Toolpath Configuration Parameters

The following six parameters that can be selected for configuring the toolpaths format:

1. Include operation comments
2. Use sequence numbers in comments
3. Generate toolpath immediately
4. Save toolpath in MC7 file
5. Assign tool numbers sequentially
6. Use tool's step, peck, coolant

Feed Calculation Parameters

Mastercam provides two modes to calculate feed: **material** and **from tool**. Feed can be assigned either using the material data table or machining data from tooling data. Maximum RPM can be assigned also. The dialog box of this category is shown below.

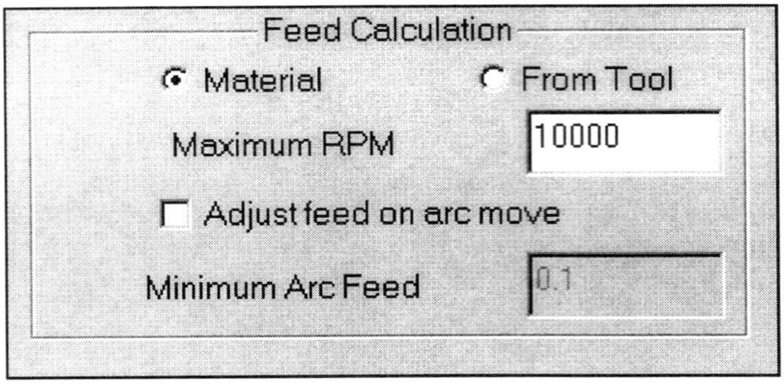

7.7 Contour definition

A contour consists of a number of connected geometric entities to form a part profile for machining. The benefit of defining a contour is to allow multiple entities of a part shape to be formed as a single entity. This facilitates profile or pocket cutting in one tool motion command.

Chaining direction

The pick point of the first entity of the contour determines the starting position of the contour and the chaining direction of the contour. The chaining direction is also the contour direction. The chaining direction starts at one entity end point, traps the end point that is closer to the picked position, and points to the other end point (Figure 7.10).

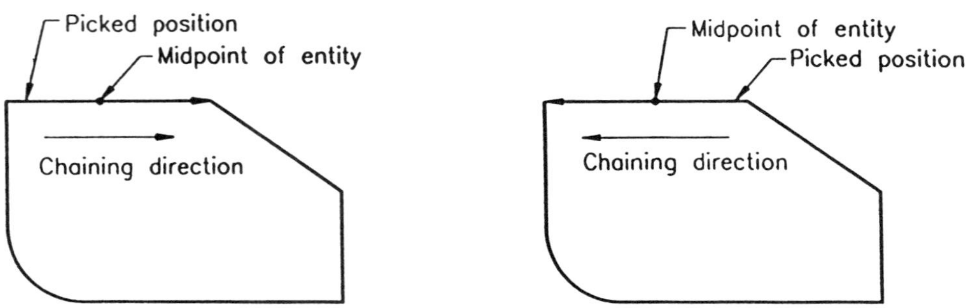

Figure 7.10

There are two types of contours: **closed** and **open**. In a closed contour, the first and last entities are connected (Figure 7.11a). In an open contour, the first and last entities are not connected (Figure 7.11b). The contours used in pocketing must be the closed type.

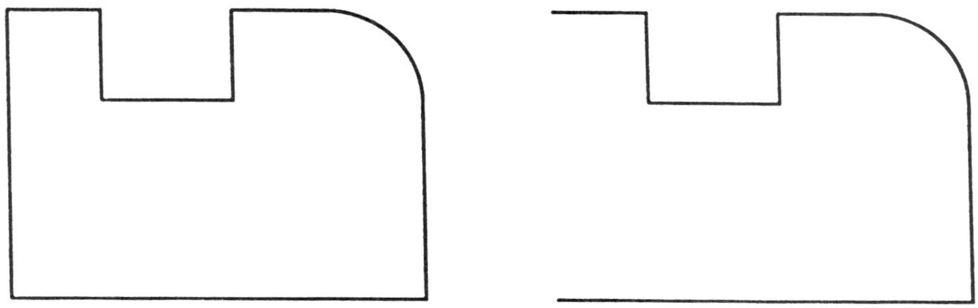

Figure 7.11

Chaining methods

Mastercam provides various methods for chaining entities into contours. Table 7.2 describes these chaining methods.

Table 7.2 Contour chaining methods

Method	Description	Illustration
Chain	defining a contour consisting of one or more connected entities.	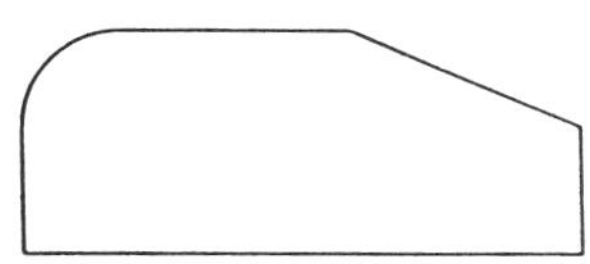
Window	defining one or more contours from those entities completely within a window.	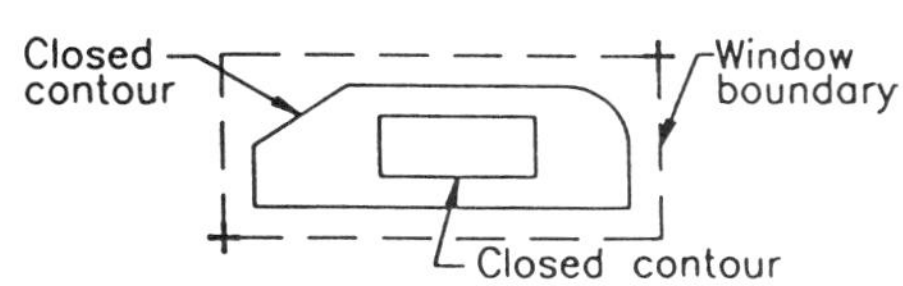
Polygon	defining one or more contours from those entities completely within a polygon.	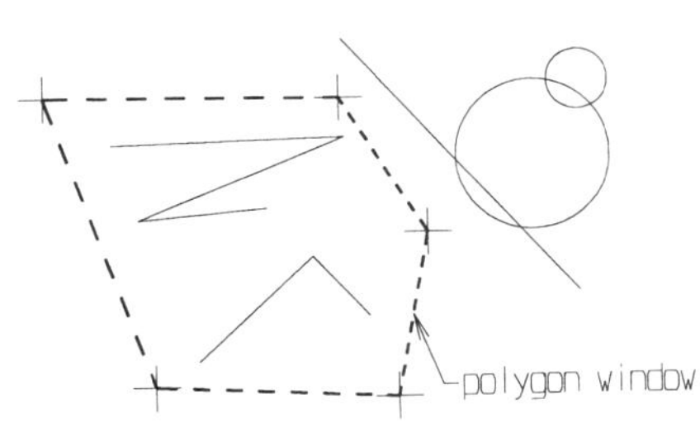

Table 7.2 continued.

Area	defining a contour from a group of contours.	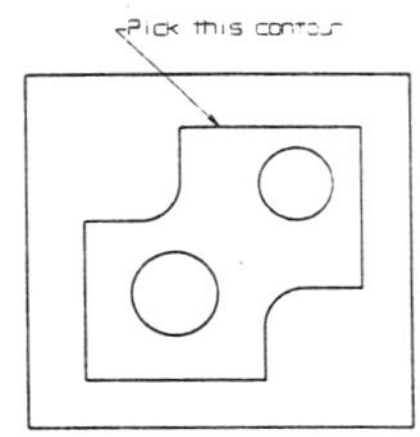
Single	defining a contour consisting of only a single entity.	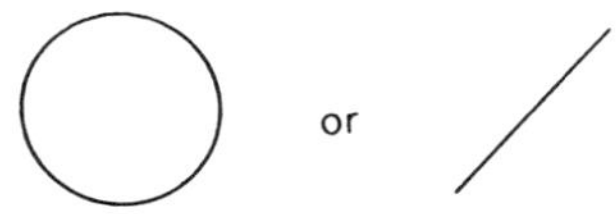
Section	defining a contour with a section of connected entities.	
Point	defining a clear point to rapid to.	
Last	recalling the last group of chained contours for new operations.	
Unselect	undoing the contour selection just made.	

Chain option

The chain option is used to automatically chain a series of connected entities as a chained contour. The picked entity becomes the first entity of the chained contour (Figure 7.12).

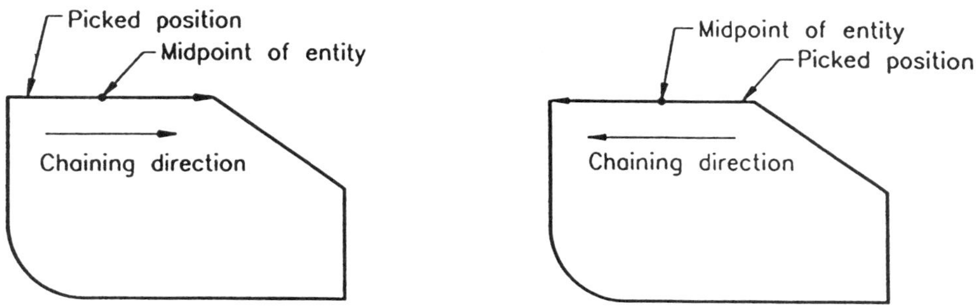

Figure 7.12

After picking the starting entity of the chained contour, Mastercam provides the following functions to modify the chaining direction and starting entity of the contour:

Reverse:	reverse the chaining direction to its opposite direction (Figure 7.13).
Start fwd:	change the starting entity to next entity in the chain (Figure 7.14).
Move back:	change the starting entity back one preceding entity in the chain (Figure 715).
Select str:	select an entity as the new starting entity of the chained contour (Figure 7.16).

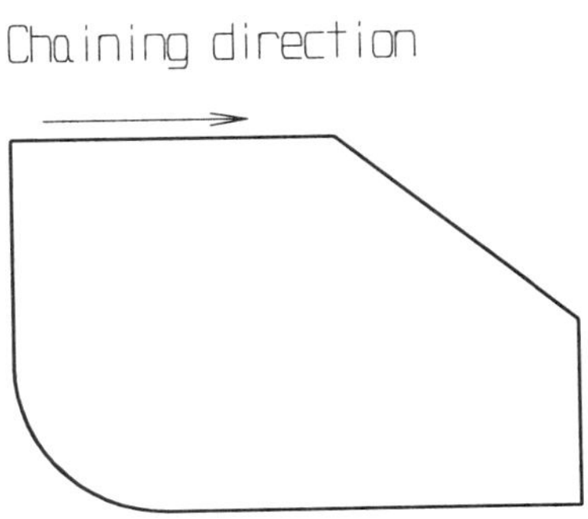

Figure 7.13a Original direction

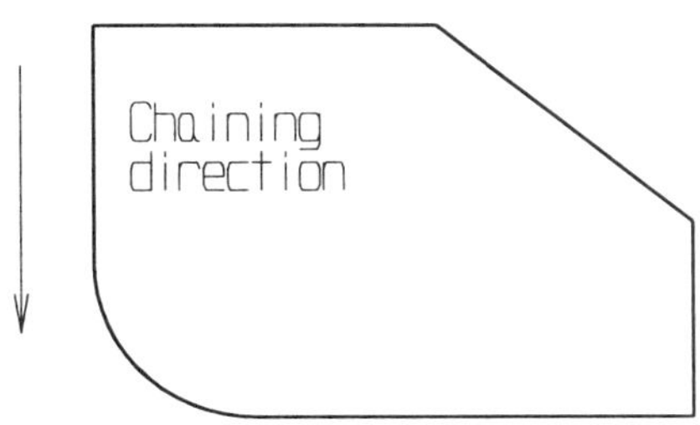

Figure 7.13b After reverse

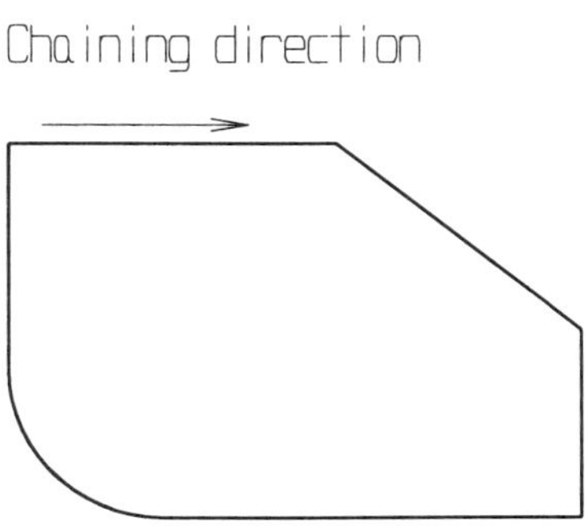

Figure 7.14a Original direction

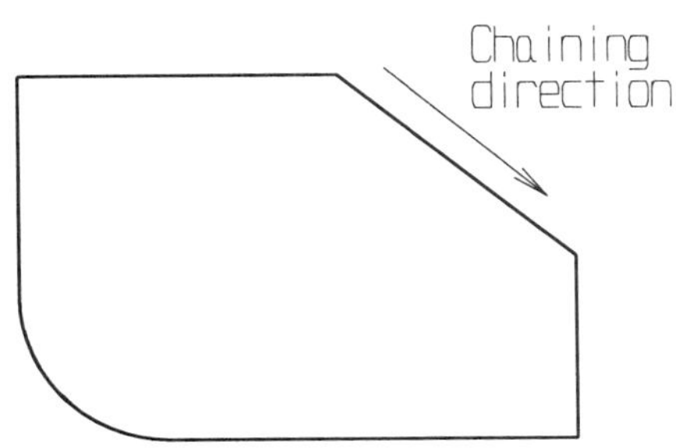

Figure 7.14b After move forward

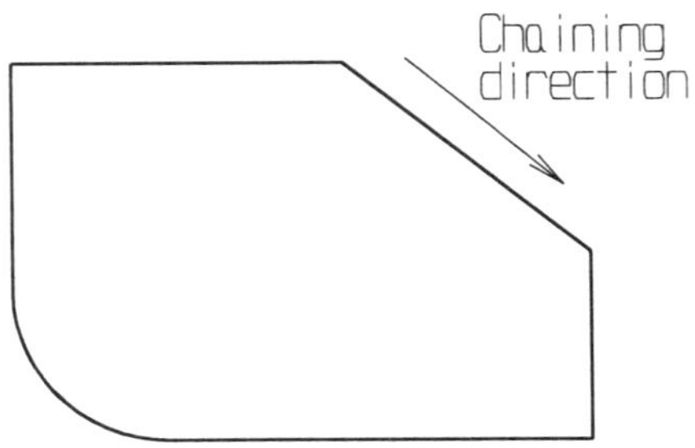

Figure 7.15a Original direction

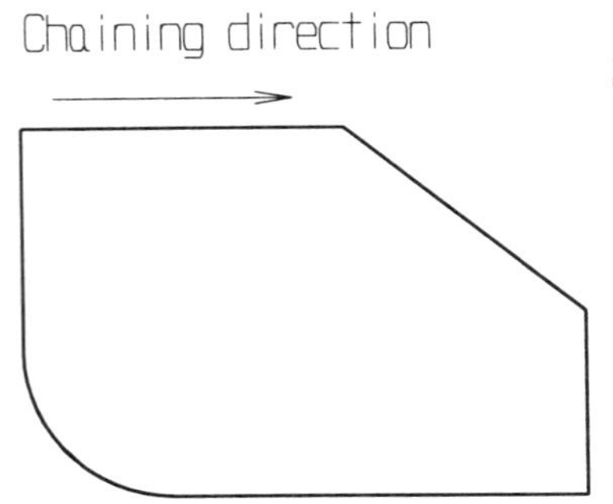

Figure 7.15b After move back

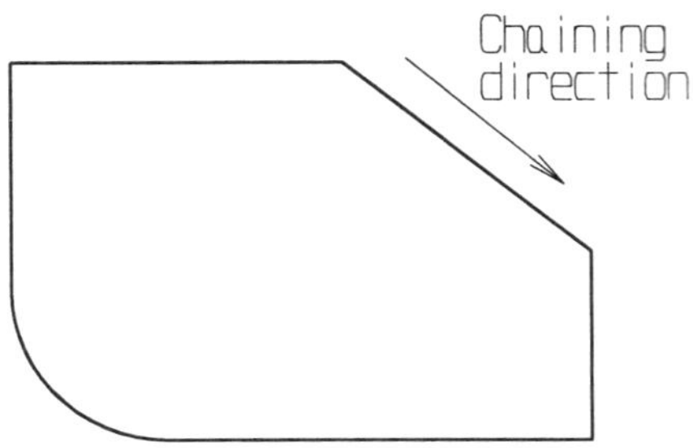

Figure 7.16a Original direction

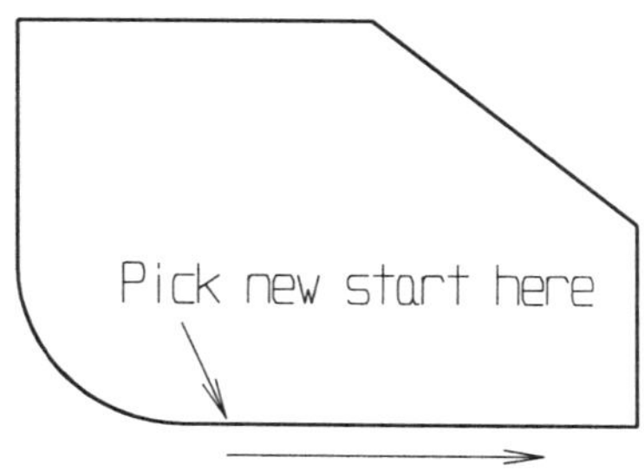

Figure 7.16b After select new start

Options

Mastercam provides various ways to mask entities to be included in the chain and other parameters to make chaining preferences. These options are grouped under Chaining Options menu as shown below.

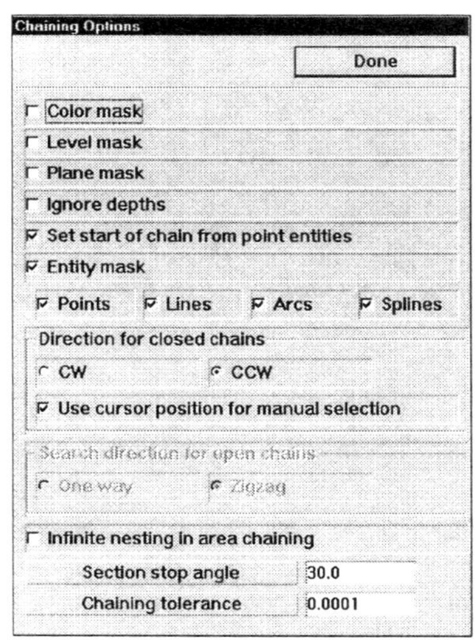

Polygon options This option allows picking a series of points for defining a polygon as the searching boundary for defining the contour. It has the following five options:

Inside:	include all entities completely inside the polygon (Figure 7.17).
In + intr:	include all entities inside or on the polygon boundary (Figure 7.18).
Intersect:	include only those entities on the polygon boundary (Figure 7.19).
Out + intr:	include all entities outside or on the polygon boundary (Figure 7.20).
Outside:	include all entities completely outside the polygon (Figure 7.21).

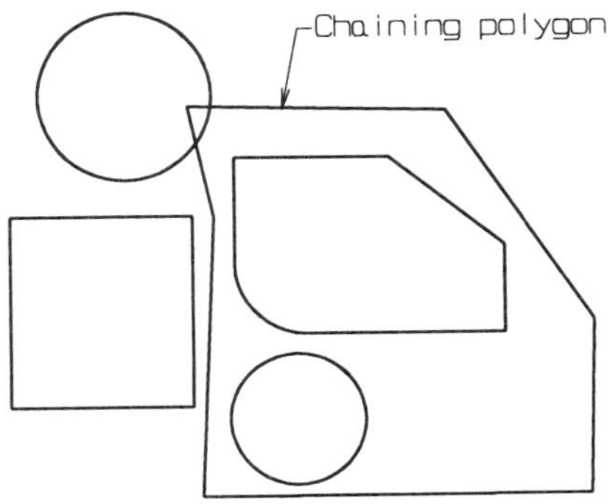

Figure 7.17a

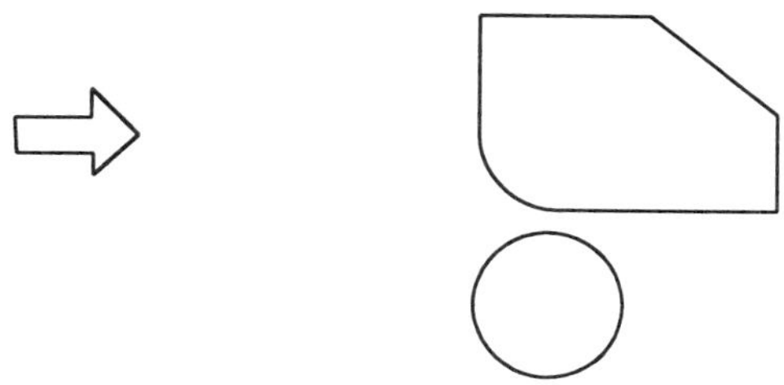

Figure 7.17b Inside polygon

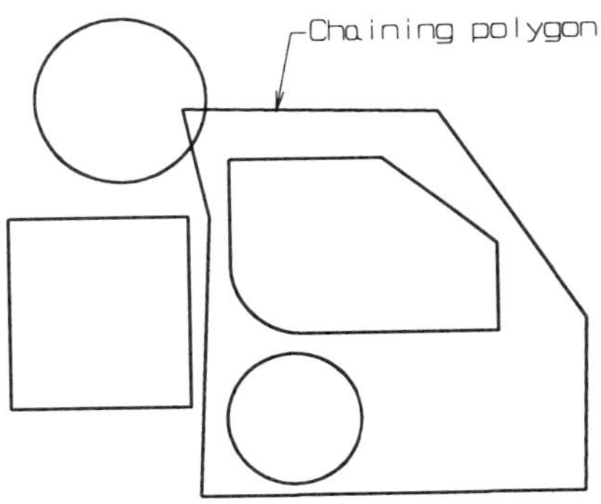

Figure 7.18a

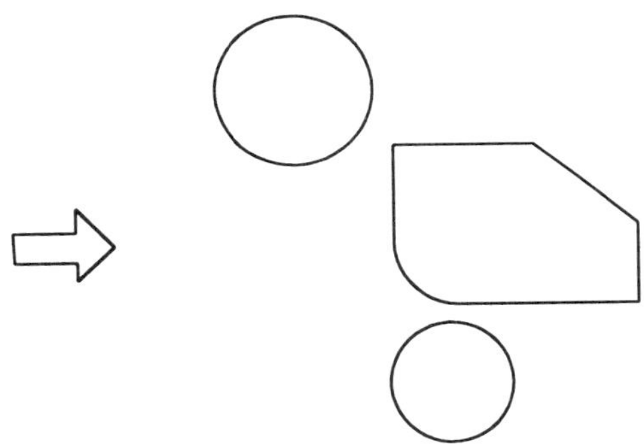

Figure 7.18b Inside and on the polygon

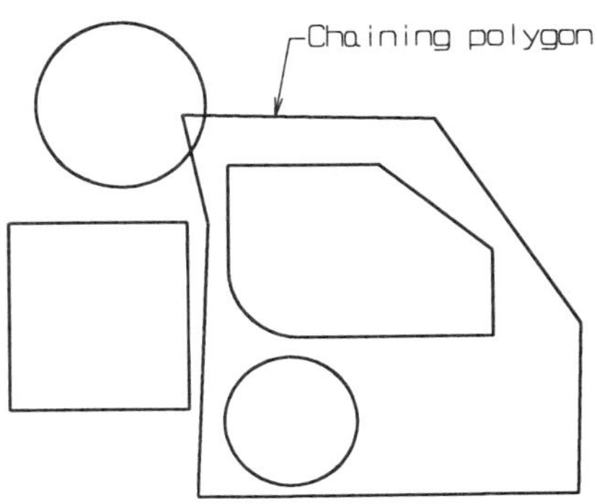

Figure 7.19a

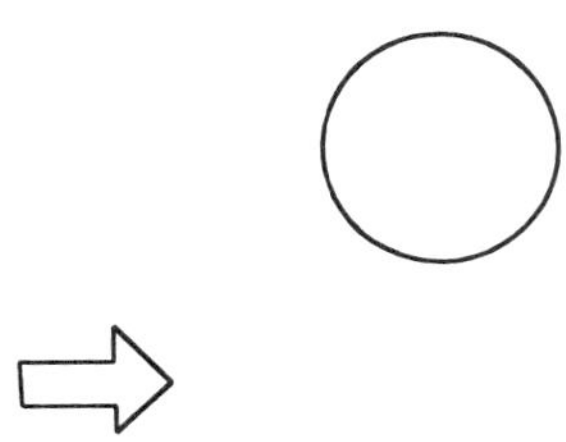

Figure 7.19b On the polygon boundary

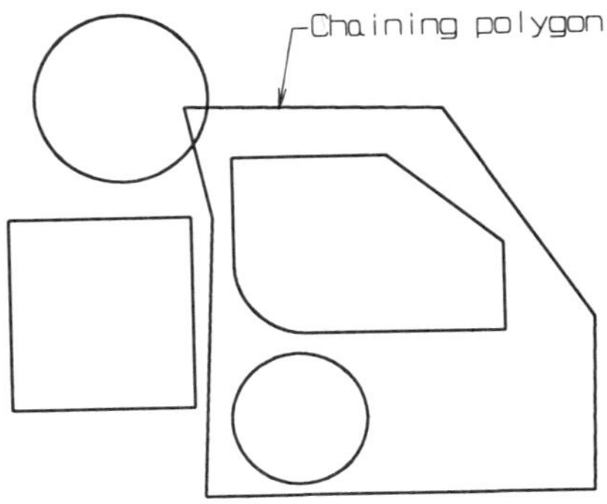

Figure 7.20a

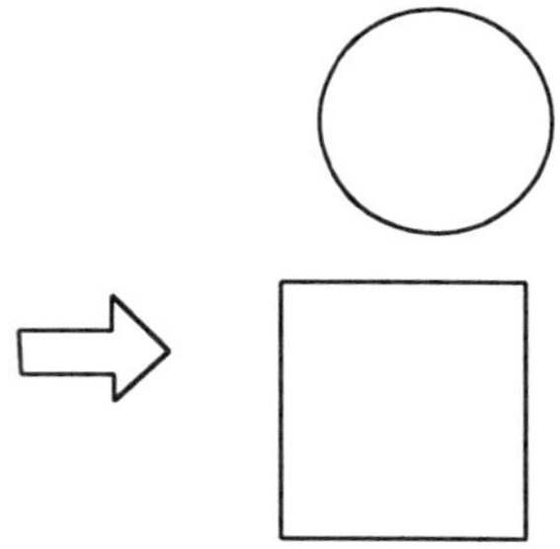

Figure 7.20b Outside and on the polygon boundary

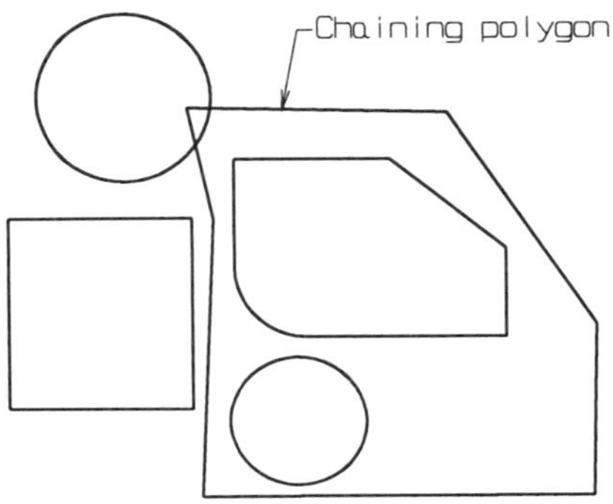

Figure 7.21a

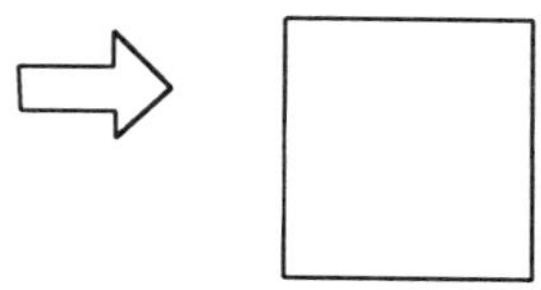

Figure 7.21b Outside the polygon

Area option This option allows picking a contour from a groups of contours. The connected entities will be included in the area (Figure 7.22).

Figure 7.22a

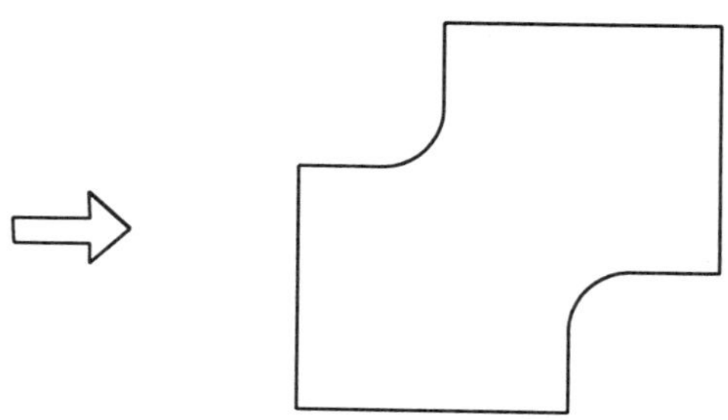

Figure 7.22b After picking an area

Single option:	This option selects a single entity as a contour.
Section option:	The section option is used to select a section of entities as a chained contour.

The range of section is determined by where you pick the entity. The section is terminated by two consecutive line entities. When a line that has an adjacent line in both ends is selected, only the selected line is included in the chained contour (Figure 7.23). Figure 7.24 shows an example that a section of entities is chained as a contour.

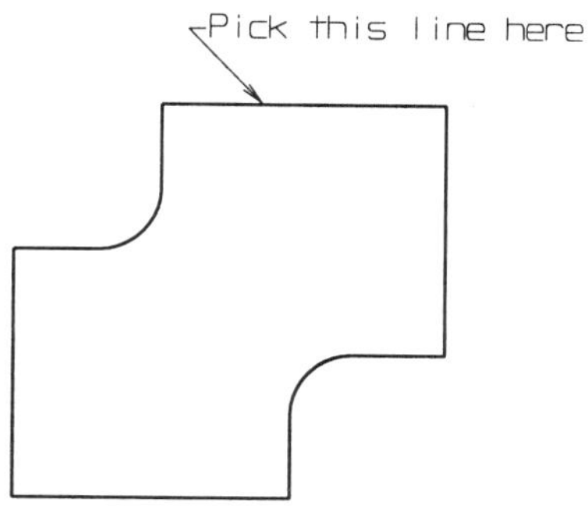

Figure 7.23a

Figure 7.23b Result of section selection

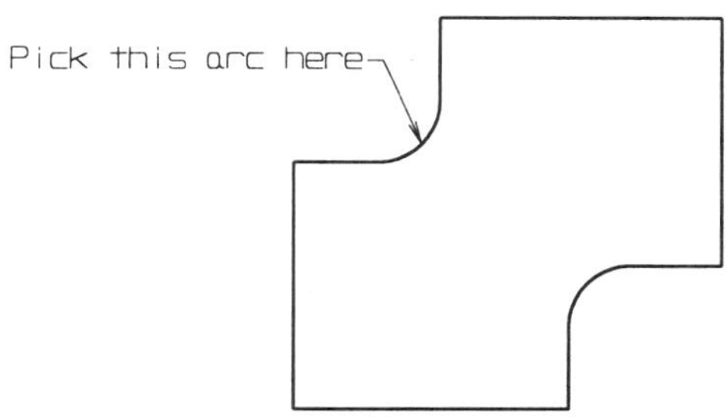

Figure 7.24a

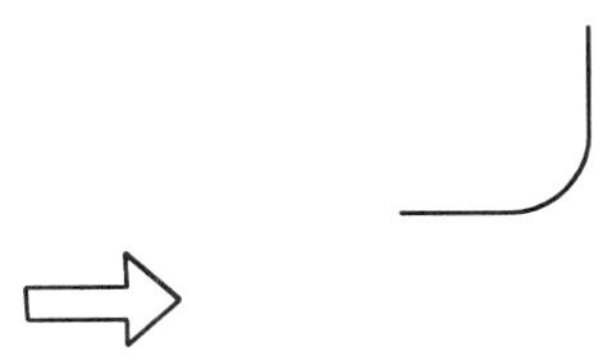

Figure 7.24b Result of selection

Point option:	The point option is to specify a single point as the contour.
Last option:	This option selects the last chained contour for the new operation.
Unselect option:	This option undo the contour selection just made.

7.8 Coordinate Setting

Mastercam uses four functions to define the work coordinates of the part program. They are **home position**, **reference point**, **rotary axis**, and **tool/construction plane**. They are described below.

Home Position

This function specifies the intermediate position for reference point return. Most CNC controls use reference return commands to generate paths for the spindle and worktable to return to machine origin. Home position dialog box appears as shown here:

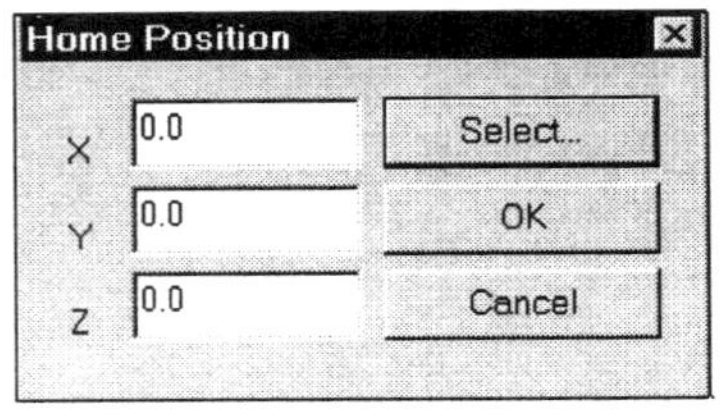

Reference point return commands have the following formats:

	G90 G28 Xx Yy Zz	(absolute positioning mode)
Or	**G91 G28 Xx Yy Zz**	(incremental positioning mode)

where G90: absolute positioning mode
G91: incremental positioning mode
G28: reference point return command
x, y, and z are the coordinate values of the intermediate point

The toolpath pattern of the reference point return G28 is shown in Figure 7.25. In fact, we arrange the reference return point command into two block statements as below:

G91 G28 Z0.0
G91 G28 X0.0 Y0.0

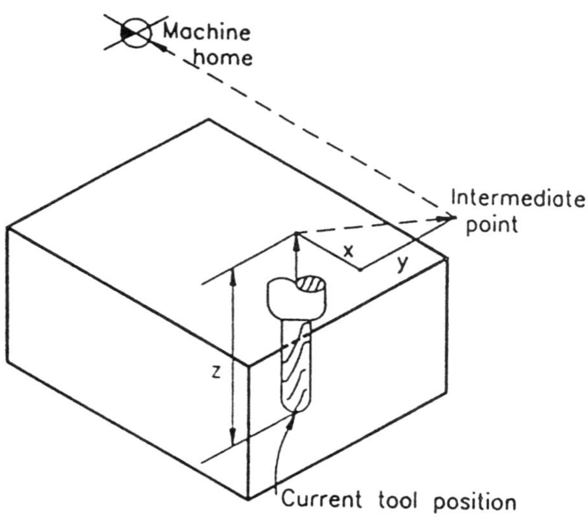

Figure 7.25

This arrangement allows the cutter to be retracted in the Z direction before the worktable moves in the X and Y plane, and avoids interference.

In Mastercam the coordinate values of the Home Position are used as the x, y, and z values of the reference return point. With the default value (X0 Y0 Z0) of home position, the reference return point commands become:

G91 G28 Z0.0
G91 G28 X0.0 Y0.0

With the coordinate value of (X1.0 Y1.0 Z2.0), the reference return point commands becomes:

G91 G28 Z2.0
G91 G28 X1.0 Y1.0

The reference point return commands are used in the following two conditions:

1. Execution of tool change. Tool change has to be implemented at the machine origin in most CNC machines.
2. At the end of the part program. The spindle and worktable should be moved to machine origin to (1) make the control ready for the next operation, and (2) load and unload the workpieces.

Tip Always use (X0 Y0 Z0) for Home Position and set the positioning system command to incremental mode in the postprocessor. This setting can be used in any workpiece machining. Care must be exercised when other coordinate values are given to this parameter, otherwise an undesirable toolpath may result.

Reference Point

This function is used to define additional reference return point beside the home position for the tool to return. Its dialog box appears as below.

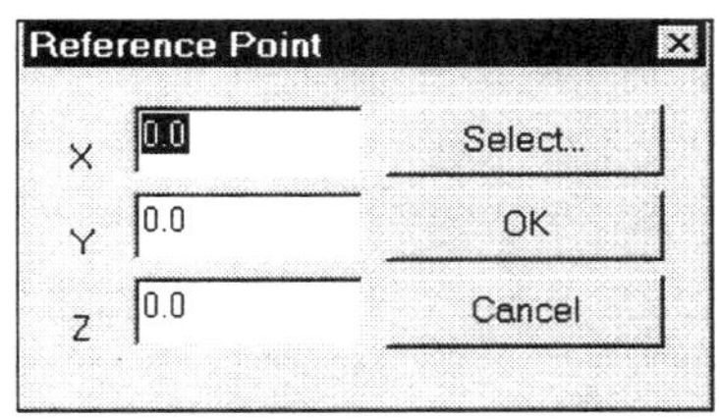

Tool Origin and Tool Plane

Mastercam allows to define three possible origins: **system origin, construction plane origin**, and **tool plane origin**. The system origin is the fixed coordinate system automatically setup by the system. The construction origin is used to redefine the origin for geometry construction. The tool plane origin redefines the tool path origin. All three origins are located at the system origin unless they are redefined.

The principle of redefining tool plane origin is the same as programming the work coordinate setting command G92. The coordinate values given in this parameter indicate the coordinate values of the system origin in the tool plane coordinate system. Figure 7.26 shows three cases of tool plane origin setup.

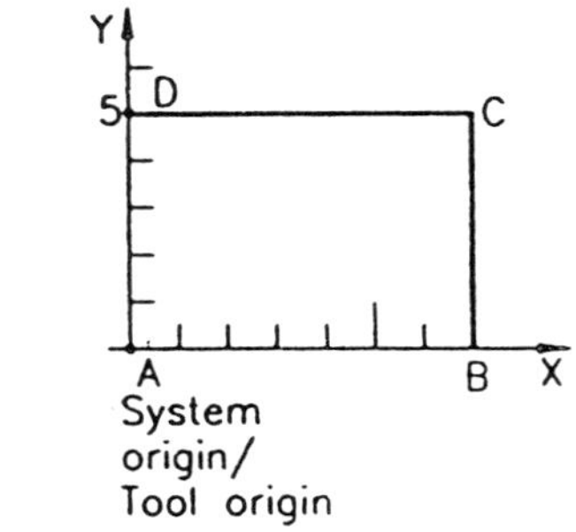

	Toolpath Coord.	
	X-Coord.	Y-Coord.
A	0	0
B	7.0	0.0
C	7.0	5.0
D	0	5.0

a. Tool origin: X0 Y0

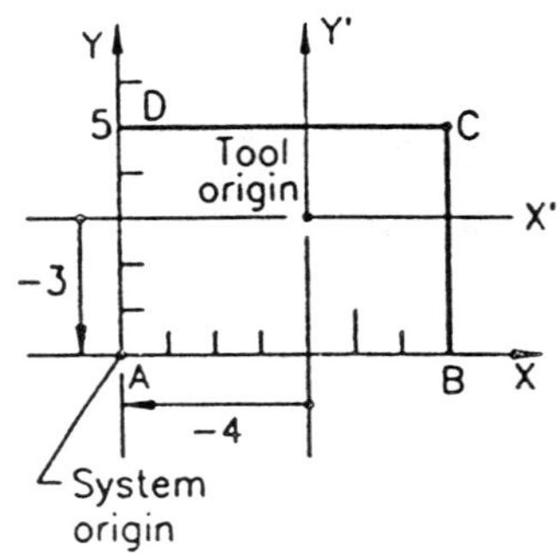

	Toolpath Coord.	
	X-Coord.	Y-Coord.
A	-4.0	-3.0
B	3.0	-3.0
C	3.0	2.0
D	-4.0	2.0

b. Tool origin: X-4.0 Y-3.0

Figure 7.26

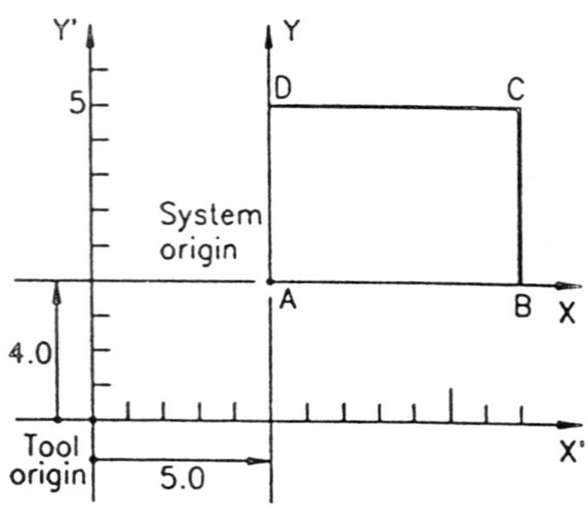

	Toolpath Coord.	
	X-Coord.	Y-Coord.
A	5.0	4.0
B	12.0	4.0
C	12.0	9.0
D	5.0	9.0

c. Tool origin: X5.0 Y4.0

The tool plane parameter is used to select the tool plane for the current operation. There are three principal tool planes: XY-plane, ZX-plane, and YZ-plane. The system will issue a plane selection command code to the part program as shown below. Figure 7.27 shows a number of examples of selecting a proper tool plane.

Plane selection	Command code
XY-plane	G17
ZX-plane	G18
YZ-plane	G19

Tool plane parameters can be toggled to these options:

Off	Tool plane defaulted to top view.
Top	Top view
Front	Front view
Side	Side view
Number	View identified by its number
2 Lines	View defined by two mutually perpendicular lines
Arc	View contained an arc
Rotate	View defined by rotating a construction plane about an axis
Normal	View which is perpendicular to a normal vector

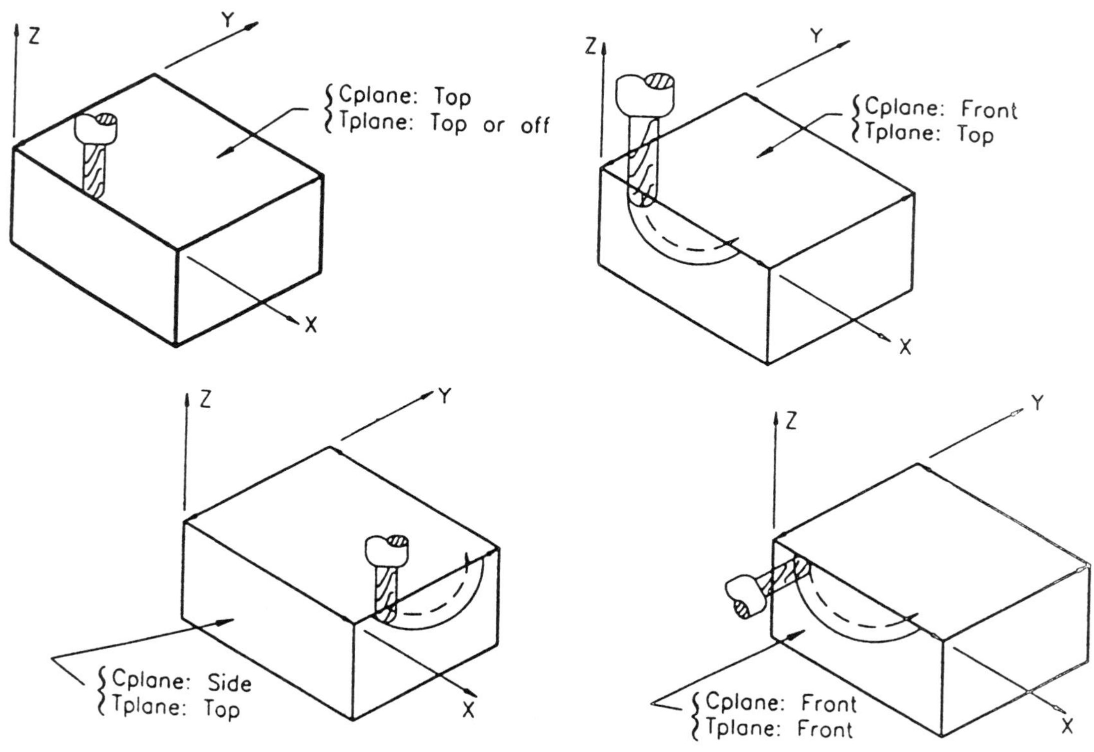

Figure 7.27

Click the "T/C planes" button at the bottom of the Tool Parameters menu to open the Tool Plane/Construction Plane dialog box as below.

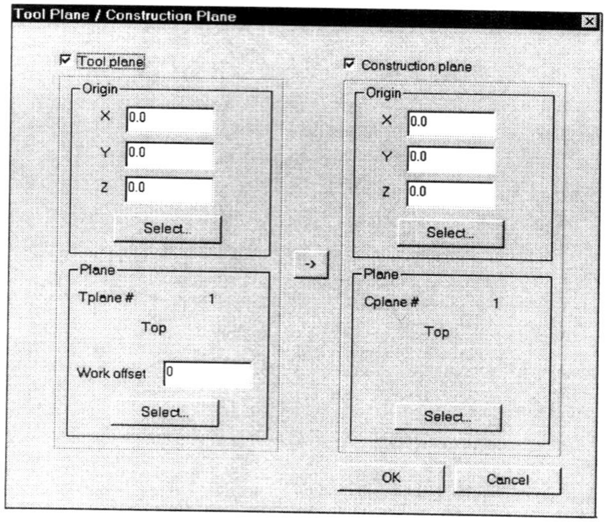

Rotary Axis

The rotary axis function is used to indicate which axis, X or Y, the rotary axis is to replace. The dialog box of rotary axis function is shown below.

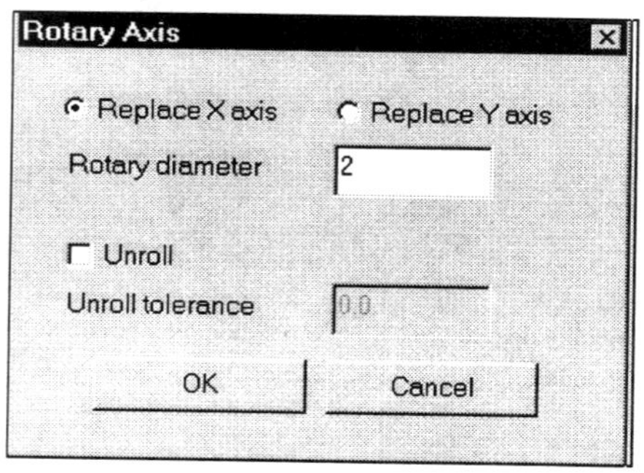

7.9 Contour Module

The contour module is used to generate cutter paths along a series of lines and arcs that form the profile of a part. Contouring is normally implemented on 2D profiles, in which the depth of cut remains constant (Figure 7.28).

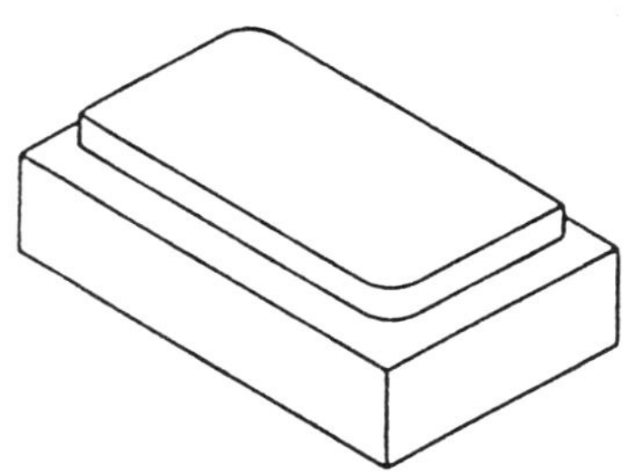

Figure 7.28

Contour Parameters

In addition to the tool parameters presented in previous sections, the contour module uses a set of contour specific parameters to define how the contouring toolpaths are generated. The contour parameters menu is shown below.

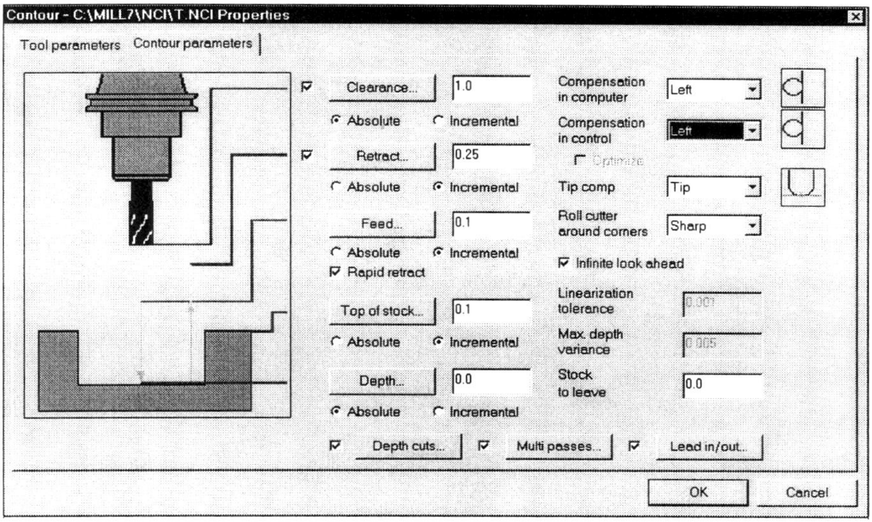

The contour parameters can be grouped into the following six categories; **Z-depth parameters, Depth cuts, Stock to leave, Multi passes, Compensations,** and **Lead in/out**.

Z-depth parameters Mastercam uses the following five parameters to define the Z-depths for generating contouring toolpaths (Figure 7.29):

Clearance:	define the clearance level at which the tool is traveled between operations.
Retract:	define the retraction level to which the tool is retracted after the end of operations.
Feed:	specify the distance above the top of stock from which the tool start to change its motion from rapid mode to feed mode.
Top of stock:	specify the Z-coordinate value of the top of stock.
Depth:	Specify the final depth of contouring toolpaths.

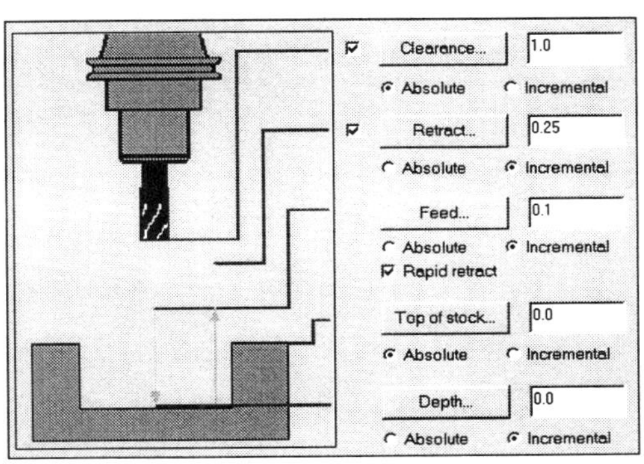

Figure 7.29

The total depth of material to be removed is determined by the two parameters; **top of stock** and **depth**. The total cutting depth is the sum of top of stock and depth.

Depth cuts The depth cuts parameters specify the number of roughing and finish cuts to be taken in the Z direction. It allows us to set the maximum roughing depth of each roughing pass and the number of finish cuts with the specified depth of each finish cut. The total number of cutting passes is the sum of the roughing cuts and finish cuts. The four parameters in depth cuts dialog box appear as here.

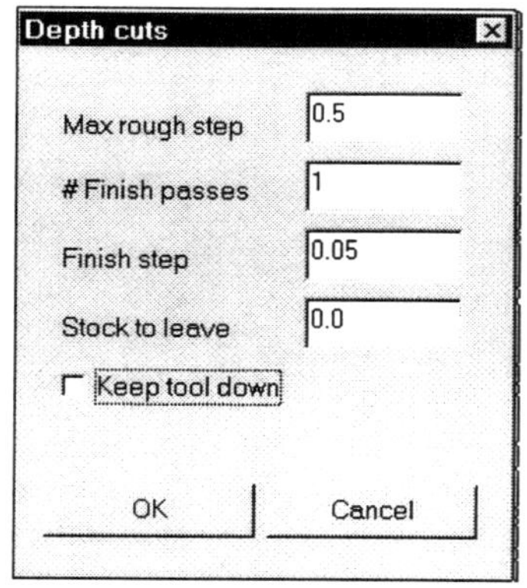

The cutting sequence is determined from the bottom up as defined below (Figure 7.30):

Last finish cut: cut at final depth.
Second to last finish cut: cut at depth that is a finish cut spacing above final depth.
Subsequent finish cut: cut at depth that is a finish cut spacing above previous finish cut.
Last roughing cut: cut at depth that is a roughing cut spacing above first finish cut.
Next to last roughing cut: cut at depth that is a roughing cut spacing above the last roughing cut.
Subsequent roughing cuts: cut at depth that is a roughing cut spacing above previous roughing cut.

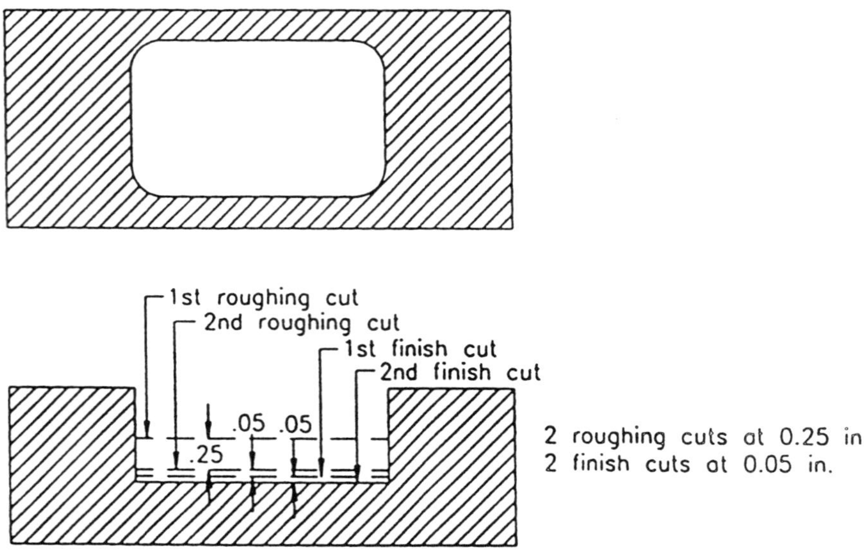

Figure 7.30

The required number of roughing passes is determined by the following formula:

$$\#\text{of roughing passes} = \frac{[\text{Total depth of cut} - (\text{Finish step x \# of finish passes})]}{\text{Max rough step}}$$

The result will be rounded to next integer number. The actual roughing step will be automatically recalculate based on the formula below:

$$\textbf{Roughing step} = \frac{\textbf{[Total depth of cut – (Finish step x \# of finish passes)]}}{\textbf{\# of roughing passes}}$$

Keep tool down The "Keep tool down" parameter is used to specify whether the tool will be retracted to "Feed" level after each roughing or finish pass. Click the check box with a (mark to keep tool down and plunge the tool from the current Z-level to the next cutting Z-level directly. Remove the (mark will retract the tool up to the "Feed" level at the end of each cutting pass. The tool plunges to the Z-depth of next cutting pass.

Stock to leave in XY-direction The "stock to leave" parameter specifies a certain amount of material to be left on the workpiece for further machining. The stock is allowed in both the XY-direction and Z direction. The stock in Z direction is specified in the "Depth cuts" dialog box. This parameter in the contour parameters dialog box is only applied to the stock in XY-direction. Leaving stock in XY-direction is shown in Figure 7.31. When a non-zero value is given to "Stock to leave" parameter, the final tool pass will leave the given amount of material on the part. The direction of stock to leave is determined by the offset side parameter. The stock is left on the left side when the compensation side is set to left, likewise, when it is set to right the stock is on the right. If the compensation side is set to Off, the stock to leave is ignored.

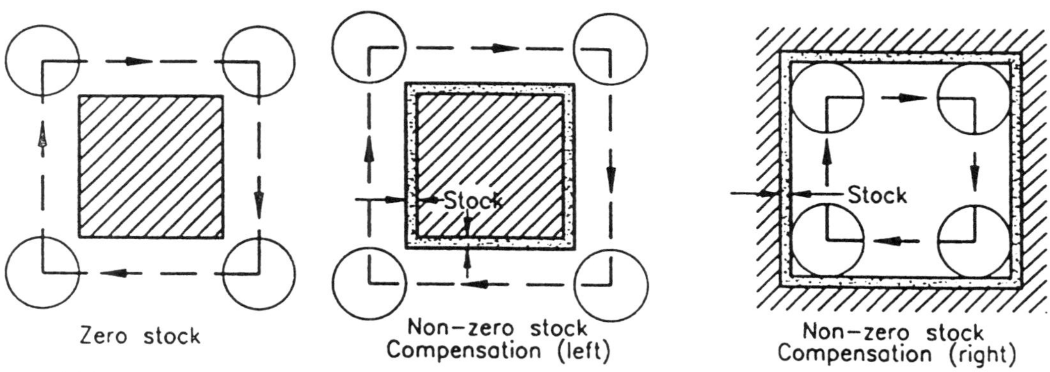

Figure 7.31

Multi passes Mastercam uses four parameters in "Multi Passes" dialog box to specify the number of roughing and finish cuts to be taken and their stepover distance in the selected cutting plane. The Multi Passes dialog box is shown here.

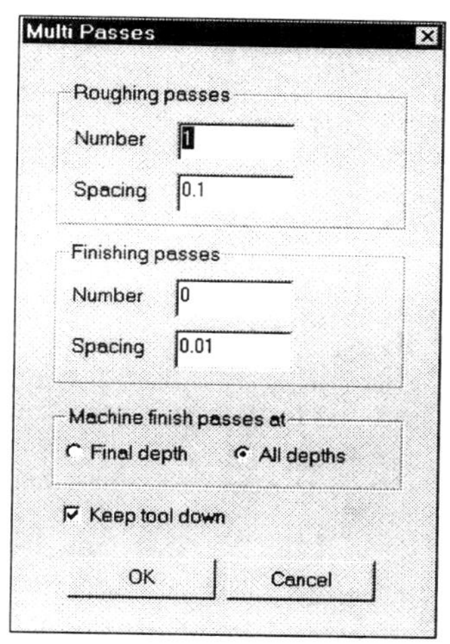

The total number of contouring passes to be taken is the sum of the number of roughing cuts and the number of finish passes. The spacing for roughing cuts is determined by the size of cutter diameter. Normally, the roughing spacing is about 60 to 75 percent of the cutter diameter. The required number of roughing cuts is determined by dividing the amount of material to be removed by the roughing spacing. If the amount of material to be removed is 1.25 in. and the roughing cut spacing is 0.7 in. (assuming 1-in. flat end mill is used), 2 (or 1.25/.7) roughing cuts should be used.

Figure 7.32 shows the toolpath pattern for the toolpath parameters having the following setting:

Number of roughing passes = 2
Spacing of roughing passes = 0.25
Number of finishing passes = 2
Spacing of finishing passes = 0.05

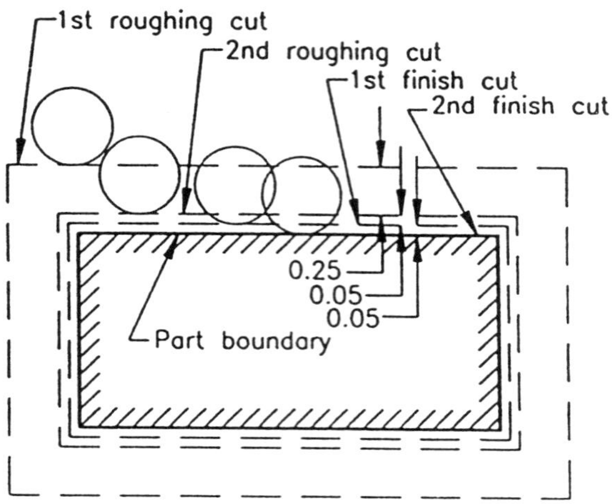

Figure 7.32

Machine finish passes at The "Machine finish passes at" parameter is used to specify whether finish passes to be implemented in final depth only or in all depths. When the "Final depth" option is selected, the finish passes are generated only at the final Z-depth passes. When the "All depths" option is selected, the finish passes are generated at each Z-depth passes. Figure 7.33 shows the contrast of these two options using the same toolpath parameters.

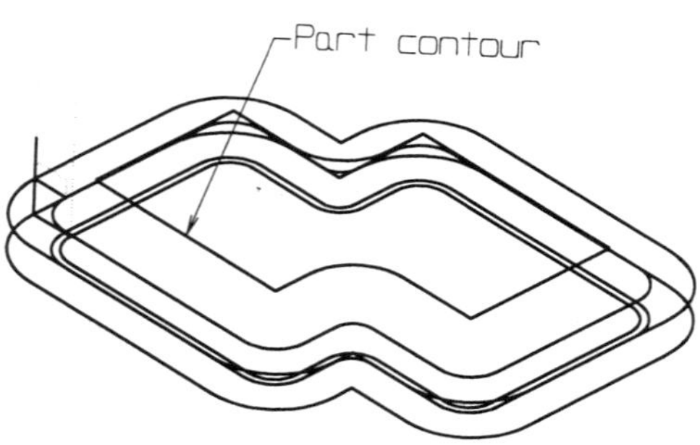

Figure 7.33a At final depth

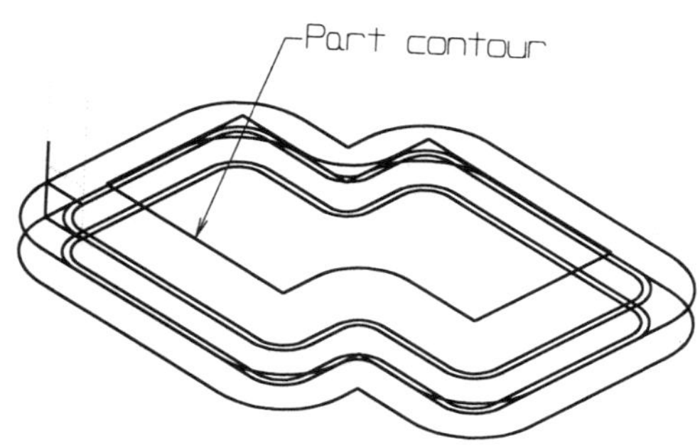

Figure 7.33b At all depths

Compensations Cutter compensation displaces the cutter center by a distance from the specified side of the programmed path. It is often referred to as cutter diameter compensation (CDC) or cutter radius compensation. It can be used in the following applications:

1. Allow the programmer to prepare the required tool path with reference to part coordinates directly.
2. Allow to use a cutter whose diameter differs from that specified by the part programmer without rewriting the program.
3. Compensate the variation in tool size due to wear, regrinding, etc.
4. Allow roughing and finishing cuts to be done with the same part program. Clearance or stock for the finishing cuts has to be set aside during the roughing cuts.

Cutter compensation parameters in Mastercam can be toggled to one of three options: tool left (CDC left), tool right (CAD right), and tool on (CDC off).

Tool left:	The cutting edge of the tool is offset to the left of the programmed path.
Tool right:	The cutting edge of the tool is offset to the right of the programmed path.
Tool on:	The cutter center is on the programmed path.

Figure 7.34 shows the effect of these three commands on the tool paths. To determine the cutter compensation option, look in the chaining direction. Use *tool left* if the cutter is offset to the left of the contour. Use *tool right* when the cutter is displaced to the right of the contour path. Use *tool on* when the cutter coincides with the contour.

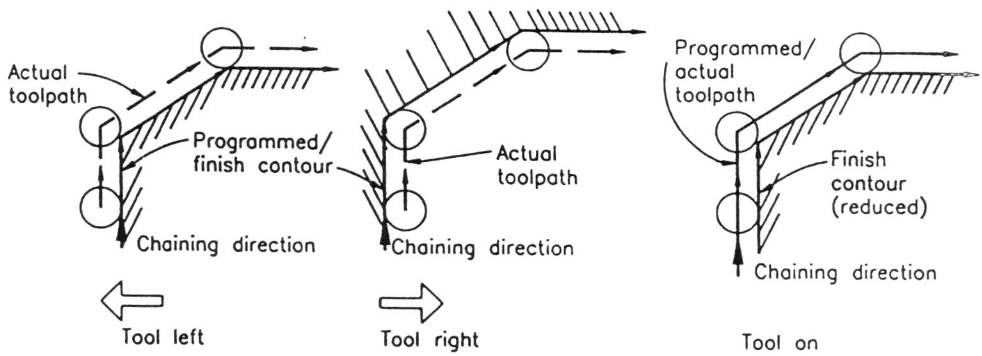

Figure 7.34

These three cutter compensation commands are converted into the following three G-codes during post processing stage:

CDC left:	**G41**
CDC right:	**G42**
CDC off:	**G40**

Mastercam uses three cutter compensation parameters to specify cutter compensation: compensation in computer, compensation in control, and tip compensation. The dialog box for these three compensations is shown here.

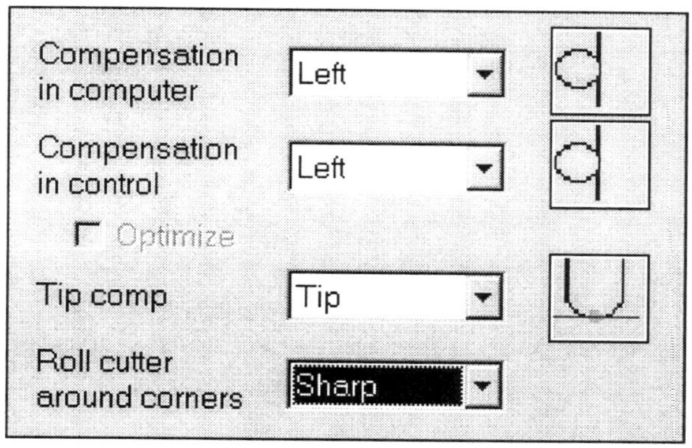

Compensation in Control This parameter generates a cutter compensation command (G40, G41, or G42) for the part program according to the selection. You can set this parameter to ""Off", "Left", or "Right". A compensation register number (Dia.ofst. n.) is assigned to the compensation in control. The compensation value is stored in the specified register. The compensation value can be (1) the actual tool diameter, or (2) the variation value between the designated tool diameter and the actual tool diameter.

Cutter compensation in control	Command in part program
Left	G41 Dd
Right	G42 Dd
Off	G40

where d is the diameter offset number (Dia. Ofst. n.).

The offset value is stored in this register in the CNC control. Figure 7.35 shows the effect of an offset value on the programmed tool paths.

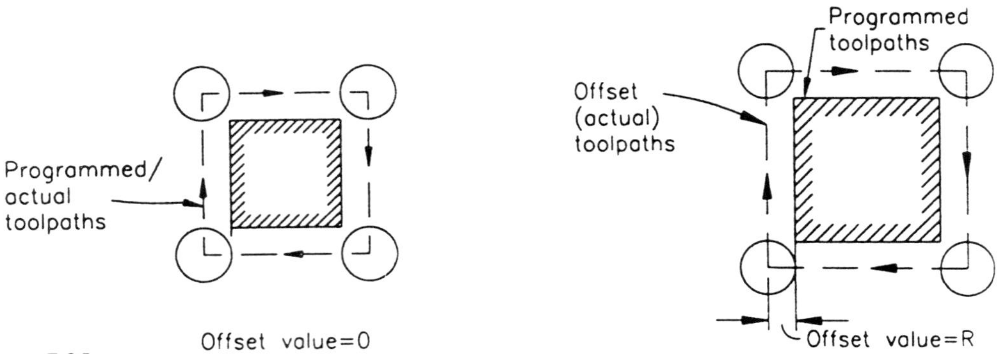

Figure 7.35

Note: On the computer screen, the cutter center does not offset even through the cutter compensation in the control is set to the right or left.

Compensation in Computer This parameter causes the cutter center to be displaced in the specified direction by the designated cutter radius distance. This parameter can be selected to left, right, or off. No cutter diameter compensation code will be inserted into the part program even though the compensation in the system parameter is toggled to the left or right. Note that this parameter changes the coordinate values of the cutter center paths. Figure 7.36 shows the effect of compensation in computer on the tool path.

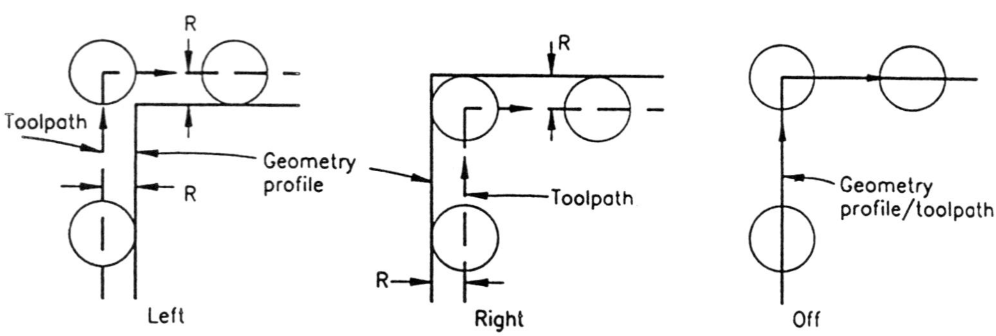

Figure 7.36

Note: Selecting the proper setting of cutter compensation parameters for a particular application is often very confusing. Two factors to be considered in selecting cutter compensation are:

(1) Is the actual cutter diameter identical to the programmed diameter?

(2) Is tool wear present?

Table 7.3 shows combinations in which two cutter compensation parameters can be applied.

Table 7.3 The use of cutter compensation in control and in system

Compensation in control	Compensation in system	CDC command	Remark	Illustration
Off	Off	None	Produces an inaccurate part profile. The dimensional error in all sides is equal to the value of the tool radius.	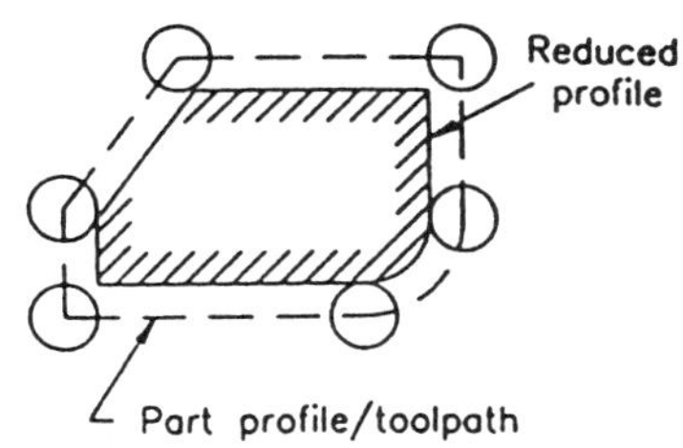
Off	On (Right or Left)	None	Actual tool diameter must be the same as designated diameter, otherwise a positional error will be encountered. The positional error is equal to one-half of the difference between the designated diameter and actual diameter.	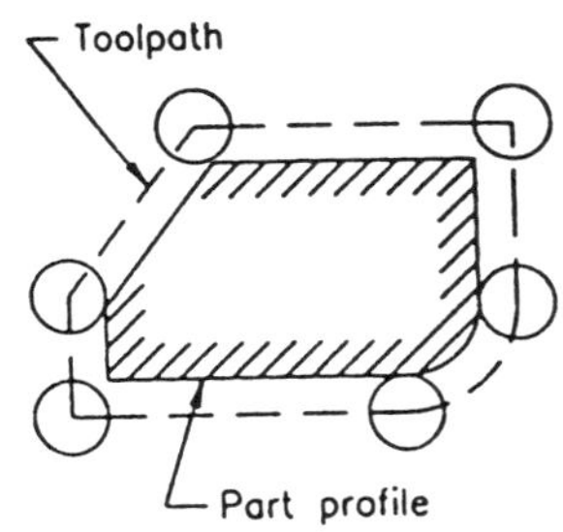
On (Right or Left)	Off	G41 Dxx or G42 Dxx	The actual cutter diameter must be input to the specified register (Dxx) to produce an accurate part profile.	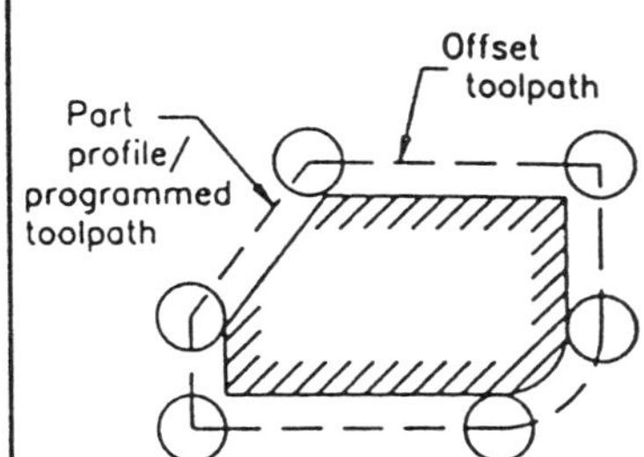
On (Right or Left)	On (Right or Left)	G41 Dxx or G42 Dxx	The difference between the actual and designated tool diameter should be input to the selected register.	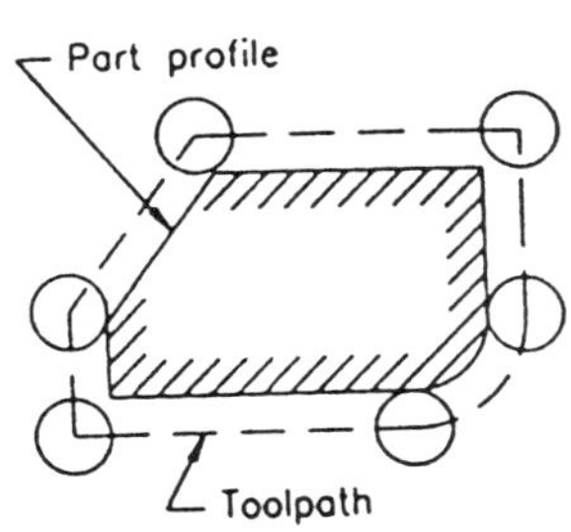

⌛**Tip** Set both compensation in computer and compensation in control to On (Right or Left). This allows the tool to be offset to the proper locations by the compensation in computer, and also permits the variation between the actual and designated cutter diameter to be compensated by using the compensation in control. The compensation value given in the register should be zero when no diameter variation exists, otherwise, the compensation value is the difference between the two diameters.

Tip Compensation This parameter allows you to select cutter compensation to the cutter's center or tip. Figure 7.37 shows the definition of cutter center and tip for three common cutter types: flat end, ball end (spherical), and bull nose. Figure 7.38 illustrates the effect of selection of cutter center and tip on 3D toolpaths.

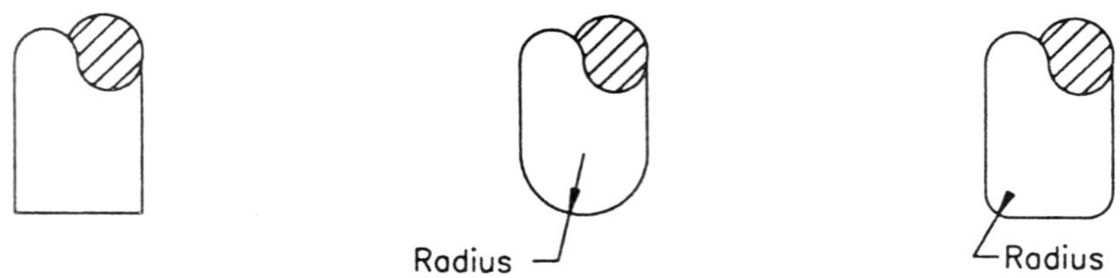

Figure 7.37a Flat end Figure 7.37b Ball end Figure 7.37c Bull nose

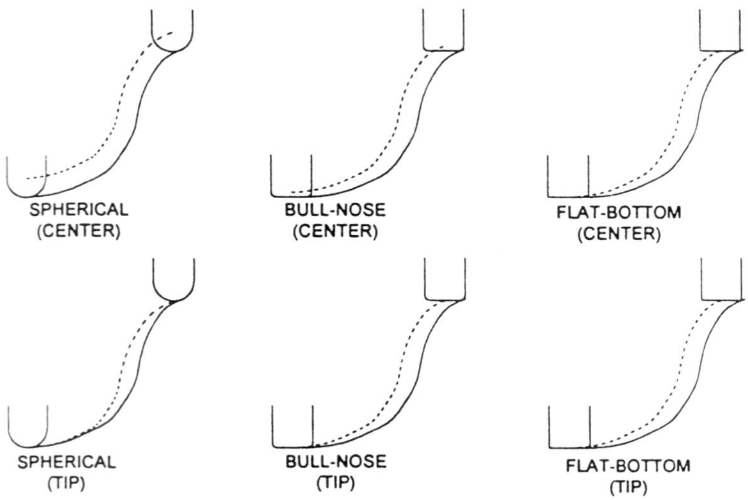

Figure 7.38 The effect of selecting the cutter center and tip on 3D toolpaths.

Roll Cutter Around Corners This parameter determines the toolpath at the corners which are formed by two joined lines. An arc move may be inserted around the corners depending on which mode is selected. The parameter can be toggled to (1) sharp corners (Sharp), (2) no corners (None), and (3) all corners (All). A sharp corner is defined as an included angle which is less than 180 (in the material side (Figure 7.39). Table 7.4 gives typical toolpaths around corners for the three modes.

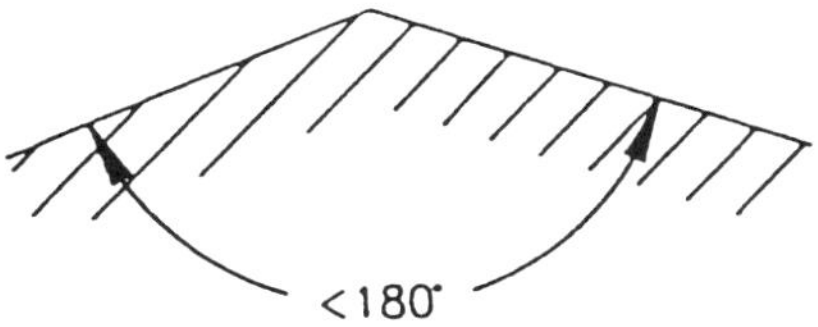

Figure 7.39a Sharp corner

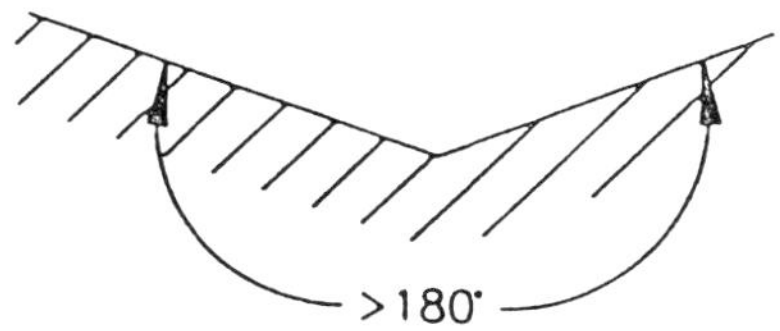

Figure 7.39b Not a sharp corner

Table 7.4 Toolpath around corners

Mode	Toolpath
Sharp corners	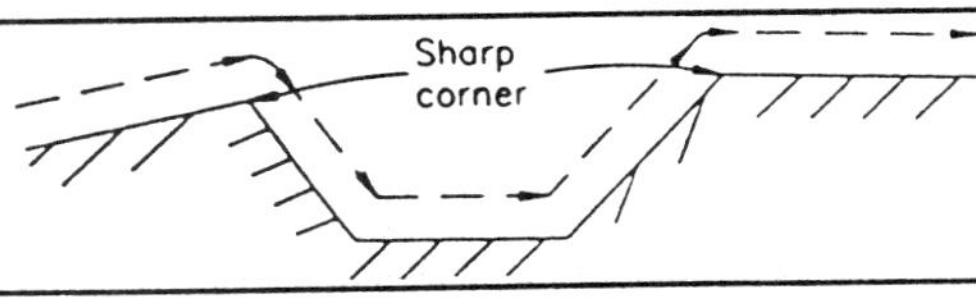
All corners	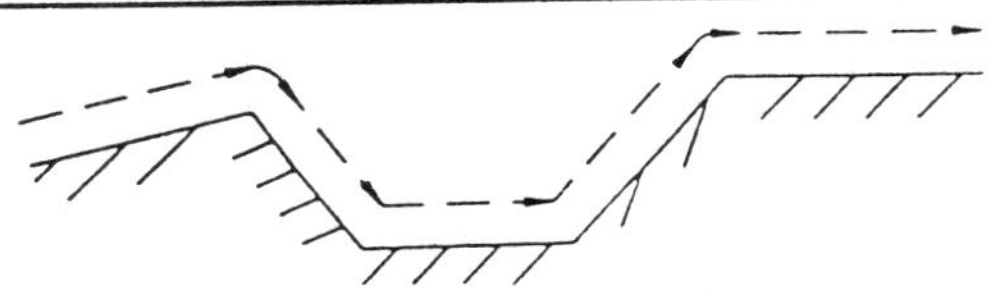
No corner	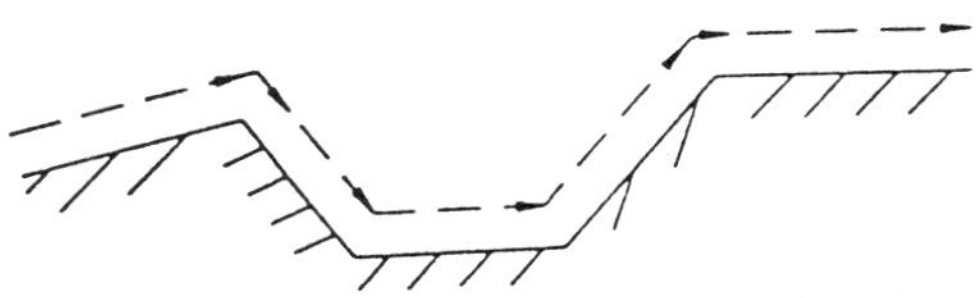

Lead in/out Mastercam allows adding a line move and/or an arc move to the beginning and/or the end of the toolpaths to smoothly engage the tool with the workpiece (Figure 7.40). The move added to the beginning of the toolpath is referred to as the lead in (or entry) move. The move added to the end of the toolpaths is called lead out (or exit) move.

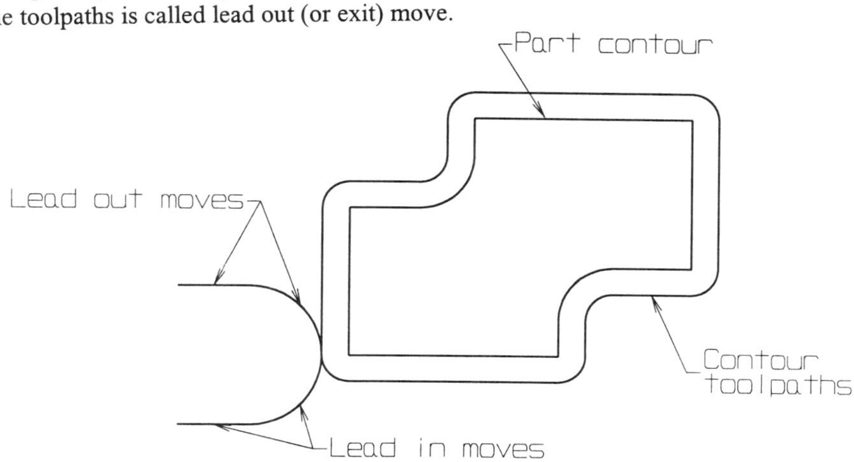

Figure 7.40

The Lead In/Out dialog box is shown below.

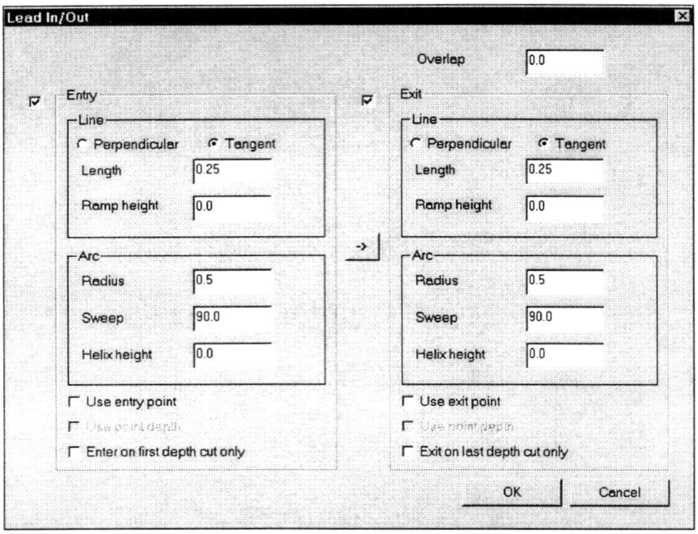

Entry/Exit line A line move can be added in two modes; perpendicular and tangent (Figure 7.41). The perpendicular mode adds the line that has its orientation perpendicular to the adjacent toolpath segment, while the tangent mode adds the line that is tangent to the adjacent toolpath segment.

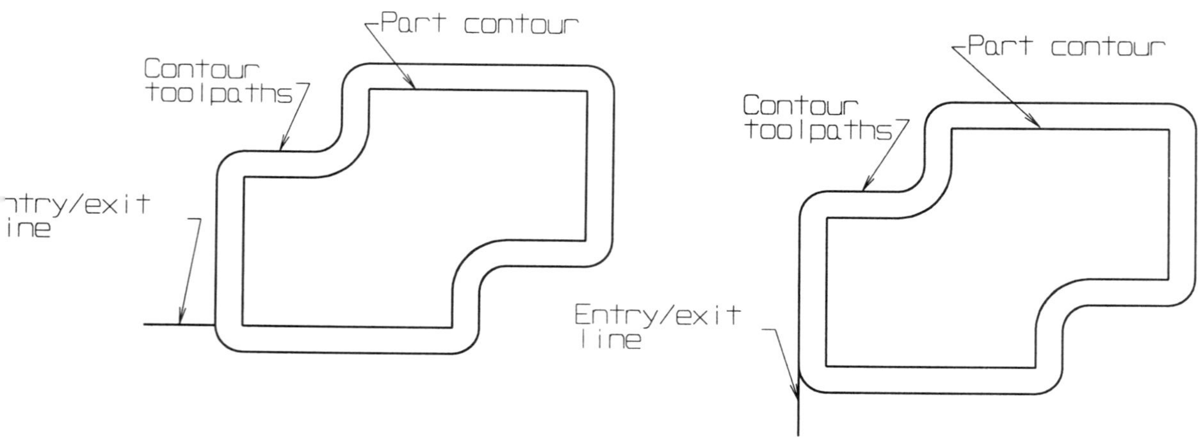

Figure 7.41a Perpendicular mode

Figure 7.41b Tangent mode

The parameter "Ramp height" specifies Z-depth for the entry move to plunge from the start of the line move to end of the move (Figure 7.42), or the Z-depth for the exit move to retract from the start of the line move to end of the move.

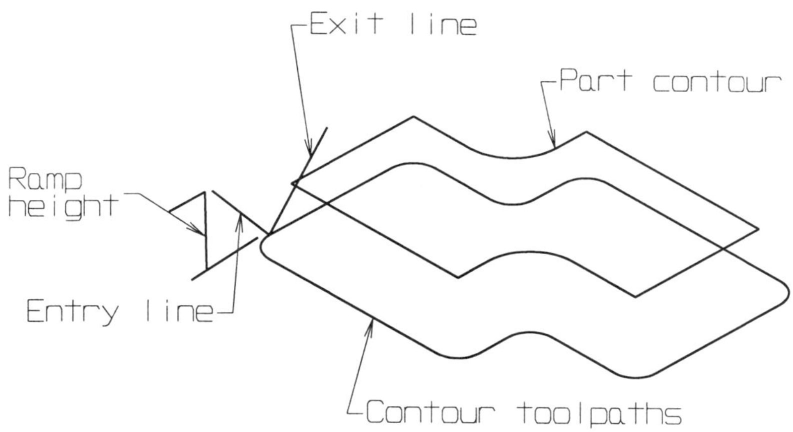

Figure 7.42

Entry/Exit arc An arc move added to the entry and/or exit of toolpaths are defined by the following three parameters (Figure 7.43):

Radius:	specify the radius value of the entry or exit arc.
Sweep:	specify the angle of the entry or exit arc.
Helix height:	specify the Z-depth change of helix spline (added arc).

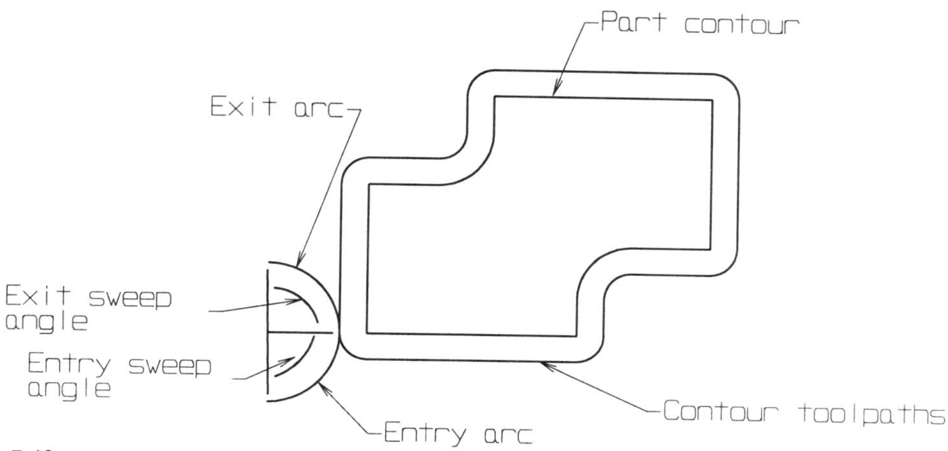

Figure 7.43

Figure 7.44 shows the effect of helix height on the entry/exit arc moves.

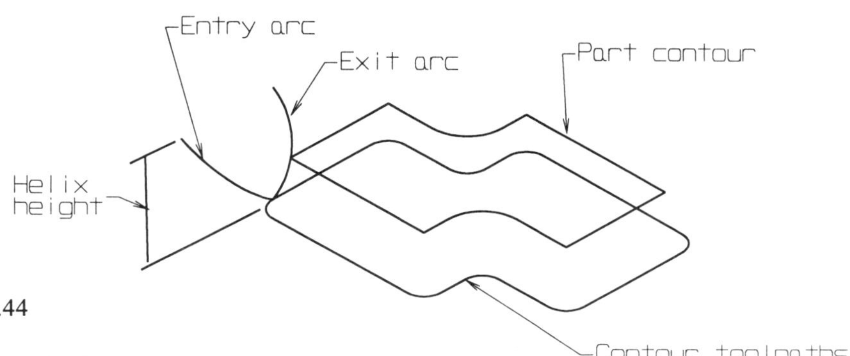

Figure 7.44

1 The remaining three parameters in Lead In/Out dialog box are briefly described below:

Use entry point:	specify the entry point.
Use point depth:	use the depth of selected point.
Enter on first depth cut only:	add entry moves only to the first depth cut.
Exit on last depth cut only:	add exit moves only to the last depth cut.

Project 1. Contouring external profile

Use the contour module to generate toolpaths to cut an external profile shown in Figure 7.45. The total depth of cut is 1-in. The raw material is the casted workpiece which is about ¼-in. larger than the finished dimensions in all directions.

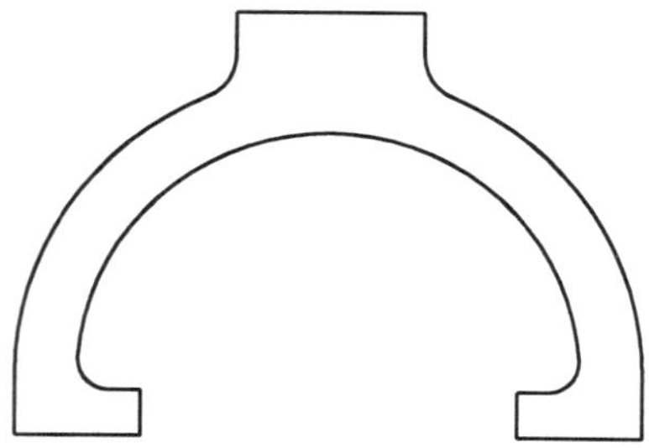

Figure 7.45a

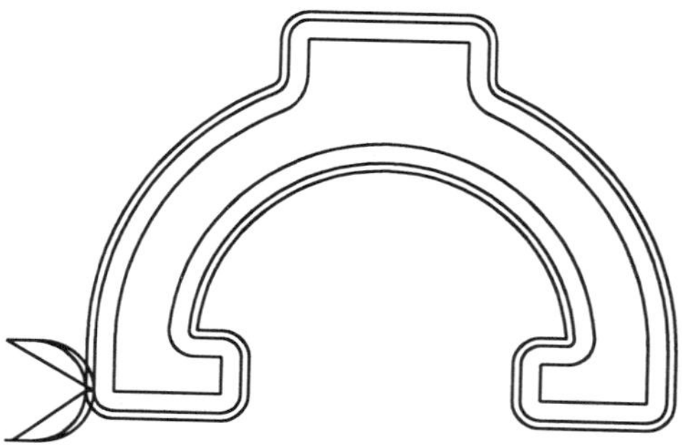

Figure 7.45b

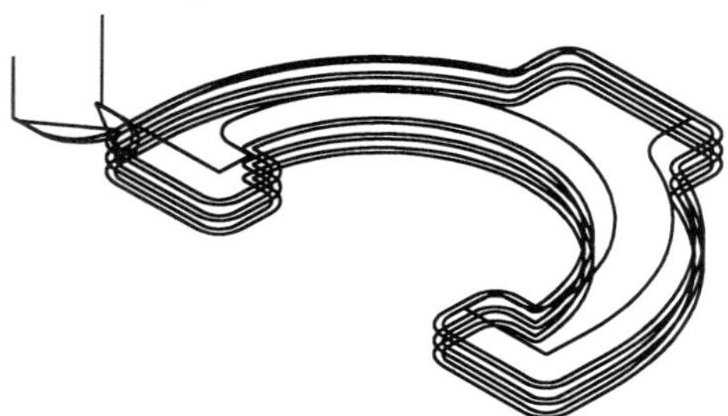

Figure 7.45c

Tips
1. Use a ¾" end mill.
2. Use one roughing cut and one finish cut for the machining taking place in the XY-plane. The stock for the finish pass is 0.1-in.
3. Use three passes (two roughing cuts and one finish pass) in the depth cut (Z) direction. The two roughing cuts take 0.35" each and the finish pass takes 0.3".
4. Set the entry/exit length to 0.5", the entry/exit arc has a radius of 1" and an angle of 90°.
5. Set cutter compensation in control to off and cutter compensation in computer to left center.

Step 1. Load the geometry file contour1.mc7.

(or create the geometric model by following the procedure given in project 1 of chapter 5.)
Select **MAIN MENU → File → Get**
File name: **contour1**

The drawing should appear as Figure 7.46.

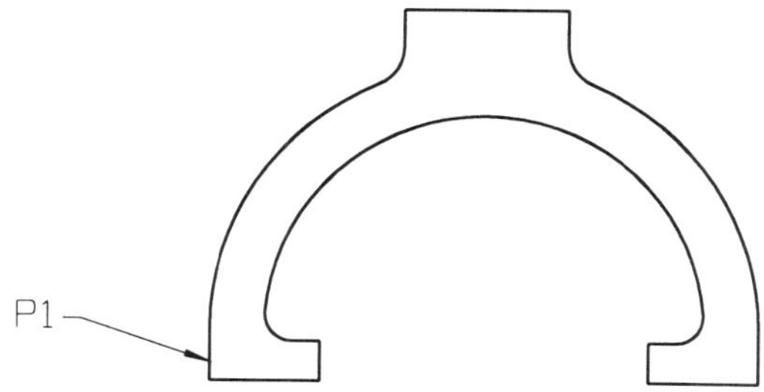

Figure 7.46

Step 2. Set both the construction plane and graphics view to Top.

Select **Cplane → Top**
Select **Gview → Top**

Step 3. Initiate the contour module.

Select **MAIN MENU → Toolpaths → Contour**
Enter file name: **contour1**
Select **Save**

Step 4. Define the contour using the pick point in Figure 7.46.

Select Chain from the chaining method menu
Pick **P1** to select the first entity of the contour
Select **Done**

Step 5. Select a tool from the tool library.

The Contour Properties dialog box should appear as below.

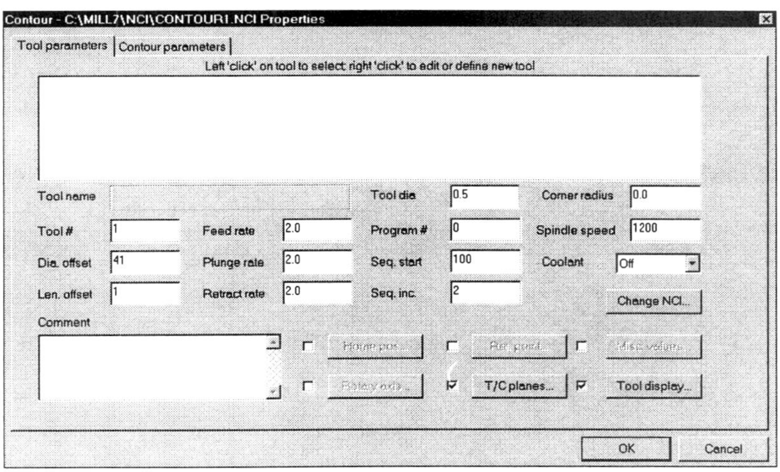

Place the mouse on the larger blank space within the dialog box, then click the right mouse button to open the selection menu as below.

Select **Get tool from library**
The Tool Manager menu appears as below.

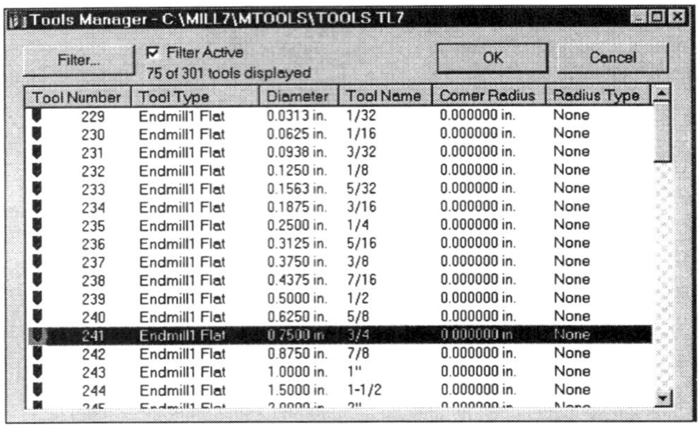

Select **3/4" end mill** from the list
Select **OK**
The 0.75" end mill has been added to the Contour Properties menu as shown below.

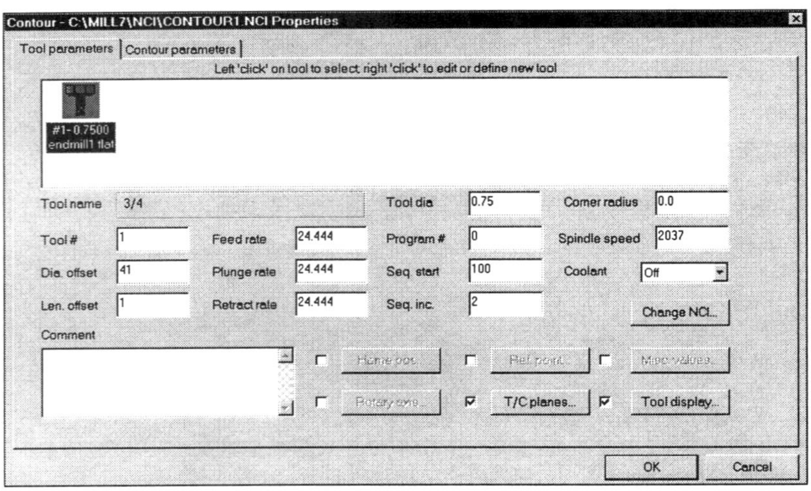

Step 6. Define tool and toolholder parameters.

Place the mouse on the tool icon (#1-0.7500 endmill flat),
then click the right mouse button to open the Define tool dialog box.
Set their parameters as shown next.

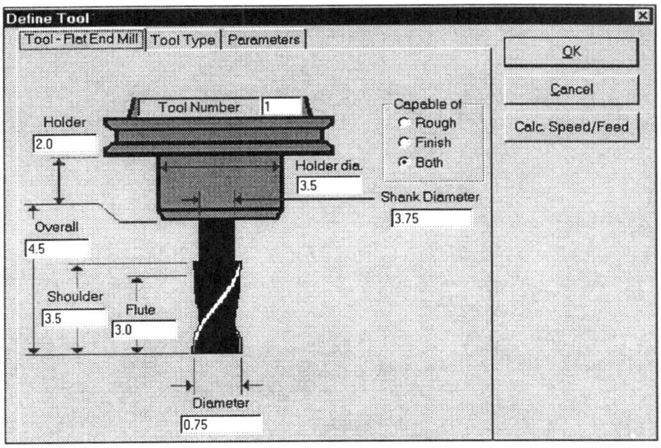

Select the Parameters button to set the tool parameters as shown below.

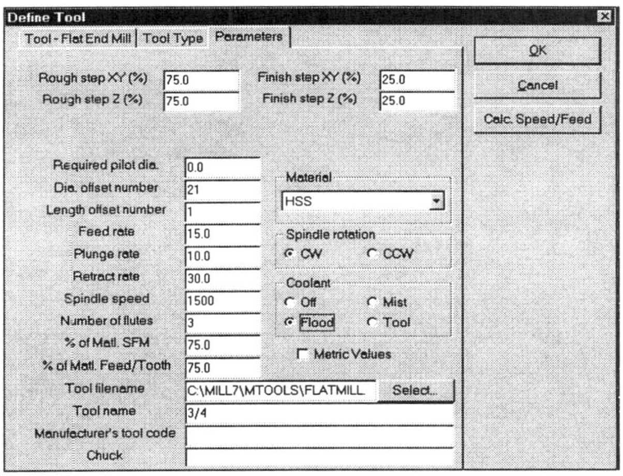

Select **OK**

Set the tool parameters as below.

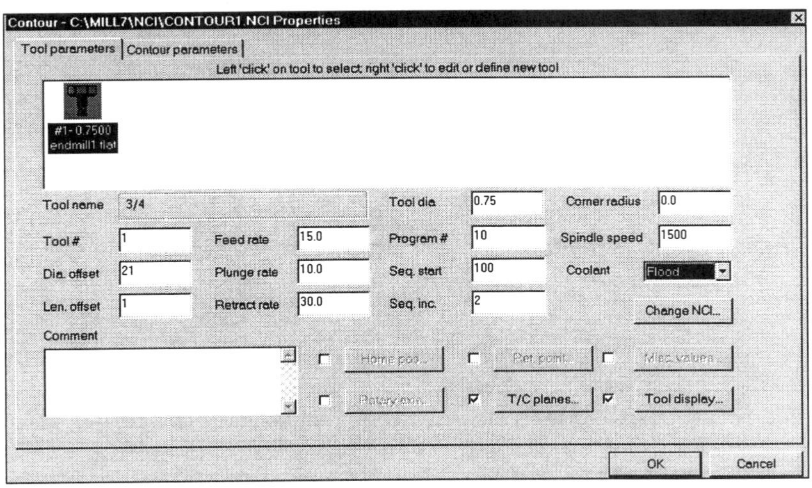

Step 7. Define the Contour parameters.

Select the **Contour parameters button**
Set the NC parameters as below.

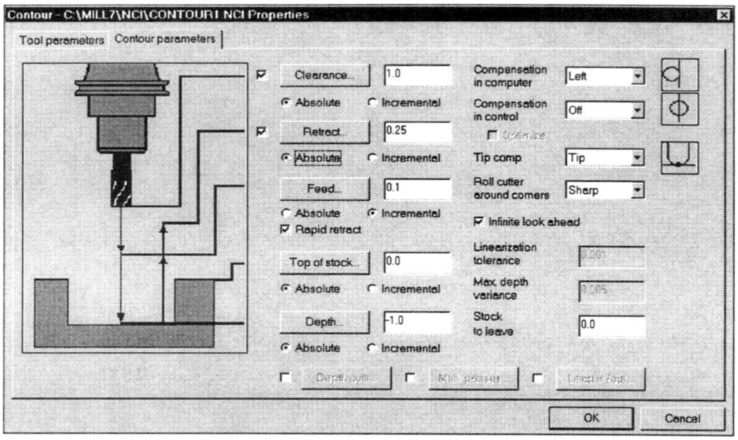

Step 8. Define the depth cuts parameters.

Click the check box of Depth Cuts, then click the **Depth Cuts** button to open its dialog box
Set depth cuts parameters as here.

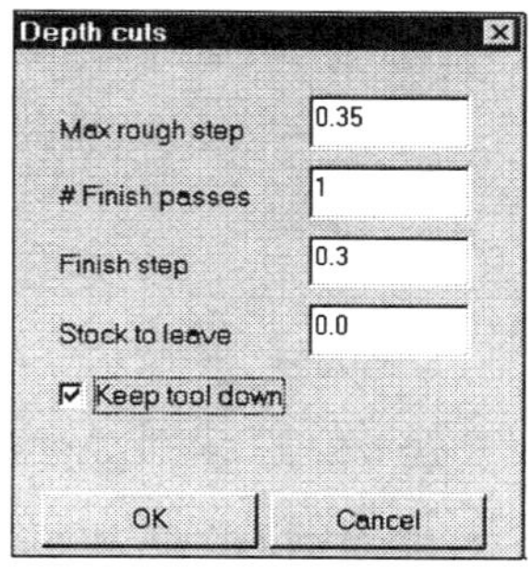

Select **OK**

Step 9. Define the multiple-passes parameters.

Click the check box of Multi passes, then click the **Multi passes** button to open its dialog box
Set the multiple passes parameters as here.

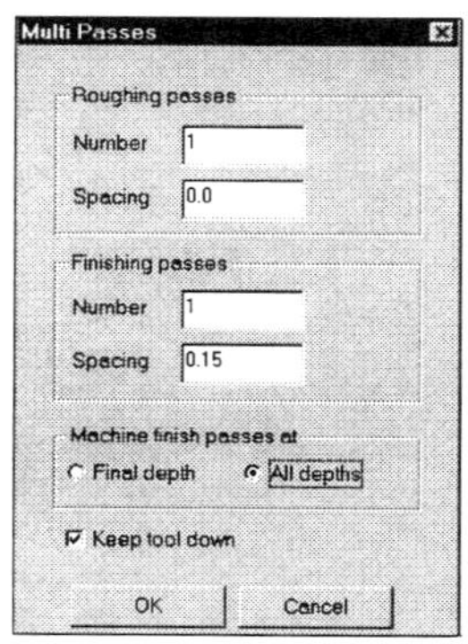

Select **OK**

Step 10. Define the lead in/out parameters.

Click the Lead in/out check box, then click **Lead in/out** button to open its dialog box

Set lead in/out parameters as below.

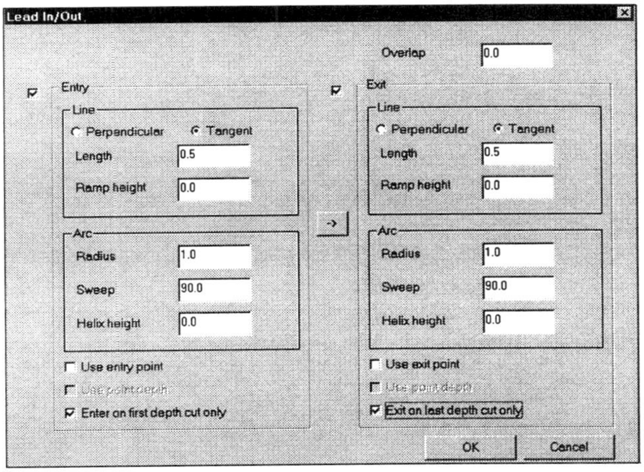

Select **OK** to return to tool parameters menu
Select **OK** to generate toolpaths
The toolpaths should appear as in Figure 7.47.

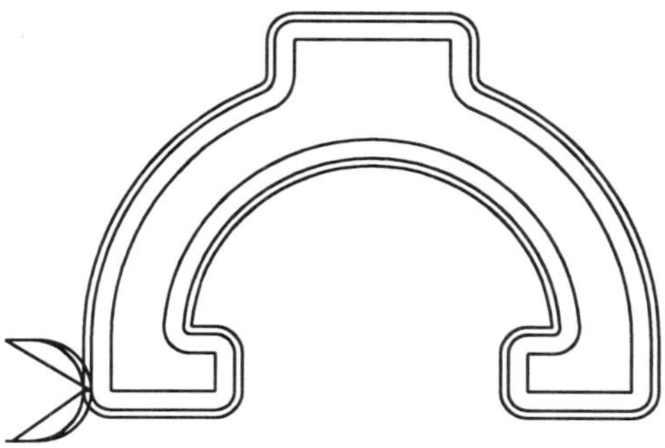

Figure 7.47

Step 11. Change Gview to Isometric

Select **Gview** → **Isometric**
The toolpath shown in isometric view appears as Figure 7.48.

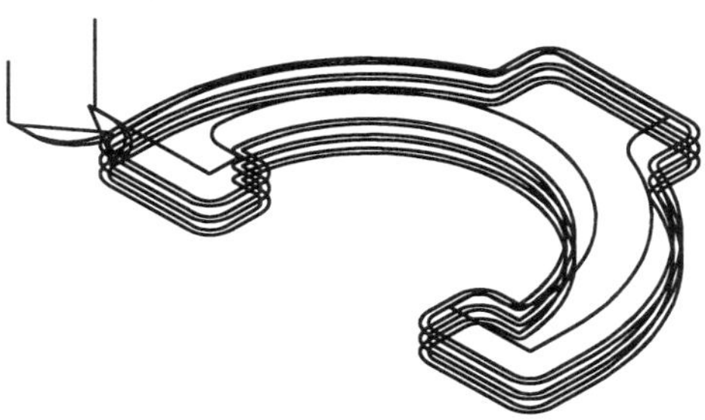

Figure 7.48

Step 12. Run the post processor.

Select **Operations**

The Operations Manager menu appears below.

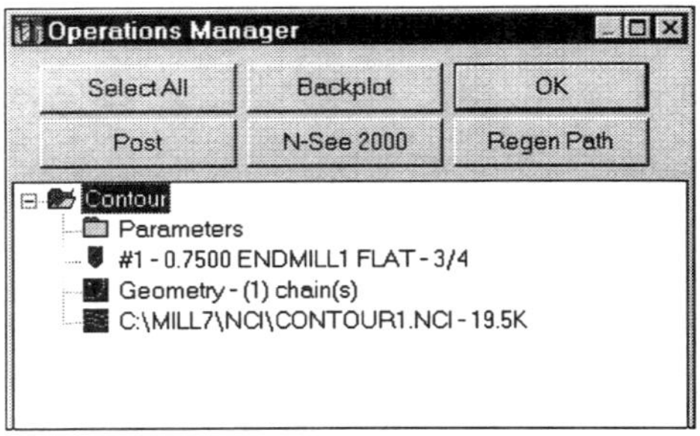

Select **Post**
Select **Yes** to "Run the post processor?"
File name for NC: **Contour1.NC**
Select **Save**

The partial program is listed below. (Your program may look somewhat different from the one listed here because your version may be using a different post processor).

```
%
(PROGRAM NAME - CONTOUR1 )
(DATE, Day-Month-Year - 12-05-98  TIME, Hr:Min - 13:12 )
( TOOL - 01   DIA. OFF. - 21   LENGTH - 01   DIA. - .7500   3D-CONTOUR )
O0010
N100 G00 G40 G49 G80 G90
/ N102 G91 G28 Z0.
/ N104 G28 X0. Y0.
/ N106 G92 X0. Y0. Z0.
N108 G0 G90 X-7.025 Y-2. S1500 M3
N110 G43 H1 Z1. M8
N112 Z.1
N114 G1 Z-.35 F10.
N116 X-6.525 F15.
N118 G3 X-5.525 Y-1. I0. J1.
N120 G1 Y0.
N122 G2 X-2.162 Y5.0844 I5.525 J0.
N124 G3 X-2.025 Y5.2915 I-.088 J.2071
N126 G1 Y6.
N128 G2 X-1.5 Y6.525 I.525 J0.
N130 G1 X0.
        -
        -
        -
N440 G1 Y-.25
N442 G2 X3. Y.125 I.375 J0.
N444 G1 X3.4911
N446 G3 X3.6157 Y.2589 I0. J.125
N448 X0. Y3.625 I-3.6157 J-.2589
N450 X-3.6157 Y.2589 I0. J-3.625
N452 X-3.4911 Y.125 I.1247 J-.0089
```

continued in next column

```
N454 G1 X-3.
N456 G2 X-2.625 Y-.25 I0. J-.375
N458 G1 Y-1.
N460 G2 X-3. Y-1.375 I-.375 J0.
N462 G1 X-5.
N464 G2 X-5.375 Y-1. I0. J.375
N466 G3 X-6.375 Y0. I-1. J0.
N468 G1 X-6.875
N470 G0 Z1.
N472 M05
N474 G91 G28 Z0. M9
N476 G90
N478 M30
%
```

Step 13. Exit file edit mode.

Click the **File list** button at the upper left corner
Select **Close** to return to the Operations Manager mode

Step 14. Backplot the toolpaths.

Click the **Backplot** button in the Operations Manager dialog box
Select **Display**
Set the display parameters as below.

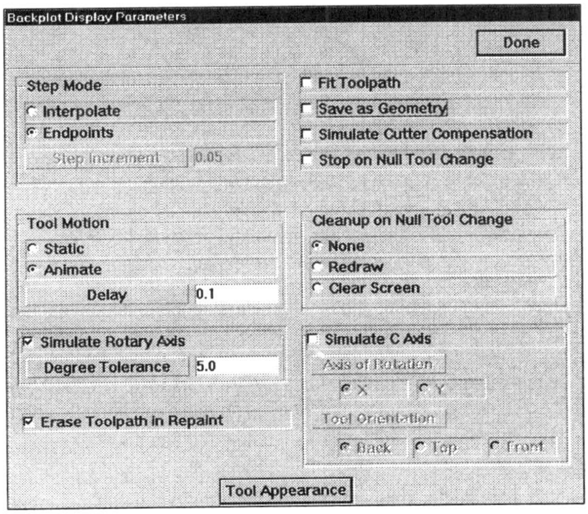

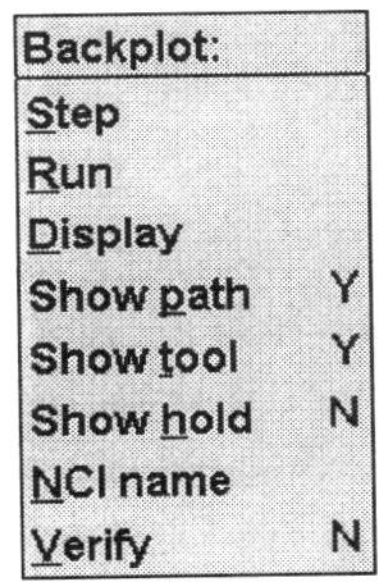

Select **Done**
Set backplot parameters as here.
Select **Run** to animate the toolpath on the screen as shown in Figure 7.49.

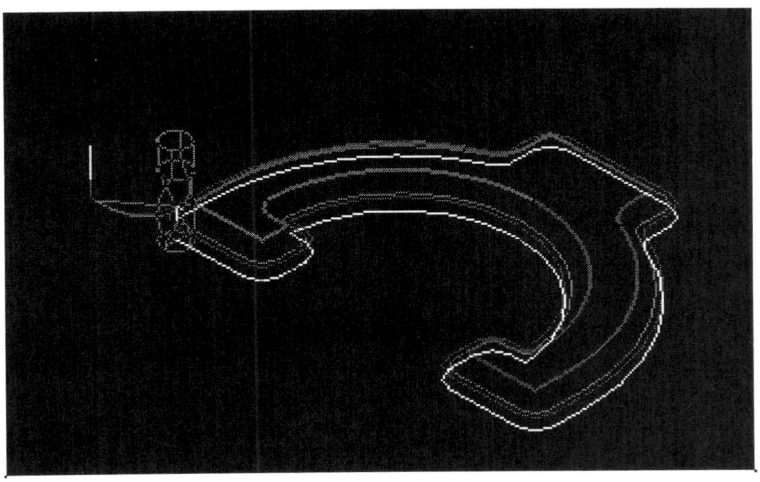

Figure 7.49

Select **MAIN MENU** to return to Operations Manager menu
Select **OK** to return back to graphic mode

Step 15. Save the project file.

Select **File → Save**
File name: **contour1t**

2 Project 2. Contouring internal profile

Use the contour module to generate toolpaths to take the cutter along the internal profile of the part shown in Figure 7.50. The workpiece has been casted to its rough size. Therefore, it requires only one finish pass to cut to the desired profile. The depth of cut in the Z direction is 0.5-in.

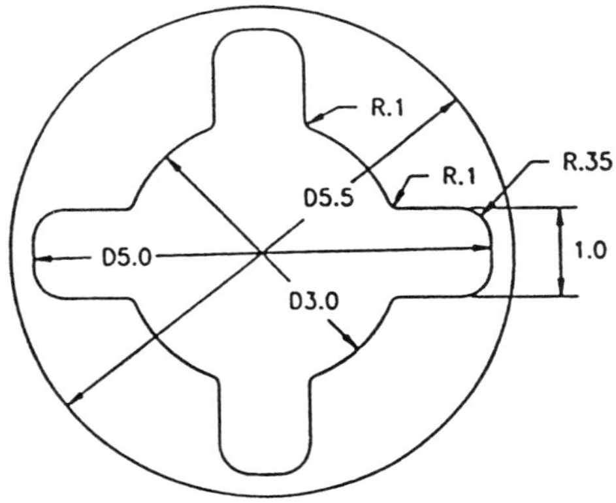

Figure 7.50a

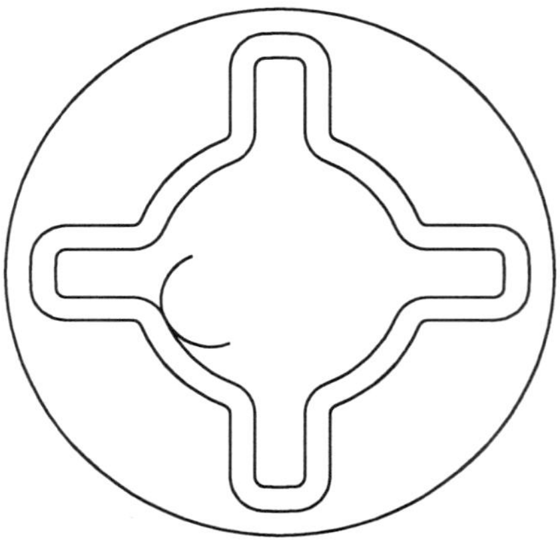

Figure 7.50b

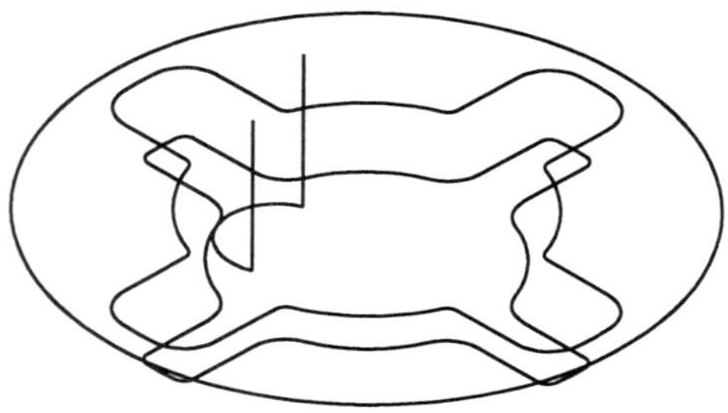

Figure 7.50c

Tips 1. Use a ½" end mill.

2. Define the contour direction to be in the counterclockwise direction to obtain climb milling for a better surface finish.
3. Set entry/exit length to 0 and arc radius to 0.5 and angle to 90(.
4. Set cutter compensation in control to left and cutter compensation in computer to left center.
5. Set rapid depth to 0.3 and contour depth to –0.5.

Step 1. Load the geometry file contour2. mc7.

(or create the geometry by following the procedure given in project 3 of chapter 6.)
Select **MAIN MENU → File → Get**
Enter file name: **contour2**

The drawing should appear as Figure 7.51.

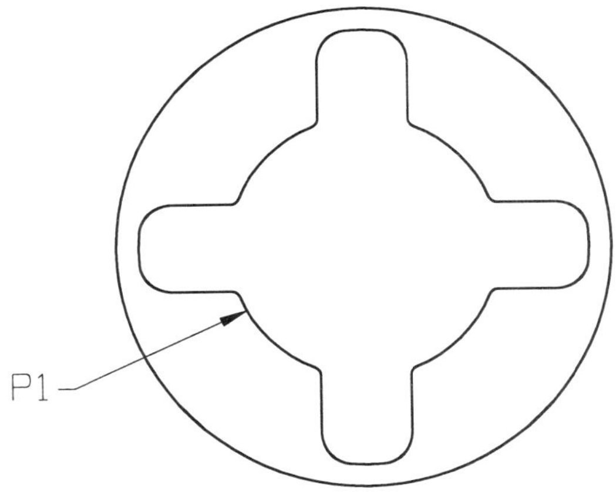

Figure 7.51

Step 2. Set both Cplane and Gview to Top view if necessary.

Select **Cplane → Top**
Select **Gview → Top**

Step 3. Initiate the contour module.

Select **MAIN MENU → Toolpaths → Contour**
Enter file name: **contour2**

Step 4. Define the Contour using the pick point in Figure 7.51.

Select **Chain**
Pick **P1** to select the starting entity of the contour
Select **Done**

Step 5. Select ½" end mill from tool library and set tool parameters.

The Contour Properties dialog box should appear on screen.
Click the right mouse button, then select **Get tool from library**
Select **tool number 239** (1/2 flat end mill)
Select **OK**
Set the tool parameters as below.

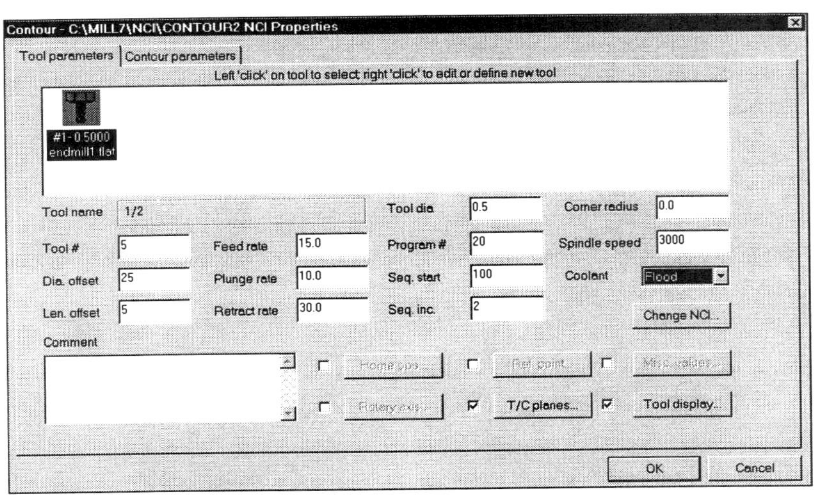

Step 6. Define the contour parameters.

Click the Contour parameters button
Set the contour parameters as below.

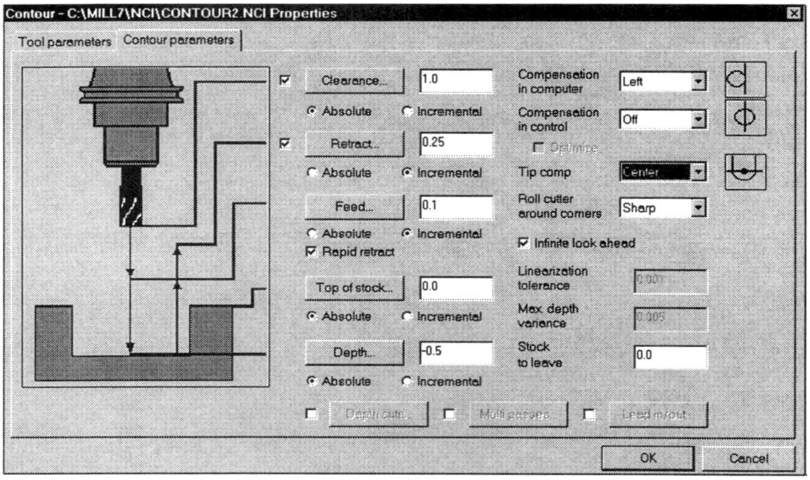

Step 7. Define lead in/out parameters.

Click the check box of Lead in/out, then click **Lead in/out** button
Set the lead in/out parameters as below.

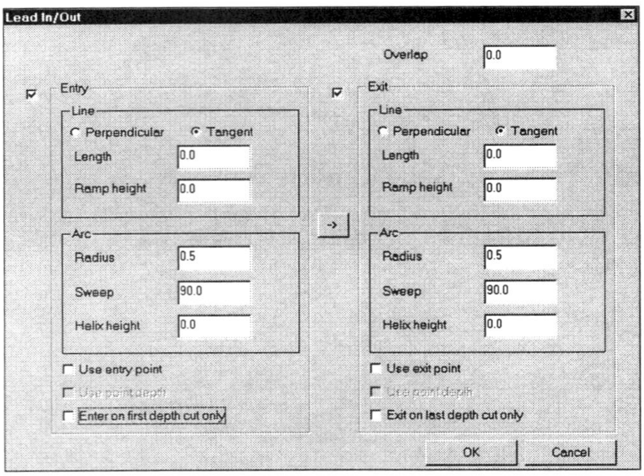

Select **OK** to return to contour parameters menu
Select **OK** to generate toolpaths
Select **OK** to "Tool #1 renumbered to #5"

The toolpaths should appear as Figure 7.52.

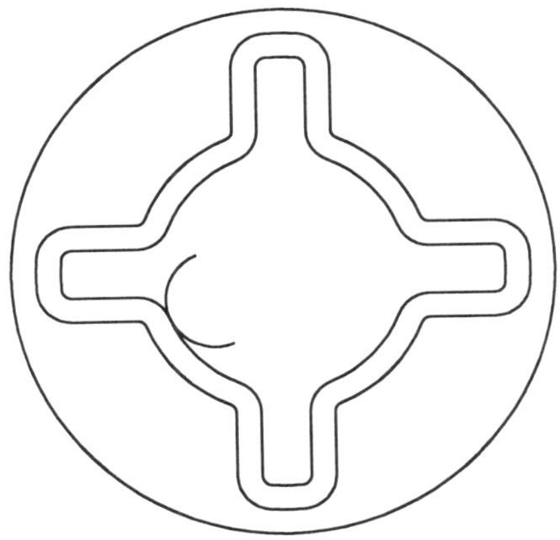

Figure 7.52

Step 8. Show the toolpaths in isometric view.

Select **Gview → Isometric**
The toolpaths shown in isometric view appear as in Figure 7.53.

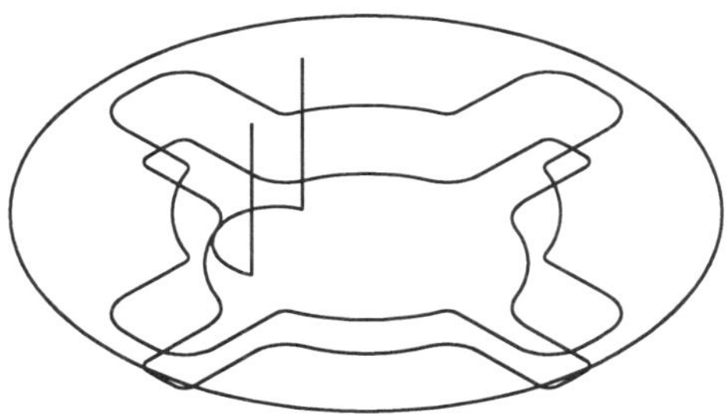

Figure 7.53

Step 9. Run the post processor.

Select **Operations** to open Operations Manager dialog box
Select **Post**
Select **Yes** to "Run the post processor"
File name for NC program: **contour2**
The part program appears on the screen.
Click the **Close button** at the upper-right corner to exit File list
Select **OK** to exit Operations Manager dialog box

Step 10. Edit the part program file.

Select **MAIN MENU → File → Edit → NC**
File name: **contour2t**

3 The NC Editor with the part program should appear as below.

```
MasterCam NC Editor and DNC Communications
File  Edit  View  NC Utils  Macros  DNC  Help
%
(PROGRAM NAME - CONTOUR2 )
(DATE, Day-Month-Year - 12-05-98  TIME, Hr:Min - 14:46 )
( TOOL - 05   DIA. OFF. - 25   LENGTH - 05   DIA. - .5000   3D-CONTOUR )
O0020
N100 G00 G40 G49 G80 G90
/ N102 G91 G28 Z0.
/ N104 G28 X0. Y0.
/ N106 G92 X0. Y0. Z0.
N108 G0 G90 X-.8828 Y.1823 S3000 M3
N110 G43 H5 Z1. M8
N112 Z.1
N114 G1 Z-.5 F10.
N116 G3 X-1.1588 Y-.4688 I.1875 J-.4635 F15.
N118 X-.8839 Y-.8839 I1.1588 J.4688
N120 X-.4688 Y-1.1588 I.8839 J.8839
N122 G2 X-.25 Y-1.4832 I-.1313 J-.3245
N124 G1 Y-2.1448
N126 G3 X-.157 Y-2.2445 I.1 J0.
N128 X0. Y-2.25 I.157 J2.2445
N130 X.157 Y-2.2445 I0. J2.25
N132 X.25 Y-2.1448 I-.007 J.0998
N134 G1 Y-1.4832
Edit Mode...                 Contour2.nc              1
```

Do all necessary editing and save the file

Step 11. Exit the NC Editor.

Select **File → Exit**

Project 3. Contouring along an open profile

This project uses the contour module to generate toolpaths for cutting an open profile. Multiple passes are used along the profile to ensure the two angle corners are removed. Figure 7.54 shows geometry and toolpaths.

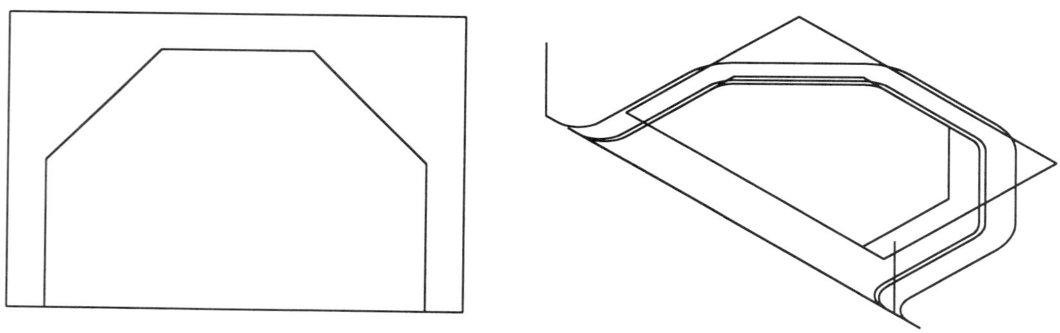

Figure 7.54

Tips 1. Use the geometry file contour3.

2. Use the contour module to generate toolpaths.

Step 1. Open the part geometry file contour3.mc7.

Select **MAIN MENU → File → Get**
Enter file name: **contour3**
The part geometry appears as in Figure 7.55.

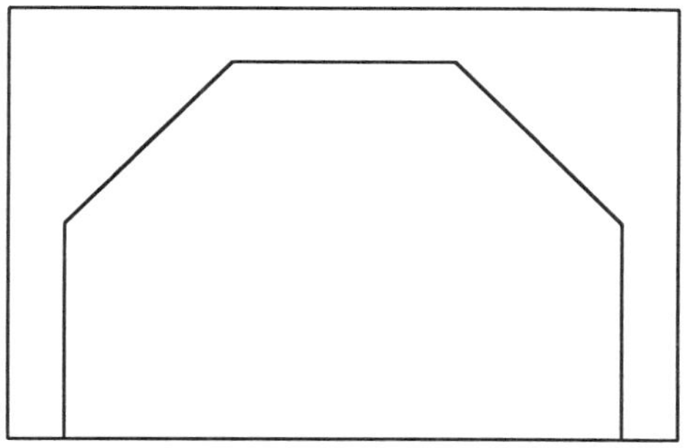

Figure 7.55

Step 2. Set Gview to isometric and Cplane to top.

Select **Gview → Isometric**
The isometric view of the part geometry appears as in Figure 7.56.

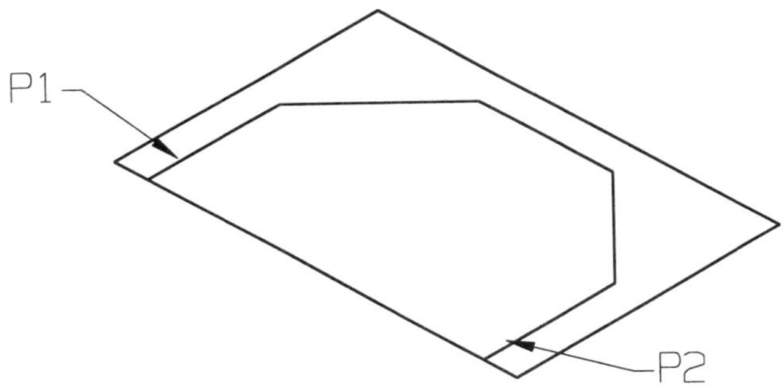

Figure 7.56

Step 3. Initiate the contour module.

Use the pick point in Figure 7.56.
Select **MAIN MENU → Toolpaths → Contour**
File name for toolpaths: **contour3**
Select **Chain → Partial**
Pick at **P1** and **P2** to select in the contour
Select **Done**

Step 4. Define the tool parameters.

Click the right mouse button, then select **Get tool from library**
Select **tool #243** (1-in. end mill)
Select **OK**

Set the tool parameters as below.

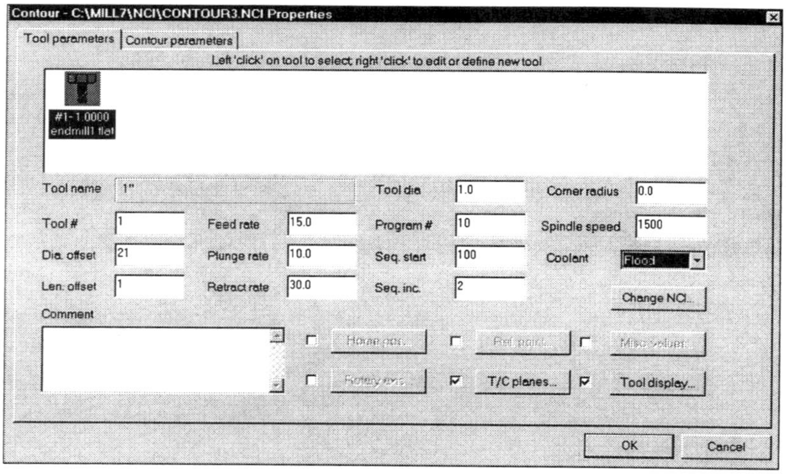

Step 5. Define the contour parameters.

Click the "Contour parameters" button
Set the contour parameters as below.

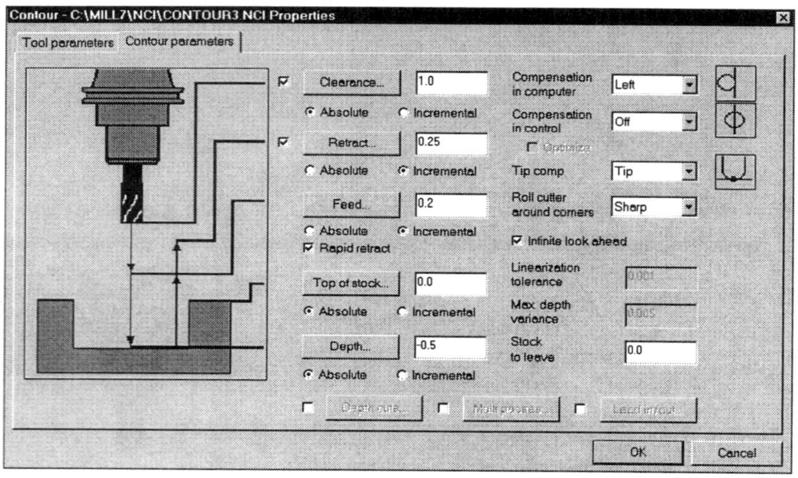

Step 6. Define the multi-pass parameters.

Click the check box of the "**Multi passes**" button
Click the Multi passes button
Set the multi passes parameters as below.

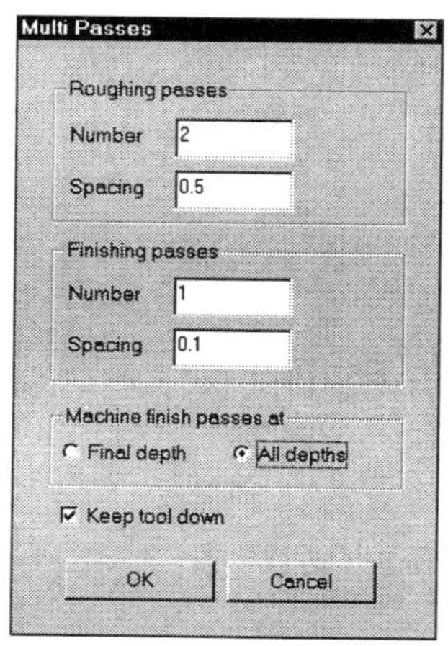

Select **OK** to exit Multi passes menu

Step 7. Define lead in/out parameters.

Click the check box of the **Lead in/out** button
Click the Lead in/out button

Set the lead in/out parameters as below.

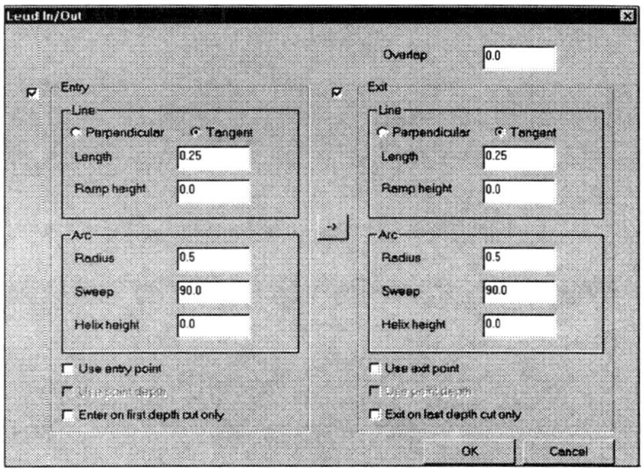

Select **OK** to exit lead in/out menu
Select **OK** to generate toolpaths as in Figure 7.57.

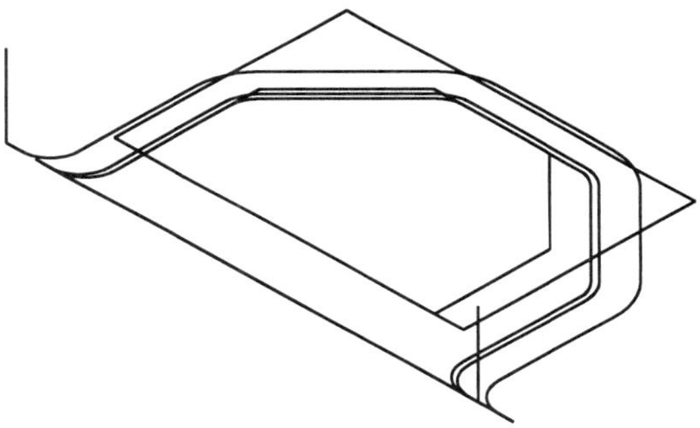

Figure 7.57

Step 8. Change to top view.

Select **Gview → Top view**
The toolpaths shown in top view appear as in Figure 7.58.

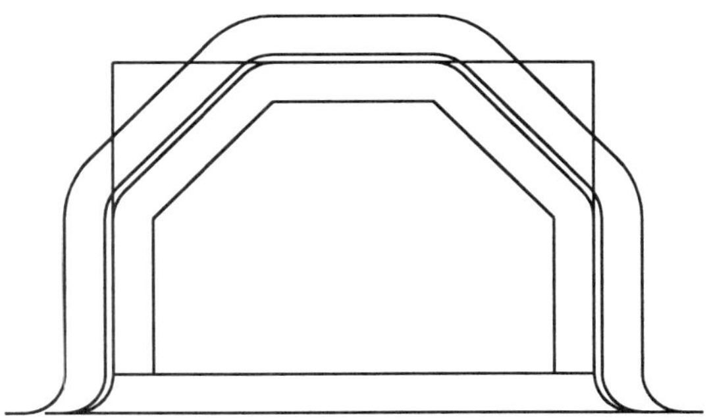

Figure 7.58

Step 9. Save the toolpaths.

Select **MAIN MENU → File → Save**
File name: **contour3t**

7.10 Pocket Module

The pocket module is used to generate a set of toolpaths to (1) remove the material enclosed by a closed contour, (2) face a flat surface, and (3) rough cut a local pocket. The pocket module has two major dialog boxes used to define pocketing and machining parameters. They are entitled as pocketing parameters and roughing/finishing parameters as below.

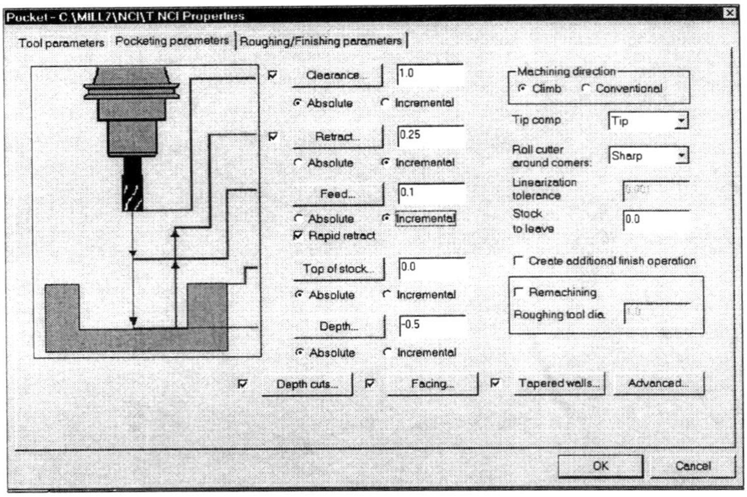

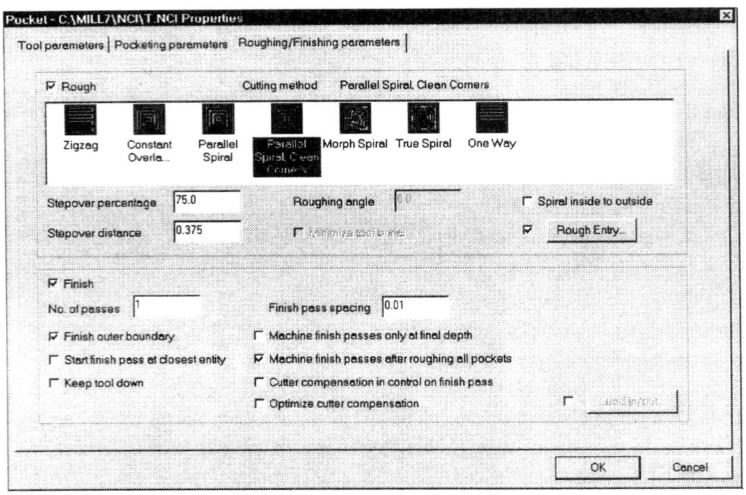

Pocketing parameters

The pocketing parameters dialog box has been shown above. It consists of the following eight groups of parameters: **Z-depth parameters, Depth cuts parameters, Facing parameters, Facing parameters, Tapered walls parameters, Advanced parameters, Machining direction**, and **Others**.

Z-depth parameters This group of parameters is used to define the Z-depth of pocketing toolpaths. They are identical to those used in the contour module. Here we only show their definition without detailed discussion (Figure 7.59).

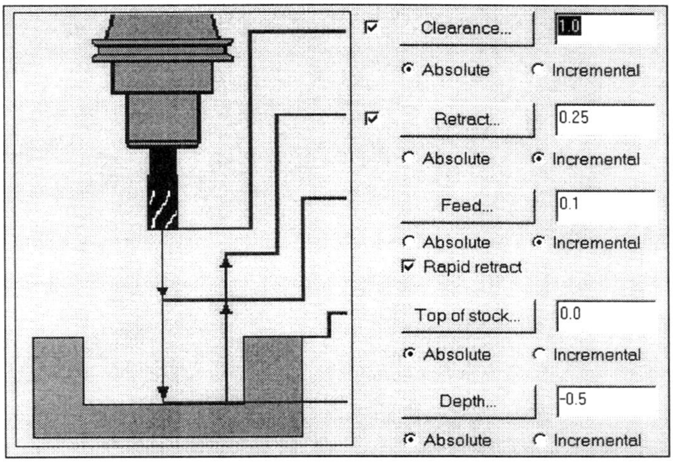

Figure 7.59

Depth cuts parameters The six parameters in the depth cuts dialog box is shown below.

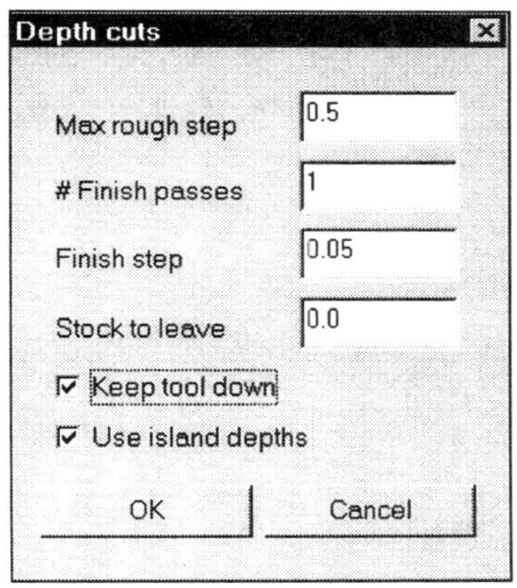

These parameters are identical to those used in the contour module except for the adding "Use island depths" parameter. The "Use island depths" parameter is to specify the pocketing depth to be set to the island depths.

Facing parameters The four facing parameters are used to extend the pocketing toolpaths to the pocketing boundary. Figure 7.60 shows the contrast between the toolpaths using facing function and without using facing function. The amount of extending toolpaths over the pocket boundary is specified either one of the following two parameters:

Overlap percentage:	the overlap amount is specified by the percentage of cutter diameter.
Overlap amount:	the overlap amount is directly specified by the value given in this parameter.

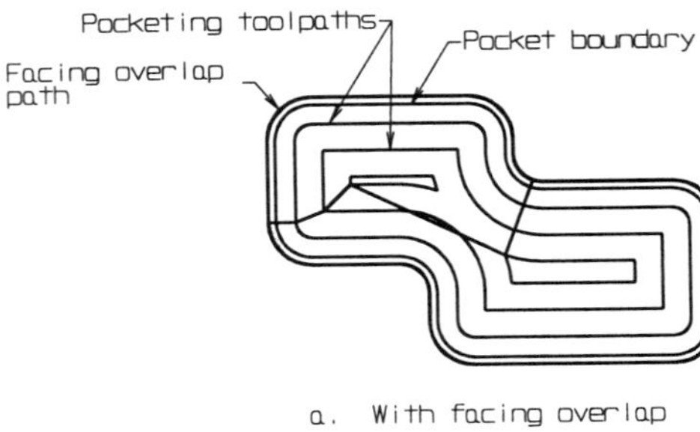

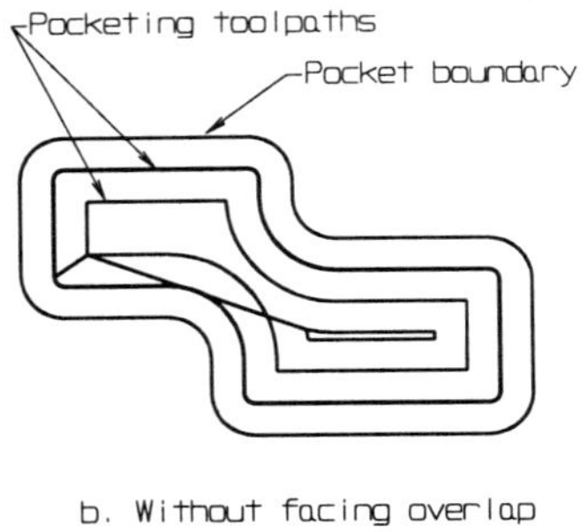

Figure 7.60a with facing overlap

Figure 7.60b Without facing overlap

Figure 7.61 shows the result of using different overlap value on the pocketing toolpaths.

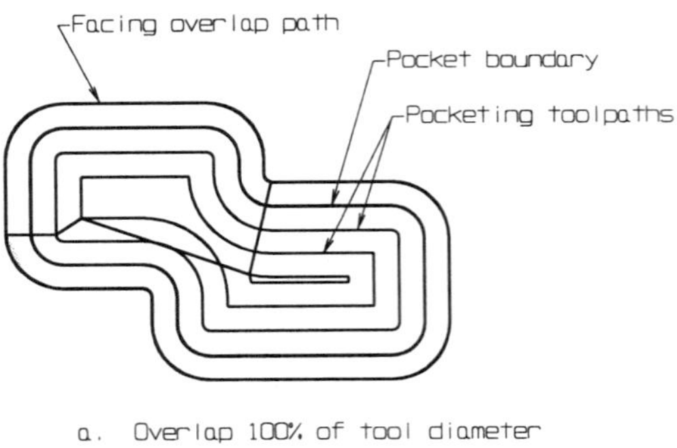

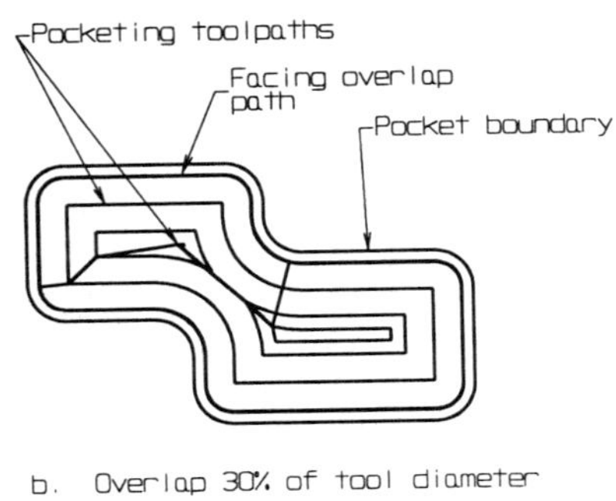

Figure 7.61a Overlap 100% of tool diameter

Figure 7.60bOverlap 30% of tool diameter

Tapered wall This parameter enables the generation of a set of toolpaths to cut a pocket with a tapered wall as shown in Figure 7.62.

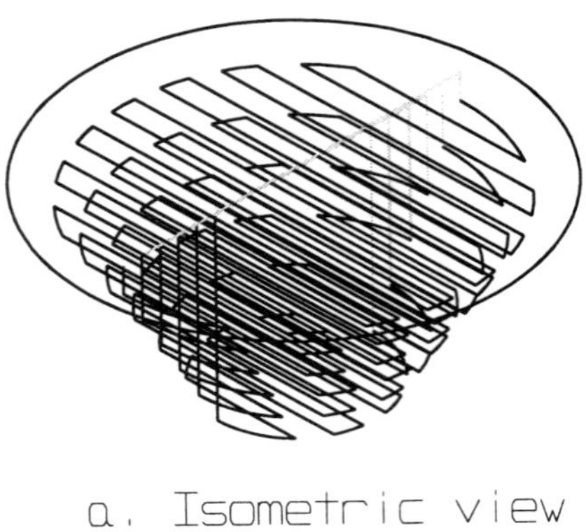

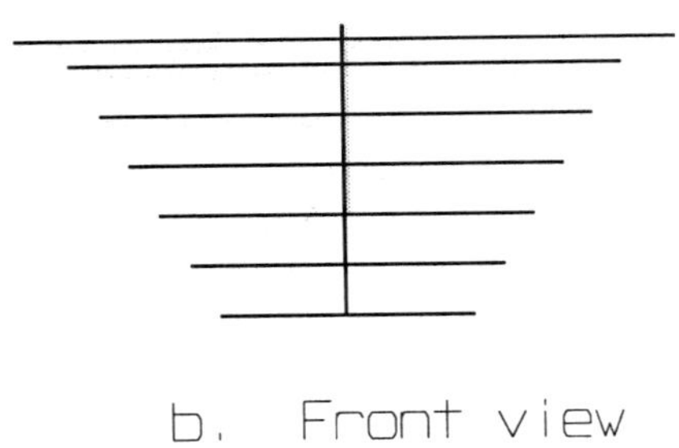

Figure 7.62a Isometric

Figure 7.62b Front view

Click on the Tapered wall button at the bottom of the Pocketing parameters dialog box to make the Tapered wall submenu appears as below.

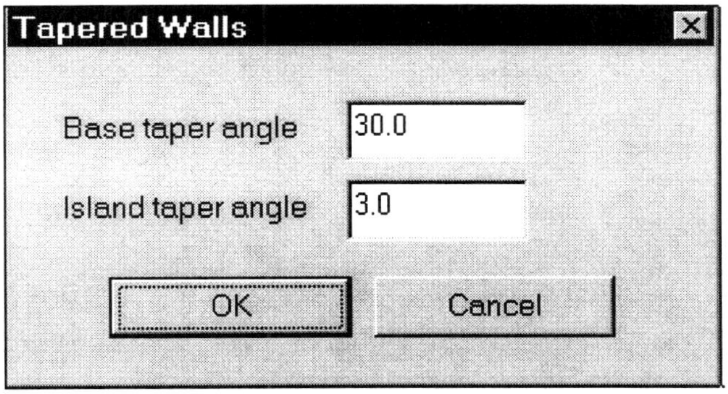

Machining direction This parameter specifies the milling type to be implemented in pocketing. It has the following two options:

Climb:	generate the pocketing toolpaths following the climb milling direction.
Conventional:	generate the pocketing toolpaths following the conventional milling direction.

In climb milling, the direction of feed is the same as the direction of tool rotation (Figure 7.63). In conventional milling, the direction of feed is opposed to the direction of cutter rotation (Figure 7.64).

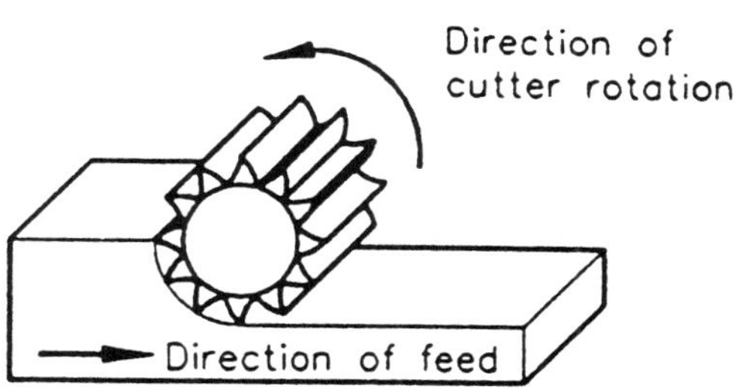

Figure 7.63a Climb milling plain milling cutter

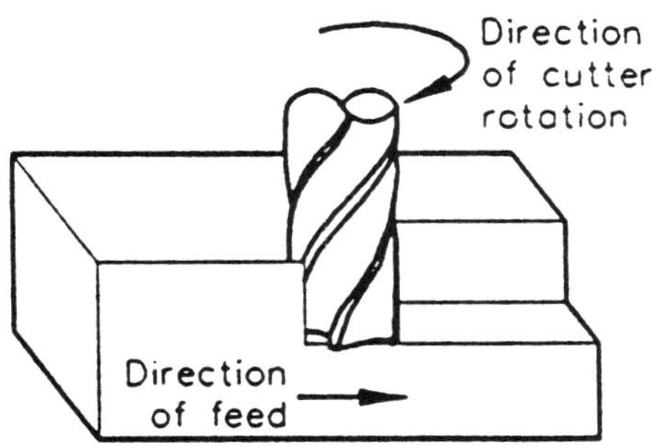

Figure 7.63b Climb milling with end mill

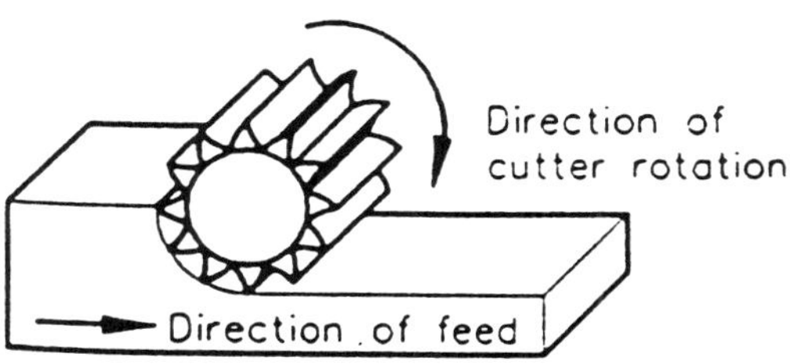

Figure 7.64a Conventional milling plain milling cutter

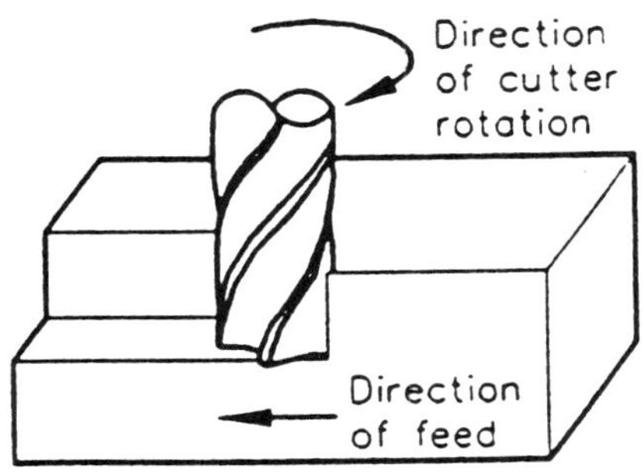

Figure 7.64b With end mill

Advanced parameters   The advanced parameters are used to specify the tolerance for remachining and constant overlap spiral. Its dialog box is shown below.

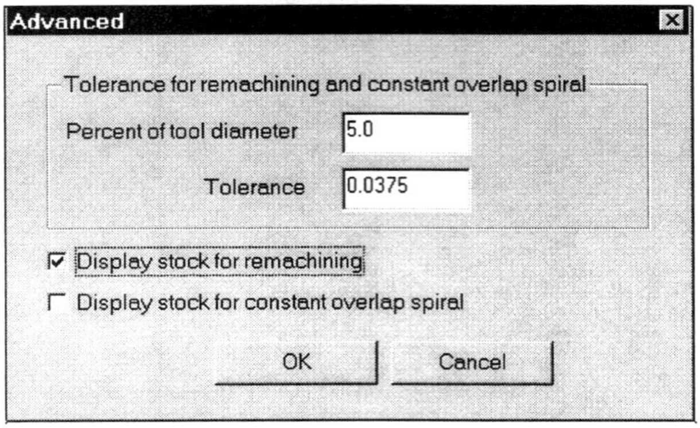

Remachining Parameter   The Remachining parameter is used to control whether the remachining function is to take place. Toggle this parameter to On√ will alter the pocketing toolpaths.

Other parameters   The remaining pocketing parameters are listed below:

Tip comp: specify the tool compensation either to Tip or Center.
Roll cutter around corners: specify the roll corners type (sharp, all, or none)
Linearization tolerance: specify the tolerance value for linearization of curves.
Stock to leave: specify the stock amount to be left for further machining.

Roughing/Finishing parameters

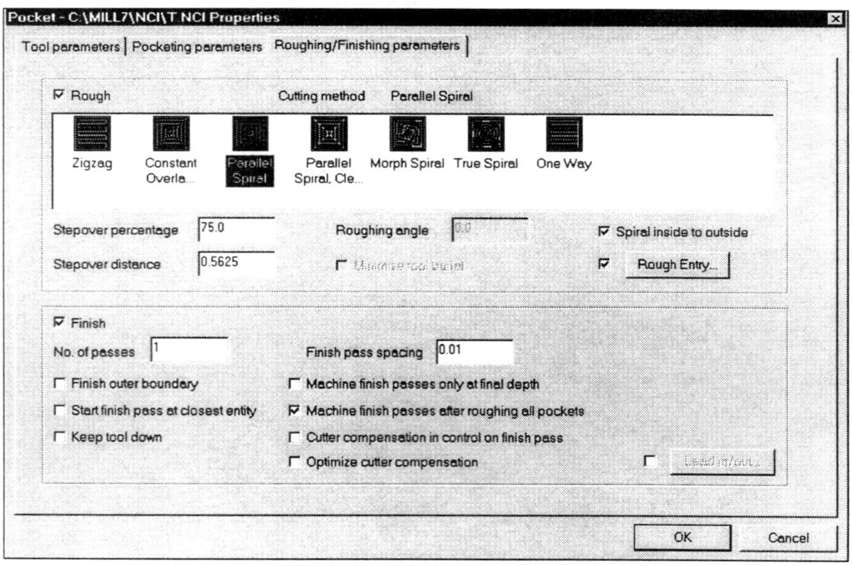

Cutting method Mastercam provides seven cutting methods for pocketing: zigzag, constant overlap spiral, constant overlap spiral, parallel spiral, parallel spiral/clean corners, morph spiral, true spiral, and one way. These seven cutting methods can be grouped under two categories: zigzag and spiral. The zigzag group has two options; zigzag and one way. The spiral group has the remaining five options.

Zigzag method This method generates a set of back and forth linear toolpaths to rough the pocket (Figure 7.65). The orientation of the toolpath is specified by the roughing angle parameter. The roughing angle also decides the start point of the pocketing toolpaths.

The cutting angle is measured from the positive X-axis and has a positive angle in the counter-clockwise direction and a negative angle in the clockwise direction (Figure 7.66).

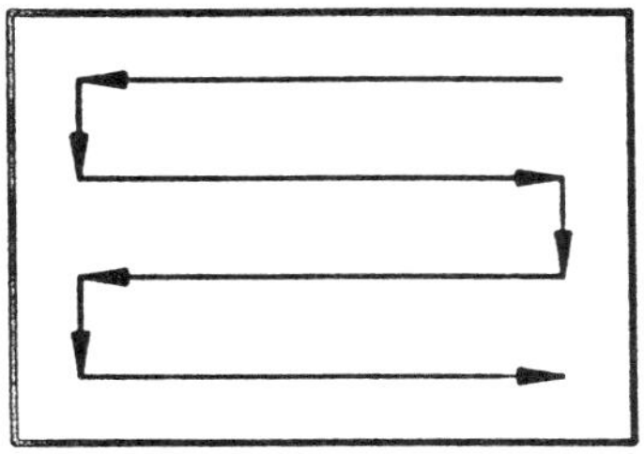

Figure 7.65

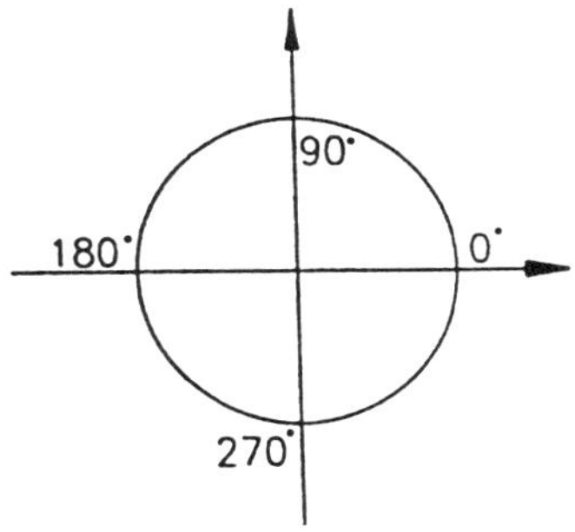

Figure 7.66

Figure 7.67 shows a number of common roughing angles and their toolpaths starting points.

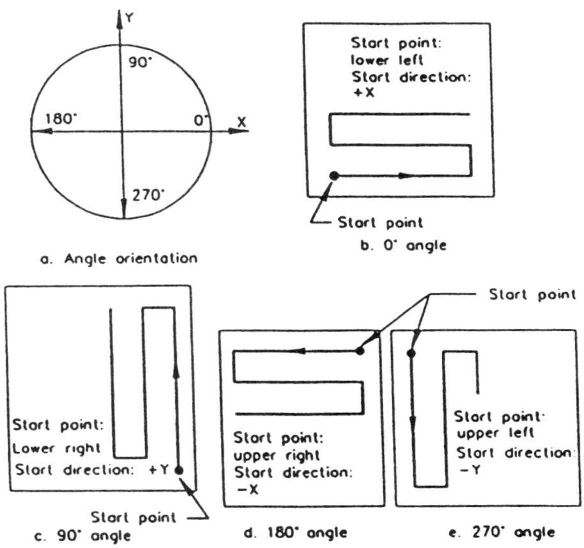

Figure 7.67

The "One Way" cutting method generates a similar set of toolpaths as the zigzag method. The difference is that one way method generates toolpaths that cut in the same direction. They make a pass, then retract in the Z direction, rapid to another starting point, and take another pass in the specified direction. The toolpath pattern is repeated until the pocket cutting is completed (Figure 7.68). The direction of the cutting paths is determined whether the climb milling or conventional milling is specified.

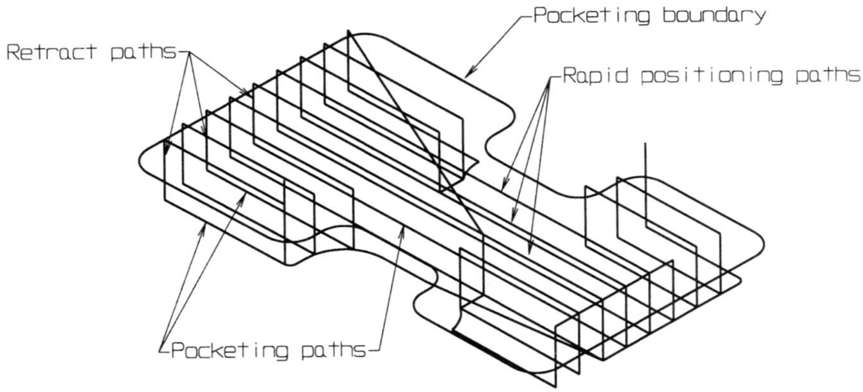

Figure 7.68

Spiral method The spiral method starts the cutter at the pocket center or specified pocket start point and spiral it to the wall of the pocket. It has the following five modes:

Constant overlap spiral:	generate pocketing toolpaths in spiral pattern with constant overlap (Figure 7.69).
Parallel spiral:	generate pocketing toolpaths in parallel-spiral pattern (Figure 7.70).
Parallel spiral, clean corners:	generate pocketing toolpaths in parallel-spiral pattern with clean corners (Figure 7.71).
Morph spiral:	generate pocketing toolpaths in morph-spiral pattern (Figure 7.72). This mode requires at least one island. It generates much more toolpath segments than other modes.
True spiral:	generate pocketing toolpaths in circular-spiral pattern (Figure 7.73).

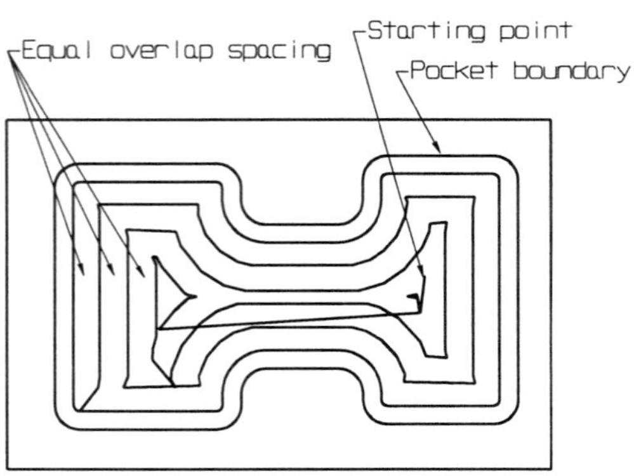

Figure 7.69

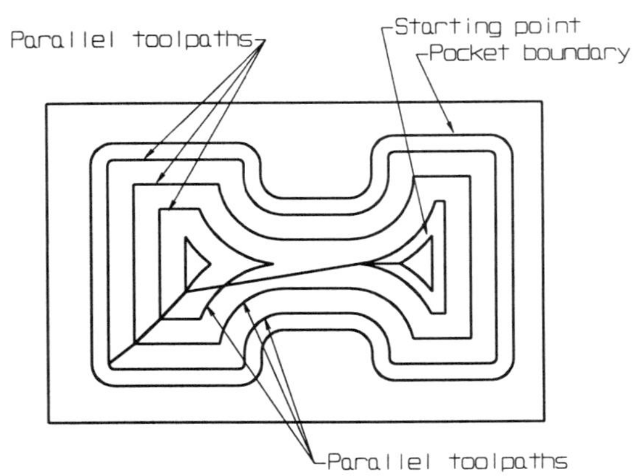

Figure 7.70

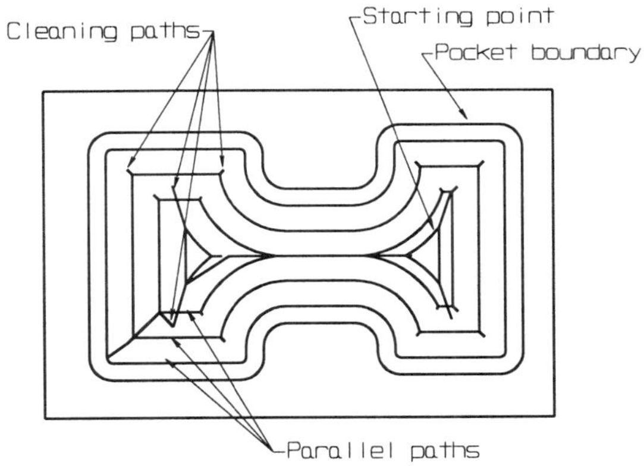

Figure 7.71

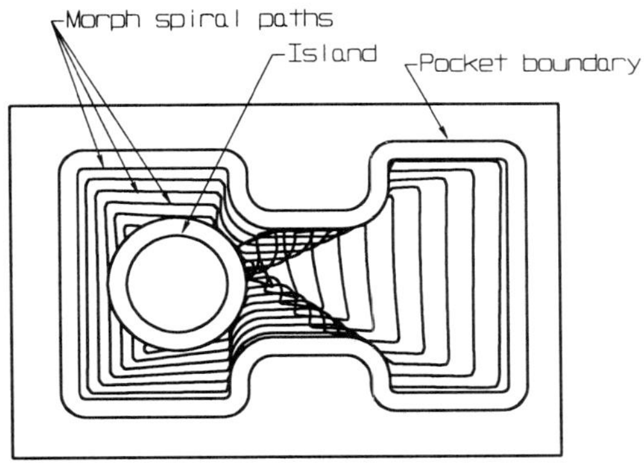

Figure 7.72

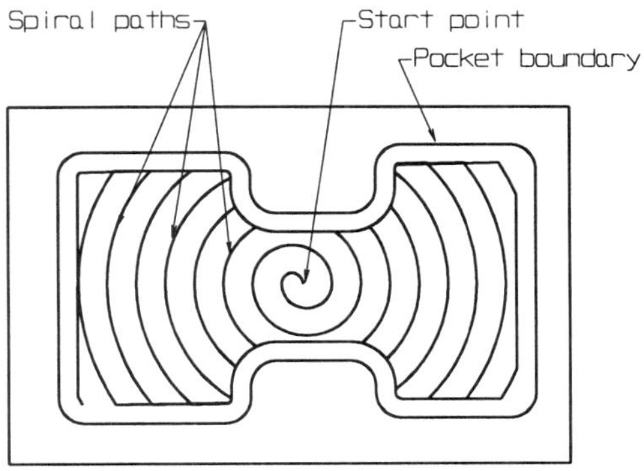

Figure 7.73

Each spiral pocketing mode has two ways to determine where to start pocketing; spiral-out and spiral-in. Mastercam uses the "Spiral inside to outside" parameter to indicate which method to use. The spiral-out method starts the cutter at the pocket center or specified pocket start point and spirals it to the wall of the pocket (Figure 7.74). The spiral-in method spirals the cutter from the outside wall of the pocket to the pocket center (Figure 7.75).

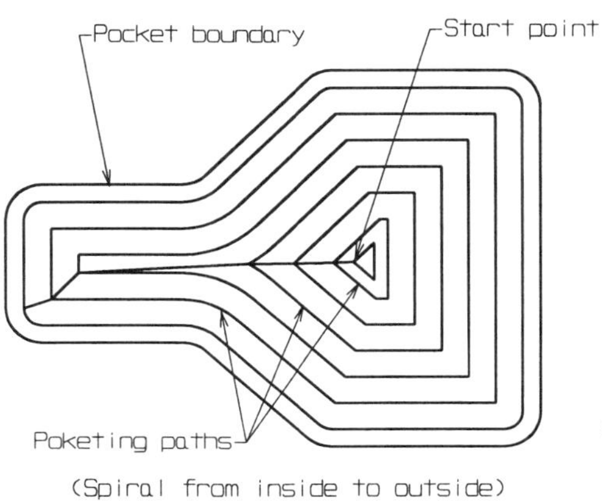

Figure 7.74

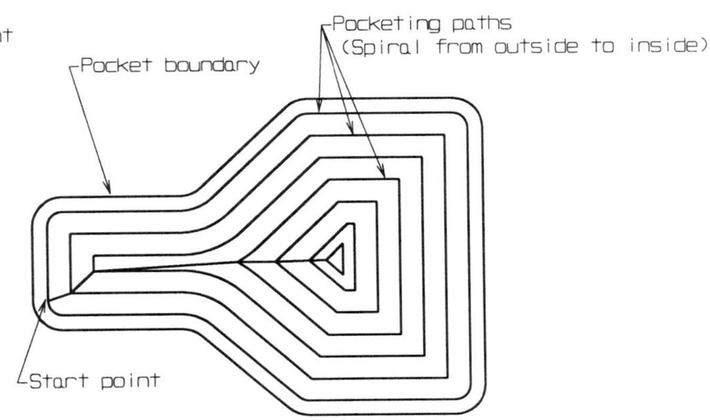

Figure 7.75

Stepover The stepover value is the distance between two adjacent pocketing paths. This value can be determined by the following two parameters:

Stepover percentage:	specify the stepover distance in the percentage of cutter diameter.
Stepover distance:	specify the stepover distance by a constant value.

The system will automatically adjust the value in the other parameter when a value is given to one parameter.

Islands and Pocket Loops

Islands are areas inside the pocket boundary that are not intended to be machined during pocketing (Figure 7.76). The islands must be closed contours. Mastercam is capable of handling multiple profiles with multiple loops that are commonly found in workpieces. A wide variety of profile looping combinations can be formed. Some examples are shown below in Figure 7.77 through 7.82.

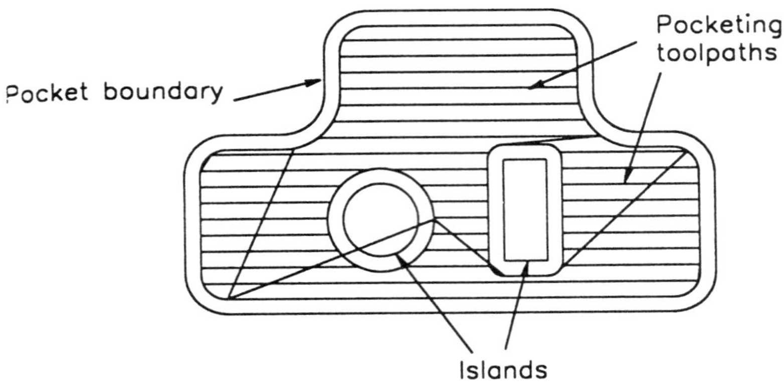

Figure 7.76

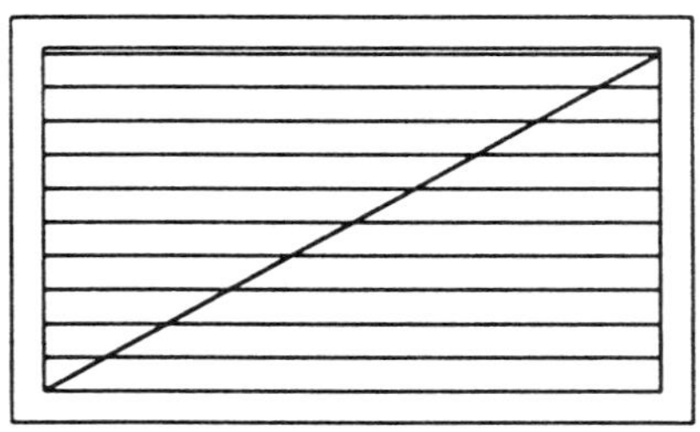

Figure 7.77

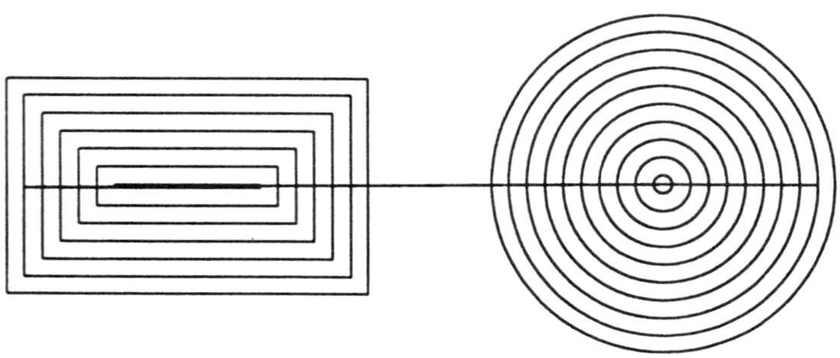

Figure 7.78

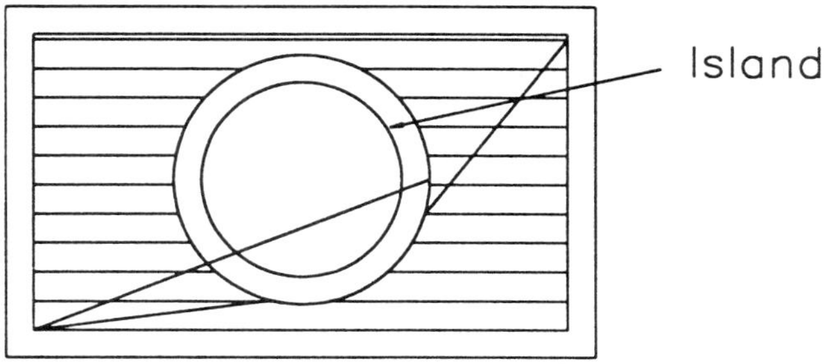

Figure 7.79

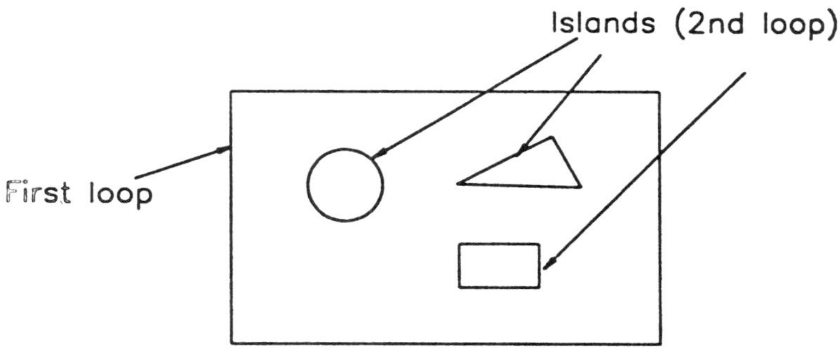

Figure 7.80

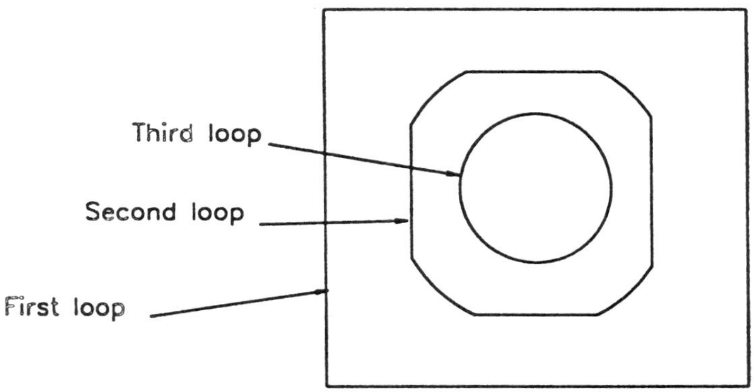

Figure 7.81

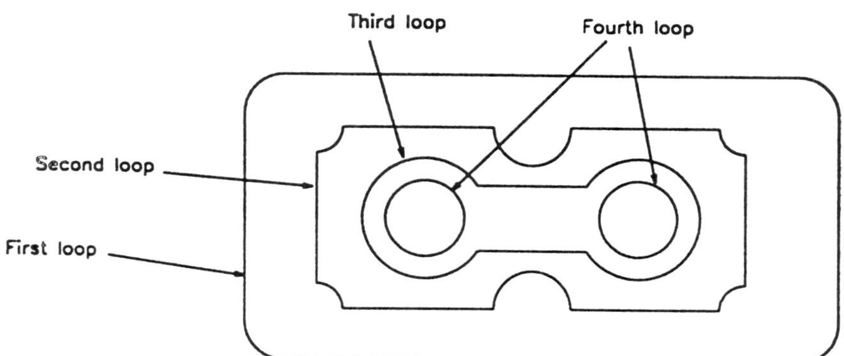

Figure 7.82

Pocketing with multiple loops can generate different sets of pocketing toolpaths depending on the pocket in which the loop is chosen. In a two-loop case, the system will prompt "click inside a pocket". If the pocket in the first loop is chosen, the pocketing is performed in the first loop, the contours in the second loop become islands (Figure 7.83). If a contour in the second loop is chosen, the pocketing is performed in all contours in the second loop (Figure 7.84).

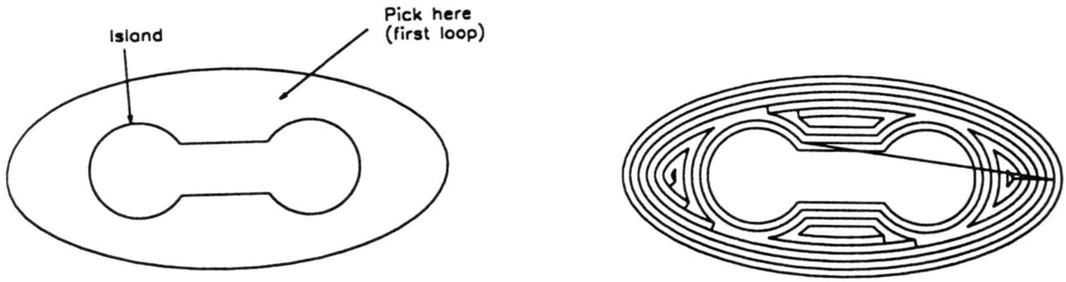

Figure 7.83

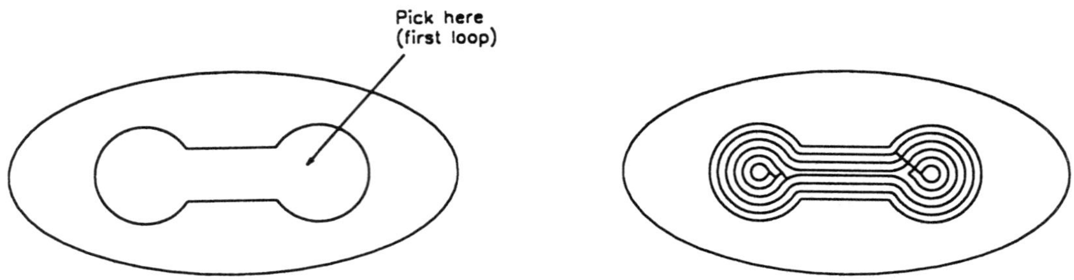

Figure 7.84

In a three-loop case, the pocketing toolpaths can be one of the three possibilities:

Click inside a pocket	**Pocketing toolpaths**
1. Selecting first loop	The pocketing is performed in the first and third loop, the second loop becomes the island (Figure 7.85).
2. Selecting second loop	The pocketing is performed in the second loop, the First and third loop become islands (Figure 7.86).
3. Selecting third loop	The pocketing is performed only in the third loop (Figure 7.87).

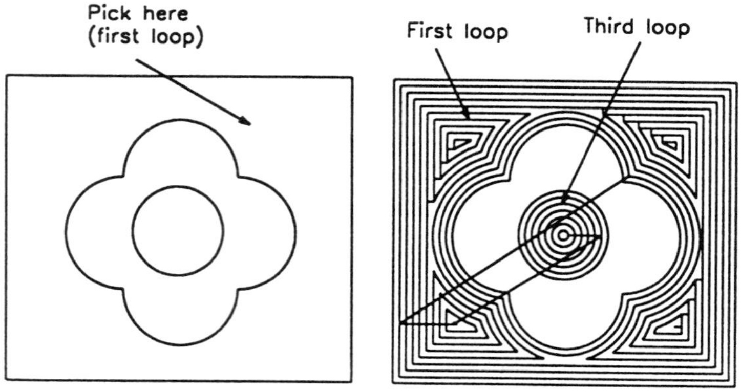

Figure 7.85

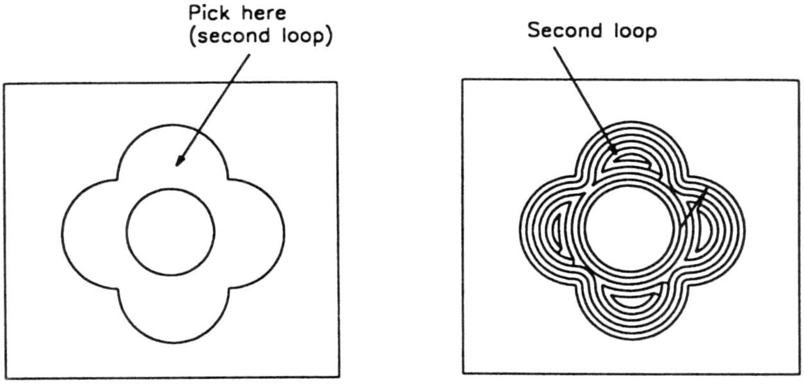

Figure 7.86

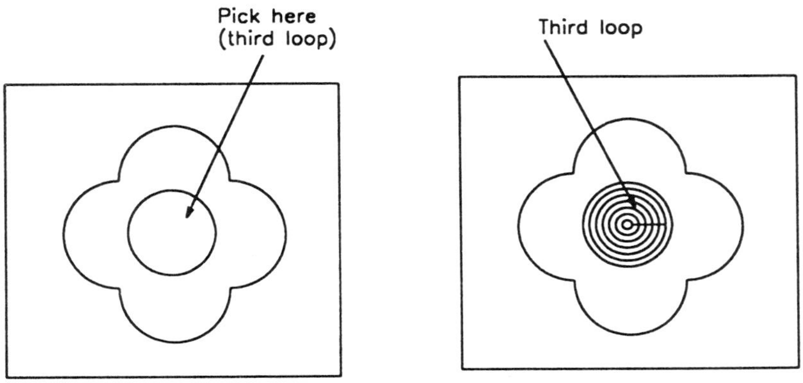

Figure 7.87

In a four-loop case, the pocketing toolpaths can be one of the following four possibilities:

Click inside a pocket	Pocketing toolpaths
1. Selecting first loop	The pocketing is performed in the first and third loop, the Second and fourth loop become islands (Figure 7.88).
2. Selecting second loop	The pocketing is performed in the second and fourth loops, and the first and third loops become islands (Figure 7.89).
3. Selecting third loop	The pocketing is performed only in the third loop, the second And fourth loops become islands (Figure 7.90).
4. Selecting fourth loop	The pocketing is performed only in the fourth loop (Figure 7.91)

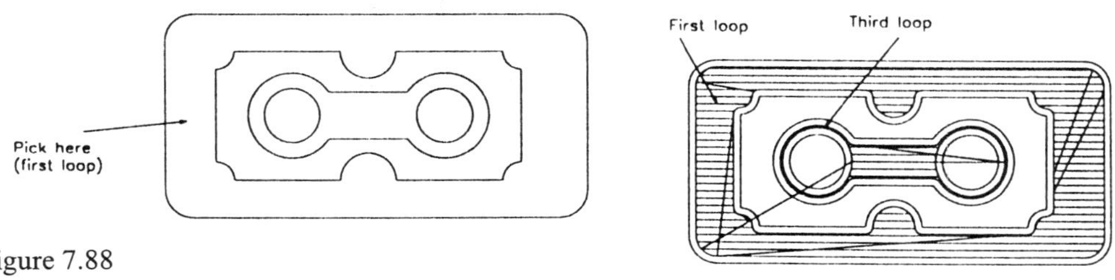

Figure 7.88

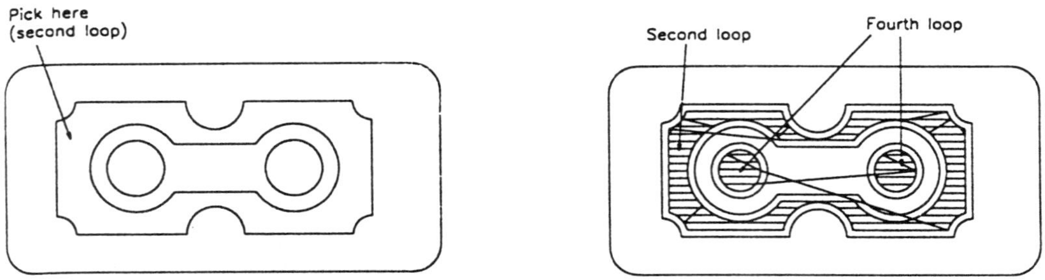

Figure 7.89

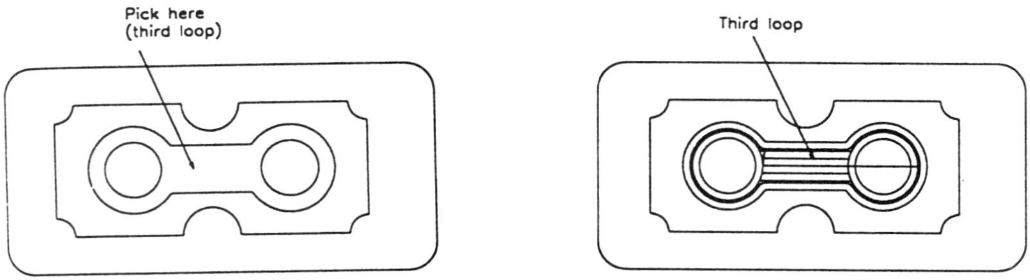

Figure 7.90

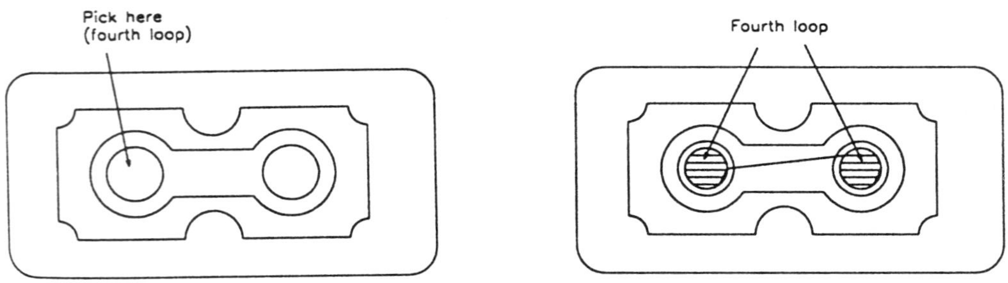

Figure 7.91

Rough Entry

The rough entry function specifies the pattern of how the cutter enters the parts. Click the "Rough Entry" button in the middle of the "Roughing/Finishing parameters" menu to open the Rough Entry dialog box. There are two forms of Rough Entry dialog box; one for helix and the other for ramp as shown next.

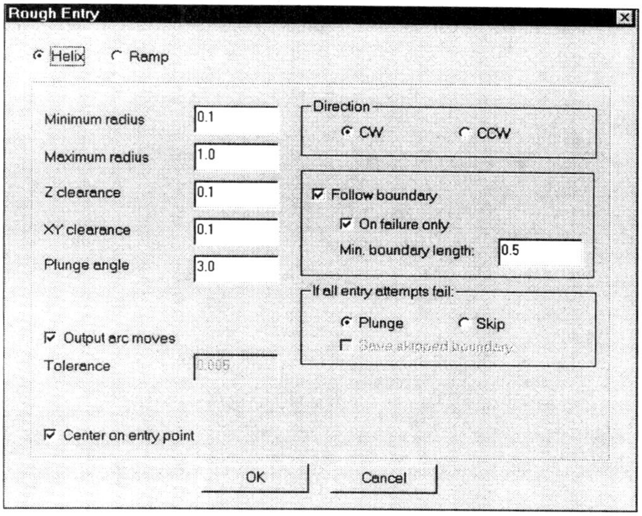

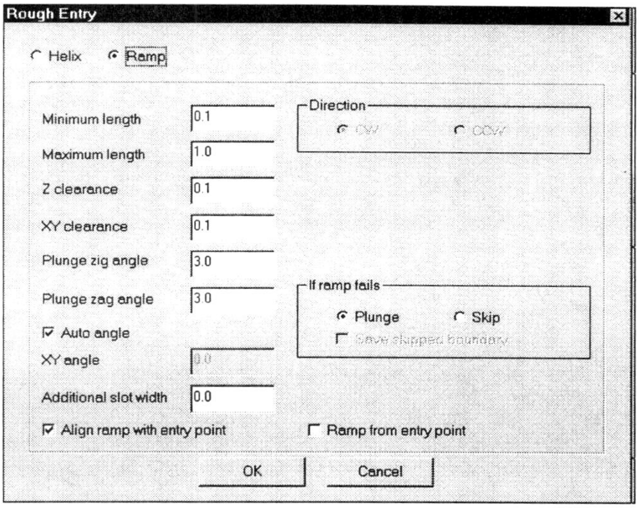

There are three rough entry patterns: **off, helix,** and **ramp**.

Off pattern In the off pattern, the tool plunges straight into the workpiece from the initial level to the desired depth (Figure 7.92). If the check box for "Rough Entry" button in "Roughing/ Finishing parameters" menu is not activated (without √), the tool entry pattern is set to off mode.

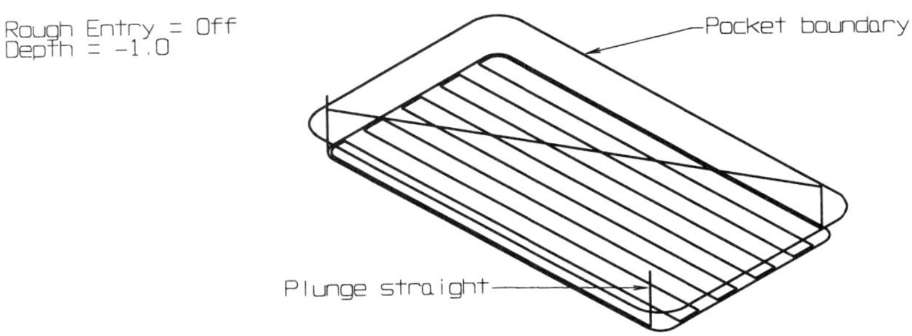

Figure 7.92

Helix mode With the helix mode, the cutter first plunges down to the starting level, then engages the workpiece in a spiral-down pattern until reaching the desired depth (Figure 7.93).

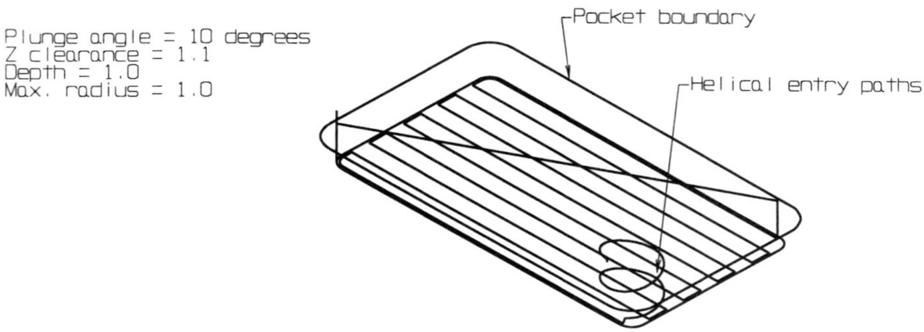

Figure 7.93a

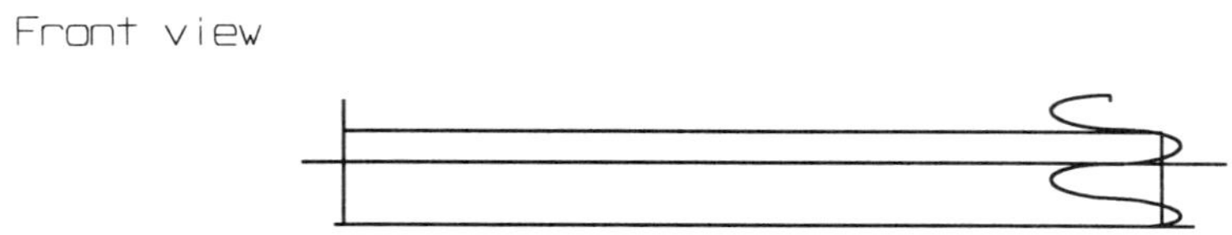

Figure 7.93b Front view

The parameters associated with the helical entry mode are described below:

Minimum radius:	specifies minimum radius of the entry helix.
Maximum radius:	specifies maximum radius of the entry helix.
Z clearance:	specifies the clearance depth of the helix.
XY clearance:	specifies the minimum clearance between the cutter and the finished pocket wall.
Plunge angle:	specifies the engaging angle of the entry helix.
Direction:	sets the helix cut direction either clockwise (CW) or counterclockwise (CCW).
Follow boundary:	sets the entry to follow the boundary when entry fails.
If all entry fail:	specifies the operation mode to either plunge or skip when all entry attempts fail.
Output arc moves:	specifies the toolpath mode of helix moves to be arc moves or linear approximated moves.
Center on entry point:	specifies the entry point to be located near the center of the pocket.

Using helix entry mode, the plunge angle parameter determines the length of the entry toolpath. The smaller the entry angle, the longer the entry toolpath (Figure 17.94).

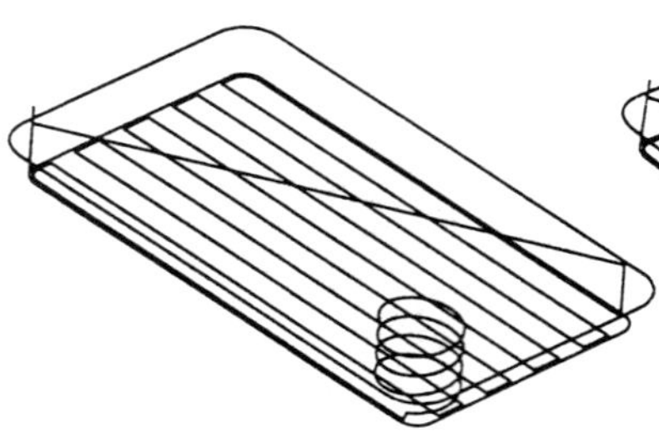

Figure 7.94a Plunge angle = 5°

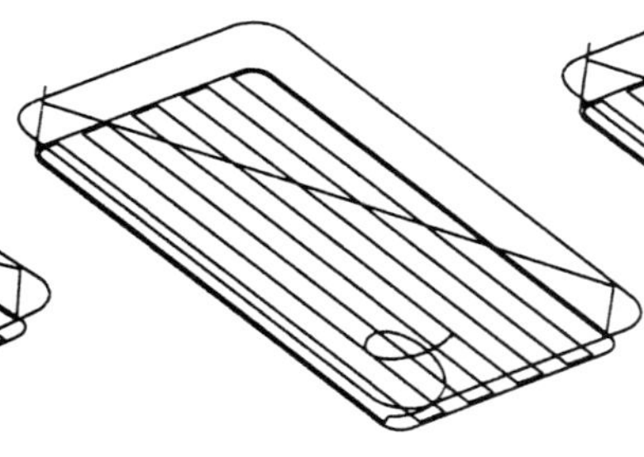

Figure 7.94b Plunge angle = 15°

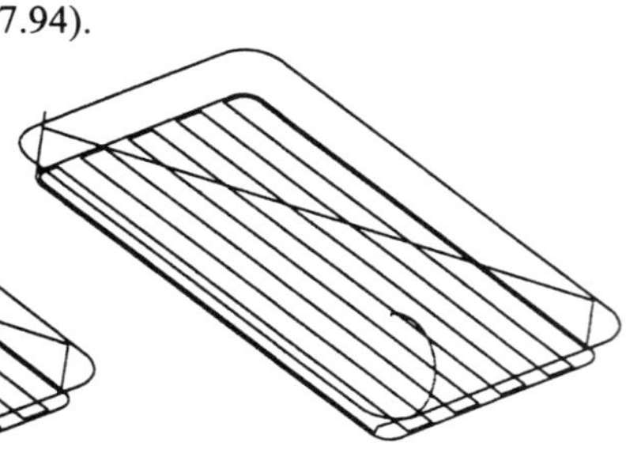

Figure 7.94c Plunge angle=30°

Tolerance parameter The tolerance parameter dictates the number of entry path segments. The helix entry path is approximated by a series of straight lines when the "Output arc moves" parameter is not toggled to On (with (mark). The smaller tolerance value results in a larger number of line segments. It is recommended that you use a larger tolerance value.

With the ramp mode, the cutter engages the workpiece in a straight ramp downward path (Figure 7.95).

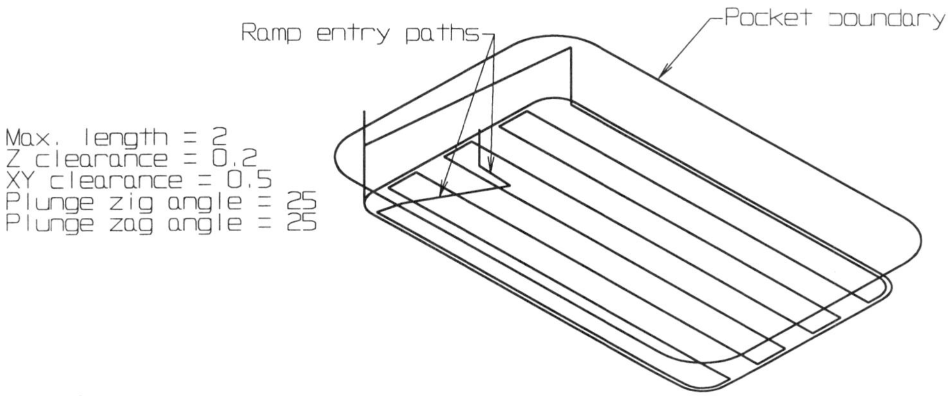

Figure 7.95a

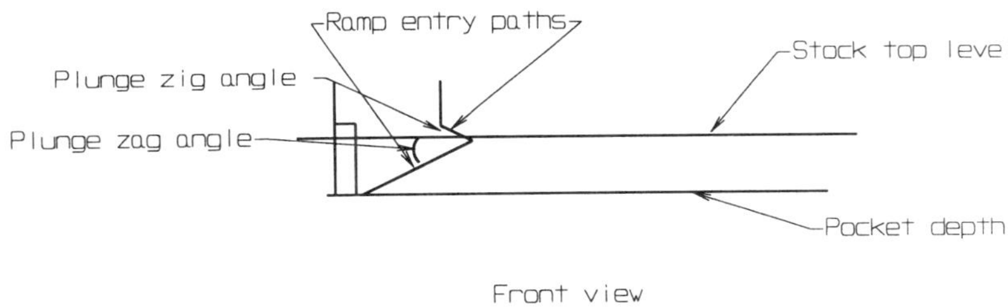

Figure 7.95b Front view

The parameters associated with the ramp entry mode are described below:

Minimum length:	specifies minimum distance of the segment of entry path.
Maximum length:	specifies maximum distance of the segment of entry path.
Z clearance:	specifies the clearance depth of the entry path. It is the distance above the top of stock.
XY clearance:	specifies the minimum clearance between the cutter the finished pocket wall.
Plunge zig angle:	specifies the plunge angle for zig path.
Plunge zag angle:	specifies the plunge angle for zag path.
Auto/XY angle:	specifies the ramping angle in XY-direction either by the system automatically or by a given value.
Additional slot width:	adds an additional amount of toolpath segment to the end of each plunge path.
Align ramp with Entry point:	aligns the entry ramp path with the entry point.
Ramp from entry point:	has the entry ramp path starting from the entry point.
If ramp fails:	specifies the operation mode to as either plunge or skip when the entry fails.

There are three parameters that dictate the number of zig-zag ramp-down segments; maximum length, plunge zig angle and plunge zag angle. Figure 7.96 shows how maximum length effects the ramp-down segments. The segments increase from 2 to 4 when the maximum length changes from 1.0 to 0.5.

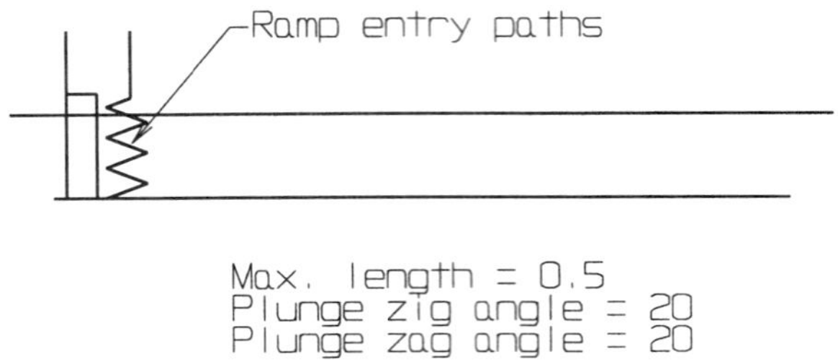

Figure 7.96a

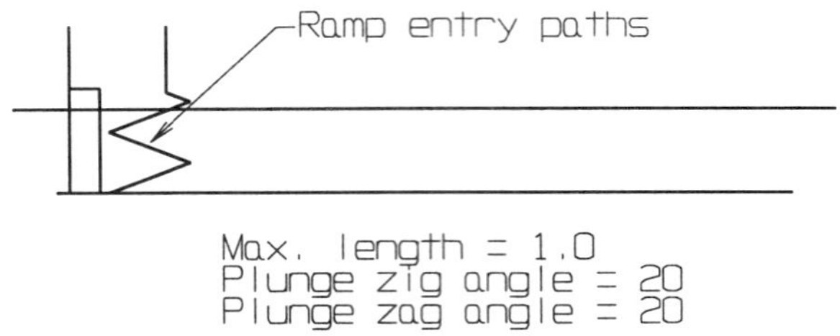

Figure 7.96b

Figure 7.97 shows the effect of plunge zig angle and plunge zag angle on the entry path. As the angle increases, the number of ramp segments reduces.

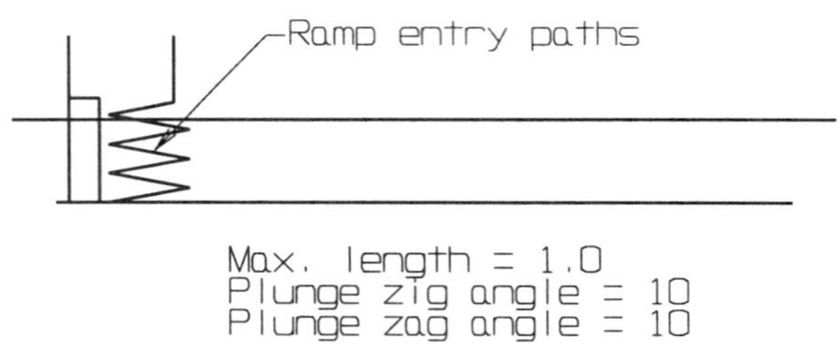

Figure 7.97a

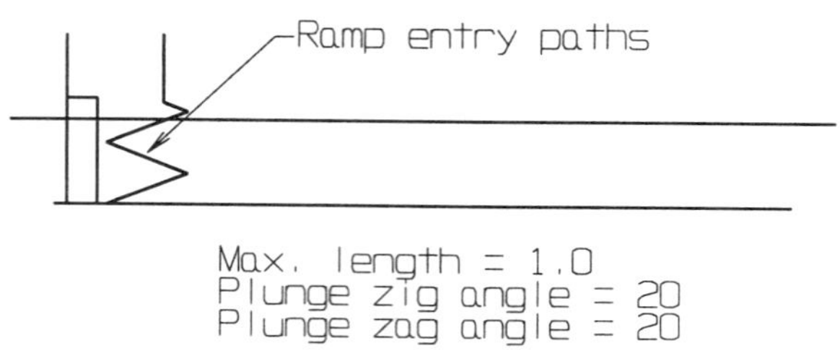

Figure 7.97b

The procedure for Selecting the Proper Rough Entry Mode

Straight end mills are often used to perform pocketing operations. Two common types of end mills are center-hole and center-cutting types. Cutting blades extend beyond the cutter in center-cutting end mills. As a result, they can be used to perform both plunging, cutting and side cutting. Center-hole type end mills are designed only for side cutting. They cannot be used for plunging operations. The following are some technical tips to help the selection of cutting engaging modes and their parameters.

> **Tips** 1. Always use helix or ramp mode. The Off (straight plunge) mode should be used only when there is a limited space in the pocket for the cutter to ramp down, and the cutter should be the center-cutting type.
> 2. It is recommended that you use a 30-degree helix or ramp angle. A small angle will takes a longer time to engage the cutter to the workpiece, while a large angle produces undesired scrapping on the cutter end.
> 3. The maximum radius width should be in a range between 1/3 to ½ of the pocket width.

Project 4. Pocketing an internal pocket

Use the pocket module to generate the toolpaths to cut the internal pocket for the part. Figure 7.98 shows the part geometry, toolpath and verification model.

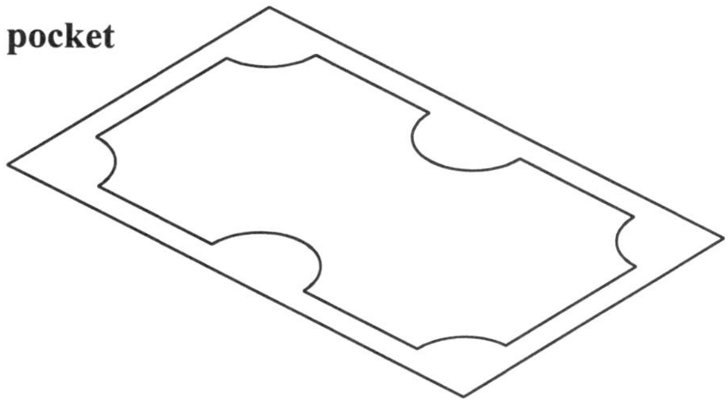

Figure 7.98a

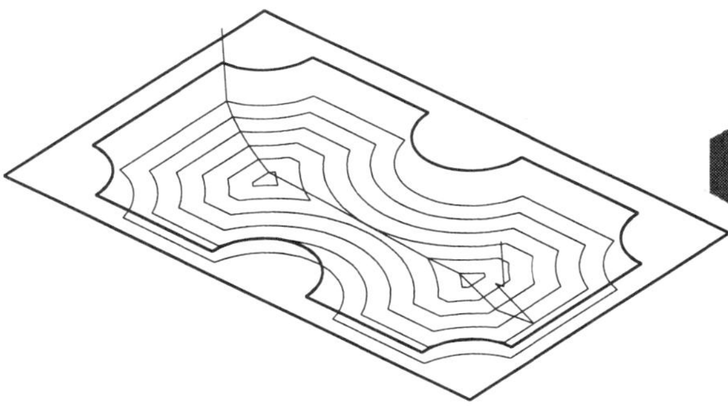

Figure 7.98b

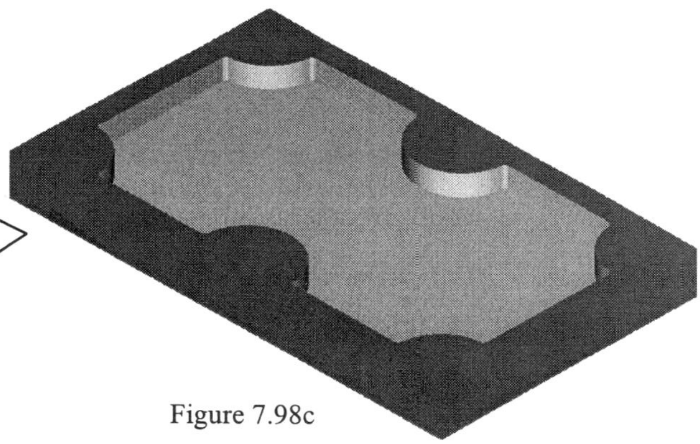

Figure 7.98c

> **Tips** 1. Define the contour in the counterclockwise direction to obtain the climb milling operations.
>
> 2. Use a spiral inside out cutting method because there is no island involved.
>
> 3. Use two cutters, 0.5" end mill for roughing cuts and 0.25" end mill for the finish pass.
>
> 4. The roughing cut spacing is 0.35" (or 0.7D).
>
> 5. The number of finish pass is 1 and finishing pass spacing is 0.1".

Step 1. Open the part geometry file pocket1.

Select **Main Menu → File → Get**
File name: **pocket1**

The part geometry should appear on the screen as Figure 7.99

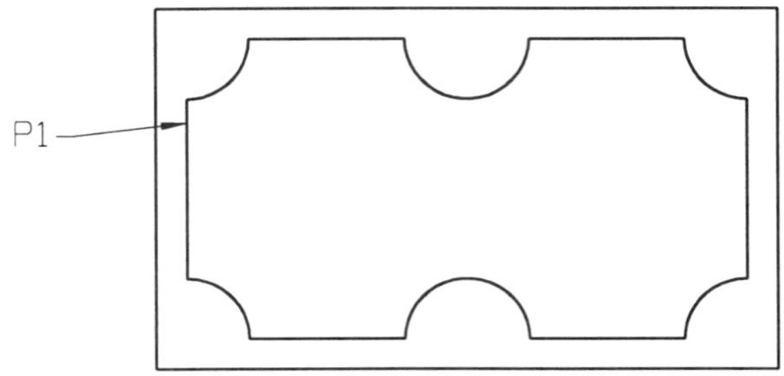

Figure 7.99

Step 2. Initiate the pocket module.

Use the pick point in Figure 7.99.
Select **MAIN MENU → Toolpaths → Pocket**
File name for toolpath: **pocket1**
Select **Chain**, then pick **P1** to automatically select the chained profile
Select **Done**

Step 3. Select a ½" end mill.

Click the right mouse button, then select **Get tool from library**
Select **tool #239** (1/2 flat end mill)
Select **OK**

Step 4. Define the tool parameters as below.

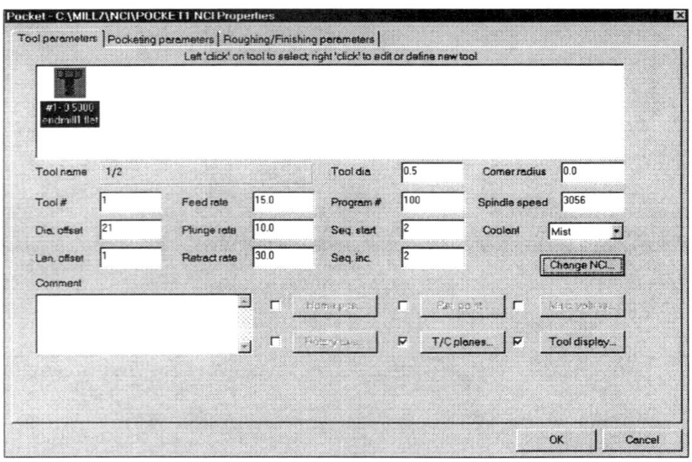

Step 5. Define the pocketing parameters.

Click the **Pocketing parameters** button

Set the pocketing parameters as below.

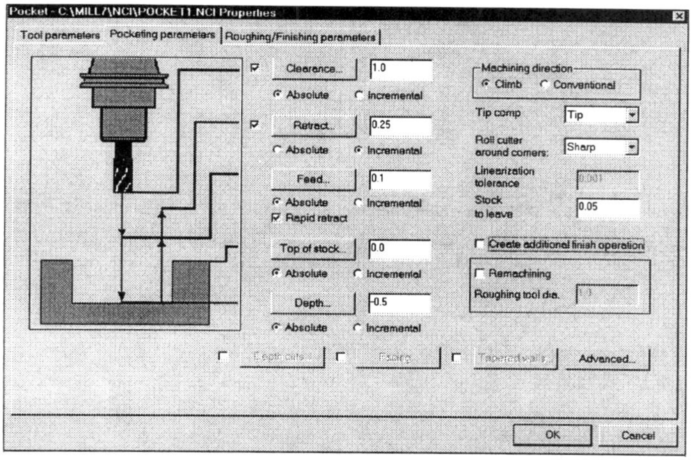

Step 6. Define the roughing/finishing parameters.

Click the **Roughing/Finishing parameters** button

Set the roughing and finishing parameters as below.

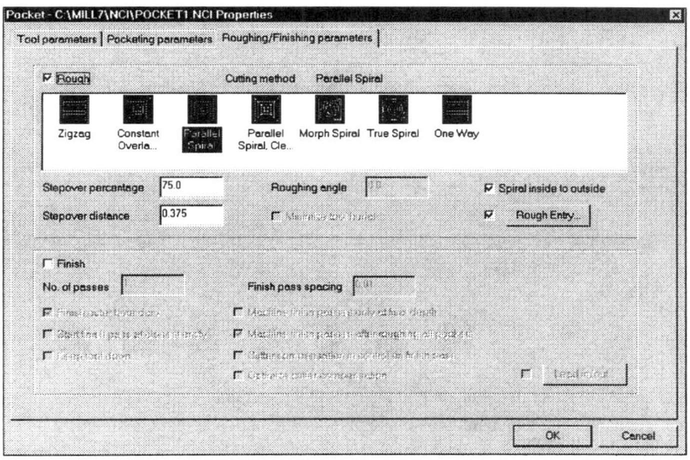

Step 7. Define the rough entry parameters.

Click the **Rough Entry** button

Set the rough entry parameters as below.

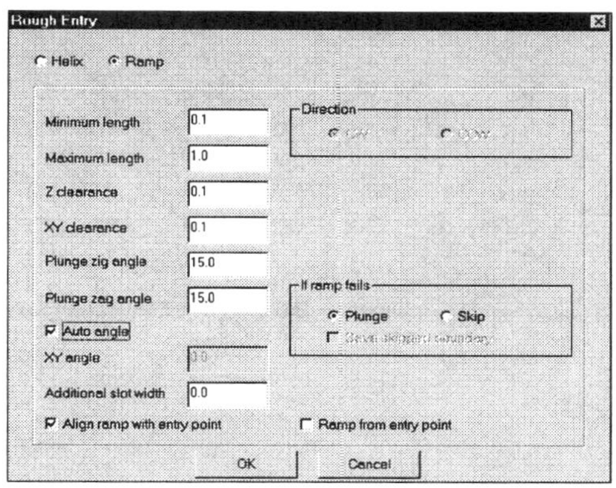

Select **OK** from Rough Entry menu

Select **OK** from Pocket menu

The pocketing toolpaths are generated as shown in Figure 7.100.

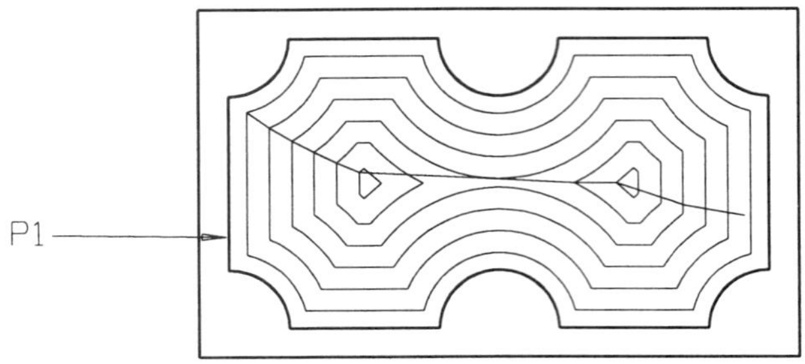

Figure 7.100

Step 8. Initiate the contour module.

Use the pick point in Figure 7.100.
Select **Contour → Chain**
Pick **P1** to select the contour
Select **Done**

Step 9. Select the finish tool.

Click the right mouse button, then select **Get tool from library**
Select **tool #234** (3/16 flat end mill)
Select **OK**
Set the tool parameters as below.

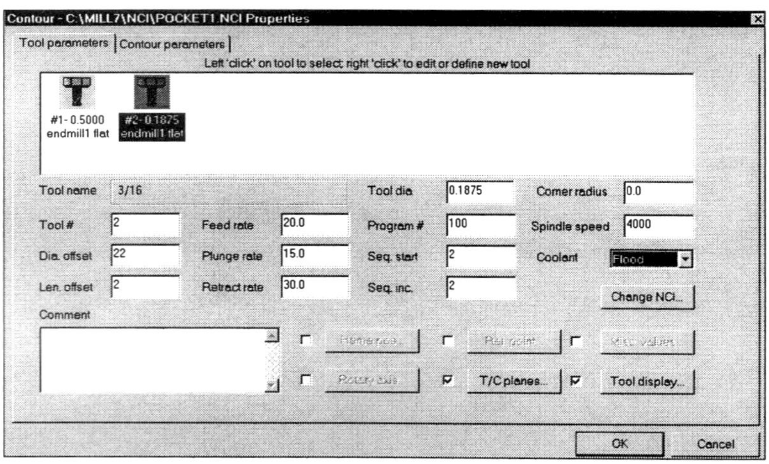

Step 10. Define the contour parameters.

Click the **Contour parameters** button

Set the contour parameters as below.

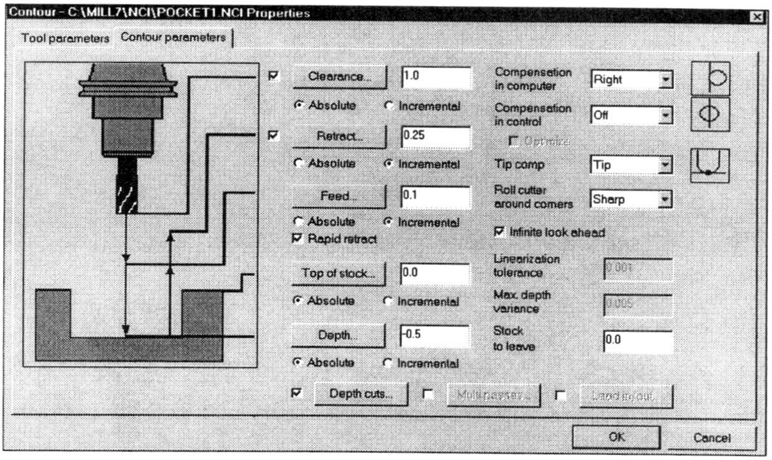

Step 11. Define the depth cuts parameters.

Click the **Depth cuts** button

Set the depth cuts parameters as here.

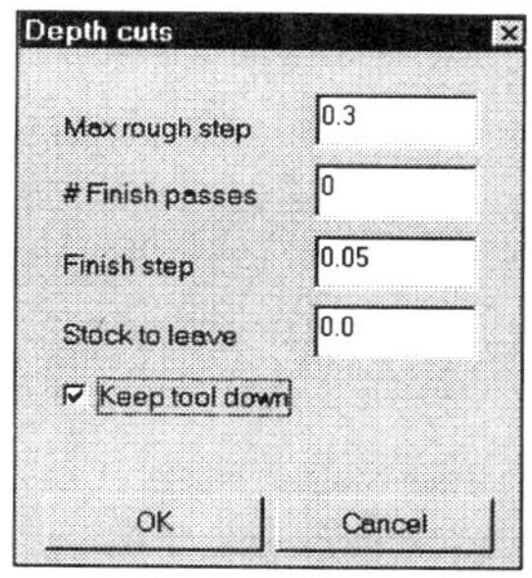

Select **OK → OK** to generate contouring toolpath

Step 12. Change to isometric view.

Select **Gview → Isometric**

The geometry model with toolpaths are shown in Figure 7.101.

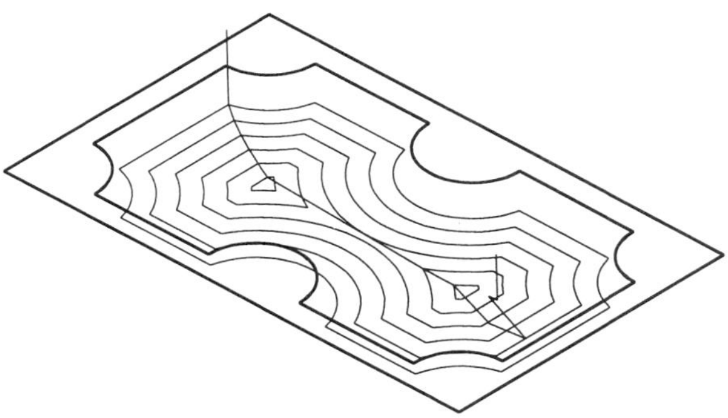

Figure 7.101

Step 13. Define the job setup.

Select **Job setup**

Set the job setup parameters as below.

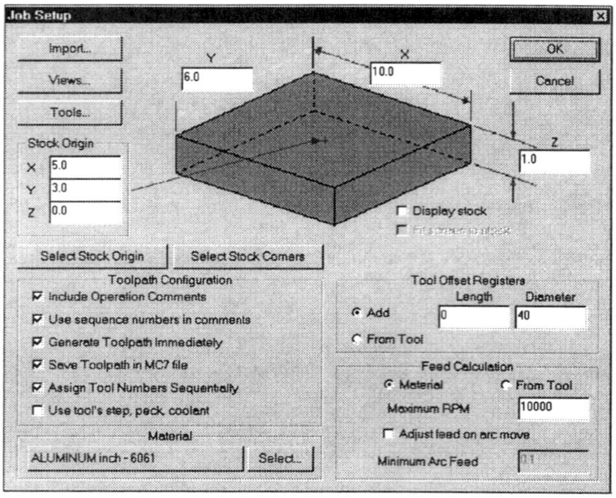

Select **OK** to exit the job setup menu

Step 14. Verify the toolpaths.

Select **Operations**

The Operations Manager menu with two sets of toolpaths should appear as below.

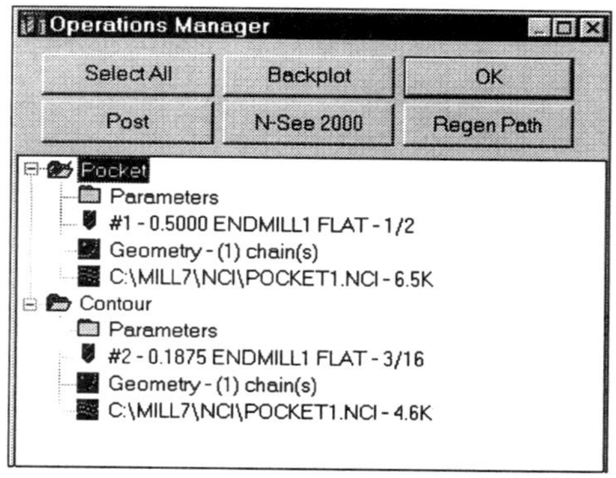

Select **Select All** to include both toolpath operations

Select **N-See 2000**

Set the "Select mode for current job" parameters as below.

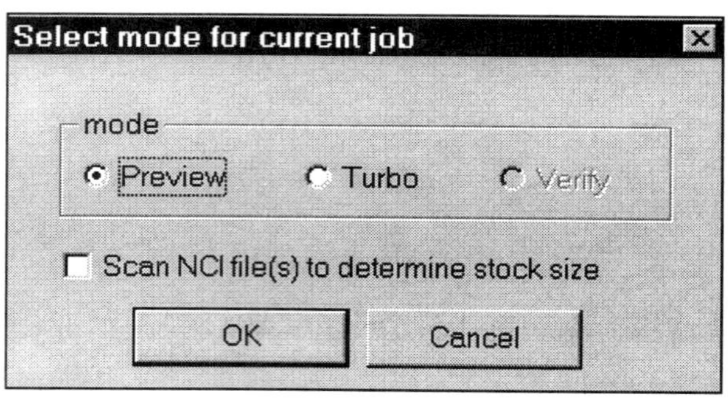

Select **OK**

A raw material block should appear on the screen.

Select **Do it**

Toolpaths with two cutters are animated on screen. Figure 7.102 shows the final verified model.

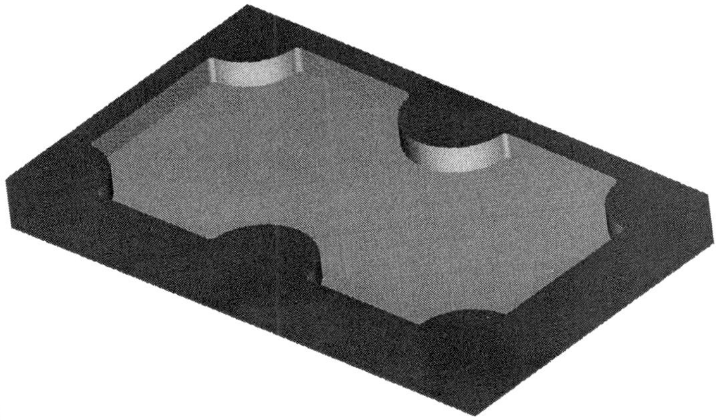

Figure 7.102

Select **BACKUP** to return back to Operations Manager menu
Select **OK** to return back to graphic mode

Step 15. Save the toolpaths.

Select **MAIN MENU → File → Save**

File name: pocket1t

Project 5. Facing top flat surface and pocketing with an island

In the part shown in Figure 7.103a, the pocket module is used three times to generate the toolpaths to (1) face the top flat surface, (2) pocket the internal profile with a circle island at the center, and (3) pocket a circular profile. The raw material is a solid circular block. The outer circular profile of the block has been premachined to the desired dimensions. One face of the block has also been faced. The thickness of the block is about 1.03". Figure 7.103b shows the three sets of pocketing toolpaths.

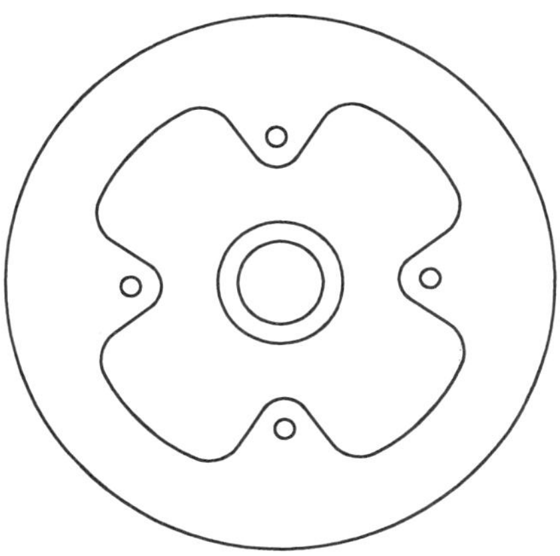

Figure 7.103a

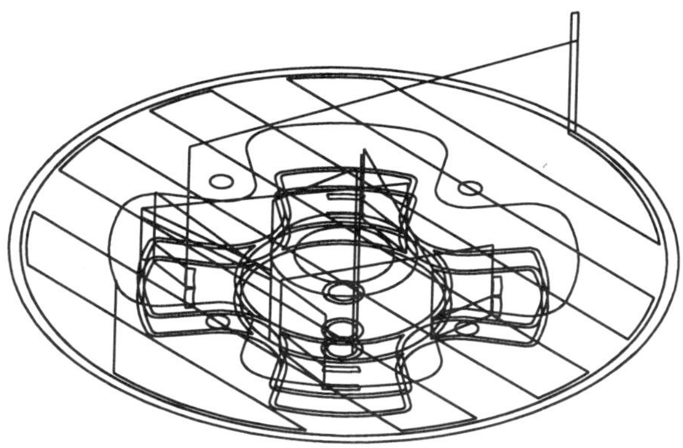

Figure 7.103b

Figure 7.103c

Tips

1. Start the operation sequence with facing the top flat surface followed by pocketing the larger internal profile, and finally pocketing the circular profile.
2. Two cutters are used including:
   1-in end mill for facing the top flat surface.
   ½-in end mill for two pocketing operations.
3. A construction circle which has a larger diameter than the outer circle should be added to serve as the outside pocket boundary for facing the top flat surface. If the original outer circle is used as the outside pocketing boundary, several pieces of uncut material may be left around the perimeter of the boundary. The diameter of this construction circle is suggested as 5.7-in.
4. Main pocketing parameters for the facing are:
   1 roughing cut and 1 finish cut
   Roughing cut spacing = 0.6"
   Cutting method = Zig zag
5. Main pocketing parameters for pocketing the larger profile are:
   Cutting method: Spiral inside out
   Roughing cut spacing = 0.35"
   Pocket depth = -0.5"
   Number of finish passes = 1
   Finishing pass spacing = 0.05"
   No entry/exit length and arc
   Machine finish passes at final depth
   Two passes of depth cut: Rough: 1 cut at 0.0 Finish: 1 cut at 0.2"
6. Main pocketing parameters for pocketing the circular profile include:
   Cutting method: spiral inside out
   Rough cut spacing = 0.35"
   Pocket depth = -1.0"
   Number of finish passes = 1
   Finishing pass spacing = 0.05"
   No entry/exit length and arc
   Machine finish passes at all depths
   Three passes of depth cut: Rough: 2 cuts at 0.4"
   Finish: 1 cut at 0.2"

Step 1. Open the part geometry file pocket2.

Select **MAIN MENU → File → Get**
File name: **pocket2**
The part geometry appears as Figure 7.104.

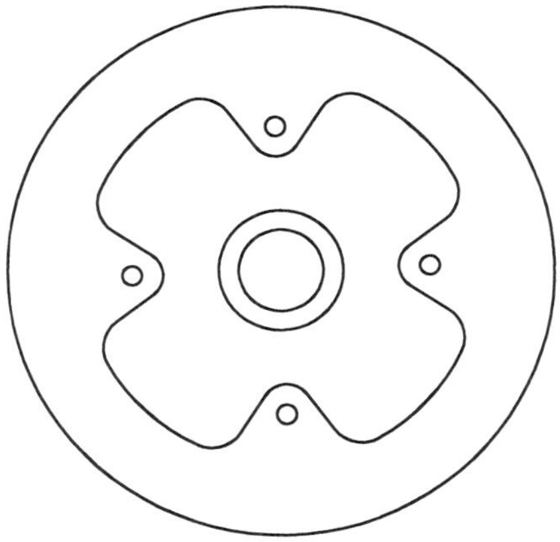

Figure 7.104

Step 2. Create a construction circle.

Select **MAIN MENU → Create → Arc → Cir pt+dia**
Enter the center point: **0,0**
Enter the diameter: **5.7**
The circle is added as in Figure 7.105.

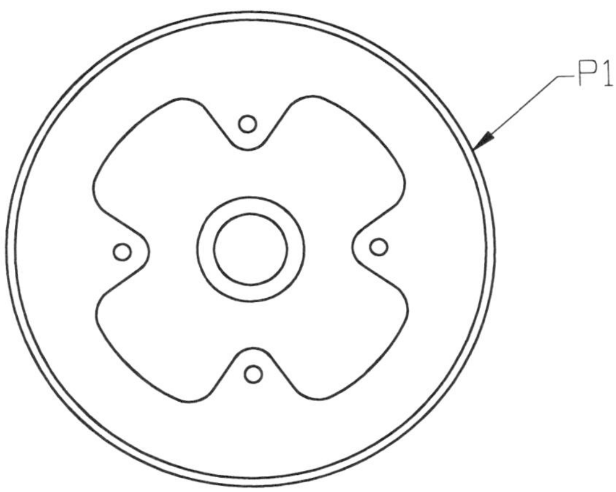

Figure 7.105

Step 3. Initiate the pocket module.

Use the pick point in Figure 7.105.
Select **MAIN MENU → Toolpaths → Pocket**
File name for toolpaths: **pocket2**
Select **Single** then pick **P1** to select the circle
Select **Done**

Step 4. Select a 1-in end mill and set tool parameters.

Click the right mouse button, then select **Get tool from library**
Select **tool #243** (1-in end mill)
Select **OK**
Set the tool parameters as below.

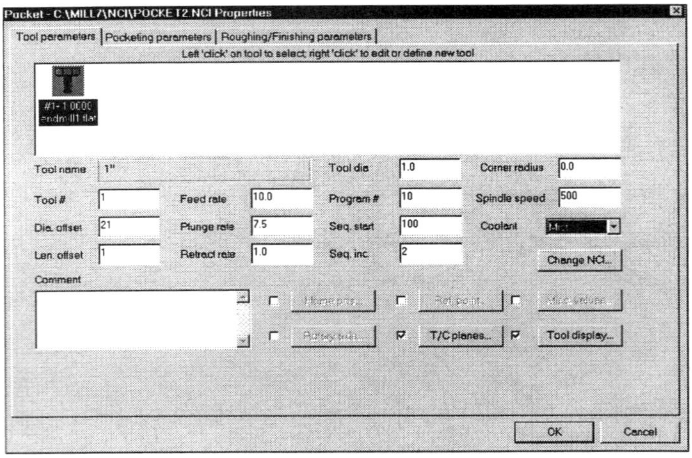

Step 5. Define the pocketing parameters.

Click the **Pocketing parameters** button
Set the pocketing parameters as below.

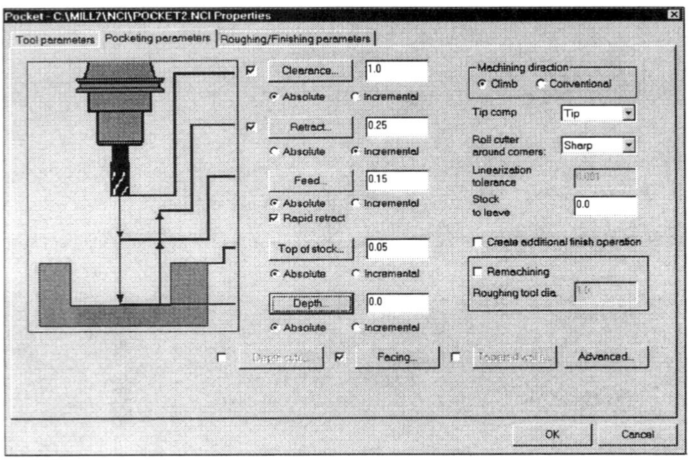

Step 6. Define the facing parameters.

Click the **Facing** button at the bottom of the menu
Set the facing parameters as here.

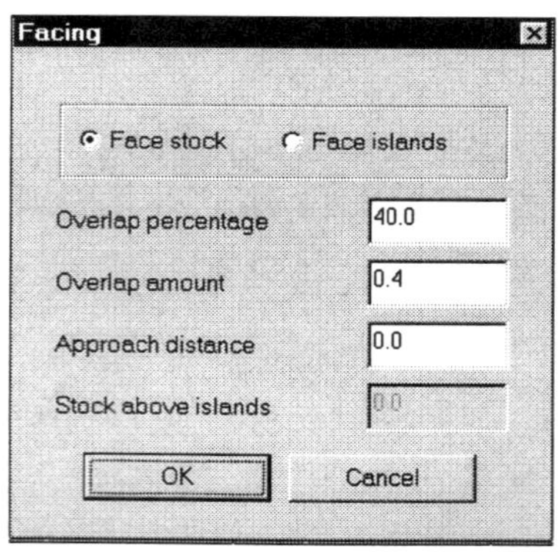

Select **OK**

Step 7. Define the roughing/finishing parameters.

Click the **Roughing/Finishing parameters** button
Set the roughing/finishing parameters as below.

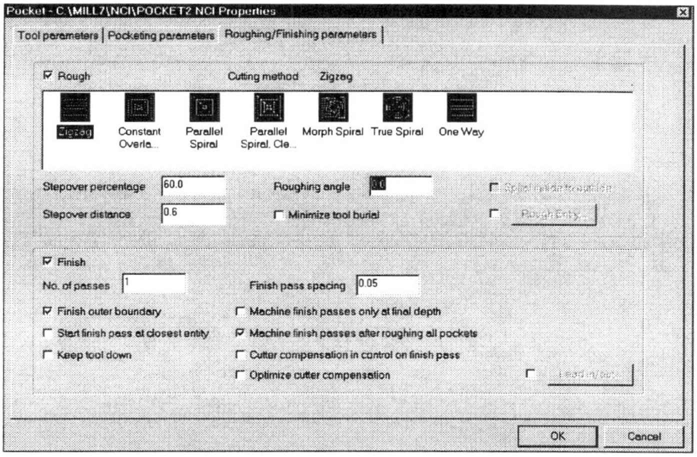

Select **OK** to generate toolpaths as shown in Figure 7.106.

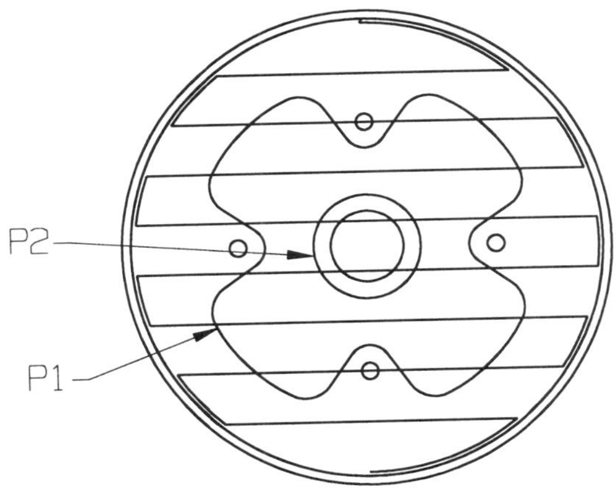

Figure 7.106

Step 8. Initiate pocket module for pocketing the larger internal profile.

Use the pick points in Figure 7.107.
Select **Pocket → Chain**
Pick **P1** to chain the contour
Select **Mode → Single**, then pick **P2** to select the circle as an island
Select **Done**

Step 9. Select a ½-in end mill and define the tool parameters.

Click the right mouse button, then select **Get tool from library**
Select **tool #239** (1/2-in flat end mill)
Select **OK**

Set the tool parameters as below.

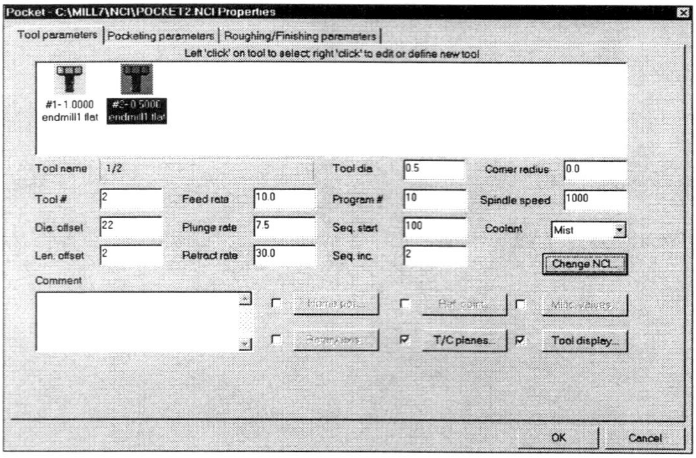

Step 10. Define the pocketing parameters.

Click the **Pocketing parameters** button

Define the pocketing parameters as below.

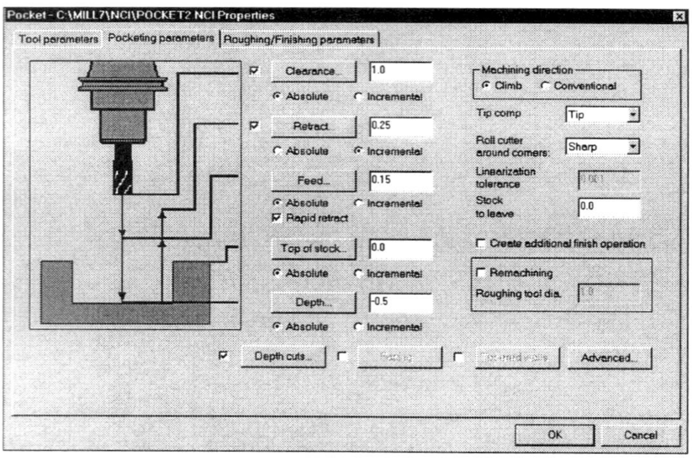

Step 11. Define the depth cuts parameters.

Click the **Depth cuts** button at the bottom of the menu

Set the depth cuts parameters as below.

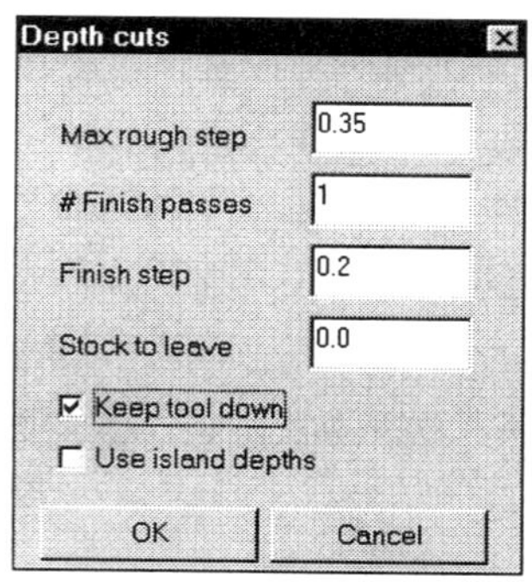

Select **OK**

Step 12. Define the roughing/Finishing parameters.

Click the **Roughing/Finishing parameters** button
Set the roughing and finishing parameters as below.

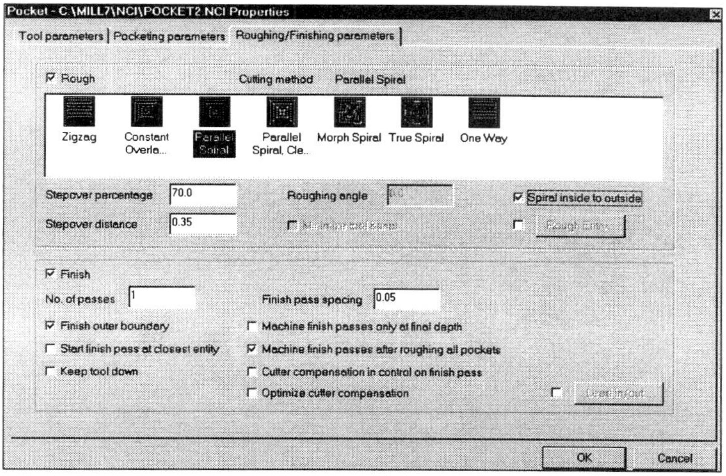

Select **OK** to generate the pocketing toolpaths as shown in Figure 7.107.

Figure 7.107

Step 13. Initiate the pocket module again.

Use the pick point in Figure 7.107.
Select **Pocket → Single**
Pick **P1** to select the inner circle, then select **Done**

Define the tool parameters as below.

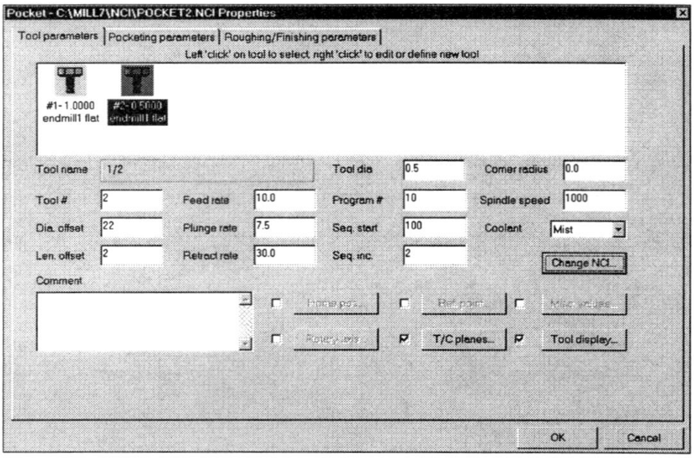

Step 14. Define the pocketing parameters.

Click the **Pocketing parameters** button

Set the pocketing parameters as below.

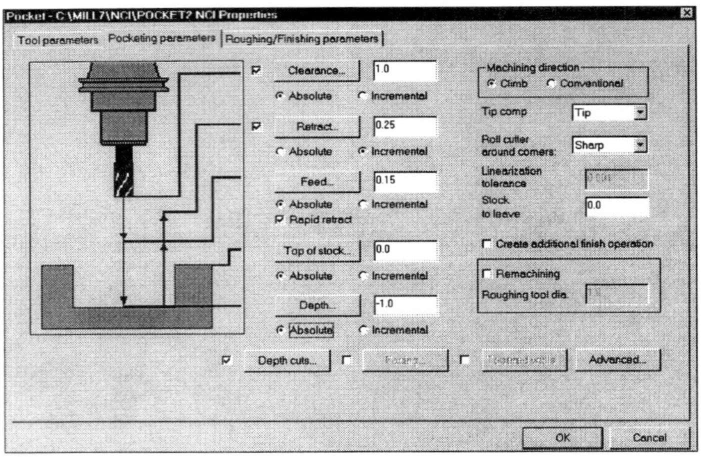

Step 15. Define the depth cuts parameters.

Select the **Depth cuts** button

Set the depth cuts parameters as below.

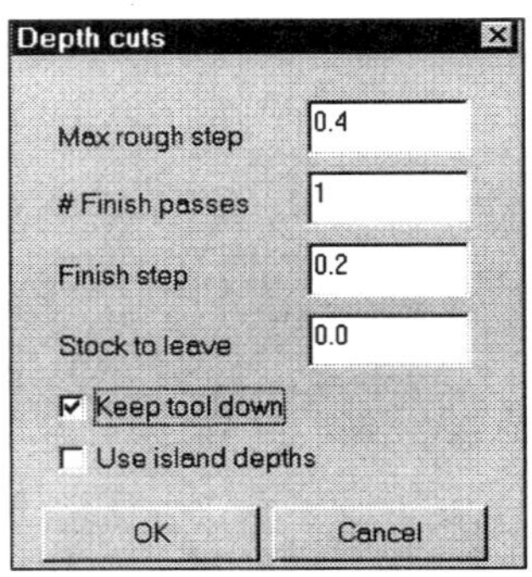

Select **OK**

Step 16. Define the roughing/finishing parameters.

Click the **Roughing/Finishing parameters** button

Set roughing and finishing parameters as shown next.

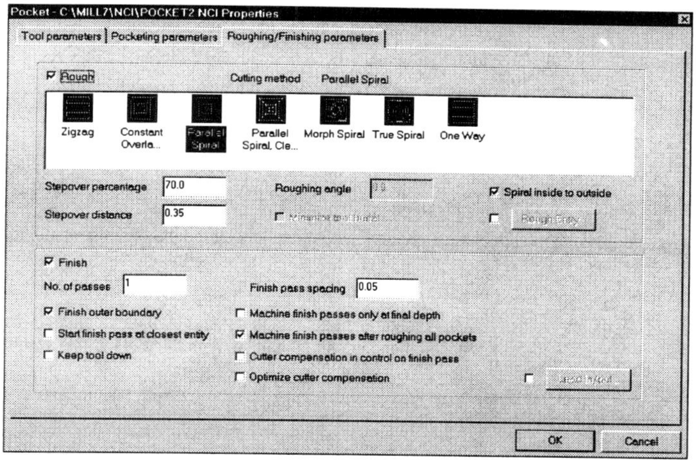

Select **OK** to generate pocketing toolpaths
Select **Gview → Isometric**
The three sets of toolpaths are displayed in Figure 7.108.

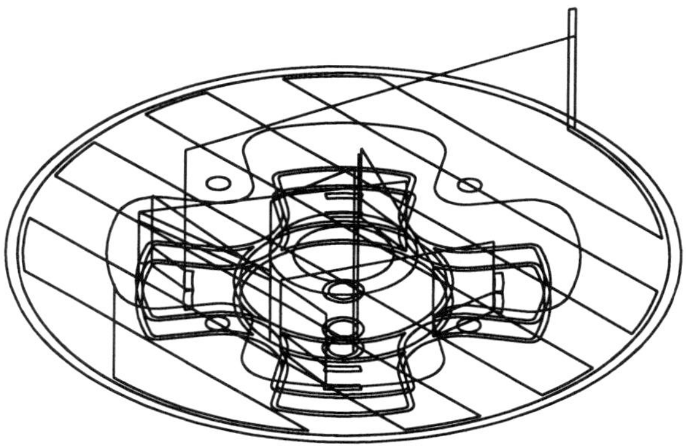

Figure 7.108

Step 17. Define the job setup parameters.

Select **Job setup**
Set the job setup parameters as below.

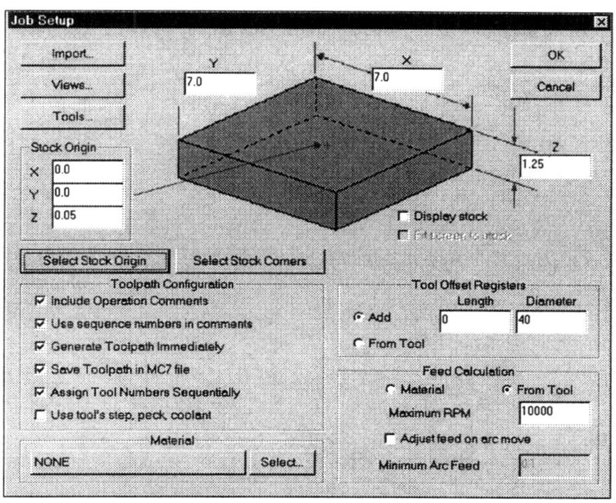

Select **OK**

Step 18. Verify the toolpaths.

Select **Operations**

The three sets of toolpaths are included in the Operations Manager menu as below.

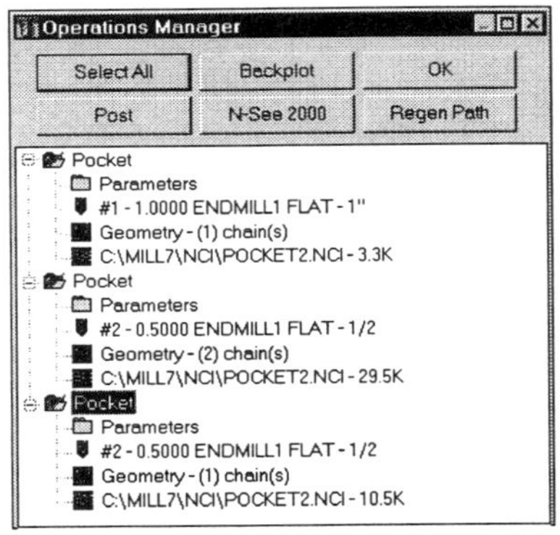

Select **Select All**
Select **N-See 2000**
Select **Preview mode**
Select **OK**

A rectangular block should appear on the screen.
Select **Do it** to verify the toolpaths
Figure 7.109 shows the verify model of this project.

Figure 7.109

Select **BACKUP** to return to Operations Manager menu
Select **OK** to exit Operations Manager menu

Step 19. Save the toolpath file.

Select **MAIN MENU → File → Save**
File name to save: **pocket2t**

7.11 Drill Module

Mastercam's drill module is used to generate toolpaths for drilling, boring, and tapping. Setting drill parameters to proper operating modes and values, and selecting points for the operation to be implemented, are very crucial to the successful execution of the drill module.

Drill Parameters

The drill parameters dialog box is shown below.

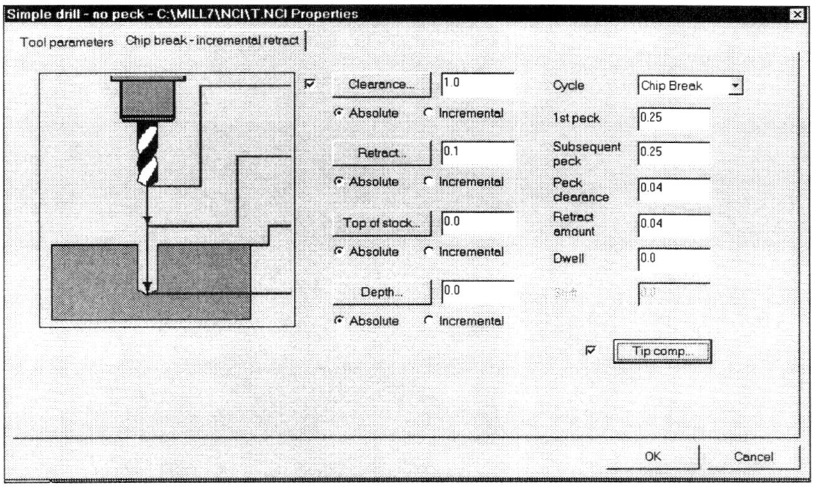

Those drilling parameters can be divided into four groups: **Z-depth, cycle mode, pecking parameters**, and **tip compensation**.

Z-depth Four Z value parameters are involved in cycle operations (Figure 7.110):

Clearance:	The cutter travels at this Z value to the specified hole center.
Retract:	The cutter moves down in rapid mode to this Z value.
Top of stock:	This level specifies the Z value for the top of stock.
Depth:	The cutter feeds down to this Z value which is the Z value of hole bottom.

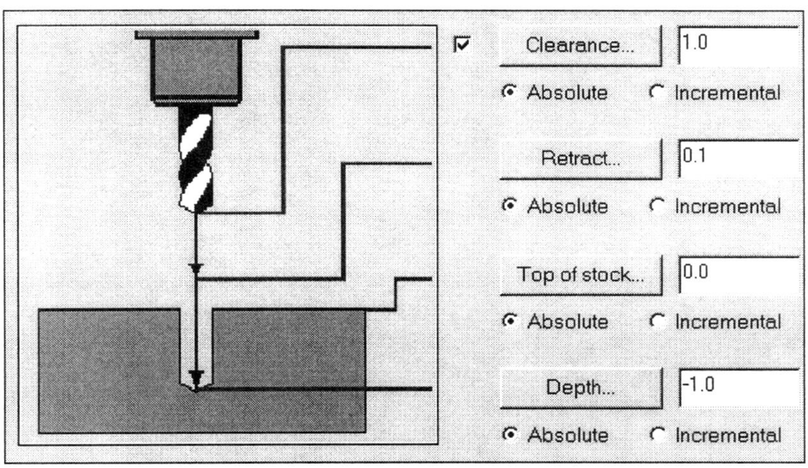

Figure 7.110

Mastercam allows Z values to be specified in either absolute or incremental mode. The depth is the distance between the selected point position to the bottom of the hole. The sign is determined as negative (-) if the hole bottom is below the selected point (Figure 7.111a) and positive (+) if the hole bottom is above the selected point (Figure 7.111b).

How the specified Z-value is measured depends on whether Incremental or Absolute mode is chosen. When it is set to Incremental mode, the Z-value is measured from the Z-coordinate of the selected point to the hole bottom as shown in Figure 7.111. If the selected point has the coordinate of (3,5,1), the following two commands define the Z-depth being at Z=-1.0: **Depth = -2.0 (Incremental)**

Depth = -2.0 Incremental

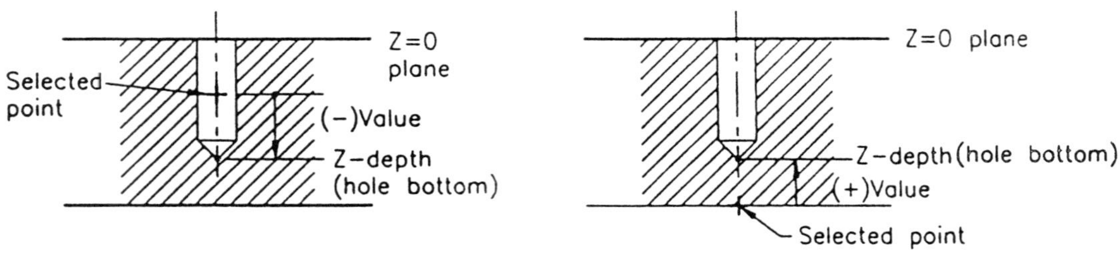

a. Negative Z value
(The hole bottom is below the selected point)

b. Positive Z value
(The hole bottom is above the selected point)

Figure 7.111 Incremental mode

In absolute mode, the Z-value is measured always from the Z-zero plane to the hole bottom (Figure 7.112). When this mode is used, the system ignores the Z-coordinate of the selected point and uses the Z-zero plane as the reference to measure the Z-depth.

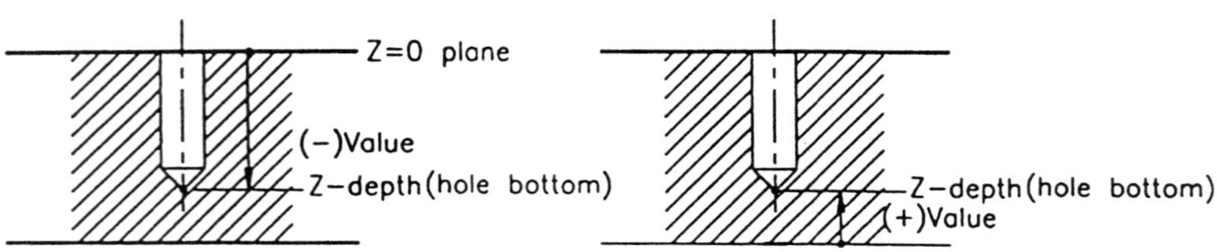

a. Z=0 plane locates on the top surface

b. Z=0 plane locates on the bottom surface

Figure 7.112 Absolute mode

> **Tip** Always use the absolute mode if possible to avoid confusion because you may not know the exact Z-vale of those selected points. Use the incremental mode only when the holes having different depths and the selected points have the actual Z-value of the hole bottoms (Figure 7.113). With the incremental mode, the same Z-depth value can be used for all holes although holes may have different depths.

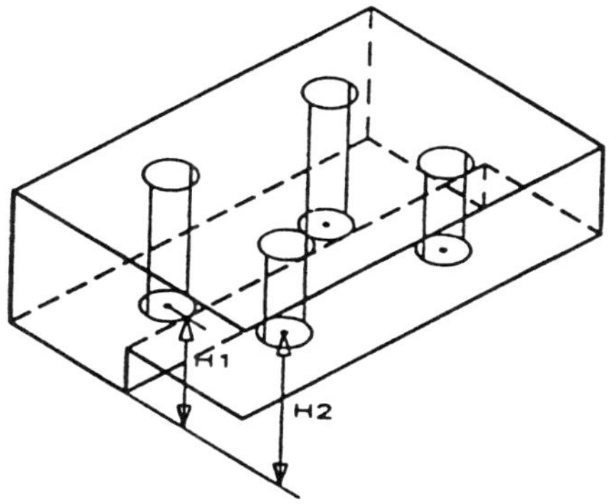

Figure 7.113

Cycle mode Mastercam provides a total of eight cycle commands with six standard types and two optional types. The two optional commands Misc. #1 and Misc. #2 are user defined cycles. They are unique and therefore are not discussed here. The six standard cycles are described in Table 7.3.

Table 7.3 Six standard cycles

Cycle Type	NC Command	Example	Typical Applications
Drill/Cbore 1. Dwell = 0 2. Dwell ≠ 0	G81 G82	G81 X1.0 Y1.0 Z-1.0 R0.2 F15.0 G82 X1.0 Y1.0 Z-1.0 R0.2 P0.5 F15.0	Drilling or counterboring holes whose depths are shorter than three times of cutter diameter.
Peck drill	G83	G83 X1.0 Y1.0 Z-3.0 Q0.7 R.2 F15.0	Drilling deep holes whose depths are longer than three times cutter diameter. Especially suited for applications where chips are difficult to remove.
Chip break	G73	G73 X1.0 Y1.0 Z-3.0 Q0.7 R.2 F15.0	Drilling deep holes whose depths are longer than three times cutter diameter.
Tap	G84	G84 X1.0 Y1.0 Z-1.0 R0.2 P0.25 F50.0	Tapping right-hand internal threads.
Bore #1 1. Dwell = 0 G85 2. Dwell ≠ 0 G89	G85	X1.0 Y1.0 Z-1.0 R0.2 F15.0 G89 X1.0 Y1.0 Z-1.0 R0.2 P0.25 F15.0	Boring holes with feed-in and feed-out paths.
Bore #2	G86	G86 X1.0 Y1.0 Z-1.0 R0.2 P0.25 F15.0	Boring holes with feed-in, spindle stop, rapid-out paths.

The operation sequence of the common drilling or boring operation is listed below. See Figure 7.114.

1. Rapid to the hole center with Z at the clearance level.
2. Rapid Z to the retract level.
3. Feed Z to the Z-depth of the hole bottom.
4. Dwell at the hole bottom for a period of time (if specified)
5. Retract Z to the retract level or clearance level.

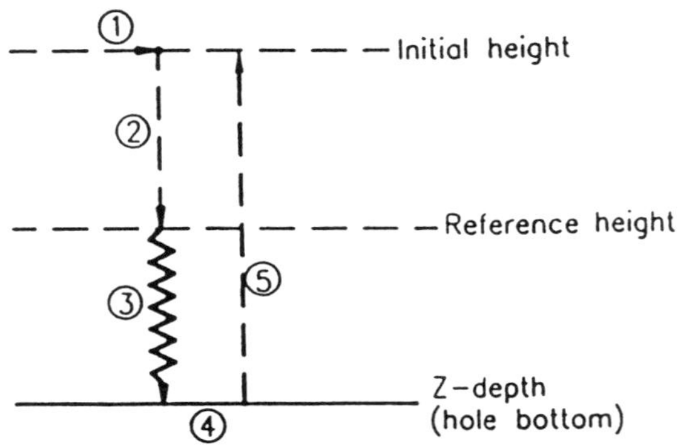

Figure 7.114

Pecking parameters Drilling deep holes are normally performed by two methods: peck drilling and chip break drilling. They are used when the depth of holes is larger than three times of the cutter diameter. Figure 7.115 illustrates the difference of these two deep hole drilling cycles.

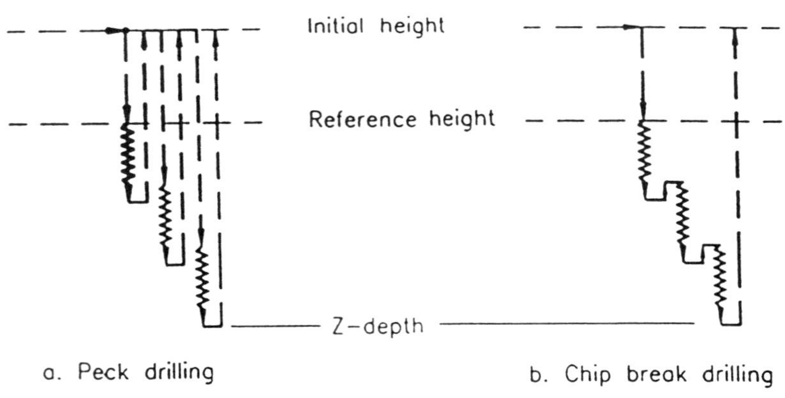

Figure 7.115

The operation sequence of the peck drilling cycle is listed below:

1. Rapid to the hole center with Z at clearance level.
2. Rapid Z to the retract level.
3. Feed Z down with one peck distance.
4. Rapidly retract Z with the retraction amount.
5. Rapid Z down to one peck clearance up form the previous drilled depth.
6. Feed Z down with one peck distance.
7. Repeat steps 4-6 until the hole bottom is reached.

Tip compensation Mastercam allows the user to compensate the drill tip which is about 118 degrees. Click "Tip comp" button at the right bottom of the drill menu to open the tip compensation dialog box as below.

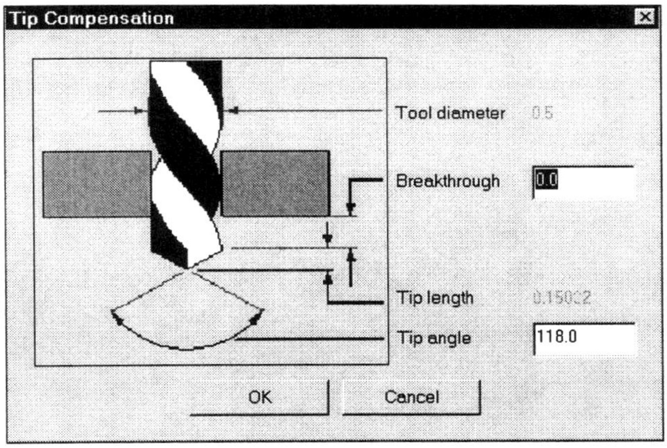

The four parameters included in tip compensation dialog box are:

Tool diameter:	specify the diameter of cutter.
Breakthrough:	specify the penetration distance of the tool.
Tip length:	specify the length of drill lip.
Tip angle:	specify the included angle of the drill lip.

Point Selection for (Drill module)

Mastercam provides a variety of methods for selecting points as the drilling center coordinates. They are briefly described below:

Add points	**Description**
Manual	manually defines the drilling center points.
Automatic	system automatically selects a series of existing points as the drilling center locations.
Entities	defines the endpoints of selected entities as the drilling center locations.
Window pts	selects all existing points within a window as the drilling center locations.
Last	uses the point set used in the last operation as the drilling center locations.
Mask on arc	selects the arc centers in the mask group as the drilling center locations.
Patterns	creates a rectangular point grid or circular pattern as the drilling center locations.

Manual method These are the options for the user to define the drilling center locations:

Values:	define drilling center locations by entering their X and Y coordinate value.
Center:	define drilling center locations by selecting existing arcs or circles.
Endpoint:	define drilling center locations by selecting the endpoints of existing entities.
Intersec:	define drilling center locations at the intersecting point of two intersecting entities.
Midpoint:	define drilling center locations at the midpoint of selecting entities.
Point:	define drilling center locations at existing points.
Last:	use the last set of points that is used in drilling operation as the center locations for new drilling operation.
Relative:	define drilling center locations by referencing to a known point.
Quadrant:	define drilling center locations at one of the four quadrants of existing arcs or circle.
Sketch:	define drilling center locations at mouse picked locations.

Automatic method The automatic method allows the system to automatically select an array of existing points as the drilling center locations. It uses the following three selection points to define the points to be included (Figure 7.116):

Select the first point:	specify the first point in the point array.
Select the second point:	specify the point to indicate the array direction.
Select the last point:	specify the last point to be included.

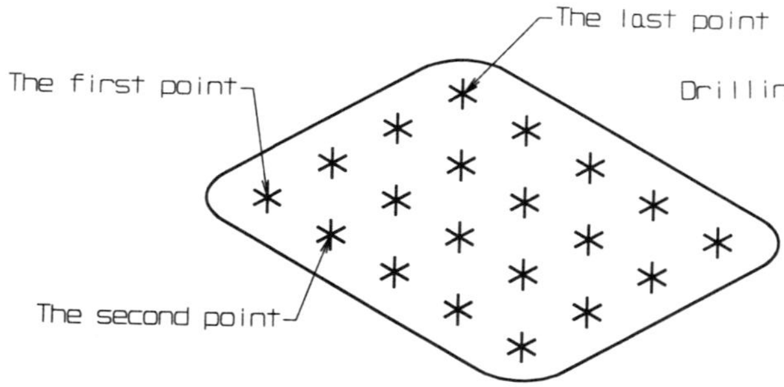

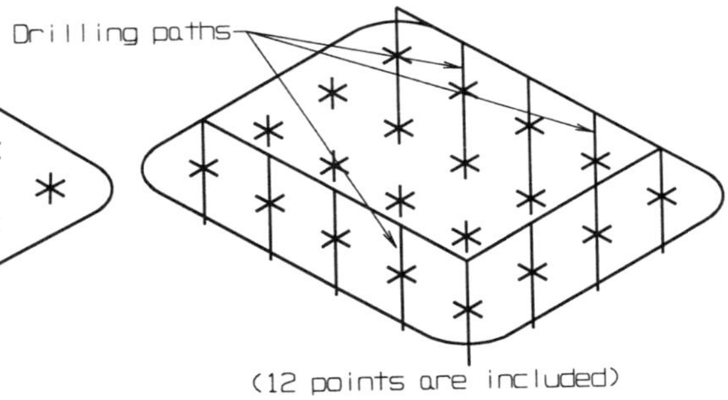

Figure 7.116a

Figure 7.116b

Entities This option allows to select the end points of a group of entities as the drilling center locations. The entities can be selected using the chain, window polygon, and area option. Figure 7.117 shows an example of using entities option to select the drilling locations.

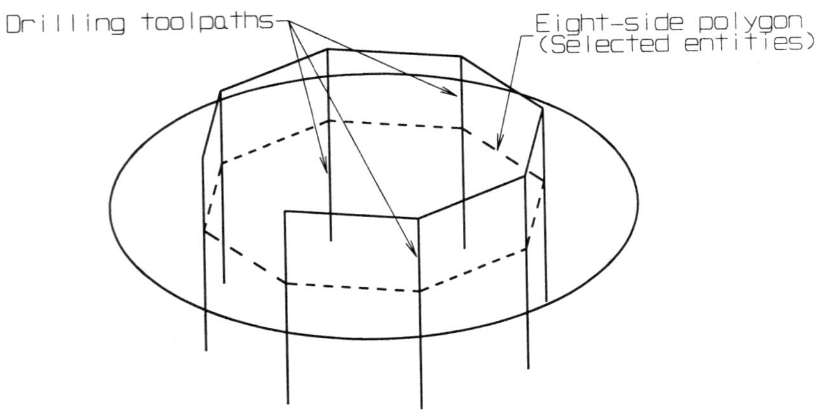

Figure 7.117

Window pts This option picks two locations to form a window for including all point entities as the drilling locations. The system will pick all points within the window and arrange the drilling sequence according to the given "Point Sorting Option". Figure 7.118 shows a drilling example in which the twenty drilling points are selected by using the "Window pts" option.

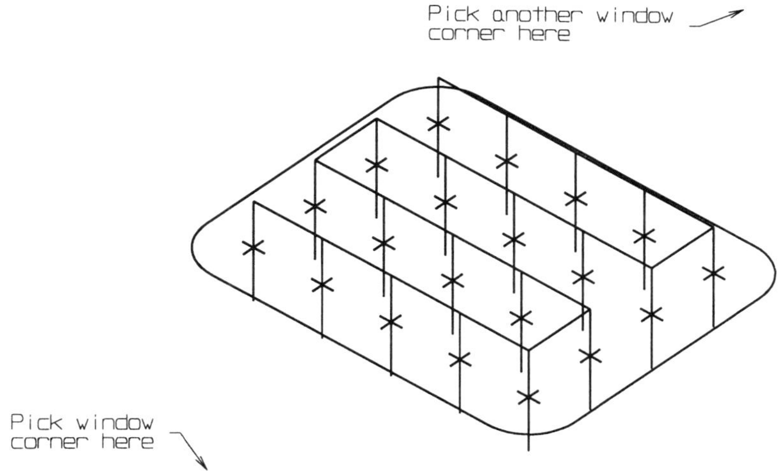

Figure 7.118

Option The option function is used to define the point sorting method for arranging the drilling sequence. Mastercam provides seventeen sorting methods to arrange the point pattern for drilling. The "Point Sorting" dialog box is shown here.

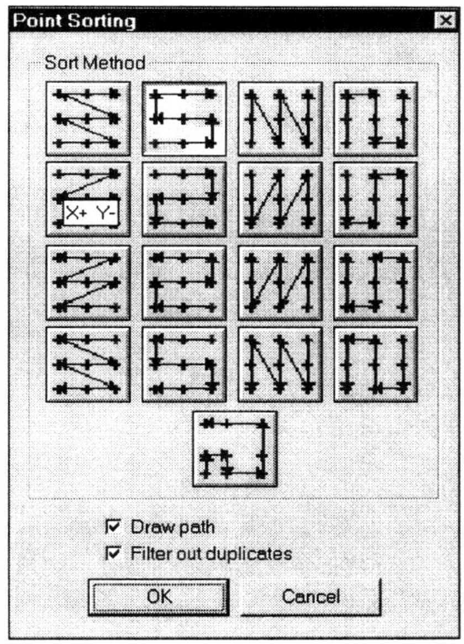

Patterns This point defining method is used to define an array of points that are arranged in either rectangular grid or circular grid pattern. It has two options; **grid pattern** and **bolt circle pattern**.

Grid pattern Mastercam uses the following parameters to define a point grid pattern (Figure 7.119):

Specify the grid origin: 0,0
Enter amount of point in X: 5
Enter X grid spacing: 1
Enter amount of point in Y: 4
Enter Y grid spacing: 1
Enter amount to shift X points: 0
Enter amount to shift Y points: 0

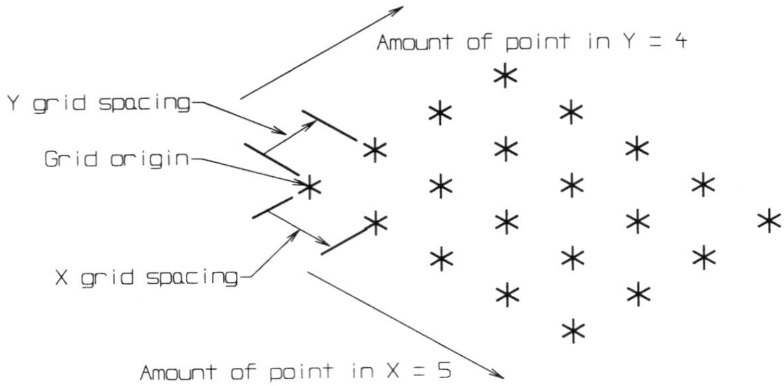

Figure 7.119

Bolt circle pattern Mastercam uses the following parameters to define a point bolt circle pattern (Figure 7.120):

> Specify the bolt circle origin: 0,0
> Enter bolt circle radius: 2
> Enter start angle (0 = 3 o'clock): 0
> Enter angle between points: 30
> Enter number of points: 12

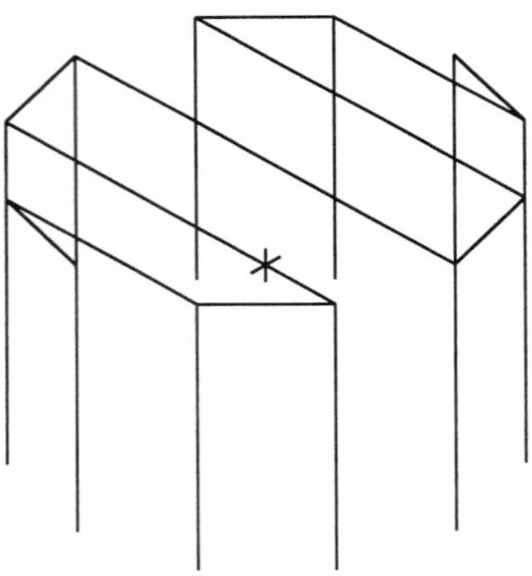

Figure 7.120a

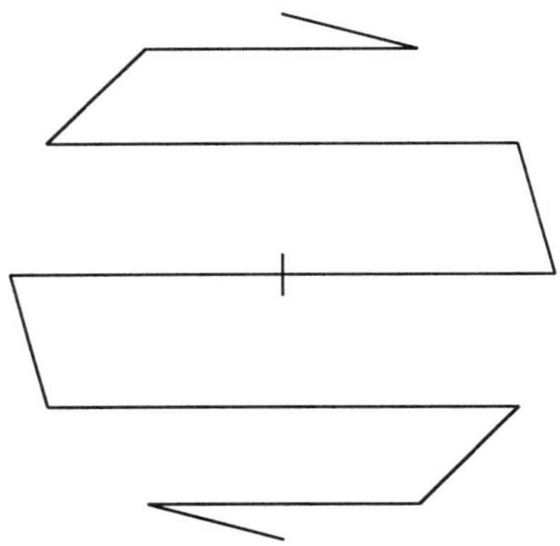

Figure 7.120b

Figure 7.121 shows how the sorting option affects the drilling sequence.

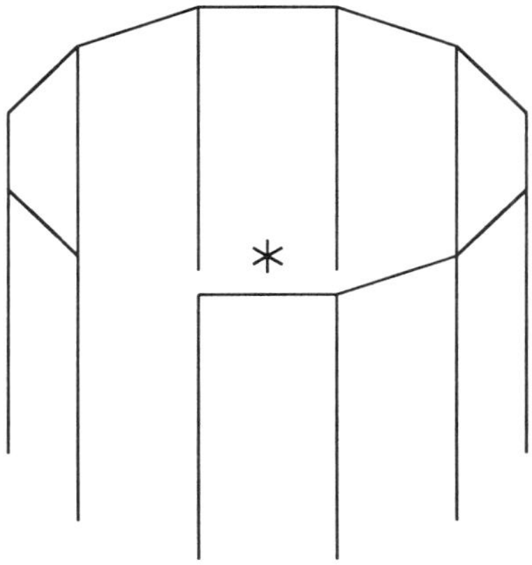

Figure 7.121a

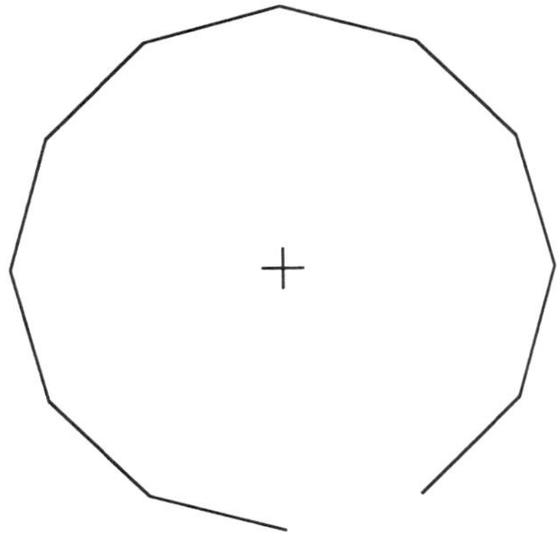

Figure 7.121b

⌛Tips for drilling operations

1. Suggestions for selecting clearance level, retract level, and Z depth.
   The clearance level must be high enough to clear any interference such as steps, clamping devices, etc.

   Retract level = 0.15" above the part surface to be drilled (for smooth surfaces)
   = 0.3" above the part surface to be drilled (for rough surfaces)

   Z depth: (a) Blind holes: (Figure 7.122a)
   Z depth = full-diameter depth + 0.3 D
   where D = drill diameter
   (b) through holes: (Figure 7.122b)
   Z depth = hole depth + 0.3 D + 0.1
   where 0.1 is the penetration (breakthrough) distance

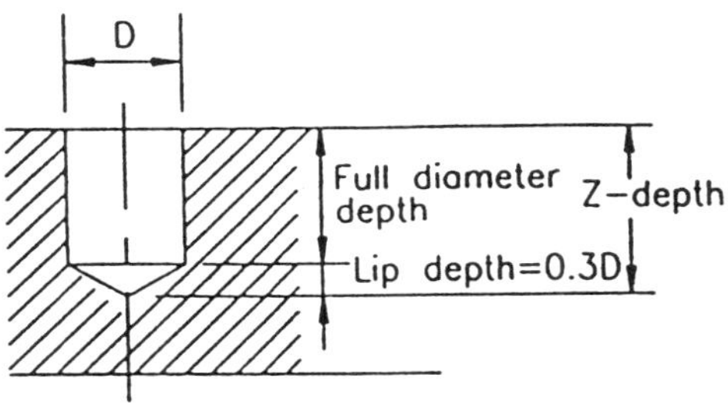

Figure 7.122a Blind hole

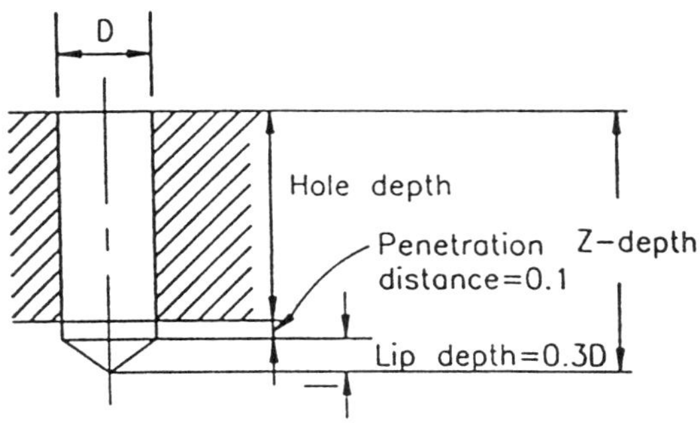

Figure 7.122b Through hole

2. Always use absolute mode to specify the Z depth (hole bottom) of the holes. The incremental mode is only recommended for drilling holes with different depths with two conditions:
   (1) the Z-value of selected points for drilling is specified and must be the exact Z-coordinate of the hole bottom and
   (2) the top surfaces are in the same horizontal plane.

Tips continued.

3. When the Z coordinate of selected points is zero, the Z depth has the same value for both incremental and absolute mode.

4. Use peck or chip break cycle when the depth of hole is longer than three times the cutter diameter. The peck drilling cycle is recommended when the chips are hard to remove from the holes. Using the chip break cycle can shorten the operation time because the drill does not retract back to clearance level or retract level. However, its chip removing ability is not as good as the peck cycle.

5. The drilling distance for each peck is about 1.5 times the drill diameter.

6. In the tapping operation, the feedrate and spindle speed must be synchronized to obtain the required thread accuracy. The following formulas can be used to obtain the proper feedrate and spindle speed:

   Feedrate (inch per minute) = Pitch x RPM
   Feedrate (inch per revolution) = Pitch
   Where Pitch = 1/number of threads per inch
   RPM = spindle speed

7. When multiple operations such as drilling, boring, and tapping, must be performed in the same set of holes, use the "Last" option to eliminate the need for repeatedly selecting points of subsequent operations.

8. Mastercam allows to define different drilling depths in one operation. Use the following commands to change the drilling depth of selected points:

   Select Edit → Edit depth
   Pick a point

   The system prompts to enter depth (absolute relative to toolplane): -0.5

   Figure 7.123 shows an example of drilling holes with different depths in one operation.

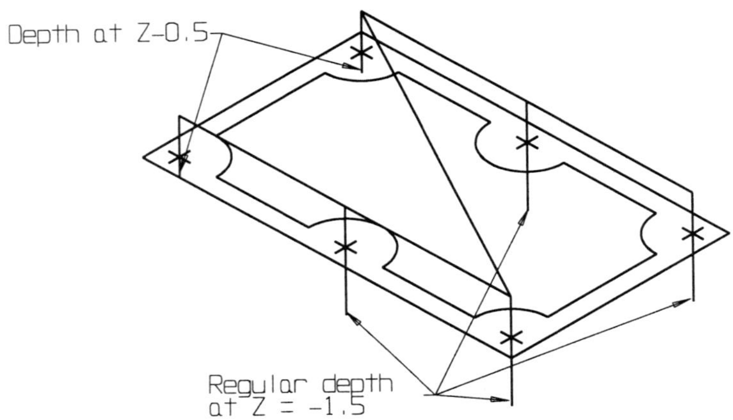

Figure 7.123

9. Use the "Edit jump" command to allow the cutter to be moved between holes at a height higher than the reference plane height. This is especially useful in avoiding interference with clamps or steps as shown in Figure 7.124.

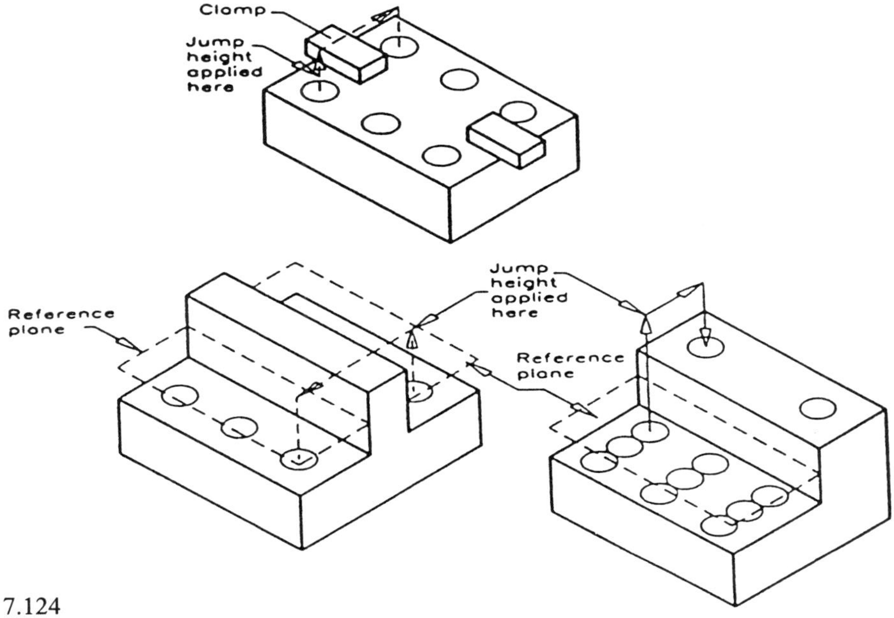

Figure 7.124

When a point is selected to apply "Edit jump" function, the system will prompt "Apply change to subsequent planar points." Select "Yes" to this prompt to cause the new jump height being applied to all subsequent points (Figure 7.125). Select "No" to keep the jump to only the selected point.

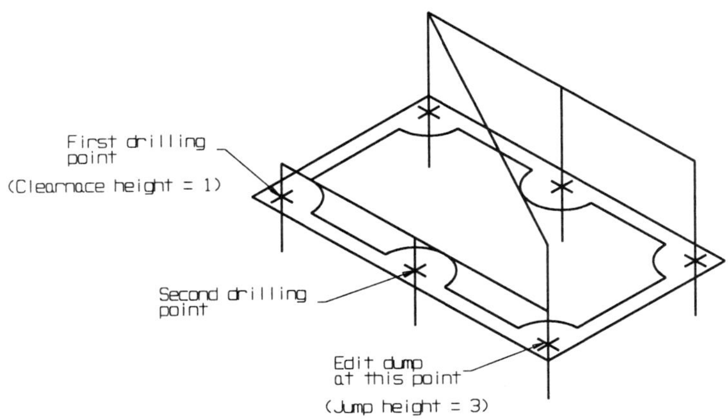

Figure 7.125

The "Rstr jump" command delete jumps in the selected points (Figure 7.126). This command often works together with the Edit jump command to control the retracting height of the drilling operations.

6

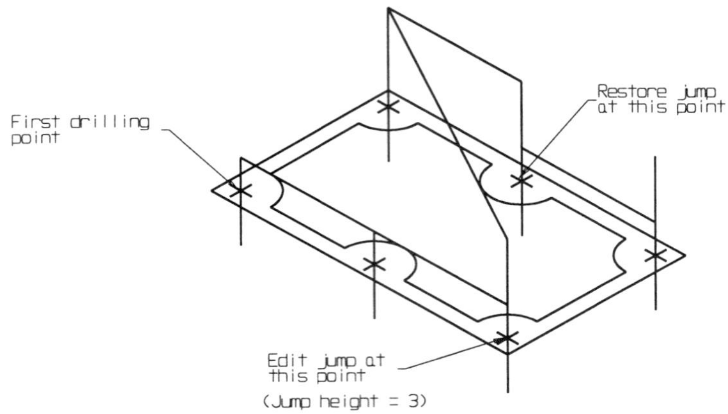

Figure 7.126

Project 6. Using the peck cycle to drill 24 deep holes

The peck drill cycle is used to drill 24 holes around three circles as shown in 7.127. The depth of the holes is 1.75-in. which is longer than 3 times hole diameter.

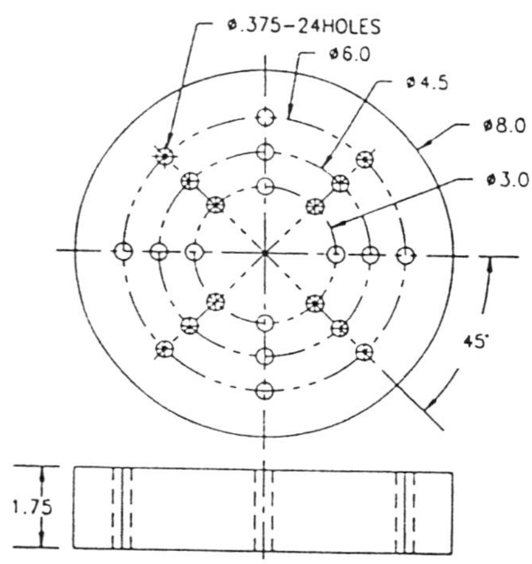

Figure 7.127a

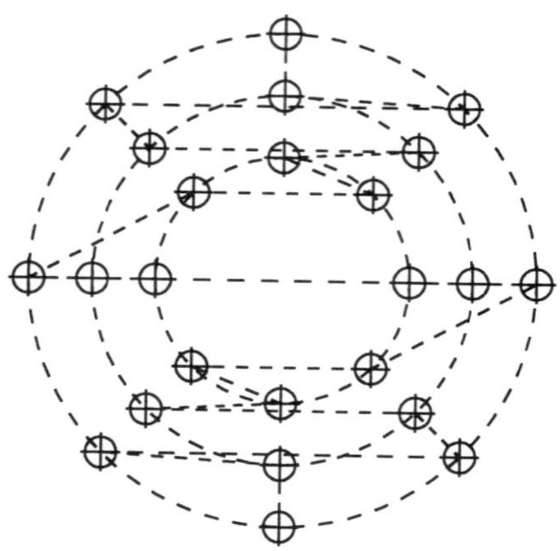

Figure 7.127b

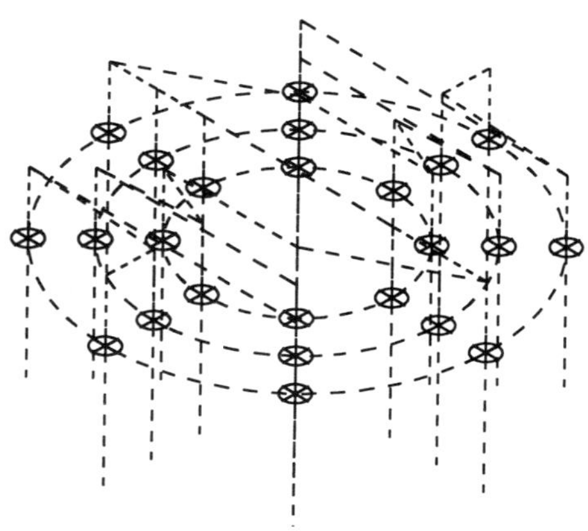

Figure 7.127c

⌛**Tips** 1. Use the peck drill cycle. The main drill parameters are set as below:

Initial height = 1.0
Reference height = 0.2
Depth = Absolute
Depth = -1.8625 (or 1.75 + 0.3 x 3/8)
First peck increment = 0.7

2. Use Window command to select points to be drilled.

Step 1. Open the part geometry file drill1.

Select **MAIN MENU → File → Get**
File name: **drill1**
The part drawing should appear as Figure 7.128.

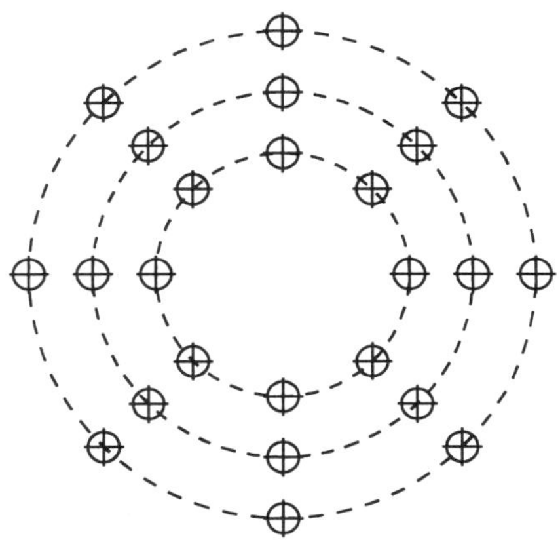

Figure 7.128

Step 2. Initiate the drill module.

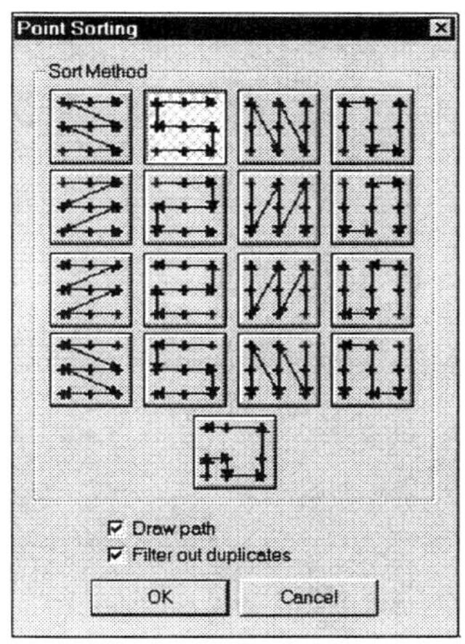

Select **MAIN MENU → Toolpaths → Drill**
File name for toolpaths: **drill1**
Select **Options**
The point sorting menu should appear as here.

Select the **X ZIG+ Y+** option which is located at second left of the top row
Select **OK**
Select **Window pts**
Pick two points to form a window including all points

The drilling paths should appear as in Figure 7.129.

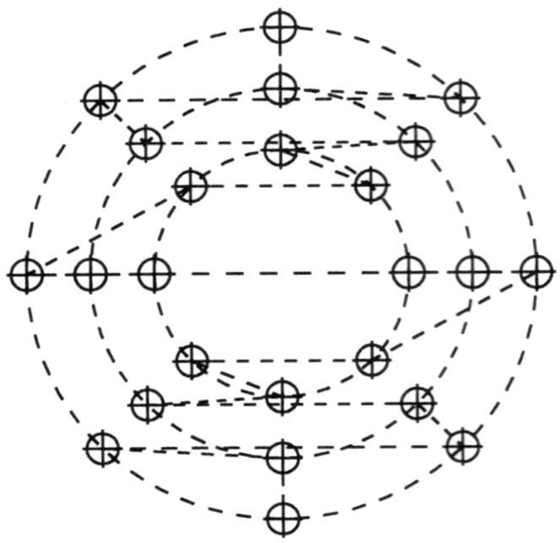

Figure 7.129

Select **Done**

Step 3. Select a 3/8" drill and define the tool parameters.

Click the right mouse button, then select **Get tool from library**
Select **tool #128** (3/8 drill)
Select **OK**
Set the tool parameters as below.

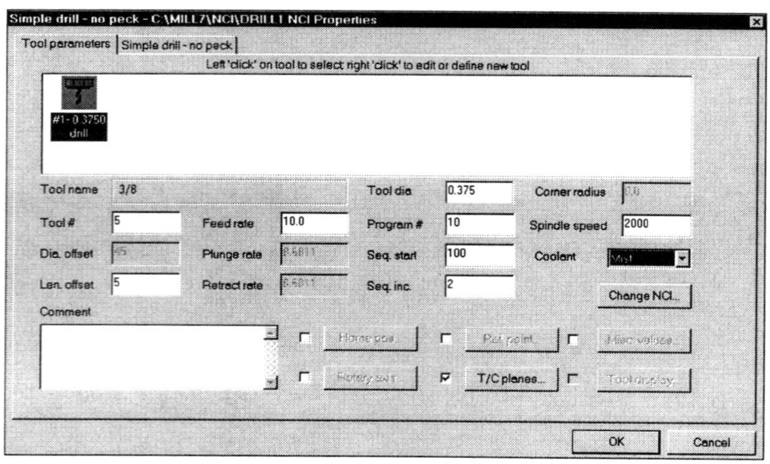

Step 4. Define the drill parameters.

Click the **Simple drill - no peck** button
Set the drilling parameters as below.

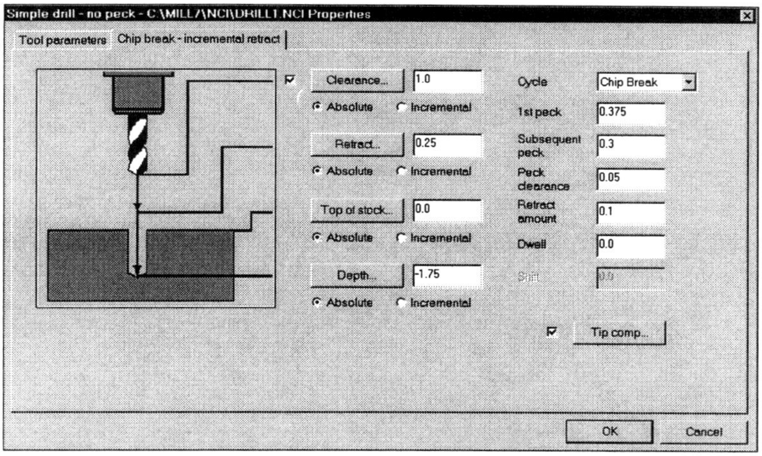

Step 5. Define the tip compensation parameters.

Click the **Tip comp** button
Set the tip compensation parameters as below.

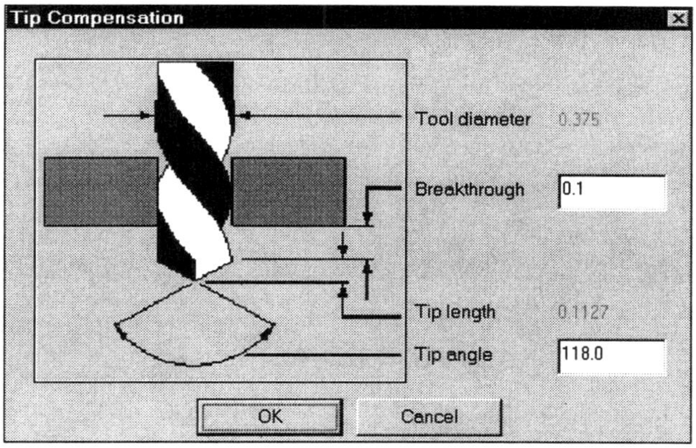

Select **OK → OK**
Select **OK** to "Tool #1 renumbered to #5"
Select **Gview → Isometric**
The drilling toolpaths are shown in Figure 7.130.

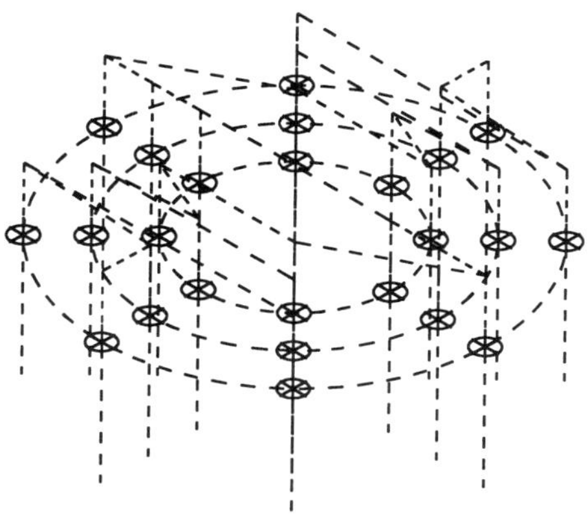

Figure 7.130

Step 6. Backplot the toolpaths.

Select **Operations**

The Operations Manager menu appears on the screen as below.

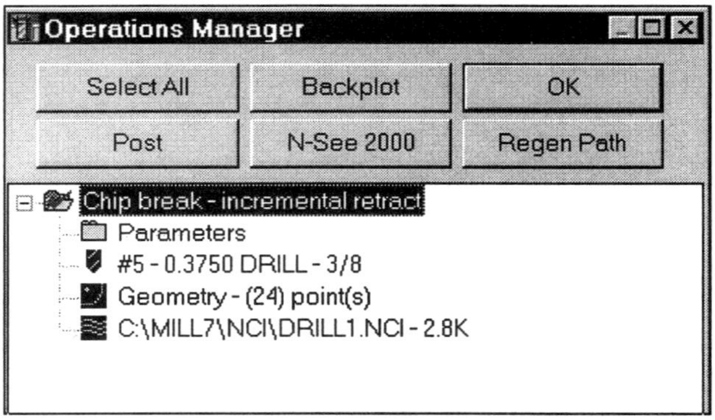

Select **Backplot → Display**

Set the display parameters as below.

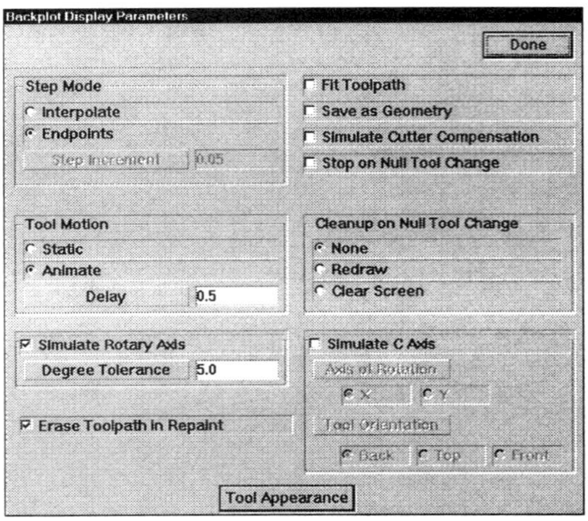

Select **Done**

Set the backplot parameters as below.

Select **Run**

The drilling toolpaths will be plotted on the screen.

You will see the sequence of drilling holes.

Select **BACKUP**

Step 7. Run the post processor.

Select **Post** from the Operations Manager menu

Select **Yes** to "Run the post processor?"

File name for NC: **drill1**

The NC program should be listed on the screen.

Select the **Close** button to close the file list menu

Step 8. Edit the part program.

Select **OK** from the Operations Manager menu

Select **MAIN MENU → File → Edit → NC**

File name: **drill1**

The NC Editor menu appears as below.

```
MasterCam NC Editor and DNC Communications
File Edit View NCUtils Macros DNC Help
%
(PROGRAM NAME - DRILL1 )
(DATE, Day-Month-Year - 16-05-98 TIME, Hr:Min - 14:09 )
( TOOL - 05 DIA. OFF. - 45 LENGTH - 05 DIA. - .3750 DRILL/MISC )
O0010
N100 G00 G40 G49 G80 G90
/ N102 G91 G28 Z0.
/ N104 G28 X0. Y0.
/ N106 G92 X0. Y0. Z0.
N108 G0 G90 X0. Y-3. S2000 M3
N110 G43 H5 Z1. M7
N112 G98 G73 Z-1.9627 R.25 Q3750 F10.
N114 Y-2.25
N116 X-2.1213 Y-2.1213
N118 X2.1213
N120 X1.591 Y-1.591
N122 X-1.591
N124 X0. Y-1.5
N126 X-1.0607 Y-1.0607
N128 X1.0607
N130 X3. Y0.
N132 X2.25
Edit Mode    Drill1.nc
```

Note: Your part program may be somewhat different from the one listed here if you use a different post processor.

Do all necessary changes to the program.

Step 9. Exit the NC editor.

Select **File → Exit**

Step 10. Save the toolpaths.

Select **MAIN MENU → File → Save**

File name: **drill1t**

Project 7. Drilling and tapping six holes

The part shown in Figure 7.131a has six 9/16-12 internal threads. Producing these six internal threads requires two operations, drilling and tapping. The tap drill size is 31/64 in. Figure 7.131b shows the drilling and tapping toolpaths.

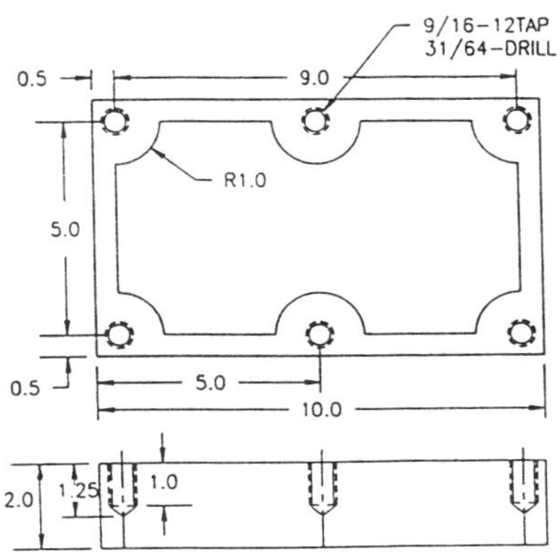

Figure 7.131a

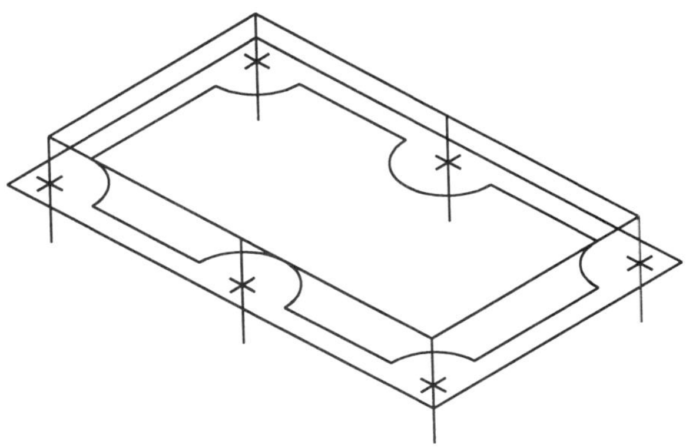

Figure 7.131b

Tips
1. The operation sequence starts with drilling all six holes and then is following by tapping.
2. Use the "Automatic" option to select the points to be drilled, then use "Repeat the points" option to select the drilled points for tapping.
3. The drilling depth is calculated as follows:
4. Drilling depth = Thread depth + 0.3 D + 0.1

   or = -(1.0 + 0.3 x (31/64) + 0.1) = -1.25

   where D is drill diameter

   0.1 is the buffer distance for tapping

Step 1. Open the part geometry file drill2.

Select **MAIN MENU → File → Get**

File name: **drill2**

The part geometry appears as in Figure 7.132.

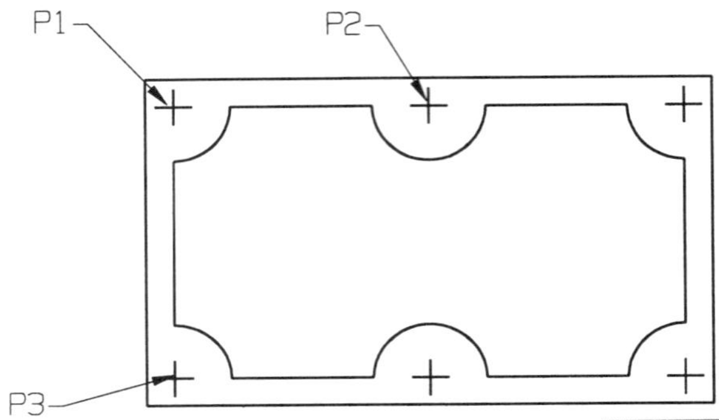

Figure 7.132

Step 2. Initiate the drill module.

Select **MAIN MENU → Toolpaths → Drill**

File name for toolpaths: **drill2**

Select **Options**

Select the **X ZIG+ Y-** option from point sorting menu as here.

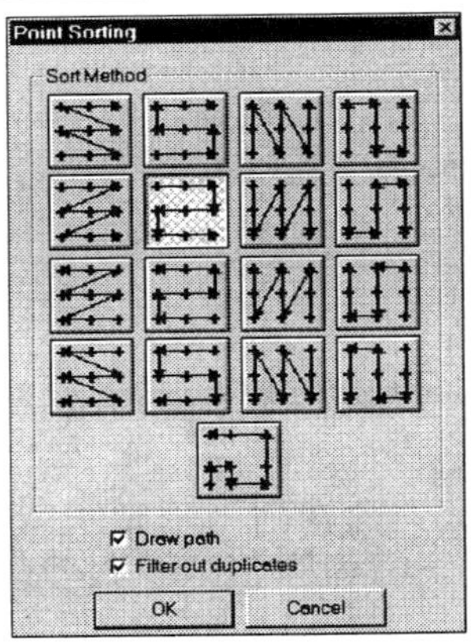

Select **OK**

Select **Automatic**

Pick **P1** as the first point

Pick **P2** as the second point

Pick **P3** as the last point

Six points are included in this selection and their path sequence is shown in Figure 7.133.

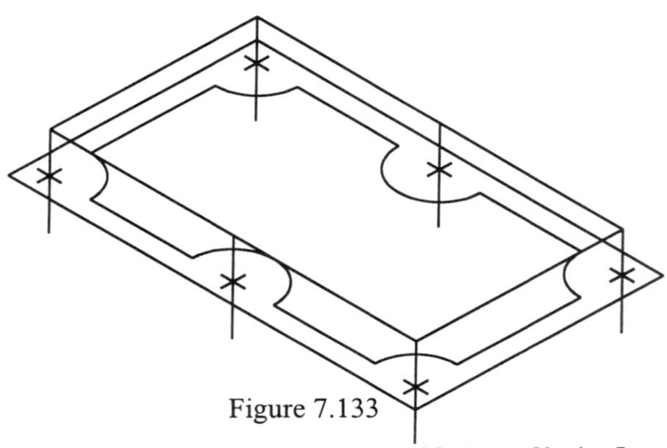
Figure 7.133

Select **Done**

Step 3. Select a 31/64" drill.

Click the right mouse button, then select **Get tool from library**
Select **tool #140** (31/64 drill)
Select **OK**
Set the tool parameters as below.

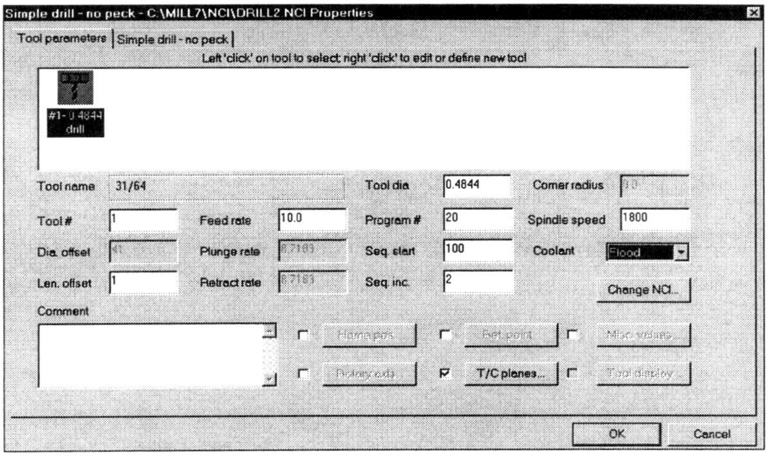

Step 4. Define drilling parameters.

Click the **Simple drill – no peck** button
Set the drilling parameters as below.

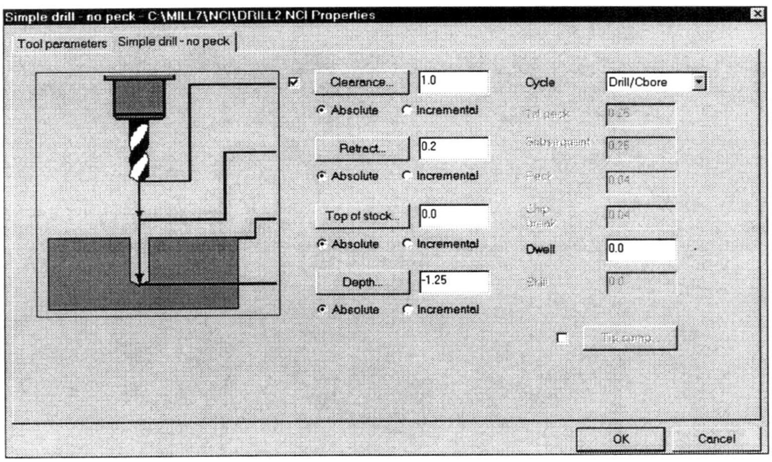

Select **OK** to generate drilling toolpaths
Select **Gview → Isometric**

The drilling toolpaths are shown in figure 7.133.

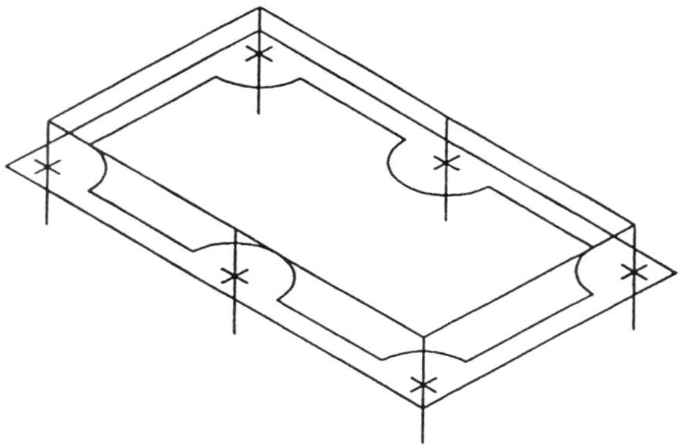

Figure 7.133

Step 5. Initiate the drill module again.

Select **Drill**
Select **Last** to use the previous point set
Select **Done**

Step 6. Select a 9/16 – 12 tap and set the tool parameters.

Click the right mouse button, then select **Get tool from library**
Select **tool #209** (9/16 – 12 right hand tap)
Select **OK**
Set the tool parameters as below.

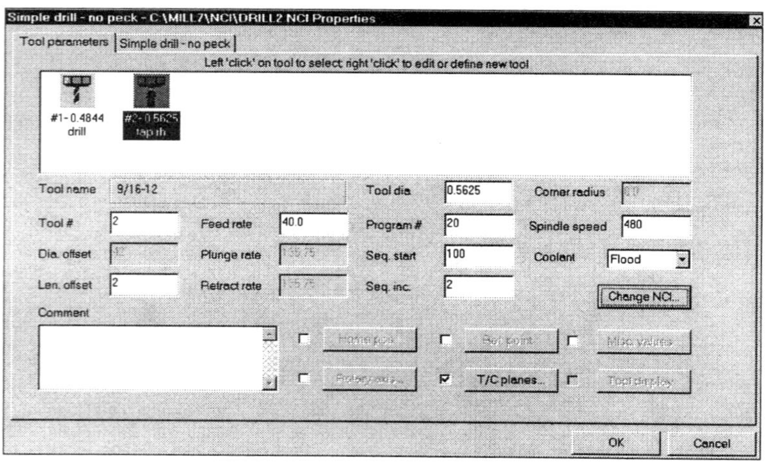

Step 7. Define the tapping parameters.

Click the **Simple drill - no peck** button

Set the tapping parameters as below.

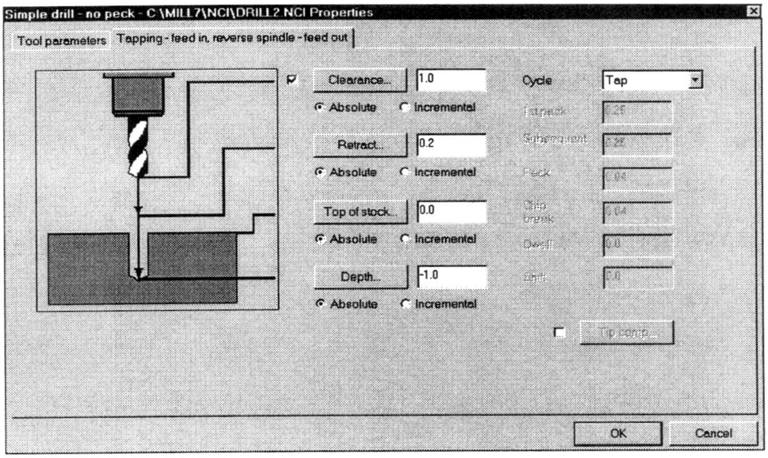

Select **OK** to generate the tapping toolpaths

Step 8. Backplot the toolpaths.

Select **Operations**

Two sets of toolpaths are included in the Operations Manager menu as below.

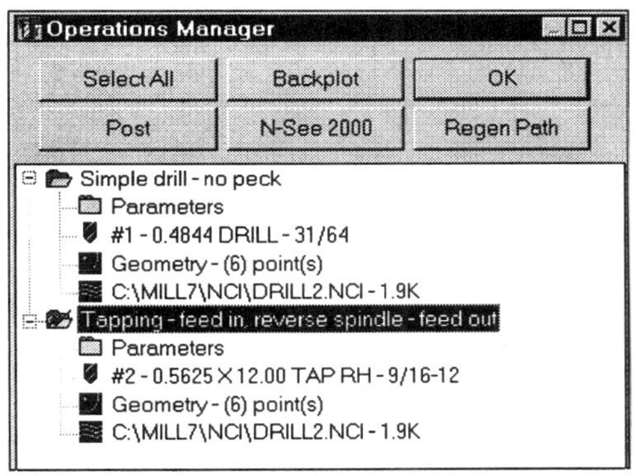

Select the **Select All** to include both sets of toolpaths

Select **Backplot**

Select **Run** to backplot the two sets of toolpaths on the screen

Select **BACKUP** to return to Operations Manager menu

Step 9. Run the post processor.

Select **Post**

Select **Yes** to "Run the post processor?"

File name for part program: **drill2**

The file list for the part program appears on the screen .

The NC program is listed below.

```
%
(PROGRAM NAME - DRILL2 )
(DATE, Day-Month-Year - 16-05-98  TIME, Hr:Min - 15:09 )
( TOOL - 01   DIA. OFF. - 41   LENGTH - 01   DIA. - .4844   DRILL/MISC )
( TOOL - 02   DIA. OFF. - 42   LENGTH - 02   DIA. - .5625   DRILL/MISC )
O0020
N100 G00 G40 G49 G80 G90
/ N102 G91 G28 Z0.
/ N104 G28 X0. Y0.
/ N106 G92 X0. Y0. Z0.
N108 T1 M06
N110 G0 G90 X.5 Y5.5 S1800 M3
N112 G43 H1 Z1. M8
N114 G98 G81 Z-1.25 R.2 F10.
N116 X5.
N118 X9.5
N120 Y.5
N122 X5.
N124 X.5
N126 G80
N128 M05
N130 G91 G28 Z0. M9
N132 T2 M06
N134 M01
N136 G0 G90 X.5 Y5.5 S0480 M3
N138 G43 H2 Z1. M8
N140 G98 G84 Z-1. R.2 F40.
N142 X5.
N144 X9.5
N146 Y.5
N148 X5.
N150 X.5
N152 G80
N154 M05
N156 G91 G28 Z0. M9
N158 G90
N160 M30
%
```

Click the **Close** button to exit the file list program

Step 10. Save the toolpaths.

Select **OK** from the Operations Manager menu
Select **MAIN MENU → File → Save**
File name: **drill2t**

Project 8. Drilling and boring four holes

This project generates toolpaths for drilling four holes with two different depths and two different retraction heights as shown in Figure 7.134. The drill has a diameter of ¾ in All four holes have the same top surface level (Z = -0.75). The Z-value of the bottom depth for holes A and B is –1.5 in. and for holes C and D is –2.25 in. This is an ideal case to use the edit depth command for defining different depths. As can be seen, there is a step between the two rows of holes. The edit jump command can be readily used to define the retract height for two Z-levels.

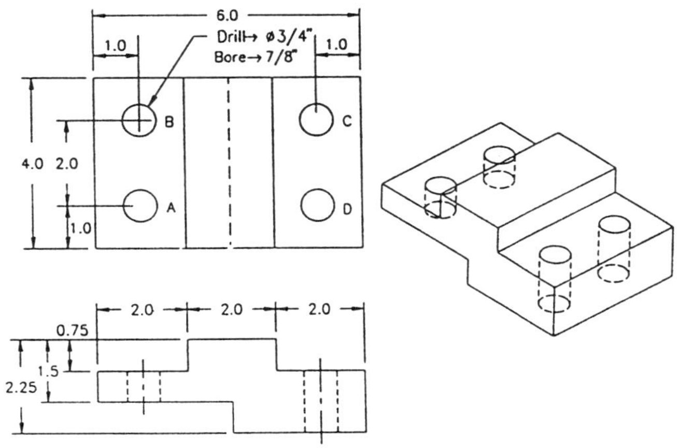

Figure 7.134a

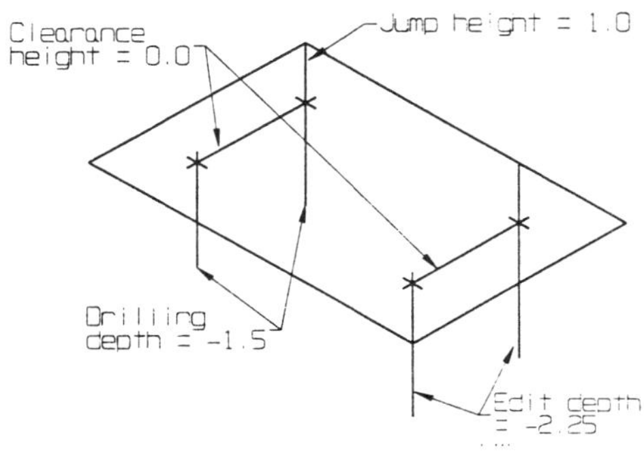

Figure 7.134b

Tips 1. Use edit depth command to change the drilling depth to Z = –2.25 at points C and D.

2. Use edit jump command to change the retract level at point B to retract the cutter higher than the step for moving to point C.

Step 1. Open the part geometry file drill3.

Select **MAIN MENU → File → Get**

File name: **drill3**

The part drawing should appear as in Figure 7.135.

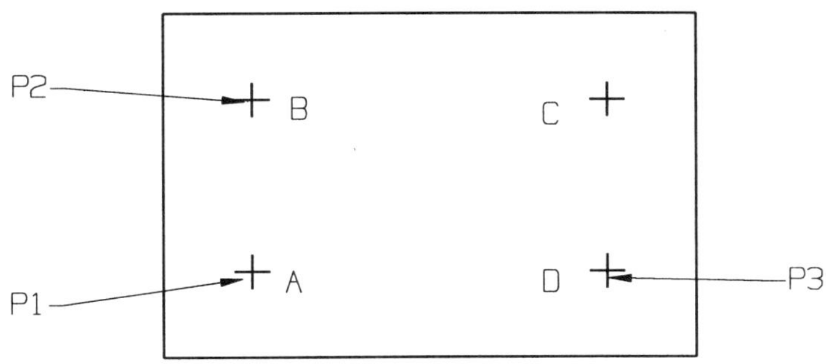

Figure 7.135

Step 2. Initiate the drill module.

Use the pick points in Figure 7.135.
Select **MAIN MENU → Toolpaths → Drill**
File name for toolpaths: **drill3**
Select **Options**
Select the **Y ZIG+ X+** option as shown here.

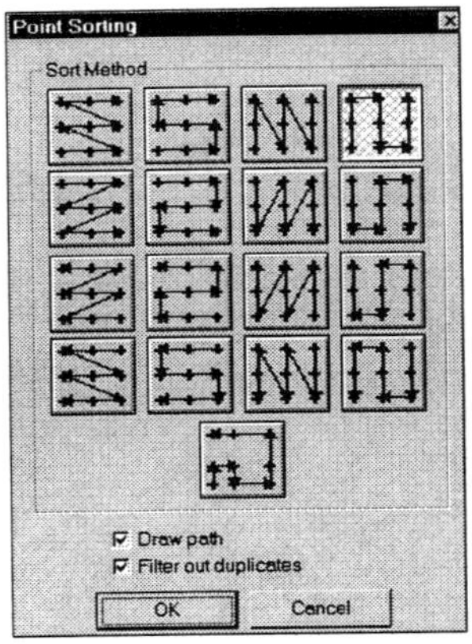

Select **OK**
Select **Automatic**
Pick **P1** as the first point
Pick **P2** as the second point
Pick **P3** as the last point
Select **Gview → Isometric**
The drilling paths are shown in Figure 7.136.

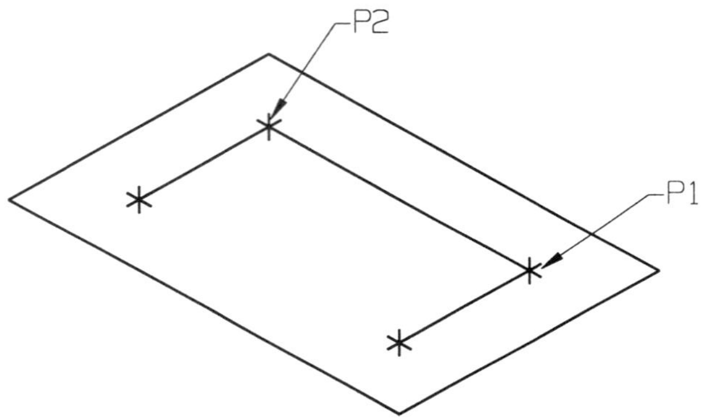

Figure 7.136

Step 3. Change the drilling depth for holes C and D.

Use the pick points in Figure 7.136.
Select **Edit → Edit depth**
Pick **P1** to select hole C
Select **Yes** to "Apply change to subsequent planar points?"
Enter depth (absolute relative to toolplane): **-2.25**
Select **BACKUP**

Step 4. Change the retract height for hole B.

Select **Edit jump**
Pick **P2** to select hole B
Select **No** to "Apply change to subsequent planar points?"
Enter jump height (absolute relative to toolplane): **1.0**
Select **BACKUP**
Select **Done → Done**

Step 5. Define the tool parameters.

Click the right mouse button, then select **Get tool from library**
Select tool # 214 (3/4 drill)
Select **OK**

Define the tool parameters as below.

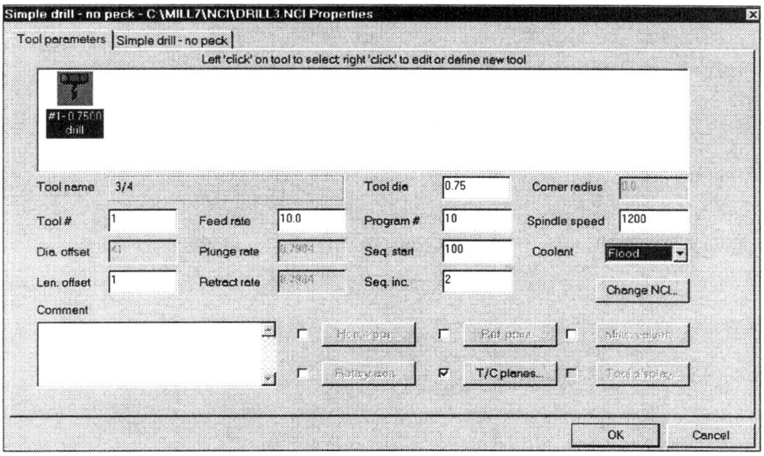

Step 6. Define the drilling parameters.

Click the **Simple drill – no peck** button
Set the drilling parameters as below.

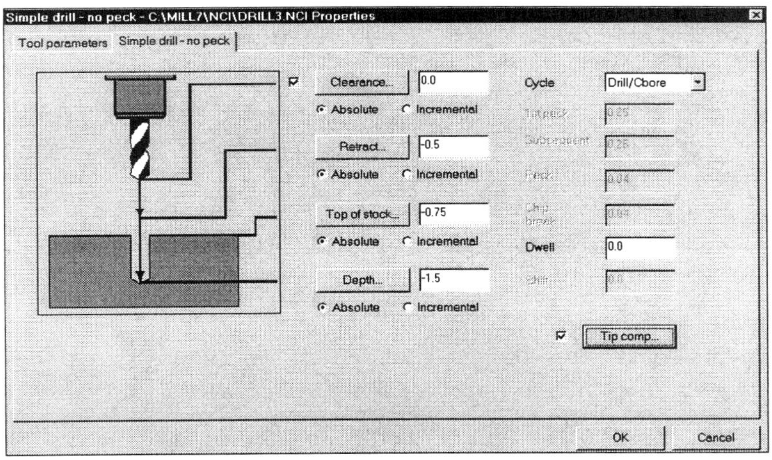

Select **OK** to generate drilling toolpaths

Drilling toolpaths with different depths and retraction levels are shown in Figure 7.137.

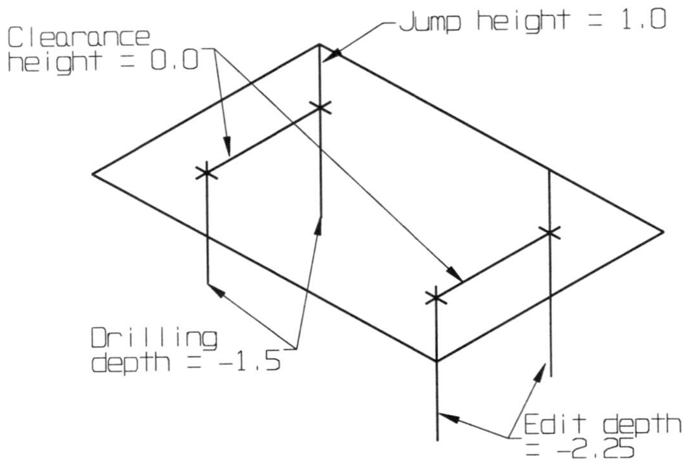

Figure 7.137

Step 7. Backplot the drilling toolpaths.

Select **Operations** to open the Operations Manager menu
Select **Backplot**
Select **Step** to plot the first toolpath
Note: The coordinate value of each toolpath end point will be displayed. Check to verify the various Z-depths.
Continue to select **Step** until the end of toolpaths
Select **OK** to "Backplot complete"
Select **BACKUP** to return to the Operations Manager menu
Select **OK** to exit the Operations Manager

Step 8. Save the toolpaths.

Select **MAIN MENU → File → Save**
File name: **drill3t**

7.12 Circmill Module

This toolpath module is used to generate a toolpath pattern for cutting a circle. Its toolpath pattern is listed below (Figure 7.138):

1. Plunge to the circle center
2. Add an entry line move
3. Add an entry arc move
4. Cut the circle
5. Add an exit arc move
6. Add an exit line move

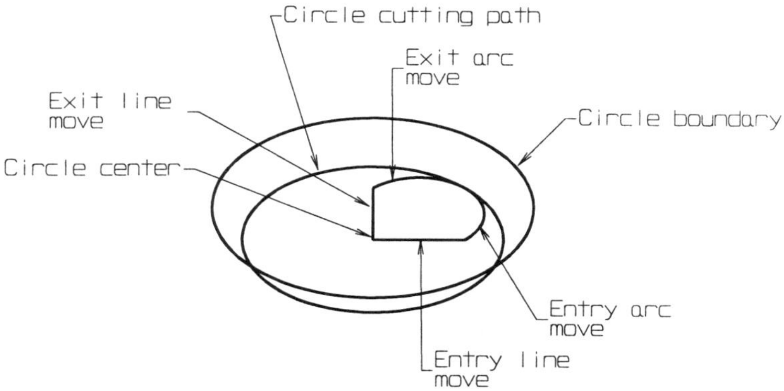

Figure 7.138a

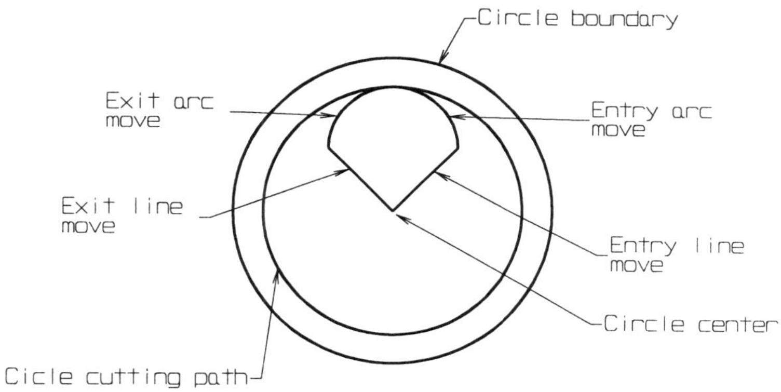

Figure 7.138b

The Circmill parameter dialog box appears as below.

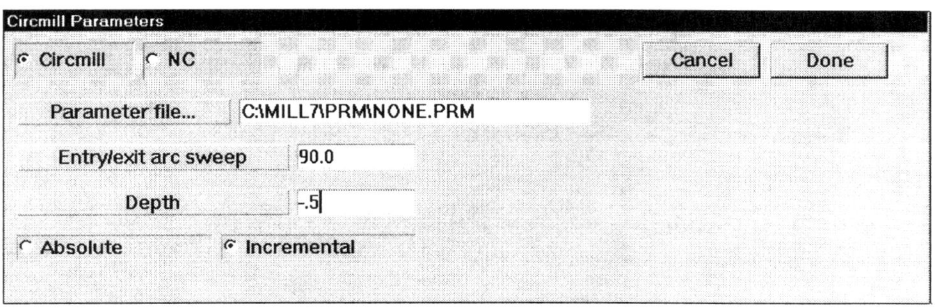

9 Project 9. Using circmill function to cut internal circle

This is a very simple project to show how to use the circmill function to generate toolpaths to cut a circle. Figure 7.139 shows the circle geometry and toolpaths.

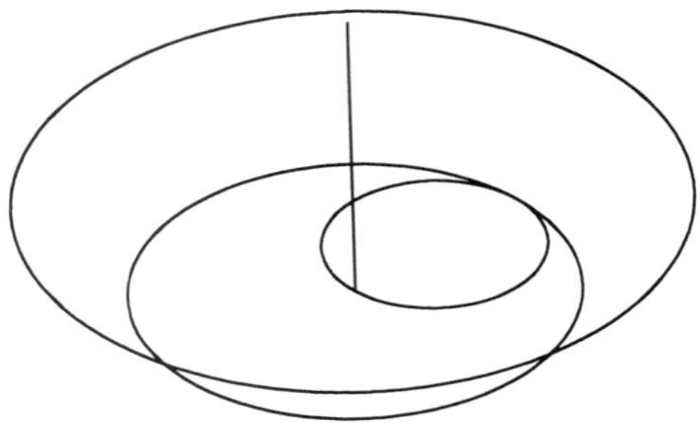

Figure 7.139

Step 1. Create a circle with its center at (0,0) and a diameter of 3-in.

Select **MAIN MENU → Create → Arc → Cir pt+dia**
Enter the center point: **0,0**
Enter the diameter: **3**
Select **Gview → Isometric**
The circle appears as in Figure 7.140.

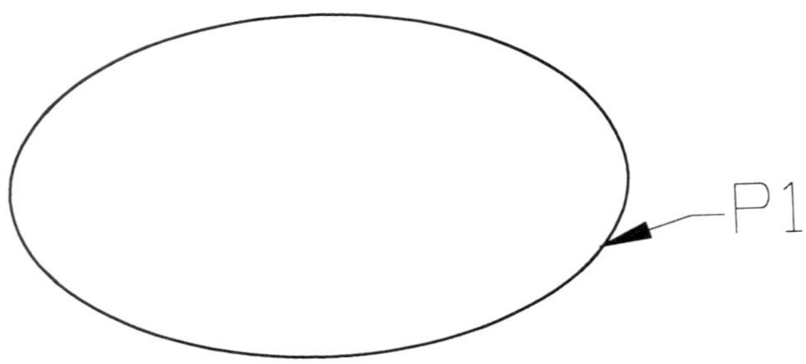

Figure 7.140

Step 2. Initiate the circmill module.

Select **MAIN MENU → Toolpaths → Next menu → Circmill**
File name for toolpaths: **cirmill**
Pick **P1** to select the circle
Select **Done**

Step 3. Define the circmill parameters.

Set the circmill parameters as below.

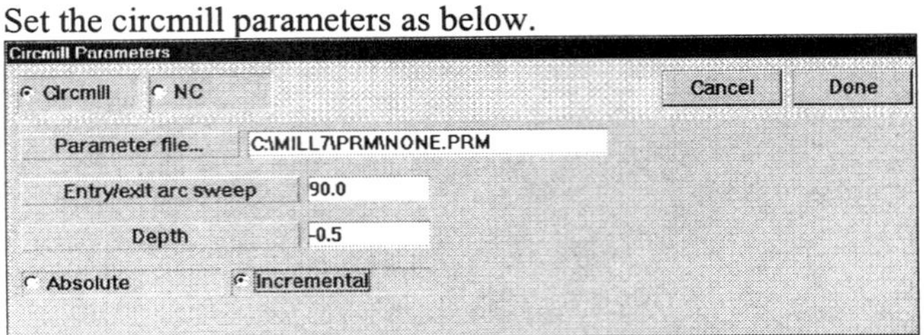

Step 4. Define the NC parameters.

Click the **NC button**
Set the NC parameters as below.

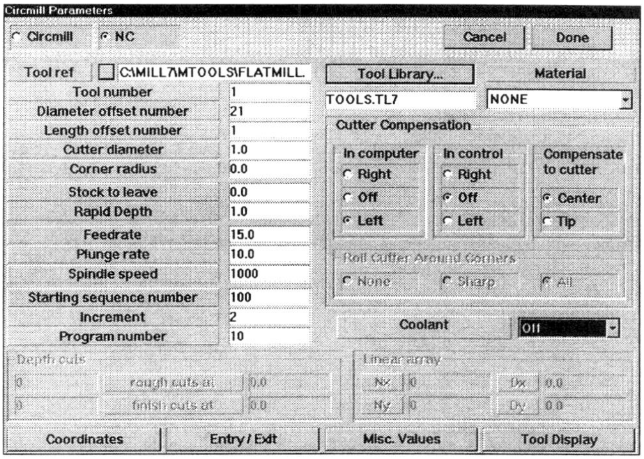

Select **Done**
The toolpaths are generated as in Figure 7.141.

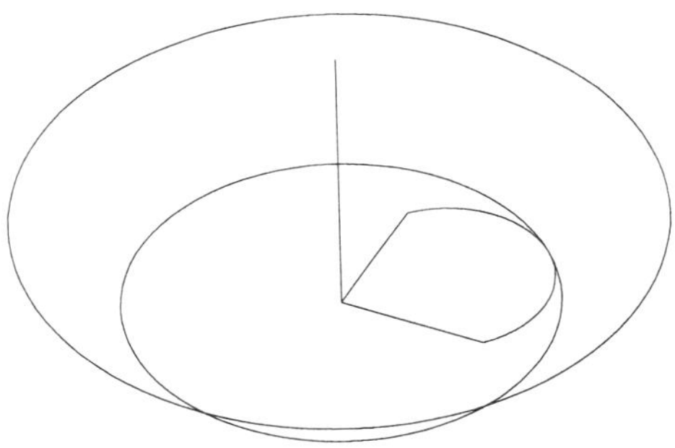

Figure 7.141

Step 5. Save the toolpath file.

Select **MAIN MENU → File → Save**
File name: **Circmillt**

7.13 NC Point Module

This toolpath module is used to generate a set of linear toolpaths that position the tool at specified locations. Its menu appears as below.

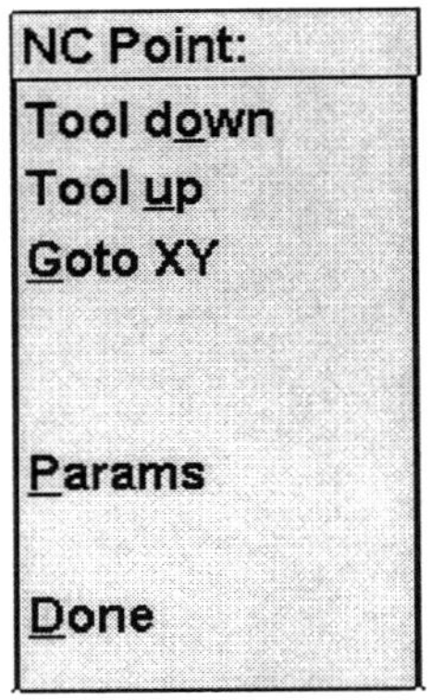

Tool down:	move the tool up.
Tool up:	move the tool down.
Goto XY:	specify the point locations to generate linear toolpaths.
Parameters:	define the tooling information and machining data.

The point parameters menu appears as below.

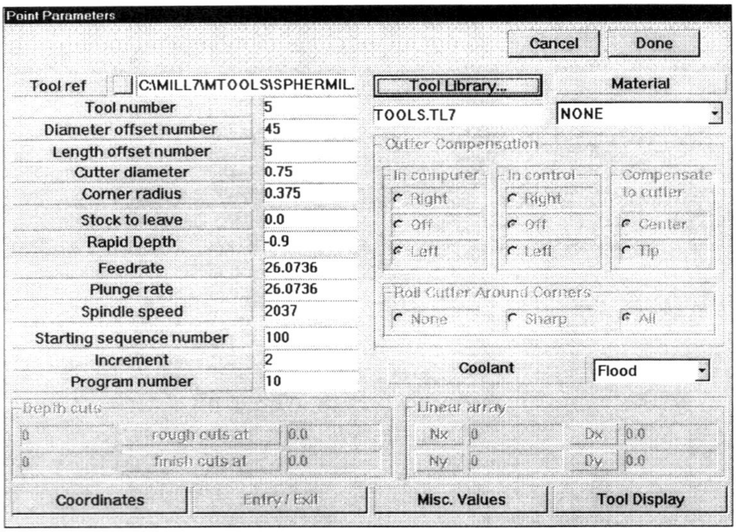

7.14 Engraving Letters 10

Engraving letters on part surfaces is a common machining application. Letters of various types and sizes can be created by using the Letters function. The contour or pocket toolpath module is then used to generate toolpaths from the existing lettering geometry. Lettering geometries can be created in two ways: **letters function** and the **edit note method**. These two methods are presented in chapter 5.

This section presents two lettering projects. The first project uses the contour and pocket modules to generate toolpaths for letters in which their geometries have been defined by using the Create → Letters commands. The second project involves using the Edit note method to create lettering geometries. These notes are modified to various fonts, sizes, and orientation. Finally the contour toolpath module is used to generate toolpaths for cutting letters.

Project 10. Using the contour and pocket module to generate toolpaths for cutting existing lettering geometries

Figure 7.142a

Figure 7.142b

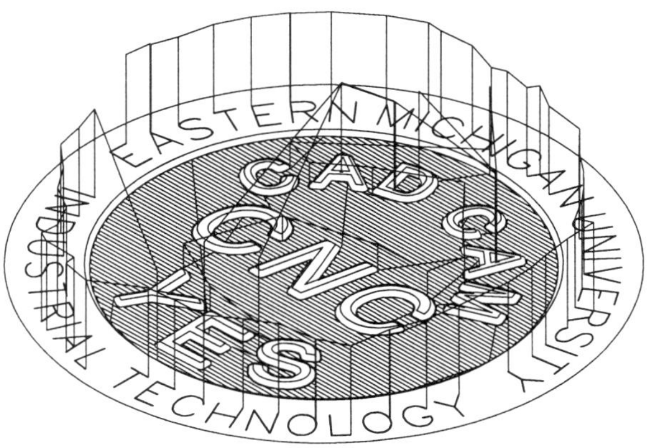

Figure 7.142c

Figure 7.142d

⌛**Tips**	1. Use the geometry file (letter2).
	2. Use the contour module to generate toolpaths for engraving letters in the outside circle.
	3. Use the pocket module to generate toolpaths for letters in the inner circle. The inner circle is used as the outside contour and profiles of these letters as islands.
	4. Verify the toolpaths.

Step 1. Open the geometry file letter2.

Select **MAIN MENU → File → Open**
File name: **letter2**
The part drawing appears as Figure 7.143.

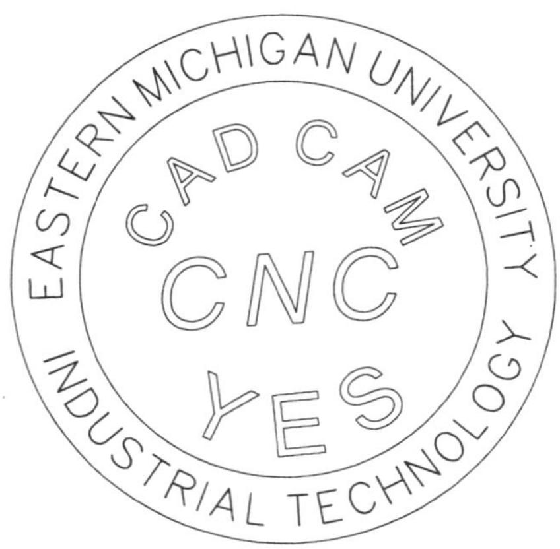

Figure 7.143

Step 2. Make levels 1 and 3 invisible.

Select **Level → Vis levels**
Toggle levels **1** and **3** to invisible (dimmed)
Select **OK** to return to graphic mode

The new drawing becomes Figure 7.144.

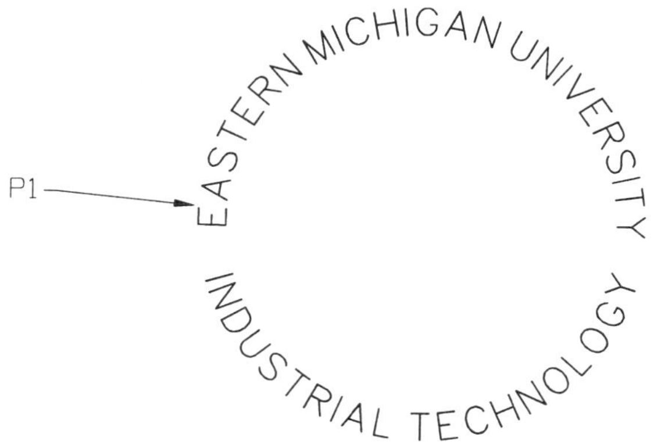

Figure 7.144

Step 3. Initiate the contour toolpath module.

Use the pick point in Figure 7.144.
Select **MAIN MENU → Toolpaths → Contour**
File name for toolpaths: **letter2**
Select **Window**
Pick two points to include all entities
Select **Endpoint**, then pick **P1** to select a search point
Select **Done**

Step 4. Select a tool and define the tool parameters.

Click the right mouse button, then select **Get tool from library**
Select **tool #248** (3/32 sphere end mill)
Select **OK**
Set the tool parameters as below.

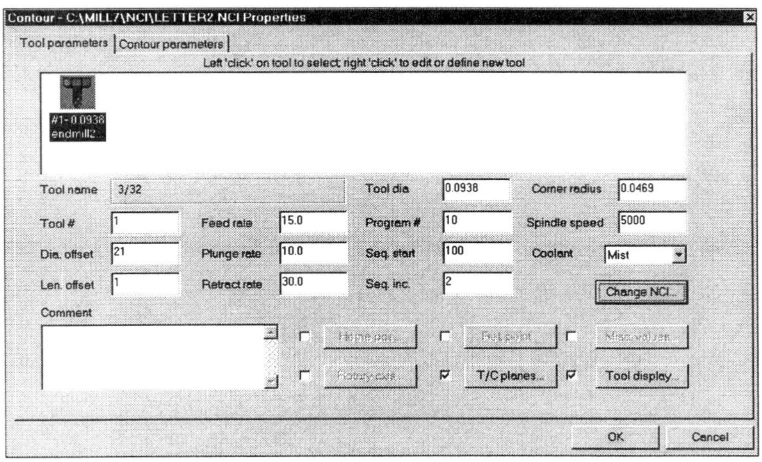

Step 5. Define the contour parameters.

Click the **Contour parameters** button

Set the contour parameters as below.

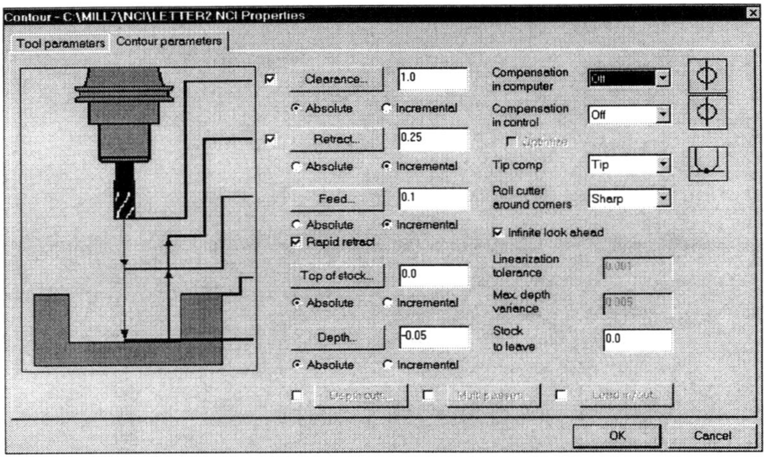

Select **OK**
The toolpaths should appear onscreen as Figure 7.145.

Figure 7.145

Step 6. Make level 2 invisible and levels 1 and 3 visible.

Select **Level → Vis. Levels**
Toggle levels **1** and **3** to visible (highlighted) and level **2** to invisible (dimmed)
The new drawings should look like Figure 7.146.
Note: the toolpaths are still visible on the screen.

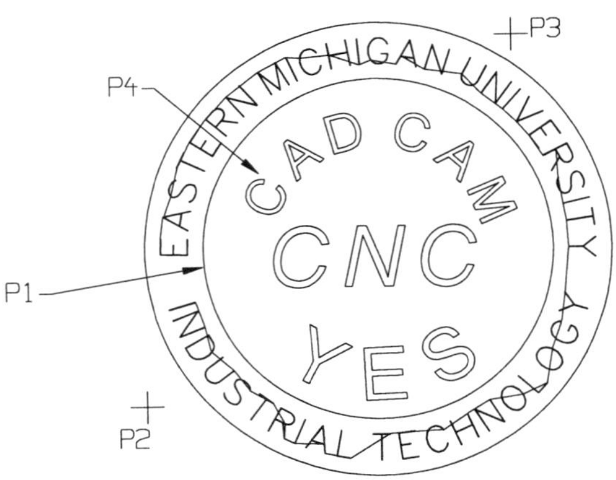

Figure 7.146

Step 7. Initiate the pocket module.

Select **MAIN MENU → Toolpaths → Pocket**
Pick **P1** to select the first contour
Select **Mode → Window**
Pick **P2** and **P3** to include all letter strings yet the inside circle is not fully included
Select **Endpoint**, then pick **P4**
Select **Done**
Set the tool parameters as below.

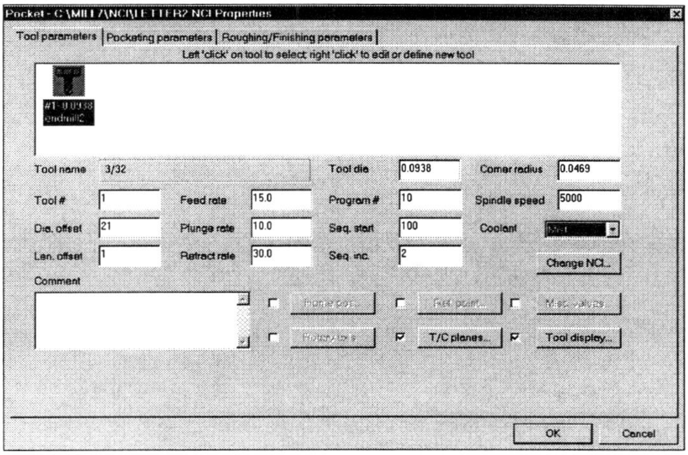

Step 8. Define the pocketing parameters.

Click the **Pocketing parameters** button
Set the pocketing parameters as below.

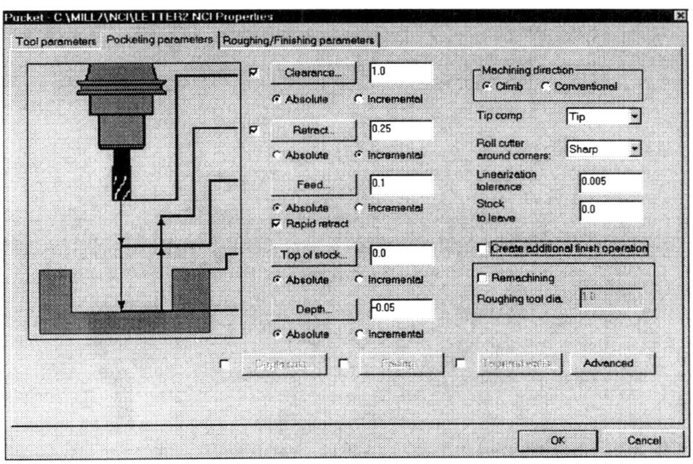

Step 9. Define the roughing/finishing parameters.

Click the **Roughing/Finishing parameters** button

Set the roughing and finishing parameters as below.

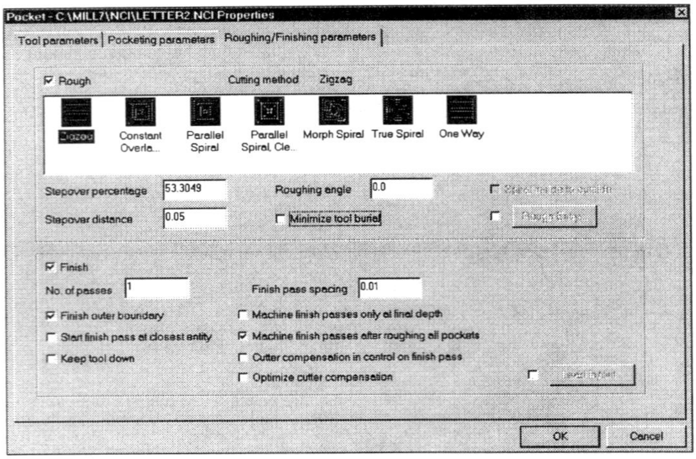

Select **OK** to generate the toolpaths as shown in Figure 7.147.

Figure 7.147

Step 10. Change to isometric view.

Select **Gview → Isometric**

The model with toolpaths shown in isometric view appear as Figure 7.148.

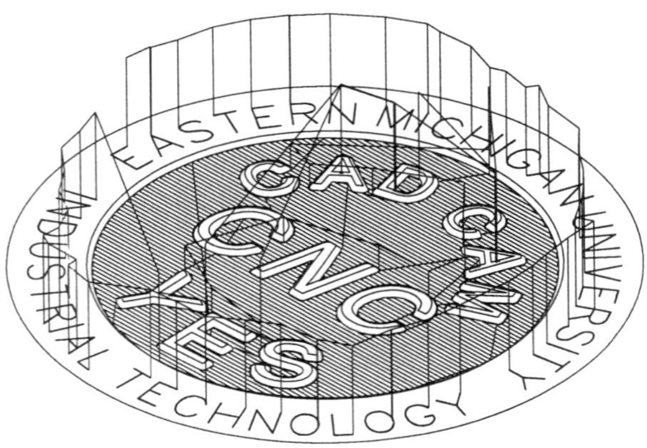

Figure 7.148

Step 11. Define the job setup parameters.

Select **Job setup**
Set the job setup parameters as below.

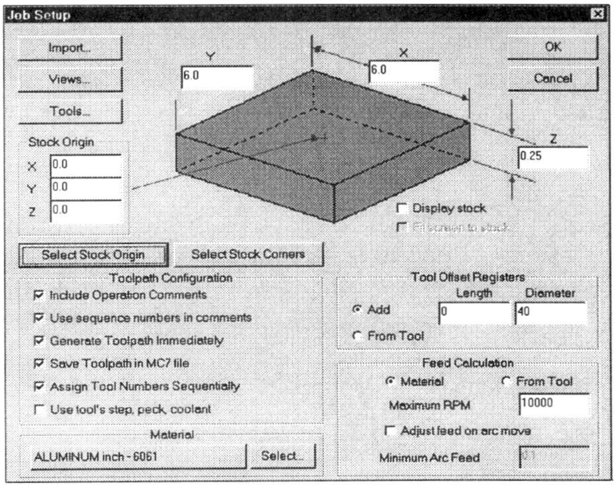

Select **OK**

Step 12. Verify the toolpaths.

Select **Operations** to open Operations Manager menu
Select **Select All**
Select **N-See 2000**
Select **Turbo mode**, then **OK**
The raw material block should appear on the screen.
Select **Do it** to verify the model
The model shown in isometric view should look like Figure 7.149.

Figure 7.149

Step 13. Show the model in the top view.

Select **Gview → Top**

12 The model shown in the top view appears as in Figure 7.150.

Figure 7.150

Step 14. Save the model.

Select **BACKUP** to return to Operations Manager menu
Select **OK** to return to graphic mode
Select **MAIN MENU → File → Save**
File name: **Letter2t**

Project 12. Using the contour module to generate toolpaths for cutting lettering geometires that are converted from notes

This project generates toolpaths to cut three strings of letters that are in different fonts and a combination of upper and lower cases. The lettering geometries must be created by the edit note method because lower case letters are involved. The specifications of these lettering strings are shown in Figure 7.151.

Modern
Font: Old English
Height = 0.4"
Aspect = 0.5
Location = (0.3,1.45)

CNC
Font: Swiss
Height = 0.6"
Aspect = 0.6
Location = (2.25,0.25)

Technology
Font: European
Height = 0.45"
Aspect = 0.5
Location = (0.5,0.1) then rotate 26.565 degrees

Figure 7.151a

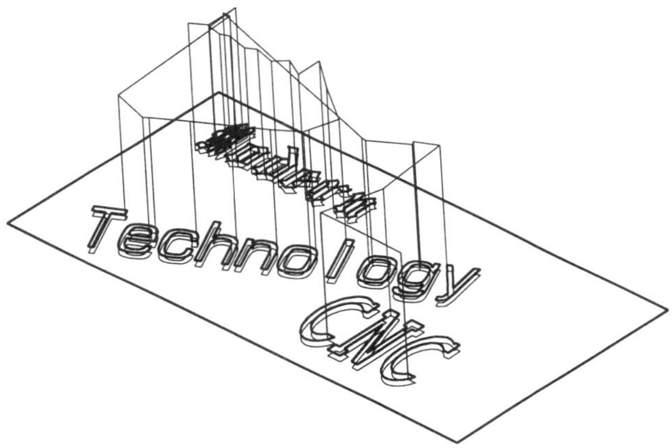

Figure 7.151b

Figure 7.151c

⏳**Tips** 1. Use the edit note method to create lettering geometries. The procedures are:

a. Create three notes using the following commands:
Create → Drafting → Note

b. Edit these three notes to their desired size, font, and orientation using commands:
Create → Drafting → Edit → Note

c. Convert these three notes to geometries by using the following commands:
Modify → Break → Note/let → Geometry

2. Use the contour toolpath module to generate toolpaths.

3. The cutter is a 1/16" end mill.

Step 1. Create a rectangle 4" x 2".

Select **MAIN MENU → Create → Rectangle → 2 points**
Enter the lower left corner: **0,0**
Enter the upper right corner: **4,2**
Press **Alt + F1** then **F2** to fit the drawing.
The rectangle should appear as in Figure 7.152.

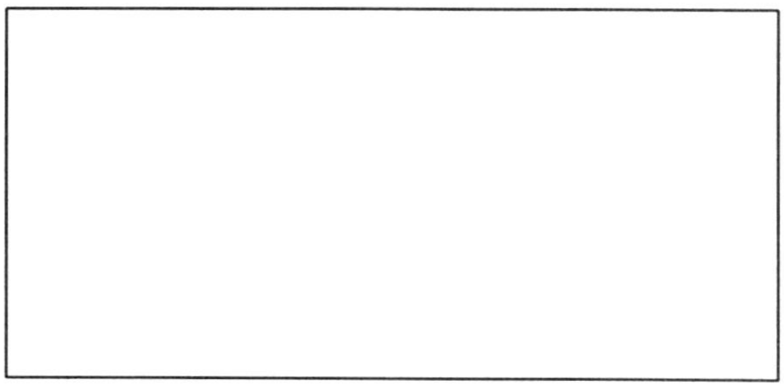

Figure 7.152

Step 2. Set the character height to 0.12" and character aspect to 0.5.

Double click **–PM-**
Select **Note Text Height** which is the top parameter on the Drafting Global parameters menu
Enter **0.12** for this parameter as shown below.

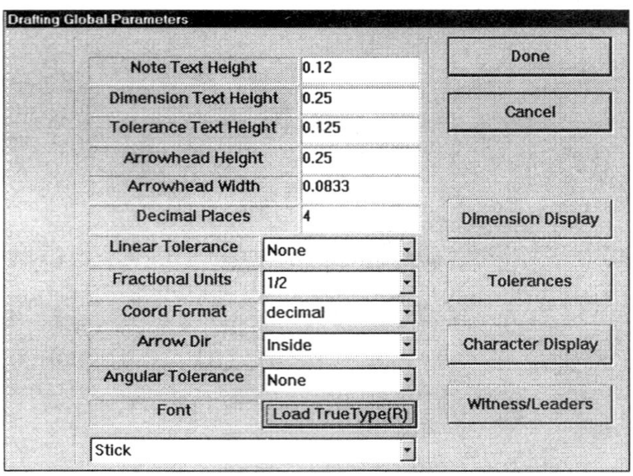

Select the **Character Display** button
Select the **Character Aspect** parameter, then enter **0.5**
Select **Done → Done** to return to graphic mode

Step 3. Create three notes.

Select **MAIN MENU → Create → Drafting → Note → Keyin**
Text: **Modern**
Then press **Enter** again to complete the note input
Press **P** for point entry
Enter coordinate value (**0.3,1.45**)
Text: **Technology**
Then press **Enter** again to complete the note input
Press **P** for point entry
Enter coordinate value (**0.5,0.1**) for the second note
Text: **CNC**
Then press **Enter** again to complete the note input
Press **P** for point entry
Enter coordinate value (**2.25,0.25**) for the third note
Press the **Esc key** to exit the note creation function
The three notes are added as shown in Figure 7.153.

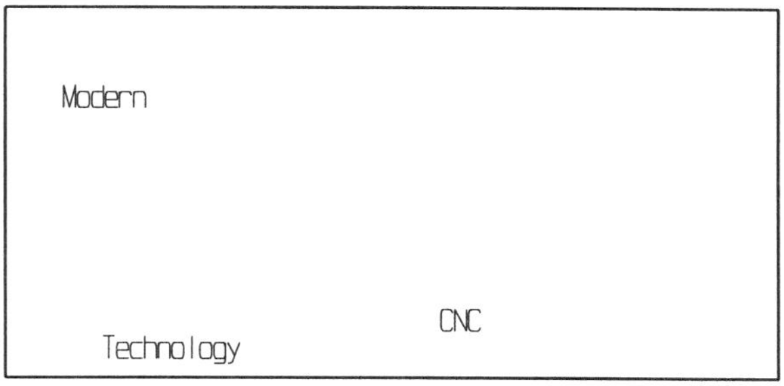

Figure 7.153

Step 4. Edit the first note "Modern".

Select **MAIN MENU → Create → Drafting → Globals edit**
Select Drafting Entities: pick the note **Modern**, then select **Done**
Change the Note Text Height and Font type as below.

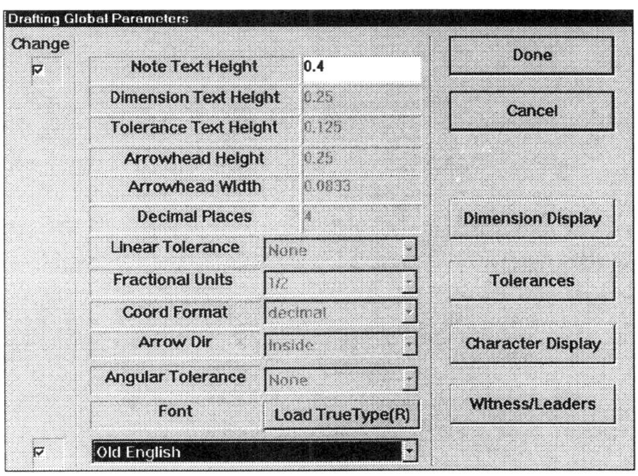

Select **Done**

The note “Modern” has been changed as shown in Figure 7.154.

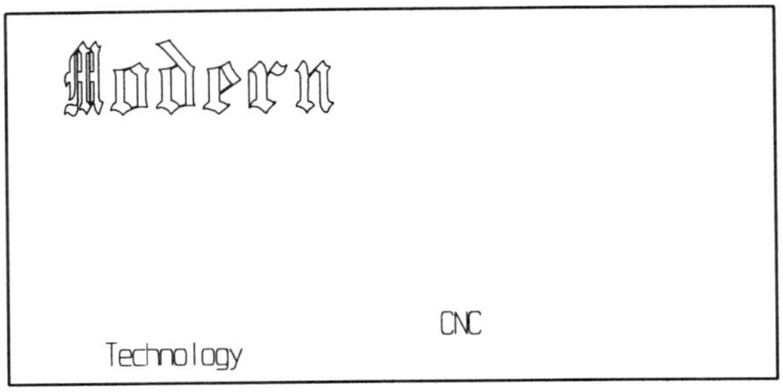

Figure 7.154

Step 5. Edit the second note “Technology”.

Select **Globals edit**
Pick the note **Technology**, then select **Done**
Change the Note height and font type as below.

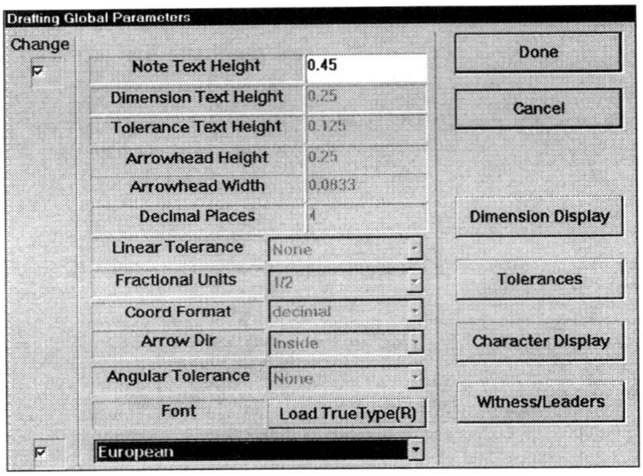

Select **Done**

The note “Technology” has been changed as shown in Figure 7.155.

Figure 7.155

Step 6. Rotate the note “Technology” by an angle of 26.565 degrees.

Select **MAIN MENU → Xform → Rotate**
Select entities to rotate: pick the note **Technology**
Select **Done → Point**
Enter the point to rotate about: **0.5,0.1**

Set the rotate parameters as below.

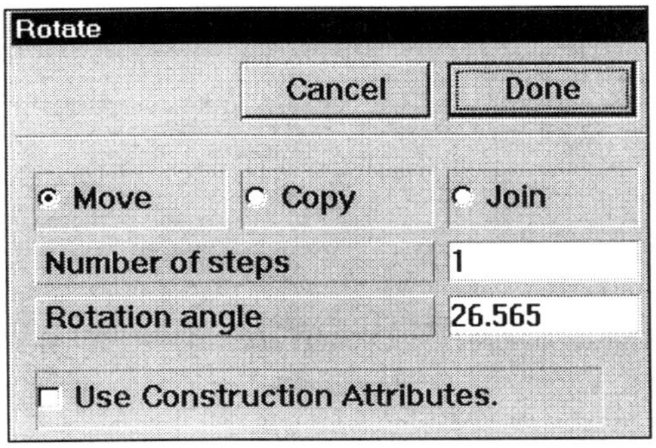

Select **Done**

The note "Technology" has been rotated to a new position as shown in Figure 7.156.

Figure 7.156

Step 7. Edit the third note "CNC".

Select **MAIN MENU → Create → Drafting → Globals edit**
Select drafting entities: pick the note **CNC**, then select **Done**
Change note height and font type as below.

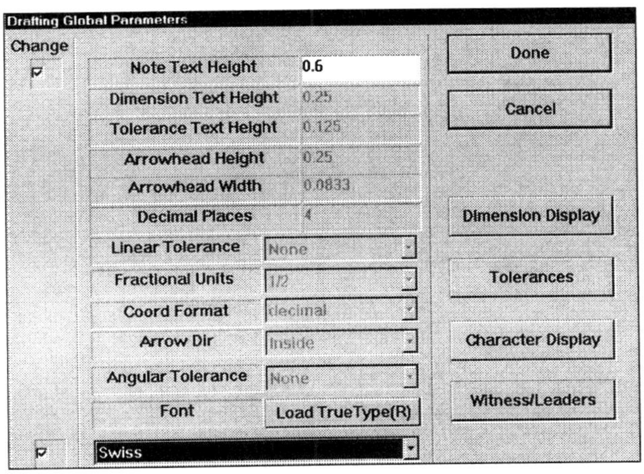

Select **Done**

The new drawing becomes Figure 7.157.

Figure 7.157

Step 8. Convert the three notes to geometries.

Select **MAIN MENU → Modify → Break → Note/let → All → Drafting → Note**
Three notes have been selected, then select **Done**
Note: These three notes have been converted to geometries. You may not see the difference graphically. The drawing is redrawn in Figure 7.158.

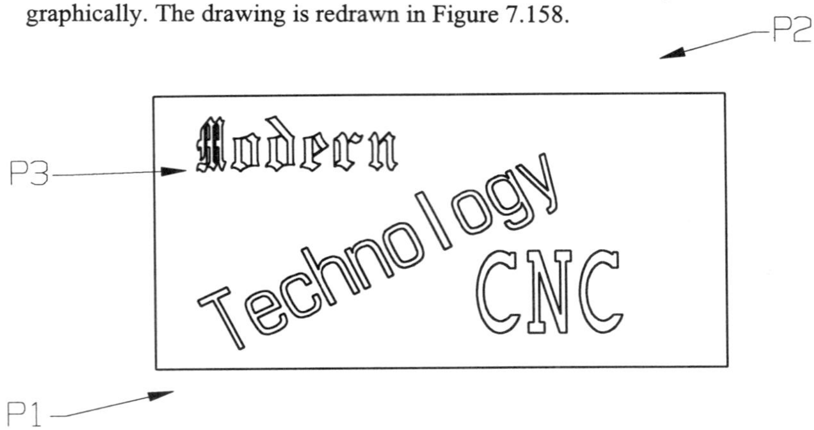

Figure 7.158

Step 9. Save the geometry file as letter3.

Select **MAIN MENU → File → Save**
File name: **letter3**

Step 10. Initiate the contour toolpath module.

Use the pick points in Figure 7.158.
Select **MAIN MENU → Toolpaths → Contour**
File name: **letter3**
Select **Window**
Pick **P1** and **P2** to include all lettering geometries
Select **Endpoint**, then pick **P3** to select the search point
Select **Done**

Step 11. Select a cutter and define the tool parameters.

Click the right mouse button, then select **Get tool from library**
Select **tool #230** (1/16 flat endmill)
Select **OK**

Set the tool parameters as below.

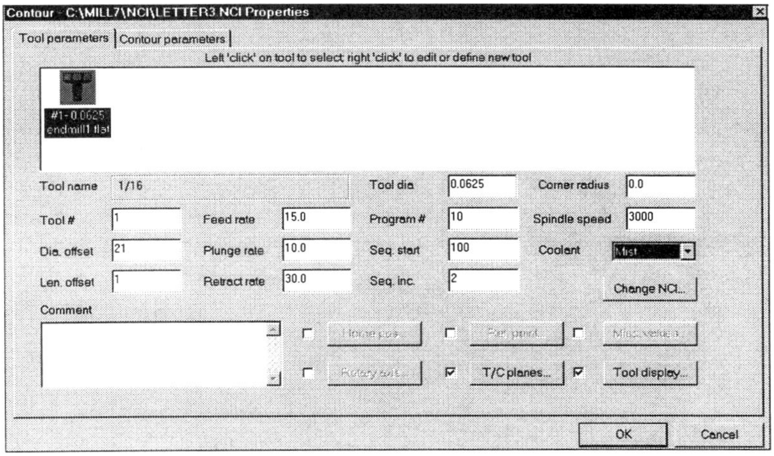

Step 12. Define the contour parameters.

Click the **Contour parameters** button

Set the contour parameters as below.

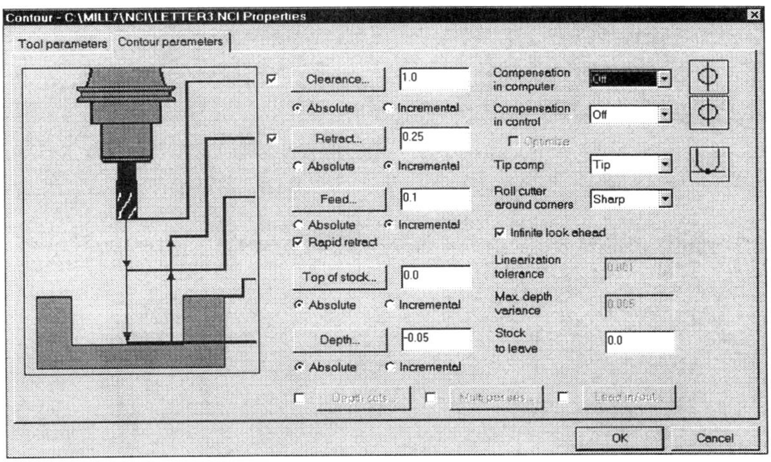

Select **OK** to generate the lettering toolpaths

Step 13. Change to isometric view.

Select **Gview → Isometric**

Select **Operations**

The geometries and toolpaths are shown in Figure 7.159.

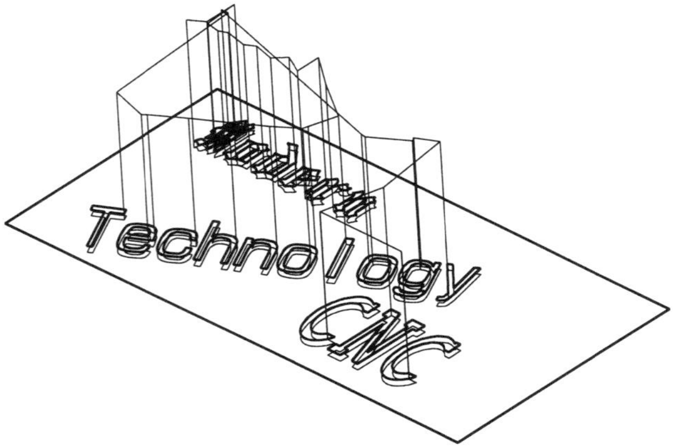

Figure 7.159

Step 14. Define the job setup parameters.

Select **MAIN MENU → Toolpaths → Job setup**

Set the job setup parameters as below.

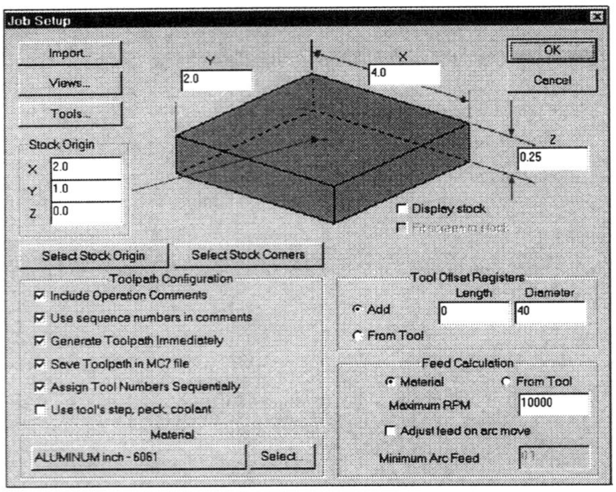

Select **OK**

Step 15. Verify the toolpaths.

Select **Operations → N-See 2000**

Select **Preview → OK** from "Select mode for current job" menu

Select **Do It** to verify the toolpaths as shown in Figure 7.160

Figure 7.160

Step 16. Exit N-See utility.

Select **BACKUP** to return to Operations Manager menu
Select **OK** to return to graphic mode
Select **MAIN MENU → File → Save**
File name: **letter3t**

Exercises

1. List the five 2-D toolpath modules in Mastercam and briefly describe what they are.
2. What are three groups of parameters used to generate toolpaths?
3. What are tool parameters?
4. List the commands to access the Tools Manager.
5. What is the operations manager?
6. List the four functions included in the operations manager.
7. List the advantages of using N-See verification utility.
8. What is the job setup?
9. What is a contour?
10. Use drawings to describe how the pick entity affects the chaining direction of the contour.

11. What are the two types of contours?

12. List the four functions Mastercam uses to define the work coordinates of the part program.

13. Explain when you should use the contour module.

14. Use a drawing to describe the following five Z-depth parameters:

Clearance	Retract	Feed
Top of stock	Depth	

15. Use a drawing to illustrate how the depth cuts parameters affect the toolpaths in Z-direction.

16. Use a drawing to illustrate how the multi passes parameters affect the toolpaths in XY-direction.

17. Use drawings to illustrate the effect of stock to leave in toolpaths.

18. Describe the purposes of cutter compensation.

19. Describe the difference between the cutter compensation in control and cutter compensation in computer.
20. Explain how the selection of cutter compensation in computer (left, right, or off) affects the toolpaths.
21. Write the proper NC command codes for the three options (right, left, and off) of cutter compensation in control with the assigned register number for diameter offset.
22. What are the purposes of using lead in and lead out moves?

23. Describe when to use the pocket module.

24. What are the seven cutting methods available in the pocket module?

25. What are the islands?

26. Use a drawing to explain how to determine the pocket loops and how the pocket loops affect toolpaths.
27. What are the two forms of rough entry?

28. Explain when you should use the drill module.

29. Use a drawing to define the following four Z-depth parameters used in the drill module:

Clearance	Retract
Top of stock	Depth

30. List the six standard cycle modes of the drill module.

31. Use a drawing to show how to create a point grid pattern.

32. Use a drawing to show how to create a point bolt circle pattern.

33. Explain how to use cirmill module.

34. Use a drawing to illustrate the toolpath pattern of cirmill operation.

35. When to use NC point module.

Problems

36. Use the contour module to generate toolpaths for machining the part shown in Figure 7.161. The raw material is a hollow plate with an outside diameter of 6.1" and an inside diameter of 2.5".

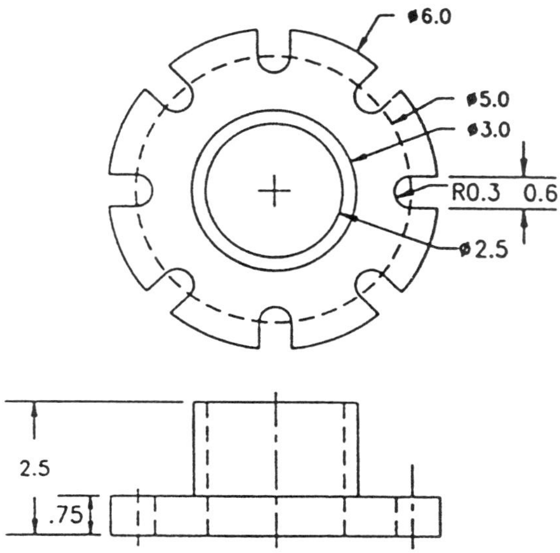

Figure 7.161

37. The raw material for the part shown in Figure 7.162 has been casted to its rough shape and size. Cut the internal profile using a 1/2" end mill to produce the profile. Only one finish pass is suggested because the material has been casted to its rough shape. The part geometry file is contour6 which is constructed in contructed in problem 5 of chapter 6.

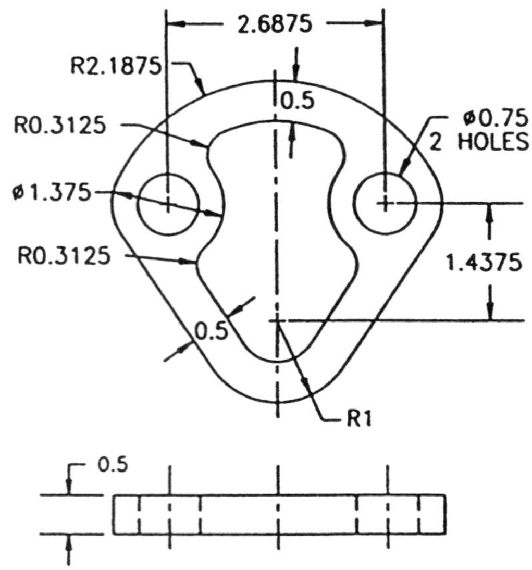

Figuer 7.162

38. The raw material for the part shown in Figure 7.163 has been casted to its rough shape. There are four features to be produced, two external profiles and two internal profiles. The contour module is used four times to generate toolpaths for cutting these four features. The part geometry file is contour7 which is created in problem 16 of chapter 6.

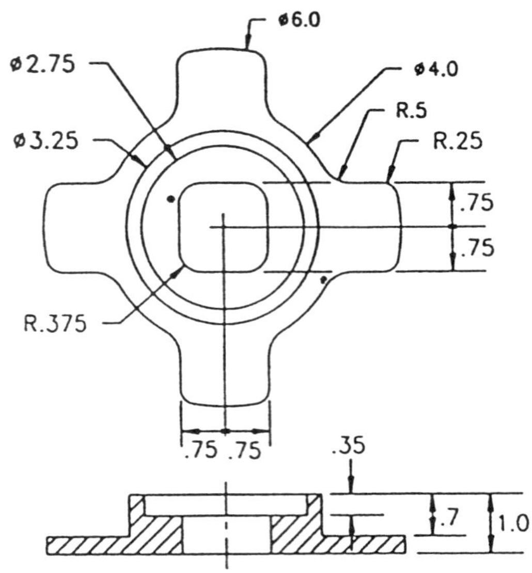

Figure 7.163

39. The part shown in Figure 7.164 has two depth changes in the profile. The depth of line profile AB linearly changes from Z-0.1 " at point A to Z-0.6" at point B. The depth remains at Z-0.6 from B to E. The depth linearly changes from E (Z-0.6) to F(Z-0.1). The part geometry file name is contour8.

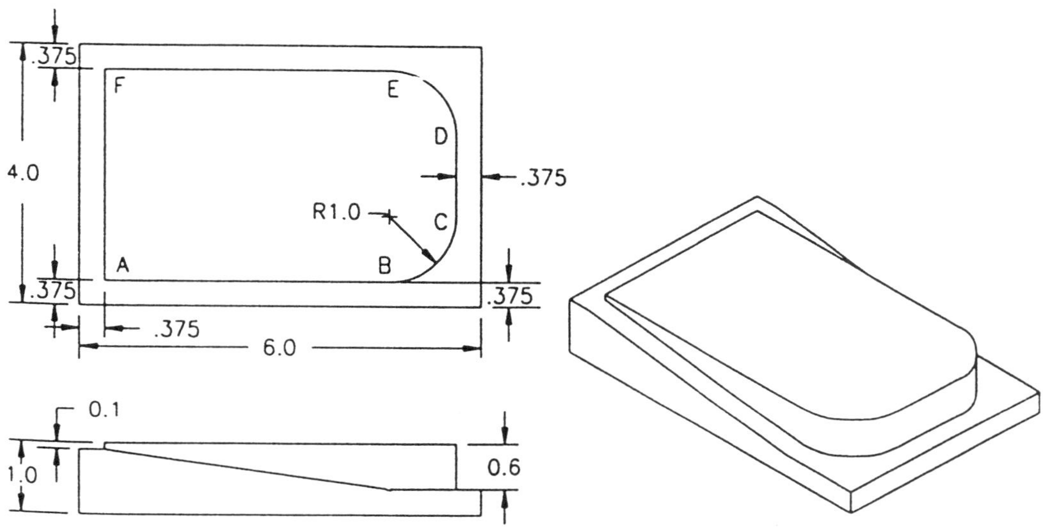

Figure 7.164

40. The profile of the part shown in Figure 7.165 has depth change between A and B. The profile has a depth of Z-0.5 " except between A and B which has Z-0.5". The part geometry file is contour9.

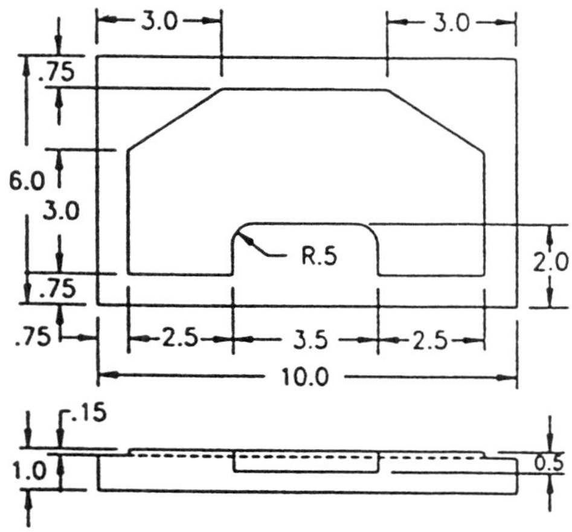

Figure 7.165

41. There are two features, top flat surface and internal pocket, to be profuced for the part shown in Figure 7.166. Pocket module can be used to produce both features. The part geometry file name is pocket3.

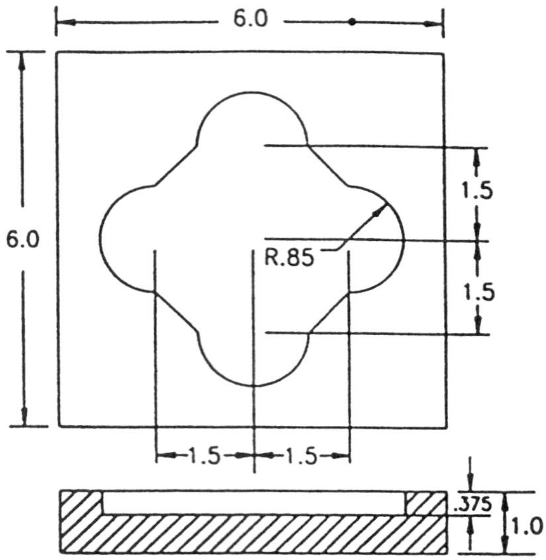

Figure 7.166

42. The part shown in Figure 7.167 consists of two internal pockets, one circular pocket in the center and one contour pocket with an island. The part geometry file name is pocket4.

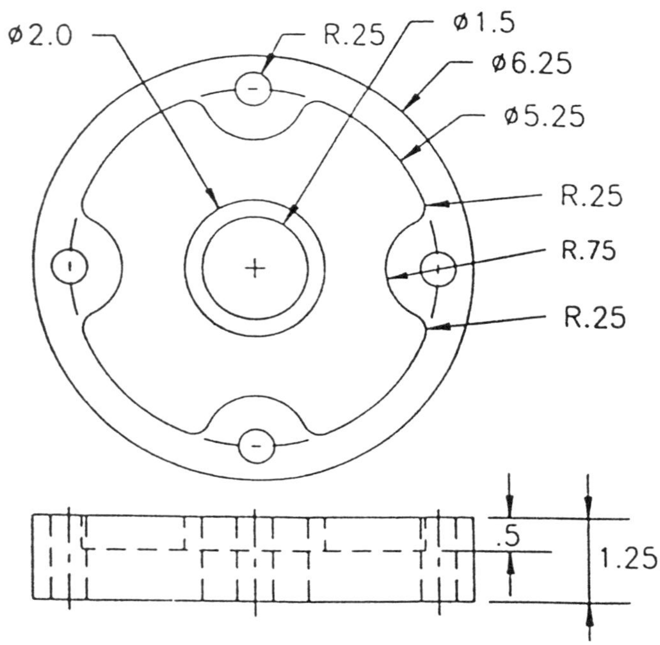

Figure 7.167

43. The part shown in Figure 7.168 consists of one internal pocket with an island. The island and the pocket profile are so close that six pocket regions are formed when a larger roughing cutter is used. The part geometry file is pocket5.

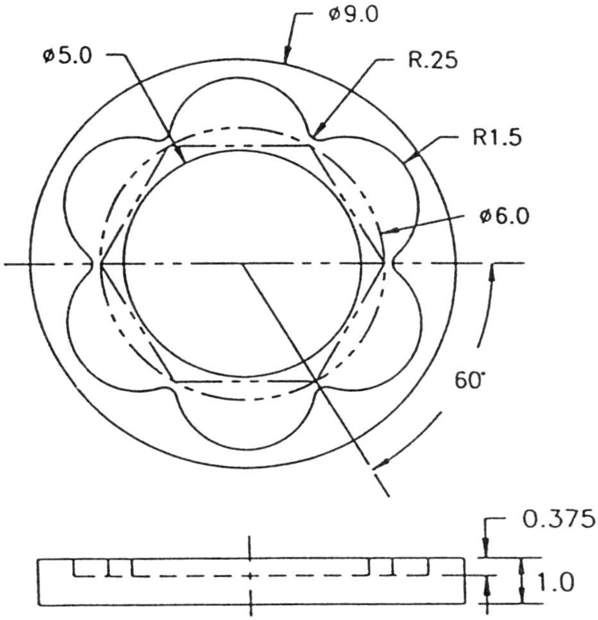

Figure 7.168

44. Four fine finish holes are required in the part shown in Figure 7.169. The holes are produed from the solid stock. Various cycle modes of the drill module should be used to produce these holes. The part geometry file is drill4.

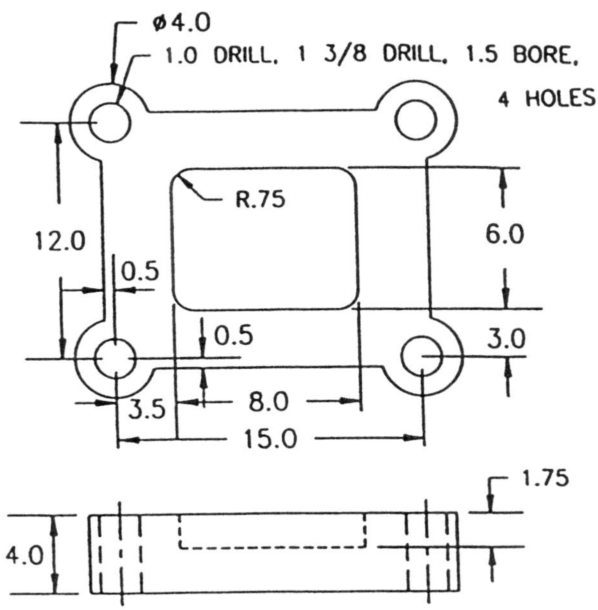

Figure 7.169

45. Three modules are used to generate toolpaths for machining the part shown in Figure 7.170. The part geometry file is comb1.

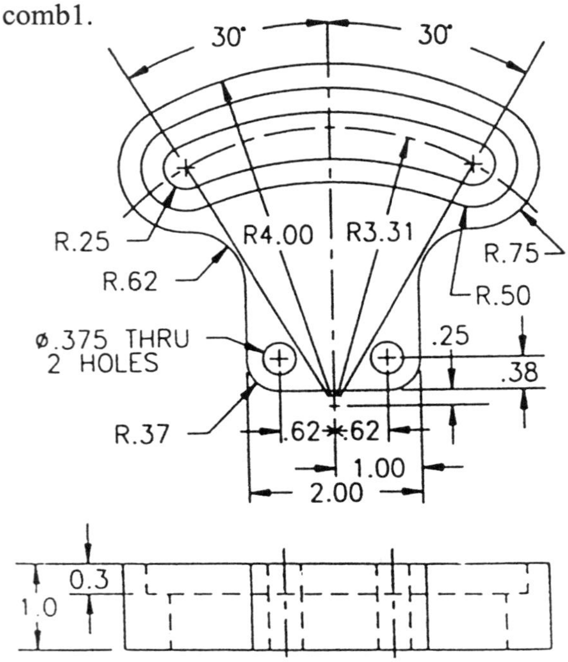

Figure 7.170

46. Five features are produced for the part shown in Figure 7.171. They include the top flat surface, two pockets, four 1/2"-holes, and six 1/4"-holes. Two toolpath modules, pocket and drill, are involved in the project. The part geometry file is comb2.

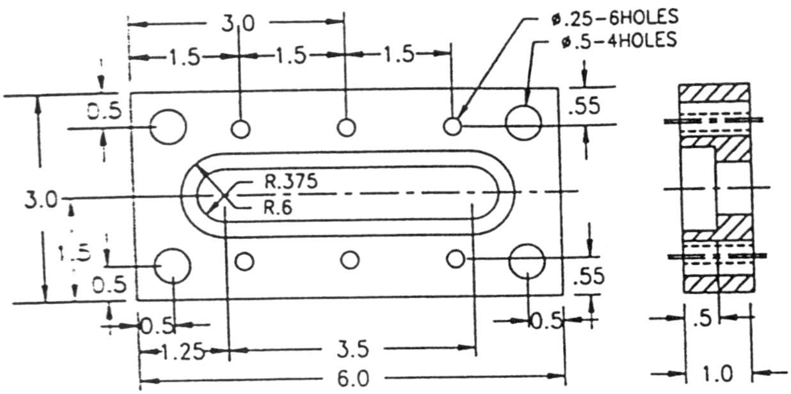

Figure 7.171

47. Six features are to be produced for the part shown in Figure 7.172. They include the external profile, two small local profiles, a slot pocket, and two holes of different size. The raw material has been casted to its rough shape. The part geometry file is comb3.

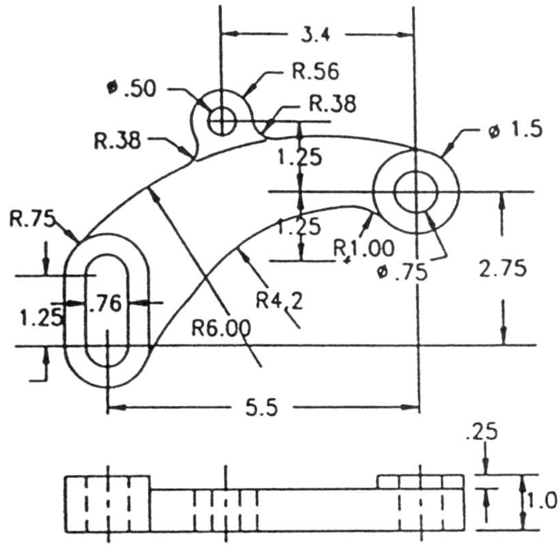

Figure 7.172

48. The part shown in Figure 7.173 consists of five features including the external profile, top flat surface, circular flange, hexagonal pocket, and two holes. The part geometry file name is comb4.

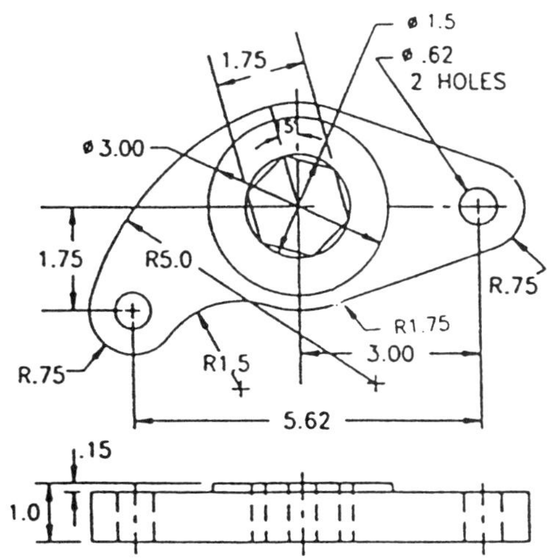

Figure 7.173

49. Five strings of letters are engraving in a circular plate as shown in Figure 7.174. The part geometry file name is letters4. Replacing the string EMU IT with your school name and department name.

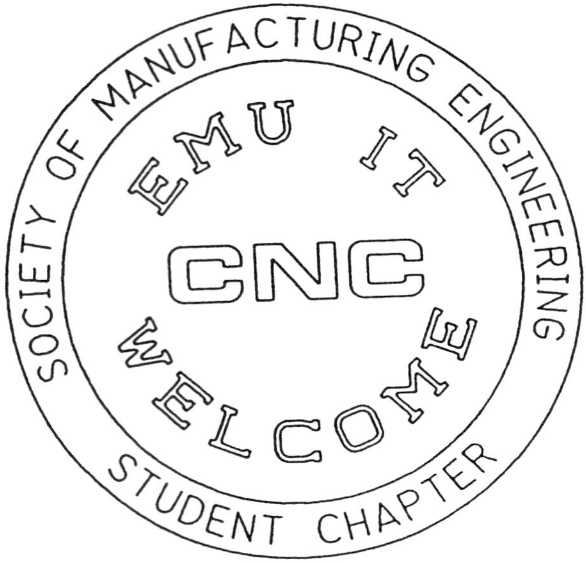

Figure 7.174

Chapter 8
Associativity and Its Applications

Objectives:

1. Principles of associativity.
2. Associativity features.
3. Modifying toolpaths using asociative features.
4. Modifying tool, holder, and machining parameters of an existing toolpath.
5. Using the chain manager to edit the chained geometries of an associative toolpath.

Overview

Often times the toolpaths must be modified or edited for some reasons after they have been generated. Mastercam provides a variety of editing functions to modify toolpaths to meet your needs. Mastercam version 7 provides a new feature "Associativity" which links geometry with toolpath, tool, material, and machining parameters to form a complete operation. We can regenerate the operation to reflect any change in parameters to other related pieces without having to recreate the whole operation. This is a very useful tool to edit an existing toolpath.

This chapter also covers file structure of toolpaths, two ways for deleting toolpaths, four toolpath editing functions, and linear array function. These editing functions can be used to significantly simplify the toolpath generation process especially for those parts having several identical features arranging in symmetrical or linear patterns.

8.1 Associativity

The term Associativity is new in Mastercam Version 7. Associativity links geometry with toolpath, tool, material, and parameter information to form a complete operation. When any part of operation changes, the other related pieces can be regenerated to reflect the change without having to recreate the whole operation. Typical information under the associativity in a project includes the following:

- Tools manager
- Tool parameters
- Chain manager
- Define tool
- Operation manager
- Job setup

All the above associativity information for a project are stored in an MC7 file. Job setup, tool manager, define tool, and tool parameter utilities are presented in chapter 7. They are briefly reviewed here in section 8.2. The Operations manager and the Chain manager are presented in detail in the following sections.

8.2 Job Setup, Tool Manager, Define Tool, and Tool Parameters

The Job Setup is the utility for **defining stock setup, NCI configuration**, and **tool offset parameters** for the current job. The job setup function has been presented in section 6 of chapter 7.

The Tool Manager provides a list of tools stored in the current MC7 file. It allows you to **select tools** from a tool library, **edit tools, delete tools**, and **open** the "Define Tool" utility to define new tools.

Define Tool is the utility used for defining a new tool including **selecting tool type, defining tool** and **holder geometry**, as well as **tooling and machining parameters**.

The Tool Parameters menu contains NC common parameters that are commonly used in various operations. Typical tool parameters include **tool number, diameter offset number, tool length offset number, feedrates, spindle speed, tool display**, etc.

8.3 Operations Manager

An operation in Mastercam is referred to as a complete machining process which includes chained geometry entities, tool, machining parameters, and toolpaths. The toolpath with its associated information generated by using a toolpath module is treated as an operation. The Operations Manager is used for managing tools to sort, edit, regenerate, and post any selected operations. It lists all operations in the current job. Follow these commands to open the "Operations Manager" menu:

Select MAIN MENU → Toolpaths → Operations

If **no operation** exists in the current job, an empty Operations Manager menu should appear as below.

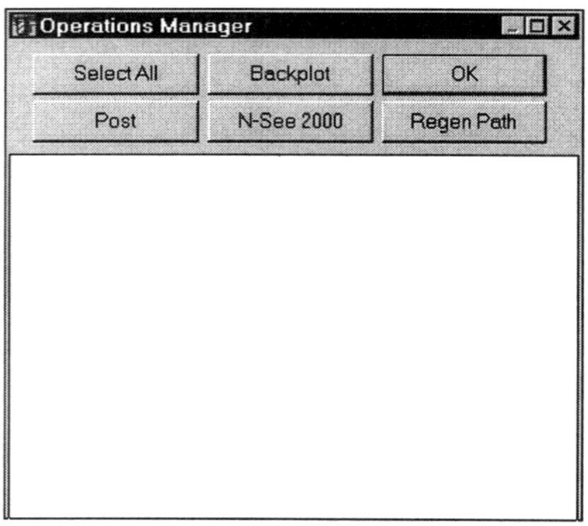

The operations will be listed in the Operations Manager menu as shown below when the current job contains any operations.

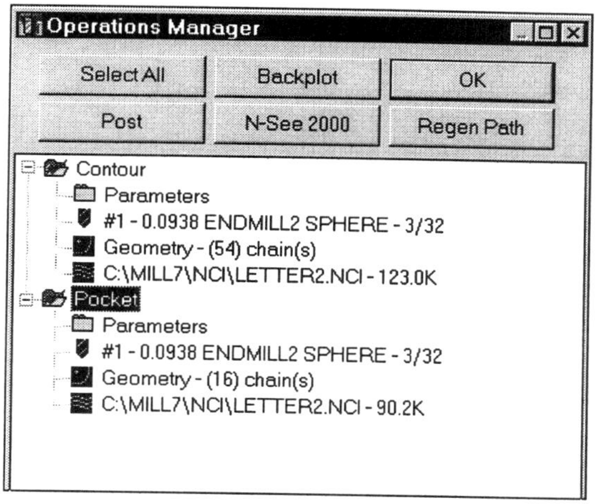

The six function buttons of the Operations Manager menu are briefly described below:

Select All:	selects all operations listed in the Operations Manager.
Post:	(1) creates an ASCII NCI file for the selected Operations; and (2) generates an NC part program from the NCI file.
Backplot:	backplots to verify the toolpaths of all selected operations.
N-See 2000:	verifies the toolpaths of the selected operations in the solid graphic mode.
Regen Path:	recreates the selected operations to reflect the changes made to the operations.
OK:	select this button to exit Operations Manager menu.

Moving Operations

The Operations Manager allows you to readily move and copy operations. Moving an operation to change the operation sequence in the current job. There are two ways to move an operation: **pick-and-place method** and **option command method.**

The procedure for using pick-and-place method for moving an operation is:

1. Click on the yellow file folder of the operation to move.

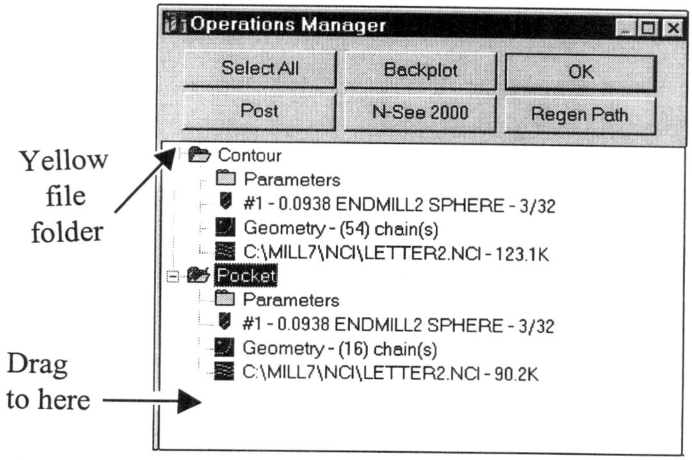

Procedure continued:

2. Drag the folder to the new position in the operation list.

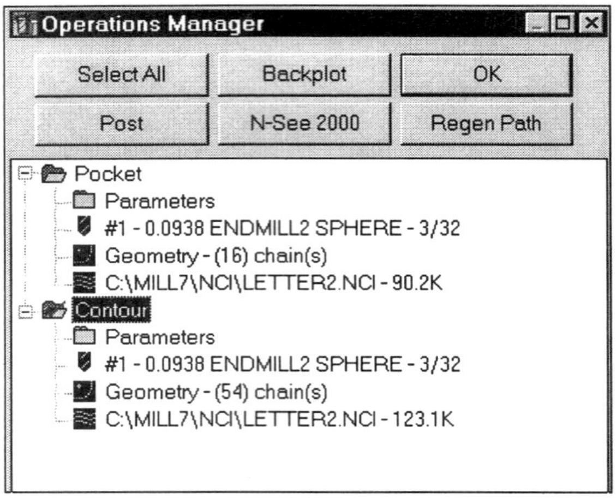

Option command method The option command menu provides the following two functions to move a selected operation to a specified location:

Move before:	moves the selected operation before the highlighted operation.
Move after:	moves the selected operation after the highlighted operation.

The procedure of using option command method for moving an operation is:

1. Right-click on the yellow file folder of the operation to move.

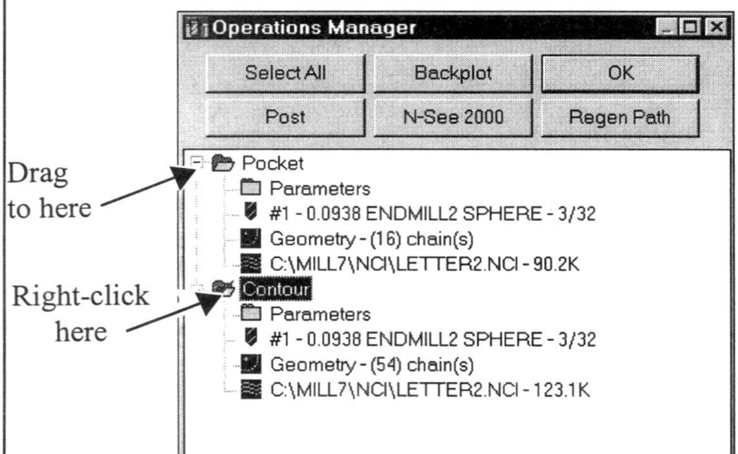

Procedure continued:

2. Drag the folder over another operation in the list, an option command menu will appear when you release the right mouse button as below.

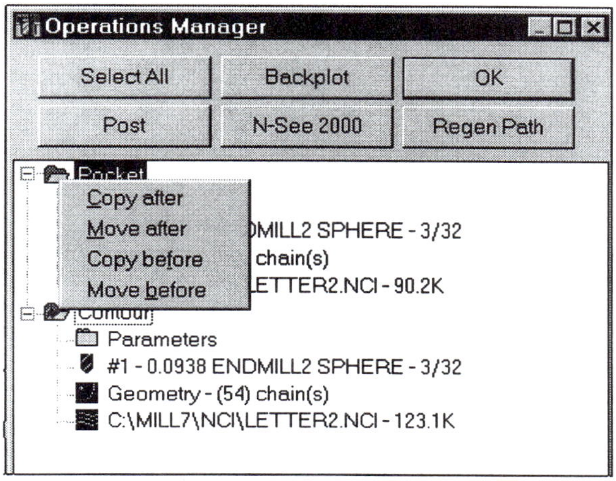

3. Select "Move before" from the list to place the selected operation as below.

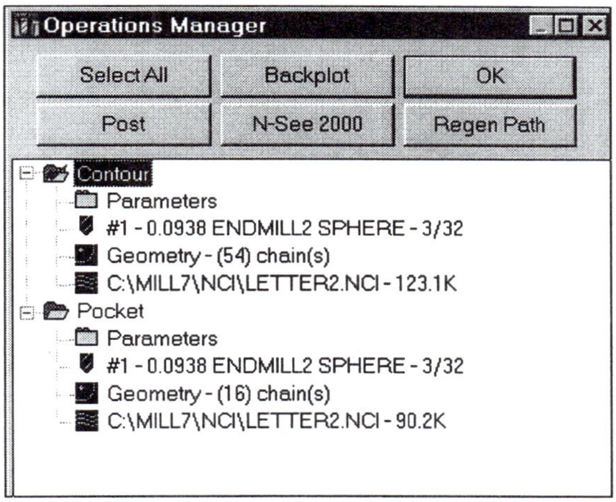

Copying Operations

The option command menu provides the following two functions to copy a selected operation to a specified location:

Copy after:	places a copy of the selected operation after the highlighted operation.
Copy before:	places a copy of the selected operation before the highlighted operation.

The procedure of copy an operation is:

1. Right-click on the yellow file folder of the operation to copy.

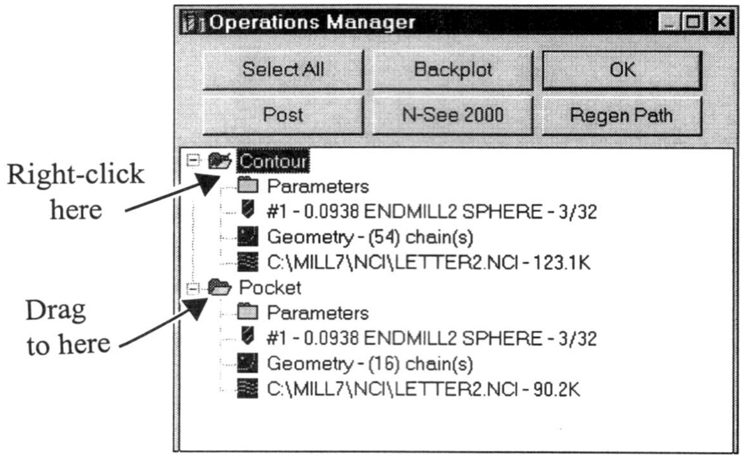

2. Drag the folder over another operation in the list, an option command menu will appear when you release the right mouse button as below.

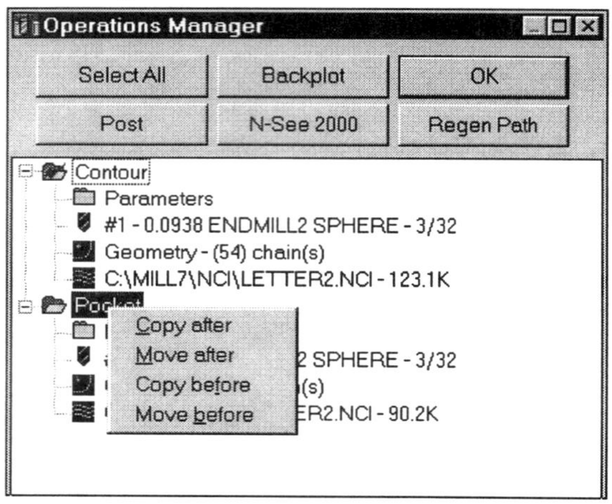

3. Select "Copy after" from the list to copy the selected operation as below.

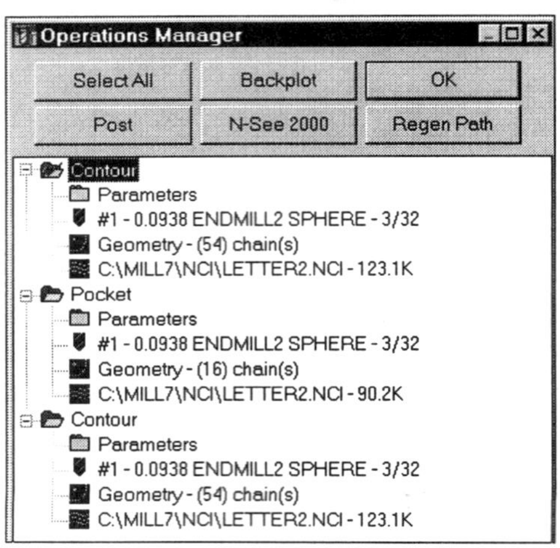

Copying Parameters

It is possible to copy parameters in one operation to another operation of the same type. Click on the gray Parameters icon for the operation to copy it and drag it on top of the Parameters icon to be replaced. The system will prompt “Copying parameters to another operation. Are you sure?”. Select “Yes” to allow the system to automatically update the toolpath parameters of the second operation to match those in the first operation.

You can only copy parameters between the same operation types (ex: contour parameters to contour parameters, pocket parameters to pocket parameters). A warning message “Copy not successfully. Operations must be of a similar type.” will be issued when you attempt to copy parameters to different type of operation.

Copying Tools

The way to copy a tool from one operation to another operation is similar to those for copying parameters. Click on the Tool Definition icon for the operation to copy and drag it on top of the Tool Definition icon for the operation to replace. The system will prompt “Copying tool parameters to another operation. Are you sure?”. Select “Yes” to update the tool parameters of the second operation to match those in the first operation.

Copying Geometry

To copy chains or drill points from one operation to another operation of a similar type, click on the Geometry icon for one operation and drag it on top of the Geometry icon for another operation. The system will prompt “Copying toolpath geometry to another operation. Are you sure?”. Select “Yes” to complete the geometry copy. Note that you can only copy chains between contour operations, pocket operations, or drill operations.

Right Click Menu

Mastercam provides a list of very useful functions for you to use to edit operations. To open this group of functions, click the right mouse button on a selected operation to open the menu as below.

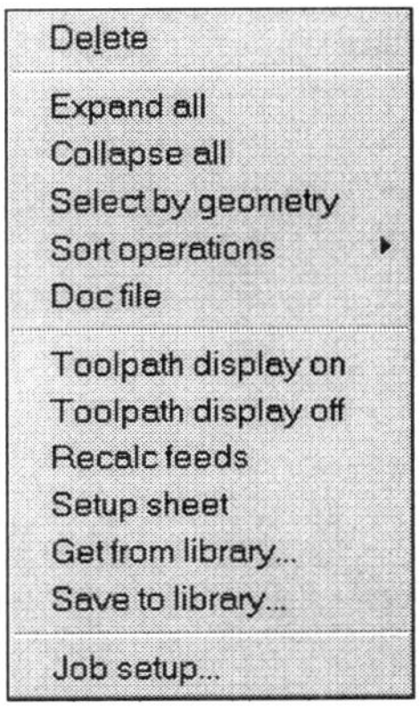

The thirteen functions in the right click menu are briefly summarized as below:

Delete: deletes the selected operation(s).
Expand all: shows all elements of the operations in the Operations Manager.
Collapse all: hides all elements of operations exceptthe file folders in Operations Manager.
Select by geometry: selects all operations associated with the chosen geometry.
Sort operations: rearranges the sequence of operations according to specified criteria.
Doc file: outputs the operations list to a document (DOC) file.
Toolpath display on: turns display of the toolpath on.
Toolpath display off: turns display of the toolpath off.
Recalc feeds: recalculates the feed rate, plunge rate, retract rate, and spindle speed after changes have been made to the toolpath.
Setup sheet: exports the setup sheet for the operation to a document (DOC) file.
Get from library: opens the Operation Import menu for selecting an operation (OP7) library.
Save to library: opens the Operation Export menu to save information to an operation library.
Job setup: display the job setup menu to allow defining job setup parameters.

Deleting operations The Delete function allows deleting one or more operations from the current job. To delete a single operation, click the yellow file folder of the Operation to be deleted, then click the right mouse button to open the right-click menu. Select "Delete" to delete the selected operation from the current job.

Click this folder

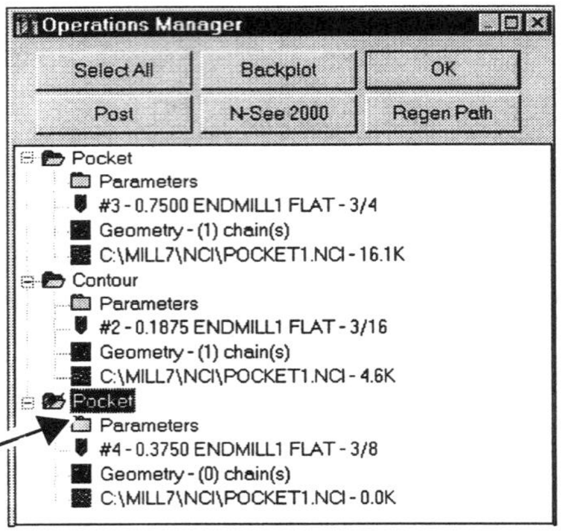

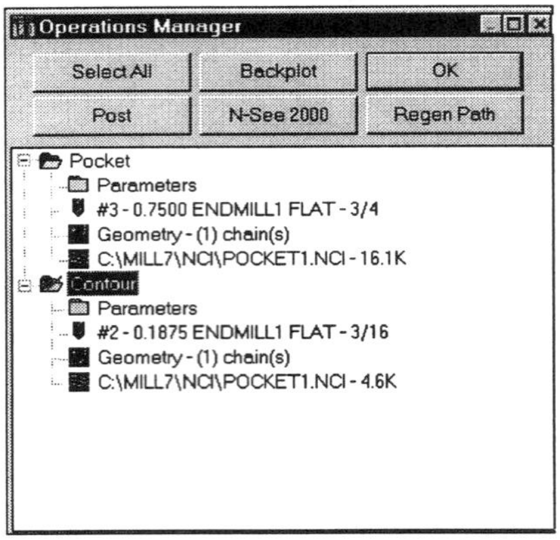

To delete all operations in the current job, select the "Select All" button then click the right mouse button to open the right-click menu. Select "Delete" to delete all operations from the current job.

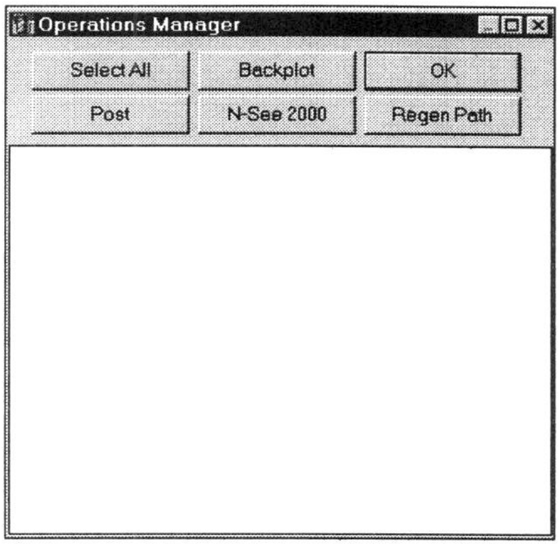

Tree directory control Mastercam uses two commands in the right-click menu to control how the elements of operations are to be shown in the operations list area. "Expand all" shows all elements of the operations and "Collapse all" condenses the tree directory to show only the file folder for operations.

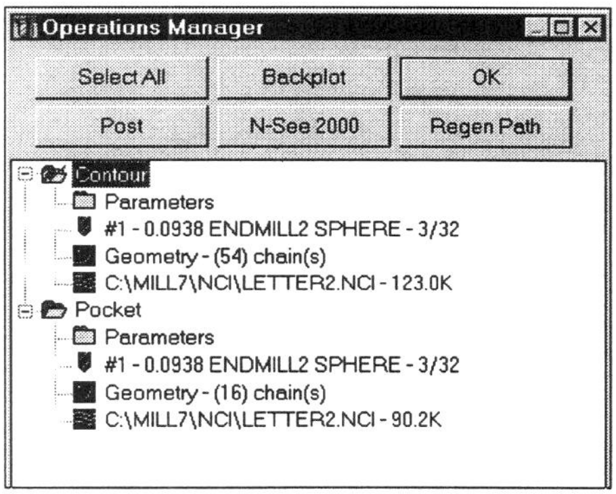

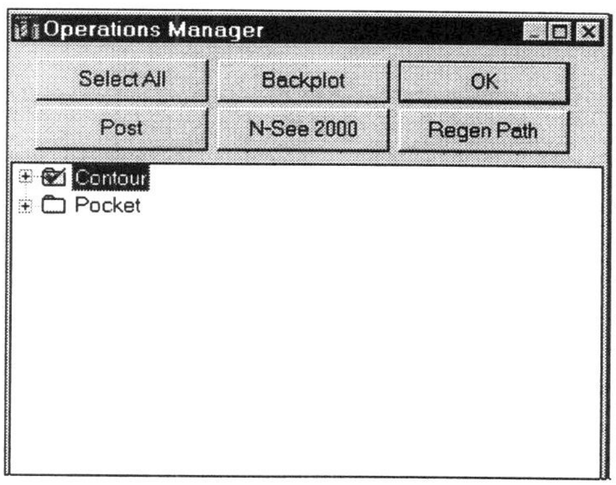

Sort operations This function resequences the operations according to specified criteria. Click this function to open its option menu as shown below.

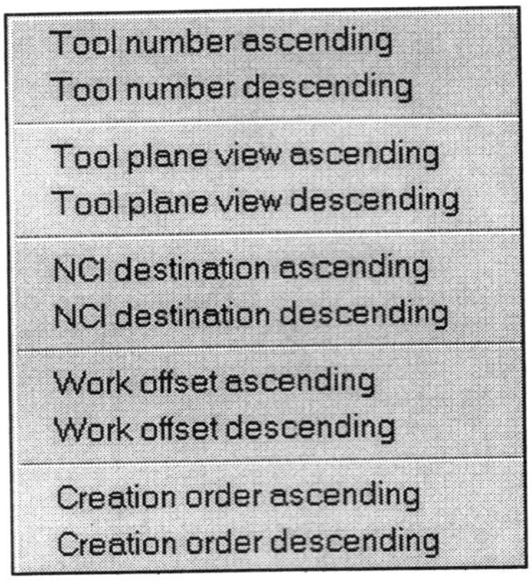

Tool number ascending:	rearranges the operations in the order of tool numbers starting from smallest number to larger number.
Tool number descending:	rearranges the operations in the order of tool numbers starting from largest number to smaller number.
Tool plane view ascending:	rearranges the operations in the order of tool plane view number starting from smallest number to larger number.
Tool plane view descending:	rearranges the operations in the order of tool plane view number starting from largest number to smaller number.
NCI destination ascending:	rearranges the operations in the order of NCI destination starting from smallest number to larger number.
NCI destination descending:	rearranges the operations in the order of NCI destination starting from the largest number to smaller number.
Work offset ascending:	rearranges the operations in the order of work offset number starting from the smallest number to larger number.
Work offset descending:	rearranges the operations in the order of work offset number starting from largest number to smaller number.
Creation order ascending:	rearranges the operations in the order of creating sequence starting from the first to last.
Creation order descending:	rearranges the operations in the order of creating sequence starting from the last to first.

DOC file This function outputs the operations list of the current job to a document (DOC) file. Click "DOC file" function to open the "Specify File Name to Write" menu as below.

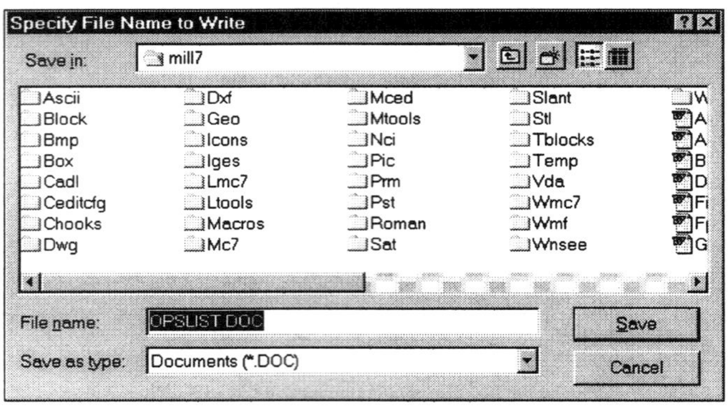

Select "Save" to save the DOC file to the specified file name and directory. Use the following commands to open the DOC file:

1. Select MAIN MENU → File → Edit → DOC
2. File name to read: opslist

The DOC file for the operation list appears as below.

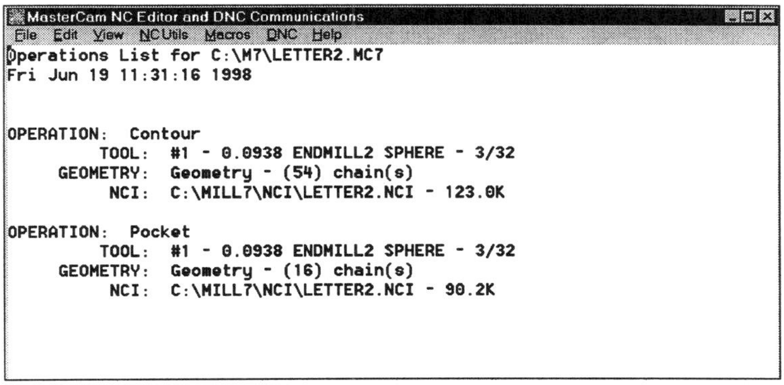


```
Operations List for C:\M7\LETTER2.MC7
Fri Jun 19 11:31:16 1998

OPERATION:  Contour
        TOOL:   #1 - 0.0938 ENDMILL2 SPHERE - 3/32
    GEOMETRY:   Geometry - (54) chain(s)
         NCI:   C:\MILL7\NCI\LETTER2.NCI - 123.0K

OPERATION:  Pocket
        TOOL:   #1 - 0.0938 ENDMILL2 SPHERE - 3/32
    GEOMETRY:   Geometry - (16) chain(s)
         NCI:   C:\MILL7\NCI\LETTER2.NCI - 90.2K
```

Toolpath display on/off Two parameters are used to control whether the toolpath is to be displayed on the screen. "Toolpath display on" shows the toolpath on the screen as shown in Figure 8.1a. "Toolpath display off" hides the toolpath from the screen (Figure 8.1b).

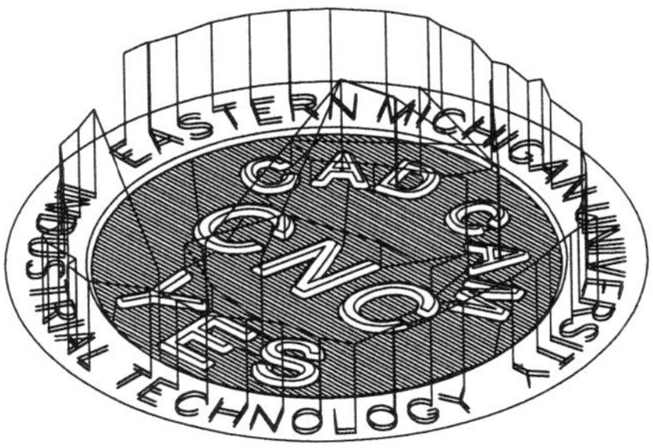

Figure 8.1a Show toolpath

Figure 8.1b Hide toolpath

Setup sheet This function exports the setup sheet for the operation to a document (DOC) file. Follow these instructions to generate the setup sheet of the current job:

1. Select "Setup sheet" from the right-click menu.
2. Select Yes to "File already exists, overwrite?" if necessary.
3. Select NO to "Run the post processor?"
4. Specify file name to read: letter2.nci
5. Specify file name to write: letter2.doc

The setup file for the current project will appear on the file list as below.

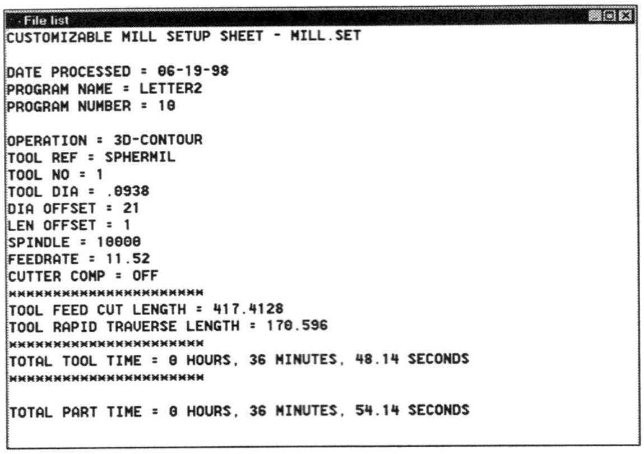

File list

CUSTOMIZABLE MILL SETUP SHEET - MILL.SET

DATE PROCESSED = 06-19-98
PROGRAM NAME = LETTER2
PROGRAM NUMBER = 10

OPERATION = 3D-CONTOUR
TOOL REF = SPHERMIL
TOOL NO = 1
TOOL DIA = .0938
DIA OFFSET = 21
LEN OFFSET = 1
SPINDLE = 10000
FEEDRATE = 11.52
CUTTER COMP = OFF
****
TOOL FEED CUT LENGTH = 417.4128
TOOL RAPID TRAVERSE LENGTH = 170.596
****
TOTAL TOOL TIME = 0 HOURS, 36 MINUTES, 48.14 SECONDS
****

TOTAL PART TIME = 0 HOURS, 36 MINUTES, 54.14 SECONDS

Job setup This function opens the job setup utility as below for you to define job setup parameters.

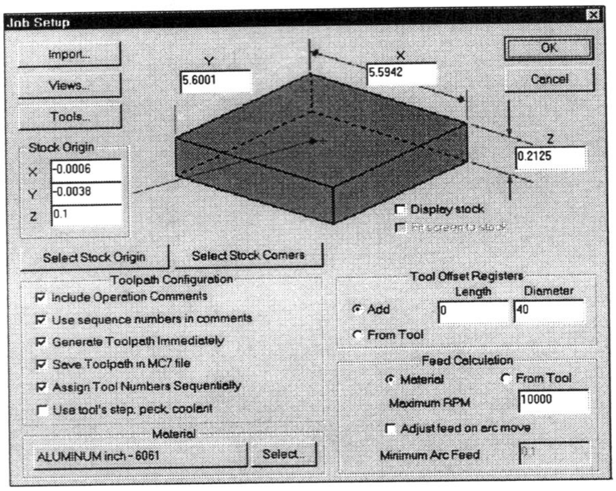

Two projects are presented in this section to show how to use various associative features to modify the existing toolpaths.

Project 1. Modifying toolpaths using associativity features

This project modifies the cutter size and machining parameters of an existing toolpath file (pocket1). Figure 8.2 shows the two sets of toolpaths before and after modification. The ½" end mill for rough pocketing is replaced by a ¾" end mill. The depth and stepover distance of the roughing pocketing are also changed.

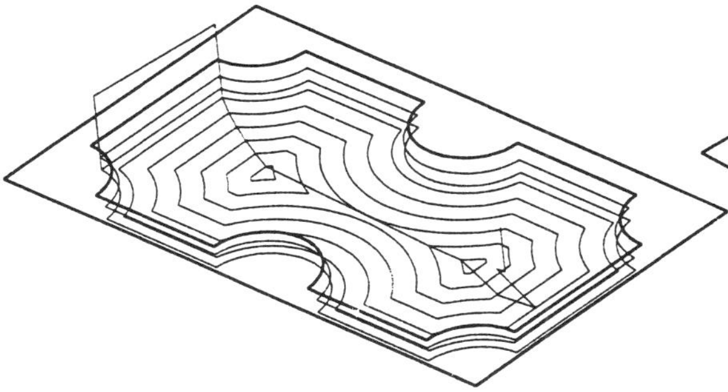

Figure 8.2a

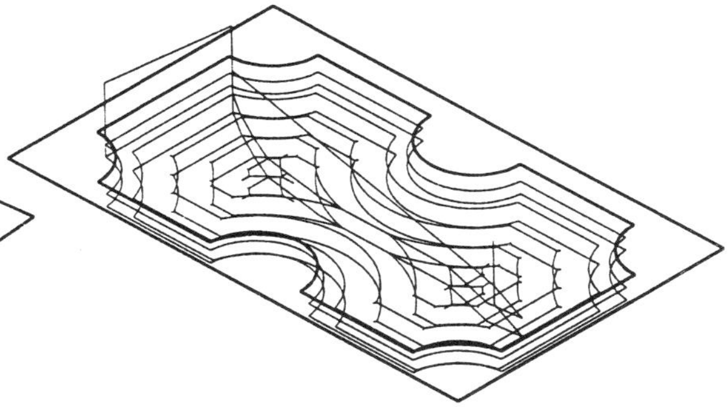

Figure 8.2b

Step 1. Open a part file with toolpath pocket1.

Select **File → Get**

File name: **pocket1**

The part geometry should appear as in Figure 8.3.

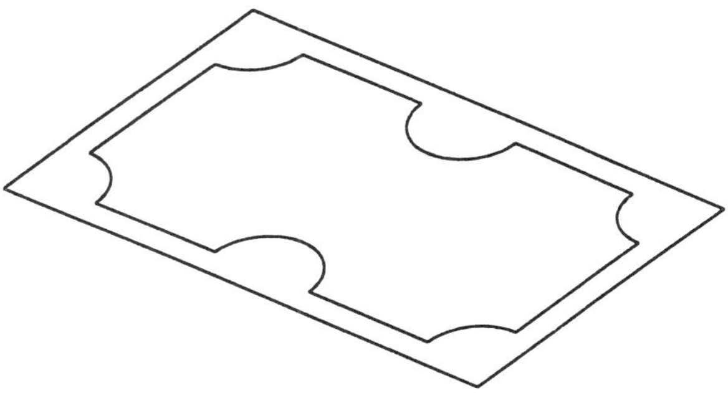

Figure 8.3

Step 2. Open the toolpaths.

Select **MAIN MENU → Toolpaths**

The existing toolpaths appear as in Figure 8.4.

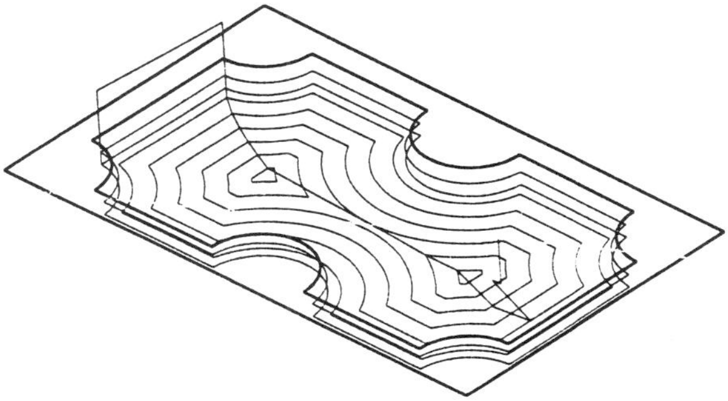

Figure 8.4

Step 3. Open the Operations Manager menu.

Select **Operations**

The Operations Manager menu with two sets of toolpaths appears as here.

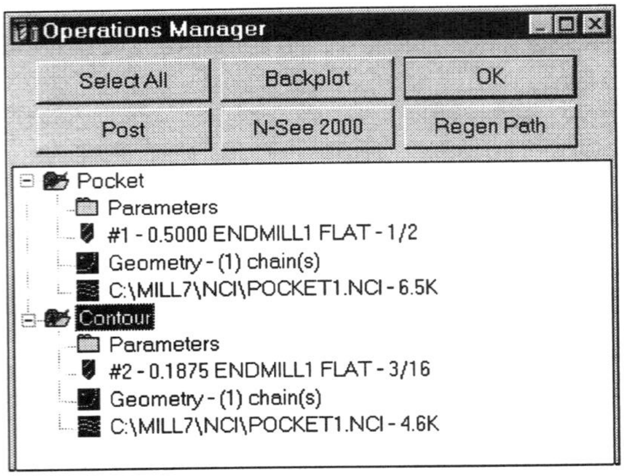

Step 4. Change the machining parameters for the pocket operation.

Click on the "**Parameters**" icon in the Pocket operation

The existing tool parameters are shown below.

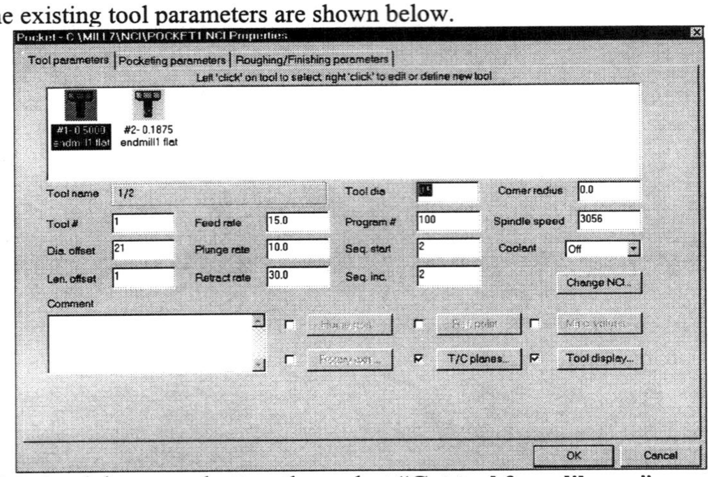

Click the right mouse button, then select "**Get tool from library**"

Select **tool #241** (3/4 flat endmill)

Select **OK**

Modify the tool parameters as below.

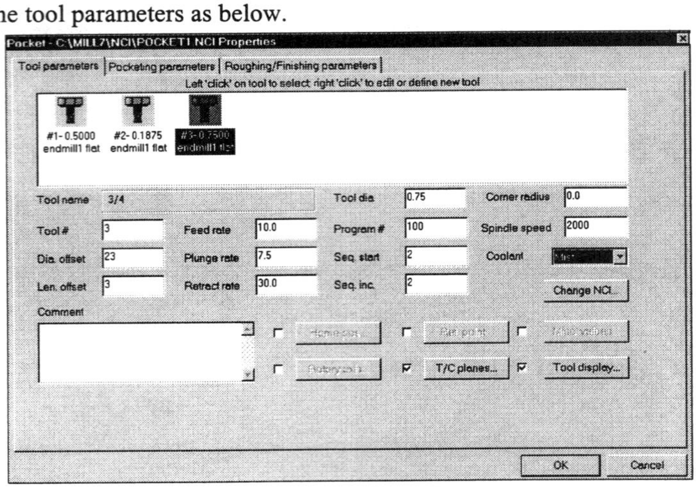

Step 5. Modify the pocketing parameters.

Click on the "Pocketing parameters" button
Set the pocketing parameters as below.

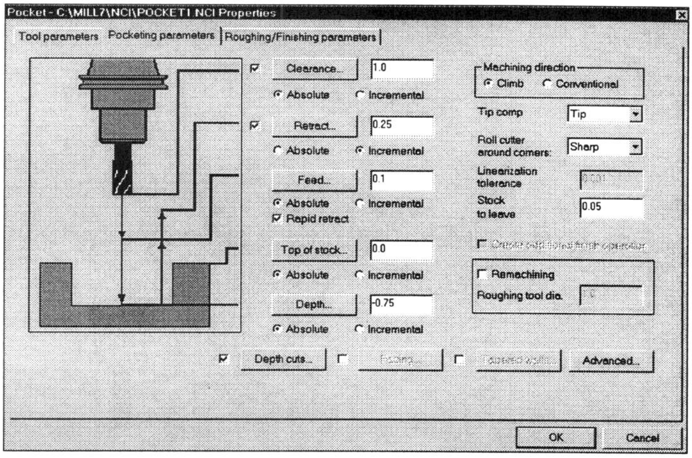

Step 6. Modify the depth cuts parameters.

Click on the "**Depth cuts**" button
Set the depth cuts parameters asshown here.

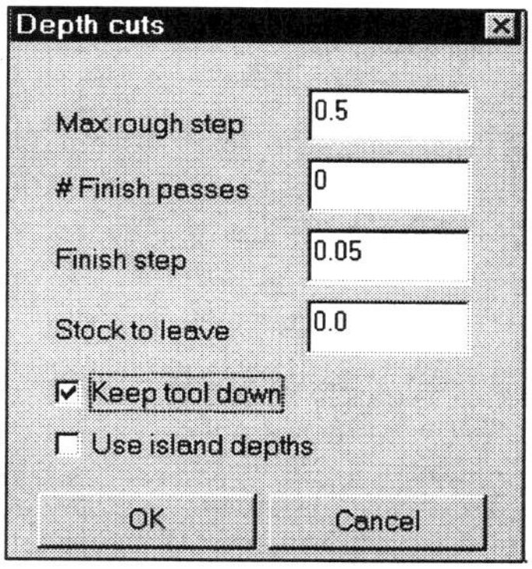

Select **OK**

Step 7. Modify roughing and finishing parameters.

Click on the "**Roughing/Finishing parameters**" button
Set the roughing and finishing parameters as below.

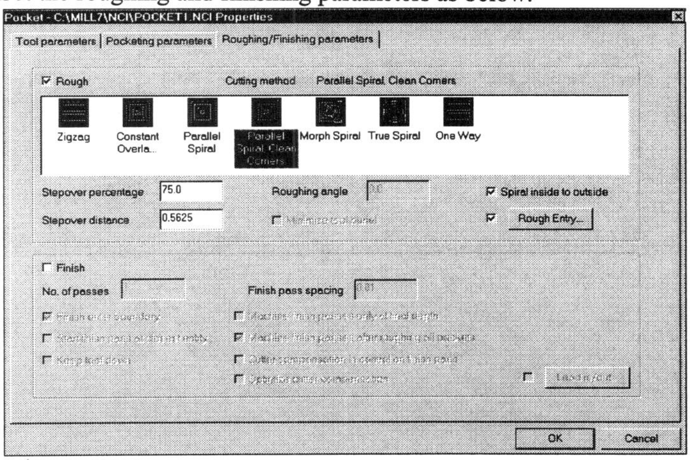

2 Step 8. Regenerate the toolpaths.

Select **Regen Path** to regenerate the pocketing toolpaths
Select **OK** to "1 associative operations regenerated successfully."
Select **OK** to exit the Operations Manager menu
The new set of toolpaths should resemble Figure 8.5.

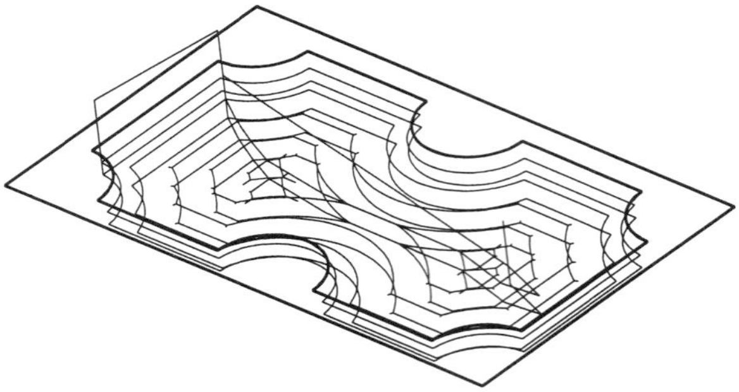

Figure 8.4

Step 9. Save the new toolpaths as pocket1n.

Select **MAIN MENU →** **File →** **Save**
File name: **pocket1n**

Project 2. Modifying tool, holder, and machining parameters of an existing toolpath

The existing toolpath file used in this project consists of three pocketing toolpaths. A ½" end mill is originally used for cutting the last two pockets. This tool is replaced by a 3/8" end mill. In addition, holder parameters and some machining parameters associated with this tool are modified. Figure 8.5 shows the toolpaths before and after modification.

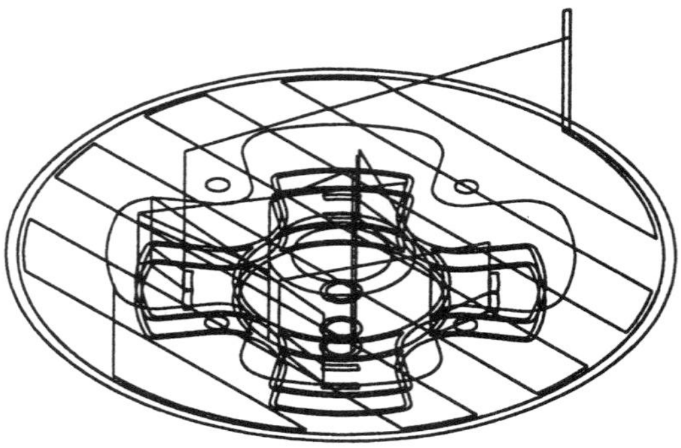

Figure 8.6a

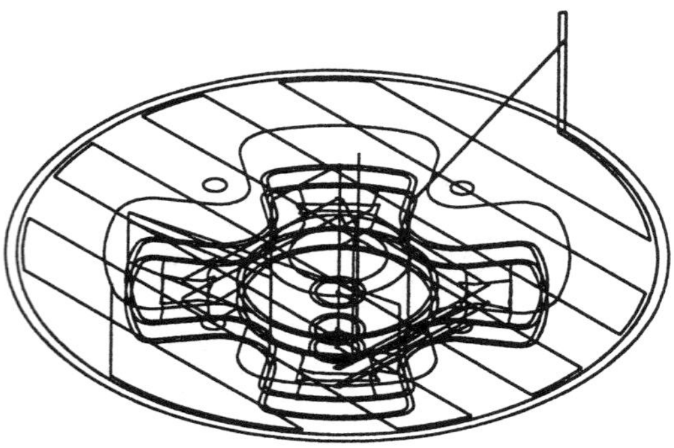

Figure 8.6b

Step 1. Open a file pocket2.

Select **MAIN MENU → File**

File name: **pocket2**

The part geometry of pocket2 should appear as Figure 8.7.

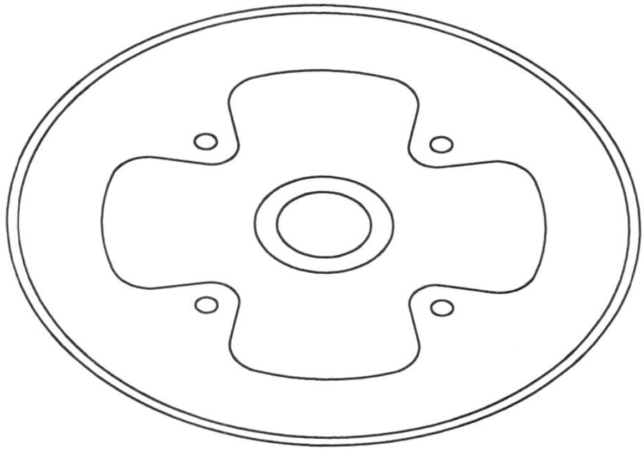

Figure 8.7

Step 2. Open the existing toolpath in the file.

Select **MAIN MENU → Toolpaths**

The existing toolpaths appear as in Figure 8.7.

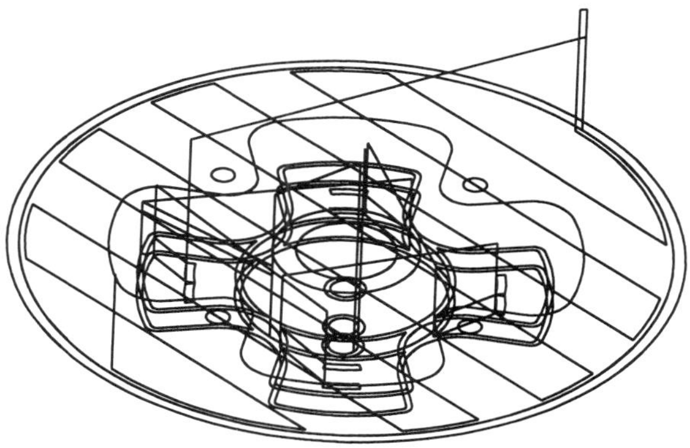

Figure 8.8

Step 3. Redefine a tool and its holder.

Select **Operations**

The toolpaths for three operations are listed in the Operations Manager menu as shown here.

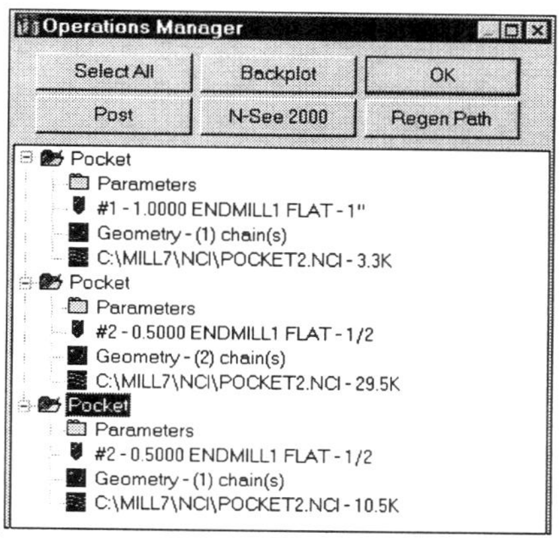

Click the tool icon for the third pocket operation

The "Define Tool" menu should appear as below.

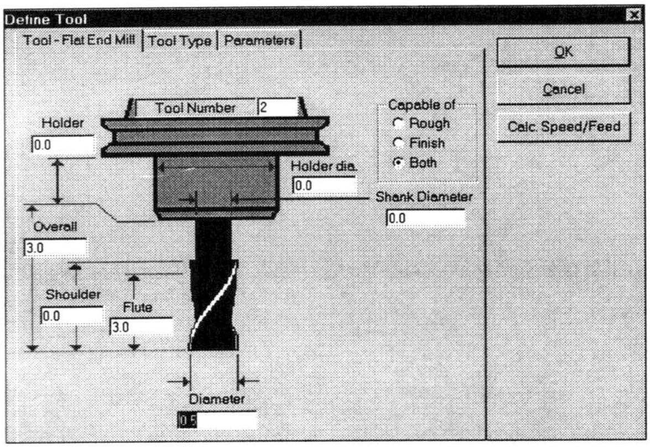

Set the tool and holder dimensions as below.

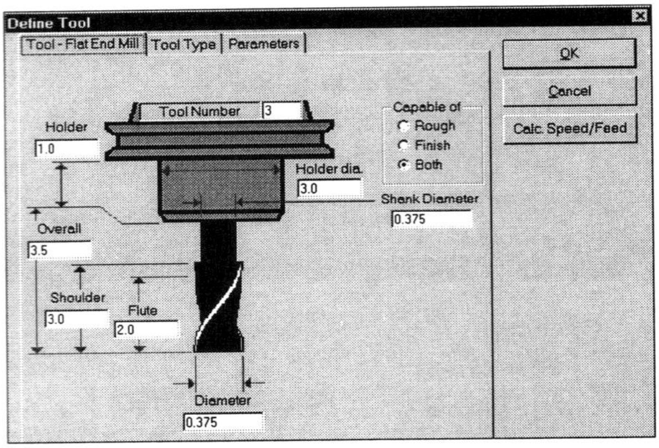

Step 4. Define the parameters.

Select the "**Parameters**" button
Set the parameters as below.

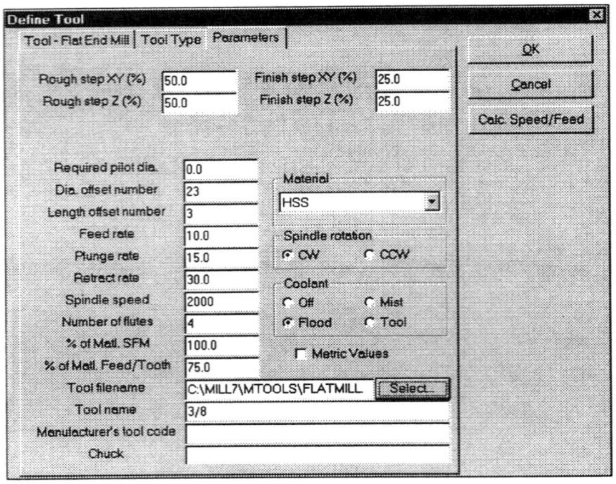

Select **OK**
Select **Yes** to "changing this tool will update your operations. Continue?"

The tool for second and third pocket operations has been changed to the new one as shown here.

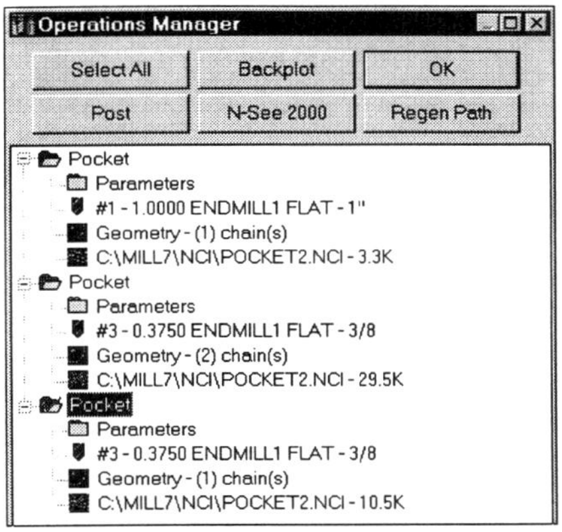

Step 5. Modify the parameters for the second pocket operation.

Click the "**Parameters**" icon in the second pocket operation
The tool parameters menu should appear on the screen
Select the "**Roughing/Finishing parameters**" button
Set the roughing and finishing parameters as below.

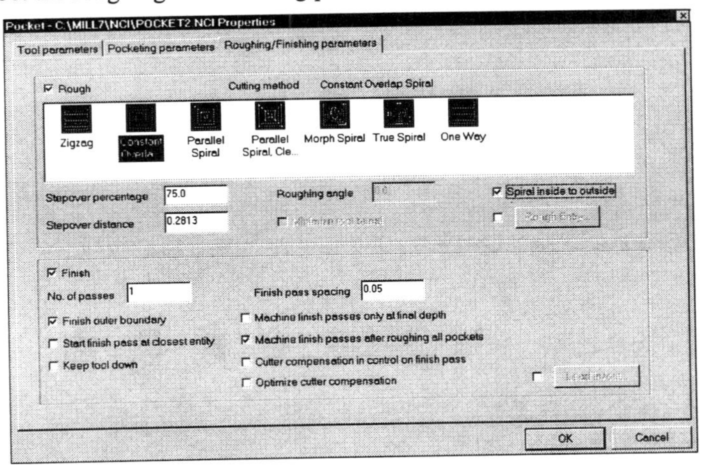

Select **OK** to return to Operations Manager menu

Step 6. Regenerate the toolpaths.

"**Select All**" to include all three operations
Select the "**Regen Path**" button to generate the toolpaths
Select **OK** to "3 associative operations regenerated successfully."
Select **OK** from the Operations Manager menu
The new toolpaths for second and third pocketing operations appear as in Figure 8.8.

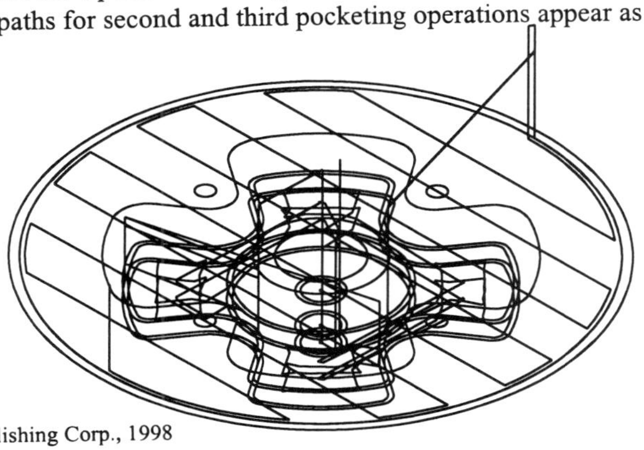

Figure 8.9

8.3 Chain Manager

The Chain Manager utility allows you to edit the chained geometry to cause changes in toolpaths.

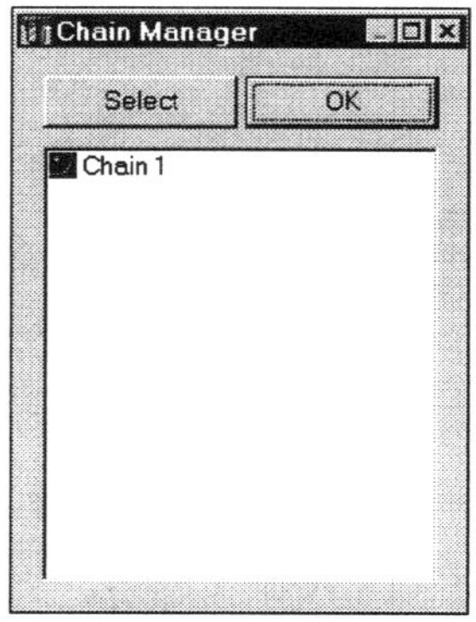

The commands to access the Chain Manager menu are:

1. Select MAIN MENU → Toolpaths → Operations to open the Operations Manager menu
2. Select the Geometry icon for a selected operation to open the Chain Manager menu as above.

The editing functions related to Chain Manager menu are grouped in a right click menu. Click the right mouse button to open the option menu as below:

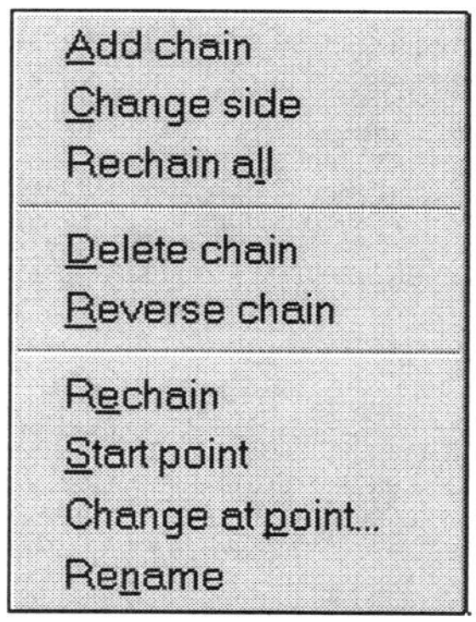

The nine functions in the option menu are briefly summarized as below:

Add chain: adds a chain to the operation.
Change side: reverses the side of cutter compensation.
Rechain all: deletes all existing chains and displays the chaining method menu to reselect all chains.
Delete chain: deletes the selected chain(s).
Reverse chain: changes the selected chain(s) to the opposite direction.
Rechain: reselects the chain in the graphics window using the chaining method menu.
Start point: returns to the graphics window to select a new start point for the chain.
Change at point: specifies a parameter change for a specific point on the geometry.
Rename: renames the selected chain.

Add chain This function allows you to add more chains to the existing operation. The toolpaths are automatically generated for the added chains without repeating the process of defining the tool and parameters. The chaining method menu will appear to define new chains when this function is selected. Figure 8.10 shows the toolpaths before and after a new chain is added.

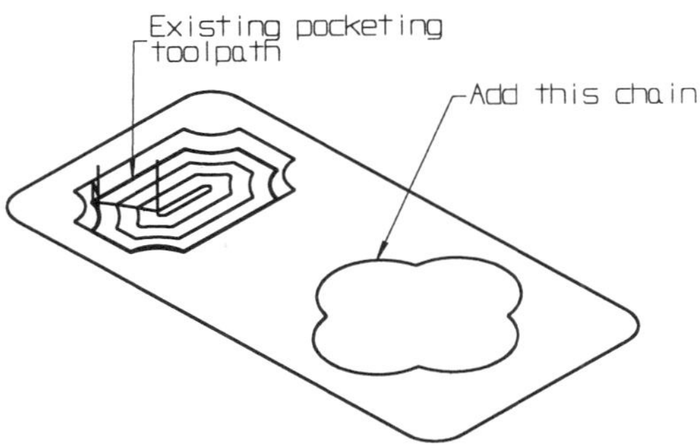

Figure 8.10a

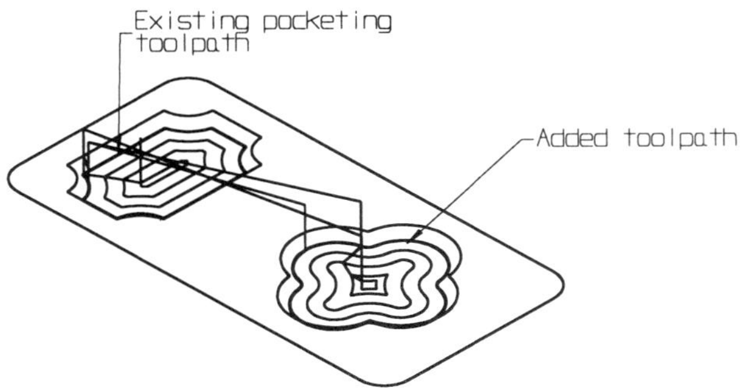

Figure 8.10b

Change side The Change Side function reverses the side of the cutter compensation. This function is only applicable to the contour module, and is not used for the pocket module. It has a significant effect on the toolpaths due to the change in the side of cutter compensation. Figure 8.11 shows the effect of changing the side on the toolpaths.

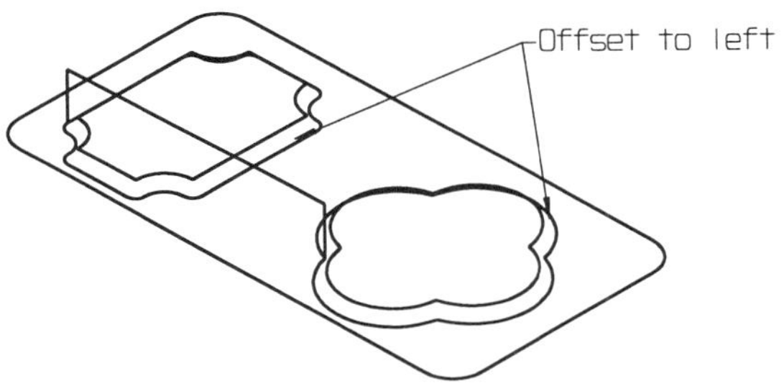

Figure 8.11a

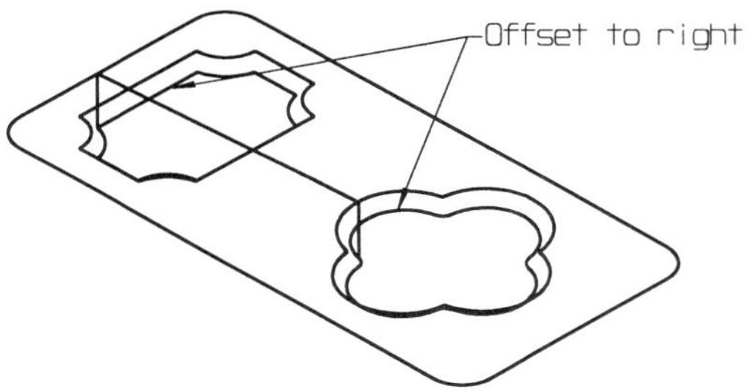

Figure 8.11b

Reverse chain This function reverses the chaining direction of the selected chain. When the chain direction is reversed, the toolpath side along the geometry is changed as shown in Figure 8.12.

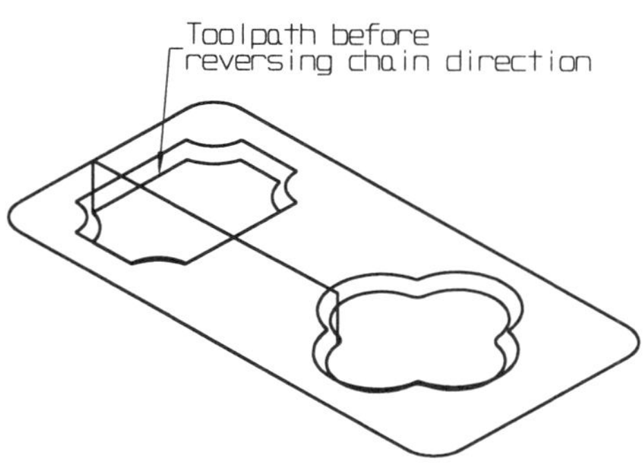

Figure 8.12a

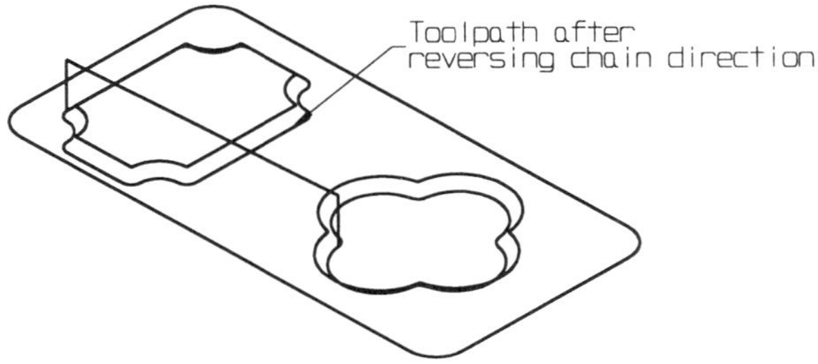

Figure 8.12b

3 **Change at point** This function allows you to change such parameters as cutter compensation, depth, feed rate, spindle speed, etc. at the selected point in the geometry. This function applies only to contour operations. Its menu appears as shown here.

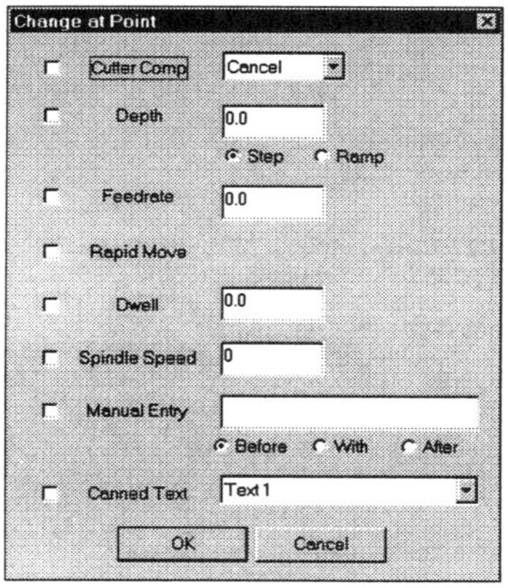

Project 3. Editing toolpaths using chain manager functions

The intent of this project is to show how to effectively use the functions of chain manager for modifying toolpaths. The part geometry file array1 is used in this project. A four-arc profile is added to the model. The contour function is used to generate a toolpath for the rectangular profile first. Use the "Add chain" function to add the four-arc chain to the contour operation. The effect of "Change side" and "Reverse chain" functions is then demonstrated. The contour operation is copied and placed after the original operation. Parameter changes are made to the second operation including tool size and stock amount for producing finishing toolpaths. Figure 8.13 shows the initial contour toolpath and edited toolpaths using chain manager functions.

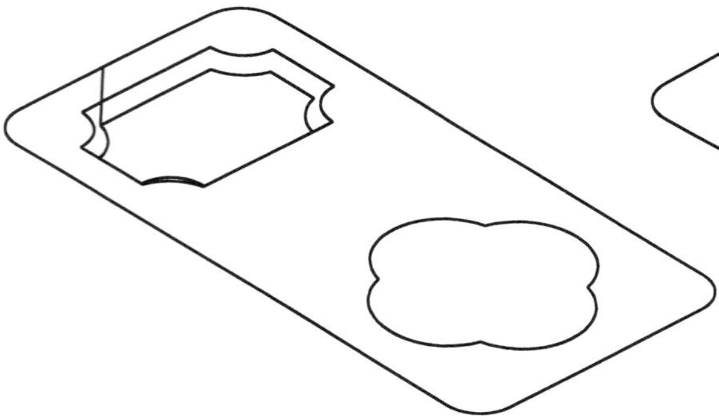

Figure 8.13a

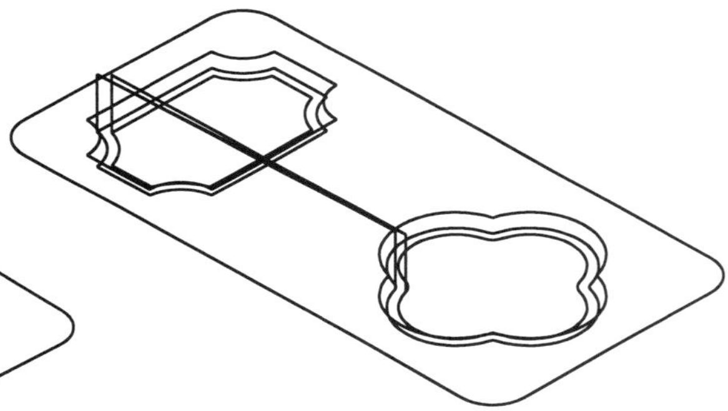

Figure 8.13b

Step 1. Open the geometry file array1.

Select **MAIN MENU → File → Get**
File name: **array1**
The part geometry appears as in Figure 8.14.

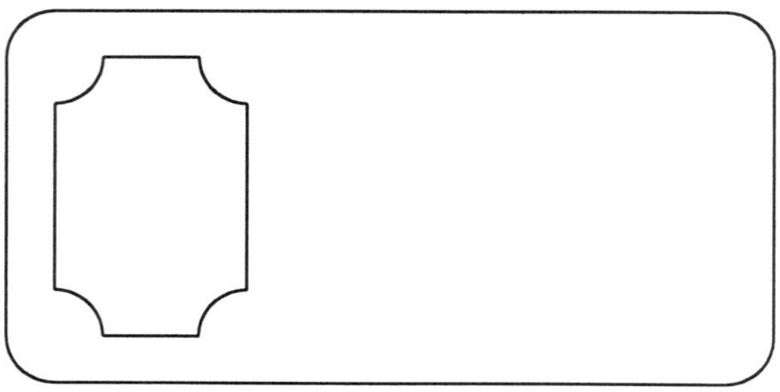

Figure 8.14

Step 2. Add four connected arcs.

Select **Level**, then enter **2**

Select **MAIN MENU → Create → Arc → Endpoints → Values**

Enter the following four sets of endpoint coordinates with the radius of 1.3:
(Note: select the second arc from outside out of the four possible arcs.)

First end point	Second end point	Radius
7.75,4.25	7.75,1.75	1.3
7.75,1.75	10.25,1.75	1.3
10.25,1.75	10.25,4.25	1.3
10.25,4.25	7.75,4.25	1.3

The four arcs are added as in Figure 8.15.

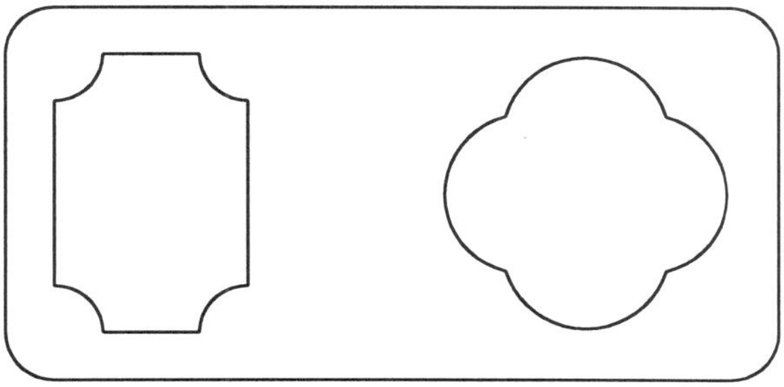

Figure 8.15

Step 3. Change to isometric view.

Select **Gview → Isometric**

The new drawing should resemble Figure 8.16.

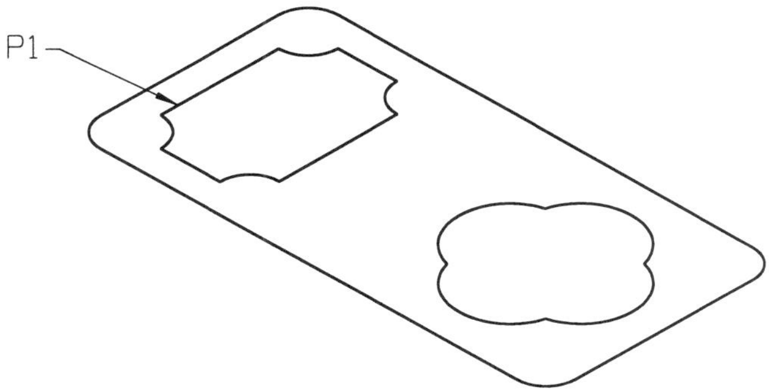

Figure 8.16

Step 4. Save the new drawing as chain.

Select **MAIN MENU → File → Save**

File name to save: **chain**

Step 5. Generate contouring toolpath for the rectangular profile.

Use the pick point in Figure 8.16.

Select **MAIN MENU → Toolpaths → Contour**

File name for NCI: **chain**

Select **Chain**, then pick **P1**

Select **Done**

Click the right mouse button, then select "Get tool from library"

Select **tool #239** (1/2” flat endmill)
Select **OK**

Step 6. Define the tool parameters as below.

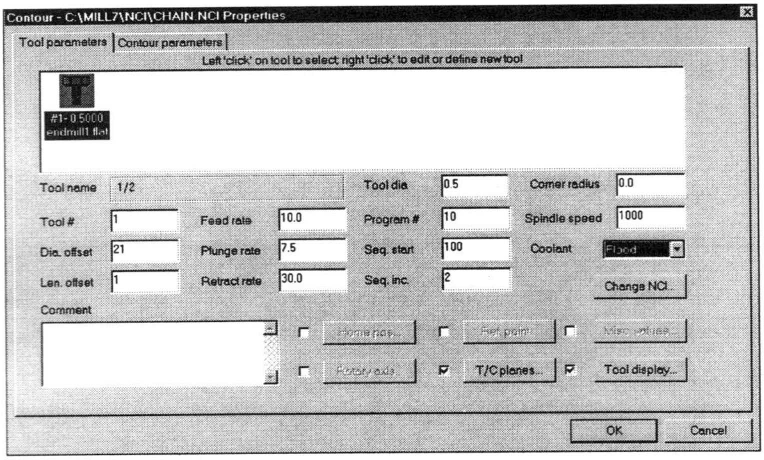

Step 7. Define the contour parameters.

Click the “Contour parameters” button
Set the contour parameters as below.

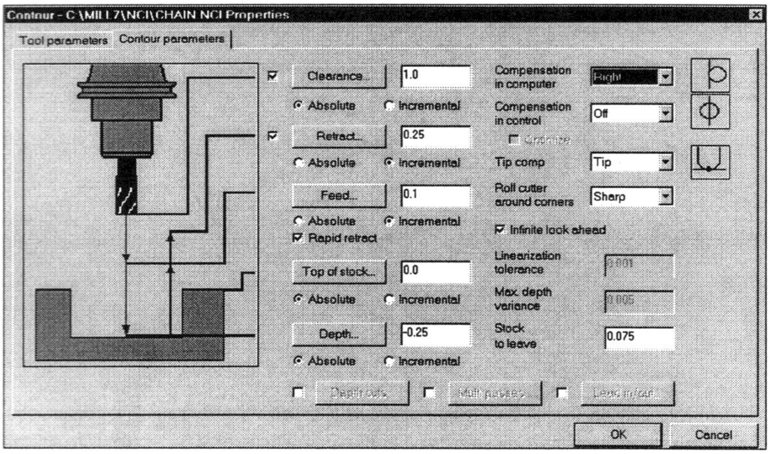

Select **OK**
The toolpath is generated as in Figure 8.17.

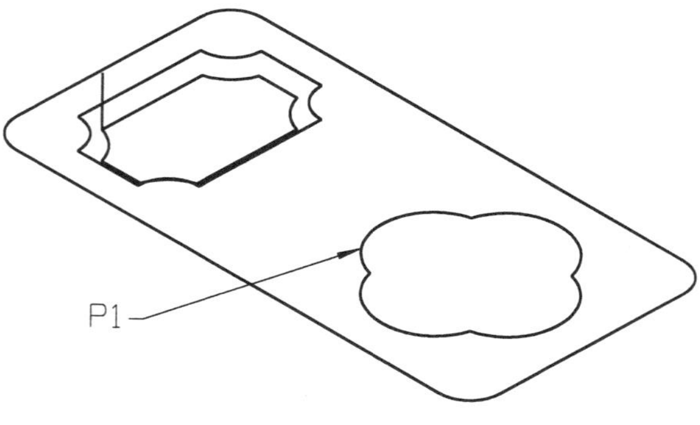

Figure 8.17

Step 8. Add a chain to the contour operation.

Use the pick point in Figure 8.17.
Select **Operations**
The Operations Manager menu appears as below.

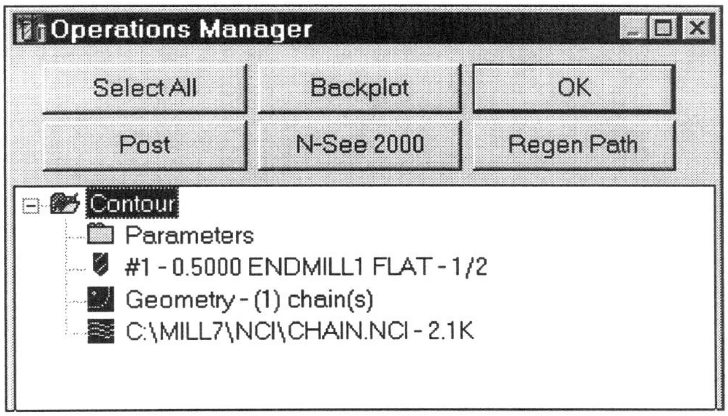

Click the green geometry icon to open the Chain Manager menu as here.

Click the right mouse button to select **Chain 1**, then select **Add chain** from the option menu
Select **Chain**, then pick **P1**
Select **Done**
The "Chain 2" is added to the Chain Manager menu as shown here.

Select **OK** to return to Operations Manager menu

Step 9. Regenerate the toolpaths.

Select **Regen Path** to regenerate the toolpaths
Select **OK** to "1 associative operations regenerated successfully."

The new toolpath is added for the second chain as shown in Figure 8.18.

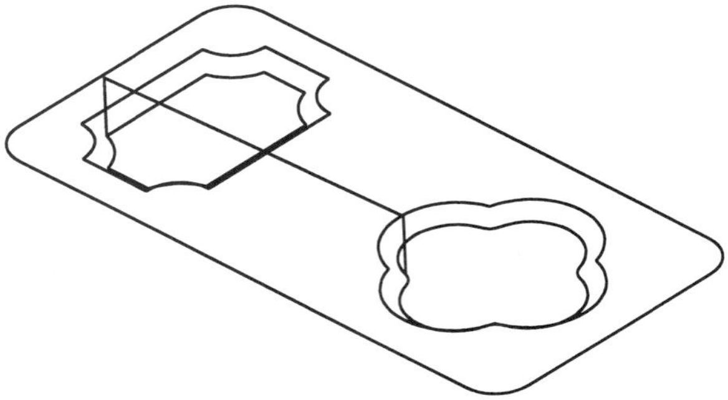

Figure 8.18

Step 10. Change side of cutter compensation.

Click the green geometry icon to open the Chain Manager menu
Click the right mouse button to select **Chain 1** to open the option menu
Select **Change side**
Select **OK** from Chain Manager menu

Step 11. Regenerate the toolpaths to reflect the side change.

Select **Regen Path** to regenerate the toolpaths
Select **OK** to "1 associative operations regenerated successfully."
The new toolpaths with new cutter compensation side are shown in Figure 8.19.

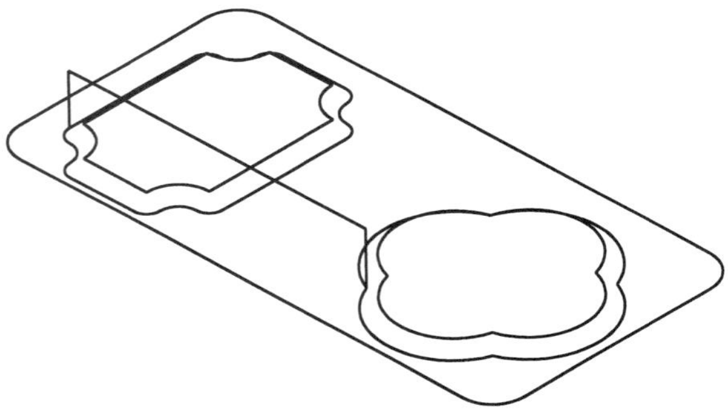

Figure 8.19

Step 12. Reverse the chain direction.

Click the green geometry icon to open the Chain Manager menu
Select **Chain 1**, then press the **Ctrl** key and select **Chain 2** to select both chains
Click the right mouse button to select **Chain 2** to open the option menu
Select **Reverse chain**
Select **OK** to return to Operations Manager menu

Step 13. Regenerate the toolpaths to reflect the reversing of chain direction.

Select **Regen Path** to regenerate the toolpaths
Select **OK** to "1 associative operations regenerated successfully."

The new toolpaths appear as in Figure 8.20.

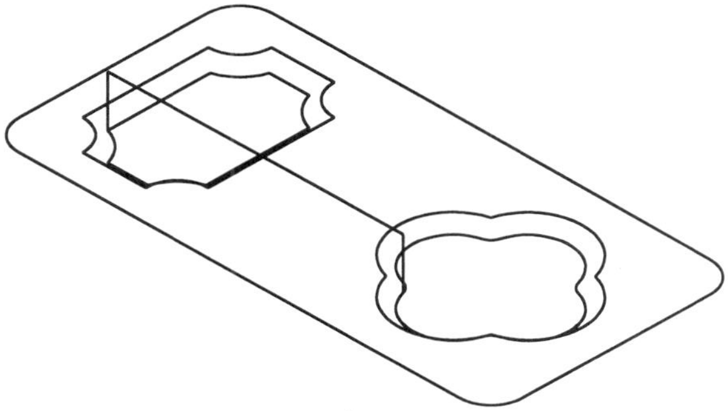

Figure 8.20

Step 14. Copy the toolpaths.

Click the right mouse button on the yellow "Contour" icon, then drag it down to the bottom of the operation list

The four-option menu should appear as here.

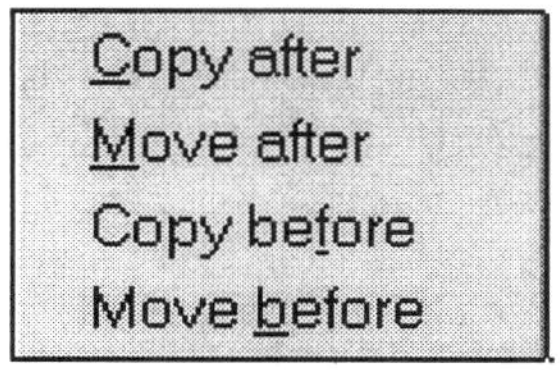

Select **Copy after** from the list

The operation has been copied as shown here.

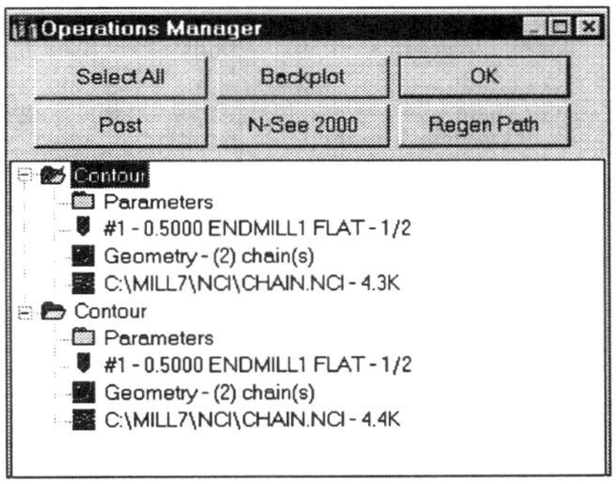

Step 15. Change the parameters for the second operation.

Click the gray parameters icon to open the parameters menu

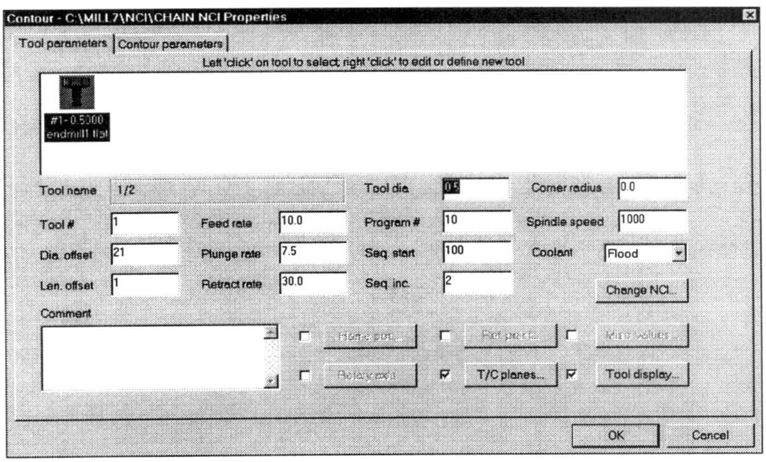

Click the right mouse button, then select “Get tool from library”
Select **tool #235** for (1/4” flat end mill)
Select **OK** to return to parameters menu
Set the tool parameters as below.

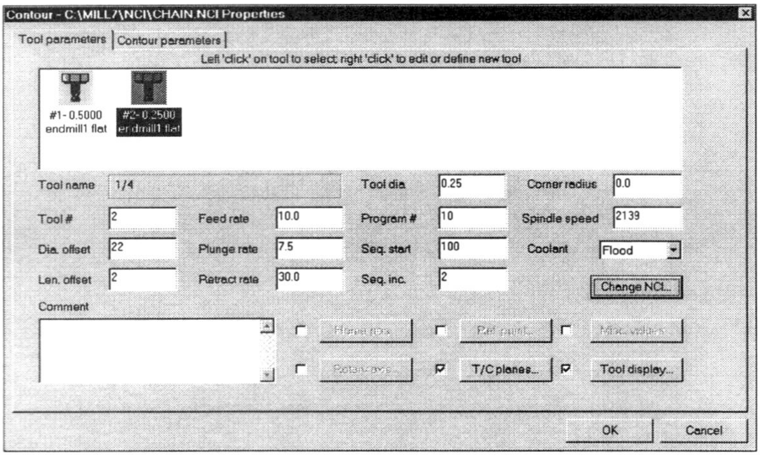

Step 16. Define the Contour parameters.

Click the “Contour parameters” button
Set the contour parameters as below.
(*Note:* only change “Stock to leave = 0.0”)

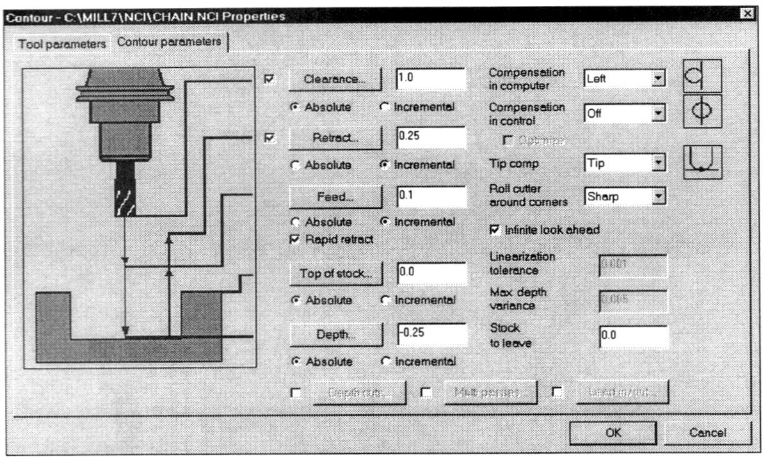

Select **OK**

Step 17. Regenerate the toolpaths to reflect the change in tool and stock.

Select **Regen Path**
Select **OK** to “1 associative operations regenerated successfully.”

The new toolpaths becomes Figure 8.21.

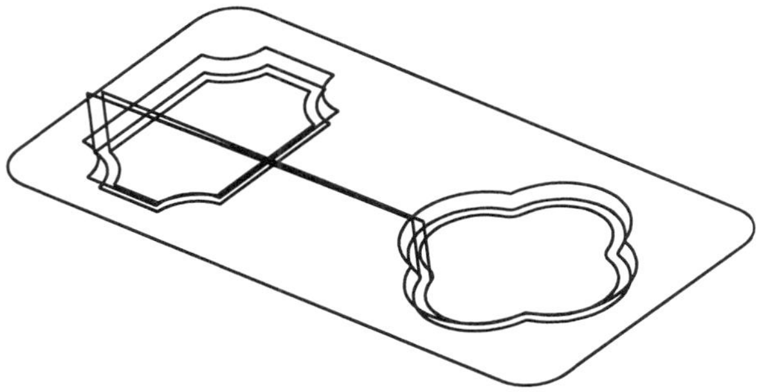

Figure 8.21

Step 18. Backplot two operations.

Select **Select All**
Select **Backplot**
Set display and backplot parameters to desired setting
Select **Run** to animate toolpaths on the screen
Note: the ½" end mill should rough cut the two chains first, followed by the ¼" end mill for finish cut.

Select **BACKUP** to return to Operations Manager menu
Select **OK** to exit Operations Manager menu

Step 19. Save the toolpath file as chain.

Select **MAIN MENU → File → Save**
File name to write: **chain**

Questions

1. What is "Associativity" in Mastercam?
2. What are the six types of associative information included in a project?
3. Define an operation in Mastercam.
4. What is the Operations Manager?
5. List the two methods of moving an operation.
6. Explain the procedure for moving an operation using the pick-and-place method.
7. Explain the procedure for moving an operation using the option command method.
8. Describe these two copy operation commands; Copy after and Copy before
9. Explain how to copy parameters between the same operation types.
10. Describe how to delete a single operation.
11. Describe how to delete all operations.
12. Explain the two tree directory control modes; Expand all and Collapse all.
13. Describe the main functions of the Chain Manager.
14. Explain the procedure to open the Chain Manager.
15. Describe the advantage of using "Add chain" function.
16. Use a drawing to show the effect of "Change side" to the toolpaths.
17. Use a drawing to show the effect of "Reverse chain" to the toolpaths.

Chapter 9

2D Toolpath Editing

Objectives:

1. Know the toolpath file structure and determine the number of toolpaths sections for various operations.
2. Delete the toolpath sections from an existing toolpath file.
3. Merge two toolpath files.
4. Know four toolpath editing functions; mirror, rotate, scale, and translate.
5. Understand the features of these toolpath editing functions and know when to apply them.
6. Apply toolpath editing functions to simplify toolpath generation process.

Overview

Toolpaths after generated can be edited in Mastercam. There are two ways to edit toolpaths; Edit NCI method and Operation Manager method. Using Operation Manager method to modify toolpaths has been presented in chapter 8. This chapter covers using Edit NCI method to modify toolpaths. Edit NCI functions include parameters, cut, copy, plot, merge, and transformation. Some of these functions can be performed in Operation Manager method. Some functions such as transformation and merge are still unique to Edit NCI methods. Transform has four functions; mirror, rotate, scale, and translate, to manipulate the existing toolpaths. This chapter starts with toolpath file structure, deleting toolpath, merging toolpaths, and editing toolpaths using four transform functions. Examples given in this chapter are not necessary the best way to generate or edit toolpaths for a particular project. Our intent is to show how to use Edit NCI functions, rather than present the best way to complete the project.

9.1 File Structure of Toolpaths

After toolpaths have been generated by using various toolpath modules, we may need to manipulate these toolpaths. Mastercam provides a variety of ways to modify toolpaths including **deleting, merging,** and **editing**. Understanding the file structure of the Mastercam toolpaths is very crucial to successfully implementing these editing features.

Mastercam organizes the toolpaths into sections so that they can be edited. The toolpath sections are assigned according to their generation sequence. The toolpath generated by one operation is normally identified as one operation or section. Therefore, a section of toolpaths is generated by using the contour, pocket, drill, or surface module. Three operations, for example, are used to machine the part shown in Figure 9.9. The operation sequence starts with using the contour module to machine the outer profile, followed by using the pocket module for pocketing the rectangular pocket and using the drill module to drill the four holes. The toolpaths in this example contain three sections and are organized as:

Section No.	**Toolpaths**
Section 1	Contour module
	-
	-
Section 2	Pocket module
	-
	-
Section 3	Drill module
	-
	-
End of file	EOF

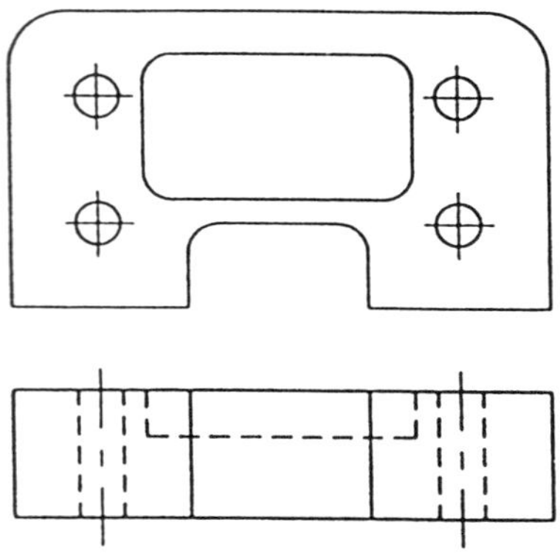

Figure 9.1

Often, more than one section is assigned to the toolpaths generated by one operation. This occurs when the contour module is used when

(1) the sum of roughing passes and finish passes is more than one or
(2) the sum of rough cuts and finish cuts in depth cut is more than one.

The number of toolpath sections for using the contour module can be calculated as:

$$NC = (NR + NF) \times (NRD + NFD)$$

Where NC = total number of toolpath sections for contouring
NR = number of rough cuts
NF = number of finish passes
NRD = number of rough passes in depth cut
NFD = number of finish passes in depth cut

Example 9.1 Number of toolpath sections in contouring

The contour module is used to cut an external profile with these cutting parameters:

Number of rough cuts (NR) = **1**
Number of finish passes (NF) = **1**
Number of rough passes in depth cut (NRD) = **0**
Number of finish passes In depth cut (NFD) = **1**

The total number of toolpath sections for this particular operation is:

$$\begin{aligned} NC &= (NR + NF) \text{ X } (NRD + NFD) \\ &= (1 + 1) \text{ X } (1 + 0) \\ &= 2 \text{ toolpath sections} \end{aligned}$$

Example 9.2 Number of toolpath sections in contouring

Find the total number of toolpath sections for contouring a profile with these cutting parameters:

Number of rough cuts (NR) = **2**
Number of finish passes (NF) = **1**
Number of rough passes in depth cut (NRD) = **2**
Number of finish passes In depth cut (NFD) = **1**

The total number of toolpath sections for this particular operation is:

$$\begin{aligned} NC &= (NR + NF) \text{ X } (NRD + NFD) \\ &= (2 + 1) \text{ X } (2 + 1) \\ &= 9 \text{ toolpath sections} \end{aligned}$$

In pocketing, the number of toolpath sections is the sum of rough cuts and finish cuts in depth cut parameters. The number of finish passes in the XY-plane does not affect the number of toolpath sections. The formula listed below can be used to find the total number of toolpath sections in pocketing:

$$\mathbf{NP = NRD + NFD}$$

Where NP = total number of toolpath sections for pocketing

Example 9.3 Number of toolpath sections in pocketing

Calculate the total number of toolpath sections in pocketing a rectangular pocket under the following cutting parameters:

Number of finish passes (NF) = **2**
Number of rough passes in depth cut (NRD) = **0**
Number of finish passes in depth cut (NFD) =**1**

The total number of toolpath sections in this pocketing operation is:

$$\begin{aligned} NP &= NRD + NFD \\ &= 0 + 1 \\ &= 1 \text{ toolpath section} \end{aligned}$$

Example 9.4 Number of toolpath sections in pocketing

Calculate the number of toolpath sections in pocketing an enclosed profile under the following cutting parameters:

Number of finish passes (NF) = **2**
Number of rough passes in depth cut (NRD) = **2**
Number of finish passes in depth cut (NFD) =**1**

The total number of toolpath sections in this pocketing operation is:

$$\begin{aligned} NP &= NRD + NFD \\ &= 2 + 1 \\ &= 3 \quad \text{toolpath sections} \end{aligned}$$

The number of toolpath segments is always **1** when the drill module is used. When a part program contains the toolpaths generated by using more than one operation (contour, pocket, drill, or surface module), the total number of toolpath sections is the sum of toolpath sections of each operation.

Example 9.5 Number of toolpath sections for multiple operations

A part program consists of the toolpaths generated by three operations (contour, pocket, and drill). Find the number of toolpath sections for the following two sets of cutting parameters:

Case 1:

Contour:	Number of roughing cuts = 0 Number of finish passes = 1 Depth cut: Rough: 0 cut at 0.0	 Finish: 1 cut at 0.0
Pocket:	Number of finish passes = 1 Depth cut: Rough: 0 cut at 0.0	 Finish: 1 cut at 0.0
Drill:	Drilling operation is always one toolpath section	

The total number of toolpath section is the sum of these three operations which is:

$$\begin{aligned} N &= 1 + 1 + 1 \\ &= 3 \quad \text{toolpath sections} \end{aligned}$$

The total number of toolpath sections for the operation conditions listed above is 3 (one for contouring, one for pocketing, and one for drilling).

Case 2:

Contour:	Number of roughing cuts = 2 Number of finish passes = 1 Depth cut: Rough: 1 cut at 0.0	 Finish: 1 cut at 0.2
Pocket:	Number of finish passes = 1 Depth cut: Rough: 0 cut at 0.0	 Finish: 1 cut at 0.0
Drill:	Drilling operation is always one toolpath section	

The contouring operation has 6 toolpath sections. The pocketing has 1 section and drilling 1 section. Therefore, the total number of toolpath sections is 8.

The Procedure to Find the List of Toolpath Sections
Use the following commands to list the toolpath sections of a toolpath file:

Select **MAIN MENU → NC utils → Edit NCI**
The Edit NCI menu should appear as below.

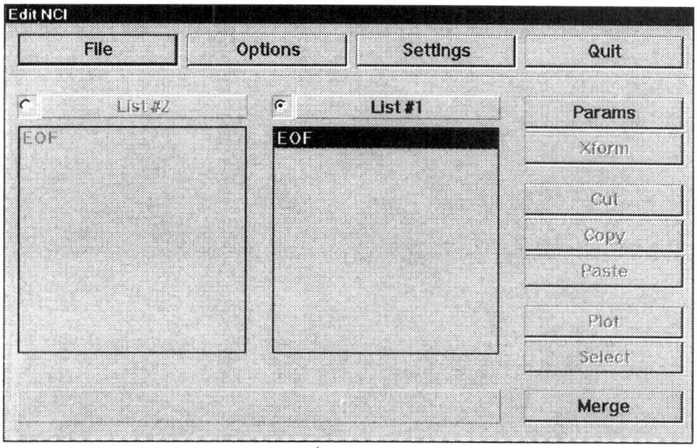

Select **File →** **Open**
Enter file name: **pocket1** (specify your own file's name)

The toolpath sections should appear under POCKET1.NCI list as shown below.

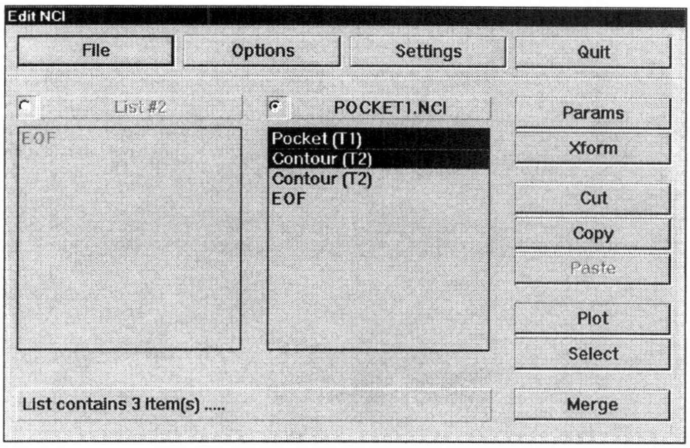

9.2 Deleting Toolpaths-Operations Manager Method

Often we need to delete the toolpaths that have become a part of the toolpath file. Mastercam uses two ways to delete the selected toolpath sections: **Operation Managers** method and the **Edit NCI** method.

The operations manager method allows deleting toolpaths for one operation or all operations. Follow the following procedure to delete the toolpaths:

The Procedure for Deleting a Single Operation Toolpath:

1. Select Toolpaths → Operations to open the Operations Manager menu.

2. Click the toolpath to be delete, then click the right mouse button to open option menu as shown here:

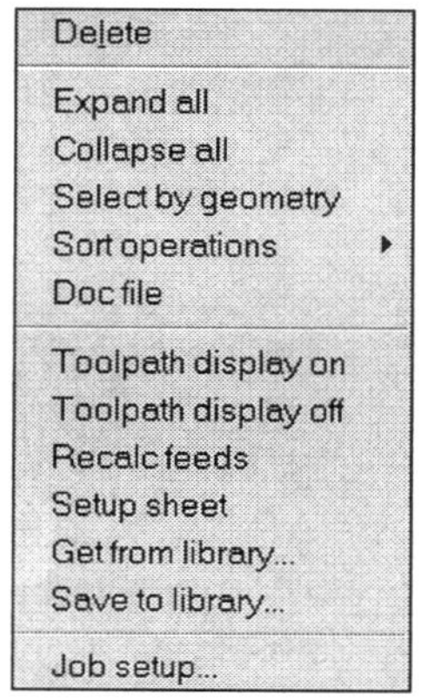

3. Select Delete, then select Yes to "(1) operations have been selected and are about to be deleted. Are you sure?"

4. Repeat steps 2 – 3 to delete toolpaths for other operations one by one.

The Procedure for Deleting the Entire Toolpath File:

1. Select Toolpaths → Operations to open the Operations Manager menu

2. Select "Select All" from Operations Manager menu

3. Click the right mouse button to open option menu

4. Select Delete, then select Yes to "(2) operations have been selected and are about to be deleted. Are you sure?"

Project 1. Delete toolpaths using operations manager method

This project uses the pocket2t project to show how to delete toolpaths for a selected operation. The toolpaths in this project consist of three pocketing operations. We delete the first pocket operation by using the single operation option, then delete the remaining two pocket operations using the entire toolpath file option. The part geometry and its existing toolpaths are shown in Figure 9.10.

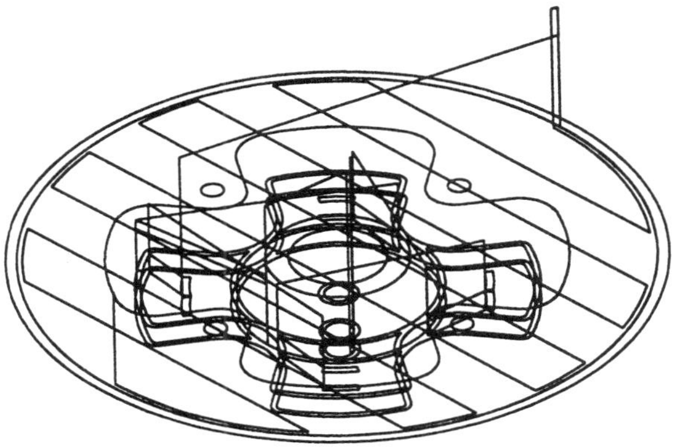

Figure 9.2

Step 1. Open the pocket2t file.

Select **MAIN MENU → File → Get**
File name: **pocket2t**
The part geometry should appear on the screen.

Step 2. Open the toolpaths.

Select **MAIN MENU → Toolpaths**
The toolpaths for three pocketing operations are displayed as in Figure 9.3.

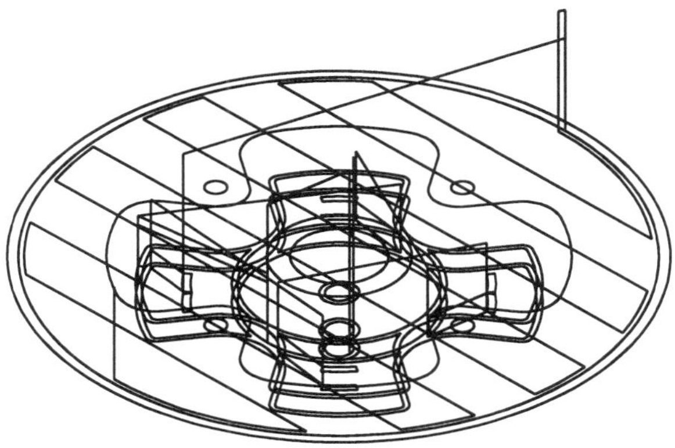

Figure 9.3

Step 3. Open the Operations Manager menu.

Select **Operations** to open the Operations Manager menu

The Operations Manager menu appear as below.

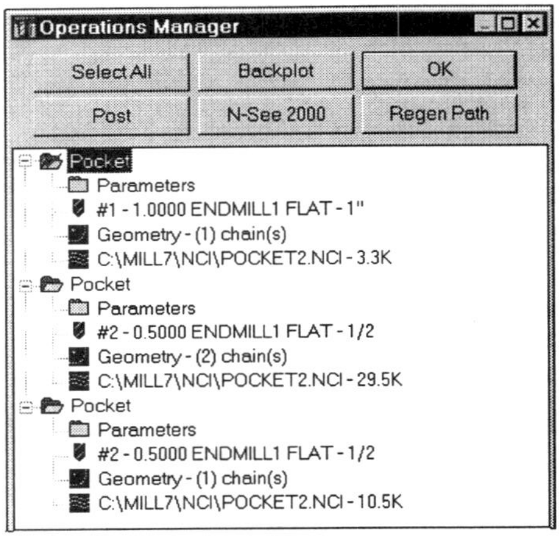

Step 4. Delete the first pocketing operation.

Click the "**Pocket**" icon of the first pocket operation
Click the right mouse button to open the option menu as here.

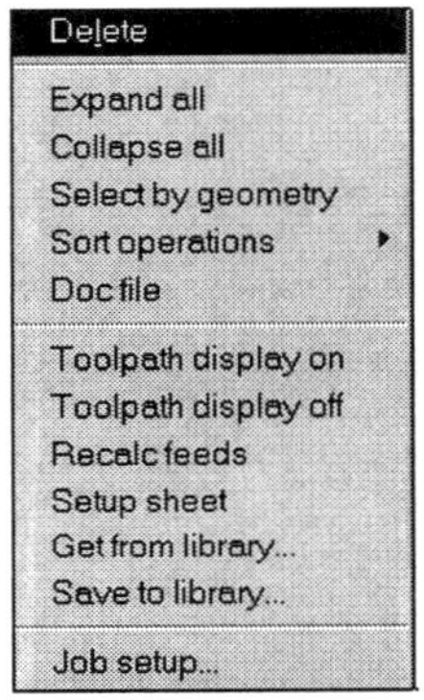

Select **Delete**
Select **Yes** to "(1) operations have been selected and are about to deleted. Are you sure?"

The toolpath of the first pocket operation has been removed as shown below.

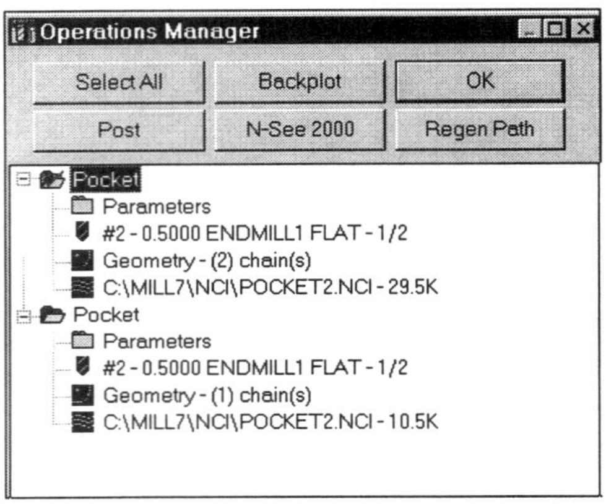

Step 5. Delete the remaining two pocketing operations.

Select the "**Select All**" button from the Operations Manager menu
Click the right mouse button, then select **Delete**
Select **Yes** to "(2) operations have been selected and are about to be deleted. Are you sure?"

The remaining two pocketing operations have been removed from the Operations Manager as shown below.

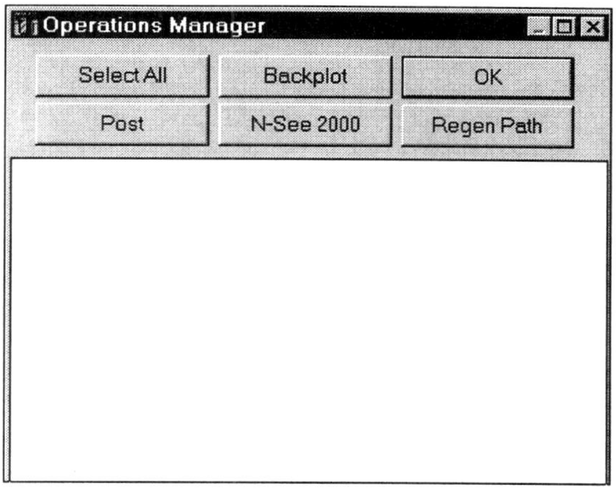

Select **OK** from Operations Manager menu

9.3 Deleting Toolpaths Using Edit NCI Method

A section or sections of toolpath can be deleted by using Edit NCI function.

The procedure for deleting toolpaths with Edit NCI method is:

1. Select NC utils → Edit NCI

2. Select Yes to "Operations have been modified. Create the NCI text file?"

3. Select Yes to "File already exists, overwrite?"

4. The Edit NCI menu with toolpath section list appears as below.

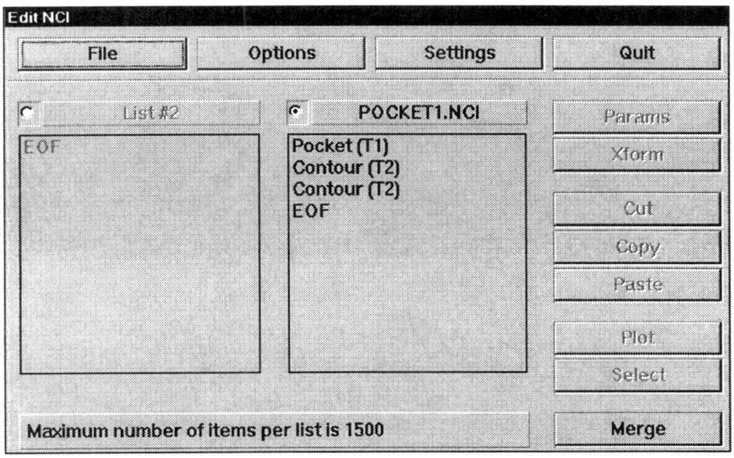

2

5. Select the toolpath section(s) to be deleted.

6. Click the toolpath section(s) to be deleted
Note: Press "Ctrl" key to select multiple sections. The selected toolpath sections will be highlighted in blue.

7. Select "Cut" from the Edit NCI menu.
The selected toolpath section has been removed from the file as shown below.

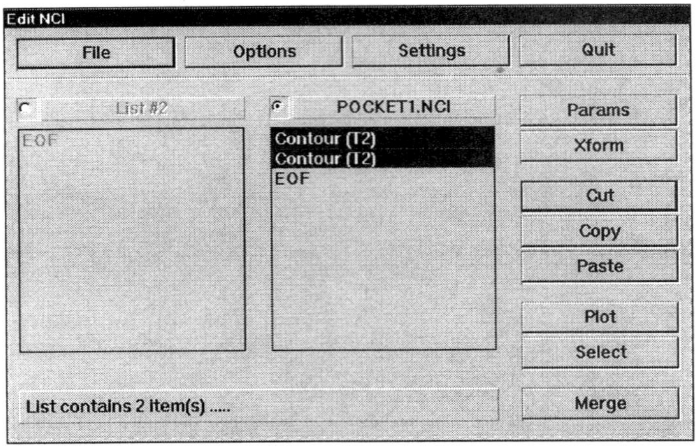

8. Save the toolpath file.

9. Select Yes to "File already exists, overwrite?"

10. Exit Edit NCI utility.

11. Select Quit to exit Edit NCI utility

Project 2. Deleting toolpath sections using Edit NCI method

The pocket1 project is used to show how to delete a toolpath section from the existing toolpath file. Figure 9.4 shows the toolpaths before and after the contouring toolpath is deleted.

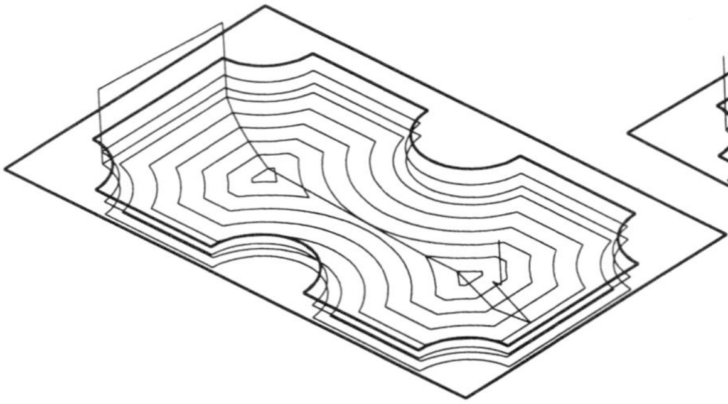

Figure 9.4a

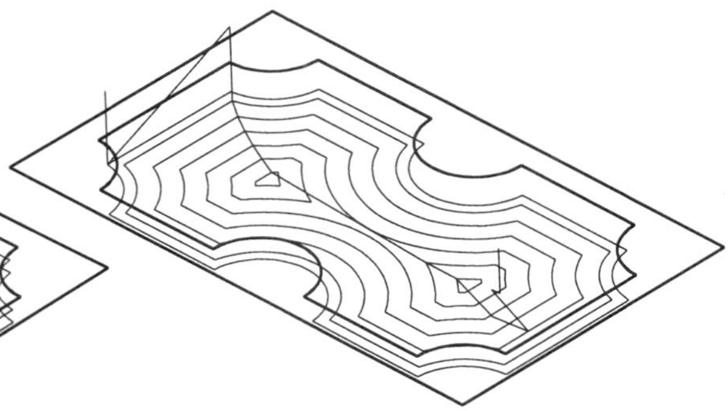

Figure 9.4b

Step 1. Open the project file pocket1.

Select **MAIN MENU → File → Get**
File name: **pocket1**
The part geometry of pocket1 shall appear on the screen.

Step 2. Open the Edit NCI utility.

Select **MAIN MENU → NC utils → Edit NCI**
Select **Yes** to "Operations have been modified. Create the NCI text file?"
Three toolpath sections in this toolpath file appear in the menu as below.

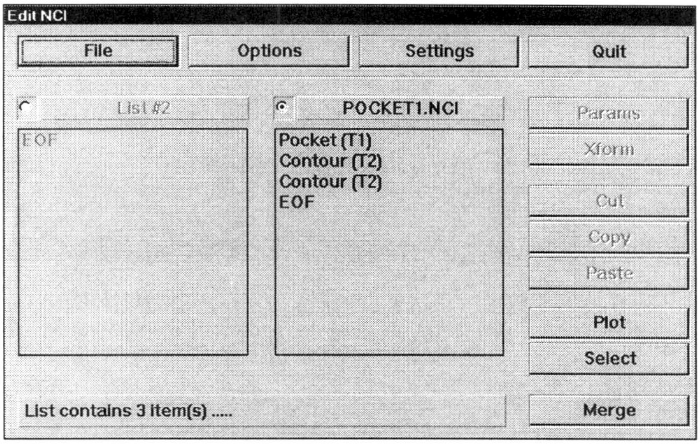

Step 3. Delete the first contour section.

Select the first contour section **"Contour (T2)"** to make it highlighted in blue as below.

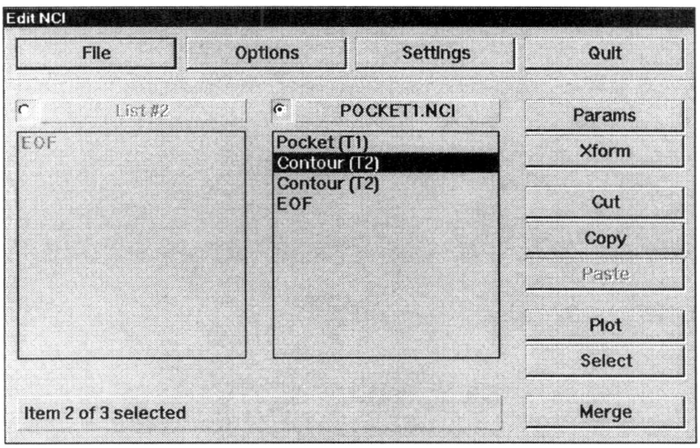

Select **Cut**

The selected toolpath section has been removed from the file and the remaining two sections appear as below.

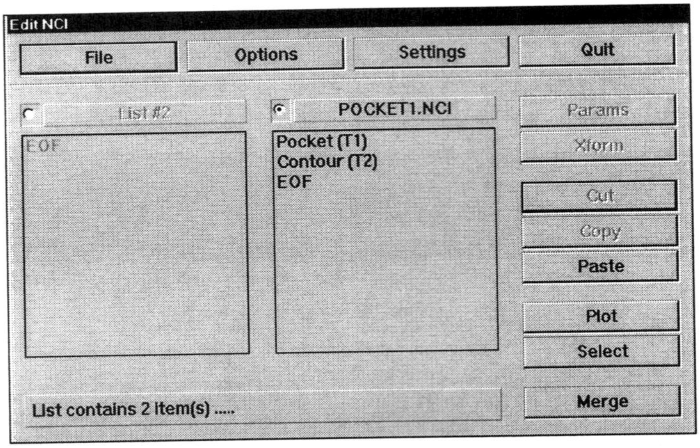

Step 4. Save the new toolpath file as delete2.

Select **File** → **Save As** from the Edit NCI menu
File name: **delete2**

Step 5. Exit the Edit NCI utility.

Select **Quit**

Step 6. Backplot the toolpath file delete2.

Select **NC utils** → **Backplot** → **NCI name**
File name: **delete2**
Select **Run** to backplot the toolpaths
The remaining two toolpath sections are shown in Figure 9.5.

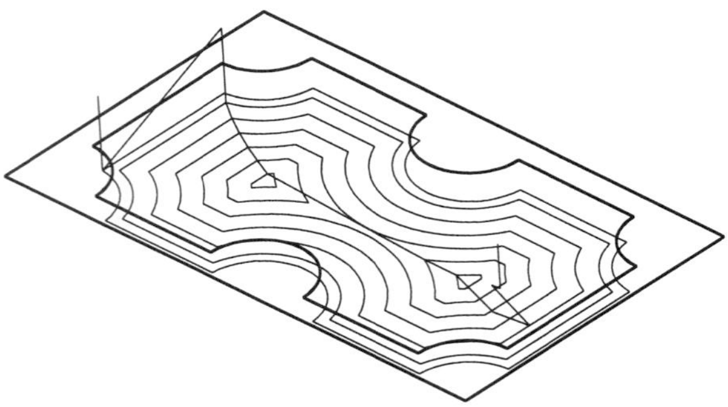

Figure 9.5

9.4 Changing the Sequence of Toolpath Sections 3

Mastercam allows the sequence of toolpath sections to be easily changed. The Cut and Paste commands in the Edit NCI menu often used for this purpose. The Cut function temporarily removes the selected toolpath section(s) from the file and places in the clipboard. The Paste function places the cut toolpath section(s) to the proper location.

Project 3. Changing the sequence of toolpath sections

There are three operations in the toolpath file of pocket2t. The sequence of existing toolpaths starts with Pocket (T1) and followed by eleven sections with Pocket (T2). In fact, the second and third pocket operations use the same tool T2. Therefore they all assigned with the same toolpath section name Pocket (T2). We want to move Pocket (T1) to become the last section of the toolpath file. Figure 9.6 shows the part model and its toolpaths.

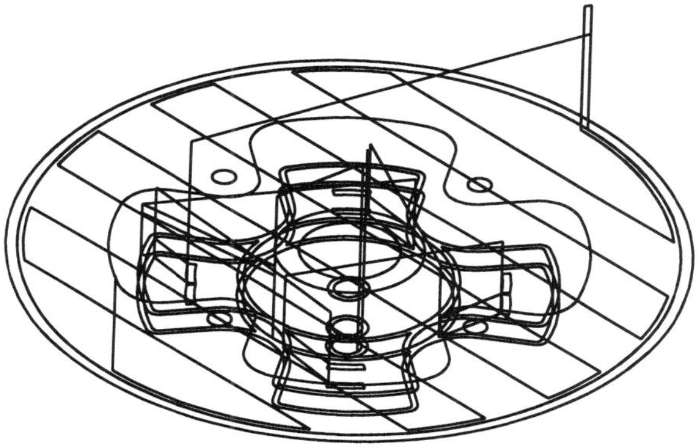

Figure 9.6

Step 1. Open the file pocket2t.

Select **MAIN MENU → File → Get à pocket2t**
The part geometry of pocket2t should appear on the screen.

Step 2. Open the toolpath file.

Select **MAIN MENU →** **NC utils →** **Edit NCI**
Select **Yes** to "Operations have been modified. Create the NCI text file?"
Twelve toolpath sections in this file appear in the Edit NCI menu as below.

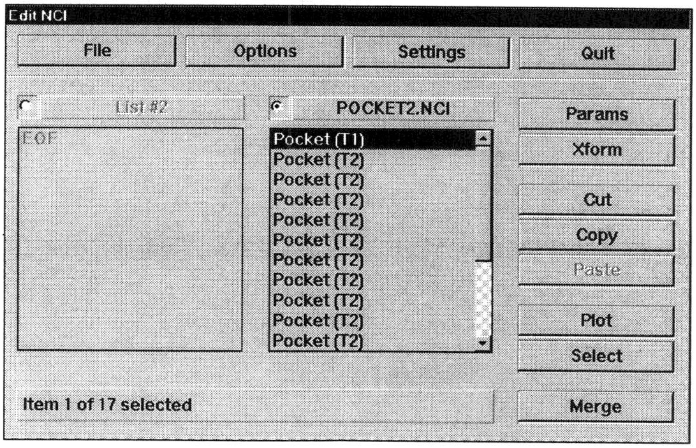

Step 3. Move the Pocket (T1) section to the last of the file.

Select the Pocket (T1) section to highlight it in blue
Select **Cut** to temporarily remove this section from the file
Scroll the section list down to the bottom
Select **Paste**
Select **EOF** as the insertion point to place the cut section before the selected section
The new sequence of the toolpath section becomes as below.

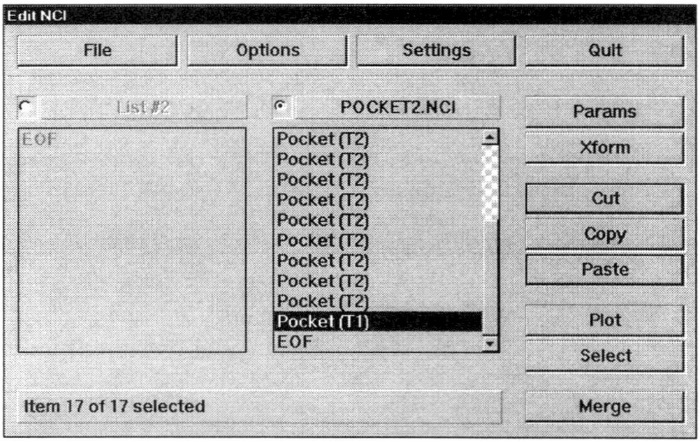

Step 4. Exit the Edit NCI utility.

Select **Quit**
Select **No** to "Save changes to current file?"

9.5 Merging Two Toolpath Files

Mastercam allows the merging of two or more toolpath files. The file name of the merged file can be a new NCI file name, or one of two file names that are to be merged. The table below illustrates how the merged file name of the three possible cases of the merged file is used.

	Use a new file name	Use File A as the merged file name	Use File B as the merged file name
File A	A	A	A
File B	B	B	B
Merged file	C	A	B

⌛Tips for merging toolpath files:

1. Use a new file name for the merged file. This allows the files to be merged remain unchanged. Later they can be used for other applications.
2. When the file name of one toolpath file to be merged is used, the toolpaths of that particular file will be altered.
3. It is possible to merge more than two toolpath files into one NCI file.
4. It is possible to include only some sections of toolpaths in an NCI file in the merged file.
5. The sequence of the toolpath files being merged determines the sequence of the machining operations. If the toolpaths of a machining operation must be performed first, enter their toolpath file first.

Project 4. Merging two toolpath files.

This project shows how to merge two toolpath files. The toolpaths for contour2t are used as one toolpath file. Use the contour module to generate a contouring toolpath for the outside circle and save as another file name. These two toolpath files are then merged. The part geometry with the merged toolpaths is shown in Figure 9.7

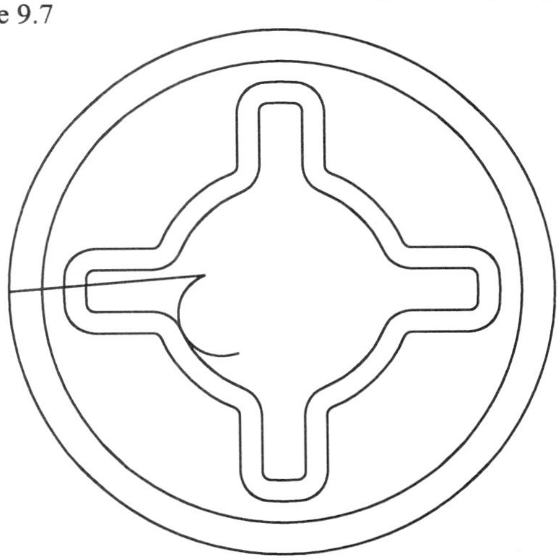

Figure 9.7

Step 1. Open the project file contour2t.

Select **MAIN MENU → File → Get→ contour2t**
Select **Save → Filename: contrur2t**
(Note: Merge function cannot support more than 8 character file names.)
Figure 9.8 shows the part geometry.

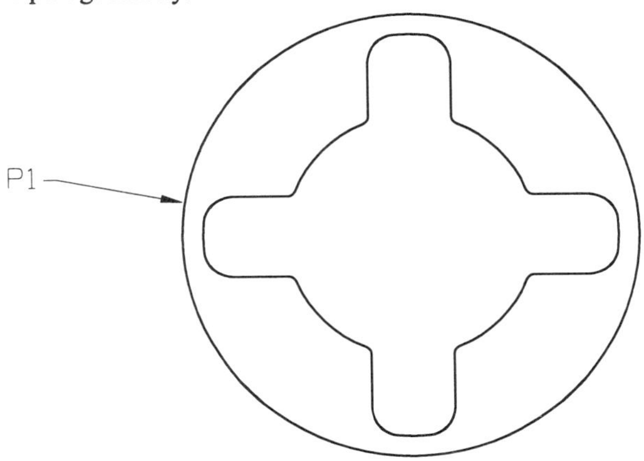

Figure 9.8

Step 2. Delete the existing toolpaths in the project.

Select **MAIN MENU →** **Toolpaths →** **Operations**

The Operations Manager menu with the contour toolpath appears below.

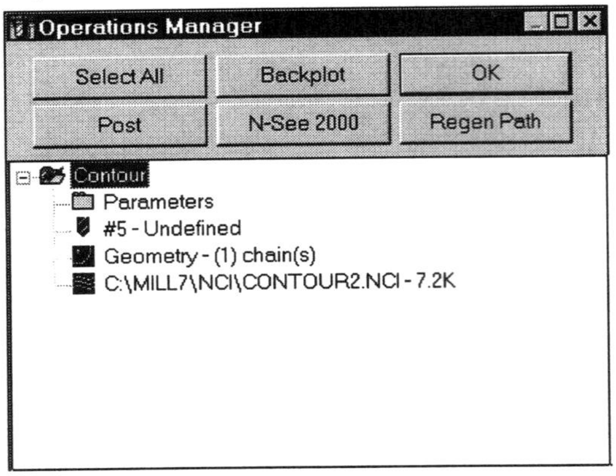

Click the toolpath section, then click right mouse button

Select **Delete**

Select **Yes** to "(1) operations have been selected and are about to be deleted. Are you sure?"

Select **OK**

Step 3. Initiate the contour module using the pick point in Figure 9.8.

Select **MAIN MENU →** **Toolpaths →** **Contour**

File name: **A**

Pick **P1**, then select **Done**

Step 4. Select a ¾" flat end mill.

Click the right mouse button, then select "**Get tool from library**"

Select **tool #241** "3/4 flat end mill"

Select **OK**

Set the tool parameters as below.

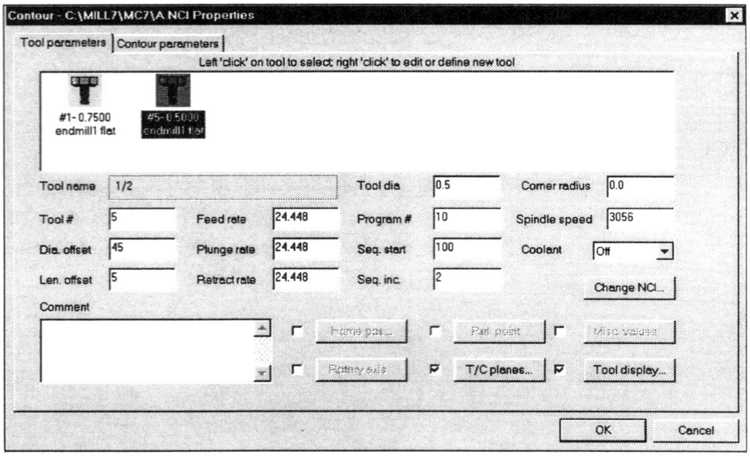

Step 5. Define the contour parameters.

Select the "**Contour parameters**" button

Set the contour parameters as below.

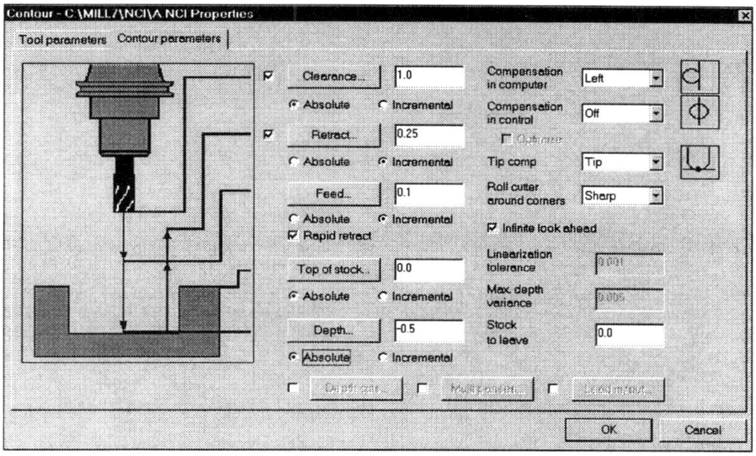

Select **OK**

The contouring toolpaths are generated as in Figure 9.9.

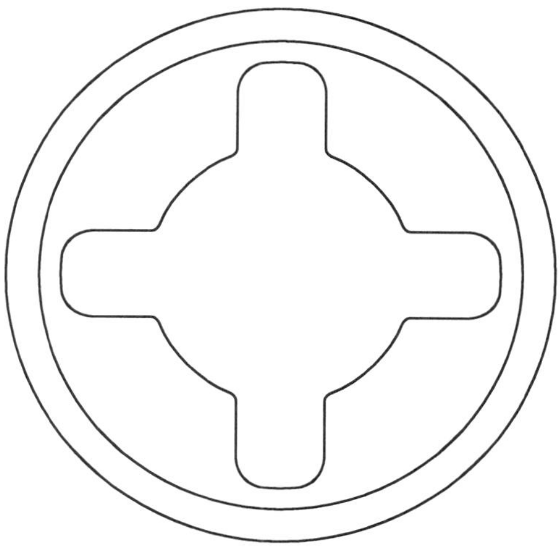

Figure 9.9

Step 6. Save the toolpath file as A.

Select **MAIN MENU →** **File →** **Save**
File name: **A**

Step 7. Initiate the Edit NCI utility.

Select **MAIN MENU →** **NC utils →** **Edit NCI**
Select **Yes** to "Operations have been modified. Create the NCI text file?"

The Edit NCI menu with the toolpath file A.NCI appears as below.

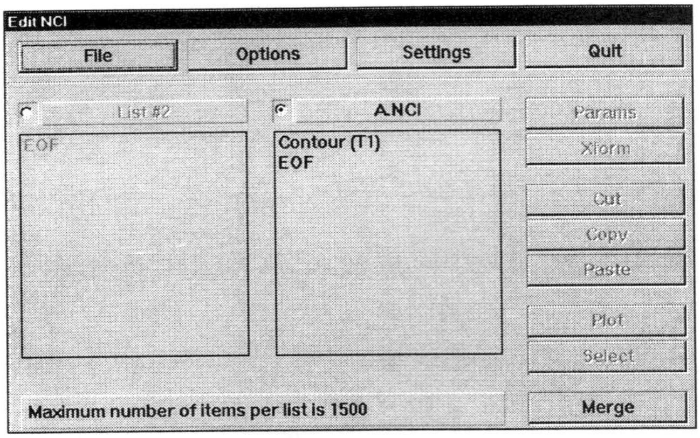

Step 7. Merge the toolpath file in conto2t.

Select **Merge** from Edit NCI menu
File name to read: **conto2t**
Select item to insert before, select **EOF**
The conto2t has been merged as shown below.

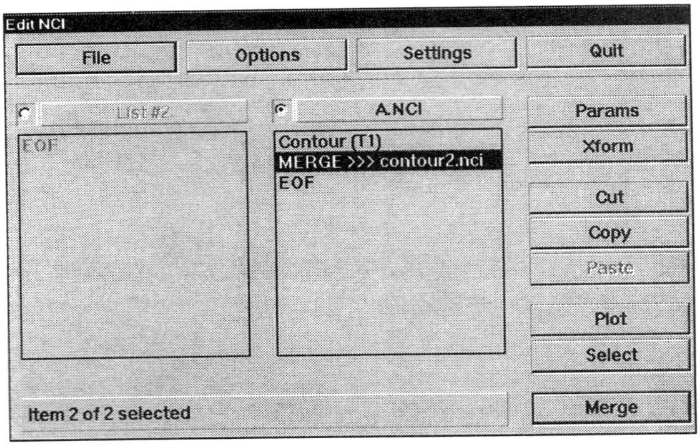

Step 8. Save the merged file as merge.

Select **File →** **Save As from Edit NCI menu**
File name: **merge**

Step 9. Exit Edit NCI utility.

Select **Quit**

Step 10. Backplot the new merged toolpaths.

Select **Backplot →** **NCI name**
File name: **merge**
Select **Run**

Toolpaths should be plotted as in Figure 9.10.

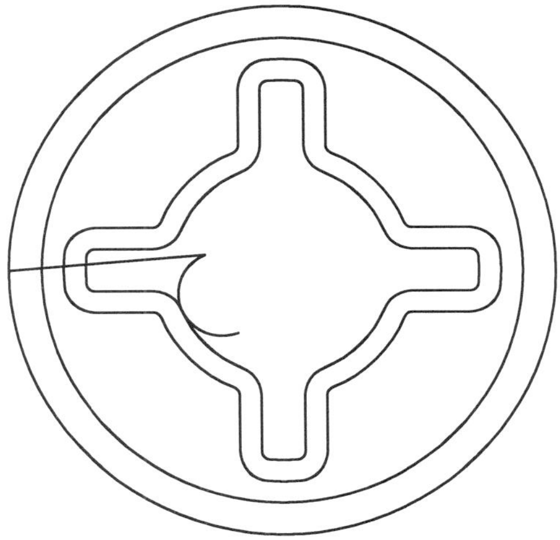

Figure 9.10

9.6 Toolpath Editing Functions

Mastercam provides four very useful toolpath editing functions to change the position, orientation, and size of existing toolpaths. These four functions are **mirror**, **rotate**, **scale**, and **translate** which are grouped under the Xform command.

Mirror: mirrors the toolpaths about the X axis, Y axis or any given line.

Rotate: rotates the toolpaths about the origin or any other point relative to the current construction plane.

Scale: increases or decreases the dimensions of toolpaths by a specified scale factor in each of three axes.

Translate: moves or copies the toolpaths to the specified new locations.

The major advantages of using toolpath editing functions are (1) eliminating the need to create the identical or similar feature geometries, and (2) eliminating the need to repeatedly use the NC modules to generate toolpaths for machining identical or similar part features.

The procedure for toolpath editing functions is:

1. Select MAIN MENU → NC utils → Edit NCI

2. Select the toolpath section(s) to be edited

3. Select Xform to open the Xform menu as below.

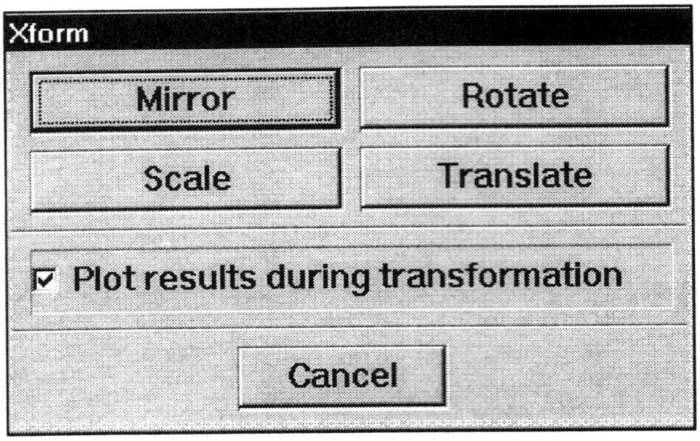

4. Select one of Xform functions (use Rotate function as an example).

5. Define the Xform – Rotate parameters.
The Xform – Rotate parameter menu should appear as below.

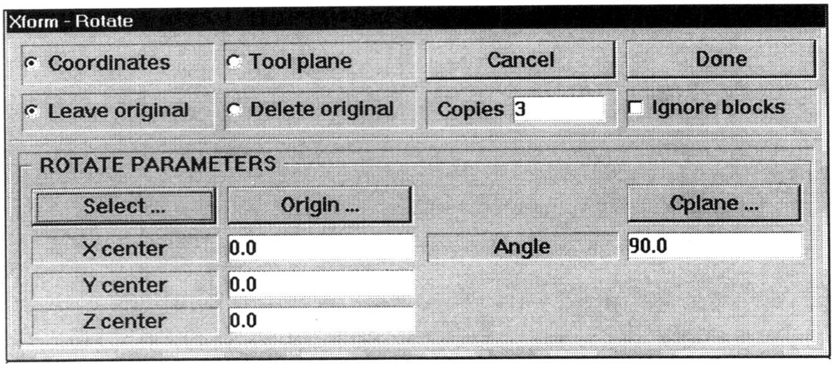

6. Select Done to implement the editing.

9.7 Mirroring Toolpaths

This function mirrors the existing toolpaths about an axis or a line. It is best suited for (1) those parts that have identical features that are symmetrical about an axis or a line (Figure 9.11a), and for (2) generating toolpaths to machine multiple workpieces that are symmetrically placed about an axis or a line (Figure 9.11b).

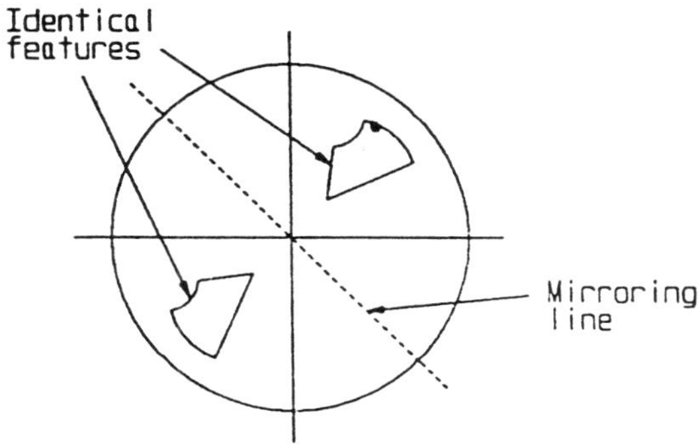

Figure 9.11a

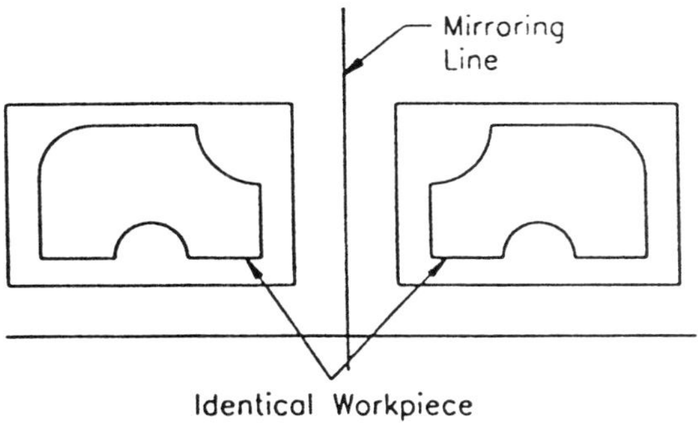

Figure 9.11b

Procedure of using the mirror function:

1. Generate the toolpaths to be mirrored. An existing toolpath should be available before using this function.
2. Select NC utils → Edit NCI to open the Edit NCI menu.
3. Select File → Open, then enter the file name.
4. Use the mouse to select the toolpath to be transformed.
5. Select Xform → Mirror
6. Define the Xform – Mirror parameters,
7. Select Done → Plot to show the mirrored toolpaths.

5 Project 5. Mirroring the toolpaths of a feature about X and Y axes to generate the toolpaths for three other locations

The part shown in Figure 9.12 has four features that are symmetrical about the X and Y axes. The Edit NCI – Mirror function is best suited for this project. We only need to create the geometry of one feature. Use the pocket module to generate the toolpaths for cutting this feature. This set of toolpaths is then copied to one adjacent side using the mirror function about the X axis. The toolpaths of two features are again copied to the other two locations by mirroring them about the Y axis.

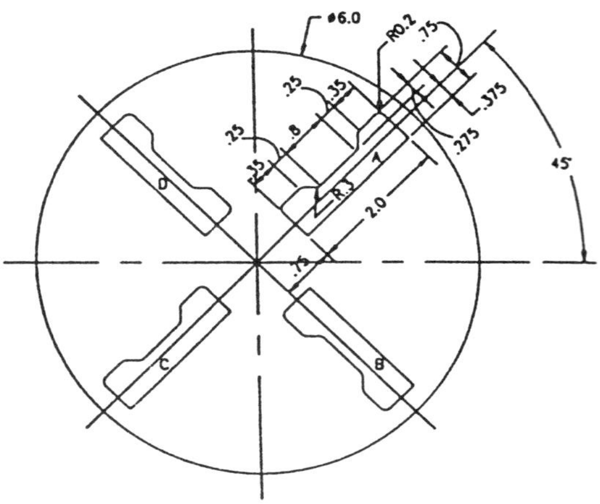

Figure 9.12a

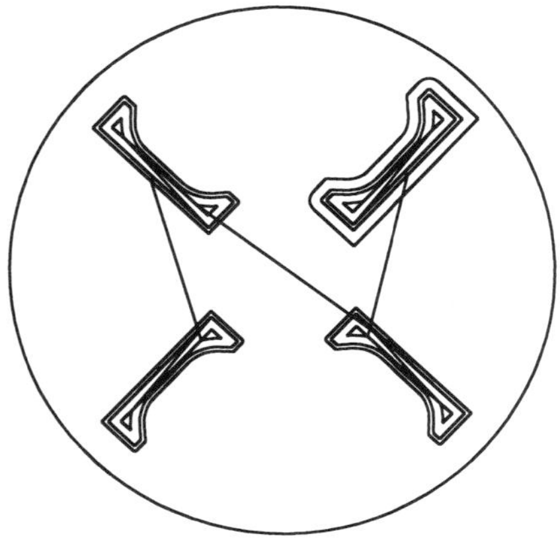

Figure 9.12b

Tips

1. Cutter diameter is 0.25".

2. Cutting parameters are:

3. Roughing cut spacing = 0.2"

4. One finish cut with spacing of 0.05"

5. Use the pocket module to generate toolpaths for feature A.

6. Use Edit NCI → Mirror function to copy the toolpaths to feature B. Mirror about X axis.

7. Mirror the toolpaths of features A and B about the Y axis to produce the other two features.

Step 1. Open the geometry file mirror1.

Select **MAIN MENU →** **File →** **Get**
File name: **mirror1**

The part drawing should appear as Figure 9.13.

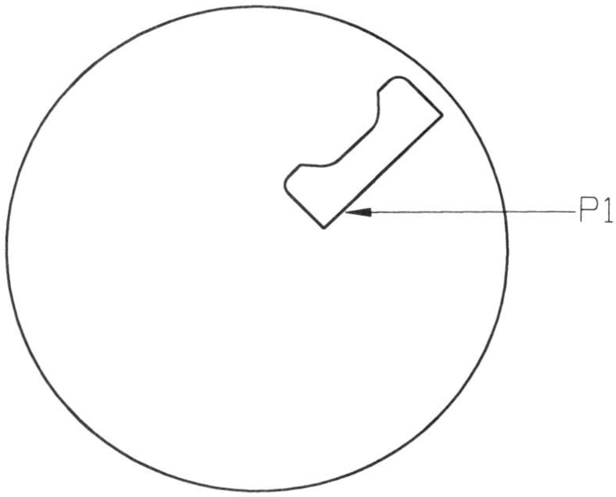

Figure 9.13

Step 2. Initiate the pocket module.

Select **MAIN MENU** → **Toolpaths** → **Pocket**
File name for toolpaths: **mirror1**
Select **Chain**, then pick **P1**
Select **Done**
Click the right mouse button, then select "**Get tool from library**"
Select **tool #235** (1/4 flat end mill)
Select **OK**
Set the tool parameters as below.

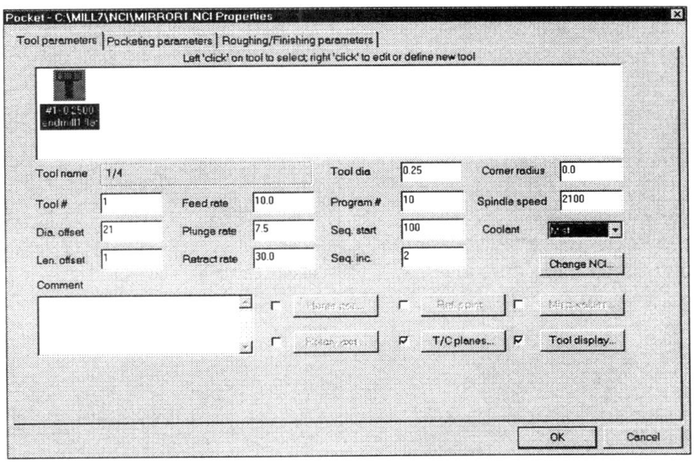

Step 3. Define the pocketing parameters.

Click the "**Pocketing parameters**" button

Set the pocketing parameters as below.

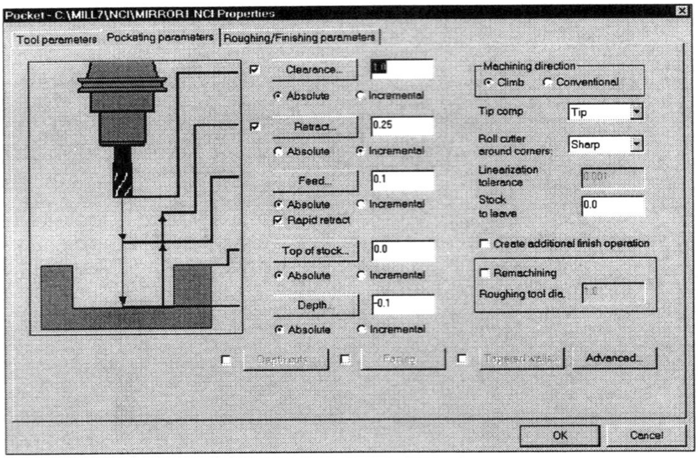

Step 4. Define the roughing and finishing parameters.

Click the "**Roughing/Finishing parameters**" button

Set the roughing and finishing parameters as below.

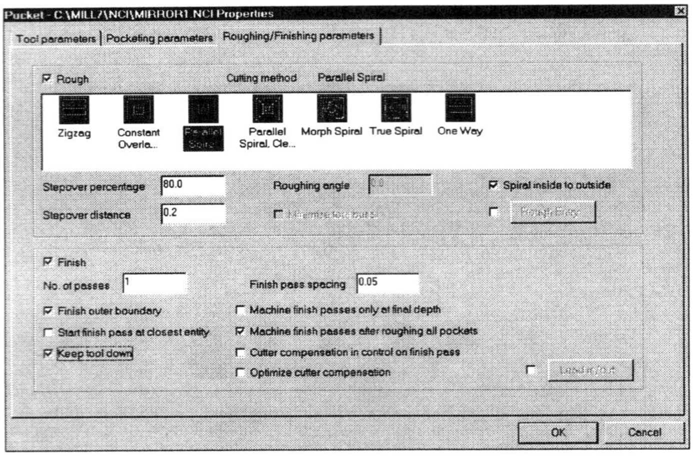

Select **OK** to generate pocketing toolpaths

The pocketing toolpaths are shown in Figure 9.14.

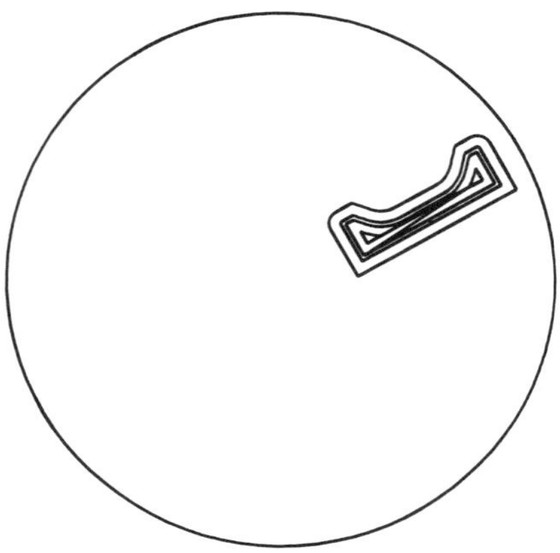

Figure 9.14

Step 5. Initiate the Edit NCI function.

Select **MAIN MENU** → **NC utils** → **Edit NCI**
Select **Yes** to "Operations have been modified. Create the NCI text file?"
Select **Yes** to overwrite already existing toolpath file
The initial Edit NCI menu should appear as below.

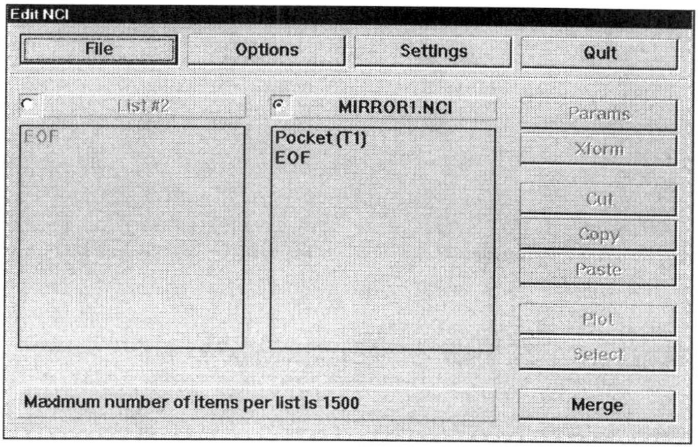

Step 6. Mirror the toolpaths about the X axis.

Click the "**Pocket (T1)**" toolpath section to highlighted it in blue
Select **Xform** from Edit NCI menu to open the Xform menu as below.

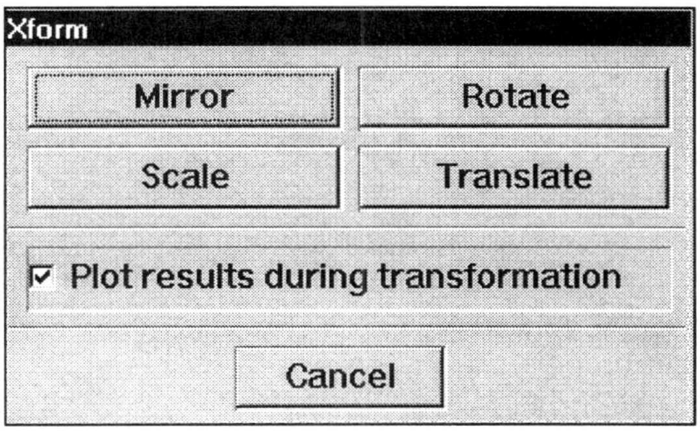

Select **Mirror**
Set the Xform – Mirror parameters as below.

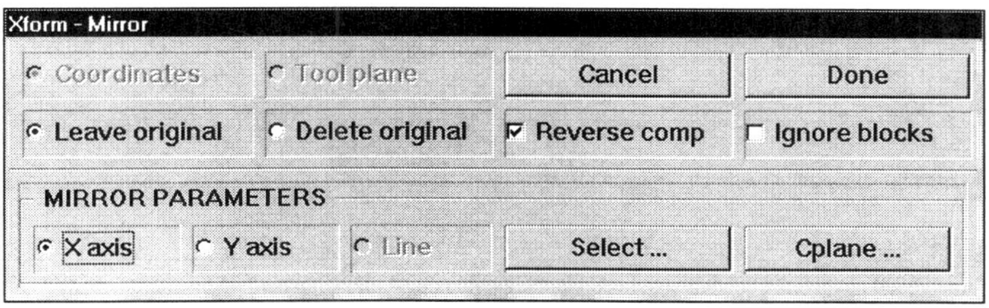

Select **Done**

The mirrored toolpaths are added as in Figure 9.15 and a new toolpath section is added to Edit NCI menu as shown below.

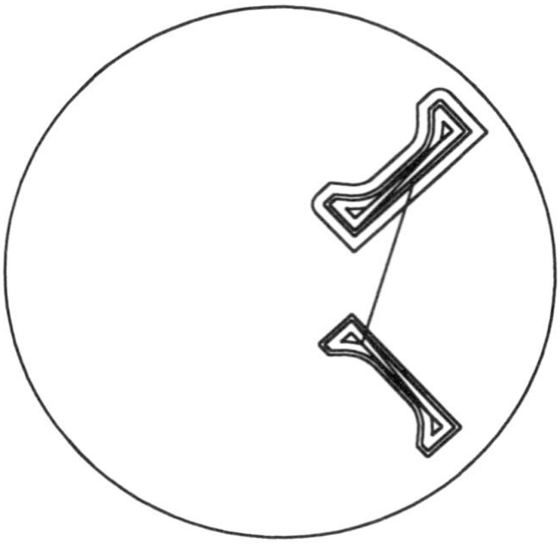

Figure 9.15

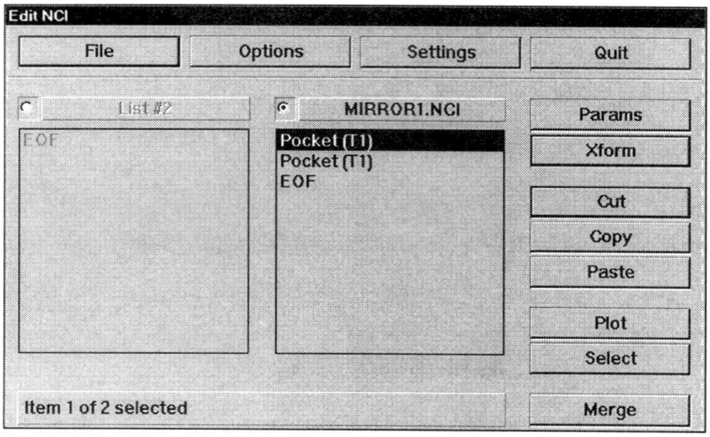

Step 7. Mirror the toolpaths for two pockets about the Y axis.

Hold down the Shift key and click on the last operation on the list to select both pocket (T1) operations

Select **Xform** → **Mirror**

Set the Xform – Mirror parameters as indicated below.

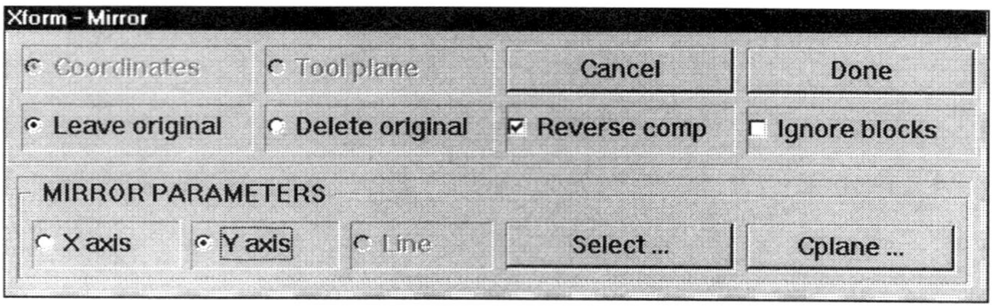

Select **Done** to complete the mirroring

The final toolpaths should resemble Figure 9.16.

Figure 9.16

Step 8. Save the toolpaths file.

Select **File** → **Save**
Select **Yes** to overwrite the existing file
Select **Quit** from Edit NCI menu

9.8 Rotating Toolpaths

The Rotate function moves (or copies) existing toolpaths of selected operations by rotating them about the origin or any given point. It is best suited to generate the toolpaths for identical patterns or features that are symmetrical about a point (Figure 9.17).

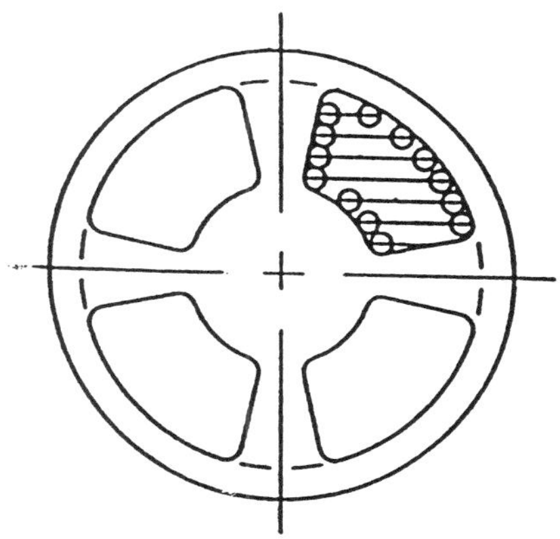

Figure 9.17

Figure 9.18 illustrates the definition of rotation angle. In Top and Front Cplane, angle is measured from the +X direction and is positive in the counterclockwise direction. In Side Cplane, the angle is measured from +Y axis.

6

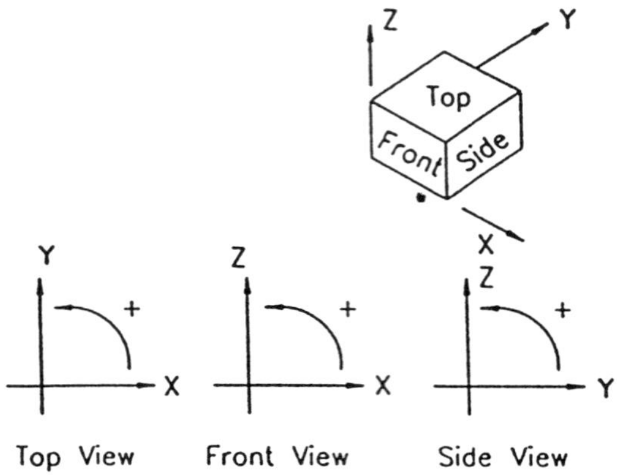

Figure 9186

Procedure of using the rotate function:
1. Generate the toolpaths for the features to be rotated.

2. Use NC utils → Edit NCI to open the Edit NCI menu.

3. Select File → Open then enter the file name.

4. Use the mouse to select the sections of the toolpath to be transformed.

5. Select Xform → Rotate.

6. Define the Xform – Rotate parameters.

7. Select Done → Plot to show the rotated toolpaths.

Project 6. Rotating toolpaths about the origin

The process of generating toolpaths for cutting the part shown in Figure 9.19 can be significantly simplified by using the Edit NCI → Rotate function. The raw material is a solid circular plate.

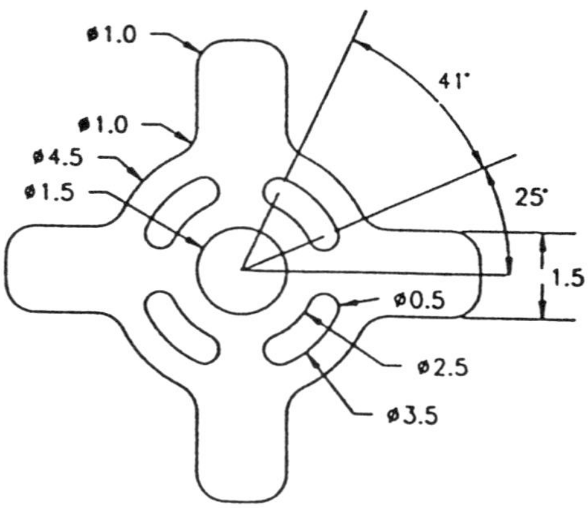

Figure 9.19a

Figure 9.19b

⌛**Tips** 1. Use the pocket module to rough cut one of the four pockets. The roughing toolpaths are then copied to the other three locations by the rotate command. This allows the final external profile to be produced by using the contour module in one pass.
2. Save the toolpaths as part1.

3. Open the geometry file (rotate1) again. Use the contour module to cut external profile.

4. Use the contour module to cut one of four circular grooves. Cutter diameter for grooving is 3/8". The rotate command is used again to copy the toolpaths to the other three positions.
5. Merge the two toolpath files and save the merged toolpath file as rotation.

Step 1. Open the part geometry file rotate1.

Select **MAIN MENU →** **File →** **Get**
File name: **rotate1**
The part geometry should appear as Figure 9.20.

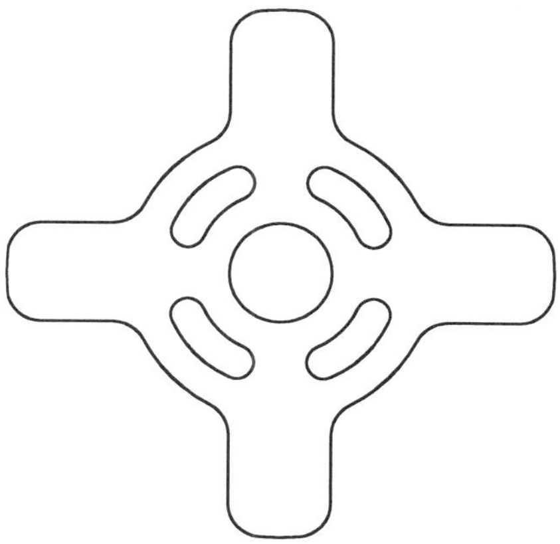

Figure 9.20

Step 2. Create a construction circle.

Select **MAIN MENU →** **Create →** **Arc →** **Cir pt+dia**
Enter the center point: **0,0**
Enter the diameter: **8.4**
The new drawing becomes Figure 9.21.

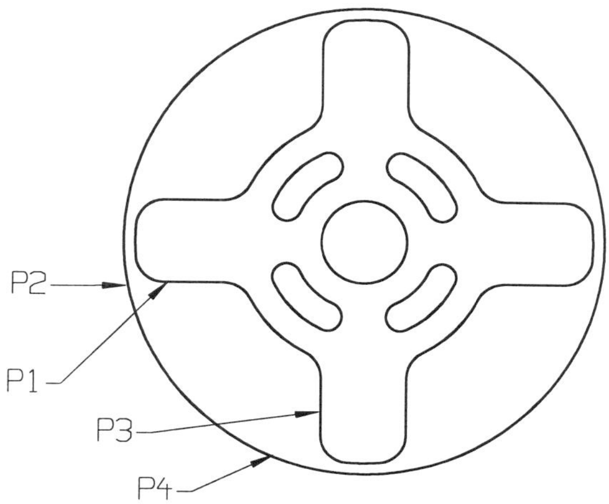

Figure 9.21

Step 3. Extend two lines to form a closed contour for pocketing.

Use the pick points in Figure 9.21.
Select **MAIN MENU →** **Modify →** **Trim →** **1 entity**
Pick **P1** to select the entity to trim
Pick **P2** to select the entity to trim to
Pick **P3** to select the entity to trim
Pick **P4** to select the entity to trim to
The two extended lines are shown in Figure 9.29.

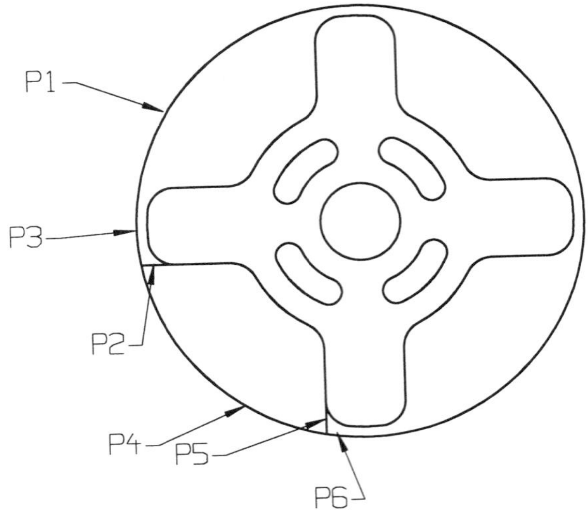

Figure 9.22

Step 4. Break the construction circle into three segments at the intersection points with the two extended lines.

Use the pick points in Figure 9.22.
Select **MAIN MENU →** **Modify →** **Break →** **2 pieces**
Pick **P1** to select the entity to break
Select **Intersec** from the Point menu
Pick **P2** and **P3** to determine the breaking point
Pick **P4** to select the entity to break
Select **Intersec**
Pick **P5** and **P6** to determine the breaking point

The drawing appearing on the screen does not change even though the outer circle has been broken into 3 pieces. The drawing is redrawn in Figure 9.23.

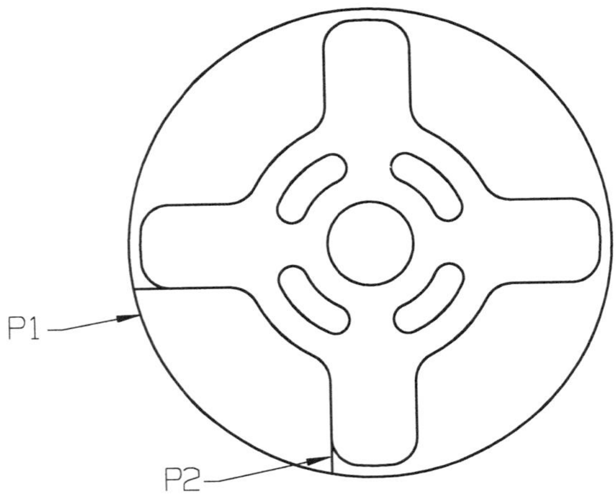

Figure 9.23

Step 5. Initiate the pocket module using pick points in Figure 8.31.

Select **MAIN MENU →** **Toolpaths →** **Pocket**
File name: **part1**
Select **Chain**, then pick **P1** and **P2**
Select **End here →** **Done**
Click the right mouse button, then select "**Get tool from library**"
Select **tool #241** (3/4 flat end mill)
Select **OK**
Set the tool parameters as below.

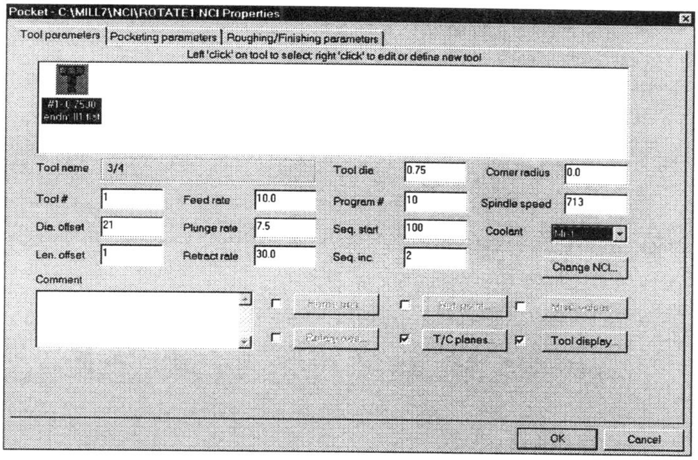

Step 6. Define the pocketing parameters.

Click the "**Pocketing parameters**" button
Set the pocketing parameters as below.

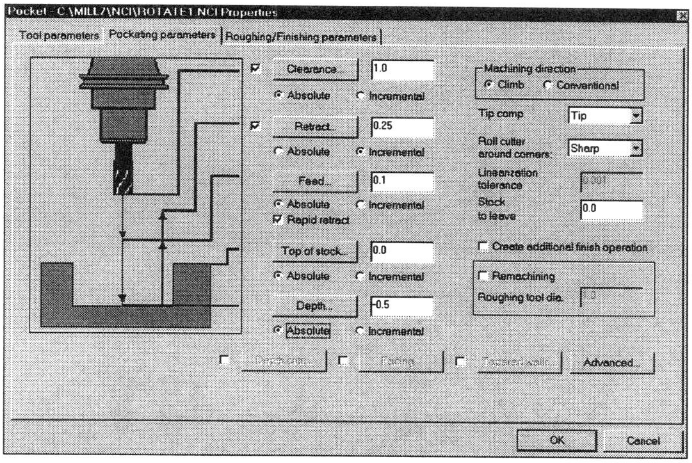

Step 7. Define the roughing and finishing parameters.

Click the "**Roughing/Finishing parameters**" button

Set the roughing and finishing parameters as below.

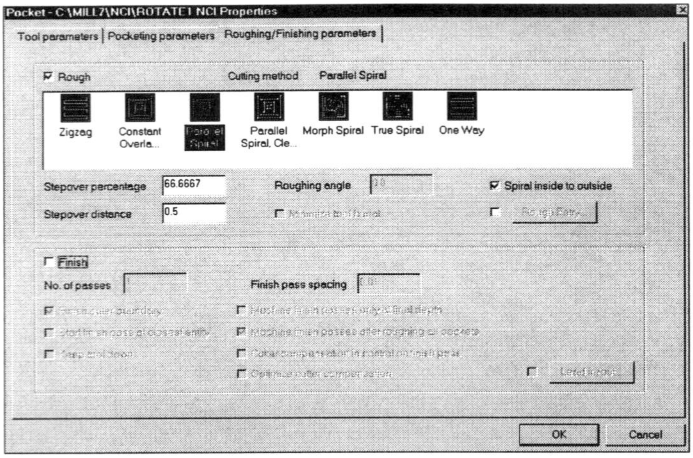

Select **OK** to generate the pocketing toolpaths as shown in Figure 8.32.

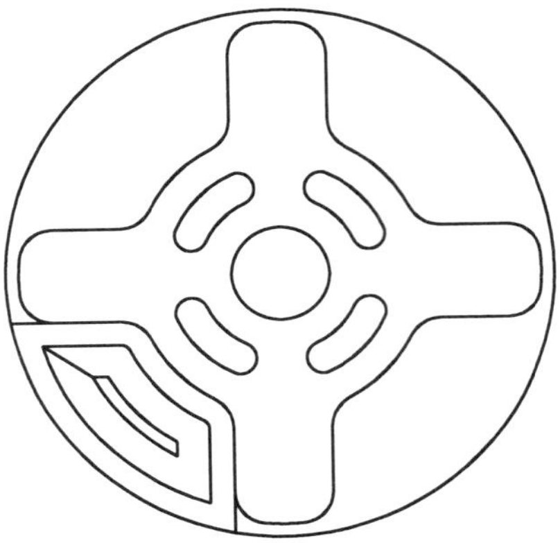

Figure 9.24

Step 8. Copy the pocketing toolpaths to three locations.

Select **MAIN MENU** → **NC utils** → **Edit NCI**

Select **Yes** to "Operations have been modified. Create the NCI tect file?"

Click the "**Pocket(T1)**" toolpath section

Select **Xform** → **Rotate**

Set the Xform – Rotate parameters as below.

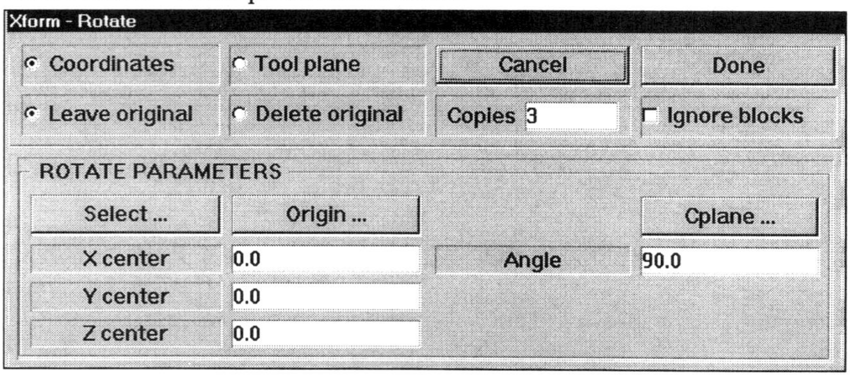

Select **Done** to copy the toolpaths to three locations
Select **Plot**
The four sets of toolpaths appear as in Figure 9.25.

Figure 9.25

Select **Done** to return to Edit NCI menu

Step 9. Save the toolpath file as part1.

Select **File** → **Save**
Select **Yes** to overwrite the existing file
Select **Quit** to exit Edit NCI menu

Step 10. Open the geometry file rotate1 again.

Select **MAIN MENU** → **File** → **Get**
File name: **rotate1**
Select **No** to "MC7 file has changed. Save it.?"
The part geometry should appear as in Figure 9.26.

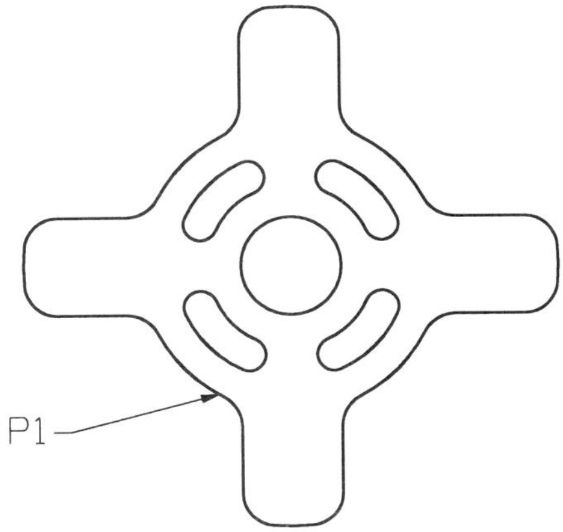

Figure 9.26

Step 11. Initiate the contour module using the pick point in Figure 9.26.

Select **MAIN MENU** → **Toolpaths** → **Contour**
File name for toolpaths: **part2**
Select **Chain**
Pick **P1**, then select **Done**
Choose **#214 Tool**

Set the tool parameters as below.

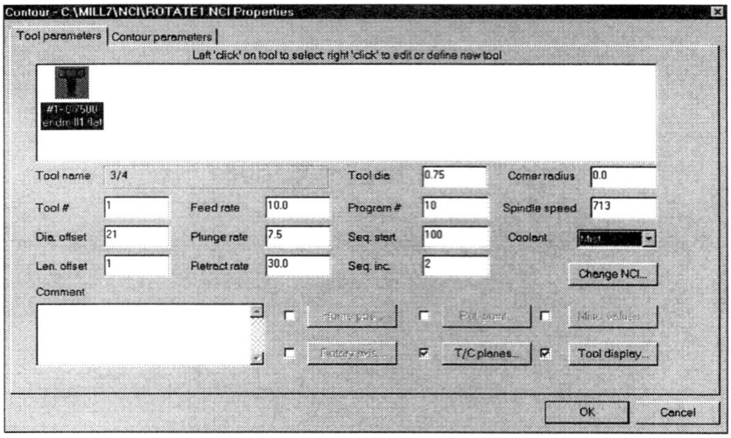

Step 12. Define the contour parameters.

Click the "**Contour parameters**" button
Set the contour parameters as below.

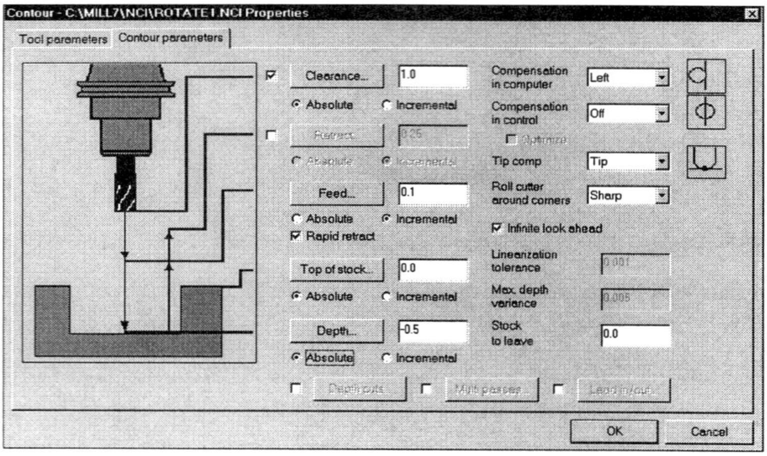

Select **OK** to generate the contouring toolpaths as shown in Figure 8.35.

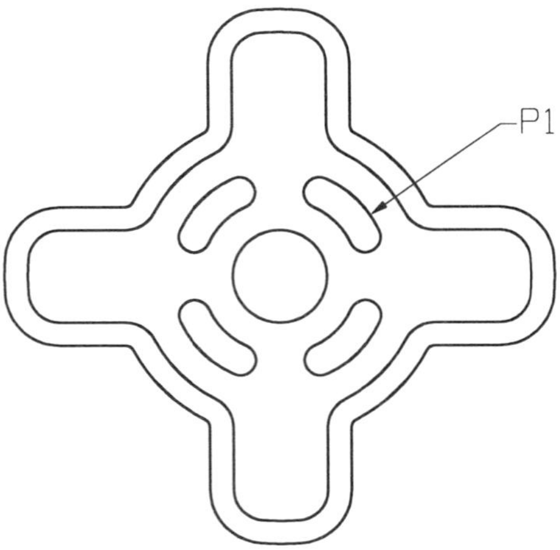

Figure 9.27

Step 13. Initiate the contour module using the pick point in Figure 8.35.

Select **Contour** → **Chain**
Pick **P1**, then select **Done**
Click the right mouse button, then select "**Get tool from library**"
Select **tool #237** (3/8 flat end mill)
Select **OK**

Set the tool parameters as below.

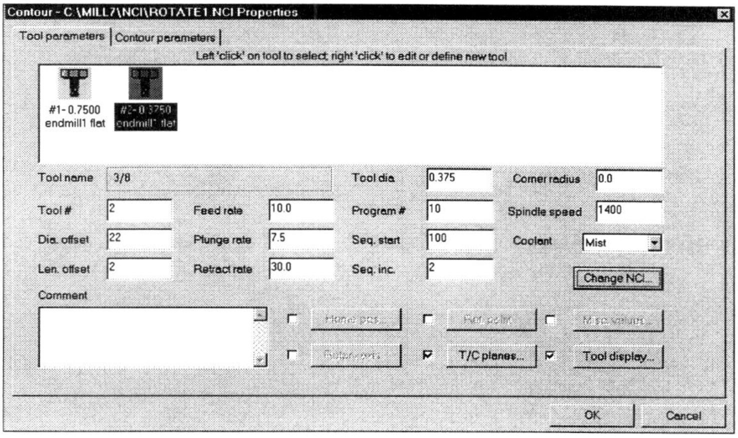

Step 14. Define the contour parameters.

Click the "**Contour parameters**" button
Set the contour parameters as below.

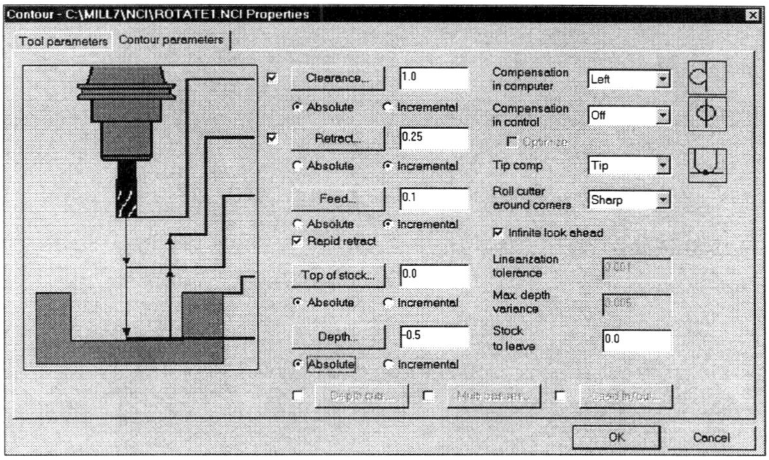

Select **OK** to generate contouring toolpaths as shown in Figure 8.36.

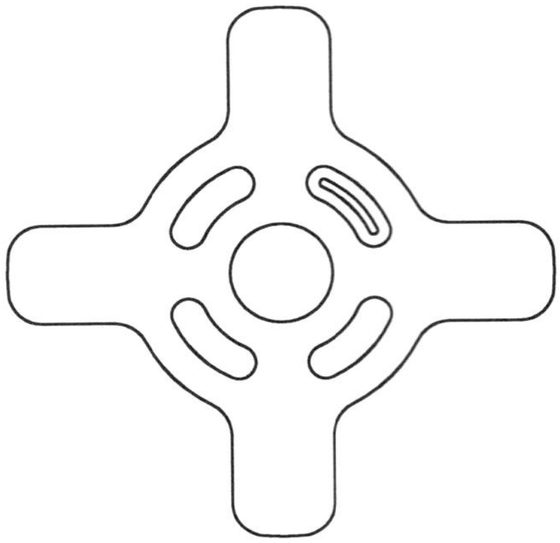

Figure 9.28

Step 15. Initiate the Edit NCI function.

Select **MAIN MENU →   NC utils →   Edit NCI**

Select **Yes** to "Operations have been modified. Create the NCI text file?"

The two toolpath sections appear on the Edit NCI menu as below.

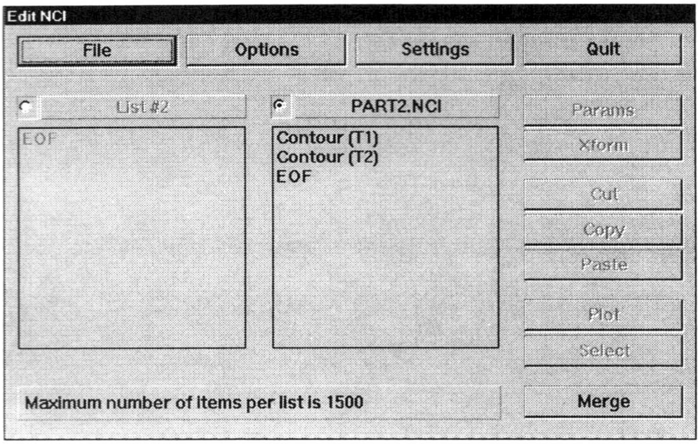

Step 16. Copy the sets of toolpaths to their other locations.

Click the (Contour (T2)) toolpath section

Select **Xform →   Rotate**

Set the Xform – Rotate parameters as below.

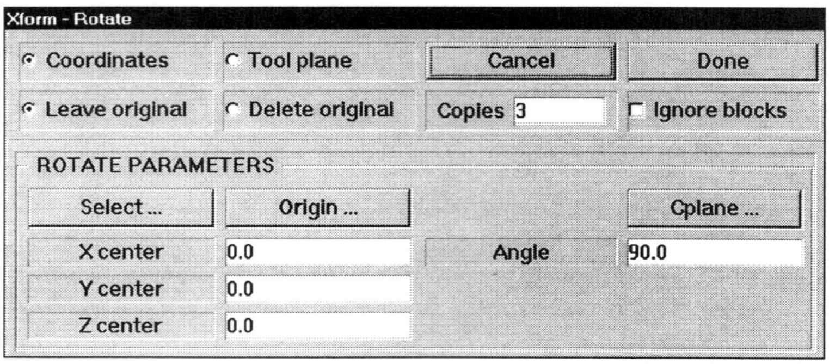

Select **Done**

The groove contouring toolpath is copied to three locations as shown in Figure 9.29 and reflects in Edit NCI menu as below.

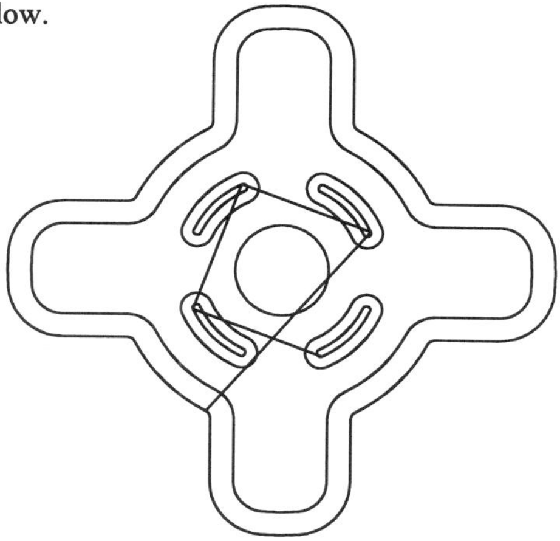

Figure 9.29

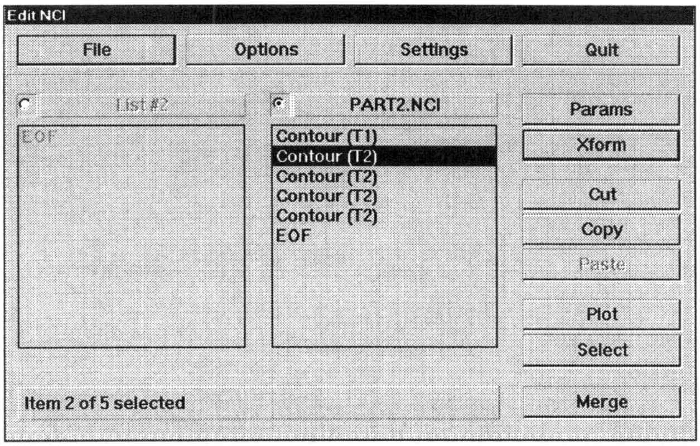

Step 17. Merge two toolpath files.

Select **Merge**
File name to read: **part1**
Click "**Contour (T1)**" to select the insertion point
The new toolpath file becomes as below.

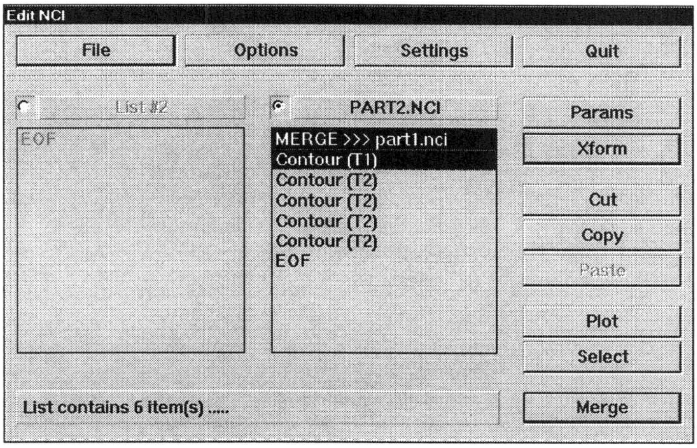

Select **Plot →** **Done**
The final toolpaths should resemble Figure 9.30.

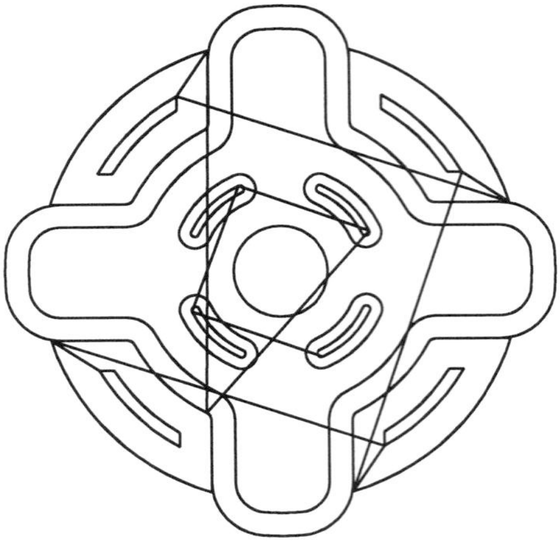

Figure 9.30

Step 18. Save the merged toolpath file as rotation.

Select **File →** **Save As**
File name for toolpath: **rotation**
Select **Quit** to exit Edit NCI menu

9.9 Scaling Toolpaths

Scale functions increase or decrease the actual dimensions of toolpaths by a specified scale factor along each of the three axes. Two important factors to be determined in scaling are the scaling center and the scaling factor in each of the three axes. The scaling center determines where the toolpaths start. The scaling factor decides which axis coordinates will be scaled and by how much.

Scale Factor:

X	Y	Z	
1	≠ 1	1	X and Z coordinates no change
≠ 1	1	1	Y and Z coordinates no change

Scaling factor > 1 enlarges the toolpath dimensions
Scaling factor = 1 toolpath dimensions do not change
Scaling factor < 1 reduce the toolpath dimensions

Tips 1. When a value of 1 is given to the scale factor of an axis, the toolpath dimensions in that particular axis do not change.

2. The location of the scaling center drastically affects the locations of the scaled toolpath. The origin and the center of the original toolpath are the two positions which can be used as the scaling center in that the scaled toolpath can be easily predicted (Figure 9.31). Using other positions as the scaling center may result in undesired toolpaths (Figure 9.32).

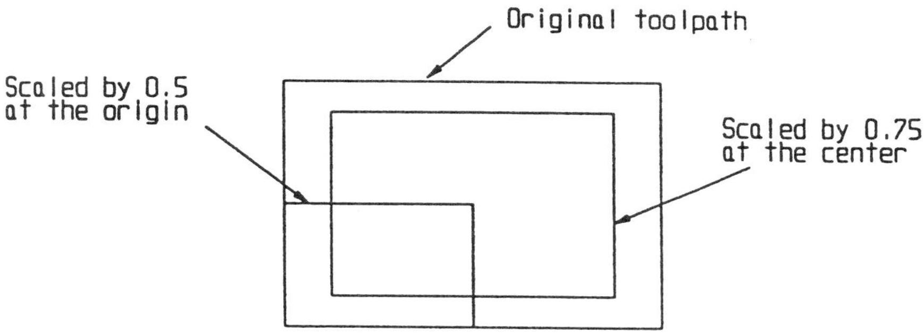

Figure 9.31

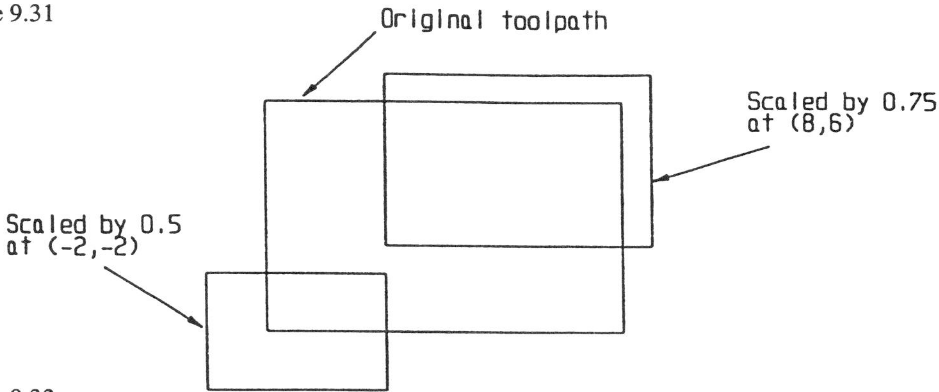

Figure 9.32

3. Do not use the scale function to modify toolpaths unless you know where the exact toolpath locations will be after being scaled.
4. Using the same cutter to cut the scaled toolpaths may result in reduced or enlarged finished parts because the offset values for the scaled toolpaths have been scaled to a smaller or larger value.

Project 7. Scaling project

The part shown in Figure 9.33 has three hexagonal pockets with different depths. The base circle of the outer pocket has a diameter of 6". The X and Y coordinates of the second pocket are scaled down by a scaling factor of 0.75. The third pocket is scaled from the second pocket by the same scaling factor of 0.75. The Z-depth in the second pocket is –0.3" which can be obtained by a scaling factor of 2 from the first pocket depth (Z = -0.15"), and the depth of the third pocket (-0.6") is scaled from the depth of the second pocket by the factor of 2.

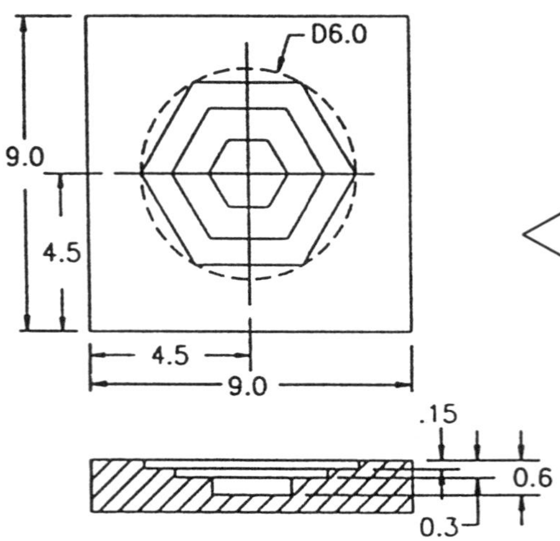

Figure 9.33a

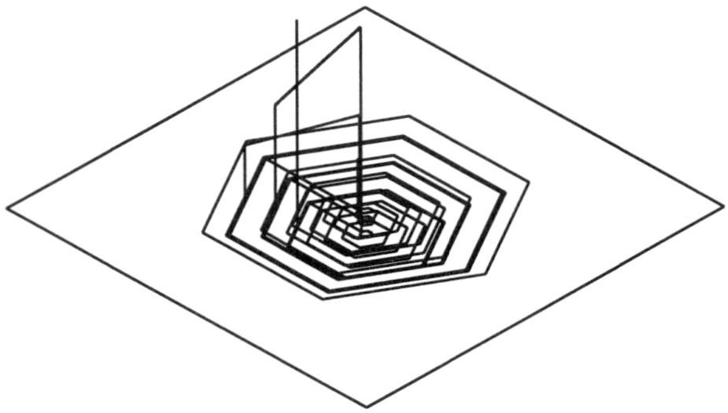

Figure 9.33b

Tips 1. Construct a larger hexagon to use as the pocketing profile. Use this hexagon to generate pocketing toolpaths.

2. Scale the pocketing toolpaths for the other two hexagonal pockets.

3. Use NC utils → Edit NCI → Xform → Scale commands to scale the pocketing toolpaths. The number of steps should be set to 2. The scaling factors are below:

Axis	Scaling factor	Scaling center
X	0.75	(0,0)
Y	0.75	
Z	2.0	

The depth of the first set of scaled toolpaths is –0.3 (or –0.15 X 2) and the second set of scaled toolpaths is –0.6 (or –0.3 x 2). Notice that the number of steps is more than one. The second set of scaled toolpaths is scaled after the first set by the scaling factor of the axis. When the second set of scaled toolpaths needs to have the same spacing as the first set of scaled toolpaths, set the number of steps to one and then repeatedly scale the original toolpaths by changing the scaling factor to the proper value.

In this project we can use two sets of scaling factors to obtain the equally spaced dimensions for the two scaled pockets:

	X	Y	Z
First scaled pocket	0.75	0.75	2.0
Second scaled pocket	0.5	0.5	3.0

3. Use the backplot function to verify the toolpaths. When verification of the toolpath coordinates, set the geometry parameter in the Backplot command to "Save the geometry". This allows a set of geometric entities to be created by using the coordinates of toolpaths. We then can use the Analyze → Entity commands to verify the coordinates of toolpaths.

Step 1. Open the part geometry file scale1.

Select **MAIN MENU →** **File →** **Get**
File name: **scale1**
The geometry appears as Figure 8.42.

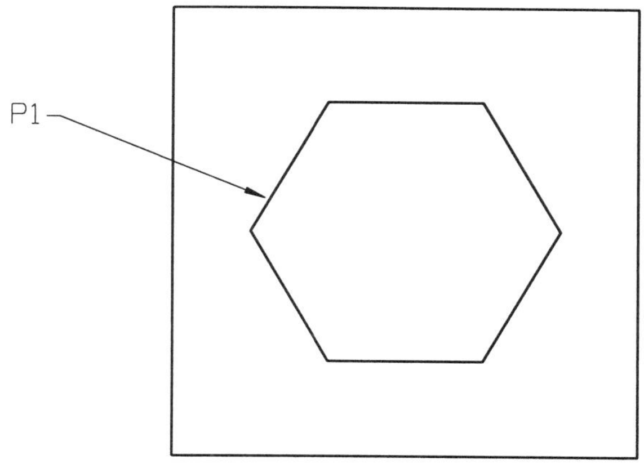

Figure 9.34

Step 2. Initiate the pocket module; use the pick point in Figure 8.42.

Select **MAIN MENU →** **Toolpaths →** **Pocket**
File name for toolpaths: **scale1**
Select **Chain**, then pick **P1**
Select **Done**
Click the right mouse button, then select **"Get tool from library"**
Select **tool #241** (3/4 flat end mill)
Select **OK**
Set the tool parameters as below.

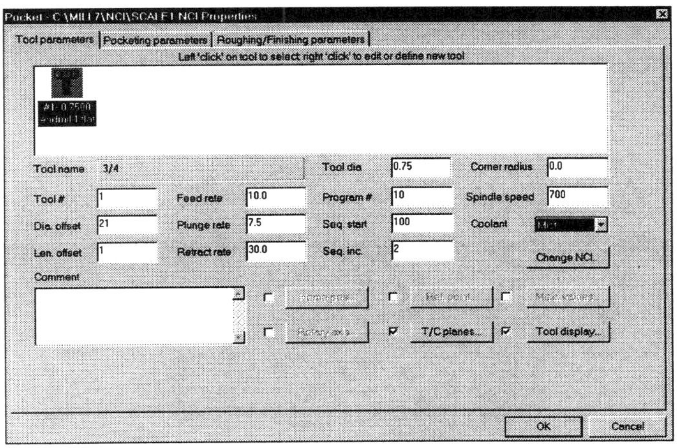

Step 3. Define the pocketing parameters.

Click the **"Pocketing parameters"** button

Set the pocketing parameters as below

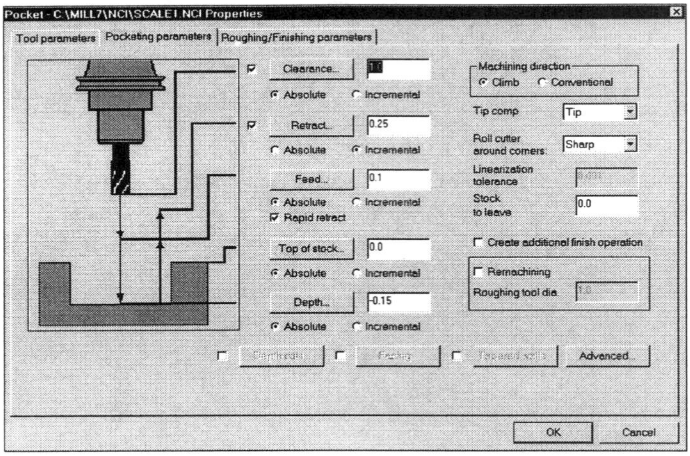

Step 4. Define the Roughing and finishing parameters.

Click on the "**Roughing/Finishing parameters**" button

Set the roughing and finishing parameters as below.

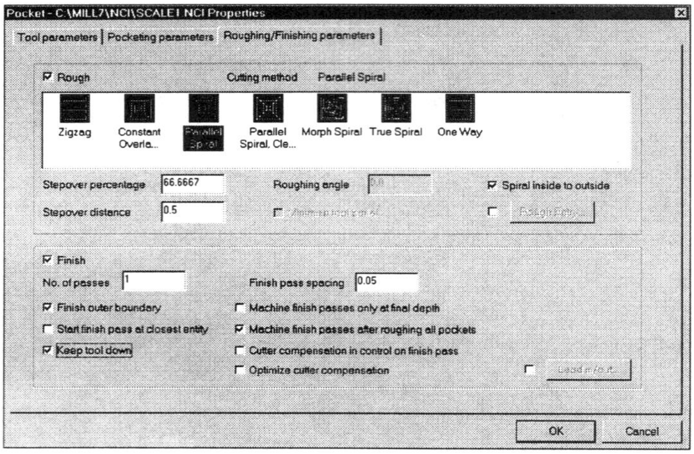

Select **OK** to generate the pocketing toolpaths as in Figure 8.43.

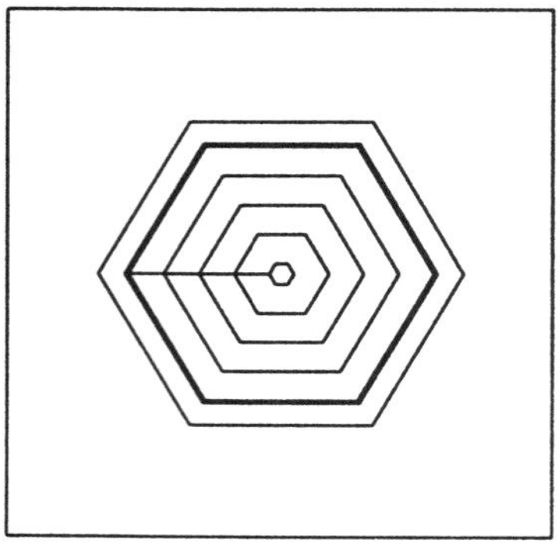

Figure 9.35

Step 5. Scale the toolpaths.

Select **MAIN MENU** → **NC utils** → **Edit NCI**

Select **Yes** to "Operations have been modified. Create the NCI text file?"

Select "**Pocket (T1)**" toolpath section

Select **Xform** → **Scale**

Set the Xform – Scale parameters as below.

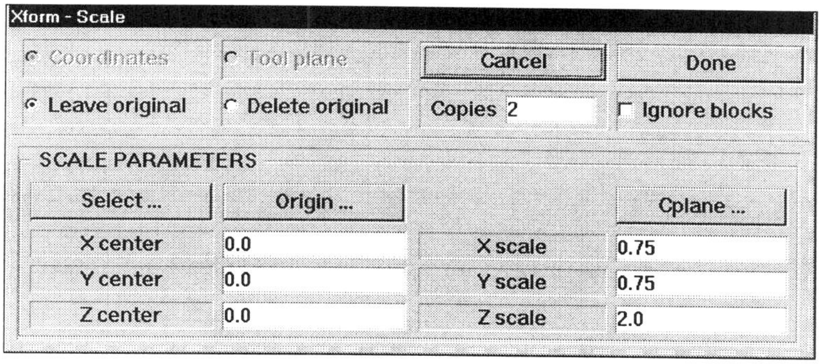

Select **Done** to generate scaled toolpaths
Two sections of toolpaths are added to the toolpath file
Select **Plot**
The two sets of scaled toolpaths should resemble Figure 8.44.

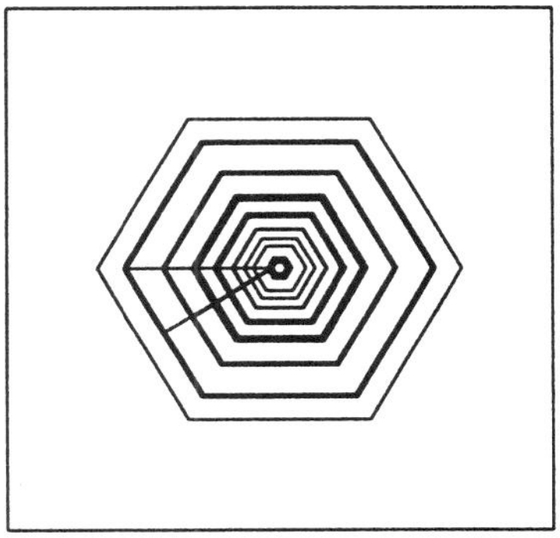

Figure 9.36

Step 6. Save the toolpath file as scale1.

Select **File** → **Save as**
File name: scale1t
Select **Quit** to exit Edit NCI menu

Step 7. Backplot the toolpaths.

Select **Gview** → **Isometric**
Select **NC utils** → **Backplot** → **Run**

The toolpaths will be sequentially plotted on the screen. The final toolpaths shown in isometric view appear as in Figure 8.45.

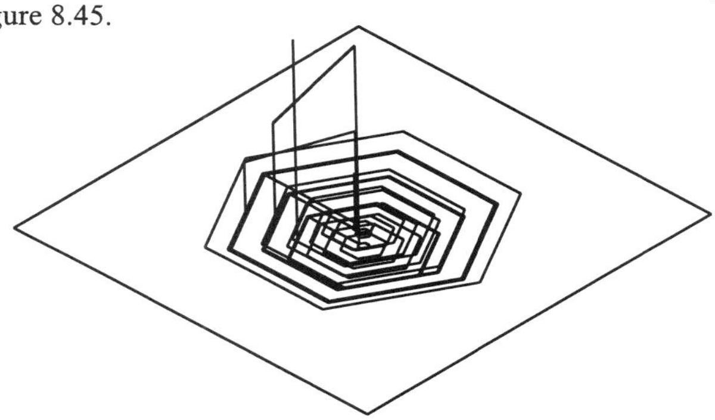

Figure 9.37

9.10 Translating Toolpaths

The translate function moves or copies the toolpath of selected operations to new locations. The locations to be moved can be defined by one of the following four methods:

Rectang:	specifies the incremental distance to be translated in the X, Y, and Z directions.
Polar:	specifies the incremental distance and the desired angle to define the translation position.
Between points:	specifies the translation distances between two points.
Between views:	translates the toolpaths from one view to another.

The translation function can be readily applied in the following three applications:

1. Change coordinate system (Figure 9.38). When the toolpaths are translated, this can be regarded as an altered coordinate system.

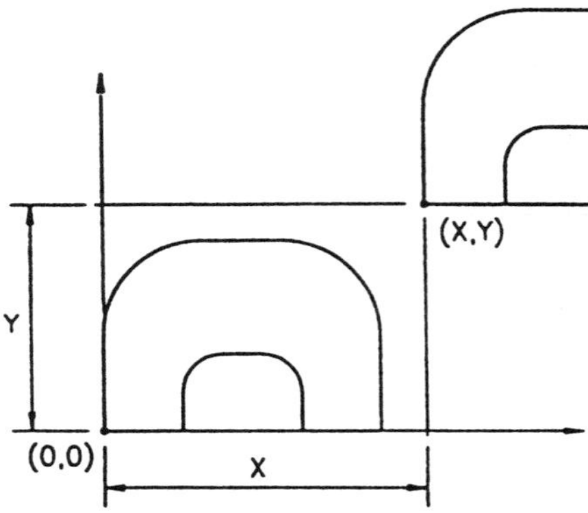

Figure 9.38

2. Generate toolpaths for identical part features located at different locations on the same workpiece (Figure 8.47).

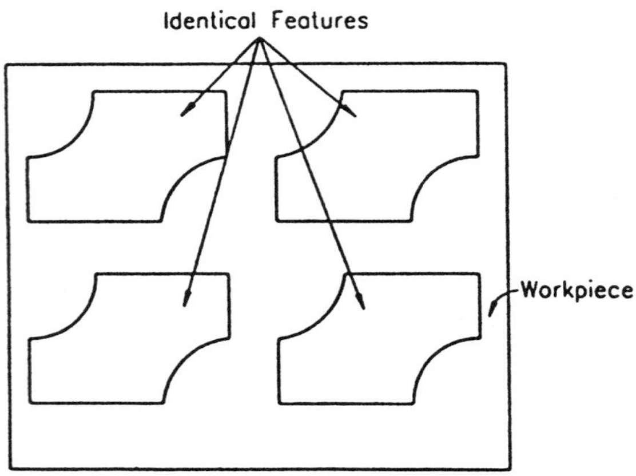

Figure 9.39

3. Generate toolpaths for producing multiple identical workpieces in one part program (Figure 9.40). This facilitates the machining of multiple workpieces in one machine setup.

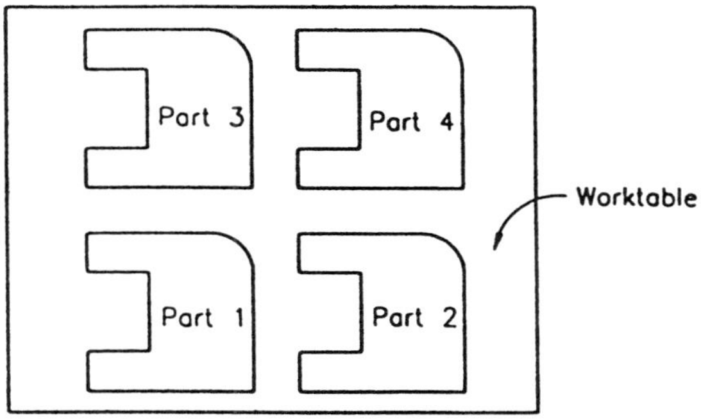

Figure 9.40

Project 10. Translating project

The part shown in Figure 8.49 has three identical features. We can generate the toolpaths for one feature and then use Edit NCI → Translate function to copy the toolpaths to the other two locations.

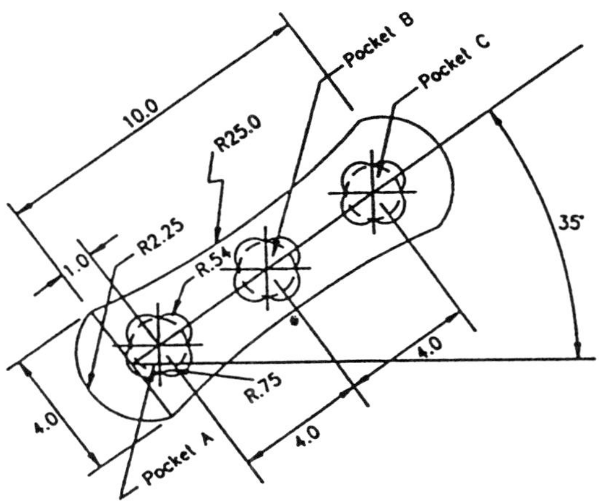

Figure 9.41a

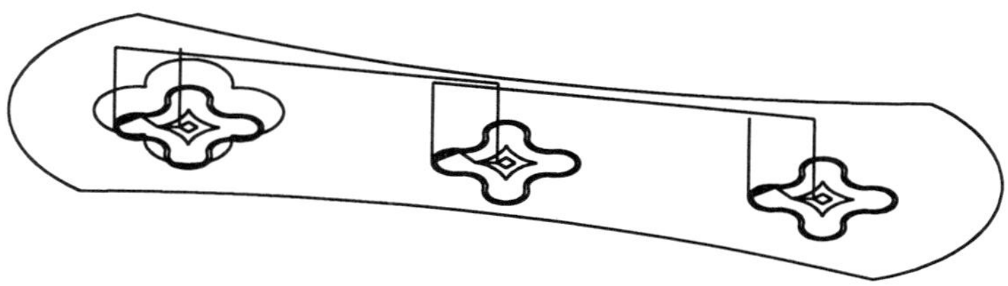

Figure 9.41b

⌛**Tips** 1. Cutter diameter = 0.5".

2. Use the pocket module to generate the toolpaths for cutting the pocket A.

3. Use Edit NCI → Xform → Translate function to copy the pocketing toolpaths to the other two locations.

Step 1. Open the part geometry file trans1.

Select **MAIN MENU → File → Get**
File name: **trans1**
The part geometry appears as in Figure 9.42.

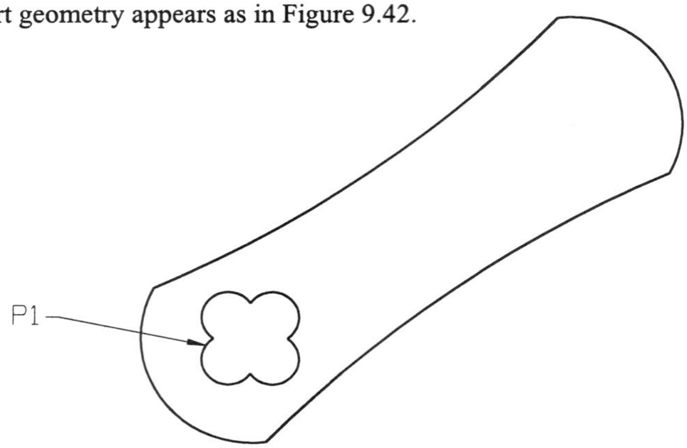

Figure 9.42

Step 2. Initiate the pocket module using the pick point in Figure 8.50.

Select **MAIN MENU → Toolpaths → Pocket**
File name for toolpaths: **trans1**
Select **Chain**
Pick **P1**, then select **Done**
Click the right mouse button, then select "**Get tool from library**"
Select **tool #239** (1/2 flat end mill)
Select **OK**
Set the tool parameters as below.

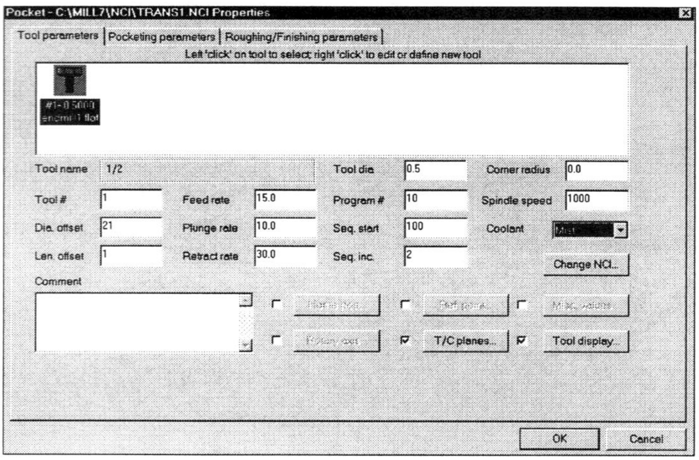

Step 3. Define the pocketing parameters.

Click on the "**Pocketing parameters**" button
Define the pocketing parameters as below.

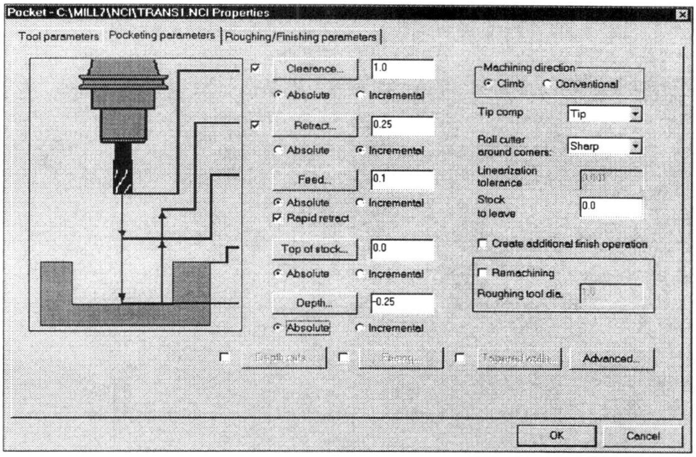

Step 4. Define the roughing and finishing parameters.

Click on the "**Roughing/Finishing parameters**" button
Set the roughing and finishing parameters as below.

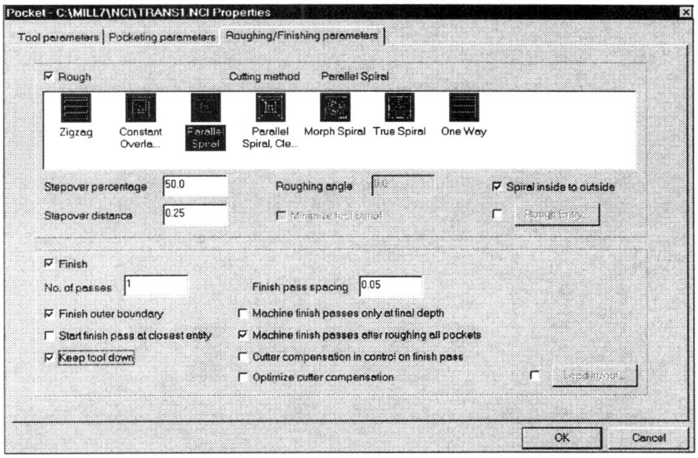

Select **OK** to generate the pocketing toolpaths as in Figure 8.51.

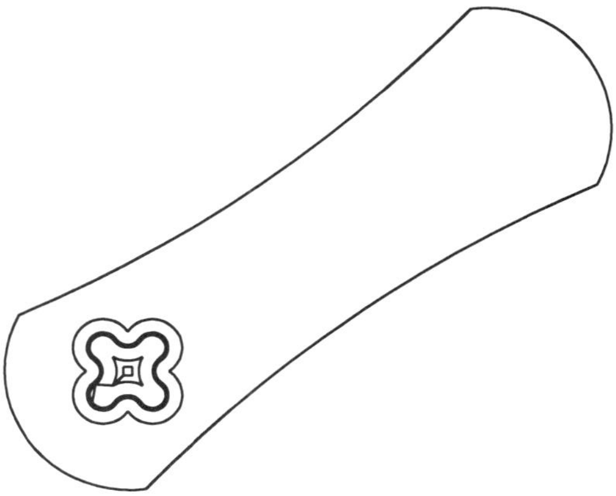

Figure 9.43

Step 5. Translate the toolpaths to two locations.

Select **MAIN MENU** → **NC utils** → **Edit NCI**
Select **Yes** to "Operations have been modified. Create the NCI text file?"
Select **"Pocket (T1)"** toolpath section
Select **Xform** → **Translate**
Set the Xform – Translate parameters to the following settings.

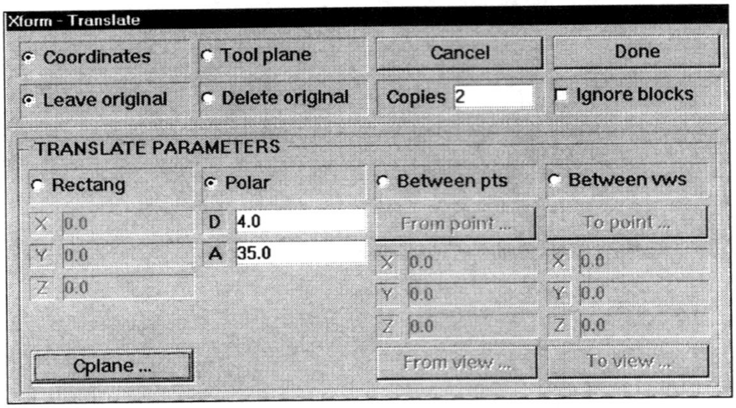

Select **Done**
The two sets of toolpaths are added as in Figure 8.52.

Figure 9.44

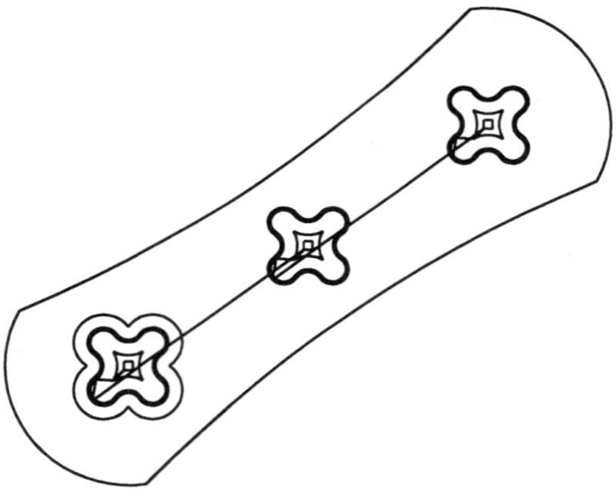

Step 6. Save the toolpath file.

Select **File** → **Save**
Enter **Yes** to overwrite the existing file
Select **Quit** to exit Edit NCI menu

Step 7. Verify the toolpaths.

Select **Gview** → **Isometric**
Select **Backplot** → **Run**
The toolpaths in isometric view should look like Figure 8.53.

Figure 9.45

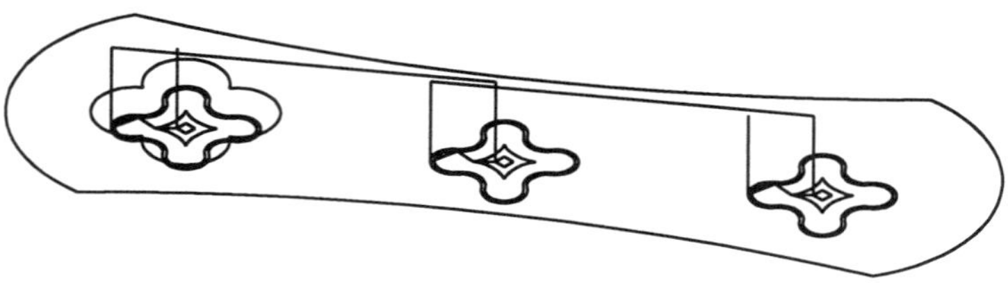

9.11 Linear Array

The linear array function allows us to generate a set of duplicated toolpaths to be located at a specified distance along the X and/or Y direction (Figure 9.54). The linear array function is not one of Edit NCI commands. It is defined by the following four parameters:

Number of steps in X:	number of times to step and repeat the toolpath along the X axis.
Number of steps in Y:	number of times to step and repeat the toolpath along the Y axis.
X distance:	spacing distance of each step in X direction.
Y distance:	spacing distance of each step in Y direction.

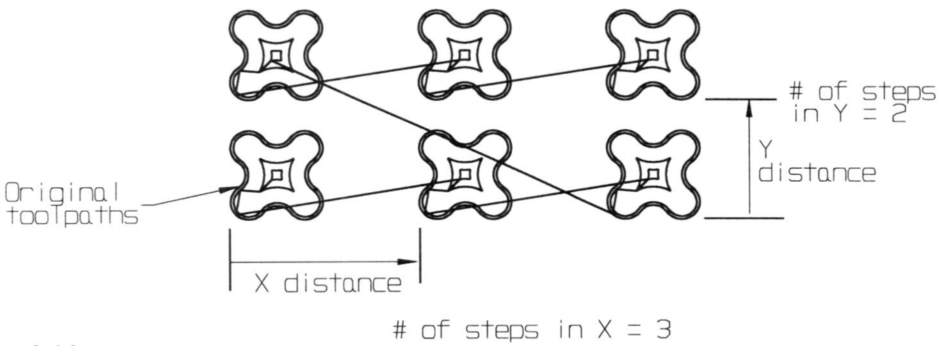

Figure 9.46

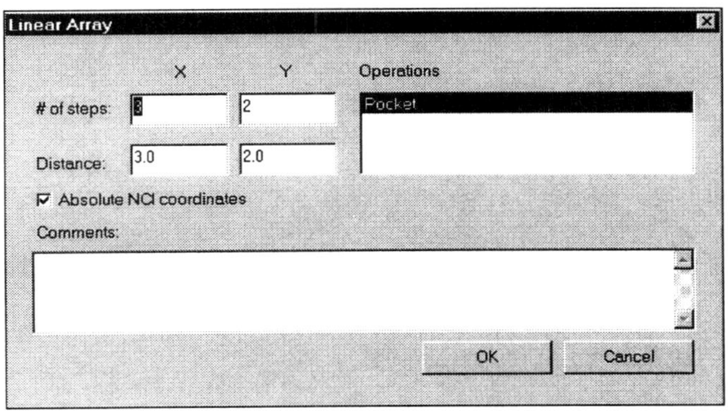

The toolpaths to be arrayed must exist before the linear array function can be used. Table 9.1 illustrates how to define the number of steps in X and number of steps in Y to generate the duplicate toolpaths.

Table 9.1 Defining number of steps in X and number of steps in Y parameters

Number of steps in X	Number of steps in Y	Description	Illustration
1	1	No duplicated toolpath is generated.	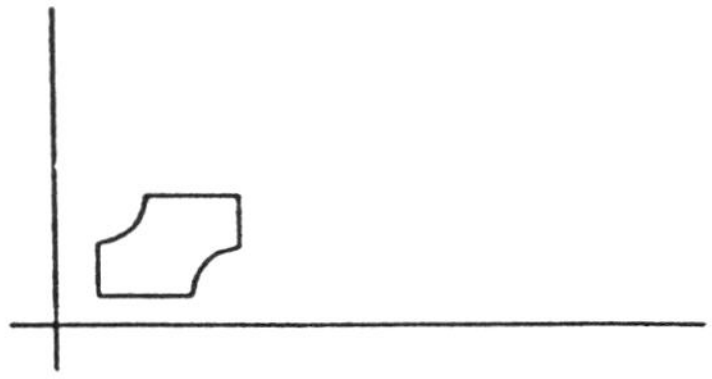
2	1	One duplicated toolpath is generated in X direction.	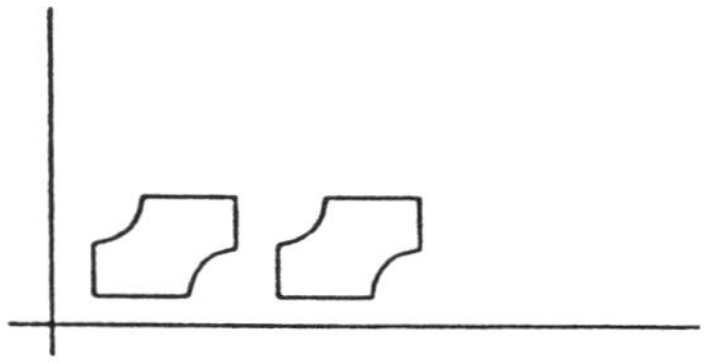
3	1	Two duplicated toolpaths are generated in X direction.	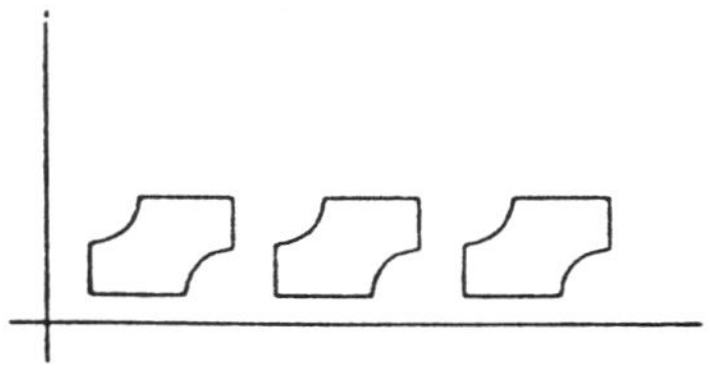
2	2	Three duplicated toolpaths are generated (one in X-direction and two in Y-direction).	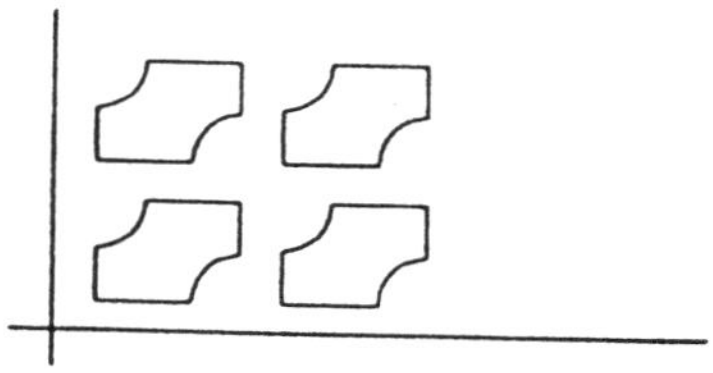
3	2	Five duplicated toolpaths are generated (two in X-direction and three in Y-direction).	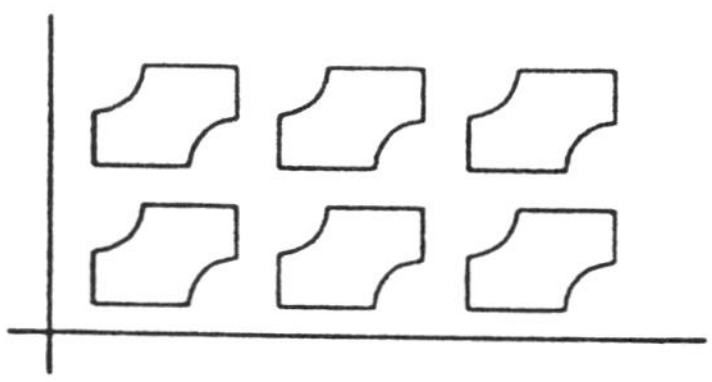

Project 9. Linear arraying toolpaths

The part shown in Figure 9.47 consists of three identical pockets that are equally spaced in the X direction. This is the ideal project for using the linear array function. The pocketing toolpaths for pocket A can be copied to the other two locations.

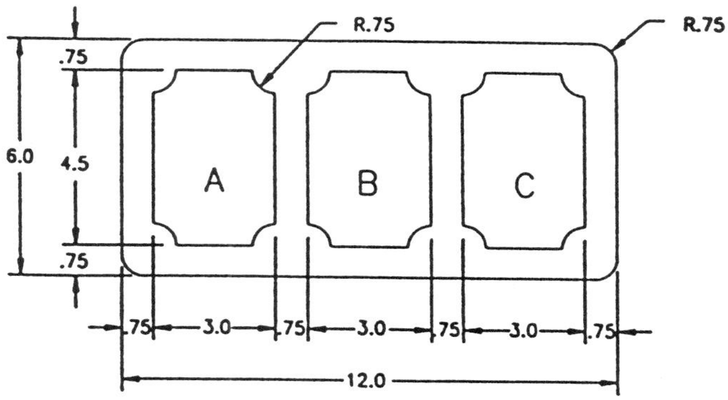

Figure 9.47a

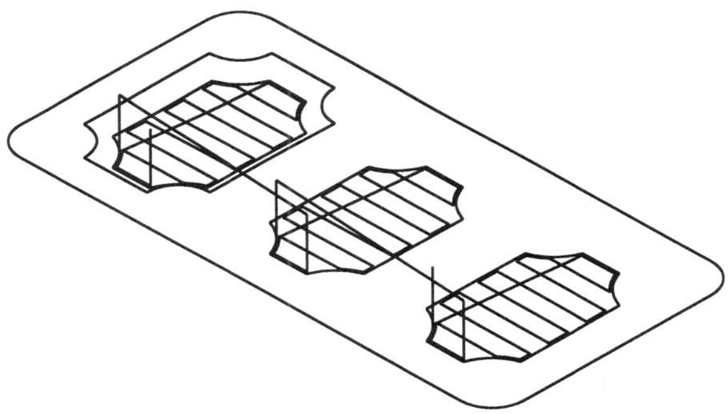

Figure 9.47b

Tips The linear array parameters should be set as:

> Number of steps in **X = 3**
> Number of steps in **Y = 1**
> X distance = **3.75**
> Y distance = **0.0**

The system will generate the roughing toolpaths for three pockets first, then will be followed by the finish toolpaths.

Step 1. Open the part geometry file array1.

Select **MAIN MENU →** **File →** **Get**
File name: **array1**

The part geometry drawing should appear as Figure 9.48.

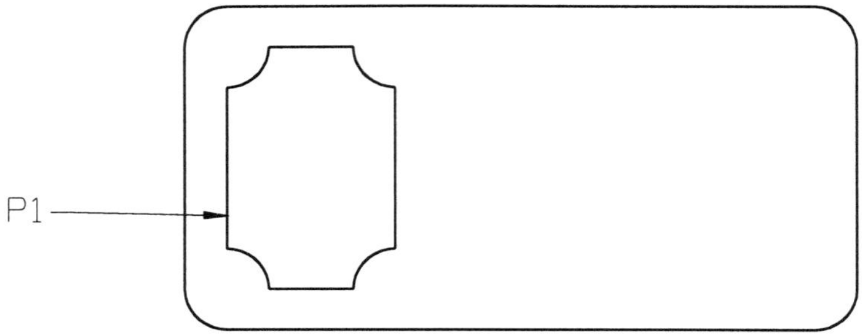

Figure 9.48

Step 2. Initiate the pocket module.

Use the pick point in Figure 8.56.
Select **MAIN MENU → Toolpaths → Pocket**
File name for toolpaths: **array1**
Select **Chain**, then pick **P1**
Select **Done**
Click the right mouse button, then select "**Get tool from library**"
Select **tool #241** (3/4 flat end mill)
Select **OK**
Set the tool parameters as below.

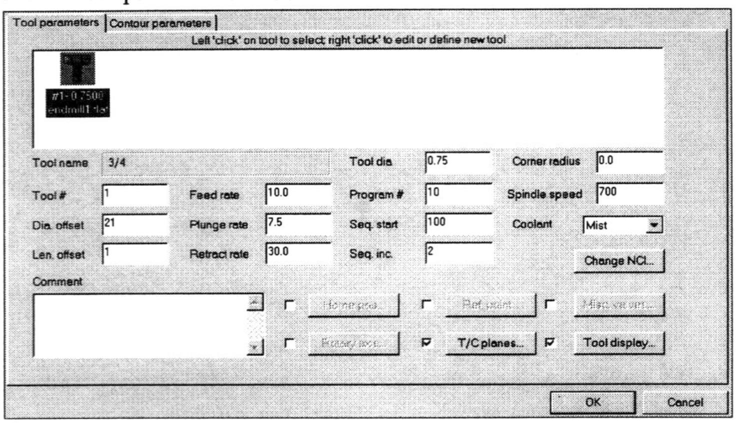

Step 3. Define the pocketing parameters.

Click "Pocketing parameters" button

Set the pocketing parameters as below.

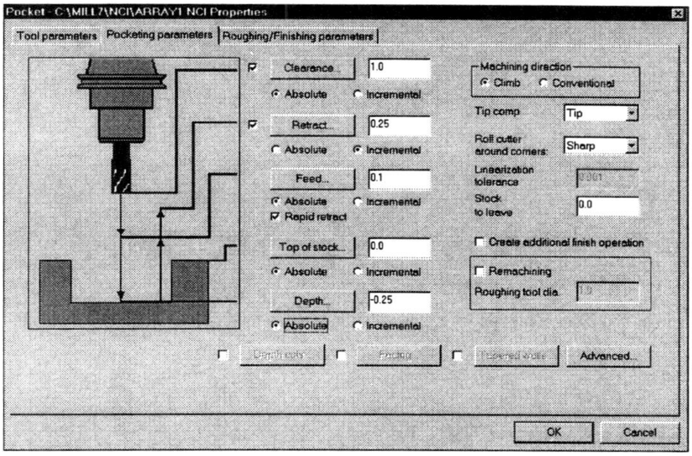

Step 4. Define the roughing and finishing parameters.

Click "Roughing/Finishing parameters" button
Set the roughing and finishing parameters as below.

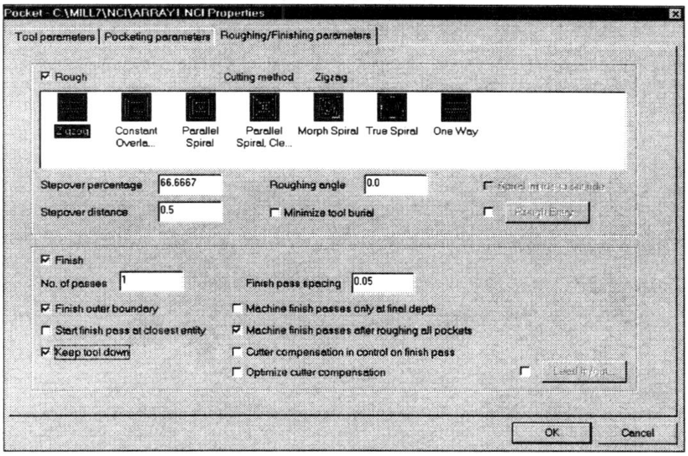

Select **OK** to generate pocketing toolpaths
The pocketing toolpaths are shown in Figure 8.57.

Figure 9.49

Step 5. Initiate the linear array function.

Select **Next menu →** **Linear array**

Set the linear array parameters as below.

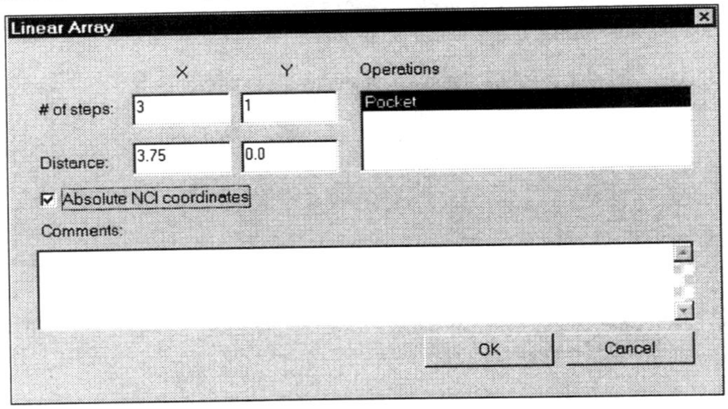

Select **OK** to execute the linear array function

The pocketing toolpaths have been copied to two locations as shown in Figure 8.58.

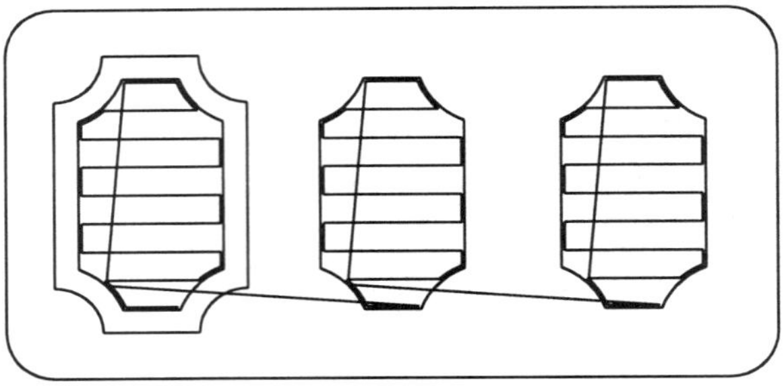

Figure 9.50

Step 6. Change to isometric view.

Select **Gview →** **Isometric**

The model shown in isometric view appears as in figure 8.59.

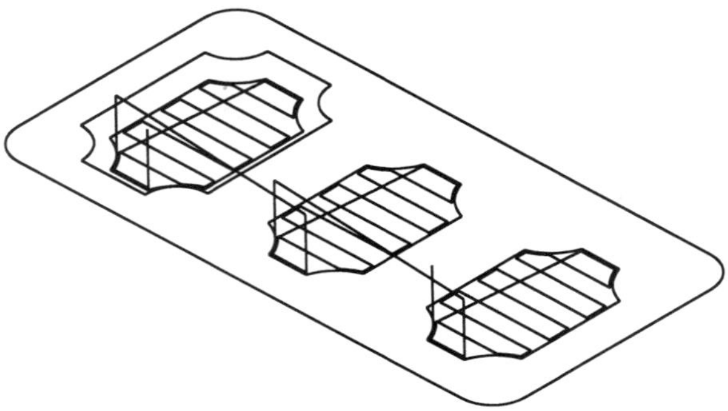

Figure 9.51

Step 7. Save the project.

Select **MAIN MENU →** **File →** **Save**

File name: **array1t**

Exercises

1. Describe how Mastercam organizes its toolpath file structure.

2. Explain how the following four parameters affect the number of toolapth sections generated in using the contour module:
   Number of roughing passes
   Number of finish passes
   Number of rough cuts in depth
   Number of finish cuts in depth

3. Determine the number of toolapth sections for using the contour module to cut an internal profile under the following conditions:
   Number of roughing passes = 2
   Number of finish passes = 1
   Number of rough cuts in depth = 2
   Number of finish cuts in depth = 1

4. What are the two main factors determining the number of toolapth sections in using the pocket module?
5. Determine the number of toolpath sections for pocketing under the following conditions:
   Number of finish passes = 1
   Number of rough passes in depth cut = 2
   Number of finish passes in depth cut = 1

6. Explain how an existing toolapth section can be deleted in Mastercam.

7. List the four toolapth editing functions in Mastercam and briefly describe what they are.

8. Describe the advantages of using toolpath editing functions.

9. Explain when to use the mirror function.

10. Explain when to use rotate function.

11. Describe the main features of the scale function.

12. Why is the scale function not recommended for modifying or editing toolpaths?

13. Under what conditions should you use the translate function?

14. Describe the features of the linear array function and list the four parameters used to define the linear array.

15. The pocket module is used twice to generate toolpaths for pocketing the larger circular pocket and pocketing one of seven small pockets as shown in Figure 9.52. The toolpaths for the small pocket are then copied to six locations by using the rotate command. The part geometry file name is rotate2 which is created in chapter 6.

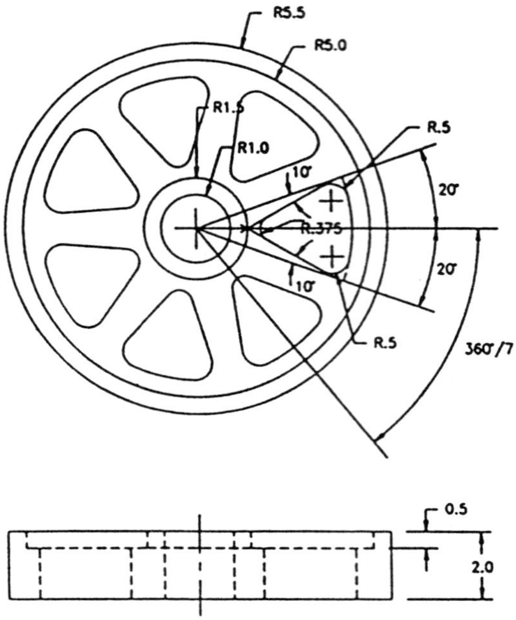

Figure 9.52

16. As illustrated in Figure 9.53, two identical parts are machined in one machine setup. These two parts are located symmetrically about a vertical line. This is the ideal case to use the mirror function. Toolpaths for producing one part are generated first, then they are duplicated for the other part by using Edit NCI → Xform → Mirror commands. The part geometry file name is mirror2.

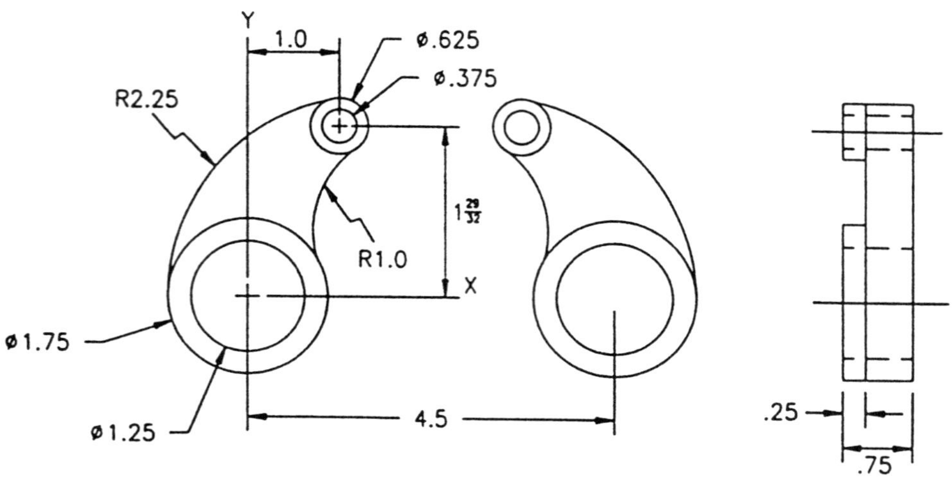

Figure 9.53

17. The scale function is sued to scale the toolpaths for pocketing a rectangle for cutting two smaller rectangular pockets as shown in Figure 9.54. The scaling center and factor are given below.

Scale about the origin

Axis	Scaling factor
X	0.75
Y	0.75
Z	2.0

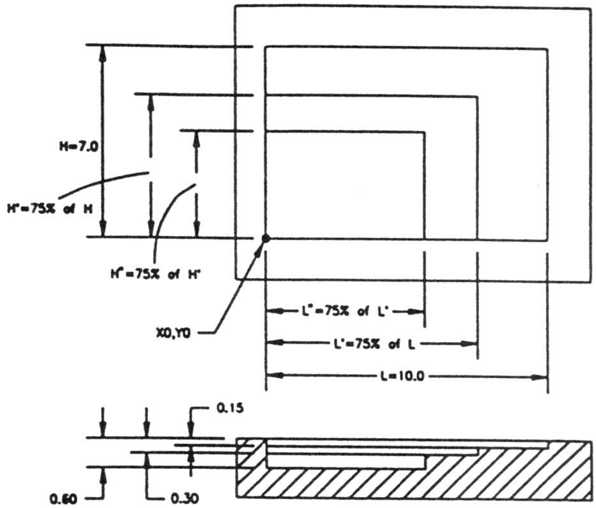

Figure 9.54

18. Two identical workpieces are to be produced in one machine setup as shown in Figure 9.55. The set of toolpaths for cutting one part is copied to another location as specified by using the translation function. The part geometry file name is trans2 which is created in chapter 5. The generation of toolpaths for machining the part includes using contour, pocket, and drill modules.

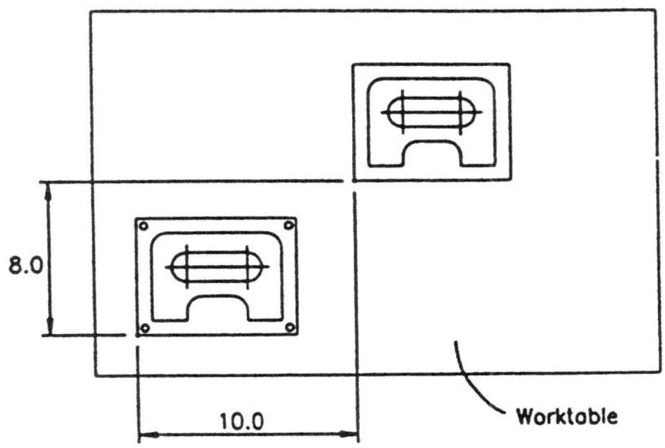

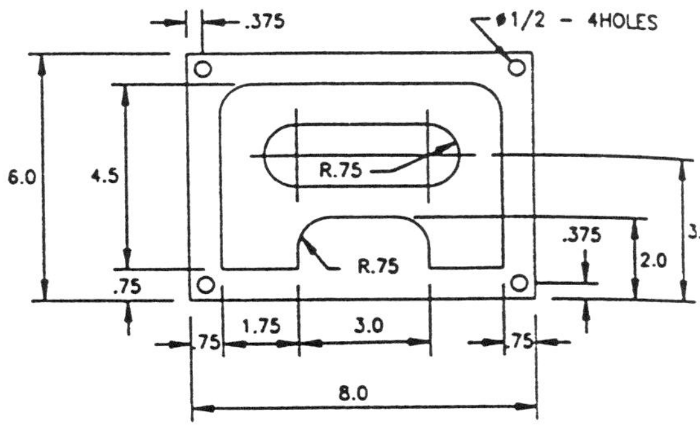

Figure 9.55

19. Use the linear array function to generate the toolpaths for cutting four identical parts in one part program. This allows four parts to be machined in one machine setup. The workholding layout of these four parts is shown in Figure 9.56. The part geometry file name is trans2 which is identical to the file used in problem 18.

Linear array: Nx, Ny = 2 2 Dx, Dy = 10.0 8.0

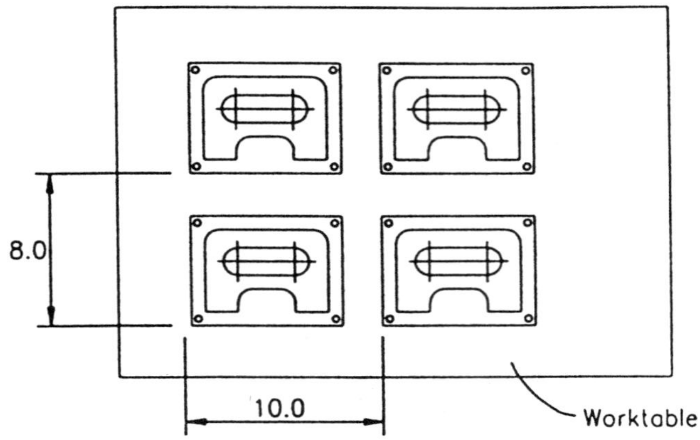

Figure 9.56

Chapter 10

Mastercam Process and Toolpath Planning

Objectives:

1. Understand toolpath generation procedure using Mastercam.
2. Identify part features to be machined from the given part and raw material drawings.
3. Select proper processes and processing sequence to machine features of the part.
4. Select proper toolpath module for the selected process to produce a particular feature.
5. Select proper cutting tools and their machining data.
6. Prepare process plan sheets.

Overview

Mastercam is a very powerful software that can be used to generate toolpaths for machining almost any parts, simple or complex. To effectively use Mastercam's power, the user must have the following knowledge:

- Be familiar with the CAD system to create part geometry
- Know basic CNC programming principles and commands
- Have a good knowledge of machining practices
- Know the CAM system (NC toolpath modules)
- Select proper tooling and machining parameters

In addition, the user must also follow a certain procedure to generate the NC part programs. The process and toolpath planning is the road map for the successful completion of the project. The benefits of good planning include: (1) avoiding errors, (2) eliminating the need for toolpath editing, and (3) serving as a record, reference guide and communication medium. The process and toolpath planning is very useful for the beginners who need to follow a logical sequence in completing any project. The planning also is important for experienced users who generate toolpaths for machining complex parts.

Figure 10.1 on the following page is a flow chart that shows the procedure for using the Mastercam system to generate a toolpath to machine a part. This flow chart indicates the input and output relationships of the major tasks in CAD/CAM NC programming.

10.1 Part and Raw Material Drawings

A part drawing describes the shape and size of a part. It provides the following useful information to the part programmer in generating the toolpath:

Part features to be produced
Dimensions, tolerances, and surface roughnesses
Material to be machined
Initial shape and size of the material to be machined
Amount of material to be removed

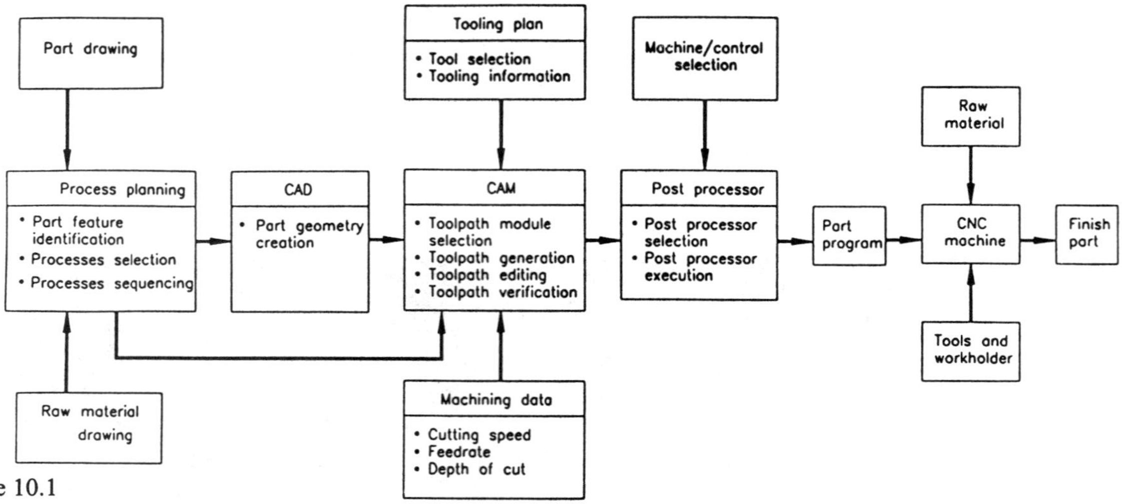

Figure 10.1

Part Features

A part feature is the distinctive shape and size to be produced in a part. Typical part features in milling operations include:

1. Flat surfaces
2. Slots
3. Shoulders or steps
4. Holes
5. Internal threads
6. Profiles (or contours)
7. Letters
8. Spline curves
9. 3-D surfaces

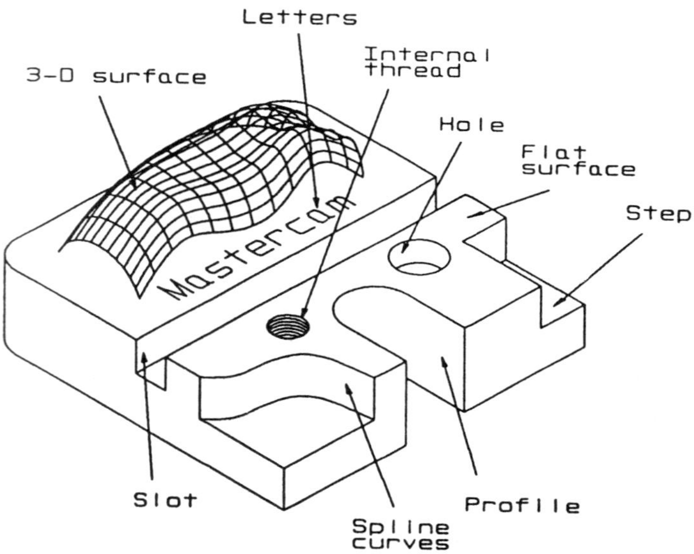

Figure 10.2

Typical part features in turning operations are:
1. End faces
2. External profiles
3. Internal profiles
4. Internal threads
5. External threads
6. Grooves
7. Holes
8. Spline curves
9. Cut-offs

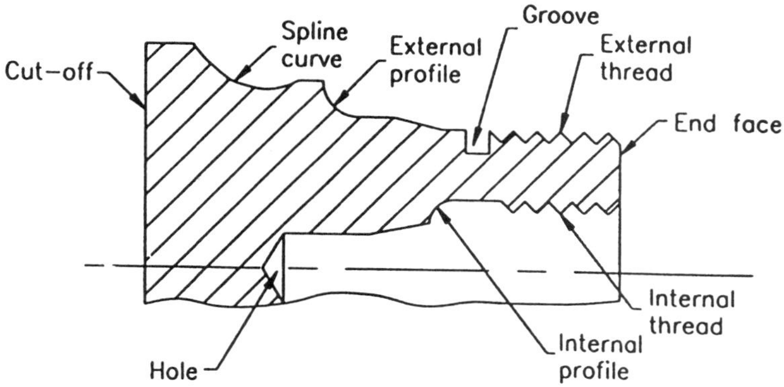

Figure 10.3

Dimensions, Tolerances, and Surface Roughnesses

Selecting a proper process to produce a part feature is dictated by the process capability. Process capability refers to positional accuracy, surface roughness, and amount of material to be removed during a particular machining process. A part drawing should provide the detailed information about dimensions, tolerances and surface roughness of a part feature.

Raw Material Drawing

A raw material drawing depicts the initial shape and size of the workpiece before it is processed. It can be an intermediate form of the part. A comparison of a part drawing and a raw material drawing should reveal the amount of mateiral to be removed to produce a part feature. The information in material removal can be further used to determine (1) the required cutter type and size, and (2) the required number of cutting passes including roughing and finishing.

Processes Selection

After part features have been identified, we need to select the proper processes to produce each feature. The commonly used processes for producing part features in milling and turning operations are listed below:

Milling Operations

Process	**Feature to be produced**
Facing	produce flat surfaces
Profiling	produce external and internal contours
Pocketing	produce internal pockets enclosed by a closed contour
Slot cutting	produce blind and through slots
Shoulder	cutting produce shoulders or steps
Drilling	produce and/or enlarge holes
Boring	enlarge holes
Tapping	produce internal threads
Surface cutting	produce various forms of 3-d surfaces
Lettering	engrave a string of letters

Turning Operations	
Process	**Feature to be produced**
Roughing	produce a rough shape of finished part
Facing	produce a flat end face
Turning	produce external and internal profiles
Grooving	produce grooves
Threading	produce external and internal threads
Drilling	produce and/or enlarge holes
Boring	enlarge holes
Tapping	produce internal threads

Processes Sequencing

The processes required to produce the part features of a piece should be arranged in a proper sequence. Some features must be produced prior to other features. The criteria in sequencing machining processes include:

1. Datum surfaces have precedence. Datum surfaces should be machined first if multiple workholding setups are required.
2. Machine larger surfaces first. Larger surfaces are more adaptable to disturbances resulting from subsequent machining operations.
3. Avoid feature interference. Feature interference happens when the machining of one feature destroys a requirement for the production of other features.
4. Pre-process must be performed first. For example, drilling must be performed before tapping threads in a hole.

Example 1.

Identify the part features to be produced and the machining process(es) to produce each feature for the part shown in Figure 10.4. Also provide the process sequence.

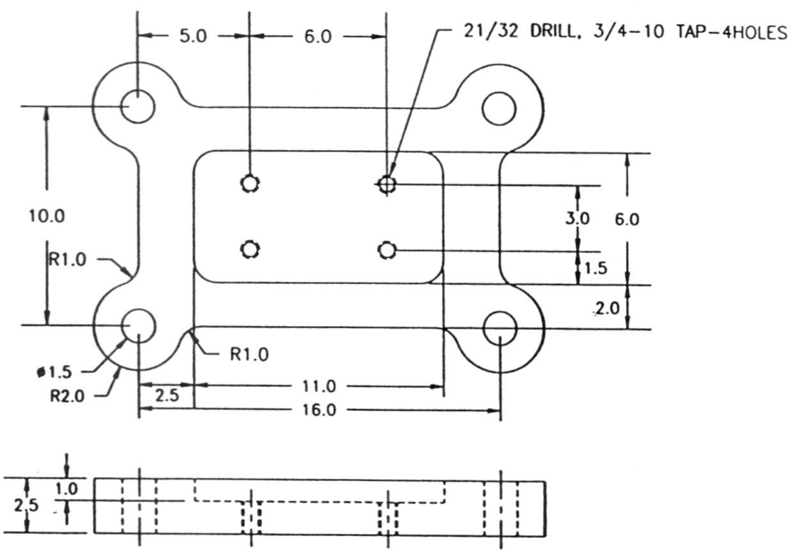

Figure 10.4

Part features:

- Flat top surface
- External profile
- Rectangular pocket
- Four holes
- Internal threads in four holes

Process selection:

Feature	Process(es)
Flat top surface	Facing
External profile	Profiling
Rectangular pocket	Pocketing
Four holes	Drilling and boring
Internal threads in four holes	Drilling and tapping

Processes sequence:

Based on the criteria given above, the suggested process sequence for this part is:

1. Facing the top surface
2. Profiling the external profile
3. Pocketing the internal pocket
4. Drilling four holes
5. Boring four holes
6. Drilling the four holes for threading
7. Tapping threads in four holes

10.2 Part Features Geometry Creation

The geometric entities that describe each part feature should be created. There are **two** types of geometric entities: true entities and construction entities. True entities are used to directly define the part features to be produced. They have the true shapes and sizes of the part features. Construction entities are used to help generating toolpaths in machining a part feature. A larger rectangle, for example, is used to define the boundary for generating the toolpaths to face a flat surface that has a smaller size than the rectangle as in Figure 10.5. The geometric entities of this rectangle are construction entities.

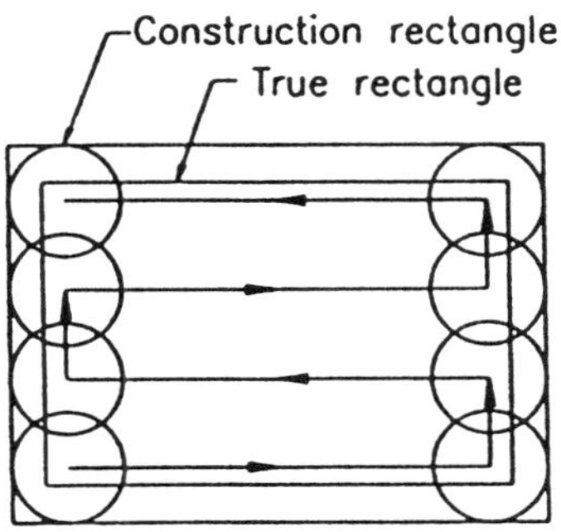

Figure 10.5

10.3 Toolpath Modules Selection

Mastercam provides a variety of toolpath modules for generating the toolpaths to produce part features. The selection of toolpath modules depends on the part feature and the process type. Table 10.3 lists the possible use of toolpath modules for various part features and processes.

Table 10.3 Toolpath Modules

Part Feature	Process	Module	Illustration	Remark
Flat surface	Facing	Pocket	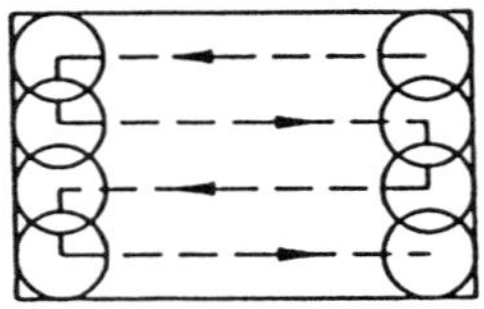	1. Use the larger face mill or end mill to shorten machining time. 2. Create a large pocket boundary to ensure all areas are cut.
Profile/contour	Profiling	Contour	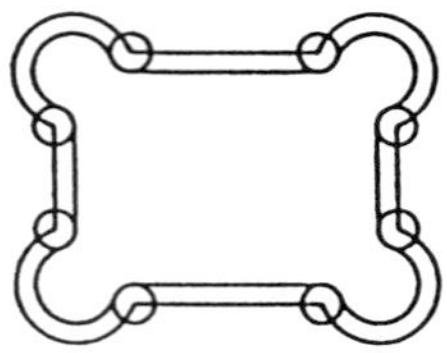	1. Use end mill to move along the part profile 2. Select proper contour direction to obtain climb or conventional milling type.
Pocket	Pocketing	Pocket	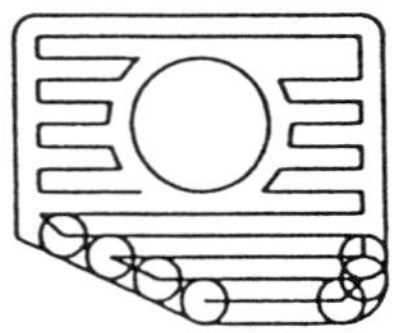	Use end mill to remove the material enclosed by a closed boundary
Slot	Slot cutting	Contour or Pocket	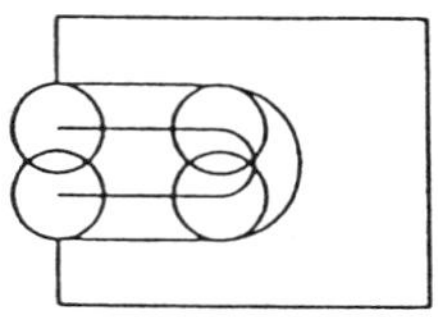	Use end mill to cut open or blind slots.
Shoulder	Shoulder cutting	Contour or Pocket	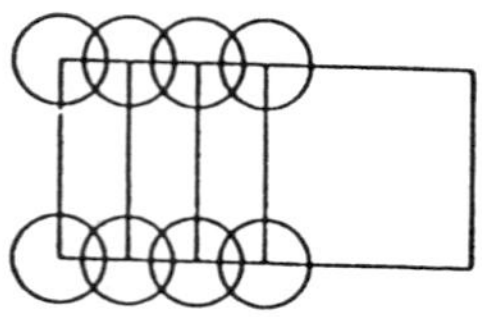	Use end mill to produce steps or shoulders.

Table 10.3 (Continued)

Part Feature	Process	Module	Illustration	Remarks
Hole	Drilling and/or boring	Drill/Bore	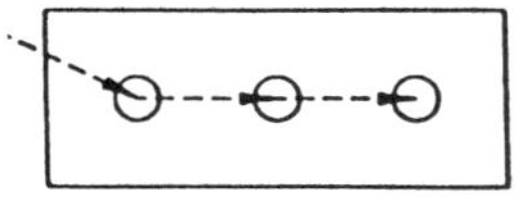	Use drill and/or boring to produce holes.
Internal thread	Drilling and tapping	Drill/Tap	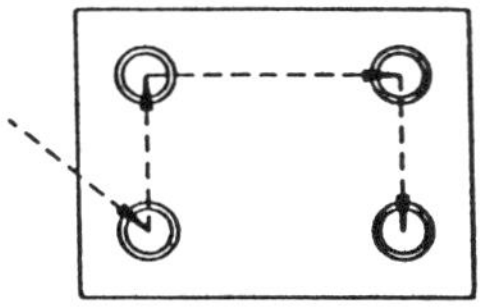	Use tap to produce internal threads of holes.
Letters	Lettering	Letters	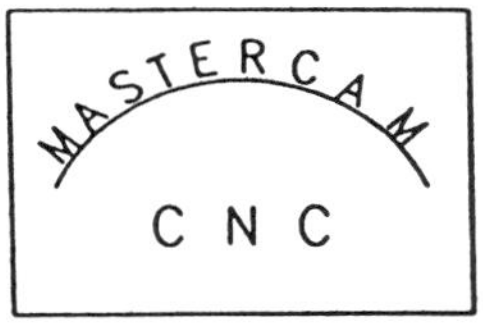	Use end mill to engrave letters on part surfaces.
Spline curves	Curve cutting	Profile or Pocket		Use end mill to cut along spline curves.
Single 3-D surface	Surface cutting	3-D toolpaths modules such as ruled, loft, swept,coons and flowline	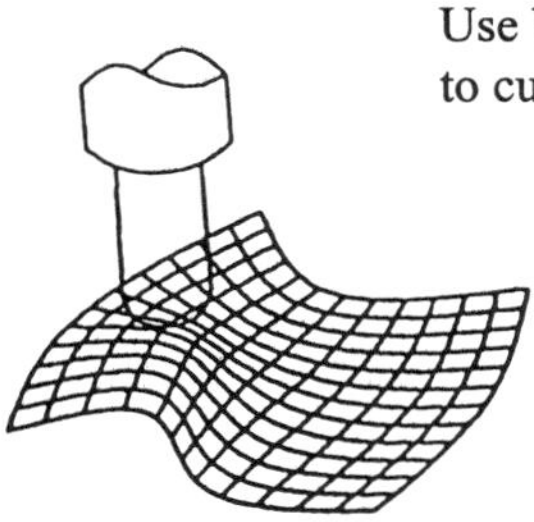	Use ball-end mill to cut 3-D surfaces
Composite surface	Surface cutting	Multisurf	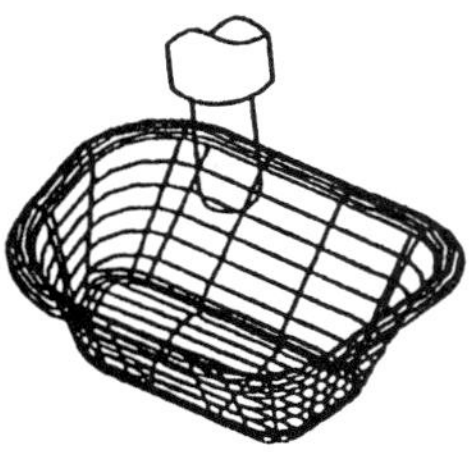	Use ball -end mill to cut multiple surfaces

10.4 Tooling Data and Machining Data

There are **two** types of information that determine the efficiency of CNC machining: **tooling data and machining data.**

- Tooling data includes information related to defining the size of the cutter, the assignment of tool number, tool length offset, and CDC offset.
- Machining data basically consists of **three** components: cutting speed, feedrate, and depth of cut.

Cutting speed, expressed in fpm, normally is not used directly in the milling operations, instead, it is used to calculate the required spindle speed (RPM) using this formula:

$$N = \frac{12 \cdot CS}{\pi \cdot D}$$

CS = cutting speed
N = Spindle speed
D = Cutter diameter

Feedrate refers to the speed of cutter moves along the workpiece. In milling, the feedrate is often expressed in the units of inches/minute.

The proper selection of tooling data and machining data is provided in chapter 2 of this book.

10.5 Process Plan Sheet Preparation

The blank sheet shown in Figure 910.6 can be used to plan the activities for machining a part. This process plan sheet includes the following important information:

Part identification and material
Machine to be used and post processor
Processes and sequencing
Process illustation
Toolpath module used in each machining process
Tools
Machining data

Example 2: Process planning

Use the sheet given in Figure 10.6 on the next page to develop a process plan for the part shown in Figure 10.7 on page 9-10. The raw material is a steel circular plate of D8.1" X 1.55".

PROCESS PLAN		PART NAME:		MATERIAL:		SHEET________OF________		
MACHINE:		POST PROCESSOR:		PREPARED BY:		DATE:		
PROCESS ILLUSTRATION	PROCESS		TOOLPATH MODULE	TOOL		MACHING DATA		
	NO.	DESCRIPTION		NO.	DESCRIPTION	CUTTING SPEED (RPM)	FEED RATE (IPM)	DEPTH OF CUT

Figure 10.6 Blank process plan sheet

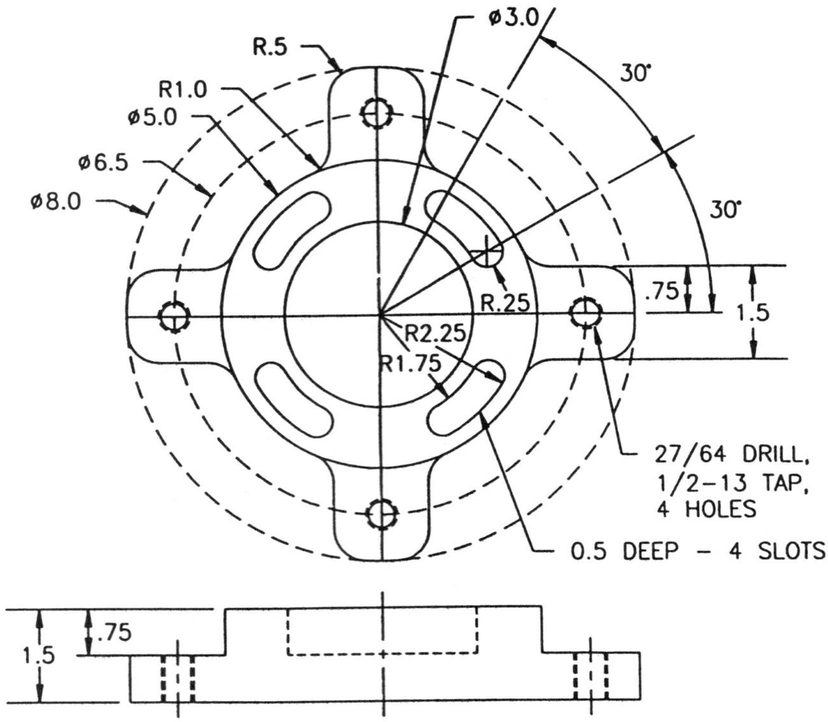

Figure 10.7

Part features:

The study of the part drawing reveals that there are **seven** part features to be produced in this piece:

1. Bottom flat surface
2. Top flat surface
3. Upper circular profile
4. External profile
5. Circular pocket
6. Four circular slots
7. Four holes with internal threads

Process Sequencing:

This project involves **two** workpiece setups. The first setup is to cut the bottom flat surface which is used as the datum for the second setup for the remaining machining operations. Thus, the machining of the bottom flat surface must be the first process. Using the sequencing criteria given in previous section, we can arrange the process sequence as below:

1. Facing the bottom flat surface
2. Facing the top flat surface
3. Cutting the upper circular profile
4. Cutting the external profile
5. Cutting the circular pocket
6. Cutting four circular slots
7. Drilling four holes for threading
8. Tapping internal threads in four holes

Module Selection

The pocket module is used for facing the bottom and top flat surfaces, circular pocket, and four circular slots. The drill module is used to drill four holes and the drill/tap option is used for tapping four holes. A careful consideration must be given to the upper circular profile and the external profile.

We have **two** ways to generate the toolpaths for cutting the upper circular profile. One way is to use the contour module and select the circle as the contour boundary. Since the material to be removed is relatively large, it requires the use of several roughing passes and one finish pass. Another way is to use the pocket module with the circle as the island. A construction circle must be created to serve as the outer pocketing boundary as shown in Figure 10.8. Finally we chose to use the contour module for cutting the upper circular profile.

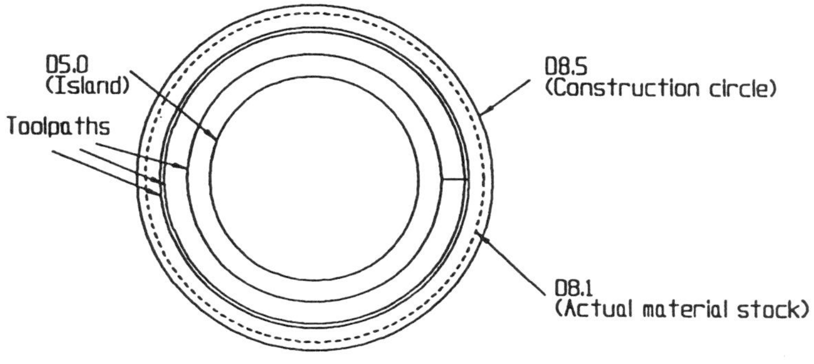

Figure 10.8

There are four local pockets formed between the four ears of the external profile. A more direct way to cut the external profile is to use the contour module with several roughing passes and one finish pass. An alternate way is to use the pocket module to cut one local pocket, then copy the toolpaths onto the other three pockets (Figure 10.9), and finally use the contour module to perform the finish cut as in Figure 10.10. In this project, we use the latter approach for cutting the external profile.

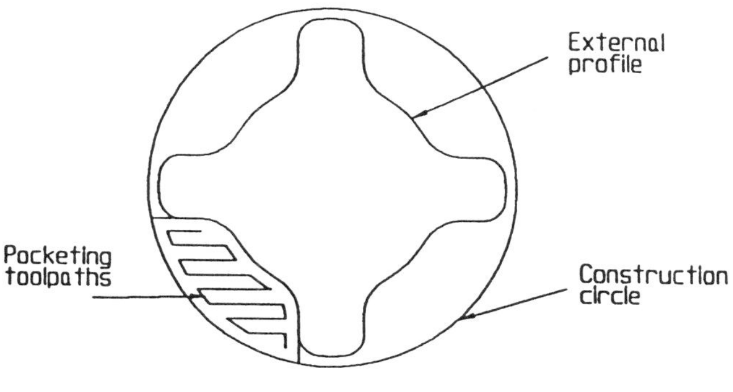

Figure 10.9

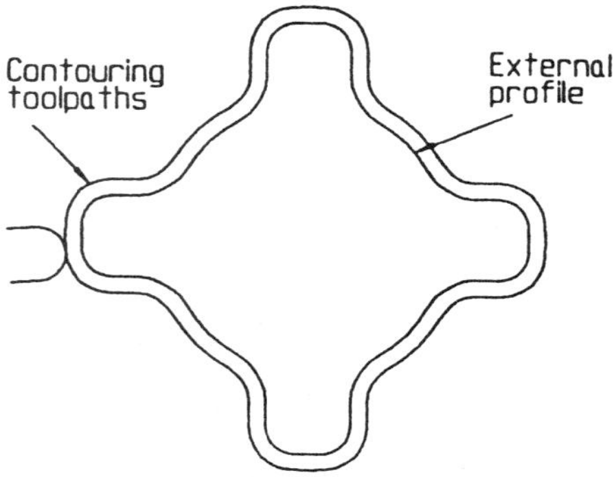

Figure 10.10

Tools and Machining Data

Six cutting tools are used in this project. They are:

- 4" face mill for facing bottom and top flat surface
- 1" end mill for cutting upper circular profile
- 1/2" end mill for cutting pockets and finish profile of the external profile, and to cut the internal circular pocket
- 1/4" end mill to cut the four circular slots
- 17/32" drill to drill four thread holes
- 5/8-11 tap to tap four holes

The machining data for each cutting tool and process is given in Figure 10.11. The completed process plan sheet for this project is given in Figure 10.11 on the next two pages.

10.6 Post Processor Selection

The toolpath file generated from the CAM system is a generic type called an NCI file in Mastercam. This file must be further processed by a software program called a post processor. The main task of a post processor is to convert the NCI file into the NC part program. The output from the post processor is the part program that is readable by a CNC controller. Since the CNC controllers of different vendors require different codes and they are used by different machines, there is no one universal post processor that can be used for all machines. In common practice, one controller/machine combination requires a dedicated post processor. The required post processor will be determined automatically once a CNC machine is chosen to machine a particular project.

Note: It is best to select the post processor you will be using **before** you begin your tool paths.

PROCESS PLAN	PART NAME: Project 5		MATERIAL: Steel		SHEET 2 OF 2		
MACHINE: LEAD-M1	POST PROCESSOR: LMC-1		PREPARED BY: J. Lin		DATE: 10-8-4		
PROCESS ILLUSTRATION	PROCESS		TOOLPATH MODULE	TOOL		MACHING DATA		
	NO.	DESCRIPTION		NO.	DESCRIPTION	CUTTING SPEED (RPM)	FEED RATE (IPM)	DEPTH OF CUT
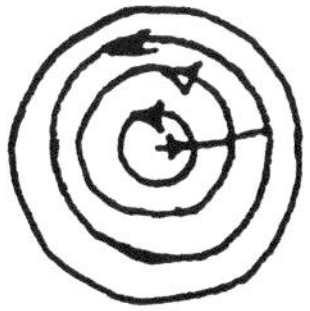	5	Cutting circular pocket	Pocket	3	1/2" end mill	600	12.5	0.2
	6	Cutting four circular slots	Pocket	4	1/4" end mill	1200	10	0.1
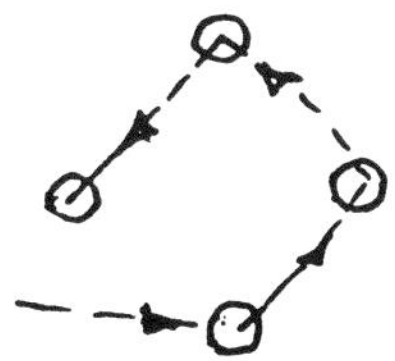	7	Drilling four holes	Drill	5	17/32 drill	500	10	—
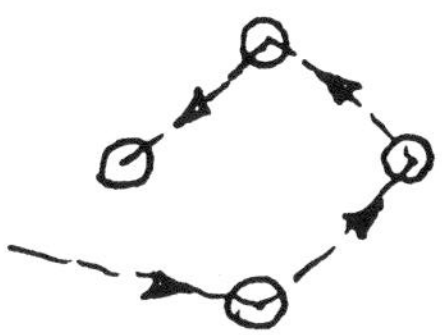	8	Tapping for internal threads	Drill	6	5/8-11 tap	200	18.18	—

Figure 10.11

PROCESS PLAN		PART NAME: Projeit 5		MATERIAL: Steal	SHEET 1 OF 2		
MACHINE: LEAD-M1		POST PROCESSOR: LMC-1		PREPARED BY: J Lin	DATE: 10-8-94		

PROCESS ILLUSTRATION	PROCESS NO.	PROCESS DESCRIPTION	TOOLPATH MODULE	TOOL NO.	TOOL DESCRIPTION	MACHING DATA: CUTTING SPEED (RPM)	FEED RATE (IPM)	DEPTH OF CUT
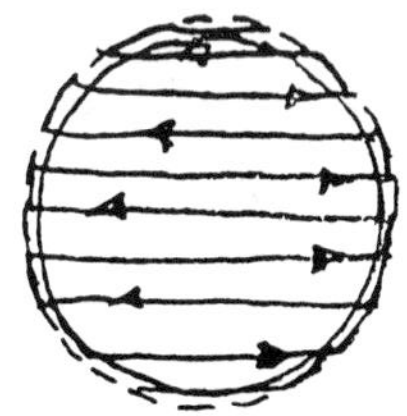	1	Facing bottom flat surface	Pocket	1	2" face mill	150	10	0.15
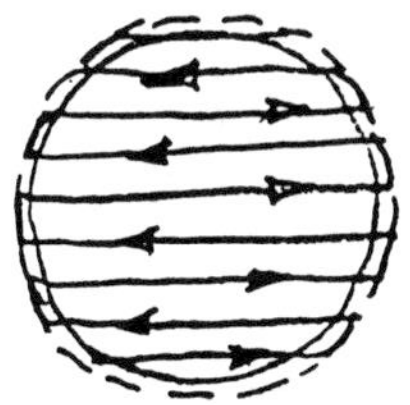	2	Facing the top surface	Pocket	1	2" face mill	150	10	0.15
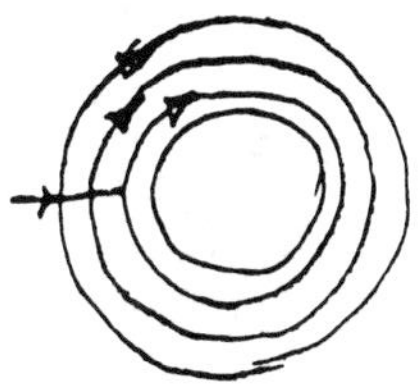	3	Cutting upper circular profile	Contour	2	1" end mill	300	12.5	0.2
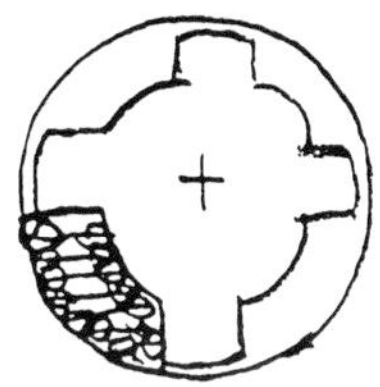	4	Cutting external profile	Pocket and Contour	3	1/2" end mill	600	12.5	0.2

Figure 10.11, continued

Exercises

1. What types of knowledge must a user have in order to effectively use a CAD/CAM system?
2. List the three benefits of good process and toolpath planning.
3. What is a part feature?
4. List at least seven common part features in milling operations.
5. List at least seven common part features in turning operations.
6. Describe how to determine the amount of material removed in producing a part feature.
7. What are the four basic criteria for sequencing machining processes?
8. What are the two types of geometric entitites used to describe part features?
9. What is tooling data?
10. What is machining data?
11. Describe the reasons for using a post processor.
12. Explain the main purpose of a post processor.
13. Use the blank process planning sheet given in Figure 9.6 to develop a process plan for the part shown in Figure 10.12.

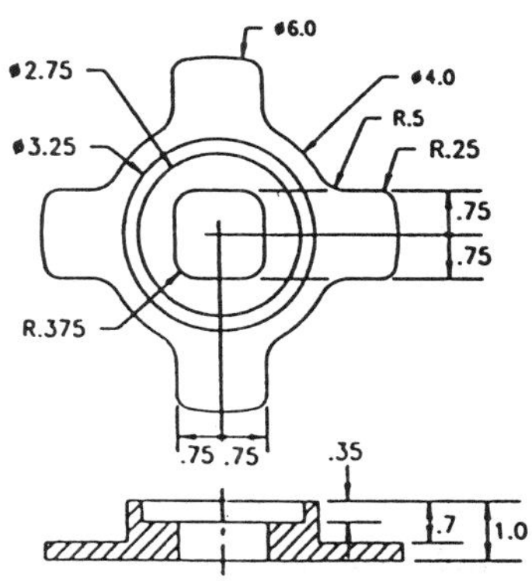

Figure 10.12

14. Use the blank process planning sheet given in Figure 9.6 to develop a process plan for the part shown in Figure 10.13.

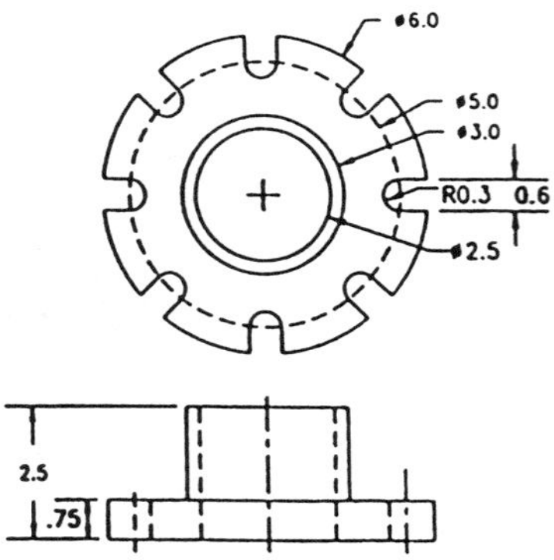

Figure 10.13

Mastercam Version 7,
Scholar's International Publishing Corp., 1998

Chapter 11
Constructing 3D Wireframe Models

Objectives:

1. Understand the features of wireframe models and surface models.
2. Know the basic elements of the surface edge profiles.
3. Select proper construction planes.
4. Use proper Z depth control.
5. Construct wireframe models.

Overview

This chapter presents important concepts and techniques in constructing wireframe models for 3D surfaces. Features of different wireframe models and surface models are included. The success in constructing a wireframe model depends on the user's ability to create profile elements, use construction planes and Z-depth control. In some cases only a partial wireframe model is needed to generate surfaces.

Sixteen examples are presented to show how the edge profiles of the surfaces are constructed. These examples are arranged in an increasing order of difficulty. They are so designed that new techniques are added in each succeeding example. These examples are used in the later chapters for creating various types of surfaces and the toolpaths to produce the surfaces.

11.1 Wireframe Modeling Fundamentals

Wireframe Models

A wireframe model is normally required to create a surface. Wireframe models represent an object by defining its edges (Figure 11.1). It is impossible to completely define surfaces with wireframe models except for simple flat surfaces. Wireframe models cannot be directly used in generating 3D surface tool paths, however, they are used as surface boundaries and cross-sectional features for developing surface models.

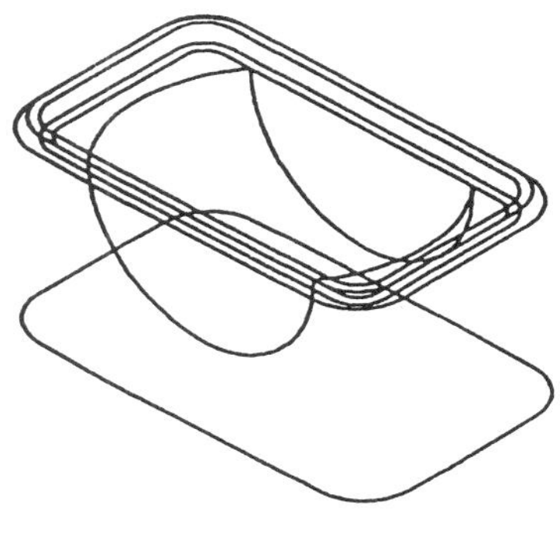

Figure 11.1

Surface Models

Surface models define surfaces, including the edges of each surface. They take the modeling of an object one step further than wireframe models. They show not only the edges of surfaces, but also the shapes. Surface models can be directly used to create a toolpath for machining surfaces. They provide more information, and can be edited and shaded. However, surface models provide no information about the weight of the workpiece. Figure 11.2 shows the surface model of its wireframe counterpart shown in Figure 11.1.

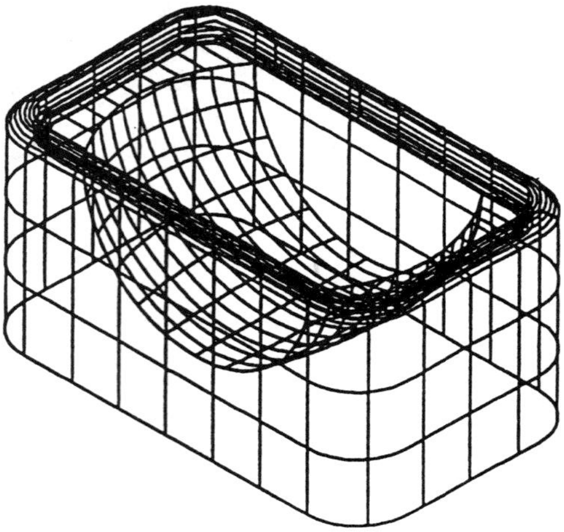

Figure 11.2

Profile Elements of Surfaces

Primitive geometric elements are normally used to form the surface edge profiles or boundaries. They include lines, arcs, splines, and ellipses (Figure 11.3). Figure 11.4 is an example in which wireframe boundaries and cross-sectional features of surfaces are defined by smooth profiles created by using these basic profile elements.

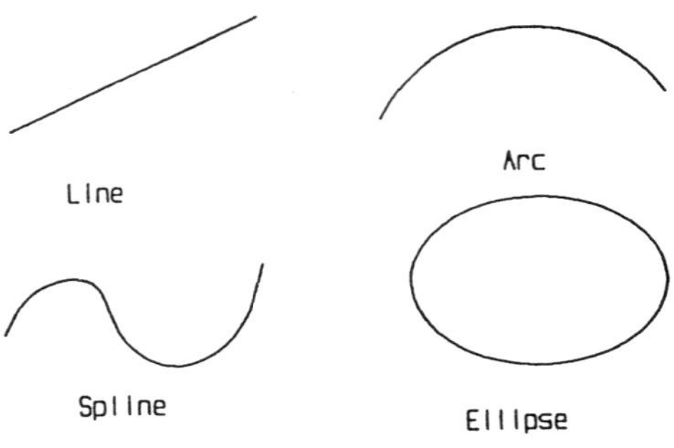

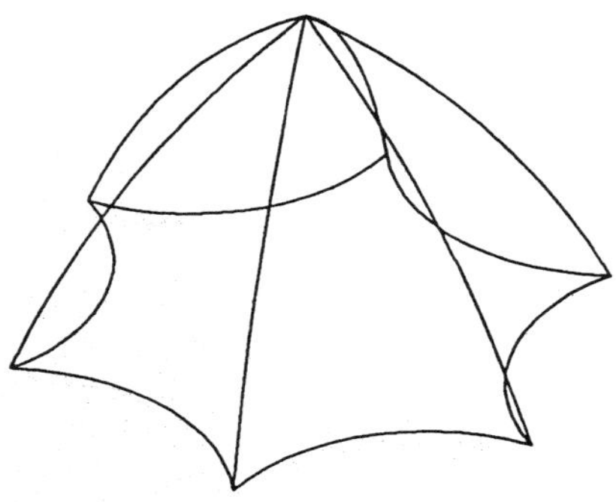

Figure 11.3

Figure 11.4

Construction Plane

A construction plane determines a plane orientation in which a geometric entity is to be placed. An arc, for example, can be constructed on a plane either parallel to the principal XY-, ZX-, or YZ-plane depending on which construction plane is chosen. A construction plane must be specified **before** any geometric entity can be created in a CAD system. Mastercam provides the following **nine standard construction planes**:

• Top Cplane	• Front Cplane	•Last
• Side Cplane	• 3D Cplane	•Entry
• Number	• Normal Cplane	•Rotate

Figure 11.5 shows the axis orientations of the **three** principal construction planes: top, front, and side. The axis orientations for the Top construction plane are the most familiar. Note that the axis assignments are changed when the construction plane is changed to the front or side. The keys to determine the axis orientation for each plane are as follows:

- The X axis is always in the horizontal direction when viewed from the direction normal to the selected plane.
- The Y axis is in the vertical direction on the selected plane.
- The Z axis is perpendicular to both the X and Y axes.

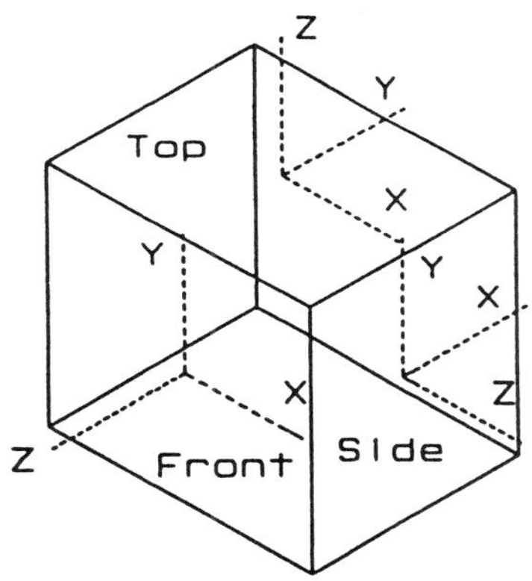

Figure 11.5

The 3D Cplane has similar axis designations to that of the Top plane. The only difference is that it allows lines to be constructed at any two specified endpoints which do not necessarily lie parallel to any one of three principal planes (Figure 11.6).

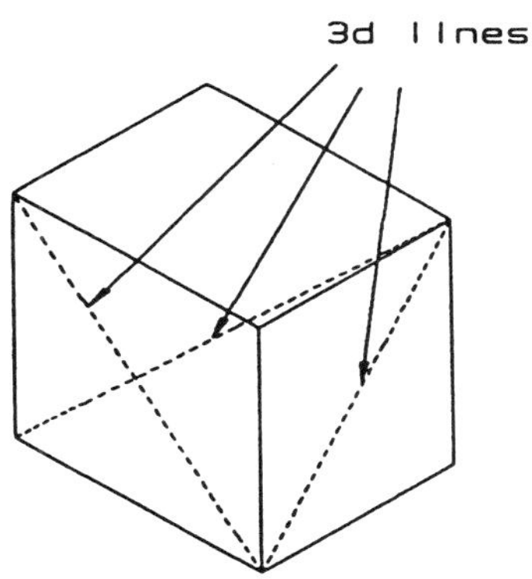

Figure 11.6

2-line Plane

Any two perpendicular lines in the space can be used to define a construction plane. The first line you pick is designated as the X axis and the second picked line becomes the Y axis. The Z axis is perpendicular to both X and Y axes (Figure 11.7).

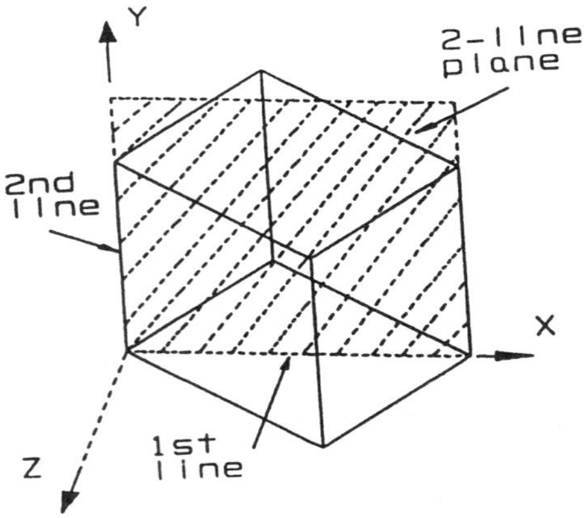

Figure 11.7

Normal Plane

A normal plane is defined by being normal (or perpendicular) to a given line at the selected point (Figure 11.8). An example of using a normal plane is illustrated in Figure 11.9. Two arcs are created using the normal plane which is perpendicular to the given line. These two arcs are located at both ends of the line.

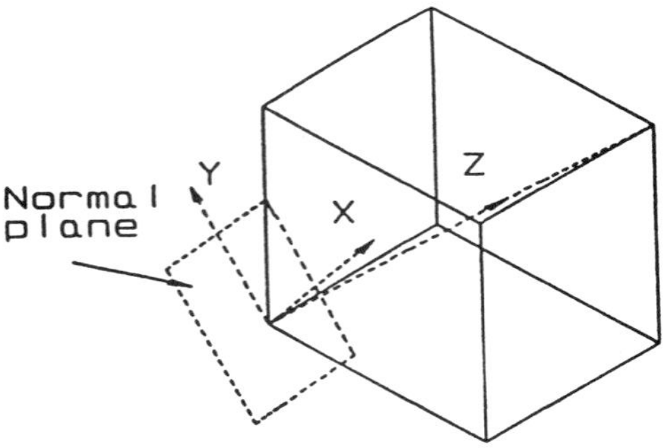

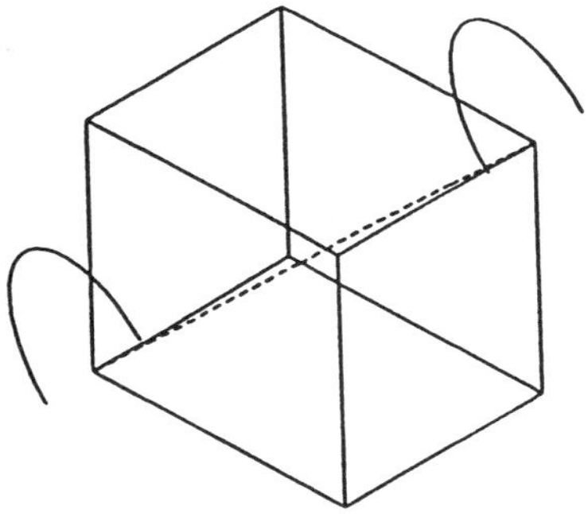

Figure 11.8

Figure 11.9

Z-Depth Control

The Mastercam system uses the Z command in the Secondary Menu to specify the Z value of the geometric entities. Figure 11.10 illustrates how to specify the Z value to properly place the construction plane in a location.

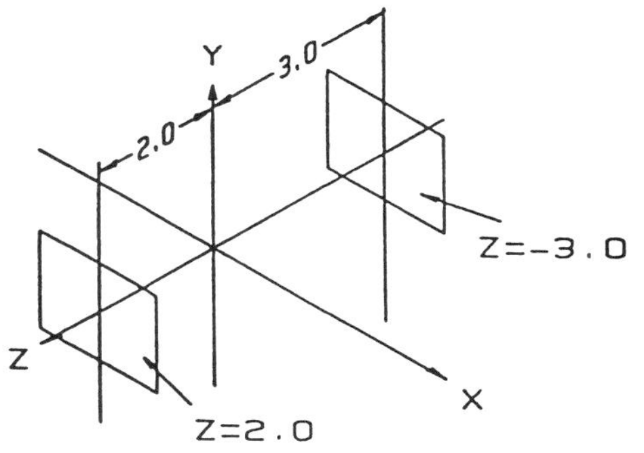

a. Front Cplane

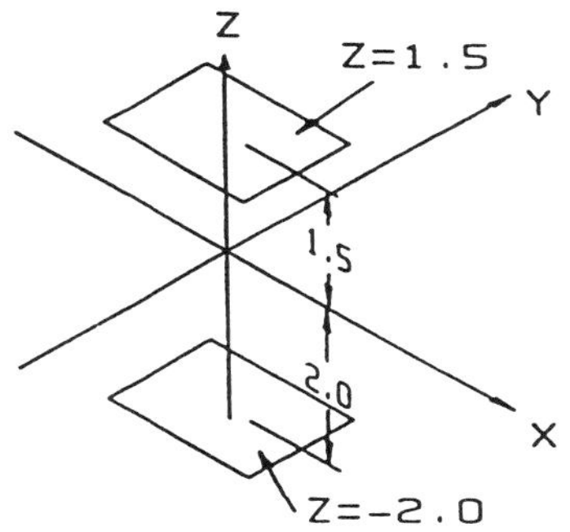

b. Top Cplane

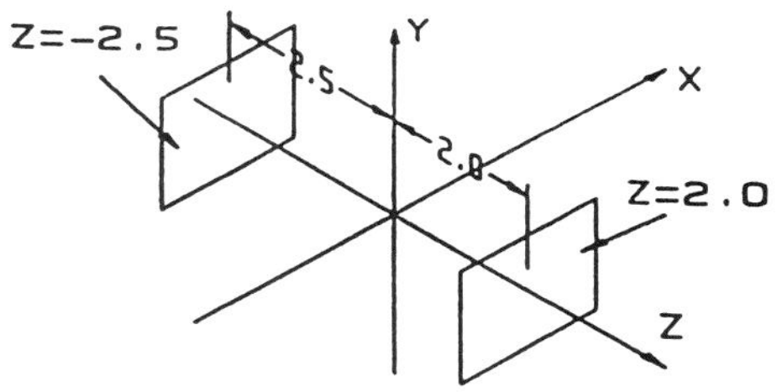

c. Side Cplane

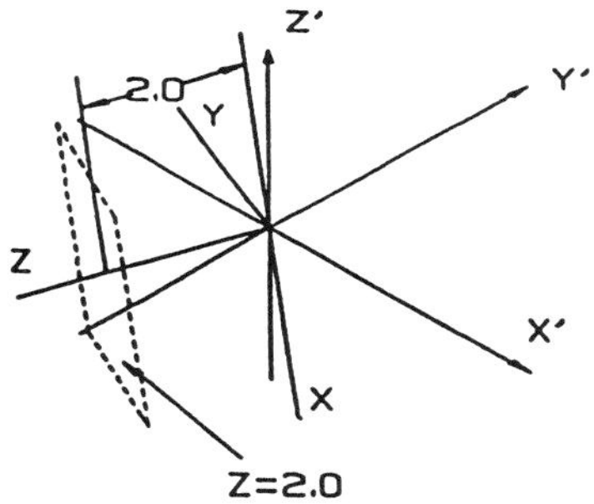

d. Normal Cplane

Figure 11.10

11.2 Wireframe Model Construction Examples

There are sixteen projects presented in this chapter. Each project gives a step-by-step procedure to complete the wireframe model. Only a partial wireframe profile is given in some projects. Useful tips for the edge profiles are provided for most projects. Each wireframe model is used to create the surface model and the toolpath to machine the surface in the following chapters.

1 **Project 1:**

In this project, you will learn to use **Front, Side, and 3D** construction planes to create 4 arcs and 2 lines as shown in Figure 11.11. These surface profile entities are then used to create two ruled surfaces
and two fillet surfaces in chapters 12 and 13, respectively.

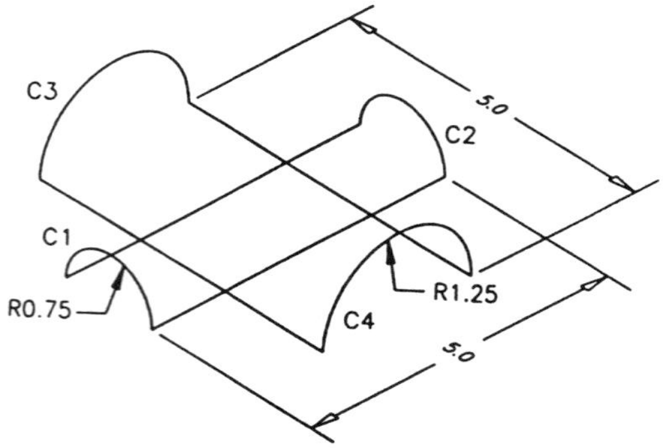

Figure 11.11a. Wireframe model

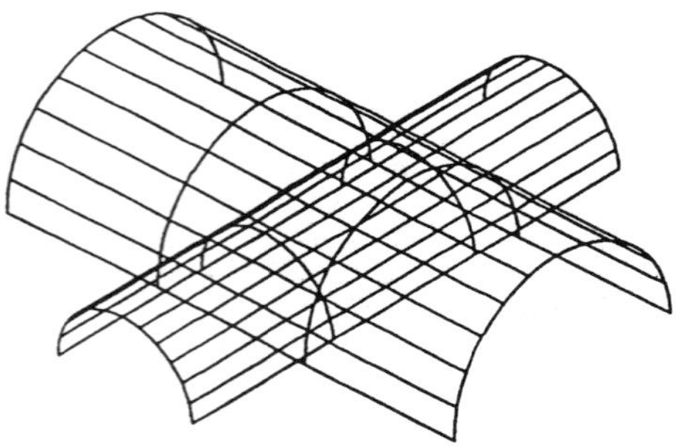

Figure 11.11b. Surface model

Tips 1. Use the Front Cplane to construct the two arcs of .75-in. radius. The front arc has a Z value of 2.5 and the rear arc has the same Z value of 2.5.
2. Use the Side Cplane to create the two arcs of 1.25-in. radius. The right and left arcs have Z values of 2.5.
3. Use the 3D Cplane to construct the four lines connecting the endpoints of the four arcs.

Step 1. Enter the Mastercam Mill.

Follow the procedure in chapter 3 to enter the Mastercam Mill 7.
Press **F9** to show the coordinate axes on the screen

The screen should look like Figure 11.12 on the next page, with the MAIN MENU on the left side and three coordinate axes in the middle.

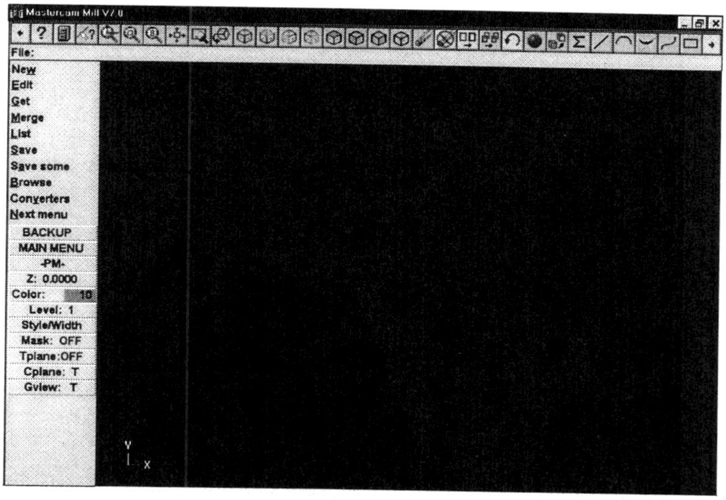

Figure 11.12

Step 2. Select front construction plane and isometric graphics view.

Select **Gview** from the Secondary Menu,
then pick **Isometric** from the Gview Menu
Select **Cplane** from the Secondary Menu,
then pick **Front** from the Cplane Menu

Step 3. Create the circle C1.

Select **Z** from the Secondary Menu, and then enter **2.5**
Select **MAIN MENU** → **Create** → **Arc** → **Polar** → **Center pt**
Enter the center point: **0,0** ←
Enter the radius (1.0): **0.75** ←
Enter the initial angle (0.0): ← to accept the default
Enter the final angle (0.0): **180** ←

Step 4. Create the circle C2.

Select **Z** from the Secondary Menu, and then enter **-2.5** ←
Enter the center point: **0,0** ←
Enter the radius (0.75): ← to accept the default
Enter the initial angle (0.0): ←
Enter the final angle (180.0): ←

Your drawing should currently look like Figure 11.13.

Figure 11.13

Step 5. Create the circle C3 using the side construction plane.

Select **Cplane** from the Secondary Menu,
then pick **Side** from the Cplane Menu
Enter the center point: **0,0** ←
Enter the radius (0.75): **1.25** ←
Enter the initial angle (0.0): ← to accept the default
Enter the final angle (180.0): ← to accept the default

Step 6. Create the circle C4.

Select **Z** from the Secondary Menu, and then enter **2.5** ←
Enter the center point: **0,0** ←
Enter the radius (1.25): ←
Enter the initial angle (0.0): ← to accept the default
Enter the final angle (180.0): ← to accept the default

The drawing appears as in Figure 11.14.

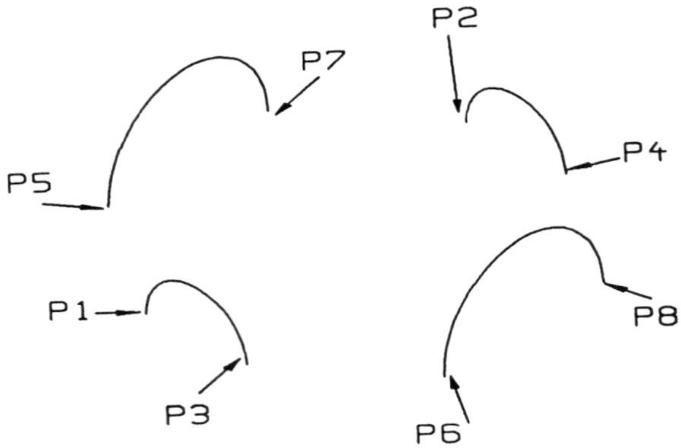

Figure 11.14

Step 7. Create four lines to connect those arcs using a 3D construction plane.

Use the pick points in Figure 11.12.
Select **Cplane → 3D**
Select **MAIN MENU → Create → Line → Endpoints → Endpoint**
Specify the first endpoint: pick **P1**
Specify the second endpoint: pick **P2** to complete the first line
Sequentially pick **P3, P4, P5, P6, P7,** and **P8** to complete the remaining three lines.

The complete drawing would look like Figure 11.15.

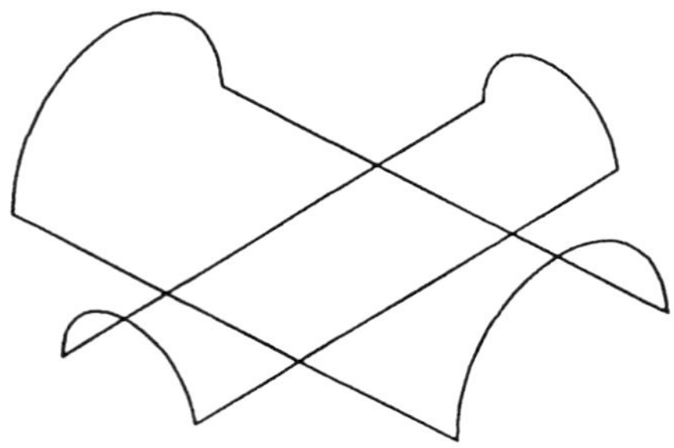

Figure 11.15

Step 8. Save the drawing (ruled1). 2

Select **MAIN MENU → File → Save**

Enter file name (C:\NC\GE3\T.GE3): **ruled1 ←**

Note: This drawing will be used in the following places:

1. For creating two ruled surfaces and two fillet surfaces in chapter 12.
2. For generating intersecting curves and trimming surfaces in chapter 13.

Project 2:

In this project, a normal construction plane is used to create two arcs that are perpendicular to a line. The drawing to be constructed is shown in Figure 11.16.

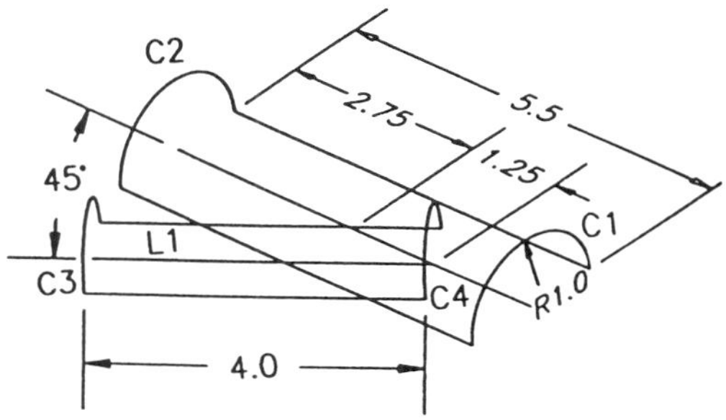

Figure 11.16a. Wireframe model

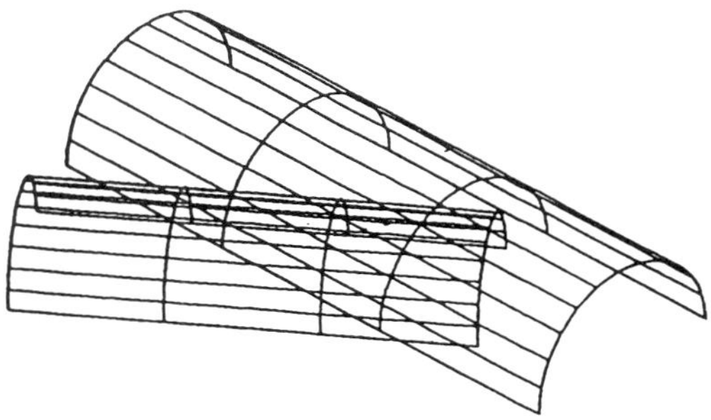

Figure 11.16b. Surface model

Tips
1. Use the Side Cplane to construct two arcs of 1-in. radius. The right arc has a Z value of 2.75 and the left arc is located at Z-2.75.
2. Use the Top Cplane to create a line L1 which has a 45 degree angle with the X axis.
3. Define a normal plane which is perpendicular to line L1.
4. Use the Normal Cplane to create the two arcs that are perpendicular to the line L1. Use **Z → Endpoint** commands and pick at the front end of the angle line to obtain the Z value for the center of the arc.
5. Use 3d Cplane to generate four lines connecting the endpoints of the four arcs.

Step 1. Create the arc C1 using the side construction plane.

First initialize the screen to begin a new start.

Select **MAIN MENU → File → New → Yes** to initialize Mastercam

Select **Gview → Isometric**

Select **Cplane → Side**

Select **Z** and then enter **2.75** ←

Select **MAIN MENU → Create → Arc → Polar → Center pt**

Enter the center point: **0,0** ←

Enter the radius (1.0): **1.0** ←

Enter the initial angle (0.0): ← to accept the default

Enter the final angle (360.0): **180** ←

Step 2. Create the arc C2.

Select **Z** and then enter **-2.75** ←

Select **BACKUP → Center pt**

Enter the center point: **0,0** ←

Enter the radius (1.0): ←

Enter the initial angle (0.0): ←

Enter the final angle (180.0): ←

The drawing of two arcs should appear as in Figure 11.17

Figure 11.17

Step 3. Create line L1 using the top construction plane.

Select **Cplane → Top**

Select **Z**, and then enter **0** ←

Select **MAIN MENU → Create → Line → Polar**

Specify an endpoint: **1.25,0** ←

Enter the angle in degrees (0.0): **215** ←

Enter the line length (1.0): **4** ←

The drawing now should look like Figure 11.18.

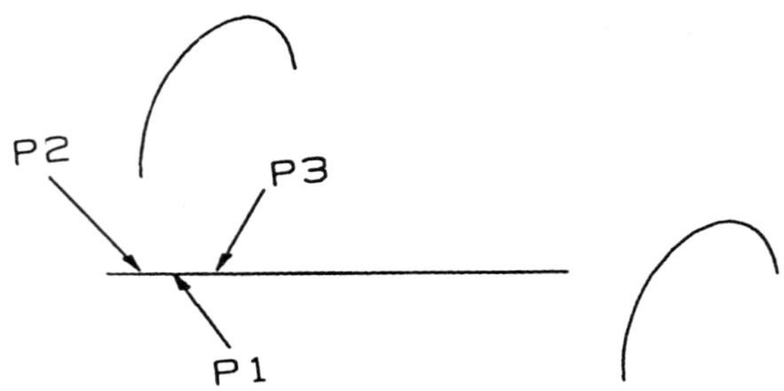

Figure 11.18

Step 4. Create arc C3 using the normal construction plane.

Use the pick points labeled in Figure 11.18.
Select **Cplane** → **Normal**
Select the normal line: pick **P1** ←
Select plane: pick **Save**
Select **Z**, and then select **Endpoint** from the point menu
Pick **P2** to trap the endpoint
Select **MAIN MENU** → **Create** → **Arc** → **Polar** → **Center pt** → **Endpoint**
Enter the center point: **P3**
Enter the radius (1.0): **0.75** ←
Enter the initial angle (0.0): **180** ←
Enter the final angle (0.0): **0** ←

Your drawing should appear as in Figure 11.19.

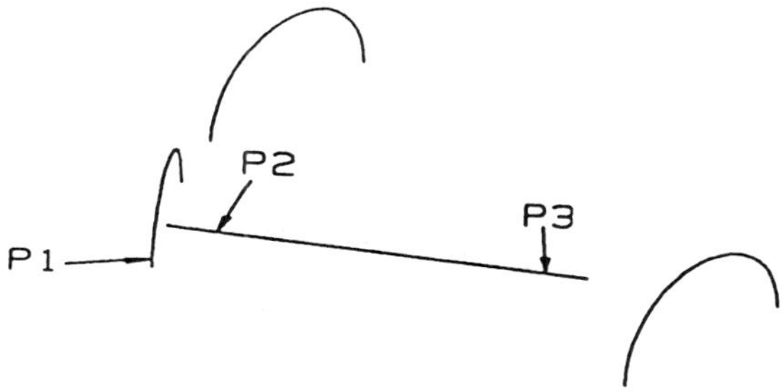

Figure 11.19

Step 5. Create the arc C4 using the transformation command.

Use the pick points in Figure 11.19 on the previous page.
Select **Cplane** → **3D**
Select **MAIN MENU** → **Xform** → **Translate** → **Only** → **Arcs**
Select an entity: pick **P1**
Select **BACKUP** → **Done** → **Between pts** →**Endpoint**
Enter the point to translate from: pick **P2**
Enter the point to translate to : pick **P3**
Set the parameters as shown
in the translate window:

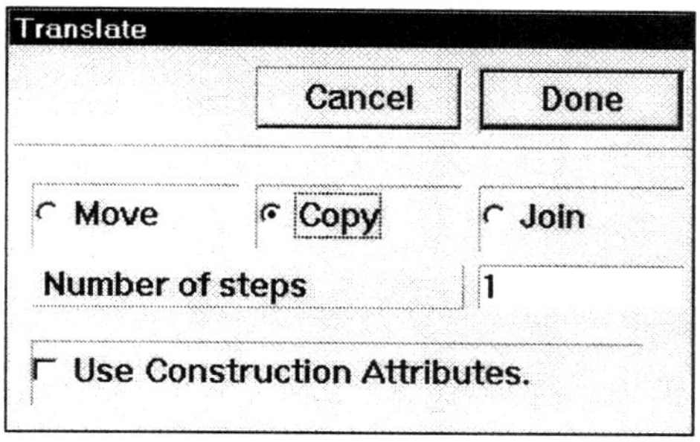

Select **Done**

The drawing with four arcs should look like Figure 11.20.

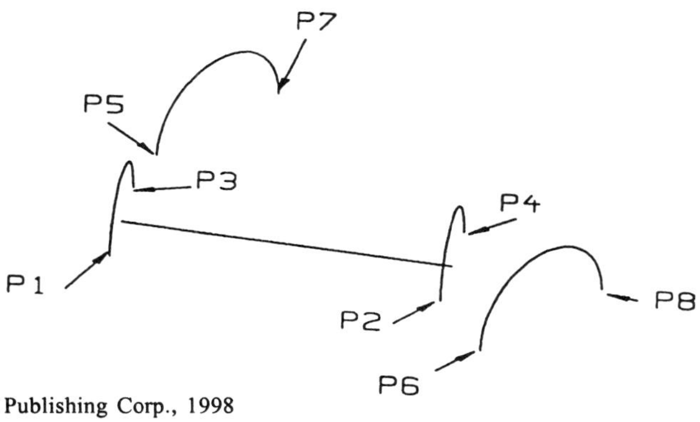

Figure 11.20

Step 6. Construct four lines.

Use the pick points in Figure 11.20.
Select **MAIN MENU → Create → Line → Endpoints**
Specify the first end point: pick **P1**
Specify the second endpoint: pick **P2** to complete the first line.
Sequentially pick the entities **P3 - P8** to complete the remaining three lines.

The complete drawing appears in Figure 11.21a.

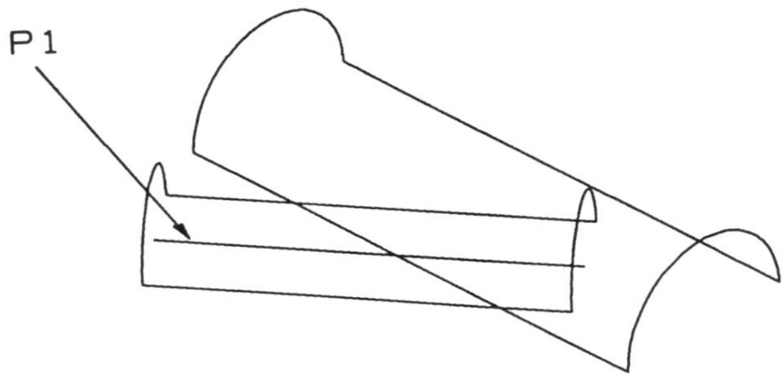

Figure 11.21a

Step 7. Delete the construction line using the pick point in Figure 11.21a.

Select **MAIN MENU → Delete**
Pick **P1** to delete the construction line.
The complete drawing should look like Figure 11.21b.

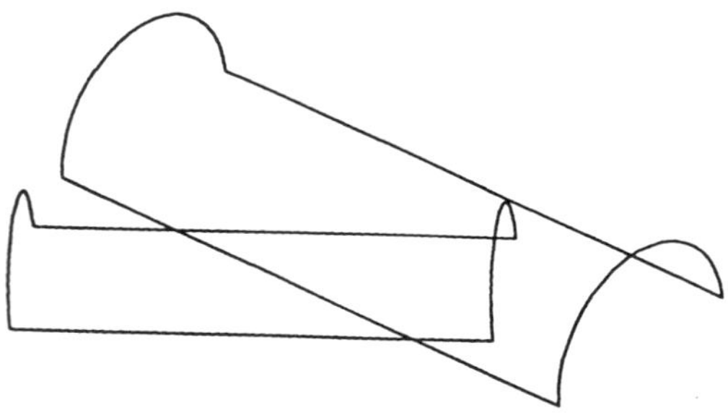

Figure 11.21b

Step 8. Save the drawing ruled2.

Select **MAIN MENU → File → Save**
Enter file name (C:\NC\GE3\T.GE3): **ruled2 ←**

Note: This drawing is used to generate ruled surfaces, and fillet surfaces with a 2variable radius in chapter 11.

Project 3:

In this project three entities are constructed at three different Z levels as shown in Figure 11.22. These three entities will be used to create a ruled surface and a loft surface, respectively, in chapter 12.

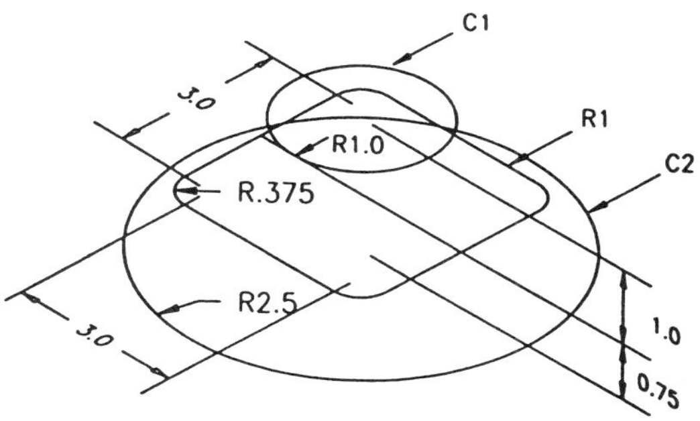

Figure 11.22a. Wireframe model

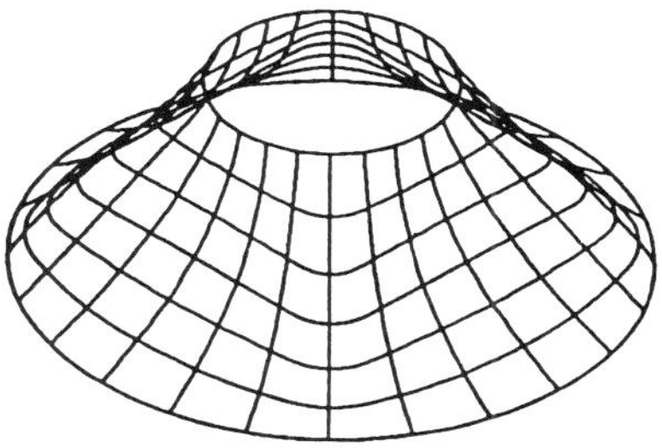

Figure 11.22b. Surface model

Step 1. Create the circle C1 using the Top construction plane.

Initialize the screen if necessary
Select **Gview** → **Isometric** to select the isometric graphics view
Select **Cplane** → **Top** to select the top construction plane
Select **Z**, and then enter **0** ← if necessary
Select **MAIN MENU** → **Create** → **Arc** → **Circ pt rad**
Enter the center point: **0,0** ←
Enter the radius (0.0): **1.0** ←

Step 2. Create the rectangle R1.

Select **Z**, and then enter **-1.0** ←
Select **MAIN MENU** → **Create** → **Rectangle** → **1 point**
Enter the lower left corner: **-1.5,-1.5** ←
Enter the width (2.0): **3** ←
Enter the height (1.0): **3** ←

Your drawing should appear as Figure 11.23.

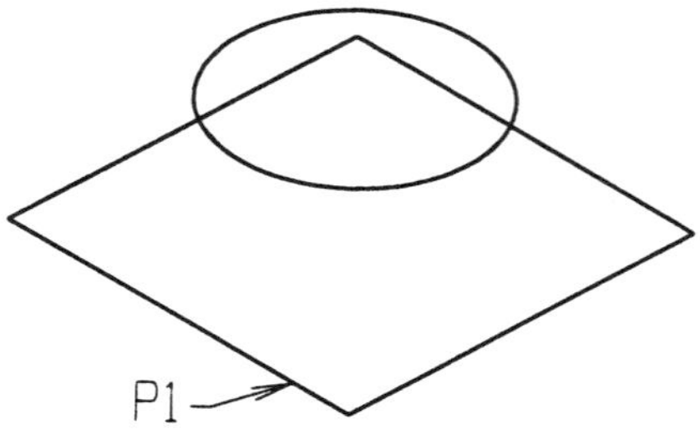

Figure 11.23

Step 3. Add fillets to the four corners of the rectangle.

Use the pick point in Figure 11.23.
Select **MAIN MENU → Modify → Fillet**
Pick **Radius** from the parameter menu
Enter the fillet radius: **0.375 ←**
Select **Chain**
Pick **P1**
Select **Done**
The four fillets are shown in Figure 11.24.

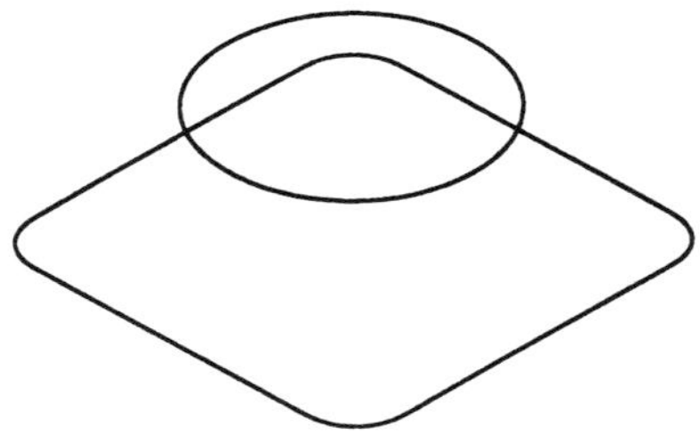

Figure 11.24

Step 4. Create the arc C2.

Select **Z**, and then enter **-1.75 ←**
Select **MAIN MENU → Create → Arc → Circ pt rad**
Enter the center point: **0,0 ←**
Enter the radius (1.0): **2.5 ←**

Your drawing would appear as Figure 11.25.

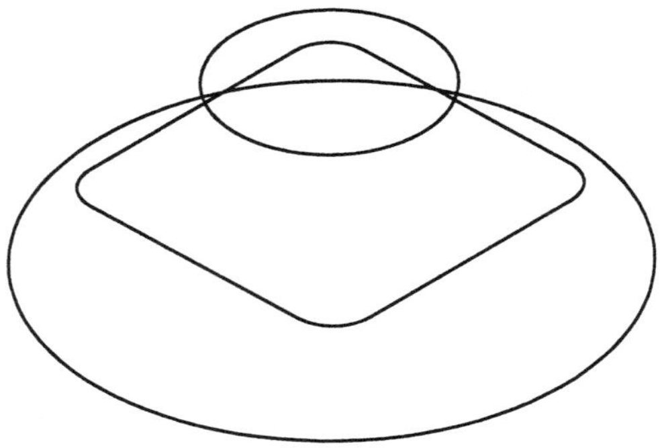

Figure 11.25

Step 5. Save the drawing using the name: 3contour. 4

Select **MAIN MENU → File → Save**

Enter the file name: **3contour ←**

Note: This drawing is used to create a ruled surface with three defining contours. It is also used to generate a loft surface in chapter 12.

Project 4:

In this example, nineteen elliptical contours are created in the side construction plane (Figure 11.26). The first and the last contours are rotated by 90° and -90°, respectively, about their end points. The rotation of these two contours must be made by using the front construction plane. These cross-sectional contours are the ideal case for creating a **loft surface.**

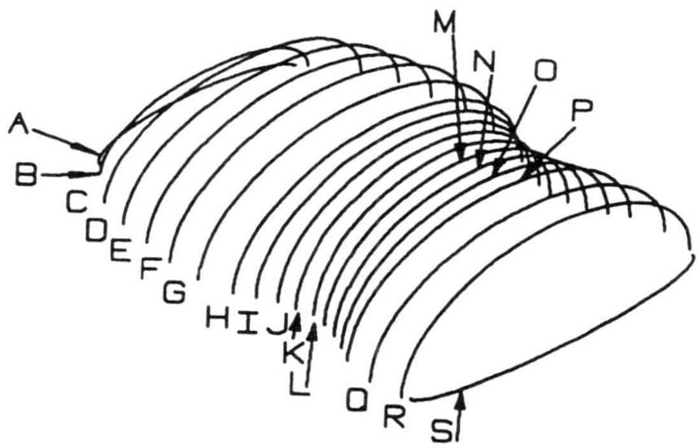

a. Wireframe model

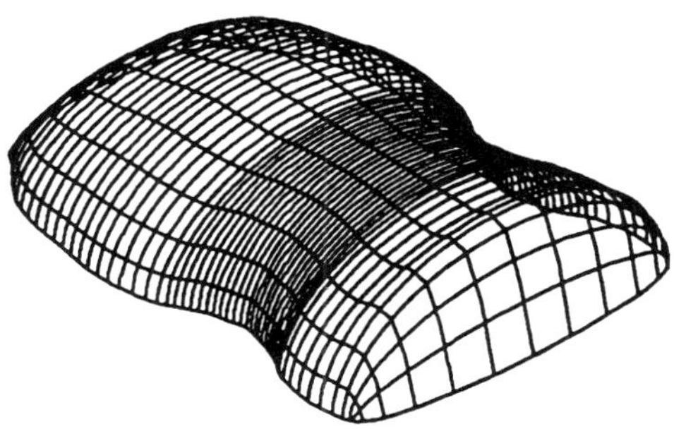

b. Surface model

Figure 11.26

The section position (Z coordinate in the side construction plane) and the axis radii of these elliptical contours at each section are tabulated below.

Section	Z-value	Major axis radius (a)	Minor axis radius (b)
A	0.2	0.8	0.2
B	0.25	0.875	0.375
C	0.5	1.083	0.563
D	0.75	1.167	0.638
E	1.0	1.2	0.7
F	1.25	1.25	0.75
G	1.5	1.25	0.75
H	1.75	1.2	0.75
I	1.875	1.125	0.75
J	2.0	1.063	0.75
K	2.125	1.03	0.75
L	2.25	1.0	0.75
M	2.375	1.03	0.75
N	2.5	1.06	0.75
O	2.625	1.125	0.75
P	2.75	1.2	0.75
Q	3.0	1.25	0.75
R	3.25	1.25	0.75
S	3.3	1.2	0.2

⌛**Tips** 1. Use Side Cplane to construct all ninteen contours.

2. Contours A and S are rotated 90° and -90°, respectively, using the Front Cplane.

Step 1. Enter Mastercam. Set the Secondary Menu to the following settings:

Initialize the screen if necessary
Select **Z**, and then enter **0.2** ←
Select **Cplane** → **Side**
Select **Gview** → **Isometric**

Step 2. Construct the first contour A.

Select **MAIN MENU** → **Create** → **Next menu** → **Ellipse**
Select A radius, enter a (X axis radius) (2.00): **0.8** ←
Select B radius, enter b (Y axis radius) (1.00): **0.2** ←
Select Start angle, enter the starting angle (0.00): ← to accept the default
Select the End angle, enter the final angle (360.00): **180** ←
Select Rot angle, enter the rotation angle (0.00): ← to accept the default
Select Center pt, enter the center: **0,0** ←

The drawing with the contour A should appear as in Figure 11.27.

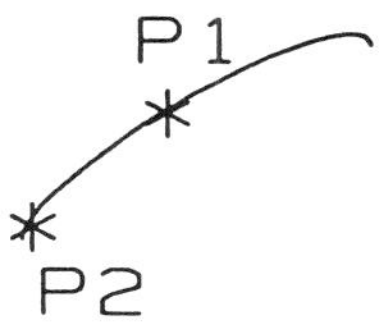

Figure 11.27

Step 3. Rotate the contour A by 90° using the Front construction plane.

Use the pick points of Figure 11.27.
Select **Cplane → Front**
Select **MAIN MENU → Xform → Rotate → Only → Splines**
Pick **P1** to select the entity
Select **BACKUP → Done → Point → Endpoint**
Pick **P2** to select the endpoint of the ellipse
Enter the rotation parameters as below:

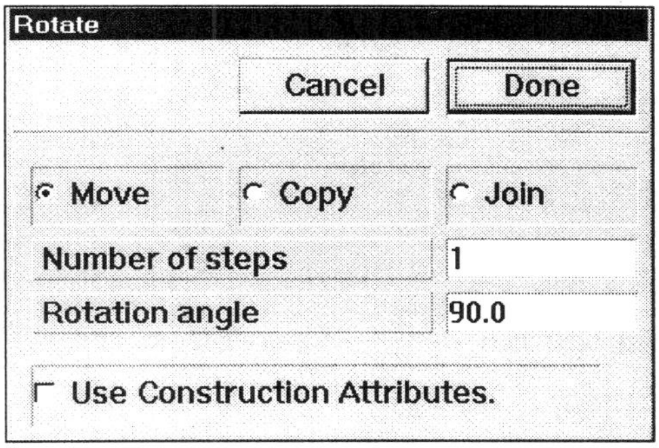

Select **Done**
The rotated ellipse contour should resemble Figure 11.28.

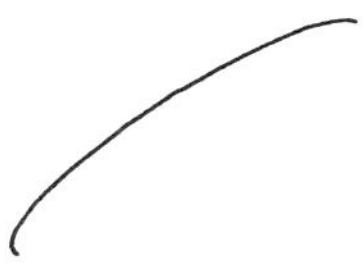

Figure 11.28

Step 4. Construct the second contour B using the side construction plane.

Select **Cplane → Side**
Select **Z**, and then enter **0.25** ←
Select **MAIN MENU → Create → Next menu → Ellipse**
Enter a: **0.875** ←
Enter b: **0.375** ←
Enter the starting angle (0.00): ← to accept the default
Enter the final angle (180.00): ← to accept the default
Enter the rotation angle (0.00); ← to accept the default
Enter the center: **0,0** ←

Step 5. Construct the remaining seventeen contours.

Repeat step 4 by using the Z value, X axis radius (a), and Y axis radius (b) given in the table on page 11-16 to complete the remaining contours.

The nineteen contours should appear as Figure 11.29.

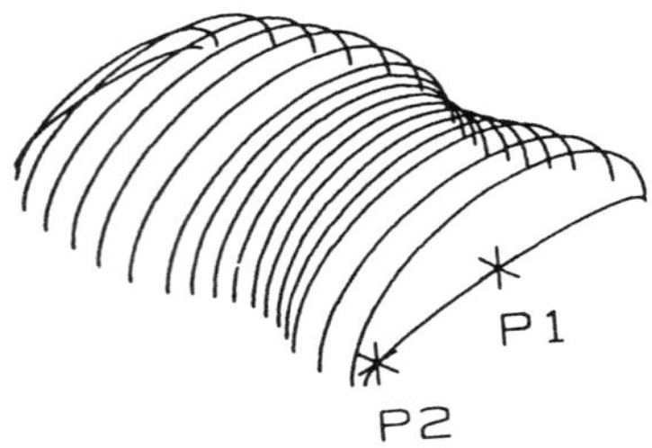

Figure 11.29

Step 6. Rotate the last contour S by -90° using the front construction plane.

Use the pick points in Figure 11.29.
Select **Cplane → Front**
Select **MAIN MENU → Xform → Rotate → Only Splines**
Pick **P1** to select the last contour **S** for rotation
Select **BACKUP → Done → Point → Endpoint**
Pick **P2** to select the end point of the contour
Set the Rotate parameters as below:

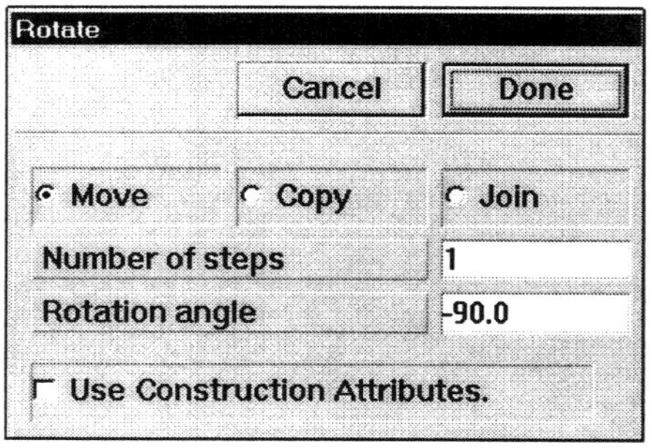

Select **Done** to complete the rotation.

Your final drawing should appear as Figure 11.30.

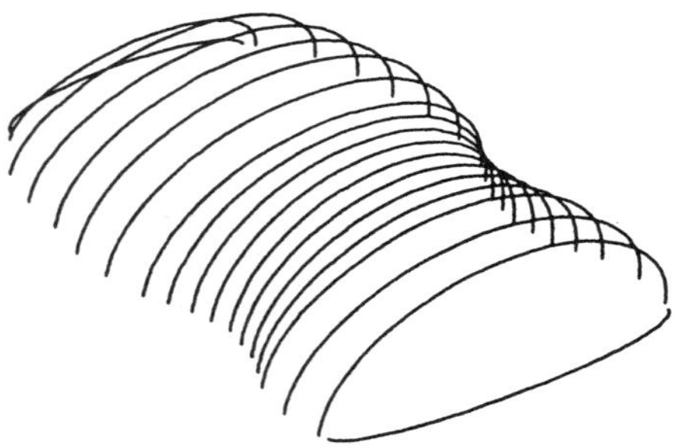

Figure 11.30

Step 7. Save the drawing using the filename loft2.

Select **MAIN MENU → File → Save**
Enter the file name: **loft2** ←
Note: This drawing will be used to generate a loft surface in chapter 12.

Project 5:

A wireframe model consisting of four contours as shown in Figure 11.31 are created in this example. A rectangular box is constructed first in the top plane. Arcs C1 and C2 are created using the front plane, and the other two contours are generated using the side plane.

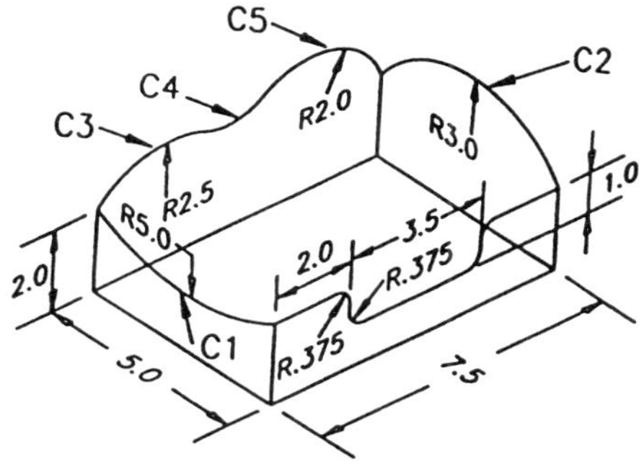

Figure 11.31a. Wireframe model

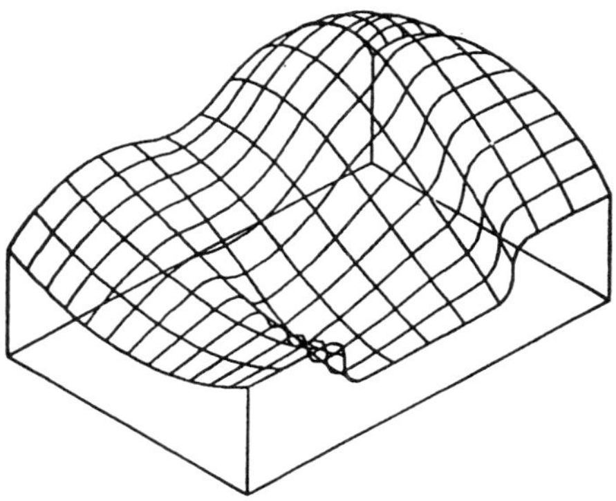

Figure 11.31b. Surface model

Tips 1. Create a rectangular box using Top Cplane.

2. Use Front Cplane to create arcs C1 and C2. Both arcs are defined by endpoints and radius.
3. Use Side Cplane to create the other two contours.

4. Generate three construction lines for creating the right contour.

5. Create a vertical construction line to help determine the endpoints of the two base arcs in the left contour.

Step 1. Enter Mastercam Mill and set the Secondary Menu to the proper settings.

Initialize the screen if necessary.
Select **Z**, and then enter **0** ← if necessary
Select **Cplane** → **Top** if necessary
Select **Gview** → **Isometric**

Step 2. Create a rectangular box.

Select **MAIN MENU** →**Create** → **Rectangle** → **2 points**
Enter **0,0** ← for the lower left corner
Enter **5,7.5** ← for the upper right corner
Press **Alt** + **F1** then **F2** to fit the drawing.
Select **MAIN MENU** → **Xform**
Select **Translate** → **All** → **Lines** → **Done** → **Rectangang**
Enter the translation vector: **Z-2** ←
Set the parameters as here:

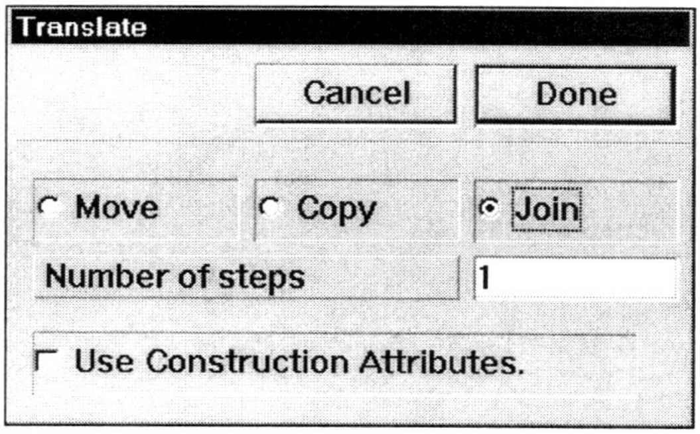

Select **Done**
The rectangular box should appear as Figure 11.32.

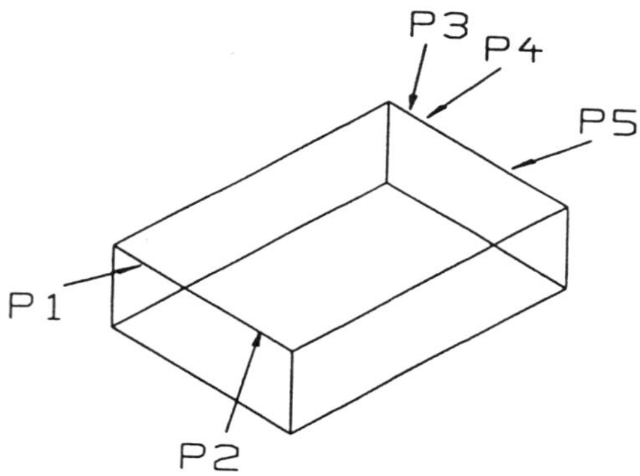

Figure 11.32

Step 3. Create the two arcs C1 and C2 using the front construction plane.

Use the pick points in Figure 11.32.
Select **Cplane** → **Front**
Select **MAIN MENU** →**Create** → **Arc** → **Endpoints** → **Endpoint**
Pick **P1** and **P2**
Enter the radius (1.00): **5** ←
Four arc segments should appear on the screen.
Use the mouse to pick the desired arc for C1 (3rd arc from the top).
Select **Z** → **Endpoint**
Pick **P3** to trap to the endpoint of the selected line
Pick **P4** and **P5** to trap the end points for the second arc

Enter the radius (5.00): **3** ←

Pick the desired arc (2nd arc from the top) to complete the arc C2

The drawing should look like Figure 11.33.

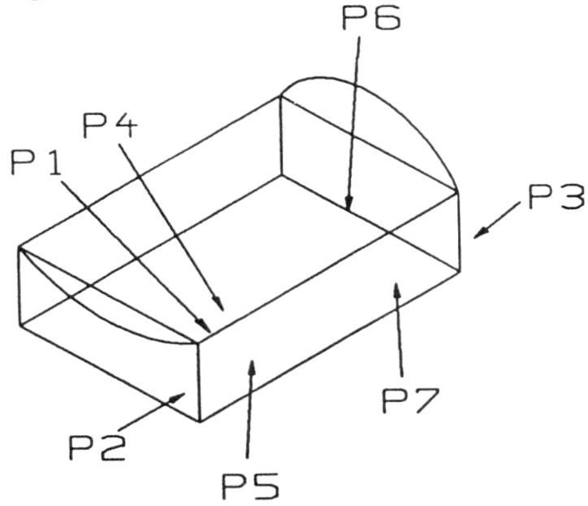

Figure 11.33

Step 4. Create three construction lines using pick points in Figure 11.33.

Select **Cplane → Side**

Select **Z → Endpoint**

Pick **P1** to obtain the Z value of the picked line (Z5.00 should appear)

Select **MAIN MENU → Create → Line → Horizontal**

Pick **P2** and **P3**, then enter **-1.0** for the Y coordinate

Select **BACKUP → Vertical**

Pick **P4** and **P5**, then enter **2.0** for the X coordinate

Pick **P6** and **P7**, then enter **5.5** for the X coordinate

The drawing should resemble Figure 11.34.

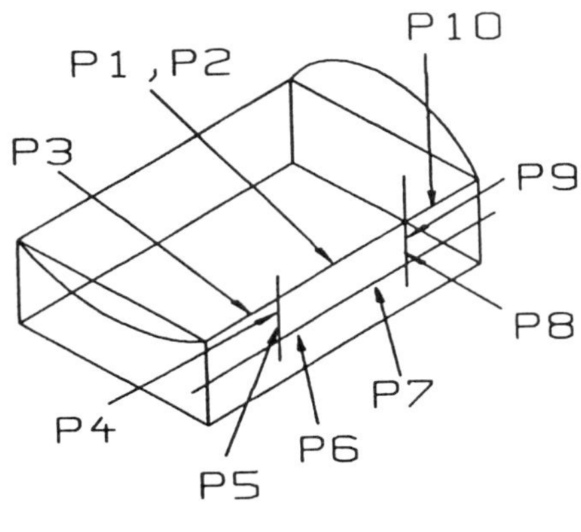

Figure 11.34

Step 5. Add four fillets. Use the pick points in Figure 11.34.

Select **MAIN MENU → Modify → Break → 2 pieces**

Pick **P1** to select the entity to break

Select the Midpoint

Pick **P2** to enter the breakpoint

Select **MAIN MENU → Modify → Fillet → Radius**

Enter the fillet radius (0.25): **0.375** ←

Sequentially pick **P3, P4, P5, P6, P7, P8, P9,** and **P10** to complete the four fillets.

The drawing should appear as Figure 11.35.

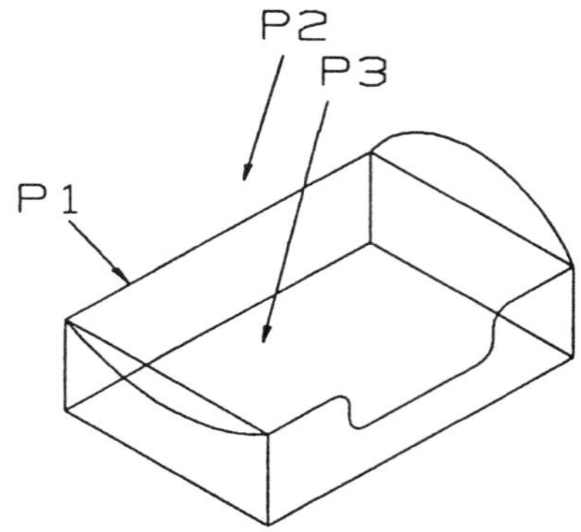

Figure 11.35

Step 6. Create a vertical construction line for creating the three arcs. C3, C4, and C5. Use the pick points in Figure 11.35.

Select **Z** → **Endpoint**
Pick **P1** to set the Z value (Z=0 should appear)
Select **MAIN MENU** → **Create** → **Line** → **Vertical**
Pick **P2** and **P3**
Enter **3.75** ← for the X coordinate

The vertical construction line should appear as Figure 11.36.

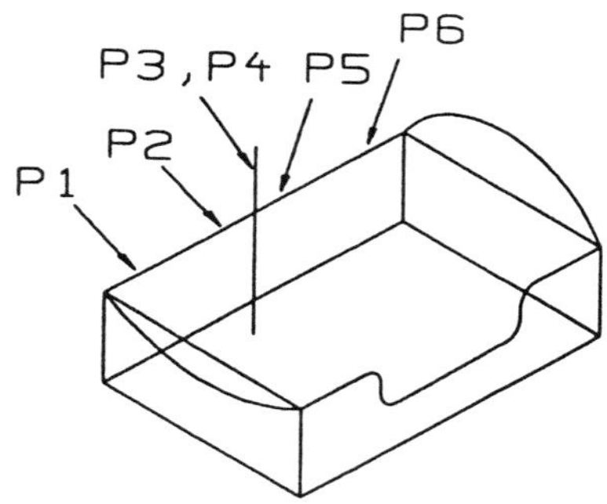

Figure 11.36

Step 7. Create two arcs C3 and C4. Use the pick points from Figure 11.36 .

Select **MAIN MENU** → **Create** → **Arc** → **Endpoints** → **Endpoint**
Pick **P1** for the first point
Select **Intersec** from the point menu
Pick **P2** and **P3** to determine the second point
Enter **2.5** ← for the radius (Four arc segments will appear.)
Use the mouse to pick the desired arc (2nd from the top) for C3
Select **Intersec**
Pick **P4** and **P5** for the first point of arc C4
Select **Endpoint** from the point menu, than pick P6 for the second point
Enter **2.0** ← for the radius
Pick the desired arc (2nd arc from the top) from the given four arc segments

The two arcs C3 and C4 should appear as in Figure 11.37.

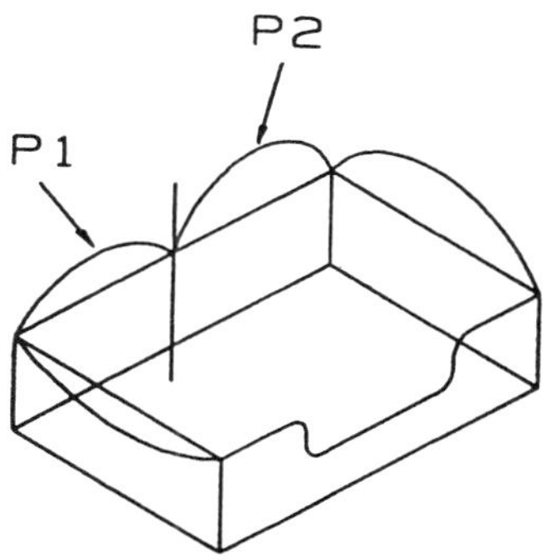

Figure 11.37

Step 8. Create a fillet C5 that is tangent to two arcs C3 and C4.

Use the pick points in Figure 11.37.

Select **MAIN MENU → Modify → Fillet → Radius**

Enter **1.5** ← for the radius

Pick **P1** and **P2** to complete the fillet

The drawing should look like Figure 11.38.

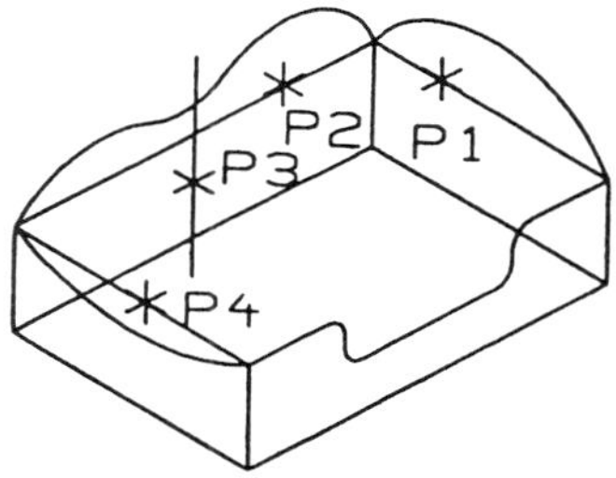

Figure 11.38

Step 9. Delete construction lines. Use the pick points in Figure 11.38.

Select **MAIN MENU → Delete**

Pick **P1, P2, P3,** and **P4** to delect four lines

The final drawing should appear as Figure 11.39.

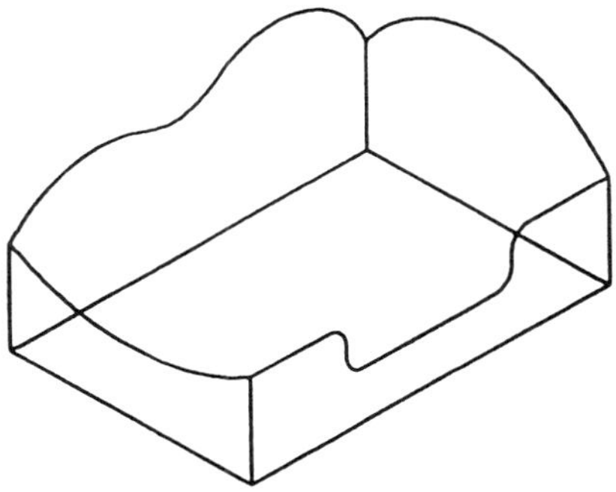

Figure 11.39

Step 10. Save the drawing in the filename coons1.

Select **MAIN MENU → File → Save**

Enter **coons1** for the file name

6 ## Project 6:

A wireframe model as shown in Figure 11.40a is constructed in this example. It is used to generate a surface shown in Figure 11.40b.

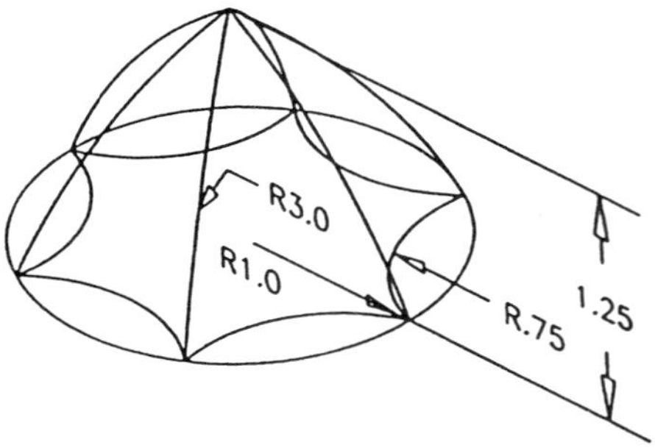

Figure 11.40a. Wireframe model

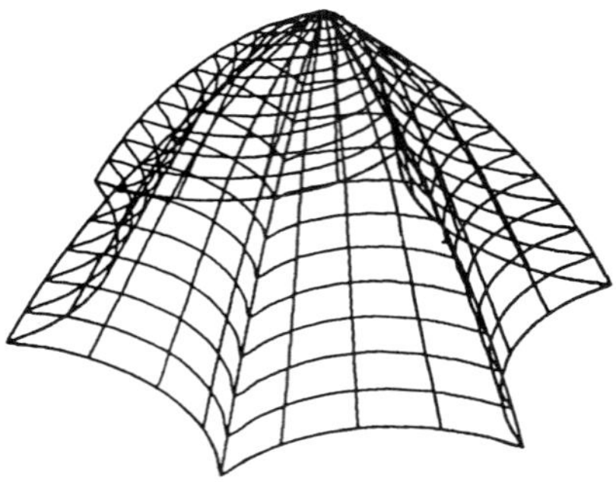

Figure 11.40b. Surface model

Tips
1. Create a base circle and a line that starts from the origin and is parallel to the X axis in the Top Cplane. Copy this line 5 times by rotating about the origin.
2. Use the intersection points between the base circle and the six lines as the endpoints to create six arcs.
3. Use Front Cplane to create a profile arc. This profile arc is then copied 5 times by rotating about the origin in Top Cplane.

Step 1. Enter the Mastercam Mill and set the Secondary Menu to the following settings if necessary:

Z=0
Cplane: Top
Gview: Top

Step 2. Create one circle and two lines.

Select **MAIN MENU →Create → Arc → Circ pt rad**
Enter the center point: **0,0** ←
Enter the radius (1.00): **1.0** ← (A circle will appear on the screen.)
Select **MAIN MENU → Create → Line → Polar**
Specify an endpoint: **0,0** ←
Enter the angle in degrees (0.00): **0** ←
Enter the line length (1.00): **1.5** ←
Specify an endpoint: **0,0** ←
Enter the angle in degrees: **60** ←
Enter the line length: **1.5** ←

The drawing should appear as Figure 11.41.

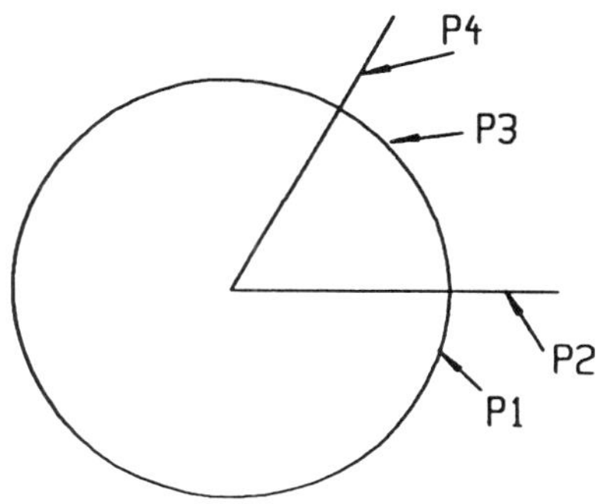

Figure 11.41

Step 3. Create an arc. Use the pick points in Figure 11.41 on the previous page.

Select **MAIN MENU → Create → Arc → Endpoints → Intersec**
Enter the first point: pick **P1** and **P2**
Select **Intersec** again
Enter the second point: pick **P3** and **P4**
Enter the radius (1.00): **0.75** ← (Four arc segments should appear.)
Pick at the desired arc (3rd arc from the right) to complete the selection.
The arc is added as shown in Figure 11.42 as shown at the top of the next page.

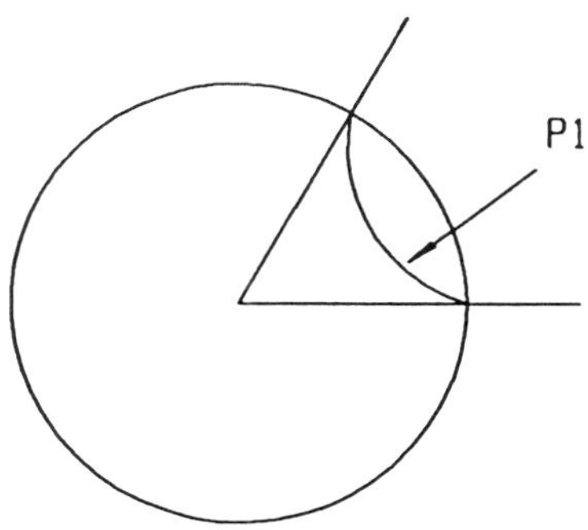

Figure 11.42

Step 4. Create the remaining five arcs.

Rotate the arc five times, at 60° intervals each.
Use the pick point in Figure 11.42.
Select **MAIN MENU → Xform → Rotate → Only → Arcs**
Pick **P1** to select the arc to rotate
Select **BACKUP → Done → Origin**
Set the Rotate parameters as below:

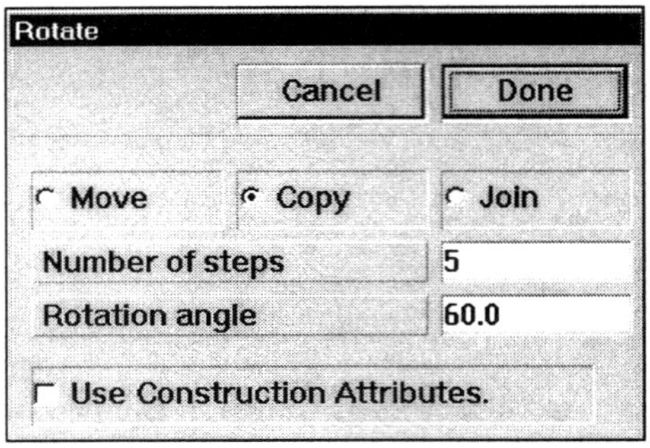

Select **Done**

Your drawing should look like Figure 11.43.

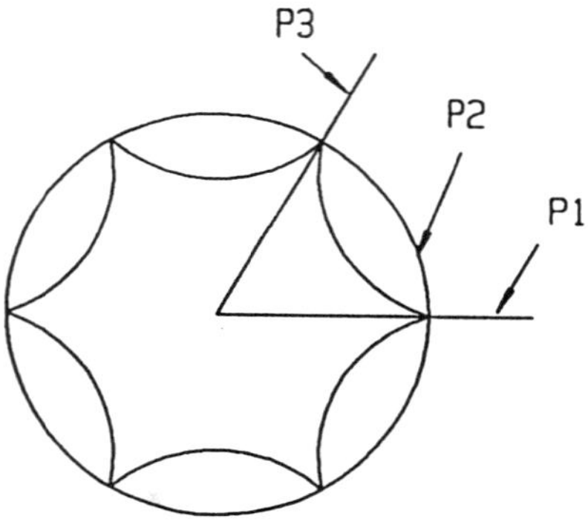

Figure 11.43

Step 5. Delete the construction lines and arc. Use the pick points in Figure 11.43.

Select **MAIN MENU → Delete**
Sequentially pick **P1 - P3** to erase 2 lines and 1 arc
Select **Gview → Isometric**

The drawing should resemble Figure 11.44.

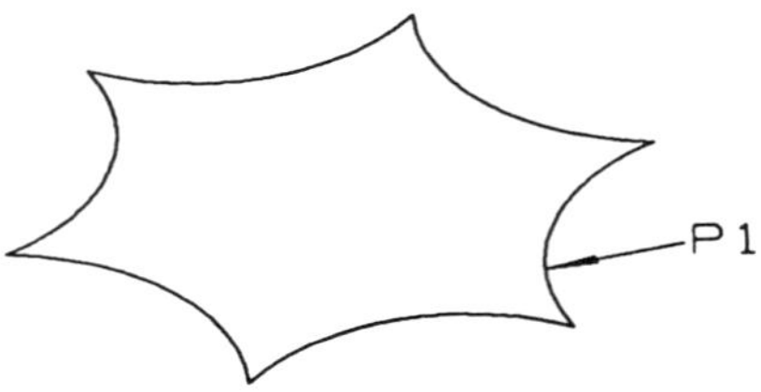

Figure 11.44

Step 6. Create the profile arc using the Front construction plane.

Use the pick points in Figure 11.44.

Select **Cplane → Front**

Select MAIN MENU →Create → Arc → Endpoints → Endpoint

Enter the first point: pick **P1**

Enter the second point: enter **0,1.25** ←

Enter the radius (.75): **3** ←

Select an arc: pick at the desired arc (the small convex arc)

The drawing should look like Figure 11.45.

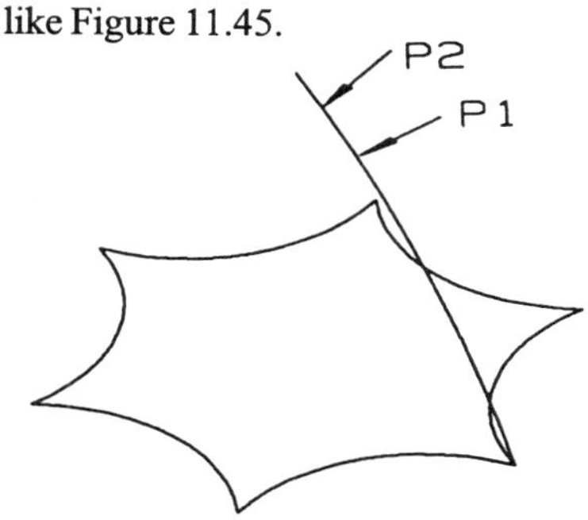

Figure 11.45

Step 7. Copy the arc profile to the other five locations using the Top construction plane. Use the pick points in Figure 11.45.

Select **Cplane → Top**

Select **MAIN MENU → Xform → Rotate**

Select an entity: pick **P1**

Select **Done → Point → Endpoint**

Pick **P2** to select the point to rotate about

Set the rotate parameters as shown here:

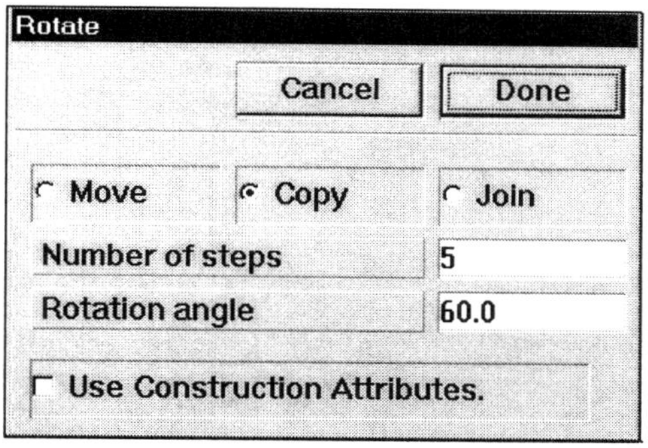

Select **Done**

The final drawing should resemble Figure 11.46.

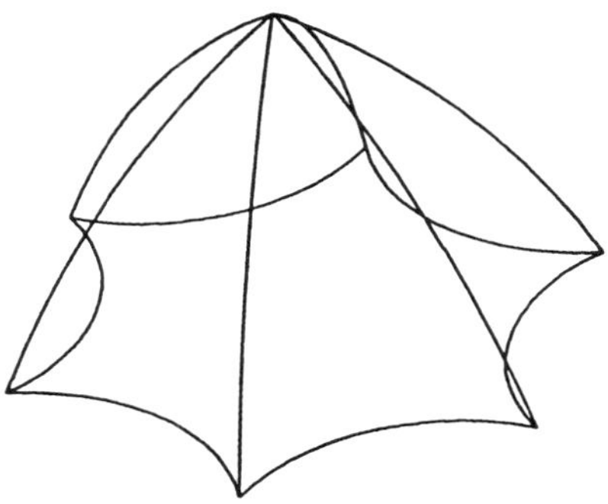

Figure 11.46

7 **Step 8. Save the drawing (coons3).**

Select **MAIN MENU → File → Save**
Enter file name: **coons3 ←**

Note: This drawing is an ideal case for creating a coons surface.

Project 7:

The wireframe model of an object with 26 faces, Figure 11.47, is presented in this example.

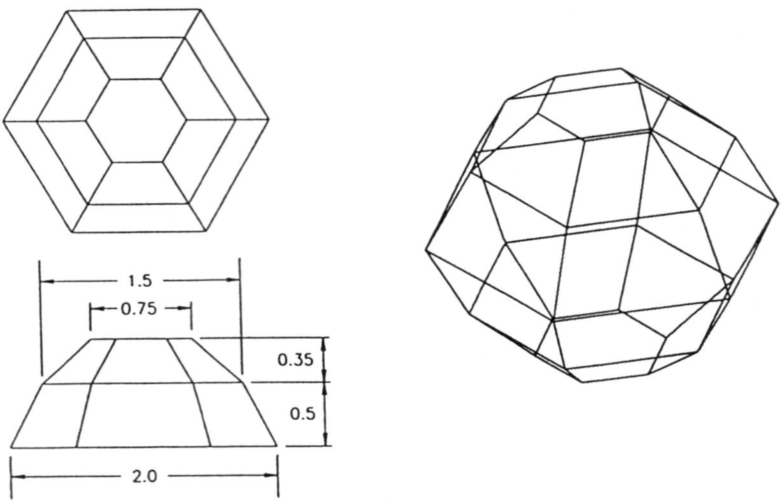

Figure 11.47

Tips 1. Create 3 construction circles and six lines to find the vertices of the three hexagons.

2. The two smaller hexagons are then translated to the proper Z positions, Z0.5 and Z0.85, respectively.
3. Use the Top Gview and the 3-d construction plane to connect the lines between the vertices. The use of the Top Gview helps in picking the right vertices which are not so easily seen in the isometric view.
4. Rotate the upper half model by 180° about the origin using the Front construction plane.

Step 1. Create three construction arcs using the Top construction plane.

Select **MAIN MENU →Create → Arc → Circ pt rad**
Enter **0,0** ← for the center point
Enter **0.375** ← for the radius to complete the first arc
Enter **0,0** ← for the center point
Enter **0.75** ← for the radius of the second arc
Enter **0,0** ← for the center point
Enter **1** ← for the radius of the third arc
Press **Alt + F1**, and then **F2** to fit the drawing.
The drawing with three arcs should resemble Figure 11.48.

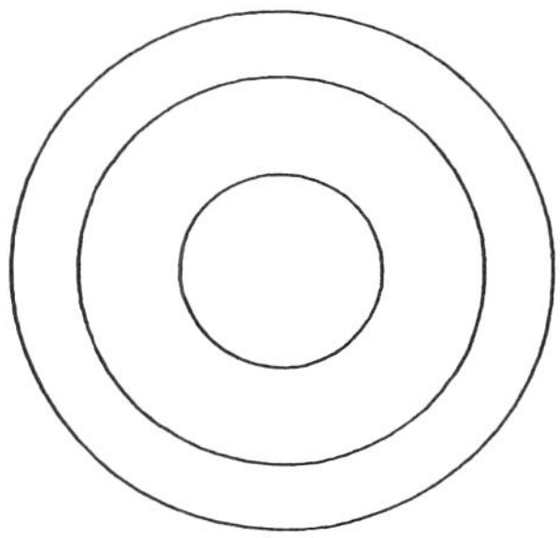

Figure 11.48

Step 2. Create six construction lines. Use the pick point in Figure 11.48.

Select **MAIN MENU → Create → Line → Polar**
Enter **0,0** ← for an endpoint
Enter **0** ← for the angle
Enter **1.25** ← for the line length to complete the first line
The new drawing should look like Figure 11.49.

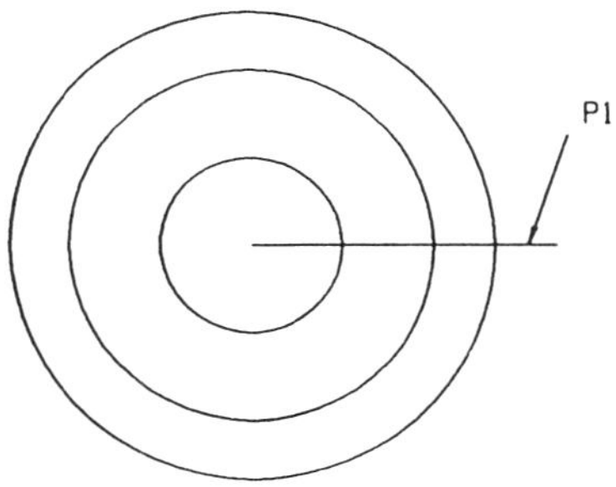

Figure 11.49

Select **MAIN MENU → Xform → Rotate → Only → Lines**
Pick **P1** to select the line to rotate from Figure 11.49
Select **BACKUP → Done → Origin**
Set the Rotate parameters as shown:

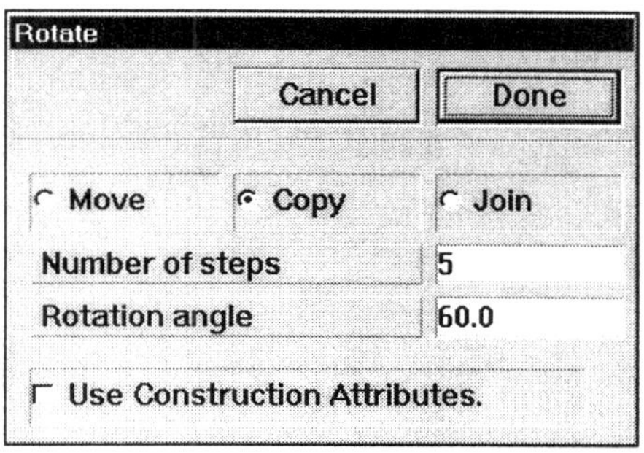

Select **Done**

The drawing should appear as Figure 11.50.

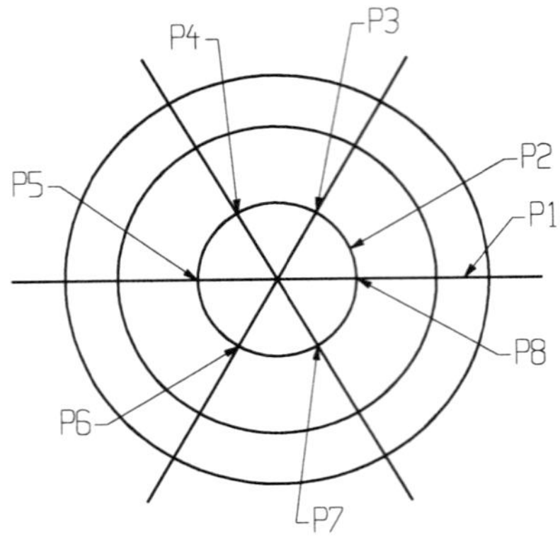

Figure 11.50

Step 3. Construct the first polygon around the smallest circle.

Use the pick points in Figure 11.50 above.

Select **MAIN MENU → Create → Line → Multi → Intersec**

Sequentially pick **P1 - P14** to complete the polygon around the smallest circle.

The first polygon should resemble Figure 11.51.

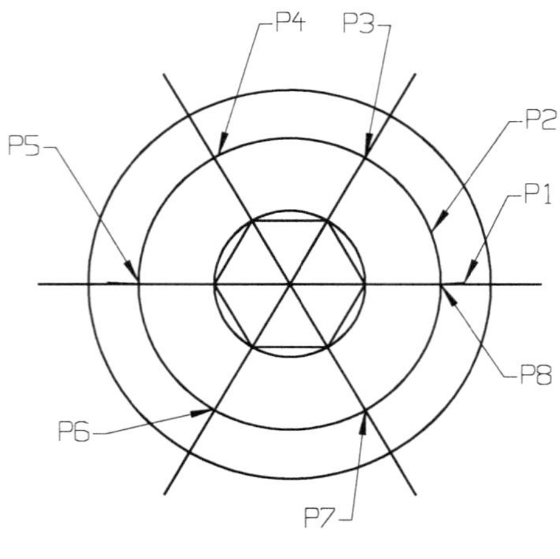

Figure 11.51

Step 4. Construct the second polygon around the mid-sized circle.

Use the pick points in Figure 11.51 on the prevoius page.

Select **BACKUP → Multi → Intersec**

Sequentially pick **P1 - P14** to complete the polygon

The new drawing should appear as Figure 11.52.

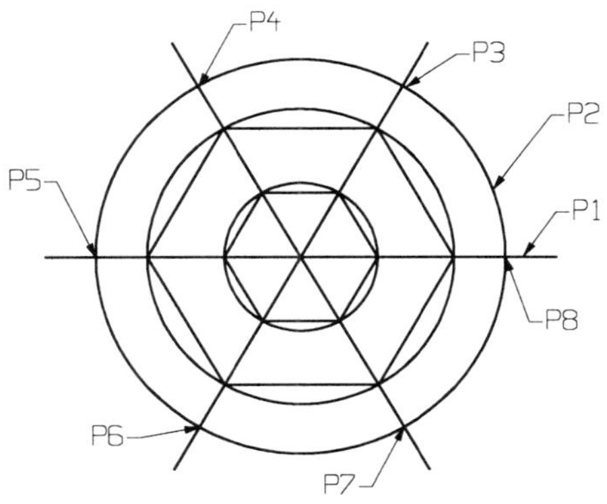

Figure 11.52

Step 5. Create a third polygon around the largest circle. Use pick points in Figure 11.52.

Select **BACKUP → Multi → Intersec**

Sequentially pick **P1 - P14** to complete the polygon

The drawing now should look like Figure 11.53.

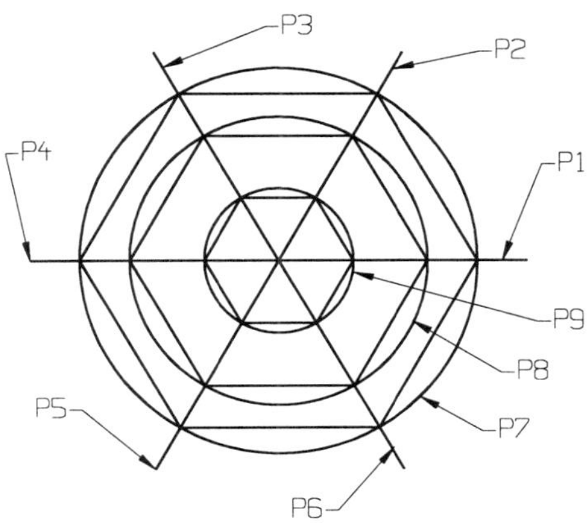

Figure 11.53

Step 6. Delete construction lines and arcs.

Use the pick points in Figure 11. 53.

Select **MAIN MENU → Delete**

Pick **P1 - P9** to delete the six construction lines and three construction circles

The new drawing appears as in Figure 11.54.

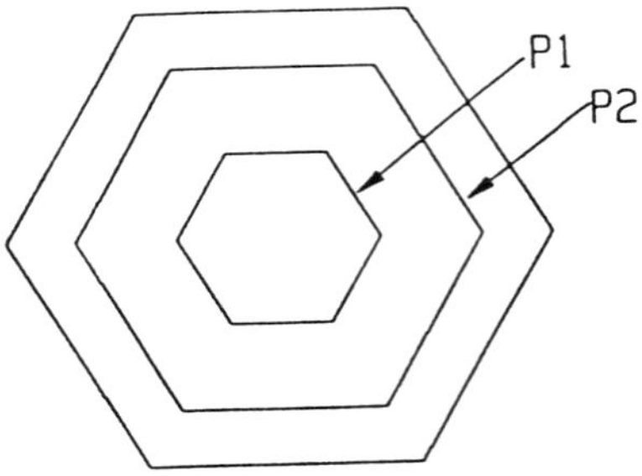

Figure 11.54

Step 7. Translate the smallest polygon to Z.85.

Use the pick points in above Figure 11.54.
Select **MAIN MENU → Xform → Translate → Chain**
Pick **P1**, then select **Done → Done → Rectang**
Enter the translation vector: **Z.85 ←** to complete the translation
Set the Translate parameters as below:

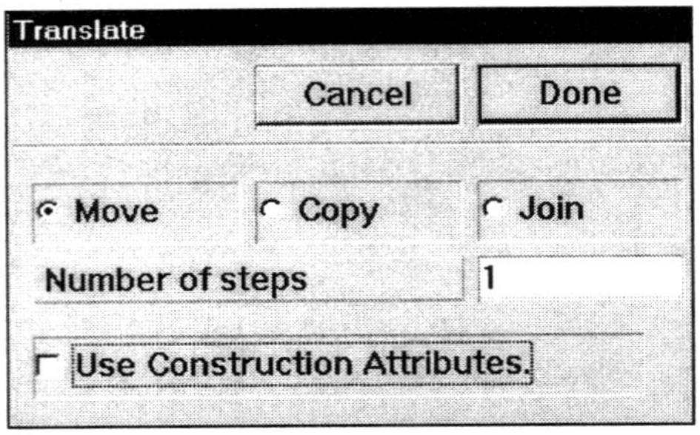

Select **Done**

Note: Your translated polygon may disappear from the screen. It will come back when you change the Gview to isometric.

Step 8. Translate the mid-sized polygon to Z.5.

Use the pick point in previous Figure 11.54.
Select **Chain**, and then pick **P2**
Select **Done → Done → Rectang**
Enter the translation vector: **Z.5 ←**
Set the Translate parameters as below:

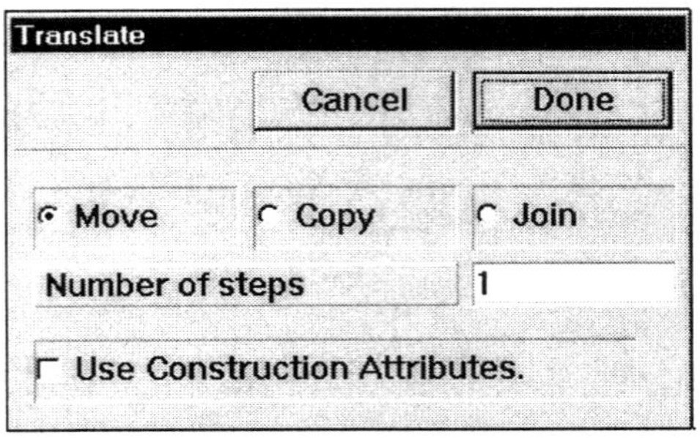

Select **Done**

Select **Gview → Isometric**

The three polygons should appear as Figure 11.55.

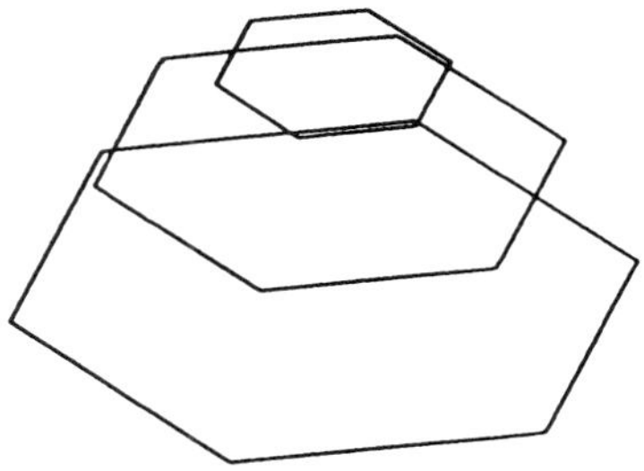

Figure 11.55

Step 9. Return the drawing to Top view to make it easier to connect the lines between the vertices.

Select **Gview → Top**

The drawing displayed in the top view should look like Figure 11.56.

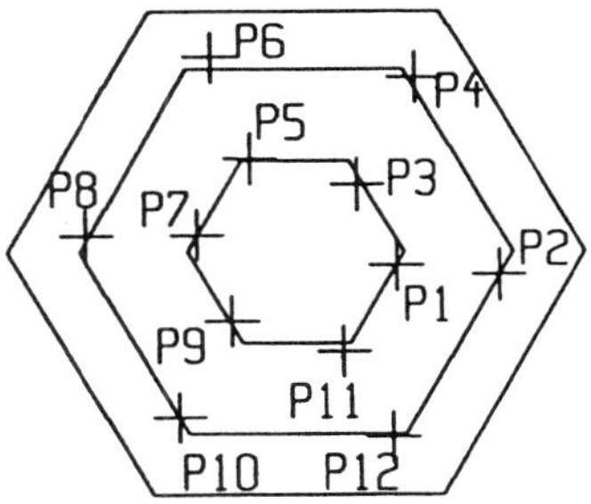

Figure 11.56

Step 10. Connect two inner polygons with lines using the 3D construction plane.

Use the pick points in Figure 11.56.

Select **Cplane → 3D**

Select **MAIN MENU → Create → Line → Endpoints → Endpoint**

Sequentially pick **P1 - P12** to complete the connecting lines

Select **Gview → Isometric**

The drawing now should look like Figure 11.57.

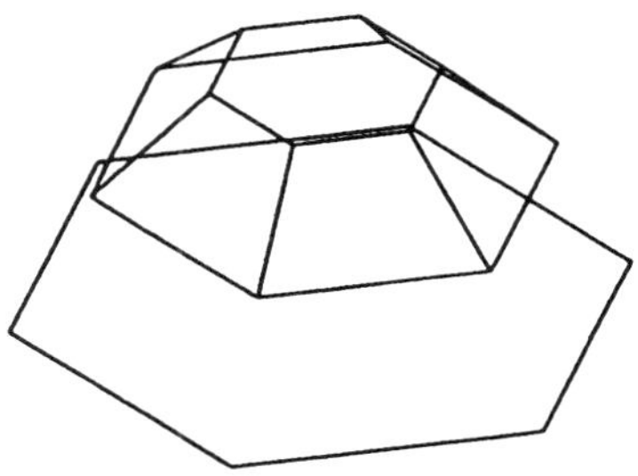

Figure 11.57

Again, change the Gview back to Top view to make picking the points easy for connecting the lines between the two outer polygons.

Select **Gview → Top**

The top view of the drawing should resemble Figure 11.58.

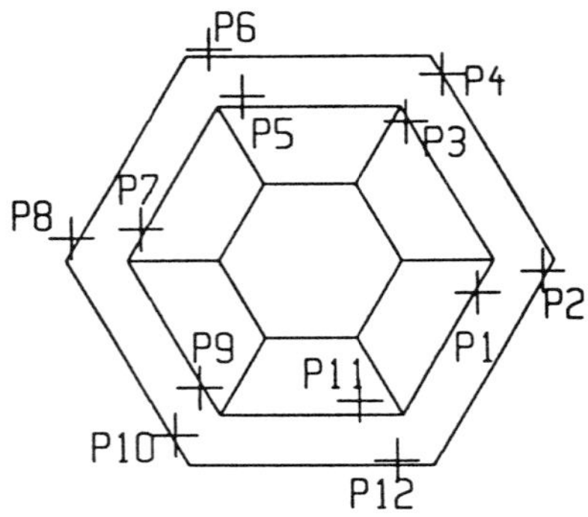

Figure 11.58

Step 11. Connect two outer polygons with lines.

Use the pick points in above Figure 11.58.
Select **BACKUP → Endpoints → Endpoint**
Sequentially pick **P1 - P12** to complete the connecting lines
Select **Gview → Isometric**

The upper half of the wireframe is done and shall look like Figure 11.59. Actually, for modeling purposes, the upper half of the model is all we need since the object is symmetrical. For visualization purposes, the entire model can be obtained by rotating the upper half of the model by 180° about the origin using the Front construction plane.

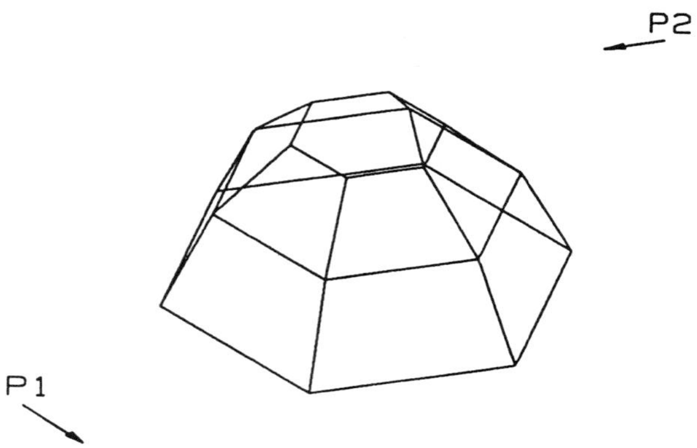

Figure 11.59

Step 12. Save the drawing coons4.

Select **MAIN MENU → File → Save**
Enter **coons4** for the file name

Step 13. Copy the upper half model to the lower half using the Front construction plane. Use the pick points in Figure 11.59.

Select **Cplane → Front**
Select **MAIN MENU → Xform → Rotate → Window**
Pick **P1** and **P2** to completely include the entire drawing
Select **Done → Origin**
Set the Rotate parameters as below:

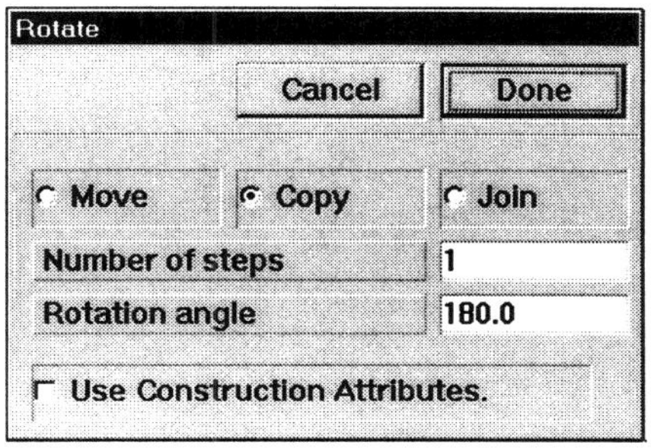

Select **Done**

The complete wireframe model is shown in Figure 11.60.

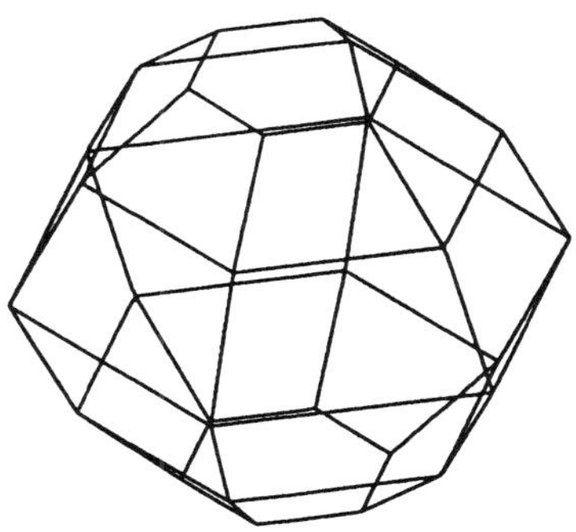

Figure 11.60

Note: This wireframe model will be used to generate two coons surfaces in the next chapter.

8 ## Project 8:

This example illustrates how to construct the wireframe surface profile for a cup shown in Figure 11.61.

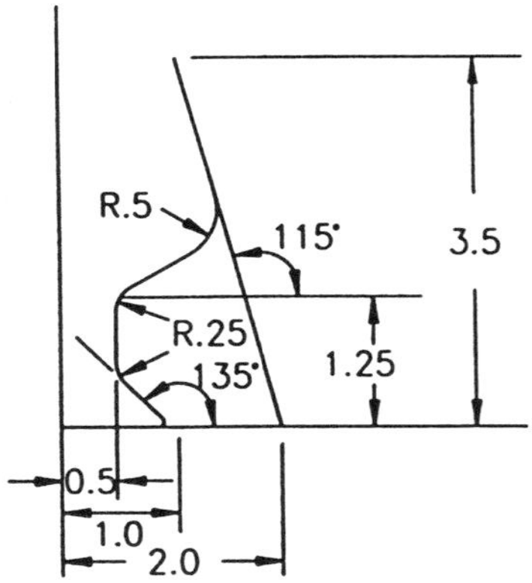

Figure 11.61a. Wireframe profile

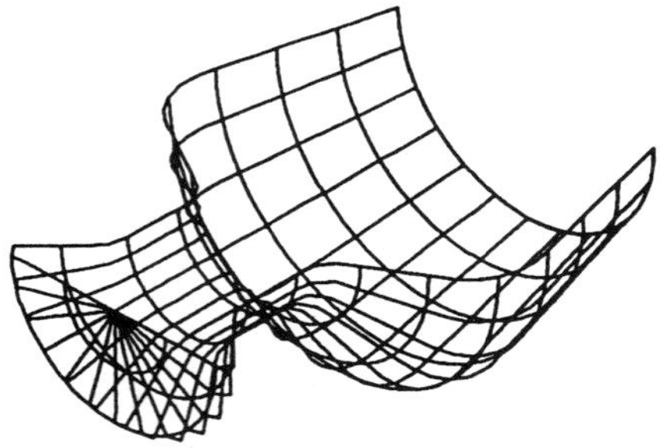

Figure 11.61b. Surface model

Tips 1. Create two slope lines using the polar method in the top construction view.

2. Create three horizontal lines and two vertical lines.

3. Create another slope line using the polar method with one intersection point as the end point.

4. Create four fillets.

5. Delete the construction entities.

Step 1. Enter the Mastercam Mill.

Set the Secondary Menu to the following settings if necessary:

Z: **0**
Cplane: **Top**
Gview: **Top**

Step 2. Create two slope lines.

Select **MAIN MENU →Create → Line → Polar**
Enter **1.0,0** ← for an endpoint
Enter **135** ← for the angle
Enter **1.5** ← for the line length to complete the first line
Enter **2.0,0** ← for an endpoint
Enter **105** ← for the angle
Enter **5** ← for the line length

Press **Alt** + **F1**, and then **F2** to fit the drawing

The drawing appears as in Figure 11.62.

Figure 11.62

Step 3. Create three horizontal lines and two vertical lines.

Select **BACKUP → Endpoints → Values**

Sequentially enter the following five pairs of point data to complete the five lines:

First end pointT	Second end point
0,0	**1,0**
0,1.25	**2,1.25**
0,3.5	**2.5,3.5**
0,-0.5	**0,4**
0.5,0.2	**0.5,2**

The drawing now should look like Figure 11.63.

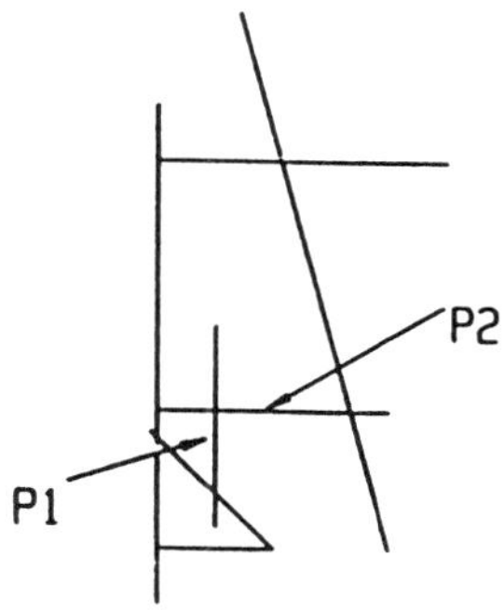

Figure 11.63

Step 4. Create a slope line that passes through the intersection point of two lines.

Use the pick points in Figure 11.63.

Select **BACKUP → Polar → Intersec**

Pick **P1** and **P2** to trap at the intersection point

Enter **30** ← for the angle

Enter **1.5** ← for the line length

The drawing now should resemble Figure 11.64.

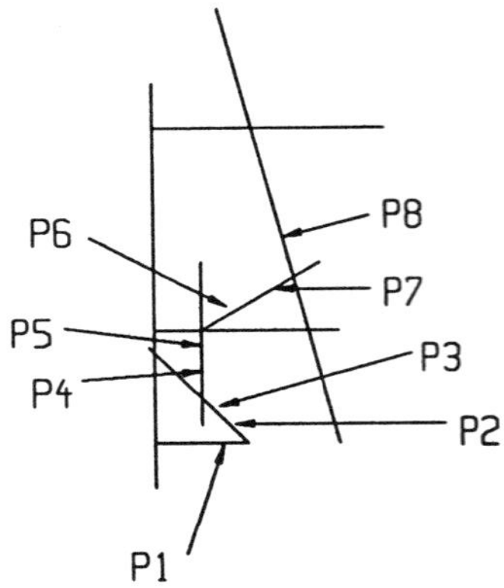

Figure 11.64

Step 5. Add four fillets. Use the pick points in Figure 11.64.

Select **MAIN MENU → Modify → Fillet → Radius**
Enter **0.05 ←** for the fillet radius
Pick **P1** and **P2** to complete the first fillet
Select **Radius**
Enter **.25 ←** for the fillet radius
Pick **P3, P4, P5,** and **P6** to complete the two fillets having .25 radius
Select **Radius**
Enter **0.5 ←** for the fillet radius
Pick **P7** and **P8** to complete the fillet of **.5** radius

The drawing should appear as Figure 11.65.

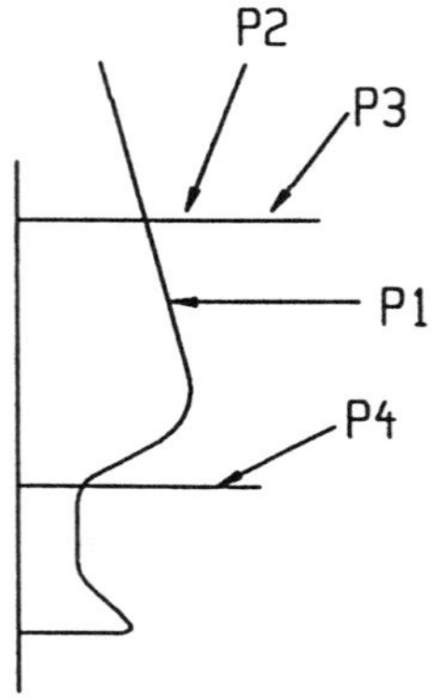

Figure 11.65

Step 6. Trim the slope line and delete two construction lines.

Use the pick points in Figure 11.65.
Select **MAIN MENU → Modify → Trim → 1 entity**
Pick **P1** and **P2** to trim the slope line
Select **MAIN MENU → Delete**
Pick **P3** and **P4** to delete the two construction lines

The final drawing should appear as Figure 11.66.

Figure 11.66

Step 7. Save the drawing. Use the file name: **cup**.

Select **MAIN MENU → File → Save**
Enter the file name: **cup**

Note: This wireframe model can be used to create the surface by using the revolved or swept command.

Project 9:

In this example, the surface profiles for a channel surface model are constructed. The cross section of the channel varies from a rectangular shape down to a circle as shown in Figure 11.67.

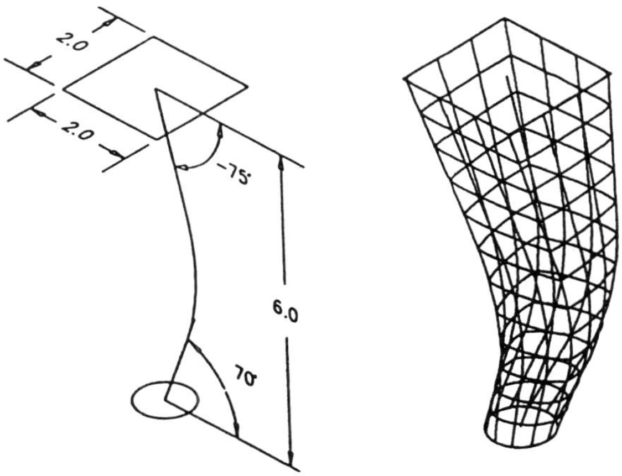

Figure 11.67

Tips 1. Use Front Cplane to construct the profile consisting of two lines and a fillet.

2. Use Top Cplane to create the rectangle and the circle.

Step 1. Construct two slope lines using Front Cplane.

Select **Gview → Isometric**
Select **Cplane → Front**
Select **Z** then enter **0** ← if necessary
Select **MAIN MENU → Create → Line → Polar**
Specify and endpoint: **0,0** ←
Enter the angle in degrees: **-75** ←
Enter the line length: **5** ← to complete the first line
Specify an endpoint: **0,-6** ←
Enter the angle in degrees: **70** ←
Enter the line length: **5** ← for the second line

The drawing of the two lines should appear as in Figure 11.68.

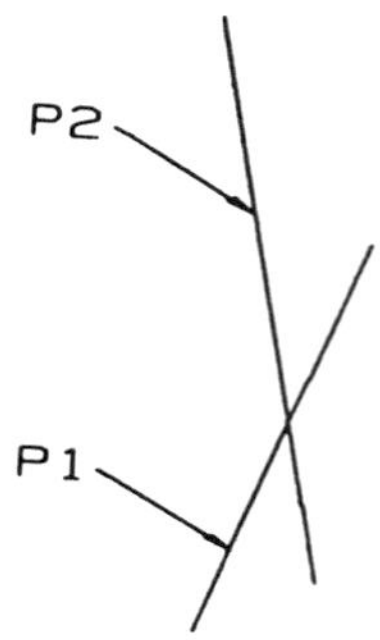

Figure 11.68

Step 2. Add a fillet using the pick points in Figure 11.68.

Select **MAIN MENU → Modify → Fillet → Radius**
Enter the fillet radius: **4** ←
Pick **P1** and **P2** to complete the fillet

The new drawing becomes Figure 11.69.

Figure 11.69

Step 3. Create a rectangle using Top Cplane.

Select **Cplane → Top**
Select **MAIN MENU → Create → Rectangle → 1 point**
Enter the lower left corner: **-1,-1** ←
Enter the width: **2** ←
Enter the height: **2** ←

The drawing should look like Figure 11.70.

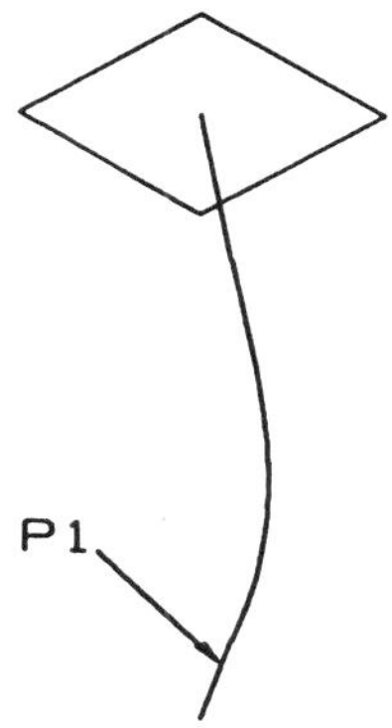

Figure 11.70

Step 4. Create a circle using the pick point in Figure 11.70.

Select **Z** → **Endpoint**
Pick **P1** to trap the Z value (Z-6.0 shall appear in the Secondary Menu)
Select **MAIN MENU** → **Create** → **Arc** → **Circ pt+dia**
Enter the center point: **0,0** ←
Enter the diameter: **1** ←

The complete wireframe model appears in Figure 11.71.

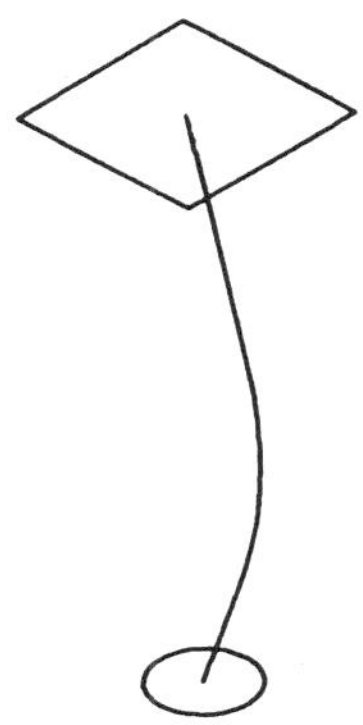

Figure 11.71

Step 5. Save the drawing. Use the file name: **Swept2**.

Select **MAIN MENU** → **File** → **Save**
Enter the file name **Swept2**

Note: This wireframe model will be used to generate a surface model using swept modeling technique in chapter 12.

🖳 10 🖳 Project 10:

This example creates a wireframe model, Figure 11.72a, of the swept surface (Figure 11.72b).

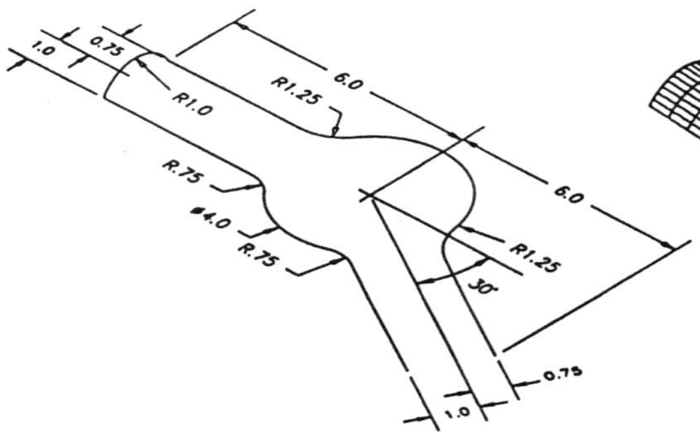

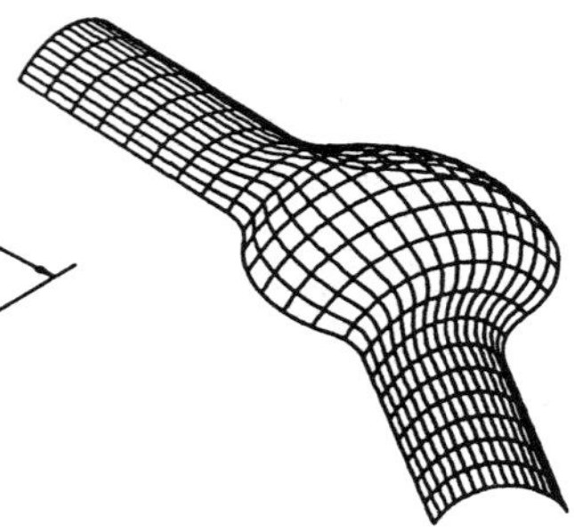

Figure 11.72a. Wireframe model Figure 11.72b. Surface model

Tips 1. Create two construction lines that start from the center of the circle. These two lines are then offset to the two sides by 0.75-in. and 1-in., respectively. 2. The circle must be broken into four pieces in order to add four fillets with proper trimming. 3. Create the across arc using the Side Cplane.

Step 1. Create an arc using Top Cplane.

Select **Cplane** → **Top**
Select **Z** then enter **0** ← if necessary
Select **Gview** → **Top**
Select **MAIN MENU** → **Create** → **Arc** → **Circ pt+dia**
Enter the center point: **0,0** ←
Enter the diameter: **4** ←

Step 2. Create two construction lines.

Select **MAIN MENU** → **Create** → **Line** → **Polar**
Specify an endpoint: **0,0** ←
Enter the angle in degrees: **-30** ←
Enter the line length: **6** ← to complete the first line
Specify an endpoint: **0,0** ←
Enter the angle in degrees: **180** ←
Enter the line length: **6** ←

The drawing should look like Figure 11.73.

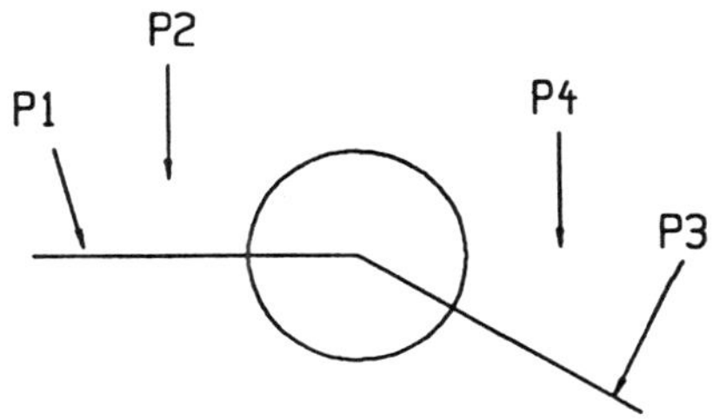

Figure 11.73

Step 3. Offset the two construction lines to the specified side by 0.75-in. using the pick points in Figure 11.73.

Select **MAIN MENU → Xform →Offset**
Set the parameters for Offset as below:

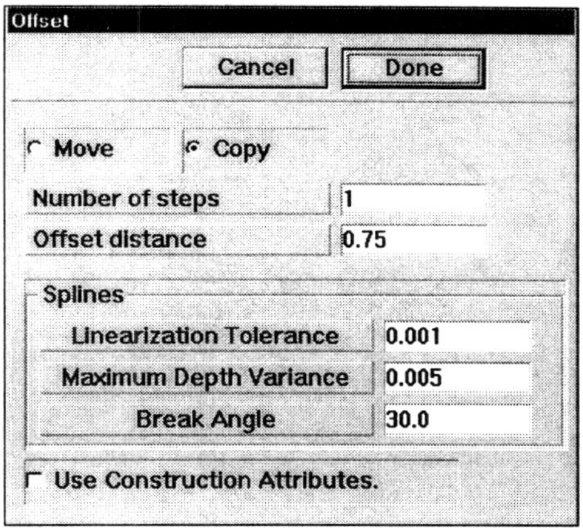

Select **Done**

Select the line or arc to offset: pick **P1**
Indicate the offset direction: pick **P2**
Select the line or arc to offset: pick **P3**
Indicate the offset direction: pick **P4**

Two offset lines will be added to the drawing as in Figure 11.74.

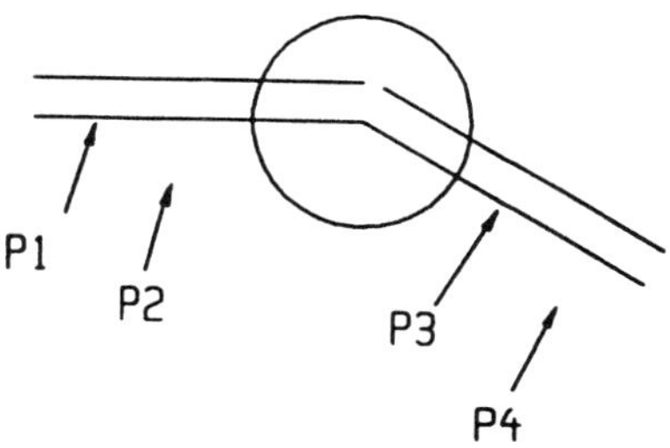

Figure 11.74

Step 4. Offset the two construction lines to the other side by 1-in.

Use the pick points in Figure 11.74.

Select **BACKUP → Offset**

Set the Offset parameters as here:

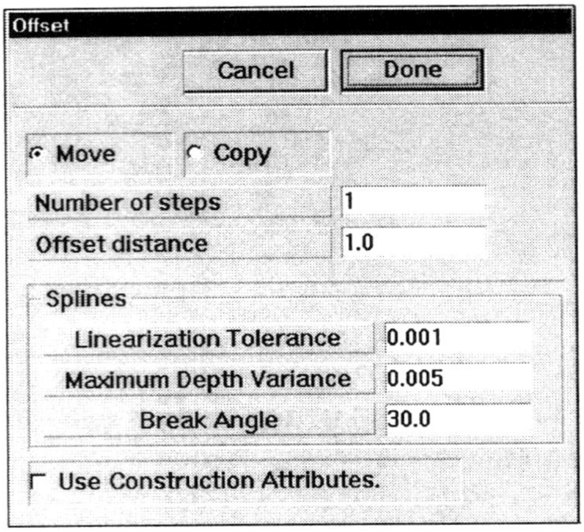

Select **Done**

Select the line or arc to offset:
 pick **P1 ←**
Indicate the offset direction:
 pick **P2 ←**
Select the line or arc to offset:
 pick **P3 ←**
Indicate the offset direction:
 pick **P4 ←**

The four offset lines should resemble Figure 11.75.

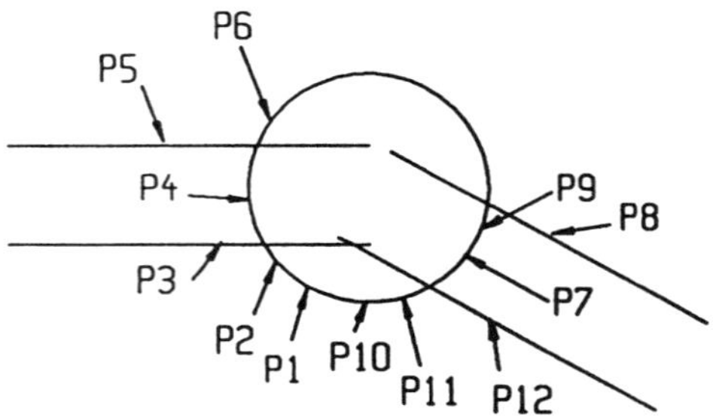

Figure 11.75

Step 5. Break the arc into four pieces using the pick points in above Figure 11.75.

Select **MAIN MENU → Modify → Break → 2 pieces**

Select an entity: pick **P1**

Select **Intersec** from the Point menu and then pick **P2** and **P3** to break the arc

Note: Select Intersec before picking two intersecting elements.

Sequentially pick **P4 - P6** to break the second time

Sequentially pick **P7 - P9** to break the third time

Sequentially pick **P10 - P12** to break the fourth time

Note: The broken arc does not look different before breaking. The drawing reappears in Figure 11.76 to show the pick points for next step.

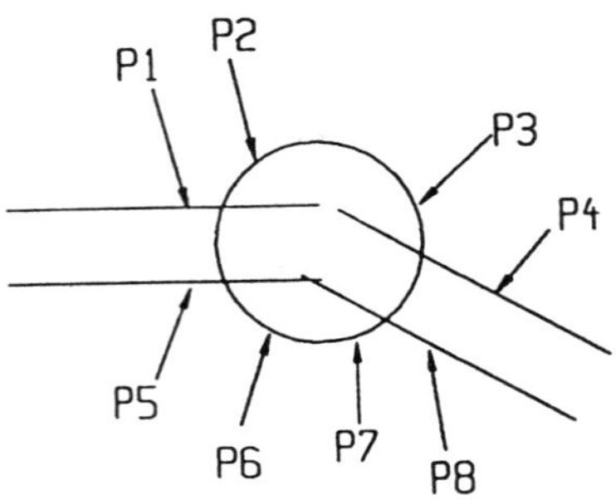

Figure 11.76

Step 6. Add four fillets using the pick points in Figure 11.76.

Select **MAIN MENU → Modify → Filler → Radius**
Enter the fillet radius: **1.25**
Pick **P1** and **P2** to complete the 1st fillet
Pick **P3** and **P4** to complete the 2nd fillet
Select **Radius** from the Fillet menu
Enter the fillet radius: **.75→**
Pick **P5** and **P6** for the 3rd fillet
Pick **P7** and **P8** for the 4th fillet

The new drawing should resemble Figure 11.77.

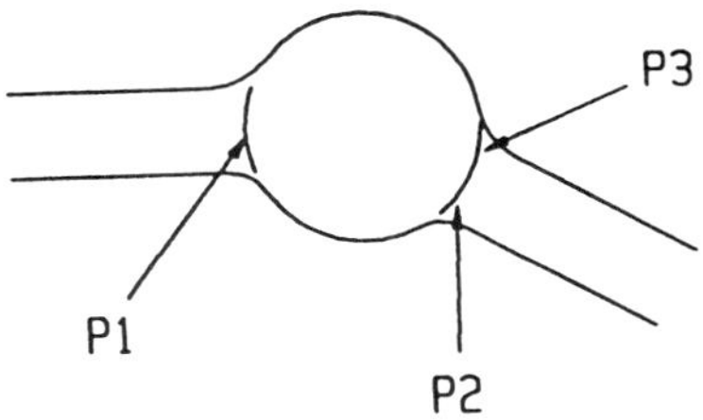

Figure 11.77

Step 7. Delete three unwanted arc segments using the pick points in Figure 11.77.

Select **MAIN MENU → Delete**
Pick **P1**, **P2** and **P3** to complete the deletion

The drawing becomes Figure 11.78.

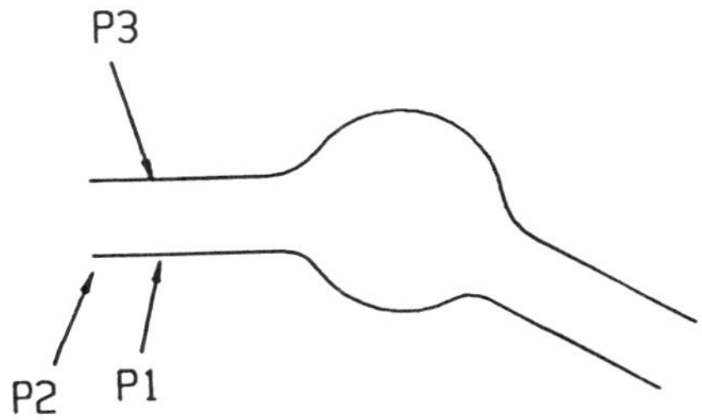

Figure 11.78

Step 8. Create an across arc using Side Cplane.

Select **Gview → Isometric**
Select **Cplane → Side**
Select **Z → Endpoint**, then pick **P1**

Z-6.0 should appear in the Secondary Menu.

Select **MAIN MENU → Create → Arc → Endpoints → Endpoint**
Pick **P2** and **P3** to select two endpoints
Enter the radius: **1**
Select an arc: pick the desired arc (2nd from the top)

11 The wireframe model should resemble Figure 11.79.

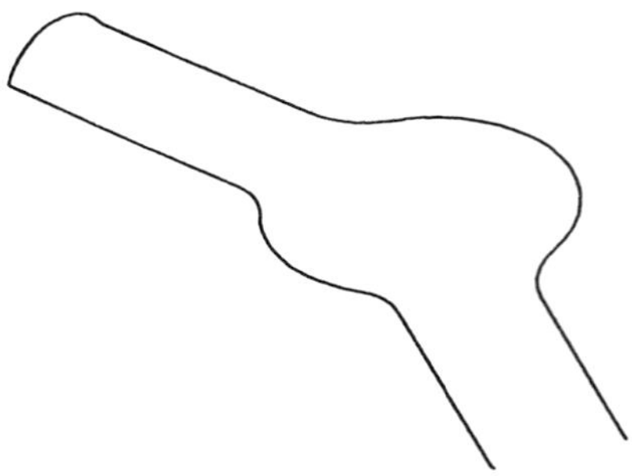

Figure 11.79

Step 9. Save the drawing. Use the file name: **Swept3**.
Select **MAIN MENU → File → Save**
Enter the file name: **Swept3**

Project 11:

The part shown in Figure 11.80 consists of **four** surfaces: a flat surface at the bottom, a wall surface, a fillet surface between the wall and the bottom, and a rim surface. The required wireframe model for these four surfaces is given in Figure 11.80a.

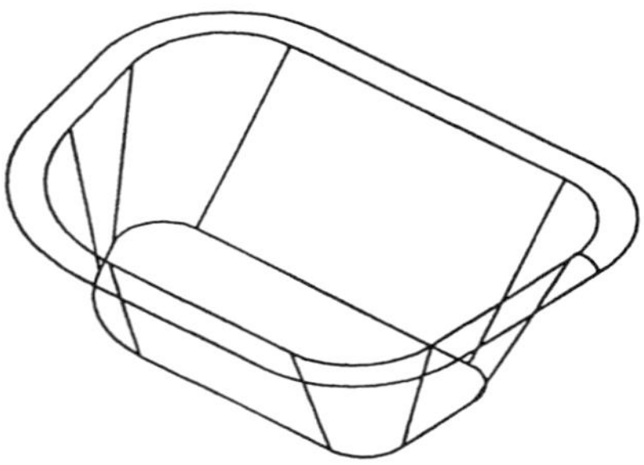

a. Wireframe model

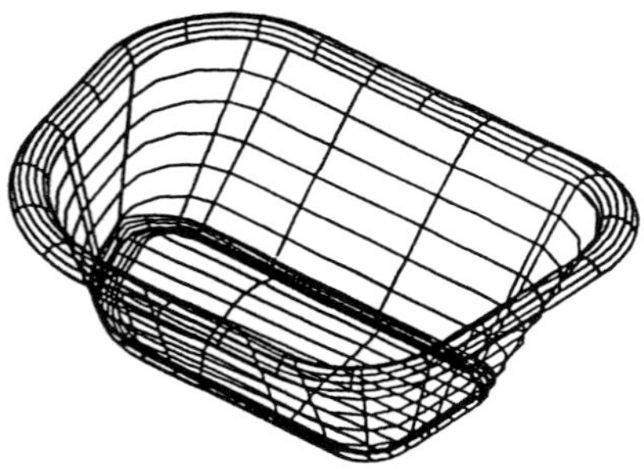

b. Surface model

Figure 11.80

Tips 1. Use the Top construction plane to construct the top and the bottom frames of the part.

2. Use the 3d construction plane to create the connecting lines between the top and the bottom frame. The connecting points of these lines are trapped at the end points of each arc.
3. Use the side construction plane to create the sweeping arc of the rim.

Step 1. Enter the Mastercam Mill.

Set the Secondary Menu to the proper settings if necessary.
Select **Cplane → Top**
Select **Gview → Top**
Select **Z** and then enter **0** ←

Step 2. Construct a rectangle.

Select **MAIN MENU → Create → Rectangle → 1 point**
Enter **0,0** ← for the lower left corner
Enter **6** ← for the width of the rectangle
Enter **4** ← for the height of the rectangle
Press **Alt** + **F1** then **F2** to fit the drawing.
A rectangle should appear as Figure 11.81.

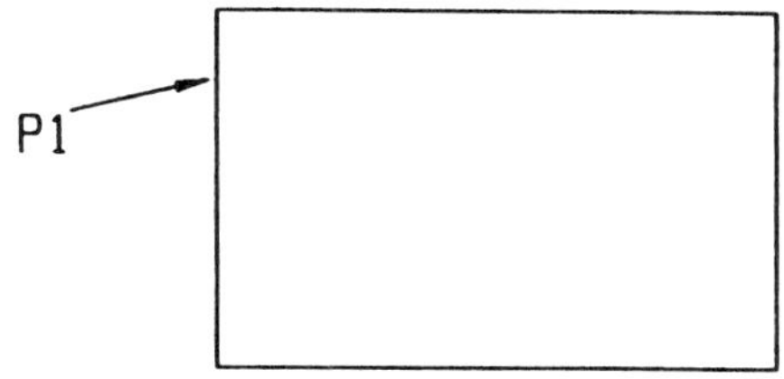

Figure 11.81

Step 3. Construct a slope line to the rectangle.

Use the pick point in Figure 11.81.
Select **MAIN MENU → Create → Line → Endpoints → Endpoint**
Pick **P1** for the first point
Enter **1,0** ← for the second point

The drawing should look like Figure 11.82.

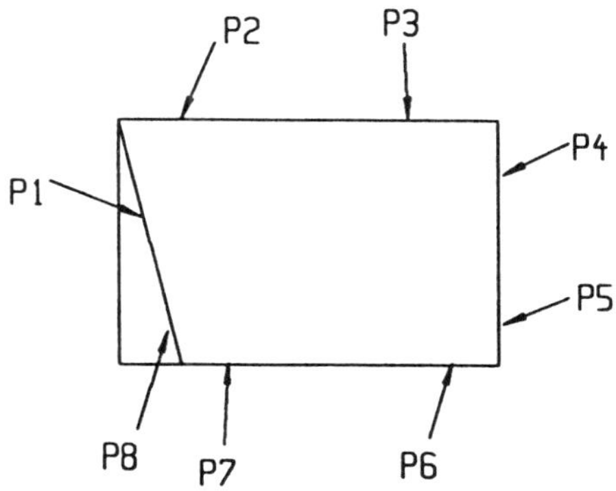

Figure 11.82

Step 4. Add four arcs at corners.

Use the pick points in Figure 11.82.
Select **MAIN MENU → Modify → Fillet → Radius**
Enter **1.0** ← for the radius value
Sequentially pick P1 - **P6** to complete the three fillets
Select **Radius**, and then enter **2.0** ← for the radius value
Pick **P7** and **P8** to complete the larger fillet

The drawing now should resemble Figure 11.83.

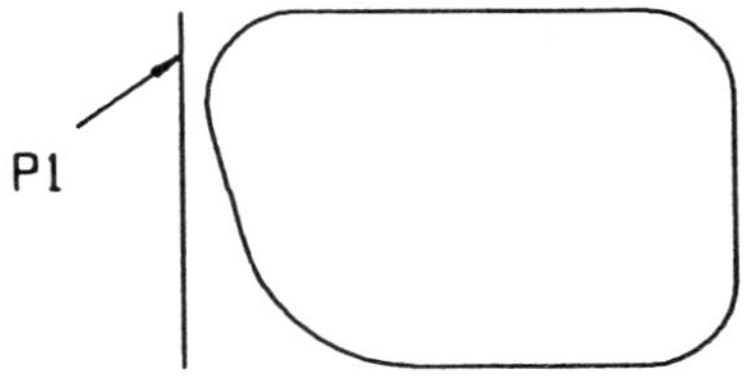

Figure 11.83

Step 5. Delete a line. Use the pick point in Figure 11.83.

Select **MAIN MENU → Delete**

Pick **P1**

The top frame appears as in Figure 11.84.

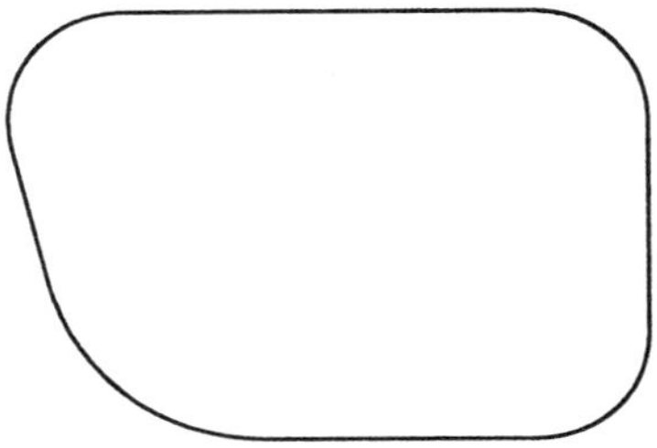

Figure 11.84

Step 6. Create the outer contour by offseting the top frame just created.

Use the pick points in Figure 11.84.

Select **MAIN MENU → Xform → Ofs ctour → Chain**

Pick any element on the contour (Be sure the contour direction runs in the clockwise direction.)

Select **Done**

Set the Offset parameters as below:

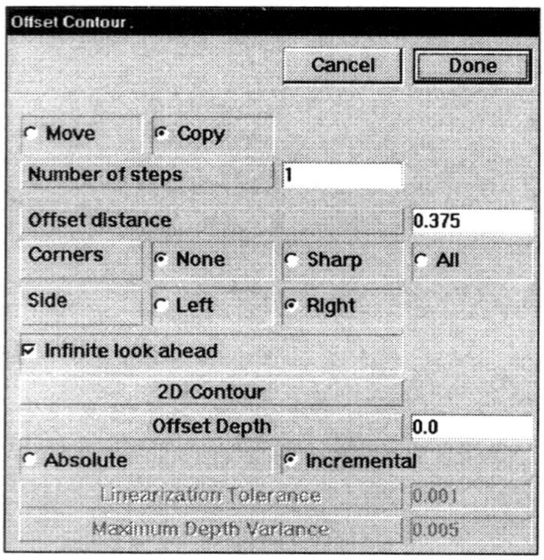

Select **Done**

The drawing now should look like Figure 11.85.

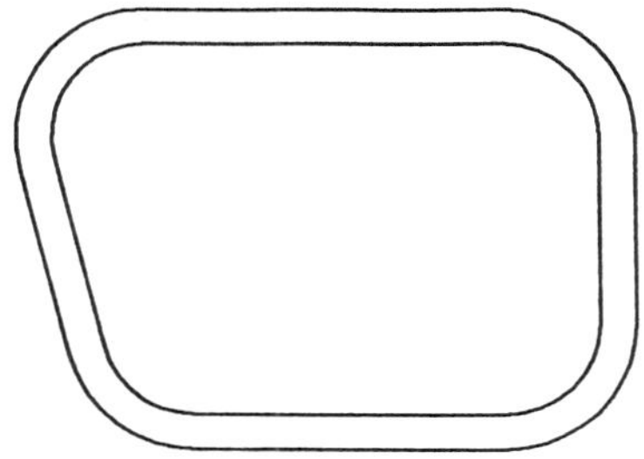

Figure 11.85

Step 7. Create the rectangle for the bottom frame.

Select **Z** and then enter **-1.5** ←
Select **MAIN MENU** → **Create** → **Rectangle** → **1 point**
Enter **0.5,0.5** ← for the lower left corner
Enter **5** ← for the width
Enter **2** ← for the height

The drawing appears as Figure 11.86.

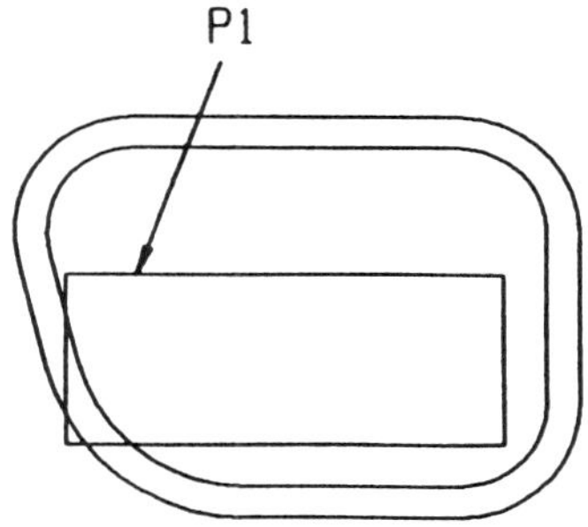

Figure 11.86

Step 8. Create a slope line to the rectangle. Use the pick point In Figure 11.86.

Select **MAIN MENU** → **Create** → **Line** → **Endpoints** → **Endpoint**
Pick **P1** to define the first point
Enter **1.5,0.5** ← for the second point

Now the drawing should look like Figure 11.87.

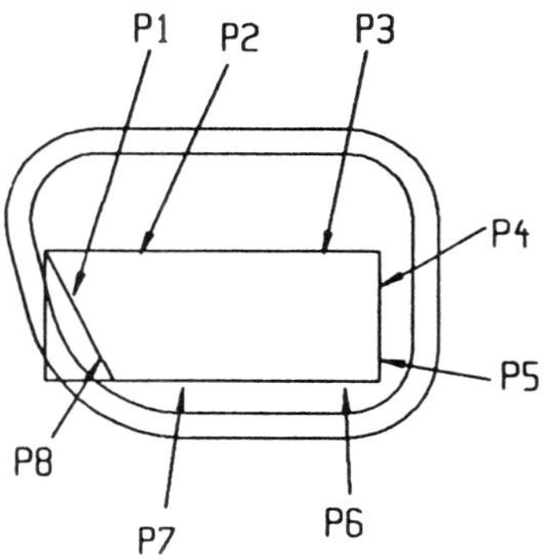

Figure 11.87

Step 9. Add fillets to four corners. Use the pick points in Figure 11.87.

Select **MAIN MENU → Modify → Fillet → Radius**
Enter **0.5 ←** for the fillet radius
Sequentially pick **P1 - P6** to complete three three fillets
Select **Radius**, and then enter **1.5 ←**
Pick **P7** and **P8** to complete the fourth fillet

The drawing should resemble Figure 11.88.

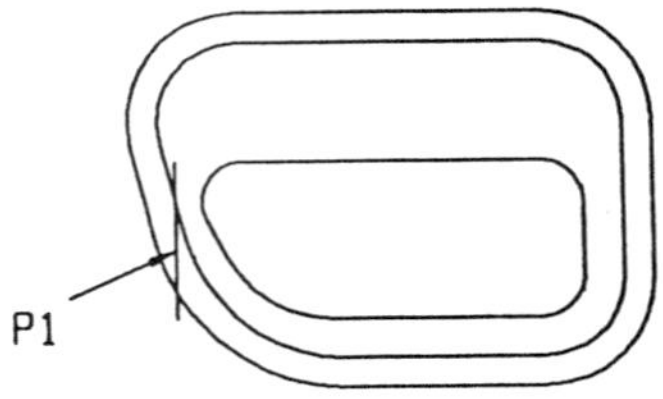

Figure 11.88

Step 10. Delete one line. Use the pick point in Figure 11.88.

Select **MAIN MENU → Delete**
Pick **P1** to delete the line

The new drawing appears as Figure 11.89.

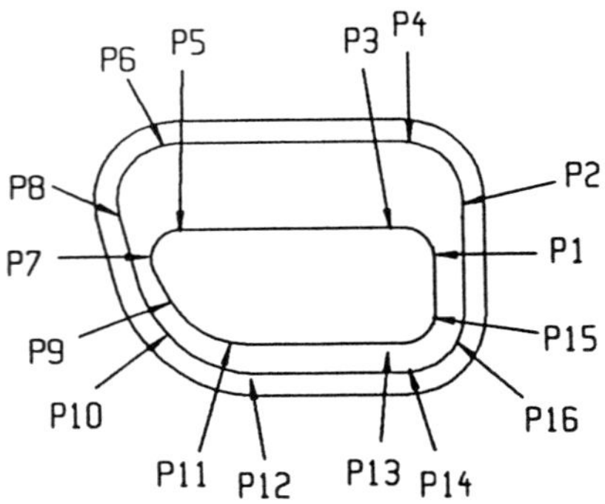

Figure 11.89

Step 11. Connect the top and bottom frames with straight lines using the 3D construction plane. Use the pick points in Figure 11.89.

Select **Cplane → 3D**
Select **MAIN MENU → Create → Line → Endpoints → Endpoint**
Sequentially pick **P1 - P16**
Select **Gview → Isometric**

Press **Alt + F1** and then **F2** to fit the drawing.

The new drawing should resemble Figure 11.90.

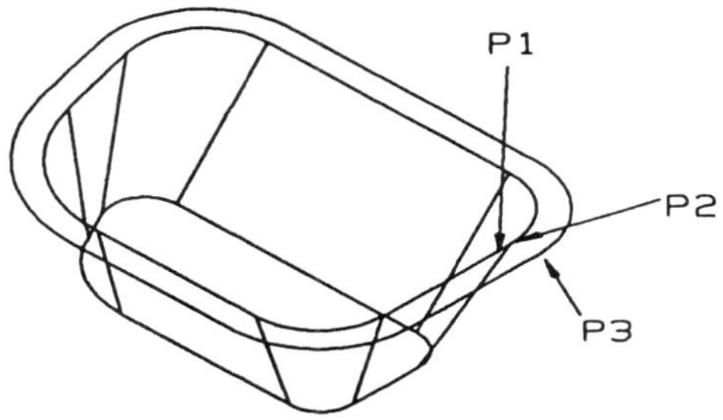

Figure 11.90

Step 12. Create the sweeping arc of the rim using the front construction plane.

Use the pick points in Figure 11.90.
Select **Cplane** → **Front**
Select **Z** → **Endpoint**
Pick **P1** to find the Z depth of the entity endpoint

Z-3.0 shall appear in the Secondary Menu.
Select **Create** → **Arc** → **Endpoints** → **Endpoint**
Pick **P2** and **P3** to define the two endpoints
Enter **0.2** ← for the rac radius
Pick at the desired arc (the second from the top)
The final drawing should resemble Figure 11.91.

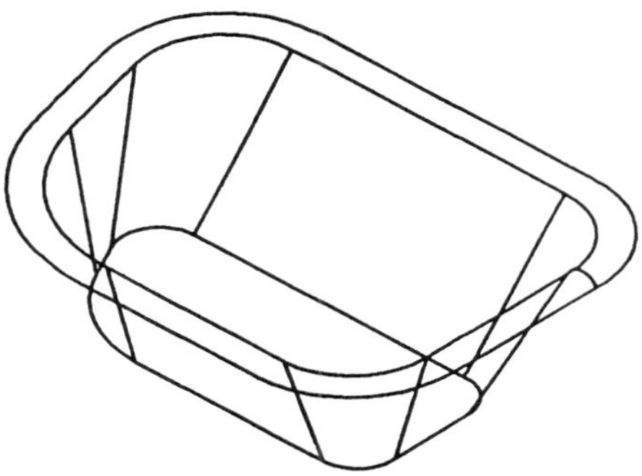

Figure 11.91

Step 13. Save the drawing. Use the file name: **basket**.

Select **MAIN MENU** → **File** → **Save**
Enter the file name: **basket**

12 Project 12: Flashlight

Construct the wireframe model of the flash light shown in Figure 11.92. The surface model consists of six surfaces: an outer frame surface, a top rim surface, a vertical wall surface, an inner top flat surface, a curved surface, and a fillet surface between the vertical wall surface and the inner top flat surface.

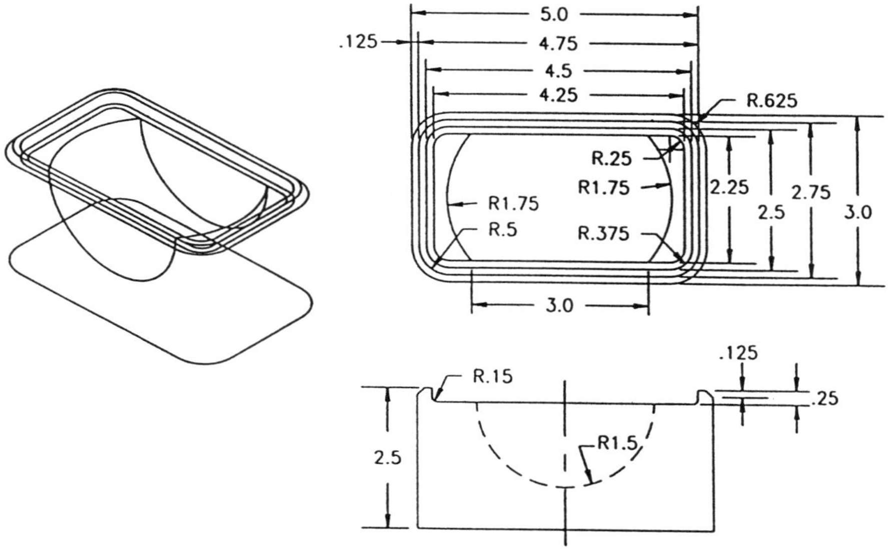

a. Wireframe model

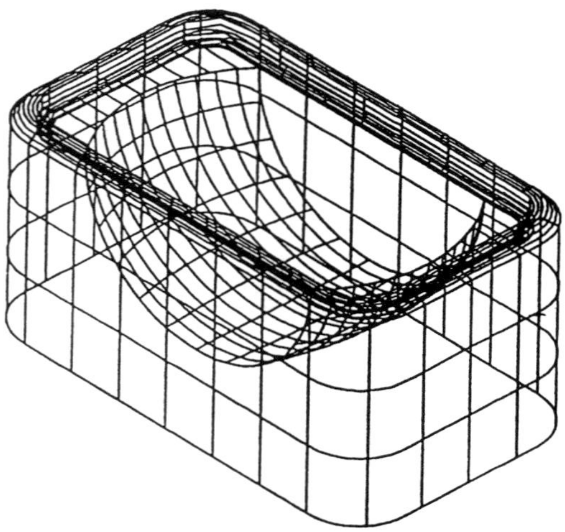

b. Surface model
Figure 11.92

Tips 1. Create four rectangles with corner arcs at the specified Z depth in the top view.

2. Translate the outer profile in the negative Z direction to form the bottom profile of the outer frame surface.
3. Construct two arcs in the top view and another two arcs in the front view to define the edge profile for the recessed surface.

Step 1. Enter the Mastercam Mill.

Set the Secondary Menu to these settings:

Cplane:	**Top**
Gview:	**Top**
Z:	**-0.125**

Step 2. Create the first rectangle.

Select **MAIN MENU →Create → Rectangle → 1 Point**
Enter the lower left corner: **-2.5, -1.5←**
Enter the width: **5←**
Enter the height: **3 ←**

The rectangle will appear on the screen like Figure 11.93.

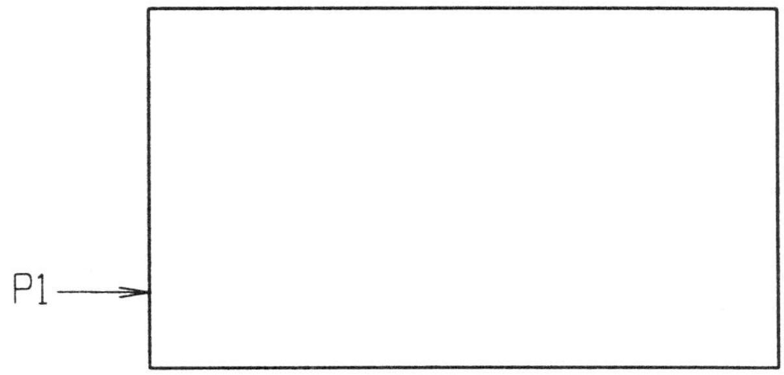

Figure 11.93

Step 3. Add four filletts using the pick points from Figure 11.93.

Select **MAIN MENU → Modify → Fillet → Radius**
Enter the fillet radius: **0.625 ←**
Select **Chain**
Select the first entity in the contour: pick **P1**
Select **Done** to complete the four fillets.

Now the drawing should look like Figure 11.94

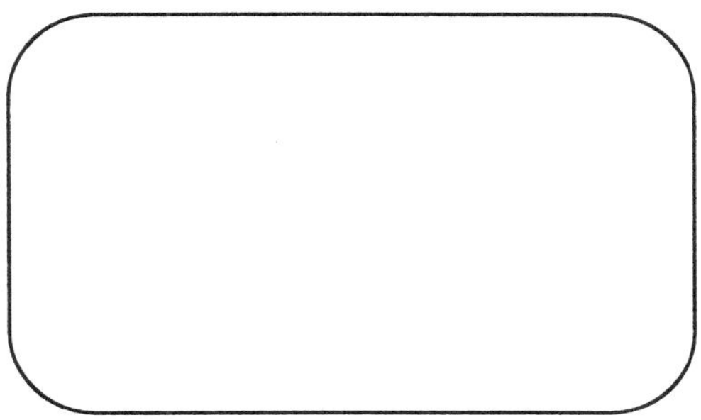

Figure 11.94

Step 4. Create the second rectangle.

Select **Z** from the Secondary Menu and then enter **0**
Select **MAIN MENU → Create → Rectangle → 1 point**
Enter the lower left corner: **-2.375,-1.375 ←**
Enter the width: **4.75 ←**
Enter the height: **2.75 ←**

The drawing should resemble Figure 11.95.

Figure 11.95

Step 5. Add four fillets to the second rectangle.

Use the pick points from Figure 11.95 on the previous page.
Select **MAIN MENU → Modify → Fillet → Radius**
Enter the fillet radius: **0.5** ←
Select **Chain**
Pick **P1**
Select **Done** to complete the four fillets.

The drawing should look like Figure 11.96.

Figure 11.96

Step 6. Create the third rectangle.

Select **MAIN MENU → Create → Rectangle → 1 point**
Enter the lower left corner: **-2.25,-1.25** ←
Enter the width: **4.5** ←
Enter the height: **2.5** ←

The drawing now should appear as in Figure 11.97.

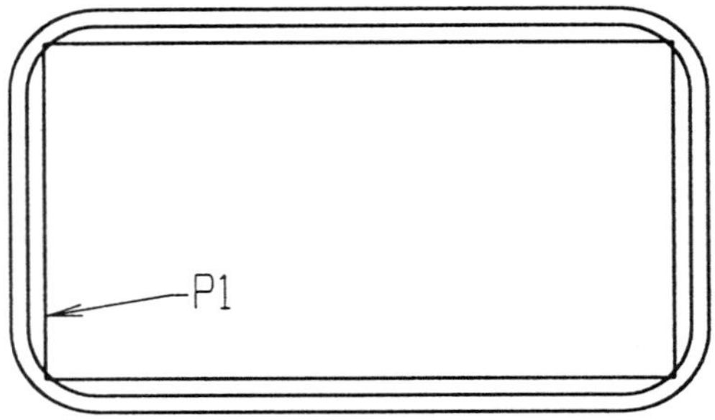

Figure 11.97

Step 7. Add four fillets to the third rectangle. Use the pick points in Figure 11.97.

Select **MAIN MENU → Modify → Fillet → Radius**
Enter the fillet radius: **0.375** ←
Select **Chain,** pick **P1**
Select **Done** to complete the four fillets.

Now the drawing should look like Figure 11.98.

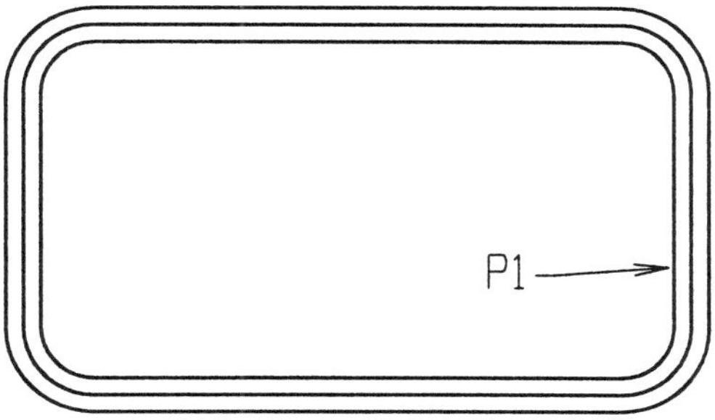

Figure 11.98

Step 8. Translate the third rectangle with fillets to Z-0.25.

Use the pick points in Figure 11.98.
Select **MAIN MENU → Xform → Translate → Chain**
Pick **P1**
Select **Done → Done → Rectang**
Enter the translation vector: **Z-0.25 ←**
Set the Translate parameters as below:

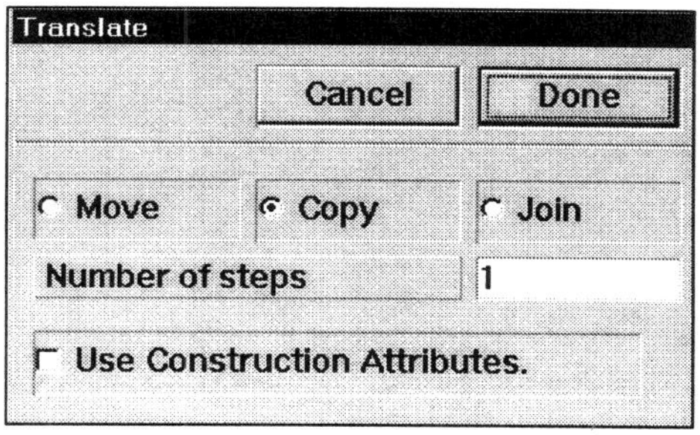

Select **Done**
Select **Gview → Isometric**

The drawing should resemble Figure 11.99.

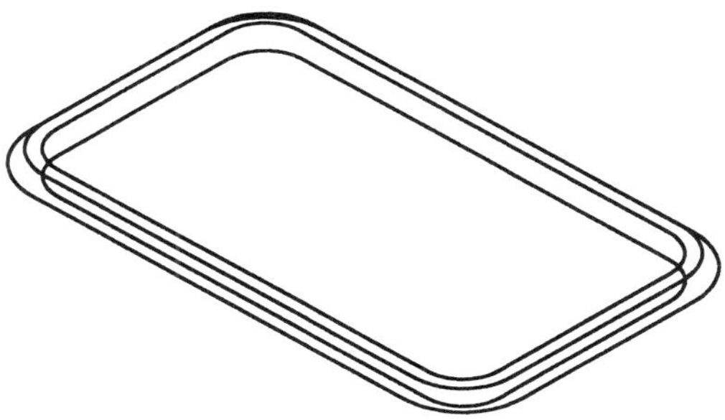

Figure 11.99

Select **Gview → Top**

Now the drawing in the top view should look like Figure 11.100.

Figure 11.100

Step 9. Create the fourth rectangle.

Select **Z** and then enter **-0.25** ←
Select **MAIN MENU** → **Create** → **Rectangle** → **1 point**
Enter the lower left corner: **-2.125,-1.125** ←
Enter the width: **4.25** ←
Enter the height: **2.25** ←

The drawing now appears as in Figure 11.101.

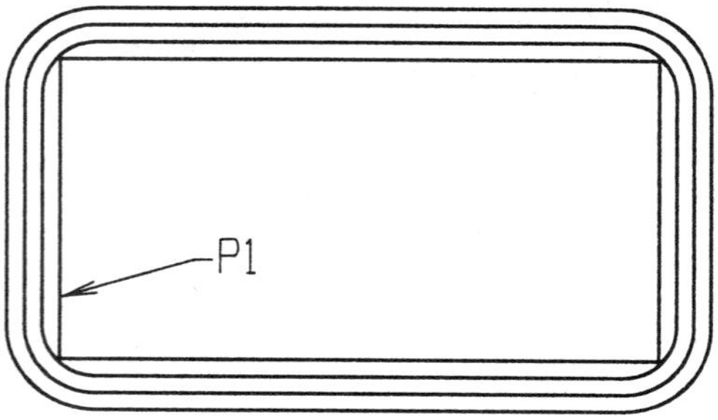

Figure 11.101

Step 10. Add four fillets to the fourth rectangle. Use the pick points shown in Figure 11.101.

Select **MAIN MENU** ← **Modify** ← **Fillet** ← **Radius**
Enter the fillet radius: **0.25** ←
Select **Chain**
Pick **P1**
Select **Done** to complete the four fillets.

The drawing should look like Figure 11.102.

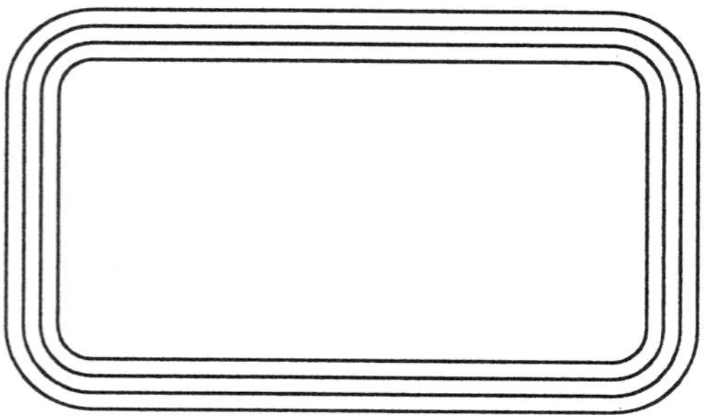

Figure 11.102

Step 11. Create two arcs on the top construction plane.

Select **MAIN MENU → Create → Arc → Endpoints**
Enter the first point: **-1.5,-1.125 ←**
Enter the second point: **-1.5,1.125 ←**
Enter the radius: **1.75 ←**
Select an arc: pick the desired arc (3rd arc from the right)
Enter the first point: **1.5,-1.125 ←**
Enter the second point: **1.5,1.125 ←**
Enter the radius: **1.75 ←**
Select an arc: pick the desired arc (2nd arc from the right)
Select **Gview → Isometric**
The drawing should resemble Figure 11.103.

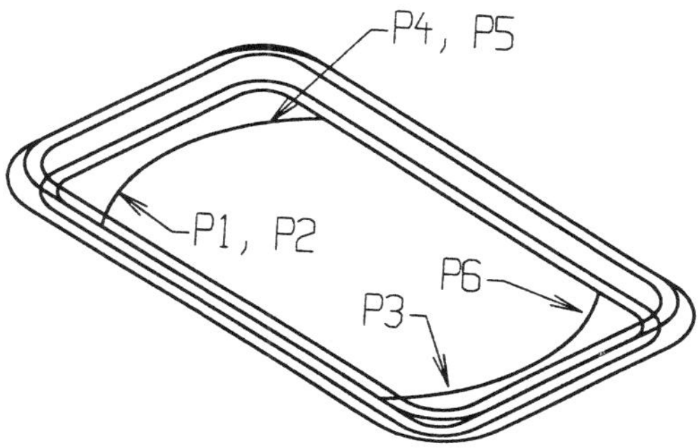

Figure 11.103

Step 12. Create the other two arcs using the front construction plane.

Use the pick points in Figure 11.103.
Select **Cplane → Front**
Select **Z → Endpoint**
Pick **P1** to obtain the Z value of the picked endpoint

Z1.125 should appear in the Secondary Menu.

Select **MAIN MENU → Create → Arc → Endpoints → Endpoint**
Pick **P2** and **P3** for the first and second point, respectively
Enter the radius: **1.5 ←**
Select an arc: pick the lower half of the arc to complete the first arc
Select **Z → Endpoint**
Pick **P4** to obtain the Z value of the picked endpoint

Z-1.125 should appear in the Secondary Menu.
Select **Endpoint**

Pick **P5** and **P6** for the first and second point, respectively
Enter the radius: **1.5 ←**
Select an arc: pick the desired arc

The drawing will appear as in Figure 11.104 .

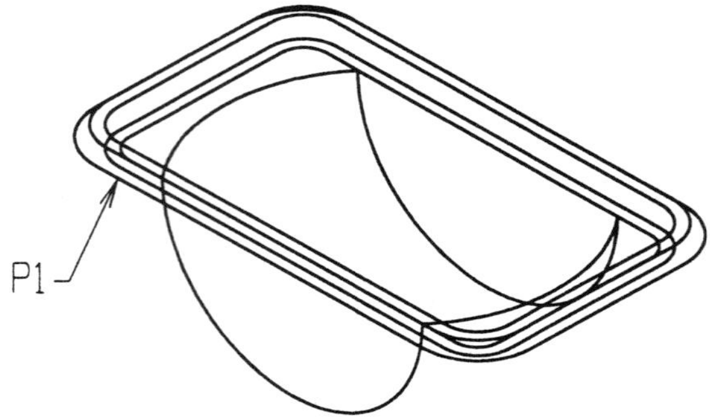

Figure 11.104

Step 13. Translate the outer rectangle to form a rectangular box.

Use the pick points in Figure 11.104.
Select **Cplane → Top**
Select **MAIN MENU → Xform → Translate → Chain**
Selete the first entity in the contour: pick **P1** ←
Select **Close → End here → Done → Rectang**
Enter the translation vector: **Z-2.375** ←
Set the Translate parameters as below:

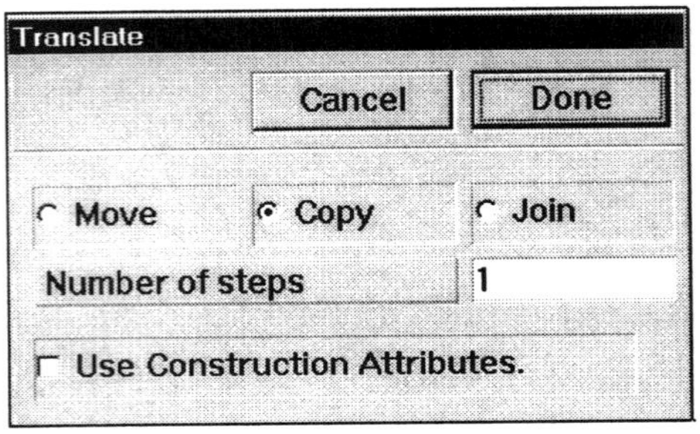

Select **Done**
The final drawing should look like Figure 11.105.

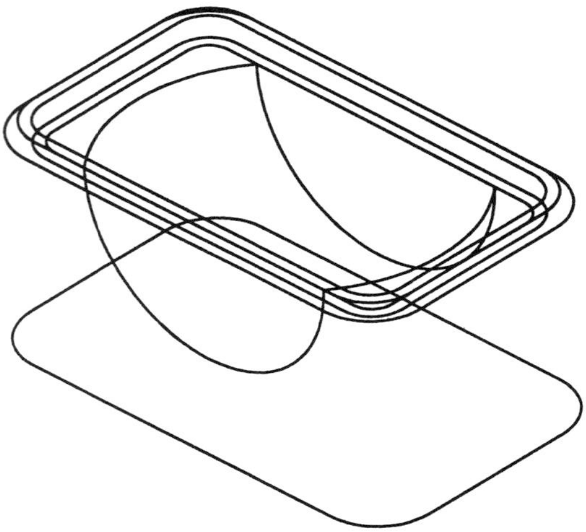

Figure 11.105

Step 14. Save the drawing. Use the file name flash.

Select **MAIN MENU → File → Save**
Enter the file name: **flash**

Project 13: Hair dryer

The hair dryer consists of three segments: handle, frame, and tube. The wireframe model is shown in Figure 11.106.

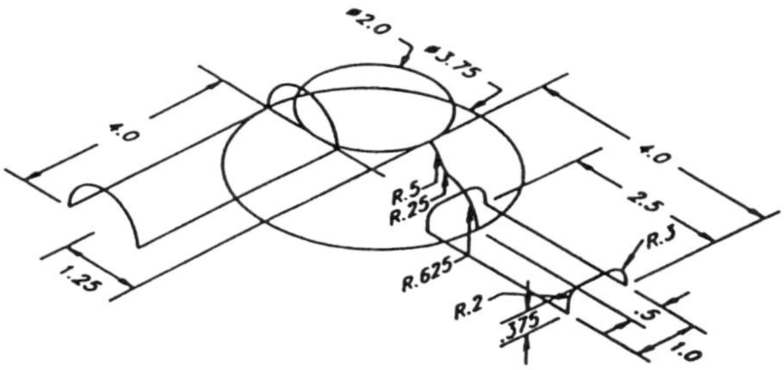

a. Wireframe model

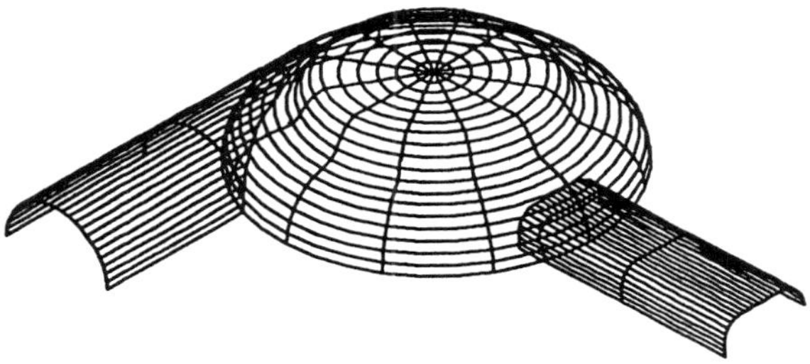

b. Surface model

Figure 11.106

Tips 1. Create three circles in the top construction plane.

2. Construct the edge profile of the frame which is formed by three tangent arcs in the front construction view.
3. Create two semi-circles for making the tube in the front construction view.

4. Construct the handle profile using the top construction view.

5. The edge profiles for the tube and the handle are made longer than needed to ensure that the surfaces intersect.

Step 1. Enter the Mastercam Mill.

Set the Secondary Menu to the following settings:

Z: **1.0**
Cplane: **Top**
Gview: **Top**

Step 2. Create three construction circles using the top construction plane.

Select **MAIN MENU →Create → Arc → Circ pt rad**
Enter the center point: **0,0** ←
Enter the radius: **1** ←
Select **Z**, and then enter **0.625** ←
Enter the center point: **0,0** ←
Enter the radius: **1.25** ←
Select **Z**, and then enter **0** ←
Enter the center point: **0,0** ←
Enter the radius: **1.875** ←
Select **Gview → Isometric**
The drawing of these three circles should look like Figure 11.107.

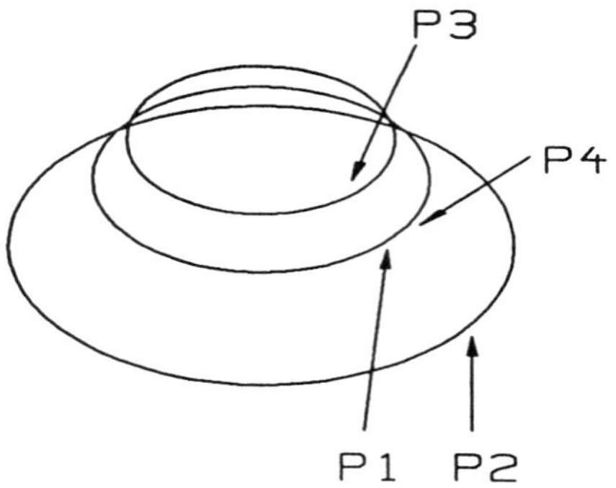

Figure 11.107

Step 3. Create the edge profile of the frame using the front consturction plane.

Use the pick points in Figure 11.107.
Select **Cplane → Front**
Select **Z** and then enter **0** ← if necessary
Select **MAIN MENU → Create → Arc → Endpoints → Endpoint**
Pick **P1** and **P2** for the first point and second point
Enter the radius: **0.625** ←
Select an arc: pick the desired arc segment (2nd from the right)
Enter the first point: pick **P3**
Enter the second point: pick **P4**
Enter the radius: **0.5** ←
Select an arc: pick the desired arc segment (2nd from the right)

The drawing should look like Figure 11.108.

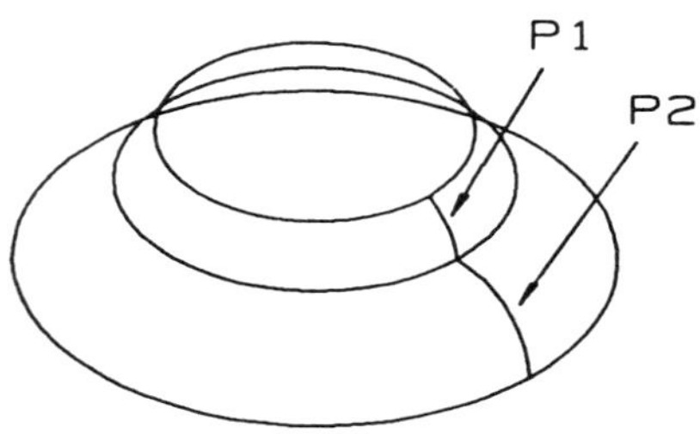

Figure 11.108

Step 4. Create an arc tangent to the two arcs.

Use the pick points from Figure 11.108.
Select **MAIN MENU → Modify → Fillet → Radius**
Enter the fillet radius: **0.25** ←
Select an entity: pick **P1**
Select another entity: pick **P2**

Now the drawing should appear as in Figure 11.109.

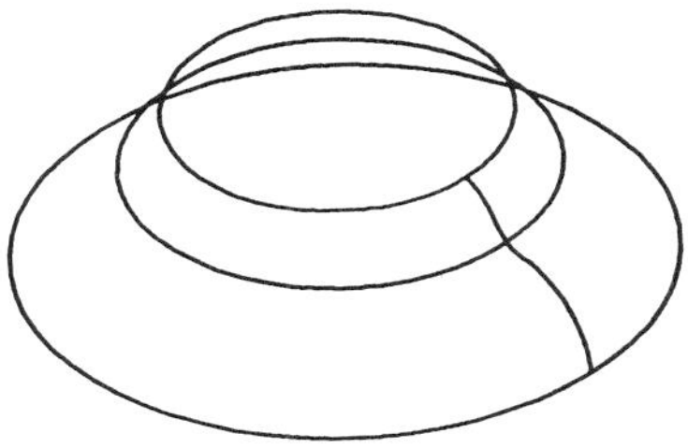

Figure 11.109

Step 5. Create two arcs for the tube.

Select **MAIN MENU → Create → Arc → Polar → Center pt**
Enter the center point: **-1.25,0** ←
Enter the radius: **0.625** ←
Enter the initial angle: **0** ←
Enter the final angle: **180** ←
Select **Z** and then enter **3.5** ←
Enter the center point: **-1.25,0** ←
Enter the radius: **0.625** ←
Enter the initial angle: **0** ←
Enter the final angle: **180** ←

The drawing should appear as in Figure 11.110.

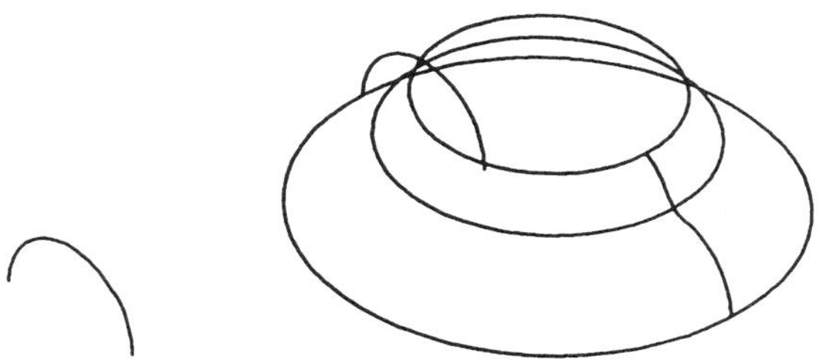

Figure 11.110

Step 6. Create the edge profile of the handle using the side construction view.

Select **Cplane → Side**
Select **Z** and then enter **4.0** ←
Select **MAIN MENU → Create → Rectangle → 2 points**
Enter the lower left corner: **-0.5,0** ←
Enter the upper right corner: **0.5,0.375** ←

The drawing should resemble Figure 11.111.

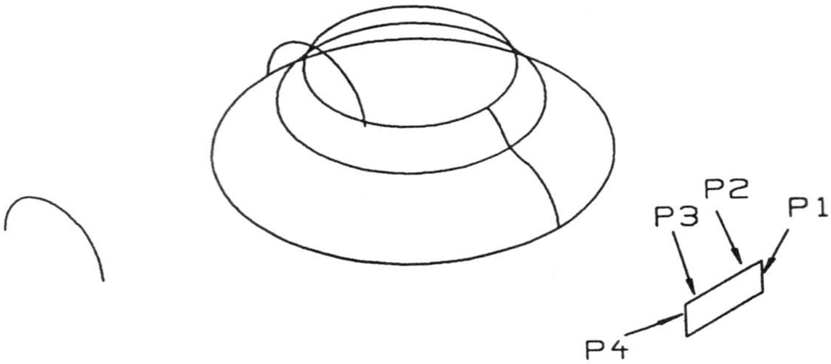

Figure 11.111

Step 7. Add two arcs. Use the pick points in Figure 11.111.

Select **MAIN MENU → Modify → Fillet → Radius**
Enter the fillet radius: **0.3** ←
Select an entity: pick **P1** ←
Select another entity: pick **P2** ←
Select **Radius**
Enter the fillet radius: **0.2** ←
Select an entity: pick **P3**
Select another entity: pick **P4**
The drawing should appear as Figure 11.112.

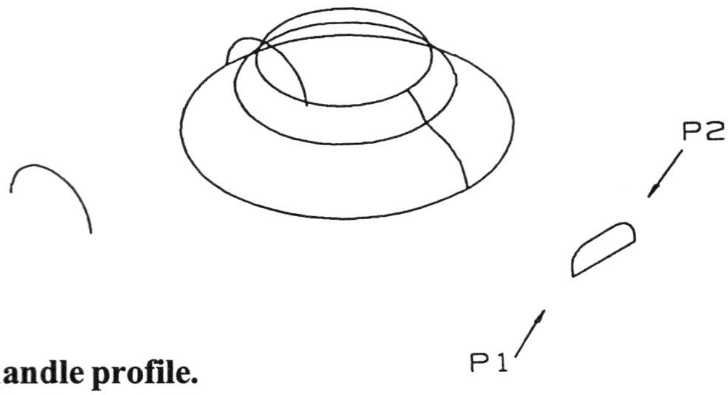

Figure 11.112

Step 8. Translate the handle profile.

Use the pick points in Figure 11.112.
Select **MAIN MENU → Xform → Translate → Window**
Enter the first corner: pick **P1**
Enter the second corner: pick **P2**
Select **Done → Rectang**
Enter the translation vector: **Z-2.5** ←
Set the Translate paramenters as here:

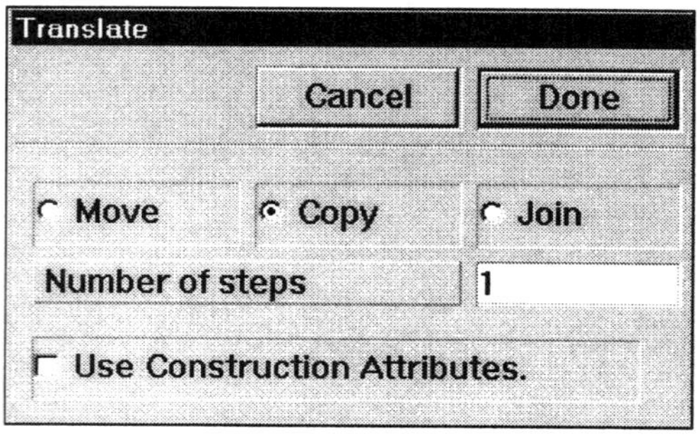

Select **Done**

The drawing should resemble Figure 11.113.

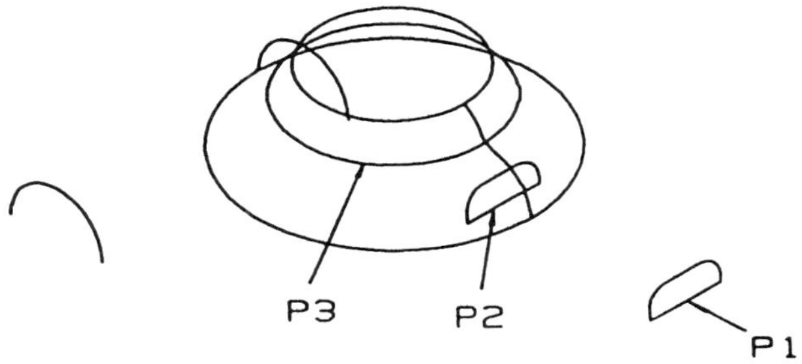

Figure 11.113

Step 9. Delete construction lines. Use the pick points in Figure 11.113.

Select **MAIN MENU → Delete**

Pick **P1, P2,** and **P3**

The new drawing appears as Figure 11.114.

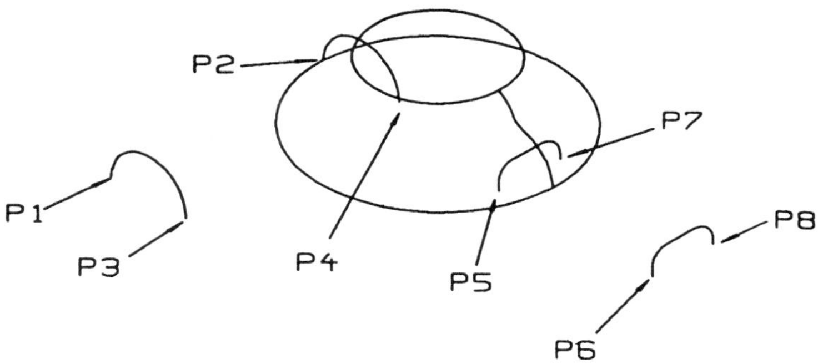

Figure 11.114

Step 10. Construct four lines to join two arcs and two handle profiles using the 3D construction plane. Use the pick points in Figure 11.114.

Select **Cplane → 3D**

Select **MAIN MENU → Create → Line → Endpoints → Endpoint**

Sequentially pick **P1 - P8** to complete the four lines

The final drawing should resemble Figure 11.115.

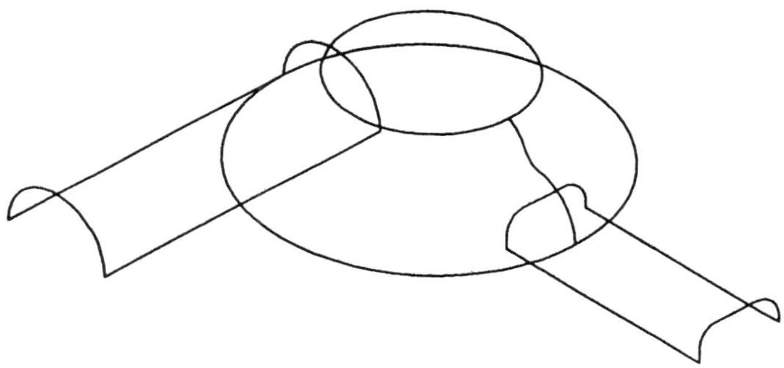

Figure 11.115

14 **Step 11. Save the drawing using the filename: dryer.**

Select **MAIN MENU → File → Save**

Enter the file name: **dryer**

Project 14:

The surface shown in Figure 11.116 is defined by **five** contours including one circle at one end, one line-profile at the other end, and three ellipses. These three ellipses are obtained by rotating a circle at a specified angle and then projecting it onto a vertical plannar surface as shown in Figure 11.117. Since the part is symmetrical about the axis, only one half of the part profile contours is required. The other half is obtained by mirroring the profile contours about the X axis. The plannar surface used for the curves to be projected onto in obtaining a surface curve can be generated as a ruled surface. Ruled surfaces are covered in chapter 12.

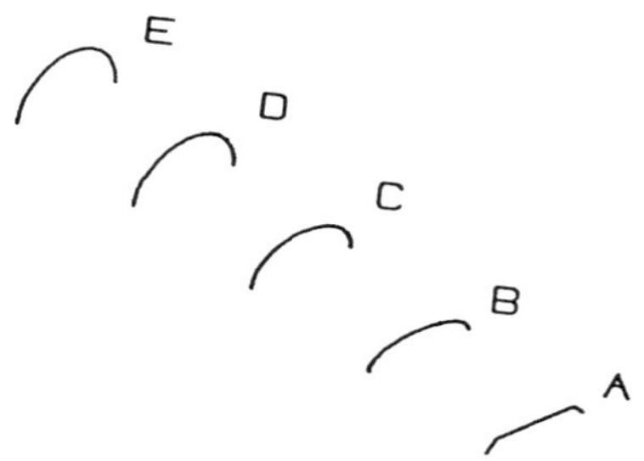

Figure 11.116a. Wireframe model

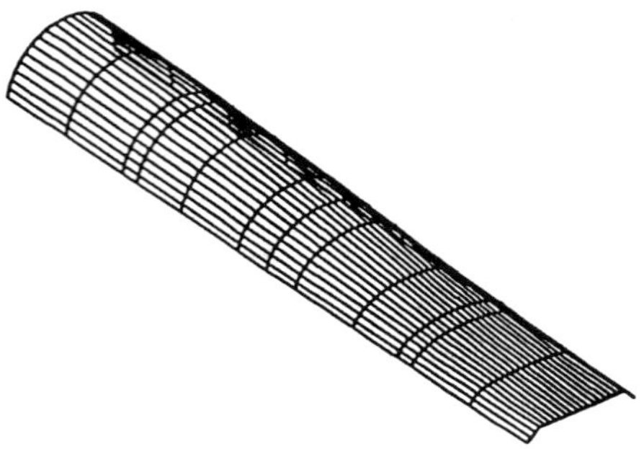

Figure 11.116b. Surface model

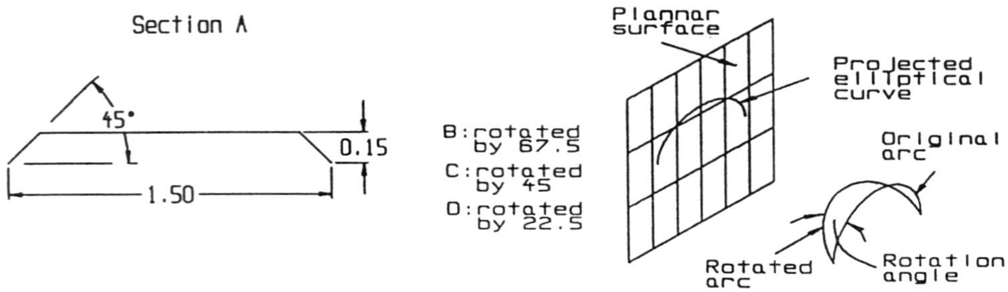

Figure 11.117

Step 1. Enter the Mastercam Mill.

Set these values: Gview to Isometric, Cplane to side plane, and Z value to 3.0.

Select **Gview → Isometric → Cplane → Side**

Select **Z** and then enter **3.0** ←

Step 2. Create a semi-circle.

Select **MAIN MENU →Create → Arc → Polar → Center pt**
Enter the center point: **0,0** ←
Enter the radius: **0.75** ←
Enter the initial angle: **0** ←
Enter the final angle: **180** ←

The drawing should resemble Figure 11.118.

Figure 11.118

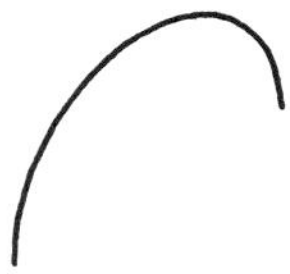

Step 3. Create two horizontal lines for generating a ruled surface.

Select **Z** and then enter **0.5** ←
Select **MAIN MENU → Create → Line → Endpoints**
Enter the first endpoint: **-1.5,1.5** ←
Enter the second endpoint: **1.5,1.5** ←
Enter the first endpoint: **-1.5,-1.5** ←
Enter the second endpoint: **1.5,-1.5** ←

These two lines now appear as in Figure 11.119.

Figure 11.119

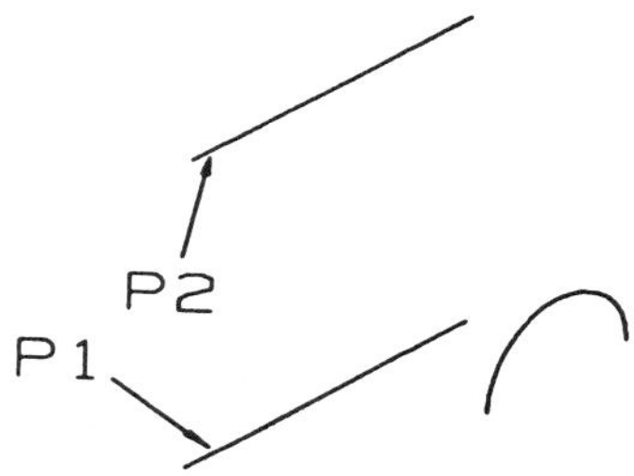

Step 4. Create a ruled surface.

Use the pick points in Figure 11.119.
Select **MAIN MENU → Create → Surface → Ruled**
Select **Single** from the chaining method menu,
then pick **P1** for contour 1
Pick **P2** for contour 2
Select **Done** to complete the selection
Toggle Surface type to **N** (for NURBS)
Select **Do it** from the ruled surface parameters menu
The ruled surface should appear as in Figure 11.120.

Figure 11.120

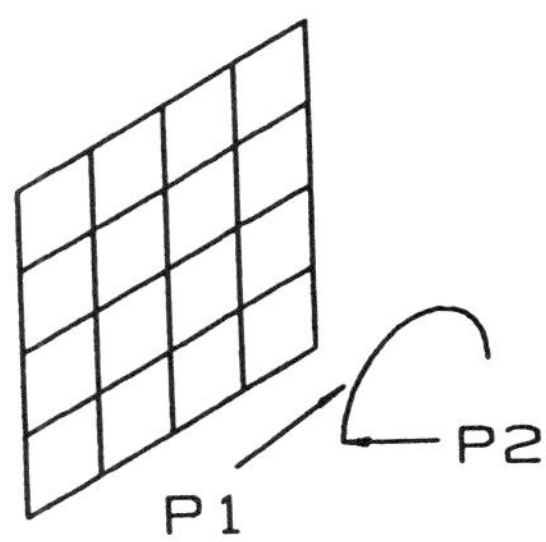

Step 5. Copy the arc twice by 22.5°, use 3 as the number of steps.

Use the pick points in Figure 11.120.
Select **Cplane → Front**
Select **MAIN MENU → Xform → Rotate → Only → Arcs**
Pick **P1** to select the entity
Select **BACKUP → Done → Point → Endpoint**
Pick **P2** to trap the endpoint of the entity
Set the Rotate parameters as here:

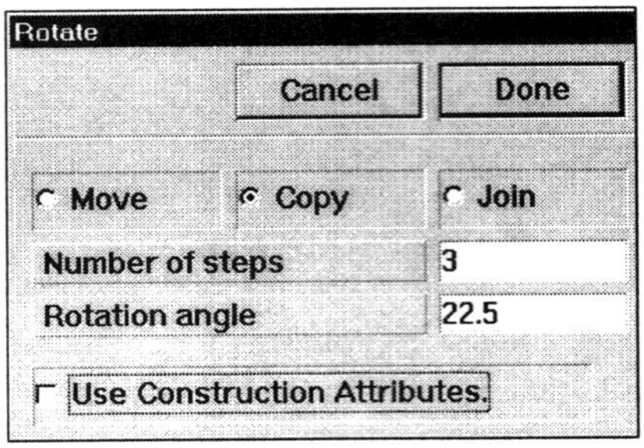

Select **Done**

The drawing is shown in Figure 11.121.

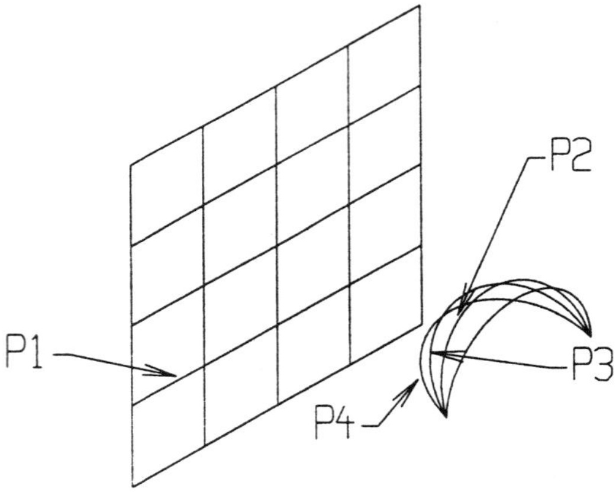

Figure 11.121

Step 6. Project the three arcs onto the plannar plane using the Side construction plane.

Use the pick points in Figure 11.121.
Select **Cplane → Side**
Select **MAIN MENU → Create → Curve → Project**

Pick **P1** to select the ruled surface
Select **Done**
Select **Single** from the chaining method menu
Pick **P2** to **P4** to select three arcs
Select **Done → Do it**

The new drawing becomes Figure 11.122.

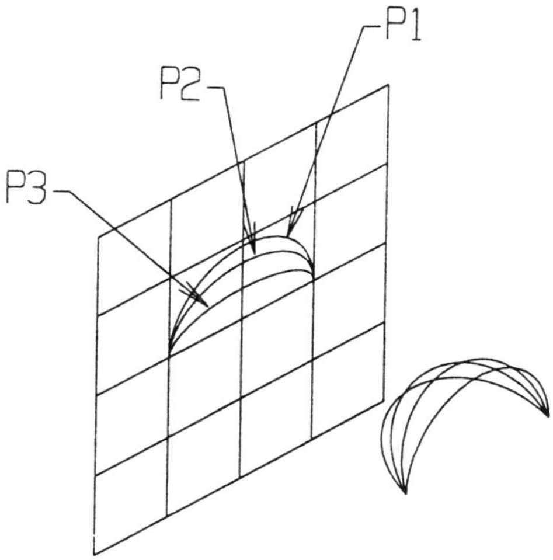

Figure 11.122

Step 7. Translate the 3 curves to their proper positions.

Use the pick points labeled above in Figure 11.122.
Select **MAIN MENU → Xform → Translate → Only → Spline**
Pick **P1** to select the entity
Select **BACKUP → Done → Rectang**
Enter the translation vector: **Z-6.5**
Set the Translate parameters as shown here:

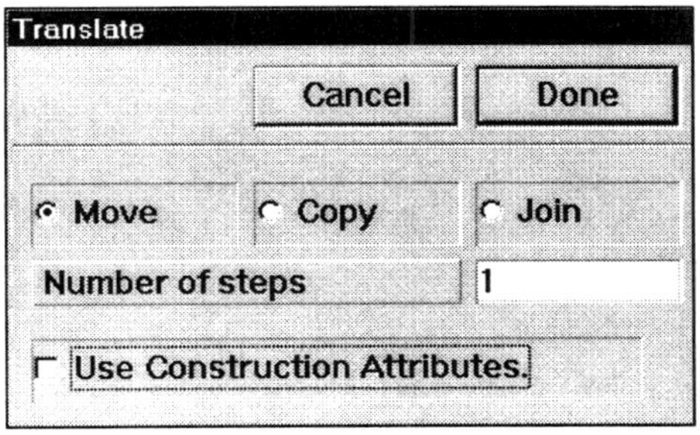

Select **Done** to move the first curve

Pick **P2** to select the second curve
Select **Done → Rectang**
Enter the translation vector: **Z-4.5**
Select **Done** from the Translation dialog box
Pick **P3** to select the third curve
Select **Done → Rectang**
Enter the translation vector: **Z-2.5**
Select **Done** from the Translate dialog box

The new drawing becomes Figure 11.123.

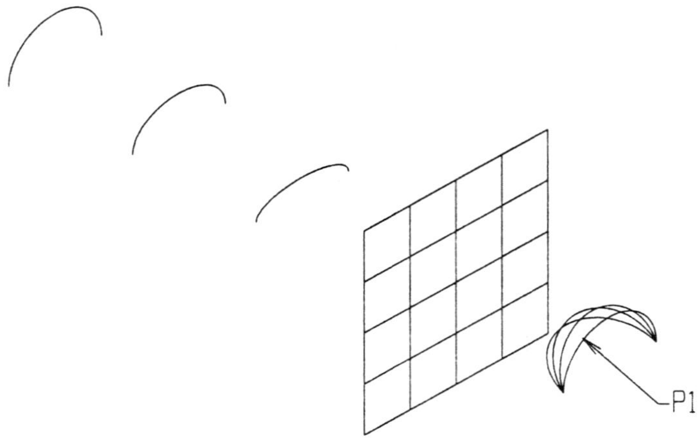

Figure 11.123

Step 8. Translate the original arc.

Use the Pick points in Figure 11.123.
Pick **P1** to select the original arc
Select **Done → Rectang**
Enter the translation vector: **Z-11**
Select **Done** from the Translate dialog box

The new drawing becomes Figure 11.124.

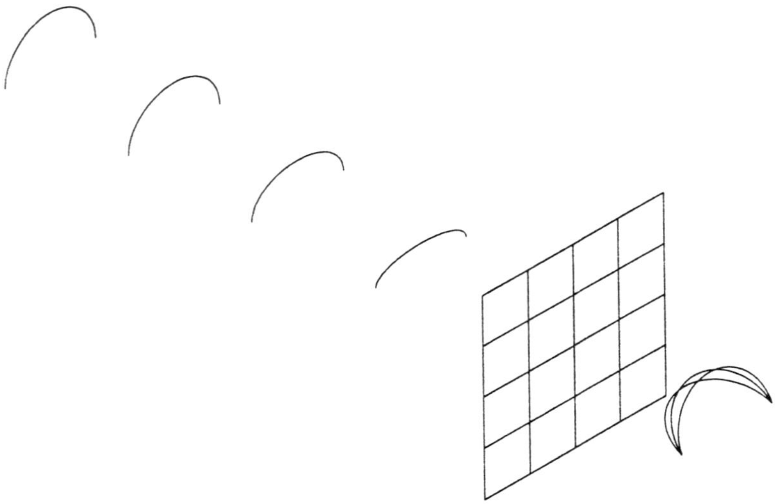

Figure 11.124

Step 9. Delete three curves, two lines and one surface. 15

Select **MAIN MENU → Delete**

Pick three curves, ruled surface, and two lines to delete from the model.

The drawing should resemble Figure 11.125.

Figure 11.125

Step 10. Construct the sectional profile at A.

Select **Z** and then enter **0** ←

Select **MAIN MENU → Create → Line → Multi**

Specify point 1: **-0.75,0** ←

Specify point 2: **-0.6,0.15** ←

Specify point 3: **0.6,0.15** ←

Specify point 4: **0.75,0** ←

The final drawing should resemble Figure 11.126.

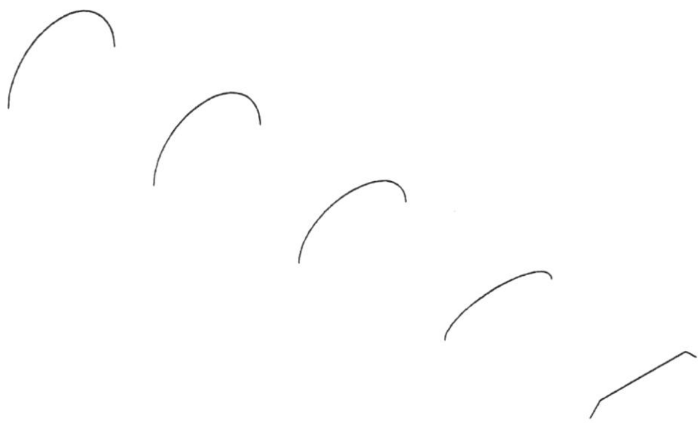

Figure 11.126

Step 11. Save the drawing. Use the Filename: loft3.

Select **MAIN MENU → File → Save**

Enter the file name: **loft3**

15 Project 15

A fan, shown in Figure 11.127, consists of seven blades that are evenly spaced around the hub. The two ends of each blade have the same cross section profile (Figure 11.128). The inside end is rotated 15° with the horizontal line and the outside end is rotated 40° with respect to the line. The end profile is curved along the hub profile.

Figure 11.127

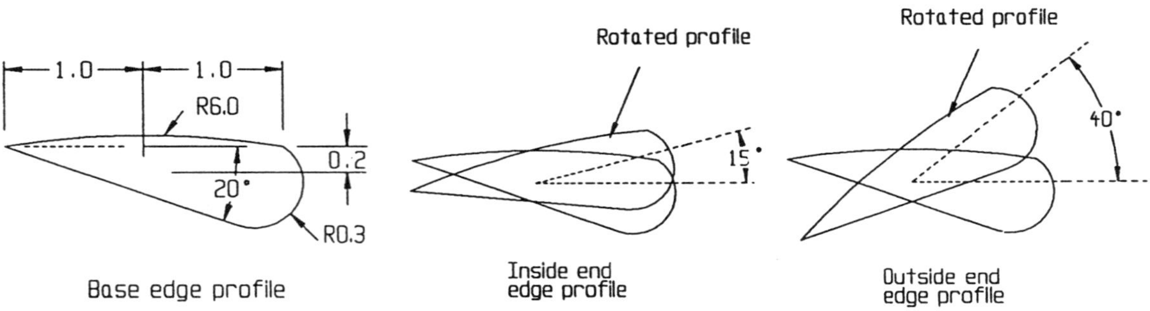

Figure 11.128

Tips 1. Create the edge profile for the hub using the Front Cplane.

2. Construct the cross section profile of the blade in the Front Cplane.

3. Create a swept surface for the outer rim which is a cylinder. This surface is used to obtain the surface curves by projecting the cross section profile onto this surface.
4. Rotate the blade edge profile by 15° with the horizontal axis, and then project it onto the outer rim surface to obtain a curved edge profile for the inside end.
5. Rotate the blade profile by 40° with the horizontal axis and then project it onto the outer rim surface to obtain the outside edge profile of the blade. This edge profile is then translated to the specified position.
6. Use different levels and colors to facilitate the creation of the wireframe model.

Step 1. Create three lines using Front Cplane. Initialize the screen if necessary.

Select **Cplane → Front**
Select **Gview → Front**
Select **MAIN MENU → Create → Line → Multi**
Specify endpoint 1: **0,1** ←
Specify endpoint 2: **0.625,1** ←
Specify endpoint 3: **0.625,0** ←
Specify endpoint 4: **2.5,1** ←

The drawing with three lines should appears as Figure 11.129.

Figure 11.129

Step 2. Create a horizontal line and a vertical line.

Select **BACKUP → Endpoints**
Specify the first endpoint: **1,1** ←
Specify the second endpoint: **4,1** ←
Specify the first endpoint: **3,1.5** ←
Specify the second endpoint: **3,-1** ←

The new drawing should look like Figure 11.130.

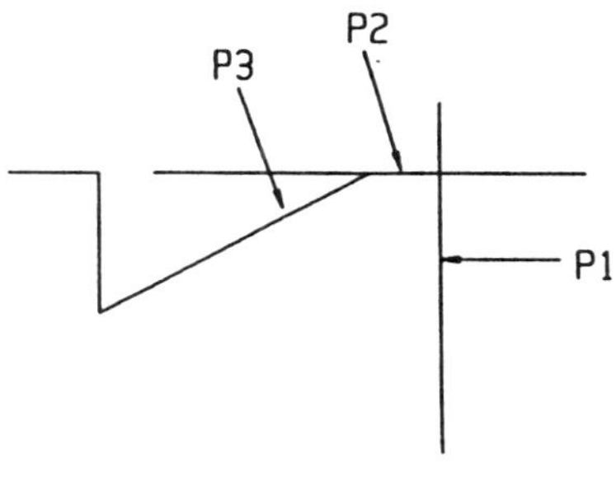

Figure 11.130

Step 3. Create an arc using the pick points in Figure 11.135.

Select **MAIN MENU → Create → Arc → Tangent → 3 ents/pts**
Pick **P1, P2,** and **P3** to select the three entities

The arc added to the drawing now appears as Figure 11.131.

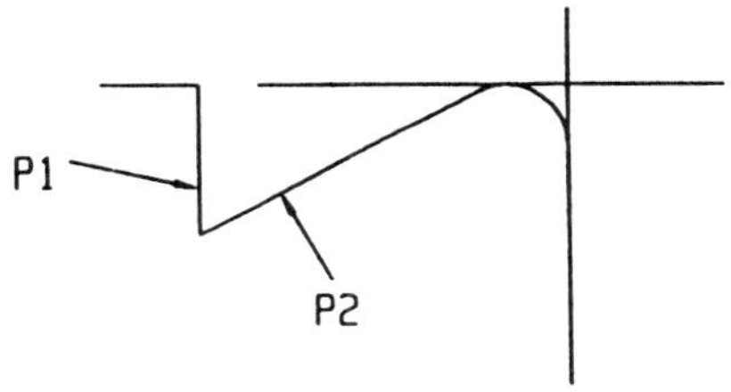

Figure 11.131

Step 4. Create a fillet using the pick points in Figure 11.131.

Select **MAIN MENU → Modify → Fillet → Radius**
Enter the fillet radius: **0.25 ←**
Pick **P1** and **P2**

The fillet is added to the drawing as shown in Figure 11.132.

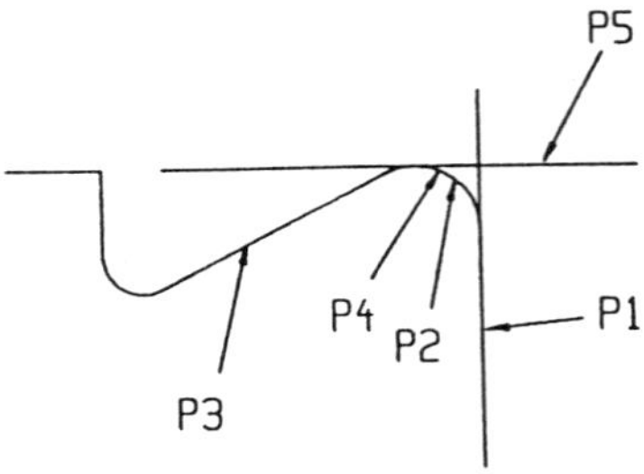

Figure 11.132

Step 5. Trim the vertical line and the slope line.

Then delete the horizontal line using the pick points in Figure 11.132 .
Select **BACKUP → Trim → 1 entity**
Pick **P1** and **P2** to trim the vertical line
Pick **P3** and **P4** to trim the slope line
Select **MAIN MENU → Delete**
Pick **P5** to delete the horizontal line

The hub profile should look like Figure 11.133.

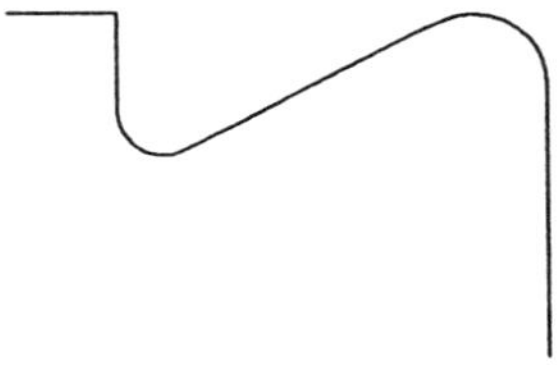

Figure 11.133

Step 6. Create a circle using Top Cplane. Change Gview to Isometric.

Select **Cplane → Top**
Select **Gview → Isometric**
Select **Z** then enter **1 ←**
Select **MAIN MENU → Create → Arc → Circ pt rad**
Enter the center point: **0,0 ←**
Enter the radius: **0.625 ←**

The hub profile should resemble Figure 11.134.

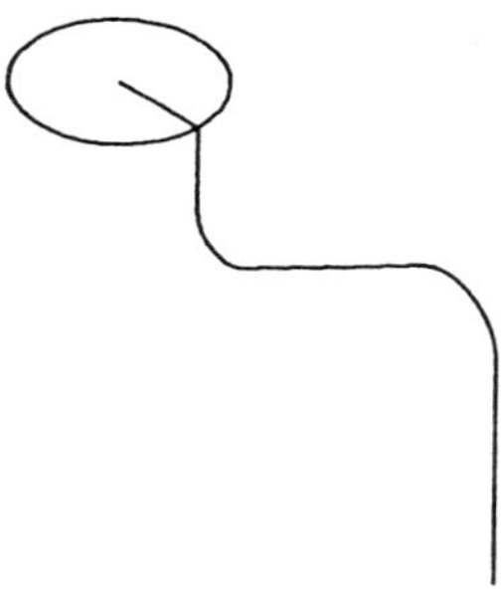

Figure 11.134

Step 7. Create the blade edge profile using Front Cplane.

Change the level to 2 and the color to 11.
Select **Level**, then enter **2** ←
Select **Color** then **11** ←
Select **Cplane** → **Front**
Select **Z** then enter **6** ←
Select **MAIN MENU** → **Create** → **Arc** → **Endpoints**
Enter the first point: **-1,0.2** ←
Enter the second point: **1,0.2** ←
Enter the radius: **6** ←
Select an arc: pick at the desired arc segment (smaller concave arc)

The arc appears on the screen as Figure 11.135.

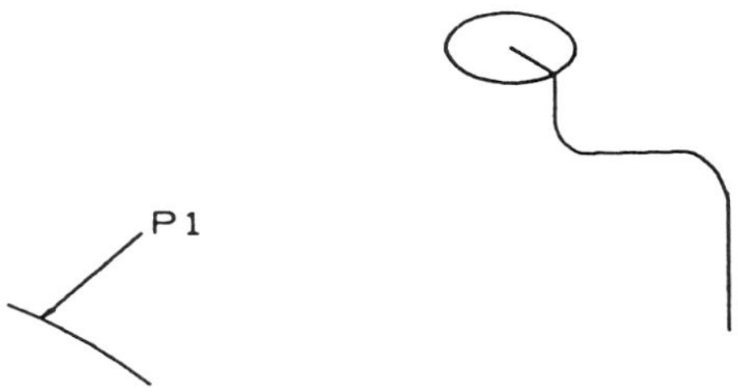

Figure 11.135

Step 8. Create a slope line using the pick points in Figure 11.135.

Select **MAIN MENU** → **Create** → **Line** → **Polar** → **Endpoint**
Pick **P1**
Enter the angle in degrees: **-20** ←
Enter the line length: **3** ←

The drawing now becomes Figure 11.136.

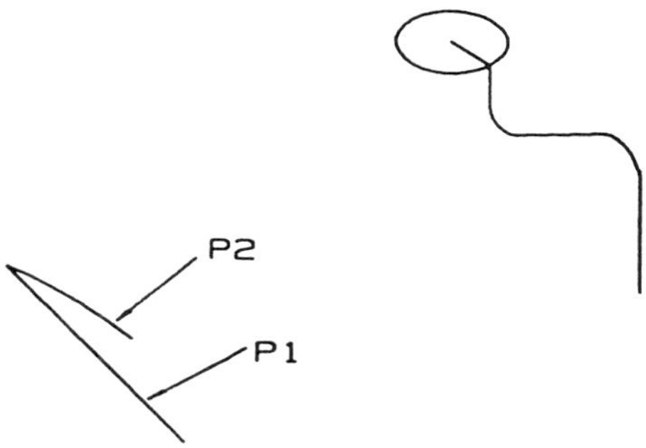

Figure 11.136

Step 9. Create an arc tangent to the slope line.

Use pick points from Figure 11.136.
Select **MAIN MENU** → **Create** → **Arc** → **Tangent** → **Point**
Pick **P1** for the arc to be tangent to
Enter the thru point: select **Endpoint** from the Point Menu
Pick **P2**
Enter the radius: **.35** ←
Select an arc: pick at the desired arc segment (2nd arc from right)

The new drawing should look like Figure 11.137.

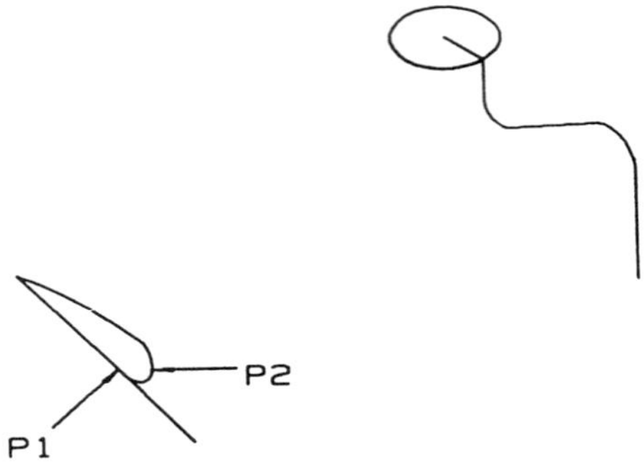

Figure 11.137

Step 10. Trim the slope line using the pick points in Figure 11.137.

Select **MAIN MENU → Modify → Trim → 1 entity**

Sequentially pick **P1** and **P2** to complete the trimming

The trimmed profile should appear as Figure 11.138.

Figure 11.138

Step 11. Extend the vertical line.

Use the pick point in Figure 11.138.

Select **MAIN MENU →Modify → Extend → Length**

Enter the length to extend: **2**

Pick **P1** to extend the line

The line is extended as in Figure 11.139.

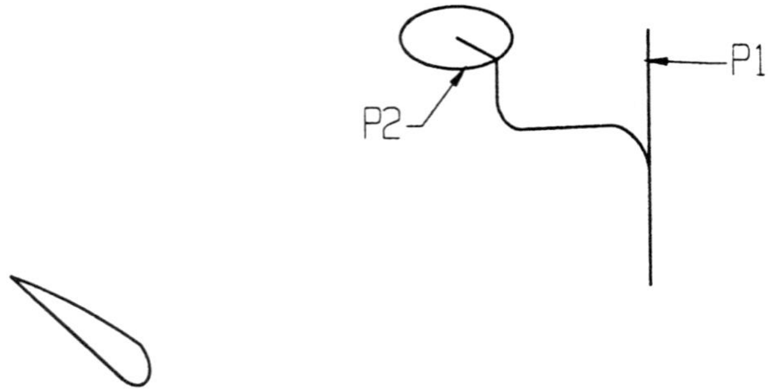

Figure 11.139

Step 12. Create a swept surface using the pick points in Figure 11.139.

Change level to 3 and color to 12.
Select **Level** then enter **3** ←
Select **Color** then enter **12** ←
Select **MAIN MENU** → **Create** → **Surface** → **Swept**
Enter the number of across contours: **1** ←
Define the across contour: select **Single** then pick **P1**
Define the along contour 1: pick **P2**
Select **Done**
Set the Swept surface parameters to the following settings:

> Surface error tolerance = **0.002**
> Surface type = **NURBS**
> **Rotate** the across contour

Select **Do it** to complete the surface

The swept surface appears as Figure 11.140.

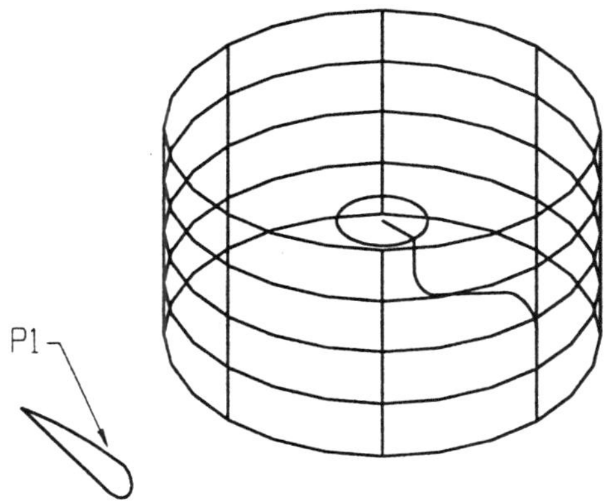

Figure 11.140

Step 13. Rotate the blade edge profile by 15°, use the pick points in Figure11.140.

Change level to 4 and color to 13.
Select **Level** then enter **4** ←
Select **Color** then enter **13** ←
Select **MAIN MENU** → **Xform** → **Rotate** → **Chain**
Pick **P1**
Select **Done** → **Done** → **Origin**
Set the Rotate parameters here:

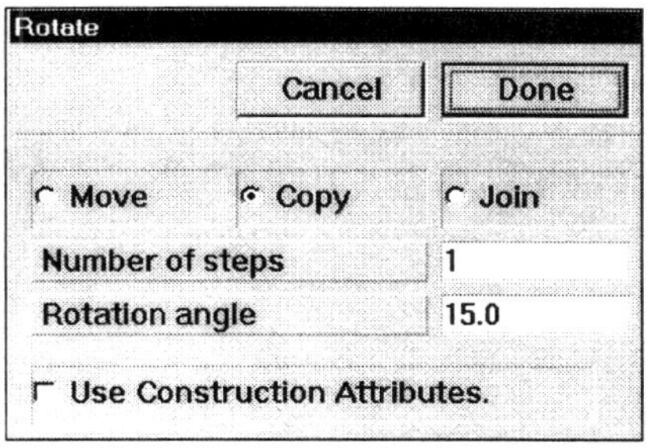

Select **Done**

The rotated profile is shown in Figure 11.141

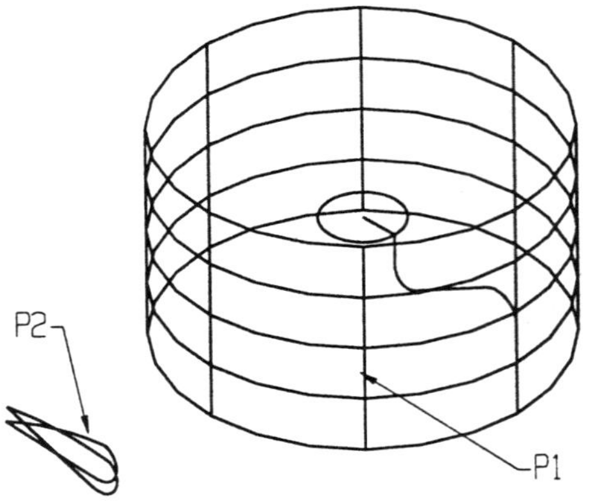

Figure 11.141

Step 14. Project the rotated profile onto the swept surface using the pick points in Figure 11.141.

Select **MAIN MENU → Create → Curve → Project**
Pick **P1** to select a surface
Select **Chain** then pick **P2**
Select **Done**
Select **Options**
Set the projection Curve parameters
as shown in this menu:

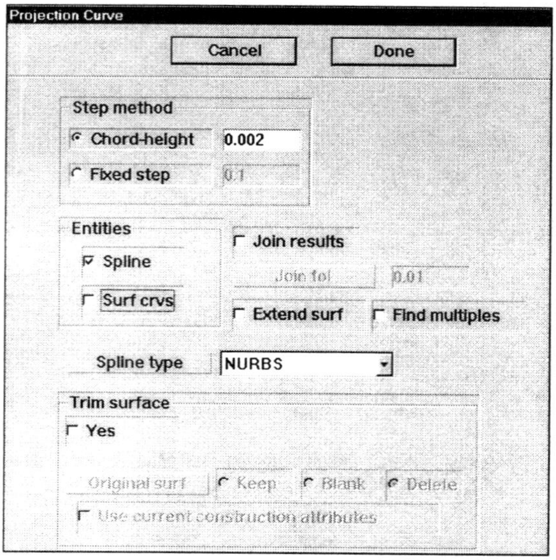

Set view/norm to **V** (for view)
Set Trim to **N** (for No)
Select **Do it**

The surface curve on the Swept surface is shown in Figure 11.142.

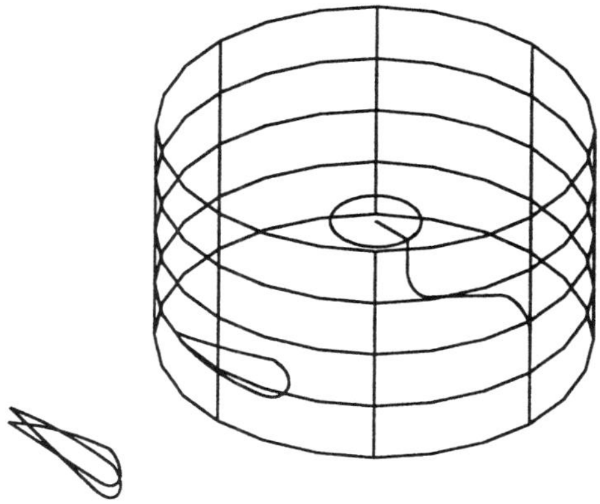

Figure 11.142

Step 15. Make level 4 invisible.

Select **Level → Vis. levels**
Click on **level 4** button, to dim
then **OK** → **OK** to return back to graphic mode

The drawing becomes Figure 11.143.

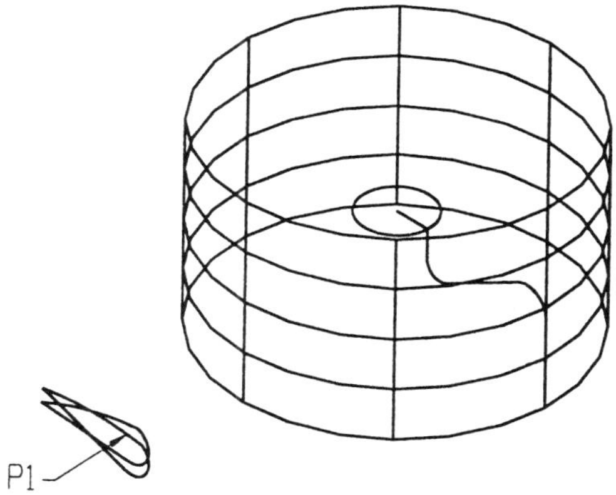

Figure 11.143

Step 16. Rotate the edge profile by 40°.

Use the pick points in Figure 11.143 on the previous page. Change level to 5.
Select **Level,** then enter **5** ←
Select **MAIN MENU → Xform → Rotate → Chain**
Pick **P1**
Select **Done → Done → Origin**
Set the Rotate parameters as below:

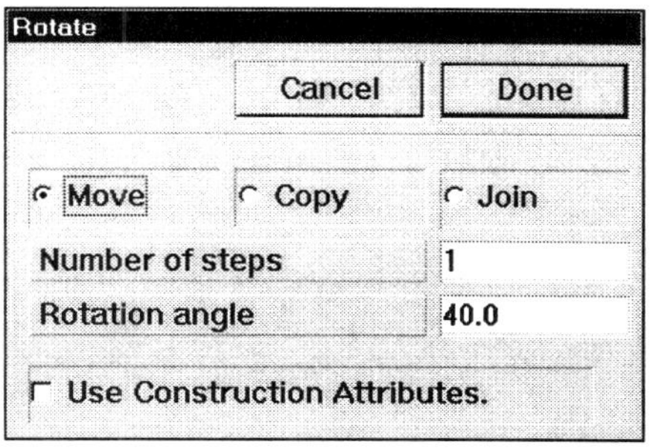

Select **Done**

The rotated profile is shown in Figure 11.144.

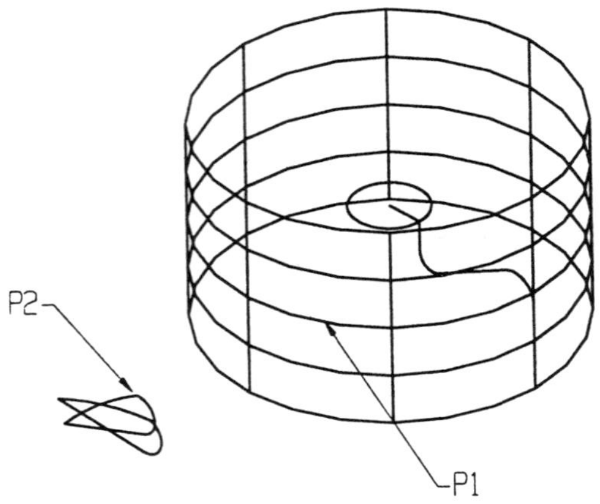

Figure 11.144

Step 17. Project the profile onto the surface using the pick points in Figure 11.144.

Select **MAIN MENU → Create → Curve → Project**
Pick **P1** to select the surface
Select **Done**
Select **Chain** then pick **P2**
Select **Done → Do it**

The drawing should resemble Figure 11.145.

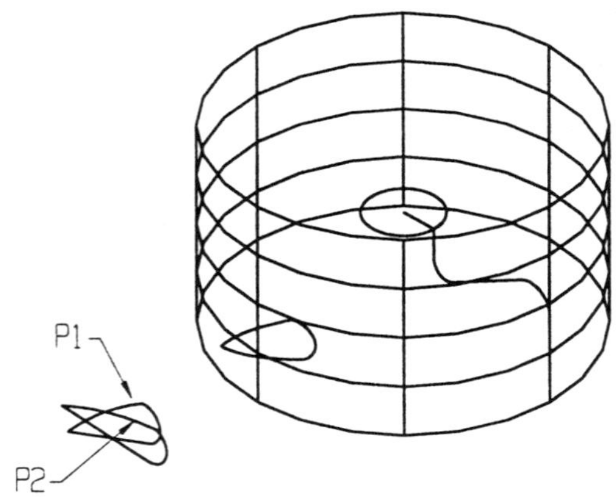

Figure 11.145

Step 18. Delete the rotated profile using the pick points in Figure 11.145.

Select **MAIN MENU → Delete →Chain**
Pick **P1** and **P2**
Select **Done** to delete the two contours

The new drawing should look like Figure 11.146.

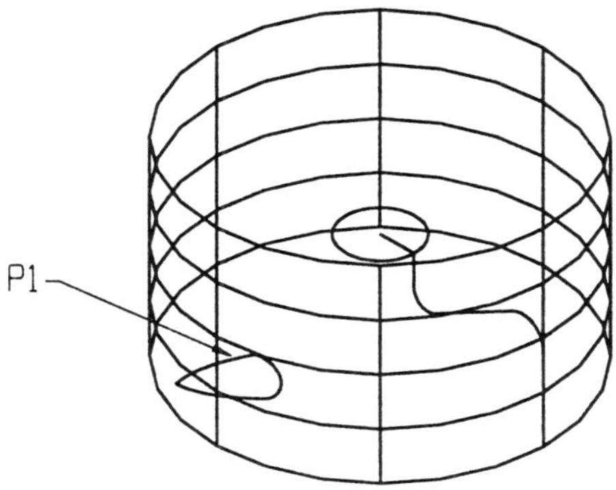

Figure 11.146

Step 19. Translate the projected curve back to the desired position using the pick points in Figure 11.146.

Select **MAIN MENU → Xform → Translate → Chain**
Pick **P1**
Select **Done → Done → Rectang**
Enter the translation vector: **Z3 ←**
Set the Translate parameters as below:

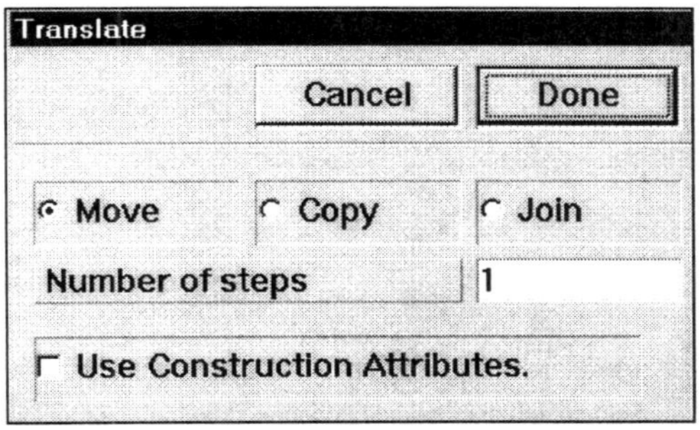

Select **Done**

The drawing becomes Figure 11.147.

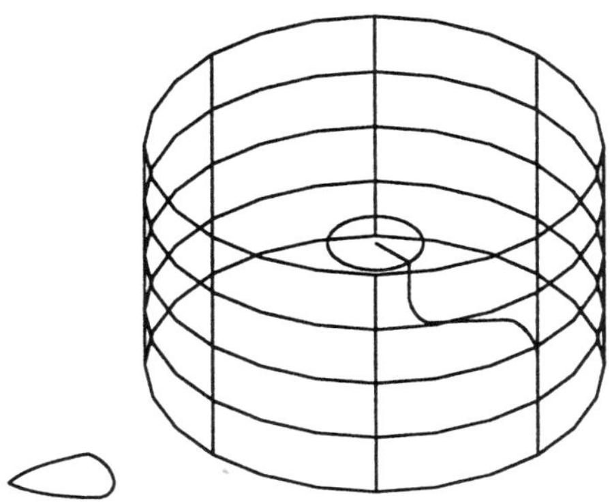

Figure 11.147

Step 20. Make level 4 visible.

Select **Level→ Vis. levels**
Click on the level 4 button (highlighted)
Click on the **OK** to return back to graphic mode
The new drawing should resemble Figure 11.148.

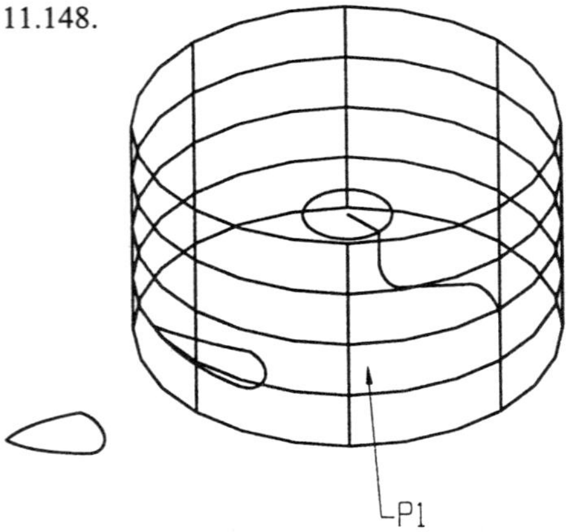

Figure 11.148

Step 21. Delete the surface curve and the swept surface using the pick points in Figure 11.148.

Select **MAIN MENU →Delete**
Pick **P1** to delete the swept surface
The drawing should look like Figure 11.149.

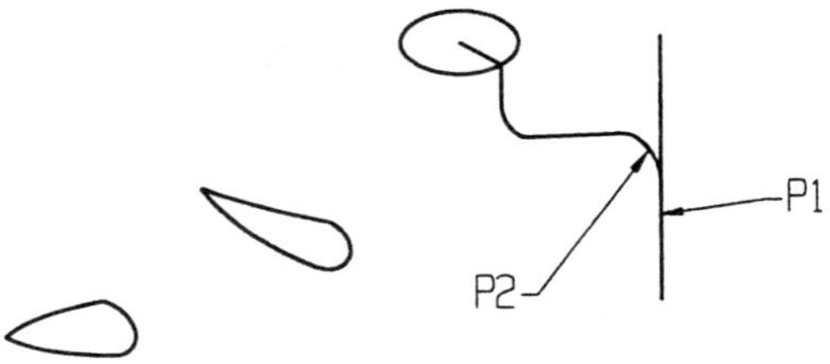

Figure 11.149

Step 22. Trim the vertical line.

Use the pick points in Figure 11.149.
Select **MAIN MENU → Modify → Trim → 1 entity**
Pick **P1** and **P2** sequentially to trim the line
The new drawing becomes Figure 11.150.

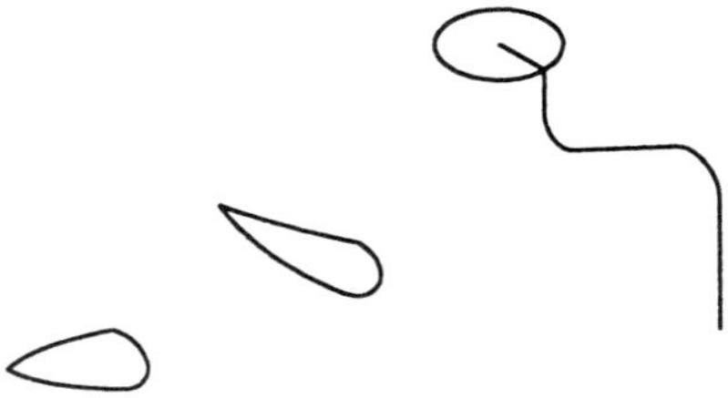

Figure 11.150

Step 23. Make level 1 invisible.

Select **Level → Vis. levels**
Click on the **level 1** button to dim the lines
Select **OK** to return back to graphic mode

The drawing becomes Figure 11.151.

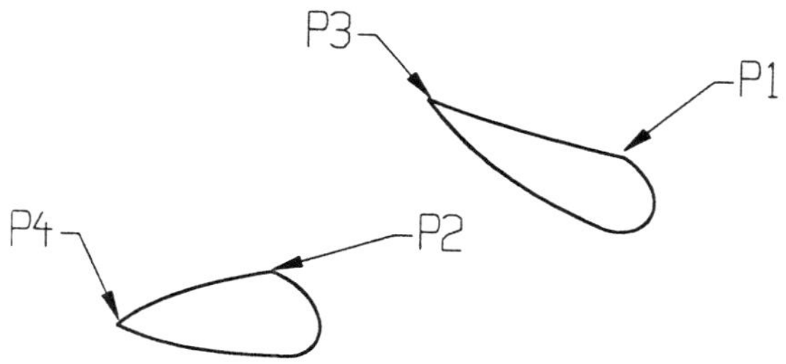

Figure 11.151

Step 24. Create two lines connecting the two profiles using the pick points in Figure 11.151. Use the 3D Cplane.

Select **Cplane → 3D**

Select **MAIN MENU → Create → Line → Endpoints → Endpoint**

Pick **P1** and **P2** for the first line

Pick **P3** and **P4** for the second line

The wireframe model needed of the blade should resemble Figure 11.152.

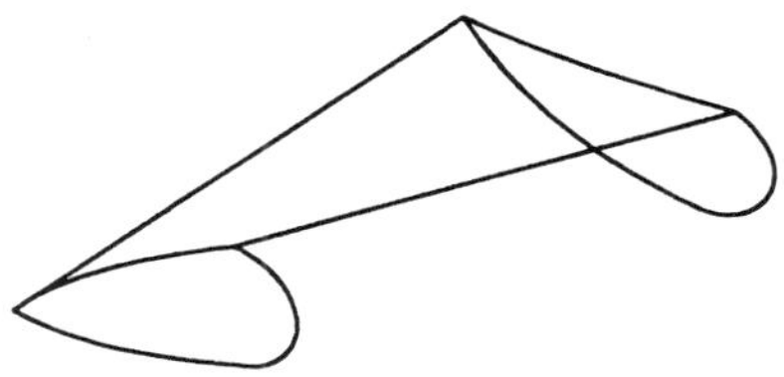

Figure 11.152

Step 25. Toggle level 1 back to visible.

Select **Level → Vis. levels**

Click on the **level 1** button to highlight

Select **OK** to return back to graphic mode

The final wireframe model should look like Figure 11.153.

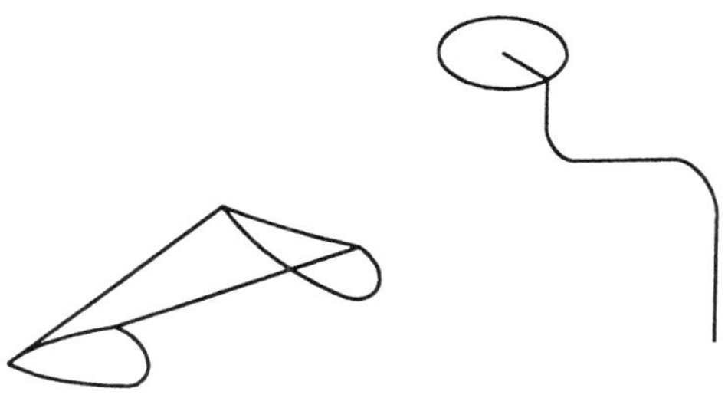

Figure 11.153

Step 26. Save the drawing file as fan.

Select **MAIN MENU → File → Save**

Enter file name: **fan** ←

16 Project 16.

Construct a wireframe model for the surface model of a car wheel (Figure 11.154b & c). The model consists of a hub, a rim, and six pockets. The two edge curves of the pockets are shown in Figure 11.154a. The coordinate values of critical points for hub and rim edge profiles are tabulated below:

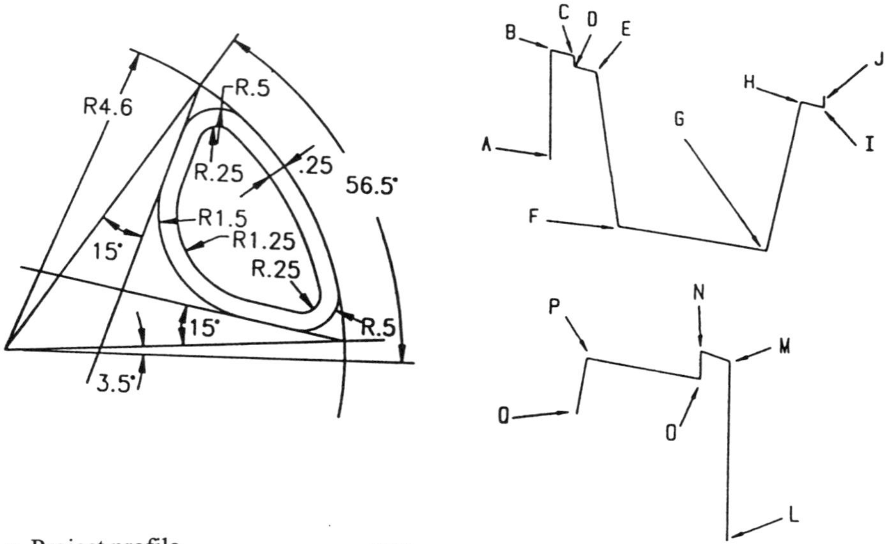

a. Project profile

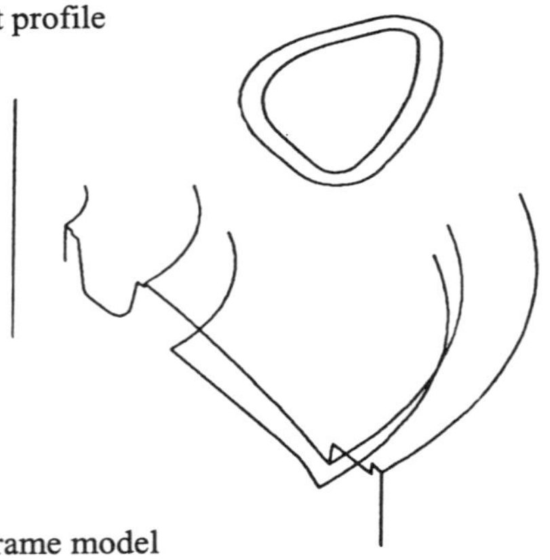

b. Wireframe model

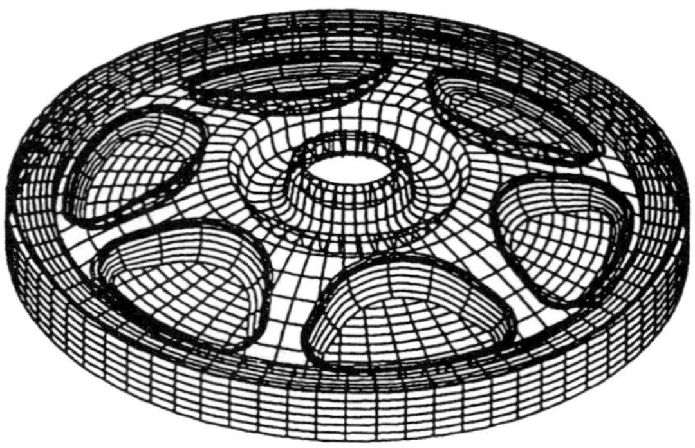

c. Surface model

Figure 11.154

Mastercam Version 7,
Scholar's International Publishing Corp., 1998

Tips 1. Use Front Cplane to construct the edge profiles of the hub, rim, and frame, as well as two upper and lower surfaces.
2. Use Top Cplane to create two of the contours for the pocket surface. The outer contour is created first. The six entities in the outer contour are then offset by a distance of 0.25-in. to obtain the inner contour. Note that these two contours are projected onto the two surfaces to obtain two surface curves for defining the pocket surface in chapter 13.

Step 1. Construct a series of lines for the hub profile using the Front construction plane.

Select **Cplane → Front**
Select **Gview → Front**
Select **MAIN MENU → Create → Line → Multi**
Specify endpoint 1: **0.8,1.4** ←
Specify endpoint 2: **0.8,1.9** ←
Specify endpoint 3: **0.9,1.875** ←
Specify endpoint 4: **0.9,1.825** ←
Specify endpoint 5: **1,1.8** ←
Specify endpoint 6: **1.1,1.1** ←
Specify endpoint 7: **1.75,1.0** ←
Specify endpoint 8: **1.9,1.675** ←
Specify endpoint 9: **2,1.65** ←
Specify endpoint 10: **2,1.7** ←

Your drawing will appear as Figure 11.155.

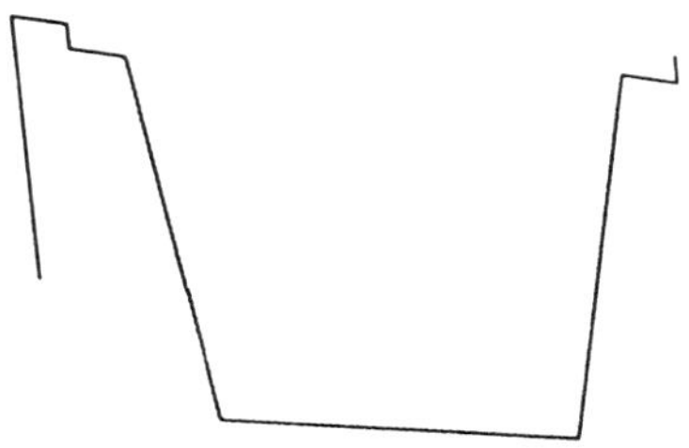

Figure 11.155

Step 2. Create another set of lines for the outer rim.

Select **BACKUP → Multi**
Specify endpoint 1: **5.65,0** ←
Specify endpoint 2: **5.65,1** ←

Press **Alt** + **F1** and then **F2** to fit the drawing in the screen

Specify endpoint 3: **5.5,1.05** ←
Specify endpoint 4: **5.5,0.9** ←
Specify endpoint 5: **4.9,1.0** ←
Specify endpoint 6: **4.85,0.7** ←

The drawing should look like Figure 11.156.

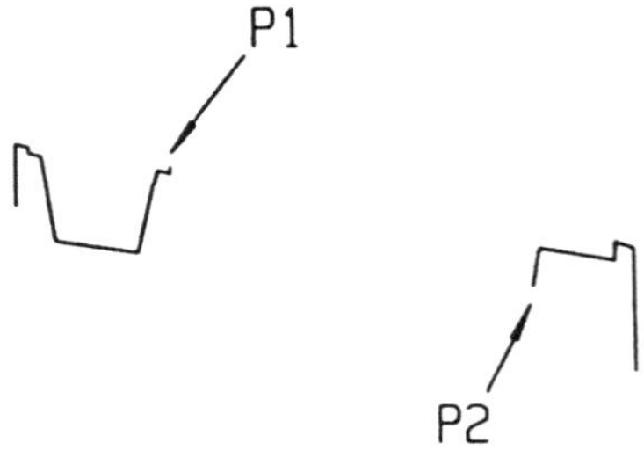

Figure 11.156

Step 3. Construct the arc for creating the top surface.

Use the pick points in Figure 11.156.
Select **MAIN MENU → Create → Arc → Endpoints → Endpoint**
Enter the first point: Pick **P1**
Enter the second point: Pick **P2**
Enter the radius: **10** ←
Select an arc: Pick the upper arc to complete the arc selection.

Your drawing should appear as Figure 11.157.

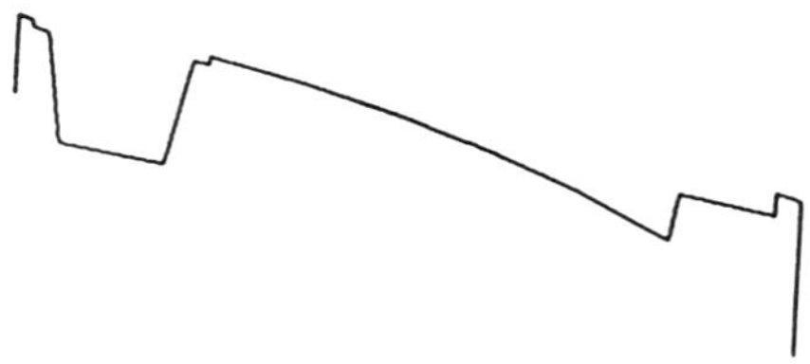

Figure 11.157

Step 4. Construct the edge profile for the lower surface.

Select **MAIN MENU → Create → Line → Polar**
Specify an endpoint: **2.4,1** ←
Enter the angle in degrees (0.00): **-12.5** ←
Enter the line length (1.00): **3** ←

The drawing should look like Figure 11.158.

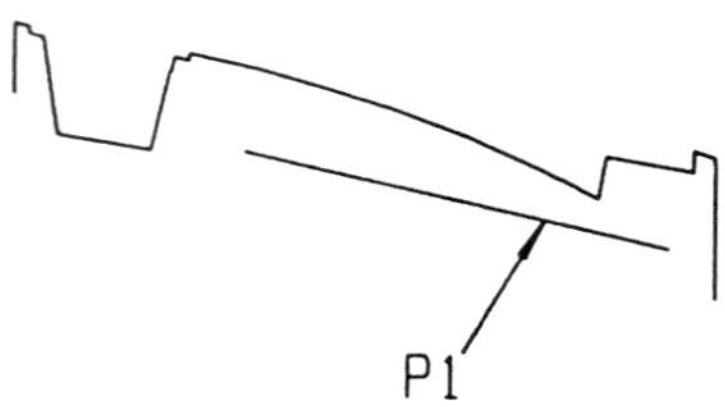

Figure 11.158

Step 5. Create the arc tangent to the line.

Use the pick points in Figure 11.158.
Select **MAIN MENU → Create → Arc → Tangent → Point**
Pick **P1** to select the entity that the arc is to be tangent to
Enter the thru point: **4.7,0.3** ←
Enter the radius: **0.8** ←
Select the right arc to complete the arc

The drawing will appear as Figure 11.159.

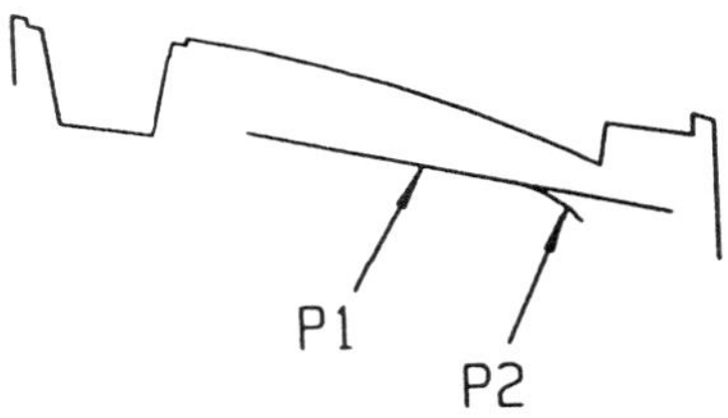

Figure 11.159

Step 6. Trim the line to the tangent point.

Use the pick points in Figure 11.159.
Select **MAIN MENU → Modify → Trim → 1 entity**
Select the entity to trim: pick **P1**
Select the entity to trim to: pick **P2**

The resulted drawing is shown in Figure 11.160.

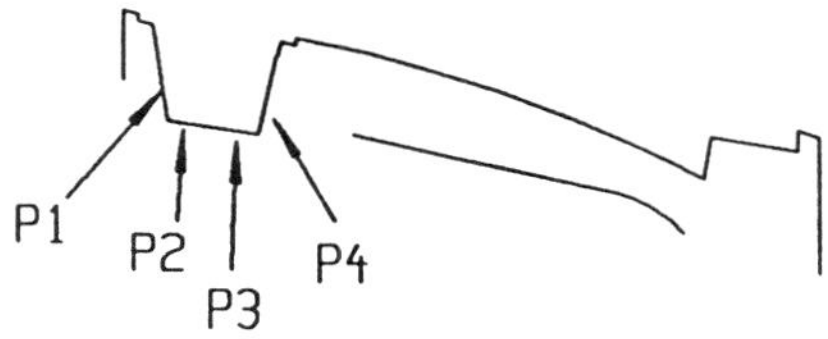

Figure 11.160

Step 7. Add two fillets. Use the pick points in Figure 11.160.

Select **MAIN MENU → Modify → Fillet**
Pick **Radius**, and then enter **0.1** ←
Pick **P1** to select an entity
Pick **P2** to select another entity to complete the first fillet
Pick **Radius**, and then enter **0.3** ←
Pick **P3** to select an entity
Pick **P4** to select another entity to complete the second fillet

The drawing will appear as Figure 11.161.

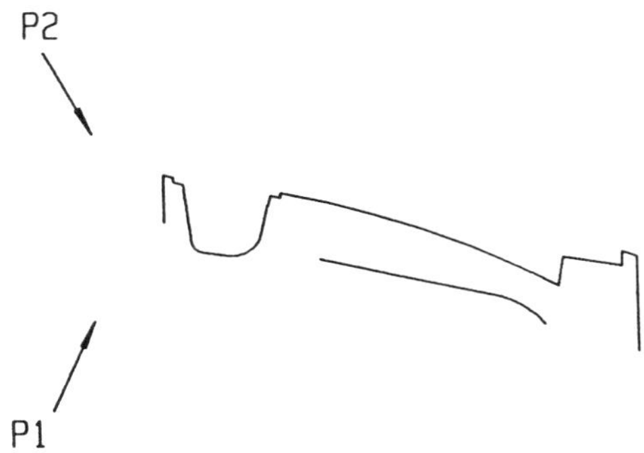

Figure 11.161

Step 8. Create a vertical line.

Use the pick points in Figure 11.161.
Select **MAIN MENU → Create → Line → Vertical → Sketch**
Pick **P1** and **P2**, and then enter **0** ← for X coordinate
Press **Alt + F1** to fit the drawing if necessary.

The drawing should appear as Figure 11.162.

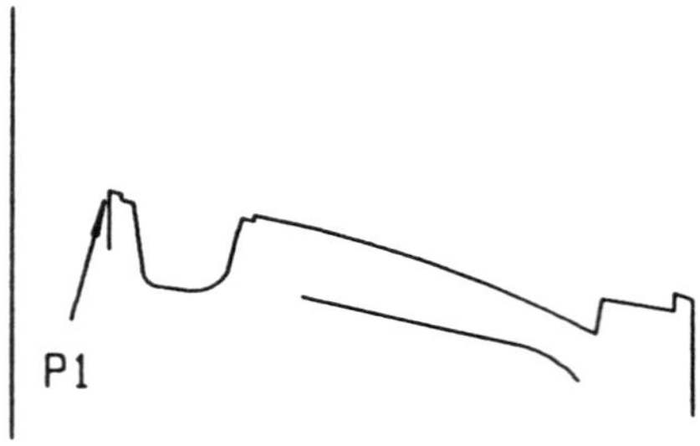

Figure 11.162

Step 9. Create six arcs using the top construction plane.

Use the pick points labeled in Figure 11.162.
Select **Cplane → Top**
Select **Gview → Isometric**
Select **Z → Endpoint** and then pick **P1** to set the Z value

Z1.9 should appear in the secondary menu

Select **MAIN MENU → Create → Arc → Polar → Center pt**
Enter the center point: **0,0** ←
Enter the radius (1.00): **0.8** ←
Enter the initial angle (0.0): press ← to accept the default value
Enter the final angle (360.0): **60** ←

The drawing now becomes Figure 11.163.

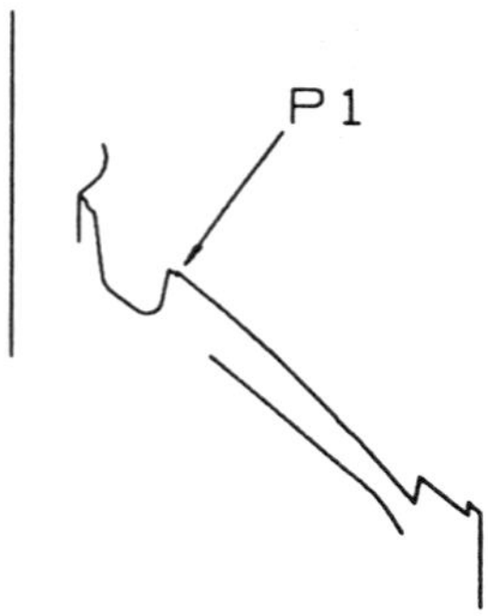

Figure 11.163

Step 10. Create the second arc using the pick points in Figure 11.163.

Pick **Z → Endpoint** and then pick **P1**
Z1.7 should appear in the Secondary menu

Select **MAIN MENU → Create → Arc → Polar → Center pt**
Enter the center point: **0,0** ←
Enter the radius (0.8): **2** ←
Enter the initial angle (0.0): ←
Enter the final angle (60.0): ←

The drawing will appear as Figure 11.164.

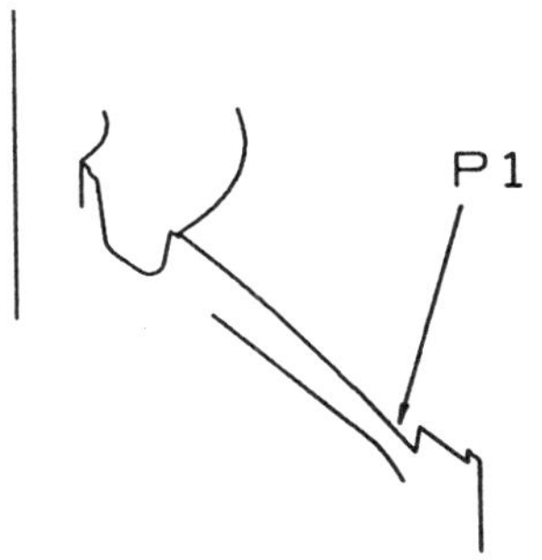

Figure 11.164

Step 11. Create the third arc.

Use the pick point in Figure 11.164.
Select **Z → Endpoint** and then pick **P1**

Z0.7 should appear in the Secondary menu

Select **MAIN MENU → Create → Arc → Polar → Center pt**
Enter the center point: **0,0** ←
Enter the radius: **4.85** ←
Enter the initial angle (0.0): ←
Enter the final angle (60.0): ←

The drawing should resemble Figure 11.165.

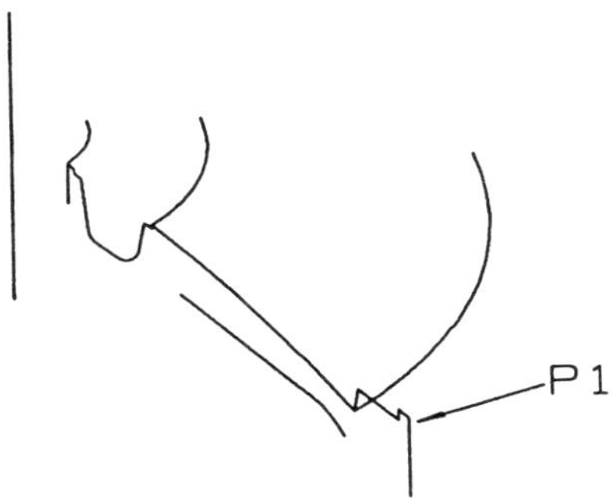

Figure 11.165

Step 12. Create the fourth arc using the pick point in Figure 11.165.

Pick **Z → Endpoint** and then pick **P1**
Z1.0 should appear in the Secondary menu

Enter the center point: **0,0** ←
Enter the radius: **5.65** ←
Enter the initial angle (0.0): ←
Enter the final angle (60.0): ←

Your drawing should appear as Figure 11.166.

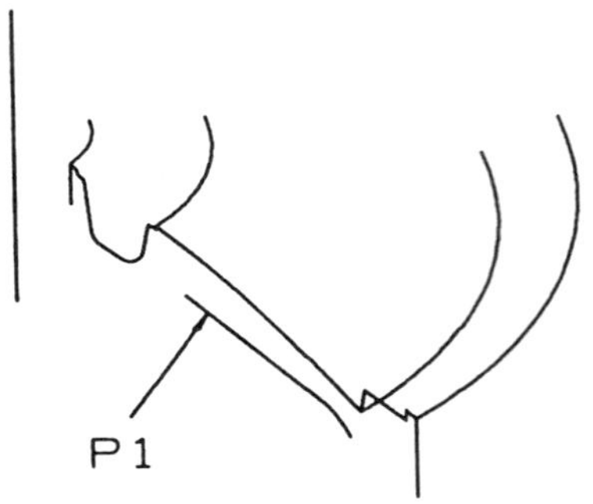

Figure 11.166

Step 13. Create the fifth arc.

Use the pick point in Figure 11.166.
Pick **Z → Endpoint** and then pick **P1**
Z1.0 should appear in the Secondary menu

Enter the center point: **0,0** ←
Enter the radius: **2.4** ←
Enter the initial angle (0.0): ←
Enter the final angle (60.0): ←

The drawing should resemble Figure 11.167.

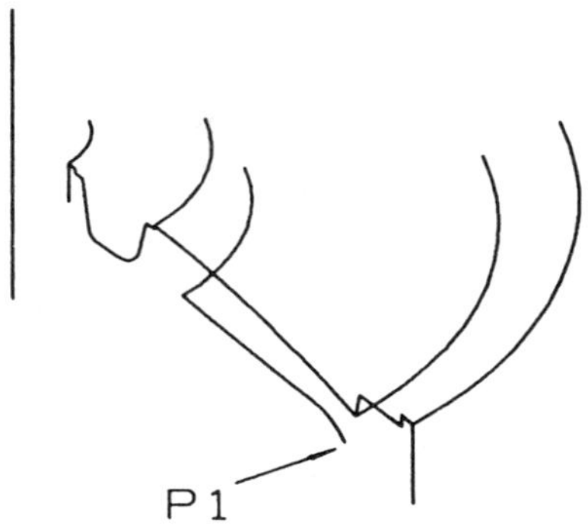

Figure 11.167

Step 14. Create the sixth arc using the pick point in Figure 11.167.

Pick **Z → Endpoint** and then pick **P1**
Z0.3 should appear in the Secondary menu

Enter the center point: **0,0** ←
Enter the radius: **4.7** ←
Enter the initial angle (0.0): ←
Enter the final angle (60.0): ←

The drawing now should look like Figure 11.168.

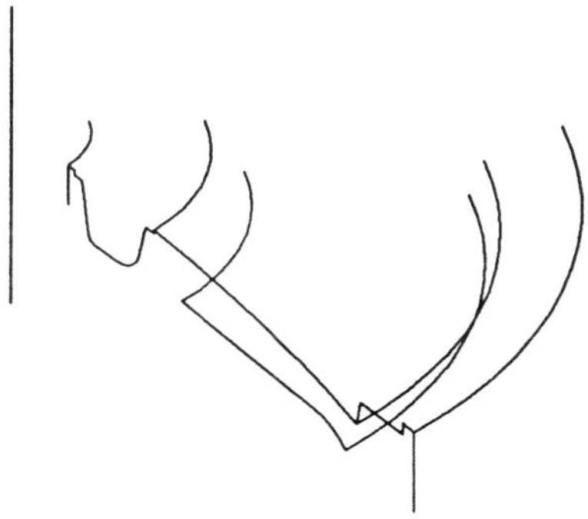

Figure 11.168

Step 15. Make level 1 invisible.

Set the Secondary menu parameters to the following settings:
Select **Level → Vis. levels**
Click on the **level 1** button (dimmed)
Select **OK → OK** to return back to graphic mode
Select **Level** and then enter **2** ←
Select **Color** and then enter **12** ←
Select **Z** and then enter **4** ←
Select **Gview → Top**

Step 16. Create an arc.

Select **MAIN MENU → Create → Arc → Polar → Center pt**
Enter the center point: **0,0** ←
Enter the radius: **4.6** ←
Enter the initial angle: **-10** ←
Enter the final angle: **70** ←

Step 17. Create two construction lines.

Select **MAIN MENU → Create → Line → Polar**
Enter coordinates: **0,0** ←
Enter the angle in degrees (0.0): **3.5** ←
Enter the line length (3.0): **5.5** ←
Enter coordinates: **0,0** ←
Enter the angle in degrees (0.0): **56.5** ←
Enter the line length (5.5): press ← to accept the default value

The drawing now will look like Figure 11.169.

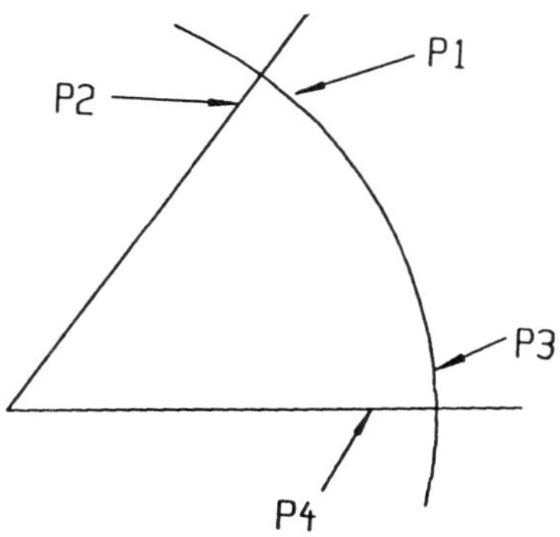

Figure 11.169

Step 18. Create another two construction lines.

Use the pick points in Figure 11.169.

Select **Intersec** then pick **P1** and **P2**

Enter the angle in degrees: **-108.5 (or 180 - 56.5 - 15)** ←

Enter the line length: **4.5** ← for the first line

Select **Intersec**

Pick **P3** and **P4**

Enter the angle in degrees: **168.5 (or 180 - 15 + 3.5)** ←

Enter the line length: **4.5** ← to complete the second line

The drawing now should resemble Figure 11.170.

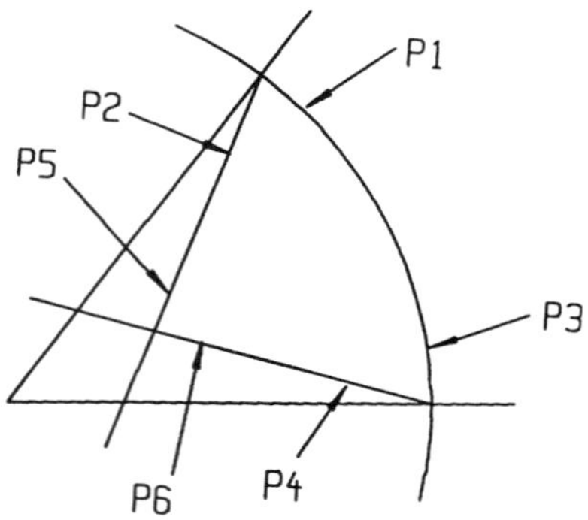

Figure 11.170

Step 19. Add three fillets.

Use the pick points in Figure 11.170.

Select **MAIN MENU → Modify → Fillet**

Select **Radius** from the parameter menu, and then enter **0.5** ← for fillet radius

Select an entity: pick **P1**

Select another entity: pick **P2** for the first fillet

Select an entity: pick **P3**

Select another entity: pick **P4** for the second fillet

Select **Radius** then enter **1.5** ←

Pick **P5** and **P6** to complete the third fillet

The new drawing will appear as Figure 11.171.

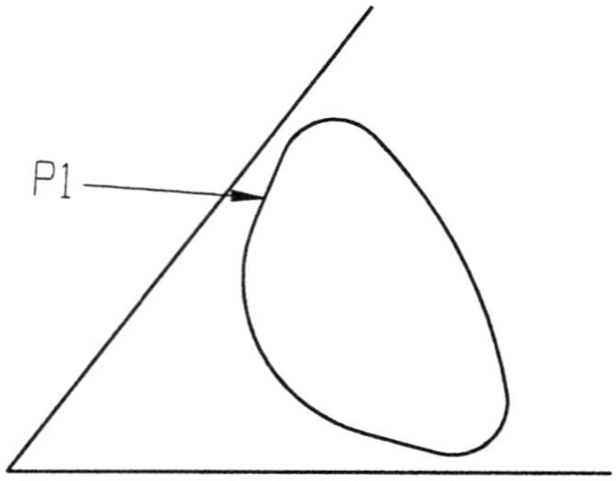

Figure 11.171

Step 20. Create the inner pocket using the offset command.

Use the pick points in Figure 11.171.
Select **MAIN MENU → Xform → Ofs ctour → Chain**
Pick **P1** to select the contour (make sure the chain direction is counterclockwise)
Select **Done**
Set the Offset Contour Parameters as shown in this menu:

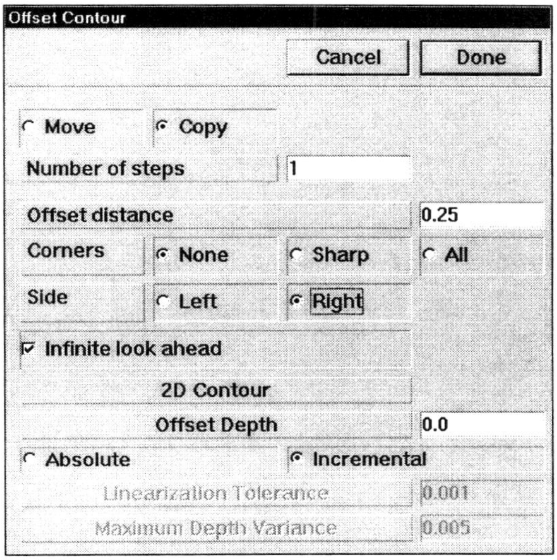

Select **Done** from the Offset Contour dialog box
The resultant inner pocket shows in Figure 11.172.

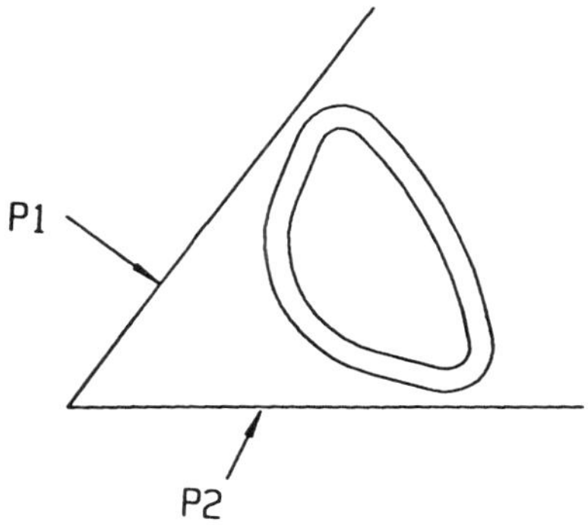

Figure 11.172

Step 21. Delete two construction lines using the pick points in Figure 11.172.

Select **MAIN MENU → Delete**
Pick **P1** and **P2**

The final drawing in Top Gview should resemble Figure 11.173.

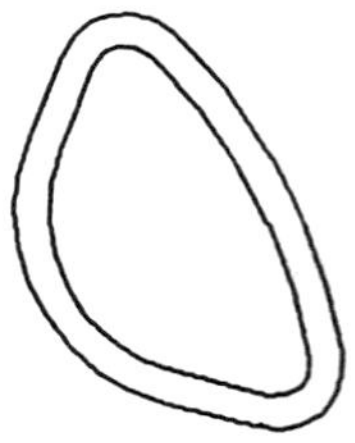

Figure 11.173

Step 22. Make level 1 visible and change Gview to isometric.

Select **Level → Vis. Levels**
Click on the **level 1** button to highlight the level
Select **OK** to return back to graphic mode
Select **Gview → Isometric**

The final drawing should look like Figure 11.174.

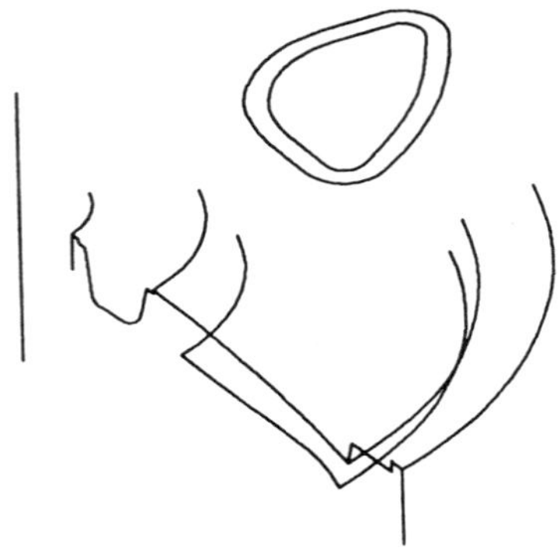

Figure 11.174

Step 23. Save the wireframe model file using the filename: wheel.

Select **MAIN MENU → File → Save**

Enter file name: **wheel** ←

11.3 Exercises

1. Explain how a wireframe model describes an object.

2. What additional information does a surface model provide over a wireframe model?

3. What is construction plane?

4. What are the three principal construction planes? Use a drawing to illustrate the definition of these three principal planes.

5. What are the six Mastercam construction planes?

6. Give the reasons we use a 3D construction plane.

7. Use a drawing to show how to define a 2-line construction plane. Explain when to use a 2-line construction plane.

8. Use a drawing to show how to define a normal construction plane; and explain when to use a normal construction plane.

9. Use drawings to show how to specify Z-depth in various construction planes.

10. Construct a wireframe model as shown in Figure 11.175. The model consists of two semi-circles, two profiles, and four lines. Save the drawing in the file name **E1**. This model can be used to generate two ruled surfaces and two fillet surfaces in chapter 12. Some helpful hints are given below.

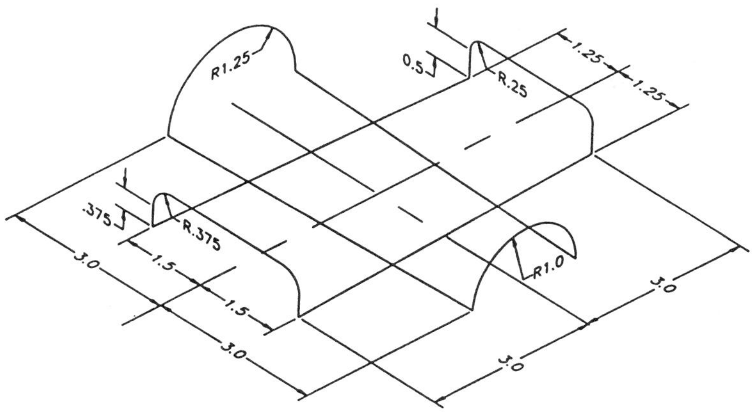

Figure 11.175

Tips 1. Follow the instructions in project 1.

2. Create two semi-circles using the side construction plane. The Z-depth is 3.0 and -3.0 for the two semi-circles, respectively.
3. Create two profiles using the front construction plane. The Z-depth is 3.0 and -3.0 for the two profiles, respectively.
4. Create four lines connecting the end points of the entities. Use the 3d construction plane.

11. Construct the wireframe model shown in Figure 11.176. This model consists of four arcs and one rectangular box. It can be used to create two ruled surfaces, generate a fillet surface, and trim the smaller ruled surface to the fillet surface. Save the file name as **E2**. Tips are suggested below.

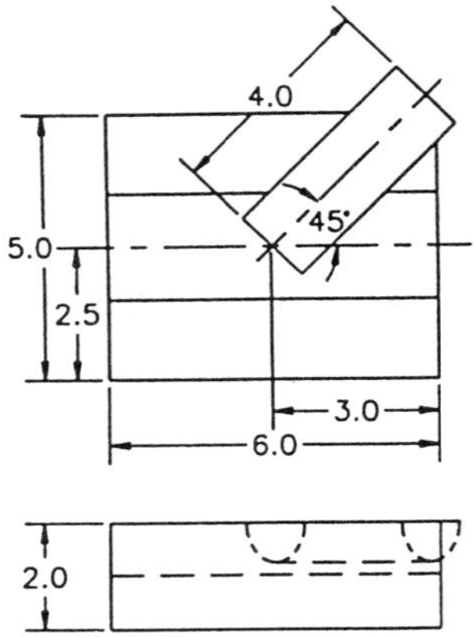

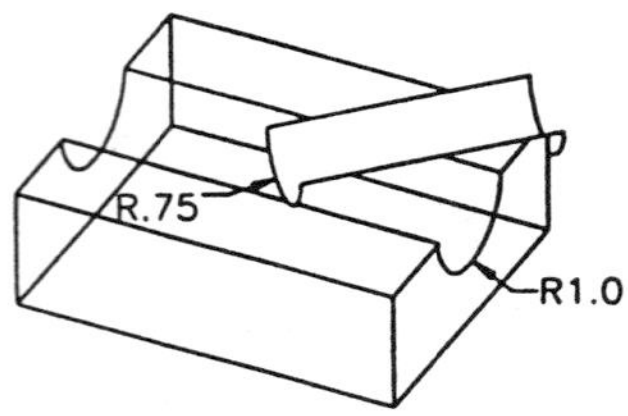

Figure 11.176

Tips 1. Study the instructions from Project 2.

2. Construct a rectangular box using the top Cplane.
3. Create the two arcs of 1.0" radius using the side Cplane.
4. Create a slope line that has a 45° with the X axis.
5. Define a normal Cplane which is perpendicular to the slope line.
6. Create two arcs of 0.75" radius using the normal Cplane.
7. Break the two upper side lines of the rectangular box into two pieces. This allows these two lines to be trimmed to the two arcs.
8. Connect four lines using 3D Cplane.

12. Construct the wireframe model consisting three cross-section profiles and four lines as shown in Figure 11.177. This model can be used to create a ruled surface, a loft surface, or a Coons surface. Save the file name as **E3**.

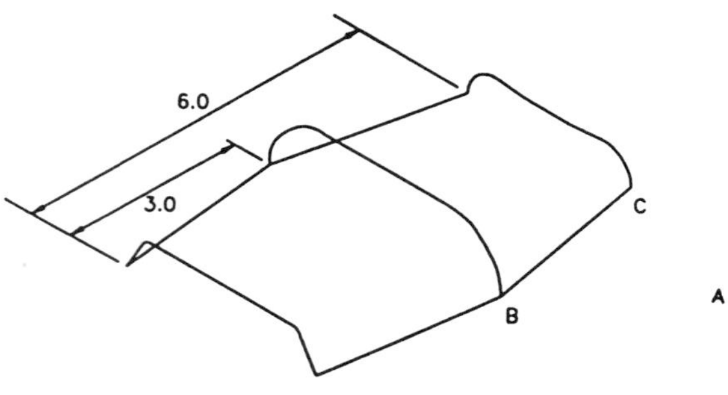

Figure 11.177a

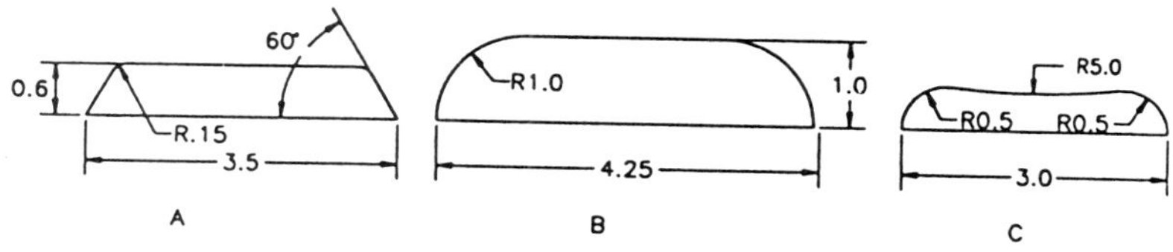

Figure 11.177b

Tips 1. Construct three profiles using Front Cplane.

2. Use the Endpoints command to create the two 0.5" radius arcs. Then use Modify → Fillet commands to create the tangent arc of 8" radius.
3. There are two ways you can place profiles B and C in the proper Z loaction. One is set Z-3.0 for profile B and Z-6.0 for profile C. The other method is to create the profile at Z0.0, then use Xform → Translate commands to move the profile to correct position.
4. Connect the four lines using the 3D Cplane.

13. Construct a wireframe model consisting of four arcs as shown in Figure 11.178. This model is used to create a Coons surface. Save the file name as **E4**. Some helpful tips are listed below.

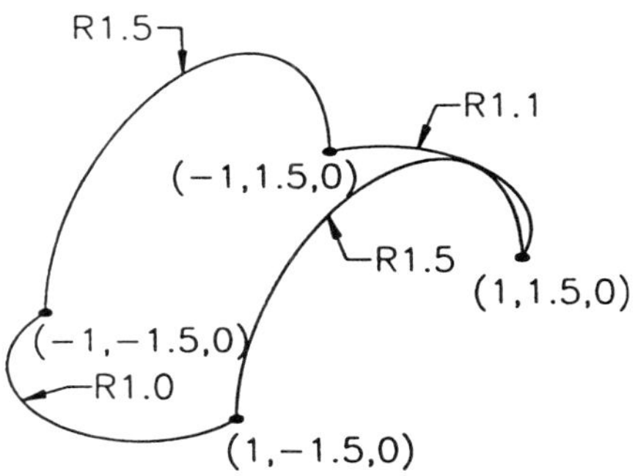

Figure 11.178

Tips 1. Create two arcs of 1.5" radius using the Side Cplane and the other two arcs in Top Cplane.

2. Use Arc → Endpoints command to construct these four arcs.

14. Construct the wireframe model shown in Figure 11.179. The model consists of four profiles set in four sides of a rectangular box. This model is used to create a Coons surface. Save the file as **E5**. Hints are provided on the next page.

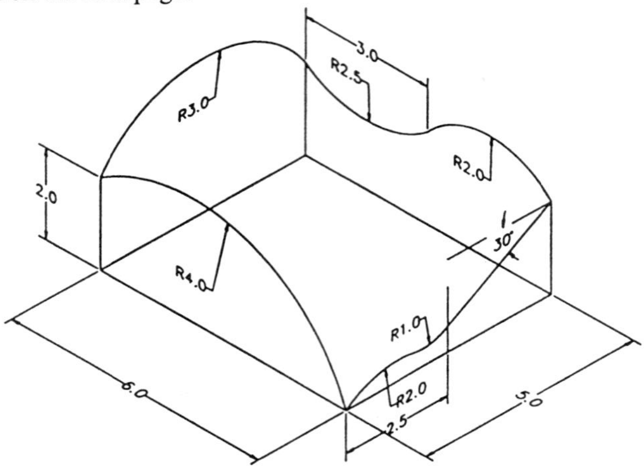

Figure 11.179

Tips 1. Study the instructions given in project 5.

2. Use Arc → Endpoints commands to construct four arcs C1, C3, C5, and C6.

3. Use Arc → Tangent commands to with Point option to create arc C2.

4. Use Modify → Fillet commands to construct arc C4.

5. Construct arcs C1, C2, and C5 using Front Cplane, and Arcs C3, C4, and C6 in Side Cplane.

15. Construct a wireframe model as shown in Figure 11.180. The model consists of eight triangular slope surfaces whose vertices joined at one point. The model can be used to create a Coons surface connecting the eight lines and the eight-sided polygon and a ruled surface on the top flat surface. Save the file as **E6**. Hints are given on below.

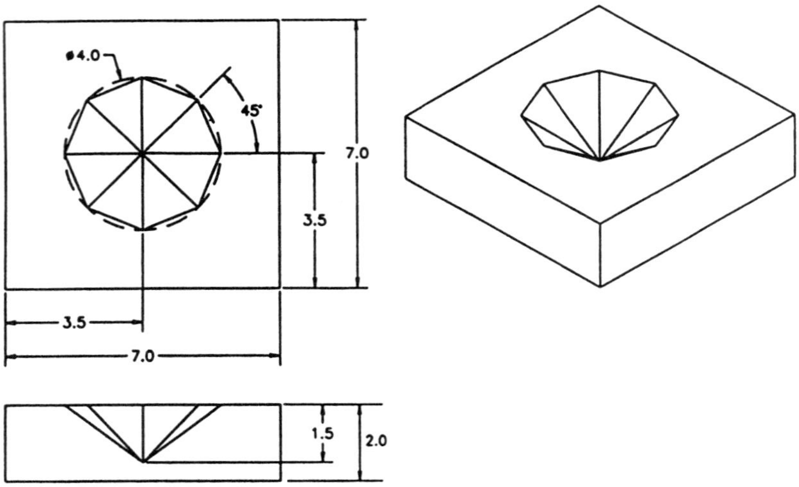

Figure 11.180

Mastercam Version 7,
Scholar's International Publishing Corp., 1998

Tips 1. Study the instructions given in projects 6 and 7.

2. Create a rectangle and an octagon using Top Cplane.

3. Create eight lines connecting the eight vertices of the octagon and the common joined point using 3d Cplane.

16. Create the wireframe model for a multiple-faced part shown in Figure 11.181. The model has two octagons at different Z levels. A total of 16 faces are formed in the upper half of the part. The bottom half also has 16 faces that can be created from the upper half by using the mirror function. Save the file as **E7**. Useful tips are given below.

Tips 1. Study the instructions given in project 7.

2. Create two construction circles and eight lines to find the vertices of the two octagons.

3. Use Top Gview and 3d Cplane to connect the lines between vertices, and between the vertices and the common join point.

4. Save the drawing of the upper half of the model.

5. Rotate the upper half model by 180° about the origin using Front Cplane to complete the entire wireframe model.

Note: Do not use the complete wireframe model for surfacing. This makes picking correct entities more difficult in surfacing because the one entity appearing in Top Gview may represent two or more entities in the model.

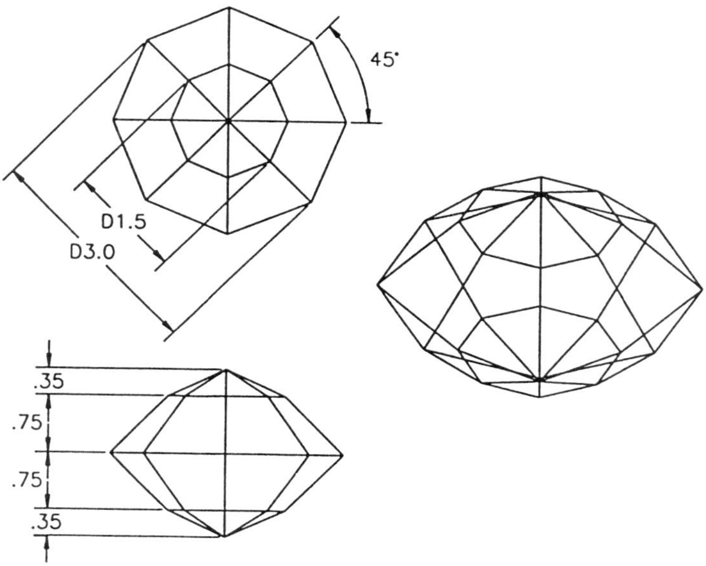

Figure 11.181

17. Construct the wireframe profile for a cup shown in Figure 11.182. The model can be used to generate a revolved surface or a swept surface. Save the file as **E8**. Tips are listed below.

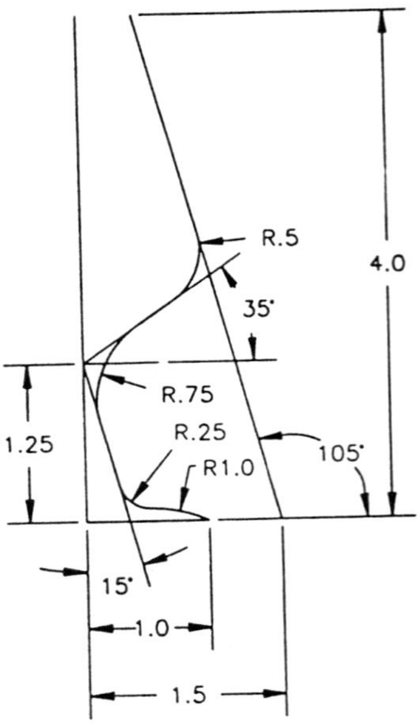

Figure 11.182

Tips 1. Study the instructions given in project 8.

2. Construct five lines, one vertical, one horizontal, and three sloped.

3. Add three fillets.

4. Use Arc → Tangent → Point commands to create the arc near the base.

18. Construct the wireframe profile for a cup shown in Figure 11.183. The model can be used to generate a revolved surface or a swept surface. Save the file as **E9**. Tips are listed below.

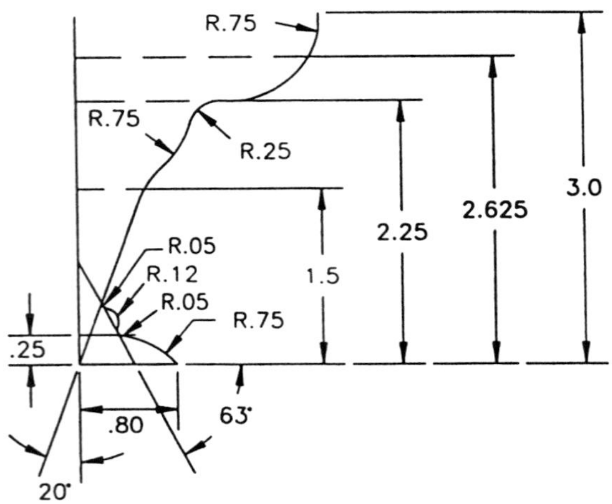

Figure 11.183

Tips 1. Study the instructions given in project 8.

2. Create necessary construction lines to help determining the end points of arcs.

3. Use Arc → Endpoints to create most of the arcs.

19. Create a wireframe model for the fly disk as shown in Figure 11.184. This model can be used to create a revolved surface or a swept surface. Save the file as **E10**. Hints are listed below.

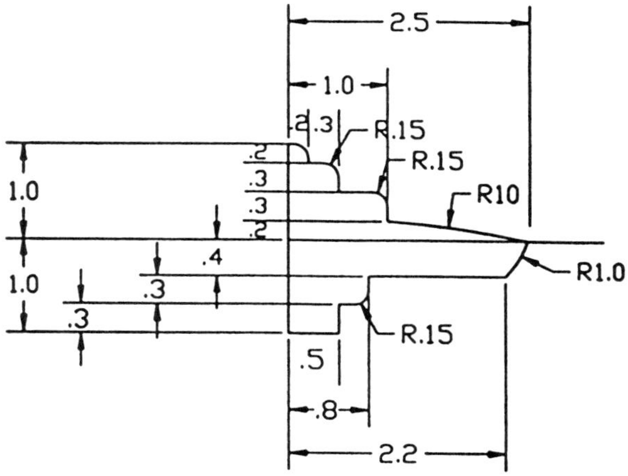

Figure 11.184

Tips 1. Create necessary construction lines to help determining the end points of arcs.

2. Use Arc → Endpoints commands to create arcs.

20. Construct the wireframe model for the part shown in Figure 11.185. The model consists of two rectangles with fillets at four corners and a section profile. One larger rectangle is located on the top to define the outer boundary of the top rim, and the smaller rectangle defines the shape of the part bottom. The section profile defines the wall and the top rim. This model is used to create a composite surface model in which multiple surfaces are blended together. Save the file as **E11**. Some hints are given below.

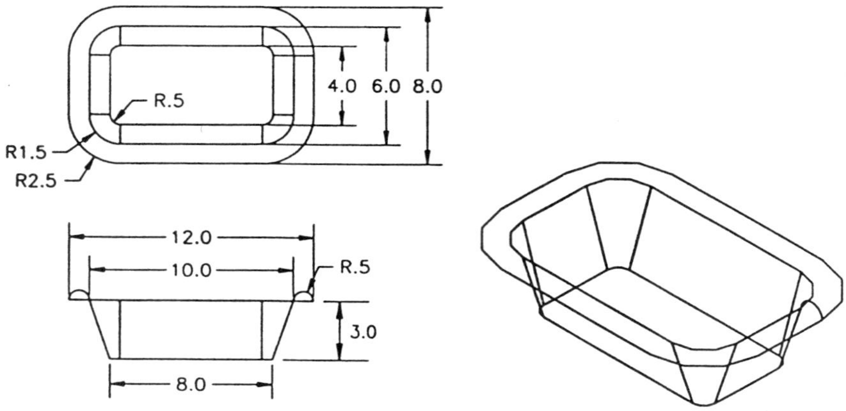

Figure 11.185

> **Tips** 1. Use Top Cplane to construct the two rectangles with fillets. Note that the two rectangles have different Z depths.
>
> 2. Create the section profile in Front Cplane.

21. Create the wireframe model for the part shown in Figure 11.186. The model consists of two circles, one profile arc, eight identical edge profiles, and eight lines connecting end points of eight edge profiles. This model is used to create a composite surface model. Save the file as **E12**. Hints are given on the next page.

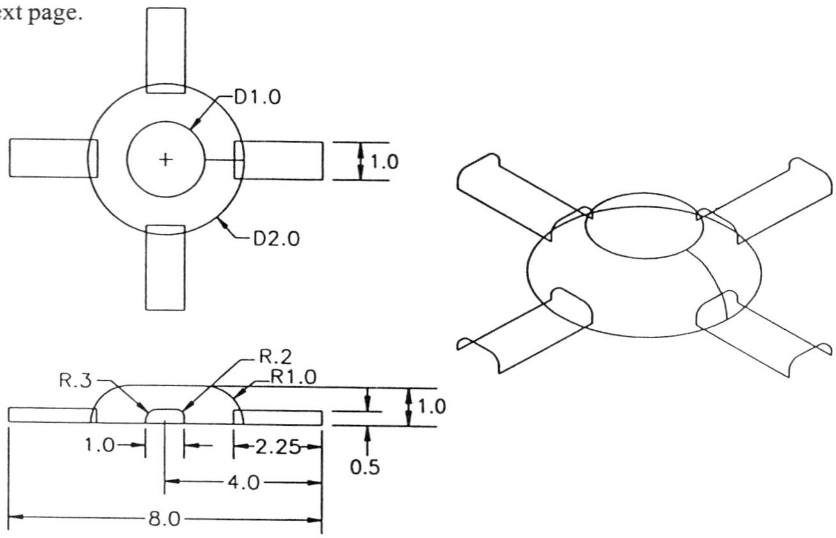

Figure 11.186

Tips 1. Construct two circles in the Top Cplane with different depths.

2. Create four edge profiles and an arc profile which connects two circles in Front Cplane.

3. Construct the other four edge profiles in Side Cplane.

4. Create eight connecting lines between eight profiles in 3d Cplane.

Chapter 12
Surfaces Modeling I: Fundamentals and Creation

Objectives:

1. Know surfaces and their applications.
2. Understand surface mathematics.
3. Identify surface types.
4. Use Mastercam surface modules to create surfaces.
5. Know what works, and what doesn't, in creating surfaces.

Overview

This chapter covers important surfacing mathematics and techniques. Four surface mathematics styles and a comparison of their features are described. Sixteen projects are presented to show how to create primitive surfaces and free-form surfaces from the wireframe models in Mastercam. Useful tips are provided to help in your understanding of the principles and procedures of each surfacing technique. Derived surfacing techniques and their examples as well as several composite surface models are presented in chapter 13.

12.1 Surfaces

A surface is the shape representation of a part's skin defined by mathematical equations. A surface normally consists of many sections or patches that are smoothly blended together to form an entity. Due to the increased computer power and the new surface modeling techniques, today's surface modeling in CAD/CAM systems can accurately and completely describe a complex part shape. In addition the multiple surfaces found in many complex parts, can be blended together to form a single surface model for design analysis and NC tool path generation. This kind of multi-surfaces model is often called the **composite surface.**

Surface modeling is widely used to describe complex objects such as a car, ship, and airplane body, as well as their dies and molds. The information of surface models can be used to perform the following engineering, design, and manufacturing functions:

- Part geometric design and representation
- Mass properties calculation
- Interference checking between mating parts
- Cross-sectioned views generation
- Finite element meshes generation
- NC tool paths generation

12.2 Surface Mathematics

All surfaces are created by using one of the following four mathematical methods: Coons surface, Bezier surface, B-spline surface, and NURBS surface. They are briefly described in this section.

Coons Surface

A Coons surface is often referred to as the **Coons patch**. A single Coons patch is a surface patch constructed by blending four boundary curves (Figure 12.1). The multiple-patches Coons surface is generated from several individual patches smoothly blended together (Figure 12.2). The blending functions used in Coons surfaces could be either bi-linear or bi-cubic.

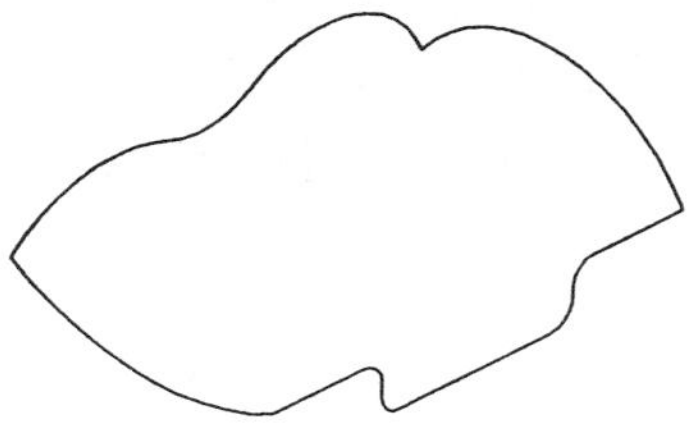

a. Wireframe model

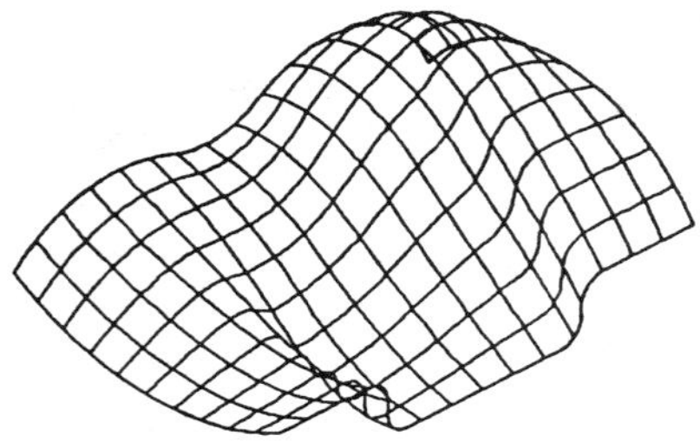

b. Surface model

Figure 12.1

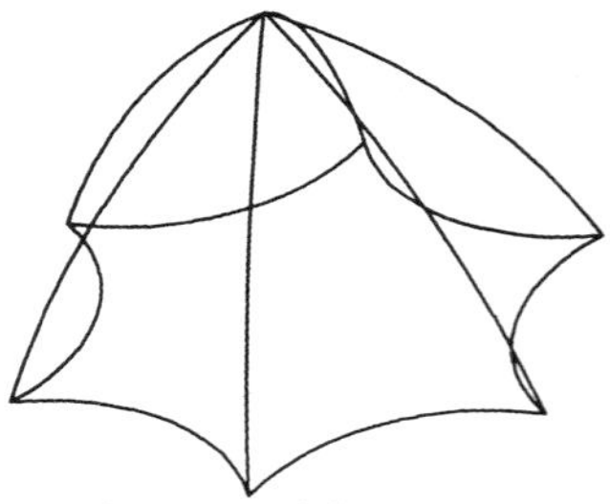

a. Wireframe model

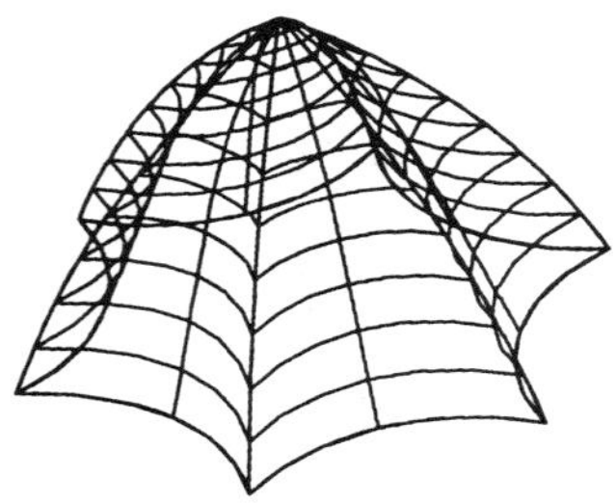

b. Surface model

Figure 12.2

The strength of the Coons surfaces is their ability to fit a smooth surface precisely throughout the wireframe curves or digitized point data. In other words, the surface must pass through all control points. The weakness is that a change of a shape of a surface requires that the control curves be altered.

Bezier Surface

A Bezier surface is created by blending all the connecting lines or facets formed by a grid of control points (Figure 12.3). Multiple-patches Bezier surfaces are formed in a way similar to Coons surfaces that smoothly blend individual Bezier patches together.

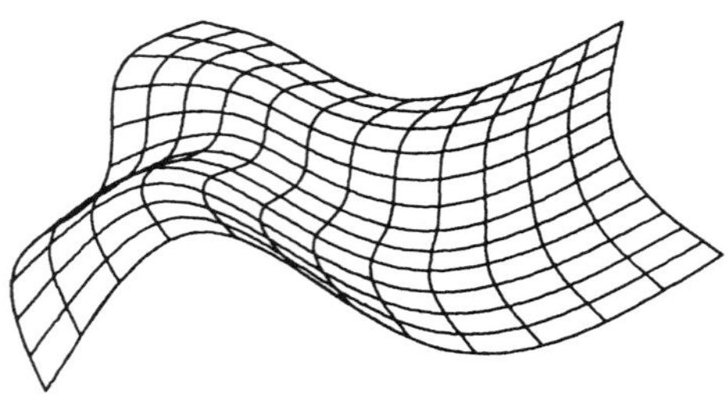

Figure 12.3

The advantage of using Bezier surfaces lies in their ability to reshape the surface by manipulating the control points. Control points can be pulled to create a new design. The weakness of Bezier surfaces is that the entire surface shape is affected simply by moving any one of the control points. They produce approximated surfaces in which specific cross-sectional shapes in particular positions are hard to obtain (if not impossible to obtain.)

B-Spline Surface

A B-spline surface possesses the combined strong features of both Coons and Bezier surfaces. Similar to the Coons patch, B-spline surfaces can be formed from a set of cross-sectional curves, and like the Bezier patch, it also has control points which can be manipulated to alter the surface texture.

A multiple-patches B-spline surface is possible and the continuity between adjacent patches can be guaranteed regardless of how the control points are moved.

The weakness of using B-spline surfaces is that primitive surfaces such as cylinders, spheres, and cones cannot be represented precisely. These surfaces can only be approximated, therefore, unacceptable dimensional errors may occur when machining these simple surfaces.

NURBS Surface

The term NURBS is an acronym for **Non-Uniform Rational B-Spline**. A rational surface is a surface in which each point described has a weight associated with it. A non-rational surface is a surface whose mathematical equations are not a rational number. NURBS surfaces are rational. They have all of B-spline surface abilities. In addition, they provide a weighting function to change the effect of the control points on the surface texture. When the weight function has a constant value of one, the NURBS surface is equivalent to a B-spline surface.

NURBS surfaces overcome the problem of the B-spline in modeling primitive surfaces. Surfaces based on conics, arcs, or spheres can be precisely represented by a NURBS surface. NURBS surface modeling is the most advanced technique of surface mathematics.

12.3 Surface Types

Surfaces can be classified into the following **three** categories: geometrical surfaces, free-form surfaces, and derived surfaces.

Geometrical Surfaces

Geometrical surfaces have constant geometrical shapes such as spheres, cones, and cyliners as well as draft surfaces and surfaces of revolution. They are generated with entities like lines, arcs, splines, and cones. Thus, there is little ambiguity in the definitions of these surfaces. Mastercam provides **two** surfacing techniques to create geometrical surfaces: draft surface modeling and revolved surface modeling. Table 12.1 on the following page summarizes these two geometrical surfacing techniques.

Table 12.1 Geometrical Surfaces

Surface type	Description	Applications	Example
Draft surface (Extruded)	A surface created by extruding a sectional shape straight along a line. The line is defined by a length and an angle.	Used to create cones, cylinders. Draft angles on molds, and tabulated cyllinders.	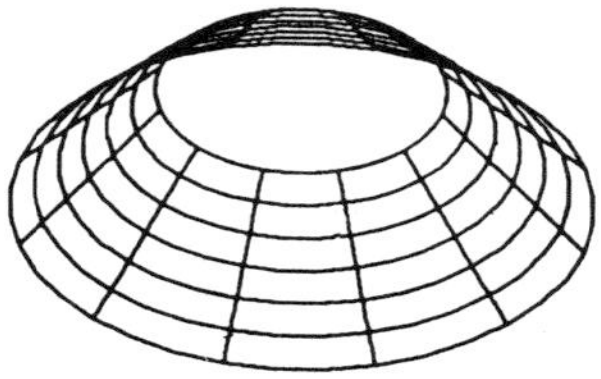
Revolved surface	A surface created by rotating a sectional shape around an axis or a line.	Used on any part that requires surfaces with arc or circular cross sections.	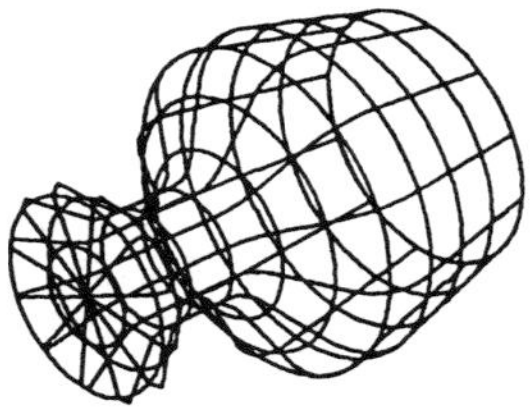

Free-Form Surfaces

Free-form surfaces follow no set geometric pattern and are normally generated from arbitrarily shaped lines and curves. These surfaces require more sophisticated surface mathematics such as Coons patches, Bezier patches, B-spline surfaces, and NURBS surfaces.

Free-form surfaces may be classified further into **two kinds** by their use: constrained surfaces and unconstrained surfaces. **Constrained surfaces** are restricted to existing data sets that may be in the form of sections or cross sections. In other words, the surfaces must pass through the given sections exactly. Coons patches is a typical constrained surface because of its direct relationship to the geometry.

Unconstrained surfaces are not restricted to pre-existing sets of data points or curves. They use control points to create the surface shape that is not necessarily passed through all pre-defined data points or curves. They are mainly used in conceptual designs. Bezier, B-spline, and NURBS surfaces are unconstrained surface types. Table 12.2 summarizes surface types, their desription, typical applications, and examples of free-form surfaces.

Derived Surfaces

Derived surfaces are surfaces that are generated from existing surfaces. They are also called edited surfaces. Table 12.3 on the next page shows **four** commonly used derived surfaces; offset, trimmed, fillet and blend.

Table 12.2 Free-form surfaces

Surface Type	Description	Applications	Example
Ruled surface	A surface created by connecting straight lines between two or more lines or curves.	Used any time a surface must be fit between two or more curves.	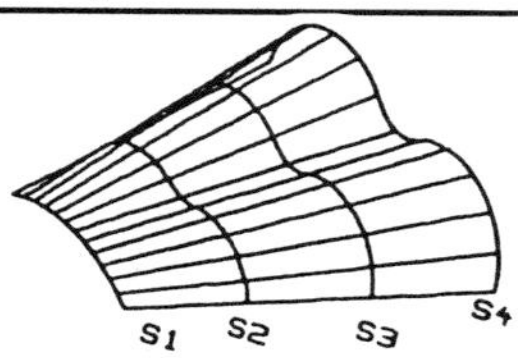
Lofted surface	A surface created by fitting through a set of cross sectional curves.	Used when a surface must be parabolically blended through more than two curves.	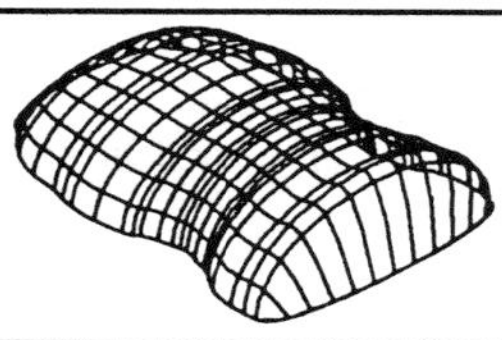

Table 12.2 Continued

Drag surface (2-D swept)	A surface created by translating or rotating a sectional profile along a drive curve.	Used when the cross section of the surface at any point remain constant.	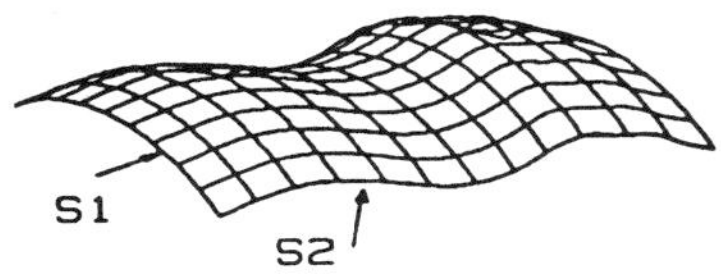
3-D swept surface (Drag with blending)	A surface created by (1) translating a sectional profile along two drive curves, (2) translating two sectional profiles along a drive curve	Used when the across sections at any section is not constant.	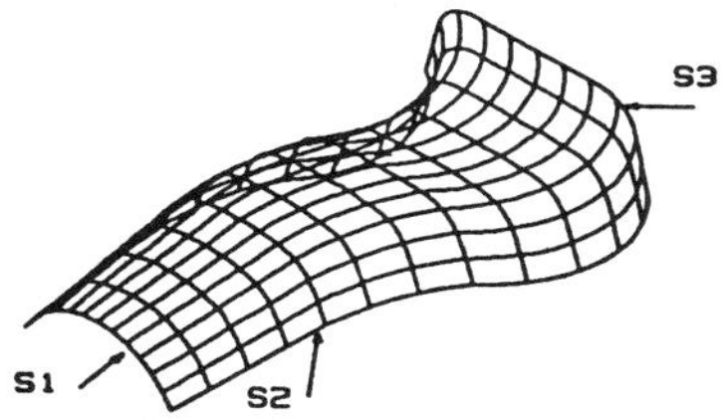
Coons surface	A surface created by blending a number of patches that have four prescribed intersecting curves which form a closed boundary.	Used when a surface is formed by a set of patches.	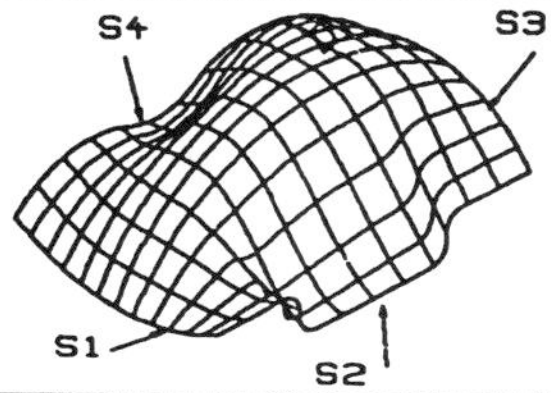

Table 12.3 Derived surfaces

Surface Type	Description	Applications	Example
Offset surface	A surface created by offsetting an existing surface by a distance. The offset is applied normal (perpendicular) to the original surface.	Used to create a new surface that is offset from the original surface.	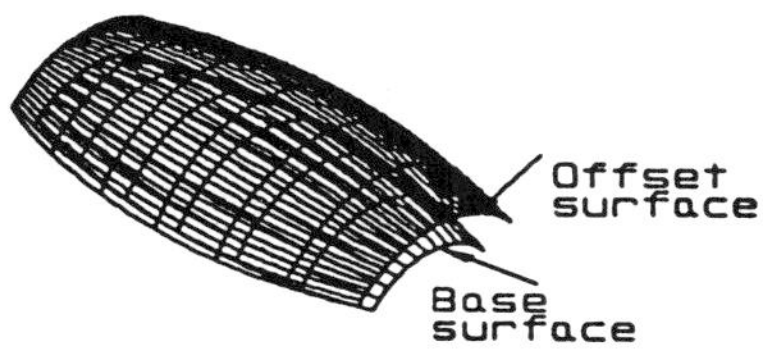
Trimmed surface	A surface created by trimming an existing surface to a specified boundary.	Used to redefine the borders of the existing surfaces.	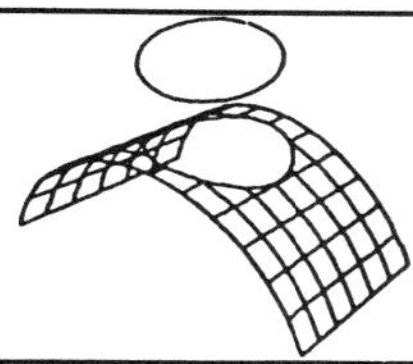
Fillet surface	A surface created by generating arc cross sections that are tangent to two surfaces.	Used to smooth sharp edges.	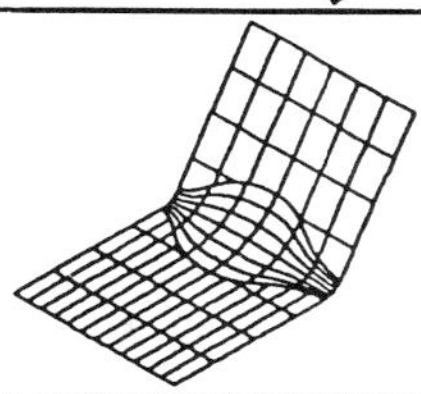
Blend surface	A surface created by joining two existing surfaces, and is tangent to each parent surface.		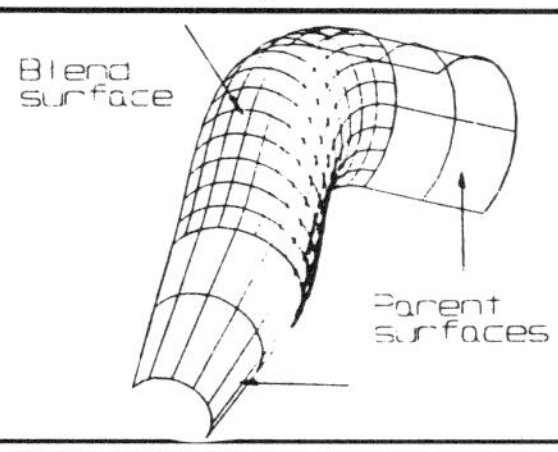

12.4 Mastercam Surfaces

The Mastercam software provides a series of very powerful surfacing techniques including:

> **two geometric** surface models: revolved and draft
> **four free-form** surface models: ruled, loft, Coons, and swept
> **three derived** surface models: fillet, offset, and trimmed.

These free-form and derived surfaces are primarily based on three surfacing mathematics principles: blend, parametric, and NURBS. Table 12.4 gives the available surfacing methods for **four** types of free-form surfaces in Mastercam.

Blend: approximates a surface by blending between the boundaries of piecewise surface contours.

Parametric:uses bi-cubic approximation to create parametric splines along and across an array of points that lie on the surface. The parametric bi-cubic surface patch connects four corner data points and utilize a bi-cublic equation.

NURBS:interpolates a surface by weighting the effect of the control points on the surface skin.

Table 12.4 Surfacing methods of free-form surfaces in Mastercam

Surface Types	Surface Methods		
	Blend	Parametric	NURBS
Loft	Yes	Yes	Yes
Coons	No	Yes	Yes
Ruled	Yes	Yes	Yes
Swept	No	Yes	Yes

Surfacing Projects

The examples given in this chapter use the wireframe models constructed in chapter 11. They are arranged in such a way that each surface modeling method begins with important tips which outline what to do for the sussessful completion of the surface model. Additional examples are used to re-enforce the use of each modeling method. The derived surfaces and composite surfaces are presented in chapter 13.

12.5 Ruled Surfaces Modeling

Mastercam's ruled surfaces modeling allows two or more contours to be linearly blended to form a surface.

Tips 1. The first pick position of each contour affects the shape of the surface (Figure 12.4). Make each contour start from the same orientation.

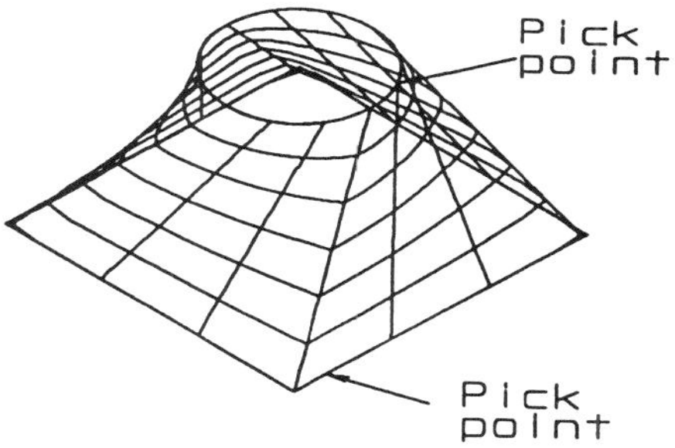

Figure 12.4a. Twisted surface shape

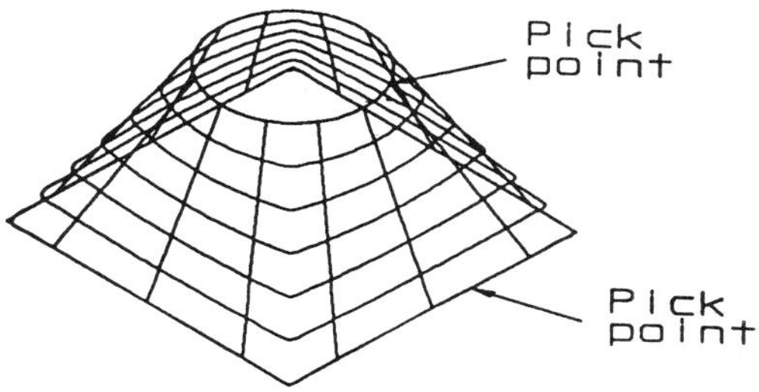

Figure 12.4b. Correct surface shape

2. An entity sometimes has to be broken into two entities in order to allow the contours to start from the same orientation. The right vertical line in Figure 12.5, for example, is broken into two segments to permit the alignment of starting point.

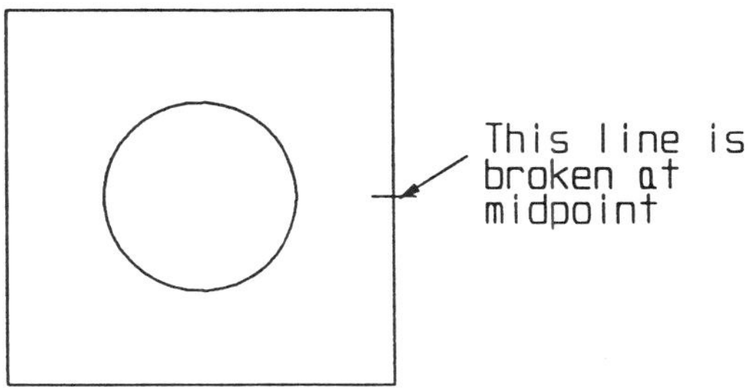

Figure 12.5a. Top view

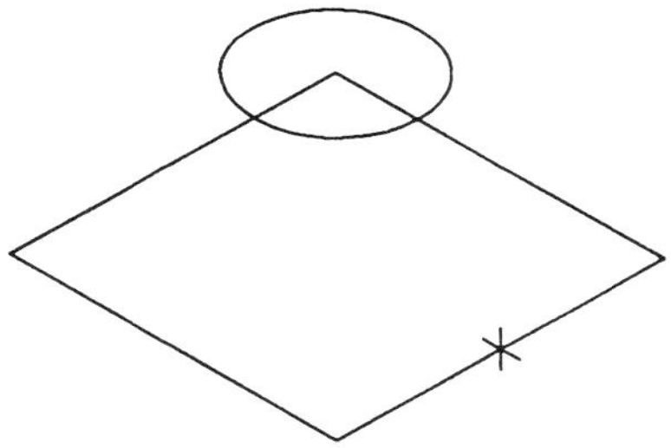

Figure 12.5b. Isometric view

3. Contours must be orderly selected. Any misplace of the picking order may result in an unacceptable surface (Figure 12.6).

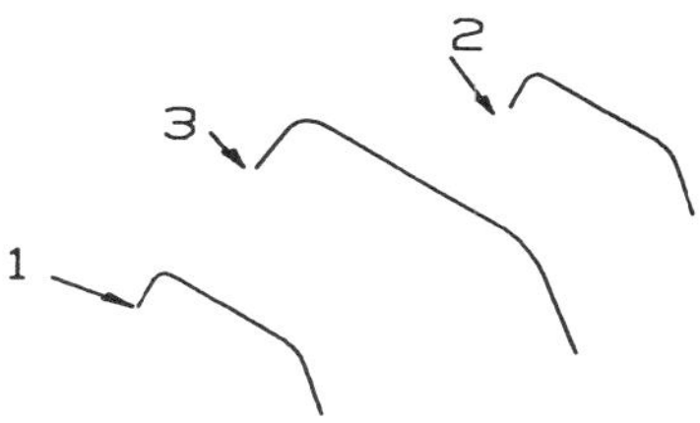

Figure 12.6a. Pick order

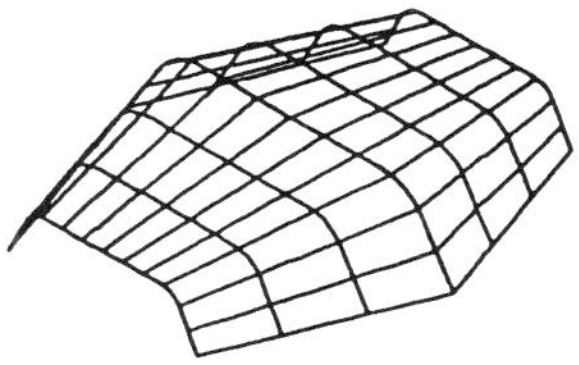

Figure 12.6b. Proper surface

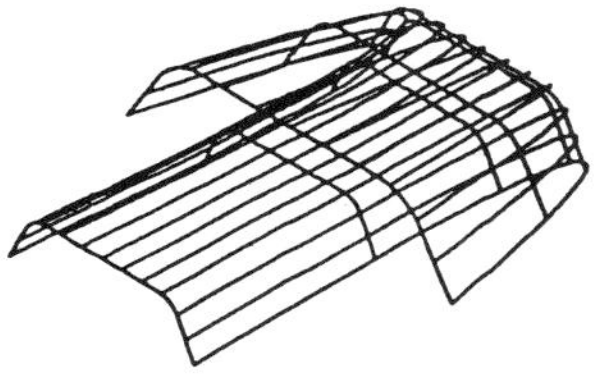

Figure 12.6c. Twisted surface

1 Tips, continued.

4. Use the Top Gview to pick the contours as the number of contours increases. Isometric Gview tends to cause confusion when the wireframe model becomes complicated. Use the Window command to automatically define the order of contours.
5. Have the same chaining direction for all contours. Reversing the chaining direction of one entity results in an improper surface (Figure 12.7).

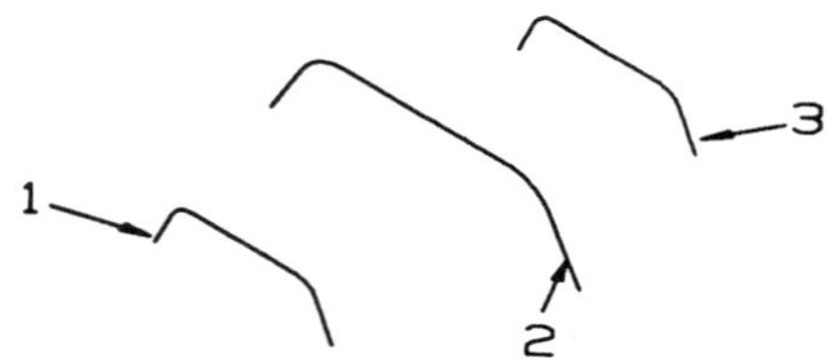

a. Contour directions

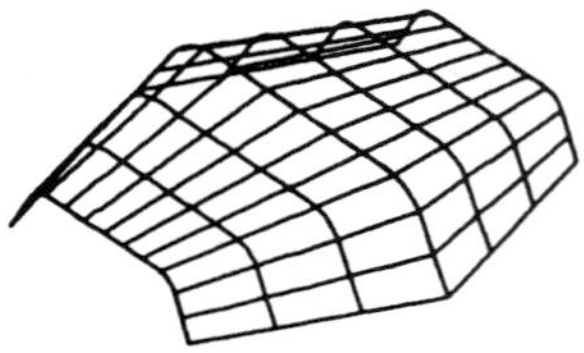

b. Proper surface

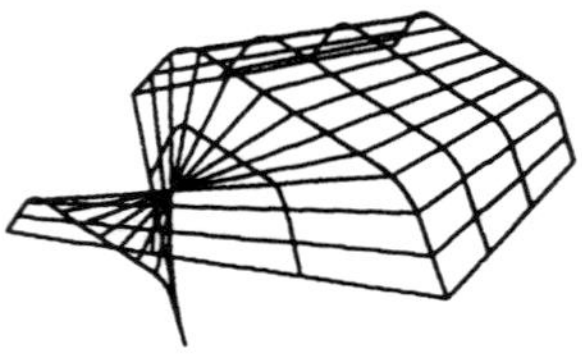

c. Twisted surface
Figure 12.7

Project 1. Creating two ruled surfaces, both formed by two contours

This example uses the wireframe model constructed in project 1 of chapter 11 to generate two ruled surfaces. The contour profiles is shown in Figure 12.8a and the finished ruled surfaces in Figure 12.8b.

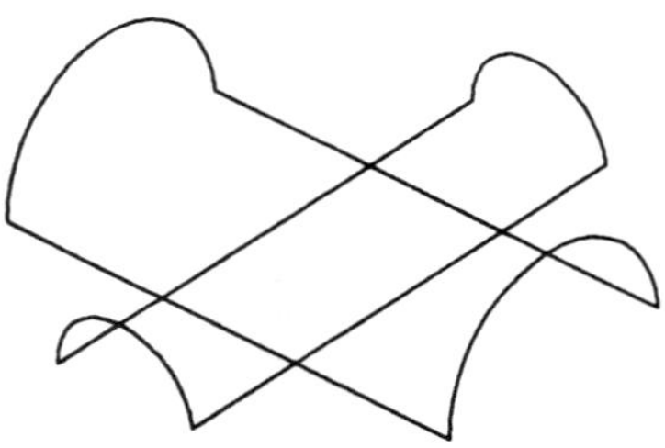

Figure 12.8a. Wireframe model

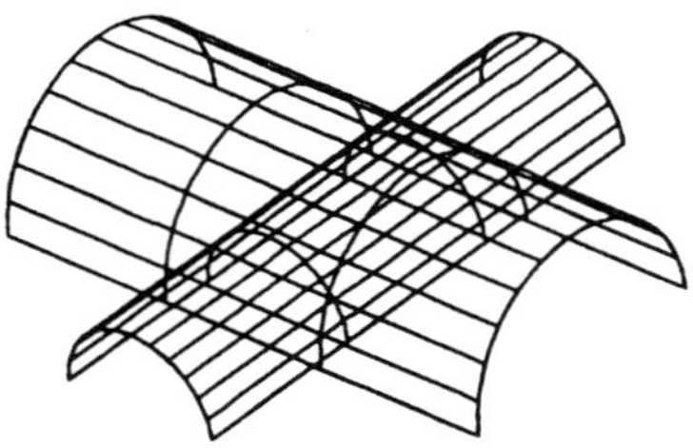

Figure 12.8b. Surface model

Step 1. Enter the Mastercam Mill and load the drawing file (ruled1).

If the wireframe model is not available, follow the step-by-step procedure given in the project 1 of chapter 11 to create the drawing.
Select **MAIN MENU → File → Get**
Enter file name: **ruled1 ←**
The drawing should appear as Figure 12.9.

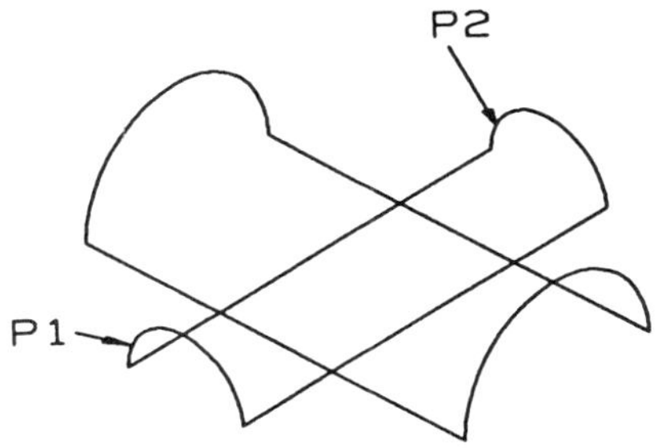

Figure 12.9

Step 2. Create the first ruled surface. Use the pick points in Figure 12.9.

Select **Level**
Enter new level number: **2 → OK**
Select **MAIN MENU → Create → Surface → Ruled**
define contour 1: pick **Single** from the chaining method menu
Pick **P1** to select the first contour
Pick **P2** to select the second contour
define contour 3: pick **Done** from the chaining method menu to complete the first ruled surface
Toggle the type parameter to **N** to set the surface type = NURBS
Select **Do it** to generate the surface

The drawing with the first ruled surface should resemble Figure 12.10.

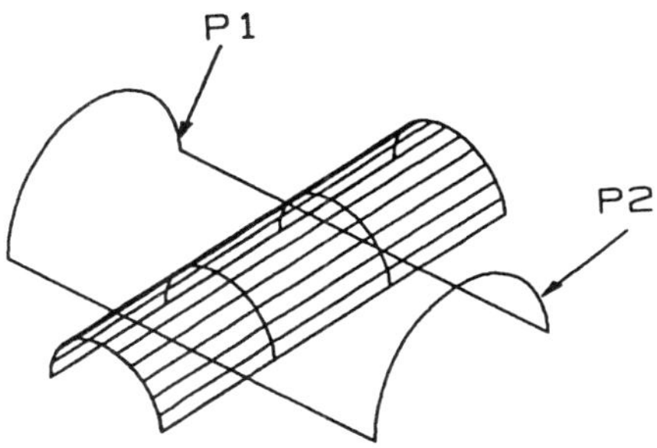

Figure 12.10

Step 3. Create the second ruled surface. Use the pick points in Figure 12.10.

From the surface menu select **Ruled**
define contour 1: select **Single** and then pick **P1**
define contour 2: select **Single** and then pick **P2**
define contour 3: select **Done** to complete the selection of the second ruled surface
Select **Do it** to generate the surface

The two ruled surfaces should look like Figure 12.11.

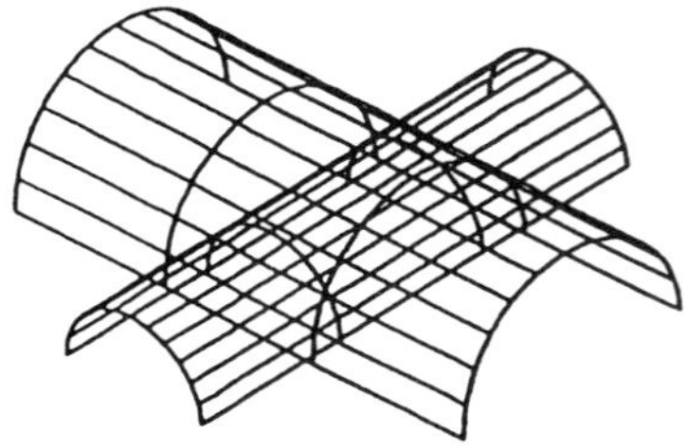

Figure 12.11

Step 4. Shade two surfaces

Select **MAIN MENU →Screen**
Select **Surf disp → Shading**
Set the Shading Setting dialog parameters to these settings:

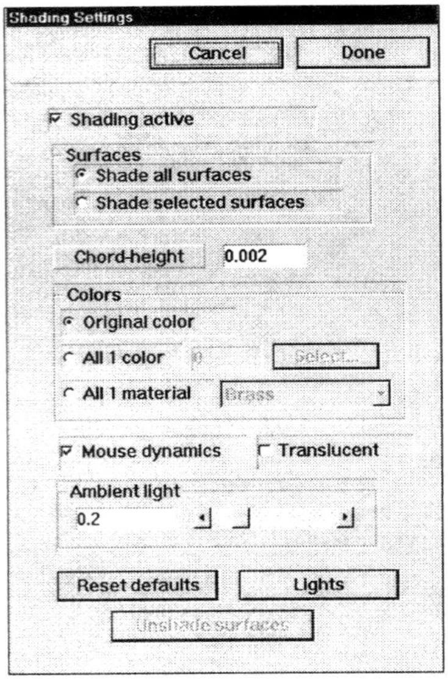

Select **Done**

Step 5. Change the Select Setting

Toggle the Shading active button to **Off** (no check mark) in the shading settings dailog box
Select **Done** to return back to the wireframe mode.
The shaded surfaces will appear on the screen as shown in Figure 12.11a.

Figure 12.11a

Step 6. Save the surfaces as ruleds1.

Select **MAIN MENU → File → Save**
Enter file name: **ruleds1**
Note: This surface is used to generate intersecting curves, fillet surfaces and trimmed surfaces in the preceeding chapters.

Project 2. Creating two ruled surfaces 2

In this example, we use the wireframe model constructed in the project 2 of chapter 11 to create two ruled surfaces. These two surfaces intersect forming an angle. The wireframe model is redrawn in Figure 12.12a, and the completed surface model is in Figure 12.12b.

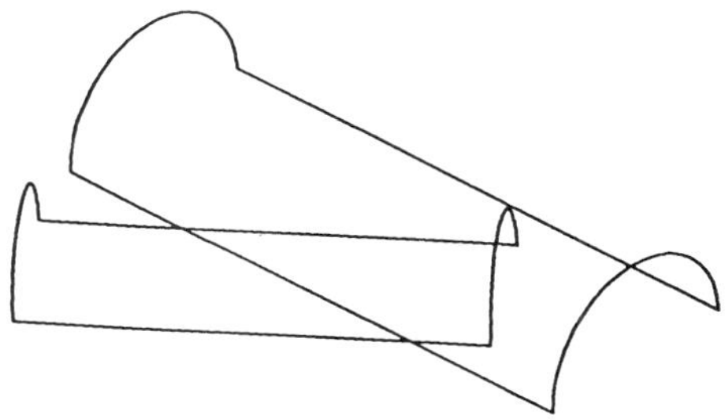

Figure 12.12a. Wireframe model

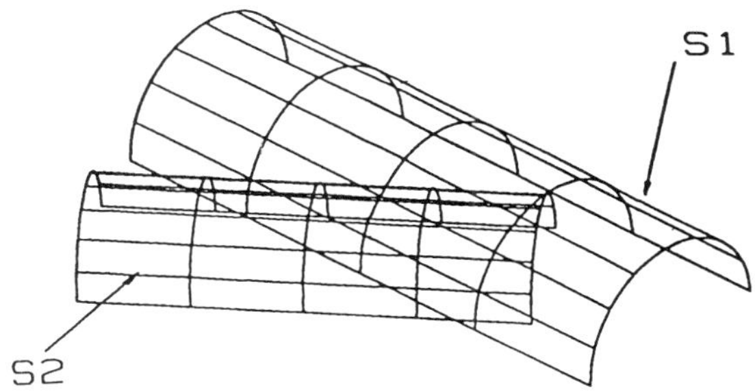

Figure 12.12b. Surface model

Step 1. Load the drawing file, or create the contour profiles by following the instructions in project 2 of chapter 11.

Select **MAIN MENU → File → Get**
Enter file name: **ruled2**

The drawing on the screen should look like Figure 12.13.

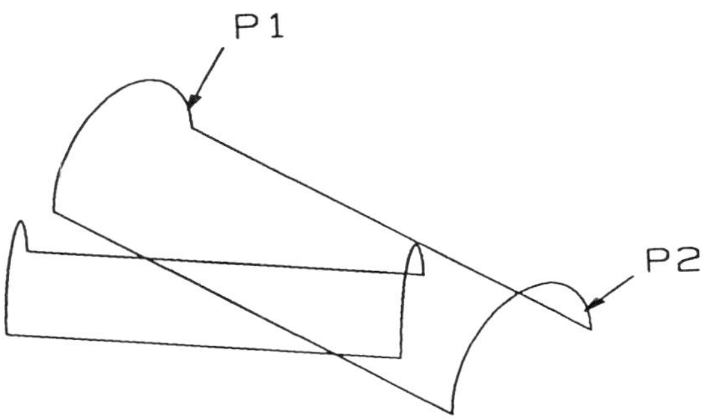

Figure 12.13

Step 2. Create the first ruled surface S1.

Use the pick points in Figure 12.13.
Select **Level**
Enter new level number: **2 → OK**
Select **MAIN MENU → Create → Surface → Ruled**
Define contour 1: select **Single** and then pick at **P1**
Define contour 2: pick at **P2**
Define contour 3: select **Done** to complete the contour selection
Toggle the type parameter to **P** for parametric surface type
Select **Tolerance**
Set the Surface Error Tolerance = **0.0**
Select **Do it**

The first ruled surface should appear as Figure 12.14.

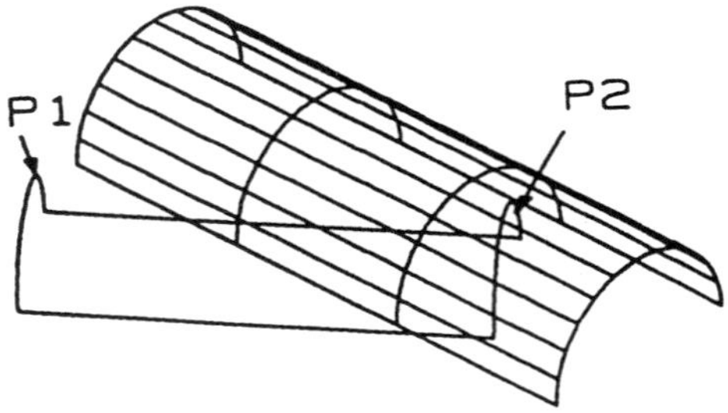

Figure 12.14

Step 3. Create the second ruled surface S2. Use the pick points in Figure 12.14.

Define contour 1: select **Single** and then pick at **P1**
Define contour 2: pick at **P2**
Define contour 3: select **Done** to complete the contour selection
Select **Do it**
The two ruled surfaces appear as Figure 12.15.

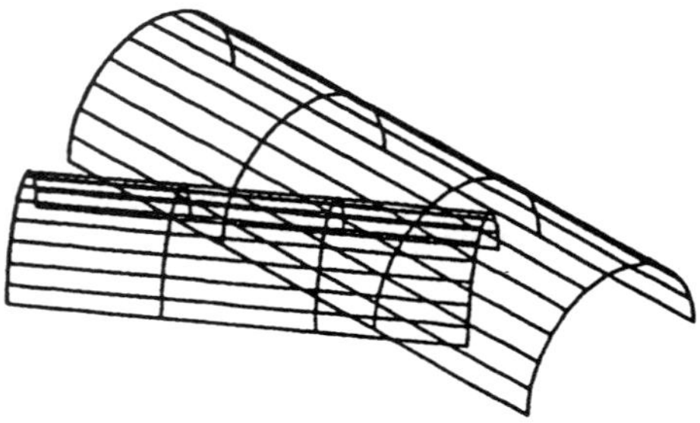

Figure 12.15

Step 4. Save the surfaces (ruleds2).

Select **MAIN MENU → File → Save**
Enter file name: **ruleds2**

Note: These two ruled surfaces are used to create two fillet surfaces with a variable radius in chapter 13.

Project 3. Creating a ruled surface formed by three contours

In this project, three contours are used to construct a ruled surface. The wireframe profiles are constructed in project 3 of chapter 11 which is redrawn in Figure 12.16a. The completed ruled surface is shown in Figure 12.16b.

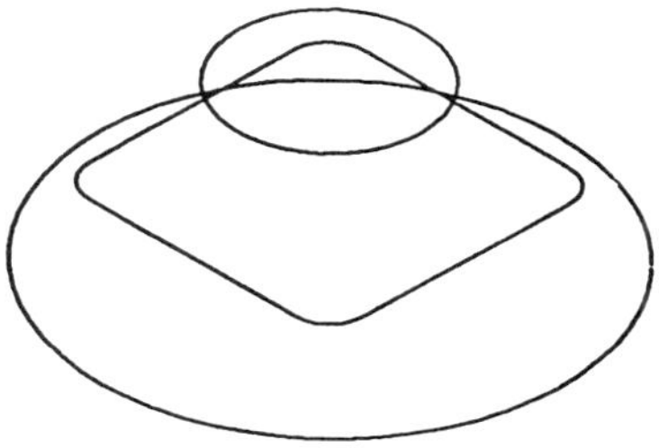

Figure 12.16a. Wireframe model

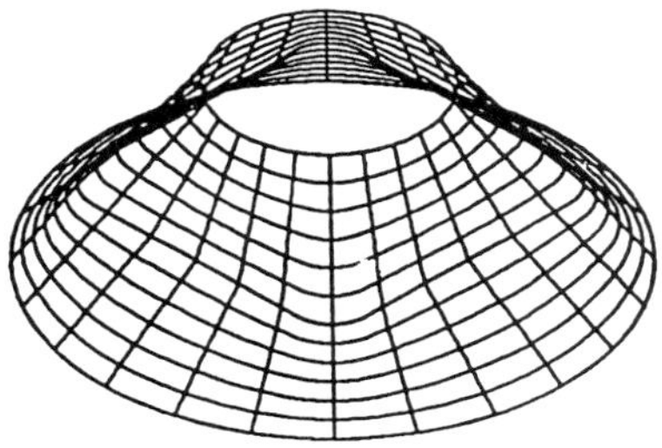

Figure 12.16b. Surface model

The keys to successfully create a ruled surface based on these three contours are:

Tips 1. Use the Top Gview to give a better view of picking at entities.

2. Break the right vertical line of the rectangular contour into two pieces. This allows each contour to start at the same orientation.
3. The pick points at each contour should be placed on the position that make contours going the same direction.

Step 1. Load the wireframe model file (3contour) or create one according to the instructions given in project 3 of chapter 11.

Select **MAIN MENU → File → Get**

Enter file name: **3contour**

The wireframe drawing should appear as Figure 12.17.

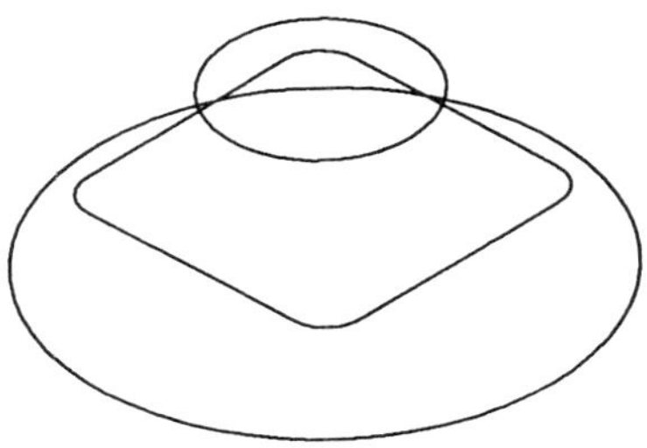

Figure 12.17

Step 2. Change to Top Gview.

Select **Gview** → **Top**

The drawing in Top Gview should resemble Figure 12.18.

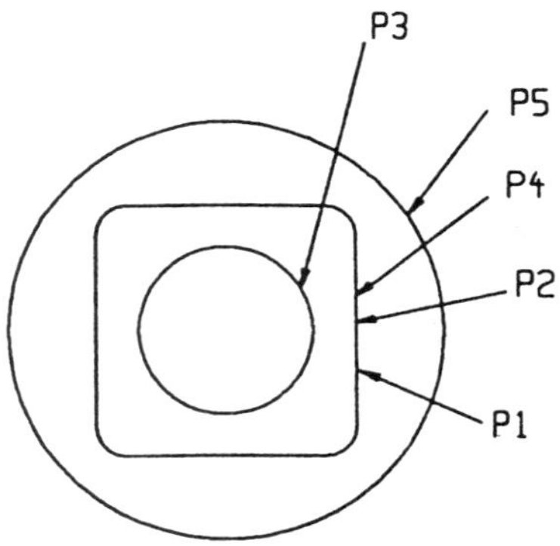

Figure 12.18

Step 3. Break the right vertical line of the rectangular contour into two pieces.

Use the pick points of Figure 12.18.
Select **MAIN MENU** → **Modify** → **Break** → **2 pieces**
Pick **P1** to select the entity to break
Select **Midpoint** from the Point Menu
Pick **P2** to complete the breaking of the line

Step 4. Create a ruled surface. Continue to use the pick points in Figure 12.18.

Select **Level**
Enter new level number: **2** → **OK**
Select **MAIN MENU** → **Create** → **Surface** → **Ruled**
Define contour 1: Select **Single** and then pick **P3** on the inside circle
Define contour 2: Select **Mode** → **Chain**
Select the rectangle: piick **P4**
Define contour 3: Select **Mode** → **Single** and then pick **P5** on the outside circle
Select **Done** to complete the contour selection
Toggle the surface type to **Nurbs**. Select **Do it**
Select **Gview** → **Isometric** to change drawing to isometric view

The surface drawing should resemble Figure 12.19 .

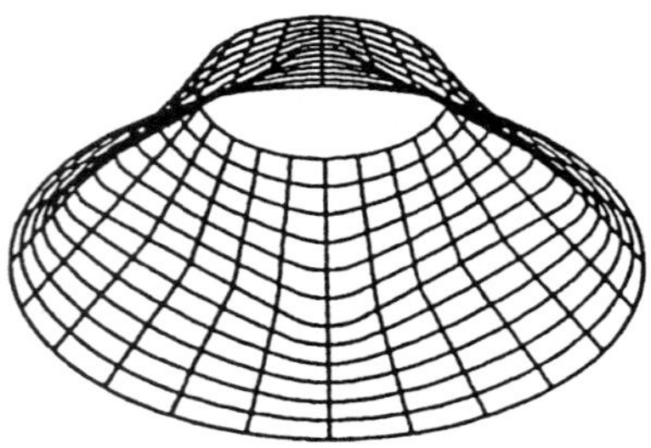

Figure 12.19

Step 5. Save the surface drawing as ruleds3.

Select **MAIN MENU** → **File** → **Save**
Enter file name: **ruleds3**

12.6 Loft Surfaces Modeling

Mastercam's loft surfaces modeling permits three or more sectional contours to be parabolically blended to form a smooth surface.

Keys to the successful completion of loft surfaces include:

Tips
1. The number of sectional contours must be more than two. When the number of contours is equal to two, the resulted surface is a ruled surface.
2. Break an entity into two pieces to allow the alignment of starting points for all contours when a contour has more than one entity. See the example in Figure 12.5.
3. Contours must be orderly selected.
4. Have the same chaining direction for all contours.
5. When the number of contours is relatively large and no contours are connected, use **Window → one way** commands to select the contours. This drastically reduces the time and the number of picking at entities and reduces the errors.

Project 4. Creating a loft surface formed by three contours

The three-contour wireframe model (3contour) is used again in this example to generate a loft surface. The contour profiles and the finished loft surface are shown in Figure 12.20.

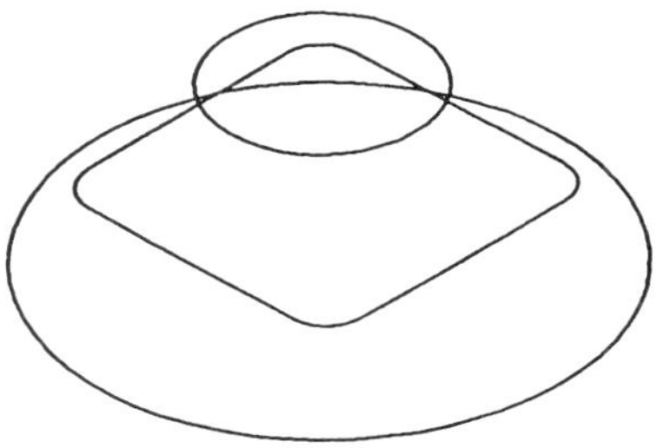

Figure 12.20a. Wireframe model

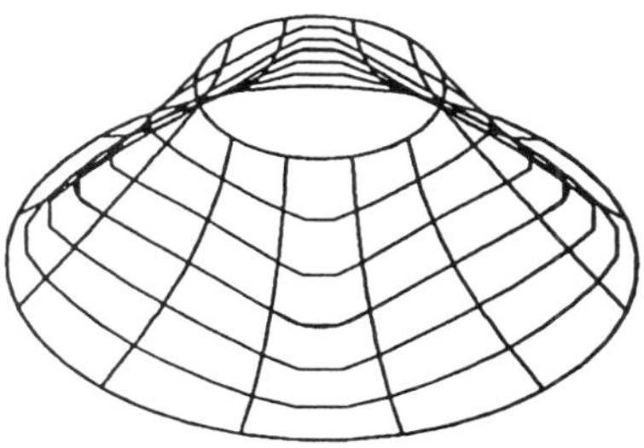

Figure 12.20b. Surface model

Tip The right vertical edge of the rectangular contour must be broken into two pieces at the midpoint.

Step 1. Load the wireframe model file (3contour)

(or follow the instructions given in project 3 of chapter 11 to create one)
Select **MAIN MANU → File → Get**
Enter file name: **3contour**
Select **Gview → Top** to change the Gview to Top view

The wireframe model on the screen appears as Figure 12.21.

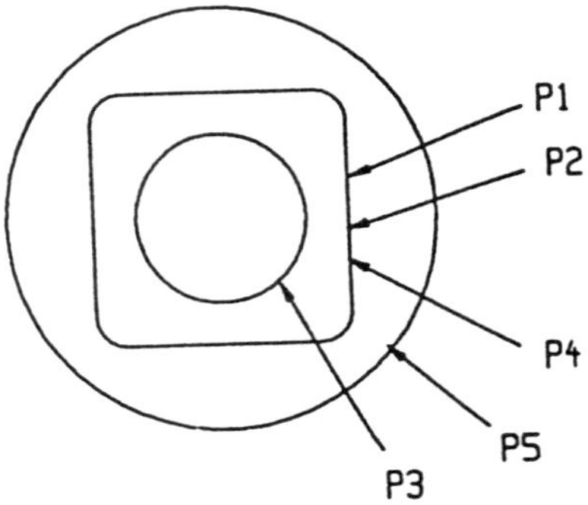

Figure 12.21

Step 2. Break the right vertical line of the rectangular contour into two pieces at the midpoint. Use the pick points in Figure 12.21.

Select **MAIN MENU → Modify → Break → 2 pieces**
Select an entity: pick **P1**
Enter the breakpoint: select **Midpoint** from the point menu and then pick **P2**

Step 3. Create the loft surface. Continue to use the pick points in Figure 12.21.

Select **Level**
Enter new level number: **2 → OK**
Select **MAIN MENU → Create → Surface → Loft**
Define contour 1: select **Single** and then pick **P3** on the inside circle
Define contour 2: select **Mode → Chain** and then pick **P4**
Define contour 3: select **Mode → Single** and then pick **P5**
Select **Done** to complete the contour selection
Toggle the surface type to **NURBS**
Select **Do it** to complete the surface

The drawing in the Top Gview should appear on the screen as Figure 12.22.

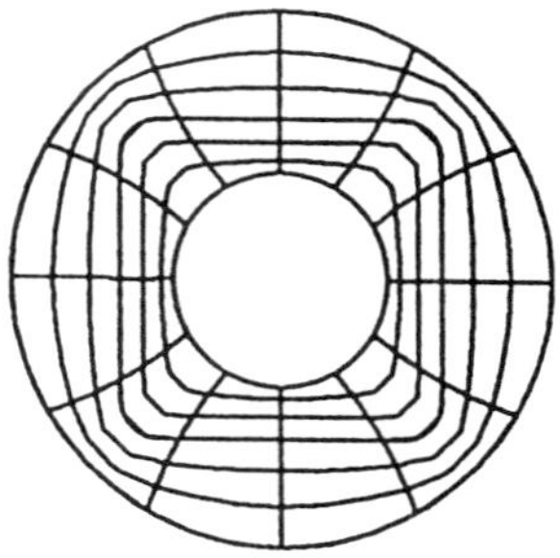

Figure 12.22

Step 4. Change the Gview to isometric. 5

Select **Gview → Isometric**

The final surface drawing should resemble Figure 12.23.

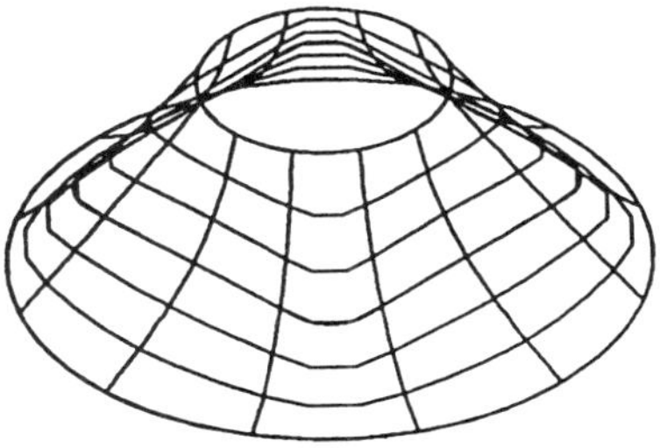

Figure 12.23

Step 5. Save the drawing file (lofts1).

Select **MAIN MENU → File → Save**
Enter file name: **lofts1**

Project 5. Creating a loft surface of ninteen sectional contours

The nineteen sectional contours created in the project 4 of chapter 11 are used to generate a loft surface. The wireframe model and the finished surface model are shown in Figure 12.24.

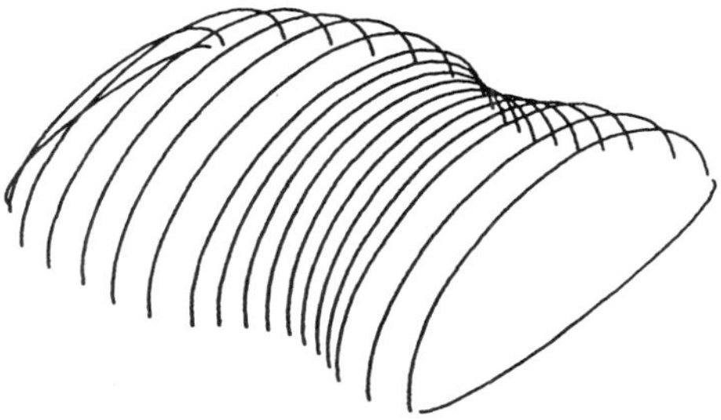

Figure 12.24a. Wireframe model

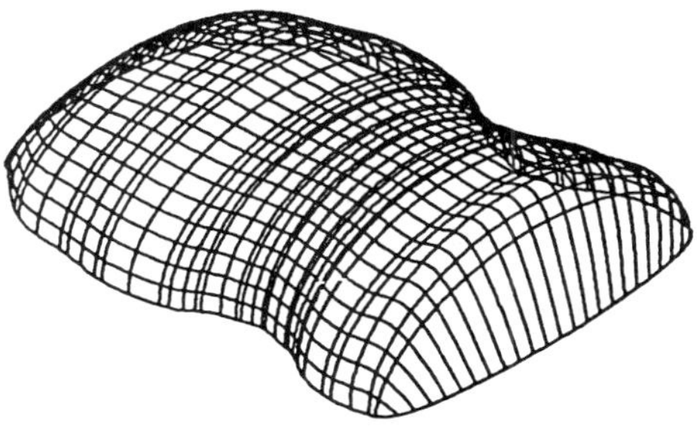

Figure 12.24b. Surface model

Tip: The Window chaining menu is used in this example to reduce the picking of contours.

Step 1. Load the wireframe model file (loft2)

(or follow the instructions in project 4 of chapter 11 to create one)
Select **MAIN MENU → File → Get**
Enter file name: **loft2**
The wireframe model should appear as Figure 12.25.

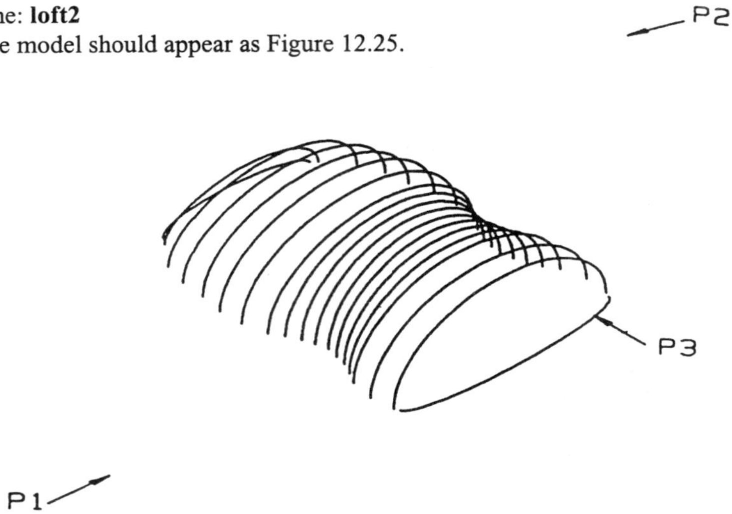

Figure 12.25

Step 2. Create the loft surface. Use the pick points in Figure 12.25.

Select **Level**
Enter new level number: **2 → OK**
Select **MAIN MENU → Create → Surface → Loft**
Select **Window → Options**
Set the Chaining Options as in the dialog box shown here:

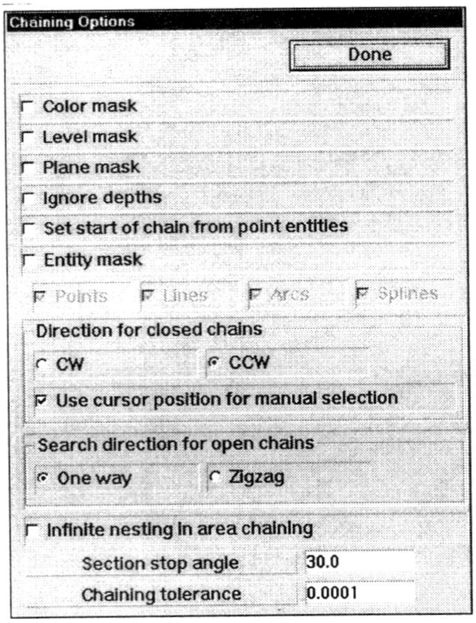

Select **Done**

Enter the first corner: pick **P1**
Enter the second corner: Pick **P2** to ensure all contours are included in the window
Enter search point: select **Endpoint** from the Point Menu and then pick **P3**
Select **Done** from the Chaining method Menu
Toggle surface type to **NURBS**
Select **Do it** to complete the surface

The loft surface should resemble Figure 12.26.

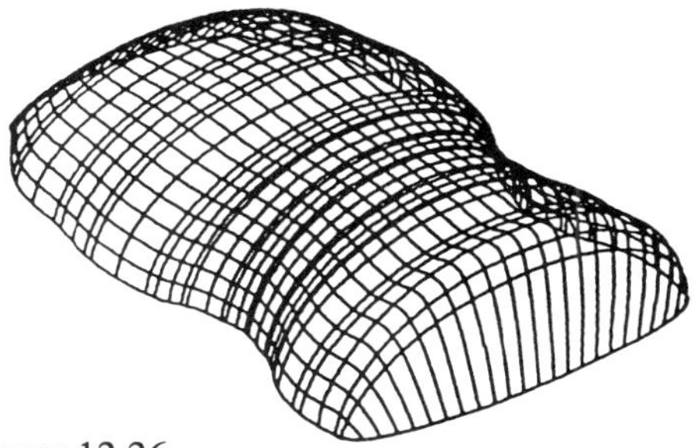

Figure 12.26

Step 3. Save the surface model file (lofts2).

Select **MAIN MENU → File → Save**
Enter file name: **lofts2**

Note: This surface model is used to create a trimmed surface in chapter 13.

Project 6. Creating a loft surface using five sectional contours

The five sectional contours constructed in the project 14 of chapter 11 are used to create a loft surface. The contours are redrawn in Figure 12.27a and the finished loft surface is in Figure 12.27b.

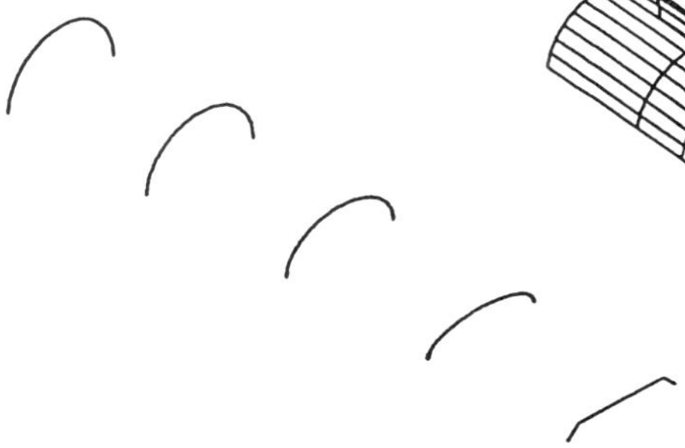

Figure 12.27a. Wireframe model

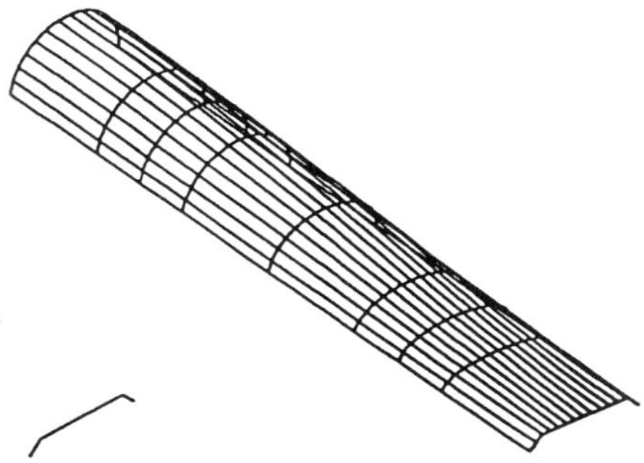

Figure 12.27b. Surface model

Tips 1. Create a loft surface based on the five sectional profiles.

2. Mirror the loft surface about the X axis to create the lower surface section. Note that the Cplane needs to be either Front or Side view.

Step 1. Load the wireframe model profiles (loft3)

(or create one by following instructions in project 14 of chapter 11.)
Select **MAIN MENU → File → Get**
Enter file name: **loft3**

The five contours should look like Figure 12.28.

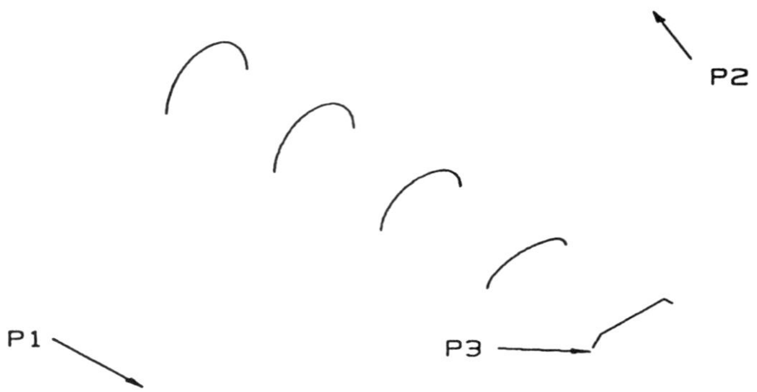

Figure 12.28

Step 2. Create a loft surface.

Use the pick points in Figure 12.28.
Select **Level**
Enter new level number: **2**
Select **MAIN MENU → Create**
Select **Surface → Loft → Window**
Select **Options**
Set the Chaining Options dialog box as here:

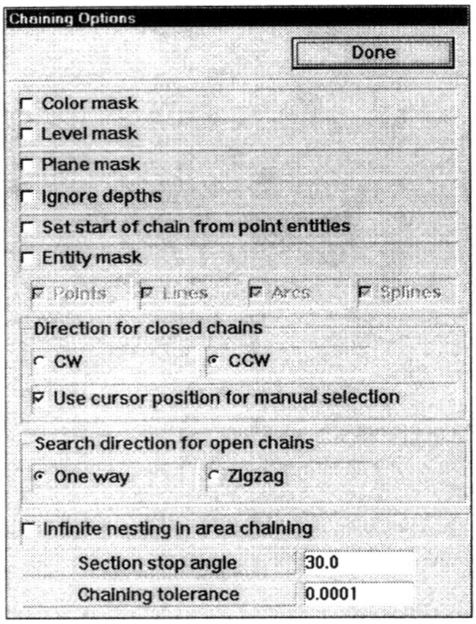

Select **Done**

Pick **P1** and **P2** to specify the window range
Select **Endpoint**
Pick **P3** to trap the endpoint for the search point
Select **Done**
Toggle surface type to **NURBS**
Set the surface error tolerance to **0.01**
Select **Do it** to complete the surface

Note: The system will display the message "Sharp corners in the Curve geometry will be ignored unless sync-ed"
Press **Enter** to generate the surface.

The loft surface should appear as Figure 12.29.

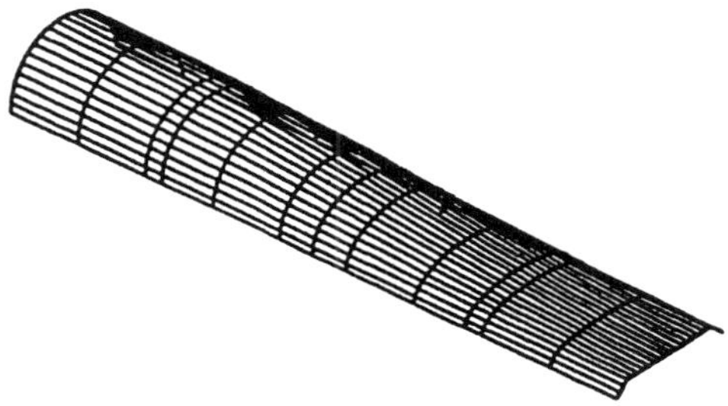

Figure 12.29

Step 3. Save the surface model file (lofts3).

Select **MAIN MENU → File → Save**

Enter file name: **lofts3**

Step 4. Mirror the surface about the X axis to create the lower surface section.

Use either Front or Side Cplane. Use the pick points in Figure 12.29.
Select **Cplane → Front**
Select **MAIN MENU → Xform → Mirror → All → Entities**
Select **Done → X axis**
Select **Copy → Done** from the Mirror parameters menu

The entire surface model now should appear as Figure 12.30.

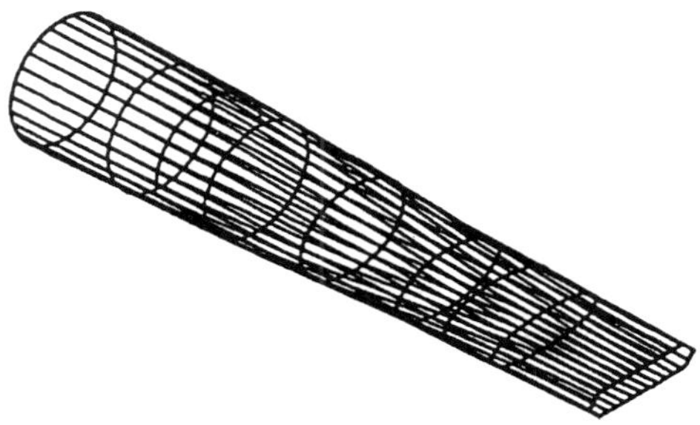

Figure 12.30

12.7 Coons Surfaces Modeling

A Coons surface is created by blending a set of surface patches, each formed by four edge curves. There are two chaining methods which are used to define surface patches; **automatic** chaining and **manual** chaining. The automatic chaining method defines the surface patch with three entities; the two curves that meet in the upper-left corner and one curve in the lower-right corner of the geometry (Figure 12.31.)

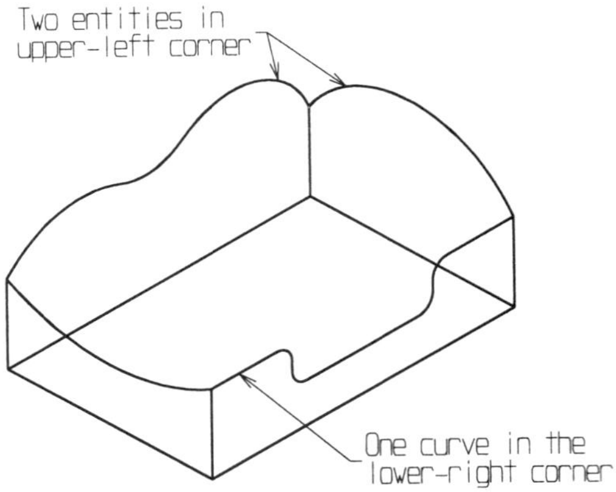

Figure 12.31a

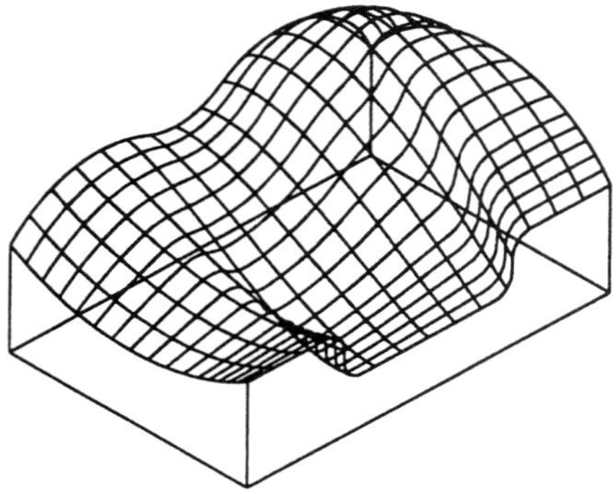

Figure 12.31b

The minimum branch angle is used to determine which of several intersecting entities to chain. Mastercam does not chain along any entity that intersects at an angle larger than the minimum branch angle.

Tips: for **automatic** chaining:

1. Mastercam may not be able to determine the patch layout for a complex chaining which has many branch points. Use the manual chaining method for a complex patch layout. In this case, an error message "Automatic Chaining Failed - Cannot reach Last Point" will appear. Figure 12.32 shows a failed example of automatic chaining due to too many branches.

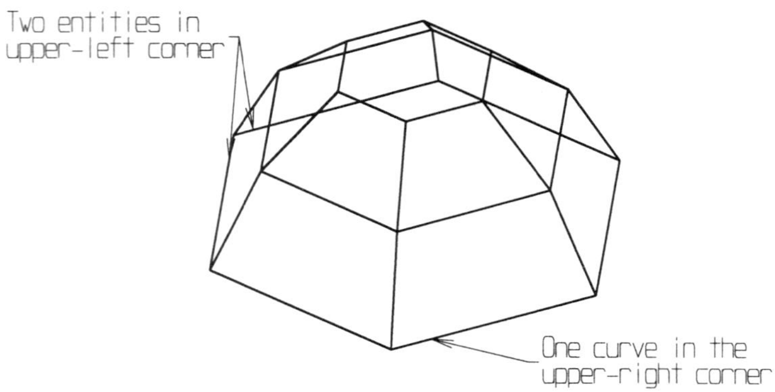

Figure 12.32

2. Automatic chaining will fail when the system cannot reach the last point. In this case, an error message "Automatic Chaining Failed - Cannot reach Last Point" appears. This error may be caused by one of these reasons:

    a. The upper-left corner was not selected (Figure 12.33.)
    b. The lower-right corner has not been selected (Figure 12.34.)
    c. The curves used for chaining are not intersecting properly.

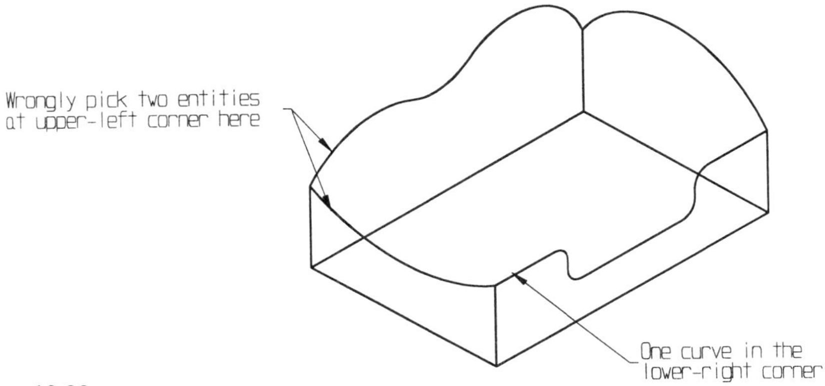

Figure 12.33

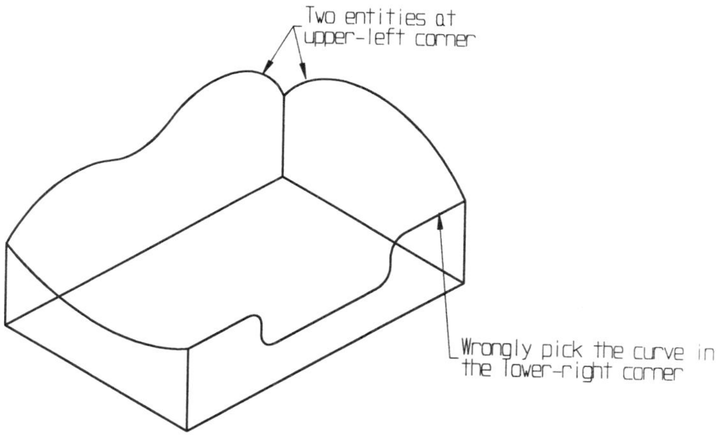

Figure 12.34

Try picking other intersecting curves to resolve the errors. If this does not work, use the manual chaining method.

The **manual** chaining method is a complicated process. These instructions should help in successfully completing a coons surface. Defining contours for Coons surfaces is a rather difficult process because they involve many more contours than other surface modeling techniques.

Tips 1. Select the start point. The start point is normally chosen at a join point of two contours. One of these two join contours becomes the first **along** contour, and the other is the first **across** contour. Figure 12.35 shows an example of selecting the start point of defining a Coons surface.

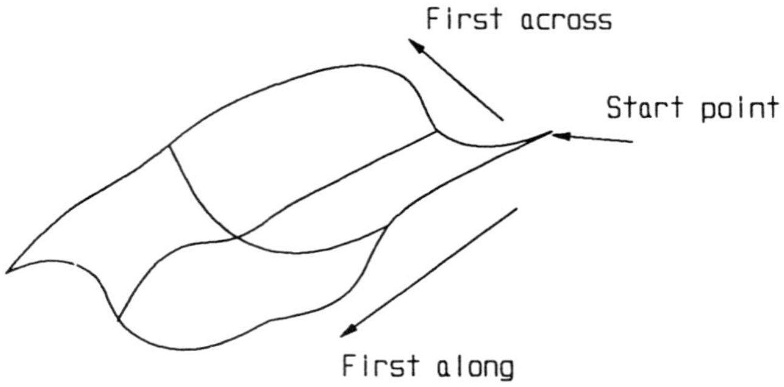

Figure 12.35

> 2. Determine the number of patches in the along direction and the number of patches in the across direction.

In the case of an open boundary where the first and the last contour are not connected as shown in Figure 12.36.

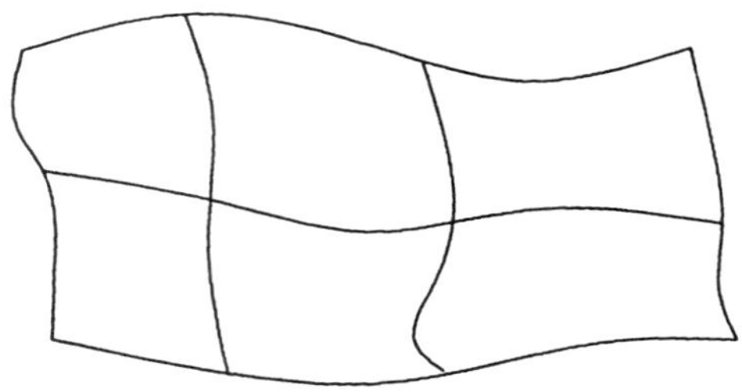

Figure 12.36

$$P_L = N_C - 1$$
$$P_C = N_L - 1$$
$$P_T = P_L \times P_C$$

where P_L = number of patches in along direction
P_C = number of patches in across direction
P_T = total number of patches
N_L = number of along contours
N_C = number of across contours

Example 12.1

Find the numbers of patches in along and across direction for the surface contours given in Figure 12.37.

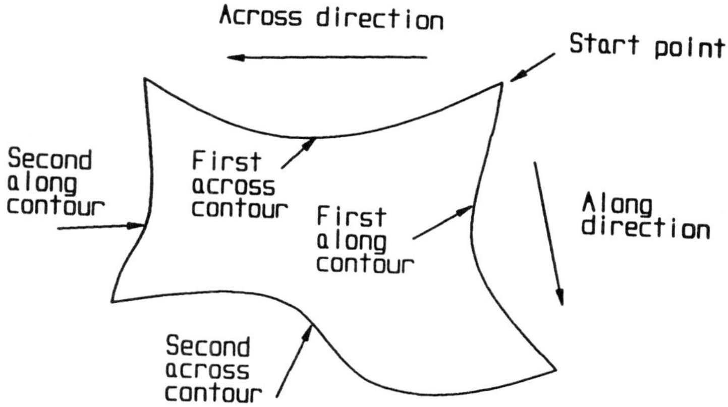

Figure 12.37

Solution:

Number of along contours $N_L = 2$
Number of across contours $N_C = 2$
Number of patches in along direction $P_L = N_C - 1 = 2 - 1 = 1$
Number of patches in across direction $P_C = N_L - 1 = 2 - 1 = 1$
Total number of patches $P_T = P_L \times P_C = 1 \times 1 = 1$

Example 12.2

Find the numbers of patches in along and across direction for the surface contours given in Figure 12.38.

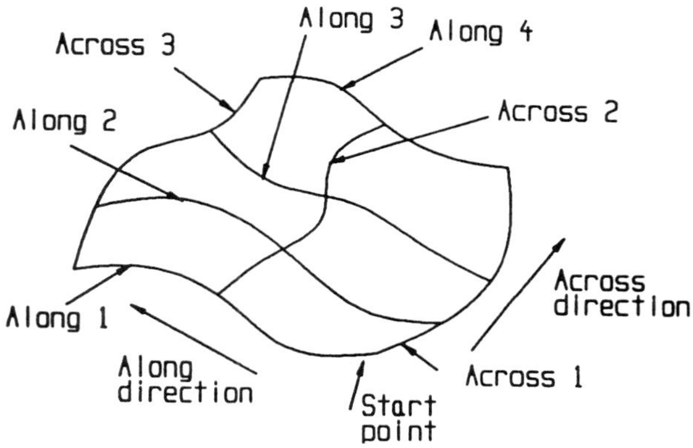

Figure 12.38

Solution:

$N_L = 4$
$N_C = 3$
$P_L = N_C - 1 \quad = 3 - 1 \quad = 2$
$P_C = N_L - 1 \quad = 4 - 1 \quad = 3$
$P_T = P_L \times P_C \quad = 2 \times 3 \quad = 6$

In the case of a close boundary where the first and the last contour are connected. Actually they are the identical contour (Figure 12.39).

The number of patches in along direction $P_L = N_C$
The number of patches in across direction $P_C = N_L - 1$

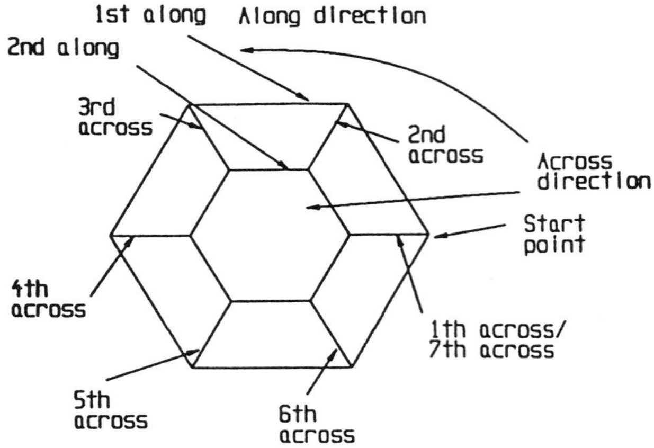

Figure 12.39

Example 12.3

Determine the number of patches in the along and across direction for the surface shown in Figure 12.40.

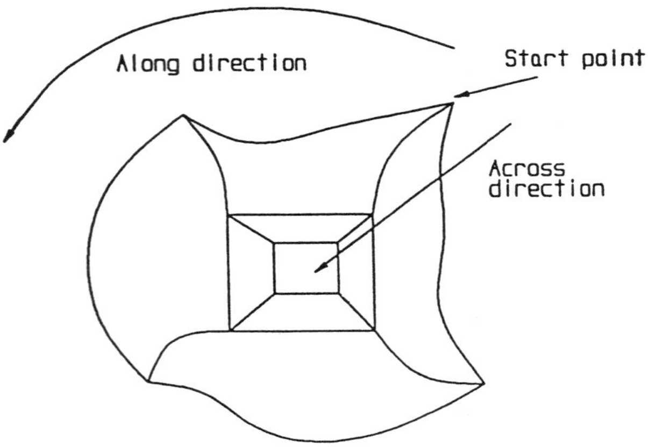

Figure 12.40

$N_L = 3$
$N_C = 4$
$P_L = N_C \quad = 4$
$P_C = N_L - 1 \quad = 3 - 1 \quad = 2$
$P_T = P_L \text{ X } P_C = 4 \text{ X } 2 = 8$

Tip 3. Assignment of along rows and across columns.

The surface patch boundaries are laid out in a grid. Along contours are assigned in rows and across contours in columns. Each contour in the grid is identified by an along row number and an across column number (Figure 12.41).

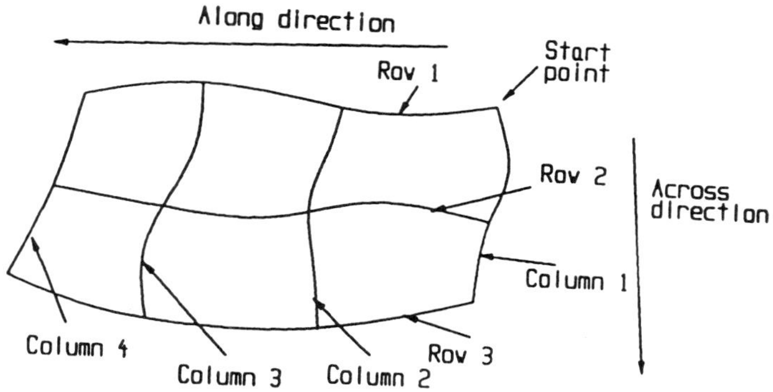

Figure 12.41

Tip 4. The order of contours selection.

The contours selection must follow a predetermined order that is along contours are sequentially selected first, followed by the across contours as follows:

Selection order	entity to be picked
1st selection	along row 1 - across column 1
2nd selection	along row 1 - across column 2
-	-
-	-
nth selection	along row 1 - across column n
n+1 selection	along row 2 - across column 1
n+2 selection	along row 2 - across column 2
-	-
-	-
2n selection	along row 2 - across column n
-	-
-	-
mn selection	along row m - across column n

Example 12.4

This example shows the contours selection sequence for the patches having an open boundary (Figure 12.42).

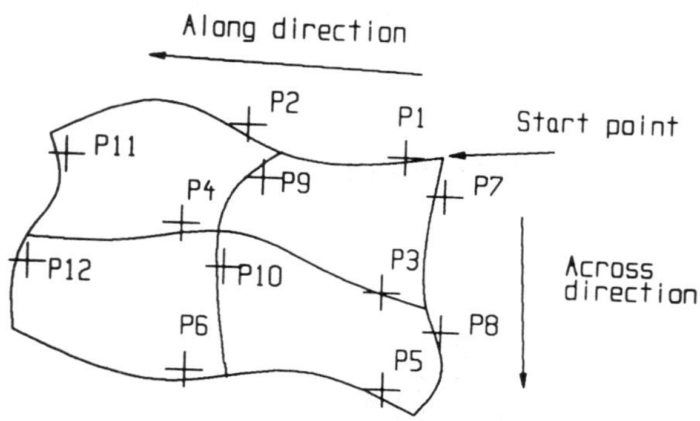

Figure 12.42

Example 12.5

In this example the contours selection sequence for the surface patches having a closed boundary is illustrated (Figure 12.43).

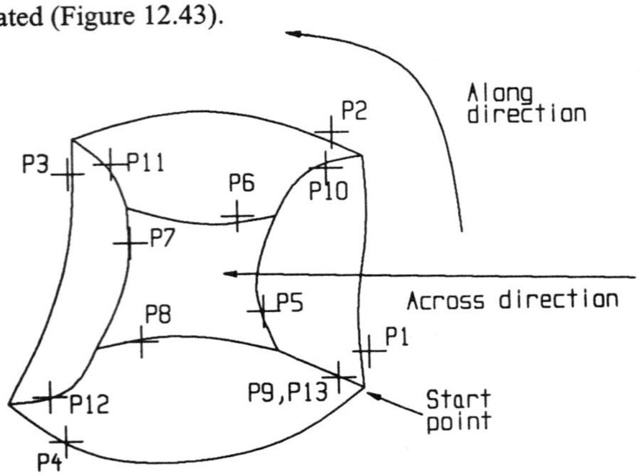

Figure 12.43

Example 12.6

Figure 12.44 shows an example where six lines are joined in one point. The patch grid layout requires two along contours and six across contours. The first along contour consists of the six sides of the hexagon. The second along contour is a point which is the common point the six lines joined.

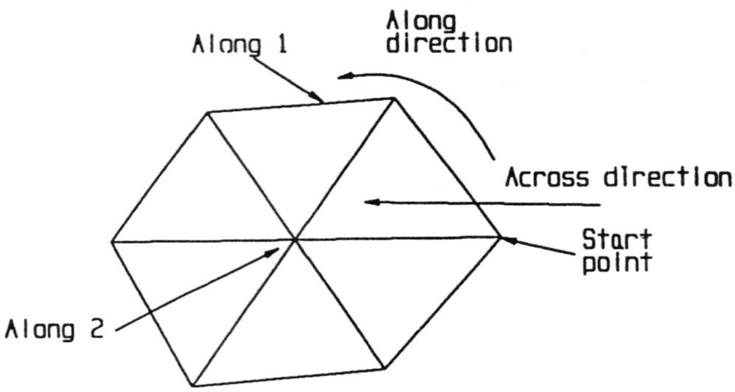

Figure 12.44

⌛**Tip**	5. Selection of the blending method There are four blending methods for generating a Coons surface:
	Linear: used when surfaces are fairly flat Parabolic: used when surfaces have greater curvatures Cubic: used when surfaces have greater curvatures Cubic with slope matching: used when parabolic or cubic produces flat spots on surfaces

Figure 12.45 compares the effect of these four blending methods on a surface.

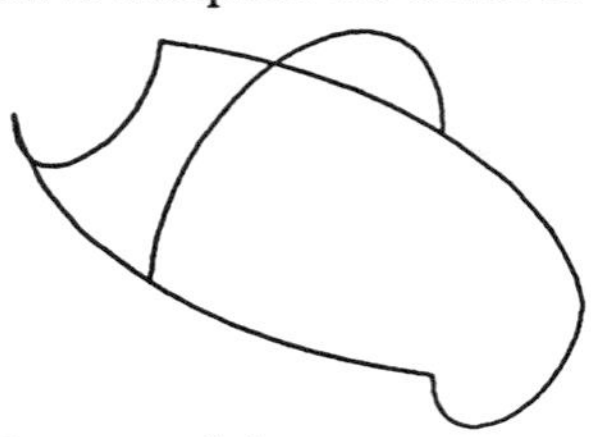

a. Wireframe model

7

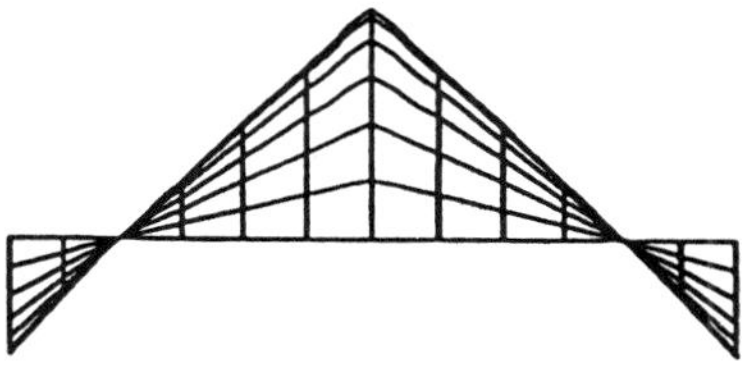

b. Linear

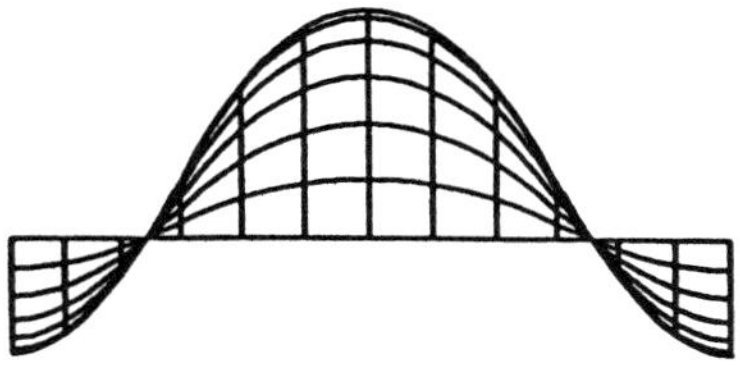

c. Parabolic

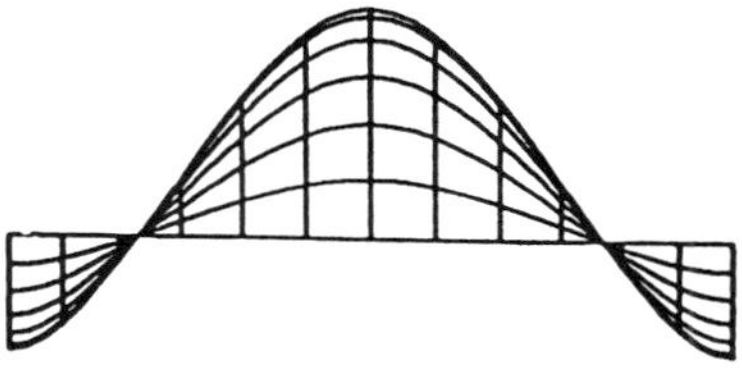

d. Cubic

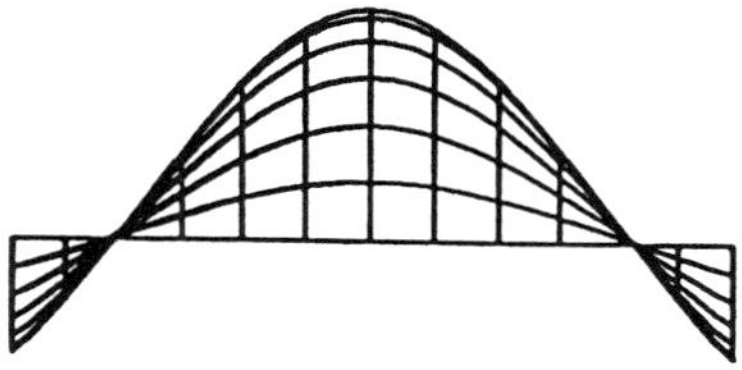

e. Cubic with slope matching

Figure 12.45

Project 7. Creating a Coons surface of one patch

This example uses the wireframe model of project 5 in chapter 11 to generate a Coons surface. The wireframe model and the final surface model are shown in Figure 12.46.

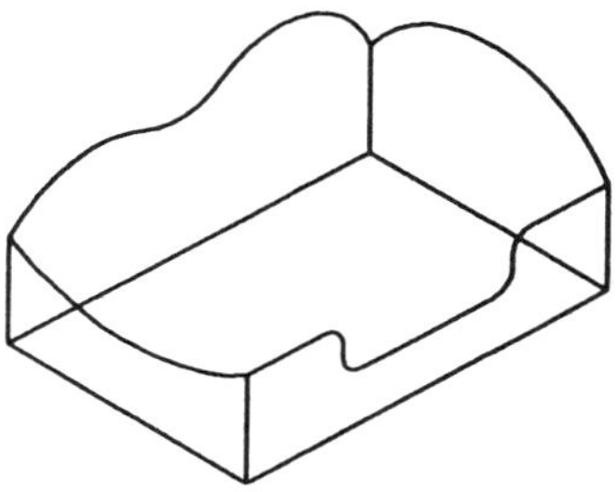

Figure 12.46a. Wireframe model

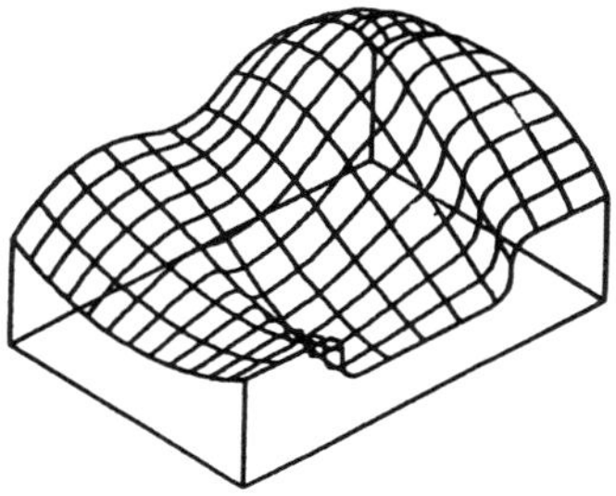

Figure 12.46b. Surface model

Tips 1. This is a single path surface.

2. Use the automatic chaining method to chain the contours.

Step 1. Load the wireframe model (coons1)

(or create one by following the instructions given in project 5 of chapter 11)
Select **MAIN MENU →File → Get**
Enter file name: **coons1**

The wireframe model on the screen should resemble Figure 12.47.

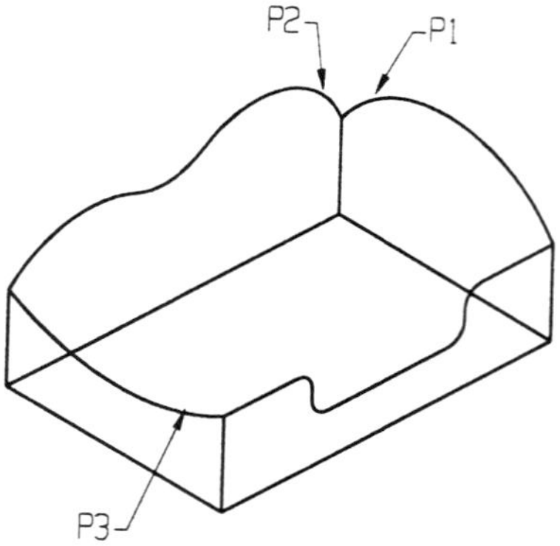

Figure 12.47

Step 2. Create the Coons surface. Use the pick points in Figure 12.47.

Select **Level**
Enter new level number: **2 → OK**
Select **MAIN MENU → Create → Surface → Coons**
Select **Yes** to use automatic coons chaining
Pick **P1** and **P2** to select the curves which intersect at the upper-left corner.
Pick **P3** to select the end of one curve at the lower-right corner.
Toggle the surface to **NURBS**
Toggle **Blending** to **Parabolic**
Select **Do it**

The newly created Coons surface should look like Figure 12.48.

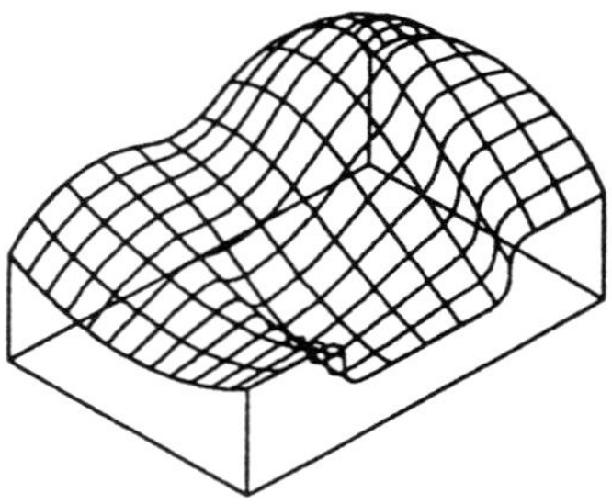

Figure 12.48

Step 3. Save the surface model file as coonss1.

Select **MAIN MENU → file → Save**
Enter file name: **coonss1**

Project 8. Creating a Coons surface of two patches

8

In this project, we still use the wireframe model of project 5 in chapter 11 except that we add an arc to form a three-along-contours surface. It is intended to show how the added contour changes the skin of the surface. The new wireframe model and the resulted surface are illustrated in Figure 12.49.

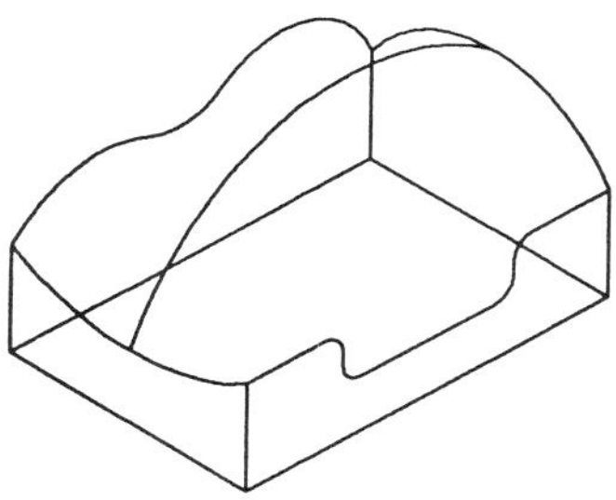

Figure 12.49a Wireframe model

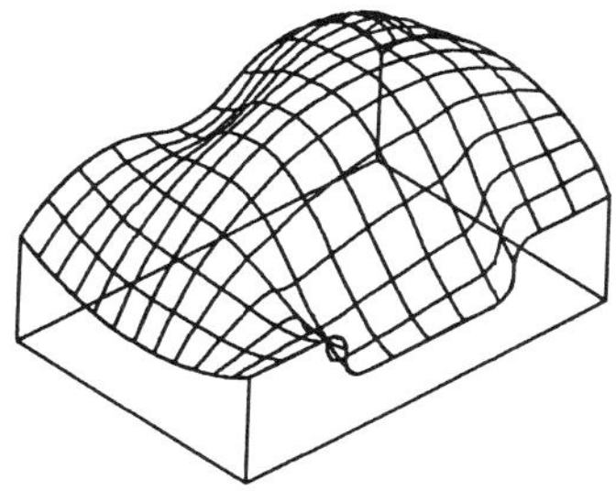

Figure 12.49b. Surface model

Tips 1. Use the Side Cplane to add an arc between the midpoint of the two arcs in the across direction.
2. The number of patches is 2.
3. Each of two across arcs must be broken into two entities at the midpoints because an along contour is added to the profile.
4. Use the automatic coons chaining method to chain contours.

Step 1. Load the wireframe model file (coons1).

Select **MAIN MENU → File → Get**
Enter file name: **coons1 ←**

The wireframe model should appear as Figure 12.50.

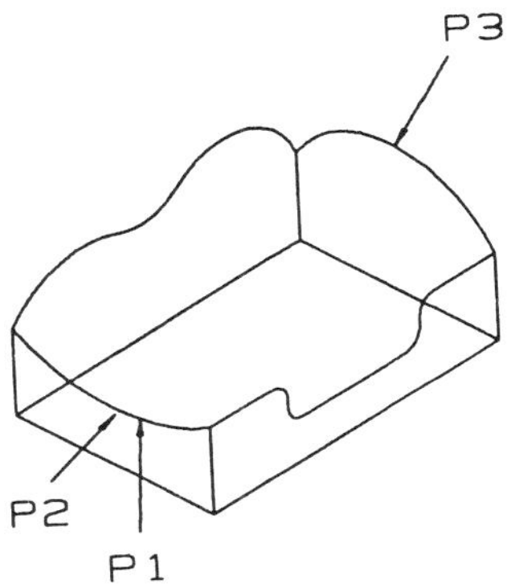

Figure 12.50

Step 2. Add an arc using the Side Cplane.

Use the pick points in Figure 12.50.
Select **Cplane → Side**
Select **Z → Midpoint** and then pick **P1**
Z2.5 should appear in the Secondary menu.
Select **MAIN MENU → Create → Arc → Endpoints → Midpoint**
Pick **P2**
Select **Midpoint,** then pick **P3**
Enter the radius: **5** ←
Pick the second arc segment from the top to complete the arc
The new wireframe model should resemble Figure 12.51.

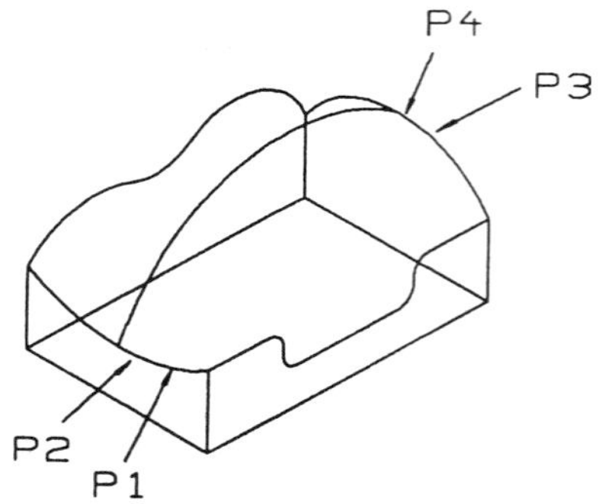

Figure 12.51

Step 3. Break the two arcs into two pieces each, using the Front Cplane.

Use the pick points in Figure 12.51.
Select **Cplane → Front**
Select **MAIN MENU → Modify → Break → 2 pieces**
Select **Midpoint,** pick **P1**
Enter the breakpoint: select **Midpoint** from the Point Menu
then pick **P2** to complete the breaking of the first arc
Select an entity: pick **P3**
Select **Midpoint**
Enter the breakpoint: pick **P4** for the breaking of the second arc

The new drawing looks identical to the one before breaking the two arcs. The drawing is redrawn in Figure 12.52.

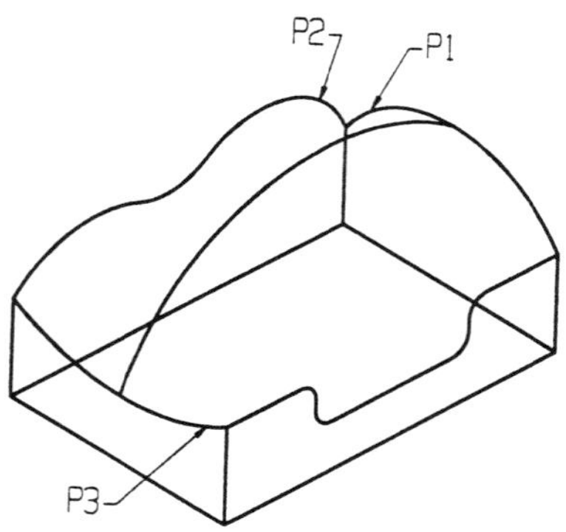

Figure 12.52

Step 4. Create the Coons surface using the pick points in Figure 12.52. 9

Select **Level,** then enter **2**
Select **MAIN MENU → Create → Surface → Coons**
Select **Yes** to use automatic coons chaining
Pick P1 and **P2** to select curves which intersect at the upper-left corner.
Pick P3 to select the end of a curve at the lower-right corner.
Set the **Coons Surface** parameters as below:

Surface error tolerance = **0.01**
Surface type = **Nurbs**
Blending = **Cubic**

Select **Do it** to complete the chaining
The surface model should resemble Figure 12.53.

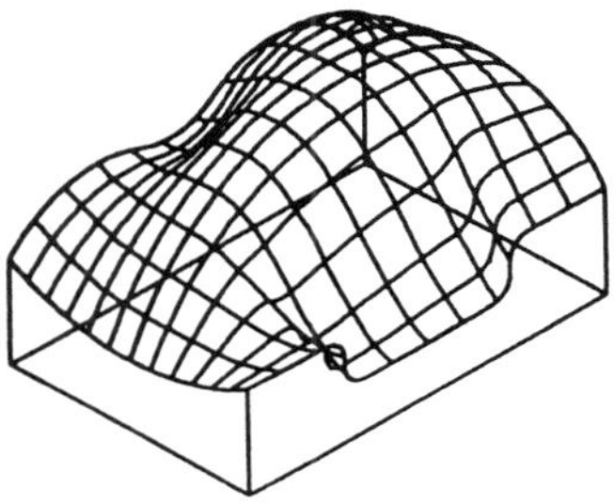

Figure 12.53

Step 5. Save the surface model file (coonss2).

Select **MAIN MENU → File → Save**
Enter file name: **coonss2**

Project 9. Creating a Coons surface with a joint point on along contours

This project uses a common join point as an along contour. The wireframe model is constructed in project 6 of chapter 11. The wireframe model and the final surface model are shown in Figure 12.54.

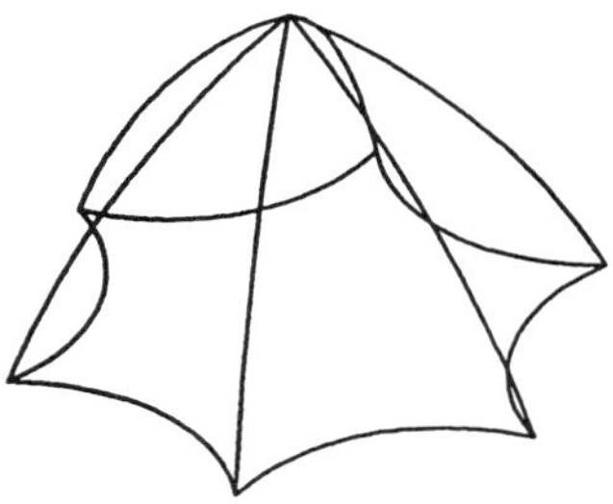

Figure 12.54a. Wireframe model

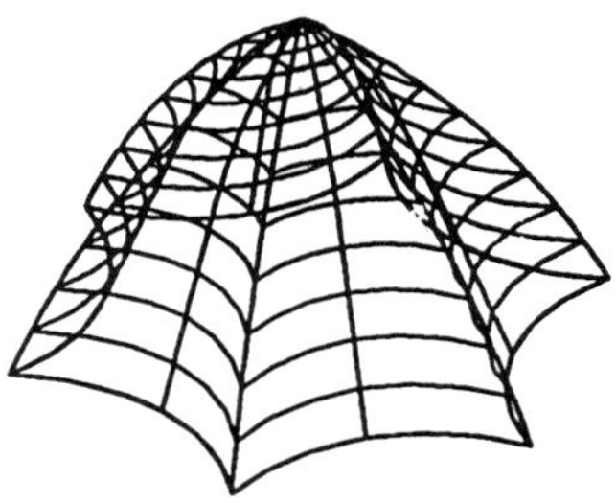

Figure 12.54b. Surface model

⌛**Tips** 1. Use Top Gview to facilitate the picking at the contours.

2. Use the common join point as one of along contours.

3. Number of patches in the along direction is 6.

4. Number of patches in the across direction is 1.

Step 1. Load the wireframe model file coons3.

(or create one by following the instructions in project 6 of chapter 11.)
The drawing should appear as Figure 12.55.)
Select **MAIN MENU→ File → Get**
Enter file name: **coons3**

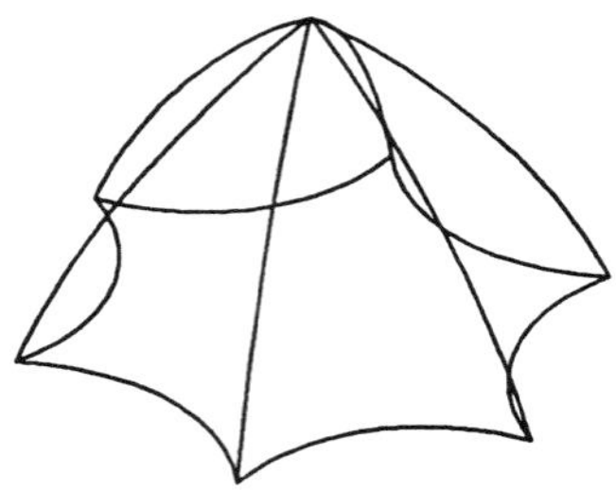

Figure 12.55

Step 2. Change the Gview to Top.

Select **Gview → Top**
The drawing becomes Figure 12.56.

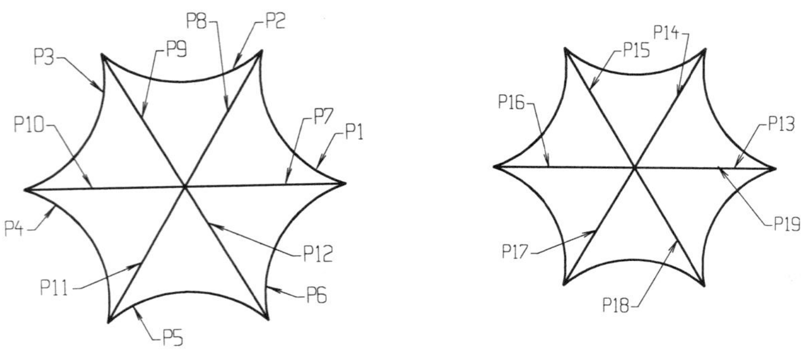

Figure 12.56

Step 3. Create the Coons surface using the pick points in Figure 12.56.

Select **Level,** then enter **2**
Select **MAIN MENU → Create → Surface → Coons**
Select **No** to use automatic chaining.

Enter the number of patches in the along direction: **6** ←
Enter the number of patches in the across direction: **1** ←
Select **Single**
Sequentially pick **P1 - P6** to complete the along contour of row 1.
Select **Mode → Point → Endpoint →** Pick **P7**
Select Point → Pick **P8** (repeat this step to the rest points:**P9-P12**)

Selecting **Mode →** **Single**
Sequentially pick **P13 - P19** to complete the across contour.

Select **Done** to complete the selection
Change the Coons surface parameters to the following settings:

Surface error tolerance = **0.05**
Surface type = **Nurbs**
Blending = **Cubic**

Select **Do it** to complete the surface
The surface model in Top Gview should appear as Figure 12.57

Figure 12.57

Step 4. Change Gview to isometric.

Select **Gview → Isometric**
The surface model shown in isometric view should resemble Figure 12.58.

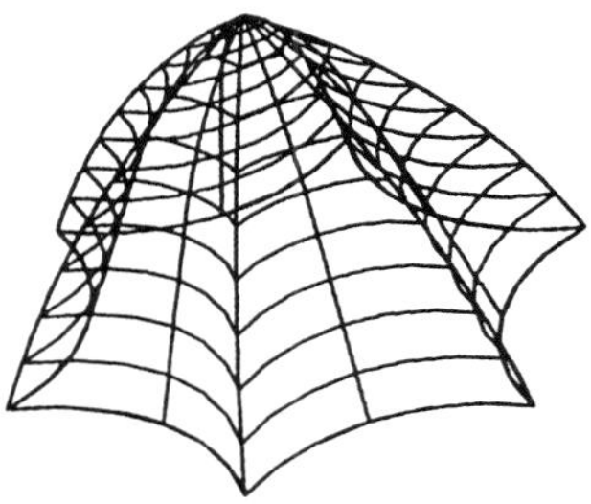

Figure 12.58

Step 5. Save the surface model file as coonss3.

Select **MAIN MENU → File → Save**
Enter file name:**coonss3**

10 Project 10. Creating a Coons surface of multiple faces

This project uses a wireframe model with thirteen faces to create a Coons surface. The wireframe model is shown in Figure 12.59a and the resultant Coons surface is illustrated in Figure 12.59b.

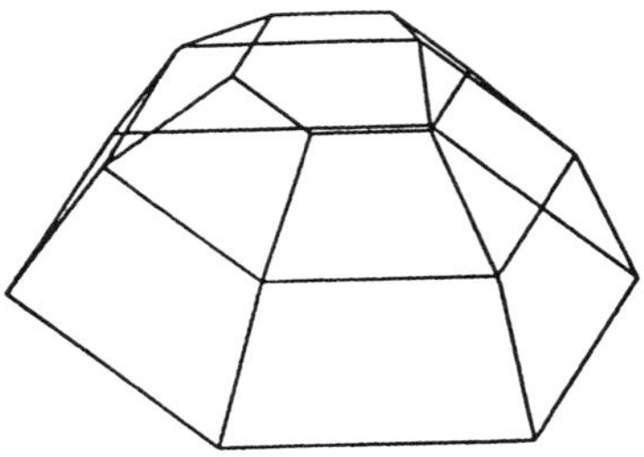

Figure 12.59a. Wireframe model

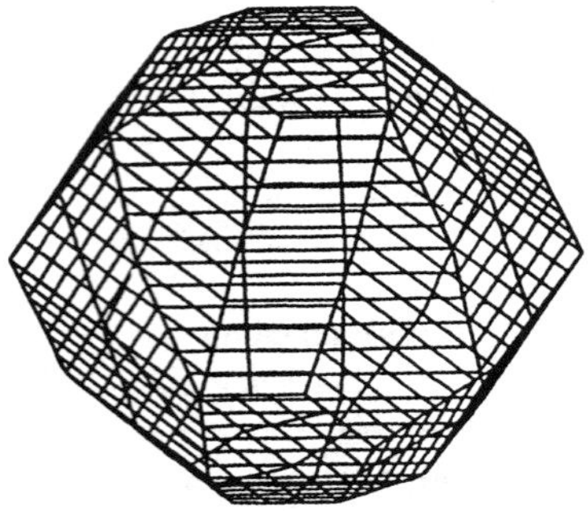

Figure 12.59b. Surface model

Tips

1. Use the Top Gview to facilitate the picking of contours.
2. Create a Coons surface based on the twelve faces.
3. The number of patches in the along direction is 6.
4. The number of patches in the across direction is 2.
5. Create a ruled surface for the top face.
6. Use separate levels and different colors for these two surfaces.
7. Mirror the two surfaces about the X axis using the Front Cplane to complete the surface model.

Step 1. Load the wireframe model file coons4.

(or create one by following the instructions in the project 7 of chapter 11.)
Select **MAIN MENU → File → Get**
Enter the file name: **coons4**

The wireframe model drawing of thirteen faces should appear on your screen as it is shown in Figure 12.60.

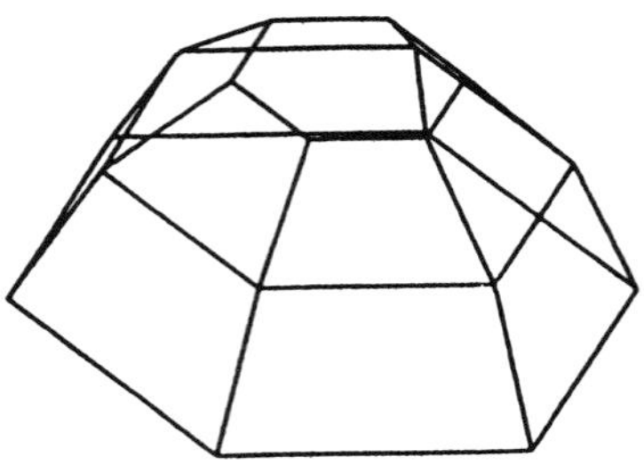

Figure 12.60

Step 2. Change the drawing to Top Gview.

Select **Gview → Top**

The drawing in the Top Gview appears as in Figure 12.61.

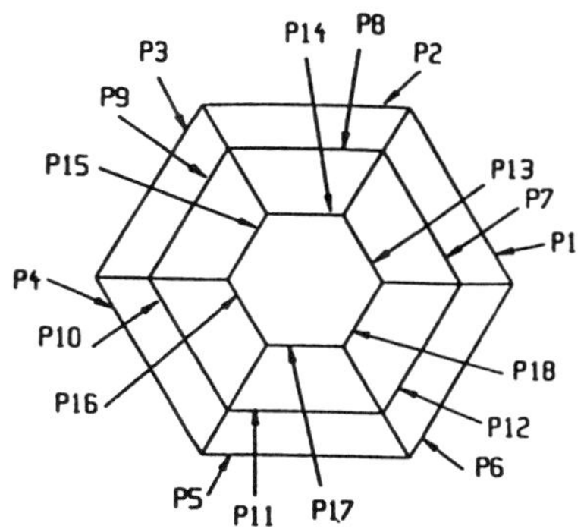

Figure 12.61a

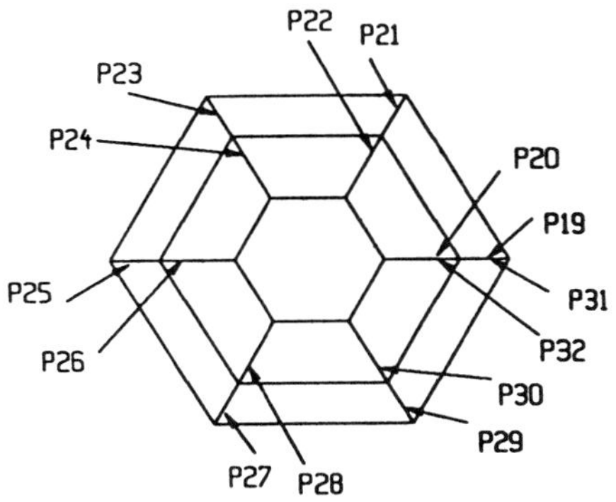

Figure 12.61b

Step 3. Create the Coons surface using the pick points in Figure 12.61.

Change the level to 2 and the color to 12.
Select **Level**, click at **2**, then select **OK**
Select **Color**, then enter **12**
Select **MAIN MENU → Create → Surface → Coons**
Select **No** to "Use automatice coons chaining?"
Enter the number of patches in the along direction: **6**
Enter the number of patches in the across direction: **2**
Select **Single**
Sequentially pick at **P1-P18** in Figure 12.61a
Pick **P19-P32** shown in Figure 12.61b to complete the selection of contours.
Select **Done**
Set the Coons surface parameters to the following settings:

Surface error tolerance = **0.005**
Surface type = **Parametric**
Blending = **Linear**

Select **Do it** to complete the surface
Select **Gview → Isometric** to display the surface in isometric view

The Coons surface should look like Figure 12.62.

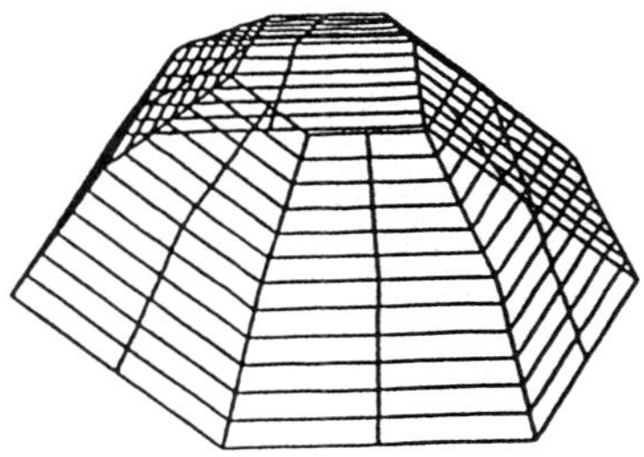

Figure 12.62

Step 4. Save the surface model file as coonss4.

Select **MAIN MENU → File → Save**
Enter file name: **coonss4**

Step 5. Make the Coons surface in Level 2 invisible.

Select **Level → Vis levels**
Toggle the **#2** button to dimmed (invisible)
Select **OK → OK** to return to the graphic mode

Step 6. Change to Top Gview

Select **Gview → Top**

The drawing on the screen should resemble Figure 12.63.

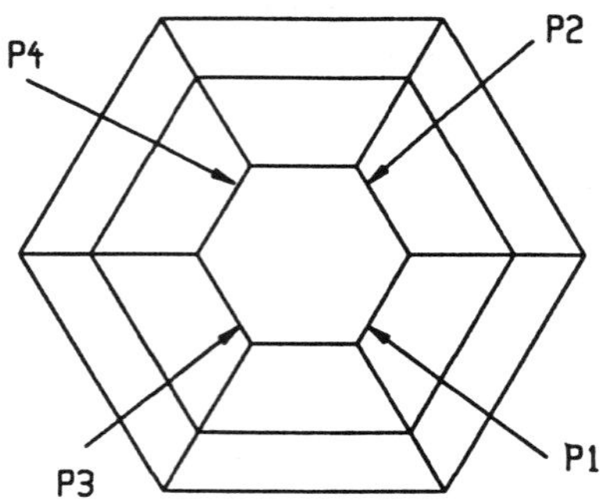

Figure 12.63

Step 7. Create a ruled surface for the top face using pick points in Figure 12.63.

Change to Level 3 and Color 13.
Select **Level**
Click the **#3** button, then select **OK**
Select **Color**, then enter **13**
Select **MAIN MENU → Create → Surface → Ruled → Sync**
The chain Synchronization Options dialog box should appear as shown here:
Set the sync option to **by Entity**

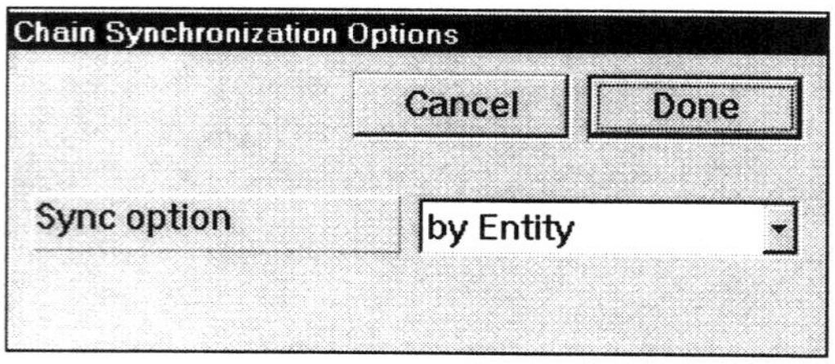

Select **Done**

Define contour 1: select chain from the Chaining method menu,
then pick **P1→ Partial→ P2** for the last entity
finally select **Done** to complete the contour selection.
Set the ruled surfaces parameters to these values:

Surface tolerance = **0.005**
Surface Type = **Parametric**

Select **Do it** to create a ruled surface.

Step 8. Change Gview to Isometric and make Level 2 visible.

Select **Gview → Isometric**
Select **Level → Vis. levels**
Click on the **#2** button to make the level visible
Select **OK** to return to the graphic mode.

The drawing with two surfaces should appear as in Figure 12.64.

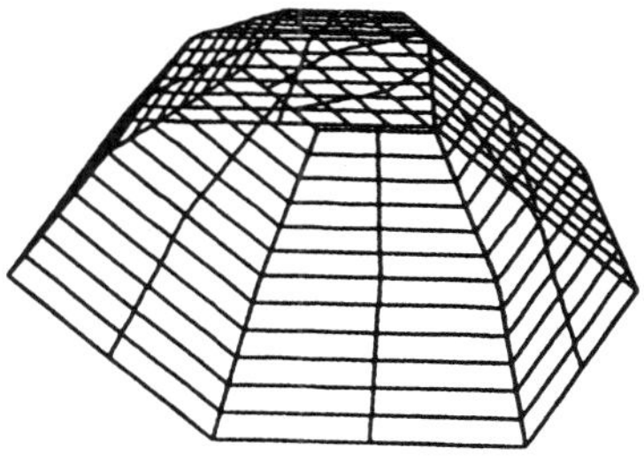

Figure 12.64

Step 9. Mirror the two surfaces about the X axis to generate the bottom half of the surface model.

Use Front or Side Cplane.
Select **Cplane → Front**
Select **MAIN MENU → Xform → Mirror → All → Surfaces → All → Lines → Done**
Select the **Xaxis**
Select **Copy → Done** from the Mirror Parameters menu to complete the Surface model.

The complete surface model should appear as in Figure 12.65.

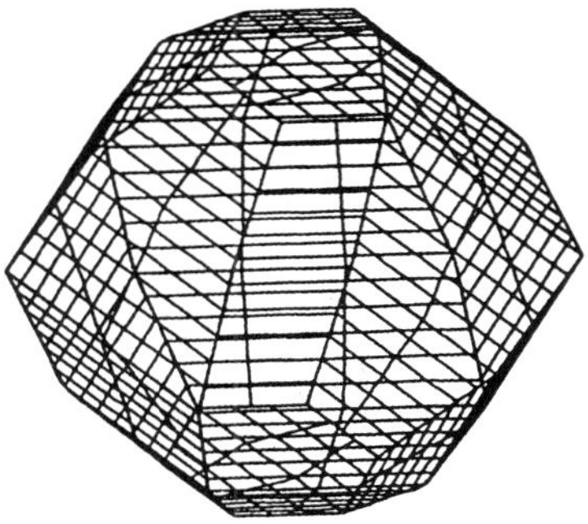

Figure 12.65

11 12.8 Revolved Surfaces Modeling

A revolved surface is created by revolving a geometric entity about an axis or a line. The geometric entity to be revolved is referred to as the generating curve, and the axis or line to be revolved about is called the revolving axis or line. The resulting surface is perpendicular to the revolving line.

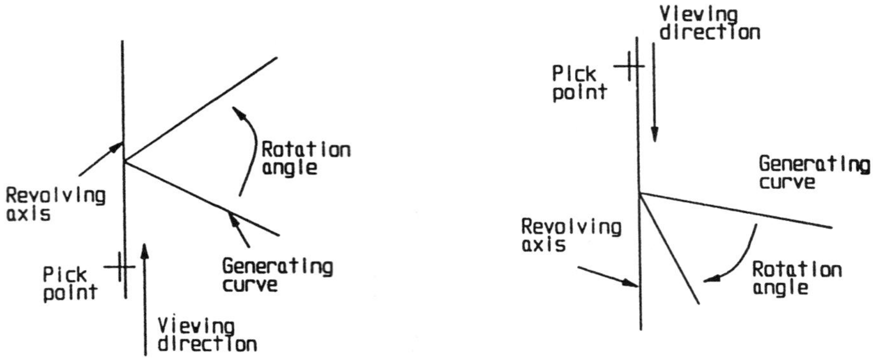

Figure 12.66

Tips 1. The revolved modeling technique generates a curve which can consist of more than one entity. You can use the Chain command to connect all entities together as a single generating curve. However, the number of resultant surfaces is eual to the number of entities included in the chained generating profile.

2. The rotation angle direction is determined by which end of the revolving axis is chosen when the user uses the mouse to pick the axis or line. A zero degree angle is assigned to the orientation of generating curve currently identified. Negative angles are invalid. The angle can rotate in either direction about the revolving axis. Figure 12.66 shows how the direction of the rotation angle is determined. The rotation direction is always in the clockwise direction when viewed from the selected end of the revolving axis toward the other end.

Project 11. Creating revolved surfaces to form a cup.

The revolved surface of a cup is created by using the wireframe model in project 8 of chapter 11. The wireframe model and the surface is shown in Figure 12.67.

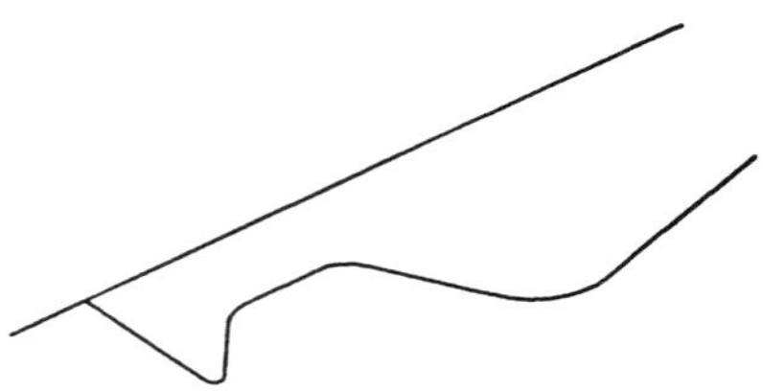
Figure 12.67a. Wireframe model

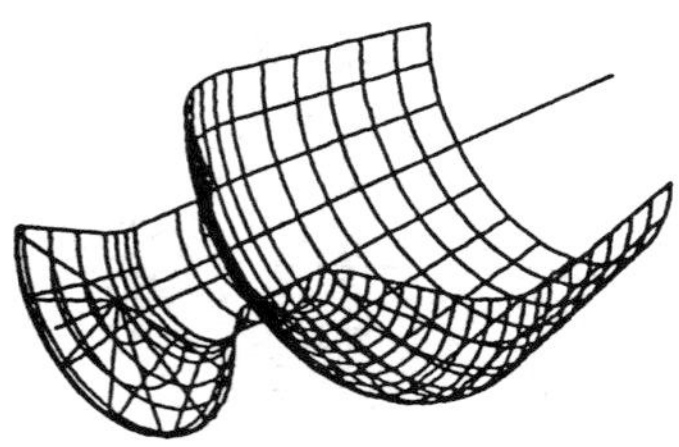
Figure 12.67b. Surface model

Tips 1. This surface model consists of nine revolved surfaces.

2. Each revolved surface is rotated 180° to form one-half of the surface model, or rotated 360° to form the complete surface model. In a manufacturing point of view, the cup mold requires one-half of the surface model.

3. The picking point on the revolving axis should be placed at the lower half segment of the line to create the correct revolving angle.

The wireframe model drawing should resemble Figure 12.68.

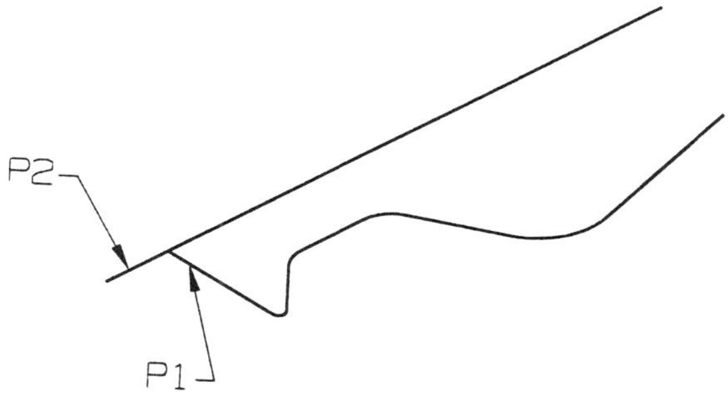

Figure 12.68

Step 2. Create the cup's first revolved surface using pick points from Figure 12.68.

Select **Level,** then enter **2**
Select **MAIN MENU → Creat → Surface → Revolved**
Select the profile entities: select **Chain**, then pick **P1**
Select **Done**
Select the axis of rotation: pick **P2**
Select Start angle, enter **0**
Select **End angle**, enter **180**
Toggle Surface Type to **N** (NURBS)
Select **Do it**

The drawing with all nine revolved surfaces appears as Figure 12.69.

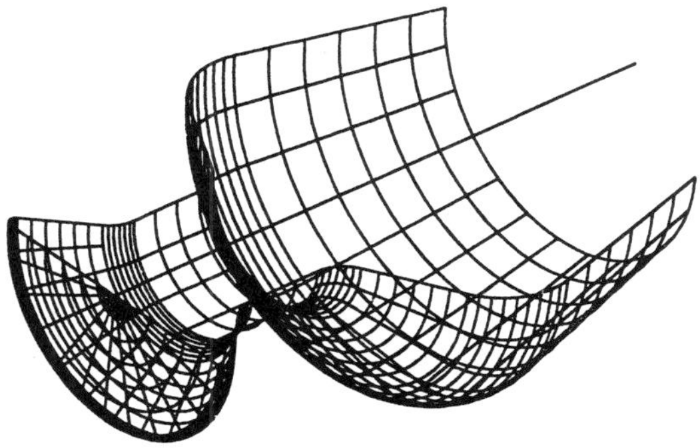

Figure 12.69

Step 3. Save the surface model file as cups.

Select **MAIN MENU → File → Save**
Enter the file name: **cups**

12.9 Draft Surfaces Modeling

A draft surface is created by extruding a sectional shape (or base curve) straight along a line (Figure 12.70). This line is defined by a length and an angle. The length is referred to as the draft length and the angle as the draft angle.

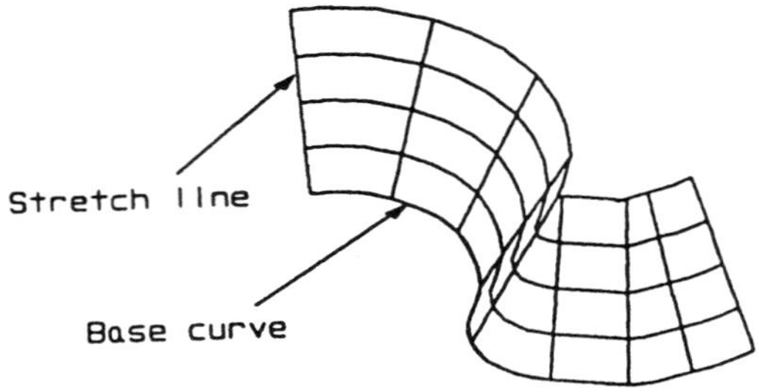

Figure 12.70

Tips 1. The base curve can be a line, an arc, a parametric spline, or a curve.

2. The draft modeling technique in Version 7 can chain more than one entity to create multiple draft surfaces. However, the number of draft surfaces is equal to the number of chained entities.
3. The draft length indicates how far the surface is to be stretched. It is measured in the direction perpendicular to the current Cplane. An arrow will appear to indicate the positive direction of the length (Figure 12.71). Entering a positive value will stretch the surface in the direction the arrow is pointing. Likewise, a negative value extends the surface in the opposite direction of the arrow.

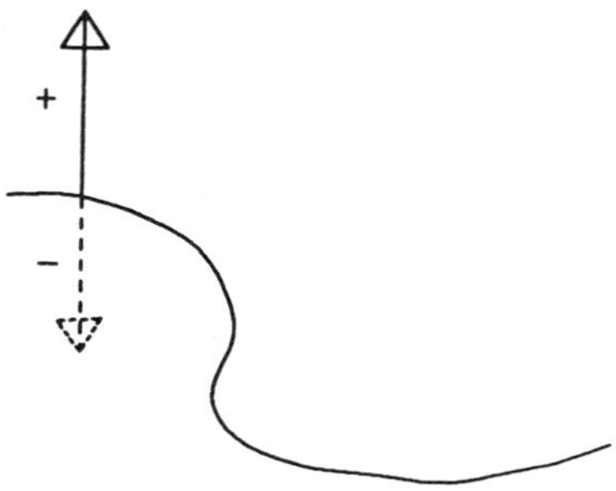

Figure 12.71

4. The draft angle specifies the orientation of the surface which in turn determines the shape of the surface. An arrow will appear to indicate the angle direction (Figure 12.72 on the next page). A positive angle will extend the surface in the direction of the angle arrow, while a negative angle value will extend the surface in the opposite direction of the indicator arrow.

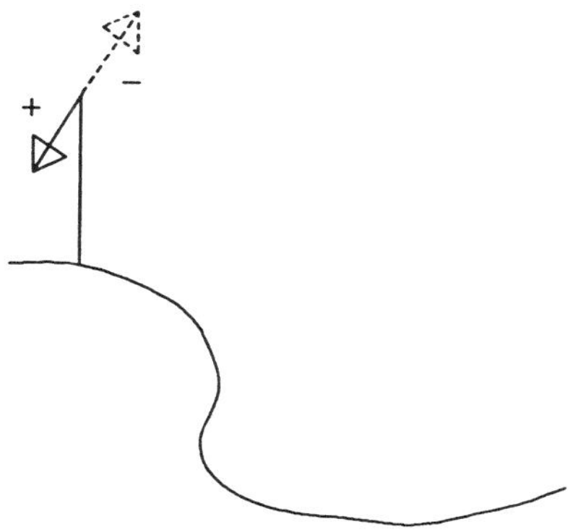

Figure 12.72

Project 12. Creating the draft surfaces to form a tabulated cylinder

This example creates a set of draft surfaces to form a tabulated cylinder based on a rectangle with a fillet at four corners as shown in Figure 12.73.

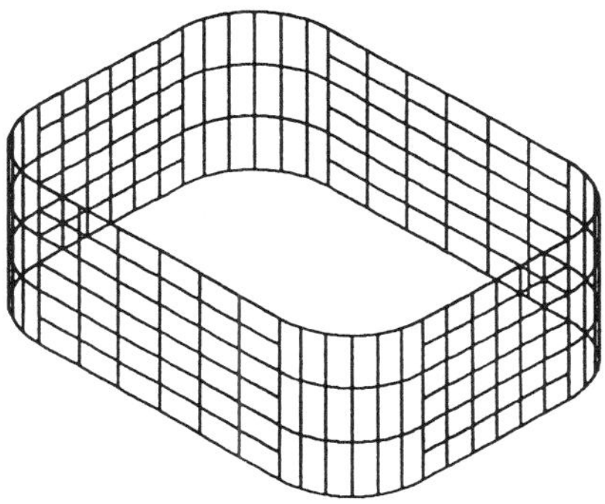

Figure 12.73

Tips 1. The base profile is a rectangle with a fillet at four corners. It is constructed in the Top Cplane.
2. The draft length is -1.5 in. and the draft angle is 0.

3. The surface model consists of eight draft surfaces.

Step 1. Create a rectangle using the Top Cplane.

Select **MAIN MENU → File → New → Yes** to initialize the screen
Select **Gview → Isometric**
Select **MAIN MENU → Create → Rectangle → 1 point**
Enter the lower left corner: **0,0** ←
Enter the width: **4** ←
Enter the height: **3** ←

The rectangle should appear on the screen as Figure 12.74.

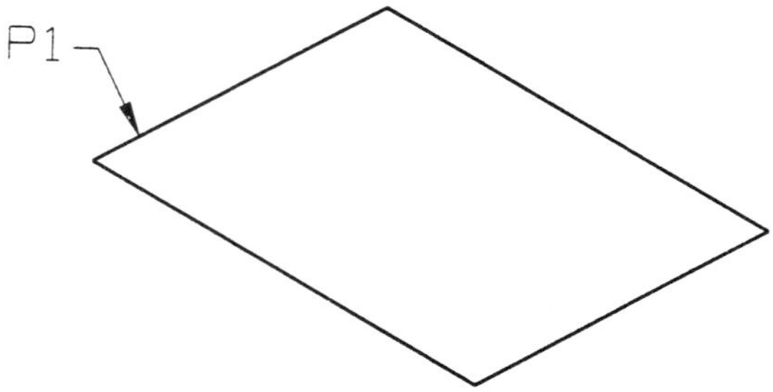

Figure 12.74

Step 2. Add four corner fillets using the pick points in Figure 12.74.

Select **MAIN MENU → Modify → Fillet → Radius**
Enter the fillet radius: **0.75** ←
Select **Chain**
Pick **P1**
Select **Done** to complete the four fillets

The new drawing should look like Figure 12.75.

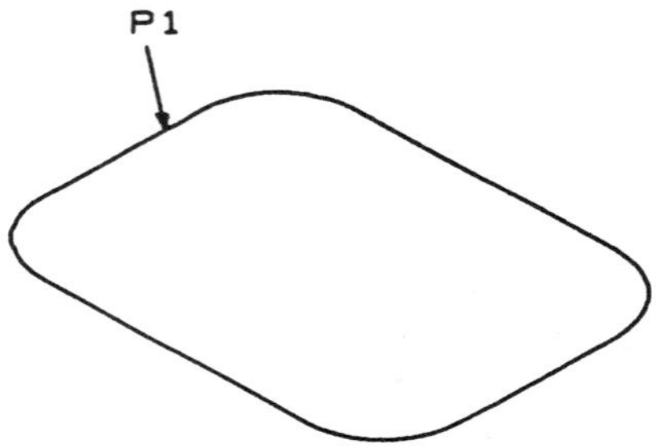

Figure 12.75

Step 3. Create eight draft surfaces using the pick points in Figure 12.71.

Select **MAIN MENU → Create → Surface → Draft**
Select the profile entities: Select **Chain** then pick **P1**
Select **Done**
Select **Length,** enter **-1.5** ←
Select **Angle**, enter **0** ←
Toggle Surface Type to **N** (NURBS)
Select **Do it**
The first draft surface should resemble Figure 12.76.

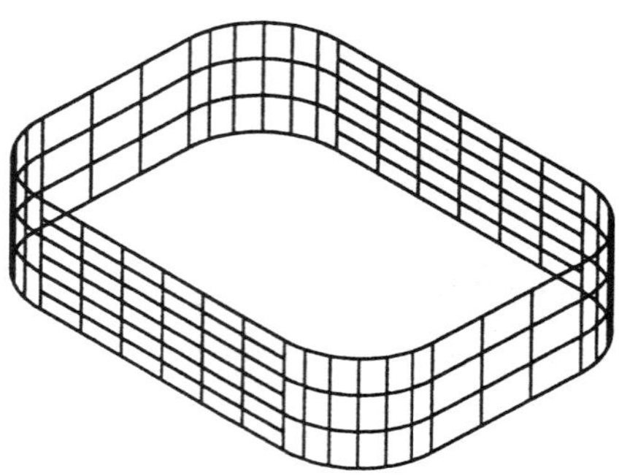

Figure 12.76

Step 4. Save the surface model as drafts1. 13

Select **MAIN MENU →File → Save**
Enter file name: **drafts1**

Project 13.

This example uses the draft surface modeling technique to create a cone surface, a spline surface, and a rectangular draft surface with four corner fillets as shown in these Figures 12.75a, b and c.

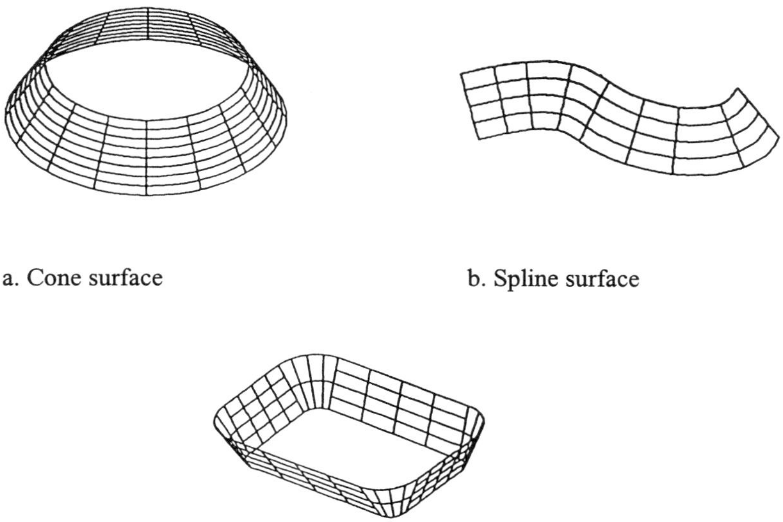

a. Cone surface b. Spline surface

c. Rectangular draft surface

Figure 12.77

Cone Surface

The cone surface has a basic circle with a 3-in. diameter. The draft length is 1-in in the downward direction and the draft angle is 30° in the outward direction.

Step 1. Create the base circle. Initialize the system if necessary.

Select **Z** then enter **0** if necessary
Select **Cplane → Top** if necessary
Select **Gview → Isometric** if necessary
Select **MAIN MENU → Create → Arc → Cir pt+rad**
Enter the center point: **0,0** ←
Enter the radius: **1.5** ←

The circle should look like Figure 12.78

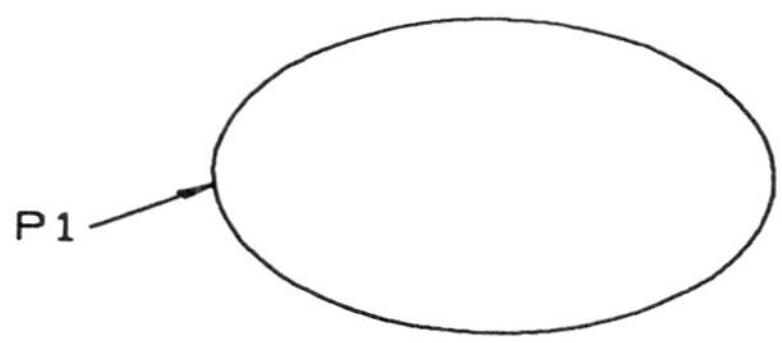

Figure 12.78

Step 2. Create the draft surface, use the pick point in Figure 12.78 on the last page.

Select **MAIN MENU → Create → Surface → Draft**
Select **Single,** then pick **P1,**
Select **Done**
Select **Length,** enter **-1** ←
Select **Angle,** enter **-30** ←
Select **Do it**
The cone surface should resemble Figure 12.79.

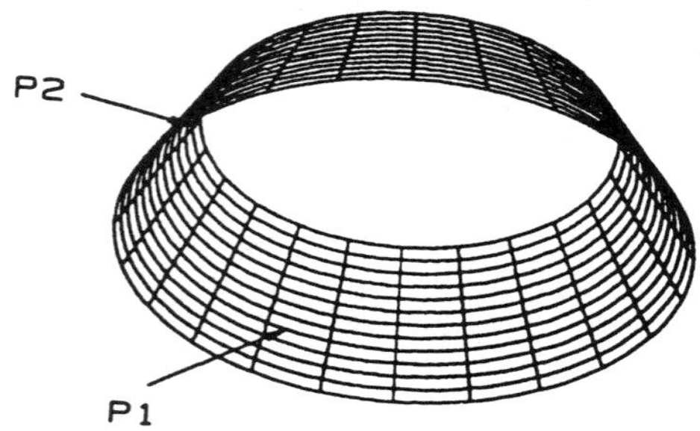

Figure 12.79

Step 3. Delete the circle and the surface using the pick points from Figure 12.79.

You may want to save the cone surface drawing for later use.
Select **MAIN MENU → Delete**
Pick **P1** and **P2**
This should give you a **clean screen** for your work.

Spline Surface

The base curve of the spline surface is a spline formed by nine points. The draft length is 1-in. in the downward direction and the draft angle is 35° in the inward direction.

Step 4. Create a spline using a set of point data.

Select **MAIN MENU → Create → Spline**
Toggle the spline type to **N (NURBS)**
Select **Manual**
Sequentially enter the following sets of point data:

0,0 ←
0.25,0.48 ←
0.5,0.85 ←
1,1.32 ←
1.75,1.5 ←
2.5,1.4 ←
3.25,1.5 ←
3.75,1.72 ←
4.15,2.25 ←
4,2.75 ←

Press **Esc** to terminate the point data entry
The spline should resemble Figure 12.80.

Figure 12.80

Step 5. Create a draft surface using the pick point in Figure 12.80.

Select **MAIN MENU → Create → Surface → Draft**
Select the base curve: pick **P1,** then select **Done**
Select **Length,** enter **-1** ←
Select **Angle,** enter **-35** ←
Select **Do it**
The draft surface should look like Figure 12.81.

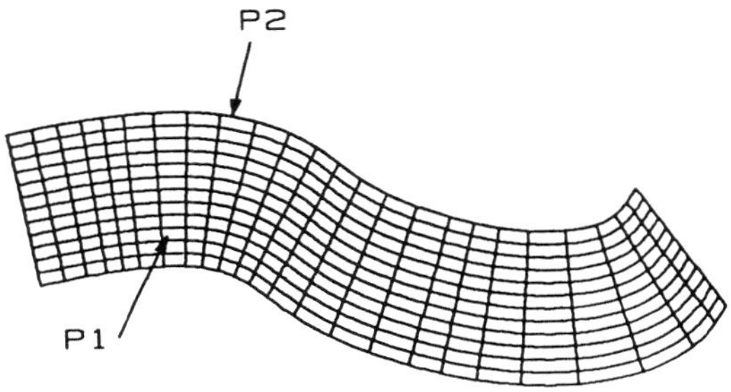

Figure 12.81

Step 6. Save the spline surface as drafts2.

Select **MAIN MENU → File → Save**
Enter file name: **drafts2**

Step 7. Delete the spline curve and surface using the pick points in Figure 12.81.

Select **MAIN MENU → Delete**
Pick **P1** and **P2**
This should give you a clean screen for your work.

Rectangular Draft Surfaces with four Corner Fillets

This surface model consists of eight draft surfaces which are extended in the downward direction by 1.25-in. and have a 25° draft angle in the inward direction.

Step 8. Create a rectangle.

Select **Main Menu →Create → Rectangle → 1 point**
Enter the lower left corner: **0,0** ←
Enter the width: **6** ←
Enter the height: **4** ←

The rectangle should appear like Figure 12.82.

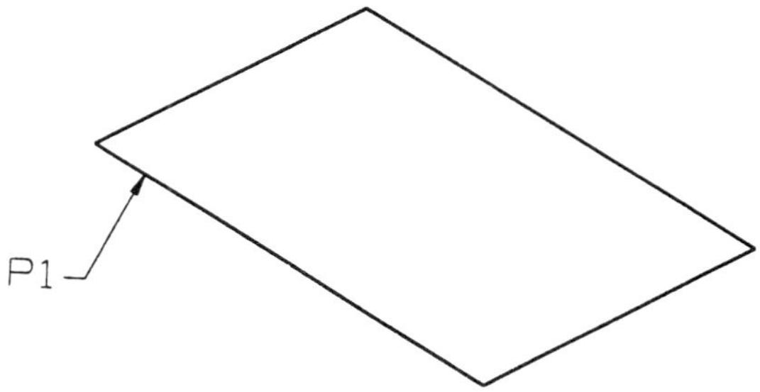

Figure 12.82

Step 9. Add four fillets using the points in Figure 12.82 on the previous page.

Select **MAIN MENU → Modify → Fillet → Radius**
Enter radius value: **1** ←
Select **Chain**, then pick **P1**
Select **Done**

The new drawing should resemble Figure 12.83.

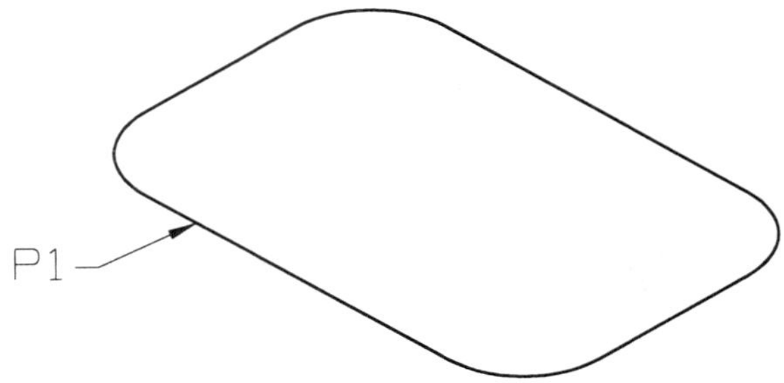

Figure 12.83

Step 10. Create eight draft surfaces. Use the pick point in Figure 12.83.

Select **MAIN MENU → Create → Surface → Draft**
Select the profile entities: Select **Chain,** then pick **P1**
Select **Done**
Select **Length,** enter **-1.25** ←
Select **Angle,** enter **-25** ←
Select **Do it**
The eight draft surfaces should appear as Figure 12.84.

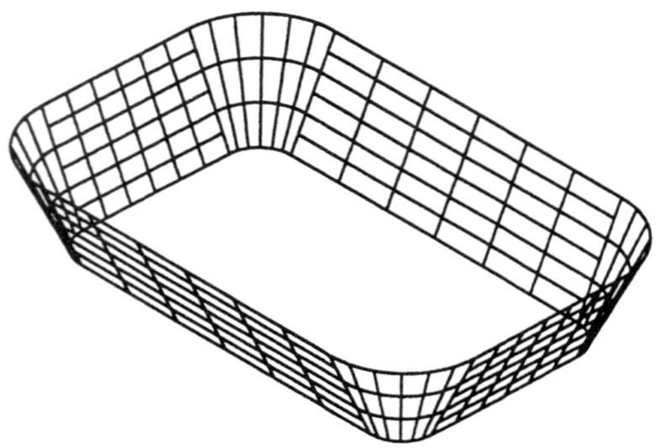

Figure 12.84

Step 11. Save the drawing as drafts3.

Select **MAIN MENU → File → Save**
Enter file name: **drafts3**

12.10 Swept Surfaces Modeling

A swept surface is created by either translating **a** sectional profile along one or two drive curves or translating **two** sectional profiles along a drive curve. Mastercam provides **three** types of swept surfaces: one across/one along, one across/two along, and two across/one along. Their descriptions and applications are given in Table 12.5.

Table 12.5 Swept surfaces modeling techniques

Surface type	Description	Application	Illustration
One across/ one along	Translate or rotate an across contour while following the along contour.	Used for a surface in which cross sections remain constant along a driving profile.	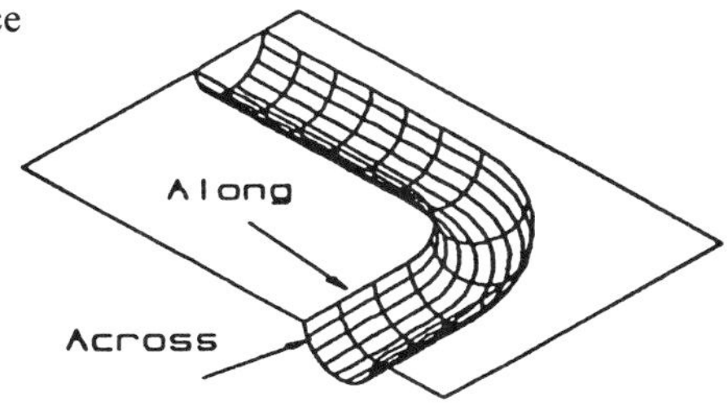
One across/ two along	Proportionally scale the across contour between the two along contours.	Used when cross sections are scaled along two driving profiles.	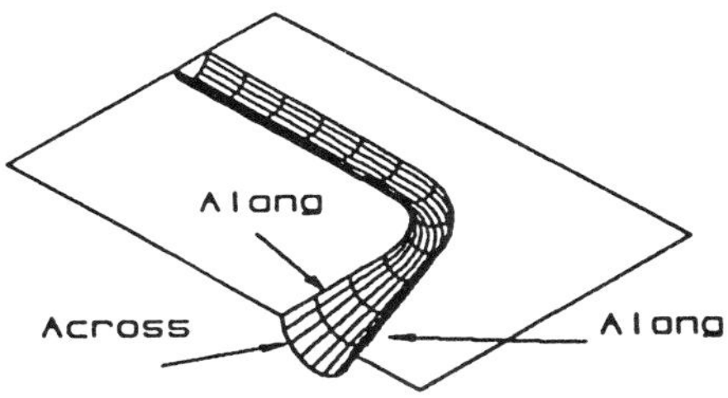
Two across/ one along	Perform a linear blend between the two across contours while following the along contour.	Used when two cross sections are linearly scaled along a driving profile.	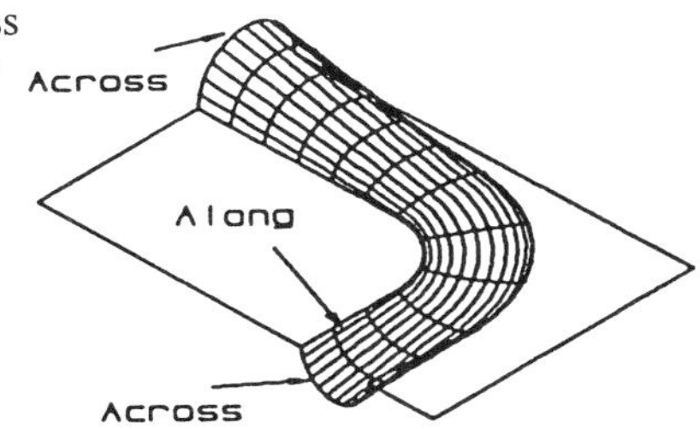

14 Project 14.

The swept surface modeling technique is used to create a surface model from the wireframe model of the cup given in project 8 of chapter 11. The advantage of modeling this cup with the swept method is that the entire
surface profile can be chained as one entity to be swept along an arc which in turn generates all surfaces but is regarded only as a single surface entity. The wireframe model and the surface model of this cup are shown in Figure 12.85.

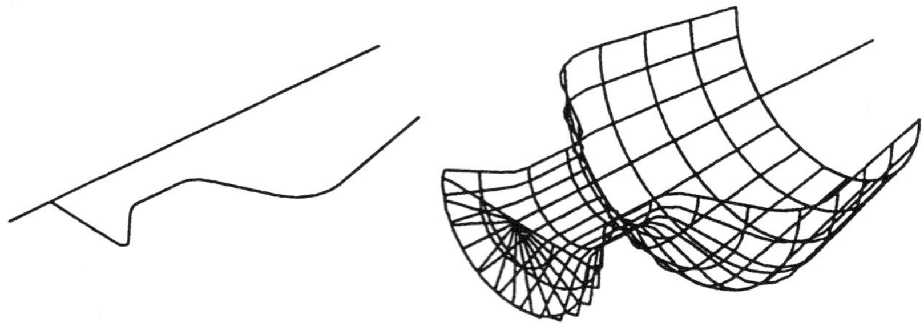

Figure 12.85

> **Tips** 1. A semi-circle has to be created in the Front Cplane to serve as the along contour in surface modeling.
> 2. Use one across/one along method using the edge profile of the cup as the across contour.

Step 1. Load the wireframe model file cup.

(or create one by following the instructions given in example 8 of chapter 11.
Select **MAIN MENU → File → Get**
Enter file name: **cup**
Select **Gview → Isometric**

The wireframe drawing appears on the screen as Figure 12.86.

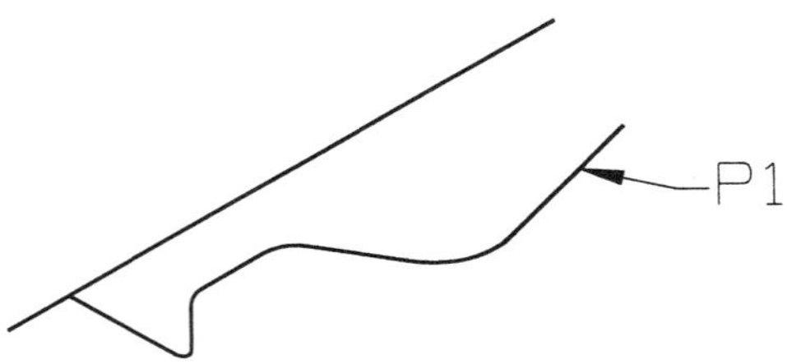

Figure 12.86

Step 2. Create an arc (semi-circle) using the Front Cplane.

Use the pick points in Figure 12.86 on the previous page.
Select **Cplane → Front**
Select **Z → Endpoint**,
then pick **1** to obtain the Z coordinate of the trapped endpoint

Z-3.5 should appear in the Secondary Menu

Select **MAIN MENU → Create → Arc → Polar → Center pt**
Enter the center point: **0,0** ←
Enter the radius: **1.062** ←
Enter the initial angle: **180** ←
Enter the final angle: **0** ←

The added arc should appear on the screen as Figure 12.87.

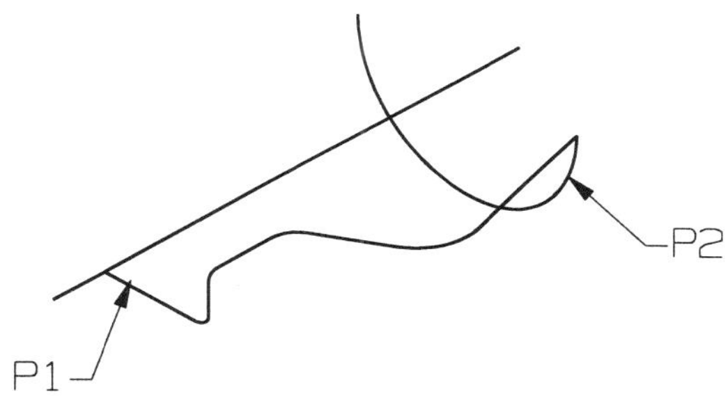

Figure 12.87

Step 3. Create a swept surface using the pick points in Figure 12.87 above.

Select **MAIN MENU → Create → Surface → Swept**
Enter the number of across contours: **1** ←
Define the across contour: select **Chain** from the Chaining method menu,
Then pick **P1** to define the across contour 1
Define the along contour 1: pick **P2**
Select **Done** to complete contours selection

Set the Swept surface parameters to the following settings:

Surface tolerance = **0.005** Surface type = **N (NURBS)** Rotate the across contour

Select **Do it** to compute the surface

15 Press Enter to display the surface model as shown here in Figure 12.88.

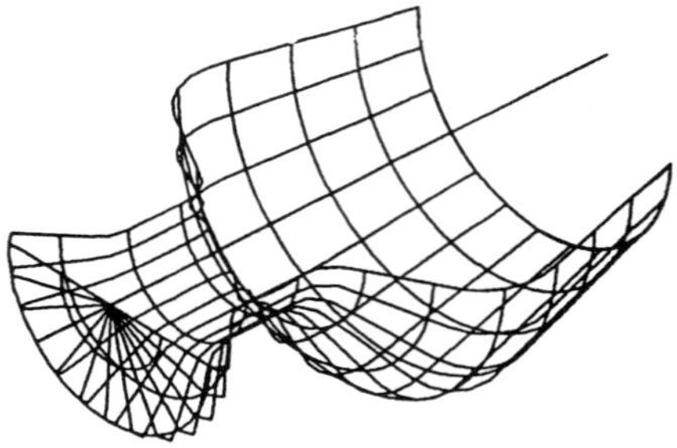

Figure 12.88

Step 4. Save the surface model swepts1.

Select **MAIN MENU → File → Save**
Enter file name: **swepts1**

Project 15.

The wireframe model of project 9 in chapter 11 is used to create a swept surface. **Two** across contours are given, a rectangle on the top and a circle in the bottom. The along contour consists of two slope lines and a fillet in between. The wireframe model and surface model are illustrated in Figure 12.89.

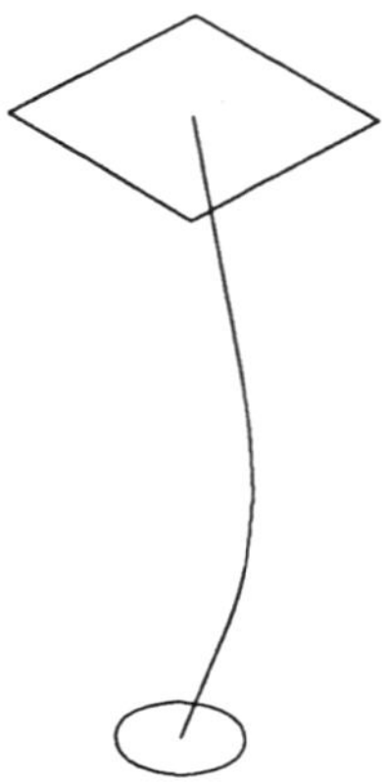

Figure 12.89a. Wireframe model

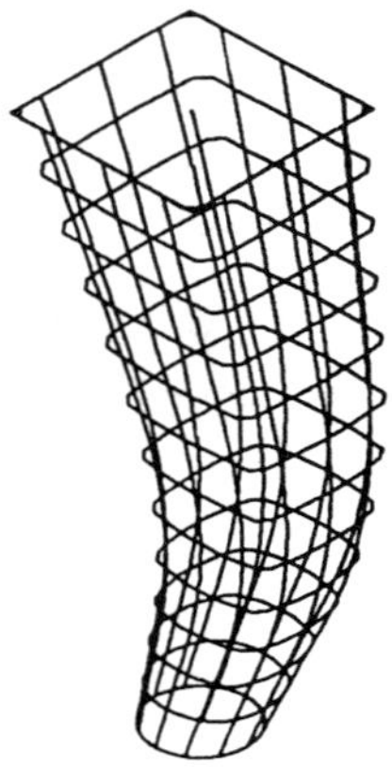

Figure 12.89b. Surface model

Tip The right vertical line of the rectangle must be broken into two pieces to obtain the orientation alignment of the two across contours. In other words, these two contours start at the same orientation to prevent the surface from twisting.

Step 1. Load the wireframe model file

(or create one following the instructions given in project 9 of chapter 11.)
Select **MAIN MENU → File → Get**
Enter file name: **swept2**

The wireframe model is shown in Figure 12.90.

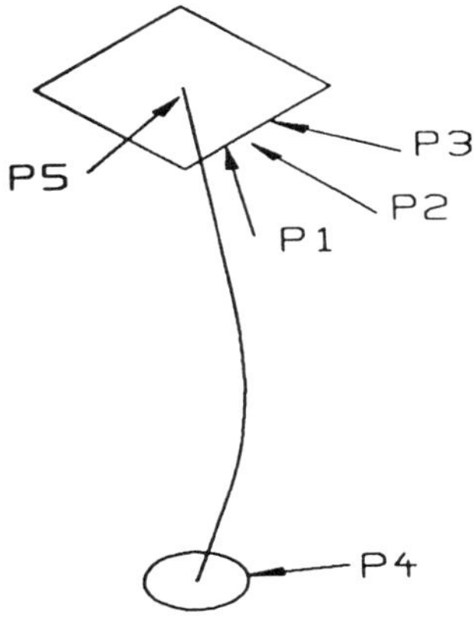

Figure 12.90

Step 2. Break the right vertical line of the rectangle into two segments using the pick points in Figure 12.90.

Select **MAIN MENU → Modify → Break → 2 pieces**
Select an entity: pick **P1**
Enter the breakpoint: select **Midpoint** from the Point Menu, and then pick **P2**

Step 3. Create the swept surface still use the pick points in Figure 12.90.

Select **MAIN MENU → Create → Surface → Swept**
Enter the number of across contours: **2** ←
Define across contour 1: select **Chain** from the Chaining method menu,
(Note: the **Chain Synchs** option must be in "**none**" mode by selecting **Syn →** "**none**")
Define across contour 2: select **Mode → Single** from the Chaining method menu,
then pick **P4**
Define the along contour: select **Chain** from the Chaining method menu,
then pick **P5**
Select **Done** to complete the contours selection
Set the Swept surface parameters to the following settings:

Surface tolerance = **0.005** Surface type = **N (NURBS)** Trans/Rot = **T** (Translate)

Select **Do it** to complete the surface

Press **Enter** to ignore the sharp corners.

16 The surface model should look like Figure 12.91.

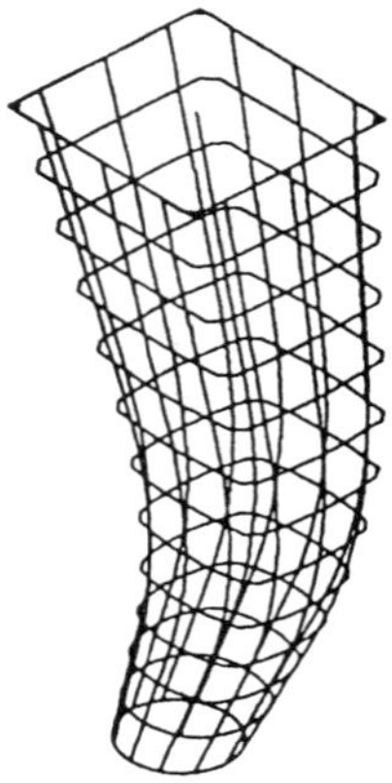

Figure 12.91

Step 4. Save the surface file as swepts2.

Select **MAIN MENU → File → Save**
Enter file name: **swepts2**

Project 16.

This example uses the wireframe model of project 10 in chapter 11 to create a swept surface. The model consists of two along contours and one across contour. The wireframe and surface model are given in Figure 12.92.

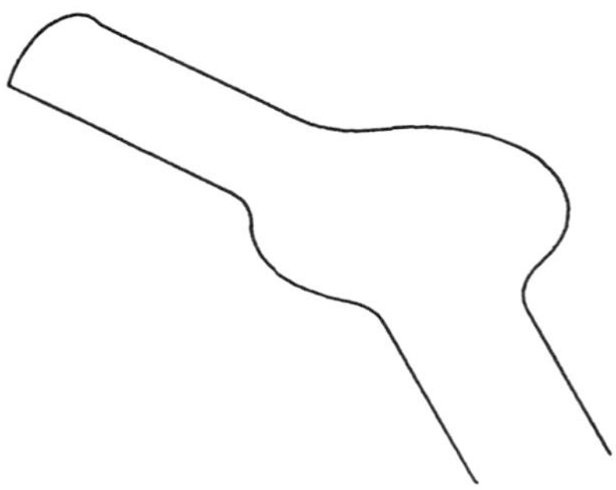

Figure 12.92a. Wireframe model

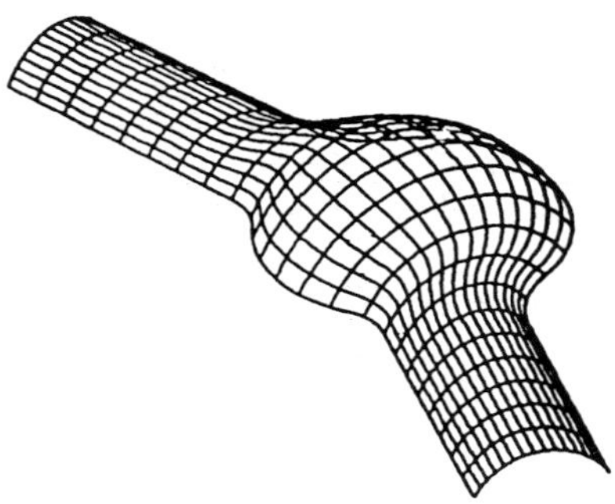

Figure 12.92b. Surface model

Step 1. Load the wireframe model file swept3.

(or create one by following the instructions of example in chapter 11.)
Select **MAIN MENU → File → Get**
Enter file name: **swept3**

The wireframe model drawing should appear as Figure 12.93.

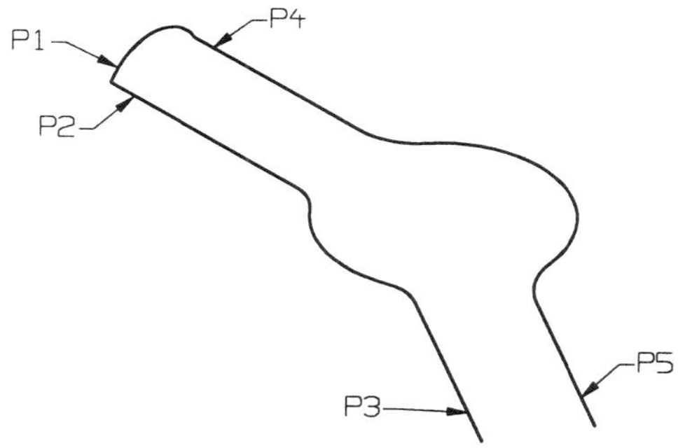

Figure 12.93

Step 2. Create a swept surface using the pick points in Figure 12.93.

Select **MAIN MENU → Create → Surface → Swept**
Enter the number of across contours: **1** ←
Define the across contour 1: select **Single** from the Chaining method menu, then pick **P1**

Define along contour 1: select **Mode → Chain → Partial**
Pick the first entity: **P2**
Pick the last entity: **P3**
Define along contour 2: select **Partial**
Pick the first entity: **P4**
Pick the last entity: **P5**
Select **Done**

Define the Swept surface parameters to the following settings:

Surface error tolerance = **0.002** Surface type = **N (NURBS)**

Select **Do it** from the parameters menu to complete the surface
Press **Enter**
The swept surface should resemble Figure 12.94.

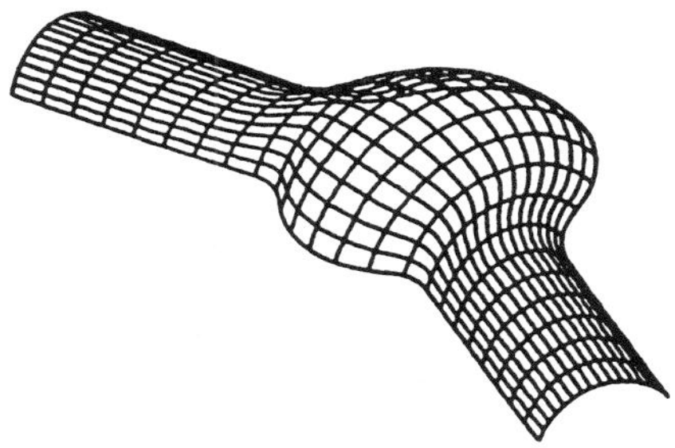

Figure 12.94

Step 3. Save the surface file as swepts3.

Select **MAIN MENU → File → Save**
Enter file name: **swepts3**

12.11 Exercises

1. What is a surface?
2. What is a composite surface model?
3. What are the four mathematical methods of modeling surfaces?
4. How is a Coons surface defined? Explain the strengths and weaknesses of a Coons surface.
5. Describe the strengths and weaknesses of Bezier surfaces.
6. Explain the strengths and weaknesses of B-spline surfaces.
7. What is NURBS surface?
8. Describe the major difference between the B-spline surface and NURBS surface.
9. List the three types of surfaces.
10. What are the two surface modeling techniques Mastercam provides to create geometrical surfaces?
11. What are free-form surfaces?
12. What are the two kinds of free-form surfaces? Describe their differences.
13. What are the four types of free-form surfaces that Mastercam provides?
14. What are derived surfaces?
15. List the three types of derived surfaces in Mastercam.
16. What are the three surfacing mathematics Mastercam uses to generate free-form and derived surfaces?
17. Use the wireframe model created in problem 11.10 to generate two ruled surfaces. The wireframe profile and the finished ruled surfaces are shown in Figure 12.95. The wireframe file is **E1**. Save the surface model file as **ES1**. Project 1 in this chapter is a similar example.

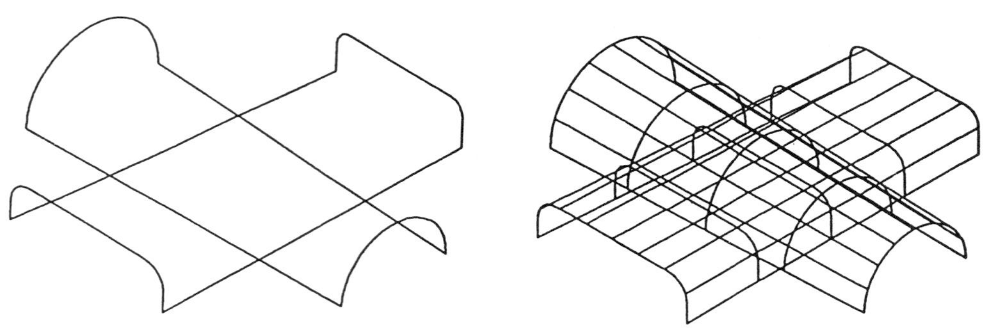

Figure 12.95

18. Use the wireframe model created in problem 11.11 to generate two ruled surfaces which intersect at an angle of 45°. The wireframe profile and the finished ruled surfaces look like Figure 12.96. The wireframe file is **E2**. Save the surface model file as **ES2**. A similar example is project 2 of this chapter.

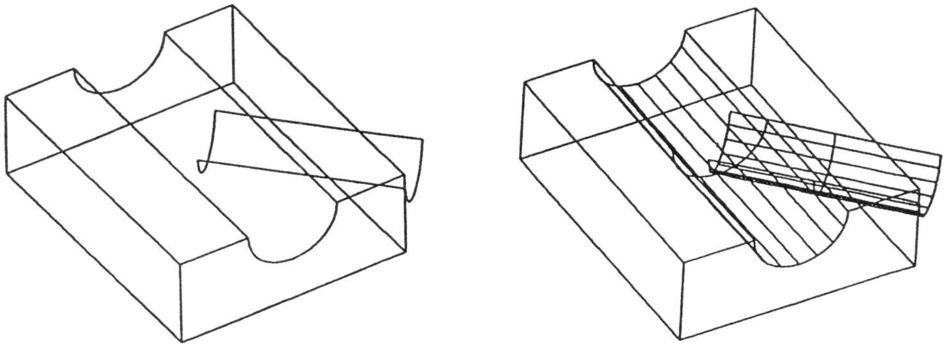

Figure 12.96

19. The three contours in problem 11.12 are used to create a ruled surface. The wireframe and finished surface model are shown in Figure 12.97. The wireframe model file is **E3**. Save the surface model file as **ES3**. A similar example in this chapter is project 3.

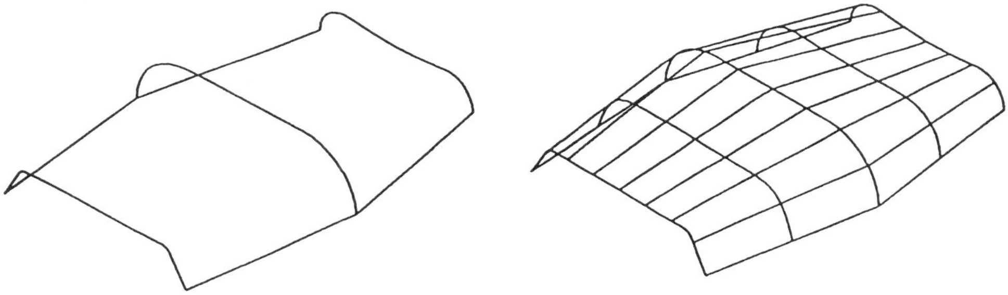

Figure 12.97

20. Use the three contours in problem 11.12 to create a loft surface. The wireframe and finished loft surface model resemble Figure 12.98. The wireframe model file is **E3**. Save the surface model file as **ES4**. A similar example is project 4 of this chapter.

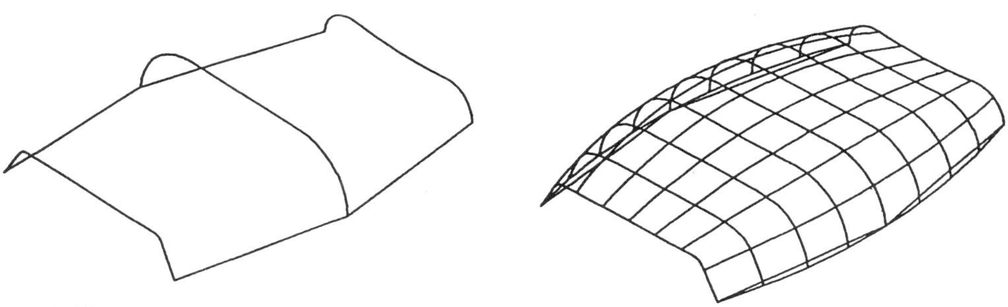

Figure 12.98

21. Use the four arcs in problem 11.13 to create a single-patch Coons surface. Both wireframe and surface models are illustrated in Figure 12.99. The wireframe model file is **E4**. Save the surface model file as **ES5**. A similar example is project 7 of this chapter.

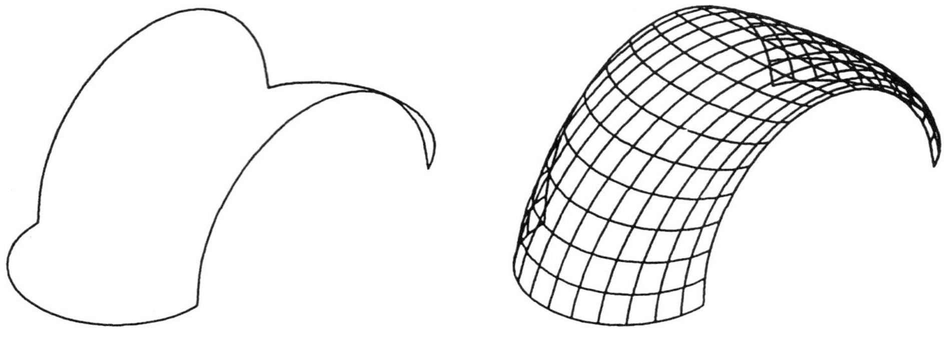

Figure 12.99

22. Create a single-patch Coons surface from the wireframe model of problem 11.14. The wireframe model file is **E5**. Save the surface model file as **ES6**. Both wireframe and surface models are given in Figure 12.100. A similar example is project 7 in this chapter.

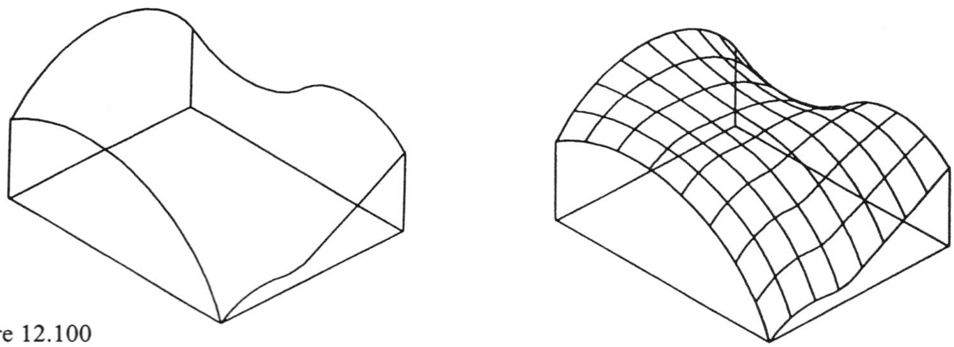

Figure 12.100

23. Use the wireframe model in problem 11.15 to create a multi-patch Coons surface. The wireframe model file is **E6**. Figure 12.101 shows both wireframe model and finished surface model. Save the surface model file as **ES7**. A similar example is project 9 of this chapter.

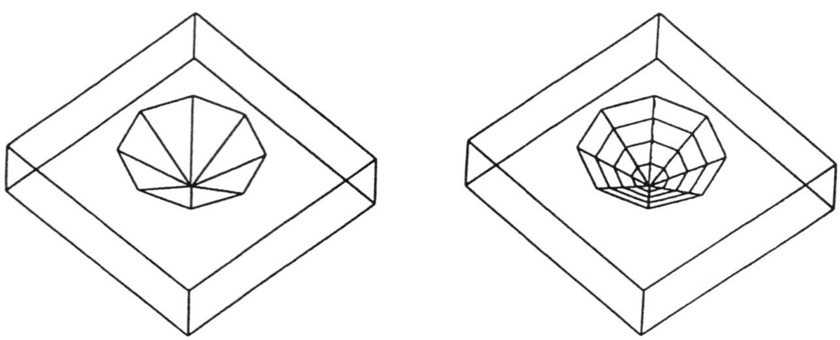

Figure 12.101

24. Use the multi-faced wireframe model given in problem 11.16 to generate a Coons surface of multiple patches. The wireframe model file is **E7**. Save the surface model file as **ES8**. A similar example is project 10 in this chapter. Both wireframe and surface models should look like Figure 12.102.

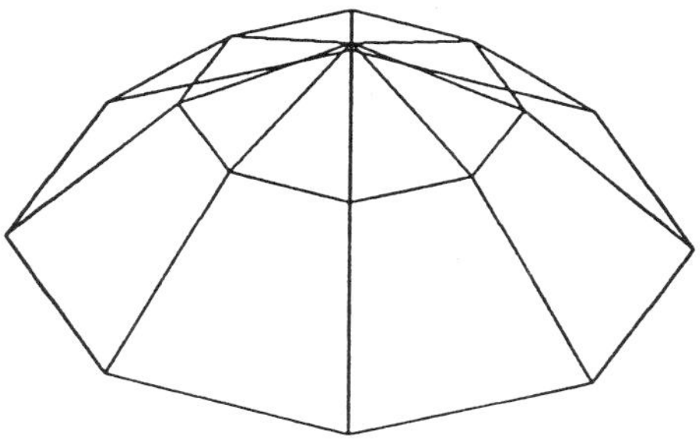

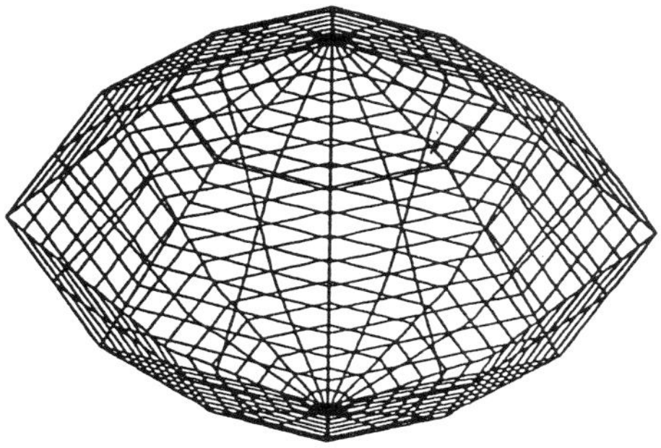

Figure 12.102

25. Use the revolved surfacing technique to creat a surface model from the wireframe model in problem 11.17. The wireframe model file is **E8**. Save the surface model file as **ES9**. Both models are illustrated in Figure 12.103. A similar example is project 11 of this chapter.

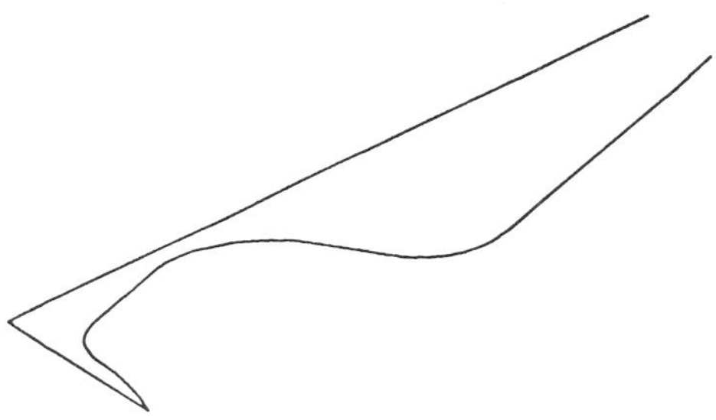

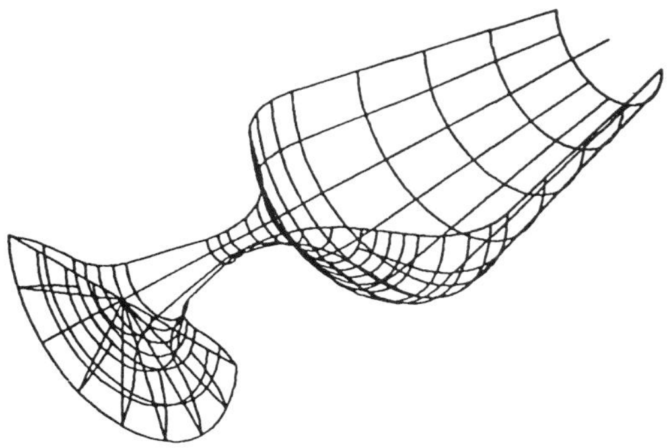

Figure 12.103

26. Use the revolved surfacing technique to create a surface model of a cup from the wireframe profiles in problem 11.18. The wireframe model file is **E9**. Save the surface model file as **ES10**. The wireframe and finished surface models are shown in Figure 12.104. A similar example is project 11 in this chapter.

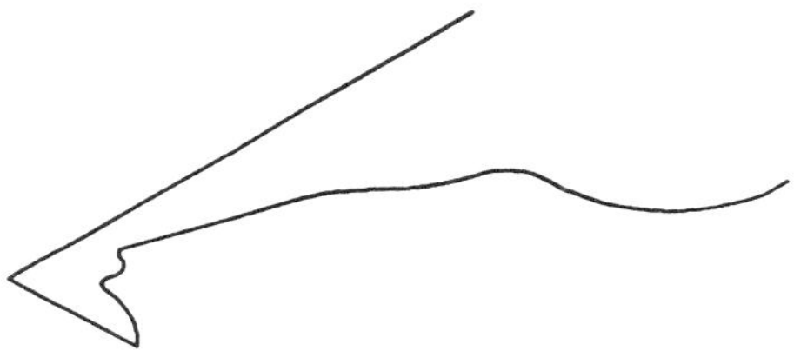

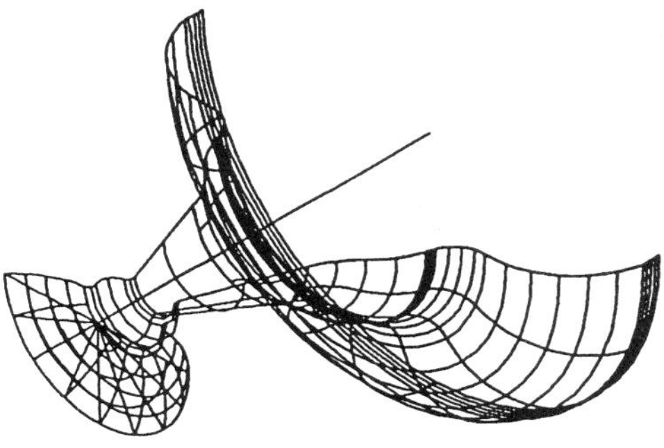

Figure 12.104

27. The wireframe model of a fly disk given in problem 11.19 is used to create a surface model by using the swept surfacing technique. The wireframe model file is **E10**. Both wireframe and surface models in front view are illustrated in Figure 12.105. Save the surface model file as **ES11**. A similar example is project 11 of this chapter.

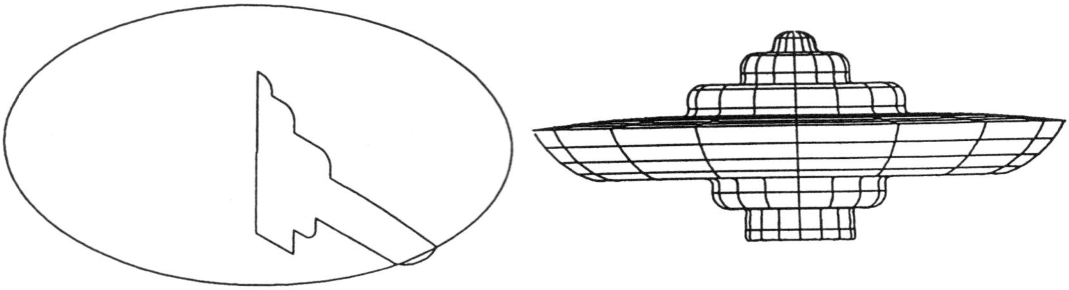

Figure 12.105

28. Create a draft surface using an 8" x 6" rectangle with a 1" fillet at four corners as the base profile. The draft length is -2" and the draft angle is 15° in the outward direction. The base profile and finished draft surfaces should resemble Figure 12.106.

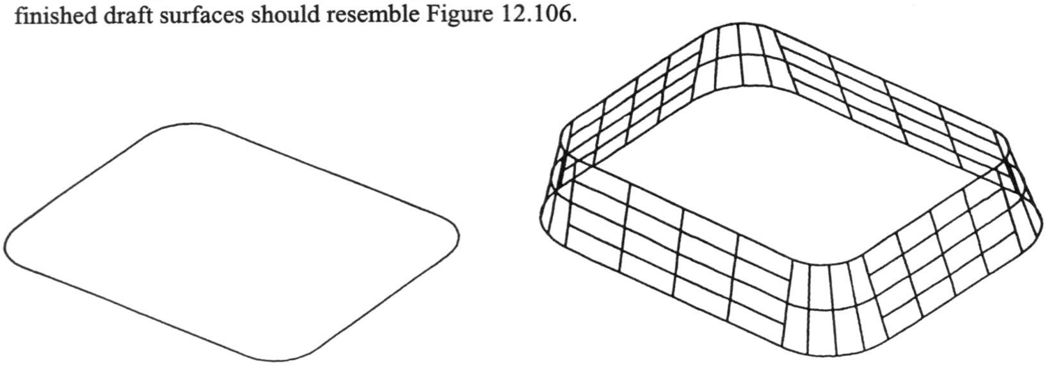

Figure 12.106

29. Create a draft surface from a spline which is defined by the the set of points given below. The draft length is 1.5" and the draft angle is 20° in the outward direction. The base spline and the finished draft surfaces are shown in Figure 12.107.

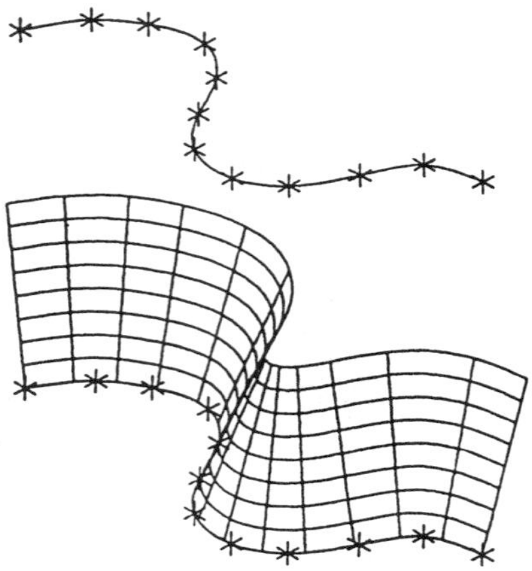

Figure 12.107

X	Y	Z
0.0	0.0	0.0
0.3	0.5	0.0
0.67	0.77	0.0
1.18	0.89	0.0
1.59	0.61	0.0
1.85	0.14	0.0
2.18	-0.24	0.0
2.69	-0.32	0.0
3.08	-0.08	0.0
3.36	0.42	0.0
3.62	0.89	0.0
4.11	1.05	0.0

Chapter 13
Surface Modeling II: Derived & Composite Surfaces

Objectives:

1. Use Mastercam to create derived surfaces from existing surfaces.
2. Create composite surface models.

Overview

Six basic surface modeling techniques and examples have been presented in chapter 12. In this chapter, four derived surfacing techniques are covered, followed by five composite surface modeling examples. Each of these five composite surface examples consists of several surfaces that are modeled by more than one surface modeling technique. They are arranged in increasing order of difficulty. Useful tips that lead to successful completion of the surface model are given in each example.

13.1 Derived surfaces Modeling

Derived surfaces are those surfaces that are generated from existing surfaces. They are used to modify or edit the existing surfaces, and because of this, they are also called **edited surfaces**. Mastercam provides **four derived surface modeling techniques**: fillet surface modeling, trimmed surface modeling, offset surface modeling, and blend surface modeling.

Fillet Surfaces Modeling

A fillet surface is created between two existing surfaces. Fillet surfaces are mainly used in two situations:

(1) adding a smooth fillet between two intersecting surface (Figure 13.1); and
(2) adding a fillet at the end of object (Figure 13.2).

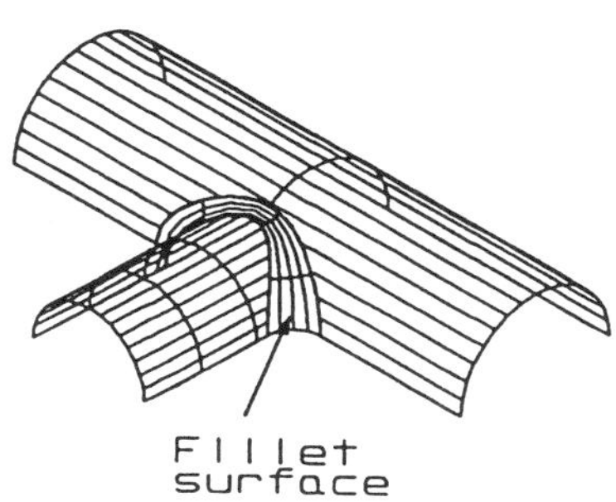

Figure 13.1

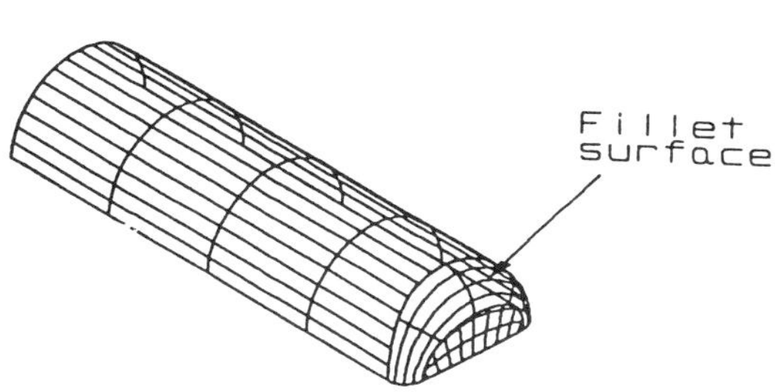

Figure 13.2

Fillet Surface Creating Methods

A fillet surface can be created between a surface and an element of one of three element types; plane, curve and surface. Table 13.1 summarizes the three methods of creating fillet surfaces.

Table 13.1 Fillet surface creating methods

Fillet Surface Method	Description	Illustration
Plane/Surf	Create a fillet surface between a plane and a surface.	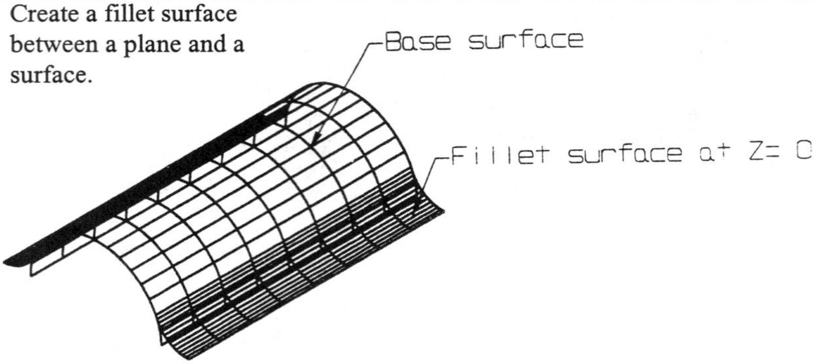
Curve/Surf	Create a fillet surface between a curve and a surface.	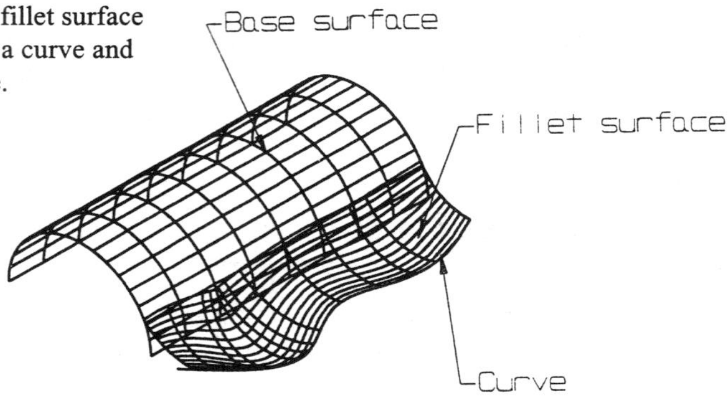
Surf/Surf	Create a fillet surface between two or more surfaces.	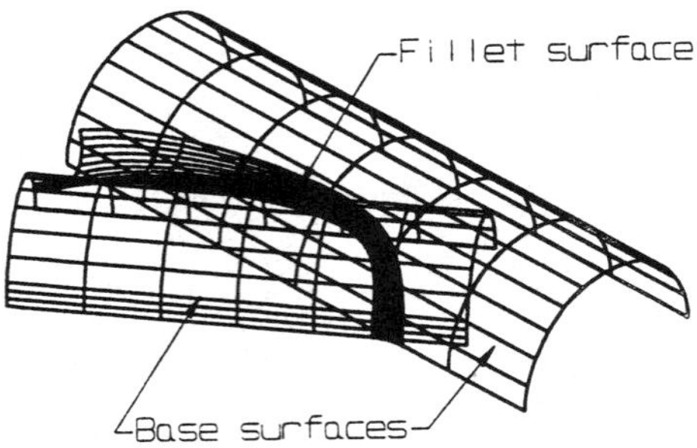

Filleting parameters

The parameters used to define the fillet surfaces are placed in the options dialog box. The option dialog boxes for these three fillet surface creating methods are shown below. The main parameters in option dialog boxes are:

Step method	Entities to be created
Fillet surface type	Join results
Find multiples	Trim surface

Plane-surface option

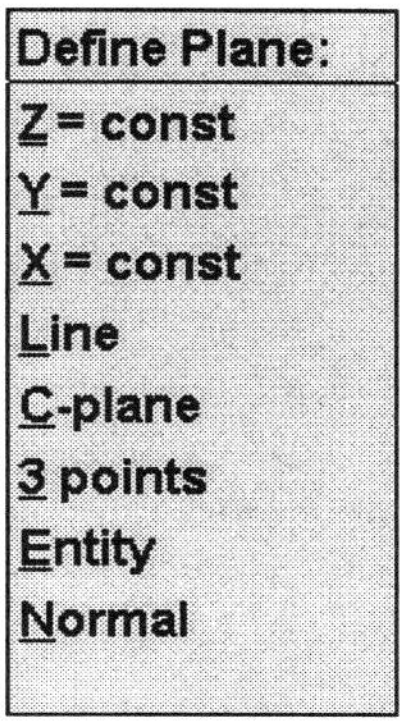

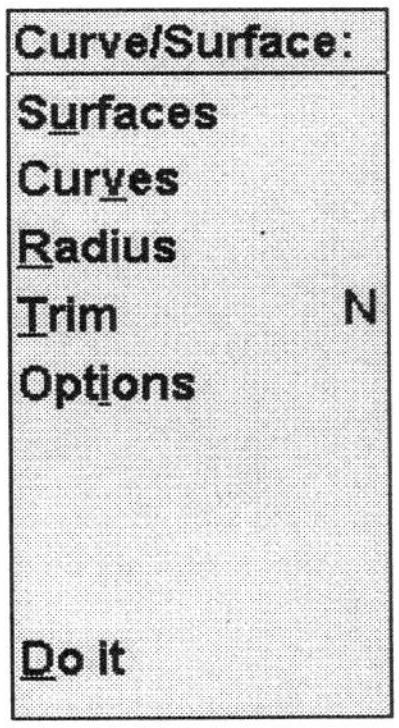

Curve-surface option

Surface-surface option

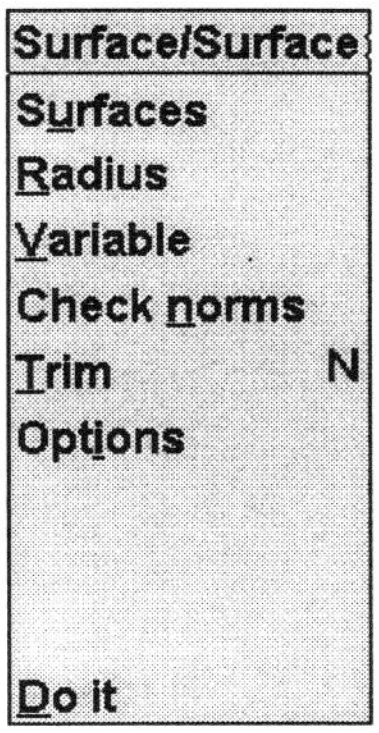

Step method

The stepping distance of the surface can be determined by two stepping methods: chord-height and fixed step. When using the chord deviation method, the given value of the stepping chord height is used to define the fillet surface. The fixed step method uses a constant stepping distance to define the fillet surface. Use fixed step method when the surface has relatively large curvature radii, has no sharp shapes, or does not require a close dimensional accuracy. Use chord-height method for those surfaces that have small curvature radii, have sharp shapes, or require a close dimensional tolerance. This method can accurately define the surface within the specified dimensional accuracy. Use smaller values for stepping parameters to tighten the accuracy of the surface. However, this will take the computer a longer amount of time to process the surface and will make the surface file bigger.

Entities to be generated

While creating a fillet surface, the system can generate the following four types of information. You can select to create any combination of the above four entity types during creating a fillet surface.

Fillet surface:	generating a fillet surface (NURBS, curve-generated, or parametric type) (Figure 13.3).
Rails:	generating two curve rails along the edges of the fillet surface (Figure 13.4).
Center:	generating a center curve of the fillet surface (Figure 13.5).
Surface curve:	generating a curve along the intersection between the existing surface and fillet surface (Figure 13.6).

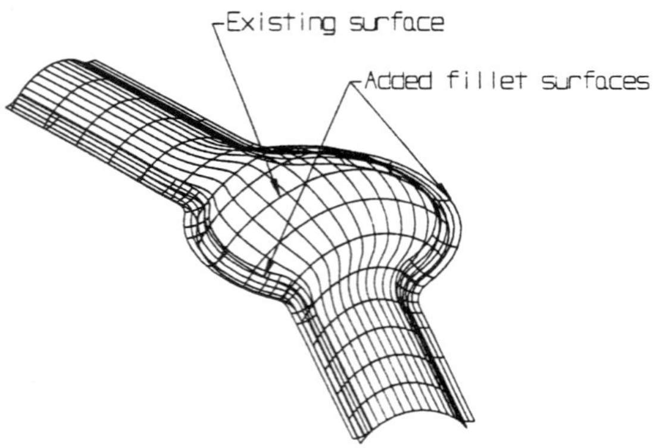

Figure 13.3

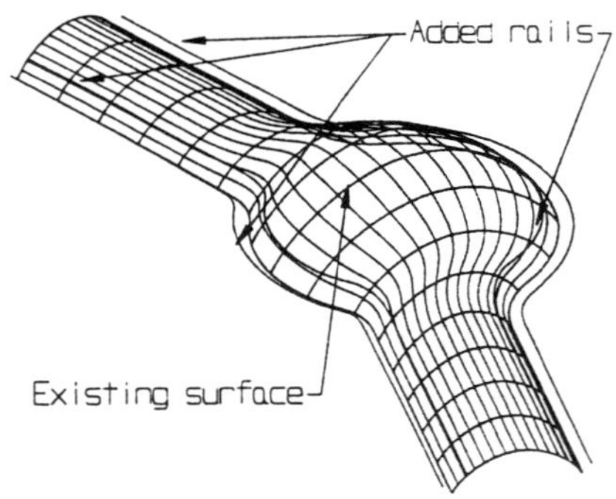

Figure 13.4

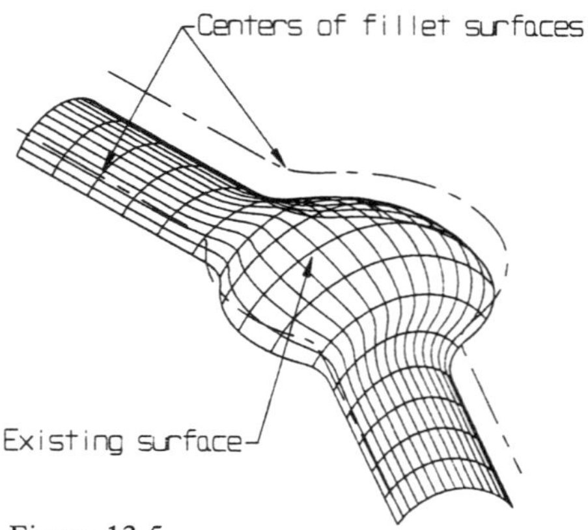

Figure 13.5

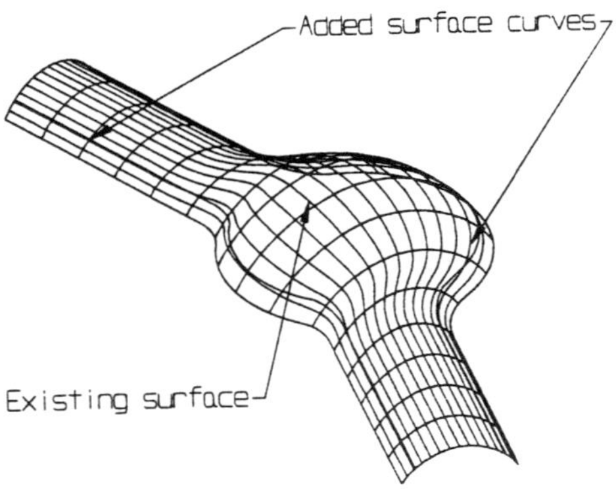

Figure 13.6

Fillet surface type

The three surface types you can select for fillet surfaces are:

Curve-generated	NURBS	Parametric

Join results

This parameter is used to join the resultant surfaces. Toggle this parameter to ON (with a check mark), the "Join tol" parameter will become active for specifying the join tolerance.

Find multiples

It is possible to generate more than one fillet surface in one operation. Mastercam uses "Find multiples" parameter to indicate whether more than one fillet surface is to be generated if possible. Toggle this parameter to ON (with a check mark), the system will generate multiple fillet surfaces (Figure 13.7).

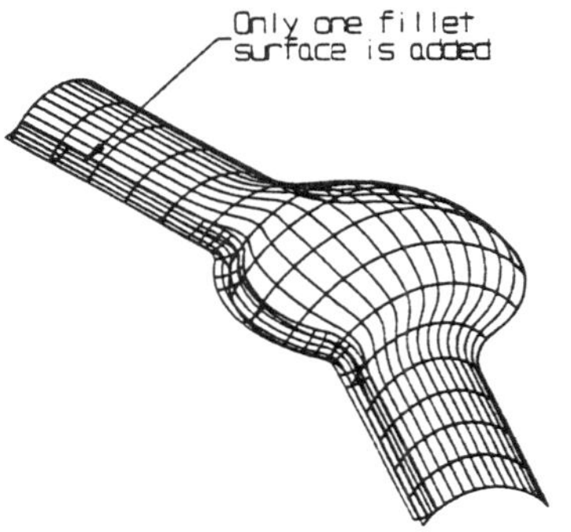

Figure 13.7a a. Find multiples = OFF

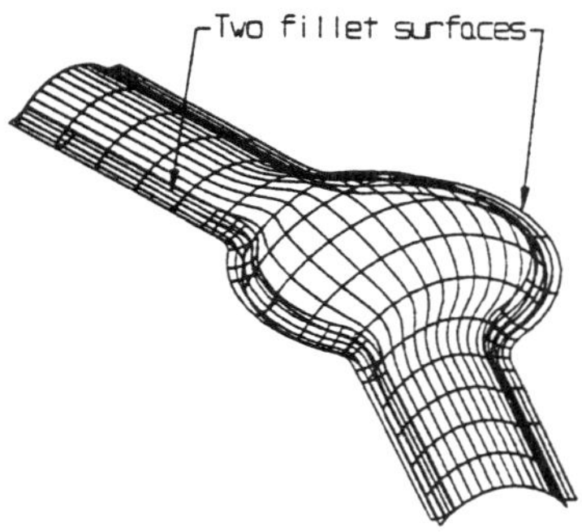

Figure 13.7b b. Find multiples = ON

Trim surface

Trim surface parameters appear somewhat different in three fillet surface creating methods. **Surface-surface** is the most commonly used method and its dialog menu is show below.

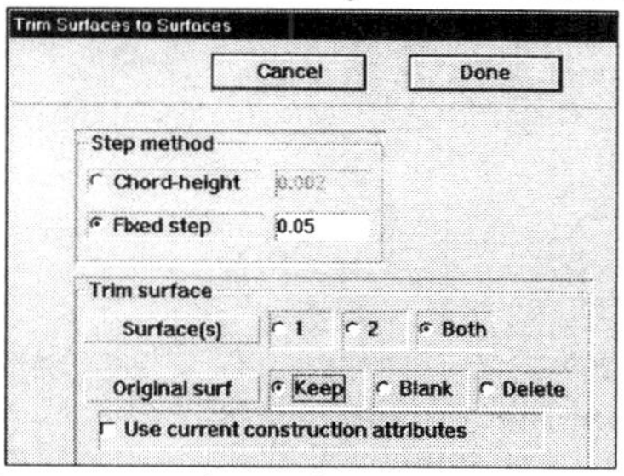

The "Yes" parameter is used to indicate whether the original surfaces are to be trimmed. Toggle this parameter to OFF (no check mark), no surface trimming will be implemented. Toggle this parameter to ON (with a check mark) to cause the original surfaces to be trimmed in the specified manner. There are two sets of surfaces can be created from the fillet surfaces creating process: fillet surfaces and trimmed surfaces of the original surfaces. The original surfaces that are used to create fillet surfaces can be kept or deleted from the model. It is somewhat confusing between "Surfaces" and "Original surfaces". The "Surfaces" are those surfaces created between the fillet surfaces and original surfaces. They are the surfaces created by trimming the original surfaces to the fillet surface boundaries. These surfaces are different from the original surfaces. Original surfaces can be handled in one of the following three ways:

keep the original surfaces after creating fillet surfaces and trimmed surfaces.

Blank: remove the original surfaces after creating fillet surfaces and trimmed surfaces.

Delete: delete the original surfaces after creating fillet surfaces and trimmed surfaces.

Mastercam has the following three options to select the surface trimming mode:

Mastercam has the following three options to select the surface trimming mode:

1:	trim only the first set of surfaces (Figure 13.8).
2:	trim only the second set of surfaces (Figure 13.9).
Both:	trim both sets of surfaces (Figure 13.10).

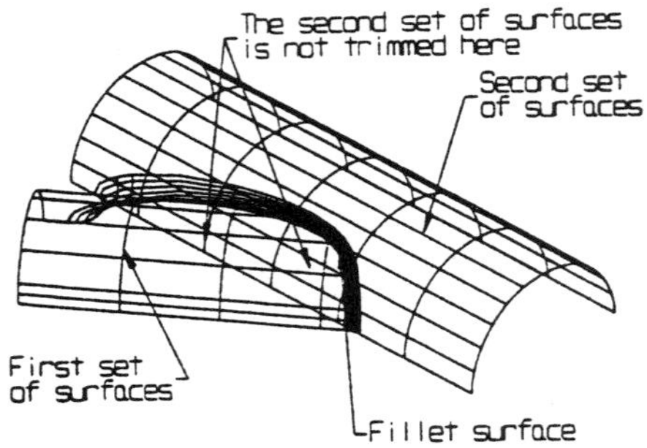

Figure 13.8

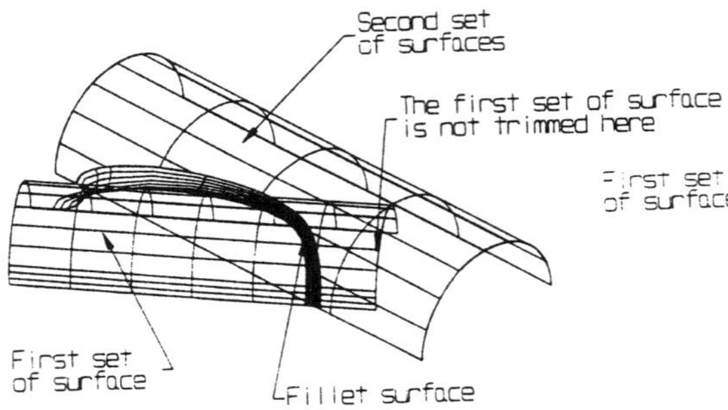

Figure 13.9

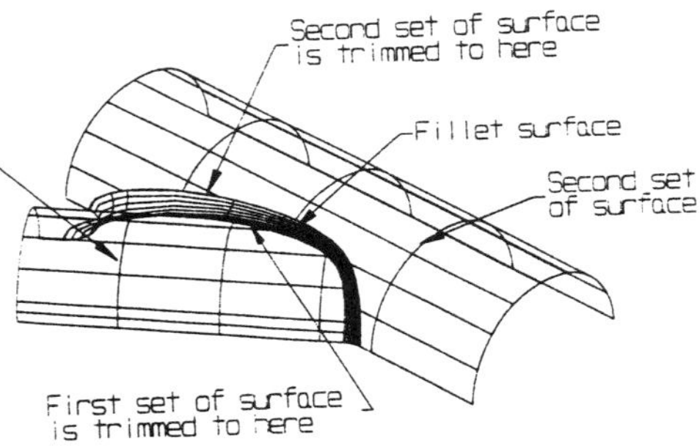

Figure 13.10

Variable Radius

There are two types of fillet surfaces: fillet surfaces with a constant radius and fillet surfaces with a variable radius. The fillet radius remains constant throughout the surface intersecting boundary for the constant radius type (Figure 13.11). The fillet radius varies along the center curve of the fillet surface in creating a fillet surface with a variable radius (Figure 13.12).

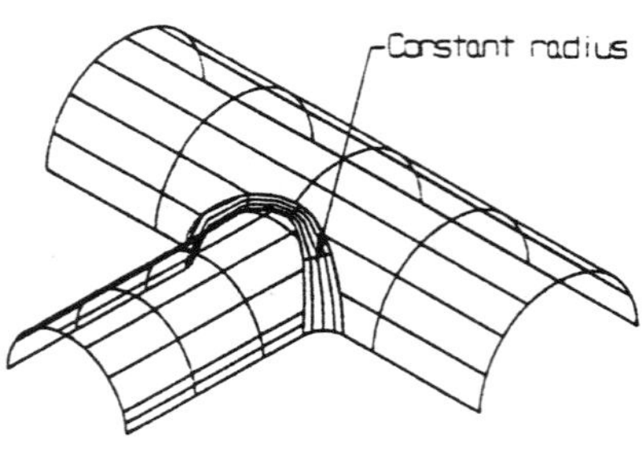

Figure 13.11a

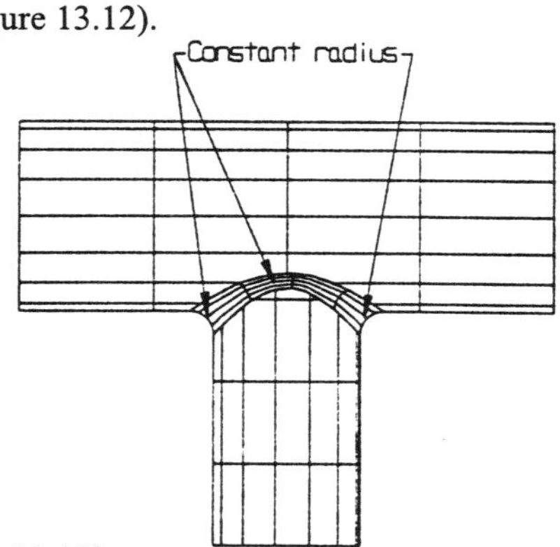

Figure 13.11b

Mastercam Version 7,
Scholar's International Publishing Corp., 1998

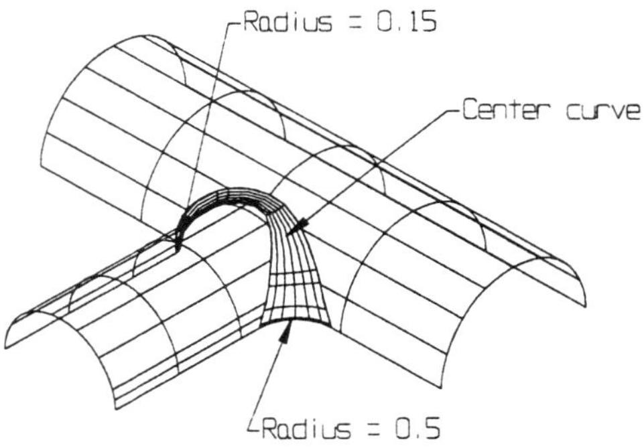

Figure 13.12a

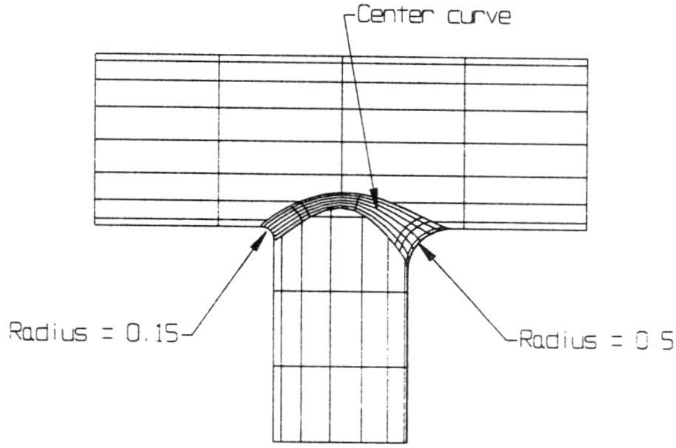

Figure 13.12b

Mastercam uses a set of control points along the center curve of the fillet surface to change the radius value of fillet curves. These control points are referred to as the radius markers in Mastercam. Each center curve of the fillet surface has two default radius markers that are located at both ends of the curve (Figure 13.13).

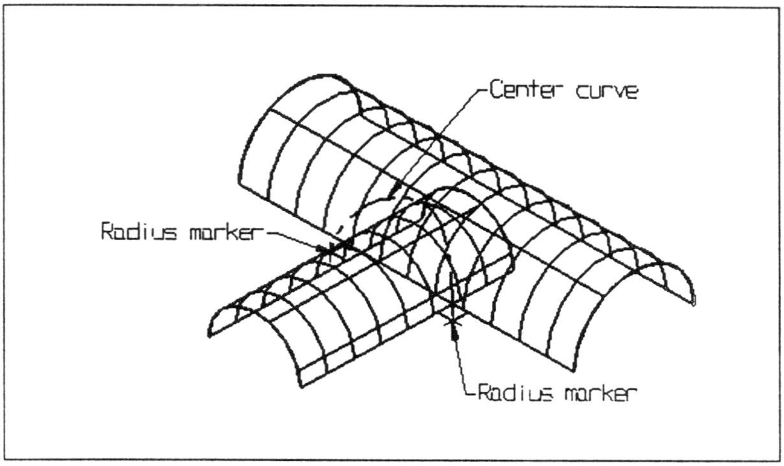

Figure 13.13

You can add more radius markers to the center curve for specifying a radius value for each radius marker. The two ways to add radius markers to the center curve are:

Insert dyn:	dynamically slide the arrow to desired location as a radius marker.
Insert mid:	add a radius marker to the midpoint between two selected radius markers.

Insert dyn mode

The procedure for inserting radius markers to the center curve is (Figures 13.14 – 13.16):

- Pick two filleting surfaces
- Enter the radius: 0.25
- Select Variable from the menu
- Select Insert dyn from the menu
- Pick a center curve
- Slide arrow to desired location and click as a radius marker
- Enter the radius: 0.5
- A new radius marker is added to the model

Repeat the above process to define as many radius markers as needed
Select **Done - Do it** to complete the fillet surface
The fillet surface with a variable radius is added as in Figure 13.16.

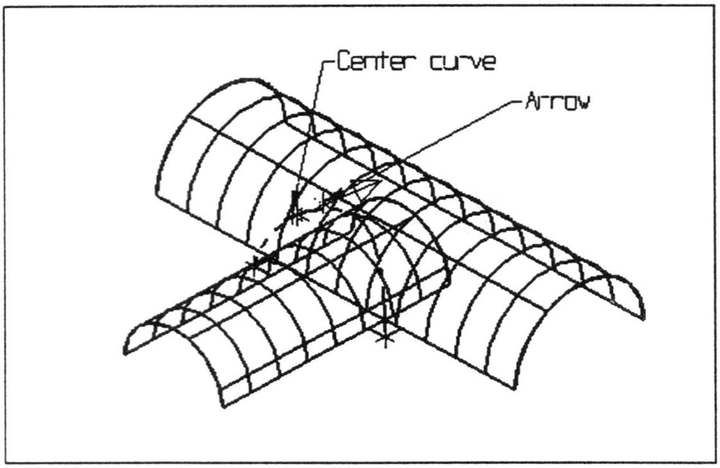

Figure 13.14

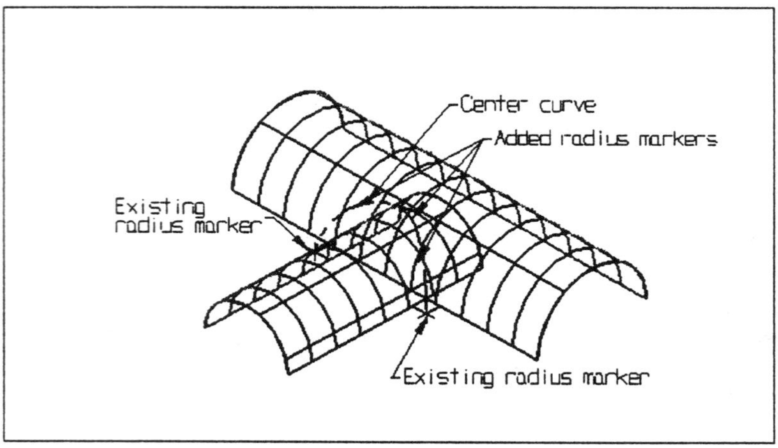

Figure 13.15

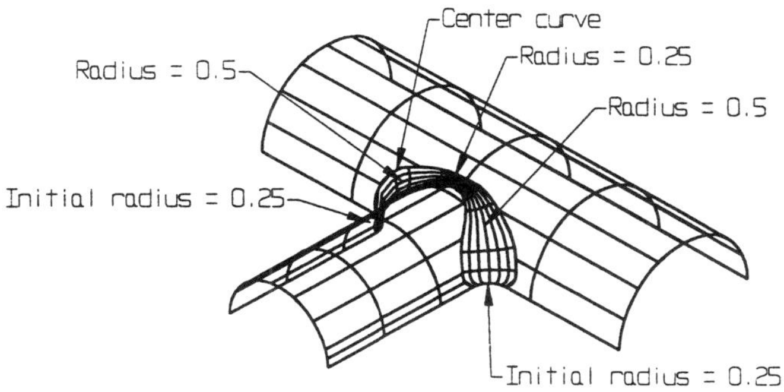

Figure 13.16

Insert mid mode

This mode adds a radius marker to the center curve at the midpoint between two selected radius markers. The second picked radius marker is referred to as "neighboring radius marker". This is a useful way to add a radius marker exactly at the midpoint of the center curve.

The procedure of adding a radius marker to the center curve is (Figures 13.17 – 13.18):

- Pick two filleting surfaces
- Enter the radius = 0.15
- Select Variable from the menu list
- Select Insert Mid from the menu
- Select a radius marker: pick the right end of center curve (Figure 13.17)
- Select a neighboring radius marker: pick the left end of center curve
- Enter the radius: 1
- Select Done
- Select Do it

The fillet surface is added to the model as in Figure 13.18.

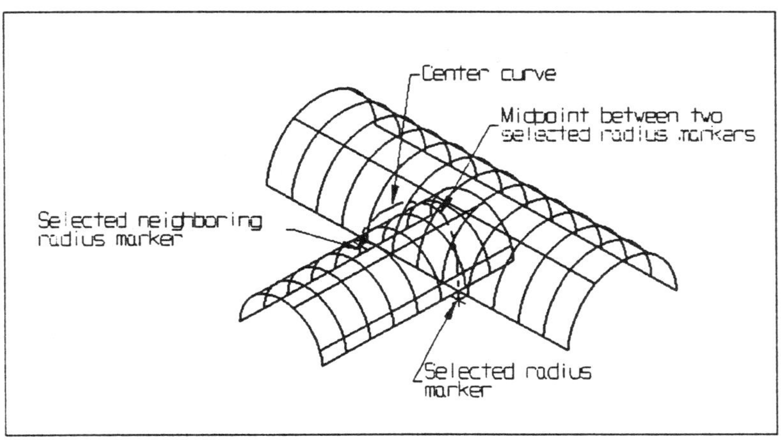

Figure 13.17

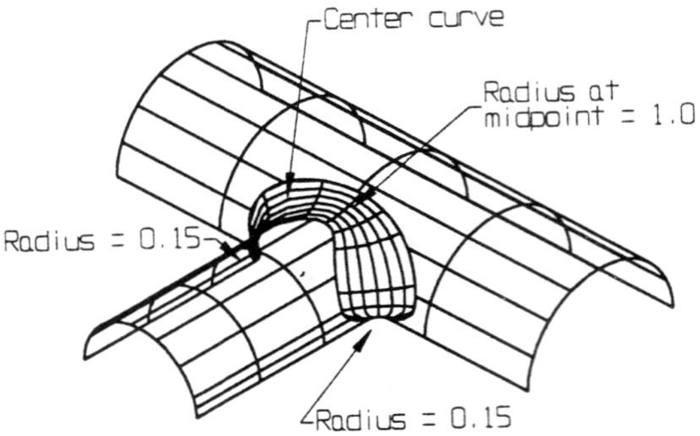

Figure 13.18

Modifying radius value at radius markers

Mastercam uses Modify command to change the fillet radius value at radius markers. Figure 13.19 shows an example of modifying the fillet radius at a radius marker. The original radius at two existing radius markers is 0.15. The radius marker at the left end of the center curve is changed to 0.5.

The procedure is:

- Select Modify from the list
- Select a radius marker: pick the radius marker at the left end
- Enter the radius = 0.5
- Select Done - Do it to complete the fillet surface

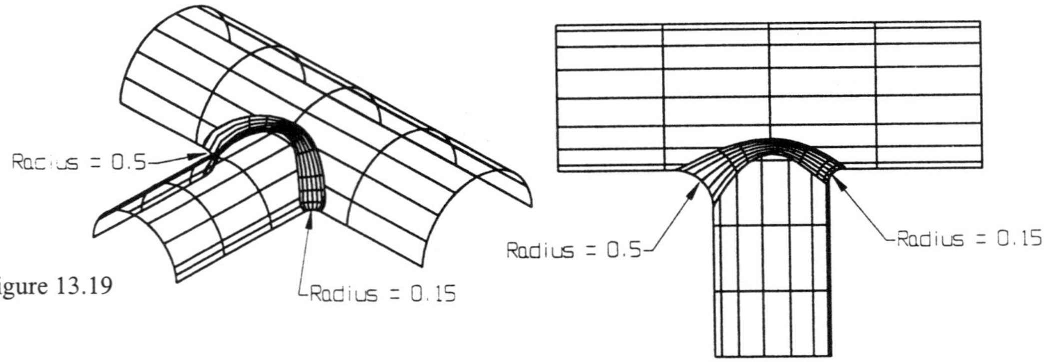

Figure 13.19

Creating a fillet surface between a plane and a surface

Mastercam allows to creating a fillet surface between an existing surface and a plane (Figure 13.20). The plane used to creating the fillet surface can be defined by one of eight methods. These eight plane defining methods are described in Table 13.2.

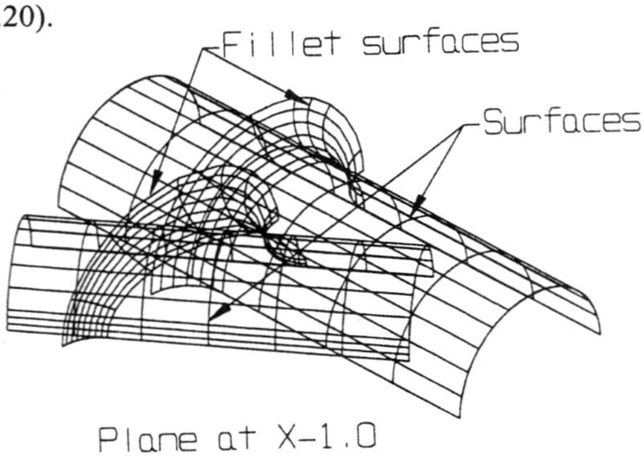

Figure 13.20

Table 13.2 Plane defining methods

Method	Description	Illustration
Z = const	A plane is defined as being parallel to the XY-plane and intersects Z axis at a given distance.	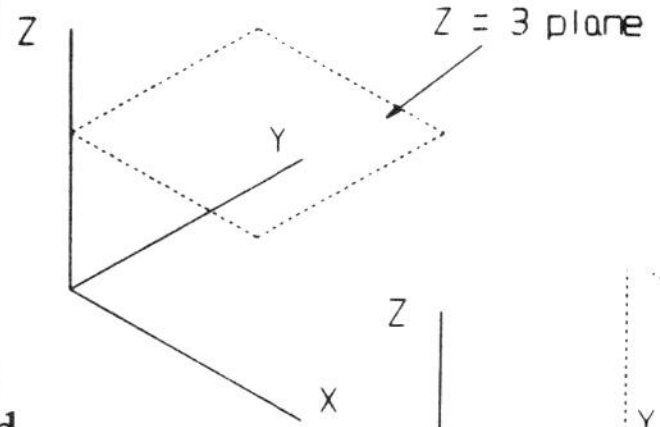
Y = const	A plane is defined as being parallel to the XZ-plane and intersects the Y axis at a given distance.	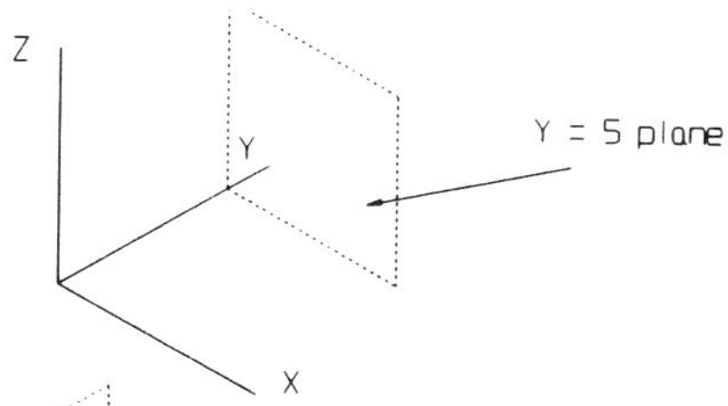
X = const	A plane is defined as being parallel to YZ-plane and intersects the X axis at a given distance.	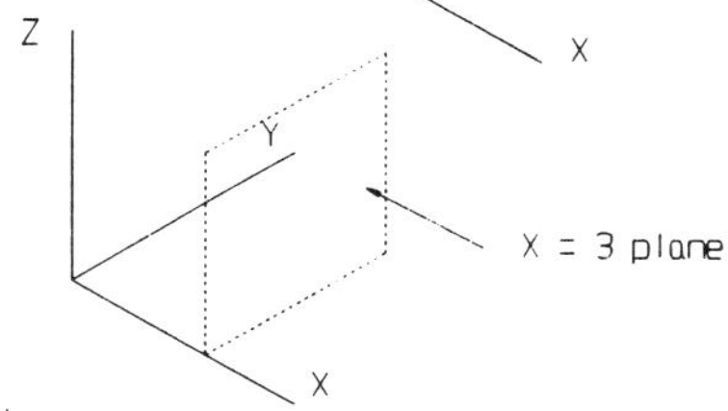
Line	A plane is defined as being co-planar with a line and perpendicular to the current Cplane.	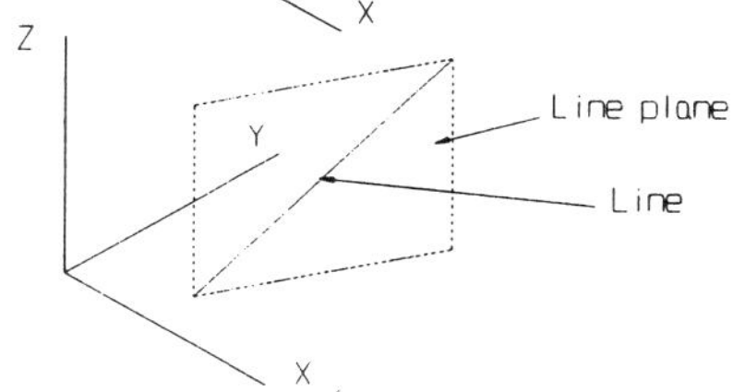
C-plane	A plane is defined as being parallel to the C-plane and intersects at a given Z-depth.	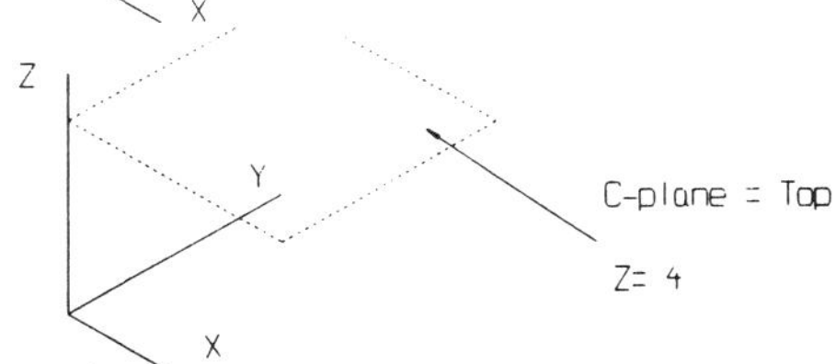
3-point	A plane is defined by three given non-collinear points.	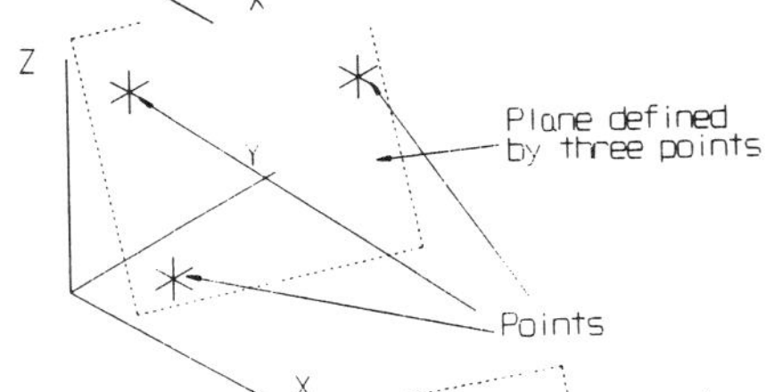
Entity	A plane is defined by: (1) an arc (2) a 2-D spline (3) two non-parallel lines (4) three non-collinear points	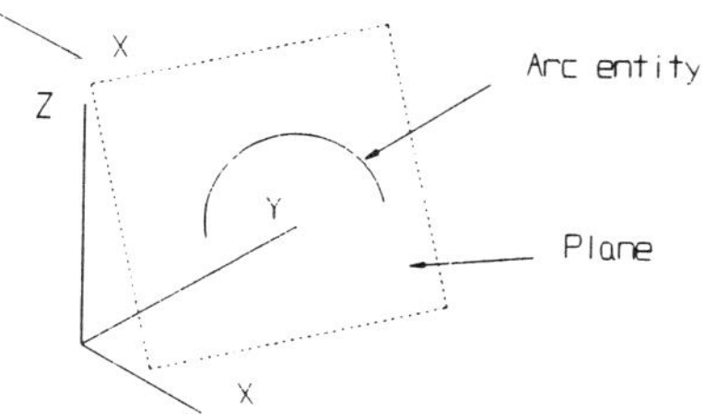
Normal	A plane is defined by being normal (perpendicular) to a given line.	

The option parameters dialog box for plane-surface method is shown here.

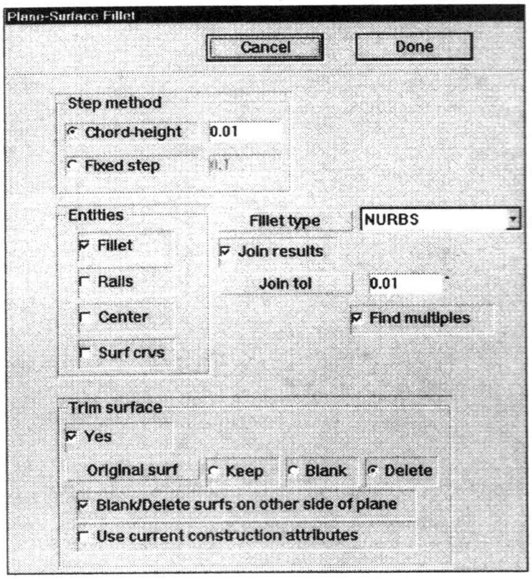

Procedure of creating a fillet surface between a plane and a surface (Figure 13.21):

- Select Create → Surface → Fillet → Plane/surf
- Pick a surface, then select Done
- Enter the radius: 0.25
- Select Plane: Select X = const
- Enter y-coordinate of plane: 0.0
- Side of Plane: select OK
- Select Do it

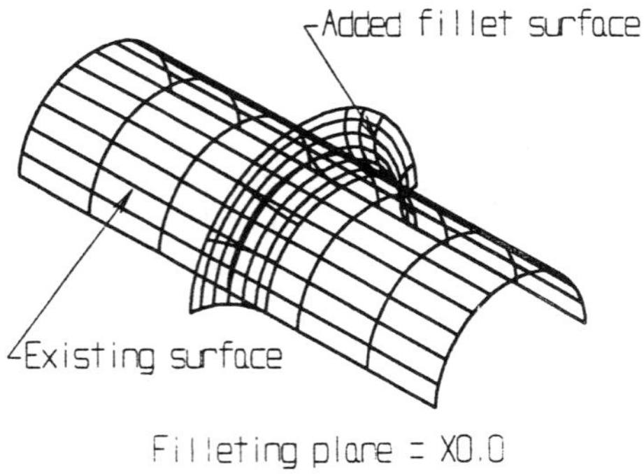

Figure 13.21

Creating a fillet surface between a curve and a surface

A fillet surface can be added between a curve and a surface (Figure 13.22). The fillet radius must be greater than the longest distance between the curve and the surface. Otherwise, it will produce partial fillet surfaces as shown in Figure 13.23. When the curve is selected, a direction arrow shall appear as in Figure 13.24. The system will prompt to select "Left" or "Right" to indicate to which side the fillet surface is added to the model (Figure 13.24).

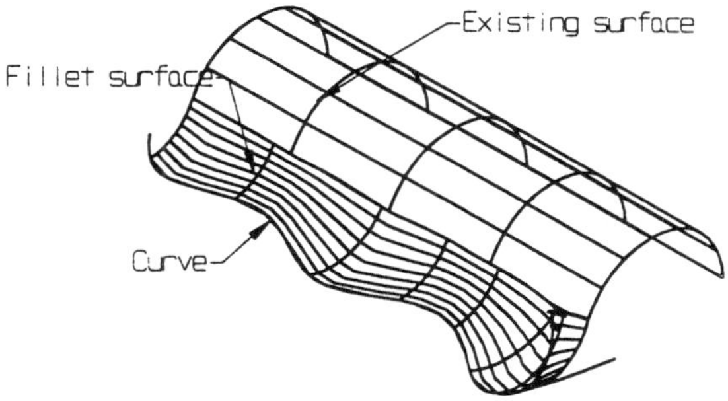

Figure 13.22

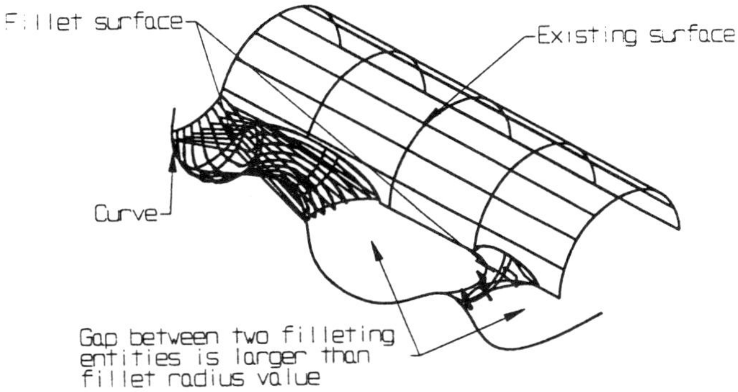

Figure 13.23

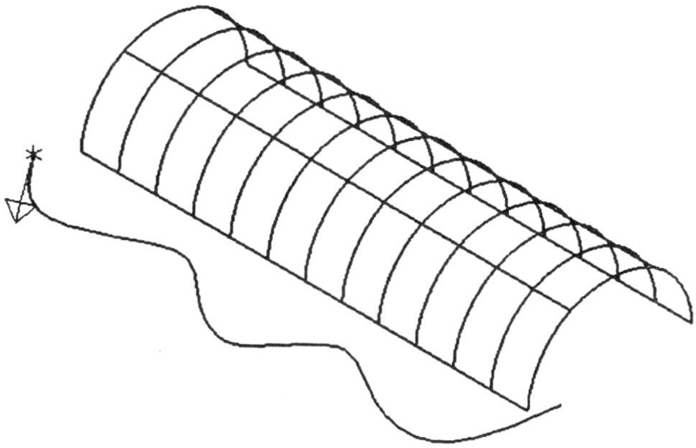

Figure 13.24

The procedure of creating a fillet surface between a curve and a surface is (Figure 13.25):

- Select Create → Surface → Fillet → Curve/surf
- Select surfaces: pick a surface, then select Done
- Enter the radius: 0.5
- Select chain 1: pick the curve, then select Done
- A direction arrow shall appear as shown in Figure 13.24.
- Select side of curve: pick Left from the list
- Select Do it to complete the fillet surface

The fillet surface is added to the model as shown in Figure 13.25.

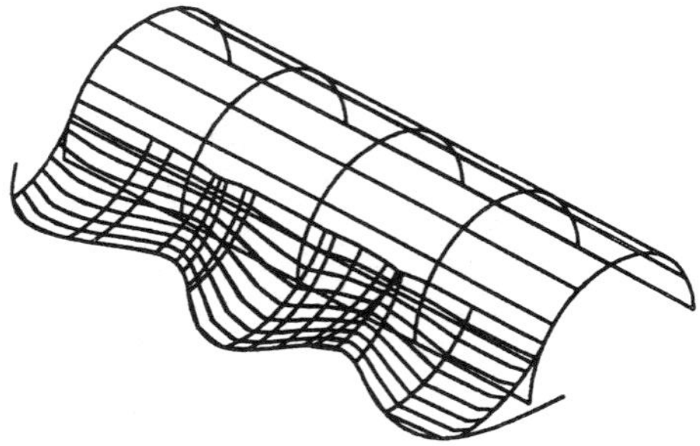

Figure 13.25

Creating a fillet surface between two surfaces

A fillet surface can be created between two existing surfaces (Figure 13.26). When two surfaces are intersected in two locations, it is possible to control whether to create only one fillet surface or two fillet surfaces (Figure 13.27). Mastercam uses "Find multiples" parameter in Options menu to control this option. With this parameter being set to Off (without a check mark), only one fillet surface is created (Figure 13.27a). With this parameter is set to On (with a check mark), two fillet surfaces are created (Figure 13.27b).

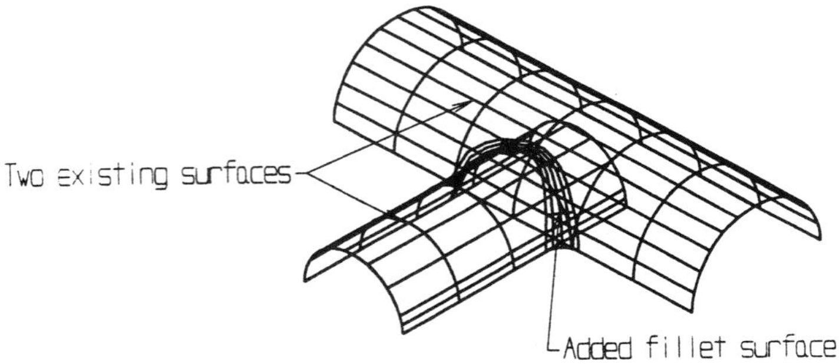

Figure 13.26

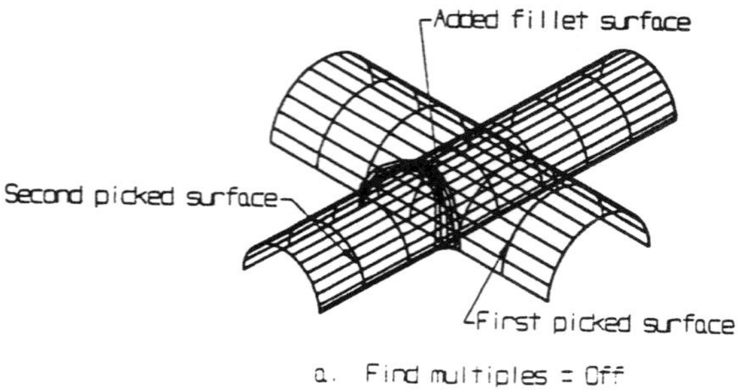

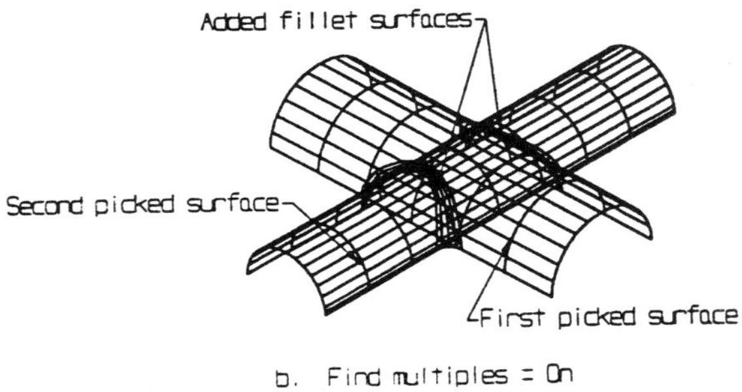

Figure 13.27a

Figure 13.27b

Actually Mastercam uses two sets of surfaces to create fillet surfaces. It is possible to have more than one surface in each set of surfaces. In this way, we can produce more than one fillet surface in one operation (Figure 13.28).

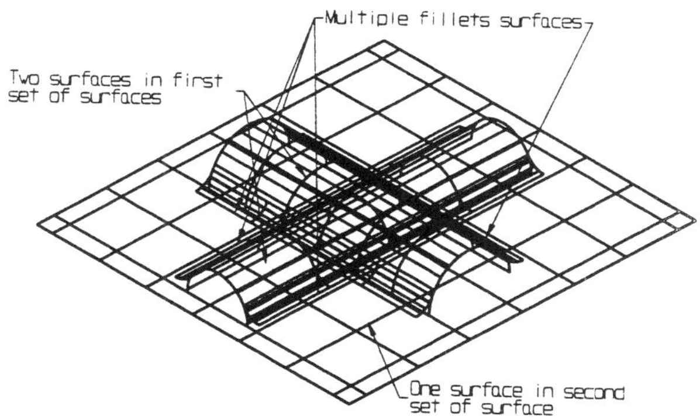

Figure 13.28

Creating a fillet surface between two existing surfaces requires the two surface normals pointing to the directions that intersect each other (Figure 13.29). If not, use Modify → Normal to set to the proper normal direction.

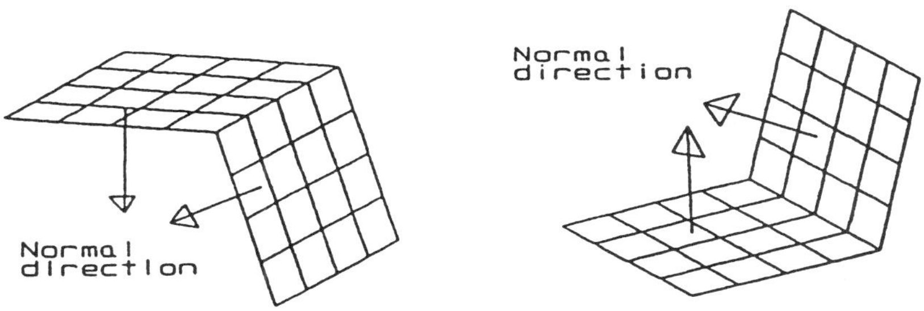

Figure 13.29

Two common problems in creating fillet surfaces are:

1. the surface normals are not in the proper direction,
2. the fillet radius may be too large to fit the two surfaces.

When a fillet surface can not be successfully generated, check the surface normals first. If the surface normals are correct and rpblem still exists, try to check if the fillet radius is too big to fit the surfaces.

Procedure of creating a fillet surface between two surfaces is (Figure 13.30):

- Select Create → Surface → Fillet → Surf/surf
- Pick the flat surface as the first set of surfaces, then select Done
- Pick the cone surface as the second set of surfaces, then select Done
- Enter the radius: 1
- Set the Options parameters if necessary
- Select Do it

1 The fillet surface is added to the model as in Figure 13.30.

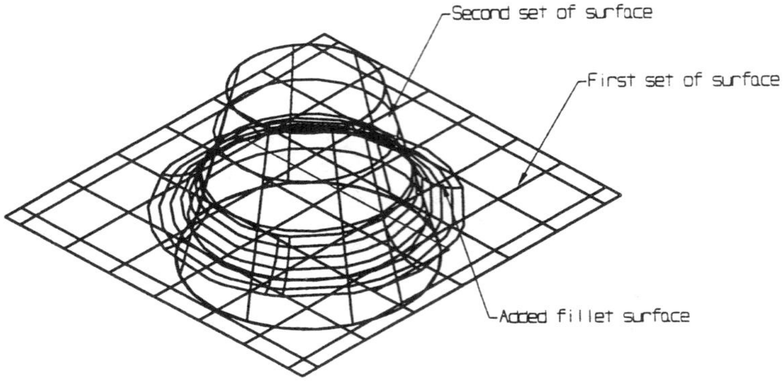

Figure 13.30

Project 1. Two fillet surfaces with a constant radius

Two fillet surfaces are created at the intersection of two ruled surfaces (Figure 13.31). The two perpendicularly intersected ruled surfaces are created in project 1 of chapter 12. These two fillet surfaces have a constant radius of 0.25-in. Use the multi-surf function to create these two fillet surfaces simultaneously.

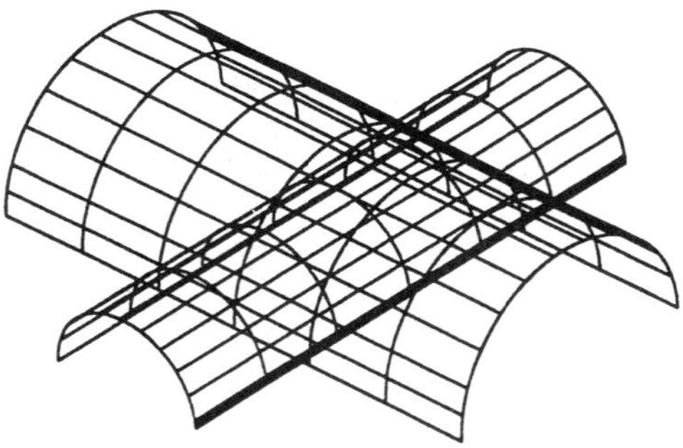

Figure 13.31a

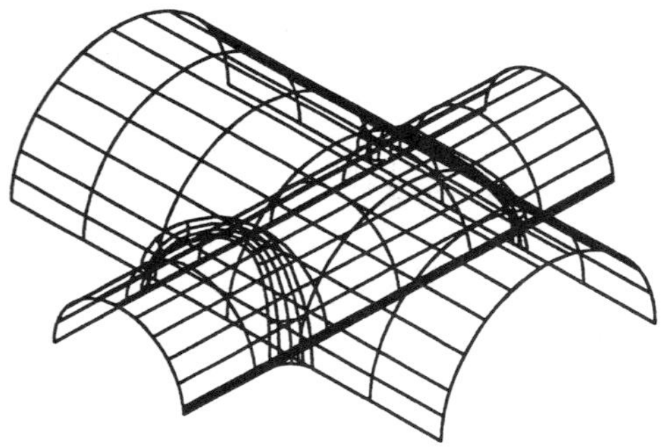

Figure 13.31b

Step 1. Load the surface model file ruleds1.

Select **MAIN MENU → File → Get**

The drawing of two ruled surfaces should appear as Figure 13.32.

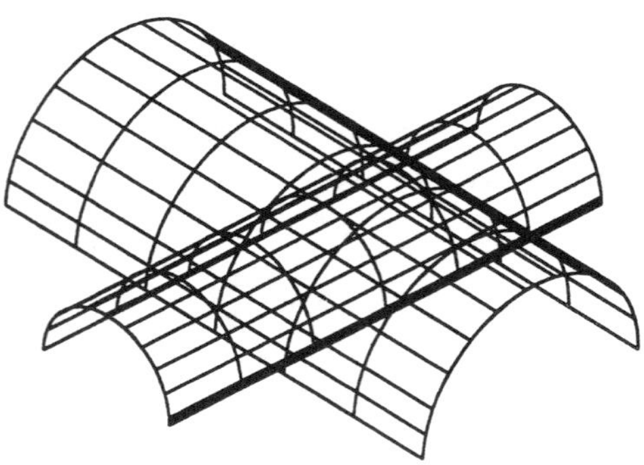

Figure 13.32

Step 2. Create the first fillet surface using the pick points in Figure 13.6.

Select **MAIN MENU → Create → Surface → Fillet → Surf/surf**
Pick the vertical surface as the first set of surface
Select **Done**
Pick the horizontal surface as the second set of surface
Select **Done**
Enter the radius: **0.25**
Select **Options**
Set the surface-surface fillet parameters as shown here.

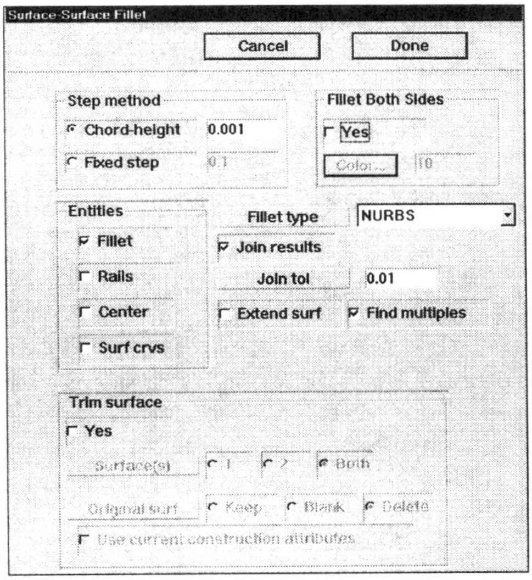

Select **Done → Do it**

The two fillet surfaces are created as shown in Figure 13.33.

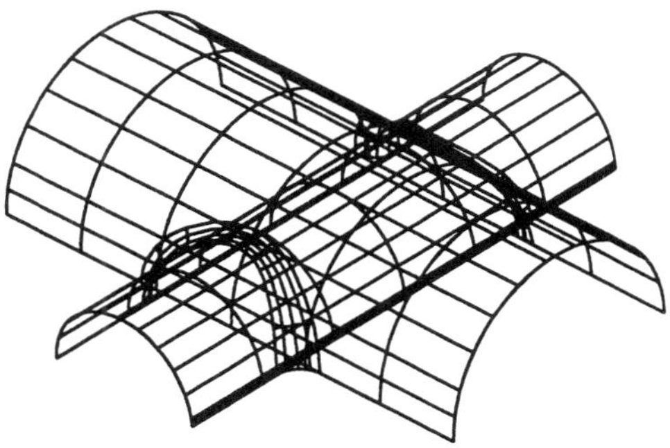

Figure 13.33

Step 3. Save the two fillet surfaces with two ruled surfaces.

Select **MAIN MENU → MAIN MENU → File → Save**
Enter file name: **fillets1**

2 Project 2. Two fillet surfaces with a variable radius

Create two fillet surfaces based on the two ruled surfaces generated in project 2 of chapter 12. Both two fillet surfaces have a variable radius. The radius of the fillet surface at the intersection of the two ruled surfaces varies in a linear pattern. The other fillet surface is added at the right end of the larger ruled surface. The radius of the second fillet surface changes in the Middle pattern. A ruled surface must be constructed at the right end before the fillet surface can be generated. Figure 13.34 shows both surface models before and after fillet surfaces are added.

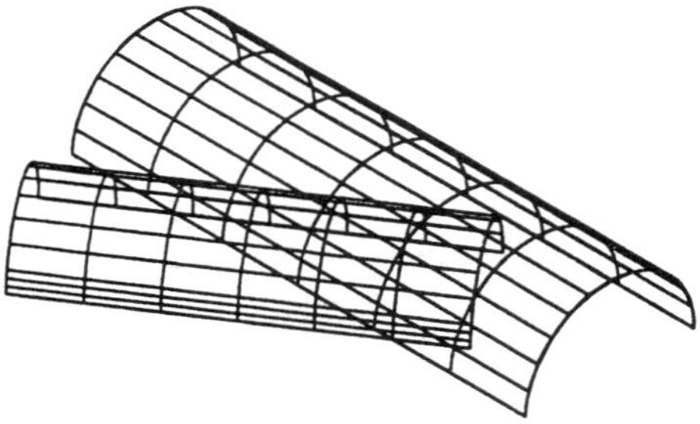

Figure 13.34a

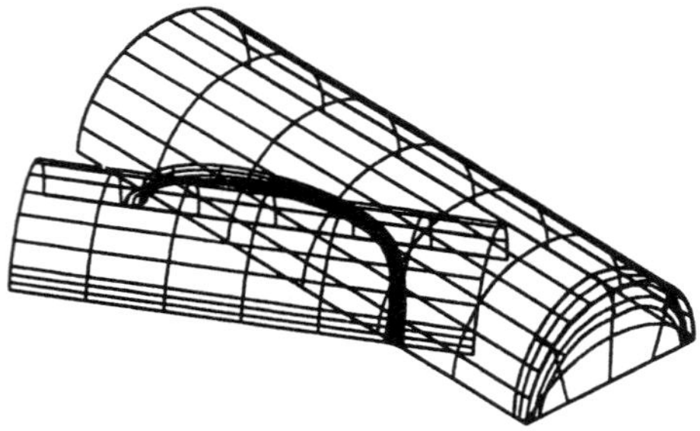

Figure 13.34b

Tips

1. Use different colors to display each surface.
2. The start fillet radius is 0.3-in and end fillet radius is 0.15-in for the fillet surface between two ruled surfaces.
3. Use the fixed step method to control the surface stepping pattern.
4. In the Surface-surface fillet dialog box, toggle the "Surf crvs" parameter to On. The two surface curves can be used to form the trimming boundary for trimming the surface in project 4 of this chapter.
5. A line should be added to the two endpoints at the right end of the larger ruled surface. This line is used with the arc to create a ruled surface.
6. The radius of the end fillet surface varies in a variable pattern. The radius starts with 0.15- in from one end and increases to 0.3-in in the middle and then decreases to 0.15-in at the other end.
7. The surface normals of both ruled surfaces for creating an end fillet surface must point toward the surfaces. Use Modify → Normal commands to change the surface normals if necessary.

Step 1. Load the surface model file ruleds2.

Select **MAIN MENU → File → Get**
Enter file name: **ruleds2**
The two ruled surfaces should appear as Figure 13.35.

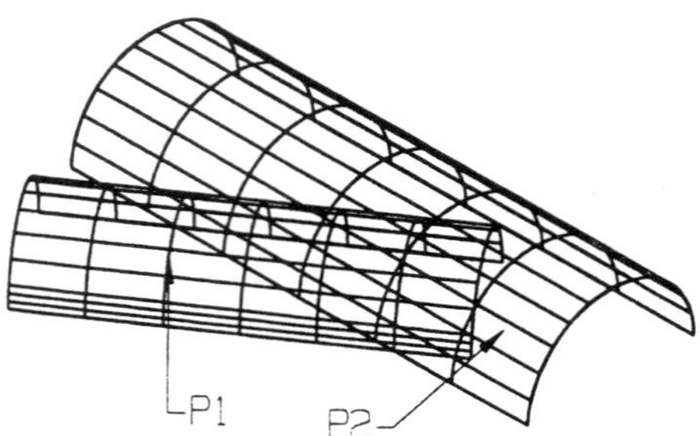

Figure 13.35

Step 2. Change color to 12.

From the Secondary menu select **Color** , then enter **12**

Step 3. Create the first fillet surface between the two ruled surfaces.

Use the pick points in Figure 13.35.
Select **MAIN MENU → Create → Surface → Fillet → Surf/surf**
Pick **P1** as the first set of surface
Select **Done**
Pick **P2** as the second set of surfaces
Select **Done**
Enter the radius: **0.3**
Select **Variable**
A center curve with two radius markers should appear as in Figure 13.36.

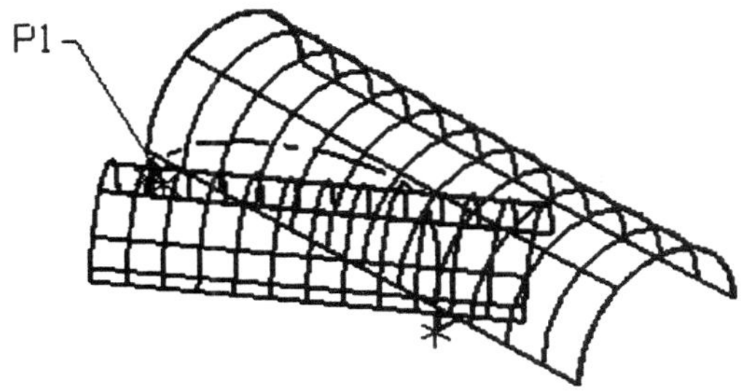

Figure 13.36

Select **Modify**
Select a Radius Marker: pick **P1** in Figure 13.36
Enter the radius: **0.15**
Select **Done → Options**
Set the surface-surface fillet parameters as below.

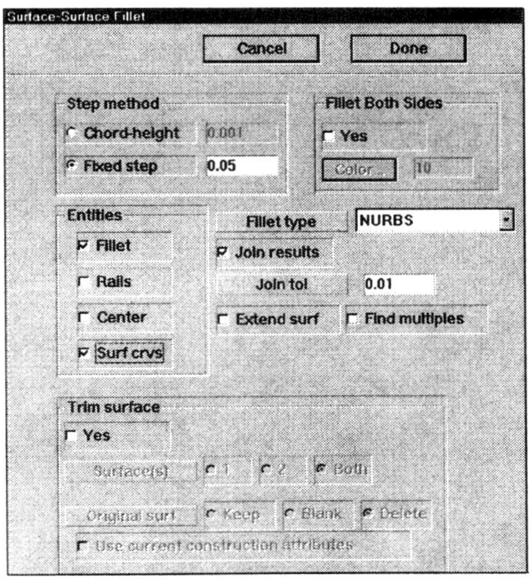

Select **Done → Do it**

The fillet surface is added as in Figure 13.37.

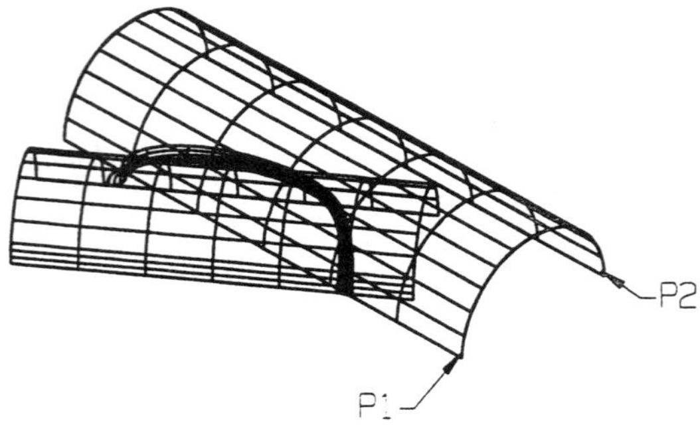

Figure 13.37

Step 4. Add a line to the right face of the larger ruled surface using 3D Cpalne.

Use the pick points in Figure 13.37.
Select **Cplane → 3D**
Select **MAIN MENU → MAIN MENU → Create → Line → Endpoints → Endpoint**
Pick **P1** and **P2** to complete the line
The line is added as shown in Figure 13.38.

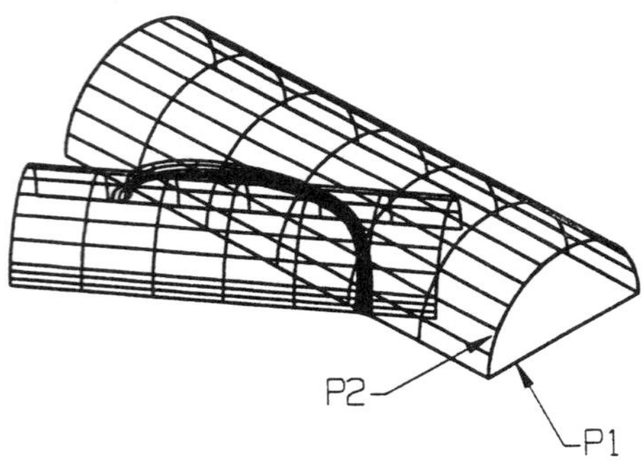

Figure 13.38

Step 5. Create a ruled surface at the right end of the semi-cone.

Use the pick points in Figure 13.38.
Select **MAIN MENU → Create → Surface → Ruled → Single**
Define contour 1: pick **P1**
Define contour 2: pick **P2**
Select **Done** to complete the contours selection
Set Surface type to **N** →NURBS)
Select **Do it** to generate the ruled surface.
The new ruled surface should appear on the screen as Figure 13.39.

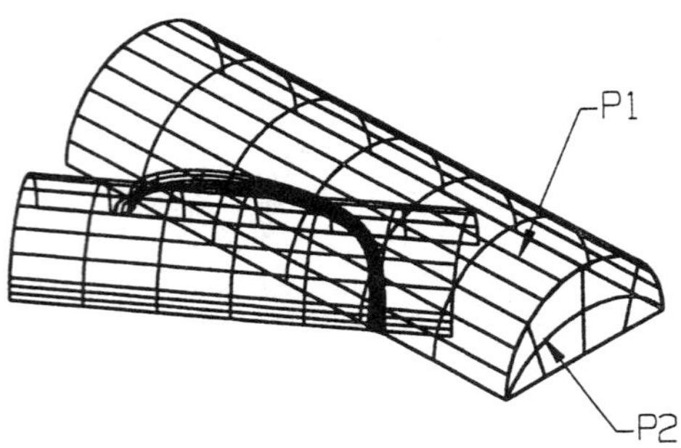

Figure 13.39

Step 6. Change the normal direction of the surfaces.

Use the pick points in Figure 13.39.
Select **MAIN MENU → Modify → Normal → Reverse**
Pick **P1** to select a surface

Note: Surface curves are dimmed when the surface normal direction is changed to point in the inward direction.

Pick **P2** to select the end surface to change the normal direction of the second surface
Note: Surface curves on both surfaces should appear dimmed.
The drawing on the screen should look like Figure 13.40.

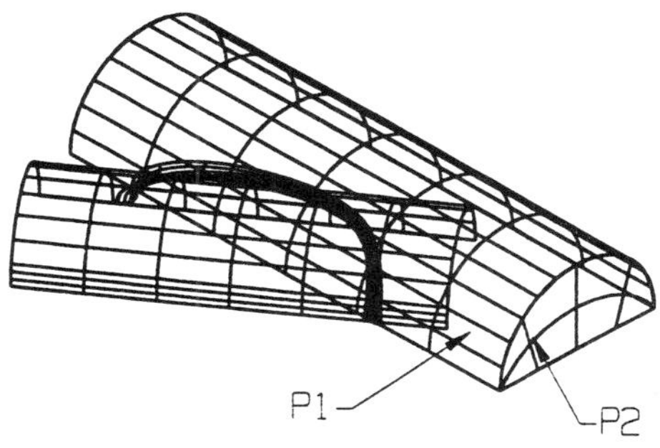

Figure 13.40

Step 7. Create a fillet with a variable radius.

Use the pick points in Figure 13.40.
From the Secondary menu select **Color**, and then enter **14**
Select **MAIN MENU → Create → Surface → Fillet → Surf/surf**
Pick **P1** to select the first set of surfaces
Select **Done**
Pick **P2** to select the second set of surfaces
Select **Done**
Enter the Radius: **0.15**
Select **Variable**

A center curve with two radius markers appear as in Figure 13.41.

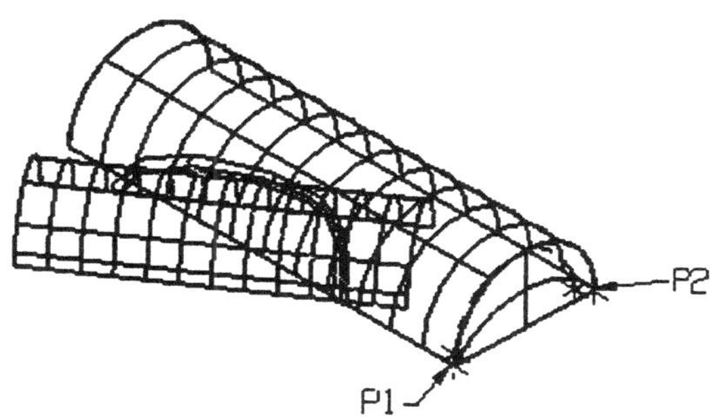

Figure 13.41

Select **Insert mid**
Select a Radius Marker: pick **P1**
Select a neighboring Radius Marker: pick **P2**
Enter the radius: **0.3**
Select **Done → Do it**
The variable fillet surface is added to the model as in Figure 13.42.

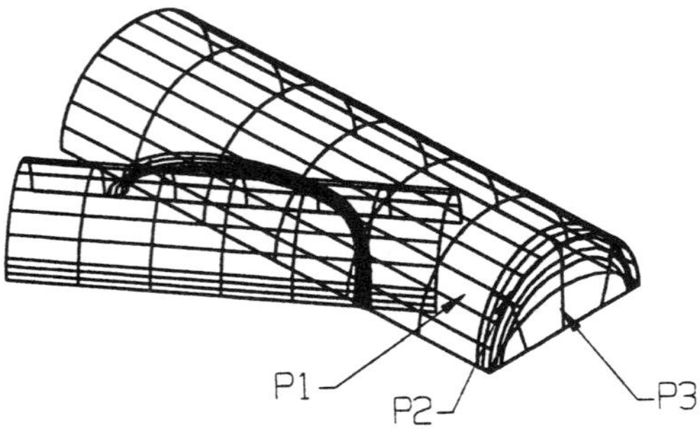

Figure 13.42

Step 8. Change three surface normals.

Use the pick points in Figure 13.42.
Select **MAIN MENU → MAIN MENU → Modify → Normal → Reverse**
Select three surfaces to change their normal direction to outward, pick **P1**, **P2**, and **P3**
The final drawing should resemble Figure 13.43.

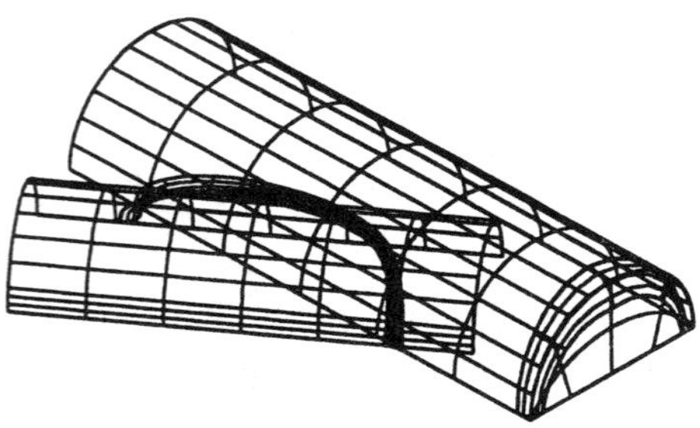

Figure 13.43

Step 9. Save the surface model file as fillets2.

Select **MAIN MENU → File → Save**
Enter file name: **fillets2**

13.2 Trim/Extend Surfaces Modeling

The Trim/Extend surface modeling technique is sued to create a trimmed surface from an existing surface (Figure 13.44). It requires an existing surface and at least one trim boundary.Table 13.4 summarizes the surface trimming methods.

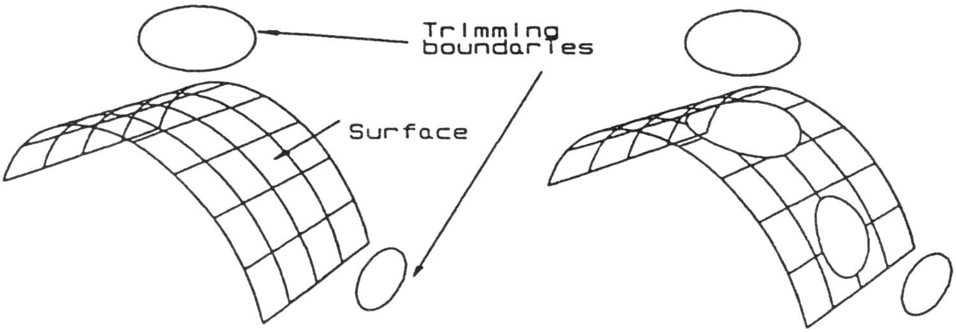

Figure 13.44a Before trimming Figure 13.44b After trimming

The command chain for the Trim/Extend is:

MAIN MENU → Create → Surface → Trim/Extend

Table 13.4 Trim/Extend surfaces modeling methods

Method	Description	Illustration	
To curves	Trim surface(s) to the given curves.	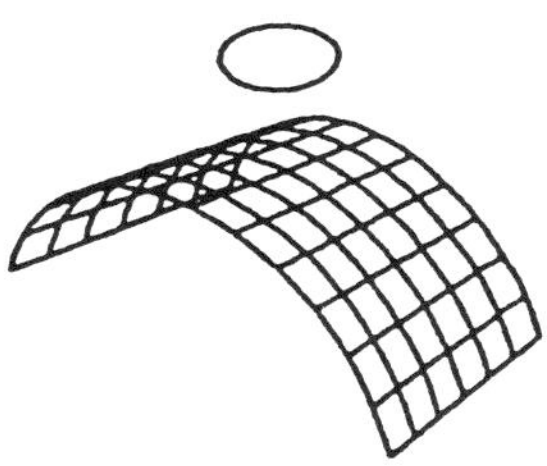	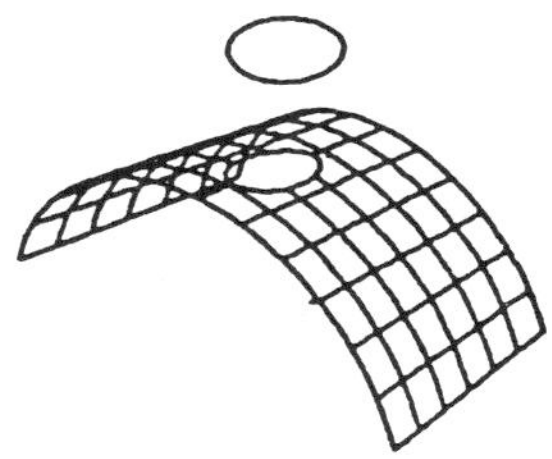
To plane	Trim surface(s) to a plane.	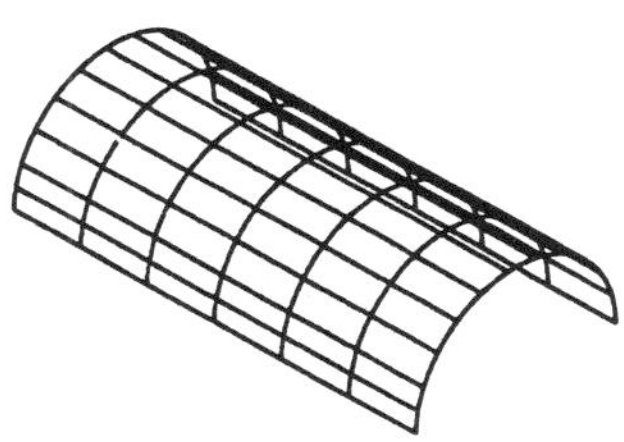 Before trimming	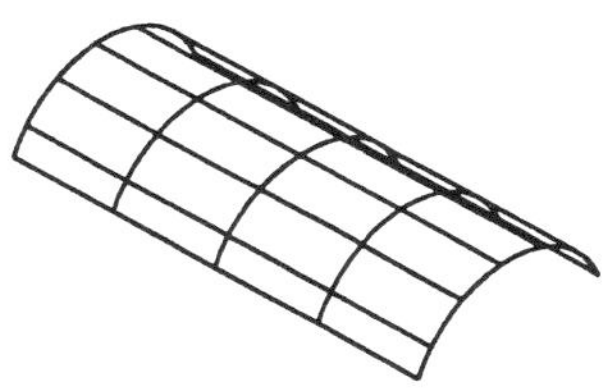 This surface is trimmed by the plane Z = 0.5

Trim/Extend surfaces modeling methods, continued.

To surfaces — Trim surface(s) to a surface.

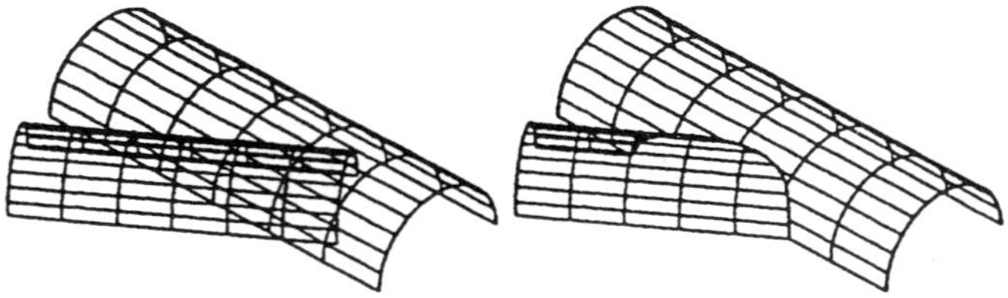

Flat bndy — Create a flat surface to the specified boundary.

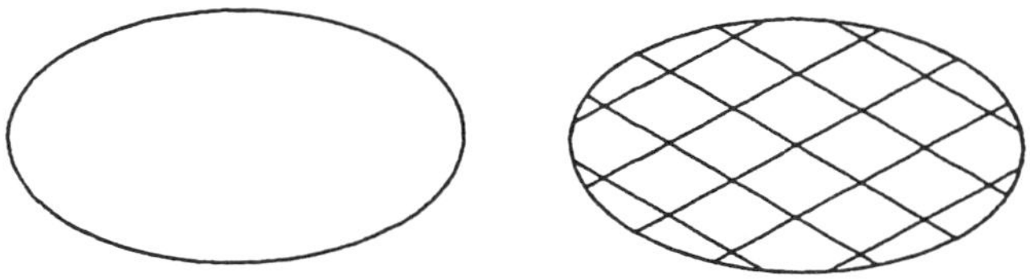

Split — Split a surface along a constant parameter into two separate surfaces.

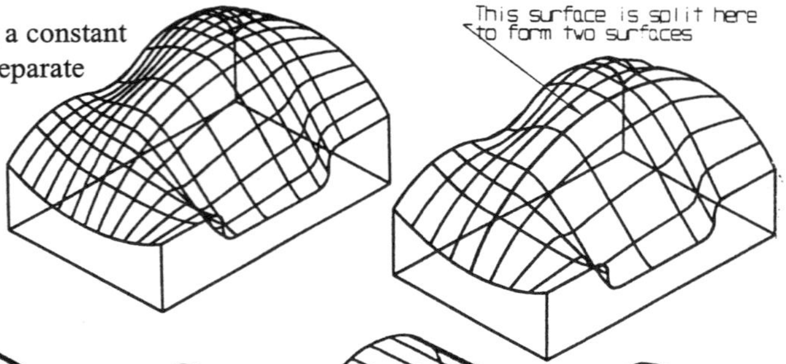

Untrim — Untrim the trimmed surfaces.

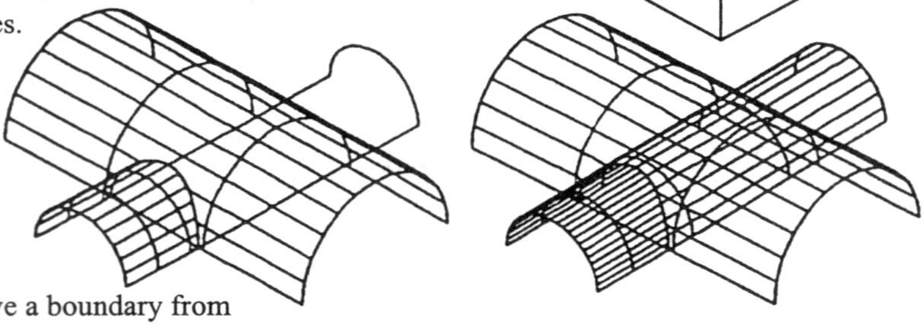

Remove bndy — Remove a boundary from a trimmed surface. The surface is extended beyond the surface.

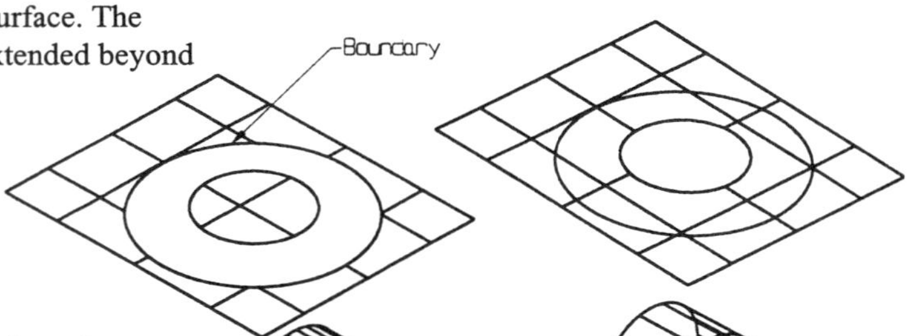

Extend — Extend a surface along one of its edges by a given distance or to a given plane.

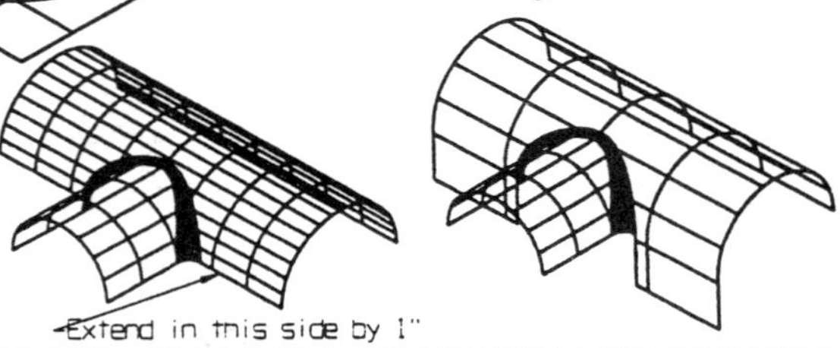

Project 3. Trimming two ruled surfaces to their intersection boundaries

Two intersecting ruled surfaces are trimmed to their intersecting boundaries. Both surface models before and after trimming are shown in Figure 13.45.

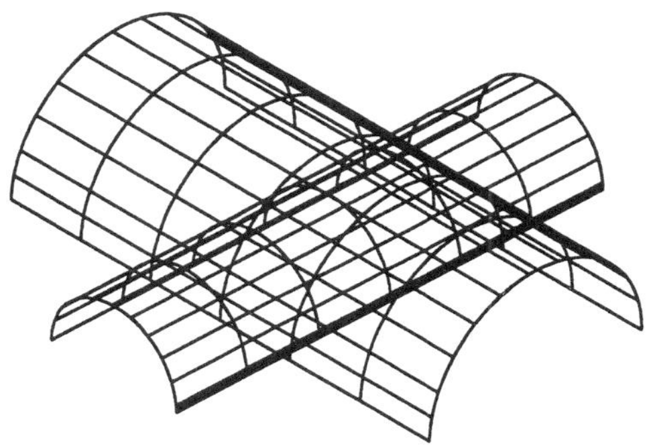

Figure 13.45a

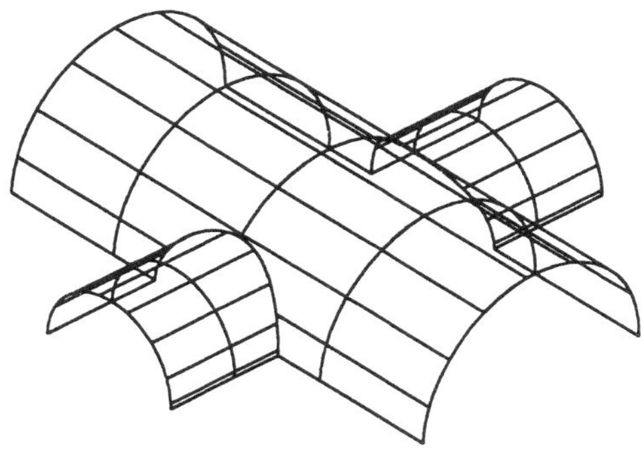

Figure 13.45b

Tips 1. The surface file to be trimmed is ruleds1.

2. Use the To surfaces method to trim both surfaces to their intersection boundaries.

3. These two ruled surfaces are intersected at two locations. Therefore, they need to be trimmed twice. After trimming at one end, the original surfaces must be kept to their original shape. The original surfaces are used again to be trimmed each other at the other end. Use the "Delete" option to delete two original surfaces in second trimming.

Step 1. Open the surface file ruleds1.

Select **MAIN MENU → File → Get**
Enter file name: **ruleds1**
The two ruled surfaces should appear as in Figure 13.46.

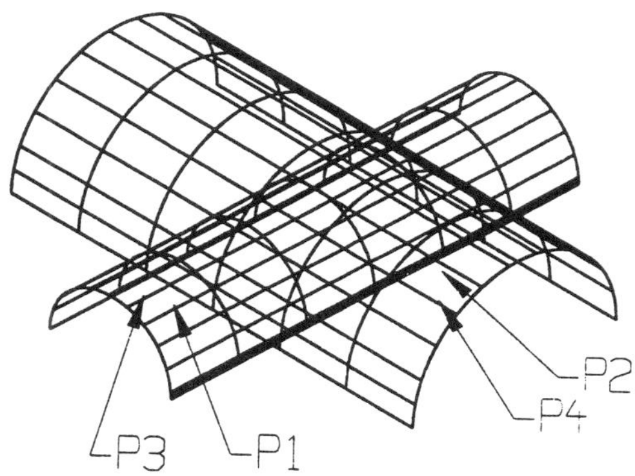

Figure 13.46

Step 2. Initiate the trimmed surface function.

Select **Level**, then enter **3**
Select **MAIN MENU → Create → Surface → Trim/Extend → To surfaces**
To select first set of surfaces, pick **P1**, then **Done**
To select the second set of surfaces, pick **P2,** then **Done**
Select **Options**

Set Trim Surfaces to Surfaces parameters
as shown here:

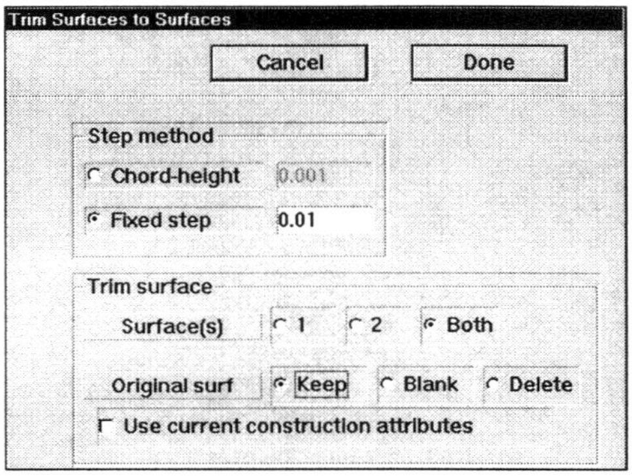

Select **Done → Do it**
Select a surface to be trimmed, pick **P1**
Indicate a location to keep after trimming, pick **P3**
Select a surface to be trimmed, pick **P2**
Indicate a location to keep after trimming, pick **P4**
The two surfaces are trimmed to their intersections as in Figure 13.47.

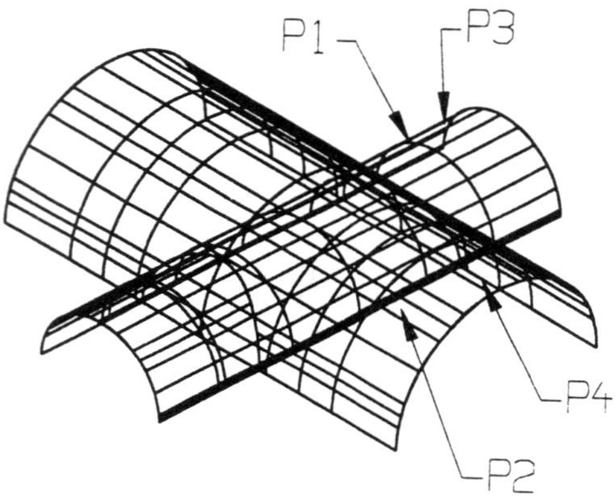

Figure 13.47

Step 3. Trim both surfaces to their intersection boundary at the other end.

Use the pick points in Figure 13.47.
Select **BACKUP → To Surfaces**
Select first set of surfaces, pick **P1** then **Done**
Select second set of surfaces, pick **P2** then **Done**
Select **Options**
Set trim surfaces to surfaces parameters
as shown here.

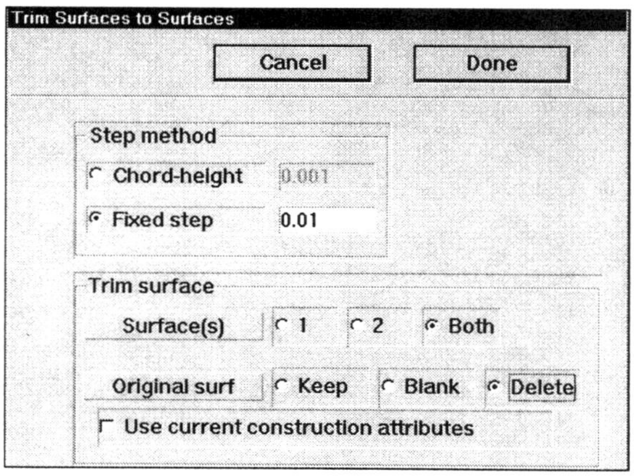

Select **Done → Do it**

Select a surface to be trimmed, pick **P1**
Indicate a location to keep after trimming, pick **P3**
Select a surface to be trimmed, pick **P2**
Indicate a location to keep after trimming, pick **P4**
New surface model becomes Figure 13.48.

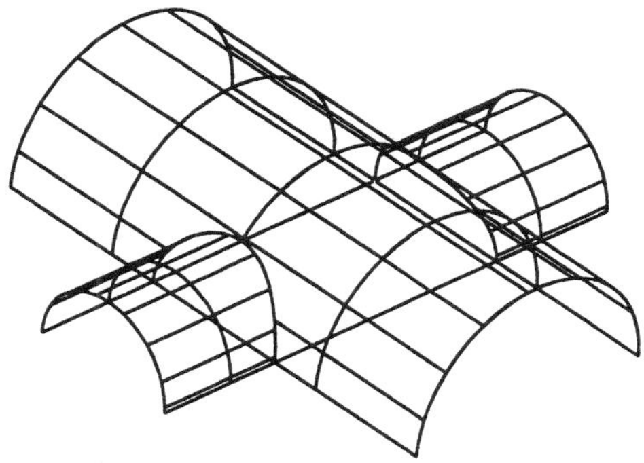

Figure 13.48

Step 4. Toggle level 1 to invisible.

Select **Level → Vis. Levels**
Click level #1 to invisible (dimmed)
Select **OK**
The final drawing appears as in Figure 13.49.

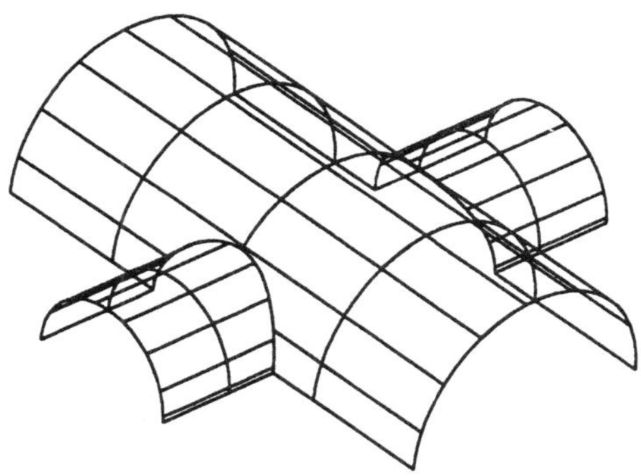

Figure 13.49

Step 5. Save the trimmed surfaces as trims1.

Select **MAIN MENU → File → Save**
Enter file name: **trims1**

4 Project 4. Trimming three surfaces to their surface boundaries

In this example, three trimmed surfaces are generated based on the surface model of project 2 in this chapter. These three ruled surfaces are trimmed to their surface boundary. The surface models before and after trimming are shown in Figure 13.50.

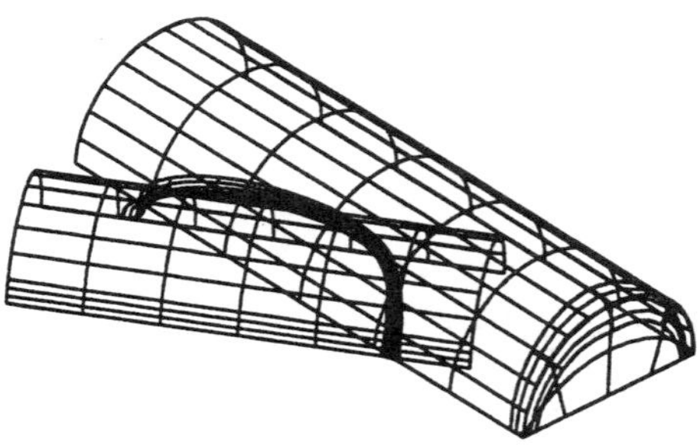

Figure 13.50a

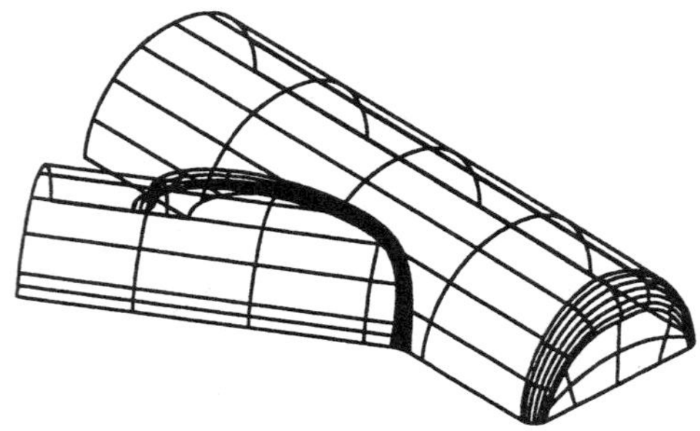

Figure 13.50b

Tips 1. Use the surface model file fillets2.

2. Use "To surfaces" option to trim two ruled surfaces to the fillet surface between them.

3. Use "To curves" option to trim the right end of the larger ruled surface and the right end surface to the surface curves of fillet surface.

Step 1. Open the surface model file fillets2.

Select **MAIN MENU → File → Get**
Enter file name: **fillets2**
The drawing should resemble Figure 13.51.

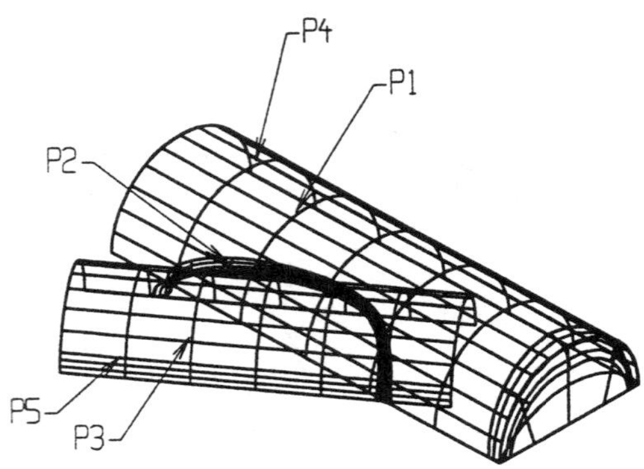

Figure 13.51

Step 2. Trim two ruled surfaces to the fillet surface.

Use the pick points in Figure 13.51.
Select **MAIN MENU → Create → Surface → Trim/Extend → To surfaces**
Select first set of surfaces: pick **P1**, then select **Done**
Select second set of surfaces: pick **P2** and **P3**, then select **Done**
Select **Options**

Set trim surfaces to surfaces parameters
as shown here.

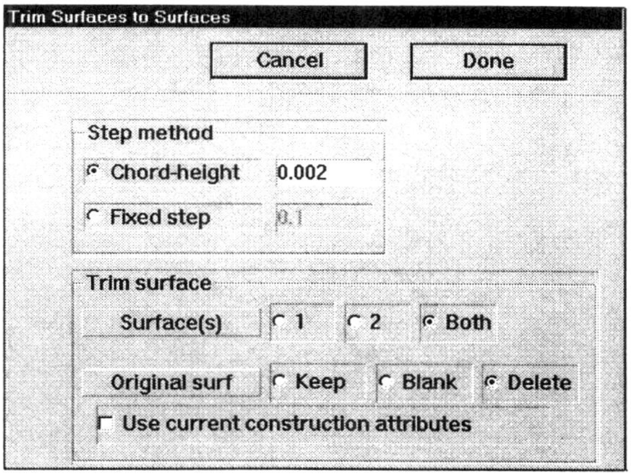

Select **Done → Do it**
Pick **P1** to select a surface, then select **P4**
Pick **P3** to select a surface, then select **P5**
The system trims two ruled surfaces to a fillet surface as shown in Figure 13.52.

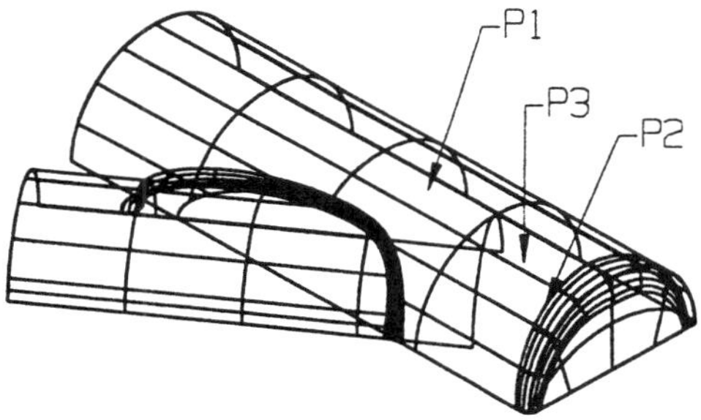

Figure 13.52

Step 3. Trim the larger ruled surface to a surface curve.

Use the pick points in Figure 13.52.
Select **BACKUP**
Select **to Curves**
Pick **P1** to select a surface, then select **Done**
Select **BACKUP → Surf crvs**
Pick **P2** to select a surface curve
Select **Done → Options**
Set trim surfaces to curves
parameters as shown here.

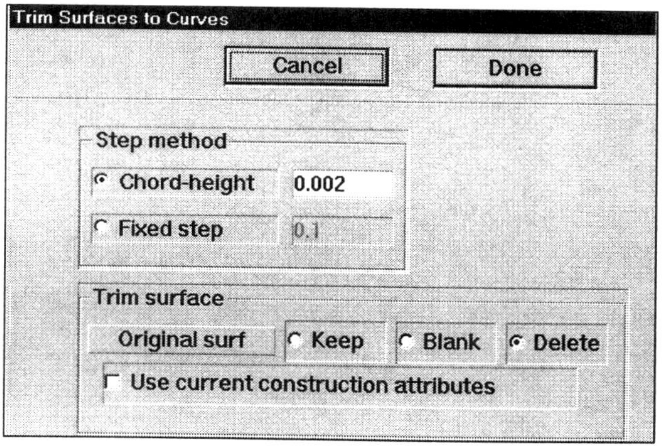

Select **Done → Do it**

Pick **P1** to select a surface to be trimmed
Pick **P3** to indicate a location to keep after trimming
The large ruled surface is trimmed as in Figure 13.53.

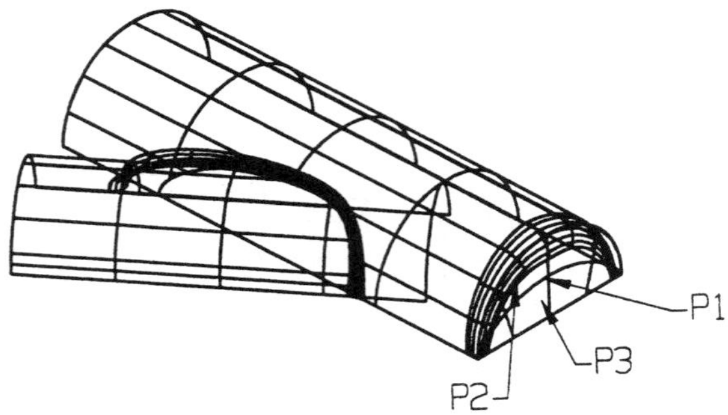

Figure 13.53

Step 4. Trim the ruled surface at the end face using the pick points in Figure 13.53.

Select **BACKUP → To curves**
Pick **P1** to select the end surface
Select **Done → BACKUP → Surf crvs**
Pick **P2** to select a surface curve
Select **Done → Do it**
Pick **P1** to select a surface to be trimmed
Pick **P3** to indicate a location to keep after trimming
The right end surface is trimmed as in Figure 13.54.

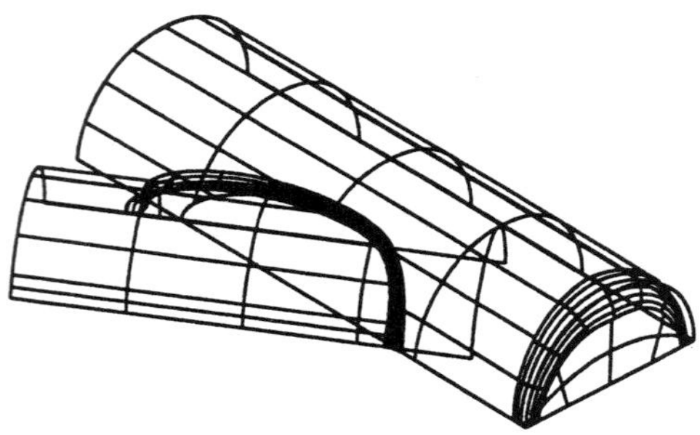

Figure 13.54

Step 5. Make level 1 invisible.

Select **Level → Vis. Level**
Click at **1** to dim
Select **OK** to return to graphic mode

The final drawing should resemble Figure 13.55.

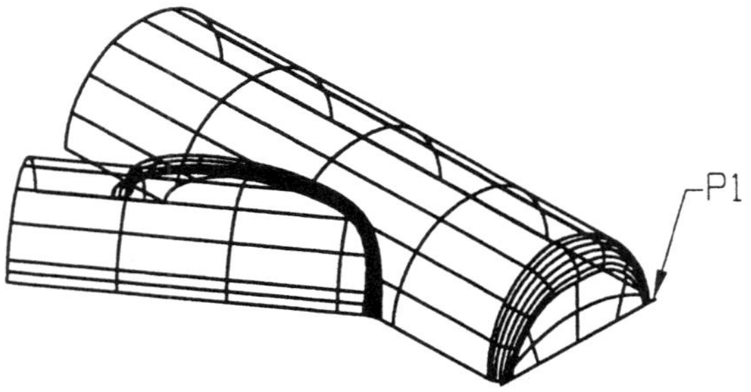

Figure 13.55

Step 6. Delete a line using the pick point in Figure 13.55.

Select **MAIN MENU → Delete**
Pick **P1** to delete a line
The final drawing appears as in Figure 13.56.

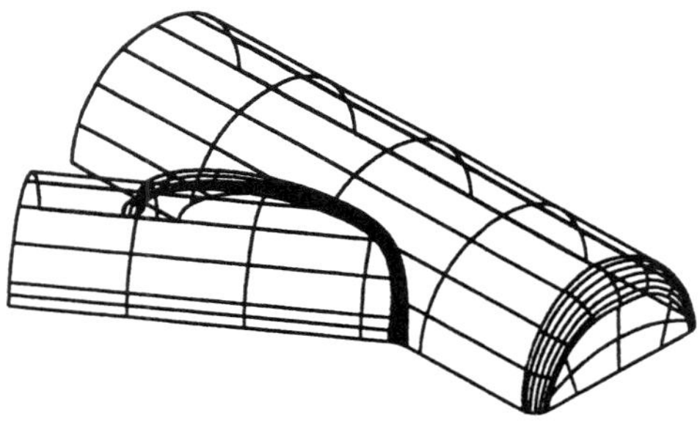

Figure 13.56

Step 7. Save the trimmed surfaces in the file trims2.

Select **MAIN MENU → File → Save**
Enter file name: **trims2**

5 Project 5. Trimming a surface using a circle

This project trims a loft surface to a curve, which is a circle of 1.5" diameter. Its center is located at (1.6,0). The surface models before and after trimming are shown in Figure 13.57.

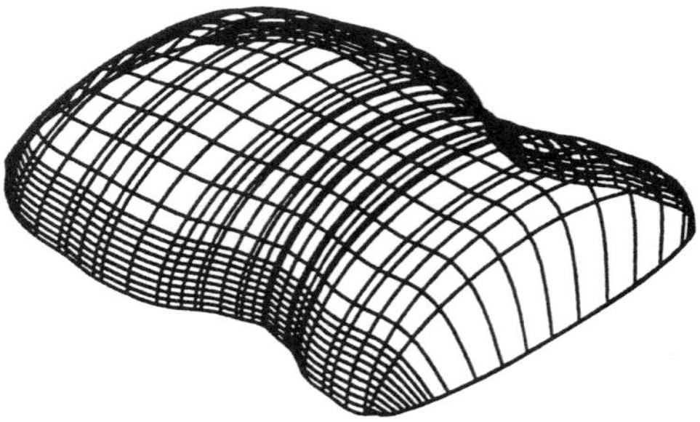

Figure 13.57a

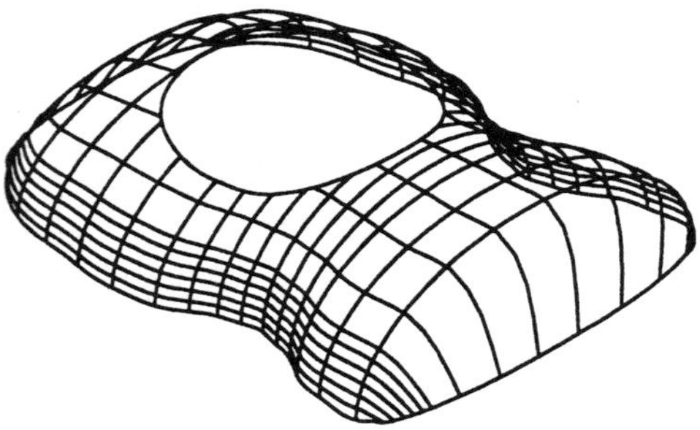

Figure 13.57b

Tips	1. Create a circle to be used as the trimming curve. The curve does not necessary have to be on the surface to be trimmed. 2. Use the "To curves" method to trim the loft surface. 3. Select the "Project normal to the construction plane" mode. The construction plane should be in the Top Cplane. If "Project normal to the surface" mode is used, the trimmed area will be altered.

Step 1. Open the surface file lofts2.

Select **MAIN MENU → File → Get**
Enter file name: **lofts2**
The loft surface should appear as in Figure 13.58.

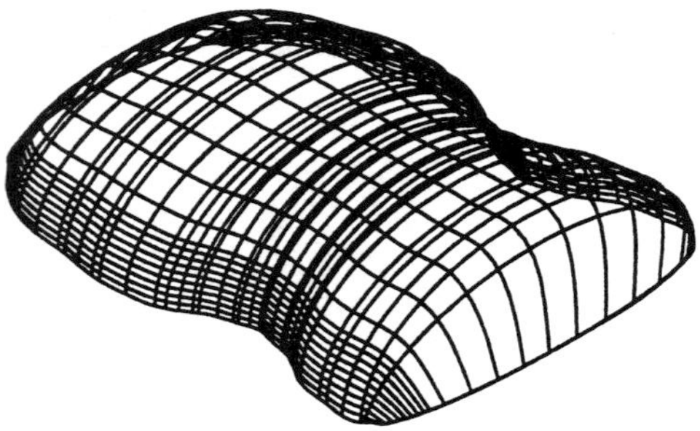

Figure 13.58

Step 2. Create a circle using Top Cplane; center located at (1.6,0), radius 0.75-in.

Select **Level**, then enter **3**
Select **Color**, then enter **14**
Select **Cplane → Top** if necessary
Select **Z**, then enter **2.5**
Select **MAIN MENU → Create → Arc → Cir pt+rad**
Enter the center point: **1.6,0**
Enter the radius: **0.75**

The circle is added to the drawing as shown in Figure 13.59.

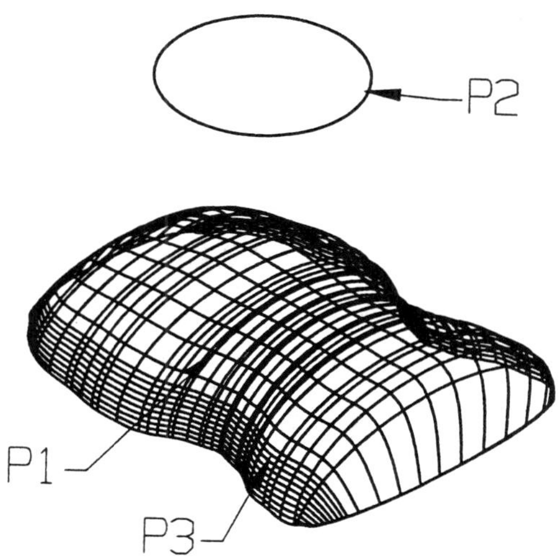

Figure 13.59

Step 3. Initiate the trim surface function.

Select **MAIN MENU → Create → Surface → Trim/Extend → To curves**
Pick **P1** to select the loft surface
Select **Done**
Select **Single** then pick **P2** to select the circle
Select **Done**
Set View/Norm to **V** (for View)
Select **Options**
Set trim surfaces to curves parameters as shown here.

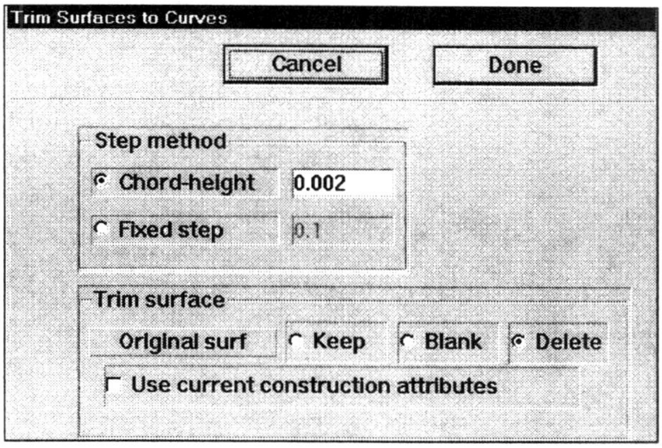

Select **Done → Do it**

Pick **P1** to select a surface to be trimmed
Pick **P2** to indicate a location to keep after trimming

The loft surface is trimmed to the circle as shown in Figure 13.60.

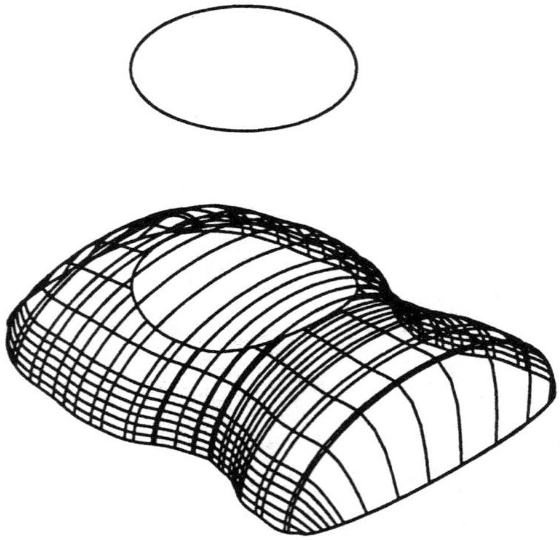

Figure 13.60

Step 4. Make levels 1 and 3 invisible.

Select **Level → Vis. Levels**
Toggle levels 1 and 3 to invisible (dimmed)
Select **OK** to return back to graphic mode
The trimmed surface is displayed as in Figure 13.61.

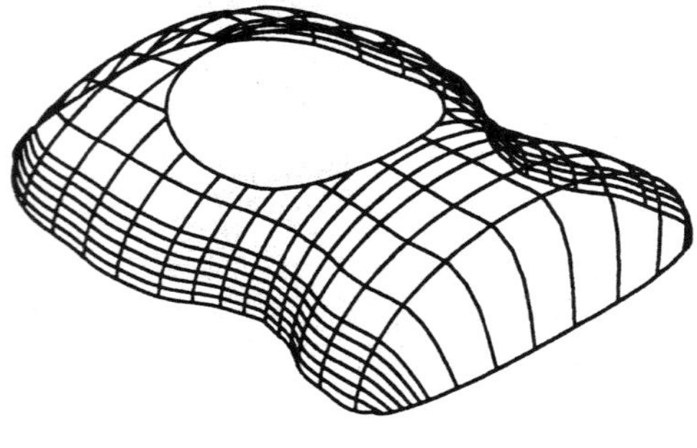

Figure 13.61

Step 5. Save the trimmed surface.

Select **MAIN MENU → File → Save**
Enter file name: **trims3**

Offset Surface Modeling

This technique creates a surface that is offset to a distance from an existing surface in the normal direction (Figure 13.62). It requires two inputs: an existing surface and an offset distance. The offset distance value can be either positive or negative. A positive offset distance value will offset the surface to the surface normal direction, while a negative value will offset to the opposite of the surface normal direction (Figure 13.63).

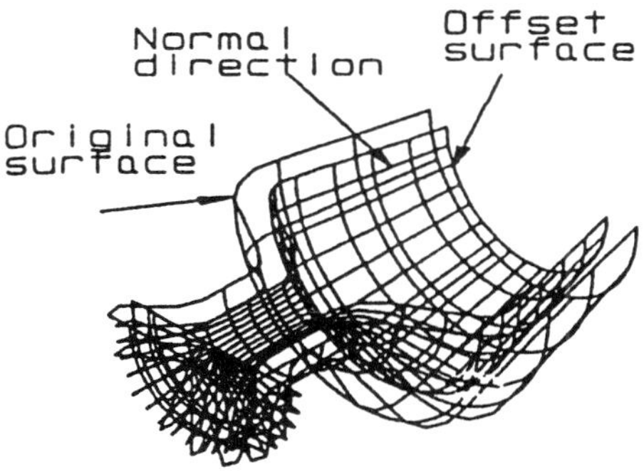

Figure 13.62

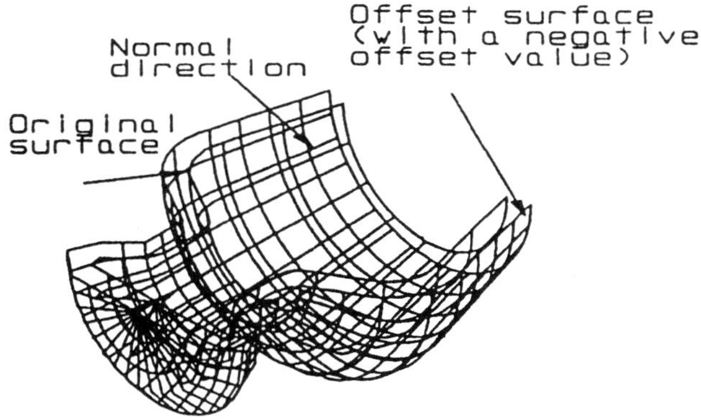

Figure 13.63

> **Tips for creating offset surfaces**
> 1. The trimmed surfaces can not be used to produce an offset surface. Only original surfaces can be used.
> 2. The surface normal direction and the sign of offset value determine the offset direction. You can use Modify → Normal commands to change the surface normal direction if necessary.

Project 6. Creating two offset surfaces.

Create two offset surfaces from the two ruled surfaces generated in project 1 of chapter 12. Both ruled surfaces are offset by 0.5-in in the outward direction. The offset surfaces are shown in Figure 13.64.

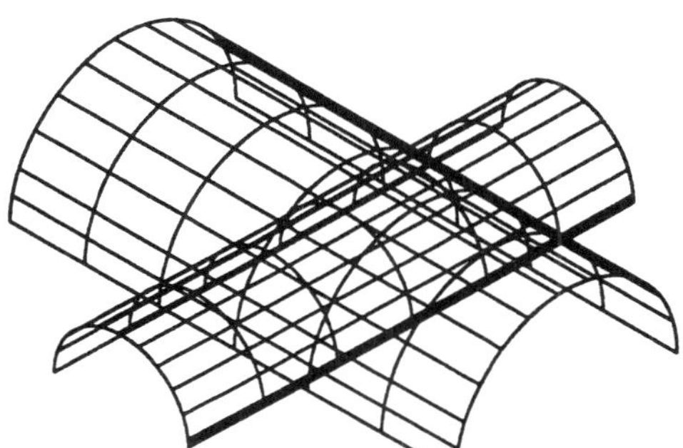

Figure 13.64a

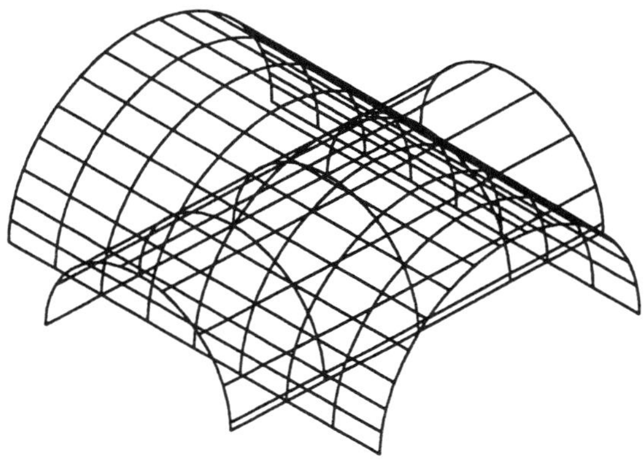

Figure 13.64b

Step 1. Open the existing surface model file ruleds1.

Select **MAIN MENU → File → Get**

Enter file name: **ruleds1**

The two ruled surfaces should appear on screen as Figure 13.65.

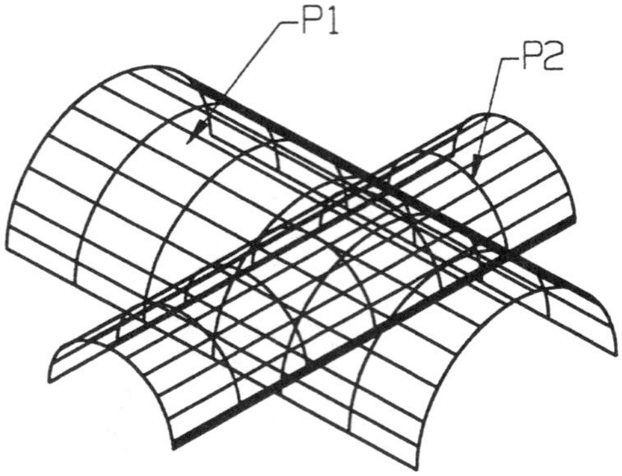

Figure 13.65

Step 2. Create two offset surfaces using the pick points in Figure 13.65.

Select **Level**, then enter **3**

Select **MAIN MENU → Create → Surface → Offset**

Select surfaces: pick **P1** and **P2**

Select **Done**

Set disPose = **K**

Select **Offset dist**

Enter offset distance: **0.5**

Select **Do it**

The two offset surfaces are added as in Figure 13.66.

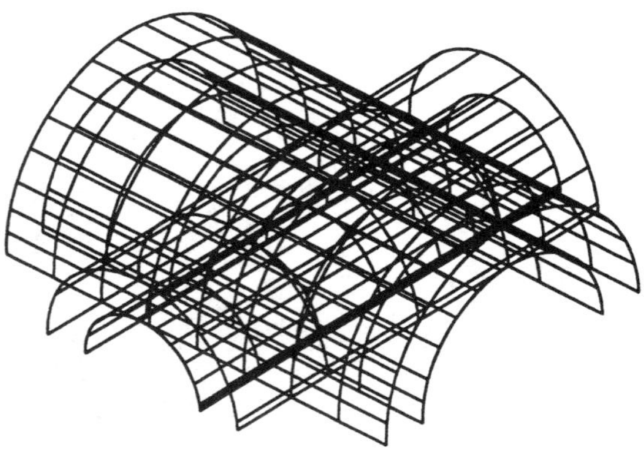

Figure 13.66

Step 3. Make levels 1 and 2 invisible.

Select **Level → Vis. Levels**

Toggle buttons 1 and 2 to dim

Select **OK** to return to graphic mode

The two offset surfaces should look like Figure 13.67.

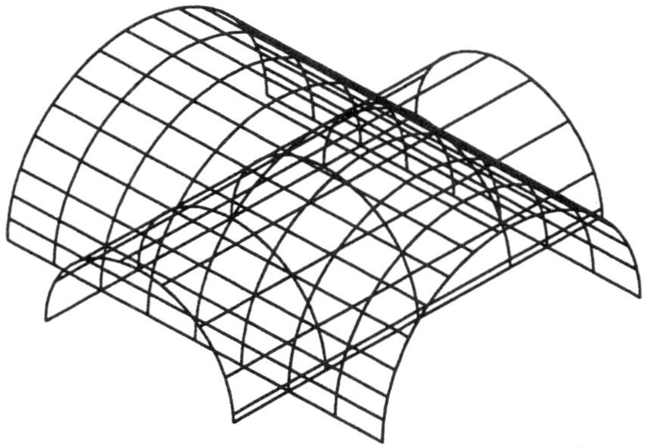

Figure 13.67

Step 4. Save the offset surface file offsets.

Select **MAIN MENU → File → Save**
Enter file name: **offsets**

Blend Surface Modeling

Blend surface modeling allows us to create a surface that smoothly joins two or three existing surfaces and is tangent to each parent surface. Figure 13.68 shows an example of adding a surface to join two intersected ruled surfaces. The two parent ruled surfaces are trimmed to the blending boundaries.

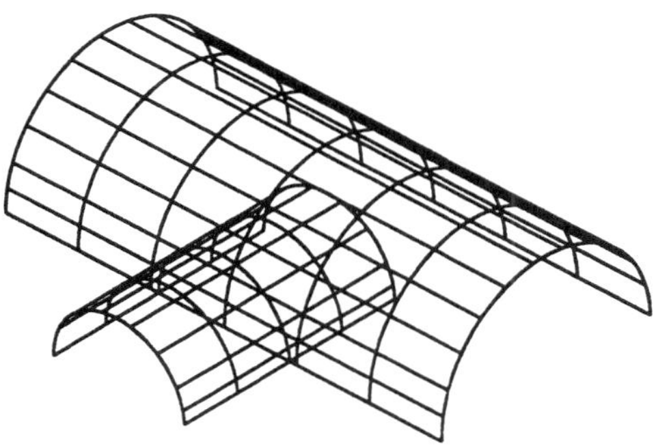

Figure 13.68a Before blending and trimming

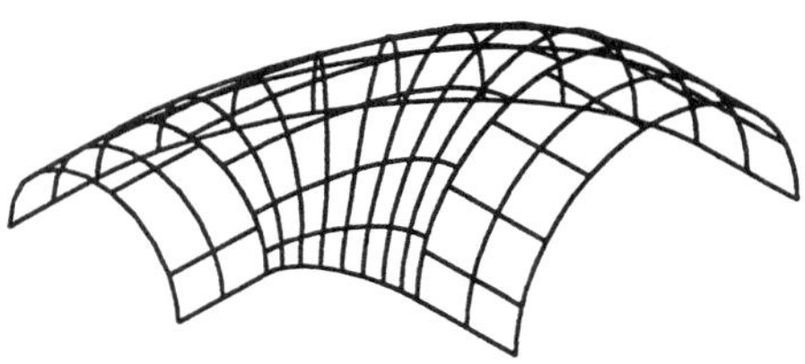

Figure 13.58b After blending and trimming

There are three surface blending methods: 2 surface, 3 surface, and Fillet blnd. They are briefly described here:

2 surface:	creates a blend surface between two existing surfaces.
3 surface:	create a blend surface between three existing surfaces.
Fillet blnd:	creates a blend surface of a three-sided blend or a six-sided blend between three existing fillet surfaces.

2-Surface Blending

The 2-surface blending method creates a blend surface between two existing surfaces. Use these commands to enter the surface blending menu:

Select **MAIN MENU → Create → Surface → Blend → 2 Surface**

The surface blending parameters are shown here:

Surf1:	The first picked surface to be blended onto.
Surf2:	the second picked surface to be blended onto.
Start mag:	Start blending magnitude on Surf1 and Surf2.
End mag;	End blending magnitude on Surf1 and Surf2.
End pts:	Indicate an end of one of blend location splines.
Reverse:	Manually reverse the blending curve direction.
Trim surfs:	Select the surface(s) to be trimmed to blending boundaries.
Keep crvs:	Select the blending curve(s) to be kept.
Surf type:	Specify the blending surface to be created being parametric or NURBS type.

⌛Tips for creating blend surfaces:

1. Theoretically, it requires two parent surfaces to create a blend surface. However, a single surface can be used to create a blend surface. This is done by carefully picking the surface twice and selecting the position to start blending. Figure 13.69 shows a blend surface created from a single ruled surface.

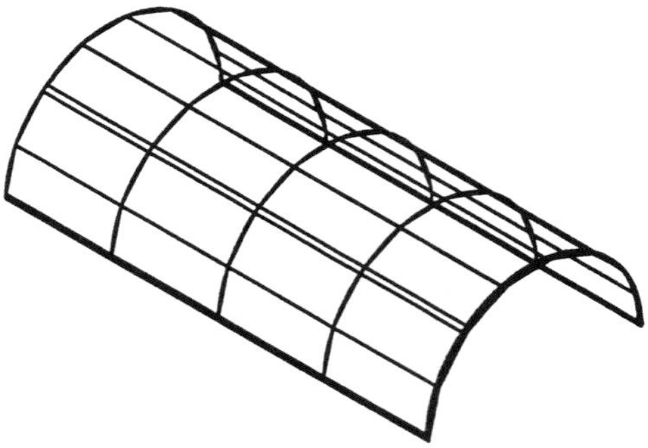

Figure 13.69a Ruled surface before blending

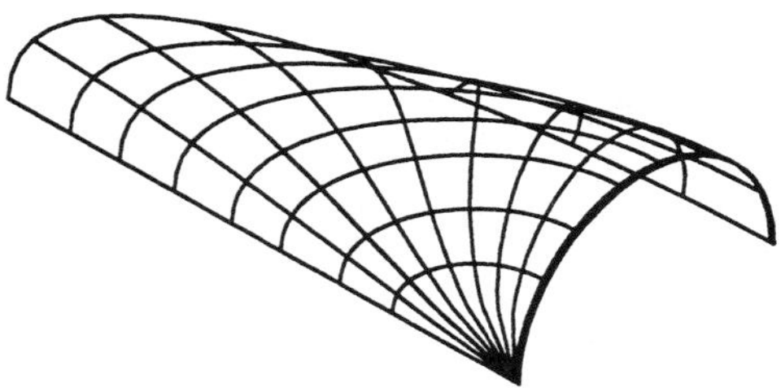

Figure 13.69b Blend surface

2. The position you pick to blend onto determines where the blend surface will be started. It also determines the size of the blend surface. Figure 13.70 and 13.71 illustrate the effect of picked locations on the blended surface.
3. The spline direction determines the orientation of the blend surface. The spline direction can be toggled to the along or across direction. The blend surface in normal (perpendicular) to the spline direction. Table 13.5 illustrates the effect of spline direction on blend surfaces.

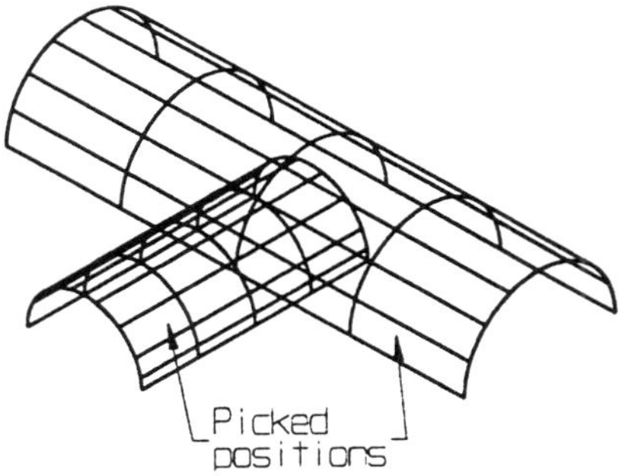

Figure 13.70a Picked positions

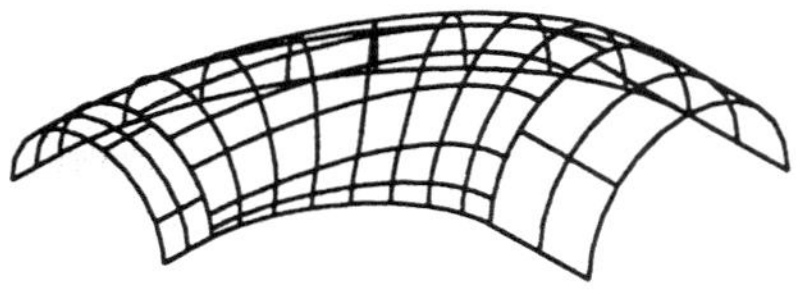

Figure 13.70b Blend surface

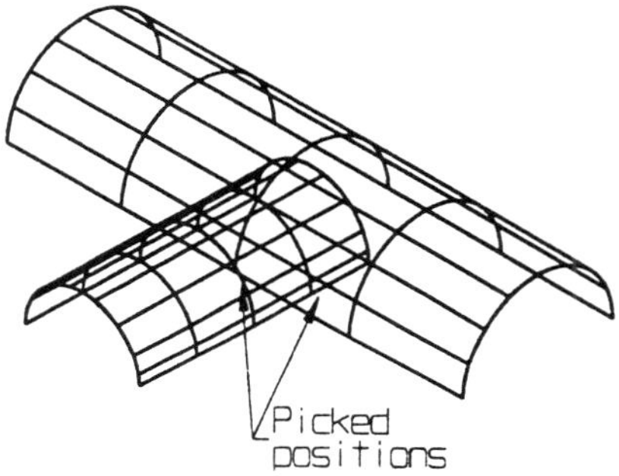

Figure 13.71a Picked positions

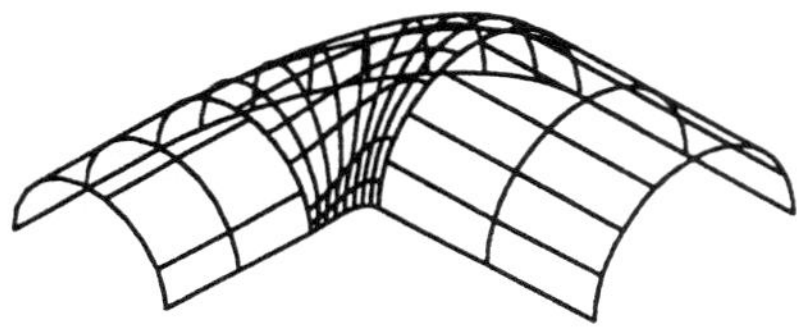

Figure 13.71b Blend surface

Table 13.5 Effects of spline direction on blend surface

Surf1	Surf2	Spline Direction	Resulted Blend Surface
Across	Across	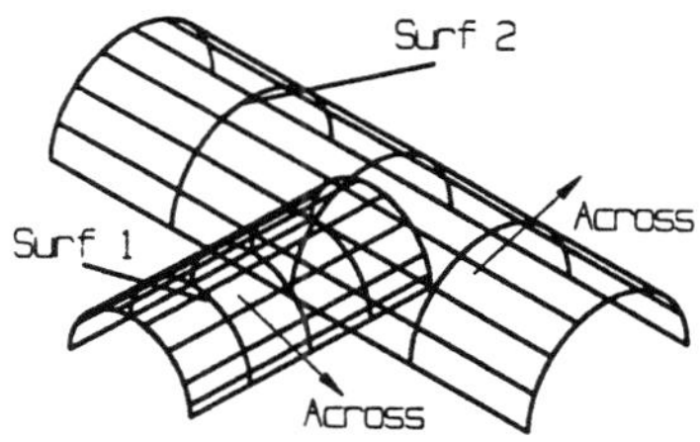	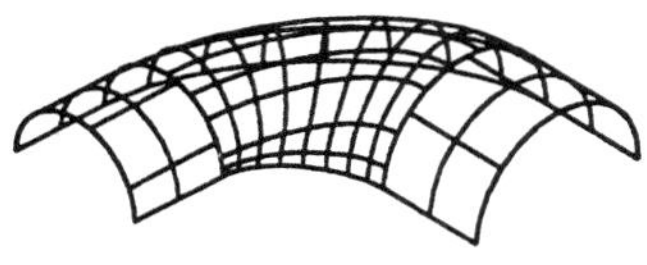
Across	Along	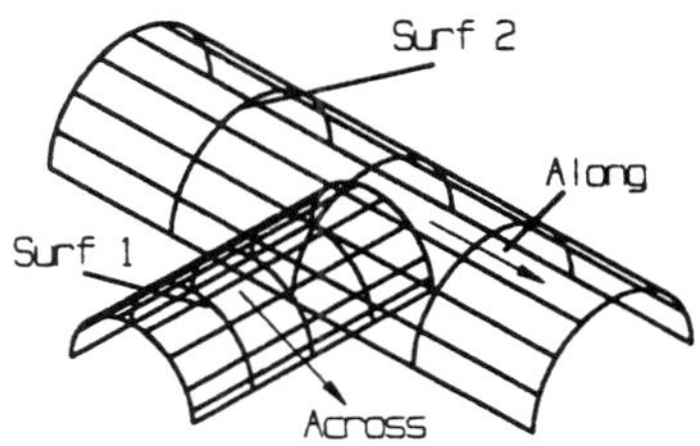	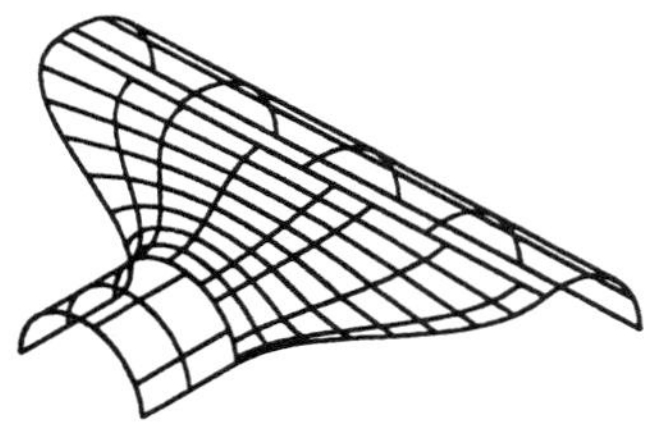
Along	Along	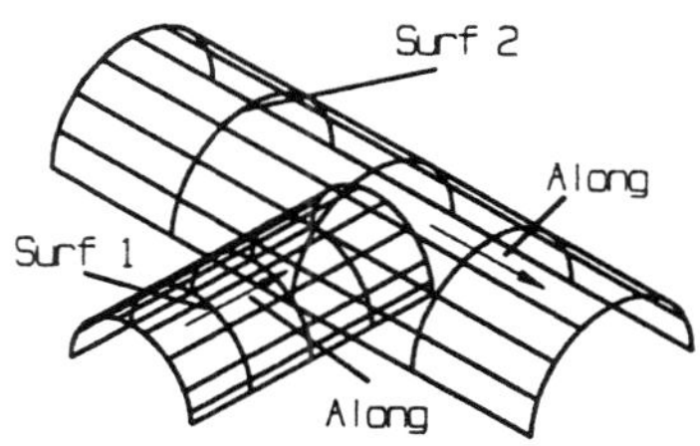	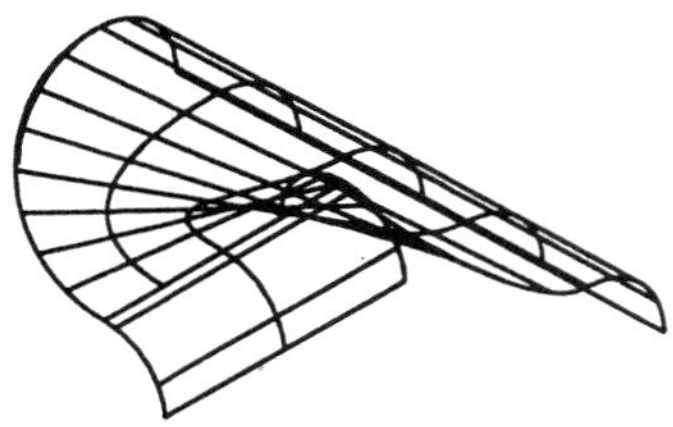

Tip	4. Blending magnitude values.There are two blending magnitude parameters for each surface to define the blend surface shape: start blending magnitude and end blending magnitude. The blending magnitude value can be regarded as the order of the curve that determines the skin form of the surface.

Magnitude Value	Surface Order
0	a plane (1st order)
1	1st order
2	2nd order
3	3rd order

Figure 13.72 shows how the magnitude value affects the blend surface.

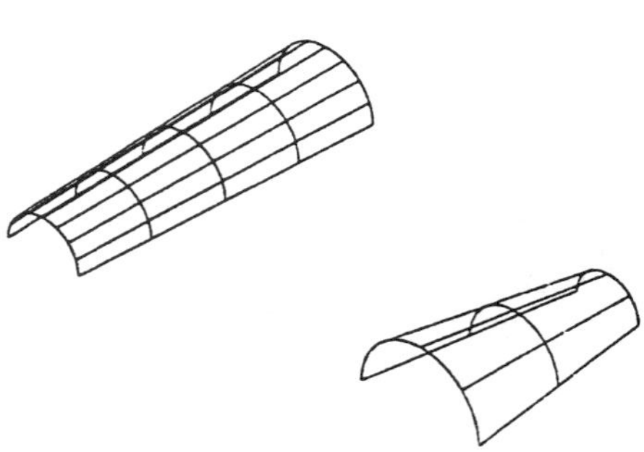

Figure 13.72a Two surfaces

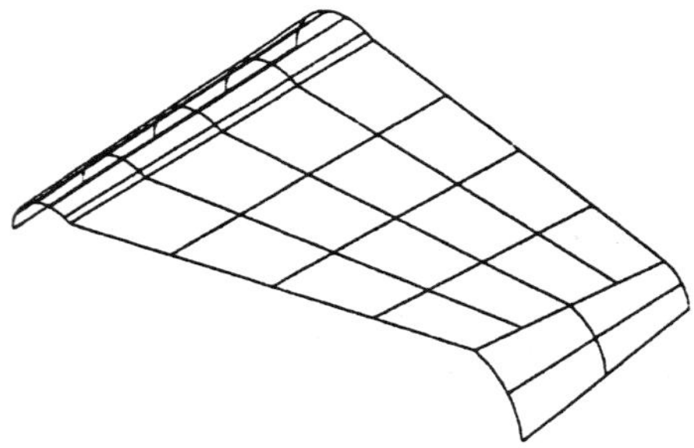

Figure 13.72b Start and end magnitudes are 0

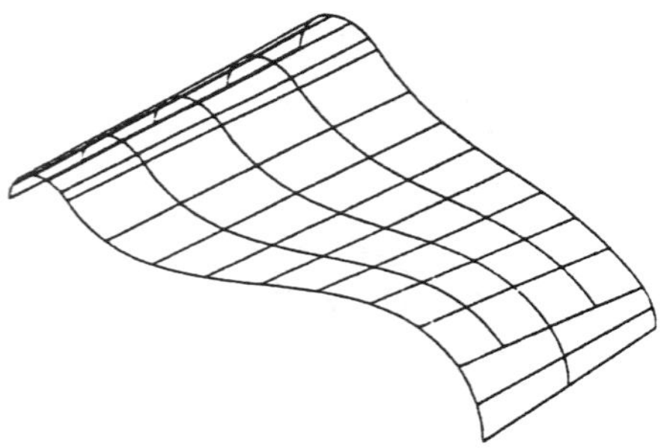

Figure 13.72c Start and end magnitudes are 1

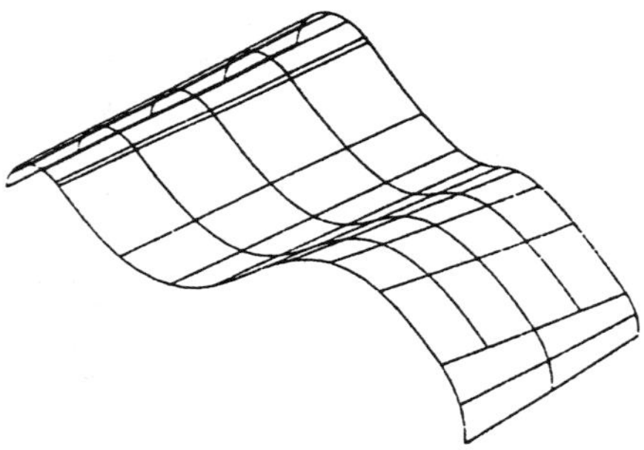

Figure 13.72d Start and end magnitudes are 2

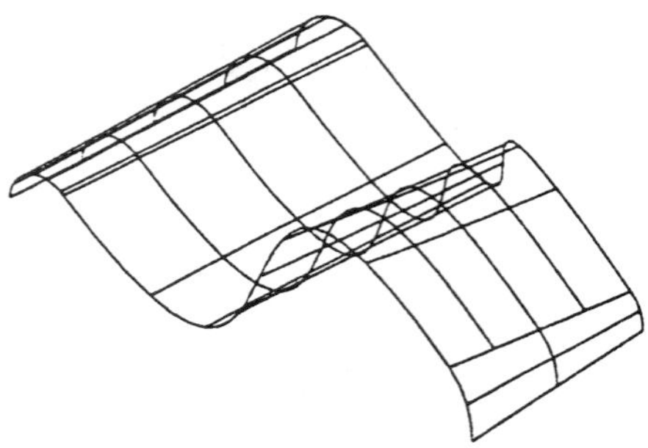

Figure 13.72e Start and end magnitudes are 3

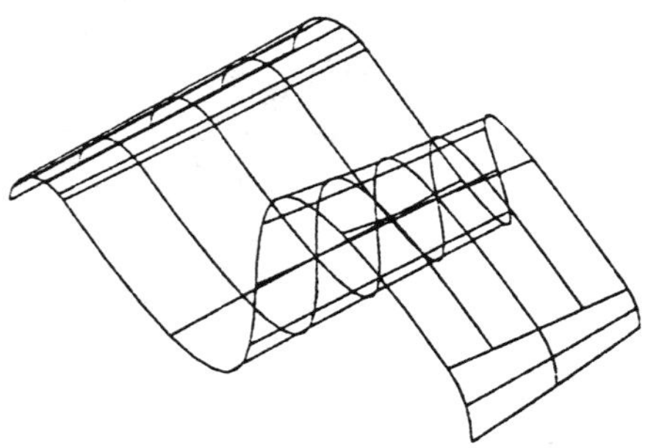

Figure 13.72f Start and end magnitudes are 4

It is possible to have different values for start and end magnitude as shown in Figure 13.73. The blend surface in Figure 13.73a has a value of 2 for the start magnitude and 1 for the end magnitude in both parent surfaces. In Figure 13.73b the start magnitude for surf1 is 3 and the remaining three magnitudes are 1.

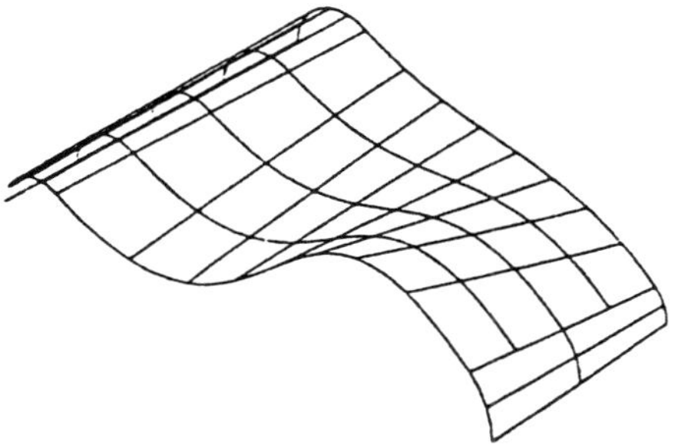

Figure 13.73a

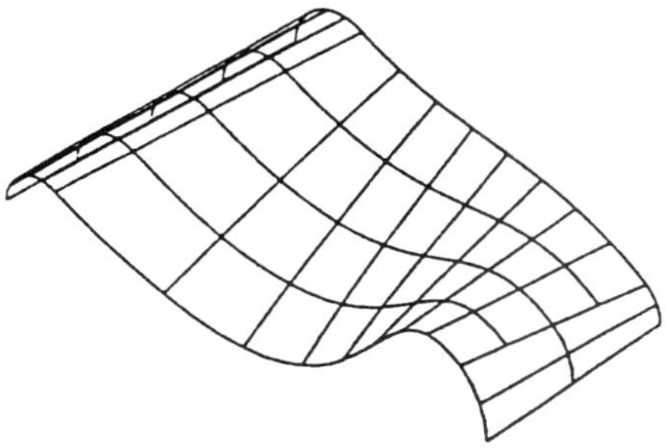

Figure 13.73b

Tip	5. The selection of surface and the kept section

Case 1: **Spline orientation is in a cross direction for both surfaces.** The direction of the blend surface and the kept section of the two parent surfaces are decided by the relationship between the two picked points located on two surfaces. The blending directions on the two parent surfaces are always opposed to each other (Figure 13.74a & a', b & b').

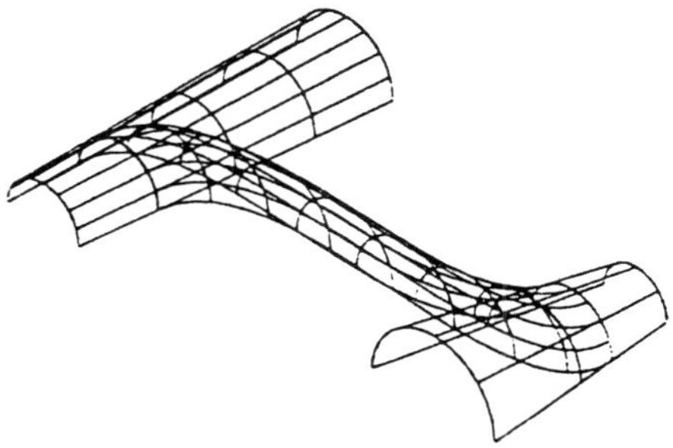

Figure 13.74a

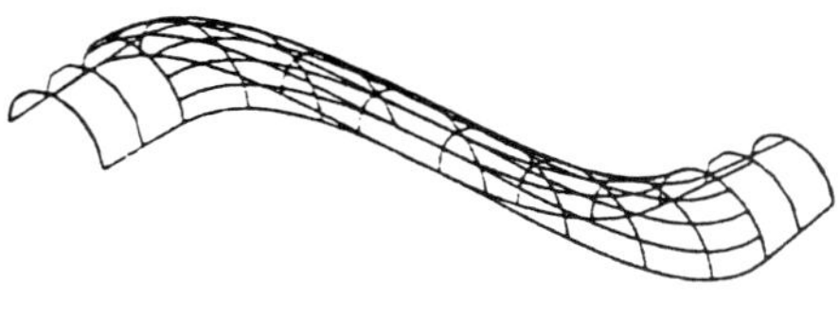

Figure 13.74a'

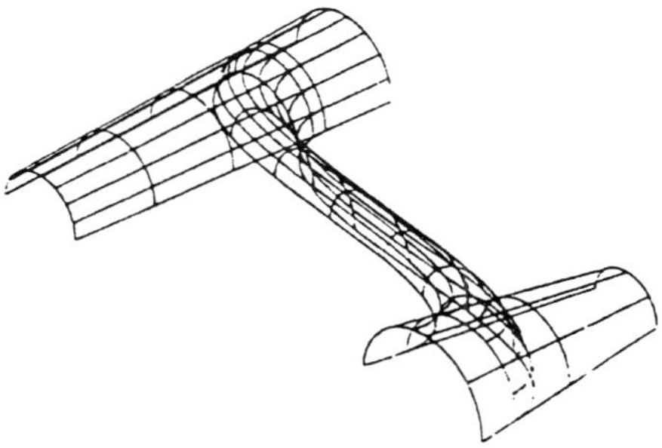

Figure 13.74b

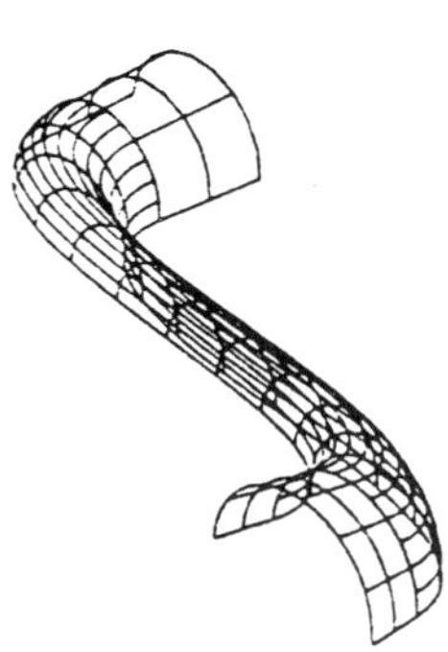

Figure 13.74b'

If the trim parameter is set for one surface or both surfaces, the kept section is the one opposite to the blend surface direction.

Case 2: Spline orientation of one surface is in along and the other in across.

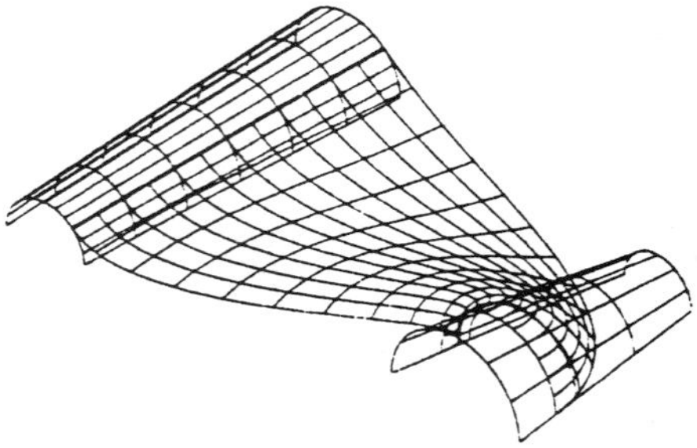

Figure 13.75a

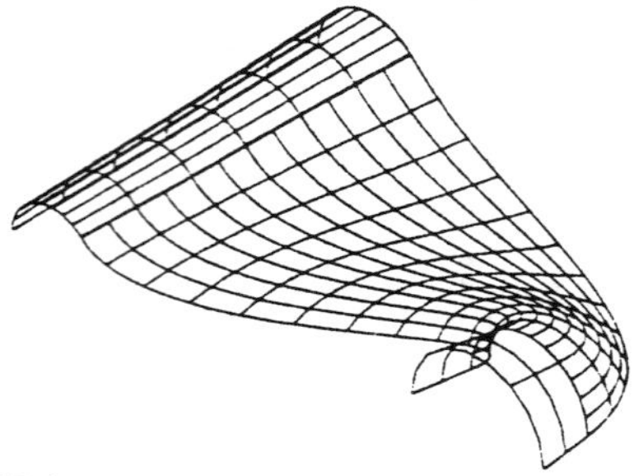

Figure 13.75a'

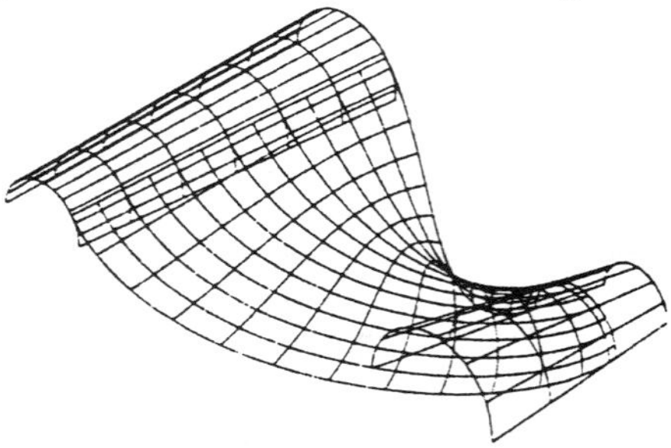

Figure 13.75b

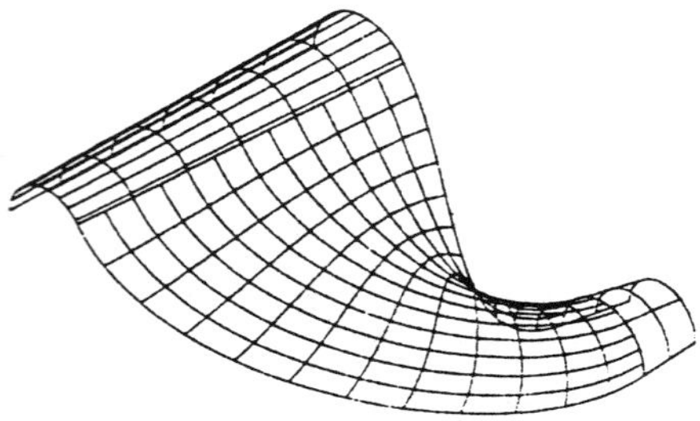

Figure 13.75b'

Case 3: Spline orientation in the along direction for both surfaces.

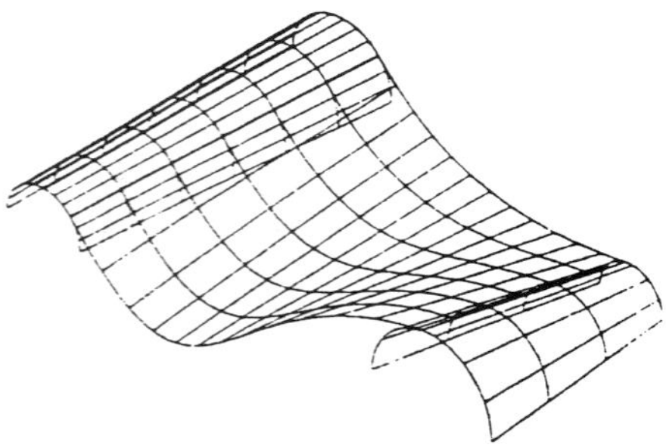

Figure 13.76a

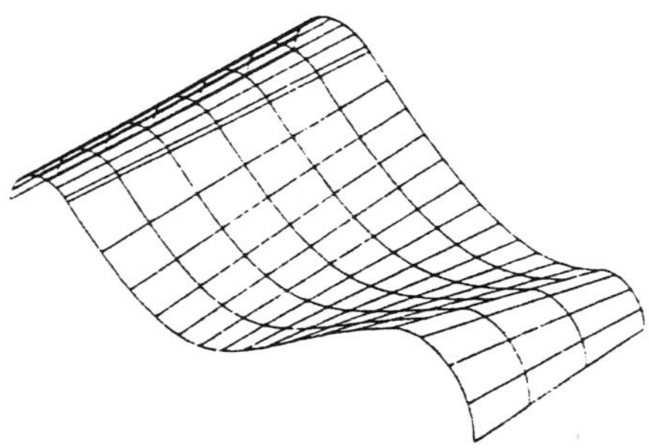

Figure 13.76b

> **Tip** 6. Use the Reverse function to change the mating ends of the blend surface on the two parent surfaces.

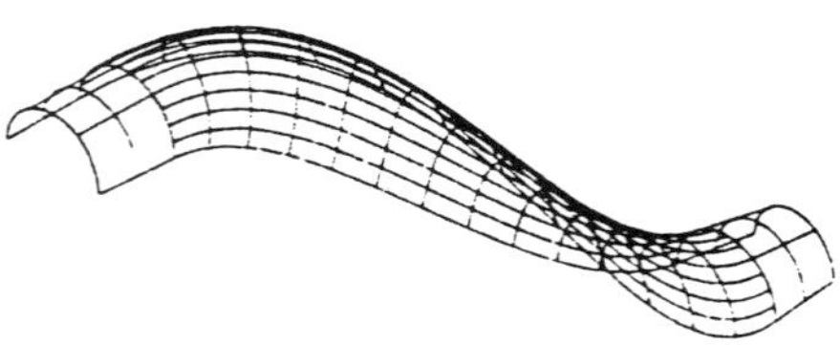

Figure 13.77a Before reverse

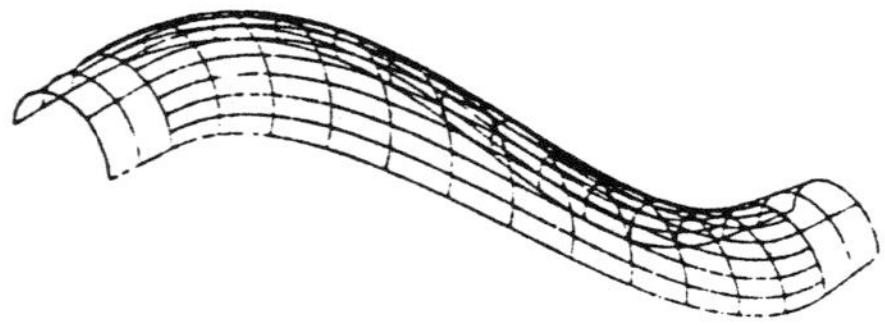

Figure 13.77a' After reverse

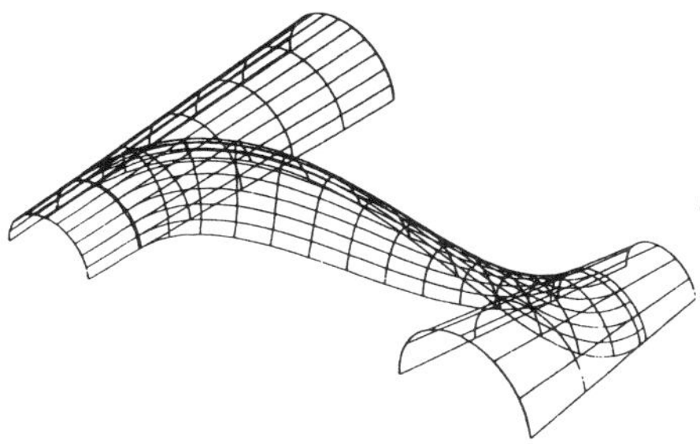

Figure 13.77b Before reverse

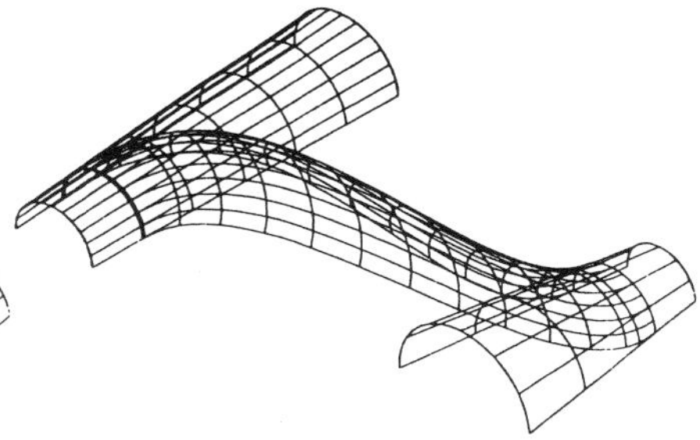

Figure 13.77b' After reverse

Project 7. Blend surfaces between two intersected surfaces

Create three blend surfaces based on the two intersected ruled surfaces generated in project 2 of chapter 12. Figure 13.78 shows original surface model and three blend surfaces.

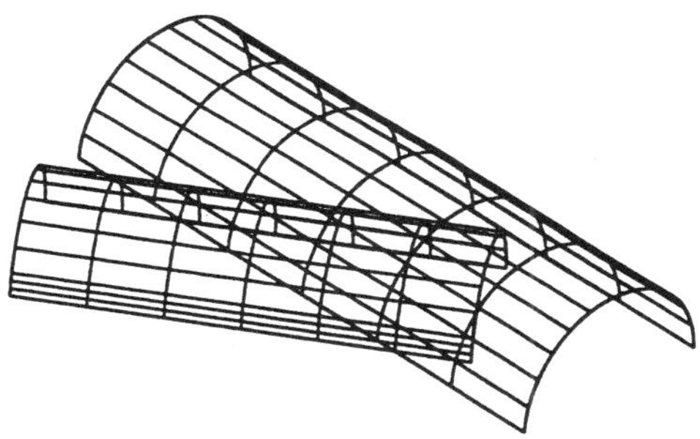

Figure 13.78a

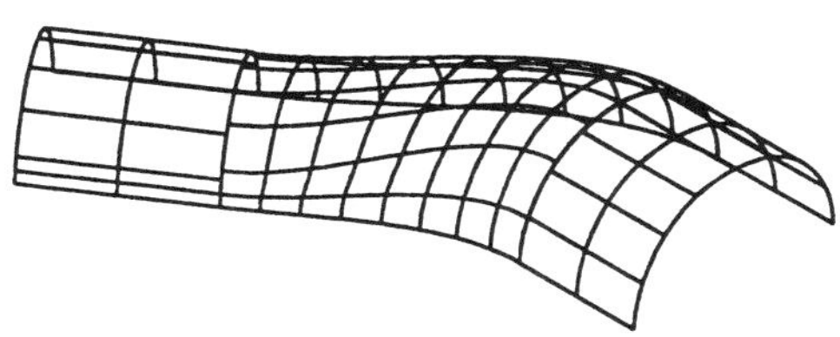

Figure 13.78b

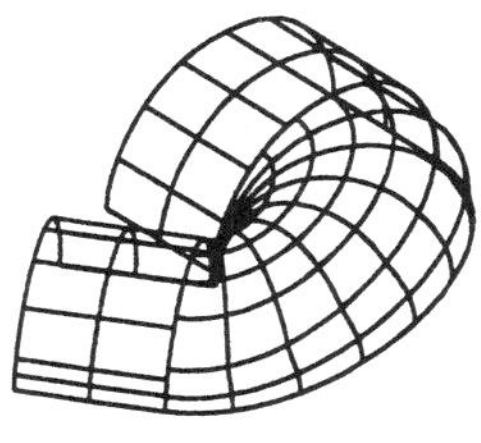

Figure 13.78c

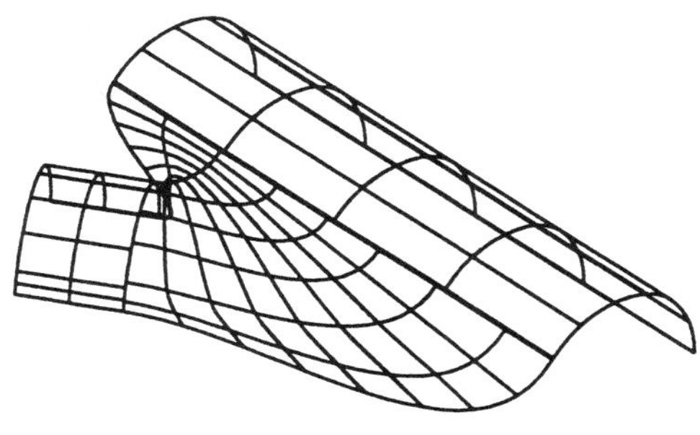

Figure 13.78d

Tips
1. The spline orientation of both parent surfaces should be set to the across direction for the first blend surface (Figure 13.78b) and second blend surface (Figure 13.78c). The third blend surface (Figure 13.78d) has the along direction in the main surface and the across direction in the other surface.
2. Set the Trim srfs parameter to B (both) to trim both parent surfaces to the spline curves.
3. Set surf type parameter to N (NURBS).

Case 1.

Step 1. Open the surface file ruleds2 and set level to 2.

Select **MAIN MENU → File → Get**

File name: **ruleds2**

Select **Level**, then enter **3**

The two ruled surfaces should appear as Figure 13.79.

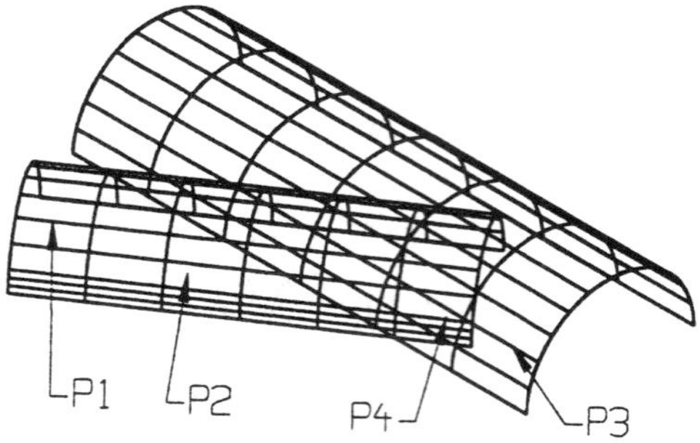

Figure 13.79

Step 2. Initiate the blend surface function.

Use pick points in Figure 13.79.

Select **MAIN MENU → Create → Surface → Blend → 2 Surface**

Pick **P1** to select a surface to blend onto

Indicate the position of the spline curve, pick **P2**

An arrow should appear to indicate the default spline orientation (in the along direction)

Select **Flip** to change the spline direction to the across direction if necessary

Select **OK** to accept the across direction

Pick **P3** to select the other surface to blend onto

Select the position of the spline curve, pick **P4**

Select **Flip** to change the spline direction to the across direction if necessary

Select **OK** to accept a spline orientation in the across direction

Set blending parameters as below:

Trim surfs:	= **B**
Keep crvs:	= **N**
Keep crvs:	= **N**

Select **Do it**

The blend surface mesh should appear as in Figure 13.80.

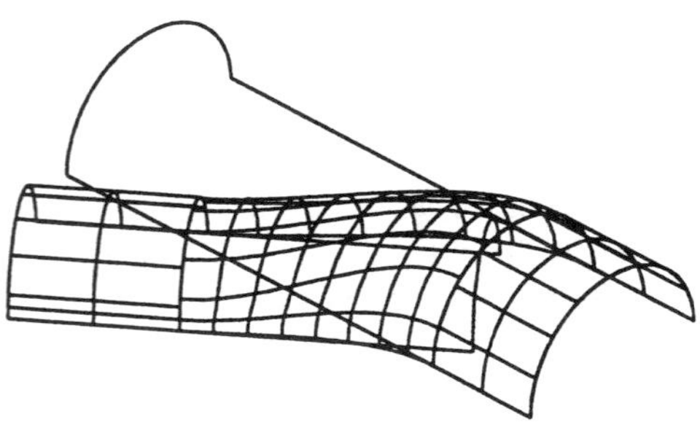

Figure 13.80

Step 3. Make level 1 to invisible.

Select **Level → Vis. Levels**
Toggle level 1 to invisible (dimmed)
Select **OK** to return back to graphic mode
The blend surface with two kept surface sections of parent surfaces are shown in Figure 13.81.

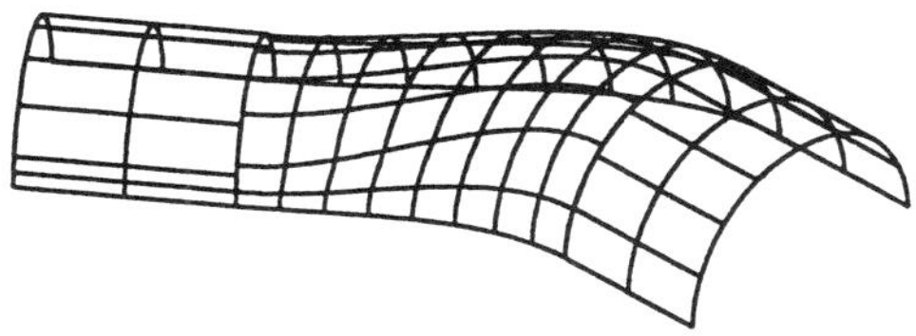

Figure 13.81

Step 4. Save the surface as blends1.

Select **MAIN MENU → File → Save**
Enter file name: **blends1**

<u>**Case 2:**</u>

Step 1. Load the surface file ruled2.

Select **Get**
Enter file name: **ruled2**
The surface model appears as Figure 13.82.

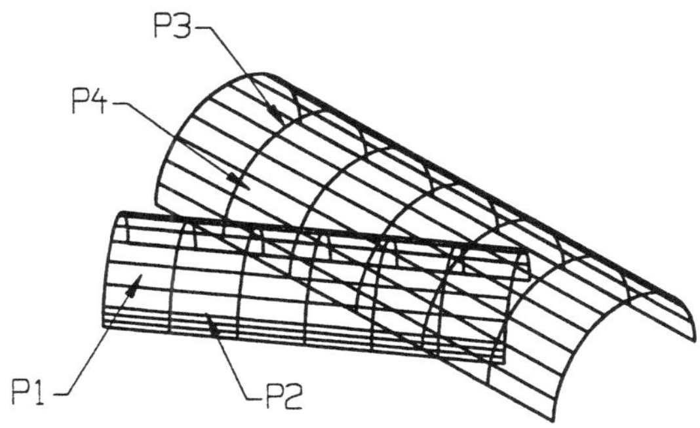

Figure 13.82

Step 2. Initiate the blend surface function.

Use the pick points in Figure 13.82.
Select **MAIN MENU → Create → Surface → Blend → 2-Surface**
Pick **P1** to select a surface to blend onto
Decide the spline location, pick **P2**
Select **Flip** to change the spline direction to across if necessary
Select **OK** to accept the spline direction (across)
Pick **P3** to select another surface
Decide the spline location, pick **P4**
Select **Flip** to change the spline to the across direction if necessary
Select **OK** to accept the across spline direction

Step 3. Define the surface Blending parameters as below.

Trim srfs	= **B**
Keep crvs	= **N**
Surf type	= **N**

Select **Do it**
The blend surface should be added as in Figure 13.83.

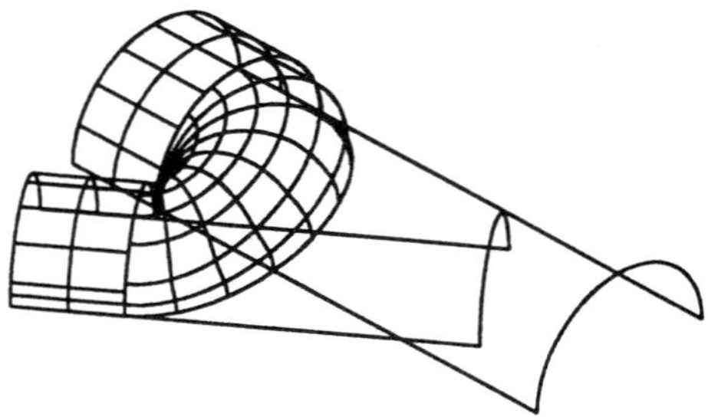

Figure 13.83

Step 4. Make level 1 invisible.

Select **Level → Vis. Levels**
Toggle level 1 button to invisible (dimmed)
Select **OK** to return to graphic mode.
The final blend surface should appear as in Figure 13.84.

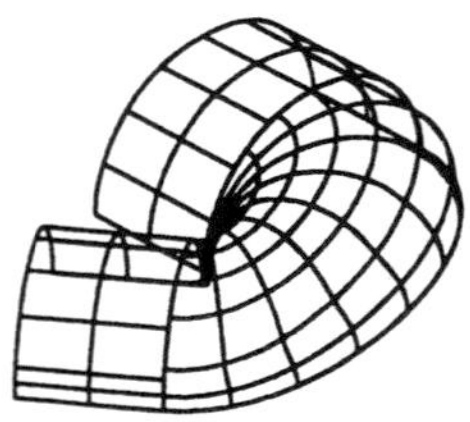

Figure 13.84

Step 5. Save the surface as blends2.

Select **MAIN MENU → File → Save**
File name: **blends2**

<u>Case 3:</u>

Step 1. Load the surface file ruleds2.

Select **Get**
Enter file name: **ruleds2**
Select **Level**, then enter **3**
The surface model appears as Figure 13.85.

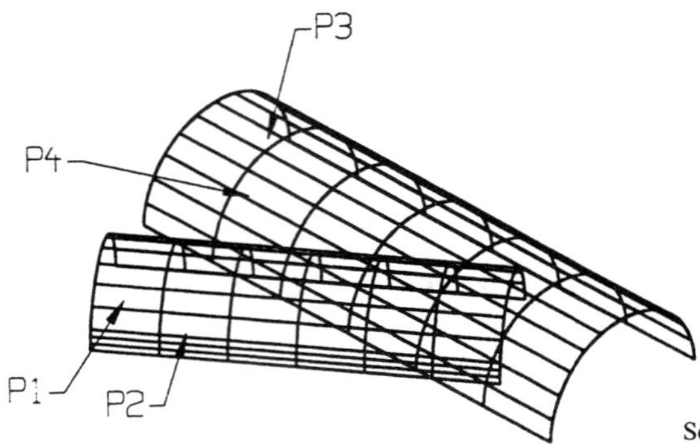

Figure 13.85

Step 2. Initiate the blend surface function and pick surfaces and spline locations.

Use the pick points in Figure 13.85
Select **MAIN Menu → Create → Surface → Blend → 2 surface**
Pick **P1** to select a surface to blend onto
Determine the spline location, pick **P2**
Select **Flip** to change the spline to the across direction if necessary
Select **OK** to accept the spline direction (across)
Pick **P3** to select another surface
Indicate the spline location, pick **P4**
Select **OK** to have the spline direction in along.

Step 3. Define the Surface Blending parameters as below.

Trim srfs	= **B**
Keep crvs	= **N**
Surf type	= **N**

Select **Do it**
The blend surface is added as in Figure 13.86.

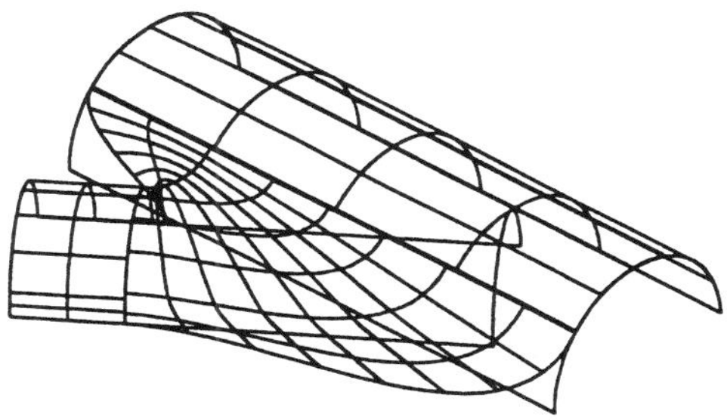

Figure 13.86

Step 4. Make level 1 invisible.

Select **Level → Vis. Levels**, then toggle the level 1 button to invisible (dimmed)
Select **OK** to return to graphic mode
The final surface model should resemble Figure 13.87.

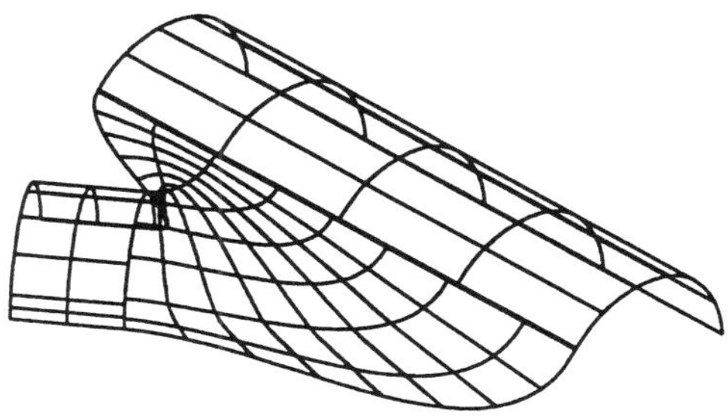

Figure 13.87

Step 5. Save the surface as blends3.

Select **MAIN MENU → File → Save**
Enter file name: **blends3**

3 Surface Blending

Mastercam provides two methods for creating a blend surface between three existing surfaces: 3-Surface and Fillet blnd. The 3 Surface method creates a blend surface from any three existing surfaces, while the Fillet blnd (three fillet blend) method creates a blend surface between three existing surface fillets.

Two examples are given in this section to show how to create a blend surface from three existing surfaces. The first example uses the 3 Surface method and the second one uses the fillet blend method.

Example 13.1 Creating blend surfaces between three surfaces

This example is intended to practice creating blend surfaces between three surfaces. Figure 13.88 shows the three stages of the model; wireframe, 3 ruled surfaces and 3 blend surfaces, each between two surfaces, and complete model.

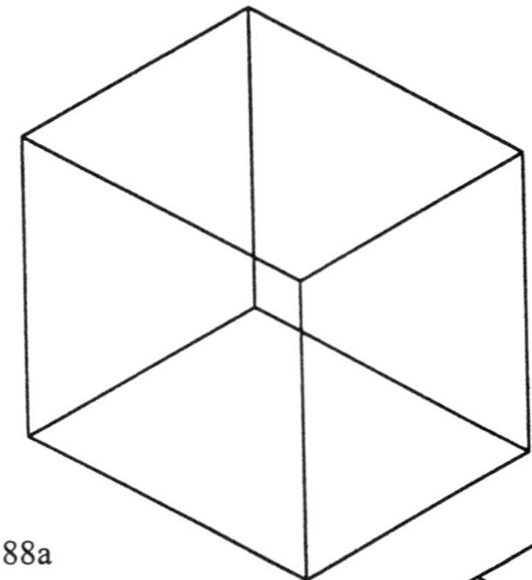

Figure 13.88a

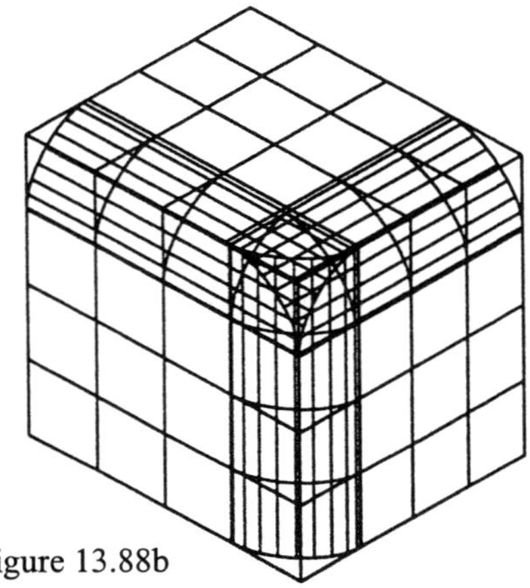

Figure 13.88b

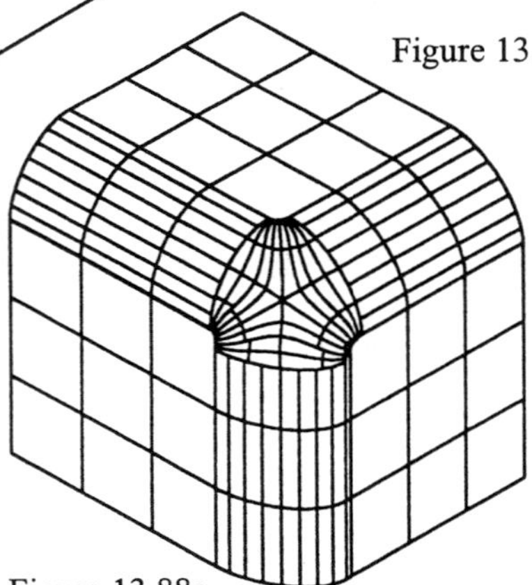

Figure 13.88c

Tips 1. Create a rectangular cube.

2. Create three flat ruled surfaces on three sides; top, front, and side.

3. Create three blend surfaces each between two ruled surfaces.

4. Trim three ruled surfaces to the surface curves of the blend surfaces.

5. Create a blend surface between three blend surfaces.

Step 1. Create a rectangle.

Select **Cplane → Top**
Select **Gview → Isometric**
Select **Create → Rectangle → 1 point**
Enter the lower left corner: **0,0**
Enter the width: **6**
Enter the height: **5**
Press **Alt+F1**, then **F2** to fit the drawing on the screen
The rectangle should appear on the screen as in Figure 13.89.

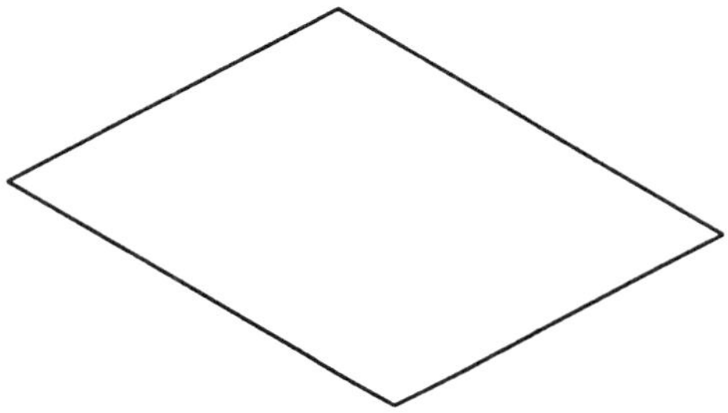

Figure 13.89

Step 2. Copy the rectangle to form a rectangular cube.

Select **MAIN MENU → Xfrom → Translate → Chain**
Pick any line on the rectangle
Select **Done → Done → Rectangle**
Enter the translation vector: **z-6**
Select **Join**
Number of Steps=**1**
Select **Done**
The rectangular cube is created as in Figure 13.90.

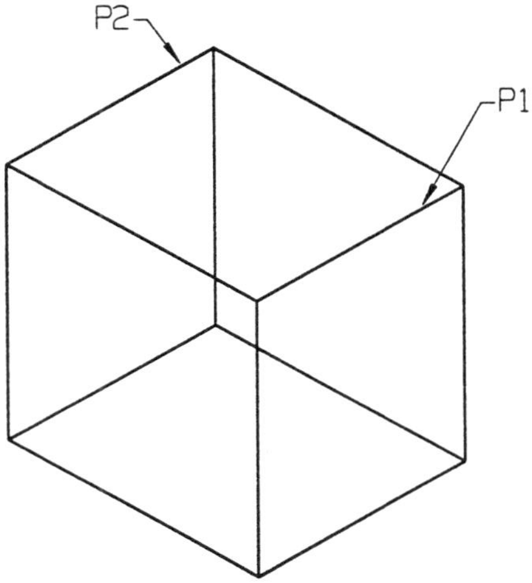

Figure 13.90

Step 3. Create a ruled surface on the top face.

Use the pick points in Figure 13.90
Select **Level**, then enter **2**
Select **Color**, then enter **10**
Select **Create → Surface → Ruled → Single**
Pick **P1** and **P2** to define two contours
Select **Done**

Set the ruled surface parameters:

Surface error tolerance =**0.005**
Surface type = **N (NURBS)**

Select **Do it**

Select **Do it**
The ruled surface is added as in Figure 13.91.

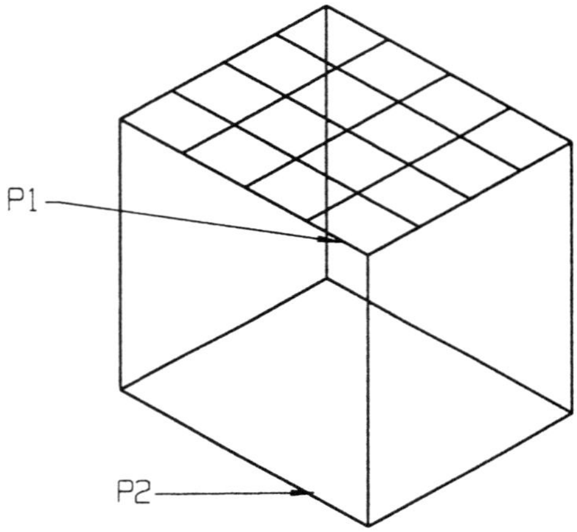

Figure 13.91

Step 4. Create a ruled surface on the front face.

Use the pick point in Figure 13.91
Select **Color**, then enter **11**
Select **Single**
Pick **P1** and **P2** to select two contours
Select **Done → Do it**
The second ruled surface is added as in Figure 13.92.

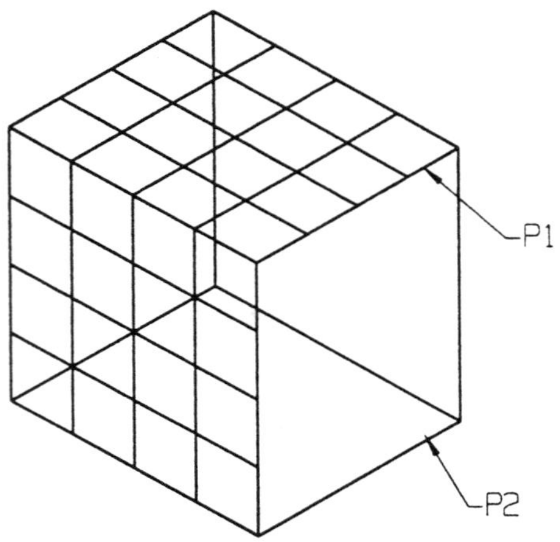

Figure 13.92

Step 5. Create a ruled surface on the side face.

Use the pick point in Figure 13.92
Select **Color**, then enter **12**
Select **Single**
Pick **P1** and **P2**
Select **Done → Do it**
The third ruled surface appears as in Figure 13.93.

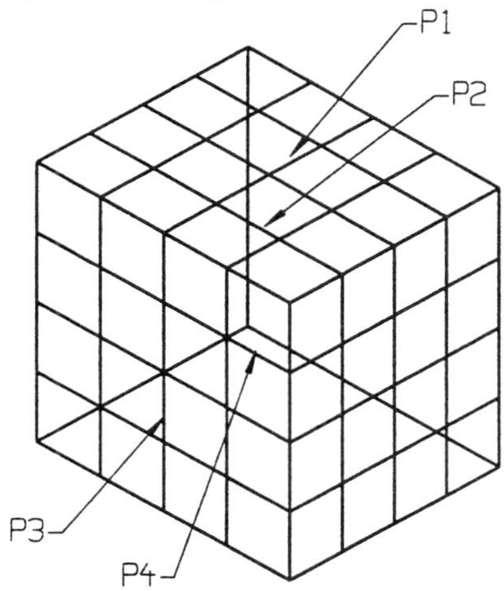

Figure 13.93

Step 6. Create a blend surface between top and front face.

Use the pick points in Figure 13.93
Select **Level**, then enter **3**
Select **Color**, then enter **13**
BACKUP → Blend → 2 surface

Pick **P1** to select a surface to blend onto
Pick **P2** to position the blend surface

Set the Spline direction parallel to the X-axis
(click on the Flip command to change the direction if necessary)
Select **OK**

Pick **P3** to select another surface to blend onto
Pick **P4** to position the blend surface
Select **Flip** to set the spline direction parallel to the X-axis
Select **OK**
Set blending parameters as below

Trim surfs= **N** Keep crvs= **B** Surf type= **N** Select **Do it**

The blend surfaces is created as in Figure 13.94.

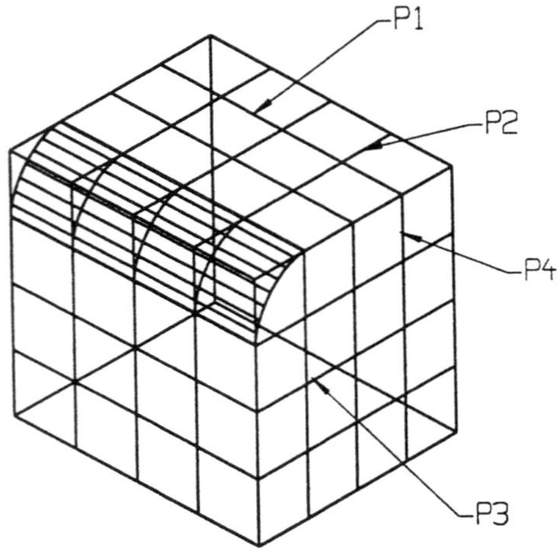

Figure 13.94

Step 7. Create a blend surface between top and side face.

Use the pick points in Figure 13.94
Select **Color**, then enter **14**
Pick **P1** to select a surface to blend onto
Pick **P2** to position the blend surface
Set the spline direction **parallel to the Y-axis**, then select **OK**
Pick **P3** to select another surface to blend onto
Pick **P4** to position the blend surface
Set the spline direction **parallel to the Y-axis**, then select **OK**
Select **Do it**
The second blend surface is added as in Figure 13.95.

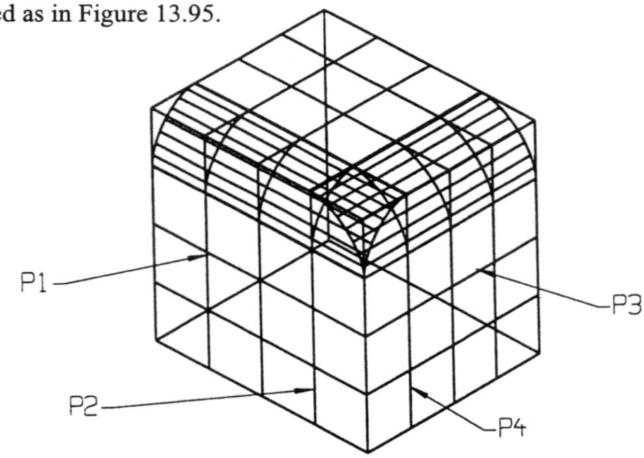

Figure 13.95

Step 8. Create a blend surface between the front and side face.

Use the pick points in Figure 13.95
Select **Color**, then enter **15**
Pick **P1** to select a surface to blend onto
Pick **P2** to position the blend surface
Set the spline direction **parallel to the Z-axis**, then select **OK**
Pick **P3** to select a surface to blend onto
Pick **P4** to position the blend surface
Set the spline direction **parallel to the Z-axis**, then select **OK**
Select **Do it**
The third blend surface is added to the drawing.

Select **Level → Vis. Levels**, then toggle Level 1 to **off**
The new drawing appears as in Figure 13.96.

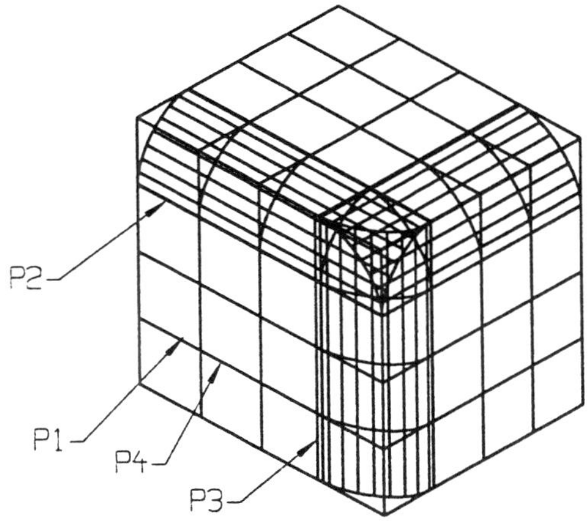

Figure 13.96

Select **MAIN MENU → File → Save**
Enter the file name: **3 blends**
Note: this file will be used in the example 2.

Step 9. Trim the front face to two curves.

Use the pick points in Figure 13.96
Select **Level**, then enter **2**
Select **Color**, then enter **10**
Select **MAIN MENU → Create → Surface → Trim/Extend**
Select **To Curves**
Pick **P1** to select the surface to be trimmed
Select **Done**
Select **Single**, then pick **P2** and **P3** to select two curves
Select **Done**

Select **Option**
Set the Trim surfaces to curves parameters as below

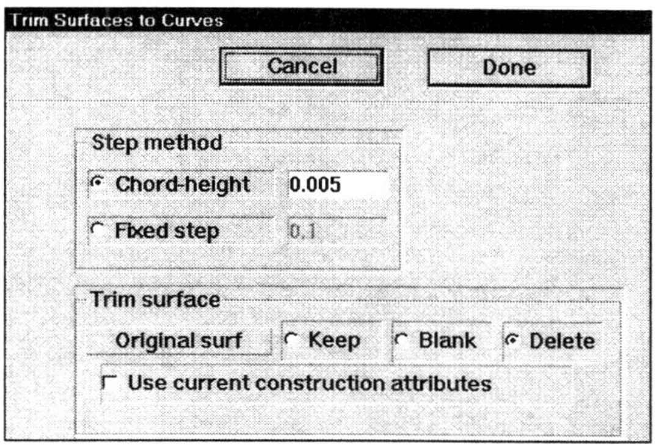

Select **Done**
Set View/Norm to **N**
Select **Do it**
Pick **P1** to select a surface to be trimmed
Pick **P4** to indicate a location to keep after trimming

The front surface is trimmed and the result is displayed in Figure 13.97.

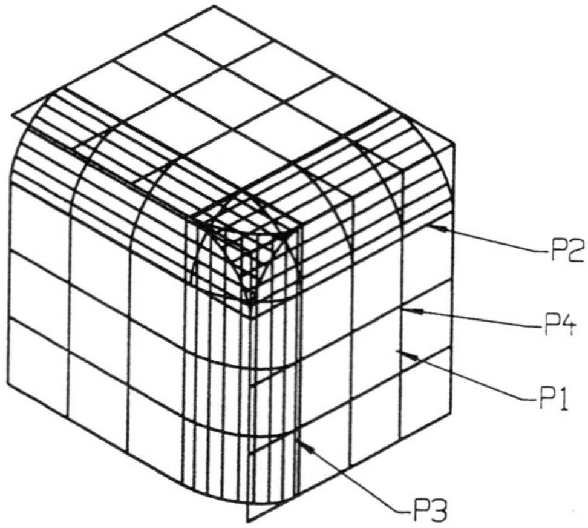

Figure 13.97

Step 10. Trim the side face to two curves.

Use the pick point in Figure 13.97
Select **BACKUP → To curves**
Pick **P1** to select the surface to trim
Select **Done**
Select **Single**, then pick **P2** and **P3** to select two curves
Select **Done → Do it**
Pick **P1** to select a surface to be trimmed
Pick **P4** to indicate the portion to keep after trimming
The side face is trimmed as shown in Figure 13.98.

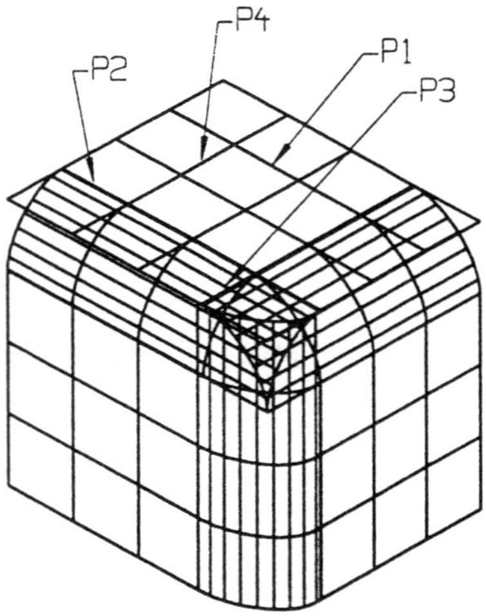

Figure 13.98

Step 11. Trim the top face to two curves.

Use the pick points in Figure 13.98
Select **BACKUP → To Curves**
Pick **P1** to select the surface to trim
Select **Done**
Select **Single**, then pick **P2** and **P3** to select two curves
Select **Done → Do it**
Pick **P1** to select a surface to be trimmed
Pick **P4** to indicate the portion to keep after trimming

The top face is trimmed and the new drawing now becomes as Figure 13.99.

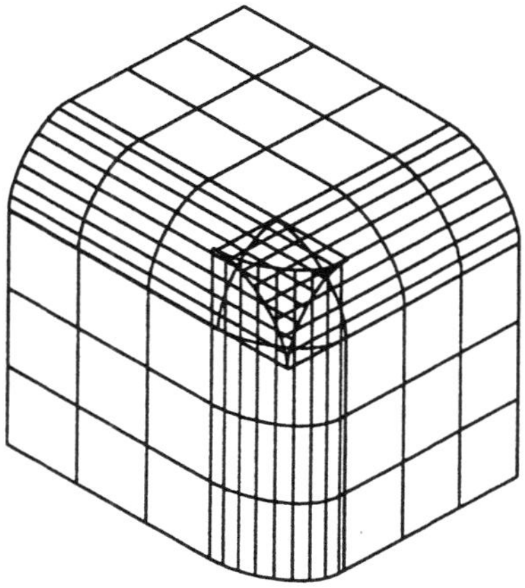

Figure 13.99

Step 12. Hide level 2.

Select **Level → Vis levels**, then toggle level 2 to **off**
Select **OK → OK** to return to graphic mode
The new drawing becomes Figure 13.100.

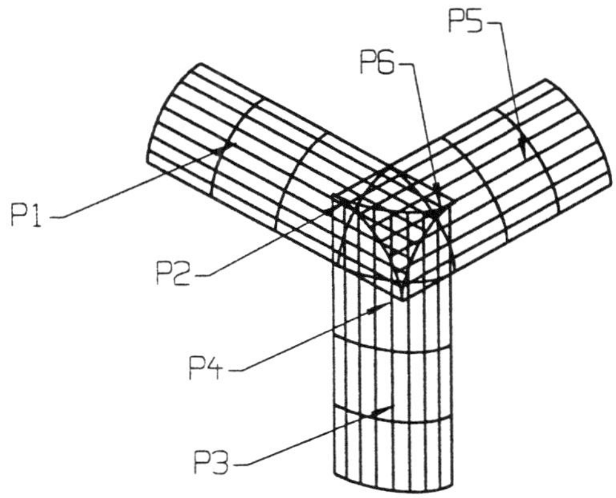

Figure 13.100

Step 13. Create a blend surface between three surfaces.

Use the pick points in Figure 13.100
Select **Level**, then enter **4**
Select **Color**, then enter **10**
Select **BACKUP → Blend → 3 Surface**
Pick **P1** to select the first surface
Pick **P2** to indicate a position to blend onto
Set the spline arrow in the **across direction**, then select **OK**
Pick **P3** to select the second surface
Pick **P4** to select a position to blend onto
Set the spline in the **across direction**, then select **OK**
Pick **P5** to select the third surface
Pick **P6** to select a position to blend onto

Set the spline in the **across direction**

Set blending parameters as below

Trim srfs = **Y** Keep crvs = **N** Surf type = **N**

Select **Do it**

Note: It is very important to pick the proper position for the surface to blend onto. Pick slightly outside the intersection zone to create the proper trimming. Undo the results if they are not what you want. Try again until you obtain the desired result.

The blend surface is created as in Figure 13.101.

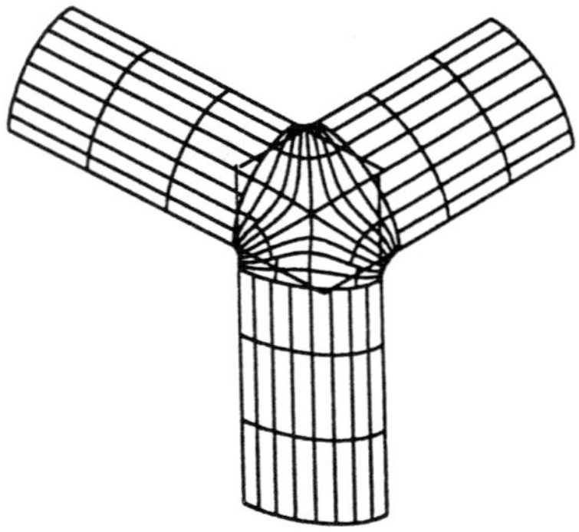

Figure 13.101

Step 14. Delete the unwanted surface curves.

Select **MAIN MENU → Delete → All → Splines**

The new drawing becomes Figure 13.102.

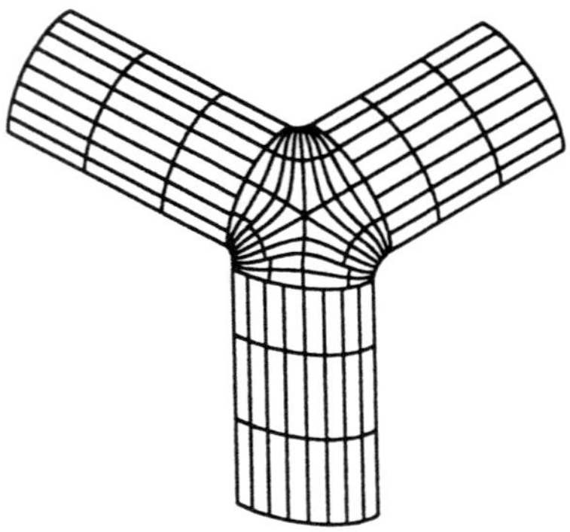

Figure 13.102

Step 15. Make level 2 visible.

Select **Level → Vis. Level**

Toggle level **2** to **ON**, then select **OK**

The complete drawing is shown in Figure 13.103.

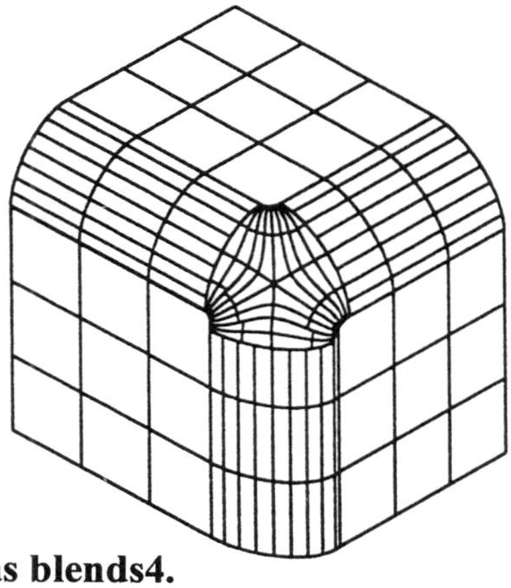

Figure 13.103

Step 16. Save the surface as blends4.

Select **MAIN MENU → File → Save**
Enter the file name: **Blends4**

Example 13.2 Creating a blend surface using three surface fillets

This example uses the three blend surfaces created in Example 1 to create a blend surface by using the Fillet blnd method. Figure 13.104 shows the surface model before and after creating a blend surface between three blend surfaces.

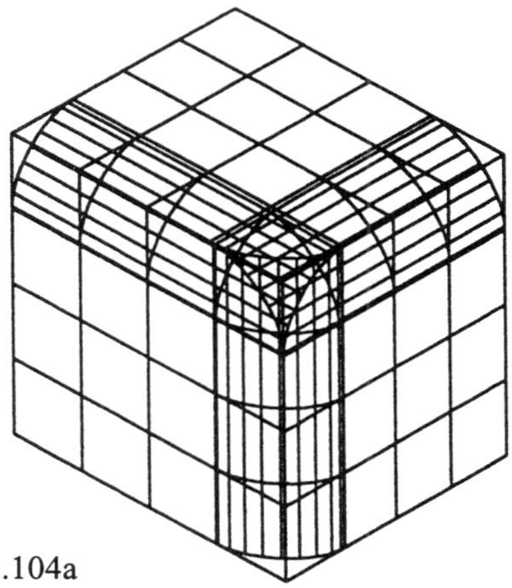

Figure 13.104a

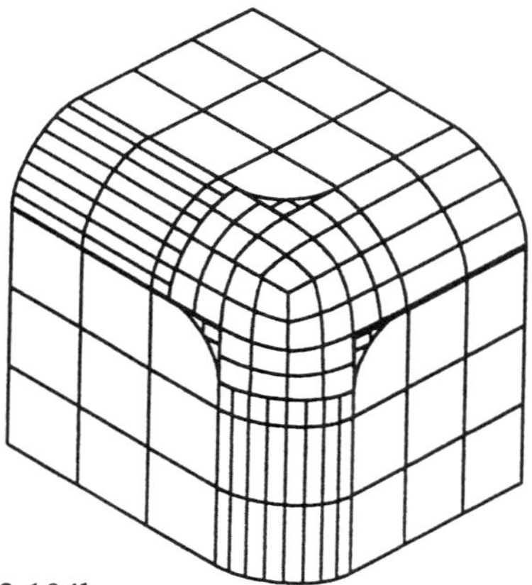

Figure 13.104b

Tips 1. Use the surface model file 3blends created in Example 1 of this section.

2. Use the fillet blnd method to create a blend surface between 3 blend surfaces.

3. Trim three ruled surfaces to the surface curves of the blend surfaces.

Step 1. Load the file 3blends.

Select **MAIN MENU → File → Get**
Enter the file name: **3blends**
If you do not have this file available, follow the instruction given in Step 1 to Step 7 of Example 1 in this section to create one.

The drawing should appear as Figure 13.105.

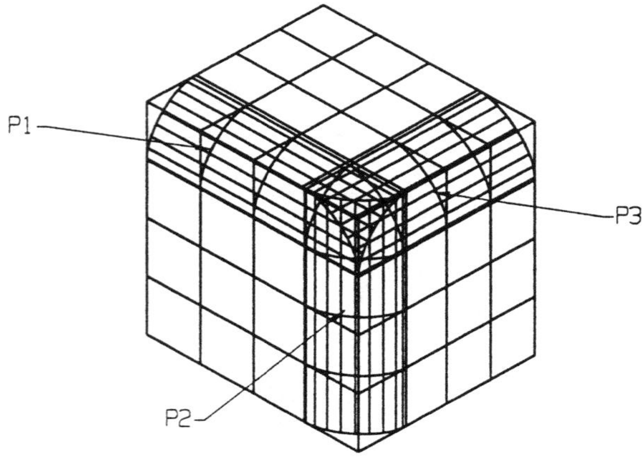

Figure 13.105

Step 2. Create a blend surface using three fillet surfaces.

Use the pick points in Figure 13.105
Select **MAIN MENU → Create → Surface → Blend → Fillet blnd**
Select the first Fillet Surface; pick **P1**
Select the second Fillet Surface; pick **P2**
Select the third Fillet Surface; pick **P3**
Set the fillet blend parameters to the following settings:

Trim = **Y**
DisPose = **D**
Edge spl = **Y**
Sides = **6**
Surf Type = **N**

Select **Do it**
The blend surface is added as shown in Figure 13.106.

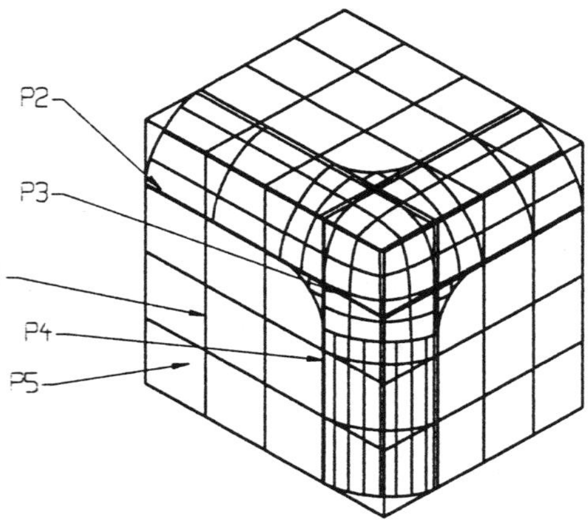

Figure 13.106

Step 3. Trim the front ruled surfaces.

Use the pick points in Figure 13.81
Select **MAIN MENU → MAIN MENU → Create → Surface → Trim/Extend**
Select **to Curves**

Pick **P1** to select the surface to trim
Select **Done**
Select **Single**, then pick **P2**, **P3** and **P4**
Select **Done**
Set View/Norm to **N**
Select **Options**
Set Trim Surfaces to Curves parameters as below

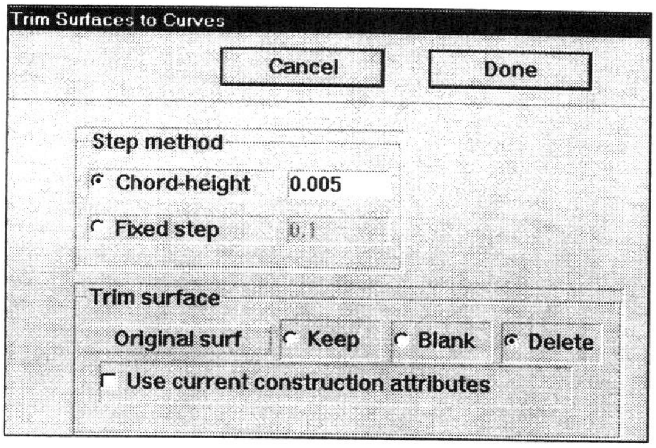

Select **Done**

Select **Do it**
Pick **P1** to select surface to trim
Pick **P5** to indicate a location to keep after trimming
The front surface is trimmed as in Figure 13.107.

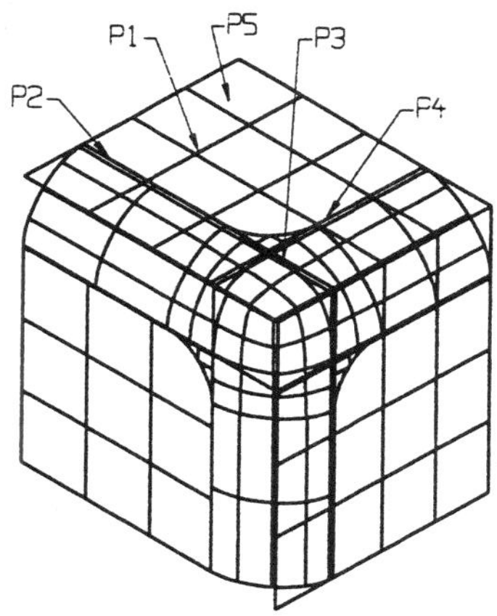

Figure 13.107

Step 4. Trim the top surface using the pick points in Figure 13.107.

Select **BACKUP → To Curves**
Pick **P1** to select the surface to trim
Select **Done**
Select **Single**, then pick **P2**, **P3** and **P4**

Select **Done → Do it**
Pick **P1** to select the surface
Pick **P5** to indicate the surface area to keep

The new drawing should resemble Figure 13.108.

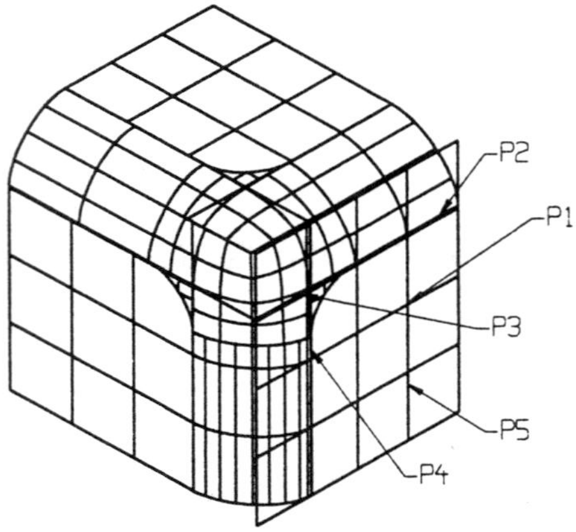

Figure 13.108

Step 5. Trim the side surface using the pick points in Figure 13.108.

Select **BACKUP** → **To Curves**
Pick **P1** to select the surfaces
Select **Done**
Select **Single**, then pick **P2**, **P3** and **P4**
Select **Done** → **Do it**
Pick **P1** to select the surface
Pick **P5** to indicate a location to keep after trimming
The drawing becomes like Figure 13.109.

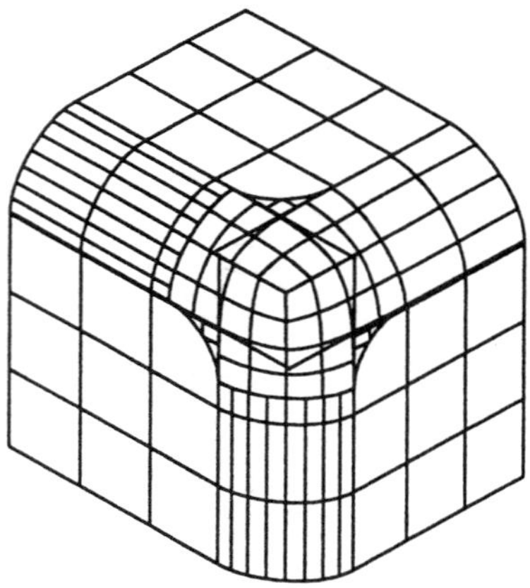

Figure 13.109

Step 6. Delete all splines.

Select **MAIN MENU** → **Delete** → **All** → **Splines**

The drawing should look like Figure 13.110.

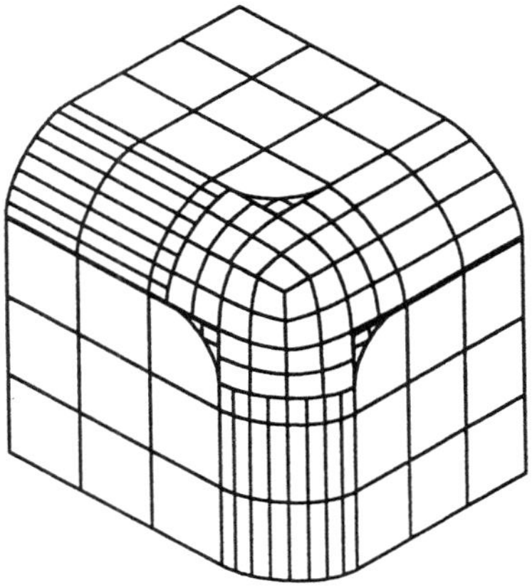

Figure 13.110

Step 7. Make level 2 invisible.

Select **Level → Vis. Levels**
Toggle level 2 to **dim**
Select **OK** to return to graphic mode
The drawing changes to Figure 13.111.

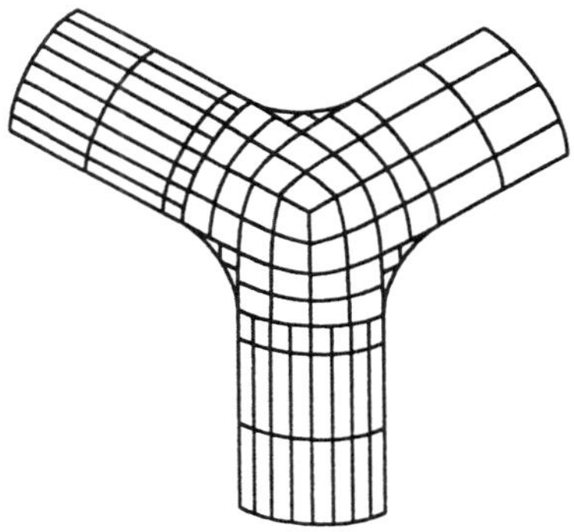

Figure 13.111

Step 8. Change to dynamic view.

Select **Gview → Dynamic**
Pick any point on the screen for drawing axes
Manipulate the mouse to dynamically view the model.

Figure 13.112 shows a dynamic view of the blend surfaces.

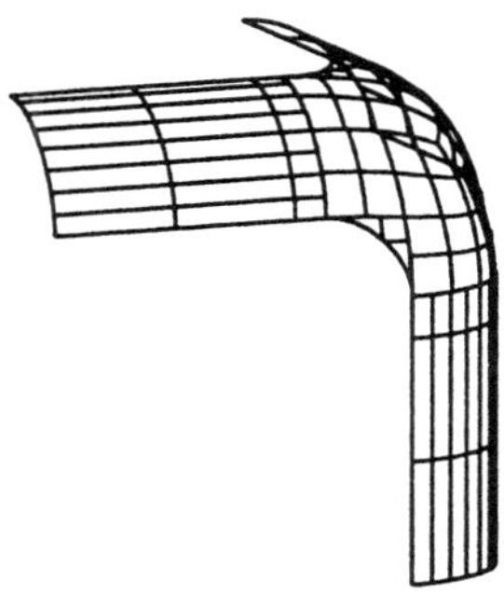

Figure 13.112

8 **Step 9. Change to isometric view.**

Select **Gview → Isometric**
Select **Level → Vis. Levels**
Make level 2 visible →highlighted)
Select **OK**
The complete model is shown in Figure 13.113.

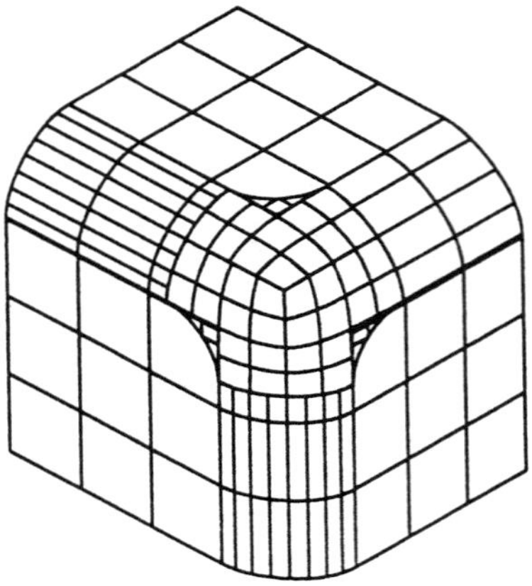

Figure 13.113

Step 10. Save the model as blends5.

Select **MAIN MENU → File → Save**
File name: **blends5**

13.2 Composite Surfaces Models

Composite surface models use more than one surfacing technique to create multiple surfaces in representing an object. In fact, most surface modeling of objects today are of the composite type. Five composite surface models are presenting in this section. They are arranged in increasing order of difficulty. Their wireframe models were presented in chapter 11.

Project 8. Basket surface model

The surface model of a basket shown in Figure 13.114 consists of four surfaces: top rim surface, wall surface surface, bottom flat surface, and fillet surface at the intersection between the wall surface and bottom flat surface.

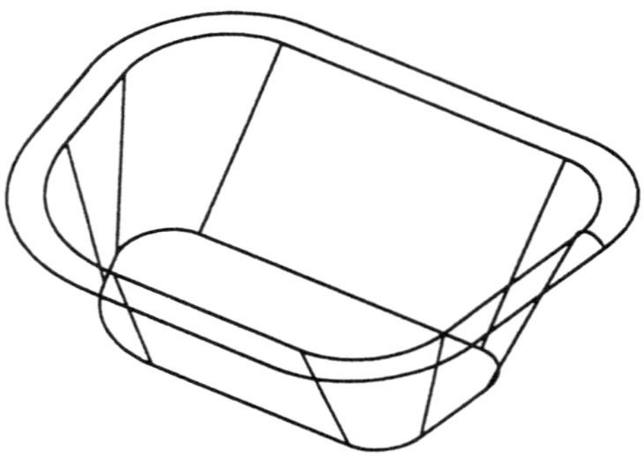

Figure 13.114a Wireframe model

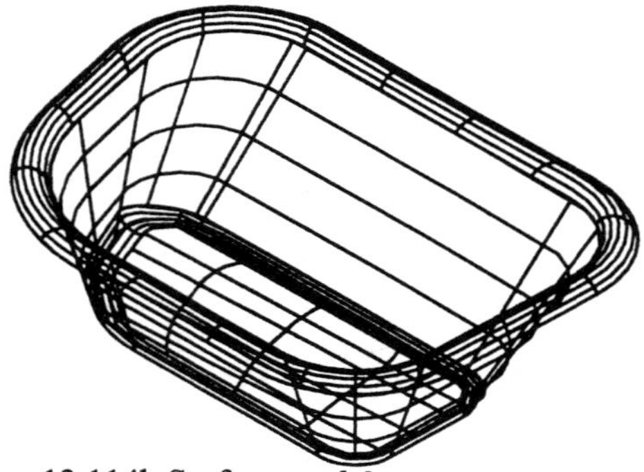

Figure 13.114b Surface model

Tips
1. Use two alone /one across swept surfacing technique to create the top rim surface. The two along contours are the two outer profiles. The across contour is the arc that encompasses these two profiles.
2. Use the Coons surfacing technique to generate the wall surface. The number of patches in the along direction is 8 and the number of patches in the across direction is 1.
3. The bottom flat surface can be modeled as a ruled surface.
4. Add a fillet surface between the wall surface and the bottom flat surface.
5. Use a different level and color for each surface.

Step 1. Load the wireframe model file basket.

Select **MAIN MENU → File → Get**
Enter file name: **basket**
The wireframe model should appear as Figure 13.115.

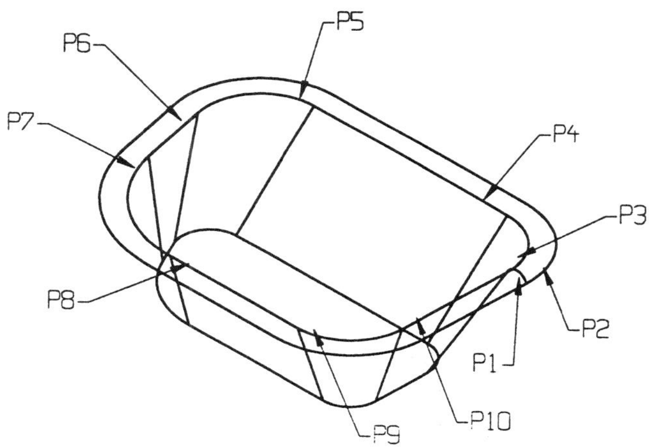

Figure 13.115

Step 2. Create the top rim surface using swept surfacing technique.

Use the pick points in Figure 13.91.
Change level 2 and color to **12**

Select **Level**, then enter **2**
Select **Color,** then enter **12**
Select **MAIN MENU → Create → Surface → Swept**
Enter the number of across contours: **1**
Define the across contour: select **Single**, then pick **P1**
Define along contour 1: Select **Mode → Chain**, then pick **P2**
Select **End here** to complete the along contour 1
Define along contour 2: select **Mode → Chain**
Sequentially pick **P3 – P10**
Select **Enter here → Done** to complete the contour selection

Set the Swept surface parameters to the following settings:

Surface error tolerance = **0.005**
Surface type = **NURBS**

Select **Do it** to complete the swept surface
The swept surface appearing on screen should look like Figure 13.116 on the next page.

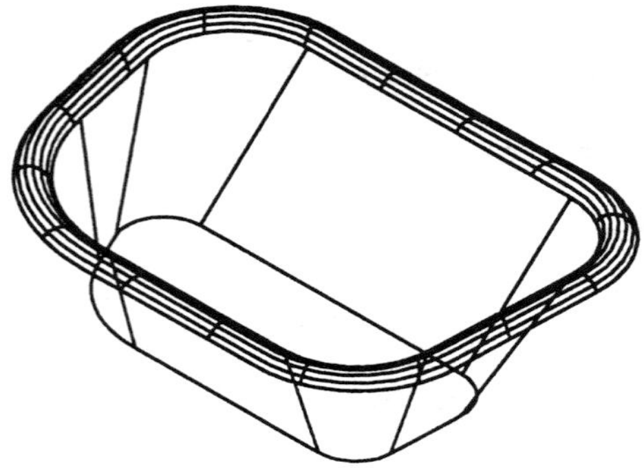

Figure 13.116

Step 3. Make level 2 invisible and change to Top Gview.

Select **Level → Vis. Levels**
Click on button 2 to set invisible (dimmed)
Select **OK → OK** to return the screen back to graphic mode
Select **Gview → Top**

Press **Alt+F1**, then **F2** to fit the drawing, if necessary
The drawing becomes Figure 13.117

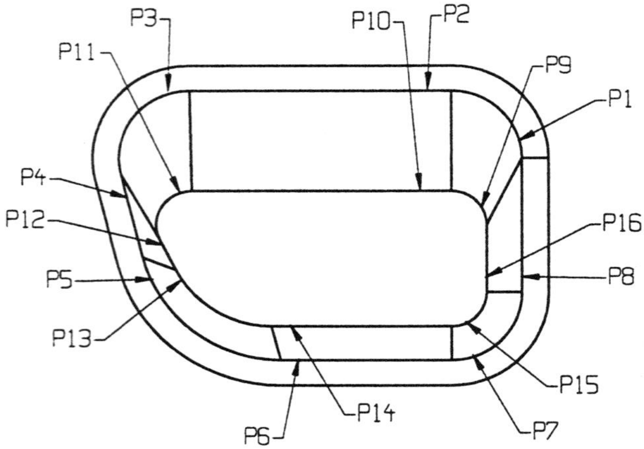

Figure 13.117a

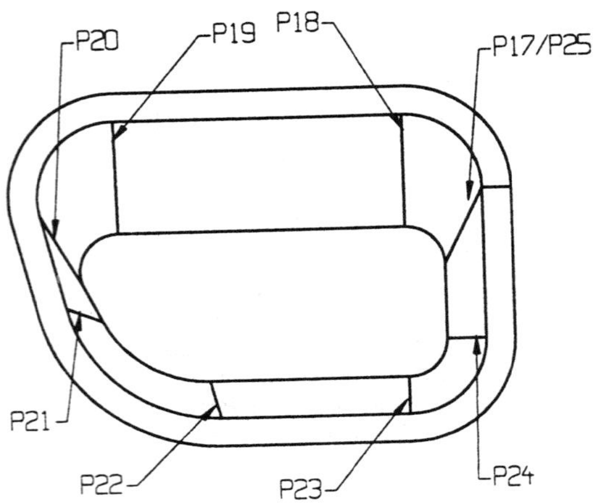

Figure 13.117b

Step 4. Create a Coons surface using the pick points in Figure 13.117.

Select **Level**, then enter **3**
Select **Color**, then enter **13**
Select **MAIN MENU → Create → Surface → Coons**
Select **No** to "Use Automatic coons chaining?"
Enter number of patches in the along direction: **8**
Enter number of patches in the across direction: **1**
Define along contour 1 of row: select **Single**, sequentially pick **P1 to P8** to complete the row 1.
Sequentially pick **P9 to P16** to complete the row 2
Sequentially pick **P17 to P25** to complete the across contour of column 1
Select **Done** to complete the chaining
Set the Coons surface parameters to the following settings:

Surface Error Tolerance = **0.005** Surface type = **NURBS** Blending = **Linear**

Select **Do it** to complete the Coons surface
The new Coons surface appears in Top Gview as in Figure 13.118.

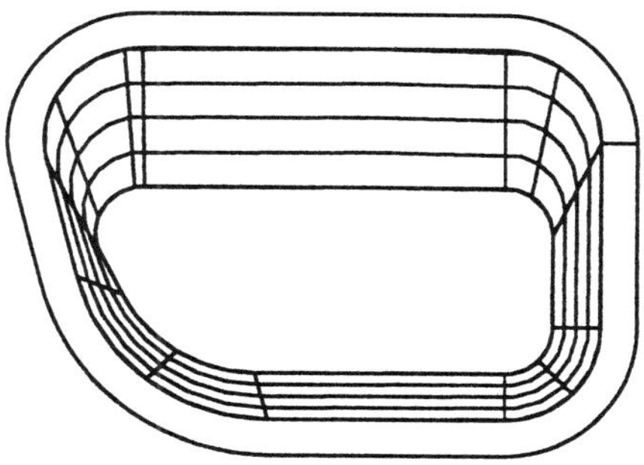

Figure 13.118

Step 5. Make level 3 invisible.

Select **Level**, then enter **4**
Select **Level → Vis.levels**
Click on button 3 to set invisible (dimmed)
Select **OK** to return to graphic mode
The drawing now should look like Figure 13.119.

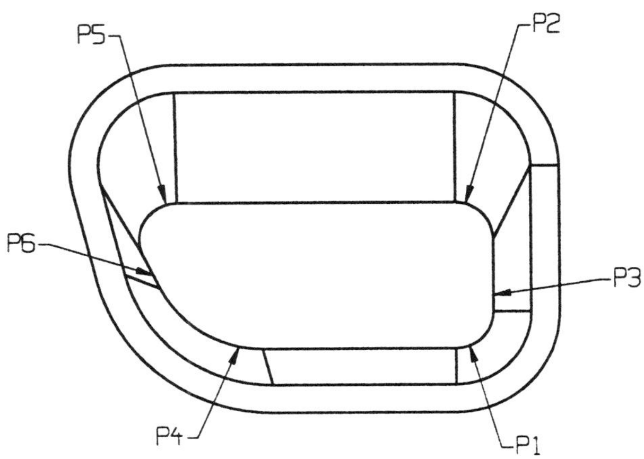

Figure 13.119

Step 6. Create a bottom ruled surface using pick points labeled in Figure 13.119.

Select **Color,** then enter **14**
Select **MAIN MENU → Create Surface → Ruled**
Define contour 1: select **Chain → Partial**
Pick **P1** as the first entity
Pick **P2** as the last entity
Pick **P3** to select new branch
Select **End here** to complete the contour 1
Define contour 2: select **Partial,** then pick **P4** as the first entity
Pick **P5** as the last entity
Pick **P6** to select new branch
Select **Done** to complete contour selection
Select **Do it**
The ruled surface should resemble Figure 13.120.

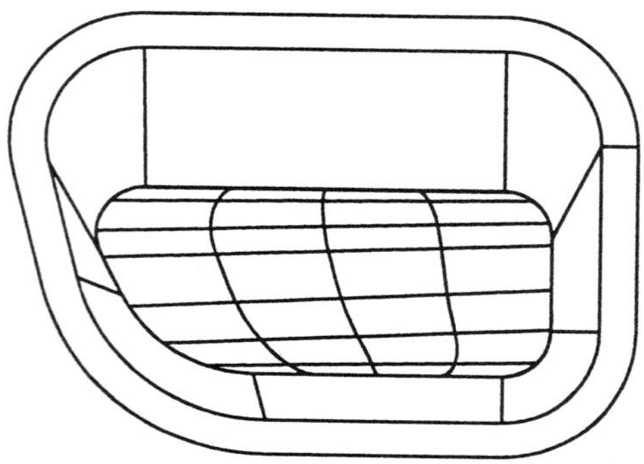

Figure 13.120

Step 7. Toggle level 3 to visible and change the level to 5.

Select **Level → Vis. Levels**
Click on button 3 to set visible →highlighted)
Click **Main**, then enter **5**
The drawing now should look like Figure 13.121.

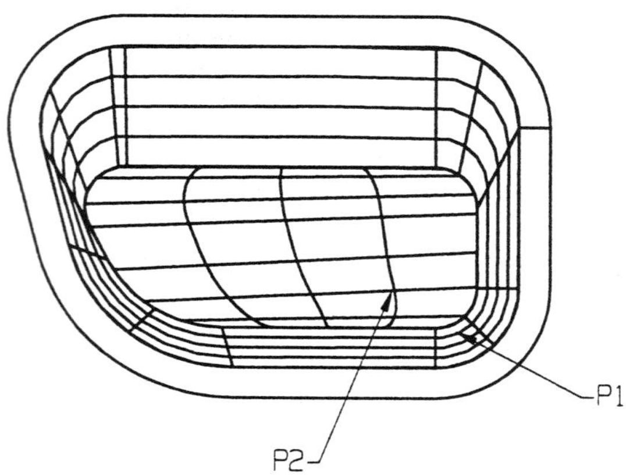

Figure 13.121

Step 8. Create a fillet surface at the intersection of the wall and bottom surfaces.

Use the pick points in Figure 13.121.
Select **Color**, then enter **15**
Select **MAIN MENU → Create → Surface → Fillet → Surf/Surf**

Pick **P1**, then **Done** to select first set of surfaces
Pick **P2** then **Done** to select second set of surfaces
Enter the fillet radius: **0.25**
Select **Options**

Set the surface fillet parameters
to the following settings:

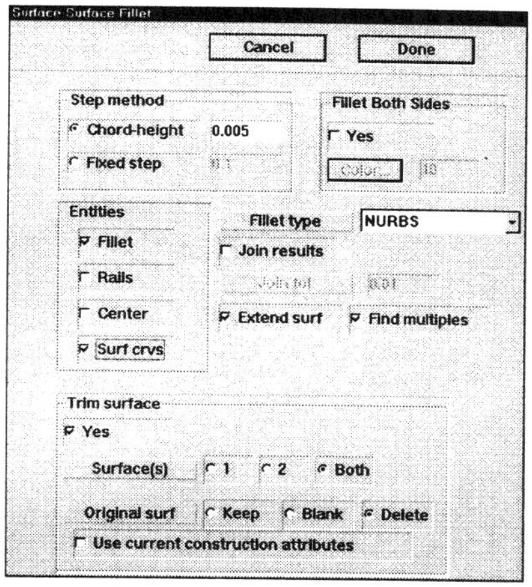

Select **Done → Do it**

The fillet surface is added to the model as in Figure 13.122.

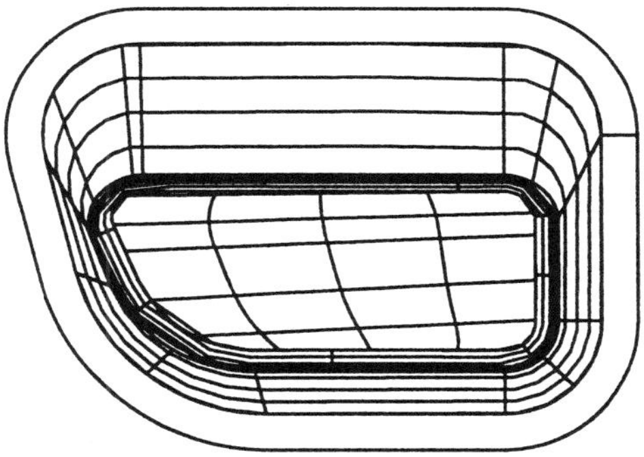

Figure 13.122

Step 9. Make all surface levels to visible and change to isometric Gview.

Select **Level → Vis. Levels**
Toggle level 2 to set visible (highlighted)
Then select **OK** to return to graphic mode
Select **Gview → Isometric**
The final surface model is shown in Figure 13.123.

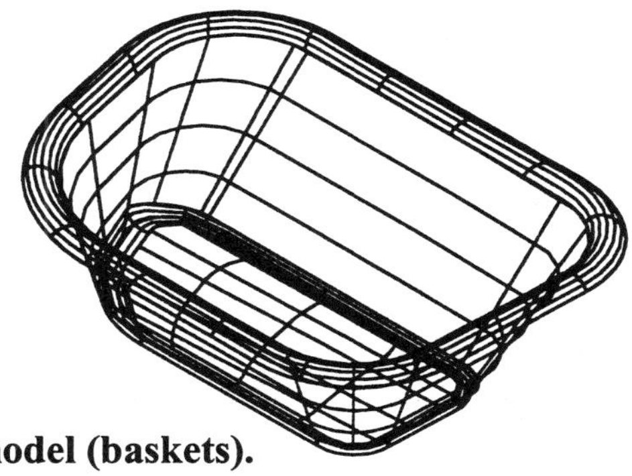

Figure 13.123

Step 10. Save the surface model (baskets).

Select **MAIN MENU → File → Save**
Enter file name: **baskets**

9 Project 9. Flash light surface model

The flash light surface model (Figure 13.124b) consists of four ruled surfaces, one coons surface and one fillet surface. The wireframe model (Figure 13.124a) is presented in project 12 of chapter 11.

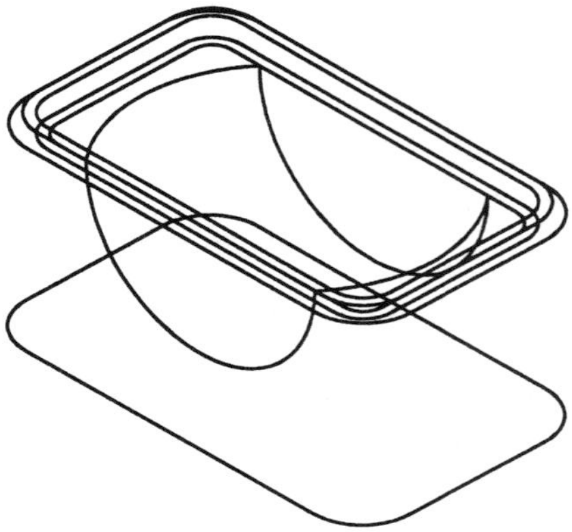

Figure 13.124a Wireframe model

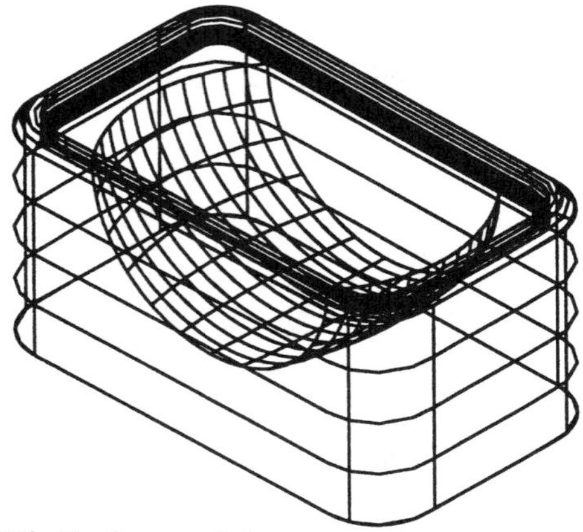

Figure 13.124b Surface model

Tips

1. Use two outer rectangular profiles to create a ruled surface for the outer frame.
2. Use three rectangular profiles to create a ruled surface for the top rim.
3. Create a vertical ruled surface for the inside wall.
4. The inner flat surface can be created as a ruled surface using the inner rectangular profile.
5. The curved surface is generated as a single-patch Coons surface.
6. The fillet surface is generated between the vertical ruled and the inner flat ruled surfaces.
7. The inner flat surface is trimmed by the surface curve created by projecting the Coons patch profile onto the inner flat ruled surface.
8. Use a different level and color for each surface.

Step 1. Load the wireframe model file "flash".

Select **MAIN MENU → File → Get**

Enter file name: **flash**

The wireframe model drawing should appear on screen as Figure 13.125.

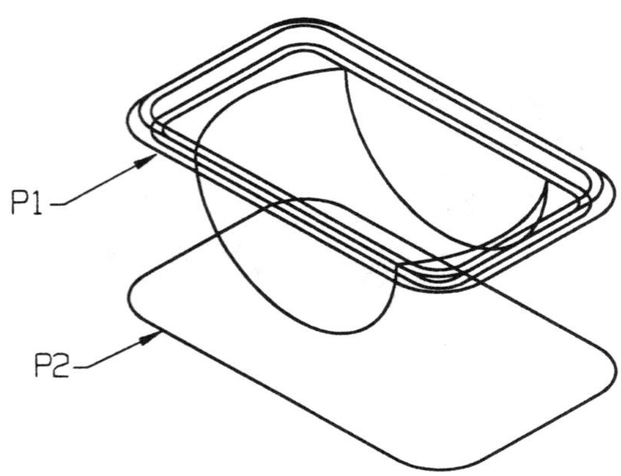

Figure 13.125

Step 2. Create a ruled surface for the outer frame.

Use the pick points labeled in Figure 13.125.
Select **Level**, then enter **2**
Select **Color,** then enter **11**
Select **MAIN MENU → Create → Surface → Ruled → Chain**
Pick **P1** to define contour 1
Pick **P2** to define contour 2
Select **Done**
Set the Ruled surface parameters as below:

Surface Error Tolerance = **0.005** Surface type = **NURBS**

Select **Do it** to complete the surface
The added ruled surface should look like Figure 13.126.

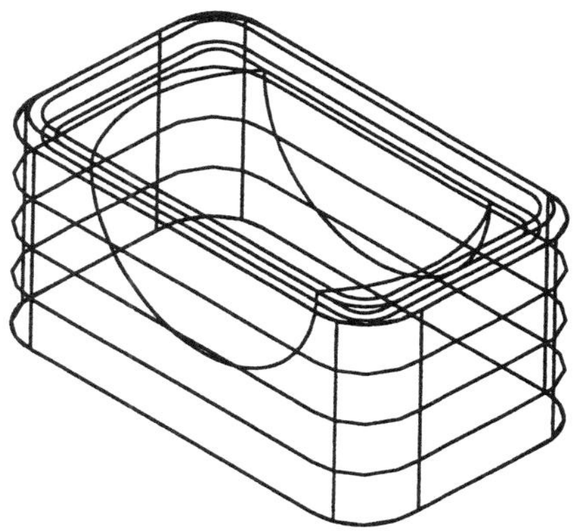

Figure 13.126

Step 3. Make level 2 invisible.

Select **Level**, then enter **3**
Select **Level → Vis.levels**
Click on the level 2 button to set invisible (dimmed)
Select **OK** to return to graphic mode
The new drawing should resemble Figure 13.127.

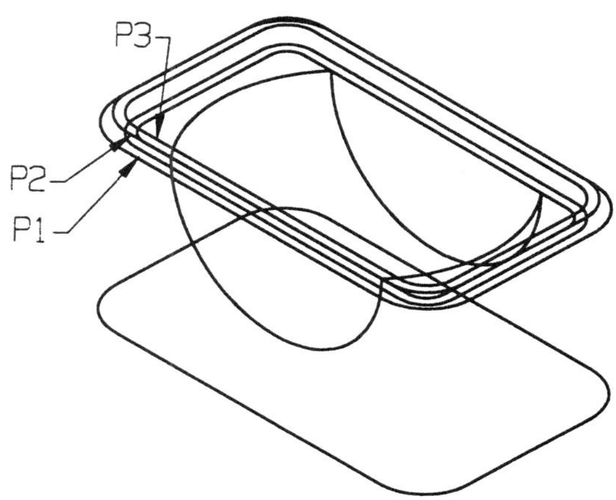

Figure 13.127

Step 4. Create a ruled surface on the top ring

Use the pick points labeled in Figure 13.127.
Select **Color,** then enter **12**
Select **MAIN MENU → Create → Surface → Ruled → Chain**
Pick **P1** define contour 1
Pick **P2** to define contour 2
Pick **P3** to define contour 3
Select **Done → Do it** to complete the ruled surface
Select **Gview → Isometric**
The new ruled surface is shown in Figure 13.128.

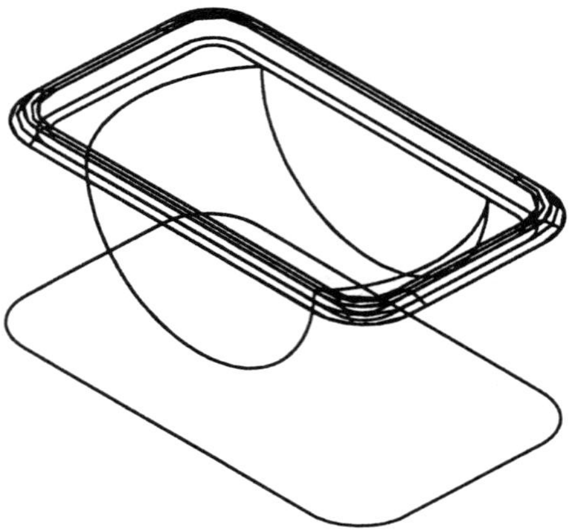

Figure 13.128

Step 5. Make level 3 invisible.

Select **Level**, then enter **4**
Select **Level → Vis. Levels**
Click on level 3 button to set to invisible (dimmed)
Select **OK** to return to graphic mode
The drawing on the screen should resemble Figure 13.129.

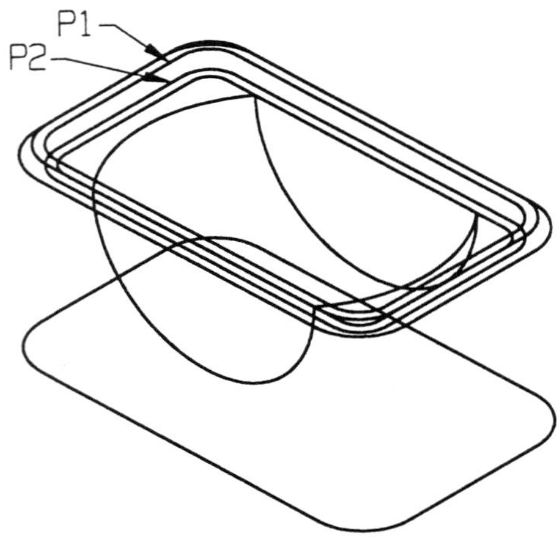

Figure 13.129

Step 6. Create a vertical ruled surface using the pick points in Figure 13.129.

Select **Color**, then enter **13**
Select **MAIN MENU → Create → Surface → Ruled → Chain**
Pick **P1** to define contour 1
Pick **P2** to define contour 2
Select **Done → Do it** to complete the surface
The drawing should resemble Figure 13.130.

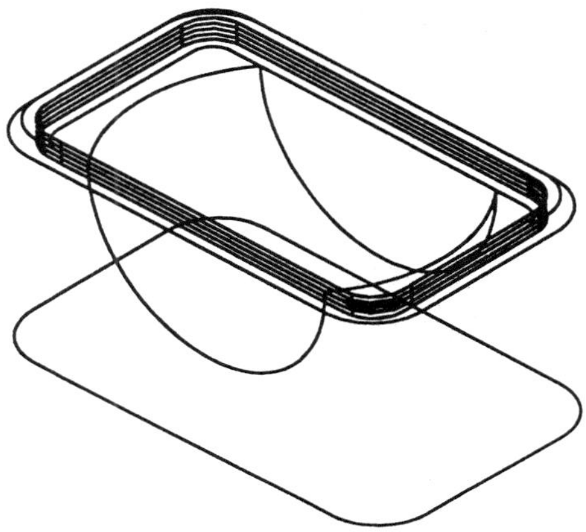

Figure 13.130

Step 7. Change to level 5 and make level 4 invisible.

Select **Level**, then enter **5**
Select **Level → Vis. Levels**
Click on the level 4 button to set to invisible (dimmed)
Select **OK** to return to graphic mode
The drawing now appears as Figure 13.131.

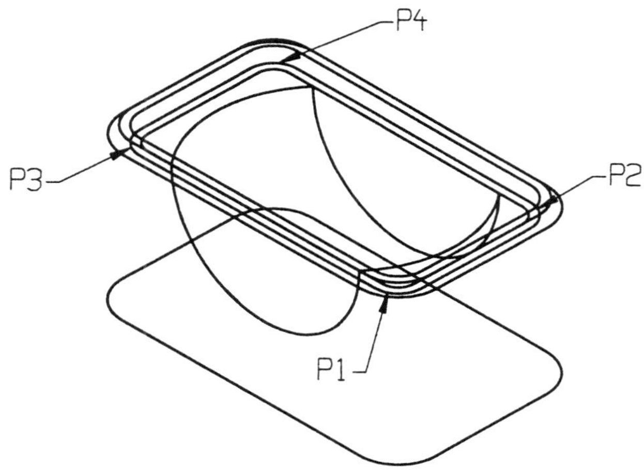

Figure 13.131

Step 8. Create a ruled surface for inner flat surface.

Use the pick points labeled in Figure 13.131.
Select **Color**, then enter **14**
Select **Ruled → Chain → Partial**

Pick **P1** and **P2** to complete contour 1
Select **Partial**
Pick **P3** and **P4** to complete contour 2
Select **Done → Do it** to complete the surface
The surface model appears as Figure 13.132.

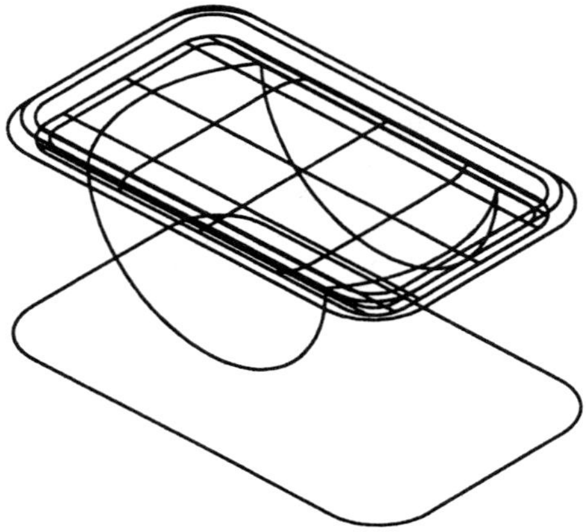

Figure 13.132

Step 9. Change to level 6 and make level 5 invisible.

Select **Level**, then enter **6**
Select **Level → Vis. Levels**
Click on the level 5 button to set to invisible (dimmed)
Select **OK** to return to graphic mode
The drawing now should resemble Figure 13.133.

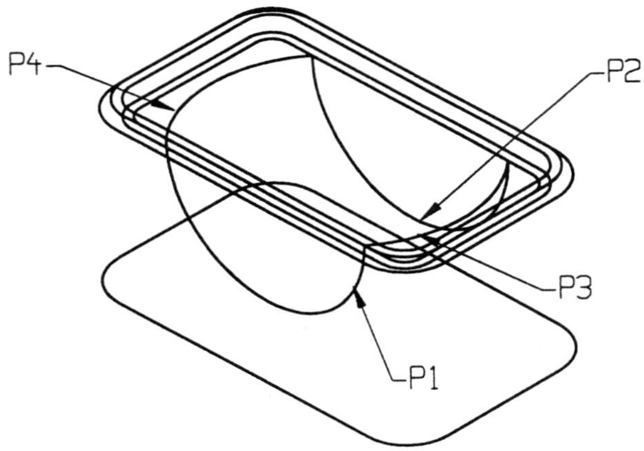

Figure 13.133

Step 10. Create a Coons surface using the pick points in Figure 13.133.

Select **Color,** then enter **15**
Select **BACKUP → Coons**
Select **No** to "Use Automatic Coons chaining ?"

Enter number of patches in the along direction: **1**
Enter number o patches in the across direction: **1**

Define along contour 1 of row 1: pick **P1**
Define along contour 1 of row 2: pick **P2**
Define across contour 1 of column 1: pick **P3**
Define across contour 1 of column 2: pick **P4**
Select **Done** to complete chaining
Set the Coons surface parameters to the following settings:

Surface Error Tolerance = **0.005** Surface Type = **NURBS** Blending = **Linear**

Select **Do it** to complete the surface
The Coons surface should appear as Figure 13.134.

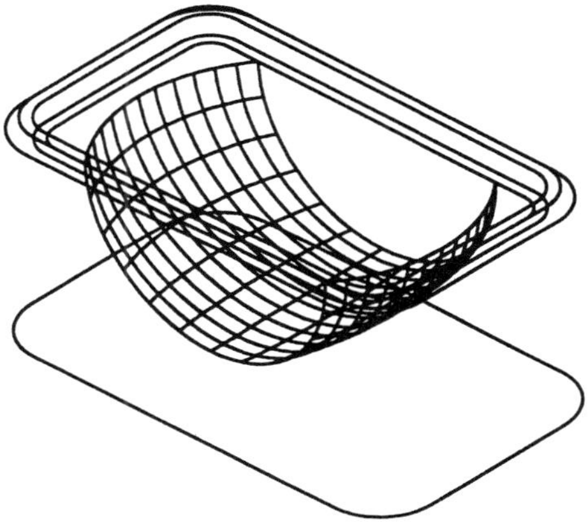

Figure 13.134

Step 11. Make level 6 invisible and level 4 and 5 visible.

Select **Level → Vis. Levels**
Toggle the level 6 to invisible (dimmed)
Toggle levels 4 and 5 to visible (highlighted)
Select **OK → OK** to return to graphic mode
The new drawing on the screen should resemble Figure 13.135.

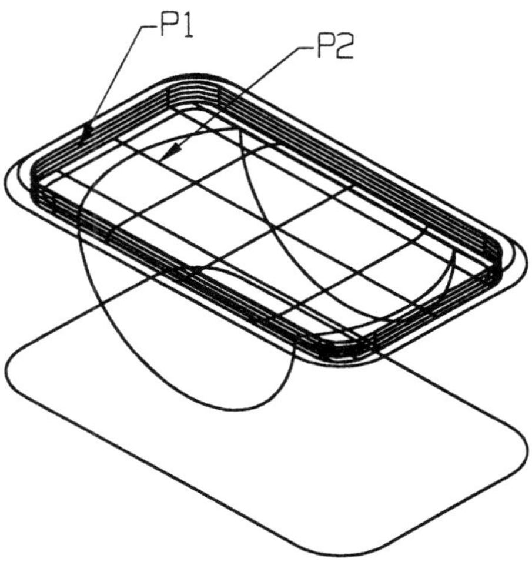

Figure 13.135

Step 12. Create a fillet surface at the intersection between the inner flat surface and the vertical wall surface.

Use the pick points in Figure 13.135.
Select **Level**, then enter **7**
Select **Color,** then enter **12**
Select **Fillet → Surf/surf**

Note: The normal direction of the vertical wall needs to be in the inward direction.
Use **Modify → Normal** commands to check if necessary.

Pick **P1**, then select **Done** to select vertical wall surface
Pick **P2** to select the inner flat surface
Enter radius: **0.1**
Select **Options**
Set **Surface → Surface Fillet** parameters as shown here

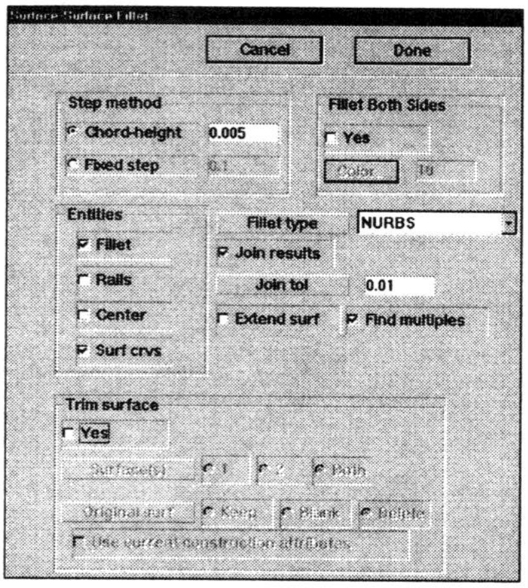

Select **Done → Do it**

The fillet surface should appear as Figure 13.136.

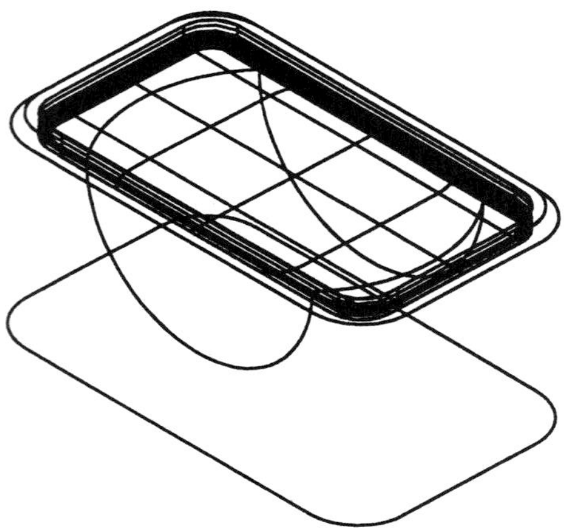

Figure 13.136

Step 13. Make levels 2, 3, 4, 6, and 7 invisible.

Select **Level → Vis. Levels**
Toggle only levels 1 and 5 to visible (highlighted) and level 7 to invisible
Select **OK → OK** return to graphic mode

The drawing should resemble Figure 13.137.

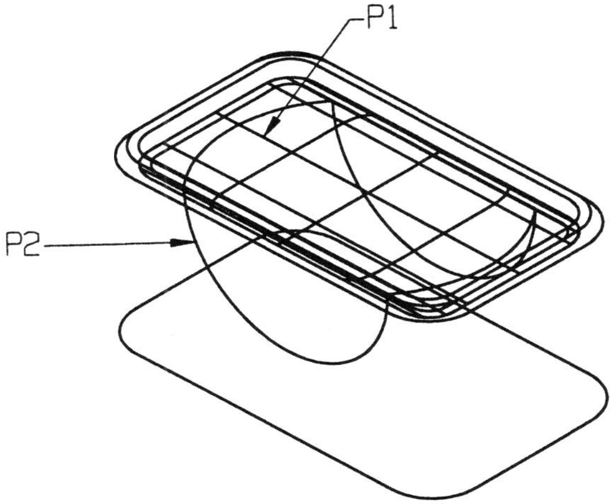

Figure 13.137

Step 14. Create the surface curve for trimming the inner flat ruled surface.

Use the pick points in Figure 13.137
Change level to **8** and color to **13**
Select **Level**, then enter **8**
Select **Color,** then enter **13**
Select **MAIN MENU → Create → Curve → Project**
Pick **P1** to select the ruled surface
Select **Done**
Select **Chain**
Pick **P2** to select the first entity
Select **Done**
Toggle "View/Norm" to select Options
Set projecting curve parameters
as shown here:

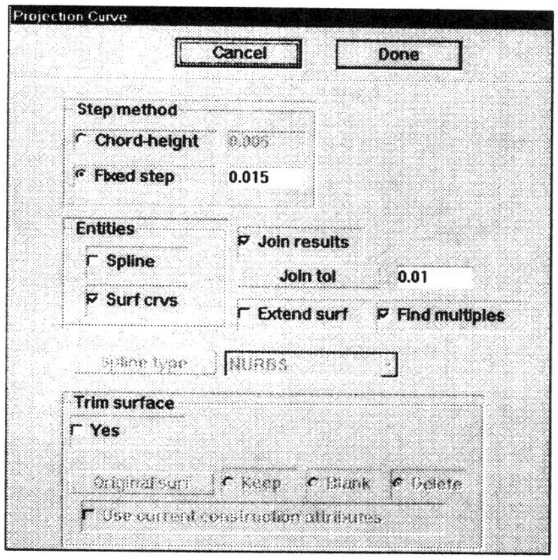

Select **Done → Do it**
The surface curve appearing on screen should look like Figure 13.138.

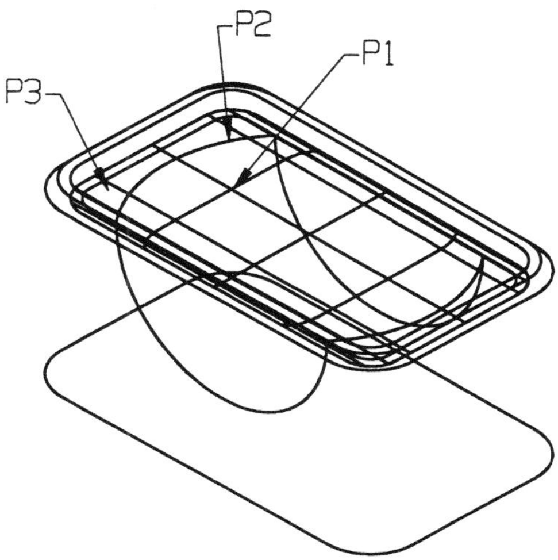

Figure 13.138

Step 15. Trim the inner flat ruled surface using the pick points in Figure 13.114.

Select **Level**, then enter **9**
Select **Color**, then enter **12**
Select **MAIN MENU → Create → Surface → Trim/Extend → To Curves**
Pick **P1** to select the surface to be trimmed
Select **Done**
Select **Chain,** then pick **P2**
Select **Done → Options**
Set the Trim surface to Curve parameters
as shown here:

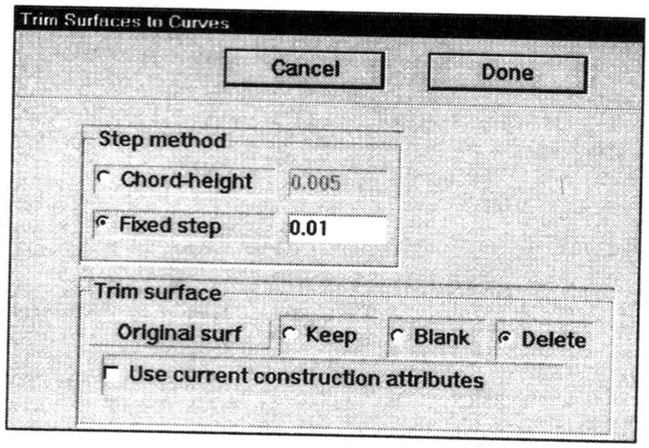

Select **Done → Do it**

Pick **P1** to select a surface to be trimmed
Pick **P3** to select a location to keep after trimming
The trimmed surface should look like Figure 13.139.

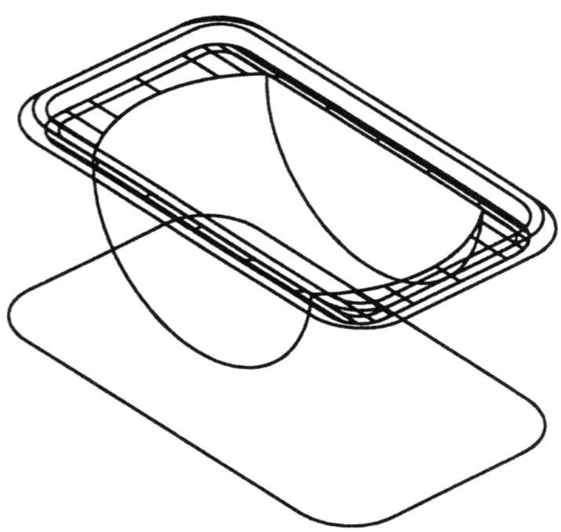

Figure 13.139

Step 16. Display all necessary surfaces.

Select **Level → Vis. Levels**
Toggle every level to visible except level 5
Press **OK** to return to graphic mode

The final surface model should look like Figure 13.140.

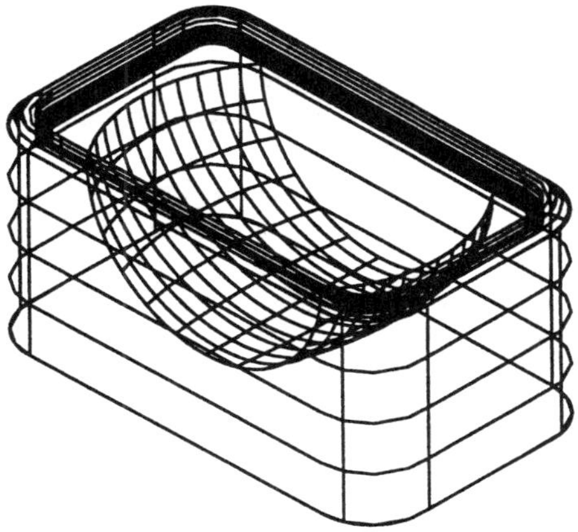

Figure 13.140

Step 17. Save the surface model →flashs).

Select **MAIN MENU → File → Save**
Enter file name: **flashs**

Project 10. Hair dryer surface model

The hair dryer surface model consists of four surfaces; two swept surfaces and two ruled surfaces (Figure 13.141). The two swept surfaces are the top surface and the frame surface. The two ruled surfaces include the tube surface and the handle surface. The two ruled surfaces are trimmed to the frame surface. These four surfaces are mirrored about the X axis in the Front Cplane to complete the surface model.

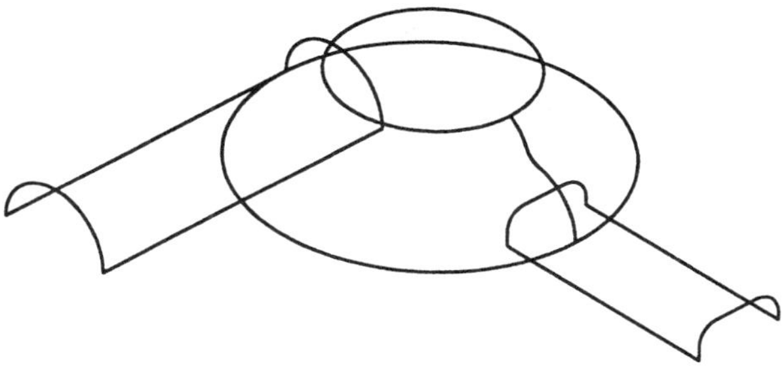

Figure 13.141a Wireframe model

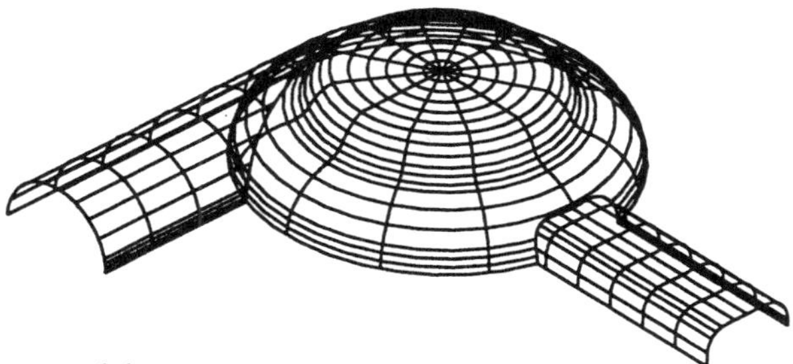

Figure 13.141b Surface model

⌛**Tips**	1. The top flat face and the frame can be formed as a single swept surface. In this case we purposely create it as two separate swept surfaces because the top flat surface can be easily machined by using a flat end mill instead of a ball end cutter. 2. In this surface model, two ruled surfaces are constructed long enough to extrude into the frame surface. Therefore, they should be trimmed. 3. Two surface curves should be created at the intersection boundary between the frame surface and the tube surface, and between the frame surface and the handle surface. These two surface curves are then used to trim the two ruled surfaces. 4. Trimming both ruled surfaces requires us to redefine the outer boundary. 5. Use the Front Cplane to mirror the upper composite surface model about the X axis to complete the modeling of the object.

Step 1. Load the wireframe model file (dryer).

Select **MAIN MENU → File → Get**
Enter file name: **dryer**
The wireframe model of hair dryer appears as Figure 13.142.

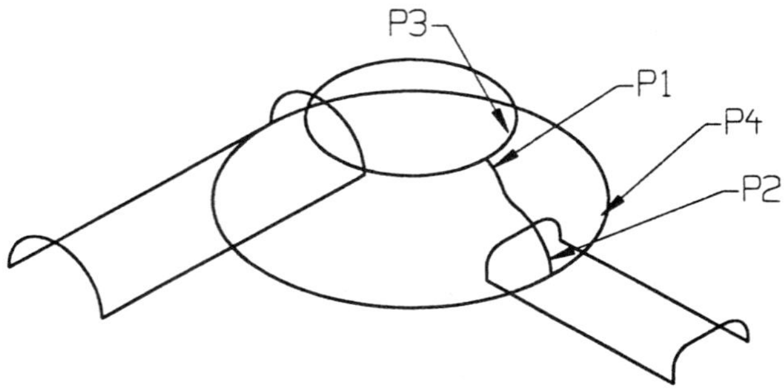

Figure 13.142

Step 2. Create a swept surface using the pick points in Figure 13.142.

Select **Level**, then enter **2**
Select **Color**, then enter **11**
Select **MAIN MENU → Create → Surface → Swept**

Enter the number of across contour: **1**
Define the across contour 1: select **Chain → Partial** from the Changing method menu
Pick **P1** and **P2**
Define along contour 1: select **Mode → Single**, then pick **P3**
Define along contour 2: pick **P4**
Select **Done** to complete contour selection
Set the Swept surface parameters to the following settings:

Surface Error Tolerance = **0.005** Surface Type = **NURBS**

Select **Do it** to complete the swept surface

The swept surface should appear as Figure 13.143.

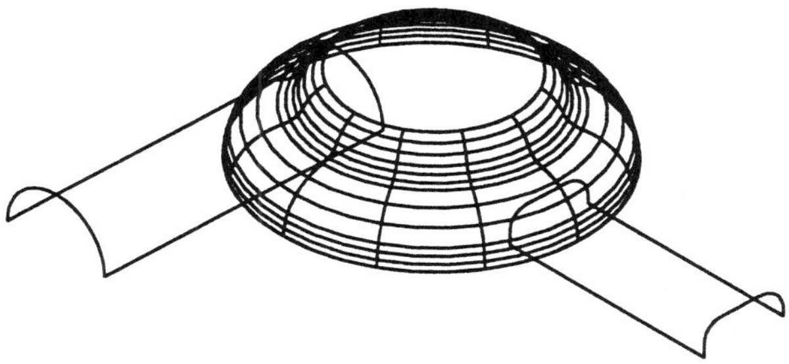

Figure 13.143

Step 3. Change to level 3 and make level 2 invisible.

Select **Level**, then enter **3**
Select **Level → Vis. Levels**
Toggle level 2 to invisible (dimmed)
Select **OK** to return to graphic mode
The drawing becomes Figure 13.144.

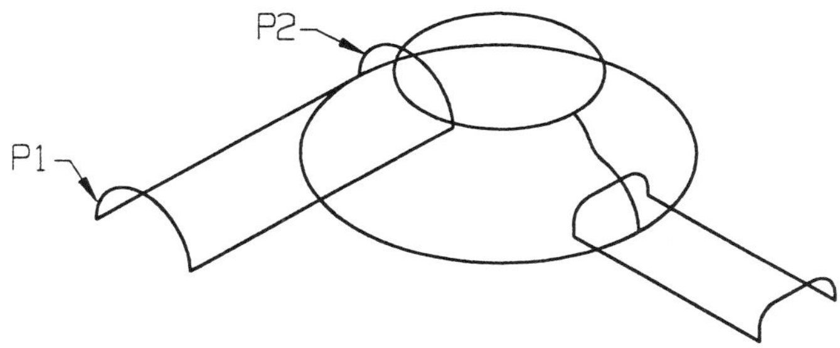

Figure 13.144

Step 4. Create a ruled surface for the tube using the pick points in Figure 13.144.

Select **Color,** then enter **12**
Select **MAIN MENU → Create → Surface → Ruled → Single**
Define contour 1: pick **P1**
Define contour 2: pick **P2**
Select **Done**
Select **Do it** to complete the ruled surface
The ruled surface should resemble Figure 13.145.

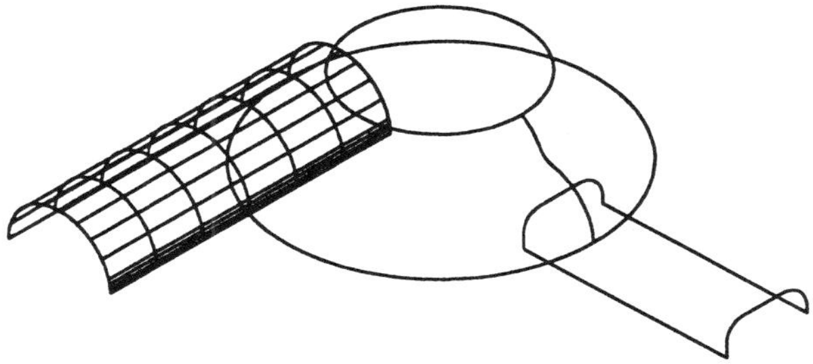

Figure 13.145

Step 5. Change to level 4 and make level 3 invisible.

Select **Level**, then enter **4**
Select **Level → Vis. Levels**
Toggle level 3 to invisible (dimmed)
Select **OK** to return to graphic mode
The drawing now should appear as Figure 13.146.

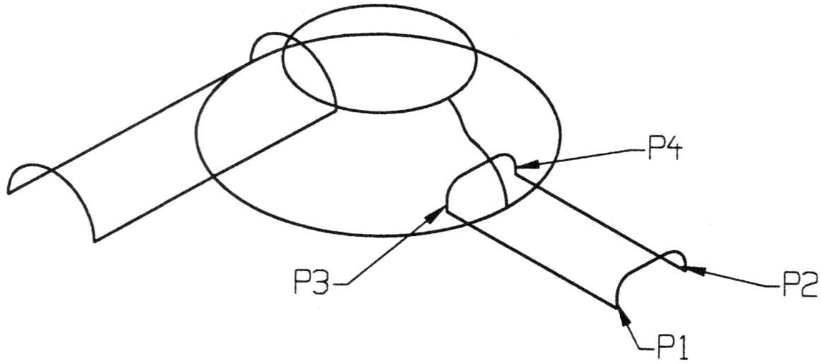

Figure 13.146

Step 6. Create a ruled surface for the handle using pick points in Figure 13.146.

Select **Color,** then enter **13**
Select **BACKUP → Ruled**
Define contour 1: select **Chain → Partial**
Pick **P1** and **P2**
Define contour 2: select **Partial**, then pick **P3** and **P4**
Select **Done**
Select **Do it** to complete the surface
The new ruled surface should resemble Figure 13.147.

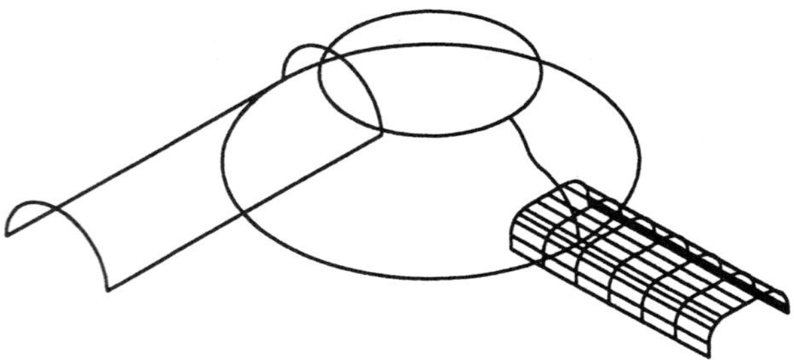

Figure 13.147

Step 7. Make levels 2 and 3 visible.

Select **Level → Vis.levels**
Toggle levels 2 and 3 to visible (highlighted)
Select **OK** to return to graphic mode

The drawing becomes Figure 13.148.

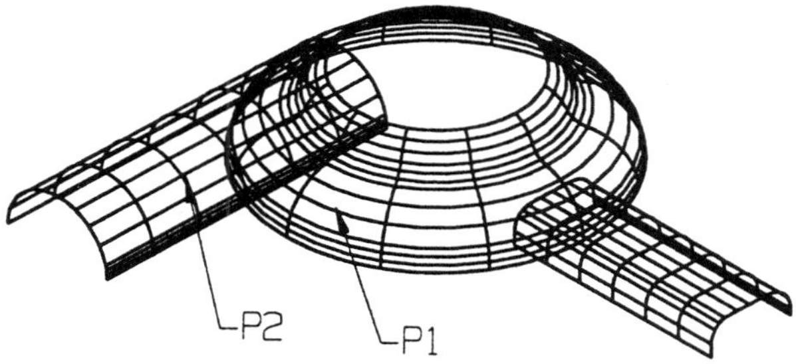

Figure 13.148

Step 8. Create a surface curve at the intersection between the frame surface and the tube surface.

Use the pick points in Figure 13.148.
Select **Level**, then enter **5**
Select **Color**, then enter **14**
Select **MAIN MENU → Create → Curve → Intersect**
Pick **P1**, then select **Done**
Pick **P2**, then select **Done**
Select **Option**
Set Intersection curve parameters as shown here:

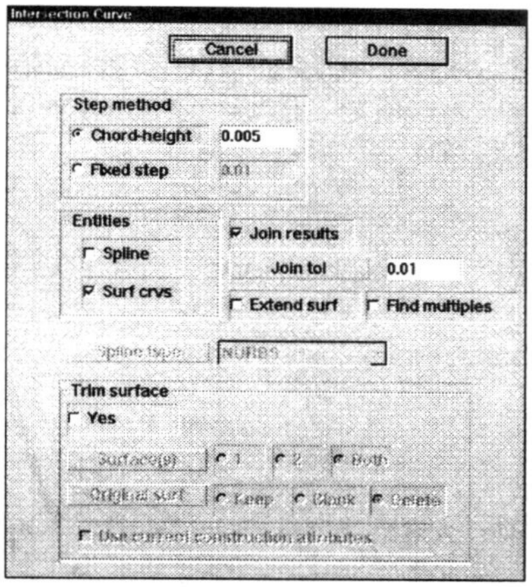

Select **Done → Do it**

The surface curve should appear as Figure 13.149.

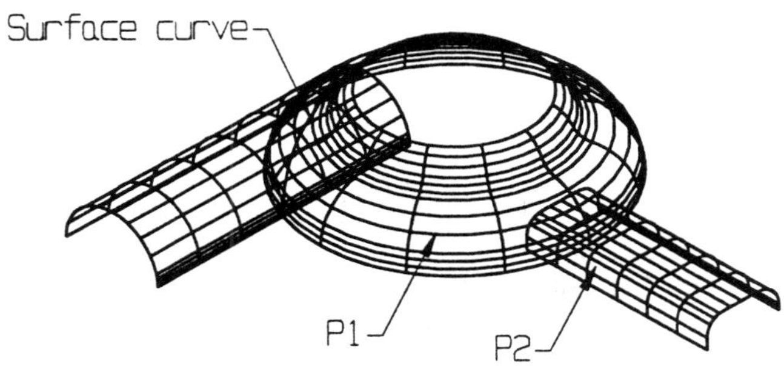

Figure 13.149

Step 9. Create a surface curve at the intersection between the frame surface and the handle surface.

Use the pick points in Figure 13.149.
Select **BACKUP → Intersect**
Pick **P1**, then **Done** to select the first set of the surfaces
Pick **P2**, then **Done** to select the second set of the surfaces
Select **Do it** to complete the surface curve
Both surface curves should appear as Figure 13.150.

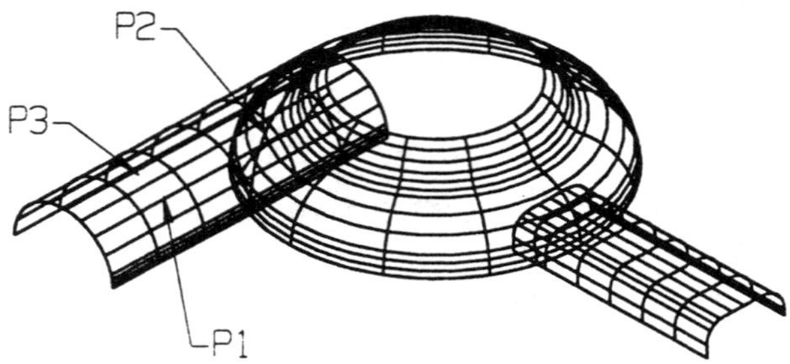

Figure 13.150

Step 10. Trim the tube surface using the pick points in Figure 13.150.

Select **Level**, then enter **6**
Select **Color**, then enter **15**
Select **MAIN MENU → Create → Surface → Trim/Extend → To Curves**
Pick **P1**, then select **Done** to select the surface to trim
Select **BACKUP → Surf crvs**
Pick **P2**, then select **Done**
Set View/Norm to **N**, then select **Do it**
Pick **P1** to select a surface to be trimmed
Pick **P3** to indicate a location to keep after trimming
The trimmed surface is shown in Figure 13.151.

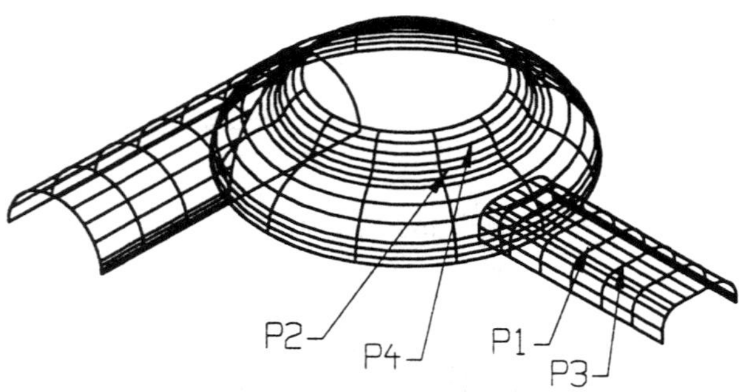

Figure 13.151

Step 11. Trim the handle surface using the pick points in Figure 13.151.

Select **BACKUP → To Surfaces**
Pick **P1**, then select **Done** to select the first set of surfaces
Pick **P2**, then select **Done** to select the second set of surfaces
Select **Options**

Set Trim Surfaces to Surfaces parameters as below

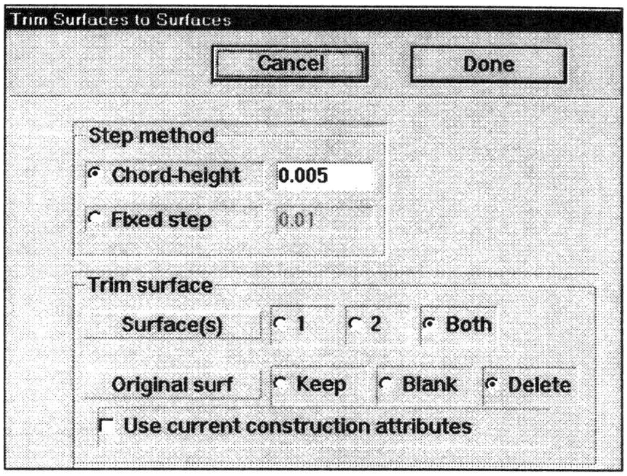

Select **Do it**
Pick **P1** to select a surface to be trimmed
Pick **P3** to indicate the portion to keep after trimming
Pick **P2** to select a surface to be trimmed
Pick **P4** to indicate the kept portion after trimming
The trimmed surface should appear as Figure 13.152.

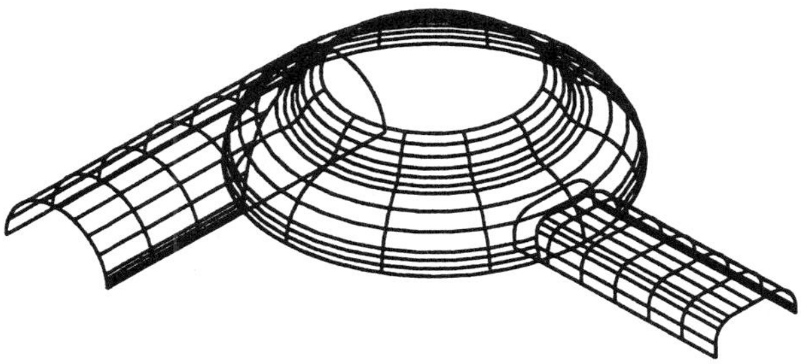

Figure 13.152

Step 12. Change to level 7 and make levels 2 to 6 invisible.

Select **Level**, then enter **7**
Select **Level → Vis.levels**
Toggle levels 2 to 6 invisible (dimmed)
Select **OK** to return to graphic mode

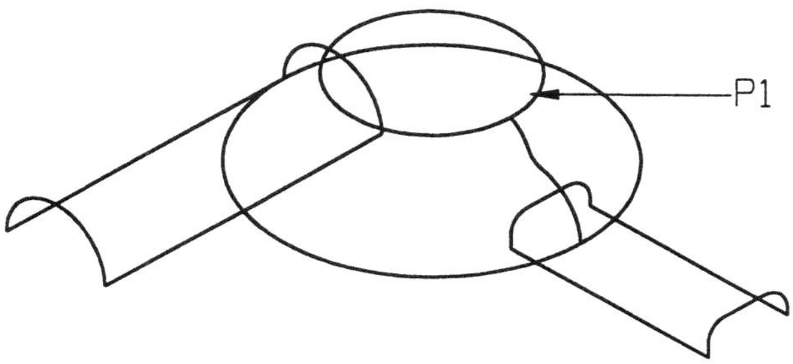

Figure 13.153

Step 13. Add a line to the top of the frame using the pick points in Figure 13.153.

Select **Color,** then enter **12**
Select **Cplane → Top** if necessary
Select **Z → Endpoint**
Pick **P1** to obtain the Z value
Z1.0 should appear in the Secondary menu
Select **MAIN MENU → Create → Line → Endpoints**
Specify the first endpoint: **0,0**
Specify the second endpoint: select **Endpoint**, then pick **P1**
The line is added to the drawing as shown in Figure 13.154.

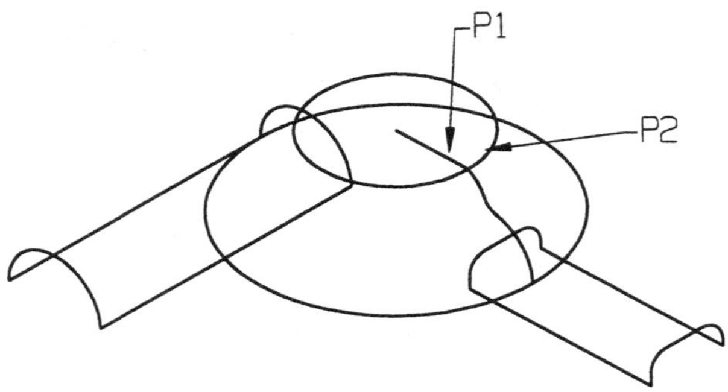

Figure 13.154

Step 14. Create a swept surface on the top frame.

Using the pick points in Figure 13.154.
Select **MAIN MENU → Create → Surface → Swept**
Enter the number of across contour: **1**
Select **Single**
Define the across contour: pick **P1**
Define along contour 1: pick **P2**
Select **Done** to complete contour selection
Set the Swept surface parameters to the following settings:

Surface Error tolerance = **0.005** Surface Type = **NURBS** Trans/Rot = **R**

Select **Do it** to complete the surface
The top swept surface should look like Figure 13.155.

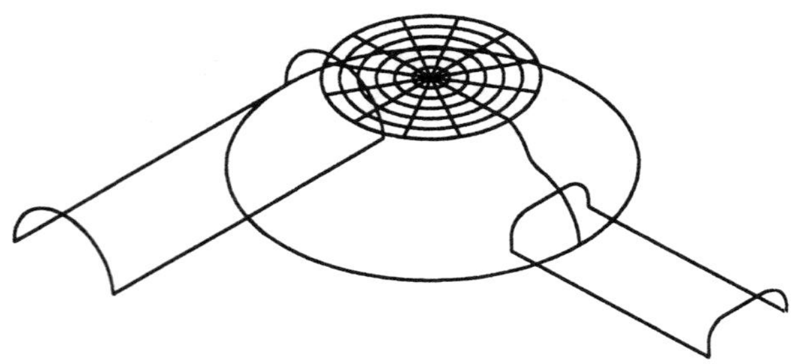

Figure 13.155

Step 15. Make all levels visible, except level 1

Select **Level → Vis. Levels → All On**
Toggle level 1 to invisible (dimmed)
Select **OK** to return to graphic mode
The drawing now appears as Figure 13.156.

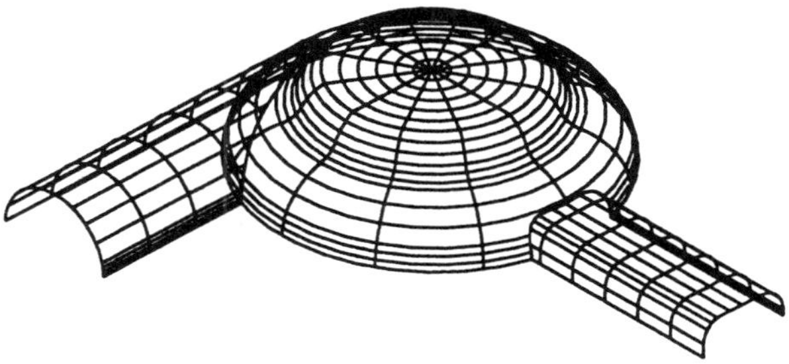

Figure 13.156

Step 16. Save the surface model.

Select **MAIN MENU → File → Save**
Enter file name: **dryers**

Step 17. Mirror the surface model about the X axis.

Use the Front Cplane.
Select **Cplane → Front**
Select **Level**, then enter **8**
Select **Color**, then enter **13**
Select **MAIN MENU → Xform → Mirror → All → Surfaces → Done → X axis**
Set the Mirror parameters to **Copy**
Select **Done**
The complete surface model should appear as Figure 13.157.

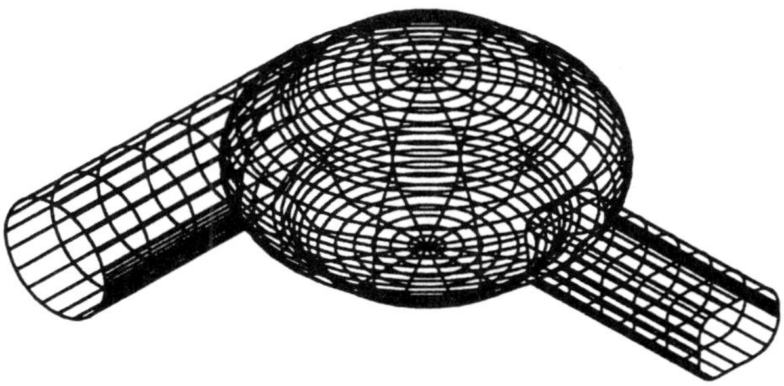

Figure 13.157

11 Project 11. Fan surface model

This surface model consists of six basic surfaces: one flat surface of the hub, one inner rim surface, one outer rim surface, and three surfaces for the blade. The three surfaces of the blade are copied to six locations to generate the surfaces of the other six blades. The wireframe model and surface model are shown in Figure 13.158a and Figure 13.158b.

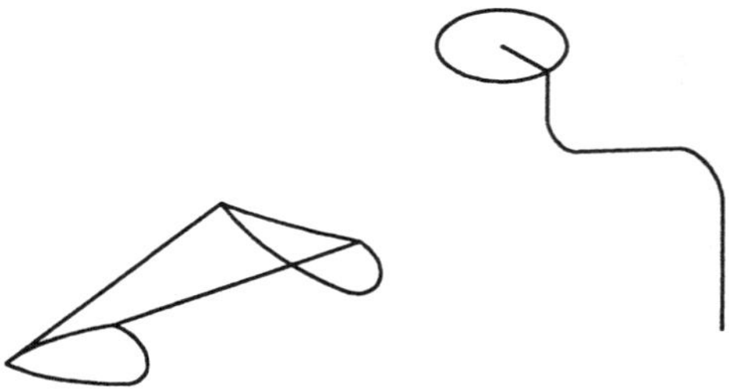

Figure 13.158a Wireframe model

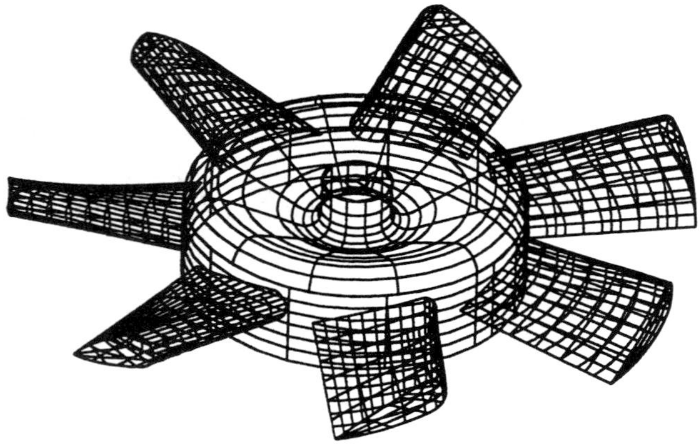

Figure 13.158b Surface model

Tips
1. The hub, rim and outer rim can be modeled as a single surface entity. However, we use three surface entities to model them to facilitate the generation of the toolpath.
2. The flat surface of the hub is created as a swept surface.
3. The inner rim surface of the hub is created as a swept surface. The across contour consists of four entities.
4. The outer rim surface can be modeled as a swept surface.
5. Both top and bottom surfaces of the blade are modeled by Coons surfacing technique. The number of patches in both along direction and across direction is one for both surfaces.
6. The outer end edge surface is modeled by the ruled surfacing technique.
7. Use Xform → Rotate commands to copy the three surfaces of the blade to six locations.
8. Use a different level and color for each surface.

Step 1. Load the wireframe model file (fan).

Select **MAIN MENU → File → Get**
Enter file name: **fan**
The wireframe model of the fan should look like Figure 13.159.

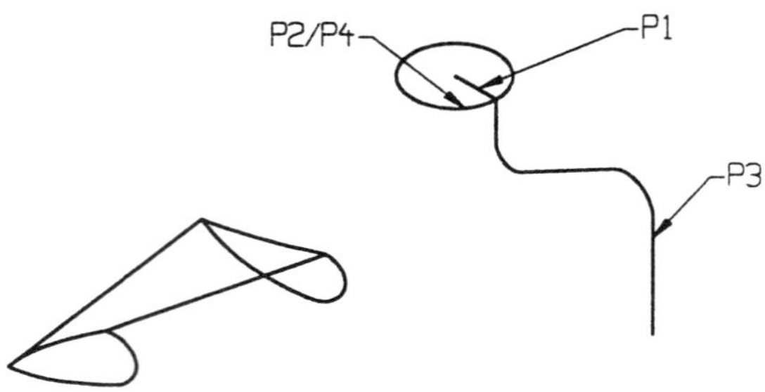

Figure 13.159

Step 2. Create two swept surfaces for the flat surface of the hub and the outer rim surface.

Use the pick points in Figure 13.159.
Select **Level,** then enter **6**
Select **Color**, then enter **14**
Select **MAIN MENU → Create → Surface → Swept**
Enter the number of across contours: **1**
Define the across contour: select **Single**, then pick **P1**
Define along contour 1: pick **P2**
Select **Done** to complete contours selection
Set the Swept surface parameters to the following settings:

Surface Error Tolerance = **0.005**
Surface Type = **NURBS**
Trans/Rot = **R**

Select **Do it** to complete the flat surface
Enter the number of across contours: **1**
Define the across contour: pick **P3**
Define the along contour 1: pick **P4**
Select **Done → Do it** to complete the outer rim surface
The flat swept surface and the outer rim surface are shown in Figure 13.160.

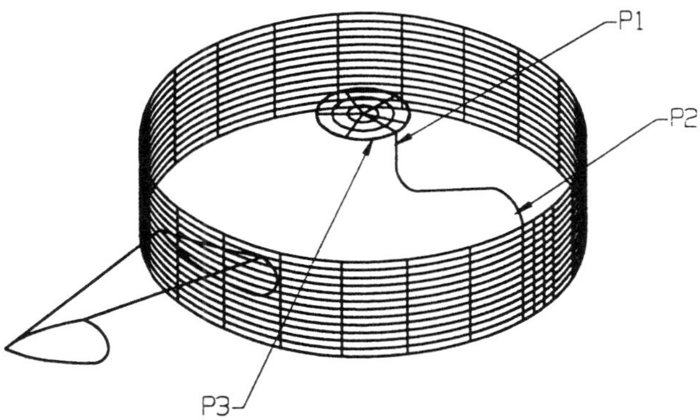

Figure 13.160

Step 3. Create a swept surface for the rim using the pick points in Figure 13.160.

Select **Color,** then enter **15**
Select **Swept**
Enter the number of across contours: **1**
Define the across contour: select **Chain → Partial**, then pick **P1** and **P2**
Define along contour 1: select **Mode → Single**, then pick **P3**

Select **Done** to complete contours selection
Set the Swept surface parameters to the following settings:

Surface Error Tolerance = **0.01**
Surface Type = **NURBS**
Trans/Rot = **R**

Select **Do it** to complete the surface
The surface should resemble Figure 13.161.

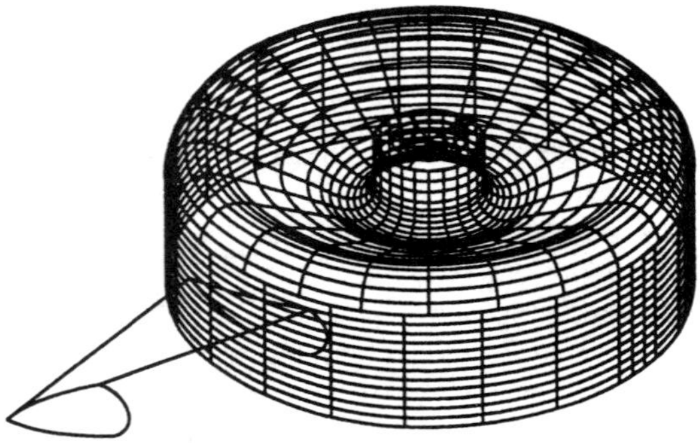

Figure 13.161

Step 4. Change to level 7 and make levels 3 and 6 invisible.

Select **Level** → Enter **7**, then select **Vis.Levels**
Toggle levels 3 and 6 to invisible (dimmed)
Select **OK** → **OK** to return to graphic mode
The drawing should look like Figure 13.162.

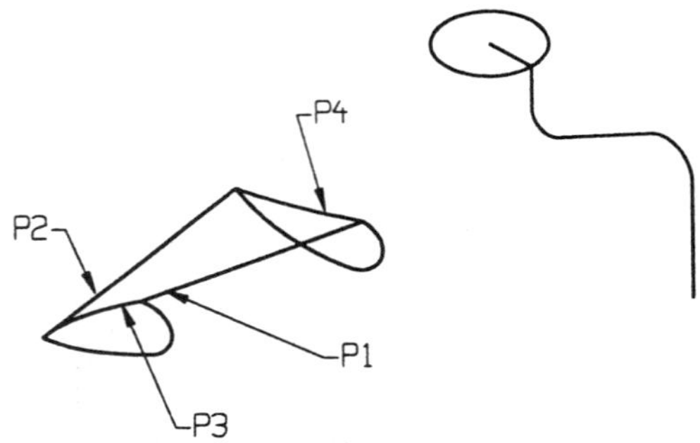

Figure 13.162

Step 5. Create a Coons surface for the top blade face

Use the pick points in Figure 13.162.
Select **Color,** then enter **11**
Select **Coons**
Select **NO** to "Use automatic Coons chaining ?"
Enter number of patches in the along direction: **1**
Enter number of patches in the across direction: **1**
Define along contour 1 of row 1: select **Single**, then pick **P1**
Define along contour 1 of row 2: pick **P2**
Define across contour 1 of column 1: pick **P3**
Define across contour 1 of column 2: pick **P4**
Select **Done** to complete contours selection
Set the Coons surface parameters to the following settings:

> Surface Error Tolerance = **0.01**
> Across cut distance = **NURBS**
> Blending = **Linear**

Select **Do it** to complete the surface

The surface should resemble Figure 13.163.

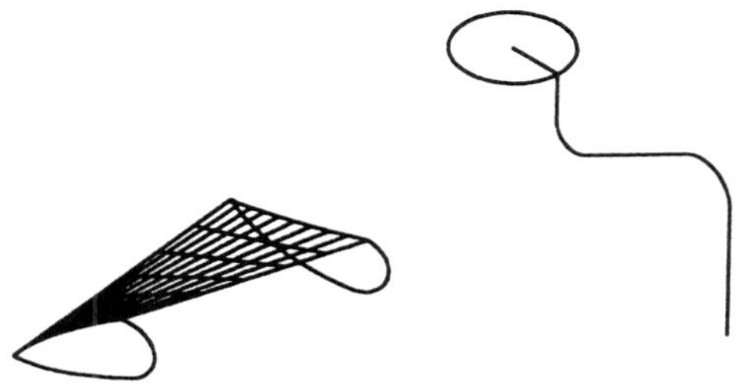

Figure 13.163

Step 6. Change to level 8 and make level 7 invisible.

Select **Level**, then enter **8**

Select **Level → Vis. Levels**

Toggle level 7 to invisible (dimmed)

Select **OK** to return to graphic mode

The drawing appears as Figure 13.164.

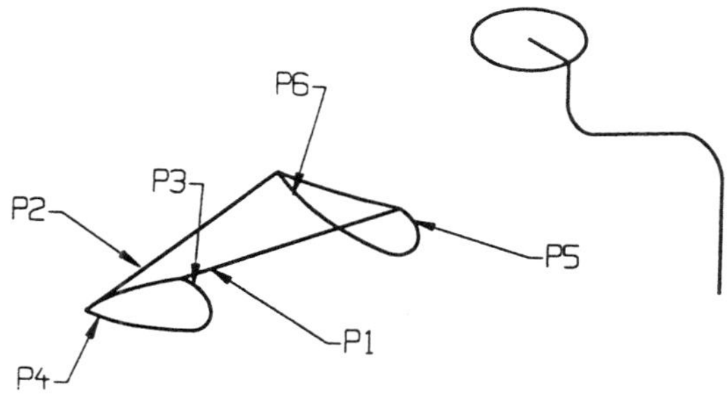

Figure 13.164

Step 7. Create a Coons surface for the bottom blade face.

Use the pick points in Figure 13.164.

Select **Color,** then enter **12**

Select **Coons**

Select **NO** to "Use automatic Coons chaining ?"

Enter number of patches in the along direction: **1**

Enter number of patches in the across direction: **1**

Define along contour 1 of row 1: select **Single**, then pick **P1**

Define along contour 1 of row 2: pick **P2**

Define across contour 1 of column 1: select **Mode → Chain → Partial**

Pick **P3** and **P4**

Define across contour 1 of column 2: select **Partial**, then pick **P5** and **P6**

Select **Done** to complete contours selection

Set the Coons surface parameters to the following settings:

Surface Error Tolerance = **0.005** Surface Type = **NURBS** Blending = **Parabolic**

Select **Do it** to complete the surface
The bottom Coons surface should appear s Figure 13.165.

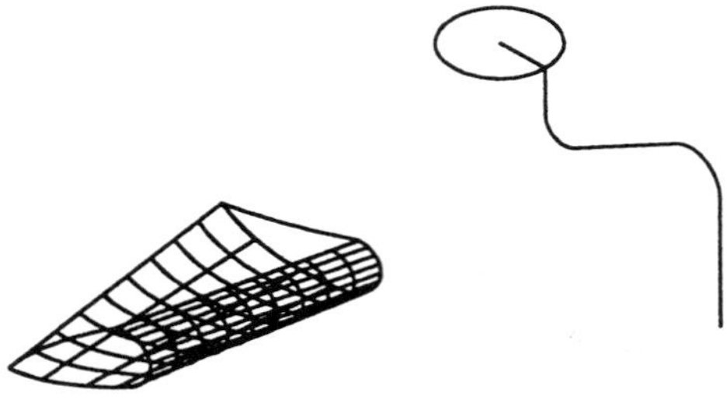

Figure 13.165

Step 8. Change to level 9 and make level8 invisible.

Select **Level**, then enter **9**
Select **Level → Vis. Levels**
Toggle level 8 to invisible (dimmed)
Select **OK** to return to graphic mode
The drawing now appears as Figure 13.166.

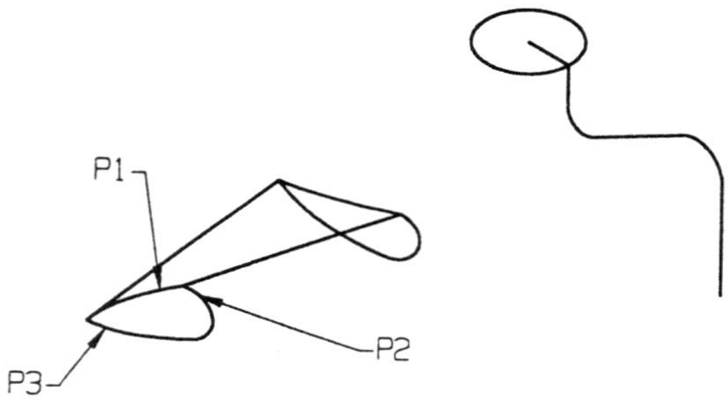

Figure 13.166

Step 9. Create a ruled surface for the outer end edge of the blade.

Use the pick points in Figure 13.166.
Select **Color,** then enter **14**
Select **Ruled → Single**
Define contour 1: pick **P1**
Define contour 2: select **Mode → Chain → Partial**
Pick **P2** and **P3** (Note: the sync mode should be on **"None"**)
Select **Done → Do it** to complete the ruled surface
The end edge surface should look like Figure 13.167.

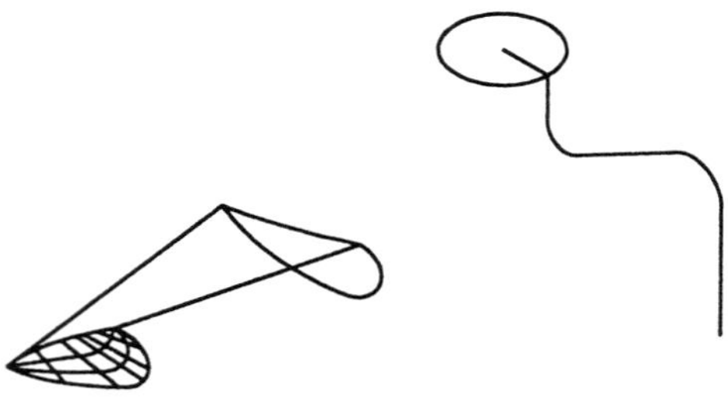

Figure 13.167

Step 10. Make levels 7 and 8 back to visible.

Select **Level → Vis. Levels**
Toggle levels 7 and 8 to visible (highlighted)
Select **OK** to return to graphic mode
The three blade surfaces should resemble Figure 13.168.

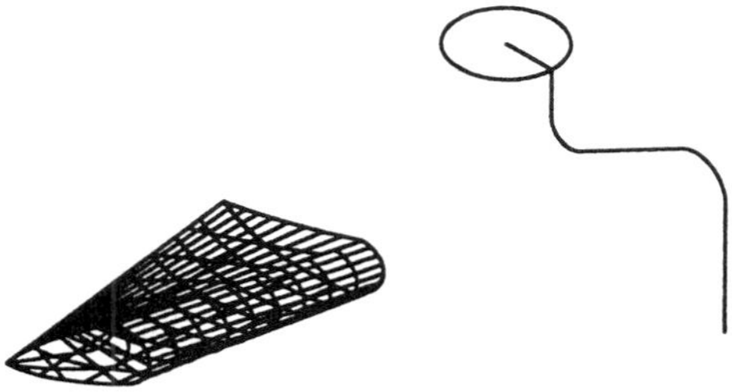

Figure 13.168

Step 11. Copy the blade surfaces to six locations using the Xform → Rotate commands.

Select **Level**, then enter **10**
Select **Color**, then enter **15**
Select **MAIN MENU → Xform → Rotate → All → Surfaces → Done → Origin**
Set the Rotate parameters as below:

Copy
Number of Steps = **6**
Rotation angle = **360/7**

Select **Done**
The three surfaces are copied to six locations as shown in Figure 13.169.

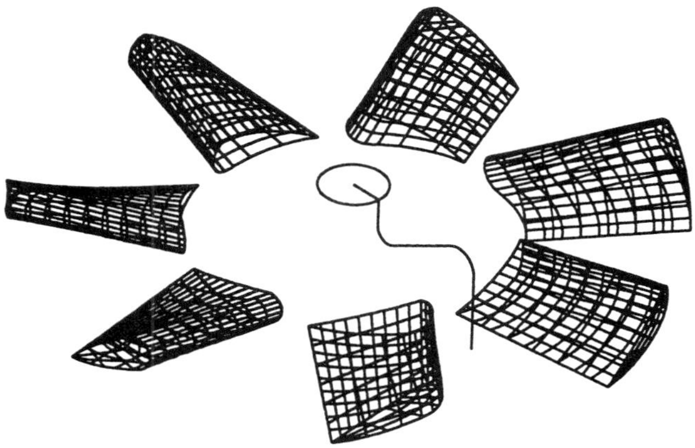

Figure 13.169

Step 12. Make levels 3 and 6 back to visible.

Select **Level → Vis. Level**
Toggle levels 3 and 6 to visible (highlighted)
Select **OK** to return to graphic mode

12 The complete surface model should resemble Figure 13.170.

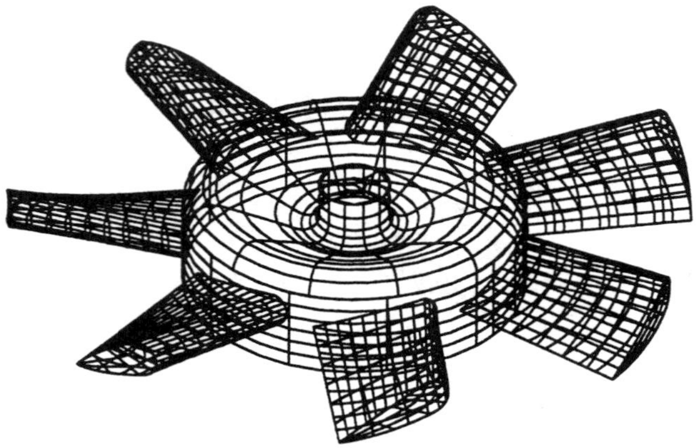

Figure 13.170

Step 13. Save the surface model in a file named fans.

Select **MAIN MENU → File → Save**
Enter file name: **fans**

Project 12. Car wheel hub

This example creates a surface model of a car wheel from the wireframe model of project 16 in chapter 11. The wireframe model and the completed surface model are shown in Figure 13.171. This is a rather complicated surface model which consists of many surfaces. The tips given on this page should help to complete the surface model.

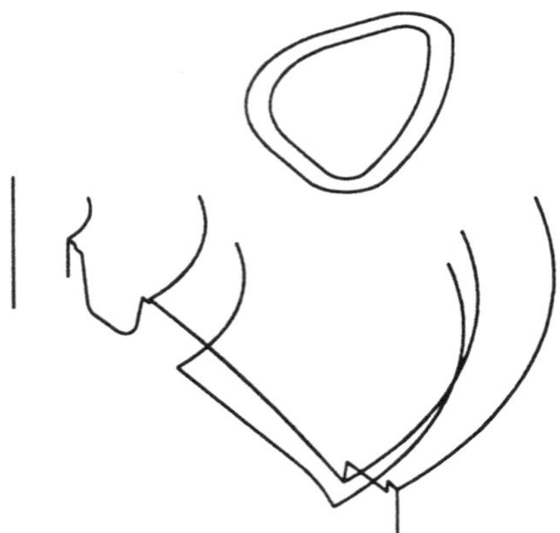

Figure 13.171a Wireframe model

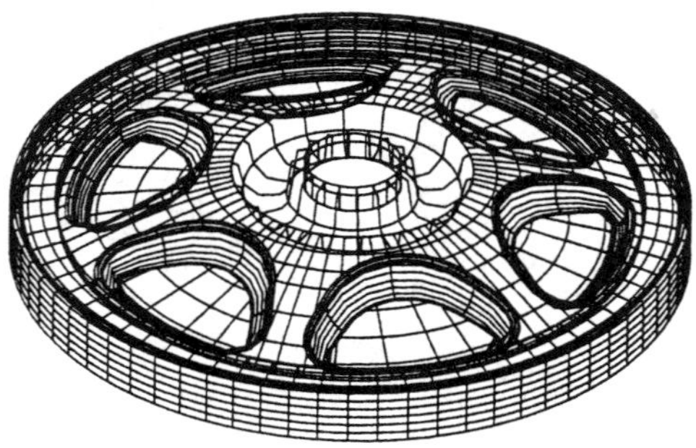

Figure 13.171b Surface model

Tips

1. Create the upper and lower surface using the swept surfacing technique.
2. The outer pocket profile projects onto the upper swept surface to generate a surface curve.
3. The inner pocket profile is projected onto the lower swept surface to generate another surface curve.
4. Create two construction lines for defining a Cplane using the "2 lines" command. This Cplane is used to create an arc as the across contour for the pocket surface.
5. Create the pocket surface using the two surface curves as the two along contours and an arc as the across contour
6. Create a fillet surface between the pocket surface and the upper swept surface.
7. Trim the upper surface to the fillet surface boundary.
8. Trim the lower surface to the pocket surface boundary.
9. Create two swept surfaces, one for the hub and the other for the rim.
10. Create two revolved surfaces, one for the inner hole and the other for the outer profile.
11. Copy all surface to five locations by using Xform → Rotate commands to complete the surface model

Step 1. Load the wireframe model (wheel).

Select **MAIN MENU → File → Get**
Enter file name: **wheel**
The wireframe model drawing should appear as Figure 13.172.

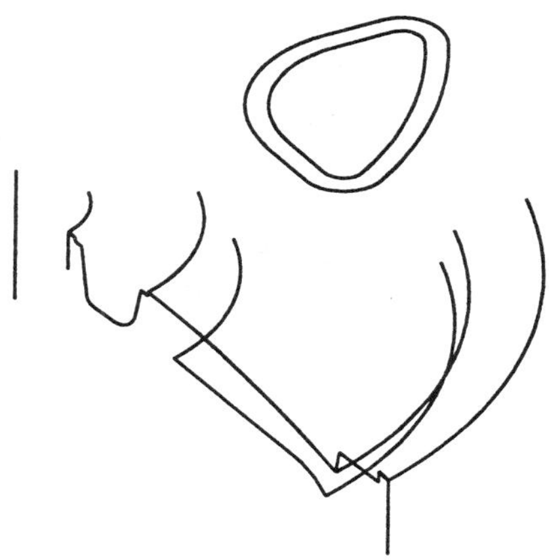

Figure 13.172

Step 2. Make level 2 invisible. Change level to 3 and color 13.

Select **Level**, then enter **3**
Select **Level → Vis. Levels**
Toggle level 2 to invisible (dimmed)
Select **Color, then enter 13**

The drawing should look like Figure 13.173.

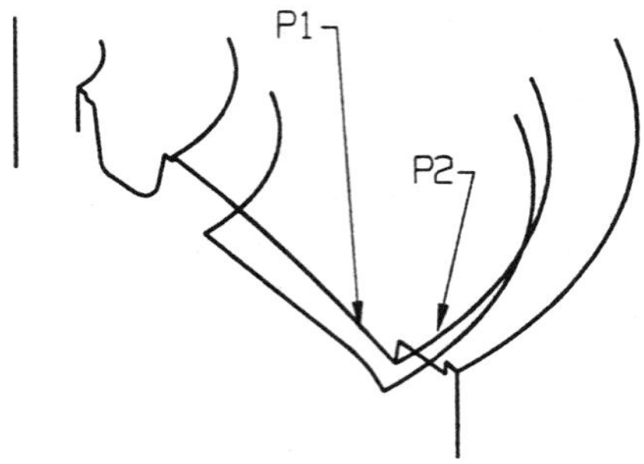

Figure 13.173

Step 3. Create the upper surface using the pick points in Figure 13.149.

Select **MAIN MENU → Create → Surface → Swept**
Enter the number of across contours: **1**
Define the across contour : select **Single**, then pick **P1**
Define along contour 1: pick **P2**
Select **Done** to complete contours selection
Set the Swept surface parameters to the following settings:

Surface Error Tolerance = **0.005**
Surface Type = **NURBS**
Trans/Rot = **R**

The surface should appear as Figure 13.174.

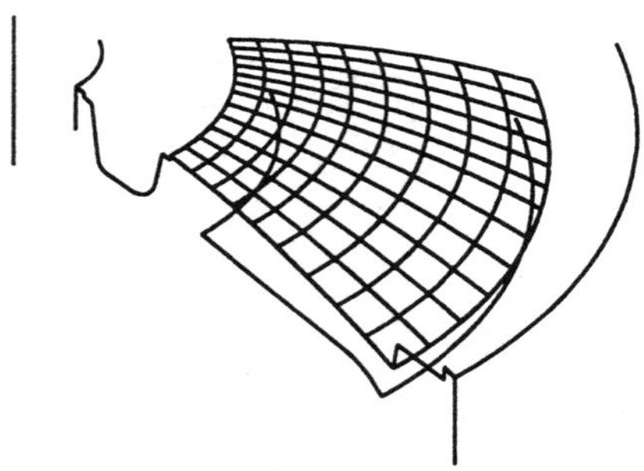

Figure 13.174

Step 4. Make level 3 invisible.

Select **Level**, then enter **4**
Select **Level → Vis.levels**
Toggle level 3 to invisible (dimmed)
Select **OK** to return to graphic mode
Select **Color**, then enter **14**

The drawing becomes Figure 13.175.

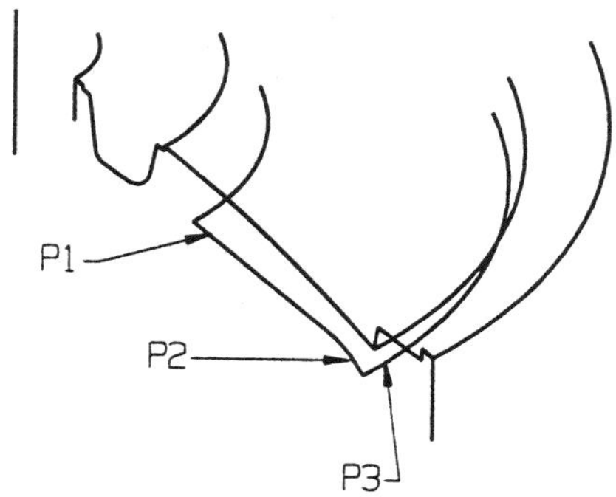

Figure 13.175

Step 5. Create the lower surface using swept surfacing technique.

Use the pick points in Figure 13.175.
Select **BACKUP → Swept**
Enter number of across contour: **1**
Define the across contour: select **Chain → Partial**
Pick **P1** and **P2**
Define along contour 1: select **Mode → Single**
Pick **P3**
Select **Done** to complete the contour selection
Select **Do it** to complete the surface
The new created surface should resemble Figure 13.176.

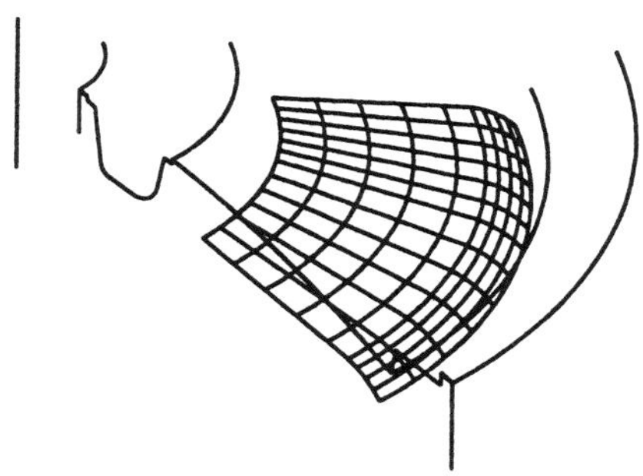

Figure 13.176

Step 6. Make level 2 visible. Change level to 5 and color to 15.

Select **Level**, then enter **5**
Select **Level → Vis. Levels**
Toggle level 2 to visible
Select **Color,** then enter **15**

The drawing now should look like Figure 13.177.

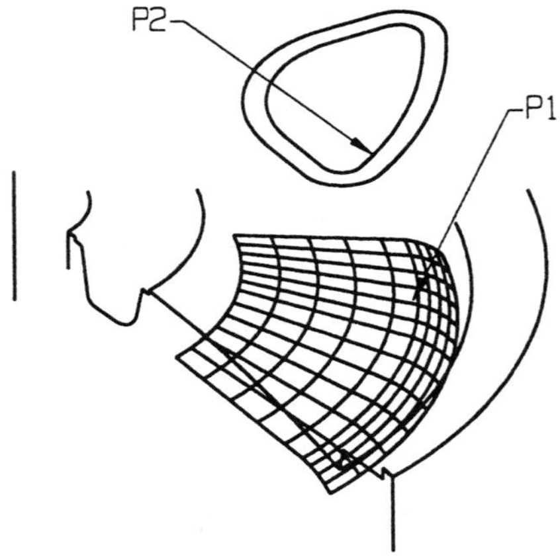

Figure 13.177

Step 7. Project the inner pocket profile to the lower surface to generate a surface curve.

Use the pick points in Figure 13.177.
Select **MAIN MENU → Create → Curve → Project**
Pick **P1** to select the surface
Select **Done**
Select **Chain,** then pick **P2**
Select **Done**
Toggle View/Norm to **V**
Select **Options**
Set the Project Curve parameters as shown here:

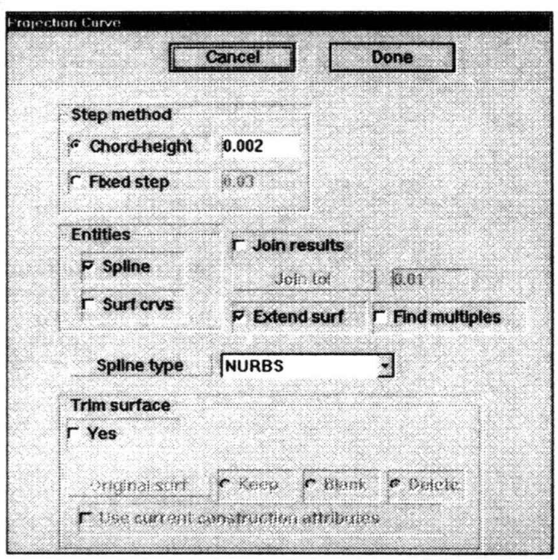

Select **Done → Do it**

The first surface curve should appear as in Figure 13.178.

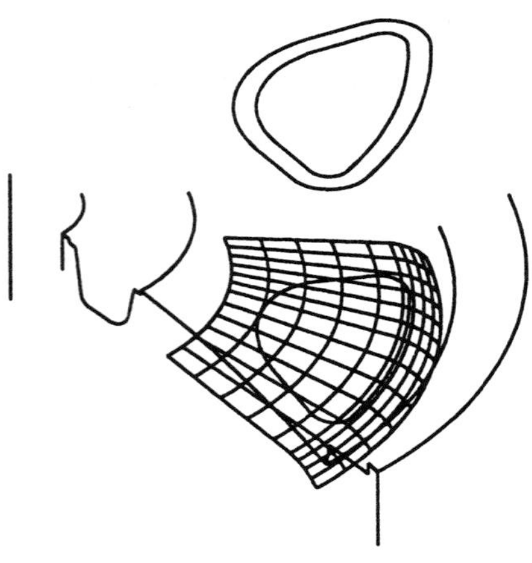

Figure 13.178

Step 8. Make level 4 invisible and level 3 visible.

Select **Level → Vis.levels**
Toggle level 4 to invisible (dimmed) and level 3 to visible (highlighted)
Select **OK** to return to graphic mode
The drawing now should look like Figure 13.179.

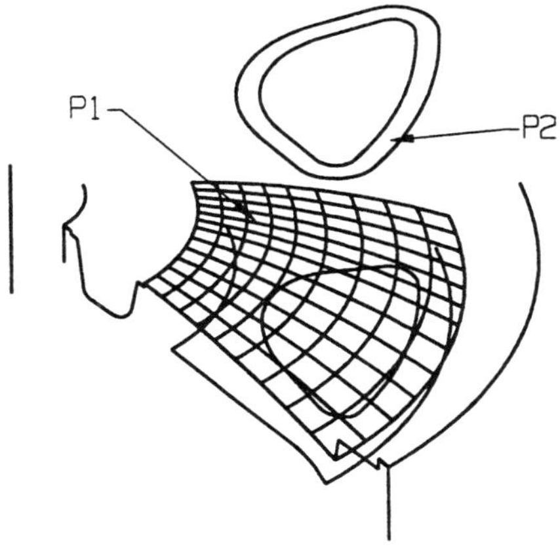

Figure 13.179

Step 9. Project the outer pocket profile to the supper surface to generate the second surface curve.

Use the pick points in Figure 13.179.
Select **BACKUP → Project**
Pick **P1** to select the surface → **Done**
Select **Chain**, then pick **P2**
Select **Done → Do it**
The second surface curve is added as shown in Figure 13.180.

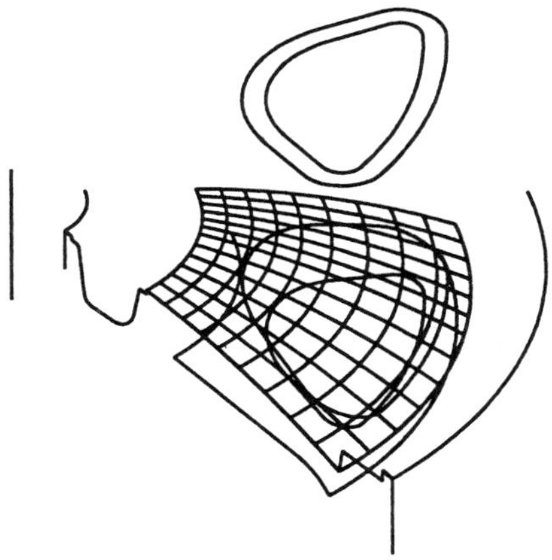

Figure 13.180

Step 10. Make levels 1,2 and 3 invisible.

Select **Level → Vis. Levels**
Toggle levels 1, 2 and 3 to invisible (dimmed)
Select **OK** to return to graphic mode

The drawing appears on the screen should now become Figure 13.181.

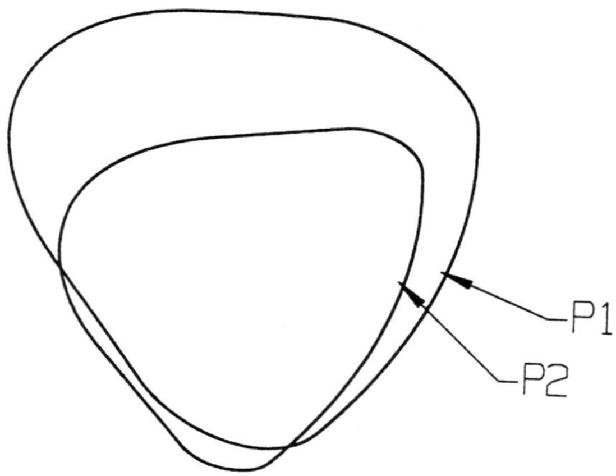

Figure 13.181

Step 11. Create a construction line using the pick points in Figure 13.181.

Select **Cplane → 3d**
Select **MAIN MENU → Create → Line → Endpoints → Midpoint → Pick P1**
Select **Midpoint**, then pick **P2**
The line is added as shown in Figure 13.182.

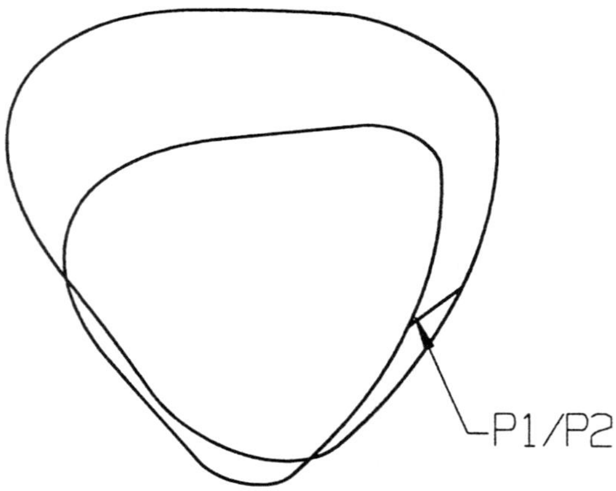

Figure 13.182

Step 12. Create another construction line using the pick points marked in Figure 13.182.

Select **Cplane → Top**
Select **Z → Endpoint**, then pick **P1**
(A value of approximately Z 0.5561 should appear in the Secondary menu)
Select **MAIN MENU → Create → Line → Endpoints → Endpoint**
Specify the first point: pick **P2**
Specify the second point: **0,0**

The drawing should appear as Figure 13.183.

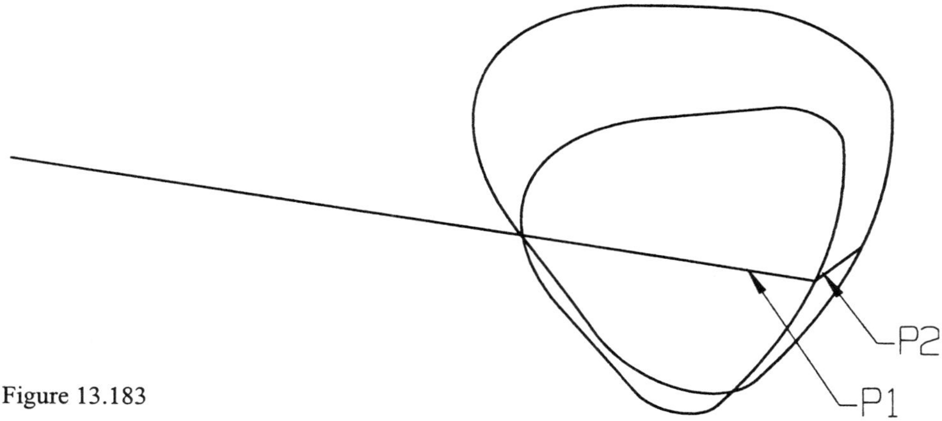

Figure 13.183

Step 13. Use the two construction lines to define a Cplane.

Use the pick points labeled in Figure 13.183.
Select **Cplane → Entity → Only → Lines**
Pick **P1** and **P2** to select the two lines
Select **Save** to accept the new Cplane
The drawing should look like Figure 13.184. (Note: the same as Figure 13.183).

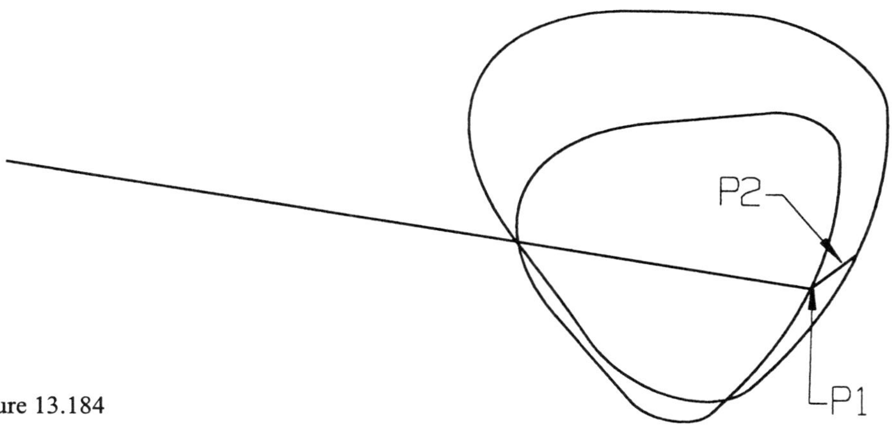

Figure 13.184

Step 14. Create an arc between two surface curves.

Use the pick points in Figure 13.184.
Select **MAIN MENU → Create → Arc → Endpoints → Endpoint**
Pick **P1** and **P2**
Enter the radius: **0.25**
Pick the desired arc →2nd arc from right)

The arc is added as shown in Figure 13.185.

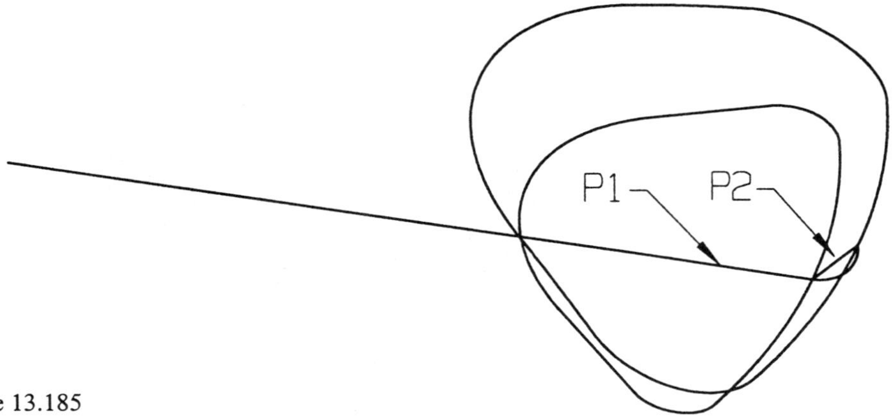

Figure 13.185

Step 15. Delete two construction lines using the pick points in Figure 13.185.

Select **MAIN MENU → Delete**
Pick **P1** and **P2**
The drawing now should resemble Figure 13.186.

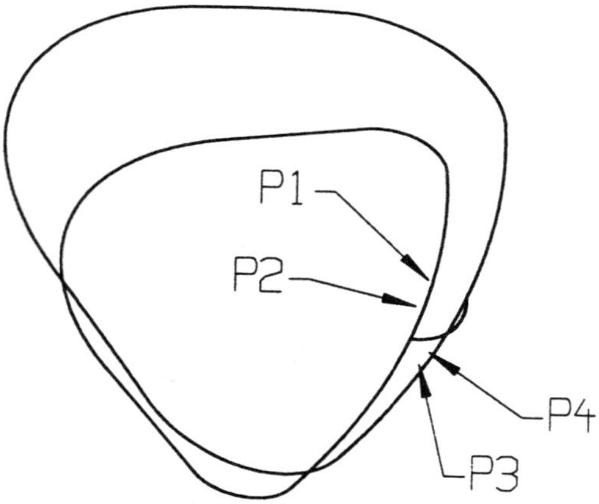

Figure 13.186

Step 16. Break two arcs into two pieces using the pick points in Figure 13.186.

Select **Cplane → Top**
Select **MAIN MENU → Modify → Break → 2 pieces**
Pick **P1** to select an entity
Select **Midpoint,** then pick **P2** to break the entity
Pick **P3** to select another entity
Select **Midpoint,** then pick **P4** to break the entity

The drawing should appear on the screen as Figure 13.187.

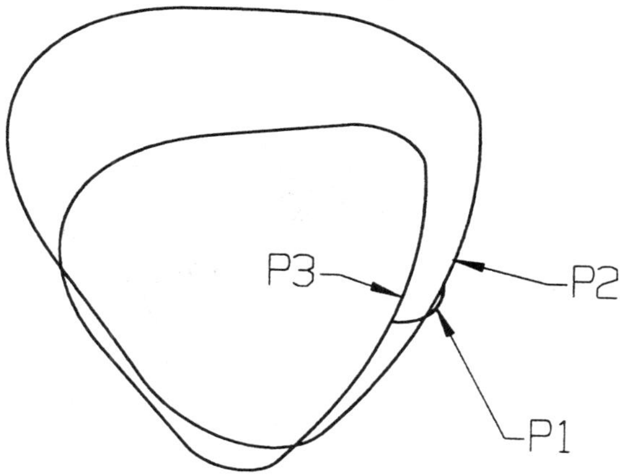

Figure 13.187

Step 17. Create the pocket surface by sweeping the arc along two surface curves.

Use the pick points in Figure 13.187.
Select **Color,** then enter **14**
Select **MAIN MENU → Create → Surface → Swept**
Enter the number of across contours: **1**
Define the across contour: select **Single**, then pick **P1**
Define along contour 1: select **Mode Chain** then pick **P2**
Select **End here**
Define along contour 2: pick **P3**
Select **End here → Done**
Set the Swept surface parameters to the following settings:

Surface Error Tolerance = **0.005** Surface Type = **NURBS**

Select **Do it** to complete the surface
The pocket surface should look like Figure 13.188.

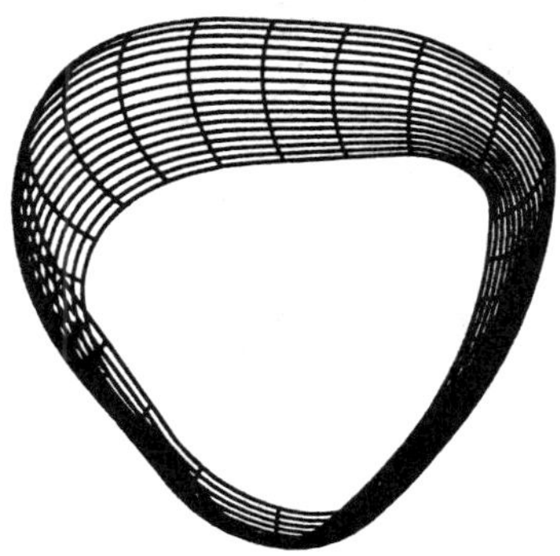

Figure 13.188

Step 18. Make level 3 visible.

Select **Level → Vis.levels**
Toggle level 3 to visible (highlighted)
Select **OK** to return to graphic mode
The drawing now becomes Figure 13.189.

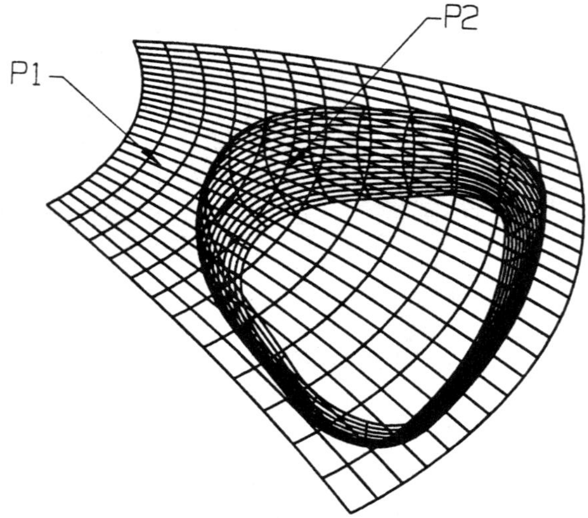

Figure 13.189

Step 19. Change the normal direction of the upper surface and the pocket surface

Use the pick points in Figure 13.189.
Select **MAIN MENU → Modify → Normal → Dynamic**
Pick **P1** and click the mouse to locate the arrow
Select **Flip** (the arrow should point upward)
Select **OK** to the normal direction for the upper surface

Pick **P2** to select the pocket surface and click the mouse to locate the arrow (the arrow should point inward), if necessary
Select **OK** for the normal direction for the pocket surface
The drawing is redisplayed in Figure 13.190.

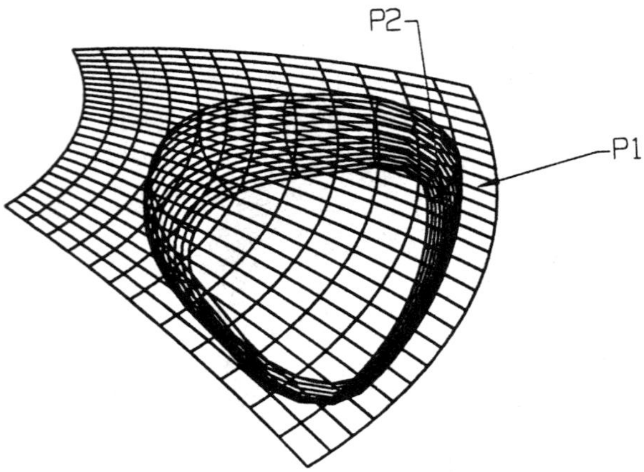

Figure 13.190

Step 20. Create a fillet surface between the upper surface and the pocket surface.

Use the pick points in Figure 13.190.
Select **Level**, then enter **6**
Select **Color**, then enter **11**
Select **MAIN MENU → Create → Surface → Fillet → Surf/surf**
Pick **P1** on the upper surface, then select **Done** for 1st set of surfaces
Pick **P2** to select the pocket surface, then select **Done** for 2nd set of surfaces
Enter the radius = **0.1**
Select **Options**
Set Surface-surface fillet parameters as shown here:

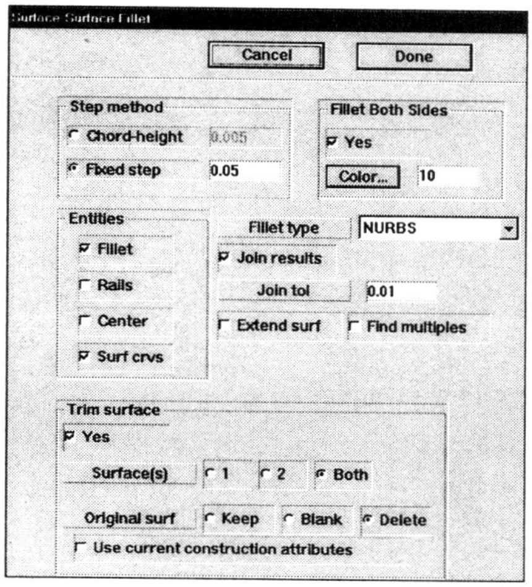

Select **Done → Do it**

The fillet surface should appear as Figure 13.191.

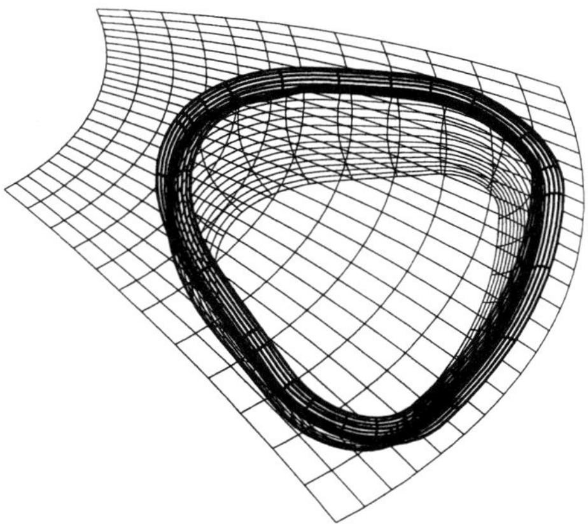

Figure 13.191

Step 21. Make only levels 4 and 5 visible.

Select **Color,** then **12**
Select **Level → Vis.levels**
Toggle levels 4 and 5 to visible (highlighted), then select **OK**
Note: levels 1, 2, 3 and 6 are visible (dimmed)
Select **Level**, then enter **7**
The new drawing becomes Figure 13.192.

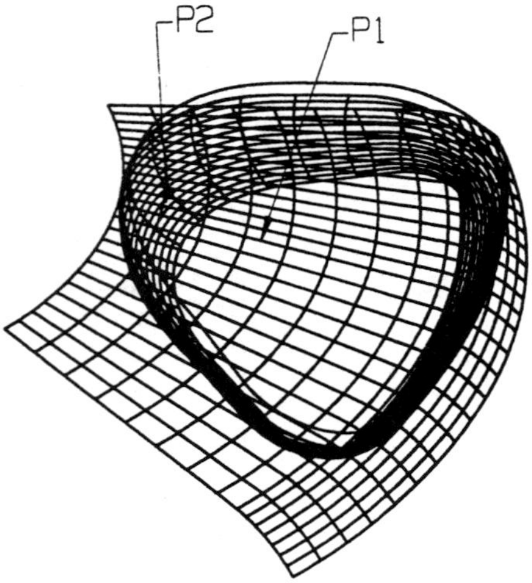

Figure 13.192

Step 22. Add a fillet surface between the lower surface and the pocket surface.

Use the pick points in Figure 13.192.
Select **MAIN MENU → Create → Surface → Fillet → Surf/surf**
Pick **P1** to select the lower surface
Select **Done**
Pick **P2** to select the pocket surface
Select **Done**
Enter radius = **0.15**
Set **Trim** on Y
Select **Do it** (Note: Turn off **"Yes"**of fillet both sides in the option menu)
The fillet surface is added and the lower surface is trimmed in Figure 13.193.

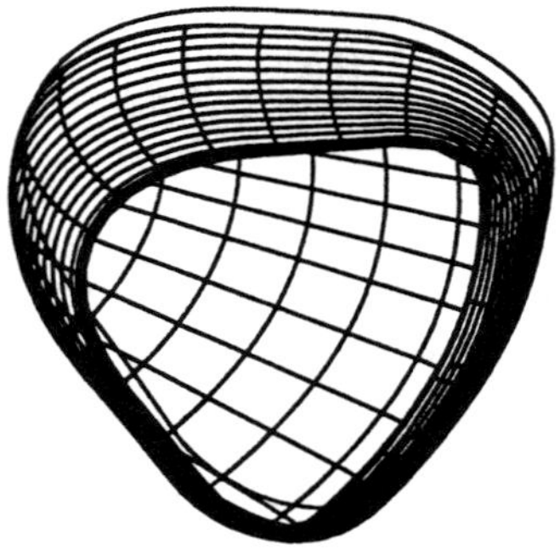

Figure 13.193

Step 23. Make levels 5, 6 and 7 to visible to show trimmed surfaces.

Select **Level → Vis.levels**
Toggle levels 3, 4, 5, 6 and 7 to visible (highlighted)
Note: levels 1 and 2 are invisible
Select **OK** to return to graphic mode
The new drawing should resemble Figure 13.194.

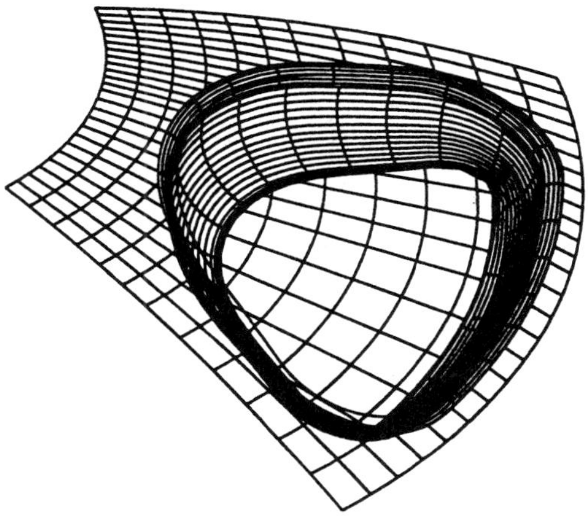

Figure 13.194

Step 24. Make only level 1 visible.

Select **Level**, then enter **8**
Select **Level → Vis.levels**
Toggle level to visible (levels 2-7 are invisible)
Select **OK** to return to graphic mode
The drawing should look like Figure 13.195.

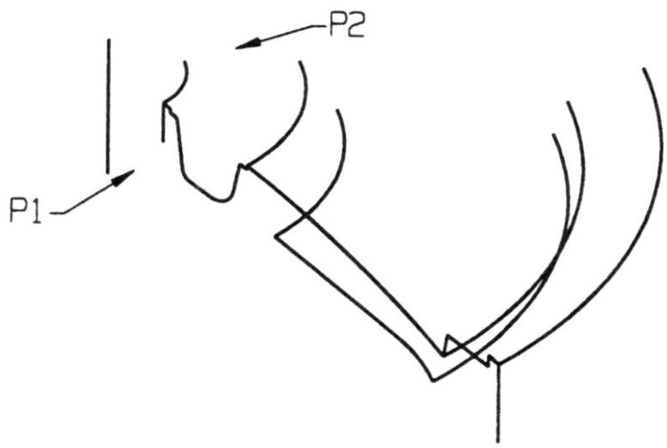

Figure 13.195

Step 25. Zoom the section profile for the hub.

Use the pick points in Figure 13.195.
Press **F1** to select the Z command
Pick **P1** and **P2** to zoom t the hub profile

The zoomed drawing should appear as Figure 13.196.

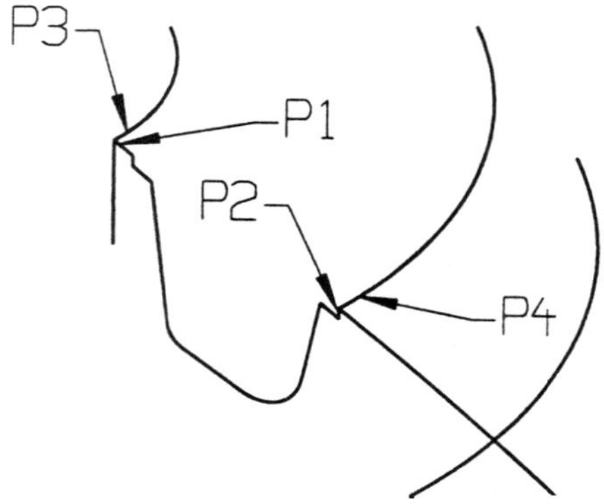

Figure 13.196

Step 26. Create a swept surface for the hub using the pick points in Figure 13.196.

Select **Color,** then enter **14**
Select **MAIN MENU → Create → Surface → Swept**
Enter the number of across contours : **1**
Define the across contour: select **Chain → Partial**
Pick **P1** and **P2**
Define along contour 1: select **Mode → Single**, then pick **P3**
Define along contour 2: pick **P4**
Select **Done** to complete contours selection

Set the Swept surface parameters as below

Surface Error Tolerance = **0.002** Surface Type = **NURBS**

Select **Do it** to complete the surface
Press **Enter** to ignore the shape corners
Press **Alt+F1** to fit the drawing
The new hub surface should look like Figure 13.197.

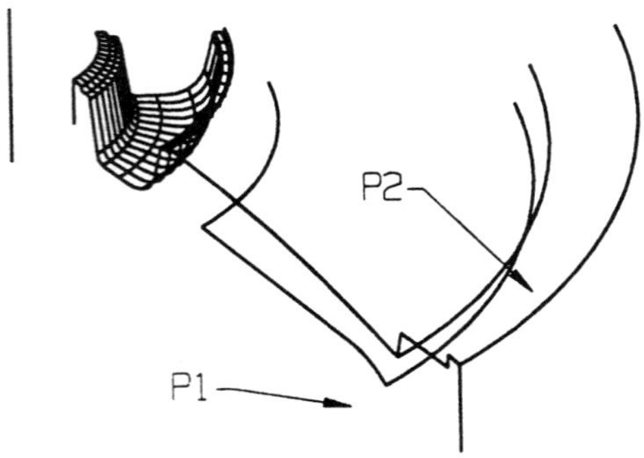

Figure 13.197

Step 27. Zoom the rim profile using the pick points in Figure 13.197.

Press **F1** to select the Zoom command
Pick **P1** and **P2** to define the zoom area

The zoomed drawing should resemble Figure 13.198.

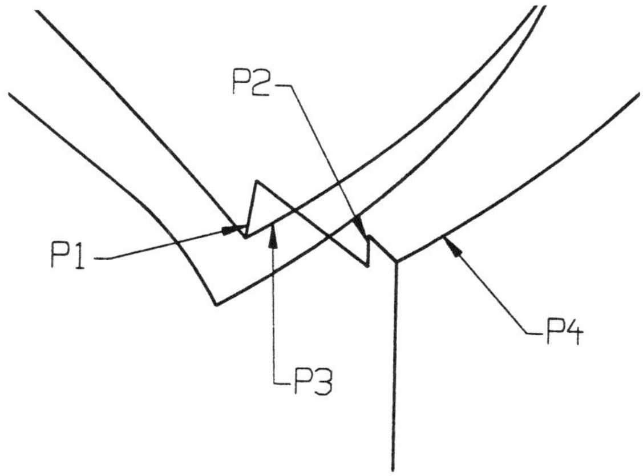

Figure 13.198

Step 28. Create a swept surface for the rim using the pick points in Figure 13.198.

Select **Swept**
Enter the number of across contours 1: **1**
Define the across contour: select **Chain → Partial**
Pick **P1** and **P2**
Define along contour 1: select **Mode → Single**, then pick **P3**

Define along contour 2: pick **P4**
Select **Done → Do it**
Press **Enter** to ignore sharp corners
Press **Alt+F1** to fit the drawing
The rim surface should appear as Figure 13.199.

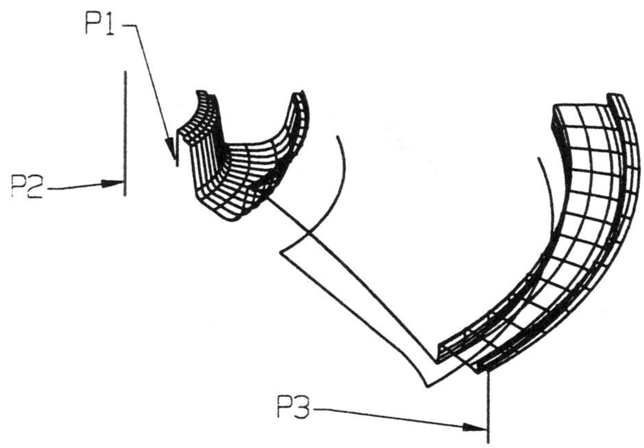

Figure 13.199

Step 29. Create two revolved surfaces using the pick points in Figure 13.199.

Select **Level**, then enter **9**
Select **Color**, then enter **15**
Select **Revolved**
Select the profile entities: select **Single**, then pick **P1→ Done**
Select the axis of rotation: pick **P2**
Enter the starting angle: **0**

Enter the final angle: **60** to complete the first surface
Select **Do it**
Select **BACKUP → Revolved**
Select the profile entities: select **Single**, then pick **P3**
Select **Done**

Select the axis of rotation: pick **P2**
Enter the starting angle: **0**
Enter the final angle: **60** to complete the second surface
Select **Do it**
The two surfaces should resemble Figure 13.200.

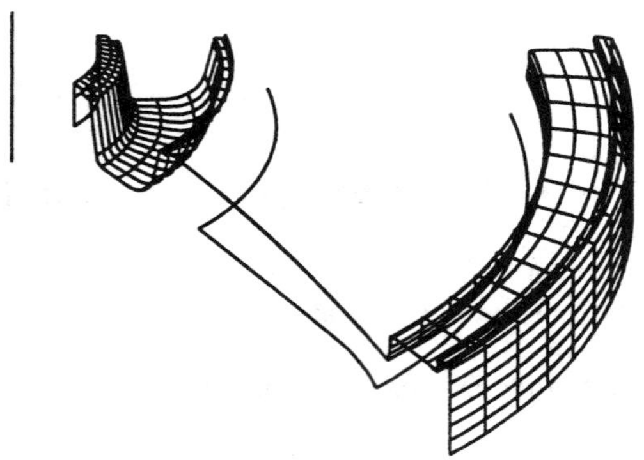

Figure 13.200

Step 30. Make levels 3 through 9 visible.

Select **Level → Vis.levels**
Toggle levels 3-9 to visible (highlighted)
Select **OK** to return to graphic mode
The complete sectional surfaces should look like Figure 13.201.

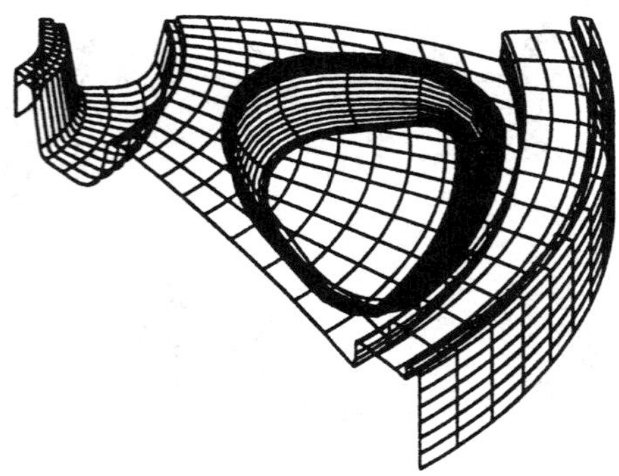

Figure 13.201

Step 31. Save the surface file wheel.

Select **MAIN MENU → File → Save**
Enter file name: **wheels**

Step 32. Copy the surfaces to five locations using Xform → Rotate commands.

Select **MAIN MENU → Xform → Rotate**

Select **Surfaces → Done → Origin**

Set the Rotate parameters as below:

Copy
Number of steps = **5**
Rotation angle = **60**

Select **Done** to complete the surface model

The final drawing should resemble Figure 13.202.

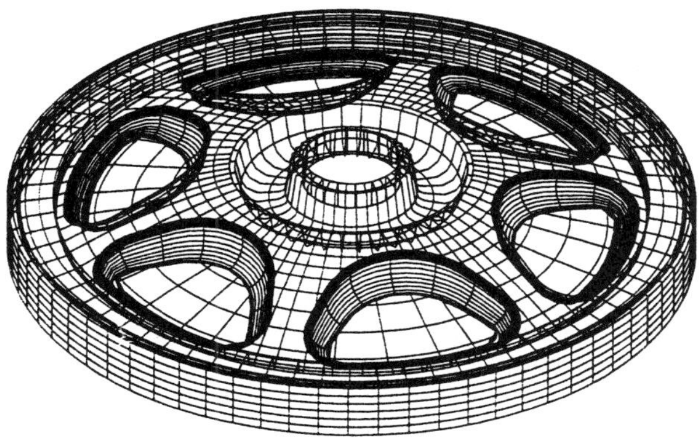

Figure 13.202

Exercises

1. What are derived surfaces ?
2. What are the three derived surface modeling techniques available in Mastercam ?
3. Explain when to use fillet surfaces ?
4. What are the two types of fillet surfaces ?
5. What are the six patterns of variable radius fillet surfaces ?
6. List the two stepping methods for specifying the stepping distance of the surface.
7. What are the three types of information to be generated during the generating of a fillet surface ?
8. What is a trimmed surface ?
9. Under what conditions does surface trimming require you to redefine the outer boundary ?
10. What is an offset surface ?
11. What are composite surface models ?

Problems

12. Create two fillet surface from the surface model created in problem 12.17. The original surface model file is ES1. Save the fillet surface model as ES14. The two fillet surfaces have a constant radius of 0.25". The fillet surfaces with the base surfaces are shown in Figure 13.203. A similar example is project 1 of this chapter.

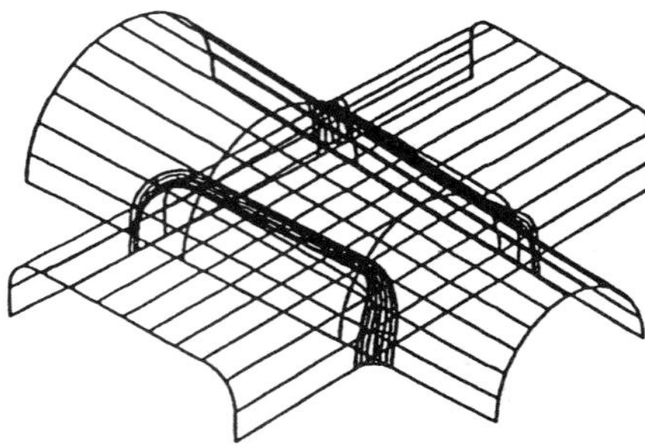

Figure 13.203.

13. Create a fillet surface at the intersection of two ruled surfaces created in problem 12.18. The radius of the fillet surface varies in a linear pattern, which starts at 0.5" at the right end to 0.35" at the other end. The fillet surface with the two base surfaces are shown in Figure 13.204. The original surface model file is ES2. Save the fillet surface model ES15. A similar example is project 2 in this chapter.

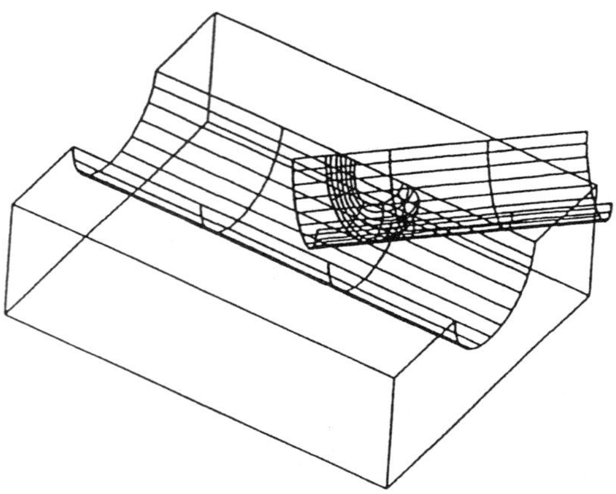

Figure 13.204

14. Create two trimmed surfaces from the surface model created in problem 12. The original surface model is ES1. Two surface curves should be created at the intersection between two ruled surfaces. These two surface curves are then used as the trimming boundary to trim two ruled surfaces. The trimmed surfaces are shown in Figure 13.205. Save the trimmed surfaces as ES16. A similar example is project 3 of this chapter.

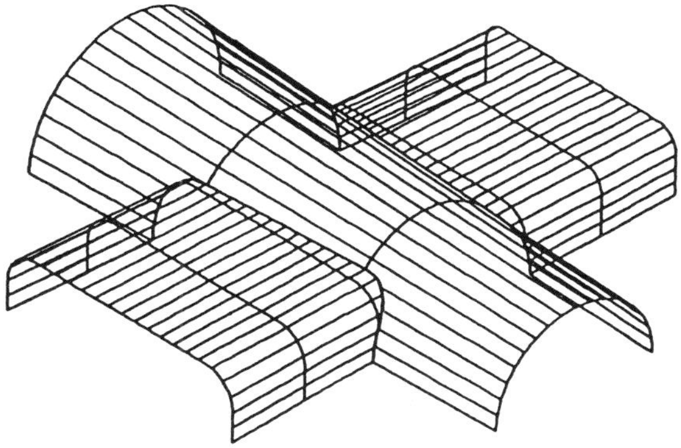

Figure 13.205

15. Create two trimmed surfaces from the surface model created in problem 13 of this chapter. The surface curves of the fillet surface are used as the trimming boundary. The base surface model file is ES15. Save the trimmed surfaces as ES17. The trimmed surfaces should look like Figure 13.206. A similar example is project 4 in this chapter.

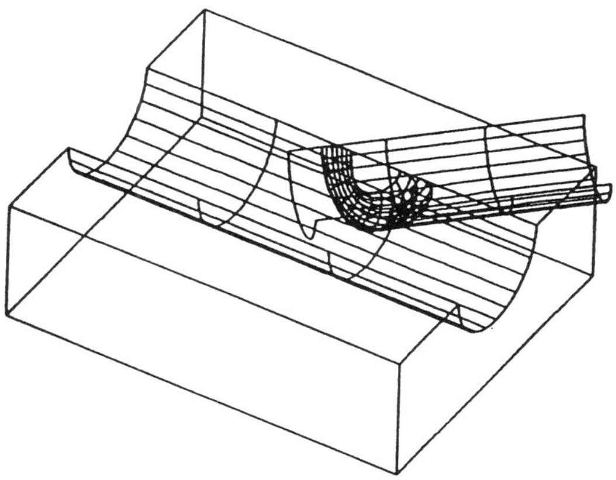

Figure 13.206

16. Generate an offset surface from the surface model created in problem 12.21. The original surface model file is ES5. The Coons surface is offset by 0.375" in the outward direction. The offset surface should resemble Figure 13.207. Save the offset surface as ES18. A similar example is project 6 of this chapter.

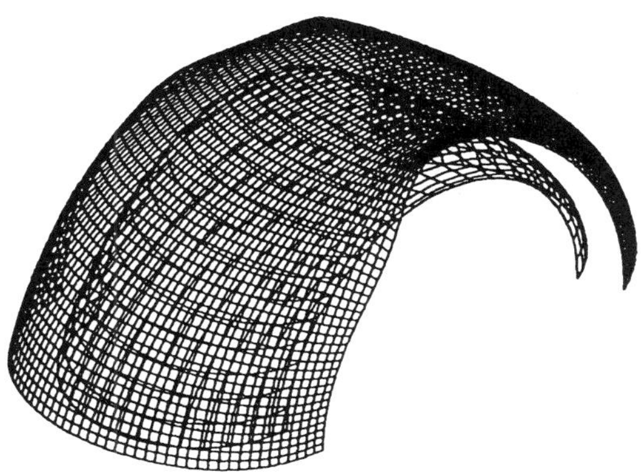

Figure 13.207

17. Create a composite surface model from the wireframe model given in problem 11.20. The wireframe model file is E11. The surface model consists of four surfaces: a ruled surface at the bottom, a swept surface for wall and top rim, and a fillet surface between the two surfaces as shown in Figure 13.208. Save the surface model as ES19. A similar example is project 7 in this chapter.

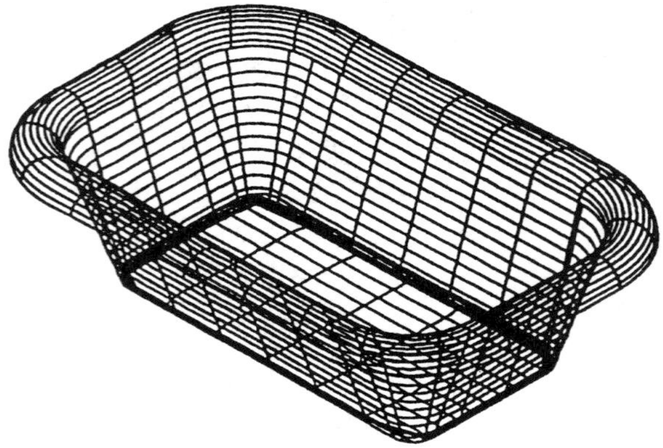

Figure 13.208

18. Create a composite surface model from the wireframe model given in problem 11.21. The wireframe model file is E12. This surface model consists of four surfaces including one swept surface on the top, one swept surface of the middle frame, and four ruled surfaces for the handles. Save the surface model file as ES20. The surface model should look like Figure 13.209. A similar example is project 9 in this chapter.

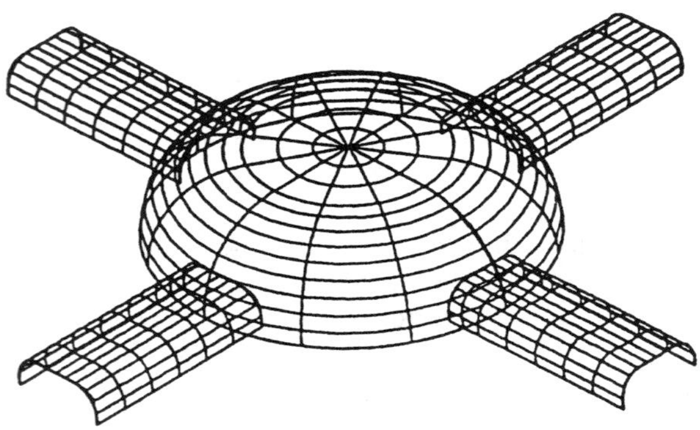

Figure 13.209

Mastercam Version 7,
Scholar's International Publishing Corp., 1998

Chapter 14

3D Toolpaths I: Generated from Wireframe Models

Objectives:

1. Know two methods of generating toolpaths to cut surfaces.
2. Understand 3-d toolpath common parameters.
3. Know 3-d toolpath modules used to generate toolpaths from wireframe models.
4. Apply 3-d toolpath modules.

14.1 Two Surface Toolpath Generation Methods

Mastercam provides **two** methods to generate toolpaths for machining various forms of surfaces: wireframe and surface. Using the wireframe method, the wireframe model is used in a 3-d toolpath module to generate the toolpaths which machine the surface. However, the surface method takes an extra step to generate the surfacing toolpaths. The wireframe model is used to create the surface model first, then this surface model is used to generate the toolpaths by the various surfacing toolpath modules. Figure 14.1 shows a flow chart of these two methods of generating toolpaths for machining surfaces.

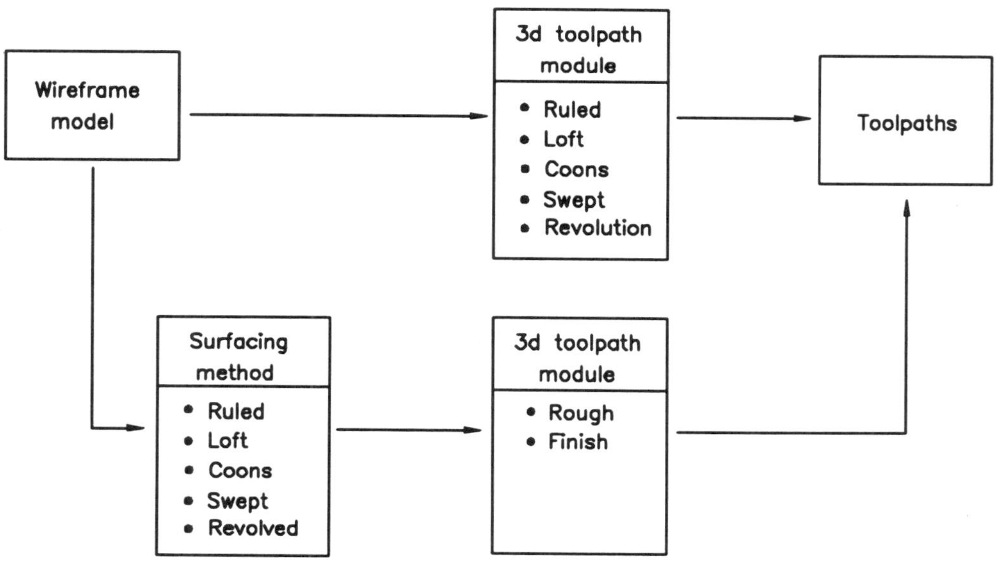

Figure 14.1

At the first glance, the wireframe method seems more straight forward and easy to use. However, we recommend using the surface method except for machining very simple surfaces. The reasons are elaborated in Table 14.1 which compares the two methods of generating surfacing toolpaths.

Table 14.1 Comparing two methods of generating 3-d surfacing toolpaths

Method	Advantages	Disadvantages
Wireframe method	1. Do not require creating a surface before generating toolpaths.	1. Can generate toolpaths for only a single surface. 2. Do not give the surface skin before toolpaths are created. 3. No surface model to be analyzed before generating toolpaths. 4. Required to define more parameters.
Surface method	1. Can generate toolpaths for multiple surfaces simultaneously. 2. Has the surface to be analyzed, examined, and edited before generating toolpaths. 3. Fewer parameters to define. 4. More flexible and easier to be edited.	1. Require an existing surface model to generate the toolpaths.

The wireframe method in generating surfacing toolpaths is presented in this chapter and the surface method is in chapter 15.

14.2 3D Toolpaths Common Parameters

As indicated in chapter 7, Mastercam uses two groups of parameters, common and module specific, to define machining and tooling data. Most common parameters presented in chapter 7 are applicable to 3-d cases. However, a number of additional parameters should be added for 3-d toolpath modules including; *along* and *across*, cutting method, stepping over distances (along cut distance, across cut distance), cutting direction, and cutter compensation.

Along and Across

Surfaces are defined by a series of joined or non-connected contours. These contours are arranged into two groups, along and across, according to their orientations. In other words, along and across are used to indicate the direction of a group of contours (Figure 14.2). Normally, the *along* direction follows the longer contours of the two directions. The *across* direction is the shorter contours.

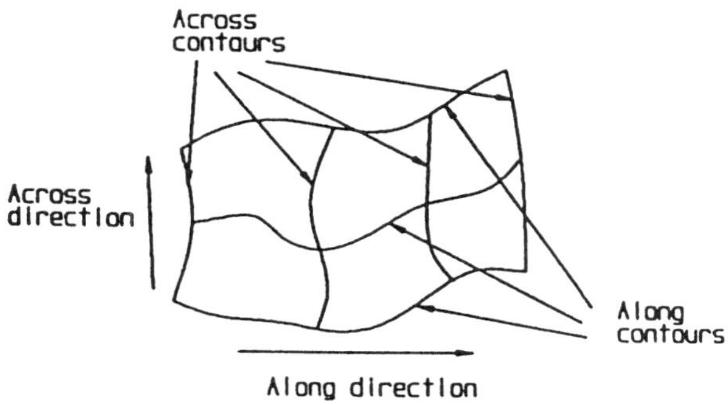

Figure 14.2

Cutting Methods

There are **four** cutting methods: zig-zag, one way, circular and 5-axis. Each method has its unique features and uses. Table 14.2 summaries the features of each cutting method.

Table 14.2 Cutting methods in 3-d surfacing

Type	Features	Illustration
Zig- zag	• Cutter moves back and forth across the part to cut the surface. The cutter makes constant contact with the surface. • Takes shorter time. • Conventional milling in one direction and climb milling in the other direction This alternate milling pattern is not desirable.	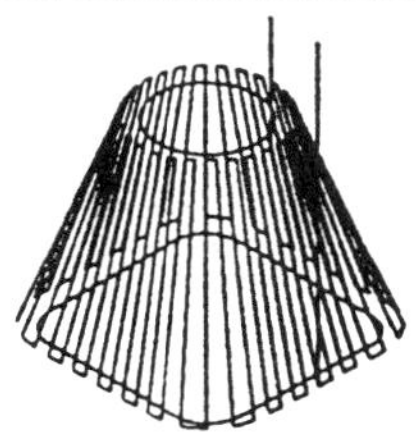
One way	• Cutter takes all passes on the surface in the same direction. It makes a pass, then retracts in Z direction, rapids to another starting point, takes another pass in the specified direction. Repeat the toolpath until completing the surface cutting. • Keep the same milling type (climb or conventional) • Take longer time due to retracting and plunging for each cutting pass.	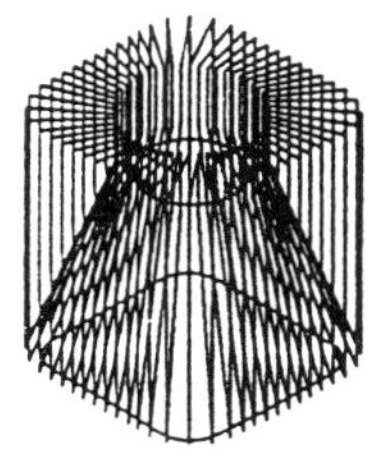
Circular	• Cutter moves along a spiral pattern to machine a surface. • Circular should only be used when closed contours are used. This means that the first and last contour are identical.	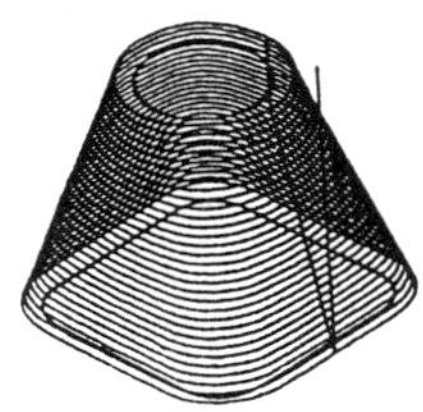
5-axis	• Cutter moves in the specified direction to machine a surface. • The tool axis is in the surface normal direction.	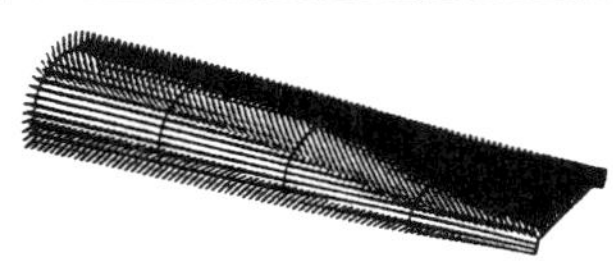

Cutting Direction

This parameter can be toggled to along or across which specifies the cutting direction of the toolpaths. In the **along** mode, the cutter cuts in the along direction while stepping over in the across direction as shown in Figure 14.3 . In the **across** mode, the cutter cuts in the across direction while stepping over in the along direction (Figure 14.4).

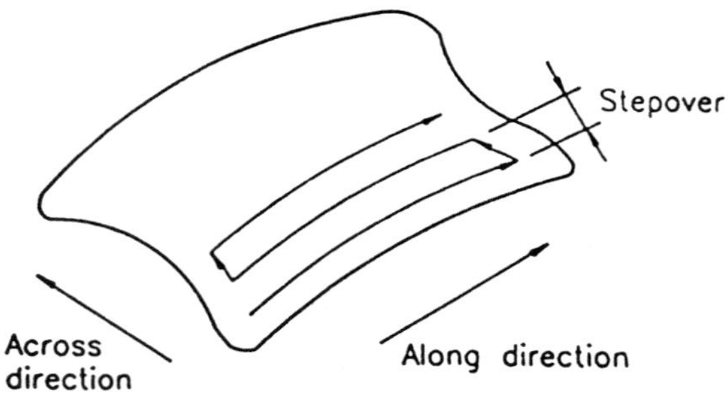

Figure 14.3

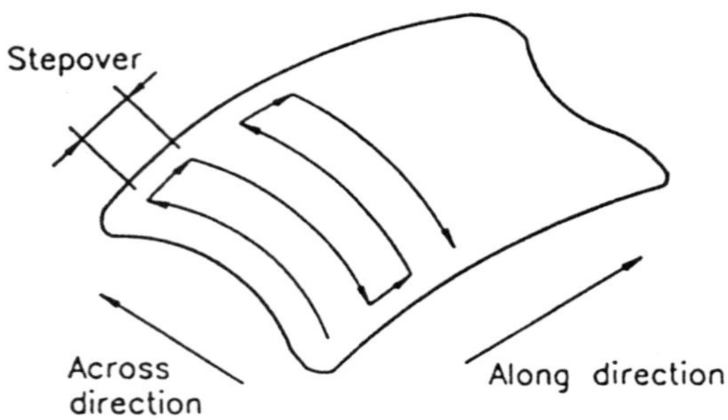

Figure 14.4

Stepping Over Distances

Surface cuttings are normally implemented in linear interpolation mode. In fact, the surface is approximated by a set of linear interpolation motion commands which step over the surface skin. Therefore, the system requires two stepping over values, one in along direction and the other in the across direction, to determine the actual coordinates of toolpaths. Mastercam uses two terms, along cut distance and across cut distance, to indicate these two stepping over values. The **along cut distance** is the cutter step-over distance in each along pass. The **across cut distance** is the cutter step-over distance between each along cut. Figure 14.5 illustrates the use of along cut distance and across cut distance in surface cutting. It should be noted that these two distances determine the cutting accuracy and the program size. The larger the distance, the bigger the surface positional error and the shorter the program size. Conversely, the smaller the distance, the smaller the surface positional error and the larger the program size.

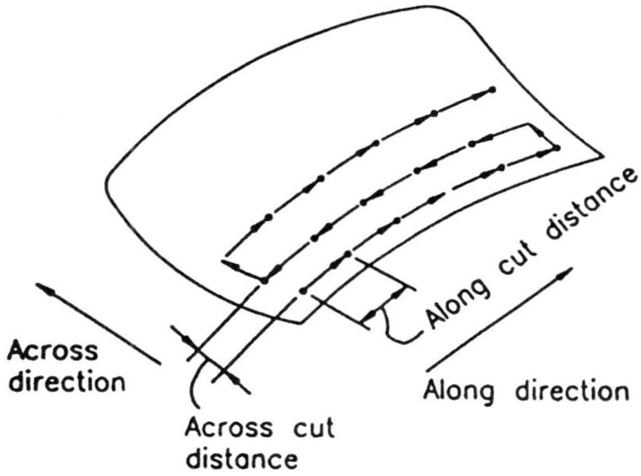

Figure 14.5

Cutter Compensation

Cutter compensation in a 3-d machining is more difficult to be determined than those in 2-d machining. The "cutter compensation in computer" parameter can be toggled to one of **five modes**: left center, left tip, right center, right tip, and off. It should be noted that ball-end mills or bull-nose mills are normally used in 3-d machining. The definition of cutter tip and cutter center for ball-end, bull-nose, and straight-end mills are illustrated in Figure 14.6. The selection of tip and center of the cutter has a significant effect on the toolpaths as shown in Figure 14.7.

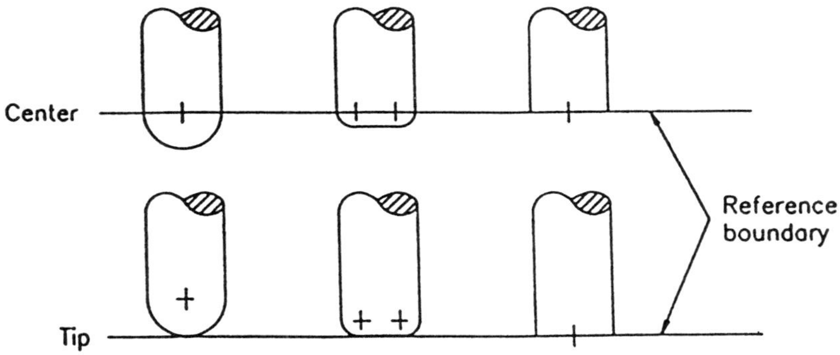

Figures 14.6

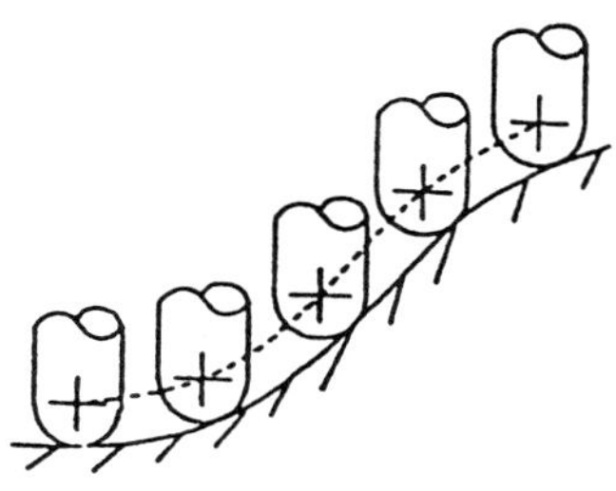

Figure 14.7a Center

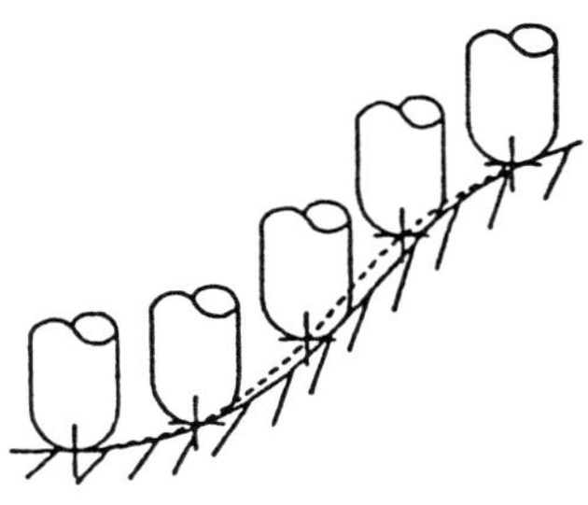

Figure 14.7b Tip

> **Tip** Mastercam actually calculates for a sphere when you specify a ball end mill so one could use a special shaped cutter if necessary.

The direction of cutter compensation can be left, right, or off. The offset direction is determined as followed:

Viewing from the first contour toward the last contour in the along direction:

> **Left:** The contours used to define the surface are located at the left side of the toolpaths (Figure 14.8a).
>
> **Right:** The contours used to define the surface are located at the right side of the toolpaths (Figure 14.8b).

Note: the cutter compensation in Figure 14.8b produces undercut throughout the surface.

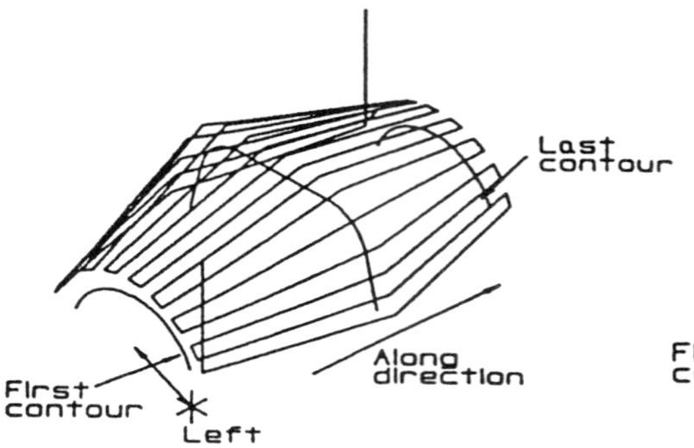

Figure 14.8a. Cutter compensation to the left

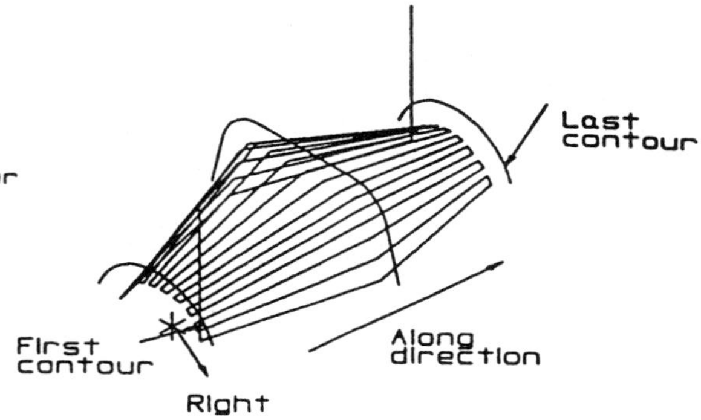

Figure 14.8b. Cutter compensation to the right

Figure 14.9 shows an example of picking the contour order reversed from that in Figure 14.8.

Note: when the picking order of the contours is reversed, the direction for cutter compensation should be changed accordingly.

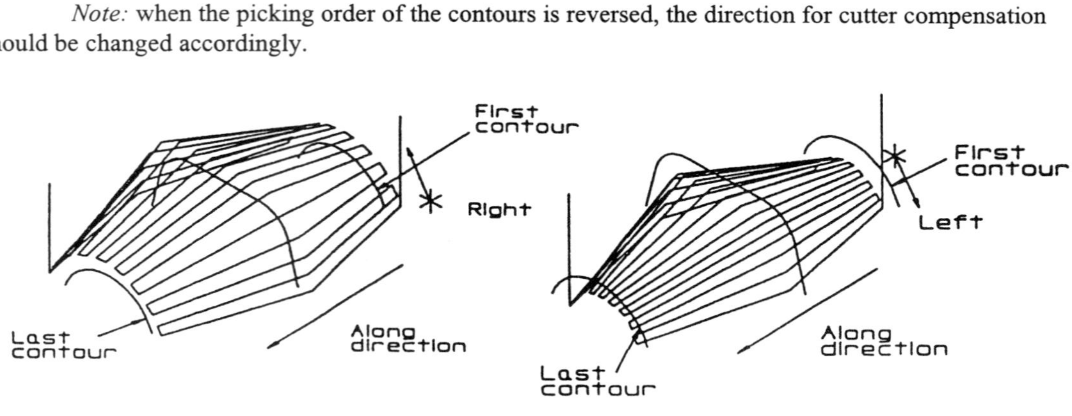

Figure 14.9

When cutter compensation is applied to the across direction, the viewing direction follows the across contour from the picking end to the other end. Then the direction of left and right is determined with the same principle as in the along direction. Figure 14.10 shows an example of cutter compensation in the across direction.

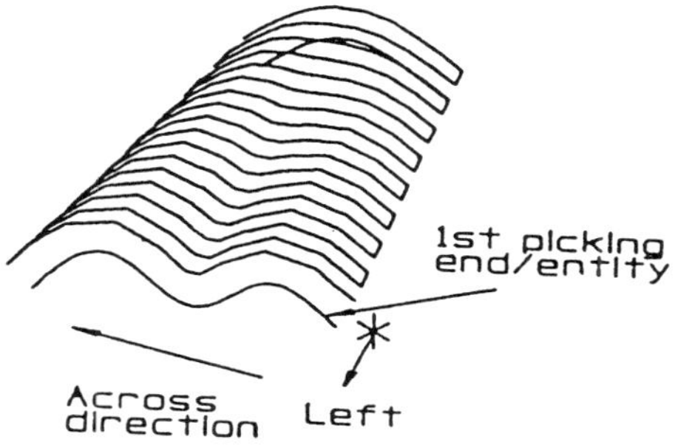

Figure 14.10a Cutter compensation to **left**

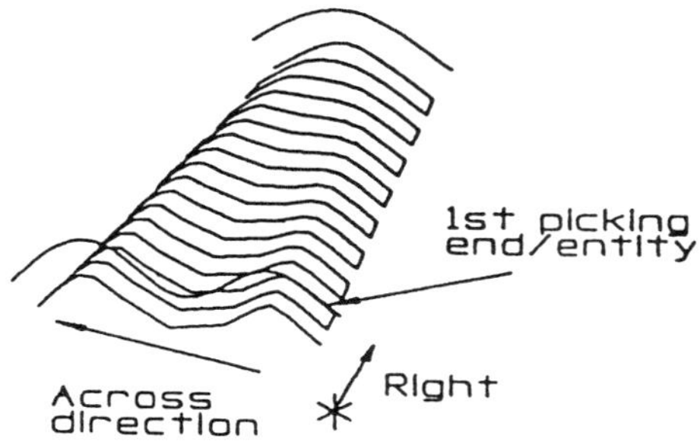

Figure 14.10b Cutter compensation to **right**

14.3 3D Toolpath Modules

Mastercam has two groups of 3-d toolpath modules. The **first group** has **five** toolpath modules which are used to generate toolpaths for cutting a single surface from a wireframe model. The **second group** has **two** subgroups oftoolpath modules that are used to generate toolpaths to rough cut or finish cut an existing surface model. In this chapter we only present the first group. The second group is covered in chapter 15.

The **five 3-d toolpath modules** for working with wireframe models include ruled, loft, Coons, swept, and revolution. The selection of a proper 3-d toolpath module mainly depends on the nature of the surface to be cut and the type and number of surface profiles available in the wireframe model. On the next page, Table 14.3 summarizes the features of these five modules.

These five toolpath modules are presented in the following five sections. Each section begins with a brief discussion of the features of the module, module specific parameters, and concluded with one or two examples.

14.4 Ruled Toolpath Module

This ruled module is used for blending two to one hundred contours to produce a linear 3D surface as shown in Figure 14.11.

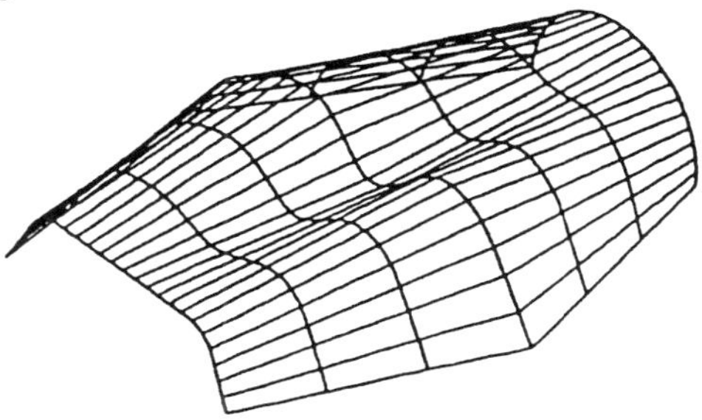

Figure 14.11

Table 14.3 3-d toolpath modules for machining surfaces from a wireframe model

Module type	Description	Illustration
Ruled	Creates the toolpaths to produce a surface formed by linearly blending at least two contours.	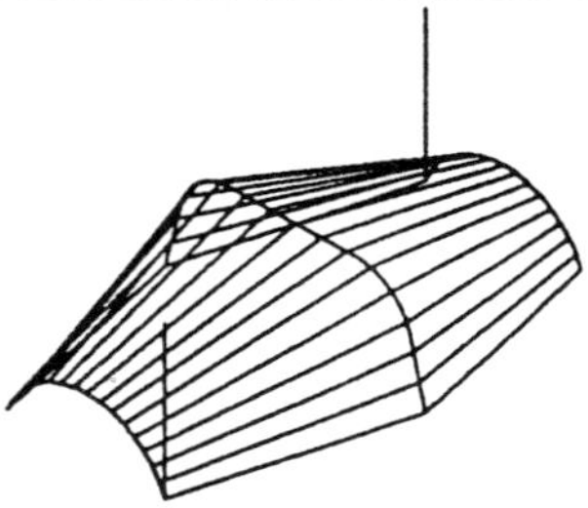
Loft	Creates the toolpaths to produce a surface formed by blending parabolically more than two contours.	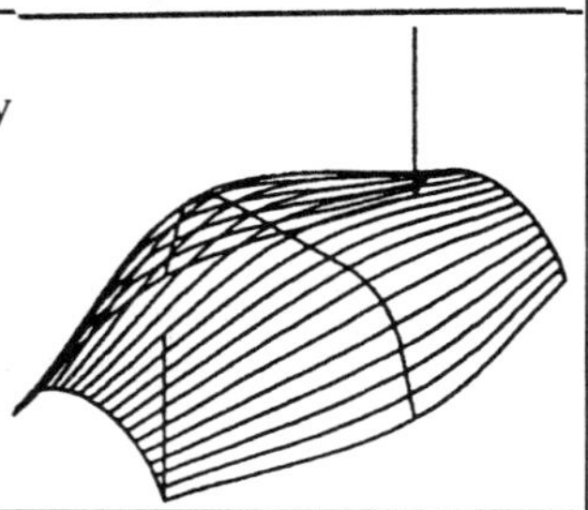
Coons	Creates the toolpaths to produce a surface that is formed by blending a grid of closed boundaries (patches).	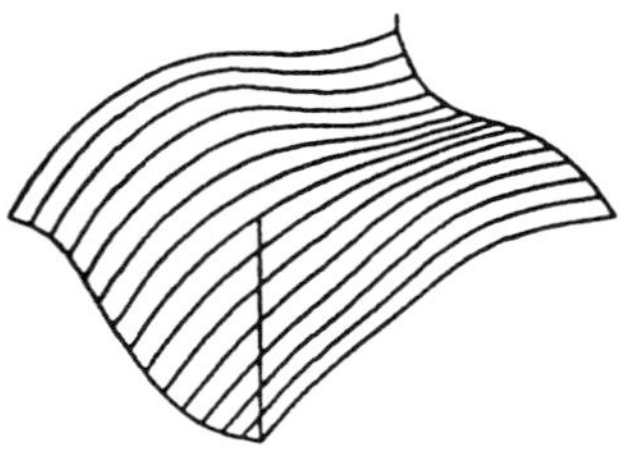
Swept 3D	Creates the toolpaths to cut a surface that is formed by sweeping one or two across contours along one or two rails (along contours).	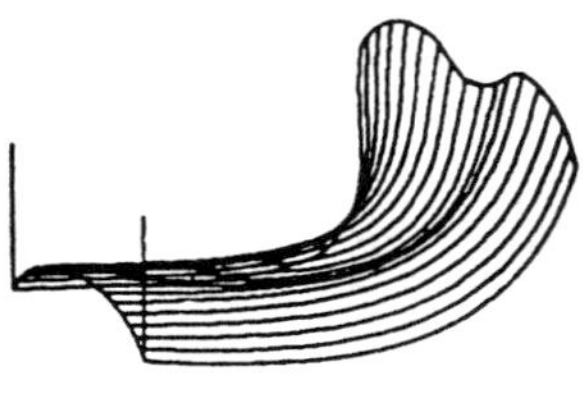
Revolution	Creates the toolpaths to produce a surface by rotating a contour about an axis of rotation.	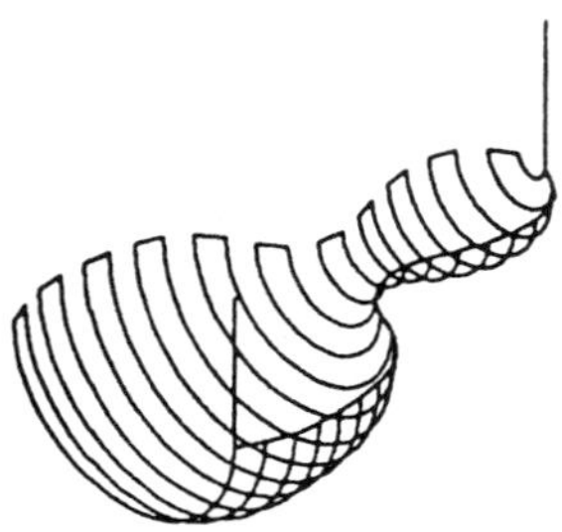

Ruled Parameters

The ruled parameters appear as below:

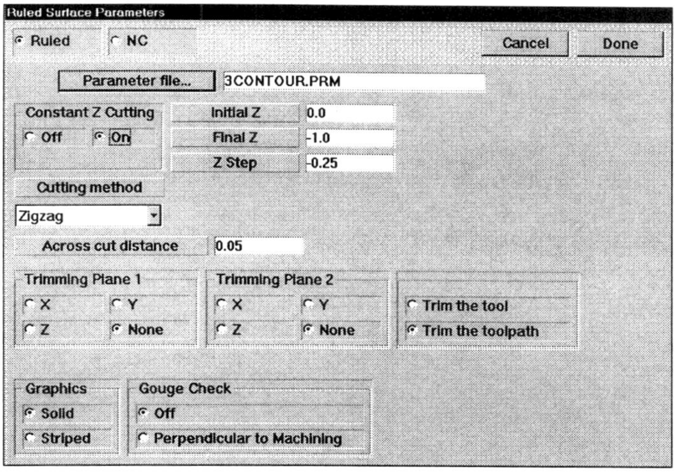

Constant Z Cutting

This parameter can be set to On or Off. When set to On, the cutter will be kept at a constant Z depth for each cut pass. The following three parameters will appear when the Constant Z cutting is set to On:

Initial Z:	specifies the Z value of top boundary
Final Z:	specifies the Z value of bottom boundary
Z step:	specifies the stepover value in Z direction of each pass

The initial Z and final Z define the constant Z cutting boundaries. These boundaries can be used to extend the toolpath beyond the defined surface or cut only a portion of the defined surface. Figure 14.12 illustrates the three parameters in constant Z cutting.

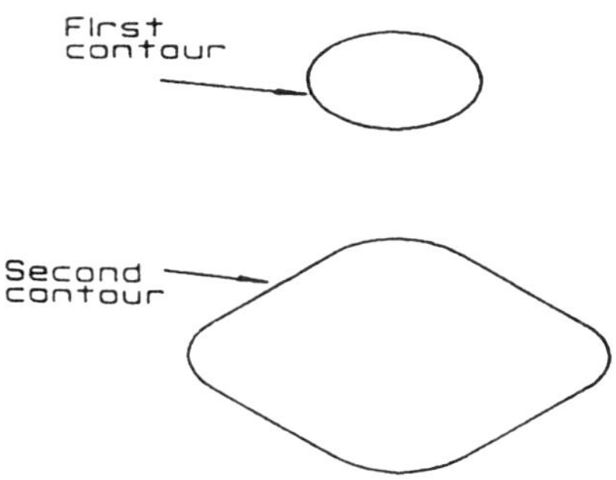

Figure 14.12a Isometric view

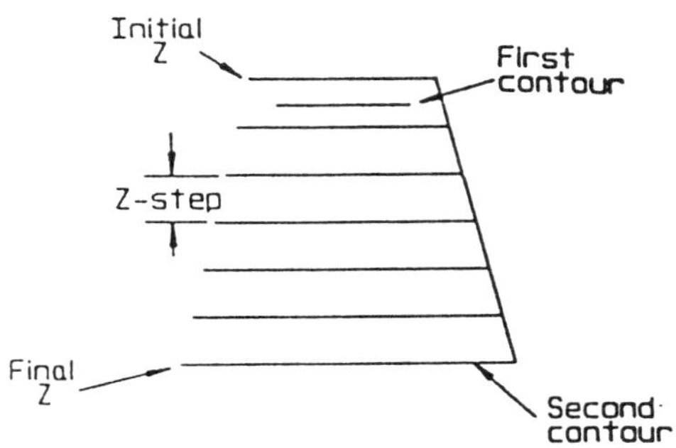

Figure 14.12b Front view

Taper Angle

This parameter specifies the angle of the surface slope for the cutting tool. It is only available for 5 axis cutting.

Trimming Planes

The ruled module allows to define two trimming planes. These trimming planes can be used to (1) extend the cut to the specified boundaries (Figure 14.13) and (2) limit the cut to pass the specified boundaries (Figure 14.14). When the trimming planes are located outside the surface boundaries, the toolpaths are extended. When the trimming planes fit inside the surface boundaries, the toolpaths are trimmed.

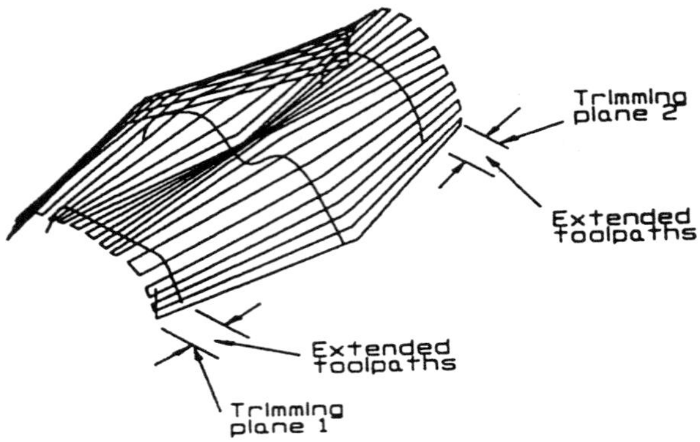

Figure 14.13 Extending

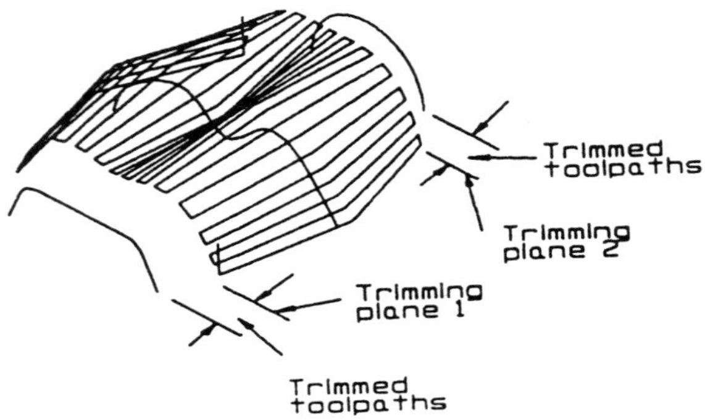

Figure 14.14 Trimming

Gouge Check Direction

This parameter can be toggled to one of two modes to determine whether the gouge check is to be performed. Gouge checking is ignored when off mode is selected. The perpendicular to machine mode assigns the group checking function to the across direction.

Project 1. Machining a ruled surface formed by two contours 1

The ruled toolpath module is used to generate toolpaths for machining two ruled surfaces as shown in Figure 14.15. The wireframe model file is **ruled1** which is created in chapter 11. These two ruled surfaces intersect in the middle. Therefore, their toolpaths can not be used without modification. Actually, we can not machine these two ruled surfaces using the toolpaths generated from this project because the toolpath in one surface cuts into the other surface. In this project we can only illustrate generating toolpaths for machining ruled surfaces. We also assume that two fillet surfaces are to be added at the two places where the ruled surfaces intersect. This is done in chapter 15. Here we create two sets of toolpaths to machine two ruled surfaces. One file is saved as Surf1 and the other as Surf2.

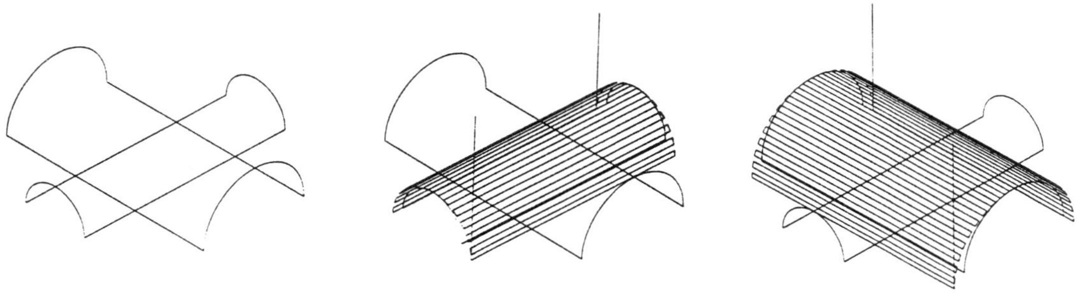

Figure 14.15

Tips 1. Cutter compensation in computer is set to **left** center for the first ruled surface and set to **right** center for the second ruled surface.

2. Cutter is 0.5" ball-end mill.

3. Save the toolpaths for each surface in a separate file, **surf1** for the first ruled surface and **surf2** for the second. These two toolpaths files can not be used without modification. They will cut through each other in the middle.

Step 1. Load the wireframe model file (ruled1.ge3) or create one by following the instructions in project 1 of chapter 11. The wireframe model should appear as in Figure 14.16.

Select **MAIN MENU → File → Get**

Enter file name: **ruled1 ←**

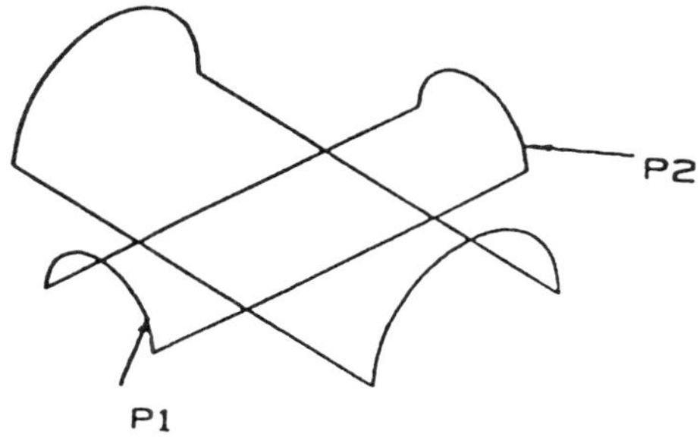

Figure 14.16

Step 2. Initiate ruled toolpath module.

Select **MAIN MENU** → **Toolpaths** → **Next menu** → **Ruled**
Enter file name: **surf1** ←

Step 3. Define the contours.
Use the pick points in Figure 14.16 on the previous page .

Select **Single** then pick at **P1**
Select **Single** then pick at **P2**
Select **Done**

Step 4. Set the ruled parameters to the following settings.

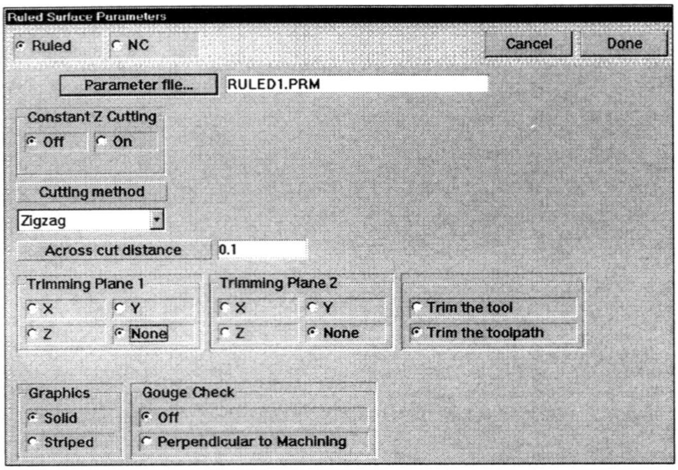

Click the **NC button** to advance to the NC parameters menu.

Step 5. Define NC parameters to the following settings.

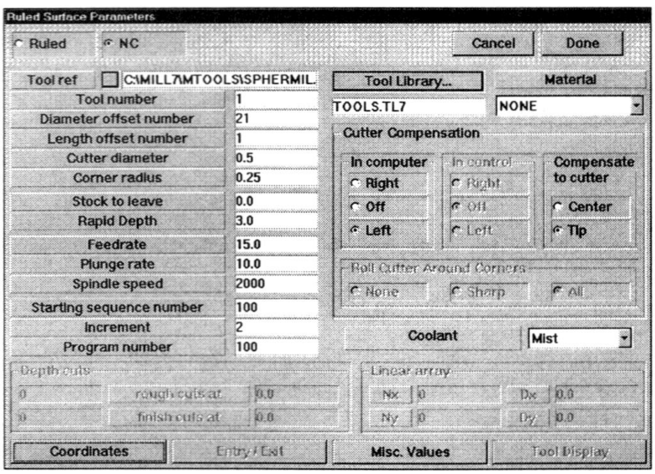

Click on the **Done button** to complete the parameter settings.

Step 6. Write and save the toolpaths.

The toolpaths should display on the screen as Figure 14.17.
Select **MAIN MENU** → **NC utils** → **Edit NCI**
Select **Yes** to "Operations have been modified. Create the NCI text file?"
Select **Quit** from the EditNCI menu

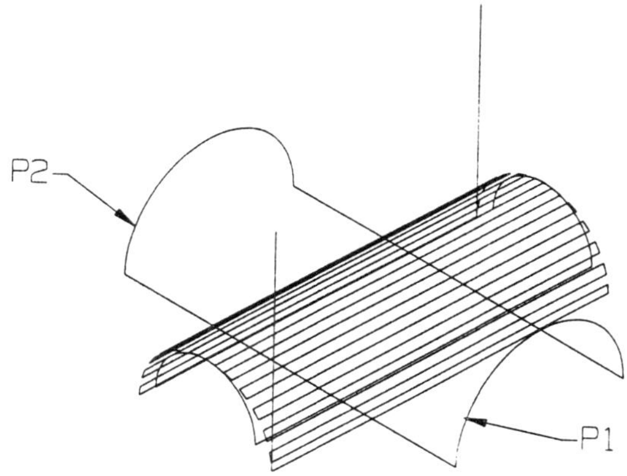

Figure 14.17

Step 7. Use ruled toolpath module again. Generate second ruled surface toolpaths.

Select **Toolpaths** → **Operations**
Click the "Ruled toolpath" with the right mouse button
Select **Delete** to delete the current toolpath → **OK**
Enter file name: **surf2** ←

Step 8. Define ruled surface contours using the pick points (Figure 14.17).

Select **Single** then pick at **P1**
Select **Single** then pick at **P2**
Select **Done**

Step 9. Define the ruled toolpath parameters to the following settings.

The Ruled parameters for this surface are the same as those in step 4.
Click the **NC** to advance to the NC parameters menu.

Step 10. Define NC parameters to the following settings.

Set the NC parameters as those given in step 5, with the exception of

Set Cutter Compensation to

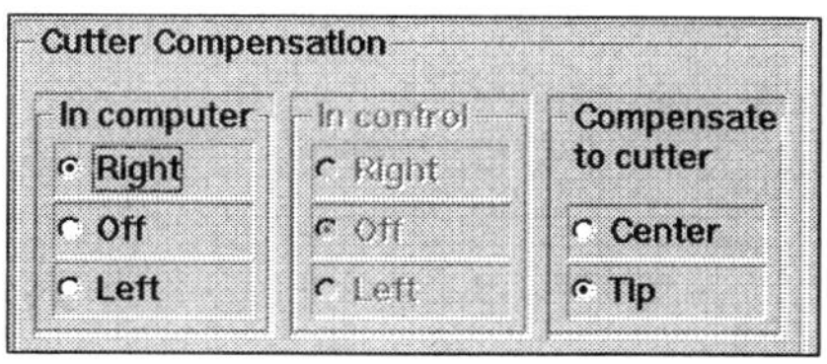

Select the **Done button** to complete the parameter settings.

Step 11. Write and accept the toolpaths.

Select **MAIN MENU** → **NC utils** → **EditNCI**
Select **Yes** to "Operations have been modified. Create the NCI text file?"
Select **Quit** from the EditNCI menu.

2 The toolpaths should resemble Figure 14.18.

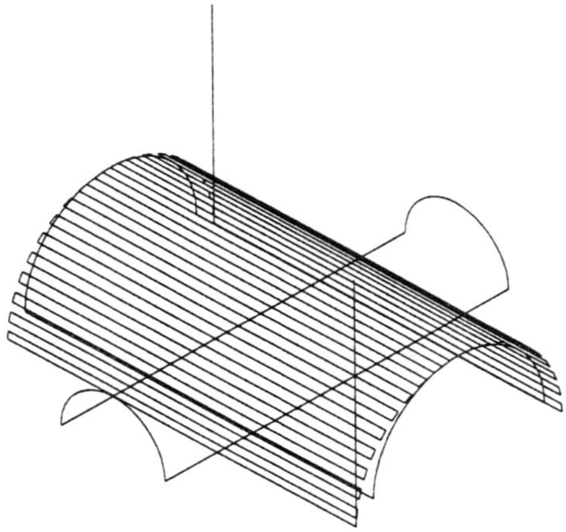

Figure 14.18

Project 2. Machining a ruled surface formed by three contours

A ruled surface is defined by a wireframe model of three contours as created in project 3 of chapter 11. The wireframe model and finished toolpaths are illustrated in Figure 14.19.

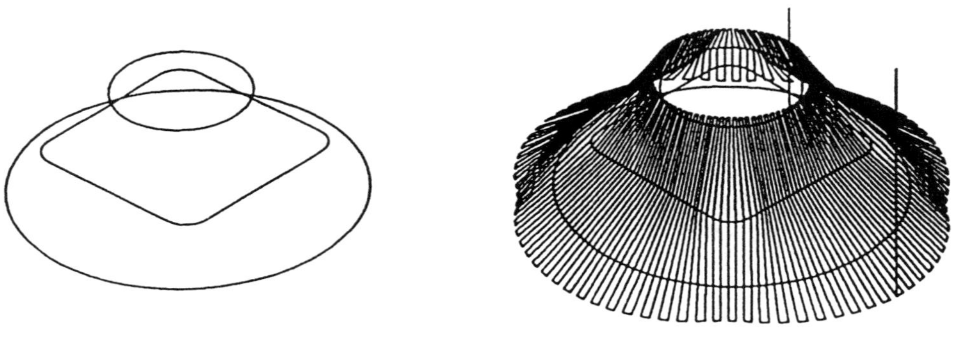

Figure 14.19

Tips 1. Use trimming planes to extend the cutting paths. The first trim plane is Z0.25 and the second plane Z-2.0.
2. The right vertical line of the rectangular contour must be broken into two pieces at the middle. This allows the alignment of the start points of three contours.
3. Picking sequence of the contours starts from the top downward. This determines the direction of toolpaths to go from top to bottom.

Step 1. Load the wireframe model file 3contour.ge3.

(or create one by following the instructions in project 3 of chapter 11.)
Select **MAIN MENU → File → Get**
Enter file name: **3contour ←**

The wireframe model should appear as Figure 14.20.

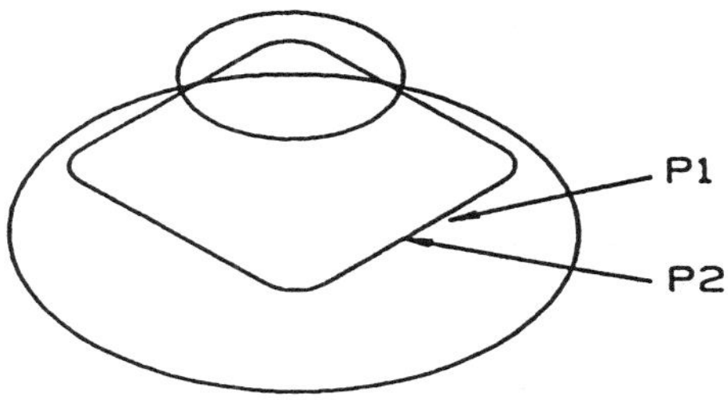

Figure 14.20

Step 2. Break the right vertical line of the rectangular contour into two pieces in the middle. Use the pick points in Figure 14.20.

Select **MAIN MENU → Modify → Break → 2 pieces**
Pick at **P1** to select the entity to break
Select **Midpoint** from the Point menu
Pick at **P2** to break the entity

The drawing does not look different before and after breaking. The drawing is redisplayed as in Figure 14.21.

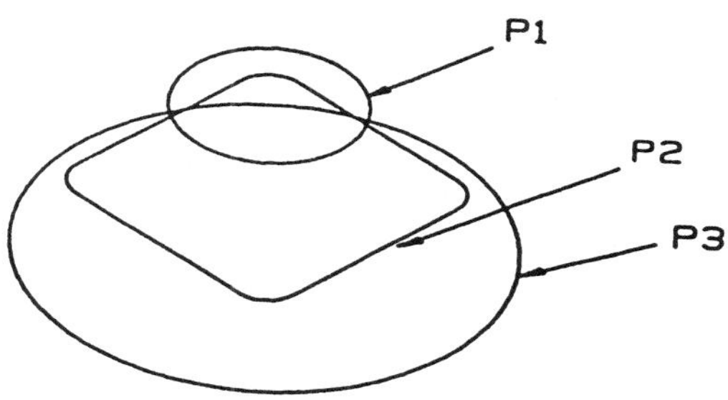

Figure 14.21

Step 3. Initiate ruled toolpath module.

Select **MAIN MENU → Toolpaths → Next menu → Ruled**
Enter file name: **ruledt2 ←**

Step 4. Define the contours using the pick points in Figure 14.21.

Select **Single** then pick at **P1** for contour 1
Select **Mode → Chain** then pick at **P2**
Select **Mode → Single** then pick at **P3** for contour 3
Select **Done** to complete defining contours

Step 5. Define ruled parameters to the following settings.

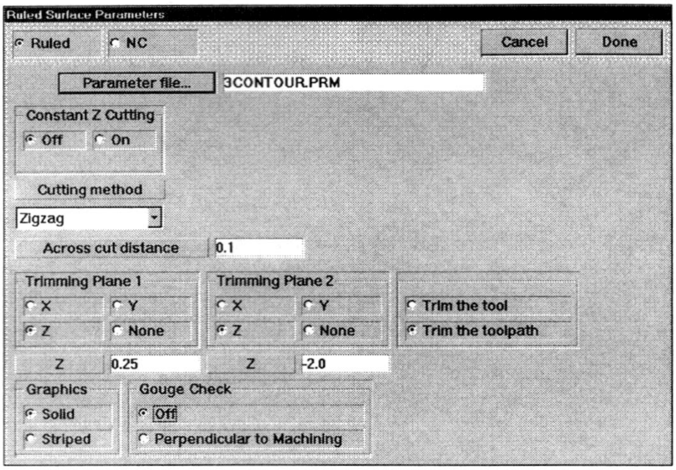

Select the **NC button** to advance to the NC parameters menu.

Step 6. Define NC parameters to the following settings.

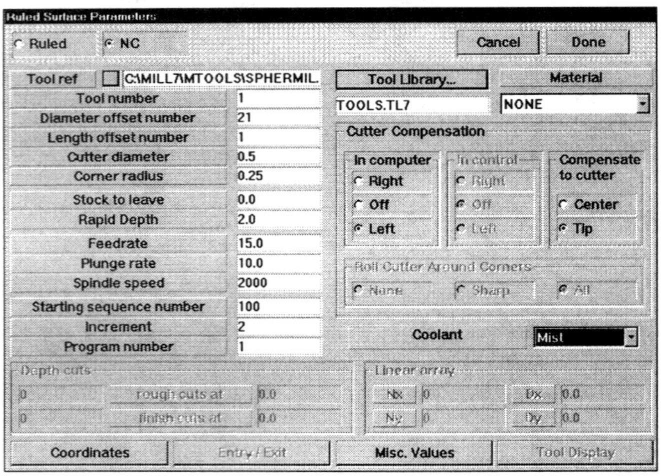

Select the **Done button** to complete the parameter settings.

Step 7. Write and save the toolpaths.

Select **MAIN MENU → NC utils → EditNCI**

Select **Yes** to "Operations have been modified. Create the NCI text file?"

Select **Quit** from the EditNCI menu.

The toolpaths should resemble Figure 14.22

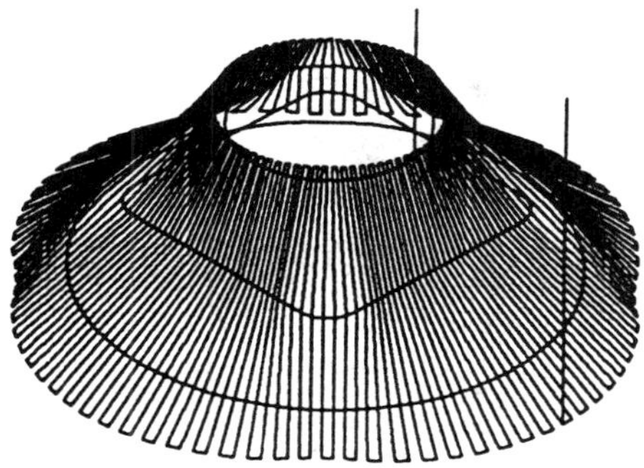

Figure 14.22

14.5 Loft Toolpath Module

This module is used to blend parabolically up to 100 contours which can be points, lines, arcs and splines or any combination of entity types. Figure 14.23 shows an example of the toolpaths generated by using the loft toolpath module.

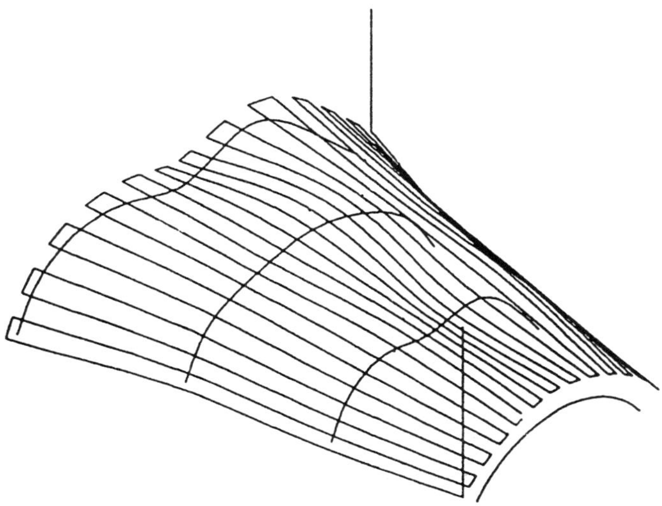

Figure 14.23

3

Loft Parameters

The five loft parameters are listed below:

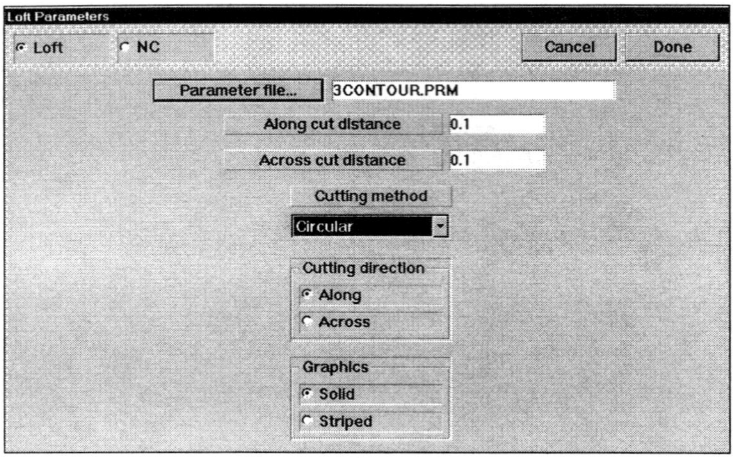

These five parameters have been discussed in previous sections.

Project 3. Machining a loft surface

The loft toolpath module is used to generate a set of toolpaths to machine a loft surface defined by 19 contours. The wireframe model for this surface is the file loft2 created in chapter 11. Figure 14.24 shows both the wireframe model and the toolpaths to cut this surface.

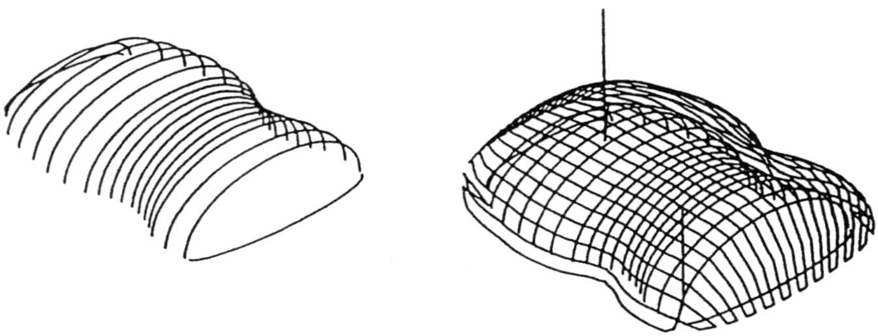

Figure 14.24

Tips 1. Wireframe model file is loft2.ge3.

2. Use Window → One Way → CW commands to orderly select contours.

3. Cutter compensation in computer should be set to right center.

Step 1. Load the part wireframe model file (loft2.ge3) or create one by following the instructions in project 4 of chapter 11.

Select **MAIN MENU → File → Get**

Enter file name: **loft2** ←

The wireframe model should appear as Figure 14.25.

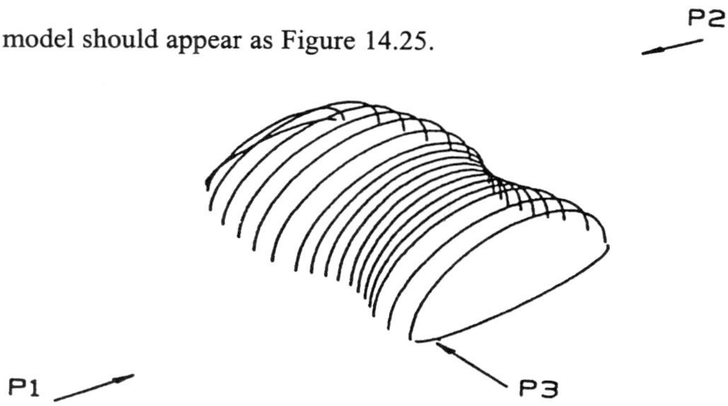

Figure 14.25

Step 2. Initiate loft toolpath module.

Select **MAIN MENU → Toolpaths → Next menu → Old tipths → Loft**

Enter file name: **loftt** ←

Step 3. Define the contours using the pick points in Figure 14.25.

Select **Window → CW → One Way → Done**

Pick at **P1** and **P2** to include all contours in the window

Select **Endpoint** then pick at **P3**

Select **Done** to complete contours selection

Step 4. Define loft parameters to the following settings.

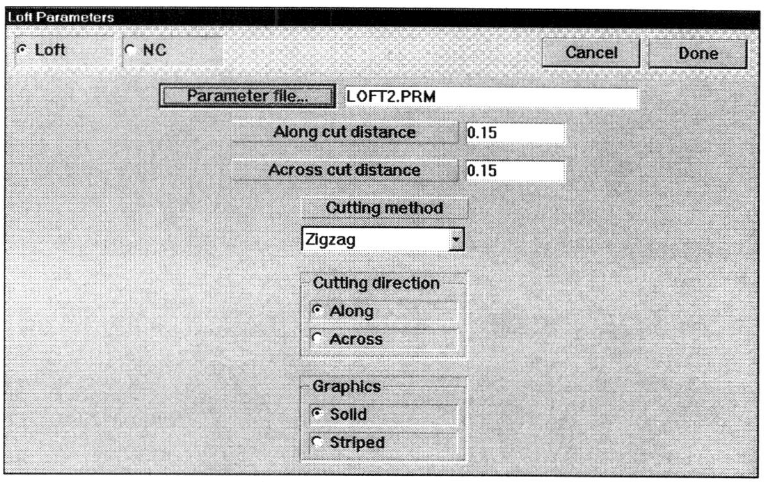

Select the **NC button** to advance to the NC parameters menu.

Step 5. Define NC parameters to the following settings.

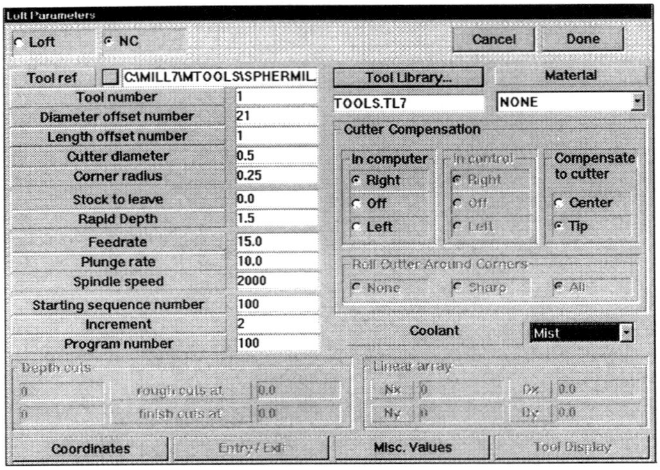

Select the **Done button** to complete the parameter settings.

Step 6. Write and save the toolpath file.

Note: The system will issue a warning to indicate that there is an undercut on 4 of 815 points, and the largest undercut = -0.25.

Press **Enter** to display the toolpaths
Select **MAIN MENU → NC utils → EditNCI**
Select **Yes** to "Operations have been modified. Create the NCI text file?"
Select **Quit** from the EditNCI menu.
The toolpaths should resemble Figure 14.26.

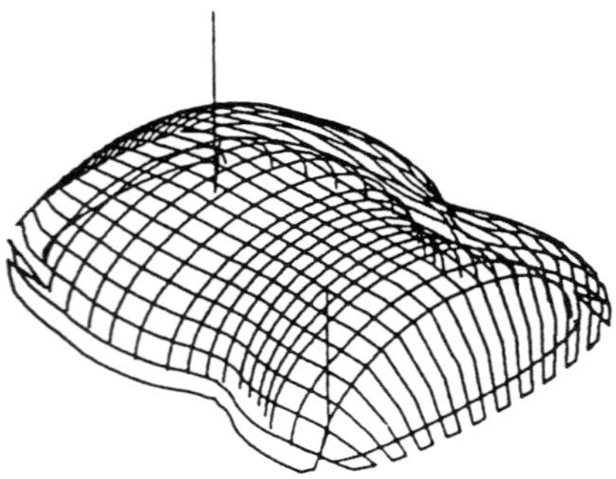

Figure 14.26

14.6 Coons Toolpath Module

The Coons module is used to generate a series of toolpaths to machine a surface defined by a single patch or multiple-patch model. Each patch normally consists of four contours. Figure 14.27 shows a surface produced by the toolpaths generated from Coons module.

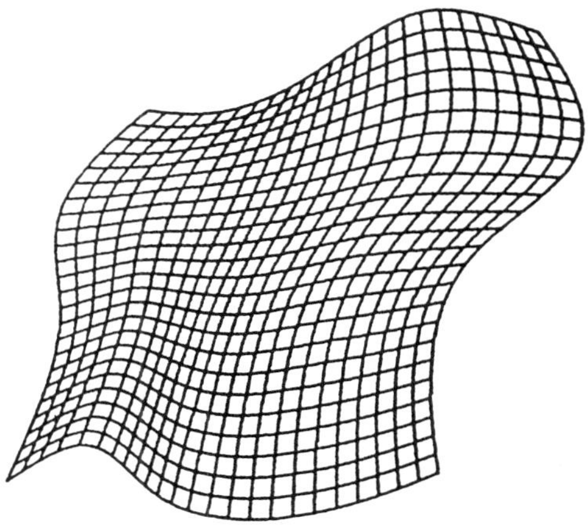

Figure 14.27

Coons Parameters

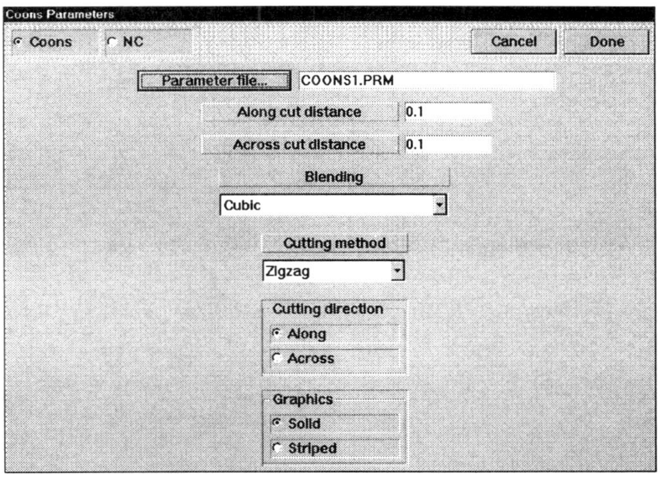

All parameters listed above, excepting the blending method, have been discussed in previous sections. Table 14.4 on the following page summarizes the features and applications of four blending methods used in Coons surfaces.

Tips
1. Refer to the instructions given for Coons surfaces in section 12.7 of chapter 12.
2. Select the starting point, along direction, and across direction.
3. Determine the number of along contours and the number of across contours.
4. Determine the number of along patches and the number of across patches.
5. Observe the picking order of selecting contours.

Table 14.4 Blending methods of Coons surfaces

Blending	Description	Application	Illustration
Linear	Patch contours are blended linearly to form a surface.	Use in single patch surfaces.	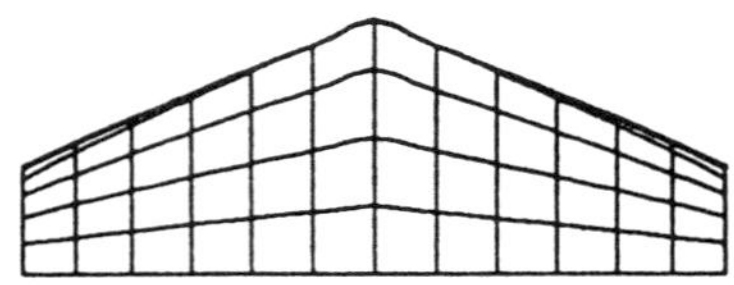
Parabolic	Patch contours are blended parabolically (2nd order) to form a surface.	Used in multiple-patch surfaces. These surfaces tend to produce flat spots on the surface.	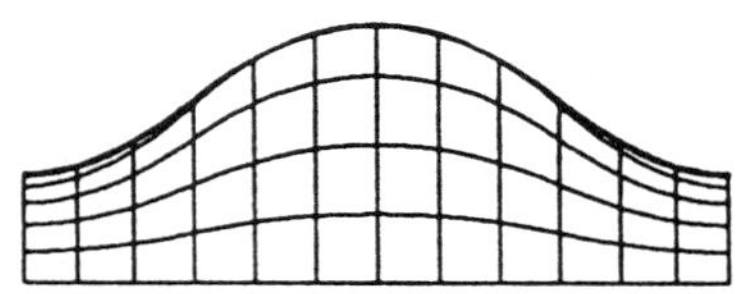
Cubic	Patch contours are blended cubically (3rd order) to form a surface.	Used in multiple-patch surfaces. These surfaces tend to produce flat spots on the surface.	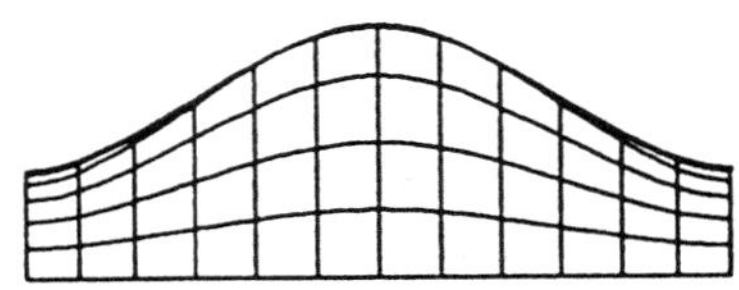
Cubic with slope matching	Patch contours are blended cubically (3rd order) with matching slope at the boundaries.	Used in multiple-patch surfaces whenever possible. The flat spots are eliminated.	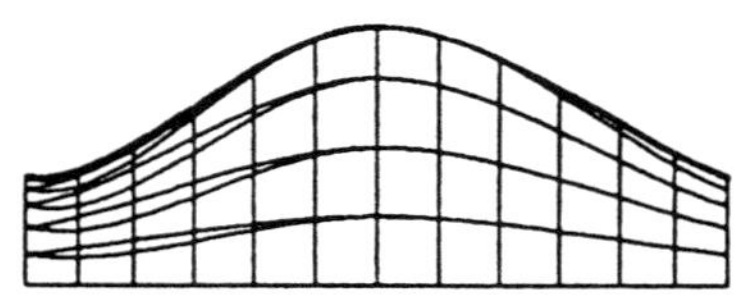

Row and Column

Mastercam uses rows and columns to identify the patch boundary grid. Along contours are assigned in rows and across contours in columns. Each contour in the grid is identified by an *along* row number and an *across* column number as shown in Figure 14.28.

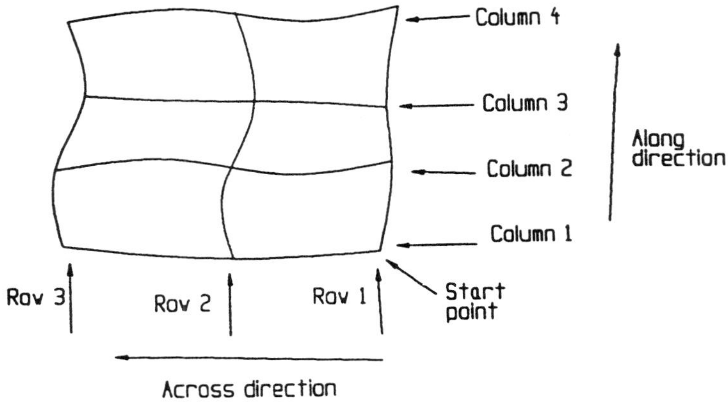

Figure 14.28

Number of Patches in Along and Across Directions

The system will ask you to enter the number of patches in the along and across directions, respectively. Whether the boundaries are closed affects your counting the number of patches. In open boundary cases, where the first and the last contour are not connected, the number of patches in the along direction is the number of across contours minus 1 and the number of patches in across direction is the number of along contours minus 1.

Figure 14.29 shows the contour profiles having an open boundary for defining a Coons surface. In this model, the start point is selected at point A and the along and across direction are as shown in the figure.

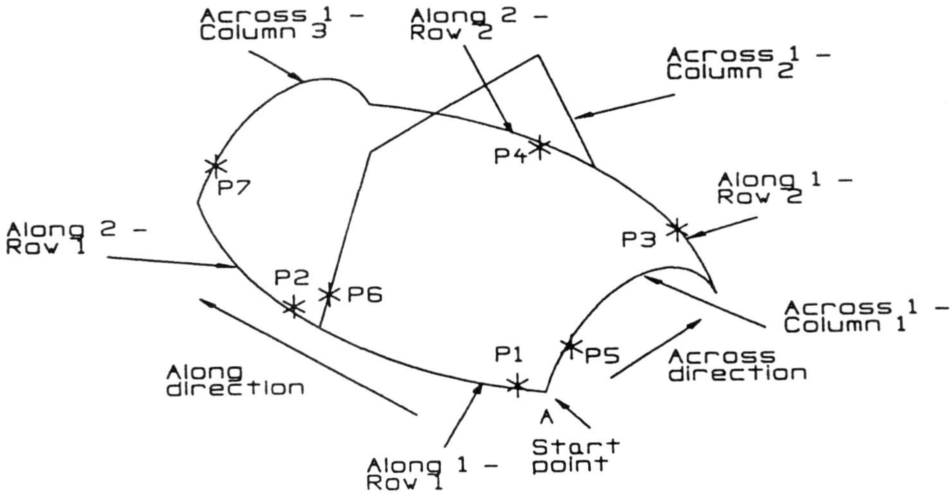

Figure 14.29

The number of along contours = 2 The number of across contours = 3 The number of along patches = The number of across contours - 1 = 3 - 1 = 2 The number of across patches = The number of along contours - 1 = 2 - 1 = 1

In close boundary cases where the first and the last contours are connected, the number of patches in the along direction is equal to the number of the across contours and the number of patches in the across direction is the number of along contours minus 1. Figure 14.30 shows an example of a closed boundary Coons surface.

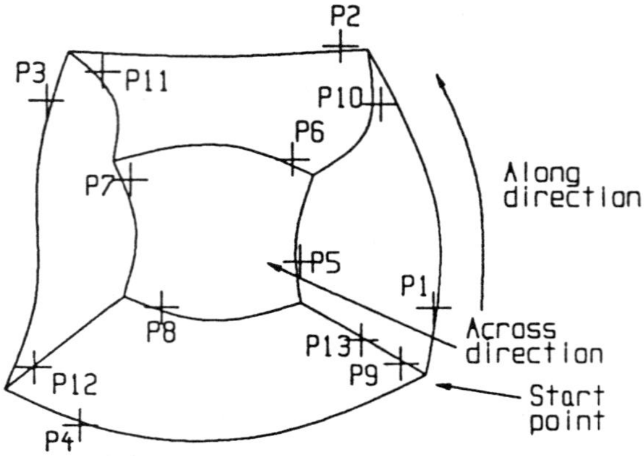

Figure 14.30

Number of along contours = 2
Number of across contours = 4
The number of patches in along direction = number of across contours = 4
The number of patches in across direction = number of along contours - 1 = 2 - 1 = 1

The Order of Contour Selection

The contours selection must follow a predetermined order that is along contours that are sequentially selected first, followed by the across contours as follows:

Selection order	Entity to be picked
1st selection	along row 1 - across column 1
2nd selection	along row 1 - across column 2
-	-
-	-
nth selection	along row 1 - across column n
n+1 selection	along row 2 - across column 1
n+2 selection	along row 2 - across column 2
-	-
-	-
2n selection	along row 2 - across column n
-	-
-	-
mn selection	along row m - across column n

Figure 14.29 on the previous page shows the contours selection sequence for an open boundary case and Figure 14.30 shows a closed boundary case.

4

Project 4. Machining a Coons surface of a single patch

The Coons toolpath module is used to generate the toolpaths for machining a surface defined by a single patch of four contours. The wireframe model and the toolpaths are illustrated in Figure 14.31.

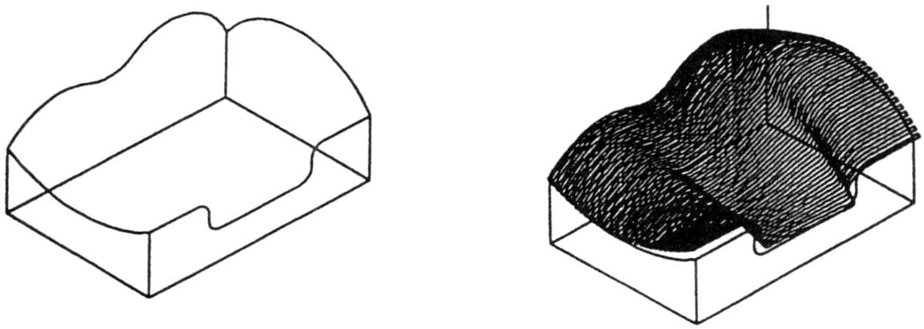

Figure 14.31

Tips 1. Use wireframe model file (coons1.ge3).

2. This is an open boundary case. The number of *along* contours is 2 and the number of *across* contours is 2. The number of patches in both along and across directions is 1 (or 2 - 1).
3. Use linear blending method because this is a single patch surface.

4. Cutter compensation in computer = left tip.

Step 1. Load the wireframe model file (coons1.ge3) or create one by following the instructions in project 5 of chapter 11.

Select **MAIN MENU → File → Get**

Enter file name: **coons1 ←**

The wireframe model should appear as Figure 14.32.

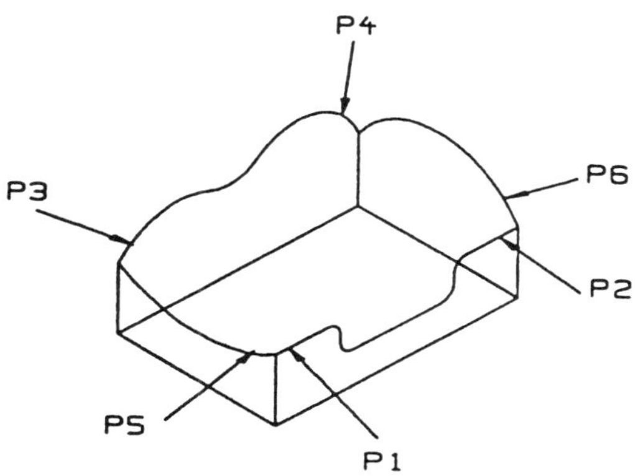

Figure 14.32

Step 2. Initiate the Coons toolpath module.

Select **MAIN MENU** → **Toolpaths** →**Next menu** →**Old tipths**→ **Coons**
Enter file name: **coonst1** ←

Step 3. Specify number of patches in along and across direction.

Enter **1** for the number of patches in the along direction
Enter **1** for the number of patches in the across direction

Step 4. Define contours using the pick points in Figure 14.32.

Select **Chain** → **Partial** then pick at **P1** and **P2** to complete along contour 1 of row 1
Select **Chain** → **Partial** then pick at **P3** and **P4** to complete along contour 1 of row 2
Select **Mode** → **Single** then pick at **P5** to define across contour 1 of column 1
Pick at **P6** to define across contour 1 of column 2
Select **Done**

Step 5. Define Coons parameters to the following settings.

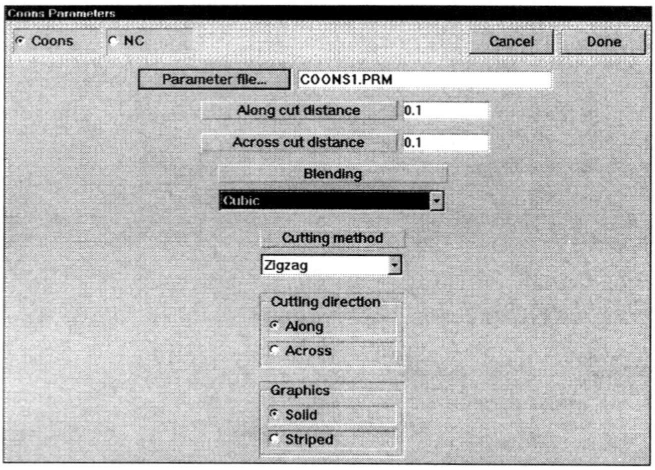

Select the **NC button** to advance to the NC parameters menu.

Step 6. Define NC parameters to the following settings.

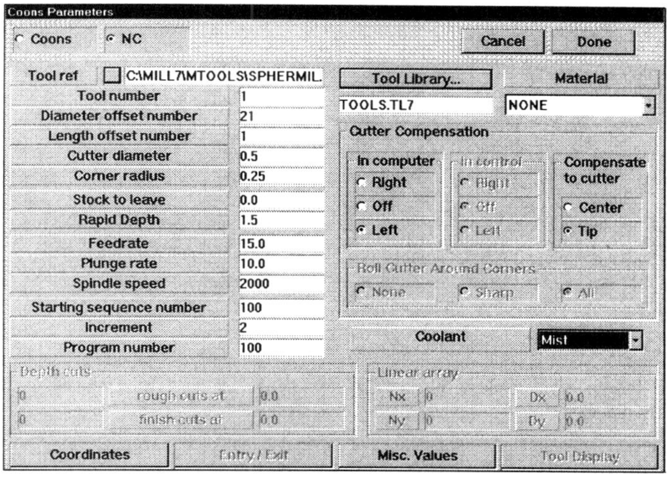

Select the **Done button** to complete the parameter settings.

Step 7. Write and save the toolpaths.

Select **MAIN MENU → NC utils → EditNCI**
Select **Yes** to "Operations have been modified. Create the NCI text file?"
Select **Quit** from the EditNCI menu.
The toolpaths should resemble Figure 14.33.

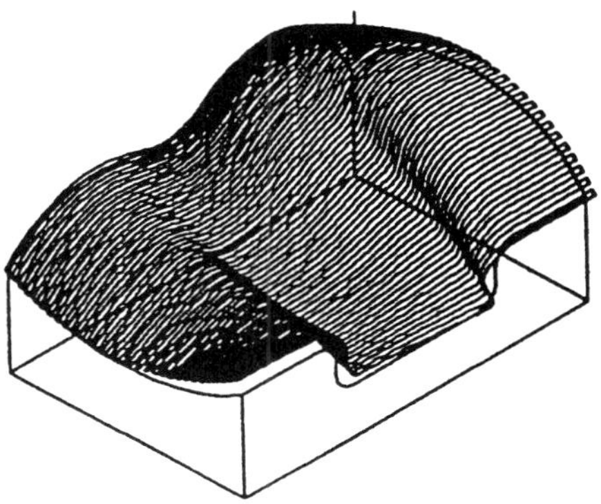

Figure 14.33

5 Project 5. Machining a Coons surface formed by multiple-patch

The Coons module is used to generate toolpaths to machine a Coons surface defined by a total of 12 patches. The wireframe model file is **coons4.ge3** created in project 7 of chapter 11. Figure 14.34 shows both the wireframe model and the toolpaths.

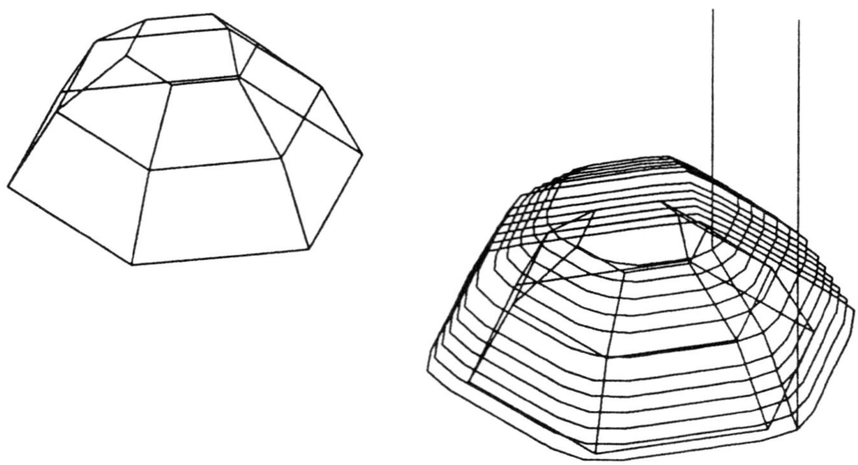

Figure 14.34

Tips 1. Use top Gview to facilitate the picking of contours.

2. The number of along contours = 3
The number of across contours = 6
The number of patches in along direction = 6
The number of patches in across direction = 3 - 1 = 2

3. Use circular cutting method to reduce the part program size.

4. Set the cutting direction to along mode.

5. Cutter compensation in computer = left tip

6. Use the filter function to significantly reduce the toolpath points.

Step 1. Load the wireframe model file (coons4.ge3) or create one by following the instructions in project 7 of chapter 11.
Select **MAIN MENU → File → Get**
Enter file name: **coons4 ←**

The wireframe model should appear as in Figure 14.35.

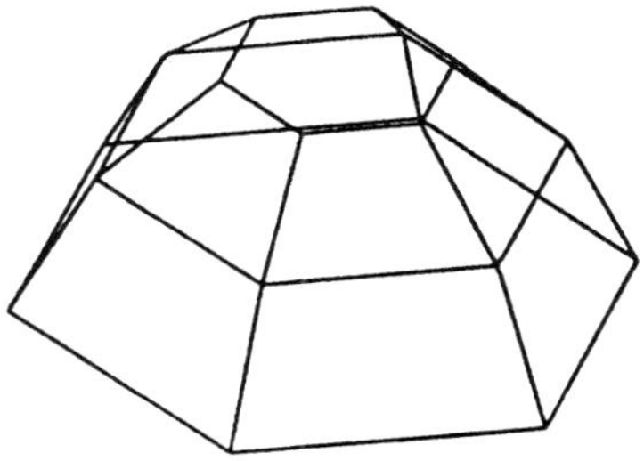

Figure 14.35

Step 2. Change Gview to top view.

Select **Gview → Top**

The wireframe model in the top view looks like Figure 14.36.

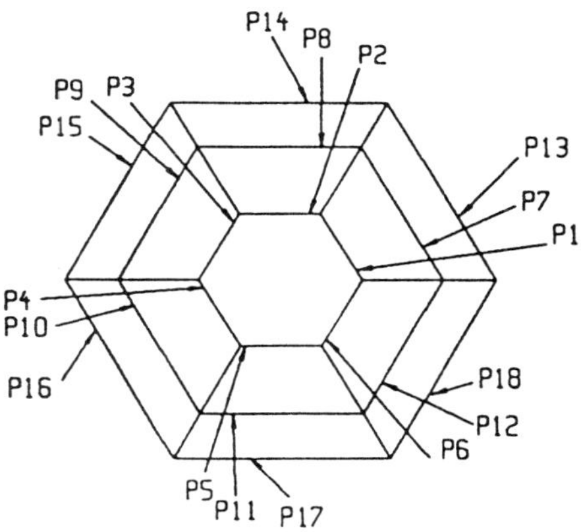

Figure 14.36a Along

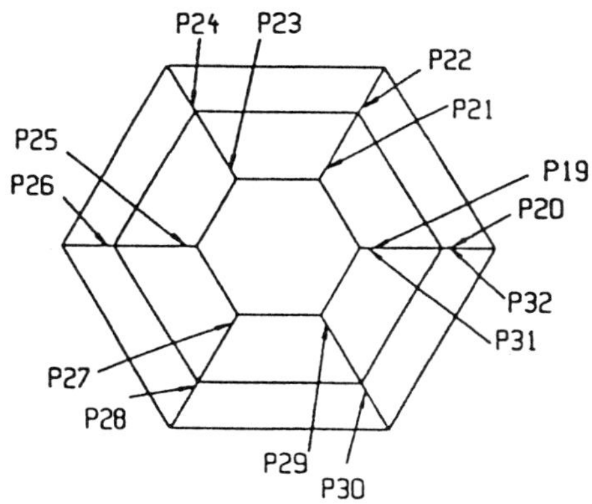

Figure 14.36b Across

Step 3. Initiate the Coons toolpath module.

Select **MAIN MENU → Toolpaths → Next menu → Oid tlpths → Coons**
Enter file name: **coonst2 ←**

Step 4. Specify the number of patches in along and across directions.

Enter **6** for the number of patches in the along direction
Enter **2** for the number of patches in the across direction

Step 5. Define the contours using the pick points in Figure 14.36.

Select **Single** then pick at **P1**
Sequentially pick at **P2 - P32**
Select **Done** to complete the contour definition

Step 6. Define Coons parameters to the following settings.

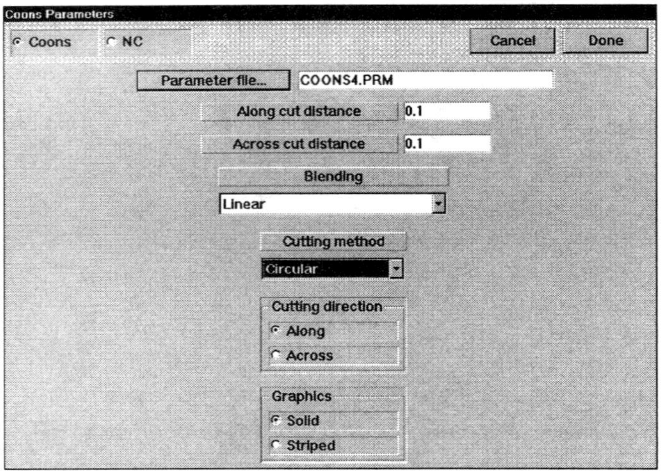

Select the **NC button** to advance to the NC parameters menu.

Step 7. Define NC parameters to the following settings.

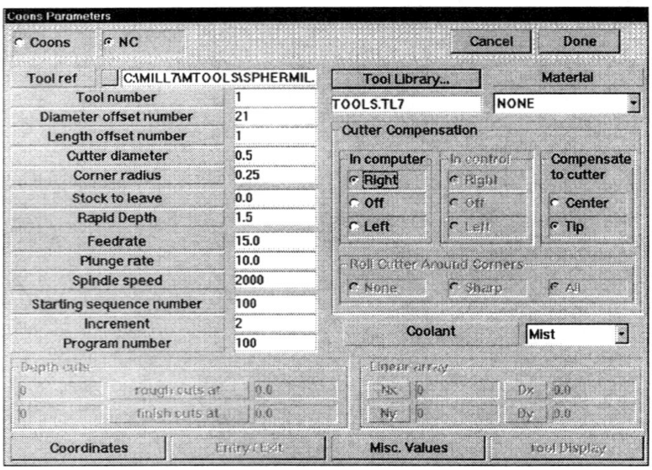

Select the **Done button** to complete the parameters settings.

Step 8. Accept and save the toolpaths.

Select **MAIN MENU → NC utils → EditNCI**
Select **Yes** to "Operations have been modified. Create the NCI text file?"
Select **Quit** from the EditNCI menu.

The toolpaths shown in top Gview should look like Figure 14.37.

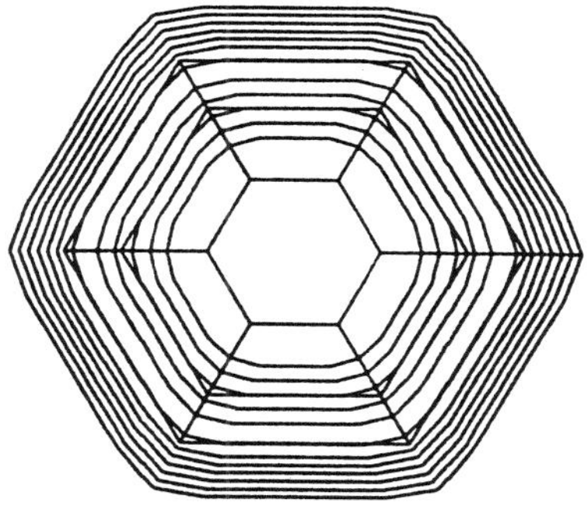

Figure 14.37

Step 9. Change Gview to Isometric.

Select **Gview → Isometric**
Select **MAIN MENU → Toolpaths**

The toolpaths are shown in isometric view as in Figure 14.38.

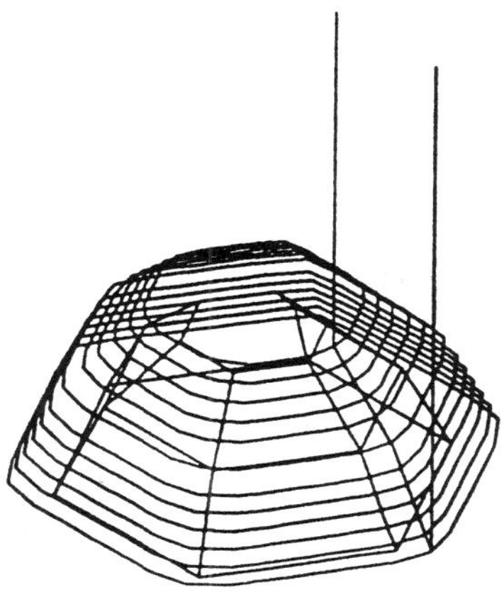

Figure 14.38

Step 10. Run the post processor.

Select **Operations → Post**
Select **Yes** to "Run the post processor?"
Filename for the NC file: **coonst2**
The part program steps are listed on the screen. The last line is N1758 M30. This part program has a total of 830 lines.

Double click the button at the upper left corner of the window to return to graphic mode.
Click **OK** from the "Operations Manager" menu.

Step 11. Run the filter function.

Select **MAIN MENU → NC utils**
Select **Filter → Settings**
Set the Filter settings as shown here:

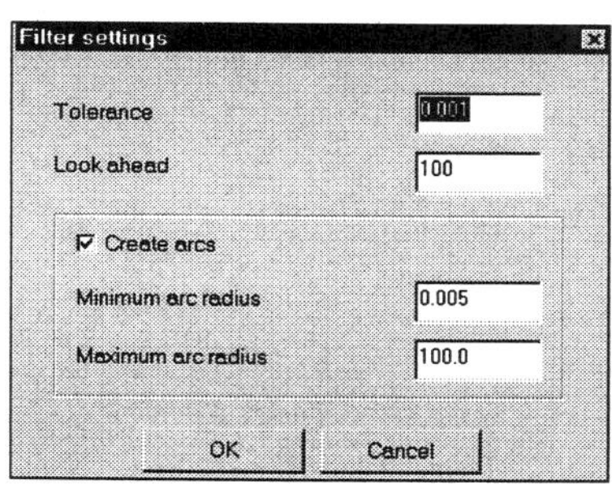

Select **Done → Do it**
File name: **coonst2.NCI**

The system will perform the filtering to remove those unwanted program blocks. The system will indicate that "Filter: 819 lines filtered to 247 lines. Reduction = 69.8%. Want to save changes?

Select **Yes**

File name to write: **coonst2.NCI**

Select **Yes** to "Delete old C:\m7\nci\coonst2.NCI ?"

Step 12. Repost process the filtered file

Select **Post proc → Run**

Filename: **coonst2.nci** for the NCI file

Filename: **coonst2.nc** for the NC file

Select **Yes** to delete the old NC file

The filtered program should be listed on the screen and the last line of the file is **N614**. This file contains a total of **255** lines (or blocks).

Step 13. Exit the Edit utility.

Double click the upper left button to exit the Edit utility.

14.7 Swept Toolpath Module

The swept module is used to generate toolpaths for cutting surfaces that are formed by either translating a sectional profile along one or two rail contours or translating two sectional profiles along a rail contour. Mastercam provides the following three modes of swept toolpath module:

One across/ one along:	translate or rotate an across contour while following the along contour.
One across/ two along:	proportionally scale the across contour between the two along contours.
Two across/ one along:	perform a linear blend between the two across contours while following the along contour.

The one across/one along mode is referred to as **2d swept in** Mastercam. In 2d mode, the along contour must lie parallel or perpendicular to the current tool plane if a tool plane is defined. Otherwise, it must parallel or perpendicular to the XY-plane. Any cross section taken normal to any part of the along contour remains constant (Figure 14.39 on the next page).

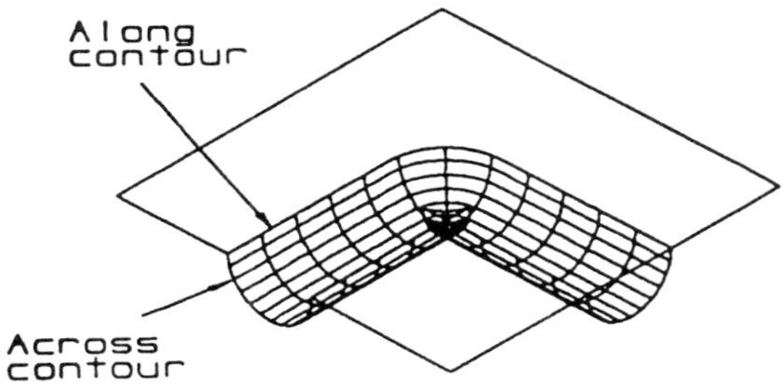

Figure 14.39

The other two modes (two across/ one along and one across/ two along) are referred to as **3d swept**. In 3d mode, contours can be in any plane, and in any orientation. Figures 14.40 and 14.41 illustrate one across/two along, and two across/one along swept surface, respectively.

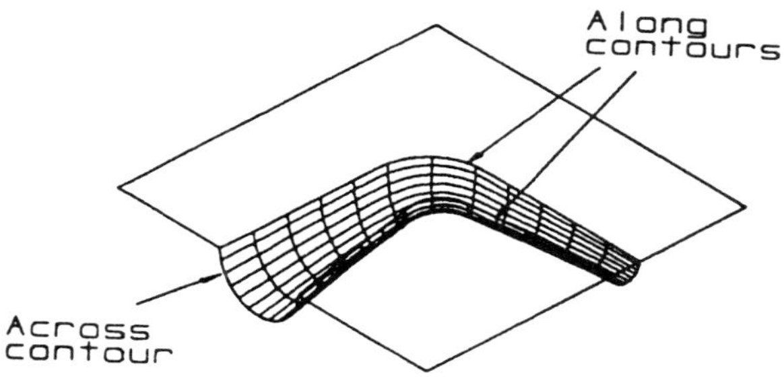

Figures 14.40

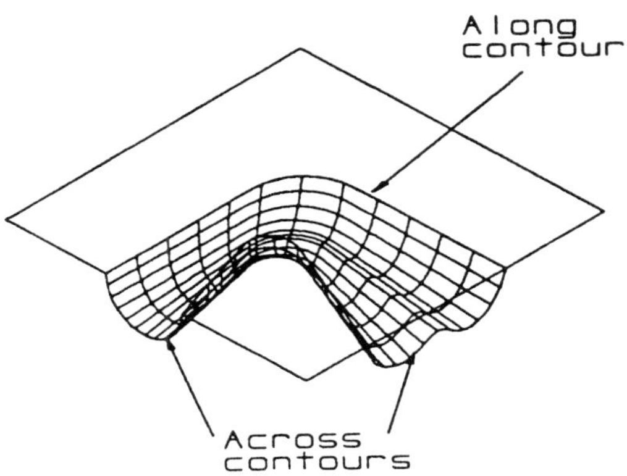

Figure 14.41

6 Project 6. Machining a 2D swept surface

Use a 2D swept module to generate toolpaths for cutting a swept surface. Figure 14.42 shows both the wireframe model and the toolpaths.

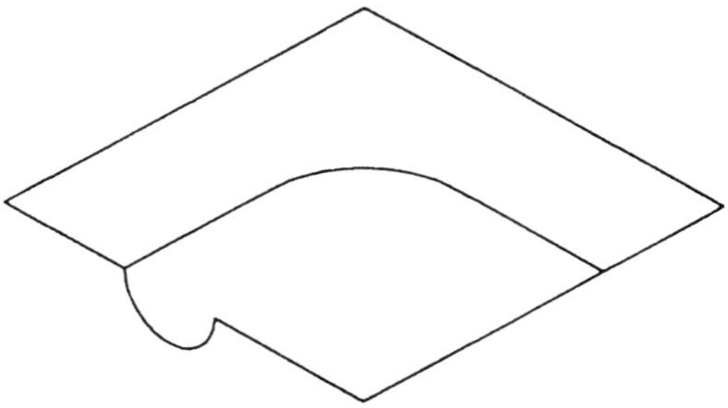

Figure 14.42a Wireframe

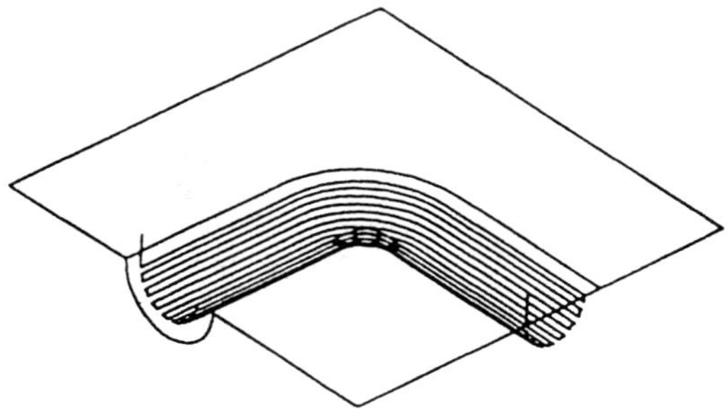

Figure 14.42b Toolpaths

> **Tips** 1. Construct a wireframe model as shown in Figure 14.42.
>
> 2. Use the Front Cplane to create an arc for across contour.
>
> 3. The front horizontal line must be broken into two pieces in the middle. This allows the line to be trimmed to the two intersection points with the arc.

Step 1. Create a rectangle using the isometric Gview.

Select **Gview** → **Isometric**
Select **Cplane** → **Top** if necessary
Select **MAIN MENU** → **Create** → **Rectangle** → **1 point**
Enter the lower left corner: **0,0** ←
Enter the width: **6** ←
Enter the height: **6** ←
Press **Alt** + **F1** simultaneously then press **F2** to fit the drawing on the screen

The rectangle should appear as Figure 14.43.

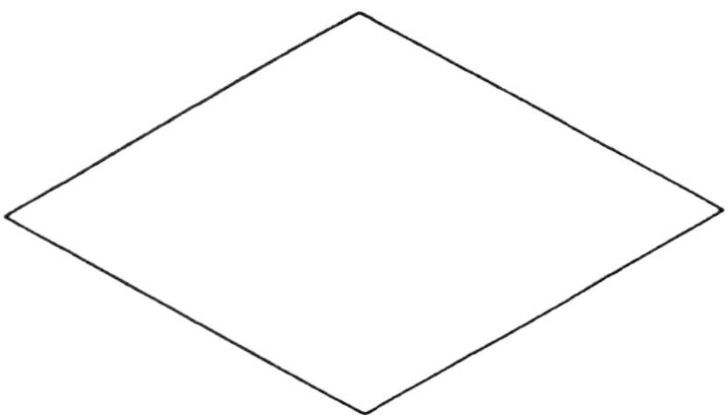

Figure 14.43

Step 2. Create two lines.

Select **MAIN MENU → Create → Line → Endpoints**
Specify the first endpoint: **2,0 ←**
Specify the second endpoint: **2,5 ←** for the vertical line
Specify the first endpoint: **6,4 ←**
Specify the second endpoint: **1,4 ←** for the horizontal line

The two lines are added as shown in Figure 14.44.

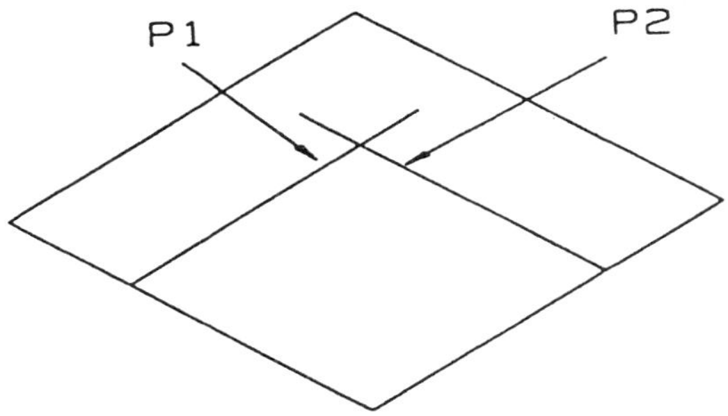

Figure 14.44

Step 3. Add a fillet to the two lines using the pick points in Figure 14.44.

Select **MAIN MENU → Modify → Fillet → Radius**
Enter radius: **1.5 ←**
Pick at **P1** and **P2**

The fillet is added to the drawing as shown in Figure 14.45.

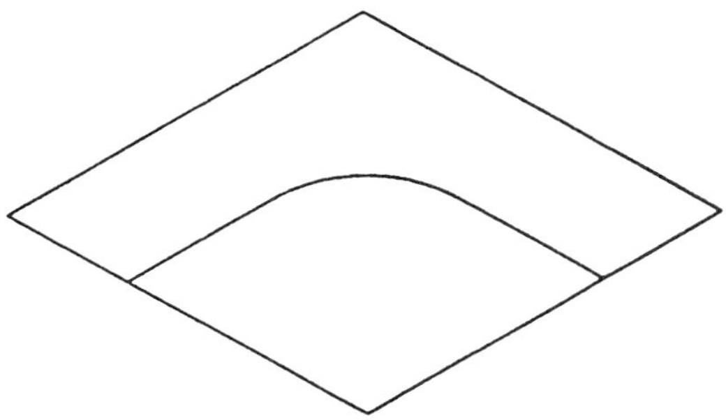

Figure 14.45

Step 4. Create an arc using the Front Cplane.

Select **Cplane → Front**
Select **MAIN MENU → Create → Arc → Endpoints**
Enter the first point: **2,0 ←**
Enter the second point: **3.5,0 ←**
Enter the radius: **0.75 ←**
Select arc: pick at the lower arc of the two

The arc is added to the drawing as shown in Figure 14.46.

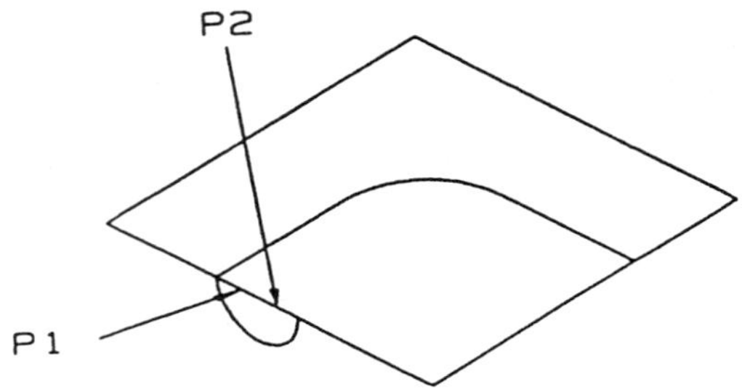

Figure 14.46

Step 5. Break the front line of the rectangle into two pieces using the pick points in Figure 14.46.

Select **MAIN MENU → Modify → Break → 2 pieces**
Pick at **P1** to select an entity
Select **Midpoint**
Pick at **P2** to enter the breakpoint

The front line is broken into two pieces but the drawing does not look different. The drawing is redrawn in Figure 14.47.

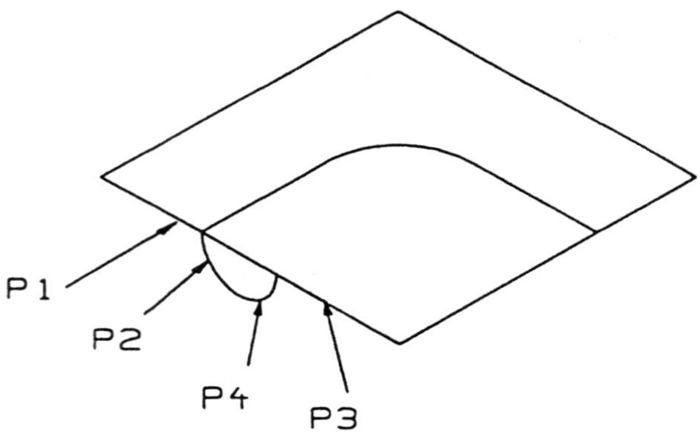

Figure 14.47

Step 6. Trim the front line using the pick points in Figure 14.47.

Change Cplane to 3D.
Select **Cplane → 3D**
Select **MAIN MENU → Modify → Trim → 2 entities**
Pick at **P1** to select the entity to trim
Pick at **P2** to select the entity to trim to
Pick at **P3** to select the entity to trim
Pick at **P4** to select the entity to trim to

The new drawing becomes Figures 14.48.

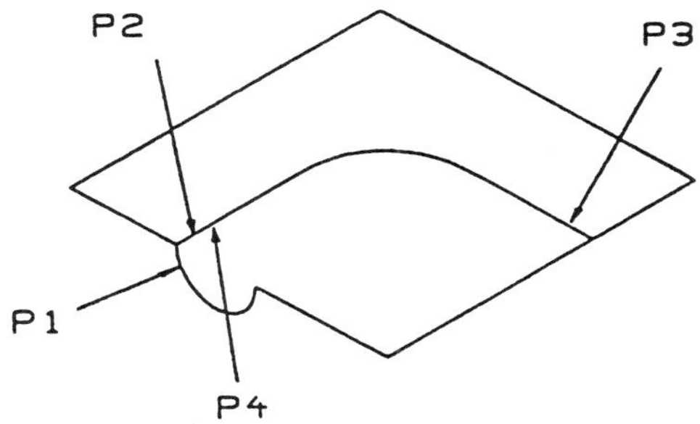

Figure 14.48

Step 7. Initiate swept toolpath module.

Select **MAIN MENU** → **Toolpaths** → **Next menu** → **Oid tlpths** → **Swept**
Enter file name: **swepttl** ←
Select **2D** from compensation method menu

Step 8. Define contours using the pick points in Figure 14.48.

Select **Single** then pick at **P1** to define the across contour
Select **Mode** → **Chain** → **Partial** then pick at **P2** and **P3**

Select **Done** to complete contour selection
Select **Endpoint** then pick at **P4** to enter the intersection of the across and along contours

Step 9. Define 2d swept parameters to the following settings.

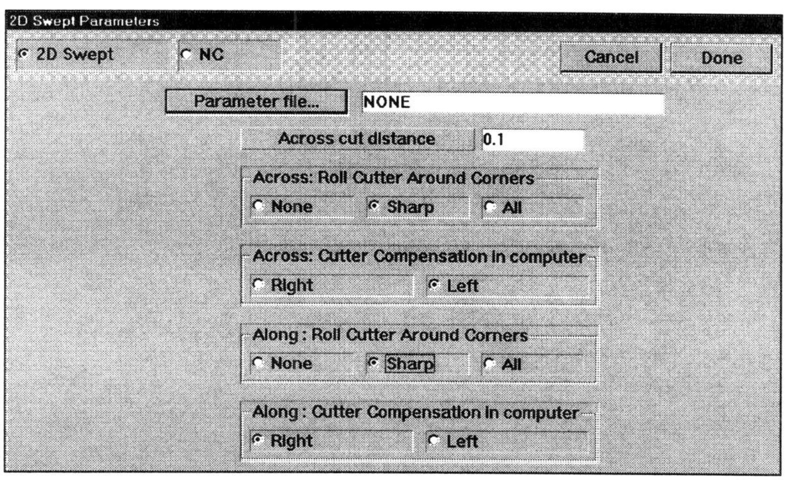

Select the **NC button** to advance to the NC parameters menu.

Step 10. Define NC parameters to the following settings.

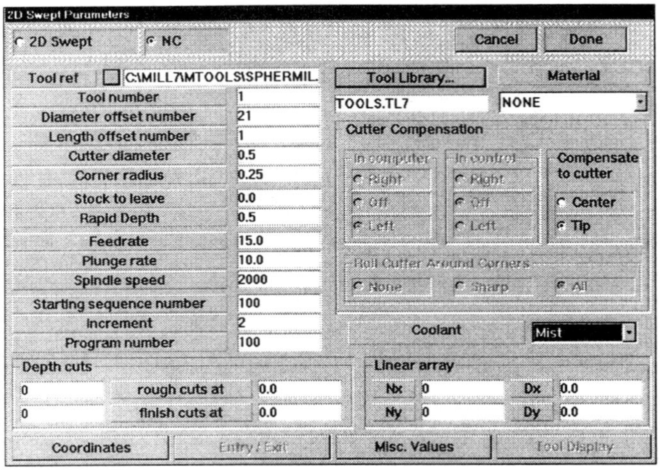

Select the **Done button** to complete the parameter settings.

Step 11. Accept and save the toolpaths.

Select **MAIN MENU → NC utils → EditNCI**
Select **Yes** to "Operations have been modified. Create the NCI text file?"
Select **Quit** from the EditNCI menu.

The toolpaths for cutting the swept surface are shown in Figure 14.49.

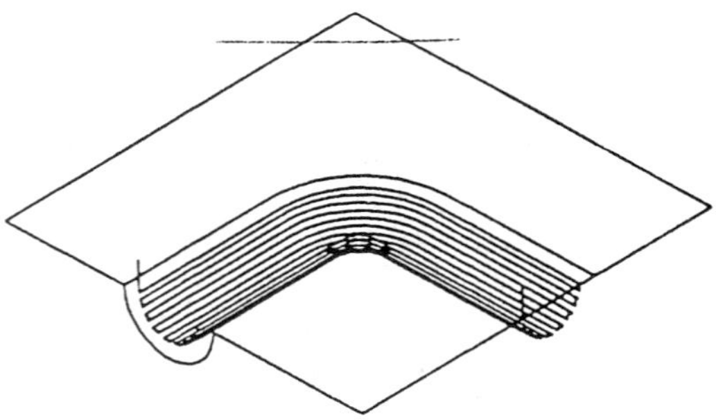

Figure 14.49

Project 7. Machining a swept surface defined by one across contour and two along contours

Use the swept toolpath module to generate a set of toolpaths to machine a swept surface defined by an across contour and two along contours. The wireframe model and the toolpaths are shown in Figure 14.50.

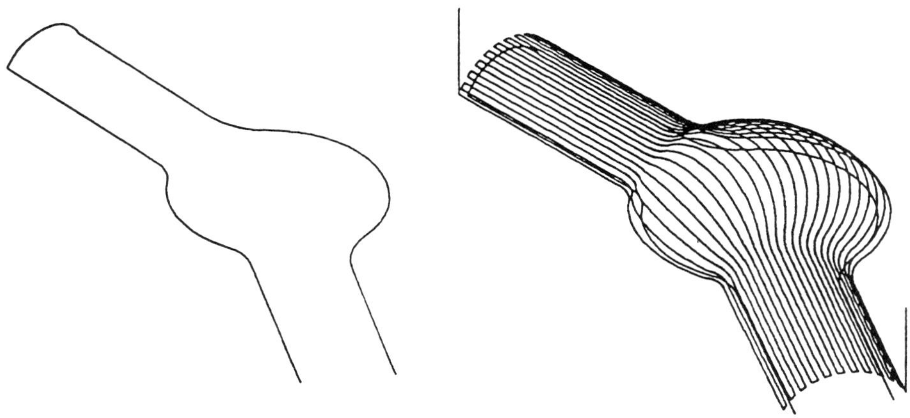

Figure 14.50

Tips 1. Use the wireframe model file swept3.ge3.

2. Use 3d swept with one across/ two along commands.

3. The syncs command is used to change the density of cutting steps of the two fillets in the first along contour. The cutting density is a ratio used to determine the step from one sync to another. One sync should be designated as the reference sync. This reference sync is defined with a cutting density of 1. Other syncs are determined by the value given to the cutting density. The section with a cutting density of 2, for example, has twice the density of the reference sync. In this project, we assign a cutting density of 5 to the two fillets, and all other sections have the density of 1.

4. Cutter compensation in computer should be set to right tip.

Step 1. Load the wireframe model file (swept3.ge3) or create one by following the instructions in project 10 of chapter 11.

Select **MAIN MENU → File → Get**

Enter file name: **swept3 ←**

The wireframe model should look like Figure 14.51 on the next page.

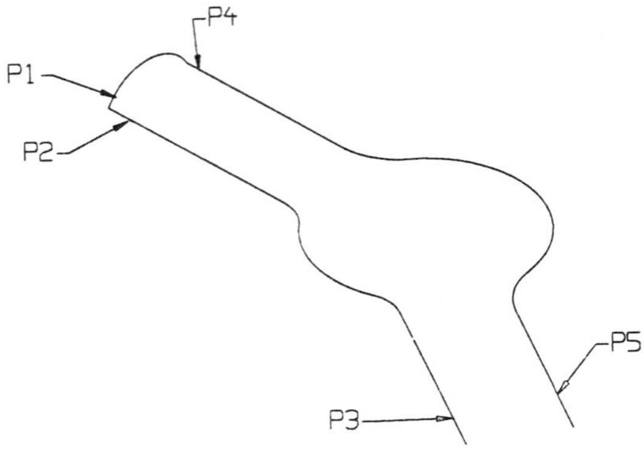

Figure 14.51

Step 2. Initiate swept toolpath module.

Select **MAIN MENU** → **Toolpaths** → **Next menu** → **Old tipths** →**Swept**
Enter file name: **sweptt2** ←
Select **3D**
Enter the number of across contours: **1** ←

Step 3. Define the across contour using the pick points in Figure 14.51.

Define the across contour: Select **Single** then pick at **P1**

Step 4. Define the two along contours.

Still use the pick points in Figure 14.51.
Select **Mode** → **Chain** → **Partial**
Pick **P2** and **P3** to define the along contour 1
Select **Partial**
Pick **P4** and **P5** to define the along contour 2
Select **Done**

Step 5. Define swept parameters to the following settings.

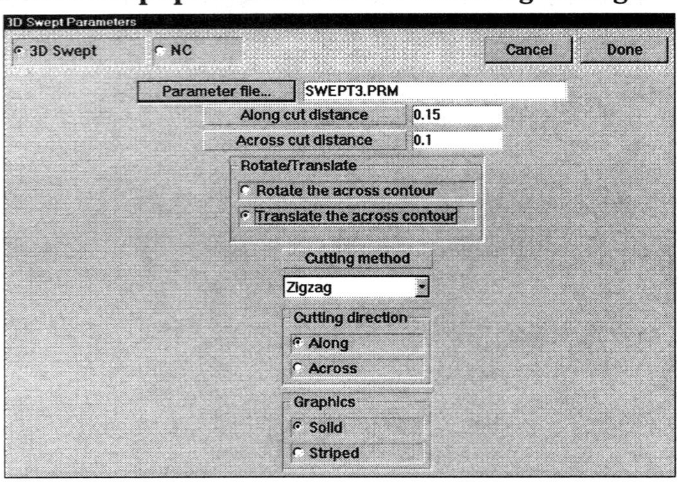

Select the **NC button** to advance to the NC parameters menu.

Step 6. Define NC parameters to the following settings.

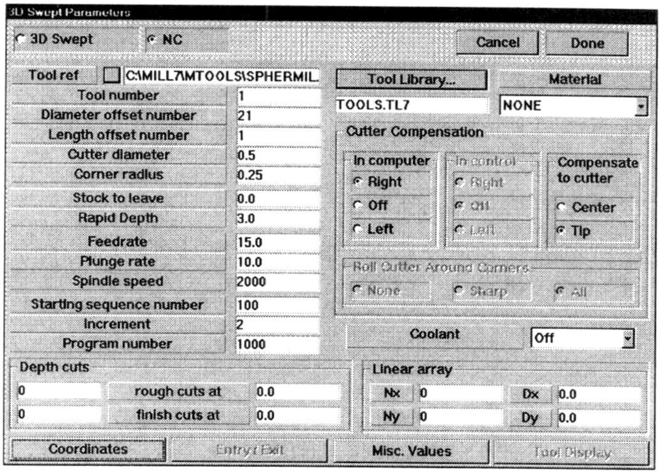

Select the **Done button** to complete the parameter settings.

Step 7. Write and save the toolpaths.

Select **MAIN MENU → NC utils → EditNCI**
Select **Yes** to "Operations have been modified. Create the NCI text file?"
Select **Quit** from the EditNCI menu.
The toolpaths should resemble Figure 14.52.

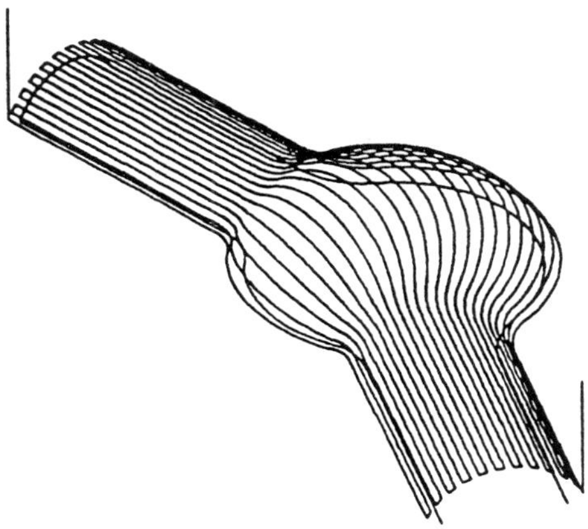

Figure 14.52

14.8 Surface of Revolution Toolpath Module

The surface of a revolution toolpath module is used to generate toolpaths to machine a surface that is defined by revolving a geometric contour about an axis. This is a very powerful tool for cutting any surface that is symmetrical about an axis. The surface of revolution parameters are:

Step size = 0.1
Axial depth = 0.0
Shape = Concave/Convex
Retract to nothing
Trim toolpath to nothing

Step size

This parameter specifies the distance between cuts in the current construction plane.

Axis depth

This parameter specifies the Z-coordinate of the axis of rotation. This Z value automatically determines the depth of the plane at which the toolpath starts being generated. Figures 14.53 and 14.54 show how the axial depth affects the toolpaths.

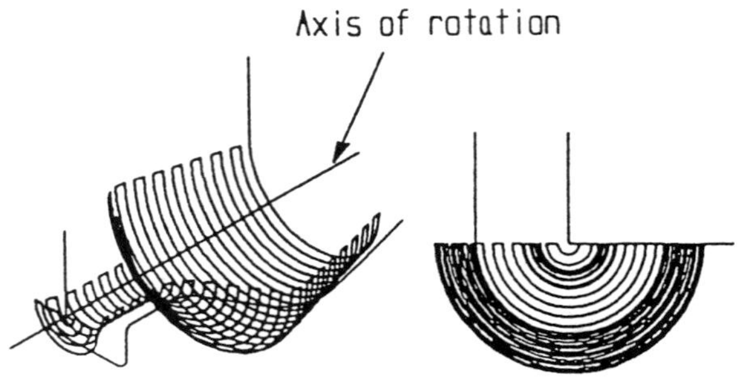

Figure 14.53 Axial depth = 0.0

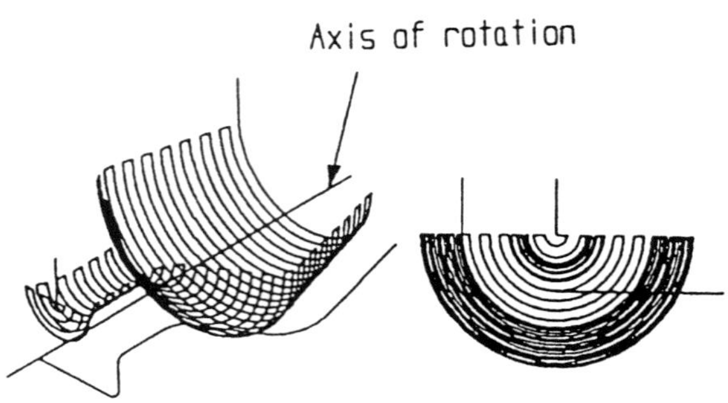

Figure 14.54 Axial depth= 0.5

Shape

This parameter allows us to select the shape of the revolved surface to be the concave or convex type. Figure 14.55 shows the toolpaths for cutting a cup in concave and convex shape.

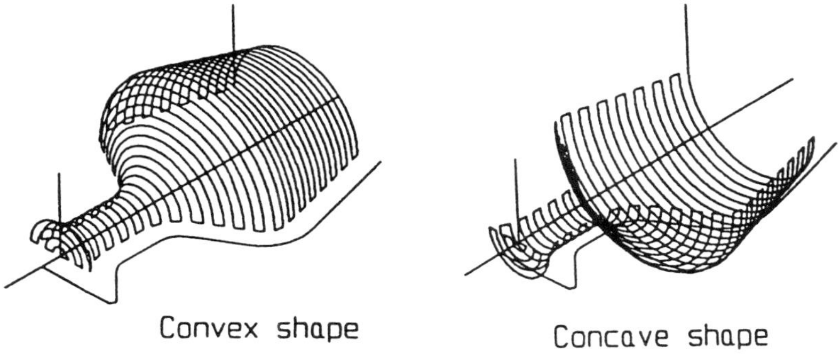

Figure 14.55

Retract to

This parameter adds a vertical wall to the surface. The system will generate a series of extended toolpaths normal to the current construction plane at surface's endpoints. At each of the surface endpoints, the tool retracts to the level specified by the Retract to parameter, then moves a stepover distance, moves down to the surface endpoint, and moves over the surface. Figure 14.56 shows the toolpath pattern of retract to parameter.

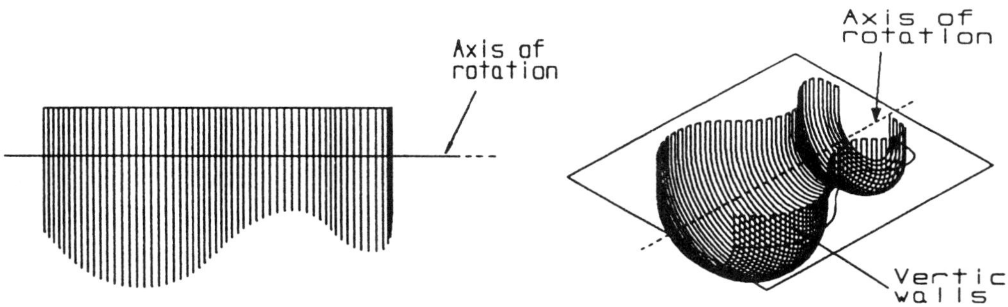

Figure 14.56

Trim to

This parameter allows the toolpaths to be trimmed or extended to a specified plane or boundary. There are two trim to modes: height and width. In trim to height mode, the toolpaths are extended to the specified height if this height is above the axis depth (axis of rotation) shown on the next page in Figure 14.57a, or the toolpaths are trimmed to the specified height if this height is below the axis depth shown in Figure 14.57b.

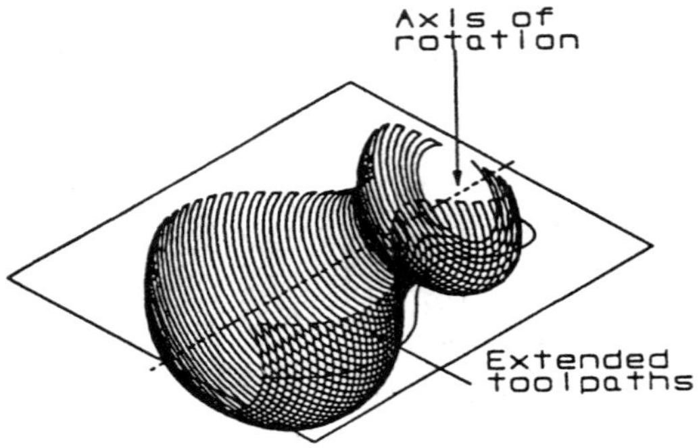

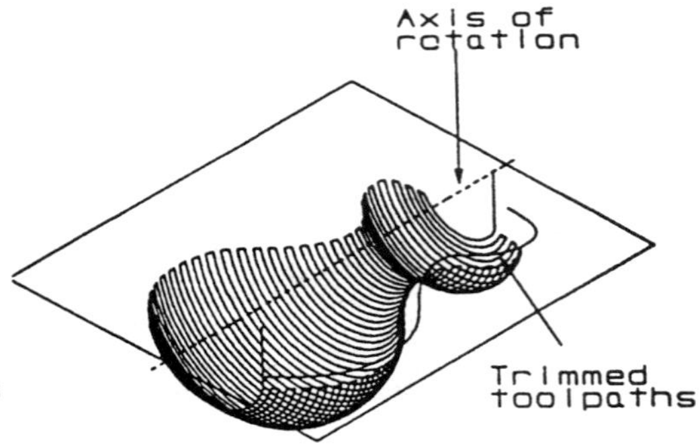

Figure 14.57a

Figure 14.57b

Note: When the toolpaths are extended above the axis depth, undercuts occur in most cases.

In the **convex cases,** the toolpaths will be trimmed when the trimming height is above the axis of rotation (Figure 14.58a), or the toolpaths will be extended when the trimming height is below the axis of rotation (Figure 14.58b).

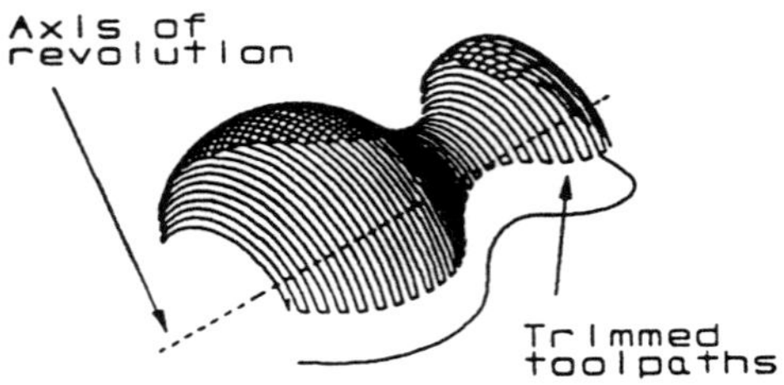

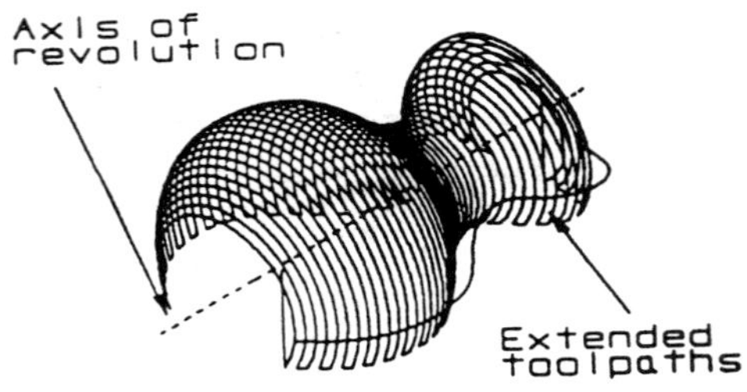

Figure 14.58a

Figure 14.58b

In trim to width mode, the toolpaths are to be trimmed to a fixed width specified by two parallel lines. Note that the toolpaths are trimmed to the tool center instead of the edge. Figure 14.59 shows a trim to width example.

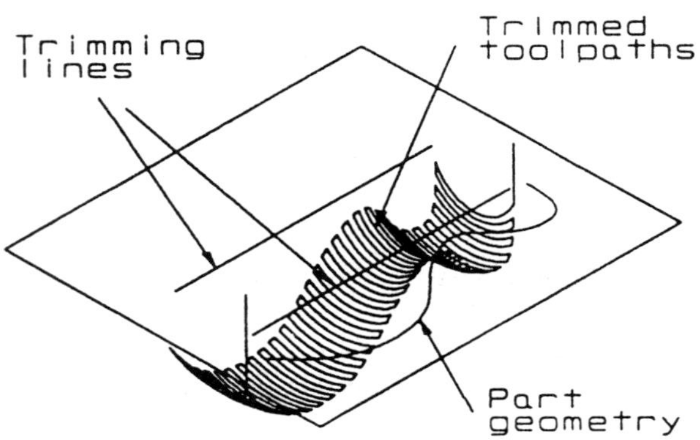

Figure 14.59

Project 8. Machining a surface of revolution 8

The revolution module is used to generate toolpaths to machine a cup with a convex shape. The wireframe model file is cup.ge3 created in project 8 of chapter 11. The wireframe model and the toolpaths are shown in Figure 14.60.

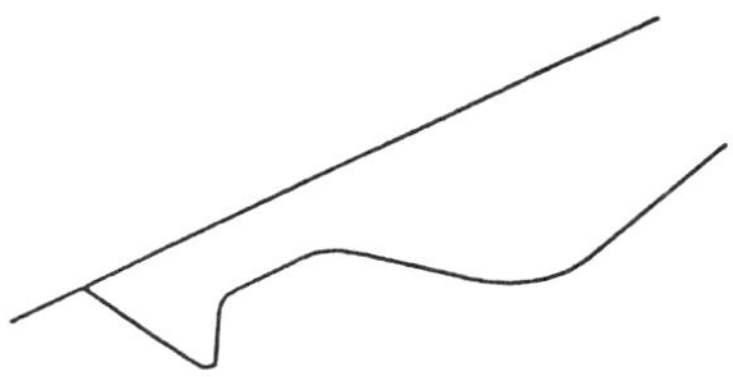

Figure 14.60a Wireframe model

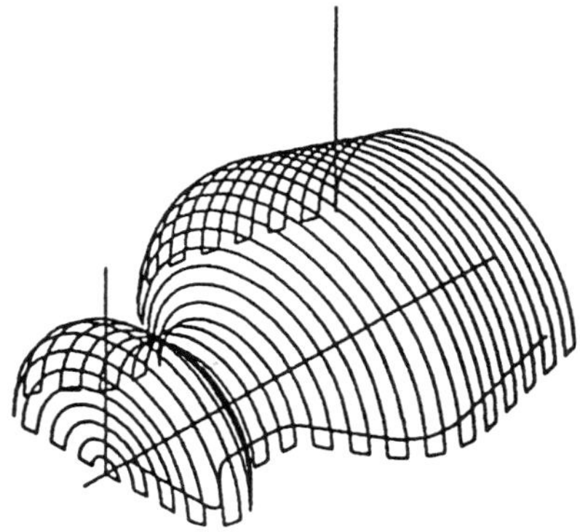

Figure 14.60b Toolpaths

Tips 1. Wireframe model file is cup.ge3.
2. Axis of rotation is Y axis.
3. Shape = Convex

Step 1. Load the wireframe model file cup.ge3.

(or create one by following the instructions in project 8 of chapter 11.)
Select **MAIN MENU** → **File** → **Get**
Enter file name: **cup** ←
Select **Gview** → **Isometric**
The wireframe model of the cup should appear as Figure 14.61.

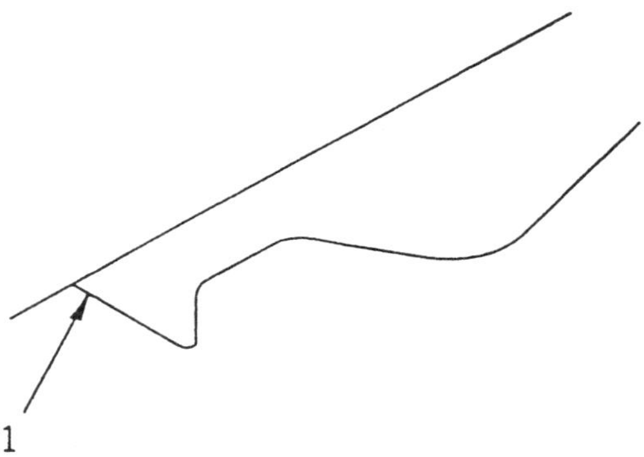

Figure 14.61

Step 2. Initiate the revolution toolpath module.

Select **MAIN MENU** → **Toolpaths** → **Next menu** → **Revolution**
Enter file name: **revolt1** ←

Step 3. Define the contours using the pick point in Figure 14.61.

Select the edge of the surface: Select **Chain** then pick at **P1**
Select **Done**
Select **Y** for the axis of rotation

Step 4. Define the surface of revolution parameters to the following settings.

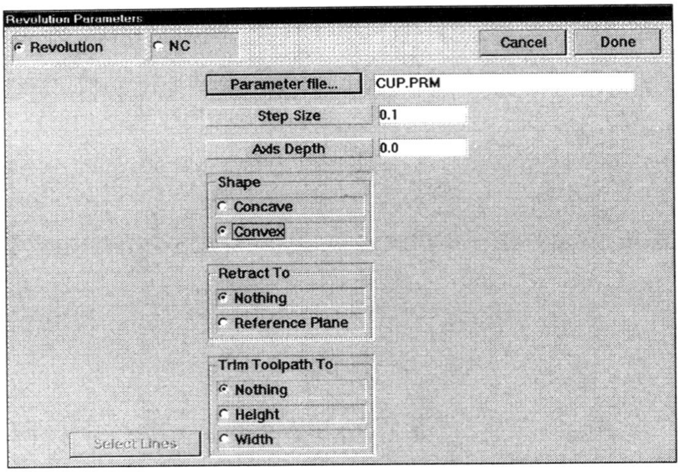

Select the **NC button** to advance to the NC parameters menu.

Step 5. Define the NC parameters to the following settings.

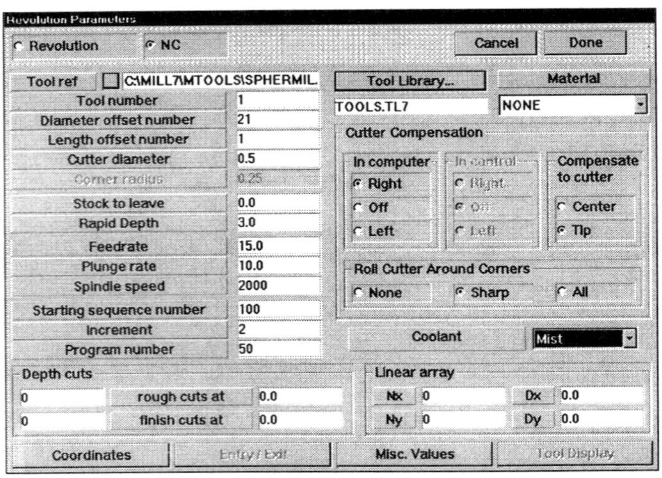

Select the **Done button** to complete the parameters settings.

Step 6. Save and close the toolpath file.

Select **MAIN MENU → NC utils → EditNCI**
Select **Yes** to "Operations have been modified. Create the NCI text file?"
Select **Quit** from the EditNCI menu.

The toolpaths should resemble Figure 14.62.

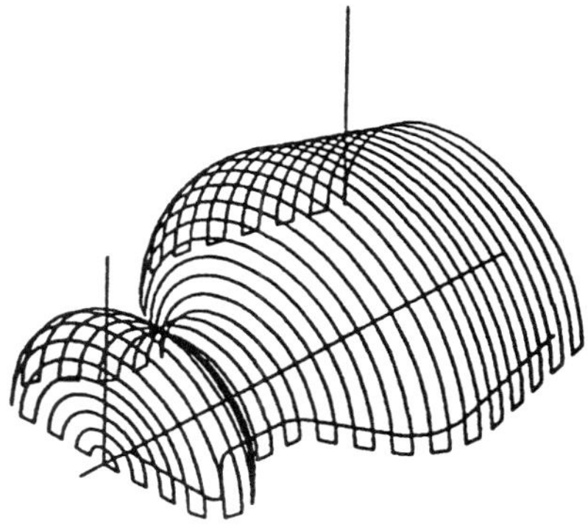

Figure 14.62

14.9 Exercises

1. What are the two methods used to generate toolpaths to cut surfaces in Mastercam? Describe the advantages and disadvantages of using these two methods, respectively.

2. Define along and across directions.

3. What are the four cutting methods in 3d surfacing?

4. Describe, with a drawing, the main features of the Zig zag cutting method.

5. Describe, with a drawing, the main features of the one way cutting method.

6. Describe, with a drawing, the main features of the circular cutting method.

7. What are the two modes of cutting direction?

8. What are the two stepping over distances used in surfacing cutting? Use drawings to illustrate these two distances.

9. Describe how the stepping over distances affects the dimensional accuracy and part program size of surface machining.

10. What are the five modes of cutter compensation in computer?

11. What are two common types of cutters used in cutting surfaces?

12. Use drawings to show how the selection of cutter tip and cutter center affect the toolpaths?

13. Describe the two groups of 3d toolpath modules in Mastercam. Explain their differences.

14. List the five 3d toolpath modules that generate toolpaths from a wireframe model.

15. What is constant Z cutting in ruled module?

16. What do initial Z and final Z parameters perform in setting constant Z cutting?

17. Describe the functions of trimming planes in ruled module.

18. What are the four blending methods used in Coons module?

Problems

19. Use the ruled toolpath module to generate the toolpaths for machining two ruled surfaces from the wireframe model created in problem 11.10. The wireframe model file is **E1.** The wireframe model and the toolpaths are illustrated in Figure 14.63.

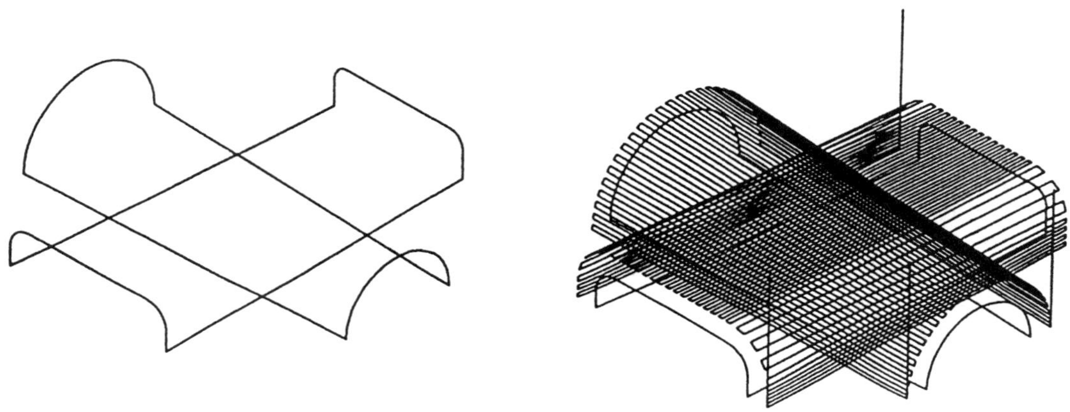

Figure 14.63

Tips 1.Wireframe model file is E1.

2. Save the toolpaths for cutting two ruled surfaces in two separate files ET1 and ET2.

3.. Cutter is 0.75" ball-end mill.

4. Cutting method = Zig zag

20. Use the loft toolpath module to generate toolpaths for cutting a loft surface defined by the wireframe model created in problem 11.12. The wireframe model file is **E3.ge3**. Both the wireframe model and toolpaths are illustrated in Figure 14.64.

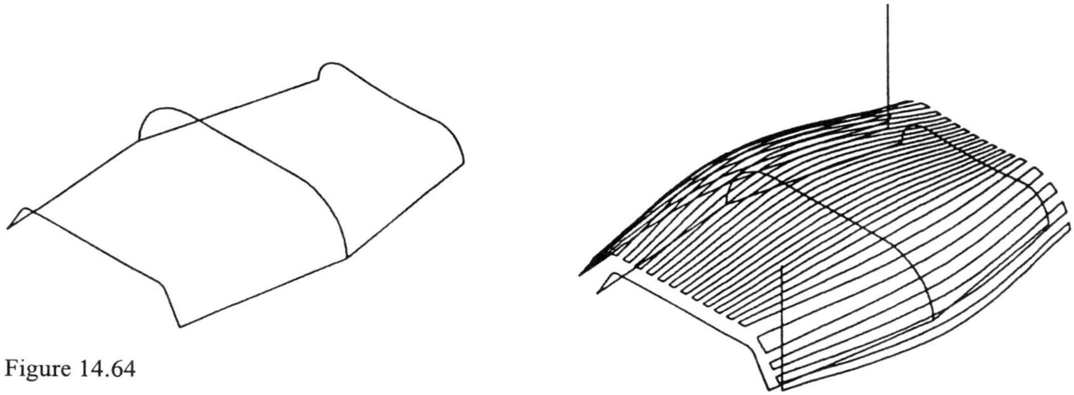

Figure 14.64

Tips 1. Wireframe model file is **E3.ge3.**

2. Pick the contours at the right end and start at contour A.

3. Set cutter compensation in computer to left tip.

21. Use the Coons toolpath module to generate toolpaths to cut the surface created from the wireframe model given in problem 11.14. This is a single patch Coons surface. The wireframe model file is **E5**. Both the wireframe model and toolpaths are shown in Figure 14.65.

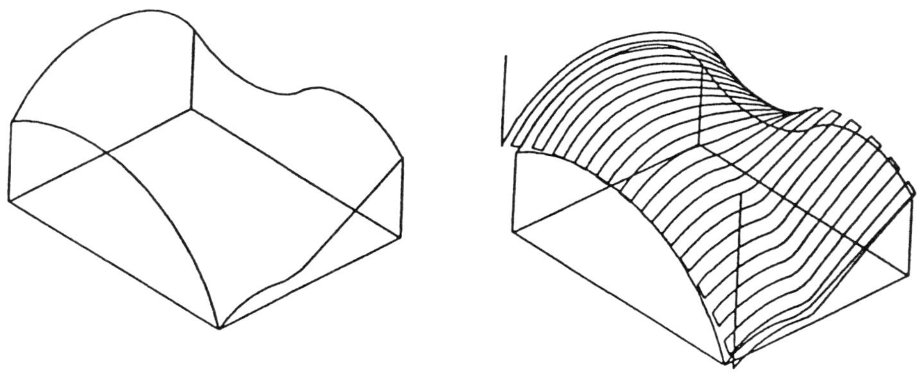

Figure 14.65

Tips 1. Wireframe model file is **E5.ge3.**

2. The number of patches in the along direction is 1.
   The number of patches in the across direction is 1.
3. Use the linear blending method because this is a single patch surface.

22. The Coons toolpath module is used to generate the toolpaths for machining a multiple-patch Coons surface. The wireframe model is created in problem 11.15 and has the name **E6.ge3**. Figure 14.66 shows both the wireframe model and the toolpaths.

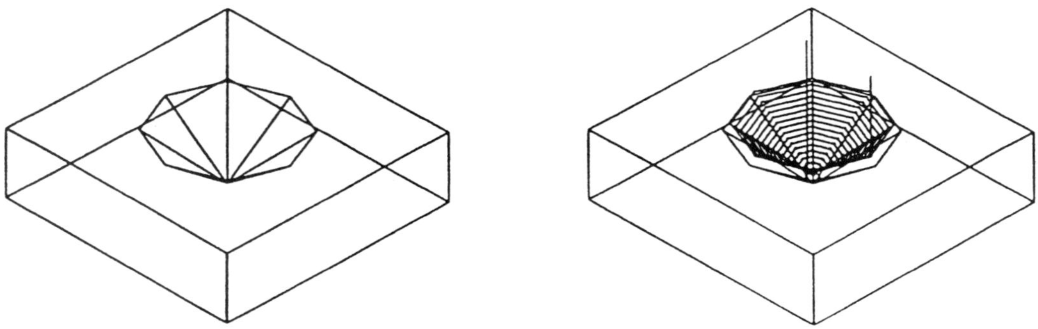

Figure 14.66

> **Tips** 1. Wireframe model file is **E6.ge3.**
>
> 2. The number of patches in the along direction is 8.
> The number of patches in the across direction is 1.
> 3. The second along contours are a common point. This point serves as the contours for the second along contour rows.
> 4. Use linear blending method because all patches are flat surfaces.

23. The revolution toolpath module is used to generate the toolpaths for machining the cup defined by the wireframe model **E8** in problem 11.17. The cup model is made using the concave shape. Figure 14.67 shows both wireframe model and toolpaths.

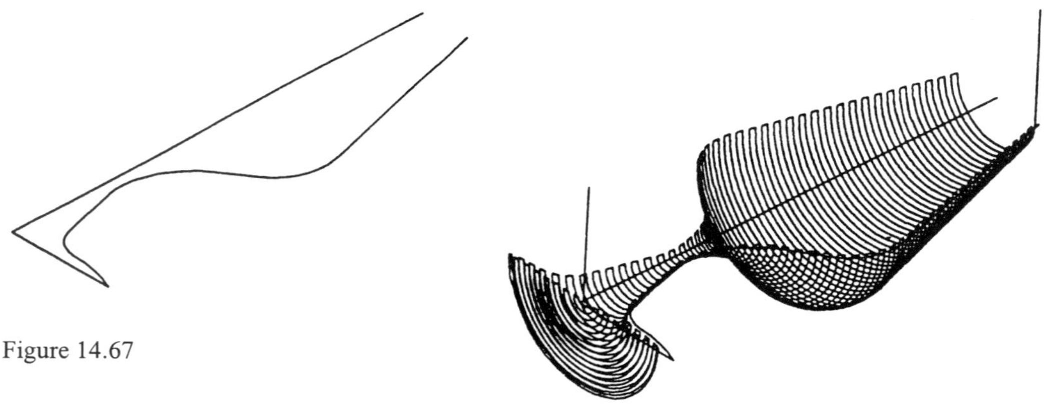

Figure 14.67

> **Tips** 1. Wireframe model file name is **E8.ge3.**
>
> 2. The axis of rotation is Y axis.
>
> 3. Surface shape is concave.
>
> 4. Set both *retraction to* and *trim to* parameters to nothing.

Mastercam Version 7,
Scholar's International Publishing Corp., 1998

24. Use the swept toolpath module to generate the toolpaths to cut a fly disk as shown in Figure 14.68. The wireframe model file is **E10**. The toolpaths for cutting the upper section of the model can be obtained by revolving the upper section profile about the Z axis. However, the bottom half of the model can not be machined in the same machine setup as the upper half. We need to flip the workpiece over and has the second setup for machining the bottom half. Therefore, it requires two toolpath files, one for the upper half and the other for the bottom half.

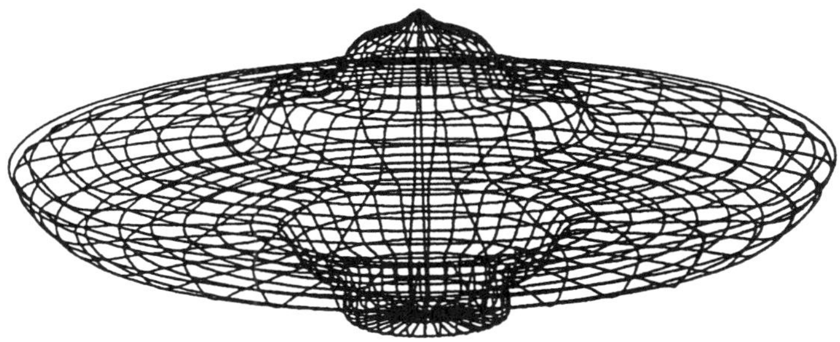

Figure 14.68

Tips 1. Use the contour profile of the upper half in the swept module to generate toolpaths and save it under one file name.
2. Change the contour profile in the bottom half to level 2. This allows the upper half contour (level 1) to be made invisible.
3. Rotate the contours in the bottom half about the X axis by 180°.
4. Use swept module to generate toolpaths for the bottom half and save under another file name.

Chapter 15

3D Toolpaths II: Generated from Surface Models

Objectives:

1. Features of seven surface roughing functions.
2. Features of eight surface finishing functions.
3. Common parameters used in surfacing toolpath functions.
4. Applying various surface toolpath functions to generate NC programs to machine surfaces.

Overview

Mastercam provides a variety of toolpath functions to generate toolpaths from existing surface models. There are two main groups of toolpath functions for cutting surfaces; **roughing functions** and **finishing functions**. There are **seven** roughing toolpath functions and **ten** finishing toolpath functions. Each toolpath function has its unique features and parameters. The intent of this chapter is to provide Mastercam users with the essential concepts and skills required to use various surfacing toolpath functions to generate roughing and finishing toolpaths to machine surface models.

15.1 Surface Toolpath Functions

All surfacing toolpath functions are grouped under the surface command. Its menu appears as below. The five surface options are briefly summarized below.

Rough: select one rough function to generate roughing toolpaths for a surface model.

Finish: select one finish function to generate finishing toolpaths for a surface model.

Recut: recut a selected toolpath file.

Rec Manager: manage the recut toolpath file.

Batch: create or modify a batch file.

15.2 Rough Functions

Most surface models require two sets of toolpaths to complete their machining; roughing and finishing. A roughing cut must be implemented prior to a finishing cut. Mastercam provides seven functions to generate roughing toolpaths for cutting surface models. These seven functions can be divided into **two main types** of roughing: **roughing around surfaces** and **roughing a pocket**. Only the pocket function is used to generate toolpaths to rough cut the material between the surfaces and material boundary. The remaining six rough functions are used to generate toolpaths to rough cut the surface profiles. Table 15.1 summaries these seven surface roughing functions. These seven roughing functions are presented, in order, after the common parameters section.

15.3 Common Parameters

Mastercam uses various types of parameters to define information required to generate toolpaths. These parameters can be classified into **two groups; common parameters** and **toolpath function specific parameters**. As their names imply, common parameters are commonly used in all toolpath functions, while function specific parameters are unique to the particular function and are not applicable to any other functions. Common parameters used in rough functions consist of two parts; tool parameters and rough parameters. Tool parameters are common to all toolpath functions including 2D and 3D surface roughing and finishing toolpath functions. Rough parameters are common to all seven rough functions.

Tool Parameters

The tool parameters dialog box for roughing surfaces is identical to the one used in 2D toolpath functions. It is redisplayed below for reference.

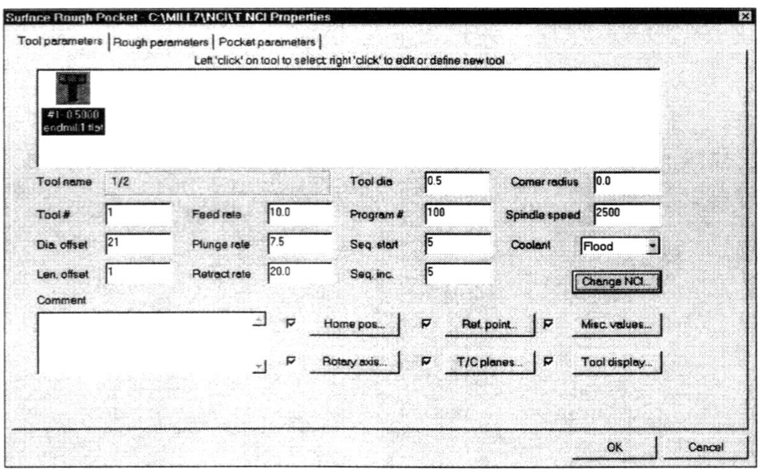

Table 15.1 Surface roughing functions

Rouging Function	Description	Illustration
Parallel	Generate roughing toolpaths that run in parallel direction specified by the machining angle parameter.	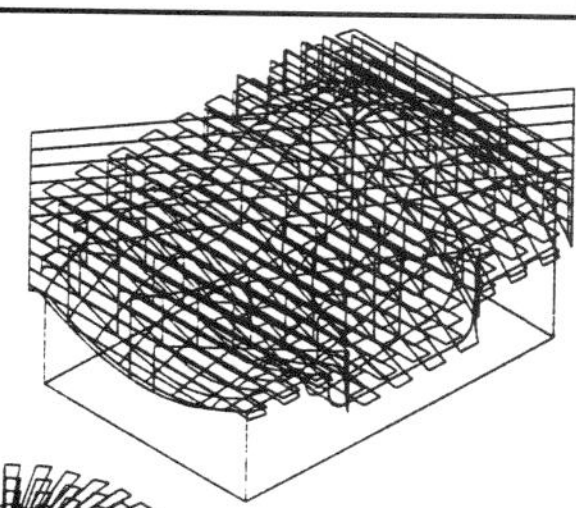
Radial	Generate roughing toolpaths that run in radial direction.	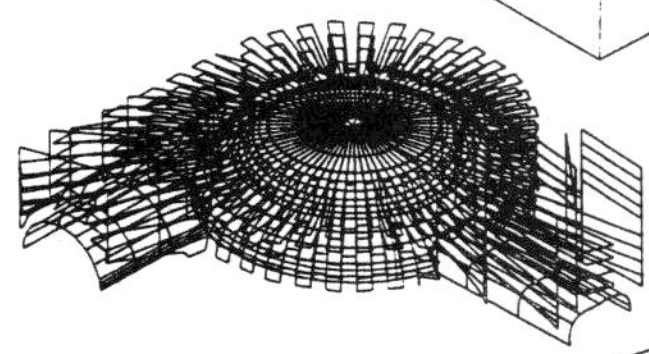
Project	Generate roughing toolpaths by projecting a set of existing toolpaths or geometry entities onto the selected surfaces.	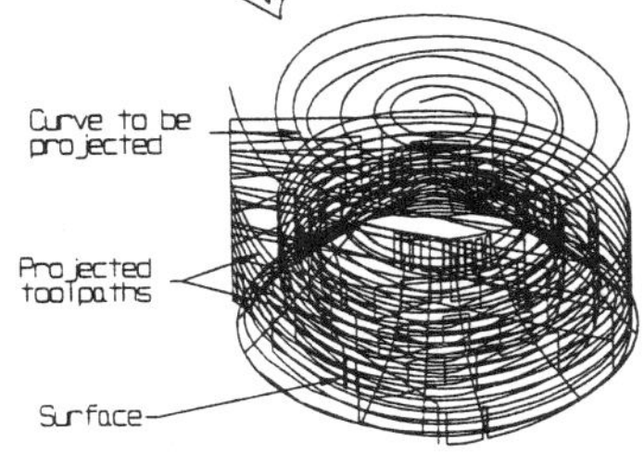
Flowline	Generate roughing toolpaths along the direction in the surface flowlines for roughing cut surface profile.	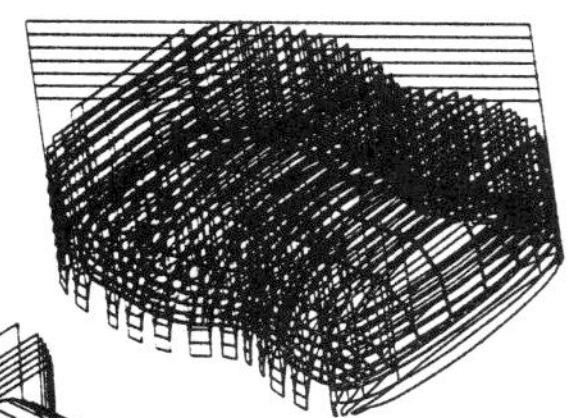
Contour	Generate roughing toolpaths along the surface contours.	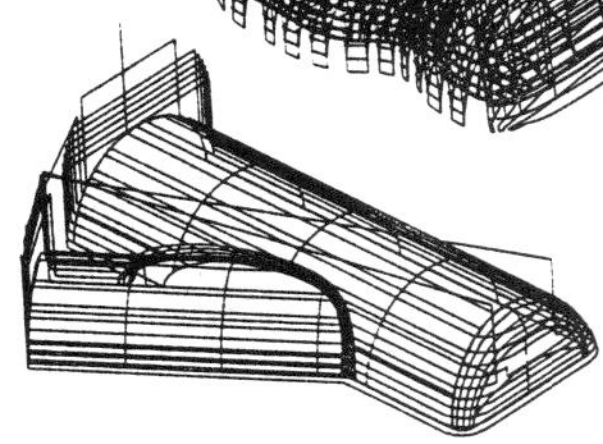
Plunge	Generate roughing toolpaths that plunge along the surface profiles in the Z direction.	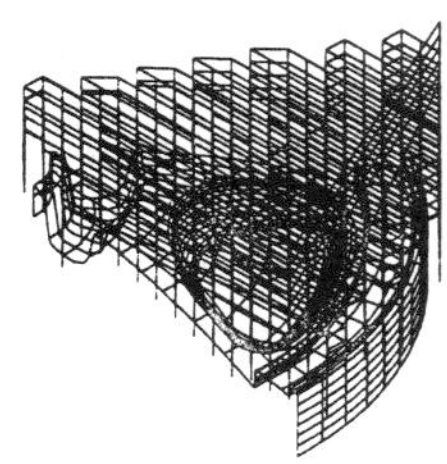
Pocket	Generate roughing toolpaths to rough out all stock between surfaces and pocket boundaries.	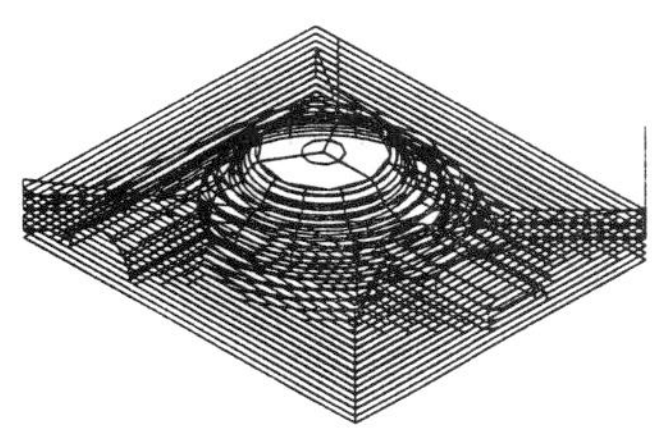

Roughing Parameters

The rough parameters dialog box is identical to all seven roughing functions. It appears as below.

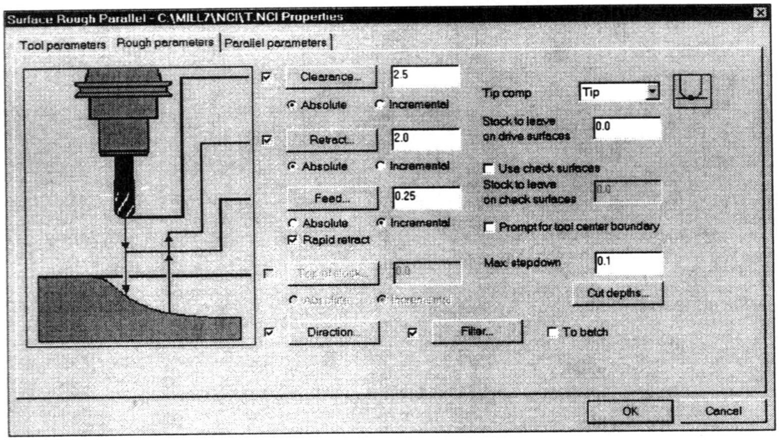

The roughing parameters can be categorized into the following eight categories: **Z depth parameters, Direction parameters, Filter parameters, Tip/center compensation, Stock, Check surfaces, Cut depths**, and **Tool center boundary.**

Z depth parameters Mastercam uses four Z depth parameters to define the toolpaths in the Z direction. These four parameters; **Clearance height, Retract height, Feed height,** and **Top of stock** are listed below and are shown in Figure 15.1.

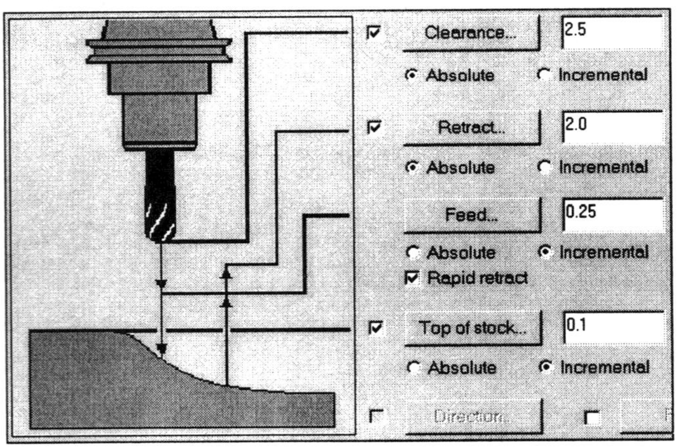

Figure 15.1

Clearance height The Clearance parameter specifies the Z-depth at which the tool moves to and from each toolpath operation. It can be set to Absolute or Incremental mode. In Absolute mode, the system places all the clearance heights at the given value by the Clearance parameter (Figure 15.2a). With Incremental mode, the system places each clearance height at a Z depth relative to the current top of the stock (Figure 15.2b).

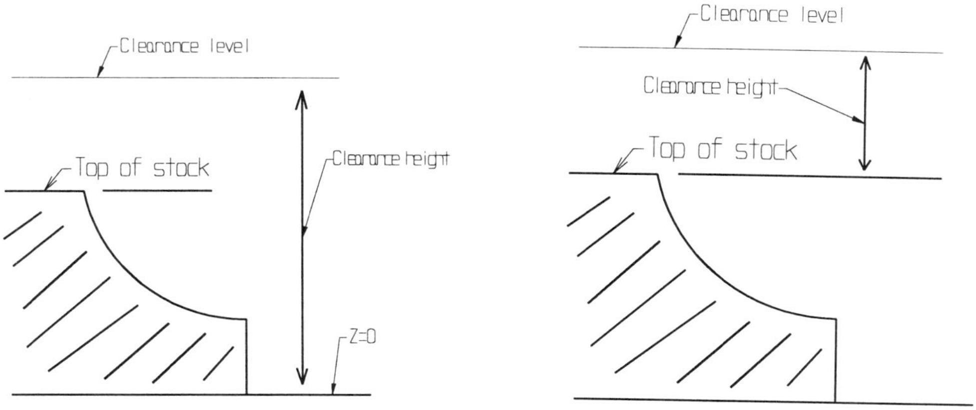

Figure 15.2

Retract height The Retract parameter specifies the Z-depth at which the tool retracts to prior to the next tool pass. The Retract height must be above the feed height in order to make it effective. It also can be set to either Absolute mode or Incremental mode. The way to determine the Retract height in these two modes are the same as in Clearance height.

Feed height The Feed parameter specifies the Z-depth that the tool moves to at a rapid rate before it changes to the plunge rate to enter the workpiece. The tool plunges to this Z-level when traveling between separate passes when the Clearance parameter is not active. This parameter also has absolute mode and incremental mode.

Top of stock The Top of stock parameter specifies the highest Z-level of the material. It has two modes to enter the value for top of stock; absolute and incremental. This parameter is only available in the Pocket function.

Direction parameters

This group of parameters define the entry move and exit move of surface roughing toolpaths. Its dialog box appears as below.

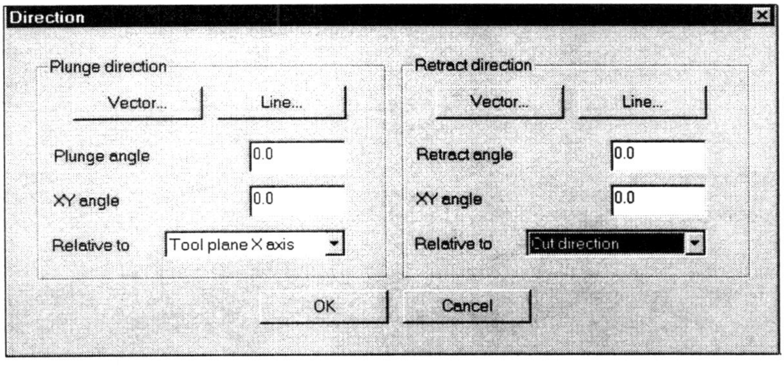

The direction of entry move and exit move can be specified in one of three ways: angle values, a vector or a line. The direction vector is defined by three direction parameters as shown below.

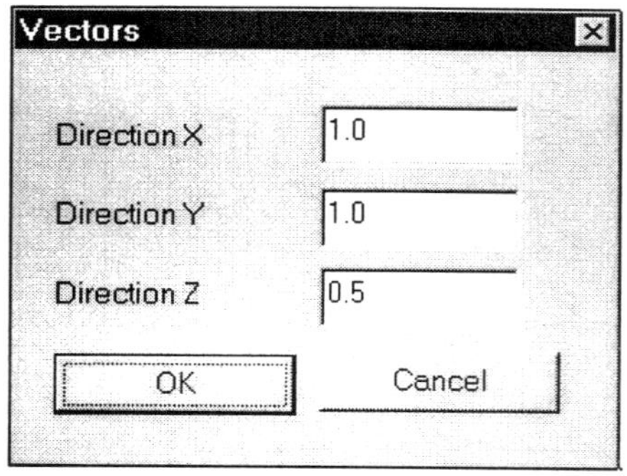

The values given to these three parameters will be reflected onto the plunge angle and XY angle in the direction dialog box. A "1.0" given to both Direction X and Direction Z as shown below makes the "Plunge angle" and "XY angle" value become 45.0 degrees and 0.0 degrees, respectively as shown.

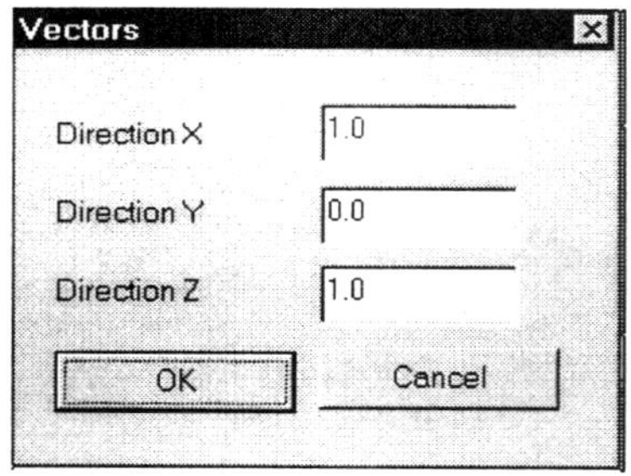

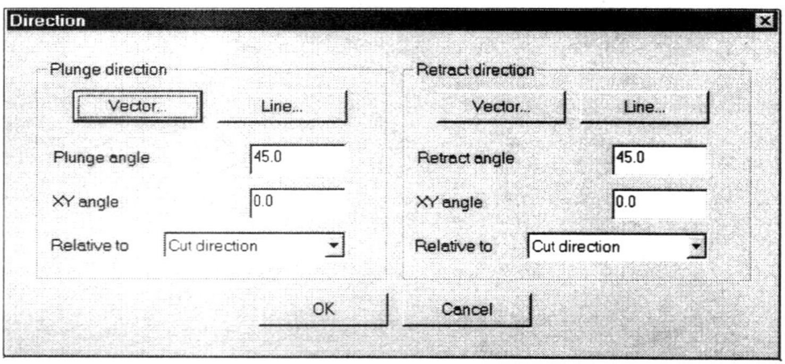

Figure 15.3 shows the effect of direction angle values on the entry/exit moves. Figure 15.3a has the direction angle of 45.0derees, and Figure 15.3b shows the direction angle of 90.0 degrees.

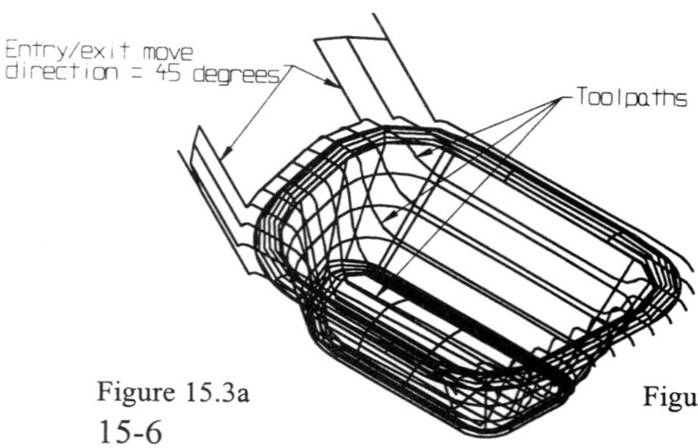

Figure 15.3a

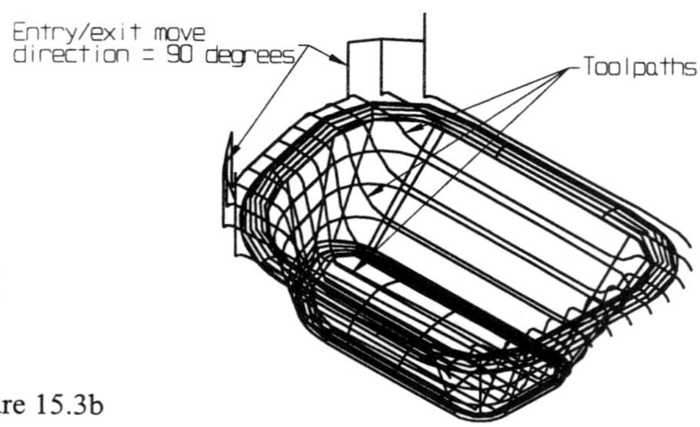

Figure 15.3b

Click the Line button, the system will goes to the graphics window for you to select a line for the direction of entry move. After selecting the line, the system will return to the Direction dialog box.

When the Direction button is toggled to Off (no check mark), the system will set the direction angle to the default value which is 90.0 degrees.

Filter parameters

This group of parameters defines the tolerance for the system to eliminate those unnecessary toolpath segments. Its dialog box appears as shown here.

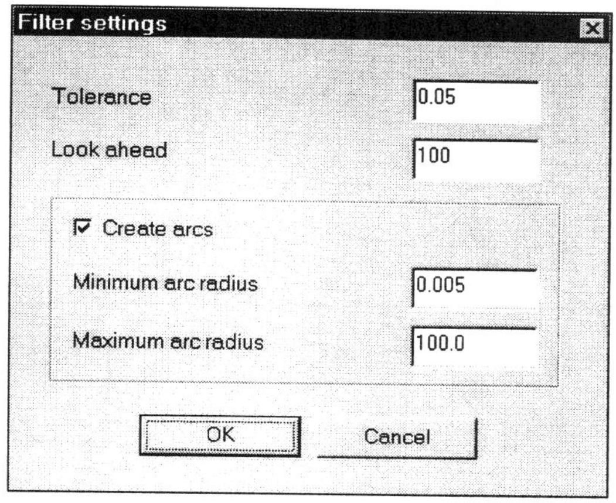

The four filter parameters are briefly described as below.

Tolerance:	specify the tolerance value for roughing toolpaths.
Look ahead:	specify the number of toolpath segments to be included in the filtering.
Minimum arc radius:	specify the minimum arc radius of the toolpath arcs.
Maximum arc radius:	specify the maximum arc radius of the toolpath arcs.

Tip/Center Compensation

This parameter specifies the cutter compensation in Z direction either to cutter tip or cutter center. Figure 15.4 shows the compensation of these two modes.

Figure 15.4a

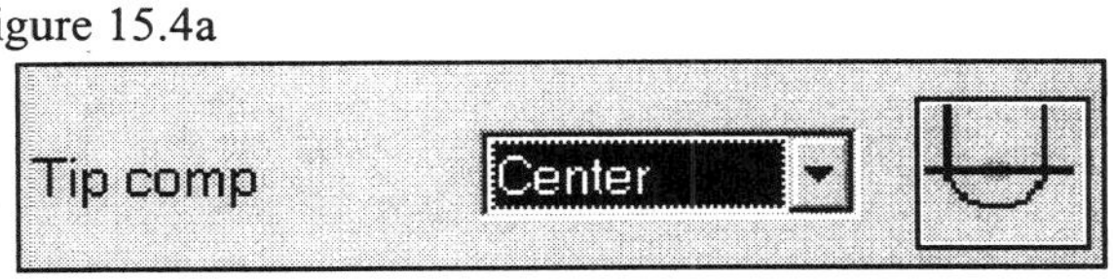

Figure 15.4b

Drive/check surfaces

Surfaces can be designated as the drive surface or the check surface. The drive surfaces are those surfaces that will be subjected to the machining operations. In other words, those surfaces wanted to be cut should be selected as the drive surfaces. The check surfaces are those surfaces that are not intended to be cut during toolpath generation for drive surfaces. This means that the system will avoid the cutting over check surfaces. Figure 15.5 shows an example of using drive/check surface function.

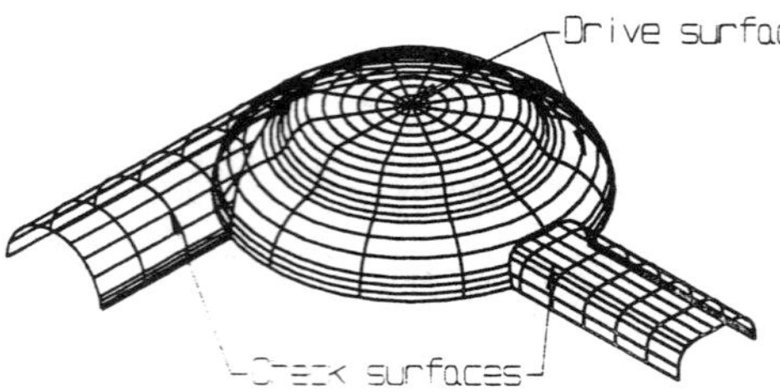

Figure 15.5a

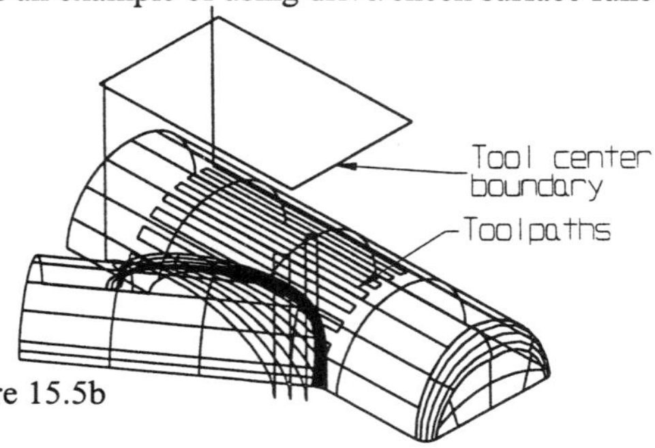

Figure 15.5b

Mastercam uses the following two parameters to specify the stock for drive surfaces and check surfaces:

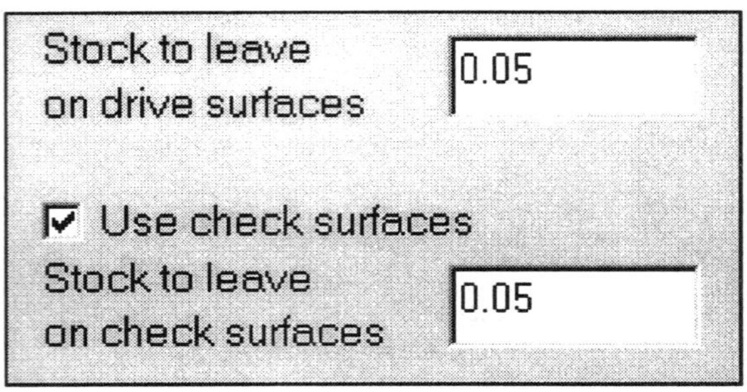

Click the "Use check surface" to On to cause the system to issue the prompt for you to select the check surfaces.

Tool center boundary

This parameter allows for the selection of a closed contour on or near the selected surfaces as the limited boundary. The tool center will be confined within the boundary during toolpath generation. Multiple confinement boundaries are allowed. Toggle the "Prompt for tool center boundary" to On to make the system prompts you to select the boundaries. When this parameter is not activated the system will not prompt you for selecting the boundaries. Figure 15.6 shows an example of using the tool center boundary.

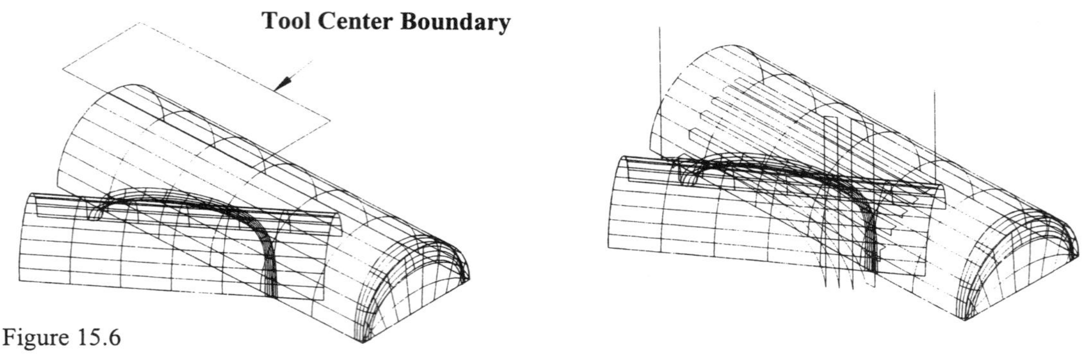

Figure 15.6

Max stepdown This parameter specifies the maximum distance between two adjacent cuts in Z-direction (Figure 15.7). A larger stepdown value produces a smaller number of roughing levels and a rougher finish. A smaller stepdown value produces a larger number of roughing levels and a smoother finish.

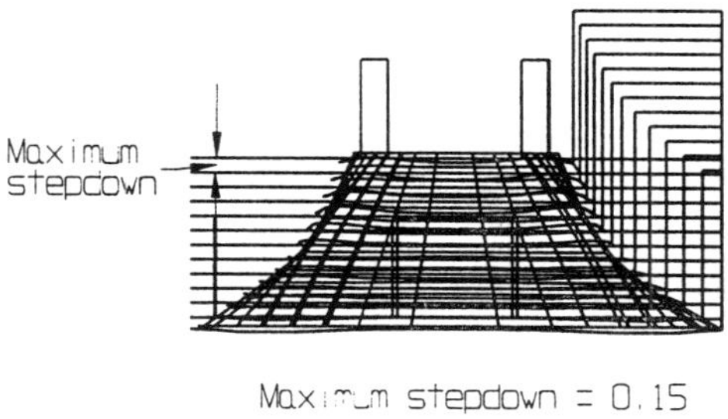

Figure 15.7a

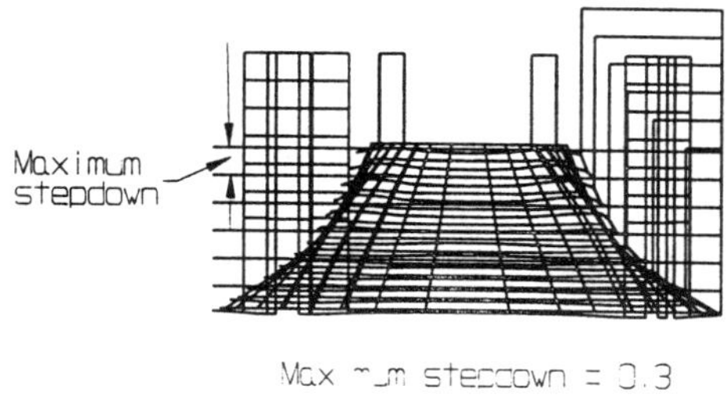

Figure 15.7b

Cut depths

This group of parameters defines the critical cut depths during roughing. These parameters make sure that certain specified depths are cut during roughing. The cut depths can be defined in absolute mode or in incremental mode. The dialog box appears different for these two modes as below.

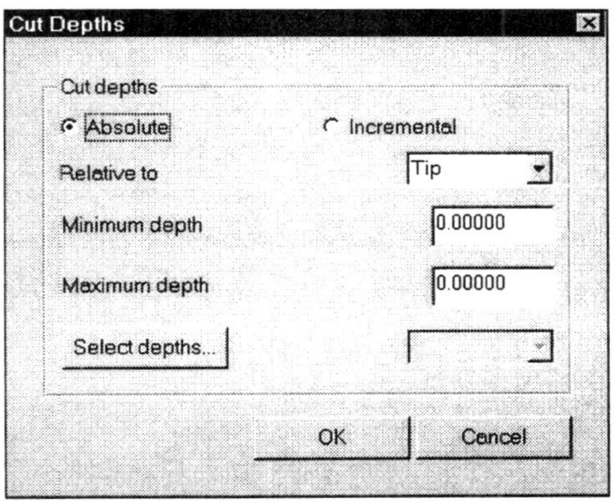

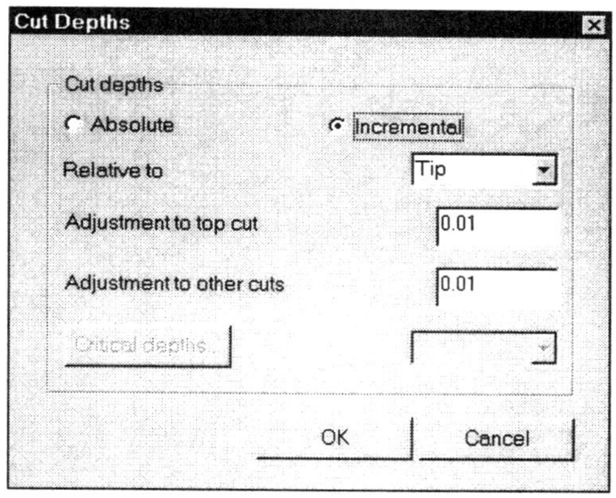

In Absolute mode, the following two parameters are used to define the critical depth (Figure 15.8):

Minimum depth:	the highest point that the tool will rise to while cutting material.
Maximum depth:	the lowest point that the tool will descend to while cutting material.

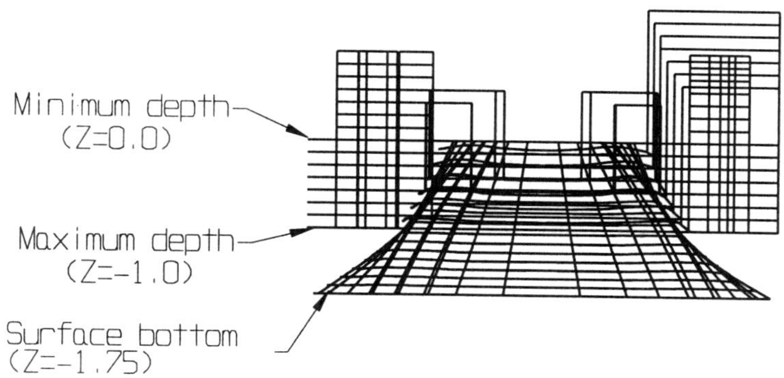

Figure 15.8

The Select depths button allows you to select graphically the minimum depth and maximum depth. Click this button, the system will move to graphic window for you to define the Z-depth.

In Incremental mode, the system places each cut at a Z-depth relative to the current surface depth. The system automatically determines the minimum and maximum depths of the toolpath based on the following three parameters (Figure 15.9):

> **Relative to:** set whether the cut depths are referred to the tip or the center of the tool.
>
> **Adjustment to top cut:** determine the distance between the minimum depth that the system calculates and where the first cut of the toolpath occurs. A positive value moves the cut to a lower level on the Z axis and a negative value moves it to a higher level on the Z axis.
>
> **Adjustment to other cuts:** determine the distance to adjust the maximum depth and all critical depth. A positive value moves the cut to a higher position on the Z axis and a negative value moves it to a lower position on the Z axis.

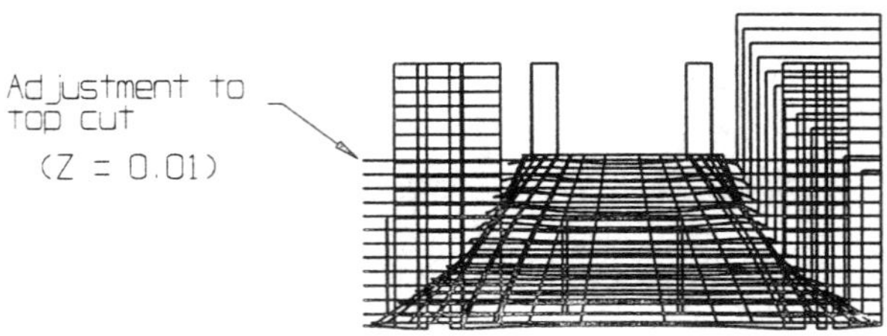

Figure 15.9a

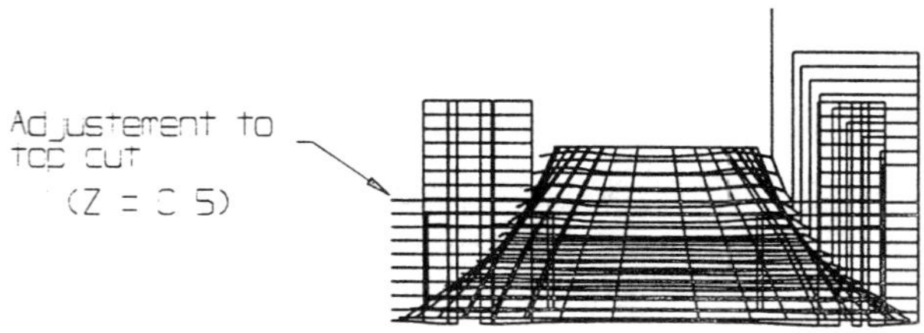

Figure 15.9b

15.4 Rough Specific Parameters

Mastercam uses four additional parameters to define the roughing toolpaths in some rough functions. They are cut tolerance, cutting method, plunge control, and Z-motion along surface. They are applicable to some rough functions only. Each rough function has its own unique parameters that are presented in their respective function.

Cut tolerance

This parameter specifies the accuracy of the surface toolpath. The smaller the cut tolerance, the more accurate the toolpath, however, it generates a longer part program. For roughing surfaces, a cut tolerance of 0.05" may be adequate for most cases. Figure 15.10 contrasts the roughing toolpaths in using different values for cut tolerance.

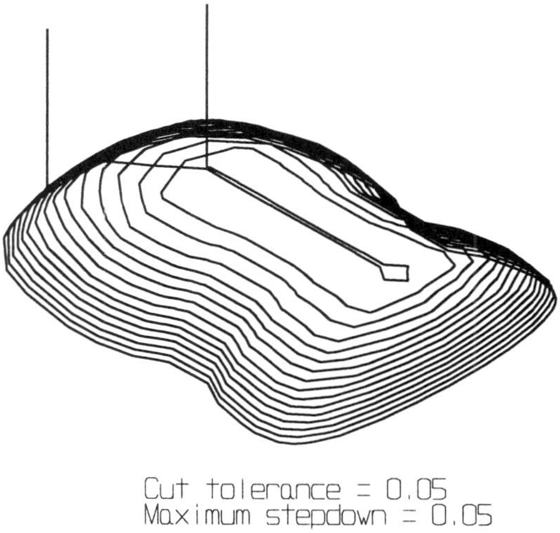

Figure 15.10a

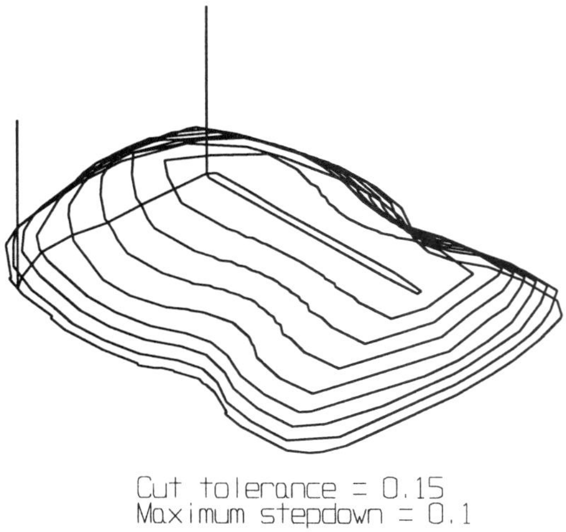

Figure 15.10b

Cutting Method

Two cutting methods are available in the roughing cut: zigzag and one way. Figure 15.11 shows the difference between these two cutting methods using the same surface model. In the zigzag mode, the cutter moves back and forth across the surfaces. In the one way mode, the cutter takes a pass, rapids up, moves back to the start of the cut, and takes another pass in the same direction.

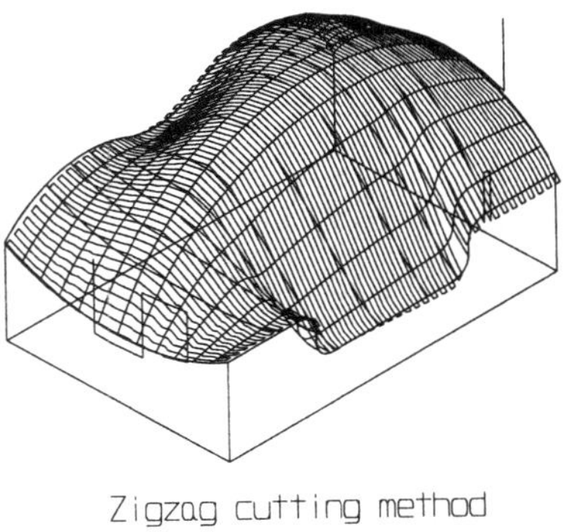

Figure 15.11a

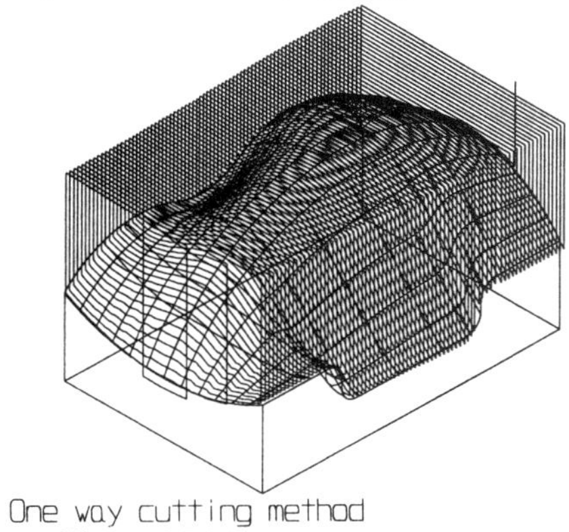

Figure 15.11b

Plunge Control

The plunge control parameters allow to select the method of plunging the tool to rough cut a multiple-surface part. The three plunge control methods are (Figure 15.12):

> **Allow multiple plunges along cut:** perform any number of tool plunges along a surface model (Figure 15.12a). Used in multiple cavities parts.
>
> **Cut from one side:** only plunge along one side of the part (Figure 15.12b).
>
> **Cut from both sides:** plunge along each side of the part (Figure 15.12c).

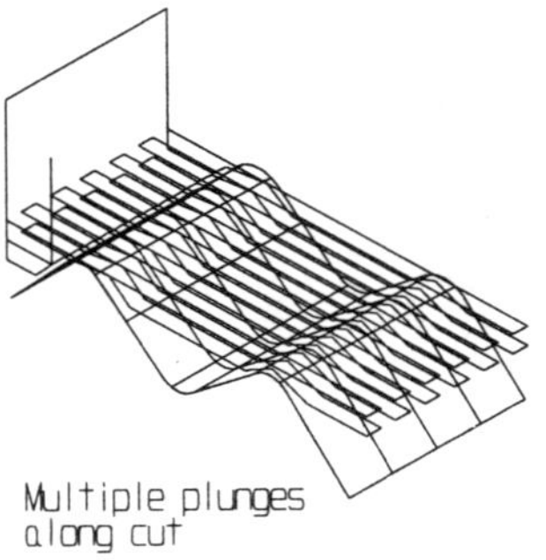

Figure 15.12a

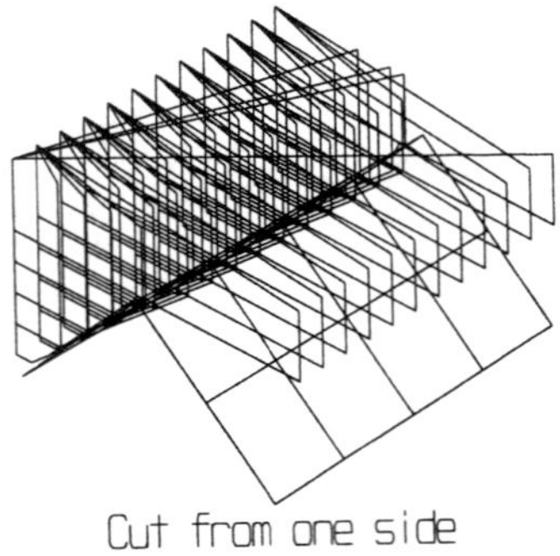

Figure 15.12b

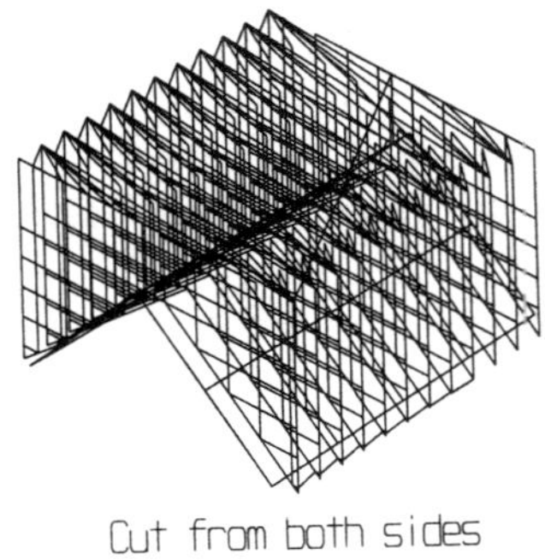

Figure 15.12c

Z Motion Control

Mastercam uses the following two parameters to control the Z motion along the surface while performing roughing cut:

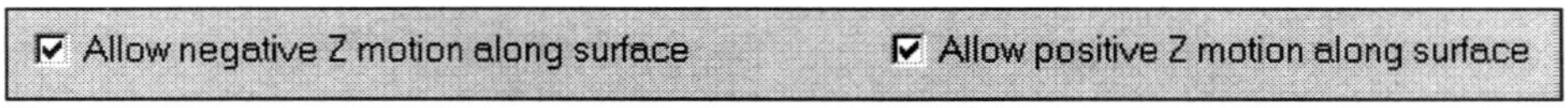

Toggle on the "Allow negative Z motion along surface" parameter makes the tool cut along the surface while plunging (Figure 15.13a). Toggle this parameter to "Off" causes the tool not to cut along the surface while plunging (Figure 15.13b).

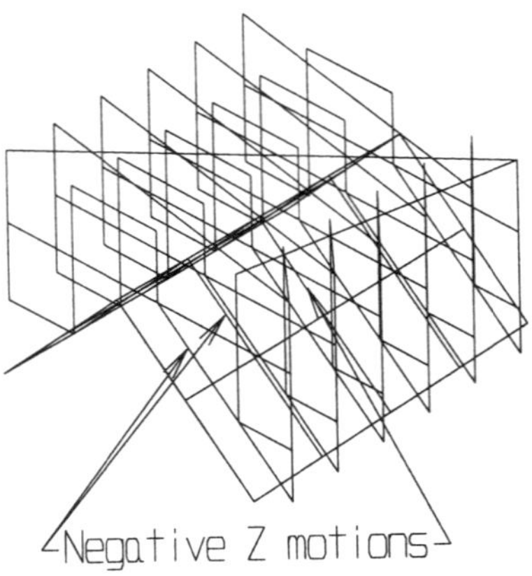

Figure 15.13a

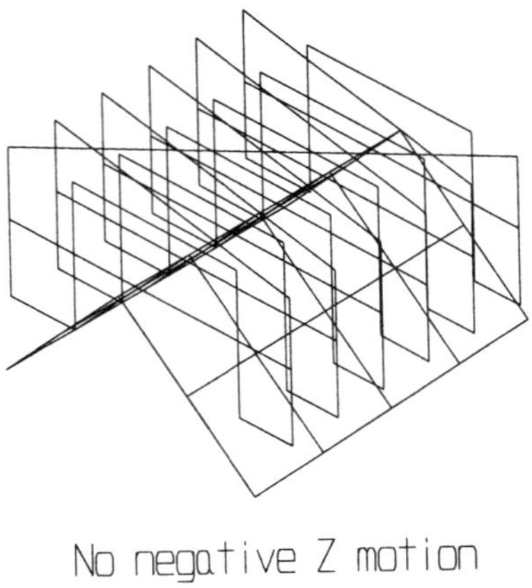

Figure 15.13b

Toggle on the "Allow positive Z motion along surface" parameter makes the tool cut along the surface while rising (Figure 15.14a). Toggle this parameter to "Off" causes the tool not to cut along the surface while rising (Figure 15.14b).

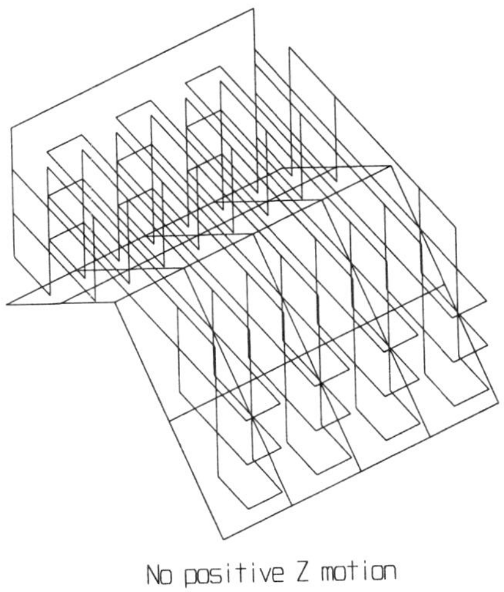

Figure 15.14a

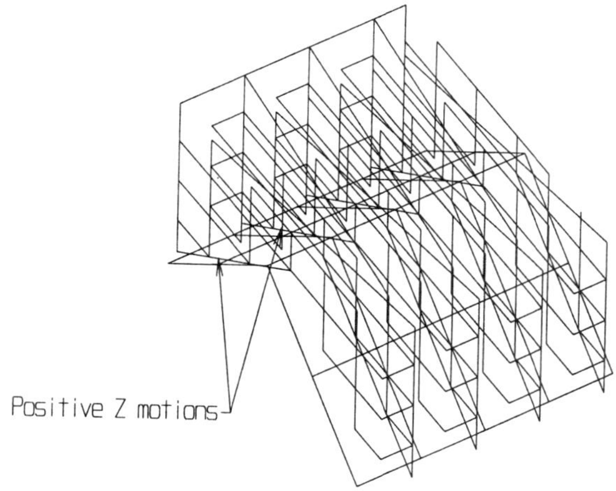

Figure 15.14b

These two Z motion control parameters can be independently set to their desired setting. Figure 15.15 shows the toolpaths that allow both positive and negative Z motions.

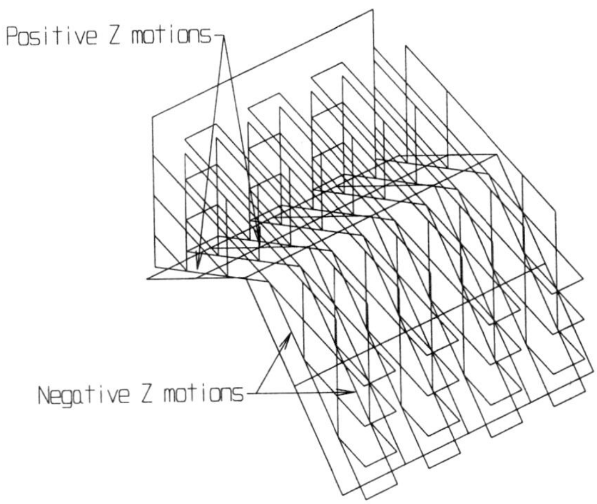

Figure 15.15

15.5 Gap Settings and Edge Settings

There are two groups of parameters that are used to control the toolpath pattern when gaps and edges are encountered.

Gap Settings

Gaps are an opening or any break in the continuity of surfaces. Gaps are normally caused by:

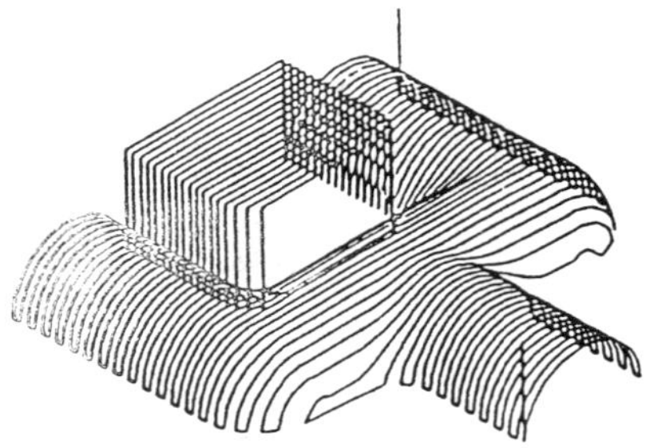

(1) adjacent surfaces that are not directly connected (Figure 15.16)
(2) trimmed areas where gaps are produced (Figure 15.17)
(3) gouge removed areas (Figure 15.18).

Figure 15.16

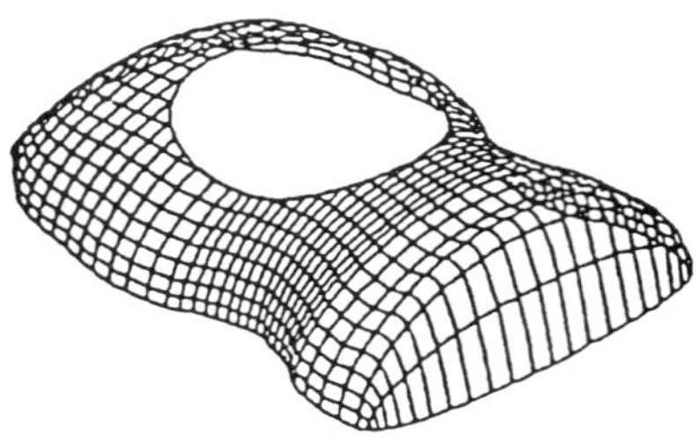

Figure 15.17

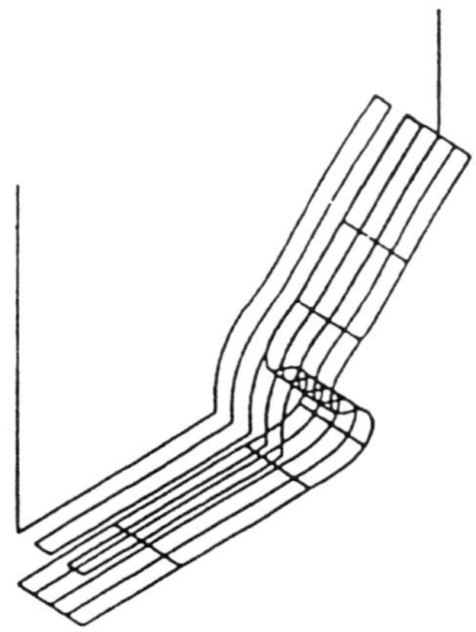

Figure 15.18

Another term you should know about is motion. **Motion** is the projected length of each cutter move onto the Cplane. A gap size is referred to as the **given gap value.** It is used to determine whether the gap is a short gap or long gap. A long gap occurs when the motion is greater than the gap size. A short gap exists when the motion is equal to, or shorter than, the gap size.

Short gap	if motion < gap size
Long gap	if motion > gap size

The value of gap size is expressed in one of the following two ways:

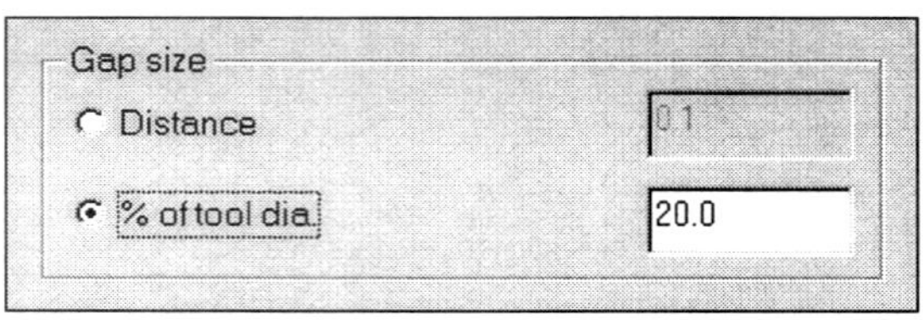

Distance:	directly specify the gap distance.
% of stepover:	specify the gap size in the percentage of the given stepover value.

Toolpath mode for short gaps (Motion < Gap Size)

Mastercam provides **four toolpath modes** for short gaps. The short gap toolpath mode menu appears as below.

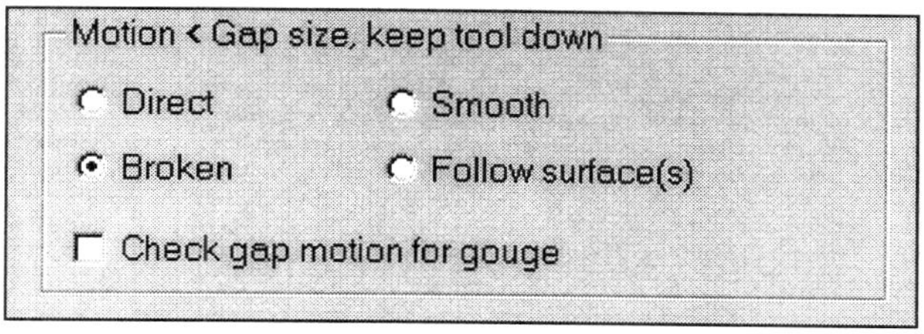

Direct Mode In the Direct mode, the cutter moves straight over the gaps in feed speed from position to position (Figure 15.19). In other words, the cutter moves from the end point of the toolpath on one surface (or move) to the start point of the toolpath on the adjacent surface (or move).

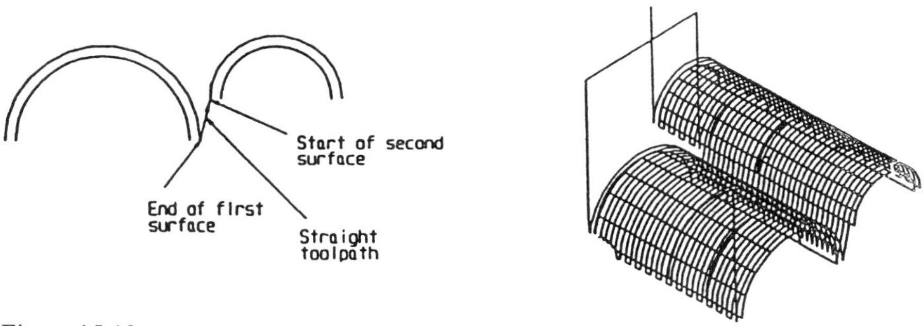

Figure 15.19

Broken Mode In the Broken mode, the toolpaths which move over gaps are broken into two segments; one with Z movement only and the other with movement in the X and/or Y direction (Figure 15.20). In other words, the cutter moves up (in the Z direction), then moves over (in the X and/or Y direction). The cutter moves over first, then moves down.

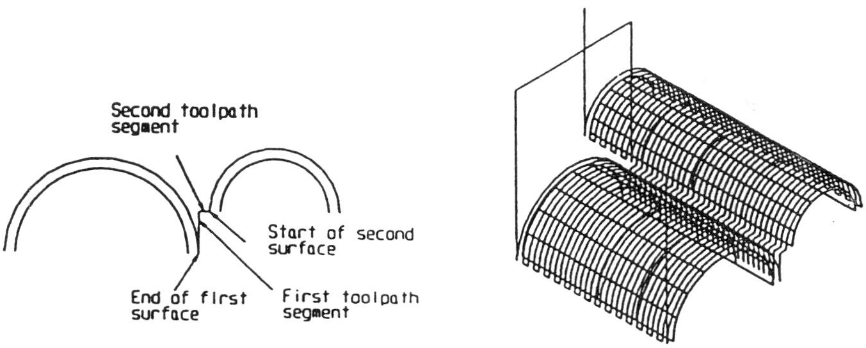

Figure 15.20

Smooth Mode In the Smooth mode, the toolpaths which move over gaps follow the fluid (smooth) motion (Figure 15.21). It is commonly used in high-speed machining.

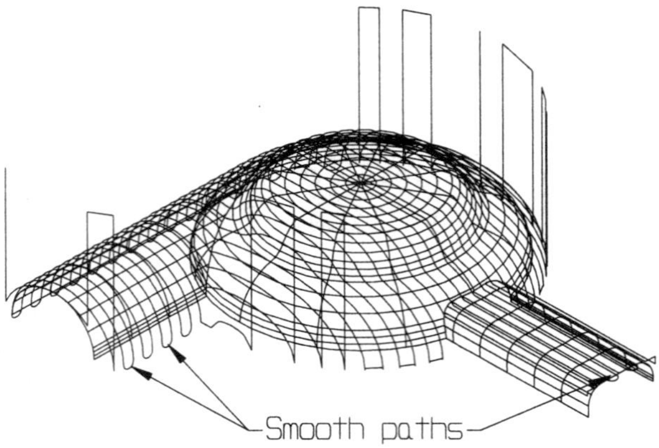

Figure 15.21

In the following surface(s) mode, the toolpaths which move over gaps follow the Z-motion of the surfaces (Figure 15.22).

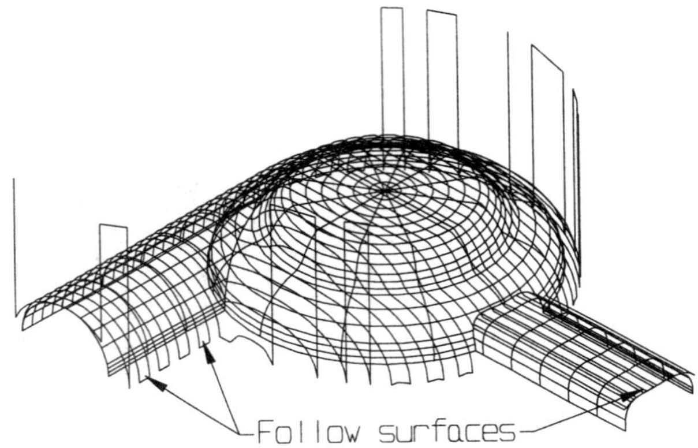

Figure 15.22

Toolpath Pattern for Long Gaps (Motion > Gap Size)

If a tool motion becomes larger than the given gap size, the system adds a retract motion to the toolpath. The toolpath pattern for long gaps following the following five steps (Figure 15.23):

(1) Cut over the first surface to one end in the specified direction.
(2) Rapidly retract to the rapid plane.
(3) Rapidly move over the gap to the start end of the second surface.
(4) Plunge to the start point of the second surface.
(5) Cut the second surface in the specified direction.

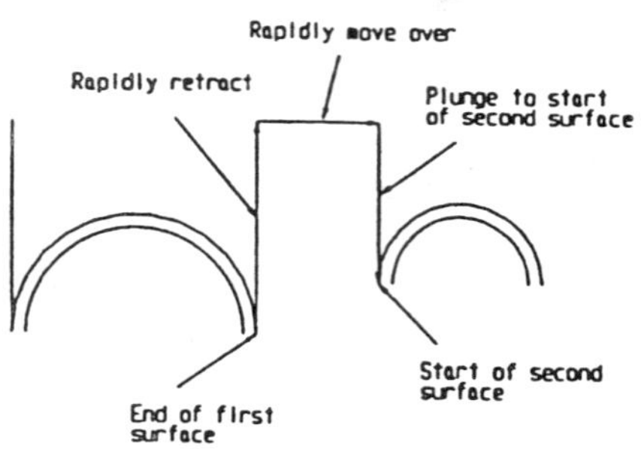

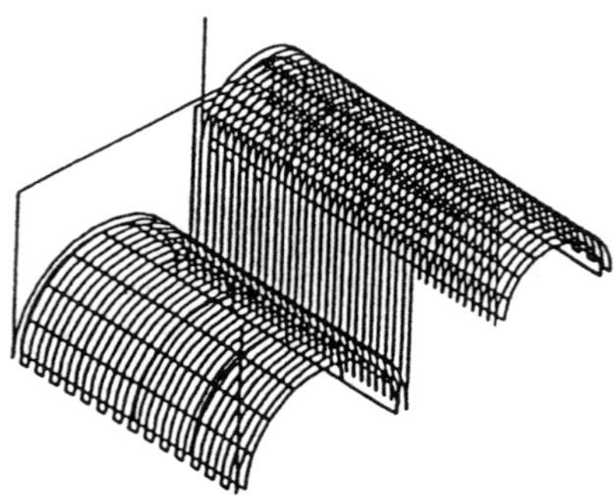

Figure 15.23

The remaining five gap setting parameters are briefly described below:

Optimize cut order: place the tool in an area and keeps it there until all cuts in the area are made.
Plunge into previously cut area: make the tool to plunge into an area of the part that was previously cleared by another cut.
Follow tool center boundary at gap: allow the tool to follow the boundary at a gap if a tool center boundary has been selected for the surface toolpath. The tool moves in XY directions to stay on the boundary.
Tangential arc radius: add an arc to the entry and exit points of a gap (Figure 15.24).

Tangential arc angle: specify the angle of the arc placed at the entry and exit points of a gap (Figure 15.24).

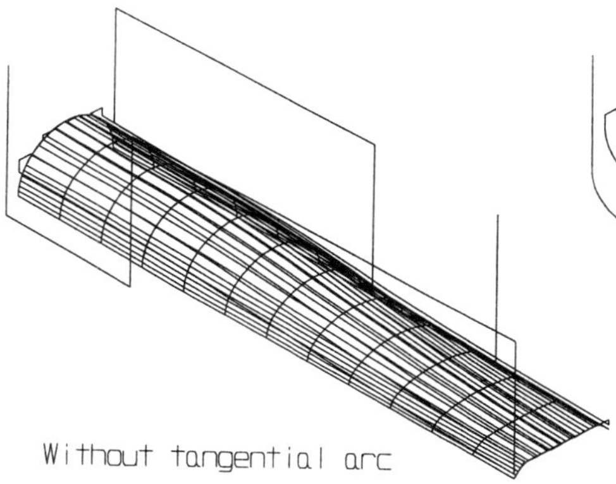

Figure 15.24a

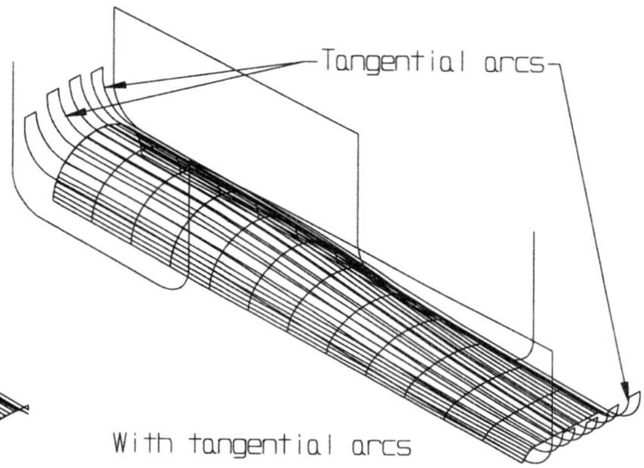

Figure 15.24b

Edge Settings

In composite surface models, some surfaces may have open edges in which the surface skin is not fully extended to cover the edges of the surfaces. Mastercam classifies the surface open edges into two categories: **open edges between surfaces** and **open edges in single surfaces** (Figure 15.25). In the between surface group, the open edges are located at the intersection of two surfaces. In a single surface group, the open edges are on a surface that is not intersected with other surfaces at the open edge boundaries.

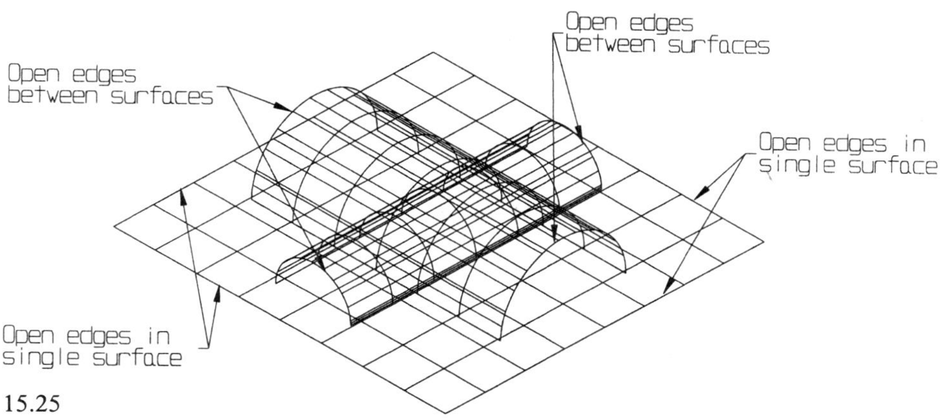

Figure 15.25

The edge settings dialog box appears as shown here.

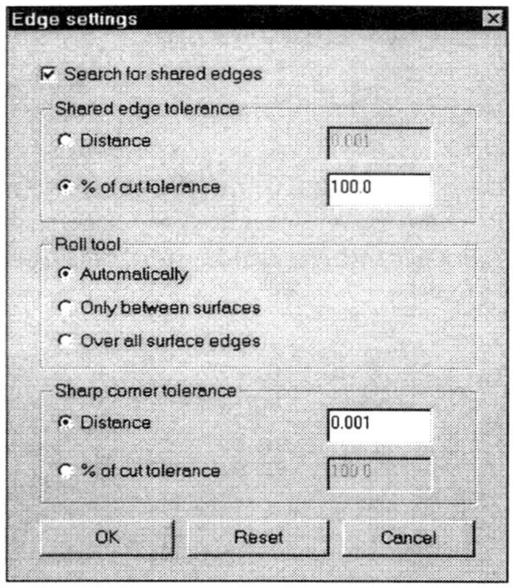

There are three parameters in the edge settings dialog box. They are; **Search for shared edges, Roll tool**, and **Sharp corner tolerance.**

Search for shared edges This parameter allows the user to look for areas where surfaces come together on the current geometry. It has two options to define the shared edge tolerance for detecting shared edges. The distance that is longer than the shared edge tolerance is qualified as a shared edge. These two options are:

Distance: specify a specific distance value as the shared edge tolerance.
% of cut tolerance: specify the tolerance value as a percentage of the cut tolerance for the toolpath.

Roll tool Mastercam uses a "Roll tool" parameter to select the edge setting option. This parameter can be set to one of the three options as below.

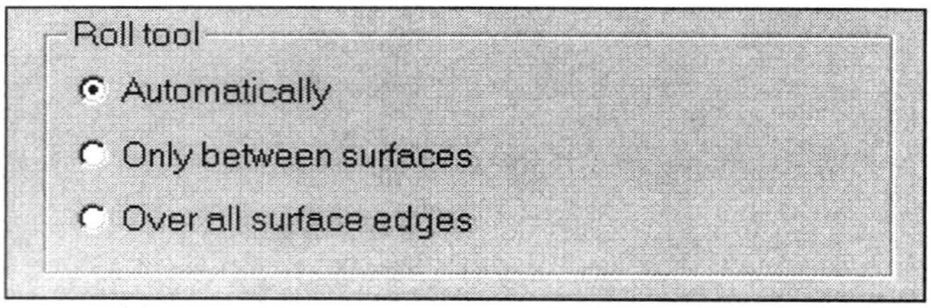

Automatically: The system automatically decides whether to roll tool at the surface edges. The tool rolls only between surfaces if no "tool center boundary" is used. This means the cutter center lies at the open edges of all surfaces (Figure 15.26a). With a tool center boundary being used, the tool rolls over all surface edges (Figure 15.26b). The "tool center boundary" parameter appears in the Rough parameters dialog box.

Only between surfaces: Roll the tool between surfaces only. Edge gougings will be removed in surfaces that are intersected with other surfaces. However, the cutter center lies at the open edges of single surfaces (Figure 15.27).

Over all surface edges: Roll the tool over all edges of the surface. Edge gougings will be removed in all surfaces including between surfaces and single surfaces (Figure 15.28).

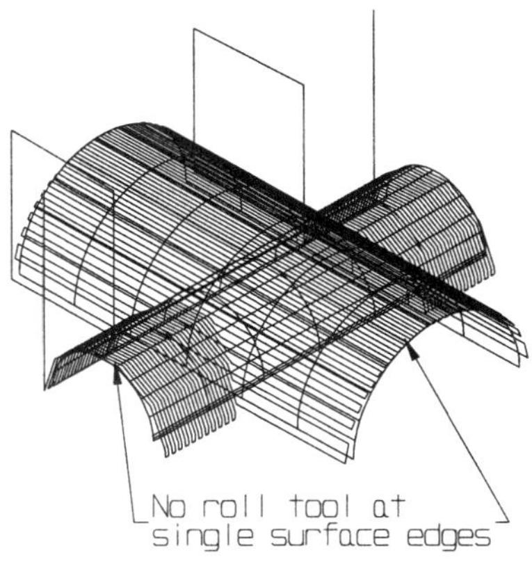

Figure 15.26a

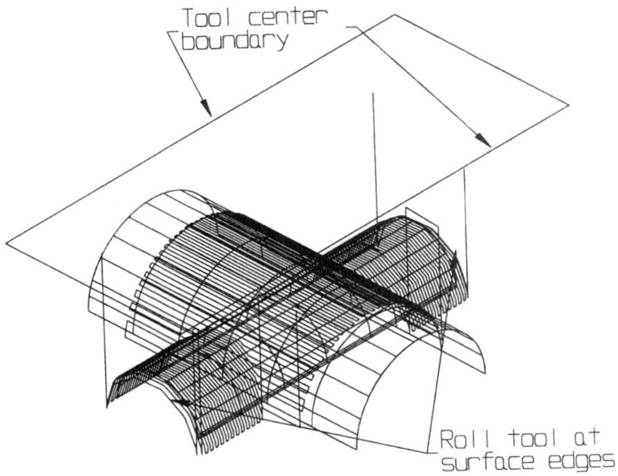

Figure 15.26b

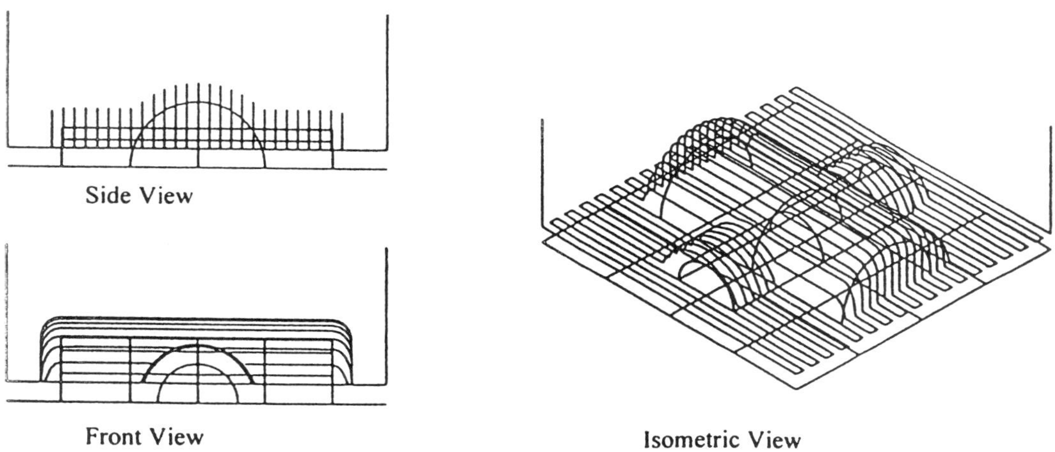

Figure 15.27

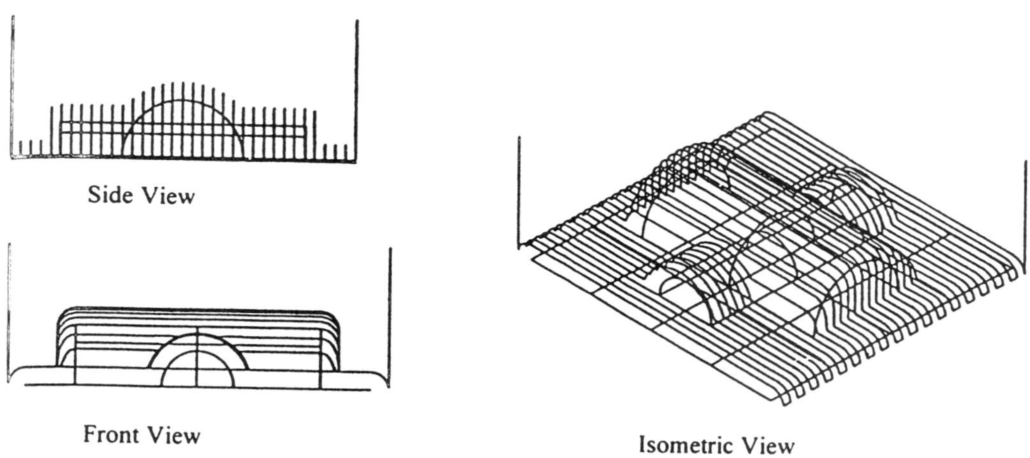

Figure 15.28

Sharp corner tolerance This parameter specifies the distance value for breaking the rolling tool motion into a set of smaller increments. A larger tolerance produces sharper corner increments (Figure 15.29a). A smaller tolerance has rounder corner increments (Figure 15.29b). The two options to specify the sharp corner tolerance are:

> **Distance:** specify a specific distance value as the sharp corner tolerance.
> **% of cut tolerance:** specify the tolerance value as a percentage of the cut tolerance for the toolpath.

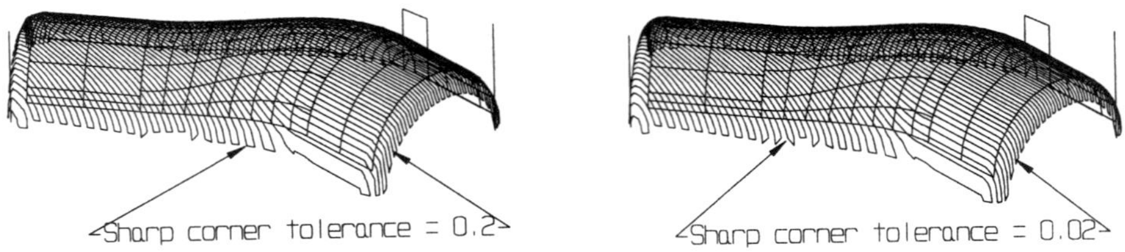

Figure 15.29

15.6 Rough Parallel Function

This roughing function generates roughing toolpaths to cut along the selected surfaces in the specified direction (Figure 15.30). The parallel parameters dialog box appears as below.

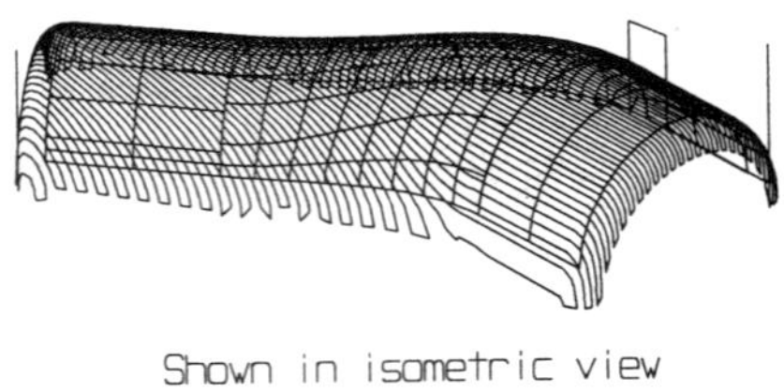

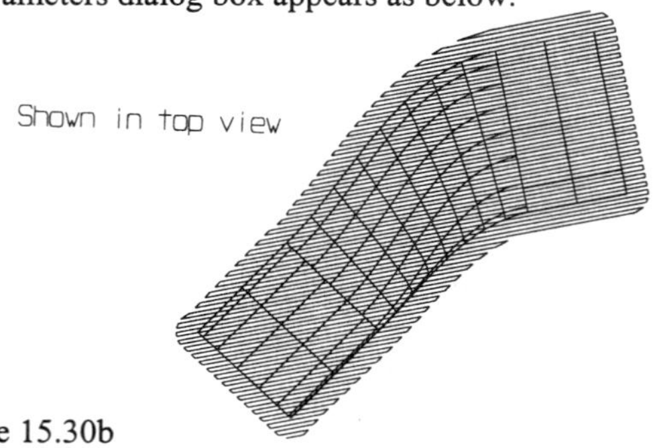

Figure 15.30a Figure 15.30b

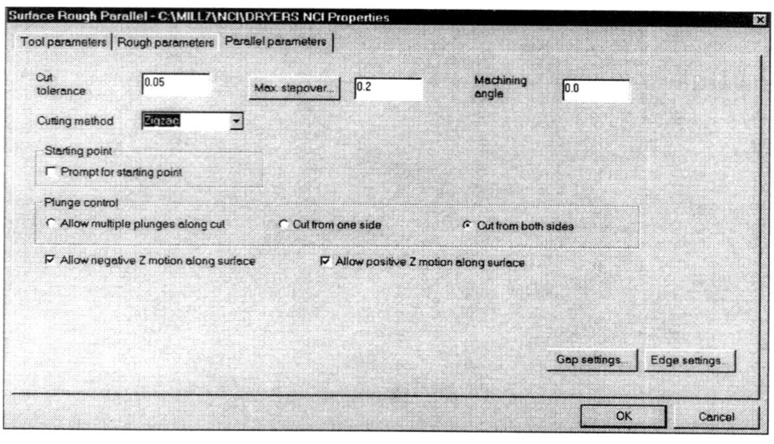

The unique parameter to this parallel function is machining angle. The machining angle is measured from the +X axis direction and is a positive value in the counterclockwise direction. Figure 15.31 shows two examples of machining angles; one in 0 degrees and the other in 45 degrees.

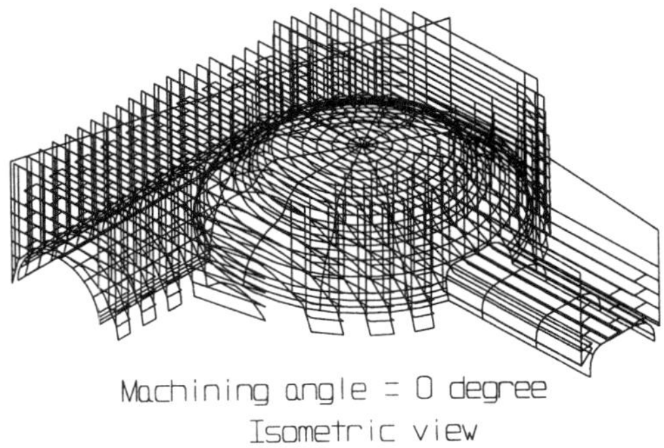

Figure 15.31a

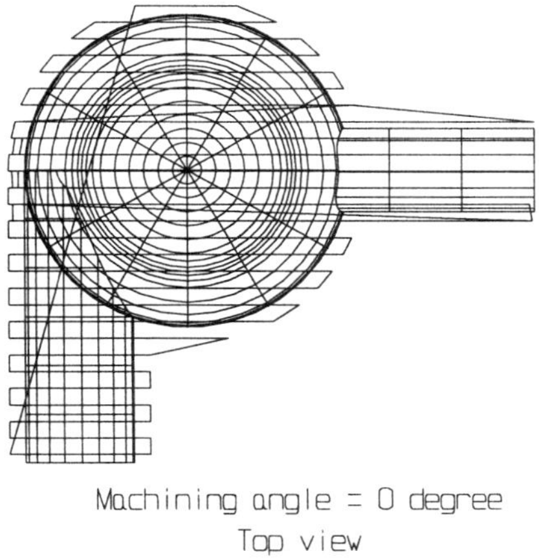

Figure 15.31a'

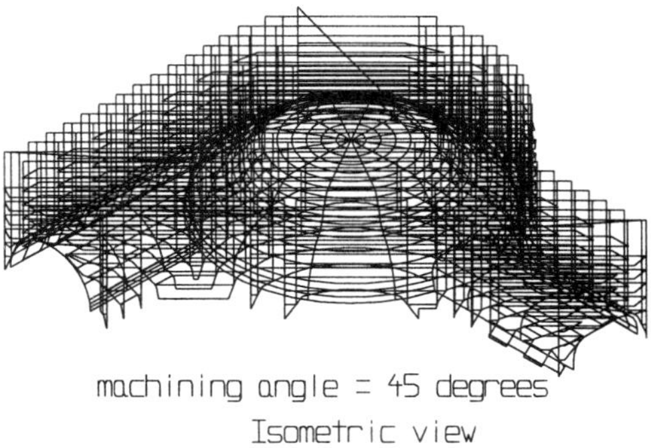

Figure 15.31b

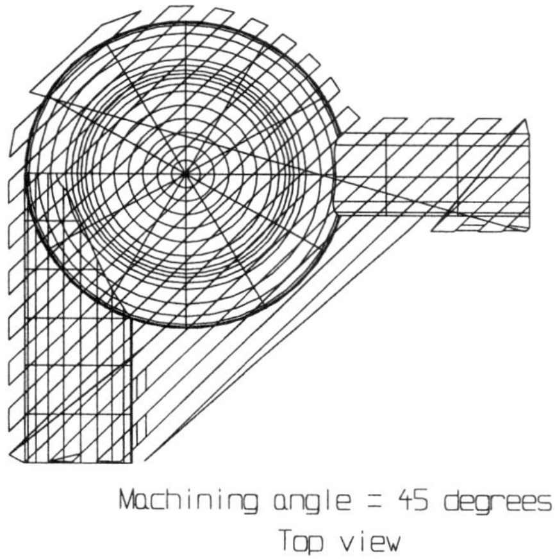

Figure 15.31b'

The maximum stepover parameter specifies the size of the stepover distance between two adjacent cuts. Click the "Max. stepover" button to open its dialog box as shown below.

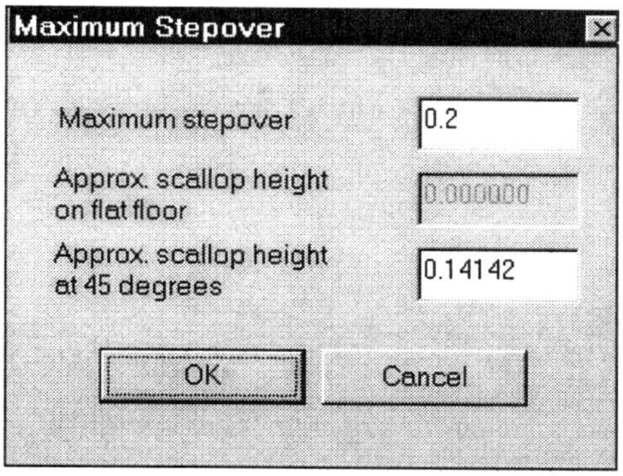

Changing the Maximum stepover value will automatically update the value for the approximate scallop height at a flat floor and the approximate scallop height at 45 degrees.

1

Project 1. Generating toolpaths for rouging cut a surface model using the parallel function

The surface rough-parallel function is used to generate the roughing toolpaths to rough cut the Coons surface shown in Figure 15.32. Both toolpath model and verification model are shown.

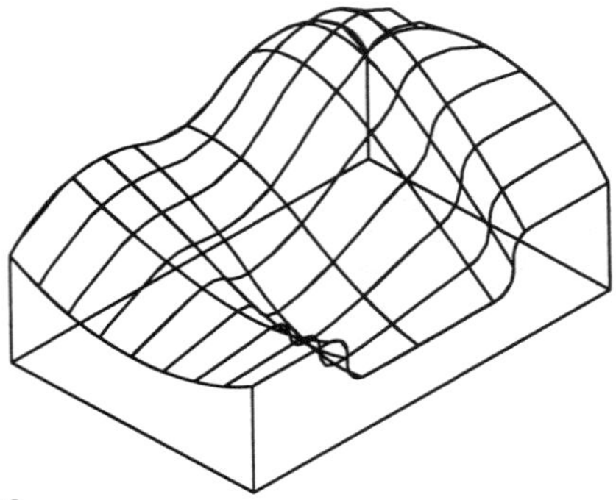

Figure 15.32a

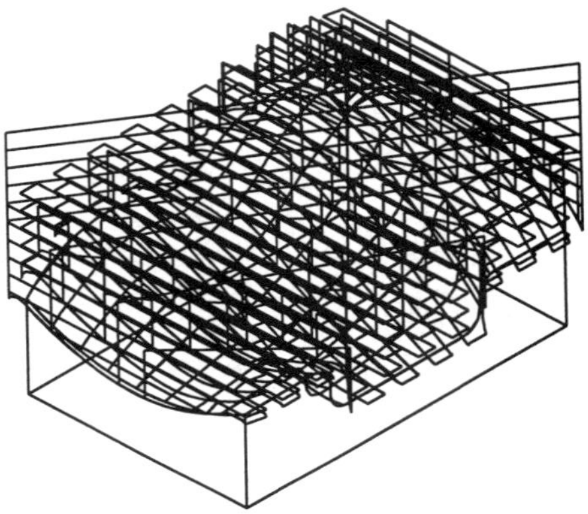

Figure 15.32b

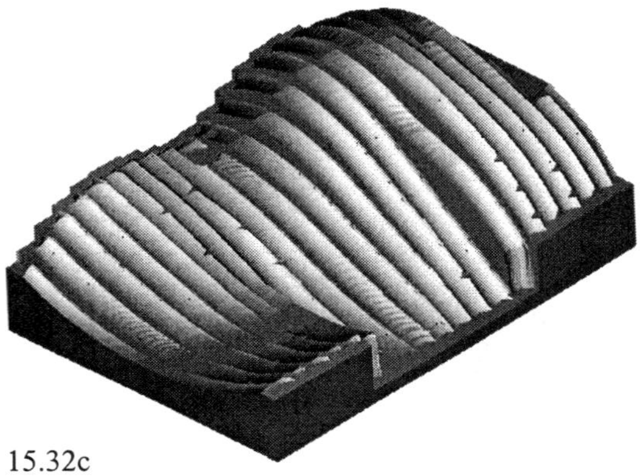

Figure 15.32c

Tips
1. Use the surface model file coonss1.
2. Use Surface-Rough-Parallel function to generate roughing toolpaths.
3. Verify the roughing toolpaths.

Step 1. Open the surface model file coonss1.

Select **File → Get**
File name: **coonss1**
The surface model appears as in Figure 15.33.

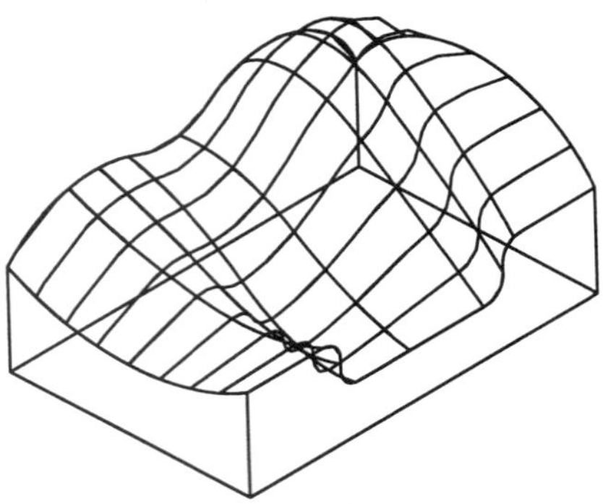

Figure 15.33

Step 2. Initiate the surface rough-parallel function.

Select **Cplane → Top**
Select **MAIN MENU → Toolpaths → Surface → Rough → Parallel**
File name for NCI file: **rough1** Pick the surface → **Done**
Click right mouse button to open the tool library
Select **tool number 235** for (1/4 flat end mill)
Select **OK**
Set the tool parameters as below.

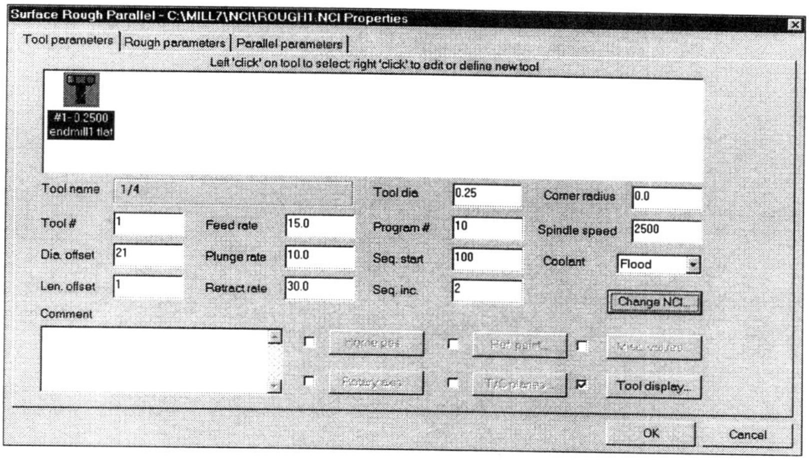

Step 3. Define the roughing parameters.

Click the "**Rough Parameters**" button to open rough parameters dialog box
Set roughing parameters as below.

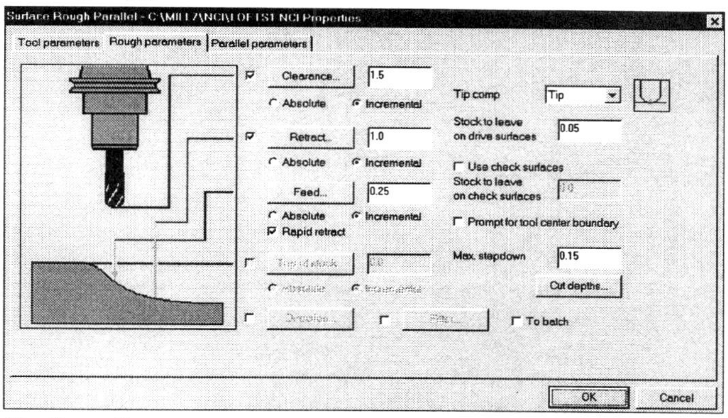

Step 4. Define the cut depth parameters.

Click the "**Cut Depths**" button to open the Cut Depths dialog box
Set cut depth parameters as shown here.

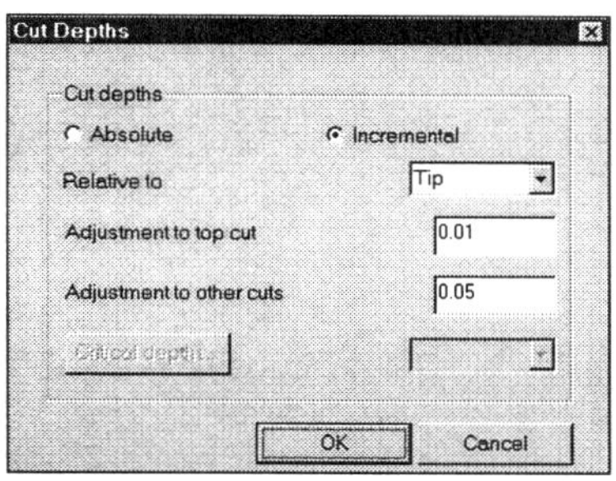

Select **OK** to return to rough parameters dialog box

Step 5. Define the parallel parameters.

Click the "**Parallel parameters**" button

Set the parameter values as below.

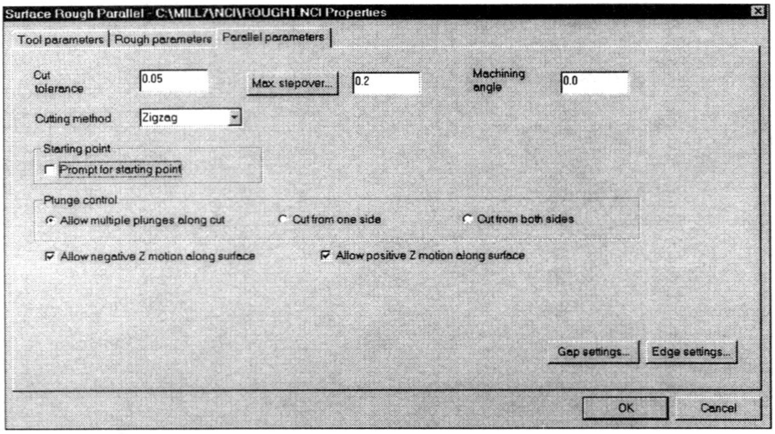

Step 6. Define the gap setting parameters.

Click the "**Gap settings**" button to open its dialog box

Set gap setting parameters as here.

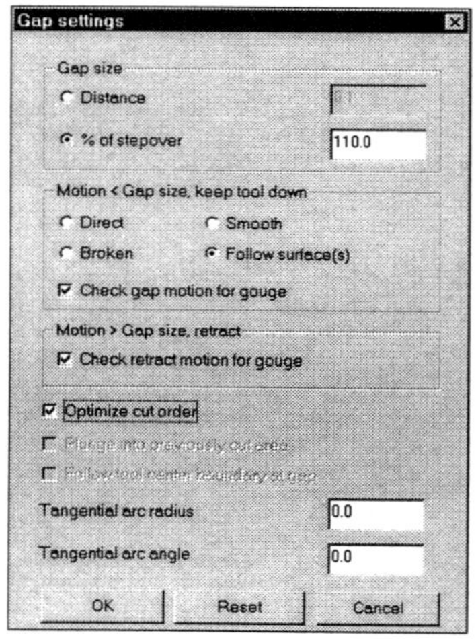

Select **OK**

Step 7. Define the edge setting parameters.

Click the "**Edge settings**" button to open its dialog box

Set edge setting parameters as below.

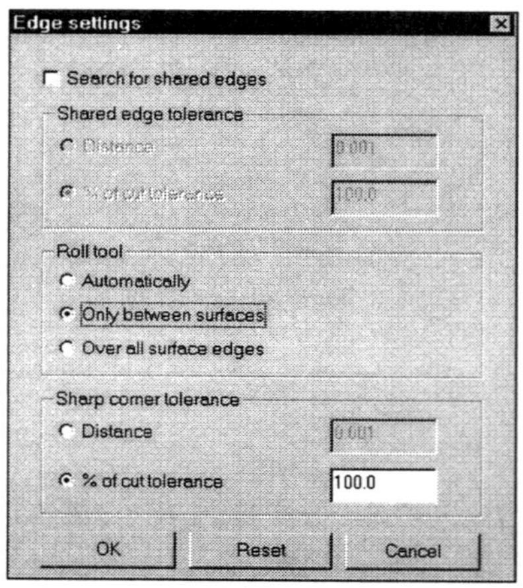

Select **OK → OK**

The roughing toolpaths are added to the model as shown in Figure 15.34.

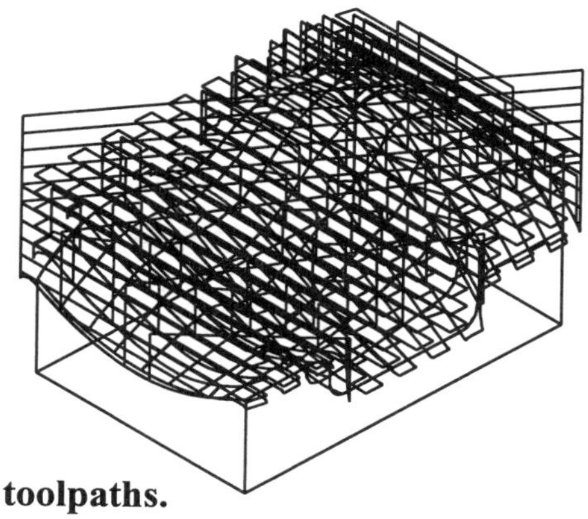

Figure 15.34

Step 8. Verify the roughing toolpaths.

Select **MAIN MENU → Toolpaths → Operations**

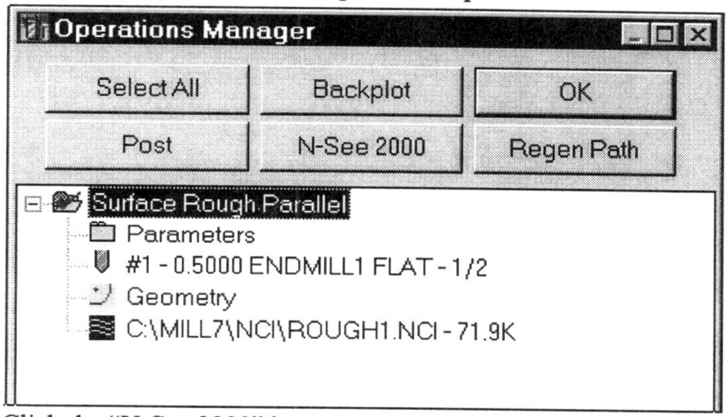

Click the "**N-See 2000**" button

Set "Select mode for current job" dialog box as shown here.

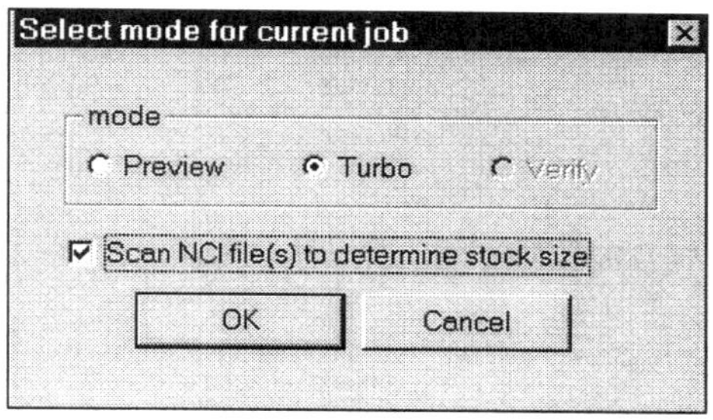

Select **OK**

Select **Do it**

The verification model should resemble Figure 15.35.

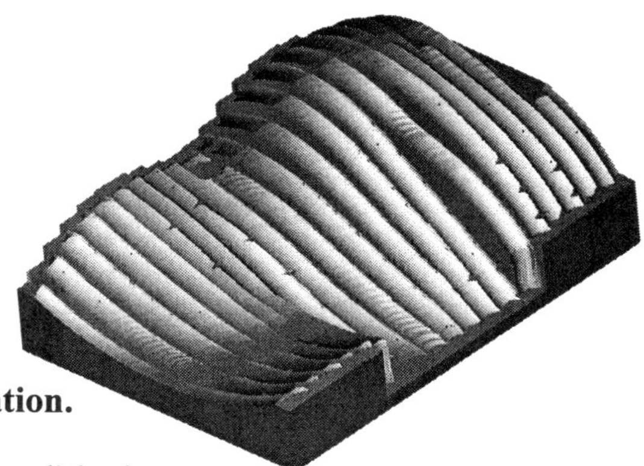

Figure 15.35

Step 9. Complete the roughing operation.

Select **BACKUP**

Select **OK** from the Operations Manager dialog box

15.7 Rough Radial Function

The radial function generates a set of toolpaths for roughing cut the surface model. The toolpaths are arranged in the radial pattern. The radial parameters dialog box is shown below.

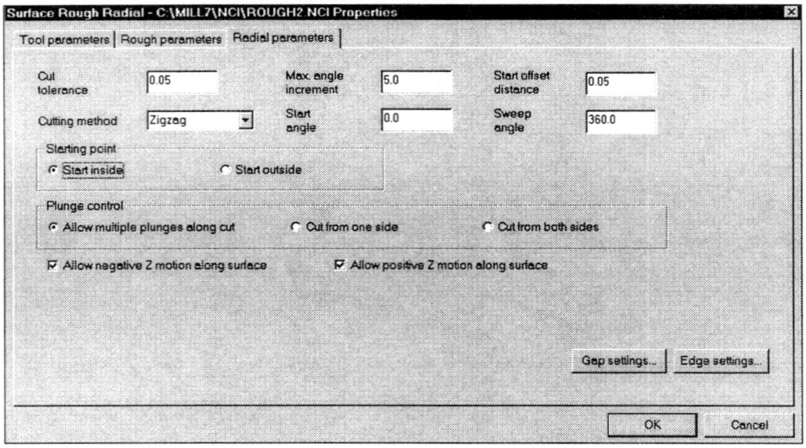

The three angle parameters to be defined in this roughing option are (Figure 15.36):

Maximum angle increment:	specify the angle value to be incremented for each path.
Start angle:	specify the starting angle of roughing paths.
Sweep angle:	specify the sweep angle range of roughing paths.

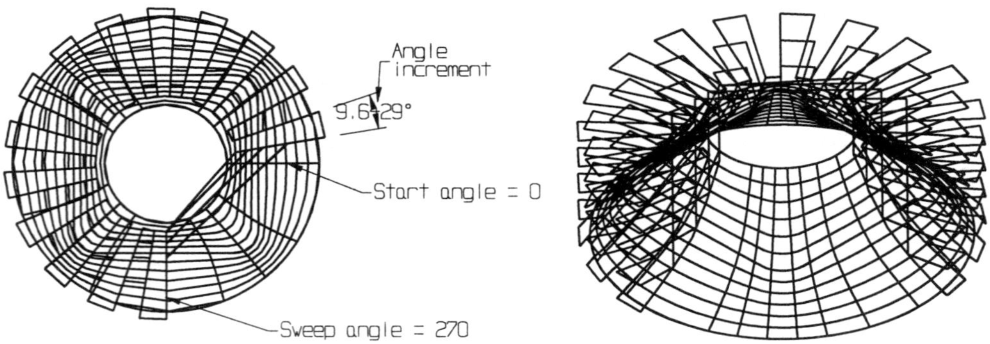

Figure 15.36

The "Starting point" parameter is used to specify the starting point and its direction of roughing paths. It has two the following two options:

Start inside: The roughing paths starts from the start point and cuts toward outside.

Start outside: The roughing paths starts from outside boundary of the starting angle and cuts toward inside.

2 Project 2. Generating roughing toolpaths for a surface model using radial function

This project uses the surface radial-rough function to generate toolpaths for roughing the dryer surface model as shown in Figure 15.37. The incremental angle is 5 degrees and maximum stepover distance is 0.2".

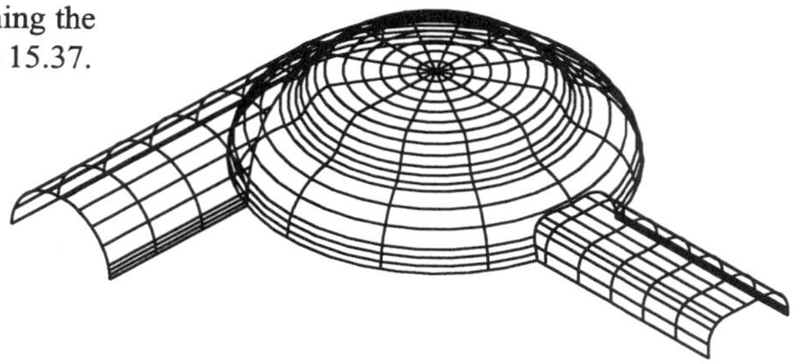

Figure 15.37a

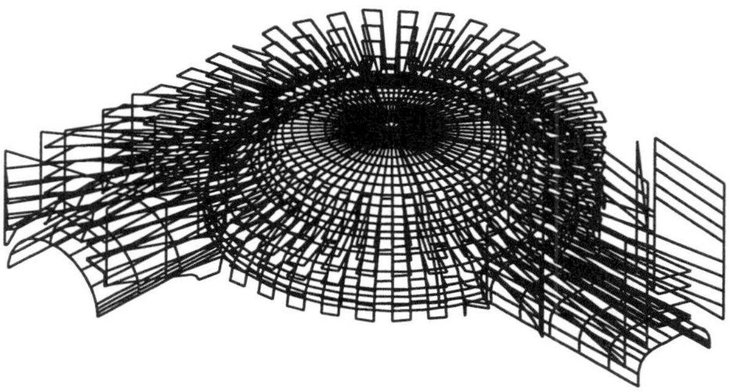

Figure 15.37b

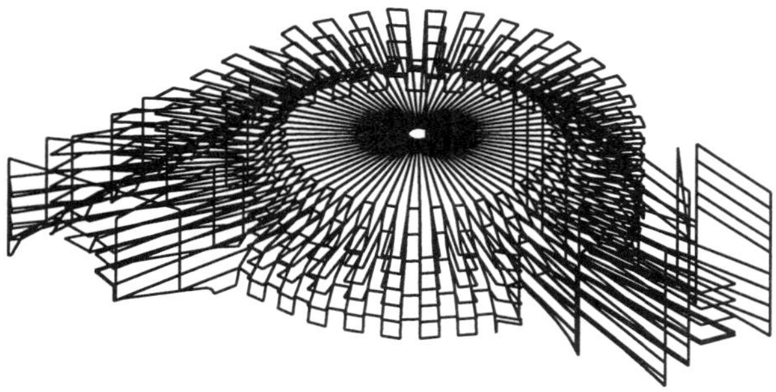

Figure 15.31c

Tips	1. Open the surface model file dryers.
	2. Use the surface radial-rough function to generate the roughing toolpaths.
	3. Use a ½" flat end mill.

Step 1. Open the surface model file "dryers".

Select **MAIN MENU → File → Get**
File name: **dryers**
The dryer surface model appears as in Figure 15.38.

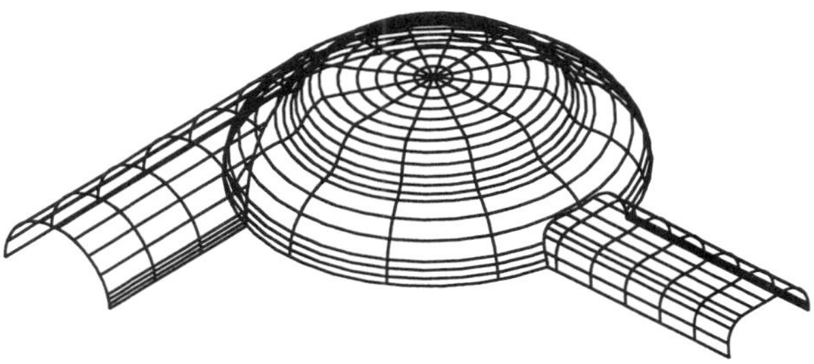

Figure 15.38

Step 2. Initiate the radial roughing function.

Select **Cplane → Top**
Select **MAIN MENU → Toolpaths → Surface → Rough → Radial**
File name: **rough2**
Select **All → Surfaces → Done**
The Surface Rough Radial dialog box should appear.
Click the right mouse button, then select **"Get tool from library"**
Select **tool number 239** (for ½" flat endmill)
Select **OK** to return back to the Tool parameters dialog box. Set tool parameters as below.

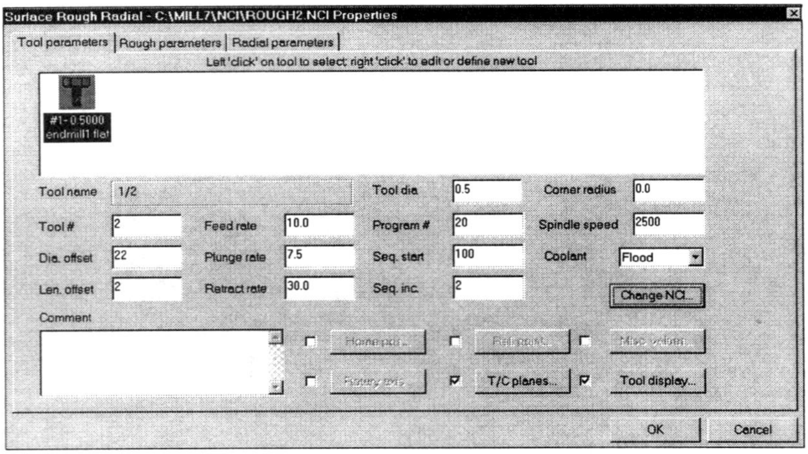

Step 3. Define rough parameters.

Click the "**Rough parameters**" button
Set rough parameters as below.

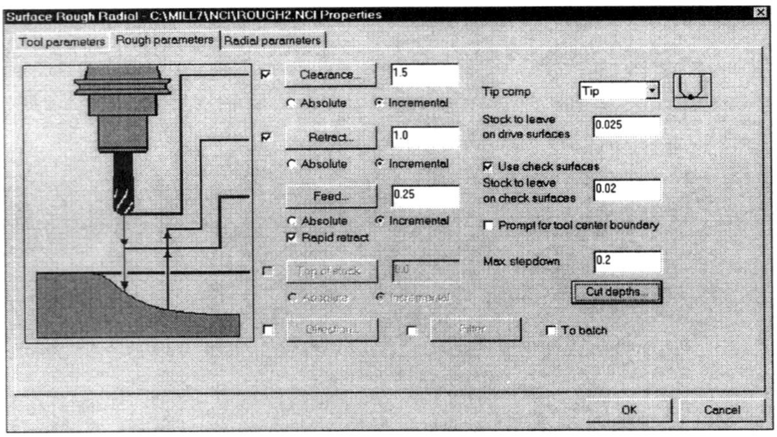

Step 4. Define the cut depth parameters.

Click the "**Cut depths**" button
Set the cut depth parameters as below.

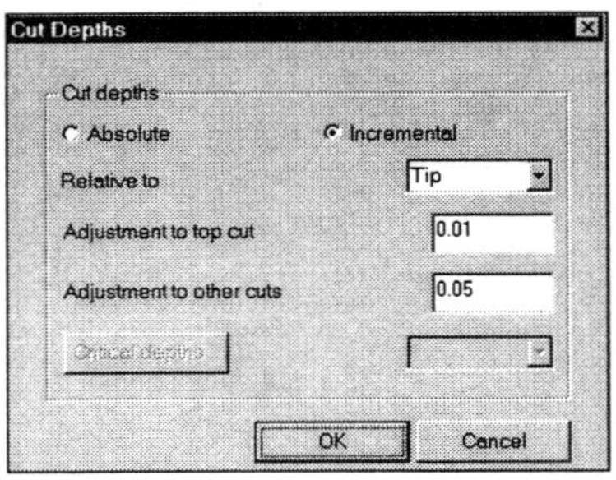

Select **OK**

Step 5. Define Radial parameters.

Click the "**Radial parameters**" button

Set radial parameters to the following settings.

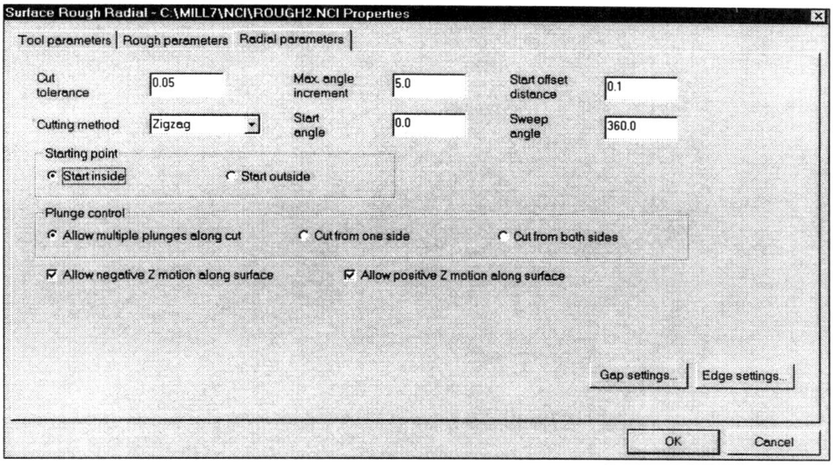

Step 6. Set gap setting parameters.

Click the "**Gap settings**" button

Set gap setting parameters as below.

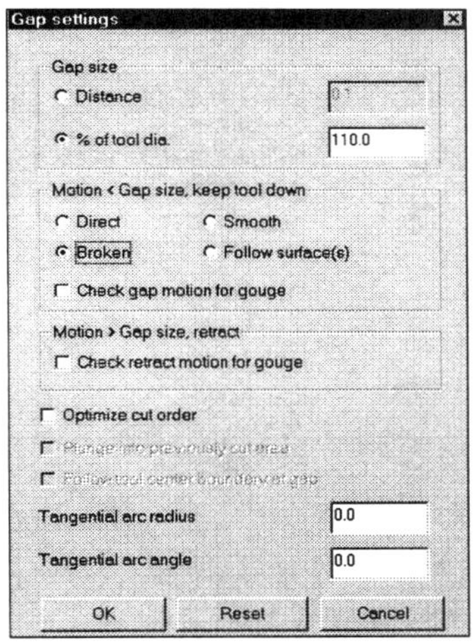

Select **OK**

Step 7. Define edge setting parameters.

Click the "**Edge settings**" button

Set edge setting parameters as below.

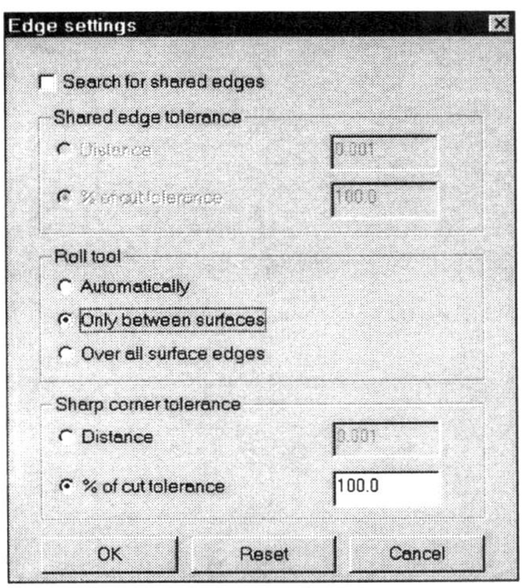

Select **OK → OK**

Step 8. Specify the rotation point.

Select **Endpoint**, then pick a line entity on the top flat surface of the model The roughing toolpaths run in radial pattern are generated as in Figure 15.39.

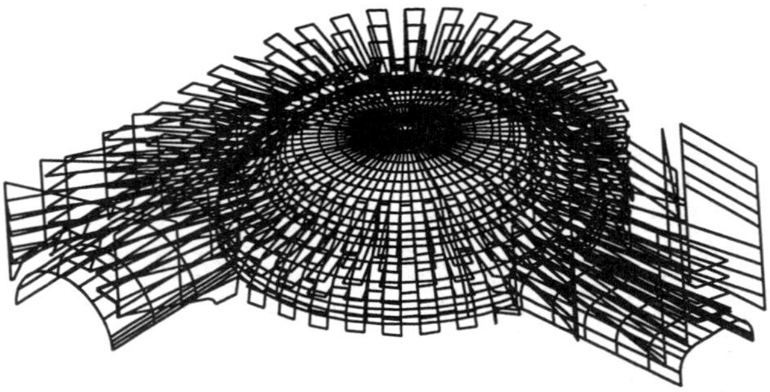

Figure 15.39

Figure 15.40 shows the roughing toolpaths without the surface model.

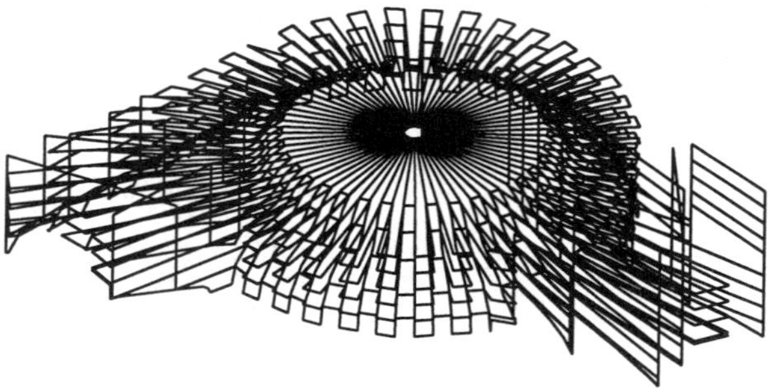

Figure 15.40

Step 9. Close the toolpath file.

Select **Operations → OK**

15.8 Rough Project Function

This rough function projects an existing set of toolpath files or geometry entities onto a surface model to generate the roughing toolpaths for cutting the model. This function provides free-form tool motion and excellent tool control. Three types of entities can be used for projection; **NCI**, **curves**, and **points**. They are described below:

NCI:	use an existing NCI file to project (Figure 15.41).
Curves:	use a curve or set of curves to project. Valid curves include splines and surface curves (Figure 15.42).
Points:	use a point or set of points to project (Figure 15.43).

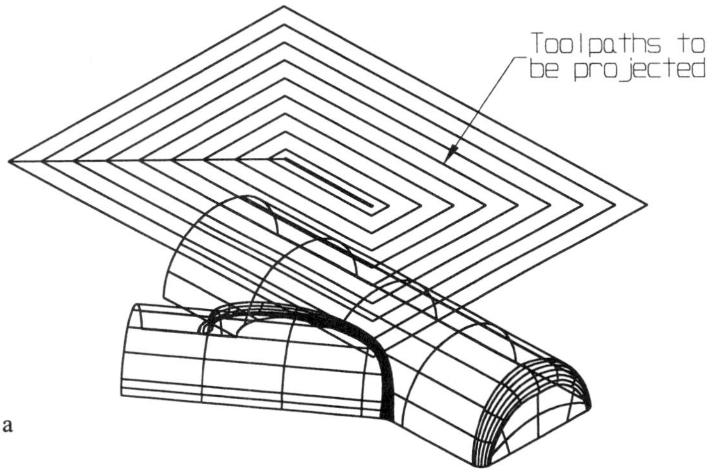

Figure 15.41a

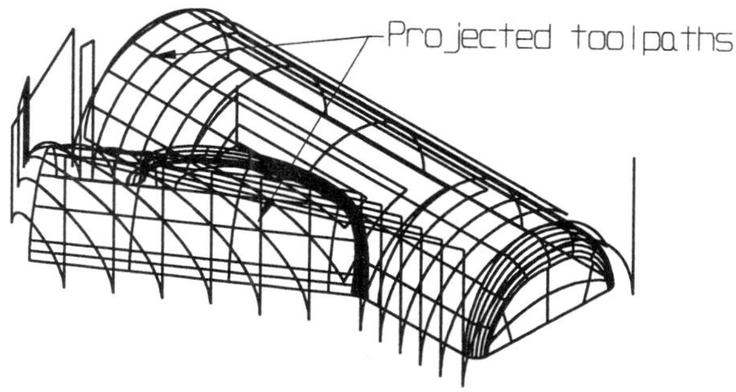

Figure 15.41b

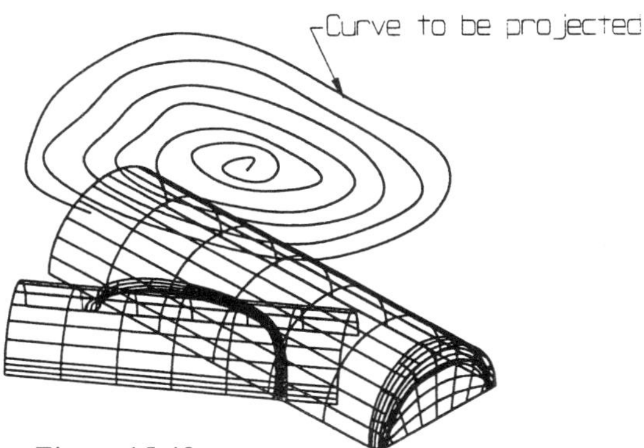

Figure 15.42a

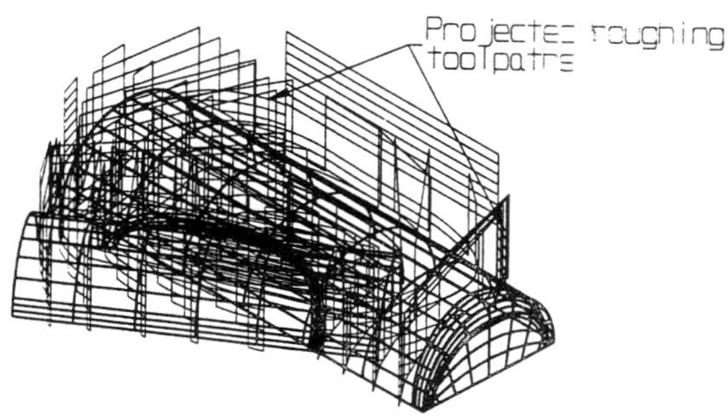

Figure 15.42b

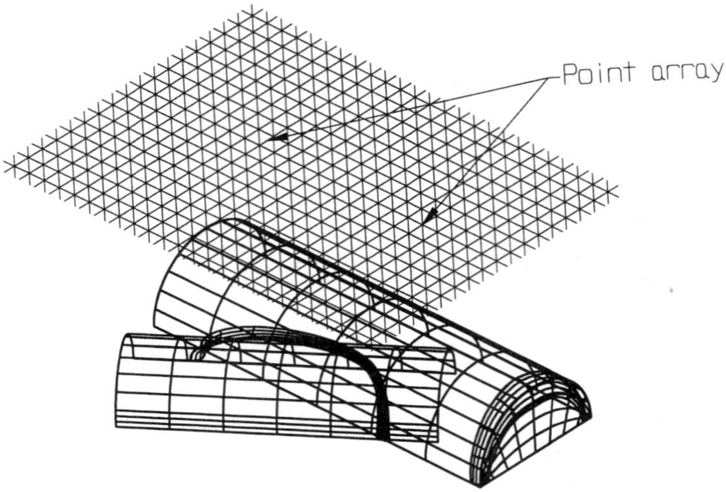

Figure 15.43a

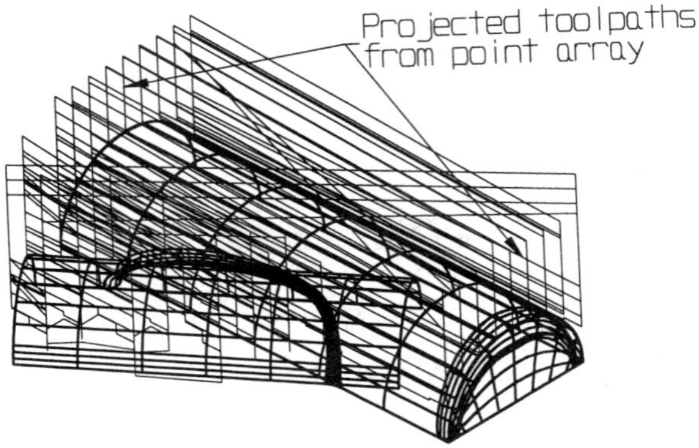

Figure 15.43b

The above three entity types used for projection must be created prior to using the project function. The dialog box for rough project function is shown below.

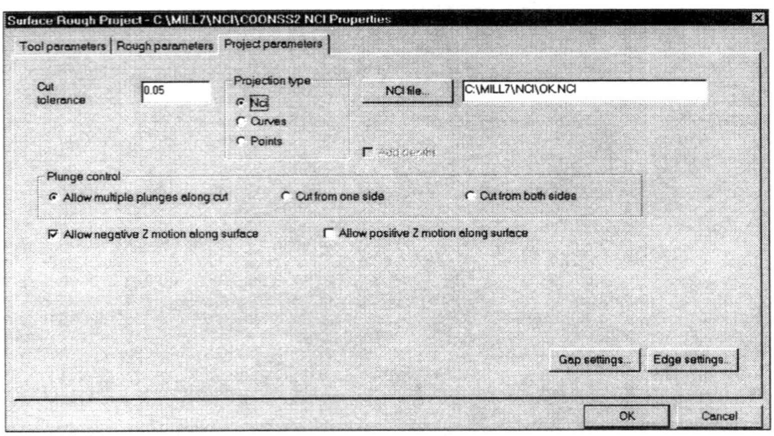

Project 3. Generating roughing toolpaths using project function

A point array is used as the projection entities to generate the toolpaths for doing a roughing cut of a Coons surface model (Figure 15.44).

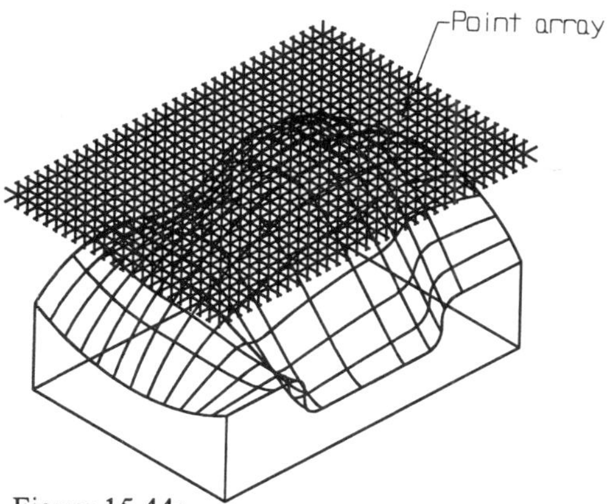

Figure 15.44a

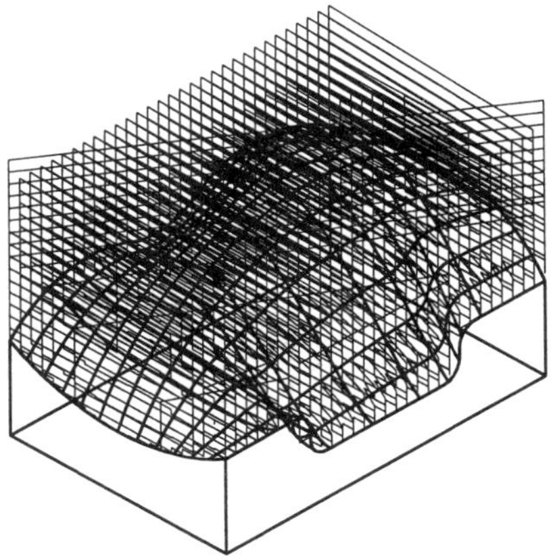

Figure 15.44b

Tips
1. Use the surface model file coonss2.
2. Create a point array with an increment of 0.25" in both X and Y directions. The number of points in horizontal direction is 22 and in vertical direction is 32.
3. Use the rough-project – point function to generate roughing toolpaths.
4. Use a ¼" flat end mill.

Step 1. Open the surface model file coonss2.

Select **MAIN MENU → File → Get**
File name: **coonss2**
The surface model appears as in Figure 15.45.

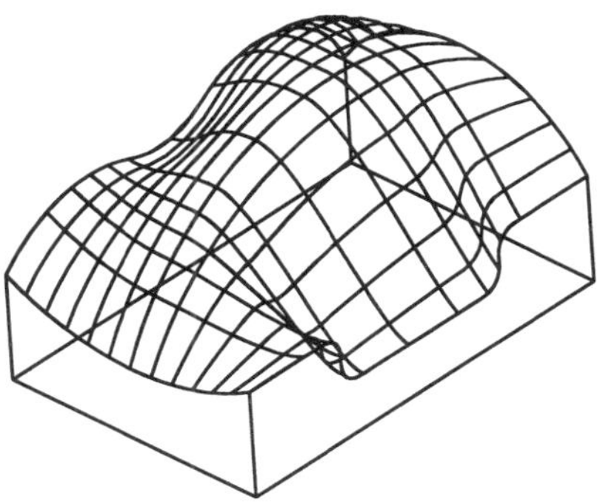

Figure 15.45

Step 2. Create a point array.

Select **Level**, then enter **3**
Select **Z**, then enter **2.5**
Select **MAIN MENU → Create → Point → Grid**
Enter the lower left corner: **-0.25, -0.25**

Enter the distance between points in the horizontal direction: **0.25**
Enter the distance between points in the vertical direction: **0.25**
Enter the angle: **0**
Enter number of points in the horizontal direction: **22**
Enter number of points in the vertical direction: **32**

The point array is added to the model as shown in Figure 15.46.

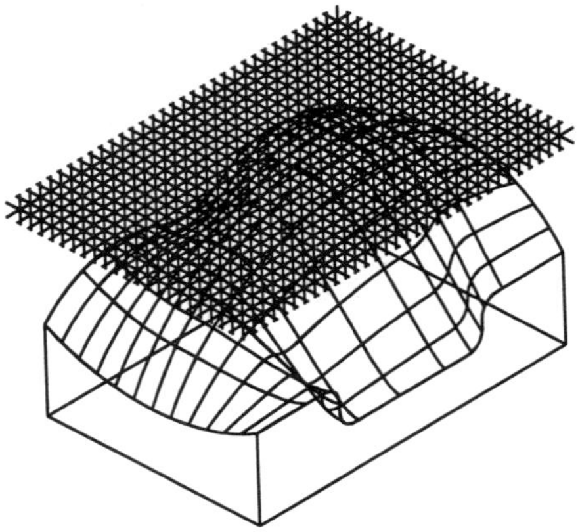

Figure 15.46

Step 3. Initiate the project function.

Select **MAIN MENU → Toolpaths → Surface → Rough → Project**
File name: **rough3**
Select **All → Surfaces → Done**
The Tool parameters dialog box should appear on the screen.
Click the right mouse button, then select **"Get tool from library"**
Select **tool number 235** (1/4 end mill)
Select **OK**
Set Tool parameters as below.

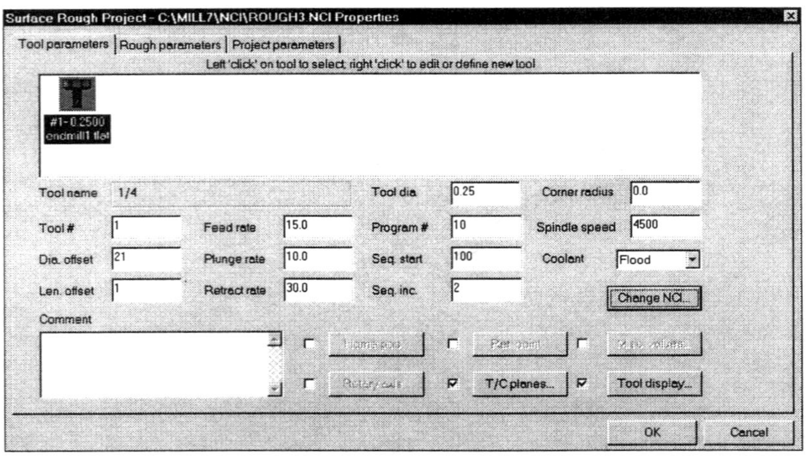

Step 4. Define rough parameters.

Click the "**Rough parameters**" button

Set rough parameters as below.

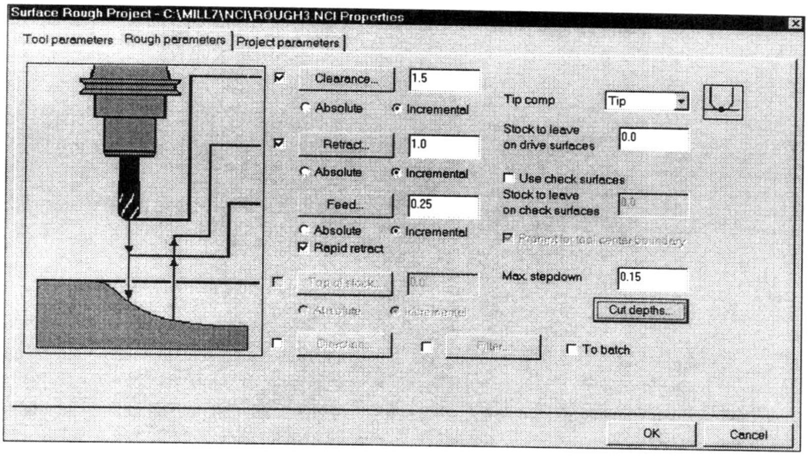

Step 5. Define project parameters.

Click the "**Project parameters**" button

Set project parameters as below.

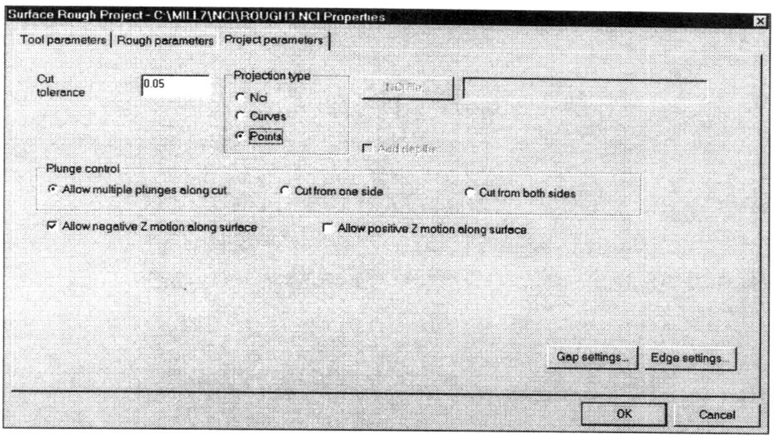

Step 6. Generate roughing toolpaths.

Select **OK**

Select **All → Points → Done**

The roughing toolpaths are generated as shown in Figure 15.47.

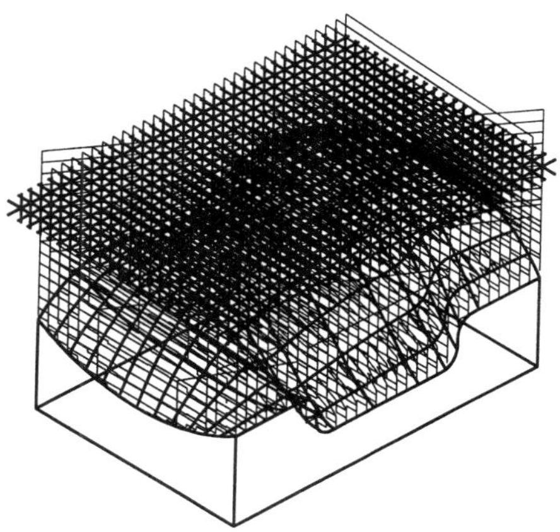

Figure 15.47

Step 7. Delete the point array.

Select **MAIN MENU → Delete → All → Points**

The surface model with the roughing toolpaths is shown in Figure 15.48.

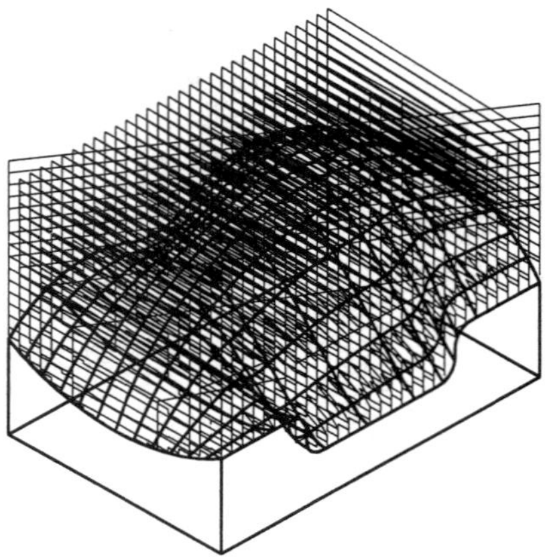

Figure 15.48

15.9 Rough Flowline Function

Rough flowline function generates a set of toolpaths for roughing a surface or set of surfaces. This surface roughing function allows precise control of the scallop height left on the surface(s). It can be used to create a smooth finish. The dialog box for flowline rough function is shown below.

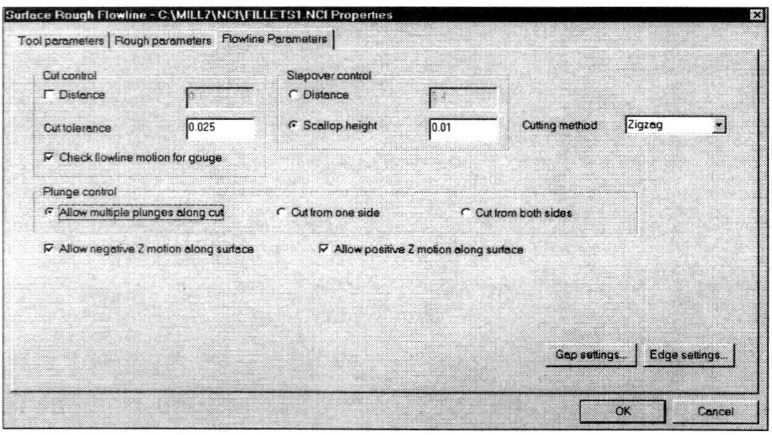

Tolerances

Surface cutting uses the principle of linear interpolation to approximate a surface. Its toolpaths can be controlled in two directions using the flowline method: **along direction** and **across direction**. Mastercam uses two parameters in this roughing function to define the tolerances in these two cutting directions: **cut control** and **stepover control**. The cut control is used to control the tool motion in the along direction, while the stepover control is used to control the tool motion in the across direction (Figure 15.49).

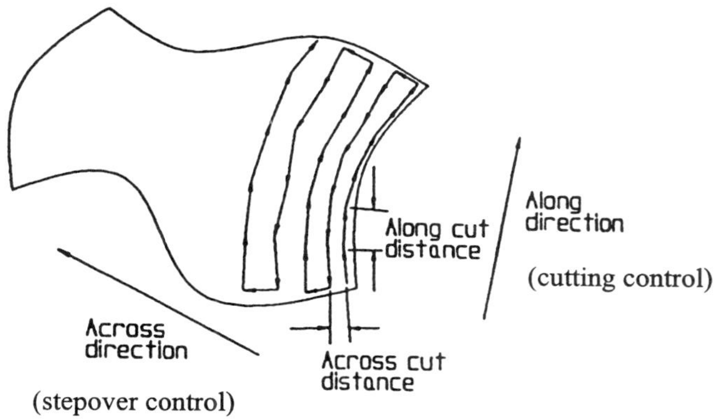

Figure 15.49

Each tolerance parameter has two methods in determining the stepping distance of the toolpath over the surfaces: **distance increment method** and **cut tolerance** (or scallop height) **method**.

Distance increment method: The "Distance in cut control" parameter specifies the stepover interval between two adjacent paths in the along direction. The "Distance in stepover control" parameter decides the stepover interval in the across direction.

Cut tolerance and scallop height method: The cut tolerance is the distance between the actual toolpath and the true surface in the along direction (Figure 15.50). This parameter is referred to as cut tolerance in Mastercam and is also commonly called as chordal deviation. The given cut tolerance value is the maximum allowable dimensional error between the toolpath and the surface. It is used to calculate the cutting increment in the along direction.

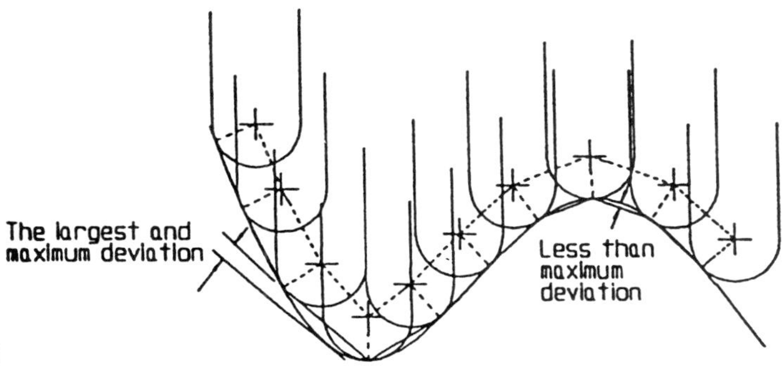

Figure 15.50

When a cutter with a non-flat end, such as a spherical end mill, is used to cut a surface in a zigzag pattern, an uncut strip results between the two adjacent cutting passes as shown in Figure 15.51. The height of these undesirable strips is called scallop height. The larger the stepover value between the two cutting passes, the bigger the scallop height. The given maximum scallop height value is used to calculate the cutter stepover distance in the across direction (or between each along cut). Mastercam uses scallop height to determine the stepping distance over surfaces.

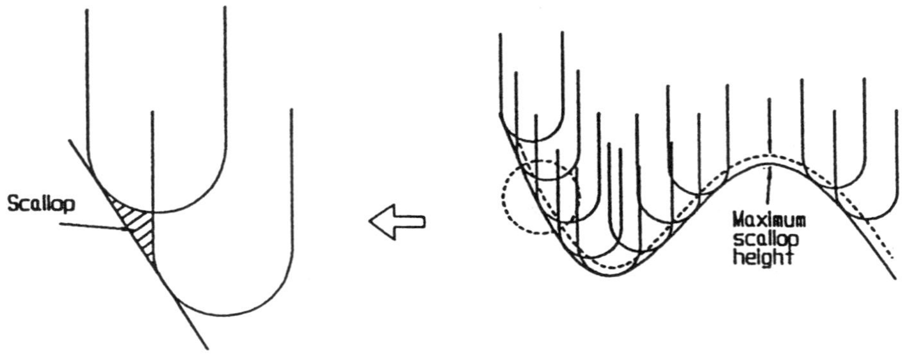

Figure 15.51

Tips for selecting the stepping over methods:

1. Use the distance increment method when the surface has relatively large curvature radii, has no sharp shapes, or does not require a close dimensional accuracy (Figure 15.52).

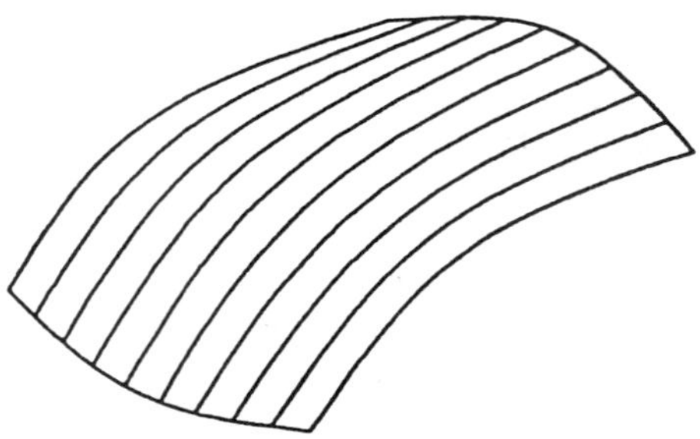

Figure 15.52

2. Use cut tolerance and scallop height method for those surfaces that have small curvature radii, have sharp shapes, or require a close tolerance (Figure 15.53). This method can accurately produce the surface within the specified dimensional accuracy.

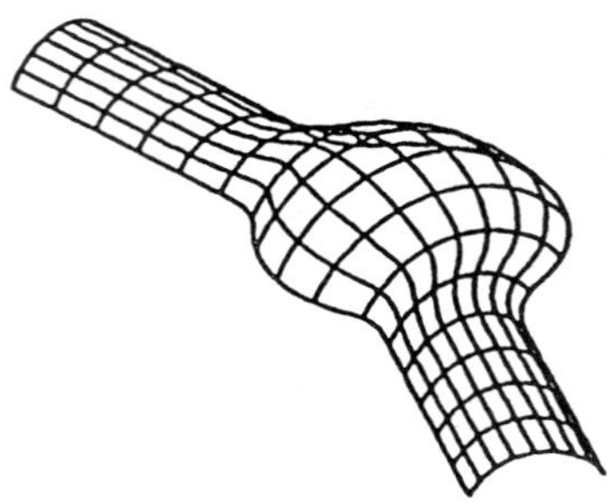

Figure 15.53

3. Computer processing time is significantly shorter when using the distance increment method than with the cut tolerance and scallop height method.

There are four flip options in flowline roughing function that allow to specify the offset direction, cut and step directions, and start point of the cutting. They are briefly described next.

Offset: flip the tool radius offset direction between the two direction of surface normal (Figure 15.54).
Cut dir: flip the toolpath direction between two cut directions, along or across (Figure 15.55).
Step dir: flip the toolpath starting corner of each surface to set the direction in which the tool movements of the flowline toolpath occur (Figure 15.56).
Start: flip the toolpath start point for each surface between two ends of cut direction of flowline (Figure 15.57).

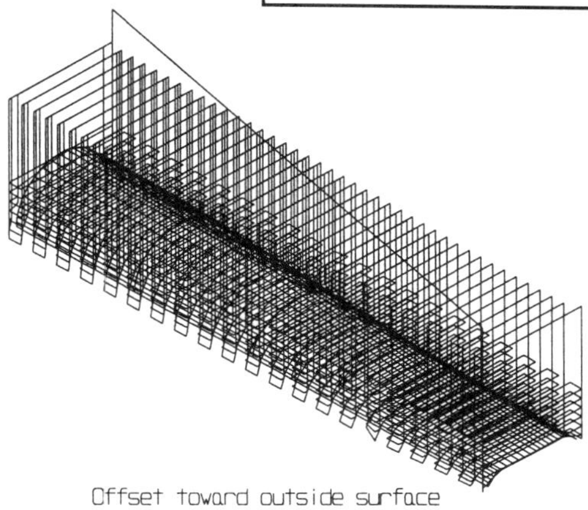

Figure 15.54a

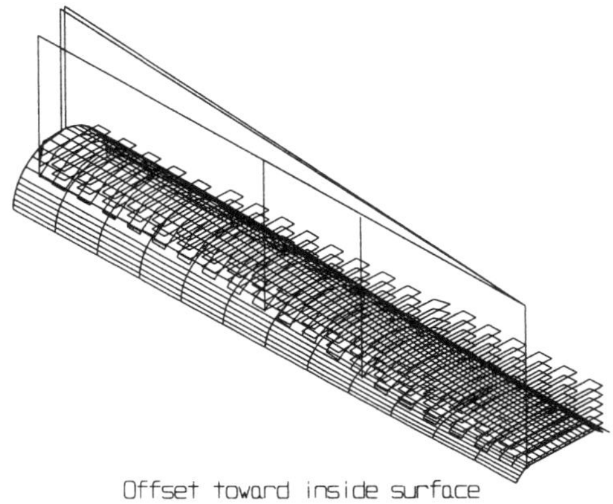

Figure 15.54b

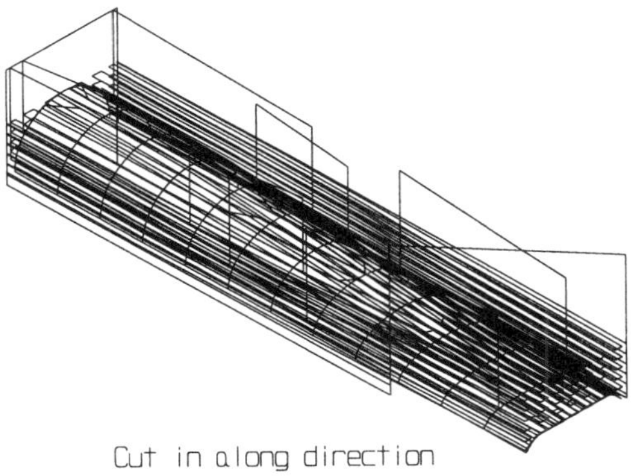

Figure 15.55a

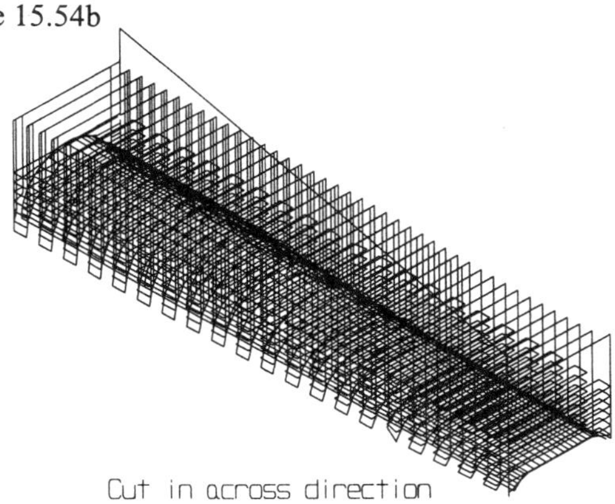

Figure 15.55b

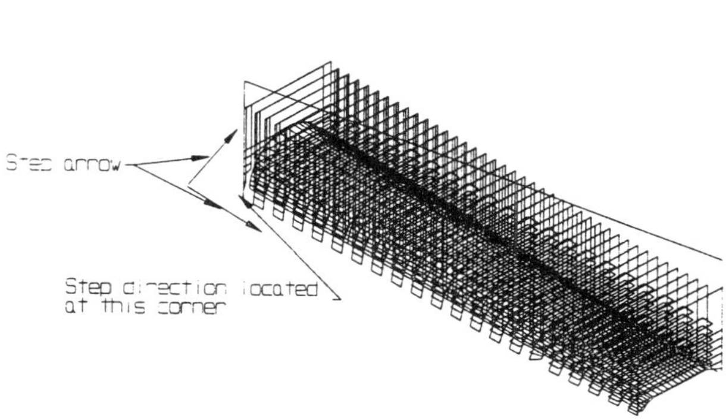

Figure 15.56a

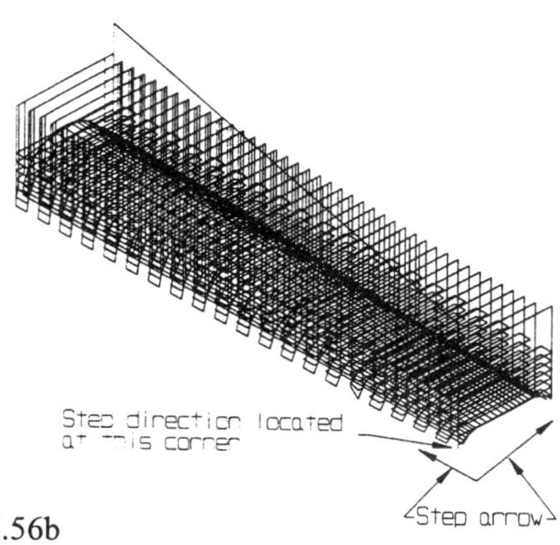

Figure 15.56b

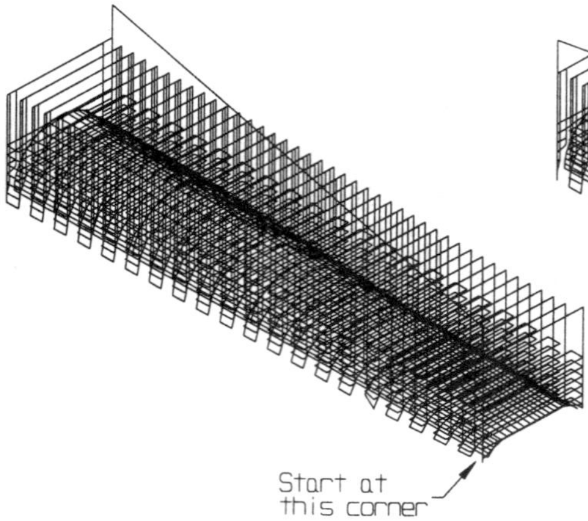

Figure 15.57a

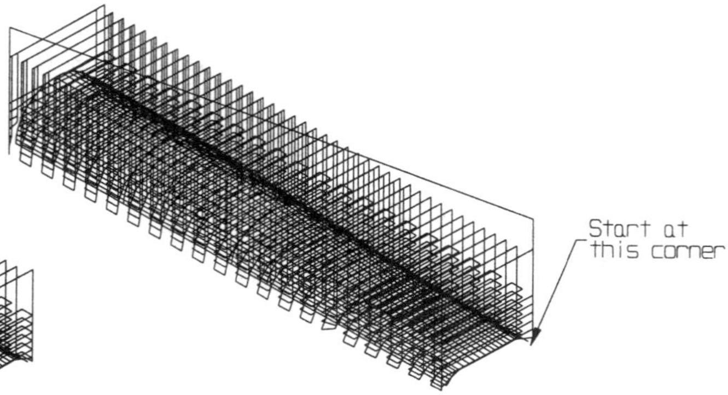

Figure 15.57b

The other parameter "Plot edges" is used to show shared surface edges and touch points using the following colors:

Color	Edges or points
Light blue lines	Free edges
Light cyan lines	Partially shared edges
Light red lines	Fully shared edges
Light blue points	Touch point projected onto adjacent surface

It is possible to simultaneously generate roughing toolpaths for multiple-surface model in one operation (Figure 15.58).

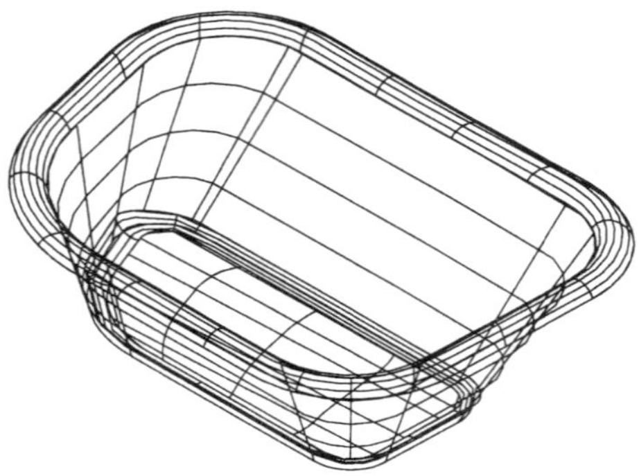

Figure 15.58a

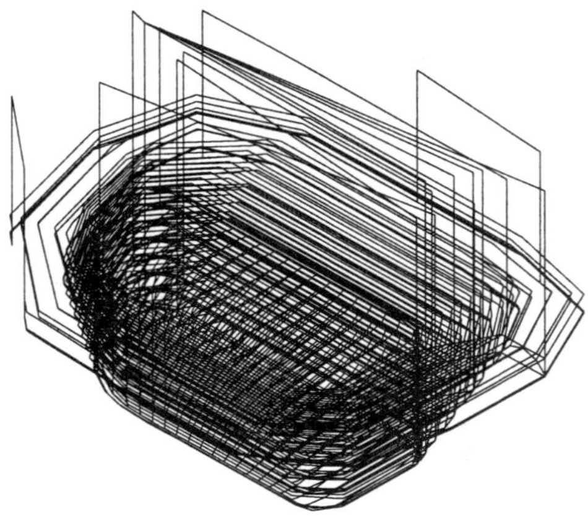

Figure 15.58b

Project 4. Generating roughing toolpaths using flowline function

4

The surface model to be rough cut consists of four surfaces including two ruled surfaces and two fillet surfaces (Figure 15.59). The rough-flowline function is used to generate toolpaths to rough cut these four surfaces simultaneously.

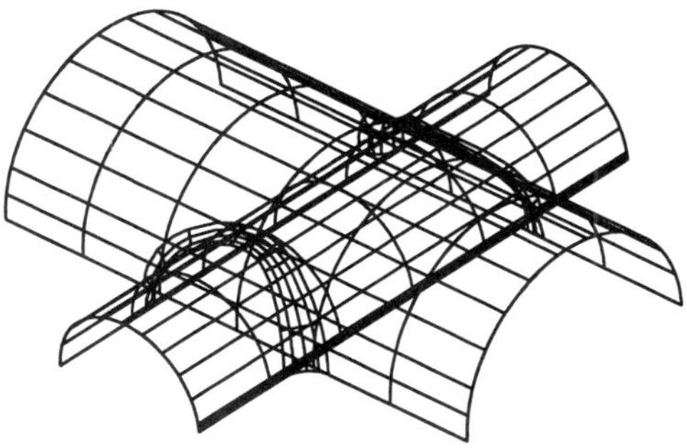

Figure 15.59a

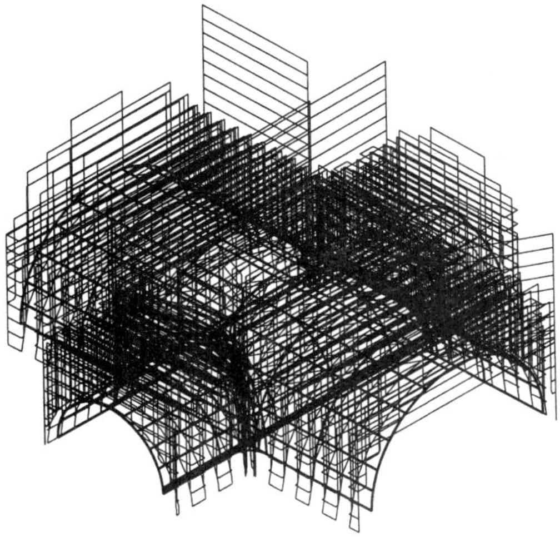

Figure 15.59b

Tips
1. Use the surface model file fillets1.
2. Use a 3/8" spherical end mill.
3. Use surface rough-flowline function.
4. Set the cut tolerance to 0.02" and maximum stepdown value 0.2".

Step 1. Open the surface model file fillets1.

Select **MAIN MENU → File → Get**
File name: **fillets1**
The surface model appears as in Figure 15.60.

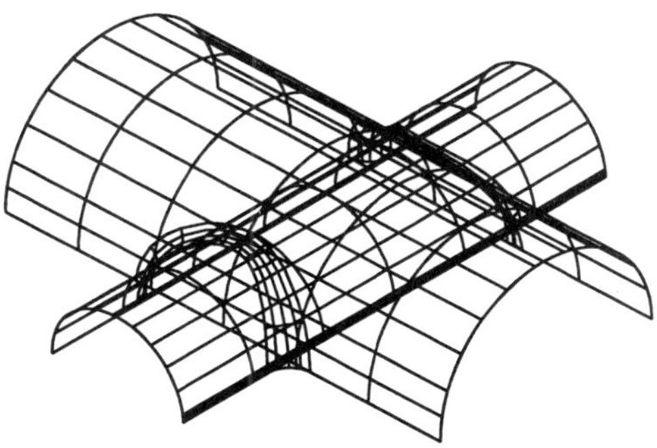

Figure 15.60

Step 2. Initiate the rough-flowline function.

Select **Cplane → Top**
Select **MAIN MENU → Toolpaths → Surface → Rough → Flowline**
File name for toolpath: **rough4**
Select **All → Surfaces → Done**

Step 3. Define the tool parameters as below.

Follow the procedure to select a **0.375" sphere endmill** (Tool **#254**)
Set the tool parameters as below.

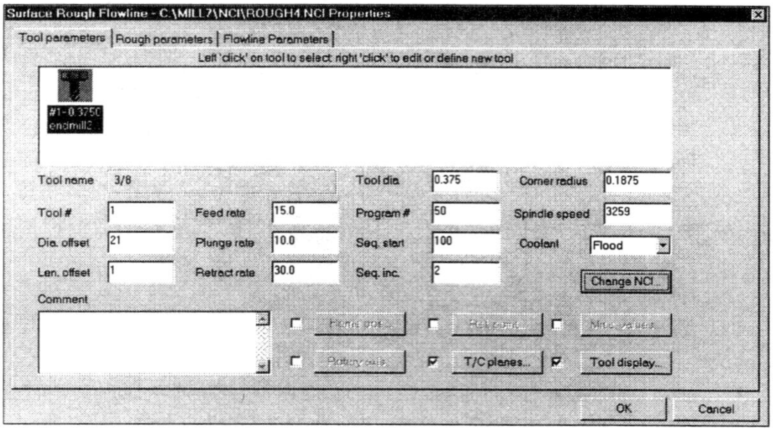

Step 4. Define the rough parameters.

Click the "**Rough parameters**" button
Define the rough parameters as below.

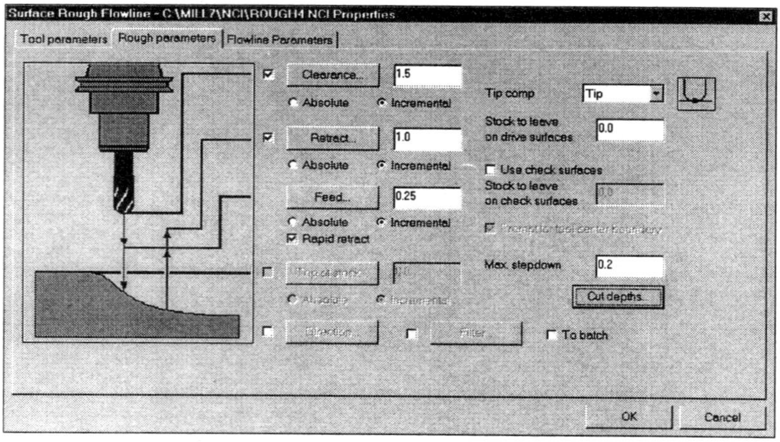

Step 5. Define the flowline parameters.

Select the "**Flowline Parameters**" button

Set the flowline parameters as below.

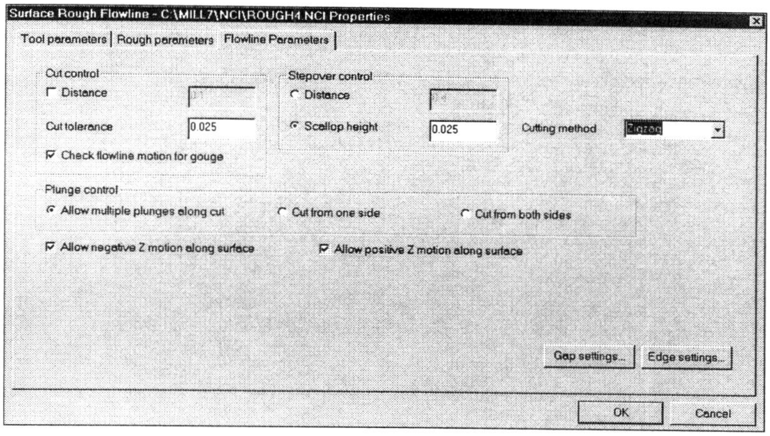

Select **OK → Do it**
The roughing toolpaths are generated as in Figure 15.61.

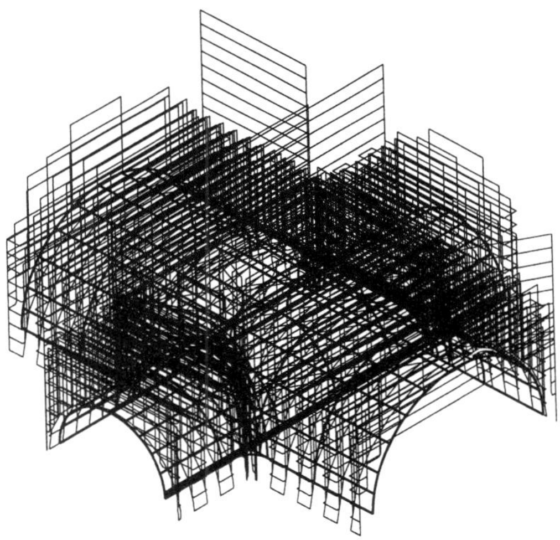

Figure 15.61

Step 6. Save the roughing toolpaths.

Select **NC utils → Edit NCI**
Select **Yes** to "Operations have been modified. Create the NCI text file?"
The Edit NCI dialog box with file ROUGH4.NCI should appear
Select **Quit** to exit the Edit NCI function

15.10 Rough Contour Function

The contour rough function generates toolpaths to rough cut a surface model around its contour (Figure 15.62). This rough function generates toolpaths to cut the surface model in only one level. It is best suited for roughing those surface models in which the workpiece has been cast or forged to approximated shape and size. The rough contour dialog box is shown below.

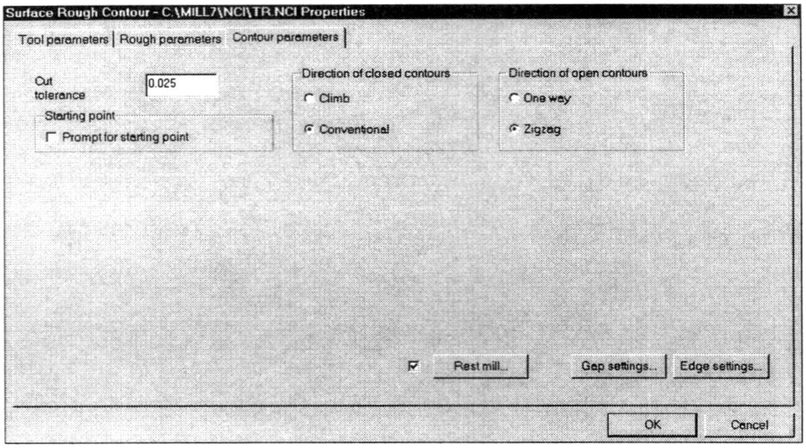

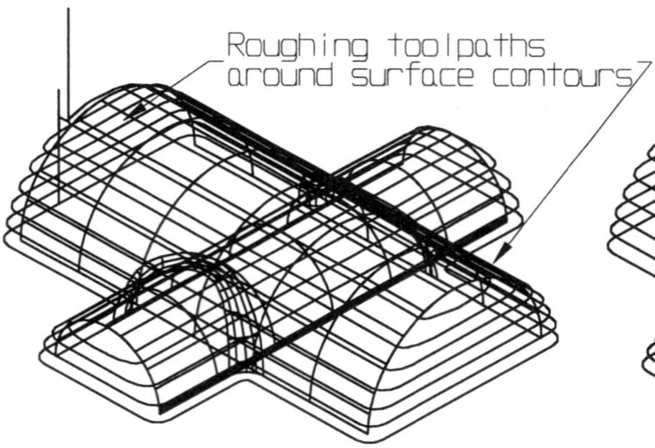

Figure 15.62a

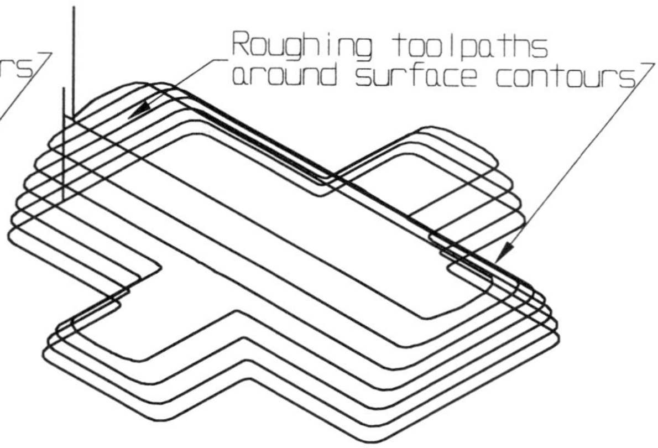

Figurte 15.62b

Three parameters that are unique to this contour rough function are:

- **Direction of closed contours**
- **Direction of open contours**
- **Rest mill**

The system will create a set of contours around the surfaces to generate toolpaths based on the given conditions. There are two types of contours: **closed contour** and **open contour**. A closed contour has its first element and last element connected (Figure 15.63). The first element and last element are not connected in an open contour (Figure 15.64). The "Roll tool" parameter in the Edge settings dialog box is the parameter which determines whether closed contours or open contours are generated.

Roll tool option	Contour type
Automatically	Open contours
Only between surfaces	Open contours
Over all surface edges	Closed contours

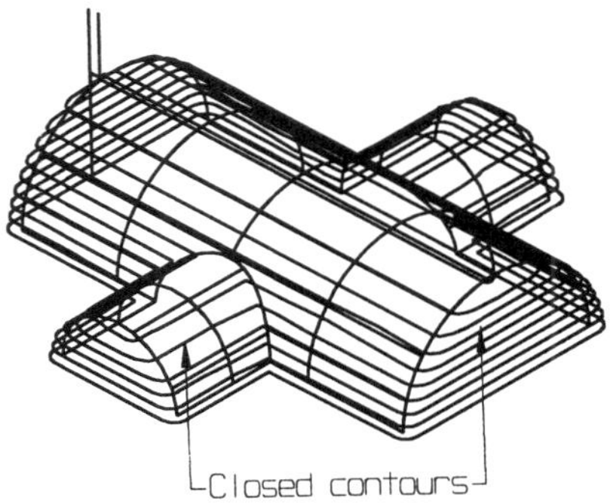

Figure 15.63

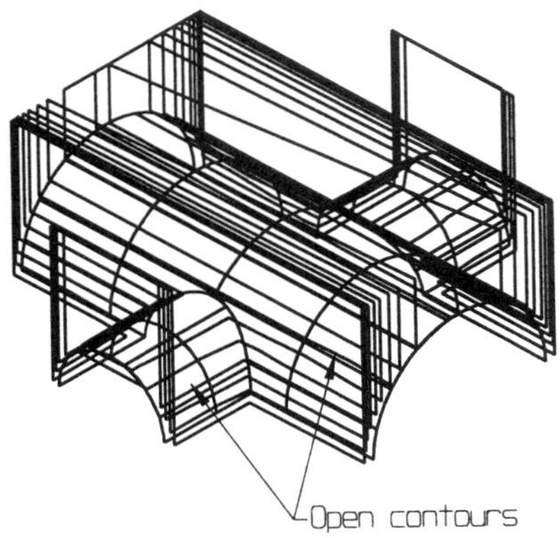

Figure 15.64

Direction of closed contours

This parameter specifies the cutting directions of the surface contour toolpaths for closed contours. It has two options: **climb** and **conventional**. In climb cuts, the tool cuts the surface contours in the direction in which the tool rotating in a direction opposite of the direction of the cutter travels. In conventional cuts, the tool cuts the surface contours in the direction in which the tool rotating in the same direction as the cutter travels.

Direction of open contours

This parameter specifies the cutting patterns of the surface contour toolpaths for open contours. It has two options: one way and zigzag.

Rest mill

This parameter provides options for cutting previously machined areas of a surface contour toolpaths. Click "Rest mill" button to open "Rest mill" dialog box as shown below.

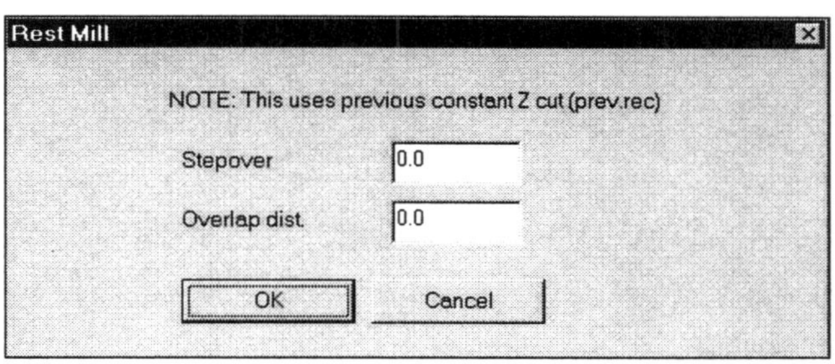

5 Project 5. Generating roughing toolpaths using rough-contour function

The rough-contour function is used to generate toolpaths for roughing a loft surface (Figure 15.65). The roughing toolpaths consist of only one level as shown in Figure 15.65c.

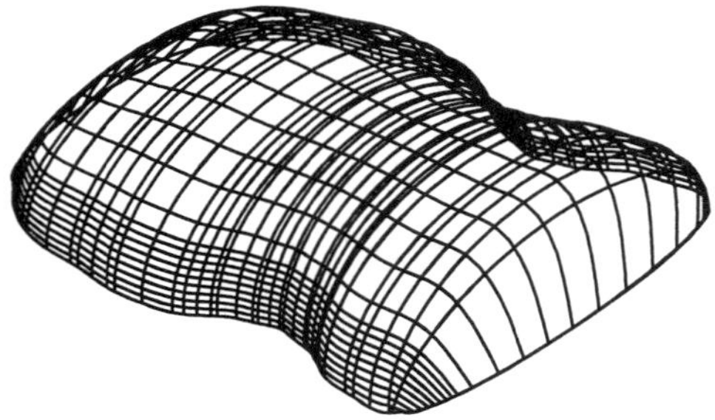

Figure 15.65a

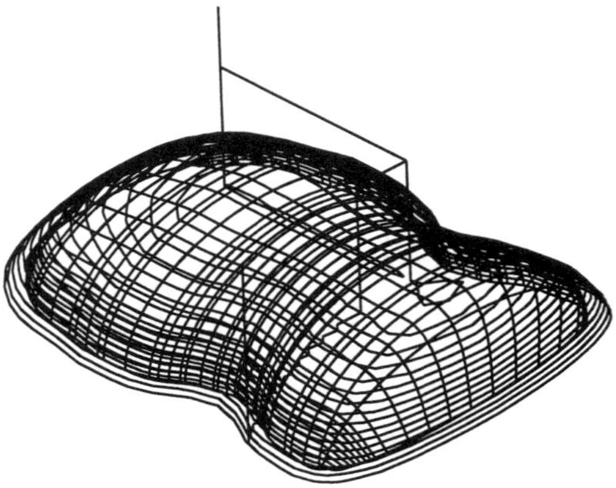

Figure 15.65b

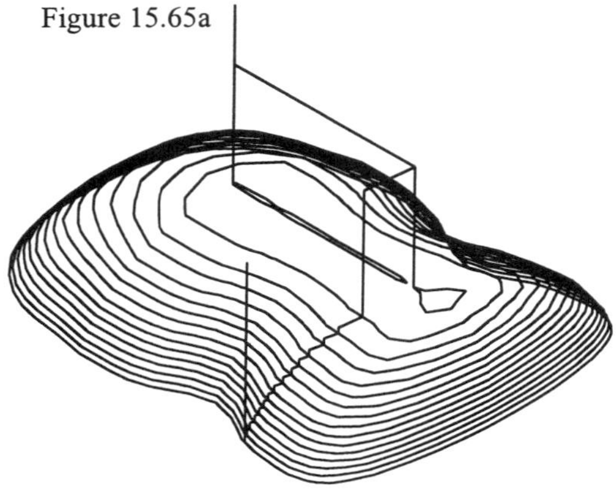

Figure 15.65c

Tips
1. Use the surface model file lofts2.
2. Use a 3/8" spherical end mill.
3. Use rough-contour function to generate roughing toolpaths.
4. Set cut tolerance to 0.025" and maximum stepdown to 0.05".

Step 1. Open the surface model file "lofts2".

Select **MAIN MENU → File → Get**
File name: **lofts2**
The loft surface model appears as in Figure 15.66.

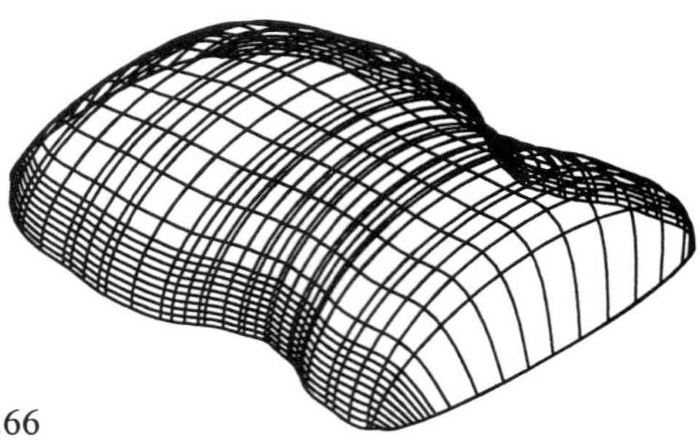

Figure 15.66

Mastercam Version 7,
Scholar's International Publishing Corp., 1998

Step 2. Initiate the contour-rough function.

Select **MAIN MENU → Toolpaths → Surface → Rough → Contour**
Enter file name for toolpaths: **rough5**
Select **All → Surfaces → Done**

Step 3. Select 3/8" sphere end mill.

Click the right mouse button , then select **"Get tool from library"**
Select **tool number 254** (3/8-sphere endmill)
Select **OK**
Set tool parameters as below.

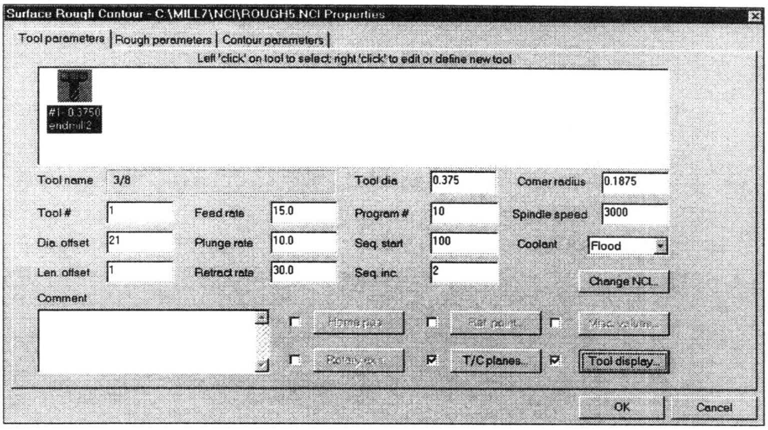

Step 4. Define rough parameters.

Click the "**Rough parameters**" button
Set the rough parameters as below.

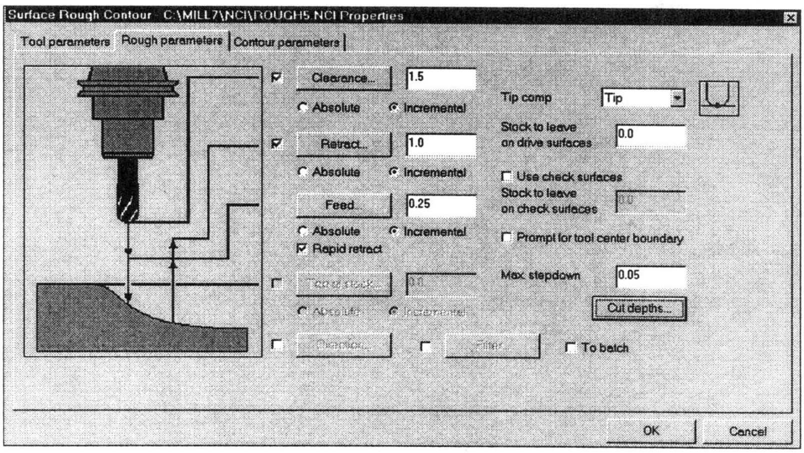

Step 5. Define the contour parameters.

Click the "**Contour parameters**" button
Set the contour parameters as below.

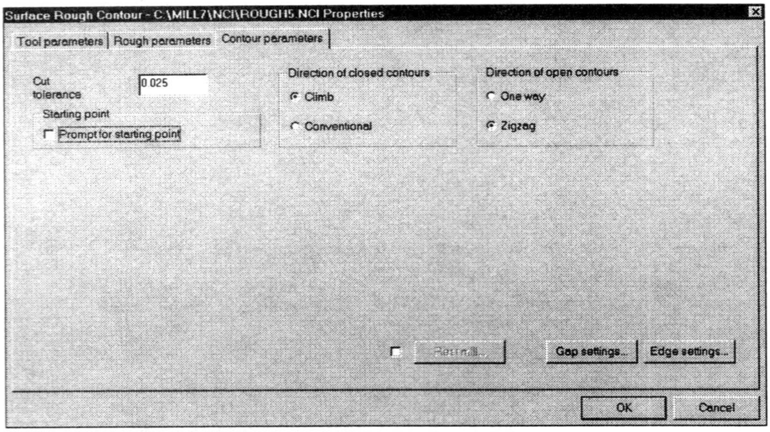

Select **OK**

The roughing toolpaths are generated as in Figure 15.67. Figure 15.68 shows only the roughing toolpaths.

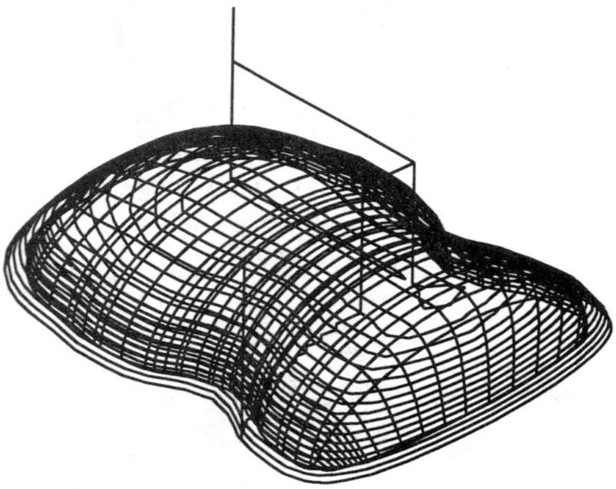

Figure 15.67

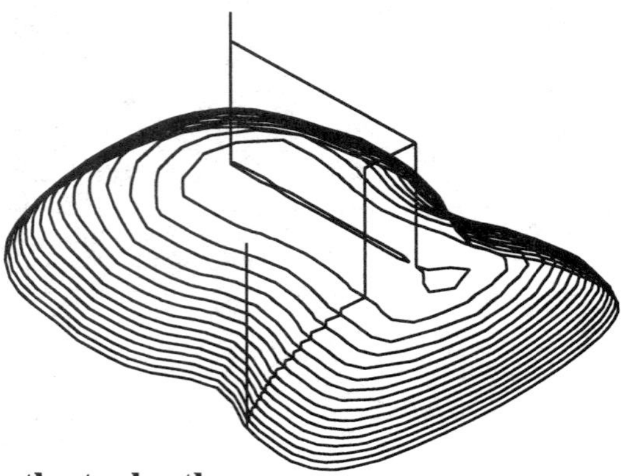

Figure 15.68

Step 6. Save the toolpaths.

Select **MAIN MENU → NC utils**
Select **Yes** to "Operations have been modified. Create the NCI text file?"

15.11 Pocket Rough Function

The pocket rough function generates a series of toolpaths to rough cut the surface model for further finish machining. This function requires a pocketing boundary to determine the pocketing rough. Figure 15.69 shows an example of using pocket rough function to generate a set of roughing toolpaths for a surface model. Figure 15.70 is an example of roughing a cavity type of surface model.

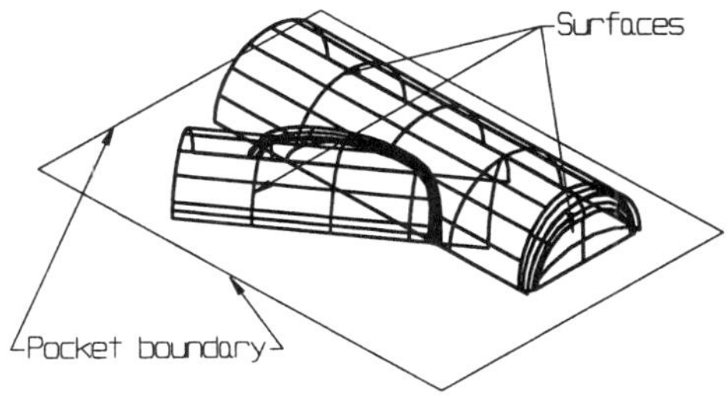

Figure 15.69a

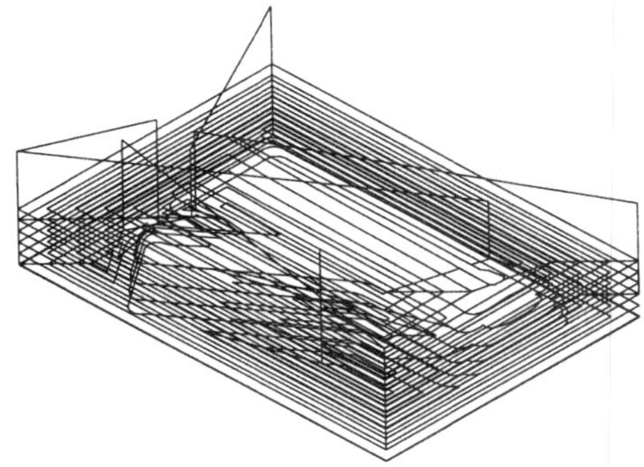

Figure 15.69b

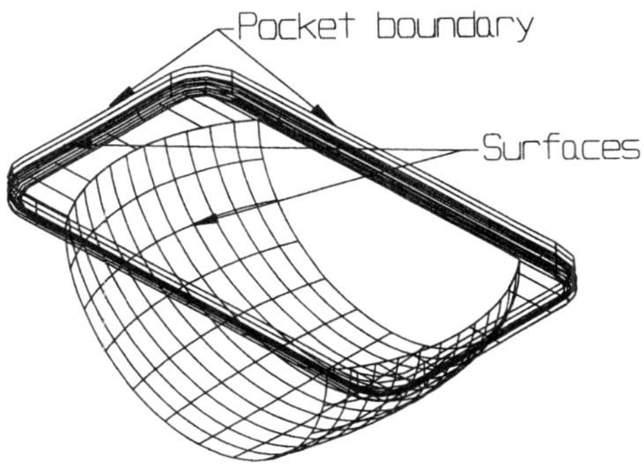

Figure 15.70a

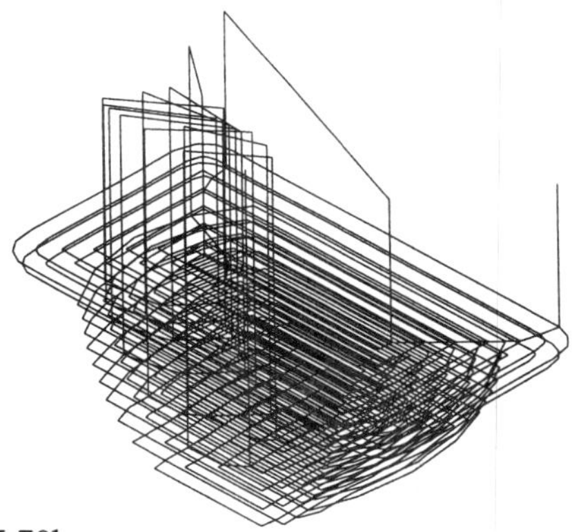

Figure 15.70b

The surface rough pocket parameters dialog box appears as below.

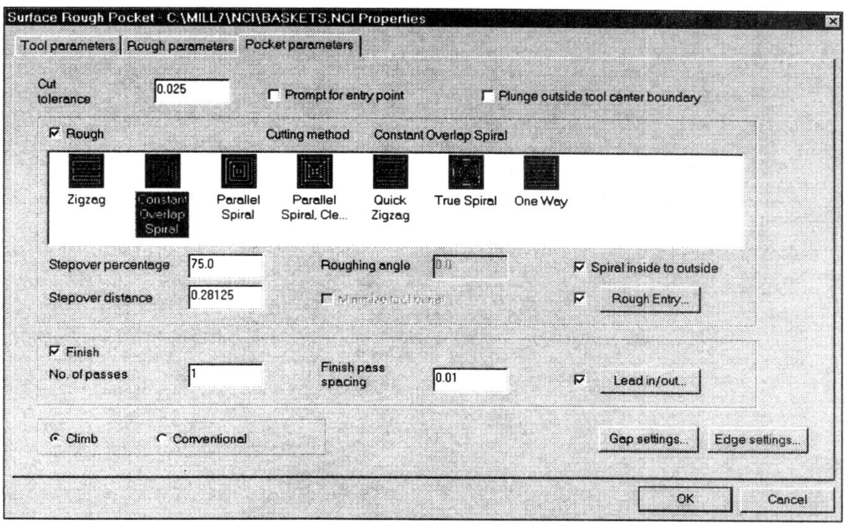

6 Cutting method

Mastercam provides the following seven cutting methods for generating toolpaths to rough a surface model:

Zigazg: rough the pocket in back and forth linear, parallel pattern according to the specified roughing angle.

Constant overlap spiral: the system calculates the stepover value based on the given stepover distance value and the remaining stock to be removed. The toolpaths are given in small linear moves.

Parallel spiral: rough the pocket in a spiral pattern that offsets the outer boundary by the stepover amount each time.

Parallel spiral, clean corners: rough the pocket in a spiral pattern that offsets the outer boundary by the stepover amount each time. In addition, it adds small cleanout moves in the corners of the pocket to remove leftover stock.

Quick zigzag: rough the pocket in a linear motion in the specified roughing angle. It is only available in surface pocket roughing function.

True spiral: rough the pocket in a circular toolpath pattern with tangent arcs. It provides a smooth motion for the tool, a short NC program, and good cleanout.

One way: rough the pocket in a linear pattern in only one direction.

Most parameters used in this rough function are identical to those parameters in 2D pocket function presented in chapter 7. The three parameters that are unique to this pocket rough functions are briefly described below.

Cut tolerance: specify the accuracy of the roughing toolpaths.

Prompt for entry point: ask for an approximate starting point for the toolpaths.

Plunge outside tool center boundary: specify a boundary from which the entry point of tool center to be placed its outside.

Project 6. Generating rough toolpaths using rough pocket function

A rectangle is created as the pocketing boundary. Use the rough pocket function to generate roughing toolpaths to rough out all material between the pocket boundary and the surface model as shown in Figure 15.71.

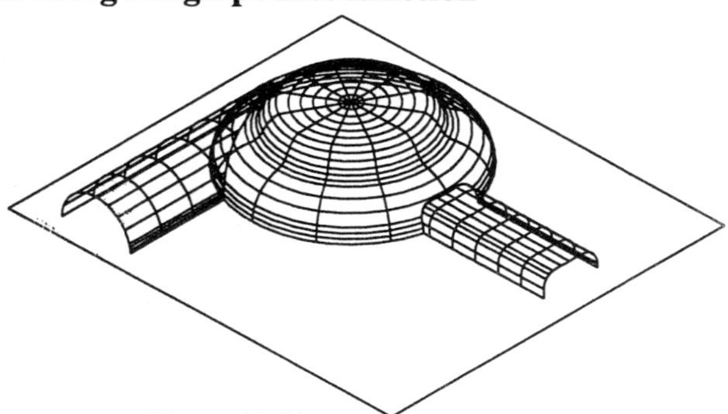

Figure 15.71a

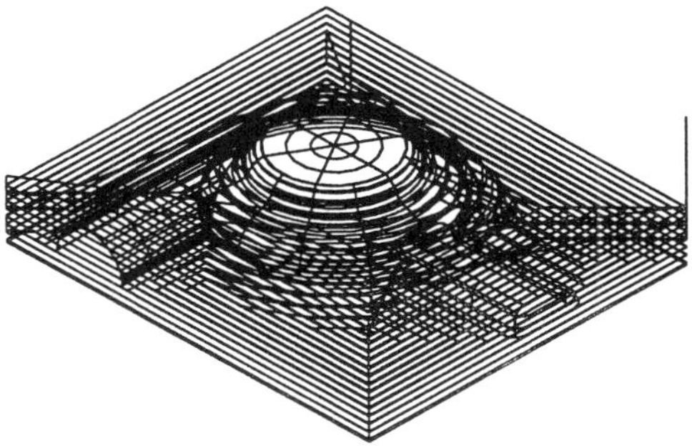

Figure 15.71b

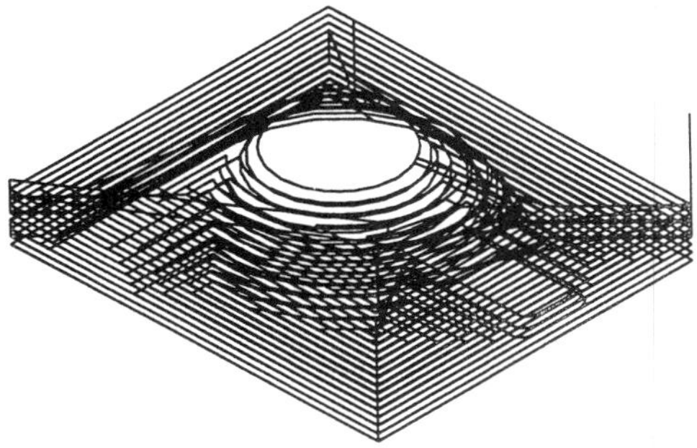

Figure 15.71c

⌛**Tips**	1. Open the surface model file dryers. 2. Create a rectangle as the pocket boundary. 3. Use surface rough-pocket function to generate roughing toolpaths. 4. Use 3/8" spherical end mill..

Step 1. Open a surface model file dryers.

Select **MAIN MENU → File → Get**
File name: **dryers**
The dryer surface model appears as in Figure 15.72.

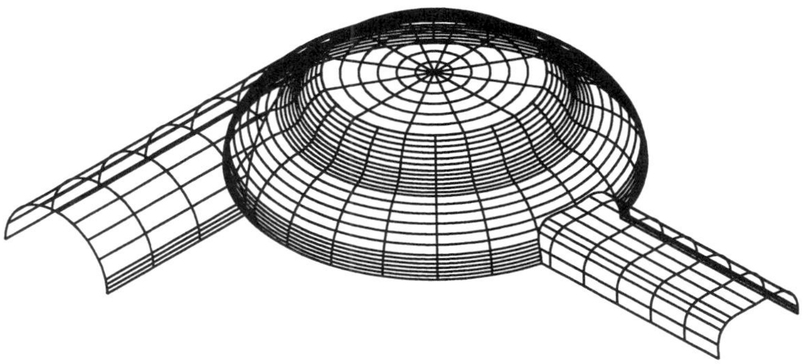

Figure 15.72

Step 2. Create a rectangle as the pocketing boundary.

Select **Cplane → Top**
Select **Level**, then enter **8**
Select **Z**, then enter **0**
Select **Create → Rectangle → 2 points**
Enter the lower left corner: **-2.5, -3.85**
Enter the upper right corner: **4.5, 2.35**

The rectangle is added as in Figure 15.73.

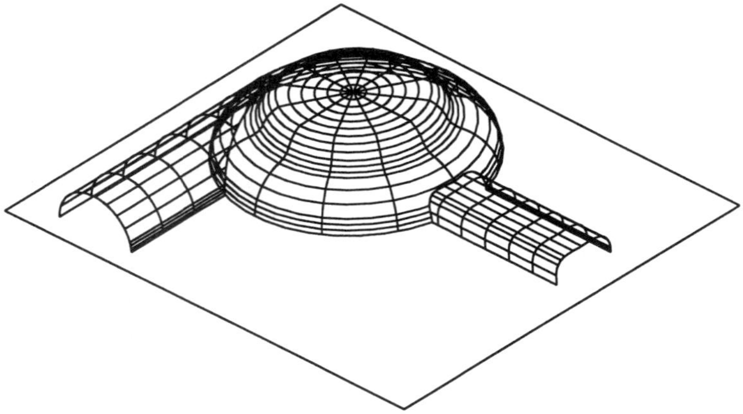

Figure 15.73

Step 3. Initiate the rough-pocket function.

Select **MAIN MENU → Toolpaths → Surface → Rough → Pocket**
Enter file name for toolpaths: **rough6**
Select **All → Surfaces → Done**

Step 4. Select a cutting tool.

Click at the right mouse button, then select **"Get tool from library"**, open the tool library
Select **tool number 254** →3/8 sphere end mill
Select **OK**
Set rough parameters as below.

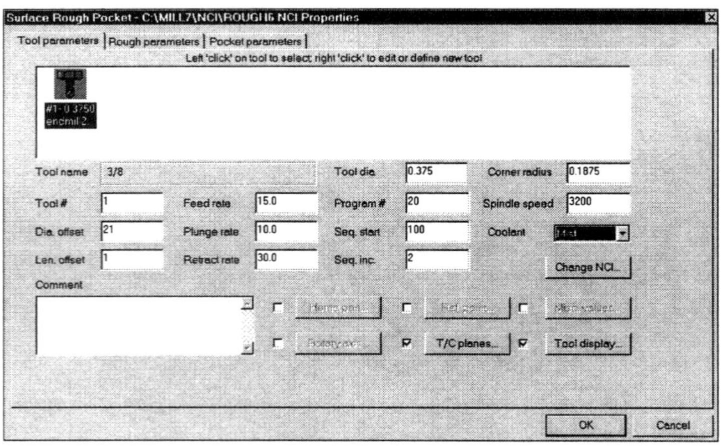

Step 5. Define the rough parameters.

Click the **"Rough parameters"** button
Set the rough parameters as below.

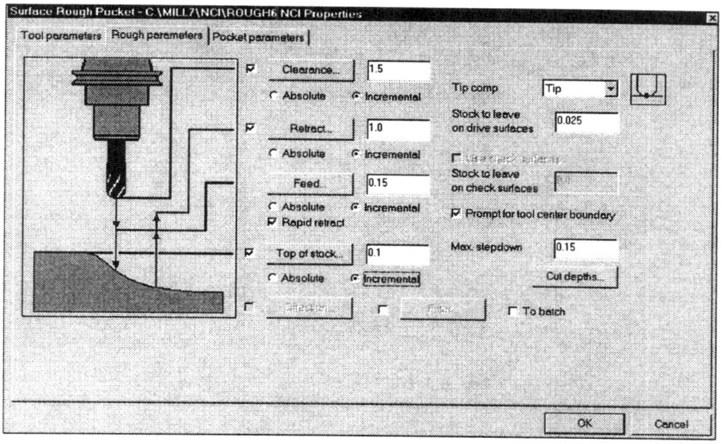

Step 6. Define the pocket parameters.

Click the "**Pocket parameters**" button

Set the pocket parameters as below.

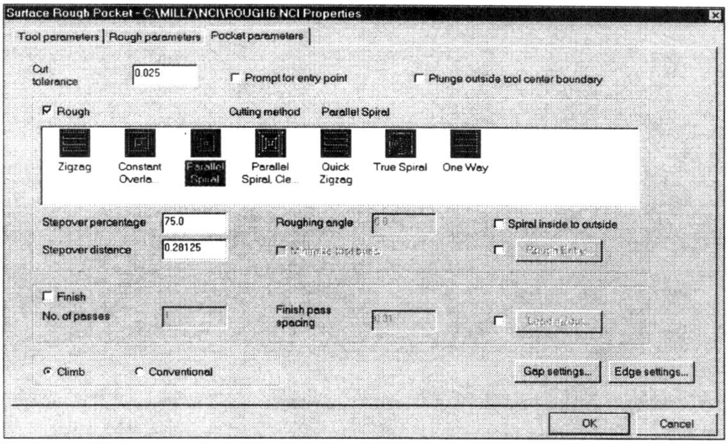

Select **OK**

Select **Chain**, then pick the front horizontal line on the rectangle

Select **Done**

The roughing toolpaths are generated as in Figure 15.74.

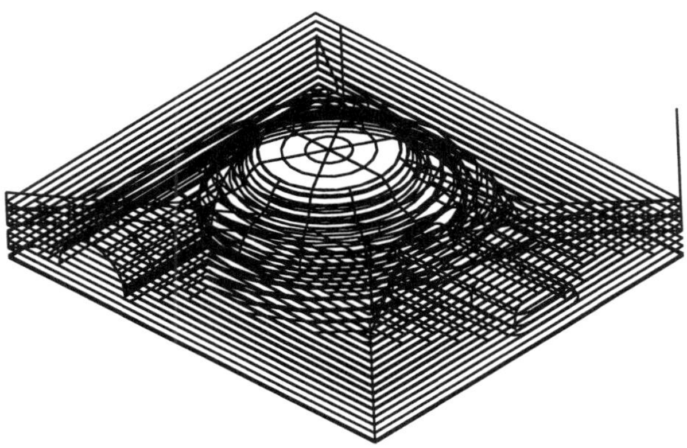

Figure 15.74

7 Figure 15.75 shows only the roughing toolpaths.

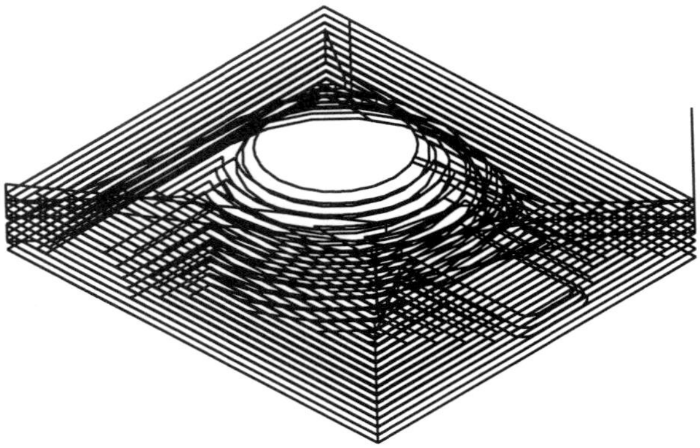

Figure 15.75

Step 7. Save the roughing toolpaths.

Select **MAIN MENU → NC utils**
Select **Yes** to "Operations have been modified. Create the NCI text file?"

Project 7. Generating toolpaths to rough a surface model using the rough-pocket function

This project uses the outside profile of the rim as the pocket boundary to generate roughing toolpaths for a basket surface model with rough-pocket function. Figure 15.76 shows the surface model and toolpaths.

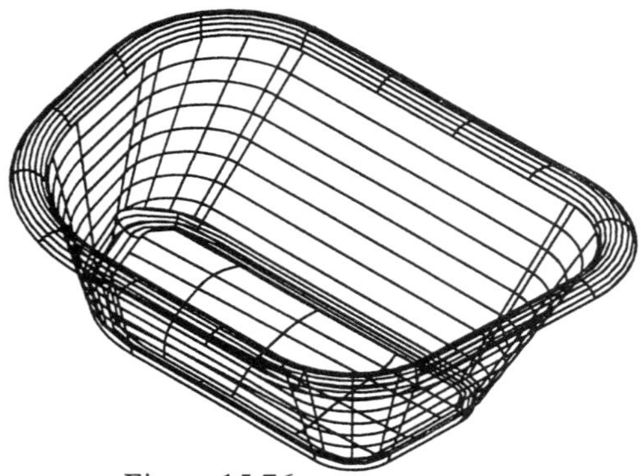

Figure 15.76a

Figure 15.76b

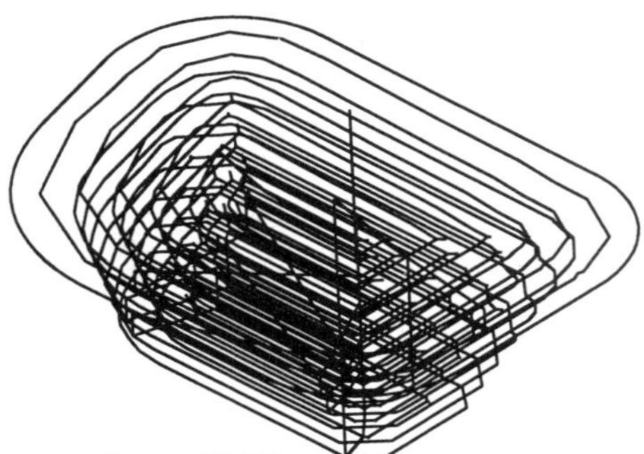

Figure 15.76b

Tips	1. Open the surface model file baskets.
	2. Use the surface rough-pocket function to generate roughing toolpaths.
	3. Use ½" sphere end mill.

Step 1. Open the surface model file baskets.

Select **MAIN MENU → File → Get**
File name: **baskets**
The basket surface model appears as in Figure 15.77.

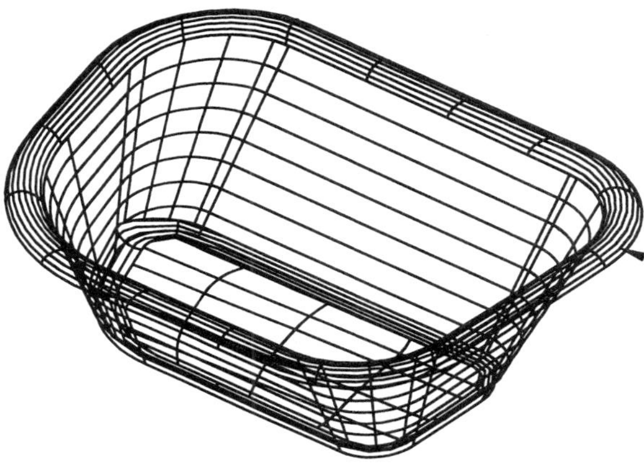

Figure 15.77

Step 2. Initiate the rough-pocket function.

Select **MAIN MENU → Toolpaths → Surface → Rough → Pocket**
Enter file name for toolpaths: **rough7**
Select **All → Surfaces → Done**
Click the right mouse button, then select "**Get** tool from library" to open tool library

Step 3. Select a tool.

Select **tool number 256** (1/2 sphere end mill)
Select **OK**
Define the tool parameters as below.

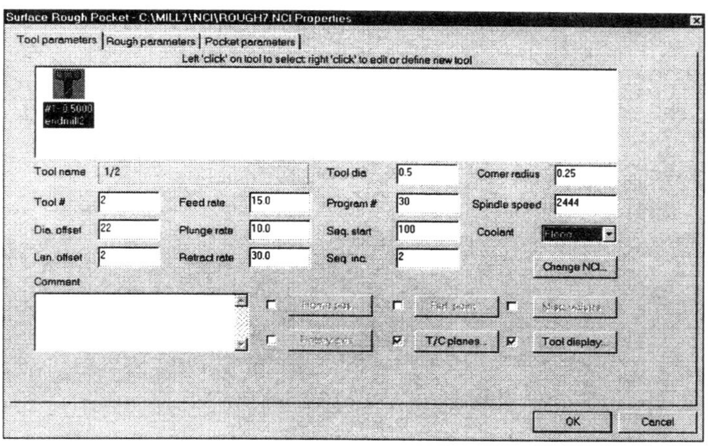
Surface Rough Pocket - C:\MILL7\NCI\ROUGH7.NCI Properties
Tool parameters | Rough parameters | Pocket parameters
Left 'click' on tool to select; right 'click' to edit or define new tool
#1 - 0.5000 endmill2
Tool name 1/2 Tool dia 0.5 Corner radius 0.25
Tool # 2 Feed rate 15.0 Program # 30 Spindle speed 2444
Dia. offset 22 Plunge rate 10.0 Seq. start 100 Coolant
Len. offset 2 Retract rate 30.0 Seq. inc 2 Change NCI...
Comment
T/C planes... Tool display...
OK Cancel

Step 4. Define the rough parameters.

Click the "**Rough parameters**" button

Set the rough parameters as below.

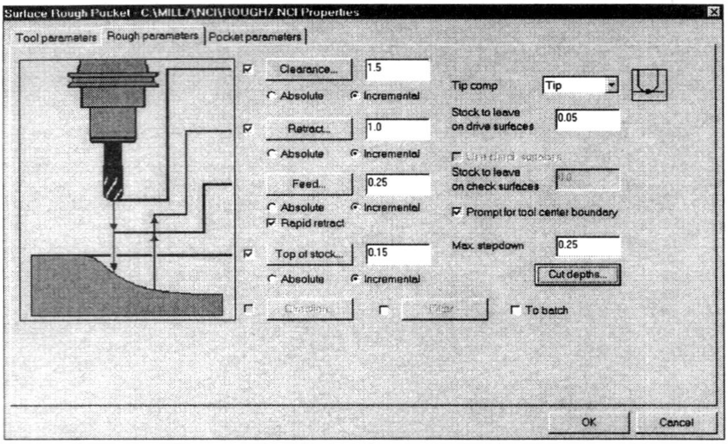

Step 5. Define the pocket parameters.

Click the "**Pocket parameters**" button

Set the pocket parameters as below.

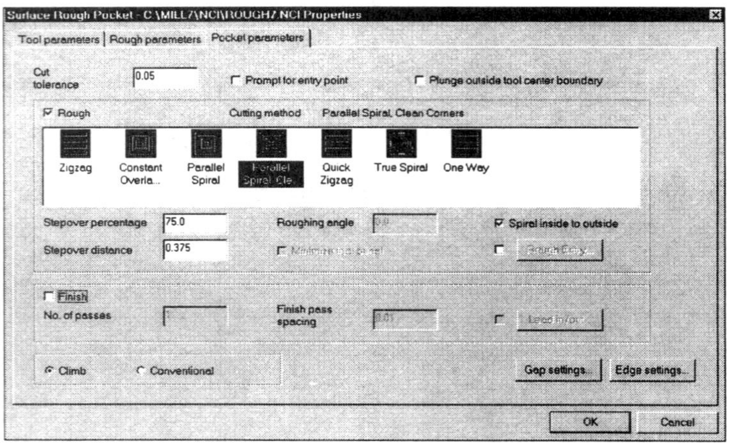

Select **OK**

Step 6. Define the outside boundary.

Select **Chain**, then pick **P1** as shown in Figure 15.77

Select **End here → Done**

Roughing toolpaths are generated as in Figure 15.78.

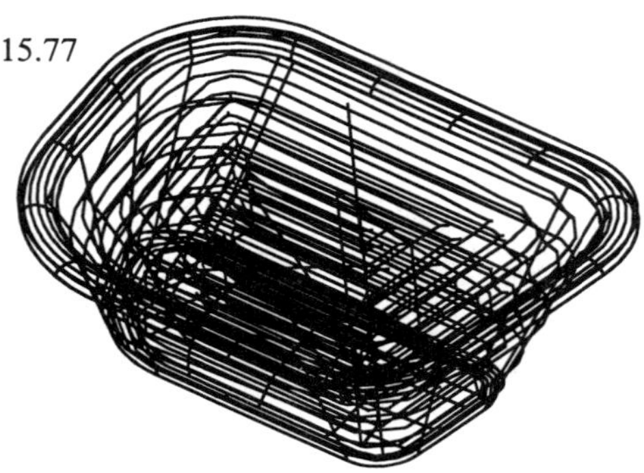

Figure 15.78

Figure 15.79 shows only the roughing toolpaths.

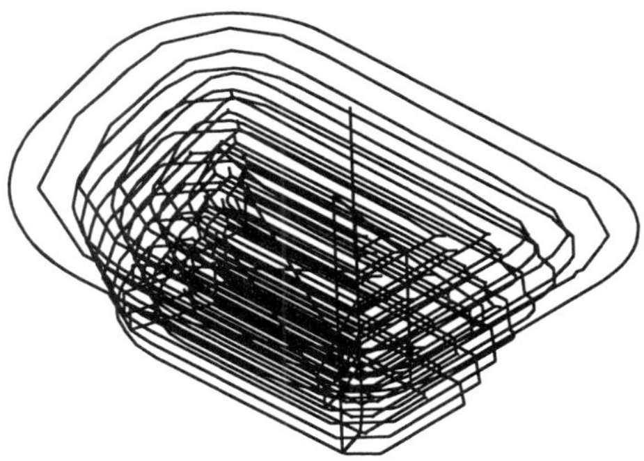

Figure 15.79

Step 7. Save the toolpath file.

Select **MAIN MENU → NC utils**

Select **Yes** to "Operations have been modified. Create the NCI text file?"

15.12 Rough Plunge Function

This surface rough function generates a set of plunging toolpaths for roughing a surface model (Figure 15.80).

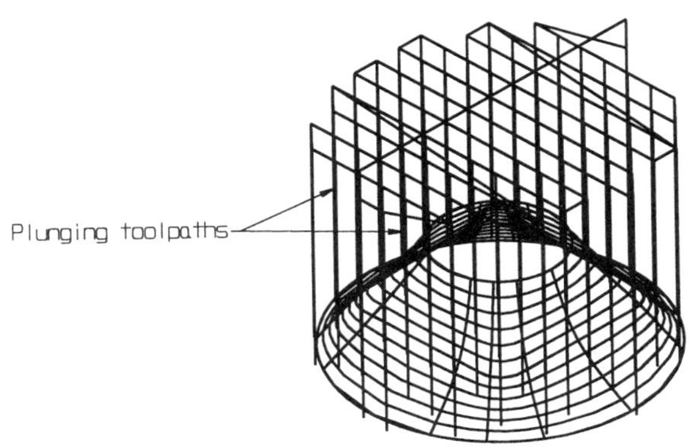

Figure 15.80

The plunge function dialog box appears as below.

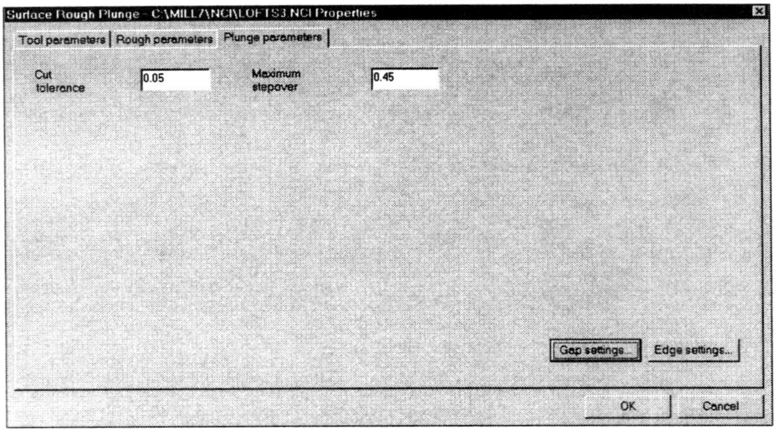

The system will prompt for the selection of two plunge points at the lower left corner and at upper right corner (Figure 15.81). These two points define the surface range to be roughed.

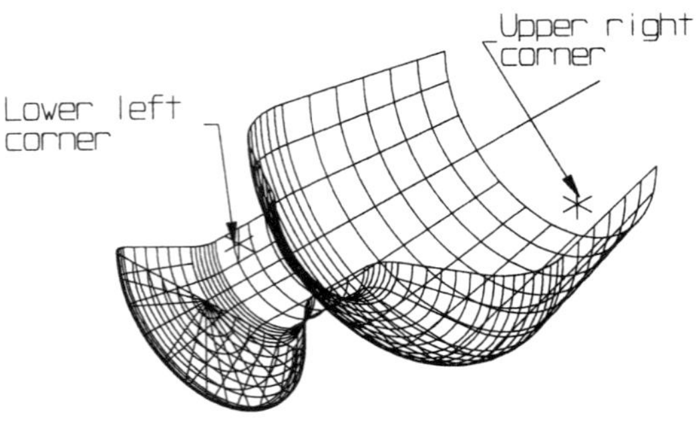

Figure 15.81a

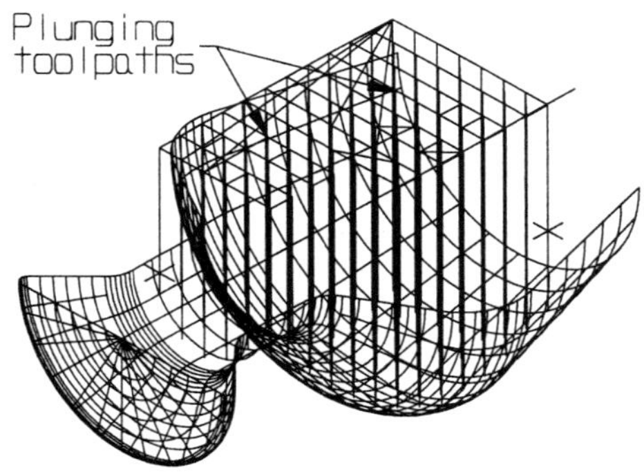

Figure 15.81b

Project 8. Generating roughing toolpaths using plunge function

The rough-plunge function is used to generate roughing toolpaths to cut the car wheel surface model as shown in Figure 15.82. Two corner points (-0.25, -0.5) and (6.0, 5.5) are used as the plunge boundary.

Tips
1. Use the surface model file wheels.
2. Use the surface rough-plunge function to generate roughing toolpaths.
3. Define two corner points at (-0.25, -0.5) and (6.0, 5.5).
4. Use a ¾" spherical end mill.

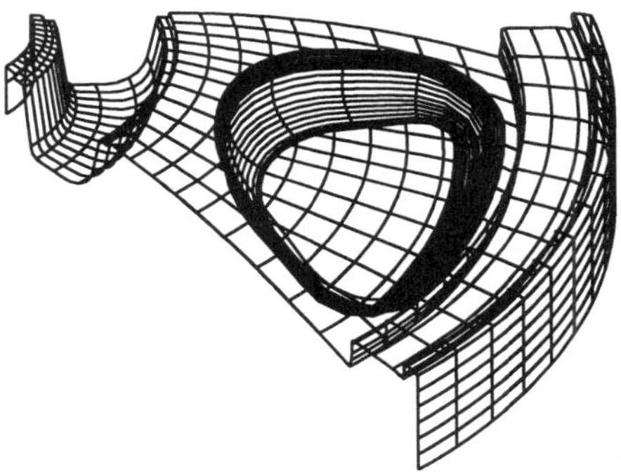

Figure 15.82a

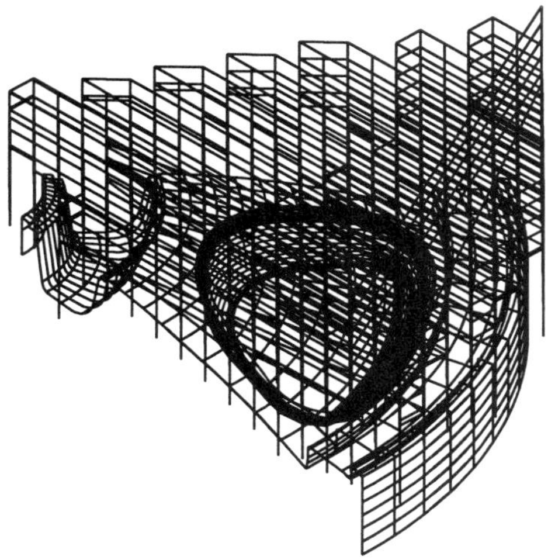

Figure 15.82b

Step 1. Open the surface model file wheels.

Select **MAIN MENU → File → Get**
File name: **wheels**
The wheel surface model appears as Figure 15.83.

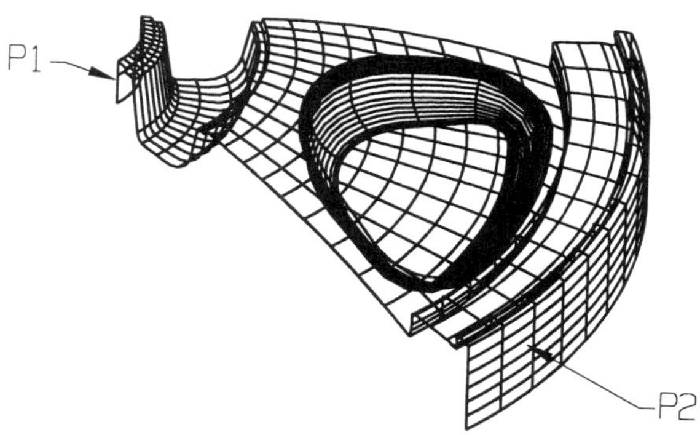

Figure 15.83

Step 2. Initiate the plunge rough function.

Use two pick points in Figure 15.83.
Select **Cplane → Top**
Select **MAIN MENU → Toolpaths → Rough → Plunge**
Enter file name for toolpaths: **rough8**
Select **All → Surfaces**
Select **Unselect**, then pick **P1** and **P2** to omit these two vertical surfaces
Select **BACKUP → Done**

Step 3. Select a tool.

Click the right mouse button, then select **"Get tool from library"**
Select **tool number 259** (3/4 sphere end mill)
Select **OK**
Define the tool parameters as below.

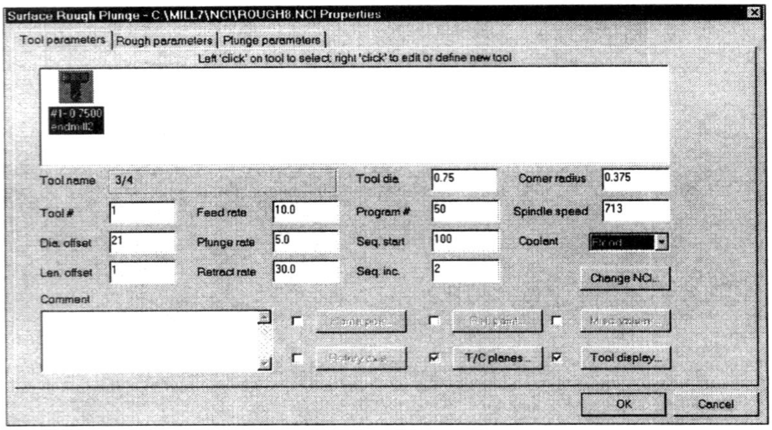

Step 4. Define the rough parameters.

Click the "**Rough parameters**" button
Set rough parameters as below.

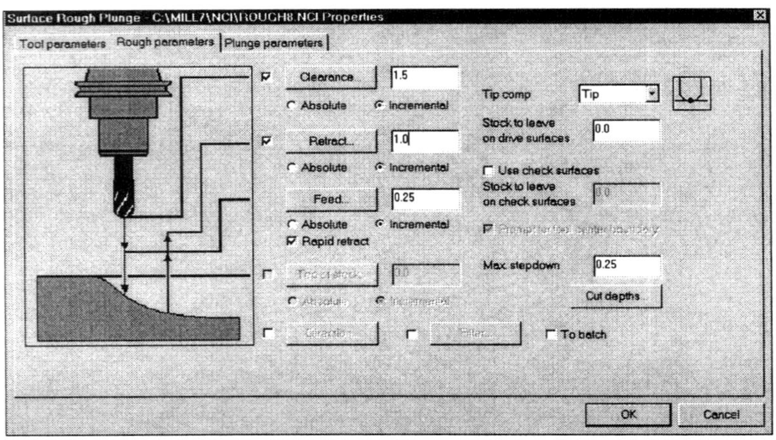

Step 5. Define the rough plunge parameters.

Click the "**Plunge parameters**" button
Set plunge parameters as below.

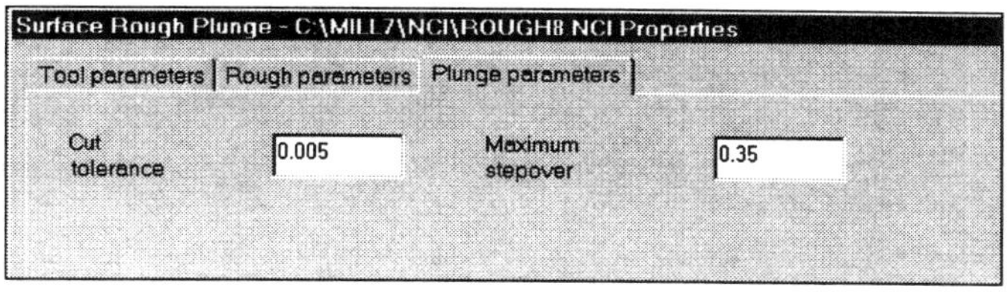

Step 6. Define two corner points.

Select **OK**
Select plunge point at lower left: **-0.25, -0.5**
Select plunge point at upper right: **6.0, 5.5**
The plunging toolpaths are generated as in Figure 15.84.

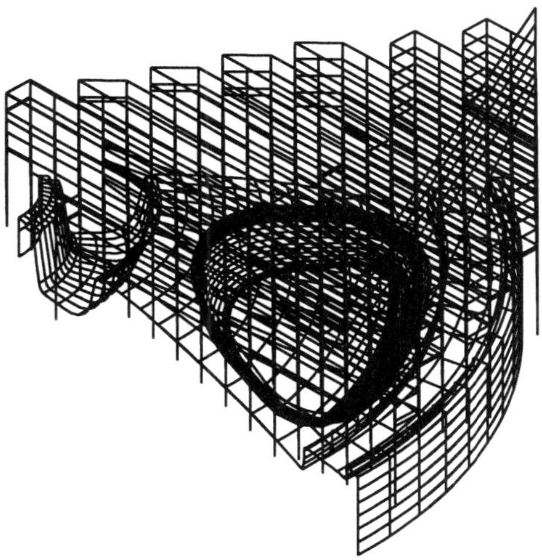

Figure 15.84

Step 7. Save the plunging toolpaths.

Select **MAIN MENU → NC utils**
Select **Yes** to "Operations have been modified. Create the NCI text file?"

15.13 Finish Functions

Mastercam provides ten functions to generate toolpaths for finishing cut a surface model. These ten functions are tabulated in table 15.2 and listed below here.

Table 15.2 Ten surface finishing functions

Finish Function	Description	Illustration
Parallel	Generate finishing toolpaths that run in parallel direction specified by the machining angle parameter.	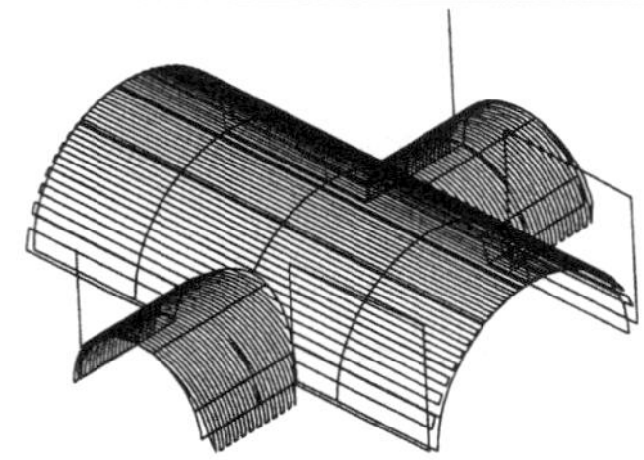
Par. Steep	Generate finishing toolpaths to clean remaining stock in the steep areas of the part. Steep areas are determined by two slope angles.	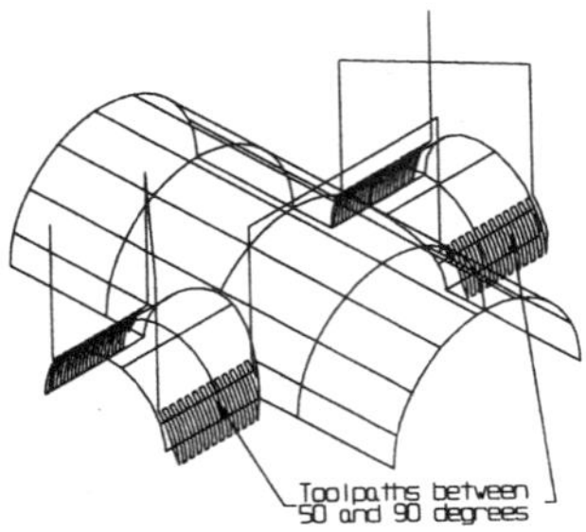
Radial	Generate finishing toolpaths that run in radial direction for cutting surfaces.	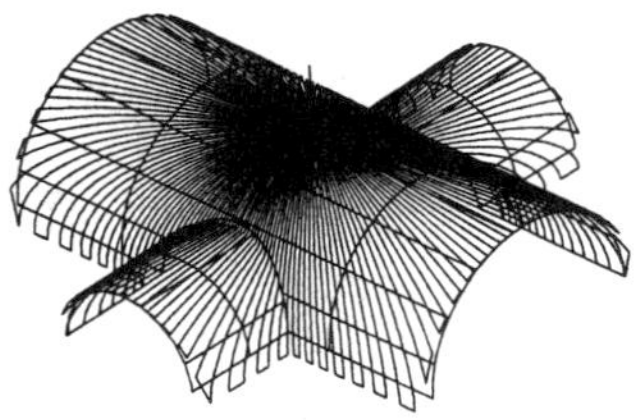
Project	Generate finishing toolpaths by projecting a set of existing toolpaths or geometry entities onto the selected surfaces.	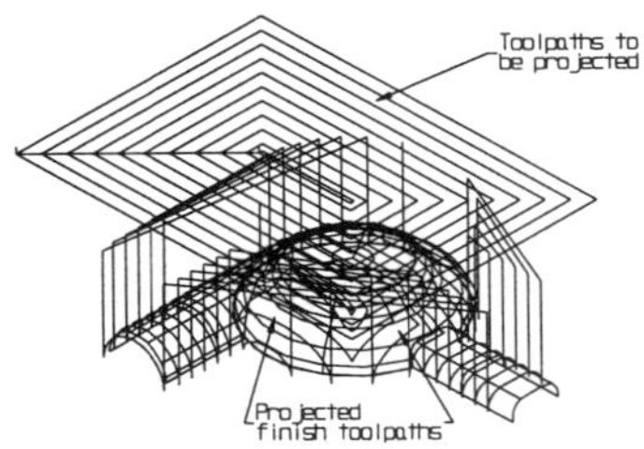
Flowline	Generate finishing toolpaths along the direction of the surface flow lines. Multiple surfaces can be used.	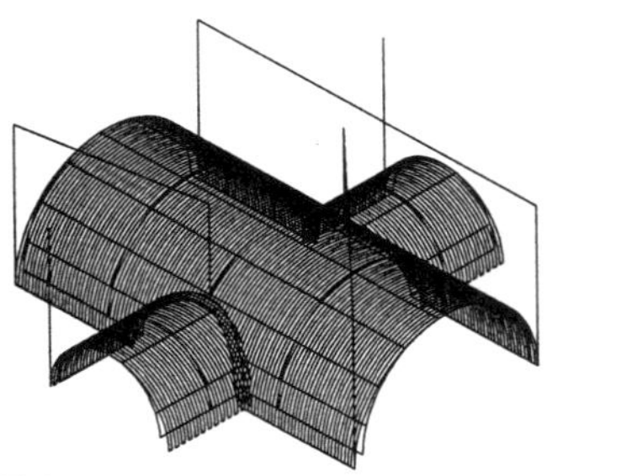

Table 15.2, continued.

Contour	Generate finishing toolpaths along the surface contours.	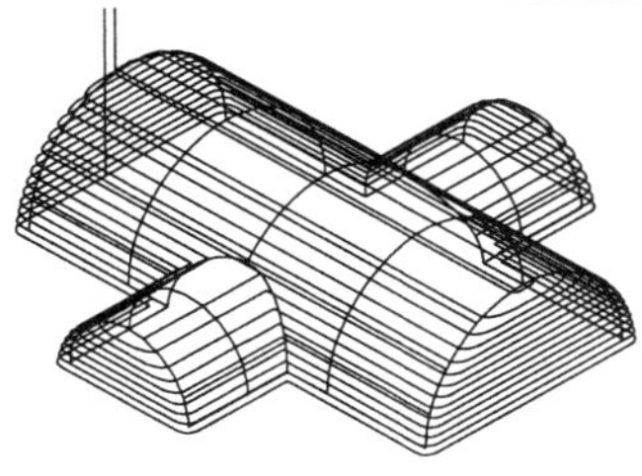
Shallow	Generate finishing toolpaths to clean remaining stock from shallow areas of the part. Shallow areas are determined by two slope angles.	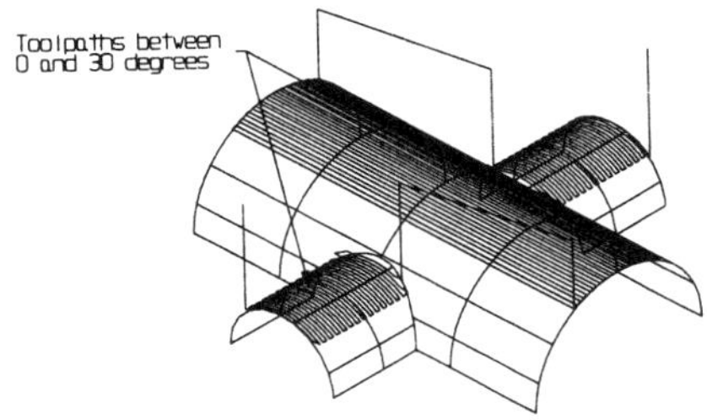
Pencil	Generate toolpaths to remove material in corners between surfaces.	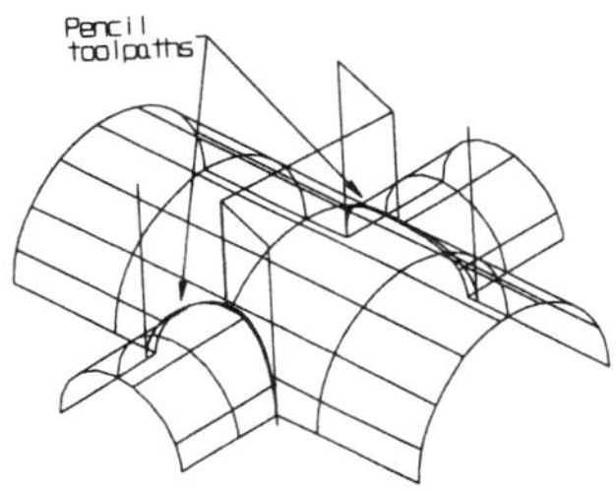
Leftover	Generate toolpaths to remove material left by a larger tool in a previous operation.	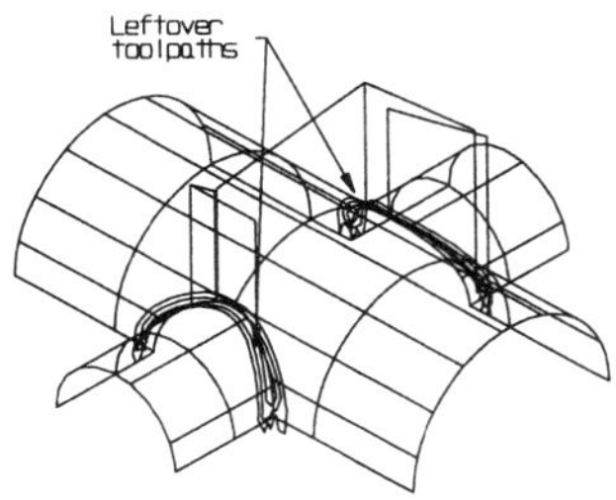 (Tool for previous operation is 1/2", new tool is 1/8")
Scallop	Generate finishing toolpaths that have consistent scallop heights over the entire set of surfaces.	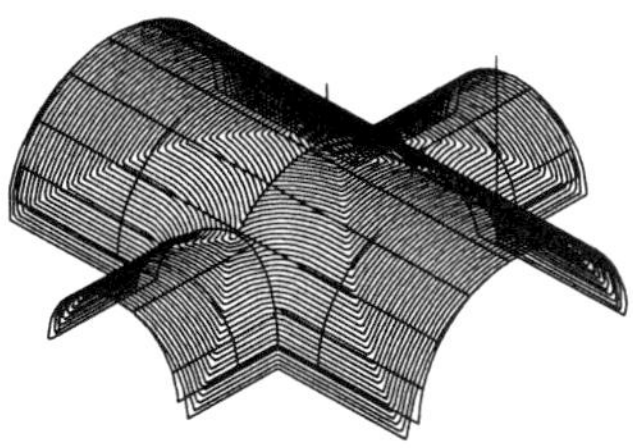

There are five finish functions that have their rough counterparts presented in previous sections. Actually, these five finish functions use the same parameters as in their rough counterparts. Rough functions uses more parameters than finish functions because they need to generate toolpaths for each roughing level. Only those five finish functions that are not covered in rough functions are discussed here in detail.

15.14 Parallel Finish Function

This function generates a set of linear, parallel toolpaths in a specified direction for the finish cut of a surface model (Figure 15.85). Its parameters dialog box appears as below.

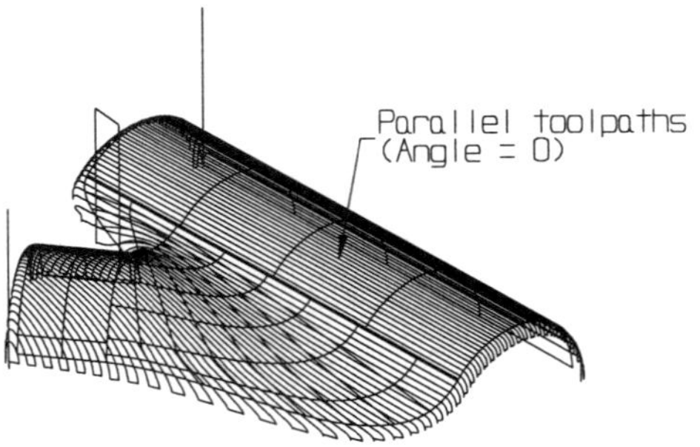

Figure 15.85a

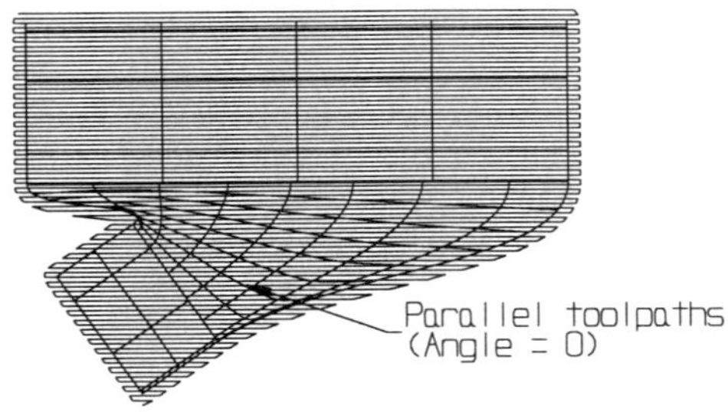

Figure 15.85b

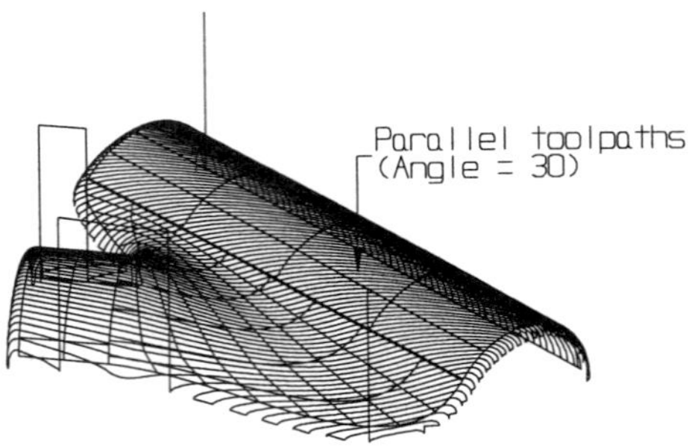

Figure 15.85c

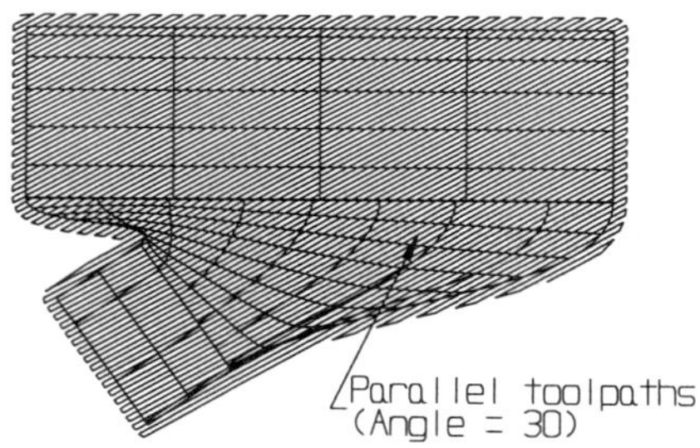

Figure 15.85d

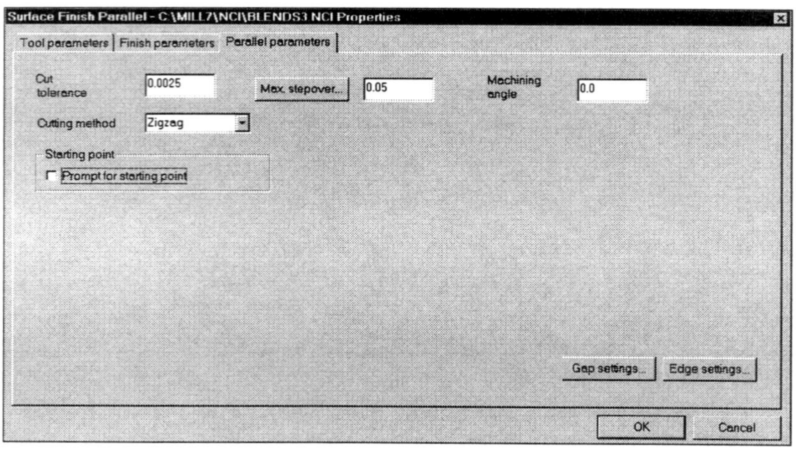

Project 9. Using parallel function

The surface finish-parallel function is used to generate finishing toolpaths to cut a flash light surface model. The external vertical wall surface is not included in the machining. Figure 15.86 shows the surface model and its finishing toolpaths.

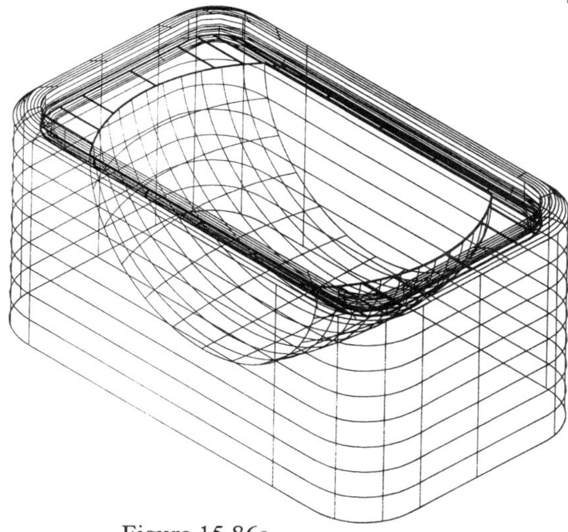

Figure 15.86a

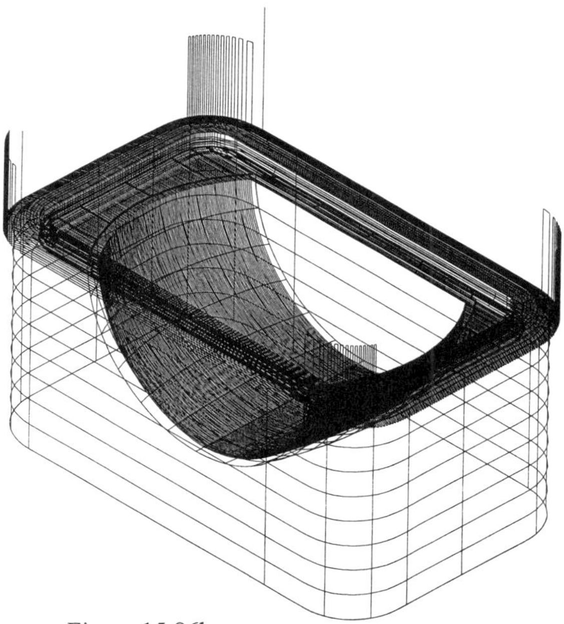

Figure 15.86b

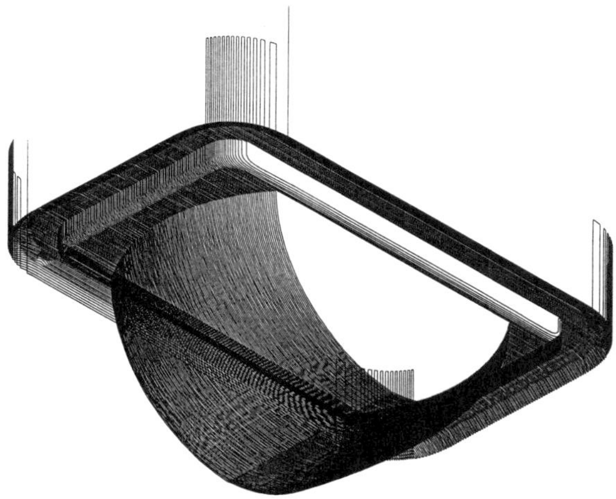

Figure 15.86c

Tips 1. Open the surface model file flashs.

2. Use surface finish-parallel function to generate finishing toolpaths.

3. Do not include the external vertical wall surface in machining.

4. Use a 3/16" spherical end mill.

Step 1. Open the surface model file flashs.

Select **MAIN MENU → File → Get**

File name: **flashs**

The flash light model appears as in Figure 15.87.

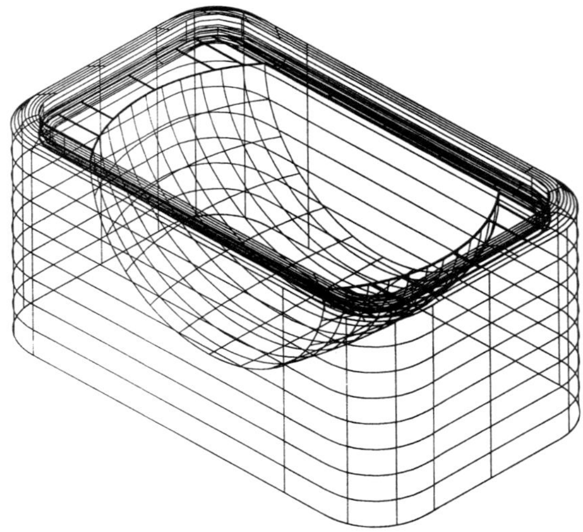

Figure 15.87

Step 2. Initiate the parallel function.

Select **MAIN MENU → Toolpaths → Surface → Finish → Parallel**
File name for toolpaths: **parallel**
Select **All → Surfaces → Unselect**
Pick the external vertical wall surface
Select **BACKUP → Done**

Step 3. Define the tool parameters.

Click the right hand button then select **"Get tool from library"**
Select **tool number 251** for (3/16 sphere end mill)
Select **OK**
Set the tool parameters as below.

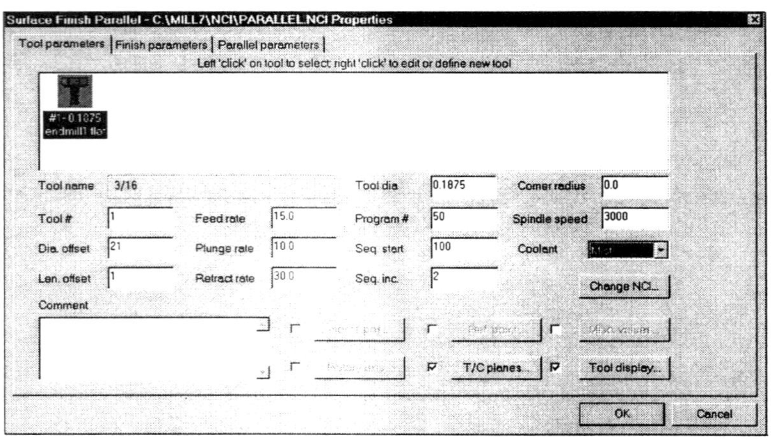

Mastercam Version 7,
Scholar's International Publishing Corp., 1998

Step 4. Define the finish parameters.

Click the "**Finish parameters**" button

Define the finish parameters as below.

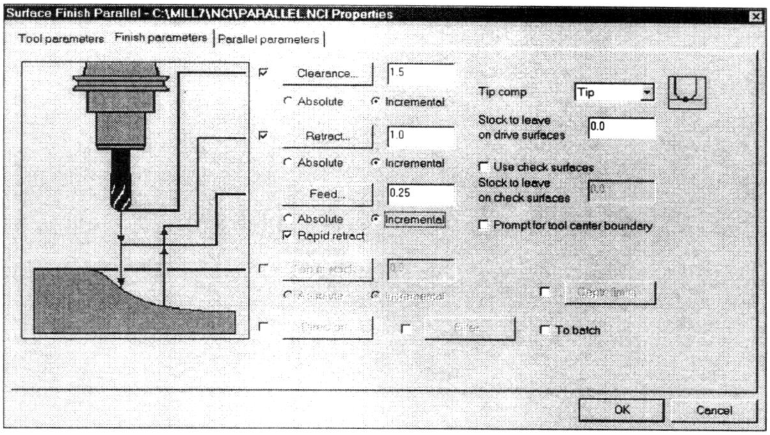

Step 5. Define the parallel parameters.

Click the "**Parallel parameters**" button

Set the parallel parameters as below.

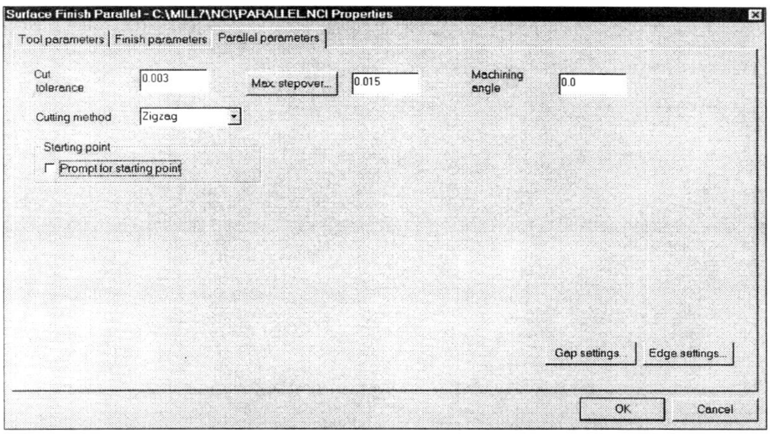

Step 6. Define gap and edge parameters.

Click the "**Gap settings**" button

Select **Smooth** for Motion < Gap size, keep tool down parameter

Select **OK**

Click the "**Edge settings**" button

Select "**Over all surface edges**" for Roll tool parameter

Select **OK** → **OK** to generate finishing toolpaths as Figure 15.88.

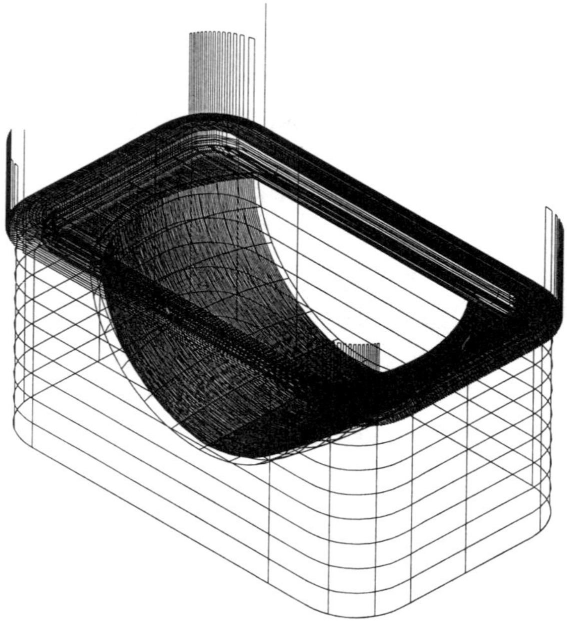

Figure 15.88

The toolpaths without showing the surface model appear as in Figure 15.89.

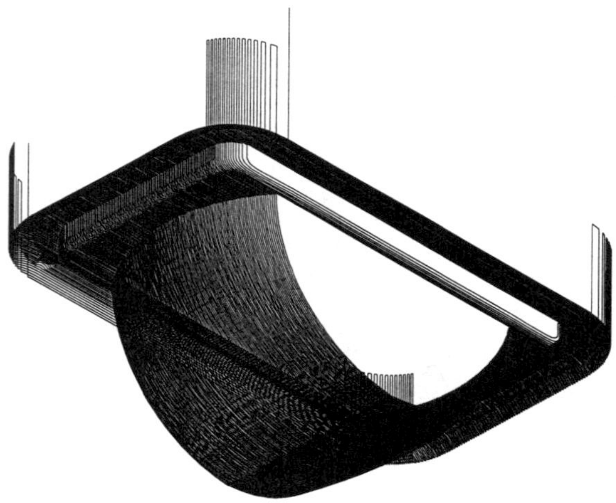

Figure 15.89

Step 7. Save the toolpaths.

Select **MAIN MENU → NC utils → Edit NCI**
Select **Yes** to "Operations have been modified. Create the NCI text file?"
Select **Quit** from Edit NCI dialog box

15.16 Parallel Steep Finish Function

This function is intended to generate a set of parallel toolpaths for the steep area of the part (Figure 15.90). The steep area is defined by two slope angles on the surface. Parallel steep parallel dialog box appears as below.

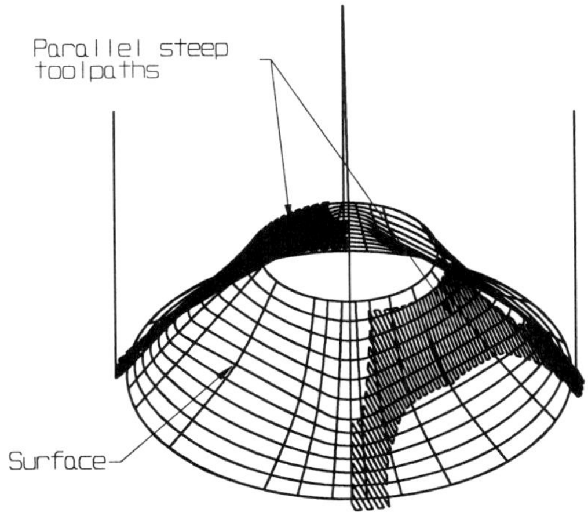

Figure 15.90

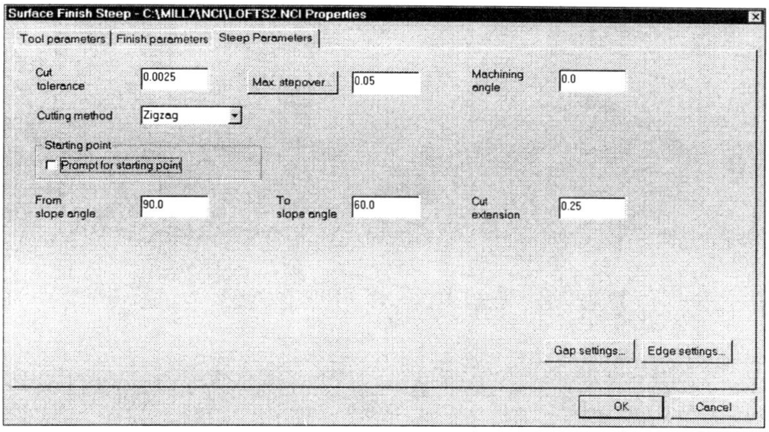

Mastercam uses two angles to define the steep area of the part; from slope angle and to slope angle. **From slope angle** specifies the minimum slope angle of the surface and **to slope angle** sets the maximum slope angle of the surface. Areas between from slope angle and to slope angle are machined (Figure 15.91).

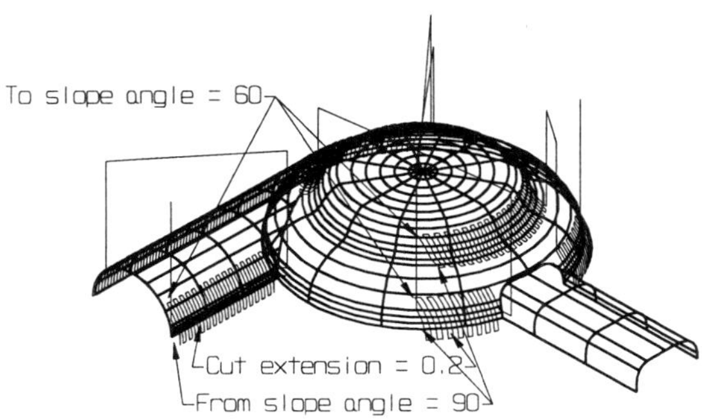

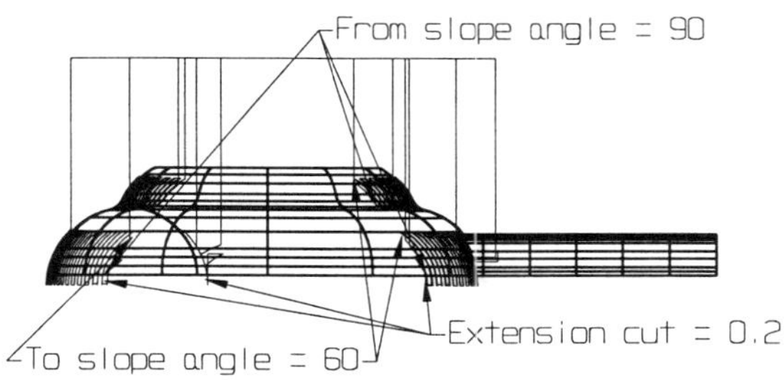

Figure 15.91a

Figure 15.91b

The "Cut extension" parameter is used to extend the cut so that the tool can plunge into a previously cut area before machining the leftover stock. The given cut extension distance is added to both ends of the toolpath and follows the curvature of the surface (Figure 15.92).

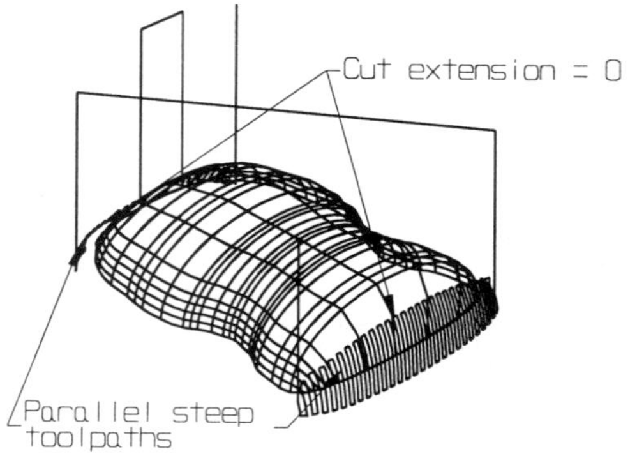

Figure 15.92a

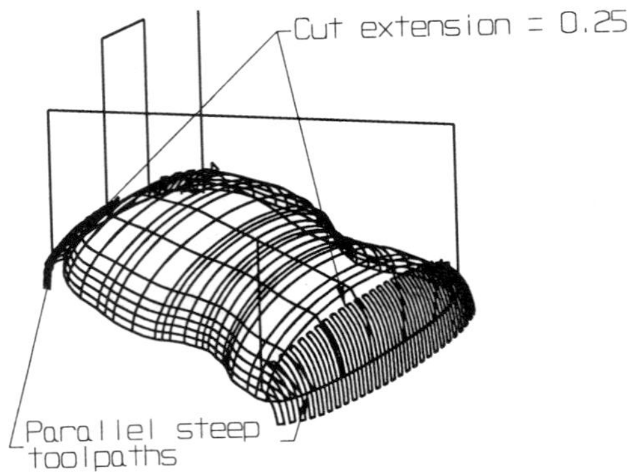

Figure 15.92b

15.17 Finish Leftover Function

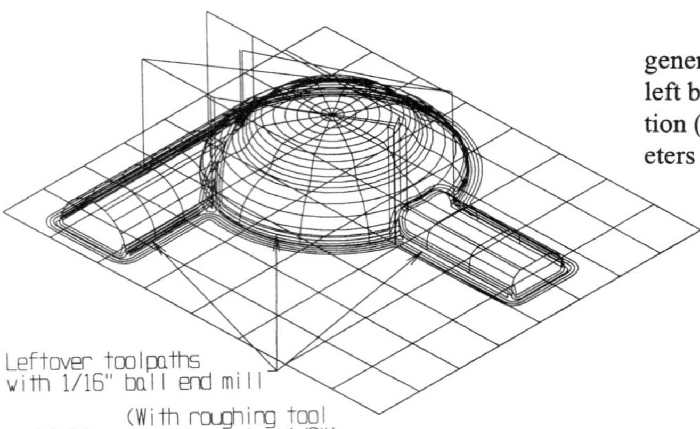

Figure 15.93

The finish leftover function generates toolpaths for removing material left by a larger tool in a previous operation (Figure 15.93). The leftover parameters dialog box appears as below.

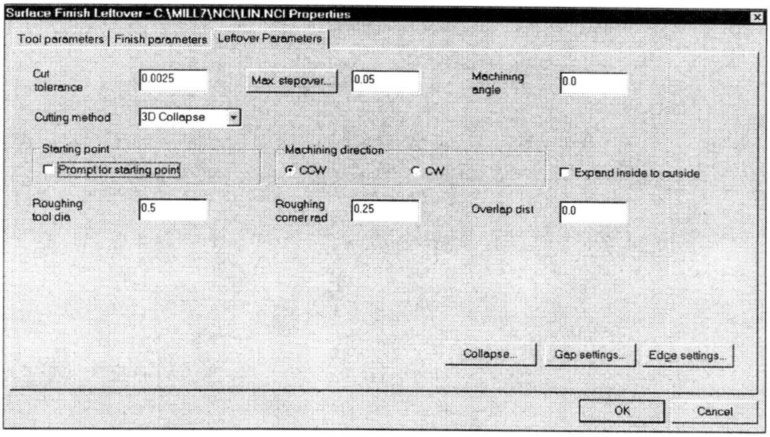

These two parameters are used to describe the cutting tool used in the previously operations:

Roughing tool dia.: specify the diameter of the tool used in the previous machining operation.
Roughing corner rad: specify the corner radius of the tool used in the previous machining operation.

The system uses these two tooling parameters to compare to the corner radius of the finishing tool to determine the leftover amount for this operation. The tool diameter for the finish leftover operation must be smaller than the roughing tool diameter.

The "Overlap distance" parameter is used to add a distance to the roughing tool's corner radius to define a larger machined area than the roughing tool diameter would allow (Figure 15.94).

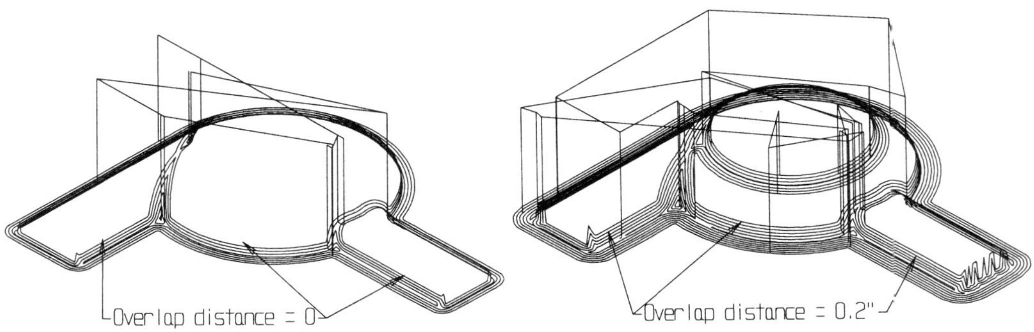

Figure 15.94a Figure 15.9
4b

10

15.18 Radial Finish Function

This function generates a set of toolpaths that run in the radial direction from a given point for the finish cut of a surface model. Its parameter dialog box appears as below. Figure 15.95 shows an example using the radial finish function for generating finish toolpaths.

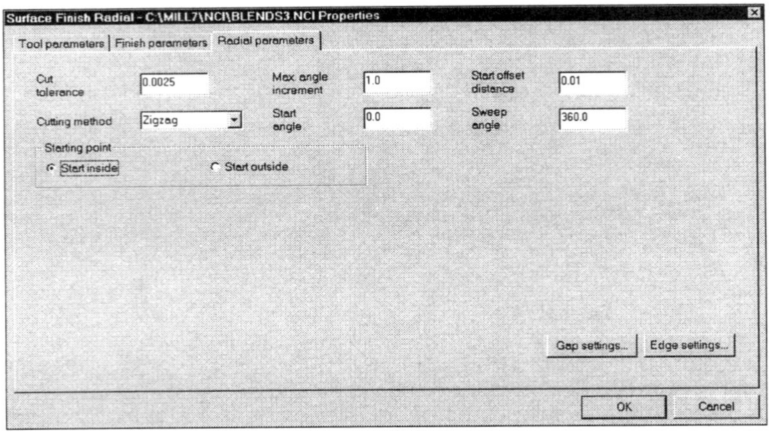

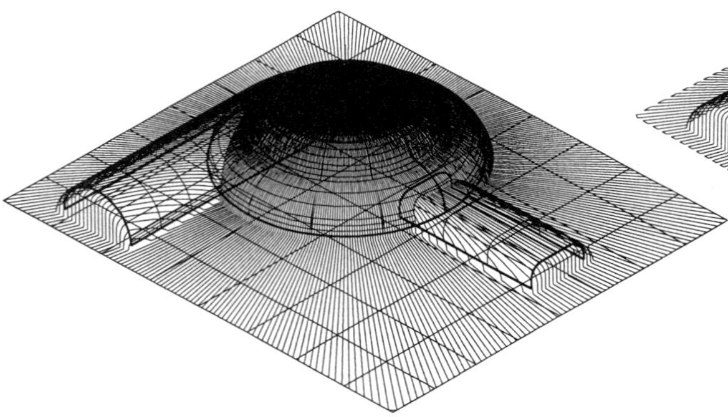

Figure 15.95a

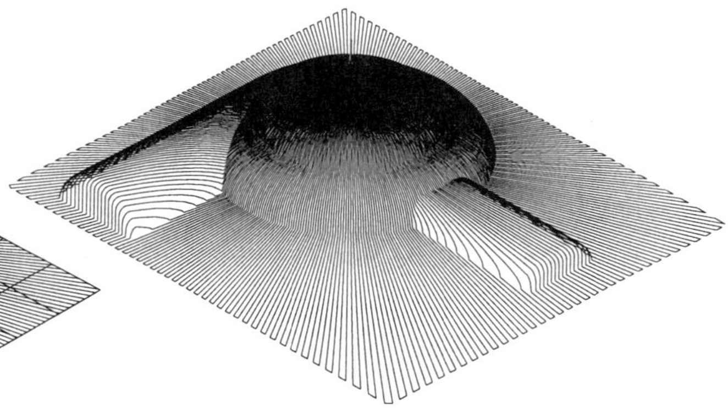

Figure 15.95b

Project 10. Using radial and leftover functions

The surface model shown in Figure 15.96a consists of three surfaces that are intersected each other. Leftover stocks will be found at intersecting corners if a spherical end mill is used. This project uses two surface finish functions to generate finishing toolpaths to machine the surface model. Radial function with a ¼" spherical end mill is used to generate finishing toolpaths. Leftover function with a 5/32" spherical end mill is used to generate toolpaths to remove leftover stock. Figure 15.96 shows toolpaths and verification model.

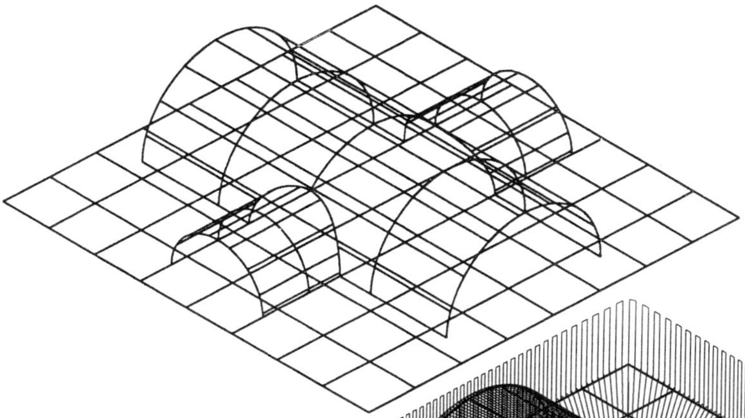

Figure 15.96a

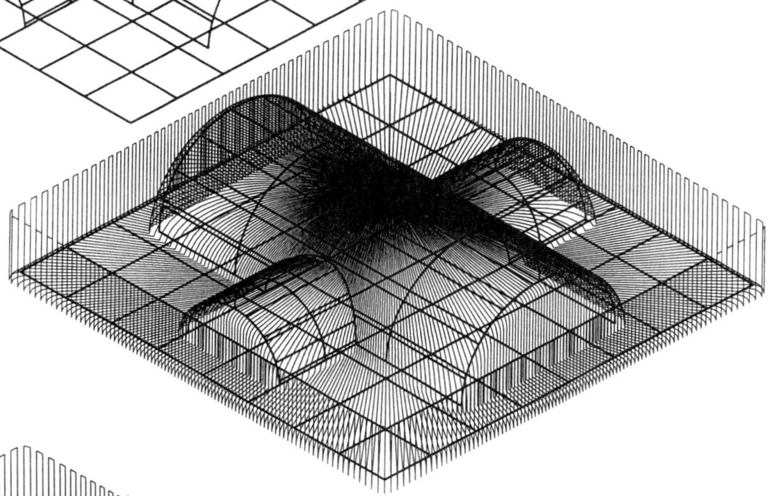

Figure 15.96b

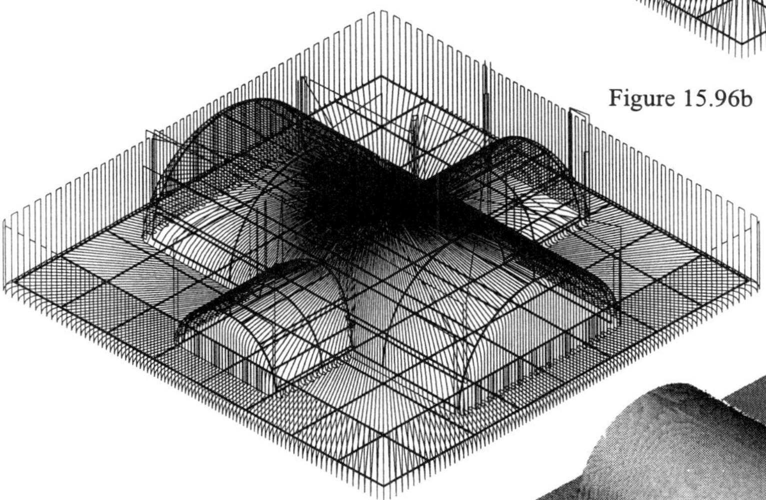

Figure 15.96c

Figure 15.96d

⌛**Tips**
1. Open the surface model file trims1.
2. Create a flat ruled surface.
3. Use the surface finish-radial function to generate finishing toolpaths.
4. Use a ¼" spherical end mill with the radial function.
5. Use the finish-leftover function to remove leftover stock.
6. Use a 5/32" spherical end mill with the leftover function.
7. Run N-See 2000 to verify the toolpaths.

Step 1. Open the surface model file trims1.

Select **MAIN MENU → File → Get**
File name: **trims1**
The surface model appears as in Figure 15.97.

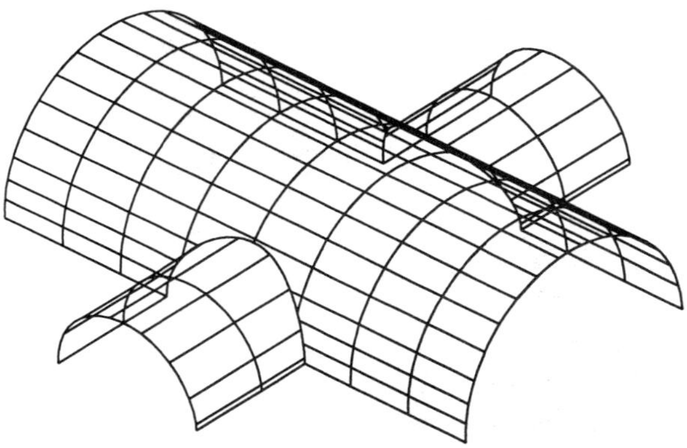

Figure 15.97

Step 2. Create a rectangle.

Select **Cplane → Top**
Select **Z**, then enter **0**
Select **Level**, then enter **3**
Select **Color**, then enter **13**
Select **MAIN MENU → Create → Rectangle → 2 points**
Enter the lower left corner: **-3,-3**
Enter the upper right corner: **3,3**

The rectangle is added to the model as in Figure 15.98.

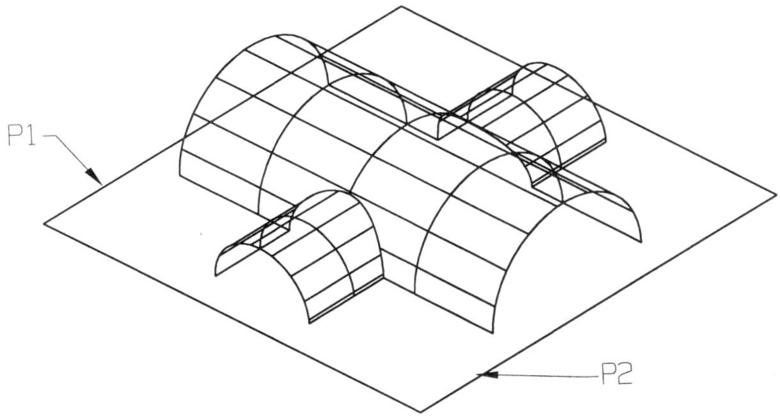

Figure 15.98

Step 3. Create a ruled surface.

Use the pick points in Figure 15.98.
Select **MAIN MENU → Create → Surface → Ruled → Single**
Pick **P1** and **P2**
Select **Done → Do it**
The ruled surface appears as in Figure 15.99.

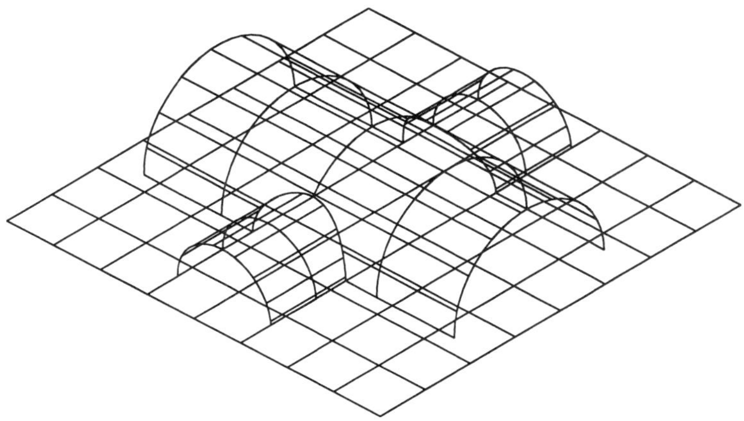

Figure 15.99

Step 4. Initiate the radial function.

Select **MAIN MENU → Toolpaths → Surface → Finish → Radial**
File name for toolpaths: **radial**
Select **All → Surfaces → Done**
Click the right mouse button, then select **"Get tool from library"**
Select **tool number 252** (1/4 sphere end mill)
Select **OK**

Set the tool parameters as below.

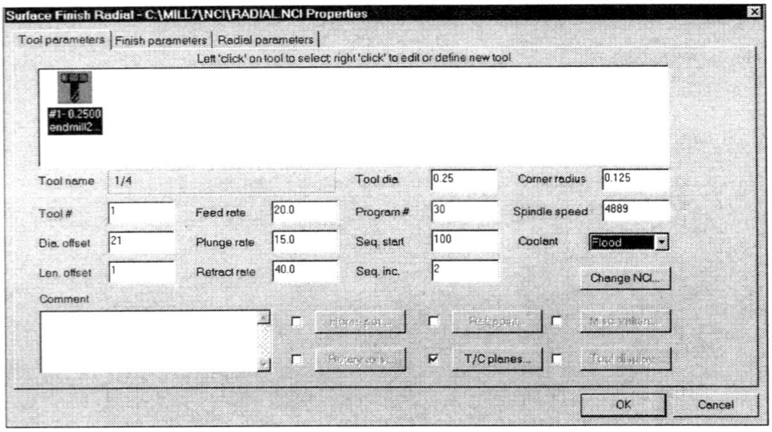

Step 5. Define the finish parameters.

Click the "**Finish parameters**" button

Set the finish parameters as below.

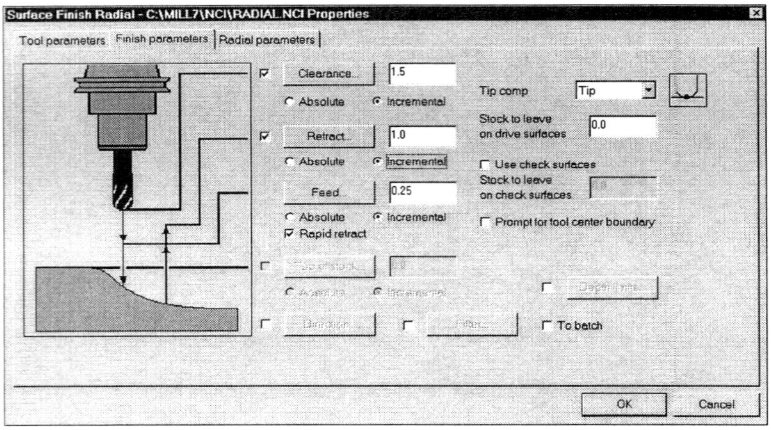

Step 6. Define the radial parameters.

Click the "**Radial parameters**" button

Set the radial parameters as below.

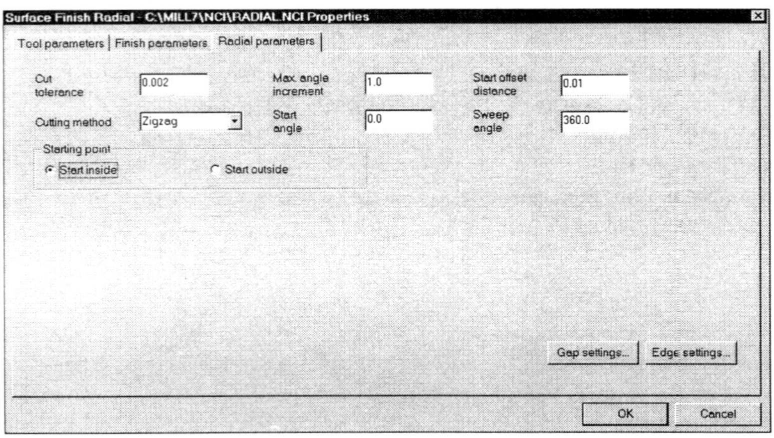

Step 7. Define gap and edge parameters.

Click the **"Gap settings"** button
Select **Smooth** for Motion < Gap size, keep tool down parameter
Select **OK**
Click the **Edge settings** button
Select the **"Over all surface edges"** for Roll tool parameter
Select **OK → OK**
Enter rotation point: **0,0**
The finishing toolpaths are generated as in Figure 15.100.

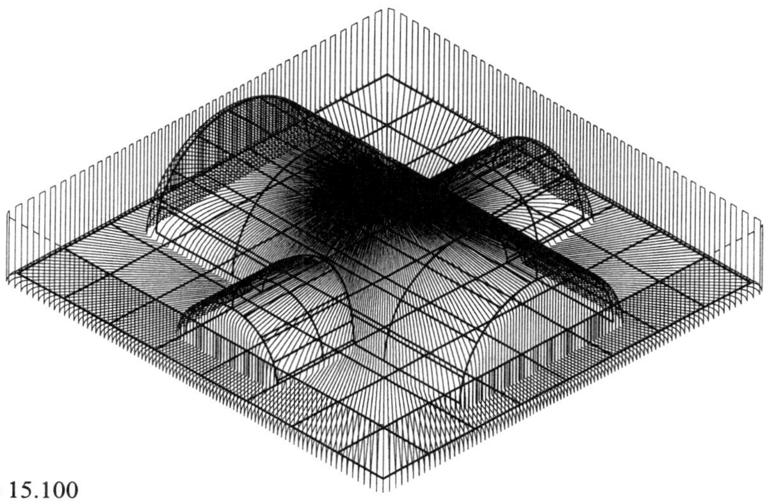

Figure 15.100

Step 8. Initiate the leftover function.

Select **Backup → Leftover → All → Surfaces → Done**
Click the right mouse button, then select **"Get tool from library"**
Select **tool number 250** (5/32 sphere end mill)
Select **OK**
Set the tool parameters as below.

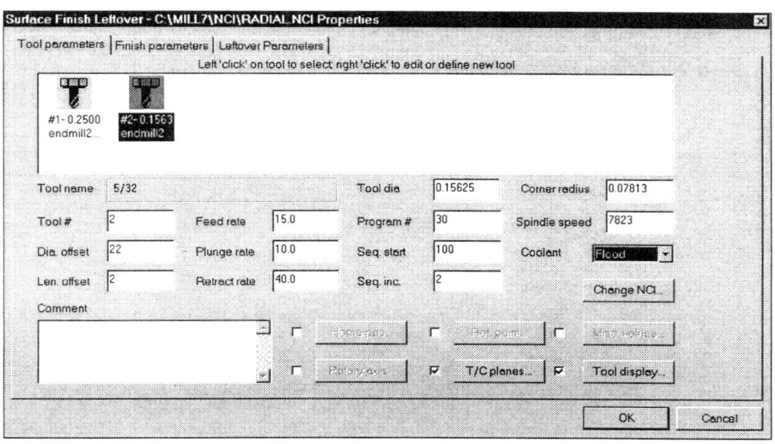

Step 9. Define the finish parameters.

Click the "**Finish parameters**" button
Set the finish parameters as below.

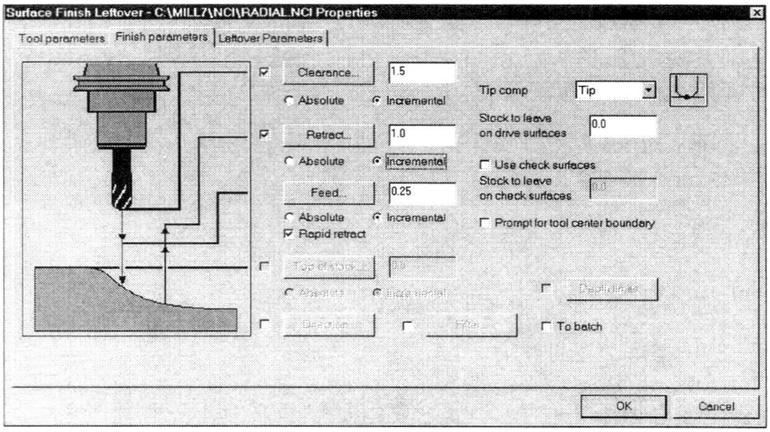

Step 10. Define the leftover parameters.

Click the "**Leftover parameters**" button
Set the leftover parameters as below.

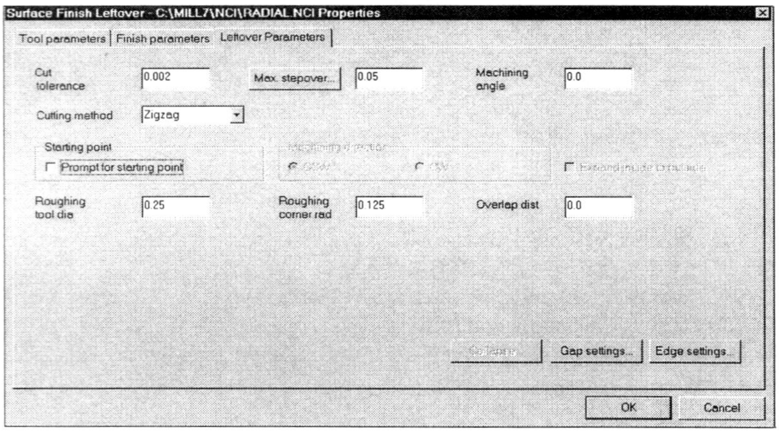

Step 11. Define gap and edge parameters.

Click the "**Gap settings**" button
Select **Smooth** for Motion < Gap size, keep tool down parameter
Select **OK**
Click the "**Edge settings**" button
Select "**Over all surface edges**" for Roll tool parameter
Select **OK → OK** to generate leftover toolpaths as shown in Figure 15.101.

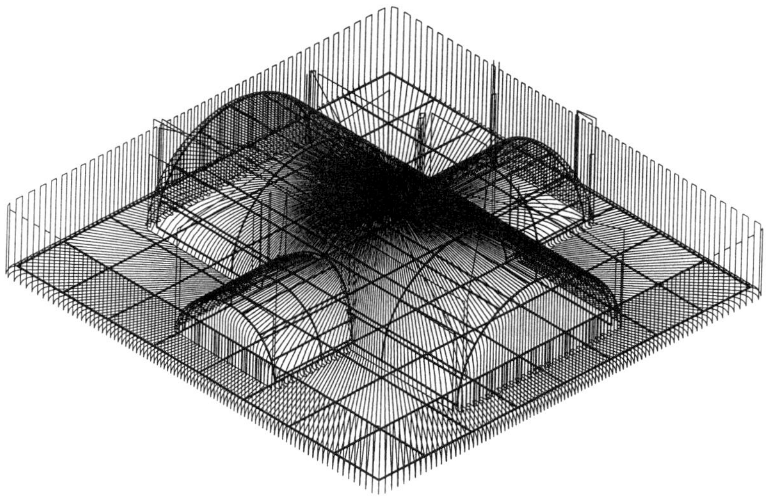

Figure 15.101

Step 12. Verify the toolpaths.

Select **BACKUP (Operations → Select All → N-See 2000**

Set the select mode parameters as below.

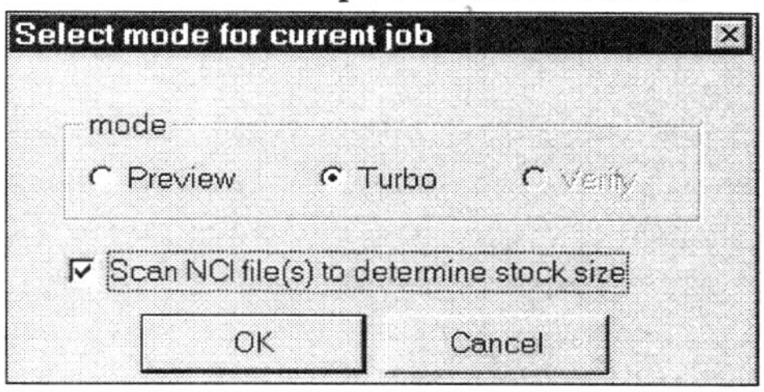

Select **OK**

Select **Do it** to verify the toolpaths

The verify model should resemble Figure 15.102.

Figure 15.102

Step 13. Save the toolpaths file.

Select **BACKUP** to return to Operations Manager dialog box
Select **OK** from Operations Manager dialog box
Select **MAIN MENU → NC utils → Edit NCI**
Select **Yes** to "Operations have been modified. Create the NCI text file?"
Select **Quit** from Edit NCI dialog box

15.19 Project Finish Function

This function generates a set of toolpaths by projecting an existing set of toolpaths for finish cutting a surface model (Figure 15.103). In addition to existing toolpaths, curves and points are also valid entities to be used for projection to obtain finish toolpaths. The project parameters dialog box appears as below.

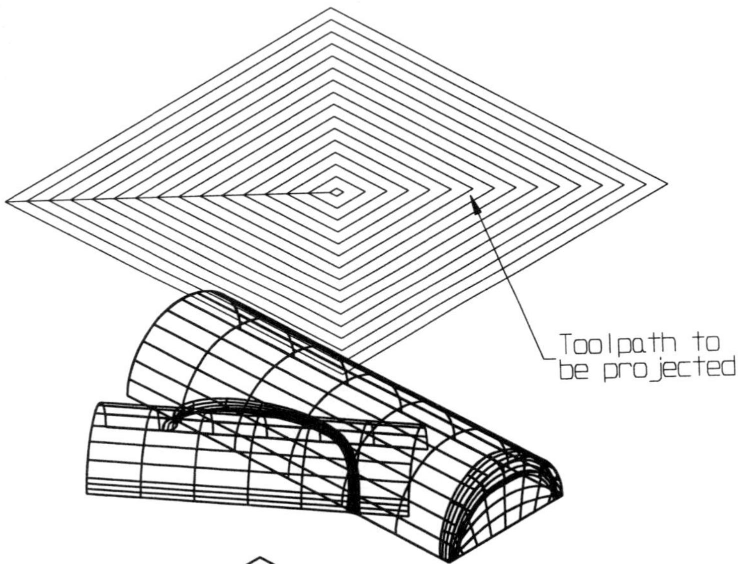

Figure 15.103a

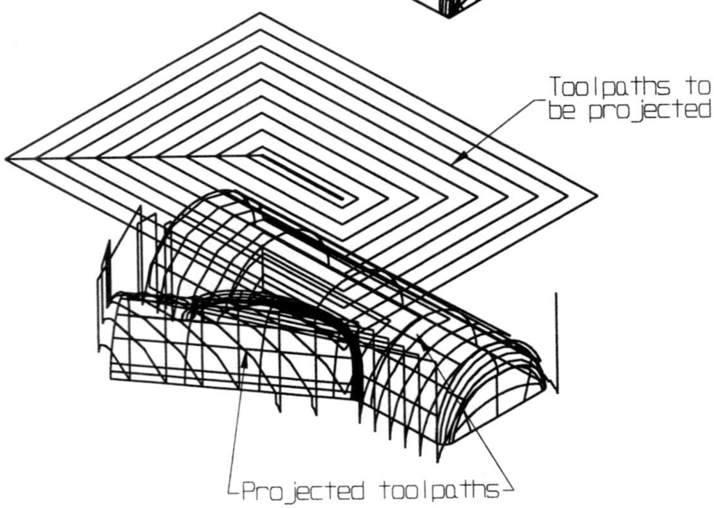

Figure 15.103b

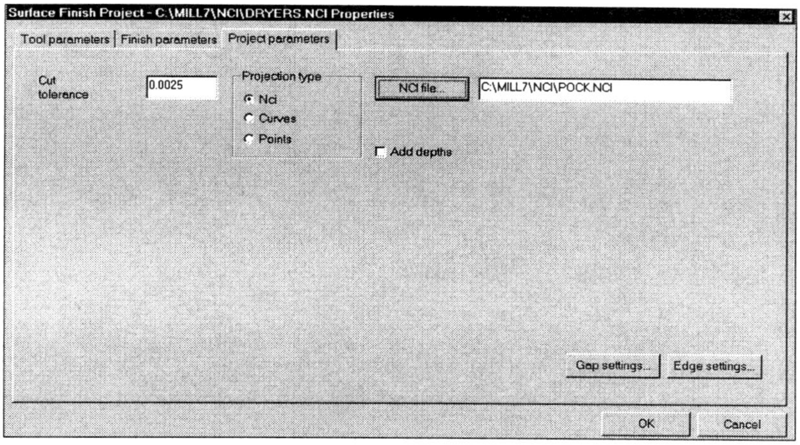

This function provides users better control of tool motions and cut pattern and orientation. The toolpaths to be projected control the spacing of cut passes and their X and Y coordinates. The surfaces to be projected onto control the Z-depth and X and Y boundary of the cut.

Add Depths

The "Add depths" parameter takes the depths from the selected NCI file and applies them to the toolpath. This means that the Z-depth of toolpaths are shifted to the existing toolpaths, rather than on the surfaces (Figure 15.104).

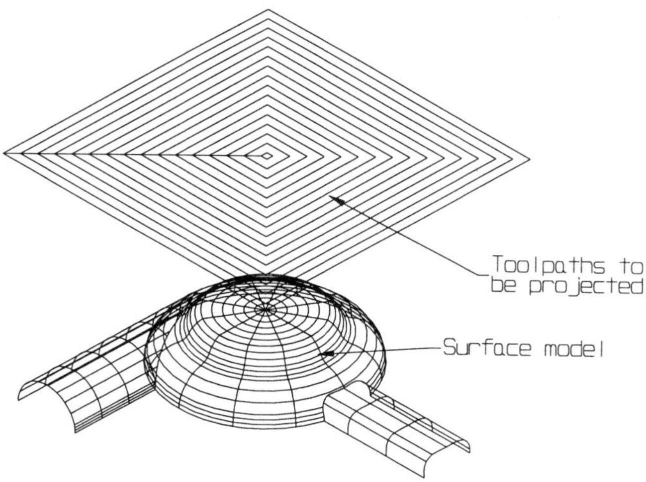

Figure 15.104a

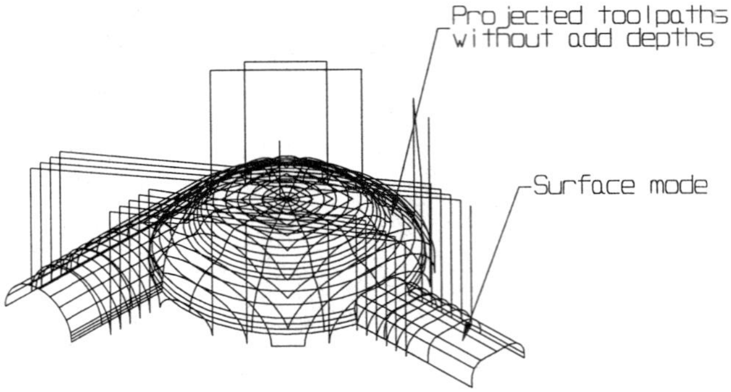

Figure 15.104b

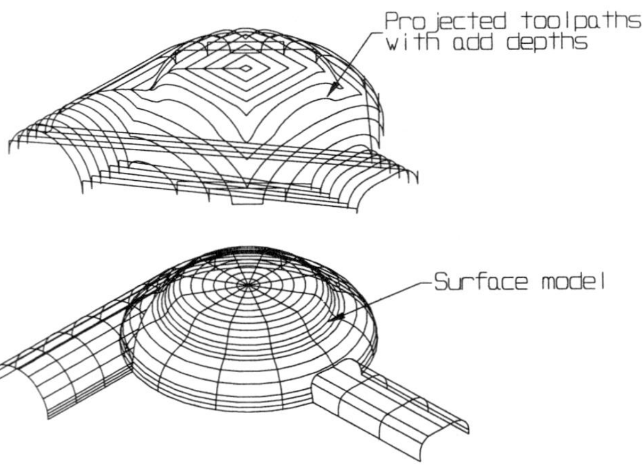

Figure 15.104c

Project 11. Using project function

This project shows how to generate finishing toolpaths to machine a surface model from an existing toolpath. A flat ruled surface is added to generate the toolpaths to be projected as shown in Figure 15.105b. This set of toolpaths is then projected onto the dryer surface model to generate the finishing toolpaths as shown in Figure 15.105c. Figure 15.105d is the verification model.

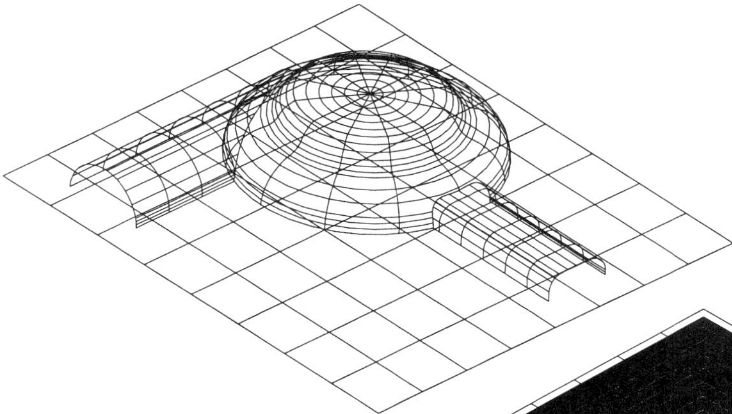

Figure 15.105a

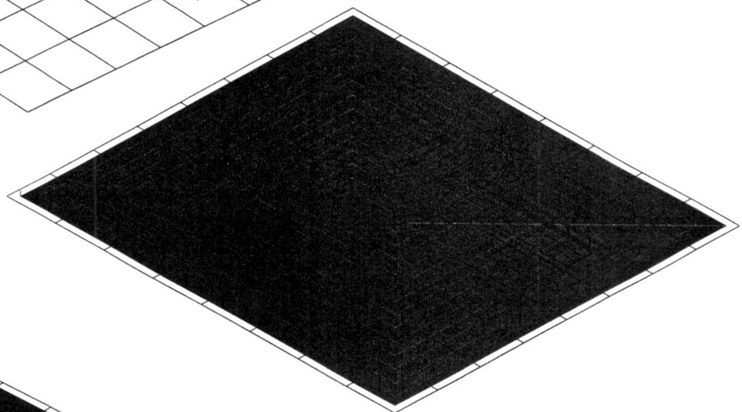

Figure 15.105b

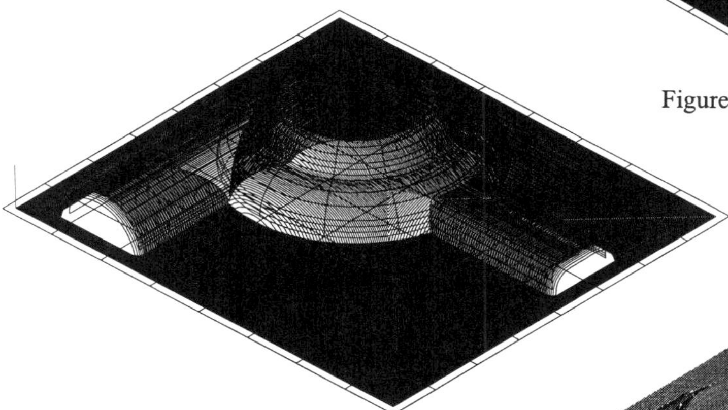

Figure 15.105c

Figuer 15.105d

Tips
1. Open the surface model file dryers.
2. Create a ruled surface from a rectangle.
3. Use the 2D pocket function to generate pocketing toolpaths with a ¼" flat end mill.
4. Save the pocketing toolpaths as proj1.
5. Use surface finish-project function to generate finish toolpaths.
6. Use a ¼" sphere end mill.
7. Verify the toolpaths using N-See 2000.

Step 1. Open the surface model dryers.

Select **MAIN MENU → File → Get**
File name: **dryers**
The dryer surface model appears as in Figure 15.106.

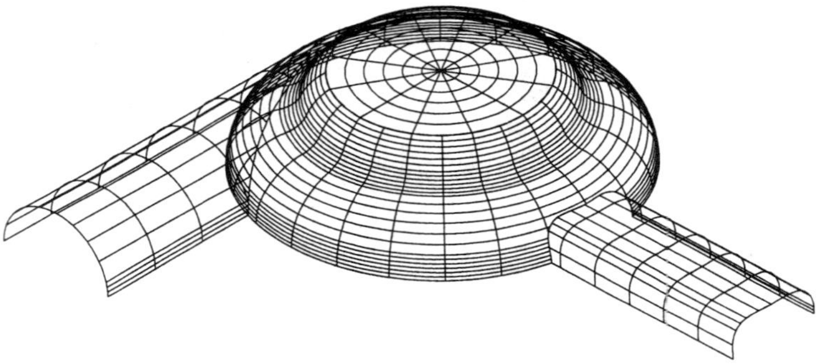

Figure 15.106

Step 2. Change graphic view to Top and set Z value to 0.0.

Select **Gview → Top**
Select **Cplane → Top**
Select **Z**, then enter **0**
The surface model shown in isometric view becomes Figure 15.107.

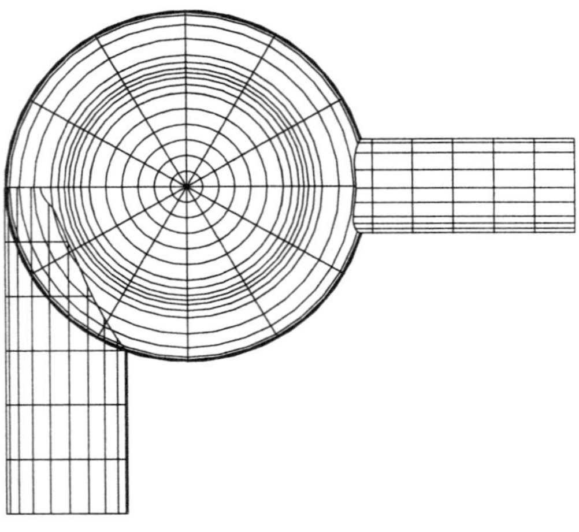

Figure 15.107

Step 3. Create a rectangle.

Select **Level**, then enter **10**
Select **MAIN MENU → Create → Rectangle → 2 points**
Enter the lower left corner: **-2.6, -4.0**
Enter the upper right corner: **4.5, 2.3**
Select **Gview → Isometric**
The rectangle is added to the model as in Figure 15.108.

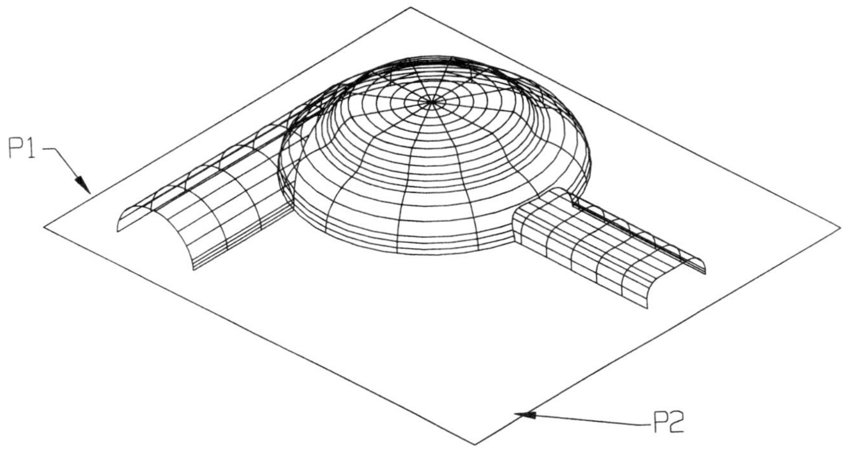

Figure 15.108

Step 4. Create a ruled surface.

Use the pick points in Figure 15.108.
Select **MAIN MENU → Create → Surface → Ruled → Single**
Pick **P1** and **P2** as shown in Figure A4
Select **Done → Do it**
The ruled surface is created as in Figure 15.109.

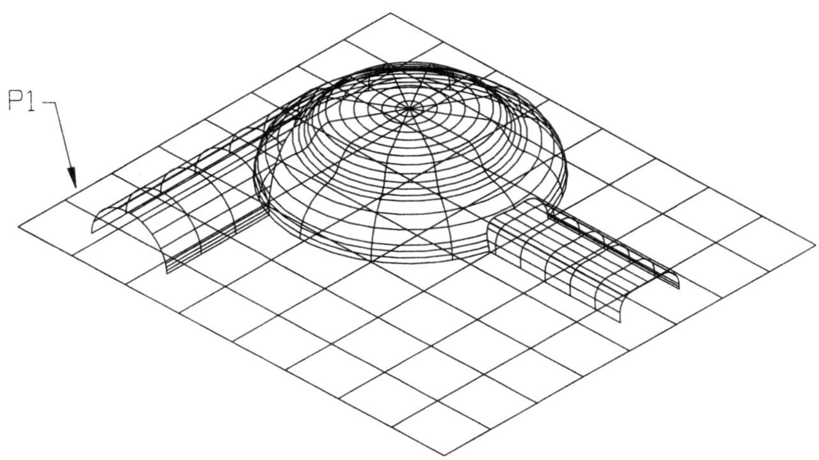

Figure 15.109

Step 5. Initiate the pocket function.

Use the pick point in Figure 15.109.
Select **MAIN MENU → Toolpaths → Pocket**
File name for toolpath: **proj1**
Select **Chain**, then pick **P1**
Select **Done**
The tool parameters dialog box should appear.
Click the right mouse button, then select **"Get tool from library"**
Pick **tool number 235** (¼ flat end mill)
Select **OK**
Set the tool parameters as below.

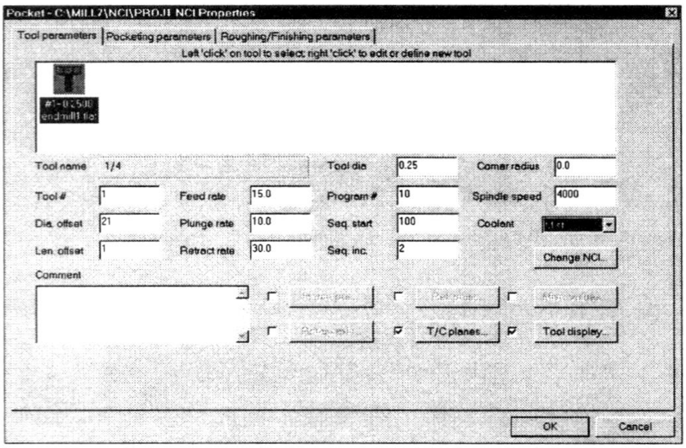

Step 6. Define pocketing parameters.

Click the **"Pocketing parameters"** button
Set pocketing parameters as below.

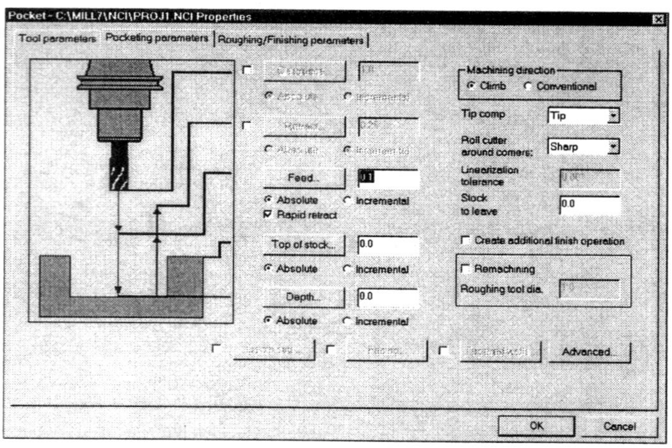

Step 7. Define the roughing/finishing parameters.

Click the "**Roughing/finishing parameters**" button
Set roughing parameters as below.

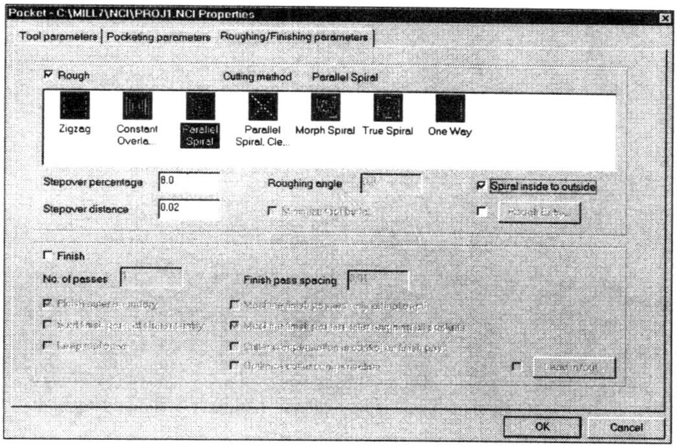

Select **OK**
The pocketing toolpaths are generated as in Figure 15.110.

Figure 15.110

Step 8. Save the toolpath file.

Select **MAIN MENU** → **NC utils** → **Edit NCI**
Select **Yes** to "Operations have been modified. Create the NCI text file?"
Select **Quit** from Edit NCI dialog box

Step 9. Initiate the finish project function.

Select **MAIN MENU** → **Toolpaths** → **New**
Select **Yes** to "Deleting all operations and tools. MC7 file has changed."
Select **Surface** → **Finish** → **Project**
File name for toolpaths: **projectf**
Select **All** → **Surfaces** → **Done**

Step 10. Define the tool parameters.

Click the right mouse button, then select **"Get tool from library"**
Pick **tool number 252** (1/4 sphere endmill)
Select **OK**
Define the tool parameters as below.

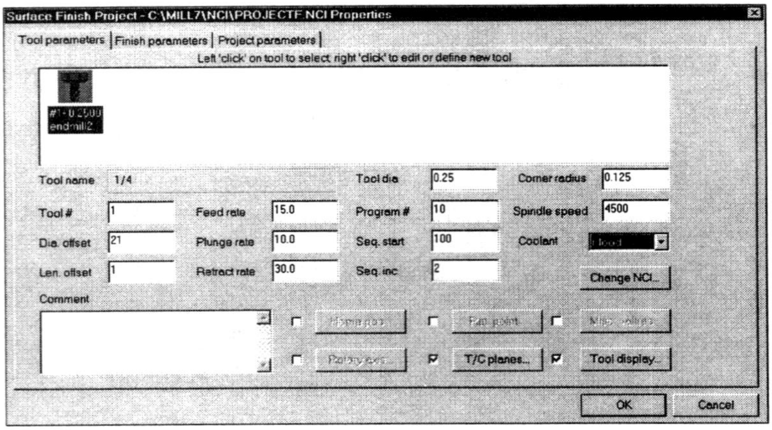

Step 11. Define the finish parameters.

Click the "**Finish parameters**" button
Define the finish parameters as below.

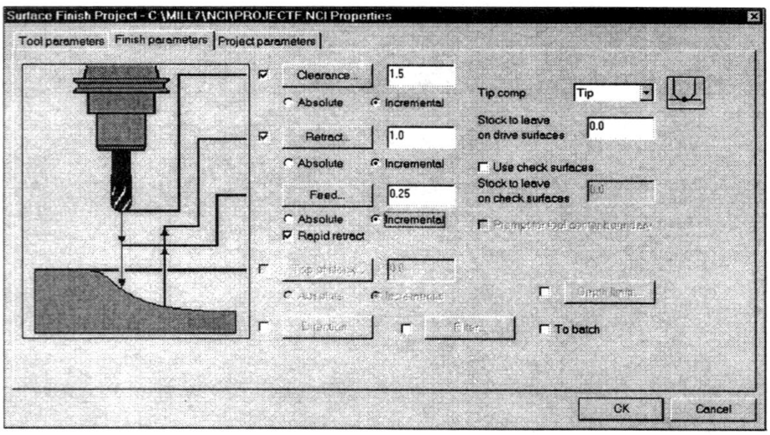

Step 12. Define the project parameters.

Click the "**Project parameters**" button
Click "**NCI**" from Projection type
Click "**NCI file**" button to open NCI files for selection
Select **Proj1.nci** for file name
Select **Save**

The project parameters dialog box appears as below.

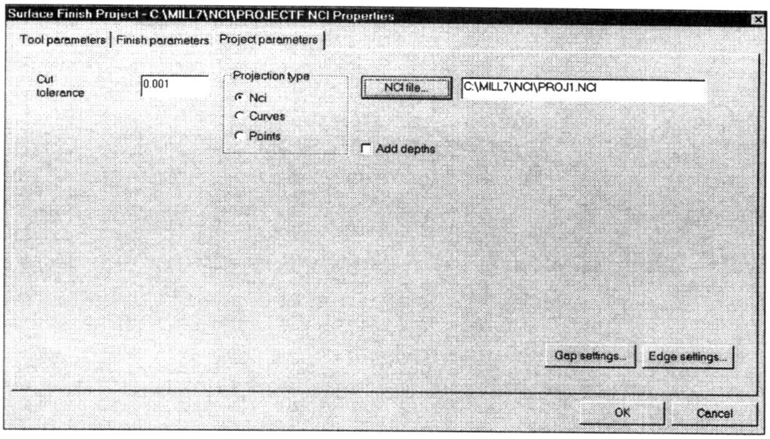

Select **OK** to generate finishing toolpaths

It takes several minutes for the computer to generate the toolpaths as shown in Figure 15.111.

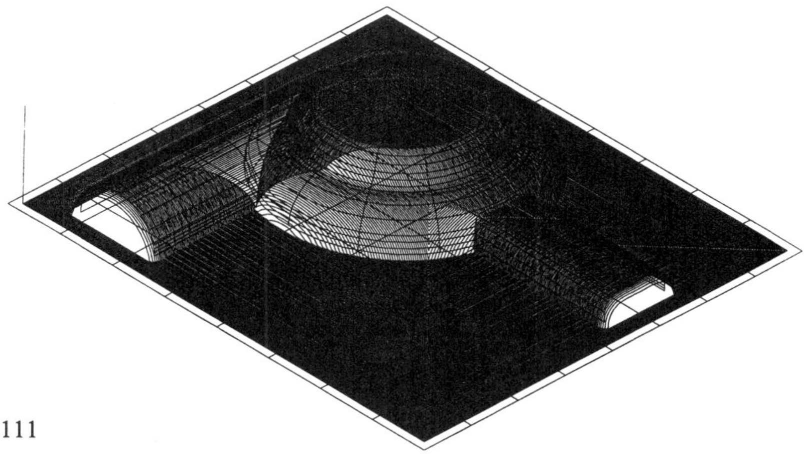

Figure 15.111

Step 13. Verify the model.

Select **Operations → N-See 2000**

Set "Select mode for current job" dialog box as below.

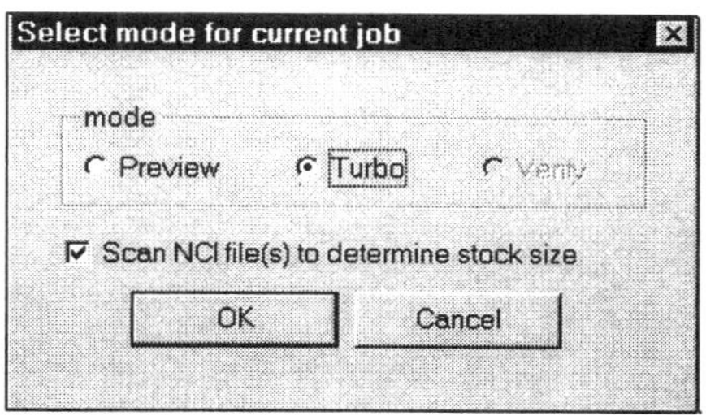

Select **OK**

Select **Do it** to verify the toolpaths

The verification model should resemble Figure 15.112.

Figure 15.112

Step 14. Save the toolpath file.

Select **MAIN MENU** to return to Operations Manager dialog box
Select **OK** to exit Operations Manager dialog box

15.20 Flowline Function

This function generates toolpaths to finish cut a surface model. The toolpaths run in the direction of surface flowline. The flowline parameters dialog box appears as below.

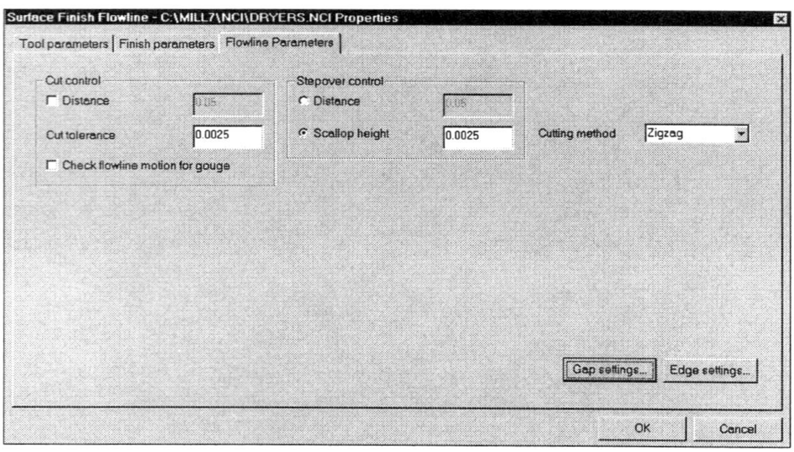

The "Check flowline motion for gouge" parameter is very important when multiple surfaces are included in generating toolpaths. When this parameter is turned to Off, gouges may occur if surfaces are not properly trimmed (Figure 15.113). When this parameter is turned to On, all potential gouges are removed (Figure 15.114).

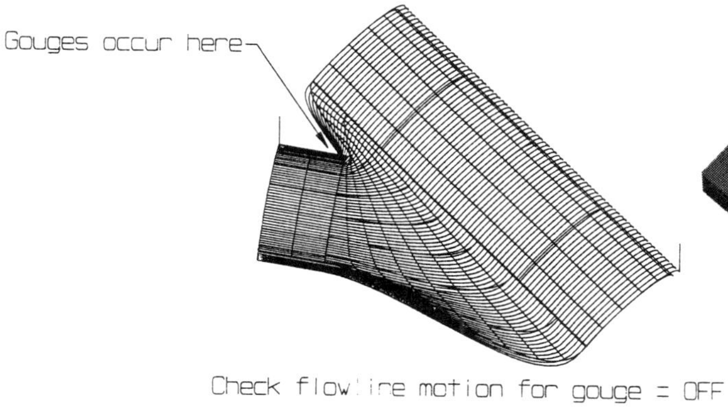

Figure 15.113a

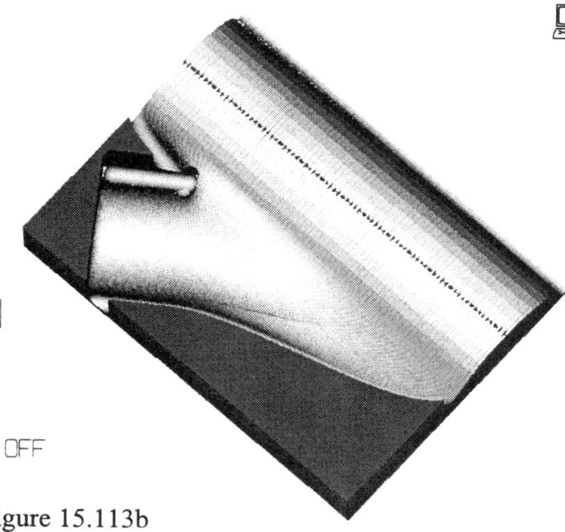

Figure 15.113b

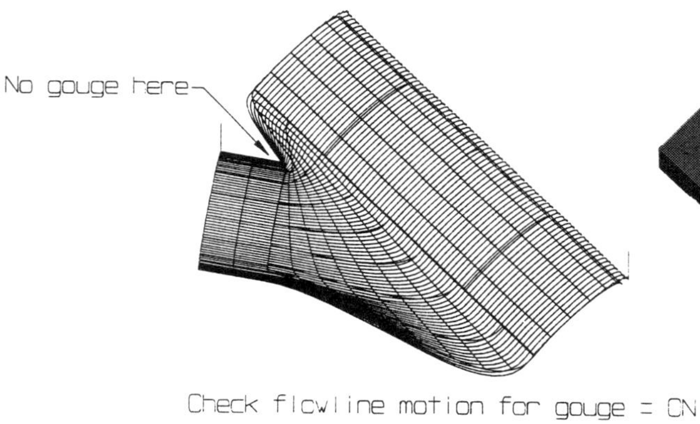

Figure 15.114a

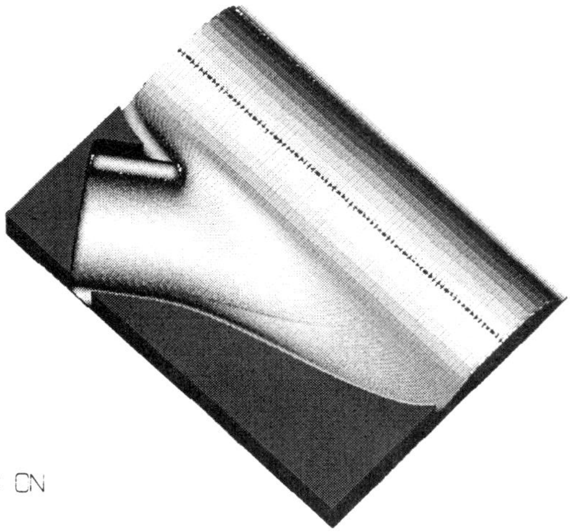

Figure 15.114b

Project 12. Using flowline function

Use the flowline function generates finishing toolpaths to cut a Coons surface as shown in Figure 15.115.

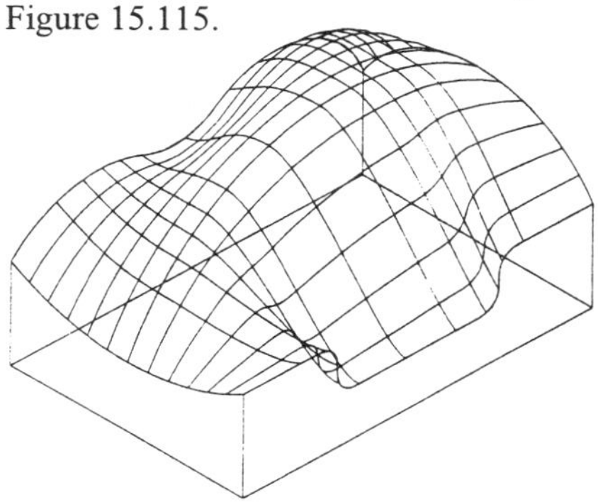

Figure 15.115a

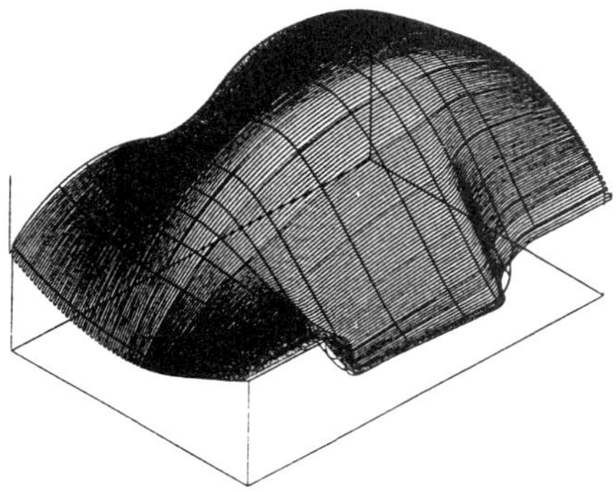

Figure 15.115b

Tips 1. Open the Coons surface model file coonnss2.

2. Use the surface finish-flowline function to generate toolpaths to cut the surface.

3. Use 3/8" sphere end mill.

Step 1. Open the coons surface model file "coonss2".

Select **MAIN MENU → File → Get**
File name: **coonss2**
The surface model appears as in Figure 15.116.

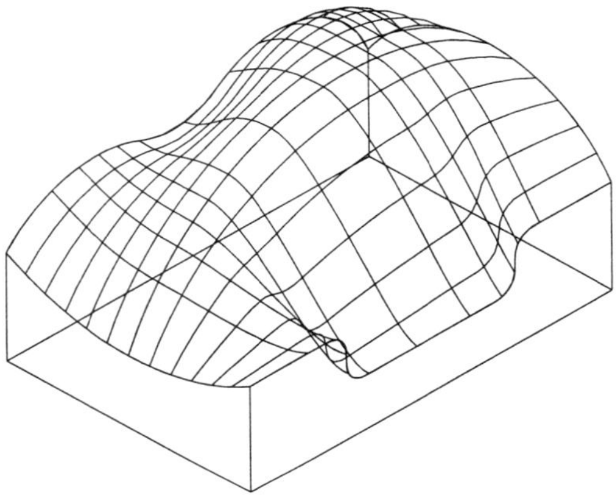

Figure 15.116

Step 2. Initiate the flowline function.

Select **MAIN MENU → Toolpaths → Surface → Finish → Flowline**
File name for toolpaths: **flowline**
Select **All → Surfaces → Done**
Click the right mouse button, then select **"Get tool from library"**
Select **tool number 254** (3/8 sphere end mill)
Select **OK**
Set the tool parameters as below.

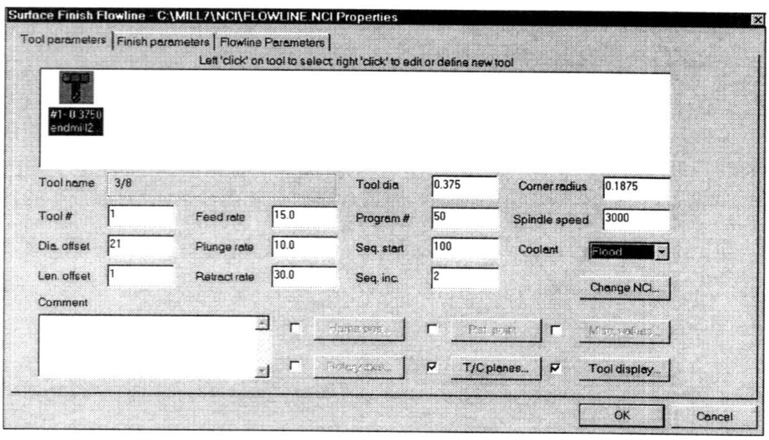

Step 3. Define the finish parameters.

Click the "**Finish parameters**" button
Set the finish parameters as below.

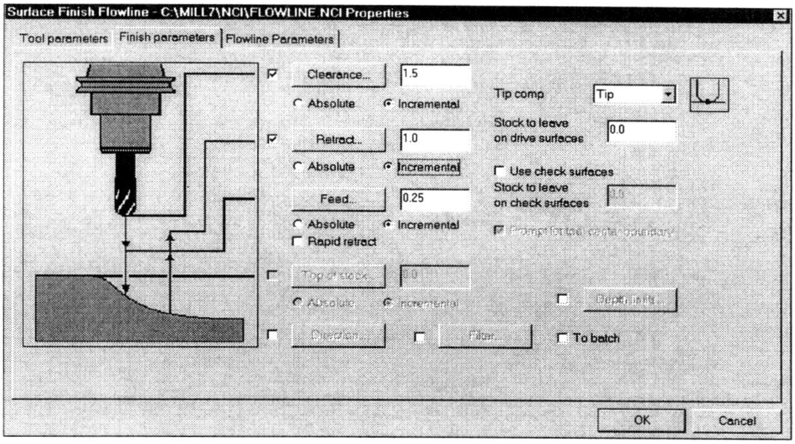

Step 4. Define the flowline parameters.

Click the "**Flowline parameters**" button
Set the flowline parameters as below.

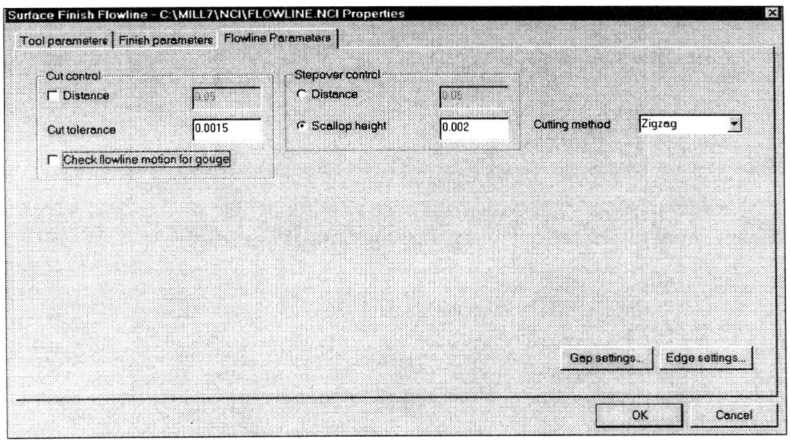

Step 5. Define gap and edge parameters.

Click the "**Gap settings**" button
Select **Direct** for Motion < Gap size, keep tool down parameter
Select **OK**
Click the "**Edge settings**" button
Select "**Over all surface edges**" for Roll tool parameter
Select **OK → OK**
The arrow to show the direction and starting location of toolpaths is initially located at the upper-right corner of the surface. The cut direction is in the X direction.
Select "**Cut dir**" to change the cut direction to the Y direction
Select "**Start**" to move the starting location to the upper-left corner
Select **Do it** to generate the toolpaths as shown in Figure 15.117.

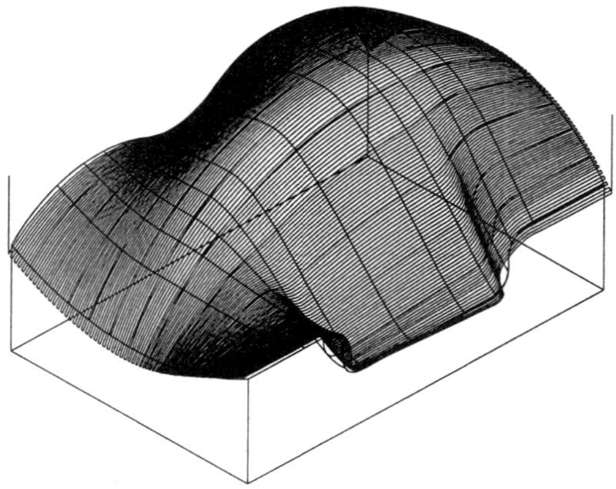

Figure 15.117

Step 6. Save the toolpath file.

Select **BACKUP** to return to Operations Manager dialog box
Select **OK** from Operations Manager dialog box
Select **MAIN MENU → NC utils → Edit NCI**
Select **Yes** to "Operations have been modified. Create the NCI text file?"
Select **Quit** from Edit NCI dialog box

15.21 Contour Function

This function generates a set of toolpaths to cut a surface model along their surface contours (Figure 15.118). The finish contour parameters dialog box appears as below.

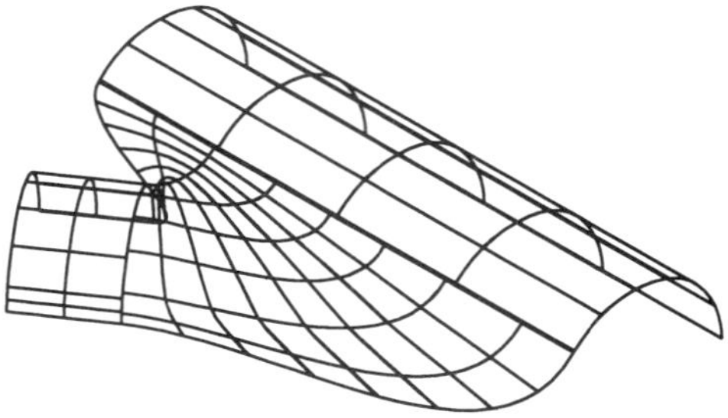

Figure 15.118a

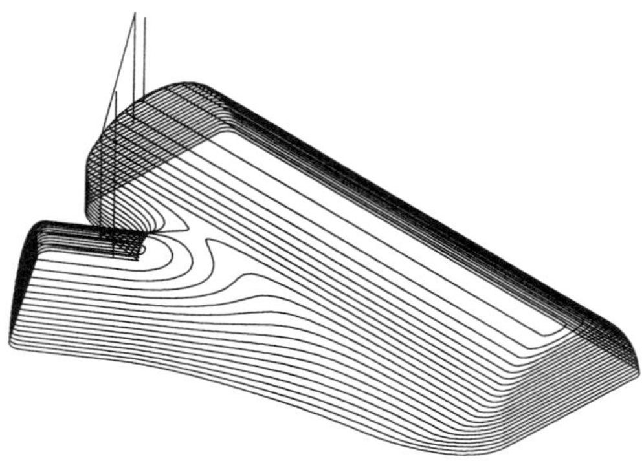

Figure 15.118b

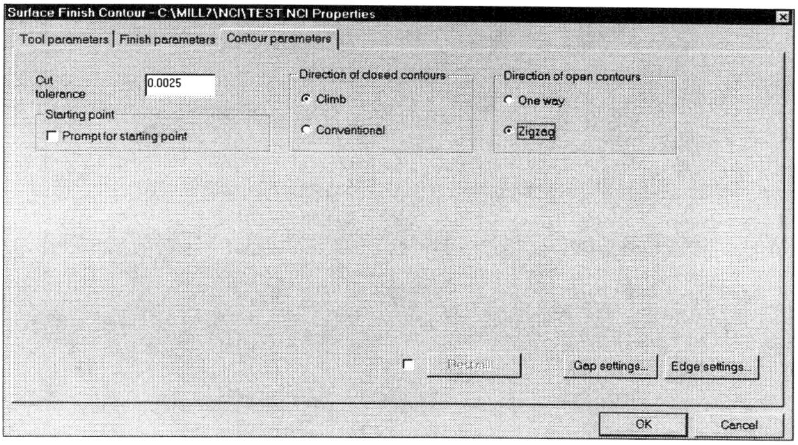

A potential problem with using the contour function is that the top flat or curve surface may not be cut and leaves a strip of uncut material as shown in Figure 15.119. The shallow function is used to generate toolpaths to remove these uncut areas.

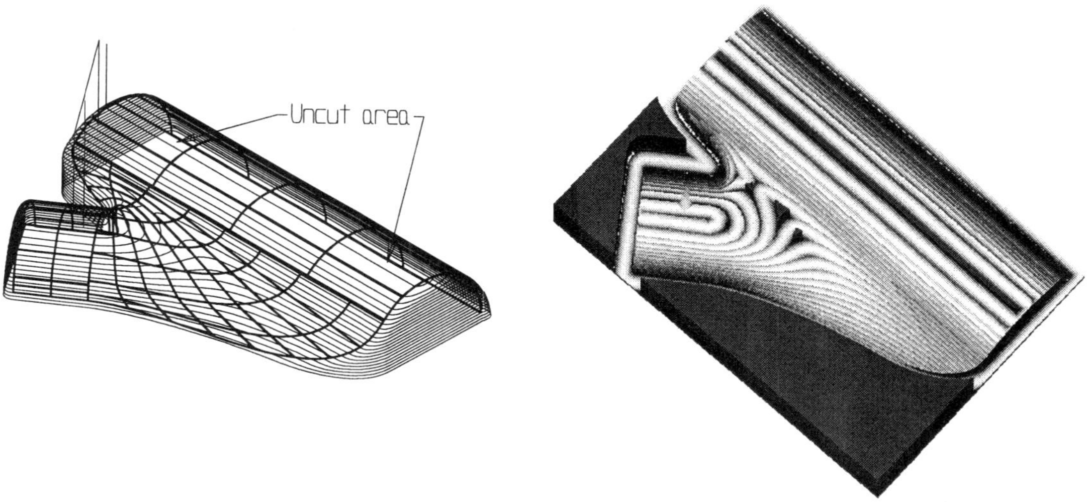

Figure 15.119

15.22 Finish Shallow Function

The shallow function generates a set of toolpaths to clean the remaining stock from shallow areas defined by two slope angles. This function is particularly useful to remove materials that are left from using a finish contour function. The finish shallow parameters dialog box appears as below.

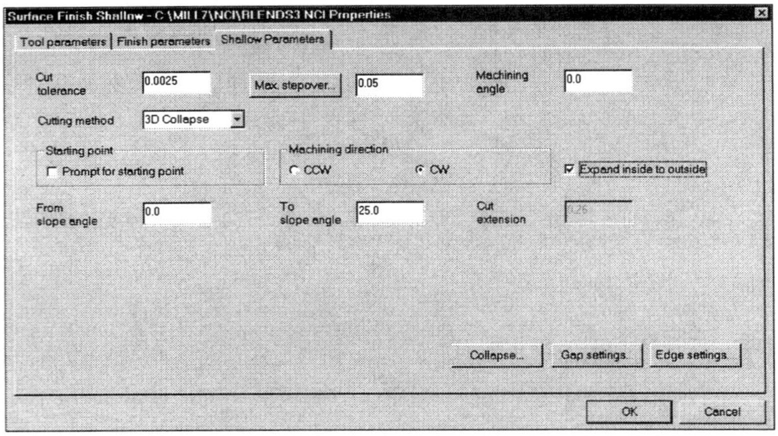

The following two angle parameters define the shallow areas (Figure 15.120):

From slope angle: specify the minimum slope angle of the shallow areas on the surfaces.

To slope angle: specify the maximum slope angle of the shallow areas on the surfaces.

The angles are measured from horizontal plane and going downward being positive angle. The horizontal plane has 0degrees.

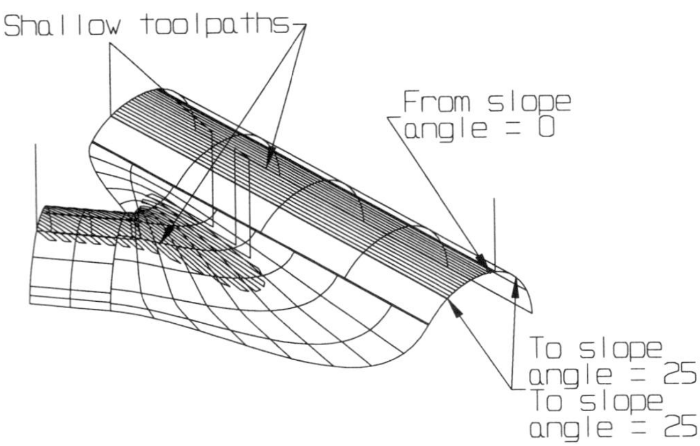

Figure 15.120

The "Cut extension" parameter is used to extend the cut in such a way that the tool can plunge into a previously cut area before machining the leftover stock. The cut extension distance adds to both ends of the toolpath and follows the curvature of the surface. Figure 15.121 shows the effect of adding cut extension.

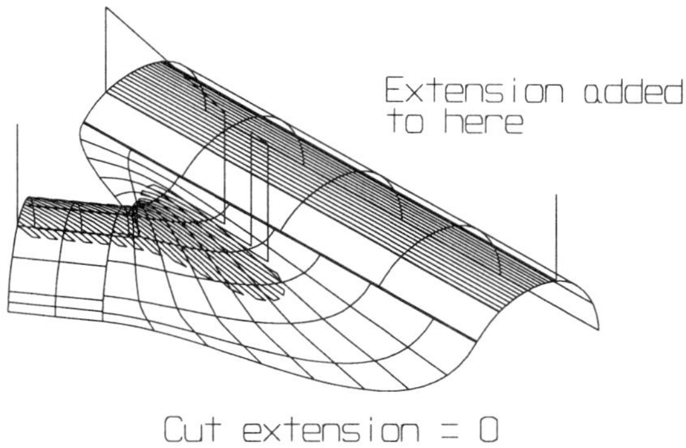

Figure 15.121a

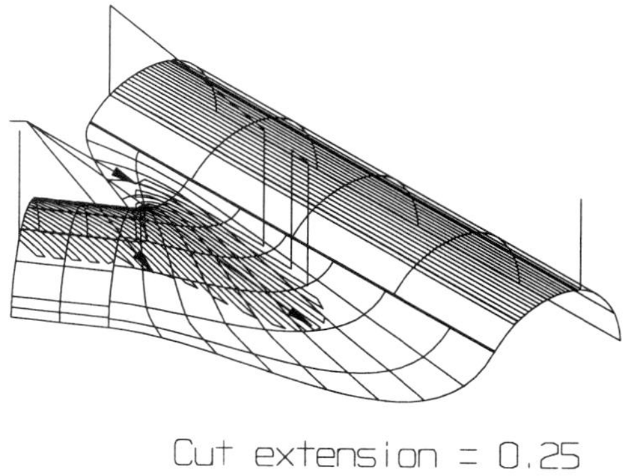

Figure 15.121b

There are three cutting methods available in this finish function: zigzag, one way, and 3D collapse. The "3D collapse" method creates a zone around the cutting area, cuts the boundary of the zone, and then steps in to create a cut that offsets the outer boundary by the maximum stepover (Figure 15.122).

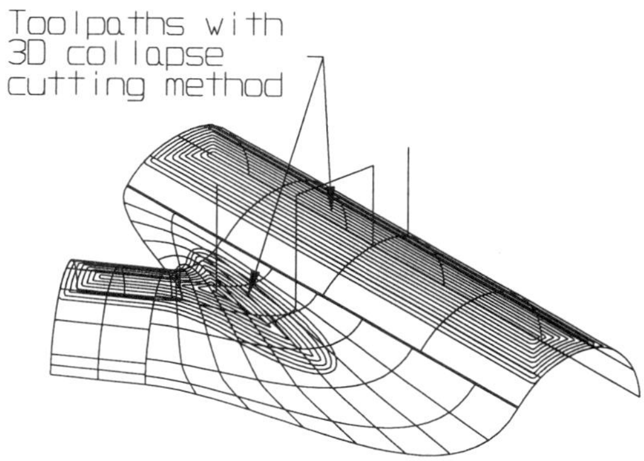

Figure 15.122

When 3D collapse cutting method is selected, the "Collapse" button becomes active to open Collapse parameters dialog box as below.

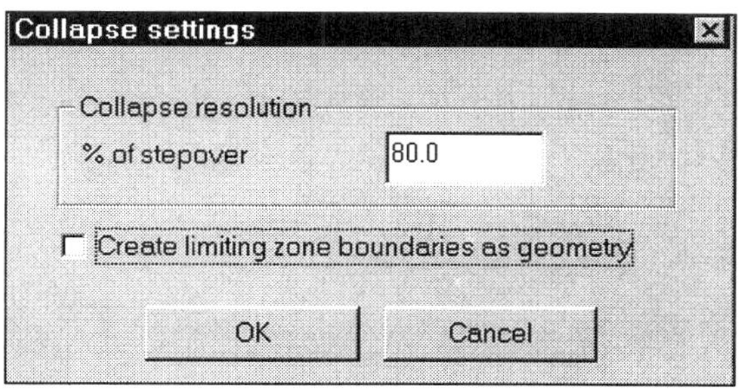

The "Collapse settings" defines how smoothly the collapse zones of a 3D collapse are created. The smaller the collapse resolution, the more accurate the toolpath. The collapse resolution is expressed in the percentage of the maximum stepover.

The "Create limiting zone boundaries as geometry" parameter is used to create geometry from the tool center boundaries of the 3D collapse.

13

Project 13. Using shallow and contour functions

This project uses two toolpath functions to generate two set of finishing toolpaths to machine a surface model. The shallow function is used to generate toolpaths to cut the areas that left from the contouring toolpaths. Figure 15.123 shows the surface model and two sets of finishing toolpaths.

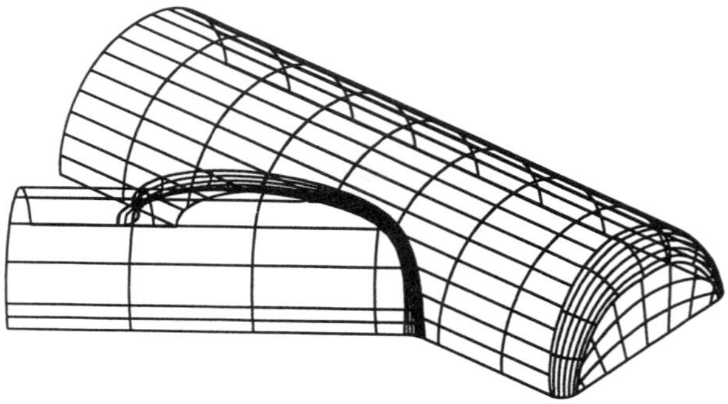

Figure 15.123a

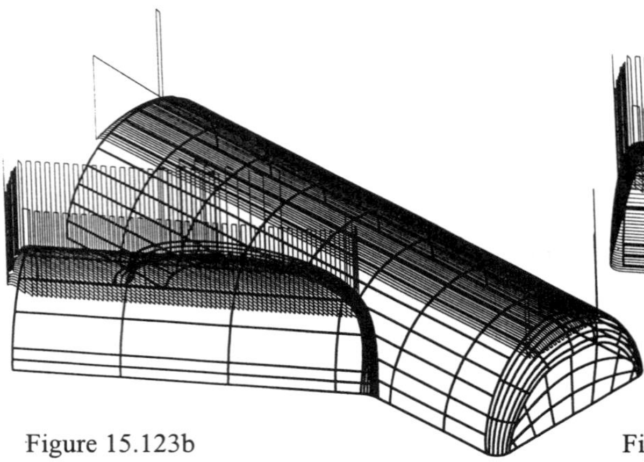

Figure 15.123b

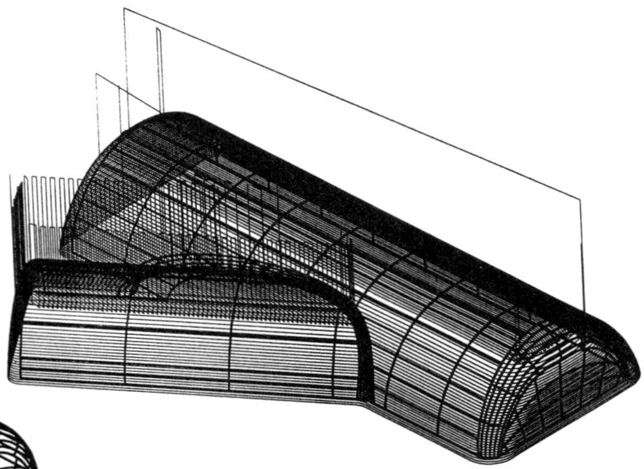

Figure 15.123c

Tips 1. Open the surface model file trims2.

2. Use the shallow function to generate toolpaths for cutting surfaces between 0→ and 25→.

3. Use a ¼" sphere end mill.

4. Use the surface finish-contour function to generate toolpaths.

5. Use the same ¼" sphere end mill.

Step 1. Open the surface model file trims2.

Select **MAIN MENU → File → Get**
File name: **trims2**

The fillet surface appears as Figure 15.124.

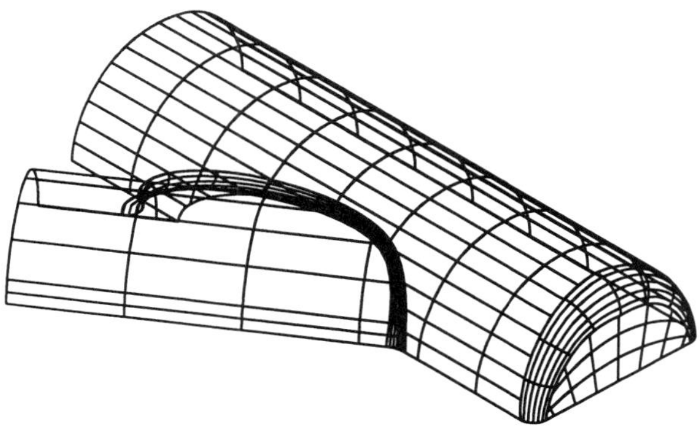

Figure 15.124

Step 2. Initiate the shallow function.

Select **Cplane → Top**
Select **MAIN MENU → Toolpaths → Surface → Finish → Shallow**
File name for toolpaths: **shallow**
Select **All → Surfaces → Done**
The tool parameters dialog box should appear on the screen.
Click the right mouse button, then select **"Get tool from library"**
Select **tool number 252** →1/4 sphere end mil
Select **OK**
Set the tool parameters as below.

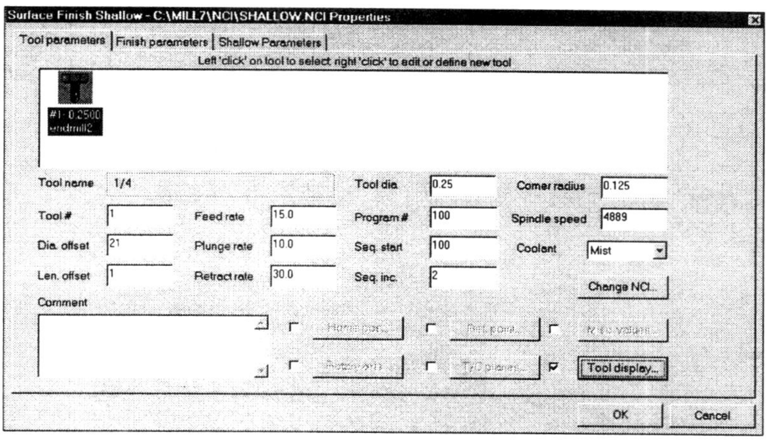

Step 3. Define the finish parameters.

Click the "**Finish parameters**" button

Set the finish parameters as below.

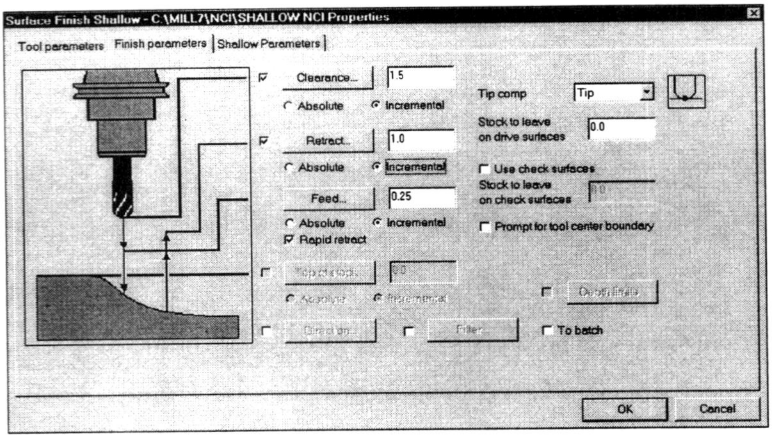

Step 4. Define the shallow parameters.

Click the "**Shallow parameters**" button

Set the shallow parameters as below.

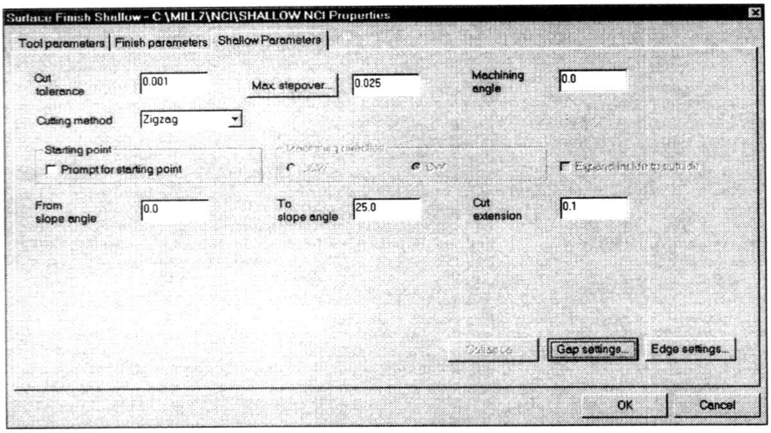

Step 5. Define the edge setting parameters.

Click the "**Edge settings**" button

Click "**Over all surface edges**" for Roll tool parameter

Select **OK** to return back to Shallow parameters dialog box

Select **OK** to generate toolpaths

The shallowing toolpaths between 0 and 25 degrees are generated as in Figure 15.125.

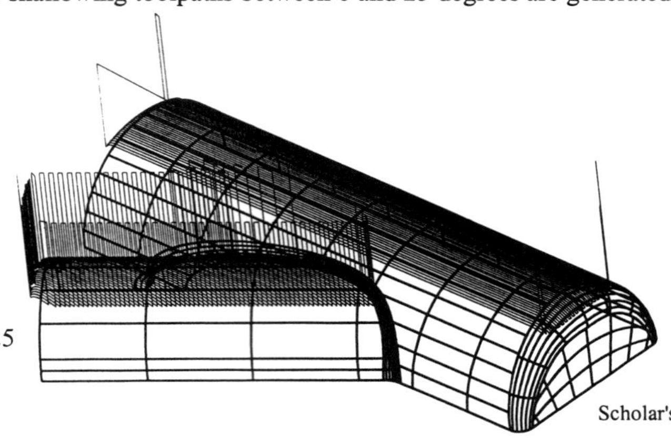

Figure 15.125

Step 6. Initiate the contour function.

Select **BACKUP → Surface → Finish → Contour**
Select **All → Surfaces → Done**
Set the tool parameters as below.

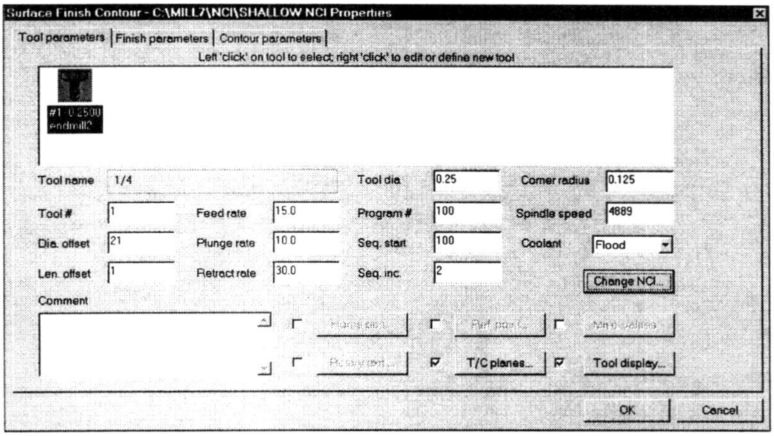

Step 7. Define the finish parameters.

Click the "**Finish parameters**" button
Set the finish parameters as below.

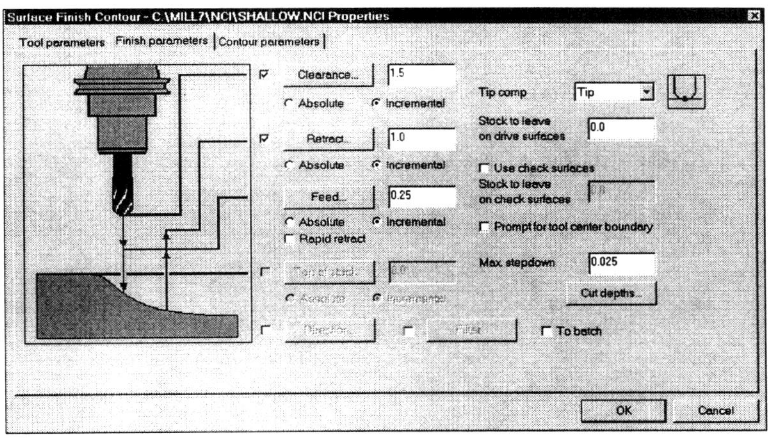

Step 8. Define the contour parameters.

Click the "**Contour parameters**" button

Set the contour parameters as below.

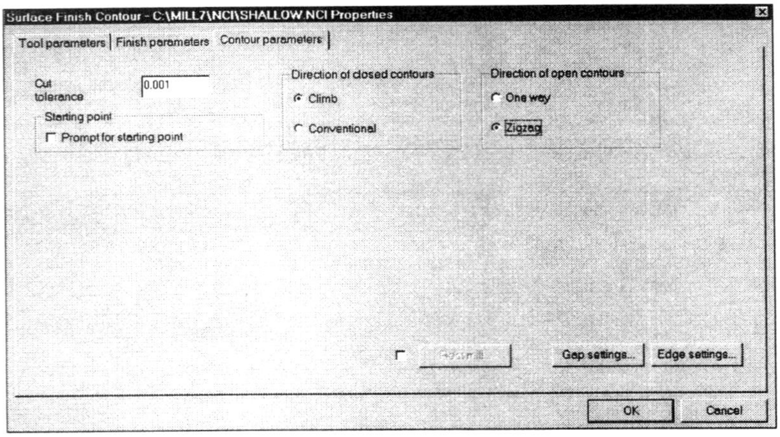

Step 9. Define the edge setting parameters.

Click the "**Edge settings**" button
Click "**Over all surface edges**" for Roll tool parameter
Select **OK** → **OK** to generate contouring toolpaths
It will take a few minutes for computer to generate the toolpaths as shown in Figure 15.126.

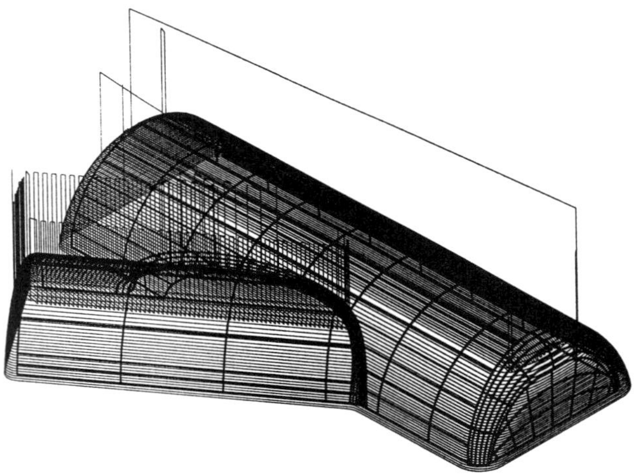

Figure 15.126

Step 10. Save the toolpaths.

Select **MAIN MENU** → **NC utils** → **Edit NCI**
Select **Yes** to "Operations have been modified. Create the NCI text file?"
Select **Quit** from Edit NCI dialog box

15.23 Finish Pencil Function

The pencil function generates a set of toolpaths for (1) a rough operation to remove material in corners so subsequent operations can machine surfaces easily, and (2) a finish operation to clean leftover material from corners (Figure 15.127). Corners are encountered mainly at the intersection of surfaces. The pencil parameters dialog box appears as below.

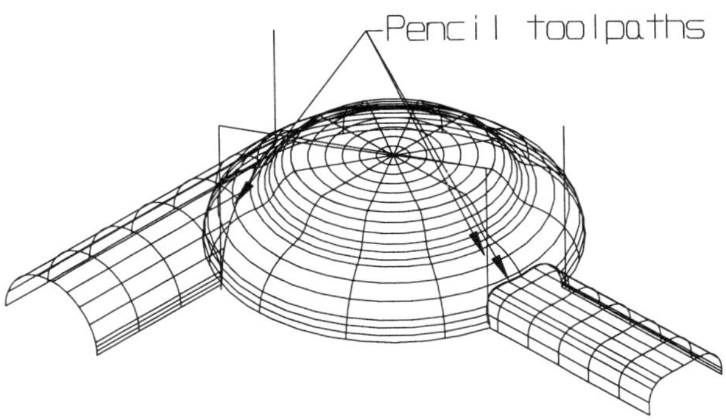

Figure 15.127

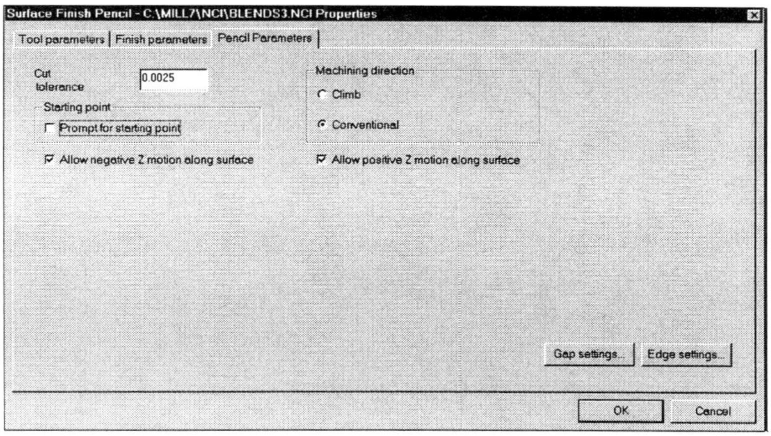

15.24 Finish Scallop Function

The scallop function generates toolpaths for machining selected surfaces. The toolpaths generated from this function have the following three distinct features (Figure 15.128):

> (1) They have consistent scallop heights over the entire set of surfaces.
> (2) They consistently touch the surfaces to minimize the retract motions.
> (3) They have a spiral pattern generated from collapse 3D cutting method.

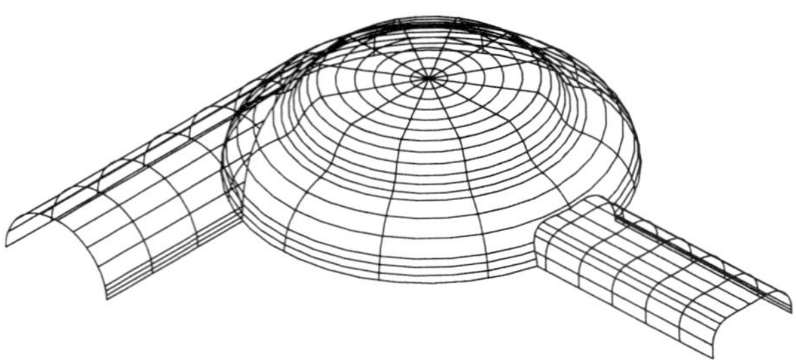

Figure 15.128a

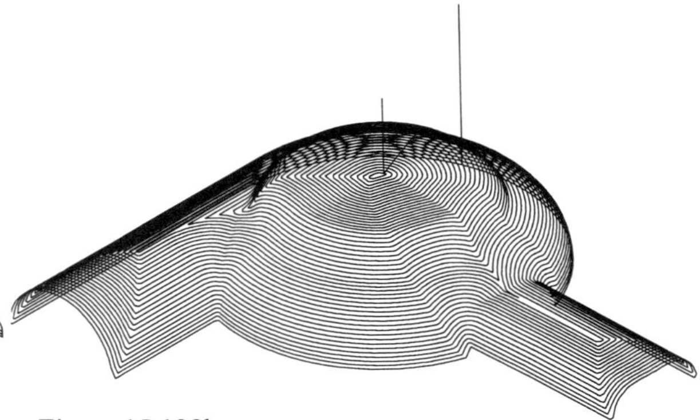

Figure 15.128b

The scallop parameters dialog box appears as below.

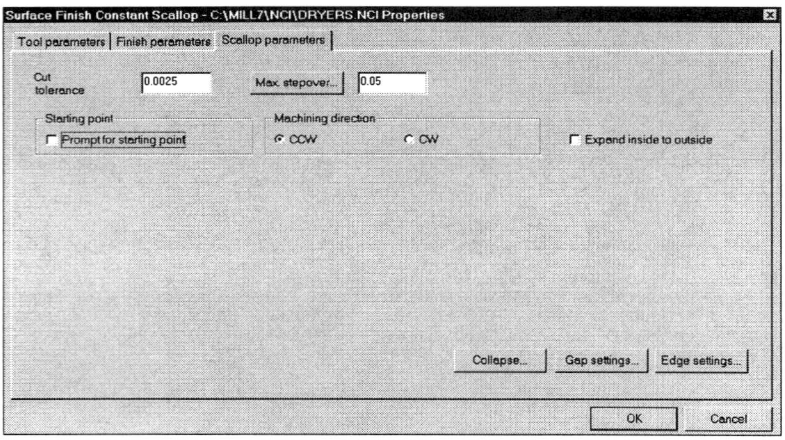

The toolpaths can be control by the following two parameters:

> **Machining direction:** specify the cutting direction either in clockwise (CW) direction or counterclockwise (CCW) direction.
>
> **Expand inside to outside:** specify the start of cutting motion
> (1) at the center of the geometry and spiraling to the outer boundary, or
> (2) at the outer boundary and spiraling toward the center.

Mastercam Version 7,
Scholar's International Publishing Corp., 1998

Project 14. Using scallop function

The scallop function is used to generate finishing toolpaths to cut the basket surface model as shown in Figure 15.129.

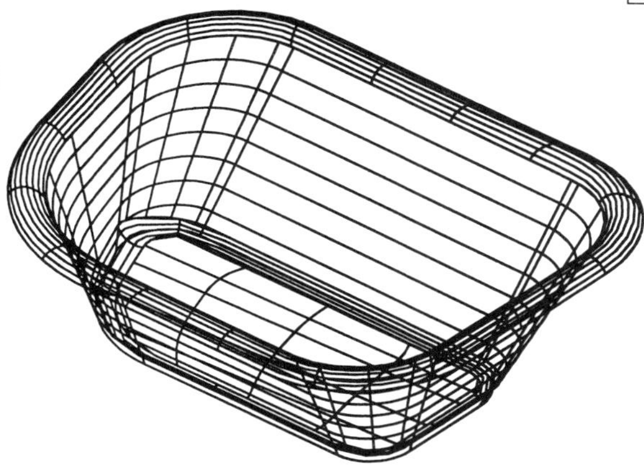

Figure 15.129a

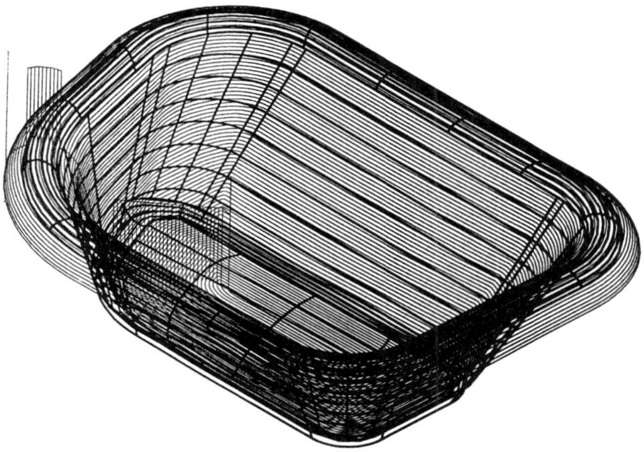

Figure 15.129b

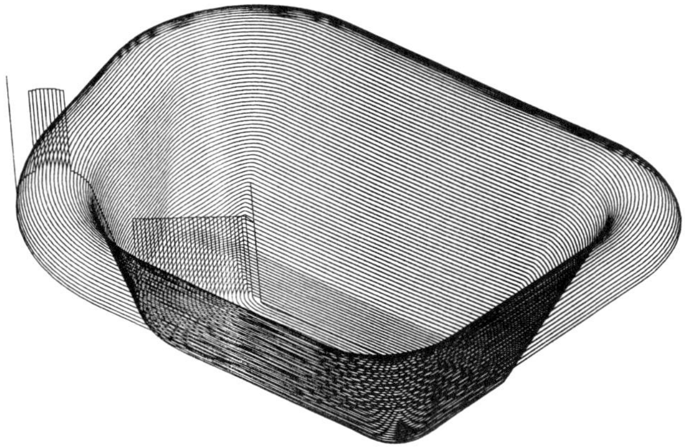

Figure 15.129c

Tips 1. Open the surface model file baskets.

2. Use the scallop function to generate finishing toolpaths.

3. Use a 3/8" sphere end mill.

Step 1. Open the surface model file baskets.

Select **MAIN MENU → File → Get**
File name: **baskets**

The basket surface model appears as in Figure 15.130.

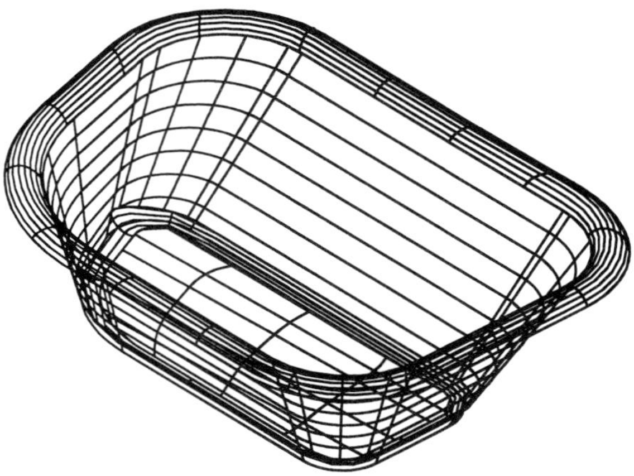

Figure 15.130

Step 2. Initiate the scallop function.

Select **MAIN MENU → Toolpaths → Surface → Finish → Scallop**
File name for toolpaths: **scallop**
Select **All → Surfaces → Done**
Click the right mouse button then select "**Get** tool from library"
Select **tool number 254** (3/8 sphere end mill)
Select **OK**
Set tool parameters as below.

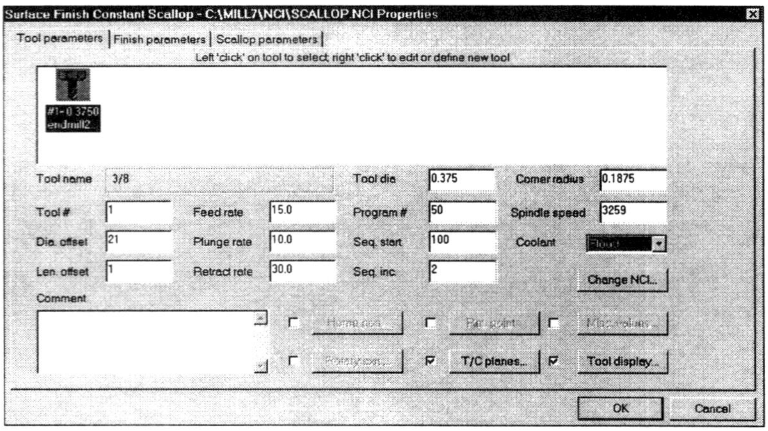

Step 3. Define the finish parameters.

Click the "**Finish parameters**" button
Set the finish parameters as on the next page.

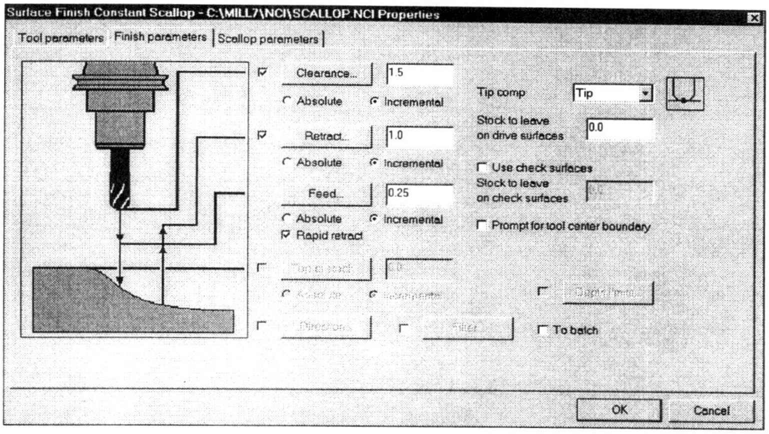

Step 4. Define the scallop parameters.

Click the "**Scallop parameters**" button
Set the scallop parameters as below.

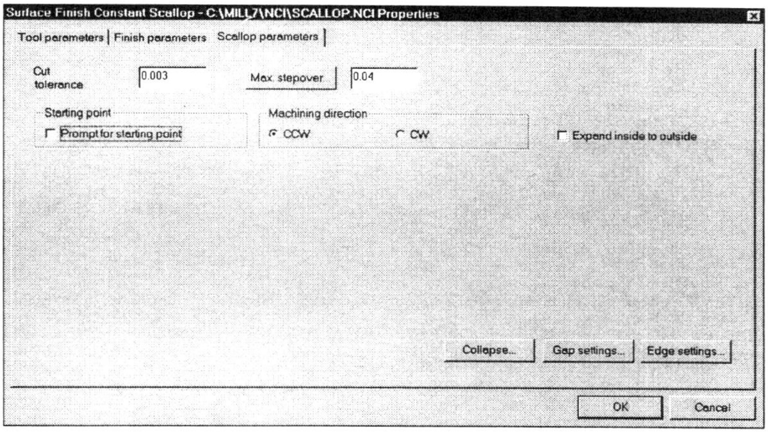

Step 5. Define the edge setting parameters.

Click the "**Edge settings**" button
Click "**Over all surface edges**" on Roll tool parameter
Select **OK → OK** to generate finishing toolpaths as shown in Figure 15.131.

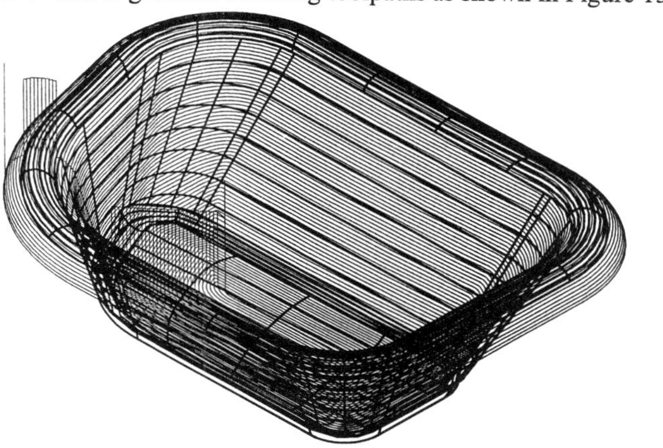

Figure 15.131

Figure 15.132 shows the toolpaths without the surface model.

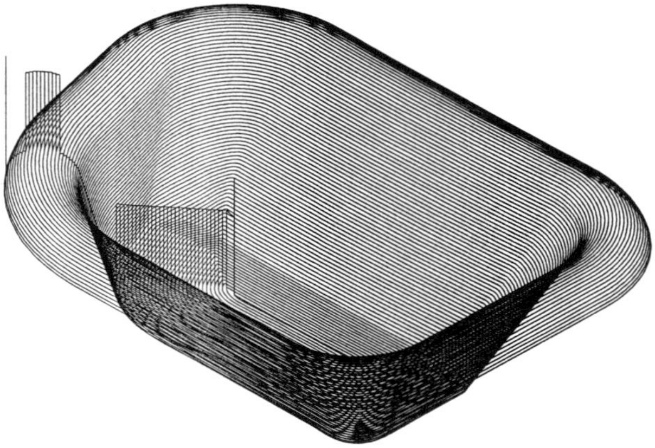

Figure 15.132

Step 6. Save the toolpath file.

Select **MAIN MENU → NC utils → Edit NCI**
Select **Yes** to "Operations have been modified. Create the NCI text file?"
Select **Quit** from Edit NCI dialog box

Project 15. Using parallel function with copy-rotate command

Generating a set of toolpaths to cut the car wheel surface model is a challenge for a Mastercam user. The complete surface model consists of 60 surfaces (some surfaces are hidden in the model.) If one of the surface finish functions is used to generate the toolpaths for the entire surface model, it may take a much longer time to complete the process of generating the toolpaths. The approach we use here is to generate the toolpaths for a partial surface model consisting of only six surfaces. This set of toolpaths is then copied to the other five locations. By doing so, the system needs only a few minutes to complete the toolpaths for the entire model. The partial surface model and complete toolpaths are shown in Figure 15.133.

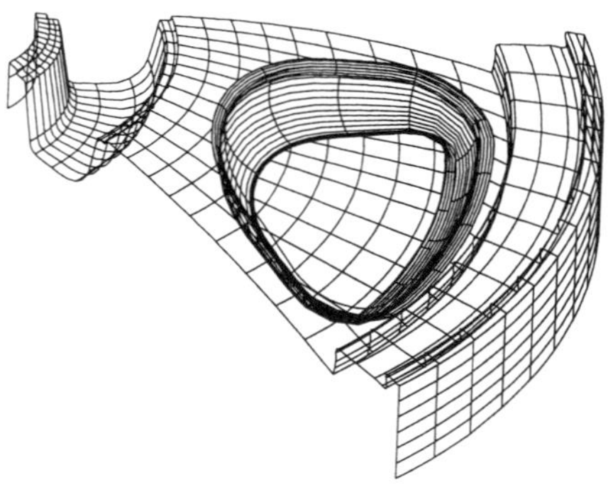

Figure 15.133a

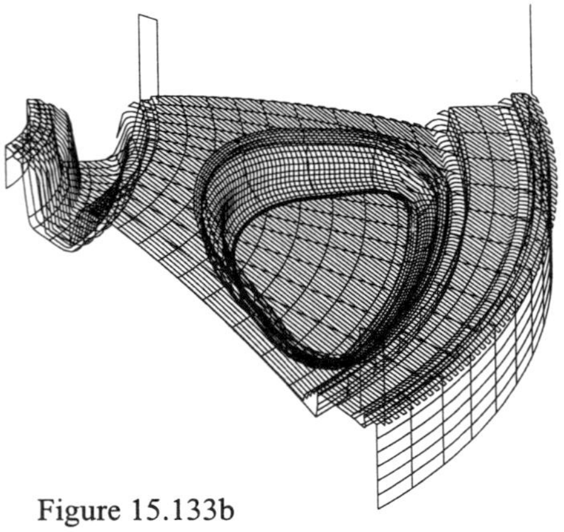

Figure 15.133b

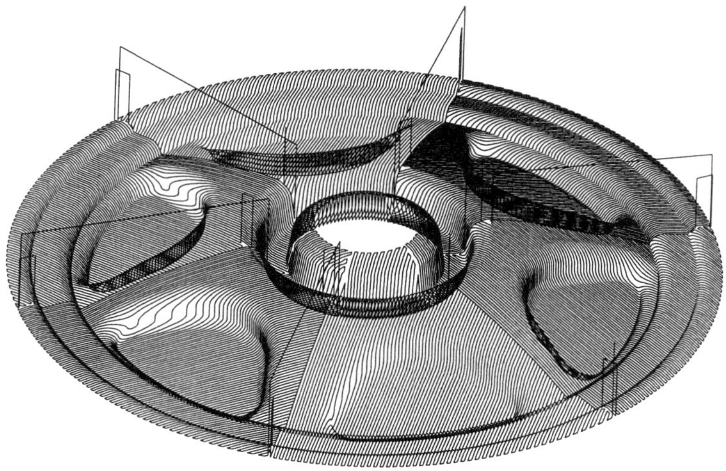

Figure 15.133c

⌛**Tips** 1. Only a section of the surface model is used to generate toolpaths. This set of toolpaths is used to copy to five locations by using NC utils → Xform → Rotate commands.

2. The inner and outer rim surfaces can be cut by using a 2D toolpath function such as contour or pocket. They do no include using the surface finish-parallel function.
3. The surface model file is wheels.
4. Use surface finish-parallel function to generate the finishing toolpaths.
5. Use 3/8" sphere end mill.
6. Use NC utils → Edit NCI → Xform → Rotate commands with the following parameters to copy the toolpaths to five locations:

Rotation angle = **60**
Number of steps = **5**
Leave the original entities

Step 1. Open the wheel surface model.

Select **MAIN MENU → File → Get**
File name: **wheels**
The wheel surface model appears as in Figure 15.134.

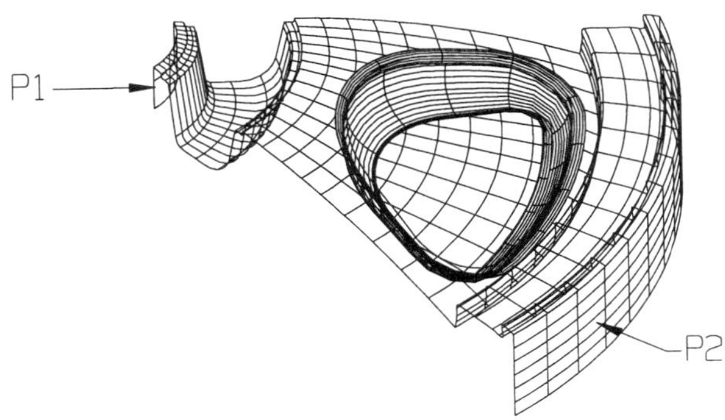

Figure 15.134

Step 2. Initiate the parallel function.

Use the pick points in Figure 15.134.
Select **Cplane → Top**
Select **MAIN MENU → Toolpaths → Surface → Finish → Parallel**
File name for toolpaths: **wheelt**
Select **All → Surfaces → Unselect**
Pick **P1** and **P2** to unselect two vertical wall surfaces
Select **BACKUP → Done**

Step 3. Define the tool parameters.

Click the right mouse button, then select **"Get tool from library"**
Select **tool number 254** (3/8 sphere end mill)
Select **OK**
Set the tool parameters as below.

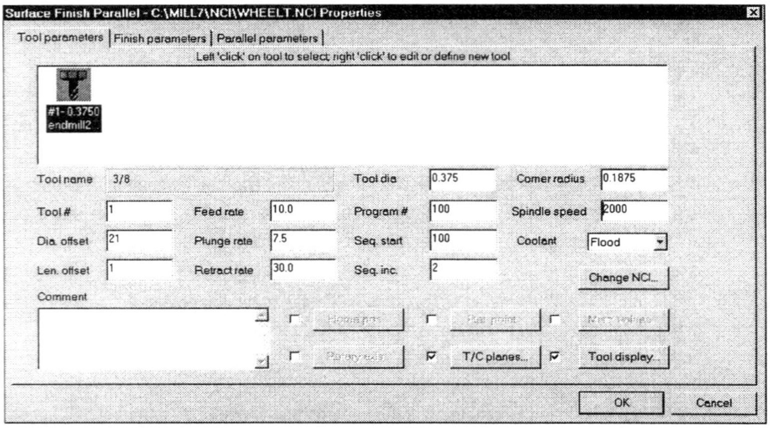

Step 4. Define the finish parameters.

Click the "**Finish parameters**" button
Set the finish parameters as below.

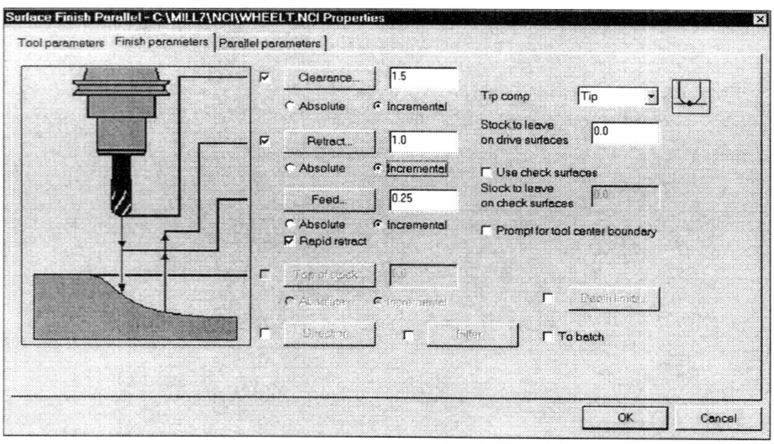

Step 5. Define the parallel parameters.

Click the "**Parallel parameters**" button
Define the parallel parameters as below.

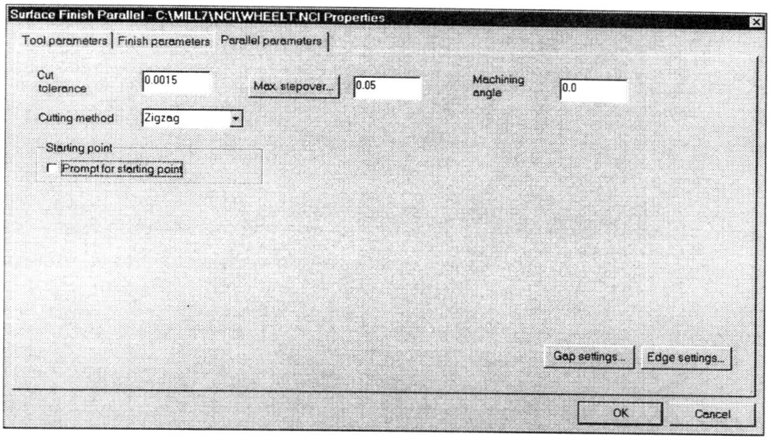

Step 6. Define the gap and edge parameters.

Click the "**Gap settings**" button
Set % of stepover to **200.0**
Select **Direct** for Motion < Gap size, keep tool down parameter
Select **OK**
Click the "**Edge settings**" button
Select **automatically** for Roll tool parameter
Select **OK → OK** to generate the toolpaths as shown in Figure 15.135.

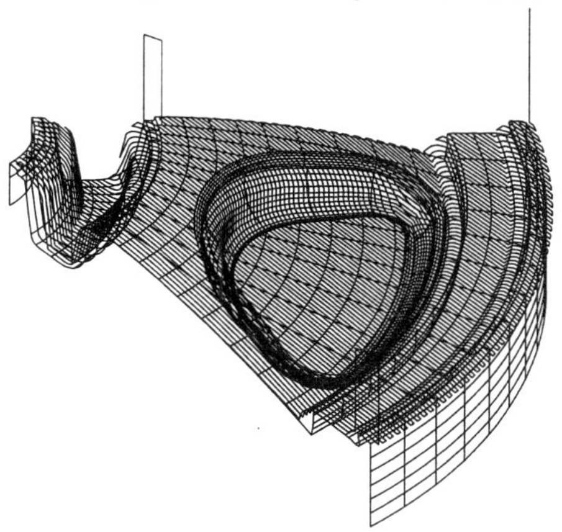

Figure 15.135

Step 7. Copy the toolpaths to the five locations using the Edit NCI → XForm → Rotate commands.

Select **MAIN MENU → NC utils → Edit NCI**
Select **Yes** to "Operations have been modified. Create the NCI text file?"

The Edit NCI dialog box should appear as below.

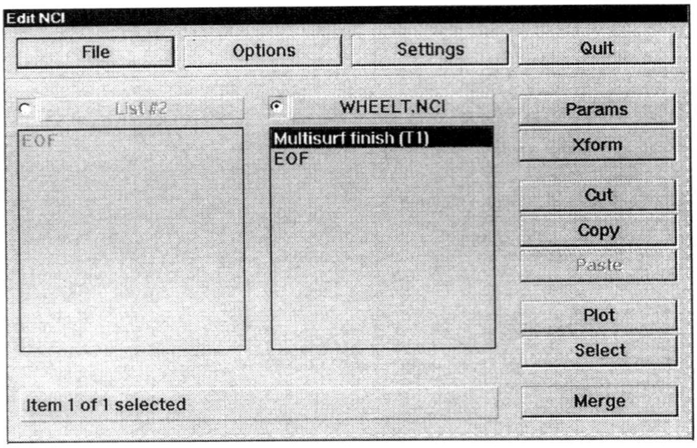

Click the **Multisurf finish [T1]** to select the toolpaths to be rotated
Select **Xform → Rotate**
Set the XForm – Rotate parameters as below.

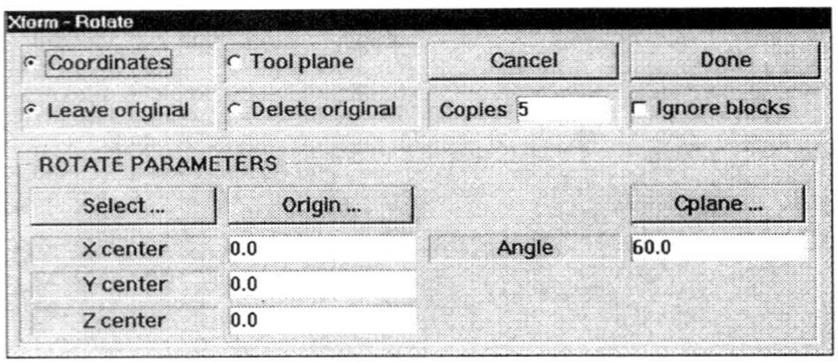

Select **Done** to copy the toolpaths to five locations
The five toolpath sections are added to the file as shown below.

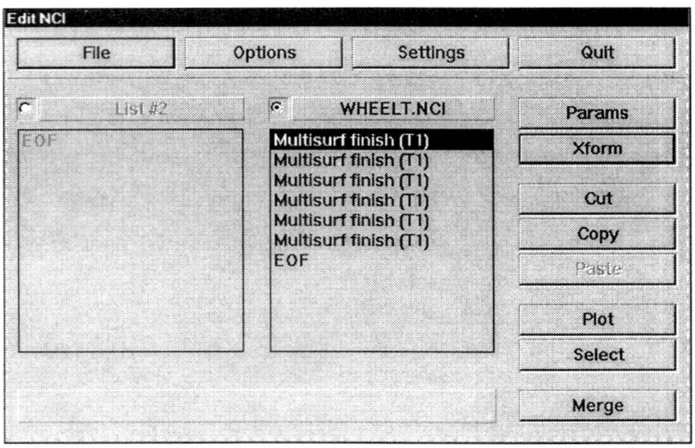

Step 8. Save the copied toolpath sections to the toolpath file.

Press the "Shift" key and click each toolpath section to highlight them
Select **File → Save**
Select **Yes** to "File already exists, overwrite?"
Select **Plot**
The toolpaths are plotted as in Figure 15.136.

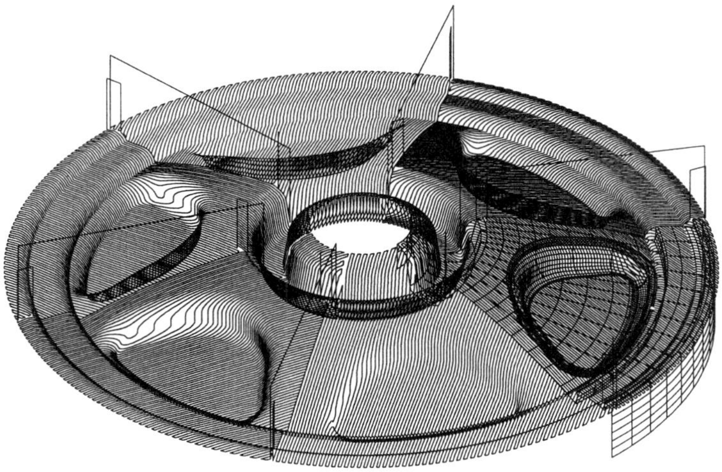

Figure 15.136

The toolpaths without showing surfaces appear as in Figure 15.137.

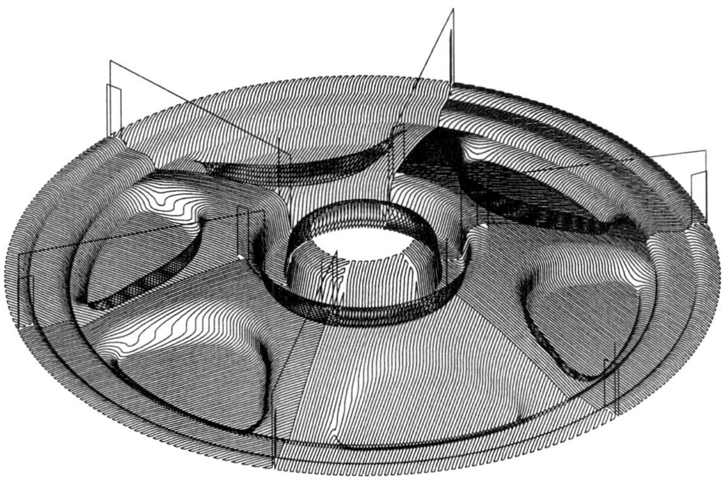

Figure 15.137

16

Project 16. Using flowline and radial functions with rotate-copy command

The fan surface model shown in Figure 15.138 has seven blades. Each blade consists of three surfaces; end ruled surface, top surface, and bottom surface. The bottom surface has a hook-shape that extends from top to bottom. In other words, we can not cut the bottom surface in one operation. This project uses the flowline function to generate toolpaths for cutting two blade surfaces from one direction. Use the vertical wall surface and the hub surface as the check surfaces. The radial function is used to cut the remaining three surfaces. The toolpaths for the blade is copied to six locations to complete the toolpaths. Figure 15.138 shows surface model, toolpaths, and verification model of this project.

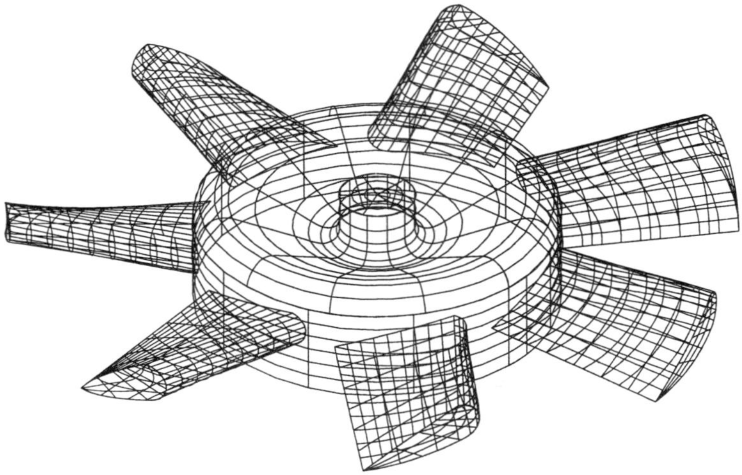

Figure 15.138a

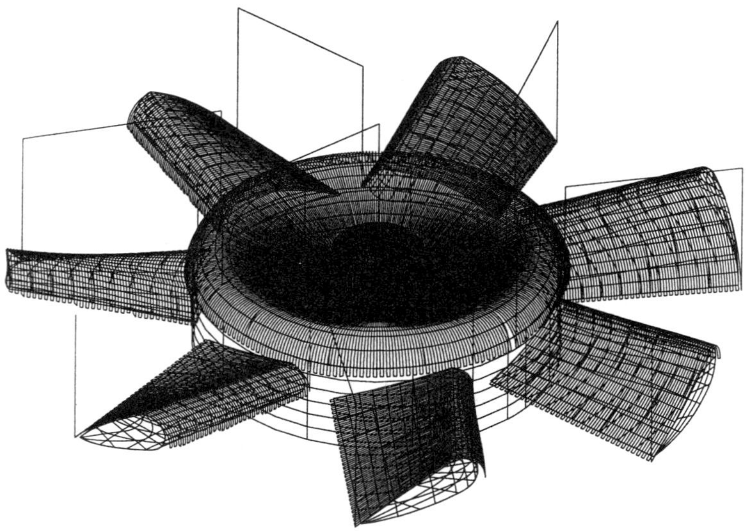

Figure 15.138b

Figure 138c

⌛**Tips** 1. Open the surface model file fans.

2. Change the direction normal for two surfaces, vertical wall surface and rim surface.

3. Use the flowline function to generate toolpaths for cutting the top section of a fan blade.

4. Use a ¼" sphere end mill.

5. Use the radial function to generate toolpaths for cutting three surfaces.

6. Use NC utils → Edit NCI → Xform → Rotate commands to copy the blade toolpaths to six locations.

7. Verify the toolpaths.

Step 1. Open the fan surface model.

Select **MAIN MENU → File → Get**

File name: **fans**

The fan surface model appears as Figure 15.139.

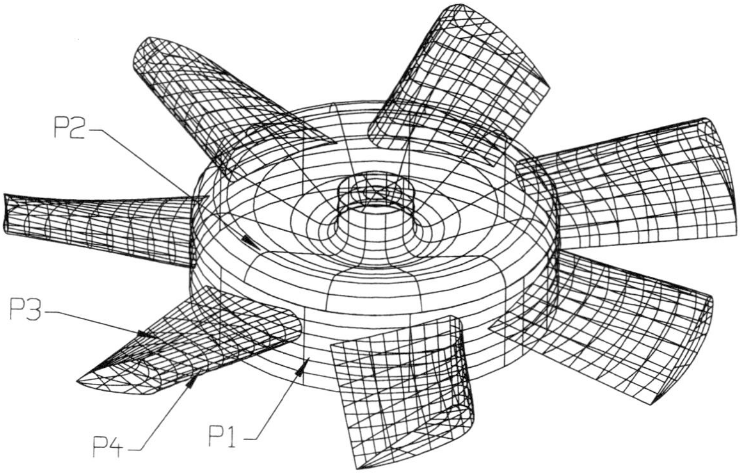

Figure 15.139

Step 2. Change the direction normal for two surfaces.

Use the pick points in Figure 15.139.
Select **MAIN MENU → Modify → Normal → Reverse**
Pick **P1** and **P2** to change the normal direction of two surfaces

Step 3. Initiate the flowline function.

Use the pick points in Figure 15.139.
Select **MAIN MENU → Toolpaths → Surface → Drive/check → On**
Pick **P1** and **P2** as two check surfaces
Select **Done → Done**
Select **Finish → Flowline**
File name for toolpaths: **fanst**
Pick **P3** and **P4** to select two drive surfaces
Select **Done**

Step 4. Define the tool parameters.

Click the right mouse button, then select **"Get tool from library"**
Select **tool number 252** →1/4 sphere end mill)
Select **OK**

Set the tool parameters as below.

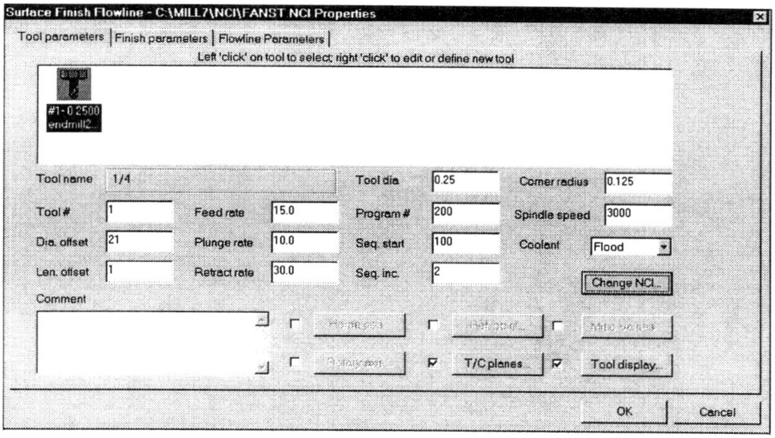

Step 5. Define the finish parameters.

Click the "**Finish parameters**" button

Define the finish parameters as below.

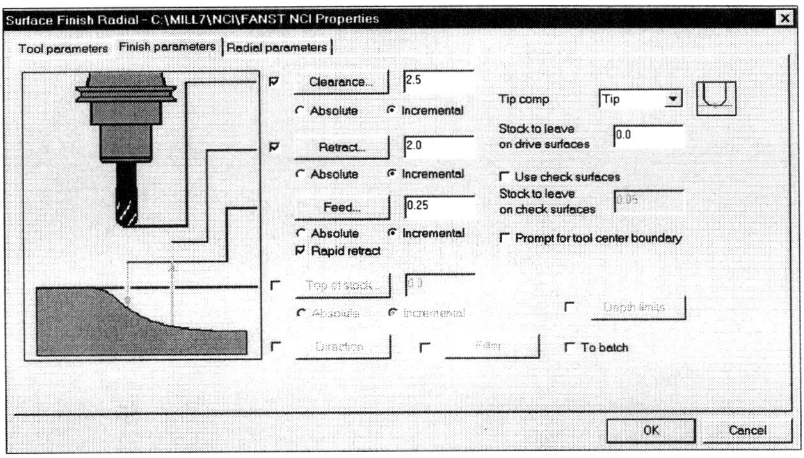

Step 6. Define the flowline parameters.

Click the "**Flowline Parameters**" button

Set the flowline parameters as below.

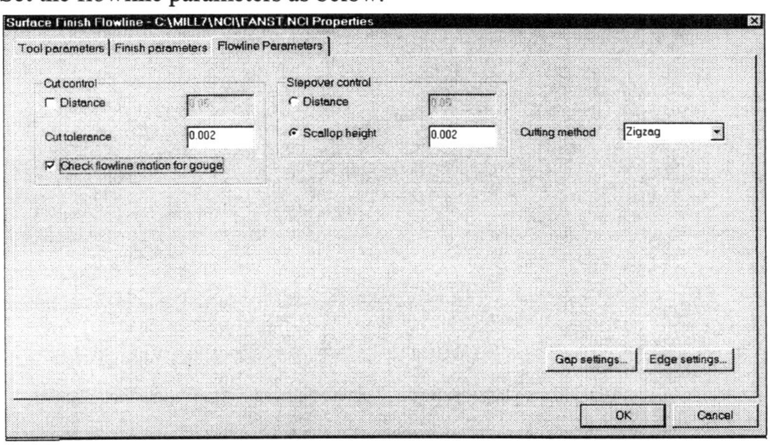

Step 7. Define the gap and edge parameters.

Click the "**Gap settings**" button
Set the gap parameters as below.

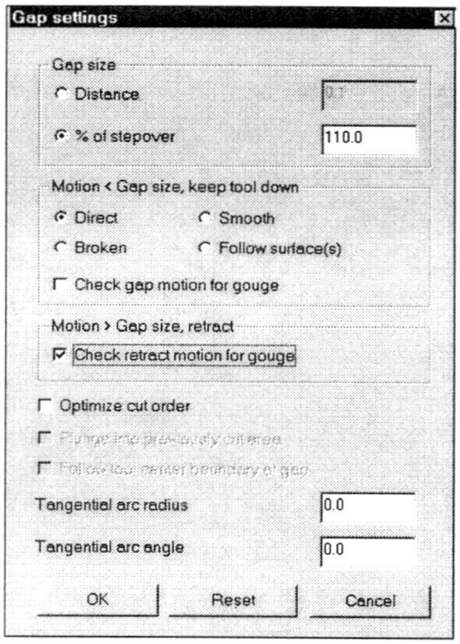

Select **OK**

Click the "Edge **settings**" button
Set the edge parameters as below.

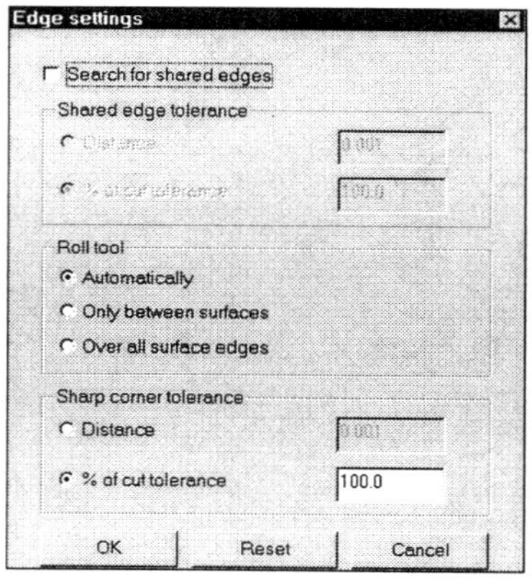

Select **OK → OK → Do it** to generate the toolpaths as shown in Figure 15.140.

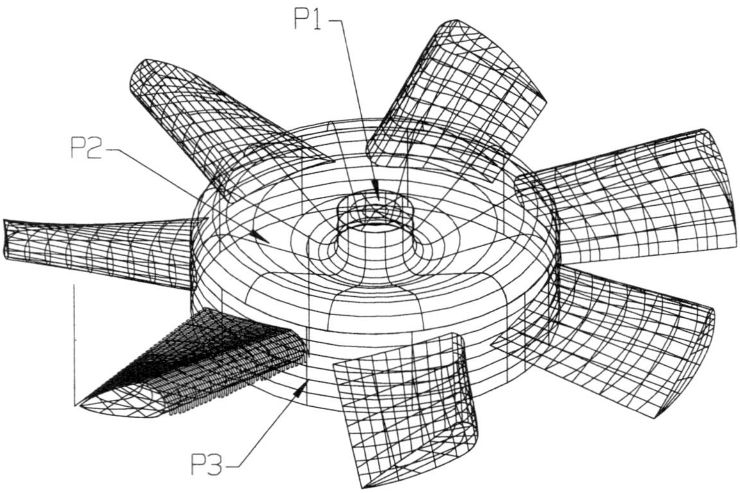

Figure 15.140

Step 8. Initiate the radial function.

Use the pick points in Figure 15.140.
Select **Finish → Radial**
Pick **P1**, **P2**, and **P3** to select three surfaces
Select **Done**
Define the tool parameters same as in step 4.

Step 9. Define the finish parameters.

Click the "**Finish parameters**" button
Set the finish parameters same as in step 5.

Step 10. Define the radial parameters.

Click the "**Radial parameters**" button
Set the radial parameters as below.

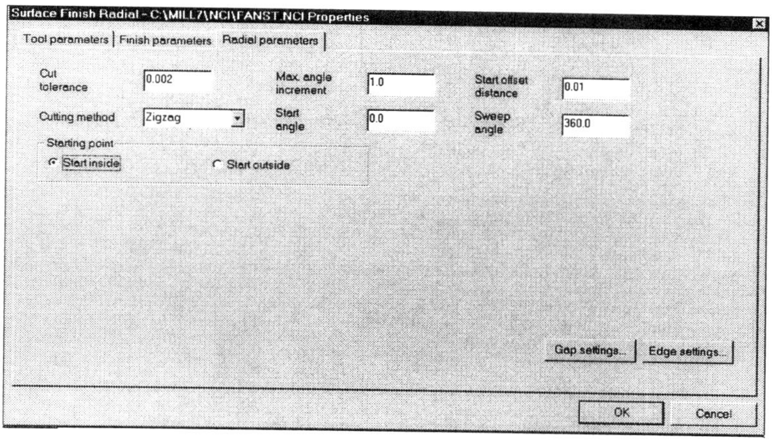

Step 11. Define the gap and edge parameters.

Set gap and edge parameters same as in step 7.
Select **OK → OK**
Enter rotation point: **0,0**
The toolpaths are generated as in Figure 15.141.

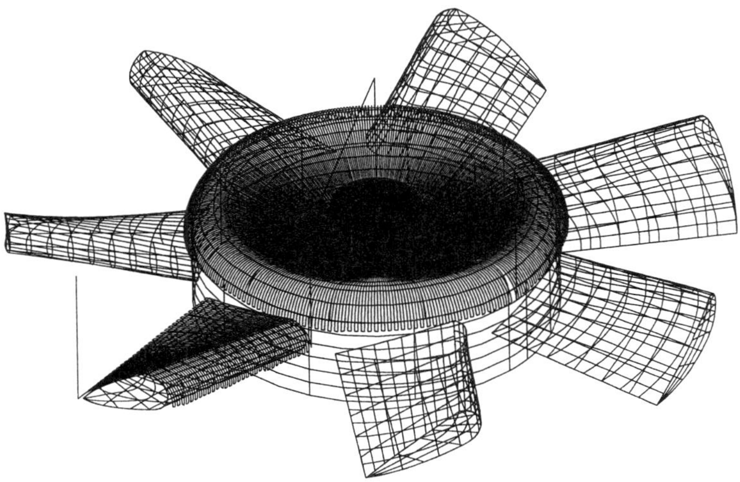

Figure 15.141

Step 12. Copy the blade toolpaths to six locations.

Select **MAIN MENU → NC utils → Edit NCI**
Select the first **Multisurf finish [T1]** from the list
Select **XForm → Rotate**
Set the XForm – Rotate dialog box as below.

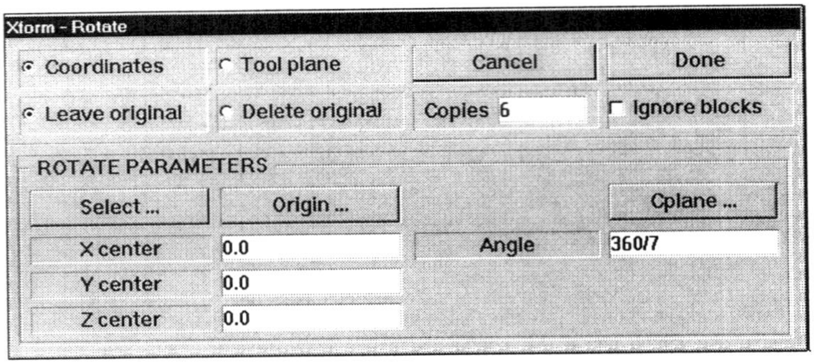

Select **Done** to copy toolpaths as shown in Figure 15.142.

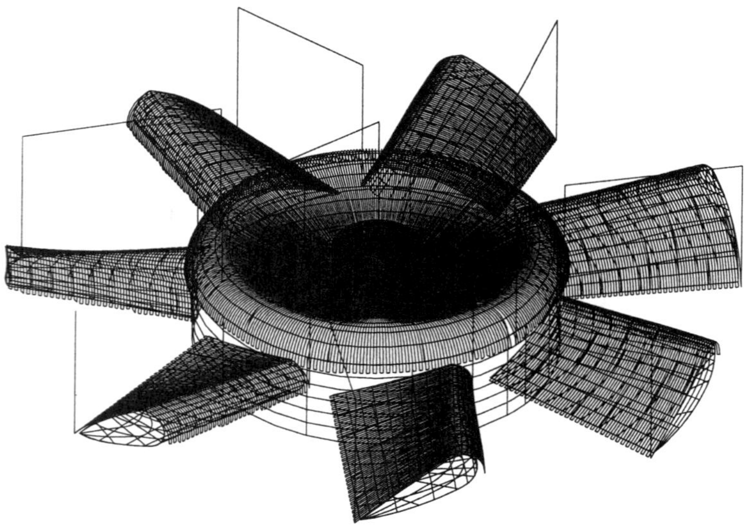

Figure 15.142

Step 13. Save the copied toolpath sections to the toolpath file.

Press the "shift" key and click each toolpath section to highlight them
Select **File → Save → Yes → Quit**

Step 14. Verify the toolpaths.

Directly select **N-See 2000** → Select **Turbo mode** → OK
Select Open NCI Open file: **fanst**
Select **OK** from "Mastercam Toolpath Verification" menu
Select **Do it**

The verification model should resemble Figure 15.143.

Figure 15.143

Step 14. Save the surface model

Select **BACKUP** to return to Operations Manager dialog box
Select **OK** from Operations Manager dialog box
Select **MAIN MENU** → **NC utils** → **Edit NCI**
Select **Yes** to "Operations have been modified. Create the NCI text file?"
Select **Quit** from Edit NCI dialog box

Exercises

1. List the five surface toolpath functions and briefly describe their function.
2. What are the two groups of parameters used in surface toolpath functions?
3. List the seven surface roughing functions.
4. What are the drive surfaces?
5. What are the check surfaces?
6. Describe the purpose of a tool center boundary.
7. What are two cutting methods in the roughing cut?
8. What are the gaps?
9. What are the motions?
10. Explain how to determine the gap either to be a short gap or a long gap.
11. What are the two categories of the surface open edges?
12. Describe the features of the rough parallel function.
13. Describe the features of the rough radial function.
14. Use a drawing to describe the three angle parameters used in rough radial function.
15. Describe the features of the rough project function.
16. What are the three types of entities that can be used in the rough project function?
17. Describe the features of the rough flowline function.
18. Describe the features of the rough contour function.
19. Explain when you should use a rough contour function.
20. Describe the features of the pocket rough function.
21. Describe the features of the rough plunge function.
22. List the ten surface finish functions.
23. Describe the features of the parallel finish function.
24. Describe the features of theparallel steep finish function.
25. When to use the finish leftover function.

26. Describe the features of the project finish function.

27. Describe the features of the finish shallow function and when to use it.

28. Describe the features of the finish pencil function and when to use it.

29. Describe the feature s of the finish scallop function.

30. Use the appropriate roughing and finish functions to generate the toolpaths for cutting the surface shown in Figure 15.144. The surface file name is ES3.

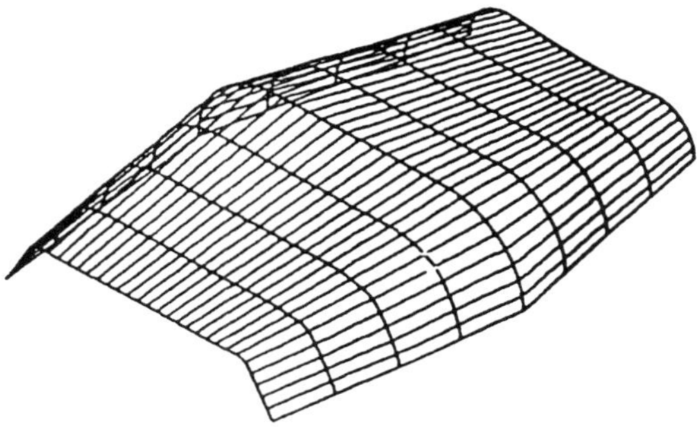

Figure 15.144

31. Use the appropriate roughing and finish functions to generate the toolpaths for cutting the surface model shown in Figure 15.145. The surface file name is ES6.

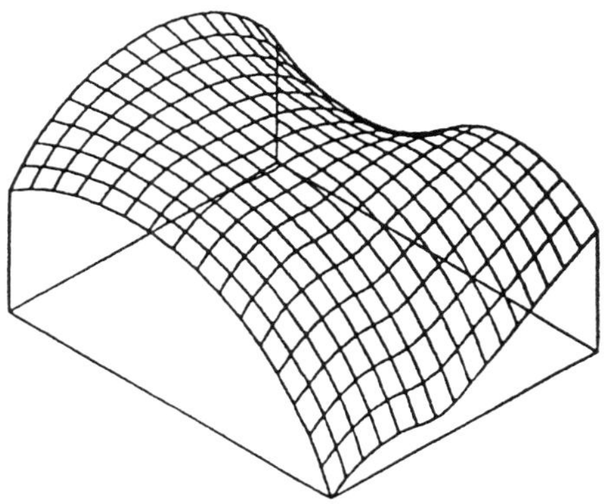

Figure 15.145

32. Use a finish function to generate the toolpaths for cutting a Coons surface of multiple patches. The surface file name is ES8. The surface model is shown in Figure 15.146.

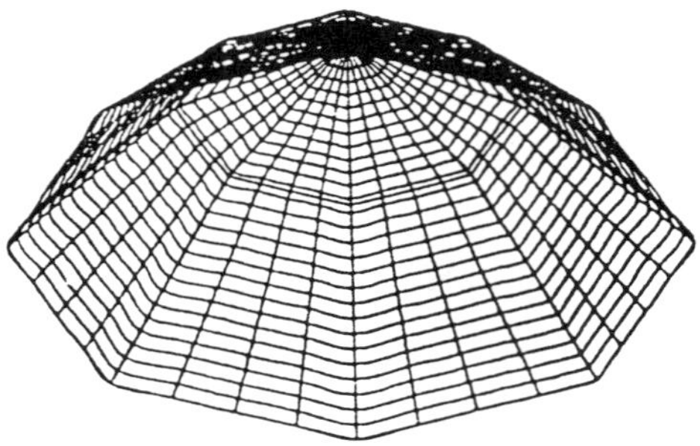

Figure 15.146

33. Use a finish function to generate the toolpaths for the fillet surface model as shown in Figure 15.147. The surface model file is ES14.

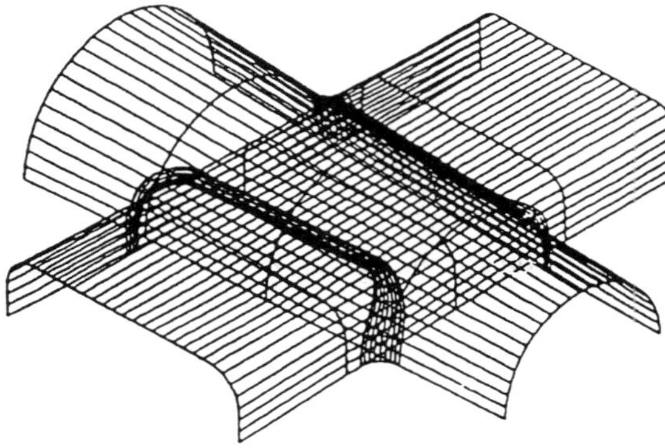

Figure 15.147

34. Use a finish function to generate the toolpaths for the surface model shown in Figure 15.148. The surface file name is ES15.

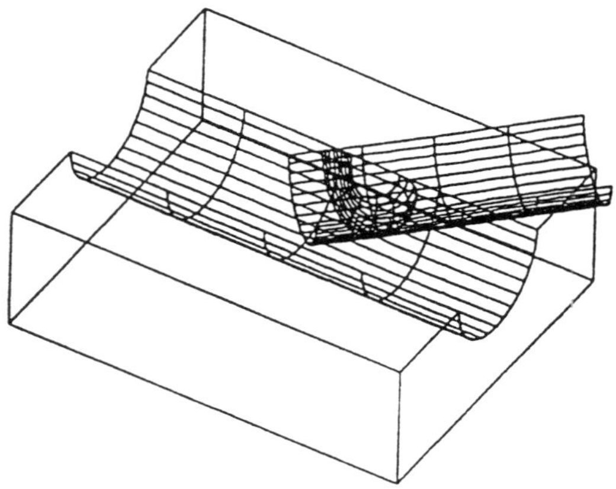

Figure 15.148

35. Use a rough and a finish function to generate the toolpaths for cutting the trimmed surface model as shown in Figure 15.149. The surface file name is ES16.

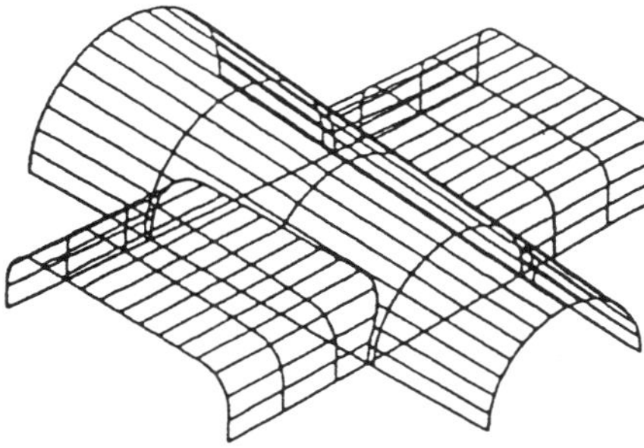

Figure 15.149

36. Use a rough and a finish function to generate the toolpaths for cutting a composite surface model shown in Figure 15.150. The surface file name is ES19.

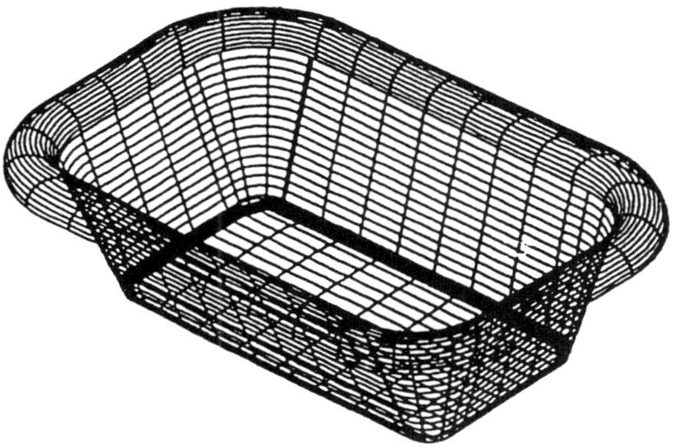

Figure 15.150

37. Generate a set of toolpaths to cut a composite surface model as shown in Figure 15.151. The surface model file is ES20.

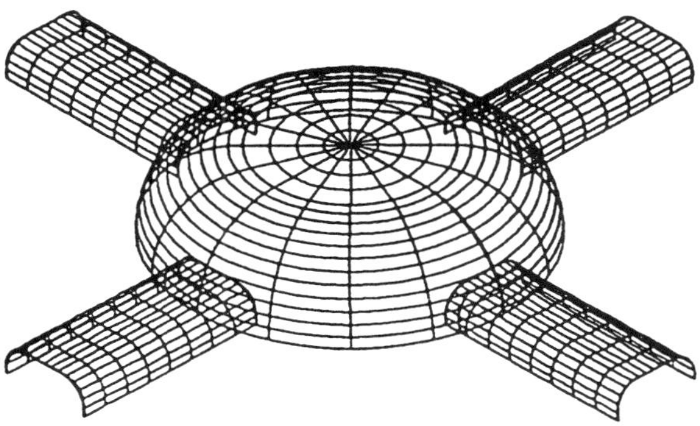

Figure 15.150

Chapter 16

Multiaxis Machining

Objectives:

1. Know four 5-axis toolpath functions.
2. Know rotary 4-axis toolpath function.
3. Apply multiaxis toolpath functions to cut surface models.

Overview

Most machining projects can be done with 3-axis machines. However, 3-axis machines may encounter difficulties or be unable to machine some complicated parts which have features such as slope planes, surfaces, undercuts, or multiple faces. In those cases, a 4-axis or 5-axis machine is more suitable to use. The programming for 4-axis and 5-axis machines is more complicated than 3-axis programming.

Mastercam is capable of generating toolpaths for 4-axis or 5-axis machining. The 4-axis machining has only one function, **Rotary 4-axis**. There are four 5-axis machining functions including **Curve 5-axis, Drill 5-axis, Swarf 5-axis**, and **Flowline 5-axis**. These multiaxis toolpath functions are used to generate toolpaths for cutting a surface model. This chapter presents these five multiaxis toolpath functions for cutting surfaces. The working principles and defining parameters of each function are covered. These are followed by several projects with step-by-step instructions.

16.1 Rotary Axes and Directions

The Electronic Industries Association has established a CNC machine axes identification standard, **EIA-267-B**. This standard defines 14 different axes, including 9 linear axes and 5 rotary axes, to describe all CNC machines, from simple to complex types. The linear axes on a machine may include 3 primary linear axes, 3 secondary linear axes, and 3 tertiary linear axes. The rotary axes may include 3 primary rotary axes and 2 secondary rotary axes. However, most CNC machines require only 3 linear axes. Some machines have one or two rotary axes in addition to the three linear axes.

Three primary rotary axes designated by the characters A, B, and C are used to indicate rotary motions about the X, Y, and Z axes, respectively in Figure 16.1. Rotary motion about the X axis is labeled with an A; rotary motion about the Y axis with B; and rotary motion about the Z axis with C.

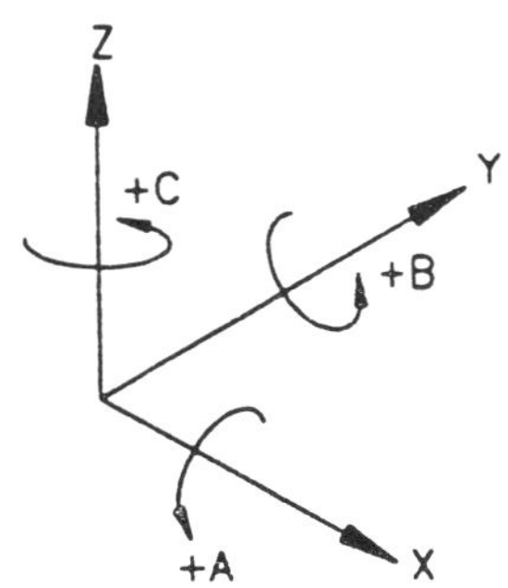

Figure 16.1

The thumb rule is used to determine the direction of the rotation. For example, with the thumb of the right hand pointing in the direction of the positive X axis, the four fingers will curl in the positive direction of the rotary A axis.

16.2 4-Axis and 5-Axis Machines

4th and 5th axis control can be implemented either on the machine tables or the spindle heads. Rotary indexing tables are common devices used to position the 4th and 5th axis on machine tables. The machine table is still controlled by three primary linear axes; X, Y, and Z. The indexing table provides 4th or 5th -axis positioning control. Figure 16.2 shows two examples using 4-axis positioning on a machine table. Figure 16.3 illustrates 5-axis machining. Rotary axes can be applied to the spindle head of machines (Figure 16.4). Profilers are the typical machines of this category.

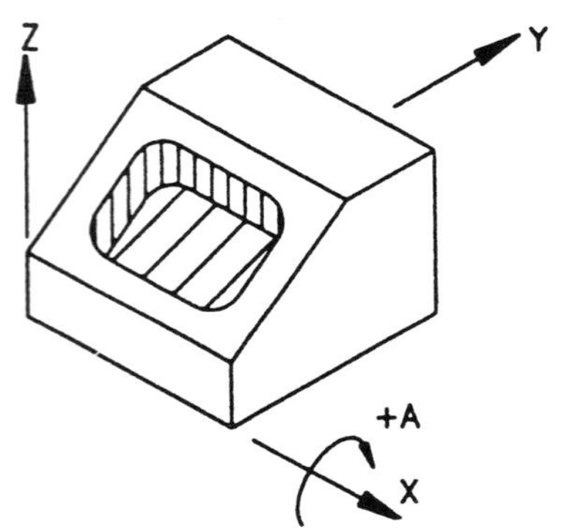

Figure 16.2a

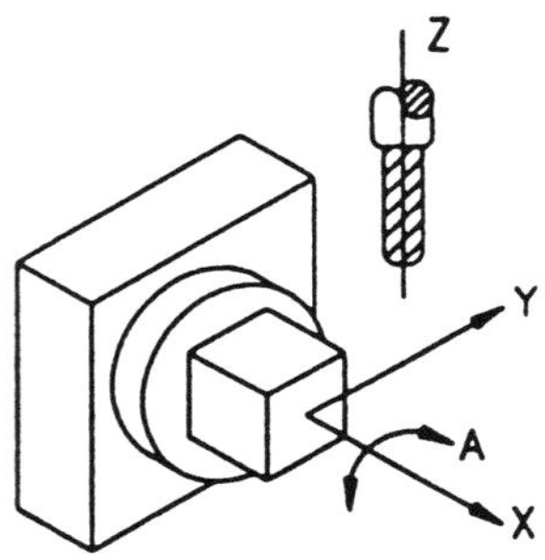

Figure 16.2b

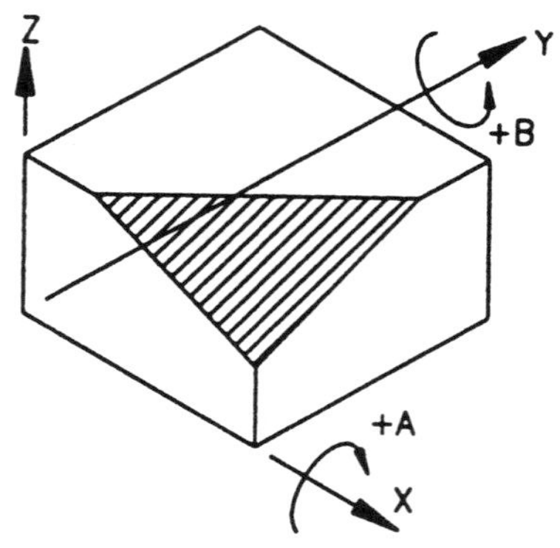

Figure 16.3

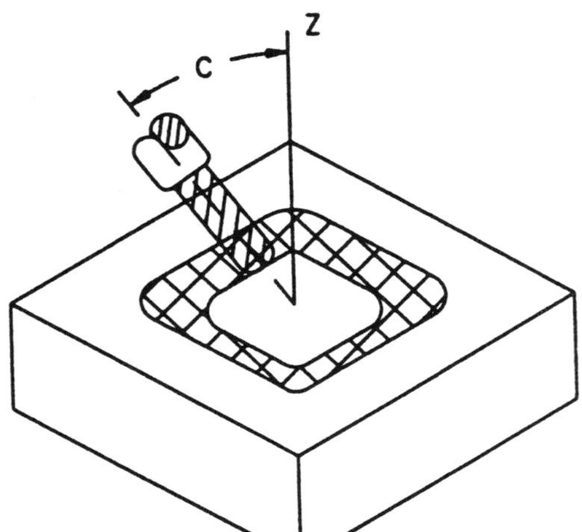

Figure 16.4

16.3 Part Features for 4th and 5th Axis Machining

A part feature is the distinctive geometric form or shape being produced from raw material. Typical part features include holes, slots, pockets, shoulders, profiles, angles, threads and surfaces. Those features that are defined in the XY-plane normally can be machined by 3-axis machines. Those features that are not lying in the XY-plane normally require using a 4- or 5-axis machine depending on the orientation of plane normal. Figure 16.5 shows an example of 4-axis machining and Figure 16.6 is an example of 5-axis machining.

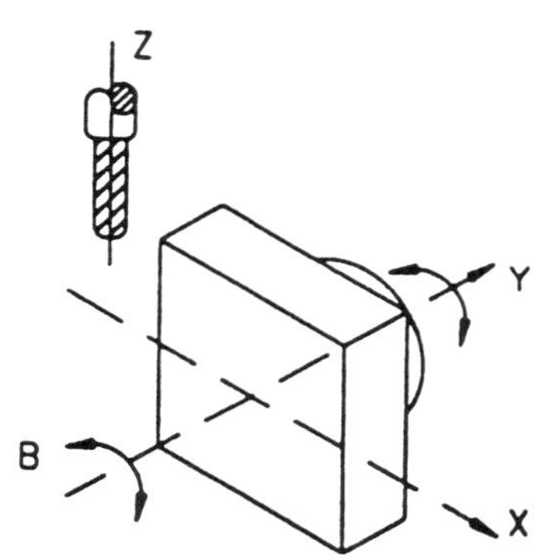

Figure 16.5

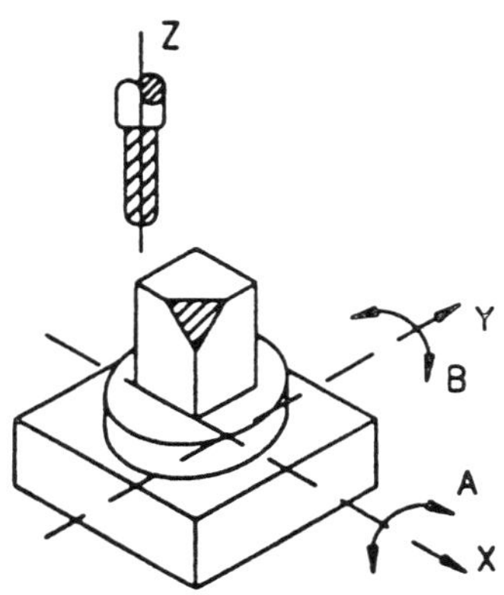

Figure 16.6

16.4 Rotary 4-Axis Function

The rotary 4-axis function generates toolpaths for cutting a surface model in a 4-axis CNC machine (Figure 16.7). Multiple-surface model can be used in rotary 4-axis function for generating toolpaths simultaneously (Figure 16.8). The rotary 4-axis parameter dialog box appears as below.

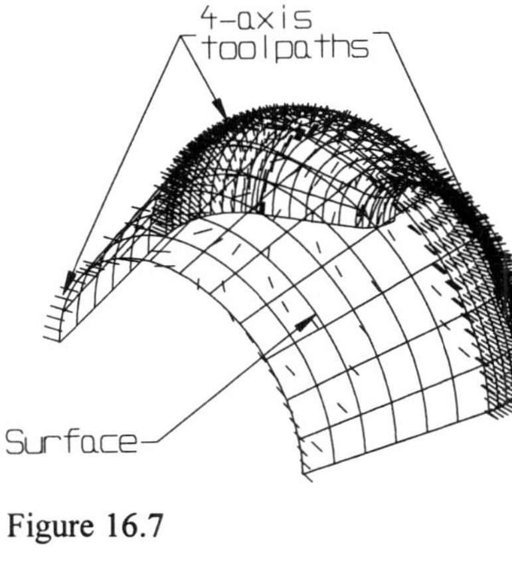

Figure 16.7

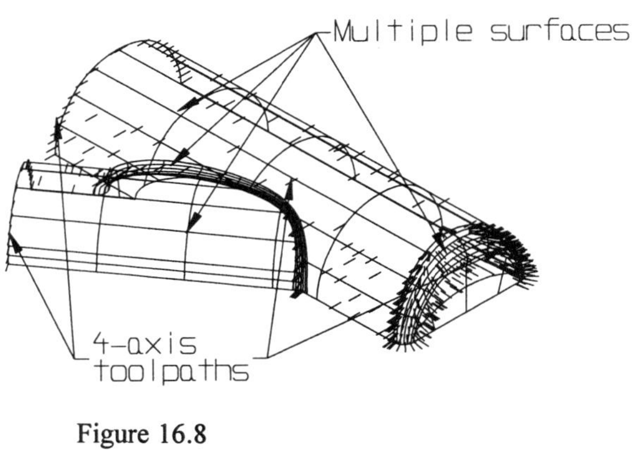

Figure 16.8

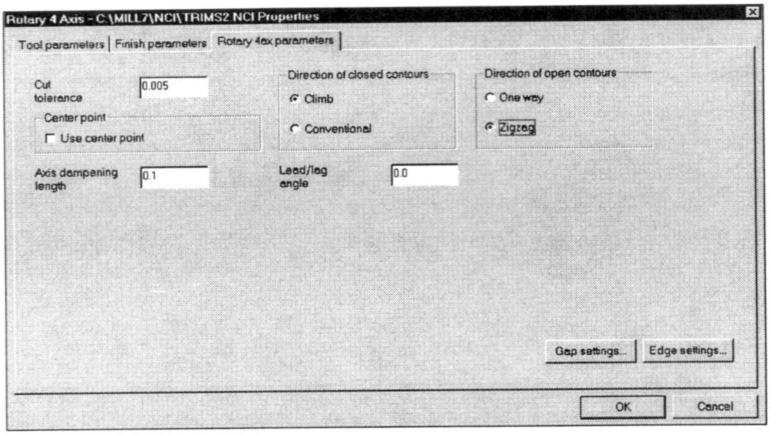

Three parameters that are unique to this toolpath function include: **Use center point, Axis dampering length,** and **Lead/lag angle**.

Use center point

This parameter uses a point at the center of the part to orient the tool axis (Figure 16.9). Mastercam will output the tool axis relative to the center point. When this parameter is set to **Off** (no check mark), the system will output the tool axis relative to the surface.

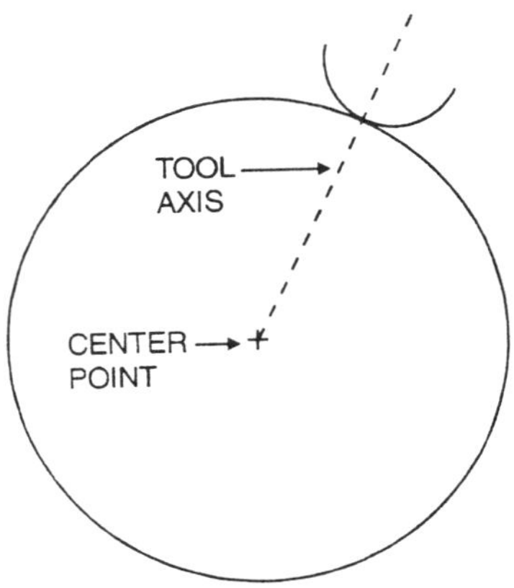

Figure 16.9

Axis dampering length

This parameter decides the position of the tool axis based on the given length along the surface of the part. This parameter becomes available only when the "Use center point" parameter is set to Off. A shorter dampering length produces more tool movement and a toolpath that adheres closely to the surface. A longer length provides less tool movement. Figure 16.10 shows the effect of axis dampering length on the toolpaths.

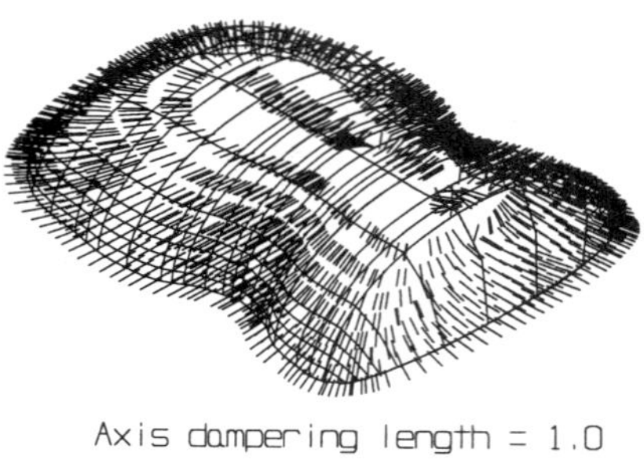

Figure 16.10a Axis dampering length = 1.0

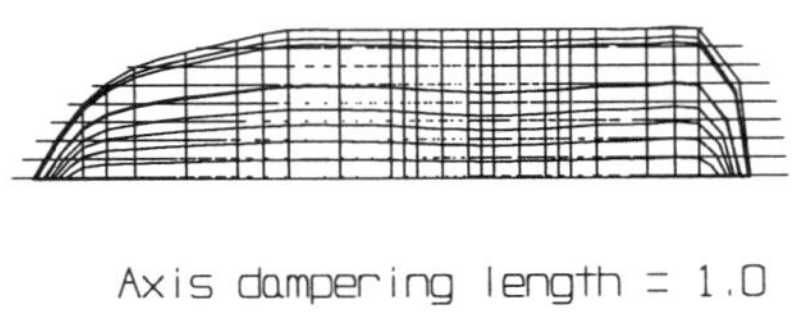

Figure 16.10b Axis dampering length = 1.0

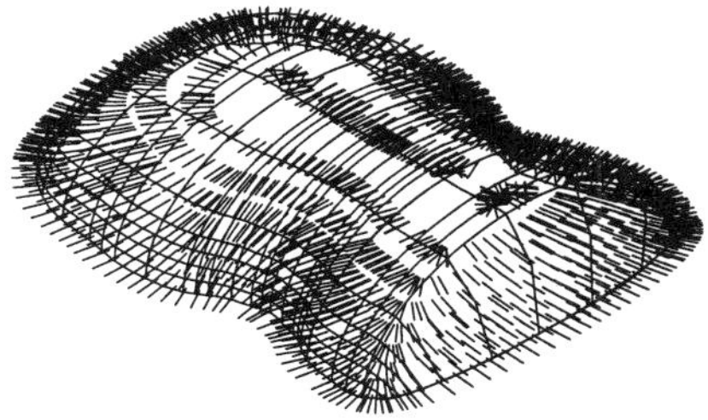

Figure 16.10c Axis dampering length = 0.1

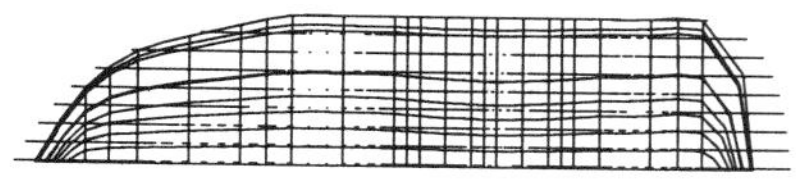

Figure 16.10d Axis dampering length = 0.1

Lead/lag angle

The "lead/lag angle" parameter specifies the relationship between tool axis and surface by an angle value. This angle can be the lead angle or lag angle. The lead angle is defined as the angle at which the tool passes over the part measured from the surface normal to the shank of the tool (Figure 16.11).

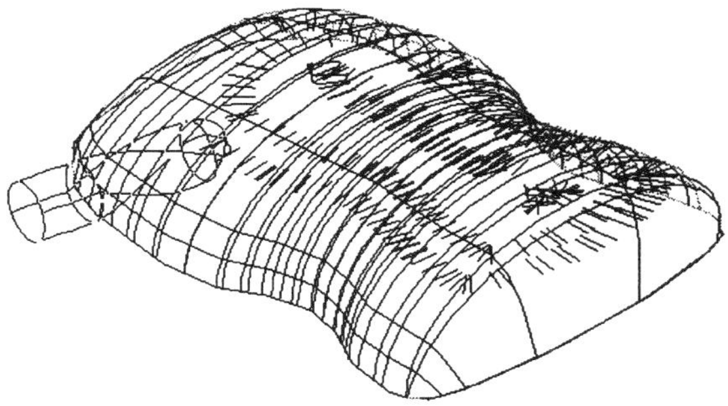

Figure 16.11a Lead angle = 0

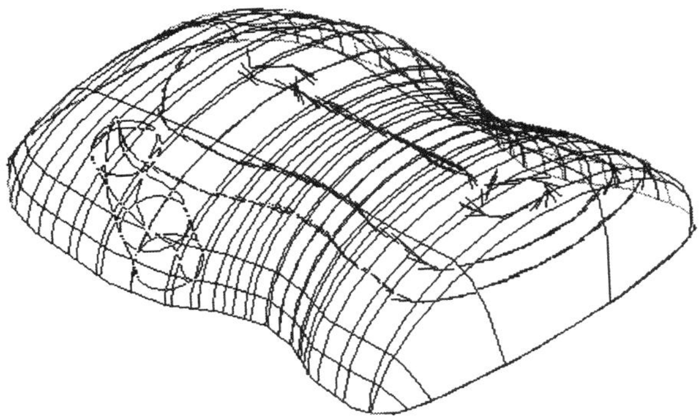

Figure 16.b Lead angle = 30°

1 Project 1. Using rotary 4-axis function to cut a single-surface model

This project shows how to create a set of rotary 4-axis toolpaths to cut a single-surface model. The loft surface to be used and its 4-axis toolpath are shown in Figure 16.12.

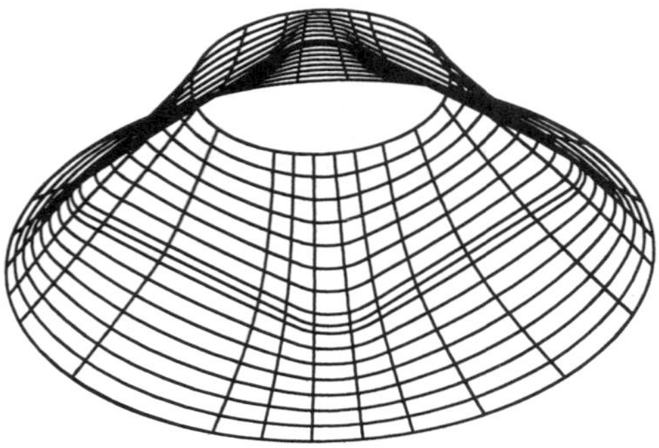

Figure 16.12a

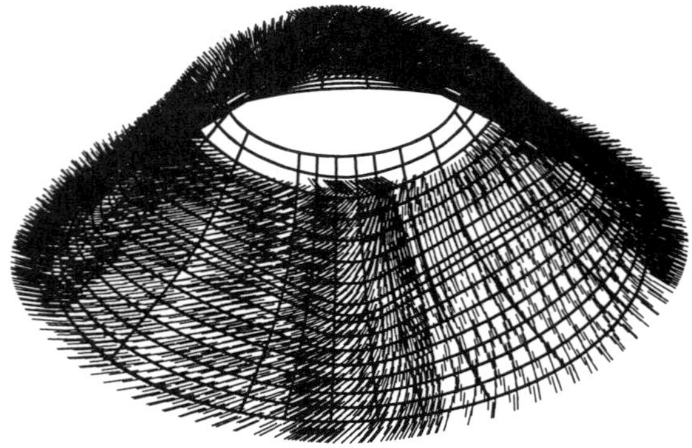

Figure 16.12b

Tips

1. Use the surface model file lofts1.
2. Use the rotary 4-axis function to generate toolpaths.
3. Use a ½" sphere end mill.

Step 1. Open the surface model file lofts1.

Select **MAIN MENU → File → Get**
File name: **lofts1**
The loft surface appears as in Figure 16.13.

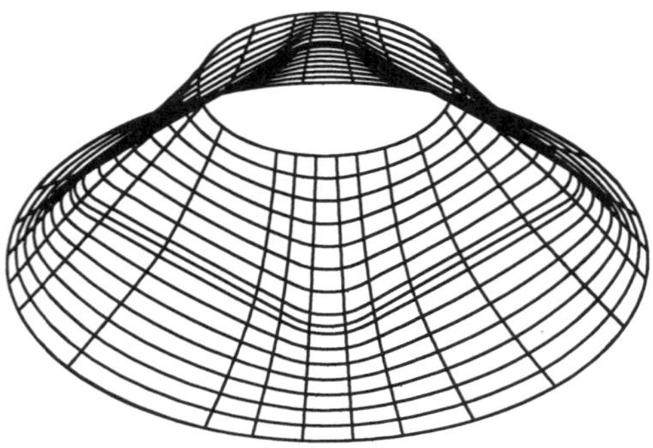

Figure 16.13

Step 2. Initiate the rotary 4-axis function.

Select **MAIN MENU → Toolpaths → Multiaxis → Rotary4ax**
File name for toolpath: **4ax1**
Pick the loft surface, then select **Done**
Click the right mouse button, then select **Get tool from library**
Select **tool number 256** (1/2 sphere endmill)
Select **OK**

Set the Tool parameters menu as below.

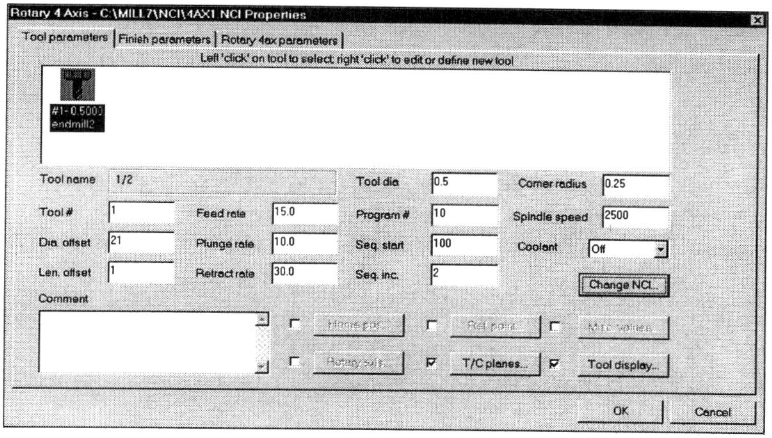

Step 3. Define the finish parameters.

Click the Finish parameters button. Set the finish parameters as below.

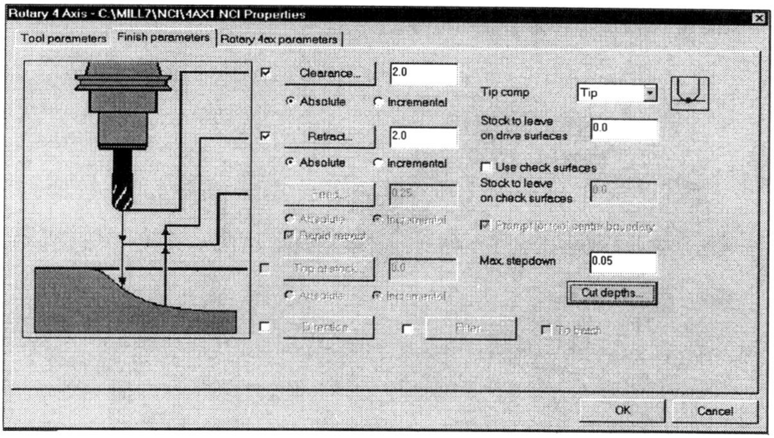

Step 4. Define the rotary 4ax parameters.

Click on the Rotary 4ax parameters. Set the rotary 4ax parameters as below.

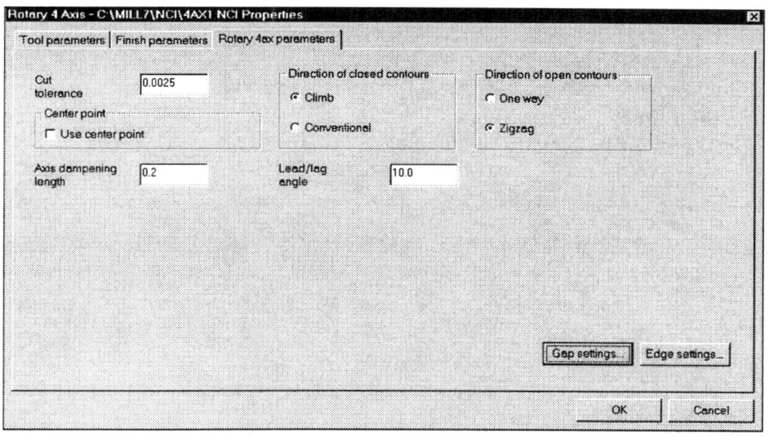

Step 5. Set gap and edge setting parameters.

Click on the Gap settings button

Set the gap setting parameters as here.

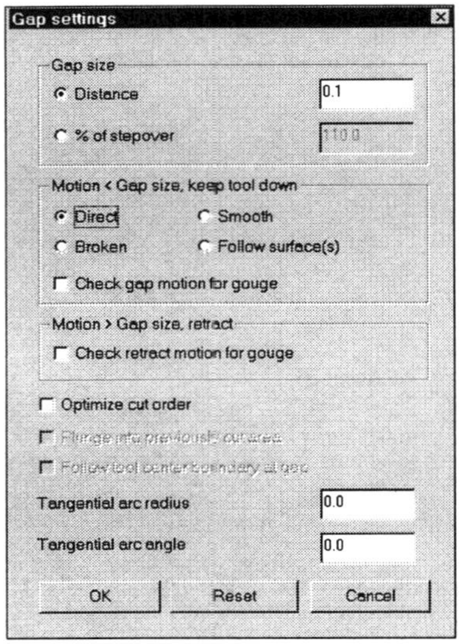

Select **OK → OK** to generate toolpaths

The 4-axis toolpaths are generated as shown in Figure 16.14.

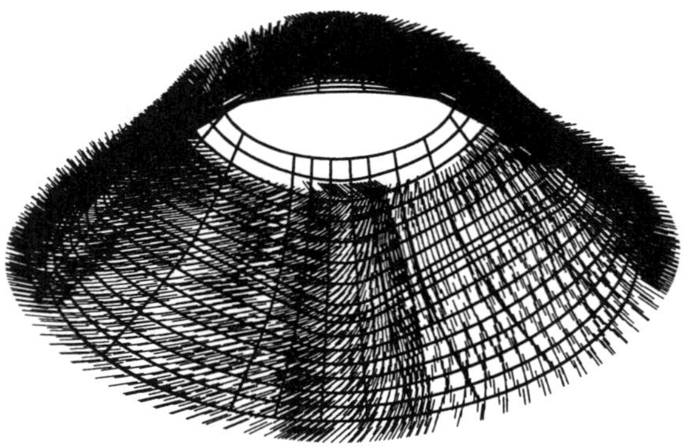

Figure 16.14

Step 6. Save the toolpath file.

Select **MAIN MENU → NC utils → Edit NCI**

Select **Yes** to "Operations have been modified. Created the NCI text file?"

Select **Quit** from the Edit NCI dialog box

Project 2. Using rotary 4-axis function for a multiple-surface model

This project use rotary 4-axis function to generate toolpaths for cutting the dryer surface model. Figure 16.15 shows both surface model and toolpaths.

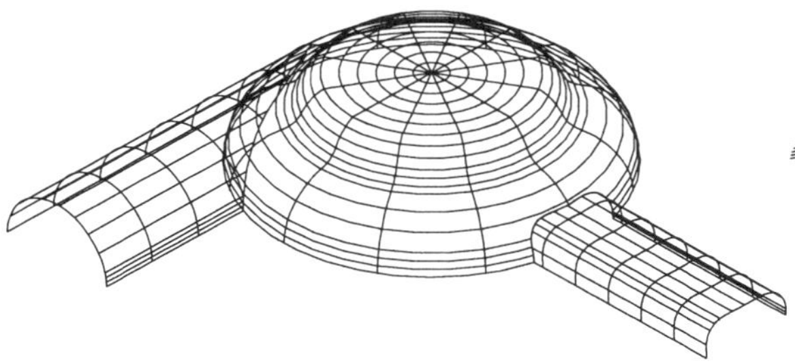

Figure 16.15a

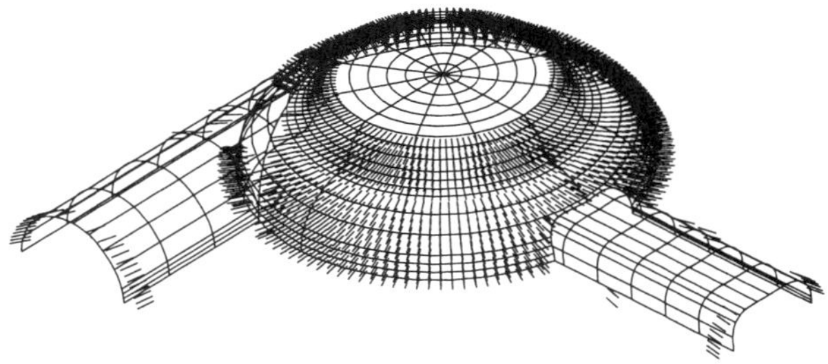

Figure 16.15b

> **Tips** 1. Use the surface model file dryers.
>
> 2. Use the rotary 4-axis function to generate toolpaths.
>
> 3. Use a 3/8" sphere end mill.

Step 1. Open the surface model file dryers.

Select **MAIN MENU → File → Get**
File name: **dryers**
The surface model appears as Figure 16.16.

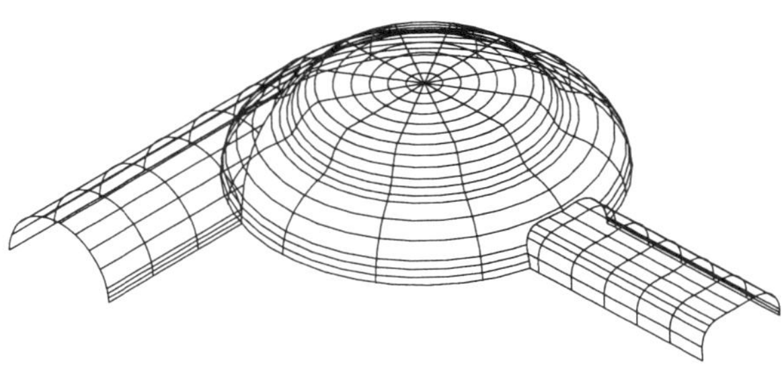

Figure 16.16

Step 2. Initiate the rotary 4-axis function.

Select **MAIN MENU → Toolpaths → Multiaxis → Rotary4ax**
File name for toolpath: **4ax2**
Select **All → Surfaces → Done**
Click the right mouse button, then select **Get tool from library**
Select **tool number 254** (3/8 sphere endmill)
Select **OK**

Set the Tool parameters as below.

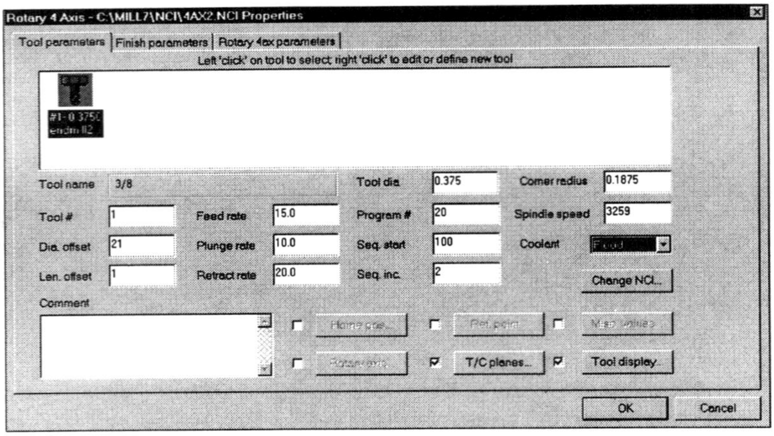

Step 3. Define the finish parameters.

Click "Finish parameters" button.
Set the finish parameters as below.

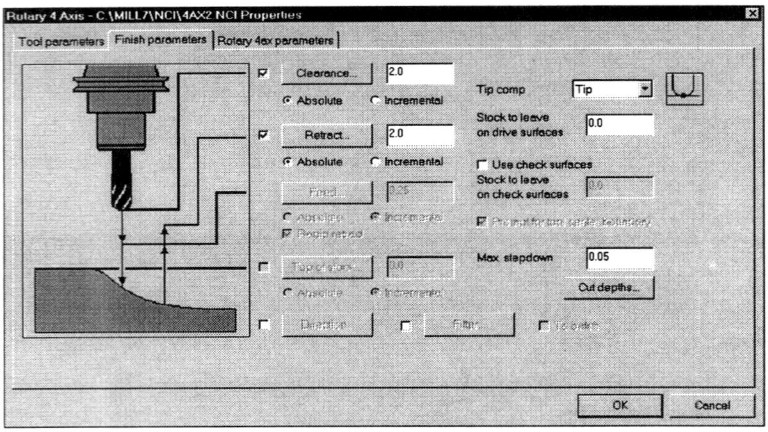

Step 4. Define the rotary 4-axis parameters.

Click "Rotary 4ax parameters" button.

Set the rotary 4-axis parameters as below.

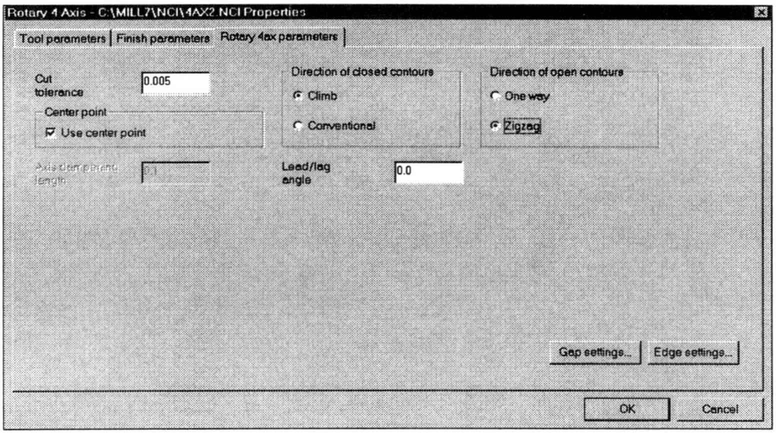

Select **OK**
Enter an approximate starting point: **0,0,0**
The 4-axis rotary toolpaths are generated as in Figure 16.17.

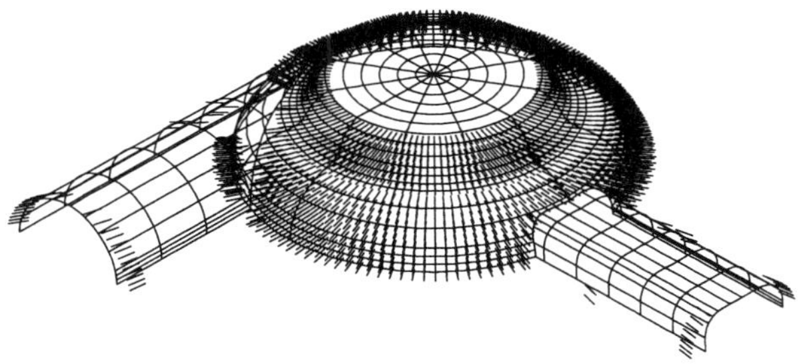

Figure 16.17

Step 5. Save the toolpath file.

Select **MAIN MENU → NC utils → Edit NCI**
Select **Yes** to "Operations have been modified. Created the NCI text file?"
Select **Quit** from the Edit NCI dialog box

16.5 5-Axis Toolpath Functions

There are four 5-axis toolpath functions. They are summarized in Table 16.1.

Table 16.1 Four 5-axis toolpath functions

Function	Description	Illustration
Curve5ax	Generate 5-axis toolpaths along surface edges, chained curves, or surface curves.	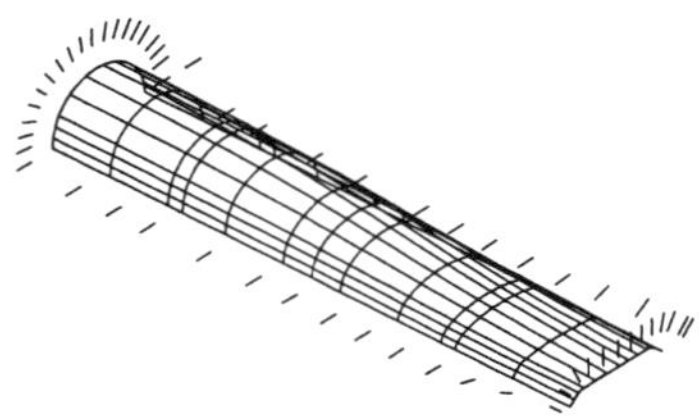
Drill5ax	Generate 5-axis drilling toolpaths that run in a specified direction and depth.	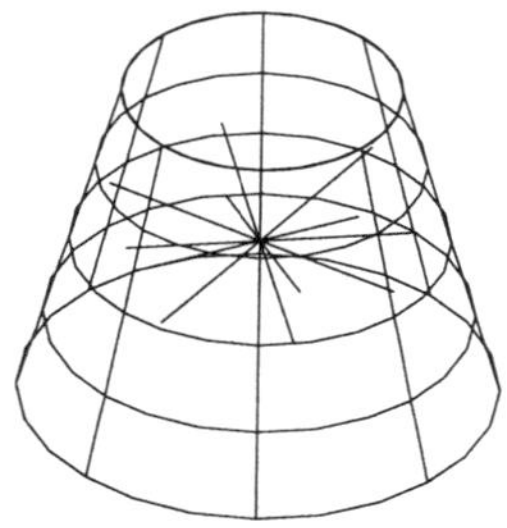
Swarf5ax	Generate 5-axis toolpaths for cutting a surface with the side of the tool.	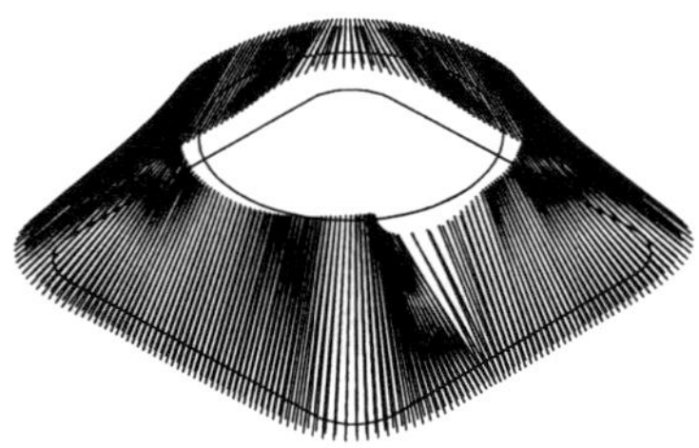
Flow5ax	Generate 5-axis toolpaths for cutting over the entire surface model.	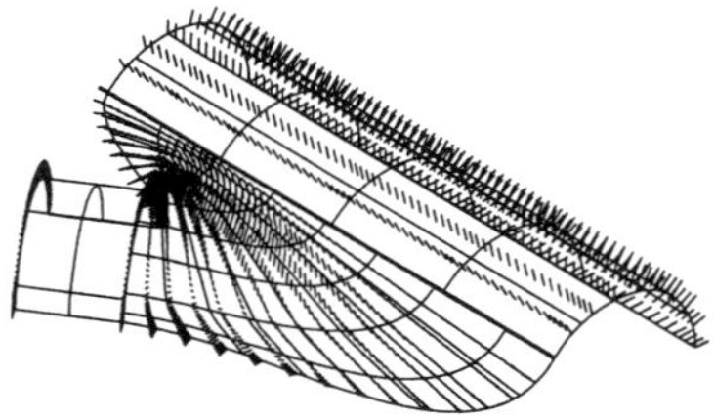

16.6 Curve 5-Axis Function

The Curve 5-Axis function is used to create a 5-axis toolpath (1) along the edges of a surface, (2) along chained curves, or (3) along projected curves on the surface. Table 16.2 summarizes the features of the three curve 5-axis functions.

Table 16.2 Three curve 5-axis functions

Function	Description	Illustration
Outer edge	Generate 5-axis toolpaths on the edges of the a selected surface.	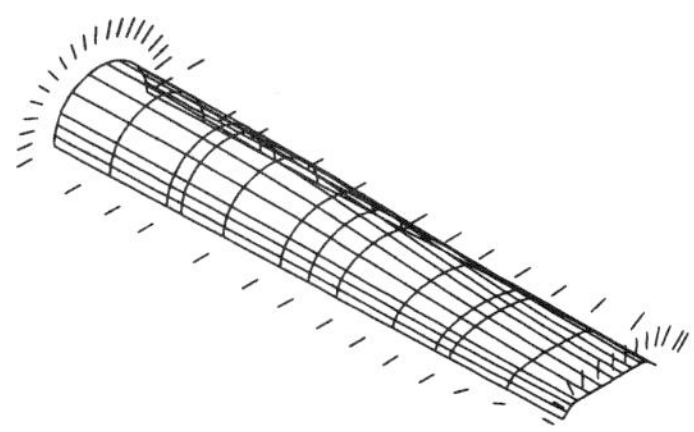
Chain crvs	Generate 5-axis toolpaths along a set of chained curves that are geometry entities not on the surface(s). The system first projects these geometry entities onto the surface(s) to generate a set of surface curves, then generates 5-axis toolpaths to cut the surface curves.	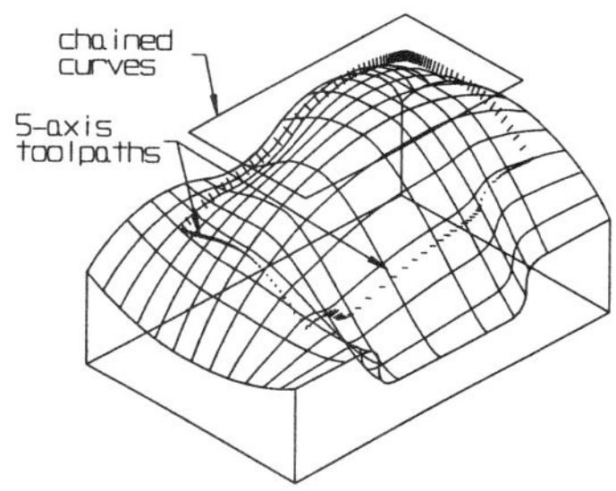
Surf crvs	Generate 5-axis toolpaths along curves projected onto the surface(s).	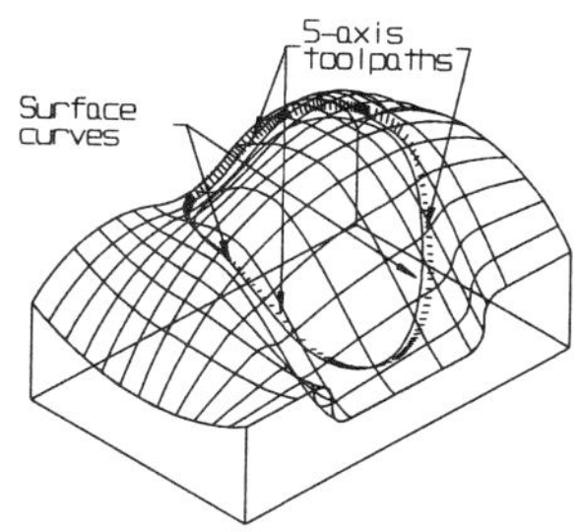

Curve 5-Axis Common Parameters

Those parameters that are commonly used in all three curve 5-axis functions are grouped under Curve 5-Axis parameter dialog box as shown below.

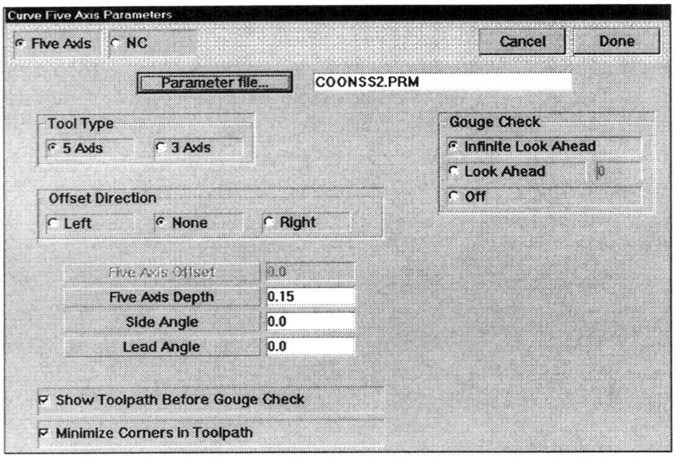

Parameter file This parameter specifies the name and directory of the parameter file used for the current toolpath.

Tool type This parameter is used to select the toolpath as either 3-axis toolpath or 5-axis toolpath. The 3-axis toolpath always has its tool axis perpendicular to the Cplane. The 5-axis toolpath has the tool axis perpendicular to the surface. Figure 16.18 shows the contrast between a 3-axis and a 5-axis toolpath on a surface.

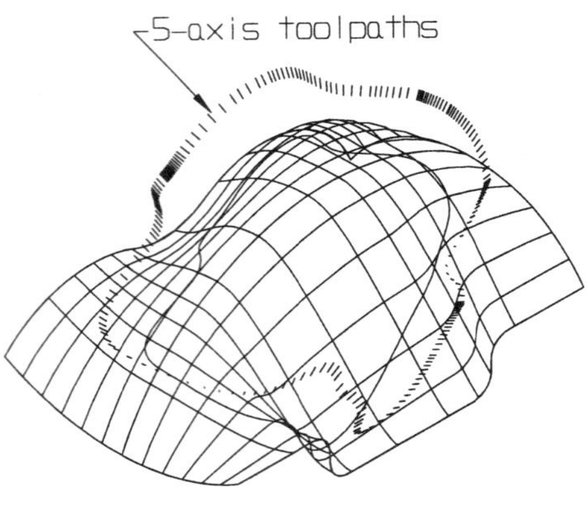

Figure 16.18a

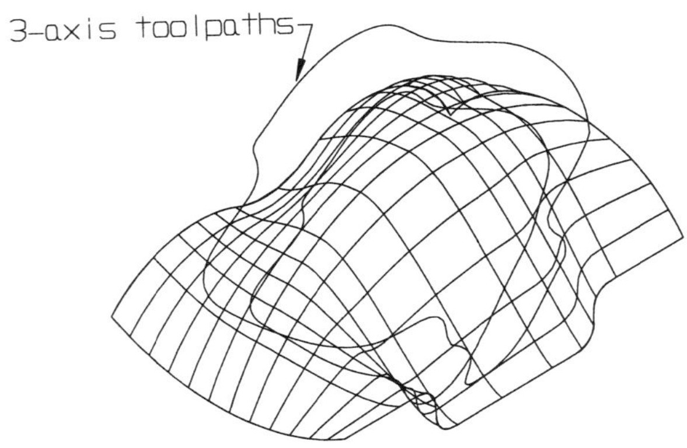

Figure 16.18b

Offset direction There is a group of parameters that are used to define the offset value and direction of the toolpaths. The Offset Direction parameter is used to set the direction for the toolpath offset from the surface edges, surface curves, or projected curves. This parameter can be set to one of the following three options (Figure 16.19).

None: The tool lies on the surface edges, surface curves, or projected curves (Figure 16.19a).
Left: The tool is offset from the left side by a given distance based on the toolpath direction (Figure 16.19b).
Right: The tool is offset from the right side by a given distance based on the toolpath direction (Figure 16.19c).

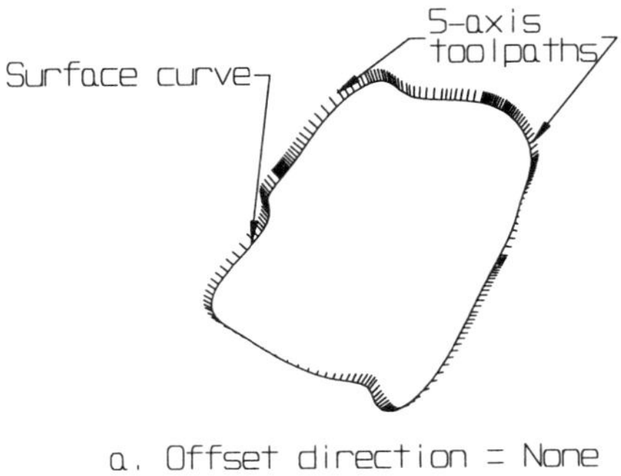

Figure 16.19a Offset direction = None

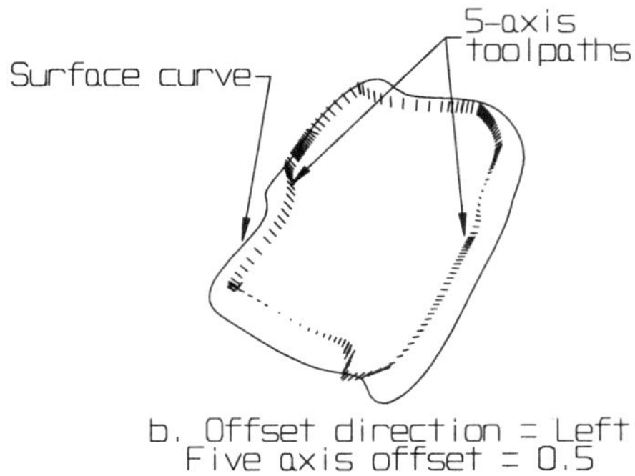

Figure 16.19b Offset direction = Left
Five axis offset = 0.5

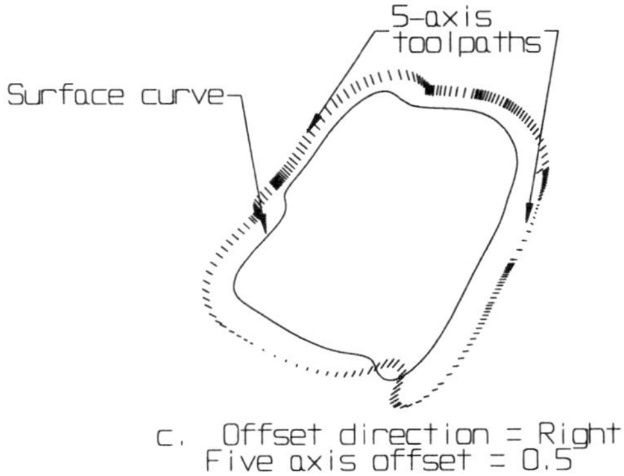

Figure 16.19c Offset direction = Right
Five axis offset = 0.5

Offset distances

Offset and depth The cutter can be offset in two directions: XY-plane and Z-direction. Mastercam uses the "Five Axis Offset" parameter to specify the offset value in the XY-plane and "Five Axis Depth" parameter to specify the offset value in the Z-direction.

Side angle and lead angle Two angle parameters also offset the tool axis orientation. The side angle tilts the tool axis to the right or left by a given angle. A positive angle tilts the tool axis to the left and a negative angle tilts it to the right (Figure 16.20).

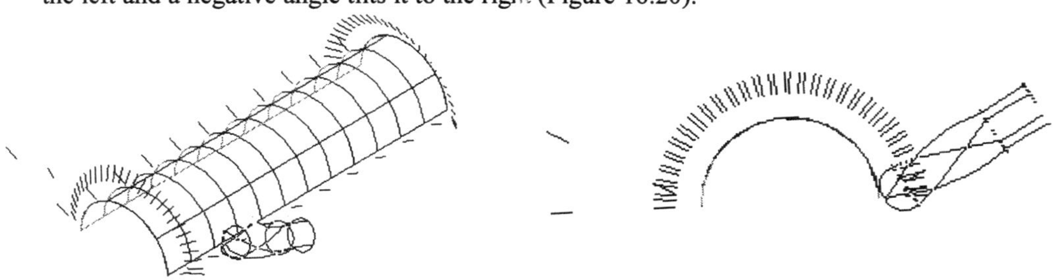

Figure 16.20 a. Side angle = 30°

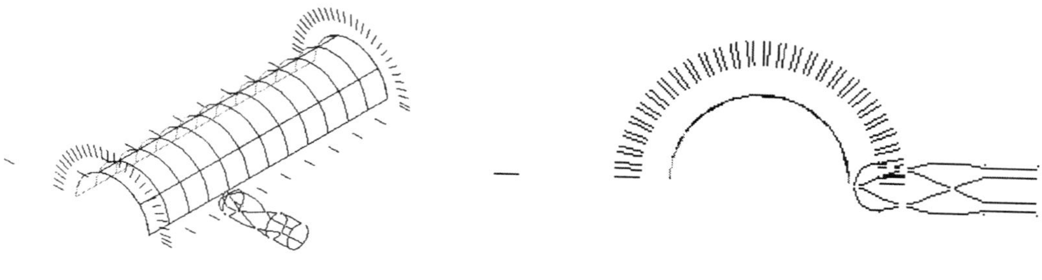

Figure 16.20b. Side angle = 0°

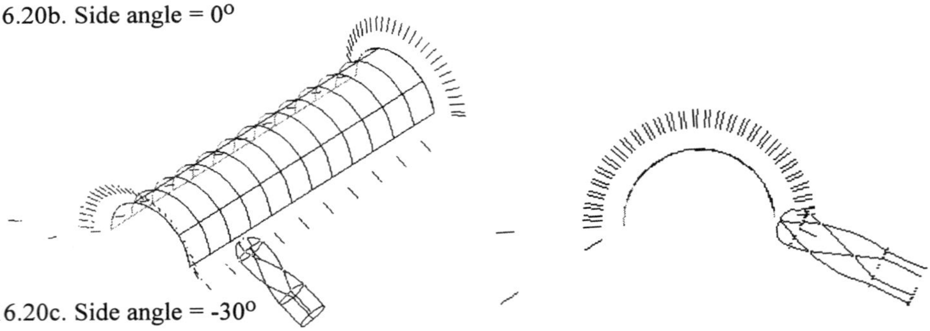

Figure 16.20c. Side angle = -30°

The lead angle tilts the tool to the front or back. A positive lead angle tilts the top of the tool forward and a negative angle tilts it backward (Figure 16.21).

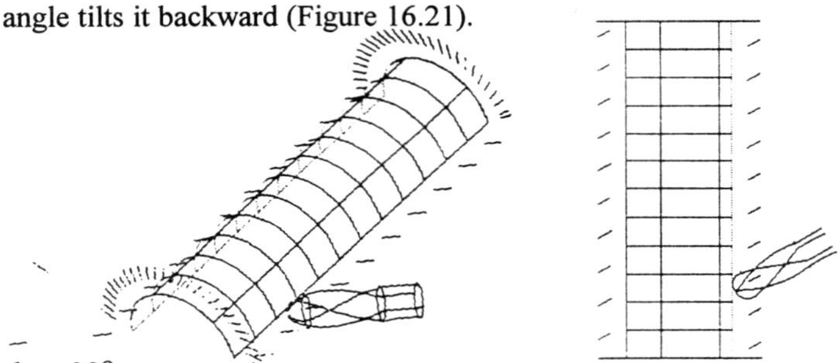

Figure 16.21a. Lead angle = 30°

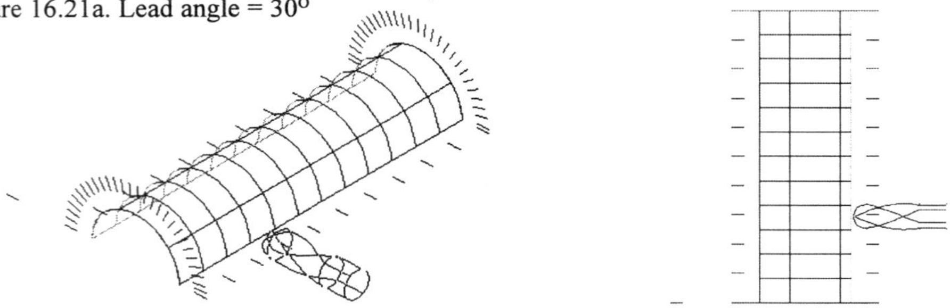

Figure 16.21b. Lead angle = 0°

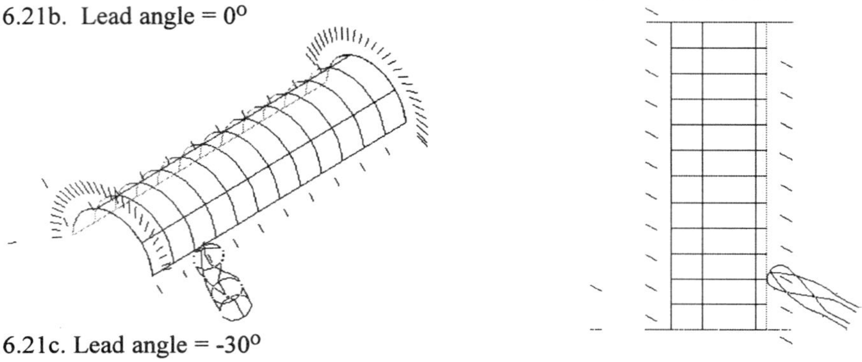

Figure 16.21c. Lead angle = -30°

Gouge check

The gouge check feature in Curve 5-Axis functions only checks for gouges on the offset toolpath. It will not check for those non-offset toolpaths. This parameter can be set to one of the following three options:

Infinite look ahead:	evaluates the entire toolpath when looking for gouges.
Look ahead:	evaluates a given number of toolpath moves ahead while looking for gouges.
Off:	turns off gouge check.

Show toolpath before gouge check

This parameter instructs Mastercam to show the toolpath before making any gouge check changes.

Minimize corners in toolpath

Selecting this option to remove the toolpath move immediately before and the toolpath move immediately after a corner in a toolpath that is offset to the outside.

16.7 Outer Edge Function

The outer edge method generates the 5-axis toolpath on the edges of the selected surface (Figure 16.22). This method is only applied to a single surface. There are two sets of surface boundary parameters dialog box depending on the type of surface you select: trimmed surface boundary and untrimmed surface boundary. They are shown below.

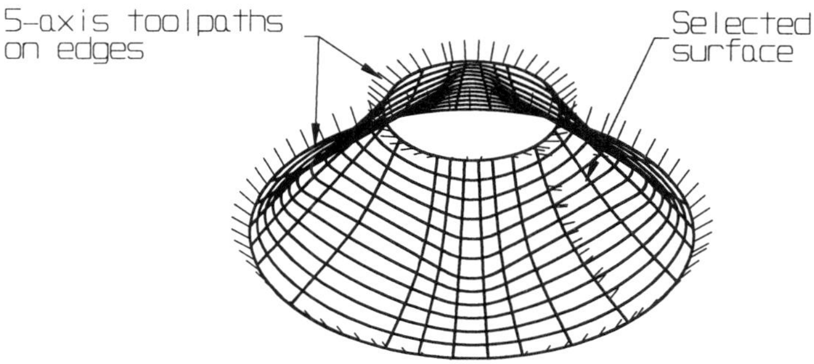

Figure 16.22

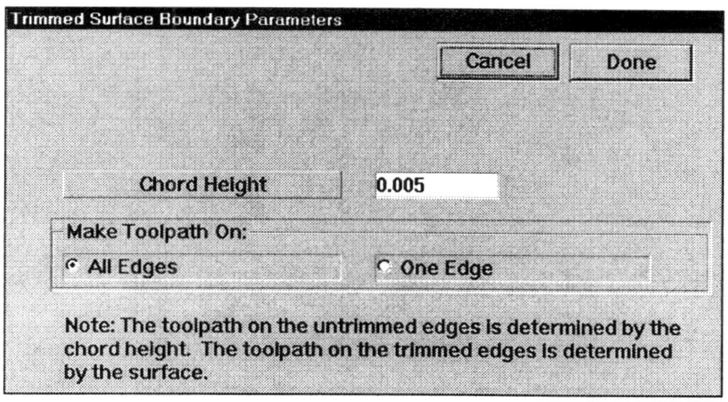

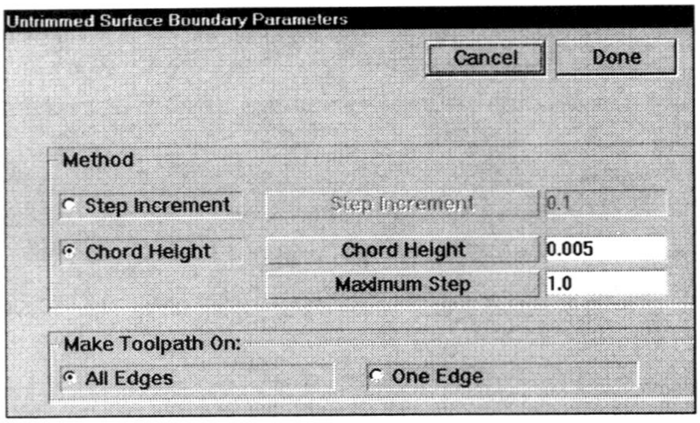

Stepping Method

Mastercam uses two methods to determine the stepping distance along the cutting surface curves: step increment and chord height. With the step increment method, the cutter advances a given distance for each of the toolpath segments disregarding the tolerance of the toolpath. This method is often used for surfaces that are relatively flat and simple.

Using the chord height method, a cutter move is determined by the following two parameters:

Chord height:	specifies the maximum distance that the toolpath can deviate from the surface.
Maximum step:	specifies the maximum distance between toolpath segments.

Make Toolpath On

This parameter uses the following two options to select one surface edge or all surface edges to generate toolpath (Figure 16.23):

All Edges:	generates toolpath along all surface edges.
One Edge:	generates toolpath along one selected surface edge.

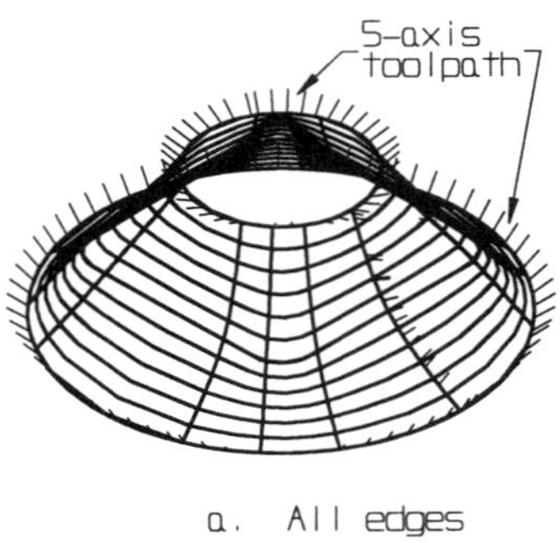

Figure 16.23a All edges

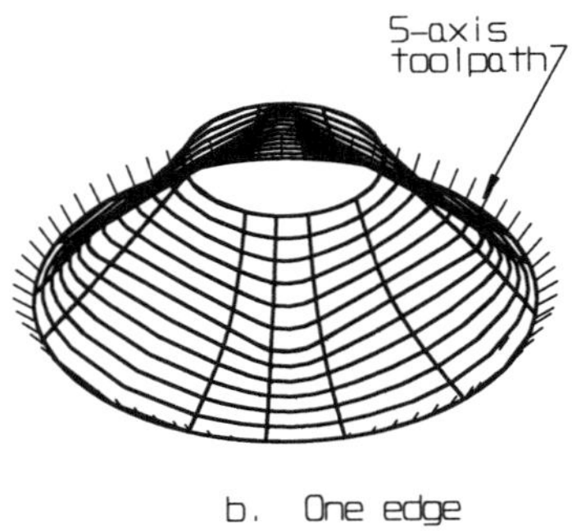

Figure 16.23b One edge

Project 3. 5-axis outer edge toolpaths

This project generates the toolpaths to machine the outer edge of a loft surface. Both 5-axis and 3-axis toolpath modes are used, respectively (Figure 16.24).

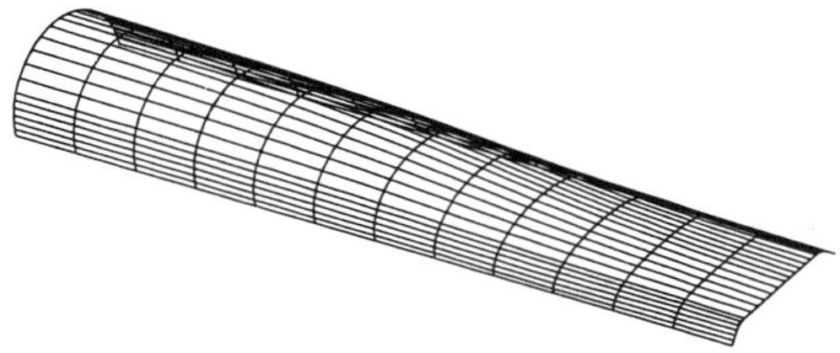

Figure 16.24a Surface

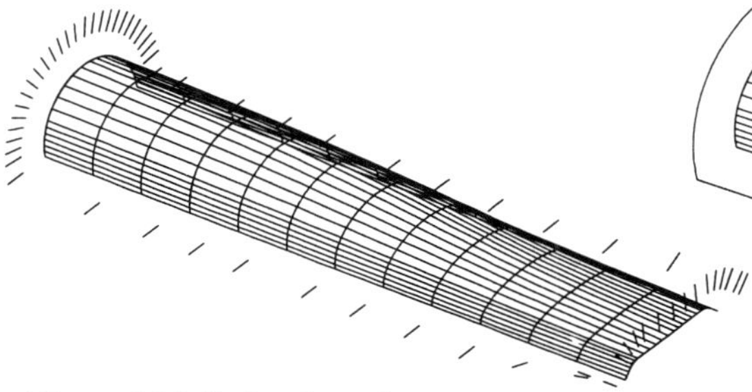

Figure 16.24b 5-axis toolpath

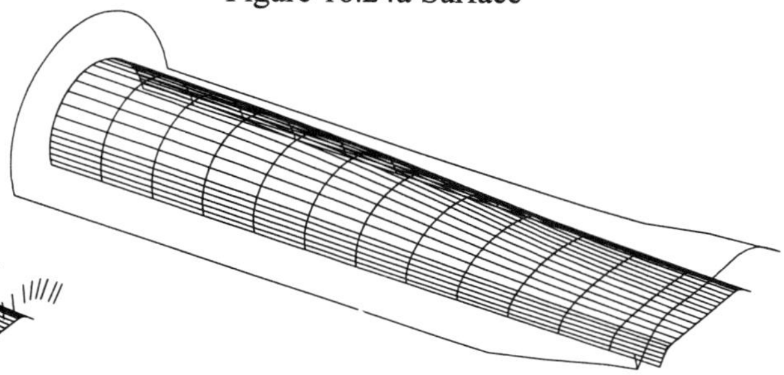

Figure 16.24c 3-axis toolpath

Tips	1. Use the loft surface file lofts3.
	2. Save the 5-axis outer edge toolpath file as 5oe.
	3. Save the 3-axis outer edge toolpath file as 3oe.

Step 1. Open the surface model file lofts3.

Select **MAIN MENU → File → Get**
File name: **lofts3**
The drawing of lofts3 will appear as Figure 16.25.

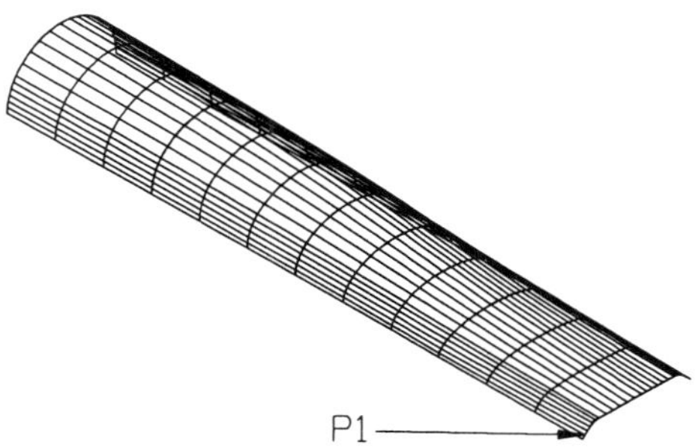

Figure 16.25

Step 2. Initiate the curve 5-axis outer edge function.

Select **Cplane → Top**
Select **MAIN MENU → Toolpaths → Multiaxis → Curve5ax**
File name for toolpath: **5oe**
Pick any point on the surface to select it
Select **Done → Outer edge**

Pick the surface again
Set the Untrimmed surface boundary parameters as below.

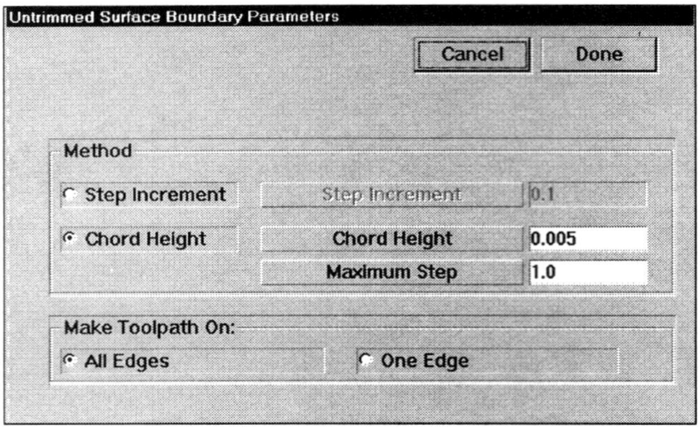

Step 3. Define curve five axis parameters.

Use the pick point in Figure 16.25.
Select **Done**
Move the cursor to the left-front corner and click **P1** as shown in Figure 16.25
The direction arrow should point toward the **+Y** direction on the screen
Select **OK** to accept this default direction
Select **Do it**
Set the Curve five axis parameters as below.

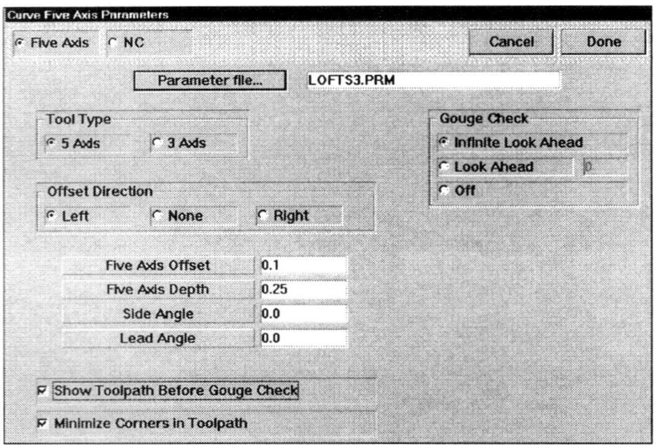

Step 4. Define the NC parameters.

Click the **NC** button

Set the NC parameters as below.

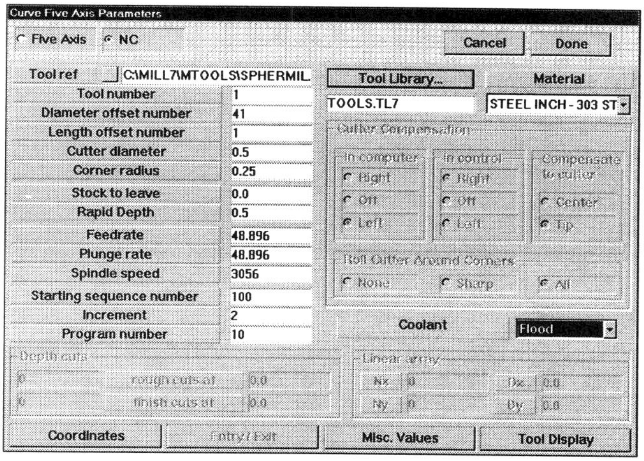

Select Done

Press <Enter> to continue

The toolpaths are generated as in Figure 16.26.

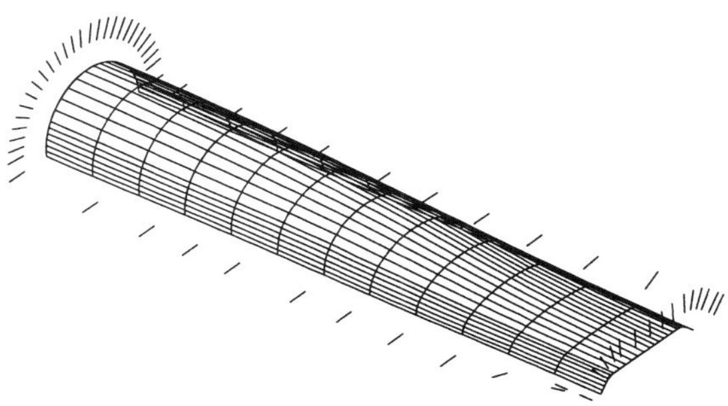

Figure 16.26

Step 5. Save the toolpath file.

Select **MAIN MENU → NC utils → Edit NCI**

Select **Yes** to “Operations have been modified. Create the NCI text file?”

Select **Quit** from Edit NCI menu

Step 6. Generate the surface outer edge toolpath for the 3-axis mode.

Follow all procedure steps 1-5 except for step 3. This time, in step 3 set the Curve Five Axis parameters as shown below.

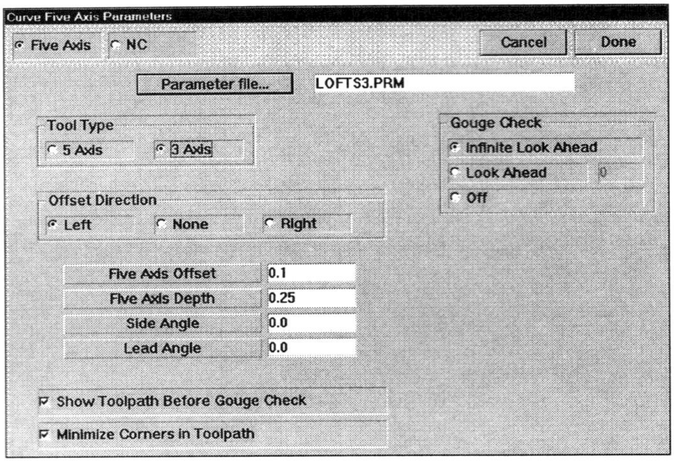

The toolpaths in 3-axis mode will appear as Figure 16.27.

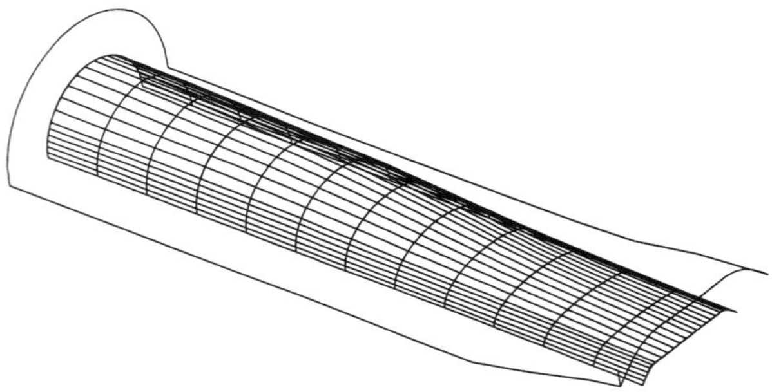

Figure 16.27

16.8 Chain Curves Function

The chain curves method generates 5-axis toolpaths along a set of chained curves that are geometry entities and not the surface. Mastercam first projects these geometry entities onto the surface to generate a set of surface curves, then generates 5-axis toolpaths to cut the surface curves (Figure 16.28).

This method can applied to both a single surface model or a multiple-surface model. The curve projection parameters dialog box appears below.

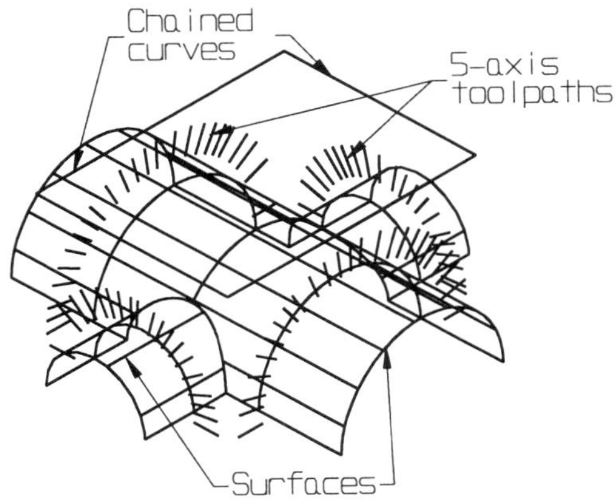

Figure 16.28

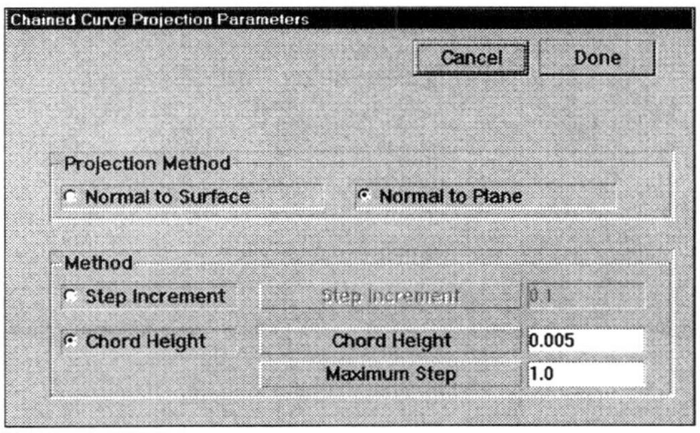

Projection Method

There are two ways to project chained entities onto the surface(s): **normal to surface** and **normal to plane**.

Normal to Surface: the chained entities are projected in the direction perpendicular to the surface.

Normal to Plane: the chained entities are projected in the direction perpendicular to the current construction plane.

4 Project 4. 5-Axis chain curve

This project generates 5-axis toolpaths to machine a curve that is created by projecting a circle onto a Coons surface. Figure 16.29 shows the surface model and a circle. Figure 16.30 shows the toolpaths generated from projecting the circle onto the surface using the normal to plane method.

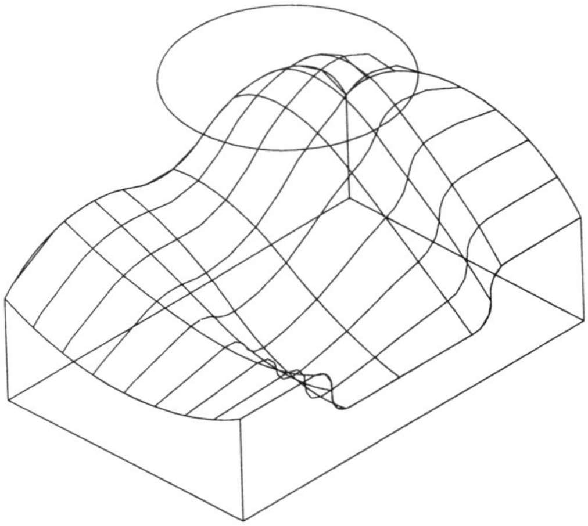

Figure 16.29 Surface and curve

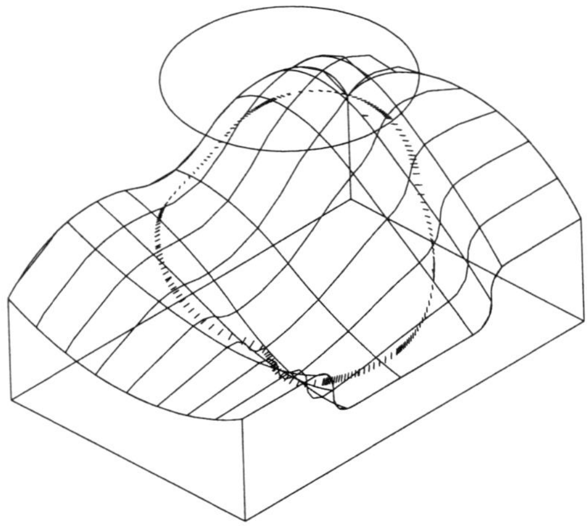

Figure 16.30 Toolpaths

Tips 1. Use the Coons surface file coonss1 as the base surface to be projected onto.

2. Create a circle having its center on (2.5, 3.75) with a diameter of 4" to use as the chain curve.

3. Use the Backplot function to visualize and verify the toolpaths.

Step 1. Open the surface model file coonss1.

Select **MAIN MENU → File → Get**

File name: **coonss1**

The Coons surface appears as Figure 16.31.

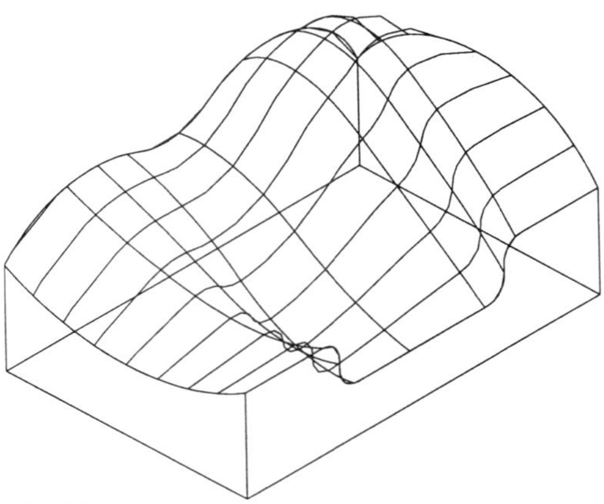

Figure 16.31

Step 2. Create a circle in level 3.

Select **Cplane → Top**
Select **Level**, then enter **3**
Select **Z**, then enter **3.5**
Select **MAIN MENU → Create → Arc → Cir pt+dia → Value**
Enter coordinates: **2.5, 3.75**
Enter the diameter: **4**
The circle is added as in Figure 16.32.

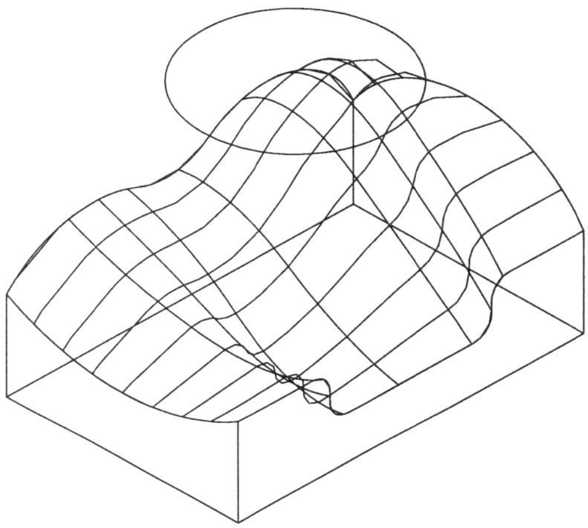

Figure 16.32

Step 3. Initiate the Curve5ax-Chain cvs function.

Select **MAIN MENU → Toolpaths → Multiaxis → Curve5ax**
File name for toolpath: **5cc**
Pick any point on the Coons surface
Select **Done → Chain cvs**
Pick the circle as the boundary
Select **Do it**
Set the Curve five axis parameters as below.

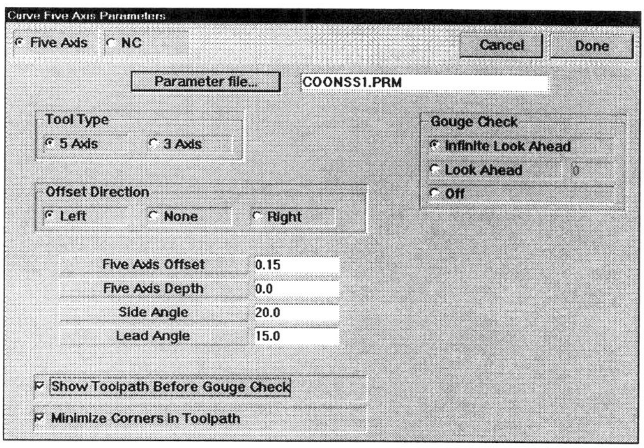

Step 4. Define the NC parameters.

Click the **NC** button
Set the NC parameters as below.

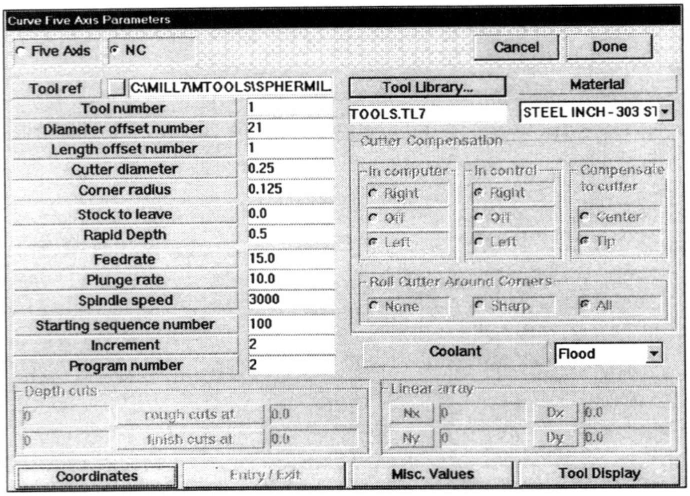

Select **Done** to generate the toolpaths
Press **<Enter>** to continue
The toolpaths are shown in Figure 16.33.

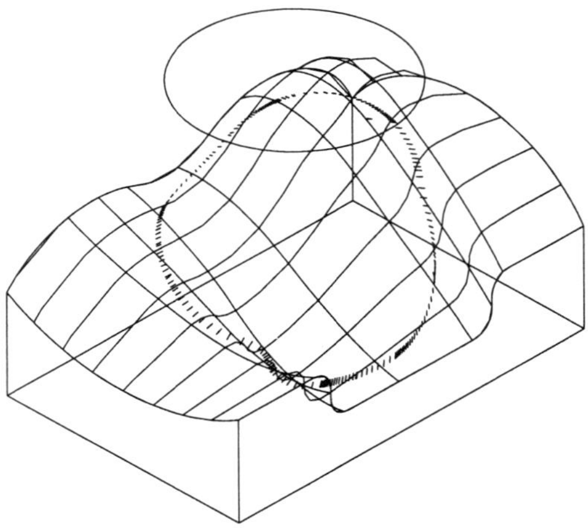

Figure 16.33

Step 5. Save the toolpath file.

Select **MAIN MENU → NC utils → Edit NCI**
Select **Yes** to "Operations have been modified. Create the NCI text file?"
Select **Quit** from the Edit NCI menu

Step 6. Backplot the toolpaths.

Select **MAIN MENU → NC utils → Backplot → Display**

Set the backplot display parameters as below.

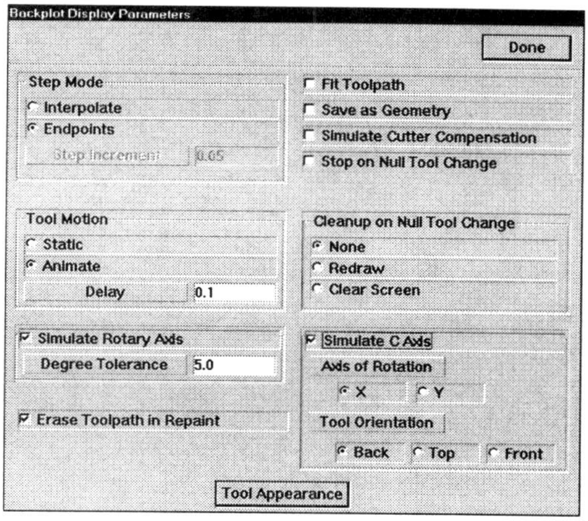

Select **Done**
Select **Run**
The toolpaths are animated on the screen.

16.9 Surface Curves Function

The surface curves method generates 5-axis toolpaths along curves that were previously projected onto the surface (Figure 16.34). This method is applied only to a single surface. Surface curves are 3D curves that lie on a surface and are defined by their location on the surface.

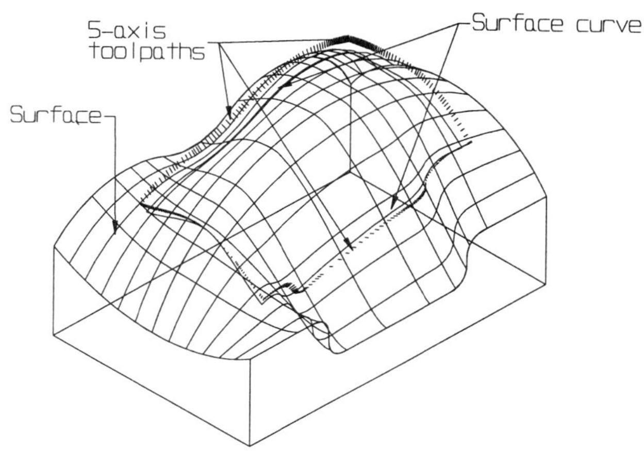

Figure 16.34

Gap Tolerance

This parameter specifies the maximum distance by which adjacent surface curves may be separated and still be chained. When the distance between two surface curves exceeds this value, the system does not chain them.

5 Project 5. Curve 5-axis-surface curve

Generate 5-axis toolpaths to machine a series of surface curves on a surface (Figure 16.35). The surface curves are created by projecting a rectangle onto a surface. Then use the Curv5ax-surf crvs function to generate 5-axis toolpaths.

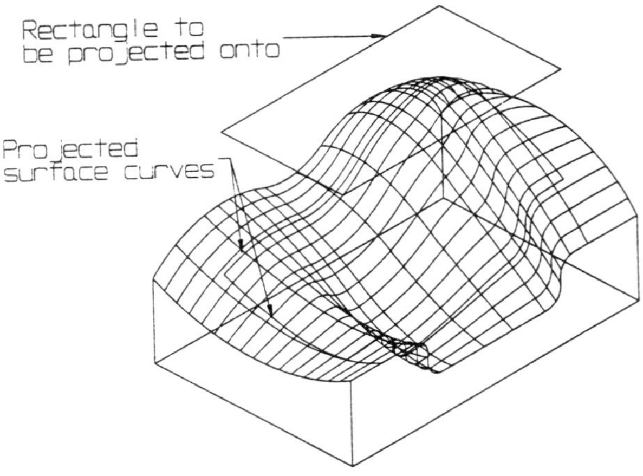

Figure 16.35a Surface curves

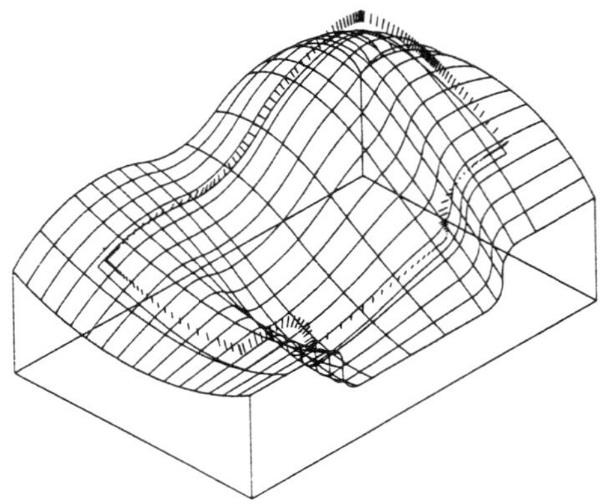

Figure 16.35b Toolpaths

Tips

1. Use the Coons surface coonss1 as the base surface.
2. Create a rectangle.
3. Project the rectangle onto the Coons surface to generate surface curves.
4. Use the Curv5ax-surf crvs function to generate toolpaths to cut surface file coonss1.

Step 1. Open the surface model file coonss1.

Select **MAIN MENU → File → Get**
File name: **coonss1**
The surface model coonss1 will appear as Figure 16.36.

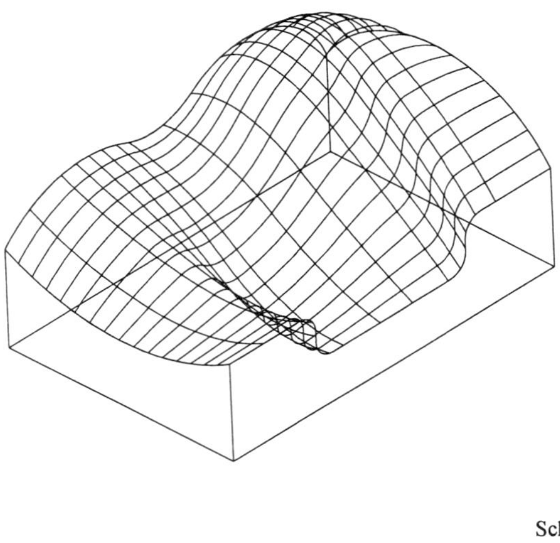

Figure 16.36

Step 2. Set the drawing environments for creating a rectangle.

Select **Level**, then enter **3**
Select **Z**, then enter **3.5**
Select **Gview → Top**
Select **Cplane → Top**
The model shown in the top view will look like Figure 16.37.

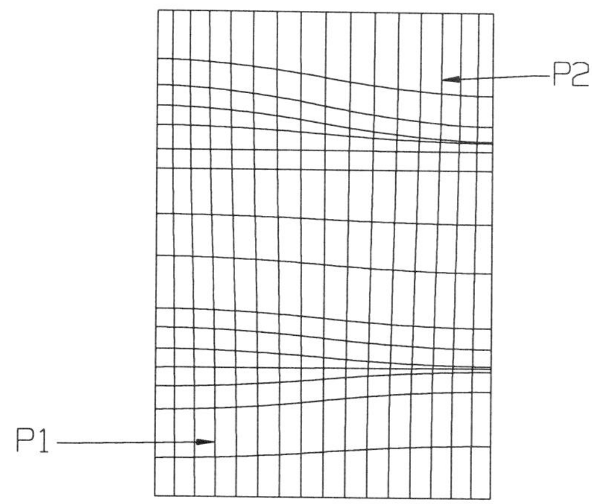

Figure 16.37

Step 3. Create a rectangle using the pick points in Figure 16.37.

Select **MAIN MENU → Create → Rectangle → 2 Points → Sketch**
Enter the lower left corner: pick **P1**
Enter the upper right corner: pick **P2**
Select **Gview → Isometric**
A rectangle is added to the model as in Figure 16.38.

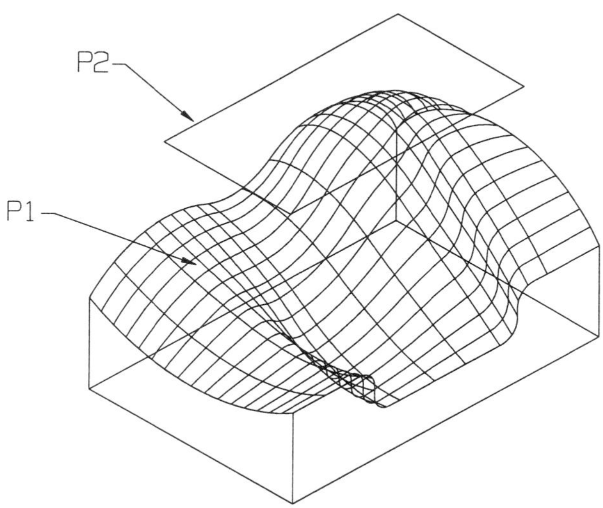

Figure 16.38

Step 4. Project the rectangle onto the surface to create surface curves.

Use the pick points in Figure 16.38.
Select **Level**, then enter **4**
Select **MAIN MENU → Create → Curve → Project**
Pick **P1** to select a surface
Select **Done**

Select **Chain**, then pick **P2**
Select **Done → Options**
Set projection curve parameters as below.

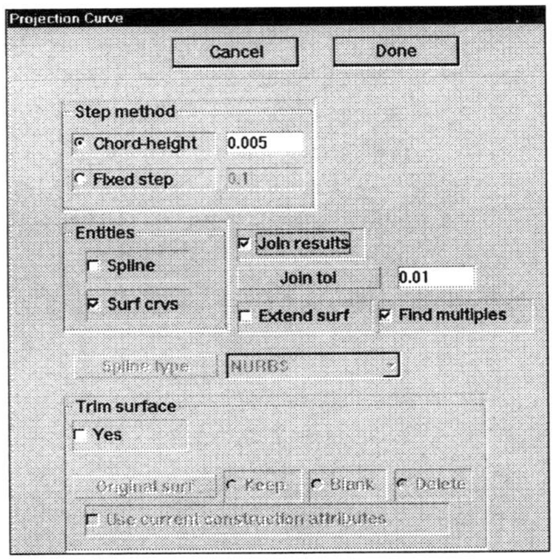

Select **Done**
Set View/norm to **V**
Select **Do it** to generate surface curves
Select **Level → Vis levels,**
toggle **3** to invisible (dimmed)
Select **OK**
The surface curves are added as in Figure 16.39.

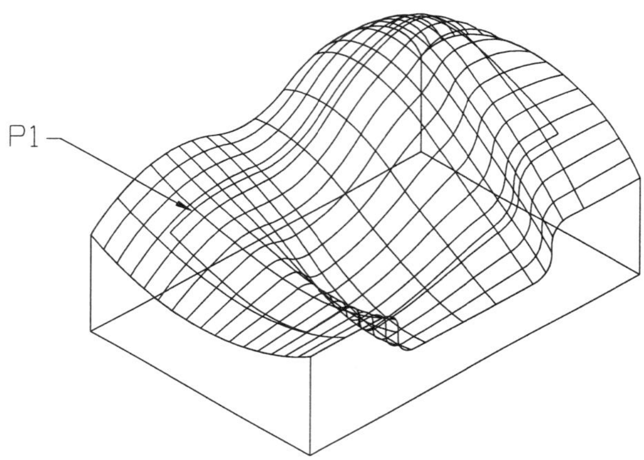

Figure 16.39

Step 5. Generate toolpaths for surface curves.

Use the pick point in Figure 16.39.
Select **MAIN MENU → Toolpaths → Multiaxis → Curve5ax**
File name: **psc**
Pick the **surface**, then select **Done**
Select **Surf crvs**
Pick **P1**
Select **Do it**

Set the curve five axis parameters as shown next.

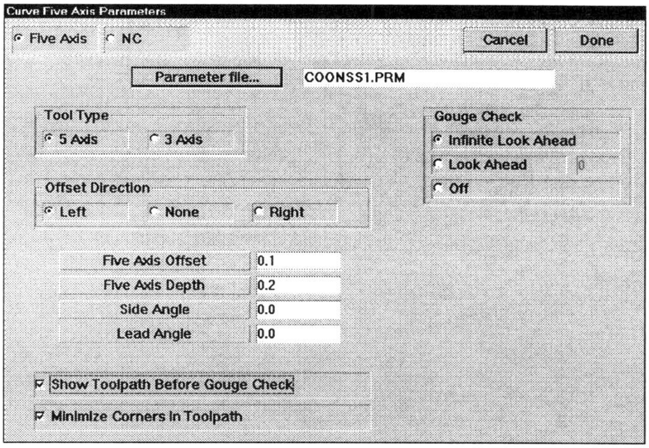

Step 6. Define the NC parameters.

Click the **NC** button. Set the NC parameters as below.

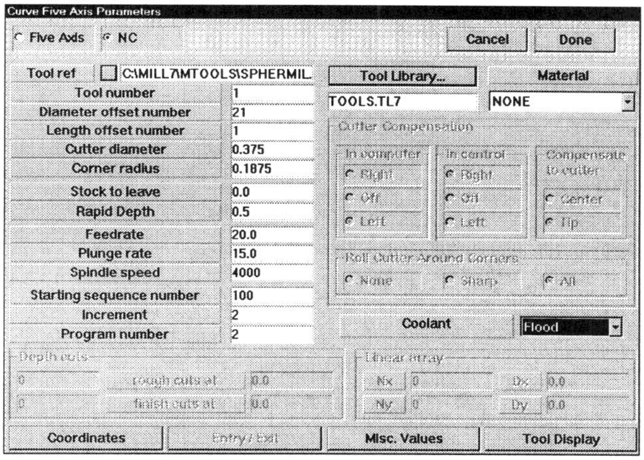

Select **Done**

The toolpaths are generated as shown in Figure 16.40.

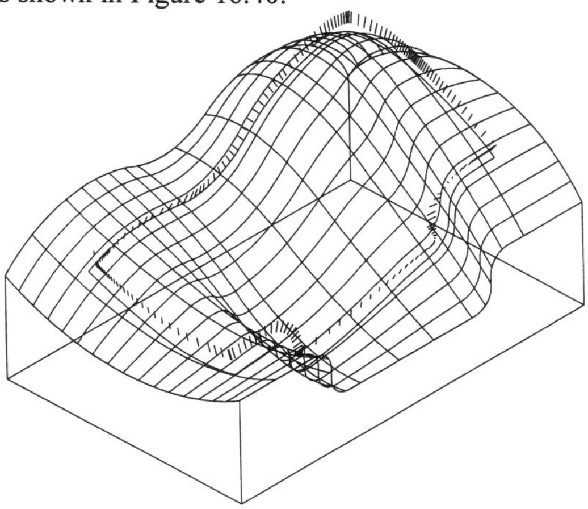

Figure 16.40

Press **<Enter>** to continue

Step 7. Save the toolpath file.

Select **MAIN MENU → NC utils → Edit NCI**

Select **Yes** to “Operations have been modified. Create the NCI text file?”

Select **Quit** from Edit NCI menu

16.10 Drill 5-Axis Function

The drill 5-axis function is used to drill holes in a specified direction. The location and direction of the drilling can be specified by two methods; points and pts/lines. With the Points method, a reference point and a projection surface or plane are used. The system projects the reference point onto the surface to obtain the drilling point on the surface, then it uses a normal vector as a reference to set the drilling direction (Figure 16.41).

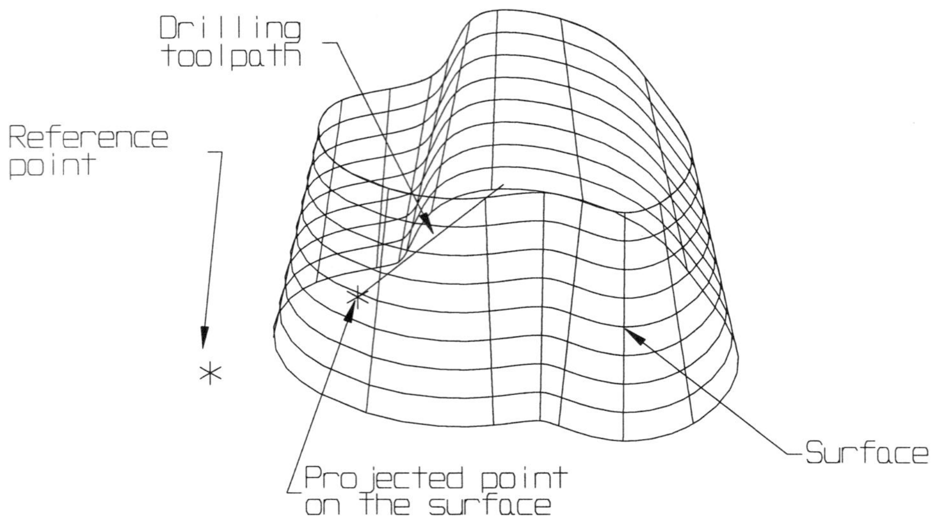

Figure 16.41

In Pts/lines method, the endpoint of a line is used as the reference point and the line defines the drilling direction (Figure 16.42).

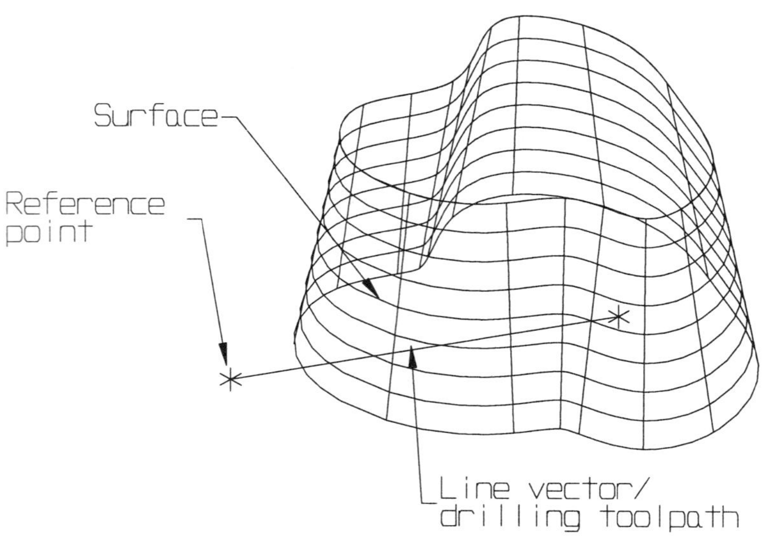

Figure 16.42

Point selection methods

The following three options are used to select points for drilling:

Manual:	manually selects or creates points for generating drilling toolpaths.
Automatic:	uses three points to automatically select a group of points for generating drilling toolpaths. The first selected point is used as the first point, the second selected point sets the search direction, and the third selected point is the stop point.
Window:	selects a series of points within the window for generating drilling toolpaths.

Project normal

This parameter selects one of the following two methods for the projection of the drill points:

Surface:	projects the points normal to the selected surface.
Plane:	projects the points normal to the current construction plane.

Drill 5-axis parameters

Drilling parameters are grouped under drill 5-axis parameters menu as shown below. The drill parameters are same as in chapter 7 for regular drilling operations. See the Drill section in chapter 7.

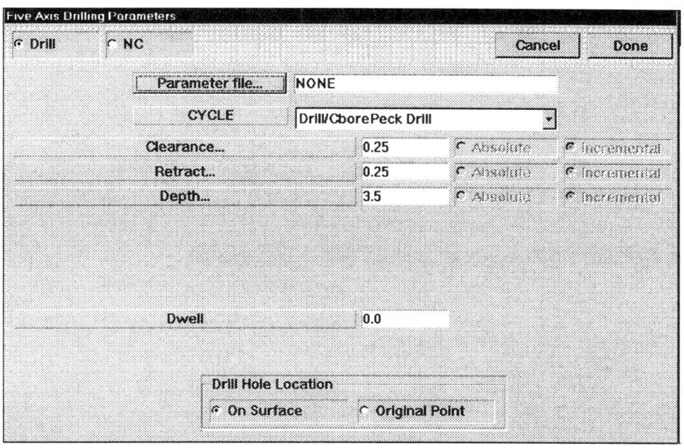

Drill hole location

This parameter is unique for drill 5-axis function and only applies to the Points method. It specifies how the selected point Mastercam uses as the reference point for drilling. This parameter has the following two options:

On Surface:	uses the projected point on the surface as the reference point (Figure 16.43). In other words, the drilling depth is measured from this point and toward the surface normal direction.
Original Point:	uses the original point above the surface as the reference (Figure 16.44). The drilling depth is measured from this point and toward the surface normal direction.

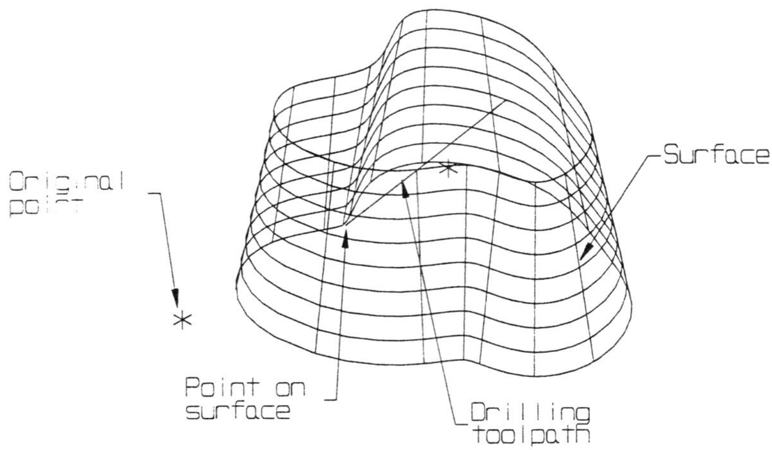

Figure 16.43

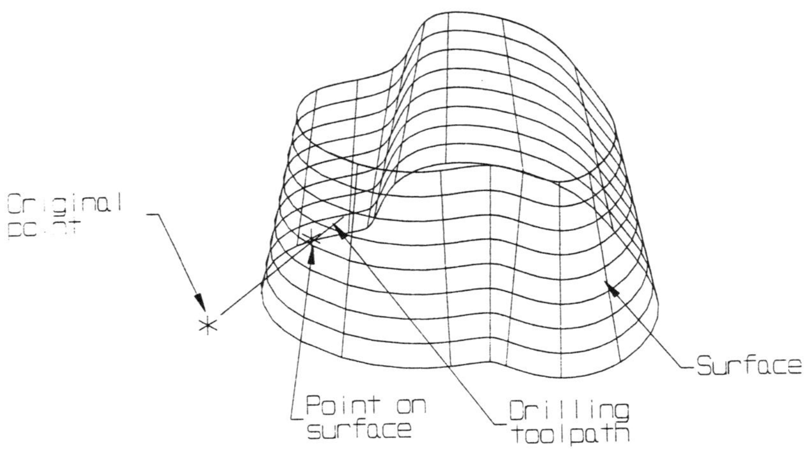

Figure 16.44

Two projects are presented in this section to demonstrate how to use two functions of the Drill 5-axis. The first project uses the points method to generate a drilling toolpath that is normal to a draft surface, then copy this toolpath to five locations around the Z axis. The second project uses the Point/ Line method to generate the toolpaths to drill two holes along the line orientation.

Project 6. Drill 5-axis with points option

This project uses the Drill 5-axis function to generate a toolpath for a point and is perpendicular to the surface. This drilling toolpath is then copied to 5 locations by using the Edit NCI-Xform-Rotate function. Figure 16.45 shows surface model and drilling toolpaths.

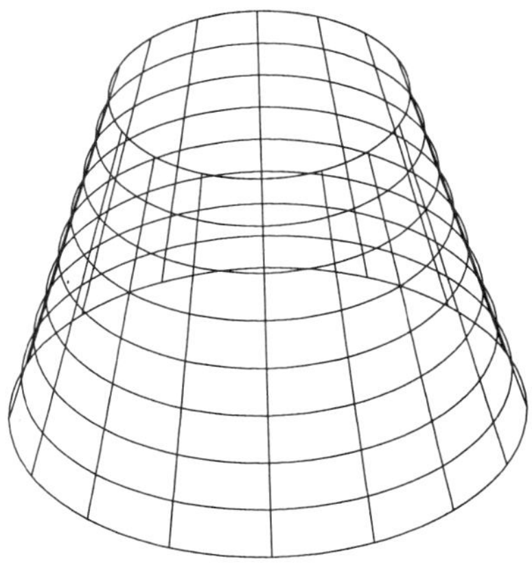

Figure 16.45a Surface

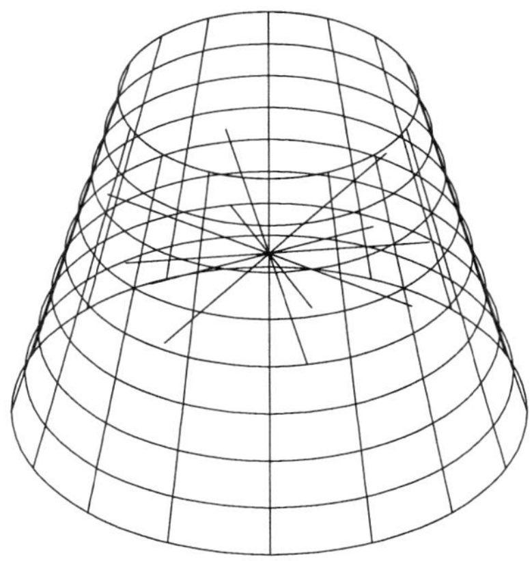

Figure 16.45b Drilling toolpaths

Tips
1. Create a cone-shaped draft surface.
2. Use the front view to define a point as the drilling location.
3. Use the Edit NCI → Xform → Rotate function to copy the drilling toolpath to five locations around the cone-shaped surface.
4. Use the Backplot function to verify the toolpaths.

Step 1. Create a circle.

Select **Cplane → Top**
Select **Gview → Isometric**
Select **Z**, then enter **0**
Select **MAIN MENU → Create → Arc → Cir pt+dia**
Enter the center point: **0,0**
Enter radius: **3**
The circle is created as in Figure 16.46.

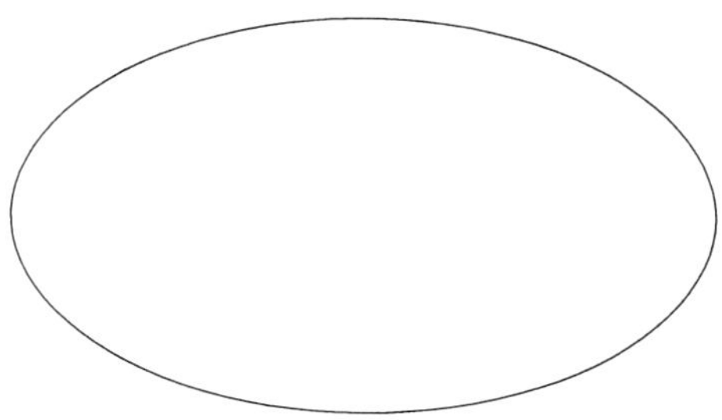

Figure 16.46

Step 2. Create a draft surface.

Select **MAIN MENU → Create → Surface → Draft**
Pick the circle to select the profile entity
Select **Done**
Ann arrow pointing upward will appear to indicate the extending direction.
Select **Length**, then enter **–4**
Select **Angle**, then enter **–15**
Select **Do it**
The draft surface is created as in Figure 16.47.

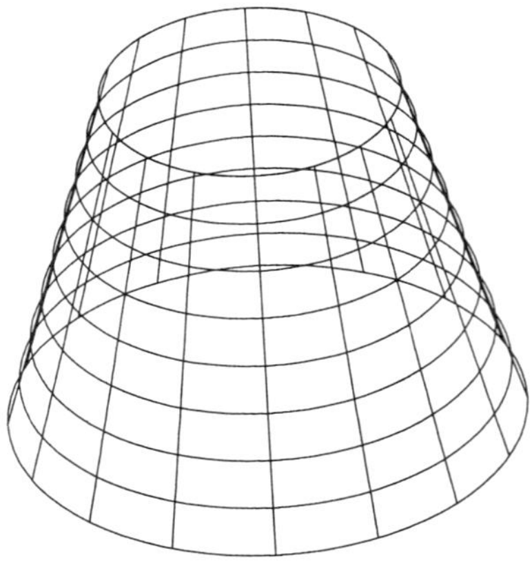

Figure 16.47

Select **MAIN MENU → File → Save**
File name: **5drl**

Step 3. Define the drilling location.

Select **Cplane → Front**
Select **MAIN MENU → Toolpaths → Multiaxis → Drill5ax**
File name for toolpath: **5drl**
Select **Points**
Set Surface to "**Y**"
Select **Manual → Value**
Enter coordinates: **0,-1.5,6**
A point will appear as in Figure 16.48.

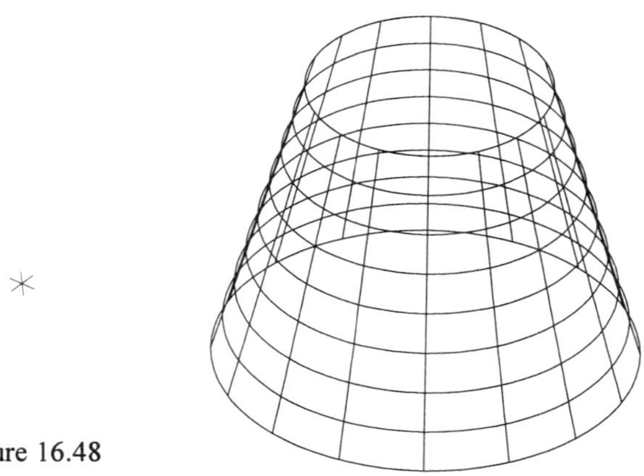

Figure 16.48

Press the **Esc key** to complete point selection
Select **Yes** to draw the path between points
Select **Yes** to "Is the path OK?"
Pick any point on the surface to select it

Step 4. Define the drilling parameters.

Set the five axis drilling parameters as below.

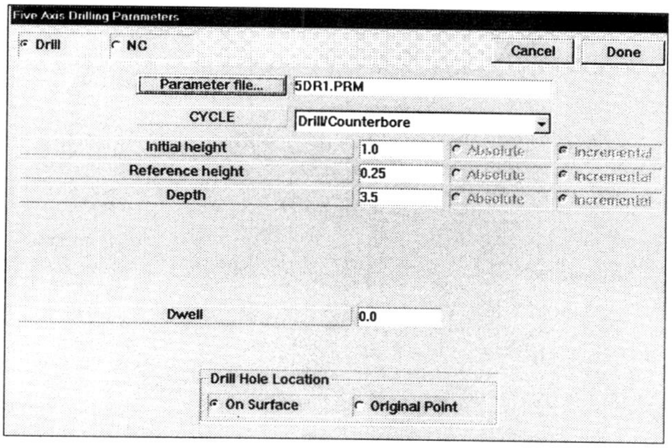

Select the **NC** button
Set the NC parameters as below.

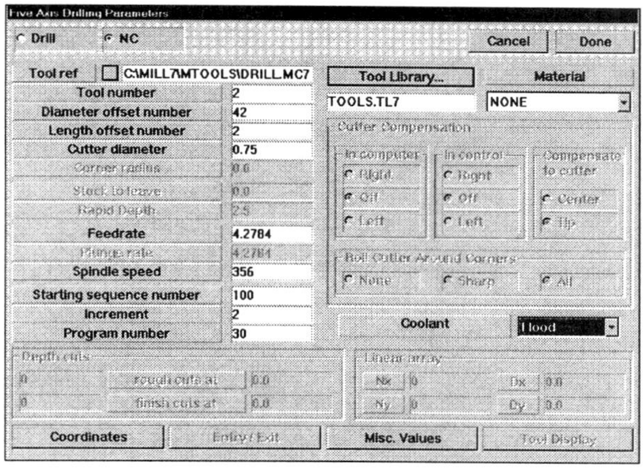

Select **Done**
The drilling path is shown in Figure 16.49.

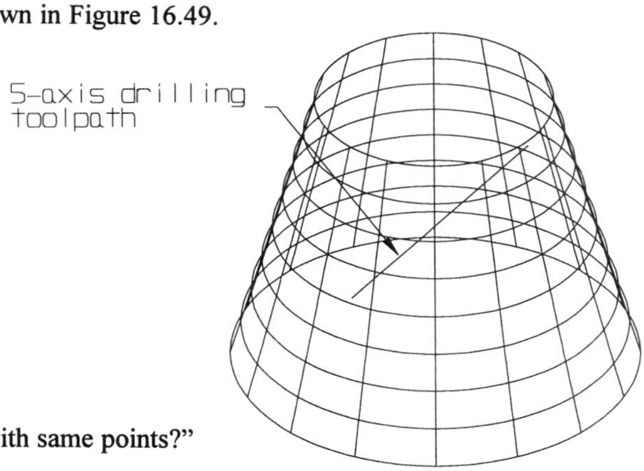

Figure 16.49

Select No to "Repeat with same points?"

Step 5. Generate five drilling toolpaths by using Xform-Rotate function.

Select **Cplane → Top**
Select **MAIN MENU → NC utils → Edit NCI**
Click Unknown **[T2]** under 5DRL.NCI
Select **Xform → Rotate**
Set the Xform – Rotate menu as below.

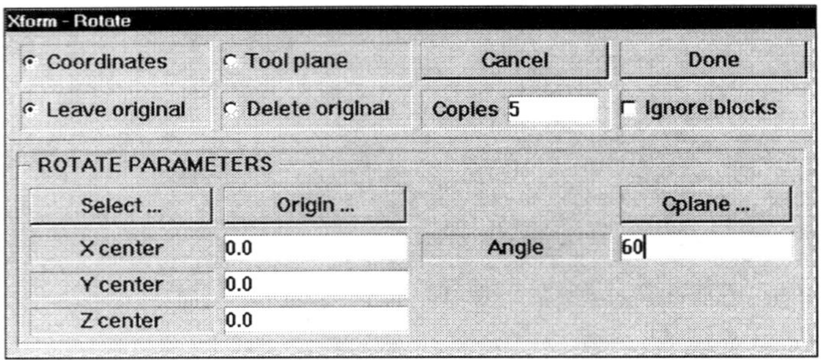

Select **Done**
The five drilling toolpaths are added to the file as shown below.

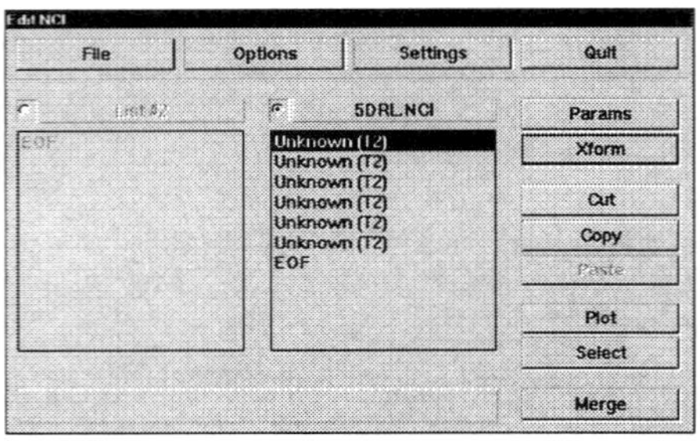

Step 6. Save the toolpath file.

Select **File → Save**
Select **Yes** to overwrite the existing file
Select **Quit** to exit the Edit NCI function
The six drilling toolpaths are shown in the model as in Figure 16.50.

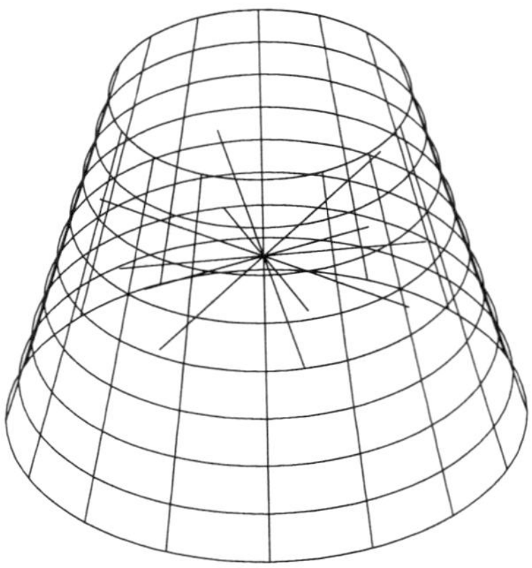

Figure 16.50

Step 7. Backplot the toolpath.

Select **MAIN MENU → NC utils → Backplot → Run**
The toolpaths are backplot on the screen.

Project 7. Drill 5-axis using point/line option

Generate two drilling toolpaths to produce two holes on a cone-shaped surface along two lines (Figure 16.51). The cone-shaped surface is created in project 6 of this chapter.

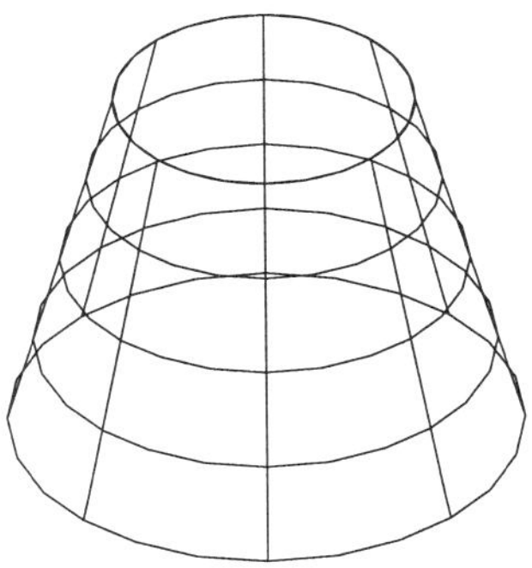

Figure 16.51a Surface

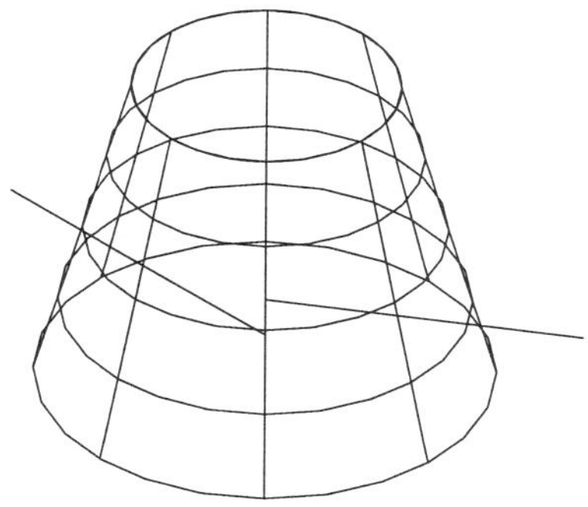

Figure 16.51b Toolpaths

Tips
1. Use the cone-shaped draft surface file 5drl.
2. Create two lines to use as the drilling direction for two holes.
3. Use Drill – pts/lines functions to generate toolpaths for two holes.
4. Backplot the toolpaths to verify results.

Step 1. Open the draft surface file 5drl.

(or create one by following the instructions in steps 1 and 2 in project 6.)
Select **MAIN MENU → File → Get**
File name: **5drl**
The draft surface appears as Figure 16.52.

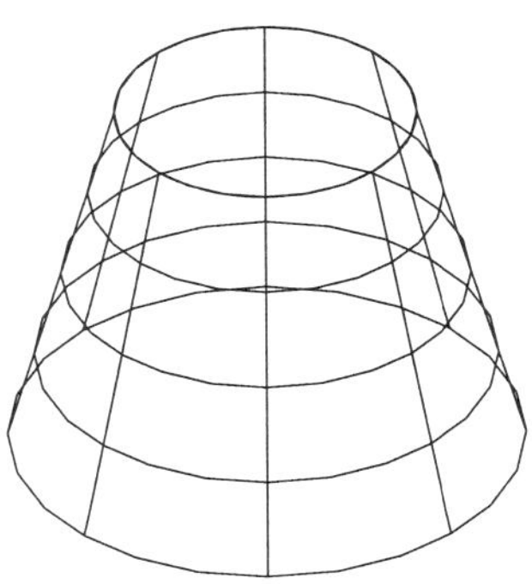

Figure 16.52

Step 2. Create two lines.

Select **MAIN MENU → Create → Line → Endpoints → Value**

Enter the following four set of coordinate values:

5,	0,	-1	
0,	0,	-3	for the first line
-4,	0,	-3.5	
0,	0,	-3.5	for the second line

The two lines are added as in Figure 16.53.

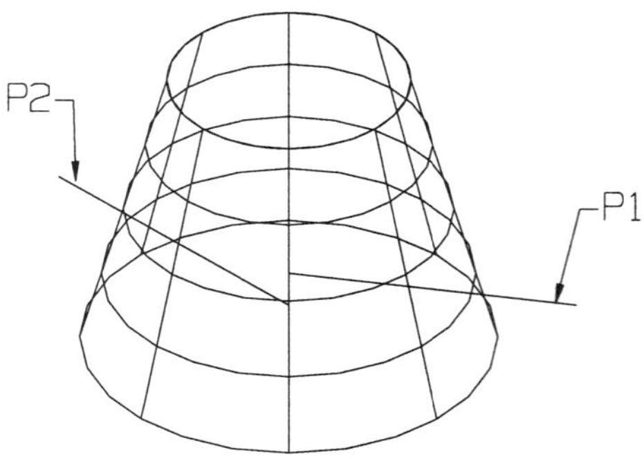

Figure 16.53

Step 3. Initiate Drill5ax – pts/lines function.

Use the pick points in Figure 16.53.
Select **MAIN MENU → Toolpaths → Multiaxis → Drill5ax**
File name for toolpaths: **5drll**
Select **Pts/Lines → Manual → Endpoint**
Pick **P1** and **P2** to select two endpoints
Press **Esc** to complete point selection
Select **Yes** to draw path between points
Select **Yes** to "Is the path OK?"

Step 4. Define the drilling parameters.

Set the five axis drilling parameters as below.

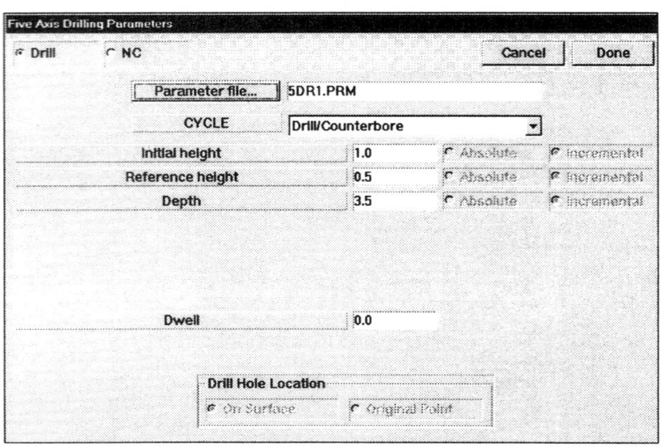

Select the **NC** button

Set the NC parameters as below.

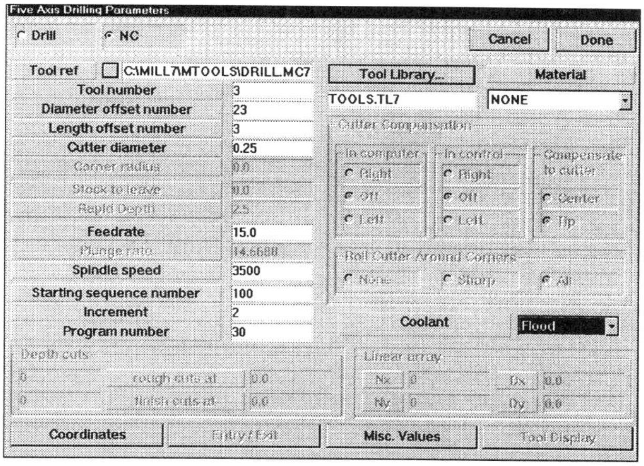

Select **Done** to generate the drilling toolpaths along two given lines
Select **No** to "Repeat with same points?"

Step 5. Backplot the toolpaths.

Select **MAIN MENU → NC utils → Backplot**
Select **Yes** to "Operations have been modified. Create the NCI text file?"
Select **Run**
Two drilling toolpaths will be animated on the screen.

16.11 Swarf 5-Axis Function

The Swarf 5-axis function generates 5-axis toolpaths for cutting a selected surface with the side of the tool (Figure 16.54). The tool axis (shank) is oriented parallel to the surface.

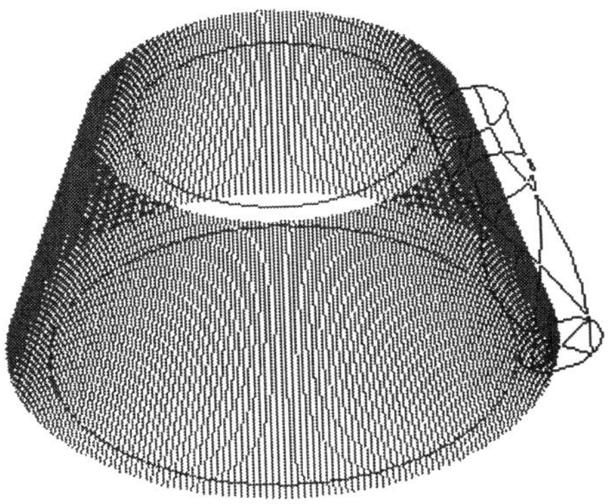

Figure 16.54

Swarf 5-axis floor

This parameter specifies the toolpath floor for generating swarf 5-axis toolpaths. The toolpath floor defines the depth of cut along the selected surface(s). It has the following two options:

Surface:	selects a surface for the toolpath floor (Figure 16.55).
Plane:	defines a plane for the toolpath floor (Figure 16.56).

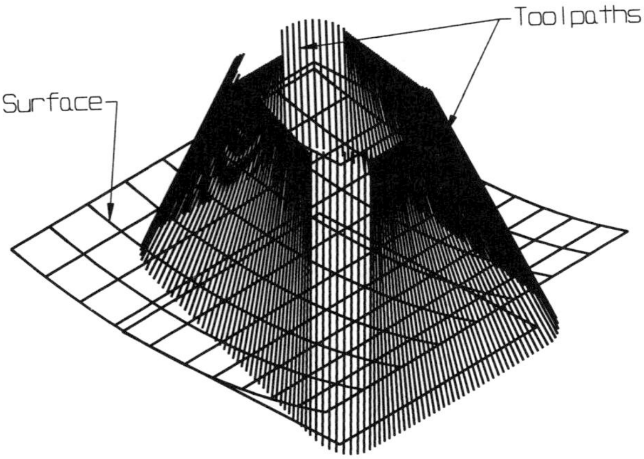

Figure 16.55

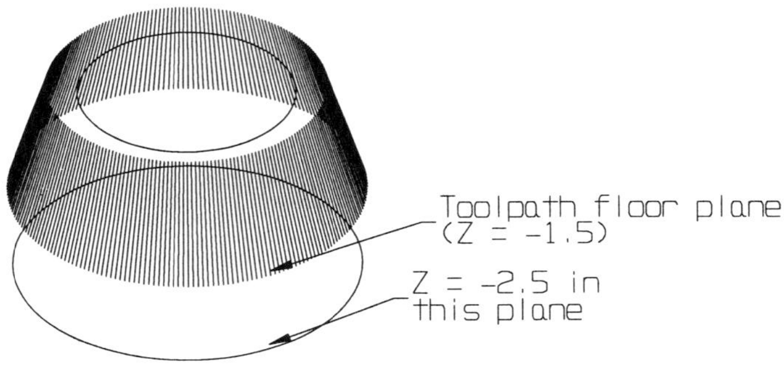

Figure 16.56

There are eight ways to define a plane. They are described in Table 13.2. Refer to page 13-10 in chapter 13 for details.

Chain wire

This parameter allows the wireframe model to be used as the driving elements for generating swarf 5-axis toolpaths (Figure 16.57). Mastercam uses two chained contours to define the wall for cutting; lower contour and upper contour. The lower chain must be defined first for the toolpath to generate properly.

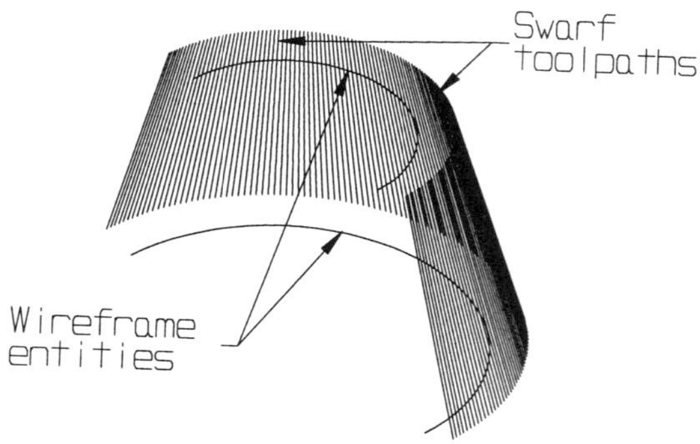

Figure 16.57

Slct walls

This parameter selects walls as the boundaries for generating swarf 5-axis toolpaths. This option can select walls on wireframe contour, surface, or combination of both. The swarf 5-axis menu appears as below.

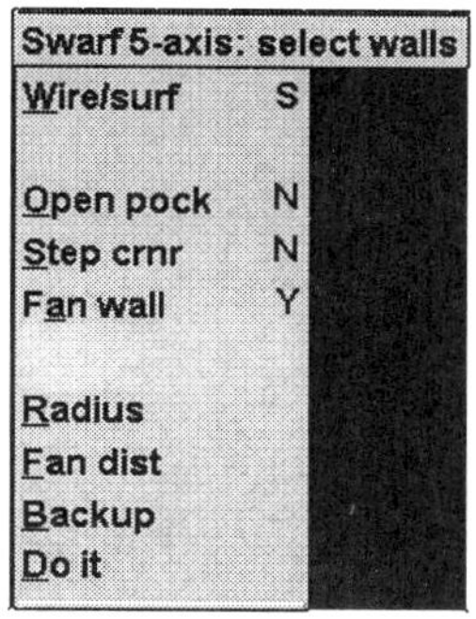

Wire/surf This parameter can be toggled to select a wireframe or a surface for the next wall of the toolpath. Toggle to "S" for surface mode and "W" for wireframe mode.

Open pock This parameter decides whether an open pocket or a closed pocket is used for generating toolpaths. A closed pocket has its starting element and ending element connected (Figure 16.58). With an open pocket, the starting element and ending element are not connected (Figure 16.59).

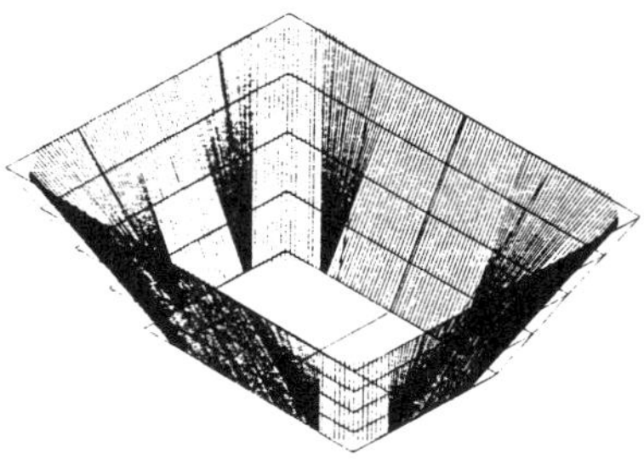

Figure 16.58 Closed pocket

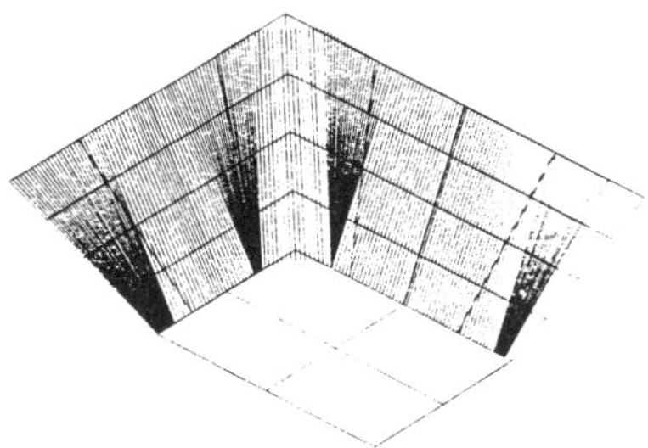

Figure 16.59 Open pocket

Step crnr This parameter determines whether the next corner of the toolpaths to move the tool in an XY direction to a parallel wall. Figure 16.60 shows the effect of this parameter on the toolpaths.

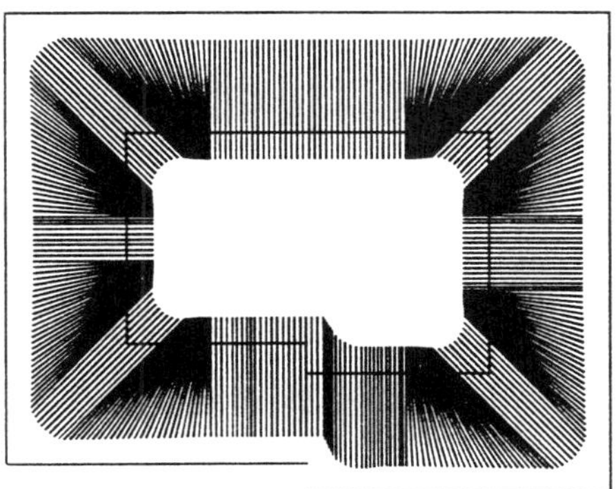

Figure 16.60

Fan wall and Fan dist The "Fan wall" parameter decides whether to place fans at the end of each wall of the toolpath. The "Fan dist" parameter specifies the fan distance for the current wall of the toolpaths. The fan distance determines the minimum distance that the tool travels between the corner position and a position where the tool is perpendicular to the floor (Figure 16.61).

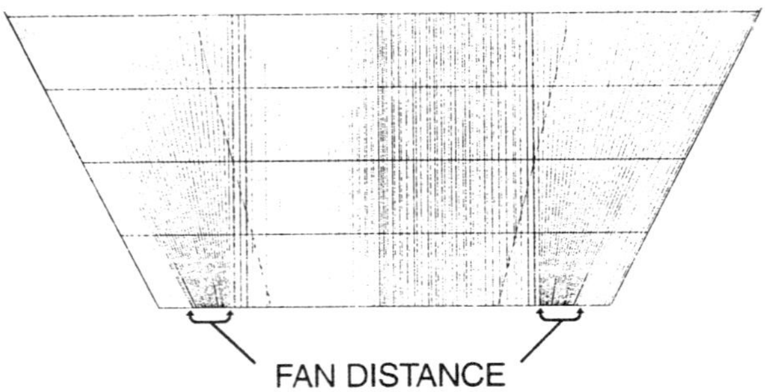

Figure 16.61

Radius This parameter specifies the radius of the next corner of the toolpath when viewed down the axis of the tool.

Swarf 5-axis parameters

Those parameters related to swarf 5-axis function is grouped under 5-axis Swarf Cutting menu as shown below.

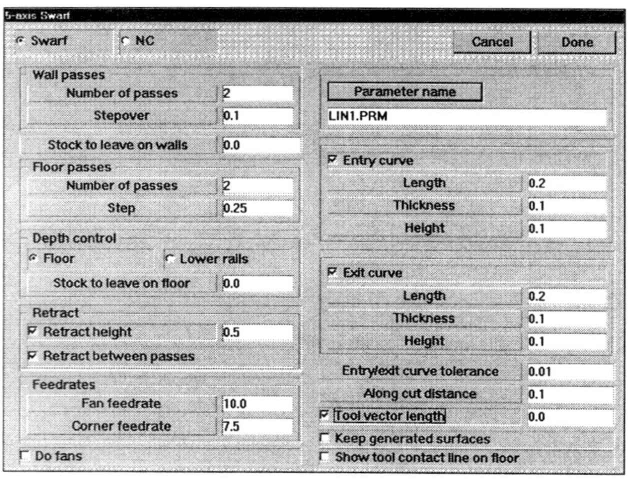

Wall passes and floor passes

The total number of toolpaths is the product of number of passes on wall and number of passes on floor. Mastercam will generate four passes of toolpaths if both numbers of passes are set to 2. When the number of passes becomes greater than one, the stepover parameter becomes active for entering proper value. Figure 16.62 shows an example of having both numbers of passes equal to 2.

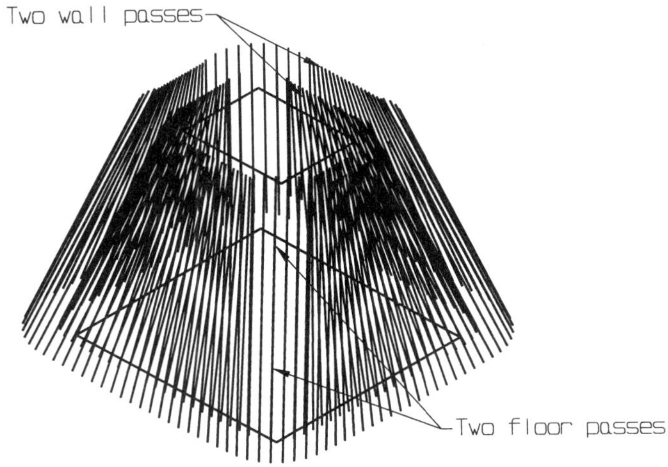

Figure 16.62

Depth control

The Depth control parameter specifies how the lowest depth of swarf toolpaths calculate. It has the following two options:

Floor:	places the lowest point of the tool on the selected floor plane.
Lower rails:	places the center of the tool in line with the lower rails when the tool rests against the walls.

Stock parameters

The following three stock parameters that allow to specify the amount of material to leave for further machining:

Stock to leave on walls:	specifies the amount of material left on the walls.
Stock to leave on floor:	specifies the amount of material left on the floor when the floor option is used.
Distance above lower rails:	specifies how far the center of the tool descends above or below the lower boundary.

Retract parameters

The following two parameters control the retraction of the tool:

Retract height:	specifies the distance above the floor or lower boundary for the initial and final tool location.
Retract between passes:	indicates whether to raise the tool to the retract height at the beginning and end of each pass. This parameter becomes active only when the retract height parameter is ON.

Feedrate parameters

The following two parameters are used to specify the feedrate for cutting fans and corners:

Fan feedrate:	specifies the feedrate for machining the fan section of the toolpaths.
Corner feedrate:	specifies the feedrate for machining the rounding corners of the toolpaths.

Do fans

This parameter enables or disables the fan capability for the entire toolpaths.

Entry and exit curves

Mastercam allows adding an entry curve and exit curve to the toolpaths. Both entry curve and exit curve have the following three parameters (Figure 16.63):

Length:	specifies the span of the entry curve along the wall in the direction the tool travels.
Thickness:	specifies the distance of the curve away from the wall.
Height:	specifies the distance of the curve away from the floor measured along the tool vector.

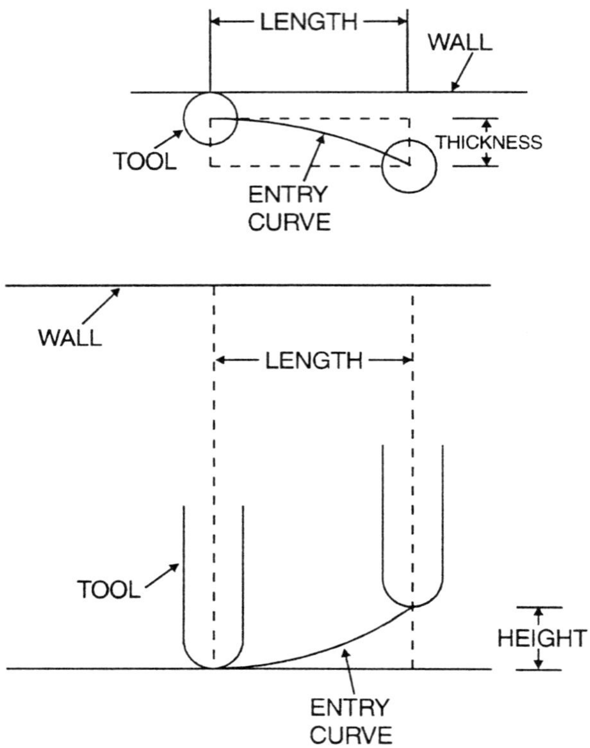

Figure 16.63

Entry/exit curve tolerance

This parameter controls the difference between a theoretical curve and its linear approximation.

Along cut distance

This parameter measures the distance between vectors in the toolpath and at the wide end of fans in the toolpath (Figure 16.64).

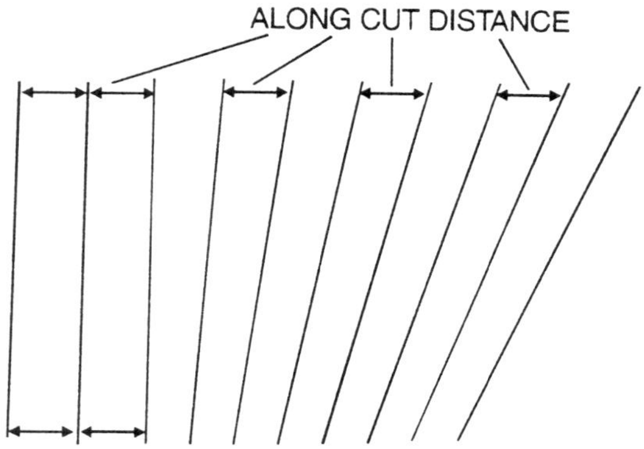

Figure 16.64

Tool vector length

This parameter sets all tool vectors in the toolpath to a selected length. Turn this parameter to Off, the system automatically controls the lengths of the vectors.

Keep generated surfaces

This parameter creates geometry from the ruled surfaces made during the toolpath creation.

Show tool contact line on floor

This parameter generates a line that represents where the tool touches the floor of the toolpath.

Two projects are presented in this section to show how to generate 5-axis swarf toolpaths. The first project uses a wireframe model as the wall for generating swarf toolpaths, and the second project uses a draft surface as the wall.

8 Project 8. Using 5-axis swarf function with wireframe model

This project uses 5-axis swarf function to generate toolpaths for cutting a slope surface defined by using two wireframe contours. Figure 16.65 shows two wireframe contours and its swarf toolpaths.

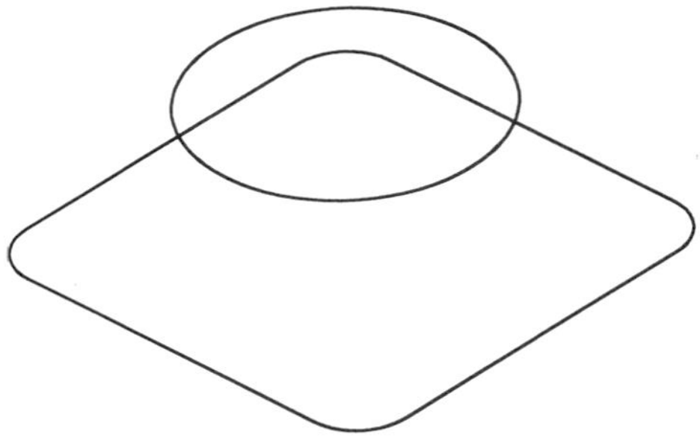

Figure 16.65a Wireframe

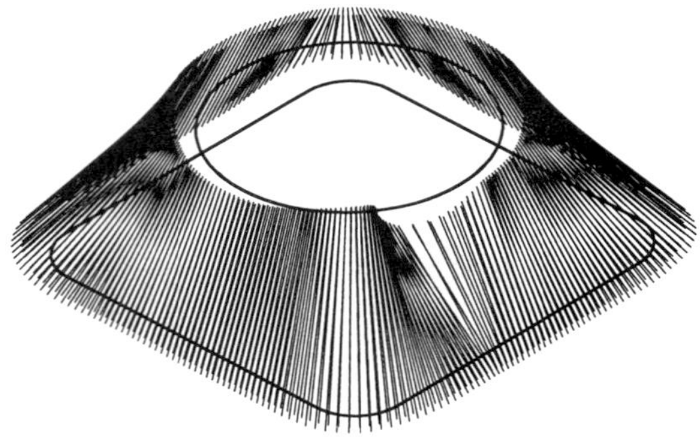

Figure 16.65b Toolpaths

Tips
1. Use the wireframe model 3contour.
2. Delete the bottom circle.
3. Break the right vertical line of the rectangle into two pieces.
4. Use Swarf5ax function to generate swarf toolpaths.
5. Backplot the toolpaths.

Step 1. Open the wireframe model 3contour.

Select **MAIN MENU → File → Get**
File name: **3contour**
The wireframe model consisting of three contours appears as in Figure 16.66.

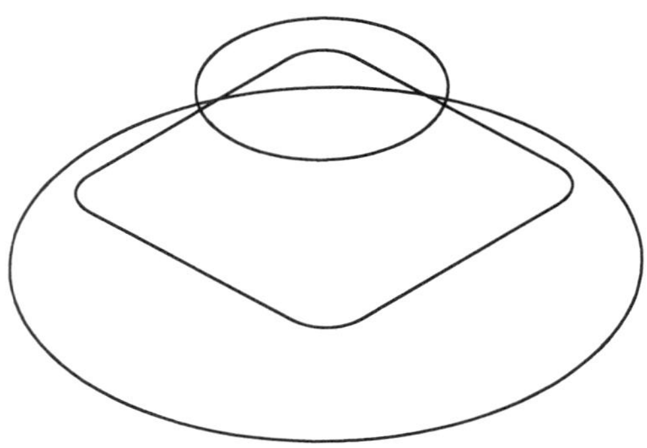

Figure 16.66

Step 2. Delete the bottom circle.

Select **MAIN MENU → Delete**
Pick the bottom circle to delete it

The new drawing becomes Figure 16.67.

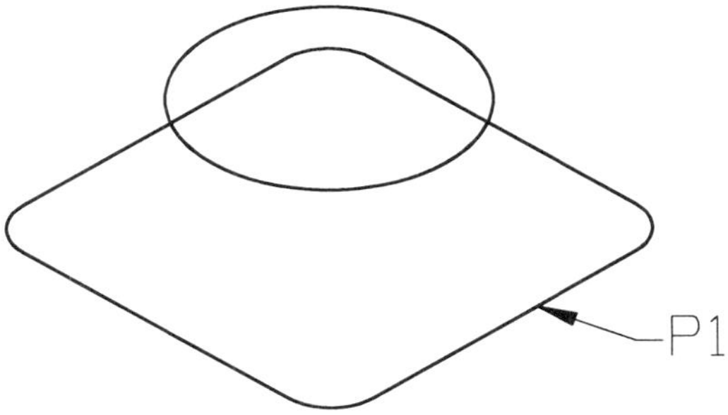

Figure 16.67

Step 3. Break the right vertical line of rectangle into two entities.

Use the pick point in Figure 16.67.
Select **MAIN MENU → Modify → Break → 2 pieces**
Pick **P1** to select the entity to break
Select **Midpoint**, then pick **P1** to break the line into 2 entities
The model is redrawn in Figure 16.68.

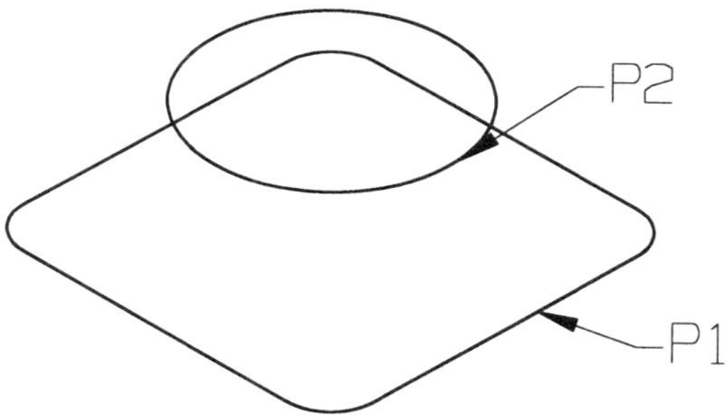

Figure 16.68

Step 4. Initiate the Swarf5ax function.

Use the pick points in Figure 16.68.
Select **MAIN MENU → Toolpaths → Multiaxis → Swarf5ax**
File name for toolpath: **swarf**
Select **Plane → z = const**
Enter z-coordiante of plane: **-1**
Select **Chain wire**
Pick **P1** as the lower contour
Pick **P2** as the upper contour
Select **Done**

Set the Swarf parameters as below.

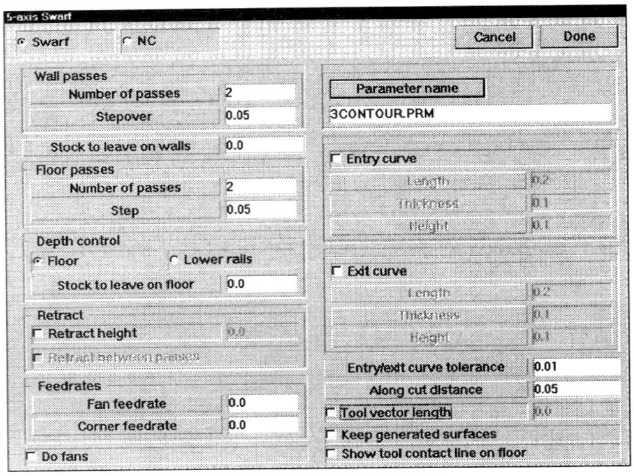

Step 5. Define the NC parameters.

Click the "**NC**" button

Set the NC parameters as below.

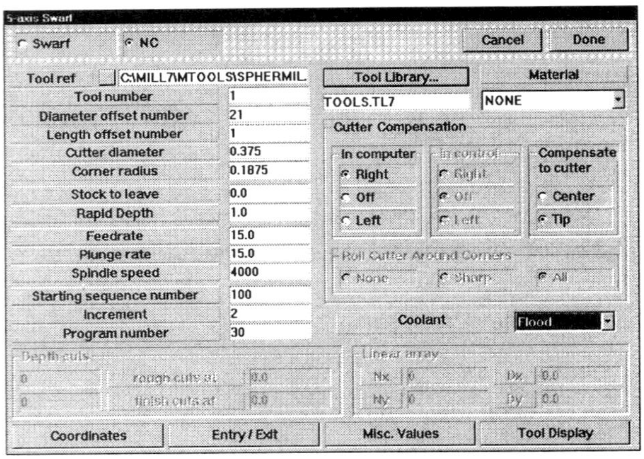

Select **Done** to generate the toolpaths as Figure 16.69.

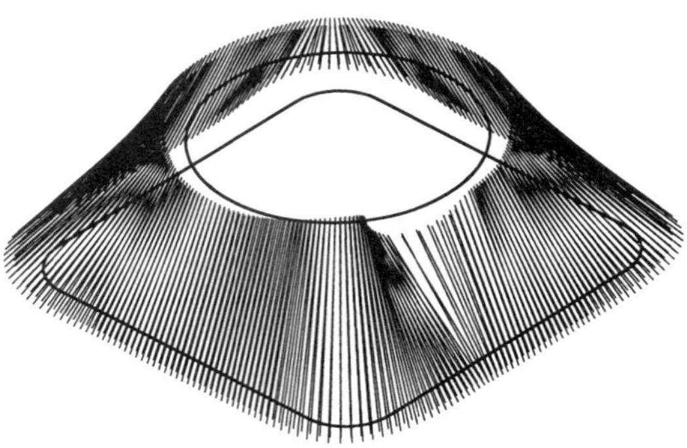

Figure 16.69

Step 6. Backplot the toolpaths.

Select **MAIN MENU → NC utils → Backplot**
Select **Yes** to "Operations have been modified. Create the NCI text file?"
Select **Run** to backplot the toolpaths on the screen

Note that there are four toolpath passes in this operation.

Project 9. Using 5-axis swarf function with a surface model

This project creates swarf toolpaths to cut a draft surface (Figure 16.70). The draft surface is created in chapter 12 and has a file name drafts2.

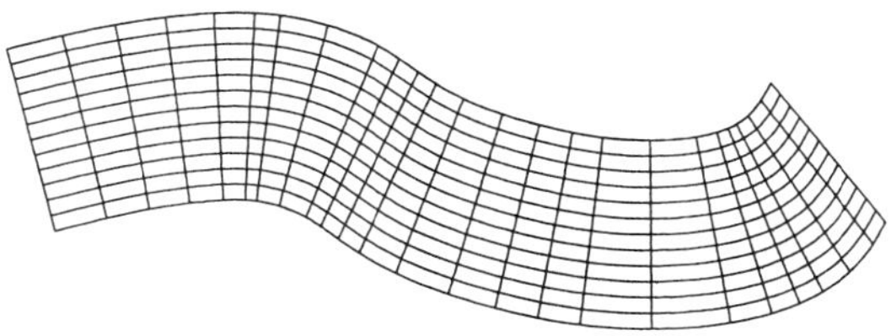

Figure 16.70a Surface

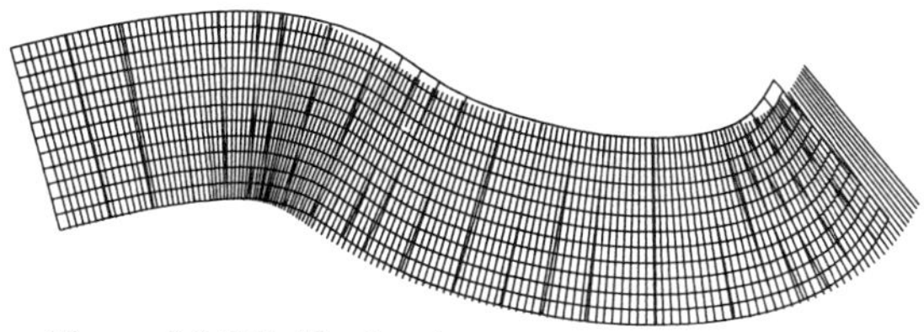

Figure 16.70b Toolpaths

Tips	1. Open the draft surface model drafts2. 2. Use the Swarf5ax function to generate toolpaths. 3. Use a ½" end mill. 4. Backplot the toolpaths to verify on the screen.

Step 1. Open the draft surface model drafts2.

Select **MAIN MENU → File → Get**
File name: **drafts2**
The draft surface appears as in Figure 16.71.

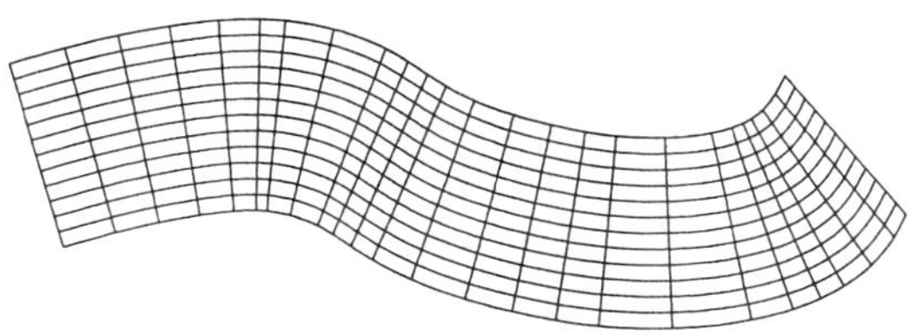

Figure 16.71

Step 2. Initiate the Swarf5ax function.

Select **MAIN MENU → Toolpaths → Multiaxis → Swarf5ax**
File name for toolpath: **swarfs**
Select **Plane → z = const**
Enter z-coordinate of plane = **-1**
Select **Slct walls**, then pick the surface

Set the parameters as below:

Wire/surf = **S**
Open pock = **N**
Step cmr = **N**
Fan wall = **Y**
Radius = **0.55**
Fan distance = **0.2**

Select **Do it**

Set the 5-axis Swarf parameters as below.

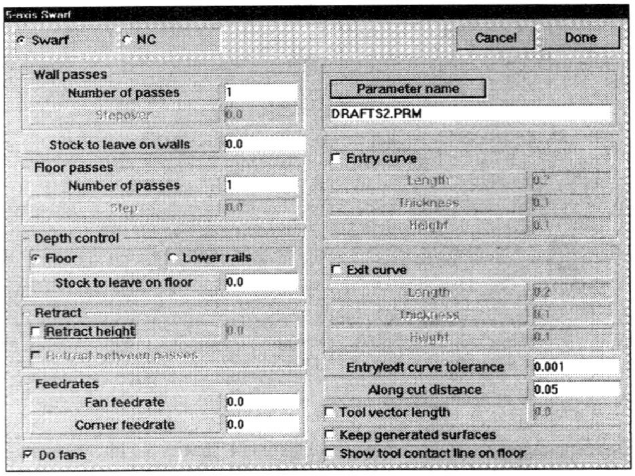

Step 3. Define the NC parameters.

Select the **NC** button

Set the NC parameters as below.

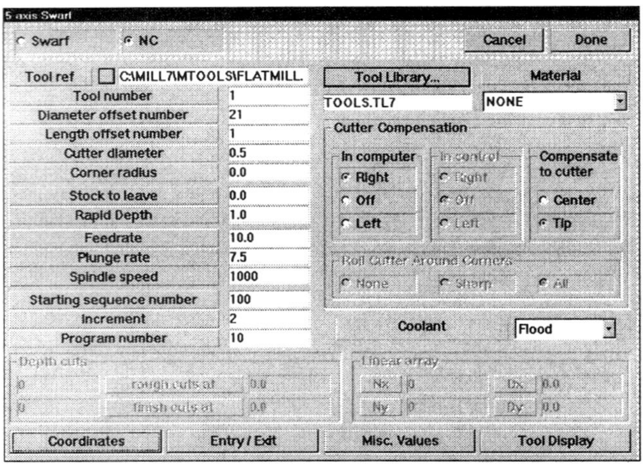

Select Done to generate toolpaths as shown in Figure 16.72.

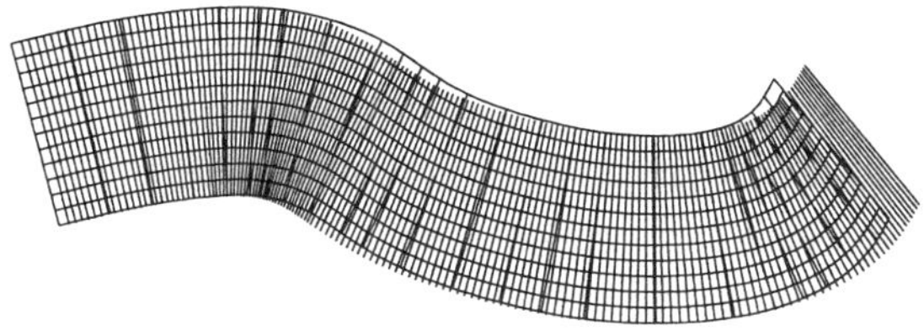

Figure 16.72

Step 4. Backplot the toolpath.

Select **MAIN MENU → NC utils → Backplot**
Select **Yes** to "Operations have been modified. Create the NCI text file?"
Select **Run** to verify the toolpaths on the screen

16.12 Flowline 5-Axis Function

The Flowline 5-axis function generates 5-axis toolpaths for cutting a surface model (Figure 16.73). This function can produce very precise and smooth finish with accurate control of the scallop height left on the part. The flowline parameter dialog box appears as below.

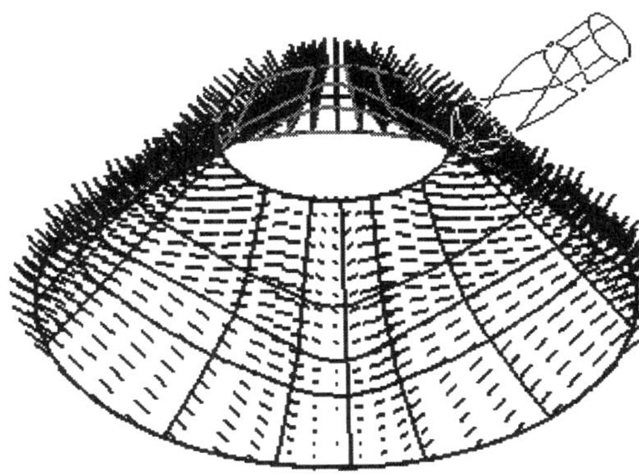

Figure 16.73

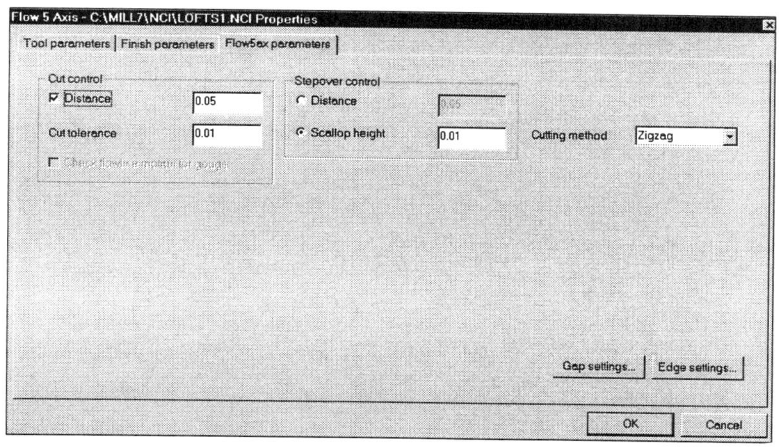

10 Project 10. Generating 5-axis flowline toolpaths

This project uses the 5-axis flowline function to generate 5-axis toolpaths to cut three surfaces in the pocket of the car wheel model. These three surfaces include two fillet surfaces and one swept surface. Figure 16.74 shows the surface model and flowline toolpaths.

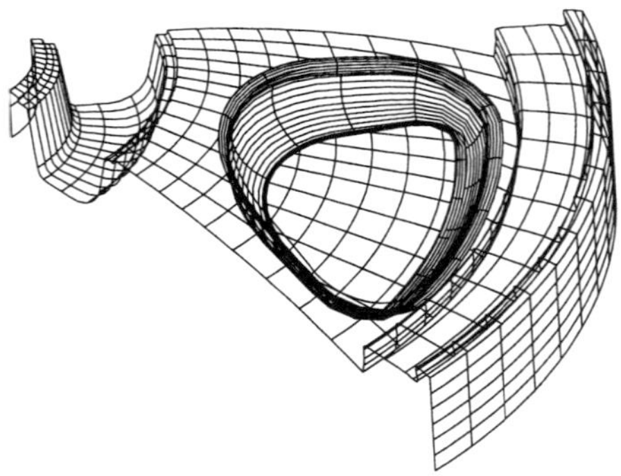

Figure 16.74a Surface model

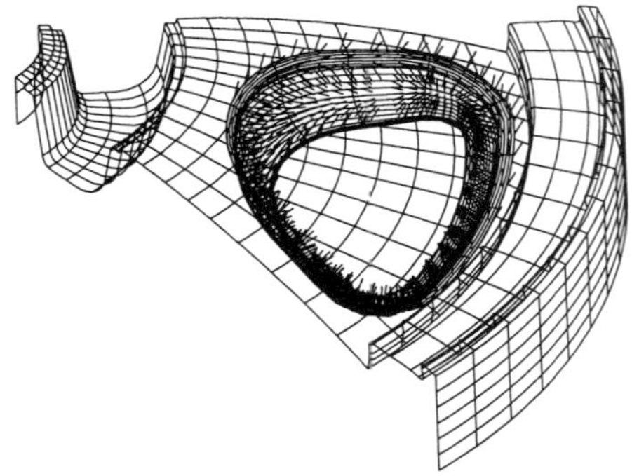

Figure 16.74b Toolpaths

Tips	1. Open the surface model file wheels.
	2. Use the flow5ax function to generate toolpaths.
	3. Select three surfaces in the concave pocket.
	4. Backplot the toolpaths to verify on the screen.

Step 1. Open the surface model file wheels.

Select **MAIN MENU → File → Get**
File name: **wheels**
The car wheel surface model appears as Figure 16.75.

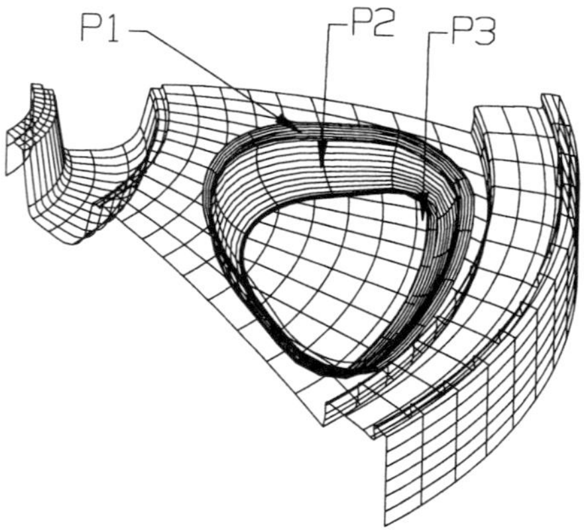

Figure 16.75

Step 2. Initiate the flow5ax function.

Use the pick points in Figure 16.75.
Select **Cplane → Top**
Select **MAIN MENU → Toolpaths → Multiaxis → Flow5ax**
File name for toolpath: **flow5ax**
Pick **P1**, **P2**, and **P3** to select three surfaces
Select **Done**
Click the right mouse button, then select **Get tool from library**
Select **tool number 254** (3/8 sphere end mill)
Select **OK**

Set the tool parameters as below.

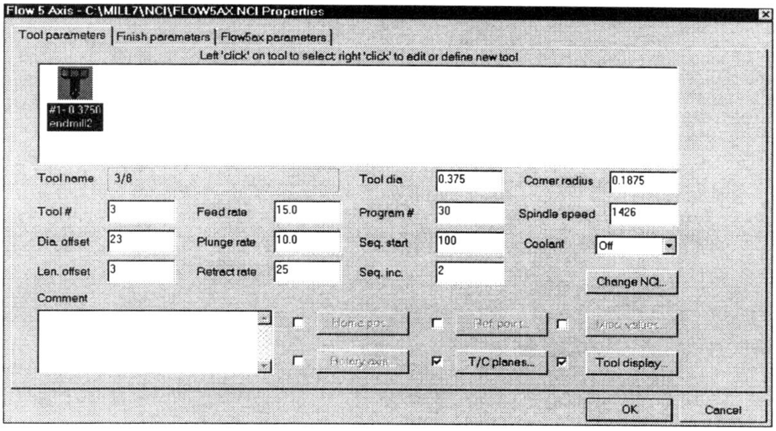

Step 3. Define the finish parameters.

Click "Finish parameters" button
Set the finish parameters as below.

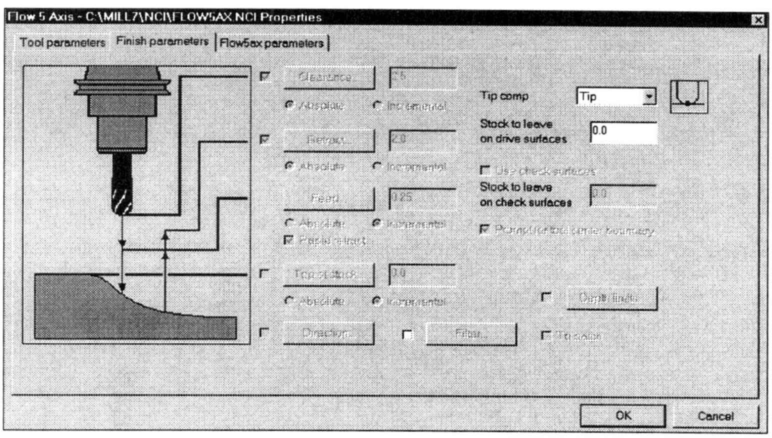

Step 4. Define the flow5ax parameters.

Click "Flow5ax parameters" button
Set the flow5ax parameters as below.

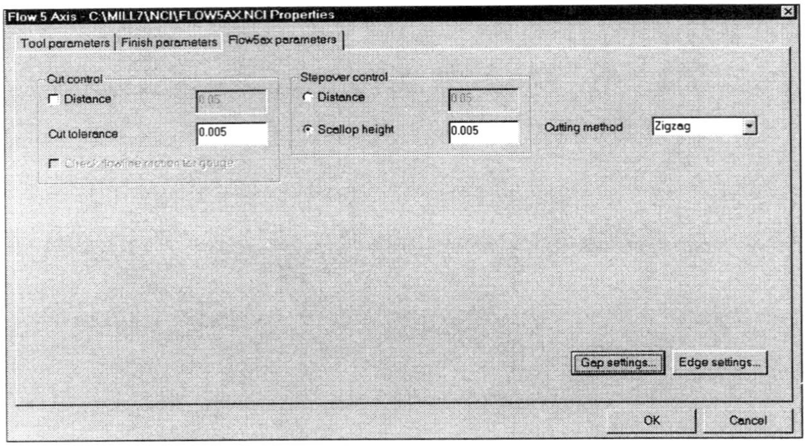

Select **OK**
Select **Do it** to generate toolpaths as shown in Figure 16.76.

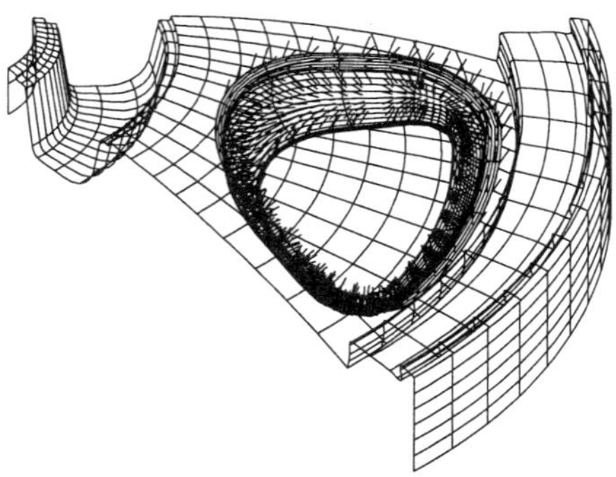

Figure 16.76

Step 5. Backplot the toolpaths.

Select **MAIN MENU → NC utils → Backplot**
Select **Yes** to "Operations have been modified. Create the NCI text file?"
Select **Run** to verify the toolpaths on the screen

Exercises

1. List the four 5-axis machining functions available in Mastercam.
2. How many axes are defined by the EIA-267-B standard?
3. Use a drawing to explain how to define the three primary rotary axes and their rotation directions.
4. Use a drawing to describe the thumb rule for determining the direction of the rotation.
5. Can the rotary 4-axis function cut multiple surfaces in one operation?
6. Use a drawing to define the lead angle in rotary 4-axis function.
7. When to use curve 5-axis function?
8. List the three options of curve 5-axis function and describe what they are.
9. Describe the difference of two tool types, 3-axis and 5-axis, in curve 5-axis function.
10. Use drawings to describe how the side angle affecting the tool axis orientation.
11. Use drawings to describe how the lead angle affecting the tool axis orientation.
12. List the two stepping methods used in outer edge function and describe what they are.
13. Use a drawing to describe the working principle of the chain curves function.
14. What are the two methods of projecting chained entities onto the surface(s)?
15. List the two methods for specifying the location and direction of the drilling in drill 5-axis function.
16. What are the main features of swarf 5-axis function?
17. List the two methods of specifying the toolpath floor in using swarf 5-axis function.
18. What is the flowline 5-axis function?

Chapter 17

3D toolpath Editing

Objectives:

1. Know two toolpath editing functions to modify toolpaths for machining 3D surfaces:
   - project and trim.
2. Understand the features of these toolpath editing functions and know when to apply them.
3. Apply these editing functions to 3D surfacing toolpath projects.

Overview

Toolpaths for cutting some surface models can be significantly simplified by using toolpath editing functions. Those toolpath editing functions given in chapter 8 are applicable to editing 3D surfacing toolpaths. **Two** additional editing functions that are particularly designed for 3D surfacing toolpaths are presented in this chapter. They are project and trim.

17.1 Project Function

Project function allows toolpaths to be projected onto a plane, cylinder, cone, sphere, cross section or 3D surface. The projected toolpaths only change the depth (Z-coordinate) of the original toolpaths; both X and Y coordinates remain the same (Figure 17.1).

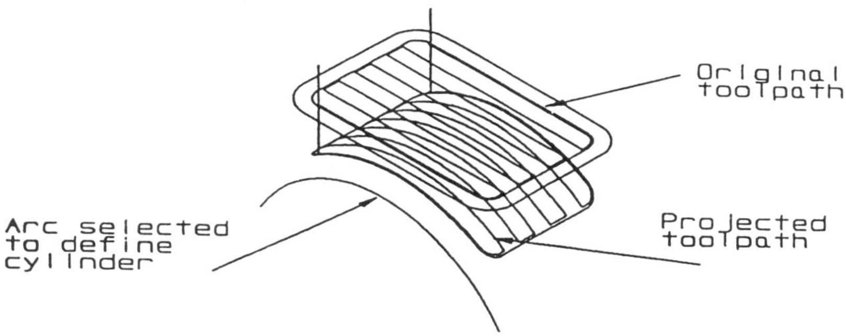

Figure 17.1

The following toolpath types can **not** be projected:

1. Drilling, boring, and taping.
2. Five axis moves.
3. Arcs in the ZX-plane and YZ-plane.

Note that arcs in the ZX-plane or YZ-plane are normally generated from surface of revolution, 2D contouring and 2D swept surface.

Table 17.1 Six Types of Toolpath Projection

Project type	Description	Illustration
Plane	Project a toolpath file onto any 3D plane defined by the construction plane.	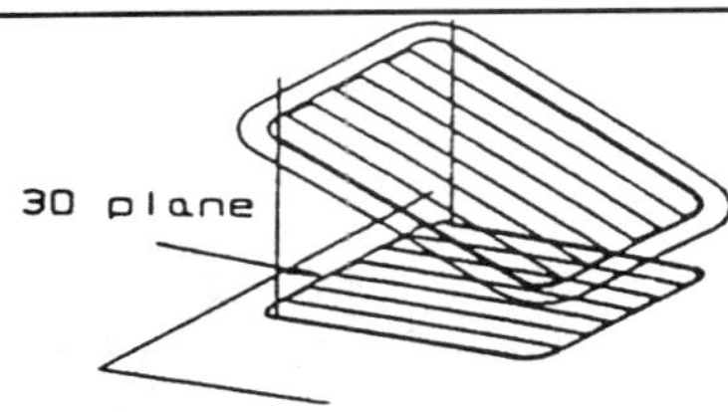
Cylinder	Project a toolpath file onto any cylinder that is defined by an arc. The axis of cylinder must be parallel to XY-plane. Concave or convex cylinders can be selected.	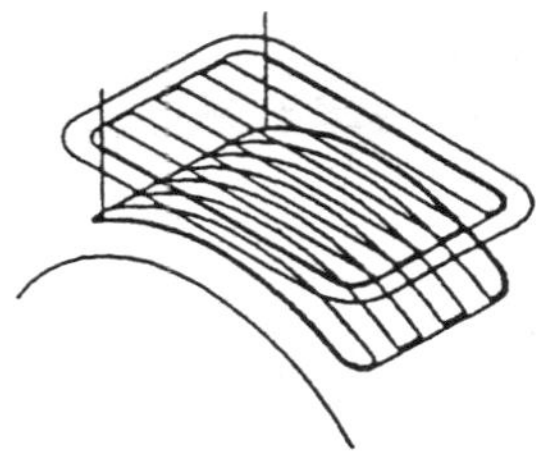
Sphere	Project a toolpath file onto any sphere. The sphere is defined by an arc. Concave or convex sphere is possible.	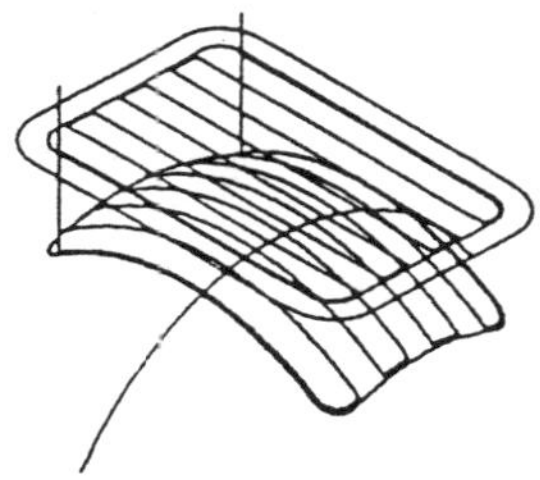
Cone	Project a toolpath file onto any cone. The cone is defined by two lines, one for the axis and the other for edge of the cone.	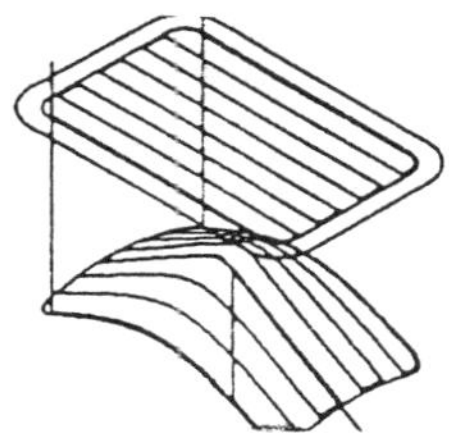
X-section	Project a toolpath file onto any cross section which is perpendicular to XY-plane or the current tool plane.	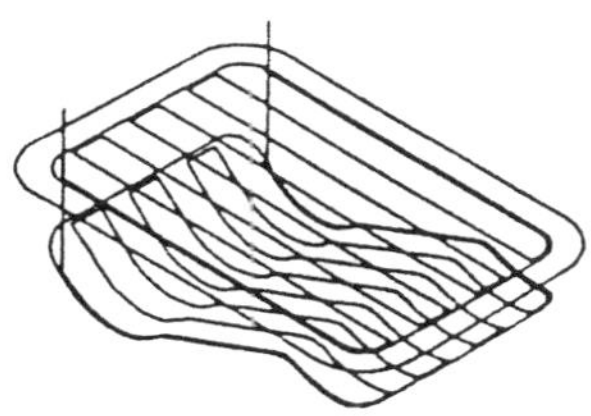

Steps for Implementing Toolpath Projects:

1. Create the profile or surface for defining the shape onto which the toolpaths are to be projected.
2. Generate the original toolpath file.
   (1) This file defines the X and Y coordinates of the toolpaths
   (2) Also the boundaries in the X and Y directions of the final toolpaths.
   (3) End program
   (4) Make sure the geometry to be projected fits on the surface.
3. Initiate the project function. Give a new name for projected path file.
4. Define the project parameters.
5. Accept the projected toolpaths.

Project 1. Projecting a set of lettering toolpaths onto a sphere

The toolpaths of a letter string which is arranged in an angular form are projected onto a sphere. Figure 17.2 shows the letter string, lettering toolpath, and projected toolpath.

Figure 17.2a

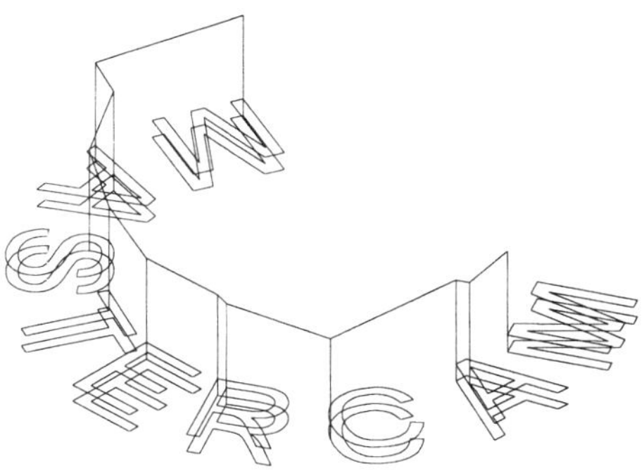

Figure 17.2b

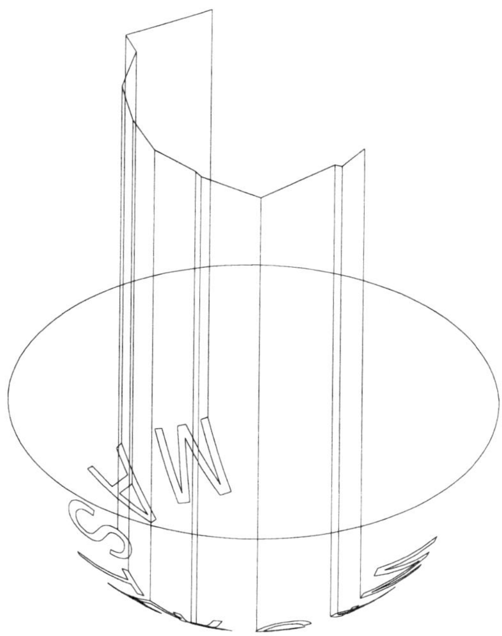

Figure 17.2c

⌛Tips

1. Create a letter string.
2. Use the contour module to generate the toolpaths for engraving letters.
3. Save the NCI file as "t1".
4. Create a new file.
5. Create a circle.
6. Project the toolpaths on to the sphere.
7. Save the projected toolpath file as "proj-1".

Step 1. Create a string of letters.

Select **Givew** → **Isometric**
Select **Z**, then enter **2.5**
Select **MAIN MENU** → **Create** → **Next menu** → **Letters** → **True Type (R)**
Set the font parameters as shown below.

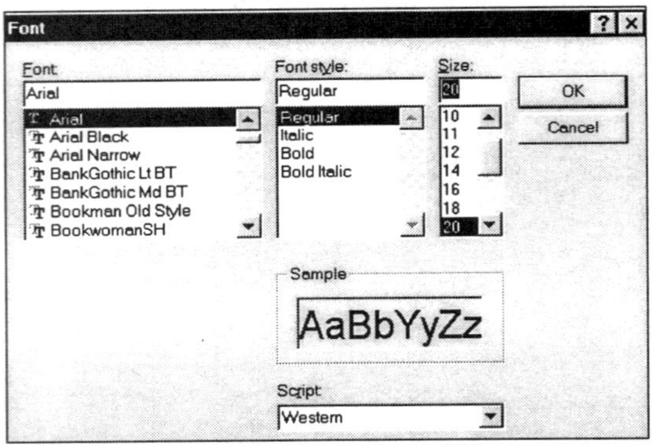

Select **OK**
Enter letters: **MASTERCAM**
Enter letter height: **0.5**
Select **Btm of arc** for the "direction to write letters?"
Enter the letter spacing: **0.15**
Enter arc radius: **1**
The letter string is added as in Figure 17.3.

Figure 17.3

Step 2. Generate the toolpaths to cut the contours of the letters.

Select **MAIN MENU → Toolpaths → Contour**
File name: **t1**
Select **window**
Pick two points to define the window for including all entities
Select **Endpoint**
Pick at the upper loft corner of first letter M
Select **Done**

Step 3. Select a tool and define the tool parameters.

Click the right mouse button, then select "Get tool from library"
Select **tool #232** (1/8" flat end mill)
Select **Done**
Set the tool parameters as below.

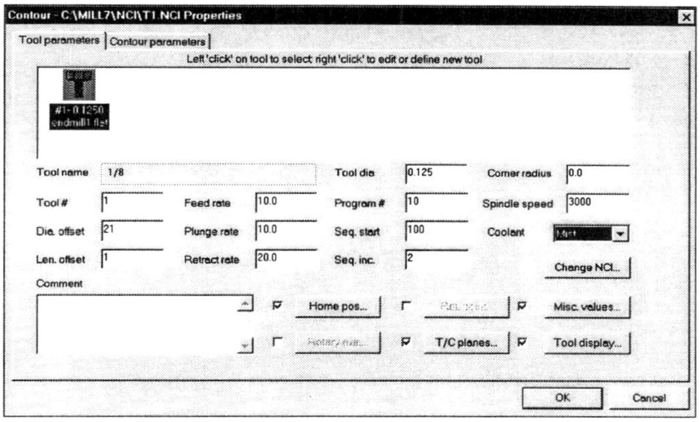

Step 4. Define the contour parameters.

Click the "Contour Parameters" button
Set the contour parameters as below.

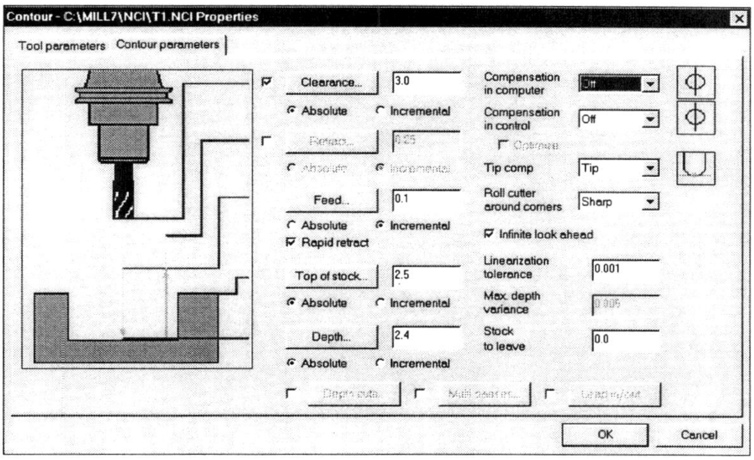

Select **Done**

The toolpaths are generated as in Figure 17.4.

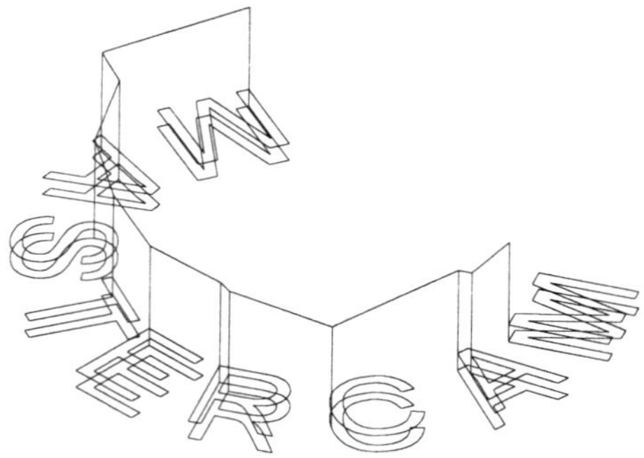

Figure 17.4

Step 5. Save the NCI file t1.

Select **MAIN MENU → Edit NCI → Backplot**
Select **Yes** to "Operations have been modified. Create the NCI text file?"
Select **MAIN MENU → File → Save**
File name: **t1.mc7**

Step 6. Create a new file.

Select **File → New**
Select **Yes** to "Are you sure you want to initialize geometry and operations?"

Step 7. Create a circle.

Select **MAIN MENU → Create → Arc → Cir pt+dia**
Enter the center point: **0,0**
Enter the diameter: **4**
Select **View → Isometric**
The circle is shown in Figure 17.5.

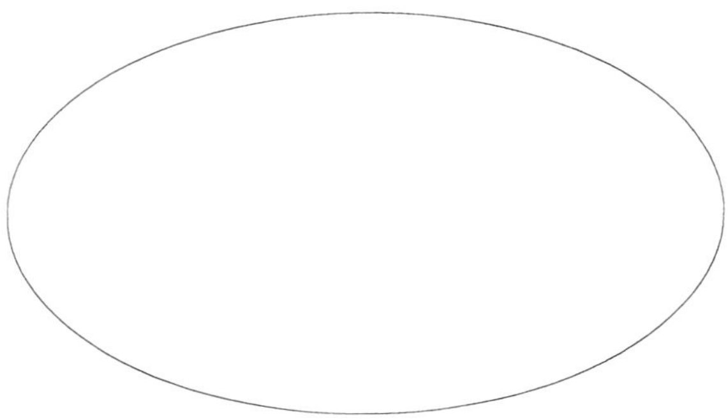

Figure 17.5

Step 8. Project the toolpaths.

Select **MAIN MENU → Toolpaths → Next menu → Project → Sphere**
Pick the circle to define the sphere
Select the "Lower" half

Set the project parameters as below.

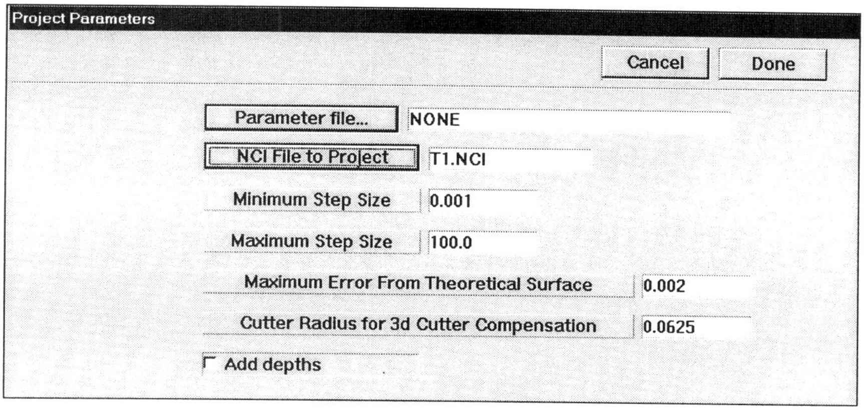

Select **Done**
Select **OK** to "#1-0.125 END MILL FLAT –1/8 has been created and added to your tool list"
The projected toolpaths are shown in Figure 17.6.

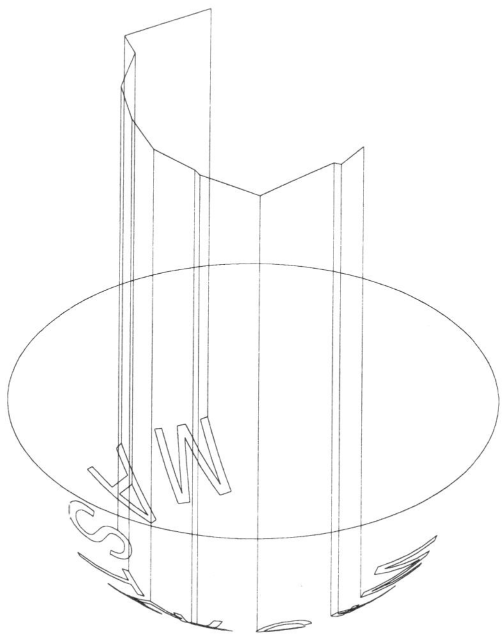

Figure 17.6

Step 9. Specify the NCI output file name.

File name to save: **proje-1**

17.2 Trim Function

The trim function is used to create a new set of toolpaths file by trimming an existing toolpath file to the specified boundaries (Figure 17.7). The original toolpath remains unchanged.

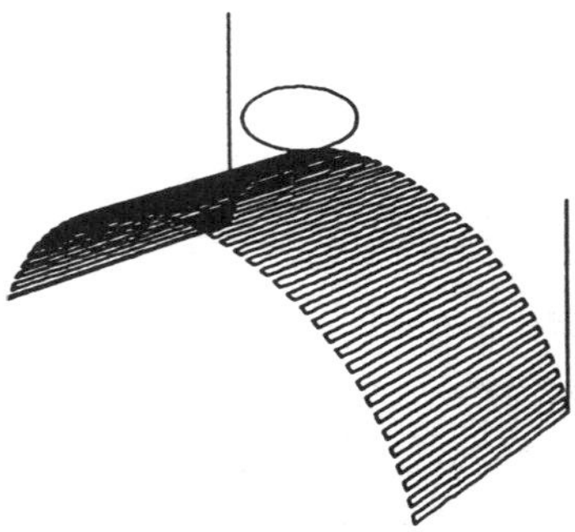

Figure 17.7a Before trimming

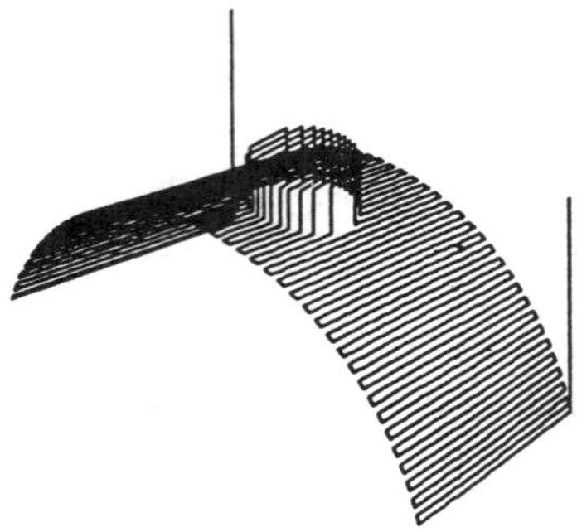

Figure 17.7b After trimming

Trimming is normally used in the following two applications:

1. To avoid islands or interferences (boss avoidance). This is especially useful in pocketing and surfacing.
2. To trim irregular boundaries at outside edges.

Trimming Boundaries

Mastercam allows us to use multiple trimming boundaries. The maximum number of boundaries is 50. The trimming boundaries must be **closed contours.** The trimming boundaries can be any shape and size and it is not necessary that they completely fall inside the toolpath range. **The trim function does not incorporate any cutter compensation. Therefore, the trimming contours should be created to reflect the center line of the cutter.**

Trimming Procedure

1. Generate the toolpath file to be trimmed and create the trimming boundaries. The toolpath (.NCI) file to be trimmed must exist before entering the Trim function.

2. Initiate the Trim function using the following commands:
   MAIN MENU → Toolpaths → Next menu → Trim

3. Enter a new name for the trimmed file name. The system issues a prompt "Enter file name:" to specify the file name for storing the trimmed toolpath.

4. Define trimming boundaries using the chain option.

5. Specify a point to indicate the side of the toolpath to keep.

6. Indicate whether the tool is up or down in the trimmed areas.

7. Enter the name of the toolpath file to trim.

8. Accept the trimmed toolpath segment.

9. Select End program to close the NCI file.

Project 2. Generating toolpaths for a surface and trimming the toolpaths to a rectangular boundary

The intent of this project is to trim the surfacing toolpaths to avoid an island of a rectangle as shown in Figure 17.13. The toolpaths are generated by using the flowline module.

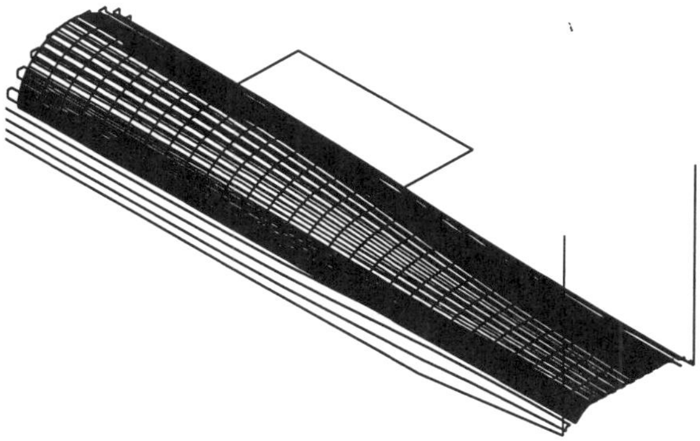

Figure 17.8a Before trimming

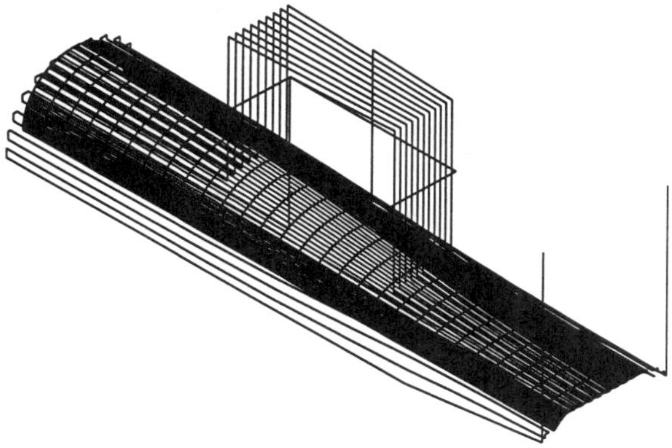

Figure 17.8b After trimming

Tips

1. The surface model used in this project is **lofts3.**
2. The island is a rectangle of 2"x 0.5". The trimming boundary for this rectangle should be 2.5"x1" because no cutter compensation is allowed in trimming. Therefore, we need to add the dimension of one-half of the cutter diameter to all sides of trimming boundary. The rectangle is centered at (-4,0) and has a height of Z1.5".
3. Use the flowline 3d toolpath module to generate the toolpaths for cutting the loft surface with a 0.5" ball end mill.
4. Initiate the trim function to trim the toolpaths to the rectangular boundary.

Step 1. Load the surface model file lofts3.

Select **MAIN MENU→ File→ Get**
Enter file pattern: **lofts3**
Select **Yes** to delete the current part

The surface model should appear on screen as in Figure 17.9.

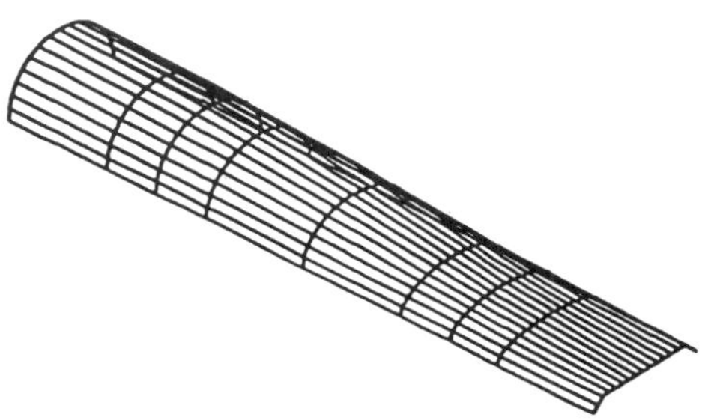

Figure 17.9

Step 2. Create a rectangle as the trimming boundary.

Select **Cplane → Top**
Select **Z** then enter **Z1.5**
Select **MAIN MENU → Create→ Rectangle→ 2 points**
Enter the lower left corner: **-5.25,-0.5**
Enter the upper right corner: **-2.75,0.5**

The rectangle is added to the drawing as shown in Figure 17.10.

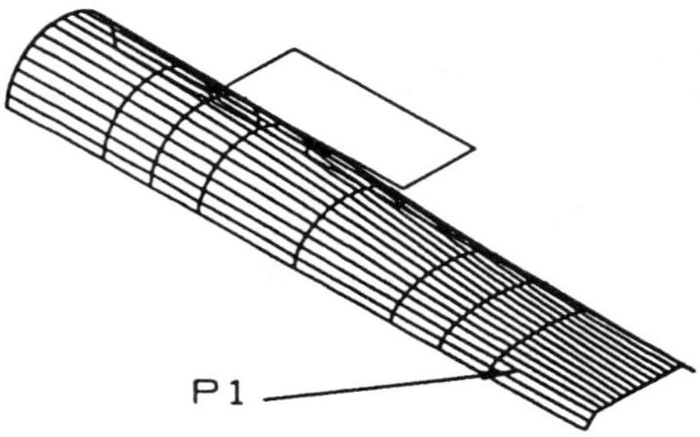

Figure 17.10

Step 3. Initiate the flowline toolpath module.

Use the pick point in Figure 17.10.
Select **MAIN MENU → Toolpaths → Surface → Finish → Flowline**
Enter file name: **lofts3**
Pick **P1** to select the surface
Select **Done**

Step 4. Select a tool and define tool parameters.

Click the right mouse button, then select “Get tool from library”
Select **tool #256** (1/2” sphere end mill)
Select **OK**
Set the tool parameters as below.

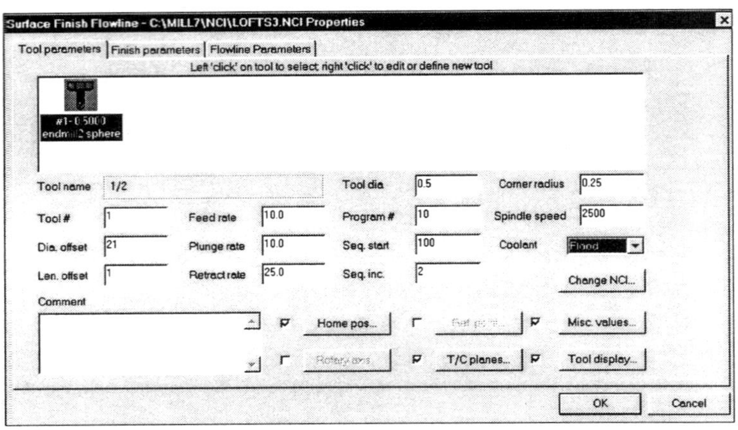

Step 5. Define the finish parameters.

Click the "Finish parameters" button
Set the finish parameters as below.

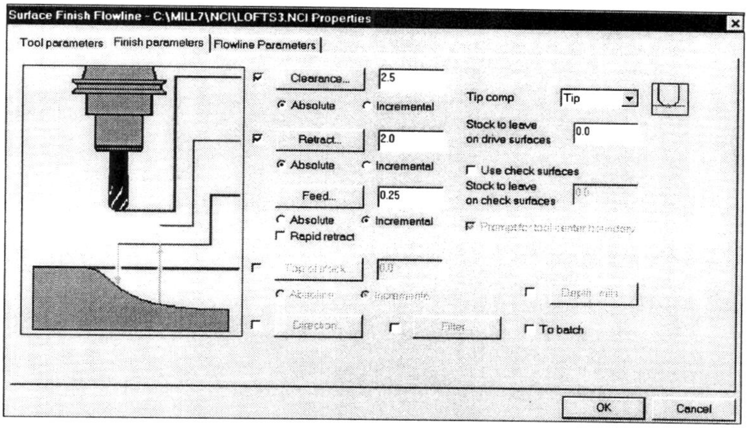

Step 6. Define the flowline parameters.

Click the "Flowline Parameters" button
Set the flowline parameters as below.

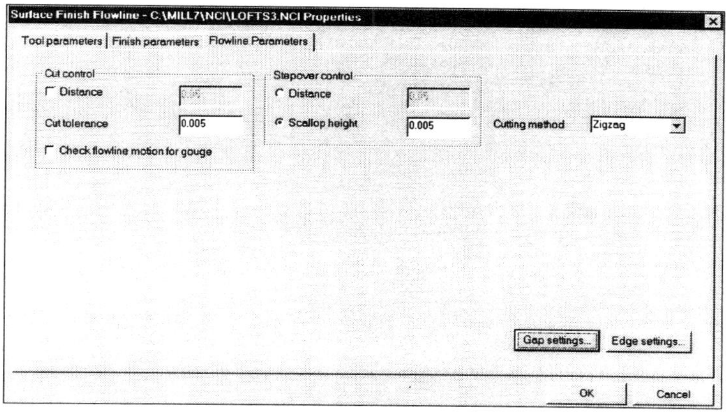

Select **OK**
Select **Cut dir**
Select **Do it**
The toolpath is generated as in Figure 17.11.

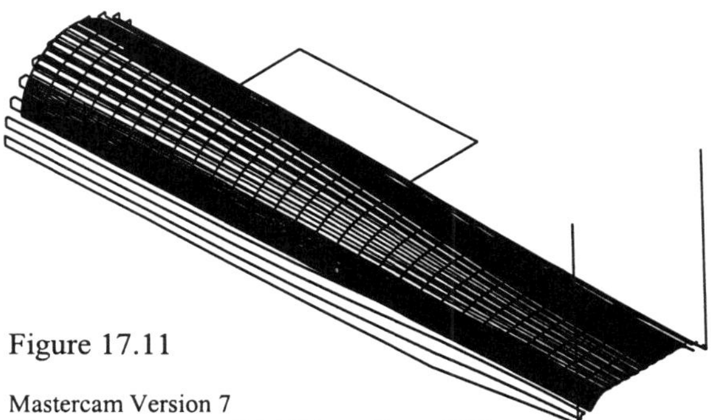

Figure 17.11

Step 7. Save the project file and toolpath file.

Select **File → Save**

File name: **lofts3.mc7**

Select **NC utils → Backplot**

Select **Yes** to "Operations have been modified. Create the NCI text file?"

Step 8. Initiate the trim function.

Select **MAIN MENU → Toolpaths → Next menu → Trim**

Enter file name: **trimt**

Define trimming boundary **1**: Select Chain, then pick any line on the rectangle

Select **Done**

Enter a point on the side to keep: pick the lower-left corner of the toolpath

Keep the tool: **select Up**

Enter file name: **lofts3**

The trimmed toolpaths should resemble Figure 17.12.

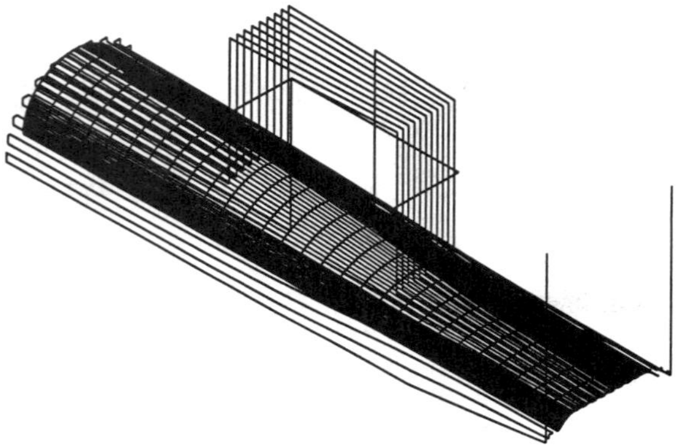

Figure 17.12

Exercises

1. What are the five toolpath editing functions commonly used in editing 3D surface toolpaths?

2. How does the project function affect the X, Y, and Z coordinate values of the toolpath ?

3. List three types of toolpaths that can not be projected.

4. Explain the main features of the trim function.

5. Identify two typical applications of the trim function.

6. What is the requirement for a trimming boundary?

Chapter 18

3D Toolpath Planning

Objectives:
1. Understand the toolpath generation procedure for 3D surfaces.
2. Identify features and surfaces of the parts.
3. Determine edge and skin profiles of a wireframe model for a surface model.
4. Select the surface modeling module and toolpath module for each surface.
5. Select proper tooling and machining parameters.

Overview

The procedure of process planning for 2D projects is presented in chapter 9. Most of the material covered in chapter 9 is applicable to 3D surfacing projects. However, there are unique features in 3D surfacing toolpath planning that warrant the discussion of this topic in a separate chapter. This chapter focuses on surface identification, wireframe model construction, surfacing module selection, toolpath generation, toolpath editing, tools and machining data selection, and NC files management. The flow chart for planning 3D surfacing toolpaths is illustrated in Figure 18.1 on the following page.

18.1 Identifying Features and Surfaces

A part feature is the distinctive shape and size to be produced in a part. Part features can be generalized as 2D and 3D features. Flat surfaces, external and internal profiles, pockets, holes, etc., are typical 2D features. Surfaces are 3D features. It is very common to have a combination of both 2D features and 3D features in a part. In this case, we need to treat 2D features and 3D features separately.

The 3D features are identified according to their types; geometric surfaces or free-form surfaces, and single surface or composite surfaces. The surface type dictates the complexity of the required wireframe model. Some surface models require a single patch edge profile, while some need multiple patches or multiple profile sections. Geometric surfaces provide an exact surface skin, while the free-form surfaces furnish approximated surface texture. In most cases, a surface can be modeled by more than one surfacing technique. The answers to the following questions should help in selecting the proper surfacing techniques which in turn determine the required wireframe model:

> Is the surface aesthetic or toleranced?
> Is it a single surface model or a composite surface model?
> How accurate is the surface skin required to be?

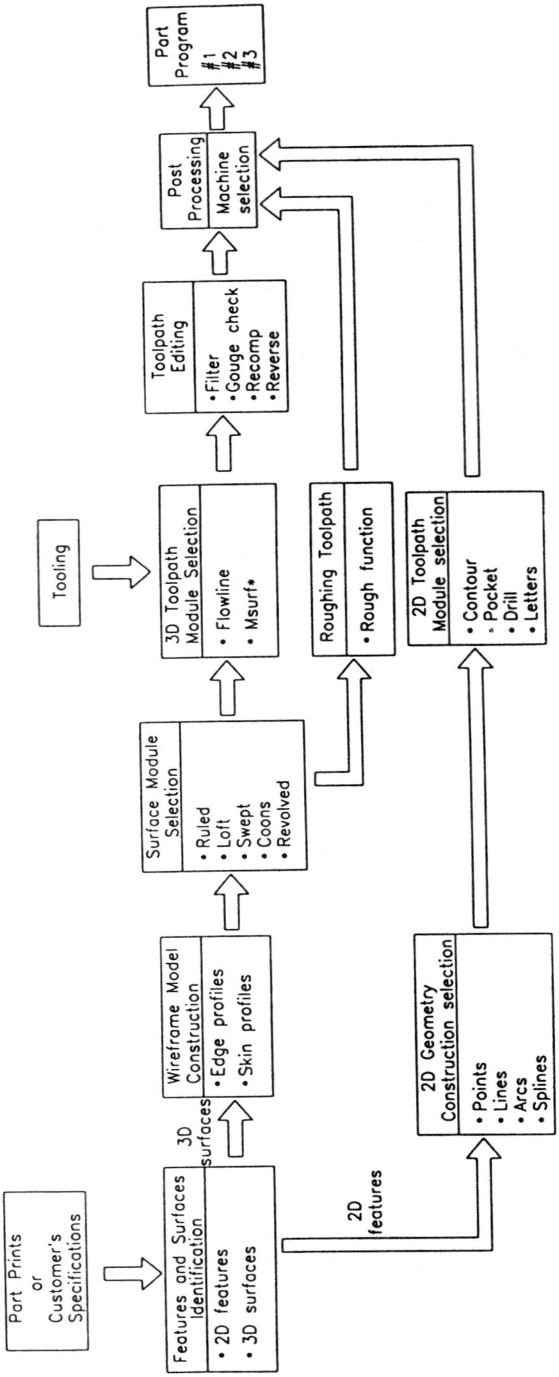

Part Prints
or
Customer's
Specifications
Features and Surfaces
Identification
• 2D features
• 3D surfaces
3D
surfaces
2D
features
Wireframe Model
Construction
• Edge profiles
• Skin profiles
Surface Module
Selection
• Ruled
• Loft
• Swept
• Coons
• Revolved
Tooling
3D Toolpath
Module Selection
• Flowline
• Msurf*
Roughing Toolpath
• Rough function
Toolpath
Editing
• Filter
• Gouge check
• Recomp
• Reverse
Post
Processing
Machine
selection
Part
Program
#1
#2
#3
2D Geometry
Construction selection
• Points
• Lines
• Arcs
• Splines
2D Toolpath
Module selection
• Contour
• Pocket
• Drill
• Letters

Figure 18.1

18.2 Wireframe Model Construction

A CAD system uses a set of edge and skin profiles to create a surface. The complete set of edge and skin profiles for a part is often referred to as the wireframe model. Actually, in most surface modeling cases only a partial wireframe model is required. The following two guidelines should help to determine how many edge and skin profiles are needed and where they are located:

Edge profiles should be defined at the outer boundaries for all sides
Skin profiles should be used to represent significant features in the surface skin

The edge profiles define the shape of the surface outer boundaries. They are definitely required. The skin profiles define the detailed texture of the surface skin. The more skin profiles used, the more accurate the surface produced.

The typical elements of edge profiles and skin profiles are points, lines, arcs, splines, and surface curves.

18.3 Surface Module Selection

Choosing proper surface modeling methods is very crucial for successfully defining surfaces. The analysis of surface features should reveal the proper surface modeling techniques to be used. The seven surface modeling modules Mastercam provides to create various forms of surfaces are:

Surface Type	Description
Ruled	at least two profiles created by connecting straight lines between profiles
Lofted	at least three profiles created by fitting parabolically through a set of cross sectional curves
Revolved	a sectional profile and a line to revolve about created by rotating a sectional shape around an axis or a line
Draft	a sectional shape created by extruding a sectional shape straight along a line
Drag (2D swept)	an along contour and an across contour created by translating or rotating a sectional profile along a drive curve
Swept	three profiles (two along and one across, or one along and two across) created by (1) translating an across profile along two drive curves (2) translating two across profiles along a drive curve
Coons	a single patch of four profiles or multiple patches created by blending a patch of three or four prescribed intersecting curves or points which form a closed boundary, or multiple patches

There are four secondary surfacing techniques used to generate surfaces from existing surfaces.

Surface	Description
Offset	an existing surface created by offsetting an existing surface by a distance
Trimmed	an existing surface created by trimming an existing surface to a specified boundary
Fillet	two existing surfaces created by generating arc cross sections that are tangent to two existing surfaces
Blend	two existing surfaces created by blending a smooth surface between two existing surfaces.

18.4 Toolpath Modules Selection

There are two ways of generating toolpaths to cut surfaces. One is directly using 3D surfacing toolpath modules to generate the toolpath from the wireframe model. The other method is to define the surface model first, then use the flowline or multisurf module to generate the toolpaths from the surface model. It is recommended that the toolpaths be generated from the surface models.

Flowline module:	generates toolpaths for cutting single surfaces
Multisurf module:	generates toolpaths for cutting multiple surfaces

18.5 Toolpath Planning

The toolpaths used to machine a part having 3D surfaces normally consists of three types: 2D toolpaths, roughing toolpaths for surfaces, and finishing toolpaths for surfaces. These three types of toolpaths should be handled separately.

1. Use the 2D toolpath modules whenever possible

The 2D toolpath modules are often used in the following operations:

contours/profiles
pockets
holes
horizontal and vertical flat surfaces

Note: Many flat planes can be defined as surfaces. But their toolpaths should be generated from 2D modules such as pocket or contour. Sloped flat planes should be treated as surfaces in generating their toolpaths.

2. Roughing toolpaths for surfaces

The roughing toolpaths for cutting surfaces normally are 2D in nature. Therefore, their part programs are relatively much shorter than the finishing toolpaths. The workpiece should be cut to approximate size and shape by roughing toolpaths. This allows the use of one single pass of finishing toolpaths to complete the surface(s). Consequently, it helps reduce the part program size and machining time.

3. Finishing toolpaths for surfaces

Make one single pass if possible

Use the largest ball end mill that the surface curvature allows.

When the surface features are symmetrical, generate the toolpaths based on the selected surface segments. Then use toolpath editing functions such as mirror, rotate, and translate to simplify the process. The larger the number of surfaces included in the multisurf function, the longer the time needed by the system to generate the toolpaths. It may take many hours for the system to generate the finishing toolpaths for cutting a composite surface model of 60 surfaces that are formed by 10 symmetrical segments about the center. The process time can be reduced to merely 20 minutes if the primary toolpaths for cutting one of ten surfacing segments is generated, and then rotated to the other nine locations.

The machining sequence for surface(s) starts with 2D machining, then is followed by roughing and finishing.

18.6 Tooling

Two types of cutters that are used extensively in machining 3D surfaces are ball-end mills and bull-corner mills. The radius of ball-end mills are one-half of the cutter diameter. The radius of the corner arc for bull-corner mills is smaller than one-half of the cutter diameter. The following tips can be used to select proper tools for machining 3D surfaces:

Use the larger cutter. The larger cutter reduces the cusp height, allows bigger stepover values, and shortens program size.

The largest cutter usable is limited by the size of the surface curvatures and surface gaps. The cutter radius must be at least slightly smaller that the smallest surface curvature or its diameter should be smaller than the smallest surface gap in the model. A gouging or undercut may occur when the cutter size is too large.

Cusp height is one of the main factors determining the roughness and tolerance of the machined surfaces. The formula given below can be used to calculate the cusp height:

$$Hc = R - [R2 - (S/2)2]\ ½$$

or

$$S = 2[R2 - (r-Hc)2]1/2$$

where Hc = cusp height

R = tool nose radius

S = stepover value between two cutting passes

Note: The cutting speed and feedrate for cutting surfaces are the same as that used in 2D cases.

18.7 Accuracy Requirement

Surface roughness and tolerance are the two major factors to be considered in determining the accuracy requirement. The tips given below can be used to obtain the required surface quality:

> Use increment mode when dimensional accuracy is not crucial or surfaces are rather flat (large curvature radius).
>
> Use chordal mode when the dimensional accuracy is important or surfaces are irregular.
>
> When chordal mode is used, the value for chordal deviation should be somewhat smaller than the required dimensional accuracy.

Use a smaller stepover value or chordal deviation value to generate the toolpaths for cutting surfaces. Then use the filter function to remove those unnecessary toolpath points. The filter function allows setting the allowed deviation or error. Any two adjacent toolpath segments that do not deviate by a value that is larger than the allowed value will be combined into one segment. This significantly shortens the part program while meeting the accuracy and tolerance requirements.

18.8 Toolpath File Management

Here are two guidelines:

> Do not combine 2D toolpaths, roughing toolpaths, and finishing toolpaths altogether in one part program.
>
> The memory size of the controller needs to be known. The program size can not be larger than the available memory size of the controller. Divide the program into several subprograms if the part program is larger than controller memory.

3D Toolpath Planning Examples

Two projects are given in this section to show how to perform toolpath planning for cutting 3D surfacing models.

Example 1. Prepare a toolpath plan for cutting a composite surface model as shown in Figure 18.2. This surface model is also project 7 of chapter 13.

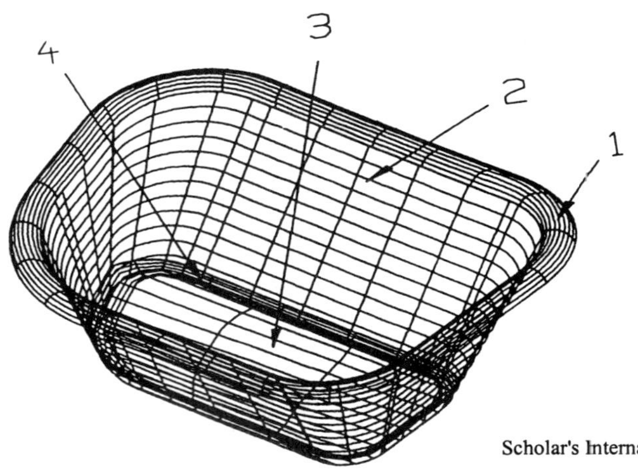

Figure 18.2

Step 1. Identify the part features and surfaces to be machined.

The following four surfaces can be identified in this model. Together they form a composite surface model that can be used to generate roughing toolpaths and finish toolpaths.

1. **Top rim surface**
2. **Wall surface**
3. **Bottom flat surface**
4. **Fillet surface**

Step 2. Select the surface modeling techniques for each surface.

The surface modeling techniques used for the four surfaces are:

1. **Top rim surface**	swept surface module with 2 along and 1 across
2. **Wall surface**	coons surface model or ruled surface module
3. **Bottom flat surface**	ruled surface
4. **Fillet surface**	fillet surface model

Step 3. Construct the wireframe model.

The complexity of the required wireframe model dictates the type of modeling techniques used and the required accuracy on the surface skin. The edge profiles an skin profiles of each surface are listed below and indicated in Figure 18.3.

Top rim surface	Edge profiles: contours 1 and 2 as well as arc 4 Skin profiles: arc 4
Wall surface	Edge profiles: contours 2 and 3 Skin profiles: lines 5-12
Bottom flat surface	Edge profile: contour 3 Skin profile: none
Fillet surface	No profile is required. Use the two existing surfaces (wall and bottom flat surfaces)

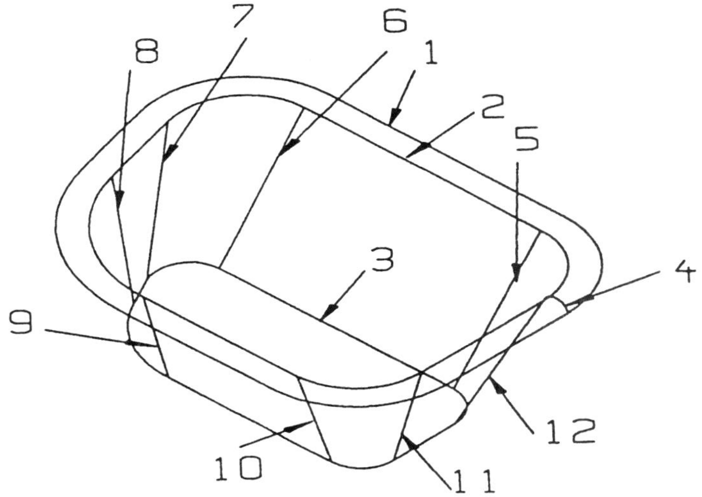

Figure 18.3

Step 4. Select toolpath modules.

The toolpaths required to machine this project consist of two parts; roughing toolpaths and finish toolpaths. Since this is a model with multiple surfaces, the best toolpath module is the Multisurf toolpath module. Use the rough function of the Multisurf module to generate the roughing toolpaths and the finish function of the Multisurf module to generate the finish toolpaths for the surface model, respectively.

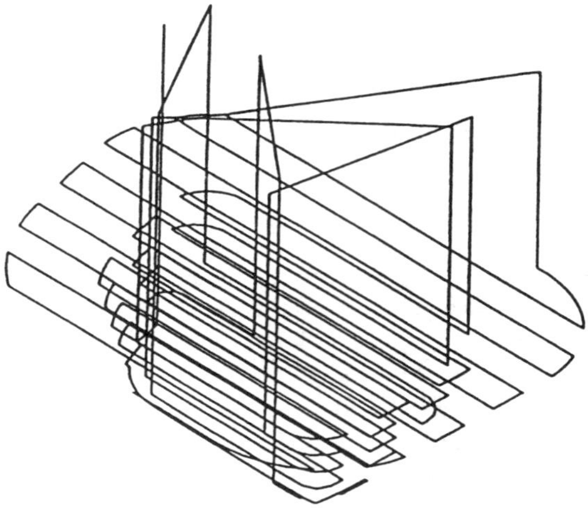

Figure 18.4

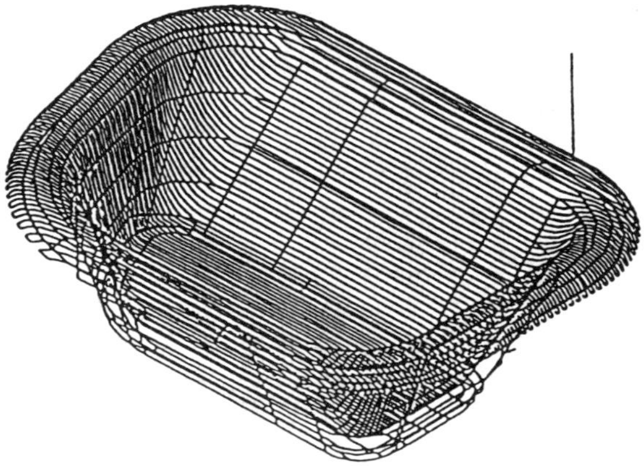

Figure 18.5

Step 5. Select the tooling and machining information.

Cutters:	Roughing	¾" end mill
	Finishing	3/8" ball end mill
Machining data:	Roughing:	Cutting speed= 350 fpm (or 2670RPM)
		Feedrate = 10 inches/min
		Depth of cut = 0.15 inches/pass
	Finishing:	Cutting speed= 250fpm (or 2500RPM)
		Feedrate = 15 inches/min
		Chordal Deviation= 0.01 inches

Mastercam Version 7,
Scholar's International Publishing Corp., 1998

Example 2.

Prepare a toolpath plan for cutting a very complicated surface model as shown in Figure 18.6. This surface model is project 11 of chapter 13. The finish toolpaths for the surface model are given in project 8 of chapter 15.

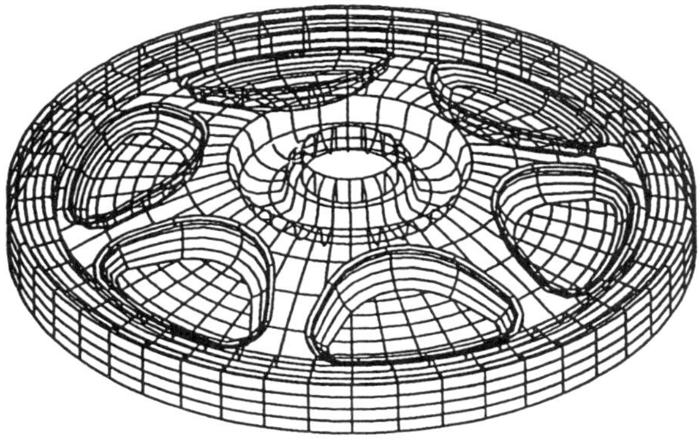

Figure 18.6

Step 1. Identify the part features and surfaces.

The complete surface model consists of 48 surfaces that are formed by six segments that are symmetric about the origin. This model can be generated by modeling a surface segment as shown in Figure 18.7 and then copying this surface segment onto five locations by rotating about the origin. Therefore, we need to define only the following eight surfaces:

1. Inner hole surface (straight circular surface)
2. Hub surface
3. Upper surface
4. Lower surface (pocket bottom surface)
5. Pocket wall surface
6. Fillet surface
7. Rim surface
8. Outer surface (straight circular surface)

Note: The upper and lower surfaces are trimmed surfaces.

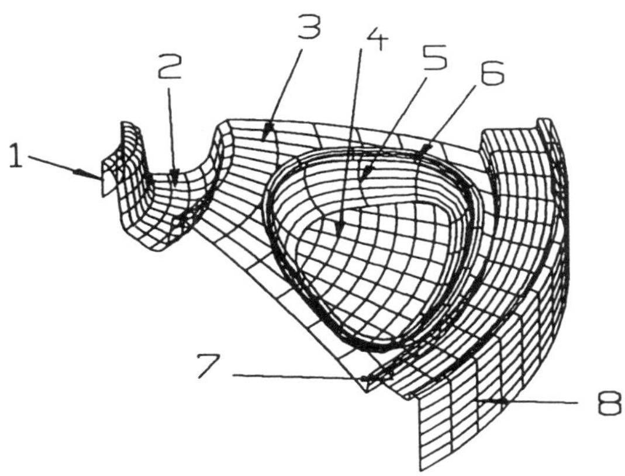

Figure 18.7

Step 2. Select the surface modeling techniques for each surface.

The surface modeling techniques used for the eight surfaces are listed below. Some surfaces can be modeled by more than one technique.

1. **Inner hole surface:**	revolved or swept surface module
2. **Hub surface:**	swept surface module (2 along and 1 across)
3. **Upper surface:**	swept surface module (2 along and 1 across) and trim function (trimmed to fillet surface)
4. **Lower surface:**	swept surface module (2 along and 1 across) and trim function (trimmed to pocket wall surface)
5. **Pocket wall surface:**	swept surface module (2 along and 1 across)
6. **Fillet surface:**	fillet surface module (between upper surface and pocket wall surface)
7. **Rim surface:**	swept surface (2 along and 1 across)
8. **Outer surface**:	revolved surface module

Step 3. Construct the wireframe model.

The required wireframe model consists of lines and arcs that are used to model the surface segment. The two defining along contours for the pocket wall surface are the two surface curves that are obtained by projecting the inner and outer pocket profiles onto the upper and lower surfaces. The required wireframe model for the basic surface segment is shown in Figure 18.8.

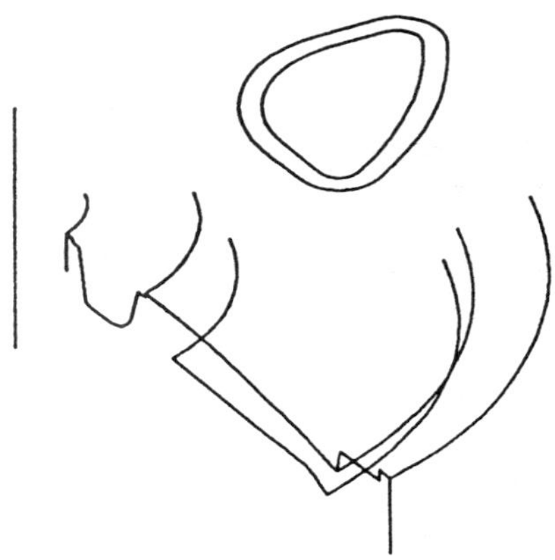

Figure 18.8

Step 4. Select the toolpath modules.

2D toolpaths:	2D pocket module to cut the inner hole surface 2D contour module to cut the outer surface
Roughing:	Use the Multisurf Rough commands to generate toolpaths for roughing the following three surfaces; hub surface, upper surface, and pocket surface. *Note:* The roughing toolpaths for the three surfaces listed above are copied to five locations by using the rotating function.
Finishing:	Use the Multisurf Finish commands to generate toolpaths for finish cutting the composite surface model that consists of six surfaces as shown in Figure 18.9.

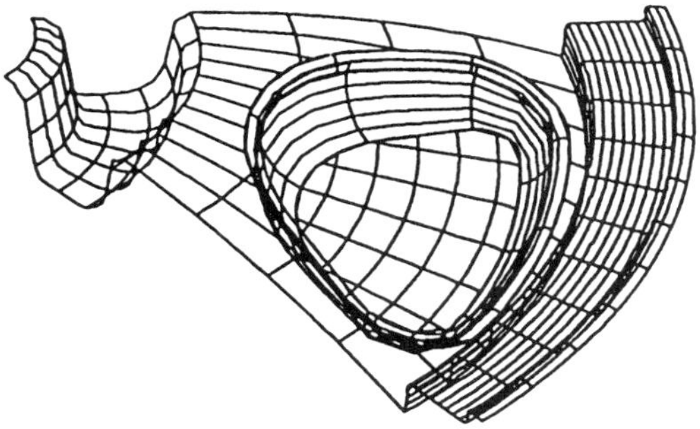

Figure 18.9

The finish toolpaths for the six surfaces should look like Figure 18.10. These finish toolpaths are then copied to five locations by using the rotating command. The finish toolpaths for the complete model are shown in Figure 18.11.

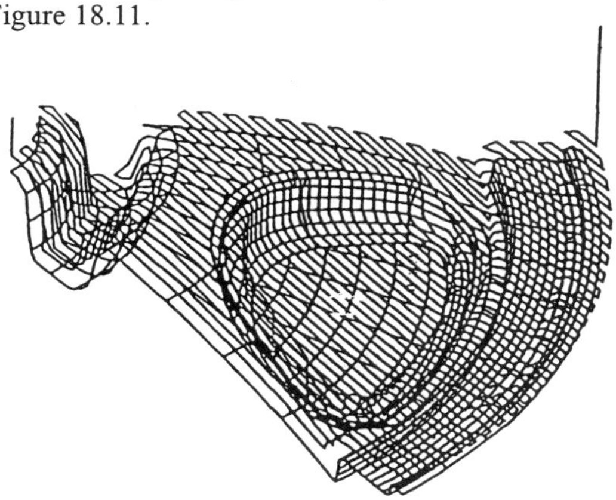

Figure 18.10

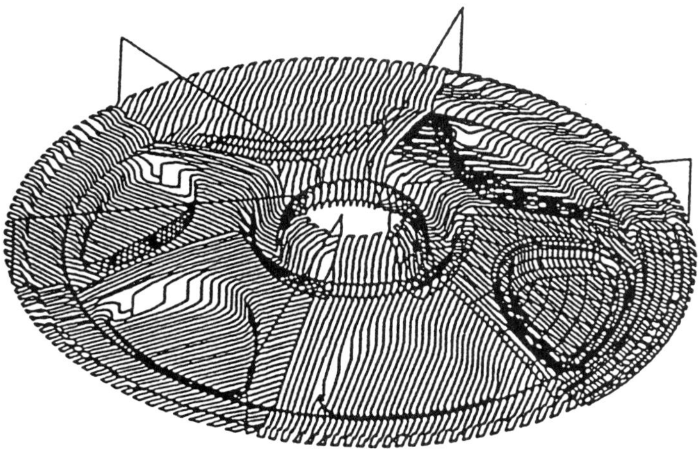

Figure 18.11

Note: It is possible to include all surfaces in a composite model to generate the finish toolpaths. However, it may take a very long time for the system to generate the toolpaths because it involves many more surfaces in the model.

Step 5. Select the tooling and machining information.

Cutters:	Roughing	1/2" end mill
	Finishing	3/8" ball end mill
Machining data:	Roughing:	Cutting speed= 350 fpm (or 2670RPM)
		Feedrate = 10 inches/min
		Depth of cut = 0.15 inches/pass
	Finishing:	Cutting speed= 250fpm (or 2500RPM)
		Feedrate = 15 inches/min
		Chordal Deviation= 0.01 inches

Exercises

1. What are two types of part features? Describe their differences.
2. What is the difference between geometric surfaces and free-form surfaces in terms of the accuracy of the surface skin?
3. What is the prime factor in determining the number of skin profiles needed in a surface model?
4. What are typical elements of edge profiles and skin profiles?
5. List the seven surface modeling modules in Mastercam. What is the required minimum number of profiles for each surface modeling module?
6. List the three secondary surfacing techniques.
7. Describe the two ways to generate toolpaths for cutting surfaces.
8. Explain when you should use the flowline and multisurf modules, respectively.
9. Explain why the 2D toolpaths, roughing toolpaths for surfaces, and finish toolpaths for surfaces should be generated separately and stored in different files.
10. What are two types of cutters that are extensively used in machining 3D surfaces?
11. Why is the larger cutter recommended in cutting surfaces? What are the limiting factors for the largest size of the cutters?
12. What are the two major factors to be considered in determining the accuracy of surfaces?

Chapter 19

Engraving Artworks

Objectives:

1. Scanning or obtaining artworks.
2. Converting artworks to vector format using Adobe Streamline programs.
3. Reducing the number of geometric entities using Interflux program.
4. Importing artworks to Mastercam.
5. Merging files in Mastercam.
6. Generating toolpaths to cut artworks.

Overview

Engraving is a major application in CNC machining. Letters and artworks are often engraved onto the parts. Artworks can be scanned and stored using the Bit Map Pixel (BMP) or other file format. These BMP files are picture image and can not be directly used in Mastercam for machining. They must be converted into the vector format. A number of software programs can be used to convert picture images to their equivalent vector form. Adobe Streamline and Corel Draw are two programs commonly used to convert images into line vector forms. The initial file normally consists of a large number of vector lines. It is impractical, if not impossible, to engrave all of the vector lines. They must be reduced to a manageable size. Adobe Streamline has various functions which smooth vector entities and reduce the number of entities. The Interflux program also can be used to reduce the large number of vector entities to a smaller number of vector lines while not significantly sacrificing image quality.

This chapter covers the procedure for converting artworks to the vector format and generating engraving toolpaths using Mastercam. Emphasis is given on to how to prepare artworks, converting drawing images to vector format using the Streamline program, reducing vector entities using the Interflux program, importing vector drawings into Mastercam, and generating engraving toolpaths to cut artworks.

19.1 Artworks and Bitmap Images

Artworks are pictorial illustrations that can be created in a wide variety of ways. Typical computer artworks include paintings, drawings, photos, sketches, and calligraphies. Artworks in any form can be readily converted into bitmap image files. These bitmap image files then can be manipulated and become readable to Mastercam for engraving. Bitmap images, also referred to raster images, use a grid of small squares known as pixels to represent graphics. A pixel, (from picture element) is the smallest visual element on a computer screen. Each pixel in a bitmap image has a specific location and color value assigned to it. When working with bitmap images, you edit a collection of pixels rather than shapes or objects.

Bitmap images can be created in one of the following ways:

- Create an image using an image-processing application software program
- Import an image from a clip-art collection
- Obtain an image by using a scanner or video digitizer

The digital bitmap image files can be saved in several formats. Some commonly used image file formats are:

BMP (Bit Map Pixel)
PCX (Windows PaintBrush)
TIFF (Tagged-Image File Format)
PSD (Photoshop)
PNT (MacPaint)

19.2 Vector Formats

The geometry types allowed in Mastercam include points, lines, arcs, splines, and surfaces. Picture image files can not be directly used in Mastercam. One way to make picture files usable in Mastercam is to convert images into the vector format. In vector format, images are represented by a series of short line elements. The vector representation of an image often requires more than ten thousand short line and arc elements. We need to carefully control the setting parameters to reduce the large number of vector elements. Figure 19.1 shows an example of bitmap image to vector drawing conversion. A comparison between bitmap images and vector artworks is summarized below

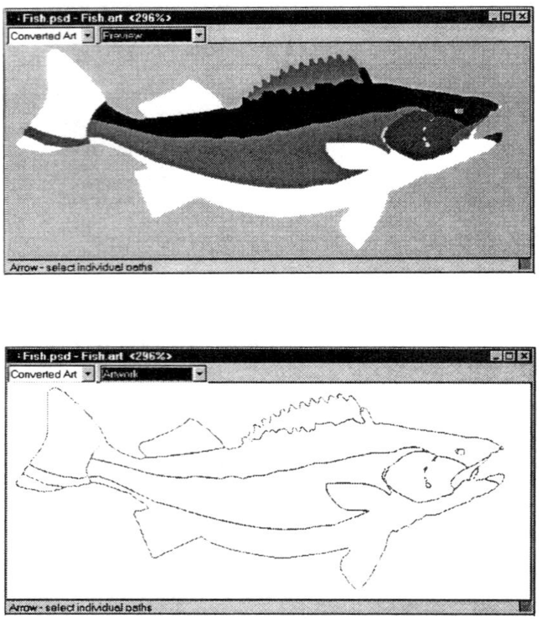

Bitmap Images

- Raster images.
- Use pixels, small square grids, to represent graphics.
- Can be distorted, lose details if they are manipulated.

Vector Artworks

- Consisting of lines and curves defined by mathematical objects called vectors.
- Vectors describe graphics according to their geometric characteristics.
- Can be moved or resized without losing the quality of the artwork.

Figure 19.1

The image file formats used depend on the conversion program used. You can save a converted image in one of the following file formats:

DXF	Metafile (Windows)	Adobe Illustrator

Two commonly used image to vector conversion programs are Adobe Streamline and Corel Draw. We only present the necessary information required to perform conversion using the Adobe Streamline program in the next section.

19.3 Adobe Streamline Program

Adobe Streamline is a computer graphic tool used for converting bitmap images into high quality vector drawings. It produces a much smaller file size than their bitmap counterparts. Adobe Streamline also offers various editing tools for changing the original image and the converted images.

You can save a converted image in one of the following file formats:

DXF	Metafile (Windows)	Adobe Illustrator

Entering Adobe Streamline

Follow these commands to open the Adobe Streamline program:

Select Start → Programs → Adobe → Streamline → Adobe Streamline

The initial menu of Streamline appears as below.

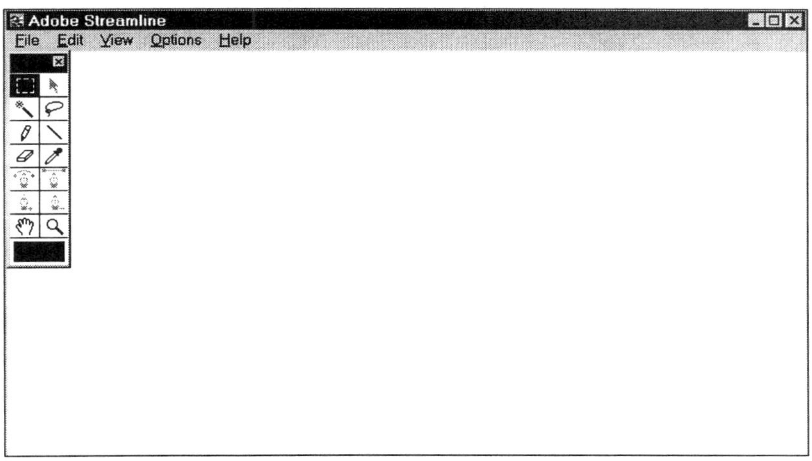

Adobe Streamline program provides three options menus for you to editing your images. They are **settings, color/B&W setup,** and **conversion setup**.

Settings menu

The Settings menu selects the image type to be converted and default parameters for each selected image type. The Settings menu appears as below.

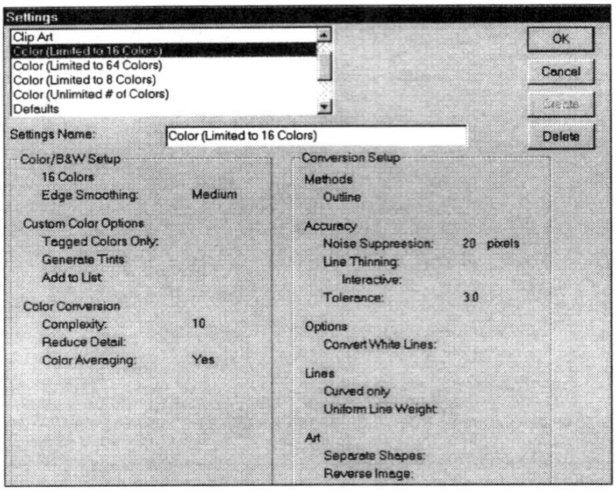

You can choose one of the following twelve image types in the list:

Blueprints	Business forms
Clip art	Color (Limited to 16 colors)
Color (Limited to 64 colors)	Color (Limited to 8 colors)
Color (Unlimited # of colors)	Default
Hand drawn sketches	Inked drawings
Outline black/white	Technical illustration

The parameters associated in this menu have default settings for each image type. You select an image type, the system automatically displays the default settings for relevant parameters.

Color/B&W Setup menu

This menu selects conversion settings and options for converting black-and-white, grayscale, and color bitmap images into vector line art. Active parameters will be highlighted when an option is selected with a Posterization parameter. The parameters menu for "Limited Colors" and "Black & White Only" options are given below.

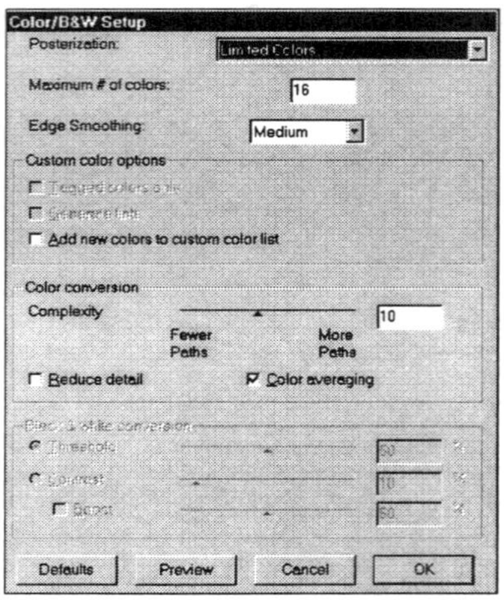

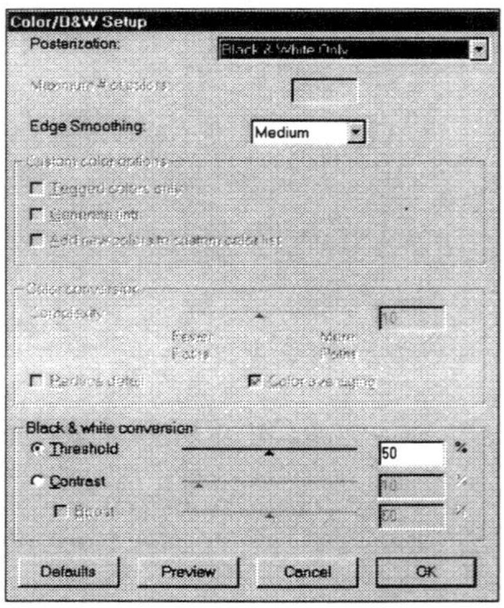

Posterization This parameter selects the image mode to be converted. It has the following four types as shown in the screen capture here.

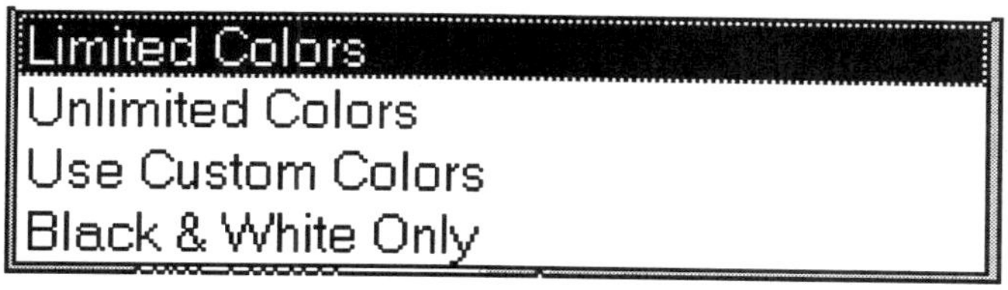

Edge smoothing This parameter allows you to control the level of edge smoothing in the converted image by limiting anti-aliasing in the original image. Anti-aliasing converts jagged edges in a bitmap image into clean edges. The higher the level of Edge Smoothing, the smoother are the paths in the converted image. Smoothing edges more than necessary can result in distorted paths.

This parameter has the following three options:

None:	no edge smoothing.
Medium:	perform average degree of edge smoothing.
Maximum:	perform maximum degree of edge smoothing.

Black & White Conversion The following three parameters are included in this group:

Threshold:	specify as a percentage the gray level above which Streamline will convert a pixel to black. For example, an 8-bit grayscale image has 256 (or 2^8) levels of gray, numbered 0 (black) to 255 (white). A threshold of 40% causes all pixels with gray-level values above 102 to be converted to black. The higher the percentage, the lower is the number of black pixels that remain.
Contrast:	specify as a percentage the contrast level above which Streamline will convert a pixel to black. Streamline compares how much each pixel contrasts with its neighboring pixels. Pixels exceeding the specified percentage are converted to black. The higher the percentage specified, the smaller is the resulting number of black pixels.
Boost:	enhance the details in the light or dark areas. It is useful when you convert color or grayscale images in which the stroke contrast is not pronounced.

Limited Colors Conversion The following parameters are used in the Limited Colors menu:

Maximum # of colors:	specify the maximum number of colors or grayscale levels to use in converting an image.
Edge smoothing:	control the level of edge smoothing in the converted image.
Color conversion:	control the way Streamline creates paths in color conversion

Color conversion has three parameters; complexity, reduce detail, and color averaging.

Complexity This parameter defines how closely Streamline examines adjacent colors in an image to determine whether they require separate paths. A higher complexity setting creates more paths and more color variation in the converted image.
Reduce detail This parameter reduces the level of detail that Streamline creates in a converted image. Streamline will double the resolution of an image before conver sion when this parameter is toggled to Off (no √ mark). The image resolution is not doubled if this parameter is set to On (with √ mark).
Color averaging This parameter controls how Streamline assigns colors to paths in a converted image. It is best suited for bitmap images consisting of solid areas of color. Color averaging will be disabled when converting continuous-tone images such as photographs or when performing multiple conversions with overlapping selections.

Conversion setup

The Conversion Setup menu allows you choose conversion methods, set line options, or reverse the bitmap image. It appears below.

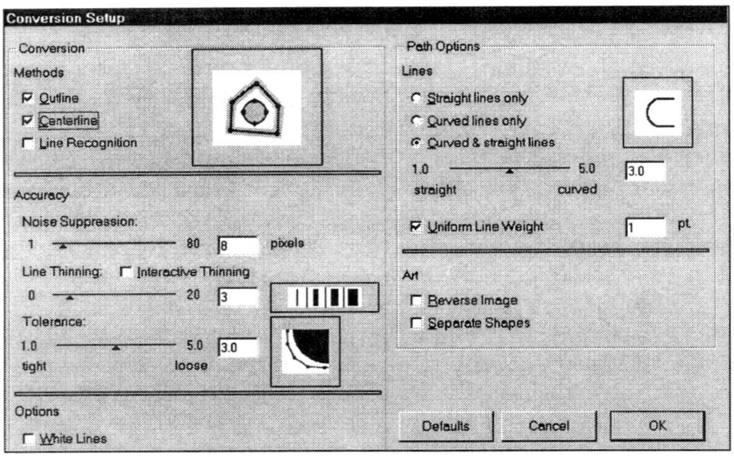

Conversion method Streamline provides the following three conversion methods:

Outline: convert images that contain filled areas and lines that vary in weight. It must be used for color images or grayscale conversions such as clip art, hand-drawn images, or photographs.
Centerline: convert images that contain consistent line weights and have no filled areas.
Line recognition: convert images that contain horizontal and vertical lines such as forms, charts, and graphs. It only recognizes and converts straight lines that are within 5% of the vertical or horizontal axis.

Path options This group of parameters allows you to select the tolerance at which a line segment becomes straight or curved in the converted image.

Lines This parameter specifies the line type to be straight, curved, or combination of straight and curved in the converted image. It has the following three options:

Straight lines only:	all entities are represented by straight lines. Use this if the original image includes only straight lines.
Curved lines only:	all entities are represented by curved lines. Use this if the original image includes only curved lines.
Curved & straight lines:	creates both straight lines and curved lines based on the given curved scale. The curved scale sets the ratio of curved to straight lines in the converted artwork. The smaller the scale value, the more **straight line** segments. The larger the scale value, the more **curved** segments.

Accuracy

Three parameters in this group are used to select the general conversion options that determine the accuracy of the conversion. They are noise suppression, line thinning, and tolerance.

Noise suppression The Noise Suppression parameter is available only when the Outline conversion method is selected. It eliminates the stray pixels (noise) introduced by scanning a poor-quality original. Areas that are smaller than the Noise Suppression pixels settings are ignored when the image is converted.

Line thinning This parameter changes the way Streamline calculates the center of the line when it converts the line to a stroked path. Increasing the line thinning value results in more pixels being shaved off of variable-weight lines, resulting in more accurately rendered artwork and a reduction in the number of junction points. However, it will shorten lines that don't meet other lines or objects. The "Interactive Thinning" option allows you to adjust the level of line thinning during the conversion process and to preview the results of line thinning as it is performed.

Tolerance This parameter allows you to control how closely Streamline converts paths that follow curved and straight lines in the original image. A loose tolerance setting creates longer line segments and fewer anchor points. Inversely, a tight tolerance setting generates shorter line segments and more anchor points to maintain the exact detail of the original image.

Art

The following two parameters are included in this group; reverse image and separate shapes.

Reverse image:	reverses the black-and-white areas of an image before it is converted.
Separate shapes:	creates a unique path for each area in the bitmap image that is completely surrounded by a stroked line.

Two projects are presented in this section. The first project converts a clip art image to vector drawing using Adobe Streamline. The second project converts a grayscale image to a vector drawing. Both vector drawing files are saved in DXF format.

1 Project 1. Converting a clip art image to vector drawing

A clip art image in black and white are imported to Adobe Streamline and converted to a vector drawing. The clip art (pilot) used in this project is directly obtained from the tutorial files that come with Adobe Streamline. The clip art image and its vector drawing are shown in Figure 19.2.

Figure 19.2

Step 1. Import the clip art file.

Select **File** → **Open**

Change file folder and select the file as below.

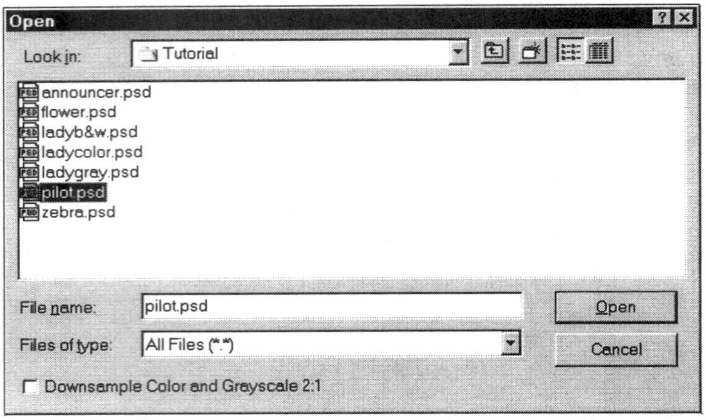

Select **Open** to import the image as shown in Figure 19.3.

Figure 19.3

Step 2. Define the setting parameters.

Select **Options → Settings**
The settings menu should appear as below.

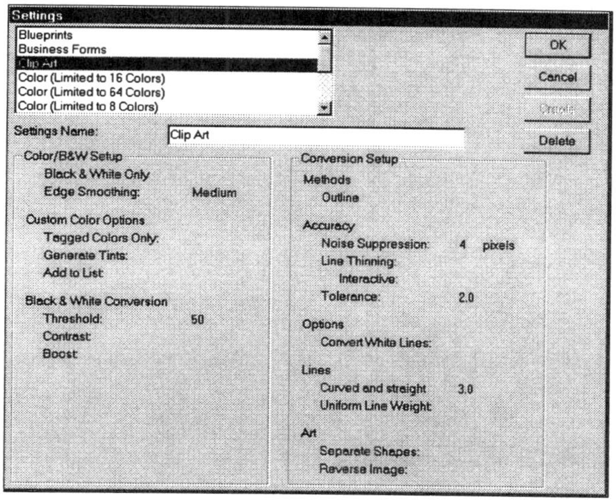

Select **Clip Art** from the settings list as above.
Select **OK**
Select **Options → Conversion Setup**
Set the conversion setup parameters as below.

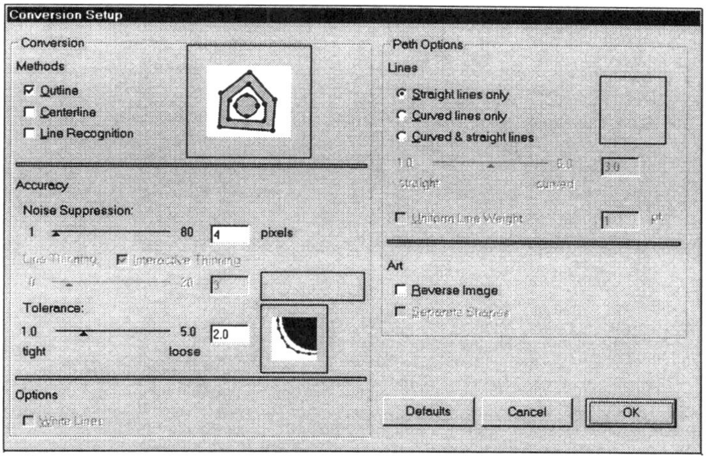

Select **File → Convert** to convert the image to vector drawing

Step 4. Display the artwork drawing.

Click the pull down icon to open the pull down menu as below.

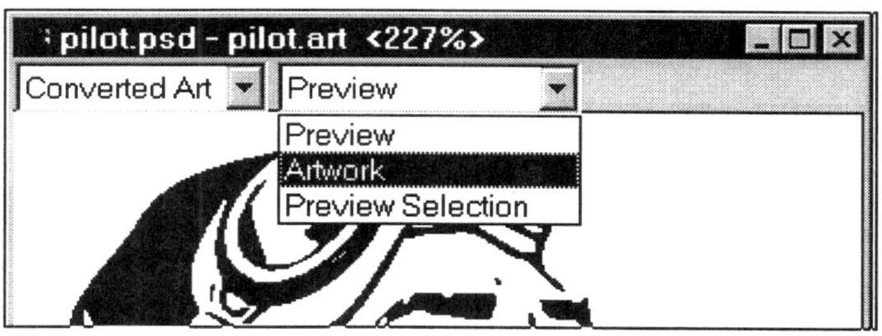

Select **Artwork** from the list
The artwork of the image
should appear as in Figure 19.4.

Figure 19.4

Step 5. Save the vector drawing.

Select **File → Save Art As**
Change the file type to DXF(*.dxf) and save the file as below.

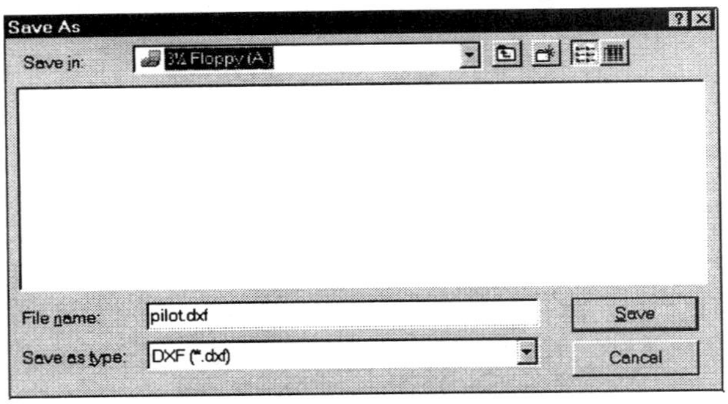

Project 2. Converting a grayscale image to vector drawing

A grayscale type bitmap image is converted to a vector drawing in this project. The bitmap image can be found in the project disk with drawing file "buck.psd". Figure 19.5 shows the bitmap image and its converted vector drawing.

Figure 19.5

Step 1. Import an image file "buck.psd".

Select **File → Open**
File name to open: **buck.psd**
The imported image appears as in Figure 19.6.

Figure 19.6

Step 2. Define setup parameters.

Select **Options → Color/B & W Setup**

Set the Color/B & W Setup parameters as below.

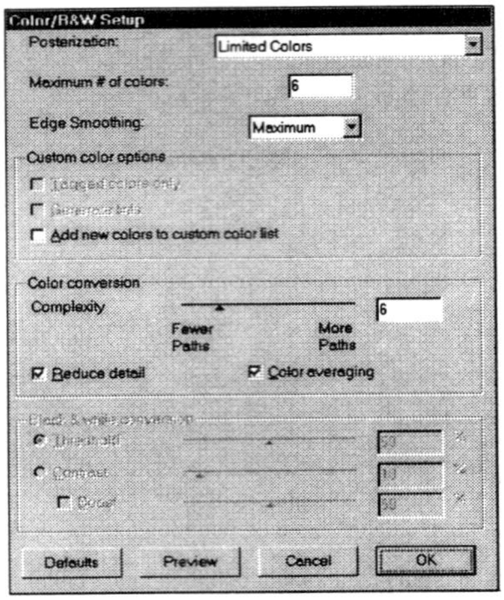

Select **OK**

Step 3. Define conversion setup parameters.

Select **Options → Conversion Setup**

Define the conversion setup parameters as below.

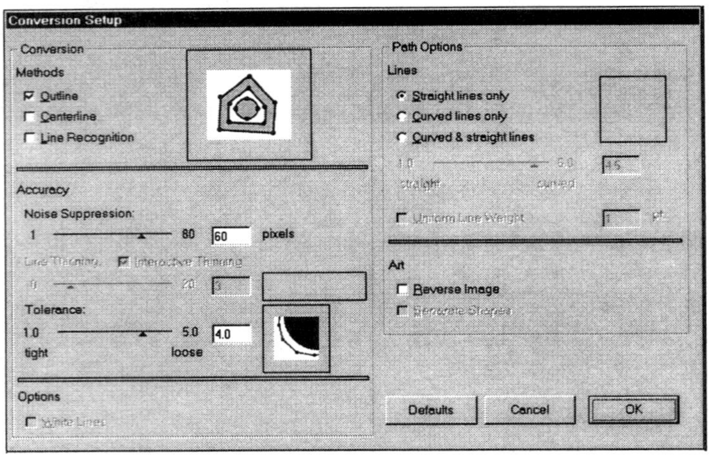

Select **OK**

Step 4. Convert the image to vector drawing.

Select **File → Convert** to convert the image to vector drawing

Select **Artwork display**

Select Pull-down icon, then select Artwork from the list

The artwork drawing appears as in Figure 19.7.

Figure 19.7

Step 5. Save the artwork file.

Select **File → Save Art As**

Set the Save As parameters as below.

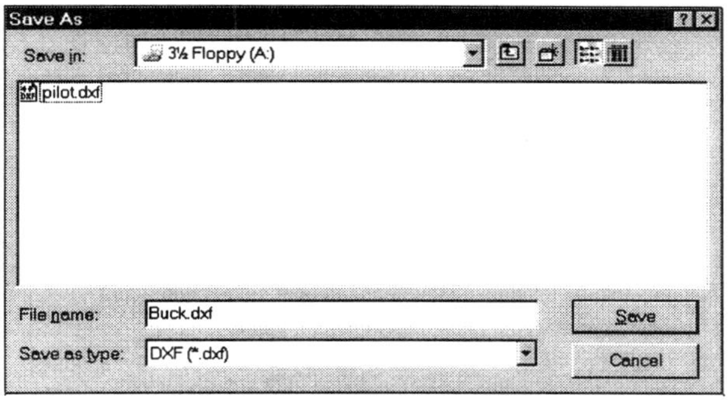

Select **Save** to save the file

19.4 Importing Vector Drawings to Mastercam

This section presents the directions for importing a vector drawing into Mastercam. The vector drawing will be temporarily placed at a location. Its size and location can be easily modified. Use the following tips to properly manipulate the imported vector drawings;

Tips

1. Place the vector drawing in a separate level and eith a separate color, so it can be readily selected by level for further manipulation.
2. Use the following Xform commands to manipulate the drawing:
   a. Use the Translate function to move the drawing to proper location.
   b. Use theScale or ScaleXYZ function to enlarge or reduce the drawing size.
   c Use the Rotate function to adjust the drawing position angularly.
3. It is possible to combine (or merge) the vector drawing with an existing Mastercam project.
4. It is possible to import more than one vector drawing file into the same project.

The procedure for importing a vector drawing to Mastercam is:

Select **MAIN MENU → File → Converters → DXF → Read File**

The vector drawings created from using Streamline may contain multiple-duplicated lines in the same area. This may create problems during generating toolpaths for engraving in Mastercam. We can use the following commands in Mastercam to eliminate the duplicated entities:

Select **MAIN MENU → Delete → Duplicate → Entities**

3 Project 3. Importing a vector drawing to Mastercam

This project imports a vector drawing file created in project 1 into Mastercam. The drawing is scaled to fit in a 2" x 4" rectangular envelop. The contour module is then used to engrave the artwork. Figure 19.8 shows the artwork and toolpath verification model.

Figure 19.8a

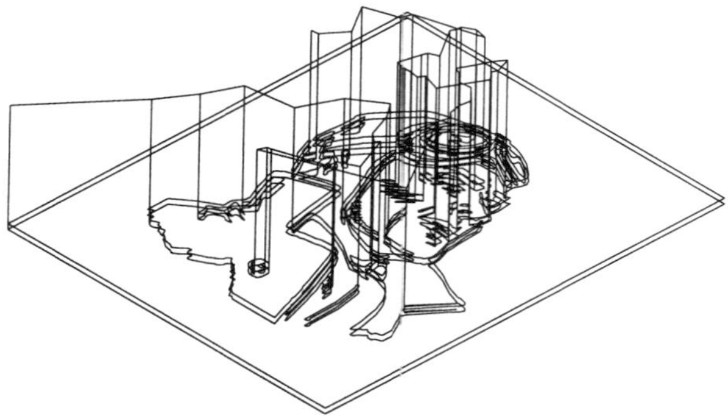

Figure 19.8b

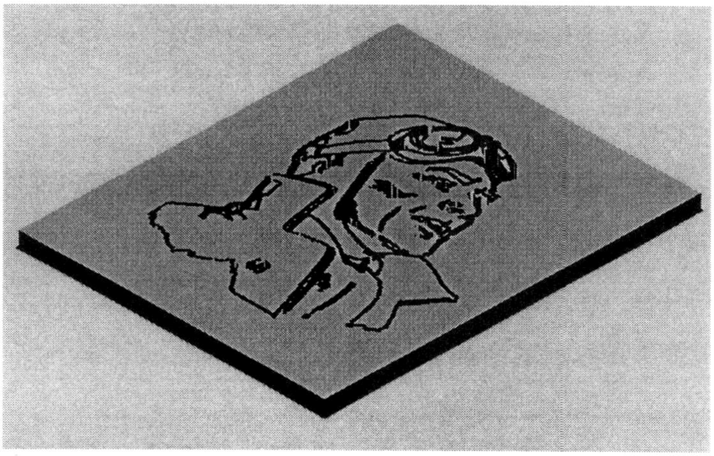

Figure 19.8c

Step 1. Open a vector drawing file (pilot).

Select **MAIN MENU → File → Converters → DXF → Read file**

File name: **pilot**

The initial drawing starts as Figure 19.9.

Figure 19.9

Step 2. Create a rectangle in level 2.

Select **Level**, then enter **2**
Select **Color**, then select **Red** (12)
Select **MAIN MENU → Create → Rectangle → 2 Points**
Enter **(0,0)** and **(3.0,3.7)** as two corner points to define a rectangle
The rectangle is added as in Figure 19.10.

Figure 19.10

Step 3. Translate entities in level 1 to a new location.

Select **MAIN MENU → Xfrom → Translate → All → Color**
Select **White** (15) for color
Select **OK → Done → Rectangle**
Enter the translation vector: **x0.5, y0.5**
Select **Move** and set Number of steps to **1**
Select **Done**
The new drawing becomes Figure 19.11.

Figure 19.11

Step 4. Initiate the contour function.

Select **MAIN MENU → Toolpaths → Contour**
File name for NCI: **pilot**
Select **Window**, then pick two points to form a window that includes all entities
Select the left-front corner as the search point
Select **Done**

Step 5. Select a 1/32" flat end mill and set tool parameters.

Click the right mouse button, then select "Get tool from library"
Select **tool #229** (1/32" flat end mill) from the list
Select **OK**
Set the tool parameters as below.

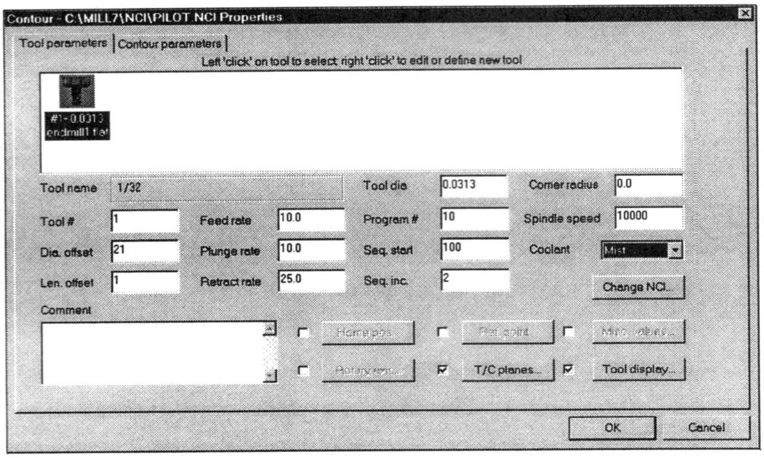

Step 6. Define the contour parameters.

Select the "Contour parameters" button
Set the contour parameters as below.

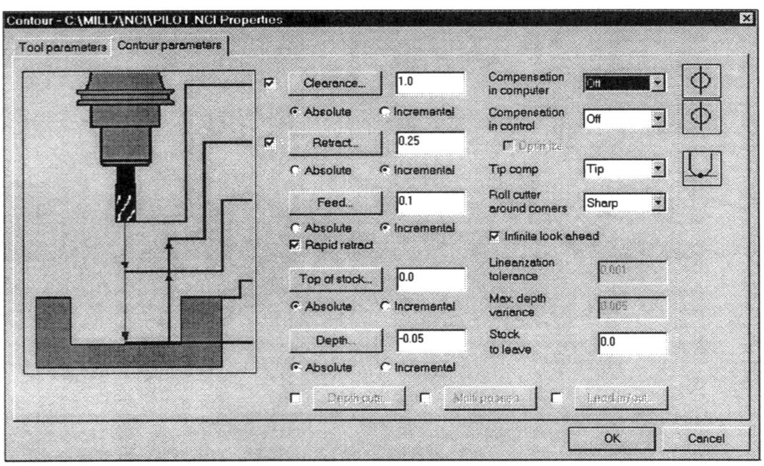

Select **OK**
Select **Gview → Isometric**
The engraving toolpaths are generated as in Figure 19.12.

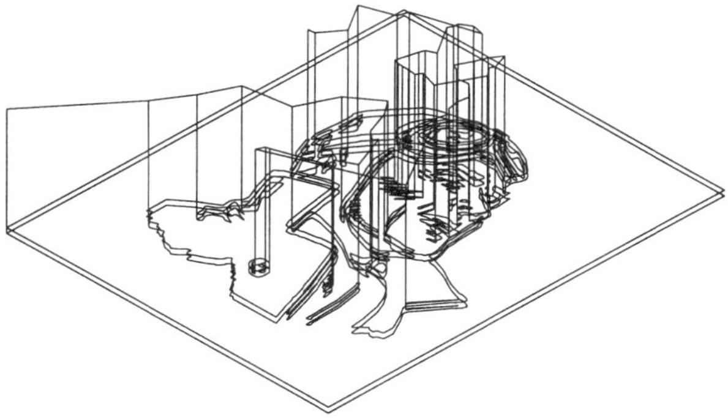

Figure 19.12

Step 7. Verify the toolpaths.

Select **Operations** to open the Operations Manager menu
Select **N-See 2000**
Select **Preview** → **OK** from "Select mode for current job menu"
Select **Do it** to verify the toolpaths
The toolpaths are animated on the screen.
The verification model should appear as Figure 19.13.

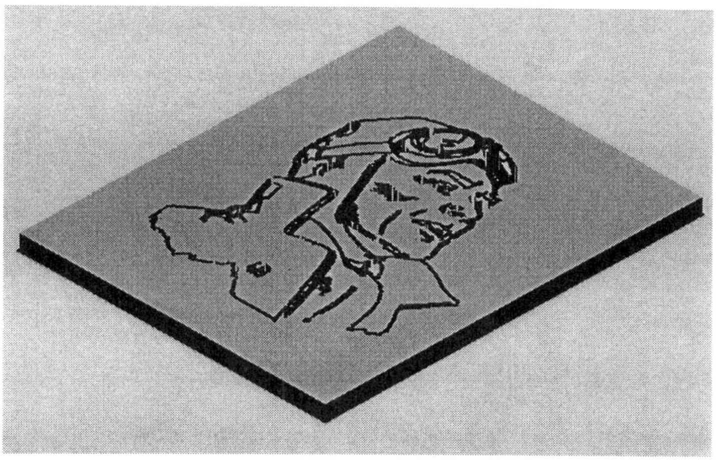

Figure 19.13

Step 8. Save the toolpath file.

Select **MAIN MENU** → **Save**

19.5 InterFlux Program

The InterFlux program developed by Northwood Designs, Inc. can be used to edit vector drawings. It can significantly reduce the number of line and arc segments by controlling the arc tolerance value and selecting the parameter settings. The main functions used in this text are grouped under Modify and Transform commands.

Modify

The Modify includes the following six functions for you to modify the vector drawing:

Arcs:	specify the arc tolerance to reduce the segment number.
Delete:	delete the selected entities.
dElete contour:	delete the selected contours.
Clean-up:	close open contours, merge between contours, or collapse small contours to points or delete them.
Reassign colors:	assign a color to selected entities.
create Polyline:	create a polyline from a series of points.

Arcs This is one of most useful functions in InterFlux for reducing the number of entities. It has these parameters:

Arc tolerance:	0.1
jaggie Cleanup:	ON/OFF
jaGgie length:	0.1
Jaggie tolerance:	0.1
Show endpoint:	ON/OFF
max arc Radius:	1000.000

The most significant parameter is "Arc tolerance". Use the larger arc tolerance value to reduce the number of segments. InterFlux will display the summary of modified results as shown here:

Original entities:	2000
Current lines:	121
Current arcs:	234
Current entities:	355
Tolerance used:	0.1
Entity reduction:	82.25%

Delete delete **entities** that are specified by using a window, polygon or color.

Delete contour delete **contours** that are specified by using a window, polygon or color.

Clean-up

cLose open contours:	make open contours becoming closed contours.
close Between contours:	merge adjacent contours.
Collapse small contours:	shrink small contours to points or totally eliminate them.
clean Move lines:	remove move lines.
Close open contours	This function makes those open contours that have a gap within the specified tolerance to become closed contours. The tolerance values are specified by the two parameters below:

Auto close tolerance:	0.2000
Manual close tolerance:	0.2500

Close between contours This function merges adjacent contours that are selected within a window, a polygon, or a color.

Collapse small contours This function can be used to reduce those small contours that are smaller than the specified bounding tolerance to point or completely eliminate them.

Its two parameters are:

Bounding tolerance:	0.1000
Modification type:	To Point/Delete

Transform

The following four parameters are used to modify the size and location of the drawing:

Scale:	resize the drawing based on the given scale factors for X and Y directions.
Force:	resize the drawing to fit the drawing to a given rectangular envelop.
Translate:	change the origin, move the drawing, and mirror or rotate the drawing.
Group:	group the selected entities.

Scale This function allows you to scale the drawing based on the given scale factors in the X and Y direction. The system will prompt "% to scale X and Y axis <X, Y>:" for you to specify scaling factors.

Force This function allows you to resize the drawing to fit in a rectangular envelop. The system will prompt "Size to force X and Y axis to <X, Y>:" for you to specify the X and Y dimensions of the rectangle.

Translate The following seven functions are included in the Translate command:

Force to origin: force the left-front corner of the rectangular drawing envelop to move to the origin.
Center on origin: force the center of the rectangular drawing envelop to move to the origin.
Absolute move: move the left-front corner of the rectangular drawing envelop to the specified X and Y location.
Relative move: move the drawing by the given X and Y distances.
Between points: move the drawing by the distance specified by two points.
Mirror/Rotate: rotate and/or mirror the drawing.

Three sub-functions are under the Mirror/Rotate function:

Rotation angle:	rotate the drawing by the specified angle.
Vertical mirror:	flip the drawing in right-left direction.
Horizontal mirror:	flip the drawing in up-down direction.

Leave original: make the original drawing remained and create a new drawing from rotate and/or mirror operation.

4 ⌛ **Tips for using InterFlux**

1. Acceptable import file formats: HPGL (.PLT)
   EPSF (.EPS)
   AISS (.SI)
   DXF (.DXF)

2. Use Transform → Force functions to fix the size of the drawing.

3. Use Transform → Translate functions to relocate the origin of the drawing.

4. Use Transform → Mirror/Rotate functions to change the drawing orientation.

5. Use Modify → Arcs → Arc tolerance functions to reduce the segment number.

6. Use Modify → Clean-up functions to edit contours

7. Acceptable export file formats: NCI
   NC
   DXF
   CDL
   INC

Project 4. Using InterFlux program to edit a vector drawing

This project uses a vector drawing provided on the project disk to show how to edit drawing using InterFlux program. The Force function is used to change the size of the drawing to a 2"x 3.5" rectangle. Both shape and size have been changed. The Modify → Arcs commands are used to reduce the number of entities. Figure 19.14 shows the original drawing, drawing after forced, and drawing after edited using the Arts command.

a. Original drawing b. Drawing after forced c. Drawing after editing
Figure 19.14

Step 1. Import a DXF file buck.dxf.

Select **File → Import → DXF**
File name: **buck**
The buck drawing appears as in Figure 19.15.

Figure 19.15

Step 2. Force the size to 2"x 3.5".

Select **Transform → Force**
Size to force X and Y axis to (X, Y): **2,3.5**
The drawing size has been forced to 2"x 3.5" and the shape is modified accordingly in Figure 19.16.

Figure 19.16

Step 3. Reduce the number of entities.

Select **Modify → Arcs**
Set the arc parameters as below:

Arc tolerance:	**0.025**
jaggie Cleanup:	**ON**
jaGgie length:	**0.05**
Jaggie tolerance:	**0.05**
Show endpoints:	**ON**
Max arc Radius:	**1000.0**

Press the **Enter** key to accept the parameters

5 The system will prompt the following menu:

Original entities:	**768**
Current lines:	**370**
Current arcs:	**106**
Current entities:	**476**
Tolerance used:	**0.025**
Entity reduction:	**38.02%**

Select **Yes** to accept this conversion
The new drawing after conversion becomes Figure 19.17.

Figure 19.17

Step 4. Export the converted file buck-new.

Select **File → Export → DXF**
Select **No** to "This file already exists. Overwrite?"
Enter a new name: **buck-new**

Step 5. Exit InterFlux program.

Select **File → Exit**

Project 5. Engraving the drawing of a buck image

This project uses the edited drawing (buck-new) in project 4 to engrave the buck image on a rectangular block. Figure 19.18 shows the drawing, toolpath and verification model of the project.

Figure 19.18a

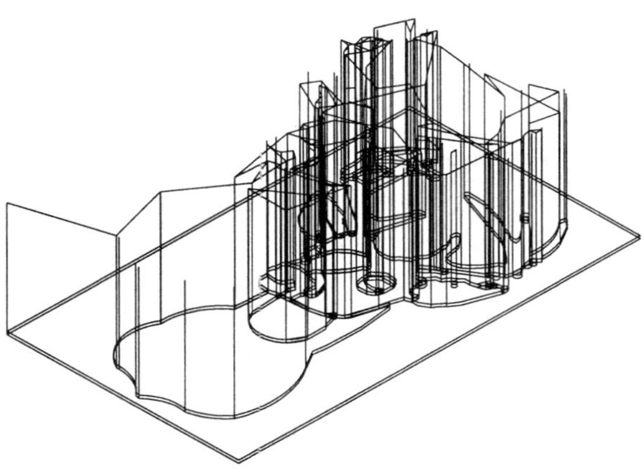

Figure 19.18b

Figure 19.18c

Step 1. Import a DXF file buck-new.

Select **MAIN MENU → File → Converters → DXF → Read file**
File name to read: **buck-new**
The vector drawing is imported as in Figure 19.19.

Figure 19.19

Step 2. Delete the duplicate entities.

Select **MAIN MENU → Delete → Duplicate → Entities**
The system will prompt "0 points, 48 lines, 2 arcs, 0 splines, 0 surfaces deleted"
Press the **Enter** key to continue

Step 3. Initiate the contour function.

Select **MAIN MENU → Toolpaths → Contour**
Enter file name for NCI: **buck**
Select **Window**, then pick two points to include all entities
Pick the lower-left corner to select the search point
Select **Done**

Step 4. Select a 1/32" ball-end mill and define the tool parameters.

Click the right mouse button, then select "Get tool from library"
Select **tool #246** (1/32" sphere end mill)
Select **OK**
Set the tool parameters as below.

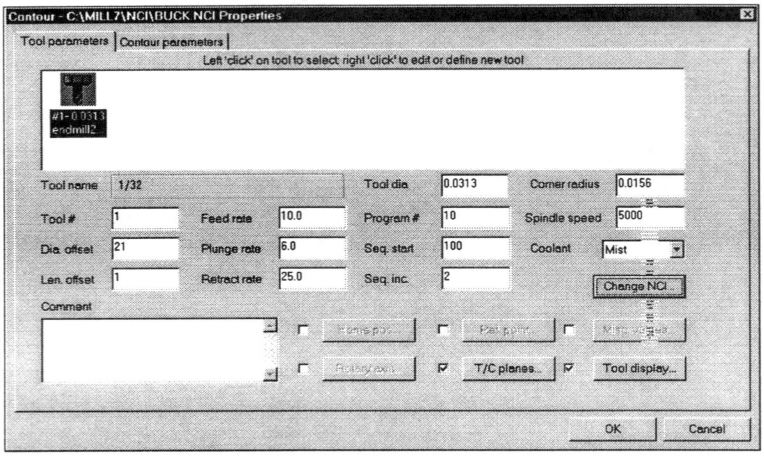

Step 5. Define the contour parameters.

Select the "Contour parameters" button
Define the contour parameters as below.

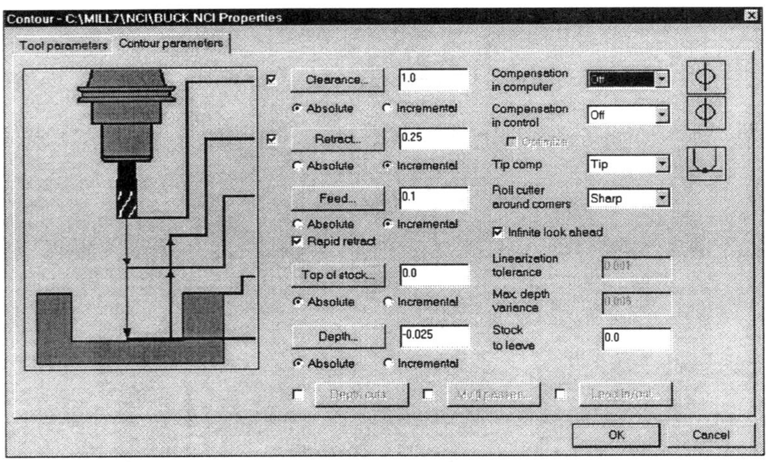

Select **OK** to generate contouring toolpaths
Select **Gview → Isometric**

The engraving toolpaths are shown in Figure 19.20.

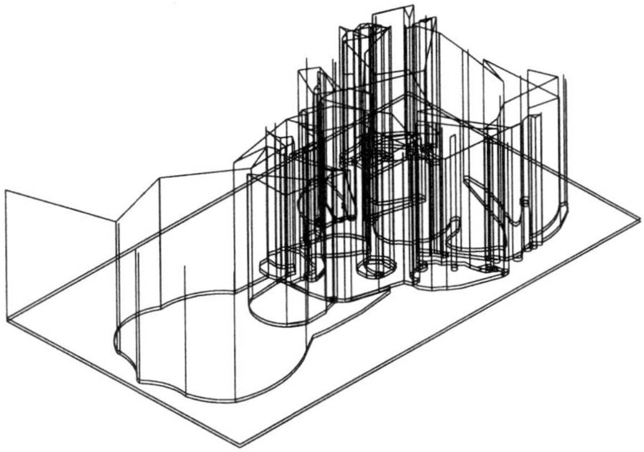

Figure 19.20

Step 6. Verify the toolpaths with N-See 2000.

Select **Operations → N-See 2000**

Select **Preview → OK** from "Select mode for current job" menu

Select **Do it** to verify the toolpaths on the screen

The toolpaths are animated on the screen and its final model should appear as Figure 19.21.

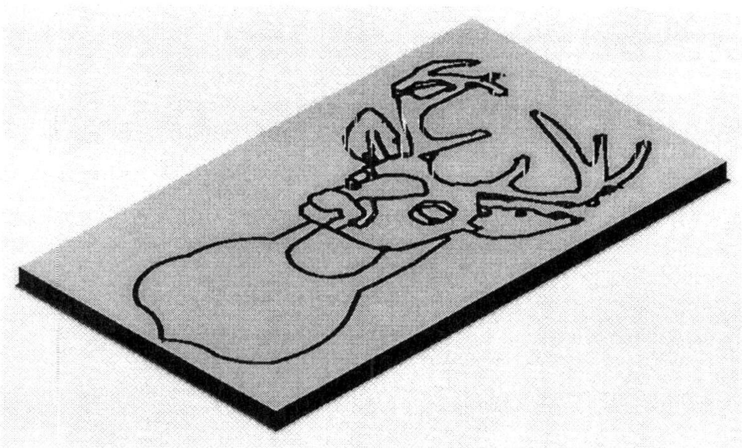

Figure 19.21

Select **BACKUP → OK** to return to graphic mode

Step 7. Save the toolpath model.

Select **MAIN MENU → File → Save**

File name to save: **buck**

Exercises

1. What are bitmap images?
2. What are the two commonly used programs for converting bitmap images into vector drawings?
3. Explain how to represent graphics in the bitmap form.
4. List at least three ways for creating bitmap images.
5. What are vector drawings?
6. Describe the contrast between bitmap images and vector artworks.
7. What is the main function of Adobe Streamline?
8. Explain the effect of three edge smoothing options.
9. Describe the function of Threshold parameter.
10. Describe the function of Boost parameter.
11. List the three conversion methods used in Adobe Streamline.
12. List the commands used to import a vector drawing to Mastercam.
13. List the commands used to delete those duplicated entities.
14. Describe the main function of using InterFlux program.
15. What is the main modify function to reduce the number of entities in InterFlux?
16. Describe the function of "close open contours".
17. Describe the function of "close between contours".
18. Describe the function of "Collapse small contours."
19. Describe the following four parameters under Transform function in InterFlux:
    Scale
    Force
    Translate
    Group

Chapter 20
Creating Part Geometry for Lathes

Objectives:

1. Lathe basics of coordinate systems, program zero, radius and diameter dimensioning.
2. Create part geometry for lathes.

Overview

Many machining operations can be performed in a CNC lathe. These operation include **facing, turning, profiling, grooving, drilling, boring, threading, chamfering, cutting off**, and **milling** (in mill-turn machines). Chapters 1 and 2 presented essential facts about CNC programming, machining, and operation. This chapter shows how to generate part programs for cutting parts with CNC lathes. It begins with lathe basics and is followed by part geometry creation, toolpath modules, common parameters, and several examples of using various toolpath modules.

20.1 Coordinate Systems of CNC Lathes

Most CNC controls for lathes provide for controlling **two basic axes**. The axis and direction designation for a two-axis lathe are illustrated in Figure 20.1. The Z axis is parallel to the spindle axis and represents the carriage travel in the longitudinal direction. The X axis is perpendicular to the Z axis and represents the cross slide travel. The direction designations for the Z and X axes are given below.

+Z	Tool carriage moves away from the spindle head
-Z	Tool carriage moves away toward the spindle head
+X	Cross slide moves away from the spindle axis
-X	Cross slide moves away toward the spindle axis

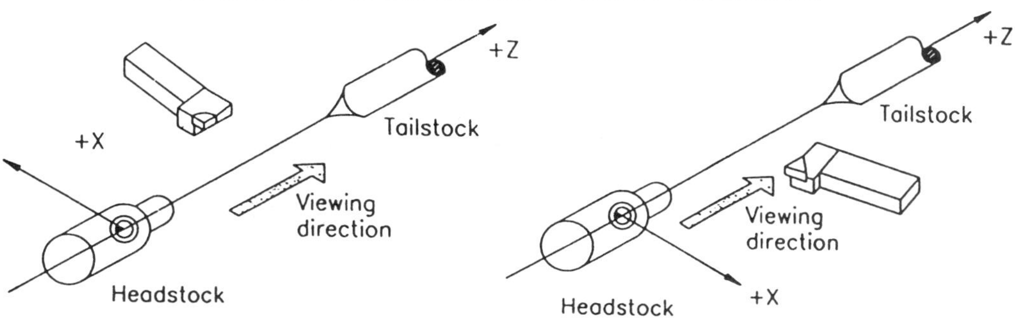

a. Left-handed (slant bed) b. Right-handed (Standard)

Figure 20.1. Coordinate System of CNC lathes

The coordinate system of a lathe can be either right-handed or left-handed, depending on which side of the spindle axis the turret is located.

Left-Handed Coordinate System

The turret is located to the left of the spindle center line (Z axis) when viewing the spindle axis from the headstock toward the tailstock (Figure 20.1a) in the left-handed coordinate system. Slant bed lathes use the left-handed coordinate system. Most CNC lathes use this left-handed coordinate system.

Right-Handed Coordinate System

The turret is located to the right of the spindle center line when observing from the headstock toward the tailstock (Figure 20.1b) in the right-handed coordinate system. Standard bed lathes use the right-handed coordinate system. Most desktop CNC lathes have the right-handed coordinate system.

20.2 Selection of Program Zero (Origin)

The program origin must be chosen before the part geometry can be created. There are two common ways to select program zero for lathe works: located at right end face of the part (Figure 20.2a) and located at the chuck fae (Figure 20.2b). The common practice in most shops is to use the right end face of the part as the program origin.

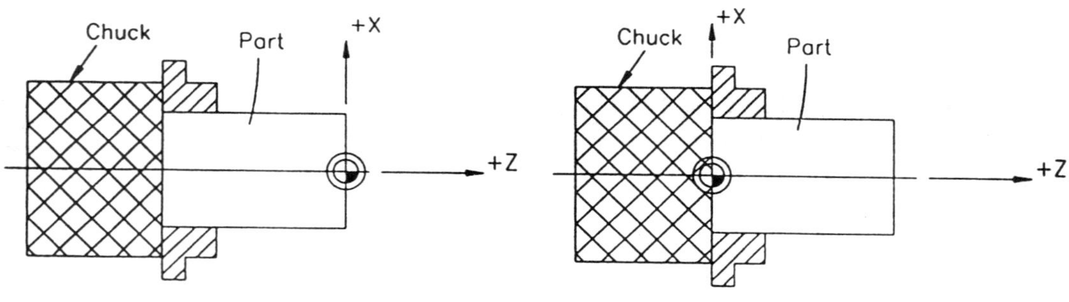

a. At Right face of the part b. At the chuck face

Figure 20.2. Selection of Program Zero

20.3 Radius and Diameter Dimensioning

The dimensions in the X direction can be specified in two ways: **radius** and **diameter dimensioning**. Mastercam uses the prefix letter X to indicate the radius value input and the letter D to specify the diameter value input. Table 1. Shows the coordinate values of the significant points for the part shown in Figure 20.3. Both radius and diameter values of X coordinates are given

Table 1. Radius and diameter dimensioning

Point	X-coordinate Radius input	X-coordinate Diameter input	Z-coordinate
O	0	0	0
A	X0.5	D1.0	0
B	X0.5	D1.0	-1.0
C	X0.75	D1.5	-1.0
D	X0.75	D1.5	-2.0
E	X1.25	D2.5	-2.0
F	X1.25	D2.5	-3.0

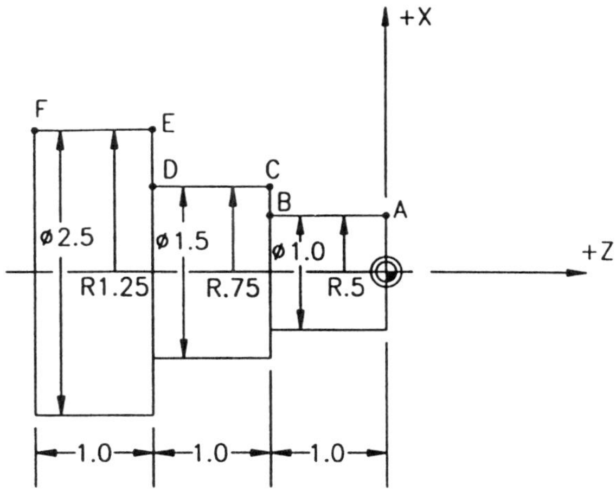

Figure 20.3. Radius and Diameter dimensioning

Mastercam provides an option parameter to specify the axis designation. It can be toggled to one of following **three options**:

Mill axis Create geometry elements in a 3-D space which is defined by three mutually perpendicular axes. The isometric view and top view of three mill axes are shown in Figure 20.4a.

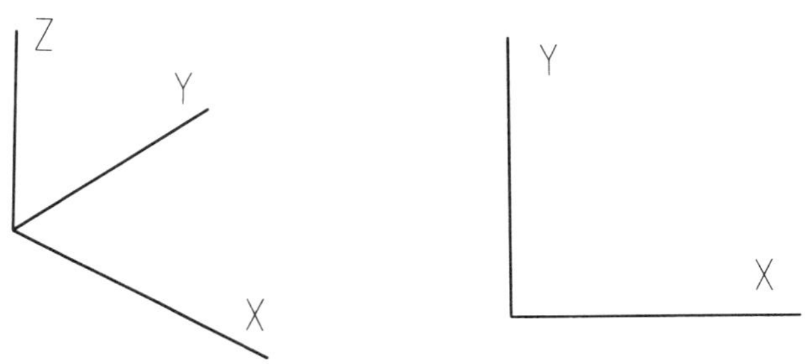

Isometric view Top view

Figure 20.4a Mill axis

Lathe Rad Create geometry for lathes in a 2-D plane which is defined by two perpendicular axes. The horizontal direction is Z axis and vertical direction X axis. The coordinate of X axis is specified in the radius value. Figure 20.4b shows the isometric view and top view of the Lathe Rad axis system.

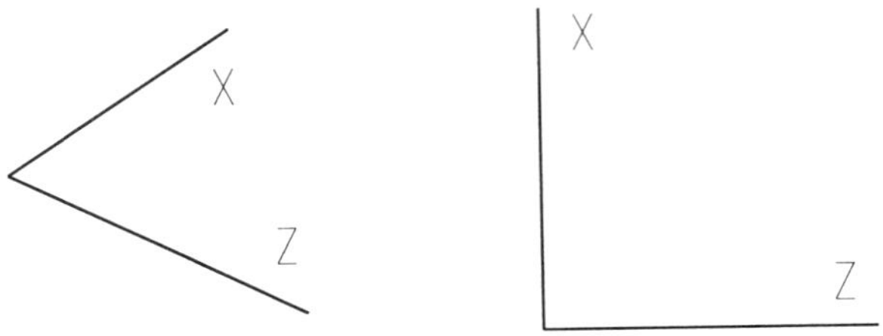

Isometric view Top view

Figure 20.4b Lathe Rad axis

Lathe Dia The Axes designation is the same as the Lathe Rad option except that the coordinate of the X axis is specified in the diameter value. Figure 20.4c shows the isometric view and top view of the Lathe Dia axis system.

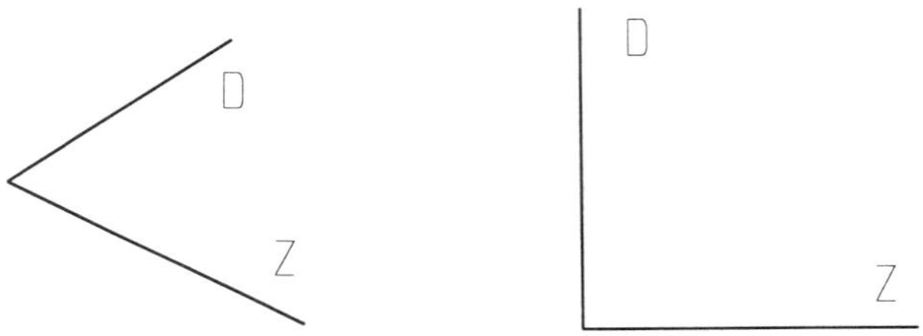

Isometric view Top view

Figure 20.4c Lathe Dia axis

Using the diameter mode is the more common practice when selecting the programming mode for the X axis in CNC lathe. Diameter programming is the default mode unless it is specified otherwise. We will use the diameter programming mode in this text.

The selection of the cplane affects the part geometry created using the same set of input data. Figure 20.5 shows an example of using four different cplanes to create the part geometry from the same input data set for the multi-line command group as below

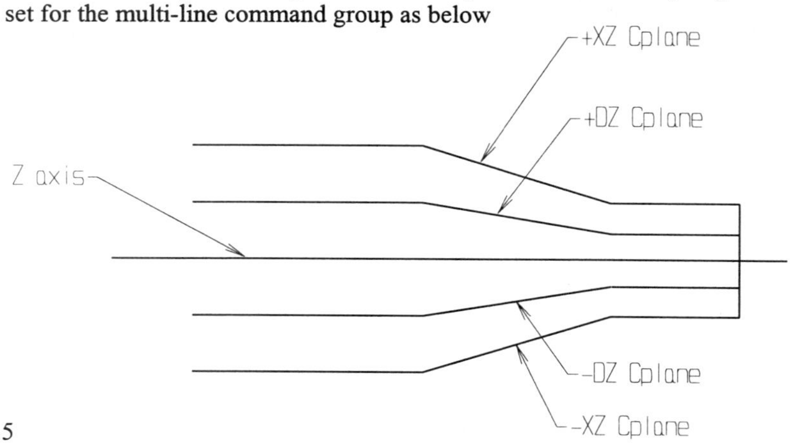

Figure 20.5

Creating Part Geometry

Most parts machined on a CNC lathe are symmetrical about the Z axis. Therefore, they require only one-half of the part geometry to be created. The techniques used in previous chapters for creating and editing part geometries for milling parts are applicable for turning except for the following two differences: 1

Only two axes (X and Z) are used
Horizontal direction represents the Z axis and the vertical direction is the X axis

Six projects with step-by-step instructions are presented in this section.

Project 1. Internal boring operation

Creating a part profile for an internal boring operation. The drawing is shown in Figure 20.6. Save the geometry as turn1.

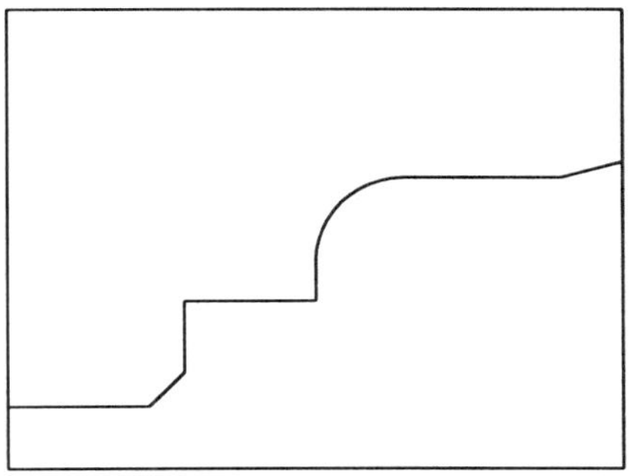

Figure 20.6

Tip

1. Set the axis to lathe diameter
2. Create an internal profile on level 1.
3. Create another external profile on level 2.
4. Save the file as turn1.

Step 1. Change the axis designation to Lathe Diameter and the view to top view.

Toggle on the word "Cplane" from the control menu
Select the **Next menu → +dz**
Toggle on the word **"Gview" → Top**

Step 2. Create five lines.

Select **MAIN MENU → Create → Line →Multi**
Sequentially input the following six sets of point coordinate value:

D value	Z value
3.5	-0.35
3.5	-1.75
2.0	-1.75
2.0	-2.5
0.75	-2.5
0.75	-3.5

Click on **Alt+F1** simultaneously then **F2** to adjust the size of the drawing
The five elements are created as in Figure 20.7.

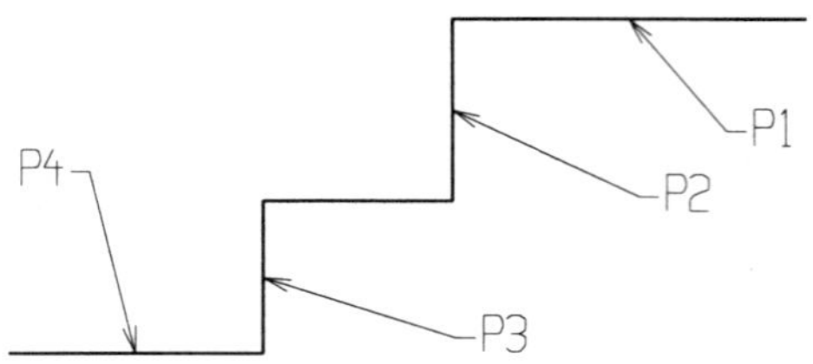

Figure 20.7

Step 3. Add a fillet and a chamfer.

Use the pick points in Figure 20.7.
Select **MAIN MENU →** **Create →** **Fillet →** **Radius**
Enter the fillet radius **0.5**
Pick **P1** and **P2** to create a fillet
Select **Back up →** **Next menu →** **Chamfer →** **Distances**
Enter the first distance **0.2**
Enter the second distance **0.2**
Pick **P3** and **P4** to complete the chamfer
The new drawing now becomes Figure 20.8.

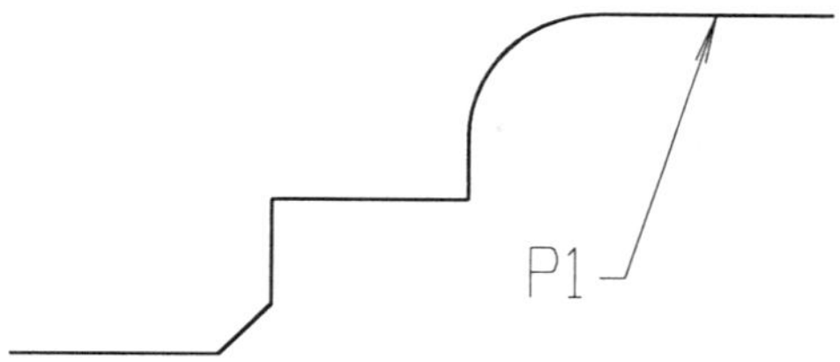

Figure 20.8

Step 4. Add a line using the pick point in Figure 20.8.

Select **MAIN MENU →** **Create →** **Line →** **Polar →** **Endpoint**
Pick **P1**
Enter the angle in degrees **15**
Enter the line length **0.75**

The slope line is added as in Figure 20.9.

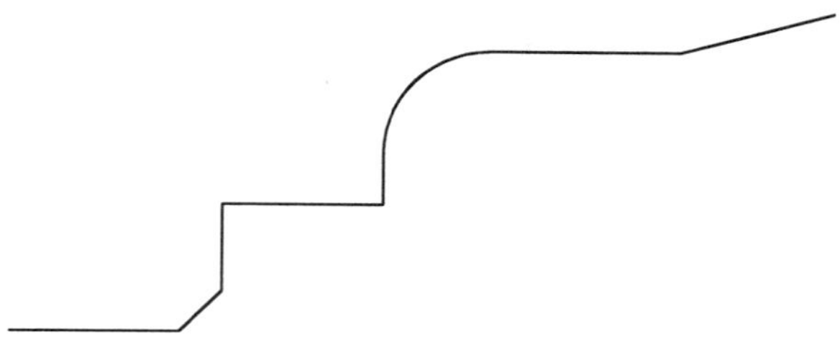

Figure 20.9

Step 5. Change level and its color.

Toggle on the word "**Level** " from the control panel
Enter **2**, then select **OK**
Toggle on the word "**Color**" from the control panel
Select **12** → Red), then select **OK**

Step 6. Add a rectangle to represent the stock.

Select **MAIN MENU** → **Create** → **Rectangle** → **2 points**
Enter the lower left corner coordinate **(0,-3.5)**
Enter the height coordinate **(5.5,0)**

The rectangle is added as Figure 20.10.

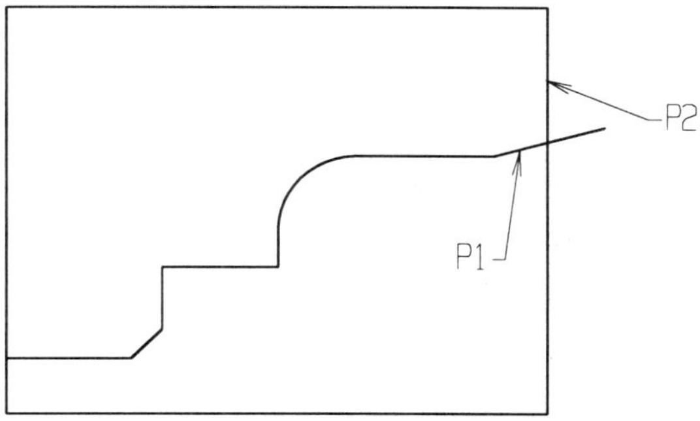

Figure 20.10

Step 7. Trim the slope line to the rectangle.

Use the pick point in Figure 20.10.
Select **MAIN MENU** → **Modify** → **Trim** → **1 entity**
Pick **P1**, then **P2**

The final drawing becomes Figure 20.11.

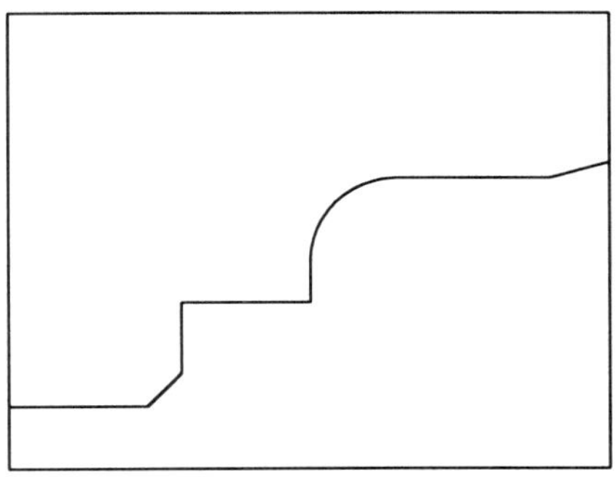

Figure 20.11

Step 8. Save the geometry model as turn1.

Select **MAIN MENU** → **File** → **Save**
File name: **turn1**

2 Project 2. Creating a profile

This project creates a profile as shown in Figure 12. The profile will be used to generate roughing and finishing toolpaths to cut the part. Save the geometry file as turn2.

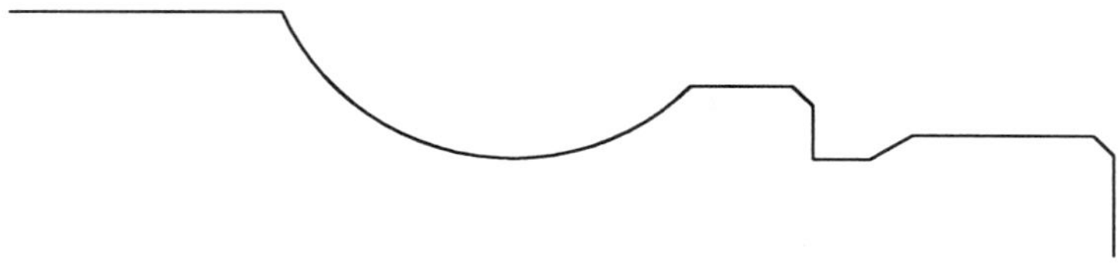

Figure 20.12.

Tip	
	1. Create the profile using various Create and Modify functions.
	2. Save the file as turn2.

Step 1. Set to the Lathe Diameter and top view.

Toggle on the word "**Cplane**" from the control menu
Select **Next menu** → **+dz**
Toggle on the word "**Gview**" → **Top**

Step 2. Create two lines.

Select **MAIN MENU** → **Create** → **Line** → **Multi**
Enter the following sets of coordinates:

D value	Z value
0.0	0.0
1.25	0.0
1.25	-1.0

Click on **Alt+F1** simultaneously, then **F2** to adjust the size of the drawing
Two lines are created as Figure 20.13.

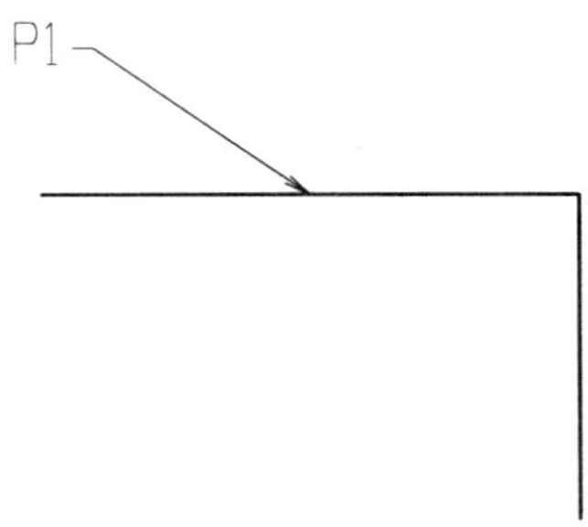

Figure 20.13.

Step 3. Create a slope line using the pick point in Figure 20.13.

Select **MAIN MENU** → **Create** → **Line** → **Polar** → **Endpoint**
Pick **P1**
Enter angle in degrees: **210**
Enter the line length: **0.3**

The slope line is added as Figure 20.14.

Figure 20.14

Step 3. Create a three-line string.

Select **Backup →** **Multi**

Enter the following sets of coordinates

D value	Z value
1.0	-0.7
1.0	-1.5
1.75	-1.5
1.75	-2.75

The three lines are added as in Figure 20.15.

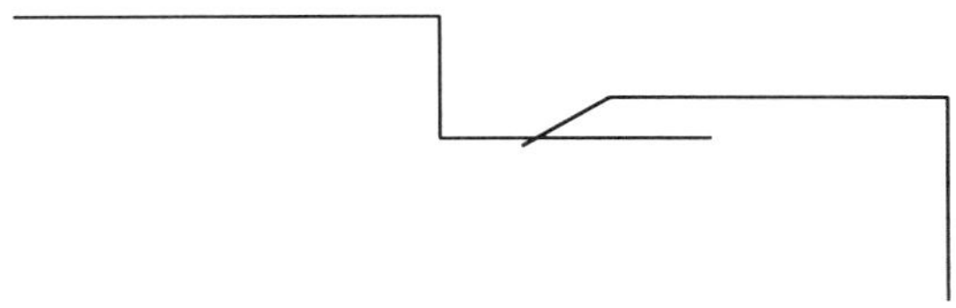

Figure 20.15

Step 4. Add another line segment.

Select **Backup →** **Endpoints**

Enter the start and end points coordinates as below

D value	Z value
2.5	-3.5
2.5	-5.5

The new drawing now becomes Figure 20.16.

Figure 20.16

Step 5. Create an arc.

Select **Backup →** **Backup →** **Arc →** **Polar →** **Center pt**

Input the following parameters to create an arc

Center point coordinate	(3.5,-3.0)
Radius	1.25
Initial angle	180
Final angle	360

The arc is added as in Figure 20.17.

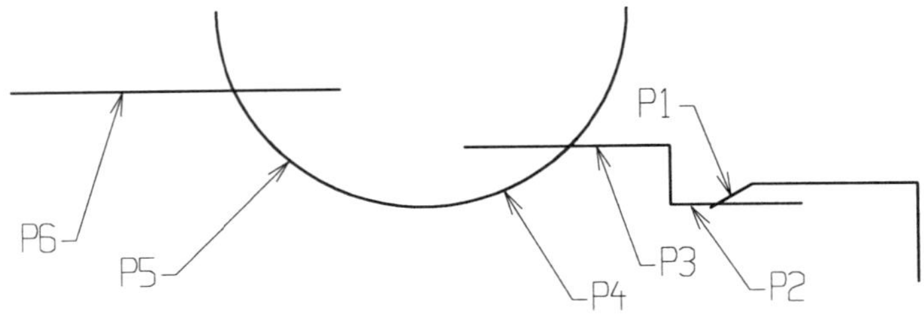

Figure 20.17

Step 6. Trim five entities.

Use the pick points in Figure 20.17.

Select **MAIN MENU →** **Modify →** **Trim →** **2 entities**

Sequentially pick **P1 – P6** to trim five entities

The result is shown in Figure 20.18.

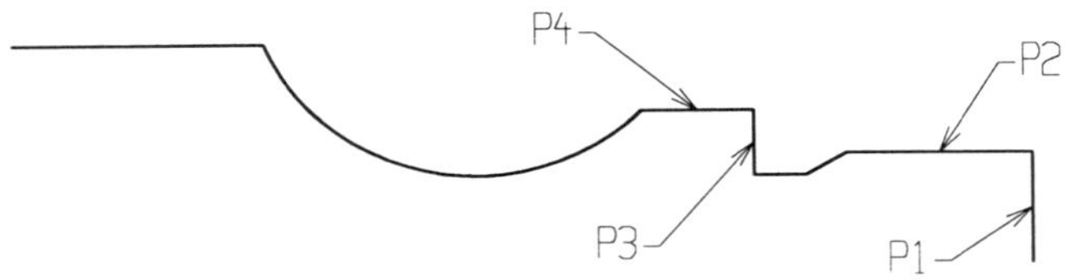

Figure 20.18

Step 7. Add two chamfers.

Use the pick points in Figure 20.18.

Select **MAIN MENU →** **Create →** **Next menu →** **Chamfer →** **Distances**

Enter the first distance: **0.1**

Enter the second distance: **0.1**

Sequentially pick **P1 – P4** to add two chamfers

The drawing appears as Figure 20.19.

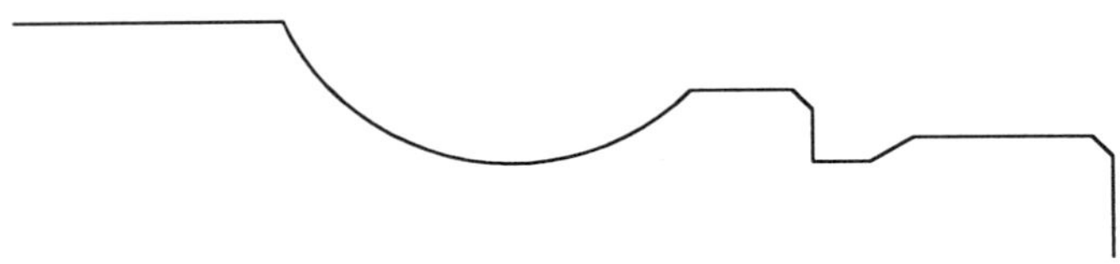
Figure 20.19

Step 8. Save the geometry files as turn2.

Select **MAIN MENU →** **Files→** **Save**

File name: **turn2**

Project 3. Internal and external profiles

Create a geometry file that consists of an internal profile and an external profile (Figure 20.20). Save the geometry file as turn3.

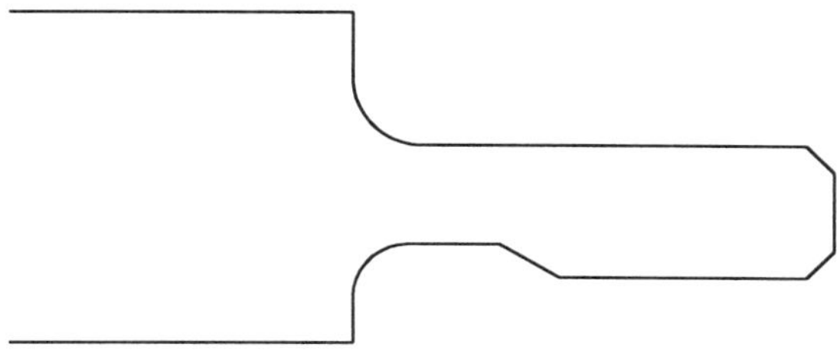

Figure 20.20

Tips
1. Create two levels; one for external profile, the other for internal profile.
2. Create the external profile in level 1.
3. Create the internal profile in level 2.
4. Save the geometry file as turn3.

Step 1. Create a four-line string.

Select **MAIN MENU** → **Create** → **Line** → **Multi**

Enter the following five sets of point coordinates:

D value	Z value
0.0	0.0
2.5	0.0
2.5	-1.75
3.5	-1.75
3.5	-3.0

Click on Alt+F1 simultaneously → F2 to adjust the size of the drawing

The four lines are created as in Figure 20.21.

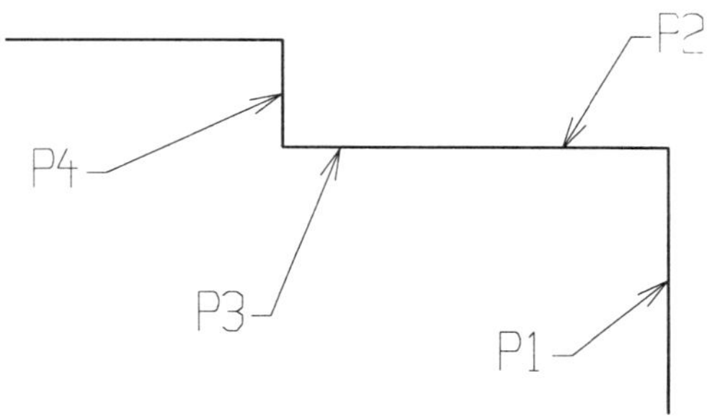

Figure 20.21

Step 2. Add a chamfer and a fillet.

Use the pick points in Figure 20.21.
Select **MAIN MENU →** **Create →** **Next menu →** **Chamfer →** **Distances**
Enter the first distance: **0.1**
Enter the second distance: **0.1**
Pick **P1** and **P2** to create a chamfer
Select **BACKUP →** **Fillet →** **Radius**
Enter the fillet radius: **0.25**
Pick **P3** and **P4** to add a fillet

The external profile should resemble Figure 20.22.

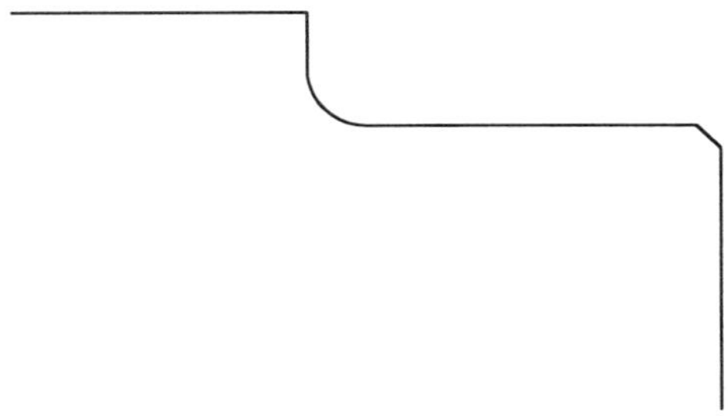

Figure 20.22

Step 3. Change level and color.

Click on the level icon from the control panel
Enter level: **2 →** **OK**

Click on the color icon from the control panel
Enter **12 →** **red) →** **OK**

Step 4. Create two lines.

Select **MAIN MENU →** **Create →** **Line →** **Endpoints**
Set the point coordinates as below for the first line

D value	Z value
1.5	0.0
1.5	-1.0

Select **BACKUP →** **Polar →** **Values**
Enter coordinate: **(1.5,-1.0)**
Enter angle in degrees: **150**
Enter line length: **0.4**

The new drawing now becomes as Figure 20.23.

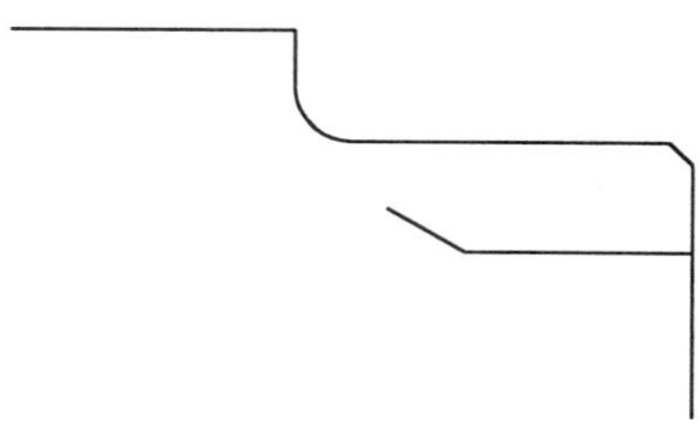

Figure 20.23

Step 5. Create a three-line string.

Select **BACKUP →** **BACKUP →** **Multi**
Enter the following four sets of point data

D value	Z value
1.75	-1.1
1.75	-1.75
1.0	-1.75
1.0	-3.0

The drawing appears as Figure 20.24.

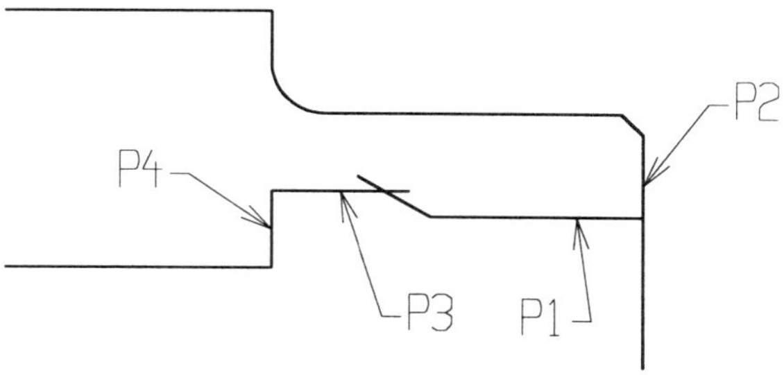

Figure 20.24

Step 6. Add a chamfer and a fillet.

Use the pick points in Figure 20.24.
Select **MAIN MENU →** **Create →** **Next menu →** **Chamfer →** **Distances**
Enter the first distance: **0.1.**
Enter the second distance: **0.1**

Pick **P1** and **P2** to add the chamfer
Select **BACKUP →** **BACKUP →** **Fillet →** **Radius**
Enter the fillet radius: **0.2**
Pick **P3** and **P4**

The drawing becomes Figure 20.25.

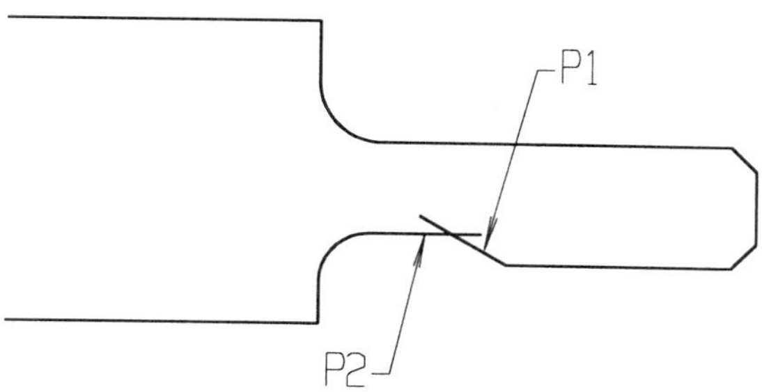

Figure 20.25

Step 7. Trim two lines.

Use the pick points in Figure 20.25.
Select **MAIN MENU →** **Modify →** **Trim →** **2 entities**
Pick **P1** and **P2**

4 The final drawing becomes Figure 20.26.

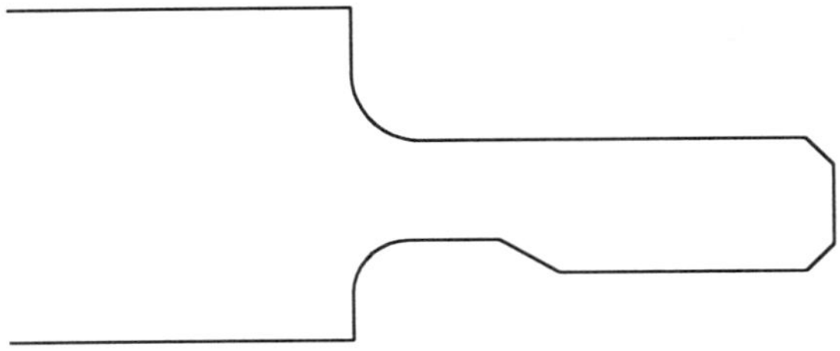

Figure 20.26

Step 8. Save the geometry file as turn3.

Select **MAIN MENU →** **File →** **Save**
File name: **turn3**

Project 4. Profile for external turning

This project creates a profile as shown in Figure 20.27 for external turning. Save the geometry file as turn4.

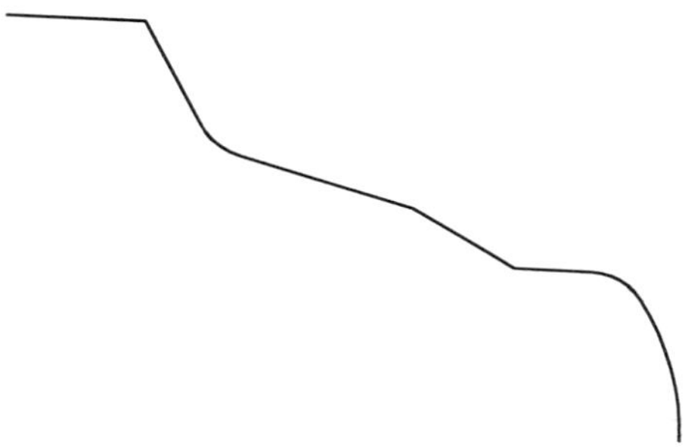

Figure 20.27

Step 1. Create an arc.

Select **MAIN MENU →** **Create →** **Arc →** **Polar →** **Center pt**
Set the center coordinate at **(0.0, -1.5)**
Set the arc parameters as below

Radius	1.5
Initial angle	0
Final angle	90

Click on **Alt+F1** simultaneously, then **F2** to adjust the size of the drawing

The arc is added as Figure 20.28.

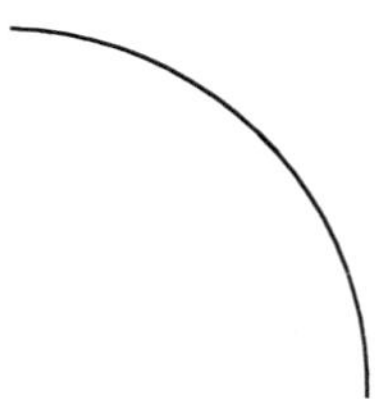

Figure 20.28

Step 2. Create two lines.

Select **MAIN MENU (Create → Line → Endpoints**

Enter the following point coordinates

D value	Z value
2.0	-0.2
2.0	-1.0

Select **BACKUP → Polar → Values**

Enter coordinate: **(2.0,-1.0)**

Enter angle in degrees: **150**

Enter line length: **0.693**

The drawing appears as Figure 20.29.

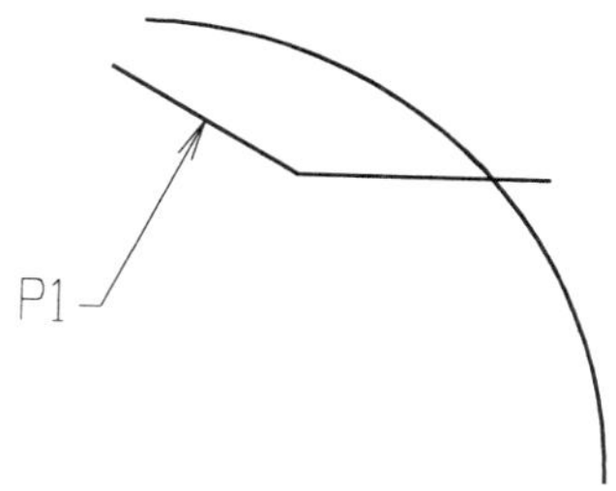

Figure 20.29

Step 3. Add two slope lines.

Use the pick points in Figure 20.29.

Select **BACKUP → Polar → Endpoint**

Pick **P1**

Enter angle in degree: **165**

Enter line length: **2.5**

Select **Values**

Enter point coordinates: **(4.8,-3.2)**

Enter angle in degrees: **-60**

Enter line length: **1.5**

The two slopes are added as Figure 20.30.

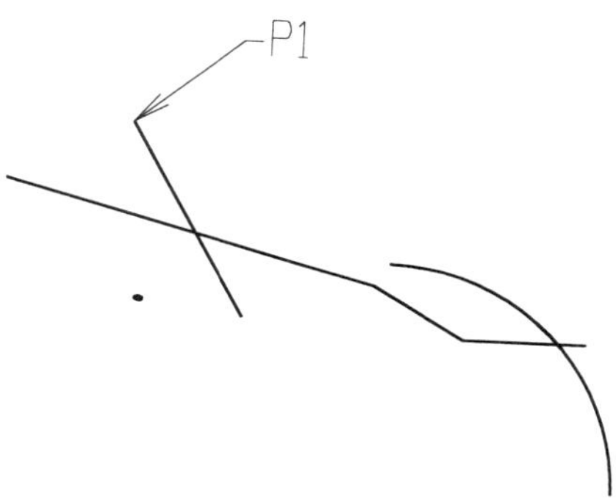

Figure 20.30

Step 4. Add a horizontal line using the pick point in Figure 20.30.

Select **MAIN MENU →** **Create →** **Line →** **Endpoints →** **Endpoint**
Pick **P1**
Enter coordinates: **(4.8,-4.0)**

The new drawing now becomes as Figure 20.31.

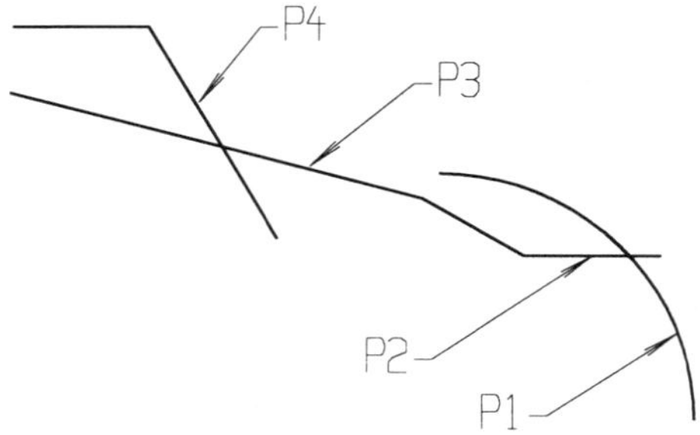

Figure 20.31

Step 5. Add two fillets.

Use the pick points in Figure 20.31.
Select **MAIN MENU →** **Create →** **Fillet →** **Radius**
Enter fillet radius: **0.35**
Pick **P1** and **P2** to add a fillet
Select **Radius**
Enter fillet radius: **0.4**
Pick **P3** and **P4**

The final drawing should look like Figure 20.32.

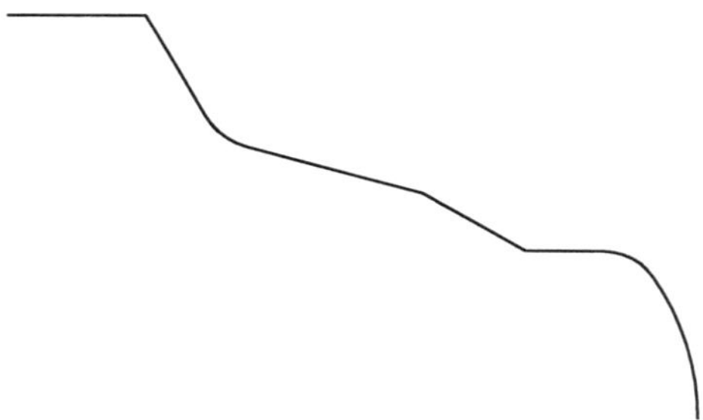

Figure 20.32

Step 6. Save the geometry file as turn4.

Select **MAIN MENU →** **File →** **Save**
File name: **turn4**

Project 5. Profile for roughing and finishing toolpaths

This project creates a profile as shown in Figure 20.33. The profile is used to generate facing, roughing and finishing toolpaths in the next chapter. Save the geometry file as turn5.

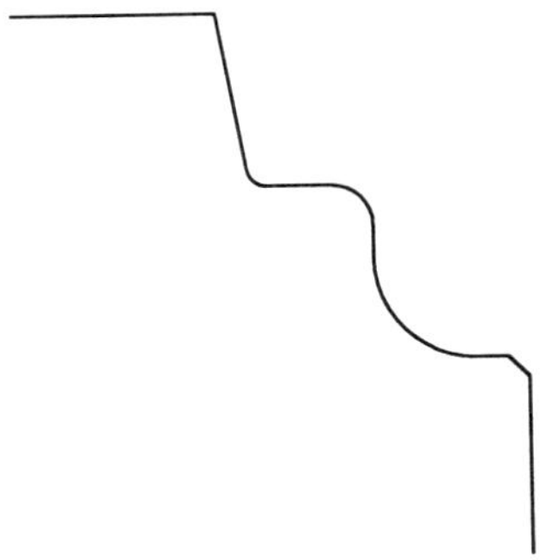

Figure 20.33

Step 1. Set the Cplane to diameter and Gview to Top view.

Toggle on the word "**Cplane**" from the control menu
Select **Next menu** → **+dz**
Toggle on the word "**Gview**" → **Top**

Step 2. Create a four-line string.

Select **MAIN MENU** → **Create** → **Line** → **Multi**
Enter the following five sets of point coordinates

D value	Z value
0.0	0.0
2.0	0.0
2.0	-0.75
3.75	-0.75
3.75	-1.5

Click on **Alt+F1** simultaneously, then **F2** to adjust the size of the drawing

The four lines appear as Figure 20.34.

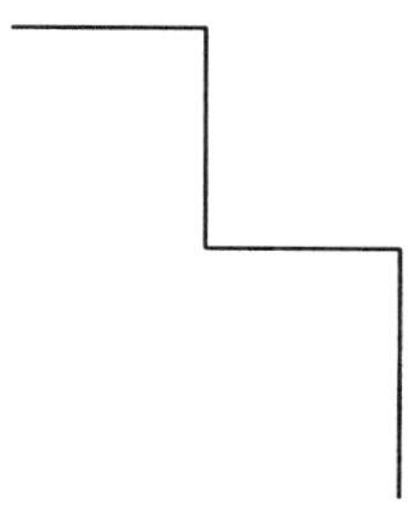

Figure 20.34

Step 3. Add two lines.

Select **BACKUP →** **Polar →** **Values**
Enter coordinates: **(5.5,-1.5)**
Enter angle in degrees: **-80**
Enter line length: **1.25** to complete the first line

Select **BACKUP →** **Endpoints**
Enter coordinates: **(5.5,-1.5)** and **(5.5,-2.5)**

The new drawing appears as Figure 20.35.

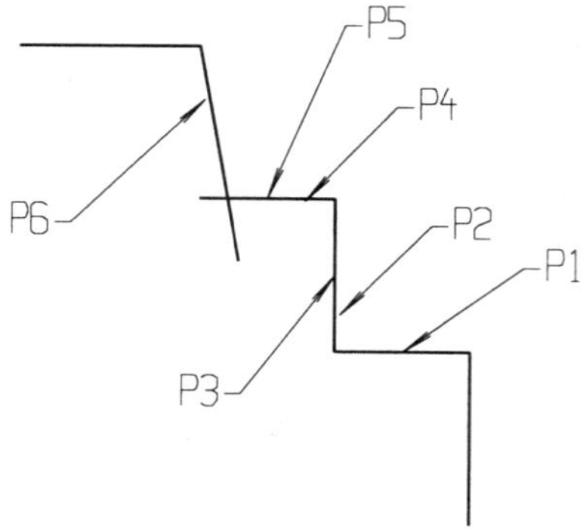

Figure 20.35

Step 4. Add three fillets using the pick points in Figure 20.35.

Select **MAIN MENU →** **Create →** **Fillet →** **Radius**
Enter fillet radius: **0.5**
Pick **P1** and **P2** to create the first fillet
Select **Radius**
Enter a new fillet radius: **0.2**
Pick **P3** and **P4** to create the second fillet
Select **Radius**
Enter fillet radius: **0.1**
Pick **P5** and **P6** to add the third fillet

The three added fillets are shown in Figure 20.36.

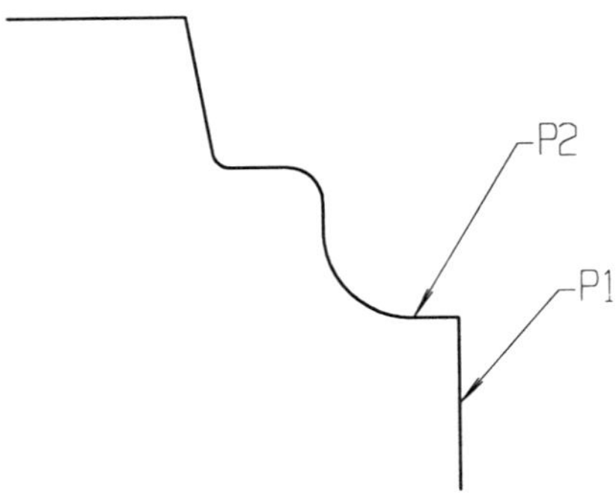

Figure 20.36

Step 5. Add a chamfer.

Use the pick points in Figure 20.36.
Select **MAIN MENU →** **Create →** **Next menu →** **Chamfer →** **Distances**
Enter the first distance: **0.1**
Enter the second distance: **0.1**
Pick **P1** and **P2**

The final drawing becomes Figure 20.37.

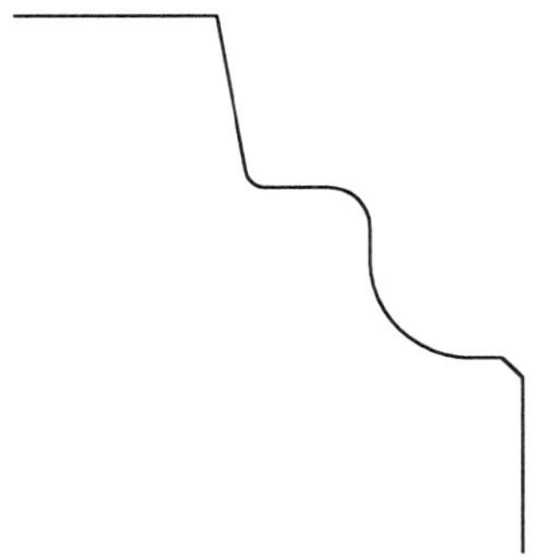

Figure 20.37

Step 6. Save the geometry file as turn5.

Select **MAIN MENU →** **File →** **Save**
File name: **turn5**

Project 6. Lathe toolpath function

This project creates a geometry model that requires the use various lathe toolpath functions to generate a toolpath to cut this part. The geometry consists of two profiles; external profile and internal profile (Figure 20.38).

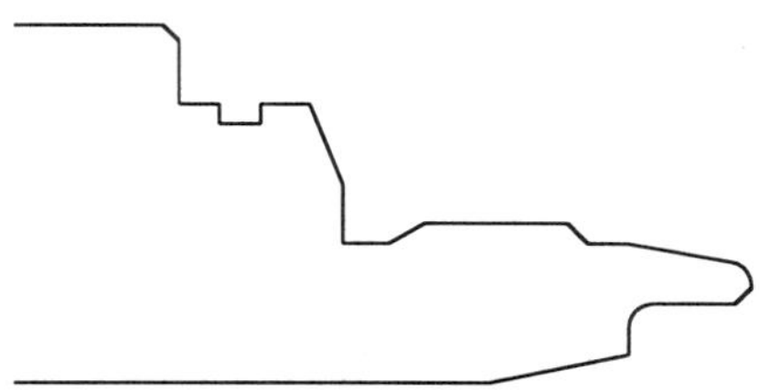

Figure 20.38.

Tip

1. Create two levels, one for an external profile, the other for an internal profile.
2. Use various Creating and Editing functions to create the external profile in level 1.
3. Create the internal profile in level 2.
4. Save the geometry file as turn6.

Step 1. Set the proper views.

Toggle on the word "**Cplane**" from the control menu
Select **Next menu →** **+dz**
Toggle on the word "**Gview**" **→** **Top**

Step 2. Create a string of five lines.

Select **MAIN MENU →** **Create →** **Line →** **Multi**
Enter the following six sets of point coordinates

D value	Z value
6.0	-4.5
6.0	-3.5
5.0	-3.5
5.0	-2.5
3.25	-2.5
3.25	-2.0

Click on **Alt+F1** simultaneously, then **F2** to adjust the size of the drawing

The five lines appear as in Figure 20.39.

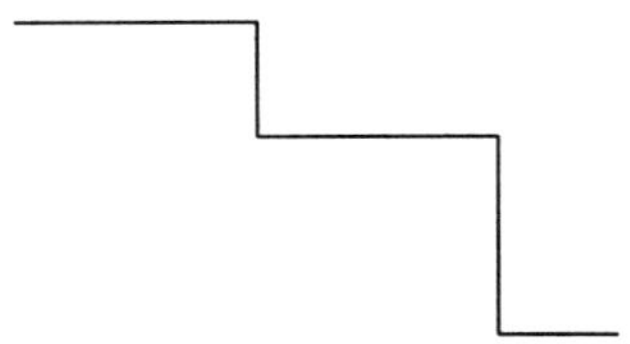

Figure 20.39

Step 3. Create two lines.

Select **MAIN MENU →** **Create →** **Line →** **Endpoints**
Enter the point coordinates: **(3.5,-2.0)** and **(3.5,-0.9)** to complete the first line
Select **BACKUP →** **Polar →** **Values**
Enter coordinates: **(3.5,-2.0)**
Enter angle in degrees: **210**
Enter line length: **0.5** to complete the second line

The new drawing becomes Figure 20.40.

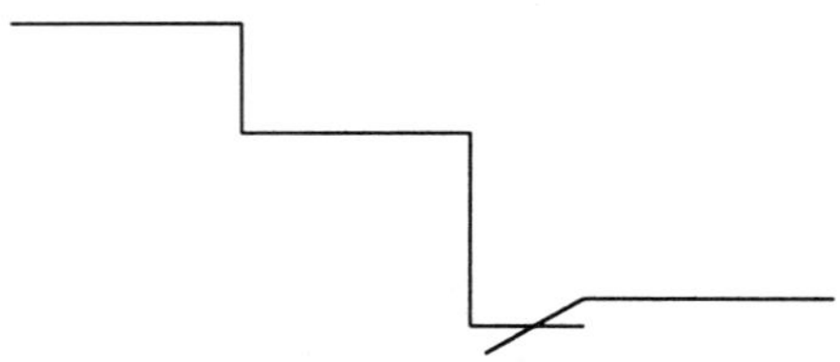

Figure 20.40

Step 4. Add three lines.

Select **BACKUP →** **Endpoints**
Enter point coordinates: **(3.25,-1.0)** and **(3.25,-0.75)** to complete the first line
Select **BACKUP →** **Polar →** **Values**

Enter coordinates: **(3.25,-1.0)**
Enter angle in degrees: **135**
Enter line length: **0.5**
Select **Values**
Enter coordinates: **(3.25,-0.75)**
Enter angle in degrees: **-10**
Enter line length: **1.5**

The three lines appear as Figure 20.41.

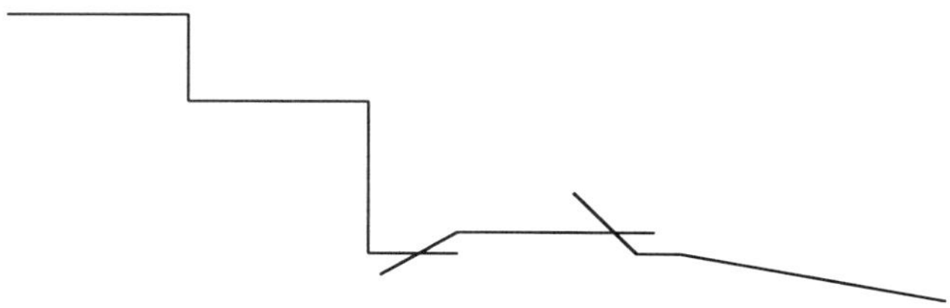

Figure 20.41

Step 5. Add a vertical line.

Select **BACKUP →** **Endpoints**
Enter the point coordinates: **(0,0)** and **(3.5,0)**

The vertical line is added as Figure 20.42.

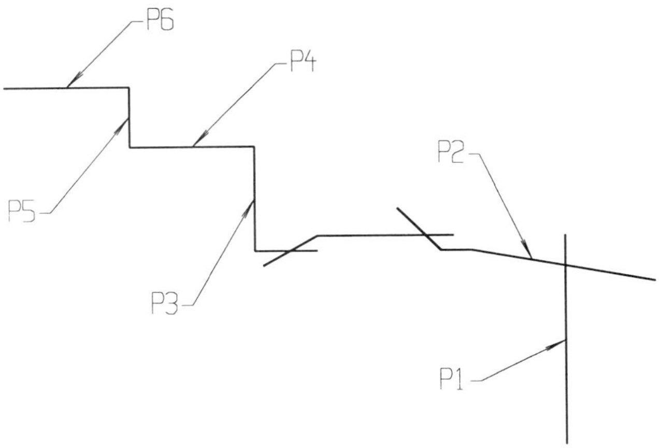

Figure 20.42

Step 6. Add a fillet and two chamfers.

Use the pick points in Figure 20.42.
Select **MAIN MENU →** **Create →** **Fillet →** **Radius**
Enter fillet radius: **0.15**
Pick **P1** and **P2** to create the fillet

Select **BACKUP →** **Next menu →** **Chamfer →** **Distances**
Enter the first distance: **0.5**
Enter the second distance: **0.2**
Sequentially pick **P3** and **P4** to create the first chamfer

Select **Distances**
Enter the first distance: **0.1**
Enter the second distance: **0.1**
Pick **P5** and **P6** to complete the second chamfer

The new drawing now becomes as Figure 20.43.

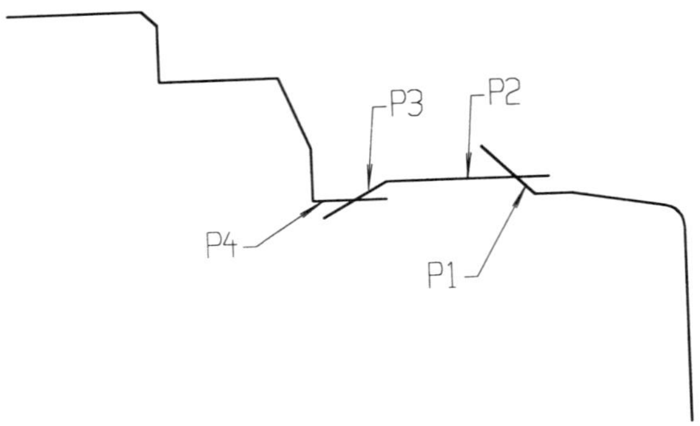

Figure 20.43

Step 7. Trim four lines.

Use the pick points in Figure 20.43.
Select **MAIN MENU →** **Modify →** **Trim →** **2 entities**
Sequentially pick **P1 – P4** to trim four lines

The new drawing resembles Figure 20.44.

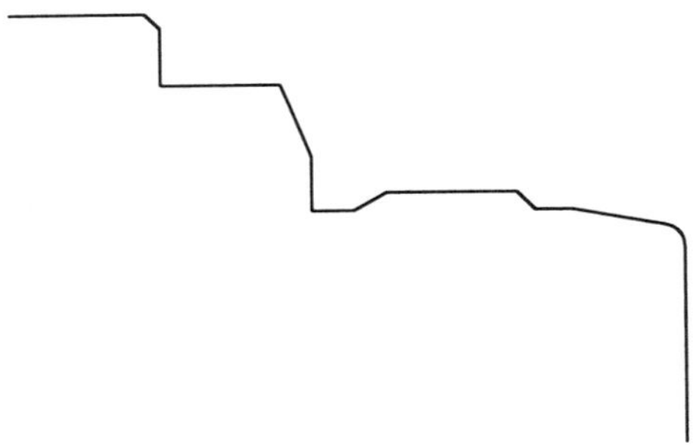

Figure 20.44

Step 8. Add three lines for grooving geometry.

Select **MAIN MENU →** **Create →** **Line →** **Multi**
Enter the following four sets of point coordinates

D value	Z value
5.25	-3.0
4.75	-3.0
4.75	-3.25
5.25	-3.25

The three lines appear as in Figure 20.45.

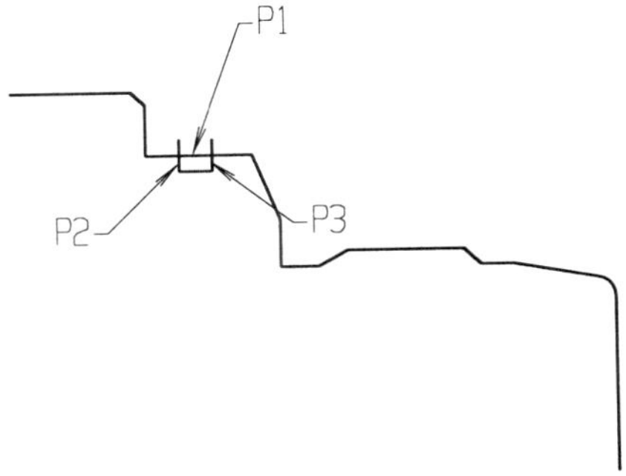

Figure 20.45

Step 9. Trim the unwanted line segment.

Use the pick point in Figure 20.45.
Select **MAIN MENU →** **Modify →** **Break →** **2 pieces**
Pick **P1** and **P2**, then again pick **P1** and **P3**

The line has been split into 2 pieces although its appearance remains the same. The new drawing is redrawn in Figure 20.46.

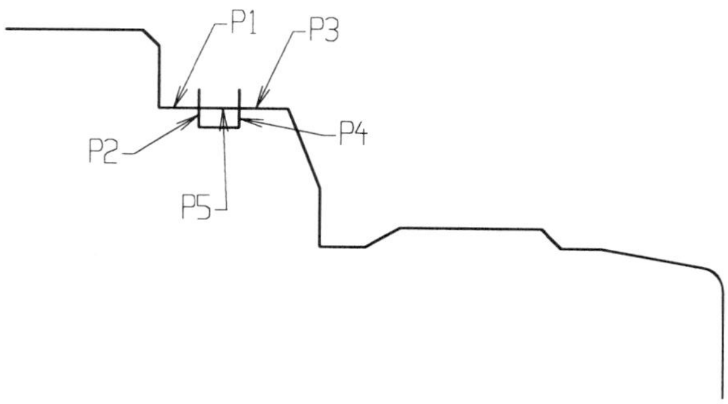

Figure 20.46

Step 10. Trim three lines using the pick points in Figure 20.46.

Select **BACKUP →** **BACKUP →** **Trim →** **2 entities**
Sequentially pick **P1 – P4**
Select **MAIN MENU →** **Delete**
Pick **P5**
The complete external profile should resemble Figure 20.47.

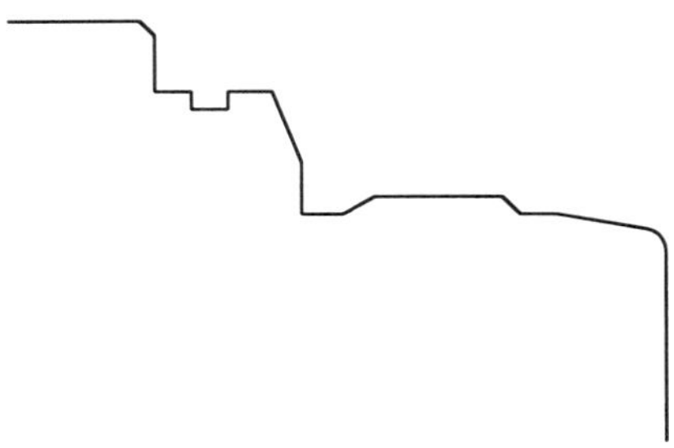

Figure 20.47

Step 11. Change settings to level 2 and red color (12) for the internal profile.

Click on **Level** from control panel, then enter **2** → **OK**
Click on **Color** from control panel, then enter **12** → **OK**

Step 12. Create a series of lines for internal profile.

Select **MAIN MENU** → **Create** → **Line** → **Multi**
Enter the following three sets of point data:

D value	Z value
2.5	0.25
2.5	-0.75
1.5	-0.75

Select **BACKUP** → **Polar** → **Values**
Enter coordinates: **(1.5,-1.6)**
Enter angle in degrees: **12**
Enter line length: **1.5**

Select **BACKUP** → **Endpoints**
Enter two point coordinates: **(1.5,-1.6), (1.5,-4.5)**

The new drawing becomes Figure 20.48.

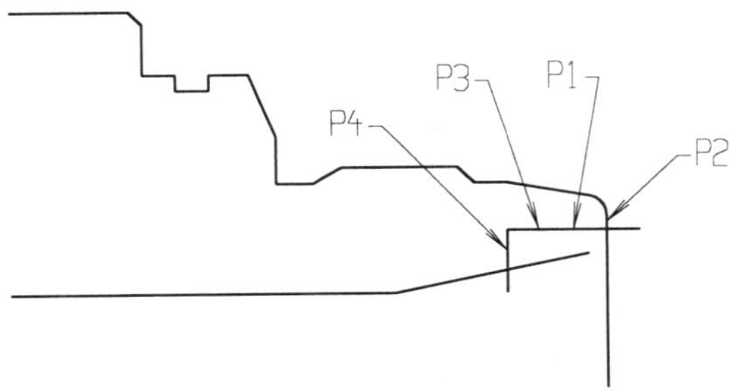

Figure 20.48

Step 12. Add a chamfer and a fillet.

Use the pick points in Figure 20.48.
Select **MAIN MENU** → **Create** → **Next menu** → **Chamfer** → **Distances**
Enter the first distance: **0.1**
Enter the second distance: **0.1**
Pick **P1** and **P2** to add the chamfer
Select **BACKUP** → **BACKUP** → **Fillet** → **Radius**
Set the fillet radius: **0.15**
Pick **P3** and **P4**

The drawing becomes Figure 20.49.

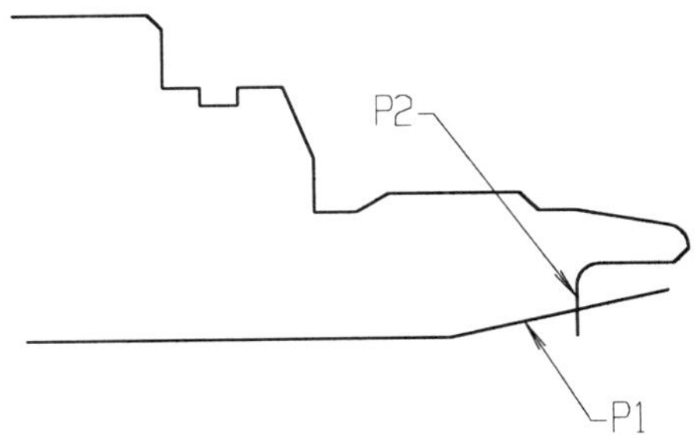

Figure 20.49

Step 13. Trim two lines using the pick points in Figure 20.49.

Select **MAIN MENU →** **Modify →** **Trim →** **2 entities**
Pick **P1** and **P2**

The final geometry model should look like Figure 20.50.

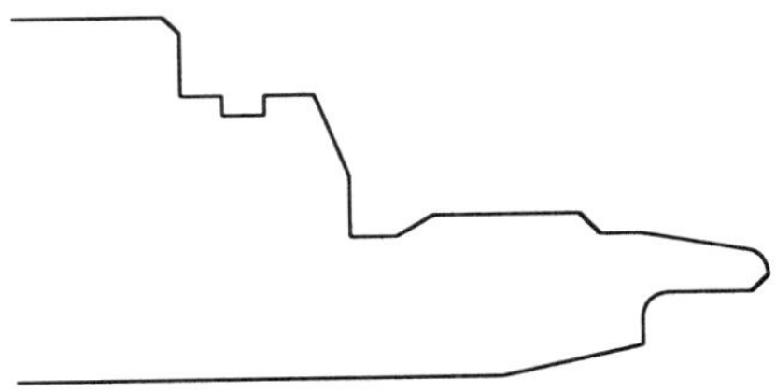

Figure 20.50

Step 14. Save the geometry file as turn6.

Select **MAIN MENU →** **File →** **Save**
File name: **turn6**

Exercises

1. Describe, with a drawing, how to determine the axis directions of a CNC lathe of the left-hand coordinate system.
2. Describe, with a drawing, how to determine the axis directions of a CNC lathe of the right-hand coordinate system.
3. What are the two methods of specifying the X coordinate values in the Mastercam lathe system?

4. Create a part geometry as shown in Figure 20.51. Save the part geometry as lathep1.

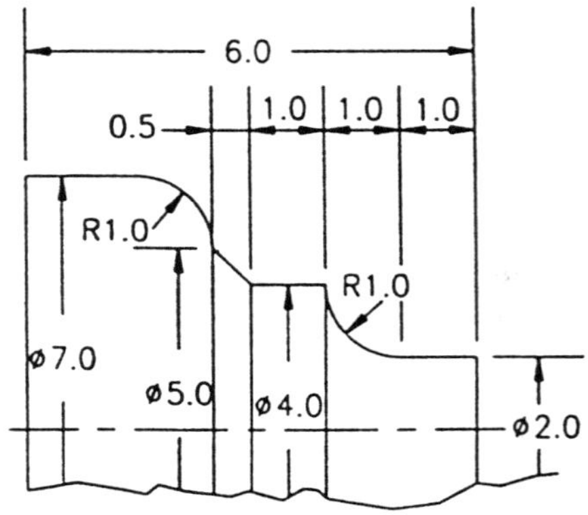

Figure 20.51

5. Create a part geometry as shown in Figure 20.52. Save the part geometry as lathep2.

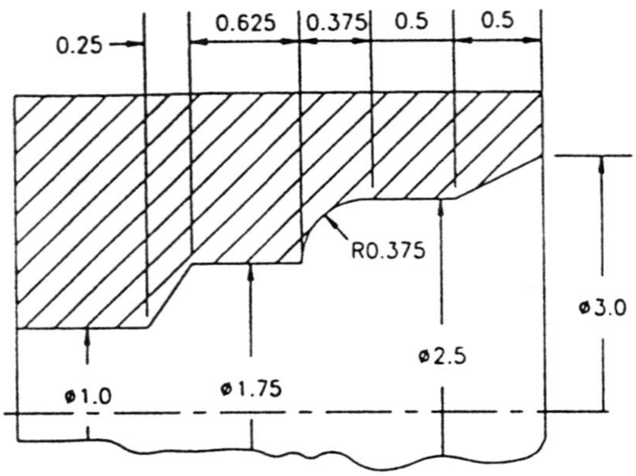

Figure 20.52

6. Create a part geometry as shown in Figure 20.53. Save the part geometry as lathep3.

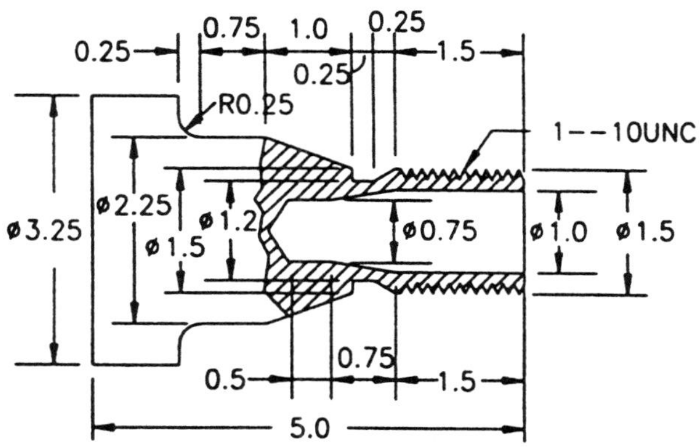

Figure 20.53

Chapter 21

Job Setup and Tool Definition

Objectives:

1. Know how to define the job setup for lathe.
2. Know various types of tools used in lathe operations.
3. Define inserts and holders for various lathe operations.

Overview

Mastercam Version 7 provides a new utility for defining job setup which allows us to specify the tool collision boundary, chuck orientation, tool clearance and offset, material, and toolpath configuration. This utility has the associativity feature to interact with the system during the toolpath generating process. Defining tools is an improved feature in Mastercam 7 allowing us to create a new tool, get a tool from tool library, and modify an existing tool. There are six tool types used in lathe operations: **general turning, boring bar, threading, grooving/parting, drill/tap/reamer**, and **custom**. A typical lathe tool consists of an insert or cutter and a holder. Mastercam has the utilities to define various types of inserts and holders to form a tool for a particular purpose. This chapter focuses on how to define a job setup and various tools with a combination of insert and holder.

21.1 Job Setup

Job setup is a new utility in Mastercam 7 for setting various parameters for the current job. It includes **stock setup, chuck orientation, tool clearance, tool offsets, toolpath configuration, material selection, feed calculation**, and **other functions**. The job setup menu appears as below.

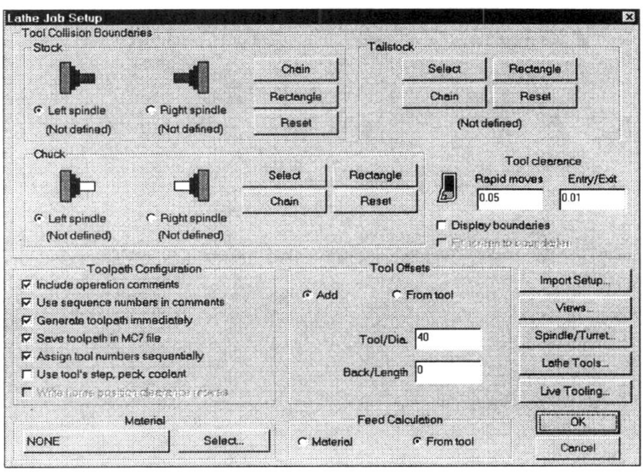

Mastercam lathe uses four parameters to define tool collision boundaries: **stock, chuck, tailstock,** and **tool clearance**. A warning message will be issued when a tool intrudes into these collision boundaries. This is a very desirous feature to prevent crushes during machining.

Stock

The stock parameter defines the stock size of the part when it is clamped on the chuck. The chuck orientation can be set to left spindle or right spindle. The stock boundary can be defined by a chained profile or a rectangle. Figure 21.1 shows the stock boundary defined by a chained profile, while Figure 21.2 is specified by a rectangle.

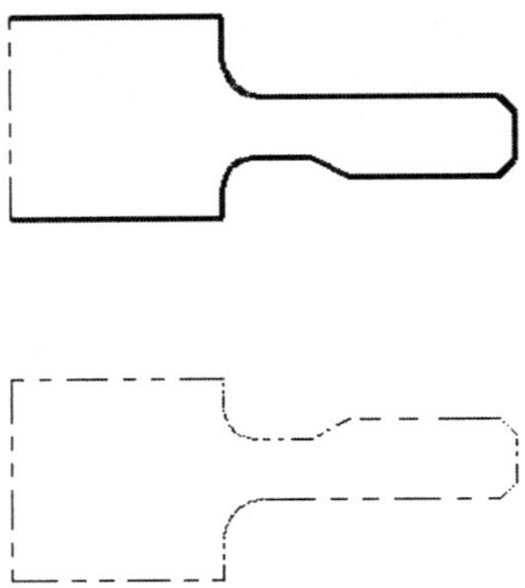

Figure 21.1 Defined by a chained profile

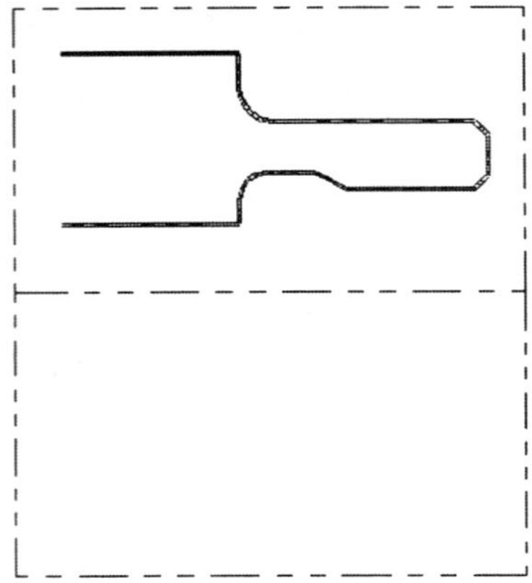

Figure 21.2 Defined by a rectangle

Chuck

The chuck parameter allows for the definition of the chuck orientation and its size. The chuck can be set to **left spindle orientation** or **right spindle orientation**. The left spindle orientation has the part clamped at the left end and extends to the right (+Z) direction. Inversely, the right spindle orientation clamps the part at the right end. The chuck boundary can also be defined by using a chained profile or a rectangle (Figure 21.3).

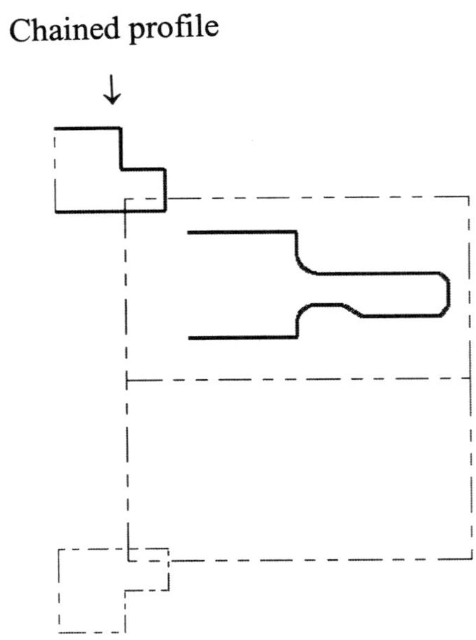

Figure 21.3

Tailstock

The tailstock parameter defines the tailstock location and size. It can be specified by a chained profile or a rectangle (Figure 21.4).

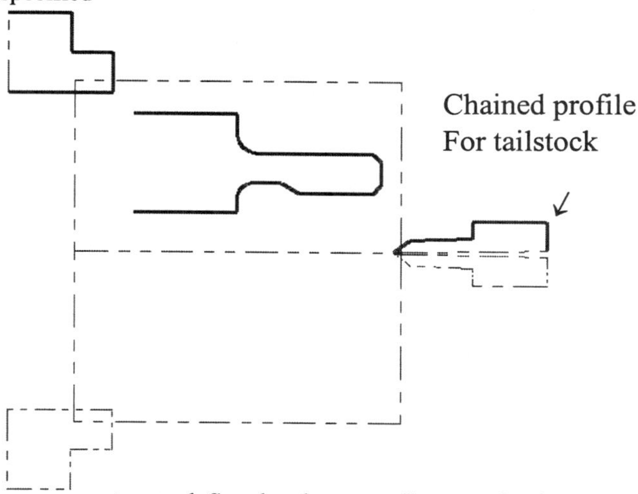

Figure 21.4

Tool clearance

Tool clearance consists of two parameters to define the clearance distances for the tool moves. They are:

Rapid moves:	the rapid move distance.
Entry/Exit:	the distance for entry move and exit move of each tool pass.

Boundary display

There are two more parameters related to tool collision boundaries: display boundary and fit screen to boundary.

Display boundary:	Toggle this parameter to On (with a √ mark) to display the boundary on the screen. A boundary will not be displayed when this parameter is toggled to Off (no √ mark).
Fit screen to boundary:	Toggle this parameter to On (with a √ mark) to fit the boundary to the entire screen.

Toolpath configuration

Mastercam lathe places a group of toolpath related parameters under Toolpath Configuration. They appear as below.

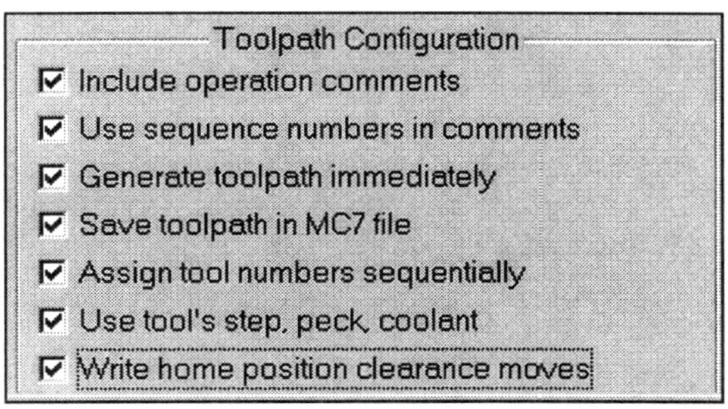

Tool offsets

This group of parameters selects how to specify the tool offset numbers or dimensions. It appears as below.

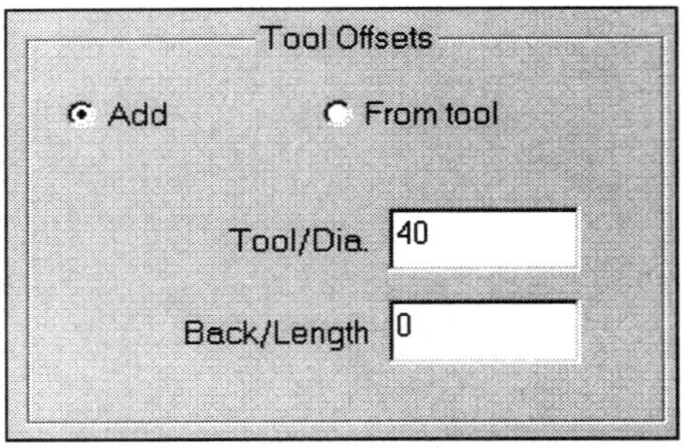

The tool offset number can be selected in two ways: **from tool** or **add**. With the "From Tool" option, the tool offset numbers or dimensions are automatically obtained from the tool parameter. When the "Add" option is used, the offset numbers or dimensions specified in this menu will be used.

Material

This parameter selects the material type to be machined. Click the "Select" button under Material to open a material list as below.

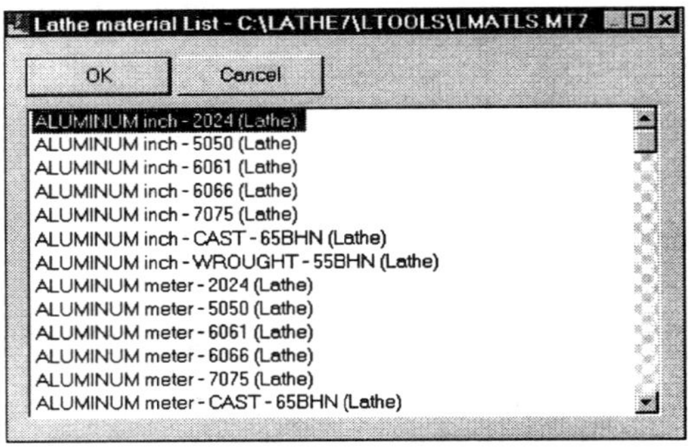

Select a material from the list and select OK to return to Job Setup menu

Feed calculation

This parameter indicates that the feeds used in cutting come from either the material table or tool information. Click the "Material" check box to use the feed data from the material table. Click the "From tool" check box to use the feed data from the tool information menu.

Miscellaneous parameters

The following five parameters are used to control some auxiliary functions in job setup:

Import Setup:	selects a setup file from an existing toolpath file.
Views:	selects an existing defined view.
Spindle/Turret:	defines orientation for turret and active spindle.
Lathe Tools:	opens tool utility for defining a lathe tool.
Live Tooling:	opens tool utility for defining a milling tool.

Import setup This parameter allows selecting an existing job setup file from a toolpath file. Click on the "Import Setup" button to open the Import menu as shown here.

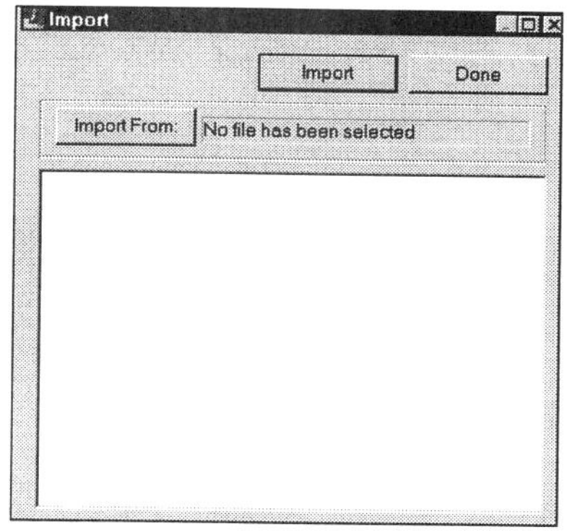

Click the "Import From" button to open project file directory. Select a project file, then select "Open" to have the import menu appear as below.

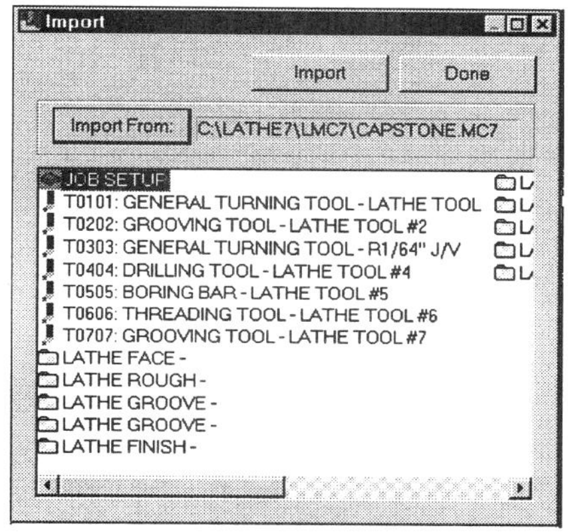

Spindle/Turret This parameter defines the orientation of turret and spindle. Its menu appears as below.

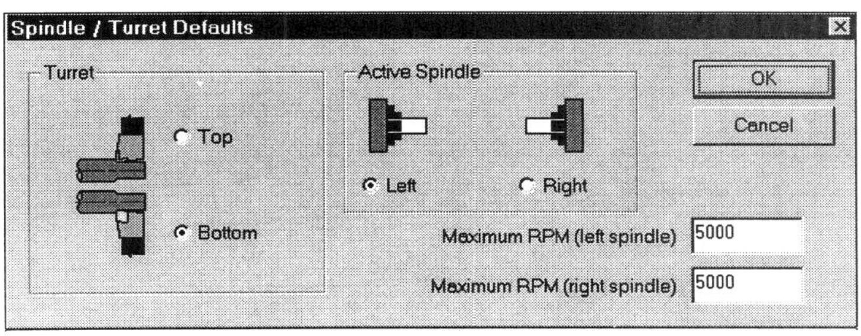

The turret orientation can be set to **top or bottom**. The "Top" option is often used in slant-bed type of turning centers. The "Bottom" option is used in flat-bed type of lathes. The spindle orientation can be set to **left or right**. The "Maximum RPM" parameters indicate the maximum spindle speed in revolution per minute for the selected spindle.

Lathe tools This parameter opens Lathe Tool Manager as below for creating a new lathe tool or selecting an existing tool from library.

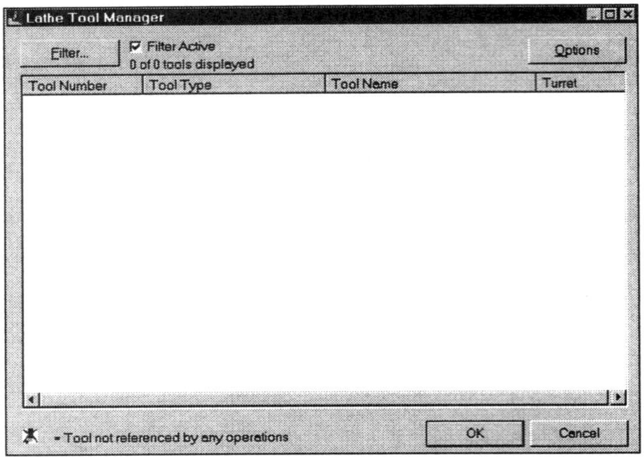

Live toolings Milling operations are allowed in mill-turn machines. Milling operations are implemented by using self-rotating (live) milling tools. Click the "Live Toolings" button to open the Live Tooling Settings menu as below.

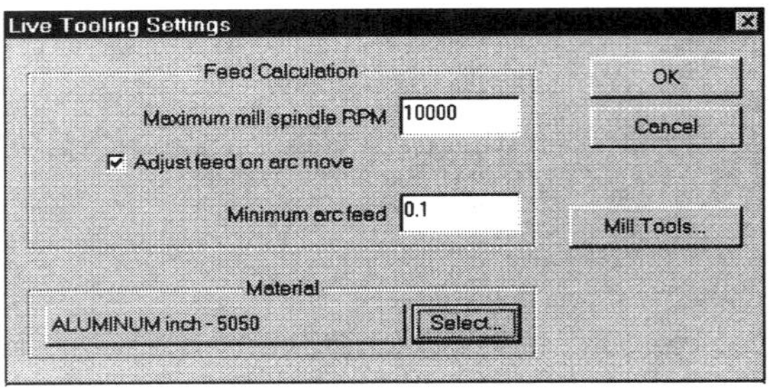

Clicking on the "Mill Tools" button will open Define Tool menu as below for you to define a milling tool.

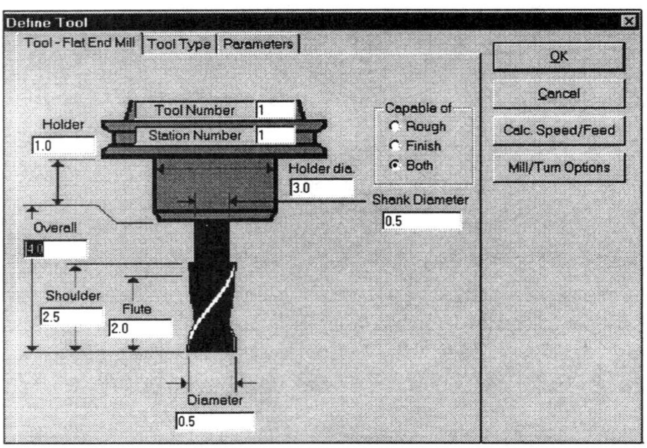

Project 1. Creating a job setup file

This project creates a job setup file for the geometry file (turn4). A geometry profile is added as the chuck boundary. The stock boundary is defined by using two points. Figure 21.5 shows the part geometry and stock boundary and chuck boundary.

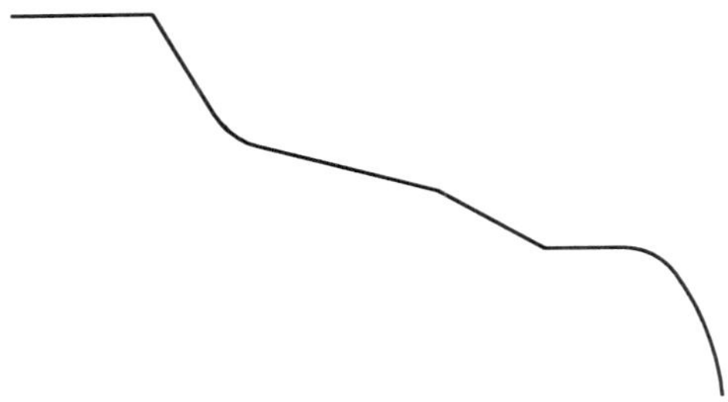

Figure 21.5a

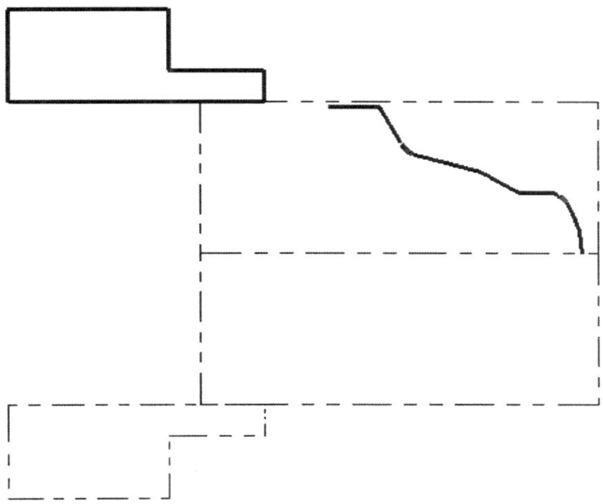

Figure 21.5b

Tips
1. Use the geometry file (turn4).
2. Create a six-line profile in level 2 as the chuck boundary.
3. Use two points (6,-6) and (0,0.25) to define the stock boundary.
4. Define the chuck boundary using the six-line profile.
5. Select the material (STEEL inch-1010-200 BHN).
6. Define the remaining parameters.
7. Save the project file with job setup as (setup).

Step 1. Open the geometry file turn4.

Select **MAIN MENU → File → Open**
File name: **turn4**

The part geometry appears as in Figure 21.6.

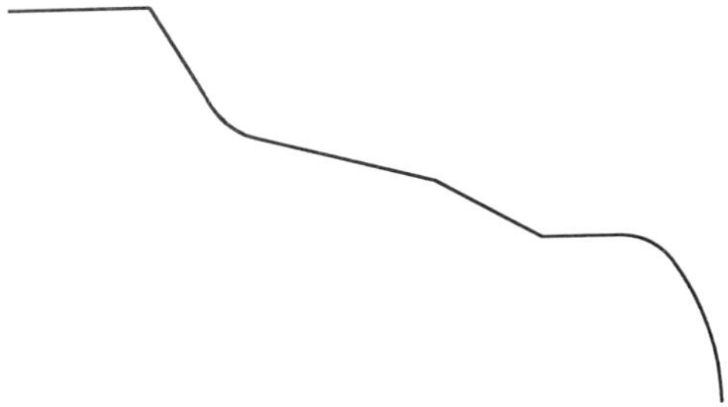

Figure 21.6

Step 2. Create a six-line profile in level2.

Select **Level**, then enter **2**

Select **MAIN MENU → Create → Line → Multi**

Enter the following point coordinate sets:

(8, -9)	(8, -6.5)	(6, -6.5)	(6, -5)	(5, -5)	(5, -9)	(8, -9)

The six-line profile is added as in Figure 21.7.

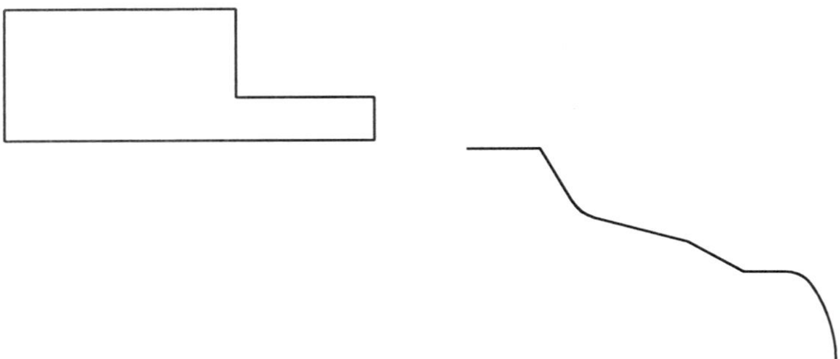

Figure 21.7

Step 3. Initiate the job setup utility.

Select **MAIN MENU → Toolpaths → Next menu → Job setup**

The initial job setup menu should appear as below.

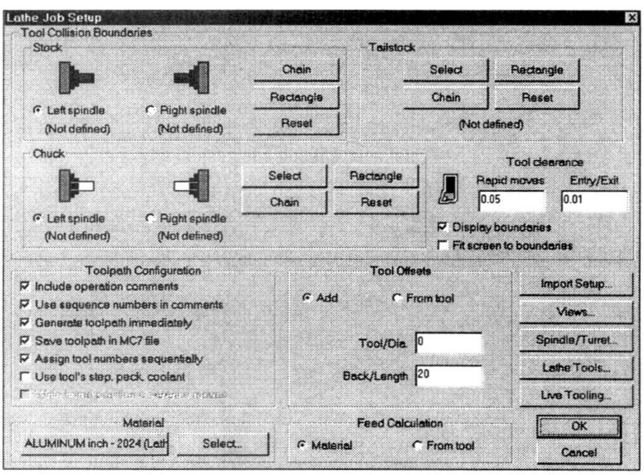

Step 4. Define the stock boundary.

Click on **Left spindle** under Stock
Select the **Rectangle** button
Select **2 points → Values**
Enter coordinates: **5,-6** as the point in one corner
Select **Values**
Enter coordinates: **0,0.25** as the second corner point
The stock boundary should look like Figure 21.8.

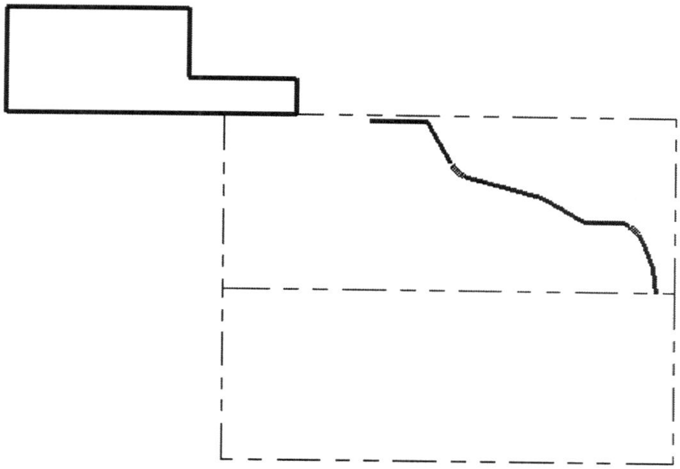

Figure 21.8

The system should return back to Lathe Job Setup menu

Step 5. Define the chuck boundary.

Click the **Left spindle** under Chuck
Select the **Chain** button
Pick any element in the upper-left profile
Select **Done**
The chuck boundary is added as in Figure 21.9.

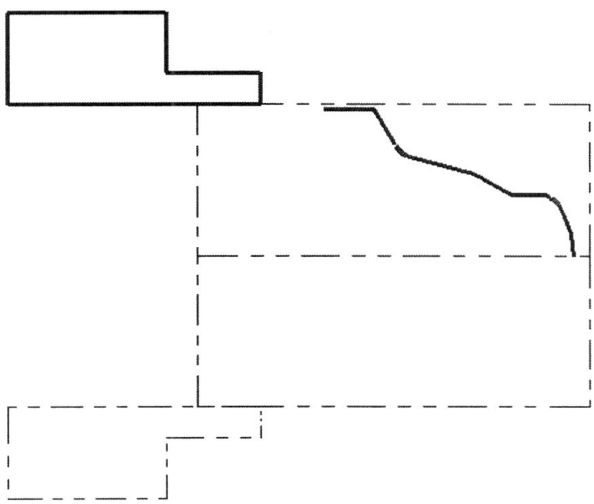

Figure 21.9

Step 6. Select a material.

Click on the **Select** button under Material

The lathe material list should appear on the screen

Scroll the list and select **STEEL inch-1010-200BHN (Lathe)** from the list as below.

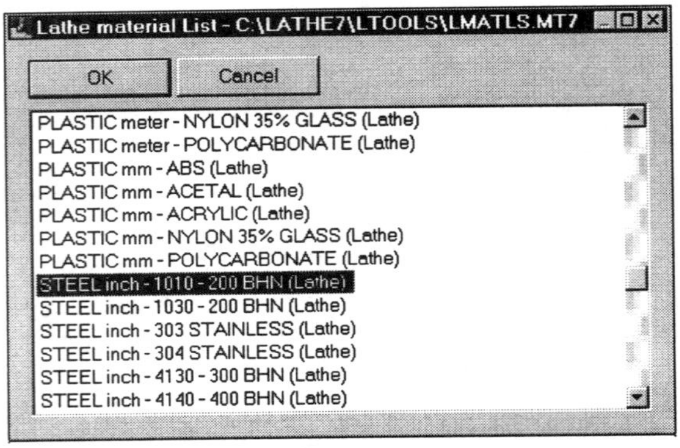

Select **OK**

Step 7. Define the remaining parameters as below.

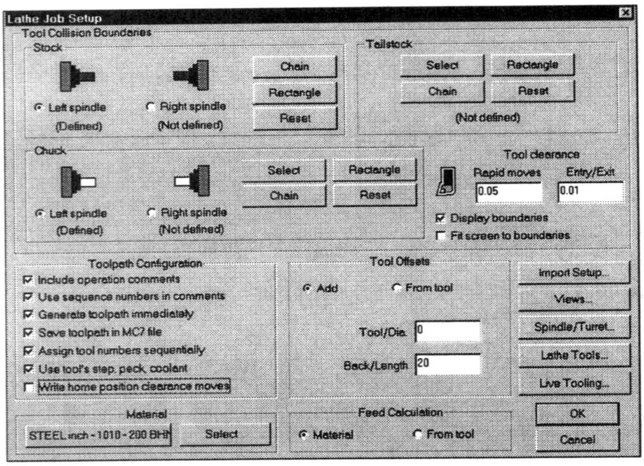

Select **OK** to return back to graphic mode

Step 8. Save the new project file as setup.

Select **MAIN MENU → File → Save**

File name: **setup**

21.2 Defining Lathe Tools

Defining a turning tool is more complicated than defining a milling tool. A complete turning tool normally consists of two components; insert or cutter and holder. There are a wide variety of inserts, cutters, and holders to choose from. You must know the turning operations as well as insert and holder specifications in order to properly define a turning tool. Insert and holder specifications have been presented in chapter 2. This section presents lathe define tool utilities and shows how to use them for creating or editing a new tool.

How to Access Define Lathe Tools Utilities

There are two ways to access Define Lathe Tools Utilities: **NC utils method** and the **on-the-fly method**.

<u>**NC utils method**</u> _ Follow these commands to open Define Lathe Tools Utilities:

1. Select MAIN MENU → NC utils → Def tools

Three options of define lathe tools appear as below for selecting a command:

Current: open the Lathe Tool Manager with the current tool.
Library: open the Lathe Tool Manager with a list of tools in the current library.
Compress: compress the tool library file.

2. Select Current or Library from the above list to open the Lathe Tool Manager menu as below.

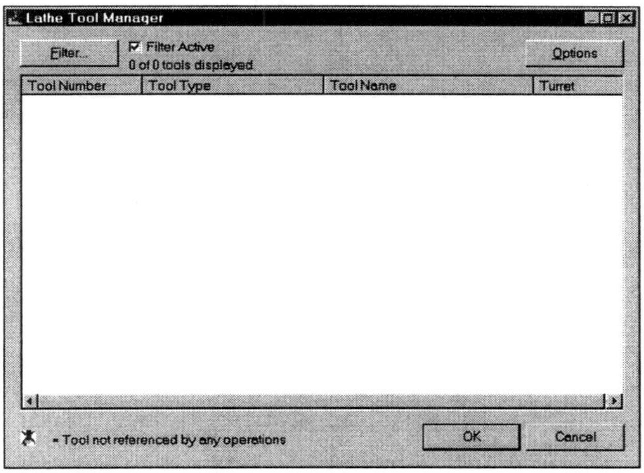

3. Click the right mouse button to open the option menu as shown here.

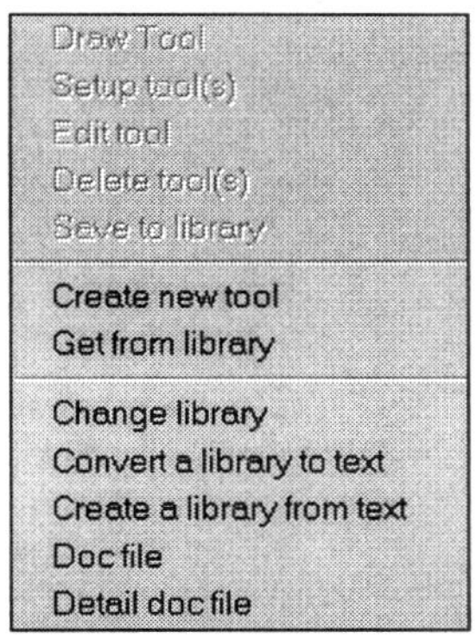

4. Select "Create new tool" from the option menu. The tool type menu appears as below.

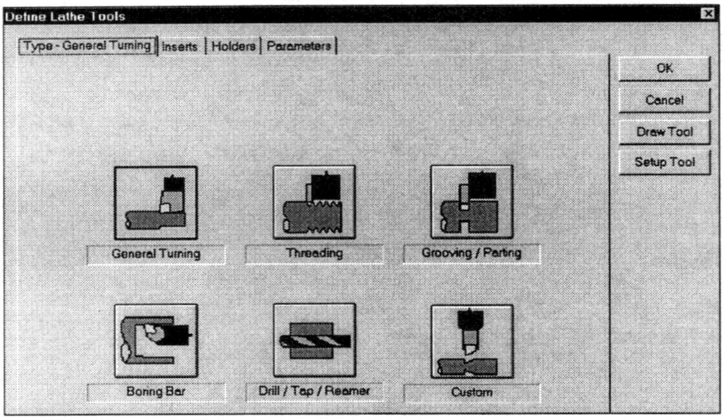

On-the-fly method The On-the-fly method creates or modifies a tool during the generating toolpath process. The procedure for using on-the-fly method for creating a new tool is:

1. Use the following commands to enter a toolpath module and chain the profile for cutting:
   - Select MAIN MENU → Toolpaths → Rough (or other toolpath module)
   - Define a chained profile for cutting boundary
   - The module parameters menu should appears as below.

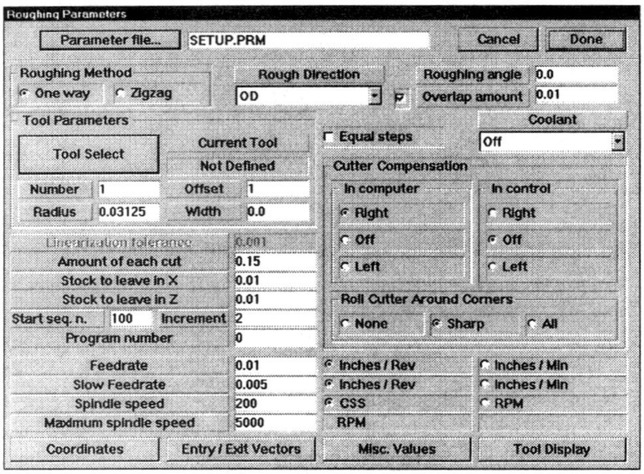

2. Click "Tool Select" button under Tool Parameters to open the Lathe Tool Manager menu as shown here.

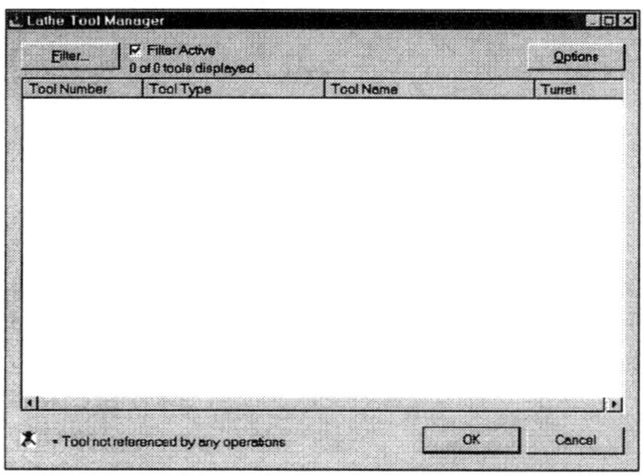

3. Click the right mouse button to open the option menu as shown here.

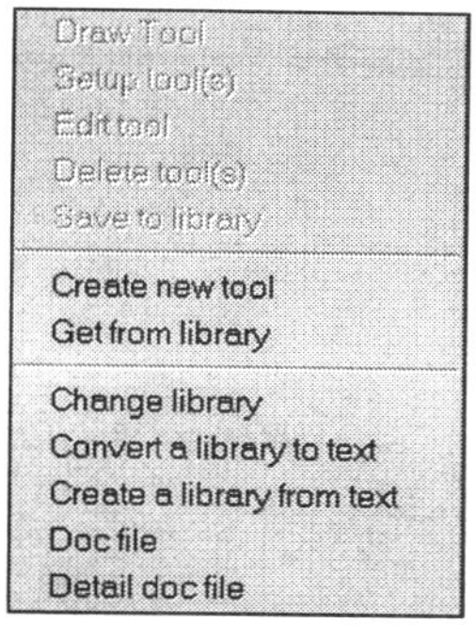

4. Highlight the words "Create new tool" from the list to open the Define Lathe Tools with insert menu as below.

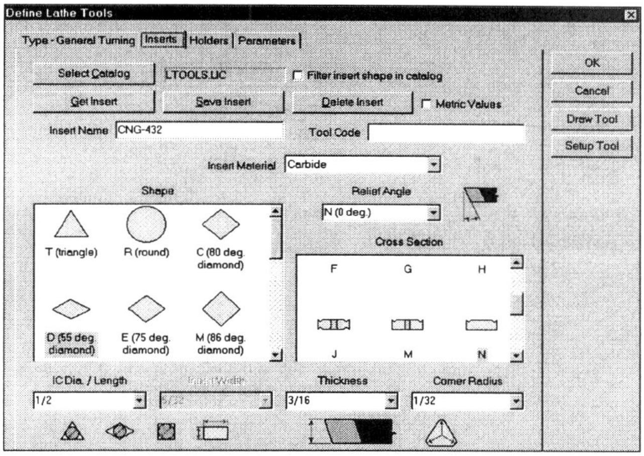

Defining a tool involves the following four steps:

1. Select the tool type.
2. Specify insert or cutter specification.
3. Specify tool holder specification.
4. Define tooling and machining parameters.

Tool type

Commonly used turning operations include external turning, facing, boring, grooving, parting, drilling, reaming, threading, and tapping. Each operation requires a special tool type. Mastercam classified all turning tools into these six categories:

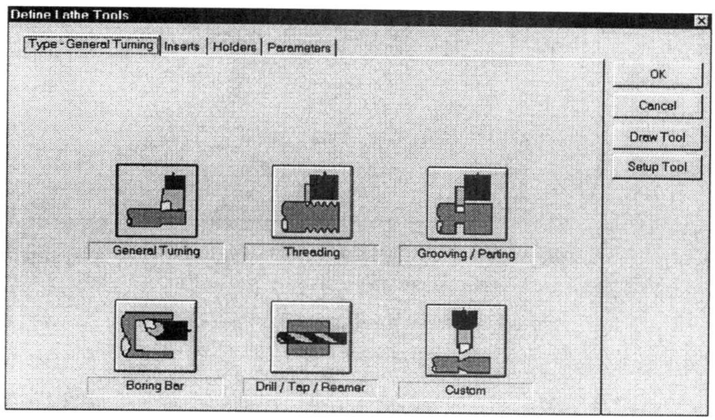

- General turning tools
- Boring tools
- Threading tools
- Drills/taps/reamers
- Grooving/parting tools
- Custom tools

Inserts for turning and boring

Most turning tools are made of carbide in the form of inserts. There is a wide variety of insert forms and sizes for various machining operations. Mastercam organizes insert define utility according to the tool type. General turning tools and boring bars have the same insert defining utility as shown below.

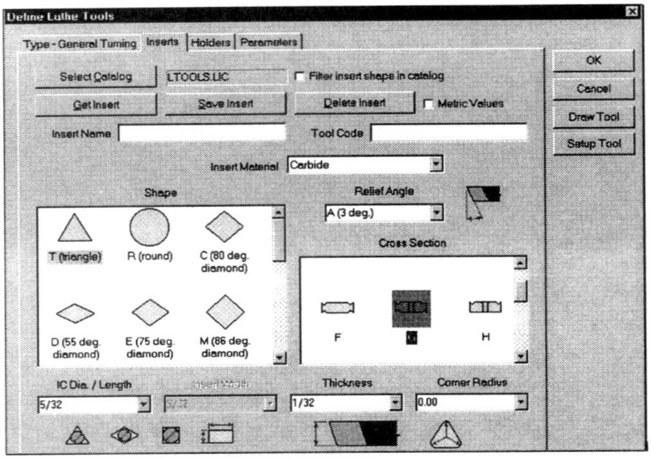

Insert shape The complete list of the insert shapes for general turning and boring is shown here. Click the desired shape to select it.

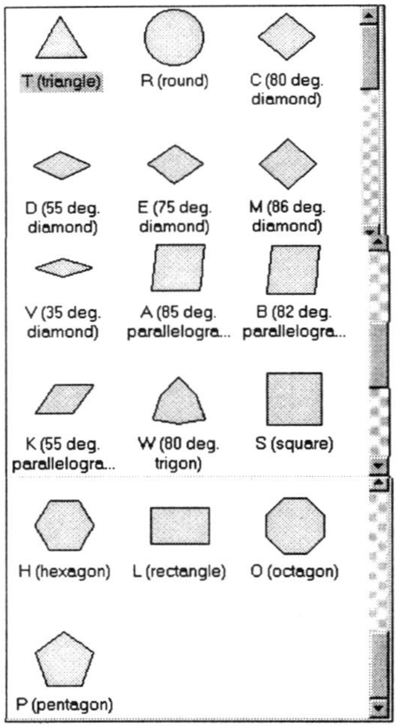

Relief angle The relief angle is the included angle between the vertical line and the front edge of the insert as shown below.

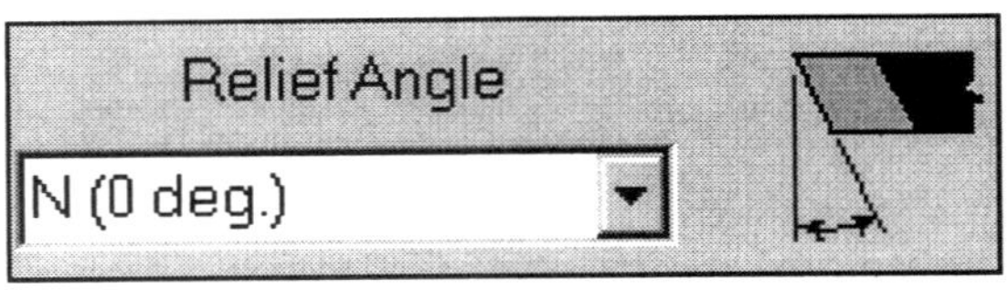

The relief angle is expressed by an alphabet code. The complete list of the relief angles is given here.

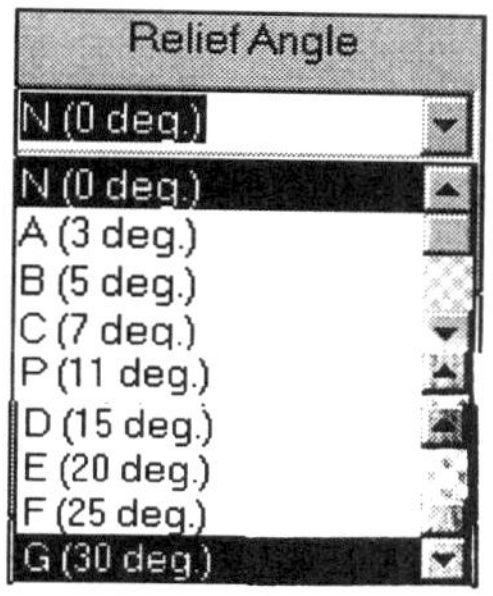

Cross section The cross section parameter defines **chip breaker** and **center hole** of the inserts. An alphabet code is used to represent a combination of chip breaker and center hole. The list of cross section is displayed here

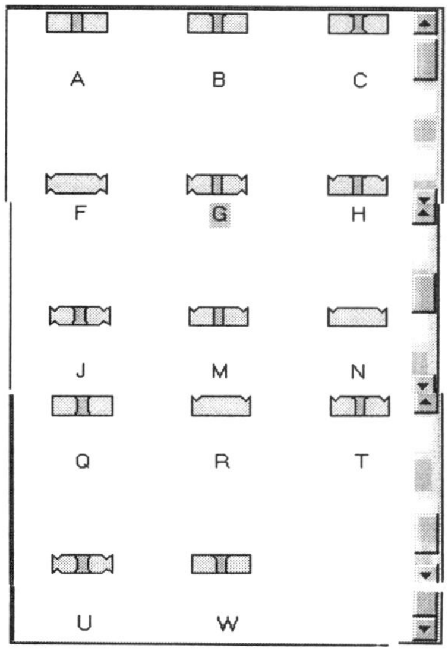

Insert size The size of an insert is expressed by the size of its **inscribed circle (IC), thickness**, and **corner radius at the cutting edge** as shown below.

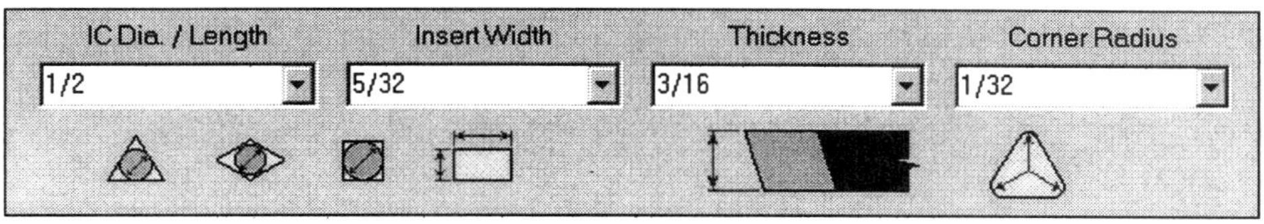

Scroll through the size list to select the proper dimensions. The selection of insert size depends on such factors as the **maximum depth of cut, feed rate, and roughing or finish machining**. The following suggestions should help to select proper insert dimensions:

1. Use carbide inserts to their maximum capacity. Do not choose an oversized insert.
2. The maximum depth of cut is about one-half the size of the inscribed circle.
3. Roughing requires a smaller insert corner radius for a reduced contact area between the cutter and part.
4. Finish cuttings uses a larger corner radius to produce a smooth surface.
5. Machining that involves heavy cuts (deep depth of cut) requires thicker inserts for sufficient strength.
6. Use commercial available inserts.

Inserts for threading

Selecting "Threading" tool type will cause the system to open the threading insert menu as below.

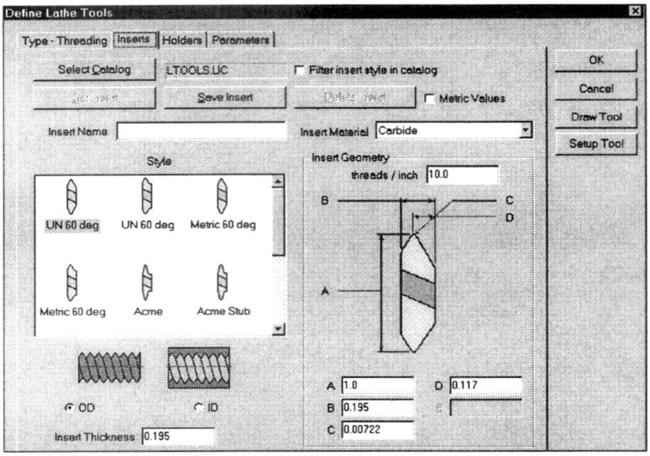

There are three main parameters in defining a threading insert: **thread style, thread type**, and **insert geometry**.

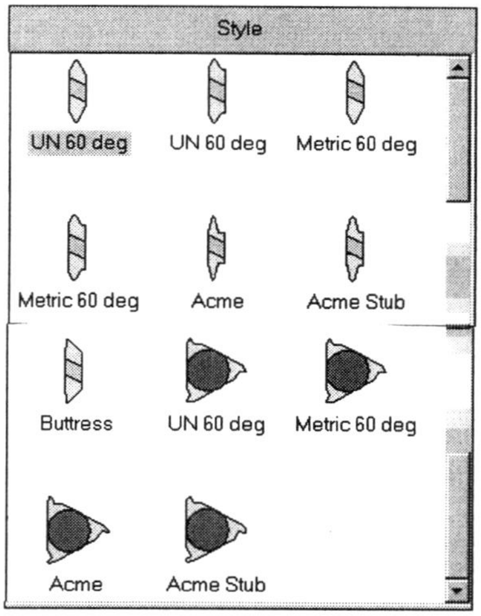

Thread form and insert style

This parameter specifies the thread form to be cut and insert style to use. Mastercam lathe allows the definition of the inserts for cutting the following thread forms:

UN 60-degree threads
Metric 60-degree threads
Acme threads
Acme stub threads

The list of combination of thread form and insert style is given here.

Thread type This parameter indicates the thread to be cut either an OD (external) thread or ID (internal) thread. Click "OD" or "ID" as shown below to select the thread type.

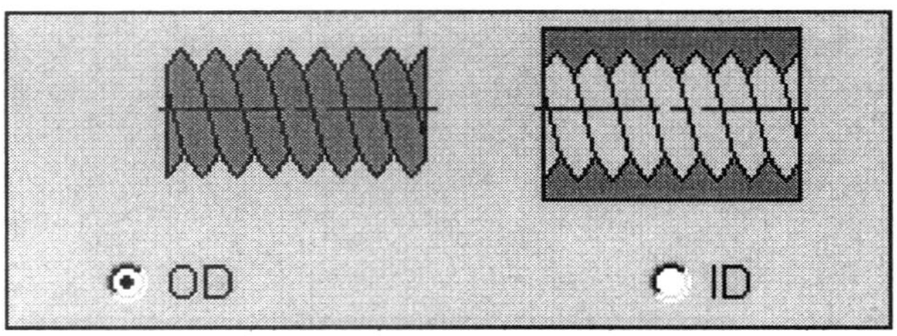

Insert thickness This parameter specifies the thickness of the threading insert

Insert geometry The threading insert can be fully defined by a group of dimensions. Depending on the threading insert style, the defining dimensions may vary slightly. The drawing shown below is the insert geometry for a UN-60 degree insert.

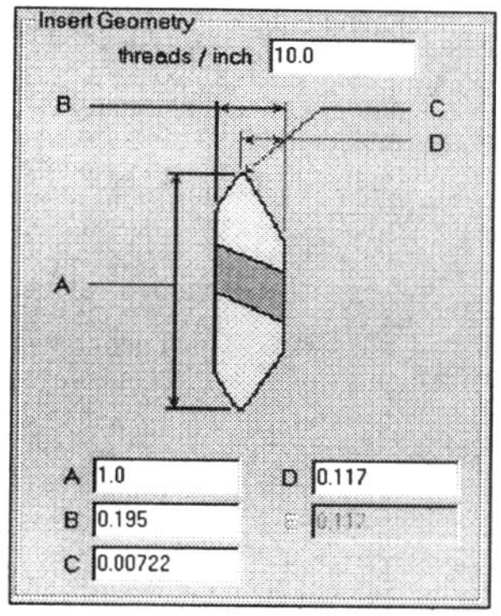

Inserts for grooving and parting

Select "Grooving/Parting" tool type will cause the system to open the grooving/parting insert menu as below.

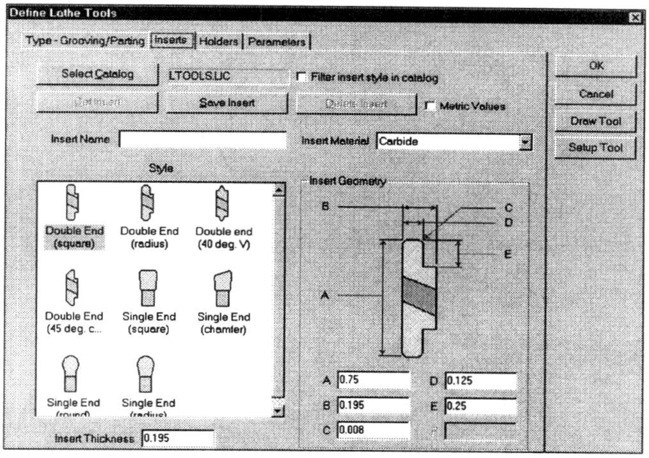

The two main parameters in defining a grooving/parting insert are **style** and **geometry.**

Style: This parameter specifies the insert form which has eight styles as shown here.

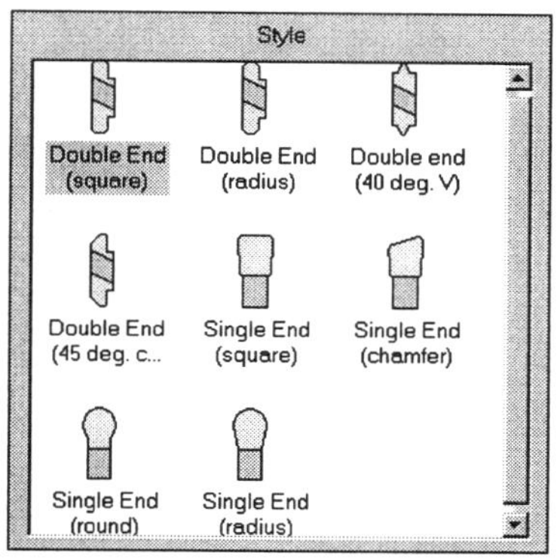

Insert thickness: This parameter specifies the thickness of the grooving/parting insert.

Insert geometry The grooving/parting insert can be fully defined by a group of dimensions. Depending on the insert style, the defining dimensions vary accordingly. The drawing shown below is the insert geometry for a single end – square insert.

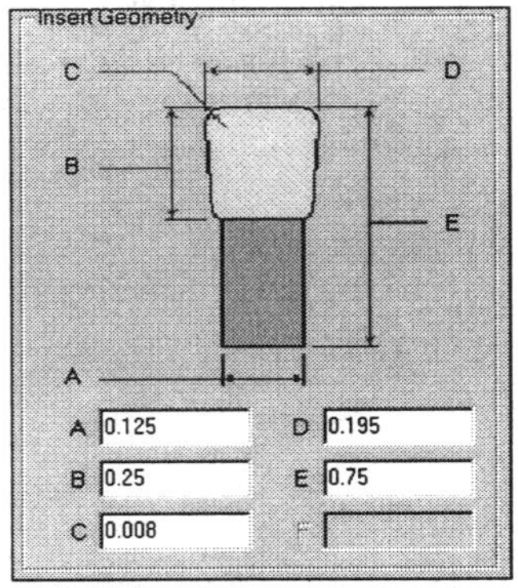

Tools for drilling/reaming/tapping

Selecting the "Drill/Tap/Reamer" tool type will cause the system to open the drilling/tapping/reaming tool menu as below.

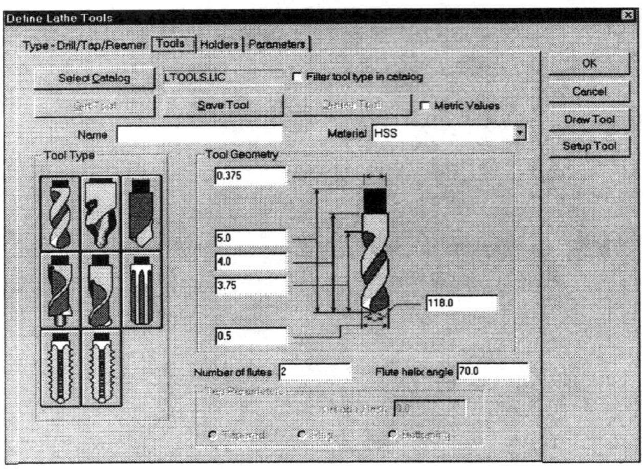

Tool type There are **eight tool types** in this category. They are:

Drill	Center drill
Countersink	Counterbore
End mill	Reamer
RH (right hand) tap	LH (left hand) tap

Their graphic pictures are shown here.

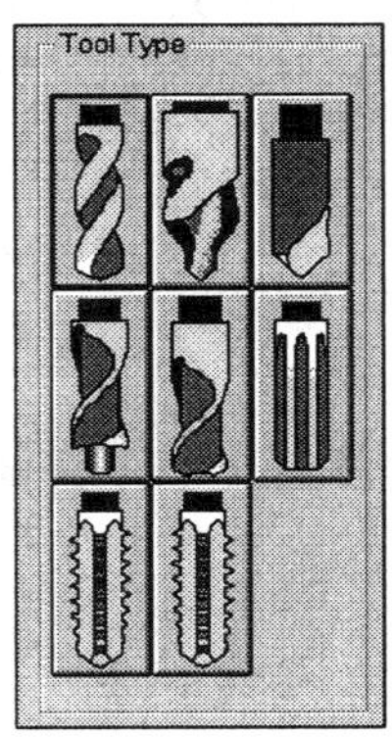

Tool geometry Each tool type has its unique dimensions for defining the tool shape and size. Tool geometry parameters for defining four selected tools are given below.

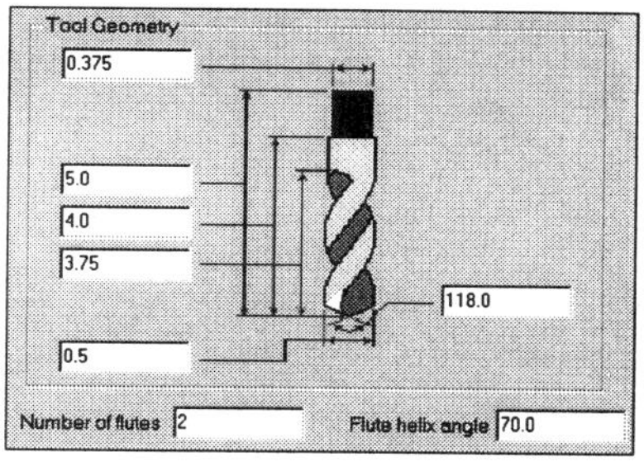

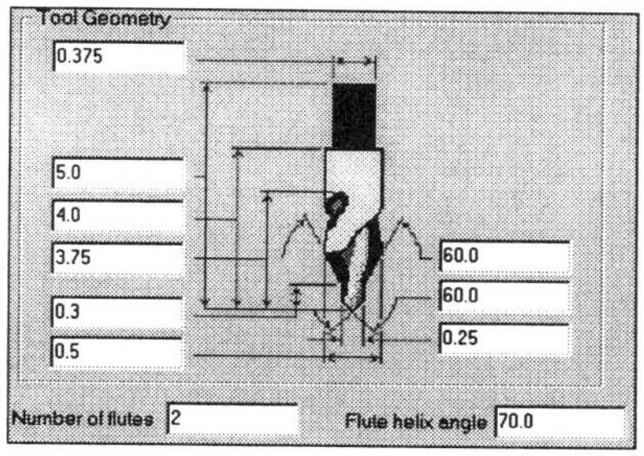

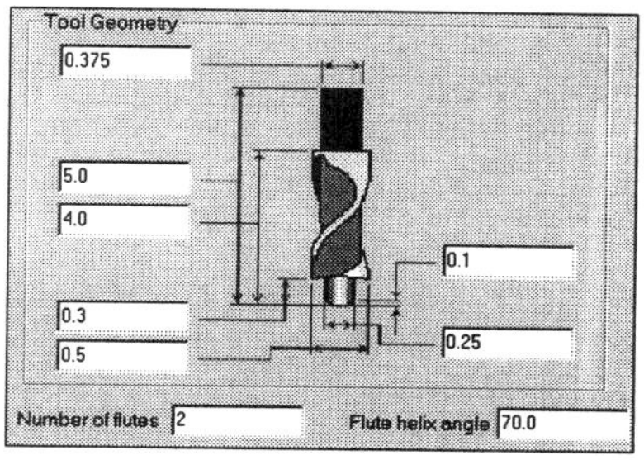

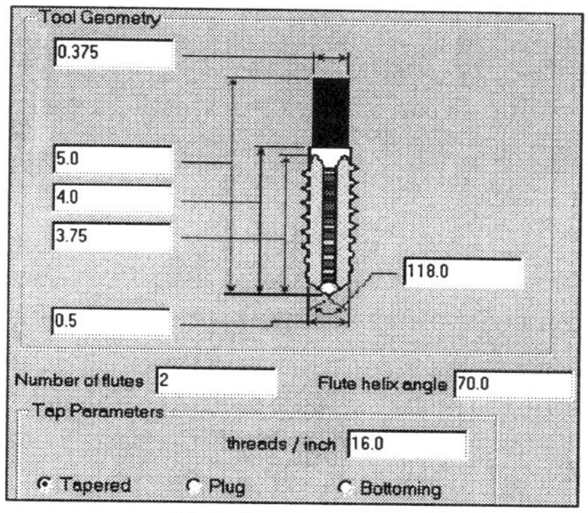

Holder specifications

The insert holders use a standard identification system which has been presented in chapter 2. Mastercam allows to either select a holder from the library or create a new holder.

The Procedure for selecting a holder from the holder library

1. Select "Get Holder" button to open the turning holders library as below.

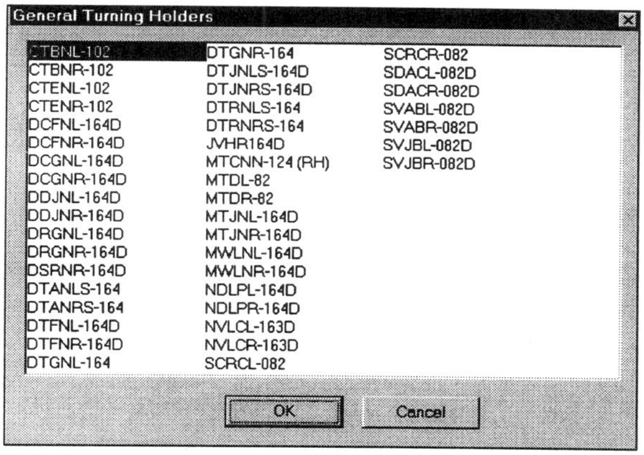

2. Select a holder (DDJNR-164D for this example) from the list.
3. Select OK from turning holders menu to return to lathe tool menu as below. Notice that the parameters defined in DDJNR-164D are reflected in the tool menu.

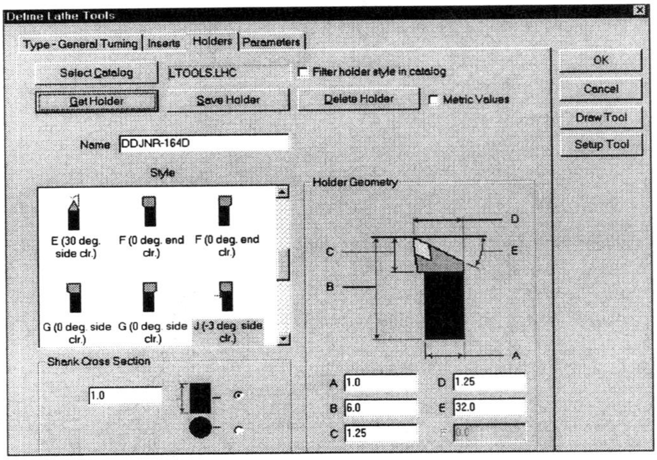

Defining a new holder for general turning

Three main parameters are used to define a holder for general turning: **holder style, shank cross section**, and **holder geometry**.

Holder style The holder style is determined by the cutting edge angle which can be a positive or negative value. The holder style is identified by an alphabetic code. Mastercam automatically associates the selected insert to the holder styles. The available holder styles will appear for selection when an insert is selected. The style menu appeared as below for is a 55° diamond insert.

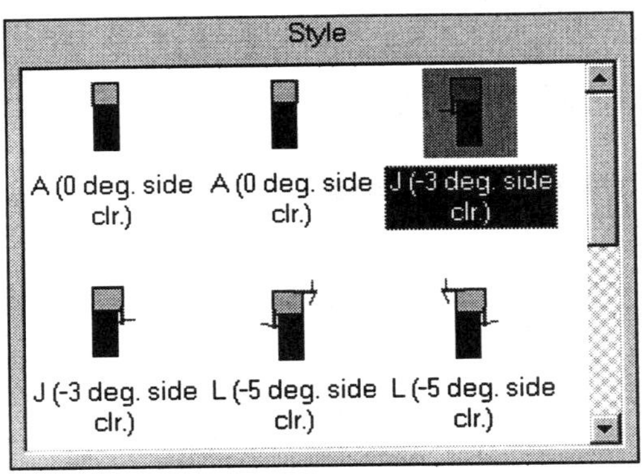

Holder geometry When a holder style is selected, the necessary geometry parameters used to define this holder will be displayed in the holder geometry area (J style holder).

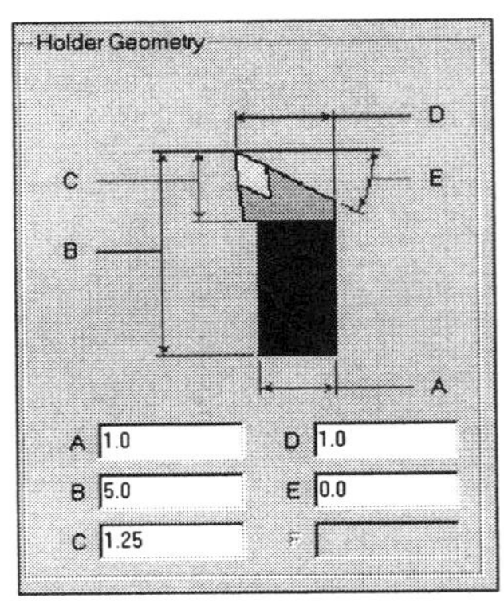

It is important to identify the proper hand type of holders. There are two hand types: **right hand** and **left hand**. Each holder style has both hand types for selection. The right-hand type has the insert pointing to the left, while the left hand style has the insert pointing to the right.

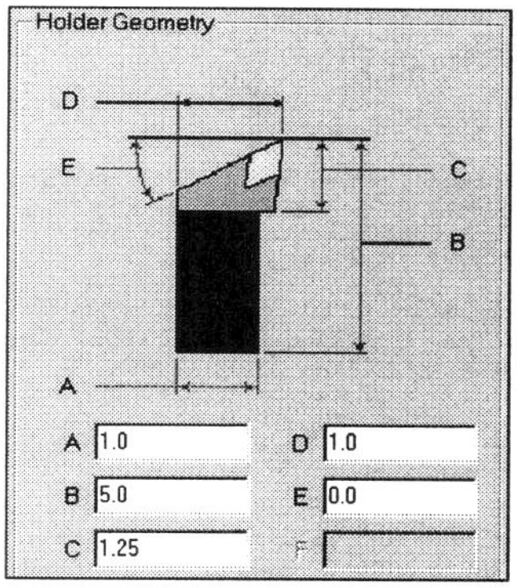

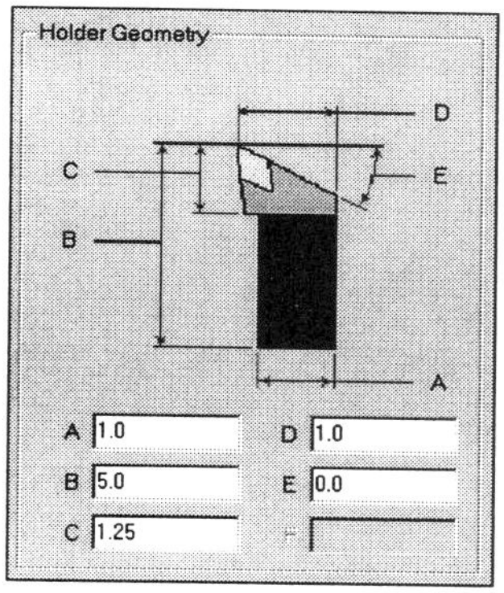

Shank cross section The cross section of the holder shank has a rectangular or circular shape. Actually, the square shape is most commonly used. Mastercam uses the shank cross section parameter as below to define the shank cross section.

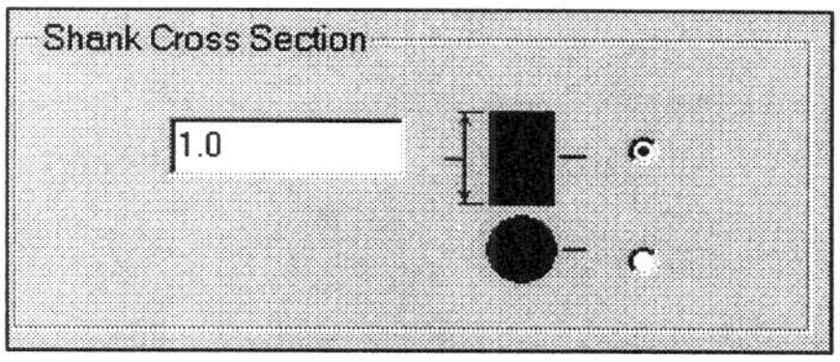

Boring bars

The holders for boring tools are often referred to as boring bars. The specifications for boring bars are similar to the holders for general turning. Mastercam automatically provides available boring bars for your selection when the insert type has been determined. Two main parameters for defining a boring bar are **style** and **holder geometry**.

Boring bar style The styles of boring bars are determined by the cutting edge angle. It uses the same alphabet code system as turning holders to represent the style. Once you have selected the insert shape, Mastercam provides all possible boring bar styles for that particular insert shape to choose from.. Some insert shapes have more boring bar styles to choose from, while other insert shapes have only one or two styles for selection. Boring bar styles for 80° diamond inserts and 55° diamond inserts are listed below for reference.

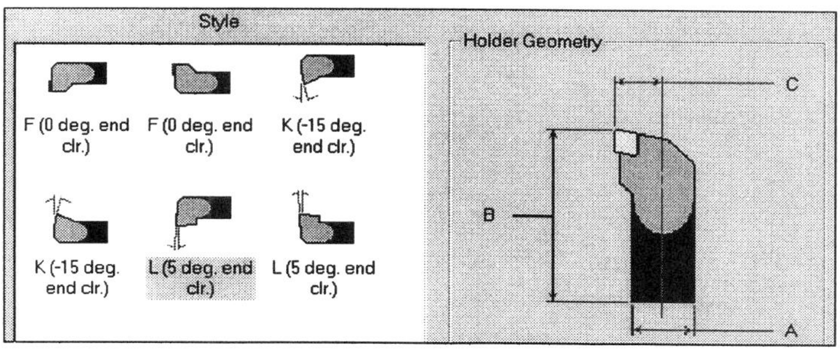

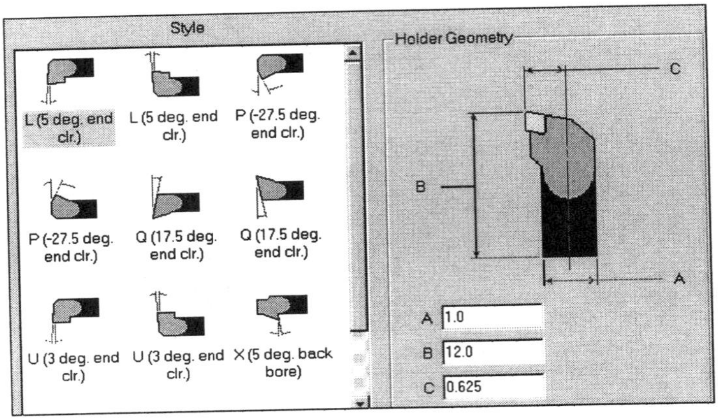

Holder geometry The size of boring bars is defined by three dimensions as shown below:

Dimension A:	diameter of the shank.
Dimension B:	overall length of the boring bar.
Dimension C:	distance from the tip of the insert to the centerline of the boring bar.

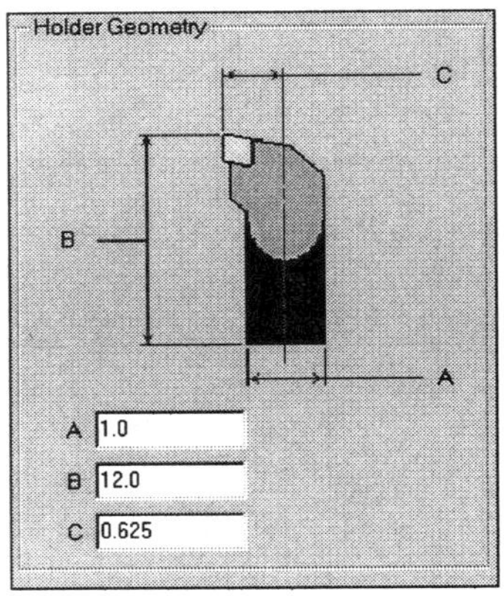

Holders for threading

There are two groups of holder styles for threading tools: **straight** and **face**. The straight holders have their shank parallel to the X direction, while face holders have their shank parallel to the Z axis. The six holder styles for threading tools as shown below.

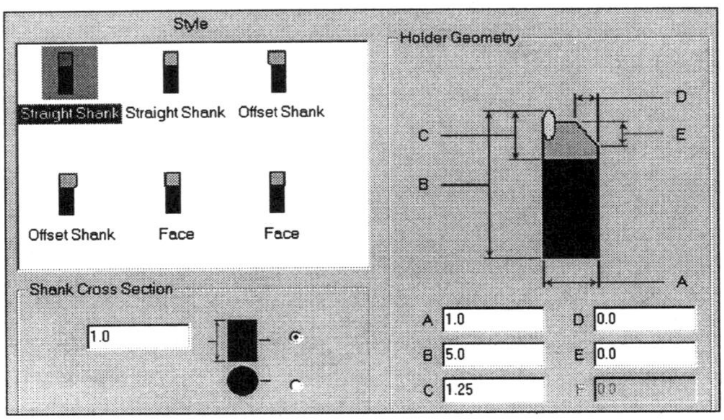

Holders for hole operations

Mastercam uses five dimensions as shown below to define the holder shape and size for those tools used in hole operations.

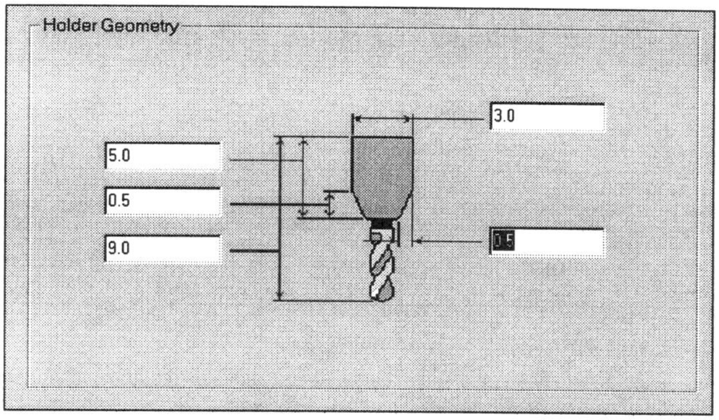

Parameters

Each tool type has a group of parameters used to define tooling and machining information. Parameters are classified under the following four groups: **Program parameters, Default cutting parameters, Toolpath parameters,** and **Miscellaneous parameters.**

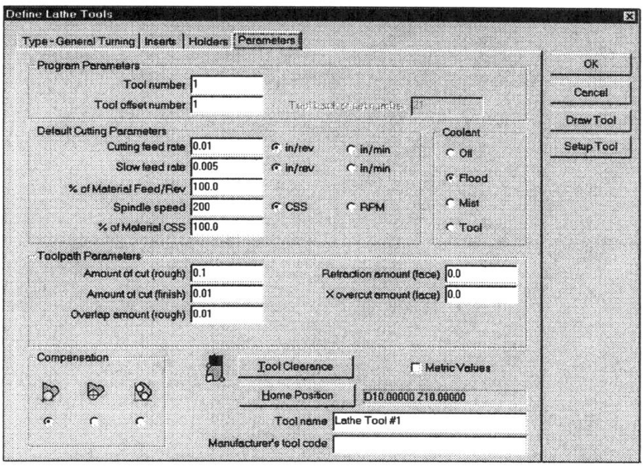

Program parameters This parameter category consists of the following three parameters:

Tool number: specifies the turret location where the tool is placed.
Tool offset number: specifies the offset number of the tool.
Tool back offset number: specifies the back offset number of the tool.

The information in these parameters will be automatically output to the part program with the T-function. A number of 2 for tool number and 2 for tool offset number will produce a T0202 command in the part program.

Default cutting parameters This parameter group specifies the cutting speed and feed rate for the operation. The cutting speed can be specified in the following two modes:

in/rev: feed in inch per revolution.
in/min: feed in inch per minute.

The following three parameters related to feed rate:

Cutting feed rate:	specifies the feed for regular cutting.
Slow feed rate:	specifies the feed for plunging cutting.
% of material feed/rev:	specifies the cutting feed rate in terms of the percentage of suggested feed for a particular material in the material table.

The spindle speed can be specified in the following two modes:

CSS:	specifies the spindle speed in terms of constant surface speed (ft/min or m/min).
RPM:	specifies the spindle speed in terms of constant spindle speed (rev/min).

Toolpath Parameters This group of parameters defines the depth of cuts of the operation. The toolpath parameters for turning and boring are listed below:

Amount of cut (rough):	depth of each roughing pass.
Amount of cut (finish):	depth of cut for finish pass.
Overlap amount (rough):	overlap amount between two successive roughing passes.
Retraction amount (face):	retraction distance for facing pass.
X overcut amount (face):	overcut distance for facing pass.

Miscellaneous Parameters This group includes the following parameters: Coolant, Tool clearance, Compensation, Home position, Tool name, Manufacturer's tool code, Metric value, and Draw tool.

21.3 Creating New Tools

A lathe or turning center has a limited number of tool slots on the turret. Small size turning centers have 12 or less tool slots. Larger turning centers have more tool slots. We need to carefully plan what tools will be installed on the turret that can be commonly used for most jobs. The following suggested tools can be used to cover a majority of turning operations:

Operations	Insert	Holder	Illustration
Rough turning and facing	80 diamond	3 or 5 lead angle	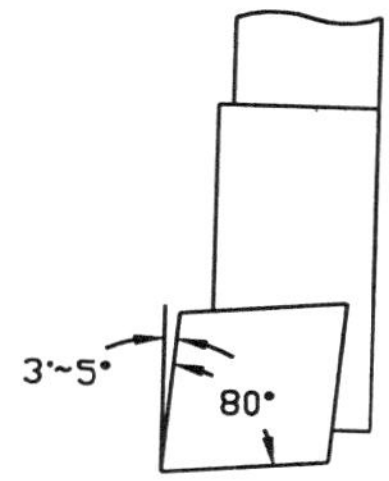
Finish turning	55 diamond	3 or 5 lead angle	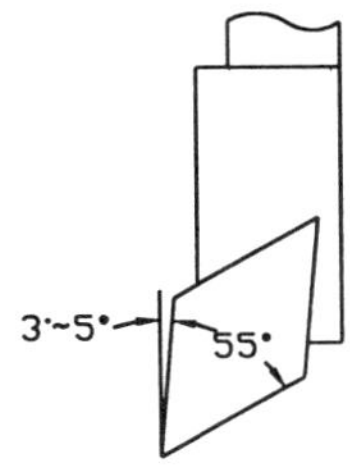
	35 diamond	3 or 5 lead angle	
Rough boring	80 diamond	3 or 5 lead angle	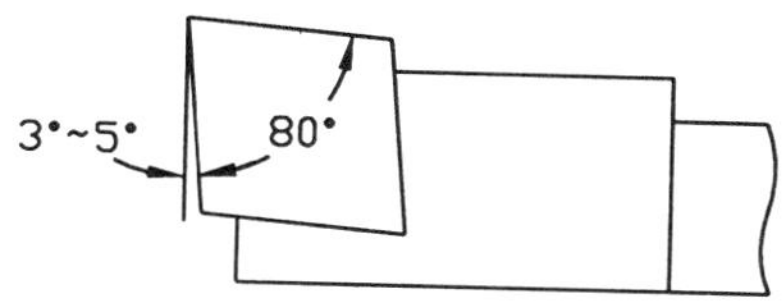
Finish boring	55 diamond	3 or 5 lead angle	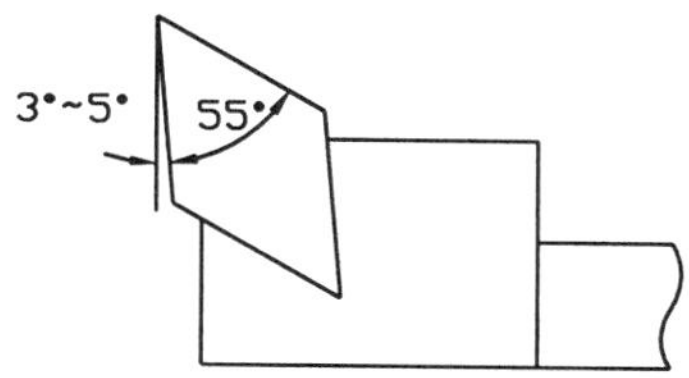
	35 diamond	3 to 5 lead angle	

External threading	60 threading	Special threading holder	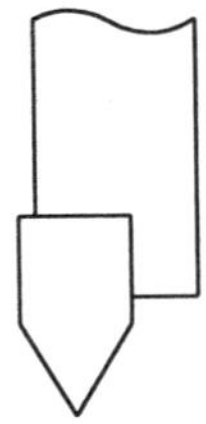
Internal threading	60 threading	Special threading holder	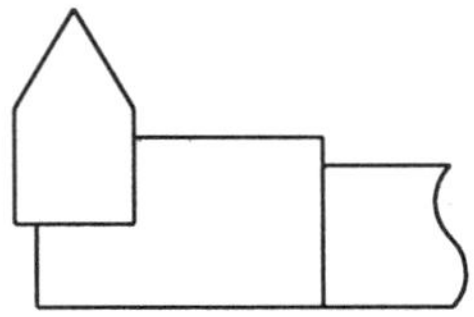
Grooving/parting	grooving insert	special holder or blade	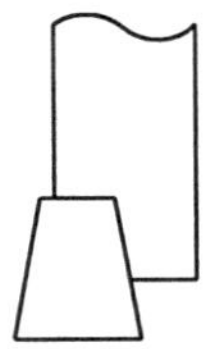
Drill	½" drill	special holder	
1" drill		special holder	

The intent of this section is to create eleven tools and save them in the tool library. These eleven tools can be used in most common turning projects without changing tool setup. The detailed information of these eleven tools are summarized below.

Turning **Tool name**	**Insert**	**Holder**	**Illustration**
Rough turn	CNMG-431 C: 80° diamond shape N: 0° relief angle M: tolerance G: chipbreaker on both sides with hole 4: IC size (1/2") 3: thickness (3/16") 1: corner radius (1/64")	DCLNR-164D D: pin and clamp clamping C: 80° diamond shape insert L: -5° lead angle N: neutral rake angle R: right hand holder 16: 1" square shank 4: IC size (1/2") D: Back and End qualified (overall length = 6")	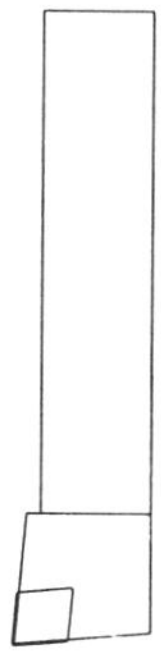
Finish turn – 55	DCMG-432 D: 55° diamond shape C: 7° relief angle M: tolerance G: chipbreaker on both sides with hole 4: IC size (1/2") 3: thickness (3/16") 2: corner radius (1/32")	DDJNR-164D D: pin and clamp clamping D: 55° diamond shape insert J: -3° lead angle N: neutral rake angle R: right hand holder 16: 1" square shank 4: IC size (1/2") D: Back and End qualified (overall length = 6")	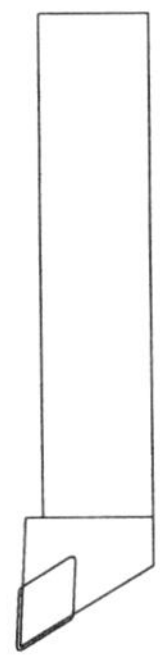
Finish turn – 35	VNMG-432 V: 35° diamond shape N: 0° relief angle M: tolerance G: chipbreaker on both sides with hole 4: IC size (1/2") 3: thickness (3/16") 2: corner radius (1/32")	DVJNR-164D D: pin and clamp clamping V: 35° diamond shape insert J: -3° lead angle N: neutral rake angle R: right hand holder 16: 1" square shank 4: IC size (1/2") D: Back and End qualified (overall length = 6")	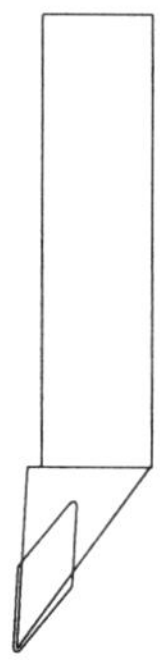

Bore Tools **Tool name**	**Insert**	**Holder**	**Illustration**
Rough bore	CNMG-321 C: 80° diamond shape N: 0°relief angle M: tolerance G: chipbreaker on both sides with hole 3: IC size (3/8") 2: thickness (1/8") 1: corner radius (1/64")	A16-MCLNR3 A: steel shank 16: 1" diameter shank M: clamping C: 80° diamond shape L: -5°lead angle N: neutral rake angle R: right hand holder 3: IC size (3/8")	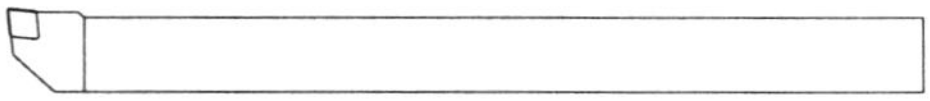
Finish bore – 55	DNMG-332 D: 55° diamond shape N: 0° relief angle M: tolerance G: chipbreaker on both sides with hole 3: IC size (3/8") 2: thickness (1/8") 2: corner radius (1/32")	A16-MDUNR3 A: steel shank 16: 1" diameter shank M: clamping D: 55° diamond shape U: -3° lead angle (front edge) N: neutral rake angle R: right hand holder 3: IC size (3/8")	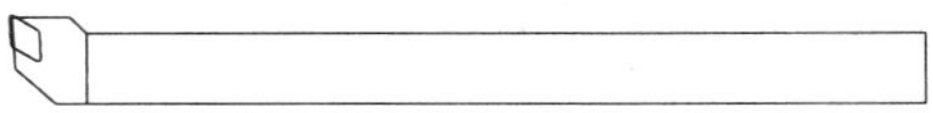
Finish bore – 35	VNMG-332 V: 35° diamond shape N: 0° relief angle M: tolerance G: chipbreaker on both sides with hole 3: IC size (3/8") 3: thickness (3/16") 2: corner radius (1/32")	A20-MVUNR3 A: steel shank 20: 1-1/4" diameter shank M: clamping V: 35° diamond shape U: -3° lead angle (front edge) N: neutral rake angle R: right hand holder 3: IC size (3/8")	

Thread **Tool name**	**Insert**	**Holder**	**Illustration**
OD thread	TNMA-43NV (Kennametal thread insert) 1/2" IC size For 6-20 OD threads per inch	MTVOR-164D 1" square shank overall length = 6" IC size (1/2")	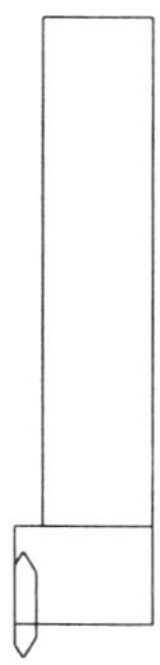

ID thread	TPMA-32NV (Kennametal thread insert) 3/8" IC size For 8-20 ID threads per inch	A20-MTHOR3 1-1/4" diameter shank 3/8" IC size Overall length = 14"	

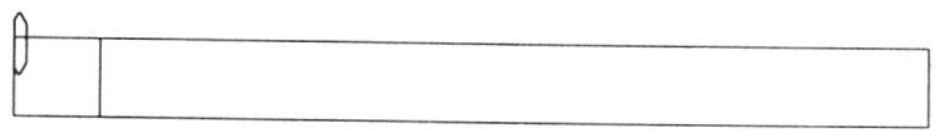

Groove

Tool name	Insert	Holder	Illustration
Groove	Groove with = 0.188" Length = 1"	1" square shank Length = 5" Groove width =0.188" Groove depth = 0.75"	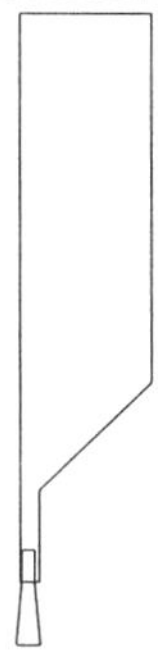

Drill

Tool name	Insert	Holder	Illustration
Drill – ½	½" drill	Special holder	

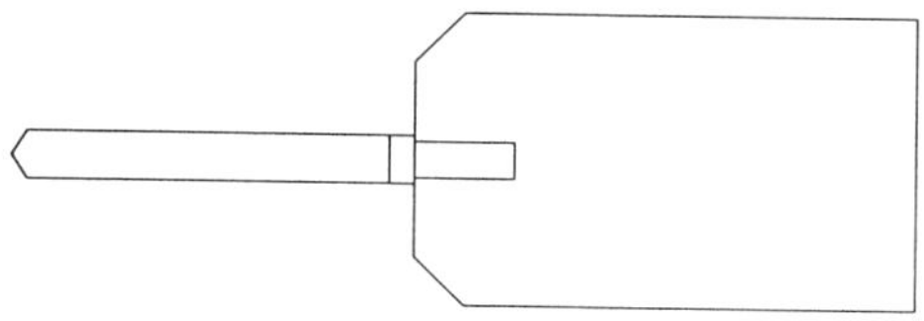

Drill – 1	1" drill	Special holder	

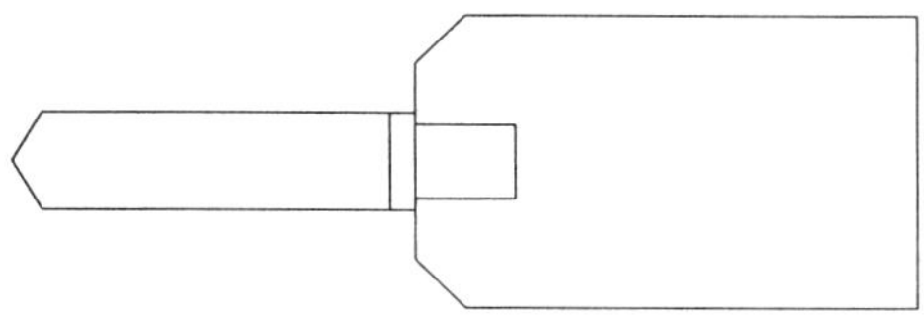

2 Project 2. Creating eleven tools

This project shows how to create a total of eleven tools that can be used in cutting a majority of lathe projects. These eleven tools are listed in the previous section. Inserts and holders of some tools are obtained directly from the library, others are created using insert and holder creation utilities. Each tool consisting of an insert or cutter and a holder that is saved in a unique name. Figure 21.10 shows the eleven tools created in this project.

a. Rough turn with 80° insert
b. Finish turn with 55° insert
c. Finish turn with 35° insert
d. Rough bore with 80° insert
e. Finish bore with 55° insert
f. Finish bore with 35°insert
g. OD threading tool
h. ID threading tool
i. Grooving tool
j. ½" drill
k. 1" drill

Step 1. Initiate the define tool utility.

Select **MAIN MENU → NC utils → Def tools → Library**

The Lathe Tool Manager menu with the tool list in the library should appear as below.

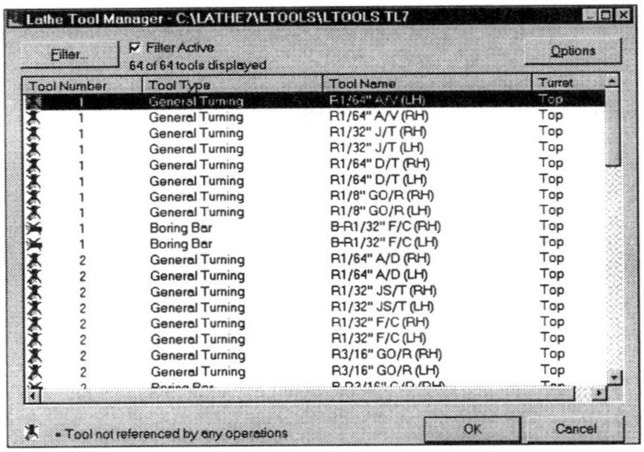

Step 2. Create a rough turn tool.

Click the right mouse button, then select **Create new tool** from the option list

The Define Lathe Tools menu appears as below.

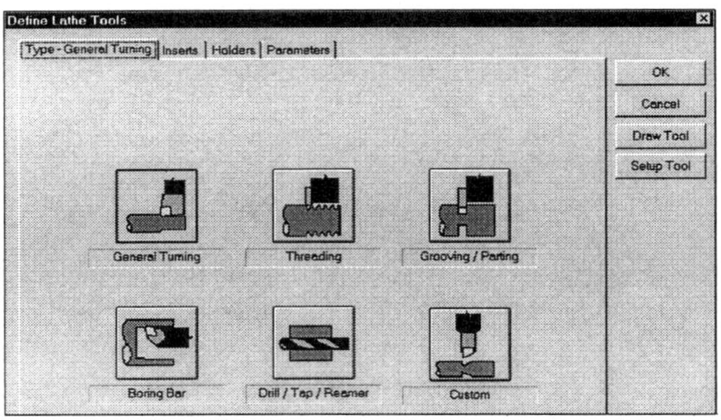

Select **General Turning tool type**
Select **Setup Tool** button
Set lathe tool setup parameters as below.

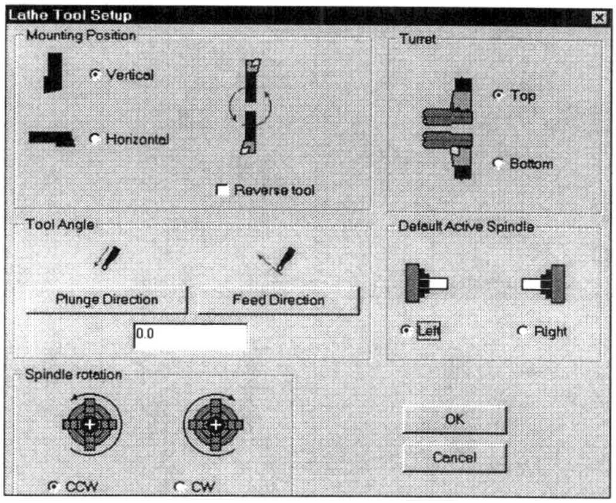

Select **OK**

Step 3. Select an insert "CNMG-431".

The initial insert menu should look like below.

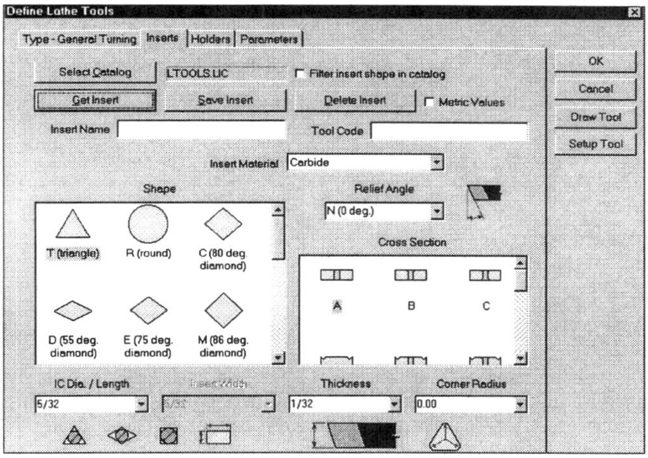

Select **Get Insert** button
The general turning/boring inserts list should appear as below.

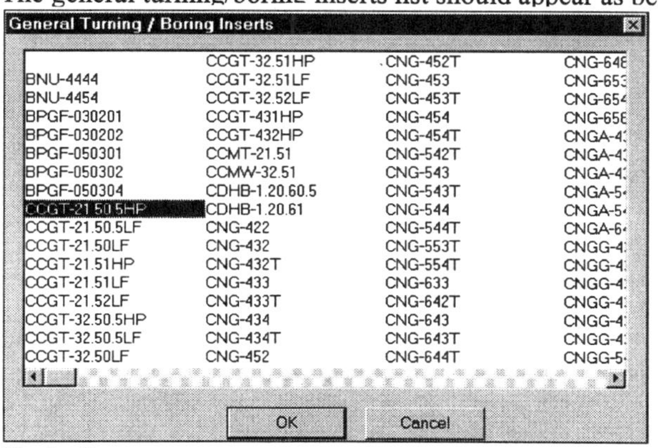

Scroll the list to find "CNMG-431"
Click on **CNMG-431** to highlight it
Select **OK**
The "CNMG-431" insert parameters are reflected on the insert menu as below.

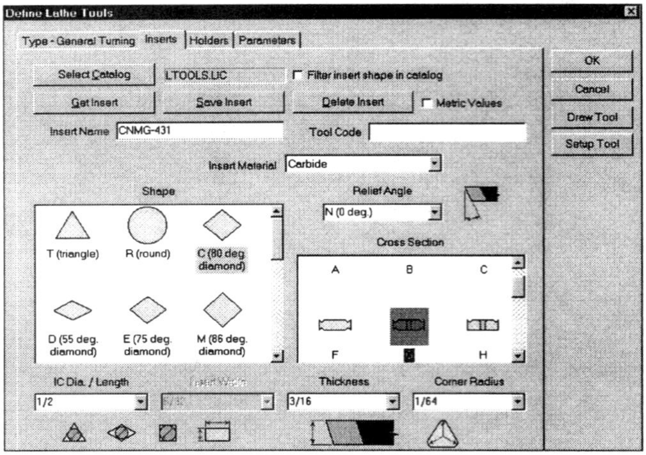

Step 4. Define a holder "DCLNR-164D".

Click the "Holders" button to open the holder menu as below.

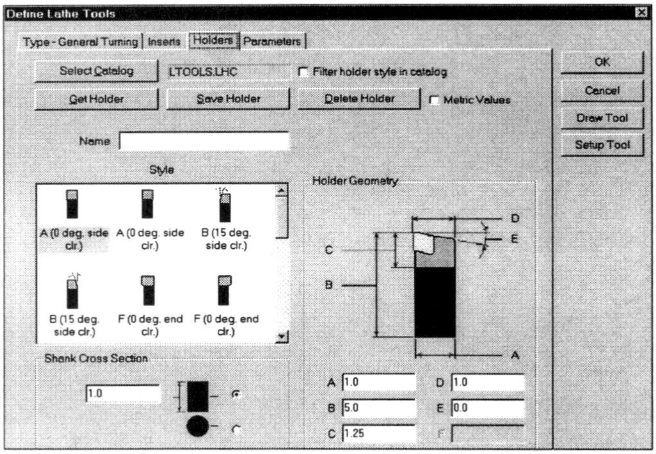

Set the holder parameters as below.

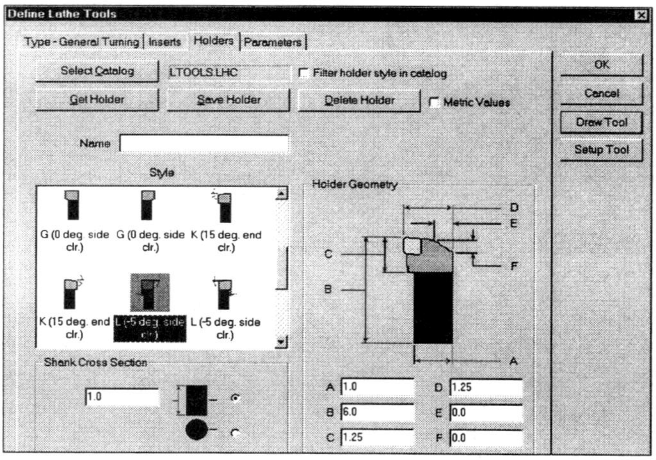

Step 5. Draw the insert and holder.

Select **Draw Tool** to view the combination of insert and holder

The insert and holder are shown in Figure 21.11.

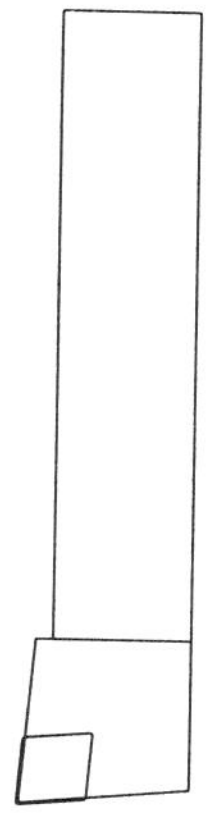

Figure 21.11

Select **Continue** to return back to Define Lathe Tool menu

Step 6. Define tooling and machining parameters.

Select **Parameters**

Set the parameters for this rough cut tool as below.

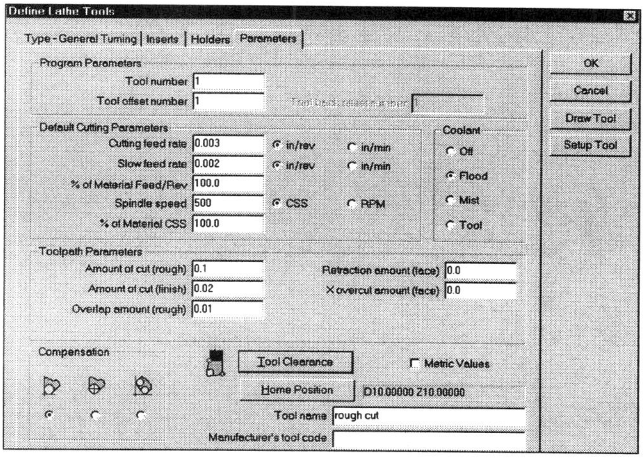

Select **OK** to complete the definition of the rough turn tool

Select **OK** to "Library updated successfully"

The rough turn tool appears on the Lathe Tool Manager menu as below.

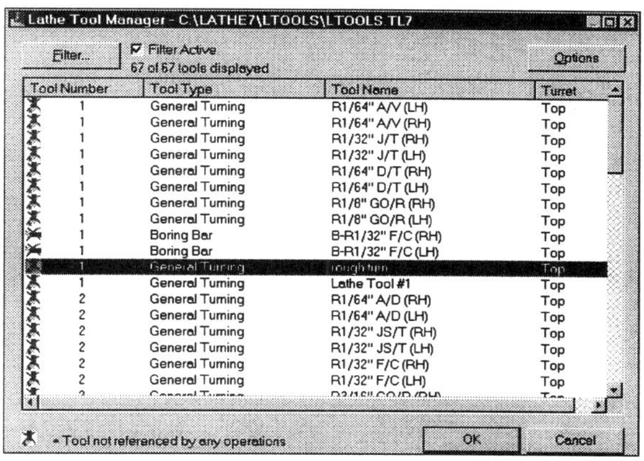

Step 7. Retrieve an existing tool "R1/32" J/D (RH)" from the library.

Scroll the tool list from the library to find "R1/32" J/D (RH)"
Click the right mouse button on **R1/32" J/D (RH)**, then select **Edit Tool** from option menu
Select the "Insert" button
The existing insert designation appears as below.

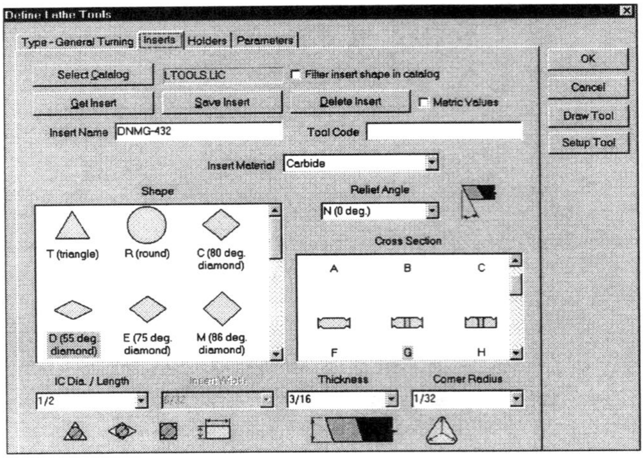

Select the "Holders" button
The existing holder designation appears as below.

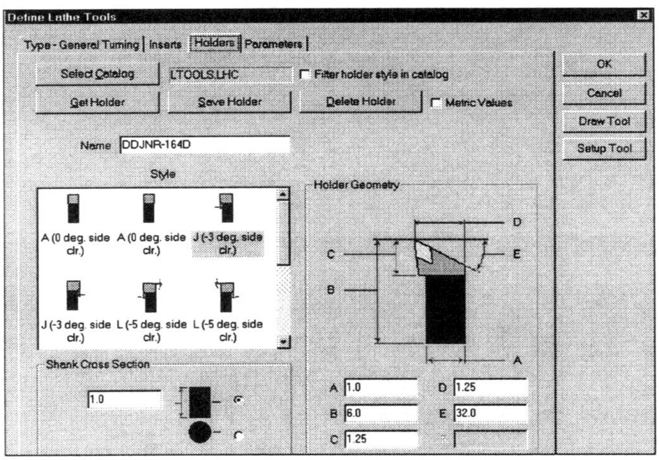

Step 8. Change the tool name to R1/2"J/D (RH) finish turn – 55.

Select the "Parameters" button

Set the parameters and tool name as below.

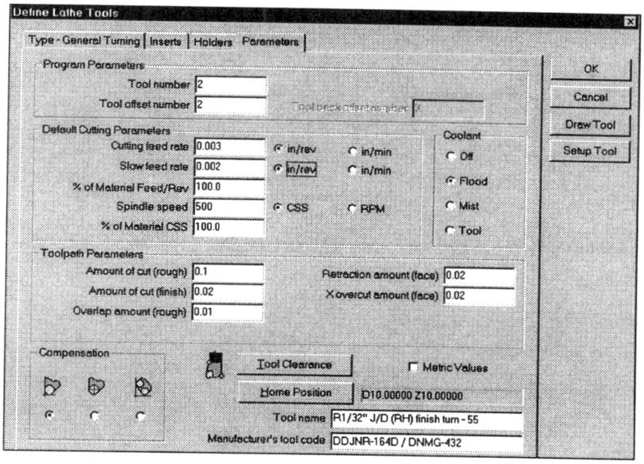

Select **OK**

The tool name of the edited tool has been changed as shown below.

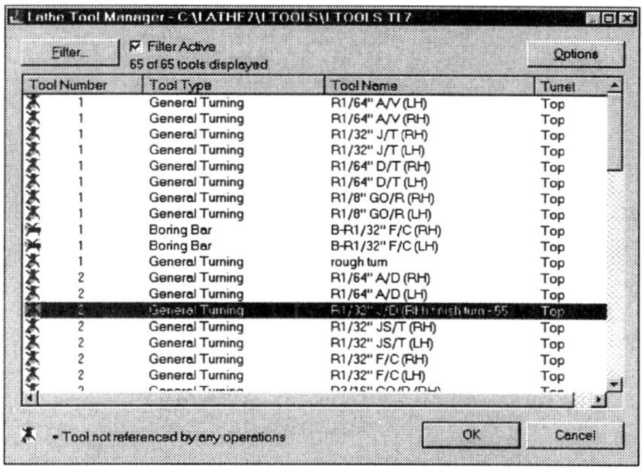

Step 9. Create a new tool for 35° diamond insert.

Click the right mouse button, then select **Create new tool** from the option menu
Select **General Turning** from the Define Lathe Tool menu
Define the insert parameters as below.

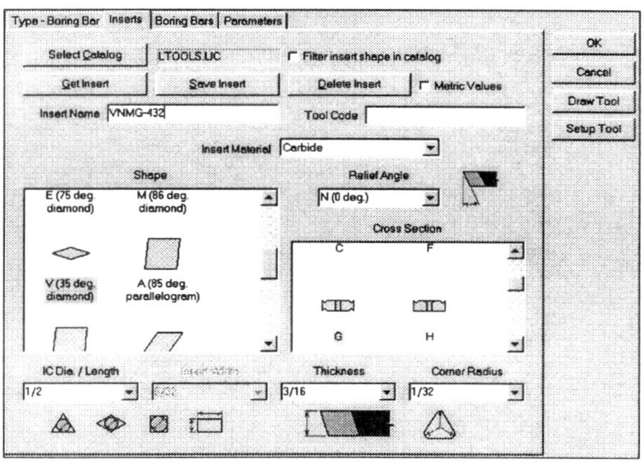

Step 10. Define the holder parameters.

Select the "Holders" button

Set the holder parameters as below.

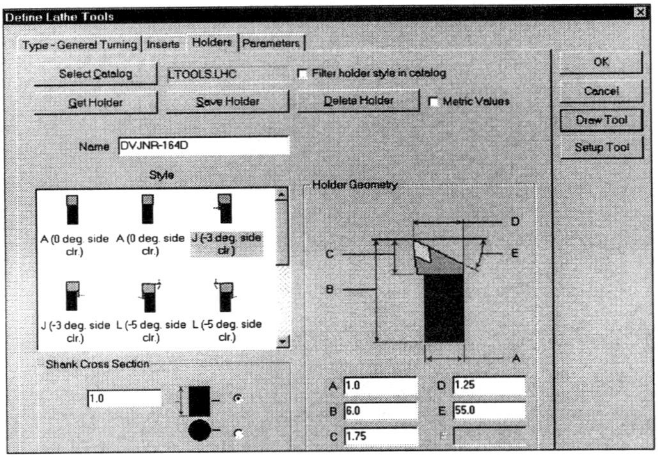

Select the **Draw Tool**

The insert and holder combination is shown in Figure 21.12.

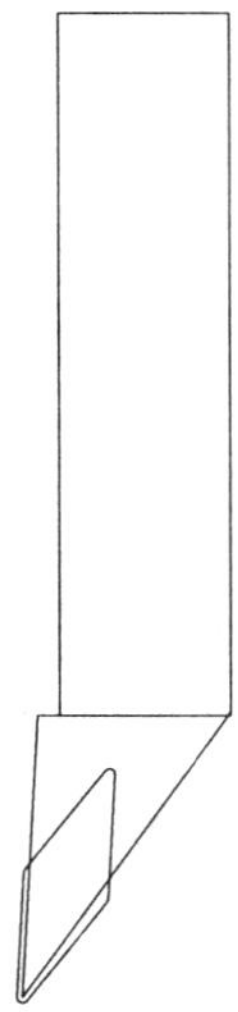

Figure 21.12

Select **Continue** to return back to holders menu

Step 11. Define the tooling and machining parameters.

Click the "Parameters" button

Set the parameters and tool name as below.

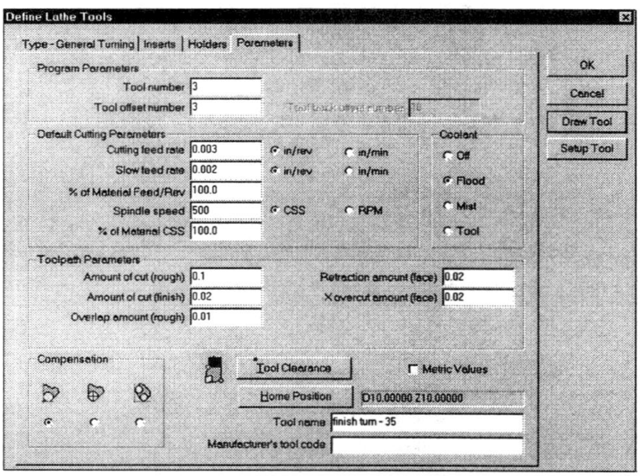

Select **OK**

Select **OK** to "Library updated successfully"

Step 12. Create a boring bar for roughing with a 80° diamond insert.

Click the right mouse button, then select **Create new tool**
Select **Boring Bar** from the tool type menu
Define the insert parameters as below.

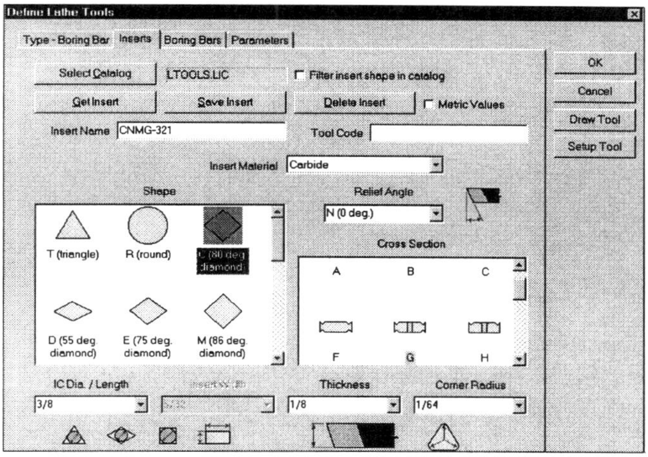

Step 13. Define the holder parameters.

Select the "Boring Bars" button
Set the holder parameters as below.

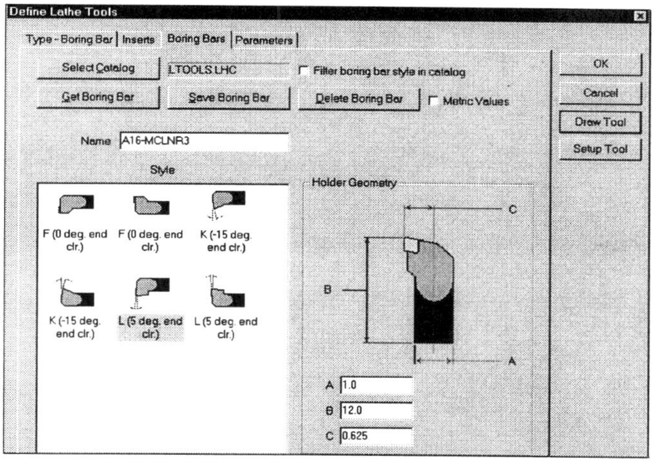

Step 14. Define the tooling and machining parameters.

Select the "Parameters" button

Set the tooling and machining parameters as below.

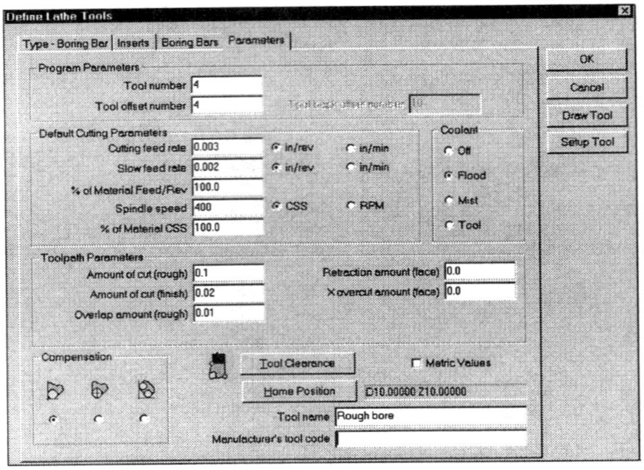

Select **Draw Tool**

The insert and holder combination appears as in Figure 21.13.

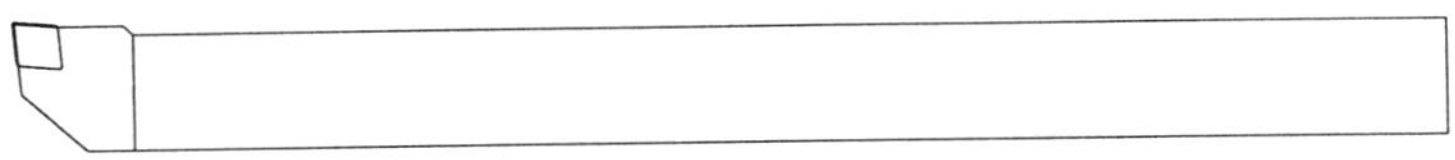

Figure 21.13

Select **Continue**

Select **OK**

Select **OK** to "Library updated successfully"

Step 15. Create a boring bar for finishing with a 55° diamond insert.

Click the right mouse button, then select **Create new tool**

Select **Boring Bar** from the tool type menu

Define the insert parameters as below.

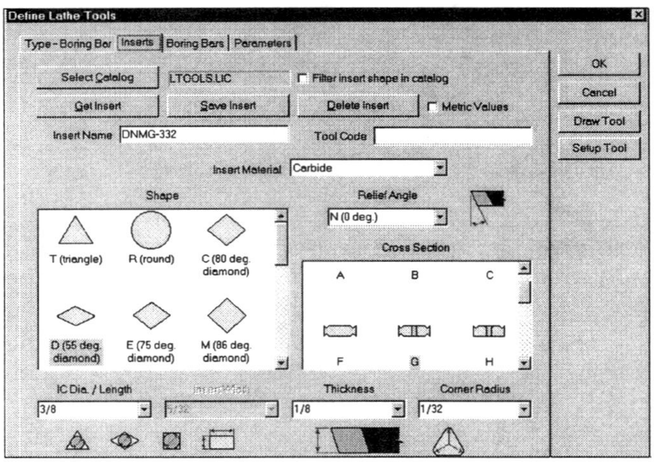

Step 16. Define the holder parameters.

Select the "Boring Bars" button

Set the holder parameters as below.

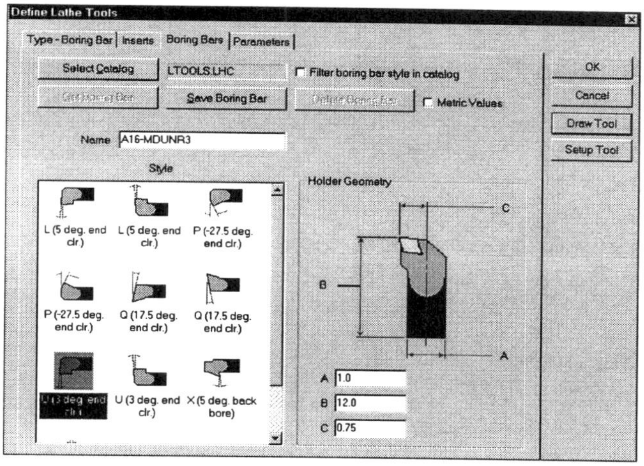

Step 17. Define the tooling and machining parameters.

Select the "Parameters" button

Set the tooling and machining parameters as below.

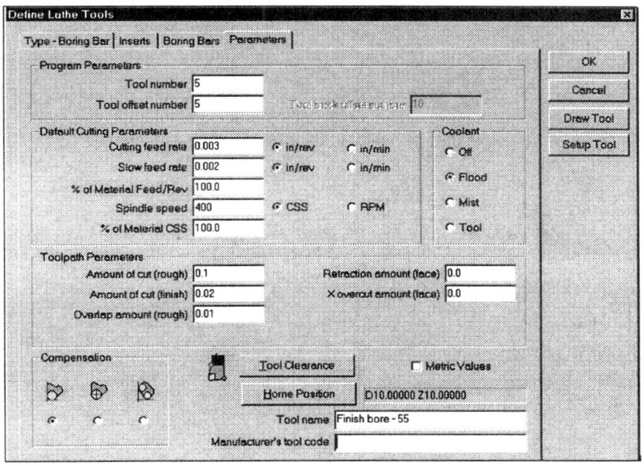

Select **OK**

Select **OK** to "Library updated successfully"

Step 18. Create a boring bar for finishing with a 35° diamond insert.

Click the right mouse button, then select **Create new tool**

Select **Boring Bar** from the tool type menu

Define the insert parameters as shown next.

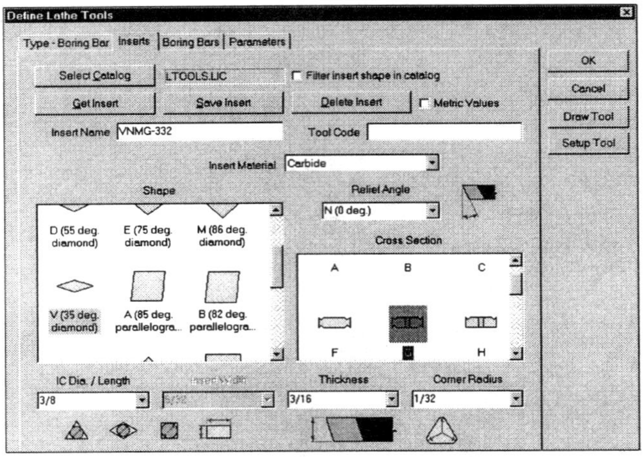

Step 19. Define the holder parameters.

Select the "Boring Bars" button

Set the holder parameters as below.

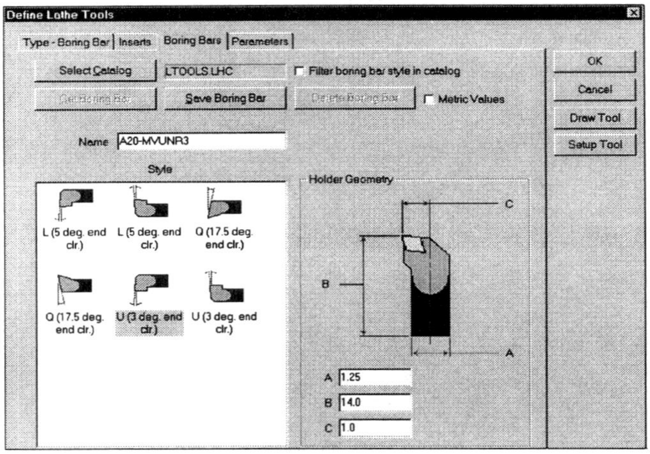

Step 20. Define the tooling and machining parameters.

Select the "Parameters" button

Set the tooling and machining parameters as below.

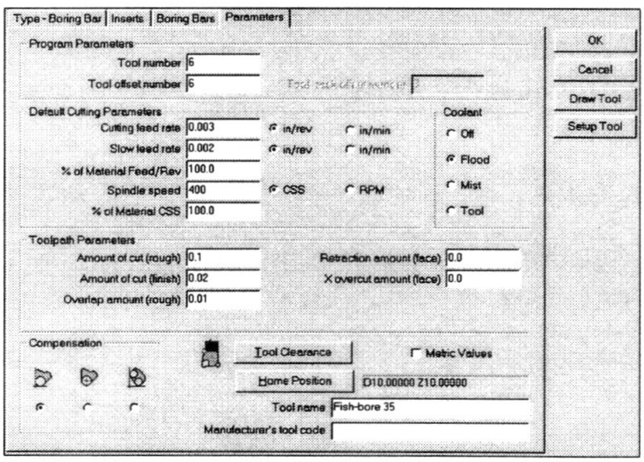

Select **OK**
Select **OK** to "Library updated successfully"

Step 21. Define an OD threading tool.

Click the right mouse button, then select **Create new tool**
Select the **Threading** tool type
Define the threading insert parameters as below.

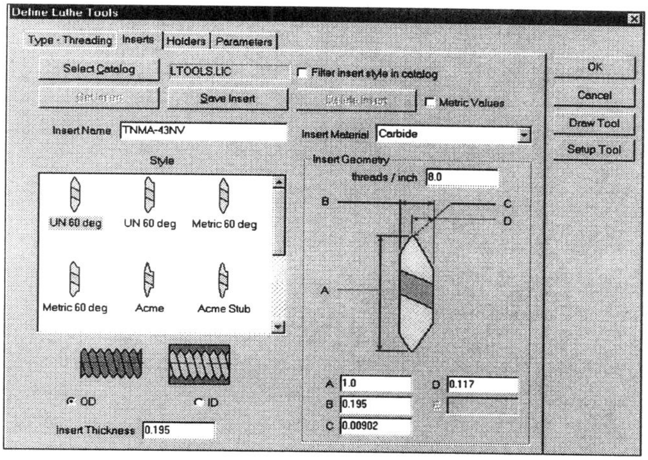

Step 22. Define threading holder parameters.

Select the "Holders" button
Set the holder parameters as below.

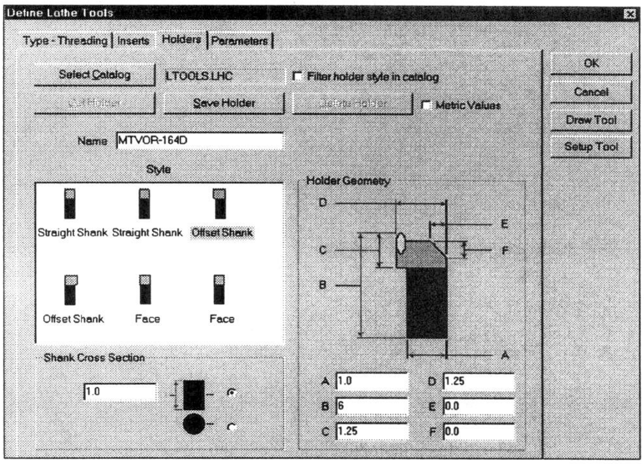

Step 23. Define the threading parameters.

Select the "Parameters" button

Set the threading parameters as below.

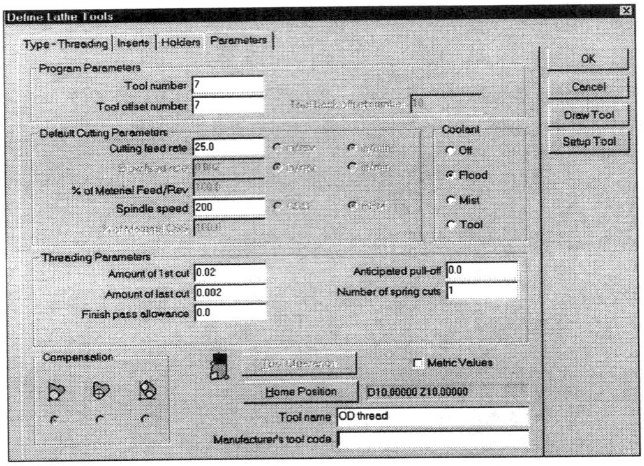

Select **OK**
Select **OK** to "Library updated successfully"

Step 24. Define an ID threading tool.

Click the right mouse button, then select **Create new tool**
Select **Threading** tool type
Define the threading insert parameters as below.

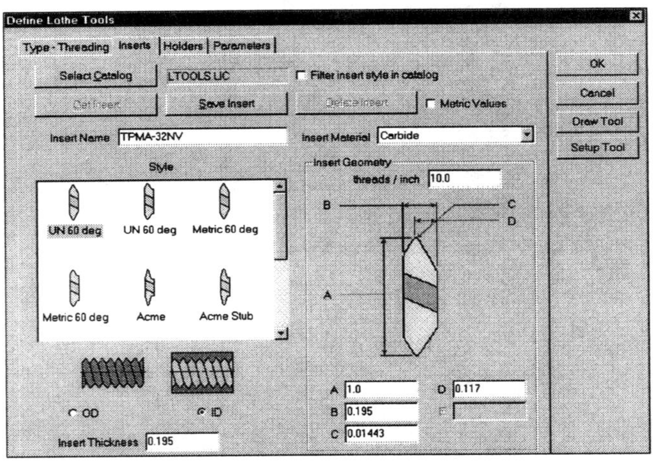

Step 25. Define threading holder parameters.

Select the "Holders" button

Set the holder parameters as below.

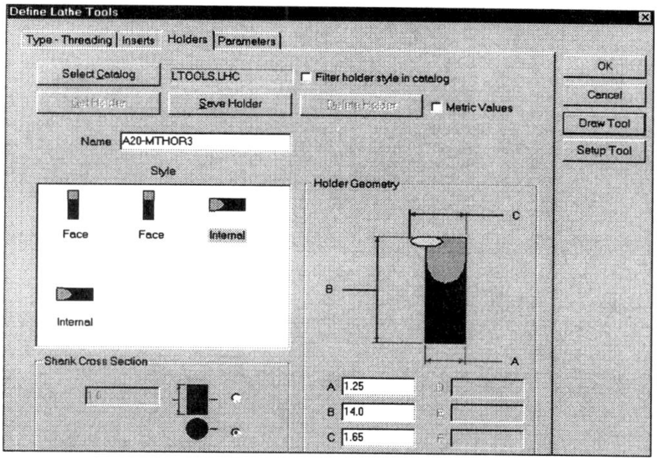

Step 26. Define the threading parameters.

Select the "Parameters" button
Set the threading parameters as below.

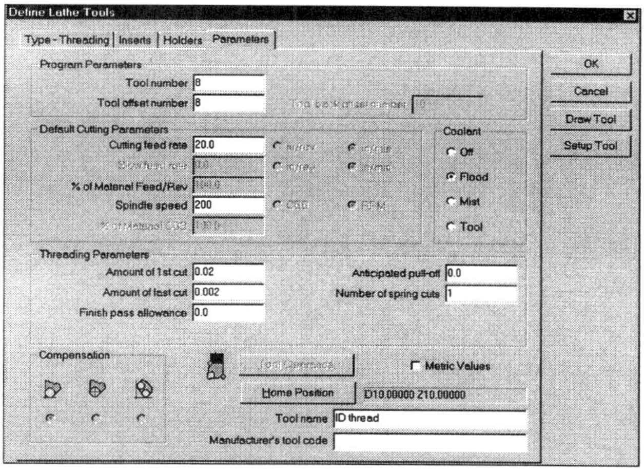

Select **OK**
Select **OK** to "Library updated successfully"

Step 27. Create a grooving tool.

Click the right mouse button, then select **Create new tool**
Select the **Grooving/Parting** tool type
Set the insert parameters as shown next.

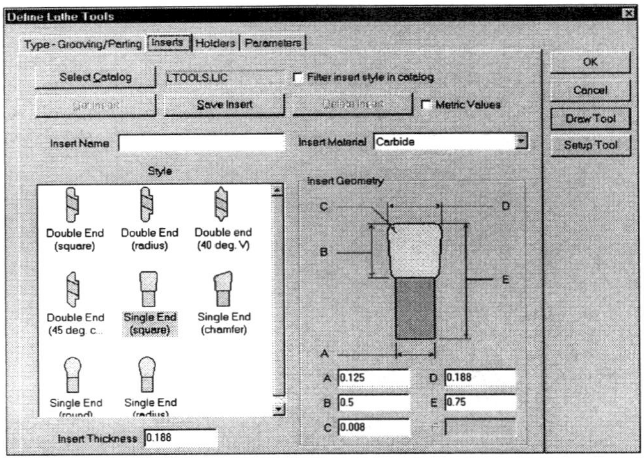

Step 28. Define the holder parameters.

Select the "Holders" button

Set the holder parameters as below.

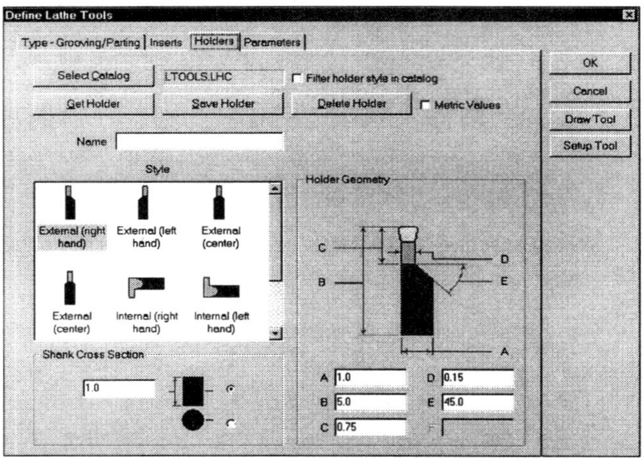

Step 29. Define the tooling and machining parameters as below.

Select the "Parameters" button

Set the tooling and machining parameters as below.

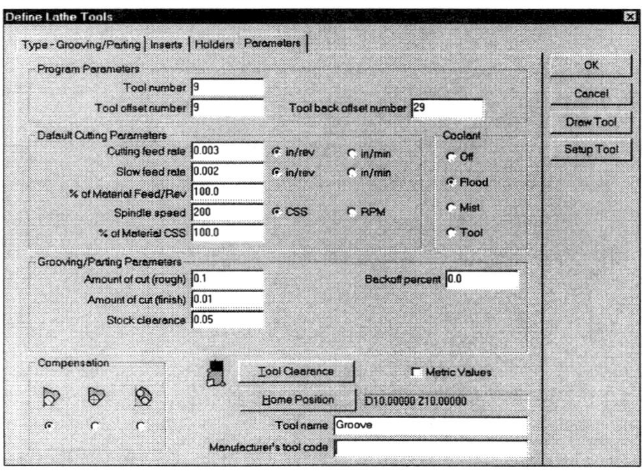

Select **OK**
Select **OK** to "Library updated successfully"

Step 30. Create a 0.5" drill.

Click the right mouse button, then select **Create new tool**
Select the **Drill / Tap / Reamer** tool type
Set the tool parameters as below.

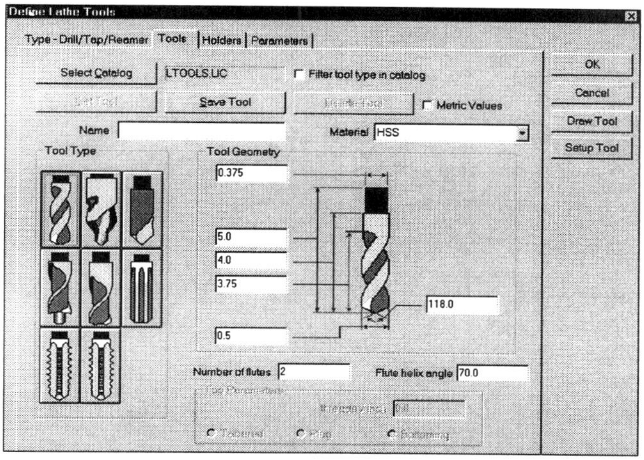

Step 31. Define the holder parameters.

Select the "Holders" button
Set the holder parameters as below.

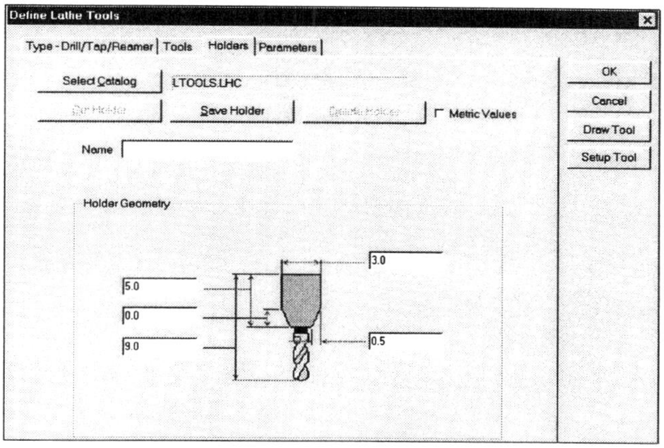

Step 32. Define the tooling and machining parameters as below.

Select the "Parameters" button

Set the tooling and machining parameters as below.

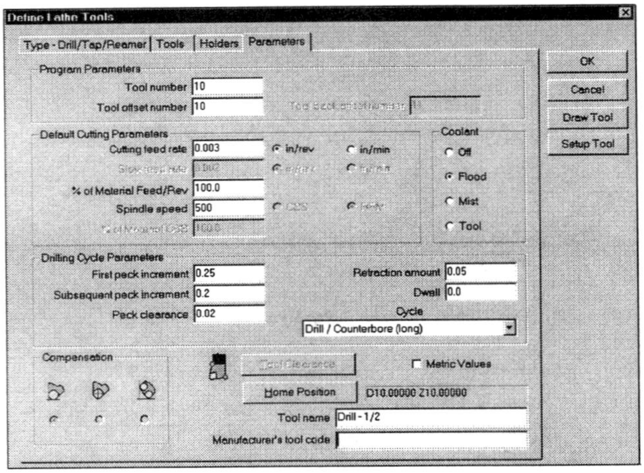

Select **OK**

Select **OK** to "Library updated successfully"

Step 33. Create a 1" drill.

Click the right mouse button, then select **Create new tool**

Select the **Drill / Tap / Reamer** tool type

Set the tool parameters as below.

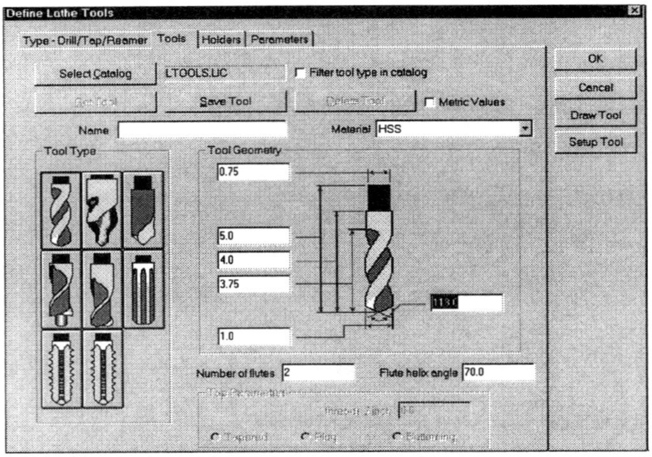

Step 34. Define the holder parameters.

Select the "Holders" button

Set the holder parameters as below.

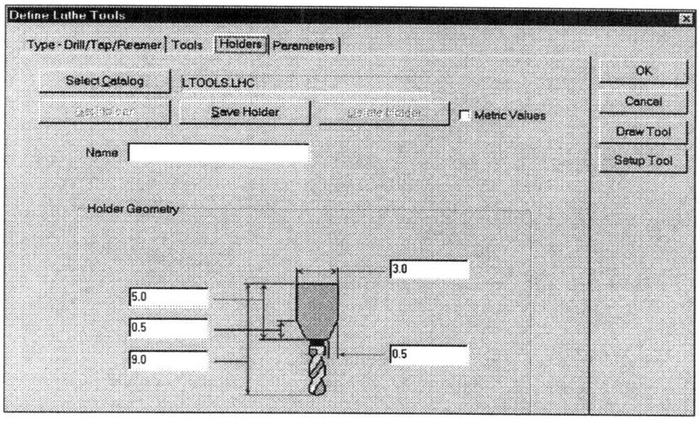

Step 35. Define the tooling and machining parameters as below.

Select the "Parameters" button
Set the tooling and machining parameters as below.

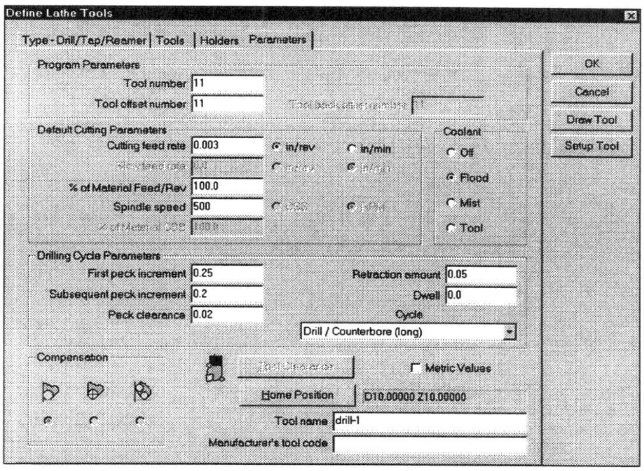

Select **OK**
Select **OK** to "Library updated successfully"

Step 36. Exit Lathe Tool Manager.

Select **OK** from the Lathe Tool Manager

Exercises

1. What is a job setup?
2. What are the four parameters Mastercam use to define tool collision boundaries?
3. Use drawings to explain the left spindle orientation and right spindle orientation of the chuck.
4. Explain how to import an existing job setup from a part file.
5. Use drawings to explain the top and bottom option of turret orientation.
6. What are the two components used to form a typical turning tool?
7. What are the two methods for accessing Define Lathe Tool utilities?
8. List the four steps involved in defining a tool.
9. List the six lathe tool categories.
10. What are the insert shapes of the following alphabet designations:
    C

    D

    T

    R

    V
11. Use a drawing to define the relief angle of an insert.
12. Use a drawing to define the inscribed circle (IC), thickness, and corner radius of an insert.
13. Explain how to determine the insert size.
14. What are the four thread forms Mastercam lathe allowed?
15. List the procedure of selecting a holder from holder library.
16. What are the three main parameters for defining a holder for general turning?
17. Explain how to define a holder style.

Chapter 22

Lathe Programming

Objectives:

1. Seven toolpath modules of lathes.
2. Common lathe parameters.
3. Applying toolpath modules to generate toolpaths.

Overview

Many machining operations can be performed in a CNC lathe. These operations include roughing, facing, turning, profiling, grooving, drilling, boring, threading, chamfering, cutting off, and milling (in mill-turn machines). Chapters 1 and 2 presented essential information about CNC programming, machining, and operation. This chapter shows how to generate part programs for cutting parts with CNC lathes. It begins with toolpath modules, common parameters, and seven lathe toolpath modules with step-by-step tutorial projects.

22.1 Lathe Toolpath Modules

The Mastercam lathe system provides two groups of toolpath modules: **turning modules** and **mill-turn modules**. The mill-turn modules generate toolpaths to perform milling operations in mill-turn machines. Mill-turn toolpath modules are covered in Chapter 23. This chapter presents the common parameters and seven turning modules. Table 22.1 on the next page summarizes the features and applications of these seven toolpath modules. The detailed presentation of these modules is given after the common parameters section.

Table 22.1 Lathe toolpath modules

Module	Description	Application	Illustration
Rough	Generate the toolpaths to rough the part to its approximated shape and size for future finishing cuts.	Roughing external and internal part contours.	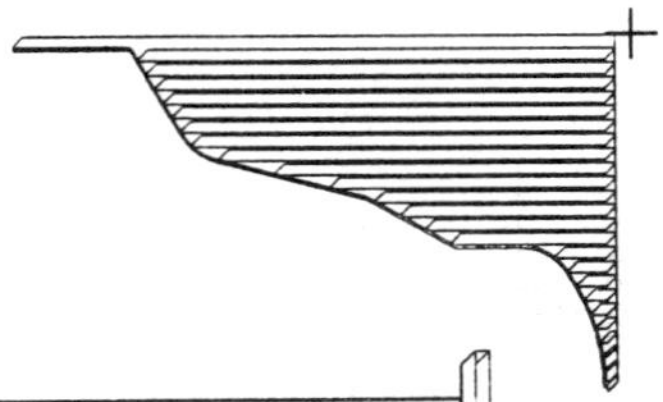
Face	Generate toolpaths to cut the end face of workpiece.	Facing the end face of the part.	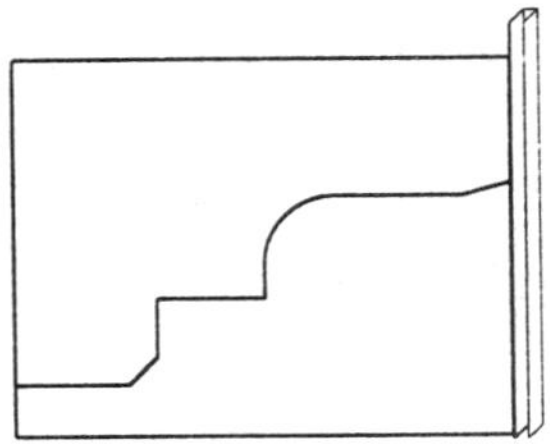
Finish	Generate the toolpaths to finishing cut the profiles.	Finishing cut along the OD, ID, or facing contours.	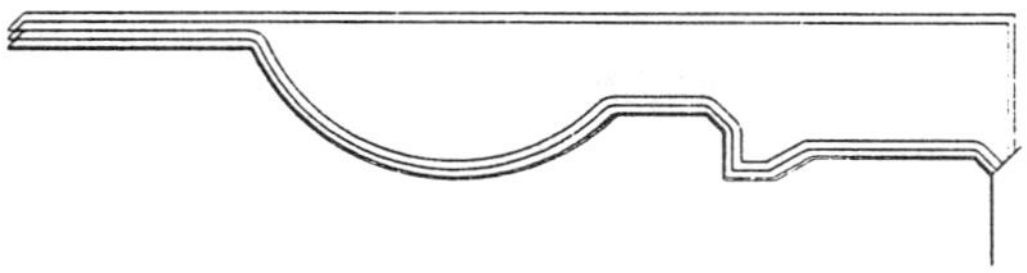
Cutoff	Generate toolpaths to parting off the finished part from the stock.	Parting off the part from the stock.	
Groove	Generate the toolpaths to rough the grooves.	Grooving external or internal grooves. Roughing a casting by using the groove module.	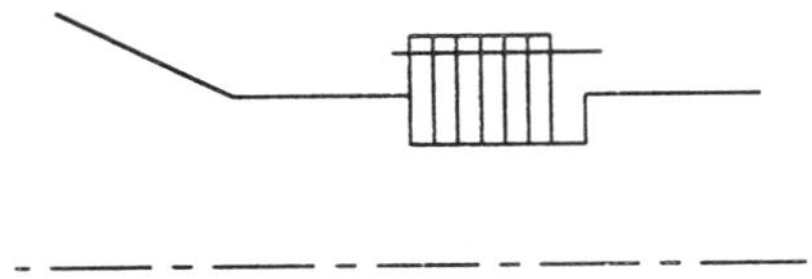
Thread	Generate the toolpaths to cut various types of threads.	Threading external or internal straight and taper threads.	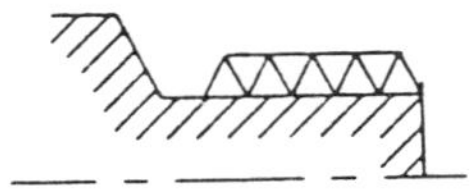
Drill	Generate the toolpaths to drill, bore, and tap holes.	Performing hole operations such as trilling, boring, and tapping.	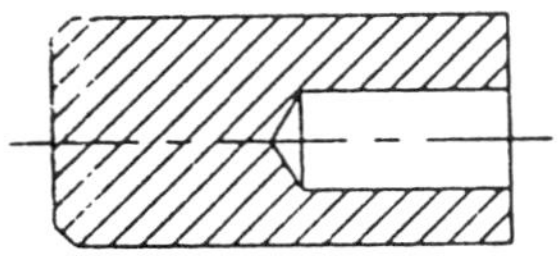

22.2 Lathe Common Parameters

Mastercam toolpath modules use two sets of parameters to define machining variables: **common NC parameters** and **module specific parameters**. As their names imply, common NC parameters are applied to all toolpath modules while module specific parameters are unique to a particular toolpath module. A sample of the lathe common NC parameter menu is shown below. Although this parameter menu is for roughing operations, you will find similar parameter menus for other operations.

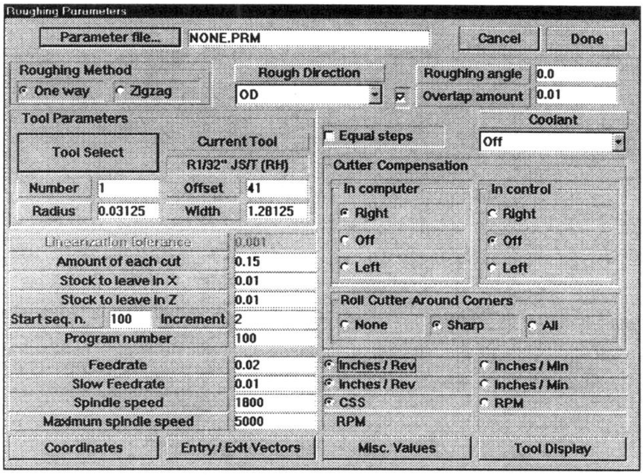

The lathe common parameters can be classified into **nine** groups:

Parameter file	Tool definition parameters
Machining parameters	Cutter compensation
Stocks	Coordinates
Entry/exit vectors	Miscellaneous
Tool display	

Parameter File

The parameter file stores all the specific parameter settings for the current operation. The system automatically names the parameter file (.PRM file) to the *.MC7 file name. For example, LATHE1.PRM is assigned as the parameter file name for a part geometry file name LATHE1.MC7. The user can change the file name by clicking on the parameter file button, then selecting a name from the list that appears.

Tool Definition Parameters

Turning tools are made with a small, rounded nose at the tool tip to increase the strength of the tip, enhance tool life, reduce stress concentration, help heat dissipation, and produce a smooth surface. This small, rounded nose is referred to as the tool nose and its radius is called the tool nose radius (Figure 22.1).

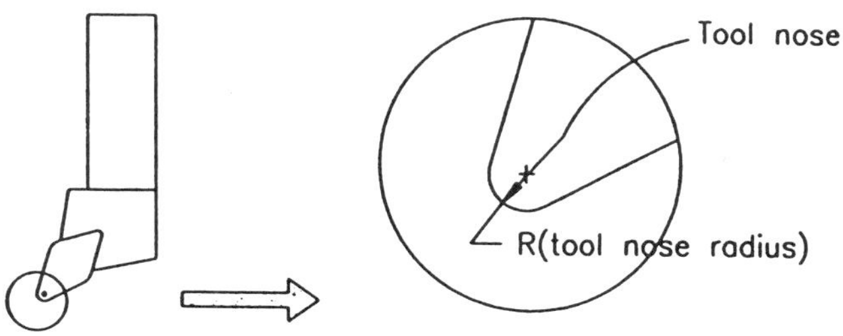

Figure 22.1

The imaginary tool nose is often used as the reference point for programming the tool path. It is defined as the intersection point between the two lines that are tangent to the tool nose and parallel to the X and Z axes, respectively (Figure 22.2). The use of an imaginary tool nose generates precise tool paths that are parallel to either the X or Z axis. However, it produces excessive cutting or insufficient cutting on taper and circular paths, depending on the orientation of the cutting vector. When the tool nose radius is very small, the cutter path error may be minute. However, as the tool nose radius becomes larger, its effect on the actual cutting path should not be ignored. These cutting path errors can be compensated by using the tool nose radius (TNR) compensation command which is controlled by the cutter compensation in control parameters.

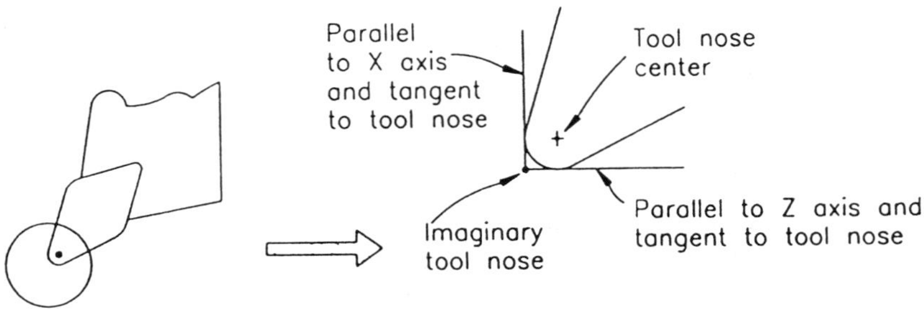

Figure 22.2

To properly use a cutting tool, it must be adequately defined by the following six variables: **Tool select, Current Tool, Number, Radius, Offset,** and **Width**.

Tool select Click the "Tool Select" button to open the "Lathe Tool Manager" menu as shown below.

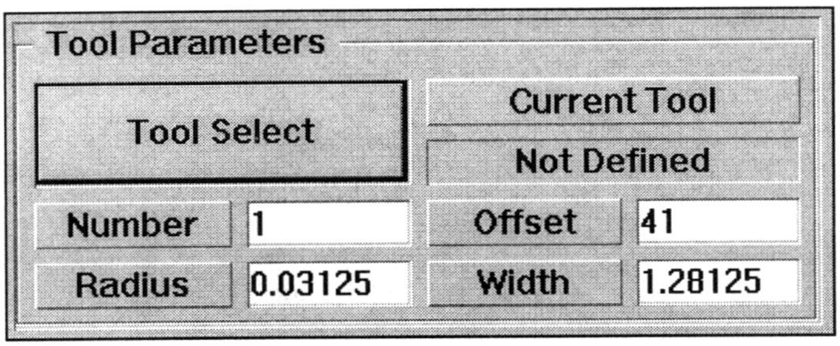

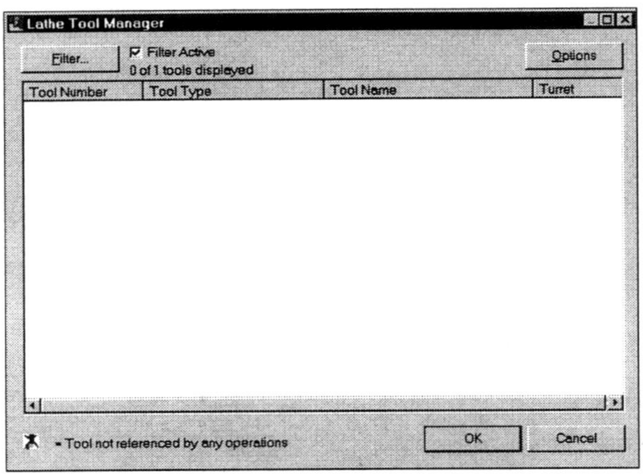

Click the right mouse button to open the option menu shown hereto either create a new tool or get a tool from the library.

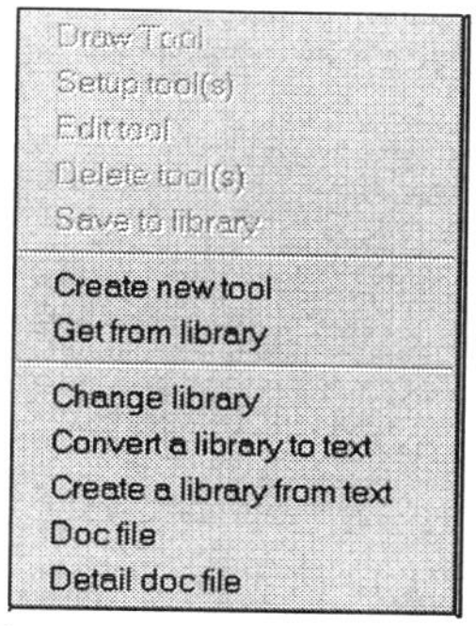

Select "Create new tool" to open the create new tool menu as below.

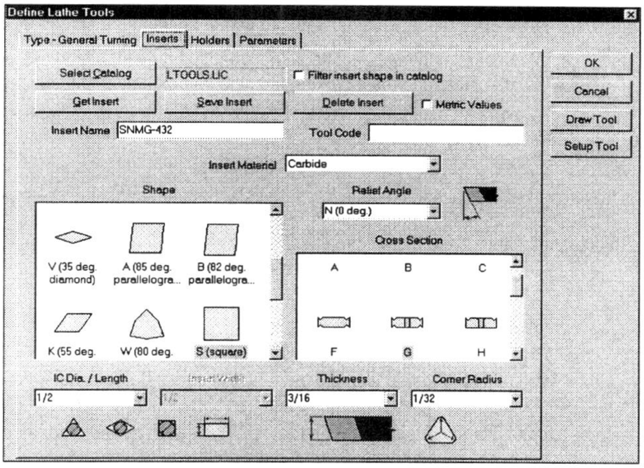

Select "Get from library" to open the get from library menu as below.

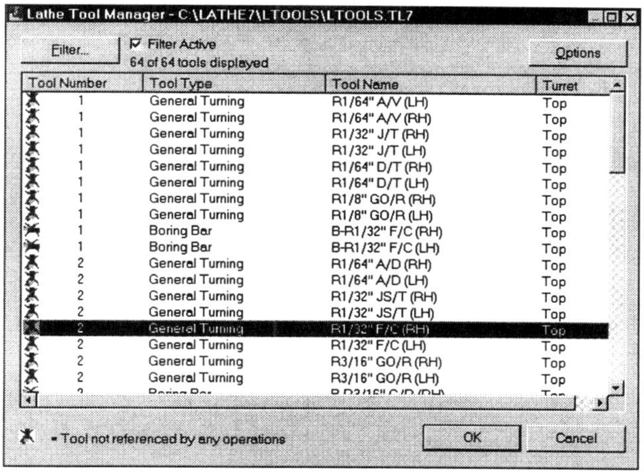

Select "R1/32" F/C (RH)" from the list
Select OK to exit the tool manager menu

The tool parameters will reflect the selected tool as shown below.

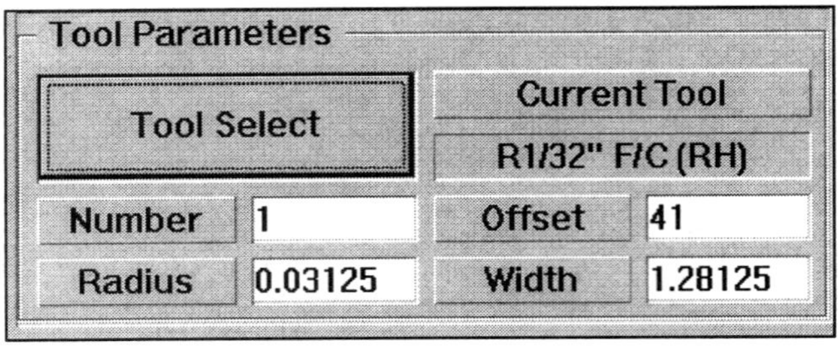

Current Tool This parameter shows the name of the selected tool. In this example, the current tool is "R1/32" F/C(RH)".

Number (Tool Number) This parameter is used to output a tool number to the part program. A number of 5, for example, will give the tool number command T05 to the part program. A tool number normally represents the tool position in the turret or tool magazine. The tool position number ranges from 6 to 24 depending on the size of the machine and the number of turret used. It is recommended that the specified tool number must match the actual tool station on the turret.

Offset (Offset Number) This parameter outputs a tool offset number to the part program. The tool offset number normally is used together with the tool number in the form:

T0101
- tool offset number
- tool number
- tool function

A tool offset number physically locates a register, which is a storage space in the control, and stores the following information. *Note:* A tool offset number can be different from the tool number (ex. T0105).

Offset Number	Offset value in X axis (OFX)	Offset value in Z axis (OFZ)	Tool nose radius comp. value (OFR)	Direction of Imaginary tool nose (OFT)
01	0	0	0.032	1
02	0.15	0.05	0.016	1

Radius (Tool Nose Radius) This parameter indicates the tool nose radius at the tool tip. Typical tool nose radii used in turning are 1/64, 1/32, 3/64, and 1/16 in.

Width The tool width in Mastercam is defined as the distance across the radii of the tool (not the distance from center to center.) See Figure 22.3.

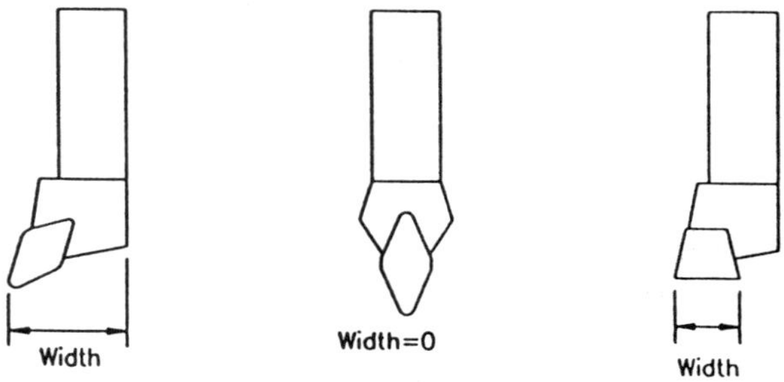

Figure 22.3

Machining Parameters

This group of parameters deals with the **depth of cut**, **feed rate**, and **cutting speed**.

Depth of cut The amount of each cut parameter specifies the depth of cut for each tool pass. This distance is measured in the direction perpendicular to the cutting direction (Figure 22.4). The X value is expressed as the radius.

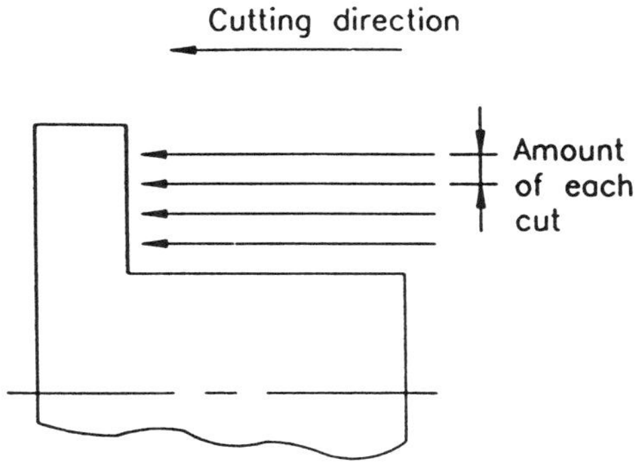

Figure 22.4a Cutting in the Z direction

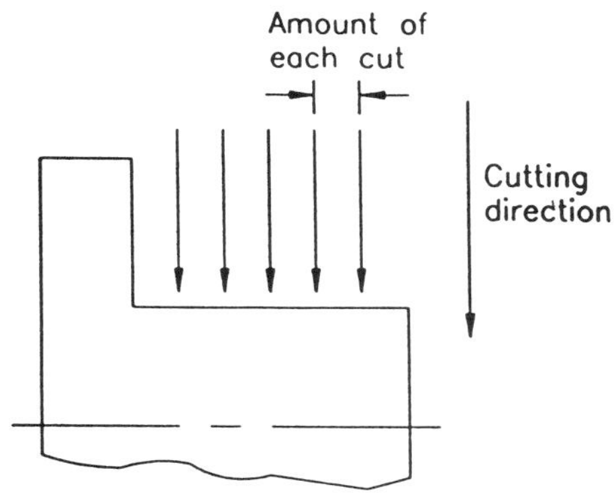

Figure 22.4b Cutting in the X direction

Feed Rate The feed rate used in lathes is normally expressed in units of inches per revolution. This parameter can be toggled to inches per revolution or inches per minute.

Cutting speed These three NC commands are used in lathe to control the spindle speed:

G50 Ss	maximum spindle speed in RPM.
G96 Ss	constant surface speed in ft/min or m/min.
G97 Ss	constant spindle speed in RPM.

The **constant surface speed** is used in turning, boring, and grooving, while the **constant spindle speed** is utilized in drilling and threading.

A maximum speed limit must be specified when the constant surface speed mode is used. Figure 22.5 shows how the two commands G50 and G96 work together to produce proper speed control.

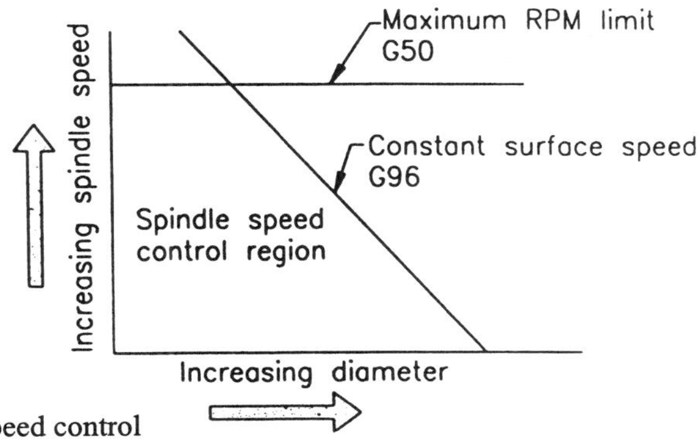

Figure 22.5 Spindle speed control

In Mastercam the spindle speed parameter can be toggled to constant RPM or constant surface speed in ft/min or m/min.

Stocks

The stock parameter specifies the amount of material to be left in both X and Z directions for subsequent finishing cuts (Figure 22.6a). Although a negative value can be assigned to the stock parameter, it is recommended that only positive stock values are used in order to produce correct toolpaths. A negative value can result in an inaccurate toolpath as shown in Figure 22.6b. *Note:* The stock parameters must be used in conjunction with the parameter of cutter compensation in computer.

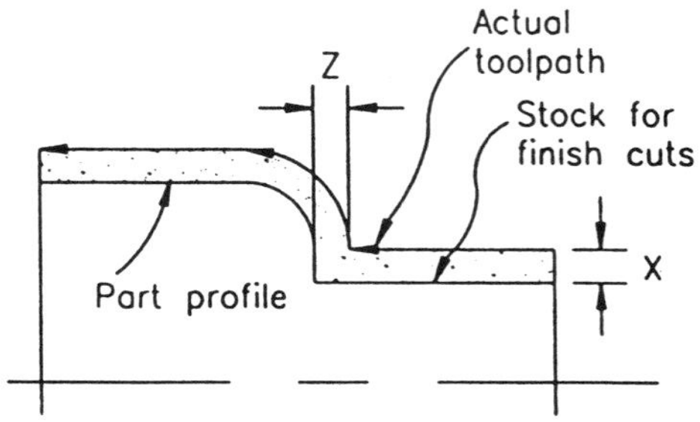

Figure 22.6a Stock in X and Z directions

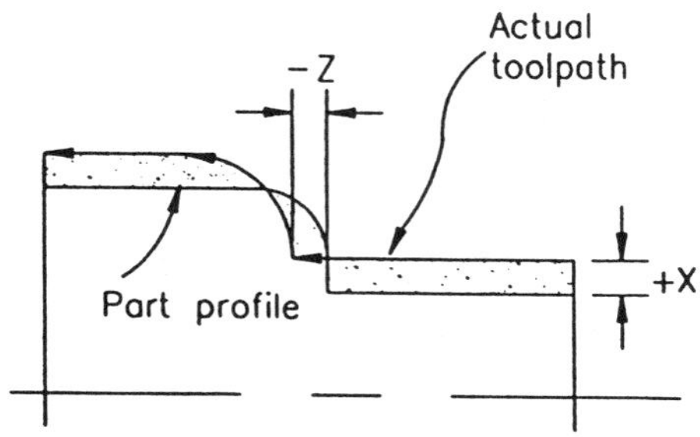

Figure 22.6b Negative stock value in Z direction

Cutter Compensation

There are two types of cutter compensation used in Mastercam: **cutter compensation in computer** and **cutter compensation in control**.

Cutter compensation in computer This parameter can be selected with three options: **Off, Left**, or **Right**. It is used to specify which side the cutter is offset in the direction of the cutting contour. The effect on the toolpaths is illustrated in Figure 22.7. When this parameter is toggled to Off, the actual toolpath coincides with the part profile even though a non-zero stock is specified (Figure 22.7a). The toolpath is displaced to the right of the part profile by a distance given in a stock parameter when this parameter is toggled to right (Figure 22.7b). *Note:* When this parameter is set to left, the toolpath is displaced to the left of the part profile (Figure 22.7c). In other words, this changes the direction of the stock in both X and Z axes.

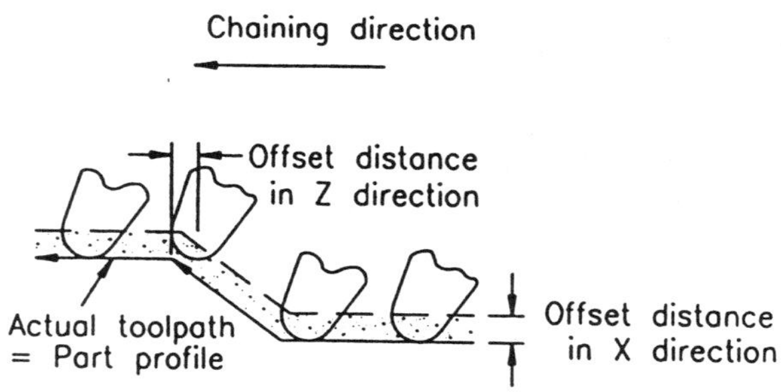

Figure 22.7a. Off

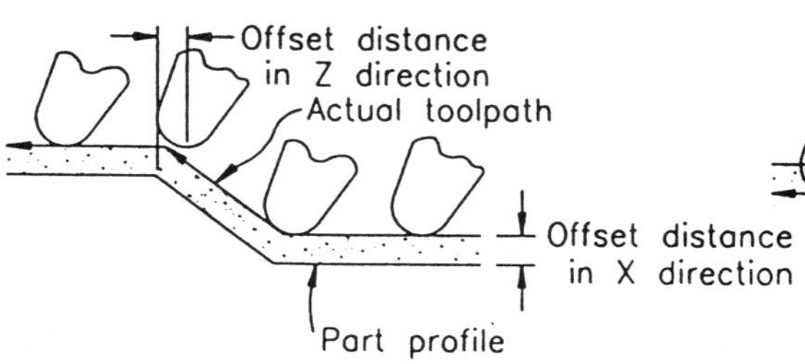

Figure 22.7b. Right

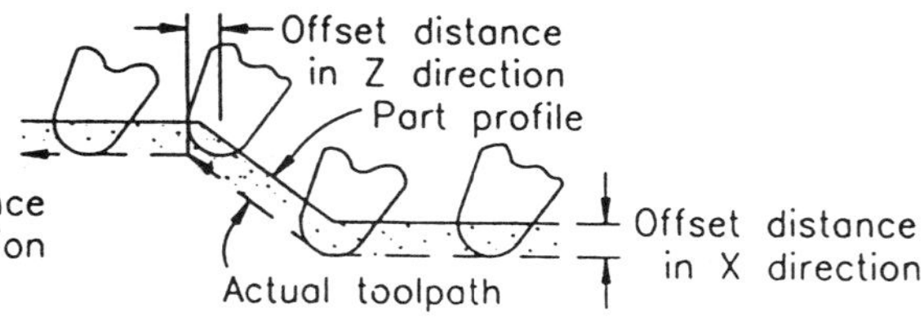

Figure 22.7c Left

The proper selection of a cutter compensation command depends on two factors: **operation type** and **chaining direction**. Table 22.3 summarizes compensation commands for various cases.

Table 22.3 Selectionof Cutter Compensation Commands

Operation type	Chaining/Cutting direction	Compensation command	Toolpath Illustration
O.D. turning (Both roughing and finishing)	← From right to left	Right	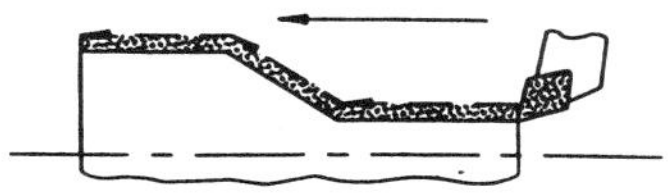
	→ From left to right	Left	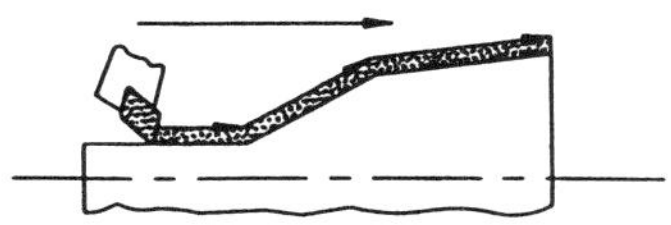
Facing	Inward ↓	Left	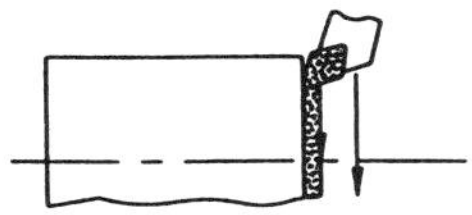
	Outward ↑	Right	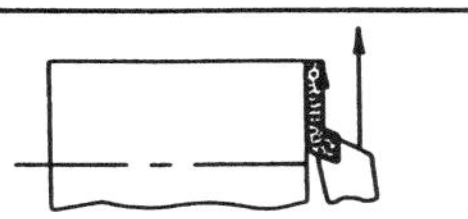
I.D. boring	← From right to left	Left	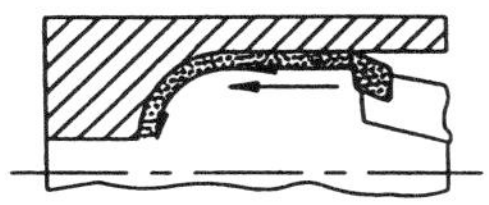
	→ From left to right	Right	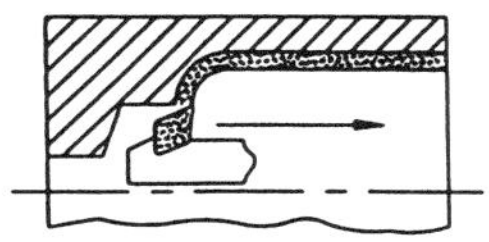
Drilling		Off	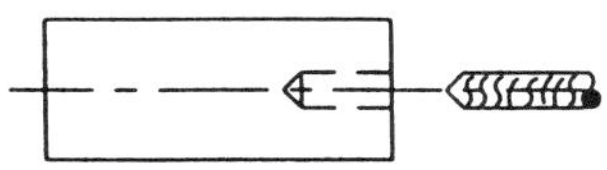

Cutter compensation in control This parameter can be selected with these options: **Off, Left**, or **Right**. It outputs a tool nose radius (TNR) compensation command to the part program. Their corresponding TNR command is given below:

Off:	G40 (TNR Off)
Left:	G41 (TNR Left)
Right:	G42 (TNR Right)

The consideration in selecting cutter compensation in control is the same as for cutter compensation in computer. Cutter compensation in control is required when turning a slope surface or a curved surface while demanding a closed dimension. Figure 22.8 on the next page illustrates position errors encountered in turning a slope surface and a curved surface without using a proper TNR compensation.

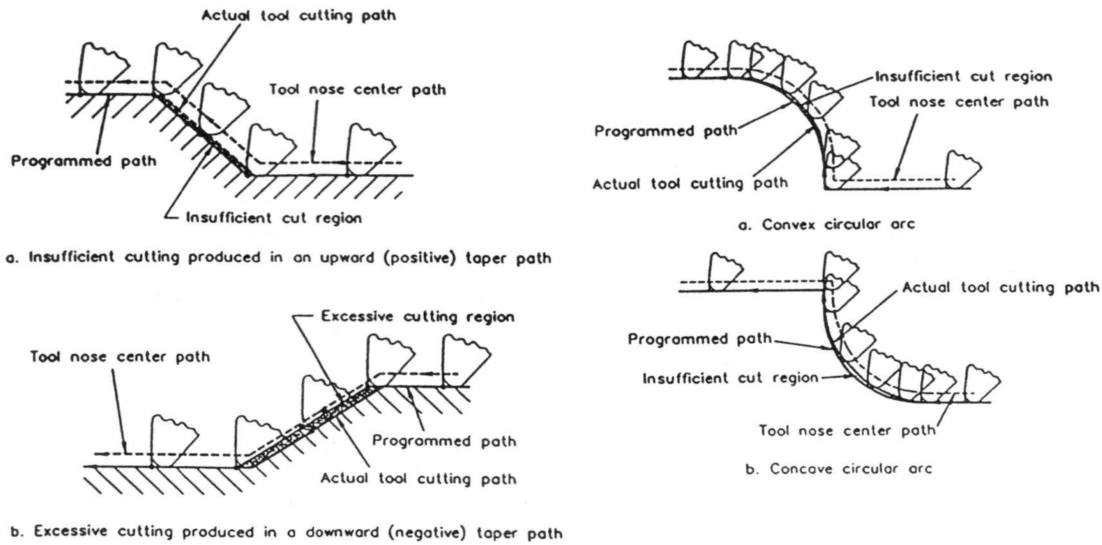

Figure 22.8

The status of this parameter does not affect the toolpath shown on the computer screen. It only inserts a TNR compensation command into the program. The tool vector and tool nose radius in the offset registers must be correctly specified in the CNC control in order to make the TNR command work properly.

Coordinates

There are three parameters under this category. The coordinate menu appears as below.

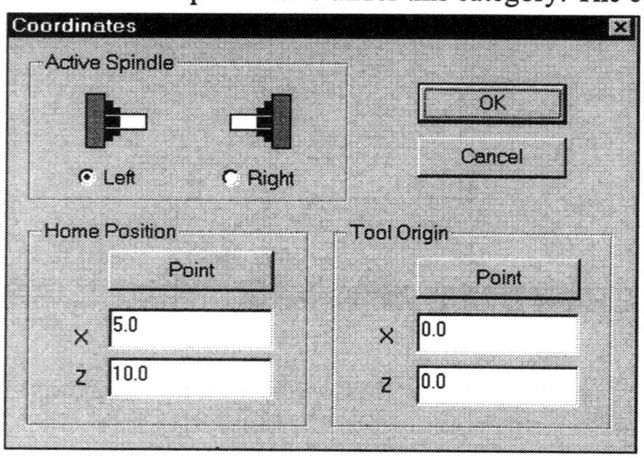

Active spindle This parameter specifies the orientation of the chuck either in the Left or Right. Normally, the chuck is in the Left orientation.

Home position This parameter specifies the home position for tool change. This parameter works with the “Toolchange on offset” parameter under Miscellaneous Integer parameter. The home position becomes the tool change position when this parameter is set to 1 (ON), otherwise, the retract location becomes the tool change location when this parameter is set to 0 (OFF). The home location is specified by its X and Z coordinate value.

Tool origin This parameter specifies the tool origin coordinates. It is defined by its X and Z coordinate value.

Entry/Exit Vectors

This group of parameters are used to add a tool move for entering or exiting the part for each cutting pass. Its parameter menu appears as below.

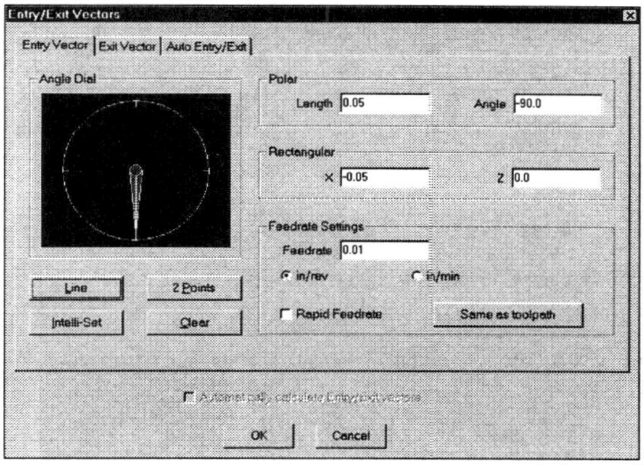

The entry or exit vector can be defined in two coordinate systems; polar coordinate system and rectangular coordinate system. In polar coordinate system, the entry or exit vector is defined by its length and angle. The angle is measured from 3 o'clock direction being 0 degree and has a positive angle in counterclockwise direction and a negative angle in clockwise direction. In rectangular coordinate system, the entry or exit vector is defined by its incremental distance in X and Z direction.

Entry vector The entry vector specifies the toolpath pattern for the tool to enter the part for each cutting pass. It is defined by either polar system or rectangular system. In the polar system, the angle value specifies the vector direction, while the length defines the actual distance of the entry vector. In the rectangular system, the direction of entry angle is indirectly defined by the two vector components, X and Z. Both positive and negative values can be used. Figure 22.9 shows some examples of using any entry vector in O.D. turning and I.D. boring.

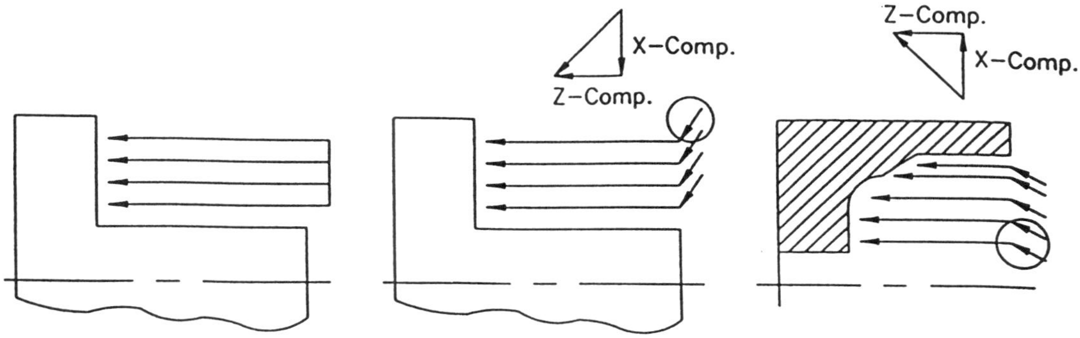

a X=0, Z= 0 b. O.D. Turning (-X, -Z) c. I.D. Boring (+X, -Z)

Figure 22.9

Exit vector This parameter defines how the tool retracts from the part at the end of each cutting pass. It also consists of two components. Some examples are given in Figure 22.10.

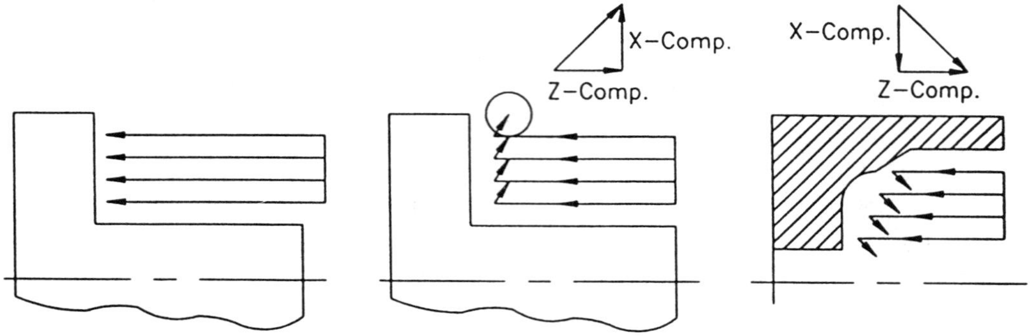

a X=0, Z= 0 b. O.D. Turning (-X, -Z) c. I.D. Boring (+X, -Z)

Figure 22.10

The speed that the tool moves along the entry vector and retraction vector can be set to rapid rate or feed rate mode.

The procedure for defining entry and/or exit vectors is:

1. Click on the "Entry/Exit Vectors" button located at the bottom of the Parameters menu. The Entry/Exit Vectors menu should appear on the screen.

2. Set the parameters to the appropriate value, then click on the Done button to return back to the Parameters menu.

Miscellaneous Parameters

There are three miscellaneous parameters: **Coolant, Program number**, and **Sequence number**.

Coolant The coolant parameter can be selected from one of these three options: **Off, Flood**, and **Mist**. The selection of coolant parameter will generate a correspondent coolant control command to the part program as shown here:

Off:	M09
Flood:	M08
Mist:	M07

Program number This parameter allows any value to be assigned to the post processor variable progno. This program number can be output to the part program for identification purpose.

Sequence number Two parameters, starting sequence number and increment, are used to set the sequence number for the NC part program.

Tool Display

This set of parameters allows you to select the display mode for the tool and the toolpath. You can select to show both the tool and the toolpath, or only display either the tool or the toolpath.

The procedure for defining tool display parameters is:

1. Click on the "Tool Display" button located at the right bottom of the parameters menu. It appears as below.

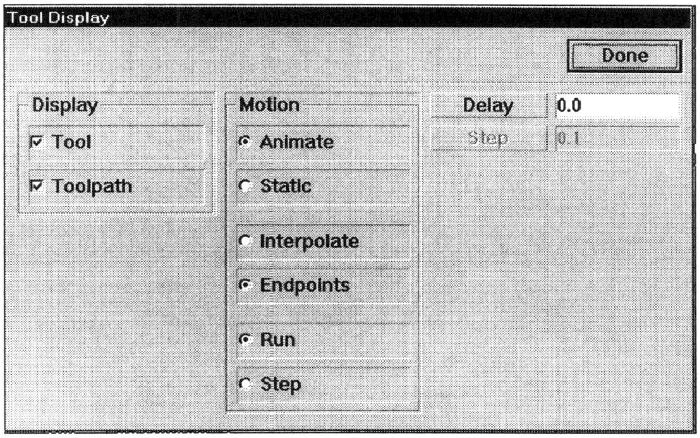

2. Set the proper setting of each parameter, then click on the Done button to return back to the Parameters menu.

Other Miscellaneous Values

There is a total of 20 miscellaneous integer and real parameters, 10 integers and 10 reals. Some parameters have been assigned to specific applications, others are not. Changing the value of a parameter will select a G-code for that particular function in the NC program. *Note*: Not every post processor uses miscellaneous values to control G-codes. Some miscellaneous values used in Fanuc-based controllers are summarized below:

Misc. Integer [1]:	work coordinate system (WCS) 0 = G50, 1-2 = home, 3 = G53, 4 = G54, 5 = G55
Misc. Integer [2]:	canned cycle 0 = OFF, 1 = Ruff, 2 = Rull/Finish
Misc. Integer [3]:	tall stock control 0 = OFF, 1 = ON
Misc. Integer [4]:	threading cycle selection 0 = G32, 1 = G92
Misc. Integer [5]:	thread chamfer 0 = OFF, 1 = ON
Misc. Integer [6]:	thread cuts 0 = OFF, 1,,,, = ON,thdmal
Misc. Integer [7]:	tool change on offset position 0 = OFF, 1 = ON
Misc. Integer [8 - 10]:	not used
Misc. real [3]:	canned cycle clearance distance
Misc. real [4]:	canned cycle peck distance
Misc. real [5]:	G76 multiple threading cycle chamfering distance factor
Misc. real [6]:	context dwell

The procedure for defining Misc. Values is:

1. Click on the "Misc. Values" button located at the middle bottom of the parameters menu to open the Miscellaneous menu as below.

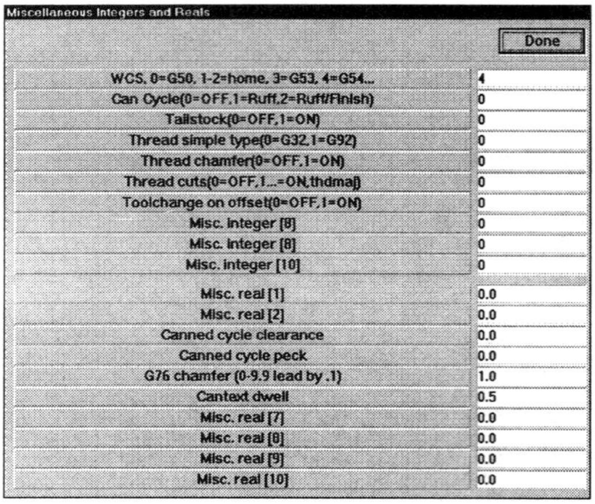

2. Set the proper setting of each parameter, then click on the Done button to return back to the parameter menu.

22.3 Rough Module

The rough module generates a set of toolpaths to rough the part to its approximate profile for subsequent finishing cuts. This module is normally applied to outside diameter (O.D.) roughing (Figure 22.11a), inside diameter (I.D.) roughing (Figure 22.11b), and face roughing (Figure 22.11c).

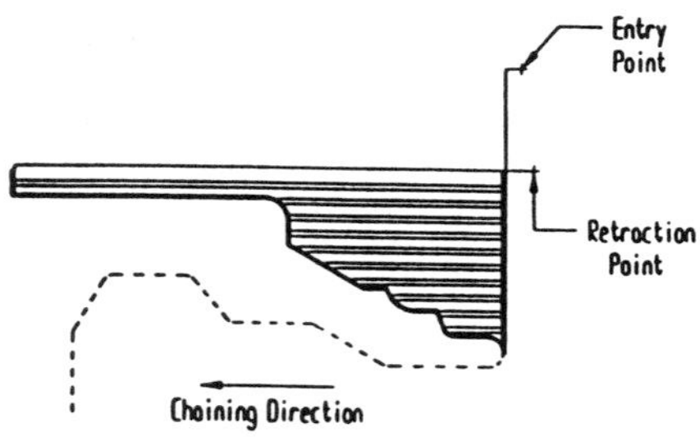

Figure 22.11a O.D. Roughing

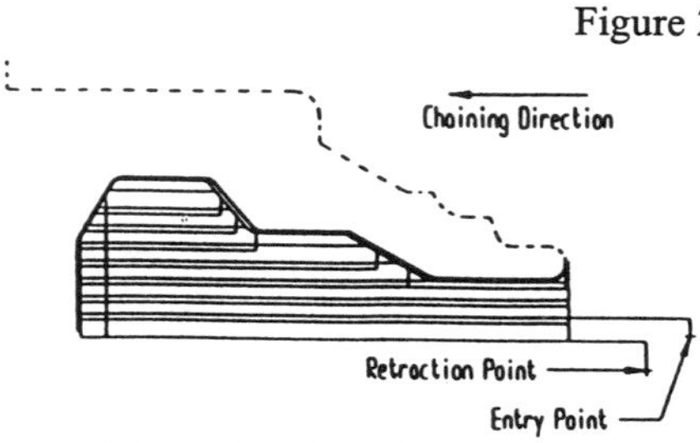

Figure 22.11b I.D. Roughing

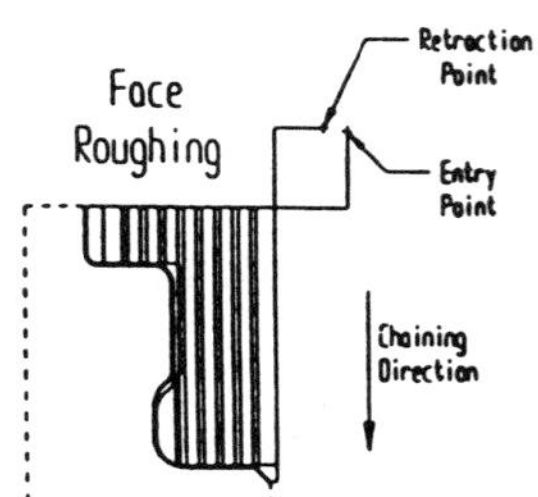

Figure 22.11c Face Rouging

Rough Specific Parameters

In addition to the common parameters, the rough module has the following four unique parameters: **Roughing method, Rough direction, Roughing angle,** and **Overlap amount.**

Roughing method This parameter selects the roughing method to be one way or zigzag. With the one way method, the tool cuts the part in one direction and retracts then moves at rapid speed in the other direction, then plunges to the level to start next cutting pass (Figure 22.12). In the zigzag method, the tool cuts the part in both direction (Figure 22.13). Only bi-directional tools are capable of cutting the parts in the zigzag pattern.

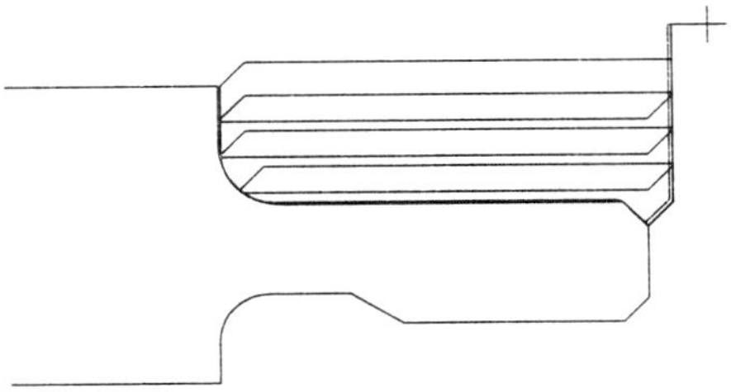

Figure 22.12

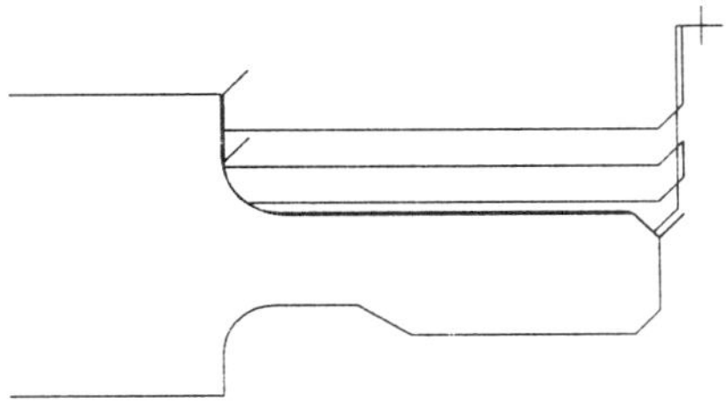

Figure 22.13

Rough direction This parameter specifies the direction of the cut to be one of these options:

ID: cut in inside diameter direction (Figure 22.14).
OD: cut in outside diameter direction (Figure 22.15).
Face: cut in facing direction (Figure 22.16).

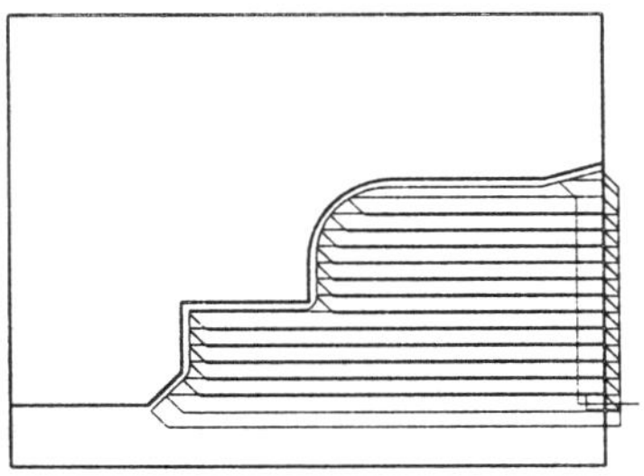

Figure 22.14

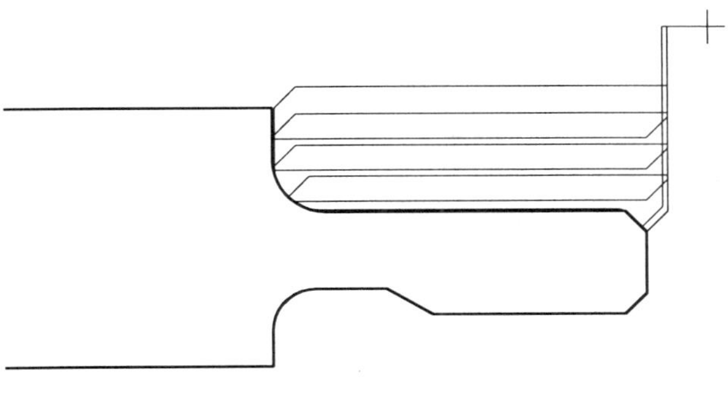

Figure 22.15

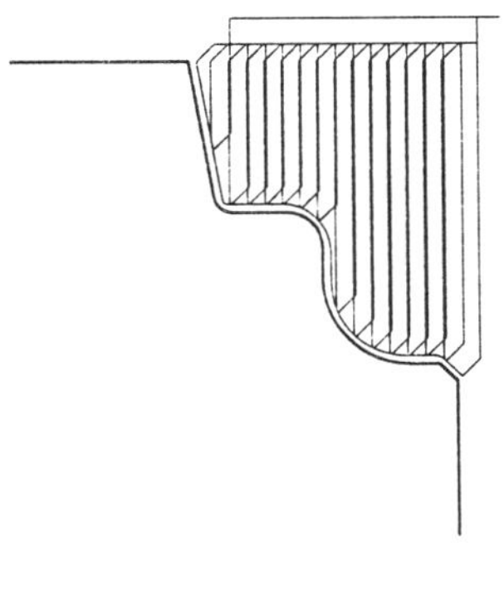

Figure 22.16

Roughing angle This parameter determines the cutting direction of roughing passes. The definition of roughing angle is shown in Figure 22.17.

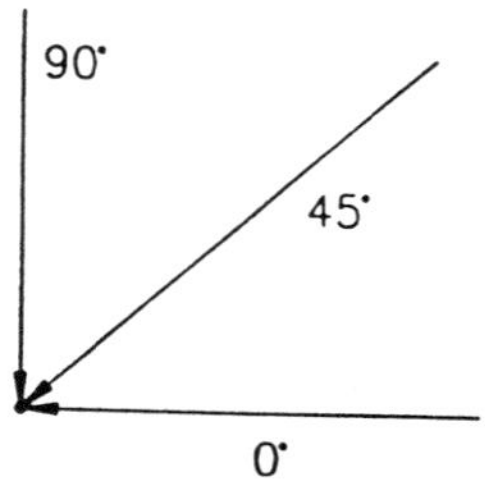

Figure 22.17

The roughing toolpaths for three roughing angles; 0°, 45°, and 90° are shown in Figure 22.18.

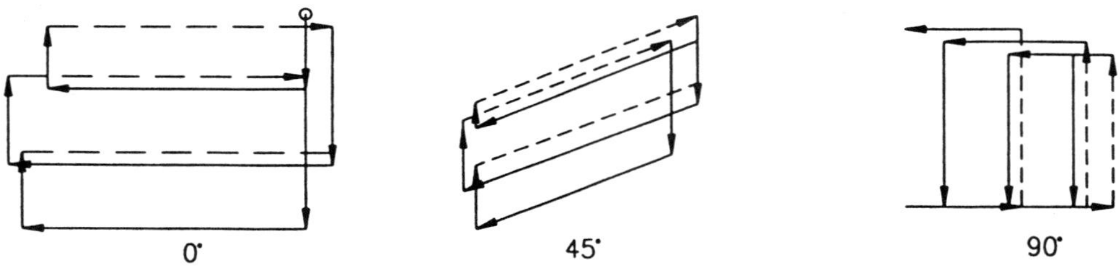

Figure 22.18

This angle can be set to any value ranging from 0 to 360°. It is recommended to use 0 for OD or ID roughing, and 90° for face roughing. In addition to the roughing angle, the roughing toolpath pattern is also affected by the chaining direction and the cutter compensation direction.

Overlap amount This parameter specifies the amount of overlap between roughing cuts. This value determines the retraction distance of each pass. Retraction distance is equal to the sum of depth of cut and overlap value (Figure 22.19). For example, roughing an OD profile with a 0.1 in. depth of cut and a 0.015 overlap would result in a 0.115 in. (or 0.1+0.015) of the retraction distance. With no overlap, it will leave scallops on the profile. These scallops will be eliminated with the use of overlap. Therefore it produces a smooth finish cut because it is cutting the same amount of stock, but not hitting hills and valleys.

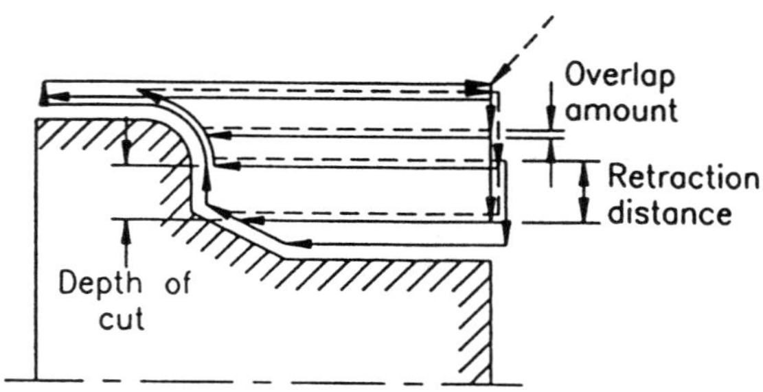

Figure 22.19

Defining the roughing stock

Mastercam uses the following two ways to define the roughing stock boundary:

1. Use the chained finish profile to determine the raw material stock
2. Use a chained profile as the raw material stock

Chained finish profile as roughing stock boundary With this option, the largest X value of the chained finish profile becomes the X coordinate of the stock boundary and the largest Z value of the chained finish profile is the Z coordinate of the stock boundary (Figure 22.20). In this way, we do not need to specify the additional boundary as the roughing stock boundary.

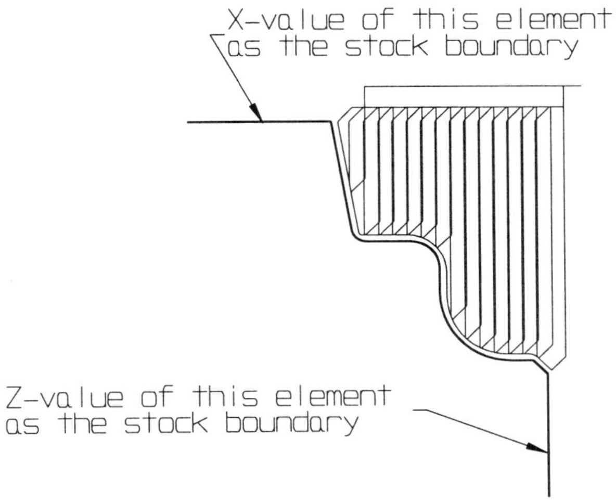

Figure 22.20

A chained profile as roughing stock boundary Mastercam allows defining a chained profile to serve as the roughing stock boundary. The area between the stock profile and finish profile is the roughing stock (Figure 22.21).

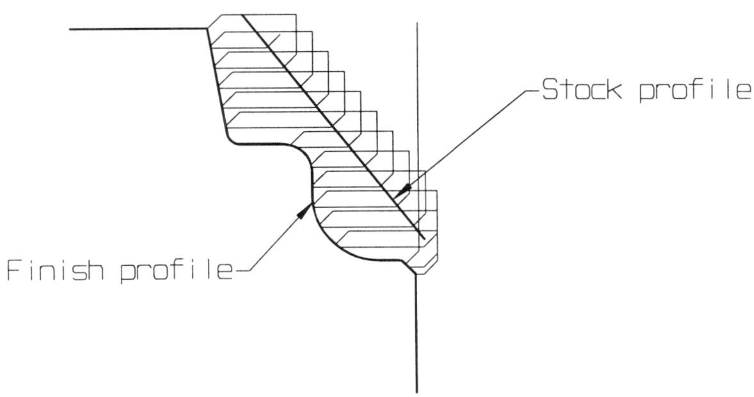

Figure 22.21

1 Project 1. Roughing a part in OD direction

The rough module is used to generate a set of toolpaths for roughing the part shown in Figure 22.22a. The toolpaths are shown in Figure 22.22b. The part geometry file is turn4.mc7.

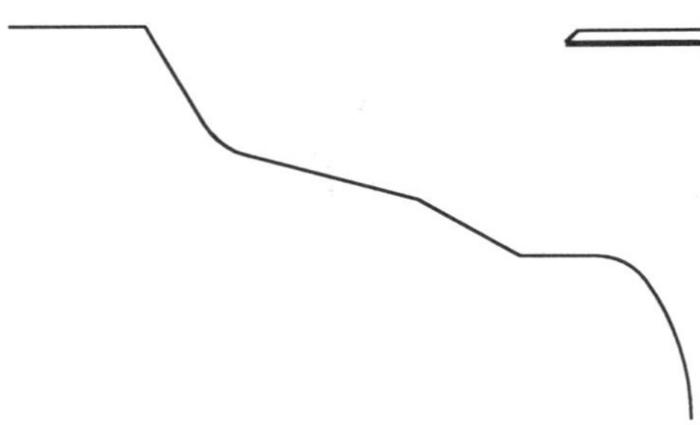

Figure 22.22a

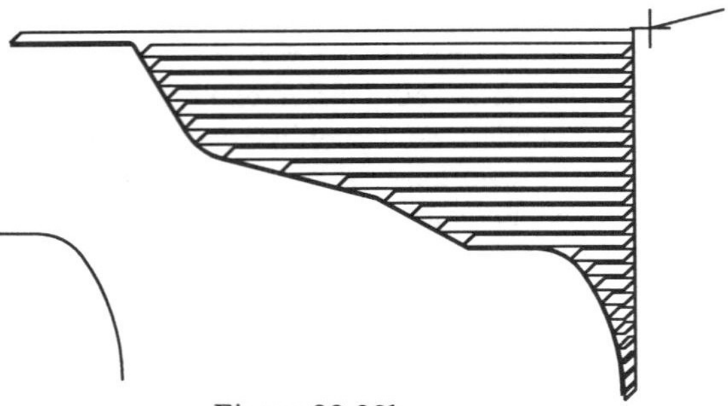

Figure 22.22b

Tips
1. Part geometry file is turn4.mc7.
2. Use the rough-OD function to generate roughing toolpaths.
3. Use a general turning tool "R1/32 J/D(RH)" from the tool library.
4. Use the point (5,0.2) as both the entry and retract points.
5. Save the toolpath file as rough-od.

Step 1. Open the part geometry file turn4.

Select **MAIN MENU → File → Get**
File name: **turn4**
The part geometry should appear as Figure 22.23.

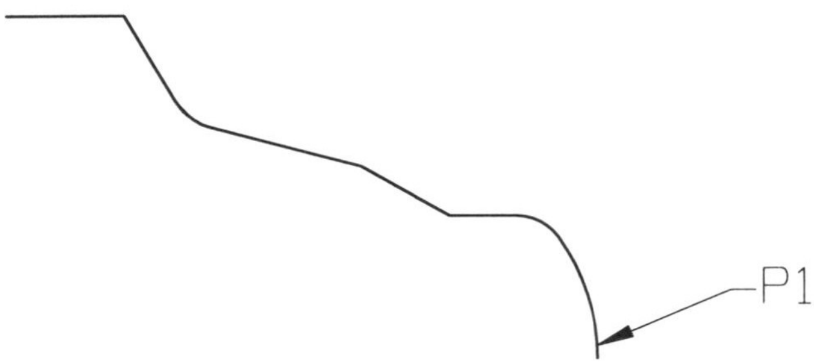

Figure 22.23

Step 2. Initiate the rough module.

Use the pick point in Figure 22.23.
Select **MAIN MENU → Toolpaths → Rough**
File name for toolpaths: **rough-od**
Select **Point → Values**

Enter coordinates: **5,0.2** as the entry point
Select **Chain**, then pick **P1**
Select **Done**
Select **Point → Values**
Enter coordinates: **5,0.2** as the retraction point
Select **Done** to open the roughing parameters menu

Step 3. Select the tool.

Click the "Tool Select" button to open lathe tool manager menu
Click the right mouse button, then select **Get from library**
Select tool (**R1/32" J/D (RH)**) from the list as below.

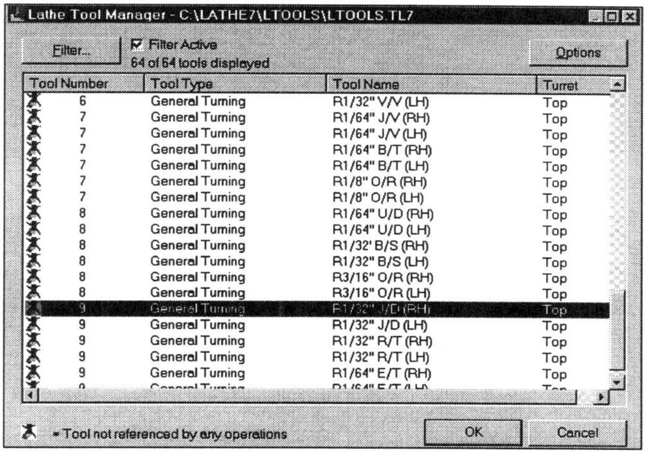

Select **OK → OK**to exit tool manager menu

Step 4. Set the roughing parameters as below.

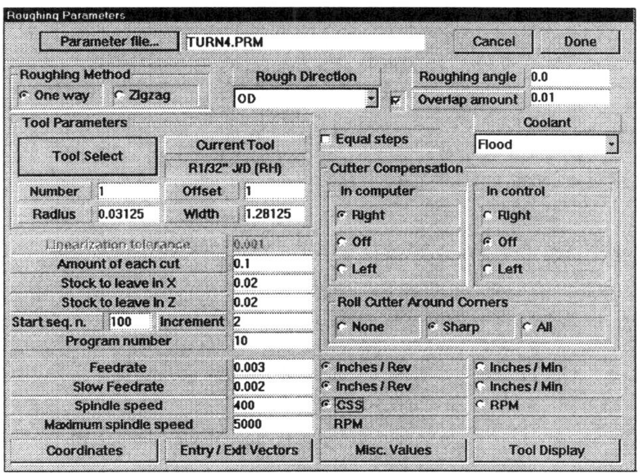

Step 5. Set the coordinate parameters.

Click the "Coordinates" button at the bottom of the menu

Set the coordinate parameters as below.

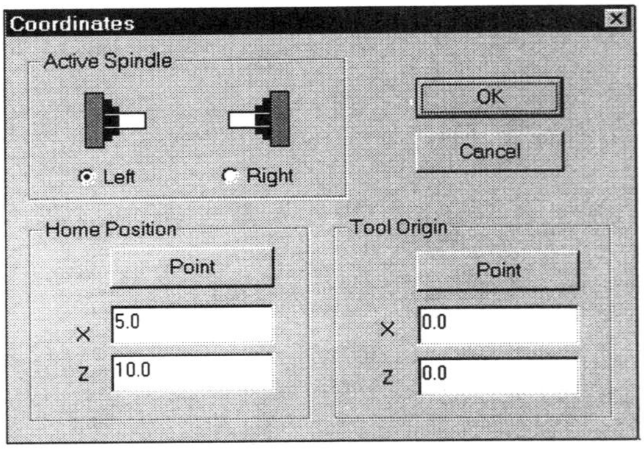

Select **OK**

Step 6. Define the entry and exit vectors.

Click the "Entry/Exit Vectors" button at the bottom of the menu
Set the entry vector parameters as below.

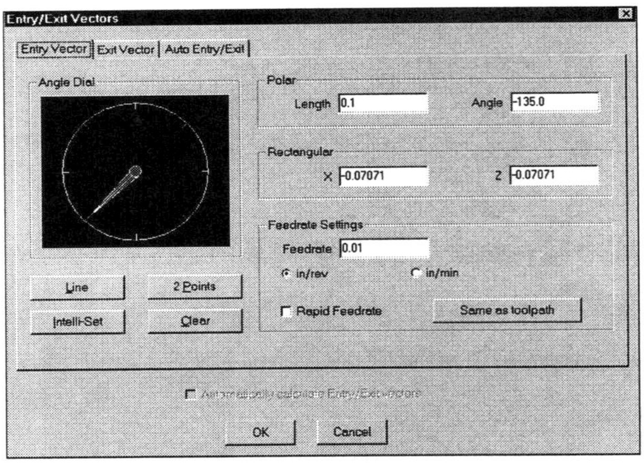

Click the "Exit Vector" button on the top of the menu
Set the exit vector parameters as below.

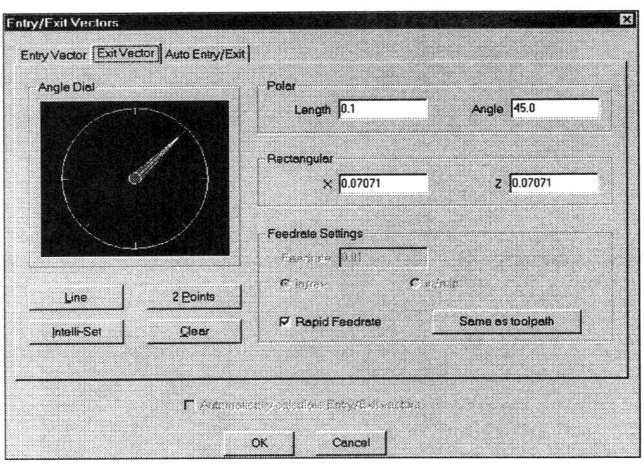

Select **OK** to return back to roughing parameters menu

Step 7. Define the miscellaneous values.

Click the "Misc. Values" button
Set the WCS value to **0** for G50 as below.

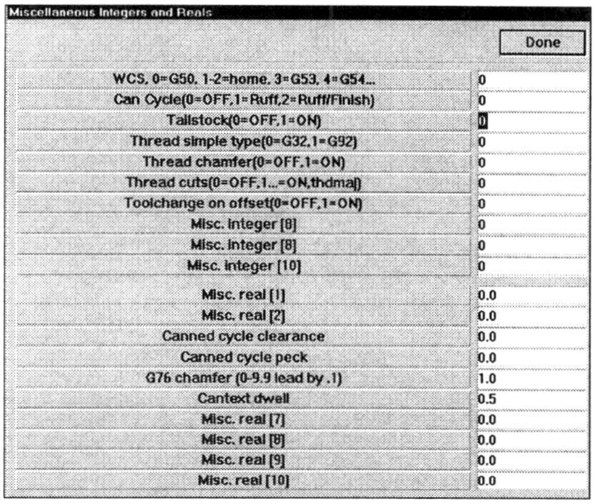

Select **Done** to return back to roughing parameters menu
Select **Done** to generate roughing toolpaths as shown in Figure 22.24.

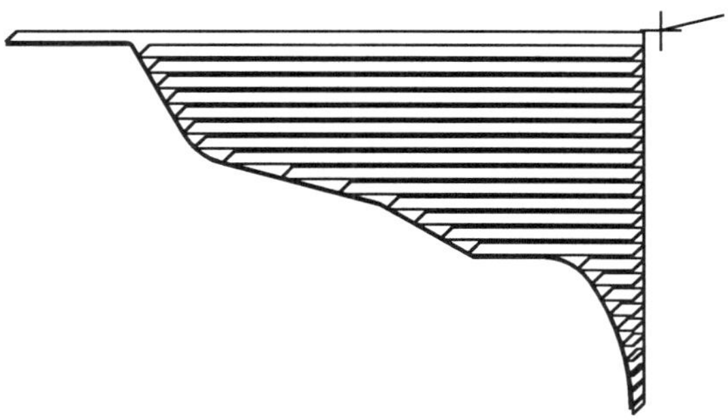

Figure 22.24

Select **Yes** to accept this toolpath segment

Step 8. Backplot the toolpaths.

Select **Operations**

The Operations Manager menu should appear as below.

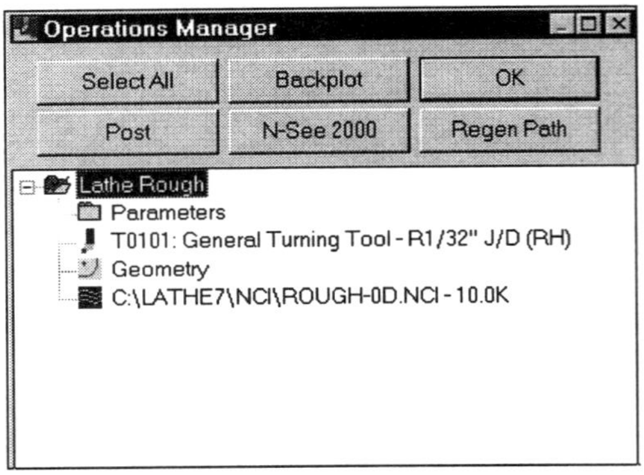

Select **Backplot**
Select **Display**
Set the display parameters as below.

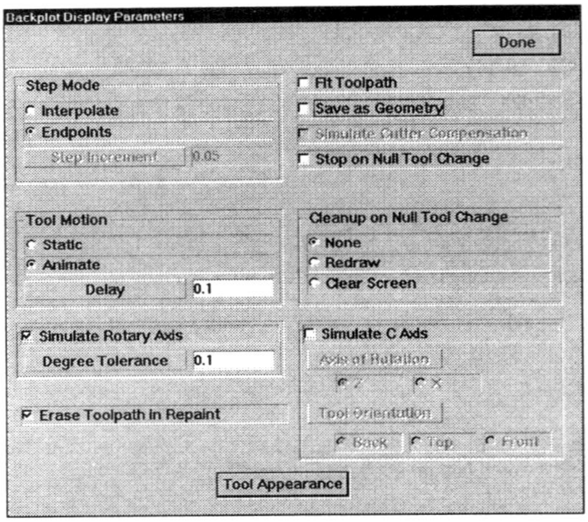

Select **Done** to exit display parameters menu
Set backplot parameters as on the right here.

Select **Run** to backplot the toolpaths
The tool and toolpaths should be animated on the screen as in Figure 22.25.

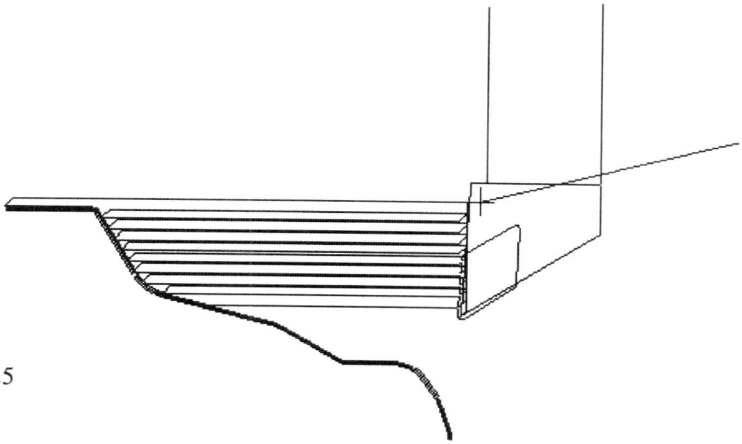

Figure 22.25

Step 9. Post process the toolpaths.

Select **BACKUP → Post**
Select **Yes** to "Run the postprocessor?"
File name to write: **rough-od**
The part program should appear on the file list menu as below.

File list

```
%
O0010(ROUGH-OD)
G20
G50X10.Z10.
G0T0101
G50S5000
G97S306M3
X5.Z.2M8
G96S400
Z.0907
X4.9814
X4.7814
G99G1X4.64Z.02F.01
Z-3.1439F.003
X4.7888Z-3.1869
G3X4.84Z-3.2313R.0513
G1Z-4.
G0X4.9814Z-3.9293
Z.0907
X4.5814
G1X4.44Z.02F.01
Z-3.0862F.003
X4.66Z-3.1497
G0X4.8014Z-3.079
Z.0907
X4.3814
```

Click the **Close** button to exit file list menu

Step 10. Exit the Operations Manager menu.

Select **OK** to exit the Operations Manager menu

Step 11. Save in a new file name rough-od.

Select **MAIN MENU → File → Save**
File name to write: **rough-od**

2 Project 2. Roughing an internal profile

This project uses the rough function to perform an ID boring operation. The part geometry is created in project 1 of chapter 20. Figure 22.26 shows the part geometry model and toolpath model, respectively. It is assumed that the workpiece has been predrilled at the center to a 1" diameter, allowing us to perform the boring operation.

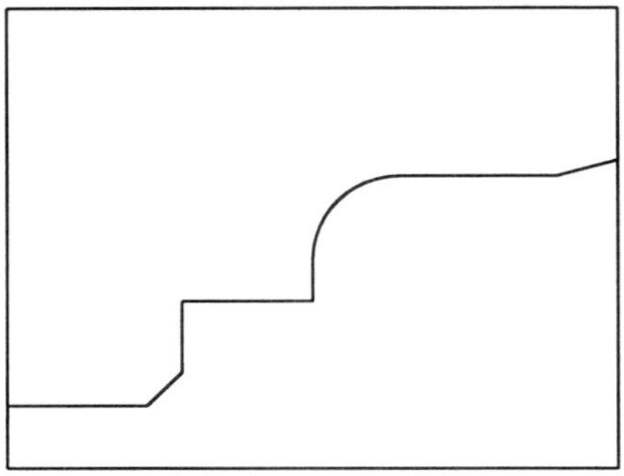

Figure 22.2a

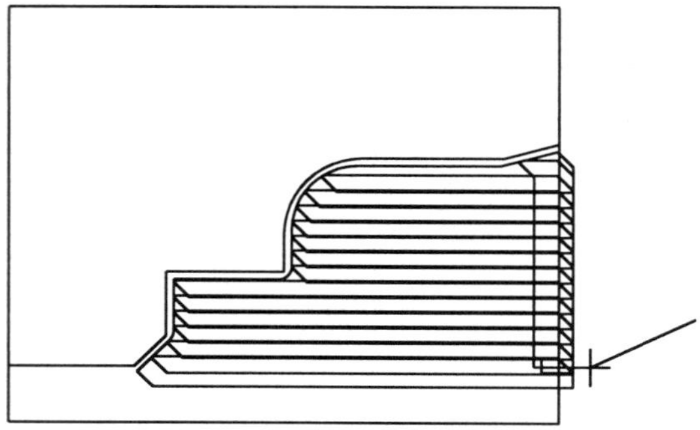

Figure 22.26b

Tips	1. Use the geometry file "turn1".
	2. Use the rough-id module to generate boring toolpaths.
	3. Use a boring tool "B-R1/32 FC(RH)" from the tool library.
	4. Save the toolpath file as "rough-id".

Step 1. Open the geometry file turn1.

Select **MAIN MENU → File → Get**
File name: **turn1**
The part geometry should look like Figure 22.27.

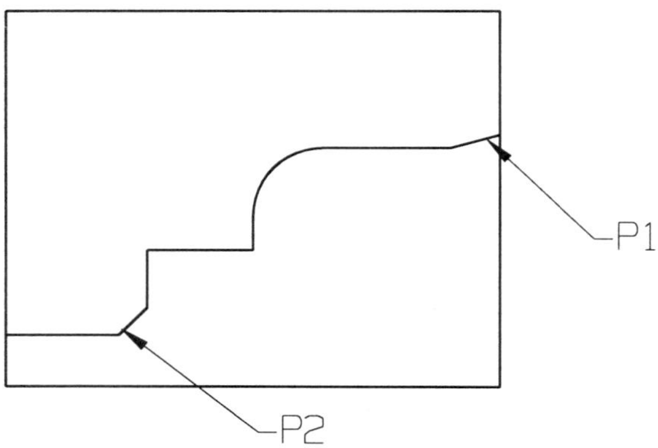

Figure 22.27

Step 2. Initiate the rough module.

Use the pick points in Figure 22.27.
Select **MAIN MENU → Toolpaths → Rough**
File name for NCI: **rough-id**

Select **Point → Values**
Enter coordinates: **0.75, 0.2** for the entry point
Select **Chain → Partial**
Pick **P1** and **P2** sequentially to define the profile
Select **Done → Point → Values**
Enter coordinates: **0.75, 0.2**
Select **Done**

Step 3. Select a boring tool.

Click the "Select Tool" button in roughing parameters menu
Click the right mouse button, then select "Get from library" to open the tool list
Select the boring tool "**B-R1/32" FC(RH)**" as shown below.

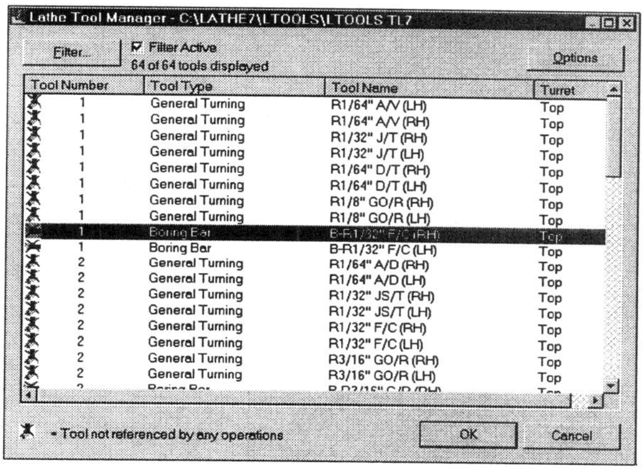

Select **OK** to return back to tool manager menu
Select **OK** to return back to roughing parameters menu

Step 4. Define the roughing parameters as below.

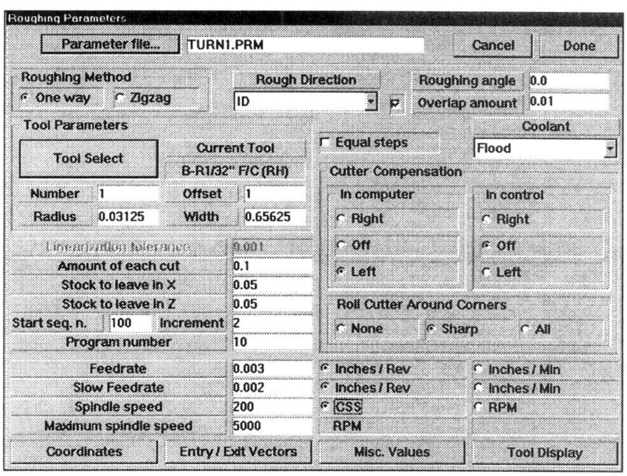

Step 5. Define the entry and exit vectors.

Click the "Entry/Exit Vectors" button

Set the entry vector parameters as below.

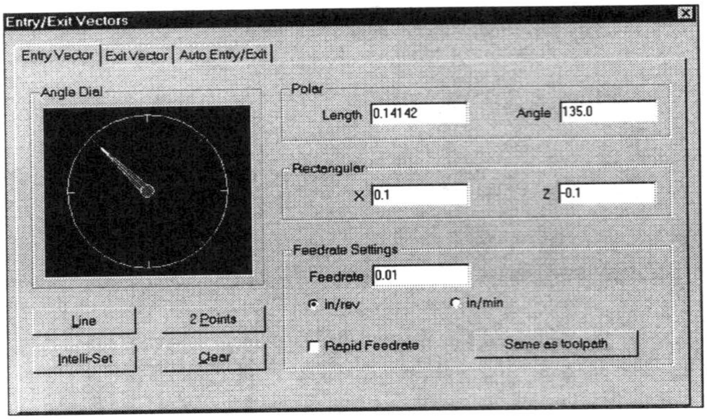

Click the "Exit Vector" button
Set the exit vector parameters as below.

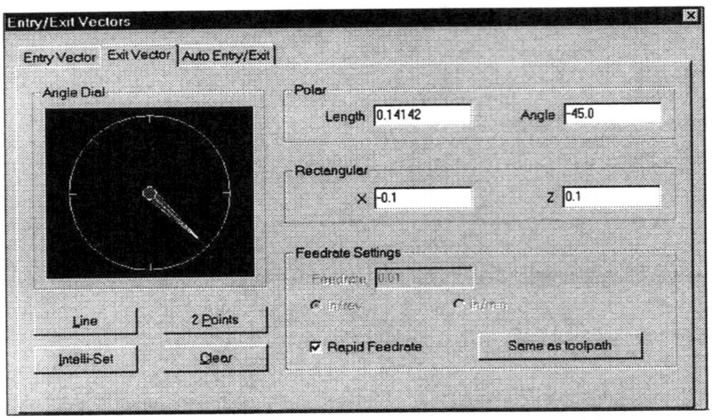

Select **OK** to return back to roughing parameters menu

Step 6. Define miscellaneous values.

Click the "Misc. Values" button
Set the miscellaneous values as below.

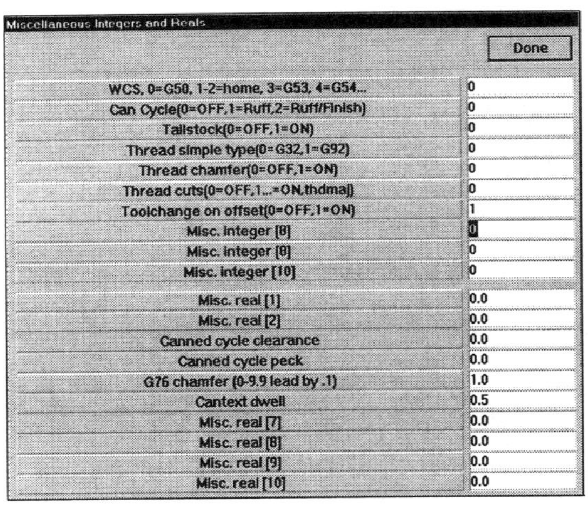

Select **Done** to return back to roughing parameters menu
Select **Done** to generate the roughing toolpaths
Select **Yes** to accept this toolpath segment

The roughing toolpaths are shown as in Figure 22.28.

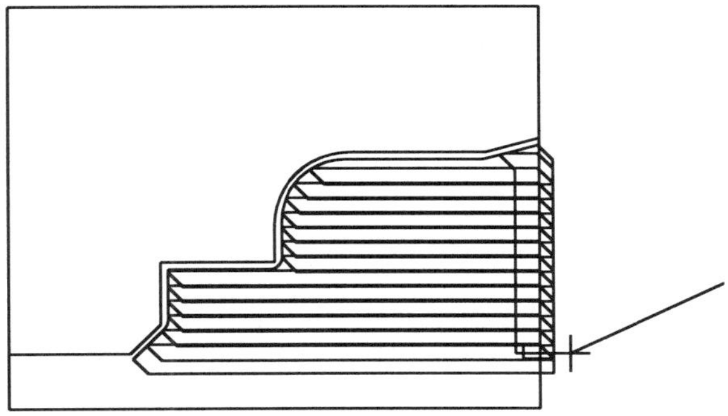

Figure 22.28

Step 7. Backplot the toolpaths.

Select **Operations** to open the operations manager menu
Select **Backplot**
Set display and backplot parameters to proper settings
Select **Run** to verify the toolpaths on the screen

Step 8. Save the project as a new file rough-id.

Select **BACKUP**
Select **OK** from Operations Manager menu
Select **MAIN MENU → File → Save**
File name to save: **rough-id**

3 Project 3. Roughing a part in face direction

This project uses the rough-face option to rough cut the part in the facing direction. The part model and toolpaths are shown in Figure 22.29.

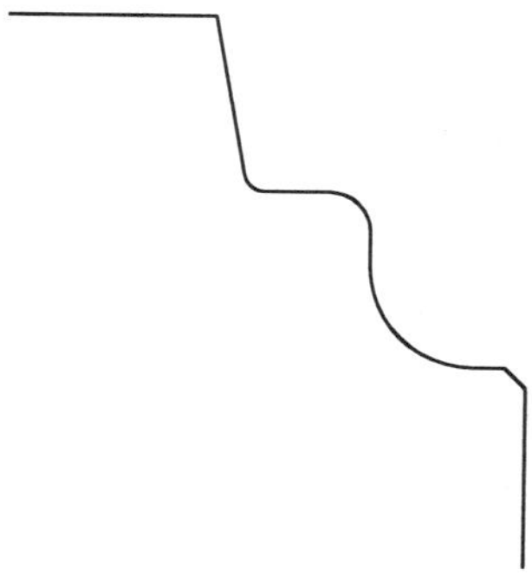

Figure 22.29a

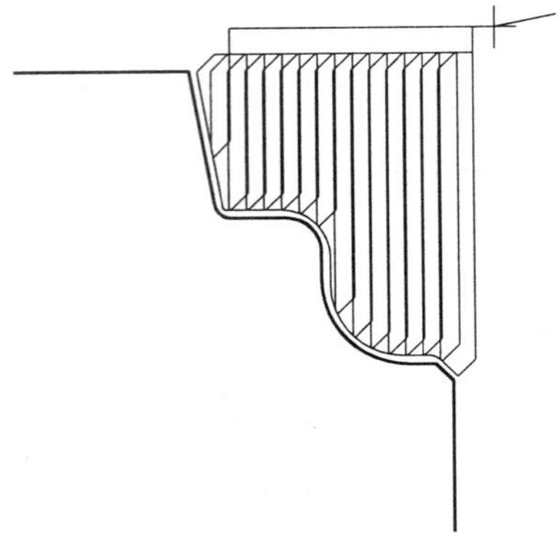

Figure 22.29b

Tips 1. Use the geometry file "turn5".

2. Use the rough-face module to generating roughing toolpaths in the facing direction.

3. Use the general turning tool "R1/32 J/D(RH)" from tool library.

4. Save the toolpath file as "rough-face".

Step 1. Open the geometry file turn5.

Select **MAIN MENU → File → Get**
File name: **turn5**
The part geometry appears as Figure 22.30.

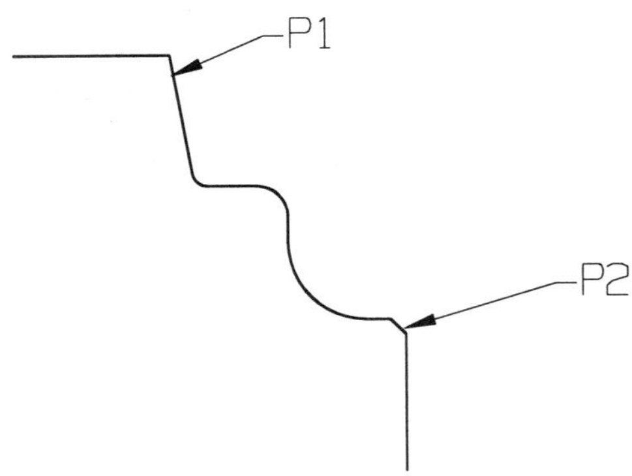

Figure 22.30

Step 2. Initiate the rough module.

Use the pick points in Figure 22.30.
Select **MAIN MENU → Toolpaths → Rough**
File name for toolpaths: **rough-face**
Select **Point → Values**
Enter coordinates: **6.0,0.25** for the entry point
Select **Chain → Partial**
Pick **P1** and **P2** to define the inner profile
Select **Done → Point → Values**
Enter coordinates: **6.0, .25** for the retraction point
Select **Done**

Step 3. Select a facing tool.

Click the "Tool Select" button
Click the right mouse button, then select **Get from library**
Select the tool **"R1/32 J/D (RH)"** from the list as below.

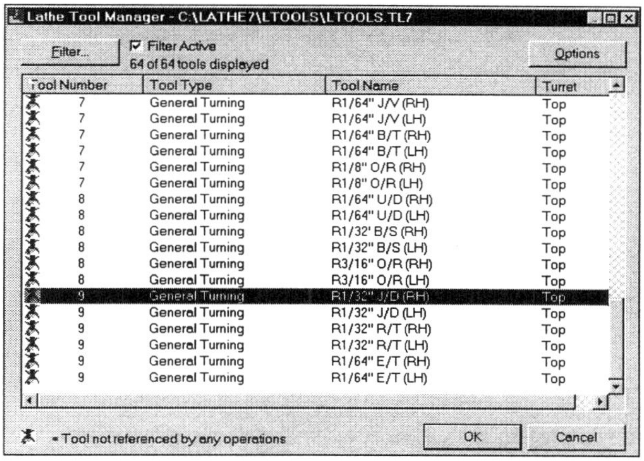

Select **OK → OK** to return to the roughing parameters menu

Step 4. Set the roughing parameters as below.

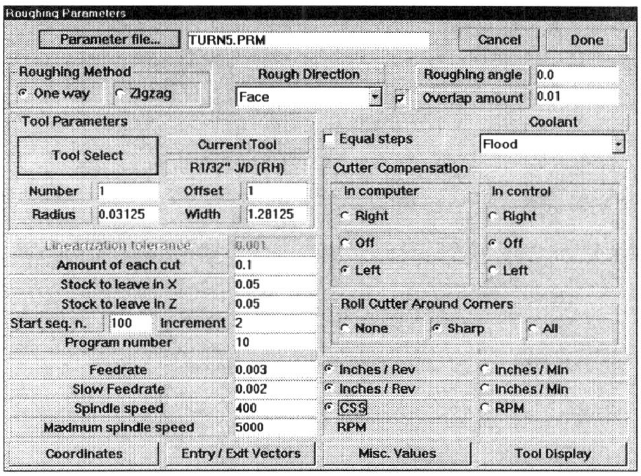

Step 5. Set the entry and exit vector parameters.

Click the "Entry/Exit Vectors" button

Set the entry vector parameters as below.

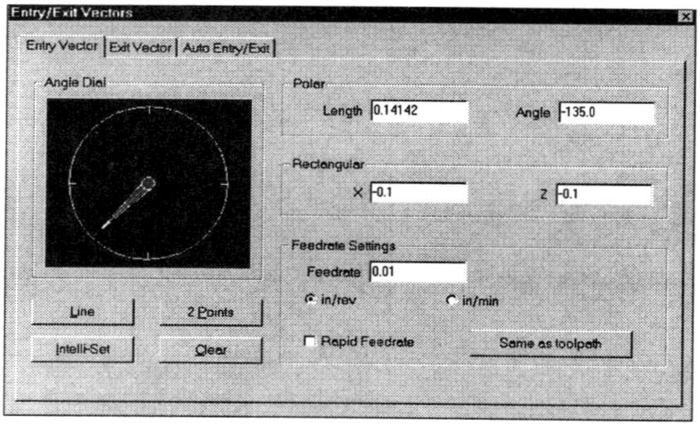

Click the "Exit Vector" button
Set the exit vector parameters as below.

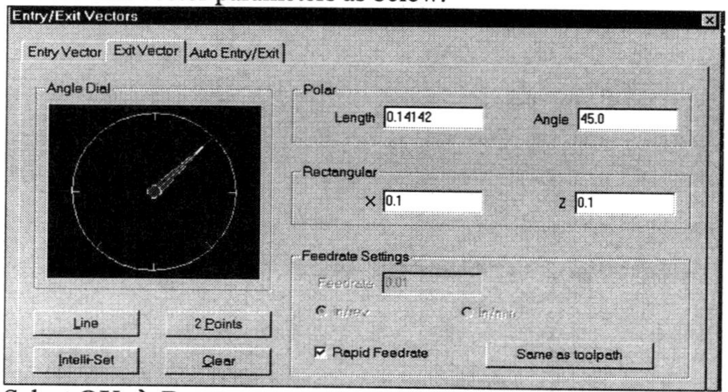

Select **OK** → **Done** to generate roughing toolpaths
Select **Yes** to accept this toolpath segment
The roughing toolpaths should look like Figure 22.31.

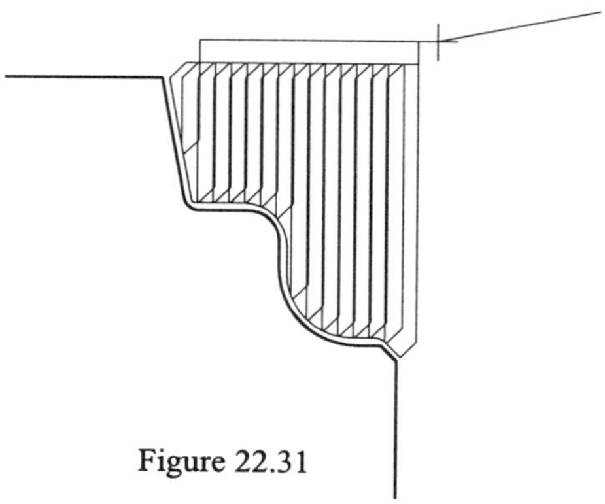

Figure 22.31

Step 6. Backplot the toolpaths.

Select **Operations** to open the Operations Manager menu
Click **Backplot**
Set display and backplot parameters to desired settings
Select **Run** to backplot the toolpaths on the screen

Step 7. Save the project as rough-face.

Select **BACKUP** to return to Operations Manager menu
Select **OK** to exit the Operations Manager menu
Select **MAIN MENU** → **File** → **Save**
File name: **rough-face**

22.4 Finish Module

The finish module creates a set of toolpaths to make one or more finish cuts along the OD, ID, or facing contours.

When to Use the Finish Module

The rough module is first used to generate the roughing toolpaths, the finish module is then used to cut the part to its final finished shape and size (Figure 22.32)

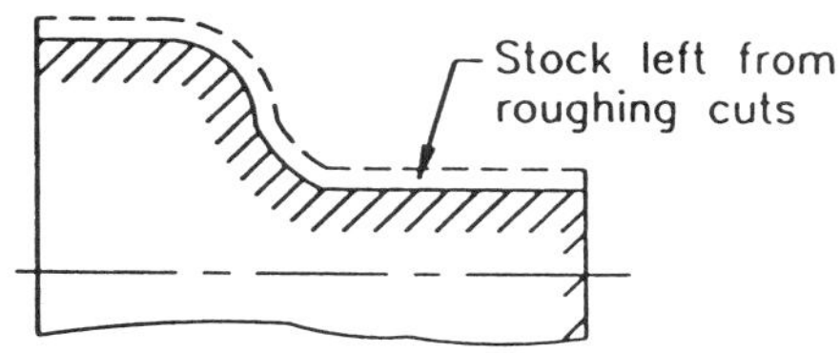

Figure 22.32

When the size of a part already has an approximated final dimension such as a casting or a forging, no roughing cuts are required. The finish module can be directly used to produce the final shape and size (Figure 22.33).

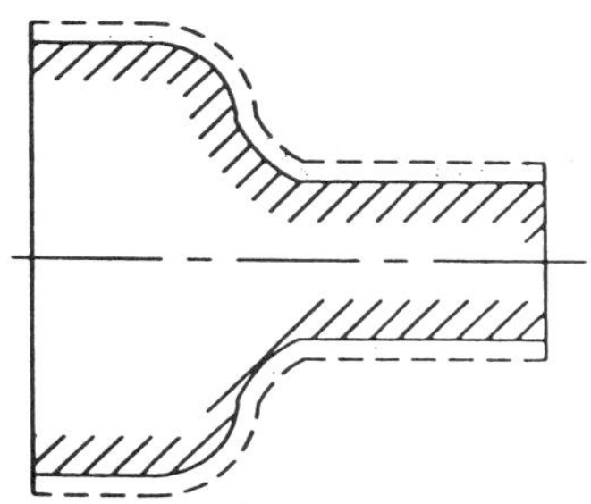

Figure 22.33

Finish Specific Parameter

There is only one unique finish parameter that specifies the number of cuts. If only one finish cut is specified, the cutter will cut to the given boundary. When the number of cuts is more than one, the cutter compensation in computer parameter should be set properly. If it is set to off, all the finishing cuts will overlap.

Cycle Parameters

Some CNC lathe controls provide a group of canned cycles for generating the toolpaths for roughing and finishing cuts. These controls are Fanuc-based and their compatible controls. The main advantage of using these canned cycles is to shorten part programs and programming time.

Mastercam lathe allows the following four roughing and finish cycles to be inserted into part programs:

G70:	Finish Cycle
G71:	Rough turning cycle
G72:	Rough facing cycle
G73:	Contour repeating cycle

Rough Turning Cycle (G71)

The rough turning cycle G71 is used to rough the part to a size that is slightly larger than its desired size in preparation for the finished cut. This cycle specifies the range of instruction blocks to be included, the depth of cut per pass, and the amount and direction of stock left for the finishing cycle. Depending on the control model, it uses one or two command blocks for G71 programming. Fanuc T-6 uses a one-block format and other models such as T-10, T-11, or O-T use a two-block format.

Use these definitions for the block format codes:

Ff	-Roughing feedrate
Ww	-Z-axis finish stock
Uu	-X-axis finish stock
Dd	-Depth of cut
Qq	-Sequence number of cycle ending block
Pp	-Sequence number of cycle starting block
Rr	-Retraction amount
Rp	-Number of repeated contours
Ui	-Distance of retraction in the X direction
Wk	-Distance of retraction in the Z direction
G##	-Cycle command

Rough turning <u>One-block format:</u>

G71 Pp Qq Dd Uu Ww Ff

Rough turning <u>Two-block format:</u>

G71 Dr Rr
└── retraction amount
G71 Pp Qq Uu Ww Ff

Figure 22.34 shows a typical toolpath pattern generated by using G71 command.

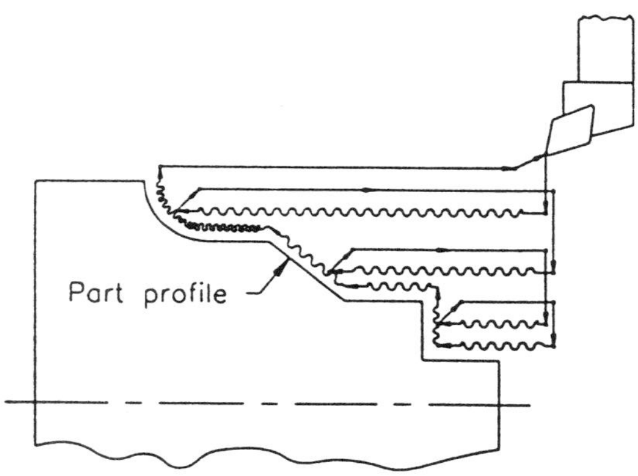

Figure 22.34

Rough Facing Cycle (G72)

The rough facing cycle G72 has a similar toolpath pattern to that of G71 except the main cutting direction is parallel to the X axis as shown in Figure 22.35.

Rough facing **One-block format:**

G72 Pp Qq Dd Uu Ww Ff

Rough facing **Two-block format:**

G72 Ww Rr

G72 Pp Qq Uu Ww Ff

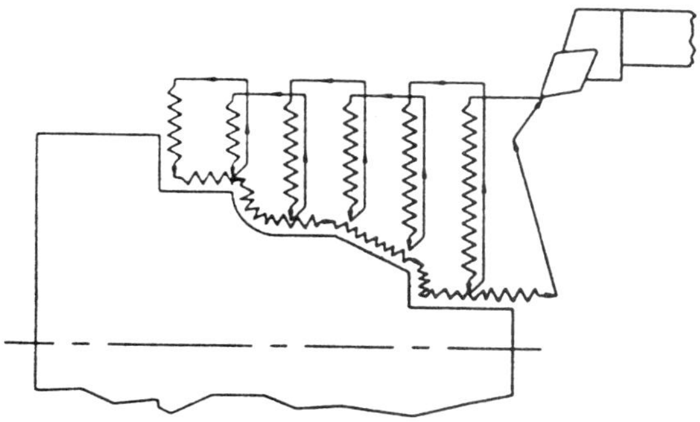

Figure 22.35

Contour Repeating Cycle (G73)

The contour Repeating Cycle (G73) generates a set of cutter paths that repeatedly move along with the part contour as many times as required. Each successive repeating path moves the cutter closer to the desired finished contour as shown in Figure 22.36.

Contour Repeating One-block format:

G73 Pp Qq Uu Ww Rp Ff

Contour Repeating Two-block format:

G73 Ui Wk Rp

G73 Pp Qq Uu Ww Ff

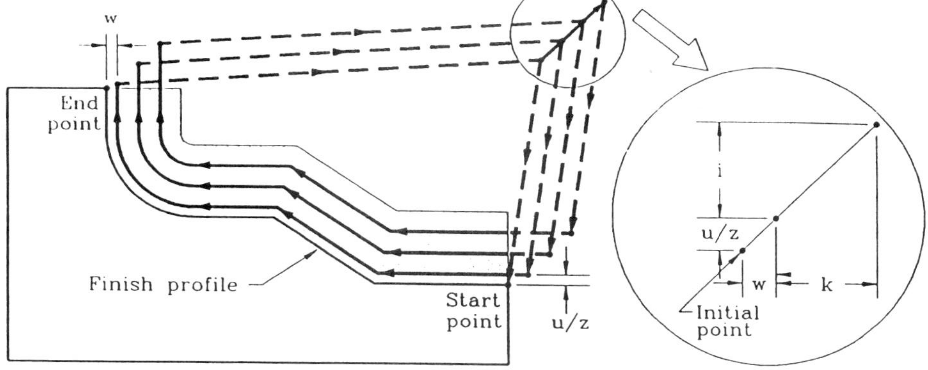

Figure 22.36

Finish Cycle (G70)

The finish cycle can be regarded as a single-pass contouring cycle. It must be used with one of two roughing cycles (G71 or G72). The G70 command is normally programmed after a roughing cycle. Its command indicates only the sequence numbers for the cycle start block and cycle ending block, and has the following format:

G70 Pp Qq

The Procedure for Using Canned Cycles G71 and G72

1. Enter the Rough toolpath module using the following commands:
   MAIN MENU → Toolpaths → Rough

2. Set roughing parameters to the following settings:
   a. Set the Roughing angle to either 0(or 90(. (Use 0(for G71 and 90(for G72).
      Select Cutter Compensation in Computer to either Left or Right.
   b. Set the entry and exit vectors if desired.
      Select the Feedrate option, otherwise they will be omitted.
   c. Set the Overlap amount to 0.
   d. Set the Miscellaneous Values to the following:
      Miscellaneous integer 2 (mi2) = Canned cycle type selection.
      The miscellaneous integer 2 (mi2) is the variable used to set the roughing toolpath either in the long or short format. The long format generates the actual command codes to rough the workpiece. The short format uses the canned cycle commands to shorten the roughing part programs.

      Mi2 = 0: do not use canned cycle (output long code)
      1: generate G71 – G73 roughing canned cycle
      2: generate G71 – G73 roughing canned cycle, and G70 finish cycle.
      Mr3 = enter value of G71-G73 clearance in canned cycle
      Mr4 = canned cycle peck clearance
   e. Accept the toolpath.

3. Select the Finish module from the toolpaths menu.
   Select Last from the chaining method menu
   Set the finishing parameters:
   a. Set the stock in both X and Z to 0
   b. Keep the same tool radius size and geometry for both roughing and finishing

   Note: Select Done to complete the Finish parameters settings.
   Select Write to generate the toolpaths.
   Select End program.

The Procedure for using canned cycle G73:

The finish module is used twice to generate a G73 for contour repeating roughing cycle and a G70 for the finish cycle. The procedure for generating G73 and G70 canned cycles are listed below.

1. Select Toolpaths → Finish

2. Set the Finish parameters to the settings specifically for generating a G73 command:
   a. Set the number of cuts and the depth of cuts to appropriate values.
   b. Set the Stock in the X and Z to the appropriate finishing Stock Value.
   c. Select Done to generate roughing paths.
   d. Accept the roughing paths.

3. Select Finish from the toolpaths menu again

4. Select Last from the chaining method menu

5. Set the Finishing parameters to the settings specifically for generating a G70 command:
   a. Set both Stock in X and Z to 0
   b. Set the number or cuts to 1

6. Generate finishing paths

7. Accept finishing paths

Change Menu

This menu writes the toolpath to the NCI file, including the options for changing feedrate at any point on the contour, inserting a rapid move at any point along a contour, and inserting comments or special codes into the NC program. This menu appears on the screen:

Change:	Effect
Write:	causes the finish toolpaths to be written to the NCI file.
Feedrate:	allows the feedrate to be changed at any point.
Rapid:	causes a rapid move to be inserted at any point along a contour.
Manual ent:	causes comments or special codes to be inserted at any point in the NC program.
Can'd Text:	allows a character string to be output with the line of code.
Spindle sp:	specifies the spindle speed.
Dwell:	Specifies the dwell time at the end of each pass.

4 Project 4. Generate finish toolpaths for an external profile

The finish module is used to generate a set of toolpaths to cut the finish profile of the part shown in Figure 22.37. The part geometry has been used in project 1 to generate the roughing toolpaths. The file name for the part geometry and rough toolpaths is rough-od.

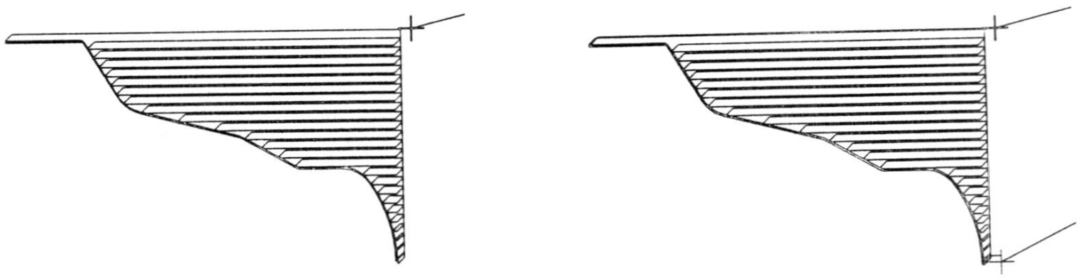

Figure 22.37

Tips	1. Use the part geometry with rough toolpath file (rough-od). 2. Use finish module to add finishing toolpaths to the existing roughing toolpaths. 3. Use the finish tool "R1/32 L/V(RH" from the tool library. 4. Save the new toolpath file as finish-od.

Step 1. Open the part file rough-od.

Select **MAIN MENU → File → Get**
File name: **rough-od**
The part geometry appears as in Figure 22.38.

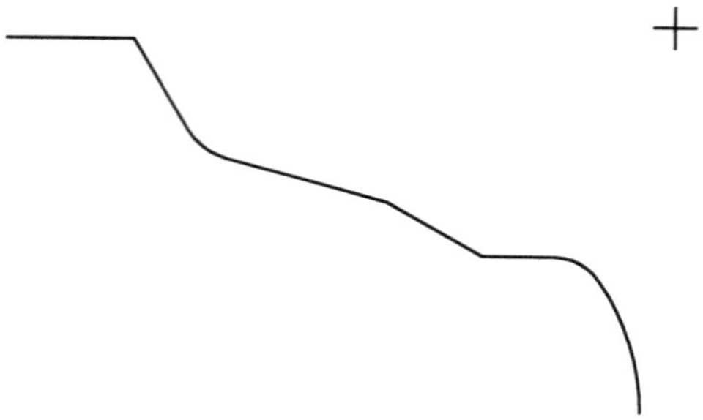

Figure 22.38

Step 2 Initiate the finish module.

Use the pick point in Figure 22.39.
Select **MAIN MENU → Toolpaths**

The existing roughing toolpaths are displayed as in Figure 22.39.

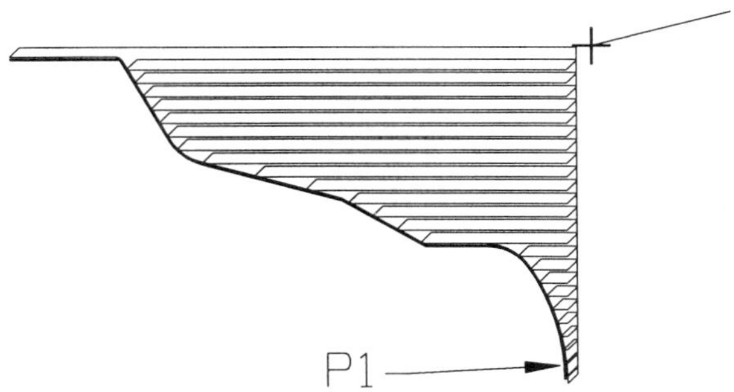

Figure 22.39

Select **Point → Values**
Enter coordinates: **0,0.2** for the entry point
Select Chain → pick **P1** in Figure 22.39 to define a contour
Select **Done → Point → Values**
Enter coordinates: **5,0.2** for the retraction point
Select **Done**

Step 3. Select a finish tool.

Click the "Tool Select" button
Click the right mouse button, then select **Get from library**
Select the tool **"R 1/32" L/V(RH)"** from the list as below.

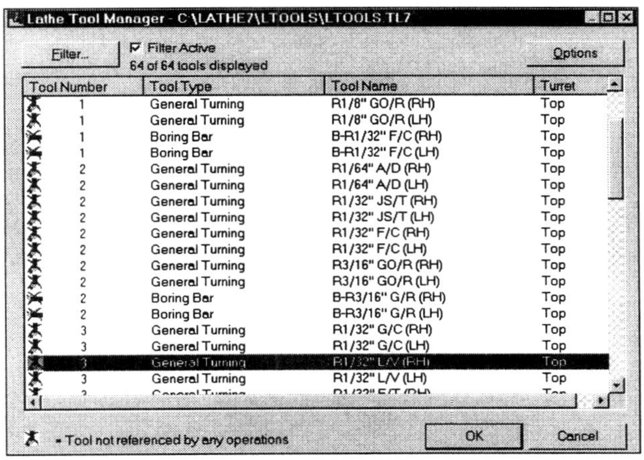

Select **OK** to exit tool library
Select **OK** to exit tool manager menu

Step 4. Define the finishing parameters as below.

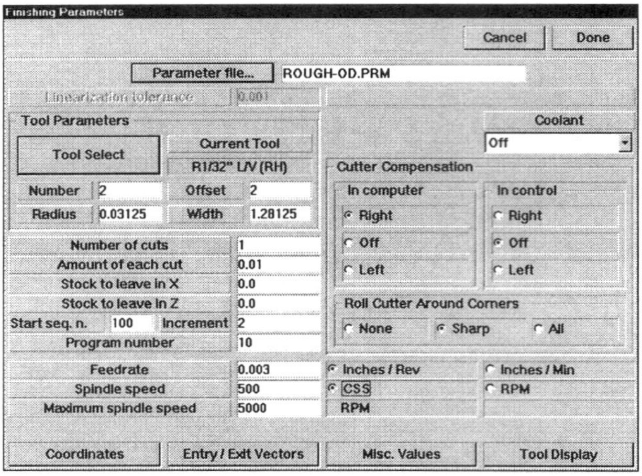

Step 5. Define the entry and exit vector parameters.

Click the "Entry/Exit Vectors" button
Set the entry vector parameters as below.

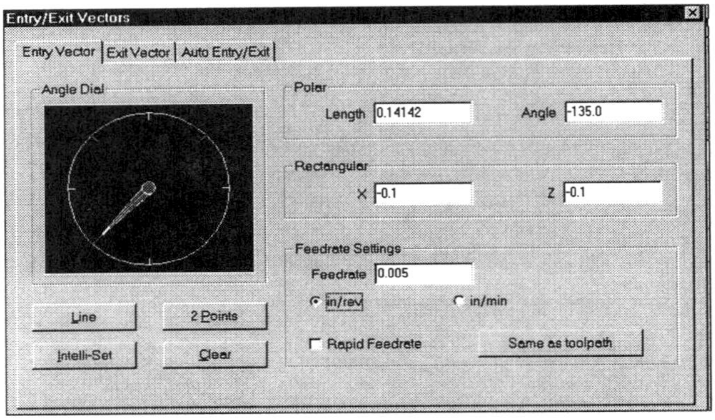

Click the "Exit Vector" button
Set the exit vector parameters as below.

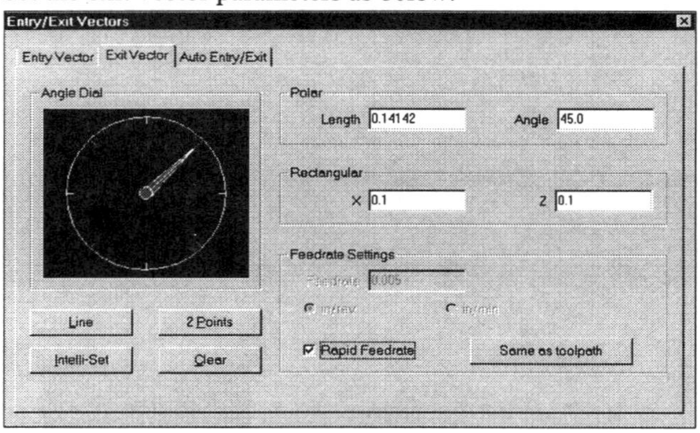

Select **OK** to return to finishing parameters menu

Step 6. Define miscellaneous valves.

Click the "Misc. Values" button
Set the miscellaneous valves as below.

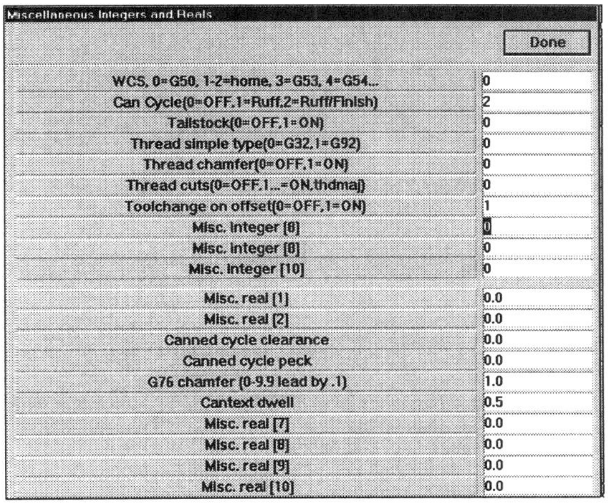

Select **Done** to return to finishing parameters menu
Select **Done** → **Write** to generate finishing toolpath
The finishing toolpath has been added as in Figure 22.40.

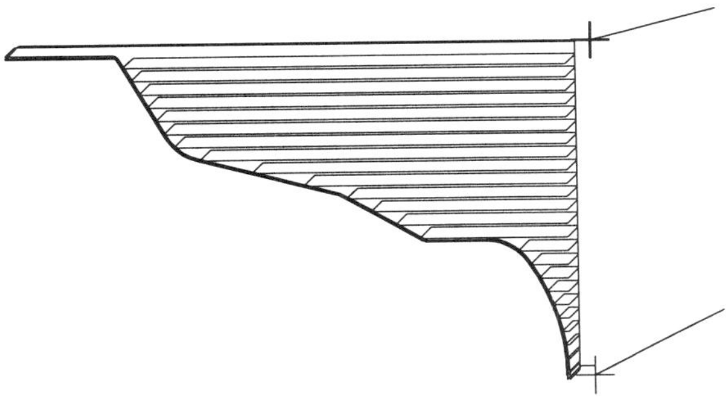

Figure 22.40

Select **Yes** to accept this toolpath segment

Step 7. Backplot both roughing and finishing toolpaths.

Select **Operations**
The toolpaths for two operations are included here.

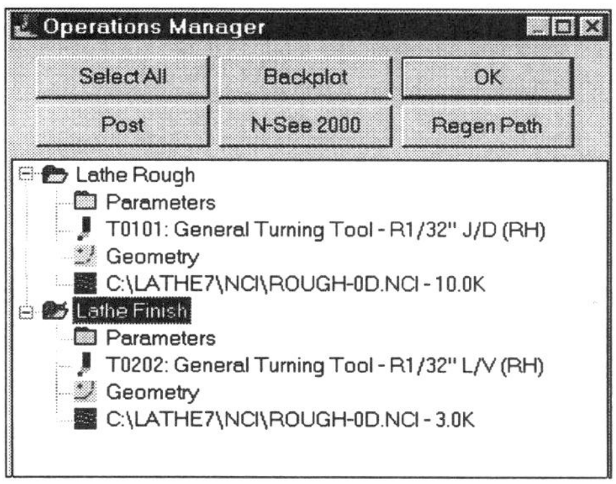

Select **Select All**
Select **Backplot**
Set display and backplot parameters to desired setting, then select **Run**
The roughing and finishing toolpaths should be animated on the screen.

5 Step 8. Postprocess the toolpaths.

Select **BACKUP** to return to Operations Manager menu
Select **Post**
Select **Yes** to overwrite the existing NCI file
Select **Yes** to run the postprocessor
File name for NC: **rough-od**
Select **Yes** to delete the old NC file
The part program should appear on the file list.
Select the **Close** button on the file list menu to return to Operations Manager menu

Step 9. Save the model with toolpaths as finish-od.

Select **MAIN MENU → File → Save**
File name: **finish-od**

Project 5. Generating finishing toolpaths for ID boring

This project adds the finishing toolpath to the roughing toolpaths file generated in project 2 of this chapter. The part geometry and roughing toolpaths are stored in a file (rough-id). Figure 22.41 shows the part geometry and toolpaths of the model.

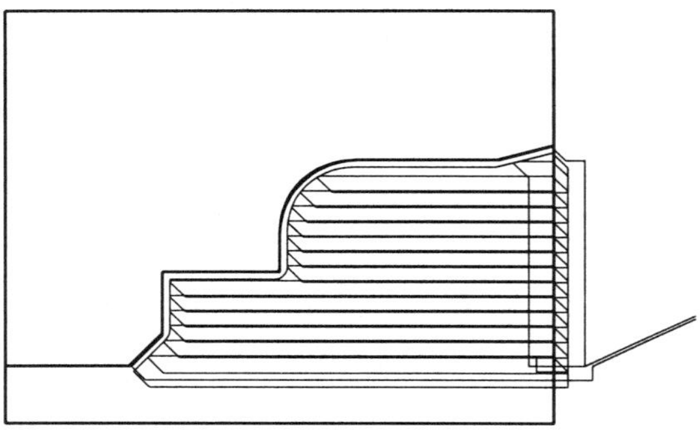

Figure 22.41

Tips 1. Use the project file (rough-id).

2. Use the finish module to add a set of boring toolpaths.

3. Use the same boring tool as the one used for rough-boring operation.

4. Save the new model file as (finish-id).

Step 1. Open the project file rough-id.

Select **MAIN MENU → File → Get**
File name: **rough-id**

The part geometry appears as Figure 22.42.

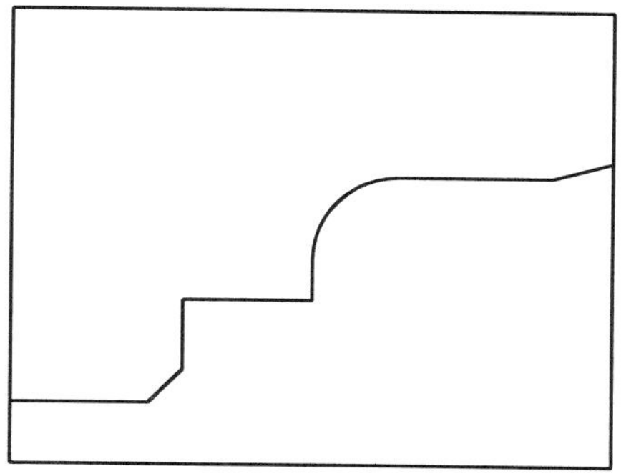

Figure 22.42

Step 2. Initiate the finish module.

Use the pick points in Figure 22.43.
Select **MAIN MENU → Toolpaths**
The existing rouging toolpaths should appear as in Figure 22.43.

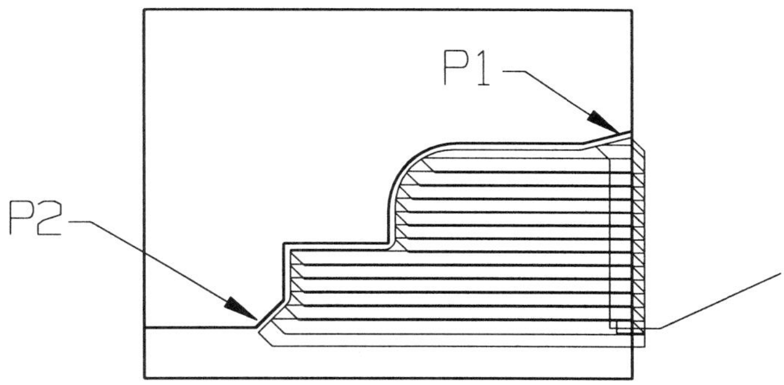

Figure 22.43

Select **Finish → Point → Values**
Enter coordinates: **3.5,0.2**
Select **Chain → Partial**
Pick **P1** to select the first entity
Pick **P2** to select the last entity
Select **Done**
Select **Point → Values**
Enter coordinates: **0.75,0.25**
Select **Done**

Step 3. Select a boring bar.

Select the "Tool Select" button to open the Tool Manager menu as below.

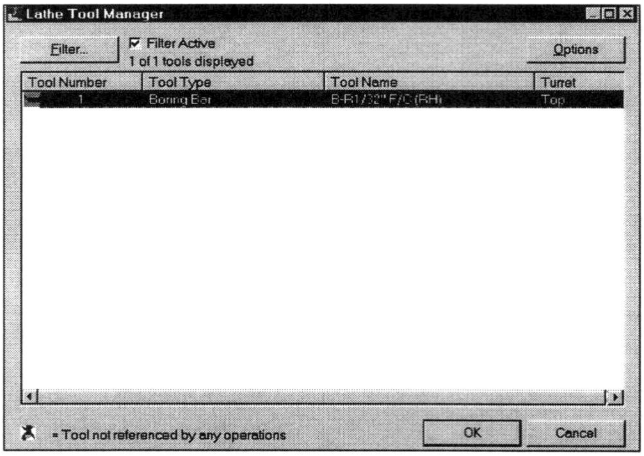

Select **OK** to use the same tool

Step 4. Set the finishing parameters as below.

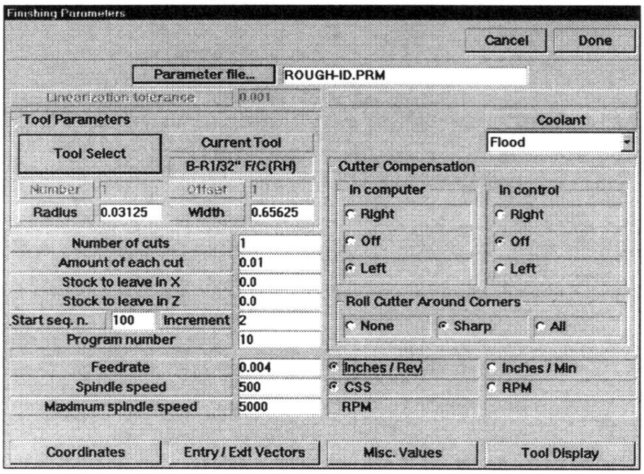

Step 5. Define entry and exit vector parameters.

Click the "Entry/Exit Vectors" button

Set the entry vector parameters as below.

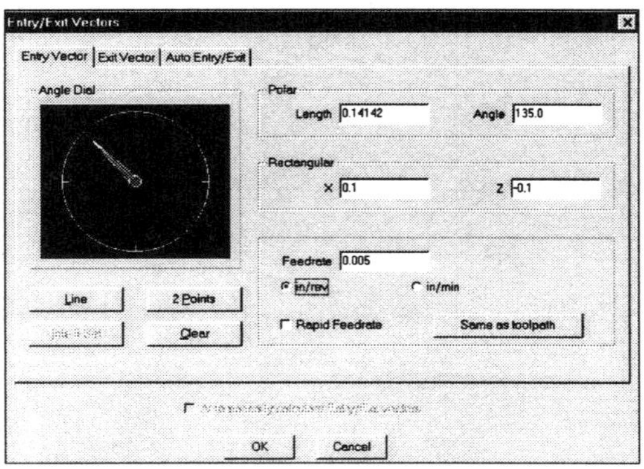

Click the “Exit Vector” button
Set the exit vector parameters as below.

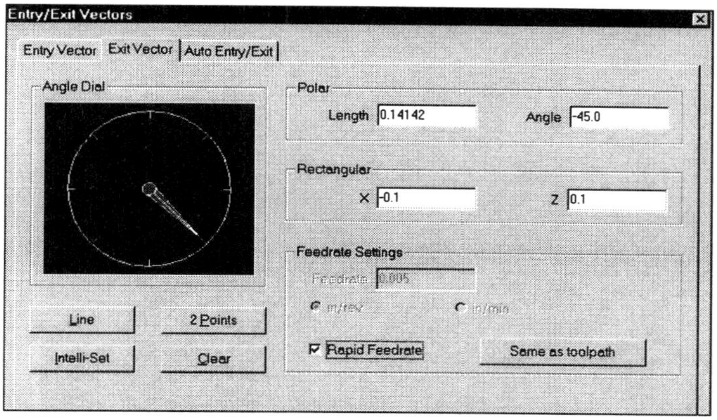

Select **OK** to return to Finishing Parameters menu
Select **Done** to generate the toolpaths
Select **Write → Yes** to accept this toolpath segment

Step 6. Backplot two sets of toolpaths.

Select **Operations** to open Operations Manager menu
Select **Select All** to select both toolpaths
Select **Backplot**
Set the display and backplot parameters to desired setting
Select **Run** to verify the toolpaths on the screen
Select **BACKUP** to return to Operations Manager menu
Select **OK**
The toolpaths should be shown as in Figure 22.44.

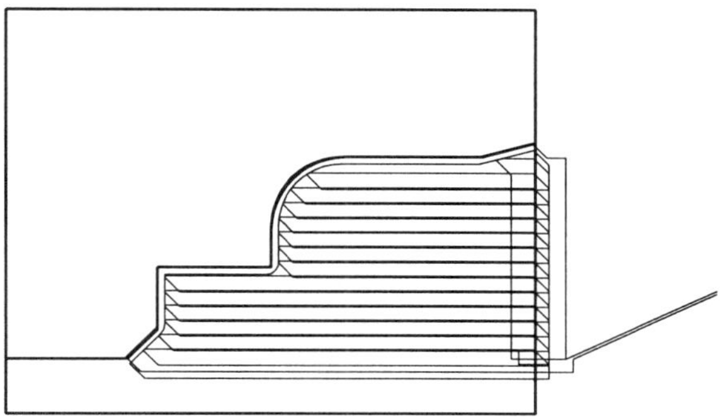

Figure 22.44

Step 7. Save the new model.

Select **MAIN MENU → File → Save**
File name: **finish-id**
Select **Yes** to delete old file

6 Project 6. Generating finishing toolpaths

This project uses the finish module to generate three toolpath passes along the finish profile. Figure 22.45 shows both the geometry model and three passes of toolpaths.

Figure 22.45a

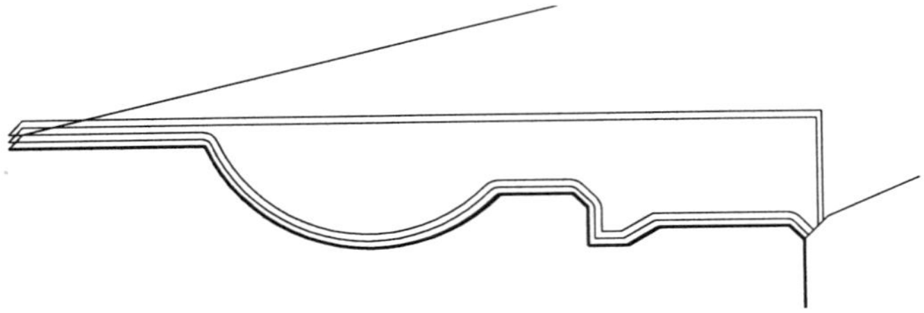

Figure 22.45b

Tips	1. Use the part geometry file "turn2". 2. Use finish module with multiple number of passes to generate finishing toolpaths. 3.Define a new turning tool with an insert "VNMG431" and holder "JVHR164D". 4. Save the toolpath file as finish.

Step 1. Open the part geometry file turn2.

Select **MAIN MENU → File → Get**
File name: **turn2**
The part geometry appears in Figure 22.46.

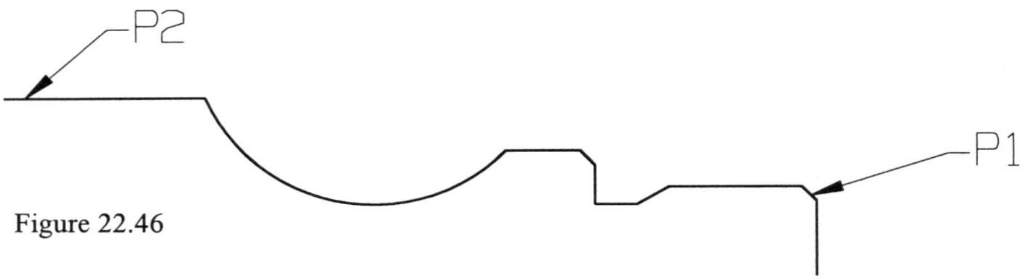

Figure 22.46

Step 2. Initiate the finish module.

Use the pick points in Figure 22.46.
Select **MAIN MENU → Toolpaths → Finish**
File name for toolpath: **finish**
Select **Chain → Partial**
Pick **P1** as the first entity
Pick **P2** as the last entity
Select **Done → Done**

Step 3. Define a new tool.

Select **Tool Select** to open Tool Manager menu
Click the right mouse button, then select **Create new tool**

Define Lathe Tools menu should appears as below.

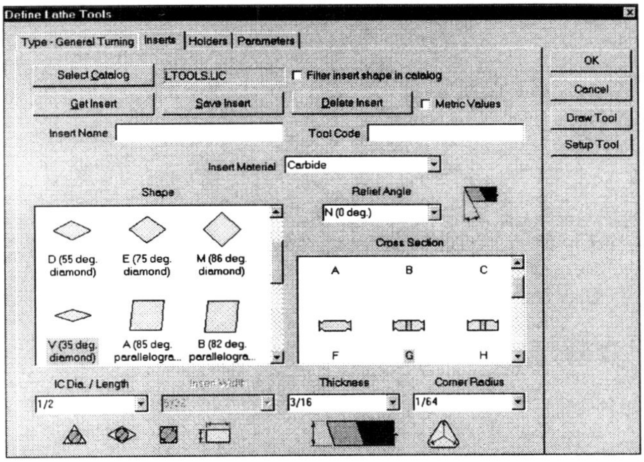

Select the "Get Insert" button to open the inserts menu as below.

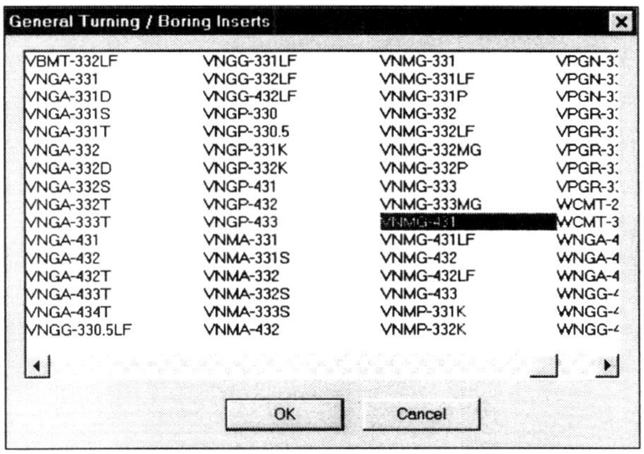

Select "**VNMG431**" from the list (you need to move to the right side of the screen)
Select **OK** to return back to insert menu as shown below.

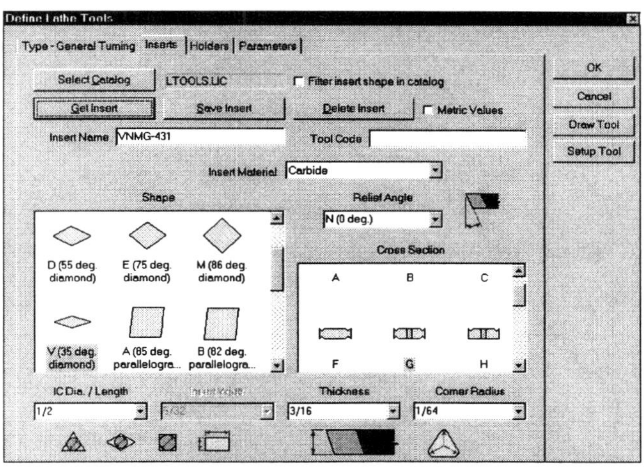

Step 4. Define the holder.

Click the "Holders" button
Click the "Get Holder" button to open the holder list as below.

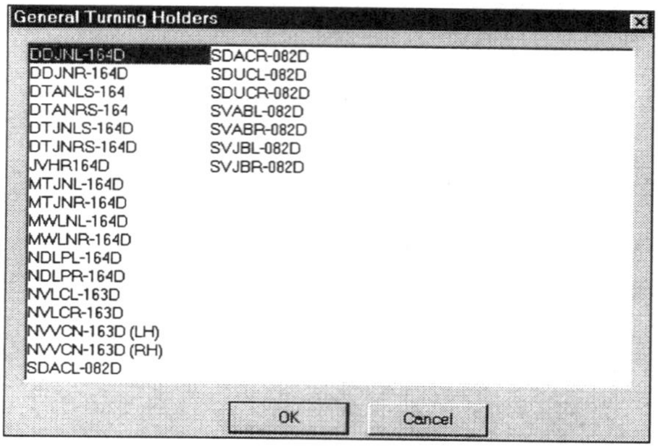

Select "**JVHR164D**" from the list
Select **OK** to return back to holders menu
Set the holder geometry as below.

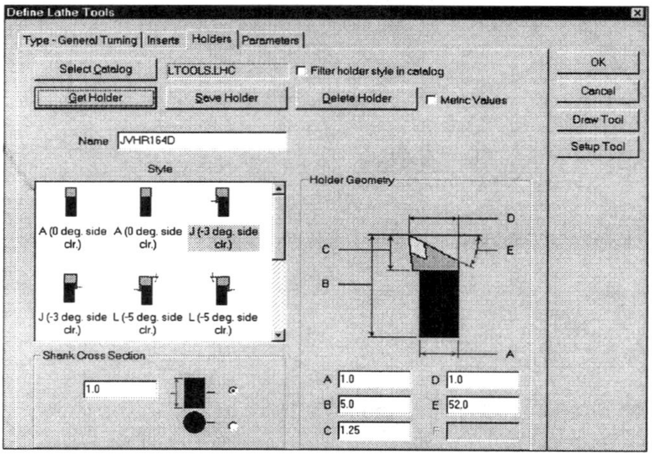

Select **OK** to return back to tool manager menu
The tool manager menu appears as below.

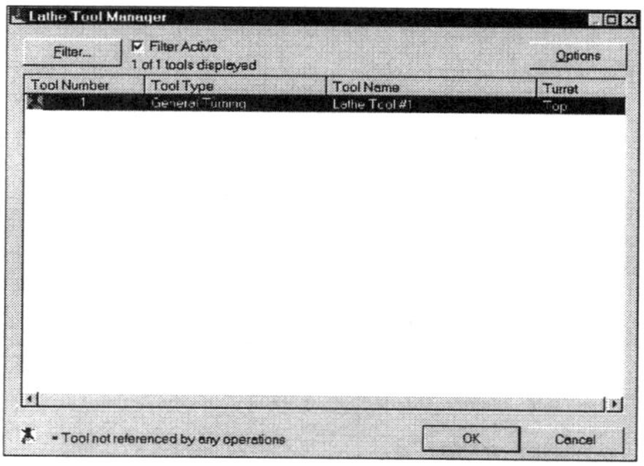

Select **OK**

Step 5. Define the finishing parameters as below.

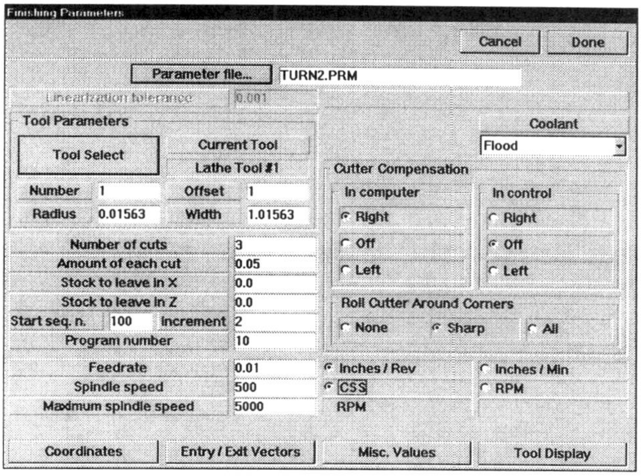

Step 6. Define the entry and exit vector parameters.

Click the "Entry/Exit Vectors" button

Set the entry vector parameters as below.

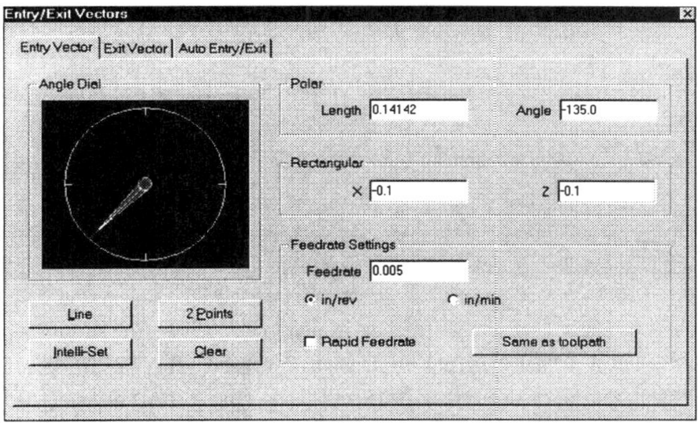

Click the "Exit Vector" button

Set the exit vector parameters as below.

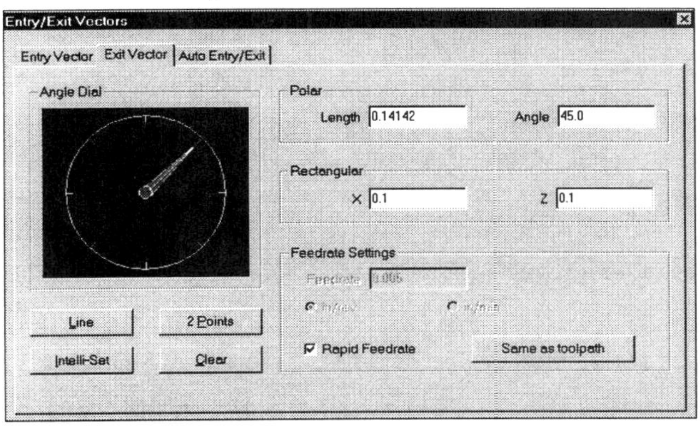

Select **OK**

Select **Done** from finishing parameters menu to generate three passes of finishing toolpaths

Select **Yes**

The toolpaths are added as in Figure 22.47.

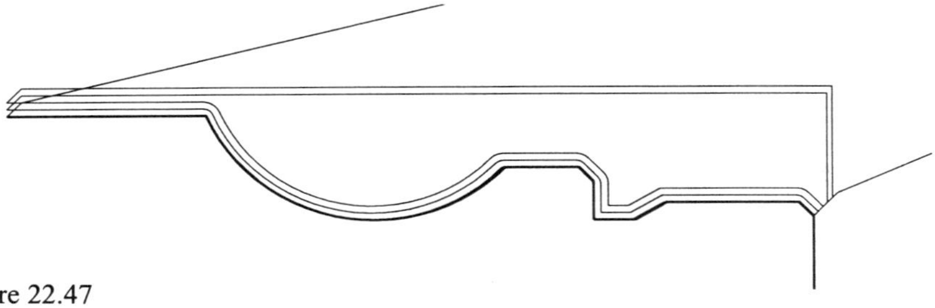

Figure 22.47

Step 7. Backplot the toolpaths.

Select **Operations → Backplot**
Set the display and backplot parameters to desired setting
Select **Run** to animate the toolpaths on the screen
Select **BACKUP** to return to Operations Manager menu
Select **OK** to exit Operations Manager menu

Step 8. Save the toolpaths.

Select **MAIN MENU → File → Save**
File name: **finish**

22.5 Face Module

The face module is used to generate a set of toolpaths for facing an end face of the part (Figure 22.48). The stock to be faced out is specified by two points which form a rectangular box (Figure 22.49). All stock in the rectangular box will be removed. The unique parameters for face module are; **Face rough**, **Face finish,** and **Cutter compensation.** The facing parameters menu appears as below.

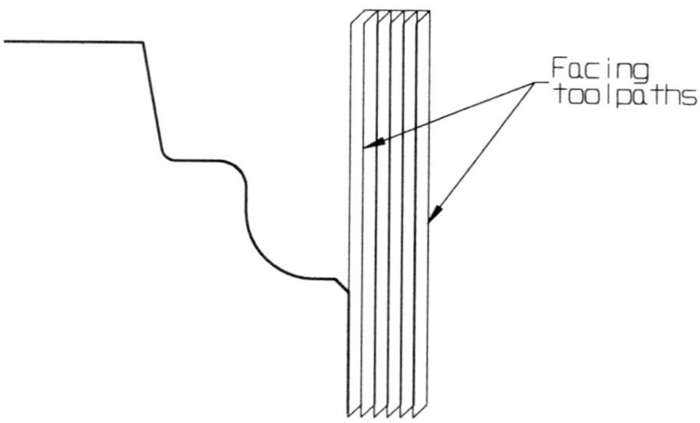

Figure 22.48 facing toolpaths

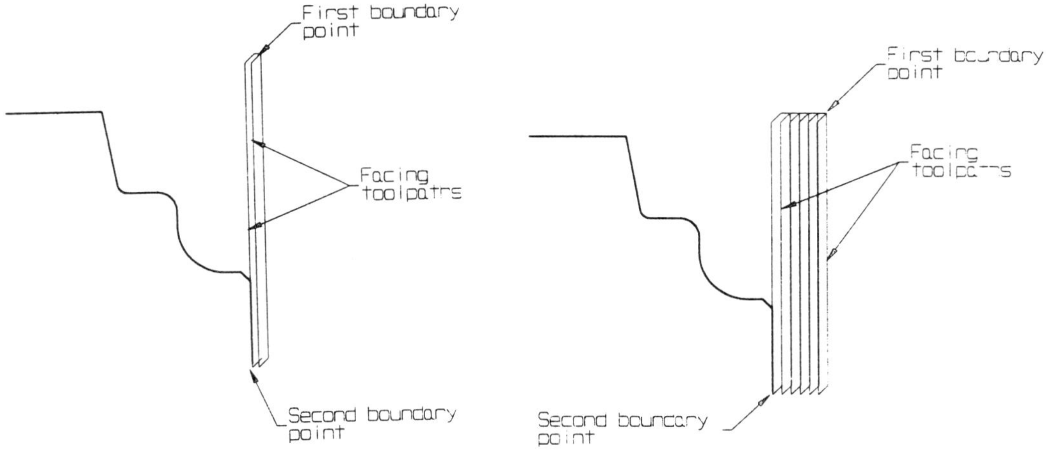

Figure 22.49 two boundary points

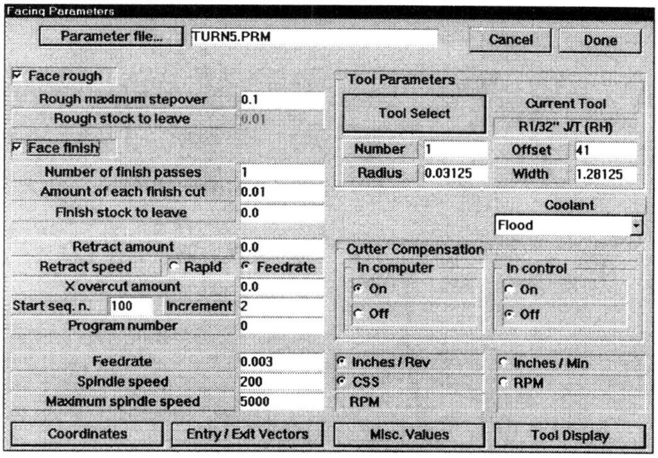

Face rough

This parameter is used to specify whether the roughing toolpaths are to be generated. Toggle this parameter to Off (no √ mark), then the system only generates a finishing toolpath (Figure 22.50 on the following page). Toggle this parameter to On (with √ mark), then the system generates a set of roughing toolpaths based on the following two parameters:

Rough maximum stepover:	the maximum stepover distance for each roughing pass.
Rough stock to leave:	the stock left for subsequent finishing cuttings. This parameter only becomes active when the "Face finish" parameter is toggled to Off (no √ mark).

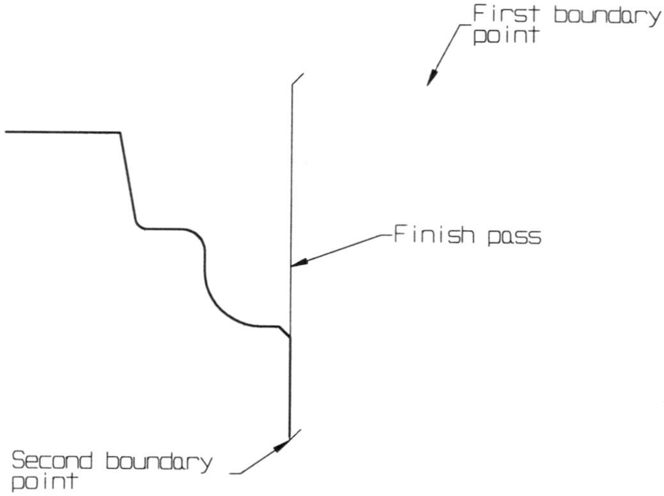

Figure 22.50 No face rough passes

Face finish

This parameter specifies whether the finish toolpaths are to be generated. Toggle this parameter to Off (no √ mark) to ignore the finishing toolpaths. With a √ mark in this parameter, the system will generate finishing toolpaths based on the following three parameters:

Number of finish passes:	specifies the number of finishing passes.
Amount of each finish cut:	specifies the distance of cut in Z direction for each pass.
Finish stock to leave:	specifies the stock amount left for subsequent operations.

Cutter compensation

The cutter compensation in computer and in control only has two options: **On** and **Off**. When it is toggled to On, the system automatically sets the compensation to the proper side.

Project 7. Facing the end face

This project uses the face module to add the facing toolpath to an existing toolpath model "finish-id" generated in projects 2 and 5 of this chapter. The new toolpath file consists of three toolpath operations with the Lathe-Rough operation being the first one. We need to change the sequence starting with the facing operation, followed by Lathe-Rough and Lathe-Finish. Figure 22.51 shows the part geometry, facing toolpaths, and complete toolpath model.

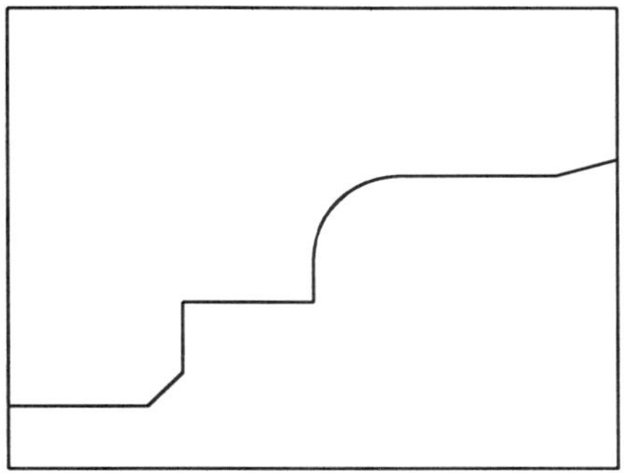

Figure 22.51a

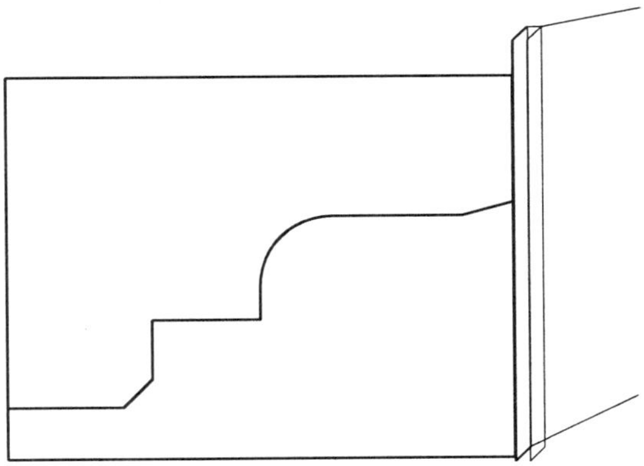

Figure 22.51b

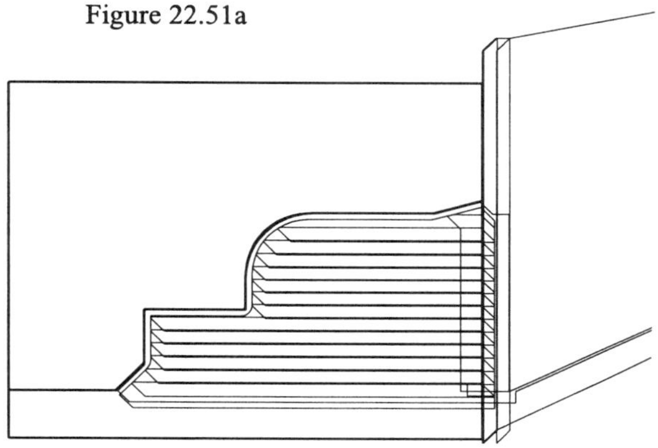

Figure 22.51c

Tips

1. Use the part model "finish-id".
2. Use the face module with the following two boundary points: (6,0.2) and (0,0).
3. Select a turning tool "R1/32 J/T(RH)" from the tool library.
4. Change the sequence of toolpath sections to start with facing, followed by roughing and finishing.
5. Save the new project file name as "face".

Step 1. Open the part geometry and toolpath model "rough-id".

Select **MAIN MENU → File → Get**
File name: **finish-id**
The part geometry appears as in Figure 22.52.

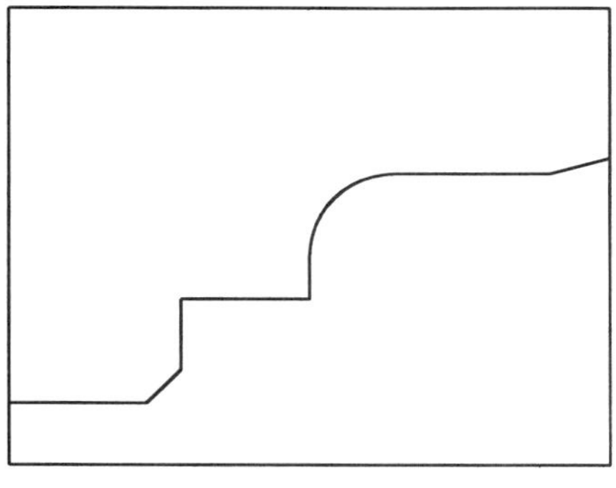

Figure 22.52

Step 2. Initiate the face module.

Select **MAIN MENU → Toolpaths**
The existing roughing and finishing toolpaths appear as in Figure 22.53.

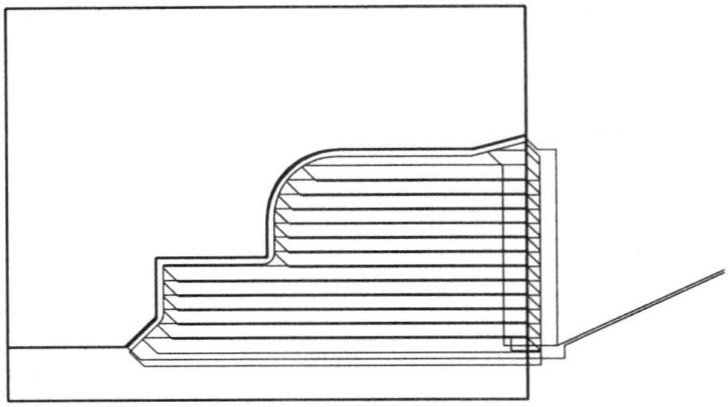

Figure 22.53

Select **Face → Values**
Enter coordinates: **6,0.2** as the first boundary point
Select **Values**
Enter coordinates: **0,0** as the second boundary point

Step 3. Select the facing tool.

Click the "Tool Select" button from the Facing Parameters menu
Click the right mouse button, then select **Get from library**
Select a turning tool "**R1/32 J/T(RH)**" as shown below.

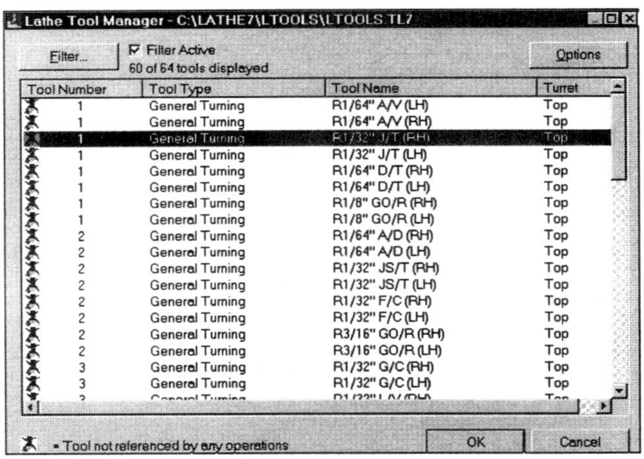

Select **OK** to return to Tool Manager menu
Select **OK** to return to Facing Parameters menu

Step 4. Define the facing parameters as below.

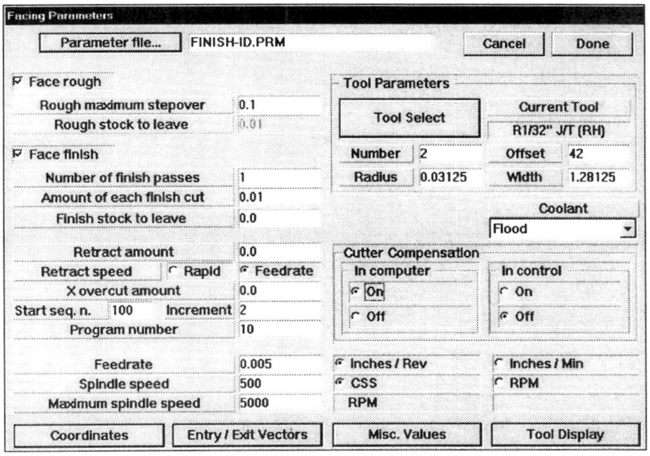

Step 5. Define the entry and exit vector parameters.

Click the "Entry/Exit Vectors" button

Set the entry vector parameters as below.

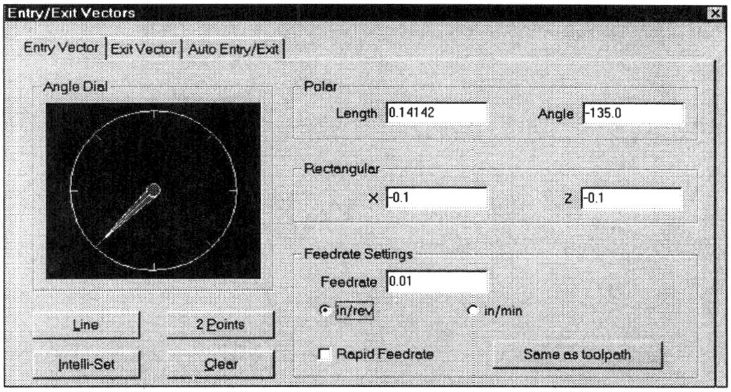

Click the "Exit Vector" button

Set the exit vector parameters as below.

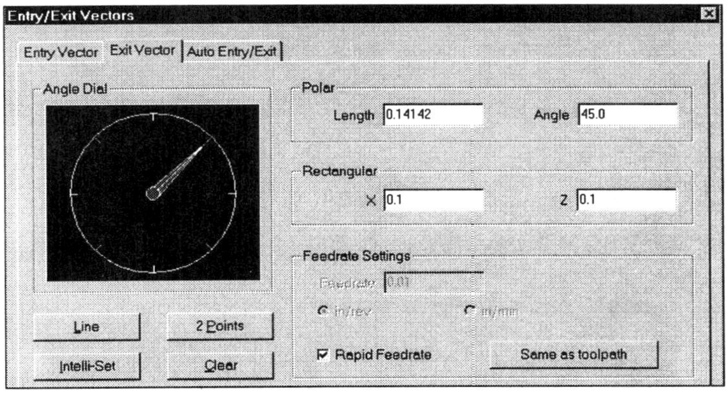

Select **OK** to return to Facing Parameters menu

Select **Done** to generate facing toolpaths

The facing toolpaths are added as in Figure 22.54.

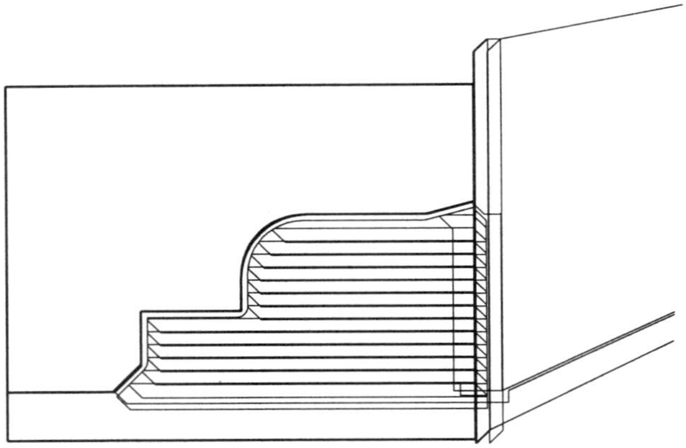

Figure 22.54

Select **Yes** to accept this toolpath segment

Step 6. Change the operation sequence.

Select **Operations**

The existing sequence of the three operations appears as below.

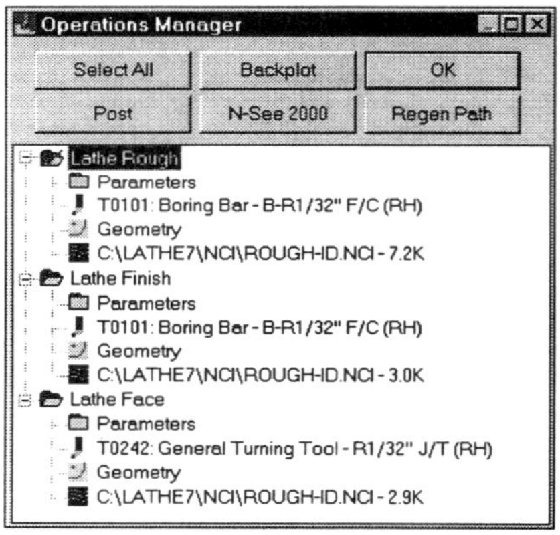

Select **Select All**, then click the right mouse button to open the option menu as shown here:

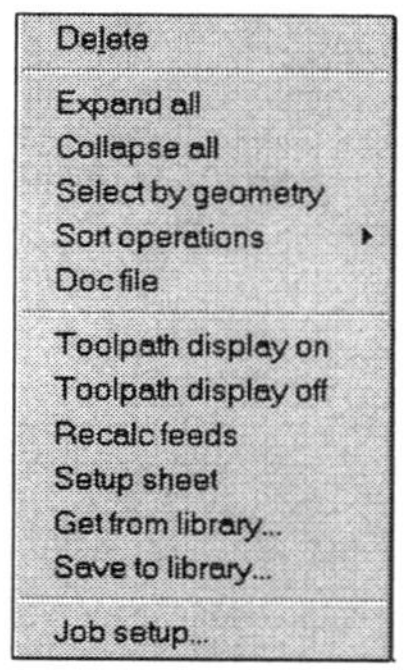

Select **Sort operations** to open a selection sub-menu as shown here:

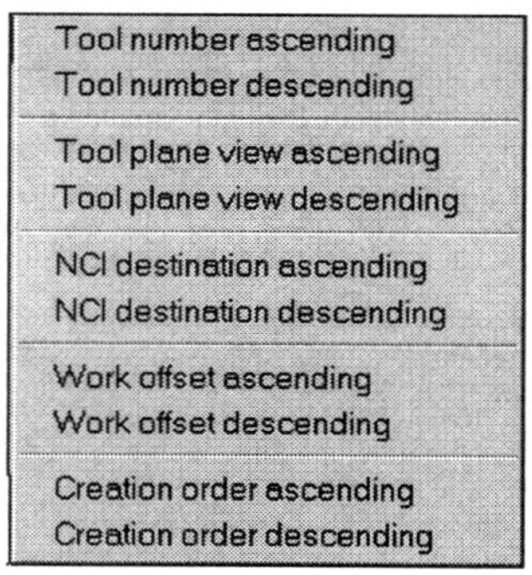

Select **Tool number descending**

The sequence for these three operations has been changes as below.

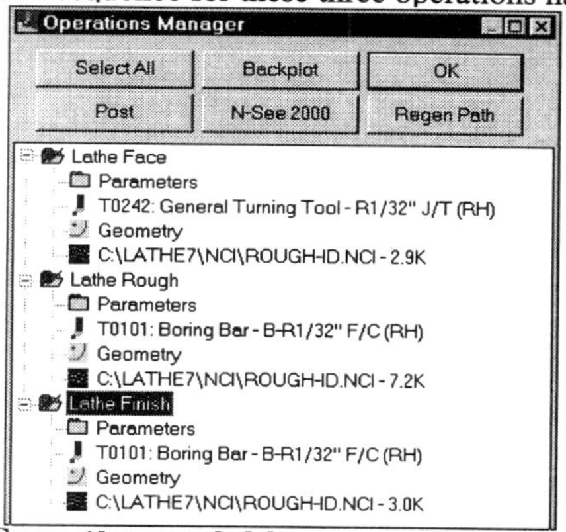

Step 7. Save the model in a new file name "face".

Select **OK** to exit Operations Manager menu

Select **MAIN MENU → File → Save**

File name: **face**

22.6 Groove Module

The groove module generates a set of toolpaths for plunging the tool into the material to rough and/or finish the part (Figure 22.55). The Grooving Parameters menu appears as below.

Figure 22.55

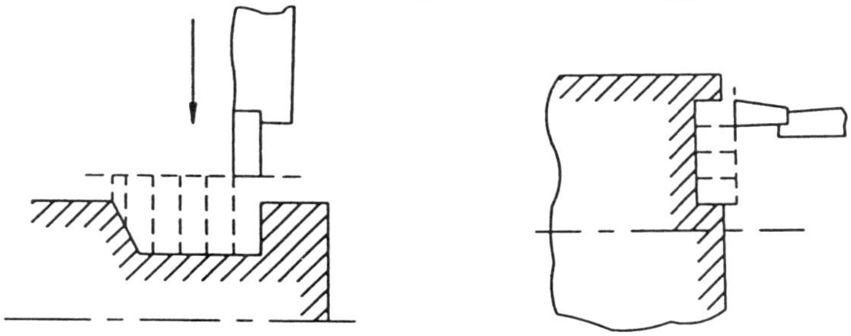

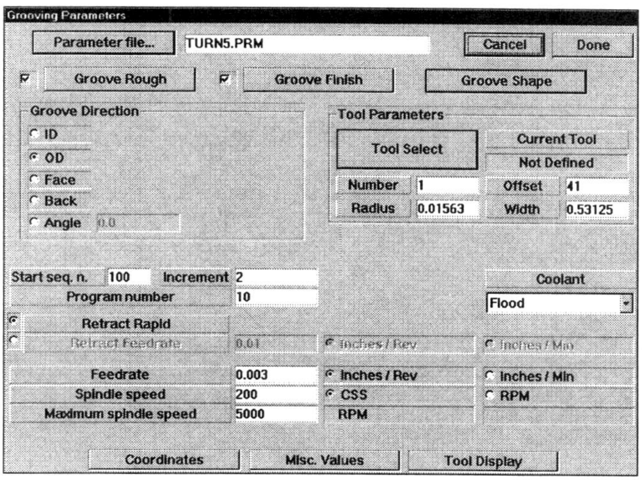

Groove Specific Parameters

The following five parameters are used to define the grooving toolpaths:

Groove rough:	generates roughing toolpaths for cutting a groove.
Groove finish:	generates finishing toolpaths for cutting a groove.
Groove direction:	specifies the cutting direction of the groove.
Groove shape:	defines the shape of four corners of the groove.
Tool parameters:	selects a grooving tool and its defining information.

Groove rough This parameter is used to indicate whether the roughing toolpath is to be generated for grooving. Toggle this parameter to On (with √ mark), the groove roughing toolpath is generated (Figure 22.56a), otherwise only groove finishing toolpath is generated (Figure 22.56b).

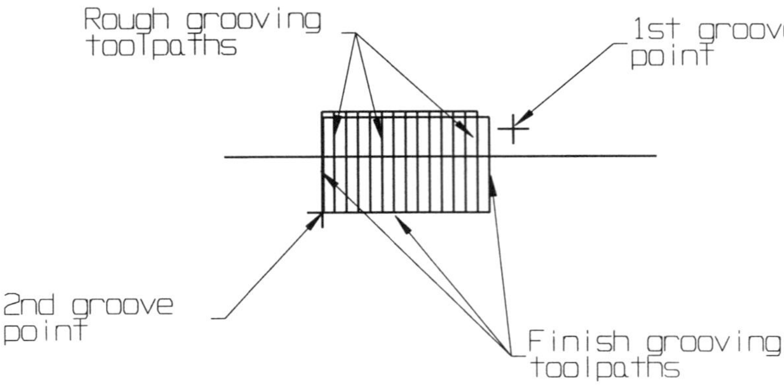

Figure 22.56a With groove roughing toolpath

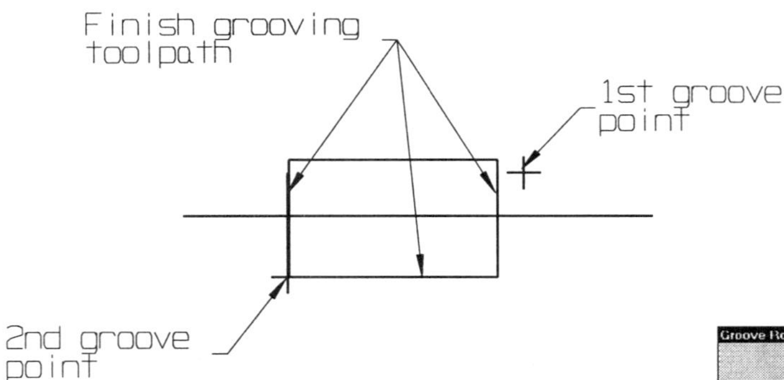

Figure 22.56b No groove roughing toolpath

The groove rough parameters menu appears like this.

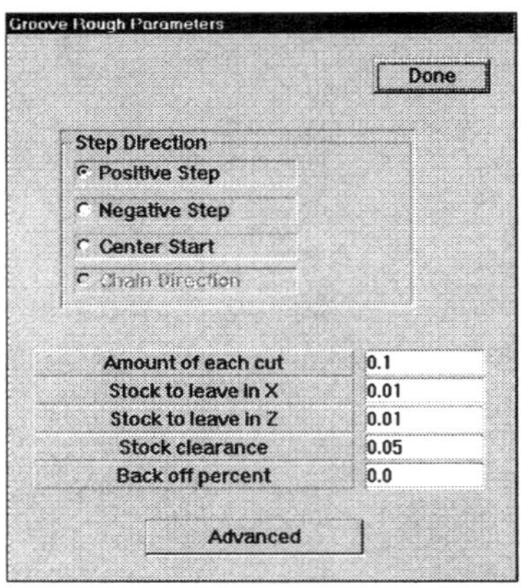

Step direction: This parameter specifies the stepping direction of the grooving toolpath. It has the following four options:

Positive step	toolpath starts from left boundary and steps in +Z direction (Figure 22.57).
Negative step	toolpath starts from right boundary and steps in –Z direction (Figure 22.58).
Center start	toolpath starts from the middle of the grooving boundary and zigzags in two directions (Figure 22.59).
Chain direction	toolpath steps in the chained direction of the grooving geometry (Figure 22.60).

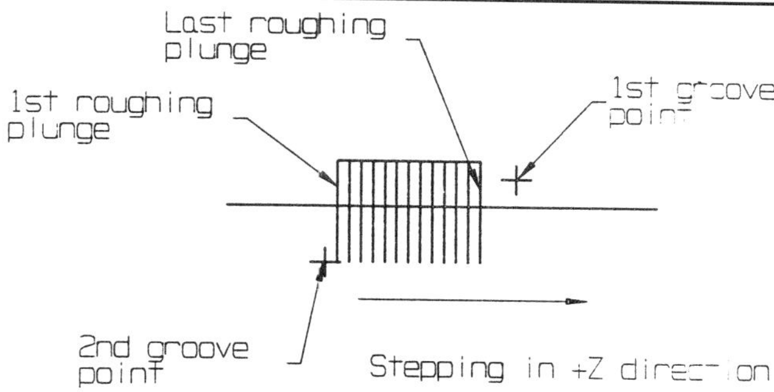

Figure 22.57 Positive step

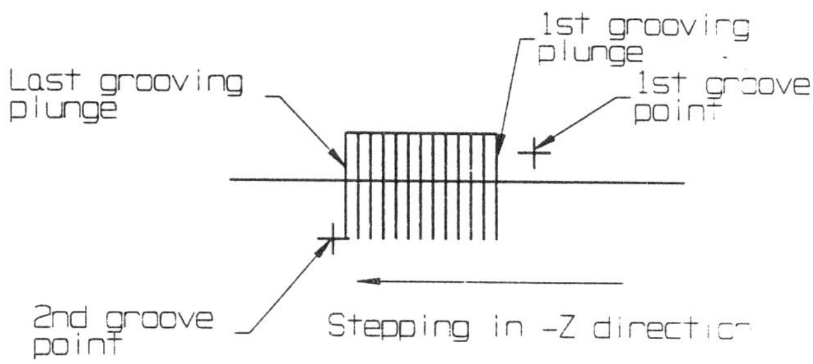

Figure 22.58 Negative step

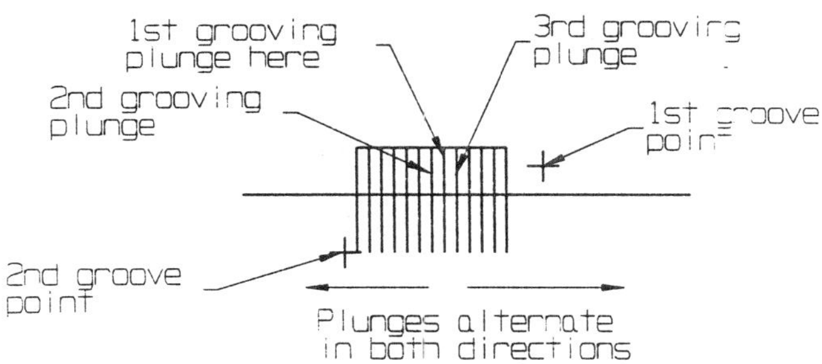

Figure 22.59 Center start

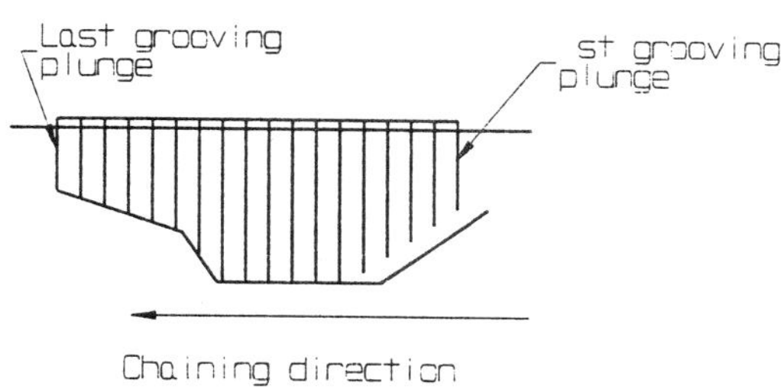

Figure 22.60 Chain direction

Amount of each cut specifies the amount of cut for each grooving plunge.

Stock to leave in X specifies the stock amount in X direction.

Stock to leave in Z specifies the stock amount in Z direction.

Stock clearance Specifies the clearance distance measured from the geometry boundary.

Back off percent Used to specify the percent of back off.

Advanced opens the Rough Advanced menu.

Rough advanced parameters Mastercam allows the grooving toolpath to be implemented in the pecking pattern and in multiple depth cuts. These parameters are grouped under the Rough Advanced menu as shown on the left.

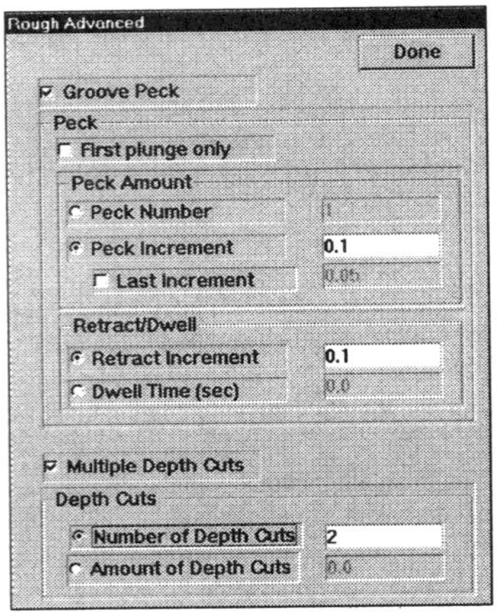

Groove finish This parameter is used to specify whether the finish toolpath is to be generated for grooving. Toggle this parameter to ON (with √ mark), the groove finish toolpath is generated, otherwise, only a groove roughing toolpath is generated.

The groove finish parameter menu appears as below.

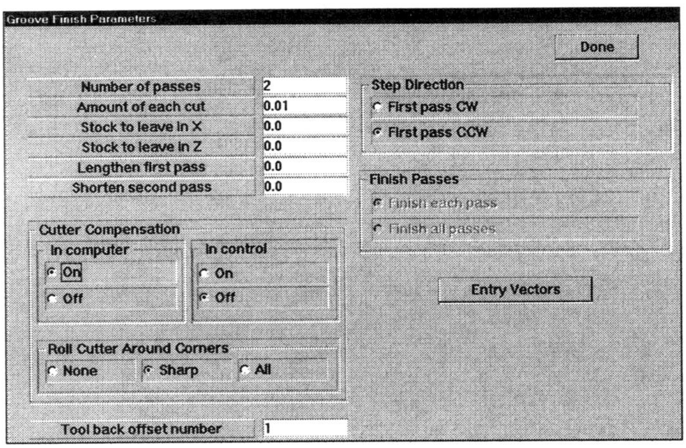

It is possible to generate both groove rough and groove finish toolpaths in one operation.

Groove direction This parameter specifies the cutting direction of the groove. The five groove direction options are:

ID:	cuts internal groove in +X direction (Figure 22.61).
OD:	cut external groove in –X direction (Figure 22.62).
Face:	cut face groove in –Z direction (Figure 22.63).
Back:	cut face groove in +Z direction (Figure 22.64).
Angle:	cut angle groove in a specified angle direction (Figure 22.65).

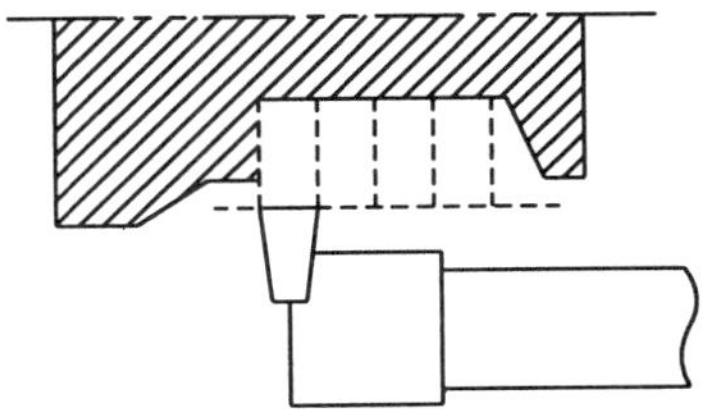

Figure 22.61 ID groove

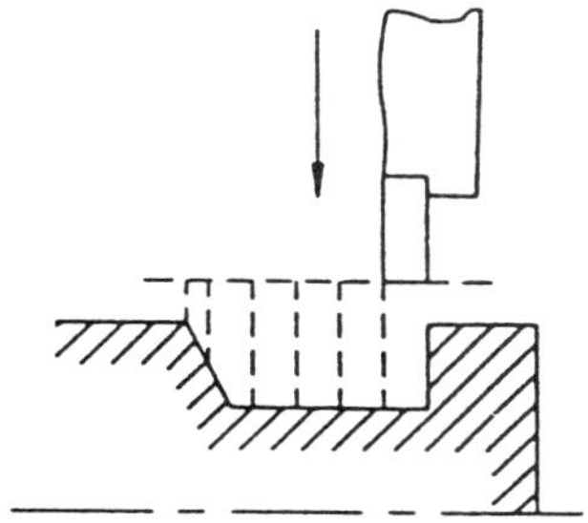

Figure 22.62 OD groove

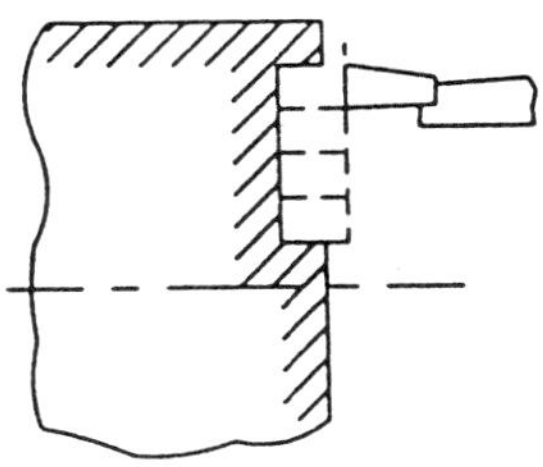

Figure 22.63 Face groove

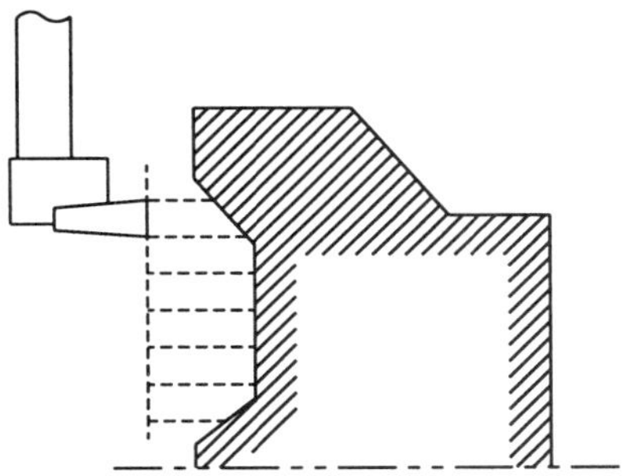

Figure 22.64 Back groove

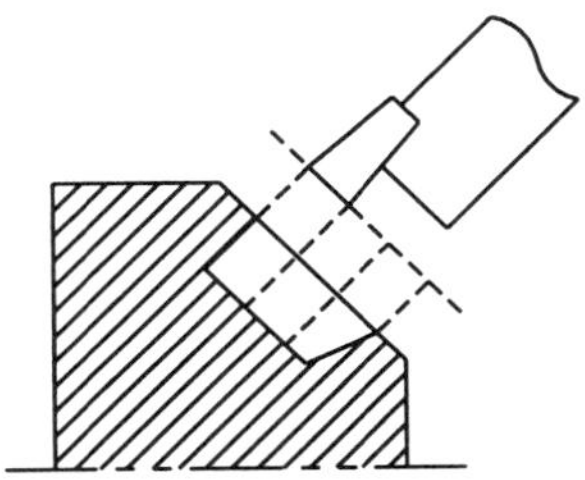

Figure 22.65 Angle groove

Groove shape Mastercam provides a number of options for you to specify the shape of the groove. The following four ways can be used to specify the groove dimensions:

1 Point: uses one point as the anchor with the given depth and width in the groove shape menu to fully define the groove size (Figure 22.66).
2 Point: uses two points to form a rectangle as the groove size (Figure 22.67).
3 Lines: uses three chained lines to from the groove shape and size (Figure 22.68).
2 Bdry: uses two chained profiles as the inner boundary and outer boundary, respectively (Figure 22.69).

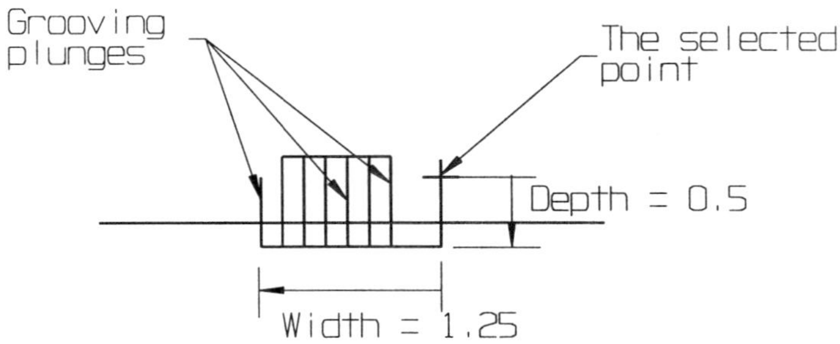

Figure 22.66 1 point

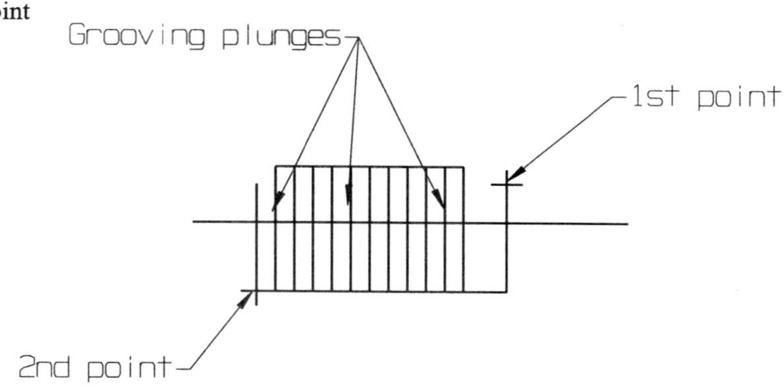

Figure 22.67 2 points

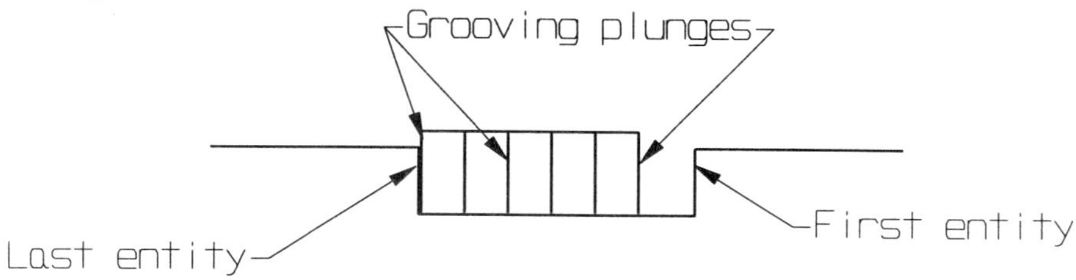

Figure 22.68 3 lines

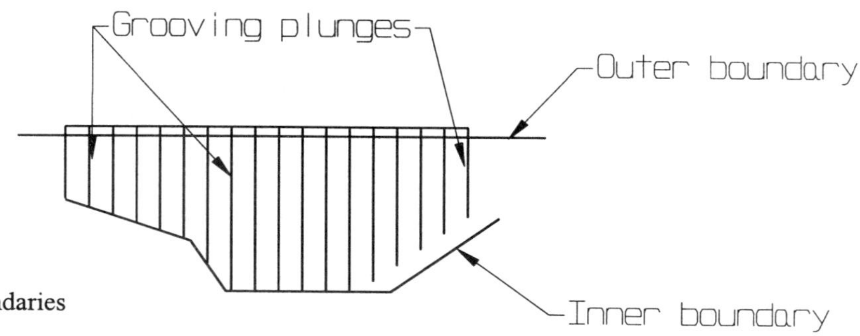

Figure 22.69 2 boundaries

In most cases, a chamfer and radius can be added to the four corners of the groove. Mastercam groups these parameters under the "Groove Shape" menu. Click the "Groove Shape" button in the Grooving Parameters menu to open the "Corner Radius/Chamfer" menu as below.

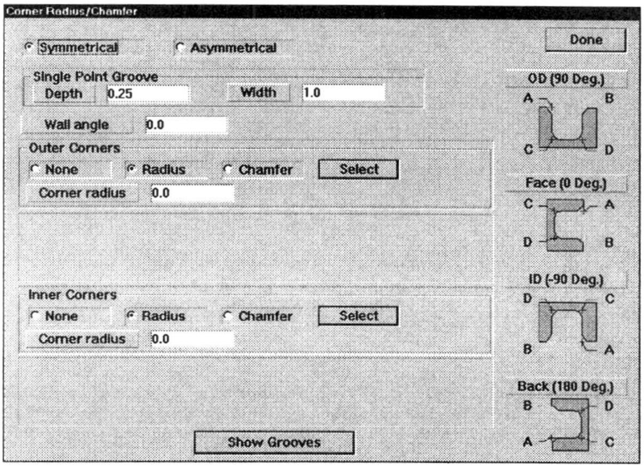

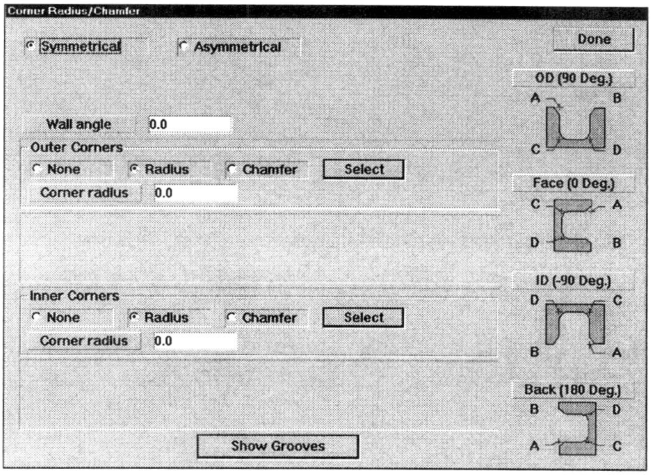

Wall angle

The wall angle parameter allows us to add a tapered angle to two sides of the groove as shown in Figure 22.70.

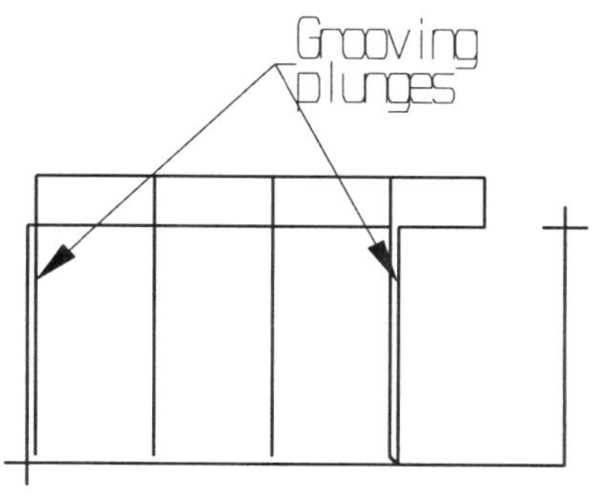

Figure 22.70 Wall angle =0°

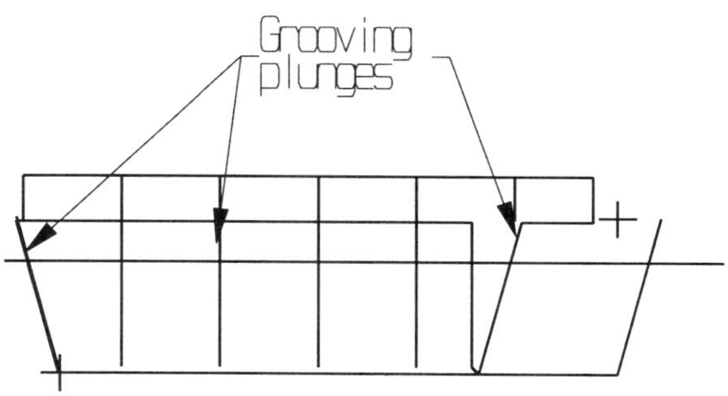

Figure 22.70b Wall angle = 15°

8 G74 and G75 canned cycles can be used for grooving and drilling. They permit the tool to be automatically relieved. The G74 canned cycle is used for ID grooving, while G75 is used for OD grooving.

These two canned cycles have the following command statement format:

Use thess definitions for the block code explanations:	
Xx Zz	- X and Z coordinate of grooving end point
Pi	- Increment in the X direction
Qk	- Increment in the Z direction
Rd	- Relief amount
Re	- Return amount

One-block format:

Ii Kk Dd

G74/G75 Xx Zz Pi Qk Rd Ff

Two-block format:

G74/G75 Re

G74/G75 Xx Zz Pi Qk Rd Ff

The Procedure for generating the Groove Canned Cycle Command G74 or G75

1. Select Toolpaths Groove
2. Define
3. Set the grooving parameters to the proper setting
4. Set the miscellaneous integer 2 to 1

Project 8. Cutting an OD groove

Define a grooving tool to cut a groove shown in Figure 22.71. The grooving tool has a width of 0.125” and a radius of 0.015” at both corners.

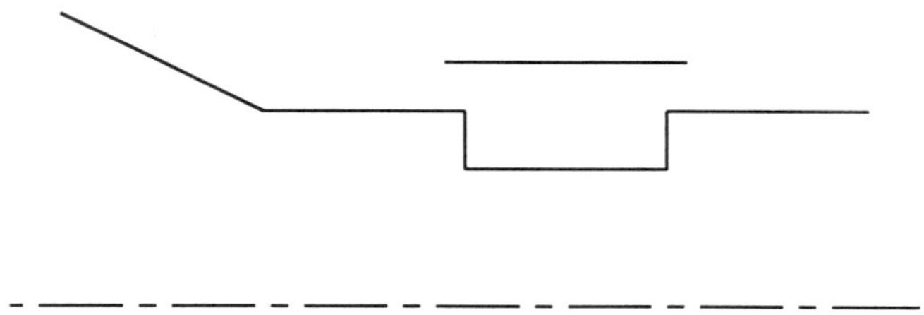

Figure 22.71a

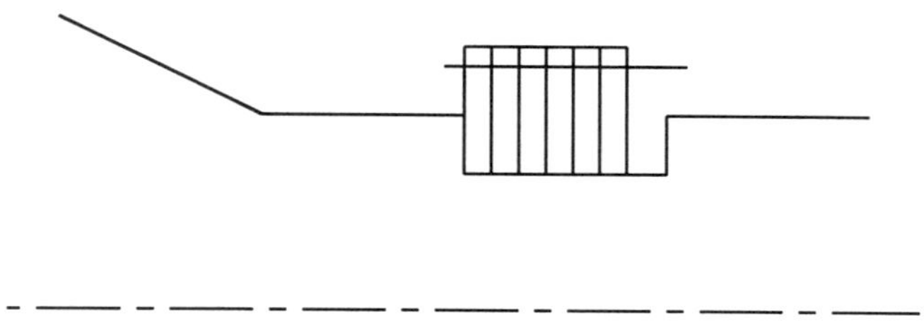

Figure 22.71b

⌛**Tips**	1. Create the inner groove profile and outer boundary. 2.Change the line type to center to create the center line of the part geometry. 3. Define a grooving tool has a width of 0.125. 4. Save the grooving toolpath as groove1.

Step 1. Create the part profile.

Select **MAIN MENU → Create → Line → Multi**
Specify endpoint 1: **2,0**
Specify endpoint 2: **2,-1**
Specify endpoint 3: **1.4,-1**
Specify endpoint 4: **1.4,-2**
Specify endpoint 5: **2,-2**
Specify endpoint 6: **2,-3**
Specify endpoint 7: **3,-4**
The part profile should look like Figure 22.72

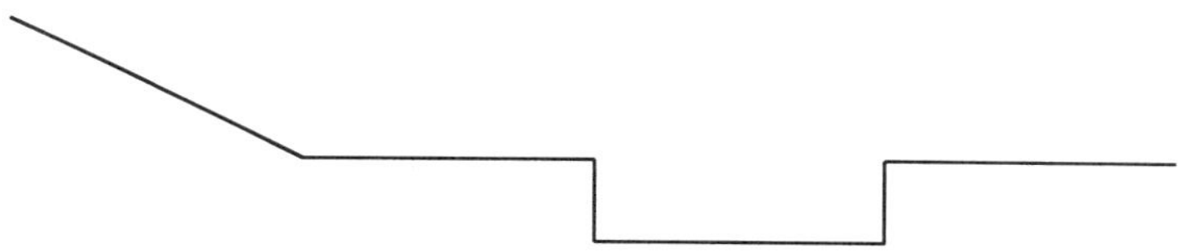

Figure 22.72

Step 2. Add a center line.

Click **Style/Width** from the left menu column
The Curve Styles/Widths menu should appear on the screen
Set "Line Style" to center as shown below.

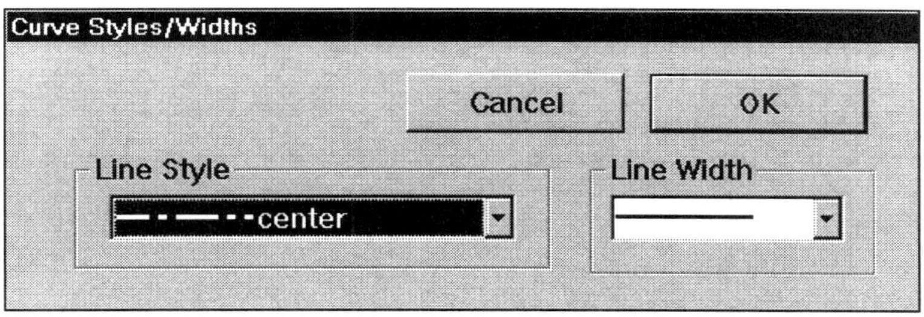

Select **OK**
Select **MAIN MENU → Create → Line → Endpoints**
Specify the first endpoint: **0,0.25**
Specify the second endpoint: **0,-4.25**

The center line is added as shown in Figure 22.73.

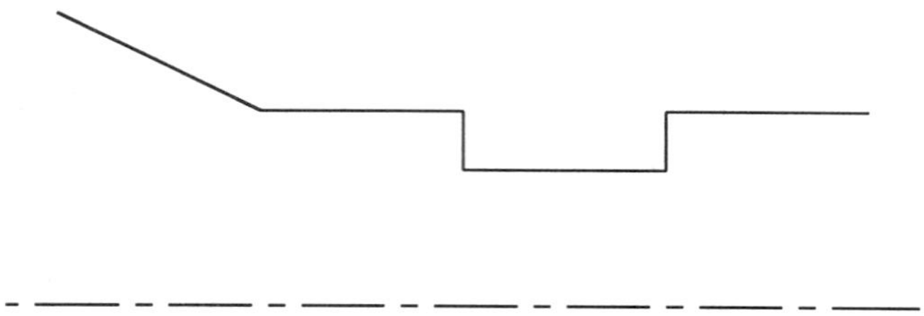

Figure 22.73

Step 3. Change line type to solid.

Click the "Style/Width" from the left menu column
Set "Line Style" to solid from the menu
Select **OK**

Step 4. Create the outer boundary line.

Select **MAIN MENU → Create → Line Endpoints**
Specify the first endpoint: **2.5,-0.9**
Specify the second endpoint: **2.5,-2.1**
The line is added as in Figure 22.74.

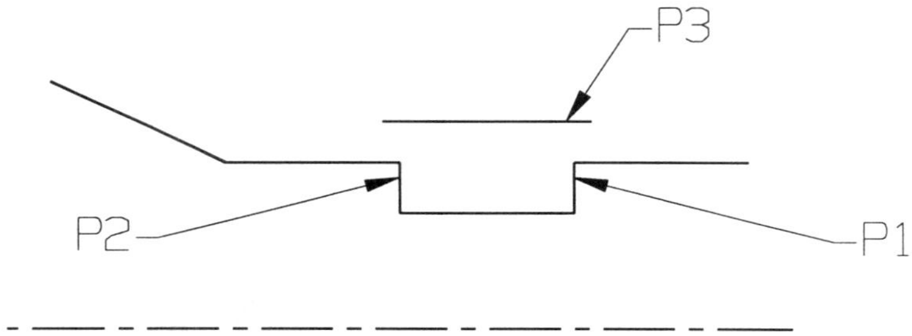

Figure 22.74

Step 5. Save the part geometry "groove1".

Select **MAIN MENU → File → Save**
File name: **groove1**

Step 6. Initiate the groove module.

Use the pick points in Figure 22.74.
Select **MAIN MENU → Toolpaths → Groove**
File name for NCI file: **groove1**
Select **2 Bdry**
Select **Chain → Partial**
Pick **P1** to select the first entity
Pick **P2** to select the last entity for the inner boundary
Select **Done → Single**
Pick **P3** as the outer boundary
Select **Done**

Step 7. Define the insert of grooving tool.

Click the "Tool Select" button in the grooving parameters menu
Click the right mouse button, then select **Create new tool**

Select “Single End (Square)" insert style and define insert geometry as below.

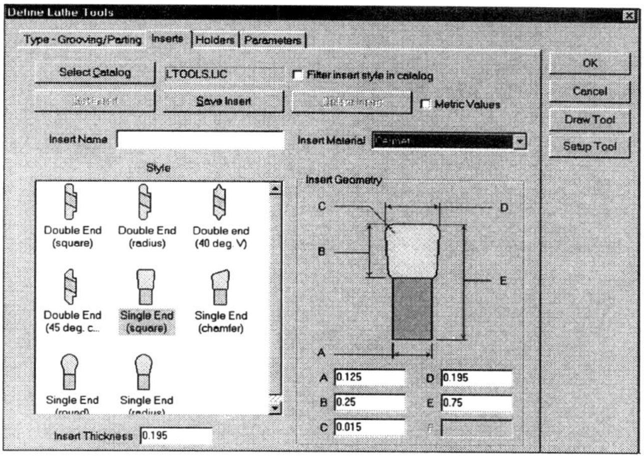

Step 8. Define the grooving tool holder.

Click the “Holders” button

Select holder style and holder geometry as below.

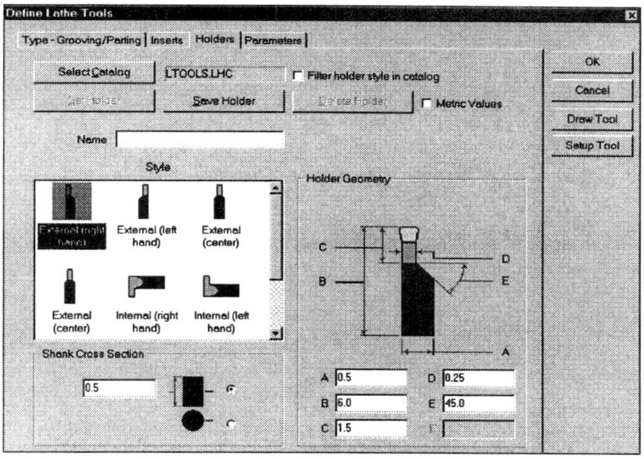

Step 9. Define the tooling and machining parameters.

Click the “Parameters” button. Set parameters as below.

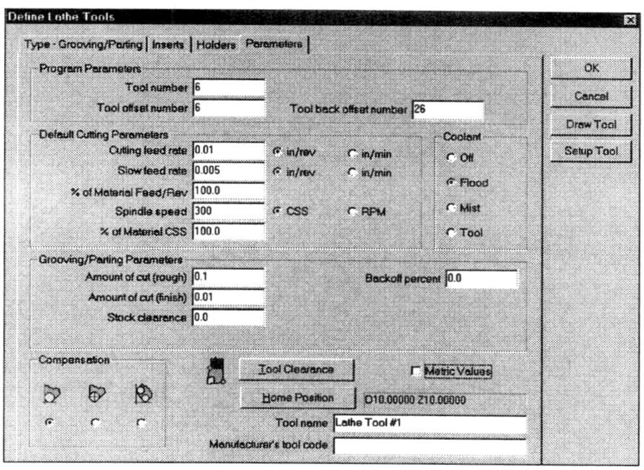

Select **Done** to return to Tool Manager menu as below.

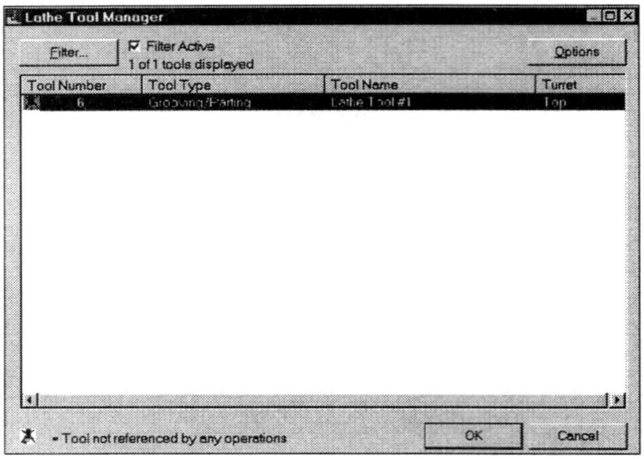

Select **OK**

Step 10. Define the groove rough parameters.

Click the "Groove Rough" button
Set the Groove Rough Parameters
as shown here.

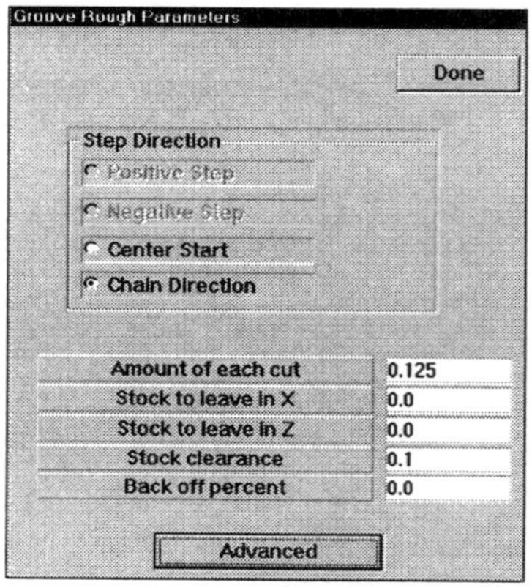

Select **Done**

Step 11. Set the grooving parameters as below.

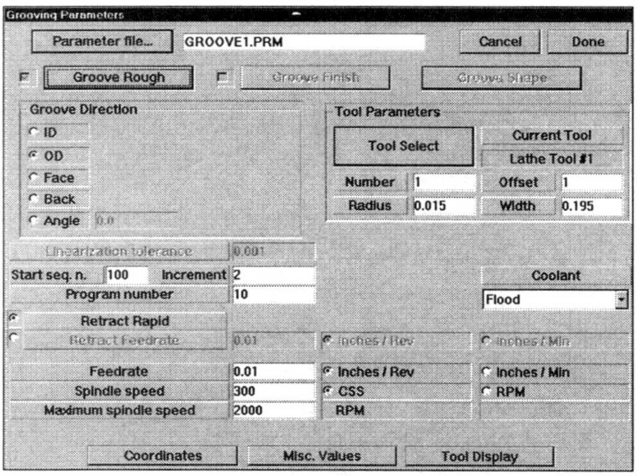

Select **Done**

The grooving toolpaths are generated as in Figure 22.75.

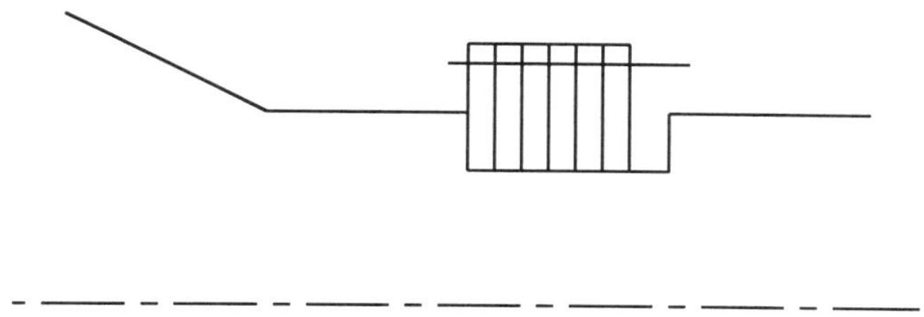

Figure 22.75

Select **Yes** to accept this toolpath segment

Step 12. Backplot the toolpaths.

Select **Operations** to open Operations Manager menu
Select **Backplot**
Set display and backplot parameters to desired setting
Select **Run** to animate the grooving toolpaths on the screen
Select **BACKUP** to return to Operations Manager menu
Select **OK** to exit Operations Manager menu

Step 3. Save the file as groove1.

Select **MAIN MENU → Save**
File name: **groove1**

Project 9. Rough cutting a non-rectangular groove

This project shows how to rough cut a non-rectangular groove. This requires to use "2 Bdry" option to define the grooving boundaries. Figure 22.76 shows the grooving boundaries and toolpaths. Use the same grooving tool as in project 8.

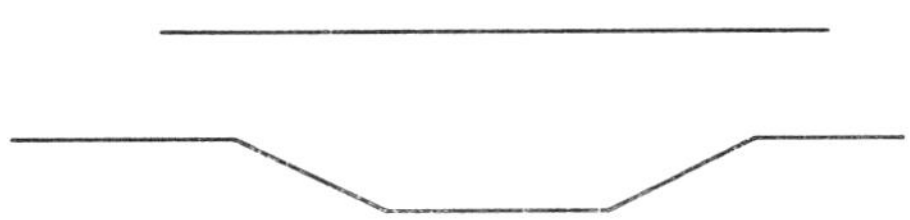

Figure 22.76a

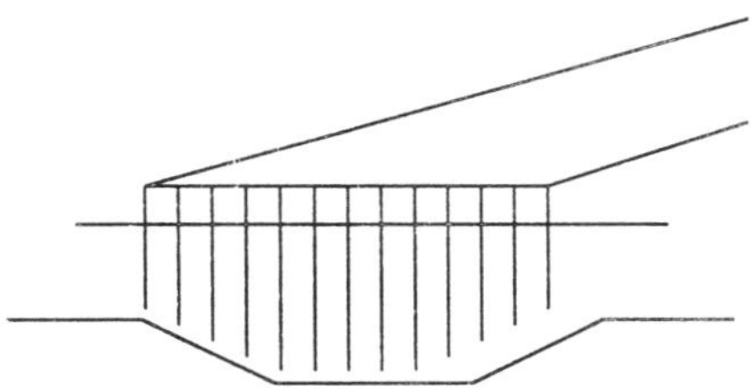

Figure 22.76b

Tips 1. Create a five-line profile and a horizontal line.

2. Use 2 boundary option to generate groove roughing toolpaths.

3. Define a OD grooving tool.

4. Save the grooving project as groove2.

Step 1. Create a five-line profile.

Select **MAIN MENU → Create → Line → Multi**
Specify endpoint 1: **2,0**
Specify endpoint 2: **2,-0.5**
Specify endpoint 3: **1.5,-1**
Specify endpoint 4: **1.5,-1.75**
Specify endpoint 5: **2,-2.25**
Specify endpoint 6: **2,-3**
The five-line profile appears as in Figure 22.77.

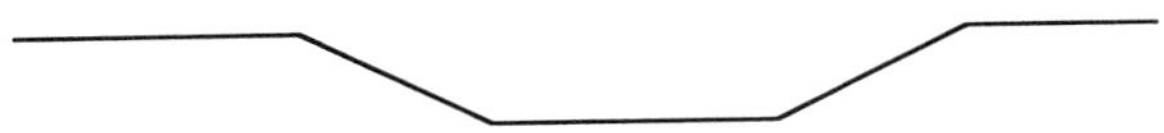

Figure 22.77

Step 2. Create a horizontal line.

Select **BACKUP → Endpoints**
Specify the first point: **2.75,-0.25**
Specify the second point: **2.75,-2.5**
The new drawing becomes Figure 22.78

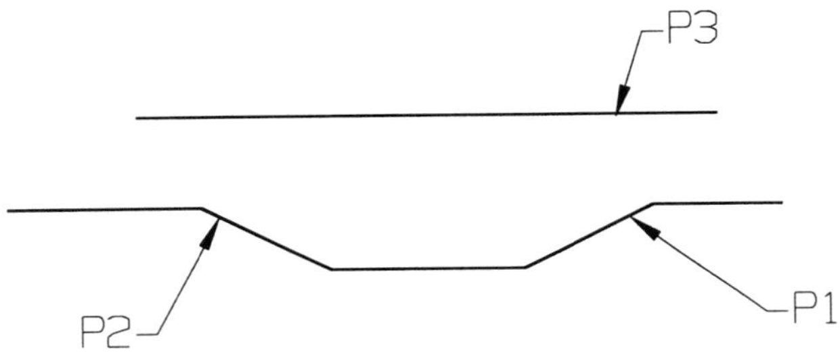

Figure 22.78

Step 3. Initiate the groove module.

Use pick points in Figure 22.78.
Select **MAIN MENU → Toolpaths → Groove**
File name for NCI: **groove2**
Select the "2 Bdry" option
Select **Chain → Partial**
Pick **P1** and **P2** to define the inner boundary
Select **Done → Single**
Pick **P3** as the outer boundary
Select **Done**

Step 4. Define a new grooving tool.

Follows steps 7-9 in project 8 to define a grooving tool.

Step 5. Define groove rough parameters.

Click the "Groove Rough" button
Set the groove rough parameters as shown here.

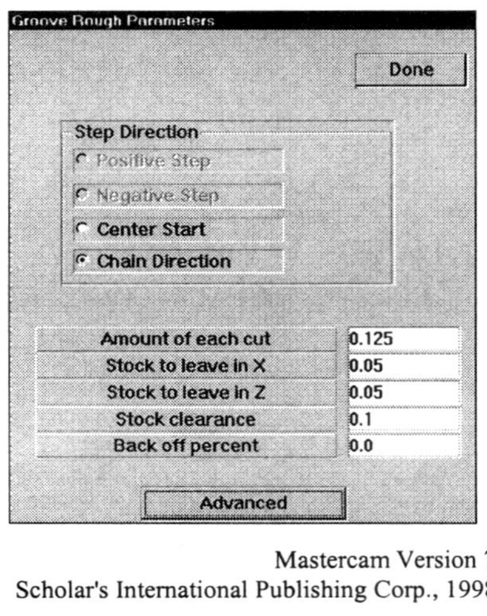

Select **Done**

Step 6. Define the grooving parameters as below.

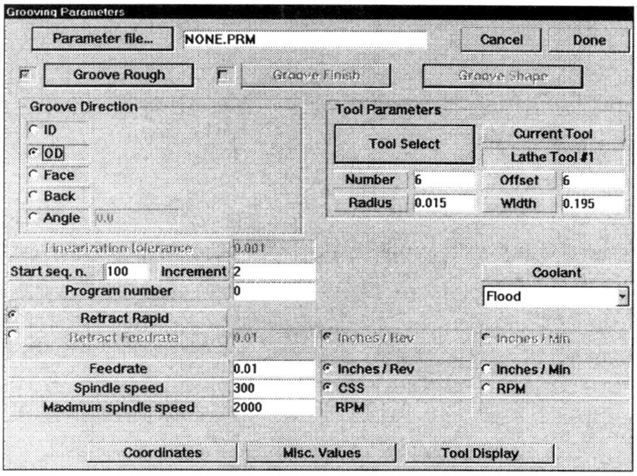

Select **Done** to generate roughing toolpaths
The roughing toolpaths are added as in Figure 22.79.

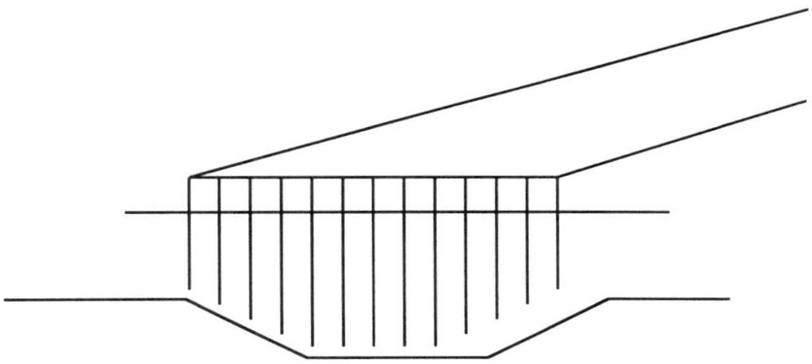
Figure 22.79

Select **Yes** to accept this toolpath segment

Step 7. Backplot the toolpaths.

Select **Operations**
Select **Backplot**
Set the display and backplot parameters to desired setting
Select **Run** to animate the grooving toolpaths on the screen

Step 8. Exit Operations Manager menu.

Select **BACKUP** to return to Operations Manager menu
Select **OK** to return back to graphic mode

Step 9. Save the project file groove2.

Select **MAIN MENU → File → Save**
File name: **groove2**

10 Project 10. Cutting a face groove using two points to define the geometry

This project is used to add a face groove at the right end face of the part shown in Figure 22.80.

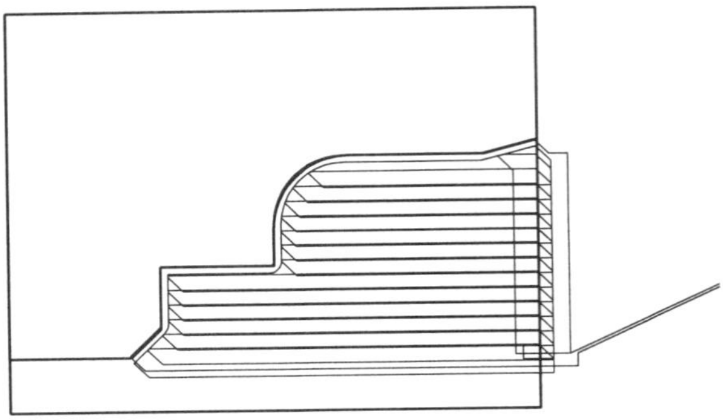

Figure 22.80a

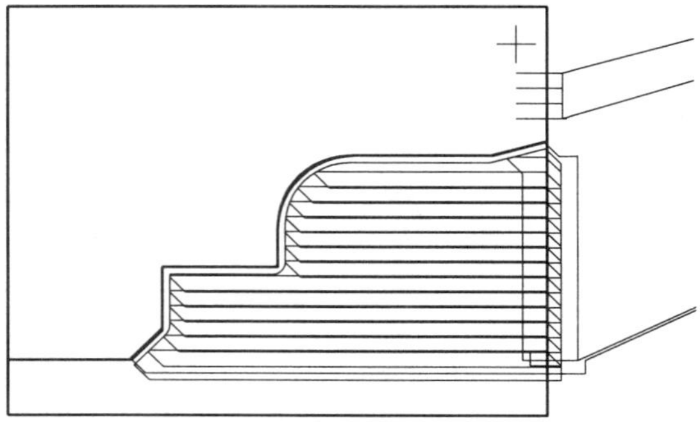

Figure 22.80b

Step 1. Open the existing project file rough-id.

Select **MAIN MENU → File → Get**
File name: **rough-id**
The part geometry appears on the screen.

Step 2. Initiate the face module.

Select **MAIN MENU → Toolpaths**
The existing toolpaths for two operations appear as in Figure 22.81.

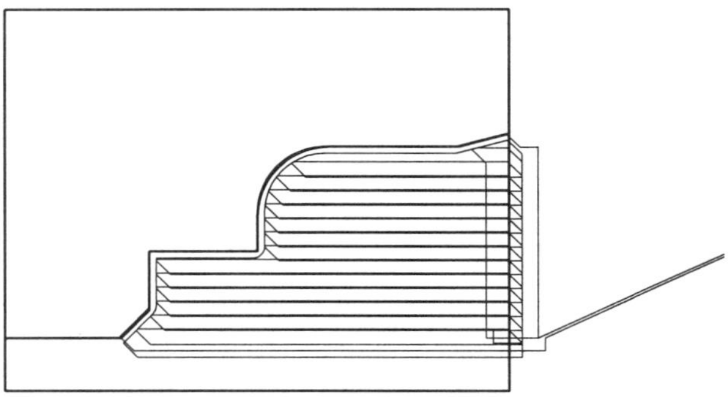

Figure 22.81

Select **Groove → 2 Point**
Select **Values**
Enter coordinates: **4.0,0** for the first point
Select **Values**
Enter coordinates: **5.0,-0.2** for the second point
Press **Esc** key

Step 3. Create a new facing tool.

Click **Tool Select**
Click the right mouse button, then select **Create new tool**

Define the insert parameters as below.

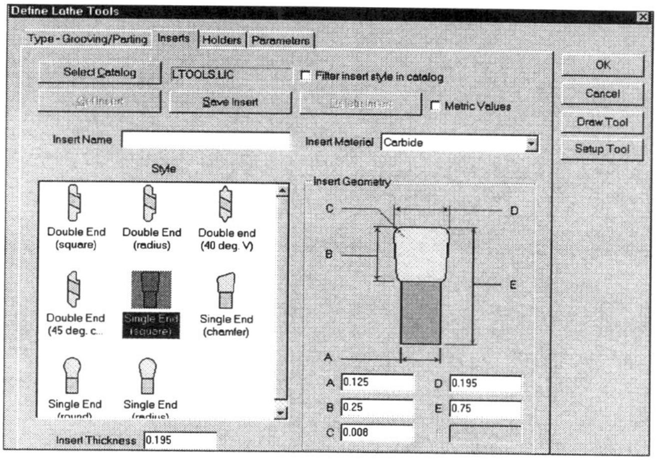

Step 4. Define the holder parameters.

Click **Holders**

Select **Face (right hand)** style

Set the holder geometry parameters as below.

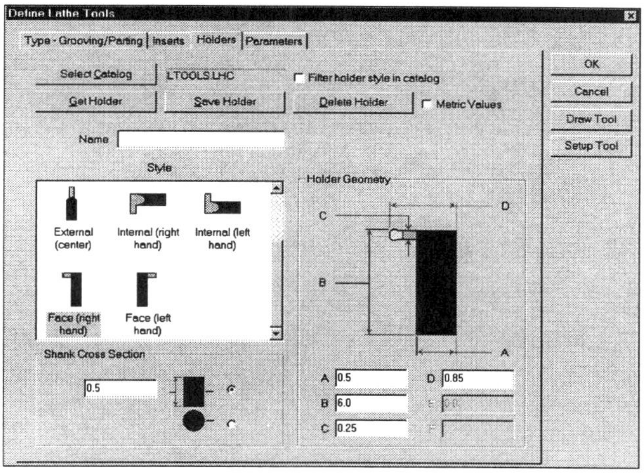

Select **OK** to return back to Tool Manager menu

Select **OK** from Tool Manager menu

Step 5. Define the groove rough parameters.

Click the "Groove Rough" button

Set groove rough parameters as shown here.

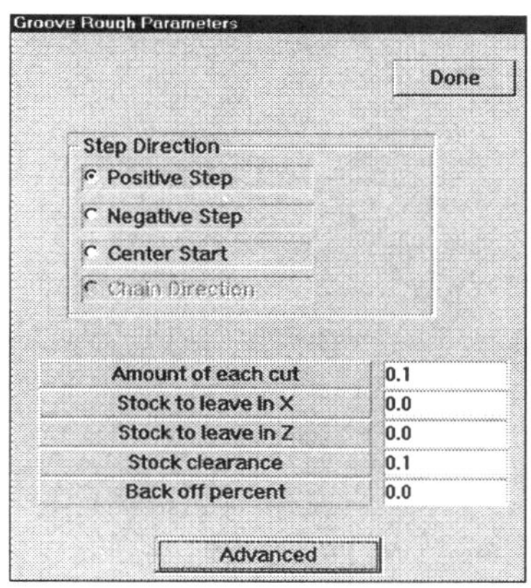

Select **Done**

Step 6. Define the grooving parameters as below.

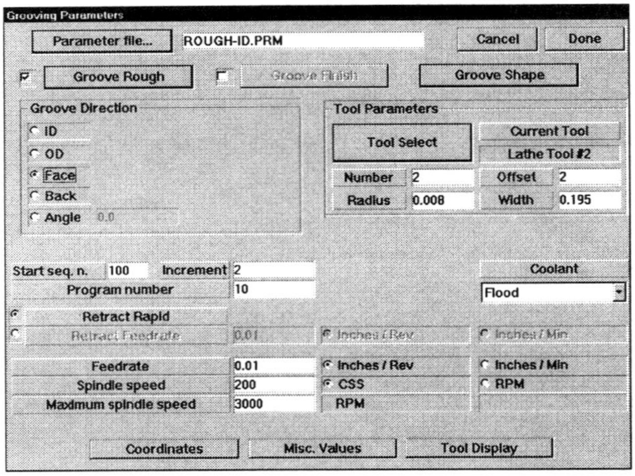

Select **Done**
The facing toolpaths are added as in Figure 22.82.

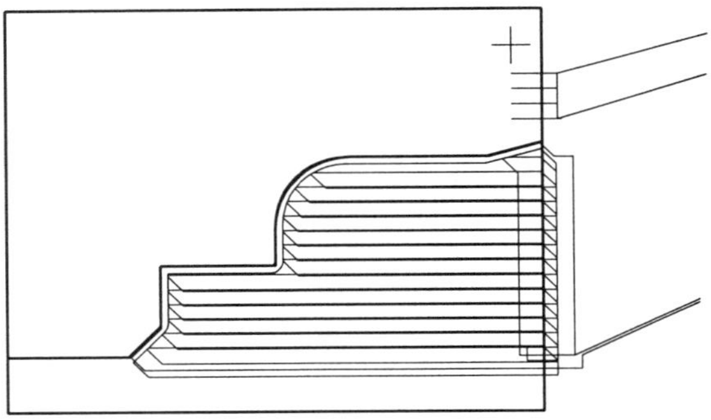

Figure 22.82

Select **Yes** to accept this toolpath section

Step 7. Backplot the toolpaths for three operations.

Select **Operations → Select All**
The toolpaths for three operations appear as here.

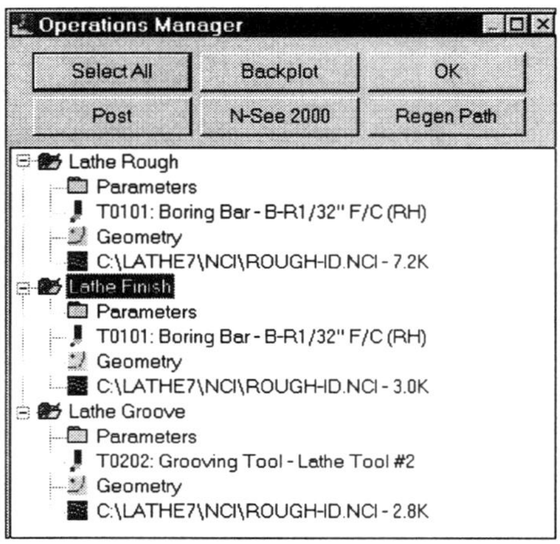

Select **Backplot**
Set display and backplot parameters to desired setting
Select **Run** to animate toolpaths on the screen

Step 8. Save the project file as face-groove.

Select **BACKUP → OK**
Select **MAIN MENU → File → Save**
File name: **face-groove**

22.7 Thread Module

The thread module is used to generate toolpaths to cut various types of threads including external and internal straight threads as well as taper threads (Figure 22.83).

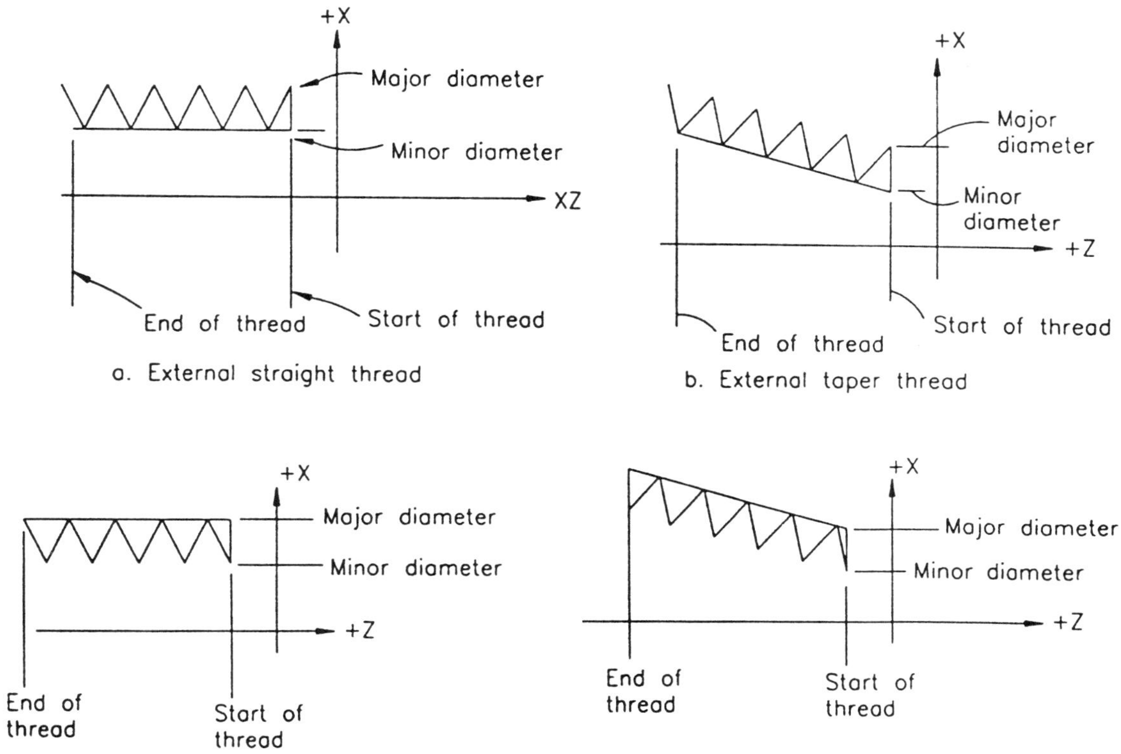

Figure 22.83

Geometric Contour for Threading

Three pieces of information must be specified in defining a geometry contour for thread cutting major diameter, minor diameter, as well as thread endpoints. Actually Mastercam does not need any geometry element to indicate the size and shape of the thread. Instead, it uses the following five parameters to define the thread size:

Major diameter:	the diameter of the thread crest.
Minor diameter:	the diameter of the thread bottom.
Start Z (thread endpoint):	the Z value of the thread starting point.
End Z (thread endpoint):	the Z value of the thread ending point.
Taper angle:	the taper angle value of the thread.

Thread Depth

The depth of threads varies according to thread form, thread series, and thread classes. Refer to Machinery's handbook or other references to obtain accurate thread dimensions. The formulas to calculate the thread height and minor diameter for two thread series, UNC and UNF, are given next:

UNC Threads:	External threads: Thread height h = 0.5952 P Minor diameter d = D - 1.1904 P where h = thread height P = thread pitch D = major diameter d = minor diameter Internal threads: Thread height h = 0.54125 P Minor diameter d = D - 1.0825 P
UNF Threads:	External threads: Thread height h = 0.599 P Minor diameter d = D - 1.198 P Internal threads: Thread height = 0.54125 P Minor diameter d = D - 1.0824 P

Example 1.

Calculate the thread height and minor diameter for the following three UNC threads.

	External thread		Internal thread	
	Thread height h=0.5952P	Minor diameter d= D-1.1904P	Thread height h=0.54125P	Minor diameter d=D-1.0825P
1/2-13-UNC	0.0458	0.4084	0.0416	0.4167
1-8-UNC	0.0744	0.8512	0.0677	0.8647
2-4½-UNC	0.1323	1.7355	0.1203	1.7594

Example 2.

Calculate the thread height and minor diameter for the following three UNF threads.

	External thread		Internal thread	
	Thread height h=0.5990P	Minor diameter d= D-1.198P	Thread height h=0.54125P	Minor diameter d=D-1.0824P
1/4-28-UNF	0.0214	0.2072	0.0193	0.2113
7/8-14-UNF	0.0428	0.7894	0.0387	0.7977
1½-12-UNF	0.0499	1.4002	0.0451	1.4098

Thread Lead

This command specifies the thread size which can be expressed in number of thread per inch or number of inches per thread.

Threading Depth

The depth of thread is one-half of the difference between the major diameter and minor diameter. As indicated previously, this depth is represented by a vertical line at the beginning of the thread. The required number of threading passes is determined by three factors: amount of first cut, amount of last cut, and the depth of the thread. Mastercam uses these three pieces of information to automatically determine the number of threading cuts and the depth of cut for each threading pass.

The two parameters that need to be specified in determining threading depth are amount of first cut and amount of last cut. The amount of first cut parameter specifies the amount of stock to be removed in the first threading pass. The amount of last cut parameter specifies the amount of stock to be removed in the last threading pass.

⌛Tips 1. The amount of the first threading cut is suggested to be in the range of 0.03" to 0.045". The larger the number of threads per inch, the smaller the amount of first threading cut.

2. The amount of the last threading cut is about 0.005".

Acceleration Length and Deceleration Length

To produce accurate threads, an acceleration length and a deceleration length should be added at the start and at the end of the threading path, respectively (Figure 22.84). Acceleration length is the allowance distance for the servo control system to accelerate the drive from zero to the specified feedrate. Deceleration length is the allowance distance for the servo system to decelerate from the threading feedrate zero.

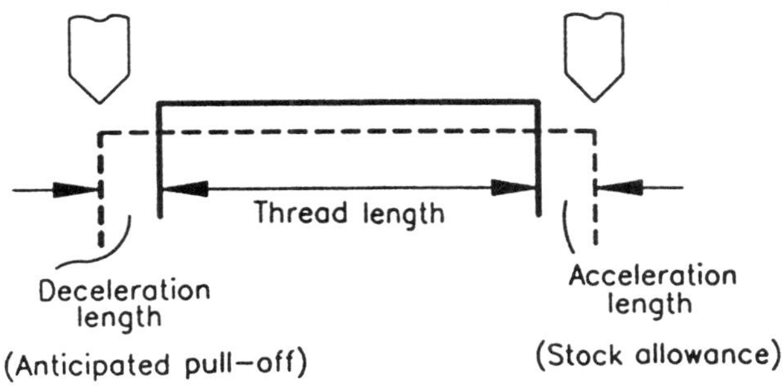

Figure 22.84

How to Determine Acceleration Length and Deceleration Length

The acceleration length (La) and deceleration length (Ld) can be found from the following two formulas:

LD = LNT/60

LA = -(1+ln a) x LD

Where L = thread lead (in.)
N = spindle speed (RPM)
T = time constant of the servo system
(T = 0.033 s, 0.05 s, 0.067 s, 0.1 s
with 0.067 s being most common)
a = thread accuracy (a = dL/L)
dL = error in the thread lead
ln = natural log

The acceleration length and deceleration length computed from the above two formulas are the **minimum** distances. Any distance greater than the computed value would satisfy the requirement.

Example 3.

Find the acceleration length and deceleration length for cutting a 1-8 UNC thread with the following operation conditions:

Time constant: 0.066 s
Spindle speed: 500 RPM
Thread accuracy: 0.01

Solution: The deceleration length is found as

LD = LNT/60 = (1/8)(500)(0.067)/60 = 0.07 in

LA = -(1+ln a) x LD = -[1 + ln(0.01)] x 0.07 = 0.252 in.

Threading Specific Parameters

The threading specific parameters are grouped under Threading Parameters menu as shown.

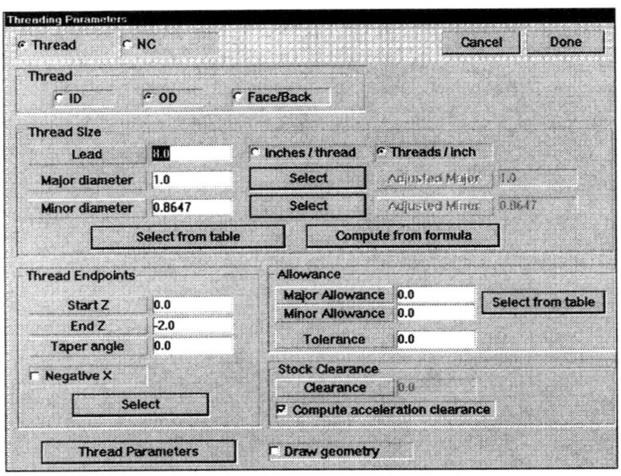

These threading parameters can be classified into the following five categories:

Thread type:	indicates the thread type to be cut.
Thread size:	indicates the diametric size of the thread.
Thread length:	specifies the thread length.
Allowances:	specifies the allowance of major and minor diameters of the thread.
Thread parameters:	defines the machining variables of the threading.

Thread Type Mastercam allows the following three thread types to be machined:

ID:	cutting internal threads.
OD:	cutting external threads.
Face/Back:	cutting face or back threads.

Thread Size The thread size has three aspects. It can be defined by its **major diameter, minor diameter**, and **lead** .

Thread lead The thread lead can be specified by either inches/threads or threads/inch. The lead of inch threads is commonly expressed in threads/inch, while the metric threads are in mm/thread.

Major diameter and minor diameter

These two parameters determine the diametric size and depth of the thread. The thread depth is the half of the difference between major diameter and minor diameter. It is very difficult to determine the thread height due to a wide variety of thread types and fit classes. Mastercam provides two ways for you to obtain data for the lead, major diameter, and minor diameter of those standardized threads: **thread table** and **thread formula**.

Thread table Click "Select from table" button in the middle of the Threading Parameters menu to open the thread table as shown below.

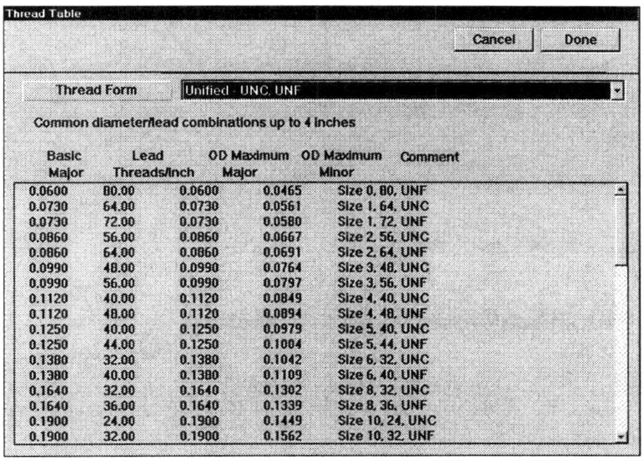
Thread Table

Cancel Done

Thread Form: Unified - UNC, UNF

Common diameter/lead combinations up to 4 inches

Basic Major	Lead Threads/Inch	OD Maximum Major	OD Maximum Minor	Comment
0.0600	80.00	0.0600	0.0465	Size 0, 80, UNF
0.0730	64.00	0.0730	0.0561	Size 1, 64, UNC
0.0730	72.00	0.0730	0.0580	Size 1, 72, UNF
0.0860	56.00	0.0860	0.0667	Size 2, 56, UNC
0.0860	64.00	0.0860	0.0691	Size 2, 64, UNF
0.0990	48.00	0.0990	0.0764	Size 3, 48, UNC
0.0990	56.00	0.0990	0.0797	Size 3, 56, UNF
0.1120	40.00	0.1120	0.0849	Size 4, 40, UNC
0.1120	48.00	0.1120	0.0894	Size 4, 48, UNF
0.1250	40.00	0.1250	0.0979	Size 5, 40, UNC
0.1250	44.00	0.1250	0.1004	Size 5, 44, UNF
0.1380	32.00	0.1380	0.1042	Size 6, 32, UNC
0.1380	40.00	0.1380	0.1109	Size 6, 40, UNF
0.1640	32.00	0.1640	0.1302	Size 8, 32, UNC
0.1640	36.00	0.1640	0.1339	Size 8, 36, UNF
0.1900	24.00	0.1900	0.1449	Size 10, 24, UNC
0.1900	32.00	0.1900	0.1562	Size 10, 32, UNF

The table can show the thread data for various thread forms. Click the "Thread Form" button on the top of the thread table to give the thread form list. The thread data will be reflected on the thread table when a particular thread form is selected. The data for major diameter, minor diameter, and lead of a selected thread in the thread table will automatically appear in the threading parameters menu.

Computer from formula (Thread Formula) The other way to obtain the thread data from the Mastercam is using the thread formula. Click "Compute from formula" button to open the "Thread Formula" menu as shown below.

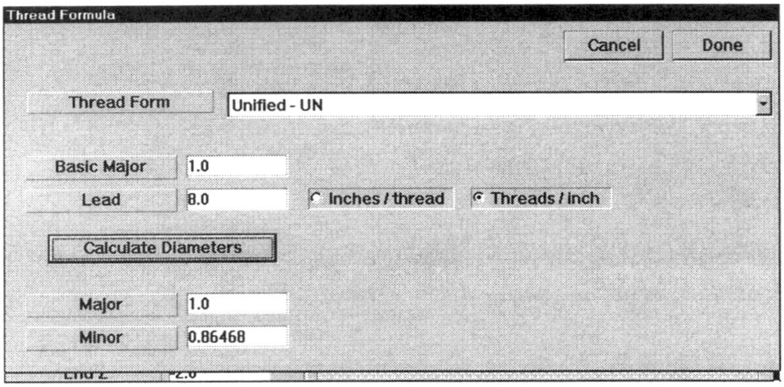

Use the "Thread Form" button to specify the thread type to cut. Enter thread data for the following two parameters:

Basic major:	the nominal diameter of the thread, normally the major diameter.
Lead:	the thread lead.

Clicking on the "Calculate Diameters" button directs the system to calculate the major diameter and minor diameter based on the given basic major diameter and lead values.

Thread length

The thread length is determined by the following two thread endpoint parameters:

Start Z:	the Z coordinate value of the threading start point.
End Z:	the Z coordinate value of the threading end point.

Allowances

There are three parameters used to specify allowances and tolerance of threads. They are:

Major allowance:	specifies the allowance of the major diameter.
Minor allowance:	specifies the allowance of the minor diameter.
Tolerance:	specifies the tolerance of the threads.

The above three parameters are determined by the thread type and fit class. Mastercam provides an allowance table for you to automatically select the allowance values for the parameters. Click on the "Select from table" button under the Allowance section to open the allowance table as shown next.

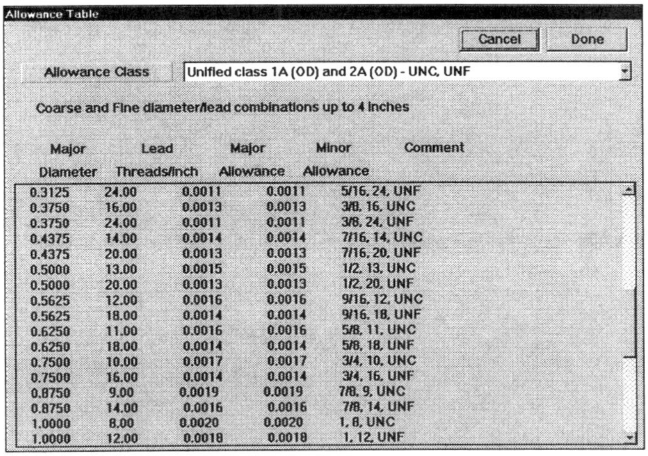

Major Diameter	Lead Threads/inch	Major Allowance	Minor Allowance	Comment
0.3125	24.00	0.0011	0.0011	5/16, 24, UNF
0.3750	16.00	0.0013	0.0013	3/8, 16, UNC
0.3750	24.00	0.0011	0.0011	3/8, 24, UNF
0.4375	14.00	0.0014	0.0014	7/16, 14, UNC
0.4375	20.00	0.0013	0.0013	7/16, 20, UNF
0.5000	13.00	0.0015	0.0015	1/2, 13, UNC
0.5000	20.00	0.0013	0.0013	1/2, 20, UNF
0.5625	12.00	0.0016	0.0016	9/16, 12, UNC
0.5625	18.00	0.0014	0.0014	9/16, 18, UNF
0.6250	11.00	0.0016	0.0016	5/8, 11, UNC
0.6250	18.00	0.0014	0.0014	5/8, 18, UNF
0.7500	10.00	0.0017	0.0017	3/4, 10, UNC
0.7500	16.00	0.0014	0.0014	3/4, 16, UNF
0.8750	9.00	0.0019	0.0019	7/8, 9, UNC
0.8750	14.00	0.0016	0.0016	7/8, 14, UNF
1.0000	8.00	0.0020	0.0020	1, 8, UNC
1.0000	12.00	0.0018	0.0018	1, 12, UNF

Stock clearance

The stock clearance parameter is used to specify the acceleration length and deceleration length. How to calculate acceleration and deceleration lengths manually has been presented in the previous section. Mastercam provides a function that can calculate acceleration clearance. Click the "Compute acceleration clearance" button to compute the acceleration length. Its result will be entered to the clearance parameter.

Thread parameters

Mastercam groups those thread cutting parameters under "Thread Parameters" menu. Click on the "Thread Parameters" button at the bottom of the Threading Parameters menu to open the thread parameters menu as shown here.

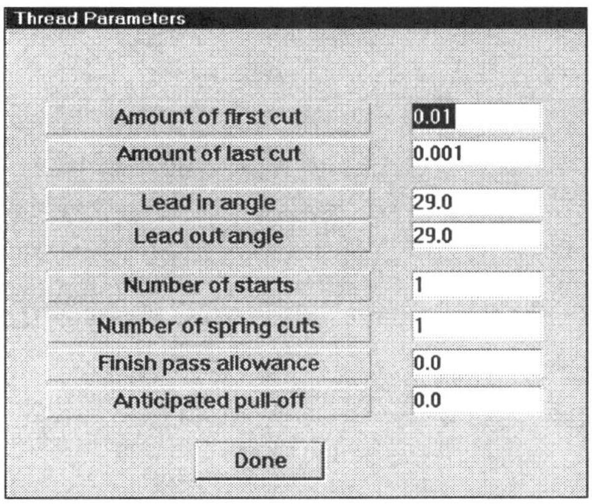

Those parameters are briefly described:

Amount of first cut:	the depth of the first threading pass.
Amount of last cut:	the depth of the last threading pass.
Lead in angle:	the angle for engaging the part in threading.
Lead out angle:	the angle for disengaging the part in threading.
Number of starts:	the number of threading heads of the thread.
Number of spring cuts:	the number of threading passes that cut the thread at the finish depth.
Finish pass allowance:	the allowance left for finish passes.
Anticipated pull-off:	the distance of pull-off during threading passes.

Lead in and lead out angles Lead in angle and lead out angle are only available when the canned cycle command is chosen. The lead in angle and lead out angle allow the cutter to engage the part in one side only (Figure 22.85).

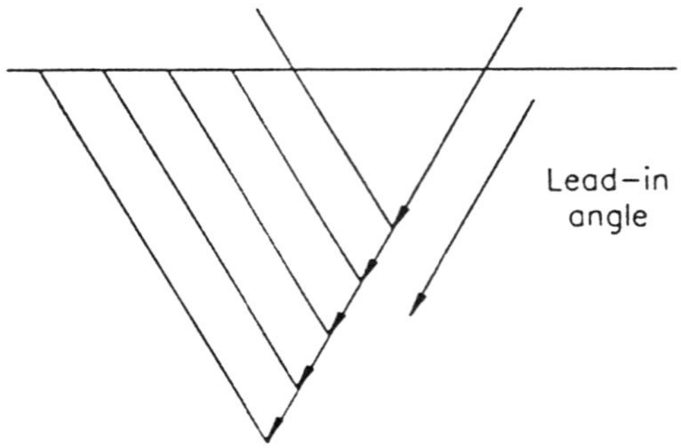

Figure 22.85

Threading Command Type

There are three common threading commands: G32, G92 and G76. G32 is the single-pass threading command and is generally used with the G00 code to complete the threading cycle. Note that some controllers use G33 as the single-pass threading command. Figure 22.86 illustrates the toolpath pattern of G32.

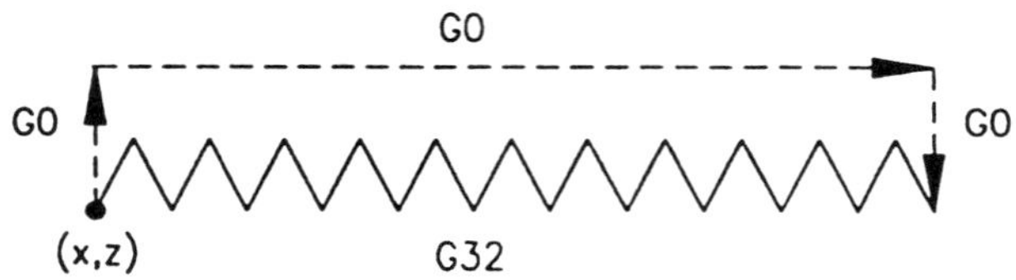

Figure 22.86

The G92 code is often referred to as a box threading cycle because it generates four toolpaths that from a box as shown in Figure 22.87. The use of G92 code reduces the number of part program blocks by 75 percent.

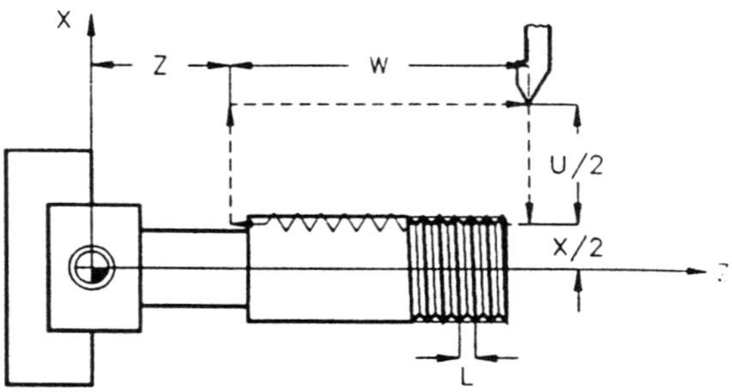

Figure 22.87

G76 is an automatic threading cycle. It generates several threading passes for cutting a thread in one G76 command block. Figure 22.88 depicts the threading toolpath pattern of G76 command.

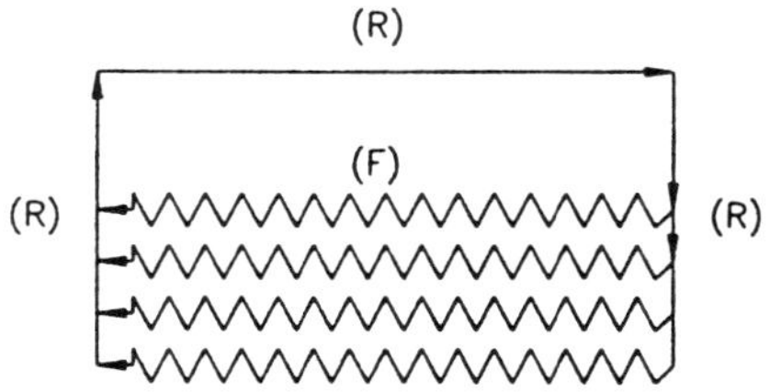

Figure 22.88a Threading path pattern

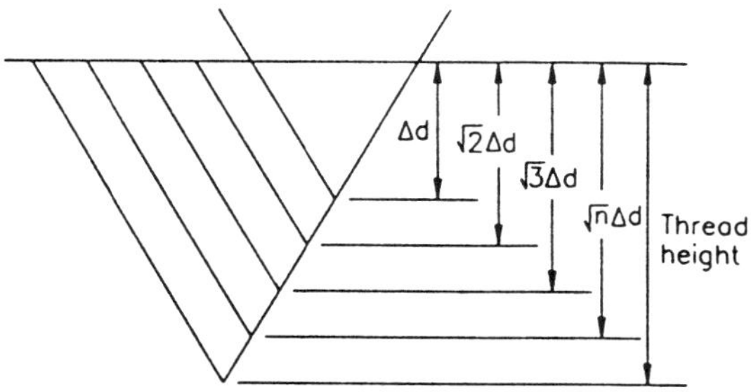

Figure 22.88b Depth of cut for threading passes

How to select Threading Command

Mastercam Lathe uses "NC Toolpath" parameter to determine the threading command type. It has the following three options:

Longhand:	selects single-pass command (G32).
Canned cycle:	selects automatic threading cycle (G76).
Box thread:	selects box-threading cycle (G92).

Note: all CNC lathe controllers have the G92 and G76 threading commands.

Project 11. Cutting external threads

Use the thread module to cut external threads 1-8-UNC as shown in Figure 22.89.

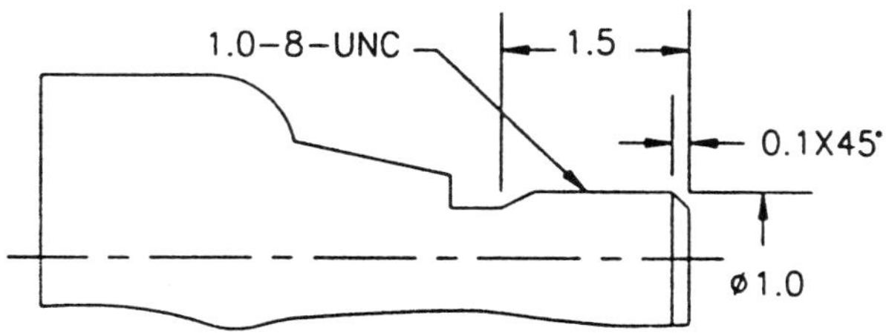

Figure 22.89a

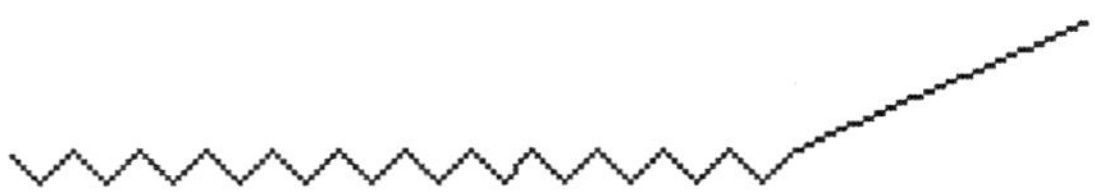

Figure 22.89b

Figure 22.89c

Step 1. Initiate the thread module.

Select **MAIN MENU → Toolpaths → Thread**

File name for NCI: **thread1**

Select the "Select from table" button in the middle of Threading Parameters menu

Select the thread form and thread size from the Thread Table as shown below.

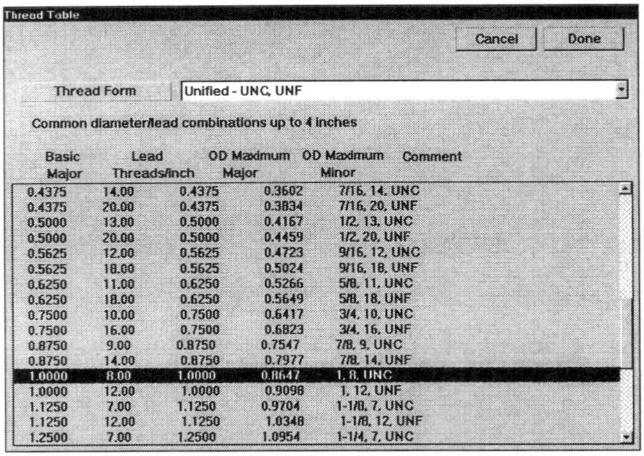

Select **Done**

Step 2. Define the thread parameters.

Click the "Thread Parameters" button at the bottom of the Threading Parameters menu

Set the thread parameters as shown here.

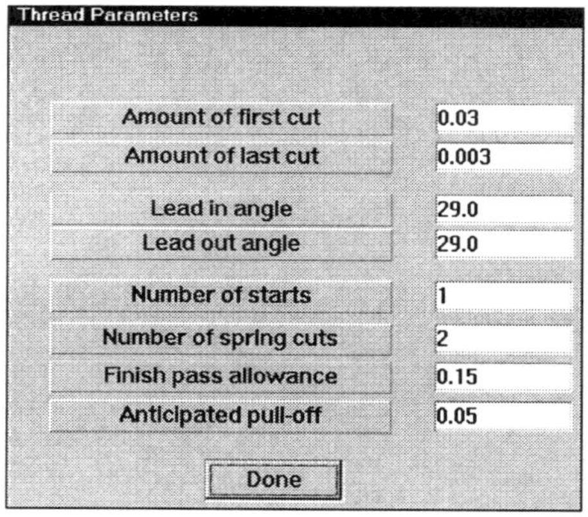

Select **Done**

Step 3. Set the threading parameters as below.

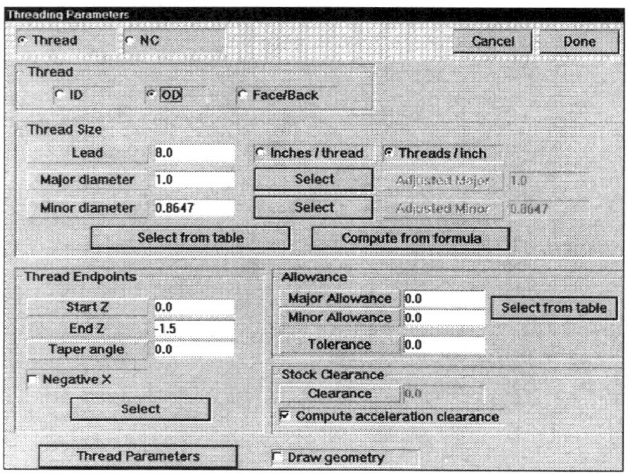

Step 4 Create a threading tool.

Select the "NC" button
Click the "Tool Select" button in NC parameters menu
Click the right mouse button, then select **Create new tool**
Set the threading insert parameters as below.

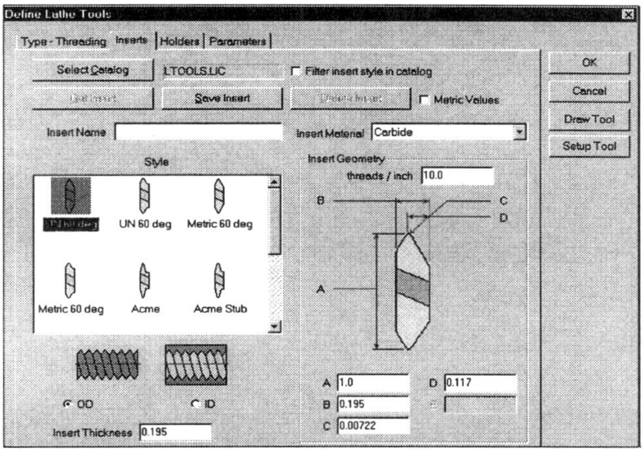

Step 5. Define the threading tool holder.

Click the "Holders" button
Set the holder parameters as below.

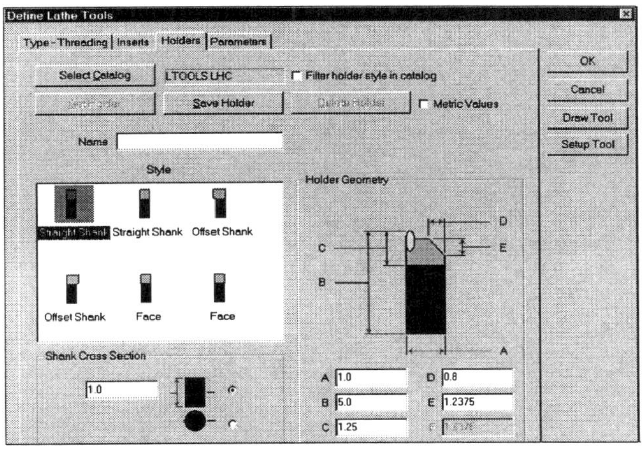

Step 6. Define the tooling and machining parameters.

Click the "Parameters" button

Set the parameters as below.

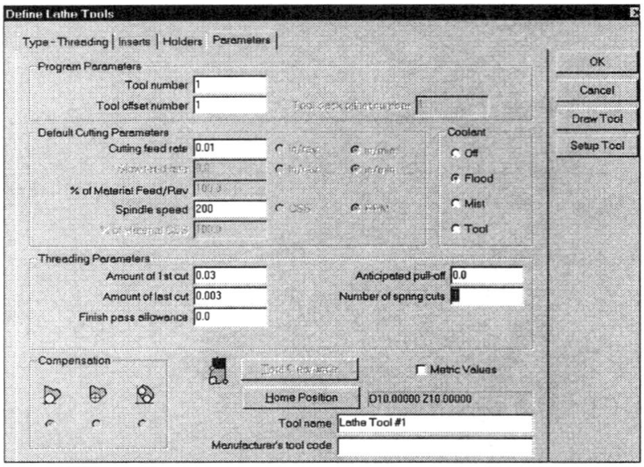

Step 7. Set the NC parameters as below.

Select **OK** from parameters menu

Select **OK** from Tool Manager menu

Set the NC parameters as below.

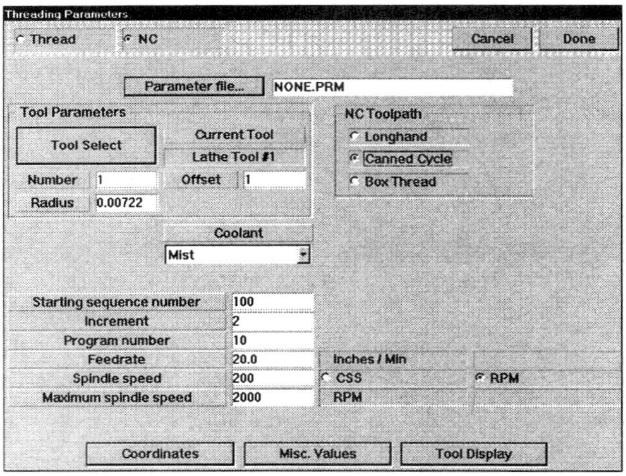

Select **Done** to generate threading toolpaths

The threading form should appear as in Figure 22.90.

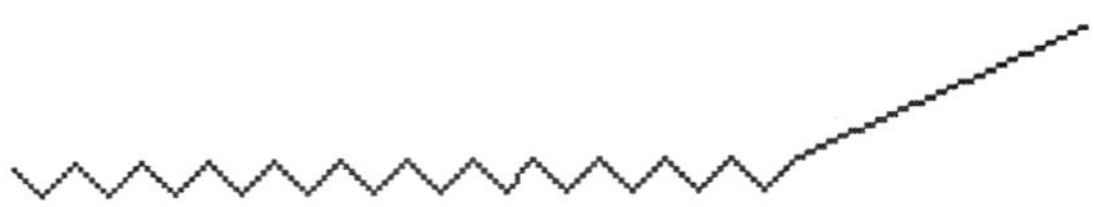

Figure 22.90

Select **Yes** to accept this toolpath section

Step 8. Backplot the threading toolpaths.

Select **Operations → Backplot**
Set display and backplot parameters to desired setting
Select **Run**
You will see that six threading passes are animated on the screen as in Figure 22.91.

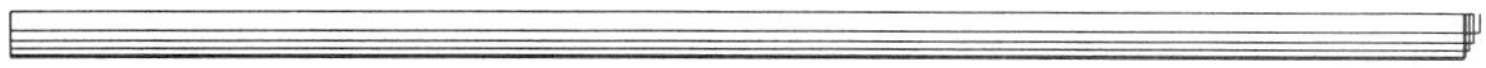

Figure 22.91

Step 9. Post process the threading toolpaths.

Select **BACKUP → Post**
Select **Yes** to "Run the post processor?"
File name for NC: **thread1**
The NC part program should appear on the file list as below.

```
File list
%
O0010(THREAD1)
G20
G28U0.W0.
G0T0101
G97S200M3
G54X1.4Z.0884M7
G76P020129Q30R.15
G76X.8647Z-1.5P677Q300R0.E.125
M9
G28U0.W0.M5
T0100
M30
%
```

Click the Close button to exit the file list menu
Select **OK** to exit Operations Manager menu

Step 10. Save the project as thread1.

Select **MAIN MENU → File → Save**
File name: **thread1**

12 Project 12. Cutting internal threads

Use the thread module to generate a part program which cuts internal threads 1-1/8-12-UNF as shown in Figure 22.92.

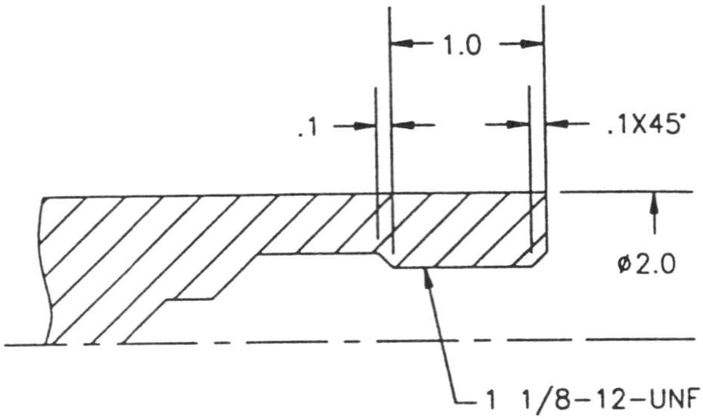

Figure 22.92a

Figure 22.92b

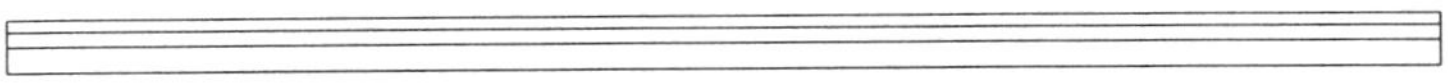

Figure 22.92c

Step 1. Initiate the thread module.

Select **MAIN MENU → Toolpaths → Thread**

File name for NCI: **thread2**

Select **Select from table** in the middle of Threading Parameters menu

Select "**1-1/8, 12, UNF**" thread from the thread table as shown below.

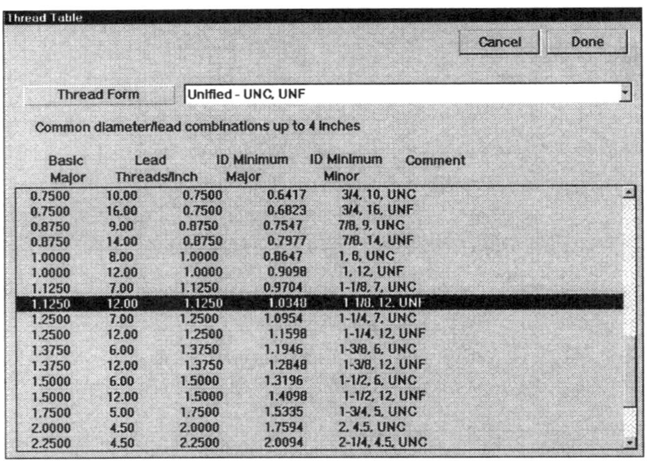

Thread Table

Cancel Done

Thread Form: Unified - UNC, UNF

Common diameter/lead combinations up to 4 inches

Basic Major	Lead Threads/inch	ID Minimum Major	ID Minimum Minor	Comment
0.7500	10.00	0.7500	0.6417	3/4, 10, UNC
0.7500	16.00	0.7500	0.6823	3/4, 16, UNF
0.8750	9.00	0.8750	0.7547	7/8, 9, UNC
0.8750	14.00	0.8750	0.7977	7/8, 14, UNF
1.0000	8.00	1.0000	0.8647	1, 8, UNC
1.0000	12.00	1.0000	0.9098	1, 12, UNF
1.1250	7.00	1.1250	0.9704	1-1/8, 7, UNC
1.1250	12.00	1.1250	1.0348	1-1/8, 12, UNF
1.2500	7.00	1.2500	1.0954	1-1/4, 7, UNC
1.2500	12.00	1.2500	1.1598	1-1/4, 12, UNF
1.3750	6.00	1.3750	1.1946	1-3/8, 6, UNC
1.3750	12.00	1.3750	1.2848	1-3/8, 12, UNF
1.5000	6.00	1.5000	1.3196	1-1/2, 6, UNC
1.5000	12.00	1.5000	1.4098	1-1/2, 12, UNF
1.7500	5.00	1.7500	1.5335	1-3/4, 5, UNC
2.0000	4.50	2.0000	1.7594	2, 4.5, UNC
2.2500	4.50	2.2500	2.0094	2-1/4, 4.5, UNC

Select **Done**

Step 2. Define the thread parameters.

Click the "Thread Parameters" button at the bottom of the Threading Parameters menu
Set the thread parameters as below.

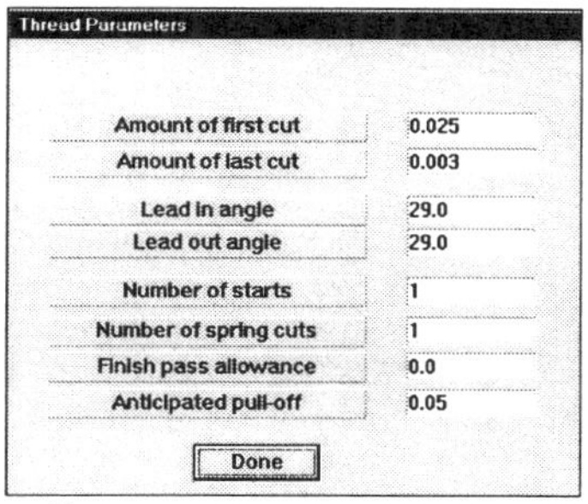

Select **Done**

Step 3. Set the threading parameters as below.

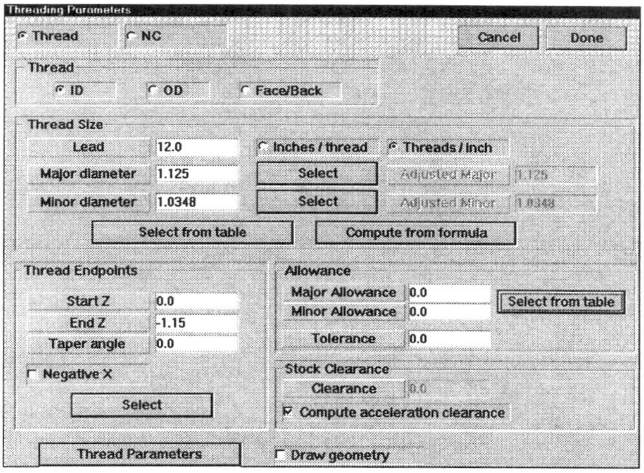

Step 4. Select an internal threading tool.

Click the "NC" button
Click the "Tool Select" button
Click the right mouse button, then select **Create new tool**
Set the insert parameters as below
Note: Need to mark the ID parameter at the bottom of the menu.

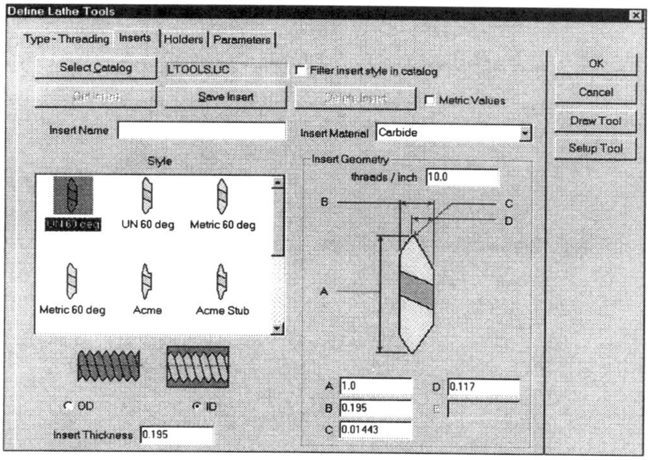

Step 5. Define the holder parameters.

Click the "Holders" button
Set the tool holder parameters as below.

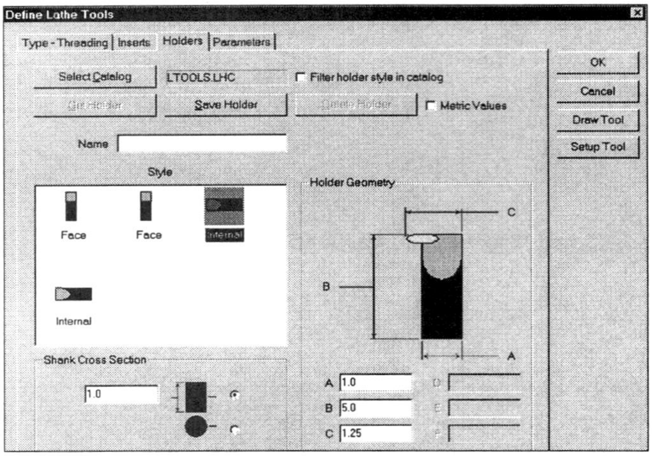

Step 6. Define tooling and machining parameters.

Click the "Parameters" button
Set parameters as below.

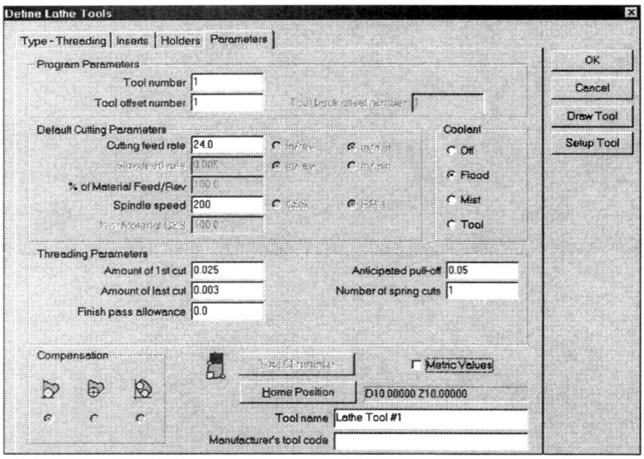

Select **OK** to return to Tool Manager menu
Select **OK** to exit Tool Manager menu

Step 7. Set NC parameters as below.

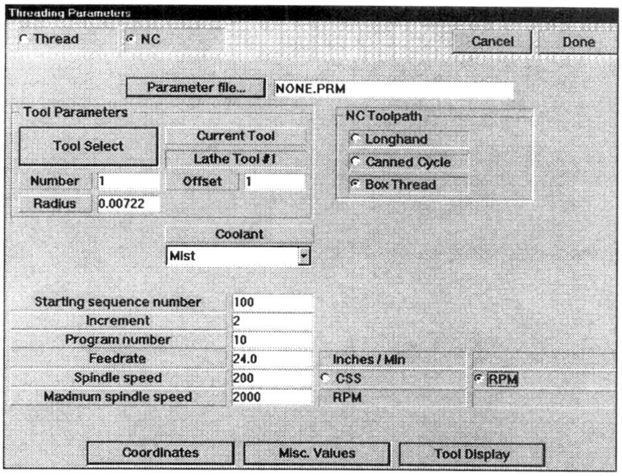

Select **Done** to generate threading toolpaths
The final thread form appears as in Figure 22.93.

Figure 22.93

Select **Yes** to accept this toolpath segment

Step 8. Backplot the toolpaths.

Select **Operations → Backplot**
Set display and backplot parameters to desired setting
Select **Run** to animate the threading toolpaths on the screen
The threading toolpaths should resemble Figure 22.94.

Figure 22.94

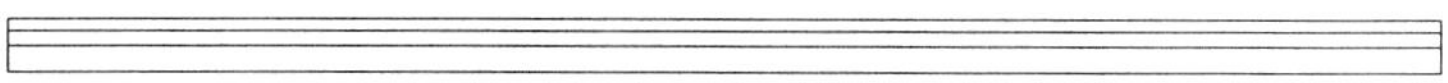

Step 9. Post process the threading toolpaths.

Select **BACKUP** to return to the Operations Manager menu
Select **Post**
Select **Yes** to "Run the post processor?"
File name for NC: **thread2**
The NC program should appear as as shown here.

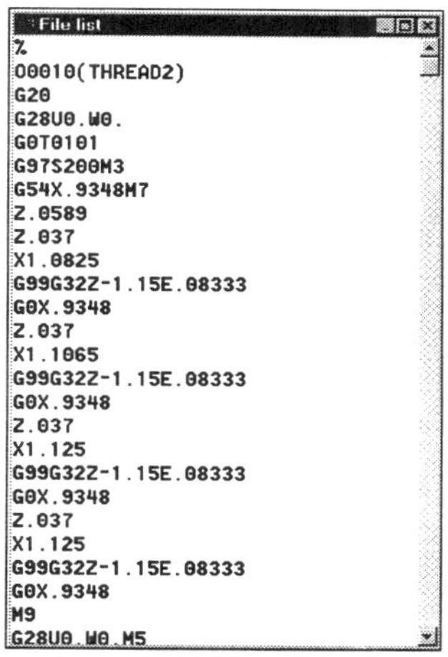

```
%
O0010(THREAD2)
G20
G28U0.W0.
G0T0101
G97S200M3
G54X.9348M7
Z.0589
Z.037
X1.0825
G99G32Z-1.15E.08333
G0X.9348
Z.037
X1.1065
G99G32Z-1.15E.08333
G0X.9348
Z.037
X1.125
G99G32Z-1.15E.08333
G0X.9348
Z.037
X1.125
G99G32Z-1.15E.08333
G0X.9348
M9
G28U0.W0.M5
```

Click the **Close** button to exit File List menu

Step 10. Save the project file as thread2.

Select **OK** to exit Operations Manager menu
Select **MAIN MENU → File → Save**
File name: **thread2**

22.8 Drill Module

The Mastercam drill module is used to generate fixed (or canned) cycle commands to perform drilling, boring, and tapping operations at the specified positions.

Drill parameters

The drill parameters can be classified into the following five groups: **Cycle type**, **X-coordinate control**, **Z-coordinate control**, **dwell**, and **peck drilling** parameters. The Drill parameters menu appears as below.

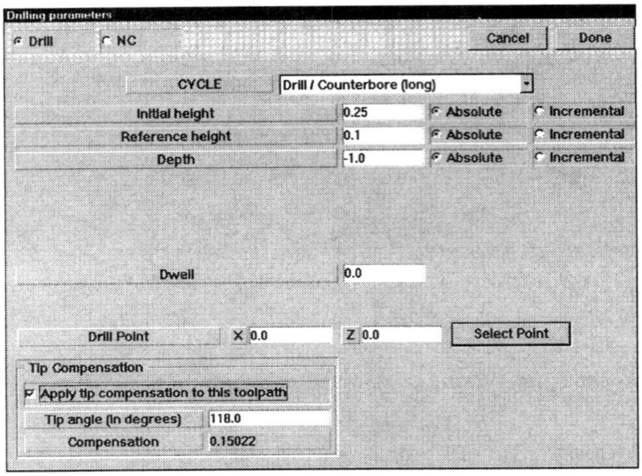

Cycle Type

There are eight fixed cycles available in Mastercam lathe including drill, peck drill, chip break, tap, bore 1, bore 2, Miscellaneous 2 as shown below.

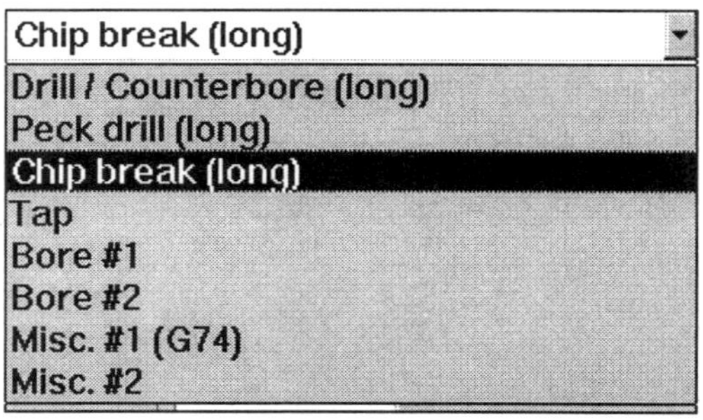

Figure 22.95 summarizes the feature and command statement of these cycle types. Note that not all lathe CNC controllers provide canned cycle commands. We can customize the post processor with G0, G1, and G4 (dwell command), and M3 (spindle clockwise), and M4 (spindle counterclockwise) commands to perform the tasks of drilling, boring, deep hole drilling, and tapping.

Cycle type	G-code	Toolpath pattern	Application
Drill/counter bore	G81 Xx Yy Zz Rr Ff G81 no dwell G82 with dwell	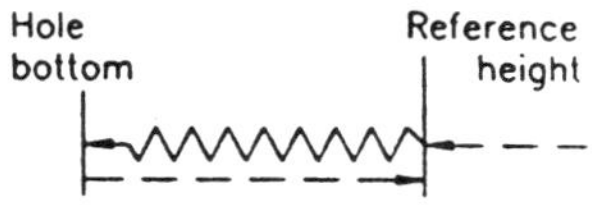	• Drilling holes
Peck drill	G83 both with/no dwell	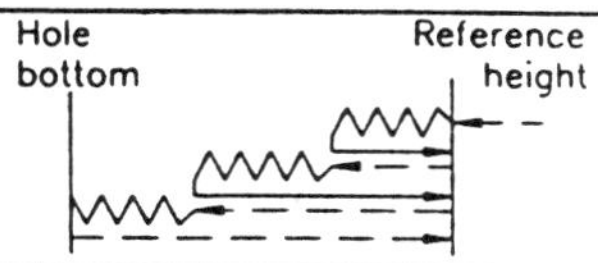	• Drilling deep holes
Chip breaker	G73 with/no dwell	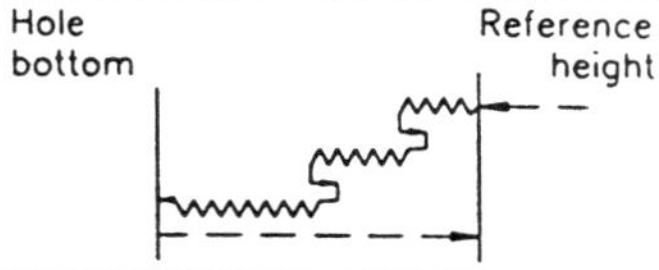	• Drilling deep holes
Tap	G84	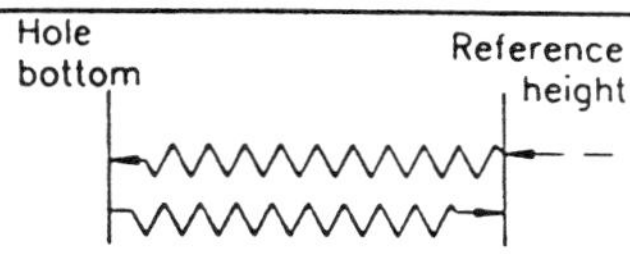	• Tapping internal threads
Bore #1	G85 – no dwell G89 – with dwell	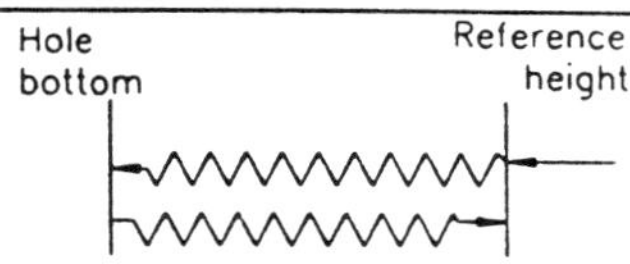	• Feed-in and feed-out
Bore #2	G86 – no/with dwell	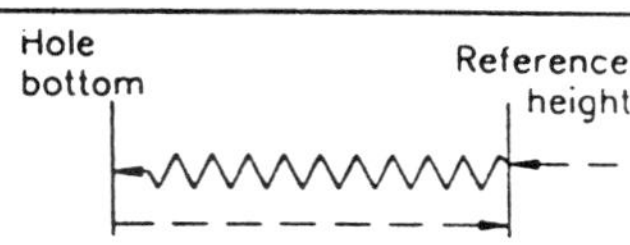	• Feed-in and rapid-out

Figure 22.95 Drill cycle types

X-Coordinate Control

Two parameters are used to control the X-coordinate values: **drill diameter** and **X drill point**. The drill diameter parameter indicates the diameter of drill to be used. This value can be used to calculate the required spindle RPM from the given CSS found in the material table.

The X drill point parameter is used to specify the X-coordinate value at which the drilling operation is performed. Normally drilling is performed at the part center that has an X-coordinate setting of zero. When drilling is not performed in the part center ($X \neq 0$), a self-rotating tool should be used and the machine spindle should be indexed to the specified position. The X-coordinate value is specified in the radius.

Z-Coordinate Control

Three Z-coordinate values are normally required in defining the toolpath pattern of fixed cycles: **initial height, reference height**, and **depth** (Figure 22.96):

Initial height:	specifies the Z level at which the tool moves rapidly from a position to the hole center.
Reference height:	indicates the level at which the feed changes from rapid rate to the programmed rate.
Depth:	indicates the Z-coordinate value of the hole bottom.

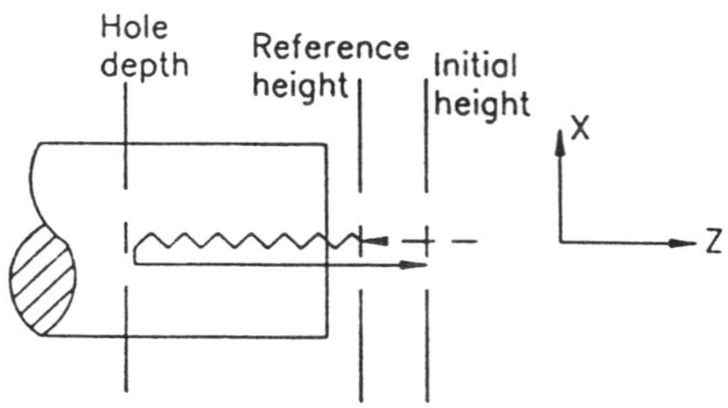

Figure 22.96

Dwell

This parameter specifies a period of time for temporary control of a total stop of the system.

Peck Drilling Parameters

This group of parameters is available for peck drilling and/or chip break cycle as shown below. The include first peck increment, subsequent peck increment, peck clearance, and retraction amount (Figure 22.97). Both peck clearance and retraction amount parameters are only available for the chip break cycle.

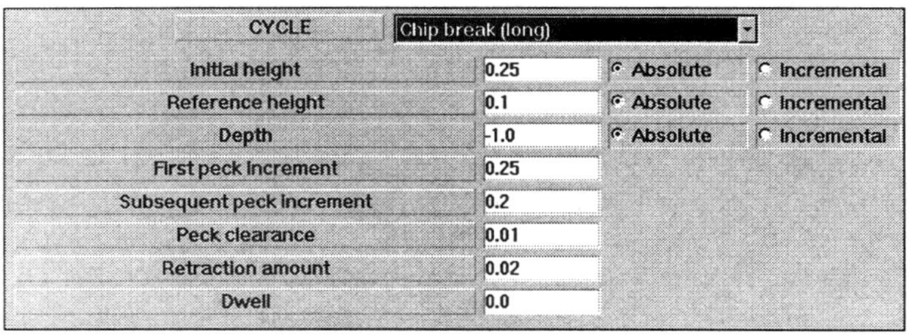

First peck increment:	specifies the drilling depth on the first peck
Subsequent peck increment:	indicates the drilling depth on each peck after the first
Peck clearance:	specifies the distance above the metal to stop moving at rapid feedrate
Retraction amount:	indicates the amount to retract the tool between pecks

Note: No geometry entity is required to define the X position and Z depth when using the drill module.

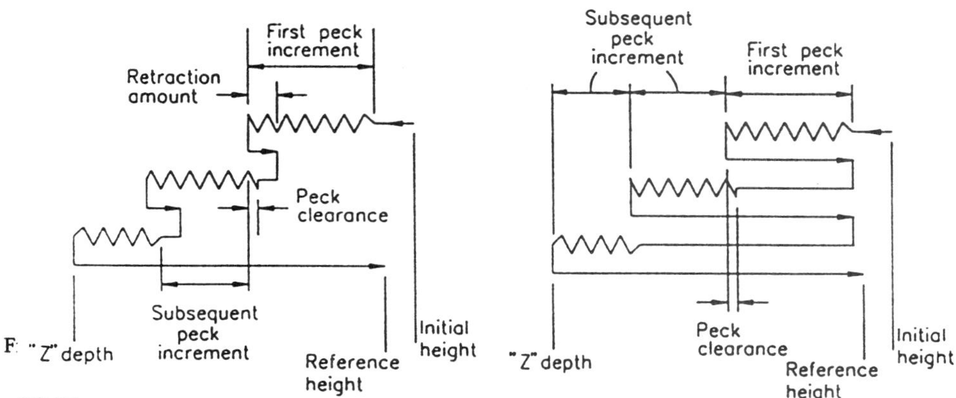

Figure 22.97

Drilling Tools

There are eight types of hole operation tools. They include **drill, center drill, countersink, counterbore, end mill, reamer, RH (right hand) tap,** and **LH (left hand) tap**. The two hole operation tool parameter menus are listed below; one for drilling/boring/reaming, and the other for tapping.

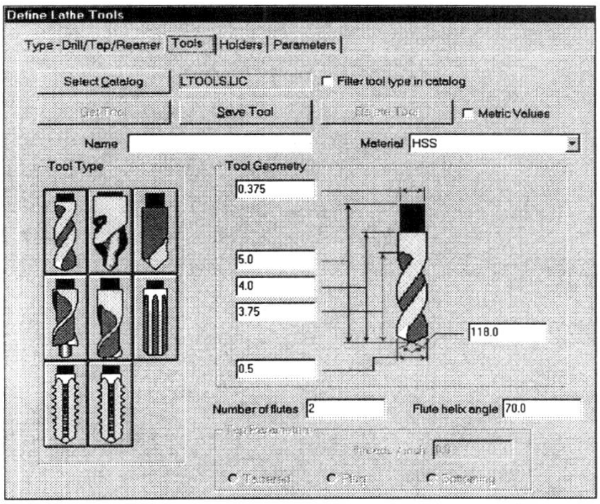

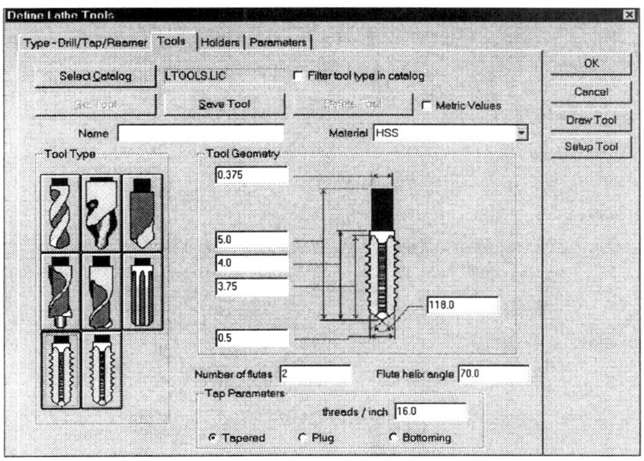

Holder

The hole operation holder can be defined by the parameters shown below.

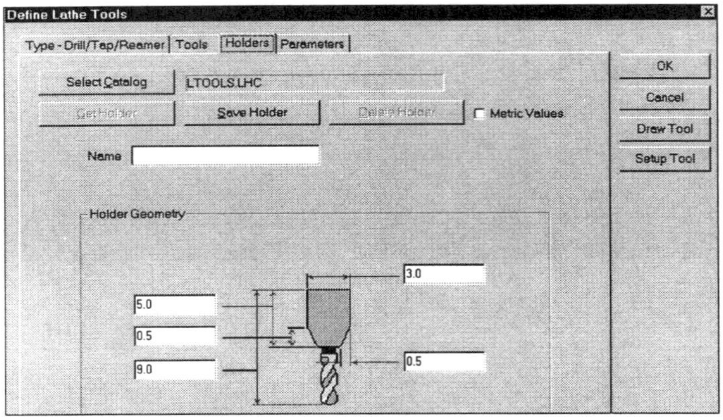

Tooling and Machining Parameters

The tooling and machining parameters related to hole operations are shown below.

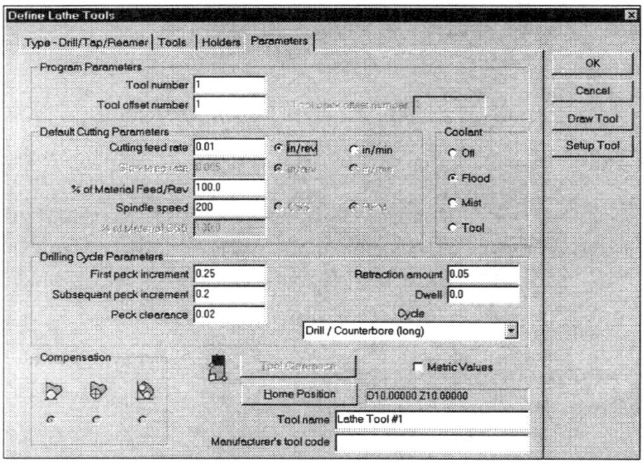

Project 13. Drilling and tapping a hole at the center

Two operations are used to produce internal threads of 5/8-11. A 17/32" drill is used to drill the base hole, then a 5/8-11 tap is used to cut the threads. The thread length is 1". Figure 22.98 shows the drilling and tapping toolpaths.

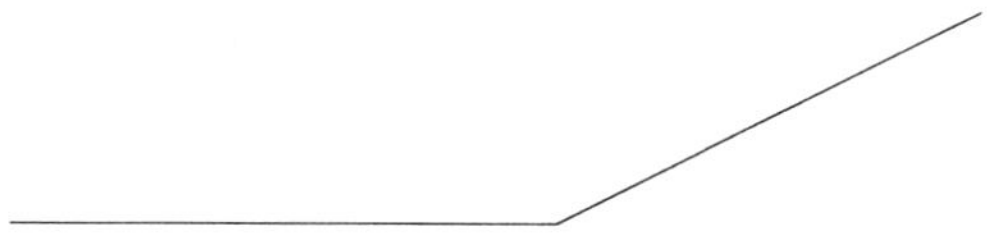

Figure 22.98

Tips Two tools are used in this project: 17/32" drill and 5/8-11 tap.
Major drilling parameters are:
Cycle = drill/counterbore (long)
X drill position = 0
Initial height = 0.5
Reference height = 0.2
Depth = -(thread length + 0.3 D + 0.1) = -(1 + 0.3(17/32) + 0.1) = -1.26
Major tapping parameters are:
Cycle = Tap
Dwell = 0.5
Initial height = 0.5
Reference height = 0.2
Depth = -1.0

Step 1. Initiate the drill module.

Select **MAIN MENU → Toolpaths → Drill**
File name: **drill**

Step 2. Set the drilling parameters as below.

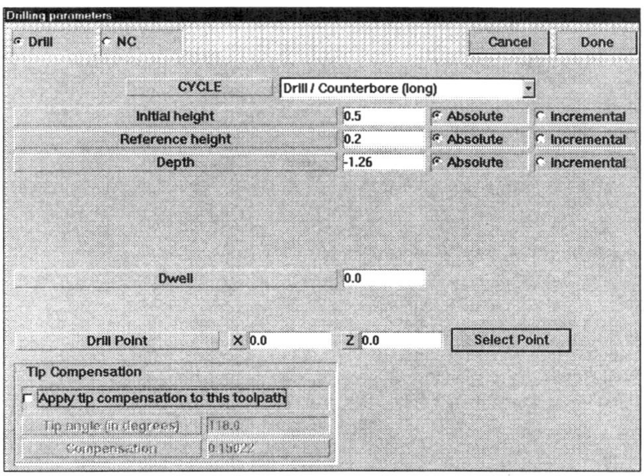

Step 3. Define a drill.

Click the "NC" button
Click the "Tool Select" button
Click the right mouse button, then select **Create new tool**

Set the drill parameters as below.

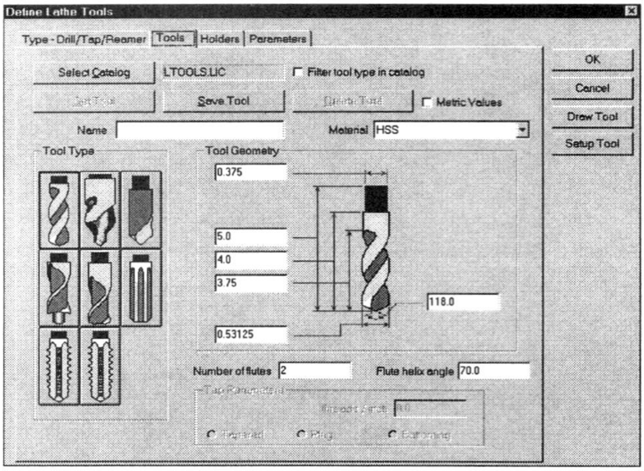

Step 4. Define the holder parameters.

Click the "Holders" button

Set the holder parameters as below.

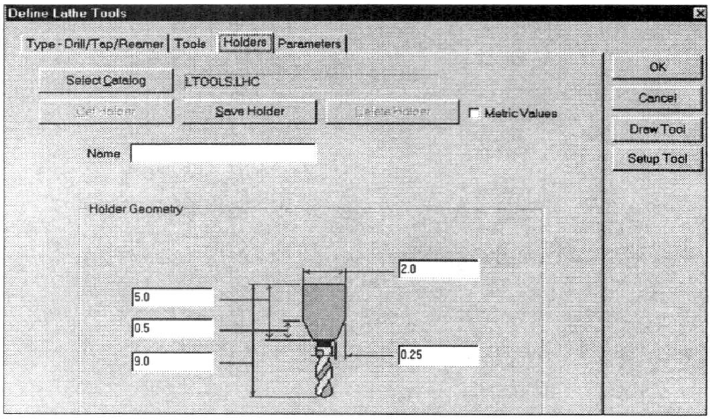

Step 5. Define the tooling and machining parameters.

Click the "Parameters" button

Set the tooling and machining parameters as below.

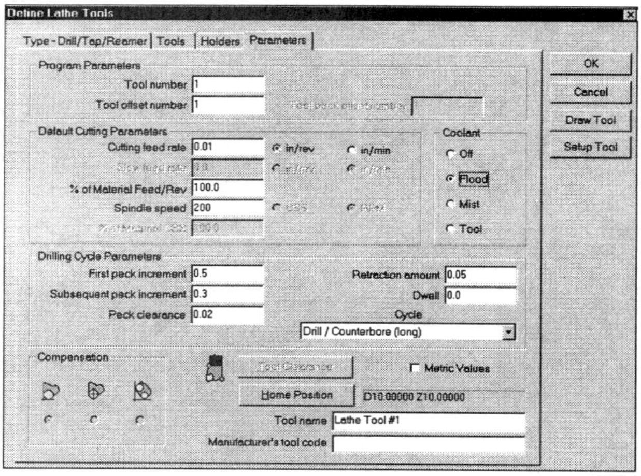

Step 6. Define NC parameters.

Select **OK → OK**

Set NC parameters as below.

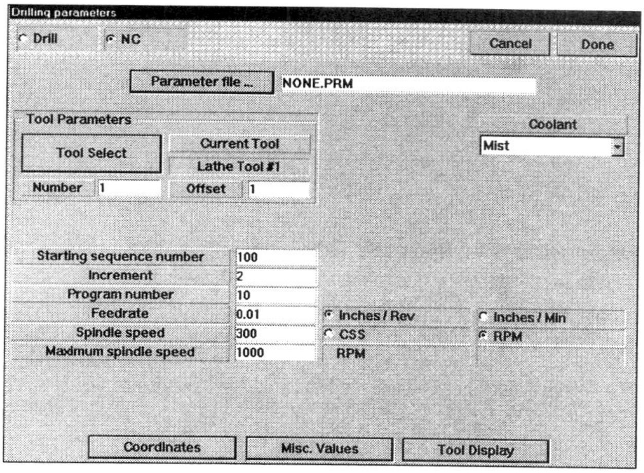

Select **Done** to generate drilling toolpath

The drilling toolpath appear as in Figure 22.99.

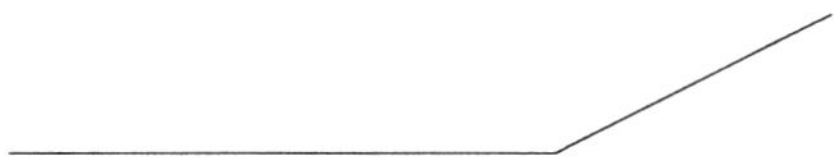

Figure 22.99

Select **Yes** to accept this toolpath segment

Step 7. Use drill module again.

Select **Drill**

Set the drilling parameters as below.

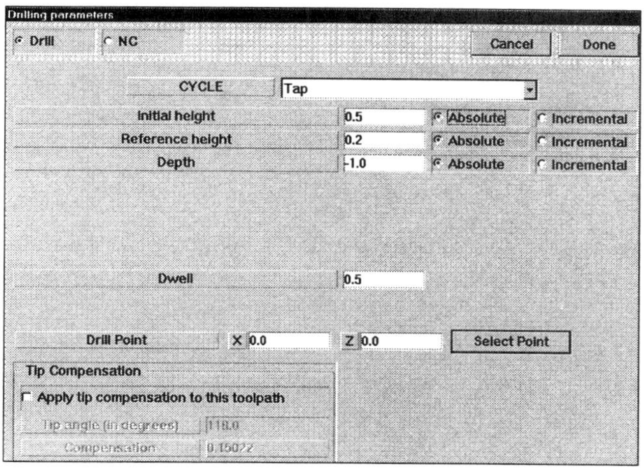

Step 8. Create a tap.

Click the "NC" button
Click the "Tool Select" button
Click the right mouse button, then select **Create new tool**
Select "**RH Tap**" icon
Set tapping parameters as below.

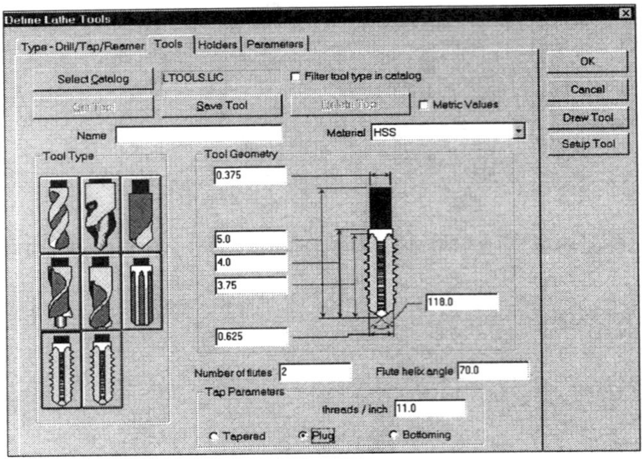

Step 9. Define tooling and machining parameters.

Click the "Parameters" button
Set the tooling and machining parameters as below.

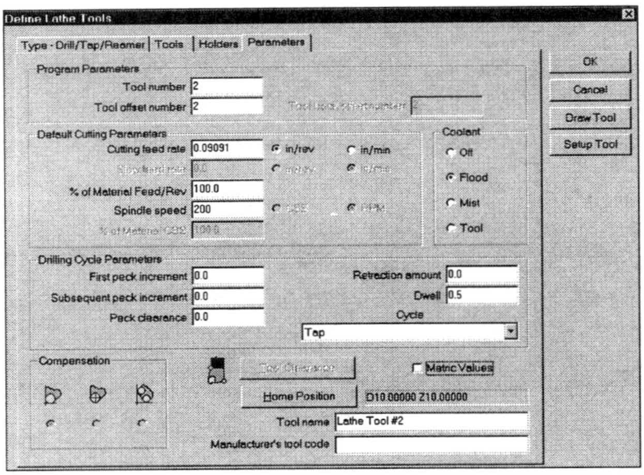

Select **OK** to return to Tool Manager menu
Select **OK**

Step 10. Set the NC parameters for tapping as below.

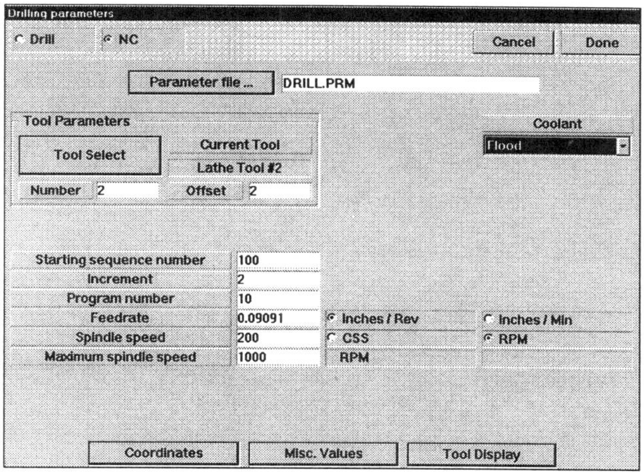

Select **Done** to generate tapping toolpath
Select **Yes** to accept this toolpath segment
Note: The tapping toolpath located at the same position as drilling. You may not see tapping toolpath has been added.

Step 11. Backplot the toolpaths.

Select **Operations** to open Operations Manager menu
Select **Select All** to select two sets of toolpaths
Select **Backplot**
Set display and backplot parameters to desired setting
Select **Run** to animate drilling and tapping on the screen
Select **BACKUP** to return to Operations Manager menu

Step 12. Post process the toolpaths.

Select **Post**
Select **Yes** to "Run the post processor?"
File name for NC: **drill**
The part program should appear on the screen. Click the Close button to exit the file list menu.

Step 13. Save the project file.

Select **OK** to exit Operations Manager menu
Select **MAIN MENU → File → Save**
File name: **drill**

22.9 Cutoff Module

The cutoff module generate a set of vertical toolpaths for cutting off the part. This function uses a boundary point to define where to cut off and its major diameter (Figure 22.100). The system starts the cut off pass from the boundary point and automatically ends at the spindle axis (X0.0). The facing parameters menu appears as below.

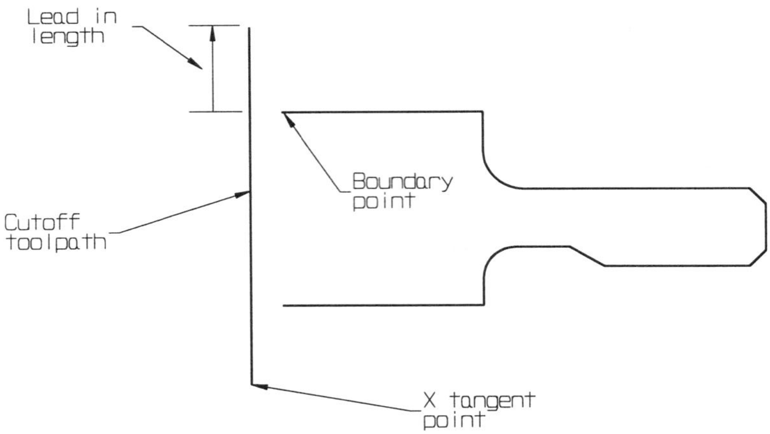

Figure 22.100

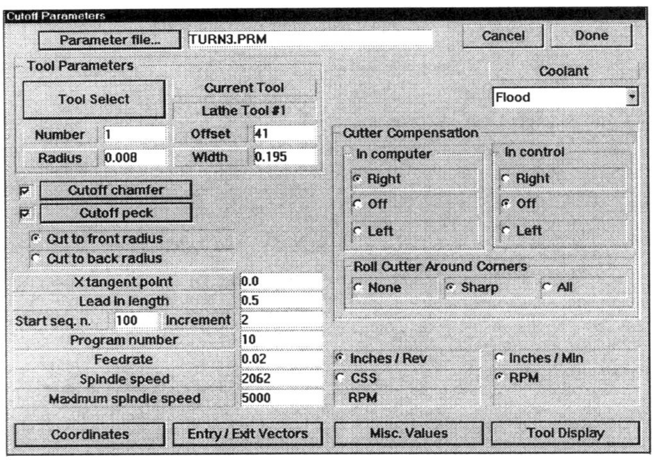

The **cutoff module specific parameters** include:

Cutoff chamfer: creates a chamfer at the start of the cutoff pass.
Cutoff peck: generates toolpaths in peck pattern.
Cut to front/back radius: selects either cut to front radius or back radius of the tool.
X tangent point: specifies the minor diameter of the cutoff pass.
Lead in length: specifies a lead in distance added to the start of the cutoff pass.

Cutoff chamfer

This parameter adds a chamfer to the start of the cutoff pass (Figure 22.101). Click "Cutoff chamfer" button to open the cutoff parameters menu as below. The chamfer size can be defined by the chamfer angle and height or width. The system also allows to select a line element for defining the chamfer.

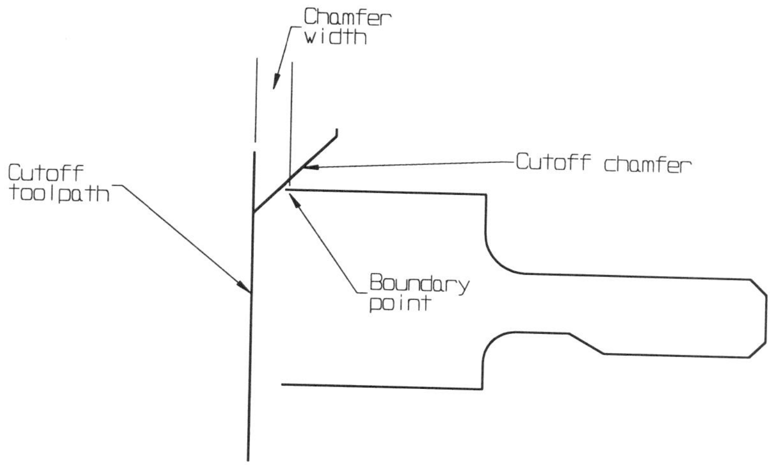

Figure 22.101

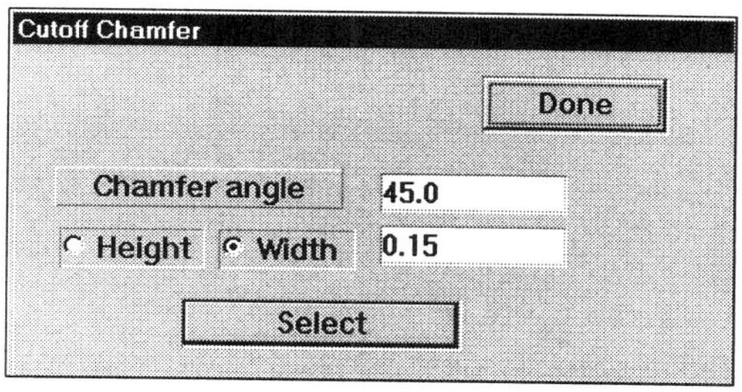

Cutoff peck

This parameter allows the plunging of cutoff pass runs in a peck pattern. This allows the system to takes more than one peck to cut off the part. The tool will retract by an amount specified by the "Retract Increment" parameter at the end of each peck before it proceeds for next peck. Click the "Cutoff peck" button to open the cutoff peck parameters menu as below.

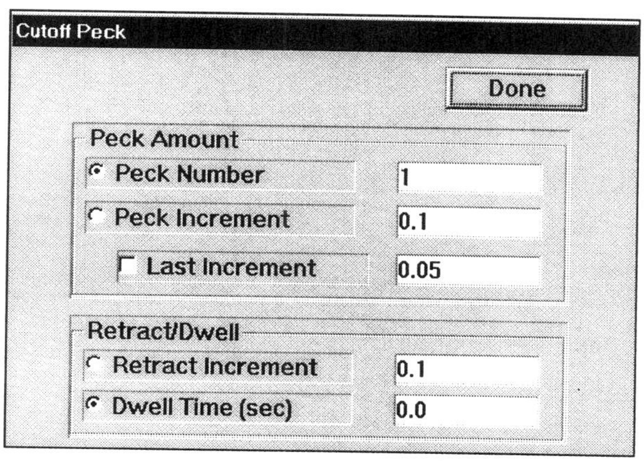

X tangent point

This parameter specifies the minor diameter of the cutoff pass. It is measured from the Z axis. Figure 22.102 shows the effect of this parameters on the cutoff toolpath. The cutoff pass extends to X = 0 when this parameter is set to 0 (Figure 22.102a). The cutoff pass stops at X = 1.0 when it is set to 0.5 (Figure 22.102b). Note that the value given to this parameter is expressed as radius, not as diameter.

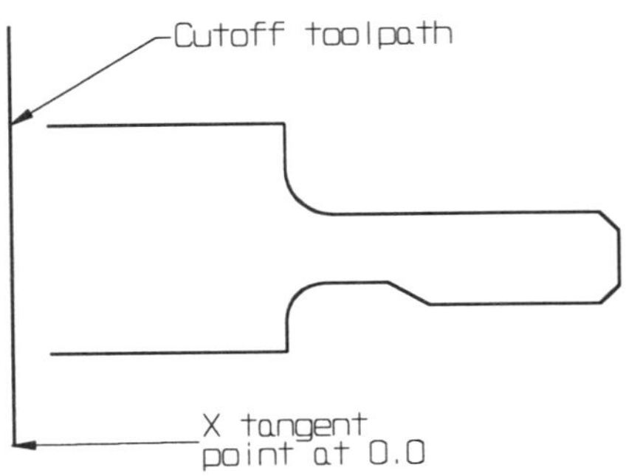

Figure 22.102a

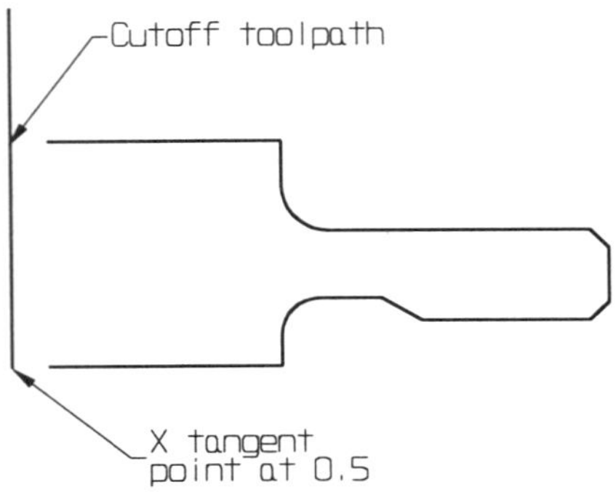

Figure 22.102b

Lead in length

This parameter extends the start of cutoff pass from the boundary point by a given distance. Figure 22.103 shows the effect of this parameter on the start of cutoff pass. The cutoff pass starts at the boundary point when this parameter is set to zero (Figure 22.103a). The cutoff pass starts at a 1" in diameter away from the boundary point when this parameter is set to 0.5 (Figure 22.103b). The given value is expressed as radius.

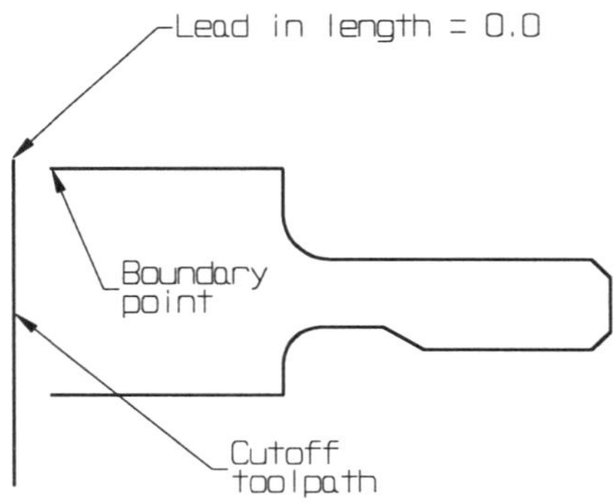

Figure 22.103a

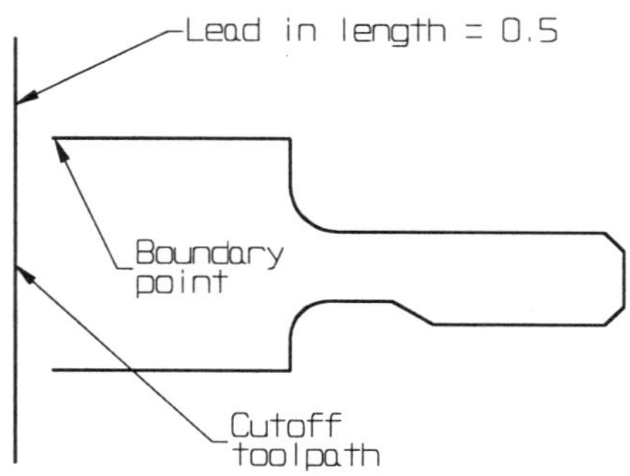

Figure 22.103b

Project 14. Cutting off a workpiece

This project shows how to generate a cutting off toolpath to an existing toolpath file for parting off the workpiece from stock. The existing toolpath file is "finish". Figure 22.104 shows the complete project with cutting off toolpath added.

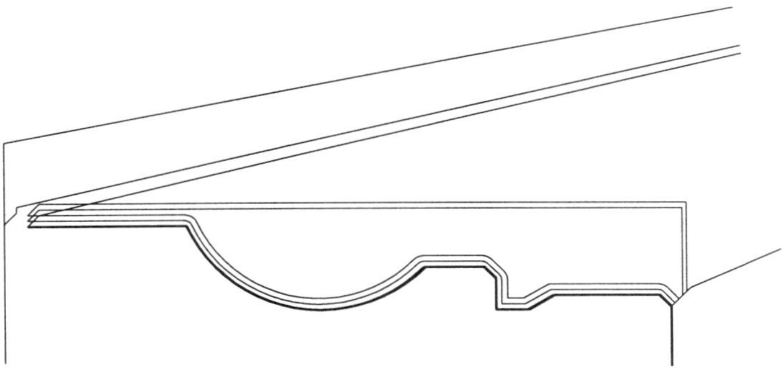

Figure 22.104

Tips 1. Use the existing toolpath model "finish".

2. Use cutoff module to add cutoff tool path.

3. Use (2.75,-5.5) as the boundary point.

4. Define a new cutoff tool.

5. Save the toolpath file as "cutoff".

Step 1. Open the existing project file finish.

Select **MAIN MENU → File → Get**
File name: **finish**
The part geometry should appear as in Figure 22.105.

Figure 22.105

Step 2. Initiate the cutoff module.

Select **MAIN MENU → Toolpaths**
The existing finishing toolpaths appear as in Figure 22.106.

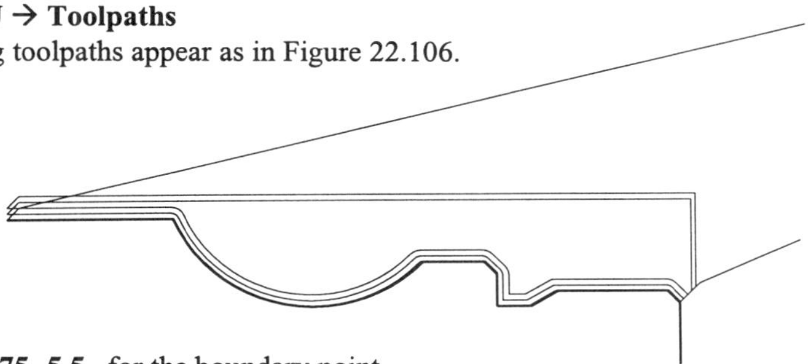

Figure 22.106

Select **Cutoff**
Select **Values**
Enter coordinates: **2.75,-5.5** for the boundary point

Step 3. Define a cutoff tool.

Select the "Tool Select" button

Click the right mouse button, then select **Create new tool**

Set the cutoff insert parameters as below.

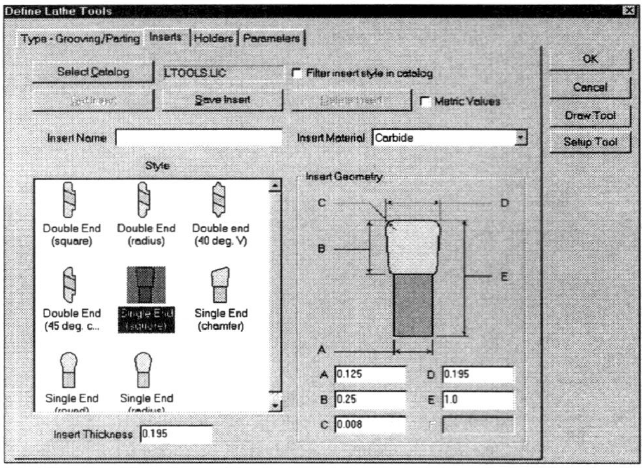

Step 4. Define the holder.

Click the "Holders" button

Set the holder parameters as below.

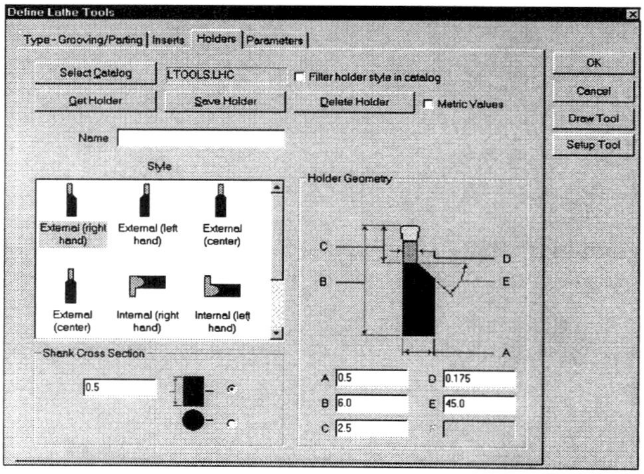

Step 5. Define tooling and machining parameters.

Click the "Parameters" button

Set tooling and machining parameters as below.

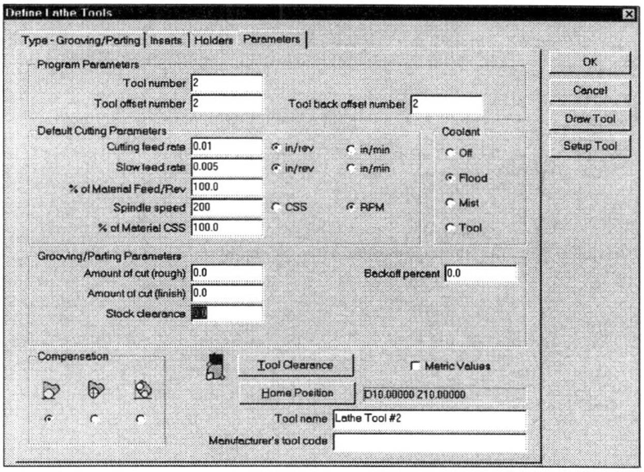

Step 6. Define the chamfer parameters.

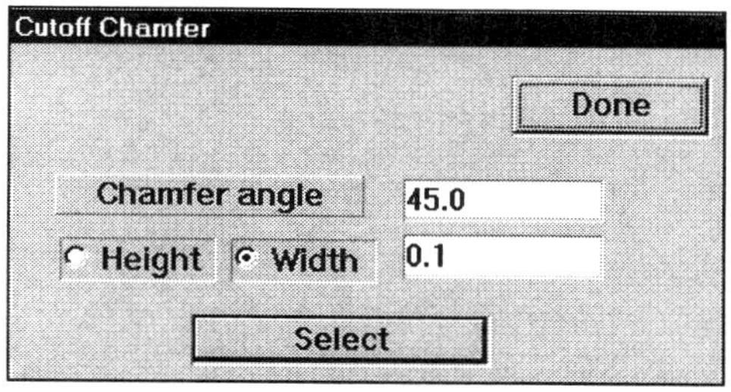

Select **OK** to return to Tool Manager menu
Select **OK** to return to Cutoff Parameters menu
Click the "Cutoff chamfer" button near the middle of Cutoff Parameter menu
Set the cutoff chamfer parameters asshown here.

Select **Done**

Step 7. Define the cutoff peck parameters.

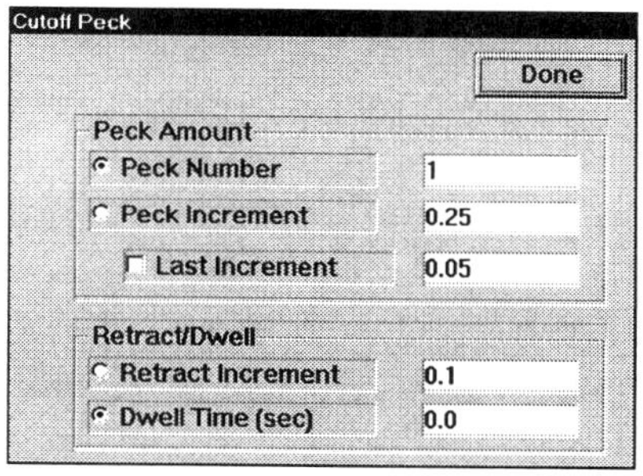

Click the "Cutoff peck" button
Set the cutoff peck parameters as shown here.

Select **Done**

Step 8. Define the exit vector parameters.

Click the "Entry/Exit Vectors" button
Click the "Exit Vector" button
Set the exit vector parameters as below, then select **OK**

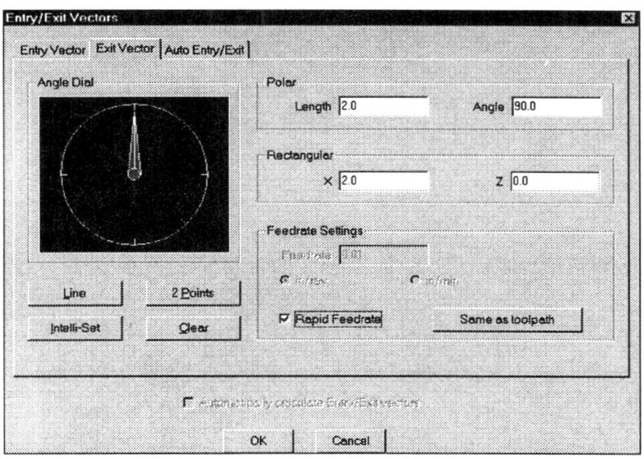

Step 9. Define the cutoff parameters.

Set the cutoff parameters as below.

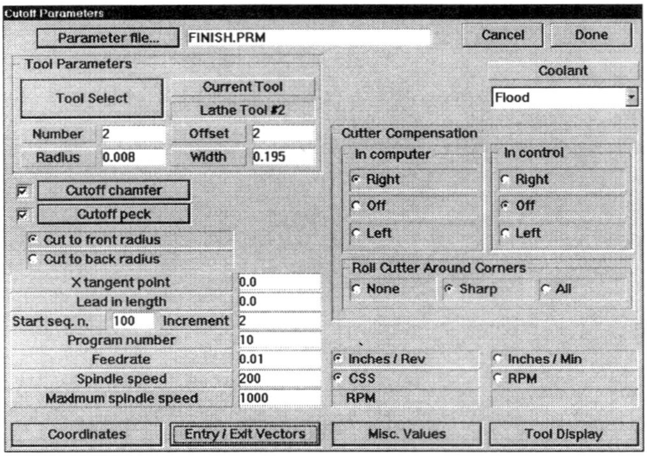

Select **Done** to generate cutoff toolpath

The cutoff toolpath has been added to the model as in Figure 22.107.

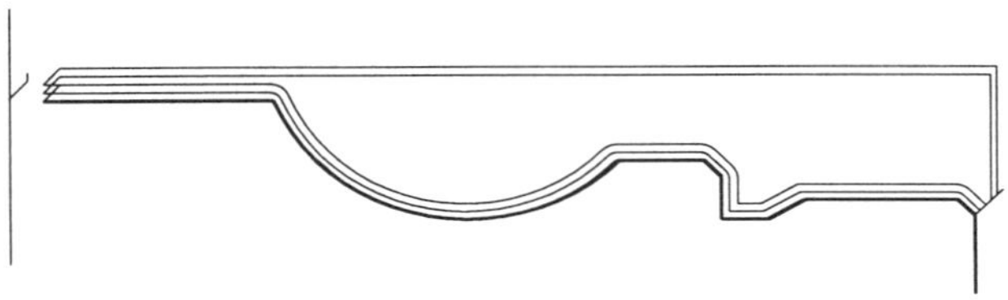

Figure 22.107

Select **Done** → **Yes** to accept this toolpath segment

Step 10. Backplot the toolpaths.

Select **BACKUP** to return to Operations Manager menu

Select **Select All**

Select **Backplot**

Set display and backplot parameters to desired setting

Select **Run** to animate toolpaths on the screen

Select **BACKUP**

Select **OK** from Operations Manager menu

Step 11. Save the file as cutoff.

Select **MAIN MENU** → **File** → **Save**

File name: **cutoff**

Project 15. Capstone project

This project is intended to use all of the toolpath modules to complete a rather complicated part which is commonly found in the actual manufacturing world. The part geometry and toolpath model are shown in Figure 22.108.

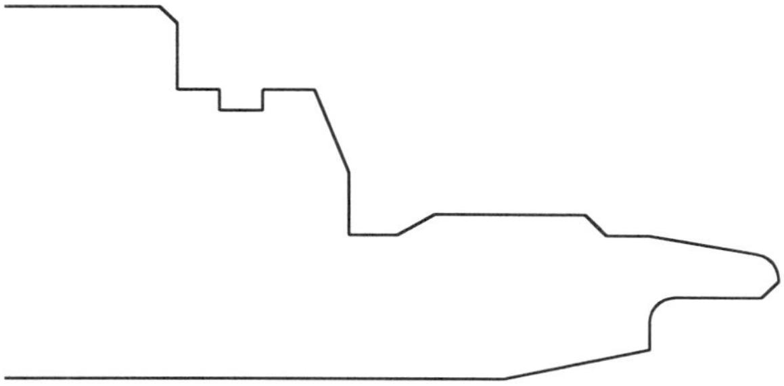

Figure 22.108a

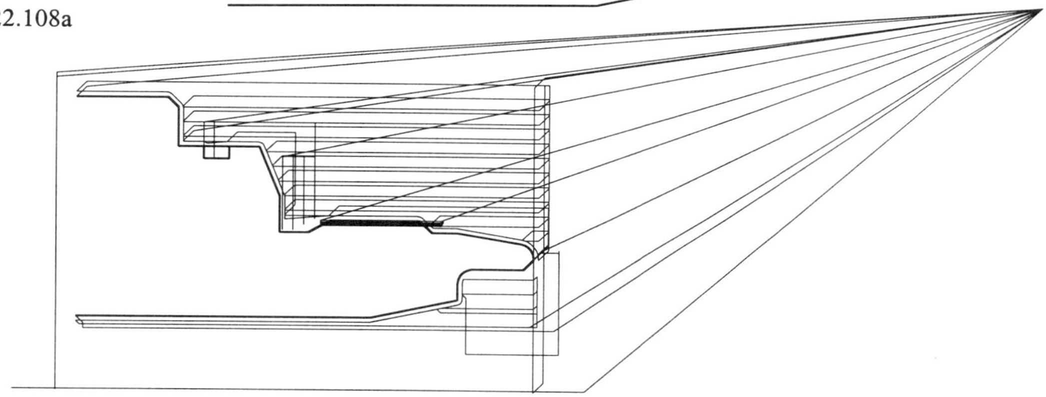

Figure 22.108b

Tips

1. Use the part geometry file "turn6".
2. Create a job setup.
3. Use the face module to create toolpath to cut the right end face with a 80^0 insert tool.
4. Use the rough module to rough cut the external profile with a 80^0 insert tool.
5. Use the groove module to cut a rectangular groove and a non-rectangular groove.
6. Use the finish module to cut the external finish profile.
7. Use the drill module to drill the center hole with a 1" drill.
8. Use the rough module to rough cut the internal profile with a boring bar.
9. Use the finish module to finish cut the internal profile.
10. Use the thread module to cut the thread.
11. Use the cutoff module to cut off the part from the stock.

Step 1. Open the part geometry file turn6.

Select **MAIN MENU → File → Get**
File name: **turn6**
The part appears as Figure 22.109.

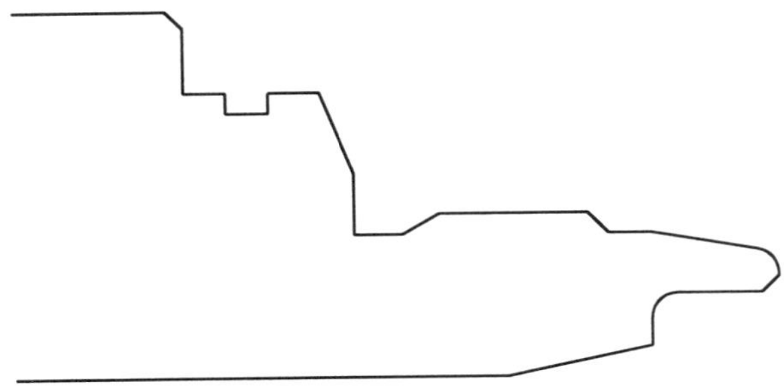

Figure 22.109

Step 2. Create a job setup.

Select **MAIN MENU → Toolpaths → Next menu → Job setup**
The initial job setup menu appears as below.

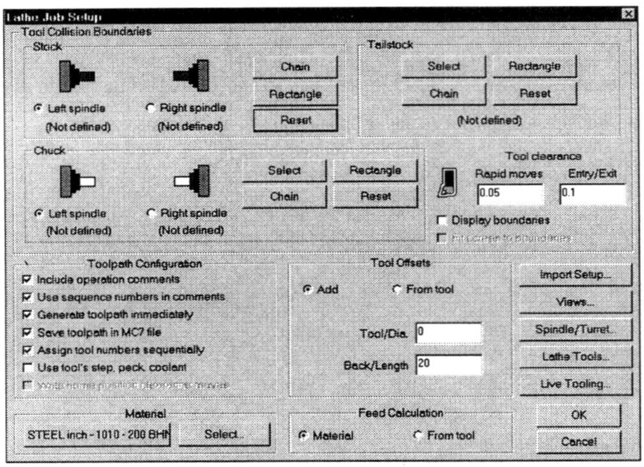

Step 3. Define the stock.

Click the "Left spindle" from Stock section
Click **Rectangle → 2 points → Values**
Enter coordinates: **0,-5** for the lower left corner
Select **Values**
Enter coordinates: **6.25,0.05** as the second point

Step 4. Select the material.

Click the "Select" button under Material which is located at the bottom of the menu
Select **STEEL inch-1010-200 BHN (Lathe)** from the list
Select **OK**

Step 5. Define job setup parameters.

Set the remaining job setup parameters as below.

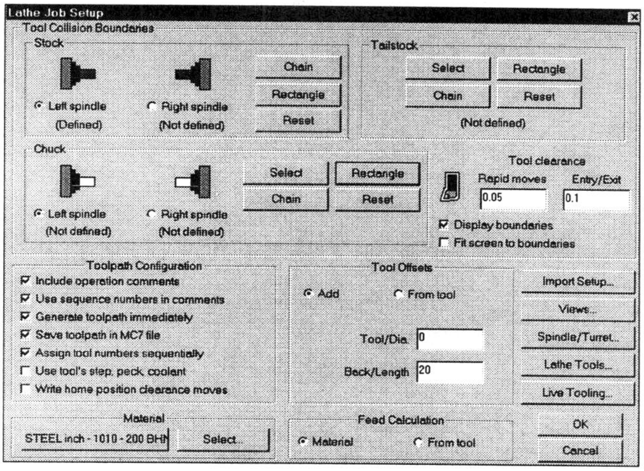

Select **OK** to return to graphic mode

Step 6. Initiate the face module.

Select **MAIN MENU → Toolpaths → Face**

File name for NCI: **capstone**

Select **Values**

Enter coordinates: **6.25,0.05** for the first boundary point

Select **Values**

Enter coordinates: **0,0** for the second boundary point

Step 7. Define a facing tool.

Select the "Tool Select" button

Click the right mouse button, then select **Create new tool**

Set insert parameters as below.

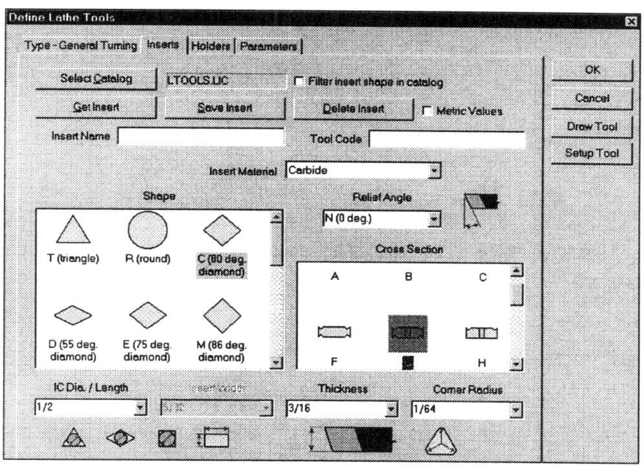

Step 8. Define the holder parameters.

Click **Holders**

Set the holder parameters as below.

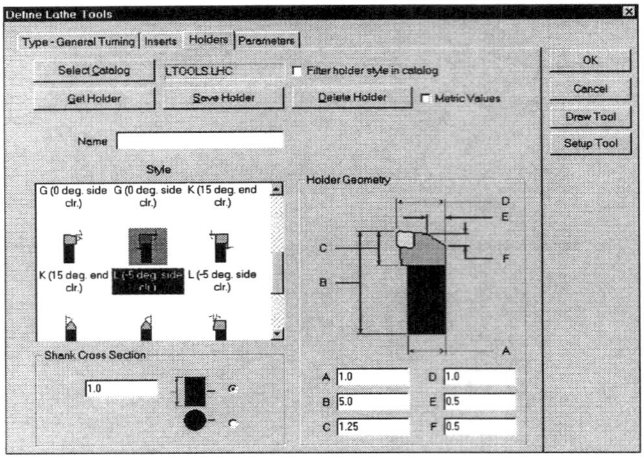

Step 9. Define the tooling and machining parameters.

Click **Parameters**

Set the tooling and machining parameters as below.

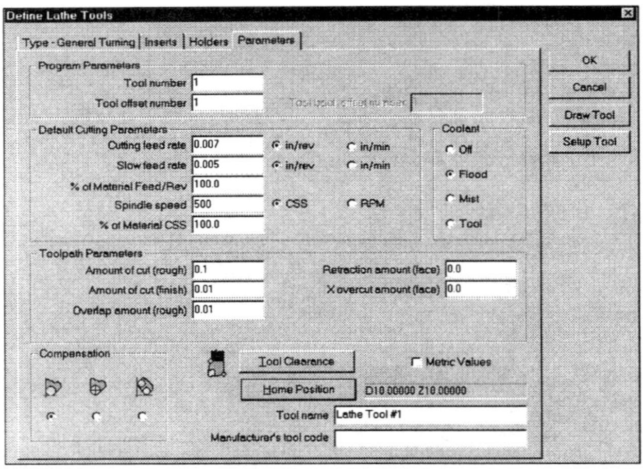

Select **OK → OK**

Step 10. Define the facing parameters as below.

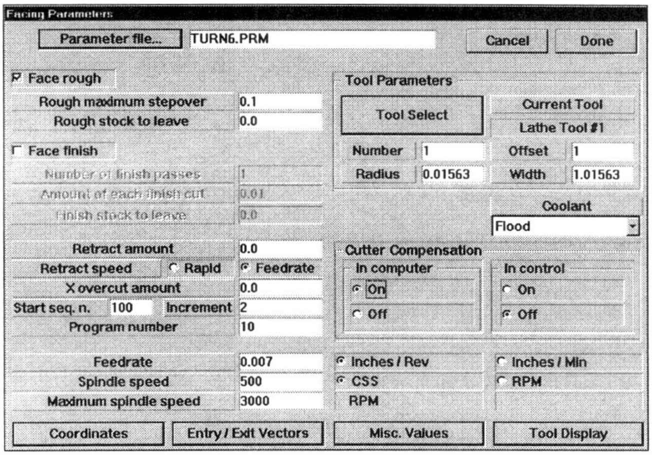

Step 11. Define coordinate parameters.

Click the "Coordinates" button

Set coordinate parameters as below. Then Select **OK**

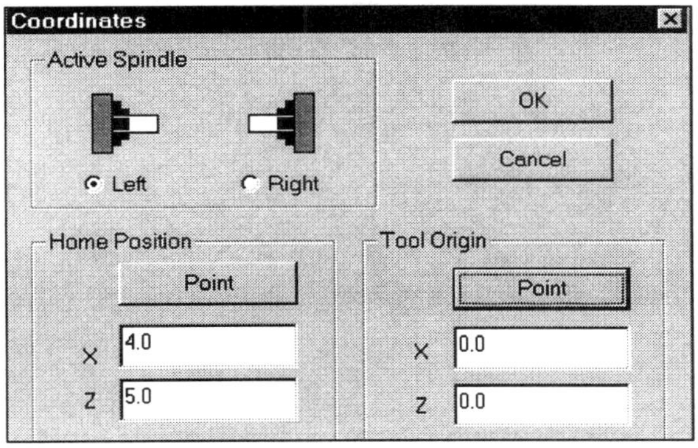

Step 12. Define the entry and exit parameters.

Click the "Entry/Exit Vectors" button

Set the entry vectors as: **X-0.1** **Z-0.1**

Click the "Exit Vector" button

Set the exit vectors as: **X0.1** **Z0.1**

Select **OK → Done**

The facing toolpath is generated as in Figure 22.110.

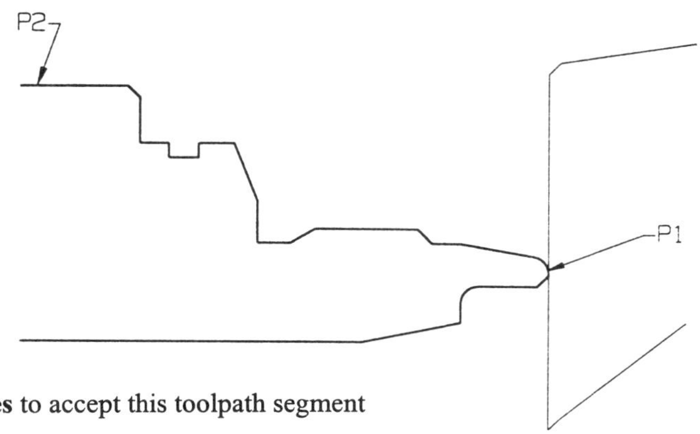

Figure 22.110

Select **Yes** to accept this toolpath segment

Step 13. Initiate rough module.

Use the pick points in Figure 22.110.
Select **Rough → Chain → Partial**
Pick **P1** as the first entity
Pick **P2** as the last entity
Select **Done → Done**

Step 14. Select a tool.

Click the "Tool Select" button
Click the existing tool: **Lathe Tool #1**
Select **OK**

Step 15. Define the roughing parameters as below.

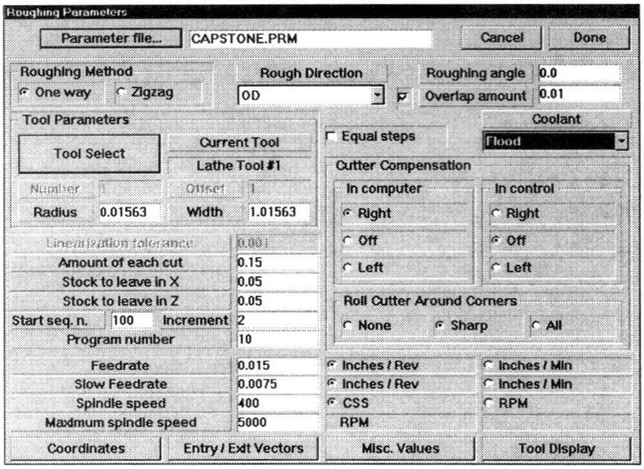

Step 16. Set coordinate values.

Click the "Coordinates" button
Set Home Position at **X4.0** **Z5.0**
Select **OK**

Step 17. Define entry and exit vector parameters.

Click the "Entry/Exit Vectors" button
Set the entry vectors as: **X-0.1** **Z-0.1**
Click the "Exit Vector" button
Set the exit vectors as: **X0.1** **Z0.1**
Select **OK → Done**
The roughing toolpaths are added as in Figure 22.111.

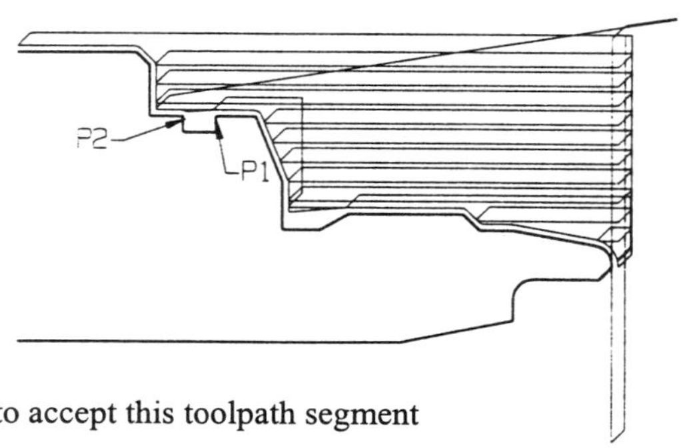

Figure 22.111

Select **Yes** to accept this toolpath segment

Step 18. Initiate the groove module.

Use the pick points in Figure 22.111.
Select **Groove → 3 Lines → Chain → Partial**
Pick **P1** as the first entity
Pick **P2** as the last entity
Select **Done**

Step 19. Create a grooving tool.

Click the "Tool Select" button
Click the right mouse button, then select **Create new tool**
Set the grooving insert parameters as below.

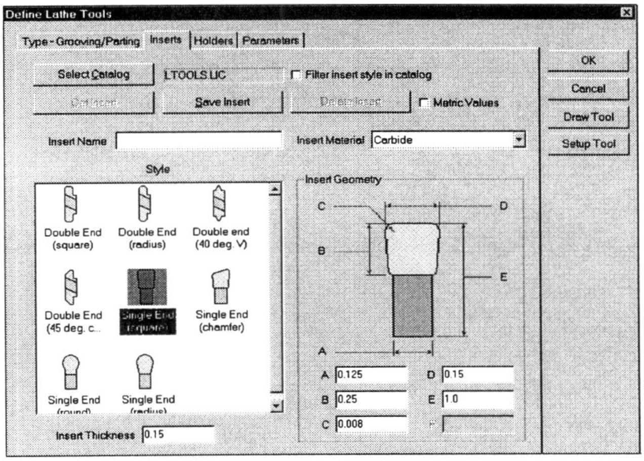

Step 20. Define the grooving holder.

Click the "Holders" button
Set the holder parameters as below.

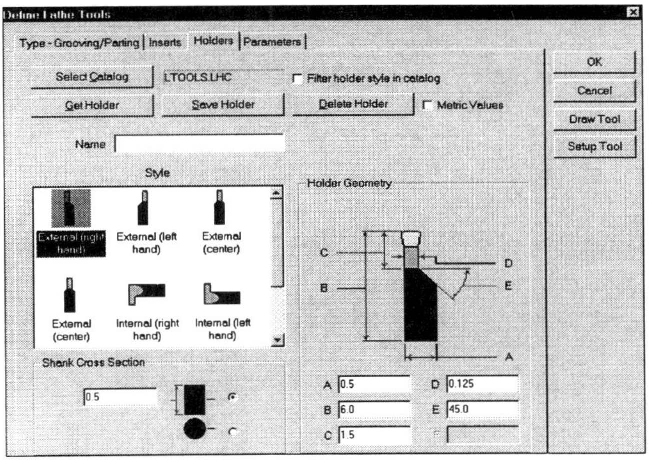

Step 21. Define the tooling and machining parameters.

Click the "Parameters" button

Set tooling and machining parameters as below.

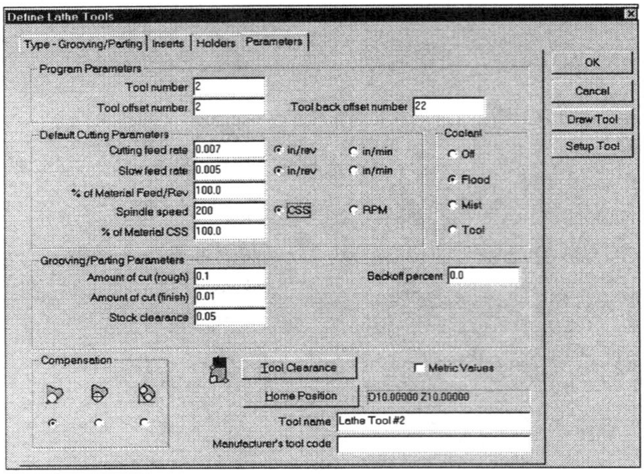

Select **Done → OK**

Step 22. Define the grooving parameters.

Click the "Groove Rough" button

Set the groove rough parameters as shown here.

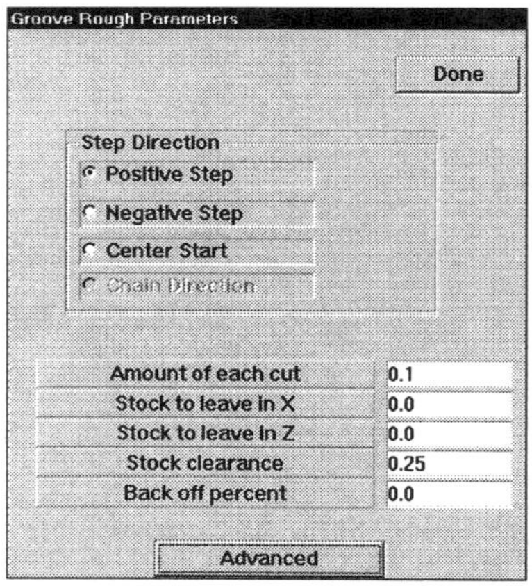

Select **Done**

Step 23. Set the coordinate values.

Click the "Coordinates" button

Set home position coordinates to **X4.0** **Z5.0**

Select **OK**

Step 24. Define the grooving parameters as below.

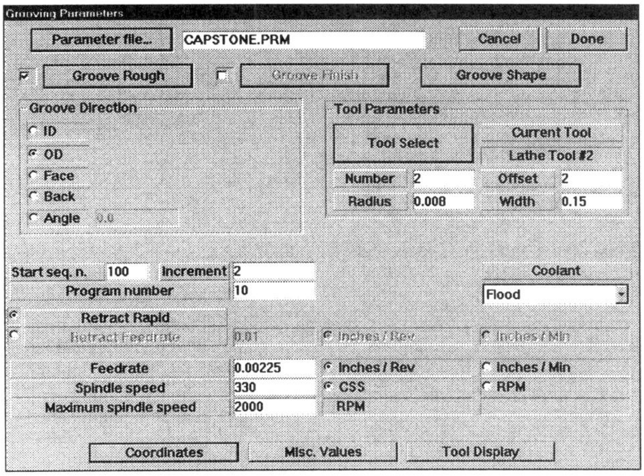

Select **Done**
The grooving toolpaths are added as in Figure 22.112.

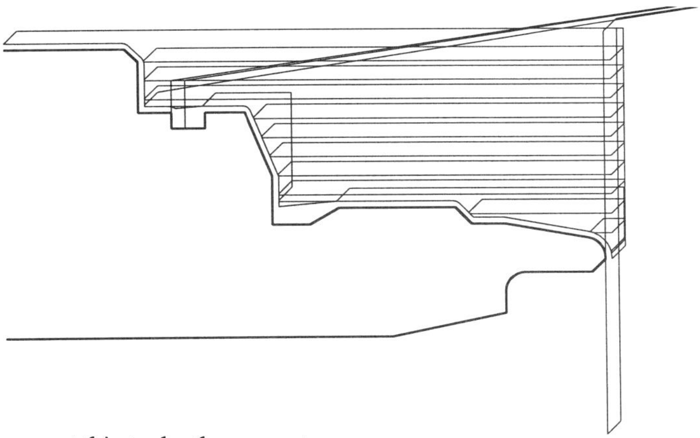

Figure 22.112

Select **Yes** to accept this toolpath segment

Step 25. Add a horizontal line.

Select **Level**, enter **3**
Select **MAIN MENU → Create → Line → Endpoints → Values**
Enter coordinates: **4.25,-1.75**
Select **Values**
Enter coordinates: **4.25, -2.75**

The line is added as in Figure 22.113.

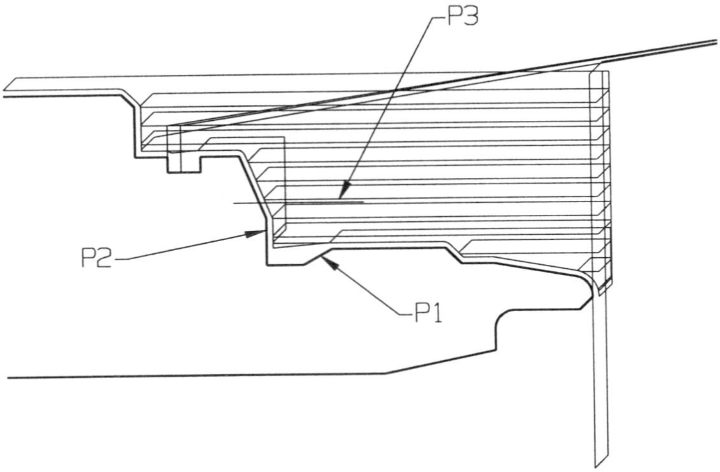

Figure 22.113

Step 26. Cut a non-rectangular groove.

Use the pick points in Figure 22.113.
Select **MAIN MENU → Toolpaths → Groove → 2 Bdry**
Select **Chain → Partial**
Pick **P1** as the first entity of the inner boundary
Pick **P2** as the last entity
Select **Done → Single**
Pick **P3** as the outer boundary
Select **Done**

Step 27. Define the coordinate values.

Click the "Coordinates" button
Set home position coordinates as **X4.0** **Z5.0**
Select **OK**

Step 28. Define the groove rough parameters.

Click the "Groove Rough" button
Set the groove rough parameters as shown here.

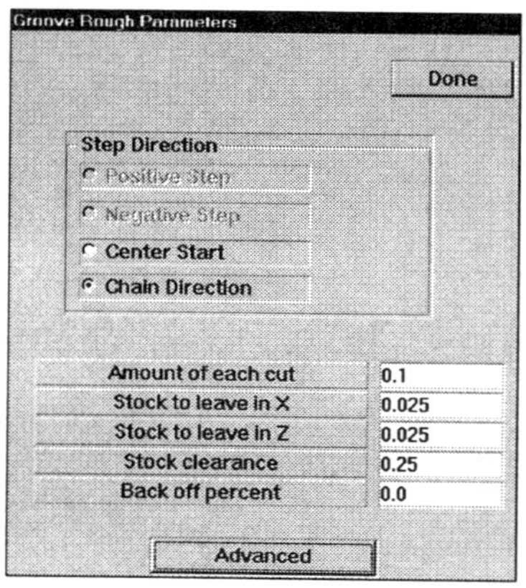

Select **Done**

Step 29. Set the grooving parameters as below.

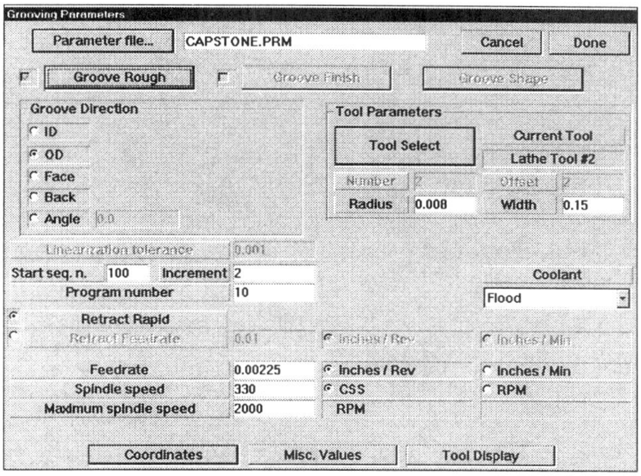

Select **Done**
The grooving toolpaths are added to the model as shown in Figure 22.114.

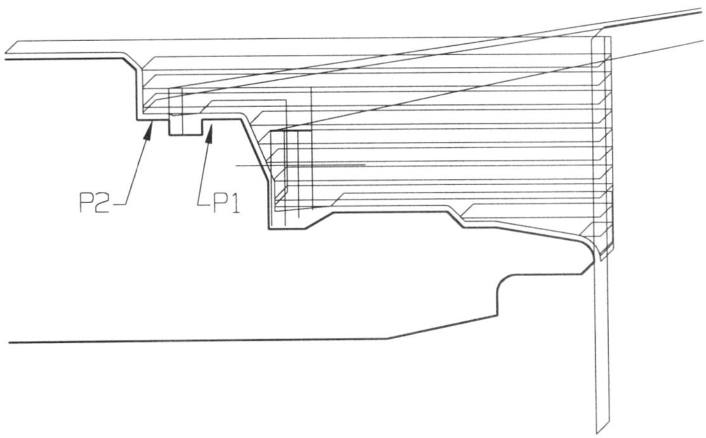

Figure 22.114

Select **Yes** to accept this toolpath segment

Step 30. Join two lines and delete a line.

Use the pick points in Figure 22.114.
Select **MAIN MENU → Modify → Join**
Pick **P1** and **P2** to join two entities into one
Select **MAIN MENU → Delete → All → Level**
Enter level: **3**

The new drawing becomes Figure 22.115.

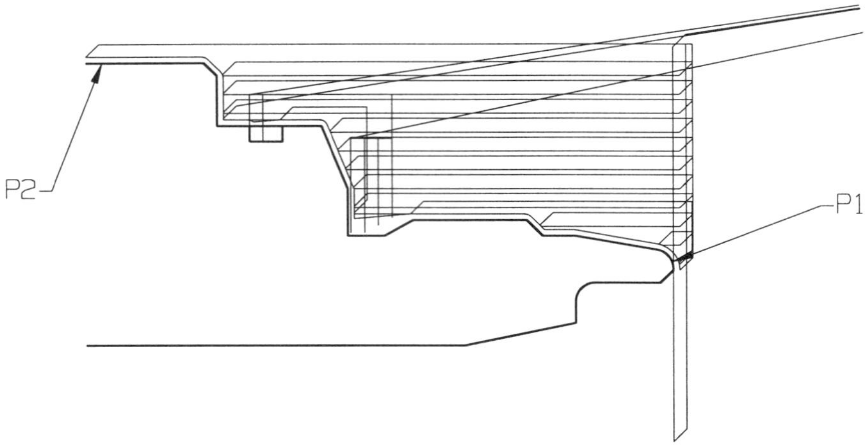

Figure 22.115

Step 31. Initiate the finish module.

Use the pick points in Figure 22.115.
Select **MAIN MENU → Toolpaths → Finish → Chain → Partial**
Pick **P1** and **P2** to define the profile
Select **Done → Done**

Step 32. Select a tool and holder assembly.

Click the “Tool Select” button
Click the right mouse button, then select **Get from library**
Select the tool **R1/64” J/V (RH)** from the tool list
Select **OK → OK**

Step 33. Define home position coordinates.

Click the “Coordinates” button
Set home position at **X4.0** **Z5.0**
Select **OK**

Step 34. Set the finishing parameters as below.

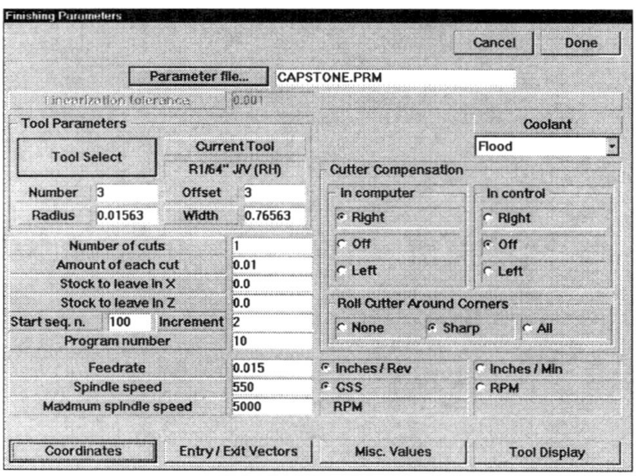

Select **Done → Write**
Select **Yes** to accept this toolpath segment
The new model with toolpaths appears as in Figure 22.116.

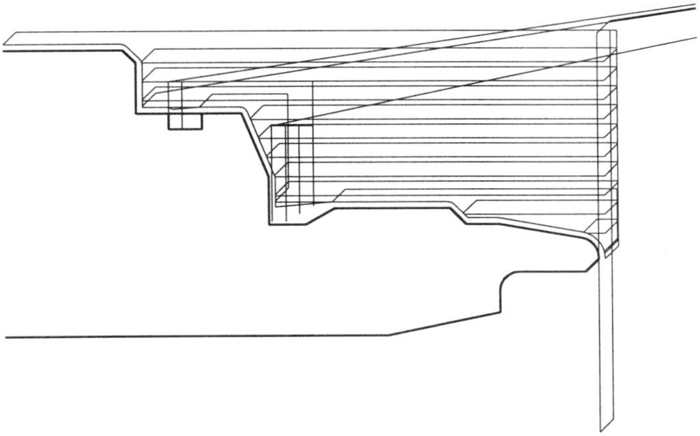

Figure 22.116

Step 35. Drill a center hole with a 1" drill.

Select **MAIN MENU → Toolpaths → Drill**
Set the drilling parameters as below.

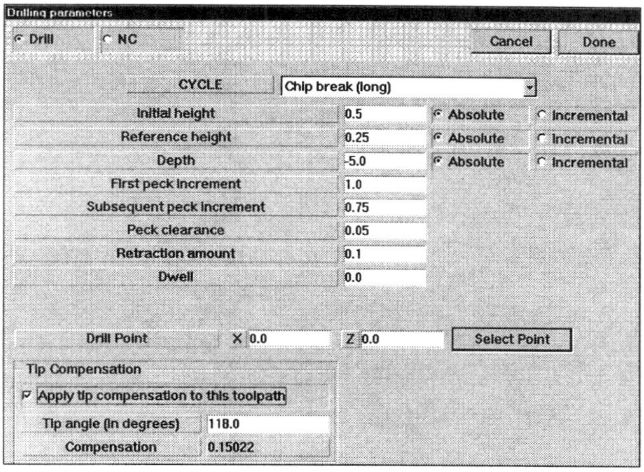

Step 36. Create a drill tool.

Click the "NC" button
Click the "Tool Select" button
Click the right mouse button, then select **Create new tool**
Select the "Drill" icon

Set the drill geometry parameters as below.

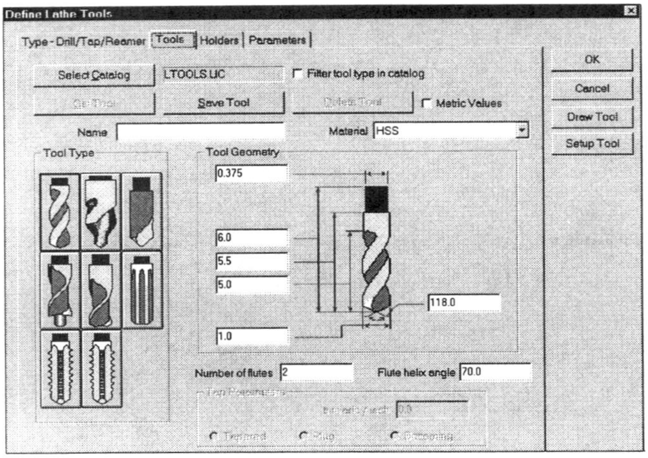

Step 37. Define the holder parameters.

Click the “Holders” button

Set the holder parameters as below.

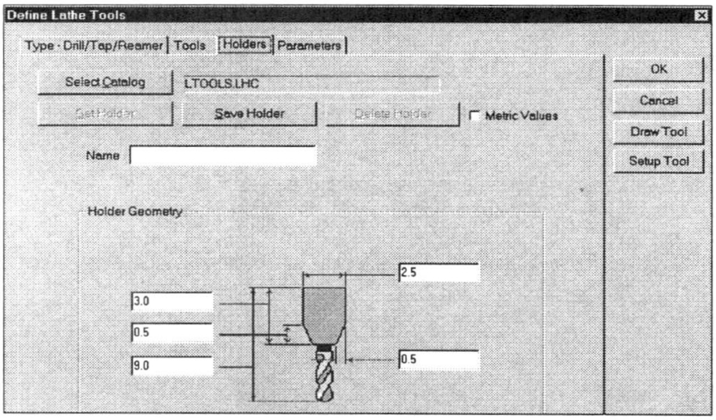

Step 38. Define the tooling and drilling parameters.

Click **Parameters**

Set the parameters as below.

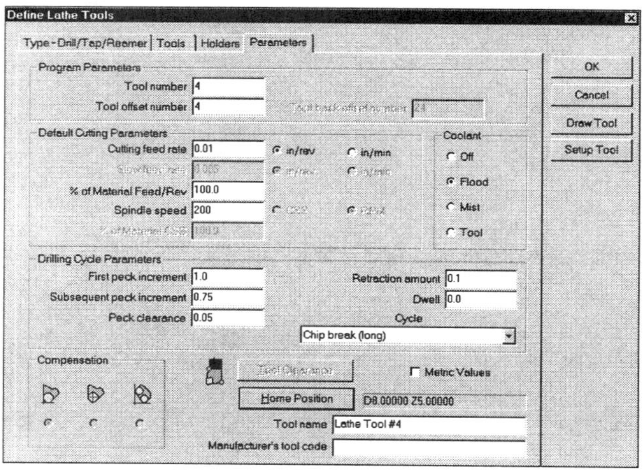

Select **OK → OK**

Step 39. Set the NC parameters as below.

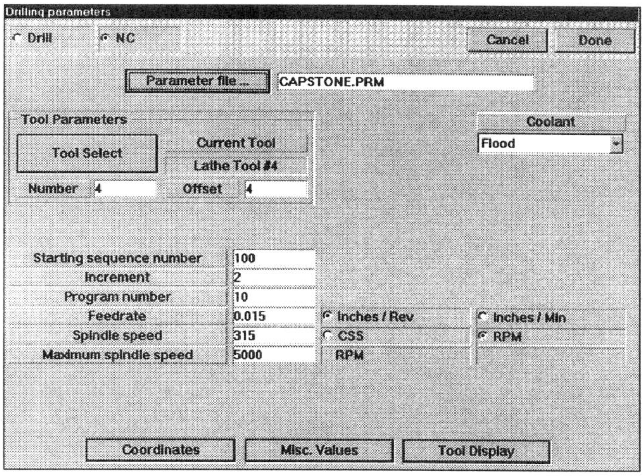

Select **Done** to generate drilling toolpath
The drilling toolpath is added to the model as in Figure 22.117.

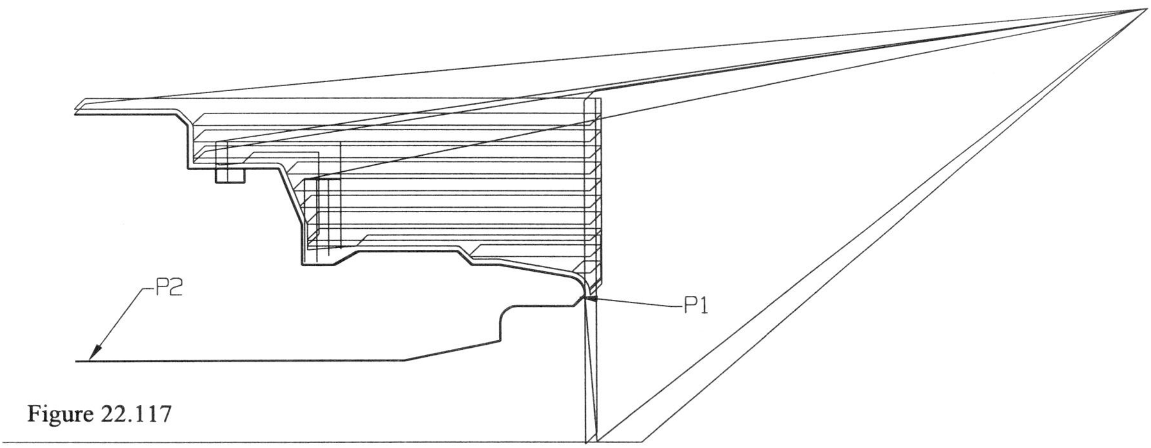

Figure 22.117

Select **Yes** to accept this toolpath segment

Step 40. Initiate the rough module for internal boring.

Select **Rough → Chain → Partial**
Pick **P1** and **P2** to define the profile
Select **Point → Values**
Enter coordinates: **0.75,0.2** as the retraction point
Select **Done**

Step 41. Define a boring tool.

Click the "Tool Select" button
Click the right mouse button, then select **Create new tool**
Click the "Type-General Turning" button
Select **Boring Bar**

Define the insert parameters as below.

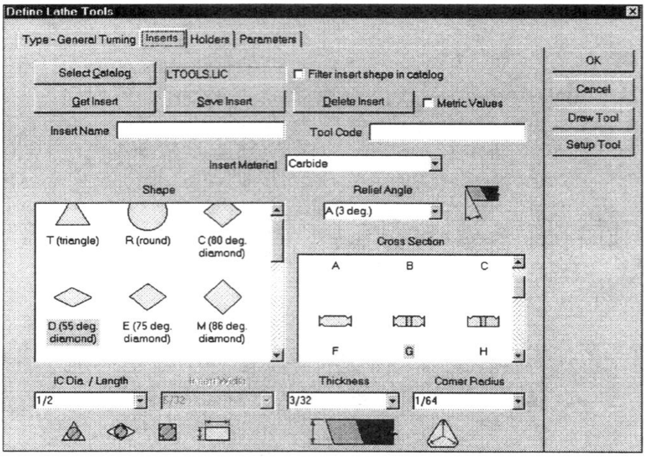

Step 42. Define the boring bar parameters.

Click the "Boring Bar" button

Set the boring bar parameters as below.

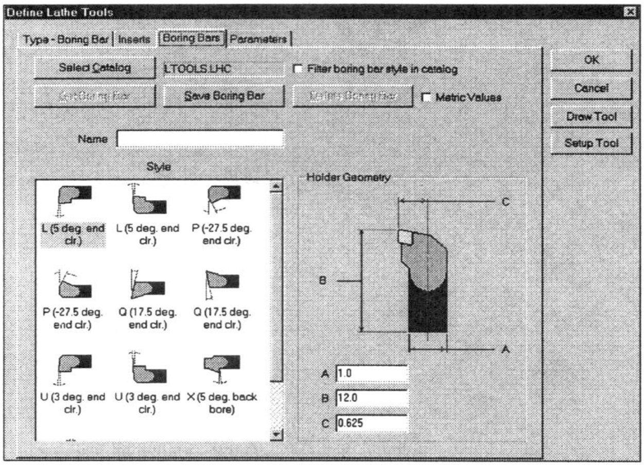

Step 43. Define the tooling and machining parameters.

Click the "Parameters" button

Set the tooling and machining parameters as below.

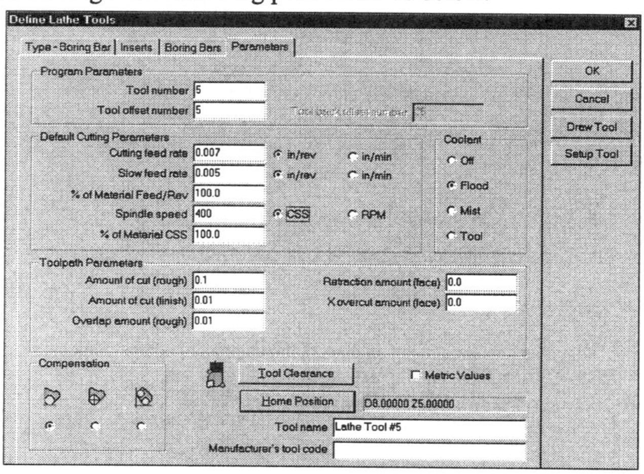

Select **OK** to return to Tool Manager menu
Select **OK**

Step 44. Define entry and exit vector parameters.

Click the "Entry/Exit Vectors" button
Set the entry vector parameters as: Length = **0.1** Angle = **-135**
Click the "Exit Vector" button
Set the exit vector parameters as: Length = **0.1** Angle = **-45**
Select **OK**

Step 45. Set the roughing parameters as below.

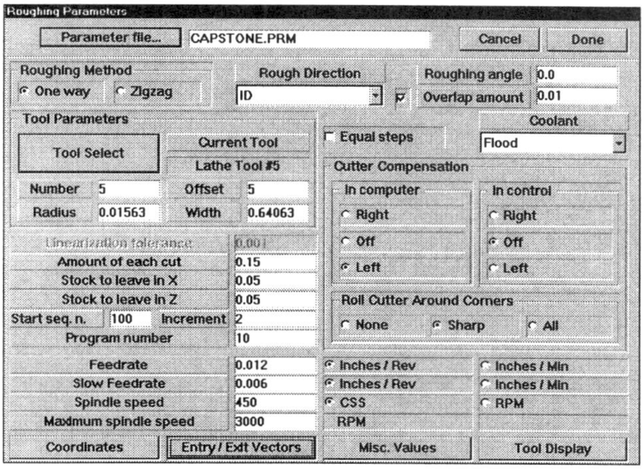

Select **Done** to generate the boring toolpaths as shown in Figure 22.118.

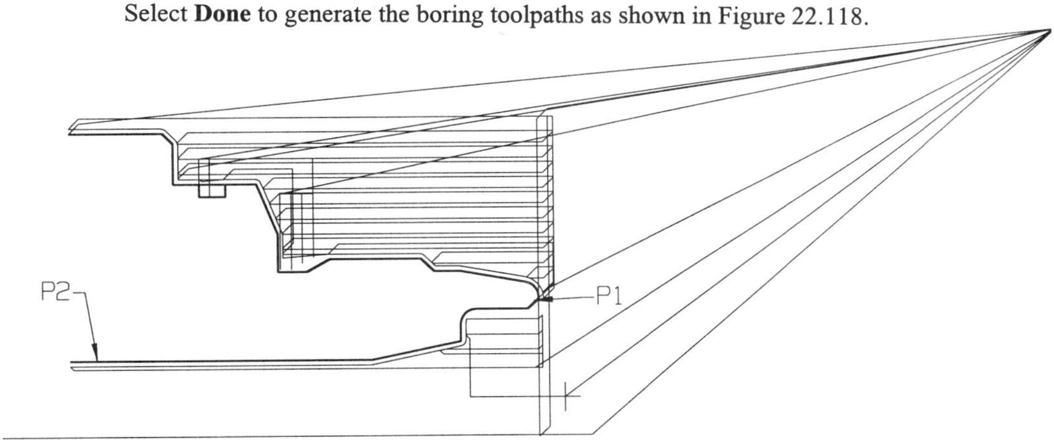

Figure 22.118

Select **Yes** to accept this toolpath segment

Step 46. Initiate the finish boring operation.

Select **Finish**
Select **Point → Values**
Enter coordinates: **2.9,0.25** as the entry point

Select **Chain → Partial**
Pick **P1** and **P2** to select the profile
Select **Done → Point → Values**
Enter coordinates: **1.25,0.2** as the retraction point
Select **Done**

Step 47. Define entry and exit vector parameters.

Click the "Entry/Exit Vectors" button
Set the entry vector parameters as: Length = **0.1** Angle = **-135**
Click the "Exit Vector" button
Set the exit vector parameters as: Length = **0.1** Angle **–45**
Select **OK**

Step 48. Set the finishing parameters as below.

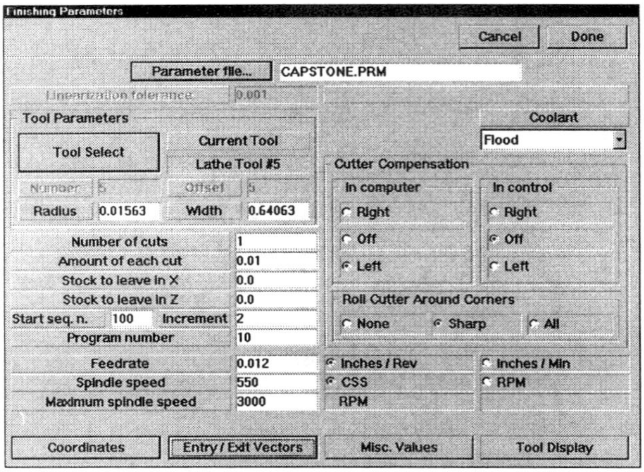

Select **Done → Write**
The boring toolpaths are added as in Figure 22.119.

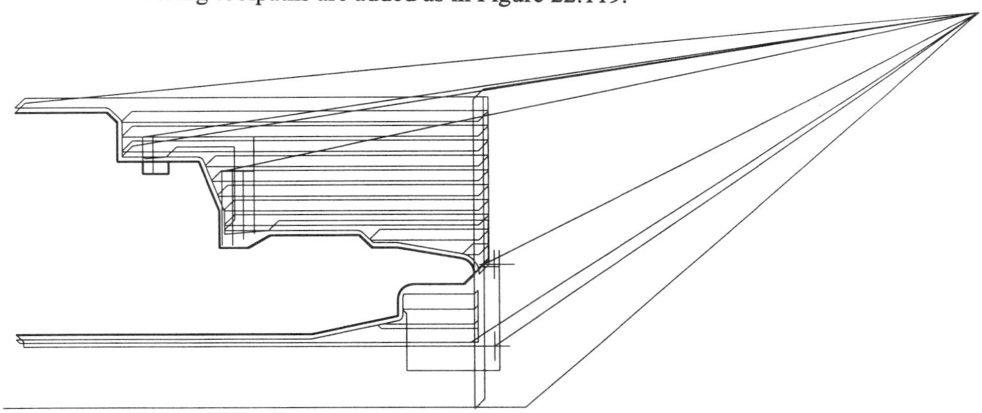

Figure 22.119

Select **Yes** to accept this toolpath segment

Step 49. Initiate the thread module.

Select **Thread**

Set threading parameters as below.

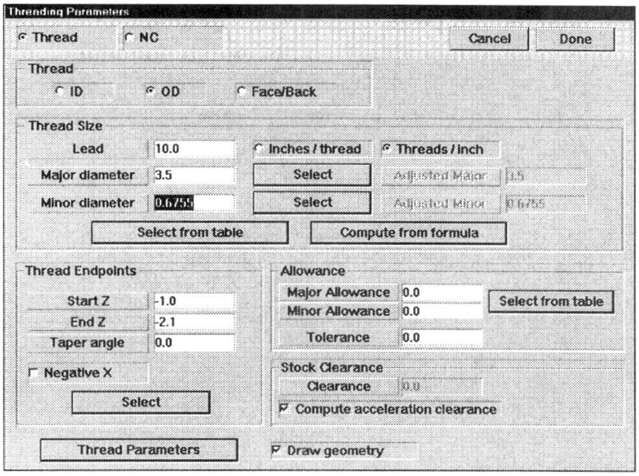

Step 50. Compute the minor diameter of threads.

Click the "Compute from formula" button

The initial thread formula menu appears as below.

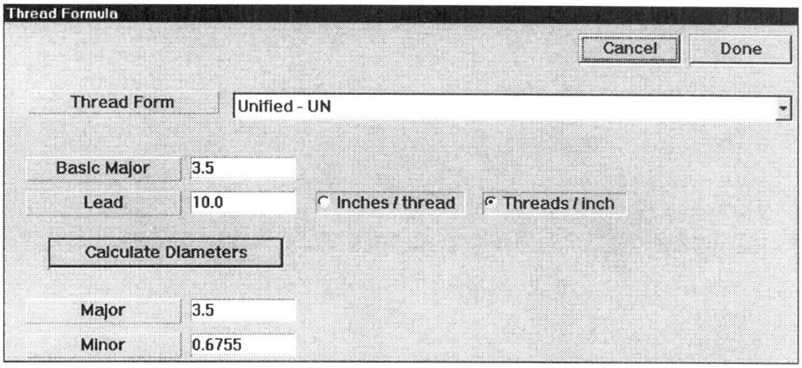

Click the "Calculate Diameters" button

The minor diameter of the threads becomes 3.39175 as below.

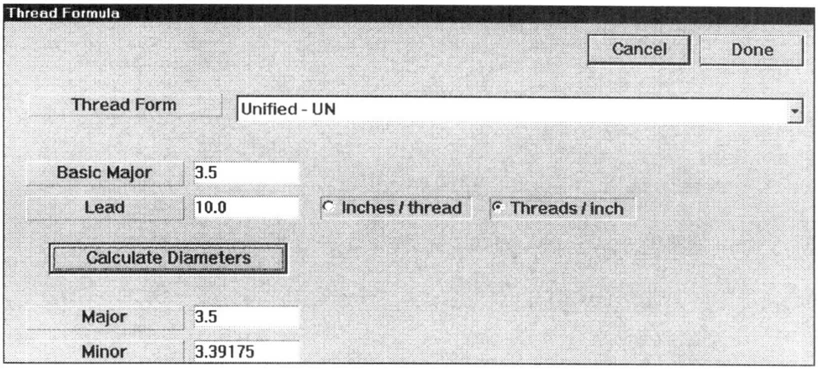

Select **Done** to return to Threading Parameters menu

Step 51. Define the thread parameters.

Click the "Thread Parameters" button

Set thread parameters as below.

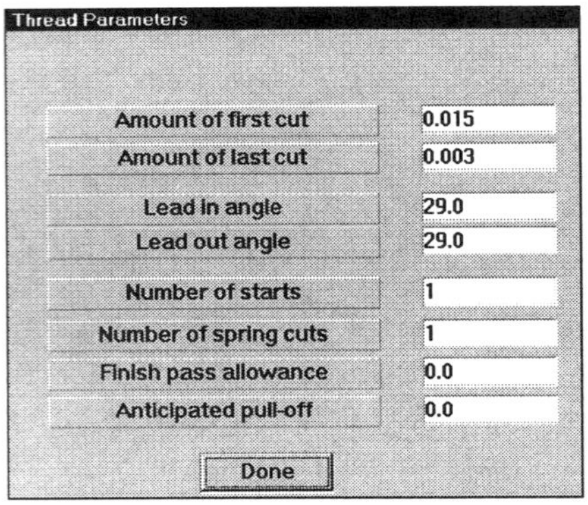

Select **Done**

Step 52. Define a thread tool.

Click the "NC" button

Click the "Tool Select" button

Click the right mouse button, then select **Create new tool**

Set the insert parameters as below.

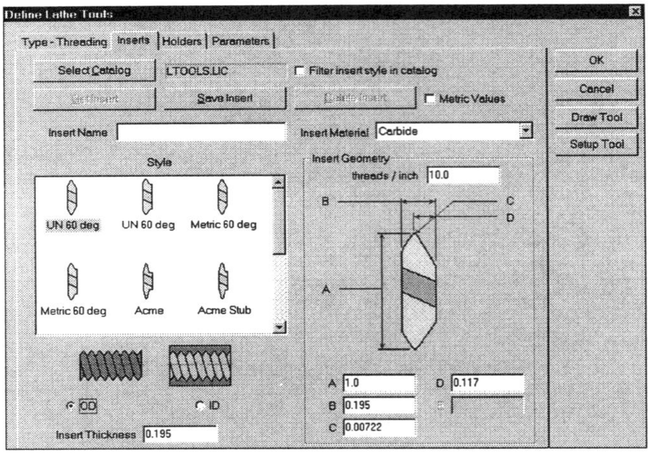

Step 53. Define holder parameters.

Click the "Holders" button

Set the holder parameters as below.

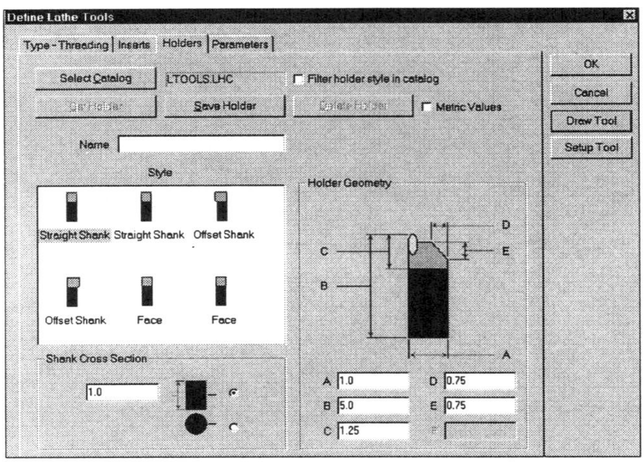

Step 54. Define tooling and threading parameters.

Click the "Parameters" button
Set the parameters as below.

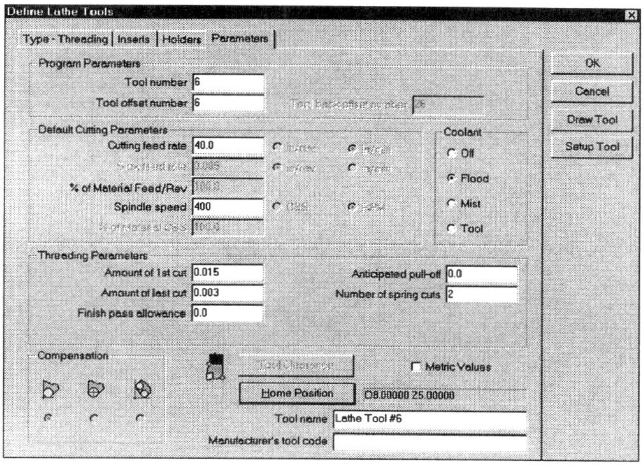

Select **OK → OK**

Step 55. Set the threading parameters as below.

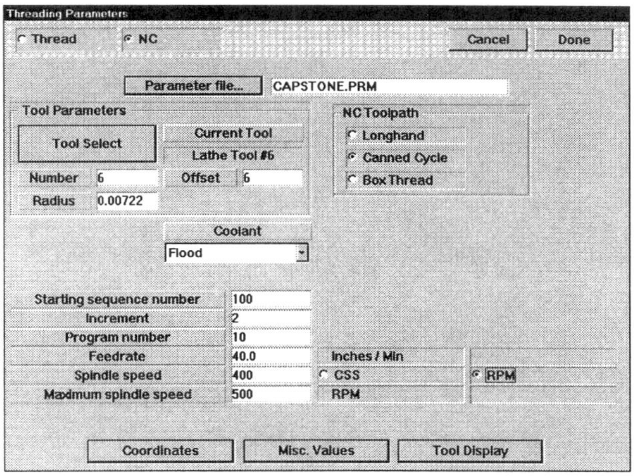

Select **Done**

The threading toolpaths are generated as in Figure 22.120.

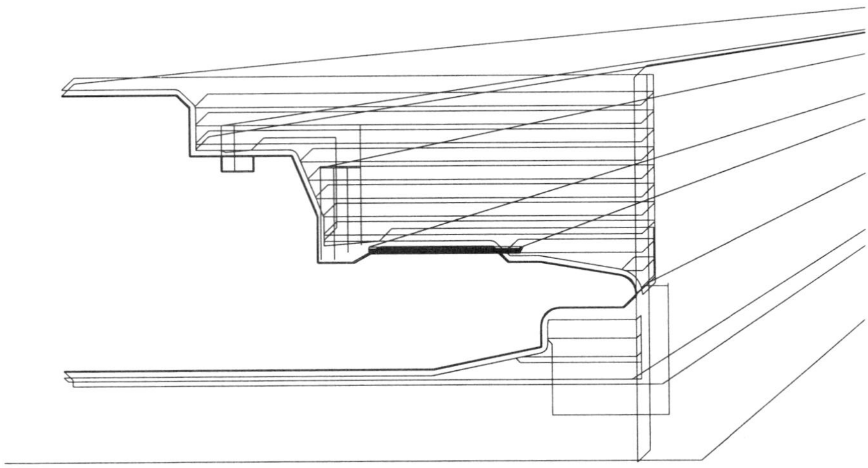

Figure 22.120

Select **Yes** to accept this toolpath segment

Step 56. Initiate the cutoff module.

Select **Cutoff**
Select **Point → Values**
Enter coordinates: **6.2,-4.5** as the boundary point

Step 57. Define a cutoff tool.

Click the "Tool Select" button
Click the right mouse button, then select **Create new tool**
Set the insert parameters as below.

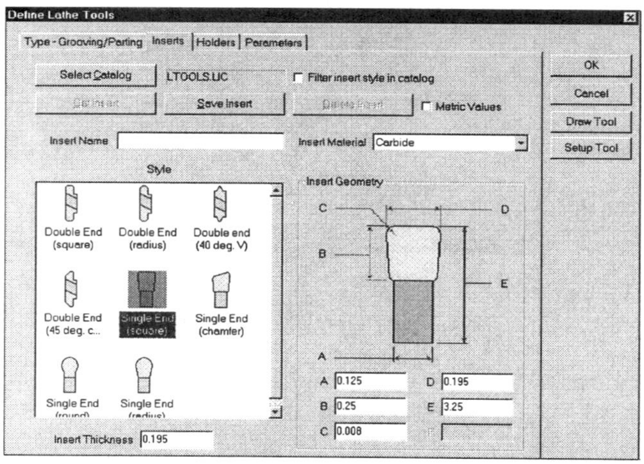

Step 58. Define the holder parameters.

Click the “Holders” button

Set the holder parameters as below.

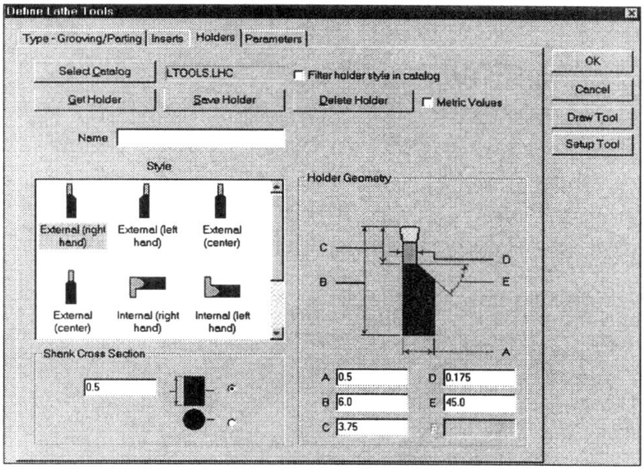

Step 59. Define the tooling and cutoff parameters.

Click the “Parameters” button

Set parameters as below.

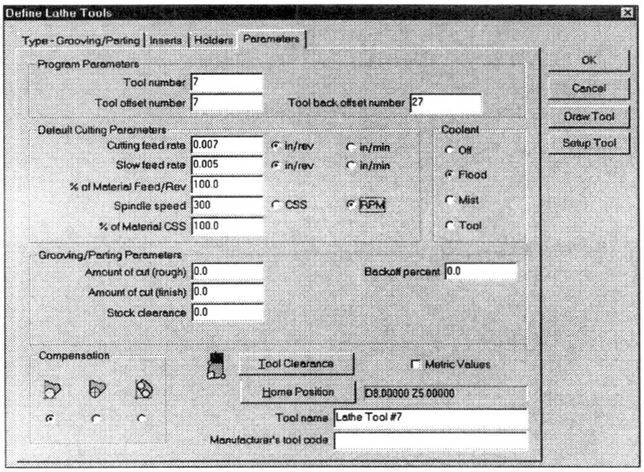

Select **OK** → **OK**

Step 60. Define the entry and exit vector parameters.

Click the “Entry/Exit Vectors” button

Set entry vector parameters as: Length = **0.1** Angle = **-90**

Click the “Exit Vector” button

Set exit vector parameters as: Length = **3.25** Angle = **90**

Select **OK**

Step 61. Define the cutoff peck parameters.

Click the "Cutoff peck" button

Set the cutoff peck parameters as below.

Select **Done**

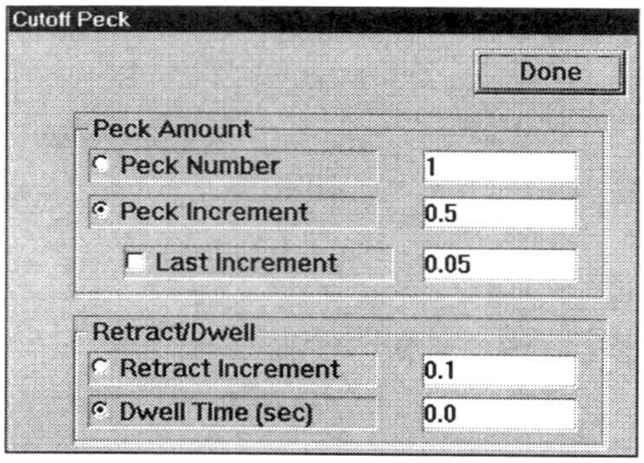

Step 62. Set the cutoff parameters as below.

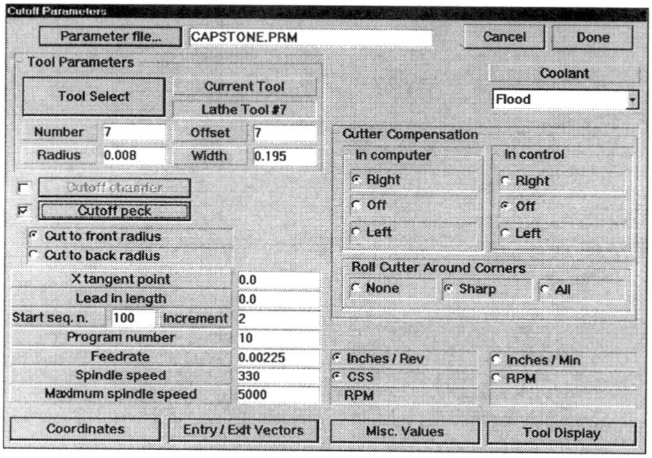

Select **Done**

The partoff toolpath is added to the left end of the part as shown in Figure 22.121.

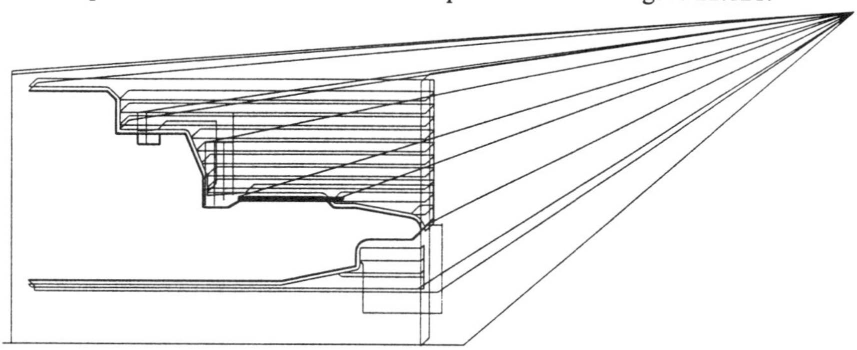

Figure 22.121

Select **Done** → **Yes** to accept this toolpath segment

Step 63. Backplot all toolpath segments.

Select **Operations** → **Select All** → **Backplot**

Set display and backplot parameters to desired setting

Select **Run** to animate the toolpaths on the screen

Step 64. Save the project file as capstone.

Select **MAIN MENU** → **File** → **Save**

File name: **capstone**

Exercises

1. Describe, with a drawing, how to determine the axis direction of a CNC lathe of the left-hand coordinate system.

2. Describe, with a drawing, how to determine the axis direction of a CNC lathe of the right-hand coordinate system.

3. What are the two methods of specifying the X coordinate values in the Mastercam lathe system ?

4. Create a part geometry as shown in Figure . Save the part geometry as lathep1.

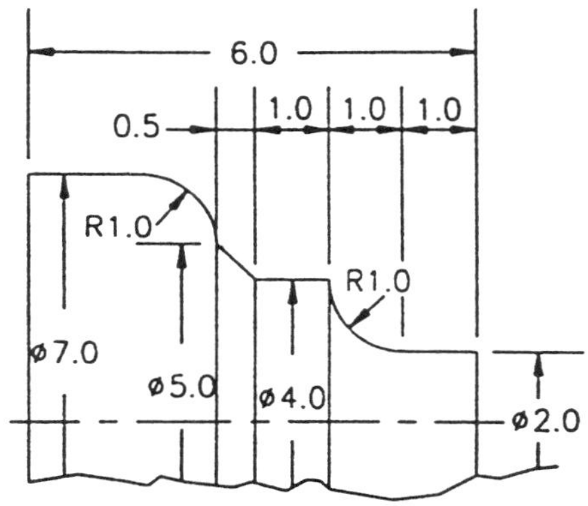

Figure 22.122

5. Create a part geometry as shown in Figure . Save the part geometry as lathep2.

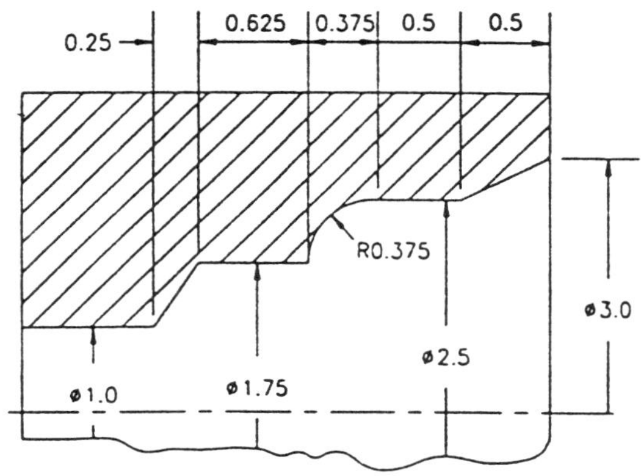

Figure 22.123

6. Create a part geometry as shown in Figure . Save the part geometry as lathep3.

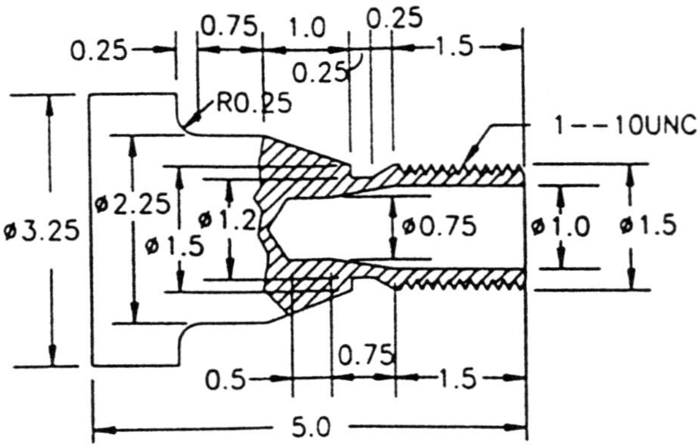

Figure22.124

7. What are the five toolpath modules used in the Mastercam lathe ? Describe when to use each of these modules.

8. What are the two sets of parameters used in the Mastercam lathe system ?

9. Describe the stock, describe, with a drawing, how the stock affects the toolpath.

10. List the two types of cutter compensation used in Mastercam.

11. List the three possible toggle modes the cutter compensation in computer parameter.

12. Write the corresponding G-codes for the following three modes of cutter compensation in computer:

    Off:
    Right:
    Left:

13. Describe, with a drawing, how to select the proper mode of cutter compensation in computer.

14. What are the three NC commands used to regulate the spindle in CNC lathes ?

15. List when to use constant surface speed.

16. List when to use constant spindle speed.

17. What are the two feedrate units used in CNC lathes ?

18. Define the imaginary tool nose.

19. Describe the meaning of the T-code followed by four digits: T0512

20. Define the following three angles in a turning tool:

    Lead angle:
    Insert angle:
    Relief angle:

21. Find the relief angle for a turning tool having a -5(lead angle and 55(insert angle.

22. What are the four parameters used to define the approaching and retracting toolpath pattern of each cutting pass ?

23. What are the three rough specific parameters ?

24. What are the proper roughing angles for longitudinal roughing and facing roughing, respectively ?

25. What are the two types of feedrate used in the rough module ? Describe when each is used.

26. Describe when to use the finish module.

27. What is the only finish specific parameter ?

28. List the types of CNC lathe controllers that provide rough canned cycles (G71 and G72) and the finish canned cycle (G70).

29. Describe the advantages of using canned cycles for roughing and finishing operations.

30. List and describe the one-block format of the rough turning cycle (G71). What type of Fanuc-controllers used the one-block format ?

31. List and describe the two-block format of the rough turning cycle (G71). What type of Fanuc-controllers used the two-block format ?

32. Use a drawing to show a typical toolpath pattern of the rough turning cycle (G71).

33. What is the major difference between the rough turning cycle (G71) and the rough facing cycle (G72) ?

34. Use a drawing to show a typical toolpath pattern of the rough facing cycle (G72).

35. Describe the statement format of the finish cycle (G70).

36. Describe the procedure to insert the finish cycle command (G70) to the part program in Mastercam lathe.

37. What is the only groove specific parameter ?

38. What are the two boundaries used in the groove module ? Explain their purpose, respectively.

39. What three pieces of information must be specified in defining the geometry contour for thread cutting ?

40. Describe how Mastercam defines the major diameter, minor diameter, and thread length.

41. Calculate the thread height and minor diameter for the following two UNC external threads:
    3/8 – 16 UNC
    1 ½ - 6 UNC

Chapter 23

Mill-turn Toolpaths

Objectives:

1. Understand the mill-turn machines.
2. Know and apply C-axis toolpath modules in Mastercam lathe.
3. Know how to generate mill operations from Mastercam lathe.

Overview

Regular lathes and turning centers are capable of performing various types of turning operations. Mill-turn machines can perform both turning and milling operations. Mill-turn machines can cut a complicated part that often requires multiple CNC machines to complete the project, in a single machine. This chapter presents the basic concept of mill-turn machines and C-axis toolpath modules in Mastercam lathe. Two projects with tutorials are provided to show how to generate mill-turn toolpaths in Mastercam.

23.1 Mill-Turn Machines

The main feature of mill-turn machines is to add milling operations to CNC turning centers. Two main functions are added to the turning centers in order to be capable of performing milling operations; **live tool** and **spindle axis control**. The cutters in regular turning centers can not rotate. The work piece is clamped on the chuck and rotates with the spindle. The cutter moves on the XZ-plane to cut the work piece while it is rotating. The live tools are referred to as the self-rotating tools that can rotate in the specified direction while still able to move in X and Z directions. Live tools include end mills, drills, taps, etc. They are used to **cut profiles, pockets**, and **holes**. The use of mill-turn machines can significantly reduce the number of machine setups, shorten setup times and machining processes for completing a project.

To allow the milling or drilling operations performed at any orientation around the cylindrical work piece, the spindle axis must be able to be oriented to any angle. The spindle axis is rotated about the Z-axis, therefore, it is assigned as the C-axis. A simple mill-turn machine has at least three control axes; X, Z, and C. X and Z axes control the tool movement on XZ-plane, while C axis control the orientation of the spindle rotation.

23.2 C-Axis Toolpaths

Mastercam Lathe Version 7 provides a group of new toolpath modules for generating toolpaths to perform milling and drilling operations in mill-turn machines. This toolpath module group is referred to as C-axis toolpaths in Mastercam Lathe. C-Axis toolpaths include the following seven functions:

Face ctr:	generates contour operation with the axis of end mill parallel to spindle axis.
Cross ctr:	generates contour operation with the axis of end mill perpendicular to spindle axis.
C-Axis ctr:	generates contour operation with the axis of end mill parallel to Y axis.
Face drl:	generates drill operation with the axis of drill parallel to spindle axis.
Cross drl:	generates drill operation with the axis of drill perpendicular to spindle axis.
Mill ctr:	generate contour operation with the axis of end mill perpendicular to the specified Tplane.
Mill drl:	generates drill operation with the axis of drill perpendicular to the specified Tplane.

The commands to access the C-axis toolpaths are:

Select Toolpaths → Next menu → C-axis

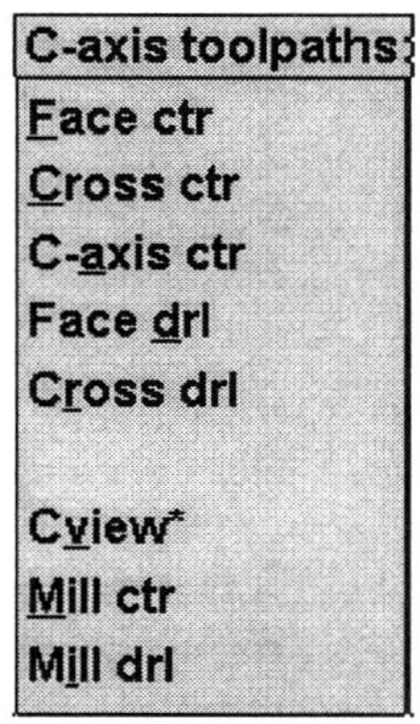

Face Contour (Face ctr)

The face contour function generates the contouring toolpath along chained entities (Figure 23.1). The Cplane and Tplane are automatically set to a side view in order to have the tool axis being parallel to the spindle axis. The axis of end mill is parallel to the spindle axis (Figure 23.2).

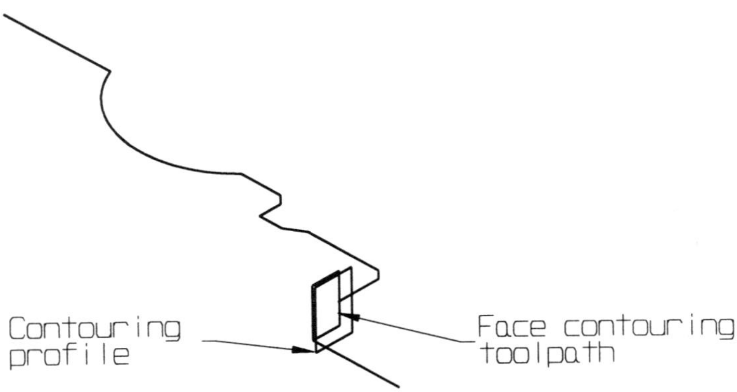

Figure 23.1

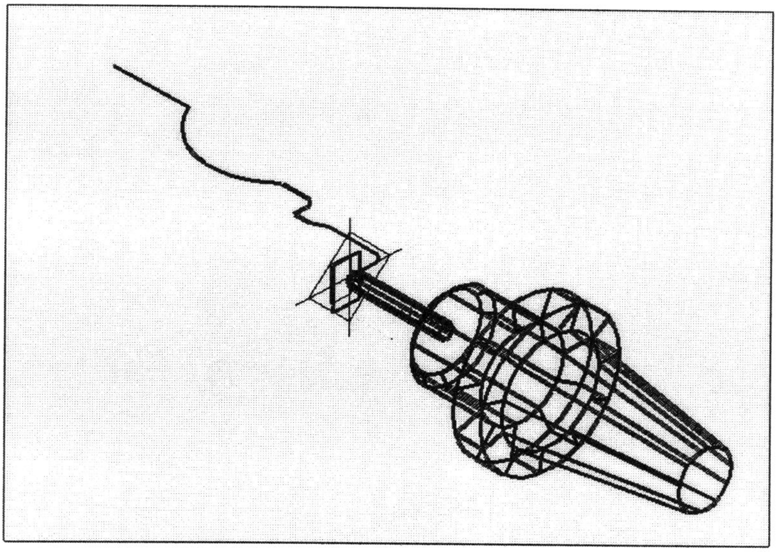

Figure 23.2

Cross Contour (Cross ctr)

The cross contour function generates the contouring toolpath along chained entities (Figure 23.3). The Cplane and Tplane are automatically set to 3 (back view) in order to have the tool axis being perpendicular to the spindle axis and parallel to horizontal plane. The axis of end mill is parallel to the Y axis (Figure 23.4).

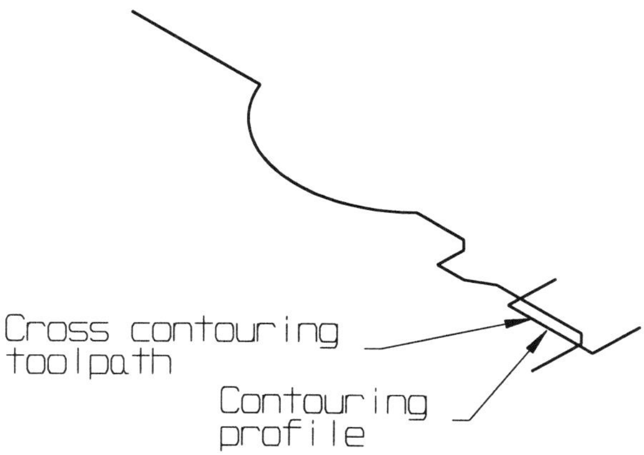

Figure 23.3

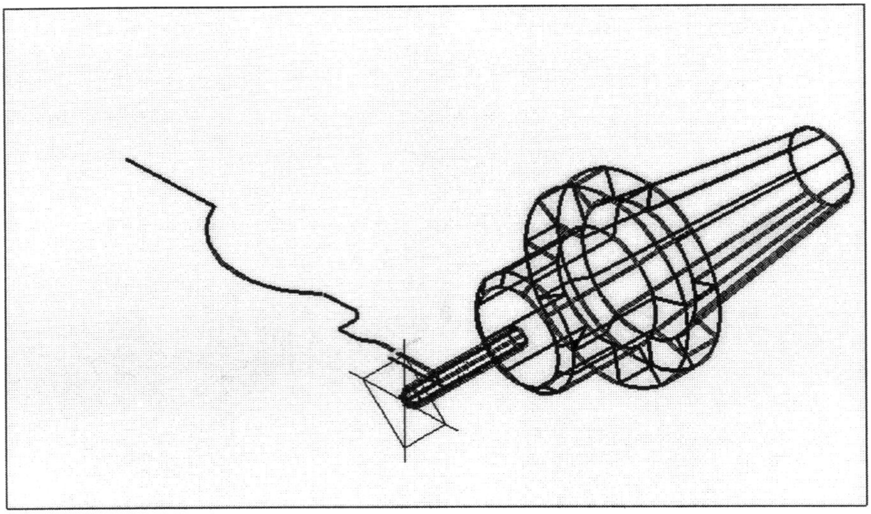

Figure 23.4

C-Axis Contour (C-axis ctr)

The C-axis contour function generates the contouring toolpath along a chained profile that can be in any orientation. Use the view defining utility to define a special view if standard views are not used. This is a useful function to generate contouring toolpaths for cutting slope profiles.

Mill Contour (Mill ctr)

The mill contour function can generate contouring toolpath along chained entities with Cplane and Tplane being set to any view orientation. This is a more versatile function that can perform all contouring functions. Figure 23.5 shows four contouring operations that use top, side, and back views as Cplane and Tplane, respectively.

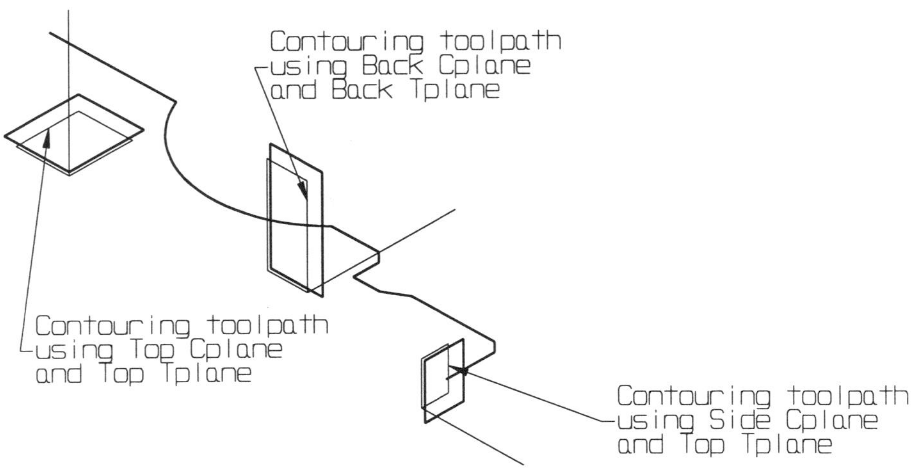

Figure 23.5

Face Drill (Face drl)

The face drill function generates drilling toolpaths for drilling a series of holes at the specified locations. The Cplane and Tplane are automatically set to Side view in order to have the axis of drill being in the spindle direction. Figure 23.6 shows an example of face drilling for eight holes.

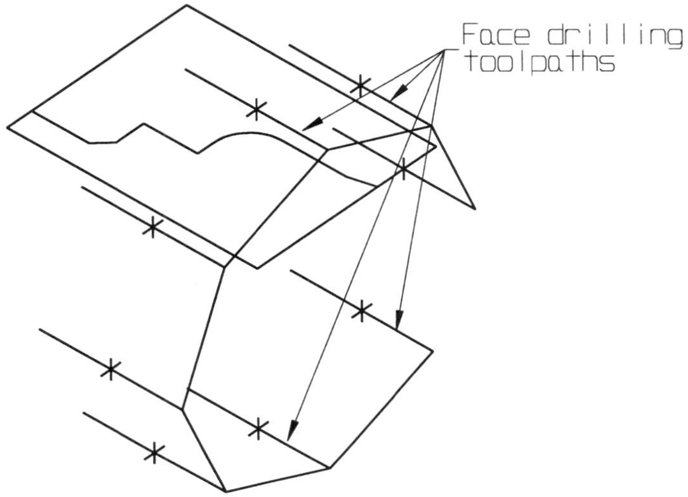

Figure 23.6

Cross Drill (Cross drl)

The cross drill function generates drilling toolpaths for drilling a series of holes at the specified locations. The Cplane and Tplane are automatically set to 3 (Back view). The orientation of the drilling points are all pointing to the axis center point (Figure 23.7).

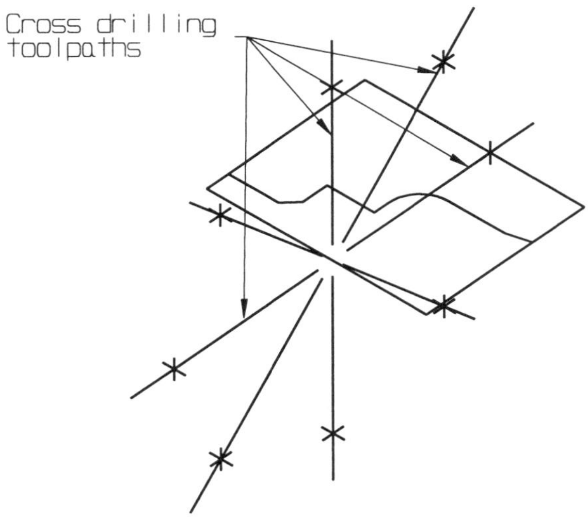

Figure 23.7

1 Mill Drill (Mill drl)

The mill drill function generates drilling toolpaths for drilling a series of holes at the specified locations at any Cplane and Tplane orientation. This is a more versatile drill function than the other two types. Figure 23.8 shows the orientation of the drilling is in the Top view.

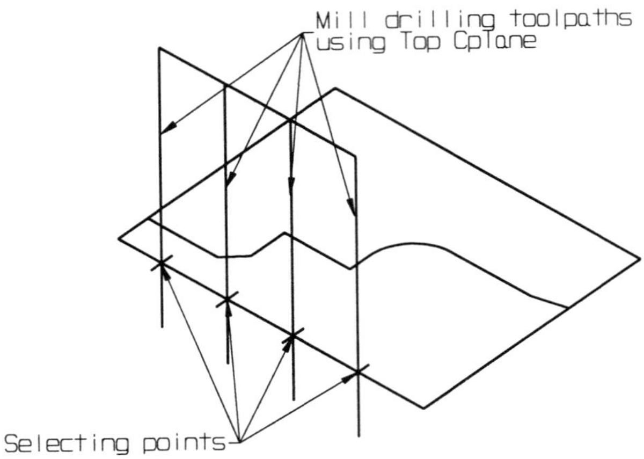

Figure 23.8

Project 1. Using C-axis functions

This project uses four C-axis functions to generate two contouring operations and two drilling operations. Figure 23.9 shows part geometry and the toolpaths for four operations.

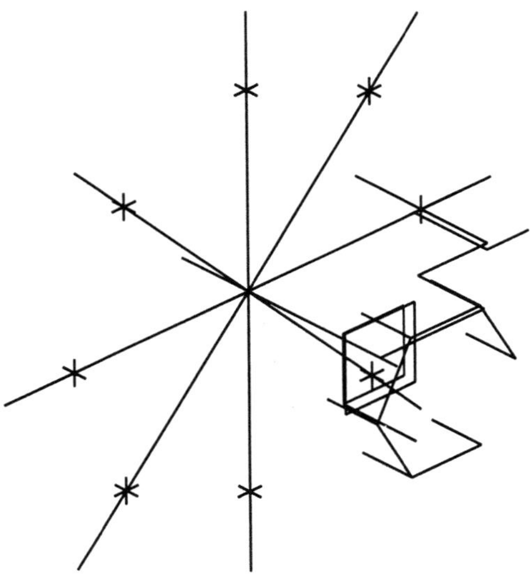

Figure 23.9

⌛Tips

1. Create a four-line profile and two lines as basic geometry.
2. Create a rectangle in the side view.
3. Create a circular array of six points in the side view.
4. Create second circular array of eight points in the side view.
5. Use the face contour function to generate toolpaths along the rectangle.
6. Use the cross contour function to generate toolpath along a line.
7. Use the face drill function to generate toolpaths for drilling six holes in the facing direction.
8. Use the cross drill function to generate toolpaths for drilling eight holes in the cross direction.
9. Backplot the toolpaths to verify the toolpath model.
10. Save the toolpath file as c-axis.

Step 1. Create a four-line profile.

Select **Create → Line → Multi → Values**

Enter the following five point coordinates:

0,0
3,0
3,-1
5,-1
5,-3

The four-line profile is created as in Figure 23.10.

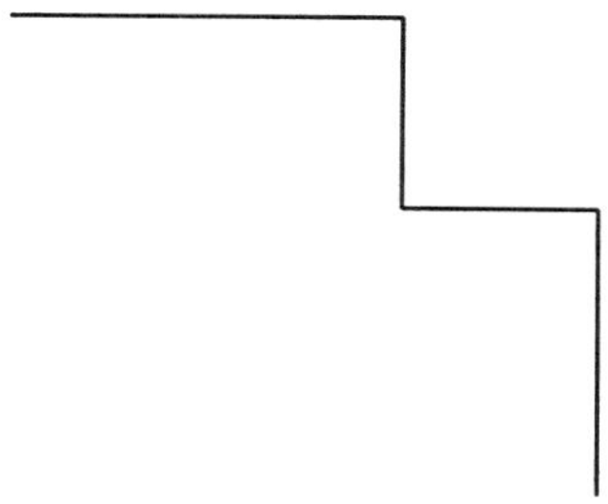

Figure 23.10

Step 2. Add two lines.

Select **BACKUP → Endpoints**

Enter **(0,0.25)** and **(0,-3)** as two endpoints for the first line

Enter **(4.8,-0.9)** and **(4.8,-2.0)** as two endpoints for the second line

Select **Gview → Isometric**

The isometric view of new drawing appears in Figure 23.11.

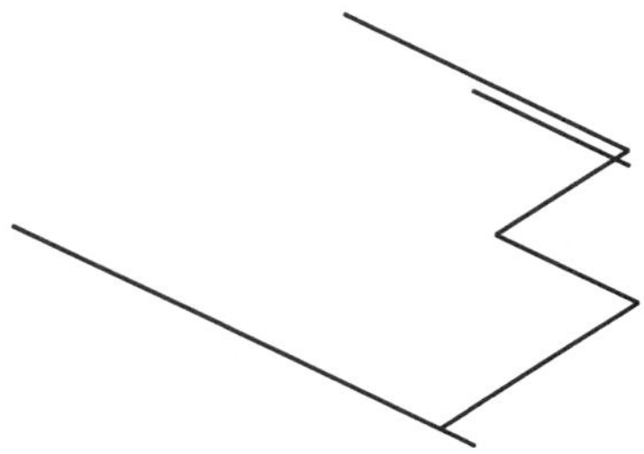

Figure 23.11

Step 3. Create a rectangle in the side view in level 2.

Select **Level**, then enter **2**
Select **Cplane → Side**
Select **MAIN MENU → Create → Rectangle → 2 points → Values**
Enter **(-0.5,-0.5)** and **(0.5,0.5)** as two corners of the rectangle
The rectangle is added as in Figure 23.12.

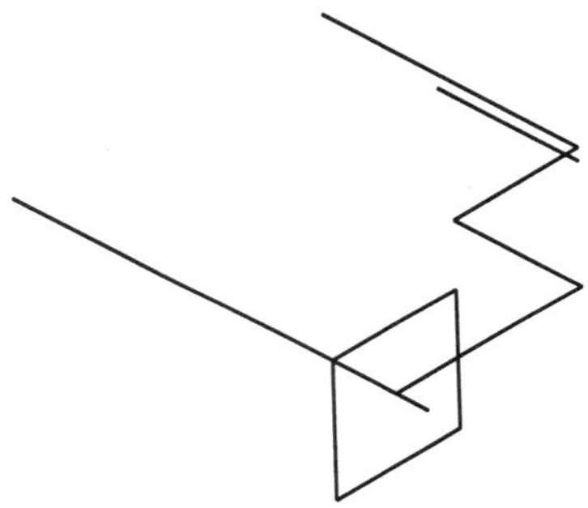

Figure 23.12

Step 4. Create a circular array of six points.

Select **Level**, then enter **3**
Select **MAIN MENU → Create → Point → Bolt circle**
Enter **(0,0)** as the center point
Enter the radius: **1**
Enter the starting angle: **0**
Enter the incremental angle: **60**
Enter the number of points: **6**
The eight points are added as in Figure 23.13.

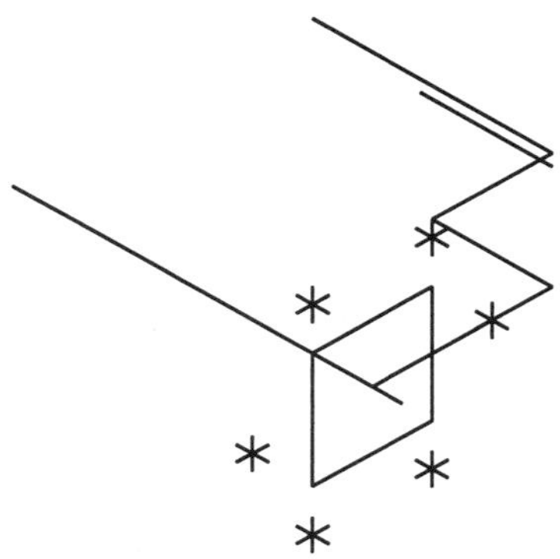

Figure 23.13

Step 5. Create another circular array of eight points.

Select **Level**, then enter **4**
Select **Z**, then enter **–2**
Select **BACKUP → Bolt circle**
Enter **(0,0)** as the center point
Enter the radius: **2.5**
Enter the starting angle: **0**
Enter the incremental angle: **45**
Enter the number of points: **8**
The new drawing becomes Figure 23.14.

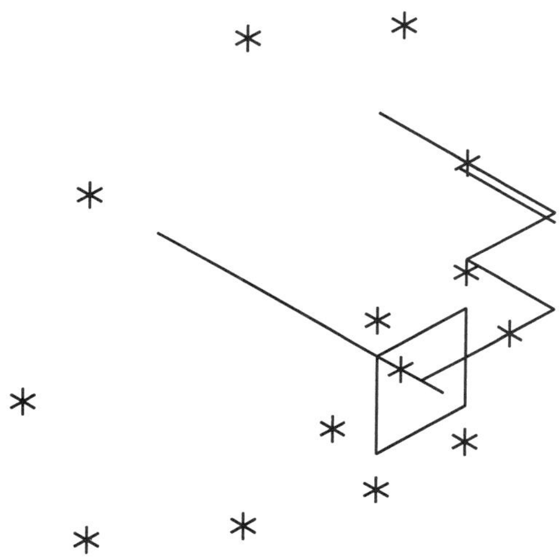

Figure 23.14

Step 6. Make levels 3 and 4 invisible.

Select **Level**, then enter **5**
Select **Vis. Levels**
Toggle levels 3 and 4 to invisible (dimmed)
Select **OK**
The new drawing becomes Figure 23.15.

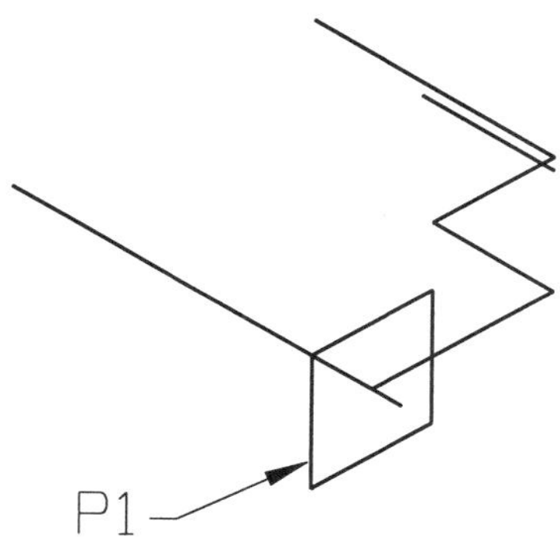

Figure 23.15

Step 7. Initiate the face contour function.

Use the pick point in Figure 23.15.

Select **MAIN MENU → Toolpaths → Next menu → C-axis → Face ctr**

File name for NCI: **c-axis**

Select **Chain**, then pick **P1**

Select **Done**

Set the contour parameters as below.

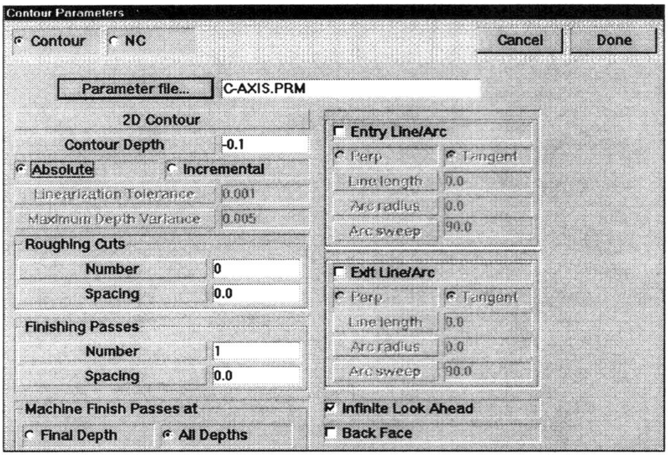

Step 8. Define the NC parameters as below.

Click the "NC" button to open NC parameters menu

Select the button next to the "Tool Ref" parameter to open the Tool Manager menu

Click the right mouse button, then select "Get from library"

Select **tool #232** (1/8" flat end mill)

Select **OK → OK**

Set the NC parameters as below.

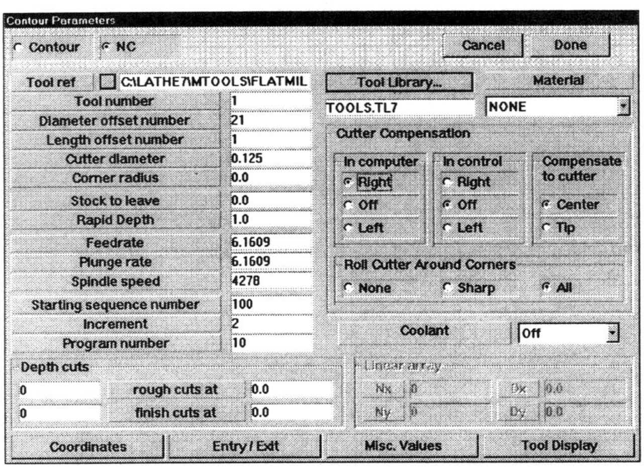

Select **Done → Write**

The face contouring paths are shown in Figure 23.16.

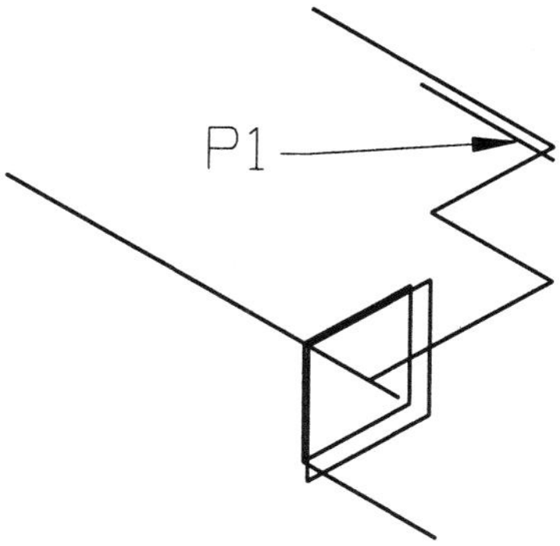

Figure 23.16

Step 9. Initiate the cross contour function.

Use the pick point in Figure 23.16.
Select **Cross ctr → Single**
Pick **P1** to select the line
Select **Done**
Set the contouring parameters as below.

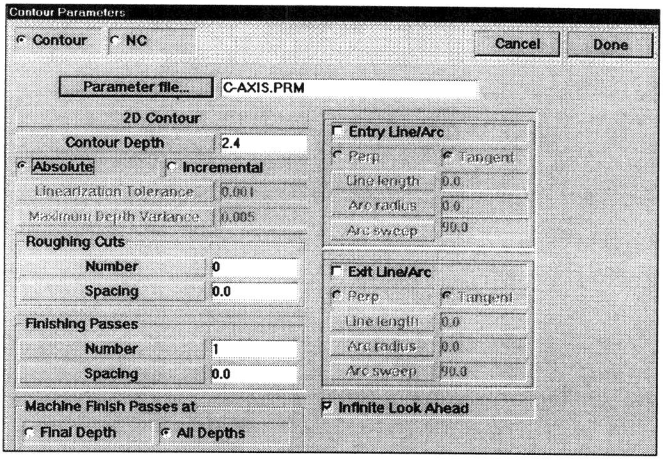

Step 10. Define the NC parameters.

Click the "NC" button
Click the button next to the Tool Ref parameter to open the Tool Manager menu
Click the right mouse button, then select "Get from library"
Select **tool #234** (3/16" flat end mill)
Select **OK**

Select tool **number 2** from the Tools Manager menu
Select **OK**

Set the NC parameters as below.

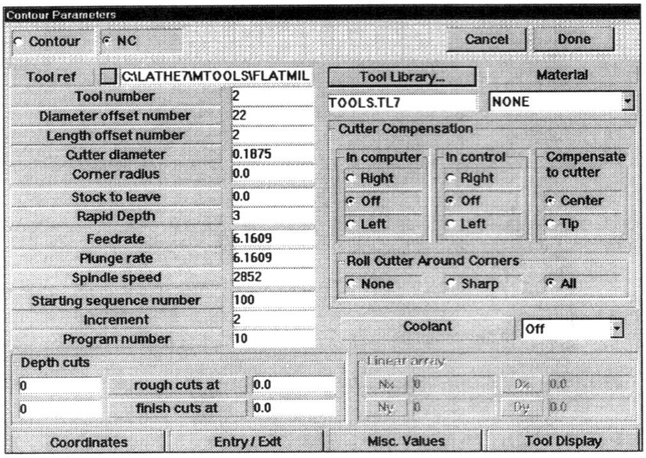

Select **Done** → **Write**
The cross contouring toolpath is added as in Figure 23.17.

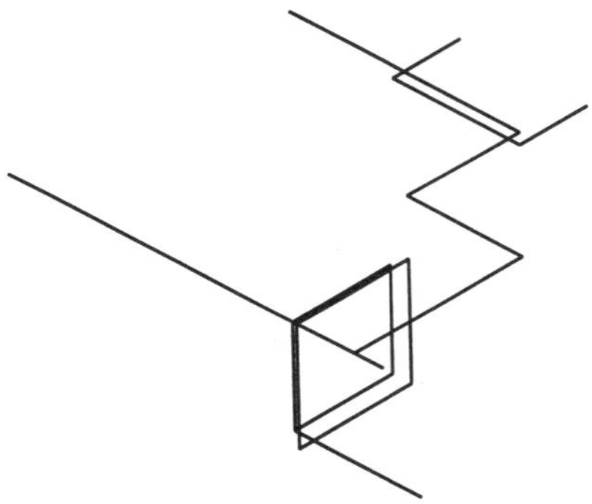

Figure 23.17

Step 11. Make level 3 visible.

Select **Level** → **Vis. levels**
Toggle level 3 to **On** (highlighted)
Select **OK** to return to graphic mode
The six points appear as in Figure 23.18.

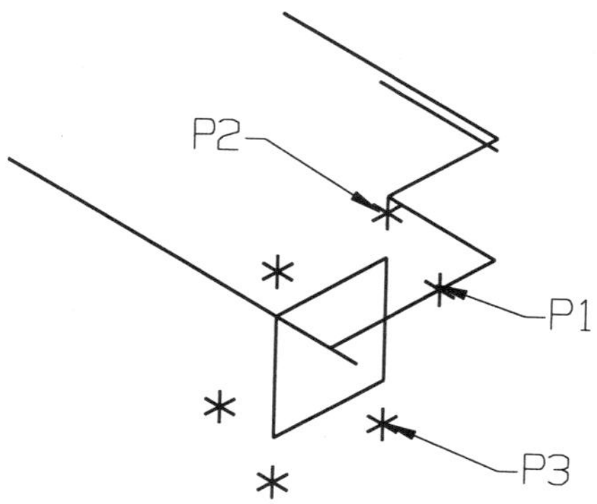

Figure 23.18

Step 11. Initiate the face drill function.

Use the pick points in Figure 23.18.

Select **MAIN MENU → Toolpaths → Next menu → C-axis → Face drl → Automatic**

Sequentially pick **P1, P2,** and **P3** to automatically select all points

Select **Yes** to "Draw the path between points?"

Select **Yes** to "Is the path OK?"

Set the drilling parameters as below.

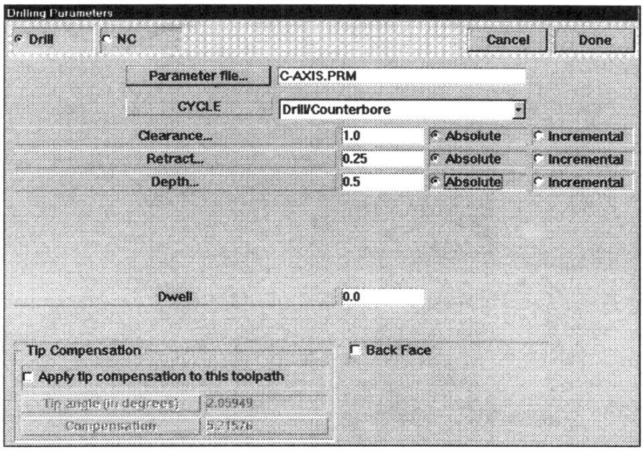

Step 12. Define the NC parameters.

Click the "NC" button

Click the button next to the "Tool ref" parameter to open the Tool Manager menu

Click the right mouse button, then select "Get from library"

Select **tool #84** (3/16 drill)

Select **OK → OK**

Set NC parameters as below.

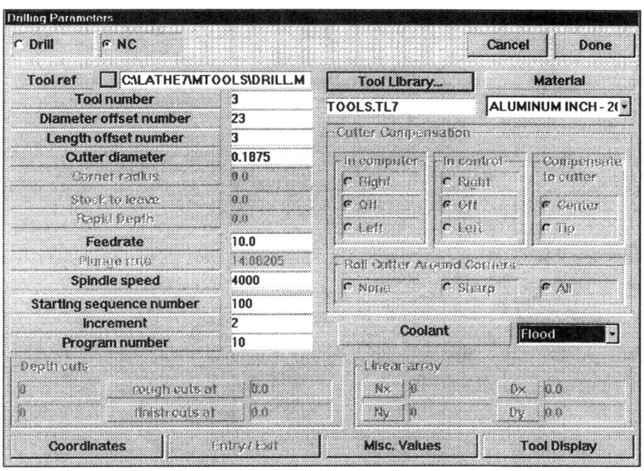

Select **Done → Write**

Select **No** to "Repeat with same points?"

The toolpaths for drilling six points in the facing direction are shown in Figure 23.19.

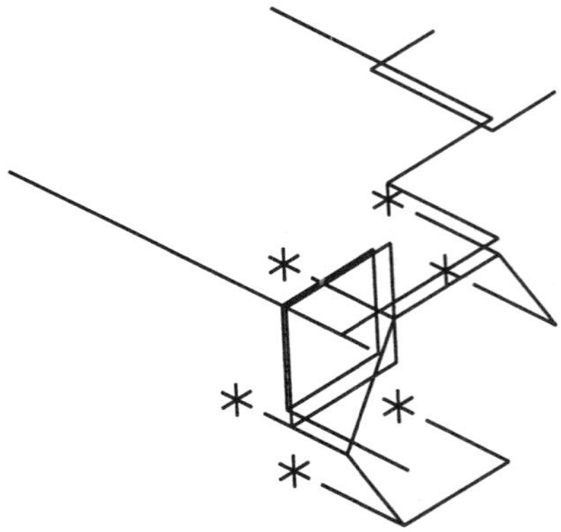

Figure 23.19

Step 13. Make level 3 invisible and level 4 visible.

Select **Level → Vis. level**
Toggle level **3** to invisible (dimmed)
Toggle level **4** to visible (highlighted)
Select **OK**
The new drawing becomes Figure 23.20.

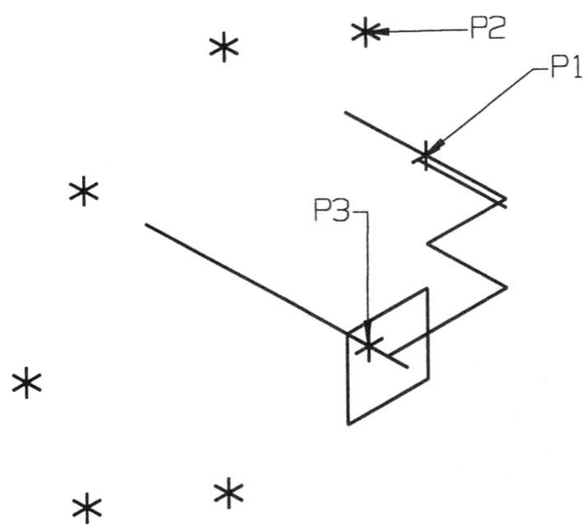

Figure 23.20

Step 14. Initiate the cross drill function.

Use the pick points in Figure 23.20.
Select **Cross drl → Automatic**
Sequentially pick **P1**, **P2**, and **P3** to select the eight points
Select **Yes** to "Draw the path between points?"
Select **Yes** to "Is the path OK?"

Set the drill parameters as below.

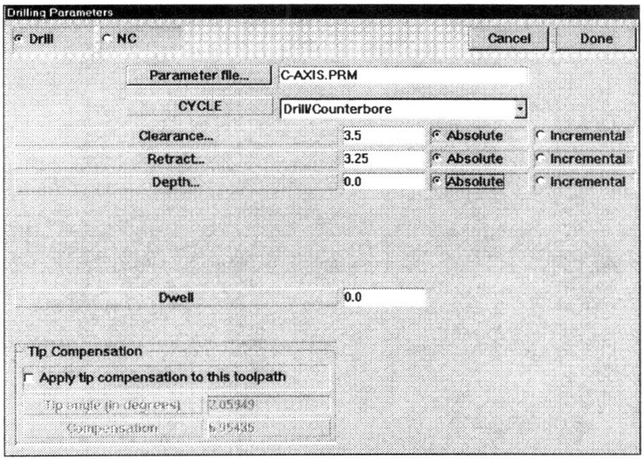

Step 15. Define the NC parameters.

Click the "NC" button
Click the button next to the "Tool ref" parameter
Click the right mouse button, then select "Get from library"
Select **tool #104** (1/4" drill)
Select **OK**
Select tool **number 4** from the Tool Manager menu, then select **OK**
Set the NC parameters as below.

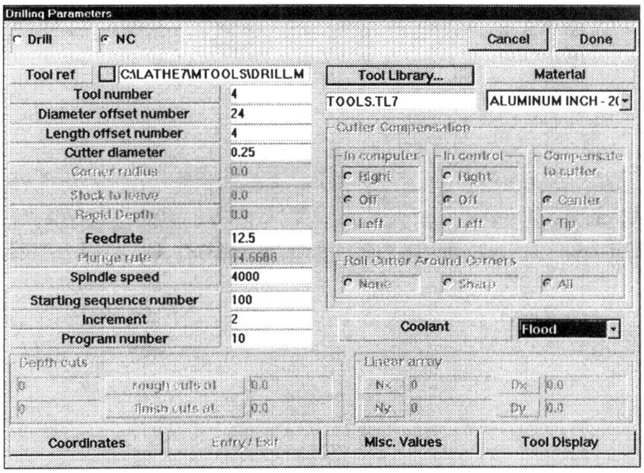

Select **Done** → **Write**
Select **No** to "Repeat with same points?"

Step 16. Make all levels visible.

Select **Level** → **Vis. levels** → **All On** → **OK**

Step 17. Backplot the toolpaths for four operations.

Select **MAIN MENU** → **Toolpaths** → **Operations to open Operations Manager menu**
Select **Select All** → **Backplot**

Set display and backplot parameters to desired settings
Select **Run**
The four operations are animated on the screen as shown in Figure 23.21.

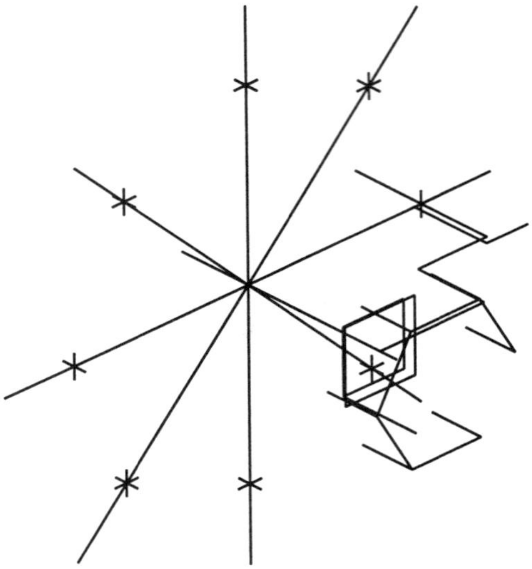

Figure 23.21

Step 18. Save the toolpaths.
Select **MAIN MENU → File → Save**
File name to save: **c-axis**

23.3 Mill Toolpaths

The mill toolpaths utility is not used to generate toolpaths for lathes, turning centers, or mill-turn machines. Instead, it uses the lathe geometry and the mill toolpath functions to generate toolpaths to be run on machining centers. When Mill Toolpaths is selected, the coordinate system will change to the regular mill coordinate system and all mill toolpath functions become available for use. The way to generate toolpaths using mill toolpath functions from the Lathe environment is identical to those given in chapters 7, 8, 9, 14, 15, and 16. The Mill Toolpaths functions are listed here.

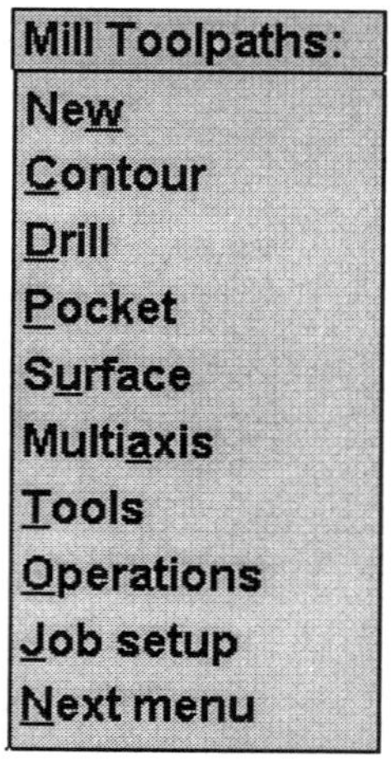

Project 2. Generating mill-pocket toolpath

This simple project shows how to use part geometry created in Mastercam Lathe and milling toolpath function in Mastercam Mill to generate toolpath. The part geometry and toolpath are shown in Figure 23.22.

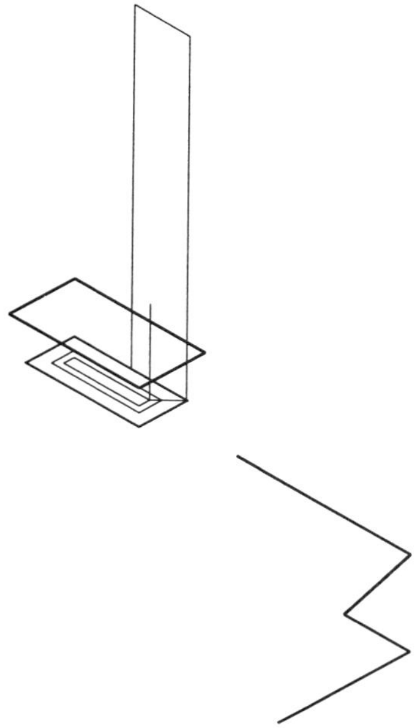

Figure 23.22

Tips 1. Create a four-line profile.

2. Create a rectangle in the top view.

3. Use the mill-pocket function to generate pocketing toolpath.

4. Backplot the pocketing toolpath to animate on the screen.

5. Save the toolpath file as mill-pocket

Step 1. Create a four-line profile.

Select **MAIN MENU → Create → Line → Multi → Values**

Enter the following five point coordinates to create a four-line profile:

0,0 3,0 3,-0.75 5,-1 5,-3

The four-line profile appears as in Figure 23.23.

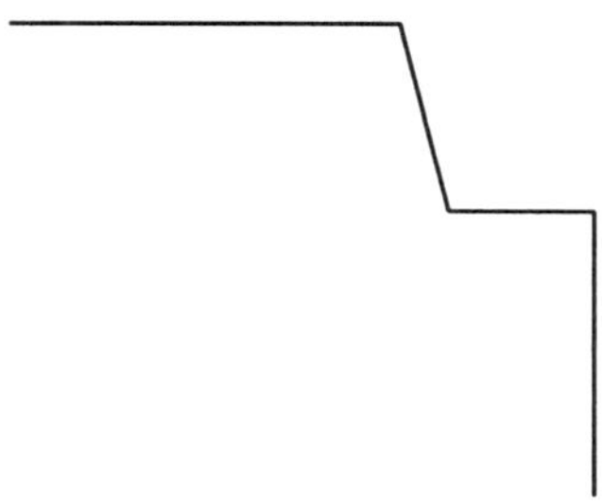

Figure 23.23

Step 2. Create a rectangle in top view and change to level 2.

Select **Level**, then enter **2**

Select **Cplane → Top**

Select **Z**, then enter **3**

Select **Gview → Isometric**

Select **MAIN MENU → Create → Rectangle → 2 points**

Enter the following two sets of point coordinates for the rectangle:

-2.75,-0.375

-1.25,0.375

The rectangle is added as in Figure 23.24.

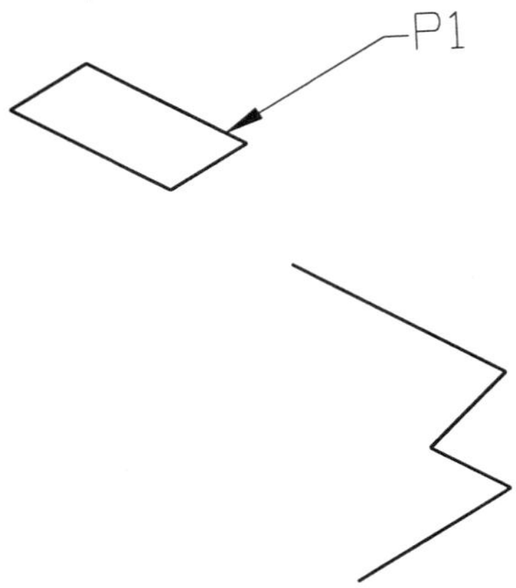

Figure 23.24

Step 3. Initiate the mill-pocket function.

Use the pick point in Figure 23.24.

Select **MAIN MENU → Toolpaths → Next menu → Mill → Pocket**

File name for NCI: **mill-pocket**

Select **Chain**, then pick **P1**

Select **Done**

Click the right mouse button, then select "Get from library"

Select **tool #234** (3/16" end mill)

Select **OK**

Set the tool parameters as below.

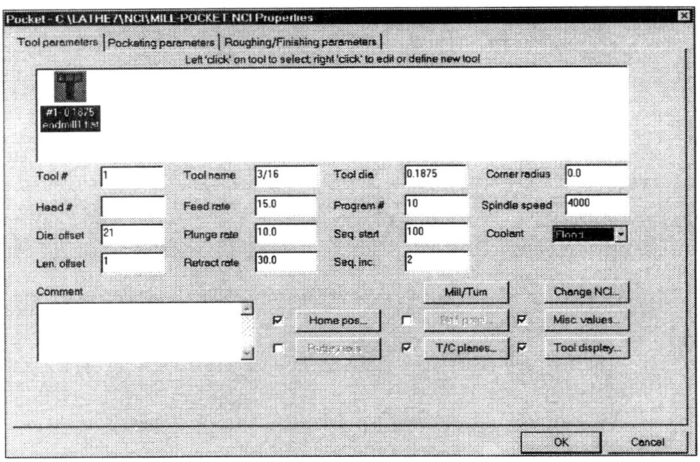

Step 4. Define the pocketing parameters.

Click on the "Pocketing parameters" button
Set the pocketing parameters as below.

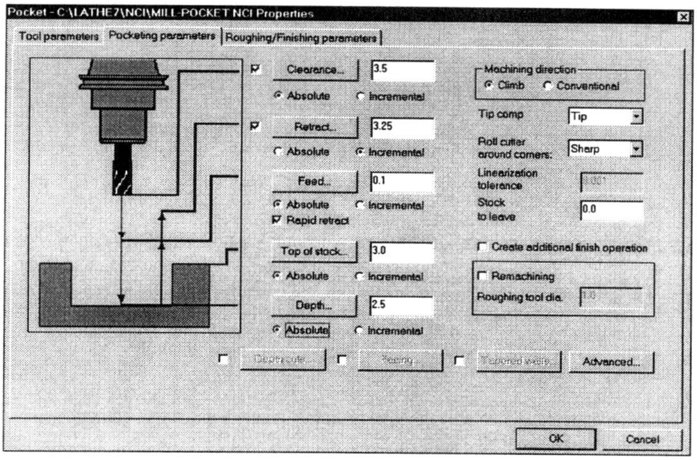

Step 5. Define the roughing and finishing parameters.

Click on the "Roughing/Finishing parameters" button
Set the roughing and finishing parameters as below.

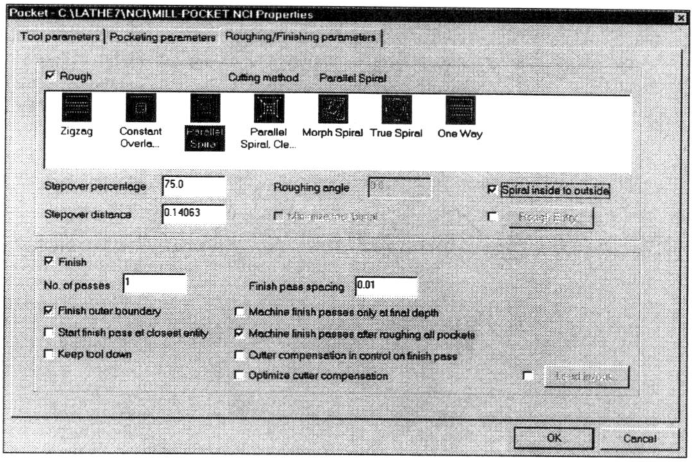

Select **OK** to generate the pocketing toolpaths

The pocketing toolpaths are added as in Figure 23.25.

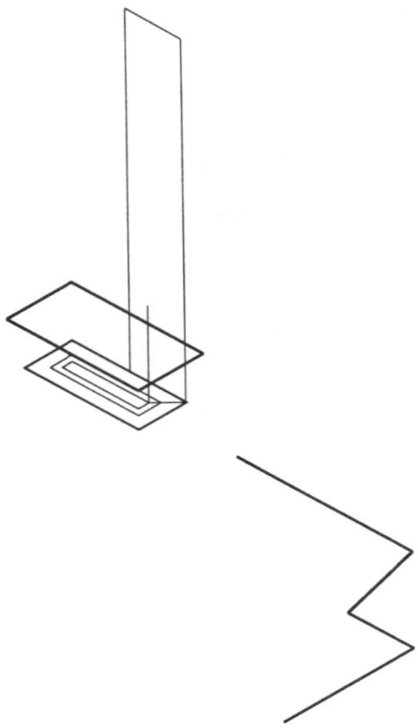

Figure 23.25

Step 6. Backplot the toolpath.

Select **BACKUP → BACKUP → Operations**
Select **Backplot**
Set the display and backplot parameters to desired settings, then select **Run**
The pocketing toolpath is animated on the screen.

Step 7. Save the toolpath file as mill-pocket.

Select **MAIN MENU → File → Save**
File name to save: **mill-pocket**

Exercises

1. What is the main feature of mill-turn machines?
2. List the two main functions added to mill-turn machines from turning center.
3. What are live tools?
4. Describe how to control the orientation of the spindle axis in mill-turn machines.
5. List and briefly describe the seven C-axis toolpath functions.
6. Describe how to generate mill operations from the Mastercam Lathe environment.

Chapter 24

File Conversion

Objectives:

1. Be familiar with the Mastercam file transfer utility.
2. Convert geometry files to and/or from another CAD/CAM system.
3. Convert the files of earlier Mastercam versions to the current version.

Overview

Each CAD/CAM system uses a particular file format to store the drawing data. Normally, the drawing file created in one CAD/CAM system can not be directly used in other CAD/CAM systems. This necessitates a file conversion utility to convert the drawing data from one format to another. For this reason, file conversion has become an important practice in today's design and manufacturing industry.

Mastercam provides file conversion facility to allow the geometry models be converted to and/or from a file format that can be used by another CAD/CAM system or earlier Mastercam releases. For most popular 3D CAD/CAM packages, Mastercam can import and export 3D lines, arcs and circles from the exchange format of the package. This exchange format is usually an ASCII file, not the standard binary file created by the package when the model is saved. For example, AutoCAD's exchange file has a .DXF extension and the normal drawing file is saved as a .DWG extension.

24.1 Mastercam File Conversion

Mastercam uses the menu tree shown in Figure 24.1 to step through the bi-direction file conversion process.

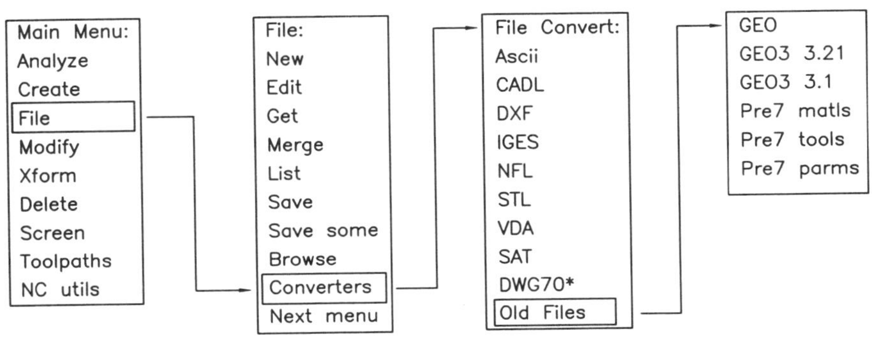

Figure 24.1

There are nine conversion utilities in Mastercam to link with popular CAD/CAM systems. The features of these utilities are summarized in Table 24.1 on the next page.

Table 24.1 Features of Mastercam file conversion facility

Utility Name	CAD/CAM System	Dimension	File Extension	Comment
ASCII	N/A	2D and 3D	.DOC	Converts XY and XYZ coordinates into points, lines or splines
CADL	CADKEY	3D	.CDL	CADL (CADKEY Advanced Design Language) is the format used by CADKEY (CADKEY, Inc.)
DXF	AutoCAD	3D	.DXF	DXF (Drawing Interchange Format File) is used by AutoCAD (Autodesk, Inc.) It is a popular way to exchange geometry files between different CAD/CAM systems.
IGES	Public Standard	3D	.IGS	IGES is a US standard and is used by many full-scale CAD systems.
NFL	Anvil	2D	.NFL	NFL is used by Anvil (MCS, Inc.)
STL	N/A	3D	.STL	Stereolithography files used by rapid prototyping
VDA	German Standard	3D	.VDA	VDA(Verband der Automobilindustrie) is a German standard.
SAT	ACIS-based Solid Models	3D	.SAT	ACIS-based solid models. Import only.
DWG70*	AutoCAD	3D	.DWG	An extra cost add-on for AutoCAD DWG files.
Old Files	Mastercam	(See the following three options)		Old Mastercam file converter for GEO, GE3 3.21 and GE3 3.1.
-GEO	Mastercam	2D	.GEO	GEO files are 2D geometry files used by Mastercam prior to V3.00.
GE3 3.21	Mastercam	3D	.GE3	These GE3 files were created by Mastercam V3.21, and can be imported and exported through this function.
GE3 3.1	Mastercam	3D	.GE3	GE3 files created by a 286 CAM system (CAM3, LATHE, FABRIX,WIRE)
Pre7	Matls			Converts material libraries created in versions of Mastrcam prior to 7.0.
Pre7	Tools			Converts tool libraries created in versions of Mastrcam prior to 7.0.
Pre7	parms			Converts parameter libraries created in versions of Mastrcam prior to 7.0.

In practice, DXF and IGES files are the most common ways to transfer files from Mastercam to another CAD/CAM system. These two conversion utilities are available in most commercial-based CAD/CAM programs.

Users should be aware that the file conversion between different CAD/CAM systems is not always perfect. In same cases, entities are incorrectly converted or simply lost in the conversion process. For example, **surface information** created by Mastercam might not be transferred to other systems. Therefore, users should verify the results after the conversion. Table 24.2 shows the entity types supported by Mastercam's conversion.

Table 24.2 Entity types supported by Mastercam

Utility Name	Entity types supported by Mastercam conversion
ASCII	Point, line and spline
CADL	Point, line, polyline, arc, circle, spline, conic, view, color, level, array, text, leader and witness
DXF	Point, line, polyline, arc, circle, trace, block, endblk, insert, vertex and sequend. Splines are not supported (use IGES).
IGES	This public standard is considerably more complex than other file formats and is used by many full-scale CAD/CAM/CAE system. Limitation: IGES does not support parametric surfaces and splines with a degree greater than three.
NFL	Point, line and circle
STL	Standard stereolithography file format
VDA	Point, pet (sequence of points), circle, curve and SURF (polynomial surface of arbitrary order) as defined in Version 2.0 of VDA. Colors and levels are not supported.
SAT	Geometry curves and surfaces
Old Files	(See the following three options)
-GEO	2D point, line and arc
GE3 3.21	Most Mastercam entities. Newer data types, such as Trimmed surfaces, are not supported.
GE3 3.1	Only read/write the GE3 file from/to Mastercam "286" data path.

1

24.2 File Conversion Projects

Six projects are presented in this section. They lead you through the step-by-step procedures to transfer drawing files between Mastercam/AutoCAD R.12, R13 and R14 and Mastercam/CADKEY 97 using the appropriate file conversion utilities. It is assumed that users already know how to load and save the drawing files in each individual package.

Project 1. Transfer a 3D drawing file to AutoCAD R.12, R13 and R14 using the DXF utility.

A geometry file (Array1.MC7) as shown in Figure 24.2 is used to convert into a DXF file. Then this file can be used in the AutoCAD system.

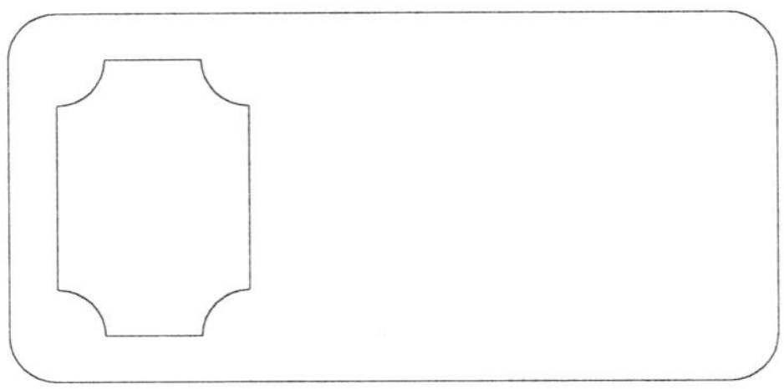

Figure 24.2

To create a DXF file from Mastercam

Step 1. Load the geometry file CAR.MC7.

Select **MAIN MENU → File → Get**
Enter file name: **array1**
Select **Yes** to save the current part

The car drawing shall appear on screen as Figure 24.3.

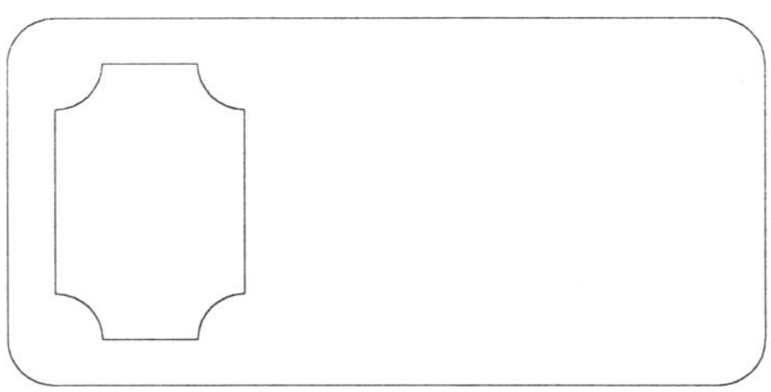

Figure 24.3

Step 2. Initiate the convert utility.

Select **MAIN MENU → File →Converters → DXF → Write file**
Enter file name: **a:\array1** *(or enter a desired file name)*

Note:You don't need to enter the file extension. Mastercam will automatically add the file extension DXF to the file.

To receive a DXF file from AutoCAD

In AutoCAD, use the following commands to read-in an ASCII-format DXF file.

Step 1. Initiate DXFIN function.

After entering AutoCAD, a command prompt should appear.
Command: **DXFIN**
(A pop-up dialogue box will ask for the DXF file name.)
File: **a:\array1** *(or enter a desired file name)*

Note: Prior to Release 11, any extension would cancel the command; after Release 11, extensions were acceptable. Here we do not need one. AutoCAD R.12, R13 and R14 will use the default file extension as DXF.

The car drawing should appear in the top view as in Figure 24.4.

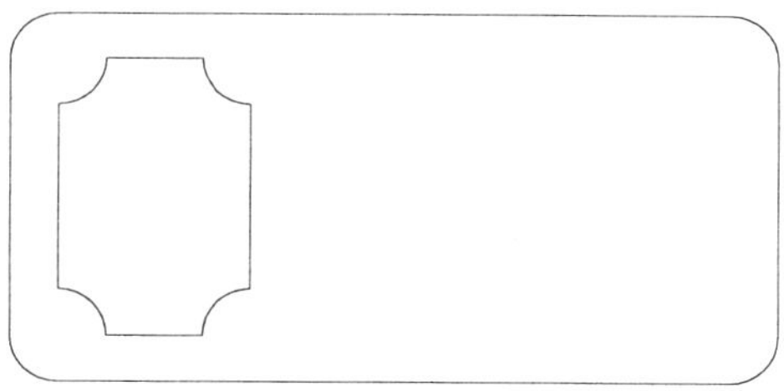

Figure 24.4

Step 2. Display the drawing in isometric view.

Command: **VPOINT**
Rotate/(View point): **1,-1,1**

The car drawing now is appeared in the isometric view as shown in Figure 24.5.

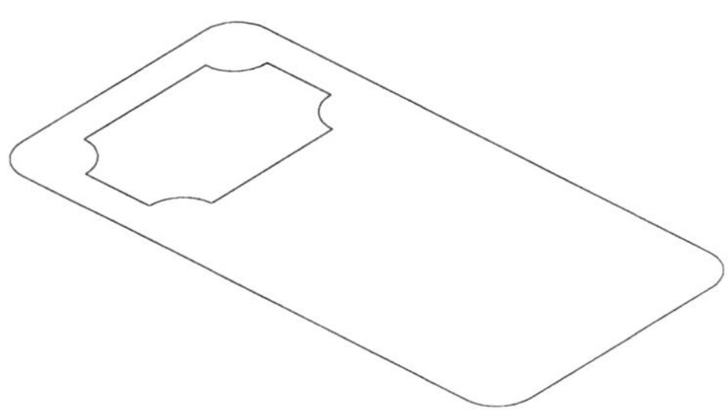

Figure 24.5

2 **Step 3. Save the drawing as CAR.**

Command: **Save**

(A pop-up dialogue box will ask for the drawing file name)

File: **CAR**

Note: During DXF transfer, parametric splines, NURB and trimmed surfaces, dimensions and notes are not converted.

Project 2. Transfer a 3D drawing file from AutoCAD R.12 to Mastercam using the DXF utility

The car drawing we imported into AutoCAD through the DXFIN command as described in project 1 becomes a DWG file. In this project, we use the same car drawing in AutoCAD but save it to the DXF format. This file is then read into Mastercam. Note that the DXF files created by AutoCAD R13 and R14 cannot be converted to MasterCAM v7 properly at the time of this writing.

To create a DXF file from AutoCAD

Step 1. Load the car drawing CAR in AutoCAD.

Command: **OPEN**

(A pop-up dialogue box will ask for the drawing name)

File: **array1**

Step 2. Initiate the DXFOUT function.

Command: **DXFOUT**

(A pop-up dialogue box will ask for the DXF file name.)

File name: **a:\array1** *(or enter a desired file name)*

Enter decimal places of accuracy (0-16)/Entities/Binary <6>: **6**

(This question is asked only by AutoCAD R12. It will allow you to select the accuracy of exported entities. In general, the default of 6 will be accurate enough.)

To receive a DXF file from Mastercam

Step 1. Initiate the convert utility.

Select **MAIN MENU → File → Converters →DXF → Read file**

Enter file name: **a:\array1** *(or enter a desired file name)*

(Mastercam will automatically enter the file extension DXF to the file.)

Select **Yes** to delete the current point.

The car drawing appearing on screen is in the top view as shown in Figure 24.6.

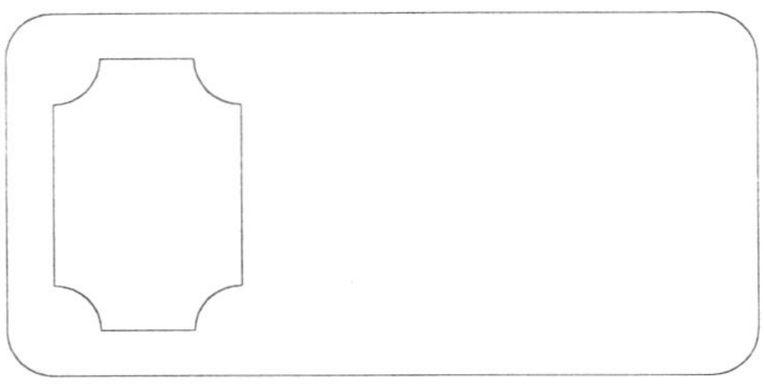

Figure 24.6

Step 2. Change Gview to isometric view.
Select **Gview → Isometric**

Press **Alt + F1** to fit the drawing on screen. The car drawing in isometric view will appear as in Figure 24.7 .

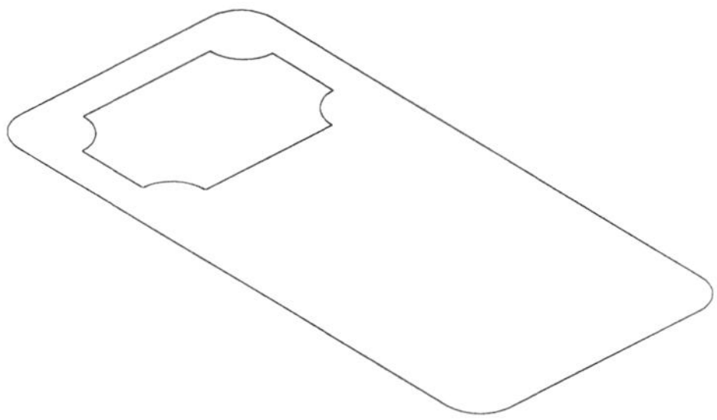

Figure 24.7

Project 3. Transfer a 3D drawing file to AutoCAD R.12 using the IGES utility.

Note: IGESin and IGESout are discontinued commands in AutoCAD R13 and R14. However, the procedure can be applied in Autodesk Mechanical Desktop.

A geometry file (fans.MC7) as shown in Figure 24.8 will be converted into an IGES file. This file is then imported into AutoCAD. Note that IGESIN and IGESOUT are discontinued commands in AutoCAD R13 and R14. However, the procedure can be applied in Autodesk Mechanical Desktop.

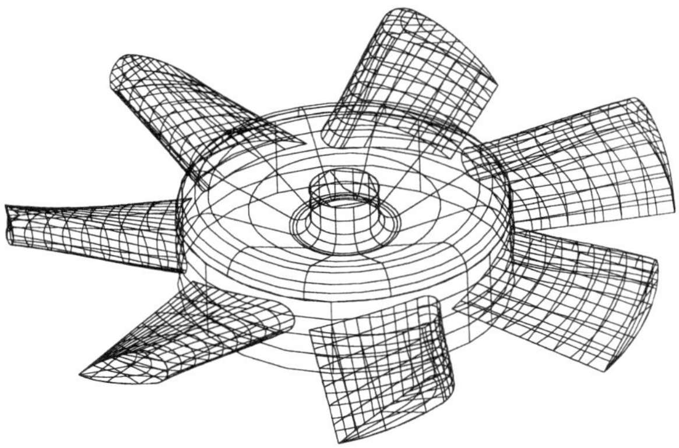

Figure 24.8

To create an IGES file from Mastercam

Step 1. Load the geometry file CALIPER.GE3.
Select **MAIN MENU → File → Get**
Enter file name: **fans**
Select **Yes** to save the current part

The caliper drawing should appear on screen as Figure 24.9 on the next page.

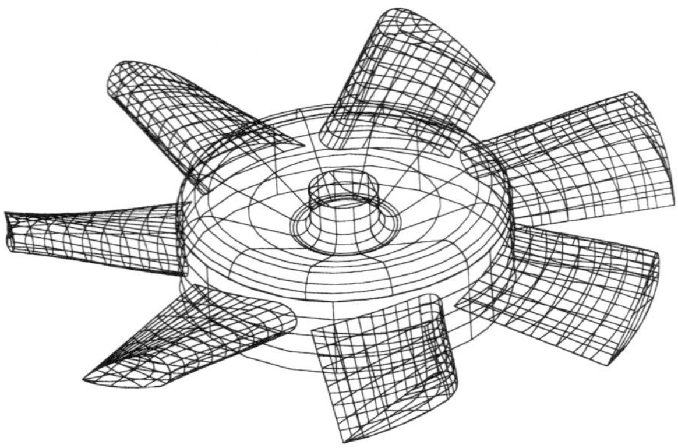

Figure 24.9

Step 2. Initiate the convert utility.

Select **MAIN MENU → File →Converters → IGES → Write file**
Enter file name: **a:\fans** *(or enter a desired file name)*
(Mastercam will automatically enter the file extension IGS to the file.)
Enter a comment: ←

To receive an IGES file from AutoCAD R.12

To receive an IGES file in AutoCAD, begin a new drawing. Then execute the IGESIN commands as list below.

Step 1. Initiate IGESIN function.

Command: **IGESIN**
(A pop-up dialogue box will ask for the IGES file name.)
File name: **a:\fans** *(or enter a desired file name)*
(AutoCAD will use the default file extension as IGS.)

The caliper drawing should appear in the top view as in Figure 24.10.

Figure 24.10

Step 2. Display the drawing in isometric view.

Command: **VPOINT**
Rotate/(View point): **1,-1,1**

The caliper drawing now appears in the isometric view as shown in Figure 24.11.

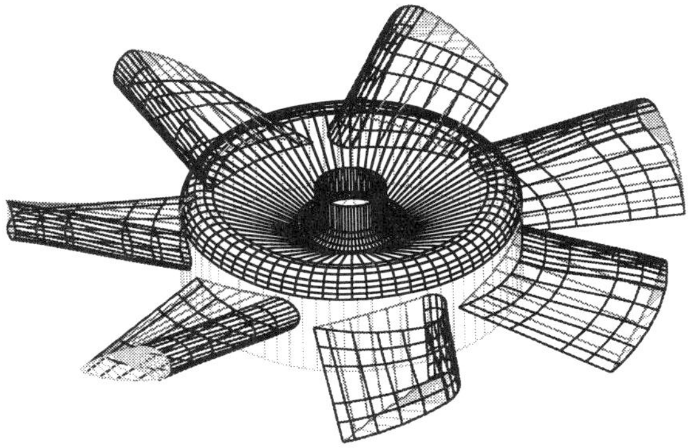

Figure 24.11

Step 3. Save this drawing as CALIPER.

Command: **SAVE**
(A pop-up dialogue box will ask for the drawing file name)
File: **fans**

Note: During IGES transfer, NURB and trimmed surfaces are not converted.

Project 4. Transfer a 3D drawing file from AutoCAD R.12 using IGES utility

Note: IGESin and IGESout are discontinued commands in AutoCAD R13 and R14. However, the procedure can be applied in Autodesk Mechanical Desktop.

The caliper drawing we imported into AutoCAD with the IGESIN command as described in project 3 becomes a DWG file. In this project, we use the same caliper drawing in AutoCAD but save it to an IGES format. This file is then read in Mastercam. Note that IGESIN and IGESOUT are discontinued commands in AutoCAD R13 and R14. However, the procedure can be applied in Autodesk Mechanical Desktop.

To create an IGES file from AutoCAD

Step 1. Load the caliper drawing CALIPER.

Command: **OPEN**
(A pop-up dialogue box will ask for the drawing file name)
File: **fans**

Step 2. Initiate the IGESOUT function.

Command: **IGESOUT**
(A pop-up dialogue box will ask for the IGES file name.)
File name: **A:\fans** *(or enter a desired file name)*
(AutoCAD will enter the default file extension IGS.)

To receive an IGES file from Mastercam

Step 1. Initiate the convert utility.

Select **MAIN MENU → File →Converters → IGES → Read file**
Enter file name: **a:\fans** *(or enter a desired file name)*
(Mastercam will automatically use the file extension IGS for the file.)

Select **Done** to use the default IGES READ parameters.
Select **Yes** to delete the current part.
Select **Yes** to save the current file, or **No** to discard it.
The caliper drawing shown in the top view should appear as in Figure 24.12.

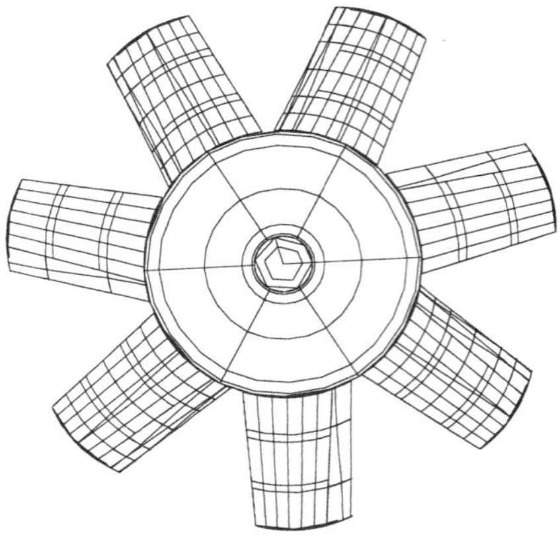

Figure 24.12

Step 2. Change Gview to isometric view.

Select **Gview → Isometric**

Press **Alt + F1** to fit the drawing on screen. The drawing shown in isometric view should resemble Figure 24.13.

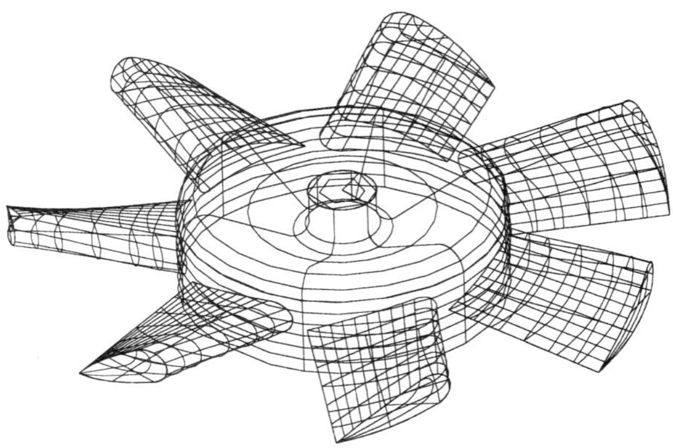

Figure 24.13

Project 5. Transfer a 3D drawing file to CADKEY 97 using the CADL utility. 5

The file (VISLAND.MC7) as shown in Figure 24.14 is used to convert into a CADL file. This file is then used in the CADKEY system.

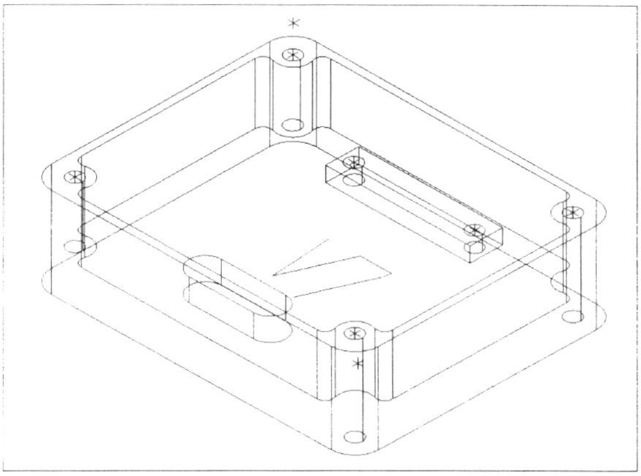

Figure 24.14

To create a CADL file from Mastercam

Step 1. Load the geometry file Visland.MC7.

Select **MAIN MENU → File → Get**
Enter file name: **visland**
Select **Yes** to delete the current part

The part drawing should appear on screen as Figure 24.14.

Step 2. Initiate the convert utility.

Select **MAIN MENU → File → Converters →CADL → Write file**
Enter file name: **a:\CADLTEST** ← *(or enter a desired file name)*
(Mastercam will automatically enter the file extension CDL to the file.)

To receive a CADL file from CADKEY

This section has to be executed in CADKEY. In CADKEY, the following commands allow you to read-in an ASCII-format CADL file, stores drawing primitives and entities and execute CADL commands.

Step 1. Initiate CADL function.

Select **APPLICATION → CADL EXECUTE.....**
Enter CADL file name: **a:\CADLTEST** ← *(or enter a desired file name)*

The part drawing should appear in the top view. Select **View →Zoom → Autoscale** to see the complete drawing as in Figure 24.15.

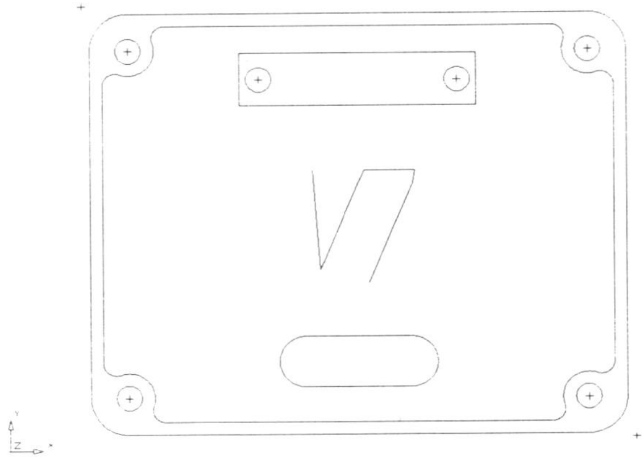

Figure 24.15

Step 2. Display the drawing in isometric view.

Select **3D Display icon** (the 14th icon in the toolbar)
Enter view number or choose menu option (1-10): **7**
Select **View →Zoom → Autoscale**

The part drawing should appear in isometric view as in Figure 24.16.

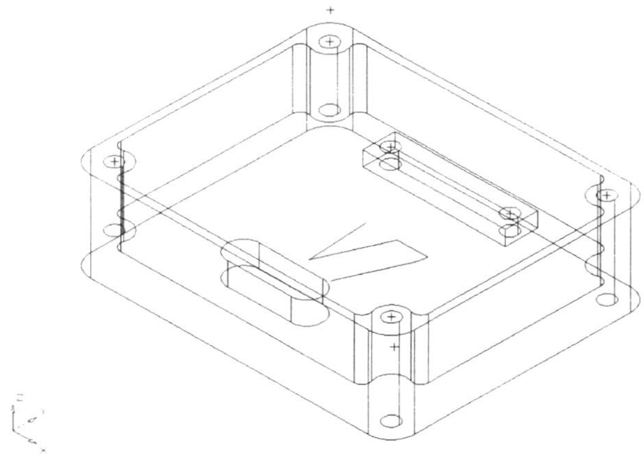

Figure 24.16

Note: During the CADL transfer, NURB and trimmed surfaces, dimensions and notes are not converted.

Step 3. Save this part drawing as CADTEST.

Select **File →Save As**
Enter part file name to save: **CADTEST**
Write the Part Description in the pop-up form and select **OK**

Project 6. Transfer a 3D drawing file from CADKEY 97 using CADL utility. 6

The part drawing we imported to CADKEY through CADL commands as described in project 5 becomes a PRT file. In this project, we use the same part drawing in CADKEY but save it to the CADL format. This file is then read into Mastercam.

To create a CADL file from CADKEY

In CADKEY, the following commands allow you to write drawing entities into an ASCII-format CADL file.

Step 1. Load the part drawing file CADTEST.

Select **File → Open.... → NO**
Enter part name to load: **CADTEST**

Step 2. Initiate the CADL function.

Select **File → Export → CADKEY CADL...**
Enter CADL file name: **B:\CADLTEST** ← *(or enter a desired file name)*
Choose output option.
Select **Select → All Ent → Done**

To receive a CADL file from Mastercam

Step 1. Initiate the convert utility.

Select **MAIN MENU → File → Converters → CADL → Read file**
Enter file name: **a:\CADLTEST** ← *(or enter a desired file name)*
(Mastercam will automatically use the default file extension CDL to retrieve the file.)
Select **Yes** to delete the current part.

The part drawing appearing on screen is in the top view as shown in Figure 24.17.

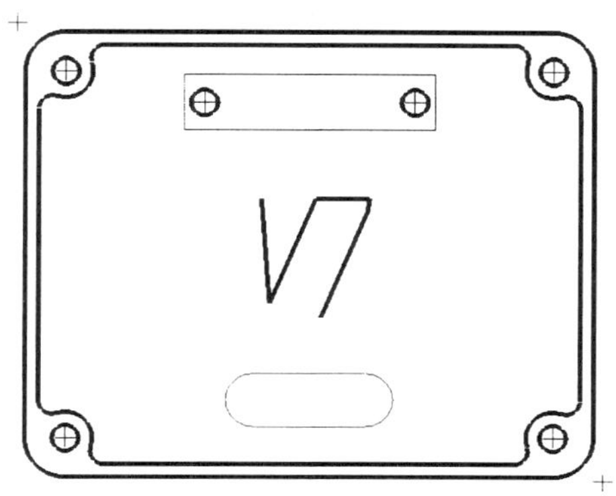

Figure 24.17

Step 2. Change the drawing to isometric view.

Select **Gview → Isometric**

Press **Alt + F1** to fit the drawing on screen. The drawing in isometric view should look like Figure 24.18.

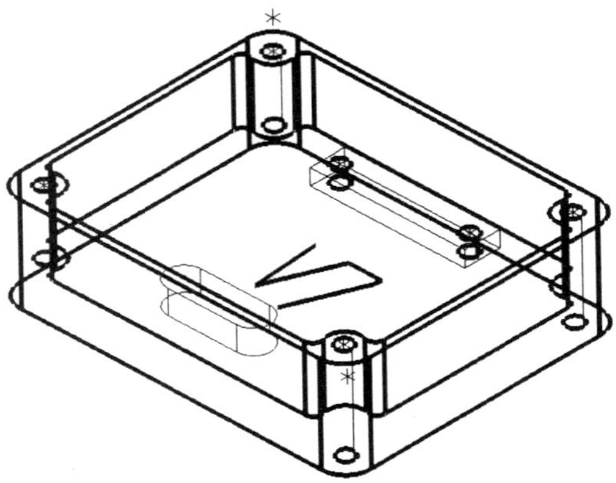

Figure 24.18

Exercises

1. How many file conversion utilities are available for Mastercam?

2. What is the name of the utility used to transfer files to/from AutoCAD?

3. What is the name of the utility used to transfer files to/from Mastercam?

4. What is the US standard for transferring drawing files between CAD/CAM systems?

5. What are the two most common file formats used to transfer drawings between different CAD/CAM systems?

6. List four entity types that can be transferred between Mastercam and AutoCAD using the DXF utility.

Chapter 25

Post Processor Customization

Objectives:

1. Know the file format of NCI and NC files.
2. Be familiar with the file structure of post processor files (.PST).
3. Know the commonly used variables for forming the NC programs.
4. Customize a post processor for a CNC mill or machining center.

Overview

The output of the CAM system is a toolpath file in generic form. The toolpath file in Mastercam is called the **NCI file**. This file can not be used directly in a CNC machine. It should be converted to the NC program acceptable to the CNC controller. The conversion of a generic toolpath file to the NC file is implemented in a software program called a **post processor**. A unique combination of machine and controller requires a dedicated post processor.

This chapter covers the structure of NCI and NC files, post processor structure, and post processor customization for a CNC mill. A sample customized post processor is given for the Fanuc-based controllers. This sample post processor is intended for 3-axis machining including rapid traverse, linear interpolation, circular interpolation, and canned cycles. Rotary-axis machining is not covered. This sample post processor is tested by a project having three machining operations including contouring, drilling, and tapping. The NC file of this project is then listed for checking its accuracy and correctness.

25.1 NCI Files and NC Files

The use of various toolpath modules in a CAM system generates a toolpath file that contains all information required to machine a part. This toolpath data is called an NCI file in Mastercam. It is written in a generic or intermediate format. NCI files are the input to all post processors. They are ASCII text files that contain all the necessary information to produce an NC program. *Note*, an NCI file can not be directly used as an input to a CNC controller. These NCI files must be converted into NC programs by a post processor which is another software program.

NCI file structure format

The data in an NCI file is arranged in pairs of lines. The first line is the operation line that contains a single number to indicate the type of operation such as a linear move, circular move, drill cycle, start of file, miscellaneous functions, etc. The second line is the data line that contains the information that defines the operation.

The data in the operation lines can be one of the following:

```
0:  rapid traverse
1:  linear interpolation
2:  circular interpolation (clockwise)
3:  circular interpolation (counter-clockwise)
11:  five axis interpolation
80:  cancel drill cycle
81:  start drill cycle
100:  drill hole
1000:  null tool change
1001:  start of file
1002:  tool change
1011:  define miscellaneous real numbers
1012:  define miscellaneous integers
1013:  define miscellaneous parameters
```

The above NCI operations can be classified into the following **four** groups:

- Motion operations
- Canned cycle operations
- File organization
- Miscellaneous operations

Motion operations

There are **two** motion operations: linear move and circular move. The linear move includes rapid traverse and linear interpolation.

Linear move (rapid and linear interpolation) The operation line contains only one digit, either 0 or 1. A zero indicates the rapid traverse and one linear interpolation. There are five pieces of information in the data line. The file format for the linear move is:

```
g (0 = rapid traverse, 1 = linear interpolation)
1  2  3  4  5
|  |  |  |  └── feedrate
|  |  |  └── Z-coordinate
|  |  └── Y-coordinate
|  └── X-coordinate
└─ cutter compensation in control
```

Keys for cutter compensation in control:

```
0 = no cutter compensation in control
40 = cancel cutter compensation in control
41 = cutter compensation in control (left)
42 = cutter compensation in control (right)
140 = last line or arc in the contour
```

Example 1:

The following pair of NCI lines defines the linear interpolation instruction that moves the cutter to a specified position (5.0,3.0,-1.0) with a feedrate of 10 inches/min and cutter compensation to left.

```
1
└──── G1 (linear interpolation)
41  5.0  3.0  -1.0  10.0
│   │    │    │     └──── F10.0
│   │    │    └──── Z-1.0
│   │    └──── Y3.0
│   └──── X5.0
└──── G41 (cutter compensation left)
```

Circular move The operation line for the circular move also contains only one digit; either 2 or 3. A two indicates clockwise direction and three indicates the counter-clockwise direction. There are **eight** pieces of information in the data line to define the circular move as shown below.

```
g (2 = clockwise, 3 = counter-clockwise)

1 2 3 4 5 6 7 8
│ │ │ │ │ │ │ └──── feedrate
│ │ │ │ │ │ └──── Z-coordinate
│ │ │ │ │ └──── Y-coordinate of arc center
│ │ │ │ └──── X-coordinate of arc center
│ │ │ └──── Y-coordiante of arc end point
│ │ └──── X-coordiante of arc end point
│ └──── cutter compensation in control
└──── plane selection
```

Keys for plane selection

0 = XY-plane
1 = YZ-palne
2 = XZ-plane

Example 2:

The following two NCI lines move the cutter in a clockwise direction to cut a circular arc to (5,3,-0.5) with the arc center at (2,3).

```
2
└──── G2 (circular move (clockwise))
0  42  4.0  3.0  2.0  3.0  -0.5  7.5
│  │   │    │    │    │    │     └──── F7.5
│  │   │    │    │    │    └──── Z-0.5
│  │   │    │    │    └──── J3.0
│  │   │    │    └──── I2.0
│  │   │    └──── Y3.0
│  │   └──── X5.0
│  └──── G42 (cutter compensation right)
└──── XY-plane selection
```

Canned cycle operations

Three operations are involved in canned cycles:

1. start drill cycle (81)
2. drill hole (100)
3. cancel drill cycle (80)

Start drill cycle (81) The operation line of the start drill cycle is 81. There are twelve pieces of information in the data line. It has the following format.

81 (Start drill cycle)

1 2 3 4 5 6 7 8 9 10 11 12

- 12 — height to retract cutter to after first peck
- 11 — height to retract cutter to between holes
- 10 — amount to retract for chip break
- 9 — safety distance for chip break
- 8 — amount of second peck increment
- 7 — amount of first peck increment
- 6 — feedrate (inches/minute)
- 5 — dwell
- 4 — Z-coordinate
- 3 — Y-coordiante
- 2 — X-coordinate
- 1 — cycle type

Keys for cycle type:

0 = simple drilling
1 = peck drilling
2 = chip break
3 = tap
4 = bore #1
5 = bore #2
6 = misc. #1
7 = misc. #2

Example 3:

The pair of NCI file lines given below initiate the peck drilling cycle to drill a deep hole located at (3.5,4.0).

81 start drill cycle

1 3.5 4.0 -2.5 0.0 7.5 0.5 0.35 0.0 0.0 0.3 0.1

- 1 — peck drilling cycle
- 3.5 — X3.5
- 4.0 — Y4.0
- -2.5 — Z-2.5
- 0.0 — Dwell = 0.0
- 7.5 — F7.5
- 0.5 — First peck amount = 0.5
- 0.35 — Q = 0.35
- 0.0 — Safety distance = 0.0
- 0.0 — M = 0.0
- 0.3 — R = 0.3
- 0.1 — E = 0.1

Drill hole (100) When a canned cycle is used to drill more than one hole with the same operating conditions, the canned cycle instruction command (ex. G81) is used in drilling the first hole only because canned cycle commands are the **modal** type; the instruction commands for subsequent holes only require the specification of the coordinates of hole centers. Mastercam uses this procedure: use the start drill cycle (81) operation to define the location and operating conditions of the first hole and use the drill hole (100) operation to specify the center coordinates of the following holes.

The data format for drill hole is:

100 drill hole

1 2 3 4 5

- 1 — not used
- 2 — X-coordinate of hole center
- 3 — Y-coordinate of hole center
- 4 — Z-depth
- 5 — not used

Example 4:

The following pair of data lines specifies that the drilling position is located at (5.5,3.0) and the drilling depth is -1.0.

```
100     drill hole

0 5.5 3.0 -1.0 0
    |   |    |
    |   |    └── Z-1.0
    |   └─────── Y3.0
    └─────────── X5.5
```

Cancel drill cycle The cancel drill cycle operation has a blank data line as shown below.

```
80      cancel drill cycle

blank line
```

File Organization

Two types of file structure data lines are used to organize the part program. One is for start of file and tool change, and the other is end of file.

Start of file (1000, 1001, 1002) The start of file data lines contain the information about tooling (size, offset, and compensation), coolant control, spindle speed, feedrate, home position, and rapid position. This set of information is required for tool change and start of part program. The start of file data lines have the following data format.

```
f         (1000, 1001, or 1002)

1 2 3 4 5 6 7 8 9 10 11 12 13 14 15 16 17 18
```

- 18 — rotary axis diameter
- 17 — rotary axis orientation
- 16 — Z-home position
- 15 — Y-home position
- 14 — X-home position
- 13 — Z-rapid position
- 12 — Y-rapid position
- 11 — X-rapid position
- 10 — coolant (0: off, 1:on)
- 9 — feedrate (inches/minute)
- 8 — spindle speed in RPM
- 7 — cutter compensation
- 6 — tool length offset number
- 5 — tool diameter offset number
- 4 — tool number
- 3 — sequence number increment
- 2 — starting sequence number
- 1 — program number

Keys for f:

1000: null tool change
1001: start of file
1002: tool change

Example 5:

The data (1001) in the operation line for the pair of data lines given below indicates that it is the start of the file. The detailed information in the data line is described by notes.

1001 start of file

10 100 5 1 21 1 0 4000 10.0 1 -0.25 0. 0.5 0. 0. 0. 0 2.

- 10 — program number (O10)
- 100 — starting sequence number (N=100)
- 5 — sequence number increment = 5
- 1 — T1 (tool number)
- 21 — D21 (tool length offset number)
- 1 — H1 (tool length offset number)
- 0 — G0 (rapid move)
- 4000 — S4000 (spindle speed 4000 RPM)
- 10.0 — F10.0 (feedrate 10.0 inches/min)
- 1 — M7 (coolant on)
- -0.25 — X-0.25 (rapid position)
- 0. — Y0. (rapid position)
- 0.5 — Z0.5 (rapid position)
- 0. — X0. (home position)
- 0. — Y0. (home position)
- 0. — Z0. (home position)
- 0 — none rotary axis
- 2. — rotary axis diameter = 2

End of file The data of the operation line for the end of file is 1003. Its data line contains only the X, Y and Z coordinates of the home position. Its data lines format is below:

1003 end of file

1 2 3

- 1 — X home position
- 2 — Y home postion
- 3 — Z home position

Miscellaneous Operations

Miscellaneous data lines are used to assign the values for miscellaneous real variables, miscellaneous integer variables, and miscellaneous parameters.
Three operation line types are:

1011 (define miscellaneous real numbers)

1012 (define miscellaneous integers)

1013 (define miscellaneous parameters)

Define miscellaneous real numbers (1011) The values of the miscellaneous real variables are assigned in this statement. The data format for defining a miscellaneous real number is:

```
1011        define miscellaneous real number

1 2 3 4 5 6 7 8 9 10
|               | |
|               | |__ value of the miscellaneous real variable 10
|               |__ value of the miscellaneous real variable 9
|             -
|         -
|     -
|__ value of the miscellaneous real variable 1
```

Define miscellaneous integers (1012) The values of miscellaneous integer variables are assigned in this statement. The data format for defining a miscellaneous integer is:

```
1012    define miscellaneous intergers

1 2 3 4 5 6 7 8 9 10
|               | |
|               | |__ value of the miscellaneous integer variable 10
|               |__ value of the miscellaneous interger variable 9
|             -
|         -
|     -
|__ value of the miscellaneous integer variable 1
```

Define miscellaneous parameters (1013) Ten miscellaneous parameters are included in this definition statement. They have the following definition format:

1013 define miscellaneous parameters

1 2 3 4 5 6 7 8 9 10

- 10 — not used
- 9 — operation code
- 8 — Z-coordinate of tool plane origin
- 7 — Y-coordinate of tool plane origin
- 6 — X-coordinate of tool plane origin
- 5 — view number
- 4 — compensation to (0: center, 1: tip)
- 3 — tool corner radius
- 2 — tool diameter
- 1 — cutter compensation

Keys for operation modes (parameter 9):

1: 2D contour
2: 3D contour
3: drill
4: pocket
5: ruled
6: 2D swept
7: 3D swept
8: revolution
9: loft
10: coons
11: fillet

Example 6:

The following pair of data lines define the miscellaneous parameters used in a part program. The detailed description of each miscellaneous parameter is provided by a note.

1013 define miscellaneous parameters

42 1.0 0. 1 0 0 0 0 1 0

- 1 — 2D contour
- 0 — Z0 (tool plane origin)
- 0 — Y0 (tool plane origin)
- 0 — X0 (tool plane origin)
- 0 — view number = 0
- 1 — compensation to tool tip
- 0. — tool corner radius = 0
- 1.0 — tool diameter = 1.0
- 42 — cutter compensation (right)

Example 7:

The NCI file of the part program for machining the part shown in Figure 25.1 is listed below. The machining processes include 2D contouring and drilling.

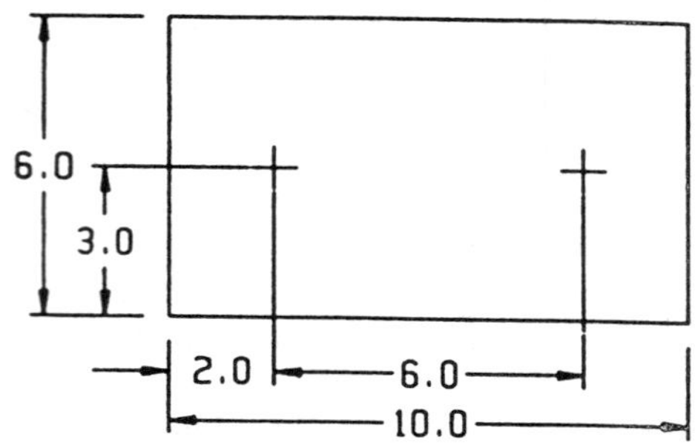

Figure 25.1

NCI file

```
1011                                        define miscellaneous real numbers
0. 118. 0. 0. 0. 0. 0. 0. 0. 0.
1012                                        define miscellaneous integers
1 0 0 0 0 0 0 0 0 0
1013                                        define miscellaneous parameters
41 1. 0. 0 0 0 0 0 1 0
1001                                        start of file
10 100 2 1 21 1 0 2000 10. 1 -0.5 -0.5 0.5 0. 0. 0. 0 2.
0                                           rapid traverse
0 -0.5 -0.5 0.5 -2.
1                                           linear interpolation
0 -0.5 -0.5 -0.5 7.5
1                                           linear interpolation
41 -0.5 6.5 -0.5 10.
1                                           linear interpolation
0 10.5 6.5 -0.5 -1.
1                                           linear interpolation
0 10.5 -0.5 -0.5 -1.
1                                           linear interpolation
140 -0.5 -0.5 -0.5 -1.
1004                                        cancel cutter compensation

0                                           rapid traverse
0 -0.5 -0.5 0.5 -1.
1011                                        define miscellaneous real numbers
0. 118. 0. 0. 0. 0. 0. 0. 0. 0.
1012                                        define miscellaneous integers
1 0 0 0 0 0 0 0 0 0
1013                                        define miscellaneous parameters
0 0.5 0. 0 0 0 0 0 3 0
1002                                        tool change
10 100 2 2 22 2 0 1000 7.5 1 2. 3. 1. 0. 0. 0. 0 2.
81                                          start drill cycle
0 2. 3. -1. 0. 7.5 0.1 0.1 0.01 0. 1. 0.2
100                                         drill hole
0 8. 3. -1. 0.
80                                          cancel drill cycle

1003                                        end of file
0. 0. 0.
```


Mastercam Version 7
Scholar's International Publishing Corp., 1998

The previous NCI file is converted into NC file by a post processor. This NC file is listed below for reference.

```
O O10
N100 G90 G80 G40 G0
N102 T1 M6
N104 G54 G0 X-.5 Y-.5
N106 S2000 M3
N108 G43 H1 Z.5 M08
N110 G1 Z-.5 F7.5
N112 G41 Y6.5 F10.0 D21
N114 X10.5
N116 Y-.5
N118 X-.5
N120 G40
N122 G0 Z.5 F7.5
N124 G91 G28 Z0 M5 M09
N126 G28 X0 Y0
N128 T2 M6
N130 G90 G80 G40 G00
N132 G54 G0 X2. Y3.
N134 S1000 M3
N136 G43 H2 Z1. M08
N138 G98 G81 X2. Y3. Z-1. R.2 F7.5
N140 X8.
N142 G91 G28 Z0 M5 M09
N144 G28 X0 Y0
N146 M30
%
```

25.2 Post Processors

A post processor is a software program that converts the generic toolpath (NCI) file into an NC part program. The combination of controller and machine requires a unique post processor. Therefore a post processor must be customized into a specific format for a particular controller/ machine. Post processors consist of two files: the executable file (MP.DLL for Mill and MPL.DLL for lathe) and an ASCII customization file (.PST). The customization file provides a means of changing the way NC programs are written for a particular controller. The structure of Mastercam's customization file is organized into the following eleven sections:

Section 1:	Information	Section 2:	debugging aids
Section 3:	format statements	Section 4:	format assignments
Section 5:	initialization	Section 6:	question defined
Section 7:	lookup table	Section 8:	string lists
Section 9:	user defined post-blocks	Section 10:	pre-defined post blocks
Section 11:	system questions		

Table 25.1 summarizes the features and includes an example of each section of the customization file of post processors.

Table 25.1 Structure of customization file.

Section	Description	Example
Information	Contains notes and information pertinent to using the post. Typical information is the title block, revision notes and feature description. This part of the file is optional. Each line starts with a remark symbol # and is ignored by the post processor.	#PST file name: MPFAN.PST #Machine model: Generic
Debugging aids	Insert variables "bug1", "bug2","bug3","bug4", and "whatno" to help debugging the post processor by displaying data on the screen.	**bug1 : 0** └─ No NC code is displayed **bug1 : 1** └─ NC code is displayed on screen **bug1 : 3** └─ NC code and leader characters are displayed on screen
Format statements	Define a numeric format to be used for variables. Always include the format statement before the format assignment.	**fs 1 2.4 l t n** - non modal t ─ leave trailing zeros l ─ leave leading zeros .4 ─ four places after decimal points 2 ─ two places before decimal points 1 ─ format number fs ─ format statement command
Format assignments	Assign a numeric format and prefix to a variable. If a variable is not output to the NC file, it is not required to format the variable.	**fmt x 1 x** x ─ variable to format 1 ─ format number x ─ prefix fmt ─ format assignment command
Initialization	Assign a specified value to a pre- or user-defined variable at the start of processing. Select canned cycles using short or long codes. Define global formulas.	**frrapid: 300** └─ 300.0 in/min └─ rapid feedrate variable **seqmax: 9999** └─ N9999 └─ maximum sequence number
Question definitions	Insert a question to be posted during processing.	**FQ 1 seqno** (Enter starting sequence number)
Lookup Table	Define a lookup table to provide a way of selecting a number from a list of integers.	**flktbl** 1 12 table#1 with 12 items 58 63 #Code 1 Match 1 59 90 #Code 2 Match 2 " " " " " " " "
String lists	Select a string based on a numeric value. String labels must Start with 'S'. A string list consists of two or more string definitions, a target variable and a string select statement.	**SMO8** **MO8** String definition **SMO9** **MO9** String definition Scool Target variable fstrsel SM09 String selection coolant scool statement

Section	Description	Example
User-defined postblocks	A postblock consists of one or more postlines used to organize the structure of an NC part program. A postline represents a single line of NC codes. The postlines form is a collection of arguments separated by commas.	**Plin # linear line movement - at feedrate** **n sccomp sgcode x y z fr** fr – feedrate z – Z-coordinate y – Y-coordinate x – X-coordinate sgcode – G-code sccomp – cutter compensation n – sequence number Ex.: N100 G41 G01 X1.0 Y9.0 F10.0
Pre-defined postblocks	Are pre-defined routines to format the most common areas of the NC program such as start of file, tool change, canned cycle, end of file, and tool move.	**peof #End of file for non-zero tool** n, "G91 G28 Z0 M5", pcooloff n, "G28 X0 Y0" n, "M30" "%"
System questions	Allow user to make slight configuration changes to the post processor.	**Rapid feedrate? 300.0** **Default X home position? 0.0** **Minimum arc length? 0.0002**

25.3 Post Processor Variables

Variables are important ingredients in a post processor. Some commonly used variables in customizing post processors are presented in this section. These variables can be classified into the following **six** groups:

- Position variables
- Compensation and offset variables
- Miscellaneous variables
- Motion and tool variables
- Canned cycle variables
- String and target variables

Position variables

X: X-coordinate of the new position
Y: Y-coordinate of the new position
Z: Z-coordinate of the new position

Xh: X-coordinate of the home position
Yh: Y-coordinate of the home position
Zh: Z-coordinate of the home position

Xr: X-coordinate of the first position in the NC program
Yr: Y-coordinate of the first position in the NC program
Zr: Z-coordinate of the first position in the NC program

I: arc center description in X-axis
J: arc center description in Y-axis
K: arc center description in Z-axis

Motion and tool variables

Gcode:	G code of the current operation
Plane:	Cutting plane of the current operation or circular move
fr:	feedrate of the current tool movement
frplunge:	feedrate for the current drilling cycle
t:	tool number

Compensation and offset variables

cc:	cutter compensation read directly from NCI file
ccomp:	cutter compensation in control status
tlngno:	tool length offset number
tloffno:	tool diameter offset number

Canned cycle variables

drillcyc:	canned drill cycle
initht:	initial height of the current drilling cycle
depth:	Z-coordinate of the current hole
dwell:	amount of dwell for the current drilling cycle
refht:	reference height of the current drilling cycle
retr:	retract amount of the current drilling cycle

Miscellaneous variables

ss:	spindle speed used for the current operation
n:	sequence number
coolant:	coolant status
progno:	program number as defined in the NC parameters
progname:	NC file name

String and target variables

sgcode:	target string for linear/circular motion G code
spdlon:	target string for spindle-on
smcool:	coolant code target string
sccomp:	cutter compensation target string
sgplane:	plane selection G-code target string
sgdrill:	target drill cycle G code

25.4 Post Processor Customization

To customize a post processor for a particular combination of controller/machine is a rather complicated task. The user must know the features, functions, and commands of the controller and the operation limitations of the machine, as well as file structure, variables, and commands of the post processor files. Fortunately, Mastercam has provided the executable files (MP.DLL for mill and MPL..DLL for lathe) and sample ASCII customization files (.PST) for most commonly used controllers. With the knowledge presented in previous sections and the reference material in the Mastercam manuals, the user should be able to modify an existing ASCII customization file to suit his own need.

In this section we modify a Fanuc generic customization file provided by Mastercam to create a new customization file. The intent is to provide a customization file that is much simpler and easy to understand than the original one. This new file is limited, it deals only with 3-axis machining and canned cycles. The main focus of modifying customization files is on user-defined postblocks and pre-defined postblocks.

User-defined Postblocks

A postblock consists of one or more postlines to implement a certain function. A postline is used to define the content of an NC program block. It consists of a collection of arguments separated by commas. Postline arguments can be of different types: boolean statements, formulas, functions, variables, forced variables, forced formulas, and special characters.

Here is a list of postlines that are used by this post processor. The lines handle cutter compensation and coolant control.

```
pccdia2        # Cutter Compensation2
               if ccomp <> 4, tloffno

pccdia         # Cutter Compensation
               if ccomp <> 0, pccdia2

pfr            # Feedrate W/O Negative Feedrates
               if fr > 0, fr

pcoolon        # Coolant on
               if coolant = 1, “M07” #FLOOD
               if coolant=2,"MO8" #MIST

pcooloff       # Coolant off
               if prv_coolant = 1, “M09” #OFF

pwcs           #G54 + coordinate setting
               if mil >=4, *sgwcs

plinm          #Linear line  movement - at feedrate
               n,sccomp,pccdia,sgcode,x,y,z,pfr,pcam
```

Pre-defined Postblocks

NC part programs can be organized into modules according to their functions. Each module contains a series of commands to implement certain tasks. These modules are referred to as pre-defined postblocks in Mastercam. They include:

- File header
- Program start
- Tool change
- Machining process
- Canned cycle
- End of program

Each module consists of a fixed pattern of command blocks to execute certain tasks. What should be included in a particular module depends on the controller/machine requirements and the user’s preference. Typical tasks performed by the above six modules are listed on the next page.

File header

- program number	O 100
- date	10/8/94
- part (or program) name	BLOCK

Program start

- safety features	G90 G80 G40 G00
- tool change	Tt M06
- work zero definition	G54 (or G92) Xx Yy
- tool length offset	G43 Zz Hh
- spindle speed control	Ss M03
- coolant control	M07

Tool change

- reference point return	G91 G28 Z0 G28 X0 Y0
- spindle stop	M05
- tool change	Tt M06
- work zero definition	G54 (or G92) Xx Yy
- tool length offset	G43 Zz Hh
- safety feature	G90 G80 G40 G00
- spindle speed control	Ss M03

Machining operation

- rapid traverse	G0 Xx Yy Zz
- linear interpolation	G1 Xx Yy Zz Ff
- circular interpolation	G2 (or G3) Xx Yy (or Zz) Rr Ff
- cutter diameter compensation	G41/G42 (or G40) Dd

Canned cycle

- cycle type	G81/G82/G83 - -/G89 Xx Yy Zz Rr Ff
- retraction mode	G98/G99
- subsequent cycles	Xx Yy Zz

Program end

- reference point return	G91 G28 Z0 G28 X0 Y0
- spindle stop	M05
- program end command	M30 (or M2)
- program end symbol	%

Project 1. Creating a post processor file

This project modifies the postlines in an existing post processor file (MPFAN.PST). Save this modified file as (LIN.PST) or any desired file name. We will use this new post processor in project 2 of this chapter. The postlines in this modified post processor are listed in step 4. The postlines are written based on the tasks listed in previous section. The user can rewrite them in different way.

Step 1. Select the post processor file to edit.

Select **MAIN MENU → File → Edit → PST**

File name to read: **MPFAN.PST**

The MasterCAM NC Editor and DNC Communications menu with PST file appears as below.

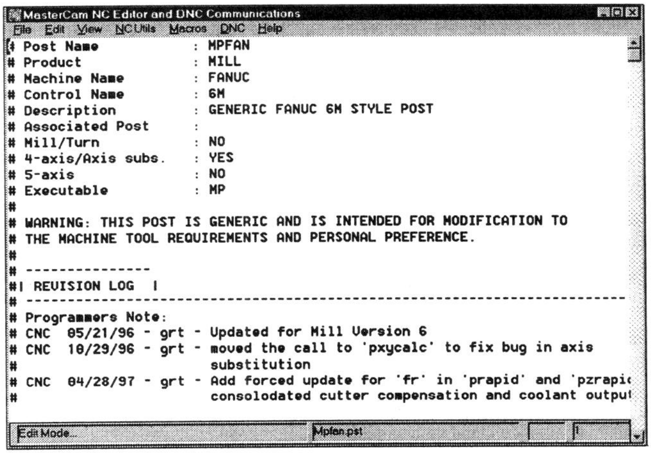

Step 2. Copy the PST file to a new file name "LIN.PST".

Select **File → Save As**

Save the file name and directory as below.

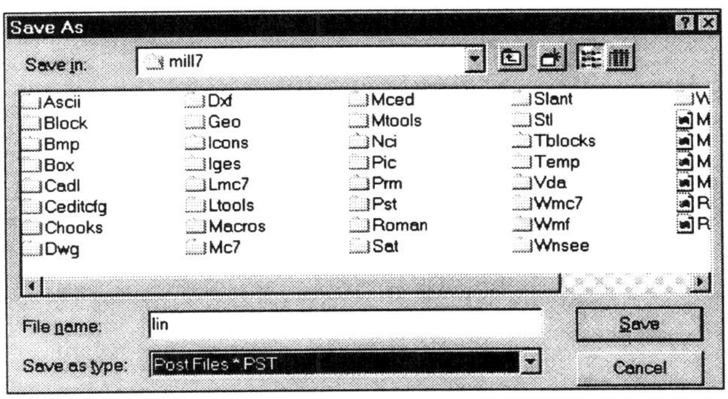

Select **Save**

Step 3. Open the new file "LIN.PST".

Select **File → Open**

File name to open: **lin**

The LIN.PST file should appear on the screen.

Scroll the screen to find "POSTLINE" section as shown below.

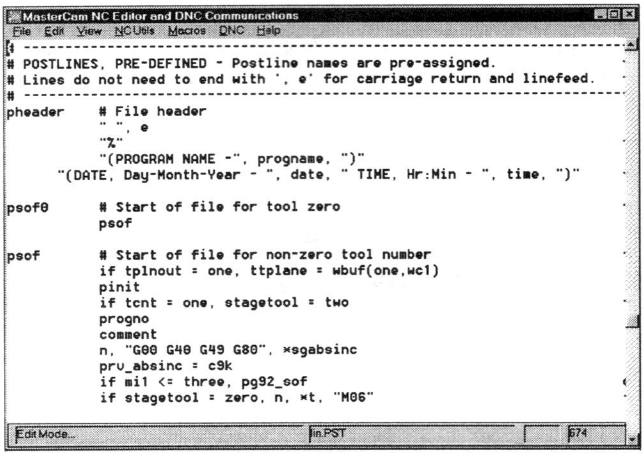

Step 4. Replace the POSTLINE section.

Change the contents in the POSTLINE section as below.

```
# ————————————————————————————————————————————————————————————#
POSTLINES, PRE-DEFINED - Postline names are pre-assigned.# Lines do not need to end with ', e'
for carriage return and linefeed.
# ————————————————————————————————————————————————————————————
pheader   # File header
      "O",progno

psof      # Start of file for non-zero tool number
          n,"G90 G80 G40 G00"
          if t<>0,n,t,"M6"n,sgwcs,"G0",*xr,*yr,*speed,*spdlon
          n,"G43",tlngno,*zr,pcoolon
ptlchg    # Tool change
          n,"G91 G28 Z0 M5",pcooloff
          n,"G28 X0 Y0"   n,t,"M6"
          n,"G90 G80 G40 G00"
          n,sgwcs,"G0",*xr,*yr,*speed,*spdlon
          n,"G43",tlngno,*zr,pcoolon

peof      # End of file for non-zero tool
          n,"G91 G28 Z0 M5",pcooloff
          n,"G28 X0 Y0"
          n,"M30"
          "%"
```

```
# ------------------------------------------------------------------------
# Axis motion
# ------------------------------------------------------------------------
prapid    # Linear line movement - at rapid feedrate
          n,sccomp,sgcode,x,y,z,pfr

plin      # Linear line movement - at feedrate
          n,sccomp,sgcode,x,y,z,pfr,pccdia

pz        # Linear movement in Z axis only - at feedrate
          n,sgcode,pzout,pfr

pcir      # Circular interpolation
          n,sgplane,sccomp,sgcode,x,y,z,arcrad,pfr
# ------------------------------------------------------------------------
# Drilling
# ------------------------------------------------------------------------
pdrill    # Canned Drill Cycle
          pdrillref
          n,drillref,sgdrill,*x,*y,*depth,*refht,pdwell,*frplunge

ppeck     # Canned Peck Drill Cycle
          pdrillref
          n,drillref,*sgdrill,*x,*y,*depth,*peck1,*refht,pdwell,*frplunge

pchpbrk   # Canned Chip Break Cycle
          pdrillref
          n,drillref,*sgdrill,*x,*y,*depth,*refht,*peck1,pdwell,*frplunge
          ptap    # Canned Tap Cycle
          pdrillref
          n,drillref,sgdrill,*x,*y,*depth,*refht,pdwell,*frplunge

pbore1    # Canned Bore #1 Cycle
          pdrillref
          n,drillref,*sgdrill,*x,*y,*depth,*refht,pdwell,*frplunge

pbore2    # Canned Bore #2 Cycle
          pdrillref
          n,drillref,*sgdrill,*x,*y,*depth,*refht,pdwell,*frplunge

pmisc1    # Canned Misc #1 Cycle (User Option)
          pdrill

pmisc2    # Canned Misc #2 Cycle (User Option)
          pdrill

pdrill_2  # Canned Drill Cycle
          n,x,y,depth

ppeck_2   # Canned Peck Drill Cycle
          pdrill_2
```

```
pchpbrk_2  # Canned Chip Break Cycle
        pdrill_2

ptap_2    # Canned Tap Cycle
        pdrill_2

pbore1_2  # Canned Bore #1 Cycle
        pdrill_2

pbore2_2  # Canned Bore #2 Cycle
        pdrill_2

pmisc1_2  # Canned Misc #1 Cycle
        pdrill_2

pmisc2_2  # Canned Misc #2 Cycle
        pdrill_2

pcanceldc  # Cancel canned drill cycle
        n,"G80"<prv_z=initht
# ----------------------------------------------------------------
# Misc. Output
# ----------------------------------------------------------------
pcomment  # Manual Entry - COMMENTS (on a block by itself) 1005,1006
      "(", scomm, ")"

pcancelcc  # Cancel cutter comp.
        #n, "G40"

# ----------------------------------------------------------------
# Tooltable Output
# ----------------------------------------------------------------
pwrtt     # Write tool table, scans entire file, null tools are negative
          if tplnout = one, ttplane = wbuf(one,wc1)
        tnote = t
        toffnote = tloffno
        tlngnote = tlngno
        if t >= zero, "(", *tnote, " ", *toffnote, " ", *tlngnote, " ", *tldia, " ",
        *sopnote, ")"
        if t >= zero, tcnt = tcnt + one
```

Step 5. Save the new file.

Select **File → Save**

Step 6. Exit the editor.

Select **File → Exit**

Project 2. Testing the customized post processor

This project uses the machining of a simple part shown in Figure 25.2 to test the newly customized post processor. The machining toolpaths consist of contouring, drilling, and tapping.

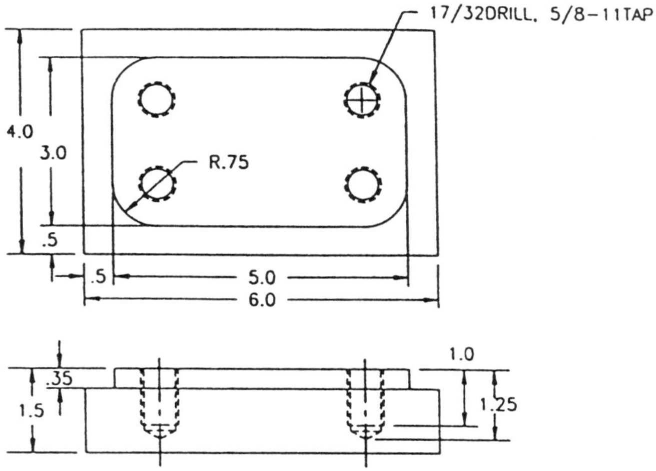

Figure 25.2

Tips 1. Use the contour module to cut the profile with tool T1 (1" end mill).

2. Use the drill/counterbore mode of the drill module to drill the four holes with tool T5 (17/32" drill).
3. Use the tap mode of the drill module to tap internal threads of the four holes with tool T7 (5/8-11 tap).

Step 1. Create two rectangles.

Select **MAIN MENU → Create → Rectangle → 2 points**
Enter the two points for the 1st rectangle: **(0,0), (6,4)**
Enter the two points for the 2nd rectangle: **(0.5,0.5), (5.5,3.5)**
Press **Alt+F1** simultaneously, and then press **F2** to fit the drawing on screen
The drawing should look like Figure 25.3.

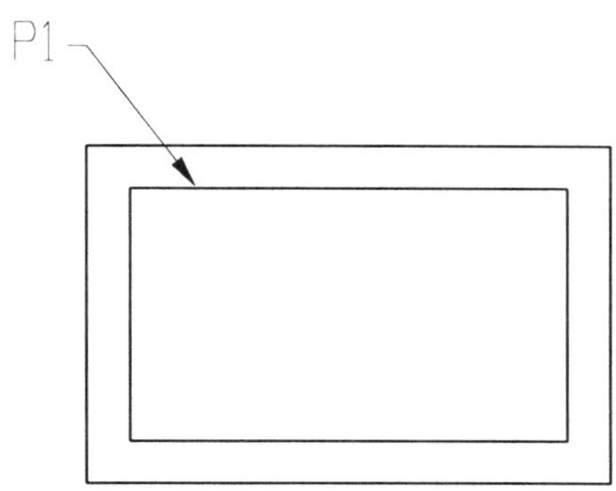

Figure 25.3

Step 2. Create four fillets at the corners of the inside rectangle.

Use the pick points in Figure 25.3.
Select **MAIN MENU → Modify → Fillet → Radius**
Enter the radius: **0.75**
Select **Chain → Pick P1,** then select **Done**
The new drawing is shown in Figure 25.4.

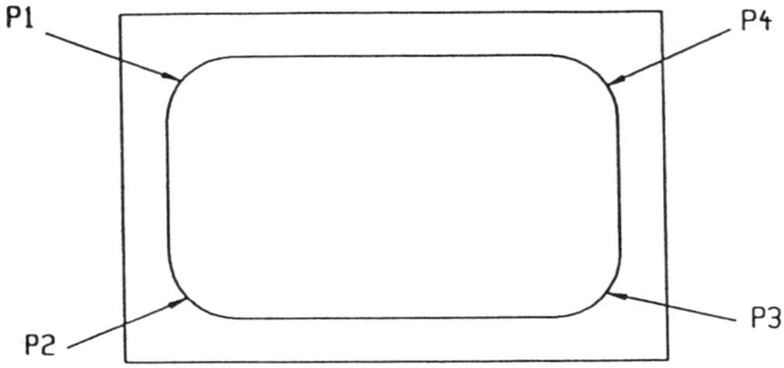

Figure 25.4

Step 3. Create four points for the hole centers using the pick points in Figure 25.4

Select **MAIN MENU → Create → Point → Position → Center**
Pick **P1 – P4** to define the four points
The four points are added as shown in Figure 25.5.

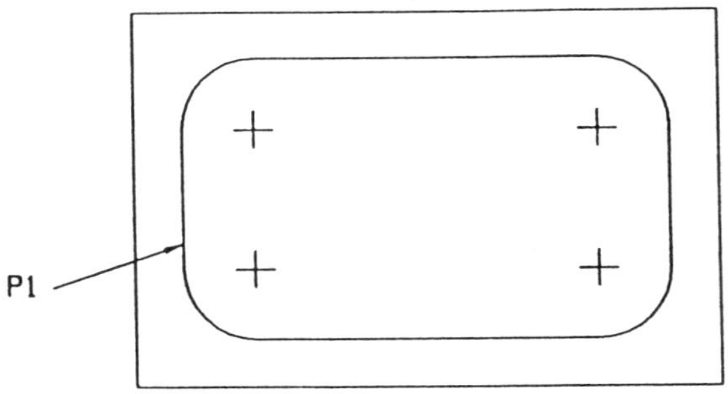

Figure 25.5

Step 4. Initiate the contour module.

Select **MAIN MENU → Toolpaths → Contour**
Enter file name: pptest

Step 5. Define the contour using the pick points in Figure 25.5.

Select **Chain** then pick **P1**
Select **Done**

Step 6. Select 1" end mill and set tool parameters.

Click the right mouse button, then select "Get tool from library"
Select **tool #243** (1" flat end mill)
Select **OK**

Set the tool parameters as below.

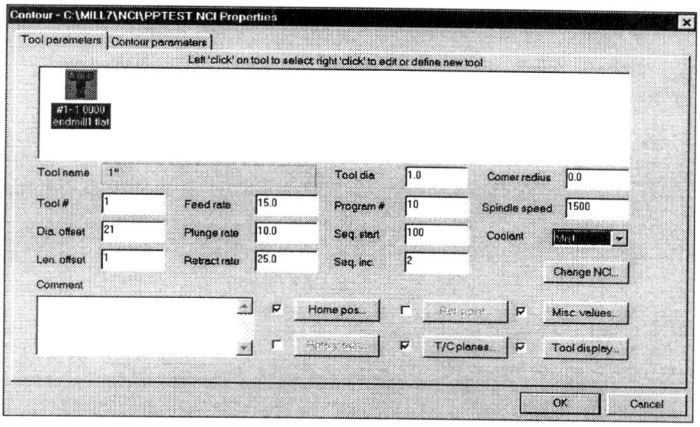

Step 7. Define the contour parameters.

Click the "Contour Parameters" button

Click the "Lead in/out" button

Set the lead in and out parameters as below.

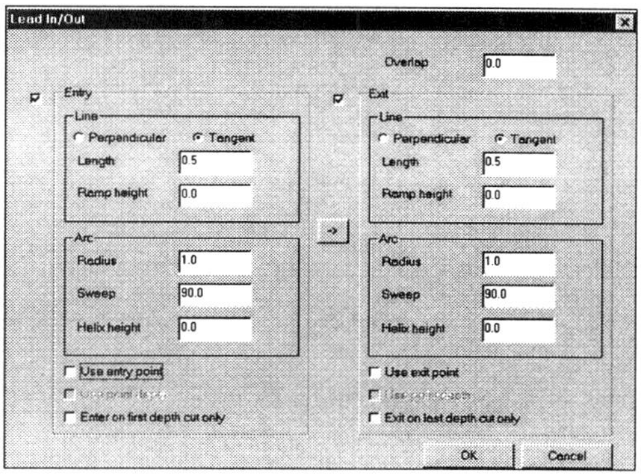

Select **OK**

Set the contour parameters as below.

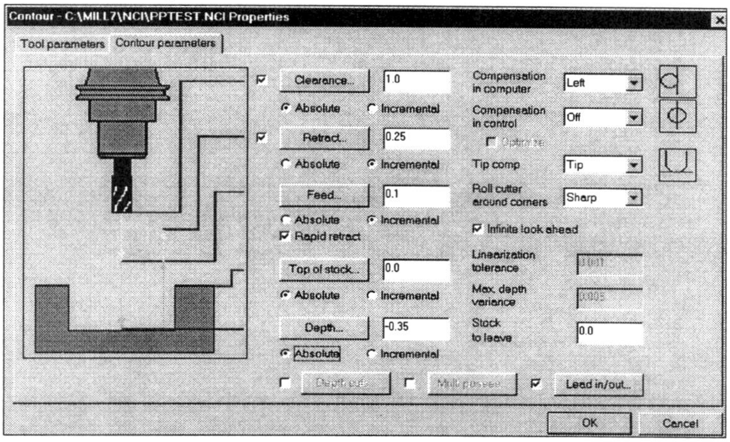

Select **OK**

The contour toolpath should resemble Figure 25.6.

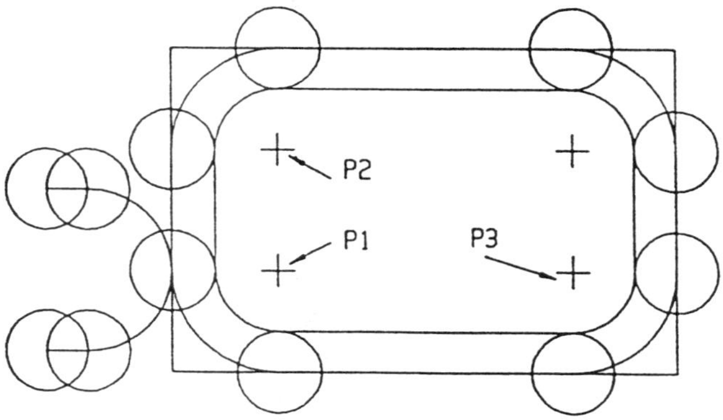

Figure 25.6

Step 8. Initiate the drill module.

Select **Drill**

Step 9. Select the points for drilling using the pick points in Figure 25.6.

Select **Automatic**
Sequentially pick **P1 – P3**
Select **Done**

Step 10. Select a drill and define tool parameters.

Click the right mouse button, and select "Get tool from library"
Select **tool #143** (17/32" drill) from the list, then select OK
Define the tool parameters as below.

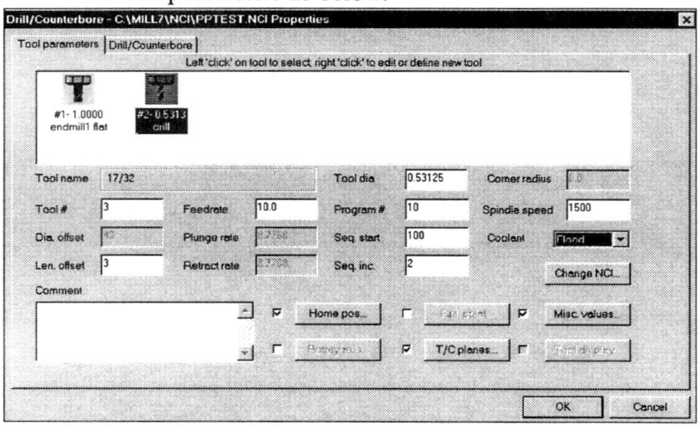

Step 11. Define the drill parameters.

Click on the "Drill/Counterbore" button

Define the drill parameters to the following settings.

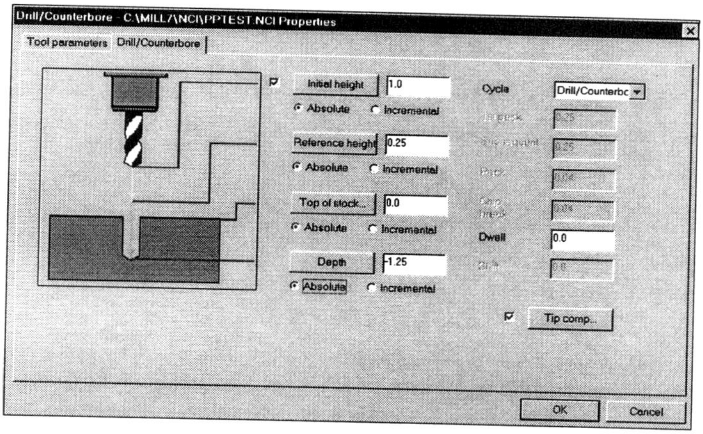

Select **OK** → **OK** to generate the drilling toolpaths
The drilling toolpaths appear on the screen.

Step 12. Initiate the drill-tap module.

Select **Drill**
Select **Last** to use the points from last operation
Select **Done**

Step 13. Select the tap and define the tool parameters.

Click on the right mouse button, then select "Get tool from library"
Select **tool #211(Tap RH- 5/8-11)**
Select **OK**
Set the tool parameters as below.

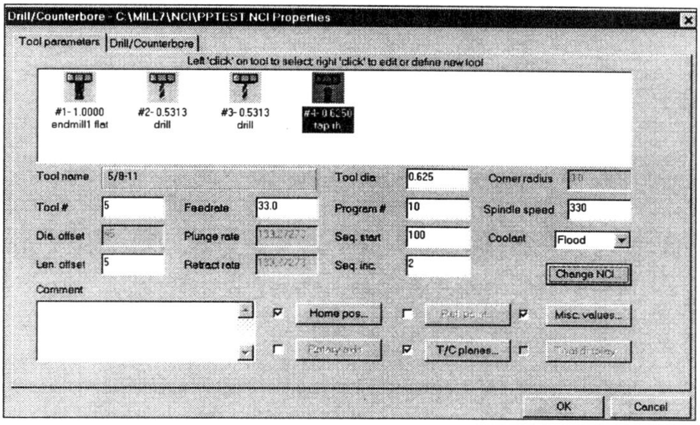

Select **OK**

Step 14. Define the drill-tap parameters.

Click the "Tap" button
Set the parameters as below.

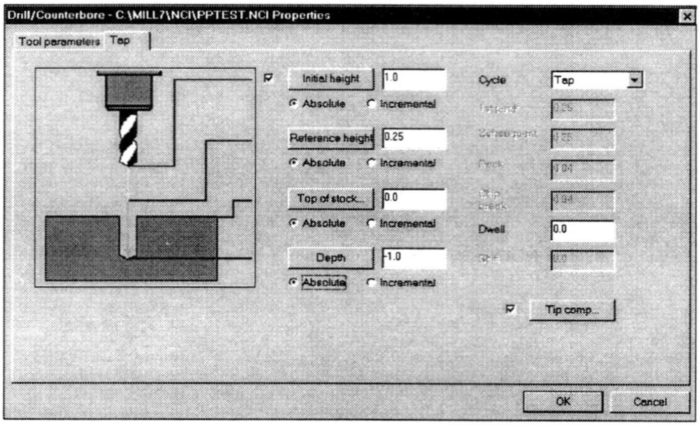

Select **OK**
The tapping toolpaths are generated and displayed on the screen.

Step 15. Select the new customized post processor (LIN.PST).

Select **MAIN MENU → NC utils → Post Proc → Change**
Enter file name (.pst): **lin**

Step 16. Run the post processor.

Select **Run**
Select "**Yes**" for Creating the NC text file
Select "**Yes**" to overwrite the "pptest.NCI"
Enter file pattern (.NCI): **pptest**
Enter file name (.NC): **pptest**

The NCI file should be converted to NCI file and listed on the screen as shoown on the next page.

```
O O0010( TOOL - 01  DIA. OFF. - 21  LENGTH - 01  DIA. - .5000  3D-CONTOUR )( TOOL - 05
DIA. OFF. - 45  LENGTH - 05  DIA. - .5000  DRILL/MISC )
( TOOL - 07  DIA. OFF. - 47  LENGTH - 07  DIA. - .5000  DRILL/MISC )
N100 G90 G80 G40 G00
N102 T1 M6
N104 G0 X-1.25 Y.25 S2500 M3
N106 G43 H1 Z.1 M7
N108 G1 Z-.35 F7.5
N110 X-.75
N112 G3 X.25 Y1.25 R1.
N114 G1 Y2.75
N116 G2 X1.25 Y3.75
N118 G1 X4.75
N120 G2 X5.75 Y2.75
N122 G1 Y1.25
N124 G2 X4.75 Y.25
N126 G1 X1.25
N128 G2 X.25 Y1.25
N130 G3 X-.75 Y2.25
N132 G1 X-1.25
N134 G91 G28 Z0 M5 M9
N136 G28 X0 Y0
N138 T5 M6
N140 G90 G80 G40 G00
N142 G0 X1.25 Y1.25 S1500 M3
N144 G43 H5 Z1. M7
N146 G98 G81 X1.25 Y1.25 Z-1.25 R2. F7.5
N148 Y2.75
N150 X4.75
N152 Y1.25
N154 G80<prv_z=initht
N156 G91 G28 Z0 M5 M9
N158 G28 X0 Y0
N160 T7 M6
N162 G90 G80 G40 G00
N164 G0 X1.25 Y1.25 S1500 M3
N166 G43 H7 Z1. M7
N168 X1.25 Y1.25 Z-1. R.2 F30.
N170 Y2.75
N172 X4.75
N174 Y1.25
N176 G80
N178 G91 G28 Z0 M5 M9
N180 G28 X0 Y0
N182 M30
%
```

Select **Close** to return back to graphic mode.

Exercises

1. What is the output file of the CAM system?

2. Explain the reason for using a post processor.

3. Describe how Mastercam uses a pair of lines to organize the data contained in NCI files.

4. Describe what the following numbers represent in the operation lines used in NCI files:

    0:
    1:
    2:
    3:
    11:
    80:
    81:
    100:
    1001:
    1002:
    1013:

5. What are the four groups of operations in NCI files?

6. Describe how the start drill cycle (81) and drill hole (100) operations are used together to specify the canned cycles for drilling, boring, or tapping multiple holes.

7. Define the term post processor.

8. What are the two files used in a post processor?

9. List the ten sections of the post processor customization files. Briefly describe what they are.

10. What are main six groups of variables used in post processors?

Mastercam 7

Index